S0-CCJ-649

INTERNATIONAL LAW

CASES AND MATERIALS

Fourth Edition

By

Lori Fisler Damrosch
Henry L. Moses Professor of Law and International Organization, Columbia University, School of Law

Louis Henkin
University Professor Emeritus, Columbia University, School of Law

Richard Crawford Pugh
Distinguished Professor of Law, University of San Diego, School of Law

Oscar Schachter
Hamilton Fish Professor Emeritus of International Law and Diplomacy, Columbia University, School of Law

Hans Smit
Stanley H. Fuld Professor of Law, Columbia University, School of Law

AMERICAN CASEBOOK SERIES®

A THOMSON COMPANY

ST. PAUL, MINN., 2001

610 Opperman Drive
P.O. Box 64526
St. Paul, MN 55164–0526
1–800–328–9352

ISBN 0–314–23764–X

1st Reprint — 2002

This book is dedicated to our predecessors in international law at Columbia University

Philip C. Jessup

Wolfgang G. Friedmann

Oliver J. Lissitzyn

*

Preface to the Fourth Edition

This edition renews and enriches a "classical" casebook on international law. It reflects our aspiration to enable teaching international law in essential continuity with the great traditions of the discipline, yet with fresh appreciation and even some radical change.

In the years since the previous edition was published, international law has been invigorated with ideas and energy from peoples around the world. Grass-roots movements, transnational networks, and non-governmental organizations have focused attention on issues where international law can make notable contributions to solution of problems affecting all humanity. New standards of conduct have been elaborated in fields as diverse as human rights, trade, the environment, and disarmament; and new institutions are coming into being to realize ambitious goals through law. No longer is international law the specialized preserve of states, governments, or diplomats: it is now put to use by activists around the globe.

The transformations in the hitherto largely state-centered nature of our discipline have been a major theme of the present revision. Along with emphasizing the centrality of human rights in contemporary international law, we have given enhanced attention to non-state actors and their influence on the theory, content, and implementation of international law, illustrated by developments since the last edition, such as the Land Mines Convention and the treaty to establish an International Criminal Court.

The electronic revolution is also working changes in the ways that we teach and research international law. Within just the last few years, the informational resources that were formerly the province of experts in international law (with access to specialized research libraries) are now instantly available around the world. Our previous edition went to press without benefit of the WorldWide Web, while today that resource forms part of every international lawyer's essential equipment.

The pace of change in the field of international law, and in the methodologies for finding and disseminating its sources, have posed challenges for the present revision. We strive in this edition to bring forward the best of the classical foundations of the discipline, while enriching the materials with suggestions for how our readers can explore at the cutting edge. The exigencies of print production have imposed a closing date of the end of calendar year 2000 for taking account of recent developments; but a new "Note on Electronic Technologies and International Law" offers a guide to finding the latest information about the topics in question.

Our editorial team has expanded to include another colleague at Columbia Law School. We have profited from suggestions received from many users of the previous editions. The result, we believe, is a casebook fit for the opening of the twenty-first century.

L.F.D.
L.H.
R.C.P.
O.S.
H.S.

*

Documents

The editors of this book have compiled a collection of documents under the title "International Law, Basic Documents," published by the same publisher, for use in connection with this book.

In most cases when this book refers to an instrument, such as a treaty or United Nations resolution, or to specific articles or parts thereof, the reader will find the original text in "International Law, Basic Documents."

Of course, the reader may also find such instruments in original sources or in other collections of documents.

*

Abbreviations

A.F.D.I. or Ann. Français — Annuaire Français de Droit International

A.J.I.L. — American Journal of International Law

Ann. de l'Institut de Droit Int. — Annuaire de l'Institut de Droit International

Ann. Dig. — Annual Digest

A.S.I.L. Proc. — American Society of International Law Proceedings

Brit. Y.B.I.L. or Brit. Y.B. Int'l Law — British Yearbook of International Law

E.J.I.L. — European Journal of International Law

E.S.C. Res. — Economic and Social Council Resolution

E.S.C.O.R. — United Nations Economic and Social Council Official Records

E.T.S. — European Treaty Series

G.A.O.R. — United Nations General Assembly Official Records

G.A. Res. — United Nations General Assembly Resolution

Gr. Brit. T.S. — Great Britain Treaty Series

Hackworth — Hackworth, Digest of International Law (1940–44)

Hyde — Hyde, International Law Chiefly as Interpreted and Applied by the United States (2nd ed. 1945)

Hudson — Hudson, International Legislation

I.C.A.O. Doc. — International Civil Aviation Organization Document

I.C.J. — International Court of Justice Reports

I.C.L.Q. — International and Comparative Law Quarterly

I.C.T.R. — International Criminal Tribunal for Rwanda

I.C.T.Y. .... International Criminal Tribunal for the Former Yugoslavia

I.L.C. .... International Law Commission

I.L.C.Rep. .... International Law Commission Reports

I.L.M. or Int'l Leg. Mat'ls .... International Legal Materials

I.L.R. .... International Law Reports

L.N.T.S. .... League of Nations Treaty Series

Malloy .... Malloy, Treaties, Conventions, International Acts, Protocols and Agreements Between the United States of America and Other Powers (1910–38)

O'Connell .... O'Connell, International Law (2nd ed. 1970)

Oppenheim .... Oppenheim, International Law, vol. 1 (9th ed. Jennings and Watts 1992), vol. 2 (7th ed. Lauterpacht 1952)

P.C.I.J. .... Permanent Court of International Justice Reports

Rec. des Cours .... Recueil des Cours, Academie de Droit International

Restatement (Third) .... Restatement (Third) of the Foreign Relations Law of the United States (1987)

Restatement (Second) 1965 .... Restatement, Second, Foreign Relations Law of the United States (1965)

S.C.O.R. .... United Nations Security Council Official Records

S.C. Res. .... United Nations Security Council Resolution

State Dept. Bull. .... State Department Bulletin

Stat. .... Statutes at Large, United States

T.D.O.R. .... United Nations Trade and Development Board Official Records

T.I.A.S. .... Treaty and Other International Act Series

U.N.C.I.O. .... United Nations Conference on International Organization

U.N.Doc. .... United Nations Document

U.N.R.I.A.A. or U.N. Rep. Int'l Arb. Awards — United Nations Reports of International Arbitration Awards

U.N.T.S. — United Nations Treaty Series

U.S.C.A. — United States Code Annotated

U.S.G.A.O. — United States General Accounting Office

U.S.T. — United States Treaties and Other International Agreements

Whiteman — Whiteman, Digest of International Law (1963–73)

Yb.I.L.C. — Yearbook of the International Law Commission

*

Acknowledgments

We acknowledge and are indebted to a large number of individuals who generously contributed their time and effort to make the Fourth Edition possible. We naturally include those people who assisted in the previous editions.

In the preparation of this edition we would like to extend our appreciation to the following present and former students at Columbia Law School for their research assistance: Jason Abel, J.D. 2001; Michael Bliss, LL.M. 1998; Karin Braverman, J.D. 2001; Seonggi Cho, J.D. 2001; Anne-Marie Corominas, LL.M. 1998; Lorna Davidson, LL.M. 2001; Cheri De Luca, J.D. Class of 2002; Michael Granne, J.D. Class of 2002; Inna Gutman, J.D. Class of 2002; Eric Hong, J.D. Class of 2002; Glen Kelley, J.D. 2001; Michael Rosenthal, LL.M. 2000; Laurent Wiesel, J.D. 2001; and Chasless Yancy-Hunter, J.D. 2001; and the following students at the University of San Diego School of Law: Kristina Kay Larsen, J.D. 1999; Laura McFarland, LL.M. 2000; and Rebecca Richards, J.D. 2000. Administrative and clerical assistance was provided by George Bareford, Debbie Cervantes, Pam Kelly, and Justine Phillips.

We extend our warm thanks for reference assistance readily and frequently given by Kent McKeever, Director of the Arthur W. Diamond Law Library at Columbia University, and the library staff.

We benefited from advice from our colleagues at Columbia, including José Alvarez, George Bermann, Richard N. Gardner, David Leebron, Petros Mavroidis, and Gerald Neuman.

We also thank the users of the previous editions who gave us comments and suggestions for improvement, including Jonathan I. Charney, Mary Coombs, and many present and former students.

Finally, we acknowledge our indebtedness to the following authors and publishers who granted us permission to reprint copyrighted material:

The American Bar Association, for permission to reprint from Salacuse, BIT by BIT, the Growth of Bilateral Investment Treaties and Their Impact, 24 International Lawyer No. 3 (1990). Reprinted by permission.

The American Law Institute, for permission to reprint from the Model Penal Code (1974); Pugh, Legal Protection of International Transactions Against Non-Commercial Risks, in Surrey and Shaw, A Lawyer's Guide to International Business Transactions (1963); Restatement (Second) of the Foreign Relations Law of the United States (1965); and Restatement (Third) of the Foreign Relations Law of the United States (1987).

The American Society of International Law, for permission to reprint from the following articles appearing in the American Journal of International Law and the Proceedings of the American Society of International Law, © The American Society of International Law: Abbott, International Relations Theory, International Law, and the Regime Governing Internal Conflicts, 93 A.J.I.L. 361 (1999); Acheson, Remarks, 57 A.S.I.L. Proceedings 9, 14 (1963); Charlesworth, Chinkin & Wright, Feminist Approaches to International Law, 85 A.J.I.L. 613 (1991); Charlesworth, Feminist Methods in International Law,

93 A.J.I.L. 379 (1999); Dunoff & Trachtman, The Law and Economics of Humanitarian Law Violations in Internal Conflict, 93 A.J.I.L. 394 (1999); Friedmann, United States Policy and the Crisis of International Law, 59 A.J.I.L. 857 (1965); Joyner, Reflections on the Lawfulness of Invasion, 78 A.J.I.L. 131 (1984); Kearney & Dalton, The Treaty on Treaties, 64 A.J.I.L. 495 (1970); McDougal, The Hydrogen Bomb Tests, 49 A.J.I.L. 357 (1955); Meeker, Defensive Quarantine and the Law, 57 A.J.I.L. 523 (1963); Moore, Grenada and the International Double Standard, 78 A.J.I.L. 145 (1984); Oxman, The 1994 Agreement and the Convention, 88 A.J.I.L. 687 (1994); Ratner, Drawing a Better Line: *Uti Possidetis* and the Borders of New States, 90 A.J.I.L. 590 (1996); Ratner & Slaughter (eds.) Symposium on Method in International Law: Appraising the Methods of International Law: A Prospectus for Readers, 93 A.J.I.L. 291 (1999); Reisman, Coercion and Self-Determination: Construing Charter Article 2(4), 78 A.J.I.L. 642 (1984); Reisman, International Law After the Cold War, 84 A.J.I.L. 859 (1990); Schachter, Compensation for Expropriation, 78 A.J.I.L. 121 (1984); Schachter, The Legality of Pro-Democratic Invasion, 78 A.J.I.L. 645 (1984); Schachter, The Twilight Existence of Nonbinding International Agreements, 71 A.J.I.L. 296 (1977); Schachter, United Nations Law in the Gulf Conflict, 85 A.J.I.L. 542 (1991); Sohn & Baxter, Responsibility of States for Injury to the Economic Interests of Aliens, 55 A.J.I.L. 545 (1961); Weil, Towards Relative Normativity in International Law?, 77 A.J.I.L. 413 (1983). Reproduced with permission from The American Journal of International Law, © The American Society of International Law.

The American Society of International Law, for permission to reprint from the following articles from Damrosch & Scheffer (eds.), Law and Force in the New International Order (1991): Chayes, The Use of Force in the Persian Gulf; Gardner, Commentary on the Law of Self-Defense; Schachter, Authorized Uses of Force by the United Nations and Regional Organizations; Scheffer, Commentary on Collective Security. Copyright © 1991 The American Society of International Law.

The American Society of International Law, for permission to reprint the international arbitral award in Texaco Overseas Petroleum, et al. v. Libyan Arab Republic, 17 I.L.M. 1 (1978); and the introductory note by Schreuer to the Brčko arbitral award, 38 I.L.M. 534 (1999).

American University Law Review, for permission to reprint from Lillich & Paxman, State Responsibility for Injuries to Aliens Occasioned by Terrorist Activities, 26 Am.U.L.Rev. 217 (1977).

Canadian Institute of International Affairs, for permission to reprint from Friedmann, The Role of International Law in the Conduct of International Affairs, 20 International Journal 158 (1965).

Cardozo Law Review, for permission to reprint from Henkin, International Human Rights as "Rights," 1 Cardozo L. Rev. 438, 446-447 (1979).

Carnegie Corporation of New York and Rowman & Littlefield, Publishers, Inc., for permission to reprint from Words Over War: Mediation and Arbitration to Prevent Deadly Conflict (Greenberg, Barton & McGuinness, eds., 2000).

Case Western Reserve Journal of International Law, for permission to reprint from Smith, Sovereignty over Unoccupied Territories–The Western Sahara Decision, in 9 Case W. Res. J. Int'l L. 135 (1977).

Columbia Journal of Transnational Law, for permission to reprint from Henkin, Act of State Today: Recollections in Tranquility, 6 Colum. J. Transnat. L. 175 (1967); and Henkin, The Invasion of Panama Under International Law: A Gross Violation, 29 Colum. J. Transnat. L. 293 (1991).

Columbia University Press, for permission to reprint from The Changing Structure of International Law by Wolfgang Gaston Friedmann, © 1964 Columbia University Press; Henkin, The Age of Rights © 1990 Columbia University Press; Henkin, The International Bill of Rights, in International Enforcement of Human Rights © 1987 Columbia University Press. Reprinted by permission of the publisher.

Council on Foreign Relations, Inc., and Foreign Affairs, for permission to reprint from Boutros-Ghali, Empowering the United Nations, 71 Foreign Affairs 89, 98-99 (Winter 1992/93). Reprinted by permission of Foreign Affairs. Copyright 1993 by the Council on Foreign Relations, Inc.

Council on Foreign Relations Press, for permission to reprint from Acevedo, The Haitian Crisis and the OAS Response: A Test of Effectiveness in Protecting Democracy, in Enforcing Restraint: Collective Intervention in Internal Conflicts (Damrosch ed., 1993); Henkin, How Nations Behave (2d ed.1979); and Henkin, The Use of Force: Law and U.S. Policy, in Right v. Might: International Law and the Use of Force (2d ed. 1991).

Duke Law Journal, for permission to reprint from Charney, Transnational Corporations and Developing International Law, in 1983 Duke L.J. 784.

Duncker & Humblot GmbH, for permission to reprint from Peters, The Position of International Law Within the European Community Legal Order, 40 German Y.B. Int'l L. 9 (1997).

Foundation Press, for permission to reprint from Human Rights (Henkin, Neuman, Orentlicher and Leebron, eds, 1999), pp. 334, 358, 370, 396, 598.

Thomas M. Franck, for permission to reprint from Franck, The Power of Legitimacy Among Nations (1990).

Hague Academy of International Law, for permission to reprint from Baxter, Treaties and Custom, 129 Rec. des Cours 25 (1970-I); Damrosch, Enforcing International Law Through Non-Forcible Measures, 269 Rec. des Cours 9 (1997); Henkin, International Law: Politics, Values and Functions, 216 Rec. des Cours 9 (1989-IV); Jiménez de Aréchaga, International Law in the Past Third of a Century, 159 Rec. des Cours 9 (1978-I); Lissitzyn, Territorial Entities Other Than Independent States in the Law of Treaties, 125 Rec. des Cours 5 (1968-III); Schachter, International Law in Theory and Practice, 178 Rec. des Cours 21 (1982-V); Waldock, General Course on Public International Law, 106 Rec. des Cours 1 (1962-II).

Harvard International Law Journal, for permission to reprint from Allott, State Responsibility and the Unmaking of International Law, 29 Harv. Int'l L. J. 1 (1988).

Harvard Law Review Association, for permission to reprint from Henkin, The Constitution and United States Sovereignty: A Century of Chinese Exclusion and Its Progeny, 100 Harv. L. Rev. 853 (1987).

Louis Henkin, for permission to reprint from Foreign Affairs and the United States Constitution, 2d edition, Oxford University Press, 1996, © Louis Henkin 1996; International Law: Politics and Values (1995).

Holt, Rinehart & Winston, for permission to reprint from Hans Kelsen, Principles of International Law 252, 450-452 (2d rev. ed. Tucker 1966).

Kluwer Law International/Kluwer Academic Publishers/Martinus Nijhoff Publishers, for permission to reprint from Henkin, International Law: Politics and Values (1995); Jiménez de Aréchaga and Tanzi, International State Responsibility in International Law, in International Law, Achievements and Prospects (Mohammed Bedjaoui ed., 1991); Macdonald & Johnson (eds.), The Structure and Process of International Law (1984); Schachter, International Law in Theory and Practice (1991), with the kind permission of Kluwer Law International/Kluwer Academic Publishers.

Lynne Rienner Publishers, Inc., for permission with respect to Falk, Evasions of Sovereignty, reprinted from Contending Sovereignties, edited by Walker and Mendlovitz, copyright © 1990 by Lynne Rienner Publishers, Inc. (later reprinted as Falk, Explorations at the Edge of Time: The Prospects for World Order, Temple University Press, 1992); and Thakur & Maley, The Ottawa Convention on Landmines: A Landmark Humanitarian Treaty in Arms Control?, in Global Governance: A Review of Multilateralism and International Affairs, vol. 5, pp. 273, 280-285 (1999), copyright © 1999 by Lynne Rienner Publishers. Reprinted with permission of the publisher.

Macmillan (U.S.)/Simon and Schuster, for permission to reprint from Philip Jessup, A Modern Law of Nations (1948).

Manchester University Press and Sir Ian M. Sinclair, for permission to reprint from Sinclair, The Vienna Convention on the Law of Treaties (2d ed. 1984).

Estate of the late Dr. F.A. Mann, for permission to reprint from Mann, Reflections on a Commercial Law of Nations, in British Year Book of International Law, Vol. 33 (1957), pp. 20, 34-39; Mann, State Contracts and International Arbitration, in British Year Book of International Law, Vol. 42, pp. 1, 27-28 (1967); and Mann, International Delinquencies Before Municipal Courts, in Studies in International Law (1973), pp. 378-380.

Michigan Law Review, for permission to reprint from Henkin, International Law as Law in the United States, 82 Mich. L. Rev. 1555 (1984); and from Schachter, The Right of States to Use Armed Force, 82 Mich. L. Rev. 1620 (1984).

New York University Journal of International Law and Politics, for permission to reprint from Monica Pinto, Fragmentation or Unification Among International Institutions: Human Rights Tribunals, 31 N.Y.U. J. Int'l L. & Pol. (1999); Bernard H. Oxman, The Duty to Respect Generally Accepted International Standards, 24 N.Y.U. J. Int'l L. & Pol. 143 (1991).

Nomos Verlagsgesellschaft, for permission to reprint from Nicolas Bratza and Michael O'Boyle, The Legacy of the Commission to the New Court Under the Protocol No. 11, in The Birth of European Human Rights Law: Studies in Honor of Carle Aage Nygaard (1998), p. 377.

Ocean Development and International Law, for permission to reprint from Oxman, Environmental Warfare, 22 Ocean Dev. & Int'l L. 433 (1991).

Oxford University Press, for permission to reprint from Allott, Eunomia: New Order for a New World (1990) © Philip J. Allott,1990, pp. 416-419, by permission of Oxford University Press; J.L. Brierly, The Law of Nations: An Introduction to the International Law of Peace, edited by Humphrey Waldock (6th edition, 1963) © Oxford University Press 1963, by permission of Oxford University Press; Ian Brownlie, Principles of Public International Law (4th edition, 1990), © Ian Brownlie 1990, by permission of Oxford University Press; H.L.A. Hart, The Concept of Law (1961) © Oxford University Press 1961, by permission of Oxford University Press; Smith, Remedies for Breaches of EU Law in National Courts: Legal Variation and Selection, in The Evolution of EU Law (Craig & de Búrca eds., Oxford University Press, 1999).

Palgrave Global Publishing at St. Martin's Press, for permission to reprint from Sol Picciotto and Ruth Mayne, Regulating International Business: Beyond Liberalization (1999), Copyright © Sol Picciotto and Ruth Mayne. Reprinted with permission of St. Martin's Press, LLC.

Pearson Education, for permission to reprint from R.Y. Jennings and A. Watts, editors, Oppenheim's International Law, 9th edition (1992). Reprinted by permission of Pearson Education Limited © Longman Group Ltd.

Princeton University Press, for permission to reprint from Wapner, Politics Beyond the State: Environmental Activism and World Civic Politics, in World Politics, Vol. 47 (1995), p. 311.

Random House, Inc./Alfred A. Knopf, for permission to reprint from Morgenthau & Thompson, Politics Among Nations (6th ed. 1985).

Regents of the University of California, for permission to reprint from Kelsen, Pure Theory of Law (Knight transl. 1967).

W. Michael Reisman, for permission to reprint from McDougal & Feliciano, Law and Minimum World Public Order (1961); and Reisman, Nullity and Revision (1971).

Royal Institute of International Affairs, for permission to reprint the following articles published in the British Yearbook of International Law: Bowett, Reservations to Non-Restricted Multilateral Treaties, [1976-1977] Brit. Y.B.I.L., vol. 48, pp. 88-90; Lauterpacht, Sovereignty Over Marine Areas, [1950] Brit. Y.B. I.L., pp. 376, 427; Rama-Montaldo, International Legal Personality and Implied Powers of International Organizations, [1970] Brit. Y.B.I.L., vol. 44, pp. 123-124.

Springer-Verlag, for permission to reprint from Henkin, The International Bill of Rights: The Universal Declaration and the Covenants, in International Enforcement of Human Rights (Bernhardt & Jolowicz eds., 1987).

Sweet & Maxwell, Ltd., for permission to reprint from Lauterpacht, International Law and Human Rights (1973), pp. 27-29; O'Connell, International Law, vol. 1 (2d ed. 1970), pp. 108-109.

Transnational Publishers, Inc., for permission to reprint from Caron, The Basis of Responsibility, Attribution and Other Transsubstantive Rules, in The Iran-United States Claims Tribunal: Its Contribution to the Law of State Responsibility (1998).

Virginia Journal of International Law, for permission to reprint from Schachter, Towards a Theory of International Obligation, 8 Va. J. Int'l L. 300, 300-304 (1968).

Virginia Law Review Association, for permission to reprint from Falk, The Adequacy of Contemporary Theories of International Law–Gaps in Legal Thinking, 50 Va. L. Rev. 231, 249-250 (1964).

Walter de Gruyter GmbH & Co. KG, for permission to reprint from Weiler, International Crimes of State: A Critical Analysis of the ILC's Draft Article 19 on State Responsibility (Weiler, Cassese & Spinedi eds., 1989), p. 232.

West Publishing Company, for permission to reprint from Jackson, Davey & Sykes, Legal Problems of International Economic Relations (3rd ed. 1995).

Zeitschrift für ausländisches öffentliches Recht und Völkerrecht, for permission to reprint from Wildhaber & Breitenmoser, The Relationship Between Customary International Law and Municipal Law in Western European Countries, Zeitschrift für ausländisches öffentliches Recht und Völkerrecht, vol. 48, pp. 163, 179-204 (1988).

Introduction to the Study of International Law

Traditionally, international law has been seen as the law of the international community of states, principally governing relations among states, the basic units in the world political system for more than 300 years. For more than half a century, however, international law has increasingly dealt also with other entities, including, notably, the individual as bearer of human rights.

That international law has been understood as the law made by states to govern relations among them implies important limitations. *Unless states have made them the subject of law between them*, non-governmental international organizations—the Catholic Church, the League of Red Cross Societies, the International Chamber of Commerce, the World Federation of Trade Unions—would not be governed by international law. Furthermore, under this theory, international law would not deal directly with multi-national corporations or other companies. It would not address other domestic matters that may be of international interest. International law is to be distinguished from national law that governs foreign and other transnational transactions and relations.

From some perspectives, no doubt, these exclusions are artificial. Some have insisted that contemporary international relations, surely, consist of much more than official relations between states or their governments; that even these relations cannot be understood in isolation from other relations involving other actors; and that the law of inter-governmental relations cannot be seen independently of other law governing other transnational relations. For these reasons, some prefer a more comprehensive perspective that includes all the law—national, international or mixed—that applies to all actors whose activities or influences cross state lines.

Certainly, for more than half a century, international law has governed relations between states and other entities and the status, rights, and duties of such entities. Ever-growing numbers of intergovernmental organizations have acquired existence and personality, rights and duties. By the beginning of the twenty-first century, sustained efforts to subject states to the authority of particular intergovernmental organizations, such as the European Union, have made notable progress. In addition, international law now protects human rights, and even accords individual human beings independent status and standing before some international bodies. International law also imposes duties on individuals and may bring them to international trial and punishment.

For purposes of study and analysis, there are good reasons for maintaining the traditional focus on interstate relations and institutions, even while recognizing that one must attend to all the other rings in the world circus as well. International law is a conceptually distinct and self-contained system of law, independent of the national systems with which it interacts. It deals with relations which individual states do not effectively govern. (The relation of international law to national law is a question with which each of them must struggle, in different ways for their different purposes. See Chapter 3.) The study of international law in the United States (and this volume too) admix some constitutional and other national laws governing the conduct of foreign relations. For example, the treaty-making powers of the President-and-Senate, and limitations on those powers in favor of States' rights or individual rights, are questions of "Foreign Relations Law of the United States" that may have important international interest and even some international legal relevance. But they are not (strictly speaking) questions of international law.

International law is a discrete, comprehensive, legal system and the law of an international political order. While international law is therefore best studied with a minimum of confusing excursions into other, related legal domains, in other respects the study of international law might profit from a broader perspective. The governance and the law of the international political order would repay study with the care and the insights devoted to national law and how national societies are governed. Students of law and jurisprudence, of politics, of sociology, or or ideas, would do well to keep ever in mind that—*mutatis mutandis*—one can, and should, ask the same questions, from the same variety of perspectives, about international law as about domestic law or law generally, though the answers might be very different and even the questions themselves might have different significance. (Feminist analysis, "critical legal studies," and law-and-economics have not overlooked international law.)

International law is not a "course"; it is a curriculum. Whether studied under one embracing rubric or spread over many, international law is a comprehensive, many-sided legal system. One can find in it the basic concepts of any legal system—property and tort, injury and remedy, status and contract. It has its own law-making and law-applying procedures. There is international commerce law and antitrust law, and a law of organizations and corporate bodies. There is law governing "public lands" and common environments, as in outer-space and the deep sea. The "public law" of the international legal system is not yet vast, as was true of the national law of even developed states only a few decades ago; nonetheless, it might well fill several courses in any comprehensive curriculum of international law, including international counterparts of constitutional law, administrative law, legislation, and judicial process. International trade law, the international law of intellectual property, international human rights law, and international environmental law have already earned study in independent courses and in courses combining national and international cases and materials.

Philosophers and other scholars of law can also impose their perspectives and ask their questions about the international legal system. There is a jurisprudence and a sociology of international law, and the beginnings of a criminology. The student of political science can—and should—consider the character of the international political system, its premises and assumptions, and how it is governed; he or she might ask whether there are legislative, executive, and judicial functions, and how they are exercised. He (she) might ask why law is made, and how it is made; whether law is enforced and what mechanisms are used to induce compliance with it; by what institutions is law interpreted, applied, developed; how are disputes settled; what is its system of administration, administrative regulation, law and procedure.

Analogies and nomenclature from domestic law are, of course, deceptive, for there are profound differences between domestic societies and international society (itself a metaphor), and between national and international law. But the concepts, the perspectives, even the nomenclature of domestic law, when used with caution and with awareness of the differences, can be directed at the international system as well. A comprehensive perspective on international law like that which is commonly applied to domestic law can benefit the student of international law.

*

Note on Electronic Technologies and International Law

The revolution in electronic information resources has fundamentally transformed the methods for researching international law, and indeed the very landscape of our subject-matter. As this casebook went to press in 2001, new databases of materials relevant to international law were being created, and "older" databases (which might have been state-of-the-art just a few months before) were being refined, improved, or replaced. These developments have vastly enhanced the accessibility of international legal materials to all interested persons.

It will be important for every student and practitioner of international law to become familiar with the techniques of computer-assisted research that are most up-to-date at the time of the inquiry in question. Yet for the foreseeable future, printed materials must continue to serve as major reference sources; and in the case of many types of materials–particularly of historical character–electronic counterparts do not yet exist. Thus the users of this casebook, especially those who are being introduced to our subject-matter for the first time, are reminded that much of what is central to international law cannot necessarily be found on the Internet or other on-line services.

For the benefit of all users, we have followed the practice of giving citations to frequently-used printed publications, such as standard treaty series, national digests of practice, and case reports. Some of these now have electronic counterparts accessible to Internet users. For example, the website of the United Nations Treaty Office serves as an electronic reference point for the United Nations Treaty Series and for the Status of Multilateral Treaties Maintained by the Secretary-General, which has been issued annually as a printed volume but is now continuously updated as a electronic database. (N.B.: At the time of this writing it was not clear which Internet resources would be continued on the basis of free access, as some providers were moving to a paid-subscriber basis.)

In view of the ephemeral nature of many Internet resources and the quickly-changing landscape of domain names and addresses, we have not found it feasible in this edition to provide references to electronic resources alongside print citations. Nonetheless, we would like users to be aware of some of the entry points for searching on the Internet for materials relevant to our subject. A list of some of the most useful websites as of the present time is provided below.

In compiling the following list, we have been mindful of the transformative potential of the Internet, not only for ease of conducting research, but even for changing our very concept of the subject-matter. With the growing connection of human beings around the globe to the raw materials of international law, it is inevitable that the subject itself will come to seem, and will become, more relevant to everyday life.

Websites are grouped below in a few convenient categories—international and regional institutions, states and governmental bodies, non-governmental organizations and professional societies, and specialized topics. The user, of course, should experiment with all these and many other available possibilities. We hasten to add that the order and grouping of these websites does not imply a hierarchy among them.

Some Useful Websites for Research in International Law

United Nations

- www.un.org

The United Nations website has much primary documentation from the U.N. system and includes a growing section on international law. Treaty documents can be accessed, and links are available to a variety of U.N. organs, including the International Court of Justice, the International Law Commission, the International Tribunal for Law of the Sea, war crimes tribunals, and human rights bodies. U.N. treaty records are available to subscribers and academic libraries at http://untreaty.un.org.

- www.icj-cij.org

The site for the International Court of Justice gives access to the Court's current docket, basic instruments, recent judgments, and transcripts of oral hearings on almost a same-day basis.

- www.unhchr.ch

The site for the U.N. High Commissioner for Human Rights is a convenient entry point to resources on human rights treaties and the work of U.N. organs and treaty implementing bodies.

- www.un.org/icty and www.ictr.org

The International Criminal Tribunals for the Former Yugoslavia and Rwanda provide much information about the workings of these bodies, including indictments, judgments, and reports.

Other Major International Institutions

- www.wto.org

This site contains essential materials about the World Trade Organization, the General Agreement on Tariffs and Trade, and related trade agreements.

- http://www.ilo.org

For information concerning the International Labour Organisation.

- www.imf.org and www.worldbank.org

For the International Monetary Fund and the International Bank for Reconstruction and Development.

Regional Institutions

- http://www.coe.fr

This is the main site for the Council of Europe.

- http://conventions.coe.int/treaty

This site has information about Council of Europe treaties, including the European Convention on Human Rights.

Judgments of the European Court of Human Rights in Strasbourg can be found at http://www.echr.coe.int.

- http://europa.eu.int

For materials on the European Union, with a link to the European Court of Justice at http://curia.eu.int

- http://www.osce.org

The website of the Organization for Security and Co-Operation in Europe.

- http://www.aseansec.org

The Association of South-East Asian Nations (ASEAN)

- www.oas.org

The Organization of American States

- www.oau-oua.org

The Organization of African Unity

States; Governments; Ministries

Many states have websites for their main organs of government, including the foreign ministry. An example is the U.S. Department of State, at www.state.gov. U.S. treaty records can be found at http://www.state.gov/www/global/legal_affairs/tifindex.html, and recent treaty actions through a link from the same site.

Illustrations for official sites in other countries include:

http://www.hmso.gov.uk (Her Majesty's Stationery Office, for government publications in the United Kingdom)

In some countries the national parliament provides electronic access to legislative materials, for example:

- http://www.assemblee-nat.fr

Non-Governmental Organizations; Professional Societies

The American Society of International Law (ASIL) publishes a variety of materials in electronic and/or print form. At the ASIL's website, www.asil.org, a guide to electronic resources is available, and links are provided to many other international sites.

The European Journal of International Law maintains a site at www.ejil.org.

Human rights organizations maintain vigorous networks for electronic communications. A sampling of current human rights sites includes www.hrw.org (Human Rights Watch) and www.lchr.org (Lawyers Committee for Human Rights). Legal information on human rights is maintained at http://diana.law.yale.edu. Resources on women and international law can be accessed through http://www.law-lib.utoronto.ca/diana.

The NGO Coalition for an International Criminal Court maintains an active network at http://www.iccnow.org, with country-by-country information on ratification and implementing legislation for the Rome Statute of the International Criminal Court.

Specialized Topics

Non-governmental organizations will often have wide-ranging electronic references on specialized topics. For example, the website of the International Committee of the Red Cross at www.icrc.org has the texts of scores of humanitarian law treaties and their party status.

Links from the U.N. website or from a specialized agency or institution can also be a good starting point for specialized research. Examples include:

- For disarmament, links from the U.N. home page at www.un.org

- For aviation (including air hijacking and sabotage), the International Civil Aviation Organization at www.icao.int

- For law of the sea, by links from the U.N. home page to www.un.org/Depts/los

- For international environmental law, links from the U.N. home page, and from the United Nations Environment Programme at www.unep.ch

See also the guide to treaties by Simon Canick at http://library.law.columbia.edu/ustreaty/, and the guide to U.N. materials by Silke Sahl at http://library.law.columbia.edu/un.

Historical Introduction*

Human history has long known tribes and peoples, inhabiting defined territories, governed by chiefs or princes, and interacting with each other in a manner requiring primitive forms of diplomatic relations and covenants of peace or alliances for war. These relations between peoples or princes, however, were not governed by any agreed, authoritative principles or rules. At various times, moreover, most of the peoples of the known world were part of large empires; and relations between them were subject to an imperial, "domestic" government and law. Empire, actual or potential, was also sometimes supported by an ideology that claimed universal authority over all peoples, or otherwise rejected the independence and equality of nations or any principles governing relations between them other than imperial law.

Thus, classical Chinese philosophy, as formulated by Confucius in the 6th Century, B.C., regarded the ruler of China as the "Son of Heaven," who governs the universe as a righteous ruler. From this conception—often greatly at variance with the division of China into many rival kingdoms and factions—developed a notion that frequently shaped Chinese attitudes toward international relations: that Chinese rulers were culturally superior "fathers" or "elder brothers" of other nations or states. This notion served to legitimate Chinese conquest and subjugation of others.

Similarly, Islam, like Christianity in its formative phase, was a crusading religion and therefore hostile to recognizing the equality and respecting the integrity of non-Islamic nations. For the Moslem jurists, the world was divided into countries under Moslem rule (*dar al Islam*) and the rest of the world (*dar al Harb*).

In medieval Christianity, the Holy Roman Empire claimed universal authority for the Pope as the spiritual, and for the Emperor as the temporal, head of the Christian nations of Europe. Thus, religious and political goals coalesced to legitimatize European efforts to conquer—and then convert—non-Christian peoples around the world. Even among the nations of Europe, as long as the concept of universal authority was ascendant, there was little need to develop rules concerning diplomatic intercourse between sovereign states, principles of territorial sovereignty, jurisdiction, treaty-making, state responsibility, and other aspects of interstate relations that form the bulk of the modern law of nations.

Ancient Judaism, ideologically committed to monotheism, did not in principle accept the equality of polytheistic nations. But Judaism has not been the ideology of a politically independent people for 2000 years until our own day, and Judaism did not develop a universalist political ideology comparable to that of Christianity or Islam.

* See generally Nussbaum, A Concise History of the Law of Nations (rev. ed. 1954); Verzijl, et al., International Law in Historical Perspective, 11 vols. (1968–1992); History of the Law of Nations, 7 Encyclopedia of Public International Law 126–273 (1984). Compare also Onuma, When Was the Law of International Society Born? An Inquiry of the History of International Law from an Intercivilizational Perspective, 2 J.Hist. Int'l L. 1–66 (2000).

Universalist ideologies and approaches to international relations were modified in recent centuries. Nation-states of different religions increasingly came into contact with each other and were compelled to deal with each other on a basis of equality and mutual respect for sovereignty. The structure and development of the modern law of nations is intimately connected with the era of sovereign national states dealing with each other as independent units. In a strict sense, therefore, the history of the modern law of nations begins with the emergence of independent nation-states from the ruins of the medieval Holy Roman Empire, and is commonly dated from the Peace of Westphalia (1648).

Origins of International Law in the Western World before Grotius

Before the Macedonian conquest, the Greek states never achieved unity; they alternated between peace and war. As a result, the Greeks, in their classical period, developed rules governing relations between the various Greek city-states, rules that more closely parallel the modern system of international law than those of any other early civilization. Any reader of Thucydides' *History of the Peloponnesian War* will detect a modern ring in the reasoning and techniques used by the Greek city-states in diplomatic practices, in treaties of alliance and in certain elementary rules of war. Disputes were sometimes submitted to arbitration. However, relations between Greeks and non-Greeks were not regulated in the same way; the latter were regarded by the Greeks as barbarians, and not as moral or legal equals.

The Roman Empire, which at its height comprised hundreds of different races, tribes and religions, could not acknowledge an international legal system in the modern sense, within the borders of an empire that comprised almost the entire civilized world. Although there were always wars at the borders of the Roman Empire, they gave rise to very few rules or usages. The significance of the Roman contribution to international law lies not in the development of any modern system of interstate legal relations, but rather in the development of *jus gentium*, a system of legal rules governing the relations between Roman citizens and foreigners. The *jus gentium* contained many principles of general equity and "natural law," some of which are similar to certain "general principles of law recognized by civilized nations"—one of the sources of contemporary international law listed in Article 38 of the Statute of the International Court of Justice. But the *jus gentium* was strictly a municipal system of law administered by a Roman magistrate, the *Praetor peregrinus*, as a system parallel to the *jus civile* applicable to relations between Roman citizens.

The Rise of the National State and the Evolution of International Law

As the medieval Holy Roman Empire disintegrated, the void was filled by a growing number of separate states, ranging from large nation-states such as England and France to hundreds of smaller kingdoms, dukedoms, principalities and city republics, especially in Germany and Italy. This multiplicity of independent political units spurred the development of a system of interstate relations.

Frederick III, German emperor from 1440 to 1493, was the last of the emperors crowned in Rome by the Pope, but at that time Europe was already divided into a large number of independent states. The collapse of the political, legal and moral authority of the emperors, and the weakening of the ecclesiastical authority of the Pope—greatly accelerated by the Reformation—made it necessary for the newly emerging independent states to develop a system of rules that could govern their mutual relations. For these legal relations, they drew predominantly upon Roman law and canon law. The professional clerks who ran the chancelleries of the newly emerging states and city republics received their training largely in universities such as Bologna, Padua or Paris, where the Renaissance had revived the study of classical civilization and, in particular, the study of Roman law. The system of the Roman law, as codified in Justinian's *Corpus Juris*, dominated the teaching of the so-called "Glossators" at these universities. Justinian's code thus spread its influence over the entire European continent, except for the Scandinavian countries. England remained largely free from the influence of Roman law both in the structure and in the substantive principles of its legal system. Although the legal systems of most of the states of continental Europe were progressively codified and modernized during the 19th and 20th centuries, they are still heavily influenced by Roman law. Some concepts of Roman law have strongly influenced international legal rules, such as those governing the acquisition of title over territory.

However, the division between the civil law world—comprising most of continental Europe, and a large number of non-European states—and the English-speaking, common law world is of relatively little significance in international legal relations. In the first place, canon law, with its essentially Romanistic conceptual framework, had an important influence on many aspects of English law. Second, the growth of international trade from the 8th century onwards led to the development of an international law merchant and, in particular, to various compilations of maritime law which gained increasing international recognition. The most famous of these are the Rhodian laws, a collection of maritime laws probably compiled between the 7th and 9th centuries, and the *Consolato del Mare,* a private collection of rules and customs of maritime law published in Barcelona during the 14th century.

The Foundations of the Modern Law of Nations

The several centuries that preceded the Thirty Years' War (1618–1648) were marked in Europe by an intensification of international trade, improvements in navigation and military techniques, and the discovery of many distant lands. These events stimulated the further development of international practices and the emergence of modern conceptions of a law of nations. In northern Europe, the Hanseatic League, founded in the 13th century by certain German city-states and comprising at its height in the early 15th century over 150 trading cities and centers, established a network of commercial and diplomatic relations which contributed substantially to the growth of international usages and customs. In Italy, city-republics, such as Venice, Genoa and Florence, developed the practice of sending resident ambassadors to the capitals of other states, thus giving rise to legal principles governing diplomatic relations and, in particular, the immunities of ambassadors and their staffs. The growth of trade led to an increasing number of commercial treaties. The discovery and subjugation of distant lands and peoples by European explorers and conquerors produced conflicting claims of sovereignty, jurisdiction and rights of trade and navigation, as well as problems of relations with indigenous populations. These difficulties stimulated juristic thought, encouraged resort to Roman law for helpful norms or analogies, and ultimately led to new practices and principles.

By the beginning of the 17th century, the growing complexity of international customs and treaties had given rise to a need for compilation and systematization. At the same time, the growing disorders and sufferings of war, especially of the Thirty Years' War, which laid waste hundreds of towns and villages and inflicted great suffering and privation on peasants and city dwellers, urgently called for some further rules governing the conduct of war. The preoccupation with war is demonstrated by the titles of the two most important treatises of the period: the De Jure Belli Libri Tres (*De Jure Belli*) (1598) by Alberico Gentili (1552–1608), the Italian-born Professor of Civil Law at Oxford, and the classic treatise of Hugo Grotius, De Jure Belli Ac Pacis Libri Tres (*De Jure Belli Ac Pacis*) (1623–1624), which is generally regarded as the foundation of modern international law.

Although the relative importance of the laws of war and the laws of peace has greatly shifted since the time of Grotius, the latter being by far the more important part of the contemporary law of nations, the importance of these classical treatises, and others, lay in their attempts to systematize the growing number of customs, usages and state practices that had developed over the previous centuries. The details of their systems are not of much contemporary importance, except for the history of international law. However, it is of interest and not without importance or reward to survey the basic ideas underlying the evolution of international law, and of the principal phases of development from the time of Grotius to the present.

Natural Law Philosophy and the Principles of International Law

Hugo Grotius (1583–1645), a Dutch jurist, historian, theologian and diplomat, who for the last ten years of his life was the ambassador of Sweden in Paris, is the best known of an important school of international jurists guided by the philosophy of natural law. Among his predecessors in this approach are the Spanish theologians Francisco de Vitoria (probably 1486–1546) and Francisco Suárez (1548–1617). The most important of the later natural law philosophers in international law is the German, Samuel Pufendorf (1632–1694), who occupied a chair for the law of nature and nations at the University of Heidelberg and whose most important work is *De Jure Naturae et Gentium* (1672). Vitoria and Suárez closely follow the natural law philosophy of St. Thomas Aquinas (1225–1274). Aquinas believed that all human laws derive from, and are subordinate to, the law of God. This law is partly reflected in the law of nature, a body of permanent principles grounded in the Divine Order, and partly revealed in the Scripture. By contrast, Grotius is a rationalist who derives the principles of the law of nature from universal reason rather than from divine authority.

Natural law adherents have been divided, throughout the ages, over the positive meaning of the laws of nature in the world of human institutions and actions. Two of the most important principles of the law of nature in Grotius' system of the law of nations are (1) that restitution must be made for a harm done by one party to another and, (2) that promises given, through signature to treaties or otherwise, must be kept (*pacta sunt servanda*). These two principles have been preserved and developed—though with many variations and modifications—throughout subsequent phases of international law, even without the doctrinal support of natural law philosophy. Another basic principle of natural law for Grotius is the freedom of the seas, a thesis expounded in an early work published in 1609, *Mare Liberum*. On this issue, he was strongly opposed by the Englishman John Selden (1584–1645), who in 1635 published a defense of the closed sea: Mare Clausum Sive De Dominio Maris (*Mare Clausum*). The opposing theses illustrate the difficulties of agreement on the concrete applications of natural law where opposing political, economic or social interests are involved. The rejection of the freedom of the seas by Selden corresponded to the interests of England, at that time navally inferior to Holland. The work of Grotius served to vindicate the interests of the Netherlands as a rising maritime and colonial power not only against England, but also against Spain and Portugal, states which claimed the right to control navigation on distant oceans and trade with the East Indies. Later, when England became dominant at sea, it also became an ardent champion of the freedom of the seas—at least in times of peace.[1]

The Turn to Positivism

No less important than the emphasis on the law of nature as a basis of the law of nations, is the distinction made by Grotius between the *jus naturale*—to which Grotius devotes his main attention—and the *jus gentium*, the customary law of nations (also called *jus voluntarium*, i.e., a body of law formed by the conduct and will of nations).

This latter aspect of the law of nations gained increasing significance as adherence to natural law philosophy declined and positivist philosophy gained. Although positivism has a number of different meanings and nuances,[2] its essential meaning in the theory and development of international law is reliance on the practice of states and the conduct of international relations as evidenced by customs or treaties, as against the derivation of norms from basic metaphysical principles. The rise of positivism in Western political and legal theory, especially from the latter part of the 18th century to the early part of the 20th century, corresponds to the steady rise of the national state and its increasingly absolute claims to legal and political supremacy. In the theory of the law of nations the shift from natural law to positivism came gradually, through increasing emphasis on the voluntary law of nations built up by state practice and custom. The most influential exponents of this turn toward positivism were the Englishman Richard Zouche (1590–1660), Professor of Civil Law at Oxford and a Judge of the Admiralty Court, and the Swiss lawyer Emerich de Vattel (1714–1767). Zouche's work, *Juris et Iudicii Fecialis, sive Juris inter Gentes* (1650), has been called the first manual of international law. Without denying the existence of the law of nature, it emphasizes the customary law of nations which he calls *jus inter gentes*. The relegation of natural law to a secondary position is made explicit by Vattel, whose treatise dominated the philosophy of international law from the middle of the 18th century to the end of the First World War. Vattel's treatise, *Le Droit des Gens, ou Principes de la Loi Naturelle, appliqués à la Conduite et aux Affaires des Nations et des Souverains* (1758), although including the *principes de la loi naturelle* in the title, distinguishes between the internal law of nations (law of conscience) and the external law (law of action). While Vattel acknowledges natural law with the assertion that "the law of nations is originally no other than the law of nature applied to nations," he considers all effective international law to have been

1. In times of war, belligerent naval powers—like Britain in the two world wars of this century—sought to restrict the freedom of the seas, especially neutral trade, to the utmost. Neutral powers stressed the freedom of the seas.

2. See Friedmann, Legal Theory, ch. 21 (5th ed. 1967).

derived from the will of nations, a presumed consent expressing itself in treaties or customs.

There is an interesting parallel between this theory and Hindu doctrine which distinguishes between *dharmasastras* (principles of right conduct) and *arthasastras* (manuals of international politics). The former corresponds to Vattel's "law of conscience" and the latter to his "law of action." As an Indian scholar has observed, "Hindu conditions presented a comparable picture to that of modern international law." [3] This approach to international law, in part foreshadowed by the German philosopher, Christian Wolff (1679–1754), in effect expresses the philosophy of the modern national state, which recognizes no international obligations other than those to which it has voluntarily agreed through practice hardening into custom, or through specific written consent expressed in treaties or other international agreements.[4]

The period between the publication of Vattel's treatise and the outbreak of the first World War in 1914 was one of phenomenal growth of international law as the diplomatic and commercial relations between nations—almost all of which were Western—multiplied and intensified. The physical volume of international law increased through a continuous growth of custom and treaties, and very few writers continued to assert the supremacy of the law of nature. The bulk of legal and political theory discussed the sovereignty of the state. It was impossible to justify international law under the state sovereignty theory, except as norms voluntarily accepted by sovereign states. Among the best known treatises reconciling the validity of international law with the concept of sovereignty are those of Georg Jellinek (1851–1911), *Allgemeine Rechtslehre* (1905), Heinrich Triepel (1868–1946), *Völkerrecht und Landesrecht* (1899), and Giorgio del Vecchio (1878–1970), *Lezioni di Filosofia del Diritto* (1929). These writers of the early 20th century sought to reconcile the sovereignty of the state with the binding nature of international law in a number of ways: by developing a doctrine of "self-limitation" of the state (Jellinek); by merging agreements made by states into an objective body of conventions which then becomes binding upon states (Triepel); or by halfheartedly reviving the natural law principle that reason demands the mutual recognition of states as equals (del Vecchio). Other positivists rejected this compromise. The English jurist, John Austin (1790–1859), whose *Province of Jurisprudence Determined* (1832) dominated jurisprudential thinking in the common law world in the 19th century, regarded a command emanating from a definite superior and punitive sanction enforcing the command as indispensable elements of law. He therefore relegated international law to the status of "positive morality." On the other hand, ideological approaches to international law were dominated by nationalist philosophy. The most influential of the nationalist philosophers, the German Georg Wilhelm Friedrich Hegel (1770–1831), in his *Philosophy of Law and State*, constructed an elaborate dialectic system, culminating in the glorification of the national (monarchic) state and denying the validity of international law (for which he substituted "The Passing of the State into World History").

3. Chacko, India's Contribution to the Field of International Law Concepts, [1958] 93 Rec. des Cours. 122.

4. Among other eighteenth century exponents of the positivist philosophy of international law are the Dutch jurist, Cornelius van Bynkershoek (1673–1743), the German jurist, Johann Jakob Moser (1701–1785), and George Friedrich von Martens (1756–1821).

From a different point of departure, Marxist doctrine challenged the national state and its legal system as an instrument of exploitation of the working class by the capitalist bourgeoisie, and called for revolution by the working classes of the world. This, of course, was incompatible with the structure of the law of nations, built on a system of sovereign national states. This philosophy influenced Soviet Communism and was proclaimed by Maoist China, but ceased to be heard in the last half of the 20th century, long before the demise of Soviet Communism.

The League of Nations and the Evolution of International Law

The most important aspect of the era of positivism and the supremacy of the national state was the freedom of the state to choose between war and peace. The Hague and Geneva Conventions of the 20th century formulated a number of rules of conduct in warfare, as distinct from principles governing the rightness or wrongness of war. Any state had the legal right to pursue its aims by means of war. This freedom meant the denial of any legally relevant distinction between just and unjust wars. A major break in this orientation came with the establishment of the League of Nations following the First World War.

In condemning "external aggression" against "the territorial integrity and existing political independence" of League members, and in providing for economic and even military sanctions to be imposed by the international community against a state violating its obligations, the League Covenant limited the legal freedom of the sovereign state to pursue war as the ultimate instrument of national policy.

The era of the League of Nations, i.e., the interwar period, was marked by another significant departure in the development of international law. The constitution of the International Labour Organisation (ILO), in association with the League of Nations, signals the end of an era in which international law was, with few exceptions, confined to the regulation of relations between the states. The ILO was the first permanent international organization concerned with the improvement of labor conditions and social welfare on a world-wide scale. At the same time the establishment of the Permanent Court of International Justice—a counterpart to the limitation on the unrestricted right of states to seek solutions to international disputes by force—was a major attempt to substitute organic methods of peaceful and legal settlement of disputes for the use of force in international affairs. Parallel to the establishment of the Permanent Court, there was a significant growth in the number of bilateral treaties requiring arbitration and other methods of peaceful settlement for disputes between states.

The noble attempt to substitute international authority for national use of force collapsed because of inadequate support from the major nations in times of crises—notably on the occasion of the Italian invasion of Abyssinia (Ethiopia) in 1935. The efforts of the ILO to achieve international standards for labor and social welfare remained severely limited by continuing divergencies in national standards. The Permanent Court of International Justice played only a marginal role in the affairs of the nations. But the world did not return to the pre-1914 state of affairs after the Second World War. It did not return to a system in which international law included no control in the use of force; nor did it abandon its halting efforts to develop an international organization of mankind for purposes of cooperation. The interwar period also brought the first major threat to the universality of the system of international law, as it had gradually developed since the time of Grotius. The original family of nations, consisting of the older European states, was, at the end of the 18th century, enlarged by the accession of the United States and, a few decades later, by the newly independent states of Latin America. Only a small number of relatively impotent non-Western states joined the family of nations. With the success of the Bolshevik Revolution and the establishment of the Soviet Union, differences of political and social ideology began to challenge the universality of the system in international law. The Soviet Union established itself essentially within the confines of the old Russia as a single major state with a radically different political and social philosophy, but it was compelled to co-exist with other states. To that extent, the Soviet challenge to the traditional system of international law was mitigated. In fact, it was the aggression-minded, fascist states of Germany, Italy and Japan that left the League of Nations and challenged the whole system of international law more immediately than did the Soviet Union.

The impact of ideological and other structural divergencies between states on the universality of the law of nations was to become a matter of major importance in the reorganization and development of international law following the end of World War II.

International Law since the Second World War

The creation of the United Nations Organization was a major development in the international political system, although the attempt in the United Nations Charter to reintroduce a system of collective security against aggression was, historically and ideologically, essentially a resumption of the League of Nations effort. However, three major developments following the end of the Second World War signaled a new departure in the evolution of international law. The first was the massive expansion of international organization for cooperative purposes, of which the ILO had been a forerunner. The United Nations, its specialized agencies and other international organizations, some on a universal and others on a regional level, marked the transition of international law from the traditional system of formal rules of mutual respect and abstention to an incipient system of organized, cooperative efforts. Organizations were formed to address a broad range of ills plaguing the world community. Most of these organizations lack executive powers and make only limited encroachments upon the traditional prerogatives of national sovereignty, but their creation confirmed a new pattern of international conduct. Their concerns include international peace and security; monetary control; international development aid; food production and distribution; universal standards of health; international communication and transport; protection of the environment; outer space and the ocean bed; and the international promotion and protection of human rights. This new phase has reflected the needs of an international society where ready communication and increased interdependence, the threat of nuclear annihilation, the growth of population and the increasing threat of exhaustion of the resources of the earth no longer permit an international attitude of laissez-faire. Consequently, international law is no longer predominantly a system of interstate diplomatic norms. It has deeply penetrated the economic and social fabrics of national life.

A second development has been the growing importance of states representing non-Western civilizations as members of the family of nations. This second major development raised the question of the compatibility of the basic cultural values and institutions of these non-Western societies with the system of international law developed by a relatively small group of Western nations. The experience with the new states of Asia and Africa has shown that this development did not fundamentally affect the system of interstate relations. Since their accession to United Nations membership, states such as India (with a long Hindu cultural tradition), Indonesia (with a Moslem background) and the new African nations (most of them emerging from tribal societies), have not adopted attitudes toward interstate relations that differ basically from the traditional attitudes of Western countries. The new states have generally accepted the traditional norms of customary law, participated in international treaties and joined a variety of international organizations. For new states, the necessity of collaboration—to face the problems of statehood and sovereignty in a divided world, the issues of war and peace, the conflicts of political and economic aspirations and the tensions between competition and cooperation in the affairs of mankind—prevailed over the diversity of cultural traditions.

The third development has been the growing gap between the economically developed and the economically less developed countries. It resulted in the creation of new types of international organization specifically designed to deal with the problems arising from the co-existence of rich and poor nations. Included among such bodies are the International Bank for Reconstruction and Development, the International Monetary Fund, and the United Nations Conference on Trade and Development (UNCTAD). The division between developed and less-developed states intensified challenges to certain norms of international law developed by the economically advanced and capital-exporting states of the West, notably for the protection of the economic interests of foreign investors. It created the demands for a New International Economic Order. It led to new arrangements in international law favored by Third World States—such as key elements in a new law of the sea; and for some forms of cooperation for economic development. But the Third World has not succeeded in obtaining significant steps towards a new international economic order. Insufficient commitment by the states of the Third World, and the competition for their favor by East and West, had the unhappy effect of politicizing and hampering various international programs—as in the protection of human rights. They have given to some Third World states some protection for violations of international law, such as acts of aggression against neighbors, or harboring hijackers or other terrorists.

Even in a divided world living in the ever-present shadow of possible nuclear destruction, the dramatic increase in the number of new states and the appearance of many problems in the economic and the social spheres have accounted for many important new developments in international law, and greatly increased both its scope and complexity. But in a larger historical context this is the continuation and intensification of an evolution that has accompanied the entire history of international law. Many norms of international law, such as the freedom of the seas, the extent of territorial waters and the principles of state responsibility, have always been the product of an adjustment between conflicting national interests.

Perhaps the most significant development of the post-war period, the addition of a new field of international cooperation and organization to the traditional system of the law of nations, has not fulfilled all its promises. But the law of nations has passed from the phase in which it was primarily an international law of co-existence—which characterized it from its birth in the early 17th century to mid-twentieth century—to a phase in which the nations of the world must develop new forms of cooperation and organization to supplement the traditional rules of interstate relations.

International Law after the Cold War

During more than four decades following the end of the Second World War, international law reflected and was shaped by ideological conflict and Cold War between nuclear superpowers, as well as the end of colonialism, the multiplication of new nations, and the emergence of the "Third World." Ideological conflict, together with divergent interests between developed and developing states ("North and South"), hampered the growth of international law and frustrated the development of international institutions—notably the United Nations Security Council and the International Court of Justice. Traditional approaches to international law were maintained, uncomfortably, alongside special attitudes of the Soviet Union, Communist China, and groupings of the "new states." New developments in the law, such as the birth of the law of human rights, had to "paper over" fundamental differences; institutions to induce compliance with the law were reduced to a very low common denominator.

However, the end of the Cold War, the demise of international Communism, the dissolution of the Soviet Empire and the fragmentation of the Soviet Union itself, have led to a radically changed world order with new opportunities and challenges for international law. Recent times have seen the law of collective security and the authority of the U.N. Security Council revisited, revived and extended. Civil wars and ethnic hostilities suggest the need to reexamine the traditional conceptions of state sovereignty and to enlarge the scope of permissible collective intervention for humanitarian assistance and protection of human rights. Political change has revived aspirations for the International Court of Justice; while alongside that venerable body, a whole constellation of new tribunals has increasingly significant jurisdiction. New needs and new perceptions have enhanced efforts to develop new norms and new institutions to protect the global environment and to reorder economic relations. Regional arrangements that once responded in part to East-West rivalry have broadened their membership and created new functions, as seen in the Organization for Security and Cooperation in Europe (OSCE) and the North Atlantic Treaty Organization (NATO). The European Community has become the European Union and continues its quest for political integration.

At the opening of the twenty-first century, the problems facing the international community are many and acute. If there is political will, if cooperation among states is pursued, new international law will surely be made in the decades ahead, as an essential tool to give effect to new solutions to new and old human problems.

Summary of Contents

Table of Contents

Table of Cases

The principal cases are in bold type. Cases cited or discussed in the text are roman type. References are to pages. Cases cited in principal cases and within other quoted materials are not included.

*

INTERNATIONAL LAW

CASES AND MATERIALS

Fourth Edition

*

Chapter 1

THE NATURE OF INTERNATIONAL LAW

SECTION 1. THE LAW OF THE INTERNATIONAL POLITICAL SYSTEM

A. INTRODUCTION: LAW AND POLITICS

HENKIN, INTERNATIONAL LAW: POLITICS AND VALUES

4–5 (1995) (footnotes omitted).

First, law is politics. Students of law as well as students of politics are taught to distinguish law from politics. Law is normative and binding, and failure to abide by legal obligations invites legal remedies and brings other legal responses; politics suggests freedom of choice, diplomacy, bargaining, accommodation. In fact, however, the distinction between law and politics is only a part-truth. In a larger, deeper sense, law *is* politics. Law is made by political actors, through political procedures, for political ends. The law that emerges is the resultant of political forces; the influences of law on state behaviour are also determined by political forces.

* * *

International law is the normative expression of a political system. To appreciate the character of international law and its relation to the international political system, it is helpful to invoke (though with caution) domestic law as an analogue. Domestic (national) law, such as the law of the Netherlands, of the United States, or of Nigeria, is an expression of a domestic political system in a domestic (national) society. A domestic society consists of people, human beings, though in developed societies law has also created artificial juristic persons (e.g., companies, associations). Domestic law is a construct of norms, standards, principles, institutions and procedures that serve the purposes of the society. Law serves, notably, to establish and maintain order and enhance the reliability of expectations; to protect persons, their property and other interests; to promote the welfare of individuals (or of some of them), and to further other societal values—justice, the good life, the good society.

Similarly, analogously, international law is the product of its particular "society," its political system. International law, too, is a construct of norms, standards, principles, institutions and procedures. The purposes of international law, like those of domestic law, are to establish and maintain order and enhance reliable expectations, to protect "persons," their property and other interests, to further other values. But the constituency of the international society is different. The "persons" constituting international society are not individual human beings but political entities, "states," and the society is an inter-state system, a system of states.

Notes

1. In this lecture, delivered in 1989, Henkin described the international political system, flatly, as "an inter-State system, a system of States". In the new century his characterization of the system might be somewhat less flat. (Even in his 1989 lecture, Henkin described the international polity as having "States as its basic constituent entities"—basic, but perhaps not exclusive.)

2. The new century is welcomed by a political system of nearly 200 states, but other actors have become prominent and have clearly diluted the impression of state exclusivity. Particularly in the age of globalization (p. 9 below), multinational companies have multiplied and grown in power and influence, have presented a challenge to state exclusivity and "sovereignty" (pp. 3–8 below), have earned a place in the process of making international law, and have influenced the subject matter and content of the law, and the means of implementing and enforcing law. Non-governmental organizations (NGOs) have joined the process of promoting and implementing law in various fields, notably human rights. Individuals also have attained a status where they may enjoy rights and incur some responsibilities directly under international law, rather than indirectly through states. See Chapter 6. But states remain "basic constituent entities" and international law continues to be described and characterized as the law of "the state system," "inter-state" law, long ago renamed "international" law.

B. THE INTERNATIONAL SYSTEM AND THE CHANGING DIMENSIONS OF SOVEREIGNTY

Any inquiry into the character and development of international law must take into account the character of international society and of the law at given times. In the international system of states, as in domestic counterparts, politics will turn to law to achieve desired ends and to promote the values of its members. Different actors, faced with different problems at different times, may desire different objectives; and both politics and the law will differ as well. To cite several examples, both law and society looked different after the Peace of Westphalia established the modern secular state and the society of such states; after the birth of international institutions, mostly since 1918; after the United Nations Charter and the advent of nuclear weapons; after the end of colonialism and the consequent proliferation of nation-states; after globalization and a revised world order, and with increasing resort to international "humanitarian intervention" at the turn of the millennium. International society (and international law) looked different during the Cold War and after it ended.

One value common to international and domestic systems throughout political history has been maintaining orderly relations among members. International law fosters the security and autonomy of states, paramount values in a "liberal" system of states; to that end, the law prohibits the threat or use of force by any state against the territorial integrity or political independence of any other state. Increasingly, the law has pursued those values through intergovernmental organizations and collective action. International institutions and collective action are instruments also for enhancing cooperation in areas of interdependence such as international environmental protection and in trade, finance, and other economic matters. For more than a half of a century, the international system has shown commitment to values that transcend purely "state values," notably to human rights, and has developed an impressive corpus of international human rights law. These changing values and new means for promoting them inevitably influence the traditional axioms and assumptions of the state system. Most notably, the concept of state "sovereignty", which was commonly noted as an implicit, axiomatic characteristic of statehood, has been increasingly challenged as outdated and exaggerated.

States and their "sovereignty"

An international (inter-state) system assumes a conception and a definition of a state; the Peace of Westphalia (1648) confirmed that conception. What is a state, and which entities having which characteristics are properly seen as states, have normally not been matters of doubt or of dispute. Other states knew a state when they "saw" and dealt with it (more precisely, when they dealt with the government that represents the state). Extraordinarily, definitions of a state and an articulation of its characteristics become a matter of political interest and controversy. See Chapter 4.

It has been an assumption of the international political system that states are "sovereign," though there was sometimes confusion as to whether sovereignty was a characteristic, an implication, a consequence, or a definition of statehood. If an entity was a state, as defined, it had the attributes of "sovereignty." Or, if a state had the characteristics that define a state (a defined territory, a government in control, a permanent population, the capacity to participate in diplomatic relations—see Chapter 4), it had the resultant attributes of statehood, principally those subsumed in "sovereignty."

Increasingly, however, the scope and significance, and the values, of state sovereignty have come into question. Challenges to the concept of sovereignty became common a half-century ago but it has been insisted on by states and their governments and was defended by eminent authority. In recent years, with globalization, the world market, cyberspace, and the human rights movement, the challenges have grown more frequent and more insistent.

CORFU CHANNEL CASE (UNITED KINGDOM v. ALBANIA)

(INDIVIDUAL OPINION BY JUDGE ALVAREZ)

International Court of Justice, 1949.
1949 I.C.J. 39, 43.

By sovereignty, we understand the whole body of rights and attributes which a State possesses in its territory, to the exclusion of all other States, and also in its relations with other States.

Sovereignty confers rights upon States and imposes obligations on them. * * *

Some jurists have proposed to abolish the notion of the sovereignty of States, considering it obsolete. That is an error. This notion has its foundation in national sentiment and in the psychology of the peoples, in fact it is very deeply rooted. The constituent instrument of the International Organization [the United Nations Charter] has especially recognized the sovereignty of States and has endeavored to bring it into harmony with the objects of that Organization (No. 1 of Art. 2).

This notion has evolved, and we must now adopt a conception of it which will be in harmony with the new conditions of social life. We can no longer regard sovereignty as an absolute and individual right of every State, as used to be done under the old law founded on the individualist regime, according to which States were only bound by the rules which they had accepted. Today, owing to social interdependence and to the predominance of the general interest, the States are bound by many rules which have not been ordered by their will. The sovereignty of States has now become an *institution,* an *international social function* of a psychological character, which has to be exercised in accordance with the new international law.

HENKIN, INTERNATIONAL LAW: POLITICS AND VALUES

8–11 (1995) (some footnotes omitted).

States are commonly described as "sovereign," and "sovereignty" is commonly noted as an implicit, axiomatic characteristic of statehood. The pervasiveness of that term is unfortunate, rooted in mistake, unfortunate mistake. Sovereignty is a bad word, not only because it has served terrible national mythologies; in international relations, and even in international law, it is often a catchword, a substitute for thinking and precision. It means many things, some essential, some insignificant; some agreed, some controversial; some that are not warranted and should not be accepted. Once there was serious debate as to whether there is, or should be, a law of nations since, it was argued, a sovereign state cannot be subject to any other authority, even to agreements of its own making or to law which it helped make or to which it consented. If today such arguments are no longer heard, states continue to argue that certain kinds of law or agreements, certain kinds of institutions, are impossible or inappropriate for "sovereign states," inconsistent with their sovereignty.*

* * *

For legal purposes at least, we might do well to relegate the term sovereignty to the shelf of history as a relic from an earlier era. To this end, it is necessary to analyze, "decompose," the concept; to identify the elements that have been deemed to be inherent in, or to derive from, "sovereignty"; and to determine which of them are appropriate and desirable for a "state" in a system of states at the turn of the twenty-first century. As applied to a state, elements long identified with "sovereignty" are inevitably only metaphors, fictions, fictions upon fictions; some of them, however, do constitute essential characteristics and indicia of statehood today. These include principally: independence, equality, autonomy, "personhood," territorial authority, integrity and inviolability, impermeability and "privacy."

* * *

The essential quality of statehood in a state system is the autonomy of each state. State autonomy suggests that a state is not subject to any external authority unless it has voluntarily consented to such authority. The state has a "will," moral authority, the power to consent, to enter into relations, to conclude agreements, to form associations. By their ability to consent, to have relations and conclude agreements, states have in effect created the international political system, by a kind of "social contract." By their ability to consent to external authority and to conclude agreements, they have created norms and institutions to govern these relations, the international law of the system. Only states can make law for the system but nothing suggests that they can make law only for themselves. States can make law for entities they create (e.g. international organizations), for entities created by individual states (e.g. companies), and for human individuals.

ALLOTT, EUNOMIA: NEW ORDER FOR A NEW WORLD

416–419 (1990).

20.18 Through the idea and ideal of democracy and through actual experience in the reality-forming of actual societies, sovereignty was socialized. It became possible to recognize that society, including its legal subsystem, was a self-willed ordering, in which the self-creating of the members of society and the self-creating of society could be reconciled.

* * *

20.20 International Society had to find its own theory. It chose to see itself as a collection of state-societies turned inside-out, like a glove. It chose to be an unsocial society creating itself separately from the development of its

* States sometimes dare even to invoke their "sovereignty" to preclude scrutiny and judgment when they are charged with violating international law and their international obligations, notably in respect of human rights. * * *

The banner of "sovereignty" also continues to frustrate the system in smaller but significant ways. For example, the International Court of Justice continues to struggle with inadequate * * * procedures because to modernize them even in modest respects, such as imposing limitations on the number of pages in a memorial or on the number of hours of oral argument, would be unthinkable since the parties are "sovereign states."

subordinate societies, ignoring the idea and the ideal of democracy, depriving itself of the possibility of using social power, especially legal relations, to bring about the survival and prospering of the whole human race.

* * *

20.21 There is no reason why international society should not reconceive itself as a society, using social power, and especially legal relations, to bring about the survival and prospering of the whole human race.

* * *

20.22 * * * International society is a self-ordering of the whole human race and of all subordinate societies. In the non-social, undemocratized and unsocialized, international society, self-ordering has taken aberrant forms. Force and the threat of force have been used as substitutes for self-ordering. The social process has been a stunted process of interaction between the public realms of state-societies, so-called international relations conducted through a vestigial will-forming system called diplomacy.

* * *

20.24 International law has been the primitive law of an unsocial international society. Itself a by-product of that unsocialization, it has contributed to holding back the development of international society as society. Failing to recognize itself as a society, international society has not known that it has a constitution. Not knowing its own constitution, it has ignored the generic principles of a constitution.

20.25 In an international society which knows itself as a society, state-societies have no natural and inherent and unlimited powers. Like any other of the myriad societies of international society, they have only the legal relations, including powers and obligations, conferred by the international constitution and by international law. Their particular status is as constitutional organs of international society, having special responsibility for the organization of its public realms, including the public realms of their own societies.

20.26 State-societies, like all other members of international society, have social power, including legal power, to serve the purposes of international society, to will and act for its survival and prospering, that is to say, for the survival and prospering of the whole human race. They are socially and legally accountable for the exercise of their powers and the carrying out of their obligations. Non-statal societies, including industrial and commercial and financial enterprises of all kinds, exercise social power and carry out obligations on the same conditions.

20.27 The new international law will be as dynamic and as rich as the law of any subordinate society, organizing human willing and acting in every field which concerns the survival and prospering of the society of which it is the law.

Notes

1. In his annual speech to the U.N. General Assembly, September 20, 1999, Secretary–General Kofi Annan said:

> State sovereignty, in its most basic sense, is being redefined by the forces of globalization and international cooperation.
>
> The State is now widely understood to be the servant of its people, and not vice versa. At the same time, individual sovereignty–and by this I mean the human rights and fundamental freedoms of each and every individual as enshrined in our Charter–has been enhanced by a renewed consciousness of the right of every individual to control his or her own destiny.
>
> * * *
>
> The Charter is a living document, whose high principles still define the aspirations of peoples everywhere for lives of peace, dignity and development. Nothing in the Charter precludes a recognition that there are rights beyond borders.
>
> Indeed, its very letter and spirit are the affirmation of those fundamental human rights. In short, it is not the deficiencies of the Charter which have brought us to this juncture, but our difficulties in applying its principles to a new era; an era when strictly traditional notions of sovereignty can no longer do justice to the aspirations of peoples everywhere to attain their fundamental freedoms.
>
> * * *
>
> This developing international norm in favor of intervention to protect civilians from wholesale slaughter will no doubt continue to pose profound challenges to the international community.
>
> Any such evolution in our understanding of State sovereignty and individual sovereignty will, in some quarters, be met with distrust, scepticism, even hostility. But it is an evolution that we should welcome.

U.N. Doc. SG/SM/7136, GA/9596 (Sept. 20, 1999).

2. At the end of 1992, then Secretary–General of the United Nations Boutros Boutros–Ghali, writing about the nature of sovereignty, suggested:

> While respect for the fundamental sovereignty and integrity of the state remains central, it is undeniable that the centuries-old doctrine of absolute and exclusive sovereignty no longer stands, and was in fact never so absolute as it was conceived to be in theory. A major intellectual requirement of our time is to rethink the question of sovereignty—not to weaken its essence, which is crucial to international security and cooperation, but to recognize that it may take more than one form and perform more than one function. This perception could help solve problems both within and among states. And underlying the rights of the individual and the rights of peoples is a dimension of universal sovereignty that resides in all humanity and provides all peoples with legitimate involvement in issues affecting the world as a whole. It is a sense that increasingly finds expression in the gradual expansion of international law.
>
> Related to this is the widening recognition that states and their governments cannot face or solve today's problems alone. International cooperation

is unavoidable and indispensable. The quality, extent and timeliness of such cooperation will make the difference between advancement or frustration and despair. * * *

Boutros–Ghali, Empowering the United Nations, 71 For.Aff. 89, 98–99 (Winter 1992/93).

3. Henkin, in a paper entitled "The Mythology of Sovereignty," concludes that "sovereignty" in itself is not a normative principle of international law. (Proceedings of the Canadian Council of International Law, 1992.) He declares that "it is time to bring 'sovereignty' down to earth, cut it down to size, discard its overblown rhetoric; to examine, analyze, reconceive the concept and break out its normative content; to repackage it, even rename it, and slowly ease the term out of polite language in international relations, surely in law." Elsewhere he has declared "Away with the S Word!" See also Henkin's paper with the same title in Essays in Honour of Wang Tieya (R.S.J. Macdonald ed., 1994), Chapter 24.

4. Professor Lillich suggested "that the concept of sovereignty in international law is an idea whose time has come and gone." In assessing the limits of the "tyrannical" concept of sovereignty, Lillich argued: " 'humanity'—is the *raison d'être* of any legal system. It goes without saying, one would think, but it needs saying nevertheless." Lillich, Sovereignty and Humanity: Can they Converge?, in The Spirit of Uppsala 406, 406–07 (Grahl–Madsen & Toman, eds. 1984).

5. In 1999, Professor Allott wrote: "International law is the self-constituting of all-humanity through law. It is the actualizing through law of the common interest of international society, the society of all societies. The legal relations of international law organize the potential willing and acting of all human beings and all human societies, including the forms of society conventionally known as 'states'." Allott, The Concept of International Law, 10 E.J.I.L. 31 (1999).

FALK, EXPLORATIONS AT THE EDGE OF TIME: THE PROSPECTS FOR WORLD ORDER

198–213 (1992).

[A]n emergent global ethos suggests the reality of a shared destiny for the human species and a fundamental unity across space and through time, built around the bioethical impulse of all human groups to *survive* and *flourish*. Such an ethos has implications for the assessment of problems, the provision of solutions, and the overall orientation of action and actors. For most people and leaders, this sense of shared destiny does not displace a persisting primary attachment to the state as a vehicle for aspiration and as an absolute, unconditional bastion of security. * * *

As interdependence grows more salient, the competence and confidence of the state tends to be eroded unless it can facilitate the development of innovative and imaginative formats for problem-solving. In a sense, the state must learn to get out of its own way if over time it is to retain, and regain the full plenum of its legitimacy. But the cumulative consequence of such adaptation is likely to be a far less state-centric global political system. Paradoxically, in order to remain potent the state must give way to a variety of alternative ordering frameworks; the more willingly and forcefully it does so, the better its legitimate sphere of authority can be eventually sustained. * * *

The state has demonstrated a remarkable degree of resilience over the several centuries of its existence, but whether it can significantly reorient its sense of sovereign prerogative from space (protecting territory) to time (contributing to a viable and desirable future) is uncertain in the extreme. * * * Only if specific persons, acting on behalf of the state, can develop the sort of understanding and backing needed can states be led away from their boundary-obsessed territorialism to a more formless contouring of authority that responds to the bewildering array of dangers and opportunities in the world today. To make this shift at all viable requires an active civil society that gives its citizens "the space" to explore "adjustments," including transnational initiatives, and depends on the secure establishment of human rights and democracy, including on the international accountability of leaders for violation of international law. * * * The natural flow of political life in response to the agenda of global concerns is to encourage evasions [of sovereignty] as a matter of deliberate tactics. Is the state flexible enough to preside over its own partial dissolution, circumvention, and reconstruction?

Notes

1. The latter decades of the 20th Century brought radical political, economic, and technological developments, and growing recognition of their transformative consequences singly and cumulatively for the international political-economic system and for international law—"globalization" and "the market"; privatization; cyberspace and the Internet.

Globalization, loosely defined, includes the expanding reaches, economic power, and influence of multinational companies, wealthier and more powerful and influential than many of the states in which they invest and conduct operations. Globalization has been enhanced by "privatization," by the demise of official socialism, and the expanding world market. Economic globalization has been accelerated by cyberspace and the Internet. Not only has the spread and development of communications technology reshaped the world economy and the market, but a virtually instant, world-wide network of world-wide communication has reshaped international diplomacy and international human rights. To the extent that the electronic revolution is breaking down traditional barriers, it may render the state and state institutions increasingly irrelevant, thereby transforming the entire system of international politics and international law.

The international human rights movement has been increasingly recognized as an erosion of traditional state sovereignty in that what happens within a society has become the legitimate concern of other states and of international institutions. The human rights movement has also brought non-governmental organizations as important new actors to the international scene, their existence and activities being recognized by states and by international bodies. See Human Rights (Henkin, Neuman, Orentlicher, & Leebron eds. 1999), Part III, Chapter 3, Section F.

See generally Schachter, The Decline of the Nation State and Its Implications for International Law, 36 Colum.J.Transnat.L. 7 (1997). Schachter presents his thesis of decline under four headings: The Impact of Global Capitalism on State Authority; The Enhanced Roles of Civil and Uncivil Society; The Resurgence of Particularism; Failed States, Illegal Regimes, and Popular Sovereignty. But Schachter concludes with a fifth section: "The Resilience of the State System."

2. In the exercise of their "sovereignty" states have accepted international law and submitted to the authority of international institutions. States have accepted norms that govern their treatment of their own inhabitants, and monitoring and investigation that intrude upon their territory. See Chapter 8 infra. States have submitted to the authority of the U.N. Security Council to issue mandatory, binding orders under Chapter VII of the U.N. Charter. See Chapters 5, 9 and 12 infra. To maintain international peace and security the Security Council has ordered measures that impinge upon territorial integrity and political independence, as with the regime imposed on Iraq after the 1991 Gulf War. New departures, seen by many as derogations from state sovereignty, have occurred in the former Yugoslavia. In 1999, NATO forces, acting to terminate and prevent the commission of genocide and to stem the tide of refugees fleeing from atrocities in Kosovo, initiated a campaign of humanitarian intervention, forcing a withdrawal of Serbian forces and overseeing the return of refugees. Other innovations have been witnessed in the U.N. authorization of a military presence in Somalia to provide a secure environment for the distribution of relief, as well as in other developments in Africa (Liberia, Sierra Leone) and Asia (Cambodia, East Timor). See Chapter 12 infra.

C. THE CHANGING INTERNATIONAL SYSTEM AND CHANGING INTERNATIONAL LAW

International law divides meaningfully between the law before and the law after the Second World War. In 1945, the Allied victory introduced a new order with important changes in international law, represented by the Charter of the United Nations and by the United Nations Organization. Article 1 of the Charter sets forth the major purposes of the United Nations:

1. To maintain international peace and security * * *
2. To develop friendly relations among nations * * *
3. To achieve international co-operation in solving international problems of an economic, social, cultural, or humanitarian character, and in promoting and encouraging respect for human rights and for fundamental freedom for all.* * *

Charter of the United Nations, done at San Francisco, June 26, 1945. The Charter established the U.N. Organization with organs empowered to carry out those purposes, principally the General Assembly, the Security Council, the Secretary General, and the International Court of Justice, See Chapters 5 and 11–12 infra.

Progress towards the realization of U.N. goals was frustrated early. For its first 40 years under the Charter, the international system suffered ideological conflict between two superpowers and their respective allies, armed with increasingly destructive nuclear weapons, and the Cold War, punctuated by only brief periods of détente, put into serious question whether there was any common bona fide commitment to U.N. purposes. The Cold War also underscored ideological differences in attitude towards international law generally, preventing or curtailing the development of new norms, institutions and procedures, and rendering others the subject of only specious agreement or of minimal value.

The decades after the Second World War also saw the transformation of the international system by the end of colonialism and the proliferation of new, mostly poor, less-developed nations, soon emerging as "the Third World." In general, these new states declared themselves ideologically "non-aligned" in the Cold War between East and West, but many of them frequently joined with the Communist bloc, both in pressing for normative change that the West resisted and in resisting developments pursued by the West. These new states also pressed their own agenda to establish principles of "economic self-determination," economic and social development, and a new international economic order.

In the late 1980s and 1990s the political cast of the international system changed dramatically. The end of the Cold War, the collapse of the Soviet empire, the splintering of the U.S.S.R., the demise of international communism, and a spreading commitment to democracy and to the market economy, have relaxed large international tensions and reordered political and economic alignments. These developments have brought and promise further important changes in international law and institutions. An early example is the renaissance of the United Nations Security Council and the extension of its authority during the Gulf War in 1991, in Somalia in 1992, in the former Yugoslavia throughout the 1990s, and East Timor in 1999. See Chapter 12.

Fragmentation of the U.S.S.R. and Yugoslavia, and realignment of multiethnic states, also fueled rivalries leading to repression and erupting into civil wars, revealing inadequacies in the laws of war, in humanitarian law and the law of human rights, especially in the protection of the rights of minorities. Resulting disorder has challenged established legal norms and the traditional commitment to state autonomy. The desperate plight of the populations in war-torn Somalia and the former Yugoslavia evoked clamor for new forms of collective action for humanitarian assistance and forms of collective intervention.

Political transformations have freed nations to attend to crying needs—the urgency of controlling the proliferation of weapons of mass destruction and trade in weapons generally; the threat of environmental catastrophe, such as climate change and related causes; the causes of incessant flows of refugees and the rights of refugees; the continuing population explosion; chaos in financial and economic relations; regulation of the movement of people, goods, capital and ideas; and control of drug smuggling, terrorism and other transnational crimes. Political change with important implications for international law continues in different regions, notably in the development and extent of the European Union, the role of NATO and of the Organization for Security and Cooperation in Europe (OSCE).

REISMAN, INTERNATIONAL LAW AFTER THE COLD WAR

84 A.J.I.L. 859, 860–64 (1990) (footnotes omitted).

The Cold War deformed the traditional international law that had developed over centuries to facilitate and regulate political, economic and other human relationships across national boundaries. It could hardly have been otherwise. For almost half a century, the world lived in a state of neither war nor peace. The independence and rights of choice of smaller states were restricted by larger neighbors in their own interest and, it was often avowed, in the interest of systemic security. The slow effort to centralize authoritative coercive force and to restrict the freedom of unilateral action, the hallmark of civilized political arrangements and the major acknowledged defect of international law, was impeded by an international security system that accorded a veto power to each of the major protagonists. That insured its ineffectiveness. Even the freedom of the oceans, one of the most venerable struts of the international system, which had reserved five-sevenths of the planet as a public highway for exchange, was attenuated to facilitate weapons development. As soon as outer space became accessible, it, too, became part of the military arena.

* * *

Some of the traditional norms and practices of international law that were suppressed during the Cold War can now be revived. As between the two blocs, the distinction between war and peace, each with its own legal regime, will be reinstated. As a consequence, there should be reduced tolerance for, hence conduct of, covert activities. There should be less international tolerance, but not necessarily less national public support, for interventions in so-called critical defense zones under rubrics such as the Brezhnev and Reagan Doctrines. * * * Nevertheless, in terms of a pre-Cold War baseline, one should expect some revival of the norm of national political autonomy.

But national political autonomy will not mean a revival of the older notion of sovereignty in its entirety. Radical changes in conceptions of the legitimacy of national authority, deriving from the international human rights program, have supplanted the older absolute notions. There is much more room for the operation of human rights norms, for the global communications system means that all of the inhabitants of the globe live in a state of electronic simultaneity, if not physical proximity. Instantaneous communication has extended the basis for symbolic, and perhaps physical, interventions into domestic processes in which gross violations of international norms are occurring. But because such humanitarian interventions, as exercises of power, are perforce reflections of the world power process, the arena of their operation will continue to be the internal affairs of smaller and weaker states.

* * *

* * * The international political system is at the threshold of a time of hope. The ending of the Cold War is a major achievement. * * * The need for international law after the Cold War will be more urgent than it was during the conflict. In many ways, what is expected of international law will be greater.

* * * The challenge to international lawyers and scholars must be to clarify continuously the common interests of this ever-changing community, drawing on historic policies but bearing in mind that the constitutive and institutional arrangements that were devised to achieve them may be no longer pertinent or effective.

Notes

1. The Cold War and "Third World non-alignment" did not prevent significant development of international law. Some new areas of law and new norms that developed during the past 50 years are now firmly established; for example, international human rights law, the fundamentals of international environmental law and the law governing outer space. But the norms and institutions developed during this period often reflected only the lowest common denominator of agreement, or concealed differences with minimal success. The heralded "New Economic Order" did not come, but a new economic order has been continually in process, an order made up of discrete steps, some small, some larger—some preferences in trade, some debt relief, some financial assistance—within the present liberal free-market system. Ten years of negotiation produced a new draft Convention on the Law of the Sea in 1982, which came into force in 1994 (though as of 2000, the United States still has not become a party to it). See Chapter 16.

2. Four decades of Cold War, the end of colonialism and the emergence of the "Third World," left marks on the literature of international law as well as on the law itself and its international institutions. The attitudes of the U.S.S.R., and to a lesser extent of Communist China, influenced the theory and content of international law, and Soviet scholars and writers, notably Professor Grigory Tunkin, were prominent in legal literature. See, e.g., Tunkin, Theory of International Law (Butler trans. 1974).

For the attitude of the Soviet Union toward international law during the Cold War, see Grzybowski, Soviet Public International Law: Doctrines and Diplomatic Practice (1970); The Soviet Impact on International Law (Baade, ed. 1965); Tunkin, The Contemporary Soviet Theory of International Law, 31 Current Legal Probs. 177 (1978).

Since the end of the Cold War, writers of the former U.S.S.R. have stressed the need for cooperation in international law. On new Russian and Eastern European thinking about international law generally, see Damrosch, Danilenko & Mullerson, Beyond Confrontation (1995), a collaborative work between the American Society of International Law and the Institute of State and Law in Moscow. This volume confirms major commonalities in East–West views on international law even during the Cold War, reveals differences which survive that period, and urges collaboration in the continuing development of the law.

3. The early attitudes of the People's Republic of China dismissive of international law were reflected in Chiu, Communist China's Attitude Toward International Law, 60 A.J.I.L. 245 (1966); Chiu & Edwards, Communist China's Attitude Toward the United Nations, 62 A.J.I.L. 20 (1968); Cohen & Chiu, People's China and International Law (1974); but following the removal of the "Gang of Four" in the late 1970's, the People's Republic of China displayed renewed interest in international law. See Selected Articles from Chinese Yearbook of International Law (Chinese Society of Int'l Law, ed. 1983). See also Chen, The People's Republic of China and Public International Law, 8 Dalhousie L.J. 3 (1984); Wang, Teaching and Research of International Law in Present Day China, 22 Colum.J. Transnat'l L. 77 (1983).

It remains unclear what effect the demise of international communism (and of the U.S.S.R.) will prove to have had on Chinese attitudes to international law. For Chinese positions at earlier points, see Chiu, Chinese Attitudes Towards International Law in the Post–Mao Era, 1978–1987, 21 Int'l Lawyer 1127 (1987);

Wang, International Law in China, 221 Rec. des Cours 195 (1990–II). Chinese spokesmen have reiterated traditional positions in respect of key international law concepts. For example, at the Vienna Conference on Human Rights in 1993, China invoked "sovereignty" in objecting to external scrutiny of compliance with international human rights standards. China also invoked respect for territorial "sovereignty" in opposing humanitarian intervention, as by NATO in Kosovo in 1999. On the other hand, in 1998, China signed the International Covenant on Civil and Political rights.

4. The expansion of the international system after the Second World War with the addition of "new states" has had important consequences for international law. The law lost its Europe-based homogeneity, but contrary to fears expressed during the early years of decolonization, international law has not been discarded and, instead, its universalism has been established. See Henkin, How Nations Behave 121–27 (2d ed. 1979).

The literature exploring the influence of "new states" on international law includes: Anand, International Law and the Developing Countries: Confrontation or Cooperation? (1987); Caribbean Perspectives on International Law and Organizations (Ramcharan & Francis, eds. 1989); Elias, Africa and the Development of International Law (2d ed. 1988); Elias, New Horizons in the Development of International Law (1980); Makonnen, International Law and the New States of Africa (1983); Third World Attitudes Toward International Law: An Introduction (Snyder & Sathirathai, eds. 1987); Norchi, Methods for Evaluating the Transcultural Applications of International Legal Prescription, 86 A.S.I.L.Proc. 570 (1992); Garcia–Amador, Current Attempts to Revise International Law–A Comparative Analysis, 77 A.J.I.L. 286 (1983); Krasner, Transforming International Regimes: What the Third World Wants and Why, 25 Int'l Studies Q. 119 (1981); Park, The Third World as an International Legal System, 7 Bost. Coll. Third World L.J. 37 (1987); Sathirathai, An Understanding of the Relationship Between International Legal Discourse and Third World States, 25 Harv. Int'l L.Rev. 395 (1984), reprinted in International Law 445 (Koskenniemi, ed. 1992); Wang, The Third World and International Law, in The Structure and Process of International Law: Essays in Legal Philosophy Doctrine and Theory 955 (Macdonald & Johnston, eds. 1983); El–Erian, International Law and the Developing Countries, in Transnational Law in a Changing Society 84 (Friedmann, Henkin & Lissitzyn, eds. 1979); Falk, The New States and International Legal Order, 118 Rec. des Cours 1 (1966). See also International Law and the Developing World: A Millennial Analysis (Symposium Issue), 41 Harv. I.L.J. (2000).

Recent scholarship has emphasized "different voices," not only of new states, but also of groups and persons within states who have been historically excluded from participation in the processes of international law. Colonial and postcolonial domination, lack of voting rights and political power on the part of women and indigenous or minority groups, and other forms of exclusion had given traditional international law a relatively narrow participatory base. With increasing democratization of politics at both the domestic and the international levels, these barriers are being overcome (or at least their salience is increasingly recognized), thereby opening up new possibilities for transforming the foundations of international law. For reflections on these possibilities, see D. Otto, Subalternity and International Law: The Problems of Global Community and the Incommensurability of Difference, 5 Social & Legal Studies 337 (1996). See also the references at pp. 40–55 infra on contemporary perspectives on international law.

5. In the Preamble to the U.N. Charter, the peoples of the United Nations, apparently in recognition of diversity among states and cultures, dedicate themselves "to practice tolerance and live together with one another as good neighbors." There have been differences among writers as to the significance of cultural diversity for international law. Adda Bozeman notes that international society is characterized by diverse cultures, political systems, and ideologies, and declares that there is no universal acceptance of Western notions of sovereignty and moral law. In fact, she notes, the word law does not translate easily into a number of foreign idea systems. Bozeman argues that Western ideals of international law can never create more than a false sense of world unity. Bozeman, The Future of International Law in a Multicultural World xii-xiii, 180–86 (1971). In contrast, others argue that a universal culture or ideology is not a prerequisite for the existence or growth of international law, since in its essentials international law responds to interests and needs common to states generally. See, e.g., Higgins, Conflict of Interests: International Law in a Divided World (1965); Jenks, The Common Law of Mankind (1958); Jessup, Diversity and Uniformity in the Law of Nations, 58 A.J.I.L. 341–358 (1964); Lissitzyn, International Law in a Divided World, International Conciliation No. 542 (March 1963). Compare Human Rights, Culture and Context: Anthropological Perspectives (Wilson ed., 1997).

6. An effort to take account of different legal cultures can be seen in the provisions for the selection of judges for the International Court of Justice. In Article 9 of the Court's Statute, electors of judges are reminded to take into account when choosing among nominees that in the Court "as a whole the representation of the main forms of civilization and of the principal legal systems of the world should be assured." According to the final report of the Committee of Jurists which drafted the Statute for the Permanent Court of International Justice (on which Article 9 of the I.C.J. Statute is based), the Article is a specific attempt to ensure "that the Bench may really and permanently represent the legal conceptions of all nations." League of Nations Doc. V.1920.2, at 710. See McWhinney, 'Internationalizing' the International Court: The Quest for Ethno–Cultural and Legal–Systemic Representativeness, in Essays in Honor of Judge Taslim Olawale Elias 277 (Bello & Ajibola, eds. 1992). For the present composition of the Court, see Chapter 11 infra.

For writing on cultural diversity and international law, see Cassese, International Law in a Divided World (1986); The Future of International Law in a Multicultural World (Dupuy, ed. 1984); McWhinney, United Nations Law Making: Cultural and Ideological Relativism and International Law Making for and Era of Transition (1984); Schachter, International Law in Theory and Practice, chapter 2 (1991); Bozeman, The International Order in a Multicultural World, in The Expansion of International Society (Bull & Weston, eds. 1984); Dore, Universality and Diversity in World Culture, in The Expansion of International Society 408 (Bull & Weston, eds. 1984); Herczegh, International Law in a Multicultural World, in 3 Questions of International Law: Hungarian Perspectives (Bokor–Szego, ed. 1986); Jennings, Universal International Law in a Multicultural World, in Liber Amicorum for Lord Wilberforce (Bos & Brownlie, eds. 1987); Joyner, Bridging the Cultural Chasm: Cultural Relativism and the Future of International Law, 20 Cal.W.Int'l L.J. 275 (1989–90); Vereshchetin & Danilenko, Cultural and Ideological Pluralism and International Law, 29 German Y.B Int'l L. (1986).

Cultural diversity became an issue during the 1993 Vienna Conference on Human Rights, and became the subject of political and intellectual controversy in that context. See Chapter 8. For a discussion of individual rights in the context of cultural diversity, see Franck, Is Personal Freedom a Western Value? 91 A.J.I.L. 593 (1997).

7. Nineteenth century positivism stressed law as science and played down the original affinity between religion and international law. The diversity of cultures and ideologies in the international system of the twentieth century has also led to reluctance to consider continuing connections between international law and religion. See generally The Influence of Religion on the Development of International Law (Janis, ed. 1991); Falk, Explorations at the Edge of Time: The Prospects for World Order 24–36 (1992).

SECTION 2. INTERNATIONAL LAW AS LAW

A. IS IT LAW?

International law has had to justify its legitimacy and its reality. Its title to law has been challenged on the ground that, by hypothesis and definition, there can be no law governing sovereign states. Skeptics have argued that there can be no international law since there is no international legislature to make it, no international executive to enforce it, and no effective international judiciary to interpret and to develop it, or to resolve disputes about it. International law, it has been said, is not "real law" since it is commonly disregarded, states obeying it only when they wish to, when it is in their interest to do so.

The jurisprudence of international law, however, has rejected the narrow definitions and unfounded assumptions implied in these challenges. The sociology of international law has denied the allegations as to how nations behave in regard to law.

The classical denial of the legal character of international law was expressed early in the 19th century by John Austin.

LAW AS COMMANDS ENFORCED BY SANCTIONS

AUSTIN, THE PROVINCE OF JURISPRUDENCE DETERMINED (1832)

133, 201 (1954 ed. Berlin, Hampshire & Wollheim, eds.).

Laws properly so called are a species of *commands*. But, being a *command*, every law properly so called flows from a *determinate* source * * *. * * * [W]henever a *command* is expressed or intimated, one party signifies a wish that another shall do or forbear: and the latter is obnoxious to an evil which the former intends to inflict in case the wish be disregarded. * * * Every sanction properly so called is an eventual evil *annexed to a command*. * * *

And hence it inevitably follows, that the law obtaining between nations is not positive law: for every positive law is set by a given sovereign to a person or persons in a state of subjection to its author. As I have already intimated, the law obtaining between nations is law (improperly so called) set by general opinion. The duties which it imposes are enforced by moral sanctions: by fear on the part of nations, or by fear on the part of sovereigns, of provoking general hostility, and incurring its probable evils, in case they shall violate maxims generally received and respected.

INTERNATIONAL LAW AND INTERNATIONAL MORALITY

HART, THE CONCEPT OF LAW

222–225 (1961).

Sometimes insistence that the rules governing the relations between states are only moral rules, is inspired by the old dogmatism, that any form of social structure that is not reducible to orders backed by threats can only be a form of "morality". It is, of course, possible to use the word "morality" in this very comprehensive way; so used, it provides a conceptual wastepaper basket into which will go the rules of games, clubs, etiquette, the fundamental provisions of constitutional law and international law, together with rules and principles which we ordinarily think of as moral ones, such as the common prohibitions of cruelty, dishonesty, or lying. The objection to this procedure is that between what is thus classed together as "morality" there are such important differences of both form and social function, that no conceivable purpose, practical or theoretical, could be served by so crude a classification. Within the category of morality thus artificially widened, we should have to mark out afresh the old distinctions which it blurs.

In the particular case of international law there are a number of different reasons for resisting the classification of its rules as "morality". The first is that states often reproach each other for immoral conduct or praise themselves or others for living up to the standard of international morality. No doubt *one* of the virtues which states may show or fail to show is that of abiding by international law, but that does not mean that that law is morality. In fact the appraisal of states' conduct in terms of morality is recognizably different from the formulation of claims, demands, and the acknowledgements of rights and obligations under the rules of international law. * * * [C]ertain features * * * might be taken as defining characteristics of social morality: among them * * * the distinctive form of moral pressure by which moral rules are primarily supported. This consists not of appeals to fear or threats of retaliation or demands for compensation, but of appeals to conscience, made in the expectation that once the person addressed is reminded of the moral principle at stake, he may be led by guilt or shame to respect it and make amends.

Claims under international law are not couched in such terms though of course, as in municipal law, they may be joined with a moral appeal. What predominate in the arguments, often technical, which states address to each other over disputed matters of international law, are references to precedents, treaties and juristic writings; often no mention is made of moral right or wrong, good or bad. Hence the claim that the Peking Government has or has not a right under international law to expel the Nationalist forces from Formosa is very different from the question whether this is fair, just, or a morally good or bad thing to do, and is backed by characteristically different arguments. No doubt in the relations between states there are halfway houses between what is clearly law and what is clearly morality, analogous to the standards of politeness and courtesy recognized in private life. Such is the sphere of international "comity" exemplified in the privilege extended to diplomatic envoys of receiving goods intended for personal use free of duty.

A more important ground of distinction is the following. The rules of international law, like those of municipal law, are often morally quite indifferent. A rule may exist because it is convenient or necessary to have some clear fixed rule about the subjects with which it is concerned, but not because any moral importance is attached to the particular rule. It may well be but one of a larger number of possible rules, any one of which would have done equally well. Hence legal rules, municipal and international, commonly contain much specific detail, and draw arbitrary distinctions, which would be unintelligible as elements in moral rules or principles. * * * Law, however, though it also contains much that is of moral importance, can and does contain just such rules, and the arbitrary distinctions, formalities, and highly specific detail which would be most difficult to understand as part of morality, are consequently natural and easily comprehensible features of law. For one of the typical functions of law, unlike morality, is to introduce just these elements in order to maximize certainty and predictability and to facilitate the proof or assessments of claims. Regard for forms and detail carried to excess, has earned for law the reproaches of "formalism" and "legalism"; yet it is important to remember that these vices are exaggerations of some of the law's distinctive qualities.

It is for this reason that just as we expect a municipal legal system, but not morality, to tell us how many witnesses a validly executed will must have, so we expect international law, but not morality, to tell us such things as the number of days a belligerent vessel may stay for refueling or repairs in a neutral port; the width of territorial waters; the methods to be used in their measurement. All these things are necessary and desirable provisions for *legal rules* to make, but so long as the sense is retained that such rules may equally well take any of several forms, or are important only as one among many possible means to specific ends, they remain distinct from rules which have the status in individual or social life characteristic of morality. Of course not all the rules of international law are of this formal, or arbitrary, or morally neutral kind. The point is only that legal rules *can* and moral rules *cannot* be of this kind.

The difference in character between international law and anything which we naturally think of as morality has another aspect. Though the effect of a law requiring or proscribing certain practices might ultimately be to bring about changes in the morality of a group, the notion of a legislature making or repealing moral rules is * * * an absurd one. A legislature cannot introduce a new rule and give it the status of a moral rule by its *fiat,* just as it cannot, by the same means, give a rule the status of a tradition, though the reasons why this is so may not be the same in the two cases. Accordingly morality does not merely lack or happen not to have a legislature; the very idea of change by human legislative *fiat* is repugnant to the idea of morality. This is so because we conceive of morality as the ultimate standard by which human actions (legislative or otherwise) are evaluated. The contrast with international law is clear. There is nothing in the nature or function of international law which is similarly inconsistent with the idea that the rules might be subject to legislative change; the lack of a legislature is just a lack which many think of as a defect one day to be repaired.

Notes

1. Professor Glanville Williams insisted that jurisprudential debate over the reality of international law is merely a debate about words. Williams, International Law and the Controversy Concerning the Word "Law," 22 Brit.Y.B.I.L. 146, 159–62 (1945). See also Professor Ian Brownlie's criticism of Austin and Hart in The Reality and Efficacy of International Law, 52 Brit.Y.B.I.L. 1 (1981).

2. There is an old but recurrent controversy as to the applicability of moral principles to the behavior of states and governments. For a rejection of the "legalistic-moralistic approach to international relations," see Kennan, American Diplomacy, 1900–1950, 95–99 (1951); see also Kennan, Morality and Foreign Policy, 64 Foreign Affairs 205 (Winter 1985–86). For a different view see Henkin, How Nations Behave 335–37 (2d ed. 1979).

3. At one time, the reality of international law was challenged in the name of state sovereignty. How can a sovereign state submit to law? The argument was disposed of in the first contentious case of the Permanent Court of International Justice, where the Court said: "The Court declines to see in the conclusion of any treaty by which a State undertakes to perform or refrain from performing a particular act an abandonment of its sovereignty. No doubt any convention creating an obligation of this kind places a restriction upon the exercise of the sovereign rights of the State, in the sense that it requires them to be exercised in a certain way. But the right of entering into international engagements is an attribute of State sovereignty." S.S. Wimbledon Case, P.C.I.J., Series A, No. 1, at 25 (1923).

To similar effect is *Prometheus* (In the Matter of an Arbitration Between the Osaka Shosen Kaisha and the Owners of the S.S. Prometheus, 2 Hong Kong L.Rpts. 207, 225 (1904)):

> It was contended on behalf of the owners of the *Prometheus* that the term "law" as applied to this recognized system of principles and rules known as international law is an inexact expression, that there is, in other words, no such thing as international law; that there can be no such law binding upon all nations inasmuch as there is no sanction for such law, that is to say that there is no means by which obedience to such law can be imposed upon any given nation refusing obedience thereto. I do not concur in that contention. In my opinion a law may be established and become international, that is to say binding upon all nations, by the agreement of such nations to be bound thereby, although it may be impossible to enforce obedience thereto by any given nation party to the agreement. The resistance of a nation to a law to which it has agreed does not derogate from the authority of the law because that resistance cannot, perhaps, be overcome. Such resistance merely makes the resisting nation a breaker of the law to which it has given its adherence, but it leaves the law, to the establishment of which the resisting nation was a party, still subsisting. Could it be successfully contended that because any given person or body of persons possessed for the time being power to resist an established municipal law such law had no existence? The answer to such a contention would be that the law still existed, though it might not for the time being be possible to enforce obedience to it.

B. THE BINDING CHARACTER OF INTERNATIONAL LAW

KELSEN, PURE THEORY OF LAW

215–17 (Knight trans. 1967).*

[G]eneral international law is regarded as [a] set of objectively valid norms that regulate the mutual behavior of states. These norms are created by custom, constituted by the actual behavior of the "states," that is, of those individuals who act as governments according to national legal orders. These norms are interpreted as legal norms binding the states, because a basic norm is presupposed which establishes custom among states as a law-creating fact. The basic norm runs as follows: "States—that is, the governments of the states—in their mutual relations ought to behave in such a way"; or: "Coercion of state against state ought to be exercised under the conditions and in the manner, that conforms with the custom constituted by the actual behavior of the states." This is the "constitution" of international law in a transcendental-logical sense.

One of the norms of international law created by custom authorizes the states to regulate their mutual relations by treaty. The reason for the validity of the legal norms of international law created by treaty is this custom-created norm. It is usually formulated in the sentence: *pacta sunt servanda.*

The presupposed basic norm of international law, which institutes custom constituted by the states as a law-creating fact, expresses a principle that is the basic presupposition of all customary law: the individual ought to behave in such a manner as the others usually behave (believing that they ought to behave that way), applied to the mutual behavior of states, that is, the behavior of the individuals qualified by the national legal orders as government organs.[80]

No affirmation of a value transcending positive law is inherent in the basic norm of international law, not even of the value of peace guaranteed by the general international law created by custom and the particular international law created by treaty. International law and—if its primacy is assumed—the subordinated national legal orders are not valid "because" and "insofar as" they realize the value that consists in peace; they may realize this value if and so far as they are valid; and they are valid if a basic norm is presupposed that institutes custom among states as a law-creating fact regardless of the content of the norms thus created. If the reason for the validity of national legal orders is found in a norm of international law, then the latter is understood as a legal order superior to the former and therefore as the highest sovereign legal order. If the states—that is, the national legal orders—are nevertheless referred to as "sovereign," then this "sovereignty" can only mean that the national legal orders are subordinated only to the international legal order.

* Some footnotes omitted.

80. The theory held by many authors (and at one time also by myself) that the norm of *pacta sunt servanda* is the basis of international law is to be rejected because it can be maintained only with the aid of the fiction that the custom established by the conduct of states is a tacit treaty.

THE REALITY OF INTERNATIONAL LAW

HENKIN, HOW NATIONS BEHAVE

25–26, 320–21 (2d ed. 1979). (footnotes omitted).

[T]o many an observer, governments seem largely free to decide whether to agree to new law, whether to accept another nation's view of existing law, whether to comply with agreed law. International law, then, is voluntary and only hortatory. It must always yield to national interest. Surely, no nation will submit to law any questions involving its security or independence, even its power, prestige, influence. Inevitably, a diplomat holding these views will be reluctant to build policy on law he deems ineffective. He will think it unrealistic and dangerous to enact laws which will not be observed, to build institutions which will not be used, to base his government's policy on the expectation that other governments will observe law or agreement. Since other nations do not attend to law except when it is in their interest, the diplomat might not see why his government should do so at the sacrifice of important interests. He might be impatient with his lawyers who tell him that the government may not do what he would like to see done.

These depreciations of international law challenge much of what the international lawyer does. Indeed, some lawyers seem to despair for international law until there is world government or at least effective international organization. But most international lawyers are not dismayed. Unable to deny the limitations of international law, they insist that these are not critical, and they deny many of the alleged implications of these limitations. If they must admit that the cup of law is half-empty, they stress that it is half-full. They point to similar deficiencies in many domestic legal systems. They reject definitions (commonly associated with the legal philosopher John Austin) that deny the title of law to any but the command of a sovereign, enforceable and enforced as such. They insist that despite inadequacies in legislative method, international law has grown and developed and changed. If international law is difficult to make, yet it is made; if its growth is slow, yet it grows. If there is no judiciary as effective as in some developed national systems, there is an International Court of Justice whose judgments and opinions, while few, are respected. The inadequacies of the judicial system are in some measure supplied by other bodies: international disputes are resolved and law is developed through a network of arbitrations by continuing or *ad hoc* tribunals. National courts help importantly to determine, clarify, develop international law. Political bodies like the Security Council and the General Assembly of the United Nations also apply law, their actions and resolutions interpret and develop the law, their judgments serve to deter violations in some measure. If there is no international executive to enforce international law, the United Nations has some enforcement powers and there is "horizontal enforcement" in the reactions of other nations. The gaps in substantive law are real and many and require continuing effort to fill them, but they do not vitiate the force and effect of the law that exists, in the international society that is.

Above all, the lawyer will insist, critics of international law ask and answer the wrong questions. What matters is not whether the international system has legislative, judicial, or executive branches, corresponding to those we have become accustomed to seek in a domestic society; what matters is whether international law is reflected in the policies of nations and in relations between nations. The question is not whether there is an effective legislature; it is whether there is law that responds and corresponds to the changing needs of a changing society. The question is not whether there is an effective judiciary, but whether disputes are resolved in an orderly fashion in accordance with international law. Most important, the question is not whether law is enforceable or even effectively enforced; rather, whether law is observed, whether it governs or influences behavior, whether international behavior reflects stability and order. The fact is, lawyers insist, that nations have accepted important limitations on their sovereignty, that they have observed these norms and undertakings, that the result has been substantial order in international relations.

Notes

1. The Restatement (Third) of the Foreign Relations Law of the United States, Part I, Chapter 1, Introductory Note, states:

> *International law as law.* The absence of central legislative and executive institutions has led to skepticism about the legal quality of international law. Many observers consider international law to be only a series of precepts of morality or etiquette, of cautions and admonitions lacking in both specificity and binding quality. Governments, it is sometimes assumed, commonly disregard international law and observe it only when they deem it to be in their interest to do so.
>
> These impressions are mistaken. International law is law like other law, promoting order, guiding, restraining, regulating behavior. States, the principal addressees of international law, treat it as law, consider themselves bound by it, attend to it with a sense of legal obligation and with concern for the consequences of violation. Some states refer to international law in their constitutions; many incorporate it into their domestic legal systems; all take account of it in their governmental institutional arrangements and in their international relations. There is reference to the "Law of Nations" in the Constitution of the United States (Article 1, section 8). It is part of the law of the United States, respected by Presidents and Congresses, and by the States, and given effect by the courts.

2. Earlier writers stressed that the authority of international law resides in the fact that the states which constitute international society recognize it as binding, and the system treats them as bound, irrespective of their individual will. See, e.g., Fitzmaurice, The Foundations of the Authority of International Law and the Problem of Enforcement, 19 Mod. L. Rev. 1, 8, 9 (1956). Compare Brierly, The Law of Nations 55–56 (6th ed. 1963); Manning, The Nature of International Society 106–107 (1962).

C. ENFORCEMENT AND COMPLIANCE

Inquiry into the "reality" of international law has been largely concerned with whether international law works: whether states act in conformity with the law. That inquiry has sometimes reflected skepticism: how can it be that states obey the law when there is no effective means of enforcing it? That in turn has encouraged inquiry as to means of enforcing international law and other inducements to comply with it.

DAMROSCH, ENFORCING INTERNATIONAL LAW THROUGH NON–FORCIBLE MEASURES

269 Rec. des Cours 19–22, 24 (1997).

A fundamental (and frequent) criticism of international law is the weakness of mechanisms for enforcement. For the sceptics and the critics of international law, a system so woefully deficient in means for compelling compliance can hardly qualify as "law", at least in the sense in which that term is used in domestic systems.

A variety of responses may be made to these objections, including along the following lines:

(1) There is much more *voluntary compliance* with international law than the critics would acknowledge. This is the argument of Louis Henkin in *How Nations Behave*: "almost all nations observe almost all principles of international law and almost all of their obligations almost all of the time". Others, notably Thomas Franck in *The Power of Legitimacy among Nations*, have shown how rules of international law differ in the extent to which they exert a normative "pull" towards compliance: actors are more likely to comply voluntarily with some kinds of rules than others, and if we understand the forces that motivate voluntary compliance, then perhaps we can improve the content of the rules, or improve the system for making rules, so that a greater portion of the system will exert a greater pull towards compliance.

(2) There are more sanctions for disobedience than is generally realized, although some of those sanctions are relatively soft. Under this heading belong claims that the force of public opinion and the "mobilization of shame" are non-trivial kinds of enforcement mechanisms. We would also include under this heading the role of non-governmental organizations (such as human rights monitoring groups) in bringing the glare of publicity on violations of international law, to mobilize public pressure for compliance.

(3) There are more *coercive* sanctions for disobedience than the critics would admit, although those sanctions are largely decentralized and non-forcible. Victims of breaches of international law can affirm their rights and obtain at least rudimentary remedies through self-help mechanisms like countermeasures and economic sanctions. For example, a State that is a victim of a material breach of a treaty can generally suspend or terminate the treaty; and the threat that it would do so serves as a deterrent to breaches, as a sanction against breaches, and to some extent as remedial mechanism. * * *

(4) There may be non-forcible remedies available in *national* courts. These could relate to the kinds of economic remedies mentioned above: for example, a victim State might use its own courts or other domestic tribunals to adjudicate claims of its nationals against the breaching State. Alternatively, it may be possible to invoke judicial remedies in third countries (wholly uninvolved in the breach) for violations of international obligations. * * *

(5) There are some *forcible* measures which provide even stronger forms of compulsion. If one State violates the rule prohibiting use of force against

another's territorial integrity or political independence, then the victim State can respond with individual or collective self-defense (within limits, which are themselves regulated by law). This is a form of enforcement of the primary rule against use of force, although the method of enforcement is largely decentralized.

(6) There are embryonic *centralized* enforcement mechanisms, both non-forcible and forcible. The primary source for these is Chapter VII of the United Nations Charter, which went virtually unused until 1990 but has witnessed a significant revival. Pursuant to decisions of the Security Council under its compulsory powers, centralized coercion has been brought to bear in a number of recent situations involving violations of international law. Collective economic sanctions have been applied, both under the authority of regional organizations and in application of the compulsory powers of the United Nations Security Council, for enforcement of international legal rules against use of force (e.g., Iraq's invasion of Kuwait), war crimes and humanitarian law (former Yugoslavia), terrorism (Libya), and serious violations of human rights (e.g. Haiti), among other instances. In several instances collective economic sanctions have laid the groundwork for the subsequent authorization by the Security Council of the use of multilateral military force for enforcement purposes, as in the cases of Iraq, Haiti and former Yugoslavia, among others.

(7) Additionally, some centralized organs now exist for the enforcement of international criminal law against individuals. The *ad hoc* International Criminal Tribunals for the Former Yugoslavia and for Rwanda have been created through the authority of the Security Council under Chapter VII of the United Nations Charter; and substantial progress has been made toward the establishment of a standing international criminal court. These bodies can supplement national criminal enforcement of international law. * * *

Furthermore, the international system is currently undergoing significant changes that could substantially transform the effectiveness of coercive enforcement. * * *

IDENTIFYING VIOLATIONS IN A DECENTRALIZED SYSTEM

FALK, THE ADEQUACY OF CONTEMPORARY THEORIES OF INTERNATIONAL LAW–GAPS IN LEGAL THINKING

50 Va.L.Rev. 231, 249–50 (1964). (footnotes omitted).

Among the most serious deficiencies in international law is the frequent absence of an assured procedure for the identification of a violation. Theoretical inquiry can clarify the problem and provide some insight into the solution. The status of controverted behavior as legal or illegal is quite problematical, in the first instance, because no central institutions exist to make judgments that will be treated as authoritative by states. This is the familiar weakness of international law that results from reliance upon self-interpretation to discern the scope of permissible behavior. How is a violation of law to be identified in a decentralized social system? National officials may help shape behavior so that it minimizes conflict with legal rules, but once behavior is undertaken, then national officials elaborate a legal argument to support the challenged action rather than attempt to reach a balanced or impartial judgment on its legality. Furthermore, the strength of psychological allegiance to one's national sovereign often seems to render non-governmental specialists incapable of divorcing their role as citizen from their role as expert. The consequence is that the international system frequently lacks the means to determine definitely that certain behavior constitutes a violation of law. This inability to identify violations is especially prominent when the action is performed by a leading international actor who is able to block censure resolutions in the political organs of the United Nations. In such event, scholars in third states might be capable of providing the most objective account, but their relative obscurity and the special interests that might underlie their outlooks act to restrict the influence of their judgment. Existing theory does not take into sufficient account this difficulty of establishing a violation of international law.

This problem has deep, as well as obvious, consequences. The obvious consequence is a conclusion that, since there is no assured way to identify what is forbidden, everything is permitted. For how can international law claim to be a system of restraint if it lacks a means to identify transgressions? This question, far from suggesting the irrelevance of international law, points toward a better understanding of its function and purpose. For, although rules of restraint are the core of the system, their influence is often realized by a combination of self-restraint and reconciliation. A state bureaucracy refrains, under routine circumstances, from violating rules and approaches them in a spirit of impartiality. Once it is alleged that restraints have been broken, the extent of adherence to applicable rules has a great bearing upon the response of the complaining party. Therefore, the degree and manner of violation may be more crucial than the fact of violation. The possibility of degrees of violation must be introduced explicitly into international legal theory. There is a need for an image of compliance and violation that draws inspiration from the idea of a spectrum or a prism, rather than insists upon a rigid dichotomy between legal or illegal conduct.

Notes

1. The need to improve procedures to deter or remedy violations of international law has placed increased emphasis on the development of international courts, quasi-judicial commissions, and alternative means of dispute resolution. See Chapter 11. The development of new norms often depends on accompanying arrangements for dispute resolution: states are more likely to agree to a norm or a particular expression of a norm if there is put in place a means for resolving disputes as to its meaning or application, but even this is no guarantee. See, e.g., the 1982 Convention on the Law of the Sea, Part XV, Arts. 279–299.

2. States may decide to violate international law in an attempt to work a change in the customary law or in the interpretation of a treaty. As Henkin explains, these violations entail risks:

> Customary international law, and even the interpretation of a treaty, may * * * change in response to new needs and new insights. A state might knowingly deviate from what had been established law (or established interpretation of a treaty) in the hope of changing the law. But that state does so at its peril. It does so at the peril that it will not succeed in changing the law and will be adjudged to have violated the law. It does so at the peril that it may succeed in destroying or eroding established law, to its later deep regret.

Henkin, The Invasion of Panama Under International Law: A Gross Violation, 29 Colum.J.Transnat.L. 293, 311 (1991). On the question whether customary law remains law despite frequent violations, see Military and Paramilitary Activities in and Against Nicaragua (Merits), 1986 I.C.J. 14, 98.

POWER AS ENFORCER OF LAW

MORGENTHAU & THOMPSON, POLITICS AMONG NATIONS

312 (6th ed. 1985).*

[W]hether or not an attempt will be made to enforce international law and whether or not the attempt will be successful do not depend primarily upon legal considerations and the disinterested operation of law-enforcing mechanisms. Both attempt and success depend upon political considerations and the actual distribution of power in a particular case. The protection of the rights of a weak nation that is threatened by a strong one is then determined by the balance of power as it operates in that particular situation. Thus the rights of Belgium were safeguarded in 1914 against their violation by Germany, for it so happened that the protection of those rights seemed to be required by the national interests of powerful neighbors. Similarly, when in 1950 South Korea was attacked by North Korea, their concern with the maintenance of the balance of power in the Far East and of territorial stability throughout Asia prompted the United States and some of its allies, such as France and Great Britain, to come to the aid of South Korea. On the other hand, the rights of Colombia, when the United States supported the revolution in 1903 which led to the establishment of the Republic of Panama, and the rights of Finland, when attacked by the Soviet Union in 1939, were violated either with impunity or, as in the case of Finland, without the intervention of effective sanctions. There was no balance of power which could have protected these nations.

ENFORCEMENT WITHOUT CENTRALIZED SANCTIONS

BRIERLY, THE LAW OF NATIONS

100–02 (6th ed., Waldock, 1963).

The international system has no central organ for the enforcement of international legal rights as such, and the creation of any such general scheme of sanctions is for the present a very distant prospect. But the most urgent part of the problem of enforcement is the subjection to law of the use of force by states, and in modern times two notable experiments, in the

* See also the Brief Edition, revised by Thompson, 1993, pp. 266–267.

Covenant of the League of Nations and the Charter of the United Nations, have been made with this end in view. These two experiments have followed different lines. The system of the Covenant relied on the fulfillment by the members of undertakings which they had severally given to take certain prescribed measures against an aggressor, but it did not set up a supranational authority; the organs of the League could be used for coordinating the actions of the individual members, but they could not issue directions as to the action these members were to take. On the other hand, the Charter has created for the first time an authority which, at least according to the letter of its constitution, is to exercise a power of this supranational kind * * *.

This absence of an executive power means that each state remains free, subject to the limitations on the use of force to be discussed later, to take such action as it thinks fit to enforce its own rights. This does not mean that international law has no sanctions, if that word is used in its proper sense of means for securing the observance of the law; but it is true that the sanctions which it possesses are not systematic or centrally directed, and that accordingly they are precarious in their operation. This lack of system is obviously unsatisfactory, particularly to those states which are less able than others to assert their own rights effectively.

But the difficulties of introducing any radical change into the present means of enforcing international law are extremely formidable. The problem has little analogy with that of the enforcement of law within the state, and the popular use of such phrases as an "international police force" tends to make it appear much simpler than it really is. Police action suggests the bringing to bear of the overwhelming force of the community against a comparatively feeble individual lawbreaker, but no action of that sort is possible in the international sphere, where the potential law-breakers are states, and the preponderance of force may even be on the law-breaking side. Even in a federation, as the experience of the United States has shown, the problem of enforcing the law against a member state has not been easy to solve.

THE UNITED NATIONS AND LAW ENFORCEMENT

The United Nations Charter, designed to establish a new world order after the Second World War, includes the most important norm of 20th Century international law: the prohibition of the use or threat of force between states, Article 2(4). That apart, the Charter itself does not and was not designed to include a code of international law. Correspondingly, the Security Council was not conceived as a body that would police and enforce international law generally, and the Charter did not create institutions to enforce international law, except in respect of the prohibition on the use of force and related threats to international peace and security.

Even that enforcement role was largely frustrated during the Cold War, but with the end of the Cold War, the role conceived for the Security Council could be and was in fact realized, as during the Gulf War (though not with U.N. forces but with voluntary contributions of force by members). But even since the end of the Cold War, the Security Council has not assumed a police power to enforce or induce compliance with international law generally, but it has taken some steps to enlarge its own "policing authority" by liberal interpretation of "threat to international peace and security" for which the Council can recommend or decide the measures to be taken. See U.N. Charter, Chapter VII, Article 39. For discussion of enforcement actions authorized by the Security Council in the 1990s, see Chapters 9 and 12 below.

Notes

1. International law has been developed by various U.N. bodies, principally the General Assembly, and the Economic and Social Council and its suborgans, committees and commissions. Inducements to comply with international law result from various programs launched by or under the auspices of the United Nations. Inducements to comply with selected international law norms such as those relating to human rights are included in the law established in such matters. See Chapter 8. The U.N. Charter also established the International Court of Justice for judicial enforcement of international law between states. See Chapter 11.

2. Both the Security Council and the General Assembly have sometimes censured states for violating Charter principles. The General Assembly rejected the credentials of South African delegations and refused to seat them because South Africa was practicing apartheid in violation of Security Council resolutions and principles of international law. In 1992, the General Assembly denied Serbia the former Yugoslavian seat in the Assembly because Serbia failed to comply with Security Council resolutions. See Blum, UN Membership of the "New" Yugoslavia: Continuity or Break?, 86 A.J.I.L. 830 (1992). Should an offending state be excluded from a treaty-based regime or from a specialized agency because that state has violated a basic rule of international law? Is the exclusion of defaulters from joint activities of the international community an effective sanction? On efforts to exclude or limit participation in international organizations as a form of sanction, see Chayes & Chayes, The New Sovereignty 68–87 (1995) (chapter on membership sanctions).

3. In the absence of compulsory jurisdiction by any international tribunal, can it be said that there exists a rule of law in international relations? Compare the following statement by Judge Dillard of the International Court of Justice:

> Law and what is legally permitted may be determined by what a court decides, but they are not only what a court decides. Law "goes on" every day without adjudication of any kind. * * *
>
> It is part of the weakness of the international legal order that compulsory jurisdiction to decide legal issues is not part of the system. To say this is not to say that decisions taken by States in conformity with their good faith understanding of what international law either requires or permits are outside a legal frame of reference even if another State objects and despite the absence of adjudication.

Separate Opinion of Judge Dillard, Legal Consequences for States of the Continued Presence of South Africa in Namibia (South West Africa) notwithstanding S.C.Res. 276 (1970), 1971 I.C.J. 138, 156.

4. For developments enhancing the prospects for centralized institutions to enforce international law, see Chapters 9, 11–12 and 15 below.

HORIZONTAL OR DECENTRALIZED ENFORCEMENT

The international system has had little capacity for centralized enforcement up through the end of 20th century. The main sanctions of international law have thus operated horizontally between states. Breaches of international law entail the possibility of reciprocal suspension of obligations owed to the breaching state, and other forms of retaliation. A state that fails to respect international law may find that other states treat it as a lawbreaker and refuse to carry on normal relations with it. For example, a state that violates its obligations toward foreign diplomats may be excluded from regular diplomatic interactions with other states. States generally want to be perceived as law-abiding, and therefore may be responsive to pressures from other states to bring their conduct into compliance with international law. The influence of public opinion contributes more generally to the processes of decentralized enforcement. See generally Damrosch, Enforcing International Law Through Non-Forcible Measures (1997), pp. 23–24 above.

Notes

1. The law against the use or threat of force may be enforced by collective action through the United Nations, but it is subject also to "horizontal enforcement" by the victim acting in self-defense or with others in collective self-defense. See Chapter 12 infra.

2. Measures that are in themselves unlawful might be permissible when taken by a state in response to a violation of law by another state. See Restatement (Third) § 905; Zoller, Peacetime Unilateral Remedies: An Analysis of Countermeasures (1984). Is the use of force ever justified as a means of enforcing international law (except as indicated in note 1)? On the present status of forcible reprisals in international law, see Chapter 12. On non-forcible measures to induce compliance or "punish" violations, see Chapters 9 and 15.

3. Who are the participants in the international sanctioning process? McDougal and Feliciano object to the fact that these participants "are customarily and summarily described as the attacking and target states and their respective allies." They argue that "[f]or purposes of precision in description * * * as well as for the application of certain sanctioning procedures such as those providing for criminal liability, one must frequently go behind the institutional abstraction 'state' and refer to the effective decision-makers * * *." McDougal & Feliciano, Law and Minimum World Public Order 12–13 (1961). The authors identify the decision-makers in the international "process of coercion":

> The authoritative decision-makers established by the public order of the world community for resolving controversies about international coercion are substantially the same as those established for other—"peacetime"—problems. Reflecting the decentralized structure of decision-making in the international community, they include not only the officials of international governmental organizations and judges of international courts and military and arbitration

> tribunals but also the officials of nation-states, whether participant or non-participant in the coercion process. Such authorized nation-state officials who respond to claims to exercise coercion may of course be the same officials who, at other times and in another capacity, assert claims to apply coercion; they may alternately be claimants making claims on their own behalf and decision-makers assessing the claims of others. This dualism in role and function, in a decentralized and primitively organized arena, permits reciprocity to operate as a sanctioning procedure and promotes recognition of the common interest in self-restraint. Conspicuous among decision-makers is, of course, the military commander who must on occasion, and at least in the first instance, pass upon the lawfulness both of his own proposed measures and of measures being taken against him.

Id. at 39–40. (footnotes omitted).

4. On the dual function of officials of states, as organs of both their national communities and of the international community, see Scelle, Le phénomène juridique de dédoublement fonctionnel, in Rechtsfragen der Internationalen Organisation, Festschrift für Hans Wehberg 324 (Schätzel ed. 1956); cf. Kelsen, General Theory of Law and State 327, 351 (1945).

5. Falk has observed that "the decentralized quality of international law places a special burden upon all legal institutions at the national level," not least domestic courts. See Falk, The Role of Domestic Courts in the International Legal Order 65–66 (1964). See also Mann, The Consequences of an International Wrong in International Law, 48 Brit.Y.B.I.L. 1 (1976–1977). Friedmann noted the "great temptation for national courts—to which they have yielded mostly—to arrive at and justify a decision that favors their own nationals." Friedmann, National Courts and the International Legal Order: Projections on the Implications of the Sabbatino Case, 34 Geo.Wash.L.Rev. 443, 453 (1966). Compare the majority and dissenting opinions in Banco Nacional de Cuba v. Sabbatino, 376 U.S. 398, 84 S.Ct. 923, 11 L.Ed.2d 804 (1964), p. 181 infra.

6. It has been suggested that what a state says about its own questionable actions, and the temptation to distort a principle of international law to justify a violation, may be more deleterious for international law than the particular violation itself. See, e.g., Henkin, The Invasion of Panama Under International Law: A Gross Violation, 29 Colum.J.Transnat'l L. 293, 314 (1991). See generally Henkin, How Nations Behave 39–87 (2d ed. 1979).

WHY STATES OBSERVE INTERNATIONAL LAW

HENKIN, HOW NATIONS BEHAVE

89–90, 92–95, 97–98 (2d Ed. 1979). (footnotes omitted).

Much of international law resembles the civil law of domestic society (torts, contracts, property); some of it is analogous to "white collar crimes" (violations of antitrust or other regulatory laws, tax evasion) sometimes committed by "respectable" elements. Like such domestic law, international law too has authority recognized by all. No nation considers international law as "voluntary."

* * *

In arguments that international law is voluntary there lies also a common confusion about the relation of law to "policy." The two are often contrasted, suggesting that law is obligatory while policy is voluntary. In fact, law and policy are not in meaningful contrast, and their relation is not simple, whether in domestic or international society. All law is an instrument of policy, broadly conceived. Law is not an end in itself: even in the most enlightened domestic society it is a means—to order, stability, liberty, security, justice, welfare. The policies served by law are sometimes articulated—in a constitution, in statutory preambles, in legislative pronouncements, in the opinions of the courts; often these policies are tacit, and commonly assumed. International law, too, serves policy, and the policies are not too different from the domestic: order and stability, peace, independence, justice, welfare.

* * *

Much is made of the fact that, in international society, there is no one to compel nations to obey the law. But physical coercion is not the sole or even principal force ensuring compliance with law. Important law is observed by the most powerful, even in domestic societies, although there is no one to compel them. In the United States, the President, Congress, and the mighty armed forces obey orders of a Supreme Court whose single marshal is unarmed.

Too much is made of the fact that nations act not out of "respect for law" but from fear of the consequences of breaking it. And too much is made of the fact that the consequences are not "punishment" by "superior," legally constituted authority, but are the response of the victim and his friends and the unhappy results for friendly relations, prestige, credit, international stability, and other interests which in domestic society would be considered "extra-legal." The fact is that, in domestic society, individuals observe law principally from fear of consequences, and there are "extralegal" consequences that are often enough to deter violation, even were official punishment lacking. * * * In international society, law observance must depend more heavily on these extra-legal sanctions, which means that law observance will depend more closely on the law's current acceptability and on the community's—especially the victim's—current interest in vindicating it. It does not mean that law is not law, or that its observance is less law observance.

There are several mistakes in the related impression that nations do pursuant to law only what they would do anyhow. In part, the criticism misconceives the purpose of law. Law is generally not designed to keep individuals from doing what they are eager to do. Much of law, and the most successful part, is a codification of existing mores, of how people behave and feel they ought to behave. To that extent law reflects, rather than imposes, existing order. * * * To say that nations act pursuant to law only as they would act anyhow may indicate not that the law is irrelevant, but rather that it is sound and viable, reflecting the true interests and attitudes of nations, and that it is likely to be maintained.

At the same time much law (particularly tort law and "white collar crimes") is observed because it is law and because its violation would have undesirable consequences. The effective legal system, it should be clear, is not the one which punishes the most violators, but rather that which has few violations to punish because the law deters potential violators. He who does violate is punished, principally, to reaffirm the standard of behavior and to deter others. This suggests that the law does not concern itself principally with "criminal elements" on the one hand or with "saints" on the other. * * * In international society, too, law is not effective against the Hitlers, and is not needed for that nation which is content with its lot and has few temptations. International law aims at nations which are in principle law-abiding but which might be tempted to commit a violation if there were no threat of undesirable consequences. In international society, too, the reactions to a violation—as in Korea in 1950 or at Suez in 1956—reaffirm the law and strengthen its deterrent effect for the future.

In many respects, the suggestion that nations would act the same way if there were no law is a superficial impression. The deterrent influence of law is there, though it is not always apparent, even to the actor himself. The criticism overlooks also the educative roles of law, which causes persons and nations to feel that what is unlawful is wrong and should not be done. The government which does not even consider certain actions because they are "not done" or because they are not its "style" may be reflecting attitudes acquired because law has forbidden these actions.

In large part, however, the argument that nations do pursuant to law only what they would do anyhow is plain error. The fact that particular behavior is required by law brings into play those ultimate advantages in law observance that suppress temptations and override the apparent immediate advantages from acting otherwise. In many areas, the law at least achieves a common standard or rule and clarity as to what is agreed. * * *

The most common deprecation of international law, finally, insists that no government will observe international law "in the crunch, when it really hurts." If the implication is that nations observe law only when it does not matter, it is grossly mistaken. Indeed, one might as well urge the very opposite: violations in "small matters" sometimes occur because the actor knows that the victim's response will be slight; serious violations are avoided because they might bring serious reactions. The most serious violation—the resort to war—generally does not occur, although it is only when major interests are at stake that nations would even be tempted to this violation. On the other hand, if the suggestion is that when it costs too much to observe international law nations will violate it, the charge is no doubt true. But the implications are less devastating than might appear, since a nation's perception of "when it really hurts" to observe law must take into account its interests in law and in its observance, and the costs of violation. * * *

Whether, in the total, there is an effective "international order" is a question of perspective and definition. Order is not measurable, and no purpose is served by attempts to "grade" it in a rough impressionistic way. How much of that order is attributable to law is a question that cannot be answered in theory or in general, only in time and context. Law is one force—an important one among the forces that govern international relations at any time; the deficiencies of international society make law more dependent on other forces to render the advantages of observance high, the costs of violation prohibitive. In our times the influence of law must be seen in the light of the forces that have shaped international relations since the Second World War.

Note

Henkin declares: "It is probably the case that *almost all nations observe almost all principles of international law and almost all of their obligations almost all of the time.*" Henkin, How Nations Behave 47 (2d ed. 1979).

COMPLIANCE WITHOUT ENFORCEMENT

Professor Harold Koh addressed "Why Do Nations Obey International Law," 106 Yale L.J. 2599 (1997), in a rich review essay of books by Abram Chayes and Antonia Chayes, and by Thomas Franck. He begins his explanation of The Roots of the Compliance Problem: "Like most laws, international rules are rarely enforced, but usually obeyed." Id. at 2603. He pursues the inquiry beginning with ancient and primitive law through a variety of approaches to international law (including Henkin's "How Nations Behave"), into the New World Order, after the Cold War. Koh concludes with his own "transnational legal process" explanation of why nations obey international law.

Notes

1. In The New Sovereignty: Compliance with International Regulatory Agreements (1995), Abram and Antonia Chayes set forth a model to explain how international regulation is accomplished through treaty regimes. They posit that three factors—efficiency, national interest, and regime norms–contribute to the general compliance of states with treaty rules. Occasional non-compliance stems from limitations on the ability of parties to carry out their undertakings, and from the ambiguity and indeterminacy of treaty language. The Chayeses present a model of international compliance based on "management," to induce compliance not through coercion but through interactive processes of justification, discourse, and persuasion. Compliance therefore may be understood as stemming not from a state's fear of coercive sanctions, but rather from processes to ensure transparency, resolve ambiguities, and strengthen states' capacity to comply with international undertakings.

For a range of perspectives on the problem of compliance with international obligations and debates over the Chayeses' managerial approach, see, e.g., Damrosch, Enforcing International Law Through Non–Forcible Measures, 269 Rec. des Cours 22–24 (1997); Weiss & Jacobson, Engaging Countries (1998); Downs, Danish & Barsoom, The Transformative Model of International Regime Design, 38 Colum. J. Transnat. L. 465 (2000).

2. Professor Thomas Franck suggests that states are likely to obey norms of international law that have a high degree of "legitimacy." Franck defines legitimacy as "a property of a rule or rulemaking institution which itself exerts a pull toward compliance on those addressed normatively because those addressed believe that the rule or institution has come into being and operates in accordance with generally accepted principles of right process." Franck, The Power of Legitimacy Among Nations 24 (1990) (emphasis omitted). He identifies four

indicators of legitimacy: "determinacy"—the ability of a rule to convey a clear message; "symbolic validation"—a ritual or signal of "pedigree" that induces compliance by communicating the authority of the rule or of its originator; "coherence"—the extent to which application of a rule is consistent and also justifiable in principled terms; "adherence"—the nexus between a "primary rule of obligation" and a "hierarchy of secondary rules" that defines how rules are to be made, interpreted and applied. Franck concludes that "to the extent a rule, or rule process, exhibits these four properties it will exert a strong pull on states to comply. To the extent these properties are not present, the institution will be easier to ignore and the rule easier to avoid by a state tempted to pursue its short-term self-interest." Id., at 49. In context, "[i]t is the community which invests legitimacy with meaning; it is in the community that legitimacy exerts its pull to rule compliance. It is because states constitute a community that legitimacy has the power to influence their conduct." Id., at 205. See also Franck's earlier article, Legitimacy in the International System, 82 A.J.I.L. 705 (1988). For a critique of Franck's concept of "legitimacy" in international law, see Alvarez, The Quest for Legitimacy: An Examination of The Power of Legitimacy Among Nations by Thomas M. Franck, 24 N.Y.U.J.Int'l L. & Pol. 199 (1991).

3. It has been suggested that states are less likely to comply with "soft" international law. Professor Prosper Weil writes:

> [A]longside "hard law," made up of the norms creating precise legal rights and obligations, the normative system of international law comprises * * * more and more norms whose substance is so vague, so uncompelling, that A's obligation and B's right all but elude the mind. One does not have to look far for examples of this "fragile," "weak," or "soft law," as it is dubbed at times: * * * the purely hortatory or exhortatory provisions whereby [states] undertake to "seek to," "make efforts to," "promote," "avoid," "examine with understanding," "take all due steps with a view to," etc. * * * Whether a rule is "hard" or "soft" does not, of course, affect its normative character. A rule of treaty or customary law may be vague, "soft"; but . . . it does not thereby cease to be a legal norm. In contrast, however definite the substance of a non-normative provision—certain clauses of the Helsinki Final Act, say, or of the Charter of Economic Rights and Duties of States—that will not turn it in to a legal norm.[7]

Weil, Towards Relative Normativity in International Law?, 77 A.J.I.L. 413, 414–15 (1983).

Weil argues that the proliferation of "soft law" weakens the international legal system by blurring the line between law and nonlaw. However, states do in fact respect and rely on "soft law" norms. Much of international environmental law, for example, is "soft law" commonly respected by states, and may be, moreover, a step towards the formulation of more precise conventional rules or customary law. See Dupuy, Soft Law and the International Law of the Environment, 12 Mich.J.Int'l L. 420 (1991); Palmer, New Ways to Make International

7. The term "soft law" is not used solely to express the vague and therefore, in practice, uncompelling character of a legal norm but is also used at times to convey the sublegal value of some non-normative acts, such as certain resolutions of international organizations * * *. It would seem better to reserve the term "soft law" for rules that are imprecise and not really compelling, since sublegal obligations are neither "soft law" nor "hard law": they are simply not law at all. Two basically different categories are involved here; for while there are, on the one hand, legal norms that are not in practice compelling, because too vague, there are also, on the other hand, provisions that are precise, yet remain at the pre- or subnormative stage. To discuss both of these categories in terms of "soft law" or "hard law" is to foster confusion.

Environmental Law, 86 A.J.I.L. 259 (1992). Can "soft law" meet Franck's definition of "determinacy?"

On "soft law" generally, see Handl et al., A Hard Look at "Soft Law," 82 A.S.I.L.Proc. 371 (1988); Bierzanek, Some Remarks on "Soft" Law, 17 Polish Y.B. Int'l L. 21 (1988); Chinkin, The Challenge of Soft Law: Development and Change in International Law, 38 I.L.C.Q. 850 (1989); Dupuy, Declaratory Law and Programmatory Law: From Revolutionary Custom to "Soft Law," in Liber Röling: Declaration on Principles–A Quest for Universal Peace 247 (Akkermans, et al., eds. 1977); Gruchalla–Wesierki, A Framework for Understanding Soft Law, 30 McGill L.J. 37 (1984); Riphagen, From Soft Law to Ius Cogens and Back, 17 Vic.U.Wellington L.Rev. 81 (1987); Sztucki, Reflections on International "Soft Law," in Festskrift till Lars Hjerner: Studies in International Law 549 (1990); Shelton (ed.) Commitment and Compliance: The Role of Non-Binding Norms in the International Legal System (2000).

For the legal character of various forms of "soft law," see Chapter 2, pp. 142–158.

4. Compliance with international law has been explained by the existence and development of a sense of legal obligation and the growth of a "culture of compliance."

For attempts to explain the sense of obligation in international law, see, e.g., 1 Oppenheim's International Law 8–13 (9th ed., Jennings & Watts, eds. 1992); Trimble, International Law, World Order and Critical Legal Studies, 42 Stan. L.Rev. 811 (1990); Brierly, The Basis of Obligation in International Law (Lauterpacht & Waldock, eds. 1958).

Professor Schachter has written:

> As a subject, the "foundation of obligation" is as old as international law itself, it had a prominent place in the seminal treatises of the founding fathers—Suarez, Vittoria, Grotius, Pufendorf et al.—and it remained a central issue in the great controversies of the nineteenth century. In our century it has had a lesser place; it was largely overtaken by the discussion of "sources" and evidence, centered around Article 38 of the Statute of the International Court. Although subordinated, it was not neglected and each of the leading scholars of the twentieth century found himself impelled to advance a fresh analysis. No single theory has received general agreement and sometimes it seems as though there are as many theories or at least formulations as there are scholars. We can list at least a baker's dozen of "candidates" which have been put forward as the basis (or as one of the bases) of obligation in international law:
>
> (i) Consent of states
>
> (ii) Customary practice
>
> (iii) A sense of "rightness"—the juridical conscience
>
> (iv) Natural law or natural reason
>
> (v) Social necessity
>
> (vi) The will of the international community (the "consensus" of the international community)
>
> (vii) Direct (or "stigmatic") intuition
>
> (viii) Common purposes of the participants
>
> (ix) Effectiveness

(x) Sanctions

(xi) "Systemic" goals

(xii) Shared expectations as to authority

(xiii) Rules of recognition

* * *

* * * [C]onceptions as to the basis of obligation arise time and again, and not only in theoretical discussion about the binding force of international law. They come up in concrete controversies as to whether a rule of law has emerged or has been terminated; whether an event is a violation or a precedent; and whether practice under a treaty is accepted as law. * * * The peculiar features of contemporary international society have generated considerable normative activity without at the same time involving commensurate use of the formal procedures for international "legislation" and adjudication.

* * *

But when we examine the arguments and the grounds for decision, we find more frequently than not that the test of whether a "binding" rule exists or should be applied will involve basic jurisprudential assumptions. Even the International Court of Justice, which is governed expressly by Article 38 of its Statute as to the sources of law, has demonstrated time and again that in their deliberative process the judges have had to look to theory to evaluate practice.

Schachter, Towards a Theory of International Obligation, 8 Va.J.Int'l L. 300, 300–04 (1968).

5. A "culture of compliance" is important to the effectiveness of international law, and the existence of such a culture has been noted at different times in the history of international law, among different political actors, in respect of particular norms. But what influences helped build such a culture, and whether and how it can be purposefully promoted, may be disputed. If a culture of compliance suggests that attitudes of compliance are contagious, violations may also be contagious.

6. What is the proper and practical role for international law in the creation of a better-ordered world community? According to Alan James, some confusion in this regard may be attributed to the phrase "law and order:"

[T]he smoothness with which it comes off the tongue can suggest that virtually all that is needed for order is the right kind of law, and in the inter-war period something of this kind was often assumed. In time the fallacy of this approach was eagerly exploded by "realistic" students of affairs, a task which was particularly easy as the word "order" was generally used in this connection to mean security. However, in their enthusiasm they threw the baby out with the bath water, and ever since students of international relations have had little time for international law. In consequence there has been a wide failure in this quarter to note that even with regard to security law can perform very useful services; that it is often a necessary means of changing and improving international society, and can sometimes make a small independent contribution towards these ends; and, above all, that the creation and maintenance of an ongoing and involved system of relationships, such as exists internationally, requires law. When, therefore, order is used to refer to such a system of relationships, it can truly be said that order is dependent on law. For order cannot exist without understandings about permissible behaviour, and the most fundamental as well as the most numerous of these understandings are unavoidably legal in character. Thus the significance of international law is enduring and vital. It does not control the ebb and flow of international politics, but it does provide an indispensable framework for the political process. Without it relations, if not minimal, could not be other than anarchical in the most drastic meaning of the word. Internationally, as elsewhere, law is a concomitant of ordered relations. *Ubi societas, ibi ius.*

James, Law and Order in International Society, in The Bases of International Order 60, 83–84 (James ed. 1973).

INTERNATIONAL LAW AND NATIONAL INTEREST

"Realist" political scientists, such as Professor Hans Morgenthau, declared the "iron law of international politics, that legal obligations must yield to the national interest." Morgenthau, In Defense of the National Interest 144 (1951). Others have suggested (e.g., the excerpt from Friedmann below) that such statements reflect a narrow view of "national interest."

Tension between respect for international law and national interest is likely to surface in particular with regard to norms that seek to regulate the use of force (Article 2 (4) of the U.N. Charter) in circumstances that plausibly engage "national security."

The Cuban Missile Crisis provides a famous illustration: In October 1962, with the Cold War at perhaps its most intense, many saw the U.S. and the U.S.S.R. on the verge of nuclear war as a result of the emplacement of Soviet nuclear missiles in Cuba. The United States responded with a quarantine of vessels headed for Cuba; this response was approved by a resolution of the Organization of American States. The crisis produced scholarly and political debates as to the relevance of law in such circumstances. See, e.g., Chayes, The Cuban Missile Crisis: International Crises and the Role of Law (2d ed. 1987), and other materials excerpted below:

FRIEDMANN, THE ROLE OF INTERNATIONAL LAW IN THE CONDUCT OF INTERNATIONAL AFFAIRS

20 Int'l J. 158, 159–62, 164–65, 168–69 (1965).*

[T]he present state of international society tends to weaken the fabric and function of international law in certain respects, and to strengthen it in others. The weakening factors are the continuing supremacy of national policy objectives over the restraints of international law with regard to the use of force, where national policy and international order conflict. This implies a narrow definition of "national interest." It excludes the question whether the "national interest" in contemporary conditions does not require the strengthening of international law and authority. The strengthening factor is the gradual emergence of an international law of cooperation, implemented by an

* Some footnotes omitted. The author has made minor changes in the text of the article as it originally appeared.

increasing number of international organizations, pursuing the common interests of mankind in the fields of economic and social development, health, communications and other matters of human welfare. Which of these two trends will prevail remains an open question, fateful for the future of mankind.

* * *

The philosophy of the supremacy of national interest over international law was recently expressed by Dean Acheson[3] in the following terms:

> "* * * those involved in the Cuban crisis of October 1962, will remember the irrelevance of the supposed moral considerations brought out in the discussions. Judgment centered about the appraisal of dangers and risks, the weighing of the need for decisive and effective actions against considerations of prudence; the need to do enough, against the consequence of doing too much."

The attitude outlined [by Mr. Acheson] expresses the prevailing instincts of most people. When the chips are down, the average Russian, Chinese, American, Frenchman, Indian or Indonesian will rally around the flag; he will respond to patriotic appeals even if it means a defiance of international legal prohibitions. Is this a simple matter of "realism" versus "wishful thinking"? It is submitted that the role of international law in our time is a more complex issue.

* * * It is the *meaning* of "national interest" which has shifted and today includes universally binding rules against aggression as an aspect of national survival. * * *

* * *

The basic defect of the Acheson thesis does not so much lie in its analysis of the present situation as in the implication that the present state of affairs should be recognized as the only "realistic" approach to the conduct of international relations. A similar argument would have appeared persuasive to the majority of contemporaries over the last eight centuries, while in one country after another central authority and law gradually established their supremacy over warring kingdoms, dukes, archbishops and city republics. * * *

What distinguishes the contemporary problem from that of previous centuries is the desperate urgency of the human condition. Just as the jet plane and the long-range missile move at speeds hundreds or thousands of times greater than that of the horse and buggy, so the need to create organized alternatives to mutual destruction * * * cannot be met with the means of earlier ages. "Co-operate or perish" is a stark fact, not an evangelistic aspiration.

3. In an address given at Amherst College, as reported in The New York Times, December 10, 1964.

Notes

1. Acheson also said about the Cuban missile crisis:

> I must conclude that the propriety of the Cuban quarantine is not a legal issue. The power, position and prestige of the United States had been challenged by another state; and law simply does not deal with such questions of ultimate power—power that comes close to the sources of sovereignty. I cannot believe that there are principles of law that say we must accept destruction of our way of life. One would be surprised if practical men, trained in legal history and thought, had devised and brought to a state of general acceptance a principle condemnatory of an action so essential to the continuation of preeminent power as that taken by the United States last October. Such a principle would be as harmful to the development of restraining procedures as it would be futile. No law can destroy the state creating the law. The survival of states is not a matter of law.
>
> However, in the action taken in the Cuban quarantine, one can see the influence of accepted legal principles. These principles are procedural devices designed to reduce the severity of a possible clash. Those devices cause wise delay before drastic action, create a "cooling off" period, permit the consideration of others' views. The importance of the Organization of American States was also procedural, and emphasized the desirability of collective action, thus creating a common denominator of action. Some of these desirable consequences are familiar to us in the domestic industrial area.
>
> In October the United States was faced with grave problems of policy and procedure in relation to its own and outside interests. The action taken was the right action. "Right" means more than legally justifiable, or even successful. The United States resolved very grave issues of policy in a way consonant with ethical restraint.

The Cuban Quarantine, Remarks by the Honorable Dean Acheson, 57 A.S.I.L.Proc. 9, 14 (1963).

2. In contrast to Acheson's view of the irrelevance of international law in the Cuban Missile Crisis, Henkin has said that persons conversant with the deliberations suggested that the constrictions of international law influenced the final decision to avoid (or mitigate) a violation of international law by implementing a quarantine rather than resorting to bombing of Cuban territory. See Henkin, How Nations Behave 286–90 (2d ed. 1979).

3. Regardless of the influence of international law on the decision-making process, would it be wise, from the point of view of the integrity of international law, to recognize certain areas as immune from the prescriptions of international law? Where policy issues are likely to be of decisive importance in determining the behavior of nations, should international law recognize sovereign prerogatives? Is aggression between states, especially when factual issues perform a major role in assessing legal implications, an area where international law should remain silent? See Chapter 12.

4. On the common view that there is continuing tension between international law and national interest:

> Of course, that statement may suggest merely the truism that nations, like individuals, balance the advantages and disadvantages of law observance and may decide to violate the law and accept the consequences. But the implica-

> tions of Mr. Morgenthau's "iron law" are broader. It seems to set up a dichotomy between law observance and national interest, to treat their concurrence as coincidental and their opposition as common. If so, it seems to see immediate tangible advantage—the gain from a violation—as the only national interest. It does not seem to consider that the law of nations may be in the interest of all nations, as the law of an enlightened society is in the interest of all its citizens. It does not see national interest in law observance—in order and stability, in reliable expectations, in confidence and credit, in the support of other nations and peoples, in friendly relations, in living up to a nation's aspirations and self image, in satisfying the "morality" of its own officials and of its own citizens. It tends to discount the national interest in avoiding other, immediate "concrete" responses to violation. The issue of law observance, I would suggest, is never a clear choice between legal obligation and national interest; a nation that observes law, even when it "hurts," is not sacrificing national interest to law; it is choosing between competing national interests; when it commits a violation it is also sacrificing one national interest to another.

Henkin, How Nations Behave 331 (2d ed. 1979). On the various national interests served by the observance of international law, see, e.g., Weston, The Logic and Utility of a Lawful United States Foreign Policy, 1 Transnat'l L. & Contemp.Probs. 1 (1991).

5. The view that international law must bow to national interest was again prominent in public discussion after international lawyers criticized the United States invasion of Grenada in 1983, and United States actions in Central America, particularly in relation to Nicaragua and Panama. Those who held the view that the NATO intervention in Kosovo in 1999 violated international law, but was undertaken at the behest of the United States and its NATO partners for reasons of their national interest, may consider the Kosovo intervention also to be an instance of international law sacrificed to national interest. See Chapter 12.

SECTION 3. CONTEMPORARY PERSPECTIVES ON INTERNATIONAL LAW

Perspectives on international law could reflect philosophical or theoretical differences as to law, e.g. between international law as natural law or as positive law. International law also has not escaped contemporary movements addressing law generally, e.g. feminist perspectives, or the critical legal studies movement, or law and economics. These may impinge on international law differently from their relevance to law generally, or to domestic law in national societies. Some writing on international law reflects perceived differences between national and international law, such as the character of international law as the law of a political system deriving from relations among states, or the reminder that international law must respect its multicultural origins and character.

A variety of methods is set forth in a symposium in the American Journal of International Law in April 1999, excerpted below. Following an overview of the methods, selected perspectives (feminism, critical legal studies, law and economics, and international relations theory) will be addressed in turn.

A. OVERVIEW OF METHODS

SYMPOSIUM ON METHOD IN INTERNATIONAL LAW: APPRAISING THE METHODS OF INTERNATIONAL LAW: A PROSPECTUS FOR READERS

Steven Ratner & Anne–Marie Slaughter (eds.) 93 A.J.I.L. 291–294, 300–301 (1999) (footnotes omitted).

[H]undreds of articles published in the *Journal* have revealed the two fundamental transformations in our field: first, the susceptibility of new areas of international affairs to treatment through international norms and institutions; and second, theoretical innovations leading to new ways of thinking about each of these issue areas. Indeed, these two developments are inseparable. As Ronald St. J. Macdonald and Douglas M. Johnston wrote in their introduction to a significant and weighty volume of theoretical essays on international law fifteen years ago, a focus on theory is increasingly needed in a field such as ours that has been driven to great degrees of both specialization and fragmentation. * * *

To elucidate the theoretical underpinnings of contemporary scholarship through recourse to the methods employed by various theories, we decided upon seven methods for appraisal: legal positivism, the New Haven School, international legal process, critical legal studies, international law and international relations, feminist jurisprudence, and law and economics. In our view, they represent the major methods of international legal scholarship today. * * *

Positivism. Positivism summarizes a range of theories that focus upon describing the law as it is, backed up by effective sanctions, with reference to formal criteria, independently of moral or ethical considerations. For positivists, international law is no more or less than the rules to which states have agreed through treaties, custom, and perhaps other forms of consent. In the absence of such evidence of the will of states, positivists will assume that states remain at liberty to undertake whatever actions they please. Positivism also tends to view states as the only subjects of international law, thereby discounting the role of nonstate actors. It remains the lingua franca of most international lawyers, especially in continental Europe.

The New Haven School (policy-oriented jurisprudence). Established by Harold Lasswell and Myres McDougal of Yale Law School beginning in the mid–1940's, the New Haven School eschews positivism's formal method of searching for rules as well as the concept of law as based on rules alone. It describes itself as a policy-oriented perspective, viewing international law as a process of decision making by which various actors in the world community clarify and implement their common interests in accordance with their expectations of appropriate processes and of effectiveness in controlling behavior. * * *

International legal process. International legal process (ILP) refers to the approach first developed by Abram Chayes, Thomas Ehrlich and Andreas Lowenfeld at Harvard Law School in the 1960's. Building on the American legal process school, it has seen the key locus of inquiry of international law as the role of law in constraining decision makers and affecting the course of international affairs. Legal process theory has recently enjoyed a domestic revival, which seeks to underpin precepts about process with a set of normative values. Some ILP scholars are following suit.

Critical legal studies. Critical legal studies (CLS) scholars have sought to move beyond what constitutes law, or the relevance of law to policy, to focus on the contradictions, hypocrisies and failings of international legal discourse. The diverse group of scholars who often identify themselves as part of the "New Stream" have emphasized the importance of culture to legal development and offered a critical view of the progress of the law in its confrontations with state sovereignty. Like the deconstruction movement, which is the intellectual font of many of its ideas, critical legal studies has focused on the importance of language.

International law and international relations. IR/IL is a purposefully interdisciplinary approach that seeks to incorporate into international law the insights of international relations theory regarding the behavior of international actors. The most recent round of IR/IL scholarship seeks to draw on contemporary developments and strands in international relations theory, which is itself a relatively young discipline. The results are diverse, ranging from studies of compliance, to analyses of the stability and effectiveness of international institutions, to the ways that models of state conduct affect the content and subject of international rules.

Feminist jurisprudence. Feminist scholars of international law seek to examine how both legal norms and processes reflect the domination of men and to reexamine and reform these norms and processes so as to take account of women. Feminist jurisprudence has devoted particular attention to the shortcomings in the international protection of women's rights, but it has also asserted deeper structural challenges to international law, criticizing the way law is made and applied as insufficiently attentive to the role of women. Feminist jurisprudence has also taken an active advocacy role.

Law and economics. In its domestic incarnation, which has proved highly significant and enduring, law and economics has both a descriptive component that seeks to explain existing rules as reflecting the most economically efficient outcome, and a normative component that evaluates proposed changes in the law and urges adoption of those that maximize wealth. Game theory and public choice theory are often considered part of law and economics. In the international area, it has begun to address commercial and environmental issues. * * *

* * * Each of the methods we consider here (with the possible exception of international law and international relations) originated in an approach to domestic law. This, of course, reinforces the conceptual connections between international law and domestic law. But the movement from the domestic to the international has not followed one trajectory; the differences between the two arenas make one model of transposition too facile. * * *

Notes

1. The symposium proceeds to address one topic–the responsibility of individuals for human rights abuses in internal conflicts–from the perspectives of the different methods.

2. Several of these methods of international law had been treated nearly 20 years earlier in a series of essays in international legal theory in The Structure and Process of International Law: Essays in Legal Philosophy Doctrine and Theory (Macdonald & Johnston, eds. 1983).

3. The continuing development of international law has attracted attention from contemporary intellectual movements, notably from feminist writers and proponents of critical legal studies. On intellectual influences giving rise to new approaches to international law in recent decades, see David Kennedy, The Disciplines of International Law and Policy, 12 Leiden J.I.L. 30 (1999). In 1999, the American Society of International Law devoted much of its annual meeting to these new approaches. For the results, see A.S.I.L. Proc. (1999).

4. In correspondence following the publication of the Symposium on Method, attention was drawn to perspectives on international law from the point of view of peoples of color, whether as a comprehensive postcolonial reconsideration of international law or as a reconceptualization from jurisprudential perspectives such as critical race theory. The symposium editors expressed the intention to include such perspectives in a forthcoming book version of the symposium. See 94 A.J.I.L. 99–101 (2000).

B. FEMINIST PERSPECTIVES ON INTERNATIONAL LAW

CHARLESWORTH, CHINKIN & WRIGHT, FEMINIST APPROACHES TO INTERNATIONAL LAW

85 A.J.I.L. 613, 615–629 (1991) (footnotes omitted).

By challenging the nature and operation of international law and its context, feminist legal theory can contribute to the progressive development of international law. A feminist account of international law suggests that we inhabit a world in which men of all nations have used the statist system to establish economic and nationalist priorities to serve male elites, while basic human, social and economic needs are not met. International institutions echo these same priorities. By taking women seriously and describing the silences and fundamentally skewed nature of international law, feminist theory can identify possibilities for change. * * *

THE ORGANIZATIONAL STRUCTURE OF INTERNATIONAL LAW

The structure of the international legal order reflects a male perspective and ensures its continued dominance. The primary subjects of international law are states and, increasingly, international organizations. In both states and international organizations the invisibility of women is striking. Power structures within governments are overwhelmingly masculine: women have significant positions of power in very few states, and in those where they do, their numbers are minuscule. Women are either unrepresented or under-represented in the national and global decision-making processes.

States are patriarchal structures not only because they exclude women from elite positions and decision-making roles, but also because they are based on the concentration of power in, and control by, an elite and the domestic legitimation of a monopoly over the use of force to maintain that control. This foundation is reinforced by international legal principles of sovereign equality, political independence and territorial integrity and the legitimation of force to defend those attributes.

International organizations are functional extensions of states that allow them to act collectively to achieve their objectives. Not surprisingly, their structures replicate those of states, restricting women to insignificant and subordinate roles. Thus, in the United Nations itself, where the achievement of nearly universal membership is regarded as a major success of the international community, this universality does not apply to women.

* * *

Women are excluded from all major decision making by international institutions on global policies and guidelines, despite the often disparate impact of those decisions on women. Since 1985, there has been some improvement in the representation of women in the United Nations and its specialized agencies. It has been estimated, however, that "at the present rate of change it will take almost 4 more decades (until 2021) to reach equality (i.e. 50% of professional jobs held by women). * * * "

The silence and invisibility of women also characterizes those bodies with special functions regarding the creation and progressive development of international law. Only one woman has sat as a judge on the International Court of Justice and no woman has ever been a member of the International Law Commission. Critics have frequently pointed out that the distribution of judges on the Court does not reflect the makeup of the international community, a concern that peaked after the decision in the *South West Africa* cases in 1966. Steps have since been taken to improve "the representation of the main forms of civilization and of the principal legal systems of the world" on the Court, but not in the direction of representing women, half of the world's population.

* * *

Why is it significant that all the major institutions of the international legal order are peopled by men? Long-term domination of all bodies wielding political power nationally and internationally means that issues traditionally of concern to men become seen as human concerns, while "women's concerns" are relegated to a special, limited category. * * * The orthodox face of international law and politics would change dramatically if their institutions were truly human in composition: their horizons would widen to include issues previously regarded as domestic—in the two senses of the word. * * *

The Normative Structure of International Law

International jurisprudence assumes that international law norms directed at individuals within states are universally applicable and neutral. It is not recognized, however, that such principles may impinge differently on men and women; consequently, women's experiences of the operation of these laws tend to be silenced or discounted.

The normative structure of international law has allowed issues of particular concern to women to be either ignored or undermined. For example, modern international law rests on and reproduces various dichotomies between the public and private spheres, and the "public" sphere is regarded as the province of international law. One such distinction is between public international law, the law governing the relations between nation-states, and private international law, the rules about conflicts between national legal systems. Another is the distinction between matters of international "public" concern and matters "private" to states that are considered within their domestic jurisdiction, in which the international community has no recognized legal interest. Yet another is the line drawn between law and other forms of "private" knowledge such as morality.

At a deeper level one finds a public/private dichotomy based on gender. One explanation feminist scholars offer for the dominance of men and the male voice in all areas of power and authority in the western liberal tradition is that a dichotomy is drawn between the public sphere and the private or domestic one. The public realm of the work place, the law, economics, politics and intellectual and cultural life, where power and authority are exercised, is regarded as the natural province of men; while the private world of the home, the hearth and children is seen as the appropriate domain of women. The public/private distinction has a normative, as well as a descriptive, dimension. Traditionally, the two spheres are accorded asymmetrical value: greater significance is attached to the public, male world than to the private, female one. * * * Its reproduction and acceptance in all areas of knowledge have conferred primacy on the male world and supported the dominance of men.

* * *

In one sense, the public/private distinction is the fundamental basis of the modern state's function of separating and concentrating juridical forms of power that emanate from the state. The distinction implies that the private world is uncontrolled. In fact, the regulation of taxation, social security, education, health and welfare has immediate effects on the private sphere. The myth that state power is not exercised in the "private" realm allocated to women masks its control.

What force does the feminist critique of the public/private dichotomy in the foundation of domestic legal systems have for the international legal order? Traditionally, of course, international law was regarded as operating only in the most public of public spheres: the relations between nation-states. We argue, however, that the definition of certain principles in international law rests on and reproduces the public/private distinction. It thus privileges the male world view and supports male dominance in the international legal order.

The grip that the public/private distinction has on international law, and the consequent banishment of women's voices and concerns from the discipline, can be seen in the international prohibition on torture. The right to freedom from torture and other forms of cruel, inhuman or degrading treatment is generally accepted as a paradigmatic civil and political right. It is included in all international catalogs of civil and political rights and is the focus of specialized United Nations and regional treaties. The right to be free from torture is also regarded as a norm of customary international law—

indeed, like the prohibition on slavery, as a norm of *jus cogens*. The basis for the right is traced to "the inherent dignity of the human person." Behavior constituting torture is defined in the Convention against Torture as

> any act by which severe pain or suffering, whether physical or mental, is intentionally inflicted on a person for such purposes as obtaining from him or a third person information or a confession, punishing him for an act he or a third person has committed or is suspected of having committed, or intimidating or coercing him or a third person, or for any reason based on discrimination of any kind, when such pain or suffering is inflicted by or at the instigation of or with the consent or acquiescence of a public official or other person acting in an official capacity.

This definition has been considered broad because it covers mental suffering and behavior "at the instigation of" a public official. However, despite the use of the term "human person" in the Preamble, the use of the masculine pronoun alone in the definition of the proscribed behavior immediately gives the definition a male, rather than a truly human, context. More importantly, the description of the prohibited conduct relies on a distinction between public and private actions that obscures injuries to their dignity usually sustained by women. The traditional canon of human rights law does not deal in categories that fit the experiences of women. It is cast in terms of discrete violations of rights and offers little redress in cases where there is a pervasive, structural denial of rights.

The international definition of torture requires not only the intention to inflict suffering, but also the secondary intention that the infliction of suffering will fulfill a purpose. Recent evidence suggests that women and children, in particular, are victims of widespread and apparently random terror campaigns by both governmental and guerrilla groups in times of civil unrest or armed conflict. Such suffering is not clearly included in the international definition of torture.

A crucial aspect of torture and cruel, inhuman or degrading conduct, as defined, is that they take place in the public realm: a public official or a person acting officially must be implicated in the pain and suffering. The rationale for this limitation is that "private acts (of brutality) would usually be ordinary criminal offenses which national law enforcement is expected to repress. *International* concern with torture arises only when the State itself abandons its function of protecting its citizenry by sanctioning criminal action by law enforcement personnel." Many women suffer from torture in this limited sense. The international jurisprudence on the notion of torture arguably extends to sexual violence and psychological coercion if the perpetrator has official standing. However, severe pain and suffering that is inflicted outside the most public context of the state—for example, within the home or by private persons, which is the most pervasive and significant violence sustained by women—does not qualify as torture despite its impact on the inherent dignity of the human person. Indeed, some forms of violence are attributed to cultural tradition. * * *

States are held responsible for torture only when their designated agents have direct responsibility for such acts and that responsibility is imputed to the state. States are not considered responsible if they have maintained a legal and social system in which violations of physical and mental integrity are endemic. * * * A feminist perspective on human rights would require a rethinking of the notions of imputability and state responsibility and in this sense would challenge the most basic assumptions of international law. If violence against women were considered by the international legal system to be as shocking as violence against people for their political ideas, women would have considerable support in their struggle.

Notes

1. Professor Charlesworth later provided an essay on feminist methodology for the Symposium on Method, pp. 41–42 above. Her essay includes:

> How do feminist methods compare to the other methodologies presented in this symposium? In principle, all the methods are capable of some response to the situation of women worldwide and, indeed, feminist international lawyers have drawn on each of these methods, from positivism to critical legal studies, in their attempts to make international law more useful to women. However, unlike these other methods, my account of feminism asserts the importance of gender as an issue in international law: it argues that ideas about "femininity" and "masculinity" are incorporated into international legal rules and structures, silencing women's voices and reinforcing the globally observed domination of women by men. None of the other methodologies represented here displays any concern with gender or, indeed, with the position of women as an international issue. The situation of over half the world's population is not seen as relevant to attempts to define universally applicable principles.
>
> Another distinction between feminist methods and many of the other contributions is in the way they view the idea of objectivity in international law. * * * Feminist methods question the possibility of objectivity in a system that effectively excludes women's voices. They are skeptical about the construction of neutral and impartial standards, seeing them as synonyms for male perspectives. Skepticism about the hunt for the objective is, of course, shared by many critical thinkers, but they have remained curiously aloof from examining the implications for gender politics, or indeed for the situation of other marginalized groups. * * *
>
> * * * Another set of methods that have had some resonance for feminist international lawyers are those of international relations. It is striking that none of the literature discussing the potential bridges between international law and international relations * * * has paid any attention to the significant influence of the rich feminist IR literature on international legal scholars and vice versa. The lack of interest in this connection underlines how eccentric and marginal feminists appear in the two disciplines.
>
> * * * Is there any point in changing the law? Some feminist theorists might dismiss reform of the law as a worthwhile strategy, arguing that this may give undue prominence to law as a site of social change. They may point out that some women will gain more from international law than others. In any event, it may be argued, even if we get the principles right, there is no guarantee that the practice will change. Feminists might point to the greater value of political campaigns or media coverage in reducing the oppression of

> women. These arguments, while powerful, do not acknowledge that international law has a symbolic, as well as a regulative, function. Claims based on international law can carry an emotional and moral legitimacy that can have considerable political force.

Charlesworth, Feminist Methods in International Law, 93 A.J.I.L. 379, 392–93 (1999).

2. For a response to the positions in the principal article, see F. Tesón, Feminism and International Law: A Reply, 33 Va. J.I.L. 647 (1993).

3. On feminist critiques of the use of force, international humanitarian law, and international human rights, see the Symposium in 12 Australian Y.B.Int'l L. (1992), especially Chinkin, A Gendered Perspective to the International Use of Force, at 279; Gardam, A Feminist Appraisal of Certain Aspects of International Humanitarian Law, at 265; Wright, Economic Rights and Social Justice: A Feminist Analysis of Some International Human Rights Conventions, at 242. See also Gardam, Women and the Law of Armed Conflict: Why the Silence? 46 I.C.L.Q. 55 (1997). For feminist perspectives on a range of issues in international law, see Dallmeyer (ed.), Reconceiving Reality: Women and International Law (1993); Charlesworth & Chinkin, The Boundaries of International Law: A Feminist Analysis (2000).

On international law and women's rights, see generally "The Human Rights of Women" in Human Rights (Henkin, Neuman, Orentlicher, and Leebron eds. 1999, pp. 358–405); see also Cook, Women's International Human Rights: A Bibliography, 24 N.Y.U.J.Int'l L. & Pol. 857 (1992). See also Ahooja–Patel, Women's Rights, in International Law: Achievements and Prospects 1105 (M. Bedjaoui, ed. 1991); Byrnes, Women, Feminism and International Human Rights–Methodological Myopia, Fundamental Flaws or Meaningful Marginalisation? Some Current Issues, 12 Australian Y.B.Int'l L. 205 (1992). A comprehensive electronic bibliography on women and international human rights is maintained at www.law-lib.utoronto.ca/diana.

4. In the 1990s, international refugee law was one of many areas of international law to undergo sustained feminist analysis and critique. In 1990 the United Nations High Commissioner for Refugees adopted a policy on the particular needs of women refugees in response to growing concerns that those needs were not being met. See UNHCR Policy on Refugee Women, U.N. Doc. A/AC.96/754 (1990). Updated references on women and refugee law are available in the electronic bibliography cited in the preceding note.

C. INTERNATIONAL LAW AND THE CRITICAL LEGAL STUDIES MOVEMENT

The critical legal studies movement has drawn attention to the discourse of international law, and to the legitimizing power of language, examining the effect of language upon ideas of rights and obligations in international relations. For example, Professor David Kennedy writes:

> Discourse about sources searches abstractly to delimit the norms which bind sovereigns in a way which relies neither on the interests of sovereigns nor on some vision of the good which is independent of state interests. The search is for a decisive discourse—not for a persuasive justification—which can continually distinguish binding from nonbinding norms while remaining open to expressions of sovereign will. The argu-

mentative moves made by those engaged in sources discourse reflect this central goal.

> The result is a discourse of evasion which constantly combines that which it cannot differentiate and emphasizes that which it can express only by hyperbolic exclusion. Pursued in this fashion, sources doctrine moves us forward from theory towards other doctrines which it supplements, remaining both authoritatively independent and parasitic. This paradoxical position between theoretical discourse and doctrines of substance and process is maintained by endlessly embracing and managing a set of ephemeral rhetorical differences. The turn to sources doctrine thus seems to provide an escape from fruitless theoretical argument, moving us towards legal order, precisely by opening up an endlessly proliferating field of legal argumentation.

Kennedy, International Legal Structures 107 (1987).

Martti Koskenniemi uses the concept of "state sovereignty" to suggest that "the use of sovereignty within international legal discourse follows from a set of contradictory assumptions which control the production of arguments within it and render it ultimately incapable of providing determinate answers to legal problems." He continues:

> Within international legal discourse "State sovereignty" is interpreted from the perspective of two conflicting assumptions. Sometimes sovereignty is taken to mean the completeness of State power within its territory which is inherent in the concept of statehood and precedes the international normative order. At other times, sovereignty is conceptualized as a "systemic" concept, determined from within the international normative system which in this sense precedes it. These two assumptions contradict each other. The former legitimizes the international normative order from the given legitimacy of State power. The latter legitimizes State power from the assumed legitimacy of the normative order. * * *
>
> International legal discourse does not establish priority between these conflicting models of legitimation. It works with a fluid conception of sovereignty which contains both simultaneously. Therefore, it is unable to produce coherent or convincing solutions to legal problems. Each disputing State's position can be expressed so as to manifest either of the legitimation models. By taking one or the other model as one's starting-point it is possible to support whatever position one needs to support. As dispute solution cannot prefer either, it will remain materially uncontrolling. What look like solutions determined by the law emerge as facade legitimation, following from adopting interpretations about the parties positions which are undetermined by the legal arguments themselves.
>
> * * *
>
> The idea of sovereignty is incoherent inasmuch as it expresses the State's subjective freedom as well as its objective submission to an international normative order. The structure of international legal discourse follows from this basic ambiguity. The dynamics of the discourse is provided by the constantly renewed effort to solve the contradiction between the two incompatible perspectives towards sovereignty. As the contradiction remains unsolved, however, the discourse remains open-

> ended. No certainty about correct norms or correct patterns of behavior can be attained within it.

Koskenniemi, Sovereignty: Prolegomena to a Study of the Structure of International Law as Discourse, 4 Kansainoikeus Ius Gentium 71, 71–72, 106 (Nos. 1/2, 1987).

Notes

1. Critical legal scholars have argued that much, if not all, of international law, is merely an ideological construct intended to secure the observance of international norms by convincing states and people that the law is politically neutral and just. See Purvis, Critical Legal Studies in Public International Law, 32 Harv.Int'l L.J. 81 (1991).

2. Critical perspectives on international law include: Carty, Critical International Law: Recent Trends in the Theory of International Law, 2 E.J.I.L. 66 (1991); Carty, The Decay of International Law: A Reappraisal of the Limits of Legal Imagination in International Affairs (1986); Koskenniemi, From Apology to Utopia: The Structure of International Legal Argument (1989); International Law (Koskenniemi, ed. 1992); Boyle, Ideals and Things: International Legal Scholarship and the Prison–House of Language, 26 Harv.Int'l L.J. 327 (1985); Kennedy, Theses About International Legal Discourse, 23 German Y.B.Int'l L. 353 (1980); Kennedy, A New Stream of International Legal Scholarship, 7 Wis.Int'l L.J., 1 (1988). For a review essay, see Trimble, International Law, World Order and Critical Legal Studies, 42 Stan.L.Rev. 811 (1990). See also A.S.I.L. Proc. (1999) for representation of a variety of critical perspectives on international law.

D. LAW AND ECONOMICS AND INTERNATIONAL LAW

A law and economics (L&E) perspective has also addressed the discipline and the study of international law. See, e.g., Dunoff & Trachtman, Economic Analysis of International Law, 24 Yale J. Int'l L. 1 (1999). In the Symposium on Method, pp. 41–42 above, Professors Dunoff and Trachtman offer a succinct exposition of L&E as applied to international law:

> Economics is the study of rational choice under conditions of limited resources. Rational choice assumes that individual actors seek to maximize their preferences. The goal of L&E analysis is to identify the legal implications of this maximizing behavior, both in and out of markets, and for markets and other institutions. While the first generation of L&E scholarship often employed cost-benefit analyses to address these issues, our focus is not just on cost-benefit analysis, but also on transaction cost analysis and game theory, and the application of these methodologies to political contexts through public choice theory.
>
> In many respects these techniques formalize, extend and contextualize insights that are familiar to most international lawyers. But this formalization is important–it allows us to focus on relevant variables, generate hypotheses, and, to some extent, empirically test these hypotheses. Furthermore, it provides a firmer and less subjective basis for argumentation than traditional international law analysis. It is less

subjective insofar as it eschews simple natural law or epithet-based argumentation, and provides the capacity to render transparent the distributive consequences of legal rules. Perhaps most important to scholars, it furnishes a basis for a progressive research program built on shared foundations, one that will seek to answer research questions and move on, rather than endlessly address the same tired questions.

* * *

[L&E analysis] is premised upon a normatively determined approach termed "methodological individualism." Under this approach, no particular outcome or norm is a priori deemed desirable; rather, individual choice, sometimes called "consumer sovereignty," is the ultimate source of values. The assumption that individuals are the ultimate source of norms sharply distinguishes L&E analysis from other approaches to international law, such as natural law theories.

When extended to the international realm, the commitment to methodological individualism has substantial normative implications. For example, given the emphasis on individual choice, L&E methods will tend to favor more, rather than less, representative institutions. Moreover, methodological individualism views the state not as a player in its own right with its own normative value, but as a mediating institution with only derivative normative value. Thus, while L&E rejects state-centered positivism, it would rehabilitate the state as an institution, just as it would validate the corporation as an institution: as a vehicle for individuals to work together more productively. Finally, the L&E approach is consistent with the legal positivism that respects the law as written because–and to the extent that–it is the product of legislative processes that reflect individual preferences better than the alternative preference-revealing mechanisms.

Dunoff & Trachtman, The Law and Economics of Humanitarian Law Violations in Internal Conflict, 93 A.J.I.L. 394, 395–398 (1999).

Note

L&E methods such as game theory have been deployed in the nature of a critique of traditional concepts of international law. For example, Jack Goldsmith and Eric Posner propose that game-theoretic models (such as a prisoner's dilemma) can be used to question conventional wisdom about whether customary international law affects state behavior. See Goldsmith & Posner, A Theory of Customary International Law, 66 U. Chicago L. Rev. 1113 (1999). Along with other approaches in international relations theory (see below), game theory has also been applied to the international law of treaties. See Setear, An Iterative Perspective on Treaties: A Synthesis of International Relations Theory and International Law, 37 Harv. Int'l L. J. 139 (1996); Setear, Responses to Breach of a Treaty and Rationalist International Relations Theory, 83 Va. L. Rev. 1 (1996). For applications of public choice theory to contemporary transnational problems, and an examination of aspects of international law that arguably bolster the influence of interest groups across national boundaries, see Benvenisti, Exit and Voice in the Age of Globalization, 98 Mich. L Rev. 167 (1999). See also Bhandari & Sykes, Economic Dimensions in International Law (1997).

E. INTERNATIONAL RELATIONS THEORY AND INTERNATIONAL LAW

Building on earlier articles, notably Slaughter–Burley, International Law and International Relations Theory: A Dual Agenda, 87 A.J.I.L. 205 (1993), and Slaughter, Tulumello, and Wood, International Law and International Relation Theory: A New Generation of Interdisciplinary Scholarship, 92 A.J.I.L. 367 (1998), Professor Kenneth Abbott has written on international relations (IR) theory and international law for the Symposium on Method, pp. 41–42 above:

ABBOTT, INTERNATIONAL RELATIONS THEORY, INTERNATIONAL LAW, AND THE REGIME GOVERNING INTERNAL CONFLICTS

93 A.J.I.L. 361–367 (1999) (footnotes omitted).

Over the last ten years, international relations (IR) theory, a branch of political science, has animated some of the most exciting scholarship in international law. If a true joint discipline has not yet emerged, scholars in both fields have clearly established the value of interdisciplinary cross-fertilization. Yet IR–like international law–comprises several distinct theoretical approaches or "methods." * * *

IR theory is most helpful in performing three different, though equally significant, intellectual tasks: *description, explanation* and *institutional design*. First, while lawyers *describe* rules and institutions all the time, we inevitably–and often subconsciously—use some intellectual template (frequently a positivist one) to determine which elements of these complex phenomena to emphasize, which to omit. The carefully constructed models of social interaction underlying IR theory remind us to choose these templates carefully, in light of our purpose. More specifically, IR helps us describe legal institutions richly, incorporating the political factors which shape the law: the interests, power, and governance structures of states and other actors; the information, ideas and understandings in which they operate; the institutions within which they interact.

IR scholars are primarily concerned with *explaining* political behavior—recently, at least, including law-related behavior. Especially within those schools that favor rationalist approaches, scholars seek to identify the actors relevant to an issue, the factors (material or subjective) that affect their behavior or otherwise influence events, and the "causal pathways" by which those factors have effect. These elements are typically incorporated in a model that singles out particular factors for study. In designing research, scholars look for ways to test explanatory hypotheses, using case studies or data analysis * * *

A scholar applying IR theory might treat legal rules and institutions as phenomena to be explained ("dependent variables") * * * Alternatively, IR might analyze legal rules and institutions—including the processes of legal decision making—as explanatory factors ("independent variables"). One might ask, has the existence of the International Criminal Tribunal for the former Yugoslavia (ICTY), or the way it has handled cases, affected the behavior of governments and other actors in the Balkans? If so, by what means?

Why should a lawyer care about questions like these? Analyses treating law as a dependent variable are valuable in many settings, for they help us understand the functions, origin and meaning of rules and institutions. Analyses treating law as an independent variable are also valuable (though unfortunately less common): they help us assess the workings and effectiveness of legal arrangements in the real world. Both forms of explanation, then, are valuable in their own rights. But explanation is at least as important for its forward-looking applications: predicting future developments and *designing institutions* capable of affecting behavior in desirable ways. It is here—constructing law-based options for the future, as the editors put it—that lawyers can play their greatest role and IR can make its most significant contribution. * * *

Clearly, interdisciplinary cross-fertilization must flow both ways. This essay suggests two important lessons for IR. First, IR scholarship has overlooked many issue areas in which international norms and institutions carry important consequences for individuals and states—as exemplified by the current *Pinochet* litigation. Second, most of these regimes are at least partially legalized, with legal rules, institutions, procedures, and discourse that modify ordinary politics. The legal character of international cooperation is itself a significant political phenomenon. * * *

Four visions of international politics are prominent in IR scholarship today. Within IR, each school views itself as foundational. Yet in studying complex phenomena like the atrocities regime, they frequently overlap, with each providing important insights. * * *

Realist theory has dominated IR since before World War II. Realists treat states as the principal actors in international politics. States interact in an environment of anarchy, defined as the absence of any central government able to keep peace or enforce agreements. Security is their overriding goal, and self-help their guiding principle. Under these conditions, differences in power are usually sufficient to explain important events. Realists concentrate on interactions among major powers and on matters of war and peace. Other issues–even related issues like war crimes—are secondary. * * *

Many *institutionalist* scholars start from a similar model of decentralized state interaction. Some share with realists a conviction that states are "real" actors with clearly specified national interests. Most, however, view states as legal fictions that aggregate the interests and preferences of their citizens; these scholars rely on state-centric analysis rather than true "methodological individualism" because it allows for more parsimonious explanation. In either case, these theorists acknowledge a broad spectrum of interests, from wealth to a cleaner environment, that depend on cooperation. Drawing on game theory, economics and other disciplines, institutionalists identify conditions that prevent states from realizing potential gains from cooperation—"market failures," in economic terms—and analyze how rules and other institutions can overcome those obstacles. Regime theory, a more expansive vein of institutionalist scholarship, incorporates information and ideas as well as power and interests, and acknowledges significant roles for private and supranational actors and domestic politics. * * *

Various forms of *liberal* IR theory have been influential for many years, but this approach has recently been given new vitality. Liberals insist on methodological individualism, viewing individuals and private groups as the fundamental actors in international (and domestic) politics. States are not insignificant, but their preferences are determined by domestic politics rather than assumed interests or material factors like relative power. This approach implies that interstate politics are more complex and fluid than realists and institutionalists assume: national preferences can vary widely and change unpredictably. It calls for careful attention to the domestic politics and constitutional structures of individual states—a daunting prospect for analysts of international relations.

Liberals, on the other hand, are developing their own theoretical generalizations, using variations in domestic governance to explain differences in international behavior. For example, scholars are exploring whether liberal democratic states—with representative institutions and a commitment to the rule of law—are more amenable to legal relationships and arguments and more prone to comply with legal rules than states with different domestic regimes. Research in this vein—exemplified by Laurence Helfer and Anne-Marie Slaughter's analysis of supranational adjudication—is also helping to identify the domestic mechanisms through which international institutions affect behavior, and thus how they can be strengthened.

Transnational liberals go further, highlighting the activities of private individuals and groups across national polities and within international institutions. Traditional interest groups like business and labor, scientific communities, advocacy groups and networks concerned with issues like the rights of women or indigenous peoples, and other private organizations all play significant roles, independently of states, in creating international rules and institutions. Such institutions may in turn function most effectively by changing the terms of domestic politics. Some liberals emphasize the role of particular organs of government—national ministries, courts, legislators—which increasingly forge their own transnational relationships.

In analyzing legal doctrine, liberals would accept traditional sources of law, but would question lawyers' easy claims of universality * * *. Transnational liberals, moreover, would reject doctrines that limit law creation to states. Asserting that the domestic-international distinction has broken down, they would urge the significance of transnational norms created by private actors and governmental units, as well as domestic norms.

Constructivist theory differs fundamentally from these rationalist accounts. Constructivists reject the notion that states or other actors have objectively determined interests that they can pursue by selecting appropriate strategies and designing effective institutions. Rather, international actors operate within a social context of shared subjective understandings and norms, which constitute their identities and roles and define appropriate forms of conduct. Even fundamental notions like the state, sovereignty and national interests are socially constructed. They are not objectively true, but subjective; their meaning is not fixed, but contingent. Hilary Charlesworth's analysis of the construction of international law on a gendered basis disadvantageous to women is a telling example. Even anarchy, the central concept of realism, "is what states make of it." Many of these ideas are shared by the "English school" of IR theory, which emphasizes the subjective elements in an international "society" of states or, for some theorists, a range of private and public actors.

Notes

1. For a bibliography of interdisciplinary scholarship on IR theory and its reciprocal influence on the study of international law, see Slaughter, Tulumello & Wood, International Law and International Relations Theory: A New Generation of Interdisciplinary Scholarship, 92 A.J.I.L. 367, 393–397 (1998). For an IR perspective on fundamental problems in international law-making, see M. Byers, Custom, Power & the Power of Rules: International Relations and Customary International Law (1999). For applications in contexts such as the use of force, see International Rules: Approaches from International Law and International Relations (R. Beck, A. Arend & R. Lugt, eds., 1996). See also J. Goldsmith, Sovereignty, International Relations Theory and International Law, 52 Stanf. L. Rev. 959 (2000); Keohane, International Relations and International Law: Two Optics, 38 Harv. I.L.J. 487 (1997).

2. The Symposium on Method, pp. 41–42 above, begins with an essay on positivism as the dominant approach to international law from the 19th through the late 20th centuries. The student of international law in the 21st century can best appreciate positivism through an examination of classical doctrines of sources of international law, which will be the subject-matter of the next chapter.

Chapter 2

SOURCES AND EVIDENCE OF INTERNATIONAL LAW

SECTION 1. SOURCES

RESTATEMENT (THIRD) § 102

Sources of International Law

(1) A rule of international law is one that has been accepted as such by the international community of states

(a) in the form of customary law;

(b) by international agreement; or

(c) by derivation from general principles common to the major legal systems of the world.

(2) Customary international law results from a general and consistent practice of states followed by them from a sense of legal obligation.

(3) International agreements create law for the states parties thereto and may lead to the creation of customary international law when such agreements are intended for adherence by states generally and are in fact widely accepted.

(4) General principles common to the major legal systems, even if not incorporated or reflected in customary law or international agreement, may be invoked as supplementary rules of international law where appropriate.

STATUTE OF THE INTERNATIONAL COURT OF JUSTICE

ARTICLE 38

1. The Court, whose function is to decide in accordance with international law such disputes as are submitted to it, shall apply:

a. international conventions, whether general or particular, establishing rules expressly recognized by the contesting states;

b. international custom, as evidence of a general practice accepted as law;

c. the general principles of law recognized by civilized nations;

d. subject to the provisions of Article 59, judicial decisions and the teachings of the most highly qualified publicists of the various nations, as subsidiary means for the determination of rules of law.

2. This provision shall not prejudice the power of the Court to decide a case *ex aequo et bono,* if the parties agree thereto.

THE DOCTRINE OF SOURCES AND THE INDUCTIVE SCIENCE OF LAW

SCHACHTER, INTERNATIONAL LAW IN THEORY AND PRACTICE

35–37 (1991).

The principal intellectual instrument in the last century for providing objective standards of legal validation has been the doctrine of sources. That doctrine which became dominant in the nineteenth century and continues to prevail today lays down verifiable conditions for ascertaining and validating legal prescriptions. The conditions are the observable manifestations of the "wills" of States as revealed in the *processes* by which norms are formed—namely, treaty and State practice accepted as law. (These are the principal processes; Article 38 of the Statute of the Court expands them to include general principles of law.) The emphasis in this doctrine on criteria of law applied solely on the basis of observable "positive" facts can be linked to those intellectual currents of the nineteenth century that extolled inductive science. It has been suggested that the sociological positivism of Comte was especially influential on juristic thinking. Not surprisingly, the conception of a positive science of law had a strong attraction in the prevailing intellectual climate.

Moreover, within the field of international law itself, the competing ideas of natural law based on moral and philosophic conceptions were increasingly perceived as irrelevant to the political order of sovereign States. It had become evident to international lawyers as it had to others that States, which made and applied law, were not governed by morality or "natural reason;" they acted for reasons of power and interest. It followed that law could only be ascertained and determined through the actual methods used by States to give effect to their "political wills". In this way, the powerful ideas of positive science and State sovereignty were harnessed to create a doctrine for removing subjectivism and morality from the "science" of international law. It was intended to make international law realistic and definite. It satisfied those concerned with the realities of State power and the importance of sovereignty. It also met the intellectual requirements of the analytical theorists of law who sought to place jurisprudence on scientific foundations. Interestingly, the doctrine of sources became acceptable to the Marxist–Leninist legal theorists despite Marxist objections to philosophical positivism. From their standpoint, the doctrine of sources properly recognized the will of sovereign States as decisive. The Soviet jurists saw international law as the product of the "coordination of wills" of the sovereign States manifested in treaties and practice *accepted* by them as law.

The doctrine of sources was more than a grand theoretical conception. It also provided the stimulus for a methodology of international law that called for detailed "inductive" methods for ascertaining and validating law. If sources were to be used objectively and scientifically, it was necessary to examine in full detail the practice and related legal convictions *(opinio juris)* of States. * * * The favored instruments of the positivist methodology were the national digests of State practice prepared by, or in close association with the government of the State concerned. * * * They were mainly systematic collections of legal conclusions and relevant facts expressed in diplomatic correspondence and in governmental officials' legal opinions * * *. It would be possible for an arbiter to conclude whether a particular decision came within the rule evidenced by the precedents in the digest. * * * However, a closer look * * * indicates that there were significant deviations from the doctrine and its methodology. These deviations suggest that the idea of an inductive, factual positive science of international law may be characterized more as myth than reality.

VOLUNTARISM AND POSITIVISM

These two terms are often used in the writings on international law relating to sources. They conceptualize theories of international law that have been widely accepted and also strongly criticized. Their significance goes beyond legal theory; they reflect conceptions of international order that influence political and legal decisions.

"Voluntarism" is the classic doctrine of state sovereignty applied to the formation of international law. It holds that international legal rules emanate exclusively from the free will of states as expressed in conventions or by usages generally accepted as law. (See the Lotus Case decision on p. __.) "Positivism" as used in this context emphasizes the obligatory nature of legal norms and the fixed authoritative character of the formal sources. It also tends to consider that to be "law," the international norm must be capable, in principle, of application by a judicial body.

The political significance of "positivist voluntarism" is brought out in the following comment by a contemporary proponent:

> This means that states are at once the creators and addressees of the norms of international law and that there can be no question today, any more than yesterday, of some 'international democracy' in which a majority or representative proportion of states is considered to speak in the name of all and thus be entitled to impose its will on other states. Absent voluntarism, international law would no longer be performing its function.

Prosper Weil, Towards Relative Normativity in International Law?, 77 A.J.I.L. 413, 420 (1983).

Supporters of "voluntarism" emphasize its necessity for a heterogeneous, pluralistic world society. Moreover, they stress the importance of maintaining a clear distinction between existing law *(lex lata)* and law in formation *(lex ferenda).* In Weil's words, the legal system must be "perceived as a self-contained, self-sufficient world." Id. at 421. Legal normativity cannot be a matter of more or less.

The material in this chapter will present various questions that bear on the voluntarist thesis. Is it realistic to consider that actual legal rules are the product of state "will" or consent in a meaningful sense? Are there not basic and axiomatic norms that are recognized as such independently of consent? Does "general acceptance" of *new* law require verifiable expressions of "will" by all states? What are the advantages and disadvantages of considering the international legal system as a "self-contained, self-sufficient world" of "positive" rules? What legal significance should be given to various types of norms and standards that do not meet the criteria of Article 38 but influence state conduct and accountability (sometimes called "soft law")?

Is international law moving toward gradations in the legal force of its rules? Do recent tendencies give greater importance to the "general will of the international community" and less to the "sovereign equality" of states in the formation of law? Do such tendencies result in increased power for a "de facto oligarchy"? What processes for determining the community "will" would support legal development in the common interest? All of these questions are implicitly raised by recent trends relating to "sources". They are not easily answered, but they merit reflection in studying the material that follows.

SOURCES AND EVIDENCE

Note that Article 38 of the Statute refers to judicial decisions and to teachings of the most highly qualified publicists as "subsidiary means for the determination of rules of law." The Restatement (Third) § 103 characterizes judicial decisions and the "writings of scholars" as "evidence" of whether a rule has become international law. It also includes as evidence the pronouncements by states that undertake to state a rule of international law when such pronouncements are not seriously challenged by other states. The Restatement notes in Comment *c* to § 103 that such pronouncements include declaratory resolutions of international organizations. See Section 6 infra.

The present chapter deals separately with each of the categories referred to in §§ 102 and 103 of the Restatement and in Article 38 of the Statute of the Court.

SECTION 2. CUSTOM

Article 38(1)(b) refers to "international custom, as evidence of a general practice accepted as law." Some writers have found this formulation curious, since it is the practice which is evidence of the emergence of a custom. However, the order of words makes little difference. What is clear is that the definition of custom comprises two distinct elements: (1) "general practice" and (2) its acceptance as law.

Clear as it may seem to be, this definition gives rise to a number of questions, many of which are highly controversial. In reading the material that follows, you should bear in mind the following questions:

(1) What constitutes state practice?

(a) Are claims or assertions of states in themselves practice or must they be accompanied by physical acts? Would assertions *in abstracto* constitute practice or must they be made in the context of particular situations? Are votes for general declarations of law in international bodies manifestations of practice?

(b) Is state practice made only by organs competent to bind or speak for states in international affairs? May national laws, municipal court judgments, or executive acts of an internal character constitute practice? Are there circumstances in which actions of non-official entities may be regarded as state practice? Are omissions and absence of action a form of practice?

(2) How much practice is required?

(a) Is repetition required or may a single act be sufficient to constitute general practice? What if a large number of states participate in a single act (e.g., a decision of a conference)? What if there is no practice contradicting the rule asserted in regard to a single act?

(b) How much time is required? What if no precedents can be found against the rule? Are there special circumstances which affect the requirement of time?

(c) How many states are needed? Is it necessary that there be "a very widespread and representative participation in the practice"? (International Court of Justice in *North Sea Continental Shelf Cases,* p. 92 infra). Must it include states specially affected? Is there a significant difference in the numbers required when there is conflicting practice or the absence of conflict? Is a greater number required to overturn an existing rule of law?

(d) Is the practice of some states more important than the practice of others? How much weight should be given to the non-participation of states with special interests?

(3) How much consistency is required?

(a) Are minor inconsistencies sufficient to negate a custom?

(b) Can one resolve apparent inconsistencies on the basis of new conditions and attitudes? Can 19th century precedents be considered as inconsistent with 20th or 21st century practice, when conditions are substantially different?

(4) Are dissenting and non-participating States bound by custom?

(a) May a state be bound if it has no practice and if the precedents did not involve it? Can a state prevent a rule of customary law from becoming binding on it? At what time must it express opposition?

(b) Are new states bound by established custom in which they had no opportunity to participate? How may they change rules to which they are opposed?

(5) Do regional and special customs involve different requirements? May a special custom (i.e., one which conflicts with general custom) bind a state which has not supported the special custom?

Is a more rigorous standard of proof required to show the existence of a special custom? Are special customs essentially similar to tacit international agreements?

(6) What evidence is required for *opinio juris,* the requirement that practice be accepted as law?

(a) Must states "believe" that something is law before it can become law?

(b) Is *opinio juris* necessary to distinguish usage from custom, legal from non-legal obligations? Can one presume *opinio juris* from consistent practice when there are no negative statements (or disclaimers) as to legal obligations?

(c) Can the requirement of *opinio juris* be met by a finding that the practice was socially necessary or suited to international needs?

(d) Is it necessary that the belief as to legal requirement be accompanied by statements that the conduct in question is obligatory? May the context provide evidence of belief in the absence of such statements?

Are such statements or positive indication required to prove an obligation to act, but not required to support a permissive rule (the freedom to act)?

(e) What significance do protests and acquiescence have for *opinio juris?*

Are isolated protests enough to prevent customary law on the basis of substantial practice? Would protest by a single state carry decisive weight if that state was the only one seriously affected?

Is failure to protest against an abstract assertion of law less significant than failure to protest concrete application of the purported rule? May protests override practice arising from physical acts (e.g., seizures) by states?

(7) May treaties be invoked as evidence of customary law? May they create customary law?

(a) Should decisive weight be given to statements in a treaty or in preparatory work to the effect that some or all provisions are declaratory of existing law?

(b) May one infer that a treaty is not declaratory of international law from the fact that it provides for withdrawal, revision, or reservations?

(c) Under what circumstances are treaty rules which are not initially declaratory likely to become part of customary law by subsequent practice?

(d) Would bilateral treaties which have similar rules and are widely adhered to constitute evidence of state practice accepted as law or of custom?

(e) What effect would a resolution of the General Assembly or of an unofficial expert body (such as the *Institut de droit international)* have on the recognition of a treaty or the draft of a treaty as customary law?

(f) Are there circumstances in which the negotiation of a treaty and drafts of treaties will substantially affect the positions of states and the *opinio juris* as to new rules?

(g) May tacit international agreements be treated as local or special custom? Does it make any difference whether treaty or custom is the basis of the obligation?

(8) Is there a normative hierarchy in customary law?

(a) Are some general principles accepted implicitly irrespective of consent as postulates of the state system (e.g., territorial integrity of a state, *pacta sunt servanda,* autonomy)?

(b) Does this mean that current state practice and *opinio juris* are no longer relevant in defining their application?

(9) Would declarations of law adopted without dissent by the U.N. General Assembly constitute presumptive evidence of accepted international law, irrespective of actual state practice?

(a) Would the rules stated in a General Assembly declaration be binding on a state that claimed it voted for the declaration on the understanding that the General Assembly had only the authority to make recommendations?

(b) Would a declaration adopted by a substantial majority that asserts the existence of a particular legal principle have evidentiary value as a statement of customary law in litigation before an international or national judicial tribunal?

(10) Would the adoption of recommended standards of conduct by the U.N. General Assembly or another representative international assembly give rise to customary law if they are generally followed by states? Would such compliance constitute state practice for purposes of establishing customary law? What factors would be relevant to showing *opinio juris* in respect of such practice?

All of the questions stated above have arisen in cases or in exchanges of views among states. They have often given rise to controversy. The material that follows will provide the answers to, or at least throw further light on, these questions.

THE PAQUETE HABANA

Supreme Court of the United States, 1900.
175 U.S. 677, 20 S.Ct. 290, 44 L.Ed. 320.

MR. JUSTICE GRAY delivered the opinion of the court:

These are two appeals from decrees of the district court of the United States for the southern district of Florida, condemning two fishing vessels and their cargoes as prize of war.

Each vessel was a fishing smack, running in and out of Havana, and regularly engaged in fishing on the coast of Cuba; sailed under the Spanish flag; was owned by a Spanish subject of Cuban birth, living in the city of Havana; was commanded by a subject of Spain, also residing in Havana. * * * Her cargo consisted of fresh fish, caught by her crew from the sea, put on board as they were caught, and kept and sold alive. Until stopped by the blockading squadron she had no knowledge of the existence of the war or of any blockade. She had no arms or ammunition on board, and made no attempt to run the blockade after she knew of its existence, nor any resistance at the time of the capture. * * *

We are then brought to the consideration of the question whether, upon the facts appearing in these records, the fishing smacks were subject to capture by the armed vessels of the United States during the recent war with Spain.

By an ancient usage among civilized nations, beginning centuries ago, and gradually ripening into a rule of international law, coast fishing vessels, pursuing their vocation of catching and bringing in fresh fish, have been recognized as exempt, with their cargoes and crews, from capture as prize of war. * * *

[The Court then describes the earliest known acts protecting foreign fishermen in time of war. In 1403 and 1406, Henry IV of England issued orders protecting fishermen of foreign states. The order of 1406 placed all fishermen of France, Flanders and Brittany, with their fishing vessels and boats and equipment, everywhere on the sea, under his special protection. As long as they were coming or going from fishing activities in good conduct, they were not to be hindered by His Majesty's officers. This practice, based upon prior agreement with the French King for reciprocal treatment, was followed in a treaty made October 2, 1521 between the Emperor Charles V and Francis I of France. In 1536, Dutch edicts permitted herring fishing in time of war. Early French practice even permitted admirals to accord fishing truces in time of war. In ordinances passed in 1681 and 1692, France curtailed this practice, apparently because of the failure of her enemies to accord reciprocal treatment.]

The doctrine which exempts coast fishermen, with their vessels and cargoes, from capture as prize of war, has been familiar to the United States from the time of the War of Independence.

On June 5, 1779, Louis XVI, our ally in that war, addressed a letter to his admiral, informing him that the wish he had always had of alleviating, as far as he could, the hardships of war, had directed his attention to that class of his subjects which devoted itself to the trade of fishing, and had no other means of livelihood; that he had thought that the example which he should give to his enemies * * * would determine them to allow to fishermen the same facilities which he should consent to grant; and that he had therefore given orders to the commanders of all his ships not to disturb English fishermen, nor to arrest their vessels laden with fresh fish * * *; provided they had no offensive arms, and were not proved to have made any signals creating a suspicion of intelligence with the enemy; and the admiral was directed to communicate the King's intentions to all officers under his control. By a royal order in council of November 6, 1780, the former orders were confirmed; and the capture and ransom, by a French cruiser, of *The John and Sarah,* an English vessel, coming from Holland, laden with fresh fish, were pronounced to be illegal. 2 Code des Prises (ed. 1784) 721, 901, 903.

Among the standing orders made by Sir James Marriott, Judge of the English High Court of Admiralty, was one of April 11, 1780, by which it was "ordered that all causes of prize of fishing boats or vessels taken from the enemy may be consolidated in one monition, and one sentence or interlocutory, if under 50 tons burthen, and not more than 6 in number." Marriott's Formulary, 4. But by the statements of his successor, and of both French and English writers, it appears that England, as well as France, during the American Revolutionary War, abstained from interfering with the coast fisheries. The Young Jacob and Johanna, 1 C.Rob. 20; 2 Ortolan, 53; Hall, § 148.

In the treaty of 1785 between the United States and Prussia, article 23 (which was proposed by the American Commissioners, John Adams, Benjamin Franklin, and Thomas Jefferson, and is said to have been drawn up by Franklin), provided that, if war should arise between the contracting parties, "all women and children, scholars of every faculty, cultivators of the earth, artisans, manufacturers, and fishermen, unarmed and inhabiting unfortified towns, villages, or places, and in general all others whose occupations are for the common subsistence and benefit of mankind, shall be allowed to continue their respective employments, and shall not be molested in their persons, nor shall their houses or goods be burnt or otherwise destroyed, nor their fields waisted by the armed force of the enemy, into whose power, by the events of war, they may happen to fall; but if anything is necessary to be taken from them for the use of such armed force, the same shall be paid for at a reasonable price." 8 Star. at L. 96; 1 Kent, Com. 91, note; Wheaton, History of the Law of Nations, 306, 308. Here was the clearest exemption from hostile molestation or seizure of the persons, occupations, houses, and goods of unarmed fishermen inhabiting unfortified places. The article was repeated in the later treaties between the United States and Prussia of 1799 and 1828. 8 Star. at L. 174, 384. And Dana, in a note to his edition of Wheaton's International Laws, says: "In many treaties and decrees, fishermen catching fish as an article of food are added to the class of persons whose occupation is not to be disturbed in war." Wheaton, International Law (8th ed.) § 345, note 168.

Since the United States became a nation, the only serious interruptions, so far as we are informed, of the general recognition of the exemption of coast fishing vessels from hostile capture, arose out of the mutual suspicions and recriminations of England and France during the wars of the French Revolution.

[The Court then surveys the measures and countermeasures taken by both governments.

[On May 23, 1806, the British government "ordered in council, that all fishing vessels under Prussian and other colors, and engaged for the purpose of catching fish * * * shall not be molested * * * " An order in council of May 2, 1810 directing the capture of certain vessels, specifically excepted "vessels employed in catching and conveying fish fresh to market * * *."]

In the war with Mexico, in 1846, the United States recognized the exemption of coast fishing boats from capture. * * *

[I]t appears that Commodore Conner, commanding the Horne Squadron blockading the east coast of Mexico, on May 14, 1846, wrote a letter * * * to Mr. Bancroft, the Secretary of the Navy, inclosing a copy of the commodore's "instructions to the commanders of the vessels of the Home Squadron, showing the principles to be observed in the blockade of the Mexican ports," one of which was that "Mexican boats engaged in fishing on any part of the coast will be allowed to pursue their labors unmolested;" and that on June 10, 1846, those instructions were approved by the Navy Department. * * *

In the treaty of peace between the United States and Mexico, in 1848, were inserted the very words of the earlier treaties with Prussia, already quoted, forbidding the hostile molestation or seizure in time of war of the persons, occupations, houses, or goods of fishermen. 9 Stat. at L. 939, 940. * * *

[The Court then notes that France had forbidden the molestation of enemy coastal fisheries during the Crimean, Italian and Prussian wars, and that England had justified destruction by her cruisers of fisheries on the Sea of Azof during the Crimean War on the ground that these were on a large scale and intended directly for the support of the Russian army.]

Since the English orders in council of 1806 and 1810, before quoted, in favor of fishing vessels employed in catching and bringing to market fresh fish, no instance has been found in which the exemption from capture of private coast fishing vessels honestly pursuing their peaceful industry has been denied by England or by any other nation. And the Empire of Japan (the last state admitted into the rank of civilized nations), by an ordinance promulgated at the beginning of its war with China in August, 1894, established prize courts, and ordained that "the following enemy's vessels are exempt from detention," including in the exemption "boats engaged in coast fisheries," as well as "ships engaged exclusively on a voyage of scientific discovery, philanthropy, or religious mission." Takahashi, International Law, 11, 178.

International law is part of our law, and must be ascertained and administered by the courts of justice of appropriate jurisdiction as often as questions of right depending upon it are duly presented for their determination. For this purpose, where there is no treaty and no controlling executive or legislative act or judicial decision, resort must be had to the customs and usages of civilized nations, and, as evidence of these, to the works of jurists and commentators who by years of labor, research, and experience have made themselves peculiarly well acquainted with the subjects of which they treat. Such works are resorted to by judicial tribunals, not for the speculations of their authors concerning what the law ought to be, but for trustworthy evidence of what the law really is. Hilton v. Guyot, 159 U.S. 113, 163, 164, 214, 215, 16 S.Ct. 139, 40 L.Ed. 95, 108, 125, 126.

Wheaton places, among the principal sources of international law, "text-writers of authority, showing what is the approved usage of nations, or the general opinion respecting their mutual conduct, with the definitions and modifications introduced by general consent." As to these he forcibly observes: "Without wishing to exaggerate the importance of these writers, or to substitute, in any case, their authority for the principles of reason, it may be affirmed that they are generally impartial in their judgment. They are witnesses of the sentiments and usages of civilized nations, and the weight of their testimony increases every time that their authority is invoked by statesmen, and every year that passes without the rules laid down in their works being impugned by the avowal of contrary principles." Wheaton, International Law (8th ed.), § 15.

Chancellor Kent says: "In the absence of higher and more authoritative sanctions, the ordinances of foreign states, the opinions of eminent statesmen, and the writings of distinguished jurists, are regarded as of great consideration on questions not settled by conventional law. In cases where the principal jurists agree, the presumption will be very great in favor of the solidity of their maxims; and no civilized nation that does not arrogantly set all ordinary law and justice at defiance will venture to disregard the uniform sense of the established writers on international law." 1 Kent, Com. 18.

[The Court then discusses the views of French, Argentine, German, Dutch, English, Austrian, Spanish, Portuguese, and Italian writers on international law, and concludes:]

This review of the precedents and authorities on the subject appears to us abundantly to demonstrate that at the present day, by the general consent of the civilized nations of the world, and independently of any express treaty or other public act, it is an established rule of international law, founded on considerations of humanity to a poor and industrious order of men, and of the mutual convenience of belligerent states, that coast fishing vessels, with their implements and supplies, cargoes and crews, unarmed and honestly pursuing their peaceful calling of catching and bringing in fresh fish, are exempt from capture as prize of war. * * *

This rule of international law is one which prize courts administering the law of nations are bound to take judicial notice of, and to give effect to, in the absence of any treaty or other public act of their own government in relation to the matter. * * *

[Finding no express intention on the part of the United States to enforce the 1898 blockade of Cuba against coastal fishermen peacefully pursuing their calling, the Court ordered the reversal of the District Court decree and the payment to the claimants of the proceeds of the sale of the vessels and cargo, together with damages and costs.

[Chief Justice Fuller argued in a dissenting opinion, in which Harlan and McKenna, JJ., concurred, that the captured vessels were of such size and range as not to fall within the exemption, and that the exemption in any case had not become a customary rule of international law but was only "an act of grace" that had not been authorized by the President.]

Notes

1. Did not the Supreme Court find inconsistencies in the practice of states in respect of the alleged rule? How many states did it refer to in support of the practice? Consider the rather small number of states in the world during the time covered. Would such support meet the requirement of a "very widespread and representative participation" as required by the International Court of Justice in the *North Sea Continental Shelf Cases* (see p. 92 infra)? Does the case show that a small number of states create a rule of customary law, if there is no practice which conflicts with the rule and no protests? Is it necessary (and realistic) to assume the acquiescence of the large majority of non-participating and silent states? Would the inconsistent conduct of one or two states be sufficient to prevent the creation of a general custom; if so, in what circumstances? See discussion of Non-Consenting States infra pp. 100–105.

2. Note the wide range of evidence of custom considered by the Court. It includes national law, executive decrees, acts of military commanders as well as judgments of national tribunals. Does this mean that states may create customary law by their unilateral acts? Does it mean that the conduct of military officers and other subordinate officials may constitute state practice? Is every official act of a state official an element of state practice? For examples, see Akehurst, Custom as a Source of International Law, 47 Brit. Y.B.I.L. 8–10 (1974–75); Wolfke, Custom in Present International Law (1964).

3. What evidence did the Court consider in arriving at its conclusions concerning the alleged "ancient usage among civilized nations"? Are executive pronouncements, legislative acts, and municipal court decisions of equal weight in "committing" a state to a given practice? What significance should be attached to the acts of military commanders, acting independently in the field? See generally Wolfke, Custom in Present International Law *passim* (1964); Waldock, General Course on Public International Law, 106 Rec. des Cours, 1, 42–43 (1962–II) and sources cited.

A recent reexamination of *Paquete Habana* takes a revisionist point of view, arguing that the U.S. Supreme Court offered unconvincing evidence for the proposition that states had acted out of a sense of legal obligation in refraining from seizing coastal fishing vessels. The authors contend that states so refrained only when it suited their national interests. Goldsmith & Posner, Understanding the Resemblance Between Modern and Traditional Customary International Law, 40 Va.J.Int'l L. 639 (2000).

4. Note the weight given by the Supreme Court to the writers on international law and the quotation from Chancellor Kent that "no civilized nation will venture to disregard the uniform sense of the established writers on international law". How objective are the leading writers? Schachter suggests that "the selective tendency of the writers to quote the generalities of other writers, meant that their statements were steps removed from the ideal of an inductive approach." International Law in Theory and Practice 38 (1991). For further comment on the role of international law scholars, see pp. 139–142 below.

5. Myres S. McDougal has described customary law "as a process of continuous interaction, of continuous demand and response, in which the decision-makers of particular nation-states unilaterally put forward claims of the most diverse and conflicting character * * * and in which other decision-makers, external to the demanding state * * * weigh and appraise these competing claims * * * and ultimately accept or reject them." In this process, McDougal observes, state officials honor each other's unilateral claims "by mutual tolerances expressed in countless decisions in foreign offices, national courts, and national legislatures—which create expectations that effective power will be restrained and exercised in certain uniformities of pattern." In a footnote, he adds that it is "the reciprocal tolerances of the external decision-makers which create the expectations of pattern and uniformity in decision, of practice in accord with rule, commonly regarded as law." McDougal emphasizes that states are influenced by "reasonableness" in their claims and reactions and he considers that the process is one in which values are clarified and "perceptions of common interest" realized. McDougal, The Hydrogen Bomb Tests, 49 A.J.I.L. 357–58 (1955). See also McDougal, Studies in World Order (1960).

6. Would states be more likely to realize common interests by negotiating multilateral law-making treaties to meet perceived needs than by relying on the case-by-case gradualism of customary law? Is customary law more responsive to

disparities in power and interest and therefore more realistic than law-making by international conferences in which all states take part on an equal footing? See comments on Treaty and Custom, pp. 115–117 below.

THE CASE OF THE S.S. LOTUS (FRANCE v. TURKEY)

Permanent Court of International Justice (1927).
P.C.I.J. Ser. A No. 10.
2 Hudson, World Ct. Rep. 20.

[A collision on the high seas between a French steamer, the Lotus, and a Turkish steamer, the Boz–Kourt in 1926 resulted in the sinking of the Turkish vessel and the death of eight Turkish nationals. When the French ship reached Constantinople (Istanbul) the Turkish authorities instituted criminal proceedings against the French officer on watch-duty at the time of the collision (Lieutenant Demons). The Turkish Court overruled Demons' objection that Turkey had no jurisdiction and after a trial sentenced him to 80 days imprisonment and a fine of 22 pounds. The French Government challenged Turkey's action as a violation of international law and demanded reparation. Following negotiations, the two states by special agreement submitted the dispute to the Permanent Court of International Justice. The arguments put forward by the two parties related exclusively to whether according to principles of international law Turkey had or had not jurisdiction to prosecute the case. Both parties recognized the applicability of the Convention of Lausanne of 1923 which provided in Article 15: "Subject to the provisions of Article 16, all questions of jurisdiction as between Turkey and the other contracting parties shall be decided in accordance with the principles of international law."]

The Court, having to consider whether there are any rules of international law which may have been violated by the prosecution in pursuance of Turkish law of Lieutenant Demons, is confronted in the first place by a question of principle which, in the written and oral arguments of the two Parties, has proved to be a fundamental one. The French Government contends that the Turkish Courts, in order to have jurisdiction, should be able to point to some title to jurisdiction recognized by international law in favour of Turkey. On the other hand, the Turkish Government takes the view that Article 15 allows Turkey jurisdiction whenever such jurisdiction does not come into conflict with a principle of international law.

The latter view seems to be in conformity with the special agreement itself, No. 1 of which asks the Court to say whether Turkey has acted contrary to the principles of international law and, if so, what principles. According to the special agreement, therefore, it is not a question of stating principles which would permit Turkey to take criminal proceedings, but of formulating the principles, if any, which might have been violated by such proceedings.

This way of stating the question is also dictated by the very nature and existing conditions of international law.

International law governs relations between independent States. The rules of law binding upon States therefore emanate from their own free will as expressed in conventions or by usages generally accepted as expressing principles of law and established in order to regulate the relations between these co-existing independent communities or with a view to the achievement of common aims. Restrictions upon the independence of States cannot therefore be presumed.

Now the first and foremost restriction imposed by international law upon a State is that—failing the existence of a permissive rule to the contrary—it may not exercise its power in any form in the territory of another State. In this sense jurisdiction is certainly territorial; it cannot be exercised by a State outside its territory except by virtue of a permissive rule derived from international custom or from a convention.

It does not, however, follow that international law prohibits a State from exercising jurisdiction in its own territory, in respect of any case which relates to acts which have taken place abroad, and in which it cannot rely on some permissive rule of international law. Such a view would only be tenable if international law contained a general prohibition to States to extend the application of their laws and the jurisdiction of their courts to persons, property and acts outside their territory, and if, as an exception to this general prohibition, it allowed States to do so in certain specific cases. But this is certainly not the case under international law as it stands at present. Far from laying down a general prohibition to the effect that States may not extend the application of their laws and the jurisdiction of their courts to persons, property and acts outside their territory, it leaves them in this respect a wide measure of discretion which is only limited in certain cases by prohibitive rules; as regards other cases, every State remains free to adopt the principles which it regards as best and most suitable.

* * *

In these circumstances, all that can be required of a State is that it should not overstep the limits which international law places upon its jurisdiction; within these limits, its title to exercise jurisdiction rests in its sovereignty.

It follows from the foregoing that the contention of the French Government to the effect that Turkey must in each case be able to cite a rule of international law authorizing her to exercise jurisdiction, is opposed to the generally accepted international law to which Article 15 of the Convention of Lausanne refers. Having regard to the terms of Article 15 and to the construction which the Court has just placed upon it, this contention would apply in regard to civil as well as to criminal cases, and would be applicable on conditions of absolute reciprocity as between Turkey and the other contracting Parties; in practice, it would therefore in many cases result in paralyzing the action of the courts, owing to the impossibility of citing a universally accepted rule on which to support the exercise of their jurisdiction.

* * *

Nevertheless, it has to be seen whether the foregoing considerations really apply as regards criminal jurisdiction, or whether this jurisdiction is governed by a different principle: this might be the outcome of the close connection which for a long time existed between the conception of supreme criminal jurisdiction and that of a State, and also by the especial importance of criminal jurisdiction from the point of view of the individual.

Though it is true that in all systems of law the principle of the territorial character of criminal law is fundamental, it is equally true that all or nearly all these systems of law extend their action to offences committed outside the territory of the State which adopts them, and they do so in ways which vary from State to State. The territoriality of criminal law, therefore, is not an absolute principle of international law and by no means coincides with territorial sovereignty.

* * *

The Court therefore must, in any event, ascertain whether or not there exists a rule of international law limiting the freedom of States to extend the criminal jurisdiction of their courts to a situation uniting the circumstances of the present case.

* * *

The arguments advanced by the French Government, other than those considered above, are, in substance, the three following:

(1) International law does not allow a State to take proceedings with regard to offences committed by foreigners abroad, simply by reason of the nationality of the victim; and such is the situation in the present case because the offence must be regarded as having been committed on board the French vessel.

(2) International law recognizes the exclusive jurisdiction of the State whose flag is flown as regards everything which occurs on board a ship on the high seas.

(3) Lastly, this principle is especially applicable in a collision case.

* * *

As has already been observed, the characteristic features of the situation of fact are as follows: there has been a collision on the high seas between two vessels flying different flags, on one of which was one of the persons alleged to be guilty of the offence, whilst the victims were on board the other.

This being so, the Court does not think it necessary to consider the contention that a State cannot punish offences committed abroad by a foreigner simply by reason of the nationality of the victim. For this contention only relates to the case where the nationality of the victim is the only criterion on which the criminal jurisdiction of the State is based. Even if that argument were correct generally speaking—and in regard to this the Court reserves its opinion—it could only be used in the present case if international law forbade Turkey to take into consideration the fact that the offence produced its effects on the Turkish vessel and consequently in a place assimilated to Turkish territory in which the application of Turkish criminal law cannot be challenged, even in regard to offences committed there by foreigners. But no such rule of international law exists. No argument has come to the knowledge of the Court from which it could be deduced that States recognize themselves to be under an obligation towards each other only to have regard to the place where the author of the offence happens to be at the time of the offence. On the contrary, it is certain that the courts of many countries, even of countries which have given their criminal legislation a strictly territorial character, interpret criminal law in the sense that offences, the authors of which at the moment of commission are in the territory of another State, are nevertheless to be regarded as having been committed in the national territory, if one of the constituent elements of the offence, and more especially its effects, have taken place there. French courts have, in regard to a variety of situations, given decisions sanctioning this way of interpreting the territorial principle. Again, the Court does not know of any cases in which governments have protested against the fact that the criminal law of some country contained a rule to this effect or that the courts of a country construed their criminal law in this sense. Consequently, once it is admitted that the effects of the offence were produced on the Turkish vessel, it becomes impossible to hold that there is a rule of international law which prohibits Turkey from prosecuting Lieutenant Demons because of the fact that the author of the offence was on board the French ship. Since, as has already been observed, the special agreement does not deal with the provision of Turkish law under which the prosecution was instituted, but only with the question whether the prosecution should be regarded as contrary to the principles of international law, there is no reason preventing the Court from confining itself to observing that, in this case, a prosecution may also be justified from the point of view of the so-called territorial principle.

* * *

The second argument put forward by the French Government is the principle that the State whose flag is flown has exclusive jurisdiction over everything which occurs on board a merchant ship on the high seas.

It is certainly true that—apart from certain special cases which are defined by international law—vessels on the high seas are subject to no authority except that of the State whose flag they fly. In virtue of the principle of the freedom of the seas, that is to say, the absence of any territorial sovereignty upon the high seas, no State may exercise any kind of jurisdiction over foreign vessels upon them. Thus, if a war vessel, happening to be at the spot where a collision occurs between a vessel flying its flag and a foreign vessel, were to send on board the latter an officer to make investigations or to take evidence, such an act would undoubtedly be contrary to international law.

But it by no means follows that a State can never in its own territory exercise jurisdiction over acts which have occurred on board a foreign ship on the high seas. A corollary of the principle of the freedom of the seas is that a ship on the high seas is assimilated to the territory of the State the flag of which it flies, for, just as in its own territory, that State exercises its authority upon it, and no other State may do so. All that can be said is that by virtue of the principle of the freedom of the seas, a ship is placed in the same position as national territory; but there is nothing to support the claim according to which the rights of the State under whose flag the vessel sails may go farther than the rights which it exercises within its territory properly so called. It follows that what occurs on board a vessel on the high seas must be regarded as if it occurred on the territory of the State whose flag the ship flies. If, therefore, a guilty act committed on the high seas produces its effects on a vessel flying another flag or in foreign territory, the same principles must be applied as if the territories of two different States were concerned, and the conclusion must therefore be drawn that there is no rule of international law prohibiting the State to which the ship on which the effects of the offence have taken place belongs, from regarding the offence as having been committed in its territory and prosecuting, accordingly, the delinquent.

This conclusion could only be overcome if it were shown that there was a rule of customary international law which, going further than the principle stated above, established the exclusive jurisdiction of the State whose flag was flown. The French Government has endeavoured to prove the existence of such a rule, having recourse for this purpose to the teachings of publicists, to decisions of municipal and international tribunals, and especially to conventions which, whilst creating exceptions to the principle of the freedom of the seas by permitting the war and police vessels of a State to exercise a more or less extensive control over the merchant vessels of another State, reserve jurisdiction to the courts of the country whose flag is flown by the vessel proceeded against.

In the Court's opinion, the existence of such a rule has not been conclusively proved.

In the first place, as regards teachings of publicists, and apart from the question as to what their value may be from the point of view of establishing the existence of a rule of customary law, it is no doubt true that all or nearly all writers teach that ships on the high seas are subject exclusively to the jurisdiction of the State whose flag they fly. But the important point is the significance attached by them to this principle; now it does not appear that in general, writers bestow upon this principle a scope differing from or wider than that explained above and which is equivalent to saying that the jurisdiction of a State over vessels on the high seas is the same in extent as its jurisdiction in its own territory. On the other hand, there is no lack of writers who, upon a close study of the special question whether a State can prosecute for offences committed on board a foreign ship on the high seas, definitely come to the conclusion that such offences must be regarded as if they had been committed in the territory of the State whose flag the ship flies, and that consequently the general rules of each legal system in regard to offences committed abroad are applicable.

In regard to precedents, it should first be observed that, leaving aside the collision cases which will be alluded to later, none of them relates to offences affecting two ships flying the flags of two different countries, and that consequently they are not of much importance in the case before the Court. The case of the *Costa Rica Packet* is no exception, for the prauw on which the alleged depredations took place was adrift without flag or crew, and this circumstance certainly influenced, perhaps decisively, the conclusion arrived at by the arbitrator.

On the other hand, there is no lack of cases in which the State has claimed a right to prosecute for an offence, committed on board a foreign ship, which it regarded as punishable under its legislation. Thus Great Britain refused the request of the United States for the extradition of John Anderson, a British seaman who had committed homicide on board an American vessel, stating that she did not dispute the jurisdiction of the United States but that she was entitled to exercise hers concurrently. This case, to which others might be added, is relevant in spite of Anderson's British nationality, in order to show that the principle of the exclusive jurisdiction of the country whose flag the vessel flies is not universally accepted.

The cases in which the exclusive jurisdiction of the State whose flag was flown has been recognized would seem rather to have been cases in which the foreign State was interested only by reason of the nationality of the victim, and in which, according to the legislation of that State itself or the practice of its courts, that ground was not regarded as sufficient to authorize prosecution for an offence committed abroad by a foreigner.

Finally, as regards conventions expressly reserving jurisdiction exclusively to the State whose flag is flown, it is not absolutely certain that this stipulation is to be regarded as expressing a general principle of law rather than as corresponding to the extraordinary jurisdiction which these conventions confer on the state-owned ships of a particular country in respect of ships of another country on the high seas. Apart from that, it should be observed that these conventions relate to matters of a particular kind, closely connected with the policing of the seas, such as the slave trade, damage to submarine cables, fisheries, etc., and not to common-law offences. Above all it should be pointed out that the offences contemplated by the conventions in question only concern a single ship; it is impossible therefore to make any deduction from them in regard to matters which concern two ships and consequently the jurisdiction to two different States.

The Court therefore has arrived at the conclusion that the second argument put forward by the French Government does not, any more than the first, establish the existence of a rule of international law prohibiting Turkey from prosecuting Lieutenant Demons.

[The Court then addressed itself to the third argument advanced by the French Government, that according to international law criminal proceedings arising from collision cases are within the exclusive jurisdiction of the state whose flag is flown. In offering this view, the French Agent pointed out that questions of jurisdiction in collision cases, which frequently arise before civil courts, rarely are presented to criminal courts. This fact led him to conclude that prosecutions only occur before the courts of the state whose flag is flown, which was proof of a tacit adherence by states to the rule of positive international law barring prosecutions by other states.

[The Court rejected this argument, explaining that even if the facts alleged were true, they would merely show that states had often abstained from instituting criminal proceedings, not that they felt obligated to do so. The Court observed that there were no decisions of international tribunals in the matter and that, of the four municipal court decisions cited by the parties, two supported the exclusive jurisdiction of the flag state and two supported the opposite contention. The Court pointed out that "as municipal jurisprudence is thus divided, it is hardly possible to see in it an indication of the existence of the restrictive rule of international law which alone could serve as a basis for the contention of the French Government." On the other hand, the Court stressed the fact that the French and German governments had failed to protest against the exercise of criminal jurisdiction by states whose flag was not being flown in the two cases cited by Turkey, and observed that the French and German governments would hardly have failed to protest if they "had really thought that this was a violation of international law."]

The conclusion at which the Court has therefore arrived is that there is no rule of international law in regard to collision cases to the effect that criminal proceedings are exclusively within the jurisdiction of the State whose flag is flown.

* * *

* * * Neither the exclusive jurisdiction of either State, nor the limitations of the jurisdiction of each to the occurrences which took place on the respective ships would appear calculated to satisfy the requirements of justice and effectively to protect the interests of the two States. It is only natural that each should be able to exercise jurisdiction and to do so in respect of the incident as a whole. It is therefore a case of concurrent jurisdiction.

* * *

FOR THESE REASONS, the Court, having heard both Parties, gives, by the President's casting vote—the votes being equally divided—judgment to the effect

(1) that, following the collision which occurred on August 2nd, 1926, on the high seas between the French steamship *Lotus* and the Turkish steamship *Boz-Kourt,* and upon the arrival of the French ship at Stamboul, and in consequence of the loss of the *Boz-Kourt* having involved the death of eight Turkish nationals, Turkey, by instituting criminal proceedings in pursuance of Turkish law against Lieutenant Demons, officer of the watch on board the *Lotus* at the time of the collision, has not acted in conflict with the principles of international law, contrary to Article 15 of the Convention of Lausanne of July 24th, 1923, respecting conditions of residence and business and jurisdiction;

(2) that, consequently, there is no occasion to give judgment on the question of the pecuniary reparation which might have been due to Lieutenant Demons if Turkey, by prosecuting him as above stated, had acted in a manner contrary to the principles of international law.

[The six dissenting judges disagreed with the proposition that France had the burden of showing a customary law rule that prohibited Turkey's exercise of jurisdiction. They took issue with the basic premise of the judgment that "restrictions upon the freedom of states cannot be presumed" and its implicit corollary that international law permits all that it does not forbid. In their view, the question was whether international law authorized Turkey to exercise jurisdiction in the particular circumstances and they concluded that customary law did not authorize a state to exercise criminal jurisdiction over a foreigner for an act committed in a foreign country or in a vessel of another state on the high seas.]

Notes

1. The *Lotus Case* has been strongly criticized for its "extreme positivism" and especially for asserting that restrictions on the freedom of states cannot be presumed. Was this principle necessary for the Court to rule on the French

contention that Turkey was not permitted under customary law to prosecute the French officer? Note that the Court's jurisdiction rested on a special agreement of the parties that asked it to decide whether Turkey acted contrary to principles of international law. Did this formulation make it reasonable for the Court to impose the burden of proof on France to show that Turkey's action violated international law rather than requiring Turkey to prove its legal right to do so?

2. If the Court found no specific customary law that either permitted or prohibited criminal jurisdiction in the given circumstances, should it have declined to decide the case? Is it necessary to assume the formal completeness of the international legal system so that there is no gap in the system? Kelsen wrote: "If there is no norm of conventional or customary international law imposing * * * the obligation to behave in a certain way, the subject is, under international law, legally free to behave as it pleases; and by a decision to this effect existing international law is applied." Kelsen, Principles of International Law 438–39 (R. Tucker ed. 1966). Some writers who agree that international law must be formally complete (i.e., every dispute must be capable of legal determination) reject the residual principle of state freedom expressed in the *Lotus Case.* They consider that every case can be decided either by existing legal rules or by deriving such rules from general principles and concepts within the legal system. See Oppenheim's International Law 12–13 (9th ed. R. Jennings & A. Watts 1992). This position expressed most influentially by Sir Hersch Lauterpacht (as a scholar and when a judge in the International Court) relies heavily on general principles and analogy to solve hard cases in order to ensure the coherence and effectiveness of the international legal system. On that view, judges cannot refuse to decide on the ground that the law is unclear (the Latin term *non liquet,* meaning "it is not clear," is sometimes used in such situations), nor can they resort to residual principles such as sovereignty. For such writers (if not for states) the system must be seen as materially (and not only formally) complete.

Other writers move beyond decisions limited to legal rules and principles. They would turn to "purposes" and "policies" of the international community (sometimes expressed as "equity" or "natural justice") for determining criteria in a balancing process. See O. Schachter, Theory and Practice in International Law 18–31 (1991); M. McDougal and M. Reisman, International Law in Policy–Oriented Perspective, in The Structure and Process of International Law 103–29 (Macdonald–Johnston eds. 1983). Can a good argument be made that an international court should decline to decide a case if the law is not clear enough *(non liquet)*? For that view, see J. Stone, *Non Liquet* and the Function of Law in the International Community, 35 Brit. Y.B.I.L. 124 (1959).

3. Notwithstanding the criticism of the *Lotus* principle, the International Court and other tribunals may still consider first whether an act that has been challenged is prohibited by existing law and, if not, sustain its validity. In effect, the presumption of freedom is then applied. However, in some cases, especially those involving maritime delimitation, the tribunals have tended to view the conflicting legal claims in terms of balancing equities. This is probably a consequence of the substantive rules that require maritime delimitation to be determined by equitable principles. But it also has been applied in cases involving territorial disputes. (See, e.g., the Island of Palmas decision, p. 316 referring to the relative strengths of the claims in regard to shared resources such as international waterways.) The freedom to use natural resources within a state—presumably a sovereign prerogative—is increasingly viewed as limited by the state's duty to take account of transborder environmental damage. Such balancing of equities or "constructivist" solutions to conflicting claims are sometimes seen as departing

from law. Judge Oda commented in a delimitation case that the I.C.J. was adopting "[t]he principle of non-principle." Oda, Diss. Op. in Tunisia–Libya Case, 1982 I.C.J. 157. Actually the I.C.J. and other international tribunals regard such decisions taken on equitable grounds as within the law, that is, as equity *infra legem* not as *ex aequo et bono*). (See p. 127 below on equity in international jurisprudence.) For a discussion of judicial reasoning sympathetic to "constructivist approaches" but critical of the claim of judicial objectivity in such cases, see M. Koskenniemi, From Apology to Utopia 220–36 (1989).

4. Referring again to the *Lotus Case,* does it seem unreasonable or unjust that Turkey should have the right to try a French captain of a French vessel for his acts outside of Turkish jurisdiction because Turkish nationals were injured in a collision between the French and Turkish vessels? Is it significant that the national courts in many countries apply their criminal law to acts committed outside the country if such acts have effects in the country? Do such municipal law cases constitute state practice? Can it be shown that they are accompanied by a belief that their acts are permissible under international law when that question does *not* arise? Is the absence of protests in such cases supportive of customary law? Suppose, as the Court says, most countries recognize the exclusive jurisdiction of the flag state even if the victims of an accident are non-nationals but a few states (for example, the United States) do not? Should exceptions weigh decisively against a customary rule of exclusive jurisdiction?

5. Why did France fail in its argument that abstention of states from exercising jurisdiction over foreign vessels or nationals involved in high seas collisions showed that there was a rule of international law restricting such jurisdiction to the flag state? What would satisfy the Court that such abstention was followed because of a conviction that it was required by international law? When does practice give rise to *opinio juris?* See p. 92 below on *opinio juris.*

6. In the *Fisheries Jurisdiction Case* between Iceland and United Kingdom (Judgment on Merits 1974), several judges of the International Court emphasized the existence of protests as refuting the claim of Iceland to an exclusive fishing zone exceeding twelve miles; other judges disagreed by noting that many interested states had not protested. How much weight is to be given isolated protests or the failure to protest? Judge Dillard's separate opinion in the *Fisheries Jurisdiction Case,* Merits, notes the importance of protest by states specially affected. Conversely, the lack of protests by non-interested states does not imply that they necessarily acquiesce in the claims. See Dillard, Separate Opinion, 1974 I.C.J. 58.

7. As the *Lotus Case* indicates, protests and acquiescence are critical factors in the formation of customary law. In that case, the Court envisaged verbal protests such as those made in diplomatic correspondence or in international conferences. They have often been regarded as effective expressions of a state's objection to an asserted rule. See, for example, *North Sea Continental Shelf Case* (infra) and *Fisheries Jurisdiction Case,* 1974 I.C.J. 47, 58, 161. Yet states sometimes consider it necessary to back their protests by physical action, as by seizing allegedly trespassing ships or sending their vessels into waters claimed by other states. For example, the U.S. rejection of the Canadian claim of competence to exclude vessels from certain Arctic waters has been emphasized by sending in a U.S. vessel without Canadian authorization. Are there good reasons to require physical acts to demonstrate the "seriousness" of the protest? Judge Read said: "The only convincing evidence of state practice is to be found in seizures where the coastal state asserts its sovereignty over trespassing foreign ships." Would such requirement increase the danger of armed conflict and give advantages to

great powers? See conflicting views in Akehurst, Custom as a Source of International Law, 47 Brit. Y.B.I.L. 1, 39–42 (1974–75), and D'Amato, The Concept of Custom in International Law 88–89 (1971).

LEGALITY OF THE THREAT OR USE OF NUCLEAR WEAPONS (ADVISORY OPINION)

International Court of Justice, 1996.
1996 I.C.J. 226.

[The U.N. General Assembly asked the I.C.J. for an advisory opinion, pursuant to Article 96(1) of the U.N. Charter, on the following question: "Is the threat or use of nuclear weapons in any circumstance permitted under international law?" The Court determined that it had jurisdiction to give a reply to the request, and likewise concluded that there were no "compelling reasons" to exercise a discretionary power to decline to answer the question.

[The Court turned to arguments pressed by some states in reliance on the *Lotus* case, including contentions that restrictions on states' freedom of action cannot be found in international law in the absence of positive law emanating from state consent. The Court also considered claims advanced by some nuclear-weapons states, to the effect that states specially affected by a purported rule of customary international law could not be presumed to be bound by such a rule without their consent and over their objections. On these points the Court said:]

21. The use of the word "permitted" in the question put by the General Assembly was criticized before the Court by certain States on the ground that this implied that the threat or the use of nuclear weapons would only be permissible if authorization could be found in a treaty provision or in customary international law. Such a starting point, those States submitted, was incompatible with the very basis of international law, which rests upon the principles of sovereignty and consent; accordingly, and contrary to what was implied by use of the word "permitted", States are free to threaten or use nuclear weapons unless it can be shown that they are bound not to do so by reference to a prohibition in either treaty law or customary international law. Support for this contention was found in dicta of the Permanent Court of International Justice in the *"Lotus"* case that "restrictions upon the independence of States cannot ... be presumed" and that international law leaves to States "a wide measure of discretion which is only limited in certain cases by prohibitive rules"* * *. Reliance was also placed on the dictum of the present Court in the case concerning *Military and Paramilitary Activities in and Against Nicaragua (Nicaragua v United States of America)* that:

> "in international law there are no rules, other than such rules as may be accepted by the State concerned, by treaty or otherwise, whereby the level of armaments of a sovereign State can be limited" (*I.C.J. Reports 1986,* p. 135, para. 269).

For other States, the invocation of these dicta in the *"Lotus"* case was inapposite; their status in contemporary international law and applicability in the very different circumstances of the present case were challenged. It was also contended that the above-mentioned dictum of the present Court was directed to the *possession* of armaments and was irrelevant to the threat or use of nuclear weapons.* * *

22. The Court notes that the nuclear-weapon States appearing before it either accepted, or did not dispute, that their independence to act was indeed restricted by the principles and rules of international law, more particularly humanitarian law * * *, as did the other States which took part in the proceedings.

Hence, the argument concerning the legal conclusions to be drawn from the use of the word "permitted", and the questions of burden of proof to which it was said to give rise, are without particular significance for the disposition of the issues before the Court.* * *

[Turning to possible sources of law, the Court surveyed various treaties and other instruments potentially bearing on the question. It addressed customary law, and the interaction between treaties and custom, in the following passages:]

52. The Court notes by way of introduction that international customary and treaty law does not contain any specific prescription authorizing the threat or use of nuclear weapons or any other weapon in general or in certain circumstances, in particular those of the exercise of legitimate self-defence. Nor, however, is there any principle or rule of international law which would make the legality of the threat or use of nuclear weapons or of any other weapons dependent on a specific authorization. State practice shows that the illegality of the use of certain weapons as such does not result from an absence of authorization but, on the contrary, is formulated in terms of prohibition. * * *

60. Those States that believe that recourse to nuclear weapons is illegal stress that the conventions that include various rules providing for the limitation or elimination of nuclear weapons in certain areas (such as the Antarctic Treaty of 1959 which prohibits the deployment of nuclear weapons in the Antarctic, or the Treaty of Tlatelolco of 1967 which creates a nuclear-weapon-free zone in Latin America), or the conventions that apply certain measures of control and limitation to the existence of nuclear weapons (such as the 1963 Partial Test–Ban Treaty or the Treaty on the Non–Proliferation of Nuclear Weapons) all set limits to the use of nuclear weapons. In their view, these treaties bear witness, in their own way, to the emergence of a rule of complete legal prohibition of all uses of nuclear weapons.

61. Those States who defend the position that recourse to nuclear weapons is legal in certain circumstances see a logical contradiction in reaching such a conclusion. According to them, those Treaties, such as the Treaty on the Non–Proliferation of Nuclear Weapons, as well as Security Council resolutions 255 (1968) and 984 (1995) which take note of the security assurances given by the nuclear-weapon States to the non-nuclear-weapon States in relation to any nuclear aggression against the latter, cannot be understood as prohibiting the use of nuclear weapons, and such a claim is contrary to the very text of those instruments. For those who support the legality in certain circumstances of recourse to nuclear weapons, there is no absolute prohibition against the use of such weapons. The very logic and construction of the Treaty on the Non–Proliferation of Nuclear Weapons, they

assert, confirm this. This Treaty, whereby, they contend, the possession of nuclear weapons by the five nuclear-weapon States has been accepted, cannot be seen as a treaty banning their use by those States; to accept the fact that those States possess nuclear weapons is tantamount to recognizing that such weapons may be used in certain circumstances. Nor, they contend, could the security assurances given by the nuclear-weapon States in 1968, and more recently in connection with the Review and Extension Conference of the Parties to the Treaty on the Non–Proliferation of Nuclear Weapons in 1995, have been conceived without its being supposed that there were circumstances in which nuclear weapons could be used in a lawful manner. For those who defend the legality of the use, in certain circumstances, of nuclear weapons, the acceptance of those instruments by the different non-nuclear-weapon States confirms and reinforces the evident logic upon which those instruments are based.

62. The Court notes that the treaties dealing exclusively with acquisition, manufacture, possession, deployment and testing of nuclear weapons, without specifically addressing their threat or use, certainly point to an increasing concern in the international community with these weapons; the Court concludes from this that these treaties could therefore be seen as foreshadowing a future general prohibition of the use of such weapons, but they do not constitute such a prohibition by themselves. As to the treaties of Tlatelolco and Rarotonga and their Protocols, and also the declarations made in connection with the indefinite extension of the Treaty on the Non–Proliferation of Nuclear Weapons, it emerges from these instruments that:

(a) a number of States have undertaken not to use nuclear weapons in specific zones (Latin America; the South Pacific) or against certain other States (non-nuclear-weapon States which are parties to the Treaty on the Non–Proliferation of Nuclear Weapons);

(b) nevertheless, even within this framework, the nuclear-weapon States have reserved the right to use nuclear weapons in certain circumstances; and

(c) these reservations met with no objection from the parties to the Tlatelolco or Rarotonga Treaties or from the Security Council.

63. These two treaties, the security assurances given in 1995 by the nuclear-weapon States and the fact that the Security Council took note of them with satisfaction, testify to a growing awareness of the need to liberate the community of States and the international public from the dangers resulting from the existence of nuclear weapons. The Court moreover notes the signing, even more recently, on 15 December 1995, at Bangkok, of a Treaty on the Southeast Asia Nuclear–Weapon–Free Zone, and on 11 April 1996, at Cairo, of a treaty on the creation of a nuclear-weapons-free zone in Africa. It does not, however, view these elements as amounting to a comprehensive and universal conventional prohibition on the use, or the threat of use, of those weapons as such.

* * *

64. The Court will now turn to an examination of customary international law to determine whether a prohibition of the threat or use of nuclear weapons as such flows from that source of law. As the Court has stated, the

substance of that law must be "looked for primarily in the actual practice and *opinio juris* of States" . . .

65. States which hold the view that the use of nuclear weapons is illegal have endeavoured to demonstrate the existence of a customary rule prohibiting this use. They refer to a consistent practice of non-utilization of nuclear weapons by States since 1945 and they would see in that practice the expression of an *opinio juris* on the part of those who possess such weapons.

66. Some other States, which assert the legality of the threat and use of nuclear weapons in certain circumstances, invoked the doctrine and practice of deterrence in support of their argument. They recall that they have always, in concert with certain other States, reserved the right to use those weapons in the exercise of the right to self-defence against an armed attack threatening their vital security interests. In their view, if nuclear weapons have not been used since 1945, it is not on account of an existing or nascent custom but merely because circumstances that might justify their use have fortunately not arisen.

67. The Court does not intend to pronounce here upon the practice known as the "policy of deterrence." It notes that it is a fact that a number of States adhered to that practice during the greater part of the Cold War and continue to adhere to it. Furthermore, the Members of the international community are profoundly divided on the matter of whether non-recourse to nuclear weapons over the past fifty years constitutes the expression of an *opinio juris*. Under these circumstances the Court does not consider itself able to find that there is such an *opinio juris*.

68. According to certain States, the important series of General Assembly resolutions, beginning with resolution 1653 (XVI) of 24 November 1961, that deal with nuclear weapons and that affirm, with consistent regularity, the illegality of nuclear weapons, signify the existence of a rule of international customary law which prohibits recourse to those weapons. According to other States, however, the resolutions in question have no binding character on their own account and are not declaratory of any customary rule of prohibition of nuclear weapons; some of these States have also pointed out that this series of resolutions not only did not meet with the approval of all of the nuclear-weapon States but of many other States as well.

69. States which consider that the use of nuclear weapons is illegal indicated that those resolutions did not claim to create any new rules, but were confined to a confirmation of customary law relating to the prohibition of means or methods of warfare which, by their use, overstepped the bounds of what is permissible in the conduct of hostilities. In their view, the resolutions in question did no more than apply to nuclear weapons the existing rules of international law applicable in armed conflict; they were no more than the "envelope" or *instrumentum* containing certain pre-existing customary rules of international law. For those States it is accordingly of little importance that the *instrumentum* should have occasioned negative votes, which cannot have the effect of obliterating those customary rules which have been confirmed by treaty law.

70. The Court notes that General Assembly resolutions, even if they are not binding, may sometimes have normative value. They can, in certain circumstances, provide evidence important for establishing the existence of a

rule or the emergence of an *opinio juris*. To establish whether this is true of a given General Assembly resolution, it is necessary to look at its content and the conditions of its adoption; it is also necessary to see whether an *opinio juris* exists as to its normative character. Or a series of resolutions may show the gradual evolution of the *opinio juris* required for the establishment of a new rule.

71. Examined in their totality, the General Assembly resolutions put before the Court declare that the use of nuclear weapons would be "a direct violation of the Charter of the United Nations"; and in certain formulations that such use "should be prohibited". The focus of these resolutions has sometimes shifted to diverse related matters; however, several of the resolutions under consideration in the present case have been adopted with substantial numbers of negative votes and abstentions; thus, although those resolutions are a clear sign of deep concern regarding the problem of nuclear weapons, they still fall short of establishing the existence of an *opinio juris* on the illegality of the use of such weapons.

72. The Court further notes that the first of the resolutions of the General Assembly expressly proclaiming the illegality of the use of nuclear weapons, resolution 1653 (XVI) of 24 November 1961 (mentioned in subsequent resolutions), after referring to certain international declarations and binding agreements, from the Declaration of St. Petersburg of 1868 to the Geneva Protocol of 1925, proceeded to qualify the legal nature of nuclear weapons, determine their effects, and apply general rules of customary international law to nuclear weapons in particular. That application by the General Assembly of general rules of customary law to the particular case of nuclear weapons indicates that, in its view, there was no specific rule of customary law which prohibited the use of nuclear weapons; if such a rule had existed, the General Assembly could simply have referred to it and would not have needed to undertake such an exercise of legal qualification.

73. Having said this, the Court points out that the adoption each year by the General Assembly, by a large majority, of resolutions recalling the content of resolution 1653 (XVI), and requesting the member States to conclude a convention prohibiting the use of nuclear weapons in any circumstance, reveals the desire of a very large section of the international community to take, by a specific and express prohibition of the use of nuclear weapons, a significant step forward along the road to complete nuclear disarmament. The emergence, as *lex lata,* of a customary rule specifically prohibiting the use of nuclear weapons as such is hampered by the continuing tensions between the nascent *opinio juris* on the one hand, and the still strong adherence to the practice of deterrence on the other.

* * *

74. The Court not having found a conventional rule of general scope, nor a customary rule specifically proscribing the threat or use of nuclear weapons *per se,* it will now deal with the question whether recourse to nuclear weapons must be considered as illegal in the light of the principles and rules of international humanitarian law applicable in armed conflict and of the law of neutrality.

[Discussion of humanitarian law and neutrality omitted]

95. Nor can the Court make a determination on the validity of the view that the recourse to nuclear weapons would be illegal in any circumstance owing to their inherent and total incompatibility with the law applicable in armed conflict. Certainly, as the Court has already indicated, the principles and rules of law applicable in armed conflict—at the heart of which is the overriding consideration of humanity—make the conduct of armed hostilities subject to a number of strict requirements. Thus, methods and means of warfare, which would preclude any distinction between civilian and military targets, or which would result in unnecessary suffering to combatants, are prohibited. In view of the unique characteristics of nuclear weapons, to which the Court has referred above, the use of such weapons in fact seems scarcely reconcilable with respect for such requirements. Nevertheless, the Court considers that it does not have sufficient elements to enable it to conclude with certainty that the use of nuclear weapons would necessarily be at variance with the principles and rules of law applicable in armed conflict in any circumstance.

96. Furthermore, the Court cannot lose sight of the fundamental right of every State to survival, and thus its right to resort to self-defence, in accordance with Article 51 of the Charter, when its survival is at stake.

Nor can it ignore the practice referred to as "policy of deterrence", to which an appreciable section of the international community adhered for many years. The Court also notes the reservations which certain nuclear-weapon States have appended to the undertakings they have given, notably under the Protocols to the Treaties of Tlatelolco and Rarotonga, and also under the declarations made by them in connection with the extension of the Treaty on the Non–Proliferation of Nuclear Weapons, not to resort to such weapons.

97. Accordingly, in view of the present state of international law viewed as a whole, as examined above by the Court, and of the elements of fact at its disposal, the Court is led to observe that it cannot reach a definitive conclusion as to the legality or illegality of use of nuclear weapons by a State in an extreme circumstance of self-defence, in which its very survival would be at stake.

[The Court then addressed the claim of an obligation expressed in Article VI of the Non–Proliferation Treaty to negotiate in good faith toward the objective of nuclear disarmament, and affirmed (paragraph 103) that "it remains without doubt an objective of vital importance to the whole of the international community today."

[In paragraph (2) of the operative portion of its judgment, the Court replied as follows to the question put by the General Assembly:]

A. Unanimously,

There is in neither customary nor conventional international law any specific authorization of the threat or use of nuclear weapons;

B. By eleven votes to three,

There is in neither customary nor conventional international law any comprehensive and universal prohibition of the threat or use of nuclear weapons as such; * * *

C. Unanimously,

A threat or use of force by means of nuclear weapons that is contrary to Article 2, paragraph 4, of the United Nations Charter and that fails to meet all the requirements of Article 51, is unlawful;

D. Unanimously,

A threat or use of nuclear weapons should also be compatible with the requirements of the international law applicable in armed conflict, particularly those of the principles and rules of international humanitarian law, as well as with specific obligations under treaties and other undertakings which expressly deal with nuclear weapons;

E. By seven votes to seven, by the President's casting vote,

It follows from the above-mentioned requirements that the threat or use of nuclear weapons would generally be contrary to the rules of international law applicable in armed conflicts, and in particular the principles and rules of humanitarian law;

However, in view of the current state of international law, and of the elements of fact at its disposal, the Court cannot conclude definitively whether the threat or use of nuclear weapons would be lawful or unlawful in an extreme circumstance of self-defence, in which the very survival of a State would be at stake; * * *

F. Unanimously,

There exists an obligation to pursue in good faith and bring to a conclusion negotiations leading to nuclear disarmament in all its aspects under strict and effective international control.

Notes

1. The seven judges voting in favor of operative paragraph 2E were: President Bedjaoui (Algeria), who cast the tie-breaking vote, Judges Ranjeva (Madagascar), Herczegh (Hungary), Shi (China), Fleischhauer (Germany), Vereshchetin (Russian Federation), and Ferrari Bravo (Italy). The seven judges voting against were: Vice–President Schwebel (United States), Judges Oda (Japan), Guillaume (France), Shahabuddeen (Guyana), Weeramantry (Sri Lanka), Koroma (Sierra Leone), and Higgins (United Kingdom). Note that the judges from nuclear-weapons states were to be found on both sides of this curiously worded paragraph.

2. Each member of the Court took advantage of the opportunity to append a declaration or a separate or dissenting opinion to the advisory opinion, in which they clarified their views on various issues. Several of these individual opinions dealt at length with the fundamental issues of international legal theory posed in the *Lotus* case, including whether international law embodies a residual principle of state freedom, whether rules of international law derive in principle from the free will of states, and if so, how acceptance of a prohibitory rule is to be proved or inferred, as well as with the problem of states claiming to be specially affected by an allegedly emergent new rule. For other questions addressed in the *Nuclear Weapons* advisory opinion, see pp. 146–147 infra (on the legal effects of General Assembly resolutions) and Chapters 11–12.

3. In an extended critique of arguments based on the *Lotus* case, Judge Shahabuddeen wrote in his dissenting opinion in *Nuclear Weapons* (1996 I.C.J. at 375, 395–396):

> The notions of sovereignty and independence which the *"Lotus"* Court had in mind did not evolve in a context which visualized the possibility that a single State could possess the capability of wiping out the practical existence both of itself and of all other States. The Court was dealing with a case of collision at sea and the criminal jurisdiction of States in relation thereto—scarcely an earth-shaking issue. Had its mind been directed to the possibility of the planet being destroyed by a minority of warring States, it is not likely that it would have left the position which it took without qualification. * * *
>
> * * * Whichever way the issue in *"Lotus"* was determined, the Court's determination could be accommodated within the framework of an international society consisting of "co-existing independent communities". Not so as regards the issue whether there is a right to use nuclear weapons. Were the Court to uphold such a right, it would be upholding a right which could be used to destroy that framework and which could not therefore be accommodated within it. However extensive might be the powers available to a State, there is not any basis for supposing that the Permanent Court of International Justice considered that, in the absence of a prohibition, they included powers the exercise of which could extinguish civilization and annihilate mankind and thus destroy the framework of the international community; powers of this kind were not in issue. To the extent that a course of action could be followed by so apocalyptic a consequence, the case is distinguishable; it does not stand in the way of this Court holding that States do not have a right to embark on such a course of action unless, which is improbable, it can be shown that the action is authorized under international law.

Judge Weeramantry's dissent elaborated additional reasons for a skeptical approach to the implications of *Lotus* (1996 I.C.J. 429, 495):

> It is implicit in *"Lotus"* that the sovereignty of other States should be respected. One of the characteristics of nuclear weapons is that they violate the sovereignty of other countries who have in no way consented to the intrusion upon their fundamental sovereign rights, which is implicit in the use of the nuclear weapon. It would be an interpretation totally out of context that the *"Lotus"* decision formulated a theory, equally applicable in peace and war, to the effect that a State could do whatever it pleased so long as it had not bound itself to the contrary. Such an interpretation of *"Lotus"* would cast a baneful spell on the progressive development of international law.

4. The argument was proffered in the Nuclear Weapons Advisory Opinion (on behalf of several of the declared nuclear weapons states) that emergence of a rule of customary international law requires the consent or acquiescence of specially affected states, that the nuclear weapons states would be "specially affected" by any purported restriction on such weapons, and that those states had strenuously and consistently maintained the lawfulness of the potential use of these weapons for deterrence of an attack (against themselves or against states under their protection). Vice–President Schwebel dissented from the Court's refusal to hold that use in extraordinary self-defense would be lawful (1996 I.C.J. at 311, 312):

> State practice demonstrates that nuclear weapons have been manufactured and deployed by States for some 50 years; that in that deployment inheres a threat of possible use; and that the international community, by

treaty and through action of the United Nations Security Council, has, far from proscribing the threat or use of nuclear weapons in all circumstances, recognized in effect or in terms that in certain circumstances nuclear weapons may be used or their use threatened.

Not only have the nuclear Powers avowedly and for decades, with vast effort and expense, manufactured, maintained and deployed nuclear weapons. They have affirmed that they are legally entitled to use nuclear weapons in certain circumstances and to threaten their use. They have threatened their use by the hard facts and inexorable implications of the possession and deployment of nuclear weapons; by a posture of readiness to launch nuclear weapons 365 days a year, 24 hours of every day; by the military plans, strategic and tactical, developed and sometimes publicly revealed by them; and in a very few international crises, by threatening the use of nuclear weapons. In the very doctrine and practice of deterrence, the threat of the possible use of nuclear weapons inheres.

This nuclear practice is not a practice of a lone and secondary persistent objector. This is not a practice of a pariah Government crying out in the wilderness of otherwise adverse international opinion. This is the practice of five of the world's major Powers, of the permanent Members of the Security Council, significantly supported for almost 50 years by their allies and other States sheltering under their nuclear umbrellas. That is to say, it is the practice of States—and a practice supported by a large and weighty number of other States—that together represent the bulk of the world's military and economic and financial and technological power and a very large proportion of its population. This practice has been recognized, accommodated and in some measure accepted by the international community. That measure of acceptance is ambiguous but not meaningless. It is obvious that the alliance structures that have been predicated upon the deployment of nuclear weapons accept the legality of their use in certain circumstances. * * *

Other judges, who dissented for the opposite reason (because they thought that the Court should have found the weapons unambiguously unlawful), rejected the proposition that nuclear weapons states were "specially affected." Judge Shahabuddeen wrote that "[w]here what is in issue is the lawfulness of the use of a weapon which could annihilate mankind and so destroy all States, the test of which States are specially affected turns not on the ownership of the weapon, but on the consequences of its use. From this point of view, all States are equally affected, for, like the people who inhabit them, they all have an equal right to exist." (Diss. Op., 1996 I.C.J. 375, 414). See also Diss. Op. Weeramantry, 1996 I.C.J. 429, 535–536 ("A balanced view of the matter is that no one group of nations—nuclear or non-nuclear—can say that its interests are most specially affected. Every nation in the world is specially affected by nuclear weapons, for when matters of survival are involved, this is a matter of universal concern.").

5. Judge Weeramantry devoted a heading of his dissent to the "Multicultural Background to the Humanitarian Laws of War," tracing the evolution of efforts to limit the destructive effects of warfare in Hindu, Buddhist, Chinese, Christian, Islamic and traditional African cultures: "These cultures have all given expression to a variety of limitations on the extent to which any means can be used for the purposes of fighting one's enemy. * * * The multicultural traditions that exist on this important matter cannot be ignored in the Court's consideration of this question, for to do so would be to deprive its conclusions of that plenitude of universal authority which is available to give it added strength—the strength

resulting from the depth of the tradition's historical roots and the width of its geographical spread." 1996 I.C.J. 429, 478 (Footnotes omitted.)

6. Another provocative issue addressed in several of the individual opinions in *Nuclear Weapons* is the problem of *non liquet*, or what the international judge should do when the evidence at hand does not clearly resolve whether a rule of customary international law governs the conduct at issue. In his declaration appended to the *Nuclear Weapons* advisory opinion, Judge Vereshchetin wrote that in an advisory proceeding the Court should "refuse to assume the burden of law-creation, which in general should not be the function of the Court. In advisory procedure, where the Court finds a lacuna in the law or finds the law to be imperfect, it ought merely to state this without trying to fill the lacuna or improve the law by way of judicial legislation. The Court cannot be blamed for indecisiveness or evasiveness where the law, upon which it is called to pronounce, is itself inconclusive." 1996 I.C.J. 279, 280.

Judge Rosalyn Higgins regretted that the Court had effectively chosen to pronounce a *non liquet*, for even if the case were one involving an "antimony" between clashing elements in the law, "the judge's role is precisely to decide which of two or more competing norms is applicable in the particular circumstances. The corpus of international law is frequently made up of norms that, taken in isolation, appear to pull in different directions—for example, States may not use force/States may use force in self-defence * * * It is the role of the judge to resolve, in context, and on grounds that should be articulated, why the application of one norm rather than another is to be preferred in the particular case. As these norms indubitably exist, and the difficulties that face the Court relate to their application, there can be no question of judicial legislation." 1996 I.C.J. 583, 592.

7. The Court in *Nuclear Weapons* searched for relevant *opinio juris,* as discussed in paragraphs 64–72 of the excerpts reprinted above and in several of the separate and dissenting opinions. Could the allegation that states had refrained after August 1945 from using nuclear weapons be explained in terms of a subjective belief that they were obliged under customary international law so to refrain?

8. A few months after the *Nuclear Weapons* advisory opinion, the U.N. General Assembly approved a Comprehensive Test Ban Treaty which was promptly signed by many states but is not yet in force. (By its terms—see Documents Supplement—ratifications on the part of 44 identified states are preconditions to entry into force.) On the occasion of the signing, President Clinton asserted that the signatures of the declared nuclear powers, along with those of the vast majority of countries, "will immediately create an international norm against nuclear testing even before the treaty formally enters into force." New York Times, Sept. 25, 1996. Could signatures of a large number of states, not necessarily followed by ratifications, create a kind of "instant custom"? Could they provide evidence of *opinio juris* accompanying an alleged custom of refraining from nuclear tests? Compare the materials below on the interaction of treaties and custom.

Two of the states that neither signed nor ratified the Comprehensive Test Ban Treaty—Pakistan and Indian—exploded nuclear devices in May and June 1998. These states denied the existence of any rule of customary international law restricting their freedom of action in nuclear matters. Could a customary rule have come into being without their consent? over their objection? Compare p. 100 infra on the "persistent objector" principle.

9. For a range of perspectives on the *Nuclear Weapons* advisory opinion, see L. Boisson de Chazournes & P. Sands (eds.), International Law, the International Court of Justice and Nuclear Weapons (1999); V. Nanda & D. Krieger, Nuclear Weapons and the World Court (1998); Symposium: Nuclear Weapons, the World Court, and Global Security, 7 Transnat. L. & Contemp. Probs. 313–457 (1997); M. Matheson, The Opinions of the International Court of Justice on the Threat or Use of Nuclear Weapons, 91 A.J.I.L. 417 (1997); Falk, Nuclear Weapons, International Law and the World Court: A Historic Encounter, 91 A.J.I.L. 64 (1997).

ASYLUM CASE (COLOMBIA v. PERU)

International Court of Justice, 1950.
1950 I.C.J. 266.

[The case concerns the institution of diplomatic asylum in Latin America. In 1949, a Peruvian political leader, Victor Raul Haya de la Torre, was given asylum in the Colombian Embassy in Lima, Peru. The Colombian Ambassador requested the government of Peru to allow Haya de la Torre to leave the country on the ground that the Colombian government qualified him as a political refugee. Peru refused to accept the right of Colombia to define unilaterally the nature of Haya de la Torre's offense. After diplomatic correspondence, the case was referred to the International Court.

In its submission, Colombia claimed the right to qualify (i.e., characterize) the nature of the offense by unilateral decision that would be binding on Peru. It based this claim on certain international agreements among Latin American states and in addition on "American international law." With respect to this latter contention, the Court said:]

The Colombian Government has finally invoked "American international law in general". In addition to the rules arising from agreements which have already been considered, it has relied on an alleged regional or local custom peculiar to Latin–American States.

The Party which relies on a custom of this kind must prove that this custom is established in such a manner that it has become binding on the other Party. The Colombian Government must prove that the rule invoked by it is in accordance with a constant and uniform usage practised by the States in question, and that this usage is the expression of a right appertaining to the State granting asylum and a duty incumbent on the territorial State. This follows from Article 38 of the Statute of the Court, which refers to international custom "as evidence of a general practice accepted as law".

* * *

It is particularly the Montevideo Convention of 1933 which Counsel for the Colombian Government has also relied on in this connexion. It is contended that this Convention has merely codified principles which were already recognized by Latin–American custom, and that it is valid against Peru as a proof of customary law. The limited number of States which have ratified this Convention reveals the weakness of this argument, and furthermore, it is invalidated by the preamble which states that this Convention modifies the Havana Convention.

Finally, the Colombian Government has referred to a large number of particular cases in which diplomatic asylum was in fact granted and respected. But it has not shown that the alleged rule of unilateral and definitive qualification was invoked or—if in some cases it was in fact invoked—that it was, apart from conventional stipulations, exercised by the States granting asylum as a right appertaining to them and respected by the territorial States as a duty incumbent on them and not merely for reasons of political expediency. The facts brought to the knowledge of the Court disclose so much uncertainty and contradiction, so much fluctuation and discrepancy in the exercise of diplomatic asylum and in the official views expressed on various occasions, there has been so much inconsistency in the rapid succession of conventions on asylum, ratified by some States and rejected by others, and the practice has been so much influenced by considerations of political expediency in the various cases, that it is not possible to discern in all this any constant and uniform usage, accepted as law, with regard to the alleged rule of unilateral and definitive qualification of the offence.

The Court cannot therefore find that the Colombian Government has proved the existence of such a custom. But even if it could be supposed that such a custom existed between certain Latin-American States only, it could not be invoked against Peru which, far from having by its attitude adhered to it, has, on the contrary, repudiated it by refraining from ratifying the Montevideo Conventions of 1933 and 1939, which were the first to include a rule concerning the qualification of the offence in matters of diplomatic asylum.

* * *

Notes

1. The *Asylum Case* deals with "American international law"—that is, regional customary law. May states of a region adopt customary law rules that derogate from general international law with respect to conduct and events within the region? Would such regional law be effective as against states outside the region? For example, may a regional group extend exclusive national jurisdiction over adjacent high seas beyond the limits established by international law? Or may they follow regional custom that gives foreign nationals doing business in the region no more than national treatment irrespective of customary law rights? See discussion of Calvo doctrine in Chapter 10.

2. Does the *Asylum Case* indicate that a state within a region is not bound by a regional custom unless it expressly agrees to be bound? Should a regional custom be treated within the regional group in the same way as general customary law—namely, binding all states that have not opposed it? Objections to regional customary law point to the difficulty of dividing the world into regions and to potential conflicts between regional and international norms. See S. Prakash Sinha, Identifying a Principle of International Law Today, 11 Can.Y.B.I.L. 106 (1973).

3. May the concept of regional custom be extended to cover special customary rules for particular groups of states? For example, could there be a rule of

restrictive sovereign immunity for one group of states and a rule of absolute immunity for another group?

4. Note the distinction drawn by the Court between practice followed for reasons of expediency and practice accepted by law. What evidence is cited for finding that the practice of diplomatic asylum lacked acceptance as law? Does the Court base its inference on subjective elements or on "objective" facts such as inconsistency, fluctuation and contradictions on practice and in statements? Under what circumstances might a uniform and general practice be sufficient to show the requisite subjective factor, the *opinio juris?* See below for further discussion of *opinio juris* and practice.

5. Charles de Visscher, a former President of the International Court, has written that "mere uniformity or external regularity never justifies a conclusion of normativity." "Governments [he wrote] attach importance to distinguishing between custom by which they hold themselves bound and the mere practices often dictated by consideration of expediency and therefore devoid of definite legal meaning. * * * The inductive reasoning that establishes the existence of custom is a tied reasoning: the matter is not only one of counting the observed regularities but of weighing them in terms of social ends deemed desirable." de Visscher, Theory and Reality in Public International Law 156–57 (Corbett trans. 1968).

SPECIAL CUSTOM

CASE CONCERNING RIGHT OF PASSAGE OVER INDIAN TERRITORY (MERITS) (PORTUGAL v. INDIA)

International Court of Justice, 1960.
1960 I.C.J. 6.

[In an application referring its dispute with India to the International Court of Justice under Article 36(2) of the Statute, the Portuguese government charged that India was unlawfully obstructing the right of passage claimed by Portugal through the Indian territory that surrounded certain Portuguese enclaves in the Indian peninsula. The Indian action, it was alleged, was in furtherance of Indian efforts to annex the Portuguese territories in India, and had made it impossible for Portugal to exercise her rights of sovereignty in the affected areas. Six preliminary objections interposed by India and going to the Court's jurisdiction were overruled.

[Turning to the merits of the Portuguese claim, the Court examined the Treaty of Poona, concluded in 1779 between Portugal and the Maratha ruler, and subsequent decrees of the latter. The Court then directed its attention to the subsequent history of the Portuguese presence in India.]

For the purpose of determining whether Portugal has established the right of passage claimed by it, the court must have regard to what happened during the British and post-British periods. During these periods, there had developed between the Portuguese and the territorial sovereign with regard to passage to the enclaves a practice upon which Portugal relies for the purpose of establishing the right of passage claimed by it.

[The Court then rejected the argument that a local custom could not have been established between only two states, and proceeded to examine whether the right of passage asserted by Portugal was established on the basis of the prevailing practice between the parties during the British and post-British periods. The Court observed that all merchandise other than arms and ammunition passed freely between Daman (a Portuguese port) and the enclaves during the periods in question, subject only to such regulation and control as were necessitated by security or revenue.]

The Court, therefore, concludes that, with regard to private persons, civil officials and goods in general there existed during the British and post-British periods a constant and uniform practice allowing free passage between Daman and the enclaves. This practice having continued over a period extending beyond a century and a quarter unaffected by the change of regime in respect of the intervening territory which occurred when India became independent, the Court is, in view of all the circumstances of the case satisfied that that practice was accepted as law by the Parties and has given rise to a right and a correlative obligation.

The Court therefore holds that Portugal had in 1954 a right of passage over intervening Indian territory between coastal Daman and the enclaves and between the enclaves, in respect of private persons, civil officials and goods in general, to the extent necessary, as claimed by Portugal, for the exercise of its sovereignty over the enclaves, and subject to the regulation and control of India.

As regards armed forces, armed police and arms and ammunition, the position is different.

[The Court then discussed an incident concerning the 1878 Treaty of Commerce and Extradition between Great Britain and Portugal which provided that the armed forces of the two governments should not enter the India dominions of the other, except for specified purposes. The Governor–General of Portuguese India stated that, following the practice of centuries of respecting treaties and according due deference to British authorities, "Portuguese troops never cross British territory without previous permission."]

It would thus appear that, during the British and post-British periods, Portuguese armed forces and armed police did not pass between Daman and the enclaves as of right and that, after 1878, such passage could only take place with previous authorization by the British and later by India, accorded either under a reciprocal arrangement already agreed to, or in individual cases. Having regard to the special circumstances of the case, this necessity for authorization before passage could take place constitutes, in the view of the Court, a negation of passage as of right. The practice predicates that the territorial sovereign had the discretionary power to withdraw or to refuse permission. It is argued that permission was always granted, but this does not, in the opinion of the Court, affect the legal position. There is nothing in the record to show that grant of permission was incumbent on the British or on India as an obligation. * * *

* * *

There was thus established a clear distinction between the practice permitting free passage of private persons, civil officials and goods in general, and the practice requiring previous authorization, as in the case of armed forces, armed police, and arms and ammunition.

The Court is, therefore, of the view that no right of passage in favour of Portugal involving a correlative obligation on India has been established in respect of armed forces, armed police, and arms and ammunition. The course of dealings established between the Portuguese and the British authorities with respect to the passage of these categories excludes the existence of any such right. The practice that was established shows that, with regard to these categories, it was well understood that passage could take place only by permission of the British authorities. This situation continued during the post-British period.

Portugal also invokes general international custom, as well as the general principles of law recognized by civilized nations, in support of its claim of a right of passage as formulated by it. Having arrived at the conclusion that the course of dealings between the British and Indian authorities on the one hand and the Portuguese on the other established a practice, well understood between the Parties, by virtue of which Portugal had acquired a right of passage in respect of private persons, civil officials and goods in general, the Court does not consider it necessary to examine whether general international custom or the general principles of law recognized by civilized nations may lead to the same result.

As regards armed forces, armed police and arms and ammunition, the finding of the Court that the practice established between the Parties required for passage in respect of these categories the permission of the British or Indian authorities, renders it unnecessary for the Court to determine whether or not, in the absence of the practice that actually prevailed, general international custom or the general principles of law recognized by civilized nations could have been relied upon by Portugal in support of its claim to a right of passage in respect of these categories. * * *

[Having found that Portugal had in 1954 a right of passage over Indian territory between Daman and the enclaves in respect of private persons, civil officials, and goods in general, the Court nevertheless then concluded that India had lawfully exercised its power of regulation and control of the Portuguese rights when it "suspended" all passage in July 1954 because of "tension" created by the overthrow of Portugal's rule in the enclaves.]

[Dissenting and separate opinions omitted.]

Note

Does the case support the argument that special or particular custom requires a higher degree of proof than general custom? Does it amount to showing tacit agreement and would that make a difference in proof?

OPINIO JURIS

NORTH SEA CONTINENTAL SHELF CASES (FEDERAL REPUBLIC OF GERMANY v. DENMARK) (FEDERAL REPUBLIC OF GERMANY v. NETHERLANDS)

International Court of Justice, 1969.
1969 I.C.J. 3.

[The cases involved a dispute over the delimitation of the Continental Shelf shared by Denmark, the Netherlands and the Federal Republic of Germany. Denmark and the Netherlands claimed that the dispute should be decided in accordance with the principle of equidistance under Article 6 of the Geneva Convention of 1958 on the Continental Shelf. The Court rejected the application of the Convention to which Germany was not a party. However, Denmark and the Netherlands also maintained that the principle in Article 6 of the Convention is part of the corpus of general international law, and in particular of customary law. The Court rejected this contention by a vote of 11 to 6 for the reasons given below.]

70. * * * [Denmark and the Netherlands argue] that even if there was at the date of the Geneva Convention no rule of customary international law in favour of the equidistance principle, and no such rule was crystallized in Article 6 of the Convention, nevertheless such a rule has come into being since the Convention, partly because of its own impact, partly on the basis of subsequent State practice * * *

71. In so far as this contention is based on the view that Article 6 of the Convention has had the influence, and has produced the effect described, it clearly involves treating that Article as a norm-creating provision which has constituted the foundation of, or has generated a rule which, while only conventional or contractual in its origin, has since passed into the general *corpus* of international law, and is now accepted as such by the *opinio juris,* so as to have become binding even for countries which have never, and do not, become parties to the Convention. There is no doubt that this process is a perfectly possible one and does from time to time occur: it constitutes indeed one of the recognized methods by which new rules of customary international law may be formed. At the same time this result is not lightly to be regarded as having been attained.

72. It would in the first place be necessary that the provision concerned should, at all events potentially, be of a fundamentally norm-creating character such as could be regarded as forming the basis of a general rule of law. Considered *in abstracto* the equidistance principle might be said to fulfill this requirement. Yet in the particular form in which it is embodied in Article 6 of the Geneva Convention, and having regard to the relationship of that Article to other provisions of the Convention, this must be open to some doubt. In the first place, Article 6 is so framed as to put second the obligation to make use of the equidistance method, causing it to come after a primary obligation to effect delimitation by agreement. Such a primary obligation constitutes an unusual preface to what is claimed to be a potential general rule of law. * * * Secondly the part played by the notion of special circumstances relative to the principle of equidistance as embodied in Article 6, and the very considerable,

still unresolved controversies as to the exact meaning and scope of this notion, must raise further doubts as to the potentially norm-creating character of the rule. Finally, the faculty of making reservations to Article 6, while it might not of itself prevent the equidistance principle being eventually received as general law, does add considerably to the difficulty of regarding this result as having been brought about (or being potentially possible) on the basis of the Convention: for so long as this faculty continues to exist, * * * it is the Convention itself which would, for the reasons already indicated, seem to deny to the provisions of Article 6 the same norm-creating character as, for instance, Articles 1 and 2 possess.

73. With respect to the other elements usually regarded as necessary before a conventional rule can be considered to have become a general rule of international law, it might be that, even without the passage of any considerable period of time, a very widespread and representative participation in the convention might suffice of itself, provided it included that of States whose interests were specially affected. In the present case however, the Court notes that, even if allowance is made for the existence of a number of States to whom participation in the Geneva Convention is not open, or which, by reason for instance of being land-locked States, would have no interest in becoming parties to it, the number of ratifications and accessions so far secured is, though respectable, hardly sufficient. That nonratification may sometimes be due to factors other than active disapproval of the convention concerned can hardly constitute a basis on which positive acceptance of its principles can be implied. The reasons are speculative, but the facts remain.

74. As regards the time element, the Court notes that it is over ten years since the Convention was signed, but that it is even now less than five since it came into force in June 1964 * * *. Although the passage of only a short period of time is not necessarily, or of itself, a bar to the formation of a new rule of customary international law on the basis of what was originally a purely conventional rule, an indispensable requirement would be that within the period in question, short though it might be, State practice, including that of States whose interests are specially affected, should have been both extensive and virtually uniform in the sense of the provision invoked;—and should moreover have occurred in such a way as to show a general recognition that a rule of law or legal obligation is involved.

75. The Court must now consider whether State practice in the matter of continental shelf delimitation has, subsequent to the Geneva Convention, been of such a kind as to satisfy this requirement. * * * [S]ome fifteen cases have been cited in the course of the present proceedings, occurring mostly since the signature of the 1958 Geneva Convention, in which continental shelf boundaries have been delimited according to the equidistance principle—in the majority of the cases by agreement, in a few others unilaterally—or else the delimitation was foreshadowed but has not yet been carried out. But even if these various cases constituted more than a very small proportion of those potentially calling for delimitation in the world as a whole, the Court would not think it necessary to enumerate or evaluate them separately, since there are, *a priori,* several grounds which deprive them of weight as precedents in the present context.

77. The essential point in this connection—and it seems necessary to stress it—is that even if these instances of action by nonparties to the Convention were much more numerous than they in fact are, they would not, even in the aggregate, suffice in themselves to constitute the *opinio juris;*—for, in order to achieve this result, two conditions must be fulfilled. Not only must the acts concerned amount to a settled practice, but they must also be such, or be carried out in such a way, as to be evidence of a belief that this practice is rendered obligatory by the existence of a rule of law requiring it. The need for such a belief, i.e., the existence of a subjective element, is implicit in the very notion of the *opinio juris sive necessitatis.* The States concerned must therefore feel that they are conforming to what amounts to a legal obligation. The frequency, or even habitual character of the acts is not in itself enough. There are many international acts, e.g., in the field of ceremonial and protocol, which are performed almost invariably, but which are motivated only by considerations of courtesy, convenience or tradition, and not by any sense of legal duty.

78. In this respect the Court follows the view adopted by the Permanent Court of International Justice in the *Lotus* case * * * [T]he position is simply that in certain cases—not a great number—the States concerned agreed to draw or did draw the boundaries concerned according to the principle of equidistance. There is no evidence that they so acted because they felt legally compelled to draw them in this way by reason of a rule of customary law obliging them to do so—especially considering that they might have been motivated by other obvious factors.

[In a dissenting opinion, Judge Lachs took issue with the Court's conclusion regarding *opinio juris.* He said, in part, 1969 I.C.J. 219, 228–231:]

All this leads to the conclusion that the principles and rules enshrined in the Convention, and in particular the equidistance rule, have been accepted not only by those States which are parties to the Convention on the Continental Shelf, but also by those which have subsequently followed it in agreements, or in their legislation, or have acquiesced in it when faced with legislative acts of other States affecting them. This can be viewed as evidence of a practice widespread enough to satisfy the criteria for a general rule of law.

* * *

Can the practice above summarized be considered as having been accepted as law, having regard to the subjective element required? The process leading to this effect is necessarily complex. There are certain areas of State activity and international law which by their very character may only with great difficulty engender general law, but there are others, both old and new, which may do so with greater ease. Where Continental Shelf law is concerned, some States have at first probably accepted the rules in question, as States usually do, because they found them convenient and useful, the best possible solution for the problems involved. Others may also have been convinced that the instrument elaborated within the framework of the United Nations was intended to become and would in due course become general law (the teleological element is of no small importance in the formation of law). Many States have followed suit under the conviction that it was law.

Thus at the successive stages in the development of the rule the motives which have prompted States to accept it have varied from case to case. It could not be otherwise. At all events, to postulate that all States, even those which initiate a given practice, believe themselves to be acting under a legal obligation is to resort to a fiction—and in fact to deny the possibility of developing such rules. For the path may indeed start from voluntary, unilateral acts relying on the confident expectation that they will find acquiescence or be emulated; alternatively the starting-point may consist of a treaty to which more and more States accede and which is followed by unilateral acceptance. It is only at a later stage that, by the combined effect of individual or joint action, response and interaction in the field concerned, i.e., of that reciprocity so essential in international legal relations, there develops the chain-reaction productive of international consensus.

* * *

In sum, the general practice of States should be recognized as prima facie evidence that it is accepted as law. Such evidence may, of course, be controverted—even on the test of practice itself, if it shows 'much uncertainty and contradiction' (Asylum, Judgment, I.C.J. Reports 1950, p. 277). It may also be controverted on the test of *opinio juris* with regard to "the States in question" or the parties to the case.

Notes

1. What evidence would satisfy the requirement of *opinio juris* under the majority opinion in the North Sea Case? Some writers maintain that an inference of *opinio juris* can only be supported by the statements of states as to legal right or obligation. On the other hand, as Judge Lachs points out, individual governments often act for convenience or utility even though their legal right to do so is unclear or non-existent. If other governments do not object and take similar actions, the general practice is recognized as a legal rule. Thus, a nascent period of formation of a rule would not exhibit the *opinio juris generalis* but with repeated instances, states come to treat the practice as law. A much cited example is the way in which the Truman Proclamation in 1945 of exclusive jurisdiction over the adjacent continental shelf—a novel position unsupported by existing law—became recognized as general customary law when other coastal states followed the U.S. action and none objected to it.

2. Kelsen points out that "in practice it appears that the *opinio juris* is commonly inferred from the constancy and uniformity of state conduct. But to the extent that it is so inferred, it is this conduct and not the state of mind that is decisive." He notes that in a period of stability, this creates no great concern. However, at a time of pervasive and rapid change, and "the equivocal nature of much state practice today," the uncertainties of law-creation through custom are much greater than in the past. H. Kelsen, Principles of International Law 450–52 (2d ed. R. Tucker 1966).

3. Has custom become less important in this time of pervasive change (as Kelsen suggests) or has its character changed in response to rapidly changing demands? Today some writers refer to "instant custom" or to "custom on

demand." Instead of emphasis on uniformities of conduct (the material element), more importance is accorded to the subjective element of *opinio juris,* particularly when declared by states collectively with reasonable expectation of future conduct conforming to the new principle. Henkin comments: "Such efforts to create new customary law by purposeful activity have included * * * resolutions adopted by international organizations * * * to promote, declare or confirm principles of law by overwhelming majorities or by consensus resolutions which discourage dissent." Henkin, International Law: Politics, Values and Functions, 216 Rec. des Cours 58 (1989–IV). (See material at pp. 142–153 on the effect of U.N. resolutions and declarations.)

4. The tendency to "find" new customary law based mainly on *opinio juris* (i.e., statements that a legal rule has now been recognized) without demonstrating uniform conduct among states in general is especially evident in regard to human rights, environmental protection, and economic development. Is this attempt to put new wine into old bottles legitimized by the felt necessity to extend law to meet social objectives, when neither treaties nor uniform practice serve that function? For varied views, see following articles in Australian Y.B.I.L. vol. 12 (1992); O. Schachter, Recent Trends in International Law–Making, pp. 1–15; A. Pellet, The Normative Dilemma: Will and Consent in International Law–Making, pp. 22–53; B. Simma and P. Alston, The Sources of Human Rights Law: Custom, Jus Cogens and General Principles, pp. 82–108. See also T. Meron, Human Rights and Humanitarian Norms as Customary Law 92–97, 134 (1989). The contradictory tendencies are emphasized by M. Koskenniemi, From Apology to Utopia 342–421 (1989).

CASE CONCERNING MILITARY AND PARAMILITARY ACTIVITIES IN AND AGAINST NICARAGUA (NICARAGUA v. UNITED STATES) (MERITS)

International Court of Justice (1986).
1986 I.C.J. 14.

[In 1984 Nicaragua instituted proceedings against the United States in the International Court of Justice, alleging unlawful military and paramilitary acts by the United States in Nicaragua (for the substance see p. 955 below). The United States contested the jurisdiction of the Court on several grounds including a reservation it had made in accepting the Court's jurisdiction that its acceptance would not apply to certain disputes arising under multilateral treaties—in this case, the U.N. Charter. Nicaragua responded that its claim was based not only on the Charter but also under rules of customary law which were similar in content to the Charter and applicable to these facts. The Court accepted the Nicaraguan contention for the reasons given below.]

182. The Court concludes that it should exercise the jurisdiction conferred upon it by the United States declaration of acceptance under Article 36, paragraph 2, of the Statute, to determine the claims of Nicaragua based upon customary international law notwithstanding the exclusion from its jurisdiction of disputes "arising under" the United Nations and Organization of American States Charters.

183. In view of this conclusion, the Court has next to consider what are the rules of customary international law applicable to the present dispute. For this purpose, it has to direct its attention to the practice and *opinio juris* of States; as the Court recently observed,

> "It is of course axiomatic that the material of customary international law is to be looked for primarily in the actual practice and *opinio juris* of States, even though multilateral conventions may have an important role to play in recording and defining rules deriving from custom, or indeed in developing them." *(Continental Shelf (Libyan Arab Jamahiriya/Malta), I.C.J. Reports 1985,* pp. 29–30, para. 27.)

In this respect the Court must not lose sight of the Charter of the United Nations and that of the Organization of American States, notwithstanding the operation of the multilateral treaty reservation. Although the Court has no jurisdiction to determine whether the conduct of the United States constitutes a breach of those conventions, it can and must take them into account in ascertaining the content of the customary international law which the United States is also alleged to have infringed.

184. The Court notes that there is in fact evidence, to be examined below, of a considerable degree of agreement between the Parties as to the content of the customary international law relating to the non-use of force and non-intervention. This concurrence of their views does not however dispense the Court from having itself to ascertain what rules of customary international law are applicable. The mere fact that States declare their recognition of certain rules is not sufficient for the Court to consider these as being part of customary international law, and as applicable as such to those States. Bound as it is by Article 38 of its Statute to apply, *inter alia,* international custom "as evidence of a general practice accepted as law", the Court may not disregard the essential role played by general practice. Where two States agree to incorporate a particular rule in a treaty, their agreement suffices to make that rule a legal one, binding upon them; but in the field of customary international law, the shared view of the Parties as to the content of what they regard as the rule is not enough. The Court must satisfy itself that the existence of the rule in the *opinio juris* of States is confirmed by practice.

185. In the present dispute, the Court, while exercising its jurisdiction only in respect of the application of the customary rules of non-use of force and non-intervention, cannot disregard the fact that the Parties are bound by these rules as a matter of treaty law and of customary international law. Furthermore, in the present case, apart from the treaty commitments binding the Parties to the rules in question, there are various instances of their having expressed recognition of the validity thereof as customary international law in other ways. It is therefore in the light of this "subjective element"—the expression used by the Court in its 1969 Judgment in the *North Sea Continental Shelf* cases *(I.C.J. Reports 1969,* p. 44)—that the Court has to appraise the relevant practice.

186. It is not to be expected that in the practice of States the application of the rules in question should have been perfect, in the sense that States should have refrained, with complete consistency, from the use of force or from intervention in each other's internal affairs. The Court does not consider that, for a rule to be established as customary, the corresponding practice must be in absolutely rigorous conformity with the rule. In order to deduce the existence of customary rules, the Court deems it sufficient that the conduct of States should, in general, be consistent with such rules, and that

instances of State conduct inconsistent with a given rule should generally have been treated as breaches of that rule, not as indications of the recognition of a new rule. If a State acts in a way prima facie incompatible with a recognized rule, but defends its conduct by appealing to exceptions or justifications contained within the rule itself, then whether or not the State's conduct is in fact justifiable on that basis, the significance of that attitude is to confirm rather than to weaken the rule.

187. The Court must therefore determine, first, the substance of the customary rules relating to the use of force in international relations, applicable to the dispute submitted to it. The United States has argued that, on this crucial question of the lawfulness of the use of force in inter-State relations, the rules of general and customary international law, and those of the United Nations Charter, are in fact identical. In its view this identity is so complete that, as explained above (paragraph 173), it constitutes an argument to prevent the Court from applying this customary law, because it is indistinguishable from the multilateral treaty law which it may not apply. In its Counter–Memorial on jurisdiction and admissibility the United States asserts that "Article 2(4) of the Charter *is* customary and general international law". It quotes with approval an observation by the International Law Commission to the effect that

> "the great majority of international lawyers today unhesitatingly hold that Article 2, paragraph 4, together with other provisions of the Charter, authoritatively declares the modern customary law regarding the threat or use of force" *(ILC Yearbook,* 1966, Vol. II, p. 247).

The United States points out that Nicaragua has endorsed this view, since one of its counsel asserted that "indeed it is generally considered by publicists that Article 2, paragraph 4, of the United Nations Charter is in this respect an embodiment of existing general principles of international law". And the United States concludes:

> "In sum, the provisions of Article 2(4) with respect to the lawfulness of the use of force *are* 'modern customary law' (International Law Commission, *loc. cit.)* and the 'embodiment of general principles of international law' (counsel for Nicaragua, Hearing of 25 April 1984, morning, *loc. cit.).* There is no other 'customary and general international law' on which Nicaragua can rest its claims."
>
> "It is, in short, inconceivable that this Court could consider the lawfulness of an alleged use of armed force without referring to the principal source of the relevant international law—Article 2(4) of the United Nations Charter."

As for Nicaragua, the only noteworthy shade of difference in its view lies in Nicaragua's belief that

> "in certain cases the rule of customary law will not necessarily be identical in content and mode of application to the conventional rule".

188. The Court thus finds that both Parties take the view that the principles as to the use of force incorporated in the United Nations Charter correspond, in essentials, to those found in customary international law. The Parties thus both take the view that the fundamental principle in this area is expressed in the terms employed in Article 2, paragraph 4, of the United

Nations Charter. They therefore accept a treaty-law obligation to refrain in their international relations from the threat or use of force against the territorial integrity or political independence of any State, or in any other manner inconsistent with the purposes of the United Nations. The Court has however to be satisfied that there exists in customary international law an *opinio juris* as to the binding character of such abstention. This *opinio juris* may, though with all due caution, be deduced from, *inter alia,* the attitude of the Parties and the attitude of States towards certain General Assembly resolutions, and particularly resolution 2625 (XXV) entitled "Declaration on Principles of International Law concerning Friendly Relations and Co-operation among States in accordance with the Charter of the United Nations". The effect of consent to the text of such resolutions cannot be understood as merely that of a "reiteration or elucidation" of the treaty commitment undertaken in the Charter. On the contrary, it may be understood as an acceptance of the validity of the rule or set of rules declared by the resolution by themselves. The principle of non-use of force, for example, may thus be regarded as a principle of customary international law, not as such conditioned by provisions relating to collective security, or to the facilities or armed contingents to be provided under Article 43 of the Charter. It would therefore seem apparent that the attitude referred to expresses an *opinio juris* respecting such rule (or set of rules), to be thenceforth treated separately from the provisions, especially those of an institutional kind, to which it is subject on the treaty-law plane of the Charter.

Notes

1. Note how the Court related *opinio juris* to evidence of practice. It found (in para. 184) "a considerable degree of agreement between the parties as to the content of the customary international law relating to the non-use of force and non-intervention." In this light, the Court referred only generally to the relevant practice. A Dutch scholar concludes from this judgment that "if there exist concordant views as to the existence of an applicable rule, less stringent proof is required to establish existence of a settled practice and *opinio juris.* * * * Where concordant views exist, the dispute will not concern the question whether a particular rule exists or whether the parties are bound by that rule but will above all concern * * * the facts, particularly * * * whether certain acts are prohibited or permitted by the rule." P. Rijpkema, Customary International Law in the Nicaragua Case, 20 Neth. Y.B.I.L. 91, 96–97 (1989). Compare this conclusion to the Court's decision in both the Lotus and the North Sea Continental Shelf Cases where one of the parties denied the existence of an applicable customary law norm. In those cases the Court looked to see if practice was accepted as law (i.e., *opinio juris*). In the Nicaragua Case, *opinio juris* (the subjective element) was not disputed and the Court states in para. 185 that it will "appraise the relevant practice" in the light of the "subjective element." Thus, *opinio juris* is established prior to appraising practice in contrast to the Lotus and North Sea judgments.

2. Is the question of state practice of less importance when the norms in question are recognized as "fundamental" and universal? The Court refers to the fact that the non-use of force, as expressed in Article 2(4), is frequently referred to

as a fundamental or cardinal principle and as a principle of *jus cogens* (peremptory norm). Is this a good reason for the Court to be less stringent in requiring proof of a general practice in conformity with the norm? See Schachter, Entangled Treaty and Custom, in International Law at a Time of Perplexity 717, 733–34 (Dinstein, ed. 1989), noting that the "higher normativity" of the rule against aggression justifies maintaining the rule even in the face of inconsistent practice.

3. After the invasion of Panama in 1990, the State Department Legal Adviser, in justifying the legality of the U.S. action, argued for a "common law approach to use of force rules" that "would take account of the circumstance of each case and avoid a mechanical application of the rules." A. Sofaer, The Legality of the United States Invasion of Panama, 29 Colum.J.Transnat'l Law 281, 282 n. 10. Henkin, in response, wrote:

> Customary international law indeed has important similarities to the common law but there are essential differences between them * * *.
>
> If the invasion of Panama, and the legal arguments to justify it, were designed to erode or modify established law, they have been rejected by the large majority of the states and of the legal communities—"the judges" of the "international common law." Indeed, the history of the common law rejects its use as an analogy to justify the U.S. invasion of Panama. When the common law proved inadequate, when society could not tolerate the law's ambiguities and uncertainties and its dependence on imperfect institutions, the law was codified, made more clear, more firm, leaving less room for violators and for reliance on an imperfect judiciary * * * Because the "common law" on the use of force failed, the law was codified, establishing clearer, firmer prohibitions, designed to leave few loopholes and little room for distortion.

Henkin, The Invasion of Panama and International Law: A Gross Violation, 29 Colum.J.Transnat'l L. 311–12 (1991). See also pp. 25–26 above.

THE POSITION OF "NON-CONSENTING" STATES

WALDOCK, GENERAL COURSE ON PUBLIC INTERNATIONAL LAW

106 Rec. des Cours 1, 49–53 (1962–II) (Some footnotes omitted).

* * * The view of most international lawyers is that customary law is not a form of tacit treaty but an independent form of law; and that, when a custom satisfying the definition in Article 38 is established, it constitutes a general rule of international law which, subject to one reservation, applies to every State. The reservation concerns the case of a State which, while the custom is in process of formation, unambiguously and persistently registers its objection to the recognition of the practice as law. Thus, in the *Anglo-Norwegian Fisheries* case the Court, having rejected the so-called ten-mile rule for bays, said:

> "In any event, the ten-mile rule would appear to be inapplicable as against Norway, inasmuch as she has always opposed any attempt to apply it to the Norwegian coast."

Similarly, in the *Asylum* case it said:

> "Even if it could be supposed that such a custom existed between certain Latin-American States only, it could not be invoked against Peru,

which, far from having by its attitude adhered to it, has on the contrary repudiated it."

These pronouncements seem clearly to indicate that a customary rule may arise notwithstanding the opposition of one State, or even perhaps a few States, provided that otherwise the necessary degree of generality is reached. But they also seem to lay down that the rule so created will not bind the objectors; in other words, that in international law there is no majority rule even with respect to the formation of customary law.

On the other hand, it is no less clear that, if a custom becomes established as a general rule of international law, it binds all States which have not opposed it, whether or not they themselves played an active part in its formation. This means that in order to invoke a custom against a State it is not necessary to show specifically the *acceptance* of the custom as law by that State; its acceptance of the custom will be presumed so that it will be bound unless it can adduce evidence of its actual opposition to the practice in question. The Court in applying a general custom may well refer to the practice, if any, of the parties to the litigation in regard to the custom; but it has never yet treated evidence of their acceptance of the practice as a *sine qua non* of applying the custom to them. The position is, of course, quite different in regard to a particular custom between two or three States, as in the *Right of Passage* case, because that is a derogation from the general law and the acceptance of the custom by the parties to the litigation themselves is the whole basis of the exceptional rule. * * *

An aspect of this question of the legal basis of custom which is of particular importance to-day is the position of the new-born State with regard to existing general rules of customary law. We know that, generally speaking, a new State begins with a clean slate in regard to treaties, although often of its own choice it takes over many of the treaty obligations formerly applicable to the territory. Logically enough on the treaty theory of custom, Communist writers maintain that the same is true for customary law; and they have strong things to say about "European" or "Western" States trying to impose norms of general international law upon the new States of Asia and Africa.

This doctrine has not been without its attraction for new States emerging from colonial régimes. But, quite apart from any theoretical difficulty about the nature of customary law, the fundamental objection to it is that it really denies the existence of a general international legal order and the new States have at least as much to lose as anyone else from a denial of the validity of existing international law. If consent is so far the basis of customary law that a new State may reject any customary rule it chooses, how can it be said that an older State is not free, vis-à-vis the new State, to reject any customary rule that it may choose? Either there is an international legal order or there is not. * * *

* * * The new States have every right to a full and equal voice both in resolving the existing controversies and in shaping the new customary law; but surely that right will itself be meaningless if it is not founded upon and given expression through a stable legal order. At any rate, it is an encouraging sign that, when controversial points in customary law are debated in the [U.N.] International Law Commission and the Sixth [Legal] Committee [of the U.N. General Assembly], a large measure of common agreement is often

reached and the divisions of opinion when they occur are on other lines than the differences between new and old States.

Notes

1. The Restatement (Third) agrees that "in principle a dissenting state which indicates its dissent from a practice while the law is still in a state of development is not bound by that rule of law even after it matures" (§ 102, Comment *d*). Presumably, a state that is silent during the period of formation would be bound by the rule when it comes into force as would a new state. Is it reasonable to apply this principle to states that had no interest in or knowledge of the conduct that developed the rule?

2. Judicial expression of a "persistent objector" rule is found in just a handful of cases, including the *Asylum* case mentioned by Waldock which arguably concerns regional (or special) custom. States have rarely claimed or been granted an exemption on the basis of the dissenting state principle (sometimes described as the principle of the persistent objector). See T. Stein, The Approach of the Different Drummer: The Principle of the Persistent Objector in International Law, 26 Harv. Int'l L.J. 457, 459–60 (1985); J. Charney, The Persistent Objector Rule and the Development of Customary International Law, 56 Brit. Y.B.I.L. 1–24 (1985). Notwithstanding the paucity of practice, Stein concludes that the principle of the persistent dissenter will be increasingly used to claim exemption from new principles of customary law developed by the majority of states. He points to the trend toward formation of new principles of customary law as a consequence of majority positions adopted in international conferences and in United Nations organs. He anticipates that the states opposing such rules will increasingly have recourse to the persistent objector principle to claim exemption. Id. at 463–69.

3. Should South Africa during the period of apartheid have been considered exempt from the customary law rule prohibiting systematic racial discrimination because it persistently dissented from that rule during the time the rule was being developed? The United Kingdom, in its pleadings in the *Anglo-Norwegian Fisheries Case,* questioned the right of a persistent dissenter to an exemption from a rule of law of fundamental importance. 1951 I.C.J. *Fisheries Case,* II Pleadings, Oral Arguments, 428–30. The Restatement (Third) implies that the persistent objector rule may not apply to peremptory norms *(jus cogens)* that permit no derogation—and it indicates that the rule against apartheid falls into the class of peremptory norms (§ 102, Comment *k* and Reporters' Note 6; § 702, Comments *i* and *n* and Reporters' Note 11). Charney has analyzed the difference of views on whether South Africa could invoke the persistent objector rule (and on whether persistent objection could ever apply in the case of *jus cogens*) and has concluded that ultimately South Africa was compelled to abide by the obligation. Charney, Universal International Law, 87 A.J.I.L. 529, 539–541 (1993); see also Byers, Custom, Power, and the Power of Rules 177–178, 194–195 (1999). On peremptory norms, see below, pp. 105–107 and Chapter 7.

4. The Restatement (Third) gives only one example of the application of the "persistent dissenter" principle. It states that the United States would not be bound by a customary law rule that prohibited deep seabed mining outside the regime established by the 1982 Convention on the Law of the Sea. It notes in

§ 523 that the U.S. rejected those principles as binding on states not parties to the Convention (see Chapter 16).

Charney, in contrast, observes that "[n]o case is cited in which the objector effectively maintained its status after the rule became well accepted in international law. * * * This is certainly the plight that befell the U.S., UK and Japan in the law of the sea. Their objections to expanded coastal state jurisdiction were ultimately to no avail, and they have been forced to accede to 12–mile territorial seas and 200–mile exclusive economic zones" (56 Brit. Y.B.I.L. at 24). Does this mean that the persistent objector "rule" is of no significance? Charney suggests that it gives an objecting state "a tool it may use over the short term with direct and indirect negotiations with the proponents of a new rule. * * * As a particularly affected state, it will have leverage in determining the evolution of the applicable rule of law and will have the theoretical advantage of invoking the persistent objector rule. * * * When the rule does settle, * * * a few states may continue to maintain their objection to a new rule of law. If they are few, they will not be able to block a finding that the new rule represents international law" (Id. 23–24). Charney has elsewhere written of the demands on the international legal system to produce universally binding international law—especially in response to universal problems, such as threats to the peace and the global environment—with no enduring exemptions for objecting states. Charney, Universal International Law, 87 A.J.I.L. 529, 538–542, 551 (1993); cf. Charney & Danilenko, Consent and the Creation of International Law, in Beyond Confrontation (Damrosch, Danilenko & Mullerson eds., 1995), at pp. 23, 47–50; compare Danilenko, Law-Making in the International Community (1993). On the pressures tending to overcome persistent objection in practice, see also Byers, Custom, Power, and the Power of Rules, pp. 102–105, 152, 177–178, 180–183 (1999).

5. Some perceive that a customary international law rule may be in the process of emerging to restrict the death penalty (or certain applications of the death penalty, e.g., as against persons under age 18 at the time of commission of the crime). If so, how would states register objections ("persistent" or otherwise) to such an emergent rule? The United States has carefully worded its acceptance of human rights obligations, notably in the form of reservations to human rights treaties, to preserve the legal position that capital punishment could be applied now or in the future by the federal or state governments. (See Chapters 7 and 8 below.) Would such reservations qualify the United States as a persistent objector to a rule in formation?

6. In the Nuclear Weapons advisory opinion, p. 77 supra, the significance of lack of consent (especially from the nuclear weapons states) was vigorously debated and addressed in several of the separate and dissenting opinions. As noted above (note 4 on pp. 84–85), Judge Schwebel considered the posture of the nuclear weapons states as a fundamental obstacle to any putative new rule, not by virtue of a "persistent objector" exception, but because of the formidable array of states opposed to such a prohibition.

7. Is the "persistent objector" rule likely to be asserted more often because of declarations by international conferences or U.N. bodies that purport to state international legal rules? Henkin comments that "efforts to make new law purposefully by custom (in effect, circumventing the multilateral treaty which requires individual consent) has given the persistent objector principle new vitality, perhaps its first real life" (216 Rec. des Cours 59 (1989–IV)). Would this new "vitality" be significantly different from the traditional requirement of *opinio juris* required of states generally and especially of those particularly affected by

the rule in question? Is the critical factor the effective power of the objecting state vis-à-vis the majority of states?

8. Does the problem of the dissenting state suggest the desirability of more individualized customary rules that make exceptions for special geographical features or other particular needs? In the Anglo–Norwegian Fisheries Case, 1951 I.C.J. 128, the Court found that Norway's practice in departing from the general rule of customary law had been condoned or acquiesced in by other states having knowledge of Norway's practice or being in a position where such knowledge was attributed to them. In this way, a state departing from a rule—in effect, violating it—may build up what is described as a historic or prescriptive right. This is not the same as a "local custom" since it comes into being not by consent of two or three states but by conduct at variance with a rule that is acquiesced in by other states. Judge Fitzmaurice wrote:

> If other States are in fact willing to acquiesce in this way and in effect to condone what are violations of the law, this can only be because they recognize that the circumstances are indeed unusual or exceptional.

Fitzmaurice, General Principles of International Law, 92 Rec. des Cours 111–12 (1957–II). See also Schachter, The Nature and Process of Legal Development in International Society, in Structure and Process of International Law 745, 779 (Macdonald & Johnston eds., 1983).

9. What is the consequence of a large number of states departing from an existing rule of law? Such departures are, in their inception, clearly violations of law. However, such violations carried out by a number of states may—and often have—resulted in new customary law. This development occurred dramatically after the 1945 Truman Proclamation as states by practice eroded the existing principle of the freedom of the seas by extending their jurisdiction over adjacent waters up to 200 miles and over the continental shelf. See Chapter 16. To determine when such new law has repealed the old rule, it is necessary to consider the same elements that are involved in creating customary law—namely, (1) the extent, consistency and frequency of the departures from old law, (2) the relation of the states concerned (both those departing and those adhering) to the subject matter of the rule, and (3) the duration of the process. *Opinio juris* must also be considered. At some point, a large number of "representative states" may conclude that their infringements have become new law, and that they will not be charged with violating existing law. Presumably, the new rule will not be opposable to states that have openly manifested their opposition to it from the start. But such states, if few, cannot prevent the adoption of a new rule. In this regard, Judge Fitzmaurice commented * * * "although such opposition may for a time, perhaps for a considerable time, prevent the rule from being opposable to themselves, it is liable in the long run to be overborne". 92 Rec. des Cours at 115.

10. May a state that was not in existence at the time a customary rule was formed object to the rule when it emerges as an independent state? Many new states have objected to particular rules of international law, in regard to state responsibility, some rules of treaty law (in particular, relating to unequal treaties), and some aspects of the law of the sea. See Anand, New States and International Law 62 (1972); Abi–Saab, The Newly–Independent States and the Rules of International Law, 8 Howard L.J. 95 (1962); Guha Roy, Is the Law of Responsibility of States a Part of Universal International Law, 55 A.J.I.L. 866 (1961); Bokor–Szego, New States and International Law (1970). These states did not reject existing customary law in its entirety. Nor did they maintain that their consent was required for every rule to be binding upon them. Their basic position was that

a rule of customary law should no longer be considered as a general rule valid for all states when most (or many) states rejected it as law. Thus the question was not whether a new state may reject a rule it did not like but rather whether the objection by a large number of states (often a majority) to a general rule must mean that that rule is no longer valid (if it ever was) for the entire international community.

Does this position mean that a number of new states may terminate any rule of customary international law they do not like? May they do this by resolution adopted by majority votes in the General Assembly? May they accomplish that goal by collectively disregarding the old rule and asserting that it is no longer law? Would they have to establish a new customary rule by general and consistent practice accompanied by *opinio juris* which other states would recognize? Would a minority of the older states be able to prevent such changes?

RELATIVE NORMATIVITY IN INTERNATIONAL CUSTOMARY LAW

PROSPER WEIL, TOWARDS RELATIVE NORMATIVITY IN INTERNATIONAL LAW?

77 A.J.I.L. 413, 421 (1983).

There is now a trend towards the replacement of the monolithically conceived normativity of the past by graduated normativity. While it has always been difficult to locate the threshold beyond which a legal norm existed, at least there used to be no problem once the threshold could be pronounced crossed: the norm created legal rights and obligations; it was binding, its violation sanctioned with international responsibility. There was no distinction on that score to be made between one legal norm and another. But the theory of *jus cogens,* with its distinction between peremptory and merely binding norms, and the theory of international crimes and delicts, with its distinction between norms creating obligations essential for the preservation of fundamental interests and norms creating obligations of a less essential kind, are both leading to the fission of this unity. Normativity is becoming a question of "more or less": some norms are now held to be of greater specific gravity than others, to be more binding than others. Thus, the scale of normativity is reemerging in a new guise, its gradations no longer plotted merely between norms and non-norms, but also among those norms most undeniably situated on the positive side of the normativity threshold. Having taken its rise in the subnormative domain, the scale of normativity has now been projected and protracted into the normative domain itself, so that, henceforth, there are "norms and norms."

JUS COGENS (PEREMPTORY NORMS)

OPPENHEIM'S INTERNATIONAL LAW

7–8 (9th ed., R.Y. Jennings and A. Watts eds. 1992).

§ 2 *Ius cogens* States may, by and within the limits of agreement between themselves, vary or even dispense altogether with most rules of international law. There are, however, a few rules from which no derogation is permissible. The latter—rules of *ius cogens,* or peremptory norms of general international law—have been defined in Article 53 of the Vienna Convention on the Law of Treaties 1969 (and for the purpose of that Convention) as norms 'accepted and recognised by the international community of states as a whole as a norm from which no derogation is permitted and which can be modified only by a subsequent norm of general international law having the same character'; and Article 64 contemplates the emergence of new rules of *ius cogens* in the future.

Such a category of rules of *ius cogens* is a comparatively recent development and there is no general agreement as to which rules have this character. The International Law Commission regarded the law of the Charter concerning the prohibition of the use of force as a conspicuous example of such a rule. Although the Commission refrained from giving in its draft Articles on the Law of Treaties any examples of rules of *ius cogens,* it did record that in this context mention had additionally been made of the prohibition of criminal acts under international law, and of acts such as trade in slaves, piracy or genocide, in the suppression of which every state is called upon to cooperate; the observance of human rights, the equality of states and the principle of self-determination. The full content of the category of *ius cogens* remains to be worked out in the practice of states and in the jurisprudence of international tribunals. * * *

The operation and effect of rules of *ius cogens* in areas other than that of treaties are similarly unclear. Presumably no act done contrary to such a rule can be legitimated by means of consent, acquiescence or recognition; nor is a protest necessary to preserve rights affected by such an act; nor can such an act be justified as a reprisal against a prior illegal act; nor can a rule of customary international law which conflicts with a rule of *ius cogens* continue to exist or subsequently be created (unless it has the character of *ius cogens,* a possibility which raises questions—to which no firm answer can yet be given—of the relationship between rules of *ius cogens,* and of the legitimacy of an act done in reliance on one rule of *ius cogens* but resulting in a violation of another such rule).

Notes

1. In its 1986 Judgment (Merits) in the Nicaragua Case (supra), the I.C.J. referred to the rule against the use of force as "a conspicuous example of a rule of international law having the character of *jus cogens.*" 1986 I.C.J. 100 [para. 190].

2. The peremptory norms mentioned above in Oppenheim are examples of rules to which no state would claim exceptions, e.g., the prohibition of genocide, slavery, aggression. Would the "international community as a whole" be likely to determine that past acts which some states have engaged in by mutual consent or without objection (e.g., environmental pollution) have now become illegal under newly created *jus cogens?*

3. Should the expression "the international community as a whole" meet a qualitative as well as a quantitative standard? Some suggest a "very large majority" is sufficient; others would require that the large majority include "essential" or "important" states. Would the latter rule (asserted by the United

States and other major powers) mean that peremptory rules would not be recognized unless accepted as such by all major powers and countries from all regions of the world? During the conference on the Law of the Sea Convention, a large majority of states declared that a peremptory norm of customary law had evolved to the effect that the sea bed beyond national jurisdiction was the common heritage of mankind and not open to exploitation by individual states except when carried out under the international regime contemplated by the 1982 Convention. The fact that important industrial states including the United States opposed this position was not considered by its proponents as sufficient to negate the new principle. A similar effort has also been made in United Nations bodies to establish the principle of "permanent sovereignty over resources" as part of *jus cogens,* in spite of the opposition of several large industrial states. Neither of these efforts have thus far resulted in acceptance of the new rules by dissenting states. Considering these examples a recent study by a Russian scholar concludes that "the emergence of effective international peremptory norms obviously requires the achievement of a genuine consensus among all essential components of the modern international community * * * opposition to a proposed norm on the part of at least one important element of the international community, whatever its numerical strength, would undermine any claim that such norm is a general peremptory rule * * * " G. Danilenko, International Jus Cogens, 2 Eur. J.Int. L. 42, 65 (1991); see also Charney & Danilenko, Consent and the Creation of International Law, in Beyond Confrontation (Damrosch, Danilenko & Mullerson eds., 1995), pp. 46–50.

4. Macdonald has suggested that it is inherent in the conception of peremptory norm that it applies against states that have not accepted the norm. See R.St.J. Macdonald, Fundamental Norms in Contemporary International Law, 25 Can. Y.B.I.L. 115, 131 (1987). See also L. Alexidze, Legal Nature of Jus Cogens in Contemporary International Law, 172 Rec. des Cours 219, 246–47, 258 (1981–III); Restatement (Third), § 102, Comments *d* and *k*; Byers, Custom, Power and the Power of Rules 183–203 (1999), and references in note 3 on p. 102 on (non)applicability of the persistent objector principle to *jus cogens*.

5. On peremptory norms in the law of treaties, see Chapter 7.

"FUNDAMENTAL" AND SUPERIOR NORMS OF GENERAL INTERNATIONAL LAW

Neither Article 38 of the Statute nor positivist doctrine draws hierarchical distinctions among customary norms. However, international tribunals and writers have done so under various headings. The International Court of Justice has referred to "fundamental principles" as a category differentiated from ordinary custom or treaty norms. See Case Concerning U.S. Hostages in Tehran (infra p. 868) and Nicaragua v. U.S. (supra). Some writers have described principles such as sovereign equality, political independence, and territorial integrity as axiomatic or constitutional in character. Henkin, for example, refers to assumptions and conceptions of axiomatic "constitutional" character as including concepts of state autonomy, *pacta sunt servanda,* and the concept of nationality. Such constitutional law, he suggests, "did not result from practice * * * they were implicit, inherent in Statehood in a State System" (Henkin, General Course, 216 Rec. des Cours 52 (1989–IV)). Schachter refers to these principles as "authoritative by virtue of the inherent necessities of a pluralist society." Such "rules of necessity" are considered as akin to "entrenched" constitutional rules that cannot be set aside by majorities whether through practice or agreements. Their emphasis on autonomy and equality as basic rights is not unlike the declarations of individual rights that reflect Western political thought. See Schachter, International Law in Theory and Practice 30–31 (1991). Although described as "implicit" and "unwritten," they have been expressed in various declarations of basic rights of states prepared by international legal bodies and in U.N. declarations (as well as in the Principles of the U.N. Charter). See, for example, the Declaration of Rights and Duties of States, prepared by the U.N. International Law Commission and adopted by the General Assembly in 1949 (Res. 375 (IV)). The much cited Declaration of Principles of International Law adopted by the U.N. General Assembly in 1970 (without dissent) is also a statement of basic principles that are mostly postulates of the state system. (See Document Supp.) Although they may be described as higher law and as axiomatic, this does not mean that their content is fixed, beyond influence of state practice and agreements.

Another category of "higher norms" is found in Article 103 of the U.N. Charter which declares that

> In the event of a conflict between the obligations of Members of the United Nations under the present Charter and their obligations under any other international agreement, their obligations under the present Charter shall prevail.

The International Court of Justice referred to Article 103 in its 1984 Judgment on Jurisdiction in Nicaragua v. U.S. pointing out that "all regional, bilateral and even unilateral arrangements that the parties have made * * * must be made always subject to the provisions of Article 103." 1984 I.C.J. 440, para. 107. Some commentators consider that treaties contrary to the Charter are null and void. A.D. McNair, The Law of Treaties 222 (1961). Others maintain that Article 103 only requires suspension or modification of treaty obligations—that it is in effect "a compatibility clause" rather than superior law comparable to peremptory norms. See W. Czaplinski and G. Danilenko, Conflicts of Norms in International Law 21 Neth.Y.B.I.L. 14–15 (1990).

SECTION 3. TREATIES AS A SOURCE OF LAW

A. THE ROLE OF TREATIES

Article 38 of the Statute of the International Court, in its list of sources according to which disputes are to be decided, gives first place to "international conventions, whether general or particular, establishing rules expressly recognized by the contracting States." Although Article 38 does not provide for a hierarchy among sources, the priority of position given to treaties reflects the understanding of states and of international lawyers that, in Lauterpacht's words:

> * * * The rights and duties of States are determined in the first instance, by their agreement as expressed in treaties—just as in the case of individuals their rights are specifically determined by any contract which is binding upon them. When a controversy arises between two or more States with regard to a matter regulated by a treaty, it is natural

> that the parties should invoke and that the adjudicating agency should apply, in the first instance, the provisions of the treaty in question.

1 Lauterpacht, International Law: Collected Papers, 86–87 (1970).

That it may be "natural" to apply a treaty in the first instance should not be taken to mean that a treaty provision necessarily prevails over a customary rule. The maxim, *lex specialis derogat generali,* the specific prevails over the general, is an accepted guide; it may give priority either to treaty or custom. The intentions of the parties are of paramount importance. They may show a common intent to replace a treaty with a customary rule; a treaty may become a dead-letter terminated by desuetude. When neither specificity nor intentions provide sufficient guidance, treaty and custom have equal weight with priority to the later in time, subject however to certain presumptions of interpretation. These presumptions operate in both directions. It is presumed that a treaty is not terminated or altered by subsequent custom in the absence of evidence that the parties had that intention. On the other hand, there is support for a general presumption that treaties are not intended to derogate from general custom. The complex interaction of treaty and custom is dealt with below and also in the chapter on the law of international agreements.

Whether treaties should logically be regarded as a source of law has been questioned by some jurists. Fitzmaurice, for example, has written that "treaties are no more a source of law than an ordinary private law contract that creates rights and obligations * * * In itself, the treaty and 'the law' it contains only applies to the parties to it. True, where it reflects (e.g., codifies) existing law, non-parties may conform to the same rules but they do so by virtue of rule of general law thus reflected in the treaty, not by virtue of the treaty itself." Fitzmaurice, Some Problems Regarding the Formal Sources of International Law, in Symbolae Verzijl 153, 157–58 (Von Asbeck, et al., eds., 1958). A distinction between treaties and "international law" (or the law of nations) is often made in popular usage and sometimes in U.S. statutes. See, for example, the Alien Tort Statute, 28 U.S.C.A. § 1350, p. 143 infra. The U.S. Constitution also refers separately to "Treaties" (Articles II, III and VI) and to the "Law of Nations" (Article I, § 8).

While it is true, as Fitzmaurice insists, that treaties have a contractual character binding only the parties, their provisions create legal obligations for the parties and may prevail over general law. Moreover, many treaties (especially multilateral treaties) lay down broad rules of conduct for states generally and are in that respect more like legislation than contracts. In international usage, treaties are generally considered as part of international law and in accordance with Article 38 of the Statute of the Court as a source of "law." When appropriate, a distinction is made between customary international law and "conventional" (i.e., treaty) international law.

That treaties govern much of international relations is evidenced by the number of such treaties and their wide scope. International agreements—the *lex scripta* of the society of states—have proliferated since the end of World War Two. More than 40,000 treaties have been registered with the United Nations since 1945. Most are bilateral agreements or agreements among a small number of states. Over 2000, it may be estimated, are multilateral. Virtually every aspect of social life affecting transnational relations and intercourse is dealt with in treaties. Nearly all treaties that have entered into force since 1946 are published in the United Nations Treaty Series. Agreements that have been adopted but have not yet come into force (pending the requisite acts of acceptance) are not available in any one collection. Many may be found in national publications such as the United States Treaties and Other International Agreements Series or International Legal Materials (published by the American Society of International Law).

Three classes of treaties may be distinguished from the standpoint of their relevance as sources of law. First is the general multilateral treaty open to all states of the world or to all members of a large regional group. Such treaties lay down rules of behavior which in the I.C.J.'s words are of a fundamentally norm-creating character such as could be regarded as forming the basis of a general rule of law *(North Sea Continental Shelf Case)*. These treaties may be codification treaties; they may be "law-making" or a combination of both.

A second category comprises treaties that establish a collaborative mechanism for States to regulate or manage a particular area of activity. They may be designed for universal adherence (for example, regulating allocation of radio frequencies) or for regional or functional groups (e.g. fishing or commodity agreements). Such treaties normally include purposes and principles and they operate through decisions by their organs (such decisions may take the form of concrete rules, orders, or recommendations). In that respect they are distinct from the "legislative type" of treaty that lays down general law. The institutional and administrative character of this group of treaties has led them to be characterized as international regimes or sometimes as international administrative law. Some comprehensive international conventions include both the first and second types of provisions. A notable example is the 1982 U.N. Convention on the Law of the Sea which contains the *corpus juris* pertaining to the seas generally and a mechanism for exploitation of seabed mineral resources. See Chapter 16.

A third category of treaties—by far the largest in number—includes bilateral agreements and, for some purposes, agreements by three or four states. Such treaties are drafted in contractual terms of mutual exchange of rights and obligations and in that respect are different from the multilateral treaties that have a more legislative form. The bilateral treaties differ widely in scope and subject matter. Many are detailed, specific and for a fixed period. Others lay down general norms and express intentions as, for example, treaties of alliance and some treaties of friendship. It is not uncommon to find standardized provisions for particular subjects, and establishing similar rights and duties for a large group of states. Many such agreements on extradition, air transport, rivers and foreign investment may create networks of obligation that are virtually general international law. However, whether they may be considered as evidence of custom and therefore binding for non-parties is another matter. On this aspect see the section on treaties and custom.

Notes

1. Are treaties superior to custom for international law-making? Richard Baxter wrote in 1970:

> As one looks at the present state of international law and attempts to see into the future, it should be quite clear that treaty law will increasingly gain paramountcy over customary international law. The treaty-making process is a rational and orderly one, permitting participation in the creation of law by all States on a basis of equity. Newly independent States, otherwise subject to a body of customary international law in the making of which they played no part, can influence the progressive development of the law or help to "codify" it in such a way as to make it more responsive to their needs and ideals. For the more established States, the codification process provides a welcome opportunity to secure widespread agreement upon norms which have hitherto been the subject of doubt or controversy or have been rejected by other States.
>
> Even in those cases in which customary international law is already clear and generally agreed upon, the treaty will strengthen that rule and simplify its application. Article 1 of the Chicago Convention confirms what is already agreed to be a State's sovereign right to exclude foreign aircraft from its airspace. The presence in bilateral treaties of a requirement of exhaustion of local remedies reminds us that the well-understood rule of customary international law has not lost its validity.

Baxter, Treaties and Custom, 129 Rec. des Cours 25, 101 (1970–I) (footnotes omitted). Tunkin maintained that treaties are the dominant and "basic source" of international law. Theory of International Law 133–36 (Butler trans. 1974).

2. What are the advantages of custom over treaty for developing law to meet new needs? Is custom more responsive to concrete situations and more malleable than multilateral treaties? Does it give more weight to power? For comment on "competition" between treaty and custom, see Schachter, Entangled Treaty and Custom, in International Law at a Time of Perplexity, 717, 720–22 (Dinstein ed. 1989).

3. Regional law-making may be preferred to global conventions as for example, in regard to trade, economic integration, migration, cultural exchange. Would such regional conventions always prevail over general international law under the *lex specialis* rule of interpretation? Could they diminish rights of non-regional states vis-à-vis the regional members?

B. TREATIES OF CODIFICATION AND PROGRESSIVE DEVELOPMENT

SCHACHTER, INTERNATIONAL LAW IN THEORY AND PRACTICE

66–69, 71–72 (1991).

The rationalist belief in the development of law through deliberate, carefully considered and well designed instruments finds expression in two closely related processes: codification and "progressive development" through multilateral law-making treaties. Both aim at achieving an international *lex scripta* through the international equivalent of a legislative process. It is easy to see advantages of that process. In place of the uncertain and slow process of custom, built upon instances that are necessarily contingent and limited, governments negotiate and collaborate in formulating rules and principles to meet perceived needs of the entire community of states. The texts bring clarity and precision where there had been obscurity and doubt. Moreover, all governments have the opportunity to take part in the legislative process and to express their consent or objection in accordance with their constitutional procedures. Neither of these opportunities was clearly available to all states in the creation of customary law.

* * *

Codification is distinct, in principle, from the so-called law-making treaty that comes within "progressive development." The Statute of the U.N. International Law Commission defined codification as "the more precise formulation and systematization of rules of international law in fields where there already has been extensive state practice, precedent and doctrine." There is almost a deceptive simplicity about this definition, as indeed there is about the act of codification.

* * *

Before the United Nations began its work in the early nineteen-fifties, sharp differences had been expressed on whether codification should be a scientific or political task. The debate on this issue reflected, in some degree, the differences concerning positivism, voluntarism, and state sovereignty. Those who saw codification as essentially scientific considered as Cecil Hurst did that its task was to "ascertain" and "declare the existing rule of international law, irrespective of any question as to whether the rule is satisfactory or unsatisfactory, obsolete or still adequate to modern conditions, just or unjust in the eyes of those who formulate it." That task could be carried out, it was assumed, solely on the basis of state practice and precedent. It was in its essence an inductive process that could and should be entrusted to independent jurists, not governments. * * *

* * *

The idea of a truly scientific, non-governmental restatement of international law did not find the requisite support in the United Nations. Nor was it generally supported by international lawyers, though there were notable exceptions. The objection to scientific, non-official codification had several grounds. There was a basic difficulty with the idea implicit in the I.L.C. definition (referred to earlier) that "extensive state practice, precedent and doctrine" would yield a rule of law. Hersch Lauterpacht commented that the absence of state practice could show the non-existence of a rule but that the converse did not hold because, in his view, the area of agreement that would be revealed by state practice "is small in the extreme." Others went further, pointing out that any attempt to formulate an explicit and clear rule, or systematizing rules based on precedent, involved elements of novelty. It assumes agreement where none may exist.

* * *

The experience of the last 25 years showed that the skepticism about the practicality of universal codification * * * was excessive. For one thing, the governments in the United Nations and the International Law Commission quickly recognized that codification involved "new law" to some degree but that it was possible and desirable to distinguish codification that had a substantial foundation in customary law from treaties that sought to formulate new principles and rules for matters previously unregulated by international law. In the former category, the drafts prepared by the Commission were mainly based on practice and precedent but often filled in lacunae and removed inconsistencies found in State practice. These elements of "progressive development" were identified in the reports of the Commission and in the *travaux préparatoires* leading to adoption by the conference of States. Since such new law generally did not involve significant conflicts of interest between States, it was regarded as essentially technical ("lawyers' law") and therefore appropriate in a codification. The fact that the codifications were drafted as treaties and passed upon in detail by conferences which included nearly all States was perceived as "settling" rather than unsettling customary law (except for the few provisions that were identified as new law in the *travaux*).

* * *

The anticipated difficulties proved less of an obstacle than had been predicted. Governments were not deterred by the fact that in reducing the unwritten law of precedents to written, generalized rules they were performing a "legislative" act that was in some measure "progressive development." They realized (as did the I.L.C.) that the customary law that they were ostensibly declaring was also being supplemented and, in a degree, modified in the light of present conditions and attitudes. Inevitably this reflected current political views and some bargaining in the negotiations at the conference. But the apprehension that codification would not be acceptable to the States "wedded to uncompromising maintenance of sovereignty" was not borne out. A considerable measure of support by all groups of States was in fact achieved in the two-stage procedure of Commission and conference. In the Commission, the draft conventions were adopted by consensus. The Commission was informed of the governmental views in the course of its work through written comments and the discussions in the Legal Committee of the General Assembly. In the conferences, most decisions were taken by consensus and compromises were reached to avoid any significant defections.

What is noteworthy is that although these texts were in the form of conventions requiring ratification or accession, they have been widely accepted as generally declaratory of existing law and therefore actually given legal effect even prior to their formal entry into force, and, when in force, applied by non-parties as well as by parties to the treaties. In this way, the old issue of "restatement" versus convention was rendered academic since the conventions were in fact regarded and used as if they were restatements except where there was persuasive evidence that a particular provision was intended to be *de lege ferenda* * * *.

* * *

There is a practical side to this conclusion that merits mention here. This relates to what might be called the bureaucratic factor in the codification process. The legal advisers and other government officials concerned with the application of law play a major part in codification. They do so mainly by way of comments on the drafts in the preparatory stages and at the conference of plenipotentiaries at which the final text is adopted. Officials who subsequently have to ascertain and involve law naturally look to the product of the process in which they or their colleagues took part. The text is, so to speak, "their" law. Moreover, the adopted text has the great advantage for busy officials of providing "black letter" law in an instrument that has been adopted by nearly all States of the world. The law is declared in a concise and definitive form that is highly convenient for lawyers and officials. In most cases there is little reason for them to search for the precedents that might underlie the rule; it is in any case difficult to challenge the validity of a rule that had received the support of their own government as well as of others. These practical and bureaucratic factors help to increase the use made of the adopted texts (whether or not the instrument has entered into force or has been ratified by the state invoking its authority). The consequences over time are two-fold: (1) the instrument generally accumulates more authority as declaratory of customary law and (2), in cases where the declaratory nature of a particular provision is shown to be contrary to the understanding of the drafters (as in the *North Sea Continental Shelf Cases),* the tendency to apply that provision will in time result in custom "grafted" upon the treaty. This latter process was described by the Court in the *North Sea Continental Shelf Cases* although the majority did not find that a customary rule had actually developed.

In suggesting that the generally accepted codification conventions tend to prevail over competing customary law I do not mean to suggest that they entirely replace customary law in the field covered. Custom may still apply to fill in the gaps that always occur or the treaty itself may recognize that exceptions to its rules are permissible in accordance with special custom. * * * In other words, a codification convention, authoritative as it may seem because of its universal (or nearly universal) acceptance, cannot entirely freeze the development of law. Changing conditions and new perceptions of interests and aims continue to operate. The existence of written codified law may impede the pace of change but it cannot prevent it.

RECENT MULTILATERAL CONVENTIONS

By the opening of the 21st century a substantial part of customary international law had been codified in multilateral conventions prepared by the International Law Commission, approved by the General Assembly, and adopted by international plenipotentiary conferences. Among the most notable of these conventions were those on the law of treaties (see Chapter 7), on diplomatic and consular immunities (see Chapter 14), and on the law of the sea (see Chapter 16).

A large number of general multilateral treaties are appropriately considered as "progressive development" or "law-making" rather than as codification of existing customary law. These treaties may be based to some degree on prior practice but by and large they are perceived as expressing new law required by states for political, social or technical reasons. They include a large number open to all states (potentially universal) and others open to all states in a major region of the globe. The United Nations alone is a depository of over 500 such multilateral treaties. Most of them were prepared and negotiated by United Nations bodies, generally expert or specialized committees broadly representative of the main political and geographical groups in the United Nations. The subject matter of the treaties is diverse; it includes matters such as outer space, dispute settlement, narcotics, status of women, refugees, human rights of various kinds, arms control, transportation, environmental protection and telecommunication. Other related United Nations bodies have also produced hundreds of treaties. There are for example, dozens of such treaties relating to intellectual property, many on education, more than 180 conventions on labor, and numerous treaties on civil aviation, shipping and broadcasting. As indicated above, many of these treaties provide for regulation of activities covered through international bodies or procedures. Others are primarily statements of rules of conduct for the states that have adhered to the instrument. Regional and functional organizations have also generated numerous treaties in their respective fields. These treaties comprise the main corpus of international law for the special subjects they deal with. They are the product, together with the more general codification treaties, of an "international legislative process" that operates through many different organizations and conferences. That process has resulted in a dense, intricate body of rules and practices followed by governments.

ENTANGLED TREATY AND CUSTOM

As already indicated, treaty rules may be accepted as customary law and therefore be binding on states not parties to the treaty in question. The International Court of Justice has noted that this would occur when one of the following conditions existed:

1. Where the treaty rule is declaratory of pre-existing custom
2. Where the treaty rule is found to have crystallized customary law in process of formation
3. Where the treaty rule is found to have generated new customary law subsequent to its adoption

The leading I.C.J. case that enunciated these conditions is the 1969 Judgment in the North Sea Continental Shelf Cases (supra). The conditions were affirmed in the 1986 Judgment of the I.C.J. in the Nicaragua Case (supra).

The Court recognized the first condition particularly in regard to certain provisions of the Vienna Convention on the Law of Treaties (see Chapter 7). See Advisory Opinion on Namibia, 1971 I.C.J. 47; Iceland Fisheries Cases (Jurisdiction), 1973 I.C.J. 18, 63.

The second condition was recognized in the North Sea Continental Shelf Cases in respect of Articles 1 to 3 of the 1958 Convention on the Continental Shelf. 1969 I.C.J. 35.

In the same case the Court dealt with the third condition. It declared that a treaty provision of a norm-creating character could have "generated a rule which, while only conventional or contractual in its origin, has since passed into the general corpus of international law and is now accepted as such by the *opinio juris,* so as to become binding even for countries which have never and do not, become parties to the Convention." (Ibid.; p. 41.)

In its Nicaragua Judgment of 1986, the Court used a different justification to support its conclusion that Articles 2(4) and 51 of the U.N. Charter were customary law. It declared:

> The Charter gave expression in this field to principles already present in customary international law and that law has in the subsequent four decades developed under the influence of the Charter to such an extent that a number of rules have acquired a status independent of it * * * [E]ven if two norms belonging to two sources of international law appear identical in content, and even if the States in question are bound by these rules both on the level of treaty-law and on that of customary law, those norms retain a separate existence.

Finding customary law identical with the Charter provisions enabled the Court to avoid the effect of a U.S. reservation that excluded from its acceptance of compulsory jurisdiction all cases involving multilateral treaties unless all treaty parties agreed to jurisdiction. Judge Jennings, in a dissent, observed that the Court did not reveal how it determined that practice since 1945 by U.N. Members was "customary" rather than treaty-based. It appeared to him as if the Court, unable to take jurisdiction in regard to the Charter, applied the Charter rules anyway by calling them customary law (see 1986 I.C.J. at 532, Jennings Diss. Op.).

Notes

1. If virtually all states are parties to a treaty—as is the case for the U.N. Charter and the Geneva Conventions on the Law of Armed Conflict—does it make any difference whether the rules are also customary as well as treaty law? Theodor Meron suggests some advantages of recognizing customary law parallel to treaty law: (1) states are not free to withdraw from customary law obligations as they might be under treaty law; (2) in many states, customary law is part of domestic law whereas treaty rules do not become domestic law unless the legislature so decides; (3) customary law—or general international law—has more weight than contractual obligations and may be a basis for the *"erga omnes"* character of the rules, allowing all states to have a legal interest in their compliance. T. Meron, Human Rights and Humanitarian Norms as Customary Law 3–10, 114–35, 192–95 (1989).

2. In the North Sea Judgment, the Court suggests that a treaty rule might be considered a customary rule of international law if the treaty has a "widespread and representative participation * * * [including] States whose interests were specially affected." 1969 I.C.J. 43 (para. 73). Would this conclusion, if applied, mean that non-parties would be subject to obligations of a treaty whenever many states have become parties? Would it not be necessary to show practice and *opinio juris* on the part of non-parties as well as parties to conclude that the non-parties are subject to the treaty rules in question? Is a convention designed to codify existing custom presumptive evidence that its rules are customary, hence applicable to all states?

3. If states not parties to a general multilateral treaty declare that some but not all of its provisions are accepted as customary law (even if of recent origin), can they claim such rights vis-à-vis parties to the treaty? The United States, which

was not a party to the comprehensive 1982 U.N. Convention on the Law of the Sea, declared in a Presidential Proclamation of March 1983 that it regards the provisions of the convention as existing customary law with the exception of provisions on the seabed beyond national jurisdiction and provisions concerned with dispute settlement and administration. It announced it will assert its rights based on the customary law provisions and reciprocally recognize such rights of others. However, other states (and commentators) question the right of non-parties to pick the provisions they like and disregard what they do not like inasmuch as the Convention contains interlinked provisions, involving a "package deal" of compromises. Should this preclude non-parties from relying on prior custom reflected in the treaty or on new rules accepted as customary during the period the treaty was negotiated? See Caminos and Molitor, Progressive Development of International Law and the Package Deal, 79 A.J.I.L. 871 (1985).

4. Consider the difference between multilateral conventions that proclaim a rule of law that virtually all states accept in principle even if they do not become parties to the treaty (for example, a treaty against torture or air hijacking) and a treaty that involves bargained-for compromise solutions such as a trade treaty or the law of the sea treaty. It has been suggested that in the former case, an inference of *opinio juris* may be made, based on statements of the governments even if actual practice is slight. However, in the latter case, an attempt to transport into customary law the substantive rules, disregarding the "deals" and compromises, may be difficult to justify. See Schachter, Recent Trends in International Law–Making, 12 Australia Y.B.I.L. 1, 7 (1992).

5. May a treaty be changed by custom? May the parties to a treaty alter its obligations by practical interpretation accepted as law? The 1958 Conventions on the Continental Shelf and on the High Seas were changed in important ways by the extension of jurisdiction by coastal states without any formal change in those treaties. Did President Reagan breach the U.S. obligations under those treaties (to which it was a party) when he proclaimed that the United States accepted as customary law many of the provisions of the 1982 Convention which the U.S. did not sign or ratify? (See Chapter 16.)

6. Many bilateral treaties include common provisions on legal rights and obligations. Examples are found in treaties on extradition, air transport, rivers, compensation for expropriation, and commercial trade. As the treaties constitute state practice, can one infer that the common provisions in many treaties are evidence of customary law? May one distinguish between those bilateral treaties which deal with matters which are clearly recognized as within the discretion of the states and those which deal with matters generally regulated by international law? In the first category, one would include extradition and aviation on the premises that states are under no customary duty to grant the rights given in the bilateral treaties. In such cases, the successive treaties, numerous as they may be, would not have the *opinio juris* necessary to establish customary law. In the other category, an example would be treaties on riparian rights as there are requirements of international customary law about riparian states' duties toward others. May one therefore conclude that such bilateral treaties are accompanied by *opinio juris* because they are in implementation of customary law? A more controversial issue is whether agreements for lump-sum compensation are evidence of the state of customary law. See Chapter.

7. A recent treaty with high potential to contribute to the development of general international law, not merely among formal parties to the treaty, is the 1998 Rome Statute for an International Criminal Court. As of 2000 the Statute

had not yet received sufficient ratifications to enter into force (60 are required), but it had already been cited by international tribunals in rulings on unresolved points of international law. For an example, see the *Tadic* decision of the International Criminal Tribunal for Former Yugoslavia, Case No. IT–94–1–AR72, (Appeal from Judgment of Conviction, July 1999), para. 223 (citing the trial chamber's *Furundzija* ruling for the proposition that the Rome Statute has "significant legal value" even prior to entry into force, e.g. with respect to determining *opinio juris*).

SECTION 4. GENERAL PRINCIPLES OF LAW AND EQUITY

A. THE BROAD EXPANSE OF GENERAL PRINCIPLES OF LAW

SCHACHTER, INTERNATIONAL LAW IN THEORY AND PRACTICE

50–55 (1991).

We can distinguish five categories of general principles that have been invoked and applied in international law discourse and cases. Each has a different basis for its authority and validity as law. They are

(1) The principles of municipal law "recognized by civilized nations".

(2) General principles of law "derived from the specific nature of the international community".

(3) Principles "intrinsic to the idea of law and basic to all legal systems".

(4) Principles "valid through all kinds of societies in relationships of hierarchy and co-ordination".

(5) Principles of justice founded on "the very nature of man as a rational and social being".

Although these five categories are analytically distinct, it is not unusual for a particular general principle to fall into more than one of the categories. For example, the principle that no one shall be a judge in his own cause or that a victim of a legal wrong is entitled to reparation are considered part of most, if not all, systems of municipal law and as intrinsic to the basic idea of law.

Our first category, general principles of municipal law, has given rise to a considerable body of writing and much controversy. Article 38(1)(c) of the Statute of the Court does not expressly refer to principles of national law but rather general principles "recognized by civilized nations". The travaux préparatoires reveal an interesting variety of views about this subparagraph during the drafting stage. Some of the participants had in mind equity and principles recognized "by the legal conscience of civilized nations". (The notion of "legal conscience" was a familiar concept to European international lawyers in the nineteenth and early part of the twentieth century.) Elihu Root, the American member of the drafting committee, prepared the text finally adopted and it seemed clear that his amendment was intended to refer to principles "actually recognized and applied in national legal systems". The fact that the subparagraph was distinct from those on treaty and custom indicated an intent to treat general principles as an independent source of law, and not as a subsidiary source. As an independent source, it did not appear to require any separate proof that such principles of national law had been "received" into international law.

However, a significant minority of jurists holds that national law principles, even if generally found in most legal systems, cannot *ipso facto* be international law. One view is that they must receive the *imprimatur* of State consent through custom or treaty in order to become international law. The strict positivist school adheres to that view. A somewhat modified version is adopted by others to the effect that rules of municipal law cannot be considered as recognized by civilized nations unless there is evidence of the concurrence of States on their status as international law. Such concurrence may occur through treaty, custom or other evidence of recognition. This would allow for some principles, such as *res judicata,* which are not customary law but are generally accepted in international law. * * *

Several influential international legal scholars have considered municipal law an important means for developing international law and extending it into new areas of international concern. For example, Wilfred Jenks and Wolfgang Friedmann have looked to a "common law of mankind" to meet problems raised by humanitarian concerns, environmental threats and economic relations. In this respect they followed the lead of Hersch Lauterpacht suggested in his classic work, *Private Law Sources and Analogies of International Law.* The growth of transnational commercial and financial transactions has also been perceived as a fruitful area for the application of national law rules to create a "commercial law of nations", referred to as a "vast *terra incognita*".

Despite the eloquent arguments made for using national law principles as an independent source of international law, it cannot be said that either courts or the political organs of States have significantly drawn on municipal law principles as an autonomous and distinct ground for binding rules of conduct. It is true that the International Court and its predecessor the Permanent Court of International Justice have made reference on a number of occasions to "generally accepted practice" or "all systems of law" as a basis for its approval of a legal rule. (But curiously the Court has done so without explicit reference to its own statutory authority in Article 38(1)(c).) Those references to national law have most often been to highly general ideas of legal liability or precepts of judicial administration. In the former category, we find the much-quoted principles of the *Chorzów Factory* case that "every violation of an engagement involves an obligation to make reparation" and that "a party cannot take advantage of his own wrong". These maxims and certain maxims of legal interpretation, as for example, *lex specialis derogat generalis,* and "no one may transfer more than he has", are also regarded as notions intrinsic to the idea of law and legal reasoning. As such they can be (and have been) accepted not as municipal law, but as general postulates of international law, even if not customary law in the specific sense of that concept.

The use of municipal law rules for international judicial and arbitral procedure has been more common and more specific than any other type of application. For example, the International Court has accepted *res judicata* as applicable to international litigation; it has allowed recourse to indirect evidence (i.e., inferences of fact and circumstantial evidence) and it has approved the principle that legal remedies against a judgment are equally open to either party. Arbitral tribunals have applied the principle of prescription (or laches) to international litigation relying on analogies from municipal law. Lauterpacht's *Private Law Sources and Analogies of International Law,* written in 1927, still remains a valuable repository of examples, as does Bin Cheng's later work on *General Principles as Applied by International Courts and Tribunals.*

But considerable caution is still required in inferring international law from municipal law, even where the principles of national law are found in many "representative" legal systems. The international cases show such use in a limited degree, nearly always as a supplement to fill in gaps left by the primary sources of treaty and custom. Waldock's conclusions expressed in 1962 at this Academy still largely hold. Referring to the corpus of "common law" applied by the International Court, he says:

> "In this corpus customary law enormously predominates and most of the law applied by the Court falls within it. But paragraph *(c)* adds to this corpus—very much in the way actually intended by its authors—a flexible element which enables the Court to give greater completeness to customary law and in some limited degree to extend it".

The most important limitation on the use of municipal law principles arises from the requirement that the principle be appropriate for application on the international level. Thus, the universally accepted common crimes—murder, theft, assault, incest—that apply to individuals are not crimes under international law by virtue of their ubiquity. In the *Right of Passage over Indian Territory* case (India v. Portugal), the Court rejected arguments that the municipal law of easements found in most legal systems were appropriate principles for determining rights of transit over State territory. Similarly, a contention that the law of trusts could be used to interpret the mandate of South Africa over South West Africa (Namibia) did not win approval as international law but it may possibly have had an indirect influence on the Court's reasoning in its advisory opinions. Lord McNair, in an individual opinion, in the 1950 Advisory Opinion on the *International Status of South West Africa,* expressed a balanced conclusion on the subject of analogies from private law that merits quotation here.

> "International law has recruited and continues to recruit many of its rules and institutions from private systems of law * * * The way in which international law borrows from the source is not by means of importing private law institutions 'lock, stock and barrel', ready-made and fully equipped with a set of rules * * * In my opinion the true view of the duty of international tribunals in this matter is to regard any features or terminology which are reminiscent of the rules and institutions of private law as an indication of policy and principles rather than as directly importing these rules and institutions".

I would subscribe to this general formulation and stress the requirement that the use of municipal law must be appropriate for international relations.

At the same time, I would suggest a somewhat more positive approach for the emergent international law concerned with the individual, business companies, environmental dangers and shared resources. Inasmuch as these areas have become the concern of international law, national law principles will often be suitable for international application. This does not mean importing municipal rules "lock, stock and barrel", but it suggests that domestic law rules applicable to such matters as individual rights, contractual remedies, liability for extra-hazardous activities, or restraints on use of common property, have now become pertinent for recruitment into international law. In these areas, we may look to representative legal systems not only for the highly abstract principles of the kind referred to earlier but to more specific rules that are sufficiently widespread as to be considered "recognized by civilized nations". It is likely that such rules will enter into international law largely through international treaties or particular arrangements accepted by the parties. But such treaties and arrangements still require supplementing their general provisions and such filling-in can often be achieved by recourse to commonly accepted national law rules. The case-law under the European Convention on Human Rights exemplifies this process. The fact that treaties and customary law now pervade most of the fields mentioned above means that the use of municipal law for specific application will normally fall within an existing frame of established international law. It would be rare that an international tribunal or organ or States themselves would be faced with the necessity of finding a specific rule in an area unregulated by international law. But there still may be such areas where injury and claims of redress by States occur in fields hitherto untouched by international regulation. Weather modification, acid rain, resource-satellites are possible examples. In these cases, municipal law analogies may provide acceptable solutions for the States concerned or for a tribunal empowered to settle a dispute.

The second category of general principles included in our list comprises principles derived from the specific character of the international community. The most obvious candidates for this category of principles are * * * the necessary principles of coexistence. They include the principles of *pacta sunt servanda,* non-intervention, territorial integrity, self-defence and the legal equality of States. Some of these principles are in the United Nations Charter and therefore part of treaty law, but others might appropriately be treated as principles required by the specific character of a society of sovereign independent members.

Our third category is even more abstract but not infrequently cited: principles "intrinsic to the idea of law and basic to all legal systems". As stated it includes an empirical element—namely, the ascertainment of principles found in "all" legal systems. It also includes a conceptual criterion—"intrinsic to the idea of law". Most of the principles cited in World Court and arbitral decisions as common in municipal law are also referred to as "basic" to all law. In this way, the tribunals move from a purely empirical municipal law basis to "necessary" principles based on the logic of the law. They thus afford a reason for acceptance by those who hesitate to accept municipal law *per se* as international law but are prepared to adopt juridical notions that are seen as intrinsic to the idea of law. Some of the examples that fall under this heading would seem to be analytical (or tautologous) propositions. *Pacta sunt servanda,* and *nemo plus iuris transfere potest quam ipse habet* (no one can transfer more rights than he possesses) are good examples. (Expressing tautologies in Latin apparently adds to their weight in judicial reasoning.) Several other maxims (also commonly expressed in Latin phrases), considered as intrinsic to all representative legal systems, are sometimes described as juridical "postulates", or as essential elements of legal reasoning. Some principles of interpretation fall in this category: for example, the *lex specialis* rule and the maxim *lex posterior derogat priori* (the later supersedes the earlier law, if both have the same source). These are not tautologies, but can be considered as "legal logic". A similar sense of lawyers' logic supports certain postulates of judicial proceedings: for example, *res judicata* and the equality of parties before a tribunal. The latter suggests that reciprocity on a more general basis may be considered as an intrinsic element of legal relations among members of a community considered equal under the law.

These various examples lend support to the theory that the general principles of law form a kind of substratum of legal postulates. In Bin Cheng's words, "They belong to no particular system of law but are common to them all * * * Their existence bears witness to the fundamental unity of law". In actual practice those postulates are established by "logic" or a process of reasoning, with illustrative examples added. The underlying and sometimes unstated premise is that they are generally accepted. They may be used "against" a State in a case because they are established law. However, if a particular principle or postulate becomes a subject of dispute regarding its general acceptance, it is likely to lose its persuasive force as an intrinsic principle. Hence, in the last analysis, these principles, however "intrinsic" they seem to be to the idea of law, rest on an implied consensus of the relevant community.

The foregoing comments are also pertinent to the next two categories of general principles. The idea of principles *"jus rationale"* "valid through all kinds of human societies" (in Judge Tanaka's words) is associated with traditional natural law doctrine. At the present time its theological links are mainly historical as far as international law is concerned, but its principal justification does not depart too far from the classic natural law emphasis on the nature of "man", that is, on the human person as a rational and social creature.

The universalist implication of this theory—the idea of the unity of the human species—has had a powerful impetus in the present era. This is evidenced in at least three significant political and legal developments. The first is the global movements against discrimination on grounds of race, colour and sex. The second is the move toward general acceptance of human rights. The third is the increased fear of nuclear annihilation. These three developments strongly reinforce the universalistic values inherent in natural law doctrine. They have found expression in numerous international and constitutional law instruments as well as in popular movements throughout the world directed to humanitarian ends. Clearly, they are a "material source" of much of the new international law manifested in treaties and customary rules.

In so far as they are recognized as general principles of law, many tend to fall within our fifth category—the principles of natural justice. This concept is well known in many municipal law systems (although identified in diverse ways). "Natural justice" in its international legal manifestation has two aspects. One refers to the minimal standards of decency and respect for the individual human being that are largely spelled out in the human rights instruments. We can say that in this aspect, "natural justice" has been largely subsumed as a source of general principles by the human rights instruments. The second aspect of "natural justice" tends to be absorbed into the related concept of equity which includes such elements of "natural justice" as fairness, reciprocity, and consideration of the particular circumstances of a case. The fact that equity and human rights have come to the forefront in contemporary international law has tended to minimize reference to "natural justice" as an operative concept, but much of its substantive content continues to influence international decisions under those other headings. Judge Sir Gerald Fitzmaurice was not far from the mark when he concluded in 1973 that there was a "strong current of opinion holding that international law must give effect to principles of natural justice" and "that this is a requirement that natural law in the international field imposes *a priori* upon States, irrespective of their individual wills or consents".

Notes

1. If "general principles of law" are a distinct and independent source of law, why would the Court tend to treat such general principles and customary law "very much as a single corpus of law" (as Waldock suggests)? Does blurring the distinction between the two sources enable the Court to imply that the "general and well-recognized principles" derived from national law have been "received into" international law?

2. Is it necessary to show that many states have recognized a principle of municipal law as appropriate to interstate relations in order to apply it in international law? Tunkin, a leading Soviet authority, argued that this was a requirement that could only be met by showing that the rule in question had been accepted by custom or treaty. G. Tunkin, op. cit. 200–01. However, Henkin suggests that "principles of law common to every developed legal system, for example, principles of property, tort and contract were in the international system from the very beginning, whenever that was." Henkin, General Course, 216 Rec. des Cours at 52. Compare Schachter's comment that the rule must be appropriate for interstate relations and Judge McNair's even more cautious view that private law rules may be regarded as "indications of policy and principles rather than directly importing them into international law." 1950 I.C.J. 148.

3. The use of analogies drawn from municipal legal systems to develop or supplement international law is as old as international law itself. International tribunals have frequently employed such analogies in deciding disputes between states. For examples, see Lauterpacht, Private Law Sources and Analogies of International Law (1927); Cheng, General Principles of Law as Applied by International Courts and Tribunals (1953).

4. If customary law is part of national law (see Paquete Habana, supra, and Filartiga v. Pena–Irala, 630 F.2d 876 (2d Cir.1980) infra), would recognition of human rights as customary law provide a stronger ground than general principles for holding states legally bound even when they were not parties to the human rights treaties? However some writers consider custom a weaker ground for human rights in view of violations and lack of uniform practice. They contend that "general principles" is a more appropriate source, based on the support of human rights in international declarations and national constitutions. B. Simma & P.

Alston, The Sources of Human Rights Law: Custom, Jus Cogens and General Principles, 12 Australia Y.B.I.L. 82 (1992).

5. For references to recent decisions by a variety of international tribunals resorting to general principles as a sources of international law, see J. Charney, Is International Law Threatened by Multiple International Tribunals?, 271 Rec. des Cours 115, 190, 196, 200–210 (1998) (citing decisions of I.C.J., Iran–U.S. Claims Tribunal and European Court of Justice, among others). Substantive principles applied as "general" principles by such tribunals have included clean hands, acquiescence, estoppel, elementary principles of humanity, duty to make reparations, equity, equality, protection of legitimate expectations, and proportionality.

6. A provocative illustration of potential uses in international jurisprudence of claims of general principles is the Case Concerning the Gabcikovo–Nagymaros Project (Hungary/Slovakia), 1997 I.C.J. 7, a dispute over the viability of a treaty dating from the socialist era to construct certain works on the Danube River. Hungary contended that the environmental risks of the project had become so grave as to create a state of "ecological necessity," such that its refusal to carry out its part of the treaty should not be viewed as wrongful. The Court's opinion takes note of a range of concepts which one or both parties had invoked as being found in legal systems in general: these included contentions that "the notion of state of necessity is . . . deeply rooted in general legal thinking" (para. 50); that a party cannot be permitted to profit from its own wrongful act (*ex injuria jus non oritur*) (paras. 57, 110, 113); that an aggrieved party has a duty to mitigate damage from another's unlawful action (paras. 68, 80–81); that if an instrument cannot be applied literally, it should be applied to approximate its primary object (paras. 75–76, citing Judge Sir Hersch Lauterpacht); and that a countermeasure to a wrongful act must be proportional to the injury suffered (paras. 83–87). The Court paraphrased the parties' reliance on claims of general principles of law but did not necessarily endorse these lines of argument, typically finding that it was unnecessary to resolve the points (e.g., para. 76) or resting its own reasoning on another source of law, such as custom (e.g., para. 52).

7. The International Criminal Tribunals for the Former Yugoslavia and for Rwanda have carried out intensive examinations of national criminals laws and procedures, to try to discern something like "general principles of law" that might guide the tribunals in resolving disputed points, in the absence of more authoritative sources. In the *Erdemovic* case, No. IT–96–22–A (Judgment on Appeal, Oct. 7, 1997), the tribunal looked in detail at national legislation from common-law and civil-law jurisdictions and at national judicial precedents, both with respect to the substantive question of whether duress can be a complete defense to a homicide and with respect to procedural points, viz., whether the defendant could withdraw a plea of guilty made with inadequate knowledge of its consequences. On the specific questions before the tribunal in *Erdemovic*, common-law and civil-law traditions seemed to differ markedly, so that no truly "general" principles could emerge. Yet, as some of the judges separately explained, "general principles of law recognized by civilized nations" might well serve as a residuum of authoritative guidance in appropriate cases. Compare Joint Sep. Op. of JJ. McDonald and Vohrah, paras. 56ff, with Sep./Diss.Op. Cassese, para. 1ff (national concepts cannot be automatically transposed to the international level).

Similarly, in the *Tadic* case, the Appellate Chamber consulted national legislation and case law relevant to participants in a common purpose, but did not find "general principles" because of a divergence in approaches among countries and major legal systems. No. IT–94–1–AR72, Judgment on Appeal from Conviction (July 15 1999), paras. 224–225.

In the *Blaskic* case, the Appellate Chamber considered whether national practice as to subpoenas, contempt of court, and other procedures claimed to be "inherent powers" of a judicial organ could be transposed to the international level, in order to fill a gap in authority that had not been explicitly conferred in the Tribunal's Statute. The Chamber observed that "domestic judicial views or approaches should be handled with the greatest caution at the international level, lest one should fail to make due allowance for the unique characteristics of international criminal procedures. * * * [T]he transposition onto the international community of legal institutions, constructs or approaches prevailing in national law may be a source of great confusion and misapprehension." No. IT–95–14–AR108*bis* (Judgment on the Request of the Republic of Croatia for Review of Decision on the Issuance of *Subpoenae Duces Tecum*, Oct. 29, 1997), paras. 23–24, 40.

MANN, REFLECTIONS ON A COMMERCIAL LAW OF NATIONS

33 Brit. Y.B.I.L. 20, 34–39 (1957).*

The general principles as a whole and the commercial law of nations in particular are determined and defined by comparative law, i.e., by the process of comparing municipal systems of law. Although publicists rarely refer in terms to comparative law as a "source" of international law, the great majority is likely to agree. This is so for the obvious reason that since the elimination of the direct influence of Roman law there does not exist any system or branch of law, other than comparative law, which could develop general principles. * * *

* * * In a sense it is quite true that all law and all legal systems incorporate and are based upon some such maxims as find expression in the maxims of English equity, in Article 1134 of the French or in s. 242 of the German Civil Code or in similar provisions of codified law. Many, if not most, of the specific rules and provisions accepted in the systems of municipal law can be said to be manifestations or applications of such maxims. Yet "general clauses," as they have been called, have been proved to be an unsatisfactory guide and dangerous to legal development. While no legal system has found it possible to do without them none has found it possible to work with them alone. They leave much room for a subjective approach by the court. They leave the result unpredictable. They lack that minimum degree of precision without which every legal decision would be wholly uncertain. They may, on occasions, be useful to fill a gap but in essence they are too elementary, too obvious and even too platitudinous to permit detached evaluation of conflicting interests, the specifically legal appreciation of the implications of a given situation. In short they are frequently apt to let discretion prevail over justice. For these reasons they cannot be the sole source of a sound and workable commercial law of nations. * * *

A principle of law is a general one if it is being applied by the most representative systems of municipal law.

* Footnotes omitted.

That universality of application is not a prerequisite of a general principle of law is emphasized by almost all authors. It should be equally clear that a single system of municipal law cannot provide a general principle within the meaning of Article 38. What is usually required is that the principle pervades the municipal law of nations in general. * * *

A principle of law is a general one even though the constituent rules of the representative systems of law are similar rather than identical. * * *

Notes

1. Disputes between states and foreign companies involving concession agreements or development contracts have involved references to principles of law common to the national legal systems of the countries involved or in a more general way to principles of law. In a well known arbitration, involving nationalization of an oil company, the sole arbitrator considered that a provision of that kind in a concession agreement brought that agreement within the domain of international law and required reference to the rules of international law, more particularly the international law of contracts. Arbitration between Libya and Texaco Overseas Petroleum Company et al. (TOPCO), Award of January 19, 1977, 17 I.L.M. 1 (1978), especially paragraphs 46–51. For more on this case see pp. 148–153 below and Chapter 10.

2. In another arbitration involving the nationalization and termination of an oil concession, the relevant agreements indicated that the applicable law included both the law common to the territorial state and the home state of the company and principles of law prevailing in the modern world. The arbitral tribunal noted that the law of the territorial state (Kuwait) also incorporated international law. However, instead of declaring that the applicable law was international law, the tribunal concluded that the three sources of law—municipal law of the state concerned, general principles, and international public law—should be considered as a common body of law. See Kuwait and American Independent Oil Company (Aminoil) Award of Sept. 26, 1977, 21 I.L.M. 976, especially paras. 6–10.

3. The tribunals that have applied "general principles" have not considered it necessary to carry out a detailed examination of the main (or "representative") systems of national law to determine whether the principles pervade "the municipal law of nations in general" (Mann, supra). They have at most referred to highly general concepts such as *pacta sunt servanda,* good faith, legitimate expectations of the parties, the equilibrium of the contract. Occasionally reference has been made to a provision of the Vienna Convention on the Law of Treaties. Query whether much would be gained by tribunals seeking to distill specific rules from several diverse legal systems in order to ascertain "general principles recognized by civilized nations." See Schlesinger, Research on the General Principles of Law Recognized by Civilized Nations, 51 A.J.I.L. 734 (1957); Friedmann, The Uses of "General Principles" in the Development of International Law, 57 A.J.I.L. 279 (1963). The Iran–U.S. Claims Tribunal has applied a large number of general principles of law, including unjust enrichment, force majeure, changed circumstances, and other doctrines. See J. Crook, Applicable Law in International Arbitration: The Iran–U.S. Claims Tribunal Experience, 83 A.J.I.L. 278, 292–299 (1989).

4. General principles of municipal law have also been relied on by the administrative tribunals established by the United Nations and other international organizations to adjudicate disputes between the organization and members of its staff. In some cases such general principles of law have been held to limit the power of the governing bodies of the international organization to alter the conditions of employment of staff members. See de Merede et al. v. The World Bank, World Bank Administrative Tribunal Reports 1981 Decision No. 1. For commentary see C.F. Amerasinghe, in The Law of the International Civil Service 151–58 (1988); Meron, The United Nations Secretariat, The Rules and Practice (1977). The body of law applied and developed by the various administrative tribunals is sometimes described as "international administrative law" or the law of the international civil service. It is not law that applies directly to states. However, since the international organizations are "international persons" (see Chapter 5), the law governing their relation to their staff has been considered by some writers as a part of international law, although quite distinct from the law governing interstate relations. See W. Friedmann, The Changing Structure of International Law 159–162 (1964). One eminent international law scholar, Suzanne Bastid, for many years the President of the United Nations Administrative Tribunal, has referred to the principles applied by administrative tribunals as a type of customary law. She wrote:

> These rules are undoubtedly inspired by the internal law of certain states, but it does not appear that they are being applied as general principles of law. "Here again one may consider that a custom is being established, which has not been contested, notably by the organs which could have recourse to the International Court of Justice against the judgments which apply the custom."

Bastid, Have the U.N. Administrative Tribunals Contributed to the Development of International Law, in Transnational Law in a Changing Society 298, 311 (Friedmann, Henkin and Lissitzyn eds., 1972).

Why would Professor Bastid prefer to regard the "general principles" as custom? Is it significant that she refers to the "internal law of certain states"? If a principle is invoked for the first time in a tribunal, and has only had application as a rule of national law, could the tribunal justifiably adopt it as "custom"?

B. CONSIDERATIONS OF EQUITY AND HUMANITY

FRIEDMANN, THE CHANGING STRUCTURE OF INTERNATIONAL LAW

197 (1964). (Some footnotes omitted.)

Probably the most widely used and cited "principle" of international law is the principle of general equity in the interpretation of legal documents and relations. There has been considerable discussion on the question of whether equity is part of the law to be applied, or whether it is an antithesis to law, in the sense in which *"ex aequo et bono"* is used in Article 38, paragraph 2, of the Statute of the International Court of Justice. A strict distinction must of course be made between, on the one hand, the Roman *aequitas* and the English equity, both separate systems of judicial administration designed to correct the insufficiencies and rigidities of the existing civil or common law, and, on the other hand, the function of equity as a principle of interpretation.

In the latter sense, it is beyond doubt an essential and all-pervading principle of interpretation in all modern civil codifications, and it is equally important in the modern common law systems, under a variety of terminologies such as "reasonable," "fair" or occasionally even in the guise of "natural justice." There is thus overwhelming justification for the view developed by Lauterpacht,[20] Manley Hudson,[21] De Visscher,[22] and Dahm,[23] that equity is part and parcel of any modern system of administration of justice. * * *

THE DIVERSION OF WATER FROM THE MEUSE (NETHERLANDS v. BELGIUM)

Permanent Court of International Justice, 1937.
P.C.I.J., Ser. A/B, No. 70, 76–78.
4 Hudson, World Ct. Rep. 172, 231–33.

[The case concerned a complaint by the Netherlands that construction of certain canals by Belgium was in violation of an agreement of 1863 in that the construction would alter the water level and rate of flow of the Meuse River. The Court rejected the Netherlands claim and a Belgian counter-claim based on the construction of a lock by the Netherlands at an earlier time. Judge Hudson, in an individual concurring opinion said:]

The Court has not been expressly authorized by its Statute to apply equity as distinguished from law. Nor, indeed, does the Statute expressly direct its application of international law, though as has been said on several occasions the Court is "a tribunal of international law". Series A, No. 7, p. 19; Series A, Nos. 20/21, p. 124. Article 38 of the Statute expressly directs the application of "general principles of law recognized by civilized nations", and in more than one nation principles of equity have an established place in the legal system. The Court's recognition of equity as a part of international law is in no way restricted by the special power conferred upon it "to decide a case *ex aequo et bono,* if the parties agree thereto". [Citations omitted.] It must be concluded, therefore, that under Article 38 of the Statute, if not independently of that Article, the Court has some freedom to consider principles of equity as part of the international law which it must apply.

It would seem to be an important principle of equity that where two parties have assumed an identical or a reciprocal obligation, one party which is engaged in a continuing non-performance of that obligation should not be permitted to take advantage of a similar non-performance of that obligation by the other party. The principle finds expression in the so-called maxims of equity which exercised great influence in the creative period of the development of the Anglo–American law. Some of these maxims are, "Equality is equity"; "He who seeks equity must do equity". It is in line with such maxims that "a court of equity refuses relief to a plaintiff whose conduct in regard to the subject-matter of the litigation has been improper". 13 Halsbury's Laws of

20. Private Law Sources and Analogies of International Law (1927), para. 28.

21. The Permanent Court of International Justice (1943), p. 617, where the task of equity is described as being "to liberalize and to temper the application of law, to prevent extreme injustice in particular cases, to lead into new directions for which received materials point the way."

22. "Contribution à L'Etude des Sources du Droit International," 60 Revue de Droit International et Législation Comparée (1933), 325, 414 et seq.

23. 1 Völkerrecht (1958), p. 40 et seq.

England (2nd ed., 1934), p. 87. A very similar principle was received into Roman Law. The obligations of a vendor and a vendee being concurrent, "neither could compel the other to perform unless he had done, or tendered, his own part".

Notes

1. While Friedmann and Hudson refer to equity as "a principle" of law, the concept of equity is used in such diverse ways by tribunals and governments that it is difficult to regard it as a single principle. Consider, for example, the following five uses of equity distinguished by Schachter:

> (1) Equity as a basis for "individualized" justice tempering the rigours of strict law.
>
> (2) Equity as consideration of fairness, reasonableness and good faith.
>
> (3) Equity as a basis for certain specific principles of legal reasoning associated with fairness and reasonableness: to wit, estoppel, unjust enrichment, and abuse of rights.
>
> (4) Equitable standards for the allocation and sharing of resources and benefits (notably, in boundary delimitation).
>
> (5) Equity as a broad synonym for distributive justice used to justify demands for economic and social arrangements and redistribution of wealth.

Schachter, International Law in Theory and Practice 55–56 (1991).

2. The use of equity to "individualize" decisions and to escape the rigors of rules is akin (as Schachter notes) to the practice of tribunals to distinguish prior cases in terms of the particular facts. In doing this they attribute weight to individual circumstances and thereby allow for exceptions to general rules. Treaty clauses that refer to equitable principles similarly permit exceptions on grounds of the particular facts. As Judge Jiménez de Aréchaga remarked in the 1982 *Tunisia-Libya Case* in the International Court:

> * * * the judicial application of equitable principles means that a court should render justice in the concrete case, by means of a decision shaped by and adjusted to the "relevant factual matrix of that case".

1982 I.C.J. 100, para. 4.

3. In discussing exceptions to rules on equitable grounds, international lawyers (especially in Europe) often refer to decisions *infra legem* (within the law), *praeter legem* (outside the law) and *contra legem* (against the law). A decision on equitable grounds that is *infra legem* typically occurs when a rule leaves a margin of discretion to a state or law-applying organ. Exercising such discretion on equitable grounds is clearly within the law. A decision that is *contra legem* would not normally be justifiable on grounds of equity, unless the tribunal had been authorized to act *ex aequo et bono*. See Judgment of International Court of Justice in Tunisia–Libya Case, 1982 I.C.J. 100, para. 71. In very exceptional circumstances, a tribunal may feel it necessary to disregard a rule of law on grounds that it is unreasonable or unfair in the circumstances. Governments may consider themselves more free than tribunals to make such exceptions.

The question of whether equity may be used to support a decision *praeter legem* arises when an issue is not covered by a relevant rule and the law appears to have a lacuna in that situation. In one view, a tribunal should hold, in that event, that it cannot decide the issue in accordance with law and therefore refrain from judgment. This distinction is designated as *non liquet* (the law is not clear enough for a decision). See discussion of the 1996 Nuclear Weapons Advisory Opinion, supra. A contrary view maintains that no court may refrain from judgment because the law is silent or obscure. Lauterpacht has argued that the principle prohibiting *non liquet* is itself a general principle of law recognized by civilized nations. Lauterpacht, The Function of Law in the International Community 67 (1933). If that position is adopted, a tribunal may be allowed to use equitable principles as a basis for decisions *praeter legem.*

4. Substantive concepts of equity such as estoppel, unjust enrichment and abuse of rights have been treated as general principles of law. On estoppel, see Temple of Preah Vihear, 1962 I.C.J. 31, 32, 39–51, 61–65; Case on Arbitral Award Made by King of Spain (Honduras v. Nicaragua) 1960 I.C.J. 192. On unjust enrichment, see Friedmann, The Changing Structure of International Law 206210 (1964). On abuse of rights, see B. Cheng, General Principles of Law Applied by International Courts 121–36 (1953). See also Schwarzenberger, "Equity in International Law" 26 Y.B. World Affs. 362 (1972).

5. Equity and "equitable doctrine" are also invoked in cases of international claims for breach of contract or taking of property by a government. The Iran–U.S. Claims Tribunal has had occasion to refer to equity as a basis for a general principle of law and also in some cases as a ground for departing from law. It declared, for example, that the concept of "unjust enrichment" has been recognized in the great majority of municipal legal systems and "assimilated into the catalogue of general principles available to be applied by international tribunals * * * Its equitable foundation makes it necessary to take into account all the circumstances of each specific situation." Sea-land Services v. Iran, 6 Iran–U.S.C.T.R. 149, 168 (1984).

In another case, the Claims Tribunal was faced with a claim of a U.S. company that shares in an Iranian company belonged to the claimant although they were registered in the name of a third party. Iran, the respondent, argued that under Iranian law the nominal registration was conclusive as to ownership. However, the tribunal majority did not accept the Iranian argument, noting that the nominal owner had acted on the basis that the shares belonged to the claimant. The tribunal concluded that a contrary result would "be both illogical and inequitable." Foremost Tehran v. Iran, 10 Iran–U.S. C.T.R. 228, 240 (1986). Was this a use of equity *contra legem?* Would the tribunal have been able to rely on a generally accepted principle such as beneficial ownership or estoppel to reach the same result?

6. Is "equity" an appropriate basis to recognize that non-performance of a contract was caused by external political events not contemplated by the parties? The dissenting opinion of an Iranian member of the Claims Tribunal called for an "equitable settlement" that would take into account such "external" events and "human factors". Gould Marketing v. Ministry of Defence, 6 Iran–U.S. C.T.R. 293–94 (1984). Is this a legitimate reason to apply equity *contra legem* as a basis for departing from strict contractual law on grounds of fairness?

7. Are there situations in which equity *contra legem* would be appropriate to allow a tribunal (or the governments concerned) to take account of circumstances that would not be germane in a purely legal adjudication? It has been suggested

that this might be the case where new international law is emerging as, for example, in regard to transborder environmental damage or access to common resources. See V. Lowe, The Role of Equity in International Law, 12 Australia Y.B.I.L. 54, 69 (1992). As an alternative, would it be more acceptable to rely on concepts that have been accepted as general principles of law as, for example, the obligation of a state "not to allow knowingly its territory to be used for acts contrary to the rights of other states" (Corfu Channel Case, 1949 I.C.J. 22). The Latin version of this *"sic utere tuo ut alienum non laedas"* (i.e., use your own so as not to injure another) is often mentioned in international legal writing and judicial decisions. (See Chapter 17 on Environmental Law.)

EQUITABLE PRINCIPLES AND SOLUTIONS: THE RELATION OF LAW AND EQUITY

1. Equitable principles and equitable solutions have become key concepts in the law governing the delimitation of maritime boundaries between states. The International Court of Justice and ad hoc arbitral tribunals have adjudicated a number of delimitation disputes based on the principle enunciated by the Court in the North Sea Continental Shelf Cases (supra) that "it is precisely a rule of law that calls for an application of equitable principles." The opinion added, "there is no legal limit to the considerations which states may take account of for the purpose of making sure that they apply equitable procedures and more often than not it is the balancing-up of all such considerations that will produce this result rather than reliance on one to the exclusion of others." 1969 I.C.J. 50.

2. In the 1982 Continental Shelf case between Tunisia and Libya, the International Court emphasized "equitable solutions" and the "particular circumstances," declaring

> Each continental shelf case in dispute should be considered and judged on its own merits, having regard to its peculiar circumstances * * * therefore no attempt should be made to over conceptualize the application of the principles and rules.

Similar emphasis on the specific circumstances can be found in the judgment of a Chamber of the Court in the Gulf of Maine Case between Canada and the United States. 1984 I.C.J. 246, 300.

3. Criticism of such "individualization" by dissenting judges and by commentators may have influenced the International Court to adopt a more "legal" view of equity. In 1985, it declared "Even though [equity] looks with particularity to the peculiar circumstances of an instant case, it also looks beyond it to principles of more general application * * * having a more general validity and hence expressible in general terms." Libya–Malta Case, 1985 I.C.J. 39.

4. The idea of "proportionality" has often been referred to as an "equitable criterion." It has been called "the touchstone of equitableness." In delimitation cases, proportionality has been generally construed to refer to the ratio between the lengths of the coasts of each state that border the marine area to be delimited. The state with the longer coastline would get the proportionally larger share of the area delimited. (The size of the area behind the coast would not be relevant at all.) The case-law has distinguished

between proportionality as an "operative" criterion and its application as a test (or corrective) of a solution reached by other criteria. The latter position was adopted by the International Court in the Libya–Malta Case of 1985. It was followed in the Gulf of Maine Case between Canada and the United States and in the 1992 decision of the Court of Arbitration established by Canada and France to delimit the marine areas between the French islands of St. Pierre and Miquelon and the opposite and adjacent coasts of Canada (31 I.L.M. 1145–1219, Sept. 1992).

In the latter case, the international tribunal declared that geographical features are at the heart of delimitation and that certain equitable criteria are prescribed by international law. The tribunal took account of the disparity in the coastal lengths of the respective territories (which was considerable) but it applied "proportionality" only as a check on the solution reached on the basis of other criteria, particularly avoidance of encroachment. In fact, the result reached by the tribunal largely reflected the disparity in the coastal lengths of the parties.

5. Should equity take account of the economic and social factors and needs in delimiting boundaries? The cases, beginning with the North Sea Shelf Cases, have all declared that delimitation should not involve "refashioning" geography and should not "compensate for the inequalities of nature". Thus in principle economic factors or needs would not be appropriate equitable criteria. However, in two recent cases this principle was somewhat attenuated. In the Gulf of Maine Case between Canada and the U.S., the judgment declared that human and economic factors were not considered as criteria to be "applied in the delimitation process itself". But it then stated that it had to assure itself that the result reached was "not radically inequitable * * * that is to say, as likely to entail catastrophic repercussions for the livelihood and well-being of the population of the countries concerned." (1984 I.C.J., para. 237.) The Court found no such consequence in that case. A similar approach was followed in the decision of the tribunal in the Canadian–French delimitation. In that case, the tribunal recognized the importance of fisheries to the parties. It found that the "full reciprocity" accorded by a treaty in force between the two states indicated that the proposed demarcation would not have a "radical impact" on the existing pattern of fishing in the area. (31 I.L.M. at 1173–74.) The tribunal also referred to possible hydrocarbon resources but concluded that it had no reason to consider potential mineral resources as relevant to the delimitation (id. at 1175). A leading expert has asked whether there is really any difference between taking account of geographical and economic factors successively and "doing it altogether at once." P. Weil, The Law of Maritime Delimitation–Reflections 262 (1989). Would the answer not depend essentially on the weight accorded to economic repercussions?

6. Equitable principles have also been considered as part of the law applicable to land frontier disputes. The tribunal in the Rann of Kutch arbitration between India and Pakistan held that the parties were free to rely on principles of equity in their arguments. 50 I.L.R. 2 (1968). However, some arbitral tribunals have considered that they could not apply equity where the *compromis* (the special agreement setting up the arbitration) required a decision based on law. See Carlston, The Process of International Arbitration 158 (1946); Feller, The Mexican Claims Commissions 223 ff. (1935). For

general discussion, see de Visscher, De L'Equité dans le Règlement Arbitral ou Judiciaire des Litiges de Droit International Public (1972); R. Lapidoth, Equity in International Law, 81 A.S.I.L. Proc. 138–47 (1987).

7. Proportionality, treated in note 4 above as relevant to principles of boundary delimitation, has been applied in various contexts by international tribunals. In the case of the Gabcikovo–Nagymaros Dam, 1997 I.C.J. 92 at paras. 85–87, the I.C.J. ruled that proportionality was a condition of the legality of countermeasures taken against a wrongful act, and that Slovakia's countermeasures against Hungary were unlawful because they had failed to respect proportionality. The dispute settlement organs of the General Agreement on Tariffs and Trade/World Trade Organization have applied a similar principle of proportionality, as well as other general principles of law (such as the equitable principle of estoppel). See D. Palmeter & P. Mavroidis, The WTO Legal System: Sources of Law, 92 A.J.I.L. 398, 408 (1998). For discussion of "reasonableness" in the jurisprudence of international courts, see O. Corten, L'Utilisation du "Raisonnable" par le Juge international (1997).

CORFU CHANNEL CASE (UNITED KINGDOM v. ALBANIA)

International Court of Justice, 1949.
1949 I.C.J. 4, 22.

[The case involved the explosion of mines in Albanian waters which damaged British warships and caused loss of life of British naval personnel on those vessels. The United Kingdom claimed Albania was internationally responsible and under a duty to pay damages. In regard to the obligations of Albania, the Court stated:]

> The obligations incumbent upon the Albanian authorities consisted in notifying, for the benefit of shipping in general, the existence of a minefield in Albanian territorial waters and in warning the approaching British warships of the imminent danger to which the minefields exposed them. Such obligations are based, not on the Hague Convention of 1907, No. VIII which is applicable in time of war, but on certain general and well-recognized principles, namely: elementary considerations of humanity, even more exacting in peace than in war; the principle of the freedom of maritime communication and every State's obligation not to allow knowingly its territory to be used for acts contrary to the rights of other States.

Notes

1. "Elementary considerations of humanity" may also be based today on the provisions of the United Nations Charter on human rights, the Universal Declaration of Human Rights, and the various human rights conventions. See the Advisory Opinion of the International Court in the Namibia Case, 1971 I.C.J. 16, 57, also discussed in note 2, p. 147 and at p. 549 infra. In its earlier decision in the

1966 *Southwest Africa Case* (2d Phase), the majority of the court declared that humanitarian considerations were not decisive and that moral principles could be considered only insofar as they are given "a sufficient expression in legal form" (1966 I.C.J. at 34).

2. Contemporary jurists who have placed high value on the role of humanitarian and moral factors in international law include such representative scholars as Hersch Lauterpacht, Myres McDougal, Hermann Mosler, and Georg Schwarzenberger.

3. The I.C.J.'s invocation of "elementary considerations of humanity" in the *Corfu Channel* case has been followed in, e.g., the *Nicaragua* case (Merits), 1986 I.C.J. 14 at 113–114, 129. Professor Meron in his treatment of the *Nicaragua* judgment has written that "[e]lementary considerations of humanity reflect basic community values whether already crystallized as binding norms of international law or not." T. Meron, Human Rights and Humanitarian Norms as Customary Law 35 (1989). In its *Nuclear Weapons* advisory opinion, 1996 I.C.J. at para. 79, the I.C.J. wrote:

> It is undoubtedly because a great many rules of humanitarian law applicable in armed conflict are so fundamental to the respect of the human person and "elementary considerations of humanity" as the Court put it in its Judgment of 9 April 1949 in the *Corfu Channel* case (*I.C.J. Reports 1949,* p. 22), that the Hague and Geneva Conventions have enjoyed a broad accession. Further these fundamental rules are to be observed by all States whether or not they have ratified the conventions that contain them, because they constitute intransgressible principles of international customary law.

Does the use of terms such as "fundamental" and "intransgressible" place "elementary considerations of humanity" in the category of hierarchically superior law?

SECTION 5. EVIDENCE OF INTERNATIONAL LAW AND SUBSIDIARY MEANS FOR DETERMINATION OF RULES OF LAW

A. JUDICIAL DECISIONS

1. International Court of Justice

Article 38 of the Statute in its paragraph 1(d) directs the Court to apply judicial decisions as "subsidiary means for the determination of rules of law." It is expressly made subject to Article 59 which states that "the decision of the Court has no binding force except between the parties and in respect of that particular case." Hence the principle of *stare decisis* is not meant to apply to decisions of the International Court. That qualification and the relegation of judicial decisions generally to a "subsidiary status" reflect the reluctance of states to accord courts—and the International Court in particular—a law-making role. The Court's decisions are supposed to be declaratory of the law laid down by the states in conventions and customary rules. In addition, the stated objection to *stare decisis* reflects a perception of international disputes as especially individual, each distinguished by particular features and circumstances.

Despite these qualifications, the decisions of the International Court of Justice are, on the whole, regarded by international lawyers as highly persuasive authority of existing international law. The very fact that state practices are often divergent or unclear adds to the authority of the Court. Its decisions often produce a degree of certainty where previously confusion and obscurity existed. A much-quoted dictum of Justice Cardozo reflects the attraction of judicial authority, especially to lawyers in the common law tradition:

> International law or the law that governs between States, has at times, like the common law within States, a twilight existence during which it is hardly distinguishable from morality or justice, till at length the imprimatur of a court attests to its jural quality.

New Jersey v. Delaware, 291 U.S. 361, 54 S.Ct. 407, 78 L.Ed. 847 (1934).

A decision of the International Court is generally accepted as the "imprimatur of jural quality" when the Court speaks with one voice or with the support of most judges. Not infrequently, the separate opinions of dissenting judges or other individual opinions contain cogent reasoning that influences subsequent doctrine more than the decision of the majority. Judgments and advisory opinions by a significantly divided court have diminished authority. This is especially true when the issues are perceived as highly political and the judges seem to reflect the positions of the states from which they come. Notable examples are the 1966 decision of the Court in the *Case Concerning South West Africa* (supra p. 133) and the 1984 decision on jurisdiction and admissibility in the case brought by Nicaragua against the United States. The fact that the key paragraph in the 1996 advisory opinion on Nuclear Weapons was decided by the president's tie-breaking vote left many commentators convinced that the judgment had done little to clarify a contested area of the law and would have little real-world impact. (For references, see p. 87 supra.)

Judgments and advisory opinions are not always compelling to states. Governments respond in various ways to decisions they consider unfounded or unwise. For example, after the *Lotus Case* (supra), many governments adopted a treaty provision which reversed the Court's ruling and prohibited a state other than the flag state from exercising criminal jurisdiction against a non-national in case of a collision or accident on the high seas. Individual states have also reacted to unfavorable decisions by altering or withdrawing their consent to jurisdiction, as the United States did after the *Nicaragua* case (see Chapter 11). After the *Nuclear Weapons* advisory opinion, U.S. officials noted that some aspects of the opinion confirmed U.S. position and that no change in U.S. nuclear policies could be expected. See the article by Deputy Legal Adviser Matheson cited in note 9 at p. 87 supra.

Notwithstanding these reactions the Court's pronouncements, especially in non-political matters, are a primary source for international lawyers. Every judgment or advisory opinion is closely examined, dissected, quoted and pondered for its implications. They are generally lengthy and learned analyses of relevant principles and practices and particular cases include opinions often amounting to more than 200–300 pages. After eight decades the case-law and associated opinions of the two "World Courts" constitute a substantial *corpus juris* relevant to many questions of international relations.

The fact that the Statute excludes *stare decisis* (Article 59) has not meant that the Court's case-law ignores precedent. The Court cites its earlier decisions and often incorporates their reasoning by reference, thereby creating a consistent jurisprudence. When the Court seems to depart from precedent, it generally distinguishes the cases and explains the reasons for the different views. See cases cited in Rosenne, The Law and Practice of the International Court, 1920–1996, Vol. III, pp. 1609–1615 (3d ed. 1996); M. Shahabuddeen, Precedent in the World Court (1996).

A more complex problem concerns the role of the Court in "developing" international law and reaching decisions that go beyond declarations of existing law. It is clear that states, by and large, do not expect or wish the Court to "create" new law. Yet as Brierly observed some years ago "the act of the Court is a creative act in spite of our conspiracy to represent it as something else." The Basis of Obligation in International Law 98 (Waldock ed., 1958). Both states and judges are aware "of the discretionary elements in the art of judging: the selection of 'relevant' facts, the need to give specific meaning to broad undefined concepts, the subtle process of generalizing from past cases, the uses of analogy and metaphor, the inevitable choices between competing rules and principles." Schachter, International Law in Theory and Practice 41 (1991). These discretionary elements are more evident in international law than in most areas of domestic law. The fragmentary character of much international law and the generality of its concepts and principles leave ample room for "creative" judicial application. On the other hand, the judges are well aware of the dangers of appearing to be "legislating" and of their precarious consensual jurisdiction (See Chapter 11). One way to meet the problem is to place emphasis on the particular facts of the case to avoid the appearance of creating new law. But there is also a pull in the opposite direction. The Court needs to show that its decisions are principled and in accord with the agreed basic concepts of international law. This requirement leads to reliance on broad doctrinal concepts and precepts taken from treatises and prior case-law. When applied to new situations, the abstractions of basic doctrine create new law. Though many governments hesitate to accept or recognize this, international lawyers acknowledge the formative role of the Court while recognizing the political necessity for the Court to appear solely as an organ for declaring and clarifying the existing law.

Notes

1. The 15 judges of the International Court are elected for 9-year terms by majority votes of political bodies, namely the Security Council and the General Assembly of the United Nations. (Statute of the Court, Articles 3–18). They are required to have the qualifications required in their respective countries for appointment to the highest judicial office or to be "jurisconsults of recognized competence in international law." (Id. Art. 2.) They are supposed to represent the "main forms of civilization and of the principal legal systems of the world." (Id. Art. 9.) This requirement is considered to be met by a geographical and political distribution of seats among the main regions of the world. Many of the judges have been well known legal scholars. In recent years, most have had prior service in their national governments, as legal advisors to the foreign office or as representatives to international bodies.

2. Does the fact that the judges are elected by political bodies and are considered likely to reflect the views of their own governments impugn or reduce

"the jural quality" of their decisions? Is it legally justifiable to minimize a judicial decision as a source of law because many of the judges have taken the same position as their own governments? How can states parties to cases before the Court seek to reduce the effect of ideological or national bias, assuming they wish to do so? Former Judge Mosler (Federal Republic of Germany) has written:

> Where there is no common agreement as to the substantive rules and especially where there is no complete agreement as to the sources of general international law, the subjective views of the individual judges assume increased importance.

The International Society as a Legal Community, 140 Rec. des Cours 293 (1974–IV). See also Suh, Voting Behaviors of National Judges in International Courts, 63 A.J.I.L. 224 (1969); S. Rosenne, The Composition of the Court, in The Future of the International Court of Justice 377 (L. Gross ed., 1976); E. Brown Weiss, Judicial Independence and Impartiality: A Preliminary Inquiry, in The International Court of Justice at a Crossroads 123–154 (Damrosch ed. 1987); Schachter at 69–73 (1991).

2. *Decisions of International Arbitral Tribunals and Other International Courts*

International decisions also embrace the numerous judgments of arbitral tribunals established by international agreement for individual disputes or for categories of disputes. Though they are not in a strict sense judicial bodies, they are generally required to decide in accordance with law and their decisions are considered an appropriate subsidiary means of determining international law. Governments and tribunals refer to such decisions as persuasive evidence of law. The International Court only occasionally identifies specific arbitral awards as precedents but it has also referred generally to the jurisprudence and consistent practice of arbitral tribunals. Governments do not hesitate to cite international arbitral decisions in support of their legal positions. Such decisions may be distinguished on the basis of the agreements establishing the tribunal or other special circumstances but in many cases they have been accepted as declaratory of existing international law.

The decisions of arbitral tribunals are published by the United Nations in Reports of International Arbitral Awards (U.N.R.I.A.A.). Other publications containing texts of arbitral decisions include the International Law Reports, an annual publication (E. Lauterpacht ed.), and International Legal Materials (published by the American Society of International Law). The Iran–U.S. Claims Tribunal, with now two decades of jurisprudence, has many volumes of published decisions. For further discussion of arbitration as a means of dispute settlement see Chapter 11.

Two European courts—the European Court of Justice (located in Luxembourg, with competence over questions arising within the framework of the European Communities/European Union) and the European Court of Human Rights (an organ of the Council of Europe, located in Strasbourg) also hand down many decisions that express or interpret principles and rules of international law. The Inter–American Court of Human Rights has a growing body of case law. The decisions of these regional courts are relevant not only to their specialized subject-matter (e.g., economic integration or human rights), but also to more general problems of international law, such as the law of treaties or of state responsibility.

The 1990s witnessed the creation of new international tribunals of specialized subject-matter jurisdiction, with growing potential to contribute to general international law. These include the International Criminal Tribunals for the Former Yugoslavia and for Rwanda, the International Tribunal for the Law of the Sea, and the dispute settlement body of the World Trade Organization. They will be dealt with in subsequent chapters, both as regards the substantive law that they apply (e.g., Chapters 15, 16, 19) and as regards general considerations of international judicial jurisdiction (Chapter 11). For present purposes it is sufficient to draw attention to two main themes relevant to the problem of sources: (1) whether these new tribunals can be expected to apply a methodology of sources similar to that indicated in Article 38 of the Statute of the I.C.J., and (2) whether their decisions will be treated by the I.C.J. and other law-applying bodies as "subsidiary means" under Article 38(1)(2) of the I.C.J. Statute, comparably to the I.C.J.'s own judgments. Commentators evaluating the early years of operation of such tribunals have ventured an affirmative answer to the first question, and have likewise predicted the inevitable influence of such tribunals on other courts, including the I.C.J. See, e.g., D. Palmeter & P. Mavroidis, The WTO Legal System: Sources of Law, 92 A.J.I.L. 398 (1998) (finding that WTO dispute settlement practice on sources is similar to that of I.C.J. Statute Art. 38, and discerning other parallels, e.g. in tendency to refer to prior rulings of the dispute settlement body as authoritative even though not formally binding); Charney, Is International Law Threatened by Multiple International Tribunals? in 271 Rec. des Cours 101, 189–236 (1998); Charney, The Impact on the International Legal System of the Growth of International Courts and Tribunals, 31 N.Y.U. J. Int'l L. & Politics 697 (1999) and related symposium articles.

The I.C.J. is not in a hierarchical relationship with such tribunals. Though I.C.J. judgments continue to have great influence, other bodies have felt free to differ with the I.C.J. when presented with similar (albeit not identical) questions. For example, the Appellate Chamber of the International Criminal Tribunal for the Former Yugoslavia explicitly disagreed with one aspect of the I.C.J.'s *Nicaragua* judgment, finding its reasoning "unconvincing." *Tadic*, Case No. IT-94-1-AR72, Appeal from Judgment of Conviction, para. 115ff. (July 15, 1999).

Other international organs perform some functions analogous to those of courts, but by virtue of their restricted competence, their authority as potential "sources" or "subsidiary means" is uncertain or disputed. As an example, the U.N. Human Rights Committee (the implementing body for the International Covenant on Civil and Political Rights) has aroused controversy for its pronouncements concerning reservations to human rights treaties; in the view of some governments, the Committee exceeded its competence in purporting to opine on the legal effects of such reservations and thus those governments contend that the Committee's opinion (expressed in the form of a "general comment") lacks authority. This controversy is addressed further below in Chapter 7 on the law of treaties and Chapter 8 on human rights. It is mentioned here as an illustration of the potentially widening domain of bodies applying at least some rules of international law, whose output might arguably (though contestedly) contribute to the sources of international law.

3. *Decisions of Municipal Courts*

The opinions in *Paquete Habana* and the *Lotus Case* (supra) cite municipal court decisions as evidence of customary law. Such municipal decisions are indicative of state practice and *opinio juris* of the state in question. However, inasmuch as national courts in many countries also apply principles and rules of international law, their decisions may be treated as a subsidiary source independently of their relation to state practice. While the authority of a national court would as a rule be less than that of an international court or arbitral body, particular decisions of the higher national courts may be the only case-law on a subject or the reasoning and learning in the decisions may be particularly persuasive. Decisions of the United States Supreme Court have been relied on by arbitral bodies and have been cited by states in support of their claims. In some areas of law such as state responsibility and sovereign immunity, national court decisions have had a prominent role. See Chapters 10 and 14.

The International Criminal Tribunal for the Former Yugoslavia (I.C.T.Y.) has referred extensively to municipal decisions, especially those applying the international laws of war. Some judges of the I.C.T.Y. have asserted that relatively greater attention should be given to the rulings of national authorities that were sitting in the capacity of an international tribunal and applying international law (e.g., the Allied military tribunals in occupied Germany after World War II) than to national courts that were merely applying local law. See, e.g, the joint separate opinion of Judges McDonald and Vohrah in *Erdemovic*, Case No. IT–96–22–A (Judgment on Appeal, Oct. 7, 1997), at paras. 42ff. In the *Nuclear Weapons* advisory opinion, a Japanese court decision was noted in some of the separate and dissenting opinions as a relevant subsidiary source under Article 38(1)(d). See, e.g., 1996 I.C.J., 375, 397 (diss. op. Shahabuddeen, citing *Shimoda v. State* (Tokyo dist. ct., 1963)).

B. THE TEACHINGS OF THE MOST HIGHLY QUALIFIED PUBLICISTS OF THE VARIOUS NATIONS

The place of the writer in international law has always been more important than in municipal legal systems. The basic systematization of international law is largely the work of publicists, from Grotius and Gentili onwards. In many cases of first impression only the opinions of writers can be referred to in support of one or the other of the opposing contentions of the parties. The extent to which writers are referred to as "subsidiary" authorities differs often according to the tradition of the court and the individual judge. Here the practice of national as well as of international courts is relevant. As a corollary to the position of precedent in common law jurisdictions, there has traditionally been judicial reluctance, more marked in the British jurisdictions than in the United States, to refer to writers. In the civilian systems reference to textbook writers and commentators ("doctrine" in continental terminology, referring to scholarship) is a normal practice, as the perusal of any collection of decisions of the German, Swiss or other European Supreme Courts will show. In France the notes appended by jurists to important decisions published in the *Recueil Dalloz* and *Recueil Sirey* enjoy high authority and often influence later decisions. A prominent example of reliance on writers in a common law court is the decision of the U.S. Supreme Court in the *Paquete Habana* case (see p. 62 supra).

The practice of the International Court of Justice and of its predecessor has typically been to refer to scholarly writings only in very general terms. Lauterpacht, The Development of International Law by the International Court 24 (1958). Lauterpacht suggests as a reason for the Court's reluctance to refer to writers: "There is no doubt that the availability of official records of the practice of States and of collections of treaties has substantially reduced the necessity for recourse to writings of publicists as evidence of custom. Moreover, the divergence of view among writers on many subjects as well as apparent national bias may often render citations from them unhelpful. On the other hand, in cases—admittedly rare—in which it is possible to establish the existence of a unanimous or practically unanimous interpretation, on the part of writers, of governmental or judicial practice, reliance on such evidence may add to the weight of the Judgments and Opinions of the Court." Id.

Although the Court itself has been reluctant to identify writers in its judgments and advisory opinions, it is evident from the pleadings and from the references in the separate and dissenting opinions of the judges that the opinions of authorities on international law have been brought to the attention of the Court and have often been taken into account by some of the judges. For a broad historical survey of the role and influence of "teachings" in the development of international law, see lectures by Judge Manfred Lachs, Teachings and Teaching of International Law, 151 Rec. des Cours 163–252 (1976–III).

The major treatises of international law usually cited by states and tribunals were generally produced by jurists of Western Europe. The citations in those treatises referred to state practice and judicial decisions in only a few countries. Most writers also relied heavily on quotations and paraphrases of statements by earlier writers. These highly selective tendencies, presented in support of broad conclusions of law were far from consistent with the prevailing doctrine of sources based on state practice accepted by law by states generally. Moreover, many of the well known treatises were written from the standpoint of national concerns and perceptions. Schachter has commented that

> many of the legal scholars had close links with their official communities and there were often pressures on them, sometimes obvious and sometimes subtle to conform to the official point of view. Even apart from such pressures, we recognize that social perspectives and values are generally shared by those in the same political and cultural community. * * * That a degree of bias is inescapable is recognized by the common assumption that more credible judgments on controversial issues of international law were more likely if made by a broadly representative body than by persons (however expert) from a single country or a particular political outlook.

Schachter, International Law in Theory and Practice at 38–39 (1991).

International bodies of "publicists" include the International Law Commission, an organ of the United Nations composed of 34 individuals elected by the U.N. General Assembly on the basis of government nominations and criteria of wide geographical representation. See Statute of the I.L.C., G.A. Res. 174–II (1947), art. 2. The I.L.C. is concerned, as indicated above (section 3) with the preparation of codification conventions and other draft treaties.

However, in the course of its work, and in its reports, positions are expressed by the Commission as a whole on existing rules of law. The I.C.J. has drawn on such reports for authority even when the I.L.C.'s study is still continuing. See, e.g., *Gabcikovo-Nagymaros* 1997 I.C.J. 7, para. 83 (citing Draft Articles on State Responsibility, adopted by I.L.C. on first reading in 1996).

A non-official body, the Institut de Droit International, established in 1873, is composed of about 120 members and associate members elected by the Institut on the basis of individual merit and published works. Its resolutions setting forth principles and rules of existing law and, on occasion, proposed rules, have often been cited by tribunals, states and writers. The biennial Annuaire de l'Institut contains its resolutions and the lengthy reports and records of discussion that preceded the resolution. For an account of its contribution from 1873 to 1973, see its centenary volume, Livre du Centenaire, Annuaire de l'Institut de Droit International (1973), particularly articles by Charles de Visscher and H. Battifol.

Another unofficial body, the International Law Association, (also founded in 1873), is organized in national branches in many countries. Resolutions adopted by majority votes at conferences of the Association are based on reports and studies of international committees. The multinational character of the Association adds weight to those of its resolutions that are adopted by consensus or large majorities representative of different regions and political systems. The biennial reports of the I.L.A. contain the resolutions and committee reports.

Another category of the writings of publicists is the Restatement of the Foreign Relations Law of the United States, prepared by recognized legal scholars and adopted after discussion by the American Law Institute, a non-official professional body. The first restatement appeared in 1965 designated curiously as the Restatement Second. A revised restatement was adopted in 1986 (Restatement Third). The Restatement contains rules of international law as it applies to the United States in its relations with other states and also rules of U.S. domestic law that have substantial significance for the foreign relations of the United States. Although this is a restatement of existing rules by a United States professional association, it does not purport to state the rules that the U.S. government would put forward or support in all cases. As stated in its introduction, "the Restatement in stating rules of international law represents the opinion of the American Law Institute as to the rules that an international tribunal would apply if charged with deciding a controversy in accordance with international law." In considering what a hypothetical international court would decide is an applicable rule, the American Law Institute adopts a standard that aims at an objective international determination of general international law.

Writings of authoritative international law scholars are published annually by the Hague Academy of International Law in its Collected Courses, often referred to by its French title, Recueil des Cours de l'Académie de Droit International (R.C.A.D.I., or Rec. des Cours). The scholars are selected by the international curatorium of the Academy on a broad geographical basis. Although Western European contributors have been heavily represented, there is increasing participation of scholars and practitioners from other areas and with diverse points of view. In addition to discussion of particular topics, the Recueil includes an annual comprehensive work by a well-known publicist under the heading of General Course. As of 2000, the Recueil includes approximately 300 published volumes. See also Schachter, Law-Making in the United Nations, in Perspectives on International Law (N. Jasentuliyana ed., 1995), pp. 119–137.

Notes

1. If "the most highly qualified publicists" are generally influenced by the interests and policies of their own states (and by their legal cultures), is their authority open to question on that ground? Would a tribunal look for majority opinions, "representative" views or "objective" data? Nardin, a political theorist, concluded that international law is founded not only on the customs of the community of states but on those of the community of international lawyers. T. Nardin, Law, Morality and the Relations of States 173 (1983). Schachter has described the "invisible college of international lawyers" as engaged in a continuous process of communication and collaboration across national lines. Schachter, The Invisible College of International Lawyers, 72 Northwestern Univ. L.Rev. 217 (1977).

2. Since the "leading" publicists are often engaged or consulted by their own governments, they influence state conduct and are in turn influenced by their governments. What advantages and drawbacks are likely in this dual role? Can the legal advisers of foreign offices meet the sometimes conflicting demands of their "clients" and the obligation to ascertain the law objectively? Do they have the double function of applying the law in the national interest and supporting the international legal system? See Report of a Joint Committee on The Role of the Legal Adviser of the State Department, 85 A.J.I.L. 358–71 (1991).

3. The vast increase in international law has naturally led to specialization. It is no longer possible for international lawyers to claim expertise on the subject as a whole. Many find it difficult to keep abreast of developments in any one of the main specialized areas. (In 2000, the American Society of International Law had more than 20 "interest groups.") Has this reduced the role of general international law? See D. Vagts, Are There No International Lawyers Anymore? 75 A.J.I.L. 134–37 (1981). Schachter argues for maintaining international law as a unified discipline. "The Invisible College of International Lawyers," supra at 221–23. See also T. Franck, Review Essay—The Case of the Vanishing Treatises, 81 A.J.I.L. 763 (1987).

SECTION 6. DECLARATIONS AND RESOLUTIONS; "SOFT LAW"

The international legal system has no organ directly comparable to a national legislature with power to make law by majority vote. The powers of the U.N. General Assembly under the U.N. Charter (arts. 13–14) are basically recommendatory. The U.N. Security Council has certain compulsory powers when acting under Chapter VII of the Charter, but only extraordinarily would it exercise these powers to prescribe rules of conduct in legislative fashion. Assertion of Security Council authority in the 1990s in an arguably law-making mode (e.g., to elaborate obligations in the wake of the 1990–91 Iraq–Kuwait conflict, or to specify aspects of humanitarian law in the context of former Yugoslavia or Rwanda) will be dealt with in Chapters 9, 12, and 15.

Pressures to fill what some perceive as a vacuum in international law-making have led to a variety of attempts at proclaiming, clarifying, or codifying standards of conduct, whether on the part of states or of other actors. Some of these modes, and the controversies surrounding them, are addressed in this section.

A. GENERAL ASSEMBLY RESOLUTIONS

FILARTIGA v. PENA–IRALA

United States Court of Appeals, Second Circuit, 1980.
630 F.2d 876.

[This was a wrongful death action which was brought in the federal district court (Eastern District, N.Y.) by two nationals of Paraguay, the father and sister of a 17–year old Paraguayan, who, it was alleged, was tortured to death in Paraguay by the defendant Pena–Irala who at the time was Inspector–General of the police. Jurisdiction was claimed principally on the basis of the Alien Tort Statute (28 U.S.C. § 1350) which provides: "The district courts shall have original jurisdiction of any civil action by an alien for a tort only, committed in violation of the law of nations or a treaty of the United States."

[The plaintiffs claimed that the conduct resulting in the wrongful death constituted torture which they contended violated the "law of nations" that is, international customary law. The District Court dismissed the complaint on jurisdictional grounds, the district judge considering himself bound by higher court decisions to construe "the law of nations" as used in the Alien Tort Law, as excluding that law which governs a state's treatment of its own citizens. On appeal, the Second Circuit Court of Appeals reversed the district court and ruled that the Alien Tort Law provides federal jurisdiction. The Court held that deliberate torture under the color of official authority violated the universal rules of international law regardless of the nationality of the parties. In reaching the conclusion that the prohibition of torture has become part of customary international law, the Court referred as evidence to the Universal Declaration of Human Rights and as particularly relevant, a 1975 U.N. General Assembly Declaration on the Protection of all Persons from Torture.

[Relevant portions of the Court's opinion follow:]

The Declaration [Against Torture] goes on to provide that "[w]here it is proved that an act of torture or other cruel, inhuman or degrading treatment or punishment has been committed by or at the instigation of a public official, the victim shall be afforded redress and compensation, in accordance with national law." This Declaration, like the [Universal] Declaration of Human Rights before it, was adopted without dissent by the General Assembly.

These U.N. declarations are significant because they specify with great precision the obligations of member nations under the Charter. Since their adoption, "[m]embers can no longer contend that they do not know what human rights they promised in the Charter to promote." Moreover, a U.N. Declaration is, according to one authoritative definition, "a formal and solemn instrument, suitable for rare occasions when principles of great and lasting importance are being enunciated." 34 U.N. ESCOR, Supp. (No. 8) 15,

U.N.Doc. E/cn. 4/1/610 (1962) (memorandum of Office of Legal Affairs, U.N. Secretariat). Accordingly, it has been observed that the Universal Declaration of Human Rights "no longer fits into the dichotomy of 'binding treaty' against 'non-binding pronouncement,' but is rather an authoritative statement of the international community." E. Schwelb, Human Rights and the International Community 70 (1964). Thus, a Declaration creates an expectation of adherence, and "insofar as the expectation is gradually justified by State practice, a declaration may by custom become recognized as laying down rules binding upon the States." 34 U.N. ESCOR, supra. Indeed, several commentators have concluded that the Universal Declaration has become, *in toto,* a part of binding, customary international law.

Turning to the act of torture, we have little difficulty discerning its universal renunciation in the modern usage and practice of nations. Smith, supra, 18 U.S. (5 Wheat.) at 160–61, 5 L.Ed. 57. The international consensus surrounding torture has found expression in numerous international treaties and accords. E.g., American Convention on Human Rights, Art. 5, OAS Treaty Series No. 36 at 1, OAS Off. Rec. OEA/Ser 4 v/II 23, doc. 21, rev. 2 (English ed., 1975) ("No one shall be subjected to torture or to cruel, inhuman or degrading punishment or treatment"); International Covenant on Civil and Political Rights, U.N. General Assembly Res. 2200 (XXI)A, U.N. Doc. A/6316 (Dec. 16, 1966) (identical language); European Convention for the Protection of Human Rights and Fundamental Freedoms, Art. 3, Council of Europe, European Treaty Series No. 5 (1968), 213 U.N.T.S. 211 *(semble).* The substance of these international agreements is reflected in modern municipal—i.e. national—law as well. Although torture was once a routine concomitant of criminal interrogations in many nations, during the modern and hopefully more enlightened era it has been universally renounced. According to one survey, torture is prohibited, expressly or implicitly, by the constitutions of over fifty-five nations, including both the United States and Paraguay. Our State Department reports a general recognition of this principle:

> There now exists an international consensus that recognizes basic human rights and obligations owed by all governments to their citizens * * *. There is no doubt that these rights are often violated; but virtually all governments acknowledge their validity.

Notes

1. After the *Filartiga* case was remanded to the district court, defendants took no part in the action (having been deported to Paraguay). A default judgment was granted and damages assessed by the U.S. district court to cover compensatory damages plus punitive damages of $5,000,000 to each plaintiff. Filartiga v. Pena–Irala, 577 F.Supp. 860 (E.D.N.Y.1984). The district court on remand also cited the General Assembly Declaration, particularly noting that it declared that the victim shall be afforded redress and compensation "in accordance with national law." Id. (These damage awards have not been collected, in the absence of assets of the defendants against which execution could be had.)

2. Did the Court's reliance on the General Assembly Declaration as evidence of a binding rule against torture have the effect of conferring on the Assembly a

degree of law-making authority inconsistent with the U.N. Charter? Does a "declaration" of a legal principle by the General Assembly have more weight than a resolution of a recommendatory character?

3. Does the Court's reference to the Universal Declaration as an "authoritative statement of the international community" imply a new "source" of international law other than treaty or custom? Would a declaration have obligatory force because it specified "with great precision" the obligations of member states under the Charter? If so, is there any reason to declare that the Declaration is customary law?

4. The Court refers to the "universal renunciation" of torture in usage and practice. However, reports of Amnesty International regularly show that torture is employed in many countries under color of official authority. Does that rebut a finding of "state practice" sufficiently consistent and general to support a finding of custom? Is "state practice" the laws prohibiting torture or the acts of torture by state officials?

5. Would the problem of inconsistent practice be avoided by treating the prohibition of torture as a general principle of law recognized in the law of all countries? Should a declaration by the General Assembly of a general principle of law be regarded as a definitive finding if adopted without dissent?

6. The Filartiga case has been widely cited in the United States for the proposition that certain human rights principles are customary law and therefore part of the law of the United States. See infra Chapter 8. Resolutions of the General Assembly have also been cited by national courts in many countries as evidence (or definitive proof) that a proposition of law expressed or implied by the resolution is binding international law. See C. Schreuer, Decisions of International Institutions before Domestic Courts (1981); L. Henkin, Resolutions of International Organizations in American Courts, in Essays on the Development of the International Legal Order (Kalshoven, Kuyper & Lammers, eds. 1980).

THE LEGAL EFFECT OF GENERAL ASSEMBLY RESOLUTIONS AND DECISIONS

The legal effect of General Assembly resolutions and other decisions has been a subject of much scholarly discussion and diverse views of governments. Article 38 of the Statute of the International Court (supra) does not mention resolutions or decisions of international organs as either a principal "source" or subsidiary means of determining applicable international law. Moreover, the U.N. Charter does not confer on the General Assembly power to enact binding rules of conduct. In contrast to the Security Council, it does not have authority to adopt binding decisions, except for certain organizational actions (such as admission of members and credentials). Such decisions can have "dispositive force and effect," as the International Court noted in its opinion in the Certain Expenses Case (1962 I.C.J. 163).

The more general problem of legal effect is raised by General Assembly resolutions and decisions that express or clearly imply legal principles or specific rules of law. The General Assembly has adopted some 8000 resolutions and numerous other decisions from 1946 to 2000. Some—probably fewer than 100—express general rules of conduct for states (as the Declaration against Torture in the Filartiga Case). They are usually formulated as "declarations" or "affirmations" of law. In many cases, they were the product of study and debate over many years and were adopted by consensus (without a vote) or by near-unanimity. Two other types of resolutions raise questions of legal effect:

1. resolutions dealing with specific situations and expressing or implying a general legal prescription for states, and

2. resolutions addressed to a particular state or states and implying that the conduct required of that state or states would be required of all states.

These resolutions, declarations or decisions may be considered by governments and by courts or arbitral tribunals as evidence of international custom or as expressing (and evidencing) a general principle of law. They may also serve to set forth principles for a future treaty (this has been the case for the Declaration against Torture and a number of other declarations in the field of human rights). The fact that a law-declaring resolution has been adopted without a negative vote or abstention is usually regarded as strong presumptive evidence that it contains a correct statement of law. A resolution that has less than unanimous support is more questionable. The size and composition of the majority, the intent and expectations of states, the political factors and other contextual elements are pertinent in judging the effect.

Notes

1. In the 1996 Advisory Opinion on Nuclear Weapons, p. 77 supra, at paras. 68–73, the I.C.J. examined a series of resolutions in which the General Assembly by large majority votes condemned nuclear weapons and characterized them as illegal. Yet the Court found that those resolutions fell short of establishing a rule of international law. What theories did the Court apply in assessing the potential legal significance of these resolutions?

Several of the separate and dissenting opinions addressed the problematic significance of General Assembly resolutions. Judge Schwebel wrote in dissent:

> In its opinion, the Court concludes that the succession of resolutions of the General Assembly on nuclear weapons "still fall short of establishing the existence of an *opinio juris* on the illegality of the use of such weapons". In my view, they do not begin to do so. * * * The continuing opposition, consisting as it does of States that bring together much of the world's military and economic power and a significant percentage of its population, more than suffices to deprive the resolutions in question of legal authority.
>
> The General Assembly has no authority to enact international law. None of the General Assembly's resolutions on nuclear weapons are declaratory of existing international law. The General Assembly can adopt resolutions declaratory of international law only if those resolutions truly reflect what international law is. If a resolution purports to be declaratory of international law, if it is adopted unanimously (or virtually so, qualitatively as well as quantitatively) or by consensus, and if it corresponds to State practice, it may be declaratory of international law. The resolutions of which resolution 1653 is the exemplar conspicuously fail to meet these criteria. While purporting to be declaratory of international law (yet calling for consultations about the possibility of concluding a treaty prohibition of what is so declared), they not

only do not reflect State practice, they are in conflict with it, as shown above. Forty-six States voted against or abstained upon the resolution, including the majority of the nuclear Powers. It is wholly unconvincing to argue that a majority of the Members of the General Assembly can "declare" international law in opposition to such a body of State practice and over the opposition of such a body of States. Nor are these resolutions authentic interpretations of principles or provisions of the United Nations Charter. The Charter contains not a word about particular weapons, about nuclear weapons, about *jus in bello*. To declare the use of nuclear weapons a violation of the Charter is an innovative interpretation of it, which cannot be treated as an authentic interpretation of Charter principles or provisions giving rise to obligations binding on States under international law. Finally, the repetition of resolutions of the General Assembly in this vein, far from giving rise, in the words of the Court, to "the nascent *opinio juris*", rather demonstrates what the law is not. When faced with continuing and significant opposition, the repetition of General Assembly resolutions is a mark of ineffectuality in law formation as it is in practical effect.

2. The International Court of Justice has referred to the General Assembly declarations on self-determination and independence of peoples in territories that have not yet attained independence as having legal effect, and as "enriching the *corpus juris gentium*." Adv. Op. on Namibia, 1971 I.C.J. 31; Adv. Op. on Western Sahara, 1975 I.C.J. 12. May these "declarations" be regarded as "authentic" interpretation of the principles of the Charter that already bind the member states and therefore as obligatory or legally authoritative for all members? Could it be plausibly argued that when such broad principles as self-determination and human rights are given more specific meaning in General Assembly declarations, they would go beyond "recommendations" and have a legislative effect beyond that authorized by the Charter? Can one assume that the governments voting in favor of such law-declaring resolutions intend to accept them as binding, rather than recommendatory? If they do not all have that intention, can the declaration be properly regarded as a binding interpretation of the Charter?

3. Does the General Assembly have law-making power when it makes a determination in specific cases? The International Court, in its 1971 *Advisory Opinion on Namibia* commented on the authority of the General Assembly to assume functions under the Mandate for South West Africa as follows: "For it would not be correct to assume that because the General Assembly is in principle vested with recommendatory powers, it is debarred from adopting in specific cases within the framework of its competence, resolutions which make determinations or have operative design" 1971 I.C.J. 50. Does this not mean that if an international body is given authority (i.e., competence to make decisions) such decisions when made by the requisite majority are binding? Would this include resolutions which recognize particular entities as states for purposes of participation in that body? Would it also include resolutions that treat items as within the competence of that body and as outside the exclusively domestic jurisdiction of a State?

4. At the San Francisco Conference of 1945 at which the Charter was drafted, a committee report noted that the General Assembly was competent to interpret the Charter, as such competence is "inherent in the functioning of any body which operates under an instrument defining its functions and powers." It then added that an interpretation of the Charter by the General Assembly would be binding on the member states if that interpretation "was generally accepted." Does this mean that the adoption of an interpretive resolution by unanimous vote (or near-unanimity) would be legally binding on the members? Would the question

arise whether the Charter was being interpreted or in effect amended? If such resolutions involve a significant modification of the rights and duties of members, should they not be required to follow the amendment procedure which involves ratification? When such broad principles as self-determination, equality of states, human rights, and political independence are construed and given more specific meaning, is there not inevitably a "legislative" component inherent in the interpretation?

Writings on this subject include Higgins, The Development of International Law Through the Political Organs of the United Nations (1963); Schachter, 178 Rec. des Cours 114–121 (1982–V); and Schachter, International Law in Theory and Practice 85–94 (1991).

TEXACO OVERSEAS PETROLEUM ET AL. v. LIBYAN ARAB REPUBLIC

International Arbitral Award, Jan. 19, 1977.
17 I.L.M. 1 (1978).

[In 1973 and 1974, Libya promulgated decrees purporting to nationalize all of the rights, interests and property of two international oil companies in Libya. The companies claimed such action by the Libyan Government violated the deeds of concession granted to them jointly by the Government. Under the arbitration clause of the concessions, the companies requested the President of the International Court of Justice to appoint a sole arbitrator to hear and determine the dispute. The Libyan Government opposed the request and filed a memorandum with the President of the Court contending, *inter alia,* that the disputes were not subject to arbitration because the nationalizations were acts of sovereignty. The President, after considering the Libyan memorandum, appointed a sole arbitrator, Professor Rene–Jean Dupuy. Libya did not take part in the subsequent proceedings, but the arbitrator specifically considered the points raised by Libya in its memorandum to the President of the Court. On January 19, 1977, the Sole Arbitrator delivered an Award on the Merits in favor of the companies. He held that the deeds of concession were binding on the parties, that the Government by adopting the nationalization decrees breached its obligations under the deeds of concession, and that the Government was bound to give the deeds full force and effect.

[In his decision, the Arbitrator considered the contention of Libya that the U.N. resolutions on permanent sovereignty over natural wealth and resources confirmed the sovereign rights to nationalize its natural resources and that the resolutions provide that any dispute related to nationalization or its consequences should be settled in accordance with the domestic law of the State concerned. In view of this contention, the Arbitrator considered the legal force of U.N. resolutions generally and specifically in respect of the resolutions on sovereignty over natural wealth and resources, including the Charter of Economic Rights and Duties of States. The text of his decision on these issues follows in unofficial English translation:]

Refusal to recognize any legal validity of United Nations Resolutions must, however, be qualified according to the various texts enacted by the United Nations. These are very different and have varying legal value, but it is impossible to deny that the United Nations' activities have had a significant influence on the content of contemporary international law. In appraising the legal validity of the above-mentioned Resolutions, this Tribunal will take account of the criteria usually taken into consideration, i.e., the examination of voting conditions and the analysis of the provisions concerned.

84. (1) With respect to the first point, Resolution 1803 (XVII) of 14 December 1962 was passed by the General Assembly by 87 votes to 2, with 12 abstentions. It is particularly important to note that the majority voted for this text, including many States of the Third World, but also several Western developed countries with market economies, including the most important one, the United States.

The principles stated in this Resolution were therefore assented to by a great many States representing not only all geographical areas but also all economic systems.

From this point of view, this Tribunal notes that the affirmative vote of several developed countries with a market economy was made possible in particular by the inclusion in the Resolution of two references to international law, and one passage relating to the importance of international cooperation for economic development. According to the representative of Tunisia:

> "* * * the result of the debate on this question was that the balance of the original draft resolution was improved—a balance between, on the one hand, the unequivocal affirmation of the inalienable right of States to exercise sovereignty over their natural resources and, on the other hand, the reconciliation or adaptation of this sovereignty to international law, equity and the principles of international cooperation." (17 U.N. GAOR 1122, U.N. Doc. A/PV. 1193 (1962).)

The reference to international law, in particular in the field of nationalization, was therefore an essential factor in the support given by several Western countries to Resolution 1803 (XVII).

85. On the contrary, it appears to this Tribunal that the conditions under which Resolutions 3171 (XXVII), 3201 (S–VI) and 3281 (XXIX) (Charter of the Economic Rights and Duties of States) were notably different:

— Resolution 3171 (XXVII) was adopted by a recorded vote of 108 votes to 1, with 16 abstentions, but this Tribunal notes that a separate vote was requested with respect to the paragraph in the operative part mentioned in the Libyan Government's Memorandum whereby the General Assembly stated that the application of the principle according to which nationalizations effected by States as the expression of their sovereignty implied that it is within the right of each State to determine the amount of possible compensation and the means of their payment, and that any dispute which might arise should be settled in conformity with the national law of each State instituting measures of this kind. As a consequence of a roll-call, this paragraph was adopted by 86 votes to 11 (Federal Republic of Germany, Belgium, Spain, United States, France, Israel, Italy, Japan, The Netherlands, Portugal, United Kingdom), with 28 abstentions (South Africa, Australia, Austria, Barbados, Canada, Ivory Coast, Denmark, Finland, Ghana, Greece, Haiti, India, Indonesia, Ireland, Luxembourg, Malawi, Malaysia, Nepal, Nicaragua, Norway, New Zealand, Philippines, Rwanda, Singapore, Sri Lanka, Sweden, Thailand, Turkey).

This specific paragraph concerning nationalizations, disregarding the role of international law, not only was not consented to by the most important Western countries, but caused a number of the developing countries to abstain.

— Resolution 3201 (S–VI) was adopted without a vote by the General Assembly, but the statements made by 38 delegates showed clearly and explicitly what was the position of each main group of countries. The Tribunal should therefore note that the most important Western countries were opposed to abandoning the compromise solution contained in Resolution 1803 (XVII).

— The conditions under which Resolution 3281 (XXIX), proclaiming the Charter of Economic Rights and Duties of States, was adopted also show unambiguously that there was no general consensus of the States with respect to the most important provisions and in particular those concerning nationalization. Having been the subject matter of a roll-call vote, the Charter was adopted by 118 votes to 6, with 10 abstentions. The analysis of votes on specific sections on the Charter is most significant insofar as the present case is concerned. From this point of view, paragraph 2(c) of Article 2 of the Charter, which limits consideration of the characteristics of compensation to the State and does not refer to international law, was voted by 104 to 16, with 6 abstentions, all of the industrialized countries with market economies having abstained or having voted against it.

86. Taking into account the various circumstances of the votes with respect to these Resolutions, this Tribunal must specify the legal scope of the provisions of each of these Resolutions for the instant case.

A first general indication of the intent of the drafters of the Charter of Economic Rights and Duties of States is afforded by the discussions which took place within the Working Group concerning the mandatory force of the future text. As early as the first session of the Working Group, differences of opinion as to the nature of the Charter envisaged gave rise to a very clear division between developed and developing countries. Thus, representatives of Iraq, Sri Lanka, Egypt, Kenya, Morocco, Nigeria, Zaire, Brazil, Chile, Guatemala, Jamaica, Mexico, Peru and Rumania held the view that the draft Charter should be a legal instrument of a binding nature and not merely a declaration of intention.

On the contrary, representatives of developed countries, such as Australia, France, Federal Republic of Germany, Italy, Japan, United Kingdom and United States expressed doubt that it was advisable, possible or even realistic to make the rights and duties set forth in a draft Charter binding upon States (Report of the Working Party on its 1st Session, U.N.Doc. TD/B/ AC.12/1 (1973), at 6).

The form of resolution adopted did not provide for the binding application of the text to those to which it applied, but the problem of the legal validity to be attached to the Charter is not thereby solved. In fact, while it is now possible to recognize that resolutions of the United Nations have a certain legal value, this legal value differs considerably, depending on the type of resolution and the conditions attached to its adoption and its provisions. Even under the assumption that they are resolutions of a declaratory nature, which is the case of the Charter of Economic Rights and Duties of States, the legal value is variable. Ambassador Castañeda, who was Chairman of the Working Group entrusted with the task of preparing this Charter, admitted that 'it is extremely difficult to determine with certainty the legal force of declaratory resolutions', that it is 'impossible to lay down a general rule in this respect', and that 'the legal value of the declaratory resolutions therefore includes an immense gamut of nuances' ('La Valeur Juridique des Resolutions des Nations Unies', 129 R.C.A.D.I. 204 (1970), at 319–320).

As this Tribunal has already indicated, the legal value of the resolutions which are relevant to the present case can be determined on the basis of circumstances under which they were adopted and by analysis of the principles which they stated:

— With respect to the first point, the absence of any binding force of the resolutions of the General Assembly of the United Nations implies that such resolutions must be accepted by the members of the United Nations in order to be legally binding. In this respect, the Tribunal notes that only Resolution 1803 (XVII) of 14 December 1962 was supported by a majority of Member States representing all of the various groups. By contrast, the other Resolutions mentioned above, and in particular those referred to in the Libyan Memorandum, were supported by a majority of States but not by any of the developed countries with market economies which carry on the largest part of international trade.

87. (2) With respect to the second point, to wit the appraisal of the legal value on the basis of the principles stated, it appears essential to this Tribunal to distinguish between those provisions stating the existence of a right on which the generality of the States has expressed agreement and those provisions introducing new principles which were rejected by certain representative groups of States and having nothing more than a *de lege ferenda* value only in the eyes of the States which have adopted them; as far as the others are concerned, the rejection of these same principles implies that they consider them as being *contra legem*. With respect to the former, which proclaim rules recognized by the community of nations, they do not create a custom but confirm one by formulating it and specifying its scope, thereby making it possible to determine whether or not one is confronted with a legal rule. As has been noted by Ambassador Casteñeda, "[such resolutions] do not create the law; they have a declaratory nature of noting what does exist" (129 R.C.A.D.I. 204 (1970), at 315).

On the basis of the circumstances of adoption mentioned above and by expressing an *opinio juris communis,* Resolution 1803 (XVII) seems to this Tribunal to reflect the state of customary law existing in this field. Indeed, on the occasion of the vote on a resolution finding the existence of a customary rule, the States concerned clearly express their views. The consensus by a majority of States belonging to the various representative groups indicates without the slightest doubt universal recognition of the rules therein incorporated, i.e., with respect to nationalization and compensation the use of the rules in force in the nationalizing State, but all this in conformity with international law.

88. While Resolution 1803 (XVII) appears to a large extent as the expression of a real general will, this is not at all the case with respect to the other Resolutions mentioned above, which has been demonstrated previously by analysis of the circumstances of adoption. In particular, as regards the Charter of Economic Rights and Duties of States, several factors contribute to denying legal value to those provisions of the document which are of interest in the instant case.

— In the first place, Article 2 of this Charter must be analyzed as a political rather than as a legal declaration concerned with the ideological strategy of development and, as such, supported only by non-industrialized States.

— In the second place, this Tribunal notes that in the draft submitted by the Group of 77 to the Second Commission (U.N. Doc. A/C.2/L. 1386 (1974), at 2), the General Assembly was invited to adopt the Charter "as a first measure of codification and progressive development" within the field of the international law of development. However, because of the opposition of several States, this description was deleted from the text submitted to the vote of the Assembly. This important modification led Professor Virally to declare:

> "It is therefore clear that the Charter is not a first step to codification and progressive development of international law, within the meaning of Article 13, para. 1(a) of the Charter of the United Nations, that is to say an instrument purporting to formulate in writing the rules of customary law and intended to better adjust its content to the requirements of international relations. The persisting difference of opinions in respect to some of its articles prevented reaching this goal and it is healthy that people have become aware of this." (La Charte des Droits et Devoirs Economiques des Etats. Notes de Lecture, 20 A.F.D.I. 57 (1974), at 59.)

The absence of any connection between the procedure of compensation and international law and the subjection of this procedure solely to municipal law cannot be regarded by this Tribunal except as a *de lege ferenda* formulation, which even appears *contra legem* in the eyes of many developed countries. Similarly, several developing countries, although having voted favorably on the Charter of Economic Rights and Duties of States as a whole, in explaining their votes regretted the absence of any reference to international law.

89. Such an attitude is further reinforced by an examination of the general practice of relations between States with respect to investments. This practice is in conformity, not with the provisions of Article 2(c) of the above-mentioned Charter conferring exclusive jurisdiction on domestic legislation and courts, but with the exception, stated at the end of this paragraph. Thus a great many investment agreements entered into between industrial States or their nationals, on the one hand, and developing countries, on the other, state, in an objective way, the standards of compensation and further provide, in case of dispute regarding the level of such compensation, the possibility of resorting to an international tribunal. In this respect, it is particularly significant in the eyes of this Tribunal that no fewer than 65 States, as of 31

October 1974, had ratified the Convention on the Settlement of Investment Disputes between States and Nationals of other States, dated March 18, 1965.

90. The argument of the Libyan Government, based on the relevant resolutions enacted by the General Assembly of the United Nations, that any dispute relating to nationalization or its consequences should be decided in conformity with the provisions of the municipal law of the nationalizing State and only in its courts, is also negated by a complete analysis of the whole text of the Charter of Economic Rights and Duties of States.

From this point of view, even though Article 2 of the Charter does not explicitly refer to international law, this Tribunal concludes that the provisions referred to in this Article do not escape all norms of international law. Article 33, paragraph 2, of this Resolution states as follows: "2. In their interpretation and application, the provisions of the present Charter are interrelated and each provision should be construed in the context of the other provisions." Now, among the fundamental elements of international economic relations quoted in the Charter, principle (j) is headed as follows: "Fulfillment in good faith of international obligations".

Analyzing the scope of these various provisions, Ambassador Castañeda, who chaired the Working Group charged with drawing up the Charter of Economic Rights and Duties of States, formally stated that the principle of performance in good faith of international obligations laid down in Chapter I(j) of the Charter applies to all matters governed by it, including, in particular, matters referred to in Article 2. Following his analysis, this particularly competent and eminent scholar concluded as follows:

> "The Charter accepts that international law may operate as a factor limiting the freedom of the State should foreign interests be affected, even though Article 2 does not state this explicitly. This stems legally from the provisions included in other Articles of the Charter which should be interpreted and applied jointly with those of Article 2." (La Charte des Droits et Devoirs Economiques des Etats. Note sur son Processus d'Elaboration, 20 A.F.D.I. 31 (1974), at 54.)

91. Therefore, one should note that the principle of good faith, which had already been mentioned in Resolution 1803 (XVII), has an important place even in Resolution 3281 (XXIX) called "The Charter of Economic Rights and Duties of States". * * *

Note

Even if the General Assembly resolutions of 1974 referred to in the arbitral award cannot be considered as declaratory of international law (because of lack of general consensus), are they significant evidence of a *lack* of consensus in support of principles previously adopted in 1962? Does the disappearance of a prior consensus erode a rule once part of customary law? May one conclude from the division of opinion (and of *opinio juris*) expressed in 1974 and prior thereto that there is no generally agreed customary law rule on the issue of the law applicable to compensation for taking of alien property? (See U.S. Supreme Court decision in

Sabbatino Case, p. 181 infra). Should the Arbitrator have considered this question in the above case?

B. CODES, GUIDELINES, STANDARDS, AND POLICY STATEMENTS

Voluntary codes and guidelines. International organizations have adopted a variety of texts, called "codes of conduct" or "guidelines," which prescribe norms for state conduct and, in some cases, for conduct of non-state entities. Such texts are recognized as "non-binding". They are usually drafted in hortatory rather than obligatory language. However, it is clear that the states voting for such non-binding codes or guidelines intend them to be followed in practice. In many cases, the texts provide for reports by governments and for periodic review by an international organ. In some cases, specific cases of non-compliance may be brought to the attention of the competent international organ.

Examples of such codes or guidelines are mainly found in economic and social fields. Foreign investment and transnational corporations have been the subject of several such texts, such as the U.N. Code on Restrictive Business Practices, 19 I.L.M. 813 (1981), and the World Bank Guidelines on the Treatment of Foreign Direct Investment 31 I.L.M. 1363 (1992). The United Nations engaged for many years unsuccessfully in work on a comprehensive code of conduct for transnational corporations. See Chapters 10 and 20.

The specialized agencies of the United Nations have relied on voluntary codes for important areas of international regulation. For example, the World Health Organization has adopted an International Code for the Marketing of Breast Milk Substitutes, 20 I.L.M. 1004 (1981), and the Food and Agriculture Organization jointly with the World Health Organization has promulgated the Codex Alimentarius for the codification of food standards.

The W.H.O. Code on Breast Milk Substitutes was adopted by the World Health Assembly in 1981 with near-unanimity, the only dissenting vote cast by the United States. The Code is concerned with a single product, infant milk substitutes. Its main object is to prohibit certain marketing and promotional activities that foster inappropriate and dangerous use of the milk substitutes in poor countries especially those with inadequate sanitation and clean water. The Code was legally a W.H.O. recommendation, not a binding set of rules. It is addressed to governments, to private firms, to institutions (such as hospitals), and to the medical and nursing professions. A few countries enacted the Code as a whole into domestic law; a considerable number gave legal effect to major parts of the Code. Some of the principal producers of the milk-substitutes at first resisted the Code, most notably Nestlé, by far the largest producer. In reaction, a group of non-governmental organizations instituted an international boycott of Nestlé which resulted in major changes by the company in its marketing and promotional activities, though some practices were still regarded as violations of the Code and as grounds for continued boycott. See N.E. Zelman, The Nestlé Infant Formula Controversy: Restricting the Marketing Practices of Multinational Corporation in the Third World, 3 Transnational Lawyer 697 (1990).

A joint project of the Food and Agriculture Organization and the World Health Organization, the Codex Alimentarius provides an institutional framework for the codification of food standards that are necessary for "protecting the health of consumers and ensuring fair practices in the food trade." Statutes, Article 1. Codex Alimentarius Commission Procedural Manual 5 (7th ed. 1989). Established in 1962, the Codex covers "all principal foods, whether processed, semi-processed or raw, for distribution to the consumer. * * * It also includes provisions of an advisory nature in the form of codes of practice, guidelines and other recommended measures." Id. at 23. Governments may respond to new standards proposed by the Codex Alimentarius Commission in one of four ways: full acceptance, target acceptance, acceptance with specific deviations, or no acceptance. Governments that refuse to accept a standard, or that prefer target acceptance, must provide an explanation of the way its own food requirements differ from the proposed ones, and must indicate whether they will allow the free distribution within their own borders of a product complying with the standard. The success of the Codex is not only to be measured by the number of acceptances for the standards, as the Codex also has exerted a powerful influence on non-accepting states, as well as food growers, packagers, transporters, and preparers. In 1979 the Codex Alimentarius Commission enacted a Code of Ethics for International Trade in Food, which recommends that "all those engaging in the international trade in food commit themselves morally to this Code and undertake voluntarily to support its implementation in the larger interest of the world community." Document CAC/RCP 20–1979, Rev. I (1985).

International standards. The conception of "generally accepted international standards" has emerged in the treaties on the law of the sea and has been extended to other fields, particularly the law of the environment. Such standards may be adopted in a treaty or by international organizations pursuant to a treaty. With respect to standards relating to marine safety and related matters, the Restatement (Third) has taken the position that "once a standard has been generally accepted, a state is obligated in particular to apply it to all ships flying its flag and to adopt any necessary laws or regulations" (section 502, Comment *c*). This obligation is said to apply to all states whether or not parties to the convention by virtue of customary law. The Restatement also declares that a similar principle requires all states to conform to international rules or standards derived from international conventions or adopted by international organizations pursuant to such conventions. Restatement (Third) section 601 and Comment *b*.

Oxman writes:

> The duty entails a legally binding obligation to observe generally accepted standards. This obligation, however, is created by general acceptance of a standard in fact, rather than by the procedure by which the standard was articulated. Thus, it creates a useful bridge between so-called "soft law" and "hard law." This, indeed, was part of its original function. Where appropriate, standards (or guidelines) can be developed in a somewhat more relaxed procedural environment which is not specifically designed to generate legally binding obligations as such; yet those same standards can become legally binding if they become generally accepted.
>
> The effect of the duty under discussion is to impose a legal obligation on a state to respect a standard which it would not otherwise be legally

> bound to respect. The consensual requirements of international law for the imposition of legal obligations are not offended by this proposition; those requirements have previously been satisfied through acceptance of the general duty either by treaty or by customary international law. It is unnecessary to restrict the scope of the duty itself to conform to such requirements.

B. Oxman, The Duty to Respect Generally Accepted International Standards, 24 N.Y.U.J.Int. L. & Pol. 143–44 (1991).

International rules of non-governmental bodies. International non-governmental organization in various fields adopt rules and standards in their respective fields of activity, many of which are given effect by official agencies, courts, and international organizations. Technical and scientific bodies in particular are authoritative sources of norms that are incorporated by reference or explicitly into rules observed by states and public agencies. Examples include the International Organization for Standardization of Weights and Measures and the International Air Transportation Association.

A more striking example of an international non-governmental legal regime is the Olympic Movement. The Olympic Charter vests "supreme authority in the International Olympic Committee (IOC)" and provides that "any person or organization belonging in any capacity to the Olympic Movement is bound by the provisions of the Charter and shall abide by the decisions of the IOC." The rules, by-laws and decisions of the IOC constitute an autonomous regime governing the relevant sports world and given effect as such by governments. A study by a European scholar in 1988 noted that "the sui generis law of the Olympic Movement is accepted, respected and applied as a State-independent body of legal rules in a growing number of municipal court decisions." Bruno Simma, quoted in J. Nafziger, International Sports Law, 86 A.J.I.L. 489, 492 (1992). When Olympic arrangements were challenged in the U.S., the Ninth Circuit declared that "[t]he Olympic Games are organized and conducted under the terms of an international agreement—the Olympic Charter. We are extremely hesitant * * * to alter an event that is staged * * * under the terms of that agreement." Martin v. IOC, 740 F.2d 670, 677 (9th Cir.1984). See also Behagen v. Amateur Basketball Ass'n of U.S., 884 F.2d 524, 527 (10th Cir.1989) (noting the centrality of the IOC in "governing structures for * * * American involvement in international amateur sports"). The decision of the IOC to exclude South African athletes from international competition between 1964 and 1991 for violating its rule against apartheid laws was effectively observed. IOC rules on substance abuse and "doping" have been accepted as binding on all, though in practice supervision has been inconsistent and some times haphazard (Nafziger at 503).

At the opening of the 21st century, the challenges of cyberspace raise new versions of problems of standard-setting in a global context. A variety of regulatory and self-regulatory functions are being handled by private bodies, such as the Internet Corporation for Assigned Names and Numbers, a non-profit corporation. A Memorandum of Understanding on the Generic Top Level Domain Name Space of the Internet Domain Name System has been signed by some 200 mainly non-governmental entities and deposited with the International Telecommunications Union (cited in Spiro, Globalization, International Law, and the Academy, 32 N.Y.U. J.Int'l L. & Politics 567, 571 n. 6 (2000)).

Political declarations and concerted acts. Governments engage in concerted acts of various kinds that express common understandings and positions but which are not recognized as treaties or customary law. Such acts may be expressed informally, as in a communiqué after an exchange of views. On occasion they are expressed in formal instruments, such as the Final Act of the Helsinki Conference in 1975. "Gentlemen's agreements" are not uncommon. They are not binding but they may be strictly observed as long as the parties consider them useful. For a further discussion of non-binding agreements, see Chapter 7.

Political declarations have been used instead of treaties in processes of settling major disputes. For example, at the end of the Second World War, the most important understandings relating to territorial disposition and post-war organization were expressed in declarations at the Yalta, Potsdam and Cairo Conferences.

It has been suggested in recent writings that the so-called purely political instruments may have legal consequences. Schachter considers that as such instruments are official acts of states, they are evidence of the positions taken by states and "it is appropriate to draw inferences that the States concerned have recognized the principles, rules, status and rights acknowledged. This does not mean that 'new law' or a new obligation is created. However, where the points of law are not entirely clear and are disputed the evidence of official positions drawn from these instruments can be significant." Schachter, International Law in Theory and Practice at 129. A non-legal text may also over time become customary law on the basis of state practice and *opinio juris*. That consequence does not depend on the original intent of the parties to the instrument.

What are the implications of non-compliance with a non-legal declaration? Schachter suggests:

> * * * States entering into a non-legal commitment generally view it as a political (or moral) obligation and intend to carry it out in good faith. Other parties and other States concerned have reason to expect such compliance and to rely on it. What we must deduce from this, I submit, is that the political texts which express commitments and positions of one kind or another are governed by the general principle of good faith. Moreover, since good faith is an accepted general principle of international law, it is appropriate and even necessary to apply it in its legal sense. Id. at 130.

A significant practical consequence of the "good faith" principle is that a party which committed itself in good faith to a course of conduct or to recognition of a legal situation would be estopped from acting inconsistently with its commitment or adopted position when the circumstances showed that other parties reasonably relied on that undertaking or position.

These problems were considered by the Institut de droit international in 1983. See reports of 7th Commission (Virally, rapporteur) and comments of members. 60–I Ann. de l'Institut de droit int'l 166–374 (1983) and 60–II id. 117–54. (1984). See also Schachter, "Non–Conventional Concerted Acts" in M.

Bedjaoui (ed.) International Law, Achievements and Prospects 265–269 (1991).

Other forms of "soft law." "Soft law" has been defined as "international law-making that is designed, in whole or part, not to be enforceable." See W.M. Reisman, The Supervisory Jurisdiction of the International Court of Justice, 258 Rec. des Cours 180–182 (1996); Reisman, The Concept and Functions of Soft Law in International Politics, in 1 Essays in Honor of Judge T.O. Elias 135 (J.A. Omotola, ed., 1992). Yet soft law may entail some legal effects, and may well elicit compliance even in the absence of direct mechanisms for enforcement.

A recent collaborative project of the American Society of International Law seeks to understand the uses of soft law and to identify factors that may make soft law effective in influencing international behavior. The project takes up case studies in diverse areas: environment and natural resources (General Assembly ban on driftnet fishing, codes of conduct on pesticides and chemicals, agreed measures concerning Antarctica); trade and finance (e.g., money laundering); human rights (protection of minorities, labor standards, principles for corporate investment in repressive societies such as South Africa under apartheid); and multilateral arms control (missile control technology regime, physical protection of nuclear materials, and land mines). The contributors also consider whether there is a conceptual distinction between binding and non-binding norms or rather a continuum. See D. Shelton (ed.), Commitment and Compliance: The Role of Non-Binding Norms in the International Legal System (2000).

Questions of compliance and enforcement—whether of "hard" or "soft" norms—will be revisited in Chapter 9.

Chapter 3

INTERNATIONAL LAW AND MUNICIPAL LAW

SECTION 1. GENERAL CONSIDERATIONS

International law is binding on the state, and the state is obliged to give effect to it, but states make and apply international law through their governments and their constitutional and legal systems. International law does not replace the domestic ("municipal") law of states; indeed international law depends on the governments of states and their legal systems. The obligation to respect and give effect to international law is upon the state, not upon any particular branch, institution, or member of its government, but the state is responsible for violations by any branch of its government or by any official (and in some contexts also for acts and omissions by private individuals). The state is responsible to assure that its constitution and its laws enable its government to carry out its international obligations.

It should go without saying that a state cannot plead its own law as a reason for non-compliance with international law. In 1887, for example, U.S. Secretary of State Bayard declared:

> [I]t is only necessary to say, that if a Government could set up its own municipal laws as the final test of its international rights and obligations, then the rules of international law would be but the shadow of a name and would afford no protection either to States or to individuals. It has been constantly maintained and also admitted by the Government of the United States that a Government can not appeal to its municipal regulations as an answer to demands for the fulfillment of international duties. Such regulations may either exceed or fall short of the requirements of international law, and in either case that law furnishes the test of the nation's liability and not its own municipal rules. * * *

[1887] U.S. Foreign Rel. 751, 753.

Article 13 of the Declaration of Rights and Duties of States prepared by the International Law Commission in 1949 provides: "Every State has the duty to carry out in good faith its obligations arising from treaties and other sources of international law, and it may not invoke provisions in its constitution or its laws as an excuse for failure to perform this duty." See Vienna Convention on the Law of Treaties, art. 46; Restatement (Third), § 311(3). There is an abundance of decisions and opinions of international courts and tribunals recognizing this principle. See, e.g., Case Concerning Certain German Interests in Polish Upper Silesia (Merits), P.C.I.J., Ser. A, No. 7, at 19, 22, 42 (1926); Case Concerning the Factory at Chorzów (Merits), P.C.I.J., Ser. A, No. 17 at 33–34 (1928); Free Zones Cases, P.C.I.J., Ser. A/B, No. 46, at 167 (1932); The Greco–Bulgarian "Communities," Advisory Opinion, P.C.I.J., Ser A, No. 17, at 32 (1930); Treatment of Polish Nationals and Other Persons of Polish Origin or Speech in Danzig Territory, Advisory Opinion, P.C.I.J., Ser. A/B, No. 44, at 24 (1932); Case Concerning Rights of Nationals of the United States of America in Morocco (France v. U.S.), 1952 I.C.J. 176; Norwegian Shipowners' Claims (Norway v. U.S.), 1922, 1 U.N.Rep. Int'l Arb. Awards 307; Shufeldt Claim (U.S.v. Guatemala), 1930, 2 U.N.Rep. Int'l Arb. Awards 1079.

Monism, dualism, and their variants.

Two principal "schools" have seen the relation of international law to municipal law differently. Dualists (or pluralists) regard international law and municipal law as separate legal systems which operate on different levels. For dualists, international law can be applied by municipal courts only when it has been "transformed" or "incorporated" into municipal law. Further, international law, as incorporated into municipal law, is subject to constitutional limitations applicable to all domestic law, and may be repealed or superseded by act of parliament for purposes of domestic law. Dualists also emphasize the international legal personality of states, rather than of individuals or other entities. Monists, on the other hand, have regarded international law and municipal law as parts of a single legal system. In a traditional version of monism, municipal law is seen as ultimately deriving its validity from international law, which stands "higher" in a hierarchy of legal norms. Therefore, international law cannot be subject to domestic law, not even to constitutional limitations. Monists find it easier to maintain that individuals have international legal personality.

There have been efforts to surmount the dichotomy between dualism and monism and to develop other approaches. See Borchard, The Relation Between International Law and Municipal Law, 27 Va.L.Rev. 137 (1940). For a general discussion, see Ferrari–Bravo, International and Municipal Law: The Complementarity of Legal Systems, in The Structure and Process of International Law (Macdonald & Johnston eds. 1983). By the late twentieth century, the dualist-monist debates had largely subsided, as particular states adopted their own variants of one school or the other, and did so not from jurisprudential persuasion but from their own historic, political and constitutional commitments.

Notes

1. The United States has never doubted the supremacy of international law in principle, but neither the President, Congress, nor the courts will give effect to a norm of customary international law or to a treaty provision that is inconsistent with the U.S. Constitution. See p. 197 infra. On several occasions, in becoming a party to human rights treaties, the United States has entered reservations or understandings to assure that it would not be undertaking international obligations that it would be unable to carry out because to do so would violate the U.S. Constitution. See Chapters 7 and 8 infra.

2. International law requires a state to carry out its international obligations but, in general, how a state accomplishes that result is not of concern to

international law or to the state system. In some instances, however, states may undertake to carry out their obligations by particular means, for example, by enacting legislation or by taking specified executive or judicial measures. See, e.g., the 1966 Covenant on Civil and Political Rights, Article 2, 999 U.N.T.S. 171. The 1948 Genocide Convention requires states parties to make genocide a crime under domestic law. Convention on the Prevention and Punishment of the Crime of Genocide, Articles V & VI, 78 U.N.T.S. 277. The Convention Against Torture and Other Cruel, Inhuman, or Degrading Treatment or Punishment provides in Article 4(1) that "each state party shall ensure that all acts of torture are offences under its criminal law." See Chapter 8.

Since a state's responsibility to give effect to international obligations does not fall upon any particular institution of its government, international law does not necessarily require that domestic courts apply and give effect to international obligations. (Of course, insofar as international law accords immunity from the jurisdiction of courts, say to a foreign state or to its diplomats, the exercise of jurisdiction by a domestic court contrary to the limitations of international law would constitute a violation by the state.) States differ as to whether international law is incorporated into domestic law and forms a part of "the law of the land," and whether the executive or the courts will give effect to norms of international law or to treaty provisions in the absence of their implementation by domestic legislation.

3. International tribunals have sometimes declared municipal legislation to be subject to international obligations. In 1999, for example, a dispute settlement panel of the World Trade Organization ruled on a petition brought by the European Union which contended that Sections 301–310 of the U.S. Trade Act were incompatible with U.S. obligations under the General Agreement on Tariffs and Trade and WTO agreements. The panel invoked the general rules of public international law for the proposition that a state is expected to ensure conformity of its domestic legislation to its international obligations. See Report of the Panel, *United States—Sections 301–310 of the Trade Act of 1974*, WT/DS152/R (Dec. 22, 1999), para. 7.80, discussed further in Chapter 9 at p. 692. In 1987 the U.S. Congress enacted the Anti–Terrorism Act containing provisions that the U.N. Secretary–General believed to be inconsistent with the U.N. Headquarters Agreement. The Secretary–General requested arbitration to resolve the dispute, as provided in the Agreement. In an advisory opinion, the International Court of Justice concluded that a dispute existed and that the United States was obliged to enter into arbitration. Applicability of the Obligation to Arbitrate Under Section 21 of the United Nations Headquarters Agreement of June 26, 1947, 1988 I.C.J. 12 (advisory opinion). International human rights tribunals have declared municipal legislation invalid as inconsistent with a state's obligations under international human rights conventions.

In many cases international tribunals have awarded damages because a state's courts have disregarded or misapplied international law. For example, an arbitral tribunal awarded damages to Great Britain for the detention or condemnation in the United States of six British vessels as prize during the American Civil War, holding that in these cases the condemnation or detention was contrary to international law, although it had been upheld by the Supreme Court as lawful. 3 Moore, International Arbitrations 3209–10 (1898); 4 id. 3902, 3911, 3928, 3935, 3950 (1898). In such cases the international tribunal normally has no power to reverse or set aside the judgment of the municipal court, which may continue to have legal effect (e.g., to pass title to property); but the international tribunal will award damages to the aggrieved state.

4. Questions of municipal law may arise in disputes between states, and international tribunals may find it necessary to interpret such law. This may happen, for example, in disputes arising out of alleged breaches of state contracts. In the *Serbian Loans* and *Brazilian Loans* cases, the Permanent Court of International Justice had to determine the meaning and effect of French legislation governing payments of debts in gold or at gold value. P.C.I.J., Ser. A, Nos. 20/21, at 5, 40–47, 93, 120–125 (1929). In construing this legislation, the Court attached controlling weight to the manner in which it had been applied by the French courts, saying:

> Once the Court has arrived at the conclusion that it is necessary to apply the municipal law of a particular country, there seems no doubt that it must seek to apply it as it would be applied in that country. . . .
>
> It follows that the Court must pay the utmost regard to the decisions of the municipal courts of a country, for it is with the aid of their jurisprudence that it will be enabled to decide what are the rules which, in actual fact, are applied in the country the law of which is recognized as applicable in a given case.

Id. at 124–25.

Where international law requires exhaustion of local remedies as a condition of pursuing international relief, see p. 755 infra, an international tribunal may consider the adequacy of a state's judicial and administrative procedures and even the judgments of its courts. In 1989, a chamber of the International Court of Justice considered Italian judicial and administrative procedures, decisions of its courts and administrative tribunals, and the weight to be given to their interpretation of Italian law. See Case Concerning Elettronica Sicula S.p.A. (ELSI) (U.S. v. Italy), 1989 I.C.J. 15.

5. International tribunals may have authority to apply or give effect to certain aspects of municipal law. For example, although the Statutes of the International Criminal Tribunals for the Former Yugoslavia and Rwanda are grounded in international law (rather than domestic criminal laws or procedures), the provisions on penalties instruct the Tribunals to take account of sentencing practices in the countries in question. See, e.g. Statute of the I.C.T.Y., art. 24(1), U.N. Doc. S/25704 (May 3, 1993), reprinted at 32 I.L.M. 1163, 1186 (1993). In the *Tadic* appeal, one of the issues considered by the I.C.T.Y.'s Appellate Chamber was the defendant's claim that the 20–year sentence imposed by the Trial Chamber was excessive in relation to the laws of the former Yugoslavia, under which a 20–year maximum sentence could be imposed only as an alternative to the death penalty. *Tadic*, Case No. IT–94–1 (Appellate Judgment of July 15, 1999).

SECTION 2. INTERNATIONAL LAW IN THE LAW OF THE UNITED STATES

A. INTERNATIONAL LAW AS "LAW OF THE LAND"

1. Reception of International Law Into U.S. Law

HENKIN, INTERNATIONAL LAW AS LAW IN THE UNITED STATES

82 Mich. L.Rev. 1555 (1984) (footnotes omitted).

"International law is part of our law." Justice Gray's much-quoted pronouncement in *The Paquete Habana* was neither new nor controversial when made in 1900, since he was merely restating what had been established principle for the fathers of American jurisprudence and for their British legal ancestors. And Gray's dictum remains unquestioned today. But, after more than two hundred years in our jurisprudence, the import of that principle is still uncertain and disputed. How did, and how does, international law become part of our law? * * *

When international law—"the law of nations"—first became part of our law can be readily stated: *how* it became our Law has been a conceptual issue not without jurisprudential implications. That it is part of federal, not state, law has been recognized only recently.

International law became part of "our law" with independence in 1776. One view has it that the law of nations came into our law as part of the common law. In the eighteenth century, the law of nations was part of the law of England, and English law, including the law of nations, applied in her colonies. With American independence, the law of England in the colonies (including the law of nations) was "received" as common law in the United States.

A different conception sees the law of nations as coming into our law not by "inheritance" but by implication from our independence, by virtue of international statehood. An entity that becomes a State in the international system is *ipso facto* subject to international law. While the obligations of international law are upon the State as an entity, a State ordinarily finds it necessary or convenient to incorporate international law into its municipal law to be applied by its courts. In the United States, neither state constitutions nor the federal Constitution, nor state or federal legislation, have expressly incorporated international law; from our beginnings, however, following the English tradition, courts have treated international law as incorporated and applied it as domestic law.

The two conceptions, and variations upon them, may bear different consequences. If international law was part of the common law that each state received from England, international law was state law. It would cease to be state law and become federal law only if the U.S. Constitution, or an act of Congress pursuant to the Constitution, so provided. On the other hand, if international law became domestic law by virtue of independence, its status as state or federal law may turn on the international character of our independence and the status of the states between 1776 and 1789. Some have insisted that during those years the states were thirteen independent states (in the international sense), each equal in status to England, France and other nations of the time, each subject to international law. Each state decided for itself whether to incorporate international law, but all of them did so, in the tradition inherited from England. On this view, as on the "common law" view, international law was state law between 1776 and 1789 and remained state law unless the federal Constitution or later federal law pursuant to the Constitution rendered it federal law.

A different view, however, concludes that the thirteen states were never independent States; that for international purposes we were from independence one nation, not thirteen. By virtue of independence and statehood, international law became binding on the United States, not on the individual states. Between 1776 and 1789, there being no national domestic law, international law could not be incorporated into national law, but the national obligations of the United States could be carried out through state law and institutions. In 1789, the obligations of the United States to give effect to international law became effectively the responsibility of the new federal government, to be carried out through federal institutions (including federal courts), through state institutions (including state courts), or both.

THE INTERPLAY OF U.S. AND INTERNATIONAL LAW

RESTATEMENT (THIRD), PART I, CHAPTER 2

Introductory Note

International law and the domestic law of the United States are two different and discrete bodies of law, but often they impinge on the same conduct, relations, and interests. The relation between international law and United States law raises complex conceptual issues that have important legal consequences.

The obligations of the United States under international law do not rest on the international plane alone: International law is, and is given effect as, law in the United States. But, like the strictly domestic law of the United States, international law as law of the United States is subject to the Constitution, and is also subject to "repeal" by other law of the United States. See § 111, Comment *a*, and § 115. When international law is not given effect in the United States because of constitutional limitations or supervening domestic law, the international obligations of the United States remain and the United States may be in default. See § 115, Comment *b*.

International law as United States law. International law was part of the law of England and, as such, of the American colonies. With independence, it became part of the law of each of the thirteen States. When the United States became a state it became subject to international law. See § 206. From the beginning, the law of nations, later referred to as international law, was considered to be incorporated into the law of the United States without the need for any action by Congress or the President, and the courts, State and federal, have applied it and given it effect as the courts of England had done. Customary international law as developed to that time was law of the United

States when it became a state. Customary law that has developed since the United States became a state is incorporated into United States law as of the time it matures into international law. Under the Supremacy Clause, self-executing treaties concluded by the United States become law of the United States as of the time they come into force for the United States. See § 111(3) and § 115, Comment *c*. As to non-self-executing treaties, see § 111(4) and Comment *h* to that section.

The Constitution declares treaties of the United States (as well as the Constitution itself and the laws of the United States) to be "the supreme Law of the Land" (Article VI), and provides that cases arising under treaties are within the Judicial Power of the United States (Article III, Section 2). The status of other international agreements and of customary international law is not clearly indicated. During the reign of Swift v. Tyson, 41 U.S. (16 Pet.) 1, 10 L.Ed. 865 (1842), State and federal courts respectively determined international law for themselves as they did common law, and questions of international law could be determined differently by the courts of various States and by the federal courts. From the beginning, the interpretation or application of United States treaties by State courts was subject to review by the Supreme Court of the United States under Section 25 of the Judiciary Act of 1789, but the Court originally thought that it could not review State court determinations or applications of customary international law. See § 111, Reporters' Note 3. Similarly, after Congress gave the inferior federal courts "federal question" jurisdiction (Section I of the Judiciary Act of 1875, 18 Stat. 470), issues arising under customary international law, unlike those arising under treaties, apparently were not considered federal questions, and therefore did not provide a basis for such jurisdiction. Claims based on customary international law in State courts (unlike those based on treaties) did not provide a basis for removal to the federal courts.

Erie R.R. Co. v. Tompkins, 304 U.S. 64, 58 S.Ct. 817, 82 L.Ed. 1188 (1938), held that, in suits based on diversity of citizenship jurisdiction, a federal court was bound to apply the common law as determined by the courts of the State in which the federal court sat. On that basis, some thought that the federal courts must also follow State court determinations of customary international law. However, a different view has prevailed. It is now established that customary international law in the United States is a kind of federal law, and like treaties and other international agreements, it is accorded supremacy over State law by Article VI of the Constitution. Hence, determinations of international law by the Supreme Court of the United States, like its interpretations of international agreements, are binding on the States. See § 111, Comment *d*, § 112(2) and Comment *a* to that section, § 326, Comment *d*. Also, cases "arising under" customary international law arise under "the laws" of the United States. They are within the Judicial Power of the United States (Article III, Section 2) and the jurisdiction of the federal courts (28 U.S.C. §§ 1257, 1331). See § 111(2) and Comment *e* to that section. * * *

Note

The views expressed by Henkin and the Restatement have been followed in numerous federal cases, and have been recognized as "settled" and characterized as the "modern position." But recently they have been challenged by some writers in some respects. See Trimble, A Revisionist View of Customary International Law, 33 U.C.L.A. L. Rev. 668 (1986); Weisburd, The Executive Branch and International Law, 41 Vand. L. Rev. 1205 (1988); Weisburd, State Courts, Federal Courts, and International Cases, 20 Yale J. Int'l L. 1 (1995); and notably, beginning in 1997, by Professors Bradley and Goldsmith in Customary International Law as Federal Common Law: A Critique of the Modern Position, 110 Harv. L. Rev. 815 (1997). For Bradley and Goldsmith, the modern doctrine "portends a dramatic transfer of constitutional authority from the state to the world community and to the federal judiciary." Id. at 846. Bradley and Goldsmith, jointly and severally, have pursued their attack on the modern position in other articles and have applied their views to challenge in particular the federal cases applying international human rights law as part of the "law of nations," such as the *Filartiga* case, p. 143. Others have responded in defense of the modern position. See, e.g., Koh, Is International Law Really State Law?, 111 Harv. L. Rev. 1824 (1998); Neuman, Sense and Nonsense About Customary International Law: A Response to Professors Bradley and Goldsmith, 66 Fordham L. Rev. 371 (1997). For more on aspects of this controversy, see pp. 169–171 below.

THE LAW OF NATIONS AS UNITED STATES LAW

MEEKER, THE LAW OF NATIONS IN THE NATIONAL GOVERNMENT

1 Whiteman 106.

In looking at the function and place of the law of nations in the national government, we are bound to begin asking how, and in what ways, the United States becomes concerned with the body of international law. * * * The Constitutional provision is familiar which gives Congress the power "To define and punish * * * Offenses against the Law of Nations;". (Art. I, sec. 8, cl. 10).

Before the Constitution, it is interesting to note, the Chief Justice of Pennsylvania stated, in Respublica v. de Longchamps, that that case was "one of first impression in the United States. It must be determined on the principles of the laws of nations, which form a part of the municipal law of Pennsylvania;". 1 Dall. 120, 123 (Pa. Oyer and Terminer, 1784). Interestingly enough, the case was a criminal prosecution for a non-statutory and uncodified offense against international law: assault upon the representative of a foreign country, France. The defendant was convicted, and sentenced to a fine, two years' imprisonment, and the posting of heavy bond for seven years to secure good behavior. The Chief Justice repeated his statement on international law, saying:

> "The first crime in the indictment is an infraction of the law of nations. This law, in its full extent, is a part of the law of this state, and is to be collected from the practice of different nations, and the authority of writers."

The Constitutional provision mentioned earlier may have brought to an end the common law of crimes against the law of nations in this country, but for purposes of civil suit the rules of international law continued applicable. The United States Supreme Court in 1815 decided in favor of private claims in a prize case by reason of the law of nations. The Nereide, 9 Cr. 388 (U.S. 1815). In the Court's opinion, Chief Justice Marshall said that in the absence of an act of Congress "the Court is bound by the law of nations which is a part of the law of the land."

Notes

1. Article VI of the United States Constitution, provides that U.S. treaties "shall be the supreme Law of the Land." See p. 195. The only reference to international law generally is that in Article I, Section 8 giving Congress power to "define and punish * * * Offences against the Law of Nations." Nonetheless, in the often-quoted language of The Paquete Habana, 175 U.S. 677, 700, 20 S.Ct. 290, 299, 44 L.Ed. 320, 328–29 (1900) (p. 62 supra): "International law is part of our law, and must be ascertained and administered by the courts of justice of appropriate jurisdiction as often as questions of right depending upon it are duly presented for their determination." American courts frequently apply customary international law.

2. On the "define and punish clause" of the U.S. Constitution, Henkin writes:

> The rule of law in relations between nations and law at sea loomed large in the minds of the Constitutional Framers, hence the explicit grant to Congress of the power to define and punish piracies, felonies on the high seas and offenses against the law of nations. Congress has made it a federal crime to commit piracy as defined by international law and has prescribed punishment for offenses committed at sea, as on American vessels, and more recently in the air, as on U.S. airplanes.
>
> The power to define and punish offenses against the law of nations has been little used and its purport has not been wholly clear. In the past, in general, traditional international law imposes duties upon states only, not upon individuals, and it was not obvious how an individual could commit an offense against the law of nations. Presumably, however, the clause would support laws that would provide punishment of U.S. officials for acts or omissions that constitute violations of international law by the United States, e.g., when they deny fundamental "justice" to an alien, arrest a diplomat, violate an embassy, fail to carry out a treaty obligation (as under human rights covenants or conventions to which the United States is party), or violate the growing customary law of international human rights. The clause would also authorize Congress to enact into U.S. law any international rules designed to govern individual behavior, for example, the humanitarian laws of war relating to the treatment of prisoners of war. Today, when international law or a treaty of the United States may apply directly to acts by individuals, Congress could implement that law by providing for punishment under this clause, as, for example, pursuant to the Genocide Convention or the Convention Against Torture.
>
> But Congress apparently, and the Supreme Court explicitly, gave the clause a broader meaning. In upholding a statute that made it a crime to counterfeit foreign currency, the Supreme Court said:
>
> > A right secured by the law of nations to a nation, or its people, is one the United States as the representatives of this nation are bound to protect. Consequently, a law which is necessary and proper to afford this protection is one that Congress may enact, because it is one that is needed to

> carry into execution a power conferred by the Constitution on the Government of the United States exclusively. . . .
>
> This statute defines the offence, and if the thing made punishable is one which the United States are required by their international obligations to use due diligence to prevent, it is an offence against the law of nations. [United States v. Arjona, 120 U.S. 479, 487–88, 7 S.Ct. 628, 30 L.Ed. 728 (1887)]

> It is perhaps under such an interpretation of the "Offences clause" that Congress long ago made it a crime to harass diplomats, to impersonate them, to damage the property of foreign governments, or to initiate activities directed against the peace and security of foreign nations. That power, then, would enable Congress also to enforce by criminal penalties any new international obligations the United States might accept, say that U.S. companies shall abide by a new international regime for the sea.

Henkin, Foreign Affairs and the U.S. Constitution 68–70 (2d ed. 1996) (footnotes omitted).

3. It has been suggested that the power of Congress to define offenses against the law of nations authorizes Congress to provide remedies in tort for such offenses instead of, or in addition to, criminal penalties. For the suggestion that Congress could legislate to that effect under its powers deriving from the sovereignty of the United States, see Henkin, The Treaty Makers and the Law Makers: The Law of the Land and Foreign Relations, 107 U.Pa.L.Rev. 903, 919–20 (1959). Cf. United States v. Curtiss–Wright Export Corp., 299 U.S. 304, 57 S.Ct. 216, 81 L.Ed. 255 (1936).

In 1791 Congress gave to U.S. district courts "original jurisdiction of any civil action by an alien for a tort only, committed in violation of the law of nations or a treaty of the United States." See Alien Tort Claims Act, codified at 28 U.S.C.A. § 1350. There has been disagreement as to whether that statute a) provided a domestic, federal forum for suits where international law itself establishes a tort with a private right of recovery; b) created a federal tort and provided a federal forum for an action that constitutes a violation of international law even though international law does not itself create the tort and the private right; or c) created a federal forum for adjudication of such claims under the law of torts (common law or statutory) of the state in which the federal court sits. Compare Filartiga v. Pena–Irala, 630 F.2d 876 (2d Cir.1980), with Tel–Oren v. Libyan Arab Republic, 726 F.2d 774 (D.C.Cir.1984), cert. denied, 470 U.S. 1003, 105 S.Ct. 1354, 84 L.Ed.2d 377 (1985). Filartiga was accepted as more persuasive in Forti v. Suarez–Mason, 672 F.Supp. 1531 (N.D.Cal.1987), reconsideration granted in part, 694 F.Supp. 707 (1988). All three cases were cited to the Supreme Court in Argentine Republic v. Amerada Hess Shipping Corp., 488 U.S. 428, 109 S.Ct. 683, 102 L.Ed.2d 818 (1989), but the Court did not address the purport or proper construction of the Alien Tort Statute. See Chapter 14 infra.

4. Citing Kansas v. Colorado, 185 U.S. 125, 146, 22 S.Ct. 552, 560, 46 L.Ed. 838, 846 (1901), some U.S. states have recognized that "international law controls the states of the United States in their relations one with the other except as modified by the federal constitution." Sinclair Pipe Line Co. v. State Com'n of Revenue and Taxation, 184 Kan. 713, 718, 339 P.2d 341, 346 (1959) (looking to international law to determine the tax status of a Delaware corporation doing business in Kansas); State v. Miller, 157 Ariz. 129, 755 P.2d 434 (App. 1988) (applying international law to determine jurisdiction over extraterritorial conduct in Colorado and Nevada).

5. For recent controversy over international law as the law of the land in the United States, see the different points of view represented in the Symposium on Foreign Affairs Law at the End of the Century, 70 U. Colo. L. Rev.1089–1594 (1999).

CUSTOMARY INTERNATIONAL LAW AS FEDERAL "COMMON LAW"

HENKIN, THE CONSTITUTION AND UNITED STATES SOVEREIGNTY: A CENTURY OF CHINESE EXCLUSION AND ITS PROGENY

100 Harv. L.Rev. 853, 867–78 (1987) (footnotes omitted).

The Constitution * * * explicitly addresses the place of treaties in our jurisprudence. It says little, however, about customary international law. It does not declare expressly whether, and if so how, customary international law is part of our law; it says nothing about how such law relates to the Constitution and to our political institutions; whether customary international law is federal or state law; whether it is supreme over state law; or whether the federal courts have jurisdiction over cases or controversies arising under international law. The Constitution expressly establishes neither the relation of treaties and customary law to each other nor that of either to the Constitution or to laws enacted by Congress. It provides no explicit direction to the courts as to what law should govern a case involving an act of Congress or an action of the President that is inconsistent with a provision in a treaty or with a principle of international law. Nor does it expressly declare that the President is obligated to respect treaties or customary law and to take care that they be faithfully executed.

The [Supreme] Court has yet to declare that the Constitution is * * * supreme over the law of nations and principles of customary law. Arguably, the fact that treaties are subject to constitutional limitations does not conclude the issue with respect to customary law. Customary law is general law binding on all nations, and no country should be able to derogate from it because of that country's particular constitutional dispositions. The law of nations antedated the Constitution, and the framers evinced no disposition to subordinate that law to the new Constitution. Nevertheless, it is unlikely that the Court would subordinate the Constitution to the law of nations and give effect to a principle of international law without regard to constitutional constraints. The Court's jurisprudence about treaties inevitably reflects assumptions about the relation between international and United States law and, at least by implication, places the United States outside the strict monist camp. Thus we can assume that, like treaties, customary international law is inferior to the United States Constitution in the hierarchy of our domestic law.

* * * During the Spanish American War, the United States Navy seized fishing vessels belonging to private Spanish citizens and condemned them as prize of war. In *The Paquete Habana,* the owners of those vessels challenged the seizure and sought recovery of the ships, asserting that under international law private fishing vessels, even if belonging to enemy aliens, were not subject to seizure as war prize. The Supreme Court examined the state of

international law, found that it indeed exempted such fishing vessels from seizure, and ordered that the proceeds of the sale of these vessels be paid to the original owners.

In supporting its conclusion, the Court made two oft-quoted statements:

> International law is part of our law, and must be ascertained and administered by the courts of justice of appropriate jurisdiction as often as questions of right depending upon it are duly presented for their determination. For this purpose, where there is no treaty and no controlling executive or legislative act or judicial decision, resort must be had to the customs and usages of civilized nations * * *

And a few pages later:

> This rule of international law is one which prize courts administering the law of nations are bound to take judicial notice of, and to give effect to, in the absence of any treaty or other public act of their own government in relation to the matter.

The statement that international law is law of the land was essential to support the judgment. The qualifying clause "where there is no treaty and no controlling executive or legislative act or judicial decision" was dictum: neither party in the case claimed that there was any relevant treaty, any "controlling executive or legislative act or judicial decision," or any "other public act of their own government" requiring a different result. In the eighty-seven years since *The Paquete Habana,* the Court repeatedly has emphasized that international law is the law of the land, and it has given effect to principles of customary international law as the law of the United States. * * *

Some * * * would construe the *The Paquete Habana* dictum as asserting that customary international law is not equal but rather is inferior to federal law. They argue that unlike treaties, which the Court has held to be equal to acts of Congress, customary international law is subject to "repeal" by subsequent acts of Congress; indeed, it cannot be given effect in the face of even an earlier act of Congress. For support, this view relies on repeated references in legal literature to customary law as "common law" which, it is argued, is inherently inferior to legislation.

I think that this argument is misconceived. * * *

Notes

1. Henkin presents arguments as to why customary law should be seen, as are treaties, as equal in stature with acts of Congress, see p. 213 below, and arguments why customary law might even be superior to statutes and treaties, but he concludes: "Despite these arguments, it is unlikely that the Supreme Court will now distinguish customary international law from treaties and declare the former supreme over federal statutory law. I see no basis, however—either in principle, in text, in history, or in contemporary practice—for interpreting *The Paquete Habana* dictum as meaning that customary international law has a status lower than that of treaties. Both treaties and customary law are law of the United States because they constitute binding international obligations of the United States. Like treaties, customary law has now been declared to be United States law within the meaning of both Article III and the Supremacy Clause."

For a view that customary international law is inferior to federal statute, see Goldklang, Back on Board The Paquete Habana: Resolving the Conflict Between Statutes and Customary International Law, 25 Va.J.Int'l L. 143 (1984). Compare Trimble, A Revisionist View of Customary International Law, 33 U.C.L.A.L.Rev. 665 (1986). The Circuit Court of Appeals for the District of Columbia has held that later statutes supersede customary international law. See Committee of U.S. Citizens Living in Nicaragua v. Reagan, 859 F.2d 929, 939 (D.C.Cir.1988); United States v. Yunis, 924 F.2d 1086, 1091 (D.C.Cir.1991). There has been no judicial discussion of whether a new rule of customary international law supersedes an earlier federal statute. For the view that some international law cannot be superseded by an act of Congress, see Paust, Rediscovering the Relationship Between Congressional Power and International Law: Exceptions to the Last in Time Rule and the Primacy of Custom, 28 Va.J.Int'l L. 393 (1988); Paust, Customary International Law: Its Nature, Sources and Status as Law of the United States, 12 Mich.J.Int'l L. 59 (1990). See also Paust, Customary International Law and Human Rights Treaties *Are* Law of the United States, 20 Mich. J. Int'l L. 301 (1999); Paust, Fitzpatrick & Van Dyke, International Law and Litigation in the U.S. (2000), Ch. 2, sec. 2.E.2 (on conflicts between federal statutes and customary international law).

2. Customary international law is treated in the United States as automatically "incorporated" from the time that the norm is deemed to have come into existence, without the need of any formal act of incorporation by Congress or the President. See Restatement (Third) § 111(3) and Part I, Chapter I, Introductory Note. Compare the distinction between "self-executing" and "non-self-executing" treaties, p. 205 below.

3. The Restatement (Third) § 115, Comment *d* states:

> *Conflict between successive international agreements or principles of customary law.* In principle, a treaty of the United States or a Congressional–Executive agreement would supersede any prior international agreement or pre-existing rule of customary law as the law of the United States. Similarly, a later principle of customary law would supersede an earlier one. However, there have apparently been no judicial decisions to that effect. A sole executive agreement that is within the President's constitutional authority (§ 303(4)) would supersede a prior sole executive agreement and probably a pre-existing rule of customary law as United States law. Whether it would supersede an earlier treaty or Congressional–Executive agreement is uncertain. It has also not been authoritatively determined whether a rule of customary international law that developed after, and is inconsistent with, an earlier statute or international agreement of the United States should be given effect as the law of the United States. In regard to the law of the sea, the United States has accepted customary law that modifies earlier treaties as well as United States statutes. See Introductory Note to Part V. Compare § 102, Comment *j*.

For a discussion of executive agreements, see p. 230 below.

2. *Judicial Application of International Law*

INTERNATIONAL LAW AND AGREEMENTS AS LAW OF THE UNITED STATES

RESTATEMENT (THIRD) § 111

(1) International law and international agreements of the United States are law of the United States and supreme over the law of the several States.

(2) Cases arising under international law or international agreements of the United States are within the Judicial Power of the United States and, subject to Constitutional and statutory limitations and requirements of justiciability, are within the jurisdiction of the federal courts.

(3) Courts in the United States are bound to give effect to international law and to international agreements of the United States, except that a "non-self-executing" agreement will not be given effect as law in the absence of necessary implementation.

DETERMINATION OF INTERNATIONAL LAW

RESTATEMENT (THIRD) § 112

(2) The determination and interpretation of international law present federal questions and their disposition by the United States Supreme Court is conclusive for other courts in the United States.

Notes

1. In 1996, Henkin wrote:

> Perhaps the Supremacy Clause cannot readily be read as declaring international law to be the law of the land; if so, international law has become law of the United States by some other route, perhaps automatically, tacitly. Prior to union, international law had been part of the common law of England and of the American Colonies, then of the states. With union, the United States became a single nation-state with rights and obligations under international law, and perhaps, with union and as a concomitant of union, "we the people," in ordaining the Constitution, tacitly recognized and accepted international law as U.S. law of extra-constitutional origin.
>
> For long, indeed, the history of international law as part of the common law of the states was a source of confusion and controversy. For many years under the Constitution, states appeared to continue to apply international law as part of their common law. But if for the states customary international law had only the status of their common law, it was presumably subject to modification or repeal by the state legislature. If so, too, state courts could decide for themselves what international law requires, and issues of customary international law, unlike questions arising under treaties, would not raise federal questions and could not be appealed to the Supreme Court for final adjudication. Fifty states could have fifty different views on some issue of international law and the federal courts might have still another view. Indeed, not only would the states be free to disregard the views of the federal courts,

> but in cases where a federal court is required to apply the law of the state in which it sits, the court would have to apply the state's view on disputed questions of international law.
>
> *Banco Nacional de Cuba v. Sabbatino*, decided in 1964, supports a better, more orderly view * * *

Henkin, Foreign Affairs and the U.S. Constitution 238 (2d ed., 1996) (footnotes omitted).

2. The Restatement (Third) accepts as established several principles that in the past had been uncertain or debated: that issues of customary law, like those arising under treaties, are matters of federal, not state, law; that matters arising under customary law "arise under the laws of the United States" for purposes of the jurisdiction of the federal courts, U.S. Constitution, Article II, and 28 U.S.C.A. § 1331, and are part of the "laws" of the United States which are supreme to state law under Article VI, clause 2 of the Constitution. See § 111, Comments *c*, *d* and *e* and Reporters' Notes 2–4.

The Restatement (Third) indicates that "customary international law is considered to be like common law in the United States, but it is federal law." § 111, Comment *d*. Compare Henkin's view, p. 163 supra.

In Bergman v. De Sieyes, 170 F.2d 360 (2d Cir.1948), removed to the federal district court from the New York state courts on the ground of diversity of citizenship, the defendant pleaded diplomatic immunity and the complaint was dismissed. In affirming, Judge Learned Hand said: "[S]ince the defendant was served while the cause was in the state court, the law of New York determines [the service's] validity, and, although the courts of that state look to international law as a source of New York law, their interpretation of international law is controlling upon us, and we are to follow them so far as they have declared themselves. Whether an avowed refusal to accept a well-established doctrine of international law, or a plain misapprehension of it, would present a federal question we need not consider, for neither is present here." Id. at 361. Judge Hand apparently thought he was following the dictates of Erie R. Co. v. Tompkins, 304 U.S. 64, 58 S.Ct. 817, 82 L.Ed. 1188 (1938), requiring a federal court in a diversity case to follow New York law as determined by New York courts.

However, in Banco Nacional de Cuba v. Sabbatino, 376 U.S. 398, 84 S.Ct. 923, 11 L.Ed.2d 804 (1964), p. 181 infra, the Supreme Court said:

> We could perhaps in this diversity action avoid the question of deciding whether federal or state law is applicable to this aspect of the litigation. * * * Thus our conclusions might well be the same whether we dealt with this problem as one of state law * * * or federal law.
>
> However, we are constrained to make clear that an issue concerned with a basic choice regarding the competence and function of the Judiciary and the National Executive in ordering our relationships with other members of the international community must be treated exclusively as an aspect of federal law. It seems fair to assume that the Court did not have rules like the act of state doctrine in mind when it decided *Erie R. Co. v. Tompkins*. Soon thereafter, Professor Philip C. Jessup, now a judge of the International Court of Justice, recognized the potential dangers were *Erie* extended to legal problems affecting international relations. He cautioned that rules of international law should not be left to divergent and perhaps parochial state interpretations. His basic rationale is equally applicable to the act of state doctrine.

Id. at 424–25, 84 S.Ct. at 938–39, 11 L.Ed.2d at 821–22.

Consider Judge Friendly's view that "by leaving to the states what ought to be left to them, *Erie* led to the emergence of a federal decisional law in areas of national concern that is truly uniform because, under the supremacy clause, it is binding in every forum * * * [T]he clarion yet careful pronouncement of *Erie* 'there is no federal common law,' opened the way to what, for want of a better term, we may call a specialized federal common law." Friendly, In Praise of *Erie*—and of the New Federal Common Law, 39 N.Y.U.L.Rev. 381, 405 (1964). See Restatement (Third), Part I, Chapter 2, Introductory Note. See generally Hill, The Law–Making Power of the Federal Courts: Constitutional Preemption, 67 Colum. L. Rev. 1024, 1042–81 (1967); Moore, Federalism and Foreign Relations, [1965] Duke L.J. 248; Henkin, The Foreign Affairs Power of the Federal Courts: *Sabbatino*, 64 Colum. L. Rev. 805 (1964); Jessup, The Doctrine of Erie R.R. v. Tompkins Applied to International Law, 33 A.J.I.L. 740 (1939).

3. The Restatement (Third) § 133, Comment *e* states:

> *Federal jurisdiction over cases "arising under" international law and agreements.* Cases arising under treaties to which the United States is a party, as well as cases arising under customary international law, or under international agreements of the United States other than treaties, are "Cases * * * arising under * * * the Laws of the United States, and Treaties made * * * under their Authority," and therefore within the Judicial Power of the United States under Article III, Section 2 of the Constitution. Civil actions arising under international law or under a treaty or other international agreement of the United States are within the jurisdiction of the United States district courts. 28 U.S.C. § 1331 (quoted in Reporters' Note 4). For the purpose of Section 1331, all valid international agreements of the United States, whatever their designation and whatever the form by which they are concluded (see § 303), are "treaties of the United States." Customary international law, like other federal law, is part of the "laws * * * of the United States."
>
> The jurisprudence implied in the phrase "arising under" is extensive and complex. (See generally Hart and Wechsler, The Federal Courts and the Federal System, Comment *d*, Chapter 7.) Some of its implications are clear. An action arises under an international agreement of the United States, or under customary international law as part of the law of the United States, if the plaintiff's complaint properly asserts a justiciable claim based upon such international law or agreement. An action does not arise under international law or agreement if the rule of international law or the provision of the agreement enters the case only by way of defense. Louisville & Nashville R.R. Co. v. Mottley, 211 U.S. 149, 29 S.Ct. 42, 53 L.Ed. 126 (1908); Wright, Miller and Cooper, Federal Practice and Procedure: Jurisdiction § 3566 (2d ed. 1984). In the latter situation, a federal court does not have jurisdiction under 28 U.S.C. § 1331; it might have jurisdiction if the action arises under some other law of the United States, for example, the Foreign Sovereign Immunities Act. See § 457, Reporters' Note 5.

4. In Zschernig v. Miller, 389 U.S. 429, 88 S.Ct. 664, 19 L.Ed.2d 683 (1968), the Supreme Court invalidated an Oregon statute which had been applied by the state courts to deny an inheritance to the heir of an Oregon resident, living in East Germany. The statute provided that non-resident aliens could inherit only if (a) there was a reciprocal right for a United States citizen to take property in the foreign country; (b) American citizens in the United States could receive payment

from an estate in the foreign country and (c) foreign heirs would receive the proceeds of the Oregon estate "without confiscation." The Supreme Court held the Oregon statute invalid as "an intrusion by the State into the field of foreign affairs which the Constitution entrusts to the President and the Congress." For discussion of this unique case, see Henkin, Foreign Affairs and the U.S. Constitution 58–59, 163–65 (2d ed.1996). For cases that apparently did not consider the Zschernig principle applicable, see, e.g., Clark v. Allen, 331 U.S. 503, 67 S.Ct. 1431, 91 L.Ed. 1633 (1947); Gorun v. Fall, 393 U.S. 398, 89 S.Ct. 678, 21 L.Ed.2d 628 (1969); De Canas v. Bica, 424 U.S. 351, 96 S.Ct. 933, 47 L.Ed.2d 43 (1976).

Despite the broad language in *Zschernig,* state and local regulation often affects foreign states, persons and property; for example, state and local measures directed against investment in South Africa, were upheld in Board of Trustees of Employees' Retirement System of City of Baltimore v. Mayor and City Council of Baltimore City, 317 Md. 72, 562 A.2d 720 (1989), cert. denied, Lubman v. Mayor and City Council of Baltimore City, 493 U.S. 1093, 110 S.Ct. 1167, 107 L.Ed.2d 1069 (1990). But see Springfield Rare Coin Galleries v. Johnson, 115 Ill.2d 221, 104 Ill.Dec. 743, 503 N.E.2d 300 (1986) (exclusion of South African coinage from tax exempt status "is an impermissible encroachment upon a national prerogative—the authority of the Federal government to conduct foreign affairs"). See generally Lewis, Dealing with South Africa: The Constitutionality of State and Local Divestment Legislation, 61 Tulane L.Rev. 469 (1987).

State and local "buy American" laws that mandate the purchase by public authorities of goods made in the United States have been upheld as having only an "incidental or indirect effect" on foreign relations. See, e.g., Trojan Technologies, Inc. v. Commonwealth of Pennsylvania, 916 F.2d 903, 913–14 (3d Cir.1990), cert. denied, 501 U.S. 1212, 111 S.Ct. 2814, 115 L.Ed.2d 986 (1991). Compare the established constitutional doctrine that the states may not burden commerce with foreign nations, and the cases holding particular state actions involving U.S. foreign affairs to have been preempted by federal action and therefore invalid under the Supremacy Clause, Article VI, clause 2 of the Constitution. See, e.g., Hines v. Davidowitz, 312 U.S. 52, 61 S.Ct. 399, 85 L.Ed. 581 (1941).

In 1995, Massachusetts enacted legislation prohibiting its public agencies from contracting with companies that do business in Burma (Myanmar). In Crosby v. National Foreign Trade Council, 530 U.S. 363, 120 S.Ct. 2288, 147 L.Ed.2d 352 (2000), the U.S. Supreme Court held that the Massachusetts law was preempted by a federal statute that had delegated to the President discretionary authority to impose a specific range of economic sanctions on Burma. The Court found the state act to be an unconstitutional interference with federal objectives and an impediment to the President's ability to develop a coherent multilateral strategy concerning Burma. The Court noted that Japan and the European Union had initiated dispute settlement proceedings over the matter at the World Trade Organization, and that the Executive Branch had consistently represented that the state measure had complicated its dealings with foreign states.

5. It has been noted that like treaties, customary international law is law for the Executive and the courts to apply, but the Constitution does not forbid the President (or the Congress) to violate international law, and the courts will give effect to acts within the constitutional powers of the political branches without regard to international law. On the other hand, the courts have enforced international law against lower federal officials not directed by the President to disregard international law. Compare Henkin, Foreign Affairs and the U.S. Constitution 241–242 (2d ed. 1996). The Restatement (Third), § 111, Comment *c* states:

That international law and agreements of the United States are law of the United States means also that the President has the obligation and the necessary authority to take care that they be faithfully executed. United States Constitution, Article II, Section 2. But under the President's Constitutional authority, as "sole organ of the nation in its external relations" or as Commander in Chief (§ 1, Reporters' Note 2), the President has the power to take various measures including some that might constitute violations of international law by the United States. * * *.

The Restatement (Third) § 115, Reporters' Note 3 explains:

President's power to supersede international law or agreement. There is authority for the view that the President has the power, when acting within his constitutional authority, to disregard a rule of international law or an agreement of the United States, notwithstanding that international law and agreements are law of the United States and that it is the President's duty under the Constitution to "take care that the Laws be faithfully executed." Article II, Section 3. Compare the authority of the President to terminate international agreements on behalf of the United States, § 339. That the courts will not compel the President to honor international law may be implied in Supreme Court statements that courts will give effect to international law "where there is no treaty, and no controlling executive or legislative act or judicial decision," and "in the absence of any treaty or other public act of their own government in relation to the matter." The Paquete Habana, 175 U.S. 677, 700, 708, 20 S.Ct. 290, 299, 302, 44 L.Ed. 320 (1900); compare Brown v. United States, 12 U.S. (8 Cranch) 110, 128, 3 L.Ed. 504 (1814). Tag v. Rogers, 267 F.2d 664 (D.C.Cir.1959), certiorari denied, 362 U.S. 904, 80 S.Ct. 615, 4 L.Ed.2d 555 (1960); and The Over the Top, 5 F.2d 838 (D.Conn. 1925) which are sometimes cited, but those cases addressed the power of Congress to act contrary to international law, not the powers of the President.

In 1986, in Garcia–Mir v. Meese, 788 F.2d 1446 (11th Cir.1986), certiorari denied, 479 U.S. 889, 107 S.Ct. 289, 93 L.Ed.2d 263 (1986), the court, relying on The Paquete Habana, gave effect to an action of the Attorney General authorizing detention of aliens although it accepted that such detention was in violation of international law. Citing this Reporters' Note (as it appeared in Tentative Draft No. 6 of this Restatement, § 135, Reporters' Note 3), the court concluded that "the power of the President to disregard international law in service of domestic needs is reaffirmed." However, the President may have power to act in disregard of international law "when acting within his constitutional authority," but the Court of Appeals failed to find any constitutional authority in the President to detain the aliens in question. See Henkin, "The Constitution and United States Sovereignty: A Century of *Chinese Exclusion* and its Progeny," 100 Harv. L.Rev. 853, 878–86 (1987).

Some courts may be disposed to treat a claim that the President was violating international law as raising a "political question" and not justiciable. See, e.g., United States v. Berrigan, 283 F.Supp. 336, 342 (D.Md.1968) affirmed, 417 F.2d 1009 (4th Cir.1969), certiorari denied, 397 U.S. 909, 90 S.Ct. 907, 25 L.Ed.2d 90 (1970). See § 1, Reporters' Note 4.

What are the sources and the scope of the President's independent constitutional authority? Are acts by the President under that authority the law of the land, equal in status and authority to acts of Congress? Could the President, acting under that authority, disregard an act of Congress or violate a treaty of the

United States? Can such Presidential constitutional authority provide authority for executive officials other than the President that violate international law?

See generally the discussion in The Authority of the United States Executive to Interpret, Articulate or Violate Customary International Law, 80 A.S.I.L. Proc. 297 (1986); Agora: May the President Violate Customary International Law, 80 A.J.I.L. 913 (1986); Agora: May the President Violate Customary International Law (cont'd), 81 A.J.I.L. 371 (1987). See also, Lobel, The Limits of Constitutional Power: Conflicts Between Foreign Policy and International Law, 71 Va.L.Rev. 1071 (1985); Glennon, Raising the *Paquete Habana:* Is Violation of Customary International Law by the Executive Unconstitutional?, 80 Nw. U.L.Rev. 322 (1985); Leigh, Editorial Comment, Is the President Above Customary International Law?, 86 A.J.I.L. 757 (1992). See also Glennon, Constitutional Diplomacy 232–48 (1990).

Compare the presidential power to make sole executive agreements, p. 230 below.

In Garcia–Mir v. Meese, supra, the district court had found that the long detention of a large number of undocumented aliens from Cuba was arbitrary, and a violation of customary international law. The court held, however, that the decision of the Attorney General was a "controlling executive act" binding on the courts. (The phrase derives from the Supreme Court's opinion in *The Paquete Habana,* p. 62 above.) The Court of Appeals affirmed, and a petition for certiorari was denied, 479 U.S. 889, 107 S.Ct. 289, 93 L.Ed.2d 263 (1986).

If international law is the law of the land and it is the President's duty to "take care that the law be faithfully executed," (U.S. Constitution Article II, Section 3), should the court refuse to give effect to international law because of a "controlling executive act"? What executive act is "controlling" for this purpose? If, as in *Garcia-Mir,* a violation of international law is not remediable in the circumstances by the courts, are other remedies available?

In the early 1990s, courts in the United States considered whether a federal court could exercise criminal jurisdiction over an accused who had been kidnapped from foreign territory by agents of the Drug Enforcement Agency. The Court of Appeals for the Ninth Circuit held that such abduction violated an extradition treaty with Mexico and consequently deprived the U.S. courts of jurisdiction. See United States v. Verdugo–Urquidez, 939 F.2d 1341 (9th Cir.1991), and United States v. Alvarez–Machain, 946 F.2d 1466 (9th Cir.1991). The U.S. Supreme Court reversed in Alvarez–Machain, 504 U.S. 655, 112 S.Ct. 2188, 119 L.Ed.2d 441 (1992), and vacated the judgment in Verdugo–Urquidez, 505 U.S. 1201, 112 S.Ct. 2986, 120 L.Ed.2d 864 (1992). The majority of the Court found that the abduction did not violate the extradition treaty, and held that the manner in which the defendant had come before the trial court was immaterial, relying on Ker v. Illinois, 119 U.S. 436, 7 S.Ct. 225, 30 L.Ed. 421 (1886). For differing views on *Alvarez-Machain,* see Agora: International Kidnaping, 86 A.J.I.L. 736, 746 (1992); Henkin, Correspondence, 87 A.J.I.L. 100 (1993). See also Schneebaum, The Supreme Court Sanctions Transborder Kidnapping in *United States v. Alvarez–Machain:* Does International Law Still Matter?, 18 Brooklyn J.Int'l L. 303 (1992). For international reactions, see Extradition, 8 Int'l Enforcement L. Rept. 444–51 (1992). See also the compilation of documents by the Mexican Secretaria de Relaciones Exteriores, Limits to National Jurisdiction: Documents and Judicial Resolutions on the Alvarez Machain Case (1992). It has been suggested that by virtue of the posture in which *Alvarez-Machain* was acted on by the Supreme Court, the only issue decided had to do with the extradition treaty and not with the authority of the executive branch to violate customary international law. See Vazquez, Misreading High Court's *Alvarez* ruling, Legal Times, Oct. 5, 1992, pp. 29–30.

6. The Restatement (Third) § 112, Comment *c* states:

> *Weight given to views of Executive Branch.* Courts give particular weight to the position taken by the United States Government on questions of international law because it is deemed desirable that so far as possible the United States speak with one voice on such matters. Compare Baker v. Carr, 369 U.S. 186, 217, 82 S.Ct. 691, 710, 7 L.Ed.2d 663 (1962), quoted in § 1, Reporters' Note 4. The views of the United States Government, moreover, are also state practice, creating or modifying international law. See § 102 and Comment *b* thereto. Even views expressed by the Executive Branch as a party before the court or as *amicus curiae* will be given substantial respect since the Executive Branch will have to answer to a foreign state for any alleged violation of international law resulting from the action of a court. The degree of respect or deference to Executive Branch views is described variously—"particular weight," "substantial respect," "great weight"—but these various expressions are not used with precision and do not necessarily imply different degrees of deference. Compare the principle that courts will give "great weight" to interpretations by the Executive Branch of international agreements of the United States, § 326 and Reporters' Note 4 thereto.

See also Restatement (Third) § 112, Reporters' Note 1:

> *Judicial and Executive determinations.* Since, in deciding cases, the Supreme Court is the final arbiter of United States law (Cooper v. Aaron, 358 U.S. 1, 17–19, 78 S.Ct. 1401, 1409–1410, 3 L.Ed.2d 5 (195[8]); United States v. Nixon, 418 U.S. 683, 703, 94 S.Ct. 3090, 3105, 41 L.Ed.2d 1039 (1974)), a determination or interpretation of international law by the Supreme Court would also bind the Executive Branch in a case to which the United States is a party for purposes of that case, and effectively for other purposes of domestic law. The President may, however, be free to take a different view of the law vis-à-vis other nations. See § 326.

7. The Restatement (Third) § 113, Comment *b* states:

> *Judicial notice of international law.* The determination of international law or the interpretation of an agreement is a question of law for the court, not a question of fact for a jury. As was stated in The Paquete Habana, 175 U.S. 677, 708, 20 S.Ct. 290, 302, 44 L.Ed. 320 (1900):
>
> > This rule of international law is one which prize courts, administering the law of nations, are bound to take judicial notice of, and to give effect to, in the absence of any treaty or other public act of their own government in relation to the matter.
>
> State courts take judicial notice of federal law and will therefore take judicial notice of international law as law of the United States. Since it is a question of law, it need neither be pleaded nor proved. But see Comment *c*.

8. *Political Questions.* The Executive Branch has sometimes resisted the adjudication of issues involving international law (or the foreign affairs power of the President) on the ground that these issues are nonjusticiable political questions.

The political question doctrine was restated and guidelines for its application were laid down in Baker v. Carr, 369 U.S. 186, 211–12, 82 S.Ct. 691, 706–07, 7 L.Ed.2d 663, 682–83 (1962). The Court stated:

> There are sweeping statements to the effect that all questions touching foreign relations are political questions. Not only does resolution of such issues frequently turn on standards that defy judicial application, or involve the exercise of a discretion demonstrably committed to the executive or legislature; but many such questions uniquely demand single-voiced statements of the Government's views. Yet it is error to suppose that every case or controversy which touches foreign relations lies beyond judicial cognizance.

369 U.S. at 211. Many "foreign affairs" issues are decided by the courts, and since *Baker* no foreign affairs issue has been held to be non-justiciable by the Supreme Court. In 1986, the Supreme Court held that the judicial interpretation of a statute of the United States, even if it involves foreign relations, is not a political question that precludes justiciability. Japan Whaling Ass'n v. American Cetacean Soc'y, 478 U.S. 221, 106 S.Ct. 2860, 92 L.Ed.2d 166 (1986). In Goldwater v. Carter, 444 U.S. 996, 100 S.Ct. 533, 62 L.Ed.2d 428 (1979), four justices thought the courts should not adjudicate an issue between the President and the Congress as to who has the authority to terminate treaties, but that was not the majority view.

In November 1990, following Iraq's invasion of Kuwait, a number of members of Congress sought to enjoin the President from initiating an armed attack against Iraq without a declaration of war or other explicit Congressional approval. Dellums v. Bush, 752 F.Supp. 1141 (D.D.C.1990). The Department of Justice, representing the President, opposed the injunction, maintaining, *inter alia* that the complaint presented a nonjusticiable political question. The Justice Department argued "that by their very nature the determination whether certain types of military actions require a declaration of war is not justiciable, but depends instead upon delicate judgments" by the executive branch. Id. at 1145. Relying on Mitchell v. Laird, 488 F.2d 611, 614 (D.C.Cir.1973), the district court held that it had the power to make the legal determination of whether the nation's military actions constituted a "war" for the purposes of the "war clause." U.S. Const., Article I, § 8. But see Crockett v. Reagan, 558 F.Supp. 893 (D.D.C.1982), aff'd, 720 F.2d 1355 (D.C.Cir.1983), cert. denied, 467 U.S. 1251, 104 S.Ct. 3533, 82 L.Ed.2d 839 (1984); Greenham Women Against Cruise Missiles v. Reagan, 591 F.Supp. 1332 (S.D.N.Y.1984), aff'd, 755 F.2d 34 (2d Cir.1985); Sanchez–Espinoza v. Reagan, 770 F.2d 202 (D.C.Cir.1985), where the lower courts applied the political question doctrine or decided that in the circumstances equitable relief was inappropriate.

Compare United States v. Sisson, 294 F.Supp. 515 (D.Mass. 1968), in which the defendant urged, as a defense to the charge of refusing induction in the armed forces of the United States, that U.S. operations in Vietnam violated international law. The court, Wyzanski, C.J., commented: "Because a domestic tribunal is incapable of eliciting the facts during a war, and because it is probably incapable of exercising a disinterested judgment which would command the confidence of sound judicial opinion, this court holds that the defendant has tendered an issue which involves a so-called political question not within the jurisdiction of this court." 294 F.Supp. at 517–18.

The courts have long refused to review some Presidential decisions (e.g., the determination of foreign political boundaries or the recognition of foreign governments) on the ground that they were political questions. Williams v. Suffolk Ins.

Co., 38 U.S. (13 Pet.) 415, 420, 10 L.Ed. 226 (1839); Jones v. United States, 137 U.S. 202, 212, 11 S.Ct. 80, 34 L.Ed. 691 (1890). See also Occidental of Umm al Qaywayn, Inc. v. A Certain Cargo of Petroleum, 577 F.2d 1196, 1201–05 (5th Cir.1978), cert. denied, 442 U.S. 928, 99 S.Ct. 2857, 61 L.Ed.2d 296 (1979); Antolok v. United States, 873 F.2d 369, 379–384 (D.C.Cir.1989). Henkin suggests that the courts did not say—or need not have said—that the issues were not justiciable, but rather that the decisions were within the President's constitutional authority to make, and therefore should be given effect by the courts. See Henkin, Is There a "Political Question Doctrine?", 85 Yale L.J. 597 (1976).

On the political question doctrine generally, see Henkin, Foreign Affairs and the U.S. Constitution 143–148 (2d ed. 1996); Charney, Judicial Deference in Foreign Relations, 83 A.J.I.L. 805 (1989); Glennon, Foreign Affairs and the Political Question Doctrine, 83 A.J.I.L. 814 (1989); Horlick, Political Questions in International Trade: A Review of Section 3017, 10 Mich. J.Int'l L. 735 (1989).

3. The Act of State Doctrine: Will Courts Apply International Law to Acts of Foreign States?

That international law is part of the law of the United States may mean it is to be given effect as United States law by the Executive Branch and by the courts. Generally, it means that international law will be applied to give effect to limitations that international law imposes upon the United States Government, as in *The Paquete Habana* and in innumerable cases recognizing sovereign or diplomatic immunity. See Note 1, p. 172 above. Compare the cases in which the courts give effect to treaty obligations assumed by the United States, p. 205 below.

In a series of cases, the issue arose whether courts in the United States should consider the validity of acts of a foreign state under international law. That question arose as an aspect of the application by U.S. courts of the American "Act of State" doctrine. The act of state doctrine developed in those cases is not a rule of international law, but a domestic rule established by the United States Supreme Court. It is a rule of judicial self-restraint, not unlike other prudential rules of judicial self-restraint. It may apply to foreign acts of state that raise no issues under international law. See pp. 181–182 below. The doctrine became a subject of controversy when it was applied to preclude scrutiny by United States courts of acts of foreign states alleged to be in violation of international law.

HENKIN, INTERNATIONAL LAW: POLITICS AND VALUES

74–75 (1995) (footnotes omitted).

A spirit of dualism tends not only to promote independence from international law for the state's own legal system, but also to foster acquiescence in such independence for other states. States are reluctant to use their institutions, particularly their courts, to compel other states to comply with international law. Compare, for example, the Act of State doctrine, which flourishes notably—but not only—in the United States. In its common formulation the doctrine declares: "The courts of one country will not sit in judgment on the acts of the government of another done within its own territory." The Act of State doctrine emerged in the United States as an expression of respect for other States, but it has been applied to give effect even to an act of a foreign state that violates international law.

There is much to be said for respect by a state for the autonomy of another state within its own territory (except where human rights are implicated). The Act of State doctrine was doubtless inspired by judicial judgment that the resolution of a dispute involving a foreign state should be left to diplomacy rather than to public adversary adjudication in national courts. But as applied where the act of a foreign state is alleged to be in violation of international law, the doctrine is one additional concession to statehood and state autonomy, one fewer weapon for inducing compliance with international law. The Act of State doctrine reminds us that behind each state are particular interests and parochial institutions. Every state can—should—do more about policing its own international obligations and maximizing the likelihood that they will be honoured; but can a state and state institutions, even courts that strive to maintain independence and impartiality, be trusted to enforce international law against another state when (as often) the forum state's own interests or those of its nationals are at issue? Political bodies, ministries, diplomats cannot avoid the tensions of that *dédoublement fonctionnel,* an inevitable consequence of applying interstate law in a state system without a comprehensive impartial, neutral judiciary. Is a national judiciary, dressed in the mantle of justice, more trustworthy than are political bodies? Even if a particular national judiciary is trustworthy, is it in fact trusted by other states?

BANCO NACIONAL DE CUBA v. SABBATINO

Supreme Court of the United States, 1964.
376 U.S. 398, 84 S.Ct. 923, 11 L.Ed.2d 804.

[In retaliation for a U.S. reduction in the import quota for Cuban sugar, the Cuban Government nationalized many companies in which U.S. nationals had interests, including Compañia Azucarera Vertientes—Camaguey de Cuba (CAV). Farr, Whitlock, an American commodities broker, had contracted to buy a shipload of CAV sugar. To obtain the now-nationalized sugar, Farr, Whitlock entered into a new agreement to buy the shipload from the Cuban Government, which assigned the bills of lading to its shipping agent, Banco Nacional. Farr, Whitlock gained possession of the shipping documents and negotiated them to its customers, but protected by CAV's promise of indemnification, Farr, Whitlock turned the proceeds over to CAV instead of Cuba. Banco Nacional sued Farr, Whitlock for conversion of the bills of lading and also sought to enjoin Sabbatino, the temporary receiver of CAV's New York assets, from disposing of the proceeds. Farr, Whitlock defended on the ground that title to the sugar never passed to Cuba because the expropriation violated international law.]

MR. JUSTICE HARLAN delivered the opinion of the Court.

* * * While acknowledging the continuing vitality of the act of state doctrine, the court [i.e., the District Court] believed it inapplicable when the questioned foreign act is in violation of international law. Proceeding on the basis that a taking invalid under international law does not convey good title, the District Court found the Cuban expropriation decree to violate such law in three separate respects: It was motivated by a retaliatory and not a public purpose; it discriminated against American nationals; and it failed to provide

adequate compensation. Summary judgment against petitioner was accordingly granted.

The Court of Appeals, 307 F.2d 845, affirming the decision on similar grounds, relied on two letters (not before the District Court) written by State Department officers which it took as evidence that the Executive Branch had no objection to a judicial testing of the Cuban decree's validity. The court was unwilling to declare that any one of the infirmities found by the District Court rendered the taking invalid under international law, but was satisfied that in combination they had that effect. We granted certiorari because the issues involved bear importantly on the conduct of the country's foreign relations and more particularly on the proper role of the Judicial Branch in this sensitive area. * * * For reasons to follow we decide that the judgment below must be reversed.

* * *

The classic American statement of the act of state doctrine * * * is found in Underhill v. Hernandez, 168 U.S. 250, where Chief Justice Fuller said for a unanimous Court (p. 252):

> "Every sovereign state is bound to respect the independence of every other sovereign state, and the courts of one country will not sit in judgment on the acts of the government of another, done within its own territory. Redress of grievances by reason of such acts must be obtained through the means open to be availed of by sovereign powers as between themselves."

Following this precept the Court in that case refused to inquire into acts of Hernandez, a revolutionary Venezuelan military commander whose government had been later recognized by the United States, which were made the basis of a damage action in this country by Underhill, an American citizen, who claimed that he had been unlawfully assaulted, coerced, and detained in Venezuela by Hernandez.

None of this Court's subsequent cases in which the act of state doctrine was directly or peripherally involved manifest any retreat from Underhill. See American Banana Co. v. United Fruit Co., 213 U.S. 347, 29 S.Ct. 511, 53 L.Ed. 826; Oetjen v. Central Leather Co., 246 U.S. 297, 38 S.Ct. 309, 62 L.Ed. 726; Ricaud v. American Metal Co., 246 U.S. 304, 38 S.Ct. 312, 62 L.Ed. 733; Shapleigh v. Mier, 299 U.S. 468, 57 S.Ct. 261, 81 L.Ed. 355; United States v. Belmont, 301 U.S. 324, 57 S.Ct. 758, 81 L.Ed. 1134; United States v. Pink, 315 U.S. 203, 62 S.Ct. 552, 86 L.Ed. 796. On the contrary in two of these cases, Oetjen and Ricaud, the doctrine as announced in Underhill was reaffirmed in unequivocal terms.

* * *

The outcome of this case, therefore, turns upon whether any of the contentions urged by respondents against the application of the act of state doctrine in the premises is acceptable: (1) that the doctrine does not apply to acts of state which violate international law; (2) that the doctrine is inapplicable unless the Executive specifically interposes it in a particular case; and (3) that, in any event, the doctrine may not be invoked by a foreign government plaintiff in our courts.

Preliminarily, we discuss the foundations on which we deem the act of state doctrine to rest, and more particularly the question of whether state or federal law governs its application in a federal diversity case.

We do not believe that this doctrine is compelled either by the inherent nature of sovereign authority, as some of the earlier decisions seem to imply, see Underhill, supra; American Banana, supra; Oetjen, supra, 246 U.S. at 303, 38 S.Ct. at 311, 62 L.Ed. 726, or by some principle of international law.

That international law does not require application of the doctrine is evidenced by the practice of nations. Most of the countries rendering decisions on the subject fail to follow the rule rigidly. No international arbitral or judicial decision discovered suggests that international law prescribes recognition of sovereign acts of foreign governments, see 1 Oppenheim's International Law, § 115aa (Lauterpacht, 8th ed. 1955), and apparently no claim has ever been raised before an international tribunal that failure to apply the act of state doctrine constitutes a breach of international obligation. If international law does not prescribe use of the doctrine, neither does it forbid application of the rule even if it is claimed that the act of state in question violated international law. The traditional view of international law is that it establishes substantive principles for determining whether one country has wronged another. Because of its peculiar nation-to-nation character the usual method for an individual to seek relief is to exhaust local remedies and then repair to the executive authorities of his own state to persuade them to champion his claim in diplomacy or before an international tribunal. * * * Although it is, of course, true that United States courts apply international law as a part of our own in appropriate circumstances, * * * the public law of nations can hardly dictate to a country which is in theory wronged how to treat that wrong within its domestic borders.

Despite the broad statement in Oetjen that "The conduct of the foreign relations of our government is committed by the Constitution to the executive and legislative * * * departments," 246 U.S. at 302, 38 S.Ct. at 311, 62 L.Ed. 726, it cannot of course be thought that "every case or controversy which touches foreign relations lies beyond judicial cognizance." Baker v. Carr, 369 U.S. 186, 211, 82 S.Ct. 691, 707, 7 L.Ed.2d 663. The text of the Constitution does not require the act of state doctrine; it does not irrevocably remove from the judiciary the capacity to review the validity of foreign acts of state.

The act of state doctrine does, however, have "constitutional" underpinnings. It arises out of the basic relationships between branches of government in a system of separation of powers. It concerns the competency of dissimilar institutions to make and implement particular kinds of decision in the area of international relations. The doctrine as formulated in past decisions expresses the strong sense of the Judicial Branch that its engagement in the task of passing on the validity of foreign acts of state may hinder rather than further this country's pursuit of goals both for itself and for the community of nations as a whole in the international sphere. Many commentators disagree with this view; they have striven by means of distinguishing and limiting past decisions and by advancing various considerations of policy to stimulate a narrowing of the apparent scope of the rule. Whatever considerations are thought to predominate, it is plain that the problems involved are uniquely federal in nature. If federal authority, in this instance this Court, orders the field of judicial competence in this area for the federal courts, and the state courts are left free to formulate their own rules, the purposes behind the doctrine could be as effectively undermined as if there had been no federal pronouncement on the subject. * * *

[We] are constrained to make it clear that an issue concerned with a basic choice regarding the competence and function of the Judiciary and the National Executive in ordering our relationships with other members of the international community must be treated exclusively as an aspect of federal law. * * * [Passage quoted on p. 173 omitted.]

If the act of state doctrine is a principle of decision binding on federal and state courts alike but compelled by neither international law nor the Constitution, its continuing vitality depends on its capacity to reflect the proper distribution of functions between the judicial and political branches of the Government on matters bearing upon foreign affairs. It should be apparent that the greater the degree of codification or consensus concerning a particular area of international law, the more appropriate it is for the judiciary to render decisions regarding it, since the courts can then focus on the application of an agreed principle to circumstances of fact rather than on the sensitive task of establishing a principle not inconsistent with the national interest or with international justice. It is also evident that some aspects of international law touch much more sharply on national nerves than do others; the less important the implications of an issue are for our foreign relations, the weaker the justification for exclusivity in the political branches. The balance of relevant considerations may also be shifted if the government which perpetrated the challenged act of state is no longer in existence, as in the Bernstein case, for the political interest of this country may, as a result, be measurably altered. Therefore, rather than laying down or reaffirming an inflexible and all-encompassing rule in this case, we decide only that the Judicial Branch will not examine the validity of a taking of property within its own territory by a foreign sovereign government, extant and recognized by this country at the time of suit, in the absence of a treaty or other unambiguous agreement regarding controlling legal principles, even if the complaint alleges that the taking violates customary international law.

There are few if any issues in international law today on which opinion seems to be so divided as the limitations on a state's power to expropriate the property of aliens. * * *

The possible adverse consequences of a conclusion to the contrary of that implicit in [our previous act of state] cases is highlighted by contrasting the practices of the political branch with the limitations of the judicial process in matters of this kind. Following an expropriation of any significance, the Executive engages in diplomacy aimed to assure that United States citizens who are harmed are compensated fairly. Representing all claimants of this country, it will often be able, either by bilateral or multilateral talks, by submission to the United Nations, or by the employment of economic and political sanctions, to achieve some degree of general redress. Judicial determinations of invalidity of title can, on the other hand, have only an occasional impact, since they depend on the fortuitous circumstance of the property in question being brought into this country. * * *

* * * If the Executive Branch has undertaken negotiations with an expropriating country, but has refrained from claims of violation of the law of nations, a determination to that effect by a court might be regarded as a serious insult, while a finding of compliance with international law would greatly strengthen the bargaining hand of the other state with consequent detriment to American interests.

* * * Considerably more serious and far-reaching consequences would flow from a judicial finding that international law standards had been met if that determination flew in the face of a State Department proclamation to the contrary. When articulating principles of international law in its relations with other states, the Executive Branch speaks not only as an interpreter of generally accepted and traditional rules, as would the courts, but also as an advocate of standards it believes desirable for the community of nations and protective of national concerns. * * *

Against the force of such considerations, we find respondents' countervailing arguments quite unpersuasive. Their basic contention is that United States courts could make a significant contribution to the growth of international law, a contribution whose importance, it is said, would be magnified by the relative paucity of decisional law by international bodies. But given the fluidity of present world conditions, the effectiveness of such a patchwork approach toward the formulation of an acceptable body of law concerning state responsibility for expropriations is, to say the least, highly conjectural. Moreover, it rests upon the sanguine presupposition that the decisions of the courts of the world's major capital exporting country and principal exponent of the free enterprise system would be accepted as disinterested expressions of sound legal principle by those adhering to widely different ideologies.

* * *

However offensive to the public policy of this country and its constituent States an expropriation of this kind may be, we conclude that both the national interest and progress toward the goal of establishing the rule of law among nations are best served by maintaining intact the act of state doctrine in this realm of its application. * * *

MR. JUSTICE WHITE, dissenting.

I am dismayed that the Court has, with one broad stroke, declared the ascertainment and application of international law beyond the competence of the courts of the United States in a large and important category of cases. I am also disappointed in the Court's declaration that the acts of a sovereign state with regard to the property of aliens within its borders are beyond the reach of international law in the courts of this country. * * *

I do not believe that the act of state doctrine, as judicially fashioned in this Court, and the reasons underlying it, require American courts to decide cases in disregard of international law and of the rights of litigants to a full determination on the merits. * * *

The reasons for nonreview, based as they are on traditional concepts of territorial sovereignty, lose much of their force when the foreign act of state is shown to be a violation of international law. * * *

Notes

1. Justice Harlan, speaking for the Court, was "constrained to make it clear that an issue concerned with a basic choice regarding the competence and function of the judiciary and the National Executive in ordering our relationships with other members of the international community must be treated exclusively as an aspect of federal law." In reaching that conclusion as to the act of state doctrine he relied on and reaffirmed the federal character of international law in the law of the United States. See p. 173 above.

2. The act of state doctrine has been less prominent (and less controversial) in U.S. jurisprudence with the waning in intervening years of the international controversies over expropriation of the properties of foreign nationals. See Chapter 10. But the doctrine has resurged with the rise of the international human rights movement and consequent efforts to engage U.S. courts to sit in judgment on foreign governments and foreign officials charged with human rights violations of international law or treaties. See generally Henkin, Foreign Affairs and the U.S. Constitution 137–40, 410–13 (2d ed. 1996).

3. The act of state doctrine as reaffirmed in *Sabbatino* was limited by act of Congress in "The Second Hickenlooper Amendment," and the ruling in the *Sabbatino* case itself, remanded to the district court, was thereby effectively reversed. See p. 190 below. On the background, the litigation and aftermath of *Sabbatino,* see Association of the Bar of the City of New York, Background Papers and Proceedings of the Seventh Hammarskjold Forum, The Aftermath of Sabbatino (1965). The international legal principles concerning the duty of a state to pay compensation for the taking of alien-owned property are discussed at pp. 745–819 infra.

In 1996 Congress sought to abolish the doctrine in respect of Cuba as to matters covered by the Helms–Burton Act. Cuban Liberty and Democracy (Libertád) Act of 1996, Pub. L. No. 104–14, March 12, 1996.

4. Restatement (Third), § 443, Comment *b* states:

> *Scope of act of state doctrine and exceptions.*
>
> * * * The *Sabbatino* case involved property taken by the government of a recognized state within its own territory, and the legal challenge to the taking was founded on a principle of customary international law as to which there was substantial controversy, not on a treaty or other unambiguous agreement. The Court said "we decide only * * * " the kind of case before it, and it is not clear whether it intended to limit application of the act of state doctrine to situations in which all of the conditions listed are present. The applicability of the doctrine where one or more of those conditions is not present should be determined in the light of the reasons for the doctrine. See Comment *a.* * * *
>
> Lower courts have been unanimous in holding that the act of state doctrine does not apply to a taking by a foreign state of property outside of its territory at the time of taking, but have been divided as to how the territorial limitations should be applied to intangible property. See Reporters' Note 4. The doctrine has been held inapplicable in the context of a challenge to a taking by a foreign state alleged to be in violation of a treaty between the United States and that state. See Reporters' Note 5. In *Sabbatino,* the Court stressed that the principles of international law on which the challenge to the foreign state's act was based were in sharp dispute, 376 U.S. at 428–30, 84

S.Ct. at 940–941, 11 L.Ed.2d at 824–25, see § 712, Reporters' Note 1; it has been argued that the doctrine was not intended to preclude review of an act of a foreign state challenged under principles of international law not in dispute * * *. No post-*Sabbatino* case has considered application of the doctrine to acts by an unrecognized state or government. A divided Supreme Court has held that the doctrine would not preclude a counterclaim against the foreign state in certain circumstances. See Reporters' Notes 2 and 9.

It is accepted that the act of state doctrine should not apply to a taking by a state of property located outside its territory at the time of the taking. Republic of Iraq v. First National City Bank, 353 F.2d 47 (2d Cir.1965), cert. denied, 382 U.S. 1027, 86 S.Ct. 648, 15 L.Ed.2d 540 (1966). Several cases have attempted to apply that exception to takings of intangibles. In various transnational financial transactions courts have sought to determine whether there has been a taking and what was the situs of the debt at the time of the taking. To determine the situs of the debt, courts have considered factors such as whether the state had jurisdiction over the debtor, the intent of the parties as to what law should govern the transaction, the currency in which the debt was denominated. See, e.g., Libra Bank Ltd. v. Banco Nacional De Costa Rica, S.A., 570 F.Supp. 870 (S.D.N.Y.1983); Callejo v. Bancomer, S.A., 764 F.2d 1101 (5th Cir.1985). See generally Restatement (Third) § 443, Reporters' Note 4; Note, The Act of State Doctrine: Resolving Debt Situs Confusion, 86 Colum. L.Rev. 594 (1986). The Restatement Reporters suggest: "In principle, it might be preferable to approach the question of the applicability of the act of state doctrine to intangible assets not by searching for an imaginary situs for property that has no real situs, but by determining how the act of the foreign state in the particular circumstances fits within the reasons for the act of state doctrine and for the territorial limitation." Is that suggestion helpful?

Lower courts have applied the act of state doctrine to cases not involving a taking of property. Several involved suits alleging conspiracies in violation of United States antitrust laws by foreign governments or by a government in conspiracy with private companies. International Association of Machinists and Aerospace Workers (IAM) v. Organization of Petroleum Exporting Countries (OPEC), 649 F.2d 1354 (9th Cir. 1981), cert. denied, 454 U.S. 1163, 102 S.Ct. 1036, 71 L.Ed.2d 319 (1982); Clayco Petroleum Corp. v. Occidental Petroleum Corp., 712 F.2d 404 (9th Cir.1983). See Restatement (Third), § 443, Reporter's Notes 3 and 7.

The act of state doctrine was held not to apply in the case of a claim based on an act alleged to be in violation of a treaty between the United States and Ethiopia. Kalamazoo Spice Extraction Co. v. Government of Socialist Ethiopia, 729 F.2d 422 (6th Cir.1984). Does the rationale of the doctrine support such a treaty exception? Should it apply where the treaty is one to which the United States is not a party? Compare Occidental of Umm al Qaywayn, Inc. v. A Certain Cargo of Petroleum, 577 F.2d 1196 (5th Cir.1978), cert. denied 442 U.S. 928, 99 S.Ct. 2857, 61 L.Ed.2d 296 (1979).

5. In Alfred Dunhill of London, Inc. v. Republic of Cuba, 425 U.S. 682, 96 S.Ct. 1854, 48 L.Ed.2d 301 (1976), a majority of the Supreme Court found that the mere refusal of a commercial agency of a foreign government to repay funds mistakenly paid to it did not constitute an act of state, since there was no reason to suppose that the agency possessed governmental as distinguished from commercial authority. Four Justices also expressed the view that repudiation by a foreign government of a commercial debt is not entitled to respect as an act of state.

"[T]he mere assertion of sovereignty as a defense to a claim arising out of purely commercial acts by a foreign sovereign is no more effective if given the label "act of State" than if it is given the label "sovereign immunity." 425 U.S. at 705, 96 S.Ct. at 1866, 48 L.Ed.2d at 318.

In W.S. Kirkpatrick & Co., Inc. v. Environmental Tectonics Corp., Int'l, 493 U.S. 400, 110 S.Ct. 701, 107 L.Ed.2d 816 (1990), the plaintiff, an unsuccessful bidder for a Nigerian military contract, alleged that the defendants had violated federal antitrust and racketeering statutes by bribing Nigerian officials in order to secure the contract. In holding that the act of state doctrine did not bar the plaintiff's claim, the Supreme Court distinguished between cases that require a court to "declare invalid the official act of a foreign sovereign performed within its own territory," and cases that require a court only to impute an "unlawful motivation" to foreign officials in the performance of official duties. Because the central issue in the case was whether the bribes had occurred, and not whether the Nigerian Government's contracts were valid, the Court ruled the act of state doctrine had no application.

6. *Human rights violations.* A restrictive view of the act of state doctrine has also been invoked in connection with human rights violations. In Forti v. Suarez–Mason, 672 F.Supp. 1531 (N.D.Cal.1987), the court held that the act of state doctrine did not bar an action for torture under the Alien Tort Statute, 28 U.S.C.A. § 1350. Id. at 1544–47. The Torture Victim Protection Act, Pub. L. 102–256, 106 Stat. 73 (Mar. 12, 1992), provides that an individual who, "under actual or apparent authority or under color of law of any foreign nation, subjects another individual to torture or extrajudicial killing shall be liable for damages in a civil action * * *." Id., § 2(a). In reporting on the legislation, the Senate Committee on the Judiciary said:

> The committee does not intend the "act of state" doctrine to provide a shield from lawsuit for [individuals]. In Banco Nacional de Cuba v. Sabbatino, 376 U.S. 398 (1964), the Supreme Court held that the "act of state" doctrine is meant to prevent U.S. courts from sitting in judgment of the official public acts of a sovereign foreign government. Since this doctrine applies only to "public" acts, and no state commits torture as a matter of public policy, this doctrine cannot shield [individuals] from liability under this legislation.

S. Rep. No. 249, 102nd Cong. 1st Sess. 8 (1991). See 138 Cong. Rec. S2667, S2668–69 (March 3, 1992).

See also Filartiga v. Pena–Irala, 630 F.2d 876, 889 (2d Cir.1980) (unauthorized torture by a state official, in violation of the law of the foreign state, could not properly be characterized as an act of state); Sharon v. Time, Inc., 599 F.Supp. 538, 544–45 (S.D.N.Y.1984) (alleged unauthorized approval of massacre by general is not an act of state). In an unreported Ninth Circuit decision, the plaintiffs had alleged various acts of kidnapping, torture, beatings, and murder carried out by the former President of the Philippines while in office and others. The district court dismissed the action on the basis of the act of state doctrine. Emphasizing that the former dictator was no longer in power, the Court of Appeals reversed and remanded for trial on the various human rights violations. Trajano v. Marcos, 878 F.2d 1439 (9th Cir.1989), disposition tabled, 878 F.2d 1439 (9th Cir.1989). Cf. Liu v. Republic of China, 892 F.2d 1419 (9th Cir.1989), cert. dismissed, 497 U.S. 1058, 111 S.Ct. 27, 111 L.Ed.2d 840 (1990) (act of state doctrine did not bar action against officials of the Republic of China on Taiwan for allegedly ordering the assassination of an American citizen in the U.S.). See generally Steinhardt, Human Rights Litigation and the "One Voice" Orthodoxy in Foreign Affairs, in

World Justice? U.S. Courts and International Human Rights 23 (Gibney, ed., 1991); Stephens & Ratner, International Human Rights Litigation in U.S. Courts (1996).

Would the act of state doctrine apply in a case where the law of a foreign state clearly authorized torture? The Restatement (Third) § 443, Comment *c* states:

> A claim arising out of an alleged violation of fundamental human rights—for instance, a claim on behalf of a victim of torture or genocide—would (if otherwise sustainable) probably not be defeated by the act of state doctrine, since the accepted international law of human rights is well established and contemplates external scrutiny of such acts.

See also id., § 443, Reporter's Note 3.

7. *Private acts of heads of state.* Republic of Philippines v. Marcos, 806 F.2d 344 (2d Cir.1986), concluded that the act of state doctrine does not apply to "purely private acts" of the head of government as distinguished from his or her "public acts." Id., at 358–59. In a related case, the Ninth Circuit reached the same conclusion. Republic of Philippines v. Marcos, 862 F.2d 1355 (9th Cir.1988) (en banc). The Second Circuit noted that the complaint alleged both public and private acts, and ruled that the defendants seeking to invoke the act of state doctrine had the burden of demonstrating that the relevant acts were public and entitled to protection from judicial scrutiny under the act of state doctrine. Can one readily distinguish between public and private acts? See Jimenez v. Aristeguieta, 311 F.2d 547 (5th Cir.1962) (act of state doctrine did not apply to private acts of embezzlement, fraud and receipt of unlawfully obtained money by former Venezuelan dictator); DeRoburt v. Gannett Co., Inc., 733 F.2d 701 (9th Cir.1984) (doctrine did not shield privately motivated, illegal loans by the former President of Nauru). See generally, Note, Defining the "Public Act" Requirement in the Act of State Doctrine, 58 U.Chi. L.Rev. 1151 (1991). Cf. W.S. Kirkpatrick & Co., Inc. v. Environmental Tectonics Corp. Int'l, 493 U.S. 400, 110 S.Ct. 701, 107 L.Ed.2d 816 (1990), p. 188 supra.

8. Can the act of state doctrine be effectively waived? By the foreign state? By private parties? The Restatement (Third) § 443, Comment *e*, states that "the doctrine cannot be 'waived' by the foreign state." It also notes that when a sovereign state has consented to adjudication in the courts of another state, the justification for applying the doctrine is "significantly weaker." Are these statements consistent?

Waiver may be asserted in a number of situations. It may be explicit or it may be inferred from a failure to plead the doctrine. Does selection of an American forum or of American law as the applicable law imply waiver of the act of state doctrine? Or does it include selection of the American act of state doctrine? The party that has allegedly waived application of the doctrine may be the state whose act is challenged or a private litigant. To the extent that the doctrine reflects judicial limitation of judicial power, should waiver be possible? To the extent that the doctrine seeks to avoid disturbing the relations of the United States with the foreign state, should a private litigant be able to waive its application?

9. In First Nat. City Bank v. Banco Nacional de Cuba, 406 U.S. 759, 92 S.Ct. 1808, 32 L.Ed.2d 466 (1972), a majority of the Supreme Court held that the act of state doctrine should not apply to bar a counterclaim. There was no opinion of the Court. Three Justices reached the result on the ground that the Executive Branch, by a letter to the Court, had suggested that the act of state doctrine should not apply in such cases and urged that the courts should follow the Executive Branch.

Justice Powell, who had joined the Court after *Sabbatino,* concurred in the judgment because he questioned the decision in that case. Justice Douglas took the view that the act of state doctrine should not be applied to counterclaims, citing National City Bank v. Republic of China, 348 U.S. 356, 75 S.Ct. 423, 99 L.Ed. 389 (1955). Justices Brennan, Stewart, Marshall and Blackmun dissented, on the ground that *Sabbatino* applied; like the concurring justices they rejected the view that the courts had to follow direction by the Executive Branch in such cases. See 406 U.S. at 776–77, 92 S.Ct. at 1817–18, 32 L.Ed.2d at 487–88.

10. Although the Court in *Sabbatino* disclaims any intimation that the courts of the United States "are broadly foreclosed from considering questions of international law" (376 U.S. at 430 n. 34, 84 S.Ct. at 941 n. 34, 11 L.Ed.2d at 824 n. 34), does its approach to the act of state issue suggest that certain issues involving aspects of international law that are unsettled and that affect sensitive national interests should be regarded as non-justiciable? Would the justiciability of the issue be influenced by whether the Executive Branch has taken a position?

On the act of state doctrine generally, see Oppenheim's International Law 365–71 (9th ed., Jennings & Watts, eds. 1992); Koh, Transnational Public Law Litigation, 100 Yale L.J. 2347 (1991).

THE SECOND HICKENLOOPER AMENDMENT

Pub. L. 89–171, 79 Stat. 653 (1964), 22 U.S.C. § 2370(e)(2).

Notwithstanding any other provision of law, no court in the United States shall decline on the ground of the federal act of state doctrine to make a determination on the merits giving effect to the principles of international law in a case in which a claim of title or other right to property is asserted by any party including a foreign state (or a party claiming through such state) based upon (or traced through) a confiscation or other taking after January 1, 1959, by an act of that state in violation of the principles of international law including the principles of compensation and the other standards set out in this subsection: *Provided,* That this subparagraph shall not be applicable (1) in any case in which an act of a foreign state is not contrary to international law or with respect to a claim of title or other right to property acquired pursuant to an irrevocable letter of credit of not more than 180 days duration issued in good faith prior to the time of the confiscation or other taking, or (2) in any case with respect to which the President determines that application of the act of state doctrine is required in that particular case by the foreign policy interests of the United States and a suggestion to this effect is filed on his behalf in that case with the court.

Notes

1. The Senate Foreign Relations Committee's Report on the Hickenlooper Amendment stated in part:

> The amendment is intended to reverse in part the recent decision of the Supreme Court in Banco de [sic] Nacional de Cuba v. Sabbatino. The act-of-state doctrine has been applied by U.S. courts to determine that the actions of a foreign sovereign cannot be challenged in private litigation. The Supreme Court extended this doctrine in the *Sabbatino* decision so as to preclude U.S. courts from inquiring into acts of foreign states, even though these acts had

been denounced by the State Department as contrary to international law. * * *

The effect of the amendment is to achieve a reversal of presumptions. Under the *Sabbatino* decision, the courts would presume that any adjudication as to the lawfulness under international law of the act of a foreign state would embarrass the conduct of foreign policy unless the President says it would not. Under the amendment, the Court would presume that it may proceed with an adjudication on the merits unless the President states officially that such an adjudication in the particular case would embarrass the conduct of foreign policy.

S.Rep. No. 1188, pt. I, 88th Cong., 2d Sess. 24 (1964).

2. Henkin has commented:

Act of state is a special rule modifying the ordinary rules of conflict of laws. If there were no act of state doctrine, a domestic court in a case like *Sabbatino* would decide it on "conflicts" principles. It would first decide what law "governed" the issues. If under accepted choice of law principles the foreign law should govern, the court could still refuse to apply that law if it were found to be contrary to the public policy of the forum. The act of state doctrine, however, says that the foreign "law" (i.e., the act of state) must govern certain transactions and that no public policy of the forum may stand in the way. * * *

* * * [Under the Supreme Court's decision, as] a substantive federal rule, [the act of state doctrine] supersedes any conflicts principle, state or federal, that might otherwise prevail. There is no room for any public policy conflicting with the policy of act of state as applied by the courts.

* * * [B]ecause the draftsmen of the Amendment did not have a clear idea of the act of state doctrine and its relation to general conflicts principles, the statute does not give a clear idea as to what is left after the Supreme Court is overruled. Did the statute intend to remove act of state from these cases? If so, are the courts left to traditional conflicts principles, and Erie R.R. v. Tompkins? Did Congress, instead, intend to prescribe new federal substantive law to govern these cases? If so, what exactly is the new law? And may Congress properly prescribe law for these transactions?

* * * The Amendment directs the courts not to "decline on the ground of the federal act of state doctrine to make a determination on the merits giving effect to the principles of international law * * *." But, first, when the courts apply act of state, they are not declining to make a "determination on the merits." There is a determination on the merits whether act of state is applied or not. The only question is which principle of conflicts and consequently which substantive law is to be applied to determine the merits. Second, act of state does not require courts to decline to give effect to international law: were there no such doctrine, courts would not give effect to international law in these cases. They would give effect to domestic principles of conflicts and the substantive law to which those principles point. International law might become relevant only if, somehow, the governing substantive law made it relevant, or if the public policy of the forum invoked it.

Perhaps the statute also sought to build on the proposition that "international law is part of the law of the United States." This proposition is established and unexceptionable; it is also irrelevant. Effectively, it means that the courts will apply international law in an appropriate case *against the*

> *United States,* the one government which is subject to the law of the United States. In a case like *Sabbatino,* however, the Government of Cuba, acting in Cuba, obviously was not subject to the laws of the United States. Of what relevance, then, is the fact that international law is part of the law of the United States? International law might have been relevant if it required the United States to respond to Cuba's violation in a particular way; for example, if international law forbade the United States to give effect to Cuba's confiscations, American courts would carry out that obligation and refuse to give them effect. But international law does not tell the United States how to react to Cuban acts that violate international law. The United States is free to condone, acquiesce in, implement, or even applaud them.
>
> International law could become relevant to a case like *Sabbatino* in the courts of the United States (as distinguished from an appropriate international tribunal) only if governing law made it relevant. For example, international law could come in through the "side-door" of public policy. Congress could declare that regardless of any principles of conflicts, or of the act of state doctrine, it is the policy of the United States not to allow its courts to apply foreign law that contravenes international law. Or Congress could pass a statute providing that in *Sabbatino*-type cases, courts shall not apply the substantive law designated either by act of state or by traditional conflicts principles, but shall apply instead a new federal substantive law, which incorporates by reference the principles of international law as Congress saw them. * * *

Henkin, Act of State Today: Recollections in Tranquility, 6 Colum.J.Transnat. L. 175, 178–82 (1967). See also Henkin, Foreign Affairs and the U.S. Constitution 137–140 (2d ed. 1996).

Is, as Henkin suggests, international law applicable to acts of a foreign state before a United States court only insofar as United States law makes international law applicable in the case? It has been argued that United States courts should consider international law applicable in its own right, as a kind of superior law to which the foreign act is subject; a foreign act should not be applied by a domestic court if that law is invalid under international law. Compare:

> [W]hen dealing with international delinquencies committed by a foreign State a municipal court ought to be bound by international law in the sense that this overrides the foreign law which, though applicable to a given set of facts, is objectionable. In other words, foreign law, *prima facie* applicable to a case, should be refused effect by a municipal court if and to such extent as public international law so requires. * * *
>
> A principle on these lines has much to commend it. In the first place it is consonant with the dignity, moral force and inherent vitality of public international law to enforce it as such, by means of direct application rather than in an oblique fashion by using public policy as a back door. If "we admit unreservedly the supremacy of international law" it would not be fitting if it had to be harnessed to the unruly horse of public policy. Secondly, the relative objectivity and uniformity of its standards, as compared with the varying notions of public policy, makes public international law a more attractive guide to judicial decision. To invoke public policy means a condemnation on grounds which are liable to create the impression of special pleading and which thus conceal, behind the interests involved in the case, the peculiarly legal quality of the issue. Thirdly, the judicial application of international law

> is, and ought to be, a matter of duty, not . . . of mere right. In other words the requirements of public international law are absolute and leave no room for the relativity of public policy. Foreign measures which do not affect the forum are not contrary to its public policy. Yet a judge who, in a case involving an international delinquency committed by State A against State B, applies the law of the former, may assist in the consummations of that delinquency and thus engage his own Sovereign's international responsibility.

Mann, International Delinquencies Before Municipal Courts, in Studies in International Law 378–80 (1973) (footnotes omitted). See also his later article, The Consequences of an International Wrong in International Law, in Further Studies in International Law, Chapter 4 (1990); The Rose Mary, [1953] I W.L.R. 246.

3. In applying the Hickenlooper Amendment, is a court required to adopt the view of international law or expropriation apparently adopted by Congress, or should it make an independent determination as to what the applicable international law provides? See Restatement (Third) § 444, Comments *b* and *d*. On expropriation in international law generally, see Chapter 10.

4. The Second Hickenlooper Amendment was applied by the district court in *Sabbatino* itself on remand and the complaint was dismissed. Banco Nacional de Cuba v. Farr, 243 F.Supp. 957 (S.D.N.Y.1965), affd, 383 F.2d 166 (2d Cir.1967), cert. denied, 390 U.S. 956, 88 S.Ct. 1038, 19 L.Ed.2d 1151 (1968).

5. In French v. Banco Nacional de Cuba, 23 N.Y.2d 46, 295 N.Y.S.2d 433, 242 N.E.2d 704 (1968), the New York Court of Appeals applied the act of state doctrine in rejecting a claim based on breach of contract by a foreign government. The court held that the Hickenlooper Amendment did not apply. "It is plain enough upon the face of the statute—and absolutely clear from its legislative history—the Congress was not attempting to assure a remedy in American courts for every kind of monetary loss resulting from actions, even unjust actions, of foreign governments. The law is restricted, manifestly, to the kind of problem exemplified by the *Sabbatino* case itself, a claim of title or other right to specific property which had been expropriated abroad." 23 N.Y.2d at 57–58, 295 N.Y.S.2d at 444–45, 242 N.E.2d at 712. See Restatement (Third) § 444, Comment *e* and Reporters' Note 4.

In West v. Multibanco Comermex, 807 F.2d 820 (9th Cir.1987), cert. denied, 482 U.S. 906, 107 S.Ct. 2483, 96 L.Ed.2d 375 (1987), the court rejected the reasoning of *French* as overly formalistic and contrary to the policies underlying the Hickenlooper Amendment. The defendants argued that ownership interests in certificates of deposit are "contractual," and thus not "tangible property" that could be expropriated within the meaning of the Amendment. The court, however, concluded that the "tangibleness" of property was not a dispositive factor and that certificates of deposits were property capable of being expropriated within the meaning of the Hickenlooper Amendment. See generally, Vandevelde, Reassessing the Hickenlooper Amendment, 29 Va. J. Int'l L. 115 (1988–89). Compare p. 187 on the "situs" of intangibles.

The reference to "property" in the Second Hickenlooper Amendment was inserted in 1965, when the Amendment was reenacted, to assure that the act of state doctrine might still be available and the courts would give effect to foreign acts that do not involve the taking of property.

6. Henkin, Note 2 above, describes the act of state doctrine as "a special rule modifying the ordinary rules of conflict of laws." Professor Anne-Marie Slaughter Burley takes the position that the Supreme Court in *Sabbatino* made "a more

fundamental statement that the act of state doctrine could not function as a conflicts rule on the particular facts of the case." Burley, Law Among Liberal States: Liberal Internationalism and the Act of State Doctrine, 92 Colum.L.Rev. 1907, 1950 (1992). Slaughter Burley suggests that the courts should apply the act of state doctrine differently in regard to "liberal" and "nonliberal" states. Is that feasible? Is it desirable?

7. *The Act of State doctrine in the courts of other states.* Restatement (Third) § 443, Reporter's Note 12, surveys the judicial application of the act of state doctrine in countries other than the United States:

> As the Supreme Court stated in *Sabbatino,* no rule of international law requires application of the act of state doctrine. Nevertheless, the courts of most states have exercised judicial restraint in adjudicating challenges to expropriation by foreign states, whether by application of the act of state doctrine, A.M. Luther v. James Sagor & Co. (U.K.), [1921] 3 K.B. 532 (C.A.); by narrow construction of the responsibility of states to alien investors, Anglo–Iranian Oil Co. Ltd. v. S.U.P.O.R. Co. (Italy), [1955] Int'l L.Rep. 23 (Civil Ct. Rome, Sept. 13, 1954); or by application of local public policy *(ordre public)* to oust normal rules of conflict of laws, Reporters' Note 1, in actions by local plaintiffs only. Soc. Minera El Teniente, S.A.v.A.G. Norddeutsche Affinerie (German Fed. Republic), 12 Int'l Leg. Mat. 251 (Hamburg, Landgericht Jan. 22, 1973). Contra: Anglo–Iranian Oil Co., Ltd. v. Jaffrate, [1953] W.L.R. 246, [1953] Int'l L.Rep. 316 (Aden Sup. Ct.); Senembah Maatschappij N.V.v. Republiek Indonesie Bank Indonesia, Ned. Jurisprudentsie 1959, No. 73, p. 218 (Amsterdam Ct. App.). For a survey of cases to 1965, see Reeves, "The Act of State—Foreign Decisions cited in *Sabbatino* Case: A Rebuttal and Memorandum of Law," 33 Fordham L.Rev. 599, 618–70 (1965). After many years of uncertainty, see Singer, "The Act of State Doctrine in the United Kingdom: An Analysis with Comparison to United States Practice," 75 Am.J.Int'l L. 283 (1981), the House of Lords decided in 1981 to adopt the United States view of the act of state doctrine, on the basis of a shared view of the nature and limits of the judicial function. Buttes Gas & Oil Co. v. Hammer, [1982] A.C. 888, 936–38 (H.L.(E.)). * * * [T]he House of Lords reaffirmed that "an English court will recognise the compulsory acquisition of a foreign state and will recognise the change of title to property which has come under the control of the foreign state and * * * the consequences of that change of title. The English court will decline to consider the merits of compulsory acquisition * * * [or to entertain an attack on the motives of the friendly sovereign state]."

For a discussion of the act of state doctrine in the jurisprudence of other states generally, see 1 Oppenheim's International Law 365–71 (9th ed., Jennings & Watts, eds. 1992); Benvenisti, Judicial Misgivings Regarding the Application of International Norms: An Analysis of Attitudes of National Courts, 4 E.J.I.L. 159 (1993).

8. Attacks on the act of state doctrine have continued. See Leigh, *Sabbatino's* Silver Anniversary and the Restatement: No Cause for Celebration, 24 Int'l Lawyer (1990). See also Halberstam, Sabbatino Resurrected: The Act of State Doctrine in the Revised Restatement of U.S. Foreign Relations Law, 79 A.J.I.L. 68, and the reply by Henkin & Lowenfeld, Act of State and the Restatement, 79 A.J.I.L. 717 (1985).

B. INTERNATIONAL AGREEMENTS IN U.S. LAW

1. *Treaties*

UNITED STATES CONSTITUTION

ARTICLE II, SECTION 2

He [the President] shall have Power, by and with the Advice and Consent of the Senate, to make Treaties, provided two-thirds of the Senators present concur * * *

ARTICLE VI

This Constitution, and the Laws of the United States which shall be made in Pursuance thereof; and all Treaties made, or which shall be made, under the Authority of the United States, shall be the supreme Law of the Land; and the Judges in every State shall be bound thereby, any Thing in the Constitution or Laws of any State to the Contrary notwithstanding.

Notes

1. Under international practice, a treaty is often signed subject to later ratification; or, especially in multilateral treaties, a state may accede to a treaty without having signed it. "Ratification" of treaties is not mentioned in the Constitution. In practice, treaties are ratified (or acceded to) by the President after the Senate has given its advice and consent. It is incorrect therefore to refer to the action of the Senate as "ratification." The President is under no duty to proceed with ratification of, or accession to, a treaty after the Senate has given its advice and consent. A number of treaties have remained "unmade" by the President after advice and consent by the Senate.

The Senate may impose conditions to its consent. It may insist that U.S. obligations under the treaty be modified. In such cases the Senate sometimes enters a "reservation" or "amendment"; technically, the Senate can neither amend the treaty nor enter a reservation to it; it can consent to the treaty on condition that the United States (through the President) enter a reservation to it. The Senate has sometimes imposed conditions that sought to control the effect of a treaty in the United States: for example, that it shall not take effect in the United States until implemented by Congress. See the discussion on self-executing treaties, pp. 205–212 below.

2. The Senate may express its understanding of a treaty provision that is arguably ambiguous. If the Senate indicates its interpretation of such a provision, the President must honor it: the treaty as so understood is the treaty to which the Senate consents. See Rainbow Navigation, Inc. v. Department of the Navy, 699 F.Supp. 339, 343–44 (D.D.C.1988), rev'd on other grounds, 911 F.2d 797 (D.C.Cir. 1990) ("Any other rule would undermine the authority of the Senate under Article 2 section 2 of the Constitution to concur or to fail to concur in treaties made by the Chief Executive."); United States v. Stuart, 489 U.S. 353, 374, 109 S.Ct. 1183, 1195–96, 103 L.Ed.2d 388, 410 (1989) (Scalia, J. concurring) ("Of course the Senate has unquestioned power to enforce its understanding of treaties."). See also ABM Treaty and the Constitution: Joint Hearings Before the Senate Comm. on Foreign Relations and Comm. on the Judiciary, 100th Cong., 1st Sess. (1987) (particularly the statements of Sen. Nunn, id. at 54, L. Henkin, id. at 81, and L.

Tribe, id. at 83); Review of ABM Treaty Interpretation Dispute and SDI: Hearing Before the Subcomm. on Arms Control, Int'l Security and Science of the House Comm. on Foreign Relations, 100th Cong. 1st Sess. (1987).

In 1985, controversy erupted when the Reagan Administration sought to give to the Anti-Ballistic Missile (ABM) Treaty an interpretation that was contrary to the Senate's understanding when it gave consent. As a result, when the Intermediate-Range Missiles (INF) Treaty came up for advice and consent in 1988, the Senate attached a condition declaring that "the United States shall interpret the Treaty in accordance with the common understanding of the Treaty shared by the President and the Senate at the time the Senate gave its advice and consent to ratification." See 134 Cong. Rec. S7277-01 (1988). See also Garthoff, Policy Versus the Law: The Reinterpretation of the ABM Treaty (1987); Kennedy, Treaty Interpretation by the Executive Branch: The ABM Treaty and "Star Wars" Testing and Development, 80 A.J.I.L. 854 (1986); Henkin, Constitutionalism, Democracy and Foreign Affairs 51-57 (1990); Glennon, Interpreting "Interpretation:" The President, the Senate, and When Treaty Interpretation Becomes Treaty Making," 20 U.C.D.L.Rev. 913 (1987).

3. Over sharp disagreement by Justice Scalia, the Supreme Court has looked to Senate pre-ratification materials for guidance in the interpretation of treaties. See United States v. Stuart, 489 U.S. 353, 109 S.Ct. 1183, 103 L.Ed.2d 388 (1989). See also Vagts, Senate Materials and Treaty Interpretation: Some Research Hints for the Supreme Court, 83 A.J.I.L. 546 (1989).

4. Article I, section 10 of the U.S. Constitution provides:

> No State shall enter into any Treaty, Alliance, or Confederation. * * *.
>
> No State shall, without the Consent of Congress, * * * enter into any Agreement or Compact with * * * a foreign Power * * *.

Article I, Section 10, cls. 1, 3.

The Restatement (Third) § 302, Comment *f*, states:

> What distinguishes a treaty, which a State cannot make at all, from an agreement or compact, which it can make with Congressional consent, has not been determined. That would probably be deemed a political decision. Hence, if Congress consented to a State agreement with a foreign power, courts would not be likely to find that it was a "treaty" for which Congressional consent was unavailing.
>
> By analogy with inter-State compacts, a State compact with a foreign power requires Congressional consent only if the compact tends "to the increase of political power in the States which may encroach upon or interfere with the just supremacy of the United States." Virginia v. Tennessee, 148 U.S. 503, 519, 13 S.Ct. 728, 734, 37 L.Ed. 537 (1893). In general, agreements involving local transborder issues, such as agreements to curb a source of pollution, to coordinate police or sewage services, or to share an energy source, have been considered not to require Congressional consent. Such agreements are not international agreements under the criteria stated in § 301(1), but other State compacts might be. See § 301, Comment *g*; compare Comment *d* to that section.

a. Applicability of Constitutional Restraints

TREATIES AND THE SUPREMACY CLAUSE

HENKIN, FOREIGN AFFAIRS AND THE U.S. CONSTITUTION

185–88 (2d ed. 1996) (footnotes omitted).

The Constitution does not expressly impose prohibitions or prescribe limits on the Treaty Power, nor does it patently imply that there are any. No provision in any treaty has been held unconstitutional by the Supreme Court and few have been seriously challenged there. It is now settled, however, that treaties are subject to the constitutional limitations that apply to all exercises of federal power, principally the prohibitions of the Bill of Rights; numerous statements also assert limitations on the reach and compass of the Treaty Power.

Once, indeed, there was extant a myth that treaties are equal in authority to the Constitution and not subject to its limitations. The doctrine, propagated even by eminent authority, found its origins, no doubt, in the language of the Supremacy Clause (Article VI, section 2):

> "This Constitution, and the Laws of the United States which shall be made in Pursuance thereof; and all Treaties made, or which shall be made, under the Authority of the United States, shall be the supreme Law of the Land * * *."

Reading that language, Mr. Justice Holmes said:

> Acts of Congress are the supreme law of the land when made in pursuance of the Constitution, while treaties are declared to be so when made under the authority of the United States. It is open to question whether the authority of the United States means more than the formal acts prescribed to make the convention. [Missouri v. Holland, p. 198 infra]

Holmes read "in pursuance of" the Constitution to mean "consistent with its substantive prohibitions" and that phrase has been generally so interpreted; if so, the language does indeed lend itself to his dictum. Long before he wrote, however, that curious language of the Supremacy Clause had been explained otherwise: to the Framers, "in pursuance of" the Constitution meant—or meant also—"following its adoption." But they wished to provide in the Supremacy Clause that treaties made before the adoption of the Constitution (principally the treaties with France and Great Britain that were being resisted in some states) should also be the law of the land and binding on the states. * * *

In 1957, Justice Black laid the issue to rest:

> no agreement with a foreign nation can confer power on the Congress, or on any other branch of Government, which is free from the restraints of the Constitution.... The prohibitions of the Constitution were designed to apply to all branches of the National Government and they cannot be nullified by the Executive or by the Executive and the Senate combined. [Reid v. Covert, 354 U.S. 1, 16–17, 77 S.Ct. 1222, 1 L.Ed.2d 1148 (1957)]

The prohibitions set forth in Article 1, section 9, then, though contained in the article devoted principally to Congress and following immediately upon the catalogue of its powers, would doubtless be held to apply to treaties as well: a treaty cannot grant a title of nobility, or lay a duty on articles exported from any state, or give preference to the ports of one state over those of another. Treaties, surely, are also subject to the Bill of Rights.*

[See Restatement (Third) §§ 302(2) and 721.]

b. Suggested Limitations: Federalism, Congressional Powers?

FEDERALISM

MISSOURI v. HOLLAND

Supreme Court of the United States, 1920.
252 U.S. 416, 40 S.Ct. 382, 64 L.Ed. 641.

MR. JUSTICE HOLMES delivered the opinion of the Court.

This is a bill in equity brought by the State of Missouri to prevent a game warden of the United States from attempting to enforce the Migratory Bird Treaty Act of July 3, 1918, c. 128, 40 Stat. 755, and the regulations made by the Secretary of Agriculture in pursuance of the same. The ground of the bill is that the statute is an unconstitutional interference with the rights reserved to the States by the Tenth Amendment, and that the acts of the defendant done and threatened under that authority invade the sovereign right of the State and contravene its will manifested in statutes. The State also alleges a pecuniary interest, as owner of the wild birds within its borders and otherwise, admitted by the Government to be sufficient, but it is enough that the bill is a reasonable and proper means to assert the alleged quasi sovereign rights of a State. * * * A motion to dismiss was sustained by the District Court on the ground that the Act of Congress is constitutional. 258 Fed. 479. * * * The State appeals.

On December 8, 1916, a treaty between the United States and Great Britain was proclaimed by the President. It recited that many species of birds in their annual migrations traversed many parts of the United States and of Canada, that they were of great value as a source of food and in destroying insects injurious to vegetation, but were in danger of extermination through lack of adequate protection. It therefore provided for specified closed seasons and protection in other forms, and agreed that the two powers would take or propose to their lawmaking bodies the necessary measures for carrying the treaty out. 39 Stat. 1702. The above mentioned act of July 3, 1918, entitled an act to give effect to the convention, prohibited the killing, capturing or selling any of the migratory birds included in the terms of the treaty except as permitted by regulations compatible with those terms, to be made by the Secretary of Agriculture. Regulations were proclaimed on July 31, and Octo-

* Even the First Amendment, though expressly addressed to Congress, and the prohibitions implied elsewhere, e.g., in the citizenship clause of the Fourteenth Amendment. * * *

An argument might be made that these prohibitions do not limit the power to make treaties, but only forbid giving them effect as law of the United States; that conceptual distinction will generally have no consequence in fact, since Presidents will not knowingly make treaties that would be unenforceable. * * *

ber 25, 1918. 40 Stat. 1812, 1863. * * * [T]he question raised is the general one whether the treaty and statute are void as an interference with the rights reserved to the States.

To answer this question it is not enough to refer to the Tenth Amendment, reserving the powers not delegated to the United States, because by Article 2, Section 2, the power to make treaties is delegated expressly, and by Article 6 treaties made under the authority of the United States, along with the Constitution and laws of the United States made in pursuance thereof, are declared the supreme law of the land. If the treaty is valid there can be no dispute about the validity of the statute under Article 1, Section 8, as a necessary and proper means to execute the powers of the Government. The language of the Constitution as to the supremacy of treaties being general, the question before us is narrowed to an inquiry into the ground upon which the present supposed exception is placed.

It is said that a treaty cannot be valid if it infringes the Constitution, that there are limits, therefore, to the treaty-making power, and that one such limit is that what an act of Congress could not do unaided, in derogation of the powers reserved to the States, a treaty cannot do. An earlier act of Congress that attempted by itself and not in pursuance of a treaty to regulate the killing of migratory birds within the States had been held bad in the District Court. United States v. Shauver, 214 F. 154. United States v. McCullagh, 221 F. 288. Those decisions were supported by arguments that migratory birds were owned by the States in their sovereign capacity for the benefit of their people, and that under cases like Geer v. Connecticut, 161 U.S. 519, [16 S.Ct. 600, 40 L.Ed. 793,] this control was one that Congress had no power to displace. The same argument is supposed to apply now with equal force.

Whether the two cases cited were decided rightly or not they cannot be accepted as a test of the treaty power. Acts of Congress are the supreme law of the land only when made in pursuance of the Constitution, while treaties are declared to be so when made under the authority of the United States. It is open to question whether the authority of the United States means more than the formal acts prescribed to make the convention. We do not mean to imply that there are no qualifications to the treaty-making power; but they must be ascertained in a different way. It is obvious that there may be matters of the sharpest exigency for the national well being that an act of Congress could not deal with but that a treaty followed by such an act could, and it is not lightly to be assumed that, in matters requiring national action, "a power which must belong to and somewhere reside in every civilized government" is not to be found. * * * [W]hen we are dealing with words that also are a constituent act, like the Constitution of the United States, we must realize that they have called into life a being the development of which could not have been foreseen completely by the most gifted of its begetters. It was enough for them to realize or to hope that they had created an organism; it has taken a century and has cost their successors much sweat and blood to prove that they created a nation. The case before us must be considered in the light of our whole experience and not merely in that of what was said a hundred years ago. The treaty in question does not contravene any prohibitory words to be found in the Constitution. The only question is whether it is forbidden by some invisible radiation from the general terms of the Tenth

Amendment. We must consider what this country has become in deciding what that amendment has reserved.

The State as we have intimated founds its claim of exclusive authority upon an assertion of title to migratory birds, an assertion that is embodied in statute. * * * If we are to be accurate we cannot put the case of the State upon higher ground than that the treaty deals with creatures that for the moment are within the state borders, that it must be carried out by officers of the United States within the same territory, and that but for the treaty the State would be free to regulate this subject itself.

As most of the laws of the United States are carried out within the States and as many of them deal with matters which in the silence of such laws the State might regulate, such general grounds are not enough to support Missouri's claim. * * * No doubt the great body of private relations usually fall within the control of the State, but a treaty may override its power. We do not have to invoke the later developments of constitutional law for this proposition; it was recognized as early as Hopkirk v. Bell, 3 Cranch 454, 2 L.Ed. 497 with regard to statutes of limitation, and even earlier, as to confiscation, in Ware v. Hylton, 3 Dall. 199, I L.Ed. 568. * * *

Here a national interest of very nearly the first magnitude is involved. It can be protected only by national action in concert with that of another power. The subject matter is only transitorily within the State and has no permanent habitat therein. But for the treaty and the statute there soon might be no birds for any powers to deal with. We see nothing in the Constitution that compels the Government to sit by while a food supply is cut off and the protectors of our forests and our crops are destroyed. It is not sufficient to rely upon the States. The reliance is vain, and were it otherwise, the question is whether the United States is forbidden to act. We are of opinion that the treaty and statute must be upheld. * * *

Decree affirmed.

MR. JUSTICE VAN DEVANTER and MR. JUSTICE PITNEY dissent.

Notes

1. Justice Holmes's suggestion that treaties may not be subject to constitutional restraints was laid to rest in Reid v. Covert. See p. 197 above.

2. Between 1950 and 1955, Senator Bricker of Ohio led a campaign to amend the Constitution so as to "reverse" *Missouri v. Holland.* A principal section would have provided that a treaty could not become law in the United States except by act of Congress which would have been valid in the absence of the treaty. See S.J.Res. 1, 83d Cong. 1st Sess., 99 Cong. Rec. 6777 (1953); Treaties and Executive Agreements, Hearings before a Subcommittee on S.J.Res. 1 and S.J.Res. 43, 83d Cong., 1st Sess. (1953); S.Rep. No. 412, 83d Cong., 1st Sess. (1953). For an extensive bibliography on the proposed amendment, see Bishop, International Law 112 n. 39 (3d ed. 1971).

For the suggestion, in regard to the International Covenant on Civil and Political Rights, that reservations and declarations seek to achieve what the failed Bricker Amendment sought to achieve generally by constitutional amendment, see Henkin, U.S. Ratification of Human Rights Conventions: The Ghost of Senator Bricker, 89 A.J.I.L. 341 (1995).

3. Henkin writes:

> Whatever the States retain in regard to foreign affairs as a matter of constitutional right must be found in * * * doctrines [other than the Tenth Amendment]. There are dicta by Justices and by writers asserting hypothetical limitations on federal power, including its foreign affairs powers, in specific constitutional guarantees to the States and in implied state sovereignty and inviolability. Justices have said that a treaty cannot cede State territory without its consent; presumably, the United States could not, by treaty or by statute for international purposes, modify the republican character of state governments or, perhaps, abolish all state militia. Under the Eleventh Amendment foreign governments and their nationals cannot sue a state in the courts of the United States without its consent. There is also something more left, too—how much cannot be said with confidence—of the sovereign immunity of the states, which would presumably limit federal regulation under foreign affairs powers as well. State immunities have shrunk radically and state activities are generally subject to federal regulation, but Mr. Justice Frankfurter said:
>
>> There are, of course, State activities and State-owned property that partake of uniqueness from the point of view of intergovernmental relations. These inherently constitute a class by themselves. Only a State can own a Statehouse; only a State can get income by taxing. These could not be included for purposes of federal taxation in any abstract category of taxpayers without taxing the State as a State.

Foreign Affairs and the U.S. Constitution 166 (2d ed. 1996) (footnotes omitted).

And elsewhere:

> * * * The states do not conduct foreign relations, but they do influence them, and the extent to which they can do so is also limited by constitutional safeguards for individual rights.
>
> In general, the rights of the individual against infringement by the states have become virtually identical with those protected against the federal government. The original Constitution forbade the states to pass any bill of attainder, *ex post facto* laws, or laws impairing the obligation of contracts (Article I, section 10). And though originally the Bill of Rights did not apply to the states, virtually all of its provisions now do, having been "incorporated" in the Fourteenth Amendment. The due process clause of that Amendment, in particular, affords procedural and substantive protections identical to those that by the same clause in the Fifth Amendment govern the federal government. States must provide due process of law to aliens and to citizens. * * *
>
> The Fourteenth Amendment forbids the states to deny the equal protection of the laws to any person, including aliens; and in respect of aliens, equal protection makes far greater demands of the states than of the federal government. * * * Discriminations and distinctions between citizens and aliens that might be reasonable if made by the federal government in the conduct of its international relations might yet constitute denials of equal protection if practiced by a state.
>
> Thus, from the early days of the Fourteenth Amendment, the Equal Protection Clause has protected aliens against state discriminations denying them equal right to common employment. A hundred years later, new doctrine giving new vitality to equal protection principles rendered state

distinctions between citizens and aliens a 'suspect classification', requiring 'compelling state interest' to support a discrimination against aliens.

Foreign Affairs and the U.S. Constitution 309–310 (1996) (footnotes omitted). See discussion of Bill of Rights safeguards, p. 236 below.

4. In the last years of the 20th century, the Supreme Court began to find in the Tenth Amendment not merely the "truism" that what was not delegated to the United States was reserved to the states, see U.S. v. Darby, 312 U.S. 100, 124, 61 S.Ct. 451, 85 L.Ed. 609 (1941), but a reservation to the states of elements of state sovereignty as a limitation on U.S. powers. See, e.g., New York v. United States, 505 U.S. 144, 112 S.Ct. 2408, 120 L.Ed.2d 120 (1992), Printz v. United States, 521 U.S. 898, 117 S.Ct. 2365, 138 L.Ed.2d 914 (1997). These cases were held to prohibit federal attempts to command state legislatures, or to co-opt and commandeer state and municipal officials. But Congress could encourage and induce states to act, as by conditional grants of federal monies. *Cf.*, South Dakota v. Dole, 483 U.S. 203, 107 S.Ct. 2793, 97 L.Ed.2d 171 (1987). Similar reinvigoration of states' "sovereign" rights and immunities appeared in the revisiting of the 11th Amendment in Seminole Tribe of Florida v. Florida, 517 U.S. 44, 116 S.Ct. 1114, 134 L.Ed.2d 252 (1996), and in new interpretations of the Commerce Clause and the section 5 of Fourteenth Amendment to place limits on the reach of congressional powers in United States v. Lopez, 514 U.S. 549, 115 S.Ct. 1624, 131 L.Ed.2d 626 (1995) and United States v. Morrison, 529 U.S. 598, 120 S.Ct. 1740, 146 L.Ed.2d 658 (2000). It remains to be seen whether "invisible radiations" from the Tenth Amendment (*cf.* Holmes, p. 199) will be held to extend to the Treaty Power and to the conduct of U.S. foreign relations.

5. The revival of constitutional constraints on federal powers in the cases cited in the preceding note has led to renewed attacks on *Missouri v. Holland*, of a sort that had not been seen since the failure of the Bricker Amendment (Note 2 above). Arguments for limiting or overruling *Missouri v. Holland* have been made by Curtis Bradley in a series of articles, including Bradley, The Treaty Power and American Federalism, 97 Mich. L. Rev. 390 (1998), and have been debated in a 1999 symposium issue of the University of Colorado Law Review (p. 169 supra). Others have risen to defend *Missouri v. Holland* against revisionist attack, showing that nationalist understandings of the treaty power long antedated Justice Holmes's opinion. See, e.g., Golove, Treaty–Making and the Nation: The Historical Foundations of the Nationalist Conception of the Treaty Power, 98 Mich. L. Rev. 1075 (2000).

CONGRESSIONAL POWER AND THE TREATY POWER

HENKIN, FOREIGN AFFAIRS AND THE U.S. CONSTITUTION

194–96 (2d ed. 1996) (footnotes omitted).

Because the President and the Congress compete for power in the conduct of foreign relations, because the treaty-makers are the President and one house of Congress but not the other, because treaties, * * * often have effect as law (as do acts of Congress), it was inevitable that questions should arise about the relations between the 'treaty-makers' and the Congress, and not surprising that these relations might suggest limitations on the scope of the Treaty Power. Early in our history, members of the House of Representatives [and Thomas Jefferson] argued that treaties could regulate only that which could not be otherwise regulated; and they could not deal with matters that were in the domain of Congress since that would exclude the House from its rightful legislative role. * * * But if the limitations suggested mean more, if they would preclude treaties on matters as to which Congress could legislate domestically, it would virtually wipe out the treaty power. Under modern, established views of the powers of Congress, there is little—or nothing—that is dealt with by treaty that could not also be the subject of legislation by Congress.

This limitation was hardly accepted by all even in our earliest days; it has now been long dead. * * * The House of Representatives has frequently bristled, but its exclusion from the treaty process was the clear constitutional plan, and the House has not been able to command the cooperation of the Senate and the President to accept modifications of their privileged prerogatives. The House has had to find consolation in that it has some voice when, as often, the President must come to Congress for appropriation of funds or other implementation of a treaty, or when the treaty-makers voluntarily leave some subjects to regulation by Congress (e.g., international tariffs and trade). * * * Presidents have also learned to take account of House sensibilities informally by consulting its leaders about major treaties.

The Treaty Power, then, is not limited by the powers of Congress, but it is assumed to be subject to other radiations from the separation of powers. It has been stated that a treaty cannot increase, diminish, or redistribute the constitutional powers of the branches of the federal government or delegate them to others—say, the power of Congress to declare war, or the President's command of U.S. armed forces, or a court's exercise of judicial power, or indeed the power of the treaty-makers to make international agreements for the United States. These examples are almost wholly hypothetical, but such issues have been raised, particularly in regard to United States participation in international organizations * * *.

Notes

1. During 200 years Congress, and the House of Representatives in particular, sought to offset its exclusion from treaty-making in various ways. Sometimes it was content to support the treaty-makers, often purporting to "authorize" the negotiation of a treaty that would come to the Senate. For an early example see Act of March 3, 1815, 13th Cong., 3d Sess., 3 Stat. 224, authorizing conventions to provide for reciprocal termination of alien discriminations. Compare ch. 1079, § 4, 32 Stat. 373 (1902); ch. 3621, § 4, 34 Stat. 628 (1906); Wright 281–82. In 1925 the House of Representatives resolved that it "desires to express its cordial approval of the [World Court] and an earnest desire that the United States give early adherence" to it with certain reservations. The House also expressed "its readiness to participate in the enactment of such legislation as will necessarily follow such approval." H.R.Res. 426, 68 Cong., 2d Sess., 66 Cong. Rec. 5404–05 (1925). Sometimes it sought to forestall a treaty by legislating: to preserve its authority over commerce it sought to enact the provisions of a treaty with Great Britain. See 5 Moore, Digest at 223. On occasion it purported to prescribe that international agreements should go to Congress for approval rather than as a treaty to the Senate alone for its consent. Compare the United Nations Participation Act of 1945, 22 U.S.C. § 287d (1988), in regard to agreements under Article 43 of the UN Charter.

Compare the argument that the Panama Canal Treaty was invalid because it disposed of "Territory or other Property belonging to the United States," a power expressly granted to Congress. (U.S. Const. Art. IV, § 3, cl. 2.) The argument was rejected in Edwards v. Carter, 580 F.2d 1055 (D.C.Cir.1978), cert. denied, 436 U.S. 907, 98 S.Ct. 2240, 56 L.Ed.2d 406 (1978).

On treaties and the legislative powers of Congress, see Restatement (Third) § 303, Comment *c*.

2. It has been suggested that giving the House of Representatives a role in treaty-making would make the treaty power more democratic. See Henkin, Treaties in a Constitutional Democracy, 10 Mich.J.Int'l L. 406, 412–23 (1989), reprinted in Henkin, Constitutionalism, Democracy and Foreign Affairs 58–68 (1990). For the distribution of power between Congress and the President in foreign affairs generally, see Special Issue, The United States Constitution in its Third Century: Foreign Affairs, 83 A.J.I.L. (October, 1989), published also as Foreign Affairs and the U.S. Constitution (Henkin, Glennon & Rogers, eds., 1990).

3. For some years, there existed the impression that in order to pass constitutional muster, a treaty had to deal with matters of "international concern," Restatement (Second) Foreign Relations Law of the United States § 117. This view had been invoked to suggest that the United States could not constitutionally adhere to human rights treaties because they involved matters of strictly domestic concern. This view has long since been abandoned. See Restatement (Third) § 302, Reporters' Note 2.

4. Henkin writes:

> If there are reasons in foreign policy why the United States seeks an agreement with a foreign country, it does not matter that the subject is otherwise "internal," that the treaty "makes laws for the people of the United States in their internal concerns", or that—apart from treaty—the matter is "normally and appropriately ... within the local jurisdiction of the States." Any treaty that has any effect within the United States, including the traditional treaties of friendship and commerce, are specifically designed to change the law of the United States that might otherwise apply, e.g., the rights of aliens here. As other policies and laws of the United States become of interest to other countries, they are equally subject to modification by treaty if the United States has foreign policy reasons for negotiating about them.
>
> If there were any basis for the [doctrine of "international concern"], and if it barred some hypothetical agreement on some hypothetical subject, surely it is not relevant where some would have invoked it—to prevent adherence by the United States to international human rights covenants and conventions. Human rights had long been of international concern and the subject of international agreements * * *.

Henkin, Foreign Affairs and the U.S. Constitution 197–198 (1996) (footnotes omitted). See also Henkin, The Age of Rights 74–80 (1990).

As of the end of the 20th Century, the United States had adhered to several human rights treaties (see Chapter 8, p. 599 below), and the constitutional propriety of United States adherence to such treaties is no longer challenged.

The Restatement (Third) has abandoned the requirement of "international concern." See § 302, Comment *c* and Reporters' Note 2.

The Foreign Affairs Manual of the Department of State (§ 311) provides: "Treaties are designed to promote United States interests by securing actions by foreign governments in a way deemed advantageous to the United States." Circular No. 175, as revised. Is that a complete statement of United States interests, particularly in multilateral treaties?

c. *Treaties as Law of the Land*

"SELF-EXECUTING" AND "NON-SELF-EXECUTING" AGREEMENTS

FOSTER AND ELAM v. NEILSON

Supreme Court of the United States, 1829.
27 U.S. (2 Pet.) 253, 7 L.Ed. 415.

[Appellants sued to recover a tract of land in Louisiana which they claimed under a grant made by the Spanish governor. The possessor of the land argued that the grant on which appellants relied was void because it was made subsequent to the transfer to France and the United States of the territory in which the land was situated. The district court upheld the defense, and the case was brought to the Supreme Court by a writ of error. The Court held that it was obliged to conform its decision on the question of sovereignty to that already reached by the executive and legislative branches of government, and that the territory had to be considered as having been part of the United States at the time of the grant. Appellants relied further, however, on Article 8 of a treaty concluded in 1819 between the United States and Spain (8 Stat. 252), which provided that "all the grants of land made before the 24th of January 1818, by his Catholic majesty, or by his lawful authorities, in the said territories ceded by his majesty to the United States, shall be ratified and confirmed to the persons in possession of the lands, to the same extent that the same grants would be valid if the territories had remained under the dominion of his Catholic majesty," arguing that the land in question formed part of the specified ceded territories. The Court found it unnecessary to decide the latter question, holding that the treaty did not operate in itself to ratify or confirm appellants' title.]

MARSHALL, C.J.: * * * Do these words [of Article 8] act directly on the grants, so as to give validity to those not otherwise valid; or do they pledge the faith of the United States to pass acts which shall ratify and confirm them?

A treaty is in its nature a contract between two nations, not a legislative act. It does not generally effect, of itself, the object to be accomplished, especially so far as its operation is infra-territorial; but is carried into execution by the sovereign power of the respective parties to the instrument.

In the United States a different principle is established. Our constitution declares a treaty to be the law of the land. It is, consequently, to be regarded in courts of justice as equivalent to an act of the legislature, whenever it operates of itself without the aid of any legislative provision. But when the terms of the stipulation import a contract, when either of the parties engages to perform a particular act, the treaty addresses itself to the political, not the judicial department; and the legislature must execute the contract before it can become a rule for the Court.

The article under consideration does not declare that all the grants made by his Catholic majesty before the 24th of January 1818, shall be valid to the same extent as if the ceded territories had remained under his dominion. It does not say that those grants are hereby confirmed. Had such been its language, it would have acted directly on the subject, and would have repealed those acts of Congress which were repugnant to it; but its language is that those grants shall be ratified and confirmed to the persons in possession, & c. By whom shall they be ratified and confirmed? This seems to be the language of contract; and if it is, the ratification and confirmation which are promised must be the act of the legislature. Until such act shall be passed, the Court is not at liberty to disregard the existing laws on the subject. Congress appears to have understood this article as it is understood by the Court. * * * [The Court then cited legislation which it construed as inconsistent with an intention on the part of Congress to preserve grants of land made by Spanish authorities.]

[Judgment of the district court affirmed.]

Notes

1. The Restatement (Third) § 111, Comment *i* states:

Constitutional restraints on self-executing character of international agreement. An international agreement cannot take effect as domestic law without implementation by Congress if the agreement would achieve what lies within the exclusive law-making power of Congress under the Constitution. Thus, an international agreement providing for the payment of money by the United States requires an appropriation of funds by Congress in order to effect the payment required by the agreement. It has been commonly assumed that an international agreement cannot itself bring the United States into a state of war. Similarly, it has been assumed that an international agreement creating an international crime *(e.g.,* genocide) or requiring states parties to punish certain actions *(e.g.,* hijacking) could not itself become part of the criminal law of the United States, but would require Congress to enact an appropriate statute before an individual could be tried or punished for the offense. It has also been suggested that a treaty cannot "raise revenue" by itself imposing a new tax or a new tariff, in view of the provision in Article I, Section 7: "All Bills for raising Revenue shall originate in the House of Representatives." Treaties of friendship, commerce and navigation, however, frequently affect tariffs and trade by "most-favored-nation," "national treatment," and analogous clauses. Compare § 801.

2. The Restatement (Third) § 111, Comment *h* states:

Self-executing and non-self-executing international agreements. In the absence of special agreement, it is ordinarily for the United States to decide how it will carry out its international obligations. Accordingly, the intention of the United States determines whether an agreement is to be self-executing in the United States or should await implementation by legislation or appropriate executive or administrative action. If the international agreement is silent as to its self-executing character and the intention of the United States is unclear, account must be taken of any statement by the President in concluding the agreement or in submitting it to the Senate for consent or to the Congress as a whole for approval, and of any expression by the Senate or by Congress in dealing with the agreement. See § 314, Comments *b* and *d*;

§ 303, Comment *d.* After the agreement is concluded, often the President must decide in the first instance whether the agreement is self-executing, *i.e.,* whether existing law is adequate to enable the United States to carry out its obligations, or whether further legislation is required. Congress may also consider whether new legislation is necessary and, if so, what it should provide. Whether an agreement is to be given effect without further legislation is an issue that a court must decide when a party seeks to invoke the agreement as law. Whether an agreement is or is not self-executing in the law of another state party to the agreement is not controlling for the United States.

Some provisions of an international agreement may be self-executing and others non-self-executing. If an international agreement or one of its provisions is non-self-executing, the United States is under an international obligation to adjust its laws and institutions as may be necessary to give effect to the agreement. The United States would have a reasonable time to do so before it could be deemed in default. There can, of course, be instances in which the United States Constitution, or previously enacted legislation, will be fully adequate to give effect to an apparently non-self-executing international agreement, thus obviating the need of adopting new legislation to implement it.

Under Subsection (3), strictly, it is the implementing legislation, rather than the agreement itself, that is given effect as law in the United States. That is true even when a non-self-executing agreement is "enacted" by, or incorporated in, implementing legislation.

Whether a treaty is self-executing is a question distinct from whether the treaty creates private rights or remedies. See Comment *g.*

3. In United States v. Percheman, 32 U.S. (7 Pet.) 51, 8 L.Ed. 604 (1833), C.J. Marshall relied in part on the Spanish text of Article 8 of the 1819 treaty to support the Court's conclusion that an adverse decision by a board of land commissioners did not foreclose claimant from pursuing judicial remedies to confirm his title to land claimed under a Spanish grant. Emphasizing that "the modern usage of nations, which has become law," demanded that private rights and property be respected upon a transfer of sovereignty over territory, Marshall held that Article 8 merely restated this principle and needed no implementing legislation.

The Spanish has been translated, and we now understand that the article, as expressed in that language, is, that the grants "shall remain ratified and confirmed to the persons in possession of them, to the same extent, & c.,"—thus conforming exactly to the universally received doctrine of the law of nations. * * * No violence is done to the language of the treaty by a construction which conforms the English and Spanish to each other. Although the words "shall be ratified and confirmed" are properly the words of contract, stipulating for some future legislative act; they are not necessarily so. They may import that they "shall be ratified and confirmed" by force of the instrument itself. When we observe that in the counterpart of the same treaty, executed at the same time by the same parties, they are used in this sense, we think the construction proper, if not unavoidable.

In the case of Foster v. Elam [*sic*] 2 Peters 253, this court considered these words as importing contract. The Spanish part of the treaty was not then brought to our view, and we then supposed that there was no variance between them. We did not suppose that there was even a formal difference of

> expression in the same instrument, drawn up in the language of each party. Had this circumstance been known, we believe it would have produced the construction which we now give to the article.

Id. at 88–89.

4. Treaties that create obligations to refrain from acting are generally self-executing. In an opinion characterized by the Supreme Court as "very able" (United States v. Rauscher, 119 U.S. 407, 427–28, 7 S.Ct. 234, 244–45, 30 L.Ed. 425 (1886)), the Court of Appeals of Kentucky said:

> When it is provided by treaty that certain acts shall not be done, or that certain limitations or restrictions shall not be disregarded or exceeded by the contracting parties, the compact does not need to be supplemented by legislative or executive action, to authorize the courts of justice to decline to override those limitations or to exceed the prescribed restrictions, for the palpable and all-sufficient reason, that to do so would be not only to violate the public faith, but to transgress the "supreme law of the land."

Commonwealth v. Hawes, 76 Ky. (13 Bush) 697, 702–03 (1878).

5. Does the Supremacy Clause (Article VI of the U.S. Constitution) suggest a presumption in favor of the self-executing nature of treaties, in the absence of clear indications to the contrary in a given treaty or the context of its approval? Since ordinarily a treaty creates international obligations for the United States from the date it comes into force for the United States, if a treaty is not self-executing the United States is obligated to act promptly to implement it. If a treaty has been in effect for some time and the Executive has not sought and Congress has not enacted implementing legislation, it may be reasonable to assume that the Executive Branch and Congress had concluded that no implementation was necessary. As to a treaty that has been in effect for some time, a finding that it is not self-executing in effect puts the United States in default on its international obligations. See Restatement (Third) § 111, Reporters' Note 5. See also Iwasawa, The Doctrine of Self–Executing Treaties in the United States: A Critical Analysis, 26 Va. J.Int'l L. 627 (1986); Paust, Self–Executing Treaties, 82 A.J.I.L. 760 (1988); Jackson, Status of Treaties in Domestic Legal Systems: A Policy Analysis, 86 A.J.I.L. 310 (1992). In Cannon v. U.S. Justice Dep't, 973 F.2d 1190, 1197 (5th Cir.1992), reh'g denied, 979 F.2d 211, the court stated that "[p]rocedural legislation which makes operation of a treaty more convenient cannot amend or abrogate a self-executing treaty."

Recent scholarship has brought out contrasting points of view as to whether Marshall's distinction between self-executing and non-self-executing treaties was well-founded in light of the framers' understanding. Compare Yoo, Globalism and the Constitution: Treaties, Non–Self–Execution, and the Original Understanding, 99 Col. L. Rev. 1955 (1999) with Flaherty, History Right? Historical Scholarship, Original Understanding, and Treaties as "Supreme Law of the Land," 99 Col. L. Rev. 2095 (1999), and Vazquez, Laughing at Treaties, 99 Col. L. Rev. 2154 (1999); see also Yoo, Rejoinder: Treaties and Public Lawmaking: A Textual and Structural Defense of Non–Self–Execution, 99 Col. L. Rev. 2218 (1999).

6. Many cases have addressed whether given treaties are non-self-executing or self-executing. Examples include:

a. Non-self-executing treaties

• Hague Convention Respecting the Law and Customs of War on Land, 1907, Art. 3, 36 Stat. 2277, 2290. See Goldstar (Panama) v. United States, 967 F.2d 965 (4th Cir.1992), cert. denied, 506 U.S. 955, 113 S.Ct. 411, 121 L.Ed.2d 335 (1992).

• United Nations Protocol Relating to the Status of Refugees, 1967, 19 UST 6223; T.I.A.S. No. 6577. See United States v. Aguilar, 883 F.2d 662 (9th Cir.1989), cert. denied, 498 U.S. 1046, 111 S.Ct. 751, 112 L.Ed.2d 771 (1991).

• Geneva Convention Relative to the Protection of Civilian Persons in Time of War, 1949, 6 UST 3516; T.I.A.S. No. 3365; Geneva Convention Relative to the Treatment of Prisoners of War, 1949, 6 UST 3316; T.I.A.S. No. 8413; Convention to Prevent and Punish the Acts of Terrorism Taking the Forms of Crime Against Persons and Related Extortion That Are of International Significance, 1971, 27 UST 3949; T.I.A.S. No. 8413. See Tel–Oren v. Libyan Arab Republic, 726 F.2d 774, 808–09 (D.C.Cir.1984) (Bork, J., concurring), cert. denied, 470 U.S. 1003, 105 S.Ct. 1354, 84 L.Ed.2d 377 (1985).

• Geneva Convention on the High Seas, 1958, 13 UST 2312; T.I.A.S. No. 5200. See United States v. Peterson, 812 F.2d 486 (9th Cir.1987).

• Geneva Convention on Territorial Sea and Contiguous Zone, 1958, 15 UST 1606, T.I.A.S. No. 5639. See United States v. Thompson, 928 F.2d 1060 (11th Cir.1991), cert. denied, 502 U.S. 897, 112 S.Ct. 270, 116 L.Ed.2d 222 (1991).

• Basel Convention on the Control of Transboundary Movements of Hazardous Wastes, 1989, reprinted in, 28 Int'l Legal Materials 657 (1989). See Greenpeace USA v. Stone, 748 F.Supp. 749 (D.Hawaii 1990), appeal dismissed, 924 F.2d 175 (9th Cir.1991).

b. Treaties held to be self-executing/directly applicable in courts

• Convention on Contracts for the International Sale of Goods, 1489 U.N.T.S. 3, Delchi Carrier SpA v. Rotorex Corp., 71 F.3rd 1024, 1027–28 (2d Cir.1995); Filanto, S.p.A. v. Chilewich Int'l Corp., 789 F.Supp. 1229, 1237 (S.D.N.Y.1992), appeal dismissed, 984 F.2d 58 (2d Cir.1993)

• Convention for the Unification of Certain Rules Relating to International Transportation by Air, 1929, T.S. 876 (1934), reprinted at, 49 U.S.C.A. § 1502 note. See Trans World Airlines, Inc. v. Franklin Mint Corp., 466 U.S. 243, 104 S.Ct. 1776, 80 L.Ed.2d 273 (1984); see also El Al Israel Airlines, Ltd. v. Tseng, 525 U.S. 155, 119 S.Ct. 662, 142 L.Ed.2d 576 (1999).

• Treaty on the Execution of Penal Sentences, 1976, 20 UST 7399; T.I.A.S. No. 8718. See Cannon v. U.S. Dep't of Justice, 973 F.2d 1190 (5th Cir.1992). See also note 7 below.

7. The United Nations Charter, and in particular its human rights provisions, have been held to be non-self-executing. See Sei Fujii v. California, 217 P.2d 481 (Cal.App.1950) rehearing denied, 218 P.2d 595 (1950), in which the California District Court of Appeal held invalid a state statute forbidding aliens ineligible for citizenship to "acquire, possess, enjoy, use, cultivate, occupy, and transfer" real property, on the ground that the statute conflicted with the United Nations Charter. On appeal, the California Supreme Court held the statute invalid under the Fourteenth Amendment, expressly rejecting the lower court's view that the Charter provisions on human rights had become the "supreme law of the land." 38 Cal.2d 718, 242 P.2d 617 (1952). Gibson, C.J., stated in part: "The fundamental provisions in the charter pledging cooperation in promoting observance of fundamental freedoms lack the mandatory quality and definiteness which would indicate an intent to create justiciable rights in private persons immediately upon ratification. Instead, they are framed as a promise of future action by the member nations." 38 Cal.2d at 724, 242 P.2d at 621–22. What legal obligations, whether or not self-executing, are actually imposed by Articles 1(3), 55 and 56 of the Charter?

In Weir v. Broadnax, 56 Empl.Prac. Dec. (CCH) 40,684 (S.D.N.Y.1990), the plaintiff's statement of claim alleging the breach of Articles 55 and 56 of the U.N. Charter, based on a pattern of systematic racial discrimination, was struck on defendant's motion. See also United States v. Caro–Quintero, 745 F.Supp. 599 (C.D.Cal.1990), aff'd sub nom. United States v. Alvarez–Machain, 946 F.2d 1466 (9th Cir.1991), rev'd, 504 U.S. 655, 112 S.Ct. 2188, 119 L.Ed.2d 441 (1992); United States v. Noriega, 746 F.Supp. 1506 (S.D.Fla.1990); Helms v. Secretary of Treasury, 721 F.Supp. 1354 (D.D.C.1989).

8. Marshall did not suggest that treaties (or treaty provisions) of a self-executing character could be rendered non-self-executing by presidential or senatorial declaration. That practice developed largely after World War II in special circumstances, on the basis of arguments for cooperation between the "treaty makers and the law makers." See Henkin, The Treaty Makers and the Law Makers: The Niagara Power Reservation, 56 Colum.L.Rev. 1151 (1956); Foreign Affairs and the U.S. Constitution 198–204, 476–78 (2d ed. 1996); Vazquez, The Four Doctrines of Self-executing Treaties, 89 A.J.I.L 695 (1995); Damrosch, The Role of the United States Concerning Self–Executing and Non–Self–Executing Treaties, 67 Chi.-Kent L. Rev. 515 (1991).

The practice became more common towards the end of the 20th century, particularly in ratifying human rights agreements. See the declarations by the Senate in connection with its consent to the United Nations Convention against Torture and Other Cruel, Inhuman or Degrading Treatment or Punishment, and the International Covenant on Civil and Political Rights, discussed in Damrosch, supra, and in Sloss, The Domestication of International Human Rights: Non–Self–Executing Declarations and Human Rights Treaties, 24 Yale. J.I.L. 129 (1999).

Declaring a treaty non-self-executing is sometimes justified on the ground that it gives a role in the treaty-making process to the House of Representatives and may make the process more "democratic" insofar as the House is a more representative body than the Senate. It sometimes appears that the President and the Senate may have declared treaties to be non-self-executing from resistance to "law-making by treaty," particularly by multilateral treaties, or in order to delay or even frustrate U.S. implementation of its undertakings. It has been suggested that since other states may have to adopt legislation to give effect to treaties, the United States too, should not enforce its obligations immediately. Compare United States v. Postal, 589 F.2d 862 (5th Cir.1979), cert. denied, 444 U.S. 832, 100 S.Ct. 61, 62 L.Ed.2d 40 (1979). But see Restatement (Third) § 111, Reporters' Note 5, declaring that view to be "misconceived."

The practice of the Senate (or the President) to declare non-self-executing a treaty that would otherwise be self-executing is being increasingly questioned. See, e.g., Damrosch, The Role of the United States Senate Concerning "Self–Executing" and "Non–Self–Executing" Treaties, 67 Chi.-Kent L.Rev. 515, 516–18 (1991); Riesenfeld & Abbott, The Scope of U.S. Senate Control Over the Conclusion and Operation of Treaties, 67 Chi.-Kent L.Rev. 571, 631 (1991); Vazquez, Treaty–Based Rights and Remedies of Individuals, 92 Colum. L.Rev. 1082 (1992). Is it implausible to argue that for the President or the Senate to declare non-self-executing a treaty that could be executed without implementing legislation is contrary to both the letter and spirit of the Constitution, and to the distribution of power between the Senate and the House intended by the Framers? See Henkin, Foreign Affairs and the U.S. Constitution 202 (2d ed. 1996). And compare, generally, the contributions by Damrosch, Glennon, Riesenfeld & Abbott, and Trimble & Weiss, in Parliamentary Participation in the Making and Operation of Treaties: A Comparative Study 205–382 (Riesenfeld & Abbott eds. 1994).

9. In Attorney–General for Canada v. Attorney–General for Ontario, [1937] A.C. 326, the Privy Council was asked to decide whether certain Canadian statutes, enacted in order to fulfill Canada's obligations under a number of International Labor Conventions, were constitutionally effective without the consent of the Canadian provinces to bring the law of those provinces into conformity with the provisions of the conventions. In the course of his opinion holding that the statutes were *ultra vires* of the Parliament of Canada under the British North America Act of 1867, Lord Atkin made the following general observations on the internal effect of treaties under the British system:

> * * * It will be essential to keep in mind the distinction between (1.) the formation, and (2.) the performance, of the obligations constituted by a treaty, using that word as comprising any agreement between two or more sovereign States. Within the British Empire there is a well-established rule that the making of a treaty is an executive act, while the performance of its obligations, if they entail alteration of the existing domestic law, requires legislative action. Unlike some other countries, the stipulations of a treaty duly ratified do not within the Empire, by virtue of the treaty alone, have the force of law. If the national executive, the government of the day, decide to incur the obligations of a treaty which involve alteration of law they have to run the risk of obtaining the assent of Parliament to the necessary statute or statutes. To make themselves as secure as possible they will often in such cases before final ratification seek to obtain from Parliament an expression of approval. But it has never been suggested, and it is not the law, that such an expression of approval operates as law, or that in law it precludes the assenting Parliament, or any subsequent Parliament, from refusing to give its sanction to any legislative proposals that may subsequently be brought before it. Parliament, no doubt, as the Chief Justice points out, has a constitutional control over the executive: but it cannot be disputed that the creation of the obligations undertaken in treaties and the assent to their form and quality are the function of the executive alone. Once they are created, while they bind the State as against the other contracting parties, Parliament may refuse to perform them and so leave the State in default. In a unitary State whose Legislature possesses unlimited powers the problem is simple. Parliament will either fulfil or not treaty obligations imposed upon the State by its executive. The nature of the obligations does not affect the complete authority of the Legislature to make them law if it so chooses. But in a State where the Legislature does not possess absolute authority, in a federal State where legislative authority is limited by a constitutional document, or is divided up between different Legislatures in accordance with the classes of subject-matter submitted for legislation, the problem is complex. The obligations imposed by treaty may have to be performed, if at all, by several Legislatures; and the executive have the task of obtaining the legislative assent not of the one Parliament to whom they may be responsible, but possibly of several Parliaments to whom they stand in no direct relation. The question is not how is the obligation formed, that is the function of the executive; but how is the obligation to be performed, and that depends upon the authority of the competent Legislature or Legislatures.

[1937] A.C. at 347–48. See the symposium on this case in 15 Canadian Bar Rev. 393 (1937), and see generally McNair, The Law of Treaties 81–110 (1961). If difficulties are expected in the process of implementing the provisions of an international agreement, what precautions might the executive of a state take in order to avoid international responsibility for defaulting on the obligations imposed by the agreement?

10. Section 34 of the Convention on the Privileges and Immunities of the United Nations, 1946, 1 U.N.T.S. 15, provides: "It is understood that, when an instrument of accession is deposited on behalf of any Member, the Member will be in a position under its own law to give effect to the terms of this convention." Article X(1) of the Interim Convention on Conservation of North Pacific Fur Seals, 1957, 8 U.S.T. 2283, 314 U.N.T.S. 105, provides: "Each Party agrees to enact and enforce such legislation as may be necessary to guarantee the observance of this Convention and to make effective its provisions with appropriate penalties for violation thereof." Article III(5) of the Treaty between the French Republic and the Federal Republic of Germany on French–German Cooperation, 2 I.L.M. 229 (1963), provides: "The present Treaty will enter into force as soon as each of the two Governments will have made known to the other that, on the domestic level, the necessary conditions for its implementation have been fulfilled." Section 15 of the Tracking Stations Agreement between the United States and Spain, 1964, 15 U.S.T. 153, 511 U.N.T.S. 61, provides: "It is understood that, to the extent the implementation of this agreement will depend on funds appropriated by the Congress of the United States, it is subject to the availability of such funds." Even a treaty that is self-executing in most of its provisions may sometimes include obligations on the parties to adopt implementing legislation. See, for example, Article 2(2) of the International Covenant on Civil and Political Rights, discussed pp. 597 and 620 below; Schachter, The Obligation to Implement the Covenant in Domestic Law, in The International Bill of Rights: the Covenant on Civil and Political Rights (Henkin ed. 1981).

11. For the different—but important—question whether an individual (in contrast to a state party to a treaty) has rights under a treaty, see Dreyfus v. Von Finck, 534 F.2d 24, 30 (2d Cir.1976). Dreyfus was a Swiss citizen who sued West German citizens in a United States court for unlawful confiscation of his property in Nazi Germany in 1938. He based his private right of action on four treaties to which the United States was a party. In concluding that Dreyfus could not sue under any of the treaties, the court said that they were not self-executing and that, in any event, it is only when a treaty "prescribes rules by which private rights may be determined, that it may be relied upon for the enforcement of such rights * * * [N]one of these [treaties] dealt with the expropriations by Germans of the property of German citizens and none conferred any private rights which were enforceable in American courts." Id. at 30. See Restatement (Third) § 111, Comment *g*. In Committee of United States Citizens Living in Nicaragua v. Reagan, 859 F.2d 929 (1988), the Court of Appeals for the D.C. Circuit held that provisions of the United Nations Charter requiring compliance with International Court of Justice decisions do not create rights that are enforceable by individuals in United States Courts. See generally Vazquez, The Four Doctrines of Self–Executing Treaties, 89 A.J.I.L. 695 (1995).

CONFLICT OF TREATY WITH UNITED STATES STATUTE

WHITNEY v. ROBERTSON

Supreme Court of the United States, 1888.
124 U.S. 190, 8 S.Ct. 456, 31 L.Ed. 386.

[Plaintiff sued to recover amounts paid under protest to the Collector of Customs at New York in satisfaction of duties assessed upon plaintiff's shipments of sugar from the Dominican Republic. Plaintiff alleged that sugar from the Hawaiian Islands was admitted free of duty into the United States, and claimed that a clause of the treaty between the United States and the Dominican Republic guaranteed that no higher duty would be assessed upon goods imported into the United States from the Dominican Republic than was assessed upon goods imported from any other foreign country. Judgment was entered for the Collector of Customs upon the latter's demurrer, and plaintiff appealed. The Supreme Court, in an opinion by Mr. Justice Field, first held that the treaty could not be interpreted to foreclose the extension by the United States of special privileges to countries such as the Hawaiian Islands which were willing in return to extend special privileges to the United States.]

FIELD, J.: * * * But, independently of considerations of this nature, there is another and complete answer to the pretensions of the plaintiffs. The act of Congress under which the duties were collected, authorized their exaction. It is of general application, making no exception in favor of goods of any country. It was passed after the treaty with the Dominican Republic, and, if there be any conflict between the stipulations of the treaty and the requirements of the law, the latter must control. A treaty is primarily a contract between two or more independent nations, and is so regarded by writers on public law. For the infraction of its provisions a remedy must be sought by the injured party through reclamations upon the other. When the stipulations are not self-executing, they can only be enforced pursuant to legislation to carry them into effect, and such legislation is as much subject to modification and repeal by Congress as legislation upon any other subject. If the treaty contains stipulations which are self-executing, that is, require no legislation to make them operative, to that extent they have the force and effect of a legislative enactment. Congress may modify such provisions, so far as they bind the United States, or supersede them altogether. By the Constitution, a treaty is placed on the same footing, and made of like obligation, with an act of legislation. Both are declared by that instrument to be the supreme law of the land, and no superior efficacy is given to either over the other. When the two relate to the same subject, the courts will always endeavor to construe them so as to give effect to both, if that can be done without violating the language of either; but, if the two are inconsistent, the one last in date will control the other: provided, always, the stipulation of the treaty on the subject is self-executing. If the country with which the treaty is made is dissatisfied with the action of the legislative department, it may present its complaint to the executive head of the government, and take such other measures as it may deem essential for the protection of its interests. The courts can afford no redress. Whether the complaining nation has just cause of complaint, or our country was justified in its legislation, are not matters for judicial cognizance.
* * *

Judgment affirmed.

Notes

1. The Restatement (Third) § 115 states:

Inconsistency Between International Law or Agreements and Domestic Law: Law of the United States

(1)(a) An act of Congress supersedes an earlier rule of international law or a provision of an international agreement as law of the United States if the purpose of the act to supersede the earlier rule or provision is clear or if the act and the earlier rule or provision cannot be fairly reconciled.

(b) That a rule of international law or a provision of an international agreement is superseded as domestic law does not relieve the United States of its international obligation or of the consequences of a violation of that obligation.

(2) A provision of a treaty of the United States that becomes effective as law of the United States supersedes as domestic law any inconsistent preexisting provision of a law or treaty of the United States.

As to conflict between statutes and customary international law, see p. 170 above. For the principle of interpretation to avoid conflict between a federal statute and international obligation, see p. 220 below.

The Restatement here states rules of United States law. For the applicable rules of international law, see Chapters 7 and 9.

2. In a Memorandum prepared for President Harding, October 8, 1921, Secretary of State Charles Evans Hughes stated, "Congress [by passing inconsistent legislation] has the power to violate treaties, but if they are violated, the Nation will be none the less exposed to all the international consequences of such a violation because the action is taken by the legislative branch of the Government." 5 Hackworth at 324–25. "Where a treaty and an act of Congress are wholly inconsistent with each other and the two cannot be reconciled, the courts have held that the one later in point of time must prevail. While this is necessarily true as a matter of municipal law, it does not follow, as has sometimes been said, that a treaty is repealed or abrogated by a later inconsistent statute. The treaty still subsists as an international obligation although it may not be enforceable by the courts or administrative authorities." Id. at 185–86. See also The Cherokee Tobacco, 78 U.S. (11 Wall.) 616, 20 L.Ed. 227 (1871); Chae Chan Ping v. United States, 130 U.S. 581, 9 S.Ct. 623, 32 L.Ed. 1068 (1889); Rainey v. United States, 232 U.S. 310, 316, 34 S.Ct. 429, 58 L.Ed. 617 (1914); and other cases cited in 5 Hackworth at 185–98. For a discussion of the jurisprudence of the Supreme Court on the hierarchy between statutes and treaties, see Henkin, The Constitution and United States Sovereignty: A Century of Chinese Exclusion and Its Progeny, 100 Harv. L.Rev. 853 (1987); Westen, The Place of Foreign Treaties in the Courts of the United States: A Reply to Louis Henkin, 101 Harv. L.Rev. 511 (1987); Henkin, Lexical Priority or "Political Question:" A Response, 101 Harv. L.Rev. 524 (1987).

3. The interplay between the treaty obligations of the United States and apparently inconsistent legislation was raised in 1987 by the Anti–Terrorism Act (22 U.S.C.A. §§ 5201–5203). The Act was construed by the Attorney General to require the closure of the P.L.O.'s Permanent Observer Mission to the United Nations. Such closure, it was assumed, would have violated U.S. obligations under the United Nations Headquarters Agreement. The dispute led to an advisory

opinion of the International Court of Justice, as well as to proceedings in the U.S. federal courts. It was resolved when the District Court ruled that the Act should be interpreted to avoid a conflict with the treaty and thus not to require closure of the mission. See Applicability of the Obligation to Arbitrate Under Section 21 of the U.N. Headquarters Agreement of June 26, 1947, 1988 I.C.J. 12; United States v. Palestine Liberation Organization, 695 F.Supp. 1456 (S.D.N.Y.1988). See also Quigley, Congress and the P.L.O. and Conflicts between Statutes and Treaties, 35 Wayne L.Rev. 83 (1988).

"A treaty will not be deemed to have been abrogated or modified by a later statute unless such purpose on the part of Congress has been clearly expressed." Cook v. United States, 288 U.S. 102, 120, 53 S.Ct. 305, 311, 77 L.Ed. 641 (1933) (Brandeis, J.). See also Steinhardt, The Role of International Law as a Canon of Domestic Statutory Construction, 43 Vand. L.Rev. 1103 (1990). Do the foregoing principles apply equally to executive agreements? See Restatement (Third) § 114, p. 220 below. See also p. 235 below.

Sohn has suggested that the United States should adopt the rule of the Netherlands and give effect to a multilateral law-codifying treaty even in the face of a later inconsistent statute. Sohn, 63 A.S.I.L.Proc. 180 (1969). Can such a principle be supported by constitutional doctrine? See Henkin, Foreign Affairs and the U.S. Constitution 485 (2d ed. 1996), suggesting that contrary to what the Supreme Court may have implied, the rule announced by Whitney v. Robertson is not compelled by the language of the Supremacy Clause, U.S. Const., Art. VI.

4. In Tag v. Rogers, 267 F.2d 664 (D.C.Cir.1959), cert. denied, 362 U.S. 904, 80 S.Ct. 615, 4 L.Ed.2d 555 (1960), the appellant argued that international practice, formalized in a rule of law, forbids the seizure or confiscation of the property of enemy nationals during time of war, at least where that property had been acquired by enemy nationals before the war and in reliance upon international agreements. In rejecting this argument the court said in part: "Once a policy has been declared in a treaty or statute, it is the duty of the federal courts to accept as law the latest expression of policy made by the constitutionally authorized policy-making authority. If Congress adopts a policy that conflicts with the Constitution of the United States, Congress is then acting beyond its authority and the courts must declare the resulting statute to be null and void. When, however, a constitutional agency adopts a policy contrary to a trend in international law or to a treaty or prior statute, the courts must accept the latest act of that agency." 267 F.2d at 668. See also The Over the Top, 5 F.2d 838 (D.Conn. 1925); Committee of United States Citizens Living in Nicaragua v. Reagan, 859 F.2d 929 (D.C.Cir.1988). As to whether the courts will give effect to executive acts that violate international law, see pp. 176–178.

In *The Paquete Habana,* p. 62 supra, the Supreme Court said: "This rule of international law is one which prize courts, administering the law of nations, are bound to take judicial notice of, and to give effect to, *in the absence of any treaty or other public act of their own government in relation to the matter.*" (Emphasis supplied.) 175 U.S. 677, 708, 20 S.Ct. 290, 302, 44 L.Ed. 320, 332; see also 175 U.S. at 700, 20 S.Ct. at 299, 44 L.Ed. at 328. In that case the Court found that the seizure of fishing boats as prize in violation of international law had not been authorized by the President, and that the President had clearly manifested a policy that the war should be conducted in accordance with international law. 175 U.S. at 712, 20 S.Ct. at 304, 44 L.Ed. at 333.

Will the courts give effect to a newly developed principle of customary law in the face of an earlier inconsistent statute, treaty, or executive action? See Restatement (Third) § 115, Reporters' Note 4.

* * *

The Supreme Court of the United States cited with approval and followed the later-in-time rule of Whitney v. Robertson in the following case:

BREARD v. GREENE; REPUBLIC OF PARAGUAY v. GILMORE

Supreme Court of the United States, 1998.
523 U.S. 371, 118 S.Ct. 1352, 140 L.Ed.2d 529.

PER CURIAM.

Angel Francisco Breard is scheduled to be executed by the Commonwealth of Virginia this evening at 9:00 pm. Breard, a citizen of Paraguay, came to the United States in 1986, at the age of 20. In 1992, Breard was charged with the attempted rape and capital murder of Ruth Dickie.... Following a jury trial in the Circuit Court of Arlington County, Virginia, Breard was convicted of both charges and sentenced to death. On appeal, the Virginia Supreme Court affirmed Breard's convictions and sentences. State collateral relief was subsequently denied as well.

Breard then filed motion for habeas relief under 28 U.S.C § 2254 in Federal District Court on August 20, 1996. In that motion, Breard argued for the first time that his conviction and sentence should be overturned because of alleged violations of the Vienna Convention on Consular Relations (Vienna Convention), April 24, 1963, (1970) 21 U.S.T 77, T.I.A.S. No. 6820, at the time of his arrest. Specifically, Breard alleged that the Vienna Convention was violated when the arresting authorities failed to inform him that, as a foreign national, he had the right to contact the Paraguayan Consulate. The District Court rejected this claim, concluding that Breard procedurally defaulted the claim when he failed to raise it in the state court and that Breard could not demonstrate cause and prejudice for this default. * * * The Fourth Circuit affirmed. * * * Breard has petitioned this Court for a writ of certiorari.

In September, 1996, the Republic of Paraguay, the Ambassador of Paraguay to the United States and the Consul General of Paraguay to the United States (collectively Paraguay) brought suit in Federal District Court against certain Virginia officials, alleging that their separate rights under the Vienna Convention had been violated by the Commonwealth's failure to inform Breard of his rights under the treaty and to inform the Paraguayan consulate of Breard's arrest, conviction, and sentence. In addition, the Consul General asserted a parallel claim under 42 U.S.C § 1983, alleging a denial of his rights under the Vienna Convention. The District Court concluded that it lacked subject-matter jurisdiction over these suits because Paraguay was not alleging a "continuing violation of federal law" and therefore could not bring its claims within the exception to Eleventh Amendment immunity established in Ex parte Young, 209 U.S. 123, 28 S.Ct. 441, 52 L.Ed. 714 (1908). Republic of Paraguay v. Allen, 949 F.Supp. 1269, 1272–1273 (E.D.Va.1996). The Fourth Circuit affirmed on Eleventh Amendment grounds. Republic of Paraguay v.

Allen, 134 F. 3d 622 (1998). Paraguay has also petitioned this Court for a writ of certiorari.

On April 3, 1998, nearly five years after Breard's conviction became final, the Republic of Paraguay instituted proceedings against the United States in the International Court of Justice (ICJ), alleging that the United States violated the Vienna Convention at the time of Breard's arrest. On April 9, the ICJ noted jurisdiction and issued an order requesting that the United States "take all measures at its disposal to ensure that Angel Francisco Breard is not executed pending the final decision in these proceedings ..." The ICJ set a briefing schedule for this matter, with oral argument likely to be held this November. Breard then filed a petition for an original writ of habeas corpus and a stay application in this Court in order to "enforce" the ICJ's order. Paraguay filed a motion for leave to file a bill of complaint in this Court, citing this Court's original jurisdiction over cases "affecting Ambassadors ... and Consuls." U.S. Const., Art. III, § 2.

It is clear that Breard procedurally defaulted his claim, if any, under the Vienna Convention by failing to raise that claim in the state courts. Nevertheless, in their petitions for certiorari, both Breard and Paraguay contend that Breard's Vienna Convention claim may be heard in federal court because the Convention is the "supreme law of the land" and thus trumps the procedural default doctrine. * * * This argument is plainly incorrect for two reasons.

First, while we should give respectful consideration to the interpretation of an international treaty rendered by an international court with jurisdiction to interpret such, it has been recognized in international law that, absent a clear and express statement to the contrary, the procedural rules of the forum State govern the implementation of the treaty in that State. * * * This proposition is embodied in the Vienna Convention itself, which provides that the rights expressed in the Convention "shall be exercised in conformity with the laws and regulations of the receiving State," provided that "said laws and regulations must enable full effect to be given to the purposes for which the rights accorded under this Article are intended." Article 36(2), [1970] 21 U.S.T., at 101. It is the rule in this country that assertions of error in criminal proceedings must first be raised in state court in order to form the basis for relief in habeas. Wainwright v. Sykes, 433 U.S. 72, 97 S.Ct. 2497, 53 L.Ed.2d 594 (1977). Claims not so raised are considered defaulted. Ibid. By not asserting his Vienna Convention claim in state court, Breard failed to exercise his rights under the Vienna Convention in conformity with the laws of the United States and Commonwealth of Virginia. Having failed to do so, he cannot raise a claim of violation of those rights now on federal habeas review.

Second, although treaties are recognized by our Constitution as the supreme law of the land, that status is no less true of provisions of the constitution itself, to which rules of procedural default apply. We have held "that an Act of Congress ... is on a full parity with a treaty, and that when a statute which is subsequent in time is inconsistent with a treaty, the statute to the extent of conflict renders the treaty null." Reid v. Covert, 354 U.S. 1, 18, 77 S.Ct. 1222, 1231, 1 L.Ed.2d 1148 (1957) (plurality opinion); see also Whitney v. Robertson, 124 U.S. 190, 194, 8 S.Ct. 456, 458, 31 L.Ed. 386 (1888) (holding that if a treaty and a federal statute conflict, "the one last in date will control the other"). The Vienna Convention—which arguably confers on an individual the right to consular assistance following arrest—has continuously been in effect since 1969. But in 1996, before Breard filed his habeas petition raising claims under the Vienna Convention, Congress enacted the Antiterrorism and Effective Death Penalty Act (AEDPA), which provides that a habeas petitioner alleging that he is held in violation of "treaties of the United States" will, as a general rule, not be afforded an evidentiary hearing if he "has failed to develop the factual basis of [the] claim in State court proceedings." 28 U.S.C.A § 2554(a), (e)(2) (Supp. 1998). Breard's ability to obtain relief based on violations of the Vienna Convention is subject to this subsequently-enacted rule, just as any claim arising under the United States Constitution would be. This rule prevents Breard from establishing that the violation of his Vienna Convention rights prejudiced him. Without a hearing, Breard cannot establish how the Consul would have advised him, how the advice of his attorneys differed from the advice the Consul could have provided, and what factors he considered in electing to reject the plea bargain that the State offered him. That limitation, Breard also argues, is not justified because his Vienna Convention claims were so novel that he could not have discovered them any earlier. Assuming that were true, such novel claims would be barred on habeas review under Teague v. Lane, 489 U.S. 288, 109 S.Ct. 1060, 103 L.Ed.2d 334 (1989).

* * *

As for Paraguay's suits (both the original action and the case coming to us on petition for certiorari), neither the text nor the history of the Vienna Convention clearly provides a foreign nation a private right of action in United States' courts to set aside a criminal conviction and sentence for violation of consular notification provisions. The Eleventh Amendment provides a separate reason why Paraguay's suit might not succeed. That Amendment's "fundamental principle" that "the States, in the absence of consent, are immune from suits brought against them ... by a foreign State" was enunciated in Principality of Monaco v. Mississippi, 292 U.S. 313, 329–330, 54 S.Ct. 745, 750–751, 78 L.Ed. 1282 (1934). * * *

Insofar as the Consul General seeks to base his claims on § 1983, his suit is not cognizable. Section 1983 provides a cause of action to any "person within the jurisdiction" of the United States for the deprivation "of any rights, privileges, or immunities secured by the Constitution and laws." As an initial matter, it is clear that Paraguay is not authorized to bring suit under § 1983. Paraguay is not a "person" as the term is used in § 1983. * * * Nor is Paraguay "within the jurisdiction" of the United States. And since the Consul General is acting only in his official capacity, he has no greater ability to proceed under § 1983 than does the country he represents. Any rights that the Consul General might have by virtue of the Vienna Convention exist for the benefit of Paraguay, not for him as an individual.

It is unfortunate that this matter comes before us while proceedings are pending before the ICJ that might have been brought to that court earlier. Nonetheless, this Court must decide questions presented to it on the basis of law. The Executive Branch, on the other hand, in exercising its authority over foreign relations may, and in this case did, utilize diplomatic discussion with Paraguay. Last night the Secretary of State sent a letter to the Governor of Virginia requesting that he stay Breard's execution. If the Governor wishes to wait for the decision of the ICJ, that is his prerogative. But nothing in our existing case law allows us to make that choice for him.

For the foregoing reason, we deny the petition for an original writ of habeas corpus, the motion for leave to file a bill of complaint, the petitions for certiorari, and the accompanying stay applications filed by Breard and Paraguay.

[Statement of Justice Souter and dissenting statements of Justices Stevens, Breyer and Ginsburg omitted.]

Notes

1. The U.S. Supreme Court, in Breard v. Greene, wrote: "If the Governor [of Virginia] wishes to wait for the decision of the ICJ, that is his prerogative. *But nothing in our existing case law allows us to make that choice for him.*" (Emphasis added.) The Court's opaque statement appears to conceal more than it declares. Was the court implying that executing Breard did not violate international law? That the State of Virginia was not bound to respect international law? That an issue of international obligation was not a federal question? Or was the Court simply concluding that it was compelled by U.S. law and procedure to acquiesce in the Governor's decision to execute? Compare Henkin, *Breard*: Provisional Measures, U.S. Treaty Obligations, and the States, in Agora: *Breard*, 92 A.J.I.L 679 (1998).

2. In an advisory opinion, the Inter–American Court of Human Rights declared that failure to inform foreign nationals at the time of arrest of the right to consult with a consular official was a violation of obligations under the Consular Convention, and (by a vote of 6–1) that inmates who had been convicted and sentenced to death without having been notified of their right to consult their consul had not been afforded due process of law. See Right to Information on Consular Assistance in the Framework of the Guarantees of the Due Process of Law, Adv. Op. OC–16/1999, Inter–Am. Ct. H.R., ser. A, No. 16 (1999). Similar issues have been raised at the I.C.J. in a case involving application of the death penalty to two German brothers, Karl and Walter LaGrand. See Case Concerning the Vienna Convention on Consular Relations (Federal Republic of Germany v. United States), 1999 I.C.J. (Prov. Measures Order), discussed at 93 A.J.I.L. 924 (1999). Should such international proceedings have legal effects in national courts?

3. In Domingues v. State, 114 Nev. 783, 961 P.2d 1279 (1998), the Nevada courts refused to stay the execution of Domingues for a murder committed when he was sixteen years old. The state courts found that the U.S. Constitution did not prohibit the execution and that a provision in a treaty to which the United States was a party (the International Covenant on Civil and Political Rights, art. 6 (5)) which prohibited capital punishment in such circumstances was not binding on the United States because it had entered a reservation to that provision. The Supreme Court of Nevada did not address an additional argument, that executing a person for juvenile crimes violated customary international law or a principle of *jus cogens*. See Chapters 2 and 8. On petition for certiorari, a brief for the United States as amicus curiae recommended that the Supreme Court deny certiorari. The brief argued that the U.S. reservation to the treaty provision precludes its applicability; that the reservation in question was not invalid as inconsistent with the object and purpose of the treaty (see p. 490 below); and that the principle in question, whatever its status as customary international law, was not binding on

the United States since the United States had persistently objected to such a principle. See the discussion of the "persistent objector" principle, Chapter 2 above. The Supreme Court denied certiorari: Domingues v. Nevada, 526 U.S. 1156, 120 S.Ct. 396, 145 L.Ed.2d 309 (1999).

4. The *Domingues* petition presented a variant on issues that had previously come to the Supreme Court concerning the juvenile death penalty, involving application of constitutional guarantees in the light of international practice. In Thompson v. Oklahoma, 487 U.S. 815, 108 S.Ct. 2687 at 2696–97, 101 L.Ed.2d 702 (1988), a plurality of the Court had taken account of foreign trends to abolish or restrict the juvenile death penalty and of major human rights treaties (at that time signed but not ratified by the United States), in the course of arriving at the conclusion that "it would offend civilized standards of decency to execute a person who was less than 16 years old at the time of his or her offense" (plurality op. of J.J. Stevens, Brennan, Marshall and Blackmun; Justice O'Connor concurred on a different ground). The next year, in Stanford v. Kentucky, 492 U.S. 361, 109 S.Ct. 2969, 106 L.Ed.2d 306 (1989), where the issue was execution of a person who had been over 16 but under 18, Justice Scalia (who had dissented in Thompson) wrote an opinion (joined by Chief Justice Rehnquist and Justices White, O'Connor and Kennedy) with the following passage concerning international practice:

> We emphasize that it is *American* conceptions of decency that are dispositive, rejecting the contention of petitioners and their various *amici* * * * that the sentencing practices of other countries are relevant. While "the practices of other nations, particularly other democracies, can be relevant to determining whether a practice uniform among our people is not merely an historical accident, but rather 'so implicit in the concept of ordered liberty' that it occupies a place not merely in our mores, but, text permitting, in our Constitution as well," [citations omitted] they cannot serve to establish the first Eighth Amendment prerequisite, that the practice is accepted among our people.

By the time of *Domingues*, the United States had ratified some of the human rights treaties drawn to the Court's attention, but with reservations addressed to their death penalty provisions. On international law aspects of treaty reservations, see Chapter 7 below.

INTERPRETATION OF STATUTE IN LIGHT OF INTERNATIONAL LAW OR AGREEMENT

RESTATEMENT (THIRD) § 114

Where fairly possible, a United States statute is to be construed so as not to conflict with international law or with an international agreement of the United States.

Notes

1. Reporters' Note 1 to the preceding provision states:

Interpretation to avoid violation of international obligation. Chief Justice Marshall stated that "an Act of Congress ought never to be construed to violate the law of nations if any other possible construction remains * * * " Murray v. Schooner Charming Betsy, 6 U.S. (2 Cranch) 64, 118, 2 L.Ed. 208 (1804). See also Lauritzen v. Larsen, 345 U.S. 571, 578, 73 S.Ct. 921, 926, 97

L.Ed. 1254 (1953). On several occasions the Supreme Court has interpreted acts of Congress so as to avoid conflict with earlier treaty provisions. Chew Heong v. United States, 112 U.S. 536, 539–40, 5 S.Ct. 255, 255–56, 28 L.Ed. 770 (1884) (later immigration law did not affect treaty right of resident Chinese alien to reenter); Weinberger v. Rossi, 456 U.S. 25, 33, 102 S.Ct. 1510, 1516, 71 L.Ed.2d 715 (1982); *cf.* Clark v. Allen, 331 U.S. 503, 67 S.Ct. 1431, 91 L.Ed. 1633 (1947) (Trading with the Enemy Act not incompatible with treaty rights of German aliens to inherit realty which were succeeded to by the United States). See also Cook v. United States, 288 U.S. 102, 53 S.Ct. 305, 77 L.Ed. 641 (1933), in which the Supreme Court found that reenactment, after a series of "liquor treaties" with Great Britain, of prior statutory provisions for boarding vessels did not reflect a purpose of Congress to supersede the effect of the treaties as domestic law. Construing an international agreement to avoid conflict with a statute is more difficult since the proper interpretation of a treaty is an international question as to which courts of the United States have less leeway. The disposition to seek to construe a treaty to avoid conflict with a State statute is less clear. Compare Nielsen v. Johnson, 279 U.S. 47, 52, 49 S.Ct. 223, 224, 73 L.Ed. 607 (1929), with Guaranty Trust Co. v. United States, 304 U.S. 126, 143, 58 S.Ct. 785, 794, 82 L.Ed. 1224 (1938).

2. Other national legal systems generally also accept the principle that, where fairly possible, domestic law should be interpreted to avoid inconsistency with international obligations. See Sorensen, Report Concerning Obligations of a State Party to a Treaty, in Human Rights in National and International Law 13 (Robertson ed. 1968); see also references from various jurisdictions collected in Benvenisti, Exit and Voice in the Age of Globalization, 98 Mich. L. Rev. 167, 191 n. 105 (1999). One U.S. writer has proposed a reexamination of the presumption of interpreting domestic law consistently with international obligations, on the theory that courts should apply a statute as the legislature enacted it and not as reconstructed to take account of external factors. Bradley, The *Charming Betsy* Canon and Separation of Powers: Rethinking the Interpretive Role of International Law, 86 Geo. L.J. 479 (1998). But U.S. cases continue to invoke the presumption to enable fulfillment of international obligations and to avoid attributing to Congress an intent to violate international law. See, e.g., United States v. Bin Laden, 92 F.Supp.2d 189, 214 (S.D.N.Y. 2000); Doe v. Unocal, 963 F.Supp. 880 (C.D.Cal. 1997); Maria v. McElroy, 68 F.Supp.2d 206, 231 (E.D.N.Y. 1999).

3. In a claim brought by the European Community against the United States, a dispute settlement panel of the World Trade Organization recently referred with favor to the *Charming Betsy* presumption and accepted the U.S. submission that U.S. authorities were required to exercise their administrative discretion in conformity with obligations under the W.T.O. agreements. By virtue of this principle of U.S. domestic law, the panel was able to find that the complaining party had not carried the burden of proving a U.S. violation of international obligations. See *United States—Sections 301–310 of the Trade Act of 1974*, WT/DS152/R (Dec. 22, 1999), paras. 7.108–7.109 and n. 681.

d. *Suspension or Termination of Treaties*

THE POWER TO "UNMAKE" TREATIES

HENKIN, FOREIGN AFFAIRS AND THE U.S. CONSTITUTION

211–214 (2d ed. 1996) (footnotes omitted).

The United States sometimes has the right to terminate a treaty by its own terms, at will or at some prescribed time after giving notice of its intention to do so. The international law of treaties permits termination for fraud or coercion in making the treaty or for important breach by the other party; a party may lawfully refuse to carry out its obligation because of a fundamental change in circumstances. International law also recognizes the power—though not the right—of a state party to break a treaty and pay damages or abide other international consequences.

No doubt, the federal government has the constitutional power to terminate treaties on behalf of the United States in all these ways and circumstances: neither the declaration in the Supremacy Clause that treaties are law of the land, nor anything else in the Constitution, denies the United States these powers which countries generally have under international law. But the Constitution tells us only who can make treaties for the United States; it does not say who can unmake them.

At various times, the power to terminate treaties has been claimed for the President, for the President-and-Senate, for President-and-Congress, for Congress. Presidents have claimed authority, presumably under their foreign affairs power, to act for the United States to terminate treaties, whether in accordance with their terms, or in accordance with, or even in violation of, international law. Franklin Roosevelt, for example, denounced an extradition treaty with Greece in 1933 because Greece had refused to extradite the celebrated Mr. Insull; in 1939 he denounced the Treaty of Commerce, Friendship and Navigation with Japan. In 1979, President Carter exercised the right which the United States had reserved to terminate the Defense Treaty with the Republic of China after a period of notice.

In principle, one might argue, if the Framers required the President to obtain the Senate's consent for making a treaty, its consent ought to be required also for terminating it; and there is eminent (if aging) dictum to support that view. But perhaps the Framers were concerned only to check the President in "entangling" the United States; "disentangling" is less risky and may have to be done quickly, and is often done piecemeal, or *ad hoc,* by various means and acts. In any event, since the President acts for the United States internationally he can effectively terminate a treaty; the Senate has not established its authority to join or veto him; it has, however, claimed the right to reserve a voice in the termination of a particular treaty as a condition of its consent.

Congress, we have seen, has some power effectively to breach a treaty. Congress is probably required (morally, constitutionally) to pass legislation necessary and proper to implement treaty obligations, but it could refuse to do so, put the United States in default, perhaps compel the President to terminate the treaty or induce the other party to do so; often Congress can achieve these ends too at a later time, by enacting legislation inconsistent with treaty obligations. Congress can also declare war and terminate or suspend treaty relations with the other belligerent.

In earlier times, Congress purported also to denounce or abrogate treaties for the United States or to direct the President to do so. Those instances, no doubt, reflected the early but recurrent claims of Congress that it has general powers to make foreign policy, supported by arguments that the maintenance or termination of treaties is intimately related to war or peace for which Congress has primary responsibility. But Congressional resolutions have no effect internationally unless the President adopts and communicates them; some Presidents have chosen to comply with Congressional wishes, but others have disregarded them.

* * *

If issues as to who has power to terminate treaties arise again, it seems unlikely that Congress will succeed in establishing a right to terminate a treaty (or to share in the decision to terminate). At the end of the twentieth century, it is apparently accepted that the President has authority under the Constitution to denounce or otherwise terminate a treaty, whether such action on behalf of the United States is permissible under international law or would put the United States in violation. With termination by the President, the treaty no longer exists in international law and ceases to be law in the United States.

The power to terminate a treaty is a political power: courts do not terminate treaties, but they may interpret political acts or even political silences to determine whether they implied or intended termination. Courts do not sit in judgment on the political branches to prevent them from terminating or breaching a treaty. Where fairly possible, the courts will interpret actions of the President or of Congress to render them consistent with the international obligations of the United States, but both President and Congress can exercise their respective constitutional powers regardless of treaty obligations, and the courts will give effect to acts of the political branches within their constitutional powers even if they violate treaty obligations or other international law. If there is a breach of a treaty by the other party, it is the President, not the courts, who will decide whether the United States will denounce the treaty, consider itself liberated from its obligations, or seek other relief, or none at all.

Notes

1. See also Henkin, Foreign Affairs and the U.S. Constitution (2d ed. 1996), at 184:

> Once the Senate has consented, the President is free to make (or not to make) the treaty and the Senate has no further authority in respect of it. Attempts by the Senate to withdraw, modify or interpret its consent after a treaty is ratified have no legal weight; nor has the Senate any authoritative voice in interpreting a treaty after it is in effect, or any part in terminating it. Of course, in its legislative capacity as one of the two houses of Congress (as distinguished from its executive role as treaty-maker) the Senate participates

in whatever Congress can do as to the legal effect of treaties in the United States.

2. In 1979, several U.S. Senators challenged the authority of the President to terminate the Mutual Defense Treaty of 1954 with the Republic of China (Taiwan). The District Court held that the power to terminate the treaty was shared between the Congress and the President, but the Court of Appeals, *en banc,* reversed, four judges holding that the President had authority to terminate the treaty in question on his own authority. The Supreme Court vacated the judgment with instructions to dismiss, four of the Justices reaching that result on the ground that the case presented a political question. (See pp. 178–180 above on political questions.) Only one justice, dissenting, reached the substantive issue and upheld the power of the President to terminate the treaty in this case as incidental to his power to recognize governments. Goldwater v. Carter (D.D.C. June 6, 1979) (Memorandum–Order), reprinted in 125 Cong. Rec. S7050 (daily ed. June 6, 1979), altered and amended, 481 F.Supp. 949 (D.D.C.1979) (granting injunctive and declaratory relief), rev'd, 617 F.2d 697 (D.C.Cir.), vacated and remanded with instructions to dismiss, 444 U.S. 996, 100 S.Ct. 533, 62 L.Ed.2d 428 (1979).

The United States Senate voted an amendment to a pending resolution in which the Senate would declare that it is the sense of the Senate that the President may not terminate any mutual defense treaty without the consent of the Senate. See 125 Cong. Rec. S7015, S7038 (daily ed. June 6, 1979). The resolution was not finally adopted.

The Senate Foreign Relations Committee had suggested instead a resolution expressing the sense of the Senate that the President should not terminate treaties on his own authority except in certain circumstances, and that the Senate may prescribe terms for termination of a particular treaty as a condition of Senate consent to its ratification. See S.Rep. No. 96–119, 96th Cong., 1st Sess. 1 (1979).

3. The Restatement (Third) § 339, Comment *a* states: "If the United States Senate, in giving consent to a treaty, declares that it does so on condition that the President shall not terminate the treaty without the consent of the Congress or of the Senate, or that he shall do so only in accordance with some other procedure, that condition presumably would be binding on the President if he proceeded to make the treaty."

TERMINATION FOR BREACH OF AGREEMENT

CHARLTON v. KELLY

Supreme Court of the United States, 1913.
229 U.S. 447, 33 S.Ct. 945, 57 L.Ed. 1274.

[Petitioner brought a writ of habeas corpus to prevent his extradition as a fugitive from justice in Italy. He argued, *inter alia,* that as a U.S. citizen he was not extraditable under the treaty since Italy had refused to extradite Italian nationals to the United States. On appeal from dismissal of the petition, the Supreme Court affirmed.]

LURTON, J.:

4. We come now to the contention that by the refusal of Italy to deliver up fugitives of Italian nationality, the treaty has thereby ceased to be of obligation on the United States. The attitude of Italy is indicated by its Penal

Code of 1900 which forbids the extradition of citizens, and by the denial in two or more instances to recognize this obligation of the treaty as extending to its citizens.

* * * If the attitude of Italy was, as contended, a violation of the obligation of the treaty, which, in international law, would have justified the United States in denouncing the treaty as no longer obligatory, it did not automatically have that effect. If the United States elected not to declare its abrogation, or come to a rupture, the treaty would remain in force. It was only voidable, not void; and if the United States should prefer, it might waive any breach which in its judgment had occurred and conform to its own obligation as if there had been no such breach. * * *

That the political branch of the Government recognizes the treaty obligation as still existing is evidenced by its action in this case. In the memorandum giving the reasons of the Department of State for determining to surrender the appellant, after stating the difference between the two governments as to the interpretation of this clause of the treaty, Mr. Secretary Knox said:

"The question is now for the first time presented as to whether or not the United States is under obligation under treaty to surrender to Italy for trial and punishment citizens of the United States fugitive from the justice of Italy, notwithstanding the interpretation placed upon the treaty by Italy with reference to Italian subjects. In this connection it should be observed that the United States, although, as stated above, consistently contending that the Italian interpretation was not the proper one, has not treated the Italian practice as a breach of the treaty obligation necessarily requiring abrogation, has not abrogated the treaty or taken any step looking thereto, and has, on the contrary, constantly regarded the treaty as in full force and effect and has answered the obligations imposed thereby and has invoked the rights therein granted. It should, moreover, be observed that even though the action of the Italian Government be regarded as a breach of the treaty, the treaty is binding until abrogated, and therefore the treaty not having been abrogated, its provisions are operative against us.

"The question would, therefore, appear to reduce itself to one of interpretation of the meaning of the treaty, the Government of the United States being now for the first time called upon to declare whether it regards the treaty as obliging it to surrender its citizens to Italy, notwithstanding Italy has not and insists it can not surrender its citizens to us. It should be observed, in the first place, that we have always insisted not only with reference to the Italian extradition treaty, but with reference to the other extradition treaties similarly phrased that the word 'persons' includes citizens. We are, therefore, committed to that interpretation. The fact that we have for reasons already given ceased generally to make requisition upon the Government of Italy for the surrender of Italian subjects under the treaty, would not require of necessity that we should, as a matter of logic or law, regard ourselves as free from the obligation of surrendering our citizens, we laboring under no such legal inhibition regarding surrender as operates against the government of Italy. Therefore, since extradition treaties need not be reciprocal, even in the matter of the surrendering of citizens, it would seem entirely sound to consider ourselves as bound to surrender our citizens to

Italy even though Italy should not, by reason of the provisions of her municipal law be able to surrender its citizens to us."

The executive department having thus elected to waive any right to free itself from the obligation to deliver up its own citizens, it is the plain duty of this court to recognize the obligation to surrender the appellant as one imposed by the treaty as the supreme law of the land and as affording authority for the warrant of extradition.

Judgment affirmed.

Note

On the right of a state to terminate a treaty because of a serious breach by the other party, see Chapter 7, Section 6.

2. *International Agreements Other Than Treaties*

AUTHORITY TO MAKE INTERNATIONAL AGREEMENTS: LAW OF THE UNITED STATES

RESTATEMENT (THIRD) § 303

(2) The President, with the authorization or approval of Congress, may make an international agreement dealing with any matter that falls within the powers of Congress and of the President under the Constitution. * * *

(4) The President, on his own authority, may make an international agreement dealing with any matter that falls within his independent powers under the Constitution.

a. Congressional–Executive Agreements

HENKIN, FOREIGN AFFAIRS AND THE U.S. CONSTITUTION

215–18 (1996) (footnotes omitted).

Since our national beginnings Presidents have made some 1600 treaties with the consent of the Senate; they have made many thousands of other international agreements without seeking Senate consent. Some were "Congressional–Executive agreements", made by the President as authorized in advance or approved afterwards by joint resolution of Congress. Many were made by the President on his own constitutional authority ("sole executive agreements").

The Constitution does not expressly confer authority to make international agreements other than treaties, but such agreements, varying widely in formality and in importance, have been common from our early history. The authority to make such agreements and their permissible scope, and their status as law, continue to be debated. Where do the President and Congress find constitutional authority to join to make international agreements? Can the President, by authority of Congress (acting by majority vote of both houses), conclude as a Congressional–Executive agreement any international agreement he might have made by treaty with the consent of two-thirds of the Senate? Where does the President find constitutional power to make any agreements on his own authority? How does one distinguish an agreement which can be made by the President alone from one requiring Senate consent or the approval of both houses of Congress? * * * Do [agreements other than treaties] have the same quality as law of the land, the same supremacy to state law, the same equality with acts of Congress?

* * *

Agreements made by joint authority of the President and Congress have come about in different ways. Congress has authorized the President to negotiate and conclude international agreements on particular subjects—on postal relations; foreign trade; lend-lease (to allies during the Second World War); foreign assistance; nuclear reactors. During the years following the Second World War, Congress authorized the President to conclude particular agreements already negotiated, as in the case of the Headquarters Agreement with the United Nations, and various multilateral agreements establishing international organizations, e.g., the International Bank for Reconstruction and Development ("the World Bank"), and the International Monetary Fund. In some instances Congress has approved Presidential agreements already made, by adopting implementing legislation or by appropriating funds to carry out the obligations assumed by the United States.

Constitutional doctrine to justify Congressional–Executive agreements is not clear or agreed. The Constitution expressly prescribes the treaty procedure, and nowhere suggests that another method of making international agreements is available * * *.

Neither Congresses, nor Presidents, nor courts, have been seriously troubled by these conceptual difficulties and differences. Whatever their theoretical merits, it is now widely accepted that the Congressional–Executive agreement is available for wide use, even general use, and is a complete alternative to a treaty: the President can seek approval of any agreement by joint resolution of both houses of Congress rather than by two-thirds of the Senate. Like a treaty, such an agreement is the law of the land, superseding inconsistent state laws, as well as inconsistent provisions in earlier treaties, in other international agreements, or in acts of Congress.

The Congressional–Executive agreement has had strong appeal. By permitting approval of an agreement by simple majority of both houses, it eliminates the veto by one-third-plus-one of the Senators present which in the past had effectively buried important treaties. It gives an equal role to the House of Representatives which has long resented the "undemocratic" anachronism that excludes it from the treaty-making process. Especially since so many treaties require legislative implementation (if only by appropriation of funds), the Congressional–Executive agreement assures cooperation by both houses, virtually eliminating the danger that the House of Representatives might later resist enacting the implementing legislation or appropriating funds. The Congressional–Executive agreement also simplifies the parliamentary process: a treaty goes to the Senate for consent and, often, to the Senate again and to the House for implementation; a Congressional–Executive agreement goes to both Houses in the first instance, and "consent" and implementation can be achieved in a single action. The Congressional–Executive agreement also eliminates issues about self-executing and non-self-executing agreements, and about the consequences of inconsistency between international agreements and statutes: all such agreements are "executed" by Congress, every agreement has Congressional sanction, and clearly the joint resolution approving it can repeal any inconsistent statutes.

[T]he Congressional–Executive agreement has not effectively replaced the treaty. * * * Perhaps the Executive has not pressed this alternative method of making international agreements because the Senate has proved sufficiently responsible "internationalist" (often more so than the House has been in related contexts); and there have appeared no important agreements which could command a majority but not two-thirds of the Senate and which the President was willing to fight for through both houses. But the constitutionality of the Congressional–Executive agreement seems established, it is used regularly at least for trade and postal agreements, and remains available to Presidents for wide, even general use should the treaty process again prove difficult.

Notes

1. The legislative branch has frequently recognized congressional–executive agreements as alternatives to treaties. After the First World War, a House Committee Report asserted the propriety of adherence to the World Court by Congressional Resolution instead of treaty, citing precedents. H.R.Rep. No. 1569, 68th Cong., 2nd Sess. 16 (1925). See also the joint resolution authorizing conclusion of the Headquarters Agreement with the United Nations, Ch. 482, 61 Stat. 756 (1947) (text of agreement included in resolution); U.N.R.R.A. Act of March 28, 1944, ch. 135, 58 Stat. 122; Bretton Woods Agreement Act (providing for participation in the International Monetary Fund and the International Bank for Reconstruction and Development), ch. 339, 59 Stat. 512 (1945); joint resolutions providing for membership and participation in the International Refugee Organization, ch. 185, 61 Stat. 214 (1947); F.A.O., ch. 342, 59 Stat. 529 (1945); U.N.E.S.C.O., ch. 700, 60 Stat. 712 (1946); W.H.O., ch. 469, 62 Stat. 441 (1948). Earlier, Congress had approved United States adherence to that part of the Versailles Treaty which established the International Labor Office, ch. 676, 48 Stat. 1182, 1183 (1934).

The U.N. Charter was approved as a treaty, but implementation was left largely to congressional–executive cooperation. See the United Nations Participation Act of 1945, ch. 583, 59 Stat. 619 (1945), as amended, 22 U.S.C.A. §§ 287–287*l*(1990); even "Article 43 agreements" to put forces at the disposal of the Security Council were to be approved by Congress, not consented to by the Senate only. See § 6, 59 Stat. 621, 22 U.S.C.A. 287d. See Chapter 12 infra on Article 43 agreements.

When the Executive Branch decided to seek approval of the U.N. Headquarters Agreement by joint resolution, it provided concerned foreign governments with an opinion of the Attorney General assuring them that the congressional–executive agreement would be the equivalent of a treaty and supreme law of the land. 40 Op.Att'y Gen. 469 (1946). While his opinion purported to speak only for the agreement in question, the arguments and authorities cited would seem to apply as well to any agreement.

The courts have approved congressional–executive agreements in a few cases involving matters within the delegated powers of Congress. In 1882 the Supreme

Court held that postal conventions have equal status with treaties as part of the law of the land. Von Cotzhausen v. Nazro, 107 U.S. 215, 2 S.Ct. 503, 27 L.Ed. 540 (1882). See comments, S.Doc. No. 244, Sen.Misc. Doc., 78th Cong., 2d Sess. (1944); 19 Op.Att'y Gen. 513 (1882). See also B. Altman & Co. v. United States, 224 U.S. 583, 32 S.Ct. 593, 56 L.Ed. 894 (1912), where the Supreme Court considered a congressional–executive agreement to be a "treaty" within the meaning of a federal statute.

For an early debate over the propriety and scope of executive agreements, see Borchard, Shall the Executive Agreement Replace the Treaty?, 53 Yale L.J. 644 (1944); McDougal & Lans, Treaties and Congressional–Executive or Presidential Agreements: Interchangeable Instruments of National Policy, 54 Yale L.J. 181, 534 (1945); Borchard, Treaties and Executive Agreements—A Reply, id. at 616. The debate has been resolved in their favor. See Restatement (Third) § 303, Comment *e*. For discussion, see Margolis, Executive Agreements and Presidential Power in Foreign Policy (1986). For a revival of the debate in the 1990s, see Note 3 below.

In recent years congressional-executive agreements have been commonly used to establish U.S. military bases in other states, and to accelerate approval of international trade agreements. In 1974 Congress enacted the Trade Act, Pub. L. 93–618, 88 Stat. 1978, 1982, 2001, 19 U.S.C.A. §§ 2101, 2111–2112, 2191, which provided for a "fast track" procedure for congressional approval of trade agreements negotiated by the Executive Branch. The "fast track" seeks to promote executive-congressional cooperation to ensure that trade agreements negotiated by the President will be implemented by Congress with appropriate legislation. This increased cooperation includes notice to Congress of an intention to conclude a trade agreement, and consultation between Executive and Congress on implementing legislation. See Koh, The Fast Track and United States Trade Policy, 18 Brooklyn J.Int'l L. 143 (1992); Holmer & Bello, U.S. Trade and Policy Series No. 20—The Fast Track Debate: A Prescription for Pragmatism, 26 Int'l Lawyer 183 (1992). Statutory authority for "fast track" trade agreements lapsed in 1994 and as of 2000 had not been renewed.

2. It has been suggested that the congressional-executive agreement might be more consistent with principles of democracy and representative government, but the U.S. Senate is not likely to agree to abandon the treaty process in which it has a special role under the Constitution. See Henkin, Constitutionalism, Democracy and Foreign Affairs (1990) pp. 58–62.

The control of Congress over congressional-executive agreements is at least as strong as that of the Senate over treaties. In 1962, Congress required the inclusion of members of prescribed congressional committees on delegations for trade agreement negotiations. See Trade Expansion Act of 1962, Pub. L. 87–794, § 243, 76 Stat. 878, 19 U.S.C.A. § 1873 (1970). In approving agreements by joint resolution Congress has sometimes entered conditions or reservations; see, e.g., the resolution approving U.S. adherence to the International Refugee Organization, ch. 185, 61 Stat. 214 (1947); also the resolution authorizing the U.N. Headquarters Agreement, ch. 482, 61 Stat. 756, 758, 767–68 (1947), Note 1 above.

Who has the power to terminate a congressional-executive agreement is unresolved, but the President's authority seems no weaker than in regard to treaties. In some cases Congress purported to reserve for itself an equal right to annul authorized arrangements independently of the President. See, e.g., The Postal Service Act of 1960, Pub. L. No. 86–682, § 6103, 74 Stat. 688. The Postal

Reorganization Act of 1970 does not contain such a provision. Pub. L. No. 91375, ch. 50, § 5002, 84 Stat. 719, 766, 39 U.S.C.A. § 5002 (1970).

3. In the 1990s, renewed attention was focused on congressional-executive agreements by virtue of their use to conclude the North American Free Trade Agreement (NAFTA) and agreements on the World Trade Organization. Some constitutional scholars, notably Professor Tribe, expressed doubts about the constitutional propriety of undertaking significant obligations in a manner other than the formal Article II treaty, which provides special safeguards for state interests through the requirement for two-thirds approval in the Senate. Professors Ackerman and Golove, on the other hand, explained the evolution of twentieth-century practice in favor of agreements other than Article II treaties: they found that alternative forms of making international agreements had achieved full constitutional equivalence with treaties and were justifiable in terms of constitutional and democratic theory. Compare Ackerman & Golove, Is NAFTA Constitutional?, 108 Harv. L. Rev. 801 (1995), with Tribe, Taking Text and Structure Seriously, 108 Harv. L. Rev. 1221 (1995). For continuation of the debate, see Golove, Treaty–Making and the Nation: The Historical Foundations of the Nationalist Conception of the Treaty Power, 98 Mich. L. Rev. 1075 (2000) and Tribe's rejoinder in his American Constitutional Law 653, n.47 (3rd ed. 2000).

b. Sole Executive Agreements

HENKIN, FOREIGN AFFAIRS AND THE U.S. CONSTITUTION

221–222, 225–226 (2d ed. 1996) (footnotes omitted)

There have indeed been suggestions, claiming support in *Belmont* [p. 232 below], that the President is constitutionally free to make any agreement on any matter involving our relations with another country, but that, for prudential reasons—especially if he will later require Congressional implementation—he will often seek Senate consent (or approval by both houses). As a matter of constitutional construction, however, that view is unacceptable, for it would wholly remove the "check" of Senate consent which the Framers struggled and compromised to write into the Constitution. One is compelled to conclude that there are agreements which the President can make on his sole authority and others which he can make only with the consent of the Senate (or of both houses), but neither Justice Sutherland nor any one else has told us which are which.* * *

Notes

1. "*Belmont* involved an agreement incidental to recognition of the Soviet Union, and Sutherland's opinion gave some emphasis to that fact. Recognition of a foreign government is indisputably the President's sole responsibility, and for many it is an 'enumerated' power implied in the President's express powers to appoint and receive Ambassadors. *Belmont,* then, might hold only that the President's specific and exclusive powers (principally his power to recognize governments and his authority as Commander in Chief) support agreements on his sole authority. * * * The whole conduct of our foreign relations, we have seen, is the President's, and that authority, too, has been claimed to be expressly 'enumerated' in the clause vesting the 'Executive Power'. Sutherland, in fact,

seemed to find authority for the Litvinov Agreement not in the President's exclusive control of recognition policy but in his authority as 'sole organ', his 'foreign affairs power' which supports not only recognition but much if not most other foreign policy." Henkin, Foreign Affairs and the U.S. Constitution 220–221 (2d ed. 1996). See also United States v. Guy W. Capps, Inc., 204 F.2d 655 (4th Cir. 1953), aff'd on other grounds, 348 U.S. 296, 75 S.Ct. 326, 99 L.Ed. 329 (1955), discussed in Henkin at 225–226.

2. Presidents have deployed U.S. forces to foreign countries in circumstances implying some executive agreement between the United States and the receiving state. In 1990, for example, President Bush sent U.S. troops to Saudi Arabia to help defend it from attack after Iraq's invasion of Kuwait. See Chapter 12.

3. "Presidents have made numerous international agreements contemplated by a treaty, or which they considered appropriate for implementing treaty obligations, and no one seems to have questioned their authority to make them. Perhaps it is assumed that Senate consent to the original treaty implies consent to supplementary agreements; perhaps by such agreements the President takes care that the treaty is faithfully executed." Henkin, Foreign Affairs and the U.S. Constitution 219 (2d ed. 1996).

4. The President has concluded numerous agreements on his own authority to settle claims between the United States and another state. In Dames & Moore v. Regan, 453 U.S. 654, 101 S.Ct. 2972, 69 L.Ed.2d 918 (1981), the Supreme Court upheld the agreement with Iran arising out of the taking of United States hostages, in which the United States agreed, *inter alia,* to terminate numerous cases in the courts of the United States and to have claims resolved by a joint arbitral tribunal. The Supreme Court upheld the validity of the agreement, noting that the power of the President to resolve international claims had been exercised for almost 200 years with Congressional acquiescence. The Court quoted Judge Learned Hand in Ozanic v. United States, 188 F.2d 228, 231 (2d Cir.1951):

> "The constitutional power of the President extends to the settlement of mutual claims between a foreign government and the United States, at least when it is an incident to the recognition of that government; and it would be unreasonable to circumscribe it to such controversies. The continued mutual amity between the nation and other powers again and again depends upon a satisfactory compromise of mutual claims; the necessary power to make such compromises has existed from the earliest times and been exercised by the foreign offices of all civilized nations."

453 U.S. at 683, 101 S.Ct. at 2988, 69 L.Ed.2d at 942. The Court postponed consideration of whether the agreement constituted a "taking" requiring compensation under the Fifth Amendment. For a note on the "taking" question, see Note, p. 237.

5. Congress has had before it numerous bills to limit or regulate sole executive agreements. In 1972, it adopted the Case Act, requiring the President to transmit to Congress all international agreements other than treaties within 60 days after their conclusion. If the President deems public disclosure of the agreement prejudicial to national security, he shall transmit it instead to the foreign affairs committees of both houses of Congress under injunction of secrecy to be removed only upon due notice from the President. See 1 U.S.C.A. § 112b. The Case Act was amended in 1977 and 1978 to make it applicable to agreements made by any department or agency of the United States government (1977) and to make it applicable to oral as well as written agreements (1978). 1 U.S.C.A. § 112b(a).

EXECUTIVE AGREEMENTS AS LAW OF THE LAND

UNITED STATES v. BELMONT

Supreme Court of the United States, 1937.
301 U.S. 324, 57 S.Ct. 758, 81 L.Ed. 1134.

MR. JUSTICE SUTHERLAND delivered the opinion of the Court.

This is an action at law brought by petitioner against respondents in a federal district court to recover a sum of money deposited by a Russian corporation (Petrograd Metal Works) with August Belmont, a private banker doing business in New York City under the name of August Belmont & Co.

* * * In 1918, the Soviet Government duly enacted a decree by which it dissolved, terminated and liquidated the corporation (together with others), and nationalized and appropriated all of its property and assets of every kind and wherever situated, including the deposit account with Belmont. As a result, the deposit became the property of the Soviet Government, and so remained until November 16, 1933, at which time the Soviet Government released and assigned to petitioner all amounts due to that government from American nationals, including the deposit account of the corporation with Belmont. Respondents failed and refused to pay the amount upon demand duly made by petitioner.

The assignment was effected by an exchange of diplomatic correspondence between the Soviet Government and the United States. The purpose was to bring about a final settlement of the claims and counterclaims between the Soviet Government and the United States; and it was agreed that the Soviet Government would take no steps to enforce claims against American nationals; but all such claims were released and assigned to the United States, with the understanding that the Soviet Government was to be duly notified of all amounts realized by the United States from such release and assignment. The assignment and requirement for notice are parts of the larger plan to bring about a settlement of the rival claims of the high contracting parties. The continuing and definite interest of the Soviet Government in the collection of assigned claims is evident; and the case, therefore, presents a question of public concern, the determination of which well might involve the good faith of the United States in the eyes of a foreign government. The court below held that the assignment thus effected embraced the claim here in question; and with that we agree.

That court, however, took the view that the situs of the bank deposit was within the State of New York; that in no sense could it be regarded as an intangible property right within Soviet territory; and that the nationalization decree, if enforced, would put into effect an act of confiscation. And it held that a judgment for the United States could not be had, because, in view of that result, it would be contrary to the controlling public policy of the State of New York. * * *

First. We do not pause to inquire whether in fact there was any policy of the State of New York to be infringed, since we are of opinion that no state policy can prevail against the international compact here involved. * * *

We take judicial notice of the fact that coincident with the assignment set forth in the complaint, the President recognized the Soviet Government, and normal diplomatic relations were established between that government and the Government of the United States, followed by an exchange of ambassadors. The effect of this was to validate, so far as this country is concerned, all acts of the Soviet Government here involved from the commencement of its existence. The recognition, establishment of diplomatic relations, the assignment, and agreements with respect thereto, were all parts of one transaction, resulting in an international compact between the two governments. That the negotiations, acceptance of the assignment and agreements and understandings in respect thereof were within the competence of the President may not be doubted. Governmental power over internal affairs is distributed between the national government and the several states. Governmental power over external affairs is not distributed, but is vested exclusively in the national government. And in respect of what was done here, the Executive had authority to speak as the sole organ of that government. The assignment and the agreements in connection therewith did not, as in the case of treaties, as that term is used in the treaty making clause of the Constitution (Art. II, § 2), require the advice and consent of the Senate.

A treaty signifies "a compact made between two or more independent nations with a view to the public welfare." B. Altman & Co. v. United States, 224 U.S. 583, 600, 32 S.Ct. 593, 596, 56 L.Ed. 894, 910. But an international compact, as this was, is not always a treaty which requires the participation of the Senate. There are many such compacts, of which a protocol, a modus vivendi, a postal convention, and agreements like that now under consideration are illustrations. * * *

* * * And while this rule in respect of treaties is established by the express language of cl. 2, Art. VI, of the Constitution, the same rule would result in the case of all international compacts and agreements from the very fact that complete power over international affairs is in the national government and is not and cannot be subject to any curtailment or interference on the part of the several states. Compare United States v. Curtiss–Wright Export Corp., 299 U.S. 304, 316, 57 S.Ct. 216, 219, 81 L.Ed. 255, 260, 261 et seq. In respect of all international negotiations and compacts, and in respect of our foreign relations generally, state lines disappear. As to such purposes the State of New York does not exist. Within the field of its powers, whatever the United States rightfully undertakes, it necessarily has warrant to consummate. And when judicial authority is invoked in aid of such consummation, state constitutions, state laws, and state policies are irrelevant to the inquiry and decision. It is inconceivable that any of them can be interposed as an obstacle to the effective operation of a federal constitutional power. Cf. Missouri v. Holland, 252 U.S. 416, 40 S.Ct. 382, 64 L.Ed. 641; Asakura v. Seattle, 265 U.S. 332, 341, 44 S.Ct. 515, 516, 68 L.Ed. 1041, 1044. * * *

Judgment reversed.

Note

In United States v. Pink, 315 U.S. 203, 62 S.Ct. 552, 86 L.Ed. 796 (1942), the United States, as assignee, sought to recover the assets in New York of a branch of a Russian corporation which had been nationalized by the Soviet Union. The

New York courts held that since, under previously enunciated New York law, the nationalization could not be given extraterritorial effect, the United States as assignee stood no better than did the Russian government and was unable to collect. In reversing the state court, the Supreme Court said in part, 315 U.S. at 222, 224–25, 228–30, 62 S.Ct. at 561–65, 86 L.Ed. at 813–18:

> * * * [T]he Belmont case is determinative of the present controversy.
>
> * * * [A]s we have seen, the Russian decree in question was intended to have an extraterritorial effect and to embrace funds of the kind which are here involved. Nor can there be any serious doubt that claims of the kind here in question were included in the Litvinov Assignment. It is broad and inclusive. It should be interpreted consonantly with the purpose of the compact to eliminate all possible sources of friction between these two great nations. * * * Strict construction would run counter to that national policy. For, as we shall see, the existence of unpaid claims against Russia and its nationals, which were held in this country, and which the Litvinov Assignment was intended to secure, had long been one impediment to resumption of friendly relations between these two great powers.
>
> * * *
>
> If the priority had been accorded American claims [over foreign claims to the assets] by treaty with Russia, there would be no doubt as to its validity. Cf. Santovincenzo v. Egan, [284 U.S. 30, 52 S.Ct. 81, 76 L.Ed. 151 (1931)]. The same result obtains here. The powers of the President in the conduct of foreign relations included the power, without consent of the Senate, to determine the public policy of the United States with respect to the Russian nationalization decrees. * * * That authority is not limited to a determination of the government to be recognized. It includes the power to determine the policy which is to govern the question of recognition. Objections to the underlying policy as well as objections to recognition are to be addressed to the political department and not to the courts. * * * Power to remove such obstacles to full recognition as settlement of claims of our nationals (Levitan, Executive Agreements, 35 Ill. L.Rev. 365, 382–385) certainly is a modest implied power of the President who is the "sole organ of the federal government in the field of international relations." United States v. Curtiss–Wright Corp., [299 U.S. at 320, 57 S.Ct. at 221, 81 L.Ed. at 262]. Effectiveness in handling the delicate problems of foreign relations requires no less. Unless such a power exists, the power of recognition might be thwarted or seriously diluted. No such obstacle can be placed in the way of rehabilitation of relations between this country and another nation, unless the historic conception of the powers and responsibilities of the President in the conduct of foreign affairs (see Moore, Treaties and Executive Agreements, 20 Pol.Sc.Q. 385, 403–417) is to be drastically revised. It was the judgment of the political department that full recognition of the Soviet Government required the settlement of all outstanding problems including the claims of our nationals. Recognition and the Litvinov Assignment were interdependent. We would usurp the executive function if we held that that decision was not final and conclusive in the courts.
>
> "All constitutional acts of power, whether in the executive or in the judicial department, have as much legal validity and obligation as if they proceeded from the legislature, * * * " The Federalist, No. 64. A treaty is a "Law of the Land" under the supremacy clause (Art. VI, Cl. 2) of the Constitution. Such international compacts and agreements as the Litvinov

Assignment have a similar dignity. United States v. Belmont, [301 U.S. at 331, 57 S.Ct. at 761, 81 L.Ed. at 1139]. See Corwin, The President, Office & Powers 228–240 (1940).

"SELF–EXECUTING" EXECUTIVE AGREEMENTS

HENKIN, FOREIGN AFFAIRS AND THE U.S. CONSTITUTION

226–228 (2d ed. 1996) (footnotes omitted).

One suggestion has had it that, granting that the President can make many sole executive agreements, and that such agreements, like the treaties, are internationally binding, unlike treaties they are not self-executing and cannot be effective as domestic law unless implemented by Congress. If they are not law of the land they cannot be given effect by the courts and they do not supersede inconsistent state law.

If there was ever any basis for that view, the *Belmont* case and *Dames & Moore* [see p. 231 supra] surely reject it as general doctrine. * * *

Again, it has been suggested that the doctrine of the *Belmont* case gives supremacy over state law only to executive agreements intimately related to the President's power of recognition, and that even such agreements will supersede only state policy not formal state laws. Neither of these limitations was expressed—or implied—in *Belmont,* or in the *Pink* case decided 5 years later by a reconstituted Supreme Court, and the language and reasoning of both cases would apply as well to any executive agreement and to any state law. * * *

At least some executive agreements, then, can be self-executing and have some status as law of the land. As with treaties, of course, a self-executing executive agreement would surely lose its effect as domestic law in the face of a subsequent act of Congress. On the other hand, in the *Capps* case, an intermediate federal court held that an executive agreement—unlike a treaty—could not prevail even against an earlier act of Congress. Yet many of the arguments why a treaty supersedes an earlier statute apply as well to executive agreements. The Supreme Court built its doctrine that treaties are equal to and can supersede acts of Congress on the Supremacy Clause of the Constitution which declares both to be supreme law of the land; executive agreements, too, are supreme law of the land. If one sees the Treaty Power as basically a Presidential power (albeit subject to check by the Senate), there is no compelling reason for giving less effect to agreements that he has authority to make without the Senate. If one accepts Presidential primacy in foreign affairs in relation to Congress, one might allow his agreements to prevail even in the face of earlier Congressional legislation. If one grants the President some legislative authority in foreign affairs—as in regard to sovereign immunity—one might grant it to him in this respect too. The issue remains unresolved.

Note

The Iran Hostage Agreement, upheld in Dames & Moore v. Regan, 453 U.S. 654, 101 S.Ct. 2972, 69 L.Ed.2d 918 (1981), also had legal effect in the United

States, closing U.S. courts to certain claims. See, e.g., Harris Corp. v. National Iranian Radio & Television, 691 F.2d 1344 (11th Cir.1982). See generally Stein, Jurisprudence and Jurists' Prudence: The Iranian–Forum Clause Decisions of the Iran–U.S. Claims Tribunal, 78 A.J.I.L. I (1984); The U.S./Iranian Hostage Settlement, 75 A.S.I.L.Proc. 236 (1981); Norton & Collins, Reflections on the Iranian Hostage Settlement, 67 A.B.A.J. 428 (1981).

C. INDIVIDUAL RIGHTS AND FOREIGN AFFAIRS

HENKIN, FOREIGN AFFAIRS AND THE U.S. CONSTITUTION

285, 288–289, 310 (2d ed. 1996) (footnotes omitted).

In principle, the Bill of Rights limits governmental authority in the conduct of foreign relations as in other federal activity. * * *

The Fourth Amendment protects only against *unreasonable* searches and seizures. The national interest in maintaining an international disarmament system, or environmental safeguards, or labor standards, might render not "unreasonable" some intrusive inspections of private establishments and records in the United States, even by international or foreign inspectors. * * *

* * * The United States could not adhere to a treaty establishing an international criminal court without considering the applicability of the rights assured to persons charged with crime by the Fourth, Fifth, Sixth and Eighth Amendments.

* * *

Respect for individual rights ranks high—perhaps highest—among the elements of U.S. constitutionalism, and despite occasional careless rhetoric, the federal government must respect those rights in its conduct of foreign affairs as in domestic governance. Foreign affairs are important national interests, but not all actions in foreign affairs are compelling. * * * Invasion of individual rights may be essential to serve a compelling public interest, but only rarely. The sovereignty of the United States, the powers of the political branches in foreign affairs, are 'plenary'—subject to individual rights.

Note

The Restatement (Third) § 721 sets forth protections provided to individuals by the Constitution in matters relating to foreign relations. See, e.g., Comments *f* and *g*:

> *f. Due process of law and equal protection of the laws.* The due process clause requires fair procedure in matters relating to foreign relations, in civil as in criminal matters, for aliens as for citizens. See § 722. What process is due, however, differs with the circumstances. Presidential decisions generally, even when they affect private interests, are not judicial in character and do not require judicial kinds of procedures. Thus, for example, a hearing is not required as of constitutional right before the President exercises his constitutional authority, or authority delegated to him by Congress, to suggest immunity from suit (see Introductory Note to Part IV, Chapter 5, Subchapter

A), to impose a tariff, to invoke the act of state doctrine (§ 444 and Comment *f* thereto), to extradite an individual for trial by a foreign country (§ 478), or to settle an international claim (§ 713, Comment *a,* and this section, Comment *g*).

The due process clause also gives some substantive protection to life, liberty, or property affected, for example, by a regulation of foreign commerce or of the right to travel. Comment *i.* To date, the due process clause has not been held to prevent deportation of an alien, even one long resident in the United States, for whatever reason Congress chooses, so long as notice, hearing, and fair procedures are provided. See § 722, Comment *i* and Reporters' Note 12.

The due process clause of the Fifth Amendment also incorporates the requirement that the federal government afford the equal protection of the laws. For equal protection of the laws as applied to aliens, see § 722, Comments *c* and *d.*

g. Taking of private property. In matters affecting foreign relations as in domestic matters, it is not always easy to distinguish a regulation that is within the police power of the United States from a taking of private property requiring just compensation under the Fifth Amendment. See § 712, Comment *g* and Reporters' Note 6. In foreign relations, the distinction must take account of the conceptions and traditions of international law. For example, under international law and practice, claims between a national or resident of the United States and a foreign state, its national or resident, are seen as claims between the United States and the other state which they can settle by international agreement. See § 713, Comment *a* and Reporters' Note 9, and § 902, Comment *i* and Reporters' Note 8. Usually, the Executive Branch consults with representatives of claimants, and Congress has generally made monies received in settlement available for distribution to the private claimants. In general, a settlement by treaty or executive agreement of foreign claims of United States nationals or residents neither deprives them of their property without due process of law (see Comment *f*) nor constitutes a taking of their property requiring compensation. In special circumstances, however, a sacrifice of private claims for a national purpose may constitute a taking requiring compensation. See Reporters' Note 8.

SECTION 3. INTERNATIONAL LAW IN THE MUNICIPAL LAW OF OTHER STATES

The United States, we have seen, developed a jurisprudence governing the place of international law within its municipal legal system, a largely dualist jurisprudence, deriving from its English antecedents varied by radical departures reflecting its federalism and its constitutional, presidential, bicameral system. The countries of Western Europe grew their own variants on dualism and monism, responding to neighborly example, political and diplomatic needs and pressures. Newer, post-colonial states have often emulated existing models but have sometimes devised their own approaches, without regard to particular constitutional or jurisprudential theory or commitment to monism or dualism or their variants (see p. 160 above).

WILDHABER & BREITENMOSER, THE RELATIONSHIP BETWEEN CUSTOMARY INTERNATIONAL LAW AND MUNICIPAL LAW IN WESTERN EUROPEAN COUNTRIES

48 Zeitschrift für ausländisches öffentliches Recht und Völkerrecht 163, 179–204 (1988) (footnotes omitted).

3.1 Constitutions with an explicit reference to customary international law

3.1.1 The Federal Republic of Germany (FRG)

Today, Art. 25 of the Basic Law (GG) is among the most favourable provisions in Western Europe with regard to customary international law:

> "The general rules of public international law shall be an integral part of federal law. They shall take precedence over the laws and shall directly create rights and duties for the inhabitants of the federal territory."

According to the practice of the Federal Constitutional Court and the predominant doctrine, the general rules of international law are norms which are recognized as binding by a predominant majority of countries (but not necessarily by the FRG itself). They include—among others—customary law (but not regional customary law) and the principles generally recognized by civilized countries. Treaty Law, on the contrary, acquires municipal validity only after a special transformation act; indeed, according to Art. 59(2) GG, "treaties which regulate the political relations of the Federation or relate to matters of federal legislation shall require the consent or participation, in the form of a federal law, of the bodies competent in any specific case for such federal legislation." Contrary to customary international law, treaty law is not superior to municipal law; likewise, however, it may be overruled by a *lex posterior*.

* * *

The constitutional principle of an interpretation and application of the municipal law in conformity with international law requests that German courts refrain from recognizing either foreign laws which violate general international law or the general reservation of the international *ordre public*, even where international law itself does not proscribe such an application.

3.1.2 Italy

Art. 10(1) of the Italian Constitution of 1948 provides that "Italy's legal system conforms with the generally recognized principles of international law."

Already three years after this provision had been adopted, the Court of Cassation said:

> "There thus exist overriding principles based upon the need to secure mutual existence among civilised States, and between the latter in relation to their nationals and to nationals of other States * * * These principles applied already before they were embodied in Article 10 * * * They require that Italian municipal law must conform to customary international law * * * "

* * * In Italy * * * the generally recognized principles of international law become an integral part of the Italian legal system only after what is called a procedure of "automatic conformance", i.e. after having been transformed into parallel Italian customary law. But this * * * position "has only the effect of a *petitio principi,* since it does not have any influence upon the practical value of the norms concerned."

* * * [T]he general principles of law, as stated in Art. 38(1) *lit.* (c) of the Statute of the ICJ are held not to fall within the scope of Art. 10(1) of the Italian Constitution. The same is true, incidentally, of international treaty law. According to * * * doctrine, there is no indirect constitutional recognition of treaties by means of the general principle of *pacta sunt servanda.* Therefore, only customary international law is within the scope of application of Art. 10(1).

The Italian Constitution does not regulate the rank of customary international law in the hierarchy of the municipal legal order. Nevertheless, according to the predominant doctrine, Art. 10(1) "implies that in the Italian legal system rules of general international law are superior to ordinary legislation, although according to most authorities they do not possess the same status as provisions of the Constitution".

3.1.3 Austria

* * * [I]n Austria customary international law may display an effect within the sphere of municipal law. Art. 9 of the Austrian Federal Constitution * * * reads: "The generally recognized principles of International Law are valid parts of the Federal Law". * * *

According to Austrian doctrine and practice, "a rule of international law does not have to be recognized unanimously by all states in order to be considered a 'generally recognized rule of international law' under Art. 9 of the Constitution". This provision is interpreted extensively as comprising the generally recognized rules of private and of administrative international law.

* * *

It is controversial whether the "generally recognized principles of international law" may be overridden by ordinary statutes. In a decision more than thirty years old, the Constitutional Court explicitly—but without any substantiation—declared that these rules ranked equally with ordinary statutes but were not on the same level as the Constitution * * *

3.1.4 Greece

In the new Greek Constitution of 1975 * * * Art. 28(1) is worded thus:

> "The generally acknowledged rules of international law, as well as international conventions as of the time they are sanctioned by law and become operative according to the conditions therein, shall be an integral part of domestic Greek law and shall prevail over any contrary provision of the law. * * * "

* * * [I]nternational agreements will only acquire internal validity after having been sanctioned by an act of Parliament. * * * During the drafting of the new Constitution, a controversy arose concerning the legal effect of treaties:

"The issue was resolved in the same manner as to both customary and conventional international law. They were given enhanced formal validity, so that they supersede both prior and subsequent acts of Parliament. * * * "

3.1.5 France

In France, * * * the fourteenth paragraph of the preamble of the Constitution of the Fourth Republic of October 27, 1946 [provides]:

"The French Republic, faithful to its tradition, abides by the rules of international law".

In several decisions, the Supreme Administrative Court [Conseil d'Etat] applied general principles of international law by way of interpretation of this preamble. According to this merely declaratory provision, which represented no modification of prior practice concerning the relationship between international law and municipal law, international law was applied *per se:*

" * * * the French tribunals have regarded the rules of customary international law as directly applicable whenever they are relevant to the adjudication of an issue of which they have jurisdiction, and concerning which there is no controlling legislative or executive act. They * * * have developed no coherent doctrine of 'adoption' or incorporation' * * * [But] they have not been influenced by the doctrines of dogmatic dualism, which would require the specific 'transformation' of a rule of international law into one of internal law as a prerequisite to its judicial application".

In the new preamble of the Constitution of the Fifth Republic of 1958 it is now stated, that "the French people hereby solemnly proclaims its attachment to the Rights of Man and the principles of national sovereignty as defined by the Declaration of 1789, reaffirmed and complemented by the Preamble of the Constitution of 1946".

Notwithstanding some doubts as to whether that preamble constituted a source of law, French courts do not hesitate to apply rules of customary international law. Indeed it is argued that an explicit reference to these rules of international law would not be necessary, "as it would merely be the expression of what is in any event a general conviction" * * *.

The predominant doctrine in France * * * regards the reference of the Constitution of 1958 to the Preamble of the Constitution of 1946 as sufficient legal basis for applying international law.

* * *

3.2 Constitutions with no explicit reference to customary international law

3.2.1 Switzerland

In the Swiss Federal Constitution, there is no explicit provision concerning the relationship between international law and municipal law. But according to unanimous doctrine, there is an unwritten rule, implicit in the Constitution, that customary international law and the general principles of international law are valid immediately and without any special procedure, i.e., that they become municipally applicable upon their international entry into force: * * *

* * *

The Federal Tribunal repeatedly confirmed this view. It held that international law had to be considered as Swiss federal law, "because its nature requires general municipal applicability, so that it has to be equated with the uniform domestic law".

In the context of judicial proceedings, the Federal Tribunal also equated the violation of customary international law with that of treaty law: * * *

* * *

Rules of customary international law have only to be completed and implemented by Swiss federal law, if they are not clear enough and therefore unfit for immediate application and execution.

With respect to treaties, no formal transformation into a federal statute is required. Treaties become municipally applicable upon their international entry into force * * *.

* * *

Although the question of the rank of international law [in relation to Swiss constitutional and statutory law] continues to be disputed in doctrine and practice, there is a strong tendency to grant both customary and conventional international law a rank above federal statutes or even the same rank as the Constitution.

* * *

3.2.3 The Netherlands

[I]n the Dutch Constitution, there has never been any provision concerning the applicability and the rank of customary international law. On the other hand, international treaties have long ago been given a most favorable position in the text of the Constitution. The previous Constitution (adopted in 1953 and revised in 1956) went even as far as to permit international treaties to modify and lawfully overrule provisions of the Constitution itself.

In the next text, passed in 1983, however, it is not quite clear whether the primacy of international law is only proclaimed with respect to statutory law, while the Constitution remains unaffected. Unquestionably, according to Art. 94 of the new Constitution, international treaties override at least statutory rules * * *.

* * *

According to their monistic legal system, the Netherlands courts apply customary international law directly and immediately as such, and not by virtue of a transformation into municipal law.

Regarding the question of the rank of customary international law in cases of conflicts with statutory law, some old decisions of domestic tribunals held that statutes which violated rules of customary international law, nevertheless had a legal validity, because an examination of their constitutionality was not provided for by the constitution. On the other hand, the domestic courts applied the traditional principle of an interpretation of municipal law in conformity with international law. Also they recognized the presumption, according to which the legislature did not intend to violate rules of customary international law, [if] such an intention was not explicitly and clearly proved. * * *

Notes

1. *International law in the municipal systems of other states.* Wildhaber and Breitenmoser address also the jurisprudence of Belgium, the principality of Liechtenstein, Portugal and Spain.

The constitutional and jurisprudential problems faced by European states arise also in the domestic law of other countries around the world. See, e.g., *Australia*—International Law in Australia (Ryan, ed. 1984); Byrnes & Charlesworth, Federalism and the International Legal Order: Recent Developments in Australia, 79 A.J.I.L. 622 (1985); McGinley, The Status of Treaties in Australian Municipal Law, 12 Adel. L.Rev. 367 (1990). *Canada*—International Law[:] Chiefly as Interpreted and Applied in Canada, Chap. 4 (4th ed., Kindred, gen. ed., 1987); Campbell, Federalism and International Relations: The Canadian Experience, 85 A.S.I.L. Proc. 125 (1991); Schwartz, The Charter and the Domestic Enforcement of International Law, 16 Man.L.J. 149 (1986). *China*—Wang, International Law in China, 221 Rec. des Cours 195 (1990—II). *Indonesia*—Hartano, The Interaction Between National Law and International Law in Indonesia, in International Law and Development (de Waart, ed. 1988). *Israel*—Lapidoth, International Law Within the Israel Legal System, 24 Israel L.Rev. 451 (1990). *Japan*—Oda, The Practice of Japan in International Law, 1961–1970 (1982); *Nigeria*—Okeke, The Theory and Practice of International Law in Nigeria (1986).

In the case of South Africa, a new constitution has provided an enlightened, "cosmopolitan" approach to the place of treaties and international law in the constitutional order. See the following provisions of Chapter 14, Title 1:

Section 231: International agreements

(1) The negotiating and signing of all international agreements is the responsibility of the national executive.

(2) An international agreement binds the Republic only after it has been approved by resolution in both the National Assembly and the National Council of Provinces, unless it is an agreement referred to in subsection (3).

(3) An international agreement of a technical, administrative or executive nature, or an agreement which does not require either ratification or accession, entered into by the national executive, binds the Republic without approval by the National Assembly and the National Council of Provinces, but must be tabled in the Assembly and the Council within a reasonable time.

(4) Any international agreement becomes law in the Republic when it is enacted into law by national legislation; but a self-executing provision of an agreement that has been approved by Parliament is law in the Republic unless it is inconsistent with the Constitution or an Act of Parliament.

(5) The Republic is bound by international agreements which were binding on the Republic when this Constitution took effect.

Section 232 Customary international law

Customary international law is law in the Republic unless it is inconsistent with the Constitution or an Act of Parliament.

Section 233 Application of international law

When interpreting any legislation, every court must prefer any reasonable interpretation of the legislation that is consistent with international law over any alternative interpretation that is inconsistent with international law.

The Constitution, Section 39, also provides that "when interpreting the Bill of Rights, a court, tribunal or forum * * * must consider international law * * *

In Eastern and Central Europe and the former Soviet Union, quite a few states have constitutionalized the principles of international law and especially of international human rights law, in some cases returning to pre-communist jurisprudential traditions. See Stein, International Law in Internal Law: Toward Internationalization of Central–East European Constitutions, 88 A.J.I.L. 427 (1994); Danilenko, The New Russian Constitution and International Law, 88 A.J.I.L. 451 (1994); Lukashuk, Treaties in the Legal System of Russia, 40 Germ. Y.B.I.L. 141 (1997); Schweisfurth & Alleweldt, The Position of International Law in the Domestic Legal Orders of Eastern and Central Europe, 40 Germ. Y.B.I.L. 164 (1997); Ziernele, The Application of International Law in the Baltic States, 40 Germ. Y.B.I.L. 243 (1997).

2. English courts have applied customary international law since before the American revolution, saying that the law of nations was "part of the law of England." See Lord Mansfield in Triquet and Others v. Bath, 97 Eng. Rep. 936, 938, 3 Burr. 1478, 1481 (K.B. 1764). In 1938, the Privy Council said: "The Courts acknowledge the existence of a body of rules which nations accept amongst themselves. On any judicial issue they seek to ascertain what the relevant rule is, and, having found it, they will treat it as incorporated into the domestic law, so far as it is not inconsistent with rules enacted by statutes or finally declared by their tribunals." Chung Chi Cheung v. The King, [1939] A.C. 160, 168 (Hong Kong) (1938). In Mortensen v. Peters, 8 Sess. Cas. (5th ser.) 93 (1906), the Scottish Court of Justiciary upheld the conviction of a Danish national, master of a Norwegian ship, for fishing in violation of a statute regulating fishing in a part of Moray Firth more than three miles from the nearest land. Appellant argued that the application of British law to foreign nationals in this place would be a violation of international law and that the statute must be presumed not to extend to foreign nationals outside of British territory. The Court expressed doubt whether it was contrary to international law to treat Moray Firth, a bay, as British territory; the following statement was made by Lord Dunedin: "In this Court we have nothing to do with the question of whether the Legislature has or has not done what foreign powers may consider a usurpation in a question with them. Neither are we a tribunal sitting to decide whether an Act of the Legislature is ultra vires as in contravention of generally acknowledged principles of international law. For us an Act of Parliament duly passed by Lords and Commons and assented to by the King, is supreme, and we are bound to give effect to its terms." After this decision, several masters of Norwegian ships were convicted, but eventually released upon Norwegian protest. In Parliament, it was stated on behalf of the British Foreign Office that the Act, as interpreted by the court, was "in conflict with international law." 170 Parl.Deb. (4th ser.) 472 (1907). Subsequently, an Act of Parliament prohibited the landing or selling in the United Kingdom of fish caught by the forbidden methods within the areas specified. 9

Edw. VIII, c. 8 (1909). For the status of international law in British law generally, see Brownlie, Principles of Public International Law 42–47 (5th ed. 1998); Mann, Foreign Affairs in English Courts (1986). Britain's entry into the European Community has had a significant effect on its legal system. See Note 3.

3. The European Court of Justice has established that European Community law not only is the law of all member states, to be directly applied by all the national courts, but that it is the higher law of the member states, prevailing over conflicting national legislation. An eminent British jurist, Lord Denning, notes that the body of community legislation penetrates the British legal system "like an incoming tide. It flows into the estuaries and up the rivers. It cannot be held back * * *. Parliament has decreed that [community law] is * * * to be part of our law." Bulmer v. Bollinger, [1974] 2 All E.R. 1226

But the Constitutional Court of the Federal Republic of Germany has held that acts of the European Community are not enforceable if (1) they are ultra vires, i.e., if they exceed the authority which the German laws ratifying the Treaty of Rome and its amendments have transferred to the Community, or (2) if they violate individual rights under the German Constitution. BVerfGE 89, 155. In its so-called "Maastricht decision" of October 1993, the German Constitutional Court reserved to itself the authority to review decisions rendered by the European Court of Justice in order to safeguard fundamental individual rights under the German Constitution. BVerfGE 89, 155 (1993). See also the decisions of the German Constitutional Court leading to the landmark Maastricht decision, BVerfGE 37, 271 (1974); BVerfGE 58, 1 (1981); BVerfGE 73, 339 (1986). See also the discussion of the Italian Corte Constituzionale, Judgement of 27 Dec. 1973, n. 183, in Giurisprudenza Constitutionale; Kommers, The Constitutional Jurisprudence of the Federal Republic of Germany 107–113 (1997).

4. Under Article 25 of the German Constitution, quoted by Wildhaber & Breitenmoser, treaty provisions would take precedence over domestic law only to the extent that they embody "general rules of international law." Contrast the Netherlands Constitution, Article 94: "Statutory regulations in force within the Kingdom shall not be applicable if such application is in conflict with provisions of treaties that are binding on all persons or of resolutions by international institutions." XI Blaustein & Flanz, Constitutions of the Countries of the World, Netherlands 23–24 (1990). Compare those distinctions between customary international law and international agreements with United States jurisprudence. See pp. 213–214 supra.

5. In most Western European countries municipal courts will give effect to customary international law in appropriate cases unless there is controlling municipal law. See, e.g., Masters, International Law in National Courts (1932); Erades & Gould, The Relation Between International Law and Municipal Law in the Netherlands and in the United States (1961). For Italy, see De Meeus v. Forzano, [1940] Foro Ital. I 336, [1938–40] Ann.Dig. 423 (Corte di Cassazione, United Sections, 1940). The situation in the Soviet Union was not clear. See Ginsburgs, The Validity of Treaties in the Municipal Law of the "Socialist" States, 59 A.J.I.L. 523 (1965), and sources there cited. See also International Law 49–62 (Tunkin & Mullerson, eds. 1990). International agreements are sometimes treated differently, as Wildhaber and Breitenmoser indicate. But in many cases, courts have resorted to techniques of avoidance or deference to the executive branch, so that judicial orders requiring national authorities to comply with international law are exceptional. See Benvenisti, Judicial Misgivings Regarding

the Application of International Norms: An Analysis of Attitudes of National Courts, 4 E.J.I.L. 159 (1993).

6. See generally Franck & Fox (eds.), International Law Decisions in National Courts (1996); Conforti & Francioni (eds.), Enforcing International Human Rights in Domestic Courts (1997); and references collected in Knop, Here and There: International Law in Domestic Courts, 32 N.Y.U. J. Int'l L. & Politics 501–501 n. 1 (2000). For earlier treatments, see 1 Oppenheim's International Law 52–86 (5th ed., Jennings & Watts, eds. 1992); Brownlie, Principles of Public International Law 49–56 (5th ed. 1998); Starke, An Introduction to International Law 71–95 (10th ed. 1989); International Law and Municipal Law (Tunkin & Wolfrum, eds. 1988); The Effect of Treaties in Domestic Law (Jacobs & Roberts, eds. 1987); Rights, Institutions and Impact of International Law According to the German Basic Law (Starck, ed. 1987); La Pergola & Del Duca, Community Law, International Law and the Italian Constitution, 79 A.J.I.L. 598 (1985); Cassese, Modern Constitutions and International Law, 192 Rec. des Cours 331 (1985–III); Ferrari-Bravo, International Law and Municipal Law: The Complementarity of Legal Systems, in The Structure and Process of International Law: Essays in Legal Philosophy Doctrine and Theory 715 (Macdonald & Johnston, eds. 1983); Kelsen, Principles of International Law 551 (2nd ed., Tucker ed. 1966); Jessup, Transnational Law (1956).

7. Recent scholarship urges reconceptualization of the role of domestic courts in relation to international law. Taking note of various writings that envisage national courts as actual or potential enforcers of international law (e.g., references in Note 6 above), Karen Knop suggests that an enforcement model unhelpfully posits that international law "binds" national judges in a hierarchical sense, and thereby obscures the creative function of judges in translating norms drawn from international sources into local contexts. She proposes understanding international law through the lens of comparative law for insight into the persuasive (rather than "binding") force of international decisions. Knop, Here and There: International Law in Domestic Courts, 32 N.Y.U. J Int'l L. & Politics 501 (2000).

THE RELATIONSHIP BETWEEN INTERNATIONAL LAW, COMMUNITY LAW, AND DOMESTIC LAW IN THE EUROPEAN LEGAL ORDER

ANNE PETERS, THE POSITION OF INTERNATIONAL LAW WITHIN THE EUROPEAN COMMUNITY LEGAL ORDER

40 Germ. Y.B. Int'l L. 9, 21–23 (1997).

Neither the EC Treaty nor the Community institutions explains the Community practice of incorporating international law (in particular international agreements) into Community law in doctrinal terms.

According to article 228(7) EC Treaty "[a]greements concluded under the conditions set out in this Article shall be binding on the institutions of the Community and on Member States." This provision presupposes the insertion of international agreements into the Community legal order, without specifically prescribing a specific technique of incorporation. An unwritten Community rule which corresponds to article 228(7) foresees the incorporation of customary international law into the Community legal order.

The ECJ has treated the incorporation of international agreements in an informal fashion. Throughout its case law, it made no difference between agreements concluded on the Community side by the Community alone * * *, those concluded by the Community and the Member States acting together * * *, and finally the GATT, which was concluded by the Member States but which became binding on the Community by succession. * * *

One could think of developing a theory of incorporation of international law (in particular international agreements) into Community law from the Member States' practice of incorporating international law into domestic law. If there existed some general principles in this respect, a Community technique tailored to these would have good chances to meet the Member States' approval. However, the Member States' regulations to ensure domestic execution of international treaties is too diverse to provide a basic Community rule. * * * [A]t first sight, practice and case law do not answer the question whether the incorporation of international law into the Community legal order occurs by transformation (within a dualist framework) or not (within a monist framework). On the contrary, practice and case law appear to be primarily guided by pragmatism. So is a theory of incorporation of international law into Community law mere theory for theory's sake? It is submitted here that it is not, because it does—due to the special characteristics of Community law—make an important difference whether international law is valid as such within the Community, or whether it is transformed into Community law.

Notes

1. In a 1997 resolution, the European Parliament asked for an amendment to the EC Treaty that would clearly establish a specific doctrine for the incorporation of international law into Community law:

[The European Parliament:]

1. Recalls that the law of the EU constitutes an autonomous legal system and recalls also the case-law of the Court of Justice of the European Communities with regard to the supremacy of Community law over national law. * * *

12. Calls, in addition, for the supremacy of Community law to be enshrined directly in the EC Treaty itself;

13. Considers that, in so far as powers which have implications for sovereignty are transferred to the EU institutions, such transfers must presuppose the recognition that the EU assumes sovereign powers which cease to fall within the exclusive ambit of the States, so that national courts cannot review the acts of the Community institutions acting within their proper competencies;

14. Calls for a clear statement of the relationship between international law and European law to be written into the EC Treaty, in terms of the EC being equated with nation states, which means that international law is applicable not directly but only after it has been declared applicable by an internal legal act of the EC or after its substance has been transposed into EC legislation;

15. Calls for the relationship with international law ultimately also to be regulated for the second and third pillars, in other words for the EU as a whole, in the same way as for the first pillar;

16. Calls for an amendment to the EU treaty to the effect that the European Union is given legal personality; * * *

Resolution of the European Parliament on the relation between international law, Community law and constitutional law of the Member States of 10 October 1997, Official Journal Eur. Comm. No. C 325 (1997).

2. Much of the doctrinal difficulty in determining the status of international law in European Community Law results from its so-called "identity crisis." One scholar has noted that "[t]he 35 years between the founding of the EEC and the creation of the European Union (EU) saw the EEC grow from a regional trading block into a supranational organization with an international identity distinct from that of its Member States." See Edwards, Fearing Federalism's Failure: Subsidiarity in the European Union, 44 Am. J. Comp. L. 537, 537–38 (1996) (discussing the EU's progress toward becoming a federal state). There has been uncertainty as to whether the European Community should be treated in the international legal context as a federal state, an intergovernmental organization, or some type of supranational entity. See Monaghan, European Union Legal Personality Disorder: The Union's Legal Nature Through the Prism of the German Federal Constitutional Court's Maastricht Decision, 12 Emory Int'l L. Rev. 1443 (1998).

3. The member states of the European Community rank international law within their domestic systems in diverse ways. The ECJ has thus been forced to determine autonomously the place of international law in the European legal hierarchy. In cases of potential conflict between a Community rule and an international agreement or customary norm, the Court has been careful to avoid concrete statements on hierarchy. It is generally agreed that international and Community laws stand in the following hierarchy: *Jus Cogens* norms, which cannot be invalidated, stand supreme, followed by the EC Treaty, followed by general international norms (arising from treaty obligations and customary international law), and finally Community legislation. See Peters, The Position of International Law Within the European Community Legal Order, 40 Germ. Y.B.I.L. 9, 37 (1997).

4. International law binding on the European Community may have an impact on the relationship between the domestic law of individual member states and Community law. For example, the German Bundesfinanzhof (Federal Financial Tribunal) argued that Community action violative of international law (in this instance the GATT) falls outside the scope of the member states' constitutional authorization of Community powers and thus does not bind the member states. This case suggests a "supremacy" or preemptive characterization of international law in the European legal order. See Order of the Bundesfinanzhof of 9 January, 1996, Europäische Zeitschrift für Wirtschaftsrecht, Bd. 7, 126 (1996).

5. For cases in which the European Court of Justice has applied international law as a standard of legality of Community or member state action, *see* Case T–115/94, Opel Austria v. Council, 1997 ECR II–39 (the Court of First Instance examined a Community regulation in light of the European Economic Area Treaty and the customary international law principle of *bona fides*); Case 175/87, Matsushita Electric v. Council, 1992 ECR I–1409; Case C–188/88, NMB (Germany) v. Commission, 1992 ECR I–1689 (individual importers sought invalidation in both cases of the European Council's basic anti-dumping regulation on the ground that

Community action violated the GATT Anti-Dumping Code); Cases 89, 104, 116, 117, 125–129/1985, Ahlström Osakeyhiö v. Commission (Wood Pulp case), 1988 ECR 5139 (court applied international law as a yardstick and held that the Commission's action of fining petitioner in a competition matter conformed to the international principle of territoriality and therefore did not breach international law); Case 21–24/72, International Fruit Company v. Produktschap voor groenten en fruit, 1972 ECR 1219 (referring court in preliminary ruling considered whether particular Community regulations were invalid on the ground of a GATT violation and determined that the Court must examine whether acts are invalid for nonconformance to a rule of international law).

6. For more on the triangular relationship between international law, European Community law and domestic law in the European Member States, *see* Weiler & Trachtman, European Constitutionalism and its Discontents, 17 Nw. J. Int'l L. & Bus. 354 (1996–1997); Eisemann, ed., The Integration of International and European Community Law into the National Legal Order: A Study of the Practice in Europe (1996); Hartley, The Foundations of European Community Law (3rd ed. 1994); Capotorti, et al. (eds.), Du droit international au droit de l'integration: Liber Amicorum Pierre Pescatore (1987); Kapteyn, The "Domestic" Law Effect of Rules of International Law Within the European Community System of Law and the Question of the Self-Executing Character of GATT Rules, 8 International Lawyer 74 (1978).

* * *

At the beginning of the 21st century, the relation between international law and municipal law largely reflects dualistic tendencies, both in the United States and elsewhere. Compare, for example, Henkin, Implementation and Compliance: Is Dualism Metastasizing? 1998 A.S.I.L. Proc. 515. But erosions of traditional "sovereignty" in respect of human rights have wrought other changes in the relation of municipal law to international law and institutions. As will be seen in Chapters 13 and 15 below (on jurisdiction and international criminal law), national courts are increasingly asserting competence under international law to adjudicate violations of some international norms, as in the proceedings in 1997–2000 in several European countries against General Pinochet of Chile, in which massive atrocities were alleged, and in national proceedings complementary to those of the several international criminal tribunals. Even within the framework of traditional dualistic approaches, domestic courts have found new avenues for the application of international law.

Chapter 4

STATES

INTRODUCTORY NOTE

SUBJECTS OF THE LAW AND INTERNATIONAL PERSONS

Subjects of international law include persons and entities capable of possessing international rights and duties under international law and endowed with the capacity to take certain types of action on the international plane. The term "international legal person" is commonly used in referring to such persons and entities. Questions of whether an entity is an international legal person arise in various contexts. Most commonly, they have related to the capacity to make treaties and agreements under international law, the capacity to make claims for breaches of international law, and the enjoyment of privileges and immunities from national jurisdiction. The question of international legal personality may also arise in regard to membership or participation in international bodies.

States are, of course, the principal examples of international persons. The attributes of statehood, as developed in customary law, provided the criteria for determining the "personality" of other entities. Indeed, at one time the generally held view was that only fully sovereign states could be persons in international law. The realities, however, were more complex and over time many different kinds of entities have been considered as capable of having international rights and duties and the capacity to act on the international plane. Such entities were often compared to states and distinctions were made by examining the degree of sovereignty they had retained or acquired. It had in fact long been evident that despite the dogma that only sovereign states could be subjects of international law, many other entities—some resembling states, others constituting organizations of states, and others not necessarily comparable to states—were regarded as international legal persons for certain purposes and in some respects. Even individuals and corporations or other juridical entities can be persons under or subjects of international law when they are accorded rights, duties and other aspects of legal personality under customary international law or an international agreement. As in any legal system, not all subjects of international law are identical in their nature or their rights and one must constantly be aware of the relativity of the concept of international legal person.

The widening of the concept of international legal personality beyond the state is one of the more significant features of contemporary international law. This broadening is particularly evident in the case of public international organizations, supranational entities such as the European Union, and insurgent communities and movements of national liberation. But these developments should not obscure the primary and predominant role of the state as the subject of international law. To quote Wolfgang Friedmann:

> The states are the repositories of legitimated authority over peoples and territories. It is only in terms of state powers, prerogatives, jurisdictional limits and law-making capabilities that territorial limits and jurisdiction, responsibility for official actions, and a host of other questions of coexistence between nations can be determined. It is by virtue of their law-making power and monopoly that states enter into bilateral and multilateral compacts, that wars can be started or terminated, that individuals can be punished or extradited. * * *
>
> At present instead of witnessing the gradual absorption of national sovereignties and legal systems, we are faced with an opposite development: the proliferation of sovereignties * * *

Friedmann, The Changing Structure of International Law 213–214 (1964).

SECTION 1. THE DETERMINATION OF STATEHOOD

A. WHAT IS A STATE?

RESTATEMENT (THIRD)

§ 201. State Defined

Under international law, a state is an entity that has a defined territory and a permanent population, under the control of its own government, and that engages in, or has the capacity to engage in, formal relations with other such entities.

Note

Restatement (Third) § 206 states that the capacities, rights and duties of states include the following:

> (a) sovereignty over its territory and general authority over its nationals;
>
> (b) status as a legal person, with capacity to own, acquire, and transfer property, to make contracts and enter into international agreements, to become a member of international organizations, and to pursue, and be subject to, legal remedies;
>
> (c) capacity to join with other states to make international law, as customary law or by international agreement.

B. WHEN DOES THE QUESTION OF STATEHOOD ARISE?

Controversies as to whether an entity should be considered as a state arise as a result of certain extraordinary political changes, particularly in the following situations:

1. Break-up of an existing state into a number of states.

2. Secession or attempted secession by part of a territory of an existing state.

3. Cases in which foreign control is exercised over the affairs of a state, whether by treaty, unilateral imposition or delegation of authority.

4. Cases in which states have merged or formed a union.

5. Claims by constituent units of a union or federation to the attributes of statehood.

6. Territorial or non-territorial communities which have a special international status by virtue of treaty or customary law and which claim statehood for certain purposes.

In the recent past issues of statehood have been generated by the break-up of the former U.S.S.R., Yugoslavia, and Czechoslovakia and the reunification of Germany. They are also raised by other contemporary situations, such as the Middle East peace process.

Controversies that arise with respect to the existence of a new state occur on both the international and national levels. On the international level, the issue is likely to arise when the entity whose status is in controversy seeks admission or the right of participation in an international body open to states alone. Issues of statehood have therefore frequently arisen in connection with applications for membership in the United Nations or its affiliated organizations or in international conferences convened under its auspices. These issues are normally decided by decision of the international body concerned. Questions of statehood have also arisen in regard to the rights of entities to become parties to multilateral treaties or agreements open only to states. In some but not all of the cases involving treaties, the issue may be resolved by a collective decision.

National governments may also have to determine whether an entity is a state for purposes of bilateral relations. Normally this determination is made by the executive branch by recognition of the entity as a state. Such recognition may be explicit and formal or it may be implied in the initiation of diplomatic relations or from conclusion of a bilateral treaty. Questions of statehood also arise in national courts, particularly in respect of entities which have not been recognized as states by the executive branch. Courts may have to decide whether an unrecognized entity should be regarded as a state for purposes of determining claims to property, issues of nationality, the right to sue, the validity of official acts, immunity from suit, and various other questions linked to statehood.

The question of whether an entity is or is not a state is distinct from the issue of whether a particular regime or authority is the government of that state. While the existence of an independent government is a requirement of statehood, governments change and conflicting claims of governmental authority may arise. In these cases, foreign governments and international organizations may have to decide which government should be considered the government of the state in question. The issues are not the same as those involved in determining statehood and are therefore treated separately in the material below.

C. THE EFFECT OF RECOGNITION ON STATEHOOD: CONSTITUTIVE AND DECLARATORY VIEWS

The question of whether an entity is a state and should be so treated has given rise to two opposing theories. One theory is that the act of recognition by other states confers international personality on an entity purporting to be a state. In effect, the other states by their recognition "constitute" or create the new state. On this "constitutive" theory an observer or a court need only look at the acts of recognition (or lack thereof) to decide whether an entity is a state.

The opposing position is that the existence of a state depends on the facts and on whether those facts meet the criteria of statehood laid down in international law. Accordingly, a state may exist without being recognized. Recognition is merely declaratory. The primary function of recognition is to acknowledge the fact of the state's political existence and to declare the recognizing state's willingness to treat the entity as an international person, with the rights and obligations of a state.

Although distinguished jurists and some judicial authorities have supported the constitutive theory, the weight of authority and state practice support the declaratory position. As stated by the authoritative *Institut de Droit International* in 1936: "The existence of a new State with all the legal consequences attaching to this existence is not affected by the refusal of recognition by one or more states." [1936] 2 Annuaire de l'Institut de Droit Int'l 300. This view is adopted by the Inter–American Convention on Rights and Duties of States, 1933, 49 Stat. 3097, T.S. No. 8811, 165 L.N.T.S. 19 (Art. 3), and the Charter of the Organization of American States, 1948, 2 U.S.T. 2416, T.I.A.S. No. 2361, 119 U.N.T.S. 3 (as amended by Protocols of 1967–1993; see renumbered Art. 13: "The political existence of the State is independent of recognition by other States."). The *ad hoc* Arbitration Commission (consisting of the Presidents of the Constitutional Courts of Belgium, France, Germany, Italy and Spain) established by the E.C.-sponsored Conference on Yugoslavia (see p. 259 infra) opined that "the existence or disappearance of the State is a question of fact; that the effects of recognition by other States are purely declaratory." Arbitration Commission Opinion No. 1, 31 I.L.M. 1494 (1992).

Some authorities, including Lauterpacht, Recognition in International Law (1947), adopt the "constitutive" theory, but contend that states have an obligation to recognize an entity that meets the qualifications of statehood. Cf. Section 1.E.

Section 202(1) of the Restatement (Third) states that although a state is not required to accord formal recognition to any other state, it is required to treat as a state an entity that meets the requirements of statehood. A state is obligated not to recognize or treat as a state an entity that has attained the qualifications of statehood as a result of a threat or use of force in violation of the United Nations Charter. Restatement (Third) § 202(2). See Section 1.E.

Thus (unless an entity has come into existence in violation of international law), in order to determine whether an entity is a state, it must be ascertained whether it meets the criteria of international law. But such application may call for the determination of difficult questions of fact and law. Is there a government with the capacity to enter into relations with other states? Is it, in that sense, independent? In ascertaining these "facts," especially when they are in dispute, states and international bodies will generally give weight to recognition *vel non* by other states. Consequently, acts of recognition or refusals to recognize may have a significant and at times decisive role in determining controversial situations. For this reason, the theoretical gap between the declaratory and constitutive views is rather less in practice than in theory. The Reporters note that the position reflected in the Restatement (Third) § 202 is closer to the declaratory than the constitutive view, but that the practical differences between the two have diminished. "Even for the declaratory theory, whether an entity satisfies the requirements for statehood is, as a practical matter, determined by other states. * * * On the other hand, the constitutive theory lost much of its significance when it was accepted that states had the obligation * * * to treat as a state any entity that had the characteristics set forth in § 201. * * * Delays in recognizing or accepting statehood have generally reflected uncertainty as to the viability of the new state * * * or the view that it was created in violation of international law. * * * " Restatement (Third) § 202, Reporters' Note 1.

It is clear that an entity that meets the conditions of statehood cannot, because of the lack of recognition, be denied its rights or escape its obligations. "Its territory cannot be considered to be no-man's-land; there is no right to overfly without permission; ships flying its flag cannot be considered stateless, and so on." Mugerwa, Subjects of International Law, in Manual of Public International Law, 269 (Sorensen ed. 1968). Nor can such a non-recognized entity evade the duties of states under international law. (In fact, non-recognized states are often charged with violations of international law and are the object of international claims by the very states refusing recognition. For example, the United States charged North Korea, which it did not recognize as a state, with illegal action when North Korea seized a United States naval vessel, the Pueblo, in 1968. 58 Dep't St. Bull. 196–97 (1968).) These legal propositions are well supported by state practice and doctrine. They confirm the essential validity of the declaratory view and therefore the relevance of the legal conditions for determining whether an entity is a state.

D. THE CONDITIONS OF STATEHOOD

1. Requirement of a Permanent Population and Defined Territory

Philip C. Jessup, then United States representative to the Security Council, advocating the admission of Israel to the United Nations, said:

> The consideration of the application requires an examination of * * * the question of whether Israel is a State duly qualified for membership. Article 4 of the Charter of the United Nations specifies the following:
>
> > Membership in the United Nations is open to * * * peace-loving States which accept the obligations contained in the present Charter

and, in the judgment of the Organization, are able and willing to carry out these obligations.

* * * My Government considers that the State of Israel meets these Charter requirements.

The first question which may be raised in analyzing Article 4 of the Charter and its applicability to the membership of the State of Israel, is the question of whether Israel is a State, as that term is used in Article 4 of the Charter. It is common knowledge that, while there are traditional definitions of a State in international law, the term has been used in many different ways. We are all aware that, under the traditional definition of a State in international law, all the great writers have pointed to four qualifications: first, there must be a people; second, there must be a territory; third, there must be a government; and, fourth, there must be capacity to enter into relations with other States of the world.

In so far as the question of capacity to enter into relations with other States of the world is concerned, * * * I believe that there would be unanimity that Israel exercises complete independence of judgment and of will in forming and in executing its foreign policy. * * *

When we look at the other classic attributes of a State, we find insistence that it must also have a Government. No one doubts that Israel has a Government. * * *

According to the same classic definition, we are told that a State must have a people and a territory. Nobody questions the fact that the State of Israel has a people. * * *

The argument seems chiefly to arise in connection with territory. One does not find in the general classic treatment of this subject any insistence that the territory of a State must be exactly fixed by definite frontiers. We all know that, historically, many States have begun their existence with their frontiers unsettled. Let me take as one example, my own country, the United States of America. Like the State of Israel in its origin, it had certain territory along the seacoast. It had various indeterminate claims to an extended territory westward. But, in the case of the United States, that land had not even been explored, and no one knew just where the American claims ended and where French and British and Spanish claims began. To the North, the exact delimitation of the frontier with the territories of Great Britain was not settled until many years later. And yet, I maintain that, in the light of history and in the light of the practice and acceptance by other States, the existence of the United States of America was not in question before its final boundaries were determined.

The formulae in the classic treatises somewhat vary, one from the other, but both reason and history demonstrate that the concept of territory does not necessarily include precise delimitation of the boundaries of that territory. The reason for the rule that one of the necessary attributes of a State is that it shall possess territory is that one cannot contemplate a State as a kind of disembodied spirit. Historically, the concept is one of insistence that there must be some portion of the earth's surface which its people inhabit and over which its Government exercises authority. No one can deny that the State of Israel responds to this requirement. * * *

3 U.N. SCOR, 383 Mtg., Dec. 2, 1948, No. 128, pp. 9–12.

Notes

1. A state does not cease to be a state because it is occupied by a foreign power. Restatement (Third) § 201, Comment *b*. Thus, Kuwait remained a state notwithstanding its occupation and putative annexation by Iraq in 1990. The United States never recognized the incorporation of Estonia, Latvia and Lithuania into the U.S.S.R. Treaties between the United States and those countries remained in force and their diplomatic representatives were regarded as duly accredited. When these countries regained their independence in 1991, the United States simply resumed full diplomatic relations. Vol. 2, No. 2 Foreign Pol'y Bull. 33 (Sept./Oct. 1991).

2. A state does not cease to exist when a previously functioning government becomes ineffective or defunct. A case in point is Somalia, the government of which no longer functioned effectively in 1992 when, under the authorization of the U.N. Security Council, a multinational force organized by the United States assisted in establishing enough stability to permit distribution of food and other humanitarian resources needed to ameliorate widespread starvation. Cambodia remained a state even when it lacked a functioning government in the traditional sense, while being administered by a Supreme National Council under the U.N.-managed political settlement process established by the 1992 Paris Accords. The SNC served as the embodiment of Cambodian national sovereignty in the transitional period leading to elections, to promote national reconciliation between four Cambodian factions. See Ratner, The Cambodia Settlement Agreements, 89 A.J.I.L. 9 (1993).

3. The requirement for a permanent population would prevent qualification of Antarctica as a state. Restatement (Third), § 201, Comment *c*. How many people does a "permanent population" imply? The proliferation of very small independent "sovereign" states, the "mini states", appears to confirm that no minimum number has been set. Nauru with 8,000 people has been considered a state as has Liechtenstein with 28,000 people. U.N. member states now include these and several others with fewer than 100,000 people. For consideration of problems created by "mini states", see J. Rapoport, Small States and Territories (a UNITAR study, 1971); Gunter, What Happened to the United Nations Ministate Problem?, 71 A.J.I.L. 110 (1977). A significant number of "permanent" inhabitants will suffice even if large numbers of nomads move in and out of the territory. Restatement (Third), § 201, Comment *c*.

The Vatican City, which has been treated as a state, has a population of about 400 citizens and 800 residents. It has entered into treaties that have a specific territorial application to the Vatican City (e.g., telecommunications). On the distinct international legal personality of the Holy See (i.e., the central administration of the Roman Catholic Church), see p. 291 below.

4. A new state does not have to extend nationality to its population as a condition of statehood. It is, however, true that when a new state is established in a territory, the inhabitants generally become nationals of that state. See Case

Concerning Acquisition of Polish Nationality, 1923 P.C.I.J., Ser. B, No. 7, at 15. See also Section 6.E below (on succession of states in relation to nationality).

5. With regard to territory, no rule prescribes a minimum. Monaco, for example, is only 1.5 square kilometers in size. One might speculate on whether an artificial installation on the sea-bed beyond national jurisdiction could have a territorial basis for a claim of statehood. See p. 1458 infra. What about a "permanent colony" in outer space? See material on sovereignty over territory in outer space, p. 1558 infra.

2. *Requirement of a Government*

LEAGUE OF NATIONS, COMMISSION OF JURISTS ON AALAND ISLANDS DISPUTE

League of Nations O.J., Spec. Supp. 4, at 8–9 (1920).

[A Commission of Jurists appointed by the League in 1920 to consider certain aspects of a dispute concerning the Aaland Islands considered when Finland attained statehood after the civil war of 1917–18 in that country. The Jurists concluded that Finland did not attain statehood until an effective government was established. In their opinion they stated that:]

> * * * for a considerable time, the conditions required for the formation of a sovereign State did not exist. In the midst of revolution and anarchy, certain elements essential to the existence of a State, even some elements of fact, were lacking for a fairly considerable period. Political and social life was disorganized; the authorities were not strong enough to assert themselves; civil war was rife; further, the Diet, the legality of which had been disputed by a large section of the people, had been dispersed by the revolutionary party, and the Government had been chased from the capital and forcibly prevented from carrying out its duties; the armed camps and the police were divided into two opposing forces, and Russian troops, and after a time Germans also, took part in the civil war * * *. It is therefore difficult to say at what exact date the Finnish Republic, in the legal sense of the term, actually became a definitely constituted sovereign State. This certainly did not take place until a stable political organization had been created, and until the public authorities had become strong enough to assert themselves throughout the territories of the State without the assistance of foreign troops. It would appear that it was in May 1918, that the civil war was ended and that the foreign troops began to leave the country, so that from that time onward it was possible to reestablish order and normal political and social life, little by little.

Notes

1. Should the standard of effective government be less stringent when a territory is granted independence by a former sovereign? No one questioned that the former Belgian Congo (later Zaire) was a state when it became independent in 1960 though, like Finland in 1917, it was in a state of civil war and virtual

anarchy. The same could be said of Burundi and Rwanda, both granted independence when they were without an effective government. See Higgins, Development of International Law Through the Political Organs of the United Nations 21–23 (1963). In contrast, Finland was engaged in a war of secession. Consider the following comment. "A new state formed by secession from a metropolitan state will have to demonstrate substantial independence, both formal and real, before it will be regarded as definitively created. On the other hand, the independence of an existing state is protected by international law rules against illegal invasion and annexation so that the state may, even for a considerable time, continue to exist as a legal entity despite lack of effectiveness. But where a new state is formed by grant of power from the former sovereign * * *, considerations of preexisting rights are no longer relevant and independence is treated as a predominantly formal criterion." Crawford, The Criteria for Statehood in International Law, 48 Brit. Y.B.I.L. 120 (1976–77).

2. The *ad hoc* Arbitration Commission established by the E.C.-sponsored Conference on Yugoslavia (see p. 252 supra and p. 259 infra) was asked by the Chairman of the Conference, Lord Carrington of the United Kingdom, to give its opinion on whether the Socialist Federal Republic of Yugoslavia continued to exist as a state. In concluding that the SFRY was in the process of dissolution, the Commission commented that "in the case of a federal-type State, which embraces communities that possess a degree of autonomy and, moreover, participate in the exercise of political power within the framework of institutions common to the Federation, the existence of the State implies that the federal organs represent the components of the Federation and wield effective power * * *." It then expressed its opinion that the "composition and workings of the essential organs of the Federation, be they the Federal Presidency, the Federal Council, the Council of the Republics and the Provinces, the Federal Executive Council, the Constitutional Court or the Federal Army, no longer meet the criteria of participation and representativeness inherent in a federal State * * *" Arbitration Commission Opinion No. 1, 31 I.L.M. 1494 (1992).

3. *Requirement of Capacity to Engage in Relations With Other States*

Comment *e* to Restatement (Third) § 201 states as follows:

> *e. Capacity to conduct international relations.* An entity is not a state unless it has competence, within its own constitutional system, to conduct international relations with other states, as well as the political, technical and financial capabilities to do so. An entity which has the capacity to conduct foreign relations does not cease to be a state because it voluntarily turns over to another state some or all control of its foreign relations * * *.

Notes

1. There have been examples in the past of states transferring control over foreign relations to another state. An example is Liechtenstein, which transferred control of its foreign relations to Switzerland, but was admitted as a party to the Statute of the International Court of Justice, for which only states qualify, and

participated in the *Nottebohm Case* (Liechtenstein v. Guatemala), 1955 I.C.J. 4, p. 430 infra. See Restatement (Third), § 201, Reporters' Note 4.

2. The establishment of the European Community did not terminate the statehood of the member states or vest the Community with statehood although the Community assumed international responsibility for certain matters, such as establishing uniform external tariffs, previously controlled by the member states. See Bermann et al., Cases and Materials on European Community Law, Part IV on External Relations and Commercial Policy (1993).

3. "Protectorates" or "protected states" predominantly of the colonial era involved agreements by local rulers conferring authority over foreign affairs or other matters on an external state, usually an "imperial power". Although "protectorates" have virtually disappeared as a distinct legal category, small or weak states may still be subject to varying degrees of foreign control of a military, economic or political character. At one time—especially during the 1950s—foreign control was cited as a ground for excluding applicants for membership in the United Nations. This was clearly bound up with political and ideological factors. In recent decades a large number of newly "independent" states have been admitted without question although they have often been heavily dependent in actuality on other powers for security and economic viability. The notable exceptions have been those "states" which have been regarded as "illegal" in the sense that their establishment was contrary to principles of international law, as for example Transkei and Rhodesia. See Section 1.E infra.

4. Emergence of Additional Criteria for Recognition of Statehood; Collective Recognition

The United States and the European Community appeared to herald a new approach to recognition of states in late 1991, in connection with the disintegration of the U.S.S.R. and the Socialist Federal Republic of Yugoslavia. In a speech before the September 1991 meeting of the Conference on Security and Cooperation in Europe (CSCE), U.S. Secretary of State Baker articulated five principles relevant to U.S. policy, in addition to the traditional criteria for statehood. Recognition was to be accorded in the light of the new states' adherence to the following:

— Determining the future of the country peacefully and democratically, consistent with CSCE principles;

— Respect for all existing borders, both internal and external, and change to those borders only through peaceful and consensual means;

— Support for democracy and the rule of law, emphasizing the key role of elections in the democratic process;

— Safeguarding of human rights, based on full respect for the individual and including equal treatment of minorities; and

— Respect for international law and obligations, especially adherence to the Helsinki Final Act and the Charter of Paris.

Testimony of Ralph Johnson, Deputy Assistant Secretary of State for European and Canadian Affairs, October 17, 1991, Vol. 2, No. 3 Foreign Pol'y Bull. 39, 42 (Nov./Dec. 1991).

In connection with the emergence of new states in Eastern Europe an extraordinary European Political Cooperation (EPC) meeting of the Foreign

Ministers of the European Community Member States issued on December 16, 1991, a Declaration on "Guidelines on the Recognition of New States in Eastern Europe and in the Soviet Union". The E.C. affirmed in the Declaration that the Community and its member states would recognize, "subject to the normal standards of international practice and the political realities in each case," those new states that had constituted themselves on a democratic basis, had accepted the appropriate international obligations, and had committed themselves in good faith to negotiations and the peaceful settlement of outstanding issues. More specifically, the E.C. Guidelines required fulfillment of the following conditions as the foundation for recognition:

— respect for the provisions of the Charter of the United Nations and the commitments subscribed to in the Final Act of Helsinki and in the Charter of Paris, especially with regard to the rule of law, democracy and human rights;

— guarantees for the rights of ethnic and national groups and minorities in accordance with the commitments subscribed to in the framework of the CSCE;

— respect for the inviolability of all frontiers which can only be changed by peaceful means and by common agreement;

— acceptance of all relevant commitments with regard to disarmament and nuclear non-proliferation as well as to security and regional stability;

— commitment to settle by agreement, including where appropriate by recourse to arbitration, all questions concerning state succession and regional disputes.

The Declaration stated that the "commitment to these principles opens the way to recognition by the Community and its Member States and to the establishment of diplomatic relations." EPC Press Release 128/91 (Dec. 16, 1991), 31 I.L.M. 1486 (1992).

In a separate Declaration on Yugoslavia, 31 I.L.M. 1485 (1992), the ministers invited all Yugoslav republics to make requests for recognition by the E.C. by December 23, 1991. Each republic seeking E.C. recognition was required to state whether:

— It wanted to be recognized as an independent state;

— It accepted the commitments included in the general E.C. guidelines on recognition;

— It accepted provisions of a draft Convention on Yugoslavia, especially those on human rights and rights of ethnic groups, developed by, and pending before, the E.C.-led Conference on Yugoslavia chaired by Lord Carrington;

— It continued to support United Nations and E.C. efforts to reach a peaceful settlement of the disputes in Yugoslavia;

— It agreed to adopt constitutional and political guarantees "ensuring that it has no territorial claims" against a neighboring E.C. country and that it would not use a name (e.g., Macedonia) that implied such claims and would conduct "no hostile propaganda activities" against a neighboring E.C. country.

Those republics that responded positively to these conditions qualified to have their applications considered by an *ad hoc* Arbitration Commission, established by the Conference on Yugoslavia and consisting of the Presidents of the Constitutional Courts of Belgium, France, Germany, Italy and Spain. The President of the French Constitutional Court (Conseil Constitutionnel), Judge Robert Badinter, was chosen to act as Chairman.

The E.C. Guidelines appear to go well beyond the traditional qualifications for statehood under customary international law and appear to imply that recognition of statehood must be "earned" by meeting the standards articulated. One commentator has observed as follows:

> This extensive catalog of criteria, far in excess of traditional standards for recognition of statehood, confirms that the Community was not applying general international law in the determination of its position. Although some of the requirements reflected objective criteria that must be fulfilled if there is to be a well-founded claim to statehood, the more specific conditions were hand tailored to fit EC interests. * * *

Weller, The International Response to the Dissolution of the Socialist Federal Republic of Yugoslavia, 86 A.J.I.L. 569, 588 (1992) (footnotes omitted).

After receiving the opinion of the E.C. Arbitration Commission, the European Community and Austria and Switzerland recognized the former Yugoslav republics of Slovenia and Croatia on January 15, 1992. Recognition of Croatia by the E.C. was reportedly jeopardized at the last minute by release of Opinion No. 5 of the Arbitration Commission on January 11, 1992, 31 I.L.M. 1503 (1992), which indicated that Croatia had not yet provided all of the constitutional guarantees of the rights of minority groups called for in the E.C. Guidelines on recognition but had otherwise met the conditions of the Guidelines. N.Y. Times, Jan. 16, 1992, p. A6, col. 1. Thus, it is unclear that the E.C. followed its own guidelines in according recognition in this instance.

On December 25, 1991, a week after the formation of the Commonwealth of Independent States to replace the former Soviet Union, President Bush made the following announcement:

> And so today, based on commitments and assurances given to us by some of these states, concerning nuclear safety, democracy, and free markets, I am announcing some important steps designed to begin this process.
>
> First, the United States recognizes and welcomes the emergence of a free, independent, and democratic Russia, led by its courageous President, Boris Yeltsin. Our Embassy in Moscow will remain there as our Embassy to Russia. We will support Russia's assumption of the U.S.S.R.'s seat as a Permanent Member of the United Nations Security Council. * * *
>
> Second, the United States also recognizes the independence of Ukraine, Armenia, Kazakhstan, Belarus, and Kirgizstan—all states that have made specific commitments to us. We will move quickly to establish diplomatic relations with these states and build new ties to them. We will sponsor membership in the United Nations for those not already members.
>
> Third, the United States also recognizes today as independent states the remaining six former Soviet Republics—Moldova, Turkmenistan, Az-

erbaijan, Tajikistan, Georgia, and Uzbekistan. We will establish diplomatic relations with them when we are satisfied that they have made commitments to responsible security policies and democratic principles, as have the other states we recognize today.

Vol. 2, Nos. 4 & 5 Foreign Pol'y Bull. 12 (Jan.-April 1992).

In connection with the emergence of new states associated with the break-up of the former Socialist Federal Republic of Yugoslavia, the United States initially declined to follow the E.C. lead on the ground that the parties to the Yugoslav conflict had first to reach a peaceful settlement through negotiation and with firm protections for minorities. N.Y. Times, Jan. 16, 1992, p. A6, col. 3. The United States did not recognize Slovenia, Croatia and Bosnia–Herzegovina until April 7, 1992, at which time the United States also announced that it was proceeding to establish diplomatic relations with each of them.

What was previously the Socialist Federal Republic of Yugoslavia thus became five separate entities: the states of Croatia, Slovenia, and Bosnia–Herzegovina, the Federal Republic of Yugoslavia (consisting of the Republics of Serbia and Montenegro) and the former Yugoslav republic of Macedonia. Although Macedonia appeared to have met the traditional criteria of statehood for some time, and it was found by the E.C. Arbitration Commission to meet the E.C. guidelines in January 1992, formal acceptance of its status as a state was deferred because of objections by Greece (a region of which is called Macedonia). It was ultimately admitted to the United Nations in April 1993 under the name of "The Former Yugoslav Republic of Macedonia."

Notes

1. The Arbitration Commission was established by the Peace Conference on Yugoslavia on August 27, 1991, as a body to which issues arising in connection with the break-up of the Socialist Federal Republic of Yugoslavia could be submitted for the rendering of opinions that would be transmitted to the Peace Conference. Through December 1992 the Commission issued ten opinions and an interlocutory decision of July 4, 1992, upholding its authority to judge its own competence in the face of a challenge thereto by Serbia and Montenegro. Opinions 1 to 3 and 8 to 10 were in response to specific questions formulated by the Chairman of the Peace Conference. Opinions 4 to 7 considered the applications for international recognition submitted by four of the republics of the former Socialist Federal Republic of Yugoslavia. The interaction between the opinions of the Commission and the political decisions of the E.C. and its member states has been complex. For example, the E.C. and its members did not fully accept the advice of the Commission when they recognized Croatia and failed to recognize Macedonia, while the E.C. and its members expressly cited the Commission's Opinion 10 of July 4, 1992, in refusing to accept the new Federal Republic of Yugoslavia (Serbia and Montenegro) as the sole successor to the former Socialist Federal Republic of Yugoslavia. See Section 6 infra.

The Commission's Opinion 10 stated in part as follows:

1. * * * In Opinion No. 8, the Arbitration Commission concluded that the dissolution of the Socialist Federal Republic of Yugoslavia (SFRY) was

complete and that none of the resulting entities could claim to be the sole successor to the SFRY.

2. On 27 April this year Montenegro and Serbia decided to establish a new entity bearing the name "Federal Republic of Yugoslavia" and adopted its constitution.

The Arbitration Commission feels that, within the frontiers constituted by the administrative boundaries of Montenegro and Serbia in the SFRY, the new entity meets the criteria of international public law for a state, which were listed in Opinion No. 1 of 29 November 1991. However, as Resolution 757 (1992) of the UN Security Council points out, "the claim by the Federal Republic of Yugoslavia (Serbia and Montenegro) to continue automatically the membership of the former Socialist Federal Republic of Yugoslavia (in the United Nations) has not been generally accepted". As the Arbitration Commission points out in its ninth Opinion, the FRY is actually a new state and could not be the sole successor to the SFRY.

3. This means that the FRY (Serbia and Montenegro) does not *ipso facto* enjoy the recognition enjoyed by the SFRY under completely different circumstances. It is therefore for other states, where appropriate, to recognize the new state.

4. As, however, the Arbitration Commission pointed out in Opinion No. 1, while recognition is not a prerequisite for the foundation of a state and is purely declaratory in its impact, it is nonetheless a discretionary act that other states may perform when they choose and in a manner of their own choosing, subject only to compliance with the imperatives of general international law, and particularly those prohibiting the use of force in dealings with other states or guaranteeing the rights of ethnic, religious or linguistic minorities.

Furthermore, the Community and its Member States, in their joint statement of 16 December 1991 on Yugoslavia and the Guidelines, adopted the same day, on the recognition of new states in Eastern Europe and in the Soviet Union, has set out the conditions for the recognition of the Yugoslav republics.

5. Consequently, the opinion of the Arbitration Commission is that:

— the FRY (Serbia and Montenegro) is a new state which cannot be considered the sole successor to the SFRY;

— its recognition by the Member States of the European Community would be subject to its compliance with the conditions laid down by general international law for such an act and the joint statement and Guidelines of 16 December 1991.

31 I.L.M. 1525 (1992).

2. One issue of central importance in the break-up of the Socialist Republic of Yugoslavia was the status of the pre-break-up frontiers of the constituent entities. The E.C. Arbitration Commission was asked to render its opinion on whether the internal frontiers between (i) Croatia and Serbia and (ii) Serbia and Bosnia–Herzegovina could be considered international boundaries under international law. Noting that Yugoslavia was in the process of dissolution, the Commission's opinion was that the new republics were entitled to the protection of their external boundaries under international law on the basis of the U.N. Charter, the Declaration on the Principles of International Law concerning Friendly Relations

and Cooperation among States, the Helsinki Final Act and Article 11 of the Vienna Convention on Succession of States in respect of Treaties. The Commission added that, in the absence of agreement to the contrary between the states concerned, the preexisting frontiers enjoyed the protection of international law on the basis of the principle of *uti possidetis juris.* This principle, originally recognized in the disposition of border issues arising out of decolonization in Spanish America, has been recognized and applied by the I.C.J. in the *Case Concerning the Frontier Dispute (Burkina Faso/Republic of Mali),* 1986 I.C.J. 554, 565, as a "general principle, which is logically connected with the phenomenon of the obtaining of independence, wherever it occurs." See also Case Concerning Land, Island and Maritime Frontier Dispute (El Salvador/Honduras; Nicaragua Intervening), 1992 I.C.J. 351, p. 334 infra. Finally, the Commission affirmed that no modification of preexisting frontiers by force would be recognized. Opinion No. 3, para. 2.

E. WHETHER THERE IS A DUTY TO RECOGNIZE OR A DUTY NOT TO RECOGNIZE

As noted above (p. 252) the Restatement (Third) adopts the view that a state is not required to accord formal recognition to any other state, but is required to treat as a state an entity that meets the requirements of statehood. As Brownlie has written,

> Recognition, *as a public act of state,* is an optional and political act and there is no legal duty in this regard. However, in a deeper sense, if an entity bears the marks of statehood, other states put themselves at risk legally if they ignore the basic obligations of state relations. Few would take the view that the Arab neighbours of Israel can afford to treat her as a non-entity: the responsible United Nations organs and individual states have taken the view that Israel is protected, and bound, by the principles of the United Nations Charter governing the use of force. In this context of state *conduct* there is a duty to accept and apply certain fundamental rules of international law: there is a legal duty to "recognize" for certain purposes at least, but no duty to make an express, public, and political determination of the question or to declare readiness to enter into diplomatic relations by means of recognition. This latter type of recognition remains political and discretionary. Even recognition is not determinant of diplomatic relations, and absence of diplomatic relations is not in itself non-recognition of the state.

Brownlie, Principles of Public International Law 90 (5th ed. 1998).

The admission of a new state to the United Nations may act as the functional equivalent of collective recognition. Such a collective decision does not entail any obligation for other members to make a formal acknowledgment of recognition, nor to enter into any form of diplomatic or other bilateral relations with the newly admitted state. But such a collective act does indicate community acceptance that the criteria for statehood are satisfied, and does require all member states to treat the new entrant in accordance with the principles embodied in the U.N. Charter. See Mosler, The International Society as a Legal Community, 140 Rec. des Cours 1, 60 (1974–IV).

On the other hand, a duty *not* to recognize may be applicable when an entity does not yet satisfy the criteria for statehood under international law, or when it has come into existence in violation of fundamental principles of international law.

1. *Premature Recognition as Unlawful Intervention*

HYDE, INTERNATIONAL LAW

152–153 (2d rev. ed. 1945).

§ 40. Prior to Recognition by Parent State

When recognition by foreign States precedes that accorded by the parent State, complaint on the part of the latter is to be anticipated. Nevertheless, the opinion has long prevailed in the United States that the propriety of recognition is not necessarily dependent upon the approval of such State. In harmony with the theory early advocated by Jefferson respecting the recognition of new governments, it has long been the accepted American doctrine that the right to accord recognition depends solely on the circumstance whether a new State has in fact come into being, and that the test of the existence of that fact is whether the conflict with the parent State has been substantially won. Statements of principle have not always drawn a sharp line of distinction between the time when the cause of the parent State was desperate or hopeless, and that when the contest was at an end. The point to be observed is, however, that the propriety of recognition, according to American theory, depends upon a fact, namely, the success of the revolutionary force, and that regardless of the illegitimacy thereof in the eyes of the parent State. Thus recognition based upon careful regard for such a fact is deemed to be consistent with the maintenance of friendly relations between the recognizing State and the parent State * * * .

The according of recognition to a country still in the throes of warfare against the parent State partakes of a different character. Such action constitutes participation in the conflict. It makes the cause of independence a common one between the aspirant for it and the outside State. Participation must be regarded as intervention, and therefore essentially antagonistic to that State.

Notes

1. United States concern about illegal recognition of the Confederacy during the Civil War was strongly expressed. See Hyde, at 153 n. 5. But the United States itself engaged in questionable recognition when it recognized Panama as a state two days after the latter declared its independence in 1903. Hyde, id., n. 6.

2. Recognition by five African governments of the secessionist territory of Biafra as a state during the Nigerian civil war of 1967–1970 was criticized as unlawful by Nigeria. See Ijalaye, Was Biafra at Any Time a State in International Law?, 71 A.J.I.L. 551–559 (1971).

3. Did third states act consistently with international law in recognizing several of the former Yugoslav republics as new states, at a time when armed conflict was still in progress and the struggle for control of territory was unre-

solved? The then-Secretary-General of the United Nations, Javier Pérez de Cuéllar, on the recommendation of his personal envoy Cyrus Vance, had warned that "any early, selective recognition could widen the present conflict and fuel an explosive situation." Report of the Secretary-General Pursuant to S.C. Res. 721(1991), U.N. Doc. S/23280 (Dec. 11, 1991), para. 25 and Annex IV, approved by the Security Council in S.C. Res. 724 (Dec. 15, 1991). By contrast, Germany and like-minded states hoped that a formal grant of recognition to Croatia would dissuade the Serbian-dominated Federal Republic from continuing to project armed force across the Serbian-Croatian frontier (by transforming that frontier from an internal to an international boundary). To what extent were legal and political considerations intertwined in the recognition decisions discussed at pp. 259–263 supra?

2. *Illegal States*

RESOLUTION CONCERNING SOUTHERN RHODESIA

U.N. Security Council, November 20, 1965.
1265th Mtg, S.C. Res. 217, 20 SCOR, Resolutions and Decisions at 8.

The Security Council,

Deeply concerned about the situation in Southern Rhodesia,

Considering that the illegal authorities in Southern Rhodesia have proclaimed independence and that the Government of the United Kingdom of Great Britain and Northern Ireland, as the administering Power, looks upon this as an act of rebellion,* * *

1. Determines that the situation resulting from the proclamation of independence by the illegal authorities in Southern Rhodesia is extremely grave, that the Government of the United Kingdom of Great Britain and Northern Ireland should put an end to it and that its continuance in time constitutes a threat to international peace and security; * * *

3. Condemns the usurpation of power by a racist settler minority in Southern Rhodesia and regards the declaration of independence by it as having no legal validity;

4. Calls upon the Government of the United Kingdom to quell this rebellion of the racist minority;

5. Further calls upon the Government of the United Kingdom to take all other appropriate measures which would prove effective in eliminating the authority of the usurpers and in bringing the minority regime in Southern Rhodesia to an immediate end;

6. Calls upon all States not to recognize this illegal authority and not to entertain any diplomatic or other relations with it;

7. Calls upon the Government of the United Kingdom, as the working of the Constitution of 1961 has broken down, to take immediate measures in order to allow the people of Southern Rhodesia to determine their own future consistent with the objectives of General Assembly resolution 1514(XV);

8. Calls upon all States to refrain from any action which would assist and encourage the illegal regime and, in particular, to desist from providing it with arms, equipment and military materiel, and to do their utmost in order

to break all economic relations with Southern Rhodesia, including an embargo on oil and petroleum products;

9. Calls upon the Government of the United Kingdom to enforce urgently and with vigour all the measures it has announced, as well as those mentioned in paragraph 8 above;

10. Calls upon the Organization of African Unity to do all in its power to assist in the implementation of the present resolution, in conformity with Chapter VIII of the Charter of the United Nations;

11. Decides to keep the question under review in order to examine what other measures it may deem it necessary to take.

Adopted at the 1265th meeting by 10 votes to none, with 1 abstention (France).

Notes

1. At the time the above resolution was adopted, Rhodesia would have met the traditional criteria of statehood. Its government was clearly the effective authority and had capacity to enter into foreign relations. Nonetheless, the Security Council resolution and previous General Assembly resolutions were accepted as definitive: Rhodesia was not recognized as a state by any government or treated as a state by any international organization. Does the decision in regard to Rhodesia confirm that a new requirement of statehood has been introduced—that a new state will not be recognized if it is a "minority regime" which violates the principle of self-determination? One commentator concluded that a new State must meet the requirement that "it shall not be based upon a systematic denial in its territory of certain civil and political rights, including in particular the right of every citizen to participate in the government of his country, directly or through representatives elected by regular, equal and secret suffrage." Fawcett, Security Council Resolutions on Rhodesia, 41 Brit. Y.B.I.L. 112 (1965–66). How can one justify a requirement for new states that does not apply to existing states? The Rhodesian problem was eventually resolved in 1979–80 with the establishment of the state of Zimbabwe, which was generally recognized.

2. The U.N. General Assembly resolution on Transkei (putatively established by South Africa during the period of apartheid, as a homeland for part of the black population) asserted both that Transkei's "independence" was sham and that the creation of Transkei was to consolidate apartheid and perpetuate white minority domination. G.A.Res. 31/6 G.A.O.R., 31st Sess., Supp. 39, p. 10 (1976). The latter point suggests that even if an independent state were created, it would be denied recognition in accordance with United Nations resolutions if its establishment was considered a means to violate basic human rights.

Compare the decisions of the General Assembly and the Security Council calling on states to recognize the illegality of South Africa's presence in Namibia (South West Africa) and to refrain from any acts and any dealings with South Africa implying recognition of the legality of the presence and administration of South Africa in Namibia. See International Court of Justice Advisory Opinion on Namibia [1971] I.C.J. 16, p. 549 infra.

3. Under international law states may not recognize "a territorial acquisition resulting from the threat or use of force." Declaration on Principles of International Law Concerning Friendly Relations and Cooperation among States in Accordance with the Charter of the United Nations, G.A.Res. 2625 (XXV) G.A.O.R., 25th Sess., Supp. 28, p. 121 (1970); 65 A.J.I.L. 243. Such recognition would be an improper interference in the internal affairs of the state of which the unlawfully acquired territory was a part. Restatement (Third) § 202(2). Thus, when following its invasion of Kuwait in August, 1990, Iraq announced a "comprehensive and eternal merger" with Kuwait, the U.N. Security Council unanimously adopted Resolution 662, calling upon "all States, international organizations and specialized agencies not to recognize that annexation, and to refrain from any action or dealing that might be interpreted as indirect recognition of the annexation." S/RES/662 (1990). See p. 342; see also pp. 1013–1023 below.

It is uncertain whether acquisition of territory by lawful force, e.g., force used in self-defense against aggression, constitutes an exception. Consider the significance of such an exception in light of the unavailability as a general matter of an authoritative international determination of the factual issues frequently present when a use of force is claimed to be lawful. Consider the following comment:

> The number of examples of entities acquiring the characteristics of statehood allegedly through violation of law has not been large. Some states, particularly after a lapse of time, have been willing to accept a *fait accompli.* On a few occasions, the United Nations Security Council, or perhaps the General Assembly, might resolve the question. Compare the resolutions declaring North Korea and China aggressors against the Republic of Korea. S.C.Res. 82–85, 5 U.N. SCOR Resolutions and Decisions (S/INF/5/Rev. 1) at 4–7 (1950); G.A.Res. 498(V), 5 U.N.G.A.O.R., Supp. No. 20A at i (1951). In most instances, the issue is not subject to authoritative determination. For example, many governments judged India's intervention in Bangladesh to be a violation of the Charter, but contrary arguments were made, justifying India's use of force as in support of self-determination or as humanitarian intervention. States generally recognized or treated Bangladesh as a state, and Bangladesh was admitted to the United Nations. See Franck & Rodley, After Bangladesh: The Law of Humanitarian Intervention by Military Force, 67 A.J.I.L. 275 (1973); Crawford, The Creation of States in International Law 115–18 (1979).

Restatement (Third) § 202, Reporters' Note 5.

4. After the Turkish invasion of Cyprus in 1974, a so-called Turkish Republic of Northern Cyprus was established on the northern part of the island several years later, which has not been recognized as a state by any state other than Turkey. The Security Council called upon all states "not to recognize any Cypriot State other than the Republic of Cyprus." S.C. Res. 541 (1983); S.C. Res. 550 (1984). Does the denial of recognition illustrate the general propositions about recognition elaborated in this section?

5. Does non-recognition based on illegality risk being ineffective in the absence of other sanctions? Can it be justified in itself as a vindication of law? Lauterpacht has suggested that non-recognition "is the minimum of resistance which an insufficiently organized but law-abiding community offers to illegality; it is a continuous challenge to a legal wrong." Lauterpacht, Recognition in International Law 431 (1947).

6. Cassese has written that "careful scrutiny of State practice shows that thus far the countermeasure most widely resorted to [for "blatant breaches of self-

determination"] is the *refusal of legal recognition* of a situation which breaches the right to self-determination." Cassese, Self–Determination of Peoples: A Legal Reappraisal 158 (1995) (citing as examples "Namibia, Southern Rhodesia, the South African *Bantustans*, the Arab territories occupied by Israel, Kampuchea, and the Turkish–Cypriot State"). On the meaning of self-determination in international law, see Section 2 below.

7. Litigation in the United States against the president of the self-proclaimed Bosnian Serb republic in Bosnia–Herzegovina, involved issues of statehood, state action, and legal consequences of non-recognition. Following a discussion of the criteria for statehood in light of the Restatement and other authorities, the court of appeals observed:

> The customary international law of human rights, such as the proscription of official torture, applies to states without distinction between recognized and unrecognized states. *See Restatement (Third)* §§ 207, 702. It would be anomalous indeed if non-recognition by the United States, which typically reflects disfavor with a foreign regime—sometimes due to human rights abuses—had the perverse effect of shielding officials of the unrecognized regime from liability for those violations of international law norms that apply only to state actors.
>
> Appellants' allegations entitle them to prove that Karadzic's regime satisfies the criteria for a state, for purposes of those international law violations requiring state action. * * * Moreover, it is likely that the state action concept, where applicable to some violations like "official" torture, requires merely the semblance of official authority. The inquiry, after all, is whether a person purporting to wield official power has exceeded internationally recognized standards of civilized conduct, not whether statehood in all its formal aspects exists.

Kadic v. Karadzic, 70 F.3d 232 (2d Cir.1995).

SECTION 2. SELF–DETERMINATION OF "PEOPLES"

The pedigree of self-determination as an international political idea is often traced to Woodrow Wilson's program for the establishment of peace after World War I, or to Lenin's revolutionary theses published in 1916 (though there are earlier antecedents, going back at least to the core idea of the American and French revolutions that sovereignty belongs to the people). See Cassese, Self–Determination of Peoples: A Legal Reappraisal 14–23 (1995). But the Versailles Treaty and related aspects of the peace settlement did not implement a coherent theory of self-determination, nor was there a legal expression of the concept in the Covenant of the League of Nations. As Cassese concludes, "on the whole, self-determination was deemed irrelevant where the people's will was certain to run counter to the victors' geopolitical, economic, and strategic interests." Ibid. p. 25. Not until the adoption of the U.N. Charter in 1945 was self-determination embraced as a "principle," and in due course became accepted as a principle of customary as well as treaty law.

In addition to its embodiment in the U.N. Charter, art. 1(2), self-determination has been treated as a principle of international law in many treaty and non-treaty instruments, e.g., the two International Covenants on

Human Rights (art. 1 of the Covenant on Civil and Political Rights and of the Covenant on Economic, Social and Cultural Rights) and the U.N. General Assembly Declaration on Principles of International Law Concerning Friendly Relations Among States in Accordance With the Charter of the United Nations, G.A. Res. 2625 (XXV) (1970) (Friendly Relations Declaration, excerpted infra). Legal issues concerning self-determination have been raised in several cases at the International Court of Justice, including the Advisory Opinion on Namibia, 1971 I.C.J. at 31; the Advisory Opinion on Western Sahara, 1975 I.C.J. 12 at 31–35; and the Case Concerning East Timor (Portugal v. Australia), 1995 I.C.J. 90; in the opinions of the Arbitration Commission on Yugoslavia, pp. 259–263 supra; and in national courts (see Reference on Secession of Quebec, p. 274 infra). In the eyes of some jurists and judges, the principle of self-determination is not only a binding rule of international law, but even enjoys the status of a peremptory norm (*jus cogens*). For discussion of the legal quality of the self-determination principle, and diverse points of view on the *jus cogens* issue, see Cassese, op.cit., pp. 133–140.

Notwithstanding its treatment in legal documents and decisions, the concept of self-determination remains fraught with uncertainty and stands in apparent tension with other equally prominent principles of international order. If the "right" of self-determination for "peoples" had a fairly well-understood meaning during most of the second half of the 20th century—that is, as a right of the people in non-self-governing territories (i.e., colonies) freely to determine their political status—its application in the post-Cold War period has been highly contested. With the winding-down of U.N.-supervised decolonization has come a resurgence of claims of self-determination on the part of ethnic minorities and other groups, which seek to control territory, to exercise autonomy, and ultimately to enjoy all the prerogatives of statehood. Whether such groups qualify as "peoples" entitled to self-determination, what a "right" of self-determination would entail (which need not mean full-fledged statehood), and how such a "right" is to be reconciled with competing principles, are among the most difficult problems for the international political and legal system in the current period.

The treatment in the present section concentrates on the evolution of legal conceptions of self-determination, but the reader should bear in mind the insights of other disciplines in understanding the powerful appeal of alternative conceptions. The rhetoric of self-determination has been deployed in attempts to align statehood with "nationalism," with ethnically-based and exclusionary conceptions of community—what some have called a "new tribalism." It is fair to ask whether the state-centered concepts of classical international law have contributed to the analytical confusion about self-determination and perhaps to some pernicious interpretations. It is also fair to ask about the trajectory of development of the international law of self-determination and whether it will be adequate to the needs of the 21st century.

In thinking about legal materials bearing on "self" and "peoples," the reader should keep in mind related questions addressed in other sections and chapters, including the territorial boundaries of a given unit (Section 5 below) and the legal concept of "nationality" which expresses the link between individual and state (see Chapter 6).

A. SELF-DETERMINATION AS A LEGAL PRINCIPLE IN THE CHARTER ERA

U.N. DECLARATION OF PRINCIPLES OF INTERNATIONAL LAW CONCERNING FRIENDLY RELATIONS AMONG STATES IN ACCORDANCE WITH THE CHARTER OF THE UNITED NATIONS ("FRIENDLY RELATIONS DECLARATION")

General Assembly Resolution A/RES 2625 (XXV)
(1970) G.A.O.R., 25th Sess., Supp. 28, at 121.

THE PRINCIPLE OF EQUAL RIGHTS AND SELF-DETERMINATION OF PEOPLES

By virtue of the principle of equal rights and self-determination of peoples enshrined in the Charter of the United Nations, all peoples have the right freely to determine, without external interference, their political status and to pursue their economic, social and cultural development, and every State has the duty to respect this right in accordance with the provisions of the Charter.

Every State has the duty to promote, through joint and separate action, realization of the principle of equal rights and self-determination of peoples, in accordance with the provisions of the Charter, and to render assistance to the United Nations in carrying out the responsibilities entrusted to it by the Charter regarding the implementation of the principle, in order:

(a) To promote friendly relations and co-operation among States; and

(b) To bring a speedy end to colonialism, having due regard to the freely expressed will of the peoples concerned;

and bearing in mind that subjection of peoples to alien subjugation, domination and exploitation constitutes a violation of the principle, as well as a denial of fundamental human rights, and is contrary to the Charter.

Every State has the duty to promote through joint and separate action universal respect for and observance of human rights and fundamental freedoms in accordance with the Charter.

The establishment of a sovereign and independent State, the free association or integration with an independent State or the emergence into any other political status freely determined by a people constitute modes of implementing the right of self-determination by that people.

Every State has the duty to refrain from any forcible action which deprives peoples referred to above in the elaboration of the present principle of their right to self-determination and freedom and independence. In their actions against, and resistance to, such forcible action in pursuit of the exercise of their right to self-determination, such peoples are entitled to seek and receive support in accordance with the purposes and principles of the Charter.

The territory of a colony or other non-self-governing territory has, under the Charter, a status separate and distinct from the territory of the State administering it; and such separate and distinct status under the Charter shall exist until the people of the colony or non-self-governing territory have exercised their right of self-determination in accordance with the Charter, and particularly its purposes and principles.

Nothing in the foregoing paragraphs shall be construed as authorizing or encouraging any action which would dismember or impair, totally or in part, the territorial integrity or political unity of sovereign and independent States conducting themselves in compliance with the principle of equal rights and self-determination of peoples as described above and thus possessed of a government representing the whole people belonging to the territory without distinction as to race, creed or colour.

Every State shall refrain from any action aimed at the partial or total disruption of the national unity and territorial integrity of any other state or country.

Notes

1. The main application of self-determination in the first half-century of the U.N. Charter period was in the decolonization of non-self-governing territories. A list of criteria for determining non-self-governing territories under Article XI of the Charter may be found in the Annex to G.A. Res. 742 (VIII), G.A.O.R., 8th Sess., Supp. 17, at 22 (1953).

2. In the Advisory Opinion on Western Sahara, 1975 I.C.J. 12 at para. 56, the I.C.J. referred to its Advisory Opinion on Namibia, 1971 I.C.J. at 31ff., as having traced the development of international law in regard to non-self-governing territories. As the Court stated:

> A further important stage in this development was the Declaration on the Granting of Independence to Colonial Countries and Peoples (General Assembly resolution 1514 (XV) of 14 December 1960), which embraces all peoples and territories which 'have not yet attained independence'.

The Court concluded:

> In the domain to which the present proceedings relate, the last fifty years, as indicated above, have brought important developments. These developments leave little doubt that the ultimate objective of the sacred trust was the self-determination and independence of the peoples concerned. In this domain, as elsewhere, the *corpus iuris gentium* has been considerably enriched, and this the Court, if it is faithfully to discharge its functions, may not ignore.

(Citations omitted.) In paragraph 57, the Court observed:

> General Assembly resolution 1514 (XV) provided the basis for the process of decolonization which has resulted since 1960 in the creation of many States which are today Members of the United Nations. It is complemented in certain of its aspects by General Assembly resolution 1541 (XV) * * *. The latter resolution contemplates for non-self-governing territories more than one possibility, namely:
>
> > (a) emergence as a sovereign independent State; (b) free association with an independent State; or (c) integration with an independent State.
>
> At the same time, certain of its provisions give effect to the essential feature of the right of self-determination as established in resolution 1514 (XV). Thus principle VII of resolution 1541 (XV) declares that: "Free association should

be the result of a free and voluntary choice by the peoples of the territory concerned expressed through informed and democratic processes."

3. The Western Sahara Advisory Opinion has contributed to the jurisprudence of self-determination, but the underlying dispute over self-determination for the people of Western Sahara has not been put to rest. Though the opinion supports the legal right of self-determination, the events which followed the opinion did not, and the matter remains one of a handful of unresolved decolonization matters on the U.N. agenda. See Franck, The Stealing of the Sahara, 70 A.J.I.L. 694 (1976); Cassese, Self–Determination: A Legal Reappraisal 214–218 (1995). The General Assembly has passed a series of resolutions on Western Sahara, and in 1991 the Security Council unanimously adopted Resolution 690 approving a schedule for holding a prompt referendum which, however, had still not been conducted as of 2000.

4. Another long-unsettled instance of imperfect decolonization also led to litigation at the I.C.J., in the Case Concerning East Timor (Portugal v. Australia), 1995 I.C.J. 90. East Timor had been a non-self-governing territory of Portugal which had not achieved self-determination when, in late 1975, Portuguese authorities withdrew from the territory and the armed forces of Indonesia intervened and occupied it. In Security Council Resolution 384 (Dec. 22, 1975), the Security Council called upon "all States to respect the territorial integrity of East Timor as well as the inalienable right of its people to self-determination"; called upon Indonesia to withdraw its armed forces from the territory; and called upon "the Government of Portugal as administering Power to co-operate fully with the United Nations so as to enable the people of East Timor to exercise freely their right to self-determination." The exhortations for Indonesian withdrawal and respect for the right of self-determination of the people of East Timor were reiterated by the Security Council the following year and by eight General Assembly resolutions between 1975 and 1982, without effect. The issue remained on the General Assembly's agenda and East Timor was maintained on the U.N. list of non-self-governing territories until after the developments of 1999 (see below).

Proceedings at the I.C.J. were initiated in 1991 by Portugal as administering power for East Timor (a capacity that had never been formally extinguished) against Australia, which had entered into a treaty with Indonesia concerning exploration and exploitation of the continental shelf in the area known as the Timor Gap. Portugal claimed that Australia had breached the principle of self-determination by dealing with Indonesia in relation to resources belonging to East Timor. For jurisdictional reasons (see Chapter 11), Indonesia could not be made a party before the Court without its consent. In 1995, the I.C.J. dismissed Portugal's suit against Australia on the threshold ground that in the absence of Indonesia, the Court could not adjudicate a dispute over the lawfulness of Indonesia's exercise of authority in and on behalf of East Timor. Thus the Court left unresolved the import of the self-determination principle as regards authority over East Timor's offshore resources.

Though the Court affirmed (in paras. 31 and 37) that "for the two Parties" East Timor remained a non-self-governing territory and its people had the right to self-determination, it declined Portugal's request to give effect to the self-determination principle as against a non-party to the suit, saying (para. 31):

> The Court notes that the argument of Portugal under consideration rests on the premise that the United Nations resolutions, and in particular those of the Security Council, can be read as imposing an obligation on States not to

> recognize any authority on the part of Indonesia over the Territory and, where the latter is concerned, to deal only with Portugal. The Court is not persuaded, however, that the relevant resolutions went so far.

Does this dictum purport to decide the substantive meaning of the resolutions, even though the Court had determined that it could not exercise jurisdiction on the merits? Does it imply anything one way or the other about whether self-determination is a right opposable *erga omnes*? Compare the discussion of *erga omnes* obligations in Chapter 9 infra.

Developments concerning self-determination for East Timor came to a head in 1999, in the aftermath of a domestic political crisis in Indonesia. In May 1999, Portugal and Indonesia asked the U.N. Secretary–General to organize and conduct a "popular consultation" to determine whether the East Timorese people accepted or rejected a special autonomy for East Timor within Indonesia. In June 1999 the U.N. Security Council established a U.N. Mission in East Timor (UNAMET) to carry out this consultation. In a ballot in which about 98% of the registered East Timorese participated, 78.5% of the voters rejected the proposed special autonomy, thereby expressing their wish for independence. Following outbreaks of violence, the Security Council in Resolution 1264 (Sept. 15, 1999) authorized a multinational force to restore peace and security (see Chapter 12). In October 1999, Indonesia formally recognized the results of the popular consultation, and the Security Council in Resolution 1272 set up a U.N. Transitional Administration in East Timor (UNTAET) to oversee the territory during a temporary period pending implementation of the separation from Indonesia. UNTAET's initial mandate was to run until January 2001.

B. SEPARATIST MOVEMENTS

The international instruments referring to a right of self-determination of "peoples" do not make clear whether the right applies outside the decolonization context, and if so, how to define "peoples" entitled to exercise the right. Sir Gerald Fitzmaurice, writing in 1973 after his retirement as a judge of the International Court, insisted that "juridically, the notion of a legal right of self-determination is nonsense, for how can an as yet juridically non-existent entity be the possessor of a legal right?" Fitzmaurice, The Future of Public International Law, in Livre du Centenaire, Ann. Inst. de Droit Int'l 1973 at 233, n. 85. Thomas Franck notes the "incoherence" of the proclaimed right since the U.N. declarations accord the right "to all peoples" but at the same time assert that the right shall not authorize or encourage action which would impair "totally or in part, the territorial integrity or political unity" of states. Franck concludes that for the right of self-determination to be seen as legitimate, the rule must make a persuasive distinction between "peoples" entitled and not entitled to self-determination. Franck, The Power of Legitimacy Among Nations 166 (1990). Compare Cassese, Self–Determination, op. cit at p. 327 (terms such as "peoples," even if not formally defined, can be inferred and are "sufficiently clear").

Are the difficulties with a legal norm of self-determination alleviated if the norm is interpreted to comprehend degrees of autonomy and/or political participation within an existing state? Legal writers have endeavored to clarify an analytical distinction between self-determination on the one hand, and separatism or secession on the other. Compare Franck, The Emerging Right of Democratic Governance, 86 A.J.I.L. 46 (1992) (examining "internal" as well as "external" self-determination and asserting that the content of the self-determination norm outside the decolonization context does not imply a right to secede). For discussion of approaches other than separate statehood, see Ruth Lapidoth, Autonomy: Flexible Solutions to Ethnic Conflicts (1997); Hurst Hannum, Autonomy, Sovereignty and Self–Determination: The Accommodation of Conflicting Rights (rev. ed. 1996); Gidon Gottlieb, Nation Against State: A New Approach to Ethnic Conflicts and the Decline of Sovereignty (1993).

The controversy over self-determination in relation to separatist aspirations became the subject-matter of an important opinion of the Supreme Court of Canada concerning Quebec:

REFERENCE RE SECESSION OF QUEBEC

[1998] 2 S.C.R. 217, 37 I.L.M. 1340.
Supreme Court of Canada, August 20, 1998.

[The Governor in Council referred the following three questions for the Supreme Court's advisory opinion:

> Question 1: Under the Constitution of Canada, can the National Assembly, legislature or government of Quebec effect the secession of Quebec from Canada unilaterally?
>
> Question 2: Does international law give the National Assembly, legislature or government of Quebec the right to effect the secession of Quebec from Canada unilaterally? In this regard, is there a right to self-determination under international law that would give the National Assembly, legislature or government of Quebec the right to effect the secession of Quebec from Canada unilaterally?
>
> Question 3: In the event of a conflict between domestic and international law on the right of the National Assembly, legislature or government of Quebec to effect the secession of Quebec from Canada unilaterally, which would take precedence in Canada?

After determining the justiciability of the questions, the Supreme Court answered Question 1 in the negative, finding that the constitutional framework would require negotiations addressing "the interests of the federal government, of Quebec and the other provinces, and other participants, as well as the rights of all Canadians both within and outside Quebec," including the rights of minorities. It also answered Question 2 in the negative, with a detailed essay on the international law of self-determination excerpted below. In view of the negative answers to both Questions 1 and 2, the answer given to Question 3 was that there was no conflict between domestic and international law to be addressed.]

Question 2

110. The argument before the Court on Question 2 has focused largely on determining whether, under international law, a positive legal right to unilateral secession exists in the factual circumstances assumed for the purpose of our response to Question 1. Arguments were also advanced to the effect that, regardless of the existence or non-existence of a positive right to unilateral secession, international law will in the end recognize effective

political realities—including the emergence of a new state—as facts. While our response to Question 2 will address considerations raised by this alternative argument of "effectivity", it should first be noted that the existence of a positive legal entitlement is quite different from a prediction that the law will respond after the fact to a then existing political reality. These two concepts examine different points in time. The questions posed to the Court address legal rights in advance of a unilateral act of purported secession. While we touch below on the practice governing the international recognition of emerging states, the Court is as wary of entertaining speculation about the possible future conduct of sovereign states on the international level as it was under Question 1 to speculate about the possible future course of political negotiations among the participants in the Canadian federation. In both cases, the Reference questions are directed only to the *legal* framework within which the political actors discharge their various mandates.

(1) *Secession at International Law*

111. It is clear that international law does not specifically grant component parts of sovereign states the legal right to secede unilaterally from their "parent" state. This is acknowledged by the experts who provided their opinions on behalf of both the *amicus curiae* and the Attorney General of Canada. Given the lack of specific authorization for unilateral secession, proponents of the existence of such a right at international law are therefore left to attempt to found their argument (i) on the proposition that unilateral secession is not specifically prohibited and that what is not specifically prohibited is inferentially permitted; or (ii) on the implied duty of states to recognize the legitimacy of secession brought about by the exercise of the well-established international law right of "a people" to self-determination.* * *

(a) *Absence of a Specific Prohibition*

112. International law contains neither a right of unilateral secession nor the explicit denial of such a right, although such a denial is, to some extent, implicit in the exceptional circumstances required for secession to be permitted under the right of a people to self-determination, e.g., the right of secession that arises in the exceptional situation of an oppressed or colonial people, discussed below. As will be seen, international law places great importance on the territorial integrity of nation states and, by and large, leaves the creation of a new state to be determined by the domestic law of the existing state of which the seceding entity presently forms a part (R.Y. Jennings, *The Acquisition of Territory in International Law* (1963) at pp. 8–9). Where, as here, unilateral secession would be incompatible with the domestic Constitution, international law is likely to accept that conclusion subject to the right of peoples to self-determination, a topic to which we now turn.

(b) *The Right of a People to Self-Determination*

113. While international law generally regulates the conduct of nation states, it does, in some specific circumstances, also recognize the "rights" of entities other than nation states—such as the right of a *people* to self-determination.

114. The existence of the right of a people to self-determination is now so widely recognized in international conventions that the principle has

acquired a status beyond "convention" and is considered a general principle of international law (A. Cassese, *Self-determination of peoples: A legal reappraisal* (1995), at pp. 171–72; K. Doehring, "Self–Determination", in B. Simma, ed., *The Charter of the United Nations: A Commentary* (1994), at p. 70). * * *

117. This basic principle of self-determination has been carried forward and addressed in so many U.N. conventions and resolutions that, as noted by Doehring, *supra,* at p. 60:

> The sheer number of resolutions concerning the right of self-determination makes their enumeration impossible. * * *

122. As will be seen, international law expects that the right to self-determination will be exercised by peoples within the framework of existing sovereign states and consistently with the maintenance of the territorial integrity of those states. Where this is not possible, in the exceptional circumstances discussed below, a right of secession may arise.

(i) Defining "Peoples"

123. International law grants the right to self-determination to "peoples". Accordingly, access to the right requires the threshold step of characterizing as a people the group seeking self-determination. However, as the right to self-determination has developed by virtue of a combination of international agreements and conventions, coupled with state practice, with little formal elaboration of the definition of "peoples", the result has been that the precise meaning of the term "people" remains somewhat uncertain.

124. It is clear that "a people" may include only a portion of the population of an existing state. The right to self-determination has developed largely as a human right, and is generally used in documents that simultaneously contain references to "nation" and "state". The juxtaposition of these terms is indicative that the reference to "people" does not necessarily mean the entirety of a state's population. To restrict the definition of the term to the population of existing states would render the granting of a right to self-determination largely duplicative, given the parallel emphasis within the majority of the source documents on the need to protect the territorial integrity of existing states, and would frustrate its remedial purpose.

125. While much of the Quebec population certainly shares many of the characteristics (such as a common language and culture) that would be considered in determining whether a specific group is a "people", as do other groups within Quebec and/or Canada, it is not necessary to explore this legal characterization to resolve Question 2 appropriately. Similarly, it is not necessary for the Court to determine whether, should a Quebec people exist within the definition of public international law, such a people encompasses the entirety of the provincial population or just a portion thereof. Nor is it necessary to examine the position of the aboriginal population within Quebec. As the following discussion of the scope of the right to self-determination will make clear, whatever be the correct application of the definition of people(s) in this context, their right of self-determination cannot in the present circumstances be said to ground a right to unilateral secession.

(ii) Scope of the Right to Self–Determination.

126. The recognized sources of international law establish that the right to self-determination of a people is normally fulfilled through *internal* self-determination—a people's pursuit of its political, economic, social and cultural development within the framework of an existing state. A right to *external* self-determination (which in this case potentially takes the form of the assertion of a right to unilateral secession) arises in only the most extreme of cases and, even then, under carefully defined circumstances. * * *

127. The international law principle of self-determination has evolved within a framework of respect for the territorial integrity of existing states. The various international documents that support the existence of a people's right to self-determination also contain parallel statements supportive of the conclusion that the exercise of such a right must be sufficiently limited to prevent threats to an existing state's territorial integrity or the stability of relations between sovereign states. [The Court then addressed the treatment of territorial integrity in the Friendly Relations Declaration, the Helsinki Final Act, and a variety of other international instruments.] * * *

130. * * * There is no necessary incompatibility between the maintenance of the territorial integrity of existing states, including Canada, and the right of a "people" to achieve a full measure of self-determination. A state whose government represents the whole of the people or peoples resident within its territory, on a basis of equality and without discrimination, and respects the principles of self-determination in its own internal arrangements, is entitled to the protection under international law of its territorial integrity.

(iii) Colonial and Oppressed Peoples

131. Accordingly, the general state of international law with respect to the right to self-determination is that the right operates with the overriding protection granted to the territorial integrity of "parent" states. However, as noted by Cassese, *supra,* at p. 334, there are certain defined contexts within which the right to the self-determination of peoples does allow that right to be exercised "externally", which, in the context of this Reference, would potentially mean secession:

> ... the right to external self-determination, which entails the possibility of choosing (or restoring) independence, has only been bestowed upon two classes of peoples (those under colonial rule or foreign occupation), based upon the assumption that both classes make up entities that are inherently distinct from the colonialist Power and the occupant Power and that their 'territorial integrity', all but destroyed by the colonialist or occupying Power, should be fully restored;

132. The right of colonial peoples to exercise their right to self-determination by breaking away from the "imperial" power is now undisputed, but is irrelevant to this Reference.

133. The other clear case where a right to external self-determination accrues is where a people is subject to alien subjugation, domination or exploitation outside a colonial context. This recognition finds its roots in the *Declaration on Friendly Relations, supra* [quotations from Friendly Relations Declaration omitted].

134. A number of commentators have further asserted that the right to self-determination may ground a right to unilateral secession in a third

circumstance. Although this third circumstance has been described in several ways, the underlying proposition is that, when a people is blocked from the meaningful exercise of its right to self-determination internally, it is entitled, as a last resort, to exercise it by secession. * * *

135. Clearly, such a circumstance parallels the other two recognized situations in that the ability of a people to exercise its right to self-determination internally is somehow being totally frustrated. While it remains unclear whether this third proposition actually reflects an established international law standard, it is unnecessary for present purposes to make that determination. Even assuming that the third circumstance is sufficient to create a right to unilateral secession under international law, the current Quebec context cannot be said to approach such a threshold. As stated by the *amicus curiae* [citation omitted] [translation]:

> 15. The Quebec people is not the victim of attacks on its physical existence or integrity, or of a massive violation of its fundamental rights. The Quebec people is manifestly not, in the opinion of the *amicus curiae,* an oppressed people.
>
> 16. For close to 40 of the last 50 years, the Prime Minister of Canada has been a Quebecer. During this period, Quebecers have held from time to time all the most important positions in the federal Cabinet. During the 8 years prior to June 1997, the Prime Minister and the Leader of the Official Opposition in the House of Commons were both Quebecers. At present, the Prime Minister of Canada, the Right Honourable Chief Justice and two other members of the Court, the Chief of Staff of the Canadian Armed Forces and the Canadian ambassador to the United States, not to mention the Deputy Secretary–General of the United Nations, are all Quebecers. * * *

136. The population of Quebec cannot plausibly be said to be denied access to government. Quebecers occupy prominent positions within the government of Canada. Residents of the province freely make political choices and pursue economic, social and cultural development within Quebec, across Canada, and throughout the world. The population of Quebec is equitably represented in legislative, executive and judicial institutions. In short, to reflect the phraseology of the international documents that address the right to self-determination of peoples, Canada is a "sovereign and independent state conducting itself in compliance with the principle of equal rights and self-determination of peoples and thus possessed of a government representing the whole people belonging to the territory without distinction". * * *

138. In summary, the international law right to self-determination only generates, at best, a right to external self-determination in situations of former colonies; where a people is oppressed, as for example under foreign military occupation; or where a definable group is denied meaningful access to government to pursue their political, economic, social and cultural development. In all three situations, the people in question are entitled to a right to external self-determination because they have been denied the ability to exert internally their right to self-determination. Such exceptional circumstances are manifestly inapplicable to Quebec under existing conditions. Accordingly, neither the population of the province of Quebec, even if characterized in terms of "people" or "peoples", nor its representative institutions, the Na-

tional Assembly, the legislature or government of Quebec, possess a right, under international law, to secede unilaterally from Canada.

139. We would not wish to leave this aspect of our answer to Question 2 without acknowledging the importance of the submissions made to us respecting the rights and concerns of aboriginal peoples in the event of a unilateral secession, as well as the appropriate means of defining the boundaries of a seceding Quebec with particular regard to the northern lands occupied largely by aboriginal peoples. However, the concern of aboriginal peoples is precipitated by the asserted right of Quebec to unilateral secession. In light of our finding that there is no such right applicable to the population of Quebec, either under the Constitution of Canada or at international law, but that on the contrary a clear democratic expression of support for secession would lead under the Constitution to negotiations in which aboriginal interests would be taken into account, it becomes unnecessary to explore further the concerns of the aboriginal peoples in this Reference.

(2) *Recognition of a Factual/Political Reality: the "Effectivity" Principle*

140. As stated, an argument advanced by the *amicus curiae* on this branch of the Reference was that, while international law may not ground a positive right to unilateral secession in the context of Quebec, international law equally does not prohibit secession and, in fact, international recognition would be conferred on such a political reality if it emerged, for example, via effective control of the territory of what is now the province of Quebec.

141. It is true that international law may well, depending on the circumstances, adapt to recognize a political and/or factual reality, regardless of the legality of the steps leading to its creation. However, as mentioned at the outset, effectivity, as such, does not have any real applicability to Question 2, which asks whether a right to unilateral secession exists.

142. No one doubts that legal consequences may flow from political facts, and that "sovereignty is a political fact for which no purely legal authority can be constituted . . .", H.W.R. Wade, "The Basis of Legal Sovereignty", [1955] *Camb. L.J.* 172, at p. 196. Secession of a province from Canada, if successful in the streets, might well lead to the creation of a new state. Although recognition by other states is not, at least as a matter of theory, necessary to achieve statehood, the viability of a would-be state in the international community depends, as a practical matter, upon recognition by other states. That process of recognition is guided by legal norms. However, international recognition is not alone constitutive of statehood and, critically, does not relate back to the date of secession to serve retroactively as a source of a "legal" right to secede in the first place. Recognition occurs only after a territorial unit has been successful, as a political fact, in achieving secession.

143. As indicated in responding to Question 1, one of the legal norms which may be recognized by states in granting or withholding recognition of emergent states is the legitimacy of the process by which the *de facto* secession is, or was, being pursued. The process of recognition, once considered to be an exercise of pure sovereign discretion, has come to be associated with legal norms. See, e.g., *European Community Declaration on the Guidelines on the Recognition of New States in Eastern Europe and in the Soviet Union,* 31 I.L.M. 1485 (1992), at p. 1487. While national interest and perceived political advantage to the recognizing state obviously play an important

role, foreign states may also take into account their view as to the existence of a right to self-determination on the part of the population of the putative state, and a counterpart domestic evaluation, namely, an examination of the legality of the secession according to the law of the state from which the territorial unit purports to have seceded. As we indicated in our answer to Question 1, an emergent state that has disregarded legitimate obligations arising out of its previous situation can potentially expect to be hindered by that disregard in achieving international recognition, at least with respect to the timing of that recognition. On the other hand, compliance by the seceding province with such legitimate obligations would weigh in favour of international recognition. The notion that what is not explicitly prohibited is implicitly permitted has little relevance where (as here) international law refers the legality of secession to the domestic law of the seceding state and the law of that state holds unilateral secession to be unconstitutional.

144. As a court of law, we are ultimately concerned only with legal claims. If the principle of "effectivity" is no more than "successful revolution begets its own legality" [citation omitted], it necessarily means that legality follows and does not precede the successful revolution. *Ex hypothesi,* the successful revolution took place outside the constitutional framework of the predecessor state, otherwise it would not be characterized as "a revolution". It may be that a unilateral secession by Quebec would eventually be accorded legal status by Canada and other states, and thus give rise to legal consequences; but this does not support the more radical contention that subsequent recognition of a state of affairs brought about by a unilateral declaration of independence could be taken to mean that secession was achieved under colour of a legal right. * * *

146. The principle of effectivity * * * proclaims that an illegal act may eventually acquire legal status if, as a matter of empirical fact, it is recognized on the international plane. Our law has long recognized that through a combination of acquiescence and prescription, an illegal act may at some later point be accorded some form of legal status. In the law of property, for example, it is well-known that a squatter on land may ultimately become the owner if the true owner sleeps on his or her right to repossess the land. In this way, a change in the factual circumstances may subsequently be reflected in a change in legal status. It is, however, quite another matter to suggest that a subsequent condonation of an initially illegal act retroactively creates a legal right to engage in the act in the first place. The broader contention is not supported by the international principle of effectivity or otherwise and must be rejected.

Notes

1. In its answer to Question 1, the Supreme Court of Canada found that a "clear expression of a clear majority of Quebecers that they no longer wish to remain in Canada" (para. 92) would entail an obligation on all sides to negotiate a reconciliation of the various interests at stake. It also commented on the connection between constitutional and international dimensions (para. 103):

To the extent that a breach of the constitutional duty to negotiate in accordance with the principles described above undermines the legitimacy of a party's actions, it may have important ramifications at the international level. Thus, a failure of the duty to undertake negotiations and pursue them according to constitutional principles may undermine that government's claim to legitimacy which is generally a precondition for recognition by the international community. Conversely, violations of those principles by the federal or other provincial governments responding to the request for secession may undermine their legitimacy. Thus, a Quebec that had negotiated in conformity with constitutional principles and values in the face of unreasonable intransigence on the part of other participants at the federal or provincial level would be more likely to be recognized than a Quebec which did not itself act according to constitutional principles in the negotiation process. Both the legality of the acts of the parties to the negotiation process under Canadian law, and the perceived legitimacy of such action, would be important considerations in the recognition process. In this way, the adherence of the parties to the obligation to negotiate would be evaluated in an indirect manner on the international plane.

2. In what international forum(s) might the content of the international law right to self-determination be adjudicated? Although Article 1 of the International Covenant on Civil and Political Rights affirms a right of self-determination of peoples, the implementing body for the Covenant (the U.N. Human Rights Committee) has not admitted petitions on behalf of groups seeking to vindicate that right, on the theory that the procedure under the Optional Protocol to the Covenant applies only to the rights of individuals and not of groups. See Mikmaq People v. Canada, Communication No. 205/1986, U.N.H.R.C., 16th Annual Report, U.N. Doc. A/39/40, p. 374; Bernard Ominayak, Chief of the Lubicon Lake Band v. Canada, Communication No. 167/1984, U.N.H.R.C., 14th Annual Report, U.N. Doc. A/45/40, p. 381.

3. In the 1990s, separatist interpretations of self-determination were asserted upon the disintegration of the former Yugoslavia. When Croatia and Bosnia–Herzegovina declared independence and achieved international recognition, substantial minority populations within those new states questioned whether they too could invoke self-determination, so that (for example) territories with high concentrations of Serbs might try either to form their own state or to unite with Serbia. Compare Opinion 2 of the Arbitration Commission on Yugoslavia, 31 I.L.M. 1497 (1992) (rejecting such an interpretation, on the rationale that "the right of self-determination must not involve changes to existing frontiers . . . except where the States concerned agree otherwise"). For discussion and critique, see Craven, The European Community Arbitration Commission on Yugoslavia, 66 Br. Y.B.I.L. 33 (1995); Frowein, Self–Determination as a Limit to Obligations Under International Law, in Tomuschat (ed.), Modern Law of Self–Determination (1993).

Out of motivations of ethnic separatism, the Republika Srpska was declared within a Serb-dominated part of Bosnia–Herzegovina; but it did not attain international recognition as a state. Rather, in the Dayton Agreement for a Bosnian peace settlement, Republika Srpska was acknowledged as one of two "entities" within the state of Bosnia and Herzegovina (the other being the Federation of Bosnia and Herzegovina, comprising the Muslim and Croat communities); the external boundaries of the state of Bosnia and Herzegovina were left intact. See General Framework Agreement for Peace in Bosnia and Herzegovina, Dec. 14, 1995, 35 I.L.M. 75.

The Kosovo crisis of 1999 did not result in the secession of an Albanian-majority region from the Federal Republic of Yugoslavia. Rather, the Security Council resolution adopted at the conclusion of the military conflict (see Chapter 12) reaffirmed "the commitment of all Member States to the sovereignty and territorial integrity of the Federal Republic of Yugoslavia"; it endorsed "substantial autonomy and meaningful self-administration for Kosovo," on the assumption that Kosovo would remain at least formally part of Yugoslavia until a political settlement of Kosovo's future status. See S.C. Res. 1244 (June 10, 1999) (preamble, para. 11, and Annex 2).

4. The Reference on Quebec leaves open the possibility that the international law right of self-determination could entail secession as a "last resort" in the case of especially severe oppression that had "totally frustrated" other channels for exercising internal self-determination. For what kinds of situations might unilateral secession be viewed as a legitimate outcome?

5. A voluminous literature addresses the claims of various kinds of self-determination movements and explores alternative approaches (other than statehood) for ethnic groups, indigenous populations, and other minorities to exercise self-government and perpetuate their cultures. In addition to the references elsewhere in this chapter, see, e.g., Halperin & Scheffer, Self–Determination in the New World Order (1992); Kymlicka, Multicultural Citizenship: A Liberal Theory of Minority Rights (1995); Kymlicka (ed.), The Rights of Minority Cultures (1995); Anaya, Indigenous Peoples in International Law (1996); Sellers, The New World Order: Sovereignty, Human Rights, and the Self–Determination of Peoples (1996); Orentlicher, Separation Anxiety: International Responses to Ethno–Separatist Claims, 23 Yale J. Int'l L. 1 (1998); and Gurr, Peoples Versus States: Minorities at Risk in the New Century (2000).

6. Do the materials in this section persuade you that claims of self-determination can be resolved within the discourse of international law? Is it necessary to rethink the foundations of the system of international law for a more inclusive approach to such questions? Compare Knop, Diversity and Self–Determination in International Law (forthcoming 2001) and extensive bibliographic references therein.

SECTION 3. ENTITIES WITH SPECIAL STATUS

Certain entities that are not states (or not generally recognized as states), or whose status is disputed or unresolved, may nonetheless enjoy attributes of international personality, at least for certain purposes. Some such entities may satisfy most of the traditional criteria for statehood—a defined territory with a population under control of a government—but their capacity to engage in independent external relations may be qualified or questionable. Others may lack one or more of the "objective" criteria, such as a given territorial base. Yet some such entities participate in at least some forms of international treaties, have been (or could be) received as participants in certain international organizations, and engage in other state-like functions. By the same token, national liberation movements speaking on behalf of populations without statehood also can have international personality.

Our focus in this section is on the practical treatment of entities whose status has provoked recent and important political-legal controversy. We need not dwell on controversies of the 19th or 20th centuries that were vivid in their time but no longer pose issues of significant interest. We will return, in later chapters, to other issues of international personality, including of international and non-governmental organizations (Chapter 5) and individuals or private companies (Chapter 6), and of capacity to engage in treaty relations (Chapter 7).

Notes

1. In a study of entities other than states that have been considered to have capacity to participate in treaty relations, Lissitzyn identified:

(a) Members of composite states (i.e., federal unions);

(b) "Dependent states" (protected states, protectorates, vassal states, "associated states," and the like);

(c) Colonial dependencies (self-governing colonies, non-self-governing colonies, condominia) and metropolitan political subdivisions;

(d) Territories administered under mandates or trusteeship agreements;

(e) Entities subject to special forms of international control or supervision other than mandates or trusteeships.

Lissitzyn, Territorial Entities Other than States in the Law of Treaties, 125 Rec. des Cours 5, 9–15, 81–82 (1968–III). On members of federal states in the law of treaties, see Chapter 7.

2. *Self-governing colonies.* Although colonies were not generally considered to have international personality, they were allowed to become parties to many multilateral treaties. The Covenant of the League allowed a "fully self-governing dominion or colony" to become a member of the League. India did so when its foreign affairs were in law and in fact under British control. Before independence in 1947, India became a party to other treaties which, in terms, were open only to states, such as the Chicago Convention on Civil Aviation. It was an original member of the United Nations and of the specialized agencies before independence. The Philippine Commonwealth was in much the same position.

3. *Mandated and trust territories.* The Mandate system was established at the end of World War I by the Allied and Associated Powers under Article 22 of the Covenant of the League of Nations. There were in all 15 mandated territories. Those in the Middle East became independent states, and the others in the Pacific and Africa (except for South West Africa) were transferred to the U.N. trusteeship system.

The U.N. trusteeship system had the same general aims as the Mandate system—namely, to promote "well-being and development" of the people and their eventual self-government or independence. The U.N. trust territories included some former mandated territories and only one additional territory, Italian Somaliland.

Trust and mandated territories were administered by an administering authority or mandatory under agreements which provided for supervision by the United Nations Trusteeship Council, or, in the case of the mandates, a League of Nations "Permanent Mandates Commission." These territories did not become part of the territory of the administering power, nor did the inhabitants acquire the nationality of the administering state. Sovereignty was considered to be vested in the people of the territory, but exercised, within strict limits of the agreements, by the administering power.

Although the mandate and trust systems have virtually disappeared, the principles of international accountability and surveillance used in the mandate and trusteeship arrangements may have application in the future. Toward the end of the 20th century, problems of collapse of governance within existing states led to suggestions for possible revival of something like a trusteeship system, for temporary conservatorship of "failed states." See Helman & Ratner, Saving Failed States, 89 Foreign Policy 3 (Winter 1992–1993); and the critique of such proposals in Gordon, Some Legal Problems With Trusteeship, 28 Cornell Int'l L.J. 301 (1995), and Richardson, "Failed States," Self–Determination, and Preventive Diplomacy: Colonialist Nostalgia and Democratic Expectations, 10 Temple Int'l & Comp. L.J. 1 (1996). On international administration in Kosovo and East Timor beginning in 1999, see pp. 1042–1043.

4. *Associated states.* Although the process of decolonization has in the great majority of cases resulted in the creation of fully independent states, some territories have passed through the status of associated states on the way to full independence, and a few retain the status of associated states. Typically, an associated state elects to combine internal independence with continued dependence upon another state in matters of foreign affairs and defense. Examples of states that have passed through the status of associated states are Antigua, St. Kitts–Nevis, Dominica, Saint Lucia, Saint Vincent and Grenada in association with the United Kingdom. All have since become independent states. The Cook Islands remain associated states with New Zealand, which is responsible for their defense and international affairs.

5. *Puerto Rico.* Puerto Rico is a Commonwealth which is essentially autonomous in internal affairs, but the United States is responsible for Puerto Rico's foreign affairs and defense. Puerto Rico has its own Constitution, tax system, and civil and criminal laws, and determines its own budget. It has a resident commissioner in the U.S. House of Representatives, who is authorized to speak but not vote. Puerto Ricans are U.S. citizens but cannot vote in presidential elections.

The special associated status of Puerto Rico was the subject of debate in the United Nations, particularly as to whether the island was a non-self-governing territory on which reports were required under Article 73(e) of the U.N. Charter. Since 1952, the United States has not submitted reports on the ground that Puerto Rico is self-governing. See Cabranes, The Status of Puerto Rico, 16 I.C.L.Q. 531–9 (1967); Reisman, Puerto Rico and the International Process (1975); Leibowitz, The Commonwealth of Puerto Rico: Trying to Gain Dignity and Maintain Culture, 11 Ga. J. Int'l & Comp. L. 211 (1981).

There has been considerable debate in Puerto Rico about whether Puerto Rico should, as an alternative to commonwealth status, become a state of, or become independent from, the United States. The position of the United States has been that Puerto Rico is self-governing and that it is for the Puerto Rican people to decide whether they prefer a change in status. (Under Art. IV of the U.S. Constitution, Congress would have to approve admission of a new state.)

6. *Micronesia, Marshall Islands and Palau.* The islands of Micronesia formerly comprised the Trust Territory of the Pacific Islands (Micronesia) established by the U.N. after World War II. Negotiations between the United States and their indigenous peoples have resulted in the creation of commonwealth status for the Northern Marianas and in free association with the United States

for the Marshall Islands, the Federated State of Micronesia, and Palau. Under the Compacts of Free Association with the United States, the associated states are self-governing and have the capacity to conduct foreign affairs, including the capacity to enter into international agreements. The United States agreed to provide economic assistance and, for at least 15 years and thereafter as agreed, it has full authority and responsibility for security and defense matters.

The Marshall Islands and Micronesia became members of the United Nations in 1991 and Palau in 1994.

A. NATIONAL LIBERATION MOVEMENTS AS REPRESENTATIVES OF PEOPLES

An especially controversial aspect of international involvement in the exercise of self-determination has been granting national liberation movements access to international forums, particularly the United Nations and international conferences of states. The General Assembly adopted as a general criterion in respect of such invitations that full participation as observers should be accorded to representatives of movements recognized by the Organization of African Unity, G.A. Res. 3280 (XXIX) G.A.O.R., 29th Sess., Supp. 31, at 5 (1974) and G.A. Res. 31/30, (XXXI) G.A.O.R., 31st Sess., Supp. 39, at 118 (1976). On this basis, African liberation movements have participated in U.N. bodies, in the specialized agencies and in international conferences on multilateral treaties convened by the United Nations. They also participated in the Diplomatic Conference on Humanitarian Law in Armed Conflicts.

Cassese has identified two bases for elevating a liberation movement to the rank of international legal subject: first, that its goals fall within the scope of the principle of self-determination (i.e., that the movement is fighting a colonial power, foreign occupier, or racist regime, with the aim of acquiring effective control over a population in a given territory), and second, that the movement is "a legitimate representative of the oppressed people," by virtue of having broad-based support among those it claims to represent. It is the attitudes of states and organizations that determine whether to accord recognition as international legal subjects to such movements (and to withhold comparable recognition from insurgencies with other kinds of objectives or without a representative base). Cassese, Self–Determination at 166–169 (1995).

Palestine Liberation Organization

Specific resolutions by the General Assembly and international conferences have accorded observer status to the Palestine Liberation Organization (PLO). See G.A. Res. 3237 (XXIX) G.A.O.R., 29th Sess. Supp. 31, at 4 (1974). The United Kingdom representative in opposing the resolution said:

> The United Nations had always been regarded as an organization of sovereign, independent States. Observer status had heretofore been confined to non-Member States and to regional organizations. The PLO was not the government of a State, was not recognized as such by anyone and does not purport to be one. Yet, under the draft resolution, it was being treated like a Member State except for the right to vote. That situation seemed to bring into question the nature of the United Nations.

11 U.N. Monthly Chronicle 39 (1974).

Over time, the PLO has gained widespread acceptance as the representative of the Palestinian people. This was the status accorded the PLO in 1974 in General Assembly Resolution 3236 (XXIX) G.A.O.R., 29th Sess., Supp. 31, at 4, calling for the invitation of the PLO to participate in all efforts, deliberations and conferences on the Middle East held under U.N. auspices. Many states have accorded recognition and full diplomatic status to the PLO. With G.A. Res. 52/250 (July 1998) the PLO's capacity to participate in General Assembly activities was upgraded to include some privileges ordinarily reserved for states. Controversy over potential Palestinian statehood (cf. "Palestinian Declaration of Independence," Nov. 15, 1988, 27 I.L.M. 1668) persisted through 2000.

The legal status of the PLO has been an issue in litigation in the United States. In United States v. Palestine Liberation Organization, 695 F.Supp. 1456 (S.D.N.Y.1988), a federal district court interpreted a statute requiring closure of PLO offices in the United States as not applicable to the PLO Observer Mission at the United Nations. See p. 214 supra. Congress has withheld portions of U.S. payments to the United Nations in relation to disputes over the PLO. See Kirgis, Admission of "Palestine" as a Member of a Specialized Agency and Withholding the Payment of Assessments in Response, 84 A.J.I.L. 218 (1990). In Klinghoffer v. S.N.C. Achille Lauro, 739 F.Supp. 854 (S.D.N.Y.1990), affirmed, 937 F.2d 44 (2d Cir.1991), the district court denied immunity to the PLO in a suit involving a terrorist act, on the ground that it did not qualify as a state under international law. For many years it was U.S. policy (codified in statute) not to deal with the PLO until the PLO renounced terrorism, recognized the right of Israel to exist, and accepted the U.N. Security Council resolutions on the framework for settlement with Israel. Those conditions were considered satisfied as of the early 1990s.

In a Declaration of Principles signed in Oslo in September 1993, 32 I.L.M. 1525, the government of Israel and the PLO agreed on a framework in which to negotiate their differences. In light of a letter from PLO Chairman Yasser Arafat making explicit commitments—inter alia that the "PLO recognizes the right of the State of Israel to exist in peace and security"—Prime Minister Yitzhak Rabin of Israel confirmed that "the Government of Israel has decided to recognize the PLO as the representative of the Palestinian people." A transitional period for interim self-government arrangements began with Israel's withdrawal from the Gaza Strip and Jericho area in 1994. Significant stages in the negotiations were consummated with further agreements in 1995, 36 I.L.M. 551, and 1998, 37 I.L.M. 1251. Final status negotiations were in progress in 2000 but were suspended shortly before this casebook went to press.

Note

For background on the controversy and differing views of self-determination as applied to the Palestinians, see Cassese, Self-Determination 230–248 (1995). On the 1993 Oslo agreement, see essays by Benvenisti, Shihadeh and Cassese at 4 E.J.I.L. 542–571 (1993).

B. ENTITIES SUI GENERIS

1. *Taiwan*

The issue of the Republic of China on Taiwan has typically been treated in international law textbooks as a problem of recognition of governments rather than of statehood. See Section 4 below. The Republic of China (ROC) had authority over both mainland China and Taiwan prior to the Communist revolution of October 1949. At that time, the People's Republic of China (PRC) was established on the mainland and the ROC government retreated to the island of Taiwan, where it continued to assert that it was the legitimate government of all of China. For decades, the ROC and the PRC each insisted that there was only one China, that Taiwan was part of China, and that their own government was the only government of all of China. The two governments vied for international recognition, for acceptance in international organizations, and for exclusion of the rival government from corresponding prerogatives. During the 1950s, 1960s, and 1970s, their competing and mutually exclusive positions were intensively debated in legal as well as political terms, under the international law of recognition of governments.

The practical and political significance of those debates seemed to wane when the PRC won the right to represent China in the United Nations in 1971 (G.A. Res. 2758, 26th Sess., Supp. No. 29, at 2) and when most major states (by the end of the 1970s) had shifted their formal recognition from the ROC to the PRC, while finding creative ways to maintain informal ties with the ROC. The United States, for example, formally recognized the PRC with effect from January 1, 1979 (the 1972 Shanghai Communique had prefigured the eventual formal shift). Yet at the same time, the U.S. executive branch and Congress developed a framework for maintaining unofficial relationships with Taiwan, as elaborated in legislation containing the following provisions:

TAIWAN RELATIONS ACT

Pub. L. No. 94–83, April 10, 1979, 22 U.S.C. 3300 et seq.
18 I.L.M. 873 (1979).

Sec. 4. (a) The absence of diplomatic relations or recognition shall not affect the application of the laws of the United States with respect to Taiwan, and the laws of the United States shall apply with respect to Taiwan in the manner that the laws of the United States applied with respect to Taiwan prior to January 1, 1979.

(b) The application of subsection (a) of this section shall include, but shall not be limited to the following:

(1) Whenever the laws of the United States refer or relate to foreign countries, nations, states, governments, or similar entities, such terms shall include and such laws shall apply with respect to Taiwan. * * *

(c) For all purposes, including actions in any court in the United States, the Congress approves the continuation in force of all treaties and other international agreements, including multilateral conventions, entered into by the United States and the governing authorities on Taiwan recognized by the United States as the Republic of China prior to January 1, 1979, and in force between them on December 31, 1978, unless and until terminated in accordance with law.

(d) Nothing in this Act may be construed as a basis for supporting the exclusion or expulsion of Taiwan from continued membership in any international financial institution or any other international organization.

* * *

Sec. 6. (a) Programs, transactions, and other relations conducted or carried out by the President or any agency of the United States Government with respect to Taiwan shall, in the manner and to the extent directed by the President, be conducted and carried out by or through—

(1) The American Institute in Taiwan, a nonprofit corporation incorporated under the laws of the District of Columbia * * *.

* * *

Throughout the 1980s and 1990s, the basic "one China" concept persisted on both sides of the Taiwan straits and continued to set the terms of relationships with third states. In general, the Taiwan question was understood to entail the aspiration of the people on both sides of the straits for eventual rapprochement and potential reunification. Texts and treatises on international law (including the previous editions of this casebook) avoided the troublesome topic of "self-determination" in relation to Taiwan by observing that the authorities on Taiwan had made no claim of the existence of separate statehood for that entity.

By the end of the 20th century, however, domestic political developments on Taiwan had altered the international calculus. In 1996, the Nationalist (Kuomintang) government that had ruled the ROC from before the 1949 schism faced its first serious challenge from a political party identified with the cause of Taiwanese independence. The PRC threatened military action if an independence program were to be pursued, and tensions mounted in the period before the March 1996 election when the Nationalist government under President Lee Teng-hui was returned to power for the next four years. Though the ROC did not abandon its one-China policy, Lee Teng-hui signaled a change in tone by referring in a 1999 interview to the relationship between China and Taiwan as a "special state-to-state relation."

In 2000 a significant change of government on Taiwan took place with the election of President Chen Shui-bian of the Democratic People's Party (a party with strong sympathy for Taiwanese independence). A head-on clash with Beijing was deflected by virtue of President Chen's cautious inaugural address, in which he pledged that unless the mainland attacked Taiwan, he would not declare independence or take other overt steps to establish Taiwan's formal independence. See "Change of Power in Taiwan is Meeting a Moderate Response From Beijing," New York Times, May 21, 2000.

The PRC government in Beijing has maintained that cross-straits differences have to be resolved on the basis of a one-China policy, but have proposed that Taiwan could retain a high degree of autonomy after reunification and could preserve its capitalist economic system. This "one country, two systems" approach would have some overlaps with the resolution of the status of Hong Kong discussed below.

Meanwhile, the ROC has been seeking for some years to gain admission (or readmission) to international organizations in parallel to the PRC, and has already been participating on its own behalf in some bodies dealing with economic and financial matters. Pragmatic legal solutions to the dilemma of membership in organizations reserved for "states" (such as the United Nations) have been proffered to preserve the aspiration for eventual reunification. As of 2000, the impending admission of the PRC to the World Trade Organization may pave the way for parallel WTO membership for Taiwan as a separate customs territory. (For comparison see below on Hong Kong and Macao.)

Notes

1. Can Taiwan properly be viewed as a self-determination unit? Some proponents of a separate Taiwanese identity argue that the issue should be viewed in the framework of decolonization. They observe that Taiwan was ceded to Japan by the Treaty of Shimonoseki of 1895 at the conclusion of a war initiated by Japan against China, was ruled from Japan through World War II, and was restored to China only with the San Francisco Peace Treaty in 1945. They point out that except for the years from 1945 to 1949, Taiwan and mainland China have had entirely different political and economic systems; there are also ethnic, linguistic, and cultural differences between the populations on the island and the mainland. What relevance should these factors have for Taiwan's status?

2. The PRC has refused to rule out the possibility of forcible reunification of Taiwan with the mainland. The United States no longer has a treaty commitment to defend the ROC (concerning the termination of the previous mutual defense treaty with the ROC, see p. 224); but the U.S. has sold arms to Taiwan under the framework of the Taiwan Relations Act and has attempted to deter the PRC from use of force against Taiwan, by leaving open a range of options to assist Taiwan in the case of an attack from the mainland. Would a formal change in Taiwan's status affect the legality of use of force by any party?

3. For different points of view on Taiwan's situation, see the Symposium on Bridging the Taiwan Strait: Problems and Prospects for China's Reunification or Taiwan's Independence, 32 N.Eng.L.Rev. 661–852 (1998); Y. Frank Chiang, State, Sovereignty and Taiwan, 23 Fordham I.L.J. 959 (2000); Su Wei, Some Reflections on the One–China Principle, 23 Fordham I.L.J. 1169 (2000).

2. *Hong Kong and Macao*

The situations of Hong Kong and Macao have their own peculiar features but in some ways resemble each other. Hong Kong had been a British colony and Macao a Portuguese colony, until their respective returns to China in 1997 and 1999. Prior to reunion with China, and continuing thereafter, they have each enjoyed a measure of international legal personality, in that they have been treated as having capacity to participate in their own behalf in certain multilateral treaty regimes and treaty-based institutions. Notably, before their return to China, both had become members (in their own names) of the General Agreement on Tariffs and Trade and World Trade Organization, under provisions of the GATT/WTO agreements allowing participation by separate customs territories; and both have continued their participation in GATT/WTO arrangements subsequent to reunification with China, even though China itself had not been admitted to GATT/WTO membership as of late 2000. Their situation in respect of international human rights treaties has also been treated as functionally equivalent to continuing membership, even though China had not ratified the treaties. A report submitted on behalf of Hong Kong under the International Covenant on Civil and Political Rights was accepted and considered by the U.N. Human Rights Committee in November 1999.

Certain aspects of the post-unification status of Hong Kong and Macao are governed by the terms negotiated with China by the United Kingdom and Portugal, respectively. The Joint Declaration on the Question of Hong Kong (U.K.-PRC), Sept. 26, 1984, 23 I.L.M. 1366, 1371, provides in Article 3(2) that after restoration to China the territory is to "enjoy a high degree of autonomy, except in foreign and defense affairs, which are the responsibility of the Central People's Government." In accordance with the Joint Declaration, Hong Kong has been designated a "Special Administrative Region" pursuant to the PRC Constitution, with its own Basic Law and its own Court of Final Appeal. The Basic Law provides that Hong Kong will maintain its distinct political, economic, and legal systems for at least 50 years.

Notes

1. On the special status of Hong Kong in international and Chinese law, see Mushkat, One Country, Two Legal Personalities: The Case of Hong Kong (1997); Ghai, Hong Kong's New Constitutional Order: The Resumption of Chinese Sovereignty and the Basic Law (1997); Chan, Fu & Ghai (eds.) Hong Kong's Constitutional Debate: Conflict Over Interpretation (2000); One Country, Two Legal Systems? The Rule of Law, Democracy, and the Protection of Fundamental Rights in Post–Handover Hong Kong, 55 Record Assn. Bar City N.Y. 325 (May/June 2000).

On Hong Kong's participation in the International Covenant on Civil and Political Rights and other treaties, see Chan, State Succession to Human Rights Treaties: Hong Kong and the ICCPR, 45 I.C.L.Q. 928 (1996); Mushkat, Hong Kong and the Succession to Treaties, 46 I.C.L.Q. 181 (1997); Yu, Succession by Estoppel: Hong Kong's Succession to the ICCPR, 27 Pepperdine L. Rev. 53 (2000).

2. At the request of the PRC, the United Nations determined in 1972 that Hong Kong and Macao were "part of Chinese territory occupied" respectively "by the British and Portuguese authorities," so that their return to China upon the expiration of the British and Portuguese leases would take place outside the framework of U.N. processes for non-self-governing territories. See Cassese, Self–Determination 79–80 (1995).

On the reporting by the United Kingdom and Portugal to the U.N. Human Rights Committee in respect of Hong Kong and Macao prior to reversion, see ibid. at 79–80, nn. 34–36.

3. U.S. policy toward Hong Kong is reflected in, inter alia, 22 U.S.C. 5712–5713 and 5722 (1994), which express the sense of the U.S. Congress that the

United States "should respect Hong Kong's status as a separate customs territory" and "should treat Hong Kong as a territory which is fully autonomous from the People's Republic of China with respect to economic and trade matters," while allowing the President to suspend U.S. laws with respect to Hong Kong if he "determines that Hong Kong is not sufficiently autonomous to justify treatment under a particular law of the United States." In Cheung v. United States, 213 F.3d 82 (2d Cir.2000), the court of appeals gave effect to an extradition agreement between the United States and the Hong Kong Special Administrative Region, which had been approved by the U.S. Senate as a treaty in October 1997, after Hong Kong's reversion to China. On other litigation involving Hong Kong in U.S. law, see pp. 311–312, 1185 infra.

4. In a recent noteworthy decision, Hong Kong's Court of Final Appeal considered a Hong Kong ordinance regulating immigration, which raised delicate constitutional questions concerning the relationship of Hong Kong law to the mainland authorities. See Ng Ka Ling v. Director of Immigration, Court of Final Appeal of the Hong Kong Special Administrative Region, Judgment of Jan. 29, 1999, 38 I.L.M. 551. For discussion of the controversy surrounding the Court's decision and subsequent developments, see "One Country, Two Legal Systems" and other references in note 1 supra.

3. The State of the Vatican City and the Holy See

As noted above (p. 255, the State of the Vatican City has been treated as a state and has entered into treaties having a specific territorial application to the Vatican. More generally, the Holy See—the central administration of the Roman Catholic Church—has engaged in international relations across a broad range of issues. The Holy See has been admitted as a full member of such specialized agencies of the United Nations as UNESCO, the World Health Organization, and the International Labour Organization, which under their constituent treaties are open only to states. Moreover, the Holy See has become a party to many of the major multinational conventions which are open to states alone. Diplomats (from many states) are accredited to the Holy See rather than to the State of Vatican City. See Graham, Vatican Diplomacy 28–30, 344–346 (1959) and Crawford, The Creation of States in International Law 152–160 (1979).

It has been the position of the Holy See that its international personality is based on its religious and spiritual authority and not its territorial enclave in Rome. The United Nations and other international organizations have taken no decision on that issue (though they use the name Holy See rather than the State of the Vatican City). To acknowledge that international personality rested on the Holy See's religious authority might give rise to similar claims by other religions, an issue that governments are not inclined to welcome. The problem has been avoided because of the ambiguity created by the fact that there is a territory, however small (and however modest its permanent population), which has been recognized by Italy as constituting the State of the Vatican City under the sovereignty of the Holy See. While no distinction is drawn by international organizations between the State of the Vatican City and the Holy See for purposes of membership or adherence to treaties, legal doctrine tends to regard them as two distinct legal persons. Consider the following comment by Hans Kelsen:

> The Head of the Church [i.e. the Holy See] is at the same time the Head of the State of the Vatican City. * * * But the State of the Vatican City, limited to a certain territory, must not be identified with the Church, which is tied to no limited territory. That means the territorial sphere of validity of the State of the Vatican City is limited, as every state territory is, whereas the territorial sphere of validity of the Roman Catholic Church is not limited.

Kelsen, Principles of International Law 252 (2d rev. ed. Tucker 1966). See also Ehler, The Recent Concordates, 104 Rec. des Cours 7–63 (1961–III).

The Holy See has been an active participant in many international meetings and negotiations, including the 1994 Cairo conference on population, the 1995 Beijing conference on women, and the 1998 Rome conference on the International Criminal Court. Its access to U.N.-sponsored events follows from the status of "Non–Member State Permanent Observer" as it has been designated for U.N. purposes. In recent years, some have questioned whether this status accords a kind of privilege not available to other religions or to other non-governmental entities. On legal aspects of this controversy, see Yasmin Abdullah, Note: The Holy See at United Nations Conferences: State or Church?, 96 Col. L. Rev. 1835 (1996). For comparisons to non-governmental organizations, see Chapter 5 infra.

SECTION 4. RECOGNITION OF GOVERNMENTS

A. CRITERIA OF RECOGNITION

Recognition of a state is not the same as recognition of its government although they often go together in the case of new states. Within existing states, governments come and go and normally the changes raise no question of recognition. When changes in government occur, foreign governments are concerned primarily with the question of whether the new regime is in fact in control of the government. When the French monarchy was replaced by a popular government, Secretary of State Thomas Jefferson instructed the U.S. envoy in Paris that "[i]t accords with our principles to acknowledge any government to be rightful which is formed by the will of the nation substantially declared. * * * With such a government every kind of business may be done." Christopher, "Normalization of Diplomatic Relations," speech at Occidental College June 11, 1977. Daniel Webster, when Secretary of State in 1852, expressed the United States' position which prevailed during the 19th century:

> From President Washington's time down to the present day it has been a principle, always acknowledged by the United States, that every nation possesses a right to govern itself according to its own will, to change its institutions at discretion, and to transact its business through whatever agents it may think proper to employ. This cardinal point in our policy has been strongly illustrated by recognizing the many forms of political power which have been successively adopted by France in the series of revolutions with which that country has been visited.

Quoted in Hyde at 159.

Although Webster was correct in expressing the position of the United States in the 19th century, the United States has later applied on occasion standards for recognition other than that of effective control by the government. The varying United States practice as to recognizing governments has been summarized as follows in Restatement (Third) § 203, Reporters' Note 1:

> United States practice long reflected the view that recognition of governments was not a matter of international obligation but could be granted or withheld at will, to further national policy. United States policy has varied as to whether recognition should be withheld from a regime that has obtained power other than through constitutional processes. The case for withholding recognition was classically stated by President Wilson on March 11, 1913, after General Huerta overthrew the government of President Madero in Mexico. Based on the premise that a "just government rests always upon the consent of the governed," Wilson's view was that a regime taking control by force should not be dealt with on equal terms by other governments. 1 Hackworth, Digest of International Law 181 (1940). It was sometimes assumed that disapproval by foreign governments would undermine such a new regime and lead to its replacement, but that assumption has not been generally borne out in fact.
>
> At other times, however, United States policy has been to recognize the government in power despite distaste for the way it acceded to power, or for its ideology, policies, or personnel. The constitutionality of a regime's coming to power was often legally and factually difficult to determine and, in any event, the inquiry might seem improper and insulting to the country involved. It could also become awkward to continue to refuse to deal with a regime that was thriving in spite of non-recognition. In particular, withholding recognition of Latin American regimes was deemed by some states to be unlawful intervention in domestic affairs and intensified resentment against the United States in that region.
>
> Since 1970 the United States has moved away from its older recognition practice. "In recent years, U.S. practice has been to deemphasize and avoid the use of recognition in cases of changes of governments and to concern ourselves with the question of whether we wish to have diplomatic relations with the new governments." [1977] Digest of U.S. Practice in Int'l L. 19–21. Repeatedly, the State Department has responded to inquiries with the statement: "The question of recognition does not arise: we are conducting our relations with the new government." [1974] *Id.* at 13: [1975] *Id.* at 34. In some situations, however, the question cannot be avoided, for example, where two regimes are contending for power, and particularly where legal consequences within the United States depend on which regime is recognized or accepted.

Notes

1. Does Jefferson's "straightforward" statement on recognition mean that "effective power" alone is the prerequisite to recognition or is there a different standard in his reference to a government "formed by the will of the nation substantially declared"? Consider the following statement of a State Department legal adviser:

> I think our present policy is more concerned with the acquiescence rather than the declaration of the will of the people. We have not generally concerned ourselves with asking, would the people, if given a free plebiscite, endorse that change of government.

United States Recognition of Foreign Governments: Hearings on S.Res. 205 Before the Comm. on For. Rel., 91st Cong., 1st Sess. 10 (1969) (Testimony of George Aldrich).

2. The criterion of constitutional legitimacy favored by Woodrow Wilson was similar to the Tobar or Betancourt Doctrine espoused in Latin America in 1907, which called for refusal to recognize any government that comes to power through extraconstitutional means until free elections are held and a government so elected assumes power. The doctrine was embodied in some treaties but in general was not followed in Latin America. However, a resolution of the Organization of American States did recommend that its member states exchange views when a government has been overthrown and take into account:

> Whether the de facto government proposes to take the necessary measures for the holding of elections within a reasonable period, giving its people the opportunity freely to participate in the consequent electoral processes.

Res. XXVI, OAS Second Special Inter–American Conference 1965, 5 I.L.M. 155 (1966). Although references were often made to this resolution, it did not preclude recognition of non-elected regimes, and many such regimes enjoyed normal relations with other governments in the Western Hemisphere during the 20th century. On developments of the 1990s, see the discussion of the Haitian crisis below.

3. During the periods in which the United States refused to recognize the U.S.S.R. (1917–1933) and the People's Republic of China (1949–1978), it asserted as a condition of recognition that governments in effective control must be able and willing to live up to their international commitments. Both governments mentioned were charged with failures to observe international obligations. In retrospect, most observers would regard the United States' objections as based on ideological and political grounds. Is the requirement, as stated, legally meaningful? Does "ability" to live up to international commitments simply mean effective power to do so? Is "willingness" more than *pro forma* since no government would deny such willingness? On the other hand, does it leave room for states to deny recognition to internationally "lawless" regimes and therefore to apply sanctions against such behavior?

4. When conflicting governments contend for power and neither has complete effective power, should other criteria be applied? Should no action be taken until the conflict is resolved? What criteria should be followed by international bodies which must decide which regime should represent the state?

5. There is a significant distinction between recognition of a government and maintaining diplomatic relations with it. Restatement (Third) § 203, Comment *d* states as follows:

> Recognition of a government is often effected by sending and receiving diplomatic representatives, but one government may recognize another yet refrain from assuming diplomatic relations with it. Similarly, breaking off relations does not constitute derecognition of the government. Some governments refrain from maintaining relations or terminate relations with each other in order to express disapproval, or from practical considerations, such as the absence of sufficient interests to warrant such relations, a lack of

necessary personnel, or a desire to save the cost. Sometimes it is judged desirable to withdraw diplomatic personnel because of concern for their safety. When relations are not maintained directly they may be carried on through diplomatic channels provided by another government. Thus, the United States terminated relations with Cuba in 1961, but is represented in Cuba by the Swiss embassy in Havana, and Cuba is represented by the Czechoslovak embassy in Washington.

Deputy Secretary of State Warren Christopher stated as follows in a speech at Occidental College on June 11, 1977:

> * * * The premise of our present policy is that diplomatic relations do not constitute a seal of approval. Winston Churchill explained it best: "The reason for having diplomatic relations is not to confer a compliment, but to secure a convenience." * * *
>
> We maintain diplomatic relations with many governments of which we do not necessarily approve. The reality is that, in this day and age, coups and other unscheduled changes of government are not exceptional developments. Withholding diplomatic relations from these regimes, after they have obtained effective control, penalizes us. It means that we forsake much of the chance to influence the attitudes and conduct of a new regime. Without relations, we forfeit opportunities to transmit our values and communicate our policies. Isolation may well bring out the worst in the new government.

THE TWO GOVERNMENTS OF CHINA

The Secretary General of the United Nations commented as follows in 1950 on the problem presented by the existence of two governments of China:

> The Chinese case is unique in the history of the United Nations, not because it involves a revolutionary change of government, but because it is the first in which two rival governments exist. It is quite possible that such a situation will occur again in the future and it is highly desirable to see what principle can be followed in choosing between the rivals. It has been demonstrated that the principle of numerical preponderance of recognition is inappropriate and legally incorrect. Is any other principle possible?
>
> It is submitted that the proper principle can be derived by analogy from Article 4 of the Charter. This Article requires that an applicant for membership must be able and willing to carry out the obligations of membership. The obligations of membership can be carried out only by governments which in fact possess the power to do so. Where a revolutionary government presents itself as representing a State, in rivalry to an existing government, the question at issue should be which of these two governments in fact is in a position to employ the resources and direct the people of the State in fulfilment of the obligations of membership. In essence, this means an inquiry as to whether the new government exercises effective authority within the territory of the State and is habitually obeyed by the bulk of the population.
>
> If so, it would seem to be appropriate for the United Nations organs, through their collective action, to accord it the right to represent the State in the Organization, even though individual Members of the Orga-

nization refuse, and may continue to refuse, to accord it recognition as the lawful government for reasons which are valid under their national policies.

Memorandum on Legal Aspects of Problems of Representation in the United Nations. U.N.Doc. S/1466 (1950).

Notes

1. When the General Assembly considered the question of criteria for choosing between rival governments, the majority of governments rejected the "objective" test proposed by the United Kingdom based on "effective control over all or nearly all of the territory" and the "obedience of the bulk of population." Instead it recommended that, "whenever more than one authority claims to be the government entitled to represent a Member State in the United Nations, and this question becomes a subject of controversy in the United Nations, the question should be considered in the light of the Purposes and Principles of the Charter and the circumstances of each case". G.A.Res. 396 (V) G.A.O.R., 5th Sess., Supp. 20, p. 24 (1950). This resolution was influenced obviously by the attitude toward Communist China, then engaged in armed hostilities against the United Nations Forces in Korea. However, the reluctance to adopt a purely factual test reflects a conception of "recognition" as involving value judgments. Such value judgments may be based on national interest in the specific sense of national policies and alliances. They may also be based on more general principles such as observance of human rights. The very broad formula adopted by the General Assembly left room for these conceptions. See Schachter, Problems of Law and Justice, in Annual Review, United Nations Affairs 1951, 200–204 (Eagleton & Swift eds. 1952).

2. As noted above (p. 287), the General Assembly decided in 1971 to accept the P.R.C. as the government with authority to represent China in the United Nations. This decision has been followed throughout the U.N. system and by other international bodies, but it did not preclude member states from maintaining a different stance in their own recognition practice. At the time of the U.N. decision, the majority of U.N. member states had already shifted their own recognition from the R.O.C. government to the P.R.C. government; but a significant minority (including the United States until 1979) continued to recognize the R.O.C.

3. As of 2000, 29 states recognize the R.O.C. rather than the P.R.C. as the government of China. See Chiang, State, Sovereignty and Taiwan, 23 Fordham I.L.J. 959, 981 n. 118 (2000). The P.R.C. does not maintain diplomatic relations with any state that recognizes the R.O.C. The P.R.C.'s sensitivities over some states' recognition of the R.O.C. may have injected an extraneous negative factor into developments far removed from China. For example, shortly before the Kosovo conflict of 1999, the fact that the Former Yugoslav Republic of Macedonia had recognized the R.O.C. was apparently a factor when the P.R.C. vetoed the renewal of the U.N. peacekeeping force that had been stationed in Macedonia in a preventive capacity. See "Security Council Fails to Extend Mandate of U.N. Preventative Deployment Force in Former Yugoslav Republic of Macedonia," U.N. Press Release SC/6648 (Feb. 25, 1999).

B. IS RECOGNITION NECESSARY?

STATEMENT OF MEXICAN FOREIGN MINISTER ESTRADA (1930)

Whiteman, Digest of Int'l Law vol. 2, 85–86 (1963).

It is a well-known fact that some years ago Mexico suffered, as few nations have, from the consequences of that doctrine, which allows foreign governments to pass upon the legitimacy or illegitimacy of the régime existing in another country, with the result that situations arise in which the legal qualifications or national status of governments or authorities are apparently made subject to the opinion of foreigners.

Ever since the Great War, the doctrine of so-called "recognitions" has been applied in particular to the nations of this continent, although in well-known cases of change of régime occurring in European countries the governments of the nations have not made express declarations of recognition; consequently, the system has been changing into a special practice applicable to the Latin American Republics.

After a very careful study of the subject, the Government of Mexico has transmitted instructions to its Ministers or Chargés d'Affaires in the countries affected by the recent political crises, informing them that the Mexican Government is issuing no declarations in the sense of grants of recognition, since that nation considers that such a course is an insulting practice and one which, in addition to the fact that it offends the sovereignty of other nations, implies that judgment of some sort may be passed upon the internal affairs of those nations by other governments, inasmuch as the latter assume, in effect, an attitude of criticism, when they decide, favorably or unfavorably, as to the legal qualifications of foreign régimes.

Notes

1. The Estrada Doctrine is generally understood to mean that recognition of governments is unnecessary once the state has been recognized. Should it not be construed more accurately as proposing (a) the sole criterion of effective control for deciding when to deal with a new government and (b) the avoidance of explicit and formal acts of recognition? What international policies would be served by this approach?

2. Baxter suggested that recognition is an "institution of law that causes more problems than it solves" and therefore should be rejected. "The partial withdrawal of law from this area of international relations will facilitate the maintenance of relations with states in which extraconstitutional changes of government are taking place, and that is a good thing." Baxter, Foreword to Galloway, Recognizing Foreign Governments p. xi (1978). If recognition in a formal sense has become unnecessary or a "non-problem," why did the People's Republic of China insist in 1979 on recognition by the United States as a condition of "normalization of relations"? Does that suggest that recognition cannot simply be replaced by the maintenance of diplomatic relations or a liaison office?

3. According to a State Department survey of 1969, "31 states indicated that they had abandoned traditional recognition policies and substituted the Estrada Doctrine or some equivalent by which they accepted whatever government was in effective control without raising the issue of recognition". Galloway at 10 and Appendix A. Mexico was among those countries, yet Mexico, the source of the Estrada Doctrine, refused relations with the Franco government of Spain for over three decades. Are many states prepared to abandon the institution of recognition as a political tool?

One study that favors the Estrada Doctrine acknowledges that most states that express allegiance to the doctrine actually consider political factors in granting or withholding recognition. Galloway at 137–138.

4. Can the Estrada Doctrine be applied when there are rival claimants to power? Should foreign governments simply deal with both sets of officials regarding problems in areas where they respectively have de facto control until the conflict is resolved? See Jessup, A Modern Law of Nations 62–63 (1948), who observed that the Estrada Doctrine will not always save foreign governments from the necessity of choosing between rival claimants.

5. In April 1980, a change in the British policy concerning recognition of governments was announced by Lord Carrington to the House of Lords as follows:

> * * * [W]e have decided that we shall no longer accord recognition to Governments. The British Government recognise States in accordance with common international doctrine.
>
> Where an unconstitutional change of régime takes place in a recognised State, Governments of other States must necessarily consider what dealings, if any, they should have with the new régime, and whether and to what extent it qualifies to be treated as the Government of the State concerned * * *.
>
> We have * * * concluded that there are practical advantages in following the policy of many other countries in not according recognition to Governments. Like them, we shall continue to decide the nature of our dealings with régimes which come to power unconstitutionally in the light of our assessment of whether they are able themselves to exercise effective control of the territory of the State concerned and seem likely to do so.

Hansard, House of Lords, vol. 408, cols. 1121–1122. As a result, the question of whether a regime qualifies in the eyes of the United Kingdom as a government "will be left to be inferred from the nature of the dealings, if any, which [the UK Government] may have with it, and in particular on whether [the UK Government] are dealing with it on a normal Government to Government basis." 985 PARL. DEB. H.C. (5th ser.) 385 (1980). See Dixon, Recent Developments in United Kingdom Practice Concerning the Recognition of States and Governments, 22 Int'l Law. 555 (1988).

6. For the point of view that the institution of recognition of governments should be preserved but governed by an effectivist rule, see Peterson, Recognition of Governments Should Not Be Abolished, 77 A.J.I.L. 32 (1983); see also Peterson, Recognition of Governments: Legal Doctrine and State Practice, 1815–1995 (1997).

7. In view of the decisions taken by the United Nations in regard to Rhodesia and Namibia which involved non-recognition, is it not realistic to expect that non-recognition will be used (or recommended) by the U.N. against regimes considered to violate standards of self-determination, human rights or nonaggres-

sion? The Governments of some member states (e.g., Hungary and South Africa) had their credentials rejected on the ground that they did not represent the people of the country.

For a general defense of the use of recognition to further international aims, see Reisman & Suzuki, Recognition and Social Change in International Law, in Toward World Order and Human Dignity 403–470 (Reisman & Weston, eds., 1976).

8. The Restatement (Third) takes the position that while a state is not required to accord formal recognition to the government of another state, a state is required to treat as the government of another state a regime that is in effective control of that state unless its control has been effected in violation of international law, in which event a state is required not to recognize or accept the regime as the government. Restatement (Third) § 203.

C. COLLECTIVE NON-RECOGNITION OF ILLEGAL REGIMES

As the foregoing materials suggest, the practice of states and international organizations and the positions of scholars have been ambivalent as regards the problem of governments whose control is "illegitimate"—whether because of interruption of constitutional governance, denial of fundamental human rights, or violation of other international norms. These issues came to a head in the Haitian crisis of 1991–1994, and have also been presented in subsequent situations.

ACEVEDO, THE HAITIAN CRISIS AND THE OAS RESPONSE: A TEST OF EFFECTIVENESS IN PROTECTING DEMOCRACY

in Enforcing Restraint: Collective Intervention in Internal Conflicts pp. 119–120, 123, 132–133 (Damrosch ed. 1993) (footnotes omitted).

In February 1991, Father Jean–Bertrand Aristide took office as the first president in the history of Haiti who had won a free and fair election. He carried with him the hopes of his supporters—an overwhelming majority of Haiti's desperately poor people—for an end to decades of abusive authoritarian rule and the beginning of a new era founded on principles of democracy and social justice.

Less than eight months later, on September 30, those hopes were dashed when President Aristide was overthrown in a military coup whose perpetrators defied not only the will of the Haitian majority but also a commitment to representative democracy undertaken on a hemisphere-wide basis through the Organization of American States (OAS). In fact, observers from the OAS, the United Nations, and nongovernmental organizations had monitored the elction that resulted in Aristide's victory. Thus the international community had established a baseline of expectations both legitimizing Aristide's government and supporting its continuation. * * *

The [OAS's] concern for the effective exercise of representative democracy took a quantum leap with approval in [June] 1991 of the Santiago Commitment to Democracy and the Renewal of the Inter–American System and a resolution on representative democracy. The latter calls for an automatic meeting of the OAS Permanent Council

> ... in the event of any occurrences giving rise to the sudden or irregular interruption of the democratic political institutional process or of the legitimate exercise of power by the democratically elected government in any of the Organization's member states, in order, within the framework of the Charter, [to convene an urgent meeting].

It further states that the purpose of any such meeting should be "to look into the events collectively and adopt any decisions deemed appropriate, in accordance with the Charter and international law."

Less than four months after their approval, the new procedures would be put to their first test, when the constitutional president of Haiti was forced from office and expelled from the country.* * *

Immediately after the coup, the OAS Permanent Council held an emergency meeting on September 30 and condemned the events that occurred in Haiti. The Council demanded adherence to the constitution and respect for the government legitimately established through the free expression of the popular will.

The ad hoc Meeting of Consultation of Ministers of Foreign Affairs, which the Permanent Council convoked in response to the situation created by the coup, condemned the disruption of the democratic process in Haiti, calling it a violation of the Haitian people's right to self-determination. The ministers demanded "full restoration of the rule of law and of the constitutional regime, and the immediate reinstatement of President Jean–Bertrand Aristide in the exercise of his legitimate authority."

The resolution the ministers of foreign affairs adopted also provided that the Organization would recognize as legitimate only representatives designated by the constitutional government of President Aristide * * *. Furthermore, the resolution recommended action to bring about the diplomatic isolation of those who held de facto power in Haiti, and the suspension, by all states, of their economic, financial, and commercial ties with Haiti, except aid for strictly humanitarian purposes. * * *

When the de facto government of Haiti refused to comply with the OAS request that President Aristide be immediately reinstated, the Meeting of Consultation passed another resolution on October 8, 1991, which strongly condemned the use of violence and military coercion, as well as the decision to illegally replace the constitutional president of Haiti. The ministers also declared that "no government that may result from this illegal situation" would be accepted and that no representative of such a government would be recognized. * * *

On October [11], 1991, the UN General Assembly "strongly condemn[ed] both the illegal replacement of the constitutional President of Haiti and the use of violence, military coercion and the violation of human rights" in Haiti, and urged UN member states "to consider the adoption of measures in keeping with those agreed on by the Organization of American States."

Notes

1. The Haitian crisis was, in the first instance, an example of hemispheric practice in the enforcement of inter-American norms of democratic governance embodied in, e.g., the O.A.S. Charter. The Santiago Commitment, O.A.S. Doc. AG/RES.1080 (XXI–0/91) (June 5, 1991), quoted in the foregoing passage, marked a hemisphere-wide undertaking to respond collectively to the overthrow of a democratic government. In the O.A.S. meetings in the first days of the crisis, the relevant organs resolved:

> 3. To recognize the representatives designated by the constitutional Government of President Jean–Bertrand Aristide as the only legitimate representatives of the Government of Haiti to the organs, agencies, and entities of the inter-American system. * * *
>
> 5. To recommend, with due respect for the policy of each member state on the recognition of states and governments, action to bring about the diplomatic isolation of those who hold power illegally in Haiti.

"Support to the Democratic Government of Haiti," OEA/Ser. F/V.1, MRE/RES.1/91 (Oct. 3, 1991); see also MRE/RES.2/91 (Oct. 8, 1991).

But the international ramifications of the situation were not confined to the hemisphere. Within days, the U.N. General Assembly condemned the coup, affirmed "as unacceptable any entity resulting from that illegal situation," and appealed to U.N. member states to support the O.A.S. measures. G.A. Res. 46/7 (Oct. 11, 1991). At almost the same time, at a meeting of the Conference on Security and Cooperation in Europe that took place in Moscow shortly after an abortive coup there, the C.S.C.E. adopted a declaration roughly comparable to the inter-American Santiago Commitment, calling for a collective response in the event of the overthrow of an elected government in Europe. See C.S.C.E., Document of the Moscow Meeting on the Human Dimension, Oct. 3, 1991, para. 17.2, reprinted in 30 I.L.M. 1670 (1991).

Collective non-recognition and other voluntary O.A.S. sanctions were insufficient to produce a restoration of the legitimate government in Haiti. Much later, the U.N. Security Council adopted a set of compulsory economic sanctions (S.C. Res. 841, June 16, 1993) and eventually authorized a military intervention (S.C. Res. 940, July 31, 1994). See Chapter 12. Was collective non-recognition a proper initial measure of nonforcible response to an illegal situation?

2. U.S. regulations implementing the O.A.S. and U.N. measures denied to the "de facto regime in Haiti" access to Haitian funds or assets in the United States. See Exec. Order 12,775 (Oct. 4, 1991); Exec. Order 12,779 (Oct. 28, 1991); Exec. Order 12,853 (June 30, 1993). These regulations represent a special case of the general practice in the United States (and elsewhere) that executive decisions on recognition of foreign governments are determinative of claims of authority to act on behalf of a foreign state, for such purposes as dealing with state property and bank accounts. On domestic legal consequences of non-recognition in other contexts, see pp. 305–312.

3. Can the collective non-recognition "precedent" in the Haitian case be generalized to other cases of overthrow of elected governments, or to other instances of interference with legitimate authority? Consider the international responses (typically fairly weak) to a variety of roughly comparable situations arising after the Haitian case. What was the relevance, in the Haitian situation, of

the fact that the international community had monitored President Aristide's election? Should a comparable factor (international supervision of an electoral process) have played a role in the international reaction in 1997 to the ouster of one of two Cambodian co-prime ministers in the government formed in 1993 as a result of U.N.-supervised elections? Would non-recognition of an irregular change of government be feasible or meaningful in such circumstances? Cf. Damrosch, Enforcing International Law Through Non–Forcible Measures, 269 Rec. des Cours 151–153 (1997); Roth, Governmental Illegitimacy in International Law (1999).

Should collective non-recognition apply to a putative government that seizes or wields effective power in defiance of a U.N.-sponsored process for political settlement of an internal or regional conflict?

4. In 1996, an Islamic movement known as the Taliban captured the capital of Afghanistan and consolidated its control over more than 90% of Afghan territory. Though a comparable degree of territorial control might well satisfy a strictly "effectivist" test for recognition of a government, most states have not recognized the Taliban as the government of Afghanistan. (As of 2000, it was reported that only three states had done so.) The U.N. General Assembly's credentials committee has not accepted the Taliban as the government of Afghanistan; instead, an alliance of opposition groups holding almost no Afghan territory continued to be accredited for U.N. purposes and held the General Assembly seat as of 2000.

To what extent should the grant or denial of recognition turn on the Taliban's attitude toward internationally protected human rights and fundamental freedoms, such as treatment of women? Measures of extreme repression and discrimination (including prohibitions on employment of women, even by international organizations and humanitarian relief groups operating in Afghan territory) have been part of the Taliban's program. Can withholding of recognition from a government that imposes such policies meaningfully advance international protection of human rights and fundamental freedoms?

In addition to withholding governmental recognition from the Taliban and refraining from engaging in diplomatic relations, the U.S. government designated the Taliban as a terrorist organization in 1999, thereby triggering provisions of U.S. antiterrorism legislation that restrict financial dealings with groups so designated. (As of 2000, however, the state of Afghanistan had not been placed on the Secretary of State's list of state sponsors of terrorism. See Chapter 12 for discussion of U.S. cruise missile attacks on terrorist bases in Afghan territory in 1998.) Do such measures to isolate and delegitimize a regime holding effective power contribute to objectives of world order?

D. UNRECOGNIZED GOVERNMENTS

1. *Capacity of Unrecognized Governments to Bind the State*

THE TINOCO CLAIMS ARBITRATION (GREAT BRITAIN v. COSTA RICA)

OPINION AND AWARD OF WILLIAM HOWARD TAFT, SOLE ARBITRATOR, 1923

1 U.N.Rep. Int'l Arbitral Awards 369, 375 (1923).

[The case involved claims by Great Britain against Costa Rica for acts of a predecessor regime (the Tinoco regime) which had come to power by a coup and maintained itself in control for two years. The Tinoco regime was recognized by some governments but not by many leading powers (including Great Britain and the United States). When the Tinoco regime fell, the restored government nullified all of the Tinoco contracts, including an oil concession to a British company. Great Britain argued that the Tinoco Government was the only government in Costa Rica when the liabilities were created and that its acts could not be repudiated. Costa Rica argued that the Tinoco regime was not a government and that Great Britain was estopped by its non-recognition of Tinoco from claiming that Tinoco could confer rights on British subjects. In discussing the issue of recognition, the Arbitrator, United States Chief Justice Taft, stated:]

The non-recognition by other nations of a government claiming to be a national personality, is usually appropriate evidence that it has not attained the independence and control entitling it by international law to be classed as such. But when recognition *vel non* of a government is by such nations determined by inquiry, not into its *de facto* sovereignty and complete governmental control, but into its illegitimacy or irregularity of origin, their non-recognition loses something of evidential weight on the issue with which those applying the rules of international law are alone concerned. What is true of the non-recognition of the United States in its bearing upon the existence of a *de facto* government under Tinoco for thirty months is probably in a measure true of the non-recognition by her Allies in the European War. Such non-recognition for any reason, however, cannot outweigh the evidence disclosed by this record before me as to the *de facto* character of Tinoco's government, according to the standard set by international law.

Second. It is ably and earnestly argued on behalf of Costa Rica that the Tinoco government cannot be considered a *de facto* government, because it was not established and maintained in accord with the constitution of Costa Rica of 1871. To hold that a government which establishes itself and maintains a peaceful administration, with the acquiescence of the people for a substantial period of time, does not become a *de facto* government unless it conforms to a previous constitution would be to hold that within the rules of international law a revolution contrary to the fundamental law of the existing government cannot establish a new government. This cannot be, and is not, true.

[The Arbitrator rejected the claim of estoppel because Great Britain by non-recognition did not dispute the *de facto* existence of the Tinoco regime and because the successor Government had not been led by British non-recognition to change its position.]

Note

In the *Tinoco* case, the *de facto* regime exercised authority throughout the country. Would the legal situation be different in respect of a *de facto* regime which controlled only a part of the country? The United States–Italian Claims Commission held that Yugoslavia was not liable for acts of the wartime state of Croatia, because Croatia was a puppet regime under German–Italian control and also because it was only a local authority with limited territorial control. Socony Vacuum Oil Co. Case, [1954] Int'l L.Rep. 55; [1956] id. 591.

2. The International Personality of Insurgent Authority in Control of Specific Territory

The category of *de facto* governments may also include organized insurgent groups which exercise governmental authority for a time over part of the territory of a state. Such groups may be regarded as "para-statal entities possessing a definite if limited form of international personality." G.G. Fitzmaurice, [1958] 2 Yb.I.L.C. at 32. Two specific attributes of such "personality" are indicated by state practice. First, the insurgent communities may be recognized as possessing belligerent rights against the *de jure* government and therefore as imposing neutrality on other states. See Lauterpacht, Recognition in International Law 187 (1947). Second, insurgent authorities in control of specific territory have also entered into agreements with governments and have therefore been considered to have treaty-making capacity. See [1958] 2 Yb.I.L.C. at 24. For example the Geneva Agreement of 1954 on the cessation of hostilities in Laos and Cambodia was signed by representatives of insurgent forces in control of some parts of the countries concerned although they were not recognized as de jure governments. However it has been argued that insurgent authorities cannot be "subjects of international law" or parties to treaties unless they represent the state "in the process of formation" and that "[a]ny detachment of insurgents cannot be entitled to such recognition. The treaties concluded with foreign authorities would have the level of a treaty only in a case where these authorities represent the State power, emerging in the course of the people's insurrection, and which is now in the process of formation." Lukashuk, Parties to Treaties—The Right of Participation, 135 Rec. des Cours 280–281 (1972–I). It is evident that this position involves an element of "legitimacy" (as well as prediction) in addition to de facto control. It therefore provides more opportunity for political considerations.

The distinction between *de facto* and *de jure* recognition of insurgents is more than a matter of form; it has significant political and legal consequences. In Lauterpacht's words: "So long as the lawful government offers resistance which is not ostensibly hopeless or purely nominal, the *de jure* recognition of the revolutionary party as a government constitutes premature recognition which the lawful government is entitled to regard as an act of intervention contrary to international law. * * * [It] constitutes a drastic interference with the independence of the State concerned". Lauterpacht, Recognition in International Law 94–95 (1947). This would not be the case for *de facto* recognition. However, *de facto* recognition of an insurgent authority has been considered as sufficient to support (as a matter of international law) sovereign immunity of the *de facto* government in the courts of the state granting such *de facto* (but not *de jure*) recognition. The Arantzazu Mendi [1939] A.C. 256.

Note

An insurgent authority with limited territorial control may nonetheless perform ordinary governmental functions in the area under its authority. It was held by a United States–Mexican Claims Commission in 1926 that the state of Mexico was liable for the acts of a local insurrectionary regime when such acts were of "purely governmental routine"—in the particular case, the sale of money orders. The Commission indicated that other types of acts by an insurrectionary regime would not subject the state to liability unless the *de facto* authority extended over a major portion of the territory of the state and over a majority of its people. Hopkins v. United Mexican States, 4 U.N.Rep. Int'l Arb. Awards 41 (1926). Is there sufficient reason to attribute to the state the responsibility for acts of a local revolutionary group which are of a routine administrative character? Is it justifiable to exclude from such attribution other "governmental acts" by the insurgents such as a contract for munitions or a large concession agreement?

E. UNRECOGNIZED GOVERNMENTS IN MUNICIPAL LAW

1. *The Validity of Acts of an Unrecognized Government*

SALIMOFF & CO. v. STANDARD OIL OF N.Y.

N.Y. Court of Appeals, 1933.
262 N.Y. 220, 186 N.E. 679.

POUND, Ch. J. The Soviet government, by a nationalization decree, confiscated all oil lands in Russia and sold oil extracted therefrom to defendants. The former owners of the property, Russian nationals, join in an equitable action for an accounting on the ground that the confiscatory decrees of the unrecognized Soviet government and the seizure of oil lands thereunder have no other effect in law on the rights of the parties than seizure by bandits. (Luther v. Sagor & Co., [1921] 1 K.B. 456; s.c., 3 K.B. 532; cited in Sokoloff v. National City Bank, 239 N.Y. 158, 164, 145 N.E. 917.) The complaints have been dismissed.

The question is as to the effect on the title of a purchaser from the unrecognized confiscating Soviet Russian government. Does title pass or is the Soviet government no better than a thief, stealing the property of its nationals and giving only a robber's title to stolen property? Plaintiffs contend that the Soviet decrees of confiscation did not divest them of title.

* * *

* * * The oil property confiscated was taken in Russia from Russian nationals. A recovery in conversion is dependent upon the laws of Russia. (Riley v. Pierce Oil Corp., 245 N.Y. 152, 154, 156 N.E. 647.) When no right of action is created at the place of wrong, no recovery in tort can be had in any other State on account of the wrong. The United States government recognizes that the Soviet government has functioned as a de facto or quasi government since 1917, ruling within its borders. It has recognized its existence as a fact although it has refused diplomatic recognition as one might refuse to recognize an objectionable relative although his actual existence could not be denied. It tells us that it has no disposition to ignore the fact that such government is exercising control and power in territory of the former Russian empire. As was said by this court in Sokoloff v. National City Bank (supra, p. 165): "Juridically, a government that is unrecognized may be viewed as no government at all, if the power withholding recognition chooses thus to view it. In practice, however, since juridical conceptions are seldom, if

ever, carried to the limit of their logic, the equivalence is not absolute, but is subject to self-imposed limitations of common sense and fairness, as we learned in litigations following our Civil War."

As a juristic conception, what is Soviet Russia? A band of robbers or a government? We all know that it is a government. The State Department knows it, the courts, the nations and the man on the street. If it is a government in fact, its decrees have force within its borders and over its nationals. "Recognition does not create the state." (Wulfsohn v. Russian S.F.S. Republic, 234 N.Y. 372, 375, 138 N.E. 24, 25.) It simply gives to a de facto state international status. Must the courts say that Soviet Russia is an outlaw and that the Provisional government of Russia as the successor of the Russian Imperial government is still the lawful government of Russia although it is long since dead? * * * The courts may not recognize the Soviet government as the de jure government until the State Department gives the word. They may, however, say that it is a government, maintaining internal peace and order, providing for national defense and the general welfare, carrying on relations with our own government and others. To refuse to recognize that Soviet Russia is a government regulating the internal affairs of the country, is to give to fictions an air of reality which they do not deserve.

Note

Should decrees of a *de facto* government be accepted as valid for transferring assets located in the state of the forum but belonging to an entity subject to the law of the *de facto* government? The New York courts denied extraterritorial effect to Soviet decrees of nationalization prior to recognition of the U.S.S.R. in 1933. Bank deposits in New York of nationalized Soviet banks remained under the control of directors of the banks chartered by the Czarist Government. See Petrogradsky Mejdunarodny Kommerchesky Bank v. National City Bank, 253 N.Y. 23, 170 N.E. 479 (1930). Similarly, the nationalization decrees of the People's Republic of China were denied effect with respect to assets of the Bank of China in the United States as long as that Government was not accorded de *jure* recognition. See Bank of China v. Wells Fargo Bank, 104 F.Supp. 59 (N.D.Cal. 1952), rev'd on other grounds, 209 F.2d 467 (9th Cir.1953).

2. *Municipal Law of Unrecognized Regime*

UPRIGHT v. MERCURY BUSINESS MACHINES CO.

Supreme Court of New York, Appellate Division, 1st Dept., 1961.
13 A.D.2d 36, 213 N.Y.S.2d 417.

BREITEL, JUSTICE PRESIDING. Plaintiff, an individual, sues as the assignee of a trade acceptance drawn on and accepted by defendant in payment for business typewriters sold and delivered to it by a foreign corporation. The trade acceptance is in the amount of $27,307.45 and was assigned to plaintiff after dishonor by defendant.

Involved on this appeal is only the legal sufficiency of the first affirmative defense. It alleges that the foreign corporation is the creature of the East

German Government, a government not recognized by the United States. It alleges, moreover, that such corporation is an enterprise controlled by and that it is an arm and instrument of such government.

On motion addressed to its sufficiency Special Term sustained the defense. For the reasons that follow the defense should have been stricken as legally insufficient * * *.

A foreign government, although not recognized by the political arm of the United States Government, may nevertheless have *de facto* existence which is juridically cognizable. The acts of such a *de facto* government may affect private rights and obligations arising either as a result of activity in, or with persons or corporations within, the territory controlled by such *de facto* government. This is traditional law (Russian Reinsurance Co. v. Stoddard, 240 N.Y. 149, 147 N.E. 703; M. Salimoff & Co. v. Standard Oil Co., 262 N.Y. 220, 186 N.E. 679, 89 A.L.R. 345 * * *.

* * *

So, too, only limited effect is given to the fact that the political arm has not recognized a foreign government. Realistically, the courts apprehend that political nonrecognition may serve only narrow purposes. While the judicial arm obligates itself to follow the suggestions of the political arm in effecting such narrow purposes, nevertheless, it will not exaggerate or compound the consequences required by such narrow purposes in construing rights and obligations affected by the acts of unrecognized governments (Sokoloff v. National City Bank, 239 N.Y. 158, 145 N.E. 917, 37 A.L.R. 712; M. Salimoff & Co. v. Standard Oil Co., supra). * * *

Applying these principles, it is insufficient for defendant merely to allege the nonrecognition of the East German Government and that plaintiffs' assignor was organized by and is an arm and instrumentality of such unrecognized East German Government. The lack of jural status for such government or its creature corporation is not determinative of whether transactions with it will be denied enforcement in American courts, so long as the government is not the suitor.[1] * * *

The extent to which courts will recognize the legal effect of transactions within the territory of an unrecognized government, even where the transaction is materially affected by the action of such government, has been dramatically demonstrated. In M. Salimoff & Co. v. Standard Oil Co., 262 N.Y. 220, 186 N.E. 679, supra, it was held that one who took property by purchase from the unrecognized Russian government which had confiscated such property from its rightful owners nevertheless had good title as against the one-time lawful owners.

* * * [The internal acts of the East German Government, insofar as they concern the parties here, should be given effect generally. At least, this is so in the absence of allegation that defendant's property was expropriated by wrongful governmental force, or that for other reasons the transaction in suit or that directly underlying it violates public or national policy.

1. For, if the unrecognized government were allowed to sue, this would be deemed recognition of jural status (Russian Socialist Federated Soviet Republic v. Cibrario, 235 N.Y. 255, 139 N.E. 259). Note that the corporation perhaps could sue (see United States v. Insurance Companies, 22 Wall. 99, 89 U.S. 99, 22 L.Ed. 816, infra).

This case does not involve the issues, tendered by defendant in its argument, of jural status of the East German corporation, or of its incapacity to transfer title, or even of its capacity to sue in our courts. These have been long recognized as issues to be resolved by reference to the actual facts—the realities of life—occurring in the territory controlled by a *de facto* government, unless, of course, the contemplated juridical consequences of such "facts" can be properly related as inimical to the aims and purposes of our public or national policy [citations omitted]. Even the power of a rebel government in one of the Confederate States to create a corporation with capacity to sue the United States Government was admitted where such creation was not directly in furtherance of the rebellion (United States v. Insurance Companies, 22 Wall. 99, 89 U.S. 99, 22 L.Ed. 816).

* * * There are many things which may occur within the purview of an unrecognized government which are not evil and which will be given customary legal significance in the courts of nations which do not recognize the prevailing *de facto* government. In a time in which governments with established control over territories may be denied recognition for many reasons, it does not mean that the denizens of such territories or the corporate creatures of such powers do not have the juridical capacity to trade, transfer title, or collect the price for the merchandise they sell to outsiders, even in the courts of nonrecognizing nations * * *.

Of course, nonrecognition is a material fact but only a preliminary one. The proper conclusion will depend upon factors in addition to that of nonrecognition. Such is still the case even though an entity involved in the transaction be an arm or instrumentality of the unrecognized government. Thus, in order to exculpate defendant from payment for the merchandise it has received, it would have to allege and prove that the sale upon which the trade acceptance was based, or that the negotiation of the trade acceptance itself, was in violation of public or national policy. Such a defense would constitute one in the nature of illegality and if established would, or at least might, render all that ensued from the infected transaction void and unenforceable. Defendant buyer cannot escape liability merely by alleging and proving that it dealt with a corporation created by and functioning as the arm of and instrumentality of an unrecognized government.

Notes

1. English courts have generally refused to give effect to legislative acts of unrecognized governments and to legal acts pursuant to such laws. They have, for example, declined to recognize Rhodesian divorce decrees emanating from courts under the non-recognized regime of Ian Smith. See Adams v. Adams [1970] 3 A.E.R. 572. However in *Luther v. Sagor,* the English Court of Appeal gave effect to a Soviet confiscation decree of 1918 after receiving a letter from the Foreign Office stating that the British Government recognized the Soviet Government as the "de *facto* Government of Russia." The Court did not regard the distinction between *de facto* and *de jure* recognition as crucial, saying that since the British Government recognized the Soviet Government "as the Government really in possession of the

powers of sovereignty, the acts of that Government must be treated with all the respect due to the acts of a duly recognized foreign sovereign State." Bankes, L.J. [1921] 3 K.B. at 543.

2. *Carl Zeiss Stiftung v. Rayner & Keeler* involved the validity of legislative and administrative acts of the East German Government (German Democratic Republic) which changed the structure of the plaintiff, the Carl Zeiss Stiftung. The Foreign Office certificate said that at the time in question the British Government recognized the Soviet Union as "*de jure* entitled to exercise governmental authority in respect of that zone * * * and have not recognized either *de jure* or *de facto* any other authority * * * in or in respect of that zone." On the basis of that certification, the Court of Appeal held that no effect could be given to the East German acts. The House of Lords reversed, holding that, since the acts of the East German Government were acts of a subordinate body exercising authority under the control of the Soviet Union as the occupying power, those acts were entitled to be regarded as the valid *lex domicilii* of the foundation *(Stiftung)* in question. [1967] 1 A.C. 853. See also Gur Corporation v. Trust Bank of South Africa Ltd., [1987] 1 Q.B. 599. Compare Carl Zeiss Stiftung v. V.E.B. Carl Zeiss, 293 F.Supp. 892 (S.D.N.Y.1968), modified, 433 F.2d 686 (2d Cir.1970), cert. denied, 403 U.S. 905, 91 S.Ct. 2205, 29 L.Ed.2d 680 (1971), in which the courts refused to give effect to the unrecognized East German Government's legislation concerning the Zeiss Foundation, distinguishing between acts of unrecognized governments "dealing solely with private, local and domestic matters," to which effect is given and acts "with respect to matters extending beyond the borders," to which it is not. 293 F.Supp. at 900. This case is cited by the Restatement (Third) in support of § 205(3), which states that "courts in the United States ordinarily give effect to acts * * * of a regime not recognized as the government of a state, if those acts apply to territory under the control of that regime and relate to domestic matters only."

3. *Access to Courts*

The traditional rule generally applied by United States courts has been that an entity not recognized as a state or a regime not recognized as a government of a state cannot institute proceedings in the courts of a foreign state. Restatement (Third) § 205. The U.S. Supreme Court in 1938 explained the principle of denial of access to a non-recognized government by stating that what government is to be regarded as the recognized representative of a foreign sovereign state is a political rather than a judicial question and is to be determined by the political department whose action in recognizing a foreign government is conclusive on all domestic courts. Guaranty Trust Co. of New York v. United States, 304 U.S. 126, 58 S.Ct. 785, 82 L.Ed. 1224 (1938).

In the *Sabbatino* case (p. 181 supra) the Supreme Court observed that the doctrine that non-recognition precluded suit by a foreign government had been much criticized and pointed out that since the precise question was not presented in the case (since Cuba was recognized, though diplomatic relations had been broken), the Court would intimate "no view on the possibility of access by an unrecognized government to United States courts." The severance of diplomatic relations did not imply the withdrawal of recognition and therefore did not preclude access: "It is the refusal to recognize which has a unique legal aspect, signifying this country's unwillingness to acknowledge that the government in question speaks as the sovereign authority for the territory it controls." The Court referred to the "possible incongruity" that would occur if a foreign power not recognized by the executive branch were accorded judicial recognition. 376 U.S. 398, 84 S.Ct. 923, 11 L.Ed.2d 804 (1964).

Loss of recognition may prevent a government from maintaining an action already commenced. See Government of France v. Isbrandtsen–Moller, 48 F.Supp. 631 (S.D.N.Y.1943). In Republic of Vietnam v. Pfizer, Inc., 556 F.2d 892 (8th Cir.1977), the court of appeals affirmed the dismissal of an antitrust suit that had been filed in 1970 by the Republic of Vietnam against several American drug companies. Although the Republic of [South] Vietnam was recognized when the suit was initiated, in 1975 the Republic surrendered to North Vietnam; and in 1976 the territory of the Republic was joined to that of North Vietnam to form a new state, the Socialist Republic of Vietnam. At the time (1976), the United States recognized no government as the sovereign authority in the territory formerly known as South Viet Nam. The District Court dismissed the action on ground that the plaintiff no longer exists and "has not been succeeded by any government, entity or person that has capacity to sue in this court." The Court of Appeals affirmed, noting that the trial court has discretion in deciding whether to suspend or dismiss a suit by a plaintiff whose recognition has been lost. In the circumstances of the case, the dismissal did not constitute an abuse of discretion.

Notes

1. In National Petrochemical Co. of Iran v. M/T Stolt Sheaf, 860 F.2d 551 (2d Cir.1988), a corporation wholly owned by Iran brought suit as a plaintiff in a U.S. federal court. The district court dismissed the claim on the ground that the United States had never extended recognition to the government of the Islamic Republic of Iran and that an entity wholly owned by an unrecognized government is not entitled to bring suit in U.S. courts. On appeal, the U.S. government entered the case as amicus curiae, urging that plaintiff be granted access to the court. In accepting the U.S. government's position, the court of appeals held that "the absence of formal recognition does not necessarily result in a foreign government being barred from access to United States courts:"

> Two reasons support this holding. First, as this century draws to a close, the practice of extending formal recognition to new governments has altered: The United States Department of State has sometimes refrained from announcing recognition of a new government because grants of recognition have been misinterpreted as pronouncements of approval. See 77 State Dep't Bull. 462–63 (Oct. 10, 1977) ("In recent years, U.S. practice has been to deemphasize and avoid the use of recognition in cases of changes of governments * * * "); Restatement 3d s 203, reporter's note 1 (commenting on recent deemphasis of formal recognition). As a result, the absence of formal recognition cannot serve as the touchstone for determining whether the Executive Branch has "recognized" a foreign nation for the purpose of granting that government access to United States courts.
>
> Second, the power to deal with foreign nations outside the bounds of formal recognition is essential to a president's implied power to maintain

international relations. Cf. United States v. Curtiss–Wright Export Corp., 299 U.S. 304, 318–20, 57 S.Ct. 216, 220–21, 81 L.Ed. 255 (1936). As part of this power, the Executive Branch must have the latitude to permit a foreign nation access to U.S. courts, even if that nation is not formally recognized by the U.S. government. This is because the president alone—as the constitutional guardian of foreign policy—knows what action is necessary to effectuate American relations with foreign governments. Cf. Sabbatino, 376 U.S. at 411 n. 12, 84 S.Ct. at 931 n. 12 (citing criticisms of any policy which would mandate formal recognition before a foreign nation could sue in U.S. courts).

This case serves as an excellent example. Relations between the United States and Iran over the past eight years have been less than friendly. Yet, the status of that relationship has not been unchanging. There have been periods of improvement, for example, release of the embassy hostages, and periods of worsening relations, most recently occasioned by the unfortunate downing of an Iranian civilian airliner by the U.S.S. Vincennes. It is evident that in today's topsy-turvy world governments can topple and relationships can change in a moment. The Executive Branch must therefore have broad, unfettered discretion in matters involving such sensitive, fast-changing, and complex foreign relationships. See Guaranty Trust, 304 U.S. at 137, 58 S.Ct. at 791 ("What government is to be regarded here as representative of a foreign sovereign state is a political rather than a judicial question, and is to be determined by the political department of the government."); Sabbatino, 376 U.S. at 410, 84 S.Ct. at 931 ("This Court would hardly be competent to undertake assessments of varying degrees of friendliness or its absence * * * "); Curtiss–Wright, 299 U.S. at 319, 57 S.Ct. at 220 ("In this vast external realm, with its important, complicated, delicate and manifold problems, the President alone has the power to speak or listen as a representative of the nation.").

The court of appeals found persuasive indications of the willingness of the U.S. government to permit the government of Iran to have access to U.S. courts in the context of the overall relationship between the United States and Iran.

2. An unrecognized government cannot bring suit in an English court. Civil law countries generally deny *locus standi* to unrecognized governments. Brownlie, Principles of Public International Law 89 (5th ed. 1998). However, in a few cases appearances by the unrecognized government have been allowed on the theory that the case involved private rather than public law. See cases cited in O'Connell, International Law 181 (2d ed. 1970).

3. Whether non-recognized governments may be defendants depends on their right to assert sovereign immunity. United States courts have taken the position that *de facto* governments in control of a state are entitled to claim sovereign immunity on behalf of the state. See Wulfsohn v. Russian Socialist Federated Soviet Republic, 234 N.Y. 372, 138 N.E. 24 (1923). The traditional rule that a foreign state may not be sued in the courts of another state without its consent must be considered in the light of the U.S. Foreign Sovereign Immunities Act, which requires denial of immunity where commercial activities conducted by the state, its instrumentalities or agents are involved. See Chapter 14 infra.

4. Unrecognized Entities in Other Contexts

Courts sometimes have to determine how to treat an unrecognized entity for purposes of laws referring generally to foreign states, governments, or countries. Particular legislation may clarify the matter, as with the Taiwan

Relations Act, p. 287 supra, which specifies that lack of recognition does not affect Taiwan's eligibility to sue and be sued or to participate in various programs and benefits. Or the executive branch may have made a determination on a matter falling within the President's competence, to which the courts will typically defer. See pp. 232–235 in Chapter 3 for cases giving effect to presidential policies in matters concerning recognition and nonrecognition. Where the legislative or executive position is unclear, however, courts may have to resolve the ambiguity.

In Matimak Trading Co. v. Khalily, 118 F.3d 76 (2d Cir.1997), cert. denied, 522 U.S. 1091, 118 S.Ct. 883, 139 L.Ed.2d 871 (1998), the issue was whether a Hong Kong company qualified as a foreign corporation for purposes of alienage jurisdiction under the federal diversity statute, 28 U.S.C. § 1332(a)(2), which confers jurisdiction over suits between Americans and citizens or subjects of foreign states. The court had to interpret the jurisdictional statute in light of the fact that the U.S. government had not recognized Hong Kong; it concluded that in the absence of executive branch recognition, diversity jurisdiction was unavailable.

In People's Mojahedin Organization of Iran v. Albright, 182 F.3d 17 (D.C.Cir.1999), two groups—the People's Mojahedin Organization of Iran and the Liberation Tigers of Tamil Eelam (LTTE)—invoked statutory procedures to challenge their designation by the Secretary of State as foreign organizations engaging in terrorist activities. One of the organizations, LTTE, claimed that it was not a "foreign organization" within the meaning of the Antiterrorism Act of 1996 but rather was a foreign government. The court observed:

> In any event, the United States replies that a court cannot make the determination the LTTE wants because recognizing foreign states is solely entrusted to the political branches, and the United States has not recognized the LTTE. "Who is the sovereign, de jure or de facto, of a territory, is not a judicial, but a political question, the determination of which by the legislative and executive departments of any government conclusively binds the judges, as well as all other officers, citizens, and subjects of that government." Jones v. United States, 137 U.S. 202, 212–13, 34 L.Ed. 691, 11 S.Ct. 80 (1890). Here, the Secretary determined that the LTTE was a foreign organization and, in the words of the statute, there is "substantial support" for her finding in the materials she has furnished us as an "administrative record."

182 F.3d at 20–21.

In Kadic v. Karadzic, 70 F.3d 232 (2d Cir.1995), defendant was described as "the President of a three-man presidency of the self-proclaimed Bosnian–Serb republic within Bosnia–Herzegovina, sometimes referred to as 'Srpska'." One issue in the case was whether Karadzic should be treated as a head of state who might be immune from judicial jurisdiction (see Chapter 14). The court of appeals concluded that the speculative possibility of future recognition should not create the functional equivalent of immunity from jurisdiction, when the U.S. government had not recognized a Bosnian Serb government or acknowledged Karadzic as a governmental official entitled to any sort of immunity.

F. GOVERNMENTS–IN–EXILE

In contrast to *de facto* governments, governments-in-exile have been accorded *de jure* recognition but lack effective control over the territory of the state. In the past, most governments-in-exile based their claim to authority on continuity with a government which had formerly been in effective control of the state. States that continue to recognize such governments generally did so on the premise that the territory had been illegally occupied and that the legitimate government would be restored to power in the foreseeable future. Several countries occupied by German forces in World War II had exile governments recognized by the United States and the United Kingdom. See Brown, Sovereignty in Exile, 35 A.J.I.L. 666 (1941).

The legal consequences of such *de jure* recognition of governments-in-exile included recognition in municipal law of the control by the exile government of assets in the recognizing state. The recognizing governments also acknowledged the authority of the government-in-exile over its nationals abroad. It was also acknowledged that certain decrees of the government-in-exile applicable to events in the occupied territory would be given effect in the municipal courts of the recognizing states. In a case concerning a wartime decree of the Netherlands government-in-exile to protective possession over securities confiscated by the Nazis in Netherlands, the United States Circuit Court of Appeals upheld the validity of the decree in its application to occupied territory. State of the Netherlands v. Federal Reserve Bank of New York, 201 F.2d 455 (2d Cir.1953).

The decrees of the governments-in-exile were not deprived of legal effect by subsequent *de jure* recognition of another government. In this connection see Gdynia Ameryka Linie v. Boguslawski, [1950] 1 K.B. 157 (1949), affirmed [1951] 1 K.B. 162 (C.A.), affirmed sub nom. Gdynia Ameryka Linie Zeglugowe Spolka Akcyjna v. Boguslawski, [1953] A.C. 11 (1952), in which the plaintiff seamen sought to recover severance pay promised to them on July 3, 1945 by a minister of the Polish government-in-exile in London. The Foreign Secretary certified to the court that the British government had recognized the Polish government-in-exile in London as the government of Poland until midnight, July 5/6, 1945, and thereafter had recognized the new Provisional Government of National Unity (Lublin Government), which had been established June 28, 1945, as the government of Poland. The court held that the recognition of the Lublin Government by England did not operate retroactively to deprive of legal effect acts done in England by the exile government while it was still recognized by England. The court relied in part on the fact that the Polish merchant fleet, including defendant's vessels, was under the effective control of the exile government at the time the promise was made.

The wartime governments-in-exile took part in many international conferences and signed international agreements on behalf of their states. See Marek, Identity and Continuity of States in Public International Law 93–94, 439–40 (1968).

In recent years, governments-in-exile have been formed by movements seeking independence. They have often designated themselves as "provisional governments" and have been accorded recognition as such by sympathetic governments and by international bodies. An early example was the revolutionary "provisional government" of Algeria established in 1958, some years before it achieved control of Algeria. See Fraleigh, The Algerian Revolution as a Case Study in International Law, in The International Law of Civil War 179, (Falk ed., 1971); Bedjaoui, Law and the Algerian Revolution 180 (1961). In 1970, Prince Sihanouk, who had been ousted as head of state in Cambodia, formed a government-in-exile in Peking which was recognized by China and by North Vietnam immediately. For an argument in favor of such recognition, see Barnes, U.S. Recognition Policy and Cambodia, in The Vietnam War and International Law, vol. 3, 149, 156 (Falk ed., 1972).

Notes

1. "National liberation movements" have generally refrained from establishing themselves as governments-in-exile. Many such "liberation movements" have been accredited to international bodies within the United Nations and regional organizations such as the Organization of African Unity. What reasons may have led them to refrain from establishing a government-in-exile in a sympathetic state?

2. Can governments-in-exile be a means to promote basic political, civil and other human rights? Two commentators have suggested that the institution of governments-in-exile "provides dissident groups with an opportunity to organize, to seek international scrutiny of the conditions within a state, and to provide alternative symbols for individuals within the state to identify with. * * * [I]t provides repositories of responsibility for the acts of regular or irregular forces of the exile government. * * * We suggest that claims for recognition * * * be granted in all those cases in which aspirant status within the state in question is denied or in which real political activity is severely sanctioned." Reisman & Suzuki, Recognition and Social Change in International Law, in Toward World Order and Human Dignity at 430 (Reisman & Weston eds., 1976). Does past experience show that such exile governments can serve the aims listed? What problems would such recognition by foreign states create?

Consider the governments-in-exile of Lithuania, Estonia, and Latvia which continued to be recognized by the United States and the United Kingdom notwithstanding the incorporation of those states in the Soviet Union. See p. 255, note 1.

G. TERMINATION OF RECOGNITION

STATEMENT OF THE UNITED STATES ON WITHDRAWAL OF RECOGNITION FROM GOVERNMENT OF THE REPUBLIC OF CHINA (TAIWAN)

80 Dep't State Bull. 26 (1979).

As of January 1, 1979, the United States of America recognizes the People's Republic of China as the sole legal government of China. On the same date, the People's Republic of China accords similar recognition to the United States of America. The United States thereby establishes diplomatic relations with the People's Republic of China.

On that same date, January 1, 1979, the United States of America will notify Taiwan that it is terminating diplomatic relations and that the Mutual

Defense Treaty between the United States and the Republic of China is being terminated in accordance with the provisions of the Treaty. The United States also states that it will be withdrawing its remaining military personnel from Taiwan within four months.

In the future, the American people and the people of Taiwan will maintain commercial, cultural, and other relations without official government representation and without diplomatic relations.

The Administration will seek adjustments to our laws and regulations to permit the maintenance of commercial, cultural, and other nongovernmental relationships in the new circumstances that will exist after normalization.

Notes

1. "A state derecognizes a regime when it recognizes another regime as the government. * * * Derecognition of one regime as the government without recognition of another regime has been rare. * * * [A] state may derecognize a regime without formally recognizing another, but any regime in effective control must be treated as the government." Restatement (Third) § 203, Comment *f*. So long as a state, as distinguished from its government, continues to meet the qualifications of statehood, its status as a state cannot be "derecognized."

2. If an entity ceases to possess the qualifications of statehood, it ceases to be a state and derecognition is unnecessary. Restatement (Third) § 202, Comment *g*. For example, derecognition of the German Democratic Republic was unnecessary when it was absorbed into the Federal Republic of Germany by accession to the Basic Law of the Federal Republic on October 3, 1990.

3. Recognition and derecognition of governments were at issue in the treatment of Cambodia (Kampuchea) by states and international organizations. Between 1975 and 1979, the Cambodian government under the Khmer Rouge regime of Pol Pot carried out a reign of terror that resulted in the deaths of some one million Cambodians. In 1979, Vietnam invaded Cambodia and set up a Vietnamese-dominated government. The United Nations refused to accept the credentials of the Vietnamese-installed government, and the U.N. seat was for some years held by representatives affiliated with the previous regime. Some states (e.g. Australia) reacted to this situation by derecognizing the Pol Pot regime and refusing to recognize any Cambodian government. See Australian statement on derecognition in 10 Austral. Yb.I.L. 263–264 (1987), quoted in Cassese, Self–Determination, at 97 n. 95 (1995).

SECTION 5. ACQUISITION OF TERRITORIAL SOVEREIGNTY

As discussed in Section 1, in order to qualify as a state, an entity must have a defined territory. Sovereignty over a specific territorial area is therefore an essential element of statehood.

There is obviously no question as to which states have acquired sovereignty over the great bulk of the earth's habitable territory, and some of the issues presented in connection with acquisition of sovereignty over territory are of more historical than contemporary significance. Nonetheless scores of controversies as to sovereignty over territory remain, including issues as to what state should be regarded as exercising sovereignty over certain islands, land areas subject to boundary disputes, and polar regions. For example, there has been a dispute between Iran and the United Arab Emirates over the islands of Abu Musa and Greater and Lesser Tunb near the Strait of Hormuz at the entrance to the Persian Gulf through which 20 percent of the world's oil is transported. Sovereignty over the northern Kurile Islands seized by the Soviet Union at the end of World War II remains in dispute between Russia and Japan. Pursuant to one of the conditions of the U.N. Security Council-supervised cease-fire ending the 1991 Persian Gulf War, the demarcation of the land frontier between Iraq and Kuwait under a 1963 agreement was handled by a special commission in the 1990s.

Longrunning disputes over territorial sovereignty have frequently escalated into armed conflict, as with the Falklands war between Argentina and the United Kingdom in 1982, the Ecuador–Peru conflict that erupted in 1995, and the fighting between Eritrea and Ethiopia in 1999. Conversely, settlement of territorial disputes on the basis of law can help the parties toward peaceful solutions. Many international arbitrations and adjudications have applied the international legal principles governing the acquisition of sovereignty over territory. This section examines those principles.

A. BASIC PRINCIPLES

ISLAND OF PALMAS CASE (UNITED STATES v. THE NETHERLANDS)

Permanent Court of Arbitration, 1928.
2 U.N. Rep. Int'l Arb. Awards 829.

[Palmas (also known as Miangas) is an isolated island of less than two square miles in area, lying about half way between Mindanao in the Philippine Islands and the most northerly of the Nanusa group in the former Dutch East Indies. It lies within the boundaries of the Philippines as ceded by Spain to the United States in 1898 by the Treaty of Paris. United States authorities learned in 1906 that the island was considered by the Netherlands to form a part of the Dutch possessions in that part of the world. After diplomatic correspondence, the United States and the Netherlands agreed in 1925 to submit to a member of the Permanent Court of Arbitration the question "whether the Island of Palmas (or Miangas) in its entirety forms a part of territory belonging to the United States of America or of Netherlands territory." The parties designated as sole arbitrator the Swiss jurist, Max Huber, who delivered his award on April 4, 1928.]

HUBER, Arbitrator: * * * The *United States,* as successor to the rights of Spain over the Philippines, bases its title in the first place on discovery. * * *

The Netherlands Government's main argument endeavours to show that the Netherlands, represented for this purpose in the first period of colonization by the East India Company, have possessed and exercised rights of sovereignty from 1677, or probably from a date prior even to 1648, to the present day. * * *

* * * [A]n element which is essential for the constitution of sovereignty should not be lacking in its continuation. So true is this, that practice, as well as doctrine, recognizes—though under different legal formulae and with certain differences as to the conditions required—that the continuous and peaceful display of territorial sovereignty (peaceful in relation to other States) is as good as a title. The growing insistence with which international law, ever since the middle of the 18th century, has demanded that the occupation shall be effective would be inconceivable, if effectiveness were required only for the act of acquisition and not equally for the maintenance of the right. If the effectiveness has above all been insisted on in regard to occupation, this is because the question rarely arises in connection with territories in which there is already an established order of things.

Territorial sovereignty, as has already been said, involves the exclusive right to display the activities of a State. This right has as corollary a duty: the obligation to protect within the territory the rights of other States, in particular their right to integrity and inviolability in peace and in war, together with the rights which each State may claim for its nationals in foreign territory. Without manifesting its territorial sovereignty in a manner corresponding to circumstances, the State cannot fulfill this duty. Territorial sovereignty cannot limit itself to its negative side, i.e. to excluding the activities of other States; for it serves to divide between nations the space upon which human activities are employed, in order to assure them at all points the minimum of protection of which international law is the guardian. * * *

Manifestations of territorial sovereignty assume, it is true, different forms, according to conditions of time and place. Although continuous in principle, sovereignty cannot be exercised in fact at every moment on every point of a territory. The intermittence and discontinuity compatible with the maintenance of the right necessarily differ according as inhabited or uninhabited regions are involved, or regions enclosed within territories in which sovereignty is incontestably displayed or again regions accessible from, for instance, the high seas. * * *

It is admitted by both sides that international law underwent profound modifications between the end of the Middle–Ages and the end of the 19th century, as regards the rights of discovery and acquisition of uninhabited regions or regions inhabited by savages or semi-civilised peoples. Both Parties are also agreed that a juridical fact must be appreciated in the light of the law contemporary with it, and not of the law in force at the time when a dispute in regard to it arises or fails to be settled. The effect of discovery by Spain is therefore to be determined by the rules of international law in force in the first half of the 16th century * * *

If the view most favourable to the American arguments is adopted—with every reservation as to the soundness of such view—that is to say, if we consider as positive law at the period in question the rule that discovery as such, i.e. the mere fact of seeing land, without any act, even symbolical, of taking possession, involved *ipso jure* territorial sovereignty and not merely an "inchoate title", a *jus ad rem,* to be completed eventually by an actual and durable taking of possession within a reasonable time, the question arises whether sovereignty yet existed at the critical date, i.e. the moment of conclusion and coming into force of the Treaty of Paris.

As regards the question which of different legal systems prevailing at successive periods is to be applied in a particular case (the so-called intertemporal law), a distinction must be made between the creation of rights and the existence of rights. The same principle which subjects the act creative of a right to the law in force at the time the right arises, demands that the existence of the right, in other words its continued manifestation, shall follow the conditions required by the evolution of law. International law in the 19th century, having regard to the fact that most parts of the globe were under the sovereignty of States members of the community of nations, and that territories without a master had become relatively few, took account of a tendency already existing and especially developed since the middle of the 18th century, and laid down the principle that occupation, to constitute a claim to territorial sovereignty, must be effective, that is, offer certain guarantees to other States and their nationals. It seems therefore incompatible with this rule of positive law that there should be regions which are neither under the effective sovereignty of a State, nor without a master, but which are reserved for the exclusive influence of one State, in virtue solely of a title of acquisition which is no longer recognized by existing law, even if such a title ever conferred territorial sovereignty. For these reasons, discovery alone, without any subsequent act, cannot at the present time suffice to prove sovereignty over the Island of Palmas (or Miangas); and in so far as there is no sovereignty, the question of an abandonment properly speaking of sovereignty by one State in order that the sovereignty of another may take its place does not arise.

If on the other hand the view is adopted that discovery does not create a definitive title of sovereignty, but only an "inchoate" title, such a title exists, it is true, without external manifestation. However, according to the view that has prevailed at any rate since the 19th century, an inchoate title of discovery must be completed within a reasonable period by the effective occupation of the region claimed to be discovered. This principle must be applied in the present case, for the reasons given above in regard to the rules determining which of successive legal systems is to be applied (the so-called intertemporal law). Now, no act of occupation nor, except as to a recent period, any exercise of sovereignty at Palmas by Spain has been alleged. But even admitting that the Spanish title still existed as inchoate in 1898 and must be considered as included in the cession under Article III of the Treaty of Paris, an inchoate title could not prevail over the continuous and peaceful display of authority by another State; for such display may prevail even over a prior, definitive title put forward by another State. * * *

In the last place there remains to be considered *title arising out of contiguity.* Although States have in certain circumstances maintained that islands relatively close to their shores belonged to them in virtue of their geographical situation, it is impossible to show the existence of a rule of positive international law to the effect that islands situated outside territorial waters should belong to a State from the mere fact that its territory forms the *terra firma* (nearest continent or island of considerable size). * * *

The Netherlands' arguments contend that the East India Company established Dutch sovereignty over the Island of Palmas (or Miangas) as early as the 17th century, by means of conventions with the princes of Tabukan (Taboekan) and Taruna (Taroena), two native chieftains of the Island of Sangi (Groot Sangihe), the principal island of the Talautse Isles (Sangi Islands), and that sovereignty has been displayed during the past two centuries.

* * *

* * * The questions to be solved in the present case are the following: *Was the island of Palmas (or Miangas) in 1898 a part of territory under Netherlands' sovereignty?*

Did this sovereignty actually exist in 1898 in regard to Palmas (or Miangas) and are the facts proved which were alleged on this subject? * * *

* * * Since the contract of 1885 with Taruna and that of 1899 with Kandahar–Taruna comprise Palmas (or Miangas) within the territories of a native State under the suzerainty of the Netherlands and since it has been established that in 1906 on the said island a state of things existed showing at least certain traces of display of Netherlands sovereignty, it is now necessary to examine what is the nature of the facts invoked as proving such sovereignty, and to what periods such facts relate. This examination will show whether or not the Netherlands have displayed sovereignty over the Island of Palmas (or Miangas) in an effective continuous and peaceful manner at a period at which such exercise may have excluded the acquisition of sovereignty, or a title to such acquisition, by the United States of America. * * *

[After a detailed examination of the acts of the Dutch East India Company and the Netherlands State tending to establish a display of sovereignty over the Island of Palmas, the arbitrator continued:]

The claim of the United States to sovereignty over the Island of Palmas (or Miangas) is derived from Spain by way of cession under the Treaty of Paris. The latter Treaty, though it comprises the island in dispute within the limits of cession, and in spite of the absence of any reserves or protest by the Netherlands as to these limits, has not created in favour of the United States any title of sovereignty such as was not already vested in Spain. The essential point is therefore to decide whether Spain had sovereignty over Palmas (or Miangas) at the time of the coming into force of the Treaty of Paris. * * *

The acts of indirect or direct display of Netherlands sovereignty at Palmas (or Miangas), especially in the 18th and early 19th centuries are not numerous, and there are considerable gaps in the evidence of continuous display. But apart from the consideration that the manifestations of sovereignty over a small and distant island, inhabited only by natives, cannot be expected to be frequent, it is not necessary that the display of sovereignty should go back to a very far distant period. It may suffice that such display existed in 1898, and had already existed as continuous and peaceful before that date long enough to enable any Power who might have considered herself as possessing sovereignty over the island, or having a claim to sovereignty, to have, according to local conditions, a reasonable possibility for ascertaining the existence of a state of things contrary to her real or alleged rights.

It is not necessary that the display of sovereignty should be established as having begun at a precise epoch; it suffices that it had existed at the critical period preceding the year 1898. It is quite natural that the establishment of sovereignty may be the outcome of a slow evolution, of a progressive intensification of State control. This is particularly the case, if sovereignty is acquired by the establishment of the suzerainty of a colonial Power over a native State, and in regard to outlying possessions of such a vassal State.

Now the evidence relating to the period after the middle of the 19th century makes it clear that the Netherlands Indian Government considered the island distinctly as a part of its possessions and that, in the years immediately preceding 1898, an intensification of display of sovereignty took place.

Since the moment when the Spaniards, in withdrawing from the Moluccas in 1666, made express reservations as to the maintenance of their sovereign rights, up to the contestation made by the United States in 1906, no contestation or other action whatever or protest against the exercise of territorial rights by the Netherlands over the Talautse (Sangi) Isles and their dependencies (Miangas included) has been recorded. The peaceful character of the display of Netherlands sovereignty for the entire period to which the evidence concerning acts of display relates (1700–1906) must be admitted.

* * *

The *conditions* of acquisition of sovereignty by the Netherlands are therefore to be considered as fulfilled. It remains now to be seen whether the United States as successors of Spain are in a position to bring forward an equivalent or stronger title. This is to be answered in the negative.

The title of discovery, if it had not been already disposed of by the Treaties of Munster and Utrecht would, under the most favourable and most extensive interpretation, exist only as an inchoate title, as a claim to establish sovereignty by effective occupation. An inchoate title however cannot prevail over a definite title founded on continuous and peaceful display of sovereignty.

The title of contiguity, understood as a basis of territorial sovereignty, has no foundation in international law. * * *

The Netherlands title of sovereignty, acquired by continuous and peaceful display of State authority during a long period of time going probably back beyond the year 1700, therefore holds good. * * *

Notes

1. Pursuant to General Assembly resolution 3292 (XXIX), the I.C.J. rendered an advisory opinion in the *Western Sahara Case,* 1975 I.C.J. 12, on two questions affecting the legal status of the Western Sahara. Question I was whether the Western Sahara (Rio de Oro and Sakiet El Hamra) was *terra nullius* at the time of its colonization by Spain. In concluding it was not, the Court stated, 1975 I.C.J. at 38–39:

> 77. In the view of the Court, for the purposes of the present Opinion, "the time of colonization by Spain" may be considered as the period beginning in 1884, when Spain proclaimed a protectorate over the Rio de Oro [on the basis of agreements entered into with the chiefs of local tribes]. * * *
>
> 79. Turning to Question I, the Court observes that the request specifically locates the question in the context of "the time of colonization by

Spain", and it therefore seems clear that the words "Was Western Sahara * * * a territory belonging to no one *(terra nullius)*?" have to be interpreted by reference to the law in force at that period. The expression *"terra nullius"* was a legal term of art employed in connection with "occupation" as one of the accepted legal methods of acquiring sovereignty over territory. "Occupation" being legally an original means of peaceably acquiring sovereignty over territory otherwise than by cession or succession, it was a cardinal condition of a valid "occupation" that the territory should be *terra nullius*—a territory belonging to no-one at the time of the act alleged to constitute the "occupation" (cf. Legal Status of Eastern Greenland, P.C.I.J., Series A/B, No. 53, pp. 44 f. and 63 f.). In the view of the Court, therefore, a determination that Western Sahara was a *"terra nullius"* at the time of colonization by Spain would be possible only if it were established that at that time the territory belonged to no-one in the sense that it was then open to acquisition through the legal process of "occupation".

80. Whatever differences of opinion there may have been among jurists, the State practice of the relevant period indicates that territories inhabited by tribes or peoples having a social and political organization were not regarded as *terra nullius*. It shows that in the case of such territories the acquisition of sovereignty was not generally considered as effected unilaterally through "occupation" of *terra nullius* by original title but through agreements concluded with local rulers. On occasion, it is true, the word "occupation" was used in a non-technical sense denoting simply acquisition of sovereignty; but that did not signify that the acquisition of sovereignty through such agreements with authorities of the country was regarded as an "occupation" of a *"terra nullius"* in the proper sense of these terms. On the contrary, such agreements with local rulers, whether or not considered as an actual "cession" of the territory, were regarded as derivative roots of title, and not original titles obtained by occupation of *terra nullius*.

81. In the present instance, the information furnished to the Court shows that at the time of colonization Western Sahara was inhabited by peoples which, if nomadic, were socially and politically organized in tribes and under chiefs competent to represent them. * * *

Can the Court's view that the Western Sahara was not *terra nullius* because it was inhabited by socially and politically organized tribes be squared with the conclusion of the Permanent Court of Arbitration in the *Island of Palmas Case* that the Netherlands could acquire sovereignty over Palmas by "occupation," when Palmas was inhabited by natives who presumably were also to some extent socially and politically organized? For a critique of the advisory opinion on the *terra nullius* issue see Smith, Sovereignty over Unoccupied Territories—The Western Sahara Decision, 9 Case W.Res. J.Int'l L. 135–143 (1977). Consider the following comment of the author (footnotes omitted):

> If a territory is not *terra nullius,* the result is that some politically organized group must be exercising traditional acts of sovereignty in relation to it. If those traditional acts include, as the court in the *Island of Palmas* case indicates, the right to exclude the activities of other States, as well as the ability to protect the rights of other nationals in the territory, then the Western Sahara Court would be hard-pressed to name the party displaying these acts of sovereignty in Western Sahara. * * * [T]he Court in the *Island of Palmas* case defines sovereignty in such a way as to disqualify all of the parties with an interest in Western Sahara. * * *

> Indeed, Morocco and Mauritania are disqualified because of the Court's determination later in the opinion that they lacked sufficient ties of territorial sovereignty *[sic]* to Western Sahara. The burden similarly cannot be placed on the tribes of Western Sahara simply because they were incapable of exercising the acts of sovereignty required by the *Palmas* decision over the vast majority of the territory. Thus, the Court's conclusion that Western Sahara was not *terra nullius* in 1884 is not consistent with the fact that there was no country or group of individuals in a position to occupy the territory at that time.

Id. at pp. 140–141. The author also suggests that the strongest argument in support of the position that the Western Sahara was not *terra nullius* is that Spain did not proceed on the basis that it was establishing sovereignty over *terra nullius,* but claimed a protectorate over Rio de Oro on the basis of agreements entered into with chiefs of the local tribes. Id. at 141–143. Note, however, the initiation of the claim of The Netherlands to sovereignty over the Island of Palmas was also based on agreements with native chieftains. What does the Court in *Western Sahara* mean when it says that such agreements with local leaders were regarded as "derivative roots of title, and not original titles obtained by occupation of *terra nullius"?*

2. How "effective" does the Dutch occupation of Palmas seem to have been? Could it be said that "effectiveness was established negatively from the absence of any competing manifestations of sovereignty, and that it was only because the Netherlands had taken more interest in the Island than Spain that it was adjudged entitled?" 1 O'Connell 472. On the problem of "effectiveness" of occupation, compare the *Eastern Greenland Case,* p. 323 infra and the *Clipperton Island* arbitration, 2 U.N.Rep. Int'l Arb. Awards 1105, 26 A.J.I.L. 390 (1931), in which France was held entitled to sovereignty over a small unpopulated guano island situated in the Pacific Ocean about 670 miles southwest of Mexico. The French claim was based on the fact that a French naval officer had in 1858 cruised to the island, proclaimed French sovereignty, made detailed geographic notes, and landed some members of his crew. The party left no sign of sovereignty on the island, but notified French and Hawaiian officials in Honolulu, and had a declaration of sovereignty published in a Honolulu journal. No further action was taken by France or any other state until 1897, when France protested to the United States the presence on the island of three persons who had raised an American flag at the approach of a French vessel. The United States disclaimed in 1898 any interest in the island, but meanwhile Mexico had sent a gunboat to the island and had had the Mexican flag raised. Mexico claimed that it had always enjoyed sovereignty over Clipperton by virtue of Spanish discovery, or in the alternative, that the French "occupation" from 1858 to 1897 had been ineffective and that the island was in 1897 *terra nullius.* The Arbitrator held that Spanish discovery had not been proved, nor had Spanish exercise of sovereign rights; the island was therefore capable of appropriation in 1858. Turning to the question whether France had effectively occupied the island, the Arbitrator held that although the exercise of effective, exclusive authority ordinarily required the establishment of an administration capable of securing respect for the sovereign's rights, this was not necessary in the case of uninhabited territory which is at the occupying state's absolute and undisputed disposition from the latter's first appearance. Should the *Clipperton Island Case* be limited to situations closely paralleling its facts; i.e., small unpopulated islands? Compare the materials on the polar regions, p. 1564 infra.

3. On April 2, 1924, Secretary of State Hughes wrote to the Norwegian Minister, H.H. Bryn, in regard to the legal effect of Amundsen's explorations in the Antarctic:

> In the penultimate paragraph of your letter you state that, in order to avoid any misunderstanding, you would add that possession of all the land which Mr. Amundsen may discover will, of course, be taken in the name of His Majesty, the King of Norway. In my opinion rights similar to those which in earlier centuries were based upon the acts of a discoverer, followed by occupation or settlement consummated at long and uncertain periods thereafter, are not capable of being acquired at the present time. Today, if an explorer is able to ascertain the existence of lands still unknown to civilization, his act of so-called discovery, coupled with a formal taking of possession, would have no significance, save as he might herald the advent of the settler; and where for climatic or other reasons actual settlement would be an impossibility, as in the case of the Polar regions, such conduct on his part would afford frail support for a reasonable claim of sovereignty. * * *

The Norwegian Minister replied on November 12, 1924, that the Norwegian Government did not intend "to invoke a possible discovery of new land as a basis for a claim to sovereignty. It only meant that the Norwegian Government claimed the right to priority in acquiring subsequently the sovereignty by settlement or by other procedure sanctioned by International Law." Both notes are quoted in 1 Hackworth 399–400. For further discussion of the issues related to acquisition of sovereignty over the Antarctic, see p. 1570 infra.

4. What is the significance of the rule of "intertemporal law" as articulated by the Arbitrator in the principal case? Is it a just criticism of this formulation that it would require every state constantly to examine its title to each portion of its territory "in order to determine whether a change in the law had necessitated, as it were, a reacquisition?" Jessup, The Palmas Island Arbitration, 22 A.J.I.L. 735, 740 (1928). See also de Visscher, Theory and Reality in Public International Law 211–12 (rev. ed. Corbett trans. 1968).

LEGAL STATUS OF EASTERN GREENLAND CASE (DENMARK v. NORWAY)

Permanent Court of International Justice, 1933.
P.C.I.J., Ser. A/B, No. 53, 3 Hudson, World Ct. Rep. 148.

[A Norwegian proclamation of 1931 purported to place portions of Eastern Greenland under Norwegian sovereignty, on the theory that the territory was *terra nullius,* rather than Danish territory. Denmark thereupon instituted proceedings against Norway in the Permanent Court of International Justice, both states being bound by the "optional clause" of the Court's Statute, asking that the Court declare the Norwegian decree invalid.

[The Court first discussed the history of Greenland, as well as the history of the Danish and Norwegian monarchies, noting that the crowns of the two countries had been united from 1380 to 1814 A.D. By the Treaty of Kiel of 1814, the King of Denmark ceded to Sweden the Kingdom of Norway, excluding, however, his rights in Greenland and other territories.]

The first Danish argument is that the Norwegian occupation of part of the East coast of Greenland is invalid because Denmark has claimed and exercised sovereign rights over Greenland as a whole for a long time and has obtained thereby a valid title to sovereignty. The date at which such Danish sovereignty must have existed in order to render the Norwegian occupation invalid is the date at which the occupation took place, viz., July 10th, 1931.

The Danish claim is not founded upon any particular act of occupation but alleges—to use the phrase employed in the Palmas Island decision of the Permanent Court of Arbitration, April 4th, 1928—a title "founded on the peaceful and continuous display of State authority over the island". It is based upon the view that Denmark now enjoys all the rights which the King of Denmark and Norway enjoyed over Greenland up till 1814. Both the existence and the extent of these rights must therefore be considered, as well as the Danish claim to sovereignty since that date.

It must be borne in mind, however, that as the critical date is July 10th, 1931, it is not necessary that sovereignty over Greenland should have existed throughout the period during which the Danish Government maintains that it was in being. Even if the material submitted to the Court might be thought insufficient to establish the existence of that sovereignty during the earlier periods, this would not exclude a finding that it is sufficient to establish a valid title in the period immediately preceding the occupation.

Before proceeding to consider in detail the evidence submitted to the Court, it may be well to state that a claim to sovereignty based not upon some particular act or title such as a treaty of cession but merely upon continued display of authority, involves two elements each of which must be shown to exist: the intention and will to act as sovereign, and some actual exercise or display of such authority.

Another circumstance which must be taken into account by any tribunal which has to adjudicate upon a claim to sovereignty over a particular territory, is the extent to which the sovereignty is also claimed by some other Power. In most of the cases involving claims to territorial sovereignty which have come before an international tribunal, there have been two competing claims to the sovereignty, and the tribunal has had to decide which of the two is the stronger. One of the peculiar features of the present case is that up to 1931 there was no claim by any Power other than Denmark to the sovereignty over Greenland. Indeed, up till 1921, no Power disputed the Danish claim to sovereignty.

It is impossible to read the records of the decisions in cases as to territorial sovereignty without observing that in many cases the tribunal has been satisfied with very little in the way of the actual exercise of sovereign rights, provided that the other State could not make out a superior claim. This is particularly true in the case of claims to sovereignty over areas in thinly populated or unsettled countries.

[The Court described the establishment of Nordic colonies in Greenland as early as the 10th century, and acknowledgments by these colonies of the sovereignty of the King of Norway. It then held that, although the original colonies disappeared at an early date, there was no abandonment by the King of his rights in Greenland. The Court then noted that a re-awakening of interest in Greenland during the 18th century led to the re-establishment of colonies in 1721, and that thereafter there was "a manifestation and exercise of sovereign rights." The Court rejected Norway's contention that in the legislative and administrative acts of the 18th century the term "Greenland" was not used in the geographic sense but only in reference to the colonized areas of western Greenland. As evidence supporting this conclusion, the Court relied on Danish treaties in which the other contracting party had agreed to the exclusion of Greenland from the scope of the treaty: this showed, said the Court, "a willingness on the part of the States with which Denmark has contracted to admit her right to exclude Greenland. * * * To the extent that these treaties constitute evidence of recognition of her sovereignty over Greenland in general, Denmark is entitled to rely upon them." After discussing Danish activity in Greenland from 1814 to 1915, the Court summarized:]

In view of the above facts, when taken in conjunction with the legislation she had enacted applicable to Greenland generally, the numerous treaties in which Denmark, with the concurrence of the other contracting Party, provided for the non-application of the treaty to Greenland in general, and the absence of all claim to sovereignty over Greenland by any other Power, Denmark must be regarded as having displayed during this period of 1814 to 1915 her authority over the uncolonized part of the country to a degree sufficient to confer a valid title to the sovereignty.

[The Court then discussed the effect of various communications which Denmark had addressed to other states between 1915 and 1921, asking recognition of Denmark's rights in Greenland, and rejected the Norwegian contentions that Denmark thereby admitted that it possessed no sovereignty over uncolonized parts of Greenland and that it was "estopped" from claiming a long-established sovereignty over the whole island.]

The period subsequent to the date when the Danish Government issued the Decree of May 10th, 1921, referred to above, witnessed a considerable increase in the activity of the Danish Government on the eastern coast of Greenland. * * *

Even if the period from 1921 to July 10th, 1931, is taken by itself and without reference to the preceding periods, the conclusion reached by the Court is that during this time Denmark regarded herself as possessing sovereignty over all Greenland and displayed and exercised her sovereign rights to an extent sufficient to constitute a valid title to sovereignty. When considered in conjunction with the facts of the preceding periods, the case in favour of Denmark is confirmed and strengthened.

It follows from the above that the Court is satisfied that Denmark has succeeded in establishing her contention that at the critical date, namely, July 10th, 1931, she possessed a valid title to the sovereignty over all Greenland.

This finding constitutes by itself sufficient reason for holding that the occupation of July 10th, 1931, and any steps taken in this connection by the Norwegian Government, were illegal and invalid.

[The Court also held, as separate and independent grounds for its conclusion, that: (1) Norway had "debarred herself from contesting Danish sovereignty over the whole of Greenland" by becoming a party to various bilateral and multilateral agreements in which Greenland had been described as Danish or in which Denmark had excluded Greenland from the operation of the agreement, and (2) Norway had given express undertakings to the Danish government by which it promised not to contest Danish sovereignty over the whole of Greenland. * * *]

Notes

1. As understood by the Court, were the numerous recognitions by *third states* of Denmark's sovereignty in Greenland mere evidence of Danish sovereignty or an actual element in the root of title? Would recognition by these third states without prior Danish occupation of parts of Greenland have aided Denmark in its claim? In the *Island of Palmas* arbitration, supra, did Spanish acquiescence in Dutch pretensions of sovereignty over the island amount, in the Arbitrator's view, to mere evidence of Dutch sovereignty or to an actual element in establishing the existence of sovereignty? Did the basis on which the Arbitrator found the island to be Dutch differ from that on which Danish sovereignty was found over Greenland? See generally Jennings, The Acquisition of Territory in International Law 36–41 (1963). If Spain could have been shown to have recognized Dutch sovereignty over Palmas, as Norway was held to have recognized Danish sovereignty in the *Eastern Greenland Case,* would Spain (and therefore the United States) have been "estopped" from contesting the rights of the Netherlands in the island? See Jennings at 41–43; McNair, The Law of Treaties 487 (1962).

2. For comment on the *Eastern Greenland Case,* see Preuss, The Dispute Between Denmark and Norway over the Sovereignty of East Greenland, 26 A.J.I.L. 469 (1932); Hyde, The Case Concerning the Legal Status of Greenland, 27 A.J.I.L. 732 (1933). For discussion of the formation of rules of international law relating to the acquisition of sovereignty over territory, see Schwarzenberger, Title to Territory: Response to a Challenge, 51 A.J.I.L. 308 (1957). Questions of treaty interpretation often affect sovereignty over territory. See the Case Concerning the Temple of Preah Vihear (Cambodia v. Thailand), 1962 I.C.J. 6; Johnson, The Case Concerning the Temple of Preah Vihear, 11 I.C.L.Q. 1183 (1962); and the Case Concerning Kasikili/Sedudu Island (Botswana/Namibia), 1999 I.C.J., p. 327 infra.

3. Disputes have arisen over the sovereignty to various small islands dotting the oceans. Although sovereignty over many has not been claimed, strategic location and possible oil and mineral reserves enhance their current attractiveness. The Spratly and Paracel Islands in the South China Sea have been claimed by Vietnam, China and the Philippines. For analysis of these claims, see Park, The South China Sea Disputes: Who Owns the Islands and the Natural Resources?, 5 Ocean Dev. & Int'l L.J. 27 (1978); Chiu & Park, Legal Status of the Parcel and Spratly Islands, 3 Ocean Dev. & Int'l L.J. 1 (1975–76); Cheng, Dispute over the South China Sea Islands, 10 Tex. Int'l L.J. 265 (1975); Clagett, Competing Claims of Vietnam and China in the Vanguard Bank and Blue Dragon Areas of the South China Sea, 13 Oil & Gas L. & Tax'n Rev. 375 (1995). Similarly, Japan and China dispute the sovereignty over the Senkaku Islands in the East China Sea. See Cheng, The Sino–Japanese Dispute Over the Tiao-yu-tai (Senkaku) Islands and the Law of Territorial Acquisition, 14 Va.J.Int'l L. 221 (1971); Charney, Central East Asian Maritime Boundaries and the Law of the Sea, 89 A.J.I.L. 724 (1995); Kim Young–Koo (ed.), Maritime Boundary Issues and Islands Disputes in the East Asian Region (1998).

On when and how sovereignty can be claimed over newly emerged islands, see Note, Eruptions in International Law: Emerging Volcanic Islands and the Law of Territorial Acquisition, 11 Cornell Int'l L.J. 121 (1978); Note, Legal Claims to

Newly Emerged Islands, 15 San Diego L.Rev. 525 (1978). On sovereignty over uninhabitable islands in relation to delimitation of maritime zones, see Charney, Rocks That Cannot Sustain Human Habitation, 93 A.J.I.L. 863 (1999).

4. Is occupation a means by which private persons can acquire sovereignty over parts of the globe? On such efforts, see Comment, To Be or Not to Be: The Republic of Minerva—Nation Founding by Individuals, 12 Colum.J.Trans. L. 520 (1973); United States v. Ray, 423 F.2d 16 (5th Cir.1970) (United States granted an injunction against the building up of a reef outside of the territorial waters of the Florida coast into an island to be known as the Grand Capri Republic or Atlantis, Isle of Gold).

5. A dispute between the United States and Haiti over an uninhabited Caribbean island known as Navassa came to public attention in 1998. Haiti claimed to have succeeded to French sovereignty over the island under the 1697 Treaty of Rijswijk between France and Spain and asserted that it was not necessary for Haiti to use the island to preserve its territorial sovereignty. Meanwhile, the United States asserted sovereignty under the Guano Islands Act of 1856; and the U.S. Supreme Court in Jones v. United States, 137 U.S. 202, 11 S.Ct. 80, 34 L.Ed. 691 (1890), had treated as dispositive the position of the U.S. executive branch that the island was U.S. territory. A California businessman had also sued the U.S. government claiming rights to mine for fertilizer. See "Whose Rock Is It? And, Yes, the Haitians Care," New York Times, Oct. 19, 1998. How should the dispute be resolved under international law?

6. Does the "ambiguity in actual cases based essentially on effective possession" suggest the question "whether the various factors contributing to building a title cannot usefully and instructively be subsumed under the one heading of a process of 'consolidation', and regarded as being for essential purposes all part of one legal process, or 'mode' of acquisition of territorial sovereignty"? Jennings, The Acquisition of Territory in International Law 23–24 (1963). On the significance of "proven long use" in consolidating title, see de Visscher, Theory and Reality in Public International Law 209 (Corbett trans. 1968). Compare Lissitzyn, International Law Today and Tomorrow 17 (1965); Blum, Historic Titles in International Law (1965); 2 Whiteman 1224–29.

B. "PRESCRIPTION" OR "TITLE FOUNDED ON LONG AND PEACEFUL POSSESSION"

CASE CONCERNING KASIKILI/SEDUDU ISLAND (BOTSWANA/NAMIBIA)

International Court of Justice, 1999.
1999 I.C.J. 39 I.L.M. 310 (2000)

[Botswana and Namibia asked the I.C.J. to determine the legal status of a small island in the Chobe River, near the headquarters of a protected wildlife reserve in Botswana. Their special agreement submitting the dispute to the I.C.J. read in part:

> "*Whereas* a Treaty between Great Britain and Germany respecting the spheres of influence of the two countries in Africa was signed on 1 July 1890 (the Anglo–German Agreement of 1890);
>
> *Whereas* a dispute exists between the Republic of Botswana and the Republic of Namibia relative to the boundary around Kasikili/Sedudu Island; * * *

ARTICLE I

The Court is asked to determine, on the basis of the Anglo–German Treaty of 1 July 1890 and the rules and principles of international law, the boundary between Namibia and Botswana around Kasikili/Sedudu Island and the legal status of the island."

The Anglo–German Agreement of 1890 specified in part that "the sphere in which the exercise of influence is reserved to Germany is bounded [by a described line, which] runs eastward along [the 18th parallel of south latitude] till it reaches the river Chobe, and descends the centre of the main channel of that river to its junction with the Zambesi, where it terminates."

The parties acknowledged the Anglo–German Agreement of 1890 to be binding on them, with Botswana as successor in interest to Great Britain (in the territory of the former British Bechuanaland Protectorate) and Namibia as successor in interest to Germany (in the territory formerly known as South–West Africa, which had been administered by South Africa under a League of Nations mandate that was later revoked by the U.N. General Assembly). They differed in the interpretations placed on the treaty term "centre of the main channel" (*Thalweg des Hauptlaufes* in German) and attributed different significance to features of the possible channels, including width, depth, velocity, discharge, and sediment transport capacity, as well as which channel had been most used for river traffic, and other factors.

After analysis of the parties' evidence bearing on interpretation of the 1890 Agreement, the Court concluded that the center of the main channel, and therefore the treaty boundary, would lie to the north of the island, so that the island would belong to Botswana. It then addressed Namibia's alternative argument founded on prescription. Excerpts from the judgment rejecting Namibia's claim follow.]

90. Namibia, however, claims title to Kasikili/Sedudu Island, not only on the basis of the 1890 Treaty but also, in the alternative, on the basis of the doctrine of prescription. Namibia argues that

"by virtue of continuous and exclusive occupation and use of Kasikili Island and exercise of sovereign jurisdiction over it from the beginning of the century, with full knowledge, acceptance and acquiescence by the governing authorities in Bechuanaland and Botswana, Namibia has prescriptive title to the Island". * * *

94. According to Namibia, four conditions must be fulfilled to enable possession by a State to mature into a prescriptive title:

"1. The possession of the ... state must be exercised *à titre de souverain.*

2. The possession must be peaceful and uninterrupted.

3. The possession must be public.

4. The possession must endure for a certain length of time."

Namibia alleges that in the present case Germany was in peaceful possession of the Island from before the beginning of the century and exercised sovereignty over it from the time of the establishment of the first colonial station in the Caprivi in 1909, all in full view and with the full knowledge of the Bechuanaland authorities at Kasane, only a kilometre or two from the Island. It states that this peaceful and public possession of the Island, *à titre de* *souverain,* was continued without interruption by Germany's successor until accession of the territory to independence. Finally, it notes that, after itself becoming independent in 1966, Botswana, which was aware of the facts, remained silent for almost two further decades. * * *

Namibia states that the authority exercised over Kasikili Island by its predecessors was implemented

> "[f]or the most part . . . through the modality of 'indirect rule,' using the chiefs and political institutions of the Masubia to carry out the directives of the ruling power, under the control and supervision of officials of that power"

and that

> "[a]lthough indirect rule was manifested in a variety of ways, its essence was that the acts of administration of the colonial authorities and those of the traditional authorities were acts of a single entity: the colonial government". * * *

95. * * * Botswana accepts the criteria for acquiring prescriptive title as set out by Namibia; it argues, however, that those criteria have not been satisfied by Namibia and its predecessors. Botswana asserts, in substance, that "there is no credible evidence that either Namibia or its predecessors exercised State authority in respect of Kasikili/Sedudu" and that even if peaceful, public and continuous possession of the Island by the people of Caprivi had been proved, it could not have been *à titre de souverain.*

Botswana does not dispute that people from the Caprivi used Kasikili/Sedudu Island at times for agricultural purposes; but it maintains that so did people living on the other side of the Chobe, in Bechuanaland, and denies that there was ever any village or permanent settlement on the Island. Botswana emphasizes that in any case "[t]he acts of private persons cannot generate title unless those acts are subsequently ratified by the State"; that no evidence has been offered to the effect that the Masubia chiefs had authority to engage in title-generating activities for the benefit of Germany or its successors; and that evidence is also lacking of any "genuine belief" in the existence of title on the part of Germany and its successors. * * *

96. The Parties agree between themselves that acquisitive prescription is recognized in international law and they further agree on the conditions under which title to territory may be acquired by prescription, but their views differ on whether those conditions are satisfied in this case. * * *

97. For present purposes, the Court need not concern itself with the status of acquisitive prescription in international law or with the conditions for acquiring title to territory by prescription. It considers, for the reasons set out below, that the conditions cited by Namibia itself are not satisfied in this case and that Namibia's argument on acquisitive prescription therefore cannot be accepted. * * *

98. * * * [T]he evidence shows that the Masubia used the Island intermittently, according to the seasons and their needs, for exclusively agricultural purposes; this use, which began prior to the establishment of any colonial administration in the Caprivi Strip, seems to have subsequently continued without being linked to territorial claims on the part of the Authority administering the Caprivi. [The Court also concluded that as soon

as Namibia's predecessor officially claimed title, Botswana's predecessor "did not accept that claim, which precluded acquiescence on its part."]

99. In the Court's view, Namibia has not established with the necessary degree of precision and certainty that acts of State authority capable of providing alternative justification for prescriptive title, in accordance with the conditions set out by Namibia, were carried out by its predecessors or by itself with regard to Kasikili/Sedudu Island.

Notes

1. An interesting aspect of the Botswana–Namibia dispute was the significance of actions or omissions on the part of South Africa at the time it controlled the territory that ultimately became the state of Namibia. Judge Fleischhauer wrote in a dissenting opinion that while he agreed with the Court's conclusion that Namibia has no title to the island based on prescription, he would have also found that South Africa (Namibia's immediate predecessor) could not have acquired prescriptive title:

> The Court should however have gone into the conditions under which title to territory may be acquired by prescription, far enough to state that South Africa could not have acquired title to the Island by prescription. South Africa, whose presence in the Caprivi Strip including the Island lasted longer than the presence there of Germany or Britain, prior to the termination of the Mandate by the General Assembly in 1966 exercised authority there not *à titre de souverain* but *à titre de mandataire.* As mandatory, South Africa certainly was vested * * * with the "full power of administration and legislation over the territory * * *"; however, as the Court observes in its Advisory Opinion on the *International Status of South West Africa* (I.C.J. Reports 1950, p. 128, at p. 132): * * * "The terms of this Mandate * * * show that the creation of this new international institution did not involve any cession of territory or transfer of sovereignty to the Union of South Africa. * * *"
>
> This perception of the nature of the Mandate is incompatible with acquisitive prescription working in favour of the Mandatory. After the termination of the Mandate, the continued presence of South Africa in South West Africa (Namibia) was no longer "peaceful", i.e., uncontested * * *
>
> I agree that the present case is not a suitable occasion for the Court to concern itself with the status of acquisitive prescription in international law or with the general conditions under which title to territory may be acquired by prescription. Nevertheless, in order to further clarify the law governing mandates or trusteeships, a statement of the Court that acquisitive prescription does not work in favour of a Mandatory would have been desirable.

2. Scholars have noted the difficulty in distinguishing between title derived from original "occupation" of territory and one founded on long and uncontested possession. As Brierly has written:

> *Prescription* as a title to territory is ill defined and some writers deny its recognition altogether. International law does appear, however, to admit that, by a process analogous to the prescription of municipal law, long possession

may operate either to confirm the existence of a title the precise origin of which cannot be shown or to extinguish the prior title of another sovereign. * * *

The principle of extinctive prescription under which the passage of time operates ultimately to bar the right of a prior owner to pursue his claim against one who, having wrongfully displaced him, has continued for a long time in adverse possession is recognized in almost all systems of municipal law and it appears equally to be admitted by international law. * * * It is a nice question as to exactly how far diplomatic and other paper forms of protest by the dispossessed state suffice to "disturb" the possession of the interloper so as to prevent the latter from acquiring a title by prescription. * * * Thus it was largely for the purpose of avoiding any risk of the extinguishment of its claims by prescription that in 1955 the United Kingdom filed a unilateral application with the International Court challenging alleged encroachments by Argentina and Chile on the Falkland Islands Dependencies.

Brierly, The Law of Nations 167–71 (6th ed. Waldock 1963).

C. PRINCIPLE OF *UTI POSSIDETIS JURIS*

The doctrine of *uti possidetis juris* has been applied to the boundaries of new states. As summarized in a recent critique:

> * * * At the core of the legal debate over the territory of new states is the principle of *uti possidetis*. Stated simply, *uti possidetis* provides that states emerging from decolonization shall presumptively inherit the colonial administrative borders that they held at the time of independence. It largely governed the determination of the size and shape of the states of former Spanish Latin America beginning in the early 1800s, as well as former European Africa and Southeast Asia beginning in the 1950s. The relevance of *uti possidetis* today is evidenced by the practice of states during the dissolution of the former Soviet Union, Yugoslavia and Czechoslovakia, apparently sanctifying the former internal administrative lines as interstate frontiers. * * *
>
> *Uti possidetis* finds its origins in the Roman law of the republican era, as one of a series of edicts that the praetor, or administrator of justice, would issue upon application of one party during the initial stage of litigation. * * * The edict came to be summarized in the phrase *Uti possidetis, ita possideatis:* "As you possess, so may you possess."

Ratner, Drawing a Better Line: *Uti Possidetis* and the Borders of New States, 90 A.J.I.L. 590, 592–593 (1996). Excerpts from Ratner's critique follow at pp. 340–341, following the excerpts from several recent cases applying the doctrine.

CASE CONCERNING THE FRONTIER DISPUTE (BURKINA FASO/MALI)

International Court of Justice, 1986.
1986 I.C.J. 554.

[Burkina Faso (previously Republic of Upper Volta) and the Republic of Mali submitted to a Chamber of the I.C.J. pursuant to a special agreement the question "[w]hat is the line of the frontier" of the Upper Volta and the Republic of Mali in "a band of territory extending from the sector Koro (Mali) Djibo (Upper Volta) up to and including the region of Béli." Prior to analyzing the evidence and drawing the line of the frontier, the Chamber (Judges Lachs, Ruda, Bedjaoui, Luchaire, Abi–Saab) commented as follows on the principle of *uti possidetis:*]

19. The characteristic feature of the legal context of the frontier determination to be undertaken by the Chamber is that both States involved derive their existence from the process of decolonization which has been unfolding in Africa during the past 30 years. Their territories, and that of Niger, were formerly part of the French colonies which were grouped together under the name of French West Africa (AOF). Considering only the situation which prevailed immediately before the accession to independence of the two States, and disregarding previous administrative changes, it can be said that Burkina Faso corresponds to the colony of Upper Volta, and the Republic of Mali to the colony of Sudan (formerly French Sudan). It is to be supposed that the Parties drew inspiration from the principle expressly stated in the well-known resolution (AGH/Res. 16 (I)), adopted at the first session of the Conference of African Heads of State and Government, meeting in Cairo in 1964, whereby the Conference solemnly declared that all member States of the Organization of African Unity "solemnly ... pledge themselves to respect the frontiers existing on their achievement of national independence", inasmuch as, in the preamble to their Special Agreement, they stated that the settlement of the dispute by the Chamber must be "based in particular on respect for the principle of the intangibility of frontiers inherited from colonization". It is clear from this text, and from the pleadings and oral arguments of the Parties, that they are in agreement as regards both the applicable law and the starting-point for the legal reasoning which is to lead to the determination of the frontier between their territories in the disputed area.

20. Since the two Parties have, as noted above, expressly requested the Chamber to resolve their dispute on the basis, in particular, of the "principle of the intangibility of frontiers inherited from colonization", the Chamber cannot disregard the principle of *uti possidetis juris,* the application of which gives rise to this respect for intangibility of frontiers. Although there is no need, for the purposes of the present case, to show that this is a firmly established principle of international law where decolonization is concerned, the Chamber nonetheless wishes to emphasize its general scope, in view of its exceptional importance for the African continent and for the two Parties. In this connection it should be noted that the principle of *uti possidetis* seems to have been first invoked and applied in Spanish America, inasmuch as this was the continent which first witnessed the phenomenon of decolonization involving the formation of a number of sovereign States on territory formerly belonging to a single metropolitan State. Nevertheless the principle is not a special rule which pertains solely to one specific system of international law. It is a general principle, which is logically connected with the phenomenon of the obtaining of independence, wherever it occurs. Its obvious purpose is to prevent the independence and stability of new States being endangered by fratricidal struggles provoked by the challenging of frontiers following the withdrawal of the administering power.

21. It was for this reason that, as soon as the phenomenon of decolonization characteristic of the situation in Spanish America in the 19th century subsequently appeared in Africa in the 20th century, the principle of *uti possidetis,* in the sense described above, fell to be applied. The fact that the new African States have respected the administrative boundaries and frontiers established by the colonial powers must be seen not as a mere practice contributing to the gradual emergence of a principle of customary international law, limited in its impact to the African continent as it had previously been to Spanish America, but as the application in Africa of a rule of general scope.

22. The elements of *uti possidetis* were latent in the many declarations made by African leaders in the dawn of independence. These declarations confirmed the maintenance of the territorial status quo at the time of independence, and stated the principle of respect both for the frontiers deriving from international agreements, and for those resulting from mere internal administrative divisions. The Charter of the Organization of African Unity did not ignore the principle of *uti possidetis,* but made only indirect reference to it in Article 3, according to which member States solemnly affirm the principle of respect for the sovereignty and territorial integrity of every State. However, at their first summit conference after the creation of the Organization of African Unity, the African Heads of State, in their Resolution mentioned above (AGH/Res. 16(I)), adopted in Cairo in July 1964, deliberately defined and stressed the principle of *uti possidetis juris* contained only in an implicit sense in the Charter of their organization.

23. There are several different aspects to this principle, in its well-known application in Spanish America. The first aspect, emphasized by the Latin genitive *juris,* is found in the pre-eminence accorded to legal title over effective possession as a basis of sovereignty. Its purpose, at the time of the achievement of independence by the former Spanish colonies of America, was to scotch any designs which non-American colonizing powers might have on regions which had been assigned by the former metropolitan State to one division or another, but which were still uninhabited or unexplored. However, there is more to the principle of *uti possidetis* than this particular aspect. The essence of the principle lies in its primary aim of securing respect for the territorial boundaries at the moment when independence is achieved. Such territorial boundaries might be no more than delimitations between different administrative divisions or colonies all subject to the same sovereign. In that case, the application of the principle of *uti possidetis* resulted in administrative boundaries being transformed into international frontiers in the full sense of the term. This is true both of the States which took shape in the regions of South America which were dependent on the Spanish Crown, and of the States Parties to the present case, which took shape within the vast territories of French West Africa. *Uti possidetis,* as a principle which upgraded former administrative delimitations, established during the colonial period, to international frontiers, is therefore a principle of a general kind which is logically connected with this form of decolonization wherever it occurs.

24. The territorial boundaries which have to be respected may also derive from international frontiers which previously divided a colony of one State from a colony of another, or indeed a colonial territory from the territory of an independent State, or one which was under protectorate, but had retained its international personality. There is no doubt that the obli-

gation to respect pre-existing international frontiers in the event of a State succession derives from a general rule of international law, whether or not the rule is expressed in the formula *uti possidetis.* Hence the numerous solemn affirmations of the intangibility of the frontiers existing at the time of the independence of African States, whether made by senior African statesmen or by organs of the Organization of African Unity itself, are evidently declaratory rather than constitutive: they recognize and confirm an existing principle, and do not seek to consecrate a new principle or the extension to Africa of a rule previously applied only in another continent.

25. However, it may be wondered how the time-hallowed principle has been able to withstand the new approaches to international law as expressed in Africa, where the successive attainment of independence and the emergence of new States have been accompanied by a certain questioning of traditional international law. At first sight this principle conflicts outright with another one, the right of peoples to self-determination. In fact, however, the maintenance of the territorial status quo in Africa is often seen as the wisest course, to preserve what has been achieved by peoples who have struggled for their independence, and to avoid a disruption which would deprive the continent of the gains achieved by much sacrifice. The essential requirement of stability in order to survive, to develop and gradually to consolidate their independence in all fields, has induced African States judiciously to consent to the respecting of colonial frontiers, and to take account of it in the interpretation of the principle of self-determination of peoples.

26. Thus the principle of *uti possidetis* has kept its place among the most important legal principles, despite the apparent contradiction which explained its coexistence alongside the new norms. Indeed it was by deliberate choice that African States selected, among all the classic principles, that of *uti possidetis.* This remains an undeniable fact. In the light of the foregoing remarks, it is clear that the applicability of *uti possidetis* in the present case cannot be challenged merely because in 1960, the year when Mali and Burkina Faso achieved independence, the Organization of African Unity which was to proclaim this principle did not yet exist, and the above-mentioned resolution calling for respect for the pre-existing frontiers dates only from 1964.

CASE CONCERNING LAND, ISLAND AND MARITIME FRONTIER DISPUTE (EL SALVADOR/HONDURAS; NICARAGUA INTERVENING)

International Court of Justice, 1992.
1992 I.C.J. 351.

[A dispute over land, island and maritime boundaries between Honduras and El Salvador festered for many years and erupted in the "Soccer War". Soccer teams from the two countries took part in a World Cup qualifying final in San Salvador in 1969. Honduran fans were beaten and the Honduran flag insulted. Mobs in Honduras beat Salvadorans. Thereafter, Salvadoran planes and warships attacked Honduran air bases and islands in the Gulf of Fonseca. Honduras responded with land and air attacks. In four days 2,000 people died, mostly Honduran civilians. Honduras forced the return of 130,000 Salvadoran migrant workers.

In 1972, after extensive negotiations, El Salvador and Honduras reached agreement on most of their land boundary which had not previously been delimited, leaving thirteen sectors unsettled. Mediation begun in 1978 led to the conclusion of a General Treaty of Peace in 1980 which defined the boundary in seven sectors of the land frontier. A Joint Frontier Commission was established to delimit the boundary in the remaining six sectors. When the Commission failed to reach agreement, the parties concluded a Special Agreement in 1986 to submit unresolved issues to a five-judge Chamber of the I.C.J.

In an exceedingly complex decision, rendered on September 11, 1992, the Chamber (Judge Sette–Camara, President; Judges Oda and Jennings; Judges ad hoc Valticos and Torres Bernardez) delimited the boundary in the six disputed sectors. It also ruled on the legal status of the islands of El Tigre, Meanguera and Meanguerita in the Gulf of Fonseca and on the legal situation of the maritime areas within and without the closing line of the Gulf of Fonseca. Nicaragua was permitted to intervene with respect to the maritime areas aspect of the case.

After the independence of Central America was proclaimed in 1821, Honduras and El Salvador were originally part of the Federal Republic of Central America, which included also Costa Rica, Guatemala and Nicaragua. When the Republic broke up in 1839, Honduras and El Salvador became independent states. It was accepted by the Chamber and the parties that the new boundaries following independence should, in accordance with the principle of *uti possidetis juris* generally applied in Spanish America, follow the administrative boundaries utilized during the colonial period.

The Chamber observed that the 1821 *uti possidetis* boundary when ascertained was not frozen for all time but was susceptible to change by subsequent adjudication, agreement, acquiescence or recognition involving the affected parties. Opinion, para. 67. For example, it concluded that one portion of the boundary was different from that of the 1821 boundary as a result of acquiescence by Honduras evidenced by its conduct from 1881 until 1972. Opinion, para. 80.

The complexities of the decision were largely attributable to the difficulties of delineating the *uti possidetis* boundary when, as in the case presented, documentary evidence is fragmentary and often ambiguous and conflicting. With respect to application of the principle of *uti possidetis juris* under such circumstances the Chamber commented as follows:]

42. * * * [I]n the Arbitral Award of the Swiss Federal Council of 24 March 1922 concerning certain boundary questions between Colombia and Venezuela, it had been observed that:

> "This general principle [of *uti possidetis juris*] offered the advantage of establishing an absolute rule that there was not in law in the old Spanish America any *terra nullius;* while there might exist many regions which had never been occupied by the Spaniards and many unexplored or inhabited by non-civilized natives, these regions were reputed to belong in law to whichever of the Republics succeeded to the Spanish province to which these territories were attached by virtue of the old Royal ordinances of the Spanish mother country. These territories, although not

occupied in fact were by common consent deemed to be occupied in law from the first hour by the new Republic * * * " (*UNRIAA,* Vol. I, p. 228.)

Thus the principle of *uti possidetis juris* is concerned as much with title to territory as with the location of boundaries; certainly a key aspect of the principle is the denial of the possibility of *terra nullius.*

43. To apply this principle is not so easy when, as in Spanish Central America, there were administrative boundaries of different kinds or degrees; for example, besides "provinces" (a term of which the meaning was different at different periods), there were *Alcaldias Mayores* and *Corregimientos* and later on, in the 18th century, *Intendencias, as* well as the territorial jurisdictions of a higher court *(Audiencias),* Captaincies–General and Vice–Royalties; and indeed the territories which became El Salvador and Honduras were, before 1821, all part of the same larger administrative area, the Captaincy–General or Kingdom of Guatemala. Furthermore, the jurisdictions of general administrative bodies such as those referred to did not necessarily coincide in territorial scope with those of bodies possessing particular or special jurisdictions, e.g., military commands. Besides, in addition to the various civil territorial jurisdictions, general or special, there were the ecclesiastical jurisdictions, which were supposed to be followed in principle, pursuant to general legislation, by the territorial jurisdiction of the main civil administrative units in Spanish America; such adjustment often needed, however, a certain span of time within which to materialize. Fortunately, in the present case, insofar as the sectors of the land boundary are concerned, the Parties have indicated to which colonial administrative divisions they claim to have succeeded; the problem is to identify the areas, and their boundaries, which corresponded to these divisions, to be referred to herein, for the sake of simplicity, as "provinces" which in 1821 became respectively El Salvador and Honduras, initially as constituent States of the Federal Republic of Central America. Moreover it has to be remembered that no question of international boundaries could ever have occurred to the minds of those servants of the Spanish Crown who established administrative boundaries; *uti possidetis juris* is essentially a retrospective principle, investing as international boundaries administrative limits intended originally for quite other purposes.

44. Neither Party has however produced any legislative or similar material indicating specifically, with the authority of the Spanish Crown, the extent of the territories and the location of the boundaries of the relevant provinces in each area of the land boundary. Both Parties have instead laid before the Chamber numerous documents, of different kinds, some of which, referred to collectively as "titles" *(titulos),* concern grants of land in the areas concerned by the Spanish Crown, from which, it is claimed, the provincial boundaries can be deduced. Some of these actually record that a particular landmark or natural feature marked the boundary of the provinces at the time of the grant; but for the most part this is not so, and the Chamber is asked, in effect, to conclude, in the absence of other evidence of the position of a provincial boundary, that where a boundary can be identified between the lands granted by the authorities of one province and those granted by the authorities of the neighbouring province, this boundary may be taken to have been the provincial boundary and thus the line of the *uti possidetis juris.* Thus it was the territorial aspect of that principle rather than its boundary aspect that was the one mainly employed by both Parties in their arguments

before the Chamber. The location of boundaries seemed often, in the arguments of the Parties, to be incidental to some "claim", or "title", or "grant", respecting a parcel of territory, within circumambient boundaries only portions of which are now claimed to form an international boundary. It is rather as if the disputed boundaries must be constructed like a jig-saw puzzle from certain already cut pieces so that the extent and location of the resulting boundary depend upon the size and shape of the fitting piece.

45. The term "title" has in fact been used at times in these proceedings in such a way as to leave unclear which of several possible meanings is to be attached to it; some basic distinctions may therefore perhaps be usefully stated. As the Chamber in the *Frontier Dispute* case observed, the word "title" is generally not limited to documentary evidence alone, but comprehends "both any evidence which may establish the existence of a right, and the actual source of that right" (*I.C J. Reports 1986,* p. 564, para. 18). In one sense, the "title" of El Salvador or of Honduras to the areas in dispute, in the sense of the source of their rights at the international level, is, as both Parties recognize, that of succession of the two States to the Spanish Crown in relation to its colonial territories; the extent of territory to which each State succeeded being determined by the *uti possidetis juris* of 1821. Secondly, insofar as each of the two States inherited the territory of particular administrative units of the colonial structure, a "title" might be furnished by, for example, a Spanish Royal Decree attributing certain areas to one of those. As already noted, neither Party has been able to base its claim to a specific boundary line on any "titles" of this kind applicable to the land frontier. * * * [T]he *titulos* submitted to the Chamber recording the grant of particular lands to individuals or to Indian communities cannot be considered as "titles" in this sense; they could rather be compared to "colonial *effectivités*" as defined by the Chamber formed to deal with the *Frontier Dispute:* "the conduct of the administrative authorities as proof of the effective exercise of territorial jurisdiction in the region during the colonial period" (*I.C.J. Reports 1986,* p. 586, para. 63). These, or some of them, are however "titles" in a third, municipal-law, sense, in that they evidence the right of the grantees to ownership of the land defined in them. In some cases, the grant of the "title" in this third sense was not perfected; but the record, particularly of any survey carried out, nevertheless remains a "colonial effectivity" which may be of value as evidence of the position of the provincial boundary. * * *

[When the Chamber found no persuasive documentary evidence of the location of the boundary at the time the states gained their independence, resort was had to other evidence. On some occasions the Chamber attached weight to a topographical feature such as a watershed that provided a readily identifiable and convenient boundary. Opinion, paras. 46, 101, 114. On another it invoked equity *infra legem* to adopt a boundary proposed in negotiations between Honduras and El Salvador in 1869 which remained unratified by the parties but was apparently not the subject of disagreement. Opinion, paras. 262–63.]

332. It is the contention of Honduras that the law applicable to the island dispute by virtue of these provisions is solely the *uti possidetis juris* of 1821. El Salvador on the other hand initially (in its Memorial) relied heavily on the exercise or display of sovereignty over the islands, contending that the island dispute was, in its view, a dispute as to attribution of territory rather

than a dispute over the delimitation of a frontier. Subsequently, however, it maintained that the dispute over the islands can be viewed in two possible ways: while it is able to rely on effective possession of the islands as the basis of its sovereignty thereof on the ground that this is a case where sovereignty has to be attributed, it is equally able to rely on historical formal title-deeds as unquestionable proof of its sovereignty of the islands in accordance with the principle of the *uti possidetis juris* of 1821. In the view of El Salvador, its rights over the islands are not merely confirmed but fortified by the combined effect of the application of the two criteria. While questioning whether Article 26 of the General Treaty of Peace is applicable to the islands at all, El Salvador also points to the final sentence of Article 26, which in its view was directed, even in the context of land boundaries, to balancing the application of Spanish colonial titles with "more modern concepts"; it concludes that the Chamber is bound to apply the modern law of the acquisition of territory, and to look at the effective exercise and display of State sovereignty over the islands as well as historical titles.

333. The Chamber has no doubt that the starting-point for the determination of sovereignty over the islands must be the *uti possidetis juris* of 1821. The islands of the Gulf of Fonseca were discovered in 1522 by Spain, and remained under the sovereignty of the Spanish Crown for three centuries. When the Central American States became independent in 1821, none of the islands were *terra nullius;* sovereignty over the islands could not therefore be acquired by occupation of territory. The matter was one of the succession of the newly-independent States to all former Spanish islands in the Gulf. The Chamber will therefore consider whether it is possible to establish the appurtenance in 1821 of each disputed island to one or the other of the various administrative units of the Spanish colonial structure in Central America. For this purpose, it may have regard not only to legislative and administrative texts of the colonial period, but also to "colonial *effectivités*" * * * In the case of the islands, there are no land titles of the kind which Chamber has taken into account in order to reconstruct the limits of the *uti possidetis juris* on the mainland; and the legislative and administrative texts are confused and conflicting. The attribution of individual islands to the territorial administrative divisions of the Spanish colonial system, for the purposes of their allocation to the one or the other newly independent State, may well have been a matter of some doubt and difficulty, judging by the evidence and information submitted. It should be recalled that when the principle of the *uti possidetis juris* is involved, the *jus* referred to is not international law but the constitutional or administrative law of the pre-independence sovereign, in this case Spanish colonial law; and it is perfectly possible that that law itself gave no clear and definite answer to the appurtenance of marginal areas, or sparsely populated areas of minimal economic significance. For this reason, it is particularly appropriate to examine the conduct of the new States in relation to the islands during the period immediately after independence. Claims then made, and the reaction—or lack of reaction—to them may throw light on the contemporary appreciation of what the situation in 1821 had been, or should be taken to have been. * * *

[The Chamber reviewed the facts, including evidences of title and colonial *effectivités,* on which El Salvador and Honduras based their claims to the islands in the Gulf and observed that many of the historical events relied on can be, and have been, interpreted in different ways and thus used to support the arguments of either Party.]

343. The difficulty with application to the present case of principles of law [relating to the acquisition of territory, invoked by El Salvador] is however that they were developed primarily to deal with the acquisition of sovereignty over territories available for occupation, i.e., *terra nullius.* Both Parties however assert a title of succession from the Spanish Crown, so that the question arises whether the exercise or display of sovereignty by the one Party, particularly when coupled with lack of protest by the other, could indicate the presence of an *uti possidetis juris* title in the Party so exercising sovereignty, where the evidence on the basis of documentary titles or colonial *effectivités* was ambiguous. * * *

345. In the present case both Parties have argued their respective claims with regard to the operation of the *uti possidetis juris* on the basis, in effect, that this is a principle the application of which is automatic: on independence, the boundaries of the relevant colonial administrative divisions are transformed into international frontiers. In the first place, it should not be overlooked that Spanish colonial divisions in Spanish America did not individually have any "original" or "historic" titles, as those concepts are understood in international law. The original title belonged exclusively to the Spanish Crown, not the internal administrative subdivisions established by it; and it was equally the Spanish Crown which had sovereignty of the colonial territories. Secondly, as the Chamber's examination of the sectors of the land boundary has shown, in practice the operation of the principle is more complex. Where the relevant administrative boundary was ill-defined or its position disputed, in the view of the Chamber the behavior of the two newly independent States in the years following independence may well serve as a guide to where the boundary was, either in their shared view, or in the view acted on by one and acquiesced in by the other * * *. This aspect of the matter is of particular importance in relation to the status of the islands, by reason of their history.

346. Shortly after independence in 1821, the newly independent Central American States were united by the Constitution of 1824 in the Federal Republic of Central America, successor of Spain in the sovereignty over, *inter alia,* the islands. Uninhabited or sparsely inhabited, the islands were left dormant for some years, since the economic value of their exploitation was little. The problem of their appurtenance to one or the other of the riparian States thus did not raise any interest or inspire any dispute until the break-up of the Federal Republic and the years nearing the mid–19th century. The well-protected waters of the Gulf of Fonseca, with its mouth extending over some 19 nautical miles, the good navigation channels, and the possibility of construction of safe and comfortable ports, had long commended the Gulf to pirates and buccaneers in search of a haven; from the 1840's onward the attention of the big powers, interested in having a foothold in Central America, began to be attracted to the islands of the Gulf.

347. Thus it was not until a number of years after the independence of the two States that the question of the appurtenance of the islands of the Gulf to the one or the other became of significant import. What then occurred appears to the Chamber to be highly material. The islands were not *terra*

nullius, and in legal theory each island already appertained to one of the three States surrounding the Gulf as heir to the appropriate part of the Spanish colonial possessions, so that *acquisition* of territory by occupation was not possible; but the effective possession by one of the Gulf States of any island of the Gulf could constitute an *effectivité,* though a post-colonial one, throwing light on the contemporary appreciation of the legal situation. Possession backed by the exercise of sovereignty may be taken as evidence confirming the *uti possidetis juris* title. The Chamber does not find it necessary to decide whether such possession could be recognized even in contradiction of such a title, but in the case of the islands, where the historical material of colonial times is confused and contradictory, and the accession to independence was not immediately followed by unambiguous acts of sovereignty, this is practically the only way in which the *uti possidetis juris* could find formal expression so as to be judicially recognized and determined.

Note

The *ad hoc* Arbitration Commission established by the European Community in 1991 to render advice on various issues relating to the dissolution of the former Socialist Republic of Yugoslavia rendered an opinion on January 11, 1992, that, in the absence of agreement of the relevant states to the contrary, the preexisting frontiers between Croatia and Serbia and Serbia and Bosnia–Herzegovina were entitled to protection under principles of international law, citing the U.N. Charter, the Declaration on the Principles of International Law concerning Friendly Relations and Cooperation among States, other international instruments, and the principle of *uti possidetis* applied by the I.C.J in the *Frontier Dispute* case. In the excerpt that follows, Professor Ratner sharply criticizes the application of the *uti possidetis* doctrine in situations like the breakup of former Yugoslavia.

RATNER, DRAWING A BETTER LINE: UTI POSSIDETIS AND THE BORDERS OF NEW STATES

90 A.J.I.L. 590–591 (1996) (footnotes omitted).

Reliance on *uti possidetis* during the post-Cold War breakups has stemmed from three arguments or assumptions. First, *uti possidetis* reduces the prospects of armed conflict by providing the only clear outcome in such situations. Absent such a policy, all borders would be open to dispute, and new states would fall prey to irredentist neighbors or internal secessionist claimants. Second, because a cosmopolitan democratic state can function within any borders, the conversion of administrative borders to international borders is as sensible as any other approach and far simpler. Third, and buttressing the other two, *uti possidetis* is asserted as a default rule of international law mandating the conversion of all administrative boundaries into international borders. This rule emerged during the decolonization of Latin America and Africa but would apply by logical extension to the breakup of states today. The most significant elaboration of this extension came from the commission chaired by Judge Robert Badinter advising the European Community on legal questions associated with the breakup of Yugoslavia.

These views seem compelling; yet the easy embrace by governments of *uti possidetis* and the suggestion that it is now a general rule of international law to govern the breakup of states lead to two distinct, yet opposite, spillover effects that endanger global order at this time of ethnic conflict. First, a policy or rule that transforms all administrative borders of modern states into international boundaries creates a significant hazard in the name of simplicity—namely, the temptation of ethnic separatists to divide the world further along administrative lines. If the Republic of Georgia's new borders must coincide with those of the former Georgian Soviet Socialist Republic, are not the future Republic of Abhazia's just as clearly those of the former Abhaz Autonomous Soviet Socialist Republic? Would the Québecois consider secession so readily if the new state had different borders from those established by Canada and the United Kingdom for the purpose of integrating Quebec into the Dominion?

Second, the extension of *uti possidetis* to modern breakups leads to genuine injustices and instability by leaving significant populations both unsatisfied with their status in new states and uncertain of political participation there. By hiding behind inflated notions of *uti possidetis,* state leaders avoid engaging the issue of territorial adjustments—even minor ones—which is central to the process of self-determination. In the case of Yugoslavia, for instance, although *uti possidetis* hardly caused the eruption of armed conflict, the assumption by states of its applicability from the outset prevented any debate over the adjustment of boundaries and limited the universe of possible borders to one—leaving those people on the "wrong" side of the border ripe for "ethnic cleansing." * * *

It is thus time to reexamine this oft-invoked principle of international law and relations. For application of *uti possidetis* to the breakup of states today both ignores critical distinctions between internal lines and international boundaries and, more important, is profoundly at odds with current trends in international law and politics. Many internal borders do merit transformation into international boundaries based on historical and other characteristics; but the assumption that all such borders must be so transformed is unwarranted.

D. CONSEQUENCES OF CONQUEST OR UNLAWFUL USE OF FORCE

Before international law prohibited the use of force in international relations, territorial changes often came about by virtue of conquest. Efforts in the 20th century to delegitimize aggression included the "Stimson Doctrine" of 1932—a policy not to recognize the validity of territorial acquisitions brought about by force used in violation of the Kellogg–Briand Pact. See Chapter 12. An articulation of a similar principle under the U.N. Charter is found in the Friendly Relations Declaration of 1970:

DECLARATION ON PRINCIPLES OF INTERNATIONAL LAW CONCERNING FRIENDLY RELATIONS AND CO–OPERATION AMONG STATES IN ACCORDANCE WITH THE CHARTER OF THE UNITED NATIONS ("FRIENDLY RELATIONS DECLARATION")

G.A. Res. 2625 (XXXV) 1970.

The General Assembly,

Having considered the principles of international law relating to friendly relations and co-operation among States,

1. *Solemnly proclaims* the following principles:

* * *

Every State has the duty to refrain in its international relations from the threat or use of force against the territorial integrity or political independence of any State, or in any other manner inconsistent with the purposes of the United Nations. Such a threat or use of force constitutes a violation of international law and the Charter of the United Nations and shall never be employed as a means of settling international issues.

* * *

The territory of a State shall not be the object of military occupation resulting from the use of force in contravention of the provisions of the Charter. The territory of a State shall not be the object of acquisition by another State resulting from the threat or use of force. No territorial acquisition by another State resulting from the threat or use of force shall be recognized as legal. Nothing in the foregoing shall be construed as affecting:

(a) Provisions of the Charter or any international agreement prior to the Charter regime and valid under international law; or

(b) The powers of the Security Council under the Charter. * * *

Notes

1. On August 1, 1990, the armed forces of Iraq invaded and occupied Kuwait. On August 2, the U.N. Security Council unanimously condemned the invasion and demanded that Iraq withdraw all forces immediately and unconditionally. S/RES/660 (1990). On August 9, 1990, the Council unanimously adopted Resolution 662 which stated, in part:

> *Gravely alarmed* by the declaration by Iraq of a "comprehensive and eternal merger" with Kuwait,
>
> *Demanding,* once again, that Iraq withdraw immediately and unconditionally all its forces to the positions in which they were located on 1 August 1990,
>
> *Determined to* bring the occupation of Kuwait by Iraq to an end and to restore the sovereignty, independence and territorial integrity to Kuwait,
>
> *Determined also* to restore the authority of the legitimate Government of Kuwait,

1. Decides that annexation of Kuwait by Iraq under any form and whatever pretext has no legal validity, and is considered null and void;

2. Calls upon all States, international organizations and specialized agencies not to recognize that annexation, and to refrain from any action or dealing that might be interpreted as an indirect recognition of the annexation;

3. Further demands that Iraq rescind its actions purporting to annex Kuwait * * *

2. In Military and Paramilitary Activities In and Against Nicaragua (Nicaragua v. United States of America), 1986 I.C.J. 14, para. 190, the I.C.J. held that the principles of the U.N. Charter relating to the threat or use of force were part of customary international law with the character of *jus cogens.* See p. 955 infra. Does this holding require U.N. members not to recognize any territorial acquisitions achieved by means of conquest? If a non-member makes such a conquest, does a member-state of the United Nations violate its obligations under the Charter by recognition of a change of sovereignty? See U.N. Charter, Art. 2(6); Jennings, The Acquisition of Territory in International Law 53–55 (1963).

3. If international law no longer permits a state to gain "title" to territory by resorting to war, what is the present status of territory conquered and annexed at a time when international law did recognize such a "title" as valid? Does the doctrine of "intertemporal law" from the *Island of Palmas* case apply? What is the present status of territory conquered and annexed by armed force in the U.N. Charter era, e.g., Goa, which was conquered and annexed by India in 1961? Will the answer depend on whether or not India's "title" has been recognized by other states? See Oppenheim at 704–705; Jennings at 61–65. What is the effect, if any, of Portugal's establishment in 1962 of a Goan government-in-exile (2 Whiteman 1144)?

4. Is the conquering state's position in any way improved through its forcing the conquered state to agree to a treaty of cession? Article 52 of the Vienna Convention on the Law of Treaties states that a treaty (including presumably a treaty of cession) is void "if its conclusion has been procured by the threat or use of force in violation of the principles of international law embodied in the Charter of the United Nations." See p. 528 infra. See also Jennings at 56–61.

5. Is there any basis for concluding that an occupation of territory by a lawful use of armed force in the exercise of the right of self-defense under Article 51 of the Charter can give rise to a valid title to territory? See Schwebel, What Weight to Conquest, 64 A.J.I.L. 344–47 (1970).

6. In the Arab–Israeli war in June 1967, Israeli armed forces occupied Gaza, the West Bank, Sinai, and the Golan Heights. In 1968, Israel began establishing civilian settlements in these territories. Was this permitted under international law? See Letter of Herbert J. Hansell, Legal Adviser to the U.S. Department of State, of April 21, 1978, 17 I.L.M. 777 (1978) (reaching the conclusion that, as a belligerent occupant, Israel had no right to establish such settlements); G.A.Res. 3215 (XXXII) (1977) at 13 (to the same effect by vote of 131 to 1, with the abstentions of Costa Rica, Fiji, Guatemala, Malawi, Nicaragua, Papua, New Guinea, and United States). On whether Israel had the right to develop new oil fields in Sinai and the Gulf of Suez, see Memorandum of Law of the U.S. Department of State of Oct. 1, 1976, 16 I.L.M. 733 (1977) (reaching a negative answer), and the Response of the Ministry of Foreign Affairs of Israel of August 1, 1977, 17 I.L.M. 432 (1978) (giving an affirmative answer). For references to the respective legal positions on the status of the occupied territories, see Cassese,

Self–Determination of Peoples 235–239 (1995). On a possible justification for Israel's actions in terms of self-defense, see p. 970 infra; see also p. 1068. Note that armed occupation is different from conquest.

7. Following the Arab–Israeli war in June, 1967, Israel took certain measures to accomplish the "administrative unification" of Jerusalem. The General Assembly, by a vote of 99 to 0, with 20 abstentions, adopted the following resolution:

> *The General Assembly,*
>
> *Deeply concerned* at the situation prevailing in Jerusalem as a result of the measures taken by Israel to change the status of the City,
>
> 1. *Considers* that these measures are invalid;
>
> 2. *Calls upon* Israel to rescind all measures already taken and to desist forthwith from taking any action which would alter the status of Jerusalem;
>
> 3. *Requests* the Secretary–General to report to the General Assembly and the Security Council on the situation and the implementation of the present resolution not later than one week from its adoption.

G.A.Res. 2253 (S–V) G.A.O.R., 5th Emerg. Spec.Sess., Supp. 1, at 4 (1967).

The action by the General Assembly was followed by a series of Security Council resolutions to the same effect, see S.C.Res. 252 (XXIII 1968) p. 9; S.C.Res. 267 (XXIV 1969) p. 3; S.C.Res. 271, id. p. 5; and S.C.Res. 298 (XXVI 1971) p. 6. The General Assembly reaffirmed its earlier resolution in G.A.Res. 31/106 (XXXI 1976) p. 50. Israel did not comply with these resolutions.

As of 2000, negotiations between Israel and the Palestine Liberation Organization aiming toward a final resolution of the status of Jerusalem, along with other interconnected problems in the Arab–Israeli conflict, were in progress with U.S. mediation but had not achieved a solution.

E. BOUNDARY DELIMITATION AND SETTLEMENT OF TERRITORIAL DISPUTES

Disputes often arise concerning the proper interpretation of agreements establishing boundaries or allocating territory. States have frequently sought the aid of third parties in resolving such disputes. Sometimes an international arbitration panel or international court is asked to decide the dispute on the basis of law, as in the cases excerpted above and many others. In other situations one or both parties have not been receptive to a juridical solution but may be willing to entertain other third-party proposals, such as through mediation. Exceptionally, the Security Council has addressed situations where territorial disputes threaten international peace and security.

Notes

1. After the 1991 Iraq–Kuwait war, a condition of the cease-fire resolution was respect for the inviolability of the international boundary as set out in a 1963 agreement between Iraq and Kuwait. S.C. Res. 687, paras. 2–4 (Apr. 3, 1991). The same resolution called upon the U.N. Secretary–General "to lend his assistance to make arrangements with Iraq and Kuwait to demarcate the boundary between

Iraq and Kuwait." The latter demarcation was effected by the U.N. Iraq–Kuwait Boundary Demarcation Commission. The Security Council adopted Resolution 773 on August 26, 1992, which stated in part:

> *Recalling* in this connection that through the demarcation process the Commission is not reallocating territory between Kuwait and Iraq, but it is simply carrying out the technical task necessary to demarcate for the first time the precise coordinates of the boundary set out in the Agreed Minutes between the State of Kuwait and the Republic of Iraq regarding the restoration of Friendly Relations, Recognition and Related Matters signed by them on 4 October 1963, and that this task is being carried out in the special circumstances following Iraq's invasion of Kuwait and pursuant to resolution 687 (1991) * * *
>
> *4. Underlines* its guarantee of the inviolability of the above-mentioned international boundary and its decision to take as appropriate all necessary measures to that end in accordance with the Charter, as provided for in paragraph 4 of resolution 687 (1991) * * *

2. The Egypt–Israel Arbitration Tribunal: Award in Boundary Dispute Concerning the Taba Area (September 29, 1988), 27 I.L.M. 1421 (1988), involved resolution of a controversy between Egypt and Israel concerning the location of nearly 100 "pillars" of demarcation originally erected in 1906 and 1907. The 1979 Israel–Egypt Treaty of Peace established that the permanent international boundary between Egypt and Israel is "the recognized international boundary between Egypt and the former mandated territory of Palestine." A joint Israeli–Egyptian Commission was established for the purpose, inter alia, of "organiz[ing] the demarcation of the international boundary." When this commission failed to agree on the location of the pillars demarcating the boundary line, the issues were submitted to arbitration. In the course of its award, the tribunal stated:

> * * * If a boundary line is once demarcated jointly by the parties concerned, the demarcation is considered as an authentic interpretation of the boundary agreement even if deviations may have occurred or if there are some inconsistencies with maps. This has been confirmed in practice and legal doctrine, especially for the case that a long time has elapsed since demarcation. Ress concludes an examination of cases with the following statement:
>
>> "If the parties have considered over a long time the demarcated frontier as valid, this is an authentic interpretation of the relevant international title." (Ress, *The Delimitation and Demarcation of Frontiers in International Treaties and Maps,* Institute of International Public Law and International Relations in Thessaloniki 1985, pp. 435–37, especially 437; see also Münch, "Karten im Völkerrecht", *Gedächtnisschrift für Friedrich Klein,* Munich 1977, p. 344). It may also be referred to the Judgment of the International Court of Justice in the *Temple* case where the Court states:
>>
>>> "In general, when two countries establish a frontier between them, one of the primary objects is to achieve stability and finality. This is impossible if the line so established can, at any moment, and on the basis of a continuously available process, be called in question, and its rectification claimed, whenever any inaccuracy by reference to a clause in the parent treaty is discovered. Such a process could continue indefinitely, and finality should never be reached so long as possible errors still remained to be discovered. Such a frontier, so far

> from being stable, would be completely precarious." (1962 *ICJ Reports* 34)

27 I.L.M. 105–106. See Kaikobad, Some Observations on the Doctrine of Continuity and Finality of Boundaries, 1983 Brit. Y.B.I.L. 119 (1983), where the author suggests that the principle of finality and stability in various manifestations constitutes one of the more fundamental and important precepts in the law of international boundaries.

3. The Beagle Channel Islands between the Atlantic and Pacific oceans were in dispute between Argentina and Chile from 1905 to 1984. Although both countries agreed in 1971 that the British Government should arbitrate their dispute (10 I.L.M. 1182 (1971)), the award of the islands to Chile (17 I.L.M. 632 (1978)) was not honored by Argentina. With war looming, Chile and Argentina agreed to mediation by the Pope, 18 I.L.M. (1979). The dispute was resolved in a treaty signed at the Vatican on January 23, 1984.

For discussion of the factors rendering the Beagle Channel dispute so difficult of solution, including reasons why Argentina did not accept the arbitral award but was willing to entertain the solution offered through papal mediation, see Laudy, The Vatican Mediation of the Beagle Channel Dispute: Crisis Intervention and Forum Building 293–320, in Words Over War: Mediation and Arbitration to Prevent Deadly Conflict (Greenberg, Barton & McGuinness, eds., 2000).

4. The Falkland Islands or Islas Malvinas have been the subject of a dispute between Argentina and the United Kingdom eventuating in armed conflict in 1982. See Franck, Dulce et Decorum Est: The Strategic Role of Legal Principles in the Falklands War, 77 A.J.I.L. 109 (1983), and Beck, The Falklands Islands as an International Problem (1988). The islands had been under British control since 1833, by virtue of successful military conquest, though Argentina never gave up its claims to territorial sovereignty. After Argentina attempted to change the status quo by sending armed forces to the islands in 1982, third-party mediation by the United States and the United Nations could not resolve the dispute. Britain then won a decisive military victory.

5. A border dispute between Ecuador and Peru has led to recurrent armed conflict between the parties and to several attempts (some at least partly successful) to bring about a solution through third-party intervention. A 1941 war between the two countries ended when four other countries—Argentina, Brazil, Chile, and the United States—agreed to serve as guarantors of a settlement embodied in a 1942 protocol concluded at Rio de Janeiro. When renewed warfare broke out over the dispute in 1995, the guarantors again sought to mediate a solution. In an agreement signed in October 1998, 38 I.L.M. 266 (1999), the parties agreed to bifurcate the issue of formal sovereignty from other issues of ownership and access. See Simmons, Territorial Disputes and Their Resolution: The Case of Ecuador and Peru (Peaceworks No. 27, U.S. Institute of Peace, 1999).

F. SOVEREIGNTY IN TERRITORIAL SEA AND AIRSPACE

1. *Territorial Sea*

State authority in offshore areas is regulated by the 1982 U.N. Convention on the Law of the Sea (UNCLOS), discussed in greater detail in Chapter 16. According to Article 2 of UNCLOS:

> 1. The sovereignty of a coastal State extends, beyond its land territory and internal waters and, in the case of an archipelagic State, its

archipelagic waters, to an adjacent belt of sea, described as the territorial sea.

2. This sovereignty extends to the air space over the territorial sea as well as to its bed and subsoil.

3. The sovereignty over the territorial sea is exercised subject to this Convention and to other rules of international law.

According to Article 3, the maximum breadth of the territorial sea is 12 nautical miles. UNCLOS rules govern innocent passage in the territorial sea and transit passage through straits used for international navigation; these rules substantially limit the sovereignty of coastal states in their territorial seas. See discussion at pp. 1401–1409 infra.

2. *Airspace*

CONVENTION ON INTERNATIONAL CIVIL AVIATION

Signed at Chicago, December 7, 1944.
61 Stat. 1180, T.I.A.S. 1591, 15 U.N.T.S. 295.

Art. 1. The contracting States recognize that every State has complete and exclusive sovereignty over the airspace above its territory.

Notes

1. 49 U.S.C.A. § 1508(a) provides: "The United States of America is declared to possess and exercise complete and exclusive national sovereignty in the airspace of the United States, including the airspace above all inland waters and airspace above those portions of the adjacent marginal high seas, bays, and lakes, over which by international law or treaty or convention the United States exercises national jurisdiction."

2. On the rights of states over the airspace above the seas adjacent to their land territory, see p. 1404 infra. Aircraft are guaranteed a "right of transit" through international straits so long as they conform to certain procedures, such as continuous monitoring of specified radio channels. See UNCLOS Articles 37–39, 42, 44, 53–54, discussed in greater detail at p. 1407 infra.

3. Since 1950, the United States has promulgated regulations establishing Air Defense Identification Zones (ADIZs) which extend at some points several hundred miles beyond the territorial sea. See 14 CFR § 99 (2000); 49 U.S.C.A. §§ 40103(b)(3), 46307 (1997). Foreign aircraft entering ADIZs are required to file flight plans and to make periodic position reports. Canada established ADIZs in 1951.

In 1956, during the Algerian conflict, France established a "zone of special responsibility," extending some eighty miles from the coast of Algeria, within which aircraft were required to file detailed information regarding their flight, to stay within assigned corridors, and to maintain contact with ground identification stations. See McDougal, Lasswell & Vlasic, Law and Public Order in Space 307–11 (1963). Some ten states other than the U.S. and Canada have maintained ADIZs.

On what basis, if any, can these extensions of jurisdiction be justified? See Note, Air Defense Identification Zones, Creeping Jurisdiction in the Airspace, 18 Va.J.Int'l L. 485, 497–505 (1978), concluding (1) that extant international conventions tend to reject claims of jurisdiction over airflights beyond the territorial sea, (2) that self-defense cannot be a justification because of the absence of an imminent threat and of proportionality, and (3) that the practice of establishing ADIZs has not become customary international law.

4. A state's authority over airspace above its territory was traditionally said to extend *usque ad coelum*. As space became exploitable, efforts have been made to define more precise limits and, specifically, to determine where airspace ends and outer space begins. For a discussion of the various criteria of delimitation that have been proposed, see U.N.Doc. A/AC. 105/C. 2/7 (1970). See also K. Gorove & E. Kamenetskaya, Tensions in the Development of the Law of Outer Space, in Beyond Confrontation: International Law for the Post–Cold War Era (Damrosch, Danilenko & Mullerson, eds., 1995), at pp. 243–248, and pp. 1559–1560 in Chapter 19.

3. Subsoil Resources

A state may have less than absolute authority over resources below the surface of its territory. For example, prevailing authority supports the rule that a state may not draw more from liquid resources below the surface that straddle national boundaries than its proportional share of the common pool. See generally Lagoni, Oil and Gas Deposits Across National Frontiers, 73 A.J.I.L. 215 (1979).

SECTION 6. STATE SUCCESSION

A. INTRODUCTION

The rights, capacities and obligations of a state appertain to the state as such and are not affected by changes in its government. If, however, a state acquires sovereignty over territory from another state, or if disintegration of a state results in the emergence of more than one state in the territory in question, issues arise relating to the extent to which the resultant states succeed to the rights, capacities and obligations of their predecessor. Issues of state succession may arise when a state absorbs all of a predecessor state, a state takes over part of the territory of another state, a state becomes independent of another state of which it had formed a part, or a predecessor state has separated into a number of states.

Most successions in the 20th century resulted from peace treaties or from decolonization. In the 1990s major successions took place at the end of the Cold War, with the disintegration of the Soviet Union and the political changes that swept Eastern and Central Europe. These included the unification of Germany in 1990 (which involved an absorption by the Federal Republic of Germany of all of the territory of the German Democratic Republic without creating a new state), the dissolution of the U.S.S.R. at the end of 1991 and the emergence of 15 states in its former territory, the violent breakup of the Socialist Federal Republic of Yugoslavia resulting in five separate states by the early 1990s, and the peaceful separation of the Czech Republic and Slovakia effective in 1993.

The Reporters of the Restatement (Third) note that "[t]he international law and the practice of states as to succession have been uncertain and confused. In recent decades several views have emerged. Some suggest that the new state succeeds to no rights or obligations of its predecessor but begins with a *tabula rasa.* At the other pole is the view that a successor state is responsible for all obligations and enjoys all rights of its predecessor. Intermediate views have distinguished different circumstances of succession and different rights and obligations." Restatement (Third) § 208, Reporters' Note 1. The view adopted in the Restatement (Third) is that "succession has varying effects on state rights and duties." Id.

Three major efforts in international law-making have sought to resolve some of the uncertainties over the legal consequences of state succession. In 1978 a Convention on Succession of States in Respect of Treaties was adopted in Vienna, U.N. Doc. A/CONF. 80/31, 72 A.J.I.L. 971 (1978), and, in 1983, a Convention on the Succession of States in respect of State Property, Archives and Debts was adopted in Vienna, A/CONF. 117/14, 22 I.L.M. 306 [hereinafter cited as 1983 Succession Convention]. Both of these treaties had been drafted by the International Law Commission. In 1999 the I.L.C. completed work on a third succession topic and recommended to the General Assembly the adoption, in the form of a declaration, of draft articles on nationality of natural persons in relation to the succession of states [hereinafter cited as Draft Articles on Nationality in Relation to Succession]. Some of the rules expressed in these instruments may be codificatory of general international law, but it cannot be assumed that this is true of the documents overall: the I.L.C. work was aimed at progressive development in controversial spheres, and its results have been skeptically received and have not yet achieved general acceptance through treaty participation. The 1978 Convention on Succession in Respect of Treaties finally entered into force in 1996 but has garnered only a relatively small number of ratifications (17 as of 2000). The 1983 Convention was not yet in force as of 2000. The United States has ratified neither of these conventions, and it voted against adoption of the latter. As of 2000, the 1999 Draft Articles on Nationality in Relation to Succession awaited action by the General Assembly.

Issues involving state succession in the context of international agreements are discussed in Chapter 7. Such issues have come before the I.C.J. in several cases of the 1990s, including cases brought by Bosnia–Herzegovina and by Croatia against the Federal Republic of Yugoslavia under the Genocide Convention, where the issue of continuity of obligations under human rights treaties has been prominent, and the dispute between Hungary and Slovakia over a Communist-era treaty for construction of a Danube River dam.

The remainder of this section surveys the effect of state succession in a variety of contexts, including membership in international organizations, the internal legal system of the successor state, public debt and other contracts, property rights, obligations arising from violations of international law, and nationality of natural persons.

CONFERENCE FOR PEACE IN YUGOSLAVIA ARBITRATION COMMISSION OPINION NO. 9

31 I.L.M. 1523 (1992).

[On May 18, 1992, the Chairman of the Arbitration Commission, the creation and function of which are discussed at p. 259 supra, received a letter from Lord Carrington, Chairman of the Conference for Peace in Yugoslavia, asking for the Commission's opinion on the following question:

Assuming that the dissolution of the former Socialist Federal Republic of Yugoslavia (SFRY) is now complete, "on what basis and by what means should the problems of the succession of states arising between the different states emerging from the SFRY be settled?"

The Commission responded in part as follows:]

1. * * * In Opinion No. 8, the Arbitration Commission concluded that the dissolution of the Socialist Republic of Yugoslavia (SFRY) had been completed and that the state no longer existed. New states have been created on the territory of the former SFRY and replaced it. All are successor states to the former SFRY.

2. As the Arbitration Commission pointed out in its first Opinion, the succession of states is governed by the principles of international law embodied in the Vienna Conventions of 23 August 1978 and 8 April 1983, which all Republics have agreed should be the foundation for discussions between them on the succession of states at the Conference for Peace in Yugoslavia.

The chief concern is that the solution adopted should lead to an equitable outcome, with the states concerned agreeing on procedures subject to compliance with the imperatives of general international law and, more particularly, the fundamental rights of the individual and of peoples and minorities.

3. In the declaration on former Yugoslavia adopted in Lisbon on 27 June 1992, the European Council stated that:

> "the Community will not recognize the new federal entity comprising Serbia and Montenegro as the successor State of the former Yugoslavia until the moment that decision has been taken by the qualified international institutions. They have decided to demand the suspension of the delegation of Yugoslavia at the CSCE and other international fora and organizations."

The Council thereby demonstrated its conviction that the Federal Republic of Yugoslavia (Serbia and Montenegro) has no right to consider itself the SFRY's sole successor.

4. The Arbitration Commission is therefore of the opinion that:

— the successor states to the SFRY must together settle all aspects of the succession by agreement;

— in the resulting negotiations, the successor states must try to achieve an equitable solution by drawing on the principles embodied in the

1978 and 1983 Vienna Conventions and, where appropriate, general international law;

— furthermore full account must be taken of the principle of equality of rights and duties between states in respect of international law;

— the SFRY's membership of international organizations must be terminated according to their statutes and that none of the successor states may thereupon claim for itself alone the membership rights previously enjoyed by the former SFRY;

— property of the SFRY located in third countries must be divided equitably between the successor states;

— the SFRY's assets and debts must likewise be shared equitably between the successor states;

— the states concerned must peacefully settle all disputes relating to succession to the SFRY which could not be resolved by agreement in line with the principle laid down in the United Nations Charter;

— they must moreover seek a solution by means of inquiry, mediation, conciliation, arbitration or judicial settlement;

— since, however, no specific question has been put to it, the Commission cannot at this stage venture an opinion on the difficulties that could arise from the very real problems associated with the succession to the former Yugoslavia.

Notes

1. In various international bodies, the Federal Republic of Yugoslavia (Serbia and Montenegro) claimed to be the successor to the former SFRY, for purposes such as the seat at the U.N. General Assembly; but this claim was not accepted. By G.A. Res. 47/1 (Sept. 22, 1992), on the recommendation of the U.N. Security Council (S.C. Res. 757, 1992), the General Assembly denied the FRY (Serbia–Montenegro) the right to succeed automatically to the U.N. membership of the SFRY. On aspects of this controversy, see the Arbitration Commission's Opinion No. 10 at p. 261 supra. Finally, after an election in fall 2000 resulting in a change of government, the Federal Republic of Yugoslavia applied for U.N. membership and was admitted by the General Assembly on November 1, 2000, upon the Security Council's recommendation. See G.A. Res. 55/12 (2000).

2. By contrast, the claim of the Russian Federation to assume the U.N. membership of the former Union of Soviet Socialist Republics, including the permanent seat on the Security Council, was generally accepted, including by the other permanent members as well as by the new states that had formerly formed part of the Soviet Union. When the Commonwealth of Independent States (CIS) was formed (consisting of the former Soviet republics, with the exception of the three Baltic states of Estonia, Latvia, and Lithuania), its founding agreement provided that the states of the CIS "support Russia's continuance of the membership of the USSR in the United Nations, including permanent membership of the Security Council, and other international organizations." See CIS Agreement reprinted at 31 I.L.M. 138, 151 (1992).

More generally, the circumstances of dissolution of the Soviet Union could be seen as entailing the essential continuity of the Russian Federation with the ex-U.S.S.R., albeit with alterations in territory, population, and government, rather than Russia becoming a successor state. On this and related points, see Mullerson, The Continuity and Succession of States, by Reference to the Former USSR and Yugoslavia, 42 I.C.L.Q. 473 (1993).

3. On state succession generally, see O'Connell, State Succession in Municipal Law and International Law (1967) [hereinafter cited as O'Connell, State Succession].

On developments in the wake of the disintegration of the U.S.S.R. and Yugoslavia, see Mullerson, Note 2 supra.

B. SUCCESSION AND A STATE'S INTERNAL LEGAL SYSTEM

With respect to the question of succession to the internal legal system of a territory, a distinction has traditionally been drawn between public law and private law. Public law, broadly, is that body of laws promulgated by the government for the effective administration of the country; it is political in character, concerns the relation of the population to the state, and pertains to the prerogatives of sovereignty. Private law, on the other hand, governs the relations between individual citizens and need not be directly affected by the administration of the country. See 1 O'Connell, State Succession 101–141.

The traditional view held that although private law survives a state succession and the rights of private parties are not affected by the change in sovereignty, public law does not survive. Id. at 104. This view, however, does not accord with state practice. An alternative approach, which seems closer to actual practice, is that if the public law of the new state and the public law of the predecessor state are consistent, succession takes place, but that if the laws are inconsistent, no succession occurs. In this view, succession is, in effect, a presumption, which can be rebutted by positive legislation of the new state. Id. at 107. State practice indicates that new states generally make legislative provision for continuity of the internal legal order, with the qualification that continuity must be consistent with the change in sovereignty. Id. at 118 et seq. Sometimes, both the predecessor state and the new state make legislative provision for succession with respect to the legal system. For instance, in the case of India, Britain provided for continuity of the legal system in the India Independence Act, 10 & 11 Geo. 6, c. 30, § 18 (1947). India provided for continuity in the Indian Constitution, Art. 372(2).

With the disintegration of the U.S.S.R., some of the successor states revived aspects of municipal law predating incorporation into the Soviet Union, notably the citizenship laws of Baltic republics. On this problem, see Mullerson, 42 I.C.L.Q. at p. 484, and pp. 357–358 infra.

C. SUCCESSION IN RESPECT OF STATE PROPERTY, ARCHIVES, AND DEBTS

When part of the territory of a state becomes territory of another state or a new state, the property of the predecessor state located in the territory concerned becomes the property of the successor state. Restatement (Third) § 209(1). Article 17 of the 1983 Succession Convention states that movable property of the predecessor state passes to the successor only if it is "connected with activity of the predecessor state in respect of territory to which the succession of states relates" 22 I.L.M. 314. "Except where the predecessor state wholly ceases to exist, property located outside the territory subject to the transfer of sovereignty (including intangibles, such as bank accounts) generally remains with the predecessor state." Restatement (Third) § 209, Reporters' Note 1.

If the successor state has violated the U.N. Charter in annexing a predecessor state with force, the unlawful successor should not be permitted to succeed to rights in property or to rights under contract, but should be responsible for the public debts of the predecessor. Restatement (Third) § 209, Comment *h*.

Public debts may be owed to another state, to an international organization, to a publicly or privately owned financial institution, or to a private person. In principle, a succession of states does not as such affect the rights and obligations of creditors with respect to public debts. 1983 Succession Convention, Art. 36, 22 I.L.M. 323. However, the issue of succession to obligations in the form of public debts is often resolved by agreement between the predecessor and successor states. See, e.g., Art. 23 of Federal Republic of Germany–German Democratic Republic: Treaty on the Establishment of German Unity, 30 I.L.M. 457, 478 (1991) and Financial and Economic Agreement between Indonesia and The Netherlands, art. 25, signed Dec. 27, 1949, 69 U.N.T.S. 252–257.

One important feature of the law in the area is the distinction drawn between the national public debt, which is owed by the state as a whole, and local public debt, which includes debts owed by the state in respect of a specific territory or specific assets and revenues and debts contracted by a political subdivision (e.g., a city or province). See generally 1 O'Connell, State Succession 369–453; Feilchenfeld, Public Debts and State Succession (1931).

In the case of national public debt, the 1983 Succession Convention provides that, in the absence of an agreement governing succession, if there is a transfer of part of the territory of a state, a separation of part of the territory of a state or a dissolution of a state, the public debt of the predecessor shall pass to the successor state "in an equitable proportion, taking into account, in particular, the property, rights and interests which pass to the successor state in relation to that * * * debt." Articles 37, 40 and 41, 22 I.L.M. 323–324. See Ottoman Public Debt Case, I R. Int'l Arb. Awards 529 (1925). If two or more states unite, the public debt of the predecessors passes to the successor. 1983 Succession Convention, Article 39. 22 I.L.M. 322. The result is the same if a state is absorbed by another state. Restatement (Third) § 209(2)(b). If the successor state were not responsible for the public debt of the predecessor(s), the creditors would have no source of payment and the successor state might be unjustly enriched by acquiring territory and assets without having to assume the debtor entity's obligations. Restatement (Third) § 209, Comment *c*. However, if the debtor entity retains fiscal independence, the debtor-creditor relationship is unaffected, and the entity remains responsible for repayment of the debt. See 1 O'Connell, State Succession 373, 375.

When Austria was made part of the German Reich in 1938, the United States delivered notes to the German Government indicating its belief that it was a general doctrine of international law that the substituted sovereign assumed the debts and obligations of the absorbed state. 1 Hackworth 545. The German Government replied that the law of state succession did not apply in the particular case because Austria had liquidated herself, that the debts were "political" in character, and that in the past the United States had failed to assume responsibility for the payment of debts. Gerner, Questions of State Succession Raised by the German Annexation of Austria, 32 A.J.I.L. 421 (1938). The United States rejected these contentions. Hyde 419. A separating state has generally not succeeded to the national (i.e., non-local) public debt of the predecessor state. See Zemanek, State Succession after Decolonization, 116 Rec. des Cours 180, 258 (1965–III).

Article 33 of the 1983 Succession Convention takes the position that the rules relating to public debt do not apply to public debt of a state held by creditors other than states and international institutions such as the World Bank. 22 I.L.M. 322. The Restatement (Third) § 209, Comment *b*, rejects this view and adopts the position that the rules also apply to public debt held by private creditors, citing the prevailing position in the International Law Commission.

Local public debts frequently take the form of obligations incurred for funds expended or used in connection with a particular project in the territory directly affected by separation or absorption. An example would be loans contracted with the International Bank for Reconstruction and Development. The Bank required that if such loans were extended to dependent territories, a separate Guarantee Agreement between the Bank and the colonial power be concluded. In most other cases, debts contracted by, or on behalf of, the separating territory are assigned to the successor state by agreement between the predecessor state and the new state. If no agreement is concluded, the new state nevertheless usually assumes the debts related to its territory which had been incurred before the separation or absorption. See Zemanek at 261–66; Feilchenfeld at 417–22.

Local debts may be obligations incurred by a fiscally autonomous governmental subdivision in the territory of the successor state before the creation of the new state. The general rule with regard to such local debts is that the change in sovereignty does not affect the local debts if the subdivision incurring those debts is unaffected by the change. If, moreover, the successor state impairs the repayment of the obligation, or causes the demise of the autonomy of the local authority which contracted the debt, the new state must assume repayment of the debt. See 1 O'Connell, State Succession at 452–54.

When the predecessor state is a party to contracts, these contracts are often governed by municipal law, and if the predecessor state remains in being (as was the case where a colony became independent), the contract between the predecessor state and a private party would remain valid, unless it was so connected with the territory of the new state that it would be impossible for the predecessor state to continue to perform the contract, in which case the successor state might be considered bound. If the private party has performed only part of the contract, but is prevented from completing performance because of the change in sovereignty, municipal law doctrines of frustration, *quantum meruit,* unjust enrichment, or restitution may become applicable. See 1 O'Connell 442–43.

If a contract between a private party and the state requires the construction and operation of public works or the extraction of minerals, it is clear that the contract is closely linked with the territory affected by change of sovereignty. However, it is also true that the successor state is not a party to the contract. Although the traditional law on this subject was unclear, compare West Rand Gold Mining Co., Ltd. v. The King, [1905] K.B. 391, with the Sopron–Koszeg Railway Case, [1929–30] Ann. Dig. 57, 59 (No. 54), economic development and concession agreements involving substantial investments by a foreign investor should be binding on the successor state. Restatement (Third) § 209, Comment *f.* Succession agreements may provide for the assumption of obligations under such agreements by the successor state.

Notes

1. Section 209(2) of the Restatement (Third) states:

(2) Subject to agreement between predecessor and successor states, responsibility for public debt of the predecessor, and rights and obligations under its contracts, remain with the predecessor state, except as follows:

(a) where part of the territory of a state becomes territory of another state, local public debt, and the rights and obligations of the predecessor state under contracts relating to that territory, are transferred to the successor state;

(b) where a state is absorbed by another state, the public debt, and rights and obligations under contracts of the absorbed state, pass to the absorbing state;

(c) where part of a state becomes a separate state, local public debt, and rights and obligations of the predecessor state under contracts relating to the territory of the new state, pass to the new state.

Comment *d* to § 209 indicates that local debt includes both indebtedness incurred by a subdivision of the state (e.g., a city or province) and debts incurred by a state to finance a project located in a given locality. "[S]ince the successor state acquires control over the assets located in that territory, it assumes corresponding obligations." Restatement (Third) § 209, Comment *d.*

2. Among the significant differences between public debts and certain other contracts is the fact that termination of an obligation to pay a debt would unjustifiably enrich the state relieved of the repayment obligation, while termination of an executory contract would not necessarily do so. With respect to succession to public debts see Report of the International Law Commission on its 31st Session, G.A.O.R. 34 Sess., Supp. No. 10 (A/34/10) (1979) p. 95.

3. There was discussion in the International Law Commission of whether a convention on state succession to debts should include articles dealing with state succession with respect to "odious" debts. For a discussion of the issues and authorities relating to odious debt issues see the Ninth Report of the Special

Rapporteur in 1977 I.L.C. Yrbk. Vol. II (Part One) p. 45. U.N. Doc. A/CN.4/301 and Add. I. The I.L.C. Report on the Work of its Thirty-third Session commented as follows on this report (footnotes omitted):

> (41) In his ninth report, the Special Rapporteur included a chapter entitled "Non-transferability of 'odious' debts". That chapter dealt, first, with the definition of "odious debts". The Special Rapporteur recalled *inter alia,* the writings of jurists who referred to "war debts" or "subjugation debts" and those who referred to "regime debts". For the definition of odious debts, he proposed an article C, which read as follows:
>
> *Article C. Definition of odious debts*
>
> For the purpose of the present articles, "odious debts" means:
>
> (a) all debts contracted by the predecessor State with a view to attaining objectives contrary to the major interests of the successor State or of the transferred territory;
>
> (b) all debts contracted by the predecessor State with an aim and for a purpose not in conformity with international law and, in particular, the principles of international law embodied in the Charter of the United Nations.
>
> (42) Second, the chapter dealt with the determination of the fate of odious debts. The Special Rapporteur reviewed State practice concerning "war debts", including a number of cases of the non-passing of such debts to a successor State, as well as cases of the passing of such debts. He further cited cases of State practice concerning the passing or non-passing to a successor State of "subjugation debts". He proposed the following article D, concerning the non-transferability of odious debts:
>
> *Article D. Non-transferability of odious debts*
>
> [Except in the case of the uniting of States,] odious debts contracted by the predecessor State are not transferable to the successor State.
>
> (43) The Commission, having discussed articles C and D, recognized the importance of the issues raised in connection with the question of "odious" debts, but was of the opinion initially that the rules formulated for each type of succession of States might well settle the issues raised by the question and might dispose of the need to draft general provisions on it. In completing the second reading of the draft, the Commission confirmed that initial view.

1981 I.L.C. Yb. Vol. II (Part Two) p. 78. The 1983 Succession Convention did not, in fact, deal with the issue of the non-transferability of odious debts.

D. SUCCESSION TO INTERNATIONAL OBLIGATIONS

Succession to obligations incurred by international agreement will be dealt with in Chapter 7, infra. The following observations concern obligations arising from violations of international law, such as the infliction of environmental or other injury.

It has been held that the successor state has no responsibility in international law for the international delicts of its predecessor. See Robert E. Brown Claim (United States v. Great Britain), American & British Claims Arbitration 187, 6 U.N.Rep. Int'l Arb. Awards 120 (1923) (Claimant sought compensation for refusal of local officials of the Boer Republics to issue licenses to exploit a goldfield. The United Kingdom contended that this was a delictual claim, and that it did not succeed to responsibility; the United States asserted that claimant's acquired rights were infringed and that Britain did succeed to the obligation to compensate Brown. The tribunal held that Brown had acquired a property right and that he had been injured by a denial of justice, but that this was a delict responsibility for which did not devolve on Britain.) See also Redward Claim (Hawaiian Claims) (Great Britain v. United States), American & British Claims, Arbitration 85, 160–61, 6 U.N.Rep. Int'l Arb. Awards 157 (1925) (Claimants had been wrongfully imprisoned by the Government of the Hawaiian Republic, which was subsequently annexed by the United States. The tribunal held that "legal liability for the wrong has been extinguished" with the disappearance of the Hawaiian Republic.) Thus if the claim has not been reduced to a money judgment, which may be considered a debt, or an interest on the part of the claimant in assets of fixed value, there is no acquired right in the claimant, and no obligation to which the successor state has succeeded. See 1 O'Connell, State Succession 482, 485–86.

Note

Why should the successor state not be responsible for an international wrong if it has been enriched by the wrongful action of its predecessor? With respect to the Brown and Redward awards, it has been observed: "These cases date from the age of colonialism when colonial powers resisted any rule that would make them responsible for the delicts of states which they regarded as uncivilized. The authority of those cases a century later is doubtful. At least in some cases, it would be unfair to deny the claim of an injured party because the state that committed the wrong was absorbed by another state." Restatement (Third) § 209; Reporters' Note 7. See generally, Czaplinski, State Succession and State Responsibility, 28 Can. Y.B.I.L. 339 (1990); Volkovitsch, Note, Righting Wrongs: Towards a New Theory of State Succession to Responsibility for International Delicts, 92 Colum. L. Rev. 2162 (1992) (arguing for a reversal of traditional doctrine and establishment of a rebuttable presumption of succession to responsibility for internationally wrongful acts).

E. SUCCESSION IN RESPECT OF NATIONALITY

Issues involving nationality of natural persons in the context of succession have arisen notably in connection with efforts of the post-Soviet and Eastern European entities to define the categories of persons entitled to exercise rights of citizenship and to reside in their territories upon the emergence (or reemergence) of new states. In the case of the Baltic republics that reassumed their former sovereignty in 1991 after a half-century of forcible incorporation into the Soviet Union, one approach was to revive their pre-incorporation citizenship laws dating from the 1930s. Such measures had the effect of conferring automatic nationality on those who had been citizens prior to World War II or who were descended from such persons, and the corresponding intent of putatively denationalizing very large segments of the population (principally ethnic Russians) who had taken up residence in those republics during the Soviet period and who were now expected to meet stringent conditions for naturalization (including mastery of the local language). These nationality policies of Estonia, Latvia and Lithuania beginning in the early 1990s came under close scrutiny and criticism from human rights groups and international organizations, on the ground of unjustifiable discrimination on the basis of ethnicity and unfair hardship to individuals and families with longstanding ties to the territory. See Mullerson, Human Rights Diplomacy 53–57, 132 (1997); Orentlicher, Citizenship and National Identity, in Wippman (ed.), International Law and Ethnic Conflict 296–325 (1998).

The Estonian, Latvian, and Lithuanian situations presented variants of a generic problem of deciding which persons are to be considered nationals of a state in the aftermath of a succession. Nationality, as the expression of the legal link between individual and state, is relevant to a host of interconnected questions, including the issue of who will form the political community for purposes of taking fundamental constitutive decisions, such as the form of government of the new state and its relationship to the predecessor state and to other states. Nationality may also be relevant to an individual's right to remain in the territory of a state or to return to it, and to questions of diplomatic protection. See Chapter 6 below.

These questions were acutely raised in the 1990s, in the former Soviet Union, former Yugoslavia, former Czechoslovkia, and elsewhere. Between 1993 and 1999, the I.L.C. understook a study of the impact of state succession on the nationality of natural persons and produced a set of draft articles on this topic in 1999. The Draft Articles on Nationality in Relation to Succession (cited at p. 349 supra; see Documents Supplement) are notable for a much greater sensitivity to human rights considerations than most earlier treatments either of nationality or of succession. The preamble affirms, for example, that "due account should be taken both of the legitimate interests of States and those of individuals," and the I.L.C.'s commentary stresses that it is "important to safeguard basic rights and fundamental freedoms of all persons whose nationality may be affected by a succession." See I.L.C. Report on Work of 51st Sess., G.A.O.R., Supp. No. 10 (A/54/10) (1999), pp. 25, 29. Substantively, the Draft Articles would establish presumptions and default rules so that no person would be left stateless by succession, and would affirm principles of respect for the will of persons concerned, family unity, and non-discrimination.

As of 2000, the I.L.C. had recommended that the U.N. General Assembly adopt the Draft Articles in the form of a declaration. Even in advance of formal adoption, the Draft Articles have made a significant contribution to the law of state succession by emphasizing the human rights of individuals affected by succession.

Chapter 5

ORGANIZATIONS: INTERNATIONAL AND NON-GOVERNMENTAL

This chapter concerns the legal status and capacity in international law of public international organizations and of non-governmental organizations. (Chapter 6 takes up the position of the individual in international law, as well as transnational corporations and other private entities.)

Organizations for purposes of the present chapter are either intergovernmental or non-governmental, a basic distinction for legal purposes. Within these categories, organizations exhibit remarkable diversity in function, structure, and effect. In international law, the term "international organization" is generally used to refer to organizations composed entirely or mainly of states and usually established by treaty. The treaty is, as a rule, the constitutive instrument. Non-governmental organizations (commonly known as NGOs) are not the creations of states but rather are formed by individuals or private groups sharing a common objective. They include worldwide organizations involved in humanitarian, health, human rights and environmental matters; professional and scientific associations; federations and international unions made up of national associations representing labor or employers; religious bodies; scientific academies; and so on. NGOs provide vehicles through which transnational "civil society" can influence the decisions and actions of states and of international organizations, and indeed the attitudes and conduct of diverse actors.

In considering the materials in this chapter, the reader should bear in mind the questions posed early in this casebook, concerning the extent to which international law has been mainly a state-centered system and the more diffuse influences that now shape that system. If international organizations came into being as the creatures of states, in what senses might they now be understood as having autonomous authority? Are non-governmental organizations able to transcend the state system and participate directly in the making and enforcement of international law?

SECTION 1. INTERNATIONAL ORGANIZATIONS

The proliferation of international organizations has been a notable feature of the period following World War II. As the 20th century progressed, not only the numbers but also the ambition and range of activities handled by such organizations increased markedly. So too did the legal issues concerning their powers, functions, membership and status.

Hundreds of international organizations are now in existence. They vary widely in scope, structure and function. The United Nations includes nearly all the states of the world as members and a wide range of functions. Linked to the United Nations are autonomous "specialized agencies," for example FAO (the Food and Agriculture Organization), WHO (World Health Organization), and ICAO (International Civil Aviation Organization). The World Bank and the International Monetary Fund are also specialized agencies of the United Nations operating under their own statutes. Many international organizations are regional bodies, either broad in scope or specialized. Still others are concerned with a particular commodity or with an activity in a particular area. Relatively recent international organizations include the World Trade Organization (established in 1994), the institutions that came into being in the 1990s with the entry into force of the U.N. Convention on the Law of the Sea in 1994, and the Organization for the Prohibition of Chemical Weapons established in 1998.

The Restatement (Third) Part II, Chapter 2, Introductory Note, states:

> International organizations are created by international agreements and are governed by the law pertaining to such agreements. The law of international organizations has become a separate subdivision of international law, much as in national legal systems the law of corporations developed independently of the law of contracts even while retaining links to it. Particularly when organs of an international organization are authorized by its constitutive agreement to make decisions, allocate funds, admit and expel members and interpret or even amend the constitutive agreement, the organization can be said to have a law of its own, a kind of "international constitutional law."

Typically, an international organization has a plenary organ in which all member states are represented, a smaller body entrusted with certain important decisions (e.g., an executive committee or council), and a secretariat or staff to carry out administrative, representative, advisory, and technical functions. The larger international organizations also have subsidiary bodies such as commissions and agencies which are under the authority of the principal organs but which often have considerable authority delegated to them. The United Nations has well over a hundred such subsidiary bodies performing executive, advisory, rule-making, and even judicial functions. Such prominent international organizations as the U.N. Children's Fund (UNICEF), the U.N. Development Program and the U.N. High Commissioner for Refugees are in this category.

A. INTERNATIONAL LEGAL PERSONALITY AND POWERS OF INTERNATIONAL ORGANIZATIONS

The attribution of international legal personality involves the capacity to perform legal acts on the international plane rather than within a municipal law system. International organizations have exercised international legal capacity in a variety of ways. "International organizations have concluded treaties, made use of the high seas with ships flying their own flag, created international peace forces, convened international conferences with representatives of States and other international organizations, organized internally the functioning and procedure of their organs, sent diplomatic representatives to member and non-member States and received permanent missions from member States, undertaken administration tasks in certain territories, presented protests to States and brought claims into the international plane, and have participated in the activities of other international organizations with envoys, observers, etc." Rama–Montaldo, International Legal Personality and Implied Powers of International Organizations, 44 Brit. Y.B.I.L. 123 (1970).

In exercising international legal capacity and correlatively in assuming international responsibility for their acts, international organizations draw a distinction in terms of legal powers and obligations between the organization and its member states. That distinction also requires that the organization possess organs capable of exercising such legal capacity and responsibilities on the international plane. Standing conferences of states under multilateral conventions or loose associations such as the British Commonwealth lack such organs and consequently do not exercise the attributes of international personality. An international organization may also have been denied such international personality by its constitutive instrument or decisions of its members. An example is the Bank for International Settlements which, though international in purpose and composition, was granted legal capacity in the municipal law of each of its member states but not international legal capacity.

Although it is now recognized that most international governmental organizations have international legal personality, there are still doctrinal controversies (with practical implications) on certain legal issues, namely:

(1) Whether international personality is an inherent (or objective) attribute of international organization or whether it depends on the constitutive instrument and the powers expressly or impliedly granted to it.

(2) Whether there is a precise category of legal rights and duties derived from the fact of international personality or whether the rights and duties depend on the powers and functions of the international organization.

(3) Whether the denial of international personality by the member states means that the entity cannot be regarded as an international organization under international law.

1. Capacity and Powers

The assassination of a U.N. emissary on a mission in the Middle East was the context for an early I.C.J. advisory opinion concerning the organization's legal capacity:

REPARATION FOR INJURIES SUFFERED IN THE SERVICE OF THE UNITED NATIONS

International Court of Justice, Advisory Opinion, 1949.
1949 I.C.J. 174.

THE COURT. * * * The first question asked of the Court is as follows:

"In the event of an agent of the United Nations in the performance of his duties suffering injury in circumstances involving the responsibility of a State, has the United Nations, as an Organization, the capacity to bring an international claim against the responsible *de jure* or *de facto* government with a view to obtaining the reparation due in respect of the damage caused (a) to the United Nations, (b) to the victim or to persons entitled through him?"

It will be useful to make the following preliminary observations:

(a) The Organization of the United Nations will be referred to usually, but not invariably, as "the Organization".

(b) Questions I(a) and I(b) refer to "an international claim against the responsible *de jure* or *de facto* government." The Court understands that these questions are directed to claims against a State, and will, therefore, in this opinion, use the expression "State" or "defendant State."

(c) The Court understands the word "agent" in the most liberal sense, that is to say, any person who, whether a paid official or not, and whether permanently employed or not, has been charged by an organ of the Organization with carrying out, or helping to carry out, one of its functions—in short, any person through whom it acts.

(d) As this question assumes an injury suffered in such circumstances as to involve a State's responsibility, it must be supposed, for the purpose of this Opinion, that the damage results from a failure by the State to perform obligations of which the purpose is to protect the agents of the Organization in the performance of their duties.

(e) The position of a defendant State which is not a member of the Organization is dealt with later, and for the present the Court will assume that the defendant State is a Member of the Organization. * * *

Competence to bring an international claim is, for those possessing it, the capacity to resort to the customary methods recognized by international law for the establishment, the presentation and the settlement of claims. Among these methods may be mentioned protest, request for an enquiry, negotiation, and request for submission to an arbitral tribunal or to the Court in so far as this may be authorized by the Statute.

This capacity certainly belongs to the State; a State can bring an international claim against another State. Such a claim takes the form of a claim between two political entities, equal in law, similar in form, and both the direct subjects of international law. It is dealt with by means of negotiation, and cannot, in the present state of the law as to international jurisdiction, be submitted to a tribunal, except with the consent of the States concerned.

When the Organization brings a claim against one of its Members, this claim will be presented in the same manner, and regulated by the same procedure. It may, when necessary, be supported by the political means at the disposal of the Organization. In these ways the Organization would find a method for securing the observance of its rights by the Member against which it has a claim.

But, in the international sphere, has the Organization such a nature as involves the capacity to bring an international claim? In order to answer this question, the Court must first enquire whether the Charter has given the

Organization such a position that it possesses, in regard to its Members, rights which it is entitled to ask them to respect. In other words, does the Organization possess international personality? This is no doubt a doctrinal expression, which has sometimes given rise to controversy. But it will be used here to mean that if the Organization is recognized as having that personality, it is an entity capable of availing itself of obligations incumbent upon its Members.

To answer this question, which is not settled by the actual terms of the Charter, we must consider what characteristics it was intended thereby to give to the Organization.

The subjects of law in any legal system are not necessarily identical in their nature or in the extent of their rights, and their nature depends upon the needs of the community. Throughout its history, the development of international law has been influenced by the requirements of international life, and the progressive increase in the collective activities of States has already given rise to instances of action upon the international plane by certain entities which are not States. This development culminated in the establishment in June 1945 of an international organization whose purposes and principles are specified in the Charter of the United Nations. But to achieve these ends the attribution of international personality is indispensable.

The Charter has not been content to make the Organization created by it merely a centre "for harmonizing the actions of nations in the attainment of these common ends" (Article 1, para. 4). It has equipped that centre with organs, and has given it special tasks. It has defined the position of the Members in relation to the Organization by requiring them to give it every assistance in any action undertaken by it (Article 2, para. 5), and to accept and carry out the decisions of the Security Council; by authorizing the General Assembly to make recommendations to the Members; by giving the Organization legal capacity and privileges and immunities in the territory of each of its Members; and by providing for the conclusion of agreements between the Organization and its Members. Practice—in particular the conclusion of conventions to which the Organization is a party—has confirmed this character of the Organization, which occupies a position in certain respects in detachment from its Members, and which is under a duty to remind them, if need be, of certain obligations. It must be added that the Organization is a political body, charged with political tasks of an important character, and covering a wide field, namely, the maintenance of international peace and security, the development of friendly relations among nations, and the achievement of international cooperation in the solution of problems of an economic, social, cultural or humanitarian character (Article 1); and in dealing with its Members it employs political means. The "Convention on the Privileges and Immunities of the United Nations" of 1946 creates rights and duties between each of the signatories and the Organization (see, in particular, Section 35). It is difficult to see how such a convention could operate except upon the international plane and as between parties possessing international personality.

In the opinion of the Court, the Organization was intended to exercise and enjoy, and is in fact exercising and enjoying, functions and rights which can only be explained on the basis of the possession of a large measure of international personality and the capacity to operate upon an international plane. It is at present the supreme type of international organization, and it could not carry out the intentions of its founders if it was devoid of international personality. It must be acknowledged that its Members, by entrusting certain functions to it, with the attendant duties and responsibilities, have clothed it with the competence required to enable those functions to be effectively discharged.

Accordingly, the Court has come to the conclusion that the Organization is an international person. That is not the same thing as saying that it is a State, which it certainly is not, or that its legal personality and rights and duties are the same as those of a State. Still less is it the same thing as saying that it is "a super-State," whatever that expression may mean. It does not even imply that all its rights and duties must be upon the international plane, any more than all the rights and duties of a State must be upon that plane. What it does mean is that it is a subject of international law and capable of possessing international rights and duties, and that it has capacity to maintain its rights by bringing international claims.

The next question is whether the sum of the international rights of the Organization comprises the right to bring the kind of international claim described in the Request for this Opinion. That is a claim against a State to obtain reparation in respect of the damage caused by the injury of an agent of the Organization in the course of the performance of his duties. Whereas a State possesses the totality of international rights and duties recognized by international law, the rights and duties of an entity such as the Organization must depend upon its purposes and functions as specified or implied in its constituent documents and developed in practice. The functions of the Organization are of such a character that they could not be effectively discharged if they involved the concurrent action, on the international plane, of fifty-eight or more Foreign Offices, and the Court concludes that the Members have endowed the Organization with capacity to bring international claims when necessitated by the discharge of its functions.

[With respect to Question I(a), the Court continued:]

* * * It cannot be doubted that the Organization has the capacity to bring an international claim against one of its Members which has caused injury to it by a breach of its international obligations towards it. The damage specified in Question I(a) means exclusively damage caused to the interests of the Organization itself, to its administrative machine, to its property and assets and to the interests of which it is the guardian. It is clear that the Organization has the capacity to bring a claim for this damage. As the claim is based on the breach of an international obligation on the part of the Member held responsible by the Organization, the Member cannot contend that this obligation is governed by municipal law, and the Organization is justified in giving its claim the character of an international claim.

When the Organization has sustained damage resulting from a breach by a Member of its international obligations, it is impossible to see how it can obtain reparation unless it possesses capacity to bring an international claim. It cannot be supposed that in such an event all the Members of the Organization, save the defendant State, must combine to bring a claim against the defendant for the damage suffered by the Organization.

The Court is not called upon to determine the precise extent of the reparation which the Organization would be entitled to recover. It may, however, be said that the measure of the reparation should depend upon the amount of the damage which the Organization has suffered as the result of the wrongful act or omission of the defendant State and should be calculated in accordance with the rules of international law. * * *

[With respect to Question I(b), the Court stated:]

* * *

The Court is here faced with a new situation. The questions to which it gives rise can only be solved by realizing that the situation is dominated by the provisions of the Charter considered in the light of the principles of international law.

The question * * * presupposes that the injury for which the reparation is demanded arises from a breach of an obligation designed to help an agent of the Organization in the performance of his duties. It is not a case in which the wrongful act or omission would merely constitute a breach of the general obligations of a State concerning the position of aliens; claims made under this head would be within the competence of the national State and not, as a general rule, within that of the Organization.

The Charter does not expressly confer upon the Organization the capacity to include, in its claim for reparation, damage caused to the victim or to persons entitled through him. The Court must therefore begin by enquiring whether the provisions of the Charter concerning the functions of the Organization, and the part played by its agents in the performance of those functions, imply for the Organization power to afford its agents the limited protection that would consist in the bringing of a claim on their behalf for reparation for damage suffered in such circumstances. Under international law, the Organization must be deemed to have those powers which, though not expressly provided in the Charter, are conferred upon it by necessary implication as being essential to the performance of its duties. This principle of law was applied by the Permanent Court of International Justice to the International Labour Organization in its Advisory Opinion No. 13 of July 23rd, 1926 (Series B., No. 13, p. 18), and must be applied to the United Nations.

Having regard to its purposes and functions already referred to, the Organization may find it necessary, and has in fact found it necessary, to entrust its agents with important missions to be performed in disturbed parts of the world. Many missions, from their very nature, involve the agents in unusual dangers to which ordinary persons are not exposed. For the same reason, the injuries suffered by its agents in these circumstances will sometimes have occurred in such a manner that their national State would not be justified in bringing a claim for reparation on the ground of diplomatic protection, or, at any rate, would not feel disposed to do so. Both to ensure the efficient and independent performance of these missions and to afford effective support to its agents, the Organization must provide them with adequate protection. * * *

* * * For that purpose, it is necessary that, when an infringement occurs, the Organization should be able to call upon the responsible State to remedy its default, and, in particular, to obtain from the State reparation for the damage that the default may have caused to its agent.

In order that the agent may perform his duties satisfactorily, he must feel that this protection is assured to him by the Organization, and that he may count on it. To ensure the independence of the agent, and, consequently, the independent action of the Organization itself, it is essential that in performing his duties he need not have to rely on any other protection than that of the Organization (save of course for the more direct and immediate protection due from the State in whose territory he may be). In particular, he should not have to rely on the protection of his own State. If he had to rely on that State, his independence might well be compromised, contrary to the principle applied by Article 100 of the Charter. And lastly, it is essential that—whether the agent belongs to a powerful or to a weak State; to one more affected or less affected by the complications of international life; to one in sympathy or not in sympathy with the mission of the agent—he should know that in the performance of his duties he is under the protection of the Organization. This assurance is even more necessary when the agent is stateless.

Upon examination of the character of the functions entrusted to the Organization and of the nature of the missions of its agents, it becomes clear that the capacity of the Organization to exercise a measure of functional protection of its agents arises by necessary intendment out of the Charter.

The obligations entered into by States to enable the agents of the Organization to perform their duties are undertaken not in the interest of the agents, but in that of the Organization. When it claims redress for a breach of these obligations, the Organization is invoking its own right, the right that the obligations due to it should be respected. On this ground, it asks for reparation of the injury suffered, for "it is a principle of international law that the breach of an engagement involves an obligation to make reparation in an adequate form"; as was stated by the Permanent Court in its Judgment No. 8 of July 26th, 1927 (Series A., No. 9, p. 21). In claiming reparation based on the injury suffered by its agent, the Organization does not represent the agent, but is asserting its own right, the right to secure respect for undertakings entered into towards the Organization.

Having regard to the foregoing considerations, and to the undeniable right of the Organization to demand that its Members shall fulfill the obligations entered into by them in the interest of the good working of the Organization, the Court is of the opinion that, in the case of a breach of these obligations, the Organization has the capacity to claim adequate reparation, and that in assessing this reparation it is authorized to include the damage suffered by the victim or by persons entitled through him.

The question remains whether the Organization has "the capacity to bring an international claim against the responsible *de jure* or *de facto* government with a view to obtaining the reparation due in respect of the damage caused (a) to the United Nations, (b) to the victim or to persons entitled through him" when the defendant State is not a member of the Organization.

In considering this aspect of Questions I(a) and (b), it is necessary to keep in mind the reasons which have led the Court to give an affirmative answer to it when the defendant State is a Member of the Organization. It has now been established that the Organization has capacity to bring claims on the international plane, and that it possesses a right of functional protection in respect of its agents. Here again the Court is authorized to assume that the damage suffered involves the responsibility of a State, and it is not called upon to express an opinion upon the various ways in which that responsibility might be engaged. Accordingly the question is whether the Organization has capacity to bring a claim against the defendant State to recover reparation in respect of that damage or whether, on the contrary, the defendant State, not being a member, is justified in raising the objection that the Organization lacks the capacity to bring an international claim. On this point, the Court's opinion is that fifty States, representing the vast majority of the members of the international community, had the power, in conformity with international law, to bring into being an entity possessing objective international personality, and not merely personality recognized by them alone, together with capacity to bring international claims.

Accordingly, the Court arrives at the conclusion that an affirmative answer should be given to Questions I(a) and (b) whether or not the defendant State is a Member of the United Nations.

Question II is as follows:

> "In the event of an affirmative reply on point I(b), how is action by the United Nations to be reconciled with such rights as may be possessed by the State of which the victim is a national?"

* * * When the victim has a nationality, cases can clearly occur in which the injury suffered by him may engage the interest both of his national State and of the Organization. In such an event, competition between the State's right of diplomatic protection and the Organization's right of functional protection might arise, and this is the only case with which the Court is invited to deal.

In such a case, there is no rule of law which assigns priority to the one or to the other, or which compels either the State or the Organization to refrain from bringing an international claim. The Court sees no reason why the parties concerned should not find solutions inspired by goodwill and common sense, and as between the Organization and its Members it draws attention to their duty to render "every assistance" provided by Article 2, paragraph 5, of the Charter.

Although the bases of the two claims are different, that does not mean that the defendant State can be compelled to pay the reparation due in respect of the damage twice over. International tribunals are already familiar with the problem of a claim in which two or more national States are interested, and they know how to protect the defendant State in such a case.

The question of reconciling action by the Organization with the rights of a national State may arise in another way; that is to say, when the agent bears the nationality of the defendant State.

The ordinary practice whereby a State does not exercise protection on behalf of one of its nationals against a State which regards him as its own national, does not constitute a precedent which is relevant here. The action of the Organization is in fact based not upon the nationality of the victim, but upon his status as agent of the Organization. Therefore it does not matter whether or not the State to which the claim is addressed regards him as its own national, because the question of nationality is not pertinent to the admissibility of the claim. * * *

Notes

1. Does the opinion of the Court rest upon the "implied powers doctrine" as many writers have assumed or does it base its conclusion on the finding of international personality in the objective characteristics of the organization? What difference does it make? Consider the following comment:

> If all these activities have their legal basis in the personality of the organization, it is sufficient that an organization should possess international personality for it to have the legal capacity to perform them. On the other hand, if they have their basis in implied powers the question will be posed in different terms for each organization. Likewise, member States will in each case possess the right to claim that certain activity of the organization does not conform to, or goes beyond, the purposes and functions expressed or implied in the constitutional provisions and therefore to refuse to collaborate financially or otherwise in its carrying out; they will be entitled to do so on the simple ground of legality, because it is their right as members to insist that the limitation of sovereignty which results from their agreement to be bound by a majority decision will only be applied in that frame of activities which they consented to grant the organization in subscribing to the constituent instrument. If all these activities are based on the international personality of the organization, they cannot be assailed simply on the ground that they are not expressly foreseen in the constitutional provisions. But, if they have their basis in the implied powers doctrine, an international tribunal might hold them to be unlawful on the ground that they do not constitute a "necessary implication" or that they are not "essential to the performance of its duties" or that they are not "within the scope of the functions of the organization".

Rama–Montaldo, 44 Brit. Y.B.I.L. at 123–124 (footnotes omitted).

2. A close reading of the Court's opinion suggests that it followed both doctrinal approaches but used each for different conclusions. It referred to the "characteristics of the organization" and to activities which "can only be based on a large measure of international personality and the capacity to operate upon an international plane." It concluded, on that basis, that the organization had the capacity to maintain its rights by international claims that is, "to negotiate, to conclude a special agreement and to prosecute a claim before an international tribunal." But after the Court reached this conclusion, it turned to a different question, to wit: whether the general right to bring a claim "comprises the right to bring the kind of international claim described in the Request for this Opinion." In answering this question, the Court did not rely on inherent legal personality; it said the answer depended on the "purposes and functions as specified or implied in its constituent documents and developed in practice." This

led the Court to consider the powers of the Organization to protect its agents as relevant to the particular claim.

3. May members act only through the organization and not independently on matters covered by the functions of the organization? This question arose in a case involving the European Community. The relevant issue was whether a treaty on European road transport (ERTA) could be negotiated by the Community. The Court of Justice of the European Community referred to the powers of the Community and said:

> This Community authority excludes the possibility of a concurrent authority on the part of member States, since any initiative taken outside the framework of the common institutions would be incompatible with the unity of the Common Market and the uniform application of Community law.

ERTA Case, 47 I.L.R. 278, 305 (1971).

Would this conclusion be appropriate for the United Nations or one of its specialized agencies?

4. Some scholars have argued that international organizations that meet certain criteria (e.g., are not under the jurisdiction of any state) have in law and practice "objective legal personality" and that they may therefore perform any international act which they are in a practical position to perform, subject only to the following legal limitations: (1) constitutional provisions forbidding acts for certain purposes or procedures; (2) the principle that the acts do not impose obligations on member states unless they have so agreed or on third parties without a special legal basis. See Seyersted, Objective International Personality of Intergovernmental Organizations (1963); also Balladore Pallieri, quoted in Rama–Montaldo, at 118–20. One difficulty in demonstrating that this position has been followed is that acts carried out by international organizations are virtually always said to be legally justified on the basis of constitutional powers and functions rather than on grounds of inherent powers. Consequently the acts, if challenged, are regarded as valid or invalid in terms of the delegated or implied purposes and competence of the organization. This has been evident in the cases brought before the International Court of Justice involving challenges to the legal authority of the United Nations. See, for example, Advisory Opinions on U.N. Administrative Tribunal, 1954 I.C.J. 47, on Certain Expenses of the United Nations, 1962 I.C.J. 151, discussed below and at p. 1028 and on Namibia, 1971 I.C.J. 16, p. 549 infra. There is little reason to expect that any international organizations will assert a general inherent legal power to perform "sovereign" international acts on grounds of their objective legal personality irrespective of the constitutional definition of their functions and powers.

2. *Authority to Act for an International Organization*

The constitutive instrument of each international organization prescribes the powers and functions of the organization and also identifies the organs entitled to exercise the powers granted to the organization. As indicated in the *Reparations Case* on p. 361 and in note 4 above, it is necessary to show that an organization has been given expressly or by implication the power to perform the acts in question. The question may also arise whether the acts in question were performed or authorized by the organs empowered to do so by the constituent instrument. If that were not the case, would the action be an act of the organization? Would it be legally effective if not taken or authorized by the proper organ?

These questions were considered in an advisory opinion of the International Court of Justice concerning Certain Expenses of the United Nations, 1962 I.C.J. 151. The "expenses" referred to were incurred by the United Nations for the United Nations peacekeeping forces in the Suez area and the former Belgian Congo (later Zaire). The General Assembly had included them in the budget as expenses of the Organization. The legality of that decision was questioned by several member states—principally, the U.S.S.R. and France, who both refused to pay. They claimed that the expenses and the underlying actions were not authorized by the proper organ of the United Nations—namely, the Security Council.

The Court, by a majority opinion, ruled that the General Assembly had the authority to decide that the expenses were those of the Organization. In regard to the contention that the action had been taken by the "wrong" organ the Court's opinion declared:

> It is agreed that the action in question is within the scope of the functions of the Organization but it is alleged that it has been initiated or carried out in a manner not in conformity with the division of functions among the several organs which the Charter prescribes. If the action was taken by the wrong organ, it was irregular as a matter of the internal structure, but this would not necessarily mean that the expense incurred was not an expense of the Organization. Both national and international law contemplate cases in which the body corporate or politic may be bound, as to third parties, by an ultra vires act of an agent.

1962 I.C.J. 151, 168.

Although this excerpt refers to the action as binding in respect of third parties, the opinion also supports the conclusion that the Assembly's action is binding on its members. One judge, Sir Gerald Fitzmaurice, thought the latter point should "not be pressed too far." He considered that the Organization may be bound by *ultra vires* acts toward parties outside the Organization but he doubted that the same principle could apply as between the Organization and the member states *inter se*. In that respect he said:

> There can be no doubt that, in principle at least, expenditures incurred in excess of the powers of the expending body are invalid expenditures. * * *. If an instrument such as the Charter of the United Nations attributes given functions in an exclusive manner to one of its organs constituted in a certain way—other and different functions being attributed to other and differently constituted organs—this can only be because, in respect of the performance of the functions concerned, importance was attached to the precise constitution of the organ concerned.

1962 I.C.J. at 200.

3. *Disputes Over Constitutional Powers (Ultra Vires Issues)*

When a dispute arises over whether a given international organization has exceeded its powers, there may not be a ready forum for authoritative resolution of the dispute. Several cases of the 1990s at the I.C.J. and other tribunals have presented variants on this problem. In the *Lockerbie* cases brought by Libya against the United States and the United Kingdom, discussed further at pp. 419–420 and 900–901 below, Libya sought orders to enjoin the U.S. and U.K. from taking coercive action against Libya in the Security Council, where those states were pressing for economic sanctions aimed at inducing Libya to surrender two individuals charged with causing a bomb to be placed on Pan Am Flight 103 that exploded over Lockerbie, Scotland. Libya's contentions included the argument that the Security Council would exceed or abuse its powers by adopting the sanctions in question. While the case was pending, the Security Council mandated the sanctions against Libya in Resolution 748 (1992). In its orders denying Libya's request for provisional measures against the U.S. and the U.K., the I.C.J. said in part:

> Whereas both Libya and the United Kingdom, as Members of the United Nations, are obliged to accept and carry out the decisions of the Security Council in accordance with Article 25 of the Charter; whereas the Court, which is at the stage of proceedings on provisional measures, considers that prima facie this obligation extends to the decision contained in resolution 748 (1992); and whereas, in accordance with Article 103 of the Charter, the obligations of the Parties in that respect prevail over their obligations under any other international agreement, including the Montreal Convention; * * *

Questions of Interpretation and Application of the 1971 Montreal Convention Arising From the Aerial Incident at Lockerbie (Libya v. United Kingdom; Libya v. United States), 1992 I.C.J. 3, 114. In the aftermath of this decision, legal commentators expounded diverse points of view on whether the I.C.J. has authority under the U.N. Charter to engage in constitutional review of actions of the Security Council as a coordinate principal organ of the United Nations, and whether the I.C.J. had in effect reviewed and affirmed the constitutionality of the Security Council's exercise of authority in the Libyan case. Compare Franck, The "Powers of Appreciation": Who Is the Ultimate Guardian of UN Legality?, 86 A.J.I.L. 519 (1992) with Reisman, The Constitutional Crisis in the United Nations, 87 A.J.I.L. 83 (1993); see also Alvarez, Judging the Security Council, 90 A.J.I.L. 1 (1996) and literature cited therein.

A similar issue arose in the case brought by Bosnia–Herzegovina against the Federal Republic of Yugoslavia (Serbia and Montenegro) under the Genocide Convention. There the applicant state claimed, among other things, that the arms embargo that the Security Council had mandated in respect of all of former Yugoslavia was illegal in its application to Bosnia–Herzegovina, as an excess of the Security Council's powers under the Charter and a derogation from Bosnia's inherent right to defend itself against aggression and genocide. The provisional measures order entered in that case was limited to an exhortation not to commit genocide and did not address the underlying questions of the scope of the Security Council's powers. Compare Application of the Convention on the Prevention and Punishment of the Crime of Genocide (Bosn.-Herz. v. FRY), 1993 I.C.J. 3; 1993 I.C.J. 325. The I.C.J. has not squarely confronted the issue of its own authority to rule on the legality of actions taken by another principal organ of the United Nations.

By contrast, the International Criminal Tribunal for the Former Yugoslavia (I.C.T.Y.) addressed and approved the legality of certain Security Council actions, in the first ruling handed down by its Appeals Chamber. In Prosecutor v. Tadic, Case No. IT–94–1–AR72, Decision on Interlocutory Appeal on Jurisdiction (Oct. 2, 1995), reprinted in 35 I.L.M. 32 (1996), the first defendant brought for trial before the I.C.T.Y. challenged the jurisdiction of the Tribunal on the ground, inter alia, that the Security Council had exceeded its powers under Chapter VII of the U.N. Charter by establishing a criminal tribunal. In rejecting the jurisdictional challenge, the Appeals Chamber took up a number of fascinating questions of constitutional character, beginning with the question of its own authority to rule on the legality of the Security Council's decision to create the I.C.T.Y. As a threshold matter, the Appeals Chamber determined that every tribunal has an inherent power to resolve challenges to its own jurisdiction: "It is a necessary component in the exercise of the judicial function and does not need to be expressly provided for in the constitutive documents of those tribunals, although this is often done. . . ." (para. 18). This inherent or incidental jurisdiction would extend to a power to determine the validity of the Tribunal's own establishment by the Security Council (para. 20).

Proceeding to the substance of defendant's jurisdictional challenge, the Tribunal addressed the issue of the scope of the Security Council's powers in the following excerpts under the heading "The Issue of Constitutionality":

PROSECUTOR v. TADIC

International Criminal Tribunal for the Former Yugoslavia, Appeals Chamber
Case No. IT–94–1–AR72.
Decision on Interlocutory Appeal on Jurisdiction, Oct. 2, 1995.
35 I.L.M. 32 (1996).

26. Many arguments have been put forward by Appellant in support of the contention that the establishment of the International Tribunal is invalid under the Charter of the United Nations or that it was not duly established by law. * * *

27. * * * These arguments raise a series of constitutional issues which all turn on the limits of the power of the Security Council under Chapter VII of the Charter of the United Nations and determining what action or measures can be taken under this Chapter, particularly the establishment of an international criminal tribunal. Put in the interrogative, they can be formulated as follows:

1. was there really a threat to the peace justifying the invocation of Chapter VII as a legal basis for the establishment of the International Tribunal?

2. assuming such a threat existed, was the Security Council authorized, with a view to restoring or maintaining peace, to take any measures at its own discretion, or was it bound to choose among those expressly provided for in Articles 41 and 42 (and possibly Article 40 as well)?

3. in the latter case, how can the establishment of an international criminal tribunal be justified, as it does not figure among the ones mentioned in those Articles, and is of a different nature?

1. The Power Of The Security Council To Invoke Chapter VII

28. Article 39 opens Chapter VII of the Charter of the United Nations and determines the conditions of application of this Chapter. It provides:

> "The Security Council shall determine the existence of any threat to the peace, breach of the peace, or act of aggression and shall make recommendations, or decide what measures shall be taken in accordance with Articles 41 and 42, to maintain or restore international peace and security." (United Nations Charter, 26 June 1945, Art. 39.)

It is clear from this text that the Security Council plays a pivotal role and exercises a very wide discretion under this Article. But this does not mean that its powers are unlimited. The Security Council is an organ of an international organization, established by a treaty which serves as a constitutional framework for that organization. The Security Council is thus subjected to certain constitutional limitations, however broad its powers under the constitution may be. Those powers cannot, in any case, go beyond the limits of the jurisdiction of the Organization at large, not to mention other specific limitations or those which may derive from the internal division of power within the Organization. In any case, neither the text nor the spirit of the Charter conceives of the Security Council as *legibus solutus* (unbound by law).

In particular, Article 24, after declaring, in paragraph 1, that the Members of the United Nations "confer on the Security Council primary responsibility for the maintenance of international peace and security", imposes on it, in paragraph 3, the obligation to report annually (or more frequently) to the General Assembly, and provides, more importantly, in paragraph 2, that:

> "In discharging these duties the Security Council shall act in accordance with the Purposes and Principles of the United Nations. The specific powers granted to the Security Council for the discharge of these duties are laid down in Chapters VI, VII, VIII, and XII." (Id., Art. 24(2).)

The Charter thus speaks the language of specific powers, not of absolute fiat.

29. What is the extent of the powers of the Security Council under Article 39 and the limits thereon, if any?

The Security Council plays the central role in the application of both parts of the Article. It is the Security Council that makes the *determination* that there exists one of the situations justifying the use of the "exceptional powers" of Chapter VII. And it is also the Security Council that chooses the reaction to such a situation: it either makes *recommendations* (*i.e.*, opts not to use the exceptional powers but to continue to operate under Chapter VI) or decides to use the exceptional powers by ordering measures to be taken in accordance with Articles 41 and 42 with a view to maintaining or restoring international peace and security.

The situations justifying resort to the powers provided for in Chapter VII are a "threat to the peace", a "breach of the peace" or an "act of aggression." While the "act of aggression" is more amenable to a legal determination, the "threat to the peace" is more of a political concept. But the determination that there exists such a threat is not a totally unfettered discretion, as it has to remain, at the very least, within the limits of the Purposes and Principles of the Charter.

30. It is not necessary for the purposes of the present decision to examine any further the question of the limits of the discretion of the Security Council in determining the existence of a "threat to the peace", for two reasons.

The first is that an armed conflict (or a series of armed conflicts) has been taking place in the territory of the former Yugoslavia since long before the decision of the Security Council to establish this International Tribunal. If it is considered an international armed conflict, there is no doubt that it falls within the literal sense of the words "breach of the peace" (between the parties or, at the very least, as a "threat to the peace" of others).

But even if it were considered merely as an "internal armed conflict", it would still constitute a "threat to the peace" according to the settled practice of the Security Council and the common understanding of the United Nations membership in general. Indeed, the practice of the Security Council is rich with cases of civil war or internal strife which it classified as a "threat to the peace" and dealt with under Chapter VII, with the encouragement or even at the behest of the General Assembly, such as the Congo crisis at the beginning of the 1960s and, more recently, Liberia and Somalia. It can thus be said that there is a common understanding, manifested by the "subsequent practice" of the membership of the United Nations at large, that the "threat to the peace" of Article 39 may include, as one of its species, internal armed conflicts.

The second reason, which is more particular to the case at hand, is that Appellant * * * no longer contests the Security Council's power to determine whether the situation in the former Yugoslavia constituted a threat to the peace, nor the determination itself. * * * But he continues to contest the legality and appropriateness of the measures chosen by the Security Council to that end.

2. The Range of Measures Envisaged Under Chapter VII

31. Once the Security Council determines that a particular situation poses a threat to the peace or that there exists a breach of the peace or an act of aggression, it enjoys a wide margin of discretion in choosing the course of action: as noted above (see para. 29) it can either continue, in spite of its determination, to act via recommendations, i.e., as if it were still within Chapter VI ("*Pacific Settlement of Disputes*") or it can exercise its exceptional powers under Chapter VII. In the words of Article 39, it would then "decide what measures shall be taken in accordance with Articles 41 and 42, to maintain or restore international peace and security." (United Nations Charter, art. 39.)

A question arises in this respect as to whether the choice of the Security Council is limited to the measures provided for in Articles 41 and 42 of the Charter (as the language of Article 39 suggests), or whether it has even larger discretion in the form of general powers to maintain and restore international peace and security under Chapter VII at large. In the latter case, one of course does not have to locate every measure decided by the Security Council under Chapter VII within the confines of Articles 41 and 42, or possibly Article 40. In any case, under both interpretations, the Security Council has a broad discretion in deciding on the course of action and evaluating the appropriateness of the measures to be taken. The language of Article 39 is quite clear as to the channelling of the very broad and exceptional powers of the Security Council under Chapter VII through Articles 41 and 42. These two Articles leave to the Security Council such a wide choice as not to warrant searching, on functional or other grounds, for even wider and more general powers than those already expressly provided for in the Charter.

These powers are **coercive** *vis-à-vis* the culprit State or entity. But they are also **mandatory** *vis-à-vis* the other Member States, who are under an obligation to cooperate with the Organization (Article 2, paragraph 5, Articles 25, 48) and with one another (Articles 49), in the implementation of the action or measures decided by the Security Council.

3. The Establishment Of The International Tribunal As A Measure Under Chapter VII

32. As with the determination of the existence of a threat to the peace, a breach of the peace or an act of aggression, the Security Council has a very wide margin of discretion under Article 39 to choose the appropriate course of action and to evaluate the suitability of the measures chosen, as well as their potential contribution to the restoration or maintenance of peace. But here again, this discretion is not unfettered; moreover, it is limited to the measures provided for in Articles 41 and 42. * * *

[The Appeals Chamber then concluded that although the establishment of an international criminal tribunal is not expressly mentioned in Articles 41 and 42, the measures set out there are merely illustrative examples which do not exclude other measures. After rejecting appellant's other objections, it held that the Tribunal had been lawfully established as a measure under Chapter VII of the Charter.]

Notes

1. Does the *Tadic* ruling clarify how to determine "inherent" powers of an international organization (such as the power of a judicial body to resolve challenges to its own jurisdiction, which the court found applicable in the situation facing it)? Is an analysis distinguishing among explicit, implicit, and inherent powers useful?

2. If the Security Council's powers are not "unfettered" but indeed bounded by law, where might the limits of those powers be discerned?

3. In addition to "inherent" power to rule on jurisdictional objections, what other powers not expressly conferred in its founding instrument might be available to an international organ such as a criminal tribunal? In Prosecutor v. Blaskic, Case No. IT–95–14–AR108*bis*, Judgment on the Request of Croatia (Oct. 29, 1997), the I.C.T.Y.'s Appeals Chamber addressed a set of questions concerning judicial powers with respect to ordering production of evidence. Croatia had requested review of a "subpoena" issued by a trial chamber, which purported to order Croatia to produce a variety of documents for inspection. The Appeals Chamber began with a clarification of terms:

> 25. The Appeals Chamber holds the view that the term "subpoena" (in the sense of injunction accompanied by threat of penalty) cannot be applied or addressed to States. This finding rests on two grounds. First of all, the International Tribunal does not possess any power to take enforcement measures against States. Had the drafters of the [I.C.T.Y.'s] Statute intended

> to vest the International Tribunal with such a power, they would have expressly provided for it. In the case of an international judicial body, this is not a power that can be regarded as inherent in its functions. * * * Secondly, * * * [u]nder present international law it is clear that States, by definition, cannot be the subject of criminal sanctions akin to those provided for in national criminal systems.

However, the Appeals Chamber did find a power to issue "binding orders" to states, which it derived from the obligation on all states to cooperate with the Tribunal, as laid down in Article 29 of the I.C.T.Y.'s Statute promulgated by the Security Council and restated in a mandatory resolution of the Council. In the event of a state's non-compliance with such a binding order, the Appeals Chamber said:

> 33. * * * As stated above, the International Tribunal is not vested with any enforcement or sanctionary power *vis-à-vis* States. It is primarily for its parent body, the Security Council, to impose sanctions, if any, against a recalcitrant State, under the conditions provided for in Chapter VII of the United Nations Charter. However, the International Tribunal is endowed with the inherent power to make a judicial finding concerning a State's failure to observe the provisions of the Statute or the Rules. It also has the power to report this judicial finding to the Security Council.
>
> The power to make this judicial finding is an inherent power: the International Tribunal must possess the power to make all those judicial determinations that are necessary for the exercise of its primary jurisdiction. This inherent power inures to the benefit of the International Tribunal in order that its basic judicial function may be fully discharged and its judicial role safeguarded. The International Tribunal's power to report to the Security Council is derived from the relationship between the two institutions. The Security Council established the International Tribunal pursuant to Chapter VII of the United Nations Charter for the purpose of the prosecution of persons responsible for serious violations of international humanitarian law committed in the territory of the former Yugoslavia. A logical corollary of this is that any time a State fails to fulfil its obligation under Article 29, thereby preventing the International Tribunal from discharging the mission entrusted to it by the Security Council, the International Tribunal is entitled to report this non-observance to the Security Council.

The consequences of non-compliance with obligations such as those addressed in *Blaskic* will be taken up in Chapter 9. For more on the I.C.T.Y.'s powers and jurisprudence, see Chapter 15.

4. *Treaty–Making Capacity*

International organizations have long assumed a capacity to enter into agreements with states, irrespective of whether that power could be found expressed or implied in its constitutive instrument. Fitzmaurice, usually cautious, concluded as far back as 1953 that: "* * * the necessary attribute of international personality, is the power to enter, directly, or mediately, into relationship (by treaty or otherwise) with other international persons." Fitzmaurice, The Law and Procedure of the International Court of Justice, 30 Brit. Y.B.I.L. 2 (1953). However, attributing treaty-making capacity to international personality does not dispose of the question whether a particular treaty falls within the purposes and competence of the international organization. For that question, one must look to the constitution and the powers granted or implied by it; it is not determined by the existence of international personality.

The U.N. Convention on Treaties Concluded Between States and International Organizations or Between Two or More International Organizations provides: "The capacity of an international organization to conclude treaties is governed by the relevant rules of that organization" (Article 6).

The International Law Commission which prepared the draft convention commented on the above article, as follows:

> A question naturally arises as to the nature and characteristics of the "relevant rules" in the matter of an organization's capacity, and it might be tempting to answer this question in general terms, particularly with regard to the part played by *practice*. That would obviously be a mistake which the text of draft article 6 seeks to avert by specifying that "the capacity of an international organization to conclude treaties is governed by the relevant rules of *that* organization".
>
> It should be clearly understood that the question how far practice can play a creative part, particularly in the matter of international organizations' capacity to conclude treaties, cannot be answered uniformly for all international organizations. This question, too, depends on the "rules of the organization"; indeed, it depends on the highest category of those rules—those which form, in some degree, the constitutional law of the organization and which govern in particular the *sources* of the organization's rules. It is theoretically conceivable that, by adopting a rigid legal framework, an organization might exclude practice as a source of its rules. Even without going as far as that, it must be admitted that international organizations differ greatly from one another as regards the part played by practice and the form which it takes, *inter alia* in the matter of their capacity to conclude international agreements. There is nothing surprising in this; the part which practice has played in this matter in an organization like the United Nations, faced in every field with problems fundamental to the future of all mankind, cannot be likened to the part played by practice in a technical organization engaged in humble operational activities in a circumscribed sector.

I.L.C.Rep. 295–96 (1981).

Note

For a discussion of the 1986 Vienna Convention on Treaties Between States and International Organizations, see Gaja, A "New" Vienna Convention on Treaties Between States and International Organizations or Between International Organizations: A Critical Commentary, 1987 Brit. Y.B.Int'l L. 253–269 (1987).

5. *Locus Standi Before International Tribunals*

Under national law, a legal person normally has the capacity to sue and be sued in national courts. International legal personality should logically involve an analogous capacity before international tribunals. This depends, however, on the law governing the tribunal or on the special agreement establishing an arbitral body.

The principal international judicial organ, the International Court of Justice, hears only states as parties in contentious proceedings. Advisory opinions may, in contrast, be requested only by certain international organizations—namely, the U.N. General Assembly and the Security Council and, when so authorized by the General Assembly, other U.N. organs and specialized agencies (Article 96 of the Charter). Although the General Assembly and Security Council may request the I.C.J.'s advisory opinion on "any legal question" (Article 96(1)), the other organs are limited to "legal questions arising within the scope of their activities" (Article 96(2)). The distinction between the two types became relevant in the I.C.J.'s response given to parallel requests concerning nuclear weapons, one from the General Assembly and one from the World Health Organization (W.H.O.): the Court addressed the General Assembly's request on the merits but found that the W.H.O.'s request was not closely enough connected with the W.H.O.'s activities to form the basis for an advisory opinion. Compare 1996 I.C.J. 226 (General Assembly request) with 1996 I.C.J. 66 (W.H.O. request).

An indirect method for overcoming one barrier to *locus standi* of international organizations before the Court is found in section 30 of the Convention on the Privileges and Immunities of the United Nations, which provides that if a difference arises between the United Nations on the one hand and a member state on the other hand in regard to the interpretation or application of the Convention, a request shall be made for an advisory opinion in accordance with the Charter. The opinion of the Court shall be accepted as decisive. Thus in effect, a dispute between the Organization and a state can be the subject of a binding decision by the Court on the basis of a proceeding which, in substance, would be akin to a contentious proceeding. For further discussion on the I.C.J.'s advisory and contentious jurisdiction, see Chapter 11.

Proposals have been made to expand the possibility for international organizations to be parties to cases at the I.C.J. and other tribunals. Such proposals would equalize the legal position of states and international organizations, and would correspond more closely to the acceptance of international organizations as subjects of international law for most purposes. They might also provide a forum for resolution of disputes that currently lack a place for authoritative settlement—for example, over monetary obligations owed by states to international organizations. On the pros and cons of such proposals, see Szasz, Granting International Organizations *Ius Standi* in the International Court of Justice, in Miller et al. (eds.), The International Court of Justice 169–188 (1997).

International organizations may be parties to arbitration proceedings in disputes with states. The Headquarters Agreement of 1947 between the United Nations and the United States provides for arbitration in case of disputes under that agreement, and many similar arbitration clauses have been introduced in agreements between international organizations and states.

6. *Responsibility of International Organizations*

Since international legal personality gives intergovernmental organizations the right to make claims and enter into treaties, it also involves legal responsibility for acts of a delictual or contractual character. If an international organization can be a "plaintiff" on the international plane, it must also be a "defendant" when the circumstances warrant it. In practice, international organizations have long accepted responsibility for tortious acts of its officials, agents, and others (such as troops) acting under their control. Most international organizations have also assumed financial responsibility for contractual obligations *vis-à-vis* states. The member states of the organizations do not, as a rule, incur individual responsibility for the acts or engagements of the organization except as they may bear the costs through the agreed procedures for meeting the financial expenses of the organization.

Questions of responsibility of international organizations have arisen most conspicuously in connection with the peacekeeping activities of the United Nations. These involved complex legal and political issues as to the financial costs incurred in the large-scale peacekeeping activities and the obligation of member states to bear these costs when they regarded the actions as ultra vires. Some of the issues were considered by the International Court in its advisory opinion on Certain Expenses of the United Nations, 1962 I.C.J. 151. Responsibility for damage and personal injuries by military forces provided by member states but acting under the authority of the United Nations was also assumed by the United Nations. Agreements with the governments which contributed troops and with the host (i.e., territorial) governments provided the terms of financial responsibility and the procedures for settling particular cases. For detailed discussions of various aspects of responsibility in respect of United Nations peacekeeping, see Bowett et al., United Nations Forces (1964). The legal issues were especially difficult in regard to the peace-keeping activities in the Congo (later Zaire) in the period 1961–1964. Their complexity is brought out in the article by Salmon, Les Accords Spaak—U Thant du 20 Fevrier 1965, 11 Ann. Francais 468 (1965). See also U.N. Jur. Yb. 41 (1965).

It is well accepted that conduct of an organ or personnel of an international organization within the territory of a state cannot, by reason of that fact alone, be attributed to the territorial state. This is recognized in agreements concluded by the organizations with the host states. For examples of agreements and analysis of legal issues, see Report of 27th Session International Law Commission relating to State Responsibility (draft article 13), [1975] 2 Yb.I.L.C. 87–91. Responsibility of the United Nations for violations of the laws of war by peace-keeping forces under its authority has been considered by the *Institut de Droit International* at its sessions in 1971 (Zagreb) and 1975 (Wiesbaden) on the basis of reports by de Visscher and Hambro. See 54–1 Ann. de l'Institut de Droit Int'l I (1971); 54–II id. 149 (1971); 56–I id. 81–117, 475–94 (1975). These questions became more acute with the proliferation, beginning in the 1990s, of U.N. peace-keeping operations of enormous difficulty and sensitivity. See Chapter 12.

The contractual responsibilities of international organizations *vis-à-vis* private persons have also generated a substantial body of law and practice especially with respect to applicable law, terms of contracts and settlement of disputes. See Valticos, Les contrats conclus par les organisations internationales avec des personnes privées, 57–I Ann. de l'Institut de Droit Int'l 1 (1977); Jenks, The Proper Law of International Organization (1962).

An issue that has attracted recent attention is the circumstances under which member states of an international organization may be secondarily or concurrently liable to third parties for debts of the organization. This issue was the focus of decisions by the English Court of Appeals in Maclaine Watson & Co. Ltd. v. Department of Trade & Indus., [1988] 3 All E.R. 257, and by the House of Lords in J.H. Rayner Ltd. v. Department of Trade & Indus., [1989] 3 W.L.R. 969, which arose out of the defaults by the International Tin Council (ITC) on contracts to purchase tin and on bank loans entered into as a part of its efforts to support the price of tin through maintenance of a buffer stock. The ITC was an international organization established with "international legal personality" by the Sixth International Tin Agreement to which more than 20 states and the European Community were parties. The Court of Appeals rejected secondary or concurrent liability of the member states, and the House of Lords affirmed.

On the basis of an examination of these English cases, the principal textual authorities, and state practice, Amerasinghe concludes that "the better view is that there is no presumption, when the constituent instrument does not indicate such an intention, that members of an international organization are concurrently or secondarily liable for its obligations. The presumption is thus the reverse. However, though there is no evidence of this in the sources, policy reasons also suggest the need to limit this rule on the basis of estoppel: the presumption of nonliability could be displaced by evidence that members (some or all of them) or the organization with the approval of members gave creditors reason to assume that members (some or all of them) would accept concurrent or secondary liability even without an express or implied intention to that effect in the constituent instrument." Amerasinghe, Liability to Third Parties of Member States of International Organizations: Practice, Principle and Judicial Precedent, 85 A.J.I.L. 259, 280 (1991).

B. IMMUNITIES AND INTERNAL AUTONOMY OF INTERNATIONAL ORGANIZATIONS; RELATION TO MUNICIPAL LAW

The Restatement (Third) § 467 states as follows:

> (1) Under international law, an international organization generally enjoys such privileges and immunities from the jurisdiction of a member state as are necessary for the fulfillment of the purposes of the organization, including immunity from legal process, and from financial controls, taxes, and duties.
>
> (2) Under the law of the United States, international organizations are entitled to the privileges and immunities provided by international agreements to which the United States is party, and organizations designated by the President under the International Organizations Immunities Act are entitled to the privileges and immunities provided in that Act.

The major international organizations enjoy the immunities referred to in subsection (1) under their charters and supplementary agreements. See the discussion in Chapter 14 beginning at p. 1295. Comments *a* and *d* of the

Restatement elaborate as follows on the scope of international organization immunities:

> *a. Privileges and immunities by international agreement and under customary law.* * * *
>
> The provisions in international agreements dealing with privileges and immunities of international organizations do not distinguish between immunity from jurisdiction to prescribe, to adjudicate, or to enforce by nonjudicial means. The immunities contemplated are principally immunities from judicial process and police interference, but immunity from any exercise of jurisdiction could be claimed if it is necessary for the fulfillment of the purposes of the organization. See also Comment *c*. Compare § 463.
>
> * * *
>
> *d. Applicability of restrictive theory of immunity.* It appears that the restrictive theory that limits the immunity of a state from legal process (see § 451) does not apply to the United Nations, to most of its Specialized Agencies, or to the Organization of American States. These organizations enjoy immunity from jurisdiction to adjudicate in all cases, both under their charters and other international agreements (see Comment *b*), and under the law of the United States. Whether other international organizations enjoy absolute or restricted immunity under international law is unclear, but at least until that question is authoritatively resolved they will probably be accorded only restricted immunity under the law of the United States. See Reporter's Note 4.

International organizations are absolutely immune from suits arising out of their internal operations, including their relations with their employees. See, e.g., Mendaro v. World Bank, 717 F.2d 610 (D.C.Cir.1983). The issue whether restrictive or absolute immunity is applicable in other situations is discussed in Oparil, Immunity of International Organizations in United States Courts: Absolute or Restrictive?, 24 Vand. J. Transnat'l L. 689 (1991). For a comprehensive comparative analysis, see Reinisch, International Organizations Before National Courts (2000).

Immunity may be waived by the organization's charter. Thus, Article VII, Section 3 of the World Bank's Articles of Agreement has been held to constitute a waiver of immunity from suits "arising out of its external commercial contracts and activities." Mendaro v. World Bank, supra at 618. Immunity may also be waived by an appropriate organ or officer of the organization. Waiver must be express. Such organ or officer may also waive the immunity of the organization in a particular case, and may agree to arbitration but, at least without specific authorization, immunity from any measure of execution may not be waived. See Restatement (Third) § 467, Comment *e*.

Notes

1. The internal autonomy of international organization has been extensively considered in the literature and in decisions of international tribunals. See

advisory opinions of the International Court of Justice on Effect of Awards of Compensation Made by the U.N. Administrative Tribunal, 1954 I.C.J. 27, on Judgments of the Administrative Tribunal of I.L.O. on Complaints against UNESCO, 1956 I.C.J. 77, and on Application for Review of Judgment of U.N. Administrative Tribunal, 1973 I.C.J. 166. See also Seyersted, Jurisdiction Over Organs and Officials of States, the Holy See and Intergovernmental Organizations, 14 I.C.L.Q. 69–71, 77–78 (1965), and Meron, The United Nations Secretariat: The Rules and Practice (1977) which reveals the tension between the legal principles of internal autonomy of the organization and the actuality of political pressure by member governments.

2. Internal judicial organs have been established within international organizations to adjudicate disputes between the organization and its staff members. The U.N. Administrative Tribunal includes within its jurisdiction not only the United Nations, but also some of the specialized agencies. The Administrative Tribunal of the I.L.O. similarly has an extended jurisdiction beyond the I.L.O. itself, including by special agreement, several of the specialized agencies located in Europe (e.g., UNESCO, FAO, and WHO). The European Economic Community did not have to create a special tribunal, since its Court of Justice had jurisdiction with respect to complaints of staff members. A considerable body of case-law has been developed by the several tribunals concerned with the rights and obligations of international organizations vis-à-vis international officials. In particular, procedural rights analogous to due process have been defined in a great variety of situations of international employment. See Bastid, Have the U.N. Administrative Tribunals Contributed to the Development of International Law in Transnational Law in a Changing Society 299–312 (Friedmann, Henkin, Lissitzyn, eds. 1972); Meron, supra.

C. MEMBERSHIP AND REPRESENTATION IN INTERNATIONAL ORGANIZATIONS

1. Membership in international organizations is generally limited to states. In some cases other governmental entities have also been admitted to membership.

States become members by:

(a) becoming parties to the constitutive treaty establishing the organization;

(b) admission through votes of one or more of the principal organs (in the United Nations, for example, an applicant state must receive the approval of the Security Council, including the affirmative vote of the five permanent members and two-thirds of the General Assembly);

(c) succession in accordance with the rules of the organization. (Generally a successor state has been required to be elected as a new member; if a successor state is admitted by virtue of succession (rather than election) it succeeds to both the rights and obligations of its predecessor.)

2. Requirements of membership

Some organizations are open to all states that accept the obligations of the constitution. Regional organizations limit membership to states within a defined region. The constitution may impose other qualifications. For example, the U.N. Charter declares (Art. 4) that membership is open to "peace-loving" states and requires that members be "able and willing to carry out the obligations of the Charter." Whether an applicant was truly independent and viable was debated in several cases. In recent years, many mini-states, including some associated states that do not conduct their own foreign relations or defense, have been admitted to membership even though it appeared that they were dependent politically and economically on other states.

3. Representation of States

States are represented in international organization by representatives or delegations appointed by the government. Changes in regime or form of government do not affect the rights or obligations of a member. In a number of instances, competing authorities have claimed to be the government with the right to represent the state. The decision as to which claimant has the right to appoint representatives is made by the organization, generally by accepting or rejecting credentials submitted by the claimants. Many states have argued that the decision should be taken on "objective" criteria, in particular, which claimant is in effective control of the state and able to employ the resources and direct the people in fulfillment of the obligations of membership. Others have maintained that the willingness of a regime to fulfill the purposes of the Organization and to abide by its principles is also relevant. See discussion in Chapter 4 at p. 292 on the recognition of governments.

The credentials of a delegation were rejected in some instances because the government in question was considered to be "unrepresentative" or to have violated principles of the constituent instrument. South Africa was denied participation in the U.N. General Assembly on these grounds. Objection to that action as illegal was registered by the United States on the ground that it was an indirect suspension of the rights of membership without conforming to the Charter's condition for such suspension, in particular, an affirmative vote by the Security Council. See Kirgis, International Organizations in their Legal Setting, 585–597, (2d ed. 1993).

On suspension of membership rights or exclusion from an organization as a sanction for violation of the obligations of membership, see Chayes & Chayes, The New Sovereignty 68–87 (1995).

4. On September 22, 1992, the U.N. General Assembly took the unprecedented step of denying the Federal Republic of Yugoslavia (Serbia and Montenegro) the right to succeed the Socialist Federal Republic of Yugoslavia as a member of the United Nations. This action was related to the former's involvement in the hostilities in Bosnia–Herzegovina. Following the change of government in the FRY in fall 2000, the FRY applied for and was admitted to U.N. membership. See p. 351.

5. Non-state entities are members of some international organizations. The Universal Postal Union, for example, includes postal administrations of territories that are not in themselves states. While representatives and delegations are normally designated by governments, the International Labour Organization constitution provides for tri-partite representation of labor, employers and governments.

D. INTERGOVERNMENTAL COMPANIES AND PRODUCERS' ASSOCIATIONS

States have also created entities of an international character to conduct financial or commercial activities, or have formed associations for economic purposes. Such entities are generally established by treaty but unlike the public international organizations may be institutions under municipal law. They may also be "mixed"—part public, part private—as to their purpose or legal form. An example of a public multinational financial institution is the Bank of International Settlements, established by a 1930 Convention of six states. It operates under a Swiss charter and is governed by Swiss law to the extent not inconsistent with the Convention. Several multinational public enterprises operate as consortia in the fields of aviation and shipping: Scandinavian Air Line and Air Afrique are examples.

An important multinational enterprise—INTELSAT, the International Telecommunications Satellite Organization—was established by a 1973 treaty among a large number of states. See 23 U.S.T. 3813, TIAS No. 7532. It is an operating organization composed of members that are public or private entities responsible for national aspects of global satellite communications. Unlike other multinational enterprises, the INTELSAT Agreement does not accept the municipal law of its headquarters state as residual law. Instead, it provides that legal disputes are to be resolved by an arbitration tribunal on the basis of the INTELSAT Agreement itself and "generally accepted principles of law."

Another form of intergovernmental organization, the intergovernmental producers association, is most prominently exemplified by the Organization of Petroleum Exporting Countries (OPEC). A number of similar organizations have been established by intergovernmental agreement of states engaged in the production of primary commodities. Examples have included producers of bauxite, copper, iron ore, and of agricultural commodities such as coffee, cocoa, bananas, and sisal. Their main objective is to secure fair (i.e., higher) prices for their product and to coordinate national action so as to increase the return to producers and to promote national control over the industry concerned. The associations engage in joint price fixing sometimes backed by export limits, production quotas, and market allocations. The developed market-economy countries have criticized such intergovernmental associations as cartel-like attempts to raise costs artificially and impose restraints on international trade.

It is not always clear whether associations of the OPEC type act independently of their members or exercise powers on the international plane (such as the power to conclude international agreements in their own right). For these reasons, investigation into the attributes and functions of a given entity would be needed in order to determine the existence or extent of international legal personality.

SECTION 2. NON-GOVERNMENTAL ORGANIZATIONS

Non-governmental organizations (NGOs) play an active role on the international scene and in some cases have a recognized legal status under treaties and other international arrangements. The Charter of the United Nations provides for consultative arrangements between the Economic and Social Council and NGOs (Article 71), and hundreds of NGOs have consultative status under that provision. Similar arrangements exist in other international organizations. The numerous international NGOs range over the entire array of human activity. They include worldwide organizations involved in humanitarian, health, human rights and environmental matters; professional and scientific associations; the federations and international unions made up of national associations representing labor or employers; religious bodies; scientific academies; and so on. Many of these organizations have been accorded the right to express their views to official international bodies and in some circumstances they perform functions delegated to them by international instruments or governmental decisions. A notable example is the distinctive role of the International Committee of the Red Cross, a non-governmental body, which has important functions under the Geneva Conventions on the Laws of the War and in delivering humanitarian supplies to areas ravaged by hostilities or famine. Some scientific bodies, though non-governmental, have also been accorded official functions by intergovernmental organizations.

NGOs have not generally been accorded the full status of international legal persons, and their legal capacity and rights are governed by applicable municipal law. But see Hondius, European Convention on the Recognition of the Legal Personality of International Non-governmental Organizations, 7 The Philanthropist 6 (1988). However, as the materials below suggest, their formal legal status may be less significant than their actual ability to influence events.

NGOs have played increasingly important roles in the human rights and environmental areas. For example, organizations such as Amnesty International and Human Rights Watch have assisted international bodies in efforts to monitor human rights violations around the world, and organizations such as Greenpeace and Friends of the Earth have played watchdog roles in identifying violators of environmental restrictions. Their multifaceted activities, in norm-creation as well as implementation, are suggested in the excerpts that follow.

THAKUR & MALEY, THE OTTAWA CONVENTION ON LANDMINES: A LANDMARK HUMANITARIAN TREATY IN ARMS CONTROL?

5 Global Governance 273, 280–285 (1999) (footnotes omitted).

* * * The coalition to ban landmines was forged by NGOs and sustained by them for over a decade. Many states remained resistant to the ban on grounds of national security. The ICBL [International Campaign to Ban Landmines], with the help and support of other NGO groups like the International Committee of the Red Cross (ICRC) and Médecins sans Frontières (MSF), called for a simple, clean, and comprehensive ban on APL [antipersonnel landmines] with no exception, reservation or loophole. * * * Their views prevailed. Working with and through states, they proved influential.

The ascendancy of realism provided a normative justification for a state-centric approach to international politics and security. Yet the state consists of rulers and citizens whose interests can come into conflict. In such circumstances, the security interests of some citizens may coincide with the goals of international government and nongovernmental organizations like the ICRC and the UN in opposition to the security and political interests of national governments. By raising the twin questions of security against what and for whom, NGOs sensitize us to definitions of security outside the realist framework of states and state interests.

The rise of a raft of transnational activists bound together by powerfully shared concerns over single issues like human rights, environment, and gender equality is the most graphic evidence of the erosion of the state-centered international order. This has important implications for the identity and shifting potency of different actors in contemporary international relations. In the words of Leon Gordenker and Thomas Weiss, NGOs are "private in . . . form but public in . . . purpose." NGO networks are neither hierarchical, like intergovernmental organizations (IGOs), nor market-based. When high-politics issues of security were dominant during the Cold War, NGO space was more circumscribed. With the greater prominence of low-politics issues of environmental degradation and humanitarian crises, NGOs have become relatively more prominent on the international landscape. * * *

* * * NGOs can serve as focal points for the mobilization and articulation of interests shared by many people living in different countries. Even in a major international forum like the UN, humanitarian NGOs have access to national delegates and Secretariat officials, provide a range of information from a broader cross-section of sources, and lobby for their preferred solutions. Liaising with the UN enables NGOs to maximize their own impact in world affairs, to express ideas and promote programs to a wider audience and on a broader platform, and to believe that they are integral parts of a global network of decisionmaking structures. The process of implementing global conference declarations and the review mechanisms usually built into them act as stimuli to the international networking of NGOs. The enhanced networking capacity of NGOs helps to offset the imbalance in relative capabilities of states and international organizations. They have also exploited advances in information and communications technology—in particular, faxes and electronic mail—to expand the range, volume, and quality of their networking activity across the globe. Electronic communication makes it feasible to forge territorially unbounded virtual communities in cyberspace based on shared values and common interests and goals.

Some of the more important NGOs, such as Amnesty International and Greenpeace, are limited *actors* in their own right. The UN is a *sovereignty-bound* actor; an NGO is a *sovereignty-free* actor. The lofty proclamations of human rights in the UN Charter suggest an expansive interest; the enabling clauses reveal a more restrictive authority conferred on the organization. The powers of humanitarian NGOs, although no more extensive, can be utilized more effectively because they are free of some of the types of inhibitions that impede the functioning of IGOs [intergovernmental organizations] that are subject to "capture" by member governments. The relationship of NGOs to governments ranges from adversarial to complementary and subservient/co-optive. Some NGOs, like Greenpeace, Amnesty International, Oxfam, CARE, and the ICRC, have achieved such longevity, scale of membership and activity, finances, and international prestige that they cannot easily be dismissed or intimidated by hostile governments. If their work is in partnership with IGOs, as is increasingly the case with developmental and humanitarian relief agencies, then attempts to subdue NGOs can lead to difficult questions being raised in IGO forums at a time when the normative importance of "civil society" and "global governance" has been greatly strengthened. * * *

The work of the NGOs in the negotiation, drafting, and adoption of the Ottawa convention can also be conceptualized as an example of social networking across national frontiers. Governments and IGOs are social organs made up of people who interact with one another and with other people outside formal roles on a variety of issues and in a range of different social contexts. Actors engage in complex or "multiplex" relationships, and informal links can be crucial to the attainment of organizational goals. The interface between formal organizations directly is provided by boundary-role occupants who mediate between the environment and their constituents. NGOs and other "boundary-role aliens" can act as linchpins or nodes through which issue-specific networks are joined. * * *

The ICBL was thus an ad hoc transnational social network whose conceptual coherence lay in what the network actors did, without reference to their structure or organizational form. It brought together operational, educational, and advocacy NGOs with governments and IGOs wedded to the same cause. * * *

The ICBL helped to raise public consciousness through seminars, lectures, and workshops involving citizens, officials, and politicians. It lobbied officials and politicians for access to funds and opportunities for agenda setting and participation in international negotiation sessions as observer-components of national delegations. NGOs offered technical expertise and research and drafting skills to governments that were relatively weak in these areas. They approached officials of international secretariats with similar requests. They mobilized public opinion and forged political coalitions within and between countries. As with the megaconferences in the 1990s on the environment and on women, any account of the Ottawa conference to sign the APL convention will be grossly deficient if NGOs are not given prominent attention. Nevertheless, international public policy even by most nonstate actors is still pursued through lobbying states. Only governments can sign binding agreements. But, as was noted above, international humanitarian law can evolve through consensus without having to rely on the consent of every state; and every state is bound by the peremptory norm of customary international law.

WAPNER, POLITICS BEYOND THE STATE: ENVIRONMENTAL ACTIVISM AND WORLD CIVIC POLITICS

47 World Politics 311–313, 318, 320, 329 (1995) (footnotes omitted).

Interest in transnational activist groups such as Greenpeace, European Nuclear Disarmament (END), and Amnesty International has been surging. Much of this new attention on the part of students of international relations is directed at showing that transnational activists make a difference in world affairs, that they shape conditions which influence how their particular cause is addressed. Recent scholarship demonstrates, for example, that Amnesty International and Human Rights Watch have changed state human rights practices in particular countries. Other studies have shown that environmental groups have influenced negotiations over environmental protection of the oceans, the ozone layer, and Antarctica and that they have helped enforce national compliance with international mandates. * * * This work is important, especially insofar as it establishes the increasing influence of transnational nongovernmental organizations (NGOs) on states. Nonetheless, for all its insight, it misses a different but related dimension of activist work—the attempt by activists to shape public affairs by working within and across societies themselves. * * *

* * * When activists work to change conditions without directly pressuring states, their activities take place in the civil dimension of world collective life or what is sometimes called global civil society. Civil society is that arena of social engagement which exists above the individual yet below the state. It is a complex network of economic, social, and cultural practices based on friendship, family, the market, and voluntary affiliation. * * * Global civil society as such is that slice of associational life which exists above the individual and below the state, but also across national boundaries. When transnational activists direct their efforts beyond the state, they are politicizing global civil society. * * *

The debate about NGOs, while important, suffered premature closure, because scholars ultimately saw NGO significance in terms of state power. That is, NGOs assumed prominence in subsequent studies only to the extent that they affected state policies; their influence on world affairs apart from this role was neglected. * * *

This article * * * eschews an understanding in which the multifarious activities of actors gain relevance only insofar as they affect states, and concentrates instead on identifying NGO activity that orders, directs, and manages widespread behavior throughout the world. One can get a sense of this through a study of transnational environmental activist groups. * * * By doing so, scholars will be able to recognize that NGOs are significant in world affairs not only because they influence states but also because they affect the behavior of larger collectivities throughout the world. They do so by manipulating governing structures of global civil society.

[The article then reviews several instances in which transnational environmental activist groups achieved change in corporate practices through techniques such as adverse publicity and consumer boycotts. In one of the examples, activist coalitions promoted the idea of "dolphin-safe" tuna labels, thereby reducing dolphin kills even before governmental and intergovernmental efforts produced legislation and international standards on the matter.]

In each instance, activist groups did not direct their efforts at governments. They did not target politicians; nor did they organize constituent pressuring. Rather, they focused on corporations themselves. Through protest, research, exposés, orchestrating public outcry, and organizing joint consultations, activists won corporate promises to bring their practices in line with environmental concerns. The levers of power in these instances were found in the economic realm of collective life rather than in the strictly governmental realm. * * *

Notes

1. How significant is the distinction, brought out in the two pieces excerpted above, between NGO activities addressed to *states* (or to organizations of states) and those directed at other segments of society? Can NGOs be said to participate directly in the processes of international law, if some of their endeavors to set standards or induce compliance bypass state organs?

2. For additional readings addressed to these themes, see Weiss & Gordenker (eds.), NGOs, the UN, and Global Governance (1996); Wapner, Environmental Activism and World Civic Politics (1996); Keck & Sikkink, Activists Beyond Borders: Advocacy Networks in International Politics (1998); Korey, NGOs and the Universal Declaration of Human Rights: A Curious Grapevine (1998); Charnovitz, Two Centuries of Participation: NGOs and International Governance, 18 Mich. J. Int'l L. 183 (1997); Steiner, Diverse Partners: Non–Governmental Organizations in the Human Rights Movement (1991); Otto, Non–Governmental Organizations in the United Nations System: The Emerging Role of International Civil Society, 18 Hum. Rts. Q. 107 (1995); Spiro, New Global Communities: Nongovernmental Organizations in International Decision–Making Institutions, 18 Wash. Q. 45 (1995); Spiro, New Global Potentates: Nongovernmental Organizations and the "Unregulated" Marketplace, 18 Cardozo L. Rev. 957 (1996); Posner, Foreword: Human Rights and Nongovernmental Organizations on the Eve of the Next Century, 66 Fordham L. Rev. 627 (1997); Esty, Non–Governmental Organizations at the World Trade Organization: Cooperation, Competition, or Exclusion, 1 J. Int'l Econ. L. 123 (1998); Korey, Human Rights NGOs: The Power of Persuasion, 13 Ethics & Int'l Affs. 151 (1999); O'Brien, et al., Contesting Global Governance: Multilateral Economic Institutions and Global Social Movements (2000).

B. ACCESS OF NGOs to INTERNATIONAL BODIES

As the preceding readings suggest, NGO influence is not limited to their impact on states or state-created international organizations. Nonetheless, much of their effectiveness stems from gaining access to arenas in which states deliberate, negotiate, decide on, and apply international standards. Through such access NGOs can participate (indirectly if not directly) in agenda-setting, information exchange, publicity, and other processes bearing on the content and implementation of international law. It is thus important for international lawyers to be aware of the procedural framework in which NGOs participate in (or are formally excluded from) the work of intergovernmental organizations. By the same token, since NGOs generally cannot be direct parties to cases in international tribunals, it is necessary to look beneath the surface to understand how they can communicate views to courts and other panels that determine substantive questions of international law.

1. Consultative Status with U.N. ECOSOC

Article 71 of the U.N. Charter provides:

The Economic and Social Council may make suitable arrangements for consultation with non-governmental organizations which are concerned with matters within its competence. Such arrangements may be made with international organizations and, where appropriate, with national organizations after consultation with the Member of the United Nations concerned.

ECOSOC's "Arrangements for Consultation with Non-Governmental Organizations," as revised in 1996, are embodied in ECOSOC Res. 1996/31, which is excerpted in the Documents Supplement (the "Arrangements"). The Arrangements are implemented through ECOSOC's Committee on NGOs (the "Committee") and the NGOs Section of the U.N. Secretariat.

NGOs in consultative relationships with ECOSOC include those at international, regional, subregional, or national levels. The Committee is instructed (para. 5) to "ensure, to the extent possible, participation of non-governmental organizations from all regions, and particularly from developing countries, in order to help achieve a just, balanced, effective and genuine involvement of non-governmental organizations from all regions and areas of the world." Where an applicant is a national NGO, the Committee is to take account of the views of the member state concerned and the response to such views from the NGO. The Arrangements contain provisions aimed at ascertaining that an NGO is representative of its members and has a governance structure with transparent decisionmaking.

The nature of consultative relationships preserves what the Arrangements characterize as a "fundamental" distinction between privileges accorded to states and international organizations on the one hand, and NGOs on the other (para. 18). The purpose of consultative status (para. 20) is to enable ECOSOC organs "to secure expert information or advice from organizations having special competence in the subjects for which consultative arrangements are made, and, on the other hand, to enable international, regional, subregional and national organizations that represent important elements of public opinion to express their views." NGOs concerned with a wide range of activities and "broadly representative of major segments of society in a large number of countries in different regions of the world" may be admitted to general consultative status, while those with more specialized scope are in special consultative status or are listed on a roster indicating their availability for consultation (paras. 21–26). The Arrangements specify the various privileges available to the respective statuses (e.g., attendance at meetings; information exchange), as well as the guidelines for NGO participation in international conferences convened by the United Nations. Provisions for suspension and withdrawal of consultative status are also specified (paras. 55–57), as where an organization "clearly abuses its status by engaging in a pattern of acts contrary to the purposes and principles of the Charter of the United Nations including unsubstantiated or politically motivated acts against Member States of the United Nations incompatible with those purposes and principles" (para. 57(b)).

Notes

1. Under the ECOSOC Arrangements, more than 100 groups have been admitted to general consultative status and more than 1000 to special consultative status as of 2000. Still, the formulation of the principles leaves room for dispute over eligibility of particular groups, as well as over whether states could prevail upon the Committee on NGOs to block admission of groups whose message they dislike. In the case of NGOs with a national rather than international base, the views of the member state concerned are one factor that the Committee considers, so that negative views of an influential state could present a significant obstacle. Also, the composition of the 19–member Committee is perceived by some human rights NGOs to be weighted with states hostile to their stance: as of 2000, its members were Algeria, Bolivia, Chile, China, Colombia, Cuba, Ethiopia, France, Germany, India, Lebanon, Pakistan, Romania, Russia, Senegal, Sudan, Turkey, Tunisia and the United States. On a controversy in spring 2000 over a move by China to deny consultative status to Freedom House, a New York-based NGO, see "Groups Fear Exclusion From the U.N.," New York Times, May 23, 2000.

2. Some NGOs (or, more broadly, members of civil society whether or not acting through organized groups) complain about the closed procedures of certain international organizations, the lack of transparency surrounding their activities, and the difficulty of gaining access to their processes. Such frustrations were part of the motivation for street protests at the Seattle meeting of the World Trade Organization in December 1999 and the meetings of the World Bank and International Monetary Fund in Washington in spring 2000 and in Prague in fall 2000. What procedural opportunities might respond to these concerns?

3. Alongside or apart from formal arrangements with U.N. bodies, NGOs have set up arenas for coordinating among themselves. Thus, in connection with the several U.N.-sponsored World Conferences of the 1990s (such as the 1995 World Conference on Women held in Beijing), parallel NGO events provided an alternative forum for airing a diversity of viewpoints.

4. As of late 2000, efforts were in progress toward a General Assembly resolution that would extend consultative arrangements for NGOs to the General Assembly, building on ECOSOC experience and regularizing what had previously been ad hoc General Assembly decisions.

2. *Participation in Tribunal Proceedings*

As will be seen in Chapter 11 on dispute settlement, NGOs typically would not have standing to be direct parties in international courts or tribunals. The jurisdiction of the I.C.J. is limited to states in contentious cases and to international organizations for advisory jurisdiction; the statutes of other bodies (such as the Dispute Settlement Understanding of the W.T.O.) limit formal participation in dispute procedures to member states; and other systems have vested the function of initiating cases in a specialized organ such as an executive commission.

Nonetheless, NGOs have contributed vibrantly to the jurisprudence of international tribunals, even of quintessentially state-centered tribunals. One method, of course, is to submit views to the tribunal through the intermediary of a sympathetic state or states. This method was used successfully in the *Advisory Opinion on Nuclear Weapons*, 1996 I.C.J. 226, where written and oral statements had to be presented by states in accordance with the I.C.J.'s Statute and Rules, but the ideas and documentation for various states' presentations had been developed with support from transnational antinuclear advocacy groups (e.g., the Lawyers Committee on Nuclear Policy or the International Alliance of Lawyers Against Nuclear Armaments). Similarly, states have sometimes adopted and submitted materials prepared by NGOs as part of their own pleadings at the W.T.O.: this was done, for example, in the *Shrimp Turtle* proceeding excerpted below, where the Appellate Body had occasion to consider more broadly the circumstances under which a dispute settlement panel has discretionary authority to receive materials from NGOs:

UNITED STATES—IMPORT PROHIBITION OF CERTAIN SHRIMP AND SHRIMP PRODUCTS

W.T.O. Appellate Body, WT/DS58/AB/R
October 12, 1998 (footnotes omitted).

98. The issues raised in this appeal by the appellant, the United States, are the following:

(a) whether the Panel erred in finding that accepting non-requested information from non-governmental sources would be incompatible with the provisions of the DSU [Dispute Settlement Understanding] as currently applied; * * *

V. Panel Proceedings and Non-Requested Information

99. In the course of the proceedings before the Panel, on 28 July 1997, the Panel received a brief from the Center for Marine Conservation ("CMC") and the Center for International Environmental Law ("CIEL"). Both are non-governmental organizations. On 16 September 1997, the Panel received another brief, this time from the World Wide Fund for Nature. The Panel acknowledged receipt of the two briefs, which the non-governmental organizations also sent directly to the parties to this dispute. The complaining parties—India, Malaysia, Pakistan and Thailand—requested the Panel not to consider the contents of the briefs in dealing with the dispute. In contrast, the United States urged the Panel to avail itself of any relevant information in the two briefs, as well as in any other similar communications. The Panel disposed of this matter in the following manner: * * *

100.* * * First, the Panel declared a legal interpretation of certain provisions of the DSU, i.e., that accepting non-requested information from non-governmental sources would be "incompatible with the provisions of the DSU as currently applied." Evidently as a result of this legal interpretation, the Panel announced that it would not take the briefs submitted by non-governmental organizations into consideration. Second, the Panel nevertheless allowed any party to the dispute to put forward the briefs, or any part thereof, as part of its own submissions to the Panel * * *.

101. It may be well to stress at the outset that access to the dispute settlement process of the WTO is limited to Members of the WTO. This access is not available, under the WTO Agreement and the covered agreements as they currently exist, to individuals or international organizations, whether governmental or non-governmental. * * * Correlatively, a panel is obliged in

law to accept and give due consideration only to submissions made by the parties and the third parties in a panel proceeding. These are basic legal propositions; they do not, however, dispose of the issue here presented by the appellant's first claim of error. We believe this interpretative issue is most appropriately addressed by examining what a panel is authorized to do under the DSU.

102. Article 13 of the DSU reads as follows: * * *

> 1. Each panel shall have the right to seek information and technical advice from any individual or body which it deems appropriate.
>
> 2. Panels may seek information from any relevant source and may consult experts to obtain their opinion on certain aspects of the matter. With respect to a factual issue concerning a scientific or other technical matter raised by a party to a dispute, a panel may request an advisory report in writing from an expert review group. * * *

104. The comprehensive nature of the authority of a panel to "seek" information and technical advice from "any individual or body" it may consider appropriate, or from "any relevant source", should be underscored. This authority embraces more than merely the choice and evaluation of the source of the information or advice which it may seek. A panel's authority includes the authority to decide not to seek such information or advice at all. We consider that a panel also has the authority to accept or reject any information or advice which it may have sought and received, or to make some other appropriate disposition thereof. It is particularly within the province and the authority of a panel to determine the need for information and advice in a specific case, to ascertain the acceptability and relevancy of information or advice received, and to decide what weight to ascribe to that information or advice or to conclude that no weight at all should be given to what has been received. * * *

107. Against this context of broad authority vested in panels by the DSU, and given the object and purpose of the Panel's mandate as revealed in Article 11, we do not believe that the word "seek" must necessarily be read, as apparently the Panel read it, in too literal a manner. That the Panel's reading of the word "seek" is unnecessarily formal and technical in nature becomes clear should an "individual or body" first ask a panel for permission to file a statement or a brief. In such an event, a panel may decline to grant the leave requested. If, in the exercise of its sound discretion in a particular case, a panel concludes inter alia that it could do so without "unduly delaying the panel process", it could grant permission to file a statement or a brief, subject to such conditions as it deems appropriate. The exercise of the panel's discretion could, of course, and perhaps should, include consultation with the parties to the dispute. In this kind of situation, for all practical and pertinent purposes, the distinction between "requested" and "non-requested" information vanishes.

108. In the present context, authority to seek information is not properly equated with a prohibition on accepting information which has been submitted without having been requested by a panel. A panel has the discretionary authority either to accept and consider or to reject information and advice submitted to it, whether requested by a panel or not. The fact that a panel may *motu proprio* have initiated the request for information does not,

by itself, bind the panel to accept and consider the information which is actually submitted. The amplitude of the authority vested in panels to shape the processes of fact-finding and legal interpretation makes clear that a panel will not be deluged, as it were, with non-requested material, unless that panel allows itself to be so deluged. * * *

110. We find, and so hold, that the Panel erred in its legal interpretation that accepting non-requested information from non-governmental sources is incompatible with the provisions of the DSU. At the same time, we consider that the Panel acted within the scope of its authority under Articles 12 and 13 of the DSU in allowing any party to the dispute to attach the briefs by non-governmental organizations, or any portion thereof, to its own submissions.

Notes

1. Why did the Appellate Body attach significance to a legal interpretation of the Dispute Settlement Understanding that would convey flexibility as regards NGO submissions, independent of party control or direct "request" emanating from the Panel? When might this interpretation make a practical difference?

2. Other international tribunals have gone much farther than the W.T.O. in encouraging NGOs to initiate participation as amicus curiae. The I.C.T.Y. has devised procedures for facilitating input from outside sources and has frequently relied on NGO amicus submissions for insight into difficult legal questions, as in the *Blaskic* ruling on subpoenas cited above and in rulings on issues of special sensitivity for women (e.g., rights of rape victims).

3. The network of human rights implementation bodies reflects more than one attitude toward NGO participation. In systems providing for individual petitions, the procedural rules governing submission of communications can sometimes be read to allow an NGO to submit on a victim's behalf (at least if the victim is unable to act personally and the organization has a sufficient link to the victim). Under Article 44 of the American Convention on Human Rights, any "person or group of persons, or any nongovernmental entity" may lodge petitions with the Inter-American Commission on Human Rights. As one commentator has written,

> This formula happens to be the broadest included in any convention. The victim and the petitioner may be different subjects in this system. Although there must be a victim for a case to be maintained, the victim need not personally bring suit. In fact, an NGO may even file a petition without the victim's consent. Because of this expanded scope, the great majority of petitioners in the Inter-American System are NGOs. One possible explanation for this phenomenon is that, with domestic courts open only to victims, civil society is seeking redress internationally.

Mónica Pinto, Fragmentation or Unification Among International Institutions: Human Rights Tribunals, 31 N.Y.U. J.Int'l L. & Pol'y 833, 837 (1999). See also Dinah Shelton, The Participation of Nongovernmental Organizations in International Judicial Proceedings, 88 A.J.I.L. 611 (1994).

4. Especially where formal implementation mechanisms for a particular set of international obligations are weak, NGOs may exert a critical influence to

induce compliance. An example is the Convention on the Elimination of All Forms of Discrimination Against Women (CEDAW), which (until the coming into force of an Optional Protocol opened for acceptance in 1999) has lacked some of the procedural means available to other human rights bodies. (See generally Chapter 8.) Meanwhile, national and international NGOs have been able to publicize the relevant treaty norms, to mobilize around reports issued under CEDAW's relatively "soft" procedures, and to focus attention on practical steps to improve the protection of women's rights in CEDAW countries. See Afsharipour, Note, Empowering Ourselves: The Role of Women's NGOs in the Enforcement of the Women's Convention, 99 Colum. L. Rev. 129 (1999).

Chapter 6

INDIVIDUALS AND PRIVATE CORPORATIONS

SECTION 1. THE STATUS OF THE INDIVIDUAL IN INTERNATIONAL LAW

As pointed out in the Historical Introduction, during its early development following the Peace of Westphalia in 1648, the law of nations was rooted in natural law. The most influential of the seventeenth century international jurists was Hugo Grotius whose classic treatise, De Jure Belli Ac Pacis Libri Tres (1623–24), was founded on natural law principles derived from universal reason rather than from the divine authority that had been looked to by some of his natural law predecessors. The law of nations, based on natural law principles, remained in the ascendency well into the 18th century before being overshadowed by the rise of positivism in the latter part of that century.

When natural law principles were looked to as its primary source, the law of nations could readily encompass individuals as well as nation-states. Thus, in 1765 Blackstone could write:

> The law of nations is a system of rules, described by natural reason, and established by universal consent among the civilized inhabitants of the world; in order to decide all disputes, to regulate all ceremonies and civilities, and to ensure the observance of justice and good faith, in that intercourse which must frequently occur between two or more independent states, and the individuals belonging to each.

W. Blackstone, 4 Commentaries on the Laws of England 66 (1st ed. 1765–1769).

The crux of the positivist view, of which the Swiss jurist Vattel was an early proponent, was that the source of the law of nations was the will of nations themselves as expressed either in international treaties or in custom.

As positivism rose to the fore, the law of nations came to be used to denote the law applicable to nation-states in their relations with one another to the exclusion of law applicable to individuals involved in transnational transactions. Political theorist Jeremy Bentham, who is generally credited with the first use of the term "international law" in lieu of the law of nations in 1789, used it to refer exclusively to relations between sovereign states. J. Bentham, An Introduction to the Principles of Morals and Legislation 296 (Burns & Hart eds. 1970).

The positivist view that international law applies only to states encouraged development of a dichotomy between public international law governing the relations between the states and "private" international law or to use Justice Story's term, the "conflict of laws," governing international transactions of private parties. J. Story, Commentaries on the Conflict of Laws, Foreign and Domestic (1st ed. 1834).

As Janis has observed:

> Positivist legal theory had taken the law of nations of the seventeenth and eighteenth centuries, a law common to individuals as well as to states, and transformed it into two international law disciplines, one "public," the other "private." The former was deemed to apply to states, the latter to individuals. * * * For most of the nineteenth and early twentieth centuries, the positivist definition of public international law as a law for states alone dominated the theory of international law.

Janis, An Introduction to International Law 242 (Little Brown, 3d ed. 1999).

Although regulating relations between states was long the dominant function of international law, defining international law as law for states alone was unrealistically narrow. In fact, individuals were implicated in a number of areas of international law even when positivist theories were ascendant. A variety of examples could be cited.

First, there were crimes under customary international law for which individuals could be tried and punished by national courts. Two leading, early examples were piracy and slave trading. In some states, including the United States, trial and conviction of such crimes in a national court were conditional on enactment of legislation making the customary international crime a crime under municipal law. See p. 1316.

Second, there have been many instances of forceful intervention by a state to protect its own nationals from mistreatment in another state. On the justifications for such uses of force, see Chapter 12.

Third, individuals (and private juridical entities such as corporations) have long been implicated under the customary international law of state responsibility. Under this regime if an alien individual is injured by a wrongful act or omission by, or attributable to, a state and if the individual is unable to obtain redress under the legal system of that state, the state of which the injured individual is a national may intercede and assert a claim against the offending state. In this way, what begins as an injury to an individual or juridical entity may be elevated to the level of a state-to-state claim in which the claimant state seeks reparation from the offending state. This was the position adopted by the Permanent Court of International Justice in Mavrommatis Palestine Concessions (Jurisdiction) (Greece v. Great Britain), P.C.I.J., Ser. A., No. 2 (1924), p. 1. The Greek Government brought a suit against Great Britain arising out of the alleged refusal of the Palestine Government, then under the sovereignty of Great Britain, to recognize rights acquired by M. Mavrommatis, a Greek national, under agreements concluded with him by the authorities of the Ottoman Empire, the predecessor sovereign in Palestine. The British Government filed a preliminary objection to the jurisdiction of the Court. In upholding its jurisdiction, the Court stated as follows, at 11–12:

> In the case of the Mavrommatis concessions it is true that the dispute was at first between a private person and a State—i.e. between M. Mavrommatis and Great Britain. Subsequently, the Greek Government took up the case. The dispute then entered upon a new phase; it entered the domain of international law, and became a dispute between two States. * * *
>
> * * * It is an elementary principle of international law that a State is entitled to protect its subjects, when injured by acts contrary to international law committed by another State, from whom they have been unable to obtain satisfaction through the ordinary channels. By taking up the case of one of its subjects and by resorting to diplomatic action or international judicial proceedings on his behalf, a State is in reality asserting its own rights—its right to ensure, in the person of its subjects, respect for the rules of international law.

Fourth, not infrequently international agreements created rights in individuals and juridical entities against foreign states. For example, treaties of friendship, commerce and navigation sometimes encompassed the right of a national of one contracting state doing business in the other to be free from discriminatory treatment and from having business property expropriated without compensation. In some cases, the rights created by treaty could be enforced against the offending state directly by the injured private party. More often, however, those rights could be enforced only by the state of which the injured individual or juridical entity was a national.

A large body of international agreements, international custom and national law has long governed transnational transactions involving private parties. Much of this was subsumed under the rubric of private international law because the rights and duties were those of private parties, not states.

In discussing the status of individuals in international law, Jessup commented as follows in 1948:

> For the purposes of this context * * * international law or the law of nations must be defined as law applicable to states in their mutual relations and to individuals in their relations with states. International law may also * * * be applicable to certain interrelationships of individuals themselves, where such interrelationships involve matters of international concern. So long, however, as the international community is composed of states, it is only through an exercise of their will, as expressed through treaty or agreement or as laid down by an international authority deriving its power from states, that a rule of law becomes binding upon an individual. When there is created some kind of international constituent assembly or world parliament representative of the people of the world and having authority to legislate, it will then be possible to assert that international law derives authority from a source external to the states. This would be true even though states might well have been the original creators of such a representative legislature. The inescapable fact is that the world is today organized on the basis of the coexistence of states, and that fundamental changes will take place only through state action * * *.

Jessup, A Modern Law of Nations 17 (1948). (Footnotes omitted.)

LAUTERPACHT, INTERNATIONAL LAW AND HUMAN RIGHTS

27–29 (1973) (footnotes omitted).

The position of the individual as a subject of international law has often been obscured by the failure to observe the distinction between the recognition, in an international instrument, of rights enuring to the benefit of the individual and the enforceability of these rights at his instance. The fact that the beneficiary of rights is not authorised to take independent steps in his own name to enforce them does not signify that he is not a subject of the law or that the rights in question are vested exclusively in the agency which possesses the capacity to enforce them. Thus, in relation to the current view that the rights of the alien within foreign territory are the rights of his State and not his own, the correct way of stating the legal position is not that the State asserts its own exclusive right but that it enforces, in substance, the right of the individual who, as the law now stands, is incapable of asserting it in the international sphere. Conversely, there seems to be no warrant for the disposition to allow the question of enforceability of rights to be influenced by the doctrine that individuals cannot be subjects of international law. The question whether individuals in any given case are subjects of international law and whether that quality extends to the capacity of enforcement must be answered pragmatically by reference to the given situation and to the relevant international instrument. That instrument may make them subjects of the law without conferring upon them procedural capacity; it may aim at, and achieve, both these objects.

The legal position in the matter is well illustrated by the question whether individuals can acquire rights directly by treaty independently of municipal legislation. Prior to the Advisory Opinion of the Permanent Court of International Justice in the case concerning the Jurisdiction of the Courts of Danzig in the matter of Danzig railway officials, that question was generally answered in the negative though even then some caution would have been indicated having regard to the law of some countries, such as the United States in which [Ed: certain] duly ratified treaties are a self-executing part of municipal law. Similarly, there had already existed treaties—such as that establishing the Central American Court of Justice, the provisions relating to the Mixed Arbitral Tribunals in the Peace Treaties of 1919, and the Polish–German Upper Silesian Convention—which conferred upon individuals direct rights of international action. However, it was the Advisory Opinion, given in 1928, in the case concerning the Jurisdiction of the Courts of Danzig, which dealt a decisive blow to the dogma of the impenetrable barrier separating individuals from international law. In that case Poland contended that the agreement between her and Danzig regulating the conditions of employment of Danzig officials whom she had taken over into her railway service was an international treaty which created rights and obligations as between Poland and Danzig only; that as that agreement had not been incorporated into Polish municipal law it did not create rights and obligations for individuals; that Poland's responsibility was limited to that owed to Danzig; and that therefore Danzig courts, before which the officials had brought an action in the matter, had no jurisdiction. The Court rejected this contention. It said:

> It may be readily admitted that, according to a well established principle of international law, the *Beamtenabkommen*, being an international agreement, cannot, as such, create direct rights and obligations for private individuals. But it cannot be disputed that the very object of an international agreement, according to the intention of the contracting Parties, may be the adoption by the parties of some definite rules creating individual rights and obligations and enforceable by the national courts. That there is such an intention in the present case can be established by reference to the terms of the *Beamtenabkommen*.

This pronouncement is among the most important rendered by the Court. On the first occasion on which it was directly confronted with the traditional argument, it rejected it * * *. It laid down, in effect, that no considerations of theory can prevent the individual from becoming the subject of international rights if States so wish. That affirmation by the Permanent Court of International Justice of the right of individuals to acquire rights directly under treaties was not an isolated event. It was followed—and the coincidence is significant—by other judicial decisions pointing in the same direction.

O'CONNELL, INTERNATIONAL LAW

Vol. 1, 108–109 (2d ed. 1970) (footnotes omitted).

* * * The individual as the end of community is a member of the community, and a member has status: he is not an object. It is not a sufficient answer to assert that the State is the medium between international law and its own nationals, for the law has often fractured this link when it failed in its purpose. For example, in the areas of black and white slavery, human rights and protection of minorities, international law has selected the individual as a member of the international community for rights and duties, even against the national State. * * *

Theory and practice establish that the individual has legally protected interests, can perform legally prescribed acts, can enjoy rights and be the subject of duties under municipal law deriving from international law; and if personality is no more than a sum of capacities, then he is a person in international law, though his capacities may be different from and less in number and substance than the capacities of States. An individual, for example, cannot acquire territory, he cannot make treaties and he cannot have belligerent rights. But he can commit war crimes, and piracy, and crimes against humanity and foreign sovereigns, and he can own property which international law protects, and he can have claims to compensation for acts arising *ex contractu* or ex *delicto*. He may not be able to pursue his claims and take action to protect his property without the intervention of his own State, but it is still his claim and still his interest which the machinery of enforcement is designed to facilitate.

The statements of doctrine of the International Court on this matter have tended to reflect the object theory which was current when they were made. The Court in the *Mavrommatis* case said that only when the national State takes up the complaint of its subject does the matter enter "the domain of international law." What, then, was the nature of the dispute before it became one between two States? It certainly was not a dispute in municipal law, because there was no municipal law on the subject. The Court would have to say that the dispute was not a legal one at all, and became such only when taken up by the Greek Government. This would be an unacceptable answer when Mavrommatis' whole position was based on the assertion that international law regulated his rights and property. In many similar instances the law officers would advise their governments that Mr. X should be compensated or his claim acknowledged, and their advice is surely in reference to law. The contention that X's claim is no claim in law at all until X's government takes it up is based upon the theory that States alone have capacity in international law and that the "object" of the law has no claim in law. The *Mavrommatis* approach on these lines demonstrates how artificial is the supposed distinction between the claim when it was a non-legal one and the claim when it became a legal one; it was still the same claim based upon the same legal propositions; the only difference was a change in the formal identity of the claimant.

Even if international law does directly create rights and duties in the individual it would not follow that the national State of the individual is no more than a technique for securing recognition of them. International law endows the national State with discretion to act in relation to these rights and duties, and if discretion to act is legal competence then it is true to say that the national State has capacity over and above the capacity of the individual.

Note

For discussion of the right of an individual to assert a claim based on violation of human rights under the European human rights regime, see p. 652. For further discussion of the status of individuals under international law see Chapters 8 and 15.

SMITH, REMEDIES FOR BREACHES OF EU LAW IN NATIONAL COURTS: LEGAL VARIATION AND SELECTION, IN THE EVOLUTION OF EU LAW 287, 288–290

(Craig & de Búrca eds., Oxford 1999) (some footnotes omitted).

Given that we are here dealing with an international compact [the 1957 European Economic Community (EEC) Treaty] among sovereign states one would probably not have expected to find the inclusion of mechanisms by which individuals could directly protect their interests. In fact, the Treaty did co-opt individuals in the task of keeping the Community institutions under control, granting them standing to seek judicial review of those Community decisions considered to be of direct and individual concern to them.[6] In addition, Article 215 provided for the award of compensation for loss caused by the tortious acts of the Community institutions or its servants. Nevertheless, the Treaty contained no explicit system for individual redress when the malefactor was a Member State as opposed to a Community institution. The

6. EC, Art. 173(4) [new Art. 230(4)].

initial enforcement mechanisms thus bore all the hallmarks of their international treaty origins: mechanisms considered appropriate by states to protect their interests from external threat, yet limiting their own exposure to third parties.

Forty years on, the enforcement and remedial provisions included in the treaty remain, on their face, largely unchanged. Member States may now be fined if they fail to bring their law into line with a Court of Justice ruling under Article 171[7] and the European Parliament and European Central Bank now explicitly have standing to seek review of Community acts which affect their prerogatives,[8] but Treaty Amendments have had a fairly peripheral impact in this context. Community legislative initiatives have been more significant and have played a particularly important role in problematic areas such as public procurement, yet such initiatives have tended to be fairly recent phenomena and essentially sector-specific.[9] This may seem surprising, particularly since the Court has looked to the legislature to complement, through harmonization, the basic structure it initially set in place to protect individual rights. Perhaps, in this, the Court was a victim of its own success, for the structure it created, with rights created at Community level yet enforced at domestic level according to domestic rules, was not only simple to implement, offering individuals immediate recourse to established remedies, it must also have appealed to Member State sensitivities by stressing the autonomy of their legal systems. Any attempt on the part of the Community legislature to regulate domestic remedies would, in challenging this autonomy, have been unlikely to find favour among the Member States.

It has thus been left to the ECJ [European Court of Justice] to engage, pretty much single-handedly, in a dramatic rebalancing and fleshing out of the original Treaty terms. On the one hand, the exposure of Community institutions to suit at the hands of individuals before the ECJ has been carefully circumscribed.[10] On the other, the Court has empowered individuals, through its expansive development of the doctrine of direct effect, to seek redress for Member State infringements of Community law in domestic courts. In the first context it has been involved in elucidation and development of specific Treaty Articles, in the latter it has had to work within the interstices of the Treaty, building up innovative mechanisms for state control without any specific Treaty base.

* * *

Regarding the role of individuals in the enforcement of Community law, it appears that the original signatories understood the Treaty as, for the most part, creating mutual obligations merely among themselves, though compliance with these obligations was admittedly to be subject to the scrutiny of independent Community institutions. Individuals were afforded limited scope to apply Community law directly in national courts: it is true that Article 189 indicated that regulations were to be directly applicable—any uncertainty as to their remit being open to clarification under the Article 177 reference

7. EC, Art. 171(2) [new Art. 228(2)].

8. EC, Art. 173(3) [new Art. 230(3)].

9. Dir. 89/655 [1989] OJ L395/33.

10. By adopting a restrictive interpretation of the standing requirements for individuals in Art. 173(4) and introducing exacting criteria for the tortious liability of Community institutions under Art. 215.

procedure—but even those Member States adopting a 'monist' approach to international law considered relatively few Treaty Articles capable of creating directly enforceable individual rights. This is apparent from the submissions made by Member States in the seminal 1963 case of *Van Gend en Loos v. Nederlandse Administratie der Belastingen.*[12] The Dutch government argued that Member State infringements were to be dealt with exclusively under the procedures set out in Articles 169–71, and was joined in its rejection of the suggestion that Article 12 might have direct internal effect by the Belgian and German governments, the latter stressing that Article 12 merely imposed an international obligation on Member States without creating individual rights. Even Advocate General Roemer concluded that the number of directly effective Treaty Articles was strictly limited.

It was the ECJ's rejection of the arguments of both the Member States and Advocate General in *Van Gend en Loos* which set about re-balancing the initial Treaty compact: individuals could look directly to Treaty Articles as a source of rights, according to criteria established by the ECJ itself, and those rights were to be rendered meaningful through enforcement in domestic courts. The ECJ's 'co-option' and empowerment of national courts in this way was certainly a policy decision of considerable audacity, given the variety of strategies which might be adopted when seeking to implement centrally determined rules within a grouping of states such as the European Community. * * *

* * *

National courts and tribunals, even the lowest in the hierarchy, were henceforth to be central to the enforcement of Community law and the success of this manoeuvre would be facilitated by their application of existing domestic procedural rules and remedies. The advantages in terms of speedy implementation and immediate familiarity were clearly apparent.

* * * [T]he impact of the Court's development of direct effect relied crucially on the willingness of national courts to give it concrete realization. As the Court noted in *Van Gend en Loos*, it was necessary to interpret the Treaty Article in dispute 'as producing direct effects and creating individual rights *which national courts must protect*.'[20] What *Van Gend en Loos* spectacularly failed to clarify was the respective roles of national and Community courts and legislatures in shaping the remedies available to individuals when enforcing Community law in domestic courts. Nor, over thirty years later, has the matter been conclusively resolved.

Note

Under the regime of the European Union (EU), there are three levels of law that may confer rights on individuals enforceable against Union institutions (EU Council or Commission) or against a member state. The first are treaty provisions

12. Case 26/62 *Van Gend en Loos v. Nederlandse Administratie der Belastingen* [1963] ECR 1, [1963] CMLR 105.

20. Case 26/62, above n.13 at (ECR), 130–1 (CMLR), italics added.

that create rights and obligations between member states themselves. These provisions can confer enforceable rights on individuals only indirectly as a consequence of the adoption of national implementing measures. A second group of treaty provisions require Union institutions to adopt implementing measures to achieve Union objectives. These fall broadly into two categories: (i) regulations applicable directly to individuals and (ii) directives addressed to member states that affect individuals only if and when further implemented by the member state. In the latter case, the individual may recover damages against its home state for its failure to implement a directive. In *Francovich and Bonifaci v. Italy*, 1991 ECR I–5357, the ECJ held that a member state is obligated to make good losses suffered by individuals as a result of a failure of a member state to adopt law implementing a directive.

The third category of provisions were initially directed to and created obligations only for member states in the area of intergovernmental cooperation, but were held by the ECJ in the *Van Gend en Loos* case to be of such a character as to produce direct effects applicable to individuals (the "direct effects" doctrine) and to confer on them rights that may override national law of a member state. See Toth, The Individual and European Law, 24 I.C.L.Q. 659, 660–62 (1975) ("Such directly applicable [European] Community provisions have an overriding effect over conflicting national rules, whether earlier or later in time, and whether laid down in ordinary statutes or in the Constitution itself."); See also Hinton, Strengthening the Effectiveness of Community Law: Direct Effect, Article 5 EC and the European Court of Justice, 31 N.Y.U.J.Int'l L. & Pol. 307 (1999); Gal–Or, Private Party Direct Access: A Comparison of the NAFTA and EU Disciplines, 21 B.C. Int'l & Comp. L.Rev. 1 (1998); O'Leary, Note: The Extension of International Law to Private Parties within the European Union, 21 B.C.Int'l & Comp.L.Rev. 219 (1998); Edwards, Fearing Federalism's Failure: Subsidiarity in the European Union, 44 Am.J. Comp.L. 537 (1996).

SECTION 2. CRIMINAL RESPONSIBILITY OF INDIVIDUALS UNDER INTERNATIONAL LAW

If a state violates international law thereby causing injury to another state, claims for such violation are properly addressed by the government of the injured state to that of the state responsible for the violation. Ordinarily, the officials, or other persons, who committed the act constituting the violation are not held personally responsible for it under international law.

In a growing number of circumstances, however, international law has recognized individual responsibility for conduct labelled as criminal under international law. There are many references, for example, to individuals committing "an offense against the law of nations." A prominent historical example, noted above, is individual responsibility for acts of piracy, which, although crimes under customary international law, have been prosecuted in national courts in the absence of an international court with jurisdiction. See, e.g., United States v. Smith, 18 U.S. (5 Wheat.) 153, 161–62, 5 L.Ed. 57 (1820), 2 Moore, International Law 951 et seq. (1906). The Constitution vests power in the U.S. Congress to define and punish "Piracies and Felonies committed on the High Seas, and Offenses against the Law of Nations." U.S. Const. Art. 1, § 8(10). Thus, U.S. courts can punish pirates only pursuant to

Congressional legislation. Under the universal principle of jurisdiction, discussed at p. 1135, international law permits any state to apply its national law to punish piracy even when the accused is not a national of the state and the act of piracy was not committed in that state's territorial waters or against one of its vessels. See the discussion of permissible bases for the exercise of legislative jurisdiction in Chapter 13. For the provision on piracy in the U.N. Convention on the Law of the Sea, see p. 1446.

Individuals accused of violations of the laws of war may be punished by the country of which they are nationals, by the enemy or by "international authorities." Ex parte Quirin, 317 U.S. 1, 63 S.Ct. 1, 87 L.Ed. 3 (1942). The four 1949 Geneva Conventions regulate the conduct of war by requiring humane treatment of sick, wounded and shipwrecked persons in the armed forces, prisoners of war and civilians. Any person who commits a grave breach under the Conventions, that is, commits one of the more serious crimes proscribed by them, is subject to trial and punishment by any state party, regardless of the nationality of the accused and the location of the crime. E.g., Geneva Convention Relative to the Protection of Civilian Persons in Time of War of 12 August 1949, Art. 147, 6 U.S.T. 3516, T.I.A.S. No. 3365, 75 U.N.T.S. 287. For a well-known instance of a trial by a U.S. military court of a U.S. army officer for his role in the My–Lai massacre during the Vietnam War, see United States v. Calley, 46 C.M.R. 1131 (A.C.M.R. 1973), aff'd, 22 C.M.A. 534, 48 C.M.R. 19 (1973), petition for writ of habeas corpus granted sub nom., Calley v. Callaway, 382 F.Supp. 650 (M.D.Ga.1974), rev'd, 519 F.2d 184 (5th Cir.1975), cert. denied, 425 U.S. 911, 96 S.Ct. 1505, 47 L.Ed.2d 760 (1976).

Provisions in the anti-terrorism conventions, such as the conventions relating to the suppression of aircraft hijacking and sabotage, frequently require any state party to make the offense punishable by severe penalties and either to investigate and prosecute, if appropriate, an alleged offender in its custody or to extradite the individual to another party having jurisdiction under the convention. E.g., Hague Convention for the Suppression of Unlawful Seizure of Aircraft, December 16, 1970, Art. 2, 22 U.S.T. 1641, T.I.A.S. No. 7192; Montreal Convention for Suppression of Unlawful Acts Against the Safety of Civilian Aviation, September 23, 1971, Arts. 3 and 7, 24 U.S.T. 564, T.I.A.S. No. 7570. See p. 1128.

A. TRIALS OF INDIVIDUALS FOR CRIMES UNDER INTERNATIONAL LAW; THE NUREMBERG TRIALS

The first instances in modern times of the trial of individuals by an international tribunal for crimes under international law were the trials of Nazi and Japanese war criminals after World War II by the multinational military tribunals in Nuremberg and Tokyo. The International Military Tribunal (IMT) at Nuremberg was established by the London Agreement of August 8, 1945 between the four victor states, France, the United Kingdom, the United States and the U.S.S.R. A Charter annexed to the agreement defined the constitution, jurisdiction, and functions of the IMT. The Tribunal was comprised of four judges, one from each of the victorious powers.

The Charter was based on the premise that major Nazi war criminals were to be held criminally responsible as individuals for:

(a) crimes against peace (planning, preparation, initiation of a war of aggression or in violation of international treaties);

(b) war crimes (violations of the laws of war);

(c) crimes against humanity; and

(d) conspiracy to commit any of the foregoing crimes.

Counsel for the accused argued, inter alia, (i) that international law is concerned only with actions of states and does not encompass punishment of individuals and (ii) when the conduct is an act of state, individuals who carry it out are not responsible. The Tribunal's Judgment rejected these arguments, stating:

> * * * In the opinion of the Tribunal, both these submissions must be rejected. That international law imposes duties and liabilities upon individuals as well as upon States has long been recognized. In the recent case of Ex parte Quirin (1942, 317 U.S. 1), before the Supreme Court of the United States, persons were charged during the war with landing in the United States for purposes of spying and sabotage. The late Chief Justice Stone, speaking for the Court, said:
>
> > From the very beginning of history this Court has applied the law of war as including that part of the law of nations which prescribes for the conduct of war, the status, rights, and duties of enemy nations as well as enemy individuals.
>
> He went on to give a list of cases tried by the Courts, where individual offenders were charged with offenses against the laws of nations, and particularly the laws of war. Many other authorities could be cited, but enough has been said to show that individuals can be punished for violations of international law. Crimes against international law are committed by men, not by abstract entities, and only by punishing individuals who commit such crimes can the provisions of international law be enforced.

International Military Tribunal (Nuremberg) Judgment and Sentences, 41 A.J.I.L. 220–21 (1947).

TRIALS OF INDIVIDUALS BEFORE THE NUREMBERG MILITARY TRIBUNALS UNDER CONTROL COUNCIL LAW NO. 10, 1946–1949, VOL. III (1951)

"The Justice Case" (Case 3), Opinion and Judgment
954, 955, 964, 970–972, 974–975, 979, 983–984.

* * * We sit as a Tribunal drawing its sole power and jurisdiction from the will and command of the Four occupying Powers. * * *

* * * As to the punishment of persons guilty of violating the laws and customs of war (war crimes in the narrow sense), it has always been recognized that tribunals may be established and punishment imposed by the state into whose hands the perpetrators fall. These rules of international law were recognized as paramount, and jurisdiction to enforce them by the injured belligerent government, whether within the territorial boundaries of the state or in occupied territory, has been unquestioned. (Ex parte Quirin, [317 U.S. 1,

63 S.Ct. 1, 87 L.Ed. 3 (1942)]; In re Yamashita, 327 U.S. 1, [66 S.Ct. 340, 90 L.Ed. 499 (1946)].) However, enforcement of international law has been traditionally subject to practical limitations. Within the territorial boundaries of a state having a recognized, functioning government presently in the exercise of sovereign power throughout its territory, a violator of the rules of international law could be punished only by the authority of the officials of that state. The law is universal, but such a state reserves unto itself the exclusive power within its boundaries to apply or withhold sanctions. Thus, notwithstanding the paramount authority of the substantive rules of common international law, the doctrines of national sovereignty have been preserved through the control of enforcement machinery. It must be admitted that Germans were not the only ones who were guilty of committing war crimes; other violators of international law could, no doubt, be tried and punished by the state of which they were nationals, by the offended state if it can secure jurisdiction of the person, or by an international tribunal if of competent authorized jurisdiction.

Applying these principles, it appears that the power to punish violators of international law in Germany is not solely dependent on the enactment of rules of substantive penal law applicable only in Germany. Nor is the apparent immunity from prosecution of criminals in other states based on the absence there of the rules of international law which we enforce here. Only by giving consideration to the extraordinary and temporary situation in Germany can the procedure here be harmonized with established principles of national sovereignty. In Germany an international body (the Control Council) has assumed and exercised the power to establish judicial machinery for the punishment of those who have violated the rules of the common international law, a power which no international authority without consent could assume or exercise within a state having a national government presently in the exercise of its sovereign powers.

* * *

C.C.Law 10 is not limited to the punishment of persons guilty of violating the laws and customs of war in the narrow sense; furthermore, it can no longer be said that violations of the laws and customs of war are the only offenses recognized by common international law. The force of circumstance, the grim fact of worldwide interdependence, and the moral pressure of public opinion have resulted in international recognition that certain crimes against humanity committed by Nazi authority against German nationals constituted violations not alone of statute but also of common international law. * * *

As the prime illustration of a crime against humanity under C.C.Law 10, which by reason of its magnitude and its international repercussions has been recognized as a violation of common international law, we cite "genocide" * * *. A resolution recently adopted by the General Assembly of the United Nations is in part as follows:

"The General Assembly therefore

Affirms that genocide is a crime under international law which the civilized world condemns, and for the commission of which principals and accomplices—whether private individuals, public officials, or statesmen, and whether the crime is committed on religious, racial, political or any other grounds—are punishable * * *."

The General Assembly is not an international legislature, but it is the most authoritative organ in existence for the interpretation of world opinion. Its recognition of genocide as an international crime is persuasive evidence of the fact. We approve and adopt its conclusions. Whether the crime against humanity is the product of statute or of common international law, or, as we believe, of both, we find no injustice to persons tried for such crimes. They are chargeable with knowledge that such acts were wrong and were punishable when committed.

The defendants contend that they should not be found guilty because they acted within the authority and by the command of German laws and decrees. Concerning crimes against humanity, C.C.Law 10 provides for punishment whether or not the acts were in violation of the domestic laws of the country where perpetrated (C.C.Law 10, art. II, par. 1(c)) * * *.

* * * The Nuremberg Tribunals are not German courts. They are not enforcing German law. The charges are not based on violation by the defendants of German law. On the contrary, the jurisdiction of this Tribunal rests on international authority. It enforces the law as declared by the IMT Charter and C.C.Law 10, and within the limitations on the power conferred, it enforces international law as superior in authority to any German statute or decree. It is true, as defendants contend, that German courts under the Third Reich were required to follow German law (i.e., the expressed will of Hitler) even when it was contrary to international law. But no such limitation can be applied to this Tribunal. Here we have the paramount substantive law, plus a Tribunal authorized and required to apply it notwithstanding the inconsistent provisions of German local law. The very essence of the prosecution case is that the laws, the Hitlerian decrees and the Draconic, corrupt, and perverted Nazi judicial system themselves constituted the substance of war crimes and crimes against humanity and that participation in the enactment and enforcement of them amounts to complicity in crime. We have pointed out that governmental participation is a material element of the crime against humanity. Only when official organs of sovereignty participated in atrocities and persecutions did those crimes assume international proportions. It can scarcely be said that governmental participation, the proof of which is necessary for conviction, can also be a defense to the charge.

Notes

1. The foregoing passage is from one of the Nuremberg trials carried out under the authority of the Allied Control Council (consisting of representatives of the four occupying powers) pursuant to Control Council Law No. 10. For these trials, the judicial machinery was part of the occupation administration for the American zone, the Office of Military Government (OM–GUS). See generally Taylor, Nuremberg Trials, International Conciliation No. 450 (1959); Taylor, Nuremberg and Vietnam (1970).

2. The General Assembly, by unanimous vote, affirmed the principles of international law recognized in the Nuremberg Charter and Judgment. G.A.Res.

95(I) U.N.Doc. A/236 (1946). Is the reasoning of the tribunals, quoted above, persuasive as to the criminal responsibility of individuals obeying state orders? See Lauterpacht, International Law and Human Rights 38–47 (1950); Schneeberger, The Responsibility of the Individual under International Law, 35 Geo. L.J. 481 (1947); Levy, Criminal Responsibility of Individuals and International Law, 12 U.Chi.L.Rev. 313 (1945); Manner, The Legal Nature and Punishment of Criminal Acts of Violence Contrary to the Laws of War, 37 A.J.I.L. 407 (1943).

3. Questions of individual responsibility for violations of the laws of war received wide public attention during the Vietnam war. The killing of prisoners in custody and the massacre of Vietnamese civilians (most notoriously in the Son My–My Lai cases) resulted in the court martial of some U.S. soldiers and stimulated demands for punishment of higher officials in both military and civilian positions. There was ample evidence that higher-ranking military commanders knew or were in a position to know that the laws of war in respect of the treatment of the civilian population and of prisoners of war were being violated in numerous situations. See Taylor, Nuremberg and Vietnam, ch. 5–7 (1970). Although no punitive action was taken against the senior military commanders, the issue of their individual responsibility was widely discussed and the precedent of Nuremberg invoked. Civilian officials, including the President and the Secretary of State, were also the targets of allegations of complicity in war crimes, most notably the bombing of civilian populations in Vietnam and Cambodia.

4. Iraq's aggression against Kuwait in August 1990 gave rise to charges that Saddam Hussein's government and military forces committed crimes against peace and war crimes, and proposals were made that the perpetrators be brought to trial, possibly in absentia. One proposal called for trial by an ad hoc tribunal established under the authority of the U.N. Security Council. Compare O'Brien, The Nuremberg Precedent and the Gulf War, 31 Va.J.I.L. 391 (1991) and Moore, War Crimes and the Rule of Law in the Gulf Crisis, 31 Va.J.I.L. 403 (1991). The U.N. Human Rights Commission appointed a Special Rapporteur in 1991 to investigate and report on human rights violations in Iraq. The Rapporteur submitted reports to the Commission and the U.N. General Assembly. See Report to the Commission on Human Rights of 18 February 1992, U.N. Doc. E/CN.4/1992/31, and an interim report on human rights violations in the southern marsh area of Iraq forwarded to the U.N. General Assembly on 10 August 1992. U.N. Doc. A/47/367.

B. THE GENOCIDE CONVENTION AND DRAFT CODE OF CRIMES AGAINST THE PEACE AND SECURITY OF MANKIND

The Convention on the Prevention and Punishment of the Crime of Genocide, Dec. 9, 1948, 78 U.N.T.S. 277, provides that persons committing genocide and related enumerated offenses "shall be punished, whether they are constitutionally responsible rulers, public officials or private individuals," and the contracting parties undertake to enact the necessary legislation to provide effective penalties for guilty persons. Articles IV and V. "Persons charged with genocide * * * shall be tried by a competent tribunal of the State in the territory of which the act was committed, or by such international penal tribunal as may have jurisdiction. * * *." Article VI. The United States has ratified the Convention and has enacted legislation rendering genocide a crime for which individuals may be tried and punished in U.S. courts. Genocide Convention Implementation Act of 1988, 18 U.S.C.A. § 1091. The first truly international criminal tribunals that have been established with competence to try serious crimes under international law, including the crime of genocide, are the ad hoc tribunals established by the U.N. Security Council to try individuals accused of atrocities in the former Yugoslavia and Rwanda. See pp. 1332–1366.

In 1950, pursuant to a request from the U.N. General Assembly, the International Law Commission (ILC) began preparation of a Draft Code of Offenses Against the Peace and Security of Mankind, including offenses that would be crimes under international law for which individuals would be responsible. [1950] 2 Yb.I.L.C. 253; [1951] 2 Yb.I.L.C. 43. A Draft Code was completed in 1954 by the ILC and submitted to the U.N. General Assembly. Because the Draft Code raised problems related to the effort to define the crime of aggression, the General Assembly postponed consideration of the Draft Code until it could consider both matters together. In 1974, the Assembly adopted a definition of aggression, G.A.Res. 3314(XXIX) G.A.O.R., 29th Sess., Supp. 31 (1974), p. 943. In 1978, the project to prepare a Draft Code of Offenses Against the Peace and Security of Mankind was reactivated, the General Assembly inviting comments on the 1954 draft. G.A.Res. 33/97(XXXIII) (1978). The United States opposed reconsideration of the Draft Code as a useless exercise. It argued that the likelihood of achieving consensus was small, a consolidated code would add nothing to existing conventions and declarations, and the General Assembly's 1974 definition of aggression was too imprecise to serve as the basis for a criminal indictment. Reply of the United States, U.N. Doc. A/35/210/Add. 1 at 11 (1980), and U.N. Doc. A/C.6/35/SR. 12 at 9 (1980).

In 1981, the Draft Code was nonetheless referred back by the General Assembly to the I.L.C., where a new controversy over individual and state criminal responsibility arose. The 1954 Draft Code was addressed to individuals and not to states (Article 1), but the I.L.C. questioned "whether new subjects of law, in the form of the State or certain other groups, have not emerged in the criminal area." [1983] I Yb.I.L.C. 22. Although the Commission divided sharply on this question, after soliciting the opinions of member states, the Commission stated it would limit criminal responsibility to individuals. [1983] I Yb.I.L.C. 23, 29–30. See Gross, Some Observations on the Draft Code of Offences Against the Peace and Security of Mankind, 13 Isr. Yb. H.Rts. 9–51 (1983); Ferencz, Current Developments: The Draft Code of Offences Against the Peace and Security of Mankind, 75 A.J.I.L. 674 (1981).

At its 43d session in 1991, the I.L.C. adopted a Draft Code of Crimes Against the Peace and Security of Mankind consisting of 26 articles, including articles on crimes under international law for which individuals could be tried and punished. Among the crimes listed were intervention; colonial domination; genocide; apartheid; systematic or mass violations of human rights; exceptionally serious war crimes; recruitment, use, financing and training of mercenaries; international terrorism; illicit drug trafficking; and wilful and severe damage to the environment. 30 I.L.M. 1584 (1991). Article 5 of the 1991 draft provided that prosecution of an individual does not relieve a State of responsibility under international law for an act or omission attributable to it. Article 6 stated that any "State in whose territory an individual alleged to have committed a crime against the peace and security of mankind is present shall either try or extradite him." 30 I.L.M. 1585 (1991). For commentary on the 1991 draft see I.L.C. Tenth Report on the Draft Code of Crimes Against the Peace and Security of Mankind at pp. 31–59, A/CN.4/L.469 20 March 1992.

Work on the Code continued, and on July 5, 1996, the I.L.C. adopted the final text of 20 draft articles constituting the Draft Code of Crimes against the Peace and Security of Mankind. The Draft Code is included in the Documents Supplement. Its cornerstone is Article 2, which provides that "[a] crime against the peace and security of mankind entails individual responsibility." The I.L.C. Commentary elaborates, in part, on Article 2 as follows:

> * * * The principle of individual responsibility and punishment for crimes under international law recognized at Nürnberg is the cornerstone of international criminal law. This principle is the enduring legacy of the Nürnberg Charter and Judgement which gives meaning to the prohibition of crimes under international law by ensuring that the individuals who commit such crimes incur responsibility and are liable to punishment.
>
> * * *

The 1996 Draft Code, which is discussed at p. 1328, includes definitions of only five crimes: aggression (Article 16); genocide (Article 17); crimes against humanity (Article 18); crimes against United Nations and associated personnel (Article 19); and war crimes (Article 20). Consideration of the Code was superseded by work on draft provisions of the statute for a permanent international criminal court. This work culminated in the adoption on July 17, 1998, of a Statute for the International Criminal Court at the U.N.-sponsored diplomatic conference in Rome discussed at p. 1367.

C. THE U.N. CRIMINAL TRIBUNALS FOR THE FORMER YUGOSLAVIA AND RWANDA

1. The International Criminal Tribunal for the Former Yugoslavia

Widespread atrocities, including mass killings and other forms of what came to be called "ethnic cleansing," committed within the territory of the former Yugoslavia, and especially in Bosnia and Herzegovina, prompted the creation of an ad hoc tribunal by the U.N. Security Council for the prosecution of individuals responsible for serious violations of international humanitarian law committed in the former Yugoslavia. On May 25, 1993, the Security Council unanimously adopted Resolution 827, to establish "an international tribunal for the sole purpose of prosecuting persons responsible for serious violations of international humanitarian law committed in the territory of the former Yugoslavia between 1 January 1991 and a date to be determined by the Security Council upon the restoration of peace and to this end to adopt the Statute of the International Tribunal [annexed to the Secretary–General's report pursuant to paragraph 2 of Security Council Resolution 808 excerpted below.]" S.C. Res 827, U.N. Doc. S/RES/827 (1993). The Security Council took this action under Chapter VII of the Charter, having found that the situation in the former Yugoslavia constituted a threat to the peace.

The International Criminal Tribunal for Yugoslavia (I.C.T.Y.) has been granted jurisdiction with respect to (1) grave breaches of the Geneva Conventions of 1949 (Article 2); violations of the laws or customs of war (Article 3); genocide (Article 4) and crimes against humanity (Article 5). What was to become the Statute of the I.C.T.Y. was set forth in a Report by the U.N. Secretary General, produced in response to Security Council Resolution 808.

REPORT OF THE U.N. SECRETARY-GENERAL PURSUANT TO PARAGRAPH 2 OF SECURITY COUNCIL RESOLUTION 808 (1993)

U.N. Doc S/2504, May 3, 1993.

B. Competence Ratione Personae (Personal Jurisdiction) and Individual Criminal Responsibility

50. By paragraph 1 of resolution 808 (1993), the Security Council decided that the International Tribunal shall be established for the prosecution of persons responsible for serious violations of international humanitarian law committed in the territory of the former Yugoslavia since 1991. In the light of the complex of resolutions leading up to resolution 808 (1993) * * * the ordinary meaning of the term "persons responsible for serious violations of international humanitarian law" would be natural persons to the exclusion of juridical persons.

* * *

52. The corresponding article of the statute would read:

Article 6

Personal jurisdiction

The International Tribunal shall have jurisdiction over natural persons pursuant to the provisions of the present Statute.

Individual criminal responsibility

53. An important element in relation to the competence *ratione personae* (personal jurisdiction) of the International Tribunal is the principle of individual criminal responsibility. * * * [T]he Security Council has reaffirmed in a number of resolutions that persons committing serious violations of international humanitarian law in the former Yugoslavia are individually responsible for such violations.

54. The Secretary-General believes that all persons who participate in the planning, preparation or execution of serious violations of international humanitarian law in the former Yugoslavia contribute to the commission of the violations and are, therefore, individually responsible.

55. Virtually all of the written comments received by the Secretary-General have suggested that the statute of the International Tribunal should contain provisions with regard to the individual criminal responsibility of heads of State, government officials and persons acting in an official capacity. These suggestions draw upon the precedents following the Second World War. * * *

* * *

58. The International Tribunal itself will have to decide on various personal defences which may relieve a person of individual criminal responsibility, drawing upon general principles of law recognized by all nations.

59. The corresponding article of the statute would read:

Article 7

Individual criminal responsibility

1. A person who planned, instigated, ordered, committed or otherwise aided and abetted in the planning, preparation or execution of a crime referred to in articles 2 to 5 of the present Statute, shall be individually responsible for the crime.

2. The official position of any accused person, whether as Head of State or Government or as a responsible Government official, shall not relieve such person of criminal responsibility nor mitigate punishment.

3. The fact that any of the acts referred to in articles 2 to 5 of the present Statute was committed by a subordinate does not relieve his superior of criminal responsibility if he knew or had reason to know that the subordinate was about to commit such acts or had done so and the superior failed to take the necessary and reasonable measures to prevent such acts or to punish the perpetrators thereof.

4. The fact that an accused person acted pursuant to an order of a Government or of a superior shall not relieve him of criminal responsibility, but may be considered in mitigation of punishment if the International Tribunal determines that justice so requires.

Note

The structure and functioning of the Tribunal are discussed in Chapter 15. Radovan Karadzic, the leader of the Bosnian Serbs, and Radko Mladic, the Serb military commander in Bosnia, have been indicted for crimes against humanity committed in the ethnic cleansing campaign in Bosnia. A number of lesser figures have been tried, convicted and sentenced, but Karadic and Mladic have not been arrested. The Tribunal's jurisdiction encompasses crimes committed in Kosovo, and Slobodan Milosevic, President of Serbia, and four other Serbian leaders have been indicted by the Tribunal for alleged crimes against humanity committed there. The indictment of President Milosevic is particularly noteworthy as the first instance in which a head of state in power has been indicted by an international tribunal.

2. The International Criminal Tribunal for Rwanda

Shortly after the assassination of Hutu President Juvenal Habyarimana of Rwanda, Hutu extremist troops, militia and mobs launched a genocidal wave of murder and rape against members of the Tutsi minority and Hutu moderates. More than half a million people were butchered between April and July 1994. On November 8, 1994, the U.N. Security Council, again finding a threat to the peace, exercised its power under Chapter VII of the Charter by establishing another ad hoc tribunal to prosecute individuals responsible for genocide and other serious violations of international humanitarian law in the territory of Rwanda during 1994. U.N. Doc. S/RES/955 (1994).

The crimes within the competence of the International Criminal Tribunal for Rwanda (I.C.T.R.) under its statute differ somewhat from those within the competence of the I.C.T.Y. The crimes for which persons may be tried by the I.C.T.R. include (1) genocide (Article 2); (2) crimes against humanity (Article 3); and (3) violations of Article 3 common to the 1949 Geneva Conventions and of Additional Protocol II (Article 4). The differences are principally attributable to the fact that the conflict in Rwanda was essentially internal while that in the former Yugoslavia involved Bosnia–Herzegovina, Croatia and Serbia.

STATUTE OF THE INTERNATIONAL CRIMINAL TRIBUNAL FOR RWANDA

Security Council Resolution 955, November 8, 1994.
U.N. Doc. S/RES/955 (1994)

Article 5

Personal Jurisdiction

The International Tribunal for Rwanda shall have jurisdiction over natural persons pursuant to the provisions of the present Statute.

Article 6

Individual Criminal Responsibility

1. A person who planned, instigated, ordered, committed or otherwise aided and abetted in the planning, preparation or execution of a crime referred to in articles 2 to 4 of the present Statute, shall be individually responsible for the crime.

2. The official position of any accused person, whether as Head of State or Government or as a responsible Government official, shall not relieve such person of criminal responsibility nor mitigate punishment.

3. The fact that any of the acts referred to in articles 2 to 4 of the present Statute was committed by a subordinate does not relieve his or her superior of criminal responsibility if he or she knew or had reason to know that the subordinate was about to commit such acts or had done so and the superior failed to take the necessary and reasonable measures to prevent such acts or to punish the perpetrators thereof.

4. The fact that an accused person acted pursuant to an order of a Government or of a superior shall not relieve him or her of criminal responsibility, but may be considered in mitigation of punishment if the International Tribunal for Rwanda determines that justice so requires.

Note

The structure and functioning of the International Criminal Tribunal for Rwanda are discussed in Chapter 15. One striking difference between the I.C.T.R. and the I.C.T.Y. is that the former has tried, convicted and punished a number of Rwandan leaders responsible for atrocities, including former Rwandan Prime

Minister Kambanda, while the principal indicted leaders allegedly responsible for the atrocities in the former Yugoslavia remained at large as of 2000. See p. 1355.

D. THE PROPOSED PERMANENT INTERNATIONAL CRIMINAL COURT

After years of groundwork by the International Law Commission and more than a year of meetings by special preparatory committees under the auspices of the U.N. General Assembly, a U.N.-sponsored conference of plenipotentiaries was convened in Rome on June 15, 1998. More than 160 countries participated with input from scores of non-governmental organizations. After five weeks of difficult negotiations, the conference adopted the Rome Statute of the International Criminal Court (I.C.C.) on July 17, 1998. The Statute was adopted over opposition by the United States by a vote of 120 to seven. The Statute will come into effect if ratified or acceded to by at least 60 states. As of December 31, 2000, 27 states had ratified.

Crimes within the jurisdiction of the Court include (1) genocide (Article 6); crimes against humanity (Article 7); war crimes (Article 8); and aggression (Article 5(1)(d)). However, aggression will be covered only if and when provisions, including a definition and specifying the conditions under which the Court may exercise jurisdiction, are adopted (Article 5(2)).

ROME STATUTE OF THE INTERNATIONAL CRIMINAL COURT

Adopted by the United Nations Diplomatic Conference of Plenipotentiaries on the Establishment of an International Criminal Court on July 17, 1998. U.N.Doc. A/CONF. 183/9 37 I.L.M. 999 (1998).

Article 25

Individual criminal responsibility

1. The Court shall have jurisdiction over natural persons pursuant to this Statute.

2. A person who commits a crime within the jurisdiction of the Court shall be individually responsible and liable for punishment in accordance with this Statute.

3. In accordance with this Statute, a person shall be criminally responsible and liable for punishment for a crime within the jurisdiction of the Court if that person:

(a) Commits such a crime, whether as an individual, jointly with another or through another person, regardless of whether that other person is criminally responsible;

(b) Orders, solicits or induces the commission of such a crime which in fact occurs or is attempted;

(c) For the purpose of facilitating the commission of such a crime, aids, abets or otherwise assists in its commission or its attempted commission, including providing the means for its commission;

(d) In any other way contributes to the commission or attempted commission of such a crime by a group of persons acting with a common purpose. Such contribution shall be intentional and shall either:

(i) Be made with the aim of furthering the criminal activity or criminal purpose of the group, where such activity or purpose involves the commission of a crime within the jurisdiction of the Court; or

(ii) Be made in the knowledge of the intention of the group to commit the crime;

(e) In respect of the crime of genocide, directly and publicly incites others to commit genocide;

(f) Attempts to commit such a crime by taking action that commences its execution by means of a substantial step, but the crime does not occur because of circumstances independent of the person's intentions. However, a person who abandons the effort to commit the crime or otherwise prevents the completion of the crime shall not be liable for punishment under this Statute for the attempt to commit that crime if that person completely and voluntarily gave up the criminal purpose.

4. No provision in this Statute relating to individual criminal responsibility shall affect the responsibility of States under international law.

Notes

1. The Rome Statute of the International Criminal Court is discussed in Chapter 15 and excerpts are set forth in the Documents Supplement.

2. Like the Nuremberg Charter and the Statutes of the U.N. Tribunals, the Rome Statute provides that individual responsibility applies equally to "all persons without any distinction based on official capacity." Article 27. Similarly, it imposes responsibility on military and other superiors. Article 28(1) provides as follows:

> In addition to other grounds of criminal responsibility under this Statute for crimes within the jurisdiction of the Court:
>
> 1. A military commander or person effectively acting as a military commander shall be criminally responsible for crimes within the jurisdiction of the Court committed by forces under his or her effective command and control, or effective authority and control as the case may be, as a result of his or her failure to exercise control properly over such forces, where:
>
> (a) That military commander or person either knew or, owing to the circumstances at the time, should have known that the forces were committing or about to commit such crimes; and
>
> (b) That military commander or person failed to take all necessary and reasonable measures within his or her power to prevent or repress their commission or to submit the matter to the competent authorities for investigation and prosecution.

Article 26 of the Statute excludes jurisdiction over persons under the age of 18.

E. INDIVIDUAL RESPONSIBILITY FOR ACTS OF TERRORISM

In recent decades, the international community has witnessed a dramatic increase in domestic and international terrorist activities. This development has been accompanied by a substantial increase in state-provided training, financing and logistical support for terrorist organizations. State-sponsored or supported terrorism has proved difficult enough to deal with, but in some ways terrorism carried out by independent groups is an even more complex challenge. Recent examples of terrorism carried out by an apparently independent group are the terrorist bombings of the U.S. Embassies in Nairobi and Dar es Salaam in 1998 which have been attributed to an organization allegedly financed by a wealthy Saudi-born Muslim fundamentalist, Osama bin Laden and his organization, Al Quaeda.

There proved to be a number of political obstacles to achieving agreement that acts of terrorism are crimes under international law, the most obvious of which is that the use of force by a revolutionary movement within a particular state has been viewed as justifiable. However, after a series of terrorist acts in 1985, the U.N. General Assembly unanimously passed a resolution which:

> 1. *Unequivocally condemns,* as criminal, all acts, methods and practices of terrorism wherever and by whomever committed, including those which jeopardize friendly relations among States and their security; * * *
>
> 4. *Appeals* to all States that have not yet done so to consider becoming party to the existing international conventions relating to various aspects of international terrorism * * *
>
> 6. *Calls upon* all States to fulfill their obligations under international law to refrain from organizing, instigating, assisting or participating in terrorist acts in other States, or acquiescing in activities within their territory directed toward the commission of such acts. * * *

U.N.G.A.Res. 40/61 G.A.O.R., 40th Sess., Supp. 53 (1985). The Security Council also adopted a resolution in December 1985 condemning all acts of hostage-taking and abduction and declaring that all states are obliged to prevent such acts. S.C.Res. 579 U.N.Doc. S/RES/579 (1985).

No overall definition of terrorism has been adopted by the international community. The only multinational agreement directed against terrorism generally is the Convention to Prevent and Punish the Acts of Terrorism Taking the Form of Crimes Against Persons and Related Extortion that are of International Significance, to which as of 2000, 23 states, including the United States, were parties. 27 U.S.T. 3949, T.I.A.S. No. 8413.

Efforts by the international community to combat acts of terrorism by individuals have led to the conclusion of a substantial number of multilateral conventions. These conventions are directed at specific types of terrorist conduct, such as aircraft sabotage and hijacking, attacks on diplomats, and hostage-taking. They oblige states to treat the designated terrorist acts as serious crimes and to prosecute an alleged offender found within their territory or to extradite him or her to another state having jurisdiction. The most significant of these conventions include the following:

1. Convention on Offences and Certain other Acts Committed on Board Aircraft (Tokyo Convention), entered into force on December 4, 1969, 20 U.S.T. 2941, T.I.A.S. No. 6768, 704 U.N.T.S. 219, 2 I.L.M. 1042;

2. Convention for the Suppression of Unlawful Seizure of Aircraft (Hague Convention), entered into force on October 14, 1981, 22 U.S.T. 1641, T.I.A.S. No. 7192, 10 I.L.M. 133 (1971);

3. Convention on the Prevention and Punishment of Crimes Against Internationally Protected Persons, including Diplomatic Agents, entered into force on February 20, 1977, 28 U.S.T. 1975, T.I.A.S. No. 8532, 13 I.L.M. 41 (1974);

4. Convention for the Suppression of Unlawful Acts against the Safety of Civil Aviation (Montreal Convention), entered into force on January 26, 1973, 24 U.S.T. 565, T.I.A.S. No. 7570, 10 I.L.M. 1151 (1971).

5. Convention against the Taking of Hostages, entered into force on June 3, 1983, T.I.A.S. No. 11081, 18 I.L.M. 1456 (1979).

6. Convention for the Suppression of Terrorist Bombings, adopted by the General Assembly on January 9, 1998, G.A. Res. 52/164, U.N. GAOR, 52nd Sess., U.N. Doc. A/Res/52/164, 37 I.L.M. 249 (1998).

A Convention for the Suppression of the Financing of Terrorism was approved by the U.N. General Assembly in G.A. Res. 54/109 (Dec. 9, 1999) and opened for signature in January 2000. 39 I.L.M. 270 (2000).

Note

Unless a state is party to a convention obliging it to prosecute or extradite an alleged terrorist, it is debatable whether the state violates international law if it offers a safe haven to such an individual. However, states allowing terrorists to use their territory as a base for their operations incur international responsibility. The well-established rule of international law forbidding states to permit their territory to be used as a base for armed bands of whatever nature to operate in the territory of another state has been suggested as a basis for international claims against states providing support for terrorists. For a discussion of state responsibility for acts of terrorism, see Lillich & Paxman, State Responsibility for Injuries to Aliens Occasioned by Terrorist Activities, 26 Am.U.L.Rev. 217 (1977), and p. 773.

1. The Obligation to Prosecute or Extradite and the Political Offense Exception

Persons accused of terrorism have frequently claimed that they are engaged in political activities and come within the "political offense" exception to extraditable crimes under many bilateral extradition treaties. See p. 1182. This claim has often been successful because of the strong tradition in many states of providing asylum and protection for individuals accused of political offenses in another country. However, the multilateral anti-terrorist conventions listed in the preceding section, which obligate the state party with custody of a suspect to investigate, and if appropriate, prosecute or extradite to another state with jurisdiction, preclude application of the political offense exception to the terrorist crimes covered. Two regional conventions also limit the application of the "political offense" doctrine to terrorist acts. See the European Convention on the Suppression of Terrorism, 15 I.L.M. 1272 (1976), and the Agreement on the Application of the European Convention for the Suppression of Terrorism (the Dublin Agreement), 19 I.L.M. 325 (1980). See also the Supplementary Extradition Treaty between the United

States and the United Kingdom, Treaty Doc. 99–8, 99th Cong., 1st Sess. (1985), which came into force as amended in 1986. For discussion, see Hannay, International Terrorism and the Political Offense Exception, 18 Col. J. Transnat'l L. 381 (1980); Note, Protecting Fugitives' Rights while Ensuring the Prosecution and Punishment of Criminals: An Examination of the New EU Extradition Treaty, 21 B.C. Int'l & Comp. L. Rev. 229 (1998), and p. 1183.

2. *Trial of Individuals Accused of Bombing Pan Am 103*

The obligation to investigate, and prosecute if the facts warrant, or to extradite an individual accused of a crime under the Montreal Convention for the Suppression of Unlawful Acts against the Safety of Civil Aviation, sometimes referred to as the Aircraft Sabotage Convention, was implicated in the events following the bombing of Pan Am 103 in 1988. Pan Am Flight 103 was en route from London to New York on December 21, 1988 when it was destroyed by a bomb over Lockerbie, Scotland, killing all 259 passengers and crew and 11 Lockerbie residents. Following a long investigation, the United States and the United Kingdom indicted two Libyan nationals, Abdelbasset Ali Mohmed Al-Megrahi and Al–Amin Khalifa Fhimah, in 1992 and demanded that they be turned over for prosecution to the United States or the United Kingdom. The Libyan Government took the position that, in the absence of an extradition treaty with either the United States or the United Kingdom, its only obligation under the 1971 Montreal Aircraft Sabotage Convention, to which all three states are parties, was to investigate and, if appropriate, prosecute, or to extradite. Libya conducted an investigation and determined that it had an inadequate basis on which to prosecute. It declined to extradite on the ground that Libya did not have extradition treaties with the United States and the United Kingdom. A similar request by the French Government for extradition of alleged Libyan terrorists allegedly involved in the destruction of UTA Flight 772 in September 1989 was also rebuffed by the Libyan Government.

On January 21, 1992, the U.N. Security Council unanimously adopted Resolution 731 urging the Libyan Government "immediately to provide a full and effective response to [the requests to cooperate fully in establishing responsibility for the terrorist acts against Pan Am flight 103 and UTA flight 772] so as to contribute to the elimination of international terrorism." S.C.Res. 731, U.N.Doc. S/RES/731 (1992). On March 31, 1992, the Security Council, by vote of 10–0 with 5 abstentions, determined that "the failure by the Libyan Government to demonstrate, by concrete actions, its renunciation of terrorism, and, in particular, its continued failure to respond fully and effectively to the requests in Resolution 731 constitute a threat to international peace and security." Acting under Chapter VII of the Charter, the Council imposed sanctions on Libya, including termination of certain air traffic, a prohibition on sale of aircraft and arms and related components and services, and a reduction in the size of Libyan diplomatic and consular missions. S/RES/748 (1992). In the absence of any change in Libya's position, the Security Council turned up the heat on November 11, 1993, by imposing additional sanctions. These included calling on member states to freeze certain assets of the Government or public authorities of Libya and to cease commercial air service to and from Libya and to embargo all aviation-related goods, services and insurance. S/RES/883 (1993).

Libya, in effect, challenged the sanctions imposed under the U.N. resolutions by instituting proceedings before the I.C.J. against the United States and the United Kingdom under the 1971 Montreal Convention. Libya v. United States, 1992 I.C.J. 114 and Libya v. United Kingdom, 1992 I.C.J. 3. The United States and the United Kingdom contended, *inter alia*, that any rights of Libya under the Montreal Convention were superseded by the Security Council resolutions, which under the U.N. Charter take precedence over any rights under the Convention. The I.C.J. denied Libya's request for provisional measures to prevent further action by the United States and the United Kingdom to compel Libya to surrender the accused, but ruled that it has jurisdiction to consider Libya's claim under the Montreal Convention. Libya v. United States, 1998 I.C.J. 115. Further proceedings are pending.

Finally, as a result of discussions involving Libya, the United States, the United Kingdom, the Netherlands and the U.N. Secretary–General, in April of 1999, Libya agreed to extradite its two indicted nationals to stand trial before Scottish judges sitting in the Netherlands. See Netherlands–United Kingdom Agreement Concerning a Scottish Trial in the Netherlands of September 18, 1998, 38 I.L.M. 926 (1999). Scottish authorities formally charged the suspects with conspiracy, murder and contravention of the Aviation Security Act of 1982, which makes it a crime "to negligently or recklessly act in a manner likely to endanger an aircraft." The suspects were tried under Scottish law before a court consisting of three Scottish judges with no jury. Dutch authorities converted a former air force base into a holding facility and courthouse, which was considered Scottish soil for the duration of the proceedings. On January 31, 2001, Megrahi was convicted of murder and was sentenced to impeachment for life. Fhimah was acquitted.

Pursuant to an undertaking of the Security Council made in a resolution adopted on August 28, 1998, the U.N. sanctions against Libya were temporarily lifted after the two suspects reached the Netherlands on April 6, 1999. S/RES/1192 (1998). The European Union sanctions, except for an arms embargo, have been lifted. 1999 O.J. European Communities (L 242) 31, 14 Sept. 1999. Under the Iran and Libya Sanctions Act of 1996, additional U.S. sanctions primarily related to investments in the oil industry will remain in force until Libya complies in full with Resolution 748. N.Y. Times, April 7, 1999 at A3. Before the U.N. sanctions will be lifted permanently, the Security Council must determine that Libya has complied with several more criteria, including renunciation of terrorism, acceptance of responsibility, cooperation with the investigators and payment of appropriate compensation. In June 1999, the Libyan government agreed to pay $40 million in compensation to the families of the victims of UTA flight 772.

Note

The United States has enacted a program of economic sanctions, including an arms embargo and denial of foreign aid and tax credits, that are automatically applied against countries that the Secretary of State determines have repeatedly provided support for acts of international terrorism. Antiterrorism and Arms

Export Amendments Act of 1989. P.L. 101–222, 22 U.S.C. § 2364. See also U.S.C. §§ 2371, 2377, 2776, 2778, and 2780.

SECTION 3. TRANSNATIONAL CORPORATIONS UNDER INTERNATIONAL LAW

In the last few decades, considerable attention has been given to the international role of private corporations that are incorporated in (and often have their headquarters in) one state and carry out operations in many countries around the world. Such transnational (or multinational) corporations (TNCs) have become the focus of considerable controversy because of their economic and, in some cases, political power, the mobility and complexity of their operations, and the difficulties they create for national states—both "home" and "host" states—which seek to exercise legal authority over them. Such corporations are most often private, nongovernmental entities; they are subject to applicable national laws, and they are not international legal persons in the technical sense. That is, they are not generally subject to obligations and generally do not enjoy rights under international law. However, in some cases they have entered into agreements with governments under which the parties have agreed that principles of public international law or general principles of law, rather than national law, will govern the transaction or investment. See p. 788. Moreover, bilateral and multilateral treaties may confer rights on a private corporation that may be enforced against the host state in its courts or, under certain circumstances, in an international arbitral tribunal or, if the corporation's claim is espoused by the state of which it is a national, before the International Court of Justice. Leading examples of such bilateral treaties would be bilateral investment treaties. See p. 808. A multilateral example would be the EEC treaty and other agreements implementing the European Union.

Under European Union law, private enterprises are accorded legal standing to participate in EU procedures. Private enterprises are accorded rights and subject to direct regulation by the Union organs with a corresponding right to appeal against acts of those organs. For a more detailed discussion of the law of the European Union, see p. 401.

For most purposes, private corporations are treated in international law as the nationals of a particular state, whether the state of incorporation, the state where the corporation's mind and management are located or the state where the corporation maintains its headquarters or registered office (*siège social*). Corporations, like individuals, must in most instances rely on the protection of the government of which they are nationals and do not have access to international legal proceedings to protect their rights. See the *Barcelona Traction Case*, 1970 I.C.J. 3, at p. 441.

THE IMPACT OF MULTINATIONAL CORPORATIONS ON THE DEVELOPMENT PROCESS AND ON INTERNATIONAL RELATIONS

Report of the "Group of Eminent Persons".
U.N.Doc. E/5500/Add 1 (1974).

Multinational corporations are enterprises which own or control production or service facilities outside the country in which they are based. Such enterprises are not always incorporated or private; they can also be cooperatives or state-owned entities.

Most countries have recognized the potential of multinational corporations and have encouraged the expansion of their activities in one form or another within their national borders. The role of foreign private investment in development is indeed acknowledged * * *. At the same time, certain practices and effects of multinational corporations have given rise to widespread concern and anxiety in many quarters and a strong feeling has emerged that the present *modus vivendi* should be reviewed at the international level.

Opinions vary on the contribution of multinational corporations to world economic development and international relations, on the problems created by them and on the ways in which they should be treated. This was amply borne out in the discussions of the Group and in the views expressed during the hearings by representatives of Governments, labour and consumer organizations, by executives of multinational corporations and by members of the academic community. All, including the multinational corporations themselves, expressed concern of one kind or another.

Home countries are concerned about the undesirable effects that foreign investment by multinational corporations may have on domestic employment and the balance of payments, and about the capacity of such corporations to alter the normal play of competition. Host countries are concerned about the ownership and control of key economic sectors by foreign enterprises, the excessive cost to the domestic economy which their operations may entail, the extent to which they may encroach upon political sovereignty and their possible adverse influence on sociocultural values. Labour interests are concerned about the impact of multinational corporations on employment and workers' welfare and on the bargaining strength of trade unions. Consumer interests are concerned about the appropriateness, quality and price of the goods produced by multinational corporations. The multinational corporations themselves are concerned about the possible nationalization or expropriation of their assets without adequate compensation and about restrictive, unclear and frequently changing government policies.

From all these expressions of concern, one conclusion emerges: fundamental new problems have arisen as a direct result of the growing internationalization of production as carried out by multinational corporations. We believe that these problems must be tackled without delay, so that tensions are eased and the benefits which can be derived from multinational corporations are fully realized.

PICCIOTTO, INTRODUCTION: WHAT RULES FOR THE WORLD ECONOMY?, IN REGULATING INTERNATIONAL BUSINESS 6–7

(Mayne & Picciotto eds. 1999).

TRANSNATIONAL CORPORATE AND CONTRACTUAL NETWORKS

The new patterns of globalization generated by post-industrial capitalism have been characterized by Manuel Castells as based on a "network society" * * *. A key element in these processes are international business networks, dominated by TNCs. The TNCs became the focus of political attention after their emergence in the 1960s and 1970s as the dominant private institutions in the world economy. The pace of internationalization of business accelerated during the 1980s and 1990s, with new trends towards internationalization in finance, services and retail sectors and in medium-sized and even smaller firms. By 1996 there were an estimated 44,000 TNCs with some 280,000 foreign affiliates, although the top 25 firms controlled over half of the outward investment stock * * *. These giant corporate groups dominate international economic flows: notably, about one-third of inter-state trade consists of internal flows between affiliates of such groups * * *.

However, business networks go well beyond corporate groups: a high degree of control is also exercised through contractual links in supply and delivery chains. Thus, technology licensing and business-format franchising enable firms such as Coca–Cola, Benetton and McDonalds to control large numbers of outlets which are owned and financed by small entrepreneurs * * *. Conversely, large retailers and firms making brand-name consumer goods source their production from hundreds or thousands of small businesses or even artisanal producers, who themselves may sub-contract to smaller workshops and even outworkers. Although the units in these supply and delivery chains are independently owned, the quantity and quality of their products are tightly supervised.

Thus, a high proportion of international economic flows is controlled by major firms which dominate business networks, and can take a longer-term strategic view of trade and investment. The central position of these firms in the global economy puts them at the heart of the issues of business standards, * * *. Much depends on whether they take advantage of inconsistencies and loopholes in international arrangements, in order to give regulatory competition a downward push, or whether accountability mechanisms can be devised to ensure that they adopt and act as a transmission-belt for high business standards. Certainly, the firms themselves can and should actively promulgate and police standards for themselves and their suppliers * * *. However, * * * the worst abuses often take place outside the formal corporate sector. Thus, a broader national and international regulatory system is necessary, to ensure that improved standards are generally disseminated * * *.

This does not necessarily mean detailed state requirements and enforcement: the important role of formal law is often to strengthen the *mechanisms of accountability*. Thus, * * * among what have been described as the core labour standards, the key ones are the right of association and free collective bargaining. It is neither economically nor morally defensible for workers in developed countries to begrudge the transfer of production to lower-paid workers in developing countries; but it can be an act of international solidarity for them to insist that the workers in those countries should have the right to form and join independent trade unions. Equally, * * * [there are] obstacles that hinder transnational legal accountability of TNCs. Since these firms gain competitive advantage from their ability to manage dispersed activities in an integrated way, they should not be allowed to shelter behind the fictions of separate legal personality and jurisdictional limits to avoid their global responsibilities.

Notes

1. In recent years, considerable emphasis has been placed on efforts to develop international measures to regulate the conduct of transnational corporations (TNCs) across national lines and to define the rights and duties of home and host states in respect of the corporation's activities. Foremost among these measures, which have not purported to set forth binding rules, have been a proposed Code of Conduct for Transnational Corporations, which was under consideration and negotiation for some years by the U.N. Commission and Centre on Transnational Corporations (see p. 1623); Guidelines on the Treatment of Foreign Direct Investment published by the World Bank Group in 1992 (see p. 1626) and an effort under the auspices of the OECD to draft a Multilateral Agreement on Investment, which has since been abandoned (see p. 1626). Proposals have also been made for a multilateral treaty under which transnational corporations which meet certain conditions would be qualified to apply for a charter from an international body which would entitle it to protection under the treaty and oblige it to comply with a set of rules and international surveillance. See, e.g., Ball, Proposal for an International Charter in Global Companies 171–172 (Ball ed. 1975). An "international companies law" of this kind does not seem likely to be realized in the foreseeable future, but the effort to develop a "code" in the form of binding rules or guidelines for transnational corporations is likely to continue.

2. One commentator notes that the international community is moving toward greater international regulation of TNCs and urges that methods be developed for expanding the role of TNCs in the process of international norm development. For example, TNCs might be accredited as non-voting participants in international conferences or TNCs might be involved in expert groups which could participate in international conferences. Such groups could observe the negotiations, participate in information exchanges, issue reports and interact with state representatives to develop new norms. Charney, Transnational Corporations and Developing International Law 1983 Duke L.J. 748, 780–783. Are such forms of informal participation likely to be fruitful? The author's conclusion is that:

> The international legal community has failed to give these [TNCs and other non-state entities possessing comparable economic power] a role because of the power struggles among nation-states and the perceived threats to the nation-state system that they represent. Continuing this conflict imposes unnecessary costs on the international legal system. The effectiveness of international law depends largely upon the legitimacy of its rules. Because the law development process is the vehicle by which these rules are legitimized, a process that excludes powerful international actors will become less legitimate

in the eyes of the excluded actors and will breed disrespect for the international system as a whole.

Id. at 787. Do you agree?

3. The commentary on the transnational corporation has been voluminous. See e.g., Regulating International Business (Mayne & Picciotto eds. 1999); Bergsten, Horst & Moran, American Multinationals and American Interests (1978); Baranson, Technology and the Multinationals (1978); Vernon, Storm over the Multinationals (1977); Conference on the Regulation of Transnational Corporations, 15 Colum.J.Transnat'l L. 367 (1976). For consideration of questions of applicable law, conflicts of jurisdiction, and international registration, see 57–I Ann. de l'Institut de Droit Int'l 266–386 (1977). The reports of the U.N. Commission on Transnational Corporations and the studies of the U.N. Centre on Transnational Corporations (CTC) are highly informative on the policies of governments and practices of multinational companies.

SECTION 4. NATIONALITY UNDER INTERNATIONAL LAW

A. NATIONALITY OF INDIVIDUALS

1. Significance of Nationality

An individual's nationality is significant under international law at a number of points. A state has jurisdiction to enact laws that apply to its nationals located outside its territory when it could not do so with respect to aliens. See p. 1111. A state may accord diplomatic protection to its national in any case in which its national has been injured by another state's violation of international law. See p. 753. It may intercede diplomatically on behalf of an alien only under special circumstances, for example, when human rights violations under a treaty or customary international law are involved. See p. 763. Extradition treaties may provide that a state need not extradite its own nationals. See p. 1182.

In 1923, the Permanent Court of International Justice in the *Tunis and Morocco Nationality Decrees Case,* P.C.I.J., Ser. B., No. 4 (1923), p. 4, held that whether a state treated an individual as its national was a matter within its exclusive domestic jurisdiction. In the intervening years some international law constraints, which are discussed in the materials that follow, have developed on the untrammelled power of a state to confer its nationality on an individual or to withdraw it.

A focus of considerable attention has been whether the individual has a right to a nationality. One aspect of this is the right to be protected from statelessness. The right also encompasses the right to change one's nationality and the right not to be arbitrarily deprived of one's nationality. See Chan, The Right to a Nationality As a Human Right, 12 Hum.Rts.L.J. 1–14 (1991).

There is significant and growing support for the proposition that a right to a nationality should be recognized as a human right protected under international law. See Restatement (Third) § 211, Comment *e*. Article 15(1) of the Universal Declaration of Human Rights provides that "[e]veryone has the right to a nationality." Article 24(3) of the Covenant on Civil and Political

Rights provides simply that "[e]very child has a right to acquire a nationality."

The American Convention on Human Rights was adopted by the Organization of American states in 1969 and came into effect on July 18, 1978. O.A.S. Official Records OEA/Ser.K/XVI/1.1. Doc. 65, Rev. 1, Corr. 1, January 7, 1970, 9 I.L.M. 101, 673 (1970), 65 A.J.I.L. 679 (1971). Article 20 provides as follows:

1. Every person has the right to a nationality.
2. Every person has the right to the nationality of the State in whose territory he was born if he does not have the right to any other nationality.
3. No one shall be arbitrarily deprived of his nationality or of the right to change it.

However, there has been substantial resistance to the recognition of a right to a nationality on the part of a number of states. In 1989, an attempt to guarantee the right to nationality in a Protocol to the European Convention on Human Rights failed. Chan, supra at p. 7.

On November 7, 1997, the European Convention on Nationality was adopted by the Committee of Ministers of the Council of Europe, which had dealt with issues of nationality for over 35 years. 37 I.L.M. 44 (1998). The Convention has been signed by 21 members of the Council of Europe and is in force for three as of 2000. The Convention recognizes a right to nationality and provides that "statelessness shall be avoided." Art. 4, 17 I.L.M. 44 (1998).

Notes

1. A stateless individual has no right to invoke the diplomatic protection of any state. If expelled by the country of residence, no state is required to accept him or her. A number of international agreements provide limited protection to stateless persons and reduce the circumstances under which statelessness can occur. The Protocol to the Convention Relating to the Status of Refugees, 19 U.S.T. 6223, T.I.A.S. No. 6577, 606 U.N.T.S. 267, 1968, to which the United States is a party, accords protection under certain circumstances to stateless refugees. The United States is not a party to the U.N. Convention relating to the Status of Stateless Persons, 360 U.N.T.S. 117 (1954), or to the U.N. Convention on the Reduction of Statelessness. U.N.Doc. A/Conf. 9/15. The latter would prohibit denationalization, except for serious acts of disloyalty, if it would render the individual stateless, and it would prohibit denationalization based on marriage to a foreign national if the result would be statelessness. The United States is also not a party to the American Convention on Human Rights.

2. The International Law Commission's Draft Articles on Nationality in Relation to the Succession of States, cited and discussed in Chapter 4, Section 6, emphasize a state's positive legal obligation to protect inhabitants from statelessness in the event of state succession. Blackman, State Successions and Statelessness: The Emerging Right to an Effective Nationality Under International Law, 19 Mich. J. Int. 1141 (1998). For discussion of the nationality policies in the Baltic Republics after their secession from the Soviet Union, see note 2 at p. 428.

3. In an advisory opinion on whether proposed amendments to the Costa Rica Constitution violated Article 20 of the American Convention on Human Rights, the Inter–American Court of Human Rights opined that nationality is an inherent right of all human beings and that a state's regulation of nationality is subject to a state's obligations to protect the human rights of individuals. Re Amendments to the Naturalization Provisions of the Constitution of Costa Rica, Advisory Opinion of 19 January 1984, OC–4/84, reported in 5 Hum.Rts.L.J. 161 (1984).

4. While nationality is a concept of international law, citizenship is a concept of the municipal law of many but not all states. Citizenship is a status that usually entails full political rights, including the right to vote and hold public office. A citizen under municipal law is usually a national under international law, but not all nationals under international law are citizens under municipal law. Restatement (Third) § 211, Comment *h* and § 212, Comment *a*.

2. *Acquisition of Nationality*

EUROPEAN CONVENTION ON NATIONALITY

Signed at Strasbourg, November 6, 1997.
17 I.L.M. 44 (1998).

ARTICLE 6—ACQUISITION OF NATIONALITY

1. Each State Party shall provide in its internal law for its nationality to be acquired *ex lege* by the following persons:

a. children one of whose parents possesses, at the time of the birth of these children, the nationality of that State Party, subject to any exceptions which may be provided for by its internal law as regards children born abroad. With respect to children whose parenthood is established by recognition, court order or similar procedures, each State Party may provide that the child acquires its nationality following the procedure determined by its internal law;

b. foundlings found in its territory who would otherwise be stateless.

2. Each State Party shall provide in its internal law for its nationality to be acquired by children born on its territory who do not acquire at birth another nationality. Such nationality shall be granted:

a. at birth *ex lege*; or

b. subsequently, to children who remained stateless, upon an application being lodged with the appropriate authority, by or on behalf of the child concerned, in the manner prescribed by the internal law of the State Party. Such an application may be made subject to the lawful and habitual residence on its territory for a period not exceeding five years immediately preceding the lodging of the application.

3. Each State Party shall provide in its internal law for the possibility of naturalisation of persons lawfully and habitually resident on its territory. In establishing the conditions for naturalisation, it shall not provide for a period of residence exceeding ten years before the lodging of an application.

4. Each State Party shall facilitate in its internal law the acquisition of its nationality for the following persons:

a. spouses of its nationals;

b. children of one of its nationals, falling under the exception of Article 6; paragraph 1, sub-paragraph a;

c. children one of whose parents acquires or has acquired its nationality;

d. children adopted by one of its nationals;

e. persons who were born on its territory and reside there lawfully and habitually;

f. persons who are lawfully and habitually resident on its territory for a period of time beginning before the age of 18, that period to be determined by the internal law of the State Party concerned;

g. stateless persons and recognised refugees lawfully and habitually resident on its territory.

Notes

1. The 1997 European Convention on Nationality is in force, having been ratified by Austria, Moldova and Slovakia. States that have signed but not yet ratified as of 2000 include Albania, Bulgaria, the Czech Republic, Denmark, Finland, France, Greece, Hungary, Iceland, Italy, Macedonia, the Netherlands, Norway, Poland, Portugal, Romania, Russia and Sweden.

The 1997 Convention supplements the 1963 Convention on the Reduction of Cases of Multiple Nationality including Military Obligations, E.T.S. No. 43, which was amended in a significant respect by a 1993 Protocol. See p. 440. Unlike the 1963 Convention, the 1997 Convention deals with all major aspects of nationality: principles, acquisition, retention, loss, recovery, procedural rights, multiple nationality, nationality in the context of state succession, military obligations and cooperation between the parties. Article 4(a) and (b). For commentary, see Citizenship and Nationality Status in the New Europe 220–252 (O'Leary & Tiilikainen eds. 1998). The Convention is set forth in the Documents Supplement, and some features of it are discussed below. Perhaps significantly, it has not been signed by Germany or the United Kingdom.

2. Among Council of Europe members that have not ratified the Convention are Latvia and Estonia. While most former Soviet republics granted citizenship to those living permanently within their territory at the time of independence, these Baltic states faced a more complicated transition. The immigration of ethnic Russians to Latvia and Estonia over the previous 50 years of Soviet rule made non-Baltic people a large percentage of the populations in these countries. In 1989, one year before gaining independence, ethnic Latvians made up 52 percent of the population and ethnic Estonians made up 61.5 percent of the population in their respective countries. These states enacted citizenship laws with an ethnic bias. Estonia automatically granted citizenship to ethnic Estonians, while requiring non-ethnic Estonians who had migrated during the Soviet occupation to meet residency requirements and pass a test on the Estonian language and Constitution before becoming naturalized. Latvia required non-ethnic residents to pass a test on the Latvian language and Constitution, meet a residency requirement of 16 years, take an oath of loyalty and renounce any other citizenship. The resulting loss of nationality for the large population of non-ethnic residents attracted

international criticism and threatened Latvia's membership in the Council of Europe. Article 2(a) of the 1997 Convention discourages ethnic origin as a basis for citizenship by stating that nationality is "the legal bond between a person and a state and does not indicate the person's ethnic origin." See Kalvaitis, Citizenship and National Identity in the Baltic States, 16 B.U. Int'l L.J. 231 (1997); Visek, Creating the Ethnic Electorate through Legal Restorationism: Citizenship Rights in Estonia, 38 Harv. Int'l L.J. 315 (1997); and Barrington, The Making of Citizenship Policy in the Baltic States, 13 Geo.Immigr.L.J. 159 (1999).

3. Restatement (Third) § 212 provides, in part, as follows:

(1) An individual is a national of the United States if he or she

(a) is a citizen of the United States under the Constitution and laws of the United States, or

(b) was born in an outlying possession of the United States.

(2) United States citizenship is acquired

(a) by birth within the United States,

(b) by naturalization, or

(c) in the case of certain categories of persons born outside the United States to parents one or both of whom are citizens of the United States, by operation of law.

Comment *b* provides, in part, as follows:

> The Fourteenth Amendment to the United States Constitution provides that "All persons born or naturalized in the United States and subject to the jurisdiction thereof are citizens of the United States." Article I, Section 8, clause 4 of the Constitution confers upon Congress the power to establish "an uniform Rule of Naturalization." That power has been exercised since 1790, currently in the Immigration and Nationality Act of 1952, as amended, codified in 8 U.S.C. § 1101 *et seq*. Citizenship is conferred by a certificate of naturalization issued by a court upon proof that the individual has complied with the requirements of that Act. * * *
>
> United States citizenship is acquired at birth outside the United States under conditions specified in § 301 of the Act (8 U.S.C. § 1401(c)-(g)), for example, when both parents are United States citizens and one of the parents had previously resided in the United States or when one of the parents was a United States citizen and had been physically present in the United States for at least five years.

3. Limits on the Conferring of Nationality

CONVENTION ON CERTAIN QUESTIONS RELATING TO THE CONFLICT OF NATIONALITY LAWS

Signed at The Hague, April 12, 1930.
179 L.N.T.S. 89, 5 Hudson, Int'l Legislation 359.

Art. 1. It is for each State to determine under its own law who are its nationals. This law shall be recognized by other States in so far as it is consistent with international conventions, international custom, and the principles of law generally recognised with regard to nationality.

Art. 2. Any question as to whether a person possesses the nationality of a particular State shall be determined in accordance with the law of that State.

Art. 3. Subject to the provisions of the present Convention, a person having two or more nationalities may be regarded as its national by each of the States whose nationality he possesses.

Note

Some states, including the United States, confer nationality on the basis of naturalization, on the basis of descent from nationals *(jure sanguinis)* or on the basis of birth within the territory of the state *(jure soli)*. Beyond these bases, what limits do "international custom" and "the principles of law generally recognised with regard to nationality" impose on the power of states to legislate matters of nationality? The Harvard Research laid down the rule in 1929 that the power of a state to confer its nationality was "not unlimited," observing that although it might be difficult to specify the limitations imposed by international law on the power of a state to confer its nationality, "it is obvious that some limitations do exist." The Law of Nationality, Art. 2, 23 A.J.I.L. Spec. Supp. 11, 24–27 (1929). The Hague Codification Conference of 1930 was unable to agree upon a more precise formulation than that adopted in Article 1 of the Convention on Certain Questions Relating to the Conflict of Nationality Laws, quoted above, but a number of participating governments asserted that states were not obligated under international law to recognize nationality conferred upon a person in the absence of some generally recognized relationship or connection between the person and the state claiming him as its national. The German government, for example, stated:

> * * * [A] State has no power, by means of a law or administrative act, to confer its nationality on all the inhabitants of another State or on all foreigners entering [its] territory. Further, if the State confers its nationality on the subjects of other States without their request, when the persons in question are not attached to it by any particular bond, as, for instance, origin, domicile or birth, the States concerned will not be bound to recognise such naturalization.

League of Nations Docs.1929.V.1, at 13.

The United States was of the opinion that there were "certain grounds generally recognised by civilised States upon which a State may properly clothe individuals with its nationality at or after birth, but * * * no State is free to extend the application of its laws of nationality in such a way as to reach out and claim the allegiance of whomsoever it pleases. The scope of municipal laws governing nationality must be regarded as limited by consideration of the rights and obligations of individuals and of other States." Id. at 145–46. Although certain governments participating in the Conference questioned the existence of rules of international law, other than those laid down in treaties, that limited a state's freedom in matters of nationality, the text of Article 1 of the Convention on Certain Questions Relating to the Conflict of Nationality Laws was adopted by an overwhelming majority. Id.

Compare Hyde 1066: "In a broad sense international law limits the right of a State to impress its national character upon an individual, or to prevent that character from being lost or transferred. The freedom of action of each member of the family of nations is, however, wide. That circumstance, as well as the modern practice of States to declare by statute what persons are deemed to be nationals by birth, and how nationality may be acquired or lost, serves to obscure from view the final test of the reasonableness of the local law." What circumstances make it "reasonable" for a state to confer its nationality upon an individual?

NOTTEBOHM CASE (LIECHTENSTEIN v. GUATEMALA)

International Court of Justice, 1955.
1955 I.C.J. 4.

[Nottebohm had been a German national from his birth in Germany in 1881 until his naturalization in Liechtenstein in 1939, shortly after the outbreak of war in Europe. In 1905, he had taken up residence in Guatemala and engaged in substantial business dealings in that country. Thereafter, he sometimes went to Germany on business, to other countries on holidays, and to Liechtenstein in order to visit a brother who lived there after 1931. In early 1939, Nottebohm went to Europe and eventually applied for naturalization in Liechtenstein on October 9, 1939. Nottebohm sought and received dispensation from residence requirements, paid his fees and gave security for the payment of taxes, and completed the naturalization process by taking an oath of allegiance on October 20, 1939. He obtained a Liechtenstein passport, had it visaed by the Guatemalan consul in Zurich, and returned to Guatemala to resume his business activities. At his request, Guatemalan authorities made appropriate changes regarding Nottebohm's nationality in the Register of Aliens and in his identity document.

[On July 17, 1941, the United States blacklisted Nottebohm and froze his assets in the United States. War broke out between the United States and Germany, and between Guatemala and Germany, on December 11, 1941. Nottebohm was arrested by Guatemalan authorities in 1943 and deported to the United States, where he was interned until 1946 as an enemy alien. He applied upon his release for readmission to Guatemala, but his application was refused. Nottebohm then took up residence in Liechtenstein, but Guatemala had in the meantime taken measures against his properties in that country, culminating in confiscatory legislation of 1949.

[Liechtenstein exercised the right of diplomatic protection on behalf of Nottebohm whom it regarded as its national, pursuant to principles of state responsibility discussed at pp. 753–764. Liechtenstein instituted proceedings against Guatemala in the International Court of Justice, asking the Court to declare that Guatemala had violated international law "in arresting, detaining, expelling and refusing to readmit Mr. Nottebohm and in seizing and retaining his property" and consequently was obligated to pay compensation as reparation. Guatemala's principal argument in reply was that the Liechtenstein claim was inadmissible on grounds of the claimant's nationality.

[The Court rejected Liechtenstein's argument that Guatemala was precluded from contesting Nottebohm's nationality because Guatemala had on several occasions acknowledged Nottebohm's claim of Liechtenstein nationality. The court then continued:]

Since no proof has been adduced that Guatemala has recognized the title to the exercise of protection relied upon by Liechtenstein as being derived from the naturalization which it granted to Nottebohm, the Court must consider whether such an act of granting nationality by Liechtenstein directly entails an obligation on the part of Guatemala to recognize its effect, namely, Liechtenstein's right to exercise its protection. In other words, it must be determined whether that unilateral act by Liechtenstein is one which can be relied upon against Guatemala in regard to the exercise of protection. The Court will deal with this question without considering that of the validity of Nottebohm's naturalization according to the law of Liechtenstein.

* * * [T]he issue which the Court must decide is not one which pertains to the legal system of Liechtenstein. It does not depend on the law or on the decision of Liechtenstein whether that State is entitled to exercise its protection, in the case under consideration. To exercise protection, to apply to the Court, is to place oneself on the plane of international law. It is international law which determines whether a State is entitled to exercise protection and to seise the Court. * * *

The practice of certain States which refrain from exercising protection in favour of a naturalized person when the latter has in fact, by his prolonged absence, severed his links with what is no longer for him anything but his nominal country, manifests the view of these States that, in order to be capable of being invoked against another State, nationality must correspond with the factual situation. * * *

The character thus recognized on the international level as pertaining to nationality is in no way inconsistent with the fact that international law leaves it to each State to lay down the rules governing the grant of its own nationality. The reason for this is that the diversity of demographic conditions has thus far made it impossible for any general agreement to be reached on the rules relating to nationality, although the latter by its very nature affects international relations. It has been considered that the best way of making such rules accord with the varying demographic conditions in different countries is to leave the fixing of such rules to the competence of each State. On the other hand, a State cannot claim that the rules it has thus laid down are entitled to recognition by another State unless it has acted in conformity with this general aim of making the legal bond of nationality accord with the individual's genuine connection with the State which assumes the defence of its citizens by means of protection as against other States. * * *

According to the practice of States, to arbitral and judicial decisions and to the opinions of writers, nationality is a legal bond having as its basis a social fact of attachment, a genuine connection of existence, interests and sentiments, together with the existence of reciprocal rights and duties. It may be said to constitute the juridical expression of the fact that the individual upon whom it is conferred, either directly by the law or as the result of an act of the authorities is in fact more closely connected with the population of the State conferring nationality than with that of any other State. Conferred by a State, it only entitles that State to exercise protection vis-à-vis another State, if it constitutes a translation into juridical terms of the individual's connection with the State which has made him its national.

* * *

Since this is the character which nationality must present when it is invoked to furnish the State which has granted it with a title to the exercise of protection and to the institution of international judicial proceedings, the Court must ascertain whether the nationality granted to Nottebohm by means of naturalization is of this character or, in other words, whether the factual connection between Nottebohm and Liechtenstein in the period preceding, contemporaneous with and following his naturalization appears to be sufficiently close, so preponderant in relation to any connection which may have existed between him and any other State, that it is possible to regard the nationality conferred upon him as real and effective, as the exact juridical expression of a social fact of a connection which existed previously or came into existence thereafter.

Naturalization is not a matter to be taken lightly. * * * In order to appraise its international effect, it is impossible to disregard the circumstances in which it was conferred, the serious character which attaches to it, the real and effective, and not merely the verbal preference of the individual seeking it for the country which grants it to him.

At the time of his naturalization does Nottebohm appear to have been more closely attached by his tradition, his establishment, his interests, his activities, his family ties, his intentions for the near future to Liechtenstein than to any other State? * * *

At the date when he applied for naturalization Nottebohm had been a German national from the time of his birth. He had always retained his connections with members of his family who had remained in Germany and he had always had business connections with that country. His country had been at war for more than a month, and there is nothing to indicate that the application for naturalization then made by Nottebohm was motivated by any desire to dissociate himself from the Government of his country.

He had been settled in Guatemala for 34 years. He had carried on his activities there. It was the main seat of his interests. He returned there shortly after his naturalization, and it remained the centre of his interests and of his business activities. He stayed there until his removal as a result of war measures in 1943. He subsequently attempted to return there, and he now complains of Guatemala's refusal to admit him. There, too, were several members of his family who sought to safeguard his interests.

In contrast, his actual connections with Liechtenstein were extremely tenuous. No settled abode, no prolonged residence in that country at the time of his application for naturalization: the application indicates that he was paying a visit there and confirms the transient character of this visit by its request that the naturalization proceedings should be initiated and concluded without delay. No intention of settling there was shown at that time or realized in the ensuing weeks, months or years—on the contrary, he returned to Guatemala very shortly after his naturalization and showed every intention of remaining there. If Nottebohm went to Liechtenstein in 1946, this was because of the refusal of Guatemala to admit him. No indication is given of the grounds warranting the waiver of the condition of residence, required by the 1934 Nationality Law, which waiver was implicitly granted to him. There is no allegation of any economic interests or of any activities exercised or to be exercised in Liechtenstein, and no manifestation of any intention whatsoever to transfer all or some of his interests and his business activities to Liechtenstein. It is unnecessary in this connection to attribute much importance to the promise to pay the taxes levied at the time of his naturalization. The only links to be discovered between the Principality and Nottebohm are the short sojourns already referred to and the presence in Vaduz of one of his brothers: but his brother's presence is referred to in his application for naturalization only as a reference to his good conduct. Furthermore other members of his family have asserted Nottebohm's desire to spend his old age in Guatemala.

These facts clearly establish, on the one hand, the absence of any bond of attachment between Nottebohm and Liechtenstein and, on the other hand, the existence of a long-standing and close connection between him and Guatemala, a link which his naturalization in no way weakened. That naturalization was not based on any real prior connection with Liechtenstein, nor did it in any way alter the manner of life of the person upon whom it was conferred in exceptional circumstances of speed and accommodation. In both respects, it was lacking in the genuineness requisite to an act of such importance, if it is to be entitled to be respected by a State in the position of Guatemala. It was granted without regard to the concept of nationality adopted in international relations.

Naturalization was asked for not so much for the purpose of obtaining a legal recognition of Nottebohm's membership in fact in the population of Liechtenstein, as it was to enable him to substitute for his status as a national of a belligerent State that of a national of a neutral State, with the sole aim of thus coming within the protection of Liechtenstein but not of becoming wedded to its traditions, its interests, its way of life or of assuming the obligations—other than fiscal obligations—and exercising the rights pertaining to the status thus acquired.

Guatemala is under no obligation to recognize a nationality granted in such circumstances. Liechtenstein consequently is not entitled to extend its protection to Nottebohm vis-à-vis Guatemala and its claim must, for this reason, be held to be inadmissible. * * *

For these reasons, the court, by eleven votes to three, holds that the claim submitted by the Government of the Principality of Liechtenstein is inadmissible.

Notes

1. Is nationality an absolute or a relative concept? Does the freedom of a state under international law to make a person its national depend on the consequences to be attached to the nationality bestowed? Would Guatemala have been under the obligation to recognize Nottebohm as a Liechtenstein national in regard to claims accrued during his actual presence in Liechtenstein?

2. The Restatement takes the position, based on the *Nottebohm* case, that states need not accept nationality conferred on an individual by another state when it is not based on a "genuine link" between the conferring state and the individual. Restatement (Third) § 211. Comment *c* notes as follows:

The precise contours of this concept, however, are not clear. Laws that confer nationality on ground of birth in a state's territory *(ius soli)* or birth to parents who are nationals *(ius sanguinis)* are universally accepted as based on genuine links. Voluntary naturalization is generally recognized by other states but may be questioned when there are no other ties to the state, *e.g.*, a period of residence in the state. The comparative "genuineness" and strength of links between a state and an individual are relevant also for resolving competing claims between two states asserting nationality, or between such states and a third state.

See Brownlie, Principles of Public International Law 411–424 (5th ed. 1998).

3. The imposition by a state of its nationality on an individual against his or her will, or if that nationality has been renounced, may violate international law. A state is not required to recognize a nationality imposed by another state on an individual against that individual's will on the basis of a link such as marriage to a national, a specified period of residence, acquisition of real property in the state's territory, bearing of a child there or having a particular ethnic or national origin. Another state is not required to recognize a nationality that the individual has renounced. Restatement (Third) § 211, Comment *d*. "However legislation that operates only prospectively and gives the alien a reasonable opportunity to avoid the imposition of nationality would probably not violate international law. Laws that provide that a woman automatically acquires her husband's nationality upon marriage are questionable if the woman objects, under the principle of gender equality now internationally recognized, *e.g.*, in the Convention on the Nationality of Women, 49 Stat. 2957, T.S. No. 875 (1934), and in the Universal Declaration of Human Rights and the principal human rights covenants." Restatement (Third) § 211, Reporters' Note 2.

4. Loss of Nationality

EUROPEAN CONVENTION ON NATIONALITY

Signed at Strasbourg, November 6, 1997.
17 I.L.M. 44 (1998)

ARTICLE 7—LOSS OF NATIONALITY *EX LEGE* OR AT THE INITIATIVE OF A STATE PARTY

A State Party may not provide in its internal law for the loss of its nationality *ex lege* or at the initiative of the State Party except in the following cases:

a. voluntary acquisition of another nationality;

b. acquisition of the nationality of the State Party by means of fraudulent conduct, false information or concealment of any relevant fact attributable to the applicant;

c. voluntary service in a foreign military force;

d. conduct seriously prejudicial to the vital interests of the State Party;

e. lack of a genuine link between the State Party and a national habitually residing abroad;

f. where it is established during the minority of a child that the preconditions laid down by internal law which led to the *ex lege* acquisition of the nationality of the State Party are no longer fulfilled;

g. adoption of a child if the child acquires or possesses the foreign nationality of one or both of the adopting parents.

2. A State Party may provide for the loss of its nationality by children whose parents lose that nationality except in cases covered by sub-paragraphs c and d of paragraph 1. However, children shall not lose that nationality if one of their parents retains it.

3. A State Party may not provide in its internal law for the loss of its nationality under paragraphs 1 and 2 of this article if the person concerned would thereby become stateless, with the exception of the cases mentioned in paragraph 1, sub-paragraph b, of this article.

ARTICLE 8—LOSS OF NATIONALITY AT THE INITIATIVE OF THE INDIVIDUAL

1. Each State Party shall permit the renunciation of its nationality provided the persons concerned do not thereby become stateless.

2. However, a State Party may provide in its internal law that renunciation may be effected only by nationals who are habitually resident abroad.

Notes

1. Restatement (Third) § 211, Comment *e* states as follows with respect to termination of nationality:

> Traditional international law did not question the authority of a state to terminate the nationality of any of its nationals. Increasingly, the law has accepted some limitations on involuntary termination of nationality, both to prevent statelessness (Comment *g*) and in recognition that denationalization can be an instrument of racial, religious, ethnic or gender discrimination, or of political repression. * * * International law does not forbid denationalization for treason, espionage, or other serious offenses against the state, or the cancellation of naturalization for fraud in obtaining it.

Article 15(2) of the Universal Declaration of Human Rights, G.A. Res. 217 (III 1948), provides that no one "shall be arbitrarily deprived of his nationality nor denied the right to change his nationality." See Lauterpacht, International Law and Human Rights (1968) at 346–350.

2. U.S. citizenship may be lost by (i) voluntary termination; (ii) cancellation of naturalization because of fraud in its acquisition; or (iii) in case of citizenship conferred by operation of law, the occurrence of conditions imposed by law as grounds for loss of such citizenship. Restatement (Third) § 212(3).

5. *Multiple Nationality*

UNITED STATES EX REL. MERGÉ v. ITALIAN REPUBLIC

Italian–United States Conciliation Commission, 1955.
3 Collection of Decisions No. 55.
14 U.N.R.I.A.A. 236.

[The claimant had acquired U.S. nationality upon her birth in New York in 1909. At the age of 24, she married an Italian national in Rome and thereby acquired, according to Italian law, Italian nationality as well. She lived in Italy with her husband until 1937, at which time she accompanied her husband to Japan, where the latter had been sent as a translator and interpreter for the Italian Embassy in Tokyo. The U.S. Consulate General there registered the claimant, at her request, as a U.S. national. The claimant remained with her husband in Japan until 1946, at which time she returned to the United States for a period of nine months on a passport issued to her by the U.S. consulate in Yokohama. She then returned to Italy to rejoin her husband. Immediately upon her arrival, she registered as a U.S. national at the American Embassy in Rome. In 1948, the United States submitted to Italy a claim based on Article 78 of the Italian Peace Treaty (February 10, 1947, T.I.A.S. 1648) for compensation for the loss, as a result of the war, of a grand piano and other personal property located in Italy and owned by the claimant. Italy rejected the claim on the ground that the claimant was an Italian national, and the dispute relating to the claimant's double nationality was submitted to the Conciliation Commission.

[The first sub-paragraph of Article 78, § 9(a), of the Italian Peace Treaty provided that the term "United Nations nationals" was to mean "individuals who are nationals of any of the United Nations." The Commission first considered whether this definition had been intended to avoid the double nationality problem, by allowing claims by all United Nations nationals whether or not they were also Italian nationals. After concluding that the treaty did not resolve the issue, the Commission considered the applicable general principles of international law:]

In this connection two solutions are possible: a) the principle according to which a State may not afford diplomatic protection to one of its nationals against the State whose nationality such person also possesses; b) the principle of effective or dominant nationality.

The two principles just mentioned are defined in [The Hague Convention on Certain Questions Relating to the Conflict of Nationality Laws of 1930]: the first (Art. 4) within the system of public international law; the second (Art. 5) within the system of private international law.

Art. 4 * * * is as follows:

> "A State may not afford diplomatic protection to one of its nationals against a State whose nationality such person also possesses."

The same Convention, in Art. 5, indicates effective nationality as the criterion to be applied by a third State in order to resolve the conflicts of laws raised by dual nationality cases. Such State "shall, of the nationalities which any such person possesses, recognize exclusively in its territory either the nationality of the country in which he is habitually and principally resident, or the nationality of the country with which in the circumstances he appears to be most closely connected."

This rule, although referring to the domestic jurisdiction of a State, nevertheless constitutes a guiding principle also in the international system. * * *

The Hague Convention, although not ratified by all the Nations, expresses a *communis opinio juris,* by reason of the near-unanimity with which the principles referring to dual nationality were accepted. * * *

It is not a question of adopting one nationality to the exclusion of the other. Even less when it is recognized by both Parties that the claimant possesses the two nationalities. The problem to be explained is, simply, that of determining whether diplomatic protection can be exercised in such cases.

A prior question requires a solution: are the two principles which have just been set forth incompatible with each other, so that the acceptance of one of them necessarily implies the exclusion of the other? If the reply is in the affirmative, the problem presented is that of a choice; if it is in the negative, one must determine the sphere of application of each one of the two principles.

The Commission is of the opinion that no irreconcilable opposition between the two principles exists; in fact, to the contrary, it believes that they complement each other reciprocally. The principle according to which a State cannot protect one of its nationals against a State which also considers him its national and the principle of effective, in the sense of dominant, nationality, have both been accepted by the Hague Convention (Articles 4 and 5) and by the International Court of Justice (Advisory Opinion of April 11, 1949 and the Nottebohm Decision of April 6, 1955). If these two principles were irreconcilable, the acceptance of both by the Hague Convention and by the International Court of Justice would be incomprehensible. * * *

The principle, based on the sovereign equality of States, which excludes diplomatic protection in the case of dual nationality, must yield before the principle of effective nationality whenever such nationality is that of the claiming State. But it must not yield when such predominance is not proved, because the first of these two principles is generally recognized and may constitute a criterion of practical application for the elimination of any possible uncertainty.

* * * In view of the principles accepted, it is considered that the Government of the United States of America shall be entitled to protect its nationals before this Commission in cases of dual nationality, United States and Italian, whenever the United States nationality is the effective nationality.

In order to establish the prevalence of the United States nationality in individual cases, habitual residence can be one of the criteria of evaluation, but not the only one. The conduct of the individual in his economic, social, political, civic and family life, as well as the closer and more effective bond with one of the two States must also be considered.

It is considered that in this connection the following principles may serve as guides:

(a) The United States nationality shall be prevalent in cases of children born in the United States of an Italian father and who have habitually lived there.

(b) The United States nationality shall also be prevalent in cases involving Italians who, after having acquired United States nationality by naturalization and having thus lost Italian nationality, have reacquired their nationality of origin as a matter of law as a result of having sojourned in Italy for more than two years, without the intention of retransferring their residence permanently to Italy.

(c) With respect to cases of dual nationality involving American women married to Italian nationals, the United States nationality shall be prevalent in cases in which the family has had habitual residence in the United States and the interests and the permanent professional life of the head of the family were established in the United States.

(d) In case of dissolution of marriage, if the family was established in Italy and the widow transfers her residence to the United States of America, whether or not the new residence is of an habitual nature must be evaluated, case by case, bearing in mind also the widow's conduct, especially with regard to the raising of her children, for the purpose of deciding which is the prevalent nationality.

United States nationals who did not possess Italian nationality but the nationality of a third State can be considered "United Nations nationals" under the Treaty, even if their prevalent nationality was the nationality of the third State.

In all other cases of dual nationality, Italian and United States, when, that is, the United States nationality is not prevalent in accordance with the above, the principle of international law, according to which a claim is not admissible against a State, Italy in our case, when this State also considers the claimant as its national and such bestowal of nationality is, as in the case of Italian law, in harmony * * * with international custom and generally recognized principles of law in the matter of nationality, will reacquire its force.

Examining the facts of the case in bar, * * * the Commission holds that Mrs. Mergé can in no way be considered to be dominantly a United States national within the meaning of Article 78 of the Treaty of Peace, because the family did not have its habitual residence in the United States and the interests and the permanent professional life of the head of the family were not established there. In fact, Mrs. Mergé has not lived in the United States since her marriage, she used an Italian passport in traveling to Japan from Italy in 1937, she stayed in Japan from 1937 until 1946 with her husband, an official of the Italian Embassy in Tokyo, and it does not appear that she was ever interned as a national of a country enemy to Japan.

Inasmuch as Mrs. Mergé, for the foregoing reasons, cannot be considered to be dominantly a United States national within the meaning of Article 78 of the Treaty of Peace, the Commission is of the opinion that the Government of the United States of America is not entitled to present a claim against the Italian Government in her behalf. * * *

[Petition of the United States rejected.]

Notes

1. In Iran v. United States, Case No. A/18, 5 Iran–U.S. Claims Tribunal Reports 251 (1984), the Tribunal held that it could exercise jurisdiction over a claim by a dual national of the United States and Iran against Iran when the claimant's U.S. nationality was dominant and effective based on all relevant factors, such as habitual residence, center of interests, family ties, participation in public life and other evidence of attachment. See Crook and Jones, Remarks at Panel on Decisions of the Iran–U.S. Claims Tribunal, A.S.I.L.Proc. 222–27 (1984). On the Tribunal generally, see discussion at p. 754.

The U.N. Compensation Commission established by the Security Council to supervise the compensation of victims of international law violations by Iraq in connection with its invasion of Kuwait, however, has ruled that Iraqi nationals may file claims if they "have bona fide nationality of any other state," evidently without having to demonstrate that the other nationality is the dominant and effective one. Brower, International Law: On the Edge of Credibility in the Wake of Iraq's Invasion and Occupation of Kuwait, A.S.I.L.Proc. 478, 480 (1992).

2. See also the Alexander Tellech Claim (United States v. Austria and Hungary), Tripartite Claims Commission, 1928 Decisions and Opinions 71, 6 U.N.R.I.A.A. 248. Claimant was born in the United States of Austrian parents in 1895, thereby acquiring both Austrian and U.S. nationality. He lived in the United States until the age of five, when he accompanied his parents to Austria. In 1914, the claimant was interned "as an agitator engaged in propaganda in favor of Russia;" after sixteen months in an internment camp, he was impressed into military service. The Commission rejected a claim, put forward by the United States on Tellech's behalf, for compensation for time lost and for alleged suffering and privation, on the ground that Tellech was a citizen of Austria as well as of the United States and that he had voluntarily taken "the risk incident to residing in Austrian territory and subjecting himself to the duties and obligations of an Austrian citizen arising under the municipal laws of Austria."

3. The Canevaro Case (Italy v. Peru), Hague Court Reports (Scott) 284 (Perm. Ct. Arb. 1912), involved a claim asserted against Peru by three individuals on whose behalf Italy had intervened. Two of the claimants were Italian nationals, but Peru contended that the third individual, Canevaro, had no right to be considered an Italian claimant. The tribunal noted that Canevaro was considered a Peruvian citizen under Peruvian law because he was born on Peruvian territory and was considered an Italian citizen under Italian law because he was born of an Italian father. It also found that Canevaro had on several occasions acted as a Peruvian citizen, both by running (successfully) as a candidate for the Senate (of which only Peruvian citizens can be members), and, particularly, by accepting the office of Consul General for the Netherlands, after having secured the authorization of both the Peruvian Government and the Peruvian Congress. It therefore held that whatever Canevaro's status as a national might be in Italy, the

Government of Peru had a right to consider him a Peruvian citizen and to deny his status as an Italian claimant.

4. In addition to the issue of whether a state of which an individual is a national may assert an international claim against another state of which the individual is also a national or against a third state, dual nationality issues may arise in the context of military service and taxation. An individual who is a national of two states is exposed to obligatory military service in each, and may be subject to taxation on worldwide income in each. The latter exposure is present only rarely, because nearly all states tax the worldwide income of only those individuals who are residents. The United States is one of a very small number of states that taxes the worldwide income of its citizens even if they reside in another state. See Gustafson, Peroni & Pugh, Taxation of International Transactions 29–32 (West 1997). For a discussion of the U.S. rules relating to dual nationality, see Kelly, Dual Nationality, the Myth of Election, and a Kinder, Gentler State Department, 23 Inter–Am.L.Rev. 421 (1991–1992).

5. The 1963 Convention on the Reduction of Cases of Multiple Nationality including Military Obligations, E.T.S. No. 43, was based on the then widely accepted position that multiple nationality was undesirable and prohibited parties from enacting domestic legislation creating multiple nationality. Subsequent developments, however, caused the Council of Europe to reconsider the policy of avoiding multiple nationality: labor migrations resulting in substantial immigrant populations, the growing number of marriages between spouses of different nationalities and freedom of movement between European Union member states. Also the principle of equality of sexes meant that men and women should be able to acquire the nationality of their spouse under the same conditions and that both spouses should be free to transfer their nationality to their children. In 1993, the Second Protocol to the 1963 Convention on Multiple Nationality withdrew the prohibition on domestic legislation creating multiple nationality. E.T.S. No. 149. The protocol is in force, having been ratified by France, Italy and the Netherlands.

B. NATIONALITY OF CORPORATIONS

CASE CONCERNING THE BARCELONA TRACTION, LIGHT AND POWER COMPANY, LIMITED (BELGIUM v. SPAIN), SECOND PHASE

International Court of Justice, 1970.
1970 I.C.J. 3.

[Proceedings were instituted before the I.C.J. against Spain by the Government of Belgium on behalf of persons (individuals and companies) of Belgian nationality, who were shareholders of Barcelona Traction, Light and Power Company, Limited, a corporation organized under the laws of, and with its registered office in, Canada. Belgium alleged that Spain should be held responsible for acts of the Spanish Government in violation of international law that caused injury, directly, to the Canadian corporation and, indirectly, to its Belgian shareholders, the value of whose shares was effectively eliminated as a consequence of the injury to the corporation. Rejecting the claim of Belgium, the court stated, in part:]

31. Thus the Court has to deal with a series of problems arising out of a triangular relationship involving the State whose nationals are shareholders in a company incorporated under the laws of another State, in whose territory

it has its registered office; the State whose organs are alleged to have committed against the company unlawful acts prejudicial to both it and its shareholders; and the State under whose laws the company is incorporated, and in whose territory it has its registered office.

32. In these circumstances it is logical that the Court should first address itself to what was originally presented as the subject-matter of the third preliminary objection: namely the question of the right of Belgium to exercise diplomatic protection of Belgian shareholders in a company which is a juristic entity incorporated in Canada, the measures complained of having been taken in relation not to any Belgian national but to the company itself.

33. When a State admits into its territory foreign investments or foreign nationals, whether natural or juristic persons, it is bound to extend to them the protection of the law and assumes obligations concerning the treatment to be afforded them. * * *

* * *

35. * * * In the present case it is therefore essential to establish whether the losses allegedly suffered by Belgian shareholders in Barcelona Traction were the consequence of the violation of obligations of which they were the beneficiaries. In other words: has a right of Belgium been violated on account of its nationals' having suffered infringement of their rights as shareholders in a company not of Belgian nationality?

36. Thus it is the existence or absence of a right, belonging to Belgium and recognized as such by international law, which is decisive for the problem of Belgium's capacity.

> "This right is necessarily limited to intervention [by a State] on behalf of its own nationals because, in the absence of a special agreement, it is the bond of nationality between the State and the individual which alone confers upon the State the right of diplomatic protection, and it is as a part of the function of diplomatic protection that the right to take up a claim and to ensure respect for the rules of international law must be envisaged." (Panevezys–Saldutiskis Railway, Judgment, 1939, P.C.I.J., Series A/B, No. 76, p. 16.)

It follows that the same question is determinant in respect of Spain's responsibility towards Belgium. Responsibility is the necessary corollary of a right. In the absence of any treaty on the subject between the Parties, this essential issue has to be decided in the light of the general rules of diplomatic protection.

37. In seeking to determine the law applicable to this case, the Court has to bear in mind the continuous evolution of international law. Diplomatic protection deals with a very sensitive area of international relations, since the interest of a foreign State in the protection of its nationals confronts the rights of the territorial sovereign, a fact of which the general law on the subject has had to take cognizance in order to prevent abuses and friction. From its origins closely linked with international commerce, diplomatic protection has sustained a particular impact from the growth of international economic relations, and at the same time from the profound transformations which have taken place in the economic life of nations. These latter changes have given birth to municipal institutions, which have transcended frontiers

and have begun to exercise considerable influence on international relations. One of these phenomena which has a particular bearing on the present case is the corporate entity.

38. In this field international law is called upon to recognize institutions of municipal law that have an important and extensive role in the international field. This does not necessarily imply drawing any analogy between its own institutions and those of municipal law, nor does it amount to making rules of international law dependent upon categories of municipal law. All it means is that international law has had to recognize the corporate entity as an institution created by States in a domain essentially within their domestic jurisdiction. This in turn requires that, whenever legal issues arise concerning the rights of States with regard to the treatment of companies and shareholders, as to which rights international law has not established its own rules, it has to refer to the relevant rules of municipal law. Consequently, in view of the relevance to the present case of the rights of the corporate entity and its shareholders under municipal law, the Court must devote attention to the nature and interrelation of those rights.

* * *

40. There is, however, no need to investigate the many different forms of legal entity provided for by the municipal laws of States, because the Court is concerned only with that exemplified by the company involved in the present case: Barcelona Traction—a limited liability company whose capital is represented by shares. * * *

41. Municipal law determines the legal situation not only of such limited liability companies but also of those persons who hold shares in them. Separated from the company by numerous barriers, the shareholder cannot be identified with it. The concept and structure of the company are founded on and determined by a firm distinction between the separate entity of the company and that of the shareholder, each with a distinct set of rights. The separation of property rights as between company and shareholder is an important manifestation of this distinction. So long as the company is in existence the shareholder has no right to the corporate assets.

* * *

44. Notwithstanding the separate corporate personality, a wrong done to the company frequently causes prejudice to its shareholders. But the mere fact that damage is sustained by both company and shareholder does not imply that both are entitled to claim compensation. Thus no legal conclusion can be drawn from the fact that the same event caused damage simultaneously affecting several natural or juristic persons. Creditors do not have any right to claim compensation from a person who, by wronging their debtor, causes them loss. In such cases, no doubt, the interests of the aggrieved are affected, but not their rights. Thus whenever a shareholder's interests are harmed by an act done to the company, it is to the latter that he must look to institute appropriate action; for although two separate entities may have suffered from the same wrong, it is only one entity whose rights have been infringed.

* * *

48. The Belgian Government claims that shareholders of Belgian nationality suffered damage in consequence of unlawful acts of the Spanish authorities and, in particular, that the Barcelona Traction shares, though they did not cease to exist, were emptied of all real economic content. It accordingly contends that the shareholders had an independent right to redress, notwithstanding the fact that the acts complained of were directed against the company as such. Thus the legal issue is reducible to the question of whether it is legitimate to identify an attack on company rights, resulting in damage to shareholders, with the violation of their direct rights.

* * *

50. In turning now to the international legal aspects of the case, the Court must, as already indicated, start from the fact that the present case essentially involves factors derived from municipal law—the distinction and the community between the company and the shareholder—which the Parties, however widely their interpretations may differ, each take as the point of departure of their reasoning. If the Court were to decide the case in disregard of the relevant institutions of municipal law it would, without justification, invite serious legal difficulties. It would lose touch with reality, for there are no corresponding institutions of international law to which the Court could resort. Thus, the Court has, as indicated, not only to take cognizance of municipal law but also to refer to it. It is to rules generally accepted by municipal legal systems which recognize the limited company whose capital is represented by shares, and not to the municipal law of a particular State, that international law refers. * * *

51. On the international plane, the Belgian Government has advanced the proposition that it is inadmissible to deny the shareholders' national State a right of diplomatic protection merely on the ground that another State possesses a corresponding right in respect of the company itself. In strict logic and law this formulation of the Belgian claim to *jus standi* assumes the existence of the very right that requires demonstration. In fact the Belgian Government has repeatedly stressed that there exists no rule of international law which would deny the national State of the shareholders the right of diplomatic protection for the purpose of seeking redress pursuant to unlawful acts committed by another State against the company in which they hold shares. This, by emphasizing the absence of any express denial of the right, conversely implies the admission that there is no rule of international law which expressly confers such a right on the shareholders' national State.

52. International law may not, in some fields, provide specific rules in particular cases. In the concrete situation, the company against which allegedly unlawful acts were directed is expressly vested with a right, whereas no such right is specifically provided for the shareholder in respect of those acts. Thus the position of the company rests on a positive rule of both municipal and international law. As to the shareholder, while he has certain rights expressly provided for him by municipal law * * *, appeal can, in the circumstances of the present case, only be made to the silence of international law. Such silence scarcely admits of interpretation in favour of the shareholder.

* * *

70. In allocating corporate entities to States for purposes of diplomatic protection, international law is based, but only to a limited extent, on an analogy with the rules governing the nationality of individuals. The traditional rule attributes the right of diplomatic protection of a corporate entity to the State under the laws of which it is incorporated and in whose territory it has its registered office. These two criteria have been confirmed by long practice and by numerous international instruments. This notwithstanding, further or different links are at times said to be required in order that a right of diplomatic protection should exist. Indeed, it has been the practice of some States to give a company incorporated under their law diplomatic protection solely when it has its seat *(siège social)* or management or centre of control in their territory, or when a majority or a substantial proportion of the shares has been owned by nationals of the State concerned. Only then, it has been held, does there exist between the corporation and the State in question a genuine connection of the kind familiar from other branches of international law. However, in the particular field of the diplomatic protection of corporate entities, no absolute test of the "genuine connection" has found general acceptance. Such tests as have been applied are of a relative nature, and sometimes links with one State have had to be weighed against those with another. In this connection reference has been made to the *Nottebohm* case. In fact the Parties made frequent reference to it in the course of the proceedings. However, given both the legal and factual aspects of protection in the present case the Court is of the opinion that there can be no analogy with the issues raised or the decision given in that case.

71. In the present case it is not disputed that the company was incorporated in Canada and has its registered office in that country. The incorporation of the company under the law of Canada was an act of free choice. Not only did the founders of the company seek its incorporation under Canadian law but it has remained under that law for a period of over fifty years. It has maintained in Canada its registered office, its accounts and its share registers. Board meetings were held there for many years; it has been listed in the records of the Canadian tax authorities. Thus a close and permanent connection has been established, fortified by the passage of over half a century. This connection is in no way weakened by the fact that the company engaged from the very outset in commercial activities outside Canada, for that was its declared object. Barcelona Traction's links with Canada are thus manifold.

* * *

76. * * * [T]he record shows that from 1948 onwards the Canadian Government made to the Spanish Government numerous representations which cannot be viewed otherwise than as the exercise of diplomatic protection in respect of the Barcelona Traction company. Therefore this was not a case where diplomatic protection was refused or remained in the sphere of fiction. It is also clear that over the whole period of its diplomatic activity the Canadian Government proceeded in full knowledge of the Belgian attitude and activity.

77. It is true that at a certain point the Canadian Government ceased to act on behalf of Barcelona Traction, for reasons which have not been fully revealed, though a statement made in a letter of 19 July 1955 by the Canadian Secretary of State for External Affairs suggests that it felt the

matter should be settled by means of private negotiations. The Canadian Government has nonetheless retained its capacity to exercise diplomatic protection; no legal impediment has prevented it from doing so; no fact has arisen to render this protection impossible. It has discontinued its action of its own free will.

* * *

79. The State must be viewed as the sole judge to decide whether its protection will be granted, to what extent it is granted, and when it will cease. It retains in this respect a discretionary power the exercise of which may be determined by considerations of a political or other nature, unrelated to the particular case. Since the claim of the State is not identical with that of the individual or corporate person whose cause is espoused, the State enjoys complete freedom of action. Whatever the reasons for any change of attitude, the fact cannot in itself constitute a justification for the exercise of diplomatic protection by another government, unless there is some independent and otherwise valid ground for that.

* * *

81. The cessation by the Canadian Government of the diplomatic protection of Barcelona Traction cannot, then, be interpreted to mean that there is no remedy against the Spanish Government for the damage done by the allegedly unlawful acts of the Spanish authorities. It is not a hypothetical right which was vested in Canada, for there is no legal impediment preventing the Canadian Government from protecting Barcelona Traction. Therefore there is no substance in the argument that for the Belgian Government to bring a claim before the Court represented the only possibility of obtaining redress for the damage suffered by Barcelona Traction and, through it, by its shareholders.

* * *

83. The Canadian Government's right of protection in respect of the Barcelona Traction company remains unaffected by the present proceedings.

* * *

88. It follows from what has already been stated above that, where it is a question of an unlawful act committed against a company representing foreign capital, the general rule of international law authorizes the national State of the company alone to make a claim.

* * *

92. Since the general rule on the subject does not entitle the Belgian Government to put forward a claim in this case, the question remains to be considered whether nonetheless, as the Belgian Government has contended during the proceedings, considerations of equity do not require that it be held to possess a right of protection. It is quite true that it has been maintained, that, for reasons of equity, a State should be able, in certain cases, to take up the protection of its nationals, shareholders in a company which has been the victim of a violation of international law. Thus a theory has been developed to the effect that the State of the shareholders has a right of diplomatic protection when the State whose responsibility is invoked is the national State

of the company. Whatever the validity of this theory may be, it is certainly not applicable to the present case, since Spain is not the national State of Barcelona Traction.

93. On the other hand, the Court considers that, in the field of diplomatic protection as in all other fields of international law, it is necessary that the law be applied reasonably. It has been suggested that if in a given case it is not possible to apply the general rule that the right of diplomatic protection of a company belongs to its national State, considerations of equity might call for the possibility of protection of the shareholders in question by their own national State. This hypothesis does not correspond to the circumstances of the present case.

94. In view, however, of the discretionary nature of diplomatic protection, considerations of equity cannot require more than the possibility for some protector State to intervene, whether it be the national State of the company, by virtue of the general rule mentioned above, or, in a secondary capacity, the national State of the shareholders who claim protection. In this connection, account should also be taken of the practical effects of deducing from considerations of equity any broader right of protection for the national State of the shareholders. It must first of all be observed that it would be difficult on an equitable basis to make distinctions according to any quantitative test: it would seem that the owner of 1 per cent. and the owner of 90 per cent. of the share-capital should have the same possibility of enjoying the benefit of diplomatic protection. The protector State may, of course, be disinclined to take up the case of the single small shareholder, but it could scarcely be denied the right to do so in the name of equitable considerations. In that field, protection by the national State of the shareholders can hardly be graduated according to the absolute or relative size of the shareholding involved.

95. The Belgian Government, it is true, has also contended that as high a proportion as 88 per cent. of the shares in Barcelona Traction belonged to natural or juristic persons of Belgian nationality, and it has used this as an argument for the purpose not only of determining the amount of the damages which it claims, but also of establishing its right of action on behalf of the Belgian shareholders. Nevertheless, this does not alter the Belgian Government's position, as expounded in the course of the proceedings, which implies, in the last analysis, that it might be sufficient for one single share to belong to a national of a given State for the latter to be entitled to exercise its diplomatic protection.

96. The Court considers that the adoption of the theory of diplomatic protection of shareholders as such, by opening the door to competing diplomatic claims, could create an atmosphere of confusion and insecurity in international economic relations. The danger would be all the greater inasmuch as the shares of companies whose activity is international are widely scattered and frequently change hands. It might perhaps be claimed that, if the right of protection belonging to the national States of the shareholders were considered as only secondary to that of the national State of the company, there would be less danger of difficulties of the kind contemplated. However, the Court must state that the essence of a secondary right is that it only comes into existence at the time when the original right ceases to exist.

As the right of protection vested in the national State of the company cannot be regarded as extinguished because it is not exercised, it is not possible to accept the proposition that in case of its non-exercise the national States of the shareholders have a right of protection secondary to that of the national State of the company. Furthermore, study of factual situations in which this theory might possibly be applied gives rise to the following observations.

97. The situations in which foreign shareholders in a company wish to have recourse to diplomatic protection by their own national State may vary. It may happen that the national State of the company simply refuses to grant it its diplomatic protection, or that it begins to exercise it (as in the present case) but does not pursue its action to the end. It may also happen that the national State of the company and the State which has committed a violation of international law with regard to the company arrive at a settlement of the matter, by agreeing on compensation for the company, but that the foreign shareholders find the compensation insufficient. Now, as a matter of principle, it would be difficult to draw a distinction between these three cases so far as the protection of foreign shareholders by their national State is concerned, since in each case they may have suffered real damage. Furthermore, the national State of the company is perfectly free to decide how far it is appropriate for it to protect the company, and is not bound to make public the reasons for its decision. To reconcile this discretionary power of the company's national State with a right of protection falling to the shareholders' national State would be particularly difficult when the former State has concluded, with the State which has contravened international law with regard to the company, an agreement granting the company compensation which the foreign shareholders find inadequate. If, after such a settlement, the national State of the foreign shareholders could in its turn put forward a claim based on the same facts, this would be likely to introduce into the negotiation of this kind of agreement a lack of security which would be contrary to the stability which it is the object of international law to establish in international relations.

* * *

99. It should also be observed that the promoters of a company whose operations will be international must take into account the fact that States have, with regard to their nationals, a discretionary power to grant diplomatic protection or to refuse it. When establishing a company in a foreign country, its promoters are normally impelled by particular considerations; it is often a question of tax or other advantages offered by the host State. It does not seem to be in any way inequitable that the advantages thus obtained should be balanced by the risks arising from the fact that the protection of the company and hence of its shareholders is thus entrusted to a State other than the national State of the shareholders.

100. In the present case, it is clear from what has been said above that Barcelona Traction was never reduced to a position of impotence such that it could not have approached its national State, Canada, to ask for its diplomatic protection, and that, as far as appeared to the Court, there was nothing to prevent Canada from continuing to grant its diplomatic protection to Barcelona Traction if it had considered that it should do so.

101. For the above reasons, the Court is not of the opinion that, in the particular circumstances of the present case, *jus standi* is conferred on the Belgian Government by considerations of equity.

* * *

103. Accordingly,

THE COURT rejects the Belgian Government's claim by fifteen votes to one, twelve votes of the majority being based on the reasons set out in the present Judgment.

Notes

1. For comment, see Higgins, Aspects of the Case Concerning the Barcelona Traction, Light and Power Company, Ltd., 11 Va.J.Int'l L. 327 (1971); Lillich, The Rigidity of Barcelona, 65 A.J.I.L. 522 (1971); Comment, 3 N.Y.U.J. Int'l L. & P. 391 (1970); Discussion in [1971] A.S.I.L.Proc. 333, 340–358, 360–365. See Jiménez de Aréchaga, International Responsibility of States for Acts of the Judiciary, in Transnational Law in a Changing Society 171–187 (Friedmann, Henkin & Lissitzyn eds. 1972), for a discussion of the merits of the case which were not reached by the Court.

2. The nationality of corporations is generally significant under international law in the same contexts as the nationality of individuals. See p. 425. However, a corporation is a legal construct which may, as in *Barcelona Traction*, be incorporated in one country and be controlled by shareholders in a second country. It may also be managed by directors and officers headquartered in a third. States sometimes define nationality of corporations in different ways for different purposes. The United States usually treats a corporation organized under the law of the United States or one of its constituent states as a domestic corporation. Civil law countries generally look to the *siège social*, the place from which the corporation is managed or controlled. Restatement (Third) § 213 Reporters' Note 5. When national security issues are involved, many states, including the United States, refer to the nationality of the owners of the corporation's stock or of those who control the corporation. Id. It has been proposed that when promotion and protection of certain national interests, such as subsidizing and safeguarding technology, are at stake, a broader "economic commitment" test should be applied to identify corporations entitled to protection. The nationality (or national identity) of a corporation would be fixed by referring to structural, organizational, and operational features of the firm, such as the nature and geographic location of its principal assets, the geographic source of its earnings, and its relationships with third-party contractors located outside of the United States. Mabry, Multinational Corporations and U.S. Technology Policy: Rethinking the Concept of Corporate Nationality, 87 Georgetown L.J. 563, 567 (1999). Would application of such a test be appropriate or feasible in the context of the issues for which the nationality of a corporation must be ascertained under international law?

3. Restatement (Second) (1965) § 172 provided as follows:

When a domestic corporation, in which an alien is directly or indirectly a shareholder, is injured by action attributable to a state that would be wrongful under international law if the corporation were an alien corporation, the state is not responsible under international law for the injury to the corporation. The state is, however, responsible for the consequent injury to the alien to the extent of his interest in the corporation, if

(a) a significant portion of the stock of the corporation is owned by the alien or other aliens of whatever nationality,

(b) the state knows or has reason to know of such ownership at the time of the conduct causing the injury to the corporation,

(c) the corporation fails to obtain reparation for the injury,

(d) such failure is due to causes over which the alien or other alien shareholders cannot exercise control, and

(e) a claim for the injury to the corporation has not been voluntarily waived or settled by the corporation.

Compare Restatement (Third) § 213, Comment *d* and Reporters' Notes 3 and 10.

4. The bulk of foreign investment is carried on by subsidiary corporations which are organized under the laws of the state where the business will be conducted and are controlled by a multinational corporation organized under the laws of another state. Capital-exporting states, including the United States, as the states of which the parent corporation is a national, have protested and made international claims when the properties of the foreign subsidiary have been expropriated by the state in which it is incorporated. See Restatement (Third) § 213, Reporters' Note 3, § 713, Comment *e* and Jones, Claims on Behalf of Nationals Who Are Shareholders in Foreign Companies, 26 Br.Y.B.I.L. 225 (1949). The 1981 Claims Settlement Declaration that set up in the Iran–United States Claims Tribunal defined "national" of Iran or the United States to include a corporation organized under the laws of Iran or the United States if, collectively, national persons who are citizens of such country held directly or indirectly a 50 percent or greater interest in its capital stock. See Flexi–Van Leasing, Inc. v. Iran, 1 Iran–U.S. C.T.R. 455 (1982).

The United States is a party to a number of treaties of friendship, commerce and navigation that usually treat companies "constituted under the applicable laws and regulations within the territories of either High Contracting Party [as] companies thereof," but they may permit each party to deny certain rights to a company controlled by nationals of a third country. See, e.g., Arts. XIII and XIV(5) of the United States–France Convention of Establishment. 11 U.S.T. 2398, T.I.A.S. No. 4625, 401 U.N.T.S. 75 (1960). They may also provide for rights in favor of alien shareholders in domestic corporations of either party. See, e.g., Article VI of the United States–Pakistan Treaty of Friendship and Commerce, 12 U.S.T. 110, T.I.A.S. No. 4683, 404 U.N.T.S. 259. Similarly, U.S. bilateral investment treaties may provide protection against expropriation of the stock or debt investments held by alien investors in a domestic corporation. See, e.g. Article IV(1) of the United States–Argentina Treaty Concerning the Reciprocal Encouragement and Protection of Investment, 31 I.L.M. 124 (1992), T.I.A.S. No. 4799, entered into force Oct. 20, 1994.

Chapter 7

THE LAW OF TREATIES

SECTION 1. DEFINITION AND GOVERNING LAW

Treaties, as noted in Chapter 2, are a principal source of obligation in international law. The term "treaty" is used generally to cover the binding agreements between subjects of international law that are governed by international law. In addition to the term "treaty," a number of other appellations are used to apply to international agreements. Some of the more common are convention, pact, protocol, charter, covenant, and declaration, as well as the words treaty or international agreement. Other terms are act, statute, *modus vivendi,* exchange of notes, memorandum of understanding, and on occasion, communiqué or agreed statement. The particular appellation given to an agreement has in itself no legal effect. Some of the terms used follow habitual uses; others are used to denote solemnity (e.g., covenant or charter) or the supplementary character of the agreement (e.g., protocol). The United Nations Charter in Article 102 requires the registration of "every treaty and every international agreement entered into by a Member of the United Nations." This applies whatever the form or descriptive name used for the agreement.

The phrase "international agreement" is sometimes used here as an alternative to "treaty." In the domestic practice of some states, the term "treaty" connotes an especially formal kind of agreement; in U.S. usage, for example, "treaty" typically signifies an agreement approved by the Senate under Article II of the Constitution, as contrasted to congressional-executive or sole executive agreements. In international usage, "treaty" is a generic term not limited by domestic particularities.

In concluding what purports or appears to be a treaty, the states concerned may sometimes intend to create only political or moral, as opposed to legal, commitments. Such "nonbinding agreements" are referred to in some cases as "gentlemen's agreements" and in other contexts as political or moral undertakings. Whether they are intended to be nonbinding in a legal sense is not always clear. Nor is it always clear what legal consequences flow from such agreements. These questions will be considered below.

A. THE VIENNA CONVENTION ON THE LAW OF TREATIES

The Vienna Convention on the Law of Treaties, concluded in 1969, is the principal authoritative source of the law of treaties, and it will therefore be the focus of this chapter. The Convention is regarded as in large part (but not entirely) declaratory of existing law. Some of its provisions have gone beyond existing law or have altered previously established rules. These provisions are generally characterized as "progressive development" in keeping with the terms used in Article 13 of the U.N. Charter and the Statute of the International Law Commission. As we shall see, the distinction between the declaratory and the "new" law of the Convention is not readily apparent from the text and is sometimes subject to conflicting assessments.

The Convention entered into force on January 27, 1980 upon ratification by the 35th state and, as of 2000, had 90 parties. The Convention had not been ratified by the United States as of 2000. However, the Department of State, in submitting the Convention to the Senate, stated that the Convention "is already recognized as the authoritative guide to current treaty law and practice." S.Exec. Doc. L., 92d Cong. 1st Sess. (1971), p. 1. Many subsequent statements of the Department of State have confirmed this view, including in U.S. briefs filed with international tribunals.

Work on the Vienna Convention was first undertaken by the International Law Commission in 1949. From its outset, it was assumed that the task was primarily that of codification and that draft articles would eventually form an international treaty. At one point, there was support for an "expository code" in lieu of a treaty. It was thought that this would allow for declaratory and expository material in the code that would not be permissible in a Convention. However, the Commission decided in 1961 (and reaffirmed in 1965) that a multilateral convention would be more effective. The Convention was concluded in 1969 in two sessions of a plenipotentiary conference of states held under United Nations auspices in Vienna. During the twenty-year period of preparation, numerous drafts and commentaries were prepared by special rapporteurs of the International Law Commission and considered in detail by the Commission and by the Legal Committee of the U.N. General Assembly. The four special rapporteurs were the leading British international lawyers of the period: James Brierly, Sir Hersch Lauterpacht, Sir Gerald Fitzmaurice and Sir Humphrey Waldock (the latter three were elected successively as judges on the International Court). The detailed reports by these rapporteurs and the summary records of the International Law Commission are a voluminous and valuable collection of the *travaux préparatoires* essential for understanding and interpretation. They have been published in the annual Yearbooks of the International Law Commission. The records of the Vienna conferences at which the treaty was finally concluded are also essential for interpretation. They have been published as U.N. documents of the United Nations Conference on the Law of Treaties, Official Records, First (and Second) Session. A useful guide to these records is contained in Rosenne, The Law of Treaties: Guide to the Legislative History of the Vienna Convention (1970). Substantive studies dealing with the legislative history of the treaty include: Sinclair, The Vienna Convention on the Law of Treaties (2d ed. 1984); Elias, The Modern Law of Treaties (1974); Haraszti, Some Fundamental Problems of the Law of Treaties (1973); Kearney & Dalton, The Treaty on Treaties, 64 A.J.I.L. 495 (1970).

THE SCOPE OF THE VIENNA CONVENTION

The Convention is limited to treaties concluded between states (Article 1). It deliberately excluded treaties between states and international organizations or between international organizations themselves. These treaties are the subject of another convention which was concluded in 1986; it is not much different in any major respects.

The Vienna Convention applies only to agreements in written form. It expressly recognizes, however, that this limitation is without prejudice to the legal force of non-written agreements or to the application to them of any of the rules set forth in the Convention to which they would be subject under international law independently of the Convention (Article 3).

The Convention declares that it is non-retroactive (Article 4). However, in this connection also it is said that the principle is "without prejudice to the application of any rules set forth in the present Convention to which treaties would be subject under international law independently of the Convention."

These latter two provisions both acknowledge the continued application of customary law and, where relevant, of general principles of law to treaties, whether covered or not by the Convention. A clause in the preamble to the Convention affirms that rules of customary international law will continue to govern questions not regulated by the Convention.

THE VIENNA CONVENTION AS CUSTOMARY INTERNATIONAL LAW

On the basis that the Vienna Convention was largely declaratory of customary international law, it has been invoked and applied by tribunals and by states even prior to its entry into force in 1980 and in regard to nonparties as well as parties. For example, in the Fisheries Jurisdiction Case (United Kingdom v. Iceland), 1974 I.C.J. 3, 18, the I.C.J. found that the principle of suspending or terminating a treaty because of a fundamental change of circumstances, as articulated in Article 62 of the Convention, along with the conditions and exceptions specified therein, "may in many respects be considered as a codification of existing customary law on the subject of the termination of a treaty relationship on account of change of circumstances." Similarly, in the Advisory Opinion on Namibia, 1971 I.C.J. 16, 47, the Court treated the rules laid down in Article 60(3) concerning termination on account of breach as a codification of existing customary law. To the same effect is the Gabcikovo–Nagymaros Dam Case (Hungary/Slovakia), 1997 I.C.J. 7, at paras. 46, 99, where the Court reaffirmed the customary character of the rules of Articles 60–62 and applied them to a dispute over a treaty concluded before the Vienna Convention had entered into force.

The principles of interpretation set forth in Articles 31 to 33 have guided many international tribunals. In Golder v. United Kingdom, (1975) E.C.H.R., Ser. A, No. 18, the European Court of Human Rights explained that even though the Convention was not then in force (and Article 4 specifies that it is not retroactive), its articles on interpretation "enunciate in essence generally accepted principles of international law." More recently, in the Case Concerning Kasikili/Sedudu Island (Botswana v. Namibia), 1999 I.C.J. (Judgment of Dec. 13, 1999), 39 I.L.M. 310 (2000) the I.C.J. noted that neither Botswana nor Namibia were parties to the Vienna Convenion but that both of them considered Article 31 applicable "inasmuch as it reflects customary international law" (para. 18). The World Trade Organization's Dispute Settlement Body has likewise treated these rules as having "attained the status of rules of customary international law." See United States—Sections 301–310 of the Trade Act of 1974, WT/DS152/R, Report of the Panel (Dec. 22, 1999), para. 7.21, reprinted at 39 I.L.M. 452, 464 (2000).

The distinction between those rules of the Convention which are customary law (or general international law) and those provisions which are extensions or changes of existing law can be made only on the basis of a particular examination of the provision in question and its relationship to existing law. In most cases where this question has arisen the answer cannot easily be given. Ian Sinclair, a leading participant and commentator, has said that: "It is only in rare cases, and then by implication rather than by express pronouncement, that one can determine where the Commission has put forward a proposal by way of progressive development rather than by way of codification" (Sinclair at p. 14).

It is perhaps more significant that states tend to refer to all of the provisions of the Convention as an authoritative source of law, thus gradually transforming its innovative features into customary law through such application. It is natural that a Convention which was concluded with virtually unanimous approval of the international community, after some two decades of study and deliberation, should be applied by legal advisors and courts as the primary source of law. It still remains possible for a nonparty state to challenge a particular provision on the ground that it goes beyond existing law and has not become part of general international law since its inclusion. However, the tendency of states and tribunals to turn to the Convention for authority makes it highly likely that it will be regarded in its entirety as having become part of general international law.

B. THE DEFINITION OF A TREATY

JIMÉNEZ DE ARÉCHAGA, INTERNATIONAL LAW IN THE PAST THIRD OF A CENTURY

159 Rec. des Cours 35–37 (1978–I) (footnotes omitted).

Although the definition of an international treaty seems at first sight to be a purely academic question, judicial experience shows that the determination of whether a certain instrument constitutes a treaty has important practical consequences.

For instance, in two cases before the International Court of Justice the question whether an instrument was a treaty had decisive significance for the establishment of the Court's jurisdiction with respect to the dispute.

In the *Anglo-Iranian Oil Co.* case the jurisdiction of the court was invoked on the basis of Iran's acceptance of the optional clause, dating from 1932, which referred to disputes "relating to the application of treaties or conventions accepted by Persia and subsequent to the ratification of this declaration."

The United Kingdom invoked as a treaty subsequent to 1932 a concession contract of 1933, signed between the Government of Iran and the Anglo–Persian Oil Company, contending that this agreement had:

> "a double character, the character of being at once a concessionary contract between the Iranian Government and the Company and a treaty between the two Governments."

The Court could not, however,

> "accept the view that the contract signed between the Iranian Government and the Anglo–Persian Oil Company has a double character. It is nothing more than a concessionary contract between a government and a foreign corporation. The United Kingdom Government is not a party to the contract; there is no privity of contract between the Government of Iran and the Government of the United Kingdom."

From this pronouncement of the Court it results that an agreement between a State and a private company, even a multinational one, even if it is (as Anglo–Iranian was then) half-owned by a government, cannot be considered as a treaty in international law, but only as a contract. The Court's dictum implies that a treaty requires that two or more States become bound *vis-à-vis* each other.

It would be wrong however to assume that the Court thus endorsed a restrictive definition of a treaty as an agreement concluded between *two or more States.*

In a subsequent decision, in 1962, the Court accepted that the notion of "treaty" also covered an agreement between a State and an international organization which constituted a subject of international law enjoying the *ius tractatum.* In the jurisdictional phase of the *South West Africa* cases, the Court decided, for the purpose of establishing its jurisdiction, that the Mandate with respect to South West Africa was a "treaty or convention" as required by Article 37 of the Statute.

The court declared that although the Mandate:

> "took the form of a resolution of the Council of the League * * * It cannot be correctly regarded as embodying only an executive action in pursuance of the Covenant. The Mandate, in fact and in law, is an international agreement having the character of a treaty or convention."

The Court further recognized that the Mandate was a treaty "to which the League of Nations itself was one of the Parties."

In the light of this judicial pronouncement it may be concluded that in contemporary international law the traditional definition of a treaty as an agreement between two or more States must be enlarged to include other types of agreement which today constitute a large percentage of the treaties concluded: agreements between States and international organizations and between international organizations *inter se.* There may also be trilateral agreements involving two States and an international organization. The traditional concept must be replaced by the notion that a treaty is an agreement between two or more subjects of international law.

The definition of a treaty as an agreement between subjects of international law is not in itself sufficient. There may be agreements between States which do not constitute international treaties. McNair gives the example of a purchase by the United Kingdom Government of one thousand tons of chilled beef from the Government of the Argentine Republic upon the basis of a standard form of contract used in the meat trade.

Another example of an interstate contract and not a treaty could be the purchase of a building or a piece of land for a legation, when this transaction is subject to the municipal law of one of the parties or to that of a third State. A third instance, involving an international organization, would be a loan or a guarantee agreement between the World Bank and a State, which, as has occurred in the past, is made subject to the laws of the State of New York. This is the reason why the codification in the Vienna Convention adds a requirement to the definition of a treaty: the agreement must be "governed by international law."

When is an agreement governed by international law? Is this a matter of choice or of intention of the parties? In principle, the intention of the parties, express or implied, would appear to be controlling. However, there are cases in which the nature and object of the agreement make it impossible to subject it to any system of municipal law; such an agreement must be governed by international law, whatever the intention of parties. A case in point is the cession of a small piece of land by France to Switzerland to permit the enlargement of Geneva Airport. Despite the comparatively trivial importance of this agreement, it had to be embodied in a treaty since it involved the transfer of sovereignty over State territory.

The deliberations at the Vienna Conference reveal that the phrase "governed by international law" is designed to cover other meanings and implications as well.

It was suggested at the Conference that it was necessary to add to the definition the requirement that to be a treaty the agreement "must produce legal effects" or must "create rights and obligations."

These suggestions were designed to exclude from the concept of "treaties" the declarations of principle, communiqués, political instruments or "gentlemen's agreements" which represent a concurrence of wills but without producing legal effects.

However, it may be unwise to exclude political declarations or joint communiqués *en bloc* and in principle from the concept of treaties. In a given case, the terms of one of those instruments may be sufficiently precise to produce legal effects under international law. It is a question to be determined in each case in the light of the circumstances.

Consequently these above-mentioned amendments were not accepted but were deemed superfluous: the production of legal effects or the creation or declaration of rights and obligations are already implicit in the phrase "governed by international law."

Notes

1. The Commission's Special Rapporteur, Sir Humphrey Waldock, commented upon the phrase "governed by international law," as follows:

> * * * [T]he element of subjection to international law is so essential a part of an international agreement that it should be expressly mentioned in the definition. There may be agreements between States, such as agreements for the acquisition of premises for a diplomatic mission or for some purely commercial transaction, the incidents of which are regulated by the local law of one of the parties or by a private law system determined by reference to conflict of laws principles. Whether in such cases the two States are *internationally* accountable to each other at all may be a nice question; but even if that were held to be so, it would not follow that the basis of their international accountability was a *treaty* obligation. At any rate, the Commission was clear that it ought to confine the notion of an "international agreement" for the purposes of the law of treaties to one the whole formation and execution of which (as well as the *obligation* to execute) is governed by international law.

[1962] II Yb.I.L.C. 32.

The Commission concluded that the element of intention is embraced in the phrase "governed by international law" and therefore it was not necessary to refer to intention in the definition.

2. How is one to know when international law applies and when it does not? A clear case for the application of international law could be an agreement whose subject-matter entails high politics between states, e.g., a treaty of alliance or cession of territory. In other cases, it has been suggested that "it is in reality the intention of the parties that determines the application of private law or of public international law. In the absence of express stipulation, that intention is to be deduced by methods similar to those employed by the private international lawyer who ascertains the 'proper law' of a contract: it depends on all the material circumstances of the case. Very clear evidence will have to be required before it can be assumed that sovereign states have contracted on the basis of private law * * *. On the other hand, it would probably not be justified to speak of a presumption that public international law applies." Mann, The Law Governing State Contracts, 21 Brit. Y.B.I.L. 11, 28 (1944). Is it possible to draw up a list of "material" circumstances that will suggest that an agreement is governed by international law? Is it material that the agreement is concluded by "two organs of government not empowered to conduct foreign relations"?

3. Are the only systems of law open to contracting states either public international law or the municipal law of one or both of the contracting states (or of a third state)? See Mann at p. 19; McNair, The Law of Treaties 4–5 (1961), suggesting that states may also enter into agreements governed by the terms of the contract, supplemented as necessary by general principles of law.

C. UNILATERAL ACTS AS A FOUNDATION FOR OBLIGATION

Although the Vienna Convention applies to agreements "between States" (Art. 1)—that is, between two or more of them—unilateral declarations of states can also form the basis for obligations on the plane of international law, and some aspects of the law of treaties are applicable by analogy to such unilateral acts. The legal consequences of unilateral statements have been considered by the I.C.J. and other international tribunals in several cases.

LEGAL STATUS OF EASTERN GREENLAND (NORWAY v. DENMARK)

Permanent Court of International Justice, 1933.
[1933] P.C.I.J. Ser. A/B, No. 53, 71.

[For background on the dispute see other excerpts from this case at pp. ___–___ in Chapter 4.]

What Denmark desired to obtain from Norway was that the latter should do nothing to obstruct the Danish plans in regard to Greenland. The declaration which the Minister for Foreign Affairs gave on July 22nd, 1919, on behalf of the Norwegian Government, was definitely affirmative: "I told the Danish Minister to-day that the Norwegian Government would not make any difficulty in the settlement of this question".

The Court considers it beyond all dispute that a reply of this nature given by the Minister for Foreign Affairs on behalf of his Government in response to a request by the diplomatic representative of a foreign Power, in regard to a question falling within his province, is binding upon the country to which the Minister belongs.

NUCLEAR TESTS CASE (AUSTRALIA & NEW ZEALAND v. FRANCE)

International Court of Justice, 1974.
1974 I.C.J. 253, 457.

[Australia and New Zealand brought applications to the I.C.J. demanding cessation of atmospheric nuclear tests being carried out by France in the South Pacific. While the case was pending, the French government announced that it had completed its series of tests and did not plan more tests. In deciding to dismiss the applications, the Court considered the relevance of the statements by the French authorities.]

43. It is well recognized that declarations made by way of unilateral acts, concerning legal or factual situations, may have the effect of creating legal obligations. Declarations of this kind may be, and often are, very specific. When it is the intention of the State making the declaration that it should become bound according to its terms, that intention confers on the declaration the character of a legal undertaking, the State being thenceforth legally required to follow a course of conduct consistent with the declaration. An undertaking of this kind, if given publicly, and with an intent to be bound, even though not made within the context of international negotiations, is binding. In these circumstances, nothing in the nature of a *quid pro quo* nor any subsequent acceptance of the declaration, nor even any reply or reaction from other States, is required for the declaration to take effect, since such a requirement would be inconsistent with the strictly unilateral nature of the juridical act by which the pronouncement by the State was made.

44. Of course, not all unilateral acts imply obligation; but a State may choose to take up a certain position in relation to a particular matter with the

intention of being bound—the intention is to be ascertained by interpretation of the act. When States make statements by which their freedom of action is to be limited, a restrictive interpretation is called for.

45. With regard to the question of form, it should be observed that this is not a domain in which international law imposes any special or strict requirements. Whether a statement is made orally or in writing makes no essential difference, for such statements made in particular circumstances may create commitments in international law, which does not require that they should be couched in written form. Thus the question of form is not decisive. As the Court said in its Judgment on the preliminary objections in the case concerning the *Temple of Preah Vihear:*

> Where * * * as is generally the case in international law, which places the principal emphasis on the intentions of the parties, the law prescribes no particular form, parties are free to choose what form they please provided their intention clearly results from it. (*ICJ Reports 1961,* p. 31.)

The Court further stated in the same case: " * * * the sole relevant question is whether the language employed in any given declaration does reveal a clear intention * * * " (*ibid.,* p. 32).

46. One of the basic principles governing the creation and performance of legal obligations, whatever their source, is the principle of good faith. Trust and confidence are inherent in international co-operation, in particular in an age when this co-operation in many fields is becoming increasingly essential. Just as the very rule of *pacta sunt servanda* in the law of treaties is based on good faith, so also is the binding character of an international obligation assumed by unilateral declaration. Thus interested States may take cognizance of unilateral declarations and place confidence in them, and are entitled to require that the obligation thus created be respected.

* * * The Court must however form its own view of the meaning and scope intended by the author of a unilateral declaration which may create a legal obligation, and cannot in this respect be bound by the view expressed by another State which is in no way a party to the text.

49. Of the statements by the French Government now before the Court, the most essential are clearly those made by the President of the Republic. There can be no doubt, in view of his functions, that his public communications or statements, oral or written, as Head of State, are in international relations acts of the French State. His statements, and those of members of the French Government acting under his authority, up to the last statement made by the Minister of Defence (of 11 October 1974), constitute a whole. Thus, in whatever form these statements were expressed, they must be held to constitute an engagement of the State, having regard to their intention and to the circumstances in which they were made.

50. The unilateral statements of the French authorities were made outside the Court, publicly and *erga omnes,* even though the first of them was communicated to the Government of Australia. As was observed above, to have legal effect, there was no need for these statements to be addressed to a particular State, nor was acceptance by any other State required. The general nature and characteristics of these statements are decisive for the evaluation of the legal implications, and it is to the interpretation of the statements that

the Court must now proceed. The Court is entitled to presume, at the outset, that these statements were not made *in vacuo,* but in relation to the tests which constitute the very object of the present proceedings, although France has not appeared in the case.

FRONTIER DISPUTE CASE (BURKINA FASO/MALI)

International Court of Justice, 1986.
1986 I.C.J. 554.

39. The statement of Mali's Head of State on 11 April 1975 was not made during negotiations or talks between the two Parties; at most, it took the form of a unilateral act by the Government of Mali. Such declarations "concerning legal or factual situations" may indeed "have the effect of creating legal obligations" for the State on whose behalf they are made, as the Court observed in the *Nuclear Tests Cases* (*ICJ Reports 1974,* pp. 267, 472). But the Court also made clear in those cases that it is only "when it is the intention of the State making the declaration that it should become bound according to its terms" that "that intention confers on the declaration the character of a legal undertaking" *(ibid.).* Thus it all depends on the intention of the State in question, and the Court emphasized that it is for the Court to "form its own view of the meaning and scope intended by the author of a unilateral declaration which may create a legal obligation" *(ibid.,* pp. 269, 474). In the case concerning *Military and Paramilitary Activities in and against Nicaragua (Nicaragua v. United States of America, Merits 1986),* the Court examined a communication transmitted by the Junta of National Reconstruction of Nicaragua to the Organization of American States, in which the Junta listed its objectives; but the Court was unable to find anything in that communication "from which it can be inferred that any legal undertaking was intended to exist" (*ICJ Reports 1986,* p. 132, para. 261). The Chamber considers that it has a duty to show even greater caution when it is a question of a unilateral declaration not directed to any particular recipient.

40. In order to assess the intentions of the author of a unilateral act, account must be taken of all the factual circumstances in which the act occurred. For example, in the *Nuclear Tests Cases,* the Court took the view that since the applicant States were not the only ones concerned at the possible continuance of atmospheric testing by the French Government, that Government's unilateral declarations had "conveyed to the world at large, including the Applicant, its intention effectively to terminate these tests" (*ICJ Reports 1974,* p. 269, para. 51; p. 474, para. 53). In the particular circumstances of those cases, the French Government could not express an intention to be bound otherwise than by unilateral declarations. It is difficult to see how it could have accepted the terms of a negotiated solution with each of the applicants without thereby jeopardizing its contention that its conduct was lawful. The circumstances of the present case are radically different. Here, there was nothing to hinder the Parties from manifesting an intention to accept the binding character of the conclusions of the Organization of African Unity Mediation Commission by the normal method: a formal agreement on the basis of reciprocity. Since no agreement of this kind was concluded between the Parties, the Chamber finds that there are no grounds

to interpret the declaration made by Mali's Head of State on 11 April 1975 as a unilateral act with legal implications in regard to the present case.

Notes

1. In 1997 the International Law Commission initiated a study on unilateral acts of states, with a view toward codification and progressive development. As of 2000, a special rapporteur had produced several reports on the topic and the Commission had solicited governmental views. An interesting issue in the Commission's consideration of the topic is how to distinguish between "legal" acts and those of "political" character: for example, would security guarantees given by nuclear-weapons states to non-nuclear-weapons states outside the framework of an international negotiation or agreement entail any obligation on the plane of international law? See I.L.C. Report, 51st Sess. (1999), G.A.O.R., 54th Sess., Supp. No. 10 (A/54/10), pp. 316, 334. To what extent should the law of treaties apply *mutatis mutandis* to unilateral declarations? Who has authority to commit the state by virtue of a unilateral statement—perhaps ministers and other high-level officials but not technicians at the working level? See discussion in *ibid.*, pp. 314–340.

2. A dispute settlement panel of the World Trade Organization addressed the legal significance of unilateral statements made by U.S. representatives, in connection with a complaint initiated by the European Union claiming that certain U.S. legislation was incompatible with GATT–W.T.O. commitments. The relevant U.S. administrative authority (the U.S. Trade Representative) had issued statements concerning the official U.S. policy to implement the challenged legislation in a manner consistent with W.T.O. obligations, and had reaffirmed that policy before the panel. The panel said:

> 7.118 Attributing international legal significance to unilateral statements made by a State should not be done lightly and should be subject to strict conditions. Although the legal effects we are ascribing to the US statements made to the DSB [Dispute Settlement Body] through this Panel are of a more narrow and limited nature and reach compared to other internationally relevant instances in which legal effect was given to unilateral declarations, we have conditioned even these limited effects on the fulfilment of the most stringent criteria. A sovereign State should normally not find itself legally affected on the international plane by the casual statement of any of the numerous representatives speaking on its behalf in today's highly interactive and inter-dependent world [citing Nuclear Test Case, excerpted above, para. 43, and other authorities] nor by a representation made in the heat of legal argument on a State's behalf. This, however, is very far from the case before us. * * *
>
> 7.121 The statements made by the US before this Panel were a reflection of official US policy, intended to express US understanding of its international obligations as incorporated in domestic US law. The statements did not represent a new US policy or undertaking but the bringing of a pre-existing US policy and undertaking made in a domestic setting into an international forum.
>
> 7.122 The representations and statements by the representatives of the US appearing before us were solemnly made, in a deliberative manner, for the record, repeated in writing and confirmed in the Panel's second hearing.

There was nothing casual about these statements nor were they made in the heat of argument. There was ample opportunity to retract. Rather than retract, the US even sought to deepen its legal commitment in this respect.

7.123 We are satisfied that the representatives appearing before us had full powers to make such legal representations and that they were acting within the authority bestowed on them. * * *

United States—Sections 301–310 of the Trade Act of 1974, WT/DS152/R, Report of the Panel (Dec. 22, 1999) (citations omitted).

D. NONBINDING AGREEMENTS

SCHACHTER, THE TWILIGHT EXISTENCE OF NONBINDING INTERNATIONAL AGREEMENTS

71 A.J.I.L. 296 (1977) (some footnotes omitted).

International lawyers generally agree that an international agreement is not legally binding unless the parties intend it to be. Put more formally, a treaty or international agreement is said to require an intention by the parties to create legal rights and obligations or to establish relations governed by international law. If that intention does not exist, an agreement is considered to be without legal effect ("sans portée juridique"). States are, of course, free to enter into such nonbinding agreements, whatever the subject matter of the agreement. However, questions have often arisen as to the intention of the parties in this regard. The main reason for this is that governments tend to be reluctant (as in the case of the Helsinki Final Act) to state explicitly in an agreement that it is nonbinding or lacks legal force. Consequently inferences as to such intent have to be drawn from the language of the instrument and the attendant circumstances of its conclusion and adoption. Emphasis is often placed on the lack of precision and generality of the terms of the agreement. Statements of general aims and broad declarations of principles are considered too indefinite to create enforceable obligations and therefore agreements which do not go beyond that should be presumed to be nonbinding.[9] It is also said, not implausibly, that mere statements of intention or of common purposes are grounds for concluding that a legally binding agreement was not intended. Experience has shown that these criteria are not easy to apply especially in situations where the parties wish to convey that their declarations and undertakings are to be taken seriously, even if stated in somewhat general or "programmatic" language. Thus, conflicting inferences were drawn as to the intent of the parties in regard to some of the well-known political agreements during the Second World War, notably the Cairo, Yalta, and Potsdam agreements.[10] No doubt

9. O'Connell, [International Law, (2d ed. 1970)] at 199–200. But other jurists have noted that vague and ill-defined provisions appear in agreements which do not lose their binding character because of such indefiniteness. See P. Reuter, Introduction au Droit des Traités 44 (1972); G.G. Fitzmaurice, Report on the Law of Treaties to the International Law Commission. [1956] 2 Y.B.Int. Law Comm. 117, UN Doc. A/CN.4/101 (1956). The latter commented that "it seems difficult to refuse the designation of treaty to an instrument—such as, for instance, a treaty of peace and amity, or of alliance even if it only establishes a bare relationship and leaves the consequences to rest on the basis of an implication as to the rights and obligations involved, without these being expressed in any definite articles." Id.

10. Statements by officials of the British and U.S. Governments indicated that they did there was a calculated ambiguity about the obligatory force of these instruments at least in regard to some of their provisions and this was reflected in the way the governments dealt with them.[11] After all, imprecision and generalities are not unknown in treaties of unquestioned legal force. If one were to apply strict requirements of definiteness and specificity to all treaties, many of them would have all or most of their provisions considered as without legal effect. Examples of such treaties may be found particularly among agreements for cultural cooperation and often in agreements of friendship and trade which express common aims and intentions in broad language. Yet there is no doubt that they are regarded as binding treaties by the parties and that they furnish authoritative guidance to the administrative officials charged with implementation. Other examples of highly general formulas can be found in the UN Charter and similar "constitutional" instruments the abstract principles of which have been given determinate meaning by the international organs (as, for example, has been done in regard to Articles 55 and 56 of the Charter).[12] These cases indicate that caution is required in drawing inferences of nonbinding intention from general and imprecise undertakings in agreements which are otherwise treated as binding. However, if the text or circumstances leave the intention uncertain, it is reasonable to consider vague language and mere declarations of purpose as indicative of an intention to avoid legal effect. Other indications may be found in the way the instrument is dealt with after its conclusion—for example, whether it is listed or published in national treaty collections, whether it is registered under Article 102 of the Charter, whether it is described as a treaty or international agreement of a legal character in submissions to national parliaments or courts.[14] None of these acts can be considered as decisive evidence but together with the language of the instruments they are relevant. The level and authority of the governmental representatives who have signed or otherwise approved the agreement may also be relevant but here too, some caution is necessary in

not consider the Yalta and Potsdam agreements as binding. For the U.K. views, see references in Münch, supra note 8, at 5 n. 22. For the U.S. position, see infra note 11. A contrary point of view was expressed in 1969 by a representative of the USSR at the Vienna Conference on the Law of Treaties. He declared that the Yalta and Potsdam agreements as well as the Atlantic Charter provided for "rights and obligations" and laid down "very important rules of international law." UN Doc. A/Conf. 39/11 Add. 1, at 226 (para. 22). Sir Hersch Lauterpacht considered that the Yalta and Potsdam agreements "incorporated definite rules of conduct which may be regarded as legally binding on the States in question." 1 Oppenheim, International Law 788 (7th ed. H. Lauterpacht, ed. 1948). On the other hand, Professor Briggs suggested that the Yalta agreement on the Far Eastern territories may be considered only as "the personal agreement of the three leaders." Briggs, The Leaders' Agreement of Yalta, 40 AJIL 376, at 382 (1946).

11. The Yalta Agreement was published by the State Department in the Executive Agreements Series (No. 498) and was also published in U.S. Treaties in Force (1963). However, in 1956 the State Department stated to the Japanese Government in an aide-mémoire that "the United States regards the so-called Yalta Agreement as simply a statement of common purposes by the heads of the participating governments and * * * not as of any legal effect in transferring territories." 35 Dept. State Bull. 484 (1956). But see Briggs, supra note 10, for statements by the U.S. Secretary of State that an agreement was concluded by the leaders.

12. See memorandum of State Department quoted infra note 24. See also L. Sohn and T. Buergenthal, International Protection of Human Rights 505–14, 946—47 (1973).

14. The appellation of an instrument has but little evidentiary value as to its legal effect in view of the wide variety of terms used to designate binding treaties and the accepted rule that form and designation are immaterial in determining their binding effect. Thirty-nine different appellations for treaties are listed in Myers, The Names and Scope of Treaties, 51 AJIL 574 (1957).

weighing the evidentiary value. Chiefs of state and foreign ministers do enter into nonbinding arrangements and lower officials may, if authorized, act for a state in incurring legally binding obligations. If a lower official, without authority, purports to conclude an agreement, the supposed agreement may be entirely void and without any effect. It would, in consequence, have to be distinguished from the kind of nonbinding agreement which is treated by the parties as an authorized and legitimate mutual engagement.

We should bear in mind that not all nonbinding agreements are general and indefinite. Governments may enter into precise and definite engagements as to future conduct with a clear understanding shared by the parties that the agreements are not legally binding. The so-called "gentlemen's agreements" fall into this category. They may be made by heads of state or governments or by ministers of foreign affairs and, if authorized, by other officials. In these cases the parties assume a commitment to perform certain acts or refrain from them. The nature of the commitment is regarded as "nonlegal" and not binding. There is nonetheless an expectation of, and reliance on, compliance by the parties. An example is the agreement made in 1908 by the United States and Japan, through their foreign ministers, relating to immigration which was observed for nearly two decades, although probably not considered binding. On the multilateral level, some gentlemen's agreements have been made by governments with regard to their activities in international organizations, particularly on voting for members of representative bodies which have to reflect an appropriate distribution of seats among various groups of states (as for instance, the London agreement of 1946 on the distribution of seats in the Security Council). It has been suggested that a gentlemen's agreement is not binding on the states because it is deemed to have been concluded by the representatives in their personal names and not in the name of their governments. This reasoning is rather strained in the case of agreements which are intended to apply to government action irrespective of the individual who originally represented the government. It seems more satisfactory to take the position, in keeping with well-established practice, simply that it is legitimate for governments to enter into gentlemen's agreements recognizing that they are without legal effect.

This still leaves us with questions as to the nature of the commitment accepted by the parties in a nonbinding agreement and what precisely is meant by stating that the agreement is without legal effect. We shall begin with the latter point.

It would probably be generally agreed that a nonbinding agreement, however seriously taken by the parties, does not engage their legal responsibility. What this means simply is that noncompliance by a party would not be a ground for a claim for reparation or for judicial remedies. This point, it should be noted, is quite different from stating that the agreement need not be observed or that the parties are free to act as if there were no such agreement. As we shall indicate below, it is possible and reasonable to conclude that states may regard a nonbinding undertaking as controlling even though they reject legal responsibility and sanctions. * * *

A second proposition that would command general (though not unanimous) agreement is that nonbinding agreements are not "governed by international law." Exclusion from the Vienna Convention on the Law of Treaties follows from the conclusion that such agreements are not governed by international law, a requirement laid down in the definition in Article 2(a). * * * The *travaux préparatoires* of the Vienna Convention on the Law of Treaties confirm the conclusion that nonbinding agreements were intended to be excluded from the Convention on the ground that they are not governed by international law.[19]

The conclusion that nonbinding agreements are not governed by international law does not however remove them entirely from having legal implications. Consider the following situations. Let us suppose governments in conformity with a nonbinding agreement follow a course of conduct which results in a new situation. Would a government party to the agreement be precluded from challenging the legality of the course of conduct or the validity of the situation created by it? A concrete case could arise if a government which was a party to a gentlemen's agreement on the distribution of seats in an international body sought to challenge the validity of the election. In a case of this kind, the competent organ might reasonably conclude that the challenging government was subject to estoppel in view of the gentlemen's agreement and the reliance of the parties on that agreement.

Still another kind of legal question may arise in regard to nonbinding agreements. What principles or rules are applicable to issues of interpretation and application of such agreements? As we have already seen, customary law and the Vienna Convention do not "govern" the agreements. But if the parties (or even a third party such as an international organ) seek authoritative guidance on such issues, it would be convenient and reasonable to have recourse to rules and standards generally applicable to treaties and international agreements insofar as their applicability is not at variance with the nonbinding nature of these agreements. For example, questions as to territorial scope, nonretroactivity, application of successive agreements, or criteria for interpretation could be appropriately dealt with by reference to the Vienna Convention even though that Convention does not in terms govern the agreements. * * * It may be useful, however, to indicate what may reasonably be meant by an understanding that an agreement entails a political or moral obligation and what expectations are created by that understanding.

Two aspects may be noted. One is internal in the sense that the commitment of the state is "internalized" as an instruction to its officials to act accordingly. Thus, when a government has entered into a gentlemen's agreement on voting in the United Nations, it is expected that its officials will

19. At the Vienna conference a Swiss amendment was proposed to exclude nonbinding agreements such as "political declarations and gentlemen's agreements." In the opinion of the Swiss legal adviser (Bindschedler), such nonbinding agreements were governed by international law and had legal consequences and therefore would not be excluded by the definition in Article 2. The amendment was not adopted presumably because most representatives thought that such nonbinding agreements were not governed by international law. Taking a different position, the USSR representative opposed the Swiss amendment because he considered that some of the agreements referred to by the Swiss delegate should be covered by the Vienna Convention (mentioning the Atlantic Charter, Yalta, and Potsdam agreements). See supra note 10. As indicated by its preparatory work, the International Law Commission intended to exclude the nonbinding agreements from the scope of the Vienna Convention and thought this would be done by the definition of international agreements as those governed by international law. See Report of the International Law Commission to the General Assembly [1959] 2 Y.B.Int. Law Comm. 96–97, UN Doc. A/4169 (1959). For earlier references, see Brierly, Report [1950] id. 228, UN Doc. A/CN.4/23 (1950); Lauterpacht, Report [1953] id. 96–99, UN Doc. A/CN.4/63 (1953).

cast their ballots in conformity with the agreement though no legal sanction is applicable. Or when governments have agreed, as in the Helsinki Act, on economic cooperation or human rights, the understanding and expectation is that national practices will be modified, if necessary, to conform to those understandings. The political commitment implies, and should give rise to, an internal legislative or administrative response. These are often specific and determinate acts.

The second aspect is "external" in the sense that it refers to the reaction of a party to the conduct of another party. The fact that the states have entered into mutual engagements confers an entitlement on each party to make representations to the others on the execution of those engagements. It becomes immaterial whether the conduct in question was previously regarded as entirely discretionary or within the reserved domain of domestic jurisdiction. By entering into an international pact with other states, a party may be presumed to have agreed that the matters covered are no longer exclusively within its concern. When other parties make representations or offer criticism about conduct at variance with the undertakings in the agreement, the idea of a commitment is reinforced, even if it is labelled as political or moral.

* * *

The fact that nonbinding agreements may be terminated more easily than binding treaties should not obscure the role of the agreements which remain operative. De Gaulle is reported to have remarked at the signing of an important agreement between France and Germany that international agreements "are like roses and young girls; they last while they last." As long as they do last, even nonbinding agreements can be authoritative and controlling for the parties. There is no *a priori* reason to assume that the undertakings are illusory because they are not legal. To minimize their value would exemplify the old adage that "the best is the enemy of the good." It would seem wiser to recognize that nonbinding agreements may be attainable when binding treaties are not and to seek to reinforce their moral and political commitments when they serve ends we value.

Notes

1. Schachter refers to the Helsinki Final Act as an example of a "nonbinding" agreement. The states that endorsed it in 1975 shared that view. See Russell, The Helsinki Declaration: Brobdingnag or Lilliput?, 70 A.J.I.L. 242 (1976). The Helsinki Final Act is reprinted in the Documents Supplement and it may be interesting to examine its terms in light of Schachter's criteria, and also to compare it to admittedly binding treaties covering similar subject matter, such as the International Covenant on Civil and Political Rights.

2. Is it possible that an agreement that was "nonbinding" at its inception could attain binding force through later developments? Consider in this regard the evolution of the processes begun at Helsinki in 1975, when the Conference on Security and Co-operation in Europe was initiated and its Final Act was adopted: these processes led some 15 years later to the establishment of the Organization for Security and Co-operation in Europe, with its complex institutions created in the 1990s and its increasingly "legal" functions. Could such developments alter the normative quality of the original Helsinki Final Act?

SECTION 2. CONCLUSION AND ENTRY INTO FORCE

A. CAPACITY

RESTATEMENT (THIRD)

§ 311 Capacity and Authority to Conclude International Agreements

(1) Every state has capacity to conclude international agreements.

(2) A person is authorized to represent a state for purposes of concluding an international agreement if (a) he produces full powers or (b) such authority clearly appears from the circumstances.

(3) A state may not invoke a violation of its internal law to vitiate its consent to be bound unless the violation was manifest and concerned a rule of fundamental importance.

Source Note:

Subsection (1) follows Article 6 of the Vienna Convention, and Subsections (2) and (3) are adapted from Articles 7(1) and 46 respectively.

Comment:

a. Agreements by subdivisions of states. The term "state" in this section, as throughout this Restatement, means a nation-state as defined in § 201. A State of the United States or a subdivision of another state is not a state having capacity to conclude an international agreement. As to the status of agreements concluded by such subdivisions, see § 301, Comment *g* and § 302, Comment *f*.

§ 301 Comment:

g. Agreements by subdivisions of states. The constitutions of some states permit the making of certain agreements by their subdivisions, such as States of the United States, German Laender, Canadian provinces, or Swiss cantons. See § 201, Reporters' Note 9. Some of those agreements are international agreements within the scope of this section. For example, if both states and subdivisions of states are parties to an agreement, the rules of this Part can apply. They can apply also to some agreements among subdivisions only. See § 486, Reporters' Note 6. For the status of agreements entered into by States of the United States, see § 302, Comment *f*.

§ 302 Comment:

f. Agreements by States of the United States. The United States Constitution provides: "No State shall enter into any Treaty, Alliance or Confederation." Article I, Section 10, clause 1. A State may, however, enter into an "Agreement or Compact ... with a foreign power" with the consent of Congress. Id., clause 3. What distinguishes a treaty, which a State cannot make at all, from an agreement or compact, which it can make with Congressional consent, has not been determined. That would probably be deemed a political decision. Hence, if Congress consented to a State agreement with a foreign power, courts would not be likely to find that it was a "treaty" for which Congressional consent was unavailing.

By analogy with inter-State compacts, a State compact with a foreign power requires Congressional consent only if the compact tends "to the increase of political power in the States which may encroach upon or interfere with the just supremacy of the United States." Virginia v. Tennessee, 148 U.S. 503, 519, 13 S.Ct. 728, 734, 37 L.Ed. 537 (1893). In general, agreements involving local transborder issues, such as agreements to curb a source of pollution, to coordinate police or sewage services, or to share an energy source, have been considered not to require Congressional consent. Such agreements are not international agreements under the criteria stated in § 301(1), but other State compacts might be. See § 301, Comment *g;* compare Comment *d* to that section.

Notes

1. *Component States of Federal Unions.* Many of the most important members of the modern community of nations are federal states; i.e., single international persons made up of entities having some degree of autonomy or sovereignty in domestic affairs. Among these are Australia, Brazil, Canada, Germany, India, Mexico, Switzerland, and the United States. The question may arise whether a constituent state of such a union, e.g., New York, has the capacity to enter into an agreement with another state. It may safely be assumed, first of all, that the capacity of one constituent state to enter into an agreement with another constituent state belonging to the same federal union is a question solely of the constitutional law of that union. The constituent states of Germany and Switzerland, for example, retain the right to conclude treaties among themselves without the consent of the central government (1 Oppenheim 176–77), while the states of the United States must receive the approval of Congress before entering into "any Agreement or Compact" (U.S. Const., Art. I, sec. 10). On the other hand, it is not clear whether the capacity of constituent states to enter into agreements with foreign states is regulated only by the union's constitutional law. Where the constituent state is authorized by the union's constitution to enter into agreements with foreign states, does the constituent state on that basis alone have capacity under international law to enter into an agreement, or does the constituent state under such circumstances act only as an agent or organ of the federal union? Under what circumstances might the answer to this question be of practical importance? Of what significance would it be that the constitutional law of the federal union required (as in Germany and the United States) that the federal legislature or executive approve agreements proposed to be concluded between constituent and foreign states, and that this procedure was followed? Note that in an American court a foreign state may not sue a state of the Union without its consent. Principality of Monaco v. Mississippi, 292 U.S. 313, 54 S.Ct. 745, 78 L.Ed. 1282 (1934).

The United States Congress is sometimes called upon to approve proposed agreements between states of the United States and foreign countries or subdivisions thereof. These typically relate to the construction or maintenance of international highways and bridges. See, e.g., P.L. 85–145 (Joint Resolution consenting to agreement between New York State and Canada providing for continued existence of the Buffalo and Fort Erie Public Bridge Authority), 71 Stat. 367 (1957); P.L.

85–877 (Act authorizing Minnesota to negotiate and enter into highway agreement with Canadian province of Manitoba), 72 Stat. 1701 (1958); Zimmerman & Wendell, The Interstate Compact since 1925, at 79–84 (1951). The State Department occasionally opposes approval of proposed agreements on the ground that they would infringe the federal treaty-making and other powers. See, e.g., 5 Hackworth 24–25; the 1956 hearings before a subcommittee of the Senate Foreign Relations Committee on the proposed Great Lakes Basin compact between two Canadian provinces and several states of the United States, 84th Cong., 2d Sess. 6–8, 13–21 (1956).

What would be the status of an agreement concluded between a state of the United States and a foreign country without the approval of Congress, where the state has represented to the foreign country that it has the capacity under United States law to enter into such an agreement, and the foreign state, not unreasonably, relies on the state's representation? Is this the same situation as one in which the head of a state falsely represents to the head of another state that he possesses the constitutional authority to bind his state in an international agreement without the consent of the legislature? See Section 5B infra.

It sometimes occurs that not only does the constitutional law of the federal union expressly permit constituent states to enter into agreements with foreign states, but that foreign states also recognize some degree of international legal personality in those states. See Triska & Slusser, The Theory, Law, and Policy of Soviet Treaties 63–64, 158–59, 427 (1962); 1 Whiteman 406–13. But see Dolan, The Member–Republics of the U.S.S.R. as Subjects of the Law of Nations, 4 I.C.L.Q. 629 (1955).

2. The International Law Commission had proposed that the article on capacity include a second paragraph providing that members of a federal union have treaty-making capacity if and to the extent provided in the federal constitution. France regarded the provision as in accord with existing practice. Strong opposition came from Canada on several grounds, in particular that it could lead to interpretation by international bodies of the constitutions of federal states. In the final stages, the paragraph was deleted. See Kearney & Dalton at 506–508.

3. *Self-Governing Territories.* What is the treaty-making capacity of political entities that have never been states and whose international relations are exercised by a dominant state, but which are more or less self-governing in respect of internal affairs? India, for example, beginning with the Treaty of Versailles in 1919, became a separate party to numerous international agreements, as did many other members of the British Commonwealth. The Philippine Commonwealth, before attaining independence, became a party to international agreements, as did Southern Rhodesia. See Lissitzyn, Territorial Entities Other Than Independent States in the Law of Treaties, 125 Rec. des Cours 5 (1968–III).

Sir Humphrey Waldock concluded that the parties to agreements with the territories do not and cannot "legally look upon the self-governing territory as a distinct juridical person and a responsible party to the treaty entirely separate from the parent State." First Report on the Law of Treaties, [1962] 2 Yb.I.L.C. 27, 37. Compare the following conclusions:

> * * * It may, indeed, be doubted that international law contains any objective criteria of international personality or treaty-making capacity. The very act or practice of entering into international agreements is sometimes the only test that can be applied to determine whether an entity has such personality or capacity, or, indeed, "statehood." * * * Perhaps the only limitation on the possession and exercise of treaty-making capacity by a

political subdivision is lack of consent to the exercise of such capacity by the dominant (or "sovereign") entity to which the subdivision is subordinate. Once such consent has been given, the capacity comes into being or is exercised whenever another entity is willing and able to enter into an agreement with the subdivision that is intended to be governed by international law. The very exercise of treaty-making capacity by a subordinate entity endows it with legal personality under international law. It makes little sense, therefore, to make possession of such personality a prerequisite to the conclusion of treaties. * * *

Lissitzyn, Efforts to Codify or Restate the Law of Treaties, 62 Colum. L.Rev. 1166, 1183–84 (1962). What are the essential elements of the process of consent described above?

4. Article 305 of the 1982 Convention on the Law of the Sea provides that the Convention is open for signature to various entities (other than states) and international organizations, provided that they have competence over matters governed by the Convention and to enter treaties in respect of these matters.

Articles 306 and 307 provide that the entities referred to in Article 305 may ratify or accede to the convention in the same way as states.

Do the foregoing provisions alter Waldock's conclusion that the parties to the treaty cannot "legally look upon the self-governing territory as a distinct juridical person and a responsible party to the treaty entirely separate from the parent state"?

B. FULL POWERS, ADOPTION, AND AUTHENTICATION

1. *Full Powers*

SINCLAIR, THE VIENNA CONVENTION ON THE LAW OF TREATIES

29–33 (2d ed. 1984) (footnotes omitted).

The first stage in the treaty-making process is to establish the authority of the representatives of the negotiating State or States concerned to perform the necessary formal acts involved in the drawing up of the text of a treaty or in the conclusion of a treaty. This authority is in principle determined by the issuance of a formal document entitled a "full power" which designates a named individual or individuals to represent the State for the purpose of negotiating and concluding a treaty. * * *

Article 7 of the Vienna Convention * * * sets out the general rule that a person is considered as representing a State for the purpose of adopting or authenticating the text of a treaty or for the purpose of expressing the consent of the State to be bound by a treaty if:

(a) he produces full powers; or

(b) it appears from the practice of the States concerned or from other circumstances that their intention was to consider that person as representing the State for such purposes and to dispense with full powers.

Thus the general rule is expressed in suitably flexible terms. Subparagraph (b) is intended to preserve the modern practice of States to dispense with full powers in the case of agreements in simplified form.

* * * Implicitly the Commission recognized that the non-production of full powers might involve a certain risk for one or other of the States concerned, in the sense that it might be subsequently claimed that an act relating to the conclusion of a treaty had been performed without authority. Partly to guard against this risk and also to respect accepted international practice, paragraph 2 of Article 7 of the Convention establishes that, "in virtue of their functions and without having to produce full powers", Heads of State, Heads of Government and Ministers for Foreign Affairs are considered as representing their State for the purpose of all acts relating to the conclusion of a treaty. Heads of diplomatic missions are likewise considered as representing their State *ex officio* and without the need to produce full powers, but only for the purpose of adopting the text of a treaty between the accrediting State and the State to which they are accredited. Finally, representatives accredited by States to an international conference or to an international organisation or one of its organs enjoy similar powers, but only for the purpose of adopting the text of a treaty in that conference, organisation or organ. * * *

An interesting point which was raised at the conference is the relationship between this rule about inherent capacity to perform certain acts relating to the conclusion of treaties and the rule set out in Article 46 of the Convention concerning the violation of provisions of internal law regarding competence to conclude treaties. It will be recalled that Article 46 establishes the principle that a State may not invoke the fact that its consent to be bound by a treaty has been expressed in violation of a provision of its internal law regarding competence to conclude treaties unless that violation was manifest and concerned a rule of its internal law of fundamental importance. The question is: does paragraph 2 of Article 7 raise an incontestable presumption as a matter of international law that the designated office-holders are *ex officio* entitled to perform the specified acts without the need to produce full powers notwithstanding that, as a matter of internal law, they are not empowered to do so? It would seem that the presumption is incontestable. * * *

Note

Is a state bound by apparent authority to conclude agreements? Two decisions of the Permanent Court of International Justice indicate that a state is bound when it is not evident to the other party that the official acting for the state has exceeded his authority. See Case on Legal Status of Eastern Greenland, 1933 P.C.I.J., Ser. A/B, No. 53, at 71, p. 458 supra; Free Zones Case, 1932 P.C.I.J., Ser. A/B, No. 46. See also discussion in Section 5 below relating to invalidity under Article 46 of the Vienna Convention.

2. *Adoption and Authentication of the Text of a Treaty*

SINCLAIR, THE VIENNA CONVENTION ON THE LAW OF TREATIES

33–36 (2nd ed. 1984).

The next stage in the conclusion of a treaty is the adoption of the text. In the Convention itself there is no definition of the term 'adoption', but it would appear to mean the formal act whereby the form and content of the proposed treaty are settled. Historically, the adoption of the text of a treaty took place by the agreement of all the States participating in the negotiations. Unanimity could therefore be said to constitute the classical rule—a rule which was considered so obvious as hardly to require stating in terms.

Unanimity must, by the nature of things, remain the unqualified rule for the adoption of the text of a bilateral treaty. If the parties to a proposed bilateral treaty have not reached agreement on the terms of the treaty, there is self-evidently no *consensus ad idem* and no text to be 'adopted'. The negotiations will obviously continue until the outstanding points in dispute have been settled and the necessary wording for the treaty agreed upon.

Unanimity likewise remains the rule for the category of treaties known, for purposes of convenience, as 'restricted multilateral treaties'. A 'restricted multilateral treaty' may be defined as a treaty whose object and purpose are such that the application of the treaty in its entirety between all the parties is an essential condition of the consent of each one to be bound by the treaty. Examples of restricted multilateral treaties are treaties establishing very close co-operation between a limited number of States, such as treaties of economic integration, treaties between riparian States relating to the development of a river basin or treaties relating to the building of a hydroelectric dam, scientific installations or the like. * * * In principle, unanimity is also required for the admission of a new member to a grouping of this nature, in the sense that the consent of all the original member States, as well as of the applicant State, to be bound by an agreement embodying conditions of admission is required as a condition precedent to admission.

Article 9 of the Convention accordingly sets out, in paragraph 1, the general rule that the adoption of the text of a treaty takes place by the consent of the States participating in its drawing up. But it is obvious that this rule is not appropriate to the process whereby the texts of treaties are adopted at international conferences. Accordingly, Article 9(2) of the Convention establishes the general rule that 'the adoption of the text of a treaty at an international conference takes place by the vote of two-thirds of the States present and voting unless by the same majority they shall decide to apply a different rule'.

* * *

We have already noted that this particular provision constitutes progressive development rather than codification. At the conference some doubts were expressed about the substance of this rule, particularly in view of the differing types of international conference to which it might be thought to be applicable. * * * There was general agreement that the rule set out in Article

9(2) did not automatically apply to treaties adopted within international organisations if the relevant rules of the organisation provided otherwise; * * *

It would accordingly seem that the rule set out in Article 9(2) applies essentially to major international conferences—that is to say, large conferences attended by a great number of States. If such conferences are convened within the framework of international organisations, then any special rules of the organisation for the adoption of treaties will apply, notwithstanding Article 9(2); * * *

C. EXPRESSION OF CONSENT TO BE BOUND

Articles 11 to 17 of the Convention deal with the ways in which states express their consent to be bound by a treaty. Article 11 lists the various means of expressing consent as signature, exchange of instruments constituting a treaty, ratification, acceptance, approval or accession. It adds to this list "any other means if so agreed." This last phrase would include for example the exchange of unsigned *notes verbales* as a means of consent to a treaty.

1. Signature

The report of the International Law Commission on the draft of the present Article 12 observes that the article deals with signature only as a means by which the definitive consent of a state to be bound by the treaty is expressed. It does not deal with signature subject to "ratification" or subject to "acceptance" or "approval."

The following comments of the Commission explain the provisions of Article 12:

> (3) *Paragraph 1* of the article admits the signature of a treaty by a representative as an expression of his State's consent to be bound by the treaty in three cases. The first is when the treaty itself provides that such is to be the effect of signature as is common in the case of many types of bilateral treaties. The second is when it is otherwise established that the negotiating States were agreed that signature should have that effect. In this case it is simply a question of demonstrating the intention from the evidence. The third case, which the Commission included in the light of the comments of Governments, is when the intention of an individual State to give its signature that effect appears from the full powers issued to its representative or was expressed during the negotiation. It is not uncommon in practice that even when ratification is regarded as essential by some States from the point of view of their own requirements, another State is ready to express its consent to be bound definitively by its signature. In such a case, when the intention to be bound by signature alone is made clear, it is superfluous to insist upon ratification; and under paragraph 1(c) signature will have that effect for the particular State in question.

[1966] II Yb.I.L.C. 196.

2. Ratification, Acceptance, and Accession

Article 14 sets out the rules determining cases where ratification is necessary in addition to signature to establish the state's consent to be bound.

The word "ratification" as used here and throughout the Convention refers only to ratification on the international plane. It is distinct and separate from the procedural act of "ratification" under municipal law such as parliamentary ratification or approval. The International Law Commission commented on the changing use of "ratification" in its report, as follows:

> (2) The modern institution of ratification in international law developed in the course of the nineteenth century. Earlier, ratification had been an essentially formal and limited act by which, after a treaty had been drawn up, a sovereign confirmed, or finally verified, the full powers previously issued to his representative to negotiate the treaty. It was then not an approval of the treaty itself but a confirmation that the representative had been invested with authority to negotiate it and, that being so, there was an obligation upon the sovereign to ratify his representative's full powers, if these had been in order. Ratification came, however, to be used in the majority of cases as the means of submitting the treaty-making power of the executive to parliamentary control, and ultimately the doctrine of ratification underwent a fundamental change. It was established that the treaty itself was subject to subsequent ratification by the State before it became binding. Furthermore, this development took place at a time when the great majority of international agreements were formal treaties. Not unnaturally, therefore, it came to be the opinion that the general rule is that ratification is necessary to render a treaty binding.
>
> (3) Meanwhile, however, the expansion of intercourse between States, especially in economic and technical fields, led to an ever-increasing use of less formal types of international agreements, amongst which were exchanges of notes, and these agreements are usually intended by the parties to become binding by signature alone. On the other hand, an exchange of notes or other informal agreement, though employed for its ease and convenience, has sometimes expressly been made subject to ratification because of constitutional requirements in one or the other of the contracting States.

Id. at 197.

It will be noted that the Convention does not take a stand on whether ratification is required when a treaty is silent on the matter. Some authorities had previously maintained that ratification is necessary when the treaty or the surrounding circumstances do not evidence an intent to dispense with ratification. The Commission had originally included a residuary rule requiring ratification if the treaty is silent on the matter. That rule was dropped after governments opposed it. The Convention, accordingly, does not adopt any presumption in favor of signature or ratification as a means of expressing definitive consent to be bound when the treaty is silent on the question. Actually, the issue is largely theoretical since as the Commission noted "total silence on the subject is exceptional."

The references in paragraph two of Article 14 to "acceptance" and "approval" were included because of an increased use of these terms for an expression of consent to be bound either without signature or after a non-binding prior signature.

Article 15 deals with accession which is the traditional means by which a state becomes a party to a treaty of which it is not a signatory. On the question of whether accession may take place prior to entry into force of the treaty, the Commission report commented:

> (2) Divergent opinions have been expressed in the past as to whether it is legally possible to accede to a treaty which is not yet in force and there is some support for the view that it is not possible. However, an examination of the most recent treaty practice shows that in practically all modern treaties which contain accession clauses the right to accede is made independent of the entry into force of the treaty, either expressly by allowing accession to take place before the date fixed for the entry into force of the treaty, or impliedly by making the entry into force of the treaty conditional on the deposit, *inter alia,* of instruments of accession. The modern practice has gone so far in this direction that the Commission does not consider it appropriate to give any currency, even in the form of a residuary rule, to the doctrine that treaties are not open to accession until they are in force.

Id. at 199 (citations omitted).

Note

A common type of provision is: "This treaty shall come into force upon the expiration of ninety days from the date of exchange of ratifications." May a state, having ratified, withdraw its ratification before ninety days have passed? Another common provision is: "This treaty shall come into force upon the receipt by the depositary of instruments of ratification of [a specified number of] states." If twelve ratifications are required, may a state which was among the first to ratify withdraw its ratification before the twelfth ratification has been received? The Universal Copyright Convention provides in Article IX(*l*) that the convention shall come into force "three months after the deposit of twelve instruments of ratification, acceptance or accession." 216 U.N.T.S. 132, 144. The Convention entered into force among the ratifying states on September 16, 1955. On August 19, 1955, the Philippine Republic deposited an instrument of accession with the Director–General of UNESCO (the depositary of the Convention). According to Article IX(2), such an instrument of accession became effective when three months had passed. On November 15, 1955 (less than a week before the date on which the Philippine accession would have become effective), the Philippine Government purported to withdraw its accession. How should the depositary act? See U.S. Dep't of State, Treaties in Force 271 n. 14 (1969). For comparable situations, see Summary of the Practice of the Secretary–General as Depositary of Multilateral Agreements, U.N.Doc. ST/LEG/7, at 28 (1959). What arguments might be made in support of, as well as in opposition to, the proposition that the Philippine Republic became and still is a party to the Universal Copyright Convention?

D. OBLIGATION NOT TO DEFEAT OBJECT OF A TREATY

What are the obligations of a state which has signed a treaty subject to ratification? The Permanent Court of International Justice appears to have taken the position that, if ratification takes place, a signatory state's misuse of its rights prior to ratification may amount to a violation of its treaty obligations. Case of Certain German Settlers in Polish Upper Silesia, 1926 P.C.I.J., Ser. A, No. 7, at 30. The International Law Commission considered that this obligation begins when a state agrees to enter into negotiations for the conclusion of a treaty. *A fortiori,* it would attach also to a state which has actually ratified, acceded, or accepted a treaty if there is an interval before the treaty enters into force.

At the Conference, the Commission proposal was criticized for imposing a duty on states which had undertaken to negotiate. It was acknowledged that this was not an existing rule. Moreover, it was suggested that the object of a treaty could not easily be determined when it was still in negotiation. States might be discouraged from entering negotiations if they were then under a vague obligation. The proposal relating to negotiations was then defeated.

Whether Article 18 as it now stands is declaratory of prior customary law is uncertain. There is some authority for that conclusion (see McNair, The Law of Treaties 199, 204 (1961)), but the matter is not free from doubt. It may be expected, nonetheless, that Article 18 will be invoked from time to time against states which have signed but not ratified and against states which have consented to be bound in the interval prior to entry into force. It should be noted that the two paragraphs have limitations. Where the state has not yet consented to be bound, the obligation continues "until it has made its intention clear not to become a party to the treaty." In the case of a state which has consented to be bound but the treaty has not yet entered into force, the obligation is made conditional on the absence of undue delay in entry into force.

Notes

1. What actions by a signatory state would defeat the object and purpose of a treaty that has not entered into force for the parties? The United States and the former U.S.S.R. signed the Strategic Arms Limitation Treaty II in 1979 but did not ratify it. Each accused the other from time to time of violating terms of the unratified treaty which imposed limits on the number of missiles.

In April 1986, the President ordered the elimination of two nuclear submarines in order to keep within the terms of the unratified treaty. Is the principle of Article 18 applicable to such actions or are they motivated by a mutual intent to comply with the treaty even if it has not entered into force legally? Would a failure to dismantle a missile scheduled to be eliminated defeat the object of the treaty if it could later be dismantled?

2. Consider Restatement (Third) § 312, Comment *i:*

> *Obligations prior to entry into force.* Under Subsection (3), a state that has signed an agreement is obligated to refrain from acts that would defeat the object and purpose of the agreement. It is often unclear what actions would have such effect. The application of that principle has raised issues with regard to the Second Strategic Arms Limitation Treaty signed in 1979 but not ratified. Testing a weapon in contravention of a clause prohibiting such a test might violate the purpose of the agreement, since the consequences of the test might be irreversible. Failing to dismantle a weapon

scheduled to be dismantled under the treaty might not defeat its object, since the dismantling could be effected later. The obligation under Subsection (3) continues until the state has made clear its intention not to become a party or if it appears that entry into force will be unduly delayed.

3. When is the obligation expressed in Article 18 extinguished? The Comprehensive Test Ban Treaty (CTBT) was opened for signature in 1996 subject to ratification, and requires ratification on the part of 44 specified states before it will enter into force. In 1999, the U.S. Senate took a vote on a resolution of advice and consent to the CTBT, but the constitutionally required two-thirds majority was not obtained. Does this vote mean that the United States has "made its intention clear not to become party to the treaty" within the meaning of Article 18(a)? President Clinton and other political leaders have indicated that the treaty might be brought to the Senate again at a more propitious time (there is no constitutional prohibition on requesting another vote after political conditions have changed).

In the case of a state that had duly ratified the CTBT, would an indefinite delay in obtaining the specified 44 ratifications required for entry into force (e.g., because of non-ratification on the part of the United States) relieve that state eventually of its Article 18 obligation?

SECTION 3. RESERVATIONS

A. WHAT IS A RESERVATION?

A reservation is "a unilateral statement, however phrased or named, made by a State, when signing, ratifying, accepting, approving or acceding to a treaty, whereby it purports to exclude or to modify the legal effect of certain provisions of the treaty in their application to that State." Vienna Convention, Article 2(1)(d). In the context of bilateral agreements, a reservation is closely analogous to a counter-offer by the reserving state, and the legal situation is clear, whether the reservation is accepted or rejected by the other state. The most difficult problems concerning reservations, however, have arisen when one or more of the parties to a multilateral treaty objects to another state's attempt to become a party subject to one or more reservations.

Notes

1. The United States and Canada concluded a treaty concerning the Niagara River which provided for the allocation as between the two countries of the hydroelectric power produced. The U.S. Senate in its resolution of advice and consent included a "reservation" that the United States reserves the right to provide by legislation for the use of the U.S. share of electric power and that no project for the use of that share should be undertaken until specifically authorized by Congress. Canada did not express any objection to the reservation, saying it was none of its concern. The N.Y. Power Authority requested a license for a project to use the U.S. share of the power, but it was refused by the Federal Power Commission on the ground that Congress had not legislated and therefore the project was contrary to the reservation incorporated into the treaty. What legal objection could be made to this opinion? See Power Authority of N.Y. v. Federal Power Commission, 247 F.2d 538 (D.C.Cir.1957), which held that the "reserva-

tion" had not the effect of law, vacated as moot, 355 U.S. 64, 78 S.Ct. 141, 2 L.Ed.2d 107 (1957). What is the basis for that decision? For critical comment, see Henkin, The Treaty Makers and the Law Makers: The Niagara Power Reservation, 56 Colum. L.Rev. 1151 (1956); see also Henkin, Foreign Affairs and the U.S. Constitution (2d ed. 1996), pp. 451–452.

2. The International Law Commission, in its commentary on Article 2(d), noted that "States not infrequently make declarations as to their understanding of some matter or as to their interpretation of a particular provision. Such a declaration may be a mere clarification of the State's position or it may amount to a reservation, according as it does or does not vary or exclude the application of the terms of the treaty as adopted. ([1966] II Yb.I.L.C. 189–90). The U.N. Convention on the Law of the Sea of 1982 excludes reservations other than those specifically authorized. However, it allows declarations of understanding provided they do not purport to exclude or modify the legal effect of provisions of the Convention. Article 309. See text below.

3. Suppose a state attaches an "interpretative statement" to its ratification which by its terms indicates that the state will become a party only if that interpretation is accepted. If the interpretation appears inconsistent with the treaty provisions, do other parties have to consider it to be a reservation and to reject it if they disagree? It has been suggested that "the better course" would be to accept the characterization of interpretation but refuse to accept the interpretation and force the issue to some form of adjudication. Bowett, Reservations to Non–Restricted Multilateral Treaties, 48 Brit. Y.B.I.L. 69 (1976–77). If an interpretative statement is not accepted by other parties, does it exclude the affected provision or prevent the treaty from entering into force between the "objecting" and "declaring" states?

4. Suppose a reservation does not purport to modify the terms of a treaty but only the legal effect of those terms? For example, a state may designate a particular area as falling within a legal category in the treaty. A Court of Arbitration ruled in 1977 that Article 2(1)(d) of the Vienna Convention also covered "statements purporting to exclude or modify the *legal effect* of certain provisions in their application to the reserving State." Arbitration between the United Kingdom and France on the Delimitation of the Continental Shelf, Decision of 30 June 1977, 18 I.L.M. 397, 418, para. 55 (1979).

5. Is a state obliged to include declarations of understanding or intent in its instrument of ratification? Strictly speaking there is no such requirement since the other party or parties need not accept understandings that are not reservations. However, states often communicate such declarations of understanding and interpretive comments to make their position clear. For bilateral treaties, the United States does this as a rule in a protocol of exchange of instruments of ratification. See Restatement (Third) § 314, Reporters' Note 1.

6. In ratifying the Statute of the International Criminal Court in 2000, France attached a statement to the effect that the treaty had no application to nuclear weapons. Was this statement a "reservation"?

B. PERMISSIBILITY OF RESERVATIONS; OBJECTIONS

RESERVATIONS TO THE CONVENTION ON GENOCIDE

International Court of Justice, Advisory Opinion, 1951.
1951 I.C.J. 15.

[After a dispute had arisen concerning the legal effect of reservations made by several states to the Genocide Convention of 1948 (78 U.N.T.S. 277), the General Assembly adopted a resolution on November 16, 1950, G.A.Res. 478 (V) (1950), asking the International Court of Justice for an advisory opinion on the questions, *inter alia:*

In so far as concerns the Convention on the Prevention and Punishment of the Crime of Genocide in the event of a State ratifying or acceding to the Convention subject to a reservation made either on ratification or on accession, or on signature followed by ratification:

I. Can the reserving State be regarded as being a party to the Convention while still maintaining its reservation, if the reservation is objected to by one or more of the parties to the Convention but not by others?

II. If the answer to Question I is in the affirmative, what is the effect of the reservation as between the reserving State and:

(a) The parties which object to the reservation?

(b) Those which accept it?

In answering these questions, the Court stated:]

It is well established that in its treaty relations a State cannot be bound without its consent, and that consequently no reservation can be effective against any State without its agreement thereto. It is also a generally recognized principle that a multilateral convention is the result of an agreement freely concluded upon its clauses and that consequently none of the contracting parties is entitled to frustrate or impair, by means of unilateral decisions or particular agreements, the purpose and *raison d'être* of the convention. To this principle was linked the notion of the integrity of the convention as adopted, a notion which in its traditional concept involved the proposition that no reservation was valid unless it was accepted by all the contracting parties without exception, as would have been the case if it had been stated during the negotiations.

This concept, which is directly inspired by the notion of contract, is of undisputed value as a principle. However, as regards the Genocide Convention, it is proper to refer to a variety of circumstances which would lead to a more flexible application of this principle. Among these circumstances may be noted the clearly universal character of the United Nations under whose auspices the Convention was concluded, and the very wide degree of participation envisaged by Article XI of the Convention. Extensive participation in conventions of this type has already given rise to greater flexibility in the international practice concerning multilateral conventions. More general resort to reservations, very great allowance made for tacit assent to reservations, the existence of practices which go so far as to admit that the author of reservations which have been rejected by certain contracting parties is nevertheless to be regarded as a party to the convention in relation to those contracting parties that have accepted the reservations—all these factors are manifestations of a new need for flexibility in the operation of multilateral conventions.

It must also be pointed out that although the Genocide Convention was finally approved unanimously, it is nevertheless the result of a series of majority votes. The majority principle, while facilitating the conclusion of multilateral conventions, may also make it necessary for certain States to make reservations. This observation is confirmed by the great number of reservations which have been made of recent years to multilateral conventions.

* * *

The Court * * * must now determine what kind of reservations may be made and what kind of objections may be taken to them.

The solution of these problems must be found in the special characteristics of the Genocide Convention. * * * The Genocide Convention was * * * intended by the General Assembly and by the contracting parties to be definitely universal in scope. It was in fact approved on December 9th, 1948, by a resolution which was unanimously adopted by fifty-six States.

The objects of such a convention must also be considered. The Convention was manifestly adopted for a purely humanitarian and civilizing purpose. It is indeed difficult to imagine a convention that might have this dual character to a greater degree, since its object on the one hand is to safeguard the very existence of certain human groups and on the other to confirm and endorse the most elementary principles of morality. In such a convention the contracting States do not have any interests of their own; they merely have, one and all, a common interest, namely, the accomplishment of those high purposes which are the *raison d'être* of the convention. Consequently, in a convention of this type one cannot speak of individual advantages or disadvantages to States, or of the maintenance of a perfect contractual balance between rights and duties. The high ideals which inspired the Convention provide, by virtue of the common will of the parties, the foundation and measure of all its provisions.

* * *

The object and purpose of the Genocide Convention imply that it was the intention of the General Assembly and of the States which adopted it that as many States as possible should participate. The complete exclusion from the Convention of one or more States would not only restrict the scope of its application, but would detract from the authority of the moral and humanitarian principles which are its basis. It is inconceivable that the contracting parties readily contemplated that an objection to a minor reservation should produce such a result. But even less could the contracting parties have intended to sacrifice the very object of the Convention in favour of a vain desire to secure as many participants as possible. The object and purpose of the Convention thus limit both the freedom of making reservations and that of objecting to them. It follows that it is the compatibility of a reservation with the object and purpose of the Convention that must furnish the criterion for the attitude of a State in making the reservation on accession as well as for the appraisal by a State in objecting to the reservation.

Any other view would lead either to the acceptance of reservations which frustrate the purposes which the General Assembly and the contracting parties had in mind, or to recognition that the parties to the Convention have the power of excluding from it the author of a reservation, even a minor one, which may be quite compatible with those purposes.

It has nevertheless been argued that any State entitled to become a party to the Genocide Convention may do so while making any reservation it chooses by virtue of its sovereignty. The Court cannot share this view. It is obvious that so extreme an application of the idea of State sovereignty could lead to a complete disregard of the object and purpose of the Convention.

On the other hand, it has been argued that there exists a rule of international law subjecting the effect of a reservation to the express or tacit assent of all the contracting parties. This theory rests essentially on a contractual conception of the absolute integrity of the convention as adopted. This view, however, cannot prevail if, having regard to the character of the convention, its purpose and its mode of adoption, it can be established that the parties intended to derogate from that rule by admitting the faculty to make reservations thereto.

It does not appear, moreover, that the conception of the absolute integrity of a convention has been transformed into a rule of international law. The considerable part which tacit assent has always played in estimating the effect which is to be given to reservations scarcely permits one to state that such a rule exists, determining with sufficient precision the effect of objections made to reservations. In fact, the examples of objections made to reservations appear to be too rare in international practice to have given rise to such a rule. * * *

* * *

It results from the foregoing considerations that Question I, on account of its abstract character, cannot be given an absolute answer. The appraisal of a reservation and the effect of objections that might be made to it depend upon the particular circumstances of each individual case.

Having replied to Question I, the Court will now examine Question II * * *.

[E]ach State which is a party to the Convention is entitled to appraise the validity of the reservation, and it exercises this right individually and from its own standpoint. As no State can be bound by a reservation to which it has not consented, it necessarily follows that each State objecting to it will or will not, on the basis of its individual appraisal within the limits of the criterion of the object and purpose stated above, consider the reserving State to be a party to the Convention. * * *

The disadvantages which result from this possible divergence of views—which an article concerning the making of reservations could have obviated—are real; they are mitigated by the common duty of the contracting States to be guided in their judgment by the compatibility or incompatibility of the reservation with the object and purpose of the Convention. It must clearly be assumed that the contracting States are desirous of preserving intact at least what is essential to the object of the Convention; should this desire be absent, it is quite clear that the Convention itself would be impaired both in its principle and in its application.

It may be that the divergence of views between parties as to the admissibility of a reservation will not in fact have any consequences. On the other hand, it may be that certain parties who consider that the assent given by other parties to a reservation is incompatible with the purpose of the Convention, will decide to adopt a position on the jurisdictional plane in respect of this divergence and to settle the dispute which thus arises either by special agreement or by the procedure laid down in Article IX of the Convention.

Finally, it may be that a State, whilst not claiming that a reservation is incompatible with the object and purpose of the Convention, will nevertheless object to it, but that an understanding between that State and the reserving State will have the effect that the Convention will enter into force between them, except for the clauses affected by the reservation.

Such being the situation, the task of the Secretary–General would be simplified and would be confined to receiving reservations and objections and notifying them.

* * *

For these reasons,

The Court is of Opinion,

In so far as concerns the Convention on the Prevention and Punishment of the Crime of Genocide, in the event of a State ratifying or acceding to the Convention subject to a reservation made either on ratification or on accession, or on signature followed by ratification,

On Question I:

by seven votes to five,

that a State which has made and maintained a reservation which has been objected to by one or more of the parties to the Convention but not by others, can be regarded as being a party to the Convention, if the reservation is compatible with the object and purpose of the Convention; otherwise, that State cannot be regarded as being a party to the Convention.

On Question II:

by seven votes to five,

(a) that if a party to the Convention objects to a reservation which it considers to be incompatible with the object and purpose of the Convention, it can in fact consider that the reserving State is not a party to the Convention;

(b) that if, on the other hand, a party accepts the reservation as being compatible with the object and purpose of the Convention, it can in fact consider that the reserving State is a party to the Convention * * *.

Notes

1. Vice President Guerrero, and McNair, Read, and Hsu Mo, JJ., joined in a dissenting opinion which argued that Question I should have been answered in the negative; i.e., that if a party to the Convention objected to a reservation made by another state, the reserving state could not be considered a party to the Convention. Question II was therefore irrelevant. The dissenters also criticized the Court's distinction between "compatible" and "incompatible" reservations on the grounds that it represented an innovation in the law of treaties and that the subjective nature of the distinction made it unworkable. The joint dissenting opinion concluded that "the integrity of the terms of the Convention [was] of greater importance than mere universality in its acceptance," and expressed skepticism that the effect of the majority opinion could be limited to the Genocide Convention, as opposed to "humanitarian" conventions generally. Id. at 46, 47.

2. The *Advisory Opinion on Reservations to the Genocide Convention was* widely endorsed by governments. It gave impetus to the adoption of the flexible system for reservations to multilateral conventions adopted in the Vienna Convention, in particular Article 20(4). The Court's opinion also emphasized the legislative character of many new multilateral conventions and especially those intended to benefit individuals. In these cases, it was deemed desirable to encourage the widest participation and therefore to allow states to participate even though they were not prepared to accept every provision. See Restatement (Third) § 313, Reporters' Note 1.

3. At the same time, both the Advisory Opinion and the Vienna Convention set limits to the permissibility of reservations. In particular, a reservation could not be accepted if it was incompatible with the object and purpose of the Convention. See Article 19 of the Vienna Convention. But query whether this test of permissibility can be maintained in the absence of an authoritative means of determining whether the reservation is compatible with object and purpose? If each state is free to make that determination, and there is no agreed means of compulsory judicial settlement or collective decision procedure, does not the test of impermissibility lose its practical significance? Judge Ruda believes it does. See Ruda, Reservations to Multilateral Conventions, 146 Rec. des Cours 95, 190 (1975–III). Bowett in contrast lays stress on the requirement of permissibility as a matter of treaty interpretation that is not dependent on the reactions of the states parties. See his comments below. Whether this is meaningful in practice would seem to depend on the readiness of states to have recourse to the Court or to other third party determinations to settle differences of views as to compatibility. States' reluctant attitudes in this regard are brought out in their practice concerning reservations to human rights treaties, discussed further below.

4. The I.C.J. Advisory Opinion highlights the character and object of the Genocide Convention. By implication it suggests that some multilateral conventions should have a different regime for reservations. What other regimes are possible? Consider the following:

(1) the "classical rule" requiring consent of every contracting state;

(2) the exclusion of all reservations;

(3) the acceptance of reservations by a decision of a collective body or by the approval of a qualified majority of parties;

(4) the rejection of reservations if a qualified majority (e.g., two thirds) of the parties object to it;

Does the Vienna Convention allow for these alternative regimes? Does it require any of them in particular treaties?

5. Can one identify certain multilateral conventions which by their character and purpose require that the treaty be applied in its entirety by all parties? See Article 20(2) of the Vienna Convention. Should this hold true only for treaties with a small number of parties? Would it apply to an arms control treaty? Is it especially applicable to economic integration treaties such as the treaties establishing common markets? See Ruda at 186.

6. Reservations have been made on several occasions by states adhering to treaties that were constituent instruments (i.e., constitutions) of international organizations. In all these cases the practice has been to refer the reservation to the body of the organization in question. The Vienna Convention now expresses this as a rule unless the treaty provides otherwise. For prior debate on this issue, see Schachter, The Question of Treaty Reservation at the 1959 General Assembly, 54 A.J.I.L. 372 (1960).

7. Reservations are most commonly made to multilateral treaties on human rights. Is a permissive flexible system desirable in these cases? See the further readings concerning reservations to human rights treaties below. Is it desirable to exclude incompatible reservations to human rights treaties by providing for the rejection of reservations if two thirds of the contracting states object to the reservation? A clause to this effect is included in the U.N. Convention on the Elimination of All Forms of Racial Discrimination 1966. 660 U.N.T.S. 195, Article 20(2).

EXCLUSION OF RESERVATIONS

Are there reasons why some general multilateral conventions of a "legislative" character should not allow any reservations at all, irrespective of compatibility? Consider the reservations clause and the accompanying clause on declarations included in the U.N. Convention on the Law of the Sea, 1982.

Article 309

No reservations or exceptions may be made to this Convention unless expressly permitted by other articles of this Convention.

Article 310

Article 309 does not preclude a State, when signing, ratifying or acceding to this Convention, from making declarations or statements, however phrased or named, with a view, *inter alia*, to the harmonization of its laws and regulations with the provisions of this Convention, provided that such declarations or statements do not purport to exclude or to modify the legal effect of the provisions of this Convention in their application to that State.

Notes

1. Why have reservations to the Law of the Sea Convention generally been prohibited? Is the element of complete reciprocity more important in this case than in other multilateral legislative treaties? Will it result in the nonparticipation

of states that object only to one or two provisions? A Report of the U.S. delegation in 1980 said:

> Since the Convention is an overall "package deal" reflecting different priorities of different states, to permit reservations would inevitably permit one State to eliminate the "quid" of another State's "quo". Thus there was general agreement in the Conference that in principle reservations could not be permitted.

Reports of the United States Delegation to the Third United Nations Conference on the Law of the Sea 83 (Nordquist & Park eds., 1983).

2. The 1998 Rome Statute on the International Criminal Court likewise prohibits reservations. Yet some states have said that reservations to certain provisions may be necessary because of requirements of their domestic constitutional law, or that the possibility of making some modest reservations might facilitate a decision to join the treaty. Is it advisable to put such states to an all-or-nothing choice by precluding reservations?

BOWETT, RESERVATIONS TO NON-RESTRICTED MULTILATERAL TREATIES

48 Brit. Y.B.I.L. 67, 88–90 (1976–77).

An examination of recent State practice on reservations suggests that there is considerable uncertainty over the operation of the rules now embodied in the Vienna Convention.

The primary source of uncertainty is the failure to perceive the difference between the issue of the "permissibility" of a reservation and the issue of the "opposability" of a reservation to a particular Party.

The issue of "permissibility" is the preliminary issue. It must be resolved by reference to the treaty and is essentially an issue of treaty interpretation; it has nothing to do with the question of whether, as a matter of policy, other Parties find the reservation acceptable or not. The consequence of finding a reservation "impermissible" may be either that the reservation alone is a nullity (which means that the reservation cannot be accepted by a Party holding it to be impermissible) or that the impermissible reservation nullifies the State's acceptance of the treaty as a whole.

The issue of "opposability" is the secondary issue and presupposes that the reservation is permissible. Whether a Party chooses to accept the reservation, or object to the reservation, or object to both the reservation and the entry into force of the treaty as between the reserving and the objecting State, is a matter for a policy decision and, as such, not subject to the criteria governing permissibility and not subject to judicial review.

It therefore follows that State practice would be clearer, and more logical, if objections to reservations stated whether the objection was based on the view that the reservation was impermissible or not. This would enable the reserving State to argue the matter of permissibility, if this were the ground of objection, whereas it cannot argue with a policy objection. It should also be incumbent upon a State objecting on the ground of impermissibility to state whether, in its view, the effect is to nullify the reservation or to nullify the acceptance of the treaty by the reserving State. Without such a statement of the legal consequences which a Party attaches to its objection on the ground of impermissibility, it is impossible to determine whether there is a treaty relationship or not.

Where the objection is not on the ground of impermissibility the matter is simpler, since Articles 20 and 21 of the Vienna Convention effectively indicate what legal consequences flow from acceptance, objection, or objection to both the reservation and any treaty relationship.

If this analysis is correct, it seems possible to formulate the following propositions which might provide useful guidance to States:

1. The test of a true reservation is whether it seeks to exclude or modify the legal effect of the provisions of the treaty to which the reservation is attached, and by this test a reservation must be distinguished from declarations or other interpretative statements however named. The latter, whilst not reservations, need not be accepted and raise an issue of treaty interpretation.

2. The permissibility of reservations under contemporary law is governed by the rules set out in Article 19 of the Vienna Convention; in essence, these rules assume the general permissibility of reservations to the non-restricted multilateral treaty except where reservations are expressly or impliedly prohibited or are incompatible with the object and purpose of the treaty. The criterion of "compatibility" does not apply to reservations which are prohibited, expressly or impliedly, or to a reservation which is expressly permitted.

3. A reservation which is expressly permitted and which requires no subsequent acceptance is one the legal effect of which is capable of being deduced from the treaty itself. Thus, a reservations clause permitting reservations to an article in general terms does not mean that all reservations to that article are *ipso facto* permissible and require no subsequent acceptance, although a reservation excluding the article *in toto* might be of this nature.

4. Therefore, in relation to reservations to an article to which reservations are allowed, the permissibility of any particular reservation will depend upon its fulfilling certain criteria, namely:

(i) that it is a true reservation;

(ii) that it is a reservation to that article and does not seek to modify the effect of some other article to which reservations are not allowed;

(iii) that it does not seek to modify rules of law which derive from some other treaty or from customary international law;

(iv) that it is not incompatible with the object and purpose of the treaty.

5. When a reservation is "impermissible" according to the rules set out in conclusions 2, 3 and 4 above, the inconsistency in the reserving State's expression of a will to be bound by the treaty and the formulation of an impermissible reservation must be resolved as a matter of construction of what the State really intended. It is suggested that the following is the proper test:

(i) a reservation not incompatible with the object and purpose of the treaty may be severed and should be disregarded as a nullity;

(ii) a reservation incompatible with the object and purpose of the treaty and not severable invalidates the State's acceptance of the treaty.

6. The question of "permissibility" is always a question to be resolved as a matter of construction of the treaty and does *not* depend on the reactions of the Parties. Therefore, though each Party may have to determine whether it regards a reservation as permissible, in the absence of any "collegiate" system it must do so on the basis of whether the treaty permits such a reservation. The issue of "permissibility" is thus entirely separate from the issue of "opposability", that is to say whether a Party accepts or does not accept a reservation which is permissible.

7. Parties may not accept an impermissible reservation.

8. As to permissible reservations, with non-restricted multilateral treaties, a reservation which is expressly authorized in the sense of conclusion 3 above requires no acceptance and takes effect with the reserving State's acceptance of the treaty. That apart, permissible reservations may meet with the following three reactions from other Parties:

(i) acceptance of the reservation: the effect is that the treaty is in force and the reservation takes full effect between the reserving and accepting States, on a reciprocal basis;

(ii) objection to the reservation: the effect is that the treaty is in force, but *minus* the provision affected by the reservation *to the extent of the reservation.* The reservation is not "opposable" to the objecting State;

(iii) objection to the reservation and an express objection to the treaty's entering into force: the effect is that the reserving and objecting States are not in any treaty relationship. Neither the treaty nor the reservation is "opposable" to the objecting State.

9. The objecting State, exercising either of the last two options set out in conclusion 8 above, is free to object on any ground: that is to say, its objection is not confined to the ground of "incompatibility" with the object and purpose of the treaty.

10. Both reservations and objections may be withdrawn in writing, taking effect on communication to the objecting or reserving State, as the case may be. The effect of withdrawal is to restore the original treaty text in the case of the withdrawal of a reservation. In the case of the withdrawal of an objection, this is equivalent to an acceptance of the reservation.

Notes

1. Bowett's point 8(ii) above restates Article 21(3) of the Vienna Convention. Does this rule mean that the legal effect is precisely the same for a state that accepts the reservation and for a state that objects to the reservation but does not object to the treaty coming into force between it and the reserving state? If a reservation excludes a particular treaty provision, both the accepting state and the objecting state are not bound by the provision. If a reservation modifies a treaty provision, the modified provision applies to the accepting state. An objecting state may exclude the provision only "to the extent of the reservation". Is the result in legal effect the same? Two leading commentators think so. See Ruda, Reservations

to Multilateral Conventions at 200, and Sinclair, The Vienna Convention on the Law of Treaties at 77.

2. If some states object to a reservation on grounds of impermissibility (e.g., incompatibility) and others accept it, is the reserving state's ratification to be counted by the depositary in determining the number of states needed to bring the treaty into force? What criteria should apply? See U.N. Secretary–General, Report on Depositary Practice in Relation to Reservations, U.N. Doc. A/5687, pp. 96–97 (1964).

IMPORTANCE OF RESERVATIONS

How important are reservations in the overall treaty relations among states? Have the new flexible rules increased participation in multilateral treaties? Neither question is easy to answer since international lawyers have rarely done research on such empirical questions. One statistical survey examined multilateral conventions that entered into force between 1919–1971. It found, surprisingly, that 85% of the 1164 conventions had no reservations at all. Even fewer reservations were found in the conventions (839) that were limited to certain states because of subject or geography; 92% had no reservations. Gamble, Reservations to Multilateral Treaties: A Macroscopic View of State Practice, 74 A.J.I.L. 372, 379 (1980).

Most reservations did not deal with the substantive provisions of the treaties. They related to dispute settlement, nonrecognition of other parties, compatibility with specific domestic laws, and colonial territories. Of the substantive reservations, the greater number were adjudged to be minor. Id. at 384–385. For similar findings, see Schachter, Nawaz & Fried, Toward Wider Acceptance of U.N. Treaties 154–156 (1971).

Although reservations are relatively infrequent to treaties generally, reservations may be significant in enabling states to join certain kinds of multilateral treaties. Most evident in that category are the human rights treaties. Many states have conditioned their ratifications of human rights treaties with reservations of highly substantive character. Some such reservations are addressed to specific and/or minor provisions of the treaties, but some (formulated more broadly) appear to go to the very heart of the treaty and raise questions about whether the reserving state intends in good faith to accept any international obligations at all.

Examples of apparently general reservations are those that qualify the state's treaty commitment by reference to its own domestic law, as the United States did in its ratification of the Genocide Convention with the following reservation:

> That nothing in the Convention requires or authorizes legislation or other action by the United States of America prohibited by the Constitution of the United States as interpreted by the United States.

A number of states registered objections to this U.S. reservation as incompatible with the object and purpose of the Genocide Convention, as vague, and as an improper attempt to circumvent the requirement of the law of treaties (see p. 497 below) that internal law may not be invoked to justify non-performance of a treaty obligation. Yet none of these states objected to the entry into force of the Genocide Convention for the United States or said that they would not consider the United States a party to the treaty.

Another rather common type of reservation to human rights treaties is a qualification in terms of principles of Islamic law or the Islamic Shari'a. Many Islamic countries have entered such reservations, either in general terms or in respect of specific provisions, when ratifying treaties such as the International Covenants or the Convention on the Elimination of Discrimination Against Women (CEDAW). Examples include:

> The Government of the Republic of Maldives will comply with the provisions of the Convention, except those which the Government may consider contrary to the principles of the Islamic Sharia upon which the laws and traditions of the Maldives are founded.
>
> The Arab Republic of Egypt is willing to comply with the content of this article [Article 2 of CEDAW], provided that such compliance does not run counter to the Islamic Sharia.
>
> It is clear that the child's acquisition of his father's nationality is the procedure most suitable for the child and that this does not infringe upon the principle of equality since it is customary for a woman to agree that the children shall be of the father's nationality. [Egypt's reservation to Article 9 of CEDAW]
>
> The Hashemite Kingdom of Jordan hereby registers its reservation and does not consider itself bound by the provisions of Article 9, paragraph 2, article 15 paragraph 4 (a woman's residence and domicile are with her husband).

For citations and discussion of these and other examples, see Christine Chinkin, Reservations and Objections to CEDAW, in Chinkin *et al.,* Human Rights as General Norms and a State's Right to Opt Out: Reservations and Objections to Human Rights Conventions 64–84 (Gardner ed., 1997); Wm. Schabas, Reservations to CEDAW and the Convention on the Rights of the Child, 3 Wm. & Mary J. of Women & L. 79 (1997); Lilly Sucharipa–Behrmann, The Legal Effects of Reservations to Multilateral Treaties, 1 Austrian Rev. Int'l & Eur. L. 67, 81 (1996); Rebecca Cook, Reservations to CEDAW, 30 Va. J.I.L. 643 (1990).

Such reservations have elicited some formal objections from states parties, as well as intense criticism from human rights groups and women's advocacy organizations. Yet the substantive import of such reservations is far from clear, since Islamic authorities have diverse views on the implications of Islamic law for particular human rights norms, especially those regarding women. It is also unclear whether such reservations are incompatible with the object and purpose of the treaty in question, and what is the status of treaty relations as between reserving and objecting states, where those states hold different views on validity of the reservation.

In the 1990s, increasing attention was focused on issues concerning reservations that had not been anticipated when the Vienna Convention was drafted. Several of the human rights treaty bodies undertook studies of the problem of reservations, notably the U.N. Human Rights Committee which in 1994 produced a General Comment on the matter, as excerpted below, and the CEDAW Committee which also issued general recommendations on reservations (cited and discussed in Chinkin, supra). At about the same time, the International Law Commission undertook a general study of reservations practice, for the first time since it had completed its work on the Vienna Convention in the 1960s. As of 2000, the I.L.C. study is still in progress, but it has already produced a series of valuable reports by its Special Rapporteur on Reservations to Treaties, Alain Pellet (with comprehensive bibliography), as well as preliminary conclusions and elements of a Draft Guide to Practice with commentary. For a summary of the work so far, and bibliographic references, see Report of the I.L.C. on the work of its 51st Session (1999), G.A.O.R., 54th Sess., Supp. No. 10 (A/54/10), pp. 200–310.

In its Preliminary Conclusions on Reservations to Normative Multilateral Treaties Including Human Rights Treaties, adopted in 1997, the I.L.C. reaffirmed the Vienna Convention regime for reservations (Articles 19–23 of the Vienna Convention) and reiterated "that, in particular, the object and purpose of the treaty is the most important of the criteria for determining the admissibility of reservations." The Commission considered that, "because of its flexibility, this regime is suited to the requirements of all treaties, of whatever object or nature, and achieves a satisfactory balance between the objectives of preservation of the integrity of the text of the treaty and universality of participation in the treaty." The Commission went on to state its view that the general rules of the Vienna Convention apply equally to human rights treaties, but it acknowledged that new legal questions had arisen in view of the establishment of monitoring bodies under human rights treaties. See Report of the I.L.C. on the work of its 49th Session (1997), G.A.O.R., 52nd Sess., Supp. No. 10 (A/52/10), pp. 126–127.

At the same time and somewhat in dialectical tension with the I.L.C. exercise, some of the human rights treaty bodies have staked out their own approaches to problems of reservations and have asserted authority to scrutinize reservations of states parties for conformity to the object and purpose of the treaty in question. The most far-reaching of these assertions came from the Human Rights Committee in its General Comment No. 24 of 1994, set forth below.

C. RESERVATIONS TO HUMAN RIGHTS TREATIES

HUMAN RIGHTS COMMITTEE GENERAL COMMENT NO. 24 ON ISSUES RELATING TO RESERVATIONS MADE TO THE ICCPR

U.N. Doc. CCPR/C/21/Rev.1/Add.6 (1994).
34 I.L.M. 839 (1995) (footnotes omitted).

1. As of 1 November 1994, 46 of the 127 States parties to the International Covenant on Civil and Political Rights had, between them, entered 150 reservations of varying significance to their acceptance of the obligations of the Covenant. * * * The number of reservations, their content and their scope may undermine the effective implementation of the Covenant and tend to weaken respect for the obligations of States Parties. * * *

5. The Covenant neither prohibits reservations nor mentions any type of permitted reservation. The same is true of the first Optional Protocol. * * *

6. The absence of a prohibition on reservations does not mean that any reservation is permitted. The matter of reservations under the Covenant and the first Optional Protocol is governed by international law. Article 19(3) of the Vienna Convention on the Law of Treaties provides relevant guidance. It stipulates that where a reservation is not prohibited by the treaty or falls within the specified permitted categories, a State may make a reservation provided it is not incompatible with the object and purpose of the treaty. Even though, unlike some other human rights treaties, the Covenant does not incorporate a specific reference to the object and purpose test, that test governs the matter of interpretation and acceptability of reservations.

7. In an instrument which articulates very many civil and political rights, each of the many articles, and indeed their interplay, secures the objectives of the Covenant. The object and purpose of the Covenant is to create legally binding standards for human rights by defining certain civil and political rights and placing them in a framework of obligations which are legally binding for those States which ratify; and to provide an efficacious supervisory machinery for the obligations undertaken.

8. Reservations that offend peremptory norms would not be compatible with the object and purpose of the Covenant. Although treaties that are mere exchanges of obligations between States allow them to reserve *inter se* application of rules of general international law, it is otherwise in human rights treaties, which are for the benefit of persons within their jurisdiction. Accordingly, provisions in the Covenant that represent customary international law (and *a fortiori* when they have the character of peremptory norms) may not be the subject of reservations. [For the Committee's views on which provisions of the Covenant represent customary international law, see additional excerpts in Chapter 8 at p. 620 below.]

10. The Committee has further examined whether categories of reservations may offend the "object and purpose" test. In particular, it falls for consideration as to whether reservations to the non-derogable provisions of the Covenant are compatible with its object and purpose. While there is no hierarchy of importance of rights under the Covenant, the operation of certain rights may not be suspended, even in times of national emergency. This underlines the great importance of non-derogable rights. But not all rights of profound importance, such as articles 9 and 27 of the Covenant, have in fact been made non-derogable. * * * While there is no automatic correlation between reservations to non-derogable provisions, and reservations which offend against the object and purpose of the Covenant, a State has a heavy onus to justify such a reservation. * * *

12. * * * Of particular concern are widely formulated reservations which essentially render ineffective all Covenant rights which would require any change in national law to ensure compliance with Covenant obligations. No real international rights or obligations have thus been accepted. And when there is an absence of provisions to ensure that Covenant rights may be sued on in domestic courts, and, further, a failure to allow individual complaints to be brought to the Committee under the first Optional Protocol, all the essential elements of the Covenant guarantees have been removed.

16. The Committee finds it important to address which body has the legal authority to make determinations as to whether specific reservations are

compatible with the object and purpose of the Covenant. [Here the Committee restates the rules of the I.C.J.'s 1951 *Genocide Convention* advisory opinion and Articles 20–21 of the Vienna Convention, on objections to reservations and the legal effect of objections.]

17. As indicated above, it is the Vienna Convention on the Law of Treaties that provides the definition of reservations and also the application of the object and purpose test in the absence of other specific provisions. But the Committee believes that its provisions on the role of State objections in relation to reservations are inappropriate to address the problem of reservations to human rights treaties. Such treaties, and the Covenant specifically, are not a web of inter-State exchanges of mutual obligations. They concern the endowment of individuals with rights. The principle of inter-State reciprocity has no place * * *. And, because the operation of the classic rules on reservations is so inadequate for the Covenant, States have often not seen any legal interest in or need to object to reservations. The absence of protest by States cannot imply that a reservation is either compatible or incompatible with the object and purpose of the Covenant. * * *

18. It necessarily falls to the Committee to determine whether a specific reservation is compatible with the object and purpose of the Covenant. This is in part because, as indicated above, it is an inappropriate task for States parties in relation to human rights treaties, and in part because it is a task that the Committee cannot avoid in the performance of its functions. * * * Because of the special character of a human rights treaty, the compatibility of a reservation with the object and purpose of the Covenant must be established objectively, by reference to legal principles, and the Committee is particularly well placed to perform this task. The normal consequence of an unacceptable reservation is not that the Covenant will not be in effect at all for a reserving party. Rather, such a reservation will generally be severable, in the sense that the Covenant will be operative for the reserving party without benefit of the reservation.

19. Reservations must be specific and transparent, so that the Committee, those under the jurisdiction of the reserving State and other States parties may be clear as to what obligations of human rights compliance have or have not been undertaken. Reservations may thus not be general, but must refer to a particular provision of the Covenant and indicate in precise terms its scope in relation thereto. * * * States should not enter so many reservations that they are in effect accepting a limited number of human rights obligations, and not the Covenant as such. So that reservations do not lead to a perpetual non-attainment of international human rights standards, reservations should not systematically reduce the obligations undertaken only to the present existing in less demanding standards of domestic law. Nor should interpretative declarations or reservations seek to remove an autonomous meaning to Covenant obligations, by pronouncing them to be identical, or to be accepted only insofar as they are identical, with existing provisions of domestic law. * * *

20. States should institute procedures to ensure that each and every reservation is compatible with the object and purpose of the Covenant. It is desirable for a State entering a reservation to indicate in precise terms the domestic legislation or practices which it believes to be incompatible with the

Covenant obligation reserved; and to explain the time period it requires to render its own laws and practices compatible with the Covenant, or why it is unable to render its own laws and practices compatible with the Covenant. States should also ensure that the necessity for maintaining reservations is periodically reviewed, taking into account any observations and recommendations made by the Committee during examination of their reports. Reservations should be withdrawn at the earliest possible moment. * * *

Notes

1. General Comment No. 24 has proven controversial in several respects. Both the United States and the United Kingdom challenged the Human Rights Committee's claim of authority to determine the validity of reservations and the legal effects of supposedly impermissible reservations. See Observations of the United States of America and of the United Kingdom on General Comment No. 24, G.A.O.R., U.N. Doc. A/50/40, Annex VI, at 131–132, 135–159 (1995), reprinted in 16 Hum.Rts.L.J. 422, 424 (1995) The U.S. observations criticized the Committee for "appear[ing] to reject the established rules * * * as set forth in the Vienna Convention on the Law of Treaties" and for giving the Committee a greater role than states parties themselves in determining the meaning of the Covenant and of their own reservations.

Concerning the standards for evaluating permissibility of reservations, the United States criticized the Committee's line of analysis in the following paragraphs:

> It is clear that a State cannot exempt itself from a peremptory norm of international law by making a reservation to the Covenant. It is not at all clear that a State cannot choose to exclude one means of enforcement of particular norms by reserving against inclusion of those norms in its Covenant obligations.
>
> The proposition that any reservation which contravenes a norm of customary international law is *per se* incompatible with the object and purpose of this or any other convention, however, is a much more significant and sweeping premise. It is, moreover, wholly unsupported by and is in fact contrary to international law. * * *
>
> With respect to the actual object and purpose of this Covenant, there appears to be a misunderstanding. The object and purpose was to protect human rights, with an understanding that there need not be immediate, universal implementation of all terms of the treaty. * * * In fact, a primary object and purpose of the Covenant was to secure the widest possible adherence, with the clear understanding that a relatively liberal regime on the permissibility of reservations should therefore be required.

With respect to the Committee's analysis of the effect of invalid reservations, and specifically whether such reservations would be severable, the United States contended:

> Since this conclusion is so completely at odds with established legal practice and principles and even the express and clear terms of adherence by many States, it would be welcome if some helpful clarification could be made.

> The reservations contained in the United States' instrument of ratification are integral parts of its consent to be bound by the Covenant and are not severable. If it were to be determined that any one or more of them were ineffective, the ratification as a whole could thereby be nullified. * * *
>
> The general view of the academic literature is that reservations are an essential part of a State's consent to be bound. They cannot simply be erased. This reflects the fundamental principle of the law of treaties: obligation is based on consent. A State which does not consent to a treaty is not bound by that treaty. A State which expressly withholds its consent from a provision cannot be presumed, on the basis of some legal fiction, to be bound by it. It is regrettable that General Comment 24 appears to suggest to the contrary.

2. Was the Committee correct in its assessment that the Vienna Convention rules on objections to reservations may be "inappropriate" or "inadequate" for human rights treaties (paras. 17–18 above)? For academic commentary to the effect that the Vienna Convention provisions "operate unsatisfactorily in human rights treaties," see, e.g., Rosalyn Higgins, The United Nations: Still a Force for Peace, 52 Mod. L. Rev. 1, 11 (1989). Professor (now Judge) Higgins served on the Human Rights Committee when General Comment No. 24 was drafted. She has more recently explained that the point is not to create a different legal regime for human rights treaties, but rather to address issues that were simply never considered or resolved in the Vienna Convention. These issues include how to apply the substantive standard of Article 19 of the Vienna Convention—incompatibility with object and purpose—in a given procedural context: namely, the existence of a monitoring body that can resolve questions of compatibility, irrespective of whether states choose to exercise their prerogative of registering objections. See Higgins, Introduction, in Chinkin *et al.,* Human Rights as General Norms, supra (Gardner ed., 1997), pp. xv-xxv.

3. The International Law Commission also responded to the claim by the Human Rights Committee that the Committee is vested with the authority to determine the validity of a reservation. In its Preliminary Conclusions on Reservations to Treaties adopted in 1997 (cited p. 490 supra), the I.L.C. said:

> 5. The Commission also considers that where these treaties are silent on the subject, the monitoring bodies established thereby are competent to comment upon and express recommendations with regard, *inter alia,* to the admissibility of reservations by States, in order to carry out the functions assigned to them;
>
> 6. The Commission stresses that this competence of the monitoring bodies does not exclude or otherwise affect the traditional modalities of control by the contracting parties * * *
>
> 8. The Commission notes that the legal force of the findings made by monitoring bodies in the exercise of their power to deal with reservations cannot exceed that resulting from the powers given to them for the performance of their general monitoring role.

4. The U.S. ratification of the Genocide Convention contained two paragraphs denominated "reservations" and other paragraphs with interpretive statements. Is it plausible in light of U.S. constitutional law to consider that the "reservation" quoted at p. 488 above may not be a reservation within the meaning of the Vienna Convention definition (if nothing in the U.S. Constitution would prevent the United States from carrying out the obligations of the treaty)?

A similar constitutional statement has been adopted by the U.S. Senate in connection with the resolutions of ratification of other human rights treaties; but in contrast to the Genocide Convention, the other statements have not been called "reservations" and have been circulated to states parties to the treaties separately from the instrument of ratification. Do these procedural differences have any significance under the Vienna Convention?

The other U.S. reservation to the Genocide Convention was addressed to the dispute settlement article (Article IX) and requires specific U.S. consent in the particular case to the submission of any disputes about the Convention to the International Court of Justice. This reservation is substantially similar to those of the Soviet-bloc countries that led to the General Assembly's request for the Advisory Opinion on Reservations to the Genocide Convention (1951) p. 479 supra.

5. For excerpts from and discussion of the U.S. reservations to other human rights treaties, see Chapter 8, pp. 616–621 infra.

6. Regional human rights organs had considered issues concerning reservations in the context of the respective regional human rights systems, even before the developments in the U.N. human rights treaty bodies and the I.L.C. described above. The Inter–American Court of Human Rights in an Advisory Opinion on Reservations, I.A.C.H.R., Ser. A, No. 2 (1982) addressed the legal effect of ratifications with reservations in the one-year period during which other states parties can object to reservations (Vienna Convention, Article 20(5)). The Court emphasized that requirements of acceptance and reciprocity were not appropriate for a human rights treaty which must be seen "for what in reality it is: a multilateral legal instrument or framework enabling states to make binding unilateral commitments not to violate the human rights of individuals within their jurisdiction." Advisory Opinion, para. 33. On this theory, reciprocity loses its relevance and reservations may be considered as authorized by the treaty provided they are not incompatible with the object and purpose of the treaty. Consequently states which ratified with reservations should be considered as legally bound from the date of their ratification.

In an Advisory Opinion on Restriction to the Death Penalty, Adv. Op. No. OC–3 (1983), Ser. A, No. 3, 23 I.L.M. 320 (1984), the Inter–American Court of Human Rights examined Guatemala's reservation to Article 4(4) of the American Convention on Human Rights, which prohibits application of the death penalty for "political offenses or related common crimes." In its reasoning, the Court emphasized the fact that derogations from Article 4 were not permitted by the Convention: "It would follow therefrom that a reservation which was designed to enable a State to suspend any of the non-derogable fundamental rights must be deemed to be incompatible with the object and purpose of the Convention and consequently not permitted by it. The situation would be different if the reservation sought merely to restrict certain aspects of a non-derogable right without depriving the right as a whole of its basic purpose." Ibid., para. 61. The Court then interpreted the reservation in a manner "most consistent with the object and purpose of the Convention," so that rather than invalidating the reservation, it gave it a limited scope.

For comments on these two advisory opinions and in particular on the linkage between non-derogability and incompatibility, see Buergenthal, The Advisory Practice of the Inter–American Human Rights Court, 79 A.J.I.L. 1, 20–33 (1985).

7. The European Court of Human Rights has also had several occasions to consider problems concerning reservations. In Belilos v. Switzerland, 132 E.C.H.R., Ser. A (1988), the Court in effect determined that a state's attempted

qualification of an obligation under the regional treaty was invalid as incompatible with the object and purpose of the treaty and could be disregarded: in other words, the state would remain a party to the treaty but without the benefit of the challenged restriction. See also Loizidou v. Turkey, 310 E.C.H.R., Ser. A (1995).

Some of the states that disagreed with the Human Rights Committee's General Comment No. 24, e.g. in relation to its treatment of questions of severability, considered that the U.N. treaty body overstepped its authority by following the general approach of regional organs, without accounting for significant differences between regional and universal systems. Is this criticism persuasive?

8. For bibliography in addition to the references noted above, see Horn, Reservations and Interpretive Declarations to Multilateral Treaties (1988); Clark, The Vienna Convention Regime and CEDAW, 85 A.J.I.L. 281 (1991); Lijnzaad, Reservations to UN Human Rights Treaties: Ratify and Ruin? (1995); Redgwell, Reservations to Treaties and Human Rights Committee General Comment No. 24, 46 I.C.L.Q. 390 (1997). See also Zemanek, General Course, 266 Rec. des Cours 175–192 (1997).

SECTION 4. OBSERVANCE, APPLICATION, AND INTERPRETATION

A. OBSERVANCE

1. *Pacta Sunt Servanda and Good Faith (Article 26)*

Lord McNair, The Law of Treaties 493 (1961) prefaces his discussion of the binding effect of treaties with the following remarks:

> In every uncodified legal system there are certain elementary and universally agreed principles for which it is almost impossible to find specific authority. In the Common Law of England and the United States of America, where can you find specific authority for the principle that a man must perform his contracts? Yet almost every decision on a contract presupposes the existence of that principle. The same is true of international law. No Government would decline to accept the principle *pacta sunt servanda,* and the very fact that Governments find it necessary to spend so much effort in explaining in a particular case that the *pactum* has ceased to exist, or that the act complained of is not a breach of it, either by reason of an implied term or for some other reason, is the best acknowledgment of that principle. * * *

The International Law Commission said in its commentary of 1966 on what became Article 26:

> (2) There is much authority in the jurisprudence of international tribunals for the proposition that in the present context the principle of good faith is a legal principle which forms an integral part of the rule *pacta sunt servanda.* * * * [T]he Permanent Court of International Justice, in applying treaty clauses prohibiting discrimination against minorities, insisted in a number of cases, that the clauses must be so applied as to ensure the absence of discrimination in fact as well as in law; in other words, the obligation must not be evaded by a merely literal

application of the clauses. Numerous precedents could also be found in the jurisprudence of arbitral tribunals.

[1966] II Y.B.I.L.C. 211.

Note

In the Case Concerning the Gabcikovo–Nagymaros Project (Hungary/Slovakia), 1997 I.C.J. 7, discussed more fully at pp. 557–559 and 574–576 infra, the I.C.J. determined that a 1977 bilateral treaty was still in force and that both parties continued to be "under a legal obligation * * * to consider, within the context of the 1977 Treaty, in what way the multiple objectives of the Treaty can best be served, keeping in mind that all of them should be fulfilled." (Para. 139.) The Court elaborated on the parties' obligations as follows:

> 142. What is required in the present case by the rule *pacta sunt servanda,* as reflected in Article 26 of the Vienna Convention of 1969 on the Law of Treaties, is that the Parties find an agreed solution within the co-operative context of the Treaty.
>
> Article 26 combines two elements, which are of equal importance. It provides that "Every treaty in force is binding upon the parties to it and must be performed by them in good faith." This latter element, in the Court's view, implies that, in this case, it is the purpose of the Treaty, and the intentions of the parties in concluding it, which should prevail over its literal application. The principle of good faith obliges the Parties to apply it in a reasonable way and in such a manner that its purpose can be realized.

2. *Internal Law and Treaty Observance (Article 27)*

The Vienna Convention restates in Article 27 the long-accepted rule of customary law that a state may not invoke its internal law as a justification for its failure to perform a treaty. See Advisory Opinion on Treatment of Polish Nationals and Other Persons of Polish Origin in Danzig Territory, 1932 P.C.I.J., Ser. A/B, No. 44, at 22. Where a state has a domestic rule of law that a later statute supersedes an earlier treaty (as is the case in the United States) a domestic court will apply the statute rather than the treaty. However, the state remains internationally bound by the treaty and responsible if it violates its provisions. Of importance in this connection is the principle widely accepted in national legal systems that domestic law should be construed insofar as possible to avoid violating a state's international obligation. See pp. 220–221 supra.

A constitutional provision has no higher status in international law than any other provision of internal law except in one respect. A state may invoke the fact that its consent to be bound by a treaty was expressed "in violation of a provision of its internal law regarding competence to conclude treaties" if (and only if) the violation was "manifest and concerned a rule of its internal law of fundamental importance." Vienna Convention, Article 46. This aspect of the problem is dealt with at pp. 523–526 infra.

Note

In Breard v. Greene, 523 U.S. 371, 118 S.Ct. 1352, 140 L.Ed.2d 529 (1998), pp. 216–219 supra and pp. 901–902 infra, the U.S. Supreme Court was asked to stay the execution of a death sentence of a Paraguayan national, pending resolution of a dispute over consequences of non-compliance with a treaty (the Vienna Convention on Consular Relations). The dispute had been brought to the International Court of Justice upon application of Paraguay, in parallel to the habeas corpus proceedings brought by the prisoner in U.S. courts. The United States government conceded in both forums that there had been a breach of the treaty, but the government's position was that neither court could accord a remedy for the breach since the petitioner had failed to raise the treaty question in the courts of the state of Virginia at the time of his trial and subsequent appeals. On this point the Supreme Court said:

> First, while we should give respectful consideration to the interpretation of an international treaty rendered by an international court with jurisdiction to interpret such, it has been recognized in international law that, absent a clear and express statement to the contrary, the procedural rules of the forum State govern the implementation of the treaty in that State. [citations to three U.S. cases omitted] This proposition is embodied in the Vienna Convention [on Consular Relations] itself, which provides that the rights expressed in the Convention "shall be exercised in conformity with the laws and regulations of the receiving State," provided that "said laws and regulations must enable full effect to be given to the purposes for which the rights accorded under this Article are intended." Article 36(2), [1970] U.S.T., at 101. It is the rule in this country that assertions of error in criminal proceedings must first be raised in state court in order to form the basis for relief in habeas. *Wainwright v. Sykes,* 433 U.S. 72 (1977). Claims not so raised are considered defaulted. Ibid. By not asserting his Vienna Convention claim in state court, Breard failed to exercise his rights under the Vienna Convention in conformity with the laws of the United States and the Commonwealth of Virginia. Having failed to do so, he cannot raise a claim of violation of those rights now on federal habeas review.

Though Paraguay eventually withdrew its I.C.J. case after Breard was executed, similar issues (concerning the relevance in international law of domestic procedural prerequisites for asserting and preserving treaty claims) were to be resolved in a comparable case brought by Germany involving execution of two of its nationals, Karl and Walter LaGrand. Case Concerning Vienna Convention on Consular Relations (Germ. v. U.S.), 1999 I.C.J. 9 (Prov. Measures). Hearings on the merits in the *LaGrand* case were held in November 2000.

B. APPLICATION

1. Non-Retroactivity and the Intertemporal Problem (Article 28)

A treaty may by its terms or by implication apply to a fact or situation prior to the entry into force of the treaty. In the absence of such provision, its provisions do not bind a party in respect of an act or fact which occurred, or a situation which ceased to exist, before the entry into force of a treaty. Article 28 makes this explicit.

But consider its application in the case of a legal or other concept which has changed its meaning over time. Should the concept be interpreted as understood at the time it was adopted or at the time of its application? Would the latter interpretation violate the rule against retroactive application?

The International Court of Justice faced this issue in its *Advisory Opinion on Namibia* (p. 549 infra) when it had to interpret terms of the Mandate for Southwest Africa. These terms included "sacred trust," and "well-being and development" of the indigenous inhabitants. The opinion of the Court included the following conclusions relating to this problem:

> Mindful as it is of the primary necessity of interpreting an instrument in accordance with the intentions of the parties at the time of its conclusion, the Court is bound to take into account the fact that the concepts embodied in Article 22 of the Covenant * * * were not static, but were by definition evolutionary, as also, therefore, was the concept of the sacred trust. The parties to the Covenant must consequently be deemed to have accepted them as such.

The Court consequently reached the following conclusion:

> * * * That is why, viewing the institutions of 1919, the Court must take into consideration the changes which have occurred in the supervening half-century, and its interpretation cannot remain unaffected by the subsequent development of law, through the Charter of the United Nations and by way of customary law.

The Court further added:

> * * * Moreover, an international instrument has to be interpreted and applied within the framework of the entire legal system prevailing at the time of interpretation.

1971 I.C.J. 31.

The interpretation of the International Court and Article 28 are aspects of the broader subject of intertemporal law. The following resolution on that subject was adopted by the *Institut de Droit International* in 1975 after several years of study and debate.

THE INTERTEMPORAL PROBLEM IN PUBLIC INTERNATIONAL LAW

Resolution adopted by the Institut de Droit International.
56 Ann. de l'Institut de Droit Int'l 537 (preamble omitted) (1975).

1. Unless otherwise indicated, the temporal sphere of application of any norm of public international law shall be determined in accordance with the general principle of law by which any fact, action or situation must be assessed in the light of the rules of law that are contemporaneous with it.

2. In application of this principle:

(a) any rule which relates to a single fact shall apply to facts that occur while the rule is in force;

(b) any rule which relates to the repetition or succession of identical facts shall apply even though only one or some of such facts should occur after the entry into force of the rule;

(c) any rule which relates to an actual situation shall apply to situations existing while the rule is in force, even if these situations have been created previously;

(d) any rule which relates to a certain period of time, or to the existence of a situation during a defined period, shall apply only to periods the initial and terminal dates of which lie within the time when the rule is in force;

(e) any rule which relates to the end of a period shall apply to any case where the period has come to an end at a time when the rule is in force;

(f) any rule which relates to the licit or illicit nature of a legal act, or to the conditions of its validity, shall apply to acts performed while the rule is in force;

(g) any rule which relates to the continuous effects of a legal act shall apply to effects produced while the rule is in force, even if the act has been performed prior to the entry into force of the rule;

(h) any rule which relates to the substance of a legal status shall apply even if the status has been created or acquired prior to the entry into force of the rule.

3. States and other subjects of international law shall, however, have the power to determine by common consent the temporal sphere of application of norms, notwithstanding the rules laid down in Paragraphs 1 and 2 and subject to any imperative norm of international law which might restrict that power.

This provision shall be without prejudice to obligations which may ensue for contracting parties from previous treaties to which they are parties and from the provisions of which they cannot depart even by common consent.

4. Wherever a provision of a treaty refers to a legal or other concept without defining it, it is appropriate to have recourse to the usual methods of interpretation in order to determine whether the concept concerned is to be interpreted as understood at the time when the provision was drawn up or as understood at the time of its application. Any interpretation of a treaty must take into account all relevant rules of international law which apply between the parties at the time of application.

5. The solution of such intertemporal problems as might arise within international Organizations is reserved.

6. In order to eliminate any cause of uncertainty or dispute, it is desirable that every international instrument should include express provisions indicating the solution which ought to be given to such intertemporal problems as might arise in the course of its application.

Note

In a variant of the intertemporal problem that arose in a recent boundary dispute between Botswana and Namibia, the International Court of Justice had to give contemporary meaning to a term in a 1890 treaty between Germany and Great Britain, which delineated their spheres of influence with reference to the "main channel" of the Chobe River. The Court said (para. 20):

> In order to illuminate the meaning of words agreed upon in 1890, there is nothing that prevents the Court from taking into account the present-day

state of scientific knowledge, as reflected in the documentary material submitted to it by the Parties * * *.

In her declaration, Judge Higgins wrote separately to clarify her position on temporal issues:

> * * * The Court is really * * * applying a somewhat general term, decided upon by the Parties in 1890, to a geographic and hydrographic situation much better understood today.
>
> 3. The Court is indeed, for this particular task, entitled to look at all the criteria the Parties have suggested as relevant. This is not to discover a mythical "ordinary meaning" within the Treaty, but rather because the general terminology chosen long ago falls to be decided today. To use contemporary knowledge and scientific data to assist in fulfilling that task is not at all inconsistent with the intertemporal rule in the *Island of Palmas* Award [pp. 316–320 supra], which was concerned with the legal rules applicable to title to territory and not with identification, through the legal technique of evaluating evidence, of a chosen term. * * *
>
> 6. We know now that the assumptions as to navigability were mistaken. For its greater part the River Chobe is not navigable; no further engineering works have been able to bring into being access to the Zambezi * * *. A fully contextual application today of treaty terms selected in 1890 should not place emphasis on elements that, to be sure, have a theoretical relevance but none in the particular realities of the case.

Case concerning Kasikili/Sedudu Island, 1999 I.C.J., excerpted in Chapter 4 at p. 327.

2. *Territorial Application (Article 29)*

SINCLAIR, THE VIENNA CONVENTION ON THE LAW OF TREATIES

89–92 (2d ed. 1984) (footnotes omitted).

The phrase "the entire territory of each party" was intended to be a comprehensive term designed to embrace all the land and appurtenant territorial waters and air space which constitute the territory of the State. * * *

It is clear that the opening words of Article 29 of the Convention impart a considerable degree of flexibility into the operation of the basic rule. But in what circumstances will a different intention appear from the treaty or be otherwise established? In other words, what exceptions are there to the residual rule?

It would appear that exceptions to the residual rule can be either express or implied. The obvious express exception is a territorial application clause in the treaty itself. But there can be other kinds of express exceptions. The device whereby, on signature or ratification, a State makes a declaration as to the territorial effect or extent of the act of signature or ratification has long been known and accepted in State practice. Thus, in ratifying the Convention on the High Seas in 1963, the United Kingdom government declared that "ratification of this Convention on behalf of the United Kingdom does not extend to the States in the Persian Gulf enjoying British protection". * * *

A word of caution is, however, necessary here. A reservation on the territorial application of certain types of treaty may be excluded because such a reservation would be incompatible with the object and purpose of the treaty. There are certain treaties, principally in the field of disarmament or humanitarian law, which are clearly intended to be world-wide in their application. It is arguable that the nature of such treaties would preclude the making of a reservation designed to limit their territorial application.

3. Application of Successive Treaties Relating to the Same Subject Matter (Article 30)

The tremendous increase in the number of treaties and the diversity of international organizations engaged in treaty-making (regional, functional, and global) have resulted in numerous treaties which overlap and sometimes create conflicting obligations. One question raised is whether inconsistent treaties *vis-à-vis* different parties are valid. The Vienna Convention bypasses this problem of invalidity and that of responsibility for breach arising from inconsistent treaties. Article 30 approaches the problem as one of priorities. It provides in substance:

(a) If a treaty says that it is subject to, or is not to be considered as incompatible with, another treaty, that other treaty will prevail.

(b) As between parties to a treaty who become parties to a later, inconsistent, treaty, the earlier treaty will apply only where its provisions are not incompatible with the later treaty.

(c) As between a party to both treaties and a party to only one of them, the treaty to which both are parties will govern the mutual rights and obligations of the States concerned.

Notes

1. Successive treaties relating to the same subject matter frequently arise in an institutional setting. For example, with respect to treaties on intellectual property or trade, the bodies charged with implementing the agreements (e.g., the World Intellectual Property Organization or the World Trade Organization) may have a role to play in clarifying apparently divergent obligations under the same general regime when successive treaties are adopted over time. However, it is not clear that the institutions of one regime are in a position to resolve conflicts between a given treaty obligation—say, in the field of trade—and another obligation in a different sphere—say, environment or human rights. Several cases before the W.T.O. Dispute Settlement Body have posed this general problem, in which a party (e.g., the United States) might argue that its obligations under a trade agreement should be interpreted to facilitate compliance with obligations under (or objectives of) a different agreement on environmental protection or human rights. See discussion of the Tuna/Dolphin and Shrimp/Turtles cases (involving issues of compatibility of trade obligations with environmental concerns, including preservation of species) at pp. 1534–1536 infra.

Do the Vienna Convention's provisions under this heading offer relevant guidance in resolving such conflicts?

2. As attitudes toward women's rights have evolved over time, differing treaties have taken divergent positions on protecting women and advancing their

equality. A notorious case is the 1919 Convention Concerning Employment of Women During the Night, adopted under the auspices of the International Labour Organisation, which generally precluded women from most nighttime work (out of what would now be considered paternalistic motivations). A more flexible definition of "night" was adopted in a 1948 amendment, without changing the underlying paternalistic philosophy. Later, with the adoption of the Convention on Elimination of All Forms of Discrimination Against Women (CEDAW), such restrictions became evidently inconsistent with CEDAW obligations on non-discrimination and promotion of equality for women. Yet some parties to CEDAW who are also parties to the earlier ILO treaties have entered reservations to CEDAW to enable continued observance of the earlier treaties. Bearing in mind the issues raised above on the Vienna Convention and human rights treaties, how should apparent incompatibility between successive treaties on women be addressed?

C. INTERPRETATION OF TREATIES

1. *Organs of Interpretation and Interpretation by the Parties*

JESSE LEWIS (THE DAVID J. ADAMS) CLAIM (UNITED STATES v. GREAT BRITAIN)

Claims Arbitration under the Special Agreement
of August 18, 1910, 1921, Nielsen Rep. 526.
6 U.N.R.I.A.A. 85.

[By the Treaty of London of 1818, 8 Stat. 248, the United States renounced for its nationals the right to fish in Canadian waters, with the proviso that American fishermen should be permitted to enter Canadian bays and harbors "for the purpose of shelter and of repairing damages therein, of purchasing wood, and of obtaining water, and for no other purpose whatever." In 1886, the American fishing schooner *David J. Adams,* having entered Canadian waters for the purpose of purchasing fresh bait, was seized by Canadian authorities for alleged violations of the Treaty of 1818 and of the applicable Canadian legislation. A Canadian court condemned the vessel, finding that it had violated the Treaty and legislation. On behalf of the vessel's owner, the United States subsequently claimed damages from the British Government on the ground, *inter alia,* that the seizure and condemnation were wrongful because based on an erroneous interpretation of the Treaty. The British agent argued, *inter alia,* that the Arbitral Tribunal was not competent to re-examine the Canadian court's interpretation.]

THE TRIBUNAL * * * Great Britain and Canada, acting in the full exercise of their sovereignty and by such proper legislative authority as was established by their municipal public law, had enacted and were entitled to enact such legislative provisions as they considered necessary or expedient to secure observance of the said Treaty; and, so far as they are not inconsistent with the said Treaty, those provisions are binding as municipal public law of the country on any person within the limits of British jurisdiction. At the time of the seizure of the *David J. Adams* such legislation was embodied in the British Act of 1819 (59 George III, C. 38), and the Canadian Acts of 1868 (31 Vict. 61), 1871 (34 Vict., C. 23).

Great Britain and Canada, acting by such proper judicial authority as was established by their municipal law, were fully entitled to interpret and apply such legislation and to pronounce and impose such penalty as was provided by the same, but such judicial action had the same limits as the aforesaid legislative action, that is to say so far as it was not inconsistent with the said Treaty.

In this case the question is not and cannot be to ascertain whether or not British law has been justly applied by said judicial authorities, nor to consider, revise, reverse, or affirm a decision given in that respect by British Courts. On the contrary, any such decision must be taken as the authorized expression of the position assumed by Great Britain in the subject matter, and, so far as such decision implies an interpretation of said treaty, it must be taken as the authorized expression of the British interpretation.

The fundamental principle of the juridical equality of States is opposed to placing one State under the jurisdiction of another State. It is opposed to the subjection of one State to an interpretation of a Treaty asserted by another State. There is no reason why one more than the other should impose such an unilateral interpretation of a contract which is essentially bilateral. The fact that this interpretation is given by the legislative or judicial or any other authority of one of the Parties does not make that interpretation binding upon the other Party. Far from contesting that principle, the British Government did not fail to recognize it. * * *

For that reason the mere fact that a British Court, whatever be the respect and high authority it carries, interpreted the treaty in such a way as to declare the *David J. Adams* had contravened it, cannot be accepted by this Tribunal as a conclusive interpretation binding upon the United States Government. Such a decision is conclusive from the national British point of view; it is not from the national United States point of view. * * * [T]he duty of this international Tribunal is to determine, from the international point of view, how the provisions of the treaty are to be interpreted and applied to the facts, and consequently whether the loss resulting from the forfeiture of the vessel gives rise to an indemnity. * * *

[The Tribunal then held that the Canadian court's interpretation and application of the Treaty had not been erroneous.]

Notes

1. A unilateral interpretation of an international agreement, whether made by the executive, legislative, or judicial organs of one of the contracting states, is not binding upon other contracting states. See McNair, The Law of Treaties 345–50 (1961); Hyde 1460–61; Degan, L'Interprétation des accords en droit international 17–18 (1963); 1 Juris–Classeur de Droit International, Fasc. 12–C, para. 7. Would it nevertheless be prudent for contracting states to protest what they believe to be an erroneous interpretation or application of a treaty by the government or courts of another contracting state? In the *Case Concerning the Temple of Preah Vihear* (Cambodia v. Thailand), 1962 I.C.J. 6, the contending states each claimed sovereignty over a small area of frontier territory in which the ruins of the ancient Temple of Preah Vihear were located. Cambodia relied on a

1907 map which showed the Temple area to be a part of French Indochina, now Cambodia. Thailand (formerly Siam) argued that the map was erroneous because it had not been drawn in accordance with a 1904 Siamese–French treaty. The Court emphasized, in holding for Cambodia, that the map had been produced by the French at Siamese request, and that the Siamese had never protested the alleged error; this was enough, the Court concluded, to amount to Siamese acquiescence in the map as drawn.

In connection with the interpretation of the Hay–Pauncefote treaty of 1901 between the United States and Great Britain, the Counselor of the Department of State (Lansing) referred in a memorandum of 1913 to a treaty concluded between the United States and Panama in 1903. The Panama Treaty was "a matter of common knowledge and a subject of public discussion," he wrote, pointing out that Great Britain had made no protest or criticism of provisions exempting Panamanian ships from canal tolls until 1912. "It may fairly be urged," concluded the Counselor, "that the Panama Treaty was a contemporaneous interpretation of the Hay–Pauncefote Treaty, and that Great Britain gave assent to the interpretation by permitting the Governments of the United States and of Panama to act under its provisions without interposing any objections." 5 Hackworth 253–54. See generally de Visscher, Problèmes d'Interprétation Judiciaire en Droit International Public 168–81 (1963); MacGibbon, The Scope of Acquiescence in International Law, 31 Brit. Y.B.I.L. 143, 146–47 (1954).

2. In 1988, the Senate included in its resolution ratifying the Intermediate Nuclear Forces Treaty between the United States and the Soviet Union a condition making executive branch statements to the Senate the main source for interpreting the agreement after the text itself. In a letter to the Senate, President Reagan registered strong disapproval of this condition. Reagan argued that the Senate had no power to alter the traditional principles of treaty interpretation by subordinating sources such as the intent of the parties, the negotiating record, and subsequent practices to the unilateral declarations of the United States. "[T]he principles of treaty interpretation recognized and repeatedly invoked by the courts may not be limited or changed by the Senate alone, and those principles will govern any future disputes over the interpretation of this treaty," concluded the President. 27 I.L.M. 1413 (1988).

3. What is the legal effect of an interpretation made by the parties to an international agreement? See Ste. Ruegger et Boutet v. Ste. Weber et Howard, [1933–34] Ann. Dig. 404 (No. 179) (Trib. civ. de la Seine, France), in which the court held itself bound by an interpretation recorded by exchange of notes between the French Minister of Foreign Affairs and the British Ambassador, of a treaty between the two countries. The Court said that although a "unilateral" interpretation had only an "advisory effect," an interpretation agreed upon by both governments had the effect of adding an additional clause to the treaty. Should *interpretation* by the parties to a bilateral treaty be regarded as an *amendment* of the treaty? What practical results might depend upon the distinction?

4. An interpretation agreed upon by all the parties to a treaty is commonly called an "authentic," as distinct from a "unilateral," interpretation. See Degan at 18–19; de Visscher, Problèmes d'Interprétation Judiciare en Droit International Public 20–21 (1963).

If a multilateral treaty is under consideration, it is ordinarily impractical to obtain the assent of every party to a given interpretation. What is the legal effect of an interpretation made by fewer than all the parties? Should nonparticipating states be bound by the interpretation made by the other contracting states if the former do not protest within a reasonable time? Should an interpretation reached by fewer than all the contracting states be given greater weight than a "unilateral" interpretation? In Philippson v. Imperial Airways, Ltd., [1939] A.C. 332, the House of Lords held that the term "High Contracting Party" as used in the Warsaw Convention on International Air Transportation, 1929, 49 Stat. 3000, 137 L.N.T.S. 11, included a state that had signed the treaty but had not yet ratified it. The British Embassy in the United States informed the Secretary of State of the decision, and stated that the British Government's interpretation of "High Contracting Party" was that the term included only states that were finally bound by the treaty's provisions. On October 6, 1939, the Secretary of State expressed his agreement with the British Government's position. 4 Hackworth 373; 5 Hackworth 199, 250–51. Could either the United States or the United Kingdom thereafter assert against the other a different interpretation of "High Contracting Party," as used in the Warsaw Convention? Would other parties to the Warsaw Convention be bound by the United States–United Kingdom interpretation if they did not protest within a reasonable time? What would be reasonable time? What would be the position of states acceding to the Convention in years subsequent to 1939? Would these be bound by the United States–United Kingdom interpretation if, upon accession, they did not reserve their position on that question?

5. May a court in a third state interpret a treaty at the request of private litigants? Would such judicial determinations contravene sovereign rights of the states that are parties to the treaty? Should the court in the third state apply the act of state doctrine? See Occidental of Umm v. A Certain Cargo of Petroleum, 577 F.2d 1196 (5th Cir.1978), cert. denied, 442 U.S. 928, 99 S.Ct. 2857, 61 L.Ed.2d 296 (1979); Buttes Gas and Oil Co. v. Hammer (House of Lords) 1982 A.C. 888, reprinted in 21 I.L.M. 92 (1982). On Act of State, see Chapter 3.

6. Which organ or organs are responsible for the interpretation of international agreements, such as the Charter of the United Nations, that serve as constitutions for international organizations? The San Francisco Conference failed to include in the Charter any specific provisions relating to the Charter's interpretation, instead leaving to the organs and member-states of the United Nations the freedom to determine for themselves the meaning of Charter provisions. The Committee on Legal Problems offered the following suggestions, which were subsequently approved by the Conference:

> In the course of the operations from day to day of the various organs of the Organization, it is inevitable that each organ will interpret such parts of the Charter as are applicable to its particular functions. This process is inherent in the functioning of any body which operates under an instrument defining its functions and powers. It will be manifested in the functioning of such a body as the General Assembly, the Security Council, or the International Court of Justice. Accordingly, it is not necessary to include in the Charter a provision either authorizing or approving the normal operation of this principle.
>
> Difficulties may conceivably arise in the event that there should be a difference of opinion among the organs of the Organization concerning the correct interpretation of a provision of the Charter. Thus, two organs may conceivably hold and may express or even act upon different views. Under unitary forms of national government the final determination of such a question may be vested in the highest court or in some other national authority. However, the nature of the Organization and of its operation would

> not seem to be such as to invite the inclusion in the Charter of any provision of this nature. If two Member States are at variance concerning the correct interpretation of the Charter, they are of course free to submit the dispute to the International Court of Justice as in the case of any other treaty. Similarly, it would always be open to the General Assembly or to the Security Council, in appropriate circumstances, to ask the International Court of Justice for an advisory opinion concerning the meaning of a provision of the Charter. Should the General Assembly or the Security Council prefer another course, an *ad hoc* committee of jurists might be set up to examine the question and report its views, or recourse might be had to a joint conference. In brief, the members or the organs of the Organization might have recourse to various expedients in order to obtain an appropriate interpretation. It would appear neither necessary nor desirable to list or to describe in the Charter the various possible expedients.
>
> It is to be understood, of course, that if an interpretation made by any organ of the Organization or by a committee of jurists is not generally acceptable it will be without binding force. In such circumstances, or in cases where it is desired to establish an authoritative interpretation as a precedent for the future, it may be necessary to embody the interpretation in an amendment to the Charter. This may always be accomplished by recourse to the procedure provided for amendments.

13 U.N.C.I.O. Docs. 709. What difficulties might be expected to arise under the above "process" of interpretation? Does the availability of an Advisory Opinion by the International Court of Justice mitigate the danger of deadlock?

7. Under the Treaty of Rome, establishing the European Economic Community, 298 U.N.T.S. 11, a Court of Justice was set up and empowered to "ensure observance of law and justice in the interpretation and application of [the] Treaty." Article 220; see also Articles 230–234. The Court's decisions are enforceable under Articles 244 and 256.

8. Many modern treaties contain clauses providing that disputes concerning the interpretation or application of the treaty shall be settled by an independent and impartial authority such as an *ad hoc* arbitral tribunal or by a permanent body such as the International Court of Justice.

In the 1998 *Breard* case noted at p. 497 above, the U.S. Supreme Court said that it should give "respectful" consideration to an interpretation rendered by an international court with jurisdiction to interpret an international treaty. If the case had arisen in a different procedural posture (without the problem of procedural default that barred Breard's federal habeas claim, and at a time when an authoritative international ruling might already be in hand before the deadline for domestic action), should the Supreme Court have considered the international court's interpretation binding?

2. *Problems and Methods of Treaty Interpretation (Articles 31–32)*

As noted above (p. 453), the I.C.J., other international tribunals, and states have treated the methodology embodied in Articles 31–32 of the Vienna Convention as declaratory of the customary international law of treaty interpretation. Those articles themselves require interpretation, however. How is the interpreter to determine the "object and purpose" of a treaty? (Compare the corresponding problems concerning "object and purpose" in relation to reservations, Section 3 above.) Does the reference to "purpose" imply a teleological (purposive) process, under which the interpreter may seek to advance the goals of the treaty beyond its literal terms? What elements are to be taken into account as the "context"? Are they limited to the items specified in Article 31(2)? Is "dynamic" interpretation implicit, e.g. in Article 31(3)'s reference to "any subsequent practice"? Is the use of "supplementary means" under Article 32 limited to the circumstances specified in that article? These and comparable problems are grist for the mill of international tribunals, which regularly deal with problems of treaty interpretation.

JIMÉNEZ DE ARÉCHAGA, INTERNATIONAL LAW IN THE PAST THIRD OF A CENTURY

159 Rec. des Cours 42–48 (1978–I) (footnotes omitted).

A divergence of views arose [at the Vienna Conference] concerning the basic approach on the interpretation of treaties.

There is a fundamental opposition between two schools of thought: the first one asserts that the primary task in the interpretation of treaties is to ascertain the common or real intention of the parties; the second school defines as the objective of treaty interpretation the determination of the meaning of a text. According to the first approach, "the prime, indeed, the only legitimate object, is to ascertain and give effect to the intentions or presumed intentions of the parties"; according to the second, the fundamental objective is "to establish what the text means according to the ordinary or apparent signification of its terms; its approach is therefore through the study and analysis of the text." The test which distinguishes at the practical level one approach from the other is the position assigned to the *travaux préparatoires* of the treaty. The first school places on the same level the text of the treaty and its *travaux préparatoires,* since both serve to determine the real intention of the parties; the second school considers the text above all as the basic material for interpretation and the *travaux préparatoires* are only taken into account as a secondary or supplementary means of interpretation.

The proposals submitted to the Vienna Conference by the International Law Commission were inspired by the textual approach; primacy was accorded to the text of the treaty as the basis for its interpretation. The Commission said in its commentary that its proposal "is based on the view that the text must be presumed to be the authentic expression of the intentions of the parties; and that, in consequence, the starting point of interpretation is the elucidation of the meaning of the text, not an investigation *ab initio* into the intentions of the parties."

PROVISIONS OF THE VIENNA CONVENTION REGARDING INTERPRETATION

Article 31, paragraph 1, of the Convention establishes what may be described as the "golden rule" of interpretation:

> "A treaty shall be interpreted in good faith in accordance with the ordinary meaning to be given to the terms of the treaty in their context and in the light of its object and purpose."

According to this and the subsequent paragraphs of Article 31, the interpretation of a treaty is to be carried out on the basis of what may be described as intrinsic materials, that is to say, texts and related instruments which have been agreed to by the parties. The process of interpretation must begin with an analysis of the specific provisions of the treaty concerning the question in dispute; it goes on to consider the context, that is to say, other provisions of the treaty, including its preamble, annexes and related instruments made in connection with the conclusion of the treaty, taking particularly into account the object and purpose of the treaty, as it appears from these intrinsic materials. It is important to remark that "the object and purpose of the treaty" is mentioned not as an independent element as in the Harvard Draft Convention but at the end of paragraph 1. This was done deliberately, in order to make clear that "object and purpose" are part of the context, the most important one, but not an autonomous element in interpretation, independent of and on the same level as the text, as is advocated by the partisans of the teleological method of interpretation. The latter method emphasizes the general purpose of the treaty, which is assigned an existence of its own, independent of the original intentions of the parties. In this way, gaps can be filled, corrections made, texts expanded or supplemented, so long as it is in furtherance of the general purpose attributed to the treaty by the interpreter.

Paragraph 3 of Article 31 then proceeds to indicate further intrinsic materials to be taken into account together with the context, and these have also been the object of the express or implied consent or consensus of the parties: subsequent agreements, subsequent practice and relevant rules of international law. This is a process of interpretation which has been aptly described by Max Huber as one of *encerclement progressif* of an agreed text: the text is departed from only gradually, in concentric circles, proceeding from the central to the peripheral. The only concession made to the "intention of the parties" school is that, according to paragraph 4, "a special meaning shall be given to a term if it is established that the parties so intended." However, as the Court has recently stressed, the party which invokes a special meaning must "demonstrate convincingly the use of the term with that special meaning."

On the other hand, and this is an essential feature of the approach proposed by the International Law Commission and adopted by the Conference, the extrinsic materials, that is to say, those which have not been the object of the specific agreement of the parties, such as the preparatory work of the treaty and the circumstances of its conclusion, are described as "supplementary means of interpretation" and are governed by a separate article. This Article 32 provides that:

> "Recourse may be had to supplementary means of interpretation, including the preparatory work of the treaty and the circumstances of its conclusion, in order to confirm the meaning resulting from the application of Article 31, or to determine the meaning when the interpretation according to Article 31,
>
> (a) leaves the meaning ambiguous or obscure; or
>
> (b) leads to a result which is manifestly absurd or unreasonable."

The separation between Articles 31 and 32 is not to be viewed as establishing two distinct and successive phases in the process of interpretation, or as providing that *travaux préparatoires* are to be only examined when, after exhausting the intrinsic materials of Article 31, an ambiguity or obscurity remains or the result is manifestly absurd or unreasonable. In the task of analysis, there need be no such succession in time and the process is largely a simultaneous one. As Sir Humphrey Waldock said in his commentary on the Article, "all the various elements, as they were present in any given case, would be thrown into the crucible and their interaction would give the legally relevant interpretation." * * *

Consequently, preparatory work is frequently examined and often taken into account. It may be difficult in practice to establish the borderline between confirming a view previously reached and actually forming it, since this belongs to the mental processes of the interpreter. In any case, the importance of *travaux préparatoires* is not to be underestimated and their relevance is difficult to deny, since the question whether a text can be said to be clear is in some degree subjective. On the other hand, the separation between Articles 31 and 32 and the restrictions contained in the latter provision constitute a necessary safeguard which strengthens the textual approach and discourages any attempt to resort to preparatory work in order to dispute an interpretation resulting from the intrinsic materials set out in Article 31.

Notes

1. In one of its first opinions, the International Court of Justice declined to "deviate from the consistent practice of the Permanent Court of International Justice, according to which there is no occasion to resort to preparatory work if the text of a convention is sufficiently clear in itself." Conditions of Admission of a State to Membership in the United Nations, Advisory Opinion, 1947–48 I.C.J. 57, 63. In a number of other cases as well, the Court displayed a readiness to assume that a treaty was clear, and consequently to dispense with preparatory work. See Lauterpacht at 121–24; Fitzmaurice, The Law and Procedure of the International Court of Justice: Treaty Interpretation and Certain Other Treaty Points, 28 Brit. Y.B.I.L. 1, 6 (1951). It is not entirely clear whether the Court has modified its attitude in more recent years so as to display a greater readiness to resort to preparatory work.

2. Is preparatory work really of any significant value in ascertaining the true intentions of the contracting parties? While the texts of many treaties often contain accidental and even deliberate ambiguities and omissions, the records of international conferences are also sometimes less than successful in depicting the true course of negotiations. See the comments by Sir Eric Beckett upon Lauterpacht's report to the Institute of International Law on the interpretation of treaties, [1950] 1 Ann. de l'Institut de Droit Int'l 435, 442–44, and Lauterpacht's reply in [1952] 1 id. 197, 214–16. Haraszti, a Hungarian jurist, emphasizes that the preparatory work has interpretative value only where it throws light on the "joint intention of the parties" and relates to the text actually agreed upon. Haraszti, Some Fundamental Problems of the Law of Treaties 122–125 (1973).

3. Disagreements over interpretation of the 1972 Anti–Ballistic Missile Treaty (U.S.-former Soviet Union) surfaced in the 1980s and persist in a somewhat different form through 2000, in relation to aspects of the Strategic Defense Initiative (colloquially known as "Star Wars") that would use exotic technologies to intercept incoming missiles. One aspect of the dispute has involved the weight

(if any) to be given to materials ancillary to the treaty that might favor a restrictive rather than permissive interpretation. The restrictive interpretation was supported by statements made by certain executive branch representatives to the Senate at the time of the debate on advice and consent to ratification. (Compare the note on the Intermediate Nuclear Forces Treaty, p. 505 supra.) A more permissive interpretation was said to be supported by the classified record of the U.S.-Soviet negotiations, in which restrictive proposals had been put forward but rejected. In terms of the methodology of the Vienna Convention, which (if any) of these materials should be taken into account? If U.S. constitutional considerations require a different interpretive methodology (perhaps because of the constitutional role of the Senate in deciding whether to approve treaty obligations), is it possible to have divergent international and domestic interpretations of a treaty? On this controversy, see generally Henkin, Foreign Affairs and the U.S. Constitution 182–184, 206 (2d ed. 1996) and references therein.

On the relevance (if any) of materials considered by the U.S. Senate but not by the treaty partner, compare U.S. v. Stuart, 489 U.S. 353, 109 S.Ct. 1183, 1195, 103 L.Ed.2d 388 (1989) (Scalia, J., concurring).

4. Should the consideration of *travaux préparatoires* be barred by the fact that not all the parties to a dispute participated in the conference or negotiations that led to the conclusion of the treaty? In the *Case Concerning the Jurisdiction of the International Commission of the River Oder,* 1929 P.C.I.J., Ser. A, No. 23, the Permanent Court of International Justice ruled that preparatory work relevant to the interpretation of disputed articles of the Treaty of Versailles was inadmissible because three of the states involved in the proceeding had not taken part in the Conference which prepared the treaty. Should the admissibility of preparatory work against a non-participating state be influenced by the fact that the materials had been published or were otherwise available for study? The rule in the *River Oder Case* is probably no longer followed by the International Court of Justice, and it has been rejected by the International Law Commission. See Rosenne, *Travaux Préparatoires*, 12 I.C.L.Q. 1378, 1380–81 (1963); International Law Commission, Commentary, [1964] II Yb.I.L.C. 205.

5. If there is no specific language on the point in controversy and no evidence of a common intention of the parties, may a tribunal seized of the dispute interpret the treaty? The International Court replied affirmatively with respect to a treaty that gave an arbitral tribunal competence to pass on claims of private persons based on the treaty. Ambatielos Case, 1953 I.C.J. 10.

6. Would the practice of single states in the application of a multilateral agreement have increased relevance if it tended to demonstrate recognition by those states of obligations later sought to be avoided by them through a narrow interpretation of the agreement? Compare the situation in which a single state, without protest from other parties, has consistently applied an agreement in such a way as to avoid obligations later sought to be imposed upon it. What are the respective roles of estoppel and acquiescence as interpretative aids in such situations? See Bowett, Estoppel Before International Tribunals and Its Relation to Acquiescence, 33 Brit. Y.B.I.L. 176 (1957).

7. May the subsequent conduct of the parties to the Treaty determine the meaning of provisions that were ambiguous? See Article 31(3) of the Vienna Convention. United States courts have often relied on subsequent conduct as evidence of the intent of the parties. See Sumitomo Shoji America v. Avagliano, 457 U.S. 176, 102 S.Ct. 2374, 72 L.Ed.2d 765 (1982). Subsequent conduct was relied on by a federal court to find that the term "accident" as used in the

Warsaw Convention on liability for aviation accidents included "hijackings." Husserl v. Swiss Air Transport Co., Ltd., 351 F.Supp. 702 (S.D.N.Y.1972). See also Day v. Trans World Airlines, Inc., 528 F.2d 31 (2d Cir.1975); Restatement (Third) § 325, Reporters' Note 5. But cf. U.S. v. Alvarez–Machain, 504 U.S. 655, 112 S.Ct. 2188, 119 L.Ed.2d 441 (1992) (Supreme Court purported to confirm its interpretation of U.S.-Mexican extradition treaty by reference to "the history of negotiation and practice under the Treaty," while the dissent, at n. 4, criticized the majority for offering no evidence from the negotiating record, ratification process, or later communications with Mexico in support of its interpretation).

8. To what extent, if at all, ought special rules to be applied in the interpretation of such international agreements as the Charter of the United Nations and other constitutive instruments of international organizations, or of multilateral conventions concerned with the regulation of matters of social or humanitarian significance? Consider the following statement of Judge Azevedo, dissenting from the Advisory Opinion Concerning the Competence of the General Assembly for the Admission of a State to the United Nations, 1950 I.C.J. 4, 23:

> * * * [T]he interpretation of the San Francisco instruments will always have to present a teleological character if they are to meet the requirements of world peace, co-operation between men, individual freedom and social progress. The Charter is a means and not an end. To comply with its aims one must seek the methods of interpretation most likely to serve the natural evolution of the needs of mankind.
>
> Even more than in the applications of municipal law, the meaning and the scope of international texts must continually be perfected, even if the terms remain unchanged.

Are the original intentions of the parties, assuming that these can be discovered, any longer relevant to an interpretation based on the "teleological" approach, or would it be more important to discover the "emergent purpose" of the treaty, i.e., the objects or purposes revealed by the operation and practical application of the treaty? Consider the statement of the European Court of Human Rights that the European Convention on Human Rights should be construed "in the light of modern-day conditions obtaining in the democratic societies of the Contracting States and not solely according to what might be presumed to have been in the minds of the drafters of the Convention." Deumeland Case, 86 I.L.R. 376, 408 (1986). See generally Fitzmaurice, The Law and Procedure of the International Court of Justice 1951–4: Treaty Interpretation and Other Treaty Points, 33 Brit. Y.B.I.L. 203, 207–09 (1957); Gordon, The World Court and the Interpretation of Constitutive Treaties, 59 A.J.I.L. 794 (1965). McDougal, Lasswell & Miller, The Interpretation of Agreements and World Public Order (1967); Schachter, Interpretation of the Charter in the Political Organs of the United Nations, in Law, State and International Legal Order (Engel & Metall eds. 1964).

9. The World Trade Organization's Dispute Settlement Body has regularly invoked the Vienna Convention methodology in addressing questions of interpretation of the GATT/W.T.O. agreements. See Palmeter & Mavroidis, The WTO Legal System: Sources of Law, 92 A.J.I.L. 398, 406, 409 (1998). In a recent dispute between the European Union and the United States, the panel said:

> 7.21 * * * Article 3.2 of the [Dispute Settlement Understanding] directs panels to clarify WTO provisions "in accordance with customary rules of interpretation of public international law". Articles 31 and 32 of the Vienna Convention on the Law of Treaties ("Vienna Convention") have attained the status of rules of customary international law. In recent years, the jurispru-

dence of the Appellate Body and WTO panels has become one of the richest sources from which to receive guidance on their application. * * *

7.22 Text, context and object-and-purpose correspond to well established textual, systemic and teleological methodologies of treaty interpretation, all of which typically come into play when interpreting complex provisions in multilateral treaties. For pragmatic reasons the normal usage, and we will follow this usage, is to start the interpretation from the ordinary meaning of the "raw" text of the relevant treaty provisions and then seek to construe it in its context and in light of the treaty's object and purpose. However, the elements referred to in Article 31—text, context and object-and-purpose as well as good faith—are to be viewed as one holistic rule of interpretation rather than a sequence of separate tests to be applied in a hierarchical order. Context and object-and-purpose may often appear simply to confirm an interpretation seemingly derived from the "raw" text. In reality it is always some context, even if unstated, that determines which meaning is to be taken as "ordinary" and frequently it is impossible to give meaning, even "ordinary meaning", without looking also at object-and-purpose.

United States—Sections 301–310 of the Trade Act of 1974, WT/DS152/R (Panel Report, Dec. 22, 1999), reprinted at 39 I.L.M. 452, 464 (2000). For the panel's application of the Vienna Convention criteria in interpreting the WTO obligations of the United States, see ibid., paras. 7.58–7.94. Among the intriguing features is the panel's position that the relevant context for interpreting WTO commitments includes "systemic" considerations, that is, potential effects on the WTO system as a whole from the construction of a given article of one of the agreements.

10. It has been suggested that the International Court of Justice has recognized and applied, in its interpretation of treaties, the "principle of maximum effectiveness." Under this rule, other things being equal, "texts are presumed to have been intended to have a definite force and effect, and should be interpreted so as to have such force and effect rather than so as not to have it, and so as to have the *fullest* value and effect consistent with their wording (so long as the meaning be not strained) and with the other parts of the text." Fitzmaurice at 28 Brit. Y.B.I.L. 8 (1951) (emphasis in original). What is the difference between the "principle of maximum effectiveness" and the "teleological" approach? See id.; Lauterpacht, Restrictive Interpretation and the Principle of Effectiveness in the Interpretation of Treaties, 26 Brit. Y.B.I.L. 48, 72–75 (1949).

In the Gabcikovo–Nagymaros Case, 1997 I.C.J. 7, p. 557 infra, Slovakia invoked Lauterpacht in arguing that Slovakia was entitled to put into place a different variant of the Danube River works than specified in the treaty in question, in view of developments including Hungary's refusal to proceed with the original plans. The Court did not find room within the treaty for as much deviation from the treaty's terms as the Slovakian variant:

75. With a view to justifying those actions, Slovakia invoked what it described as "the principle of approximate application," expressed by Judge Sir Hersch Lauterpacht in the following terms:

"It is a sound principle of law that whenever a legal instrument of continuing validity cannot be applied literally owing to the conduct of one of the parties, it must, without allowing that party to take advantage of its own conduct, be applied in a way approximating most closely to its primary object. To do that is to interpret and to give effect to the instrument—not to change it." [citation to separate opinion of Judge Lauterpacht, 1956 I.C.J. 46]

It is claimed that this is a principle of international law and a general principle of law.

76. It is not necessary for the Court to determine whether there is a principle of international law or a general principle of law of "approximate application" because, even if such a principle existed, it could by definition only be employed within the limits of the treaty in question. In the view of the Court, Variant C does not meet that cardinal condition with regard to the 1977 Treaty.

11. Interesting problems of interpretation—in some respects typical, in other respects novel—were raised in the Case Concerning Kasikili/Sedudu Island, 1999 I.C.J. pp. 327–330 supra, in which the I.C.J. was asked to determine a boundary line between Botswana and Namibia, on the basis of a 1890 treaty between Great Britain and Germany delimiting their respective spheres of influence in Africa. After reaffirming that the provisions of Articles 31–32 of the Vienna Convention reflect the customary international law of treaty interpretation (para. 18), the Court examined "ordinary meaning" (paras. 20ff.) in light of "object and purpose" (paras. 43ff.), with attention to *travaux préparatoires* (paras. 46ff.) and "subsequent agreement" or "subsequent practice" (paras. 49ff.). The parties disagreed on the consequences to be drawn from the facts of the case, including the significance (if any) of certain reports and correspondence prepared by their colonial predecessors. In relation to some of these points, the Court said:

55. The Court shares [Namibia's] view that the Eason Report [a document prepared by a British captain in 1912] and its surrounding circumstances cannot be regarded as representing "subsequent practice in the application of the treaty" of 1890, within the meaning of Article 31, paragraph 3(b) of the Vienna Convention. It notes that the Report appears never to have been made known to Germany [Namibia's predecessor in interest] and to have remained at all times an internal document. The Court observes, moreover, that the British Government itself never took the Report any further * * *.

Later, after control of South–West Africa (in the territory that later became Namibia) had passed from Germany to South Africa, British and South African authorities had exchanges of correspondence concerning the disputed area. Each party relied on those documents as tending to show "subsequent practice" under the 1890 treaty, but drew opposite inferences from the evidence. The Court, after recounting these differences, observed:

63. From all of the foregoing, the Court concludes that the above-mentioned events, which occurred between 1947 and 1951, demonstrate the absence of agreement between South Africa and Bechuanaland with regard to the location of the boundary around Kasikili/Sedudu Island and the status of the Island. Those events cannot therefore constitute "subsequent practice in the application of the treaty [of 1890] which establishes the agreement of the parties regarding its interpretation" (1969 Vienna Convention on the Law of Treaties, Art. 31, para. 3(b)). *A fortiori,* they cannot have given rise to an "agreement between the parties regarding the interpretation of the treaty or the application of its provisions" (*ibid.,* Art. 31, para. 3(a)).

Still later, after the U.N. General Assembly had revoked South Africa's mandate to administer South–West Africa:

64. In October 1984 an incident during which shots were fired took place between members of the Botswana Defence Force and South African

soldiers who were travelling by boat in the Chobe's southern channel. At a meeting held in Pretoria on 19 December 1984 between representatives of various South African and Botswanan ministries, it emerged that the incident had arisen out of differences of interpretation as to the precise location of the boundary around Kasikili/Sedudu Island. At this meeting, reference was made to the terms of the 1890 Treaty and it was agreed "that a joint survey should take place as a matter of urgency to determine whether the main Channel of the Chobe River is located to the north or the south of the Sidudu/Kasikili Island."

The joint survey was carried out at the beginning of July 1985, by a team of technical experts. Thereafter Botswana and South Africa exchanged diplomatic notes concerning the joint survey, in which Botswana insisted that the matter had been resolved in Botswana's favor and the South African authorities proposed further discussions. The I.C.J. judgment continues:

67. In these proceedings, Botswana contends that the decision taken in December 1984 to carry out a joint survey, and all the documents relating to that decision—including the survey of July 1985 itself—constitute an "inter-governmental agreement ... between the parties regarding ... the application" of the 1890 Treaty * * * . Botswana points out *inter alia* that "general international law do[es] not require any particular formality for the conclusion of an international agreement" and that "[t]he only criterion is the intention of the parties to conclude a binding agreement and this can be inferred from the circumstances."

Namibia categorically denies that the discussions conducted between the Botswana and South African authorities in 1984–1985 led to an agreement on the boundary; it stresses in this connection that the July 1985 joint survey was not "self-executing" and was devoid of any legally binding status unless the parties concerned took the appropriate measures to confer such status upon it. Namibia points out that, once the United Nations General Assembly had terminated South Africa's mandate over South West Africa in 1966, neither South Africa nor Botswana could in any case conclude any kind of agreement on the boundaries of this territory.

68. Having examined the documents referred to above, the Court cannot conclude therefrom that in 1984–1985 South Africa and Botswana had agreed on anything more than the despatch of the joint team of experts. In particular, the Court cannot conclude that the two States agreed in some fashion or other to recognize themselves as legally bound by the results of the joint survey carried out in July 1985. * * *

69. The Court has reached the conclusion that there was no agreement between South African and Botswana "regarding the ... application of the [1890 Treaty]." This is in itself sufficient to dispose of the matter. It is unnecessary to add that in 1984 and 1985 the two States had no competence to conclude such an agreement, since at that time the United Nations General Assembly had already terminated South Africa's Mandate over South West Africa * * *.

Several of the separate and dissenting opinions discussed the principles of interpretation involved in this case at great length.

3. *Treaties in Plurilingual Texts (Article 33)*

Many international agreements are drawn up in more than one language. Where each version is formally authenticated (e.g., through signature), and the parties have not provided that one version should prevail in the event of disagreement, are all versions equally authoritative? The parties often expressly provide that all versions are equally authoritative (see, e.g., multilateral conventions drawn up under the auspices of the United Nations). When the parties have not otherwise provided, there is considerable authority for the proposition that the two or more texts should be interpreted with reference to one another so as to give corresponding provisions a common meaning. See generally Hardy, The Interpretation of Plurilingual Treaties by International Courts and Tribunals, 37 Brit. Y.B.I.L. 72 (1961); International Law Commission, Commentary, [1966] II Yb.I.L.C. 224–26.

The Permanent Court of International Justice expressed itself on the question of reconciling versions in the different languages in the *Mavrommatis Palestine Concession Case,* P.C.I.J., Ser. A, No. 2 (1924). It stated that "where two versions possessing equal authority exist, one of which appears to have a wider bearing than the other, it [the Court] is bound to adopt the more limited interpretation which can be made to harmonize with both versions and which, as far as it goes, is doubtless in accordance with the common intention of the Parties." P.C.I.J., Ser. A, No. 2, p. 10.

In *Nicaragua v. U.S.* (Jurisdiction) (1984), the International Court of Justice relied in part on the French text of Article 36(5) of the Statute of the International Court to resolve an issue of interpretation which the judges considered as equivocal, and which was left open in the English text. 1984 I.C.J. 406–407 (paras. 30, 31).

Should a different approach be taken where it can be shown that the parties used one language in negotiating and establishing the text, even though the treaty itself declared the texts in all the languages as authentic? In the *Mavrommatis Case,* the Permanent Court supported its choice of the more restrictive text (which was the English version) by noting also that the original text was English. Even jurists who strongly favor equality of all language texts recognize that, if no common meaning can be found, a text used in the negotiations would reflect the intention of the parties more than the versions in translation. The problem of ascertaining which text was used is complicated when a negotiating conference, such as those under U.N. auspices, have versions in 6 languages distributed to the delegates, all of which are declared equally authentic. See Haraszti, Some Fundamental Problems of the Law of Treaties 183 (1973). Germer, Interpretation of Plurilingual Treaties, 11 Harv. Int'l L.J. 400, 413 (1970).

Notes

1. U.S. courts sometimes need to interpret a U.S. treaty obligation by reference to the French text of the treaty (or a French term in the English version). The Warsaw Convention on limitation of liability of air carriers has presented various instances: for example, in Eastern Airlines v. Floyd, 499 U.S. 530, 111 S.Ct. 1489, 113 L.Ed.2d 569 (1991), concerning the issue of whether mental injury unaccompanied by physical manifestation could be compensable, the Supreme Court considered the French legal meaning of "lésion corporelle" for guidance as to the shared expectations of the parties to the Warsaw Convention, which had been drafted in French by continental jurists.

2. In Sale v. Haitian Centers Council, 509 U.S. 155, 113 S.Ct. 2549, 125 L.Ed.2d 128 (1993), the Court construed U.S. obligations under a treaty on refugees, in relation to refugees apprehended on the high seas. The treaty provision provided that no state shall "expel or return ('refouler') a refugee" to a state where he would be persecuted. In holding that the treaty did not have extraterritorial application, the Court gave the French term a narrow meaning, with reference to French-language dictionaries. (International authorities do not agree with the Supreme Court's interpretation, however: see p. 622 infra.)

D. TREATIES AND THIRD STATES

A third state, in international law usage and as defined in the Vienna Convention, is any state not a party to the treaty in question (Article 2(1)(h)). In principle a treaty creates neither obligations nor rights for third states without their consent. The maxim *pacta tertiis nec nocent nec prosunt* is often quoted. The principle is firmly established as a general rule but questions have arisen as to possible exceptions with respect both to rights and to obligations. The International Law Commission and the Vienna conference considered that the basic principle should be maintained without any exception. They sought to meet the cases of possible exceptions through doctrinal explanation and flexible articles. The following excerpts from the report of the Commission express the rationale for Articles 34 to 38.

1. Obligations for Third States (Article 35)

(1) The primary rule, formulated in the previous article, is that the parties to a treaty cannot impose an obligation on a third State without its consent. That rule is one of the bulwarks of the independence and equality of States. The present article also underlines that the consent of a State is always necessary if it is to be bound by a provision contained in a treaty to which it is not a party. Under it two conditions have to be fulfilled before a non-party can become bound: first, the parties to the treaty must have intended the provision in question to be the means of establishing an obligation for the State not a party to the treaty; and secondly, the third State must have expressly agreed to be bound by the obligation. The Commission appreciated that when these conditions are fulfilled there is, in effect, a second collateral agreement between the parties to the treaty, on the one hand, and the third State on the other; and that the juridical basis of the latter's obligation is not the treaty itself but the collateral agreement. However, even if the matter is viewed in this way, the case remains one where a provision of a treaty concluded between certain States becomes directly binding upon another State which is not and does not become a party to the treaty. [1966] II Yb.I.L.C. 227.

Notes

1. Is there an implied exception to the rule enunciated above in Article 2, paragraph 6 of the U.N. Charter? The International Court of Justice in its advisory opinion in the *Namibia Case,* p. 549 infra, declared that the nonmember states of the U.N. must "act in accordance with" the decisions of the United Nations which terminated the mandate for South–West Africa (Namibia) and

declared the presence of South Africa in Namibia illegal. See Advisory Opinion, 1971 I.C.J. 16. See Article 2(6) of U.N. Charter.

2. May obligations be imposed by a treaty on an aggressor state which is not a party? See Article 75 of the Vienna Convention.

3. Would a treaty for demilitarization of a territory be binding on third states? See Antarctic Treaty. The concept of an "objective régime" is considered at p. 519 below.

4. As of 2000, the United States has maintained that it will not become a party to the 1998 Rome Statute for the International Criminal Court, and has criticized the Rome Statute for purporting to affect the rights and interests of non-parties without their consent. See Chapter 15. Is this concern well-founded? Can it be analyzed (or understood) under the Vienna Convention's provisions on third parties?

2. *Rights of Third States Under Treaties (Article 36)*

(7) *Paragraph 1* lays down that a right may arise for a State from a provision of a treaty to which it is not a party under two conditions. First, the parties must intend the provision to accord the right either to the particular State in question, or to a group of States to which it belongs, or to States generally. The intention to accord the right is of cardinal importance, since it is only when the parties have such an intention that a legal right, as distinct from a mere benefit, may arise from the provision. Examples of stipulations in favour of individual States, groups of States or States generally have already been mentioned in paragraph (2). The second condition is the assent of the beneficiary State. The formulation of this condition in the present tense "and the State assents thereto" leaves open the question whether juridically the right is created by the treaty or by the beneficiary State's act of acceptance. In one view, as already explained, the assent of the intended beneficiary, even though it may merely be implied from the exercise of the right, constitutes an "acceptance" of an offer made by the parties; in the other view the assent is only significant as an indication that the right is not disclaimed by the beneficiary. The second sentence of the paragraph then provides that the assent of the State is to be presumed so long as the contrary is not indicated. This provision the Commission considered desirable in order to give the necessary flexibility to the operation of the rule in cases where the right is expressed to be in favour of States generally or of a large group of States. * * *

(8) *Paragraph 2* specifies that in exercising the right a beneficiary State must comply with the conditions for its exercise provided for in the treaty or established in conformity with the treaty. The words "or established in conformity with the treaty" take account of the fact that not infrequently conditions for the exercise of the right may be laid down in a supplementary instrument or in some cases unilaterally by one of the parties. For example, in the case of a provision allowing freedom of navigation in an international river or maritime waterway, the territorial State has the right in virtue of its sovereignty to lay down relevant conditions for the exercise of the right provided, of course, that they are in conformity with its obligations under the treaty. * * *

[1966] II Yb.I.L.C. 229.

Notes

1. Will states be discouraged from creating rights in favor of third states (*e.g.*, freedom of transit through the Panama Canal) by fear they would be limiting their action in the future? If the parties may freely revoke such rights of third states, the "rights" may be more nominal than legal. Is the compromise, as set forth in Article 37(2), satisfactory from the standpoint of third states?

2. In a case relating to the Kiel Canal, the Permanent Court of International Justice held that the Versailles treaty which provided that the Canal was to be open to all vessels of nations at peace with Germany had provided a "treaty guarantee * * * for the benefit of all nations of the world." The S.S. Wimbledon, 1923 P.C.I.J., Ser. A, No. 1, at 22. Would Germany have the right to close the Canal to any non-party under Article 37(2)?

3. Are rights in third states to most-favored nation treatment revocable by the parties?

3. Objective Régimes Created by Treaty

(4) The Commission considered whether treaties creating so-called "objective régimes", that is, obligations and rights valid *erga omnes,* should be dealt with separately as a special case. Some members of the Commission favoured this course, expressing the view that the concept of treaties creating objective régimes existed in international law and merited special treatment in the draft articles. In their view, treaties which fall within this concept are treaties for the neutralization or demilitarization of particular territories or areas, and treaties providing for freedom of navigation of international rivers or maritime waterways; and they cited the Antarctic Treaty as a recent example of such a treaty. Other members, however, while recognizing that in certain cases treaty rights and obligations may come to be valid *erga omnes,* did not regard these cases as resulting from any special concept or institution of the law of treaties. They considered that these cases resulted either from the application of the principle in [Article 36] or from the grafting of an international custom upon a treaty under the process which is the subject of the reservation in the present article. Since to lay down a rule recognizing the possibility of the creation of objective régimes directly by treaty might be unlikely to meet with general acceptance, the Commission decided to leave this question aside in drafting the present articles on the law of treaties. It considered that the provision in Article [36], regarding treaties intended to create rights in favour of States generally, together with the process mentioned in the present article, furnish a legal basis for the establishment of treaty obligations and rights valid *erga omnes,* which goes as far as is at present possible. Accordingly, it decided not to propose any special provision on treaties creating so-called objective régimes.

[1966] II Yb.I.L.C. 231.

Notes

1. Can it be said that the Antarctic Treaty, p. 1570, imposes obligations *erga omnes* by virtue of "custom" when only a small number of states have become

parties to the treaty? What is the legal basis for states which have made a territorial arrangement outside of their national jurisdiction to consider that arrangement to be binding on non-parties? If a substantial number of non-party states express approval of the treaty provisions (such as those on demilitarization and environmental protection) but deny that the treaty expresses customary law, can it be maintained that the treaty is binding on those states? For positions of governments on this issue, see U.N. Secretary General, Report on Antarctica, U.N. Doc. A/39/583 Part II (1984).

2. If two states enter into a treaty for cession of territory, are third states free to refuse to recognize the effects of the treaty as, for example, on the nationality of the inhabitants? Are such treaties "dispositive," as suggested by McNair, The Law of Treaties 256–59 (1961)? Would the Antarctic Treaty regime be opposable to third states on the ground that the states party to the treaty include all those which have claims to territorial sovereignty? For discussion of sovereignty claims, see Chapter 19. See also Antarctic Resources Policy: Scientific, Legal and Political Issues (Vicuña, ed., 1983); Cahier, Le Problème des Effets des Traités a L'Égard des États Tiers, 143 Rec. des Cours 595, 660–79 (1974–III).

3. What is the effect of Article 2(6) of the United Nations Charter on states that are not members of the Organization?

E. AMENDMENT AND MODIFICATION OF TREATIES

KEARNEY & DALTON, THE TREATY ON TREATIES

64 A.J.I.L. 495, 523–525 (1970) (footnotes omitted).

Article 40 provides residuary rules that safeguard the rights of parties to a treaty to participate in the amending process by requiring notification to all parties of any proposed amendment and by specifying their right to participate in the decision to be taken on the proposal and in the negotiation and conclusion of any amendatory agreement. The right to become party to the new agreement is also extended to every state entitled to become a party to the treaty.

Paragraphs 4 and 5 contain a much needed clarification of the relationships between the various parties to an original treaty and a series of amending agreements, particularly with regard to a state that becomes a party to an amended treaty. In that case, the state, unless it expresses a different intention, becomes both a party to the treaty as amended and a party to the unamended treaty vis-à-vis any party to the treaty not bound by the amendment.

The distinction between Article 40 on amendments and Article 41 on modification is based upon whether the proposal to change the treaty is directed to all the parties or only a part of them. The Commission's rationale for Article 41 was that it dealt not with the amendment of a treaty but with an *inter se* agreement "in which two or a small group of parties set out to modify the treaty between themselves alone without giving the other parties the option of participating in it. * * * " The commentary indicates considerable dubiety in the Commission regarding such agreements: "An *inter se* agreement is more likely [than an amendment] to have an aim and effect incompatible with the object and purpose of the treaty. History furnishes a number of instances of *inter se* agreements which substantially changed the regime of the treaty and which overrode the objections of interested States. * * * ''

Notes

1. In 1963, an international arbitration tribunal in a dispute between France and the United States concerning the bilateral Air Transport Services Agreement of 1946 concluded that the subsequent practice of the two parties was relevant not only to the interpretation of the treaty but also to its modification by tacit consent. The Tribunal found that the conduct of the parties (in particular, the acts of officials concerned with aviation services) established a right ''not by virtue of the Agreement of 1946 but rather by virtue of an agreement that implicitly came into force at a later date.'' Decision of Arbitration Tribunal concerning International Air Transport Services Agreement between France and the United States, digested in 58 A.J.I.L. 1016–1030 (1964); see especially 1023–1027. The full text of the decision is in 3 I.L.M. 668 (1964).

2. Whether all parties to a treaty had the right to participate in negotiation of a revision was a disputed question prior to the Vienna Convention. Some writers said that there was no such right. See Hoyt, The Unanimity Rule in the Revision of Treaties (1959). The International Law Commission declined to accept that view. It considered that ''the very nature of the legal relations established by a treaty requires that every party should be consulted in regard to any amendment or revision of the treaty.'' The fact that this has not always happened, the Commission stated, was not a sufficient reason to set aside the principle. [1966] II Yb.I.L.C. 233. The Commission was also concerned to assure all parties to a treaty that they would be notified when some parties intend to include an agreement to modify the treaty as between themselves alone. See Article 41(2).

3. Multilateral agreements, especially those which are the constituent instruments of international organizations, nearly always contain specific rules for amendment. Generally, these rules permit amendment by approval of a qualified majority (often, two-thirds of the parties). In most of the constituent instruments of international organizations states which do not accept the amended treaty are required by the terms of the treaty to cease to be parties. In the absence of a provision to this effect, the non-assenting parties are in principle unaffected by the amendment in their relations with the amending parties. The U.N. Charter states that amendments shall come into force for all members when they have been adopted and ratified by two-thirds of the members, including all the permanent members of the Security Council (Article 108).

4. The United States has sometimes had concerns about treaty amendment procedures that might allow an amendment to come into effect without the consent of the U.S. Senate. Would senatorial consent to the underlying treaty serve as prospective consent to amendments concluded pursuant to such procedures? Is it necessary (or sufficient) for a state to be given a right to ''opt out'' of a future amendment adopted without a new consent given through domestic constitutional procedures?

Concerns about amendment procedures were among the U.S. objections to the 1982 Law of the Sea treaty. A 1994 agreement modifying Part XI of UNCLOS went some distance toward alleviating these concerns, by clarifying that amendment to the deep seabed regime could not be adopted without U.S. consent. See Oxman, Law of the Sea Forum: The 1994 Agreement and the Convention, 88

A.J.I.L. 687, 695 (1994). Nonetheless, the Senate had not acted on the treaty as of 2000. See Chapter 16.

5. The 1998 Rome Statute for the International Criminal Court specifies procedures for amendment. Notably, some of the thorny issues that could not be resolved at Rome—e.g., a definition of the crime of aggression—were put aside for an amendment to be adopted at a future date. See Rome Statute, Article 5(2) on aggression, cross-referencing Articles 121 and 123.

SECTION 5. INVALIDITY OF TREATIES

A. GENERAL PROVISIONS RELATING TO INVALIDITY

The International Law Commission considered it important to provide that the validity of a treaty may be impeached only through the application of the Vienna Convention (Article 42). It was also considered desirable to state explicitly that a state which is no longer bound by a treaty because of invalidity or termination does not escape an obligation to which it is subject under international law independently of the treaty (Article 43).

Prior to the Vienna Convention, there was some doubt whether an invalid provision of a treaty may be struck out without declaring the entire treaty invalid. Some judges in separate opinions in the *Norwegian Loans,* 1957 I.C.J. 9, and *Interhandel,* 1959 I.C.J. 6, cases had favored separability in the case of the alleged nullity of a unilateral declaration under Article 36(2) of the Statute of the Court by reason of an allegedly invalid reservation. The Commission favored separability provided that it did not materially upset the balance of interests on the basis of which the parties consented to be bound. This is made clear in Article 44(3). In cases of fraud and corruption only the victim state may invoke invalidity, and then it has the option of invalidating the whole treaty or only the clauses to which the fraud or corruption relate (Article 44(4)). In cases where the treaty is absolutely void (as in cases of coercion or conflict with *jus cogens*) there is no separability; the treaty is entirely null and void (Article 44(5)).

The Commission was aware that provisions on invalidity involved possible abuse. A party may become aware of a ground for invalidity but "continue with the treaty and only raise the matter at a much later date when it desires for quite other reasons to put an end to its obligations under the treaty." [1966] II Yb.I.L.C. 239. Article 45 seeks to meet that situation. A state is prohibited from claiming invalidity if after becoming aware of the facts it has agreed that the treaty remains in force or by reason of its conduct must be considered to have acquiesced in the validity of the treaty or its continuation in force. This rule does not apply where the treaty is absolutely void as in cases of coercion or *jus cogens.*

The principle of acquiescence played a role in two cases before the International Court of Justice: the case of the Arbitral Award of the King of Spain, 1960 I.C.J. 192, 213–214 and the case of The Temple of Preah Vihear, 1962 I.C.J. 6, 23–32.

Note

Exclusivity of grounds for invalidity, suspension or termination. In the Case Concerning the Gabcikovo–Nagymaros Project (Hungary/Slovakia), 1997 I.C.J. 7, discussed more fully at pp. 557–559 and 574–576 infra, Hungary argued that a 1977 treaty was not in force between the two states. Hungary put forward a number of grounds for considering that the treaty was without legal effect. Some of those grounds were based in the law of treaties as codified in the Vienna Convention (material breach in Article 60; supervening impossibility in Article 61; fundamental change of circumstances in Article 62). Other grounds were claimed outside the framework of the Vienna Convention—notably, Hungary's arguments that a "state of ecological necessity" justified suspension or termination of obligations under the treaty, and that new norms of international environmental law had developed since the treaty's conclusion. The Court evaluated certain of Hungary's claims not under the law of treaties but rather under another body of law, the law of state responsibility that pertains to the consequences of wrongful acts. (See Chapter 9.) In respect of the proposition that grounds for invalidating, suspending or terminating a treaty as such could be found in addition to those specified in the Vienna Convention, the Court said:

> 47. * * * [T]he Vienna Convention of 1969 on the Law of Treaties confines itself to defining—in a limitative manner—the conditions in which a treaty may lawfully be denounced or suspended; while the effects of a denunciation or suspension seen as not meeting those conditions are, on the contrary, expressly excluded from the scope of the Convention by operation of Article 73.

Later, in its discussion of the particular grounds invoked by Hungary (see pp. 557–559) below, the Court stressed that the "stability of treaty relations" requires that the grounds specified in the Vienna Convention be applied in accordance with their strict conditions, and that it "would set a precedent with disturbing implications for treaty relations and the integrity of the rule *pacta sunt servanda*" if a party could unilaterally set aside a treaty on grounds other than those so specified. Thus, the treaty could be terminated "only on the limited grounds enumerated in the Vienna Convention." See paras. 100, 104, 114.

B. ULTRA VIRES TREATIES

As we saw earlier, a state may not invoke its internal law as justification for failure to perform a treaty. This general principle is qualified, however, by the rule stated in Article 46 of the Vienna Convention. That provision permits a state to assert as a ground of invalidity of a treaty the fact that its consent to be bound was expressed in violation of a provision of its internal law concerning the competence to conclude treaties. A state may invoke that fact only if "the violation was manifest and concerned a rule of internal law of fundamental importance." Article 46. Accordingly, in the special circumstances stated, the question of constitutional competence to conclude a treaty—a matter of internal law—becomes internationally relevant. The rule, it should be noted, may be relied upon only by the state whose consent was expressed in contravention of its own constitutional provision or other rule of fundamental importance.

The requirement that the violation must be "manifest" is of particular interest. Article 46(2) says that "a violation is manifest if it would be objectively evident to any State dealing with the matter in accordance with normal practice and good faith." Article 46(2). It is conceivable that a head of state might enter into a treaty in contravention of an unequivocal and well-known fundamental principle of his national law. But such cases are rare. See [1966] II Yb.I.L.C. 241–42. Normally when a head of state or government ratifies or accedes to a treaty, a strong presumption exists that he or she has acted within constitutional authority. Even if doubts were expressed in that respect, it is unlikely that another state would find a violation "manifest" or objectively evident.

Studies of treaty practice have confirmed the perception that constitutional incompetence has not actually resulted in invalidating treaties. Hans Blix, in a study prior to the Vienna Convention, concluded that in fact "no treaty has been found that has been admitted to be invalid or held by an international tribunal to be invalid, because concluded by a constitutionally incompetent authority or in an unconstitutional manner * * *. Furthermore, there is no lack of treaties made in violation of constitutions, or by constitutionally incompetent authorities, and yet admitted to be valid in international law." Blix, Treaty–Making Power 373–374 (1960). A similar conclusion was reached by a later study. See Wildhaber, Treaty–Making Power and Constitutions 146–82 (1971). The latter also observes on the basis of an comparative analysis that the constitutional competences to enter into treaties "are almost never really clear." Id. at 181.

The provision in the United States Constitution that the President may not enter into a "treaty" without the advice and consent of the Senate is of particular interest. McNair commented that that requirement possesses "an international notoriety so that other states cannot hold a State bound by a treaty when in fact there has been no compliance with constitutional requirements of this type." McNair, The Law of Treaties 63 (1961). A different conclusion is drawn by Henkin in the following comment:

> But the power of the President to make many agreements without the Senate casts some doubt on "the fundamental importance" of Senate consent; in any event, failure to obtain such consent cannot be a "manifest" violation of the Constitution since no one can say with certainty when it is required.

Henkin, Foreign Affairs and the U.S. Constitution 500 (2d ed. 1996).

The Restatement (Third) contains the following comment on this point:

> Some agreements such as the U.N. Charter or the agreement creating NATO are of sufficient dignity, formality and importance that, in the unlikely event that the President attempted to make such an agreement on his own authority, his lack of authority might be regarded as "manifest".

Restatement (Third) § 311, Comment *c*.

Notes

1. As of 2000, Article 46 has not been invoked before an international tribunal as a basis for a claim of invalidity. However, the article was invoked in

the U.S. Senate in connection with two bilateral agreements to which the United States adhered. One was an agreement between the United States and Israel in 1975 connected with the withdrawal of Israel from the Sinai peninsula, which involved a number of commitments by the United States with respect to meeting Israeli's supply needs and defense requirements. The Legislative Counsel to the Senate took the position that since the agreement was concluded without the advice and consent of the Senate, it was without force under domestic law. Moreover, since it violated in that respect a rule of fundamental importance and since Israel should reasonably have known of this constitutional defect, the agreement was without force in international law. The State Department rejected that position and no action was taken by the Senate. The Department of State memorandum is reproduced in 15 I.L.M. 198 (1976). For an analysis of the issues, see Meron, Article 46 of the Vienna Convention on the Law of Treaties (*ultra vires* treaties), 49 Brit. Y.B.I.L. 175–199 (1978).

2. The question of constitutional competence was also raised in the Senate in regard to the agreement between the United States and Panama concluded in 1977 with respect to the Panama Canal. In this case, the issue related to an alleged violation by Panama of its constitutional requirements for entering into an agreement of the character of the Canal treaty. A group of U.S. Senators contended that the Panama constitution clearly required a plebiscite to approve a treaty. They asserted that the plebiscite conducted prior to ratification did not meet that requirement because subsequently the United States, on the advice of the Senate, included a number of reservations, conditions and understandings in the instruments of ratification. While these were accepted by the President of Panama, they were not submitted to a second plebiscite. Several Senators argued that the violation was "manifest" and concerned a rule of fundamental importance. They maintained that unless this was corrected by renegotiation, Panama would be able in the future to claim invalidity because of the constitutional defect. Sen. Exec. Report 95–12 of the Comm. on Foreign Relations, 95 Cong., 2d Sess. (1978); see also 71 A.J.I.L. 635–43 (1978). The Government of Panama responded that under Panamanian law, a second plebiscite was not required. Panama had accepted the Senate's conditions, reservations and understandings but regarded them as interpretations of the treaties, not as alterations or amendments. The Executive Branch of the U.S. Government considered the legal position of Panama as "reasonable." They did not see any violation of Panamanian law and certainly no manifest violations within the meaning of Article 46. Meron, at 190.

Would there be a basis for a future Panamanian Government to seek to invalidate the agreements on the ground of Article 46? Would Article 45 apply in that event?

3. The reluctance of tribunals to look behind the ostensible authority of a foreign minister to commit his state was evidenced in the *Eastern Greenland Case* decided by the Permanent Court of International Justice in 1933. P.C.I.J., Ser. A/B, No. 53. The case involved a dispute between Norway and Denmark regarding Norwegian occupation of parts of Greenland. The Norwegian Foreign Minister had informed Denmark orally that the "Norwegian Government would not make any difficulty in the settlement of this question." Before the court, Norway contended that under its constitution the foreign minister could not enter into a binding international agreement on "matters of importance" without approval of the "King in Council." The Court rejected the Norwegian claim that this constitutional limitation invalidated the commitment of the foreign minister. It was sufficient, the Court found, that the foreign minister acted "within his province" in replying to an inquiry of the Danish Government. Presumably, the Court

meant "within his province" under international customary law (see Full Powers). In view of that oral statement, Norway was held bound to refrain from contesting Danish sovereignty and from occupying any part of Greenland.

C. ERROR, FRAUD, AND CORRUPTION

1. *Error (Article 48)*

In regard to error as a ground of invalidity, the International Law Commission had the following comments:

> (1) In municipal law error occupies a comparatively large place as a factor which vitiates consent to a contract. Some types of error found in municipal law are, however, unlikely to arise in international law. Moreover, treaty-making processes are such as to reduce to a minimum the risk of errors on material points of substance. In consequence, the instances in which errors of substance have been invoked as affecting the essential validity of a treaty have not been frequent. Almost all the recorded instances concern geographical errors, and most of them concern errors in maps. In some instances, the difficulty was disposed of by a further treaty; in others the error was treated more as affecting the application of the treaty than its validity and the point was settled by arbitration. * * *
>
> (7) Under paragraph 1 error affects consent only if it was an essential error in the sense of an error as to a matter which formed an essential basis of the consent given to the treaty. Furthermore, such an error does not make the treaty automatically void, but gives a right to the party whose consent to the treaty was caused by the error to invoke the error as invalidating its consent. On the other hand, if the invalidity of the treaty is established in accordance with the present articles, the effect will be to make the treaty void *ab initio.*
>
> (8) *Paragraph 2* excepts from the rule cases where the mistaken party in some degree brought the error upon itself. The terms in which the exception is formulated are drawn from those used by the Court in the sentence from its judgment in the *Temple* case * * *. The Commission felt, however, that there is substance in the view that the Court's formulation of the exception "if the party contributed by its own conduct to the error, or could have avoided it, or if the circumstances were such as to put that party on notice of a possible error" is so wide as to leave little room for the operation of the rule. This applies particularly to the words "or could have avoided it." Accordingly, without questioning the Court's formulation of the exception in the context of the particular case, the Commission concluded that, in codifying the general rule regarding the effect of error in the law of treaties, those words should be omitted.
>
> (9) *Paragraph 3,* in order to prevent any misunderstanding, distinguishes errors in the *wording* of the text from errors in the treaty. The paragraph merely underlines that such an error does not affect the validity of the consent and falls under the provisions of article 74 relating to the correction of errors in the texts of treaties.

[1966] II Yb.I.L.C. 243–244.

For more detailed discussion of error, see Elias, The Modern Law of Treaties 154–61 (1974).

2. *Fraud (Article 49)*

Fraud as a ground for invalidity was separated from error because in the Commission's words:

> Fraud, when it occurs, strikes at the root of an agreement in a somewhat different way from innocent misrepresentation and error. It does not merely affect the consent of the other party to the terms of the agreement; it destroys the whole basis of mutual confidence between the parties.

[1966] II Yb.I.L.C. 244.

The Commission noted a "paucity of precedents" in international law with regard to fraud. However, it decided against defining fraud and stated that it proposes only a broad concept comprised in the term "fraud" ("dol" in French and "dolo" in Spanish) rather than the detailed connotations the term has in domestic law. It added that the expression "fraudulent conduct" ("conduite frauduleuse") is designed "to include any false statements, misrepresentations or other deceitful proceedings by which a State is induced to give a consent to a treaty which it would not otherwise have given." Id. at 245.

3. *Corruption (Article 50)*

Although some members of the International Law Commission considered that corruption fell within the category of fraud, the majority considered that corruption was sufficiently distinct and required a special article. The Commission commented:

> (4) The strong term "corruption" is used in the article expressly in order to indicate that only acts calculated to exercise a substantial influence on the disposition of the representative to conclude the treaty may be invoked as invalidating the expression of consent which he has purported to give on behalf of his State. The Commission did not mean to imply that under the present article a small courtesy or favour shown to a representative in connexion with the conclusion of a treaty may be invoked as a pretext for invalidating the treaty.
>
> (5) Similarly, the phrase "directly or indirectly by another negotiating State" is used in the article in order to make it plain that the mere fact of the representative's having been corrupted is not enough. The Commission appreciated that corruption by another negotiating State, if it occurs, is unlikely to be overt. But it considered that, in order to be a ground for invalidating the treaty, the corrupt acts must be shown to be directly or indirectly imputable to the other negotiating State.

Id.

D. COERCION

1. *Coercion of a Representative (Article 51)*

The Commission considered coercion of a representative of such gravity that the consent of a state so obtained shall be without any legal effect. It referred to a case of "third-degree methods of pressure" against the President and Foreign Minister of Czechoslovakia in 1939 to extract their signatures to a treaty creating a German protectorate over Bohemia and Moravia. It also referred generally to instances in which members of legislatures were coerced to procure ratification of a treaty. Id. at 246. Coercion was also used to include a threat to ruin the career of a representative by exposing a private indiscretion as well as a threat to injure a member of his family.

2. *Coercion of a State (Article 52)*

The Commission considered this principle as established law. It said:

> (1) The traditional doctrine prior to the Covenant of the League of Nations was that the validity of a treaty was not affected by the fact that it had been brought about by the threat or use of force. However, this doctrine was simply a reflection of the general attitude of international law during that era towards the legality of the use of force for the settlement of international disputes. With the Covenant and the Pact of Paris there began to develop a strong body of opinion which held that such treaties should no longer be recognized as legally valid. The endorsement of the criminality of aggressive war in the Charters of the Allied Military Tribunals for the trial of the Axis war criminals, the clear-cut prohibition of the threat or use of force in Article 2(4) of the Charter of the United Nations, together with the practice of the United Nations itself, have reinforced and consolidated this development in the law. The Commission considers that these developments justify the conclusion that the invalidity of a treaty procured by the illegal threat or use of force is a principle which is *lex lata* in the international law of to-day.
>
> (2) Some jurists, it is true, while not disputing the moral value of the principle, have hesitated to accept it as a legal rule. They fear that to recognize the principle as a legal rule may open the door to the evasion of treaties by encouraging unfounded assertions of coercion, and that the rule will be ineffective because the same threat or compulsion that procured the conclusion of the treaty will also procure its execution, whether the law regards it as valid or invalid. These objections do not appear to the Commission to be of such a kind as to call for the omission from the present articles of a ground of invalidity springing from the most fundamental provisions of the Charter, the relevance of which in the law of treaties as in other branches of international law cannot today be regarded as open to question.

Id. at 246.

The proposed article led to a major confrontation at the Vienna Conference when a number of states proposed an amendment to define "force" to include "economic or political pressure" (referred to as the nineteen-state amendment). An account by the U.S. representative to the Vienna Conference and his colleague follows:

> The proponents of the amendment made it quite clear in the committee of the whole that their amendment was directed toward "economic needs." The representative of Tanzania described "the withdrawal of economic aid or of promises of aid [and] the recall of economic experts" as

the type of conduct which should be prohibited. The Algerian representative advanced the thesis:

> * * * the era of the colonial treaty was past or disappearing, but there was no overlooking the fact that some countries had resorted to new and more insidious methods, suited to the present state of international relations, in an attempt to maintain and perpetuate bonds of subjection. Economic pressure, which was a characteristic of neo-colonialism, was becoming increasingly common in relations between certain countries and the newly independent States.
>
> Political independence could not be an end in itself; it was even illusory if it was not backed by genuine economic independence. That was why some countries had chosen the political, economic and social system they regarded as best calculated to overcome under-development as quickly as possible. That choice provoked intense opposition from certain interests which saw their privileges threatened and then sought through economic pressure to abolish or at least restrict the right of peoples to self-determination. Such neo-colonialist practices, which affected more than two-thirds of the world's population and were retarding or nullifying all efforts to overcome under-development, should therefore be denounced with the utmost rigour.

Statements of this character reinforced the already deep misgivings as to the effect of the amendment held by the states concerned with the stability of treaties.

The scope of the phrase "threat or use of force" in Article 2, paragraph 4, of the United Nations Charter, as is well known, has been for many years the source of acrimonious dispute. The legislative history of the San Francisco Conference is clear as to its original intent. The Chilean delegate made that point:

> * * * The Brazilian delegation to the 1945 San Francisco Conference had proposed the inclusion of an express reference to the prohibition of economic pressure, and its proposal had been rejected. Consequently, any reference to the principles of the Charter in that respect must be a reference to the kind of force which all the Member States had agreed to prohibit, namely, physical or armed force.

The discussions were complicated by the fact that the United Nations Special Committee on Principles of International Law concerning Friendly Relations and Cooperation Among States had been studying the "threat or use of force" issue since 1964, and action by the Conference could only cut across the deliberations of that body. The question was also raised whether the conference was attempting to amend the United Nations Charter. The basic problem was well summed up by the Dutch representative:

> In itself, the rule stated in article [52] was perfectly clear and precise. He supported the principle underlying the article, namely, the principle that an aggressor State should not, in law, benefit from a treaty it had forced its victim to accept. Nevertheless, it must be borne in mind that there was a fundamental difference of opinion as to the meaning of the words 'threat or use of force' in Article 2,

> paragraph 4, of the United Nations Charter. If those words could be interpreted as including all forms of pressure exerted by one State on another, and not just the threat or use of armed force, the scope of article [52] would be so wide as to make it a serious danger to the stability of treaty relations.
>
> The course of the debate had made it clear that if the amendment were put to the vote it would carry by quite a substantial majority. On the other hand, in private discussions it had been made quite clear to the proponents that adoption could wreck the conference because states concerned with the stability of treaties found the proposal intolerable.
>
> To reduce tension, discussion of the article was adjourned and private negotiations resorted to. A compromise solution was reached after some days of cooling off. The amendment was withdrawn. In its place, a draft declaration condemning threat or use of pressure in any form by a state to coerce any other state to conclude a treaty was unanimously adopted by the committee. Although at one point during the plenary it appeared that the compromise might be unraveling, it was adhered to by both sides. The declaration finally approved by the conference in 1969 is annexed to the Final Act.

Kearney & Dalton, 64 A.J.I.L. at 533–535 (footnotes omitted).

The International Law Commission also considered that a treaty imposed by illegal force should be void, as opposed to voidable. It said in this connection:

> Even if it were conceivable that after being liberated from the influence of a threat or of a use of force a State might wish to allow a treaty procured from it by such means, the Commission considered it essential that the treaty should be regarded in law as void *ab initio*. This would enable the State concerned to take its decision in regard to the maintenance of the treaty in a position of full legal equality with the other State. If, therefore, the treaty were maintained in force, it would in effect be by the conclusion of a new treaty and not by the recognition of the validity of a treaty procured by means contrary to the most fundamental principles of the Charter of the United Nations.

[1966] II Yb.I.L.C. 247.

The question of the time element in the application of the article was dealt with by the Commission in the following comments:

> The Commission considered that there is no question of the article having retroactive effects on the validity of treaties concluded prior to the establishment of the modern law. "A juridical fact must be appreciated in the light of the law contemporary with it." The present article concerns the conditions for the valid conclusion of a treaty—the conditions, that is, for the *creation* of a legal relation by treaty. An evolution of the law governing the conditions for the carrying out of a legal act does not operate to deprive of validity a legal act already accomplished in conformity with the law previously in force. The rule codified in the present article cannot therefore be properly understood as depriving of validity *ab initio* a peace treaty or other treaty procured by coercion prior to the establishment of the modern law regarding the threat or use of force.

(8) As to the date from which the modern law should be considered as in force for the purposes of the present article, the Commission considered that it would be illogical and unacceptable to formulate the rule as one applicable only from the date of the conclusion of a convention on the law of treaties. As pointed out in paragraph (1) above, the invalidity of a treaty procured by the illegal threat or use of force is a principle which is *lex lata.* Moreover, whatever differences of opinion there may be about the state of the law prior to the establishment of the United Nations, the great majority of international lawyers to-day unhesitatingly hold that article 2, paragraph 4, together with other provisions of the Charter, authoritatively declares the modern customary law regarding the threat or use of force. The present article, by its formulation, recognizes by implication that the rule which it lays down is applicable at any rate to all treaties concluded since the entry into force of the Charter. On the other hand, the Commission did not think that it was part of its function, in codifying the modern law of treaties, to specify on what precise date in the past an existing general rule in another branch of international law came to be established as such. Accordingly, it did not feel that it should go beyond the temporal indication given by the reference in the article to "the principles of the Charter of the United Nations."

Id.

Notes

1. Would the seizure of hostages for the purpose of coercing their government to grant certain concessions and benefits to the state that seized the hostages constitute a use of force or threat of force against the political independence of the state whose nationals were seized? Would an agreement granting the benefits demanded be void under Article 52?

2. When the United States and Iran reached agreements (known as the Algiers Accords) in 1980 that called for the release of U.S. diplomats and other U.S. nationals who had been held hostage in Iran, were those agreements void under Article 52 because they were procured by the use of force against the United States? Could either side have refused to perform on the ground that the treaty was void *ab initio?* The main provisions of the agreement provided for the release of the hostages plus a declaration of nonintervention by the U.S. and the unblocking of Iranian assets frozen in the U.S. in response to the seizure. The United States gave nothing to Iran beyond releasing Iranian assets. In fact Iran received back less than its assets, since a part was placed in escrow to pay creditors and other claimants of United States nationality. See Chapter 9, pp. 739, and Chapter 10, p. 754. Can one say that an arrangement of this kind was "procured by" the use of threat of force, even if force was initially used against the United States? See Schachter, International Law in the Hostages Crisis in American Hostages in Iran 325, 369–373 (Christopher, *et al.,* 1985).

3. In the aftermath of the Kosovo crisis of 1999, some critics who viewed the NATO intervention as a use of force in violation of the U.N. Charter also thought that the subsequent arrangements to settle the situation might have been tainted, and that Yugoslavia could potentially have invoked the Vienna Convention's

coercion provision to impeach the validity of the settlement. See, e.g., Nambiar, India: An Uneasy Precedent, in Kosovo and the Challenge of Humanitarian Intervention (Schnabel & Thakur eds., 2000). See Chapter 12. Does the Security Council's approval of the Kosovo arrangements in Resolution 1244 (June 10, 1999) render moot the issue of whether Yugoslavia was "coerced" for purposes of the law of treaties?

E. CONFLICT WITH A PEREMPTORY NORM (JUS COGENS)

INTERNATIONAL LAW COMMISSION REPORT

[1966] II Yb.I.L.C. 169, 247–249.

(1) The view that in the last analysis there is no rule of international law from which States cannot at their own free will contract out has become increasingly difficult to sustain, although some jurists deny the existence of any rules of *jus cogens* in international law, since in their view even the most general rules still fall short of being universal. The Commission pointed out that the law of the Charter concerning the prohibition of the use of force in itself constitutes a conspicuous example of a rule in international law having the character of *jus cogens*. Moreover, if some Governments in their comments have expressed doubts as to the advisability of this article unless it is accompanied by provision for independent adjudication, only one questioned the existence of rules of *jus cogens* in the international law of today. Accordingly, the Commission concluded that in codifying the law of treaties it must start from the basis that to-day there are certain rules from which States are not competent to derogate at all by a treaty arrangement, and which may be changed only by another rule of the same character.

(2) The formulation of the article is not free from difficulty, since there is no simple criterion by which to identify a general rule of international law as having the character of *jus cogens*. Moreover, the majority of the general rules of international law do not have that character, and States may contract out of them by treaty. It would therefore be going much too far to state that a treaty is void if its provisions conflict with a rule of general international law. Nor would it be correct to say that a provision in a treaty possesses the character of *jus cogens* merely because the parties have stipulated that no derogation from that provision is to be permitted, so that another treaty which conflicted with that provision would be void. Such a stipulation may be inserted in any treaty with respect to any subject-matter for any reasons which may seem good to the parties. The conclusion by a party of a later treaty derogating from such a stipulation may, of course, engage its responsibility for a breach of the earlier treaty. But the breach of the stipulation does not, simply as such, render the treaty void (see article 26). It is not the form of a general rule of international law but the particular nature of the subject-matter with which it deals that may, in the opinion of the Commission, give it the character of *jus cogens*.

(3) The emergence of rules having the character of *jus cogens* is comparatively recent, while international law is in process of rapid development. The Commission considered the right course to be to provide in general terms that a treaty is void if it conflicts with a rule of *jus cogens* and to leave the full content of this rule to be worked out in State practice and in the jurispru-

dence of international tribunals. Some members of the Commission felt that there might be advantage in specifying, by way of illustration, some of the most obvious and best settled rules of *jus cogens* in order to indicate by these examples the general nature and scope of the rule contained in the article. Examples suggested included (a) a treaty contemplating an unlawful use of force contrary to the principles of the Charter, (b) a treaty contemplating the performance of any other act criminal under international law, and (c) a treaty contemplating or conniving at the commission of acts, such as trade in slaves, piracy or genocide, in the suppression of which every State is called upon to co-operate. Other members expressed the view that, if examples were given, it would be undesirable to appear to limit the scope of the article to cases involving acts which constitute crimes under international law; treaties violating human rights, the equality of States or the principle of self-determination were mentioned as other possible examples. The Commission decided against including any examples of rules of *jus cogens* in the article for two reasons. First, the mention of some cases of treaties void for conflict with a rule of *jus cogens* might, even with the most careful drafting, lead to misunderstanding as to the position concerning other cases not mentioned in the article. Secondly, if the Commission were to attempt to draw up, even on a selective basis, a list of the rules of international law which are to be regarded as having the character of *jus cogens,* it might find itself engaged in a prolonged study of matters which fall outside the scope of the present articles.

* * *

(6) The second matter is the non-retroactive character of the rule in the present article. The article has to be read in conjunction with article [64] (Emergence of a new rule of *jus cogens),* and in the view of the Commission, there is no question of the present article having retroactive effects. It concerns cases where a treaty is void *at the time of its conclusion* by reason of the fact that its provisions are in conflict with an already existing rule of *jus cogens.* The treaty is wholly void because its actual conclusion conflicts with a peremptory norm of general international law from which no States may derogate even by mutual consent. Article [64], on the other hand, concerns cases where a treaty, valid when concluded, becomes void and terminates by reason of the subsequent establishment of a new rule of *jus cogens* with which its provisions are in conflict. The words *"becomes* void and *terminates"* make it quite clear, the Commission considered, that the emergence of a new rule of *jus cogens* is not to have retroactive effects on the validity of a treaty. The invalidity is to attach only as from the time of the establishment of the new rule of *jus cogens.* The non-retroactive character of the rules in articles [53] and [64] is further underlined in article [71], paragraph 2 of which provides in the most express manner that the *termination* of a treaty as a result of the emergence of a new rule of *jus cogens* is not to have retroactive effects.

Notes

1. Although the draft article on peremptory norms generated much controversy at the Vienna conference, a revised draft was adopted by a vote of 72 in favor, 3 against, and 18 abstentions. Three changes were made to meet objections:

— The words "at the time of its conclusion" were added to make clear the non-retroactive character of the rule.

— It was made explicit that the peremptory norms were the norms recognized by the international community as a whole as those from which no derogation was permitted.

— It was agreed that a party to a dispute involving *jus cogens* may submit it to the International Court for a decision in all cases in which the procedures for settlement (indicated in Article 65) have failed to produce a solution within twelve months.

The adoption of this compulsory jurisdiction compromissory clause made it possible for states apprehensive over the possible destabilizing effect of the *jus cogens* article to support the adoption of the Vienna Convention. For detailed accounts, see Sinclair, The Vienna Convention on the Law of Treaties 203–226 (2d ed. 1984); Elias, The Modern Law of Treaties 177–187, 192–194 (1974); Sztucki, *Jus Cogens* and the Vienna Convention (1974).

2. What are the rules of *jus cogens* today? A former President of the International Court of Justice has suggested the following answer:

> The substantive contents of *jus cogens* are likely to be constantly changing in accordance with the progress and development of international law and international morality. *Jus cogens* is not an immutable natural law but an evolving concept: the last phrase in the definition envisages the modification of *jus cogens* by the same process which led to its establishment.
>
> Such subsequent rules may originate in a treaty whose norms become generally accepted. A treaty of this nature, containing a new rule of *jus cogens,* would not be void, even if some of its provisions conflicted with an established rule of *jus cogens:* the new rules of *jus cogens* would simply modify or replace the old ones. Otherwise, international society would be deprived of the necessary means of development of its notions of public policy through processes of international legislation. For instance, the traditional definition of piracy may be extended to cover hijacking of aeroplanes or the opium and drug conventions expanded to include synthetic drugs.

Jiménez de Aréchaga, 159 Rec. des Cours 9, 64–67 (1978–I). See Chapter 2 supra, pp. 105–108.

SINCLAIR, THE VIENNA CONVENTION ON THE LAW OF TREATIES

222–224 (2d ed. 1984) (footnotes omitted).

Whatever their doctrinal point of departure, the majority of jurists would no doubt willingly concede to the sceptics that there is little or no evidence in positive international law for the concept that nullity attaches to a treaty concluded in violation of *jus cogens*. But they would be constrained to admit that the validity of a treaty between two States to wage a war of aggression against a third State or to engage in acts of physical or armed force against a third State could not be upheld; and, having made this admission, they may be taken to have accepted the principle that there may exist norms of international law so fundamental to the maintenance of an international legal order that a treaty concluded in violation of them is a nullity.

Some (among whom may be counted your author) would be prepared to go this far, but would immediately wish to qualify this acceptance of the principle involved by sketching out the limits within which it may be operative in present-day international law. In the first place, they would insist that, in the present state of international society, the concept of an "international legal order" of hierarchically superior norms binding all States is only just beginning to emerge. Ideological differences and disparities of wealth between the individual nation States which make up the international community, combined with the contrasts between the objectives sought by them, hinder the development of an over-arching community consensus upon the content of *jus cogens.* Indeed, it is the existence of these very differences and disparities which constitute the principal danger implicit in an unqualified recognition of *jus cogens;* for it would be only too easy to postulate as a norm of *jus cogens* a principle which happened neatly to serve a particular ideological or economic goal. In the second place, they would test any assertion that a particular rule constitutes a norm of *jus cogens* by reference to the evidence for its acceptance as such by the international community as a whole, and they would require that the burden of proof should be discharged by those who allege the *jus cogens* character of the rule. Applying this test, and leaving aside the highly theoretical case of a treaty purporting to deny the application of the principle *pacta sunt servanda,* it would seem that sufficient evidence for ascribing the character of *jus cogens* to a rule of international law exists in relation to the rule which requires States to refrain in their international relations from the threat of force against the territorial integrity or political independence of any other State. There is ample evidence for the proposition that, subject to the necessary exceptions about the use of force in self-defence or under the authority of a competent organ of the United Nations or a regional agency acting in accordance with the Charter, the use of armed or physical force against the territorial integrity or political independence of any State is now prohibited. This proposition is so central to the existence of any international legal order of individual nation States (however nascent that international legal order may be) that it must be taken to have the character of *jus cogens.* Just as national legal systems begin to discard, at an early stage of their development, such concepts as "trial by battle," so also must the international legal order be assumed now to deny any cover of legality to violations of the fundamental rule embodied in Article 2(4) of the Charter.

Beyond this, uncertainty begins, and one must tread with considerable caution. The dictates of logic, and overriding considerations of morality, would appear to require that one should characterise as *jus cogens* those rules which prohibit the slave trade and genocide; but the evidence is ambivalent, since the treaties which embody these prohibitions contain normal denunciation clauses. Of course, it may be argued that the presence or absence of normal denunciation clauses should not be taken as being decisive; denunciation clauses are regularly embodied in treaties for traditional, rather than practical, reasons. In any event, it is likely that the prohibitions may now be taken to form part of general international law binding all States regardless of whether they are parties to the treaties embodying them. The unenforceability of any treaty contemplating genocide or the slave trade is further assured by the fact that such a treaty would contravene the Charter of the United Nations, which prevails in the event of conflict.

To sum up, there is a place for the concept of *jus cogens* in international law. Its growth and development will parallel the growth and development of an international legal order expressive of the consensus of the international community as a whole. Such an international legal order is, at present, inchoate, unformed and only just discernible. *Jus cogens* is neither Dr. Jekyll nor Mr. Hyde; but it has the potentialities of both. If it is invoked indiscriminately and to serve short-term political purposes, it could rapidly be destructive of confidence in the security of treaties; if it is developed with wisdom and restraint in the overall interest of the international community it could constitute a useful check upon the unbridled will of individual States.

Notes

1. Recall Chapter 2, pp. 105–108 supra, for an overview of *jus cogens*. What is meant by "international community of states" in Article 53?

2. Although Article 66 of the Vienna Convention provides for compulsory adjudication of disputes concerning the application of Articles 53 and 64, there is little or no case-law involving invocation of *jus cogens* to impeach the validity of a treaty. In the Case Concerning the Gabcikovo–Nagymaros Project (Hungary/Slovakia), 1997 I.C.J. 7, pp. 557–559 and 571–576 infra, Hungary argued that "new requirements of international law for the protection of the environment" had come into existence after the conclusion of a 1977 treaty concerning works on the Danube River and that those new requirements negated the obligations of the treaty. However, Hungary did not argue that these environmental norms were peremptory norms, and thus the Court did not have to consider Articles 53 or 64 of the Vienna Convention. It rejected Hungary's argument on the effect of new environmental norms on treaty obligations as unfounded in the law of treaties.

3. Is the principle of self-determination a *jus cogens* norm? If so, could a third state obtain judicial invalidation of a treaty between two other states on a claim that the treaty conflicted with a people's right to self-determination? The Case Concerning East Timor (Portugal v. Australia), 1995 I.C.J. 90, pp. 272–273 supra, involved issues along these lines. Portugal, on behalf of East Timor, claimed that a treaty between Australia and Indonesia concerning offshore resources in the so-called Timor Gap violated the right to self-determination of the people of East Timor. The Court dismissed the case on a threshold ground (absence of Indonesia as an indispensable party), without reaching the merits. If that jurisdictional problem had been surmountable, what reasoning might have been used to resolve the *jus cogens* issue under the Vienna Convention standard? See Cassese, Self–Determination: A Legal Reappraisal 133–140 (1995).

4. Jurists and governments have not been hesitant to propose their own ideas of peremptory norms. For examples see Sinclair at 217. The International Law Commission suggested such norms in a proposed list of international crimes. See Chapter 9, pp. 697–701. At the U.N. Conference on the Law of the Sea, a number of governments maintained that the principle of the common heritage of mankind with respect to areas beyond national jurisdiction had acquired the character of a peremptory norm. However, a proposal to that effect was not included in the Convention on the Law of the Sea. See Chapter 16. The General Assembly adopted a resolution in 1979 declaring that the agreements between Egypt and Israel (known as the Camp David Agreements) "have no validity." G.A.Res. 34/65 B (XXXIV 1979). The legal premise appeared to be that the agreements were considered to violate *jus cogens* norms. See Gaja, *Jus Cogens* Beyond the Vienna Convention, 172 Rec. des Cours 279, 282 (1981–III).

5. Would the compulsory adjudication clause of Article 66 of the Vienna Convention significantly reduce the risk that Articles 53 and 64 would "destroy the security of treaties"? Would it restrain governments from attacking treaties regarded by them as unjust? Could they not use Article 66 to impugn treaties which are alleged to be contrary to such Charter principles as sovereign equality, or such "fundamental principles" as the non-acquisition of territory by the threat or use of force? (See Chapter 4, Section 6.) Would the International Court now have wide latitude to declare treaties to be void on the basis of such principles?

6. It has been suggested that the concept of *jus cogens* has inspired the distinction between international delicts and international crimes proposed in the International Law Commission's Draft Articles on State Responsibility. An international crime was defined as a violation of an "international obligation so essential for the protection of fundamental interests of the international community that its breach is recognized as a crime by that community as a whole." Article 19 of the Draft Articles. [1976] II Yb.I.L.C. The Commission observed, however, that the "category of international obligations admitting of no derogation is much broader than the category of obligations whose breach is necessarily an international crime." Id. at 120. On the controversy about "international crimes," see pp. 697–701 in Chapter 9.

7. Article 64 deals with the emergence of a new rule of *jus cogens*. The treaty becomes void but, as stated in Article 71, the termination does not affect any right, obligation, or legal situation created through the execution of the treaty "provided that those rights, obligations or situations may thereafter be maintained only to the extent that their maintenance is not in itself in conflict with the new peremptory norm of general international law." Does this proviso throw doubt on executed settlements?

8. The International Law Commission suggested that any alteration of a rule of *jus cogens* would probably be effected by conclusion of a general multilateral treaty. But would not such a treaty when concluded contravene unlawfully the rule of *jus cogens* it purports to alter? Does this make the idea of *jus cogens* almost meaningless in that context?

9. The Restatement (Third) accepts the provisions of Articles 53 and 64 as customary law. However, it adds that inasmuch as the United States is not a party to the Convention and therefore the judicial safeguards do not apply to it, "the United States is likely to take a particularly restrictive view of these doctrines, and they can be applied as international law accepted by the United States only with caution." § 331, Reporters' Note 4. The Restatement also declares in § 331, Comment *e*, that in view of the uncertainty as to the scope of *jus cogens*, there is a particularly strong need "for an impartial determination of its applicability. A domestic court should not on its own authority refuse to give effect to an agreement on the ground that it violates a peremptory norm."

SECTION 6. TERMINATION OR SUSPENSION OF TREATIES

A. TERMINATION OR WITHDRAWAL UNDER THE TERMS OF A TREATY OR BY CONSENT

Most treaties today contain clauses specifying (a) their duration, or (b) the date of termination, or (c) an event or condition to bring about termination, or (d) a right to denounce or withdraw from the treaty. The clauses themselves are varied. Whether they apply in a particular case is a matter of interpretation. Article 54 of the Vienna Convention contains the self-evident rule that a treaty may be terminated in accordance with its own provisions. It also provides that a treaty may be terminated at any time by consent of all its parties.

Notes

1. Who has the right to act for a state in terminating a treaty? In principle, this is left to municipal law just as is the competence to express consent to be bound. But suppose the termination of the treaty is declared by an organ of the state lacking constitutional authority to take such action definitively. The Vienna Convention does not deal with this question. In Article 67, it mentions only the state officials who do not have to produce full powers for acts of termination; it follows in this respect the general principle of Article 7. Article 46 deals with the violation of domestic law regarding competence to conclude a treaty. It has been suggested that a similar rule should be applied in case of termination. See Haraszti, Some Fundamental Problems of the Law of Treaties 251–253 (1973). Haraszti (a Hungarian) cites as an instance of unlawful termination the denunciation of the Warsaw Pact by Hungary "at the time of the counter-revolution of 1956." In 1979, when President Carter terminated the Mutual Defense Treaty with the Republic of China (Taiwan) by giving one year's notice in accordance with the terms of the treaty, his right to do so without obtaining the advice and consent of the Senate was challenged by a Senator who brought a judicial proceeding. However, the Supreme Court dismissed the case without reaching the merits of the constitutional claim, so that the notice of termination took effect. See Goldwater v. Carter, 444 U.S. 996, 100 S.Ct. 533, 62 L.Ed.2d 428 (1979), p. 224 supra.

2. Does a clause providing for unilateral termination of a treaty give a party a right to terminate one or more clauses of the treaty without abrogating the rest of the treaty? When the other party or parties refused to accept such partial termination, termination of the entire agreement was necessitated. See 5 Hackworth 309–14; McNair, The Law of Treaties 476–478 (1961).

3. What happens if the denunciations or withdrawals reduce the parties to a multilateral treaty to a number below that required for its entry into force? The Vienna Convention (Article 55) states that that fact alone shall not result in termination. If the negotiating states consider that a minimum number should be necessary for maintaining the treaty in force, it should be so stated.

4. Many agreements have special provisions for withdrawal or release under particular circumstances. These are often preferred to general unilateral withdrawal provisions because they indicate an awareness of contingencies under which release from obligations would be acceptable. In some cases they provide for special procedures under which a party can seek to be released from some or all of its obligations. See General Agreement on Tariffs and Trade (GATT) Articles XXV(5), XXVIII. When agreements identify the circumstances that would trigger release, the determination whether those circumstances have occurred may be left to the party itself or referred to an international organ authorized to grant a waiver to the party. The latter type is found in the International Monetary Fund Agreement and various commodity agreements. For a general review of withdraw-

al and release provisions in international agreements, see Bilder, Managing the Risks of International Agreement 52–55, 98–104 (1981).

5. May a denunciation or withdrawal be revoked before the end of the period when it would take effect? Article 68 of the Vienna Convention answers in the affirmative. In proposing this rule, the International Law Commission commented that the right to revoke the notice is implicit in the rule that it is not to become effective until a certain date and other parties should take that into account. Accordingly, there would be no grounds for requiring consent of the other parties.

6. In 1993–1994 a dispute arose over the compliance of the Democratic People's Republic of Korea (North Korea) with a safeguards agreement under the Nuclear Non–Proliferation Treaty (NPT). Article X, paragraph 1 of the NPT has a clause (similar to that in other arms control agreements) allowing unilateral withdrawal, as follows:

> Each Party shall in exercising its national sovereignty have the right to withdraw from the Treaty if it decides that extraordinary events, related to the subject matter of this Treaty, have jeopardized the supreme interests of its country. It shall give notice of such withdrawal to all other Parties to the Treaty and to the United Nations Security Council three months in advance. Such notice shall include a statement of the extraordinary events it regards as having jeopardized its supreme interests.

On March 12, 1993, North Korea gave three months' notice of withdrawal under Article X. In the same month, the Director–General of the International Atomic Energy Agency (IAEA) reported North Korea's continuing noncompliance with the safeguards agreement. Within the three-month period, the U.N. Security Council adopted a resolution calling on North Korea to comply with the agreement. S.C. Res. 825 (May 11, 1993). Security Council members stepped up pressure to keep North Korea within the NPT framework, and the possibility of U.N. sanctions was under consideration. Following high-level talks between North Korea and the United States held June 2–11, 1993, North Korea announced that it had suspended its notice of withdrawal and would consider itself in "special status" under the NPT.

Over the ensuing year, the General Assembly called on North Korea to fulfill its NPT obligations. G.A. Res. 48/14 (Nov. 1, 1993); the vote was 140 to 1 (North Korea voting against) with 9 abstentions. The crisis eased (at least for the time being) when former President Carter negotiated a formula for resolution of North Korea's concerns, later embodied in an "Agreed Framework" between the United States and North Korea announced Oct. 21, 1994 (reprinted at 34 I.L.M. 603). See generally Dorn & Fulton, Securing Compliance with Disarmament Treaties: Carrots, Sticks, and the Case of North Korea, 3 Global Gov. 21 (1997).

As of 2000, North Korea remains a party to the NPT.

B. DENUNCIATION OR WITHDRAWAL FROM A TREATY WHICH CONTAINS NO PROVISION REGARDING TERMINATION

Article 56 of the Vienna Convention contains a provision permitting denunciation or withdrawal where such a right "may be implied by the nature of the treaty." Examples sometimes given of such cases are treaties of alliance and of commerce. Conversely, the nature of other categories of treaties is clearly perpetual, such as those for territorial cession or settlement of a boundary. See International Law Commission, Commentary, [1966] II Yb. I.L.C. 169, 250–251; Sinclair, Vienna Convention, at 102.

Some human rights treaties have no termination clause. Should they be considered denunciable or not? The Human Rights Committee dealt with this issue in General Comment No. 26 adopted in 1997:

GENERAL COMMENT NO. 26 ON ISSUES RELATING TO THE CONTINUITY OF OBLIGATIONS TO THE INTERNATIONAL COVENANT ON CIVIL AND POLITICAL RIGHTS

CCPR/C/21/Rev.1/Add.8/Rev.1.
Adopted October 29, 1997.

1. The International Covenant on Civil and Political Rights does not contain any provision regarding its termination and does not provide for denunciation or withdrawal. Consequently, the possibility of termination, denunciation or withdrawal must be considered in the light of applicable rules of customary international law which are reflected in the Vienna Convention on the Law of Treaties. On this basis, the Covenant is not subject to denunciation or withdrawal unless it is established that the parties intended to admit the possibility of denunciation or withdrawal or a right to do so is implied from the nature of the treaty.

2. That the parties to the Covenant did not admit the possibility of denunciation and that it was not a mere oversight on their part to omit reference to denunciation is demonstrated by the fact that article 41(2) of the Covenant does permit a State party to withdraw its acceptance of the competence of the Committee to examine inter-State communications by filing an appropriate notice to that effect while there is no such provision for denunciation of or withdrawal from the Covenant itself. Moreover, the Optional Protocol to the Covenant, negotiated and adopted contemporaneously with it, permits States parties to denounce it. Additionally, by way of comparison, the International Convention on the Elimination of All Forms of Racial Discrimination, which was adopted one year prior to the Covenant, expressly permits denunciation. It can therefore be concluded that the drafters of the Covenant deliberately intended to exclude the possibility of denunciation. The same conclusion applies to the Second Optional Protocol in the drafting of which a denunciation clause was deliberately omitted.

3. Furthermore, it is clear that the Covenant is not the type of treaty which, by its nature, implies a right of denunciation. Together with the simultaneously prepared and adopted International Covenant on Economic, Social and Cultural Rights, the Covenant codifies in treaty form the universal human rights enshrined in the Universal Declaration of Human Rights, the three instruments together often being referred to as the International Bill of Human Rights. As such, the Covenant does not have a temporary character typical of treaties where a right of denunciation is deemed to be admitted, notwithstanding the absence of a specific provision to that effect.

4. The rights enshrined in the Covenant belong to the people living in the territory of the State party. The Human Rights Committee has consistently taken the view, as evidenced by its long-standing practice, that once the people are accorded the protection of the rights under the Covenant, such protection devolves with territory and continues to belong to them, notwithstanding change in government of the State party, including dismemberment

in more than one State or State succession or any subsequent action of the State party designed to divest them of the rights guaranteed by the Covenant.

5. The Committee is therefore firmly of the view that international law does not permit a State which has ratified or acceded or succeeded to the Covenant to denounce it or withdraw from it.

Notes

1. The background to General Comment No. 26 includes the following facts, as summarized in the U.S. Department of State's Report on Human Rights Practices for 1997 (Country Report on Democratic People's Republic of Korea):

> On August 22 [1997], the U.N. Subcommission on Prevention of Discrimination and Protection of Minorities adopted a resolution criticizing the DPRK for its human rights practices. On August 27, the DPRK announced that it would withdraw from the International Covenant on Civil and Political Rights (ICCPR), calling the resolution an attack on its sovereignty. On October 29 [1997], the U.N. Human Rights Committee, during its 61st session, issued a statement criticizing the attempt by North Korea to withdraw from the ICCPR.

See also "U.N. Blocks Rights Move by North Korea," New York Times, Oct. 31, 1997.

The Secretary–General of the United Nations, as depositary for the International Covenant, had to determine how to exercise depositary functions in view of the DPRK's notice of withdrawal. The matter was handled as follows:

> On 25 August 1997, the Secretary–General received from the Government of the Democratic People's Republic of Korea a notification of withdrawal from the Covenant, dated 23 August 1997.
>
> As the Covenant does not contain a withdrawal provision, the Secretariat of the United Nations forwarded on 23 September 1997 an aide-mémoire to the Government of the Democratic People's Republic of Korea explaining the legal position arising from the above notification.
>
> As elaborated in this aide-mémoire, the Secretary–General is of the opinion that a withdrawal from the Covenant would not appear possible unless all States Parties to the Covenant agree with such a withdrawal.
>
> The above notification of withdrawal and the aide-mémoire were duly circulated to all States Parties under cover of C.N.467.TREATIES–10 of 12 November 1997.

As of 2000, the DPRK continues to be treated as a party to the Covenant, both by the Secretary–General as depositary (see Status of Multilateral Treaties Maintained by the Secretary–General) and by the Human Rights Committee. Indeed, the DPRK seems to have accepted the U.N. position, as it did file a report under the Covenant in 2000. See CCPR/C/PRK/2000/2 (May 4, 2000).

2. In the Case Concerning the Gabcikovo–Nagymaros Project (Hungary/Slovakia), 1997 I.C.J. 7, pp. 557–559 and 574–576 infra, Hungary attempted to terminate a bilateral treaty without the other party's consent. The subject-matter of the treaty was construction of works for navigation, flood control, and hydroelectric power along the Danube River. After unsuccessful efforts between 1989 and early 1992 to renegotiate the plans for the works and other developments,

Hungary gave a notice of termination on May 19, 1992 with purported effect as of May 25, 1992. In holding that Hungary could not terminate the treaty in this manner, the I.C.J. said:

> 100. The 1977 Treaty does not contain any provision regarding its termination. Nor is there any indication that the parties intended to admit the possibility of denunciation or withdrawal. On the contrary, the Treaty establishes a long-standing and durable régime of joint investment and joint operation. Consequently, the parties not having agreed otherwise, the Treaty could be terminated only on the limited grounds enumerated in the Vienna Convention. * * *
>
> 109. In this regard, it should be noted that, according to Hungary's Declaration of 19 May 1992, the termination of the 1977 Treaty was to take effect as from 25 May 1992, that is only six days later. Both Parties agree that Articles 65 to 67 of the Vienna Convention on the Law of Treaties, if not codifying customary law, at least generally reflect customary international law and contain certain procedural principles which are based on an obligation to act in good faith. * * *
>
> The termination of the Treaty by Hungary was to take effect six days after its notification. On neither of these dates had Hungary suffered injury from acts of Czechoslovakia. The Court must therefore confirm its conclusion that Hungary's termination of the Treaty was premature.

UNITED NATIONS CONFERENCE ON INTERNATIONAL ORGANIZATION

Commission I: Commentary on Withdrawal.
San Francisco, 1945. 1 U.N.C.I.O. Docs. 616–617.

The Committee adopts the view that the Charter should not make express provision either to permit or to prohibit withdrawal from the Organization. The Committee deems that the highest duty of the nations which will become Members is to continue their cooperation within the Organization, for the preservation of international peace and security. If, however, a Member because of exceptional circumstances feels constrained to withdraw, and leave the burden of maintaining international peace and security on the other Members, it is not the purpose of the Organization to compel that member to continue its cooperation in the Organization.

It is obvious, however, that withdrawal or some other forms of dissolution of the Organization would become inevitable if, deceiving the hope of humanity, the Organization was revealed to be unable to maintain peace or could do so only at the expense of law and justice.

Nor would it be the purpose of the Organization to compel a Member to remain in the Organization if its rights and obligations as such were changed by Charter amendment in which it has not concurred and which it finds itself unable to accept, or if an amendment duly accepted by the necessary majority in the Assembly or in a general conference fails to secure the ratification necessary to bring such amendment into effect.

It is for these considerations that the Committee has decided to abstain from recommending insertion in the Charter of a formal clause specifically forbidding or permitting withdrawal.

Notes

1. Commission I's Rapporteur stated on June 23, 1945 that "the absence of * * * [a withdrawal] clause is not intended to impair the right of withdrawal, which each state possesses on the basis of the principle of the sovereign equality of the members. The Commission would deplore any reckless or wanton exercise of the right of withdrawal but recognizes that, under certain exceptional circumstances, a state may feel itself compelled to exercise this right." 6 U.N.C.I.O. Doc. 5, 149. The Plenary Session of the Conference approved the Report. The sole objection was raised by the Soviet delegate, who interpreted the Commentary as "condemn[ing] beforehand the grounds on which any state may find it necessary to exercise its right of withdrawal from the Organization. Such right is an expression of state sovereignty and should not be reviled, in advance, by the International Organization." I U.N.C.I.O. 619–20. What weight should be assigned to the above statements, as well as to the Commentary on Withdrawal, in the interpretation of the Charter? See Kelsen, The Law of the United Nations 127 (1950). For a discussion of contemporaneous United States views on the problem of withdrawal, see id. at 129 n. 1. See, in general, Feinberg, Unilateral Withdrawal from an International Organization, 39 Brit. Y.B.I.L. 189 (1963).

On the withdrawal of Indonesia from the United Nations in 1965 and its return in 1966, see 4 I.L.M. 364 (1965); Livingstone, Withdrawal from the United Nations—Indonesia, 14 I.C.L.Q. 637 (1965); Schwelb, Withdrawal from the United Nations: The Indonesian Intermezzo, 61 A.J.I.L. 661 (1967).

2. In recommending acceptance by the United States of the Constitution of the World Health Organization, Congress included in its Joint Resolution a reservation to the effect that, "in the absence of any provision * * * for withdrawal from the Organization, the United States reserves its right to withdraw from the Organization on a one-year notice * * * " 62 Stat. 441–42. See 19 Dep't St. Bull. 310 (1948). The World Health Assembly unanimously accepted the United States reservation by a Resolution of July 2, 1948. See Feinberg at 202–203. In 1949 and 1950, a number of states of the Soviet bloc announced their withdrawal from WHO, but their notifications to the Director–General were rejected on the ground that the WHO Constitution made no provision for withdrawal. The Organization continued to regard the absent states as members, and when the Soviet Union and the other "inactive members" began to resume full participation in 1957, it was agreed that the Organization would accept a token payment of five percent in settlement of the absentee states' financial obligations for the intervening years. See generally id. at 202–208, and sources cited. After a number of states had withdrawn from and then returned to UNESCO, the Organization's Constitution was amended in 1954 to provide specifically for withdrawal. Id. at 209–11. In all the remaining Specialized Agencies of the United Nations, withdrawal is specifically authorized under the conditions stated.

3. The United States gave notice of withdrawal from the International Labour Organisation in 1975 and returned in 1980. It withdrew from UNESCO in 1984 and had not returned as of 2000. See 1980 Digest of U.S. Practice in International Law 76–78, 84 Dep't State Bull. No. 2083, 41 (1984).

4. Consider the Human Rights Committee's position on non-terminability of human rights treaties in light of the distinction between the substantive norms of the treaties and their implementation within an institutional setting. Do the

foregoing materials on withdrawal from international institutions support drawing such a distinction in the case of human rights bodies? Should parties to institutional treaties be considered to have an implied right of withdrawal, or would some institutions be perpetual and their membership likewise locked in to indefinite participation? What reasons might a state have for wishing to withdraw from an institutional treaty? What reasons might there be for discouraging unilateral withdrawal? Compare Hirschman, Exit, Voice and Loyalty (1970). Do human rights institutions have special features compared to other institutions as to which a right of withdrawal has been explicitly granted or considered implicit?

5. The Treaty of Rome that established the European Economic Community had no provision on withdrawal, and differing legal positions were developed as to its potential denunciability. See, e.g., Weiler, Alternatives to Withdrawal from an International Organization: The Case of the EEC, 20 Israel Law Review 282 (1985). From time to time, dissatisfaction in some member states with the operation of European institutions has made the possibility of unilateral withdrawal seem more than a hypothetical question. Does the more tightly integrated European Union of the 1990s and beyond suggest a negative answer to whether a right of denunciation "may be implied by the nature of the treaty" within the meaning of Vienna Convention Article 56(1)(b)?

C. TERMINATION OF A TREATY AS A CONSEQUENCE OF BREACH

INTERNATIONAL LAW COMMISSION REPORT

[1966] II Yb.I.L.C. 169, 253–255.

(1) The great majority of jurists recognize that a violation of a treaty by one party may give rise to a right in the other party to abrogate the treaty or to suspend the performance of its own obligations under the treaty. A violation of a treaty obligation, as of any other obligation, may give rise to a right in the other party to take nonforcible reprisals, and these reprisals may properly relate to the defaulting party's rights under the treaty. Opinion differs, however, as to the extent of the right to abrogate the treaty and the conditions under which it may be exercised. Some jurists, in the absence of effective international machinery for securing the observance of treaties, are more impressed with the innocent party's need to have this right as a sanction for the violation of the treaty. They tend to formulate the right in unqualified terms, giving the innocent party a general right to abrogate the treaty in the event of a breach. Other jurists are more impressed with the risk that a State may allege a trivial or even fictitious breach simply to furnish a pretext for denouncing a treaty which it now finds embarrassing. These jurists tend to restrict the right of denunciation to "material" or "fundamental" breaches and also to subject the exercise of the right to procedural conditions.

(5) The Commission was agreed that a breach of a treaty, however serious, does not *ipso facto* put an end to the treaty, and also that it is not open to a State simply to allege a violation of the treaty and pronounce the treaty at an end. On the other hand, it considered that within certain limits and subject to certain safeguards the right of a party to invoke the breach of a treaty as a ground for terminating it or suspending its operation must be recognized. Some members considered that it would be dangerous for the

Commission to endorse such a right, unless its exercise were to be made subject to control by compulsory reference to the International Court of Justice. The Commission, while recognizing the importance of providing proper safeguards against arbitrary denunciation of a treaty on the ground of an alleged breach, concluded that the question of providing safeguards against arbitrary action was a general one which affected several articles. It, therefore, decided to formulate in the present article the substantive conditions under which a treaty may be terminated or its operation suspended in consequence of a breach, and to deal with the question of the procedural safeguards in article [65].

(6) *Paragraph 1* provides that a "material" breach of a bilateral treaty by one party entitles the other to *invoke* the breach as a ground for terminating the treaty or suspending its operation in whole or in part. The formula "invoke as a ground" is intended to underline that the right arising under the article is not a right arbitrarily to pronounce the treaty terminated. If the other party contests the breach or its character as a "material" breach, there will be a "difference" between the parties with regard to which the normal obligations incumbent upon the parties under the Charter and under general international law to seek a solution of the question through pacific means will apply. The Commission considered that the action open to the other party in the case of a material breach is to invoke either the termination or the suspension of the operation of the treaty, in whole or in part. The right to take this action arises under the law of treaties independently of any right of reprisal, the principle being that a party cannot be called upon to fulfill its obligations under a treaty when the other party fails to fulfil those which it undertook under the same treaty. This right would, of course, be without prejudice to the injured party's right to present an international claim for reparation on the basis of the other party's responsibility with respect to the breach.

(7) *Paragraph 2* deals with a material breach of a multilateral treaty, and here the Commission considered it necessary to distinguish between the right of the other parties to react jointly to the breach and the right of an individual party specially affected by the breach to react alone. Subparagraph (a) provides that the other parties may, by a unanimous agreement, suspend the operation of the treaty or terminate it and may do so either only in their relations with the defaulting State or altogether as between all the parties. When an individual party reacts alone the Commission considered that its position is similar to that in the case of a bilateral treaty, but that its right should be limited to suspending the operation of the treaty in whole or in part as between itself and the defaulting State. In the case of a multilateral treaty the interests of the other parties have to be taken into account and a right of suspension normally provides adequate protection to the State specially affected by the breach. Moreover, the limitation of the right of the individual party to a right of suspension seemed to the Commission to be particularly necessary in the case of general multilateral treaties of a law-making character. Indeed, a question was raised as to whether even suspension would be admissible in the case of lawmaking treaties. The Commission felt, however, that it would be inequitable to allow a defaulting State to continue to enforce the treaty against the injured party, whilst itself violating its obligations towards that State under the treaty. Moreover, even such treaties as the

Genocide Convention and the Geneva Conventions on the treatment of prisoners of war, sick and wounded allowed an express right of denunciation independently of any breach of the convention. The Commission concluded that general lawmaking treaties should not, simply as such, be dealt with differently from other multilateral treaties in the present connexion. Accordingly, subparagraph (b) lays down that on a material breach of a multilateral treaty any party specially affected by the breach may *invoke* it as a *ground* for suspending the operation of the treaty in whole or in part *in the relations between itself and the defaulting State.*

(8) *Paragraph 2(c)* is designed to deal with the problem raised in the comments of Governments of special types of treaty, e.g. disarmament treaties, where a breach by one party tends to undermine the whole régime of the treaty as between all the parties. In the case of a material breach of such a treaty the interests of an individual party may not be adequately protected by the rules contained in paragraphs 2(a) and (b). It could not suspend the performance of its own obligations under the treaty vis-à-vis the defaulting State without at the same time violating its obligations to the other parties. Yet, unless it does so, it may be unable to protect itself against the threat resulting from the arming of the defaulting State. In these cases, where a material breach of the treaty by one party radically changes the position of every party with respect to the further performance of its obligations, the Commission considered that any party must be permitted without first obtaining the agreement of the other parties to suspend the operation of the treaty with respect to itself generally in its relations with all the other parties. Paragraph 2(c) accordingly so provides.

(9) *Paragraph 3* defines the kind of breach which may give rise to a right to terminate or suspend the treaty. Some authorities have in the past seemed to assume that any breach of any provision would suffice to justify the denunciation of the treaty. The Commission, however, was unanimous that the right to terminate or suspend must be limited to cases where the breach is of a serious character. It preferred the term "material" to "fundamental" to express the kind of breach which is required. The word "fundamental" might be understood as meaning that only the violation of a provision directly touching the *central* purposes of the treaty can ever justify the other party in terminating the treaty. But other provisions considered by a party to be essential to the effective execution of the treaty may have been very material in inducing it to enter into the treaty at all, even though these provisions may be of an ancillary character. Clearly, an unjustified repudiation of the treaty—a repudiation not sanctioned by any of the provisions of the present articles—would automatically constitute a material breach of the treaty; and this is provided for in sub-paragraph (a) of the definition. The other and more general form of material breach is that in sub-paragraph (b), and is there defined as a violation of a provision essential to the accomplishment of any object or purpose of the treaty.

Notes

1. At the Vienna conference, paragraph 5 was added to the draft of the Commission. Its objective was to ensure that the rules providing for termination

as a consequence of breach would not cause the termination or suspension of the many conventions of a humanitarian character which protect the "human person." Reference was made to the Geneva Conventions for the Protection of Victims of War and to conventions relating to refugees and human rights. It was considered desirable to make it clear that a material breach in these cases should not lead to abrogation or suspension of the treaty. The general view is that such treaties are essentially for the benefit of individuals and they involve obligations which should not be dependent on reciprocal performance by the states parties. Compare the reasoning of the International Court in its *Advisory Opinion on Reservations to the Convention on Genocide,* p. 479 supra.

2. A state may choose to ignore a violation by another state of a treaty to which both are parties. See Charlton v. Kelly, 229 U.S. 447, 33 S.Ct. 945, 57 L.Ed. 1274 (1913), where the Supreme Court held that inasmuch as the executive branch of government had waived its "right to free itself from the obligation to deliver up its own citizens" pursuant to an extradition treaty with Italy that had been interpreted by Italian authorities as excluding the extradition from Italy of Italian citizens, the courts were compelled to recognize the treaty as binding and in full force.

3. Does a violation by one party of a single article or group of articles of an agreement justify another party in regarding itself as freed of all obligations under the agreement? In his report to the Security Council on problems concerning the Armistice Agreements concluded between Israel and various Arab states in 1949, the Secretary–General stated:

> 16. As a matter of course, each party considers its compliance with the stipulations of an armistice agreement as conditioned by compliance of the other party to the agreement. Should such a stand be given the interpretation that any one infringement of the provisions of the agreement by one party justifies reactions by the other party which, in their turn, are breaches of the armistice agreement, without any limitation as to the field within which reciprocity is considered to prevail, it would in fact mean that the armistice regime could be nullified by a single infringement by one of the parties. Although such an interpretation has never been given from responsible quarters, it appears to me that a lack of clarity has prevailed. From no side has it been said that a breach of an armistice agreement, to whatever clause it may refer, gives the other party a free hand concerning the agreement as a whole, but a tendency to regard the agreements, including the cease-fire clauses, as entities may explain a feeling that in fact, due to infringements of this or that clause, the obligations are no longer in a strict sense fully binding, and specifically that a breach of one of the clauses, other than the cease-fire clause, may justify action in contravention of that clause. * * *
>
> 18. The very logic of the armistice agreements shows that infringements of other articles cannot serve as a justification for an infringement of the cease-fire article. If that were not recognized, it would mean that any one of such infringements might not only nullify the armistice régime, but in fact put in jeopardy the cease-fire itself. For that reason alone, it is clear that compliance with the said article can be conditioned only by similar compliance of the other party.

11 SCOR, Supp. Apr.-June 1956, at 34–35, U.N.Doc. S/3596, at 6–7 (1956). See the International Law Commission's comment on the separability of treaty provisions, [1966] II Yb.I.L.C. 237–39 (Art. 41).

4. In *Rainbow Warrior* (New Zealand v. France), 82 I.L.R. 499 (1990), a French–New Zealand Arbitration Tribunal addressed the question of whether a state can justify breach of treaty obligations by referring to exceptions within the law of state responsibility, such as *force majeure,* distress, and necessity. (The topic of circumstances precluding wrongfulness in the law of state responsibility is treated in Chapter 9.) The Tribunal answered this question in the affirmative, holding that both the customary law of treaties and the customary law of state responsibility were relevant and applicable in ascertaining the consequences, if any, of a breach of treaty:

> The reason is that the general principles of International Law concerning State responsibility are equally applicable in the case of breach of treaty obligation, since in the international law field there is no distinction between contractual and tortious responsibility, so that any violation by a State of any obligation, of whatever origin, gives rise to State responsibility and consequently, to the duty of reparation.

Id. at 551. To similar effect on the relationship between the law of treaties and the law of state responsibility, see Gabcikovo–Nagymaros Project (Hungary/Slovakia), 1997 I.C.J. 7, at paras. 47–48 (see excerpts at pp. 557–559 and 574–576 infra).

In *Gabcikovo*, Hungary's contentions included an allegation of material breach by the other party, as Slovakia had put into place a variant of the Danube River plans to which Hungary had not consented. The Court concluded that even if Slovakia had thereby breached the underlying treaty, it had done so in response to Hungary's prior wrongful actions:

> 110. * * * Hungary, by its own conduct, had prejudiced its right to terminate the Treaty; this would still have been the case even if Czechoslovakia, by the time of the purported termination, had violated a provision essential to the accomplishment of the object or purpose of the Treaty.

5. In 1998–1999, issues of material breach in the context of a cease-fire agreement were given prominence when Iraq refused to comply with obligations concerning elimination of capabilities for weapons of mass destruction, in accordance with the framework established at the conclusion of the 1991 Persian Gulf war by Security Council Resolution 687 (1991). After Iraq expelled the U.N. inspectors and repudiated the supervisory regime, President Clinton ordered cruise missile strikes against Iraqi targets. Among the possible legal arguments to justify this new use of force was that Iraq's material violation of the cease-fire terms revived the legal situation of collective self-defense of Kuwait that had prevailed prior to Resolution 687. See Chapter 12, p. 1022. In terms of the matters dealt with in the present chapter, to what extent should one party's breach of a cease-fire agreement warrant a legal conclusion that another party can treat the cease-fire as suspended or terminated? For discussion of Vienna Convention issues in this context, see Wedgwood, The Enforcement of Security Council Resolution 687: The Threat of Force Against Iraq's Weapons of Mass Destruction, 92 A.J.I.L. 724 (1998). Compare Note 3 above.

ADVISORY OPINION ON NAMIBIA

International Court of Justice, Advisory Opinion, 1971.
1971 I.C.J. 16.*

[In 1966, the General Assembly adopted a resolution in which, *inter alia,* it decided that South Africa's Mandate from the League of Nations to what

* The complete title of this opinion is: Legal Consequences for States of the Continued Presence of South Africa in Namibia (South West Africa), notwithstanding Security Council Resolution 276 (1970).

became known as Namibia (South West Africa) was terminated. G.A.Res. 2145 (XXI) (1966). This resolution was predicated on the General Assembly's assessment that South Africa had breached the Mandate by introducing the system of *apartheid* into South West Africa. When the General Assembly's action did not succeed in inducing South Africa to terminate or relax its control of the territory or to abandon *apartheid* in South West Africa, the situation was put on the agenda of the Security Council, which on January 30, 1970, reaffirmed the General Assembly resolution and declared, *inter alia,* "that the continued presence of the South African authorities in Namibia is illegal and that consequently all acts taken by the Government of South Africa on behalf of or concerning Namibia after the termination of the Mandate are illegal and invalid." S.C.Res. 276, U.N.Doc. S/INF/25, at 1. South Africa remained adamant and refused to cooperate with the U.N. Council for Namibia which had been set up by the General Assembly in 1967 and which had begun to issue Travel Documents and Identity Certificates for inhabitants of Namibia. On July 29, 1970, the Security Council adopted a resolution submitting to the International Court of Justice for an advisory opinion the following question: "What are the legal consequences for States of the continued presence of South Africa in Namibia, notwithstanding Security Council resolution 276 (1970)?" S.C.Res. 284.

On June 21, 1971, the Court answered this question as follows:]

by 13 votes to 2,

(1) that, the continued presence of South Africa in Namibia being illegal, South Africa is under obligation to withdraw its administration from Namibia immediately and thus put an end to its occupation of the Territory;

by 11 votes to 4,

(2) that States Members of the United Nations are under obligation to recognize the illegality of South Africa's presence in Namibia and the invalidity of its acts on behalf of or concerning Namibia, and to refrain from any acts and in particular any dealings with the Government of South Africa implying recognition of the legality of, or lending support or assistance to, such presence and administration;

(3) that it is incumbent upon States which are not Members of the United Nations to give assistance, within the scope of subparagraph (2) above, in the action which has been taken by the United Nations with regard to Namibia.

1971 I.C.J. 16, at 58.]

93. In paragraph 3 of the operative part of the resolution the General Assembly "*Declares* that South Africa has failed to fulfil its obligations in respect of the administration of the Mandated Territory and to ensure the moral and material well-being and security of the indigenous inhabitants of South West Africa and has, in fact, disavowed the Mandate". In paragraph 4 the decision is reached, as a consequence of the previous declaration "that the Mandate conferred upon His Britannic Majesty to be exercised on his behalf

by the Government of the Union of South Africa is *therefore* terminated * * * ". (Emphasis added.) It is this part of the resolution which is relevant in the present proceedings.

94. In examining this action of the General Assembly it is appropriate to have regard to the general principles of international law regulating termination of a treaty relationship on account of breach. For even if the mandate is viewed as having the character of an institution, as is maintained, it depends on those international agreements which created the system and regulated its application. As the Court indicated in 1962 "this Mandate, like practically all other similar Mandates" was "a special type of instrument composite in nature and instituting a novel international régime. It incorporates a definite agreement * * * " (I.C.J. Reports 1962, p. 331). The Court stated conclusively in that Judgment that the Mandate " * * * in fact and in law, is an international agreement having the character of a treaty or convention" (I.C.J. Reports 1962, p. 330). The rules laid down by the Vienna Convention on the Law of Treaties concerning termination of a treaty relationship on account of breach (adopted without a dissenting vote) may in many respects be considered as a codification of existing customary law on the subject. In the light of these rules, only a material breach of a treaty justifies termination, such breach being defined as:

(a) a repudiation of the treaty not sanctioned by the present Convention; or

(b) the violation of a provision essential to the accomplishment of the object or purpose of the treaty (Art. 60, para. 3).

95. General Assembly resolution 2145 (XXI) determines that both forms of material breach had occurred in this case. By stressing that South Africa "has, in fact, disavowed the Mandate", the General Assembly declared in fact that it had repudiated it. The resolution in question is therefore to be viewed as the exercise of the right to terminate a relationship in case of a deliberate and persistent violation of obligations which destroys the very object and purpose of that relationship. * * *

96. It has been contended that the Covenant of the League of Nations did not confer on the Council of the League power to terminate a mandate for misconduct of the Mandatory and that no such power could therefore be exercised by the United Nations, since it could not derive from the League greater powers than the latter itself had. For this objection to prevail it would be necessary to show that the mandates system, as established under the League, excluded the application of the general principle of law that a right of termination on account of breach must be presumed to exist in respect of all treaties, except as regards provisions relating to the protection of the human person contained in treaties of a humanitarian character (as indicated in Art. 60, para. 5, of the Vienna Convention). The silence of a treaty as to the existence of such a right cannot be interpreted as implying the exclusion of a right which has its source outside of the treaty, in general international law, and is dependent on the occurrence of circumstances which are not normally envisaged when a treaty is concluded.

* * *

101. It has been suggested that, even if the Council of the League had possessed the power of revocation of the Mandate in an extreme case, it could not have been exercised unilaterally but only in cooperation with the mandatory Power. However, revocation could only result from a situation in which the Mandatory had committed a serious breach of the obligations it had undertaken. To contend, on the basis of the principle of unanimity which applied in the League of Nations, that in this case revocation could only take place with the concurrence of the Mandatory, would not only run contrary to the general principle of law governing termination on account of breach, but also postulate an impossibility. For obvious reasons, the consent of the wrongdoer to such a form of termination cannot be required.

Note

Was the Court correct in saying that there is a general principle of law that a right of termination on account of breach must be presumed to exist in respect of all treaties? Briggs has noted that the Court produces no evidence in support. Moreover, he finds that Article 60 does not recognize that proposition. In the case of multilateral treaties, a material breach may be invoked only *as a ground for termination or suspension* under paragraph 2(a). Paragraphs 2(b) and 2(c) permit invocation of a material breach only as a ground for suspension, not termination. Briggs points out that the International Law Commission stated that "the breach of a treaty, however serious, does not *ipso facto* put an end to the treaty and * * * it is not open to a state simply to allege a violation of the treaty and pronounce the treaty at an end * * *." (See [1966] II Yb.I.L.C. at 253–255 quoted supra, p. 507.) The statement of the Court, according to Briggs, is *obiter dicta* since the *Namibia Case* did not involve a claim by a state of a unilateral right to terminate a treaty for breach. The analogy should have been with the collective right of termination set forth in paragraph 2a of Article 60. See Briggs, Unilateral Denunciation of Treaties, 68 A.J.I.L. 51, 56–57 (1974).

APPEAL RELATING TO THE JURISDICTION OF THE ICAO COUNCIL (INDIA v. PAKISTAN)

International Court of Justice, 1972.
1972 I.C.J. 46.

[Pakistan had brought a complaint against India before the Council of the International Civil Aviation Organization (ICAO) on the ground that India had violated provisions of the 1944 Chicago Convention on International Civil Aviation and the International Air Services Transport Agreement. The basis for the complaint was that India had unilaterally suspended flights of Pakistan aircraft over Indian territory. The ICAO Council assumed jurisdiction on the basis of the jurisdictional clauses in the treaties. India appealed to the International Court of Justice charging that the treaties had been suspended by India on ground of a breach by Pakistan (in particular, the hijacking of an Indian plane, allegedly with compliance of Pakistan). Therefore, it claimed the ICAO Council had no jurisdiction.

Pakistan objected to the Court's taking jurisdiction on the ground that India's contention that the treaties were not in force or in operation meant that India did not have standing to bring a case on the basis of the treaty jurisdictional clauses. The Court rejected the Pakistan challenge and in so doing declared:]

Nor in any case could a merely unilateral suspension per se render jurisdictional clauses inoperative, since one of their purposes might be, precisely, to enable the validity of the suspension to be tested. If a mere allegation, as yet unestablished, that a treaty was no longer operative could be used to defeat its jurisdictional clauses, all such clauses would become potentially a dead letter, even in cases like the present, where one of the very questions at issue on the merits, and as yet undecided, is whether or not the treaty is operative i.e., whether it has been validly terminated or suspended. The result would be that means of defeating jurisdictional clauses would never be wanting.

[With respect to the jurisdiction of the ICAO Council, India claimed that its right to unilateral termination or suspension for material breach had been properly exercised and accordingly the treaties no longer were in force. It followed that the ICAO Council could not have jurisdiction. India's conduct in suspending Pakistan flights was therefore outside of, not under, the treaties. In regard to this, the Court stated:]

* * * it involves a point of principle of great general importance for the jurisdictional aspects of this—or of any—case. This contention is to the effect that since India, in suspending overflights in February 1971, was not invoking any right that might be afforded by the Treaties, but was acting outside them on the basis of a general principle of international law, "therefore" the Council, whose jurisdiction was derived from the Treaties, and which was entitled to deal only with matters arising under them, must be incompetent. Exactly the same attitude has been evinced in regard to the contention that the Treaties were suspended in 1965 and never revived, or were replaced by a special régime. The Court considers however, that for precisely the same order of reason as has already been noticed in the case of its own jurisdiction in the present case, a mere unilateral affirmation of these contentions—contested by the other party—cannot be utilized so as to negative the Council's jurisdiction. The point is not that these contentions are necessarily wrong but that their validity has not yet been determined. Since therefore the Parties are in disagreement as to whether the Treaties ever were (validly) suspended or replaced by something else; as to whether they are in force between the Parties or not; and as to whether India's action in relation to Pakistan overflights was such as not to involve the Treaties, but to be justifiable *aliter et aliunde*;—these very questions are in issue before the Council, and no conclusions as to jurisdiction can be drawn from them, at least at this stage, so as to exclude *ipso facto* and *a priori* the competence of the Council.

32. To put the matter in another way, these contentions are essentially in the nature of replies to the charge that India is in breach of the Treaties: the Treaties were at the material times suspended or not operative, or replaced,—hence they cannot have been infringed. India has not of course claimed that, in consequence, such a matter can never be tested by any form of judicial recourse. This contention, if it were put forward, would be equivalent to saying that questions that prima facie may involve a given treaty, and

if so would be within the scope of its jurisdictional clause, could be removed therefrom at a stroke by a unilateral declaration that the treaty was no longer operative. The acceptance of such a proposition would be tantamount to opening the way to a wholesale nullification of the practical value of jurisdictional clauses by allowing a party first to purport to terminate, or suspend the operation of a treaty, and then to declare that the treaty being now terminated or suspended, its jurisdictional clauses were in consequence void, and could not be invoked for the purpose of contesting the validity of the termination or suspension,—whereas of course it may be precisely one of the objects of such a clause to enable that matter to be adjudicated upon. Such a result, destructive of the whole object of adjudicability, would be unacceptable.

Notes

1. As in the *Advisory Opinion on Namibia,* the Court in the above case relied on the Vienna Convention on the Law of Treaties as authoritative even prior to the entry into force of that Convention.

2. Briggs commented on the decision as follows:

> The court properly confined itself to upholding its own jurisdiction and that of the ICAO Council; but it may be noted that much of the rationale advanced by the Court to restrict claims of a unilateral right under general international law to terminate or suspend jurisdictional treaties for breach would appear to have cogency in relation to all treaties, whether or not they contain jurisdictional clauses.

Briggs, Unilateral Denunciation of Treaties: The Vienna Convention and the International Court of Justice, 68 A.J.I.L. 60–61 (1974).

3. Is a party affected by a breach obliged to continue performance of a treaty which the other party is violating during the period when the required process of dispute settlement is in progress? Is the aggrieved party restricted in taking counter-measures (including non-compliance) when the treaty itself provides for negotiation, arbitration or other means of settlement? These questions were considered by an arbitral tribunal in a dispute between France and the United States concerning an Air Services Agreement. The tribunal held that the aggrieved state (the United States) was entitled to take counter-measures including suspension of its performance under the treaty when such measures were not disproportionate to the breach, notwithstanding the agreement for arbitration. Case Concerning the Air Services Agreement between France and the United States, Award of December 9, 1978. 18 U.N.R.I.A.A. 417. The decision is dealt with in more detail below in Chapter 9, Section 7 on countermeasures. See also Damrosch, Retaliation or Arbitration—or Both?, 74 A.J.I.L. 785 (1980).

D. FUNDAMENTAL CHANGE OF CIRCUMSTANCES

INTERNATIONAL LAW COMMISSION REPORT

[1966] II Yb.I.L.C. 169, 256–258.

(1) Almost all modern jurists, however reluctantly, admit the existence in international law of the principle with which this article is concerned and which is commonly spoken of as the doctrine of *rebus sic stantibus.* Just as

many systems of municipal law recognize that, quite apart from any actual *impossibility* of performance, contracts may become inapplicable through a fundamental change of circumstances, so also treaties may become inapplicable for the same reason. Most jurists, however, at the same time enter a strong *caveat* as to the need to confine the scope of the doctrine within narrow limits and to regulate strictly the conditions under which it may be invoked; for the risks to the security of treaties which this doctrine presents in the absence of any general system of compulsory jurisdiction are obvious. The circumstances of international life are always changing and it is easy to allege that the changes render the treaty inapplicable.

* * *

(6) The Commission concluded that the principle, if its application were carefully delimited and regulated, should find a place in the modern law of treaties. A treaty may remain in force for a long time and its stipulations come to place an undue burden on one of the parties as a result of a fundamental change of circumstances. Then, if the other party were obdurate in opposing any change, the fact that international law recognized no legal means of terminating or modifying the treaty otherwise than through a further agreement between the same parties might impose a serious strain on the relations between the States concerned; and the dissatisfied State might ultimately be driven to take action outside the law. The number of cases calling for the application of the rule is likely to be comparatively small. As pointed out in the commentary to article [54], the majority of modern treaties are expressed to be of short duration, or are entered into for recurrent terms of years with a right to denounce the treaty at the end of each term, or are expressly or implicitly terminable upon notice. In all these cases either the treaty expires automatically or each party, having the power to terminate the treaty, has the power also to apply pressure upon the other party to revise its provisions. Nevertheless, there may remain a residue of cases in which, failing any agreement, one party may be left powerless under the treaty to obtain any legal relief from outmoded and burdensome provisions. It is in these cases that the *rebus sic stantibus* doctrine could serve a purpose as a lever to induce a spirit of compromise in the other party. Moreover, despite the strong reservations often expressed with regard to it, the evidence of the acceptance of the doctrine in international law is so considerable that it seems to indicate a recognition of a need for this safety-valve in the law of treaties.

(7) In the past the principle has almost always been presented in the guise of a tacit condition implied in every "perpetual" treaty that would dissolve it in the event of a fundamental change of circumstances. The Commission noted, however, that the tendency to-day was to regard the implied term as only a fiction by which it was attempted to reconcile the principle of the dissolution of treaties in consequence of a fundamental change of circumstances with the rule *pacta sunt servanda.* In most cases the parties gave no thought to the possibility of a change of circumstances and, if they had done so, would probably have provided for it in a different manner. Furthermore, the Commission considered the fiction to be an undesirable one since it increased the risk of subjective interpretations and abuse. For this reason, the Commission was agreed that the theory of an implied term must be rejected and the doctrine formulated as an objective rule of law by which,

on grounds of equity and justice, a fundamental change of circumstances may, under certain conditions, be invoked by a party as a ground for terminating the treaty. It further decided that, in order to emphasize the objective character of the rule, it would be better not to use the term *"rebus sic stantibus"* either in the text of the article or even in the title, and so avoid the doctrinal implication of that term.

Notes

1. Consider the five conditions that have to be met under Article 62 before a "fundamental change of circumstances" can be invoked as a ground of termination:

— The change must have been of a fundamental character.

— The change must have been unforeseen (if the treaty contains provisions for certain contingencies, e.g., economic hardships, the condition is not unforeseen).

— The circumstances which have changed must have been "an essential basis of the consent to be bound by the treaty."

— The effect of the change must be to transform radically the extent of the obligations of the party invoking the change as a ground of termination.

— The obligations in question are "still to be performed under the treaty" (hence, the article does not apply to treaties whose provisions have been fully executed).

2. Would the principle of Article 62 apply to settlements of a territorial nature? Note the explicit exclusion of a treaty if it "establishes a boundary." The International Law Commission rejected suggestions that the exception for boundary treaties might be inconsistent with the principle of self-determination. It considered that if a boundary treaty were not excepted, the rule "might become a source of dangerous friction." But the Commission also said: "By excepting treaties establishing a boundary from its scope, the present article would not exclude the operation of the principle of self-determination in any case where the conditions for its legitimate operation existed." [1966] II Yb.I.L.C. 259. A territorial settlement need not establish a boundary, e.g., it may transfer an island or a zone such as the Canal Zone. Since these actions would not establish a boundary, the issue would be whether the treaty was fully executed or whether in some respects it is executory. In the *Free Zones Case* (P.C.I.J., Ser. A/B, No. 46), Switzerland claimed that *rebus sic stantibus* did not apply to the territorial clauses which had been executed. France, however, noted that certain personal rights were created and that France, for example, had a continuing obligation to abstain from levying customs duties on individuals. The Court did not find it necessary to pass on this point but it exemplifies the case of a continuing obligation as part of a territorial settlement.

3. May a state invoke a fundamental change which has resulted from its own acts? An example mentioned in the International Law Commission was whether a state which had transformed itself from an agricultural to an industrial country could claim that change as a ground for terminating a treaty which was based on the previous agricultural character of the country. Since it could not be said that industrialization was a breach of the treaty, the exception in paragraph 2(b) of

Article 62 would not apply. However, when a change is the result of a breach by a party, that party cannot invoke the change as a ground for termination.

4. Does Article 62 apply to treaties which have a fixed duration? Under customary international law, *rebus sic stantibus* was considered inapplicable to treaties containing a fixed term, however long the duration. See Jiménez de Aréchaga, 159 Rec. des Cours at 48. But the Commission considered that a fundamental change of circumstances may occur when a treaty has a fixed term and that it was desirable to apply the rule to such treaties wherever the necessary conditions were met. Is Article 62 in that respect *de lege ferenda?*

5. Does Article 62 permit an automatic extinction of a treaty? Does it provide for an unchallengeable unilateral right to terminate? By its terms, Article 62 confers a right to call for termination. Procedural requirements are laid down for this, as for other grounds of termination, in Articles 65 and 66. These provisions come into play if the claim to termination is disputed. They require that negotiation or other procedures of settlement be used as agreed by the parties. If no solution is reached, a compulsory conciliation procedure may be instituted by any party to the dispute; however, the Conciliation Commission's conclusions are not binding on the parties (Annex V of Vienna Convention). Accordingly, it remains open to a party to maintain its right to terminate on grounds of Article 62, provided that it has complied with the notification and procedural requirements. How effective this will prove in limiting claims based on fundamental change remains to be seen. The Vienna Convention does, however, exclude the right to an absolutely unlimited right to unilateral termination, such as was apparently asserted by the United States in 1941 when the President suspended the operation of the International Load Line Convention of 1930 on grounds of changed shipping conditions brought about by the war in Europe. See 5 Hackworth 355–56; Briggs, The Attorney–General Invokes Rebus Sic Stantibus, 36 A.J.I.L. 89 (1942).

6. International tribunals, while recognizing the principle of *rebus sic stantibus,* have generally avoided terminating treaties on this ground, usually by finding that it did not apply on the facts of the case. This is borne out by the two cases most often cited in this connection. The first is the *Case of the Free Zones* between France and Switzerland decided by the P.C.I.J. in 1932 (see p. 555 supra), in which the Court found that the circumstances which had changed were not those on the basis of which the parties entered into the treaty. The second case is the *Fisheries Jurisdiction Case* between the United Kingdom and Iceland decided by the International Court of Justice in 1973. In that case, the Court considered the applicability of the principle of fundamental change of circumstances in the light of the Vienna Convention. Excerpts from the decision of the Court are given below.

For a detailed treatment of doctrine and state practice prior to the Vienna Convention, see Haraszti, Treaties and the Fundamental Change of Circumstances, 146 Rec. des Cours I (1975–III).

7. May a private party invoke the doctrine of changed circumstances to defeat the application of a treaty? A claimant in a suit against an airline for loss of cargo argued that the limits on liability of the Warsaw Convention of 1929 did not apply because fundamental changes of circumstances had occurred since its conclusion. The U.S. Supreme Court recognized that a party to a treaty might invoke changed circumstances as an excuse for terminating its treaty obligations. However, when the states parties continue to assert the vitality of the treaty, a private person who finds the continued existence of the treaty inconvenient may

not invoke the doctrine of changed circumstances. Trans World Airlines, Inc. v. Franklin Mint, 466 U.S. 243, 104 S.Ct. 1776, 80 L.Ed.2d 273 (1984).

CASE CONCERNING THE GABCIKOVO–NAGYMAROS PROJECT (HUNGARY/SLOVAKIA)

International Court of Justice, 1997.
1997 I.C.J. 7.

[In 1977, when both Hungary and Czechoslovakia were under Communist rule, the two countries concluded a treaty for the construction and operation of a system of locks on the Danube River, comprising *inter alia* a reservoir, dam, bypass canal, hydroelectric power plants, and navigational and flood control improvements. The Danube forms the border between the two countries for a stretch affected by these works and elsewhere flows through their respective territories. Both were expected to benefit from the project. Construction began in 1978 but was not completed.

Beginning in 1989, major transformations took place in the political and economic systems of both countries. Along with these came a heightened environmental consciousness and awareness of potential risks from carrying through with the plans. New political leadership in the two countries expressed objections to the project as originally conceived: the Hungarian government said it was a "mistake" and the Czechoslovak President called it a "totalitarian, gigomaniac monument which is against nature" but emphasized that it was already partly built.

In response to increased criticism of the project among its public, Hungary first suspended its parts of the works in 1989 and later abandoned them. Negotiations between the parties for a mutually satisfactory solution were unsuccessful. Czechoslovakia began work in 1991 on an alternative to the original plan, known as Variant C. This variant was unacceptable to Hungary, which in May 1992 gave notice of termination of the treaty; see p. 542 supra.

Effective January 1, 1993, Czechoslovakia dissolved into two states; Slovakia became independent. Later in 1993, Hungary and Slovakia asked the I.C.J. to decide on the basis of international law several questions, including whether Hungary was entitled to suspend and subsequently abandon its part of the works.

Among Hungary's claimed grounds for termination was changed circumstances, as well as an argument of impossibility. The portions of the Court's judgment dealing with those issues follow.]

102. Hungary also relied on the principle of the impossibility of performance as reflected in Article 61 of the Vienna Convention on the Law of Treaties. Hungary's interpretation of the wording of Article 61 is, however, not in conformity with the terms of that Article, nor with the intention of the Diplomatic Conference which adopted the Convention. * * *

103. Hungary contended that the essential object of the Treaty—an economic joint investment which was consistent with environmental protection and which was operated by the two contracting parties jointly—had permanently disappeared and that the Treaty had thus become impossible to perform. It is not necessary for the Court to determine whether the term "object" in Article 61 can also be understood to embrace a legal régime as in

any event, even if that were the case, it would have to conclude that in this instance that régime had not definitively ceased to exist. The 1977 Treaty * * * actually made available to the parties the necessary means to proceed at any time, by negotiation, to the required readjustments between economic imperatives and ecological imperatives. The Court would add that, if the joint exploitation of the investment was no longer possible, this was originally because Hungary did not carry out most of the works for which it was responsible under the 1977 Treaty; Article 61, paragraph 2 of the Vienna Convention expressly provides that impossibility of performance may not be invoked for the termination of a treaty by a party to that treaty when it results from that party's own breach of an obligation flowing from the treaty.

* * *

104. Hungary further argued that it was entitled to invoke a number of events which, cumulatively, would have constituted a fundamental change of circumstances. In this respect it specified profound changes of a political nature, the Project's diminishing economic viability, the progress of environmental knowledge and the development of new norms and prescriptions of international environmental law.

The Court recalls that, in the *Fisheries Jurisdiction* case (*I.C.J. Reports 1973,* p. 63, para. 36), it stated that,

> "Article 62 of the Vienna Convention on the Law of Treaties . . . may in many respects be considered as a codification of existing customary law on the subject of the termination of a treaty relationship on account of change of circumstances."

The prevailing political situation was certainly relevant for the conclusion of the 1977 Treaty. But the Court will recall that the Treaty provided for a joint investment programme for the production of energy, the control of floods and the improvement of navigation on the Danube. In the Court's view, the prevalent political conditions were thus not so closely linked to the object and purpose of the Treaty that they constituted an essential basis of the consent of the parties and, in changing, radically altered the extent of the obligations still to be performed. The same holds good for the economic system in force at the time of the conclusion of the 1977 Treaty. Besides, even though the estimated profitability of the Project might have appeared less in 1992 than in 1977, it does not appear from the record before the Court that it was bound to diminish to such an extent that the treaty obligations of the parties would have been radically transformed as a result.

The Court does not consider that new developments in the state of environmental knowledge and of environmental law can be said to have been completely unforeseen. What is more, the formulation of [the treaty articles] designed to accommodate change, made it possible for the parties to take account of such developments and to apply them when implementing those treaty provisions.

The changed circumstances advanced by Hungary are, in the Court's view, not of such a nature, either individually or collectively, that their effect would radically transform the extent of the obligations still to be performed in order to accomplish the Project. A fundamental change of circumstances must have been unforeseen; the existence of the circumstances at the time of the

Treaty's conclusion must have constituted an essential basis of the consent of the parties to be bound by the Treaty. The negative and conditional wording of Article 62 of the Vienna Convention on the Law of Treaties is a clear indication moreover that the stability of treaty relations requires that the plea of fundamental change of circumstances be applied only in exceptional cases.

THE FISHERIES JURISDICTION CASE(UNITED KINGDOM v. ICELAND)

International Court of Justice, 1973.
1973 I.C.J. 3.

[On April 14, 1972, the United Kingdom filed an Application before the International Court of Justice instituting proceedings against Iceland challenging the proposed extension of Iceland's exclusive fisheries jurisdiction from 12 to 50 miles around its shores. The United Kingdom founded the Court's jurisdiction on Article 36, paragraph 1, of the Court's Statute and a March 11, 1961, Exchange of Notes between the two countries under which the United Kingdom recognized Iceland's claim to a 12–mile fisheries limit in return for Iceland's agreement that any dispute as to the extension of Icelandic fisheries jurisdiction beyond the 12–mile limit "shall, at the request of either party, be referred to the International Court of Justice." Iceland, however, was not willing to have the I.C.J. hear the dispute in 1972 and absented itself from the proceedings. In a letter to the Registrar of the Court dated May 29, 1972, Iceland asserted that because of changed circumstances the 1961 Exchange of Notes was no longer applicable.

With respect to questions relating to fundamental change of circumstances, the decision of the Court contained the following paragraphs:]

31. * * * The argument of Iceland appears * * * to be that, because of the general trend of development of international law on the subject of fishery limits during the last ten years, the right of exclusive fisheries jurisdiction to a distance of 12 miles from the baselines of the territorial sea has been increasingly recognized and claimed by States, including the applicant State itself. It would then appear to be contended that the compromissory clause was the price paid by Iceland for the recognition at that time of the 12–mile fishery limit by the other party. It is consequently asserted that if today the 12–mile fishery limit is generally recognized, there would be a failure of consideration relieving Iceland of its commitment because of the changed legal circumstances. * * *

32. While changes in the law may under certain conditions constitute valid grounds for invoking a change of circumstances affecting the duration of a treaty, the Icelandic contention is not relevant to the present case. The motive which induced Iceland to enter into the 1961 Exchange of Notes may well have been the interest of obtaining an immediate recognition of an exclusive fisheries jurisdiction to a distance of 12 miles in the waters around its territory. It may also be that this interest has in the meantime disappeared, since a 12–mile fishery zone is now asserted by the other contracting party in respect of its own fisheries jurisdiction. But in the present case, the object and purpose of the 1961 Exchange of Notes, and therefore the circumstances which constituted an essential basis of the consent of both parties to

be bound by the agreement embodied therein, had a much wider scope. That object and purpose was not merely to decide upon the Icelandic claim to fisheries jurisdiction up to 12 miles, but also to provide a means whereby the parties might resolve the question of the validity of any further claims. This follows not only from the text of the agreement but also from the history of the negotiations, that is to say, from the whole set of circumstances which must be taken into account in determining what induced both parties to agree to the 1961 Exchange of Notes.

34. It is possible that today Iceland may find that some of the motives which induced it to enter into the 1961 Exchange of Notes have become less compelling or have disappeared altogether. But this is not a ground justifying the repudiation of those parts of the agreement the object and purpose of which have remained unchanged. Iceland has derived benefits from the executed provisions of the agreement, such as the recognition by the United Kingdom since 1961 of a 12-mile exclusive fisheries jurisdiction, the acceptance by the United Kingdom of the baselines established by Iceland and the relinquishment in a period of three years of the preexisting traditional fishing by vessels registered in the United Kingdom. Clearly it then becomes incumbent on Iceland to comply with its side of the bargain, which is to accept the testing before the Court of the validity of its further claims to extended jurisdiction. Moreover, in the case of a treaty which is in part executed and in part executory, in which one of the parties has already benefited from the executed provisions of the treaty, it would be particularly inadmissible to allow that party to put an end to obligations which were accepted under the treaty by way of *quid pro quo* for the provisions which the other party has already executed.

* * *

35. In his letter of 29 May 1972 to the Registrar, the Minister for Foreign Affairs of Iceland refers to "the changed circumstances resulting from the ever-increasing exploitation of the fishery resources in the seas surrounding Iceland." * * *

37. One of the basic requirements embodied in [Article 62 of the Vienna Convention, which the Court considers customary law] is that the change of circumstances must have been a fundamental one. In this respect the Government of Iceland has, with regard to developments in fishing techniques, referred in an official publication on *Fisheries Jurisdiction in Iceland,* enclosed with the Foreign Minister's letter of 29 May 1972 to the Registrar, to the increased exploitation of the fishery resources in the seas surrounding Iceland and to the danger of still further exploitation because of an increase in the catching capacity of fishing fleets. The Icelandic statements recall the exceptional dependence of that country on its fishing for its existence and economic development. * * *

39. The Applicant, for its part, contends that the alterations and progress in fishing techniques have not produced in the waters around Iceland the consequences apprehended by Iceland and therefore that the changes are not of a fundamental or vital character. In its Memorial, it points out that, as regards the capacity of fishing fleets, increases in the efficiency of individual trawlers have been counter-balanced by the reduction in total numbers of vessels in national fleets fishing in the waters around Iceland, and that the

statistics show that the total annual catch of demersal species has varied to no great extent since 1960.

40. The Court, at the present stage of the proceedings, does not need to pronounce on this question of fact, as to which there appears to be a serious divergence of views between the two Governments. If, as contended by Iceland, there have been any fundamental changes in fishing techniques in the waters around Iceland, those changes might be relevant for the decision on the merits of the dispute, and the Court might need to examine the contention at that stage, together with any other arguments that Iceland might advance in support of the validity of the extension of its fisheries jurisdiction beyond what was agreed to in the 1961 Exchange of Notes. But the alleged changes could not affect in the least the obligation to submit to the Court's jurisdiction, which is the only issue at the present stage of the proceedings. It follows that the apprehended dangers for the vital interests of Iceland, resulting from changes in fishing techniques, cannot constitute a fundamental change with respect to the lapse or subsistence of the compromissory clause establishing the Court's jurisdiction. * * *

43. Moreover, in order that a change of circumstances may give rise to a ground for invoking the termination of a treaty it is also necessary that it should have resulted in a radical transformation of the extent of the obligations still to be performed. The change must have increased the burden of the obligations to be executed to the extent of rendering the performance something essentially different from that originally undertaken. In respect of the obligation with which the Court is here concerned, this condition is wholly unsatisfied; the change of circumstances alleged by Iceland cannot be said to have transformed radically the extent of the jurisdictional obligation which is imposed in the 1961 Exchange of Notes. The compromissory clause enabled either of the parties to submit to the Court any dispute between them relating to an extension of Icelandic fisheries jurisdiction in the waters above its continental shelf beyond the 12–mile limit. The present dispute is exactly of the character anticipated in the compromissory clause of the Exchange of Notes. Not only has the jurisdictional obligation not been radically transformed in its extent; it has remained precisely what it was in 1961.

* * *

44. In the United Kingdom Memorial it is asserted that there is a flaw in the Icelandic contention of change of circumstances: that the doctrine never operates so as to extinguish a treaty automatically or to allow an unchallengeable unilateral denunciation by one party; it only operates to confer a right to call for termination and, if that call is disputed, to submit the dispute to some organ or body with power to determine whether the conditions for the operation of the doctrine are present. In this connection the Applicant alludes to Articles 65 and 66 of the Vienna Convention on the Law of Treaties. Those Articles provide that where the parties to a treaty have failed within 12 months to achieve a settlement of a dispute by the means indicated in Article 33 of the United Nations Charter (which means include reference to judicial settlement) any one of the parties may submit the dispute to the procedure for conciliation provided in the Annex to the Convention.

45. In the present case, the procedural complement to the doctrine of changed circumstances is already provided for in the 1961 Exchange of Notes,

which specifically calls upon the parties to have recourse to the Court in the event of a dispute relating to Iceland's extension of fisheries jurisdiction. * * *

E. WAR BETWEEN CONTRACTING PARTIES

The Vienna Convention does not contain any provision concerning the effect of the outbreak of hostilities upon treaties. (Compare Article 73, that the Convention "shall not prejudge any question" arising from the outbreak of hostilities.) The International Law Commission explained that it:

> * * * considered that the study of this topic would inevitably involve a consideration of the effect of the provisions of the Charter concerning the threat or use of force upon the legality of the recourse to the particular hostilities in question; and it did not feel that this question could conveniently be dealt with in the context of its present work upon the law of treaties.

[1966] II Yb.I.L.C. 176 (para. 29).

Case-law and scholars have, however, dealt with such questions, as indicated in the following materials.

TECHT v. HUGHES

Court of Appeals of New York, 1920.
229 N.Y. 222, 128 N.E. 185, cert. denied, 254 U.S. 643, 41 S.Ct. 14, 65 L.Ed. 454.

[An American citizen died intestate in New York, where he owned real property, on December 27, 1917, twenty days after the outbreak of war between the United States and Austria–Hungary. One of the decedent's two daughters, Mrs. Techt, had previously married a citizen of Austria–Hungary and had, under Federal legislation then in force, thereby lost her United States citizenship and acquired that of her husband. The New York statute allowed citizens and "alien friends" to take and hold real property. Mrs. Techt's sister claimed the whole property on the ground that Mrs. Techt was an "alien enemy," but the Appellate Division pointed out that neither Mrs. Techt nor her husband had been interned or subjected to other restrictions as enemy nationals and held that Mrs. Techt was an "alien friend." 188 App. Div. 743, 177 N.Y.S. 420 (First Dep't 1919). On the sister's appeal, Mrs. Techt also relied on the Treaty of 1848 between the United States and Austria, 9 Stat. 944, which provided that nationals of either state could take real property by descent, sell it within two years, and remove the proceeds thereof. The Court of Appeals decided that Mrs. Techt, despite the absence of restrictions, was not an alien friend and not entitled to the statute's protection. Her claim therefore depended entirely upon the continuing effectiveness, despite the state of war, of the Treaty of 1848.]

CARDOZO, J. * * * The support of the statute failing, there remains the question of the treaty. The treaty, if in force, is the supreme law of the land (Const. U.S. art. 6) and supersedes all local laws inconsistent with its terms * * *. The plaintiff has an estate of inheritance, if the treaty is in force.

The effect of war upon the existing treaties of belligerents is one of the unsettled problems of the law. The older writers sometimes said that treaties ended ipso facto when war came. 3 Phillimore, Int. L. 794. The writers of our own time reject these sweeping statements. 2 Oppenheim, Int. L. § 99; Hall, Int. L. 398, 401; Fiore, Int.L. (Borchard's Transl.) § 845. International law today does not preserve treaties or annul them, regardless of the effects produced. It deals with such problems pragmatically, preserving or annulling as the necessities of war exact. It establishes standards, but it does not fetter itself with rules. When it attempts to do more, it finds that there is neither unanimity of opinion nor uniformity of practice. "The whole question remains as yet unsettled." Oppenheim, supra. This does not mean, of course, that there are not some classes of treaties about which there is general agreement. Treaties of alliance fall. Treaties of boundary or cession, "dispositive" or "transitory" conventions, survive. Hall, Int.L. pp. 398, 401; 2 Westlake, Int.L. 34; Oppenheim, supra. So, of course, do treaties which regulate the conduct of hostilities. Hall, supra; 5 Moore, Dig. Int. L. 372; Society for Propagation of the Gospel v. Town of New Haven, 8 Wheat. 464, 494, 5 L.Ed. 662.

Intention in such circumstances is clear. These instances do not represent distinct and final principles. They are illustrations of the same principle. They are applications of a standard. When I ask what that principle or standard is, and endeavor to extract it from the long chapters in the books, I get this, and nothing more: That provisions compatible with a state of hostilities, unless expressly terminated, will be enforced, and those incompatible rejected.

> Treaties lose their efficacy in war only if their execution is incompatible with war. Les traités ne perdent leur efficacité en temps de guerre que si leur exécution est incompatible avec la guerre elle-même.

Bluntschli, Droit International Codifié, sec. 538.

That in substance was Kent's view, here as often in advance of the thought of his day:

> All those duties, of which the exercise is not necessarily suspended by the war, subsist in their full force. The obligation of keeping faith is so far from ceasing in time of war that its efficacy becomes increased, from the increased necessity of it.

1 Kent, Comm. p. 176.

That, also, more recently, is the conclusion embodied by the Institute of the International Law in the rules voted at Christiania in 1912, which defined the effects of war on international conventions. In these rules, some classes of treaties are dealt with specially and apart. Treaties of alliance, those which establish a protectorate or a sphere of influence, and generally treaties of a political nature, are, it is said, dissolved. Dissolved, too, are treaties which have relation to the cause of war. But the general principle is declared that treaties which it is reasonably practicable to execute after the outbreak of hostilities must be observed then, as in the past. The belligerents are at liberty to disregard them only to the extent and for the time required by the necessities of war. * * *

This, I think, is the principle which must guide the judicial department of the government when called upon to determine during the progress of a war whether a treaty shall be observed, in the absence of some declaration by the political departments of the government that it has been suspended or annulled. A treaty has a two-fold aspect. In its primary operation, it is a compact between independent states. In its secondary operation, it is a source of private rights for individuals within states. Head Money Cases, 112 U.S. 580, 598, 5 Sup.Ct. 247, 28 L.Ed. 798. Granting that the termination of the compact involves the termination of the rights, it does not follow, because there is a privilege to rescind, that the privilege has been exercised. The question is not what states may do after war has supervened, and this without breach of their duty as members of the society of nations. The question is what courts are to presume that they have done. * * *

President and Senate may denounce the treaty, and thus terminate its life. Congress may enact an inconsistent rule, which will control the action of the courts. * * * The treaty of peace itself may set up new relations, and terminate earlier compacts, either tacitly or expressly. The proposed treaties with Germany and Austria give the victorious powers the privilege of choosing the treaties which are to be kept in force or abrogated. But until some one of these things is done, until some one of these events occurs, while war is still flagrant, and the will of the political departments of the government unrevealed, the courts, as I view their function, play a humbler and more cautious part. It is not for them to denounce treaties generally en bloc. Their part it is, as one provision or another is involved in some actual controversy before them, to determine whether, alone or by force of connection with an inseparable scheme, the provision is inconsistent with the policy or safety of the nation in the emergency of war, and hence presumably intended to be limited to times of peace. The mere fact that other portions of the treaty are suspended, or even abrogated, is not conclusive. The treaty does not fall in its entirety unless it has the character of an indivisible act. * * *

To determine whether it has this character, it is not enough to consider its name or label. No general formula suffices. We must consult in each case the nature and purpose of the specific articles involved. * * *

I find nothing incompatible with the policy of the government, with the safety of the nation, or with the maintenance of the war in the enforcement of this treaty, so as to sustain the plaintiff's title. We do not confiscate the lands or goods of the stranger within our gates. If we permit him to remain, he is free during good behavior to buy property and sell it. Trading with Enemy Act Oct. 6, 1917, 40 Stat. 411, c. 106. * * * A public policy not outraged by purchase will not be outraged by inheritance.

The plaintiff is a resident; but even if she were a nonresident, and were within the hostile territory, the policy of the nation would not divest her of the title whether acquired before the war or later. Custody would then be assumed by the Alien Property Custodian. The proceeds of the property, in the event of sale, would be kept within the jurisdiction. * * *

I do not overlook the statements which may be found here and there in the works of authors of distinction (Hall, supra; Halleck, Int. L. [4th Ed.] 314; Wheaton, Int. L. [5th Ed.] 377) that treaties of commerce and navigation are to be ranked in the class of treaties which war abrogates or at least suspends. Commerce is friendly intercourse. Friendly intercourse between nations is impossible in war. Therefore treaties regulating such intercourse are not operative in war. But stipulations do not touch commerce because they happen to be embodied in a treaty which is styled one to regulate or encourage commerce. We must be on our guard against being misled by labels. Bluntschli's warning, already quoted, reminds us that the nature and not the name of covenants determines whether they shall be disregarded or observed. * * *

Restrictions upon ownership of land by aliens have a history all their own, unrelated altogether to restrictions upon trade. * * * When removed, they cease to exist for enemies as well as friends, unless the statute removing them enforces a distinction. * * * More than that, the removal, when effected by treaty, gives reciprocal privileges to the subjects of each state, and is thus of value to one side as much as to the other. For this reason, the inference is a strong one, as was pointed out by the Master of the Rolls in Sutton v. Sutton, 1 Russ. & M. 664, 675, that the privileges, unless expressly revoked are intended to endure. Cf. 2 Westlake, p. 33; also Halleck, Int. L., supra. There, as in Society for Propagation of the Gospel v. Town of New Haven, 8 Wheat. 464, 494, 5 L.Ed. 662, the treaty of 1794 between the United States and England, protecting the citizens of each in the enjoyment of their landed property, was held not to have been abrogated by the war of 1812. Undoubtedly there is a distinction between those cases and this, in that there the rights had become vested before the outbreak of the war. None the less, alike in reasoning and in conclusion, they have their value and significance. If stipulations governing the tenure of land survive the stress of war, though contained in a treaty which is described as one of amity, it is not perceived why they may not also survive, though contained in a treaty which is described as one of commerce. In preserving the right of inheritance for citizens of Austria when the land inherited is here we preserve the same right for our citizens when the land inherited is there. * * * Congress has not yet commanded us, and the exigencies of war, as I view them, do not constrain us, to throw these benefits away.

No one can study the vague and wavering statements of treaties and decision in this field of international law with any feeling of assurance at the end that he has chosen the right path. One looks in vain either for uniformity of doctrine or for scientific accuracy of exposition. There are wise cautions for the statesmen. There are few precepts for the judge. All the more, in this uncertainty, I am impelled to the belief that, until the political departments have acted, the courts, in refusing to give effect to treaties, should limit their refusal to the needs of the occasion; that they are not bound by any rigid formula to nullify the whole or nothing; and that, in determining whether this treaty survived the coming of war, they are free to make choice of the conclusion which shall seem the most in keeping with the traditions of the law, the policy of the statutes, the dictates of fair dealing, and the honor of the nation.

Judgment affirmed.

Note

What did the court mean by its reference to the "compatibility" of the treaty with "the policy or safety of the nation in the emergency of war"? How is this "compatibility" related to the intentions of the parties? What standards of "compatibility" did the court have in mind, and to what sources of policy did it look? Would the following statement of Secretary of State Lansing, if it had been brought to the court's attention, have required a different result? "[I]n view of the present state of war between the United States and Austria–Hungary and Germany, the Department does not regard these provisions [relating to inheritance of real property] as now in operation." Letter to the Alien Property Custodian, September 10, 1918, 5 Hackworth 379. The Supreme Court stated in Clark v. Allen, 331 U.S. 503, 513, 67 S.Ct. 1431, 1437, 91 L.Ed. 1633 (1947), that "[w]here the relevant historical sources and the instrument itself give no plain indication that it is to become inoperative in whole or in part on the outbreak of war, we are left to determine as *Techt v. Hughes,* supra, indicates, whether the provision under which rights are asserted is incompatible with national policy in time of war." The court held that a treaty provision similar to that involved in *Techt v. Hughes* was not incompatible with national policy. Compare Karnuth v. United States ex rel. Albro, 279 U.S. 231, 49 S.Ct. 274, 73 L.Ed. 677 (1929), in which Article III of the Jay Treaty of 1794, 8 Stat. 116, which provided for the free passage and repassage of British and United States citizens across the Canadian border, was held to have been abrogated by the war of 1812. The Court pointed out that the treaty provision was "wholly promissory and prospective and necessarily ceases to operate in a state of war, since the passing and repassing of citizens or subjects of one sovereignty into the territory of another is inconsistent with the condition of hostility." The Court held that the "provision belongs to the class of treaties which does not survive war" between the parties. 279 U.S. at 240, 49 S.Ct. at 277, 73 L.Ed. at 682.

THE EFFECTS OF ARMED CONFLICTS ON TREATIES RESOLUTION OF THE INSTITUT DE DROIT INTERNATIONAL

Adopted 1985 (Helsinki Session).

Article 1

For the purposes of this Resolution, the term "armed conflict" means a state of war or an international conflict which involve armed operations which by their nature or extent are likely to affect the operation of treaties between States parties to the armed conflict or between States parties to the armed conflict and third States, regardless of a formal declaration of war or other declaration by any or all of the parties to the armed conflict.

Article 2

The outbreak of an armed conflict does not *ipso facto* terminate or suspend the operation of treaties in force between the parties to the armed conflict.

Article 3

The outbreak of an armed conflict renders operative, in accordance with their own provisions, between the parties treaties which expressly provide that they are to be operative during an armed conflict or which by reason of their nature or purpose are to be regarded as operative during an armed conflict.

Article 4

The existence of an armed conflict does not entitle a party unilaterally to terminate or to suspend the operation of treaty provisions relating to the protection of the human person, unless the treaty otherwise provides.

ARTICLE 5

The outbreak of an armed conflict does not *ipso facto* terminate or suspend the operation of bilateral treaties in force between a party to that conflict and third States.

The outbreak of an armed conflict between some of the parties to a multilateral treaty does not *ipso facto* terminate or suspend the operation of that treaty between other contracting States or between them and the States parties to the armed conflict.

ARTICLE 6

A treaty establishing an international organization is not affected by the existence of an armed conflict between any of its parties.

ARTICLE 7

A State exercising its right of individual or collective self-defence in accordance with the Charter of the United Nations is entitled to suspend in whole or in part the operation of a treaty incompatible with the exercise of that right, subject to any consequences resulting from a later determination by the Security Council of that State as an aggressor.

ARTICLE 8

A State complying with a resolution by the Security Council of the United Nations concerning action with respect to threats to the peace, breaches of the peace or acts of aggression shall either terminate or suspend the operation of a treaty which would be incompatible with such resolution.

ARTICLE 9

A State committing aggression within the meaning of the Charter of the United Nations and Resolution 3314 (XXIX) of the General Assembly of the United Nations shall not terminate or suspend the operation of a treaty if the effect would be to benefit that State.

ARTICLE 10

This Resolution does not prejudge rights and duties arising from neutrality.

ARTICLE 11

At the end of an armed conflict and unless otherwise agreed, the operation of a treaty which has been suspended should be resumed as soon as possible.

Notes

1. What are the implications of the distinction drawn in the above resolution between rights of states acting in self-defense and rights of aggressor states? If contradictory claims as to legality are made by the parties to armed conflicts and no authoritative determination is made by the U.N. Security Council, would states in conflict be entitled to determine unilaterally whether they may suspend treaties

considered incompatible with their exercise of the right of self-defense? Would the practical effects be different if the above resolution were followed instead of the rationale in *Techt v. Hughes?*

2. The resolution adopted by the *Institut* in 1985 followed several years of study and discussion. For reports and comments see Annuaire de l'Institut, volumes 59–I, p. 201–284 (1981), 59–II, p. 175–244 (1981), 61–I, p. 1–25 (1985), 61–II (1986).

3. The hostilities between the United States and Iran following the Iranian Revolution in 1979 raised some question of whether their bilateral treaties still remained in force. Concurring in Sedco, Inc. v. National Iranian Oil Company and the Islamic Republic of Iran, 84 I.L.R. 521 (Iran–U.S.C.T.R. Mar. 27, 1986), Judge Brower rejected Iran's claim that the Treaty of Amity, Economic Relations, and Consular Rights between the United States and Iran was no longer applicable because of the souring of relations. Judge Brower pointed to statements by Iran subsequent to the Iranian Revolution referring to the continued validity of the treaty and Iran's failure to give notice of termination pursuant to the terms of the treaty.

4. Did agreements between Iraq and other states survive the outbreak of military conflict with Kuwait in 1990 and with the U.N.-authorized coalition in 1991? The Security Council several times called upon Iraq to comply with its obligations under international treaties, especially those having to do with the laws of war and warfare and with control of weapons of mass destruction. See, e.g., S.C. Res. 664 (1990); S.C. Res. 687 (1991). However, the economic sanctions imposed on Iraq beginning with Resolution 661 (1990), which were continued in effect with Resolution 687 (1991) on the terms for ending the hostilities, interrupted normal commercial and financial relationships with Iraq. Measures ordered by the Security Council in the exercise of its compulsory powers in relation to international peace and security would prevail over any inconsistent treaty obligation. See U.N. Charter, Article 103.

As of 2000, Iraq remains under the compulsory sanctions regime stemming from the 1990–1991 hostilities. See Chapters 9 and 12.

SECTION 7. STATE SUCCESSION IN RESPECT OF TREATIES

A. GENERAL COMMENTS ON SUCCESSION TO TREATY OBLIGATIONS AND RIGHTS

1. Introduction

"Succession of states" refers to the fact of replacement of one state by another in the responsibility for the international relations of territory. That factual event is to be distinguished from its legal consequences, such as the transfer of rights or obligations on the occurrence of that event. This section deals with the rights and obligations in respect of treaties which derive from the factual change in the state responsible for international relations of a territory.

The replacement of one state by another is different, of course, from the changes in government which take place without affecting the legal identity of the state (see Chapter 4). Even a "social revolution" is considered only to change the régime and not the continuity of the state.

Succession of states has been a persistent feature of international history. The consolidation of national states, the creation of empires and their break-up, the secession of states, annexation, merger and consolidation, and, after the Second World War, decolonization are the historical events which have given rise to the legal questions of inheritance or devolution of rights and obligations in regard to treaties. From 1950 through the 1980s, the problems of state succession were most prominently associated with decolonization and the legal answers were largely addressed to those problems.

In the 1990s, new problems of succession arose, particularly in Europe. The unification of the two German states in 1990 raised questions of succession with respect to hundreds of treaties of practical importance. Even more complicated were the treaty succession issues presented by the dissolution of the Soviet Union in 1991 into 15 states, with perhaps more to come. The break-up of Yugoslavia into 5 states in 1992 and the splitting of Czechoslovakia into two in 1993 also raised problems of treaty succession that included novel aspects. Secessionist movements are on the increase in many countries and it is almost certain that new states will emerge. It is also safe to anticipate that some existing states will merge or be absorbed into other states and that some boundaries will be changed. Treaty succession questions will require solutions for all such cases.

The legal consequences of state succession arise in respect of matters other than treaties. For example, questions arise in regard to the "inheritance" of state property, fiscal claims, public debt, state contracts and concessions, nationality and transmissibility of state responsibility. These matters are dealt with separately from questions concerning treaties. See Chapters 4, 6 and 9.

Note

The terminology of succession can be confusing or ambiguous in some situations. For example, although numerous succession problems arose from the disintegration of the USSR, they are not all of the same character and it may be misleading to apply the same terms to them. The Russian Federation asserted that it was a "continuing state" or "continuator" of the USSR rather than, strictly speaking, a "successor" to it: in other words, it remained the same subject of international law (though with smaller territory and population after the dissolution). With the agreement or acquiescence of the other constituents of the ex-USSR and its treaty partners, the Russian Federation "continued" on the international plane the legal subjectivity of the USSR and all its treaty relationships. However, one will often encounter the term "successor" as applied to the Russian Federation, notwithstanding Russia's own preference for the concept of "continuator." Analytically, the notion of a *state* as "continuator" is distinct from a "continuity theory" of certain treaty relationships in respect of new subjects of international law. See generally Mullerson, The Continuity and Succession of States, by Reference to the Former USSR and Yugoslavia, 42 I.C.L.Q. 473, 475–480 (1993); Hafner & Kornfeind, The Recent Austrian Practice of State Succession: Does the Clean Slate Rule Still Exist?, 1 Austrian Rev. Int'l & Eur. L. 1, 10–13 (1996).

As noted in Chapter 4, in the case of the disintegration of Yugoslavia, no one of the resulting republics was accepted as a continuator or sole successor to the former Socialist Federal Republic of Yugoslavia (SFRY); rather, all five were viewed as successor states. Some of them affirmed continuity of the treaties of the SFRY, while in other cases new instruments of accession were registered. These legal distinctions raise questions with important practical consequences: for example, if there had been any gap in the applicability of human rights treaties within the several successors to the SFRY, such a lapse might affect the possibility of bringing claims under them. The Human Rights Committee and the International Court of Justice have confirmed the essential continuity of obligations under the human rights treaties of the SFRY throughout the territories of all the successor states. See Human Rights Committee, General Comment No. 26, p. 540 supra; compare Case Concerning Application of the Genocide Convention (Bosnia–Herzegovina v. Federal Republic of Yugoslavia (Serbia–Montenegro)), 1996 I.C.J. 595, 610–612 (Jurisdiction); see also Mullerson, pp. 489–492.

2. *Devolution Agreements*

In a number of cases, predecessor and successor states have made agreements concerning the "devolution" of rights and obligations under treaties. Such agreements were generally used by the United Kingdom when transferring sovereignty to former colonial territories. Some other colonial powers also had such agreements. Under their terms, they deal only with the transfer of treaty rights and obligations from predecessor to successor. They do not in themselves bind other states parties to the predecessor's treaties. The International Law Commission has commented on such agreements, as follows:

> (18) The practice of States does not admit, therefore, the conclusion that a devolution agreement should be considered as by itself creating a legal nexus between the successor State and third States parties, in relation to treaties applicable to the successor State's territory prior to its independence. Some successor States and some third States parties to one of those treaties have undoubtedly tended to regard a devolution agreement as creating a certain presumption of the continuance in force of certain types of treaties. But neither successor States nor third States nor depositaries have as a general rule attributed automatic effects to devolution agreements. Accordingly, State practice as well as the relevant principles of the law of treaties would seem to indicate that devolution agreements, however important as general manifestations of the attitude of successor States to the treaties of their predecessors, should be considered as *res inter alios acta* for the purposes of their relations with third States.

[1974] II (I) Yb.I.L.C. 186.

In the case of the reunification of Germany, the problems of treaty succession of the two states were dealt with principally by three treaties entered into by the two German states. One of the treaties, the Treaty of Final Settlement of 1990, was also signed by the four main allies of World War Two; it terminated the rights and responsibilities of the four powers and the quadripartite treaties relating to Germany. 29 I.L.M. 1186 (1990). This treaty (also known as the Two Plus Four treaty) also provided that the current external borders of the two states shall be final. The right of united Germany to belong to alliances was also recognized.

Another treaty, the Treaty on Unification of September 18, 1990, recognized that the treaties in force in the Federal Republic (i.e., West Germany) before unification now extend to the territory of the former East German state (G.D.R.). With respect to treaties of the former G.D.R. the Unification Treaty calls for consultation with the other parties to settle the questions of continuity, adjustment or termination. A third treaty (the "State Treaty") established the union between the two parts of Germany and laid down fundamental constitutional principles. As indicated, these treaties on unification still leave open for consultation which treaties of the former GDR will continue in force for that territory. It is recognized that "GDR treaties with ideological-political contents inconsistent with the attitude of the unified state are no longer valid." H. Steinberger, Germany Reunified: International and Constitutional Problems. 1992 Brigham Young U.L.Rev. 23.

Note

The situation of dissolution of the USSR was factually more complex, but an analogue to an agreement between predecessor and successors could be found in several instruments concluded just before and shortly after dissolution, among the republics that agreed to form the Commonwealth of Independent States. These included a memorandum of understanding on issues of succession to treaties. See 32 I.L.M. 138 (1992) and documents cited in Mullerson, 42 I.C.L.Q. at 479–480 (1993); Hafner & Kornfeind, 1 Austrian Rev. Int'l & Eur. L. at 10–13 (1996).

3. Unilateral Declarations by Successor States

A number of newly independent states have made unilateral declarations of a general character regarding the continuation of treaties of their predecessor states. Such declarations have varied in form but have generally provided for the provisional application of such treaties during a period in which the new state would examine the treaties and determine which would be adopted and which terminated. Such declarations were designed to avoid sudden discontinuity and also to avoid an assumption of universal succession. They came to be known as "pick and choose" declarations. For examples of such declarations, see [1974] II (I) Yb.I.L.C. 188–192. The International Law Commission described the legal effect of such agreements, as follows:

> Accordingly, the legal effect of the declarations seems to be that they furnish bases for a *collateral* agreement in simplified form between the newly independent State and the individual parties to its predecessor's treaties for the provisional application of the treaties after independence. The agreement may be express but may equally arise from the conduct of any individual State party to any treaty covered by the declaration, in particular from acts showing that it regards the treaty as still having application with respect to the territory.

[1974] II (I) Yb.I.L.C. 192.

4. The Vienna Convention on the Succession of States in Respect of Treaties

The comprehensive Vienna Convention on the Succession of States in Respect of Treaties was concluded in 1978 by a conference convened by the

United Nations. One hundred states participated in the conference. The Vienna Convention on Succession in Respect of Treaties was the culmination of work commenced by the International Law Commission in 1962 and carried out by the Commission and governments on the basis of draft articles and commentaries prepared by special rapporteurs during the decade 1964 to 1974. It entered into force on November 6, 1996, after 15 states had finally ratified or acceded to it.

As of 2000, only 17 states were parties to the Succession Convention. This meager number of adherences casts doubt on whether states have accepted it as reflecting customary international law. Of those 17 states, a total of 5 ex-Yugoslav, 2 ex-Czechoslovak, and 2 ex-Soviet states make up a majority; most other regions are represented by at most one or two states. Like the Vienna Convention on the Law of Treaties, the Succession Convention was in large part intended to codify customary law, but it cannot be presumed that all articles are declaratory. The U.S. State Department Legal Advisor stated that the rules of the Vienna Convention were "generally regarded as declarative of existing customary international law by the United States." Robert Owen quoted in M. Leich, Digest of US Practice (1980) 1041 n. 43. In at least some aspects, international courts have treated it as codificatory of customary law. See the 1997 *Gabcikovo* case, pp. 574–576 infra. In other respects, however, the existence of state practice to validate the claim that it reflects custom is questionable.

The Convention by its terms applies only in respect of a succession of states which has occurred after the entry into force of the Convention except as otherwise agreed. Agreements to apply the Convention to earlier treaties may be made by declarations of successor states in relation to any other state accepting such declaration (Article 7). The Convention includes the "saving clause" that the non-retroactivity provision is without prejudice to the application of any rules to which states would be subject under international law independently of the Convention.

The material which follows will deal with the major features of the new Convention. Explanatory material is taken largely from the authoritative commentary of the International Law Commission in its report of 1974. That report and earlier special reports of the rapporteurs also contain extensive material on cases and treaty practice. References to articles in the material that follows are to the articles of the Convention.

5. *The Restatement (Third)*

Section 210 of the Restatement (Third) provides:

Section 210. State Succession: International Agreements

(1) When part of the territory of a state becomes territory of another state, the international agreements of the predecessor state cease to have effect in respect of that territory and the international agreements of the successor state come into force there.

(2) When a state is absorbed by another state, the international agreements of the absorbed state are terminated and the international agreements of the absorbing state become applicable to the territory of the absorbed state.

(3) When part of a state becomes a new state, the new state does not succeed to the international agreements to which the predecessor state was party, unless, expressly or by implication, it accepts such agreements and the other party or parties thereto agree or acquiesce.

(4) Preexisting boundary and other territorial agreements continue to be binding notwithstanding Subsections (1)-(3).

The above text is generally consistent with the Vienna Convention but varies from it in certain respects. For example, it rejects the distinction made in the Vienna Convention between newly independent states emerging from colonialism and states ensuing from separation of parts of a State. See Section C–D below.

B. TREATIES NOT AFFECTED BY SUCCESSION OF STATES (TERRITORIAL TREATIES)

INTERNATIONAL LAW COMMISSION REPORT

[1974] II (I) Yb.I.L.C. 157, 196, 201, 206.

(1) Both in the writings of jurists and in State practice frequent reference is made to certain categories of treaties, variously described as of a "territorial," "dispositive," "real" or "localized" character, as binding upon the territory affected notwithstanding any succession of States. The question of what will for convenience be called in this commentary "territorial treaties" is at once important, complex and controversial. In order to underline its importance the Commission need only mention that it touches such major matters as international boundaries, rights of transit on international waterways or over another State, the use of international rivers, demilitarization or neutralization of particular localities, etc.

* * *

(17) The weight of the evidence of State practice and of legal opinion in favour of the view that in principle a boundary settlement is unaffected by the occurrence of a succession of States is strong and powerfully reinforced by the decision of the United Nations Conference on the Law of Treaties to except from the fundamental change of circumstances rule a treaty which establishes a boundary. Consequently, the Commission considered that the present draft must state that boundary settlements are not affected by the occurrence of a succession of States as such. Such a provision would relate exclusively to the effect of the succession of States on the boundary settlement. It would leave untouched any other ground of claiming the revision or setting aside of the boundary settlement, whether self-determination or the invalidity or termination of the treaty. Equally, of course, it would leave untouched any legal ground of defence to such a claim that might exist. In short, the mere occurrence of a succession of States would neither consecrate the existing boundary if it was open to challenge nor deprive it of its character as legally established boundary, if such it was at the date of the succession of States.

* * *

Running through the precedents and the opinions of writers are strong indications of a belief that certain treaties attach a régime to territory which continues to bind it in the hands of any successor State. Not infrequently other elements enter into the picture, such as an allegation of fundamental change of circumstances or the allegedly limited competence of the predecessor State, and the successor State in fact claims to be free of the obligation to respect the régime. Nevertheless, the indications of the general acceptance of such a principle remain. * * * The evidence does not, however, suggest that this category of treaties should embrace a very wide range of so-called territorial treaties. On the contrary, this category seems to be limited to cases where a State by a treaty grants a right to use territory, or to restrict its own use of territory, which is intended to attach to territory of a foreign State or, alternatively, to be for the benefit of a group of States or of all States generally. There must in short be something in the nature of a territorial régime.

CASE CONCERNING THE GABCIKOVO–NAGYMAROS PROJECT (HUNGARY/SLOVAKIA)

International Court of Justice, 1997.
1997 I.C.J. 7.

[For the factual background of this case, see pp. 557–559.]

117. The Court must first turn to the question whether Slovakia became a party to the 1977 Treaty as successor to Czechoslovakia. As an alternative argument, Hungary contended that, even if the Treaty survived the notification of termination, in any event it ceased to be in force as a treaty on 31 December 1992, as a result of the "disappearance of one of the parties". On that date Czechoslovakia ceased to exist as a legal entity, and on 1 January 1993 the Czech Republic and the Slovak Republic came into existence.

118. According to Hungary, "There is no rule of international law which provides for automatic succession to bilateral treaties on the disappearance of a party" and such a treaty will not survive unless another State succeeds to it by express agreement between that State and the remaining party. * * * It contended that it had never agreed to accept Slovakia as successor to the 1977 Treaty. Hungary referred to diplomatic exchanges in which the two Parties had each submitted to the other lists of those bilateral treaties which they respectively wished should continue in force between them, for negotiation on a case-by-case basis; and Hungary emphasized that no agreement was ever reached with regard to the 1977 Treaty.

119. Hungary claimed that there was no rule of succession which could operate in the present case to override the absence of consent. Referring to Article 34 of the Vienna Convention of 23 August 1978 on Succession of States in respect of Treaties, in which "a rule of automatic succession to all treaties is provided for", based on the principle of continuity, Hungary argued not only that it never signed or ratified the Convention, but that the "concept of automatic succession" contained in that Article was not and is not, and has never been accepted as, a statement of general international law.

Hungary further submitted that the 1977 Treaty did not create "obligations and rights ... relating to the regime of a boundary" within the meaning of Article 11 of that Convention, and noted that the existing course of the boundary was unaffected by the Treaty. It also denied that the treaty was a "localized" treaty, or that it created rights "considered as attaching to [the] territory" within the meaning of Article 12 of the 1978 Convention, which would, as such, be unaffected by a succession of States. The 1977 Treaty was, Hungary insisted, simply a joint investment. * * *

120. According to Slovakia, the 1977 Treaty * * * remains in force between itself, as successor State, and Hungary. * * * It relied * * * on the "general rule of continuity which applies in the case of dissolution"; it argued, secondly, that the Treaty is one "attaching to [the] territory" within the meaning of Article 12 of the 1978 Vienna Convention, and that it contains provisions relating to a boundary. * * *

122. * * * According to Slovakia, [Article 12] can be considered to be one of those provisions of the Vienna Convention that represent the codification of customary international law". The 1977 Treaty is said to fall within its scope because of its "specific characteristics ... which place it in the category of treaties of a localized or territorial character". Slovakia also described the Treaty as one "which contains boundary provisions and lays down a specific territorial régime" which operates in the interest of all Danube riparian States, and as "a dispositive treaty, creating rights *in rem*, independently of the legal personality of its original signatories". * * *

123. The Court does not find it necessary for the purposes of the present case to enter into a discussion of whether or not Article 34 of the 1978 Convention reflects the state of customary international law. More relevant to its present analysis is the particular nature and character of the 1977 Treaty. An examination of the Treaty confirms that, aside from its undoubted nature as a joint investment, its major elements were the proposed construction and joint operation of a large, integrated and indivisible complex of structures and installations on specific parts of the respective territories of Hungary and Czechoslovakia along the Danube. The Treaty also established the navigational régime for an important sector of an international waterway, in particular the relocation of the main international shipping lane to the bypass canal. In so doing, it inescapably created a situation in which the interests of other users of the Danube were affected. Furthermore, the interests of third States were expressly acknowledged in Article 18, whereby the parties undertook to ensure "uninterrupted and safe navigation on the international fairway" in accordance with their obligations under the Convention of 18 August 1948 concerning the Régime of Navigation on the Danube.

In its Commentary on the Draft Articles on Succession of States in respect of Treaties, adopted at its twenty-sixth session, the International Law Commission identified "treaties of a territorial character" as having been regarded both in traditional doctrine and in modern opinion as unaffected by a succession of States [citation omitted]. The draft text of Article 12, which reflects this principle, was subsequently adopted unchanged in the 1978 Vienna Convention. The Court considers that Article 12 reflects a rule of customary international law; it notes that neither of the Parties disputed this. Moreover, the Commission indicated that "treaties concerning water rights or navigation on rivers are commonly regarded as candidates for inclusion in the category of territorial treaties" (*ibid.,* p. 33, para. 26). The Court observes that Article 12, in providing only, without reference to the treaty itself, that rights and obligations of a territorial character established by a treaty are unaffected by a succession of States, appears to lend support to the position of Hungary rather than of Slovakia. However the Court concludes that this formulation was devised rather to take account of the fact that, in many cases, treaties which had established boundaries or territorial régimes were no longer in force (*ibid.*, pp. 26–37). Those that remained in force would nonetheless bind a successor State.

Taking all these factors into account, the Court finds that the content of the 1977 Treaty indicates that it must be regarded as establishing a territorial régime within the meaning of Article 12 of the 1978 Vienna Convention. It created rights and obligations "attaching to" the parts of the Danube to which it relates; thus the Treaty itself cannot be affected by a succession of States. The Court therefore concludes that the 1977 Treaty became binding upon Slovakia on 1 January 1993.

Notes

1. Was it consistent for newly independent states to demand freedom to continue or terminate treaties of predecessor states but insist that boundary treaties remain in force? Even when boundary disputes have arisen between a newly independent state and another state, the new states have not claimed they were free from the obligation to respect boundaries made in treaties of their predecessor colonial rulers. See Charter of the Organization of African Unity Art. III(3) and Chapter 4, pp. 327–334.

2. Does Article 11 bar a successor state from challenging an existing boundary based on a treaty? What grounds might be advanced for such challenge?

3. Article 12 relates to "other territorial régimes" not affected by succession. Why did not this Article (and Article 11) simply provide for succession, i.e., continuity of rights and obligations, instead of declaring that the territorial régime is not affected by succession? In either case, there would be a rule of continuity. Is it not artificial to separate succession in respect of the territorial régime from succession in respect of the treaty establishing that régime? On the other hand, does it favor stability if the territorial régime (or boundary régime) is regarded as established by an executed treaty and that this legal situation rather than the treaty passed to the successor state? For discussion see [1974] II (I) Yb.I.L.C. 201 (paragraphs 18–20) and 206 (para. 36.)

4. Note that paragraph 3 of Article 12 excludes from that article treaties for the establishment of foreign military bases. Would such treaties otherwise have been binding on successor states? The United Kingdom had in 1941 granted to the United States military bases in British colonies in the West Indies. When these colonies were approaching independence, the United States declared that the future of the bases must be a matter of agreement with the newly independent states. Would the U.S. have had legal grounds to insist on the retention of the bases irrespective of the successor's consent? See Esgain, Military Servitudes and the New Nations, in The New Nations in International Law and Diplomacy 42–97 (O'Brien ed. 1963).

5. Is the analysis of the I.C.J. in the *Gabcikovo* Case applicable to other treaties concerning the Danube, such as the 1948 Convention concerning the Régime of Navigation on the Danube mentioned in paragraph 123? The 1948 Danube Convention figured prominently in a 1999 controversy over responsibility

for clearing wreckage from a stretch of the Danube flowing through Serbia, in the aftermath of the NATO bombardment of Danube bridges during the Kosovo crisis. Are obligations under the 1948 Convention (e.g., to keep the navigational channel clear) ones "attaching to" the territory through which the Danube flows? See "A Plan to Rebuild Danube Bridges Widens Gap on Aid to Serbs," New York Times, Nov. 1, 1999.

C. THE NEWLY INDEPENDENT STATE: "CLEAN STATE"?

A newly independent state is defined in Article 2, paragraph 1(f). To meet the definition, the new state must have been a "dependent territory for the international relations of which the predecessor state was responsible." In these essentially colonial situations, the drafters of the Vienna Convention favored a "clean slate" approach, whereas in other cases of separating states a "continuity" approach was preferred. (See Section D, p. 581 infra.) The Commission explained as follows the application of the "clean slate" metaphor to newly independent states:

INTERNATIONAL LAW COMMISSION REPORT

[1974] II (I) Yb.I.L.C. 157, 211–217, 237, 239.

(2) The question of a newly independent State's inheritance of the treaties of its predecessor has two aspects: (a) whether that State is under an *obligation* to continue to apply those treaties to its territory after the succession of States, and (b) whether it is *entitled* to consider itself as a party to the treaties in its own name after the succession of States. These two aspects of succession in the matter of treaties cannot in the view of the Commission be treated as if they were the same problem. If a newly independent State were to be considered as automatically bound by the treaty obligations of its predecessor, reciprocity would, it is true, require that it should also be entitled to invoke the rights contained in the treaties. And, similarly, if a newly independent State were to possess and to assert a right to be considered as a party to its predecessor's treaties, reciprocity would require that it should at the same time be subject to the obligations contained in them. But reciprocity does not demand that, if a State should be *entitled* to consider itself a party to a treaty it must equally be *bound to* do so. Thus, a State which signs a treaty subject to ratification has a right to become a party but is under no obligation to do so. In short, the question whether a newly independent State is under an *obligation* to consider itself a party to its predecessor's treaties is legally quite distinct from the question whether it may have a *right* to consider or to make itself a party to those treaties.

Clearly, if a newly independent State is under a legal *obligation* to assume its predecessor's treaties, the question whether it has a right to claim the status of a party to them becomes irrelevant. The first point, therefore, is to determine whether such a legal obligation does exist in general international law, and it is this point to which the present article is directed.

(3) The majority of writers take the view, supported by State practice, that a newly independent State begins its life with a clean slate, except in regard to "local" or "real" obligations. The clean slate is generally recognized to be the "traditional" view on the matter. It has been applied to earlier cases of newly independent States emerging either from former colonies (i.e., the

United States of America; the Spanish American Republics) or from a process of secession or dismemberment (i.e., Belgium, Panama, Ireland, Poland, Czechoslovakia, Finland). * * *

(6) The metaphor of the clean slate is a convenient way of expressing the basic concept that a newly independent State begins its international life free from any *obligation* to continue in force treaties previously applicable with respect to its territory simply by reason of that fact. But even when that basic concept is accepted, the metaphor appears in the light of existing State practice to be at once too broad and too categoric. It is too broad in that it suggests that, so far as concerns the newly independent States, the prior treaties are wholly expunged and are without any relevance to its territory. The very fact that prior treaties are often continued or renewed indicates that the clean slate metaphor does not express the whole truth. The metaphor is too categoric in that it does not make clear whether it means only that a newly independent State is not *bound* to recognize any of its predecessor's treaties as applicable in its relations with other States, or whether it means also that a newly independent State is not *entitled* to claim any right to be or become a party to any of its predecessor's treaties. As already pointed out, a newly independent State may have a clean slate in regard to any *obligation* to continue to be bound by its predecessor's treaties without it necessarily following that the new independent State is without any *right to* establish itself as a party to them.

* * * Moreover, although modern depositary and State practice does not support the thesis that a newly independent State is under any general obligation to consider itself a successor to treaties previously applicable in respect of its territory, it does appear to support the conclusion that a newly independent State has a general *right of option* to be a party to certain categories of multilateral treaties in virtue of its character as a successor State. A distinction must, however, be drawn in this connexion between multilateral treaties in general and multilateral treaties of a restricted character, for it is only in regard to the former that a newly independent State appears to have an actual right of option to establish itself as a party *independently of the consent of the other States parties and quite apart from the final clauses of the treaty.*

(9) * * * If the conclusions drawn by the Commission from the modern practice are correct what the principle confers upon a newly independent State is simply a *right of option* to establish itself as a separate party to the treaty in virtue of the legal nexus established by its predecessor between the territory to which the succession of States relates and the treaty. It is not a right to "succeed" to its predecessor's participation in the treaty in the sense of a right to step exactly, and only to step exactly, into the shoes of its predecessor. The newly independent State's right is rather to *notify its own consent to be considered as a separate party to the treaty.* In short, a newly independent State whose territory was subject to the régime of a multilateral treaty at the date of the State's succession is entitled, simply in virtue of that fact, to establish itself as a separate party to the treaty.

* * * If in the case of many multilateral treaties that legal nexus appears to generate an actual right for the newly independent State to establish itself

as a party or a contracting State, this does not appear to be so in the case of bilateral treaties.

* * *

(12) From the evidence adduced in the preceding paragraphs, the Commission concludes that succession in respect of bilateral treaties has an essentially voluntary character: voluntary, that is, on the part not only of the newly independent State but also of the other interested State. On this basis the fundamental rule to be laid down for bilateral treaties appears to be that their continuance in force after independence is a matter of agreement, express or tacit, between the newly independent State and the other State party to the predecessor State's treaty.

Notes

1. Is the definition of "newly independent state" in Article 2(1)(f) adequate to distinguish between separation of a part of a state (Article 34) and the creation of a newly independent state? What criteria apply in case of secession?

2. Are newly independent states entitled to automatic admission to international organizations of which their predecessor states were members? Article 4 of the Convention provides that the rules of the international organization concerning acquisition of membership shall apply. See commentary of International Law Commission on Article 4 in [1974] II (I) Yb.I.L.C. 177–180. In practice, the United Nations and the specialized agencies have recognized that a new state would have to apply for membership irrespective of its inclusion in a member state. When British India, a U.N. member split into India and Pakistan, the U.N. General Assembly decided that India (the larger part) continued as the U.N. member whereas Pakistan was required to apply for membership. On the basis of an opinion by the U.N. Legal Department, the Legal Committee of the General Assembly declared that as a general principle a member state did not cease to be a member because its boundary or constitution had been changed. It would be necessary to show that it ceased to exist as a legal personality before it would lose its membership. The new state formed from the territory would have to submit a new application for membership. See Schachter, 25 Brit. Y.B.I.L. (1948) at 101–109. For the treatment of Yugoslavia in the 1990s, see Chapter 4, pp. 349–351. On November 1, 2000, the Federal Republic of Yugoslavia (Serbia–Montenegro) was admitted to the United Nations as the fifth new state formed on the territory of the former Yugoslavia, which had been an original U.N. member. G.A. Res 55/12.

3. When the USSR dissolved in 1990, Russia, the largest and most important Republic, was accepted as a continuing member. It was also accepted by the General Assembly and the Security Council as the successor to the USSR under Article 23, thus confirming permanent membership and the veto right on Russia. The actual text of the article was not amended; it still includes the Union of Soviet Socialist Republics. Ukraine and Belarus (formerly Byelorussia) that had been original members of the U.N. continued as members. All of the other Republics were admitted by separate votes to membership. They were also admitted to most of the specialized agencies of the United Nations through the normal admission procedure.

4. Are the successor states to the Soviet Union "newly independent states" and therefore not bound to maintain in force its predecessor's treaties in their

respective territories? In view of the actual conditions of the USSR is it plausible to conclude that since none of the *component* states had been truly self-governing, they were now "newly independent" and therefore the "clean slate" rule applied? An alternative view would be that although state power in the USSR was concentrated in the Communist Party and Russia was dominant, the other republics were not excluded as such from having its citizens take part in the central government. They could appropriately be distinguished from colonies ruled by a metropolitan power. On this premise, they would be "separating" states and the rule of continuity would apply—that is, any treaty in force in respect of the entire territory of the USSR would continue in force for each successor state (See infra).

5. The Restatement (Third) (written prior to the USSR dissolution) would apply the clean slate rule to any new state that separated from the predecessor state. See § 210(3). Reporters' Note 4 to that section says that the distinction between former colonies and other new states

> does not reflect consistent practice and would be difficult to apply. Moreover, some "dependent territories", such as the British dominions, had a greater voice in making international agreements applicable to their territory than some "separated states" such as Bangladesh.

6. When a newly independent state chooses to become a party, does it inherit the reservations, acceptances, and objections of the predecessor exactly as they were at the date of the succession? Is it free to withdraw in regard to itself any such reservation or objection of the predecessor? See Article 20 of the Convention. For state practice, see commentary of the Commission in [1974] II (I) Yb.I.L.C. 222–227.

7. Although the "clean slate" metaphor applies to bilateral treaties (since the successor state as stated in Article 24 has neither an obligation nor a right to become a party), in actual practice there has been a considerable measure of continuity in respect of bilateral treaties in certain categories. Such *"de facto* continuity" is frequent in regard to agreements on air transport, trade, technical assistance, tax, visa requirements and powers of consuls. The International Law Commission took note of such continuity but concluded that the continuity derived from mutual consent and not from a sense of a legal rule. They noted that the unilateral declarations (supra) and the devolution agreements assumed that, in general, bilateral treaties required the consent of the other contracting party for their continuance in force. See commentary in Commission report of 1974, id. at 236–241.

8. Article 24 provides that consent to continuity of a bilateral treaty may be inferred from conduct of the two states concerned. Would this mean that the two states need only continue to apply the treaty without any formalities as to its continuance? Would a mere listing of a treaty as in force constitute evidence of consent? Consider the relation of this clause to the principle of good faith and acquiescence as expressed in Article 45 of the Vienna Convention on the Law of Treaties.

9. Has the international trend in the period after decolonization supported a presumption of continuity in cases of dissolution or secession rather than the rupture sanctioned by the clean slate theory? Should a presumption of continuity make allowance for negotiation in particular cases for exceptions? See comments of Crawford and Williamson in 86 Proc. Am. Soc. Int. L. 10–23 (1992). For an interesting analysis of how Austria—a proponent since its own independence of a "clean slate" approach—shifted toward a continuity policy in the light of Europe-

an developments of the 1990s, see Hafner & Kornfeind, The Recent Austrian Practice of State Succession: Does the Clean Slate Rule Still Exist?, 1 Austrian Rev. Int'l & Eur. L. 1, 19–31, 42–43 (1996).

D. UNITING AND SEPARATION OF STATES: CONTINUITY IN TREATY RELATIONS?

1. *Uniting of States*

INTERNATIONAL LAW COMMISSION REPORT

[1974] II (I) Yb.I.L.C. 157, 253–258.

(1) These articles deal with a succession of States arising from the uniting in one State of two or more *States,* which had separate international personalities at the date of the succession. They cover the case where one State merges with another State even if the international personality of the latter continues after they have united. The case of the emergence of a newly independent State from the combining of two or more territories, not already States at the date of the succession, has been dealt with separately in part III, article 29. The transfer of a mere *territory* to an existing State also falls under an earlier provision of the draft articles, namely the moving treaty-frontier rule set out in article [15].

(2) The succession of States envisaged in the present articles does not take into account the particular form of the internal constitutional organization adopted by the successor State. The uniting may lead to a wholly unitary State, to a federation or to any other form of constitutional arrangement. In other words, the degree of separate identity retained by the original States after their uniting, within the constitution of the successor State, is irrelevant for the operation of the provisions set forth in these articles.

(3) Being concerned only with the uniting of two or more States in one *State,* associations of States having the character of intergovernmental organizations such as, for example, the United Nations, the specialized agencies, OAS, the Council of Europe, * * * etc., fall completely outside the scope of the articles; as do some hybrid unions which may appear to have some analogy with a uniting of States but which do not result in a new *State* and do not therefore constitute a succession of *States.*

* * *

(27) In the light of the above practice and the opinion of the majority of writers, the Commission concluded that a uniting of States should be regarded as in principle involving the continuance in force of the treaties of the States in question *ipso jure.* This solution is also indicated by the need of preserving the stability of treaty relations. As sovereign States, the predecessor States had a complex of treaty relations with other States and ought not to be able at will to terminate those treaties by uniting in a single State. The point has particular weight today in view of the tendency of States to group themselves in new forms of association.

(28) Consequently, the Commission formulated the rule embodied in article [31] as the corresponding article of the 1972 draft, on the basis of the *ipso jure* continuity principle duly qualified by other elements which need also

to be taken into account; i.e. the agreement of the States concerned, the compatibility of the treaties in force prior to the uniting of the States with the situation resulting from it, the effects of the change on the operation of the treaty and the territorial scope which those treaties had under their provisions.

Notes

1. When Texas, then an independent state, was admitted to the United States in 1845, the United States considered that Texas's pre-union treaties lapsed. However, Great Britain and France objected, arguing that Texas could not, by joining the U.S., exonerate itself from its existing treaties. Later, the U.S. view seems to have been accepted by Great Britain. [1974] II (I) Yb.I.L.C. 254.

2. Recent examples of union of sovereign states are those of Egypt and Syria in 1958 into the United Arab Republic (later dissolved) and of Tanganyika and Zanzibar into the United Republic of Tanzania (1964). In both cases, the treaties of the individual constituent states were continued in force within their regional limits.

3. May the evolution of the European Economic Community into the European Union lead to its being treated as a union of states for purposes of Article 31? Although the Community has treaty-making authority in some areas, it is not at present regarded as a state and *a fortiori* it is not a successor state in respect of treaties of its member states. The pre-Community treaties of member states are dealt with by the Treaty of Rome (the constituent instrument of the EEC) in terms of the compatibility of obligations of successive treaties relating to the same subject matter. See Article 234 of the Treaty of Rome (renumbered Article 307 effective in 1999). When new members have joined the EEC/EU they have been required to become bound by certain prior treaties made by the EEC/EU. This is therefore a matter of express agreement rather than by operation of law consequent on succession.

4. The Restatement (Third), distinguishes between absorption of one state by another and the merger of two or more states into a new state that is a federal union. Section 210, Comment *c* states:

> *Federal union.* It is sometimes difficult to distinguish between an absorption of one state by another and the merger of two or more states into a federal union. See Reporters' Note 2. In a federal union, the effect on preexisting obligations may depend on the constitutional character of the union and the nature of the preexisting rights and obligations. If the constituent entities have no power under the union to maintain pre-existing agreements, their obligations terminate when the union comes into effect. If the agreement remains within the power of a constituent entity, the agreement continues in force in the territory of that entity.
>
> In general, when the constituent states merging to form a federal union had each been a party to a multilateral agreement, the federal union becomes a party to the agreement and the constituent entities cease to be parties. However, membership in an international organization is generally not treated as automatic for a new federal union but must be conferred, even if the constituent entities had all been members of the organization.

2. *Separation of States*

INTERNATIONAL LAW COMMISSION REPORT

[1974] II (I) Yb.I.L.C. 157, 260, and 265.

(23) From a purely theoretical point of view, there may be a distinction between dissolution and separation of part of a State. In the former case, the predecessor State disappears; in the latter case, the predecessor State continues to exist after the separation. This theoretical distinction might have implications in the field of succession in respect of treaties, but it does not necessarily follow that the effects of the succession of States in the two categories of cases must be different for the parts which become new States. In other words, it is possible to treat the new States resulting from the dissolution of an old State as parts separating from that State.

* * *

(25) * * * The Commission concluded that although some discrepancies might be found in State practice, still that practice was sufficiently consistent to support the formulation of a rule which, with the necessary qualifications, would provide that treaties in force at the date of the dissolution should remain in force *ipso jure* with respect to each State emerging from the dissolution. The fact that the situation may be regarded as one of "separation of part or parts of a State" rather than one of "dissolution" does not alter this basic conclusion.

(27) The available evidence of practice during the United Nations period appears to indicate that, at least in some circumstances, the separated territory which becomes a sovereign State may be regarded as a newly independent State to which in principle the rules of the present draft articles concerning newly independent States should apply. * * *

Notes

1. Who determines whether a separated part of a state shall be considered as a newly independent state or as governed by Article 34? When Singapore separated from Malaysia in 1965, it chose to act as a newly independent state not bound by the treaty obligations of its predecessor except insofar as it consented. Assuming the Convention was in force, could Singapore's action have been challenged on the ground that it had not been a "dependent territory" of the Federation of Malaysia and therefore could not release itself from treaty obligations in accordance with Article 34?

2. Consider contemporary examples of territorial units in which separatist movements are strong. If successful, would the new states have grounds to characterize themselves as "newly independent" for purposes of the Convention on Succession of States in Respect of Treaties? Would they have reasons to favor application of Article 34 instead?

3. Practice of the 1990s illustrates strong pressures for continuity in treaty relationships. For example, in their policies concerning recognition of the new states of the former USSR and former Yugoslavia, both the United States and the European Community stressed the importance of fulfillment of treaty obligations

of the predecessor state by the states that sought recognition. (See Chapter 4 on recognition.) In addition to human rights obligations (see p. 258 supra), the United States attached special significance to continuity in respect of arms control treaties. The fact that nuclear weapons were based not only in Russia but also in Ukraine, Belarus and Kazakhstan lent special urgency to continuity of the arms control regime.

Unique problems have arisen with respect to certain arms control treaties, e.g. whether the ex-Soviet republics with nuclear arms on their territories could succeed to the Nuclear Non–Proliferation Treaty as non-nuclear-weapons states (while Russia remained party as a nuclear-weapons state), and how to proceed with the Strategic Arms Reduction Treaty negotiated between the U.S. and the USSR, which had not been ratified at the time of dissolution. See generally Bunn & Rhinelander, Who Inherited the Former Soviet Union's Obligations Under Arms Control Treaties With the United States? Memorandum for the U.S. Senate Foreign Relations Committee (1992); Mullerson, 42 I.C.L.Q. at 488 (1993). As of 2000, an unresolved controversy surrounded the U.S.–Soviet Anti-Ballistic Missile Treaty of 1972: some members of the U.S. Senate contended that the treaty did not survive dissolution or that new senatorial consent would be required for its transformation from a bilateral to a multilateral treaty.

4. If the continuity theory applies, the question of renewed parliamentary approval for treaties of the predecessor should not arise, either for the successor states or for their treaty partners. However, in connection with certain U.S.-Soviet arms control treaties, concerns have been registered in the U.S. Senate that the effect of dissolution has been to produce a new network of treaty relationships, so that the Senate should have the opportunity to consent to each set of bilateral obligations on renewed terms. The Executive Branch has not accepted this view of Senatorial prerogatives as a matter of constitutional principle. The international legal dimensions of the matter are also far from clear.

By way of comparison, in certain European parliamentary democracies with constitutional rules on parliamentary approval of treaties, it is an interesting question whether an international rule of continuity could avoid the need for parliamentary action. See Hafner & Kornfeind, 1 Austrian Rev. Int'l & Eur. L. at 6, 43–47.

E. TRANSFERS OF TERRITORY: THE "MOVING TREATY–FRONTIERS" RULE

INTERNATIONAL LAW COMMISSION REPORT

[1974] II (I) Yb.I.L.C. 157, 208.

(1) [Article 15] concerns the application of a rule, which is often referred to by writers as the "moving treaty-frontiers" rule, in cases where territory not itself a State undergoes a change of sovereignty and the successor State is an already existing State. The article thus concerns cases which do not involve a union of States or merger of one State with another, and equally do not involve the emergence of a newly independent State. The moving treaty-frontiers principle also operates in varying degrees in certain other contexts. But in these other contexts it functions in conjunction with other rules, while in the cases covered by the present article—the mere addition of a piece of territory to an existing State—the moving treaty-frontiers rule appears in pure form. Although in a sense the rule underlies much of the law regarding

succession of States in respect of treaties, the present case constitutes a particular category of succession of States, which the Commission considered should be in a separate part.* * *

(2) Shortly stated, the moving treaty-frontiers rule means that, on a territory's undergoing a change of sovereignty, it passes automatically out of the treaty régime of the predecessor sovereign into the treaty régime of the successor sovereign. It thus has two aspects, one positive and the other negative. The positive aspect is that the treaties of the successor State begin automatically to apply in respect of the territory in question as from the date of the succession. The negative aspect is that the treaties of the predecessor State, in turn, cease automatically to apply in respect of such territory as from that date.

Notes

1. Paragraph (a) of Article 15 provides that treaties of the predecessor state cease to be in force in respect of the territory to which the succession relates. It does not affect the continued application of the treaties of the predecessor apart from their territorial scope. However, would the predecessor state still be bound by a treaty if the separated territory was a large or important area for the application of the treaty? What rule would provide a ground for termination?

2. Assuming the factual conditions for the application of the "moving treaty-frontier" rule in accordance with Article 15, would the successor be bound to consider the treaties of the predecessor state as in force for the territory transferred?

Chapter 8

HUMAN RIGHTS

The second half of the 20th century has been described as the "Age of Rights." That characterization reflects the view that, with the end of the Second World War, the idea of human rights has become a universal political ideology and a central aspect of an ideology of constitutionalism. The ideology of human rights, of course, is a municipal ideology, to be realized by states within their national societies through national constitutional law and implemented by national institutions. But beginning with the promises made during the Second World War in the plans for a new world order, human rights became a matter of international concern and progressively a subject of international law.

The international law of human rights seeks to establish minimum international standards for national human rights as international norms which states are required "to respect and to ensure." See International Covenant on Civil and Political Rights, Article 2. Following the Nuremberg Charter and the judgment of the Nuremberg tribunal (and Tokyo counterpart), the international system, largely under the aegis of the United Nations and of regional bodies in Europe, in the Americas, and in Africa, also promoted new institutions for monitoring and inducing compliance with international norms. In time, with the end of the Cold War, the international system also developed the authority of existing institutions, notably that of the U.N. Security Council, to address human rights violations that threaten international peace and security. See Chapter 12.

That international law was traditionally seen as governing only relations between states did not preclude the early development of customary norms or conventional international obligations dealing with the condition and treatment of individuals in whom states had an interest—notably their diplomats or nationals. In principle, such duties and obligations were seen as owing by one state to another state, although, of course, they redounded to the benefit of individuals. State responsibility for injury to aliens (Chapter 10), for example, was not seen as creating rights for the alien under international law; he or she would benefit because the law sees an offense to the individual as an offense against the state whose nationality the individual bears; remedies for violation of these norms are accorded to the state, although the individual has to exhaust local remedies under domestic law before his government may pursue its remedies under international law. Diplomatic privileges and immunities (Chapter 14), provisions about the rights of nationals commonly found in treaties of friendship, commerce and navigation, limitations and safeguards in extradition treaties, restrictions on prescriptive jurisdiction, the laws of war, all in fact afford protection to individuals, although in principle the obligation and the remedies for violation run from state to state. The fact that these norms and agreements reflected very largely a state's interests in protecting its own nationals against other states confirmed the identification of an individual with his own state, and discouraged any tendency to grant independent status to the individual. That, in turn, rendered it unthinkable that international law should concern itself with protecting the interests of the individual against his own government, even less that it might give the individual international remedies against his own government.

What was once unthinkable had become normal by the end of the 20th century.

THE ORIGINS OF CONTEMPORARY INTERNATIONAL HUMAN RIGHTS LAW

HENKIN, THE INTERNATIONALIZATION OF HUMAN RIGHTS

Proceedings of the General Education Seminar.
Vol. 6, No. 1 (Fall 1977) p. 7–9.

Historically, how a state treated persons within its territory was its own affair, implicit in its sovereignty over its own territory and in the freedom to act there as it would unless specifically forbidden by international law. International law developed one early exception when it recognized that how a country treats an alien is the proper concern of the government whose nationality he/she bore. The exception might be seen as essentially political, not humanitarian. Long ago, we know, a government which offended a citizen of Rome offended Rome, and if an American is abused elsewhere today, the United States is offended. (It was widely accepted, therefore, that injustice to a stateless person was not a violation of international law since no state was offended; surely, there was no state that could invoke a remedy for such injustice.) But even if that exception is seen as a political expression of our nation-state system, rather than humanitarian, it is significant that governments were offended by violations of the "human rights" of their nationals. In our day this law has been controversial insofar as it has been invoked to protect alien property, but it is not commonly challenged as regards treatment of the alien person, and at least some security for at least some property is also widely recognized as a human right.

In order to determine whether an alien was mistreated, there had to be some standard of treatment, and traditional international law, at least as seen in the West, developed the idea of an international standard of justice. I know of no accepted philosophical foundation for this international standard and no agreed legal definition of its contents, nor are there enough cases from which one might derive a clear sense of what it imports. Americans would probably recognize in it something very like "fairness." In any case, this international notion of justice obviously long antedated the universalization of human rights. The standard for the treatment of aliens invoked by their national governments and acquiesced in by host governments was often higher than that applied by these countries to their own citizens at home. The international standard, then, was not a universal human rights standard, and governments that invoked it did not suggest that it applied also to how governments treated their own citizens. That treatment was not the concern of international law or the business of other governments, and in fact governments rarely concerned themselves with domestic injustice elsewhere. The few major-power intercessions, for example, that of the United States in the nineteenth century in response to Russian pogroms, did not invoke international law. In that instance as in other examples of "quiet diplomacy," intercession invoked a general morality and occurred only when violations were egregious and dramatic, and when there was a demand for it by a domestic constituency with affinity for the victims in the other country (as in the United States, for example, the Irish, the Jews, and others).

The treatment of aliens was not the only exception to the principle that how a government acts at home is a matter of local concern only. In the seventeenth century, Catholic princes negotiated agreements about the treatment of Catholics by Protestant princes, and vice versa, and later, governments began to negotiate protections for ethnic minorities with which they identified, even those who as a matter of law held the nationality of the country in which they lived. In the late nineteenth and early-twentieth century, minority treaties were virtually imposed by the major powers on smaller ones in Central and Eastern Europe because it was believed that violation of minority rights led to intervention and war. The mandate system of the League of Nations, following World War I, required a commitment by the mandatory power to promote the welfare of the local population. It has been argued that such clauses did not reflect *bona fide* concern for human rights but were only a "sop" to justify keeping "the natives" in continued tutelage; whatever the reason, "primitive" human rights provisions appeared in international legal documents. (Such a clause in the mandate for South West Africa became the basis for a suit in the International Court of Justice and contributed to the termination of the mandate and the emergence of Namibia.) A clear example of early internationalization of human rights is slavery; in the nineteenth century, when major countries abolished slavery in their own countries, an international standard developed that slavery was unacceptable and the slave trade was outlawed.

The contribution of the International Labor Organization also should not be overlooked. The ILO was organized after World War I to promote common basic standards for labor and social welfare. Sixty years later we have more than a hundred international conventions promulgated by the ILO, widely adhered to and fairly well observed. Again, one might find political-economic rather than humanitarian motivations for what the ILO achieved: perhaps, indeed, the ILO was the West's fearful answer to socialism which had gained its first bridgehead in the USSR; perhaps the convention reflected a desire by developed states to reduce "unfair competition" from countries with substandard labor conditions. Whatever the reason(s), international human rights were planted and grew.

Real, full-blown internationalization of human rights came in the wake of Hitler and World War II. ["Crimes against humanity" were among the charges in the Nuremberg Charter. See p. 929 below.] The United Nations

Charter includes legal obligations in respect to human rights and virtually all states today are parties to the Charter. The Universal Declaration has achieved universal recognition, and the two principal international covenants, one on Civil and Political Rights, the other on Economic, Social and Cultural Rights, have now come into effect. There are other conventions dealing with particular rights, and the Genocide Convention and the Convention on the Elimination of all Forms of Racial Discrimination have many adherents. Corresponding programs have internationalized human rights on a regional basis in Europe and Latin America.

Notes

1. In the above essay, written in 1977, Henkin says: "I know of no accepted philosophical foundation for this international standard [of justice] and no agreed legal definition of its contents, nor are there enough cases from which one might derive a clear sense of what it imports." In light of developments through the year 2000, should the statement be modified?

2. Since the above was written, the Organization of African Unity adopted the Charter on Human and Peoples' Rights (The Banjul Charter) and has established a commission to promote the aims of the Charter. See p. 671 below. In the year 2000 an African human rights court is an early prospect.

3. "Human rights" has been a term in common usage but not authoritatively defined. Such rights were said to include those "moral-political claims which, by contemporary consensus, every human being has or is deemed to have upon his society or government," claims which are recognized "as of right," not by love, or grace, or charity. Henkin, Rights: American and Human, 79 Colum.L.Rev. 405 (1979); Henkin, The Rights of Man Today 1–3 (1978); Henkin, The Age of Rights (1990).

From 1948, the Universal Declaration has been recognized as the authoritative articulation and enumeration of the essential human rights of individuals. (On the rights of juridical persons, see note 5.) Rights of peoples to self-determination and to "economic self-determination" were added by the International Covenants. There have been suggestions also of additional "generations" of rights, e.g., rights to peace, a healthful environment, economic and political development. See, e.g., Crawford, The Rights of Peoples 159–166 (1988); Alston, A Third Generation of Solidarity Rights: Progressive Development or Obfuscation of International Human Rights Law?, 29 Neth. Int'l L.Rev. 307 (1982); Marks, Emerging Human Rights: A New Generation for the 1980s?, 33 Rutgers L.Rev. 435 (1981). See also Henkin, International Law: Politics and Values 184–202 (1995).

4. It is common practice to distinguish, and to treat as a separate subject, "humanitarian law," applicable during hostilities. See Chapter 12 infra. In fact, the two bodies of law overlap and individuals in war and hostilities enjoy rights under the law of human rights as well. See generally Meron, Human Rights and Humanitarian Norms as Customary Law (1989). See also the symposium on Human Rights and Humanitarian Law, in 91/1 Bull. Human Rts. 1–61 (1992). Beginning in the 1990s, some humanitarian law and some human rights law are within the jurisdiction of new international criminal tribunals. See Chapter 15.

5. International Human Rights generally, the Universal Declaration, and, notably, the International Covenant on Civil and Political Rights, address the

rights of natural persons only. (The Covenant on Economic, Social, and Cultural Rights, however, recognizes some rights for trade unions. Article 8(1).) Compare the European Convention for the Protection of Human Rights and Fundamental Freedoms, some of whose provisions apply also to juridical persons. Article 25 of that Convention expressly accords a right of petition to "any person, nongovernmental organization or group of individuals claiming to be a victim of a violation." The First Protocol to the Convention provides: "[e]very natural or legal person is entitled to the peaceful enjoyment of his possessions." Article 1. See also Respect for the Right of Everyone to Own Property Alone as Well as in Association with Others and Its Contribution to the Economic and Social Development of Member States, G.A.Res. 45/98 (22 January 1991). See Buergenthal, To Respect and to Ensure: State Obligations and Permissible Derogations, in The International Bill of Rights 72, 73 (Henkin ed. 1981). See Restatement (Third) § 701, Reporters' Note 6.

6. International human rights law cuts across all states and many different cultures. This has given rise to an examination of the nature of human rights from different cultural perspectives. See, e.g., Human Rights in Cross–Cultural Perspectives: A Quest for Consensus (An–Na'im, ed. 1992). And see the discussion of "cultural relativism," in Human Rights (Henkin, Neuman, Orentlicher & Leebron, eds. 1999), Part I; see also Donnelly, Universal Human Rights in Theory and in Practice 109–114 (1989); Yash Ghai, Human Rights and Asian Values, 9 Public L. Rev. 168 (1998); The East Asian Challenge to Human Rights (Joanne R. Bauer & Daniel A. Bell, eds., forthcoming, 2000).

7. The literature on international human rights is voluminous and continues to grow. See generally Power & Allison (eds.), Realizing Human Rights: Moving from Inspiration to Impact (2000); Weston & Marks (eds.), The Future of International Human Rights (1999); Henkin & Hargrove (eds.), Human Rights: An Agenda for the Next Century (1996); Forsythe, The Internationalization of Human Rights (1991); Cassese, Human Rights in a Changing World (1990); Henkin, the Age of Rights (1990); Donnelly, Universal Human Rights in Theory and Practice (1989); Vincent, Human Rights of Mankind: An Introduction to the International Legal Code of Human Rights (1985); Human Rights in International Law: Legal and Policy Issues (Meron, ed. 1984); The International Dimensions of Human Rights (Vasak, ed. 1982); McDougal, Lasswell & Chen, Human Rights and World Public Order (1980). For earlier writings see Henkin, The Rights of Man Today, Chapter 3 (1978); Lauterpacht, International Law and Human Rights (1950, 1973). Books designed for teaching international rights include Henkin, Neuman, Orentlicher & Leebron (eds.), Human Rights (1999); Alston & Steiner, International Human Rights in Context: Law, Politics, Morals (2000); Lillich & Hannum, International Human Rights: Problems of Law, Policy and Practice (3rd ed. 1995); Newman & Weissbrodt, International Human Rights: Law, Policy and Process (2nd ed., 1996). There is also specialized literature, for example, on the European Convention, the American Convention, the African Charter. See pp. 650–674 infra. For compilations of human rights documents, see the Basic Documents supplement to Human Rights, Henkin, Neuman, Orentlicher & Leebron (eds.); Brownlie, Basic Documents on Human Rights (3rd ed. 1992); Center for the Study of Human Rights, Columbia University, Twenty Five Human Rights Documents (1994); and Human Rights: A Compilation of International Instruments (United Nations Publication, Doc. No. ST/HR/7/REV.5 (Vol. II, 1997). See

also United Nations Action in the Field of Human Rights, U.N. Doc. ST/HR/2/Rev. 4 (1994).

SECTION 1. INTERNATIONAL HUMAN RIGHTS LAW

A. THE SUBSTANTIVE LAW OF HUMAN RIGHTS

The international law of human rights includes numerous (and increasing) international agreements and other instruments, as well as a recognized corpus of principles of customary law. Three principal instruments—the Universal Declaration of Human Rights, the International Covenant on Civil and Political Rights (ICCPR), and the International Covenant on Economic, Social and Cultural Rights (ICESCR), have, together, acquired the designation "the International Bill of Rights."

The international law of human rights begins with the United Nations Charter.

1. *Charter of the United Nations*

Article 55

With a view to the creation of conditions of stability and well-being which are necessary for peaceful and friendly relations among nations based on respect for the principle of equal rights and self-determination of peoples, the United Nations shall promote:

a. higher standards of living, full employment, and conditions of economic and social progress and development;

b. solutions of international economic, social, health, and related problems; and international cultural and educational co-operation; and

c. universal respect for, and observance of, human rights and fundamental freedoms for all without distinction as to race, sex, language, or religion.

Article 56

All Members pledge themselves to take joint and separate action in cooperation with the Organization for the achievement of the purposes set forth in Article 55.

Notes

1. See also the references to human rights in the Preamble to the U.N. Charter, Articles 1(3), 62(2), 68, 76(c). And see Article 13(1)(b), providing that the General Assembly "shall initiate studies and make recommendations for the purpose," *inter alia,* of "assisting in the realization of human rights and fundamental freedoms * * *."

2. There has been continuing controversy as to whether the human rights provisions of the U.N. Charter create binding legal obligations on member States to respect the human rights of their inhabitants and, if so, which rights are the subject of this obligation. Compare Re Drummond Wren, [1945] O.R. 778, [1945] 4 D.L.R. 674 (Ontario High Court), in which the court declared a restrictive racial covenant void, *inter alia,* as against public policy, citing the Charter provisions on human rights as indicative of public policy, with Sei Fujii v. California, 217 P.2d 481, rehearing denied, 218 P.2d 595 (Cal.App.1950). In the latter case, the California District Court of Appeal held the California Alien Land Law invalid in

that it conflicted with the human rights provisions of the United Nations Charter. On appeal, however, the California Supreme Court held the statute invalid under the Fourteenth Amendment, but expressly rejected the lower court's view that the Charter provisions on human rights had become the "supreme law of the land." 38 Cal.2d 718, 722–25, 242 P.2d 617, 621–22 (1952). The California Supreme Court observed that the Charter provisions lacked the mandatory quality and definiteness that would indicate an intent to create enforceable rights. *Sei Fujii,* also discussed p. 209 supra. Compare also Oyama v. California, 332 U.S. 633, 649–50, 673, 68 S.Ct. 269, 27677, 288, 92 L.Ed. 249, 259 (1948), in which the Court held a section of the Alien Land Law unconstitutional as violative of the Fourteenth Amendment; in concurring opinions, however, Justices Black, Douglas, Rutledge and Murphy referred to the section's inconsistency with the United Nations Charter. Efforts to invoke the human rights provisions of the U.N. Charter in U.S. courts have not been successful, the Charter being held not to be self-executing. See p. 209 above. It has been urged that the issue be reexamined. See, e.g., Newman, Keynote Address, Conference on Human Rights Law in State and Federal Courts, 17 U.S.F.L.Rev. 2 (1982); Strossen, Recent U.S. and International Judicial Protection of Individual Rights: A Comparative Legal Process Analysis and Proposed Synthesis, 41 Hastings L.J. 805 (1990).

The issue has also been recast as whether the provisions of the Charter, taken together with later developments, notably the Universal Declaration of Human Rights, various covenants and conventions, resolutions of the U.N. General Assembly and of other international bodies, and the practices and declarations of states, have created binding legal obligations. Those who find such legal obligation argue either that the documents and developments have filled out and concretized the obligations left inchoate or undefined by the Charter; or that the Charter, together with what came after, have created a customary law of human rights. See Schwelb, The International Court of Justice and the Human Rights Clause of the Charter, 66 A.J.I.L. 337 (1972); Sohn, Protection of Human Rights through International Legislation, in 1 René Cassin, Amicorum Discipulorumque Liber 325 (1969); also Lauterpacht, International Law and Human Rights 145–60 (1950, 1973). On this view, all members of the United Nations are legally bound, and the binding obligations would require respect for at least those rights that are not disputed, for example, those which international law had always included in the concept of "justice" not to be denied to an alien, as well as freedom from slavery, systematic racial discrimination and genocide, perhaps also from systematic patterns of torture and arbitrary detention. See, for example, the numerous resolutions of the General Assembly and those of the Security Council declaring apartheid to be contrary to the principles of the Charter; see also the Draft Articles on State Responsibility, in the Report of the International Law Commission, 51 GAOR Supp. 10 (A/51/10)at p.131 (1996), discussed in Chapter 9 infra. Article 19(3)(c) of the Draft Articles would provide that an international crime may result from "a serious breach on a widespread scale of an international obligation of essential importance for safeguarding the human being, such as those prohibiting slavery, genocide and apartheid." See generally Schachter, International Law in Theory and Practice 335–42 (1991).

The customary law of human rights is discussed in Restatement (Third), Part VII, Introductory Note, and §§ 702, 703. See p. 602 below.

3. It has been suggested that the U.N. Charter should be seen together with the Nuremberg Charter, the latter judging the past, the U.N. Charter prescribing for the future. The Nuremberg Charter applied a customary international law of human rights in charging the Nazi war criminals, with *inter alia,* "crimes against

humanity." See Charter of the International Military Tribunal, August 8, 1945, 59 Stat. 546–47. See p. 930 below. The U.N. Charter codified that customary law and rendered applicable to all States at least such human rights law as was invoked at Nuremberg. Telford Taylor, Nuremberg and Vietnam: An American Tragedy 78–79 (1970).

2. The International Bill of Rights: The Declaration and the Covenants

UNIVERSAL DECLARATION OF HUMAN RIGHTS

Adopted and Proclaimed by G.A.Res. 217A (III) (10 Dec. 1948).

[See Documents Supplement]

Notes

1. The Universal Declaration was adopted on December 10, 1948, by a vote of 48 to 0 with eight abstentions: Byelorussian S.S.R., Czechoslovakia, Poland, Saudi Arabia, Ukrainian S.S.R., U.S.S.R., Union of South Africa, and Yugoslavia. The Communist states of Europe later accepted the Universal Declaration, expressly in the Final Act of the Conference on Security and Cooperation in Europe (Helsinki 1975). No state or government that has come into existence has questioned or expressed reservations to the Universal Declaration, and it continues to be cited with unanimous approval or acquiescence in resolutions of international bodies.

2. There has been debate about the legal status of the Declaration. At the time of its adoption, the U.S. representative in the General Assembly said: "It is not a treaty; it is not an international agreement. It is not and does not purport to be a statement of law or of legal obligation." 19 Dep't State Bull. 751 (1948). See also Lauterpacht, International Law and Human Rights 408–417 (1950, 1973). But compare the following, from Sohn & Buergenthal, International Protection of Human Rights 518–19, 522 (1973):

> The duty to "observe faithfully and strictly" not only the provisions of the Charter but also of the Universal Declaration was proclaimed by the General Assembly in the 1960 Declaration on the Granting of Independence to Colonial Countries and Peoples. Similarly, the 1963 Declaration on the Elimination of All Forms of Racial Discrimination recognized that every State shall "fully and faithfully observe the provisions of . . . the Universal Declaration of Human Rights." Both declarations were adopted unanimously.
>
> Taking the above mentioned developments into account, the unofficial Assembly for Human Rights, which met in Montreal in March 1968, stated that the "Universal Declaration of Human Rights constitutes an authoritative interpretation of the Charter of the highest order, and has over the years become a part of customary international law." Montreal Statement of the Assembly for Human Rights 2 (New York, 1968); reprinted in 9 Journal of the International Commission of Jurists, No. 1, p. 94, at 95 (June 1968). In the Declaration of Teheran, the official International Conference on Human Rights, which met at Teheran in April–May 1968, reached a similar conclusion and proclaimed that the "Universal Declaration of Human Rights states a common understanding of the peoples of the world concerning the inalienable and inviolable rights of all members of the human family and constitutes

an obligation for the members of the international community." Final Act of the International Conference on Human Rights 3, at 4, para. 2 (UN Doc. A/CONF. 32/41; UN Publ. E.68.XIV.2). The General Assembly of the United Nations in December 1968 endorsed the Proclamation of Teheran "as an important and timely reaffirmation of the principles embodied in the Universal Declaration of Human Rights." General Assembly, Resolution 2442 (XXIII), 19 Dec. 1968; 23 GAOR, Suppl. No. 18 (A/7218), at 49. See also the statement by the Secretary–General emphasizing the proclamation by the Teheran Conference that the Universal Declaration constitutes "an obligation for the members of the international community." Introduction to the Annual Report of the Secretary–General on the Work of the Organization, Sept. 1968, 23 GAOR, Suppl. No. 1A (A/7201/Add.1), at 13.

* * *

The Secretary–General, in his 1971 Survey of International Law (A/CN.4/245, at 196), noted that the "Universal Declaration is not in terms a treaty instrument;" he pointed out, however, that:

> "During the years since its adoption the Declaration has come, through its influence in a variety of contexts, to have a marked impact on the pattern and content of international law and to acquire a status extending beyond that originally intended for it. In general, two elements may be distinguished in this process: first, the use of the Declaration as a yardstick by which to measure the content and standard of observance of human rights; and, second, the reaffirmation of the Declaration and its provisions in a series of other instruments. These two elements, often to be found combined, have caused the Declaration to gain a cumulative and pervasive effect."

See Schwelb, The Influence of the Universal Declaration of Human Rights on International and National Law, 53 A.S.I.L.Proc. 217 (1959). See also the separate opinion of Vice President Ammoun in Advisory Opinion on the Continued Presence of South Africa in Namibia (South West Africa), [1971] I.C.J. 16, 76; Lillich, Civil Rights, in Human Rights in International Law (Meron ed. 1984); Nickel, Making Sense of Human Rights: Philosophical Reflections on the Universal Declaration of Human Rights (1987); Ramcharan, The Concept and Present Status of International Protection of Human Rights: Forty Years after the Universal Declaration (1989); Humphrey, No Distant Millennium: The International Law of Human Rights (1989); Schachter, The Genesis of the Declaration: A Fresh Examination, 11 Pace Int'l L. Rev. 51 (1999).

3. The Restatement concludes: "Few states would agree that any action by a state contrary to any provision of the Declaration is, for that reason alone, a violation of the Charter or of customary international law. On the other hand, almost all states would agree that some infringements of human rights enumerated in the Declaration are violations of the Charter or of customary international law. See § 702." Restatement (Third), Introductory Note to Part VII. See p. 602 below.

4. Though the Universal Declaration was originally not intended to be law, there has been an increasing propensity to attribute legal character to many of its provisions. Virtually uncontested and frequently repeated acceptance of the Declaration has led some to argue that these provisions have the force of customary law. See Hannum, The Status of the Universal Declaration of Human Rights in National and International Law, 25 Ga. J. Int'l & Comp. L. 287 (1995–96).

5. It has been suggested that the Universal Declaration is, after the U.N. Charter, the most influential instrument of the second half of the twentieth century. It underlies the entire international law of human rights, but, as the Declaration itself contemplated, its principal influence may have been to secure the recognition of human rights by states and instill the idea and the principles of human rights into the national constitutions and laws of virtually all states. The Universal Declaration has been copied or incorporated by reference in numerous constitutions of new states.

"The significance of the Universal Declaration lies in four achievements:

> 1. It helped convert a discredited philosophical idea ("natural rights") into a dominant political ideology.
>
> 2. It defined a vague colloquialism ("human rights") in an authoritative code, a triple "decalogue" of thirty articles of fundamental rights.
>
> 3. It universalized human rights, promoting a constitutional ideology accepted in a few countries into a standard of constitutionalism for all countries.
>
> 4. It internationalized human rights, transferring matters that had been subject to exclusive domestic jurisdiction—"sovereignty"–into matters of international concern, putting them permanently on the international political agenda, and providing the foundation for a sturdy edifice of international norms and institutions.
>
> The Declaration established the human rights idea as the ideology of our times. It is the holy writ to which all pay homage, even if sometimes the homage of hypocrisy. Eschewing—in its quest for universality—explicit reliance on divine inspiration or on natural rights, the Declaration provided the idea of human rights with a universally acceptable foundation, a supreme principle, that of *human dignity*."

See Henkin, Human Rights: Ideology and Aspiration, Reality and Prospect, in Realizing Human Rights: Moving From Inspiration to Impact (Samantha Power & Graham Allison eds., 2000), pp. 3, 11.

THE PRINCIPAL COVENANTS

HENKIN, THE INTERNATIONAL BILL OF RIGHTS: THE UNIVERSAL DECLARATION AND THE COVENANTS

in International Enforcement of Human Rights 6–9, Bernhardt & Jolowicz, eds. (1987).

After the Universal Declaration was adopted, there were various views as to how best to secure its "universal and effective recognition and observance." Although some continued to insist that a binding international law of human rights was neither desirable nor feasible, the view that prevailed was that the Declaration should be converted into an international human rights covenant that would clearly be of binding character in international law.

* * *

* * * [T]he Universal Declaration was bifurcated into two distinct and different covenants, a Covenant on Civil and Political Rights, and another Covenant on Economic, Social, and Cultural Rights. Over the objection of the

more developed states, which questioned the relevance and propriety of such provisions in covenants on human rights, both Covenants begin with the right of peoples to self-determination and to sovereignty over their natural resources. Then the two covenants go different ways.

In the Covenant on Civil and Political Rights states undertake to respect and ensure the rights recognized by the Covenant for all persons subject to their jurisdiction and to enact any laws and adopt any other measures necessary to that end. The rights recognized in the Covenant, following the first twenty-one articles of the Universal Declaration, generally spell out the same rights in greater detail and sometimes with qualifications. Unlike the Declaration, however, the Covenant includes a right not to be imprisoned for debt, and makes special mention of the rights of children and of minorities; it also requires states to prohibit propaganda for war or incitement to racial hatred. On the other hand, the right to enjoy private property and not to be arbitrarily deprived of one's property, found in Article 17 of the Universal Declaration, is missing from the Covenant. That omission doubtless was not a rejection of the essential right but was the result of sharp disagreement on the scope and definition of the right, and perhaps a spill-over of the controversy over the protection of properties of foreign nationals.

The Covenant also spells out permissible limitations on particular rights when necessary for national security, public order *(ordre public)*, public health and morals or the rights and freedoms of others. Article 4 permits derogation from most (not all) rights in time of proclaimed public emergency which threatens the life of the nation, to the extent strictly required by the exigencies of the situation.

Unlike the Declaration, the Covenant, since it created legal obligations, addressed the need to provide measures for their enforcement. While in legal principle every state party is a promisee and entitled to request compliance by any other state party, ordinarily no other state has any interest in doing so and is especially reluctant to demand compliance or threaten sanctions for violation at the expense of its friendly relations and diplomatic capital.

It has been necessary, therefore, to develop special "enforcement machinery" that would monitor compliance and bring to bear international influence and world opinion so as to help deter or terminate violations. The International Covenant on Civil and Political Rights established a Human Rights Committee of experts as its principal monitoring body. Within one year of adherence to the Covenant, and [periodically] thereafter, states parties are required to report to the Committee on measures taken to give effect to the rights recognized in the Covenant. In addition, member states may, if they wish, declare that they agree to be subject to complaints to the Committee by other state parties. (Article 41.) Under a separate, optional protocol to the Covenant, member states may agree to submit to communications—i.e., complaints—to the Committee lodged against them by or on behalf of private persons claiming to be victims of violation. [See pp. 626–632 below.]

Notes

1. The drafters of the Covenants initially intended only one instrument. The original drafts included only political and civil rights, but economic and social

rights were added early. Western States then fought for, and obtained, a division into two covenants. They insisted that economic and social rights were essentially aspirations or plans, not rights, since their realization depended on availability of resources and on controversial economic theory and ideology. These, they said, were not appropriate subjects for binding obligations and should not be allowed to dilute the legal character of provisions honoring political-civil rights; states prepared to assume obligations to respect political-civil rights should not be discouraged from doing so by requiring of them impossible social-economic commitments. There was wide agreement and clear recognition that the means required to enforce or induce compliance with social-economic undertakings were different from the means required for civil-political rights. See Henkin, Introduction, The International Bill of Rights 9–10 (1981).

The Covenant on Civil and Political Rights is drafted in terms of the individual's rights, whereas the Covenant on Economic, Social and Cultural Rights speaks to the obligations of states. Is that significant? Under the Covenant on Civil and Political Rights, states parties are obligated to respect and ensure the rights recognized in the Covenant without delay or exception. A state party to the Covenant on Economic, Social and Cultural Rights undertakes "to take steps to the maximum of its available resources, with a view to achieving progressively the full realization of the rights recognized" (Article 2).

The Covenant on Civil and Political Rights came into effect on March 23, 1976, and the Covenant on Economic, Social and Cultural Rights on January 3, 1976. As of 2000, 144 States have adhered to the Covenant on Civil and Political Rights, and 95 States have adhered to the first Optional Protocol. (On March 27, 2000, the Government of Trinidad and Tobago denounced the Optional Protocol in accordance with Article 12.) The Second Optional Protocol to the Covenant on Civil and Political Rights, aiming at the abolition of the death penalty, entered into force on July 11, 1991; as of 2000, 42 States have adhered to it. As of 2000, 142 States have adhered to the Covenant on Economic, Social and Cultural Rights.

2. By Article 2 of the International Covenant on Civil and Political Rights, states parties undertake to respect and ensure the rights indicated "to all individuals within its territory and subject to its jurisdiction." Is the Covenant violated if a state party fails to respect or ensure the rights of persons when they are on the high seas? In the territory of another state? See Buergenthal, To Respect and Ensure: State Obligations and Permissible Derogations, in The International Bill of Rights 73–77 (Henkin ed. 1981). Compare Sale v. Haitian Centers Council, Inc., 509 U.S. 155, 113 S.Ct. 2549, 125 L.Ed.2d 128 (1993) (issue of applicability of Protocol on Status of Refugees to actions on high seas), at p. 622 infra.

The obligation of states "to respect and ensure" the rights recognized by the Covenant on Civil and Political Rights apparently includes an obligation to protect individuals against violations of their human rights by private persons. Contrast the principle in U.S. constitutional jurisprudence that the Constitution protects only against "state action." See Tribe, American Constitutional Law, chapter 18 (3d ed. 2000). Compare the provision in the Restatement (Third) § 702, that a state violates customary law if, as a matter of state policy, it "encourages or condones" certain infringements of human rights. See p. 602 below. Does a state party violate the Covenant if it kidnaps a person in the territory of another state and brings him or her back for trial? See United States v. Alvarez–Machain, 504 U.S. 655, 112 S.Ct. 2188, 119 L.Ed.2d 441 (1992); Lutz, State Sponsored Abductions: The Human Rights Ramifications of Alvarez–Machain, 9 World Pol'y J. 687

(1992). See also the discussion of that case in Chapter 3, p. 177 above and Chapter 13 below.

3. The Covenant on Economic, Social and Cultural Rights obligates States to recognize and achieve progressively the following rights: the right to work (Art. 6); to just and favorable working conditions (Art. 7); to form and join trade unions (Art. 8); to social security (Art. 9); to protection of and assistance to the family, mothers and children (Art. 10); to adequate food, clothing and housing (Art. 11); to the highest attainable standard of physical and mental health (Art. 12); to education (Art. 13); and the right to take part in cultural life, to enjoy the benefits of scientific progress and its applications, and to benefit from the protection of the moral and material interests resulting from any scientific, literary or artistic production of which a person is the author (Art. 15). What obligations do parties to the Covenants assume? To whom? See Schachter, International Law in Theory and Practice 345–51 (1991).

By Article 2(1) of the International Covenant on Economic, Social and Cultural Rights, states undertake to realize the rights indicated "individually and through international assistance and cooperation, especially economic and technical." Does this provision create obligations for a state party to assist other states parties to realize the economic and social and cultural rights of their inhabitants? Compare the arguments of advocates of a "right to development," some of whom suggest that persons in need have claims upon wealthy nations for assistance. Rich, The Right to Development as an Emerging Human Right, 23 Va.J.I.L. 287 (1983); Espiell, The Right of Development as a Human Right, 16 Tex. I.L.J. (1981). See generally the U.N. Declaration on the Right of Development, G.A.Res. 41/128 (1986), G.A.O.R. 41st Sess., Supp. 53, at 86, which recognized the "right of development" as "an inalienable human right." (Article 1). The Declaration on the Right of Development was adopted by a vote of 146 to 1 (the U.S.), with eight abstentions (including Japan and Great Britain); and there has been uncertainty whether it was intended to state the customary law. For a discussion of the right to development, and of the possible tension between individual and collective rights, see Schachter, International Law in Theory and Practice 331–32 (1991); Henkin, The Age of Rights 191–93 (1990). See also Crawford, The Rights of Peoples 65–66 (1988); International Law and Development (De Waart, Peters & Denters, eds. 1988); International Law of Development (Snyder & Slinn, eds. 1987).

4. For comprehensive guidance to interpretation of the Covenants, see The International Bill of Rights: The Covenant on Civil and Political Rights (Henkin, ed., 1981); Nowak, U.N. Covenant on Civil and Political Rights: CCPR Commentary (1993); Sohn, Guide to the Interpretation of the International Covenant on Economic, Social and Cultural Rights (1993) (new edition pending); Eide, Krawe & Rosas, Economic, Social & Cultural Rights (1995).

5. A few international human rights agreements were concluded before the Covenants, e.g., The Slavery Convention of 1926 and the Genocide Convention of 1948. A substantial number of human rights conventions have been adopted since, generally to develop and expand the protections provided in the Covenant on particular subjects. The following are the principal agreements:

Table of International Human Rights Instruments

As of 1999*

	Date	No. of Parties	U.S. a Party?	Citation
The Covenants and their Protocols				
International Covenant on Economic, Social and Cultural Rights	12/16/66	139	No	993 UNTS 3
International Covenant on Civil and Political Rights	12/16/66	141	Yes	999 UNTS 171
Optional Protocol on Civil and Political Rights	12/16/66	95	No	999 UNTS 171
Second Optional Protocol on Civil and Political Rights (death penalty)	12/15/89	35	No	A/Res./44/128
Genocide, War Crimes, Crimes Against Humanity				
Convention on the Prevention and Punishment of the Crime of Genocide	12/9/48	127	Yes	78 UNTS 277
Convention on the Non–Applicability of Statutory Limitations to War Crimes Against Humanity	1/26/68	43	No	754 UNTS 73
Slavery and Forced Labor				
Slavery Convention of 1926, as amended by 1953 Protocol	9/25/26 amended 12/7/53	94	Yes	182 UNTS 51; 212 UNTS 17
Supplementary Convention on the Abolition of Slavery	9/7/56	117	Yes	266 UNTS 3
Convention for the Suppression of Traffic in Persons and of the Exploitation of the Prostitution of Others	3/21/50	72	No	96 UNTS 271
ILO Convention on the Abolition of Forced Labor	6/25/57	133	Yes	320 UNTS 291
Refugees and Stateless Persons				
Convention Relating to the Status of Refugees	7/28/51	132	No	189 UNTS 137
Protocol Relating to the Status of Refugees	1/31/67	132	Yes	606 UNTS 267
Convention Relating to the Status of Stateless Persons	9/28/54	44	No	360 UNTS 131
Racial Discrimination				
International Convention on the Elimination of All Forms of Racial Discrimination	12/21/65	152	Yes	660 UNTS 195

* from Human Rights, Henkin, Neuman, Orentlicher & Leebron, eds. (1999), p. 334.

	Date	No. of Parties	U.S. a Party?	Citation
International Convention on the Suppression and Punishment of the Crime of Apartheid	11/30/73	101	No	1015 UNTS 243
Rights of Women and Children				
Convention on the Political Rights of Women	12/20/52	111	Yes	193 UNTS 135
Convention on the Nationality of Married Women	2/20/57	66	No	309 UNTS 65
Convention on the Elimination of All Forms of Discrimination Against Women	12/18/79	163	No	G.A. Res. 34/180
Convention on the Rights of the Child	11/20/89	191	No	G.A. Res. 44/25
Other				
Geneva Conventions [Conduct of War]	8/12/49	188	Yes	77 UNTS 31, 85, 135, 287
Convention Against Torture and Other Cruel, Inhuman or Degrading Punishment	12/10/84	110	Yes	G.A. Res. 39/46
Convention Against Discrimination in Education	12/14/60	85	No	429 UNTS 93
Convention on the International Right of Correction	3/31/53	14	No	439 UNTS 191
International Convention on the Protection of the Rights of All Migrant Workers	12/18/90	10	No	G.A. Res. 45/158

The United Nations and some of its Specialized Agencies have also promoted other human rights conventions, declarations and guidelines, e.g.,

— Discrimination (Employment and Occupation) Convention;

— Convention Against Discrimination in Education;

— Equal Remuneration Convention;

— Convention on the Reduction of Statelessness;

— Universal Declaration on the Eradication of Hunger and Malnutrition;

— Standard Minimum Rules for the Treatment of Prisoners;

— Declaration on the Protection of all Persons from Being Subjected to Torture and Other Cruel, Inhuman or Degrading Treatment or Punishment;

— Declaration on the Granting of Independence to Colonial Countries and Peoples;

— Declaration on the Elimination of Discrimination Against Women;

— Declaration on Territorial Asylum;

— Declaration of the Rights of the Child;

— Declaration on the Promotion among Youth of the Ideals of Peace, Mutual Respect and Understanding between Peoples;

— Declaration on Social Progress and Development;

— Declaration on the Rights of Mentally Retarded Persons;

— Declaration of the Principles of International Cultural Co-operation;

— Declaration on the Elimination of all Forms of Intolerance and of Discrimination Based on Religion or Belief;

— Declaration on Race and Racial Prejudice;

— Convention Concerning Minimum Standards of Social Security;

— International Convention on the Protection of the Rights of Migrant Workers and Members of Their Families;

— Convention Concerning Employment Policy;

— Convention on Consent to Marriage and Minimum Age for Marriage and Registration of Marriages;

— International Convention Against Apartheid in Sports.

The texts of many of these instruments are collected in Human Rights, A Compilation of International Instruments (United Nations Publication, Doc. No. ST/HR/7/REV. 5 (Vol. II), 1997).

6. Since it came into existence after the First World War, the International Labour Organization (originally the International Labour Office) has promoted more than 100 conventions dealing with conditions of labor and other social conditions; a number of them have been widely ratified. International Labour Office, International Labour Conventions and Recommendations, chart of ratifications, Jan. 1, 1993. See generally N. Valticos and G. Von Potobsky, International Labor Law (2d. Ed., 1995); Galenson, The International Labour Organisation: An American View (1981). For a summary and review of the structure of the ILO, see International Labour Office, International Labour Standards 197–204 (1982). See also, International Labour Organization, Handbook for Procedures relating to International Labour Conventions and Recommendations (1995). UNESCO has also promoted agreements on human rights matters within its particular jurisdiction, e.g., the UNESCO Convention Against Discrimination in Education, 429 U.N.T.S. 93 (1960).

7. The Covenants were designed to transform the provisions of the Universal Declaration into binding treaties, but there are significant differences between the Declaration and the Covenants. Some of the rights set forth in the Declaration, notably Article 14 (asylum) and Article 17 (property), have no counterpart in the Covenants. Failure to include a right to property may have reflected principally international differences, particularly intense at the time, as to the obligation of states to compensate aliens for nationalized properties. See Chapter 10. On the other hand, the Covenant on Civil and Political Rights includes the right of peoples to self-determination and to freely dispose of their natural resources (Article 1); procedural protections for aliens against expulsion (Article 13); the right not to be compelled to testify against oneself (Article 14(3)(g)); compensation for miscarriage of justice (Article 14(6)); freedom from double jeopardy (Article 14(7)); the prohibition of propaganda for war or advocacy of national, racial or ethnic hatred (Article 20); the right of a child to a name and a nationality (Article 24); protection for cultural, religious and linguistic rights of minorities (Article 27). The Covenant also spells out limitations on rights referred to in the Declaration (Art. 29(2)). See p. 606 below and Restatement (Third) § 701, Reporters' Note 6. The socio-economic provisions in the Declaration are much expanded in the Covenant on Economic, Social and Cultural Rights. (That Covenant also includes a right of peoples to self-determination and to their natural resources in terms identical to the provisions in Article 1 of the other Covenant.)

Some of the differences between the Declaration and the Covenants reflect differences between a declaration and international agreements, and what states sought to achieve by each. The differences reflect also the changing composition of international society; 58 states were members of the United Nations in 1948, and 122 in 1966 when the Covenants were adopted. Most of the additional members were new states that had recently been colonies, and their admission into the international system changed the balance between traditional and new states, between developed and developing, between "libertarian," "socialist," and various "mixed" societies.

The right to self-determination was included in Article 1 of the Covenant on Economic, Social and Cultural Rights and in Article 1 of the Covenant on Civil and Political Rights over objections that these are political principles, not legal rights; that, in any event, they are not rights of individuals but of "peoples," and not a continuing responsibility of a State towards its own inhabitants. Note the reservation of the United Kingdom to Article 1 of the Covenant on Civil and Political Rights. But see Jenks, Human Rights, Social Justice and Peace: The Broader Significance of the ILO Experience, in International Protection of Human Rights, Proceedings of the Seventh Nobel Symposium 227 (Eide & Schou eds. 1967). On the meaning of the right of self-determination in the Covenant, see Cassese, Self–Determination of Peoples: A Legal Reappraisal 141–146 (1995). On self-determination generally, see Chapter 4, p. 268. Do the provisions for implementation provided in the Covenants, p. 626 infra, apply as well to this right?

3. *Customary International Law of Human Rights*

The international law of human rights consists primarily of multilateral conventions, covenants and other international agreements largely concluded in the aftermath of the Second World War. But the proliferation of human rights agreements has not prevented the growth of important customary international law on human rights. Customary law was the foundation for "crimes against humanity" under the Nuremberg Charter. Customary human rights law has bound states that have been unwilling to accept treaties or that have done so with the inclusion of debilitating reservations. In a celebrated example, the international system produced customary international law outlawing apartheid and other forms of systematic racial discrimination, and has indeed given that norm peremptory character (*jus cogens*). Whereas many international treaties have codified and developed pre-existing customary principles of international law, human rights covenants and conventions have helped to shape customary legal norms. Compare North Sea Continental Shelf cases, p. 92 above.

RESTATEMENT (THIRD) § 702

A state violates international law if, as a matter of state policy, it practices, encourages or condones

(a) genocide,

(b) slavery or slave trade,

(c) the murder or causing the disappearance of individuals,

(d) torture or other cruel, inhuman or degrading treatment or punishment,

(e) prolonged arbitrary detention,

(f) systematic racial discrimination, or

(g) a consistent pattern of gross violations of internationally recognized human rights.

Notes

1. The Restatement (Third) comments on this section include:

a. Scope of customary law of human rights. This section includes as customary law only those human rights whose status as customary law is generally accepted * * * and whose scope and content are generally agreed. See § 701, Reporters' Note 6. The list is not necessarily complete, and is not closed: human rights not listed in this section may have achieved the status of customary law, and some rights might achieve that status in the future. See Comments *j, k,* and *l.*

* * *

j. Systematic religious discrimination. The United Nations Charter (Articles 1, 13, 55) links religious discrimination with racial discrimination and treats them alike; to the extent that racial discrimination violates the Charter religious discrimination does also. Religious discrimination is also treated identically with racial discrimination in the principal covenants and in the constitutions and laws of many states. There is as yet no convention on the elimination of religious discrimination, and there has been no concerted attack on such discrimination comparable to that on *apartheid,* but there is a strong case that systematic discrimination on grounds of religion as a matter of state policy is also a violation of customary law. See Reporters' Note 8.

k. Right to property. The Universal Declaration of Human Rights includes the right to own and not to be arbitrarily deprived of property. See § 701, Reporters' Note 6, and § 711, Comment *d.* There is, however, wide disagreement among states as to the scope and content of that right, which weighs against the conclusion that a human right to property generally has become a principle of customary law. All states have accepted a limited core of rights to private property, and violation of such rights, as state policy, may already be a violation of customary law. Invasions of rights in private property that have not achieved the status of customary law may nonetheless violate a particular international agreement or, where the victim is a foreign national, the principles of customary law governing state responsibility to foreign nationals. See §§ 711–713.

l. Gender discrimination. The United Nations Charter (Article 1(3)) and the Universal Declaration of Human Rights (Article 2) prohibit discrimination in respect of human rights on various grounds, including sex. Discrimination on the basis of sex in respect of recognized rights is prohibited by a number of international agreements, including the Covenant on Civil and Political Rights, the Covenant on Economic, Social and Cultural Rights, and more generally by the Convention on the Elimination of All Forms of Discrimination Against Women, which, as of May 1987, had been ratified by 91 states and signed by a number of others. The United States had signed the Convention but had not yet ratified it. See Introductory Note to this Part. The domestic laws of a number of states, including those of the United States, mandate equality for, or prohibit discrimination against, women generally or in various respects. Gender-based discrimination is still practiced in many states in varying degrees, but freedom from gender discrimination as state policy, in many matters, may already be a principle of customary international law. Discrimination by a state that does not constitute a violation of customary law may violate a particular international agreement if practiced by a state party.

m. Consistent pattern of gross violations of human rights. The acts enumerated in clauses (a) to (f) are violations of customary law even if the practice is not consistent, or not part of a "pattern," and those acts are inherently "gross" violations of human rights. Clause (g) includes other infringements of recognized human rights that are not violations of customary law when committed singly or sporadically (although they may be forbidden to states parties to the International Covenants or other particular agreements); they become violations of customary law if the state is guilty of a "consistent pattern of gross violations" as state policy. A violation is gross if it is particularly shocking because of the importance of the right or the gravity of the violation. All the rights proclaimed in the Universal Declaration and protected by the principal International Covenants (see § 701, Reporters' Note 6) are internationally recognized human rights, but some rights are fundamental and intrinsic to human dignity. Consistent patterns of violation of such rights as state policy may be deemed "gross" *ipso facto.* These include, for example, systematic harassment, invasions of the privacy of the home, arbitrary arrest and detention (even if not prolonged); denial of fair trial in criminal cases; grossly disproportionate punishment; denial of freedom to leave a country; denial of the right to return to one's country; mass uprooting of a country's population; denial of freedom of conscience and religion; denial of personality before the law; denial of basic privacy such as the right to marry and raise a family; and invidious racial or religious discrimination. A state party to the Covenant on Civil and Political Rights is responsible even for a single, isolated violation of any of these rights; any state is liable under customary law for a consistent pattern of violations of any such right as state policy.

Reporters' Note 10 adds:

"Consistent pattern of gross violations." This phrase derives from Res. 1503 of the United Nations Economic and Social Council, which authorized the Subcommission on Prevention of Discrimination and Protection of Minorities of the Commission on Human Rights to appoint a "working group" to consider communications "which appear to reveal a consistent pattern of gross and reliably attested violations of human rights and fundamental freedoms," even by states not parties to any relevant international agreement. Res. 1503, 48 U.N. ESCOR Supp. No. 1A at 8–9. The Subcommission has been implementing that resolution annually since that time. See the annual reports of the United Nations Commission on Human Rights to the Economic and Social Council. See also, for example, the action taken in respect of Chile, Report of the United Nations Commission on Human Rights on its 32d session, 60 U.N. ESCOR Supp. No. 3 (1976); the report dealing with Malawi, Report of the United Nations Commission on Human Rights on its 36th session, U.N. ESCOR Supp. No. 3 (1980). United Nations bodies have recommended measures against particular "consistent patterns of gross violation," notably *apartheid.* See § 703, Reporters' Note 10.

2. Does the practice of states support § 702 of the Restatement? The Reporters' Notes to § 701 state:

> 1. *Human rights law and sources of international law.* Ordinarily, international law does not assume restrictions on state autonomy. But the universal acceptance of human rights in principle, and active international concern with human rights, has led to some readiness to conclude that states have assumed human rights obligations. There is a disposition to find legal obligation in indeterminate language about human rights in international agreements, *e.g.*, the United Nations Charter (see Introductory Note to this Part). There is some willingness to find that the practice of states, perhaps under constitutional, political, or moral impetus, is practice with a sense of international legal obligation creating a customary international law of human rights, even though many states sometimes violate these rights, see § 102(2). Absorption into international law of principles common to national legal systems generally is only a secondary source of international law (§ 102(4)), but there is a willingness to conclude that prohibitions common to the constitutions or laws of many states are general principles that have been absorbed into international law.
>
> 2. *Practice creating customary human rights law.* International human rights law governs relations between a state and its own inhabitants. Other states are only occasionally involved in monitoring such law through ordinary diplomatic practice. Therefore, the practice of states that is accepted as building customary international law of human rights includes some forms of conduct different from those that build customary international law generally. See § 102, Comment *b*. Practice accepted as building customary human rights law includes: virtually universal adherence to the United Nations Charter and its human rights provisions, and virtually universal and frequently reiterated acceptance of the Universal Declaration of Human Rights even if only in principle; virtually universal participation of states in the preparation and adoption of international agreements recognizing human rights principles generally, or particular rights; the adoption of human rights principles by states in regional organizations in Europe, Latin America, and Africa (see Introductory Note to this Part); general support by states for United Nations resolutions declaring, recognizing, invoking, and applying international human rights principles as international law; action by states to conform their national law or practice to standards or principles declared by international bodies, and the incorporation of human rights provisions, directly or by reference, in national constitutions and laws; invocation of human rights principles in national policy, in diplomatic practice, in international organization activities and actions; and other diplomatic communications or action by states reflecting the view that certain practices violate international human rights law, including *condemnation* and other adverse state reactions to violations by other states. The International Court of Justice and the International Law Commission have recognized the existence of customary human rights law. See Case Concerning the Barcelona Traction, Light & Power Co., Ltd. (Belgium v. Spain), [1970] I.C.J. Rep. 32, quoted in § 703, Reporters' Note 3; § 702, Reporters' Notes 3, 4. See, generally McDougal, Lasswell and Chen, Human Rights and World Public Order 266 *et seq.*, 313 *et seq.* (1980). Some of these practices may also support the conclusion that particular human rights have been absorbed into international law as general principles common to the major state legal systems. See § 702, Reporters' Note 1.

Compare Chapter 2 supra.

3. Section 702 of the Restatement has been invoked in U.S. courts by undocumented aliens whom the United States was unable to deport and who were in detention. They claimed, *inter alia,* that they were being arbitrarily detained in violation of international law. The Court so held in Rodriguez Fernandez v. Wilkinson, 505 F.Supp. 787 (D.Kan.1980), aff'd, 654 F.2d 1382 (10th Cir.1981). See also Fernandez–Roque v. Smith, 600 F.Supp. 1500 (D.Ga.1985), rev'd sub nom., Garcia–Mir v. Smith, 766 F.2d 1478 (11th Cir.1985), cert. denied, 475 U.S. 1022, 106 S.Ct. 1213, 89 L.Ed.2d 325 (1986). For a discussion of U.S. constitutional protections afforded aliens, see pp. 236–237 above. The Circuit Court of Appeals apparently accepted that the detention violated international law, but held that the courts could not give relief against such a violation. See p. 177 supra.

In Garcia–Mir, the Circuit Court of Appeals for the Eleventh Circuit relied on "controlling" legislative, executive, and judicial acts which, in the court's view, superseded the customary international law prohibition on prolonged arbitrary detention. More than a decade later, a substantial number of Mariel Cubans remained in indefinite immigration detention, theoretically awaiting an eventual removal to Cuba. Courts have continued to follow the reasoning of Garcia–Mir in rejecting challenges to their detention on international law grounds. See, e.g., Guzman v. Tippy, 130 F.3d 64 (2d. Cir.1997); Barrera–Echavarria v. Rison, 44 F.3d 1441 (9th Cir.), cert. denied, 516 U.S. 976, 116 S.Ct. 479, 133 L.Ed.2d 407 (1995); Gisbert v. U.S. Attorney General, 988 F.2d 1437 (5th Cir.1993).

For additional discussion of these issues, see Chapter 3.

4. An early invocation of a customary law of human rights is found in the Nuremberg Charter, which charged Nazi leaders with "crimes against humanity." See pp. 929–930 below.

For an application of customary law of human rights in a suit against a foreign official, see *Filartiga,* p. 143.

5. Are human rights norms *jus cogens?* See Restatement (Third) § 702, Comment and Reporters' Note 11; Schachter, International Law in Theory and Practice 342–45 (1991). On *jus cogens* generally, see Chapter 2, p. 105 and Chapter 7, p. 532.

6. What limitations upon the scope of rights do international instruments permit? Henkin writes:

> As in even the most enlightened and libertarian national rights systems, most of the rights in the Covenant [on Civil and Political Rights] are not absolute. The freedom of expression, in the classic reference, does not permit one falsely to cry "fire" in a crowded theater; the most libertarian societies do not permit slander; all countries impose some limits on freedom of movement in some circumstances to protect national security or public order. In the rights jurisprudence of the United States these permissible limitations are not expressed in the Constitution, although sometimes read into general phrases: search and seizure is forbidden only if "unreasonable," punishment only if "cruel and unusual," infringements on liberty only if they deny "due process of law."
>
> The Framers of the Covenant sought to define the permissible scope of limitations as strictly as possible, although inevitably in general phrases. For example, the freedom of movement within a country or the right to leave it "shall not be subject to any restrictions except those which are provided by law, are necessary to protect national security, public order *(ordre public),*

> public health or morals, or the rights and freedoms of others, and are consistent with the other rights recognized" in the Covenant (Article 12(3)). Or, "the Press and the public may be excluded from all or part of a trial for reasons of morals, public order *(ordre public)* or national security in a democratic society, or when the interest of the private lives of the parties so requires, or to the extent strictly necessary in the opinion of the court in special circumstances where publicity would prejudice the interests of justice" (Article 14(1)). One can debate the merits of these and other limitations or their particular formulations, but few would question that in principle some such limitations are inevitable and probably desirable. The limitations themselves, however, are governed by law, not by the whim of the state. Whether a particular limitation on a right is permissible under the Covenant is a question of international law, and the state's action can be scrutinized and challenged as a violation of the Covenant. * * *

Introduction, The International Bill of Rights: The Covenant on Civil and Political Rights 21–22 (Henkin ed. 1981). See also Kiss, Permissible Limitations on Rights, id. at 290.

Limitations on rights are to be distinguished from derogations from rights permissible in times of public emergency.

DEROGATIONS FROM RIGHTS IN EMERGENCIES

INTERNATIONAL COVENANT ON CIVIL AND POLITICAL RIGHTS

999 U.N.T.S. 171, 6 I.L.M. 368.

ARTICLE 4

1. In time of public emergency which threatens the life of the nation and the existence of which is officially proclaimed, the States Parties to the present Covenant may take measures derogating from their obligations under the present Covenant to the extent strictly required by the exigencies of the situation, provided that such measures are not inconsistent with their other obligations under international law and do not involve discrimination solely on the ground of race, colour, sex, language, religion or social origin.

2. No derogation from articles 6, 7, 8 (paragraphs 1 and 2), 11, 15, 16 and 18 may be made under this provision.

3. Any State Party to the present Covenant availing itself of the right of derogation shall immediately inform the other States Parties to the present Covenant, through the intermediary of the Secretary–General of the United Nations, of the provisions from which it has derogated and of the reasons by which it was actuated. A further communication shall be made, through the same intermediary, on the date on which it terminates such derogation.

Notes

1. Paragraph 2 of Article 4 prohibits derogations from, among others, guarantees to the right to life (Article 6), against torture (Article 7), and against slavery and servitude (Article 8).

2. Does the availability of derogations from human rights obligations render the agreements that embody them ineffectual? Henkin comments:

> A different question is whether the derogations and limitations permitted by the agreements are so large as to render the undertakings illusory, especially since they are, in the first instance at least, interpreted and applied by every acting state for itself, and—to date—no other state (or international body) scrutinizes that interpretation and application in fact. Those are subjects for fuller exposition another day, but, in a preliminary word, I do not think these and other "loopholes" render the undertakings illusory, or derogate from the quality of any rights created. In my view the derogation clauses are not destructive of the obligations (or the rights) so long as they are in fact interpreted and applied as written and intended, and the other states and the international bodies scrutinize their interpretation and application. Similarly, I do not consider undertakings to realize economic, social, and cultural rights "progressively" as essentially illusory. The economic-social undertakings were made legal obligations in order to establish the idea of economic-social benefits as rights and to increase the likelihood of their enjoyment; it was not clear what else was expected to flow [from] making them legal obligations. Even those purposes may be sufficient to support law and rights; the future may show whether there are in fact other purposes and consequences for seeing, and continuing to see, international covenants as law and as creating rights.

Henkin, International Human Rights as "Rights," 1 Cardozo L. Rev. 446–47 (1979).

3. Is derogation permissible for a principle of human rights that has the character of *jus cogens?* See Restatement (Third) § 702, Comment *n*. See generally Chapter 7, p. 532.

LAWLESS CASE

[1961] European Court of Human Rights, Ser. A. no. 1.

As to whether, despite Articles 5 and 6 of the [European Convention for the Protection of Human Rights and Fundamental Freedoms], the detention of G.R. Lawless was justified by the right of derogation allowed to the High Contracting Parties in certain exceptional circumstances under Article 15 of the Convention.

20. *Whereas* the Court is called upon to decide whether the detention of G.R. Lawless from 13th July to 11th December 1957 under the Offences against the State (Amendment) Act, 1940, was justified by the right of derogation * * *

21. *Whereas* Article 15 reads as follows:

"(1) In time of war or other public emergency threatening the life of the nation any High Contracting Party may take measures derogating from its obligations under this Convention to the extent strictly required by the exigencies of the situation, provided that such measures are not inconsistent with its other obligations under international law.

(2) No derogation from Article 2, except in respect of deaths resulting from lawful acts of war, or from Articles 3, 4 (paragraph 1) and 7 shall be made under this provision.

(3) Any High Contracting Party availing itself of this right of derogation shall keep the Secretary–General of the Council of Europe fully informed of

the measures which it has taken and the reasons therefor. It shall also inform the Secretary–General of the Council of Europe when such measures have ceased to operate and the provisions of the Convention are again being fully executed."

22. *Whereas* it follows from these provisions that, without being released from all its undertakings assumed in the Convention, the Government of any High Contracting Party has the right, in case of war or public emergency threatening the life of the nation, to take measures derogating from its obligations under the Convention other than those named in Article 15, paragraph 2, provided that such measures are strictly limited to what is required by the exigencies of the situation and also that they do not conflict with other obligations under international law; whereas it is for the Court to determine whether the conditions laid down in Article 15 for the exercise of the exceptional right of derogation have been fulfilled in the present case;

(a) *As to the existence of a public emergency threatening the life of the nation.*

23. *Whereas* the Irish Government, by a Proclamation dated 5th July 1957 and published in the Official Gazette on 8th July 1957, brought into force the extraordinary powers conferred upon it by Part II of the Offences against the State (Amendment) Act, 1940, "to secure the preservation of public peace and order;"

24. *Whereas,* by letter dated 20th July 1957 addressed to the Secretary–General of the Council of Europe, the Irish Government expressly stated that "the detention of persons under the Act is considered necessary, to prevent the commission of offences against public peace and order and to prevent the maintaining of military or armed forces other than those authorized by the Constitution;" * * *

27. *Whereas* the Commission, following the investigation carried out by it in accordance with Article 28 of the Convention, expressed a majority opinion in its Report that in "July 1957 there existed in Ireland a public emergency threatening the life of the nation within the meaning of Article 15, paragraph 1, of the Convention;"

28. *Whereas,* in the general context of Article 15 of the Convention, the natural and customary meaning of the words "other public emergency threatening the life of the nation" is sufficiently clear; whereas they refer to an exceptional situation of crisis or emergency which affects the whole population and constitutes a threat to the organised life of the community of which the State is composed; whereas, having thus established the natural and customary meaning of this conception, the Court must determine whether the facts and circumstances which led the Irish Government to make their Proclamation of 5th July 1957 come within this conception; whereas the Court, after an examination, find this to be the case; whereas the existence at the time of a "public emergency threatening the life of the nation," was reasonably deduced by the Irish Government from a combination of several factors, namely: in the first place, the existence in the territory of the Republic of Ireland of a secret army engaged in unconstitutional activities and using violence to attain its purposes; secondly, the fact that this army was also operating outside the territory of the State, thus seriously jeopardising the relations of the Republic of Ireland with its neighbour; thirdly the steady

and alarming increase in terrorist activities from the autumn of 1956 and throughout the first half of 1957;

29. *Whereas,* despite the gravity of the situation, the Government had succeeded, by using means available under ordinary legislation, in keeping public institutions functioning more or less normally, but whereas the homicidal ambush on the night of 3rd to 4th July 1957 in the territory of Northern Ireland near the border had brought to light, just before 12th July—a date, which, for historical reasons is particularly critical for the preservation of public peace and order—the imminent danger to the nation caused by the continuance of unlawful activities in Northern Ireland by the IRA and various associated groups, operating from the territory of the Republic of Ireland;

30. *Whereas,* in conclusion, the Irish Government were justified in declaring that there was a public emergency in the Republic of Ireland threatening the life of the nation and were hence entitled, applying the provisions of Article 15, paragraph 1, of the Convention for the purposes for which those provisions were made, to take measures derogating from their obligations under the Convention;

(b) *As to whether the measures taken in derogation from obligations under the Convention were "strictly required by the exigencies of the situation".*

31. *Whereas* Article 15, paragraph 1, provides that a High Contracting Party may derogate from its obligations under the Convention only "to the extent strictly required by the exigencies of the situation;" whereas it is therefore necessary, in the present case, to examine whether the bringing into force of Part II of the 1940 Act was a measure strictly required by the emergency existing in 1957; * * *

35. *Whereas* it was submitted that in view of the means available to the Irish Government in 1957 for controlling the activities of the IRA and its splinter groups the Irish Government could have taken measures which would have rendered superfluous so grave a measure as detention without trial; whereas, in this connection, mention was made of the application of the ordinary criminal law, the institution of special criminal courts of the type provided for by the Offences against the State Act, 1939, or of military courts; whereas it would have been possible to consider other measures such as the sealing of the border between the Republic of Ireland and Northern Ireland;

36. *Whereas,* however, considering, in the judgment of the Court, that in 1957 the application of the ordinary law had proved unable to check the growing danger which threatened the Republic of Ireland; whereas the ordinary criminal courts, or even the special criminal courts or military courts, could not suffice to restore peace and order; whereas, in particular, the amassing of the necessary evidence to convict persons involved in activities of the IRA and its splinter groups was meeting with great difficulties caused by the military, secret and terrorist character of those groups and the fear they created among the population; whereas the fact that these groups operated mainly in Northern Ireland, their activities in the Republic of Ireland being virtually limited to the preparation of armed raids across the border was an additional impediment to the gathering of sufficient evidence; whereas the sealing of the border would have had extremely serious repercussions on the

population as a whole, beyond the extent required by the exigencies of the emergency;

Whereas it follows from the foregoing that none of the above-mentioned means would have made it possible to deal with the situation existing in Ireland in 1957; whereas, therefore, the Administrative detention—as instituted under the Act (Amendment) of 1940—of individuals suspected of intending to take part in terrorist activities, appeared, despite its gravity, to be a measure required by the circumstances;

37. *Whereas,* moreover, the Offences against the State (Amendment) Act of 1940, was subject to a number of safeguards designed to prevent abuses in the operation of the system of administrative detention; whereas the application of the Act was thus subject to constant supervision by Parliament, which not only received precise details of its enforcement at regular intervals but could also at any time, by a Resolution, annul the Government's Proclamation which had brought the Act into force; whereas the Offences against the State (Amendment) Act 1940, provided for the establishment of a "Detention Commission" made up of three members, which the Government did in fact set up, the members being an officer of the Defense Forces and two judges; whereas any person detained under this Act could refer his case to that Commission whose opinion, if favourable to the release of the person concerned, was binding upon the Government; whereas, moreover, the ordinary courts could themselves compel the Detention Commission to carry out its functions;

Whereas, in conclusion, immediately after the Proclamation which brought the power of detention into force, the Government publicly announced that it would release any person detained who gave an undertaking to respect the Constitution and the Law and not to engage in any illegal activity, and that the wording of this undertaking was later altered to one which merely required that the person detained would undertake to observe the law and refrain from activities contrary to the 1940 Act; whereas the persons arrested were informed immediately after their arrest that they would be released following the undertaking in question; whereas in a democratic country such as Ireland the existence of this guarantee of release given publicly by the Government constituted a legal obligation on the Government to release all persons who gave the undertaking;

Whereas, therefore, it follows from the foregoing that the detention without trial provided for by the 1940 Act, subject to the above-mentioned safeguards, appears to be a measure strictly required by the exigencies of the situation within the meaning of Article 15 of the Convention;

38. *Whereas,* in the particular case of G.R. Lawless, there is nothing to show that the powers of detention conferred upon the Irish Government by the Offences against the State (Amendment) Act 1940, were employed against him, either within the meaning of Article 18 of the Convention, for a purpose other than that for which they were granted, or within the meaning of Article 15 of the Convention, by virtue of a measure going beyond what was strictly required by the situation at that time; * * *

Notes

1. The substantive provisions of the European Convention are similar to those in the International Covenant on Civil and Political Rights. See p. 596 above. Article 15 of the Convention provides for derogation from rights in emergency but forbids derogations from the right to life (Article 2), and the guarantees against torture (Article 3), slavery (Article 4), or *ex post facto* criminal law (Article 7).

2. For a comprehensive study of derogations, see Despouy, The Administration of Justice and the Human Rights of Detainees: Question of Human Rights and States of Emergency, U.N.Doc. E/CN.4/Sub. 2/1992/23/Rev. I (2 November 1992); International Commission of Jurists, States of Emergency: Their Impact on Human Rights (1983). See also Higgins, Derogation Under Human Rights Treaties, 48 Brit. Y.B. I.L. 281 (1975–76); Buergenthal, To Respect and to Ensure: State Obligations and Permissible Derogations, in The International Bill of Rights 72, 78–86 (Henkin ed., 1981); Chowdhury, The Rule of Law in a State of Emergency: The Paris Minimum Standards of Human Rights Norms in a State of Emergency (1989); Grossman, States of Emergency: Latin America and the United States, in Constitutionalism and Rights 176–96 (Henkin & Rosenthal eds., 1990); Oraa, Human Rights in States of Emergency in International Law (1992); Fitzpatrick, Human Rights in Crisis: The International System for Protecting Human Rights during States of Emergency (1994).

3. In *Silva v. Uruguay*, the Human Rights Committee expressed its views on the derogations clause of Article 4(1) of the Covenant on Civil and Political Rights, stating:

> According to Article 4(1) of the Covenant, the States Parties may take measures derogating from their obligations under that instrument in a situation of public emergency which threatens the life of the nation and the existence of which has been formally proclaimed * * *.
>
> Although the sovereign right of a State Party to declare a state of emergency is not questioned * * * the Human Rights Committee is of the opinion that a State, by merely invoking the existence of exceptional circumstances, cannot evade the obligations which it has undertaken by ratifying the Covenant. Although the substantive right to take derogatory measures may not depend on a formal notification being made pursuant to Article 4(3) of the Covenant, the State Party concerned is duty-bound to give a sufficiently detailed account of the relevant facts when it invokes Article 4(1) of the Covenant in proceedings under the Optional Protocol. * * * If the respondent Government does not furnish the required justification itself, as it is required to do under Article 4(2) of the Optional Protocol and Article 4(3) of the Covenant, the Human Rights Committee cannot conclude that valid reasons exist to legitimise a departure from the normal legal regime prescribed by the Covenant.

Silva v. Uruguay, 1 Selected Decision H.R.C. 65 (1981). See also General Comment 5, in Report of the Human Rights Committee, U.N. GAOR Human Rights Comm., 36th Sess., Annex VII, U.N. Doc. A/36/40 at 110 (1981). For derogations in the Inter–American System, see I/A Court H.R., Advisory Opinion OC–8/87, Habeas Corpus in Emergency Situations (Arts. 27(2), 25(1), and 7(6) of the American Convention on Human Rights) (30 January 1987).

In 1984 at Siracusa, Italy, a colloquium sponsored by the American Association of the International Commission of Jurists (a nongovernmental body) produced the Siracusa Principles on the Limitation and Derogation Provisions in the International Covenant on Civil and Political Rights.

4. Should derogations from human rights treaties be permitted? Would states ratify the treaties if derogations were not permitted? What is the effect of continuous or repeated derogations? Henkin writes:

> The relation of rights to remedies to enjoyment raises other questions for the international law of human rights. In principle, whether the human rights agreements are being honored, whether the individuals are in fact enjoying the human rights promised, is not immediately legally (or philosophically) relevant. For the short term, at least, failure of one or more states to carry out their international human rights undertakings does not vitiate the character of the undertakings as legal obligations, or the rights and duties they create. But if international human rights obligations fail to make any difference in fact over an extended time; if the states that undertook these obligations act continuously and consistently as though they had not, or as if they were not legal obligations; if the promisee-states do not seek to have the undertakings enforced, and otherwise acquiesce in violations and act as though no obligations exist—then one would have to consider whether there are legal obligations and consequent rights and duties.

Henkin, International Human Rights as "Rights," 1 Cardozo L. Rev. 446 (1979).

B. INTERNATIONAL HUMAN RIGHTS LAW FOR THE UNITED STATES

The United States was a major player in the promulgation of the Universal Declaration of Human Rights and in transforming the Declaration into the principal human rights Covenants. As of 2000, however, the United States is a party to only one of the two Covenants and to few other international human rights conventions. Some conventions which the President of the United States has signed have not been ratified. The instruments which have been ratified have been subjected to extensive reservations, understandings and declarations.

HENKIN, THE AGE OF RIGHTS

74–77 (1990) (footnotes omitted).

From the beginning, the international human rights movement was conceived by the United States as designed to improve the condition of human rights in countries other than the United States (and a very few like-minded liberal states). United States participation in the movement was also to serve the cause of human rights in other countries. To that end, the United States promoted and actively engaged in establishing international standards and machinery. It did not strongly favor but it also did not resist the move to develop international agreements and international law, but, again, it saw them as designed for other states. * * *

The reasons why the United States has maintained its distance from the international human rights agreements are not obvious. At one time, some lawyers in the United States questioned the constitutional authority of the treaty makers to adhere to such agreements: it was said that the agreements dealt with matters that under the United States Constitution were reserved to the States; or were delegated exclusively to Congress; or were not a proper subject for a treaty because they were only of "domestic concern." Each of these legal objections was long ago refuted. Thirty-five years ago some feared that United States adherence to international human rights agreements would threaten then-existing institutions and practices, such as racial segregation; now, Americans are happy to say, those practices are outlawed, independently of international agreements. Thirty-five years ago Senator Bricker's proposed constitutional amendment sought to prevent the use of treaties to "nationalize" human rights matters and to give Congress authority to deal with them. Today, as a result of new constitutional interpretations, individual rights are already national, Congress already has power to legislate about them.

And yet, resistance to United States adherence remains strong. In some measure, resistance to United States participation builds on differences between constitutional rights and international human rights. In particular, American constitutional rights are individualistic and deeply democratic in their eighteenth-century conception. Self-government is the basic right on which all others depend: *Representative government is freedom,* Thomas Paine said. In contemporary international human rights, on the other hand, popular sovereignty does not imply any particular system of government; individual participation in government is only one right among others, and the form of participation is not defined. * * *

But the resistance in the United States is deeper. There is resistance to imposing national standards on some matters that have long been deemed "local"; even more, there is resistance to accepting international standards, and international scrutiny, on matters that have been for the United States to decide. A deep isolationism continues to motivate many Americans, even some who are eager to judge others as by interceding on behalf of human rights in other countries.

Notes

1. The Introductory Note to Part VII, Protection of Persons (Natural and Juridical), of the Restatement (Third) provides, in part:

> *Human rights in United States foreign relations law.* The United Nations Charter and the Charter of the Organization of American States, both of which include human rights provisions, are treaties of the United States. The human rights conventions to which the United States is a party (see § 701, Comment *e*, and chart above) are also treaties of the United States. Obligations assumed by the United States in these agreements are law of the land, either directly if the provisions are self-executing or upon implementation by Congress. See § 111. The customary international law of human rights, § 702, is also law of the United States. § 111(1). Federal statutes refer to "internationally recognized human rights" and have legislated national policy toward governments guilty of "consistent patterns of gross violations" of such rights. See § 702, Reporters' Note 10. The United States has frequently reiterated its acceptance of the Universal Declaration, and whatever legal character it has applies to the United States.
>
> * * * In 1978, President Carter transmitted to the Senate the International Covenant on Civil and Political Rights, the International Covenant on Economic, Social and Cultural Rights, the Convention on the Elimination of

All Forms of Racial Discrimination, and the American Convention on Human Rights. In 1980, President Carter submitted to the Senate the Covenant on the Elimination of All Forms of Discrimination against Women. If the Senate consents and the President proceeds with ratification of these treaties, they will become law of the United States. Even in the absence of ratification by the United States, some provisions of these covenants and conventions reflect principles of customary international law and thus are part of the law of the United States. * * *

Restatement (Third), Introductory Note to Part VII 149–50 (footnotes omitted).

2. As of 2000, the U.S. Senate has consented to the ratification of four major human rights agreements. The principal human rights Covenants were opened for signature in 1966, but the United States did not sign them until 1977. The Covenant on Civil and Political Rights lay before the Senate until 1992, and the Covenant on Economic, Social and Cultural Rights is still before the Senate as of 2000. Neither the Bush Administration nor the Clinton Administration asked for Senate action on that Covenant or on two other conventions signed and transmitted to the Senate by President Carter. The four main agreements ratified by the United States are:

a. Genocide. The Convention on the Prevention and Punishment of the Crime of Genocide was signed by President Truman in 1948 and was before the United States Senate from 1949 to 1986. In February 1986, the Senate gave its consent, subject to several reservations and other conditions. One of these required the President to delay ratification until Congress enacted legislation, required by the Convention, to make genocide a crime. Congress passed the Genocide Convention Implementation Act in 1988 and the U.S. ratified the Convention in 1989. The Genocide Convention has been referred to by U.S. courts. See Beanal v. Freeport–McMoran, 969 F.Supp. 362 (E.D.La.1997), aff'd, 197 F.3d 161 (5th Cir.1999) (plaintiff sued defendant mining company, alleging cultural genocide in the operation of a mine in Indonesia); Ntakirutimana v. Reno, 184 F.3d 419 (5th Cir.1999), cert. denied, 528 U.S. 1135, 120 S.Ct. 977, 145 L.Ed.2d 929; Kadic v. Karadzic, 70 F.3d 232 (2d Cir. 1995), cert. denied, 518 U.S. 1005, 116 S.Ct. 2524, 135 L.Ed.2d 1048 (1996); Princz v. F.R.G., 26 F.3d 1166 (D.C.Cir. 1994), cert. denied, 513 U.S. 1121, 115 S.Ct. 923, 130 L.Ed.2d 803 (1995); Matter of Extradition of Demjanjuk, 612 F.Supp. 544 (N.D.Ohio 1985), and related cases at 612 F.Supp. 571 (N.D.Ohio 1985) (denying writ of habeas corpus), 776 F.2d 571 (6th Cir.1985), cert. denied, 475 U.S. 1016, 106 S.Ct. 1198, 89 L.Ed.2d 312 (1986). See also Lippman, The Convention on the Prevention and Punishment of Genocide: Fifty Years Later, 15 Ariz. J. Int'l & Comp. L. 415 (Spring 1998).

b. Torture. In 1988 the United States signed the U.N. Convention Against Torture and other Cruel, Inhuman or Degrading Treatment or Punishment. The Senate gave consent in 1990 with reservations and required the President to delay ratification until Congress had adopted implementing legislation. See 136 Cong. Rec. S17486, 101st Cong., 2d Sess. (Oct. 27, 1990). In 1992 Congress enacted the Torture Victim Protection Act, Pub. L. 102–256, March 12, 1992, 106 Stat. 73, 28 U.S.C.A. § 1350), but the Act was not intended to, and did not in fact, implement the Torture Convention. In 1994, Congress enacted the Torture Convention implementation legislation, 18 U.S.C. §§ 2340–2340B, whereupon the United States ratified the Convention.

The Torture Convention has been cited numerous times by U.S. courts before and after final ratification. See In re Estate of Marcos, 25 F.3d 1467 (9th Cir.1994), cert. denied, 513 U.S. 1126, 115 S.Ct. 934, 130 L.Ed.2d 879 (1995);

Xuncax v. Gramajo, 886 F.Supp. 162 (D.Mass.1995); Tel–Oren v. Libyan Arab Republic, 726 F.2d 774 (D.C.Cir.1984). See also Weissbrodt & Hortreiter, The Principle of Non–Refoulement: Article 3 of the Convention Against Torture and Other Cruel, Inhuman or Degrading Treatment or Punishment in Comparison with the Non–Refoulement Provisions of Other International Human Rights Treaties, 5 Buff. Hum. Rts. L. Rev. 1 (1999); Cohen, Implementing the U.N. Torture Convention in U.S. Extradition Cases, 26 Denv. J. Int'l & Pol'y 517 (Summer, 1998).

c. Civil and Political Rights. In 1992, President Bush requested Senate consent to ratification of the Covenant on Civil and Political Rights with a number of reservations, understandings and declarations (RUDs). The Senate gave its consent and the United States ratified the Covenant subject to the RUDs quoted and discussed below.

d. Convention on Elimination of Racial Discrimination. In 1993, Secretary of State Warren Christopher announced that the Clinton Administration intended to seek Senate approval of the Convention on the Elimination of All Forms of Racial Discrimination (CERD), the Convention on the Elimination of All Forms of Discrimination Against Women (CEDAW), the American Convention on Human Rights, and the International Covenant on Economic, Social and Cultural Rights (ICESCR). In 1994, the Senate gave its consent to CERD, accompanied by RUDs, including a declaration that the Convention was not self-executing. As of 2000, Congress has passed no implementing legislation.

For a critical response to the United States package of RUDs to the CERD, see International Human Rights Law Group, U.S. Ratification of the International Convention on the Elimination of All Forms of Racial Discrimination (1994); Gay McDougall, Toward a Meaningful International Regime: The Domestic Relevance of International Efforts to Eliminate All Forms of Racial Discrimination, 40 Howard L. J. 571 (1997), and additional articles in this symposium volume on CERD.

In 1994, the Senate Committee on Foreign Relations recommended Senate consent to CEDAW, subject to a series of RUDs, including a declaration that the convention was not self-executing. (See p. 210 above.) As of 2000, the full Senate has not acted on CEDAW. Also as of 2000, there has been no Senate action on the American Convention or on the ICESCR.

No U.S. action had been taken on the Convention on the Rights of the Child as of 2000, leaving the United States alone with Somalia as the only two states not to have ratified this major human rights treaty.

Difficulties in U.S. ratification of human rights treaties are suggested by the RUDs required by the U.S. Senate in connection with ratification of the Civil and Political Covenant:

U.S. RESERVATIONS, UNDERSTANDINGS AND DECLARATIONS TO ITS RATIFICATION OF THE INTERNATIONAL COVENANT ON CIVIL AND POLITICAL RIGHTS

138 Cong. Rec. S4781, S4783 (April 2, 1992).

Resolved (two-thirds of the Senators present concurring therein), That the Senate advise and consent to the ratification of the International Covenant on Civil and Political Rights, adopted by the United Nations General Assembly on December 16, 1966, and signed on behalf of the United States on October

5, 1977 (Executive E, 95–2), subject to the following reservations, understandings, declarations and proviso:

I. The Senate's advice and consent is subject to the following reservations:

(1) That Article 20 does not authorize or require legislation or other action by the United States that would restrict the right of free speech and association protected by the Constitution and laws of the United States.

(2) That the United States reserves the right, subject to its Constitutional constraints, to impose capital punishment on any person (other than a pregnant woman) duly convicted under existing or future laws permitting the imposition of capital punishment, including such punishment for crimes committed by persons below 18 years of age.

(3) That the United States considers itself bound by Article 7 to the extent that "cruel, inhuman or degrading treatment or punishment" means the cruel and unusual treatment or punishment prohibited by the Fifth, Eighth and/or Fourteenth Amendments to the Constitution of the United States.

(4) That because U.S. law generally applies to an offender the penalty in force at the time the offense was committed, the United States does not adhere to the third clause of paragraph 1 of Article 15.

(5) That the policy and practice of the United States are generally in compliance with and supportive of the Covenant's provisions regarding treatment of juveniles in the criminal justice system. Nevertheless, the United States reserves the right, in exceptional circumstances, to treat juveniles as adults, notwithstanding paragraphs 2(b) and 3 of Article 10 and paragraph 4 of Article 14. The United States further reserves to these provisions with respect to individuals who volunteer for military service prior to age 18.

II. The Senate's advice and consent is subject to the following understandings, which shall apply to the obligations of the United States under this Covenant:

(1) That the Constitution and laws of the United States guarantee all persons equal protection of the law and provide extensive protections against discrimination. The United States understands distinctions based upon race, colour, sex, language, religion, political or other opinion, national or social origin, property, birth or any other status—as those terms are used in Article 2, paragraph I and Article 26—to be permitted when such distinctions are, at minimum, rationally related to a legitimate governmental objective. The United States further understands the prohibition in paragraph I of Article 4 upon discrimination, in time of public emergency, based "solely" on the status of race, colour, sex, language, religion or social origin not to bar distinctions that may have a disproportionate effect upon persons of a particular status.

(2) That the United States understands the right to compensation referred to in Articles 9(5) and 14(6) to require the provision of effective and enforceable mechanisms by which a victim of an unlawful arrest or detention or a miscarriage of justice may seek and, where justified, obtain

compensation from either the responsible individual or the appropriate governmental entity. Entitlement to compensation may be subject to the reasonable requirements of domestic law.

(3) That the United States understand[s] the reference to "exceptional circumstances" in paragraph 2(a) of Article 10 to permit the imprisonment of an accused person with convicted persons where appropriate in light of an individual's overall dangerousness, and to permit accused persons to waive their right to segregation from convicted persons. The United States further understands that paragraph 3 of Article 10 does not diminish the goals of punishment, deterrence, and incapacitation as additional legitimate purposes for a penitentiary system.

(4) That the United States understands that subparagraphs 3(b) and (d) of Article 14 do not require the provision of a criminal defendant's counsel of choice when the defendant is provided with court-appointed counsel on grounds of indigence, when the defendant is financially able to retain alternative counsel, or when imprisonment is not imposed. The United States further understands that paragraph 3(e) does not prohibit a requirement that the defendant make a showing that any witness whose attendance he seeks to compel is necessary for his defense. The United States understands the prohibition upon double jeopardy in paragraph 7 to apply only when the judgment of acquittal has been rendered by a court of the same governmental unit, whether the Federal Government or a constituent unit, as is seeking a new trial for the same cause.

(5) That the United States understands that this Convention shall be implemented by the Federal Government to the extent that it exercises legislative and judicial jurisdiction over the matters covered therein, and otherwise by the state and local governments; to the extent that state and local governments exercise jurisdiction over such matters, the Federal Government shall take measures appropriate to the Federal system to the end that the competent authorities of the state or local governments may take appropriate measures for the fulfillment of the Convention.

III. The Senate's advice and consent is subject to the following declarations:

(1) That the United States declares that the provisions of Articles 1 through 27 of the Covenant are not self-executing.

(2) That it is the view of the United States that States Party to the Covenant should wherever possible refrain from imposing any restrictions or limitations on the exercise of the rights recognized and protected by the Covenant, even when such restrictions and limitations are permissible under the terms of the Covenant. For the United States, Article 5, paragraph 2, which provides that fundamental human rights existing in any State Party may not be diminished on the pretext that the Covenant recognizes them to a lesser extent, has particular relevance to Article 19, paragraph 3, which would permit certain restrictions on the freedom of expression. The United States declares that it will continue to adhere to the requirements and constraints of its Constitution in respect to all such restrictions and limitations.

(3) That the United States declares that it accepts the competence of the Human Rights Committee to receive and consider communications under Article 41 in which a State Party claims that another State Party is not fulfilling its obligations under the Covenant.

(4) That the United States declares that the right referred to in Article 47 may be exercised only in accordance with international law.

IV. The Senate's advice and consent is subject to the following proviso, which shall not be included in the instrument of ratification to be deposited by the President:

Nothing in this Covenant requires or authorizes legislation, or other action, by the United States of America prohibited by the Constitution of the United States as interpreted by the United States.

Notes

1. President Carter had recommended generally similar reservations to the Covenant on Civil and Political Rights in 1978. See Message from the President of the United States Transmitting Four Treaties Pertaining to Human Rights, 95th Cong., 2d Sess. iii-xxiii (Feb. 23, 1978). See also Int'l Human Rights Law Group, U.S. Ratification of the Human Rights Treaties 85–103 (Lillich, ed. 1981).

In seeking Senate consent to ratification of the Covenant, the Bush Administration indicated that it would not seek implementing legislation because none was necessary, even though the United States declared the Covenant non-self-executing. Was the position of the Bush Administration legally defensible? Was implementing legislation in fact unnecessary? Note that the Clinton Administration also did not seek implementing legislation, apparently acquiescing in the conclusion that none was necessary. See generally Sloss, The Domestication of International Human Rights: Non–Self–Executing Declarations and Human Rights Treaties, 24 Yale J. Int'l l. 129 (1999); Louis Henkin, U.S. Ratification of Human Rights Conventions: The Ghost of Senator Bricker, 89 Am. J. Int'l L. 341 (1995); Symposium: The Ratification of the International Covenant on Civil and Political Rights, 42 Depaul L. Rev. 1167 (1993). For the effect of a Senate declaration that a treaty is not to be self-executing, see Chapter 3.

Some have suggested that the Bush Administration package is inconsistent with the object and purpose of the treaty and therefore makes ratification nugatory. Do you agree? See Chapter 7 supra.

For the texts of reservations and declarations to the Covenant by other states, see Note by the Secretary–General, Reservations, Declarations, Notifications and Objections Relating to the International Covenant on Civil and Political Rights and the Optional Protocol Thereto, U.N.Doc. CCPR/C/2/Rev.3 (12 May 1992).

2. *The Human Rights Committee's reaction to the U.S. RUDs.* In its Consideration of Reports Submitted by States Parties Under Article 40 of the Covenant: Comments of the Human Rights Committee, 53d Sess., 1413th mtg., at 4 U.N. Doc. CCPR/C/79/Add.50 (1995), the Human Rights Committee criticized the extent of the U.S. RUDs, and asserted that some of them were incompatible with the object and purpose of the Covenant:

> 14. The Committee regrets the extent of the State party's reservations, declarations, and understandings to the Covenant. It believes that, taken together, they intended to ensure that the United States has accepted what is

> already the law of the United States. The Committee is also particularly concerned at reservations to article 6, paragraph 5, and article 7 of the Covenant, which it believes to be incompatible with the object and purpose of the Covenant. * * *
>
> 27. The Committee recommends that the State party review its reservations, declarations and understandings with a view to withdrawing them. * * *

The Human Rights Committee's review of the U.S. Report under the ICCPR was preceded by the issuance of General Comment No. 24 on issues relating to reservations, as discussed in Chapter 7 at pp. 490–496 above. In that General Comment, the Committee asserted:

> 8. Reservations that offend peremptory norms would not be compatible with the object and purpose of the Covenant. Although treaties that are mere exchanges of obligations between States allow them to reserve *inter se* application of rules of general international law, it is otherwise in human rights treaties, which are for the benefit of persons within their jurisdiction. Accordingly, provisions in the Covenant that represent customary international law (and *a fortiori* when they have the character of peremptory norms) may not be the subject of reservations. Accordingly, a State may not reserve the right to engage in slavery, to torture, to subject persons to cruel, inhuman or degrading treatment or punishment, to arbitrarily deprive persons of their lives, to arbitrarily arrest and detain persons, to deny freedom of thought, conscience and religion, to presume a person guilty unless he proves his innocence, to execute pregnant women or children, to permit the advocacy of national, racial or religious hatred, to deny to persons of marriageable age the right to marry, or to deny to minorities the right to enjoy their own culture, profess their own religion, or use their own language. And while reservations to particular clauses of Article 14 may be acceptable, a general reservation to the right to a fair trial would not be.
>
> 9. Applying more generally the object and purpose test to the Covenant, the Committee notes that * * * a reservation to the obligation to respect and ensure the rights, and to do so on a non-discriminatory basis (Article 2(1)) would not be acceptable. Nor may a State reserve an entitlement not to take the necessary steps at the domestic levels to give effect to the rights of the Covenant (Article 2(2)). * * *
>
> 11. The Covenant consists of not just the specified rights, but of important supportive guarantees. These guarantees provide the necessary framework for securing the rights in the Covenant and are thus essential to its object and purpose. Some operate at the national level and some at the international level. Reservations designed to remove these guarantees are thus not acceptable. * * *

On this view, would the United States be bound to respect and ensure rights that are "excluded" by the RUDs attached to ratification? See, e.g., Domingues v. State, 114 Nev. 783, 961 P.2d 1279 (1998), cert. denied, 526 U.S. 1156, 120 S.Ct. 396, 145 L.Ed.2d 309 (1999). See p. 220 supra. Is the Committee's interpretation persuasive? How might General Comment No. 24 affect U.S. ratification of human rights treaties in the future?

Compare the Committee's enumeration (in paragraph 8 quoted above) of "provisions in the Covenant that represent customary international law" with the

Restatement's treatment of the customary international law of human rights (at pp. 602–606 supra). What could account for the differences in the two catalogues?

3. Are the following arguments on RUDs and U.S. policy in respect of the ratification of human rights conventions convincing? Henkin writes:

> By adhering to human rights conventions subject to these reservations, the United States, it is charged, is pretending to assume international obligations but in fact is undertaking nothing. It is seen as seeking the benefits of participation in the convention (e.g., having a U.S. national sit on the Human Rights Committee established pursuant to the Covenant) without assuming any obligations or burdens. The United States, it is said, seeks to sit in judgment on others but will not submit its human rights behavior to international judgment. To many, the attitude reflected in such reservations is offensive: the conventions are only for other states, not for the United States.

Henkin, U.S. Ratification of Human Rights Conventions: The Ghost of Senator Bricker, 89 A. J. Int'l L. 341, 344 (1995).

Consider also:

> Human rights experts critical of the United States' reservations to the CCPR have described them as designed to ensure that the U.S. was taking on no new obligations, beyond what its constitution and laws already required. [citing Henkin, supra] This rhetoric should not be misunderstood. The U.S. certainly identified a series of respects in which the CCPR would have imposed new obligations, and sought to avoid them. But the reservations contain no systematic exclusion of new obligations, and the U.S. did not explicitly reserve against every aspect of the CCPR that went beyond existing law.

Neuman, The Global Dimension of RFRA, 14 Const. Commentary 33, 43 n. 58 (1997).

4. One international human rights agreement that has been frequently invoked in the United States is the Protocol Relating to the Status of Refugees (see p. 646 below). The definition of refugee contained in the Protocol was before the Supreme Court in I.N.S.v. Stevic, 467 U.S. 407, 104 S.Ct. 2489, 81 L.Ed.2d 321 (1984). Whether the Protocol is self-executing (see p. 209 below), and whether some of its provisions were violated, was argued in the challenge to the Haitian Interdiction Program, Haitian Refugee Center, Inc. v. Gracey, 600 F.Supp. 1396 (D.D.C.1985), affirmed, 809 F.2d 794 (D.C.Cir.1987), and in several proceedings brought by Cuban nationals claiming asylum, e.g., Fernandez–Roque v. Smith, 567 F.Supp. 1115 (N.D.Ga.1983), and subsequent proceedings. See also Bertrand v. Sava, 684 F.2d 204 (2d Cir.1982); Pierre v. United States, 525 F.2d 933, 935 (5th Cir.1976), vacated and remanded to dismiss as moot, 434 U.S. 962, 98 S.Ct. 498, 54 L.Ed.2d 447 (1977).

Litigation concerning the interdiction of Haitian boats continued into the 1990s. One of the grounds of appeal relied upon by lawyers for the Haitian asylum-seekers concerned interpretation of U.S. legislation intended to reflect the provision in the Protocol to the Refugee Convention concerning the obligation not to return refugees to a place where they fear persecution ("*non-refoulement*"). Circuit courts of appeal were divided as to whether the interdiction program was consistent with the legislation giving effect to the Protocol. Compare Haitian Refugee Center, Inc. v. Baker, 953 F.2d 1498 (11th Cir.1992), cert. denied, 502 U.S. 1122, 112 S.Ct. 1245, 117 L.Ed.2d 477 (1992) (interdiction program was consistent with the legislation), with Haitian Centers Council, Inc. v. McNary, 969

F.2d 1350 (2d Cir.1992). The Supreme Court granted certiorari in the *McNary* case and reversed the judgment *sub nom.* Sale v. Haitian Centers Council, Inc., 509 U.S. 155, 113 S.Ct. 2549, 125 L.Ed.2d 128 (1993). The Court held, *inter alia*, that Article 33 of the Convention Relating to the Status of Refugees, which provides that no state shall expel or return ("*refouler*") a refugee to a state where his or her life or freedom is threatened because of race, religion, nationality or political beliefs, was not intended to have extraterritorial effect. The U.S. interdiction program was not in violation of Article 33 because it took place outside U.S. territorial waters. The Court stated the interdiction program may "violate the spirit of Article 33," but because "* * * the text of Article 33 cannot reasonably be read to say anything at all about a nation's actions toward aliens outside its own territory, it does not prohibit such actions."

The U.N. High Commissioner for Refugees issued a statement critical of the *Sale* decision, expressing the opinion that the *non-refoulement* obligation of Article 33 applied also outside a state's own borders. See UN High Commissioner for Refugees Responds to U.S. Supreme Court Decision in Sale v. Haitian Centers Council, 32 I.L.M 1215 (1993). The Inter–American Commission on Human Rights later expressed its conclusion that the interdiction program upheld in *Sale* violated Article 33 of the Refugee Convention, as well as several provisions of the American Declaration of the Rights and Duties of Man. See Haitian Centre for Human Rights v. United States, Case 10.675, Inter–Am. Comm'n H.R. 550, OEA/Ser.L/V/II.95 Doc. 7 rev. (1997). The United States Government has continued to assert that Article 33 does not apply extraterritorially.

In 1998, however, Congress enacted a rider forbidding the use of appropriated funds for extraterritorial *refoulement* of refugees, and also establishing a policy of applying *non-refoulement* as required by the Torture Convention (see p. 615, note 2, b. supra) without regard to geographical location. See Pub. L. No. 105–277, §§ 2241, 2242, 112 Stat. 2681–821 (1998) (22 U.S.C. § 1231 note).

For comparison, note that the ICCPR requires parties to respect and ensure "to all individuals within its territory and subject to its jurisdiction" the enumerated rights. That phrasing has been interpreted as including responsibilities to individuals who are outside that state's territory but subject to its jurisdiction. See Meron, Extraterritorial Violation of Human Rights by the United States, 9 Am. U. J. Int'l L. & Pol. 213 (1994); Buergenthal, To Respect and Ensure: State Obligations and Permissible Derogations, in The International Bill of Rights 73–77 (Henkin ed. 1981).

5. December 10, 1998 marked the fiftieth anniversary of the Universal Declaration. In connection with the commemoration of this event, President Clinton issued an Executive Order on Implementation of Human Rights Treaties. Exec. Order No. 13107, 63 Fed. Reg. 68,991 (1998). The order declares it to be the "policy and practice of the Government of the United States * * * fully to respect and implement its obligations under the international human rights treaties to which it is a party, including the ICCPR, the CAT [Convention Against Torture], and the CERD." The Executive Order directs executive departments and agencies to perform their functions in a manner that respects relevant human rights obligations. It also creates an Interagency Working Group on Human Rights Treaties to provide guidance, oversight and coordination in such matters. The significance of the Interagency Group remains to be seen. The Order expressly states that it does not create any rights or benefits enforceable by any party, or create any justiciable obligations.

6. Restatement (Third) § 701, Reporters' Note 7, states:

Courts in the United States have increasingly looked to international human rights standards as law in the United States or as a guide to United States law. See cases cited in § 702, Reporters' Notes 5 and 6; compare Reporters' Note 5 to this section. There are numerous references to the Universal Declaration, *e.g.*, Zemel v. Rusk, 381 U.S. 1, 14, n. 13, 85 S.Ct. 1271, 1279, n. 13, 14 L.Ed.2d 179 (1965); Kennedy v. Mendoza–Martinez, 372 U.S. 144, 161, n. 16, 83 S.Ct. 554, 564, n. 16, 9 L.Ed.2d 644 (1963). Several cases have cited the United Nations Standard Minimum Rules for the Treatment of Prisoners (10 GAOR, U.N.Doc. A/Conf. 6/C.1/L.1, 1955), to help determine rights under the due process and the cruel and unusual punishment clauses of the United States Constitution. See Estelle v. Gamble, 429 U.S. 97, 103–104 and n. 8, 97 S.Ct. 285, 290–291 and n. 8, 50 L.Ed.2d 251 (1976); Detainees of Brooklyn House of Detention for Men v. Malcolm, 520 F.2d 392, 396 (2d Cir.1975); Morgan v. LaVallee, 526 F.2d 221 (2d Cir.1975); Lareau v. Manson, 507 F.Supp. 1177, 1187 and n. 9 (D.Conn.1980), affirmed in part, 651 F.2d 96 (2d Cir.1981); see also United States *ex rel.* Wolfish v. Levi, 439 F.Supp. 114, n. 20 (S.D.N.Y.1977), affirmed in part and reversed in part, 573 F.2d 118 (2d Cir.1978), reversed, Bell v. Wolfish, 441 U.S. 520, 99 S.Ct. 1861, 60 L.Ed.2d 447 (1979). In Sterling v. Cupp, 290 Or. 611, 625 P.2d 123 (1981), the Supreme Court of Oregon enjoined prison officials from assigning female guards to certain duties in relation to male prisoners, citing the United Nations standards and other international human rights instruments to support its conclusion that "needlessly harsh, degrading, or dehumanizing treatment of prisoners" violated the Oregon Constitution. 625 P.2d at 131, n. 21.

7. The United States has been the respondent in a number of petitions filed with the Inter–American Commission alleging violations of the American Declaration of the Rights and Duties of Man. Some of these have involved application of the death penalty, e.g. to persons under the age of 18 at the time of commission of the crime. In view of the fact that the United States has not ratified the American Convention on Human Rights, the Inter–American Commission has had to consider the extent to which the American Declaration and American Convention reflect customary international law. On the Inter–American human rights system, see generally pp. 662–671 infra, and for petitions involving the United States, see p. 670.

C. IMPLEMENTATION AND ENFORCEMENT OF HUMAN RIGHTS

RESTATEMENT (THIRD), INTRODUCTION TO PART VII

International human rights law and agreements have the same status and the same binding character as other international law and agreements. However, international law generally is largely observed because violations directly affect the interests of states, which are alert to deter, prevent, or respond to violations. See Introductory Note to Part I, Chapter 1. Violations of the international law of human rights, on the other hand, generally injure the inhabitants of the violating state; ordinarily, other states are not directly affected by such violations and their concern for human rights in other states has been uneven. Moreover, states are generally reluctant to submit their actions in respect to human rights to scrutiny by other states. Special international "machinery" has been created to monitor compliance with international human rights law, but the effectiveness of those bodies and procedures in helping induce compliance has been variable. (The European Convention regime has had conspicuous success.) The condition of human rights varies widely even among states that have adhered to international human rights agreements.

1. *Enforcement of International Agreements*

Enforcement has long been seen as the weak link in the international legal system, and it is surely the weak link of international human rights law. As a subject mainly concerned with relations between the state and the individual, rather than with inter-state relations, human rights have presented special problems of responsibility and enforcement. For example, in respect of remedies for violations of international law generally, it has been traditionally posited that only states with a legal interest to bring a claim for a breach of international norms have standing to seek enforcement. By contrast, the interests directly affected by human rights violations are those of individual victims, not of states, and of a variety of individuals under the "sovereign" control of the state committing the breach of international law. The injury suffered by a state and, by implication, the legal interest to bring a claim, in the case of human rights, necessitates a variation in traditional conceptions of injury, remedy and implementation. Because the victims of violations are the violating state's own inhabitants, "horizontal enforcement" (p. 29) is generally inapplicable. The international system has had to develop an "enforcement system," largely unprecedented.

Rights, it is commonly assumed, imply remedies. If human rights are claims upon society (as suggested in the previous section), society is required to provide means to realize them, to assure that they are respected, and to provide compensation and other remedies to individuals whose rights are violated. Thus international human rights conventions typically require states parties not only to respect but also to ensure that those rights are protected through national law. While the International Covenant for Civil and Political Rights and its regional counterparts provide for the establishment and operation of treaty bodies to monitor compliance by states parties, the machinery established by human rights conventions is designed above all to secure compliance through the effective operation of national law and procedures.

Though largely codified by treaties met with virtually universal ratification, customary international human rights law has been recognized and likewise calls upon the international system to develop adequate means of enforcement. A number of international human rights bodies have been established through means other than the provisions of human rights treaties. These include, in particular, the Commission on Human Rights of the United Nations, and various other mechanisms established by that body and by the United Nations Secretary General. The regional systems have also played a significant role; these contributions are dealt with below at p. 650.

Ordinarily, when violations of international human rights obligations have been established, the responsible actor is the state that failed to meet its obligations. But international law also imposes some human rights obligations directly on individuals, making them liable for criminal punishment. The principle of individual responsibility was first recognized and enforced in the aftermath of World War II, when Allied countries established tribunals in Nuremberg and Tokyo to prosecute major war criminals. The work of these tribunals provided the foundation for two international tribunals established by the U.N. Security Council in 1993 and 1994 in Yugoslavia and Rwanda, respectively. See Chapter 15.

CONVENTION ON THE PREVENTION AND PUNISHMENT OF THE CRIME OF GENOCIDE

General Assembly of the United Nations, December 9, 1948.
78 U.N.T.S. 277.

Article VIII

Any Contracting Party may call upon the competent organs of the United Nations to take such action under the Charter of the United Nations as they consider appropriate for the prevention and suppression of acts of genocide or any of the other acts enumerated in article III.

Article IX

Disputes between the Contracting Parties relating to the interpretation, application or fulfillment of the present Convention, including those relating to the responsibility of a State for genocide or for any of the other acts enumerated in article III, shall be submitted to the International Court of Justice at the request of any of the parties to the dispute.

Notes

1. There have been efforts to persuade one or more states to bring a proceeding against Cambodia in respect of genocide by Pol Pot and the Khmer Rouge, and later against Iraq (on account of its actions towards the Kurds). In 1993 Bosnia and Herzegovina brought an application to the I.C.J. charging genocide against the Federal Republic of Yugoslavia (FRY), and Croatia charged genocide in its application against the FRY in 1999. (As of 2000 the International Court of Justice has not addressed the merits on either of these applications.) What deters states generally from instituting proceedings charging genocide?

On May 25, 1993, the Security Council established an International Criminal Tribunal to prosecute persons responsible for serious violations of international humanitarian law, committed in the territory of the former Yugoslavia since 1991, including "mass killing, organized and systematic detention and rape of women, and the continuance of the practice of 'ethnic cleansing' * * *" S.C.Res. 827 (May 25, 1993). See p. 1332 infra. In 1994, the Security Council took similar action and established a second tribunal with jurisdiction over international crimes committed in Rwanda earlier that year. See p. 1352 infra.

In ratifying the Genocide Convention, the United States reserved the right not to go to the Court unless the U.S. agreed to do so in a particular case. See Chapter 11.

2. A human rights issue reached the International Court of Justice in the South West Africa Case, in which Ethiopia and Liberia instituted proceedings against the Republic of South Africa charging violation of the undertaking in Article 27 of the Mandate "to promote to the utmost the material and moral well-being and the social progress of the inhabitants" of South West Africa. In its first

judgment, 1962 I.C.J. 319, a majority of the Court found that the Mandate was an international agreement and that any member of the League of Nations could object to violations and bring the dispute to court as one between them and the Mandatory power. But in its final judgment the majority held that the petitioner states had not established any legal rights or interest appertaining to them in the subject matter of the present claims. 1966 I.C.J. 6.

In *Barcelona Traction*, a case unrelated to human rights, the International Court of Justice modified the implications of its 1966 judgment. See generally p. 694 infra. In oft-cited dicta, the Court stated that a distinction should be drawn between the obligations of a state towards the international community as a whole and those arising vis-à-vis another state. The former, concerning all states by their very nature, derive, *inter alia*, from the outlawing of acts of aggression, and of genocide, as also from the principles and rules concerning the basic rights of the human person, including protection from slavery and racial discrimination. See Barcelona Traction, Light and Power, Ltd. (Belgium v. Spain) Second Phase, 1970 I.C.J., 3, at 33.

3. Building on the legacy of the tribunals established in Germany and Japan after World War II and on the work of the ad hoc tribunals (see Note 1 above), a diplomatic conference was convened in Rome in 1998 to finalize a text of an agreement for a permanent International Criminal Court (ICC). The new permanent tribunal, like its ad hoc predecessors, will establish the principle of individual responsibility for genocide, war crimes, and crimes against humanity. The statute for the ICC was adopted with affirmative votes of 120 states; seven countries, including the United States, voted against it. As of 2000, more than 25 states have ratified the treaty. The ICC will come into existence when 60 states have ratified the statute. For a detailed discussion of the ICC, see p. 1367 infra.

INTERNATIONAL COVENANT ON CIVIL AND POLITICAL RIGHTS

General Assembly of the United Nations, December 16, 1966.
999 U.N.T.S. 171, 6 I.L.M. 368 (1967).

Article 40

1. The States Parties to the present Covenant undertake to submit reports on the measures they have adopted which give effect to the rights recognized herein and on the progress made in the enjoyment of those rights: (a) within one year of the entry into force of the present Covenant for the States Parties concerned and (b) thereafter whenever the Committee so requests.

2. All reports shall be submitted to the Secretary–General of the United Nations who shall transmit them to the Committee for consideration. Reports shall indicate the factors and difficulties, if any, affecting the implementation of the present Covenant.

3. The Secretary–General of the United Nations may after consultation with the Committee transmit to the specialized agencies concerned copies of such parts of the reports as may fail within their field of competence.

4. The Committee shall study the reports submitted by the States Parties to the present Covenant. It shall transmit its reports and such general comments as it may consider appropriate to the States Parties. The Committee may also transmit to the Economic and Social Council these comments

along with the copies of the reports it has received from States Parties to the present Covenant.

5. The States Parties to the present Covenant may submit to the Committee observations on any comments that may be made in accordance with paragraph 4 of this article.

ARTICLE 41

1. A State Party to the present Covenant may at any time declare under this article that it recognizes the competence of the Committee to receive and consider communications to the effect that a State Party claims that another State Party is not fulfilling its obligations under the present Covenant. Communications under this article may be received and considered only if submitted by a State Party which has made a declaration recognizing in regard to itself the competence of the Committee. No communication shall be received by the Committee if it concerns a State Party which has not made such a declaration. * * *

ARTICLE 42

1. (a) If a matter referred to the Committee in accordance with article 41 is not resolved to the satisfaction of the States Parties concerned, the Committee may, with the prior consent of the States Parties concerned, appoint an *ad* hoe Conciliation Commission (hereinafter referred to as "the Commission"). * * *

ARTICLE 44

The provisions for the implementation of the present Covenant shall apply without prejudice to the procedures prescribed in the field of human rights by or under the constituent instruments and the conventions of the United Nations and of the specialized agencies and shall not prevent the States Parties to the present Covenant from having recourse to other procedures for settling a dispute in accordance with general or special international agreements in force between them.

ARTICLE 45

The Committee shall submit to the General Assembly, through the Economic and Social Council, an annual report on its activities.

Notes

1. Article 28 of the Covenant on Civil and Political Rights provides for the establishment of the Human Rights Committee, the Covenant's principal organ of implementation. The Committee consists of eighteen members, nationals of states parties, who serve in their personal capacities. The Committee considers the reports submitted by states parties under Article 40.

The Committee has established guidelines for the form and content of reports. See U.N.Doc. A/40/600 (1985). The first part of the report should describe the general legal framework within which civil and political rights in the state are protected. The second part is to deal with the legislative, administrative and other measures in force to protect each of the rights under the Covenant, and include information about limitations or restrictions on their exercise. See United Nations Centre for Human Rights/United Nations Institute for Training and Research, Manual on Human Rights Reporting, U.N.Doc. HR/PUB/91/1 (1991). The Manual not only covers reporting under the Civil and Political Covenant, but also canvasses reporting under the Covenant on Economic, Social and Cultural Rights; the Convention on the Elimination of All Forms of Discrimination; the Convention on the Suppression and Punishment of the Crime of Apartheid; the Convention on the Elimination of All Forms of Discrimination Against Women; and the Convention Against Torture and Other Cruel, Inhuman or Degrading Treatment or Punishment.

The Committee invites states to send representatives to discuss their reports and to answer questions. The Committee also considers information from other sources. During the Cold War there had been controversy within the Committee as to what sources of information may be used.

The Committee is authorized only to make general comments on reports. The states concerned are not required to take any action on the Committee's comments, nor are the Committee's conclusions submitted to an authoritative political organ empowered to make formal and specific recommendations to the government concerned. Pursuant to Article 45 the Committee submits to the General Assembly an annual report on its activities. In these reports, the Committee has not restricted itself to reporting compliance of states, but has included general comments on the substance of particular articles of the Covenant. See, e.g., Report of the Human Rights Committee, G.A.O.R. 54th Sess. No. 40 (A/47/40) (1999). For a compilation of comments by the Committee, see Compilation of General Comments and General Recommendations Adopted by Human Rights Treaty Bodies 1–35, U.N.Doc. HRI/GEN/1/Rev. 3 (15 Aug. 1997). As of 2000, the Human Rights Committee has made 28 general comments covering many of the Covenant's substantive guarantees including, *inter alia*, equality between the sexes, the right to life, the right to freedom of thought, conscience and religion, as well as a controversial comment on reservations to the ICCPR. See p. 490 supra. The Committee continues to add to its collection of general comments. At its sixty-second session, the Committee received a draft general comment on Article 12. At its sixty-sixth session, the Committee completed the second reading of the draft and began consideration of a draft general comment on Article 4. Other general comments which the Committee has agreed to prepare will deal with Articles 2, 21 and 22. See Report of the Human Rights Committee, G.A.O.R. 54th Session, No. 40 (A/54/40) at para. 378–381 (1999).

2. For parties that have agreed, pursuant to Article 41, the Committee may receive and consider communications by one state party claiming that another state party is in violation of the Covenant. This procedure assumes that bilateral negotiations have failed and domestic remedies exhausted. The Committee is to make available its "good offices" to help settle the dispute. If a settlement is not achieved, the Committee is required to submit a report which is to be confined to a brief statement of the facts and the Committee's view on the possibilities of an amicable solution. The parties then have three months to decide whether to accept the Committee's report. As of 2000, 47 states (including the United States) have elected to declare recognition of the Committee's competence under Article 41. Through the year 2000, no parties to the treaty have made use of this mechanism providing for the "horizontal" implementation and enforcement of the Covenant.

If the state is a party to the Optional Protocol, the Committee also receives and considers communications from individuals claiming a violation by a state. See p. 631 infra.

3. The United Nations meets the expenses of and provides services to the Human Rights Committee; but, strictly, the Committee is not a U.N. agency; it is a body established by the states parties to the Covenant. (It is not to be confused with the Human Rights Commission, a United Nations agency and sub-organ of the Economic and Social Council.) Analogous committees have been established by other human rights conventions, notably the Committee on the Elimination of Racial Discrimination (CERD), established by the Convention on the Elimination of All Forms of Racial Discrimination; the Committee on the Elimination of Discrimination Against Women (CEDAW), established by the Convention on the Elimination of All Forms of Discrimination Against Women; the Committee Against Torture (CAT), established by the Convention Against Torture and Other Cruel, Inhuman or Degrading Treatment or Punishment; and the Committee on the Rights of the Child, (CRC) established by the Convention on the Rights of the Child. About the Treaty Committees, Henkin has written:

> The impressive array of international standards adopted in the various covenants and conventions indicates the readiness of the international state system in principle to sacrifice state values of autonomy and impermeability in order to promote the human values of human rights. On the other hand, the character of the enforcement machinery established by the agreements indicates how strong still is the commitment to state values, and how resistant states still are to derogations from their autonomy and to the penetration of their society, even for purposes of promoting the human values they have willingly embraced. International agreements, developed by state representatives committed to state values, have eschewed "intrusive" means of enforcement. The Genocide Convention (1948), still following a pattern established for treaties generally, provided for resort to the International Court of Justice by any party to the Convention against another party as to a dispute between them relating to the "interpretation, application or fulfillment of the present Convention". * * * The principal international covenants and conventions do not contain such a compromissory clause or any comparable provision for compulsory dispute resolution. They do not provide for institutions with authority to take initiative to monitor compliance and investigate possible violations. They do not provide generally for a body that might receive complaints of violation, examine them, and issue a judgment and a directive to a state found guilty of a violation to "cease and desist" or provide another remedy.
>
> * * *
>
> With small differences, treaty committees follow a pattern established for the Human Rights Committee in the Covenant on Civil and Political Rights and the Committee on Racial Discrimination in the Convention on the Elimination of Racial Discrimination. Committee members are elected by the states parties. They are to be nationals of states parties but may not include more than one national of the same state, with consideration being given to equitable geographical distribution [of membership] and to the representation of the different forms of civilizations as well as of the principal legal systems. Committee members are to be persons of "high moral character and recog-

nized competence in the field of human rights" and serve in their personal capacities, not as government representatives.

* * *

State reporting is the least "intrusive" enforcement machinery, reflecting the international system's strong commitment to values of state autonomy and impermeability. (It reflects too some abiding feeling that a "sovereign state" is not to be accused or adjudged, surely not without its consent.) State values are respected also in the limitations on committee consideration of the reports. The Human Rights Committee "shall study the report". It may make only "general comments" and its comments (and the "observations" of the state party) are reported to the Economic and Social Council, a political body. State values and inter-State political forces have been reflected also in various aspects of the committee's operations: in the rules of procedure adopted by the committee; in the kind and degree of attention given to reports by committee members. The committee members serve in their personal capacity and solemnly declare their impartiality, yet the kind and amount of "cross-examination" of state representatives about the reports often differs with the degree of independence which the member enjoys from his (her) own government in fact, and with relations between that government and the reporting state. The process is inevitably influenced by the disposition of political forces in the system generally—"Cold War" or "*détente*", considerations of "Third World solidarity" and "non-alignment".

Political forces have moved enforcement small steps beyond reporting, in different measure for different conventions. Differences reflect the degree of the international system's commitment to the particular rights involved in a particular convention, and corresponding political pressures to accept more intrusive monitoring. The time at which a convention was adopted may be significant, as later draftsmen learned from experience under earlier bodies, and states were reassured (or habituated) by that experience. Thus, the Covenant on Civil and Political Rights, applying to all rights, had to settle for the reporting system as the lowest common denominator of agreement. * * *

The slow development of enforcement machinery reflects the tensions in the international system between its new commitment to human values and its traditional commitment to values of State autonomy and impermeability. Slowly the treaty committees—notably the Human Rights Committee and the Committee on Racial Discrimination—have gained experience, confidence and acceptance, becoming less "politicized" and more effective. Slowly more States have accepted the jurisdiction of these committees to consider private complaints. States have not become much more willing to scrutinize or be scrutinized by other States; they have become less unwilling to respond to intercession by a respected multilateral body in limited circumstances.

Experience has afforded important lessons in the politics of enforcement of the special law of human rights. It had been anticipated that States would be reluctant to submit to complaints that they were violating their obligations under the Covenant and other conventions, but that they would be less reluctant to submit to State complaints than to private complaints. Therefore, the Convention on the Elimination of Racial Discrimination provided for inter-State complaints but made submission to private complaint optional. The Covenant made both procedures optional, but relegated State submissions to private complaint to a separate protocol so as not to discourage adherence to the Covenant.

> Many States, we must conclude, remain reluctant to submit to individual complaints—because they resist penetration of the State veil, are unwilling to have their citizens act independently in the international arena, and fear they might be embarrassed by accusations. But slowly an increasing number of States are becoming less unwilling to submit to the possibility of such complaints before a respected international body in a discreet process. On the other hand, States remain unwilling to expend political capital and to jeopardize their friendly relations by complaining of human rights violations by another State; states are unwilling to invite such complaints against themselves. States have made significant steps towards accepting third party resolution of disputes involving traditional state interests; they have not yet recognized that human rights everywhere are every state's proper interest.

Henkin, International Law: Politics and Values 208–214 (1995).

OPTIONAL PROTOCOL TO THE INTERNATIONAL COVENANT ON CIVIL AND POLITICAL RIGHTS

General Assembly of the United Nations, December 16, 1966.
999 U.N.T.S. 171, 6 I.L.M. 383 (1967).

Article 1

A State Party to the Covenant that becomes a Party to the present Protocol recognizes the competence of the Committee to receive and consider communications from individuals, subject to its jurisdiction, claiming to be victims of a violation by that State Party of any of the rights set forth in the Covenant. No communication shall be received by the Committee if it concerns a State Party to the Covenant which is not a Party to the present Protocol.

Notes

1. Compare Part II of the International Convention on the Elimination of All Forms of Racial Discrimination, 660 U.N.T.S. 195, 1966, which provides for a Committee on the Elimination of Racial Discrimination, requires parties to report to the Committee on compliance, and provides for state complaints against other states. In addition, Article 14 provides that a state may by declaration recognize the competence of the Committee to consider communications from individual victims or groups of victims.

2. Although the Protocol to the International Covenant on Civil and Political Rights speaks of "communications from individuals * * * claiming to be victims of a violation," the Human Rights Committee early concluded that it may receive communications on behalf of such individuals from other persons or organizations. See Report of the Human Rights Committee, 32 GAOR Supp. 44 (A/32/44) at i (1977). That is now reflected in Rule 90(1)(b) of the Committee's Rules.

3. Since the Committee began its work under the Optional Protocol at its second session in 1977, 911 communications have been placed before it (as of 2000). See 54 U.N.G.A.O.R. Supp. No. 40 at 160, U.N.Doc. A/54/40 (1999). Of the 911 communications, 333 were concluded by Committee views expressed under Article 5(4) of the Optional Protocol; 274 were declared inadmissible; 129 were discontinued or withdrawn; 175 were declared admissible but have not yet been concluded; and 139 were pending at the pre-admissibility stage. See generally

Helfer & Slaughter, Toward a Theory of Effective Supranational Adjudication, 107 Yale L. J. 273 (1997); Pocar, Legal Values of the Human Rights Committee's Views, 1991–92 Canadian Hum. Rts. Y.B. 119 (1992); Opsahl, The Human Rights Committee, in The United Nations and Human Rights: A Critical Appraisal 369 (Alston, ed. 1992); McGoldrick, The Human Rights Committee: Its Role in the Development of the International Covenant on Civil and Political Rights (1991); Higgins, The United Nations: Still a Force for Peace, 52 Mod. L.Rev. I (1989).

The Committee defines and clarifies the Optional Protocol as it presents its views on the cases it finds admissible. For example, the Committee has required authors of communications to justify their authority to act on behalf of an alleged victim. It has declared that only individuals, not organizations, may submit communications. The Committee has also explained its understanding of many of the substantive provisions of the Covenant on Civil and Political Rights, including the right to life (Art. 6), the right not to be subjected to torture (Art. 7), the right to liberty and security of person (Art. 9), the rights to family life and protection of the family (Articles 17 and 23), and others. See generally Compilation of General Comments and General Recommendations adopted by Human Rights Treaty Bodies, HRI/GEN/1/Rev.3, 15 August 1997.

4. Since 1991, the Human Rights Committee has sometimes requested States to submit "emergency" reports when events indicated that the enjoyment of Covenant rights had been seriously affected. See Joseph, New Procedures Concerning the Human Rights Committees Examination of State Reports, 13 Netherlands Q. Hum. Rts. 5 (1995).

INTERNATIONAL COVENANT ON ECONOMIC, SOCIAL AND CULTURAL RIGHTS

General Assembly of the United Nations, December 16, 1966.
993 U.N.T.S. 3, 6 I.L.M. 360 (1967).

Article 16

1. The States Parties to the present Covenant undertake to submit in conformity with this part of the Covenant reports on the measures which they have adopted and the progress made in achieving the observance of the rights recognized herein.

2. (a) All reports shall be submitted to the Secretary–General of the United Nations who shall transmit copies to the Economic and Social Council for consideration in accordance with the provisions of the present Covenant.

(b) The Secretary–General of the United Nations shall also transmit to the specialized agencies copies of the reports, or any relevant parts therefrom, from States Parties to the present Covenant which are also members of these specialized agencies in so far as these reports, or parts therefrom, relate to any matters which fall within the responsibilities of the said agencies in accordance with their constitutional instruments.

Article 19

The Economic and Social Council may transmit to the Commission on Human Rights for study and general recommendation or as appropriate for information the reports concerning human rights submitted by States in accordance with articles 16 and 17, and those concerning human rights submitted by the specialized agencies in accordance with article 18.

Notes

1. In the light of the growing maturity and success of the Human Rights Committee, the Economic and Social Council established a Committee on Economic, Social and Cultural Rights to consider the reports submitted by the states parties. G.A. Res. 1985/17 (1985). The character and function of this Committee parallel those of the Human Rights Committee established by Article 28 of the Covenant on Civil and Political Rights.

2. Does the Economic and Social Committee "monitor" compliance? Could the Committee determine whether a state is "achieving progressively the full realization of the rights" set out in the Covenant? Could the Committee determine the optimal use of a state's "available resources" and the "appropriate means" to bring about the realization of the rights recognized in the Covenant?

3. The Committee on Economic, Social and Cultural Rights has developed the practice, following the Human Rights Committee, of adopting "general comments." By 2000, the Committee had adopted 13 such comments, the most recent on the right to education (Art 13). See Committee on Economic, Social and Cultural Rights, General Comment No. 13, U.N. Doc. E/C.12/1999/10. Other comments have dealt with, *inter alia*, international technical assistance measures, the right to adequate housing, the rights of persons with disabilities, forced evictions, and the right to adequate food.

4. Like other U.N. human rights treaty bodies, the Committee on Economic, Social and Cultural Rights has faced the problem of persistent failure by states parties to satisfy their reporting obligations. In the Committee's words, "a situation of persistent non-reporting by states parties risks bringing the entire supervisory procedure into disrepute, thereby undermining one of the foundations of the Covenant." See Committee on Economic, Social and Cultural Rights, Report on the Sixteenth and Seventeenth Sessions (Sessional/Annual Report of Committee), U.N. Doc. E/1998/22, at para. 42. To address this problem, the Committee decided that it would begin scheduling "very much overdue" reports to be considered at future sessions and would notify the states parties concerned. If that state failed to provide a report, the Committee would proceed, in the absence of a report, "to consider the status of economic, social and cultural rights in the light of all the available information." Id. at 44.

5. Since 1990, the Committee on Economic, Social and Cultural Rights has considered developing an optional protocol to the ICESCR, modeled after the first optional protocol to the ICCPR. The Committee on Economic, Social and Cultural Rights, at its 15th session held in Geneva in 1996, concluded its consideration of a draft Optional Protocol to the International Covenant on Economic, Social and Cultural Rights granting the right of individuals or groups to submit communications (complaints) concerning non-compliance with the Covenant. The elaboration of the draft optional protocol was recommended by the World Conference on Human Rights. See Annual Report of the Committee on Economic, Social and Cultural Rights on its 14th and 15th Sessions, U.N. Doc. E/1997/22, Annex IV.

6. In addition to the comprehensive Covenants, the United Nations has adopted a number of Conventions concerned with specific rights. See p. 599 supra. Numerous specialized conventions have also been adopted by regional organizations. See p. 650 infra. The following report addresses some of the problems associated with the multiplication of treaties and treaty bodies within the U.N.

system, while also providing a broader perspective on the effectiveness of U.N. human rights treaty systems.

FINAL REPORT ON ENHANCING THE LONG–TERM EFFECTIVENESS OF THE UNITED NATIONS HUMAN RIGHTS TREATY SYSTEM

U.N. Doc. E/CN.4/1997/74.

1. This report is submitted by the independent expert, Mr. Philip Alston, appointed by the Secretary–General.

* * *

7. * * *

(d) The number of overdue reports has increased by 34 percent [since 1993] and the delays experienced by States parties between the submission and examination of their reports have increased to the point where some States will wait almost three years before their reports are examined;

(e) The number of communications being processed under the various complaints procedures has greatly increased and existing backlogs are unacceptably high. At the same time, there is a clear need to create additional complaints systems in order to ensure that due attention is paid to economic, social and cultural rights and to the full range of women's rights. Specific proposals in relation to both the Convention on the Elimination of All Forms of Discrimination against Women and the International Covenant on Economic, Social and Cultural Rights are currently under consideration;

(f) The resources available to service this sizeable expansion in the system have actually contracted rather than expanded and there have been consistent calls, escalating in volume and intensity, * * * for increased resources and improved servicing to be made available; * * *

8. The extent of the shortcomings inherent in the treaty monitoring system has led some observers to propose radical solutions. Thus, for example, in 1994 one commentator proposed, *inter alia,* that States which do not satisfy a set of minimum requirements drawn from the relevant treaties should be expelled from the treaty regime; the system of State reporting should be discontinued; the treaty bodies should undertake onsite fact-finding in every State party; and acceptance of a right to petition under all six treaties should be made mandatory.* Writing in August 1996, in a report for the International Law Association, the same commentator considered there to be an "implementation crisis * * * of dangerous proportions".** In her view, "the treaty regime has been depreciated by chronic levels of non-compliance, both with

* Bayefsky, "Making the Human Rights Treaties Work:, in L. Henkin and J.L. Hargrove (eds.), *Human Rights: An Agenda for the Next Century*, Studies in Transnational Legal Policy No. 26 (Washington D.C., American Society of International Law, 1994) p. 229 at p. 264.

** Bayefsky, "Report on the UN Human Rights Treaties: Facing the Implementation Crisis", in *First Report of the Committee on International Law and Practice,* International Law Association, Helsinki Conference (1996), p. 11.

the substantive terms of the treaties, and with existing enforcement mechanisms".***

* * *

9. The present report is based upon several premises. The first is that the basic assumptions of the treaty supervisory system are sound and remain entirely valid. In other words, the principle of holding States accountable for non-compliance with their treaty obligations by means of an objective and constructive dialogue, on the basis of comprehensive information and inputs from all interested parties, has been vindicated in practice and has the potential to be an important and effective means by which to promote respect for human rights. * * *

10. The fourth premise is that the present system is unsustainable and that significant reforms will be required if the overall regime is to achieve its objectives.

* * *

37. Most of the committees continue to express concern over the consequences of the large number of significantly overdue reports.* * *

38. In its 1996 annual report * * * the Committee against Torture noted * * * that there were 96 States parties and * * * that there were 55 States with overdue reports [some of which were more than four years late]. * * * The Committee took two measures in response. The first was to issue a separate document listing overdue reports. The second was to give wide publicity to the list at its end of session press conferences.

39. In its 1996 annual report * * * the Human Rights Committee expressed "its serious concern" that "more than two thirds of all States parties * * * were in arrears with their reports". * * *

41. * * * [R]esponses might include an easing of the reporting requirements under certain circumstances. * * * The Human Rights Committee decided in 1996 that, "under very exceptional circumstances", when a report is overdue "because of material difficulties", the State party could be invited to send a delegation to discuss those difficulties or be asked to submit a provisional report dealing only with certain aspects of the Covenant. * * *

Another approach * * * would be to eliminate the obligation to provide comprehensive periodic reports. * * *

* * *

45. The key question * * * is what types of measures designed to raise the costs of non-compliance [with reporting obligations] might be appropriate, potentially productive in terms of upholding the integrity of the system, consistent with the legal framework of the relevant treaty, and politically and otherwise acceptable. Various palliatives are available. * * * They include: the elimination of reporting and its replacement by detailed questions to which answers must be given; the preparation of a single consolidated report to satisfy several different requirements; and the much wider use of a more professional advisory services programme designed to assist in the preparation

*** Ibid., p. 12.

of reports. Ultimately, however, none of these might make a difference in hard-core cases. Under those circumstances the only viable option open to the treaty bodies is to proceed with an examination of the situation in a State party in the absence of a report. This has been done for a number of years by the Committee on Economic, Social and Cultural Rights and the Committee on the Elimination of Racial Discrimination has adopted a very similar approach. * * *

* * *

47. In implementing such an approach, the experience of the Committee on Economic, Social and Cultural Rights is instructive. Ample notice has been given to the States concerned and, in a majority of the cases taken up so far, reports which had been dramatically overdue have suddenly materialized. For the rest, it is particularly important that the Committee is in a position to undertake detailed research work and to be able to base its examination upon a wide range of sources of information. * * *

48. The present supervisory system can function only because of the large-scale delinquency of States which either do not report at all, or report long after the due date. * * *

49. * * * [I]f every State party with a report overdue under either of the Covenants were to submit that report tomorrow, the last to be received could not be considered, on the basis of existing arrangements, before the year 2003. At that point, the relevant committee would be considering an eight-year-old report and would have a huge backlog of subsequent reports pending.

* * *

90. [One possible option for addressing the reporting backlog is] the preparation of a single consolidated report by each State party, which would then be submitted in satisfaction of the requirements under each of the treaties to which the State is a party. * * *

* * *

91. Another proposal * * * would be to eliminate the requirement that States parties' periodic reports should be comprehensive. Such an approach would clearly not be appropriate in relation to initial reports. * * *

[The report also recommends the convening of an expert group to consider the consolidation (reduction) of the number of treaty bodies.]

Note

The preceding report considers treaty bodies established to monitor conventions adopted under U.N. auspices and notes a range of proposals that have been put forth to address the problem of persistent delays by states parties in meeting their obligations under the various treaties. Which of these proposals merit support? What other possible reforms should be considered? For an analysis of the effectiveness of human rights treaty regimes, see The U.N. Human Rights Regime: Is it Effective?, 1997 A.S.I.L. Proc. 460–484. See Alston & Crawford, The Future of U.N. Human Rights Treaty Monitoring (2000).

INTERSTATE ENFORCEMENT

All international human rights agreements make some provision for the settlement of disputes between parties about the interpretation or application of the agreement. The Covenant on Civil and Political Rights includes an optional clause (Article 41) by which a State may declare that it recognizes, on a reciprocal basis, the competence of the Human Rights Committee to receive and consider "communications" that it is not fulfilling its obligations under the Covenant. See p. 627 supra. The Convention on the Elimination of all Forms of Racial Discrimination (CERD) and the Convention Against Torture include similar provisions, but the CERD provision (Article 11) is not optional and requires no special declaration.

Do these provisions supplement or replace the ordinary interstate remedies for violations of international law?

HENKIN, HUMAN RIGHTS AND "DOMESTIC JURISDICTION"

(in Human Rights, International Law and the Helsinki Accord 21, 29–31, 33 (Buergenthal ed. 1977).

Breach of a human rights obligation, like violation of any international legal obligation, is an international wrongful act for which the international legal system provides remedies. It has been suggested, however, that the only remedies for the violation of a human rights agreement are those specified in the agreement. In particular, unless expressly so provided, one party does not have a remedy against another for failure to live up to the agreement. That view is ill-founded.

The duty to carry out international obligations is the heart of the international legal system; and that prime duty implies an ancillary duty to cease and desist from a violation and to give other satisfaction to the state or states to which the obligation was due. The injured state may seek reparation and ask that the violator take measures to prevent repetition, offer an apology, punish the persons who committed the violation, pay a symbolic sum of money, or afford other relief.

Except for the few universal obligations, enforceable perhaps by any state (in a kind of *actio popularis*), a breach of an international obligation is a wrong to the particular state or states to which that obligation is due, and only such state or states may enforce that obligation and seek a remedy for its violation. An international agreement creates obligations between parties and gives each party a legal interest in having it carried out; it may be enforced by one party against another even if it is an agreement for the benefit of a third entity not party to the agreement. * * *

The argument that human rights agreements are not directly enforceable between the parties * * * seems to be based * * * on the view that, as a matter of interpretation, human rights agreements in general, and particular human rights agreements, contemplate no remedies between parties, but only whatever remedies are expressly provided. It is assumed that states are willing to enter into agreements about human rights but are unwilling to have them enforced among the parties; the quest for special enforcement machinery, it is said, also reflects the intention that ordinary interstate remedies be excluded.

These arguments are not persuasive. International human rights agreements are like other international agreements, creating legal obligations between the parties and international responsibility for their violation. They are essentially mutual undertakings among states for the benefit of third parties (the inhabitants of the countries party to the agreement) and in principle are enforceable by the promisees, that is, the other parties to the agreement. *Prima facie,* surely, and in the absence of any expressed or clearly implied intention to supersede them, the usual remedies for breach of an international obligation are available here. * * *

No human rights agreements, even those that establish elaborate enforcement machinery, expressly or by clear implication exclude the ordinary interstate remedies. In fact, the principal human rights agreements clearly imply the contrary: that every party to the agreement has a legal interest in having it observed by other parties and can invoke ordinary legal remedies to enforce it.

* * *

There is no suggestion * * * that the human rights of all individuals everywhere can be protected by all states. Human rights agreements generally do not create universal legal interests for all states: they create legal interests for the parties to the agreement by virtue of the legal obligations assumed by them *inter sese.* The remedies to be invoked are not by way of some extraordinary *actio popularis;* they are the ordinary remedies available to parties to an agreement against violation by another party. The distinction is fundamental and clear. In the *South West Africa* Cases, for example, the majority denied the standing of Ethiopia and Liberia to enforce the human rights provisions of the mandate because they "were not parties to them * * * Not being parties to the instruments of mandate, they could draw from them only such rights as are unequivocally conferred." The implication is that, even for the majority of the court, had the petitioners been parties to the mandate agreement they would have had a legal interest to enforce it and could have availed themselves of the usual remedies for vindicating that interest.

Notes

1. For a contrary view, see Frowein, The Interrelationship between the Helsinki Final Act, the International Covenants on Human Rights, and the European Convention on Human Rights, in Human Rights, International Law and the Helsinki Accord 71, 78–80 (Buergenthal ed. 1977). See Restatement (Third) § 703, Reporters' Note 2.

2. In the *Soering* case, the European Court of Human Rights ruled that under Article 3 of the European Convention on Human Rights (which prohibits torture, inhuman or degrading treatment) the United Kingdom could not extradite a person to the United States to be tried for a capital offense because of the possibility that upon conviction the person would be confined on "death row" which is inhuman and degrading and would violate Article 3. The Soering Case,

[1989] Eur. Ct.H.R., Ser. A. No. 161. See p. 656 infra. But see Pratt and Morgan v. Jamaica, Communications Nos. 210/1986 and 225/1987, in Report of the Human Rights Committee, U.N.G.A.O.R., 44th Sess., Supp. No. 40 (A/44/40) at 215, 231, where the Committee held that the Covenant on Civil and Political Rights was not violated by a lengthy stay on death row.

For state enforcement of human rights upon violation by other states, see p. 641.

INDIVIDUAL RIGHTS AND REMEDIES UNDER INTERNATIONAL AGREEMENTS

HENKIN, INTERNATIONAL HUMAN RIGHTS AS "RIGHTS"

1 Cardozo L. Rev. 438 (1979) (footnotes omitted).

Because the international law of human rights is made by states assuming obligations (the state as legislator), the international instruments focus at first on the state's obligations: it is the state's undertaking that creates the law. But under that law after it is in effect, the focus shifts sharply. The instruments are designated as dealing with the "rights" of individuals and there is reference to individual "rights" in every article. But the state's obligation and the individual's right are not necessarily correlative, or even in the same legal order. There are different possible perspectives on the relation between them:

1. The simple, undaring view sees international human rights agreements essentially, if not exclusively, in interstate terms. The agreements constitute undertakings by each state-party to every other state-party, creating rights and obligations between them. * * *

In this perspective the only rights and duties created by international human rights agreements are the duty of every state-party to act as it had promised, and the right of every other state-party to have that promise to it kept. The individual has no international legal rights; he is only the "incidental beneficiary" of rights and duties between the state-parties. The individual has no international remedies; he is only the "incidental" beneficiary of the remedies available between states-parties. * * *

2. A second perspective would see the international agreements, while creating rights and duties for the states-parties, as also giving the individual rights against his society under international law (in addition to any rights he has under his national constitutional-legal system). The language of the agreements clearly declares these individual rights in every clause: "Every human being has the inherent right to life"; "No one shall be held in slavery;" "Everyone has the right to liberty and security of the person;" "Everyone shall be free to leave any country, including his own." The individual has these international legal rights even though they are enforceable only by interstate remedies, by governments or international bodies acting in his behalf. Under the Optional Protocol to the Covenant on Civil and Political Rights providing for consideration by the Human Rights Committee of individual complaints, or under the provision in the European Convention that the European Commission "may receive petitions" from any person

claiming to be the victim of a violation, the individual enforces his own right by his own remedy.

* * *

3. A third perspective, which is independent of but might be combined with either of the two set forth, would suggest that the states-parties, as legislators, have legislated "human rights" into international law giving them status as affirmative independent values. That status is supported and furthered by the rights and duties which were established, whether the rights be those of states or of individuals. While directly creating status or values, independent of rights and duties, is an unusual conception in international law, since law is made wholly by way of states assuming obligations, one can say, perhaps, that every state-party assumes two different kinds of obligations corresponding to the two roles I have described. Acting with other states (the state as legislator), each state agrees to recognize and give legal status in the international system to "human rights" as claims that every individual has— or should have upon his own society. In addition, each state (the state as obligor) undertakes to respect and ensure these values for its own citizens, thereby also creating rights in other states, and perhaps in individuals.

Note

Compare the opinion of Judge Bork in Tel–Oren v. Libyan Arab Republic, 726 F.2d 774 (D.C.Cir.1984), p. 648 infra.

2. *Enforcement of Customary Law of Human Rights*

RESTATEMENT (THIRD) § 703

Comment *b* and Reporters' Notes 3 and 4

b. Remedies for violation of customary law of human rights. Since the obligations of the customary law of human rights are *erga omnes* (obligations to all states), § 702, Comment *o*, any state may pursue remedies for their violation, even if the individual victims were not nationals of the complaining state and the violation did not affect any other particular interest of that state. For the remedies available to individual victims against the state or state officials, see Comment *c*.

* * *

3. *Remedies for violation of customary law of human rights.* Ordinarily, violations of customary law entail remedies for the state that is the victim of the violation. The customary law of human rights, however, protects individuals subject to each state's jurisdiction, and the international obligation runs equally to all other states, with no state a victim of the violation more than any other. Any state, therefore, may make a claim against the violating state. Where the complaining and the accused states have agreed to means for settling disputes between them generally—for example, by accepting the jurisdiction of the International Court of Justice or submitting to arbitration—such means are available for alleged violations of this section.

In the *Barcelona Traction* case, Reporters' Note 2, at 32, the International Court of Justice said:

> In particular, an essential distinction should be drawn between the obligations of a State towards the international community as a whole, and those arising vis-à-vis another State in the field of diplomatic protection. By their very nature the former are the concern of all States. In view of the importance of the rights involved, all States can be held to have a legal interest in their protection; they are obligations *erga omnes*.
>
> Such obligations derive, for example, in contemporary international law, from the outlawing of acts of aggression, and of genocide, as also from the principles and rules concerning the basic rights of the human person, including protection from slavery and racial discrimination. Some of the corresponding rights of protection have entered into the body of general international law * * *; others are conferred by international instruments of a universal or quasi-universal character.
>
> Obligations the performance of which is the subject of diplomatic protection are not of the same category. It cannot be held, when one such obligation in particular is in question, in a specific case, that all States have a legal interest in its observance.

The Court seemed to distinguish diplomatic protection in general, including protection for ordinary violations of human rights, which is available only for nationals of the complaining state (see Reporters' Note 2), from protection against violations of the "basic rights of the human person" set forth in this section, as to which "all States can be held to have a legal interest in their protection."

4. *Remedies regardless of nationality of individual victim.* Remedies available to states parties under international human rights agreements (Subsection (1)), and remedies available to all states for violation by any state of the customary law of human rights (Subsection (2)), do not depend on the nationality of the individual victim. But see Reporters' Note 2, distinguishing between interstate claims and diplomatic protection under international human rights agreements. In practice, states are more likely to intercede on behalf of individuals who are their own nationals or with whom they have other links. But see the South West Africa cases, Reporters' Note 1.

Notes

1. There have been suggestions that a state may intervene by force in another state that commits gross human rights violations. Is this consistent with Article 2(4) of the U.N. Charter? "Humanitarian intervention" has in effect been authorized by the Security Council when it found a threat to international peace and security. The legitimacy of collective intervention by groupings such as NATO became an issue in 1999 in respect of Kosovo. See the discussion in 93 A.J.I.L. 831–869 (1999) and Chapter 12 infra.

2. The Restatement (Third) § 703, Comment *f* adds the following:

> *State sanctions for human rights violations by another state.* A state may criticize another state for failure to abide by recognized international human rights standards, and may shape its trade, aid or other national policies so as

to dissociate itself from the violating state or to influence that state to discontinue the violations.

3. On obligations and remedies *erga omnes* generally, see Schachter, International Law in Theory and Practice 208–13 (1991); Henkin, International Law: Politics and Values 216–217 (1995); see also Meron, Human Rights and Humanitarian Norms as Customary Law (1989) and Chapter 9 infra, pp. 694–697.

ENFORCEMENT BY POLITICAL BODIES

By the end of the 20th century consideration of human rights violations by, or under the auspices of the U.N. Commission on Human Rights has become established practice, with the Commission designating "rapporteurs" and working groups to consider violations in particular countries, or to consider patterns of violations in several countries. See e.g. the Resolution designating a Rapporteur for Zaire, E/CN.4/Res/1994/87, and the Resolution designating a Rapporteur on the human rights of migrants, E/CN.4/Res/1999/44.

See generally the discussion of political enforcement by the United Nations, in Philip Alston, The Commission on Human Rights, in the United Nations and Human Rights, a Critical Appraisal (Alston ed. 1992).

HENKIN, INTERNATIONAL LAW: POLITICS AND VALUES

217–218 (1996) (footnotes omitted). Also at 216 Rec. des Cours 9, 265–67 (1989–IV).

International human rights law benefits significantly from enforcement also by political bodies. In general, international political bodies have attended only to the enforcement of international legal norms of extraordinary political significance, such as the law of the Charter on the use of force, but political bodies have devoted extraordinary efforts to promoting law on human rights and for that and other reasons they have not avoided the demands of enforcement of—inducing compliance with—that law.

If law is politics, enforcement of law in the inter-state system is also heavily political. Political influence brought to bear in the organs and suborgans of the United Nations determined the enforcement machinery that found its way into covenants and conventions. (Political forces, I have suggested, influenced also how that machinery has worked.) But United Nations bodies themselves have also been an arena for charges of human rights violations, sometimes evoking resolutions of condemnation.

The Members of the United Nations have been divided as to their readiness to address charges of specific human rights violations. Some states have resisted the airing of such charges on the ground that these were not the proper business of the Organization, which is forbidden "to intervene in matters which are essentially within the domestic jurisdiction of any state" (Art. 2(7)). In fact, United Nations practice long ago rejected that objection, in effect reflecting the conclusion that human rights violations were not a matter of domestic jurisdiction, or that United Nations discussion of them is not intervention, or both. United Nations practice in this regard has been determined not according to legal principle but by negotiation and majority vote.

Sensitivity to state values, reluctance to scrutinize and be scrutinized, have generally discouraged United Nations consideration of charges of specific violations. For a while, dominant forces in the Organization succeeded in preventing consideration of the thousands of complaints of human rights violations that poured into the United Nations Secretariat. In time, the Economic and Social Council was moved to authorize a subcommission of the Human Rights Commission to appoint a "working group" to meet for a short period each year, in confidence, to consider communications "which appear to reveal a consistent pattern of gross violations of human rights and fundamental freedoms." In time, the proceedings became less limited and less confidential and increasingly the United Nations Human Rights Commission has been appointing "rapporteurs,", adopting resolutions, and issuing reports. At all times, moreover, some charges of violation have made their way to the agenda of the larger United Nations bodies, the Economic and Social Council and the General Assembly, and—especially since the end of the Cold War—also the Security Council.

One cannot appraise these activities with precision or with confidence, but clearly they have served as some inducement to terminate or mitigate violations, perhaps even as some deterrent. Political bodies, however, are subject to their own political laws. The larger bodies—notably the United Nations General Assembly—are more visible, more newsworthy, therefore more "politicized," therefore less likely to apply human rights norms judicially, impartially. In such bodies, human rights are more susceptible to being subordinated to non-human rights considerations. There, voting, including "bloc-voting", has led to "selective targeting" of some states, sometimes exaggerating their violations, and overlooking those of other states, including some that are guilty of gross violations. Smaller political bodies, such as the Human Rights Commission, are also inhabited by government representatives concerned for state values and friendly relations, but increasingly they are able to be somewhat less "political," more evenhanded, as well as more activist in the cause of human rights.

QUESTION OF THE VIOLATION OF HUMAN RIGHTS AND FUNDAMENTAL FREEDOMS, INCLUDING POLICIES OF RACIAL DISCRIMINATION AND SEGREGATION AND OF APARTHEID, IN ALL COUNTRIES, WITH PARTICULAR REFERENCE TO COLONIAL AND OTHER DEPENDENT COUNTRIES AND TERRITORIES

Economic and Social Council, 1967.
E.S.C.Res. 1235, 42 ESCOR Supp. I (E/4393) at 17.

* * *

2. *Authorizes* the Commission on Human Rights and the Sub–Commission on Prevention of Discrimination and Protection of Minorities, in conformity with the provisions of paragraph i of the Commission's resolution 8 (XXIII), to examine information relevant to gross violations of human rights and fundamental freedoms, as exemplified by the policy of apartheid as practised in the Republic of South Africa and in the Territory of South West Africa under the direct responsibility of the United Nations and now illegally occupied by the Government of the Republic of South Africa, and to racial

discrimination as practised notably in Southern Rhodesia, contained in the communications listed by the Secretary–General pursuant to Economic and Social Council resolution 728 F (XXVIII) of 30 July 1959; * * *

PROCEDURE FOR DEALING WITH COMMUNICATIONS RELATING TO VIOLATIONS OF HUMAN RIGHTS AND FUNDAMENTAL FREEDOMS

Economic and Social Council, 1970.
E.S.C.Res. 1503, 48 ESCOR Supp. 1A (E/4832/Add. 1) at 8 (footnotes omitted).

Noting resolutions 7 (XXVI) and 17 (XXV) of the Commission on Human Rights and resolution 2 (XXI) of the Sub–Commission on Prevention of Discrimination and Protection of Minorities,

1. *Authorizes* the Sub–Commission on Prevention of Discrimination and Protection of Minorities to appoint a working group consisting of not more than five of its members, with due regard to geographical distribution, to meet once a year in private meetings for a period not exceeding ten days immediately before the sessions of the Sub–Commission to consider all communications, including replies of Governments thereon, received by the Secretary–General under Council resolution 728 F (XXVIII) of 30 July 1959 with a view to bringing to the attention of the Sub–Commission those communications, together with replies of Governments, if any, which appear to reveal a consistent pattern of gross and reliably attested violations of human rights and fundamental freedoms within the terms of reference of the Sub–Commission; * * *

Notes

1. Under what authority did the Economic and Social Council adopt this procedure? Is the assumption that "gross violations of human rights" constitute violations of the U.N. Charter or of other international agreements? Of customary law? Is the authority of the working group limited to charges against states members of the U.N., or states that have adhered to the international covenants on human rights or other relevant conventions? See Buergenthal, Human Rights, International Law, and the Helsinki Accord (1977); Sohn, Human Rights: Their Implementation by the United Nations, in Human Rights in International Law (Meron ed. 1984).

2. Human rights questions considered by the U.N. Human Rights Commission of the Economic and Social Council frequently come also to the U.N. General Assembly. (For years, the Assembly had on its agenda apartheid in South Africa.)

For a discussion of U.N. bodies concerned with human rights, see Farer & Gaer, The UN & Human Rights: At the End of the Beginning, in United Nations, Divided World 245 (Roberts & Kingsbury, eds. 2d ed. 1993) Meron, Human Rights Law–Making in the United Nations (1986). The General Assembly has considered human rights issues in the context of other subjects within its jurisdiction—because they endangered relations between states and international peace and security (e.g., the issue of Indians in South Africa, G.A. Res. 44 (1946); apartheid, G.A. Res. 721 (1953)); because they raised questions under principles of international law (e.g., the case of the Russian wives, G.A. Res. 285 (1949)); because they raised questions under peace treaties or under principles of the Charter (violations by Bulgaria and Hungary, G.A. Res. 272 (1949) and G.A.Res. 385 (1950)).

See also the Security Council Resolution imposing a mandatory arms embargo against the Republic of South Africa in response to racial repression, p. 727 infra.

3. It was doubtless the issue of apartheid that galvanized support for U.N. implementation of human rights as reflected in Resolutions 1235, and 1503; apartheid brought other "consistent patterns of gross violations" in its wake.

With the end of apartheid will there be less support for consideration of complaints of violations? Or has U.N. consideration become accepted practice?

3. National Enforcement of International Human Rights Obligations

Since human rights are to be enjoyed and implemented within national societies, the enforcement of international human rights norms (or their national equivalents) becomes largely the responsibility of national institutions, whether such institutions enforce the international norm directly, as by incorporating treaty provisions into domestic law or by enacting the substance of such norms in national constitutions or legislation.

HENKIN, INTRODUCTION

in The International Bill of Rights: The Covenant on Civil and Political Rights 7 (Henkin, ed. 1981) (footnote omitted).

The international law of human rights parallels and supplements national law, superseding and supplying the deficiencies of national constitutions and laws; but it does not replace, and indeed depends on, national institutions. The constituency in every society that supports human rights law is different from the constituency that supports, say, international trade agreements, or military alliances, or peaceful settlements, or even international organization and cooperation. The pressures on a government to adhere to international human rights law are also different from those to adhere to other law, and indeed, a state's adherence to human rights conventions is far less important if in fact it behaves at home, toward its own, consistently with their terms.

In other respects, too, international law and politics see human rights in the context of the international political system. Although human rights are universal, they are the claims of an individual upon his society, not on other societies. Although the society in which one lives may be crucial to life and dignity, although a right to change one's society might well be deemed fundamental, the individual does not have an absolute right to join another society and seek his rights there. Even those who are oppressed at home do not yet have an international human right to asylum elsewhere; those who are starving at home do not have an internationally recognized human right to be taken in by the more affluent societies or to be fed by them.

INTERNATIONAL COVENANT ON CIVIL AND POLITICAL RIGHTS

999 U.N.T.S. 171, 6 I.L.M. 368 (1967).

ARTICLE 2

1. Each State Party to the present Covenant undertakes to respect and to ensure to all individuals within its territory and subject to its jurisdiction the rights recognized in the present Covenant, without distinction of any kind, such as race, colour, sex, language, religion, political or other opinion, national or social origin, property, birth or other status.

2. Where not already provided for by existing legislative or other measures, each State Party to the present Covenant undertakes to take the necessary steps, in accordance with its constitutional processes and with the provisions of the present Covenant, to adopt such legislative or other measures as may be necessary to give effect to the rights recognized in the present Covenant.

3. Each State Party to the present Covenant undertakes:

(a) To ensure that any person whose rights or freedoms as herein recognized are violated shall have an effective remedy, notwithstanding that the violation has been committed by persons acting in an official capacity;

(b) To ensure that any person claiming such a remedy shall have his right thereto determined by competent judicial, administrative or legislative authorities, or by any other competent authority provided for by the legal system of the state, and to develop the possibilities of judicial remedy;

(c) To ensure that the competent authorities shall enforce such remedies when granted.

Notes

1. Human rights norms recognized as customary international law (p. 602 above) are law in the United States and can be enforced in appropriate proceedings. For the suggestion that such cases arise under U.S. law and are therefore within the general jurisdiction of U.S. federal courts under § 1331, see Restatement (Third) § 703. Reporters' Note 7. For a discussion of the extent to which international human rights law is part of U.S. law generally, see p. 163 above. For the view that the courts will not compel the President to respect customary international law, see p. 176, Chapter 3.

Whether U.S obligations under treaty obligations can be enforced in courts may depend on whether the treaties are viewed as self-executing. For cases holding that the human rights provisions of the U.N. Charter are not self-executing, see Frolova v. Union of Soviet Socialist Republics, 761 F.2d 370 (7th Cir.1985), and cases cited there at 374 n. 5. And see Chapter 3, p. 209 above. The U.S. is a party to the Protocol Relating to the Status of Refugees, 1966, and this Protocol has been invoked in United States courts. See I.N.S. v. Stevic, 467 U.S. 407, 104 S.Ct. 2489, 81 L.Ed.2d 321 (1984); compare Sale v. Haitian Centers Council, discussed at p. 622 supra. On the problem of non-self-executing declarations attached to U.S. instruments of ratification, see pp. 210–211 supra.

2. In some situations, aliens may obtain a remedy in United States courts for human rights violations by foreign officials. See Filartiga v. Peña–Irala, 630 F.2d 876 (2d Cir.1980). Dr. Joel Filartiga and his daughter, Dolly, Paraguayan nationals residing in the United States, brought suit in the Eastern District of New York against Americo Peña–Irala (Peña), a former police official in Paraguay who was in New York on an expired visa. Filartiga claimed that Peña had kidnapped and tortured his son to death in retaliation for the father's political opposition to the Paraguayan government. Alleging that such torture was a violation of international law, they invoked the jurisdiction of the district court under the Alien Tort Statute, 28 U.S.C. § 1350, which gives the district court jurisdiction over a civil action by an alien for a tort only, committed in violation of the law of nations or a treaty of the United States. The district court dismissed the claim for lack of jurisdiction. On appeal, the Court of Appeals for the Second Circuit reversed, It said in part:

> In light of the universal condemnation of torture in numerous international agreements, and the renunciation of torture as an instrument of official policy by virtually all of the nations of the world (in principle if not in practice), we find that an act of torture committed by a state official against one held in detention violates established norms of the international law of human rights, and hence the law of nations. * * *
>
> * * * Accordingly, we must conclude that the dictum in Dreyfus v. von Finck, supra, 534 F.2d at 31, to the effect that "violations of international law do not occur when the aggrieved parties are nationals of the acting state," is clearly out of tune with the current usage and practice of international law. The treaties and accords cited above, as well as the express foreign policy of our own government, all make it clear that international law confers fundamental rights upon all people vis-a-vis their own governments. While the ultimate scope of those rights will be a subject for continuing refinement and elaboration, we hold that the right to be free from torture is now among them. * * * [W]e believe it is sufficient here to construe the Alien Tort Statute, not as granting new rights to aliens, but simply as opening the federal courts for adjudication of the rights already recognized by international law. * * *
>
> Although the Alien Tort Statute has rarely been the basis for jurisdiction during its long history, there can be little doubt that this action is properly brought in federal court. This is undeniably an action by an alien, for a tort only, committed in violation of the law of nations. * * *
>
> * * * In the modern age, humanitarian and practical considerations have combined to lead the nations of the world to recognize that respect for fundamental human rights is in their individual and collective interest. Among the rights universally proclaimed by all nations, as we have noted, is the right to be free of physical torture. Indeed, for purposes of civil liability, the torturer has become—like the pirate and slave trader before him—*hostis humani generis*, an enemy of all mankind. Our holding today, giving effect to a jurisdictional provision enacted by our First Congress, is a small but important step in the fulfillment of the ageless dream to free all people from brutal violence.

Id. at 880–890 (footnotes omitted). For other excerpts, see pp. 143–144 supra.

Compare Tel–Oren v. Libyan Arab Republic, 517 F.Supp. 542 (D.D.C.1981). In that case, representatives of twenty-nine persons who died in a terrorist attack on a bus in Israel filed suit in a United States district court against Libya, the P.L.O., the Palestine Information Office, the National Association of Arab Americans and the Palestine Congress of North America. The complaints charged the defendants with torts in violation of both international law and criminal statutes of the United States. The plaintiffs asserted that the district court had jurisdiction under the Alien Tort Claims Act, 28 U.S.C.A. § 1350. Addressing the jurisdictional issue, the district court said:

> For jurisdiction to vest under § 1350, three elements must be present: 1) the claim must be made by an *alien*, 2) it must be for a *tort*, and 3) the tort must be *in violation of the law of nations or the treaties of the United States.*
>
> * * *
>
> * * *[§ 1350] serves merely as an entrance into the federal courts and in no way provides a cause of action to any plaintiff. Somewhere in the law of nations or in the treaties of the United States, the plaintiffs must discern and plead a cause of action that, if proved, would permit the Court to grant relief. The plaintiffs cite no cause of action given to them by the law of nations or by treaties of the United States. Just as discussed under § 1331, an action predicated on a treaty or on more general norms of international law must have at its basis a specific right to a private claim. Plaintiffs have demonstrated no such entitlement. "[T]o interpret international human rights law to create a federal private right of action overstates the level of agreement among nations on remedies for human rights violation." Note, Torture as a Tort in Violation of International Law: Filartiga v. Pena–Irala, 33 Stan. L.Rev. 353, 357 (1981). * * * In short, unless treaties to which the United States is a party or even the law of nations generally provide a private right of action, no jurisdictional grant, be it § 1331 or § 1350, can aid a plaintiff seeking relief in federal district court.
>
> * * *
>
> * * * [I]t behooves the court to discern promptly in cases such as the instant whether international law has expressly or impliedly entrusted individuals with the authority to enforce its precepts. Because that determination may ultimately cloak a court with potent authority over a foreign land, the query is jurisdictional, not merely a demurrer to the plaintiffs complaint. Absent the clear indication, not present here, that nations intend to subject themselves to such worldwide jurisprudential assaults, jurisdiction under § 1350 will not vest.

517 F.Supp. at 548–50.

The judgment of the district court was affirmed, 726 F.2d 774 (D.C.Cir.1984), cert. denied, 470 U.S. 1003, 105 S.Ct. 1354, 84 L.Ed.2d 377 (1985). There was no opinion of the court. While Judge Edwards' analysis of § 1350 generally followed that of the court in *Filartiga*, Judge Bork argued that Congress gave the federal courts jurisdiction only when international law created a private tort. *Filartiga* was followed in other cases, see e.g., Forti v. Suarez–Mason, 672 F.Supp. 1531 (N.D.Cal.1987). See p. 168, Chapter 3. Congress may have implicitly confirmed the

Filartiga interpretation when it enacted the Torture Victim Protection Act, see note 3 below. On the Alien Tort Statute, see Randall, Federal Jurisdiction Over International Law Claims: Inquiries into the Alien Tort Statute, 18 N.Y.U. J. Int'l L. & Pol. 1 (1985); Casto, The Federal Court's Protective Jurisdiction Over Torts Committed in Violation of the Law of Nations, 18 Conn. L. Rev. 467 (1986); Slaughter Burley, The Alien Tort Statute and the Judiciary Act of 1789: A Badge of Honor, 83 A.J.I.L. 461 (1989). For a comprehensive survey of the cases under the Alien Tort Statute, see Stephens & Ratner, International Human Rights Litigation in U.S. Courts (1996).

As of 2000, the *Filartiga* case has been followed in some 20 cases but has not been considered by the U.S. Supreme Court. The cases have resulted in judgments for substantial sums of money but rarely in actual recovery since the defendants have not had recoverable assets. The efforts to enforce a judgment against the estate of former Philippine President Marcos (still pending in 2000) could represent the exceptional case where assets may actually be available, though they have been tied up with competing claims from other parties. Efforts to sue a foreign government (rather than a foreign official) have been frustrated by the principle of sovereign immunity. See, e.g., Saudi Arabia v. Nelson, 507 U.S. 349, 113 S.Ct. 1471, 123 L.Ed.2d 47 (1993), excerpted in Chapter 14.

3. Section 1350 provides jurisdiction for suits by aliens only. Could a citizen bring a suit under 28 U.S.C.A. § 1331, on the ground that a suit in tort for torture in violation of international law is a case arising under the laws of the United States? See Restatement (Third) § 131, Comment *e* and Reporters' Note 4. The argument was rejected in Handel v. Artukovic, 601 F.Supp. 1421 (D.C.Cal.1985). In 1992, however, Congress enacted the Torture Victim Protection Act, Pub. L. 102–256,106 Stat. 73 (Mar. 12,1992), codified at, 28 U.S.C.A. § 1350, providing a remedy in damages for victims of torture. The Act applies whether the victim is an alien or a U.S. national. The Act does not expressly indicate the constitutional basis for the jurisdiction of the federal courts but presumably it confers jurisdiction pursuant to Article III, Section 2 of the Constitution, on the basis that the cases would be arising under the laws of the United States. Does this suggest that Congress considers torture (and by implication other violations of customary international law) to be violations of U.S. law and therefore within 28 U.S.C.A. § 1331?

4. Congress has provided sanctions for violations of human rights in other countries by denying economic aid and military sales to "any country which engages in a consistent pattern of gross violations of internationally recognized human rights, including torture or cruel, inhuman, or degrading treatment or punishment, prolonged detention without charges, or other flagrant denial of the right to life, liberty and the security of the person." 22 U.S.C.A. § 2151n(a). See also 22 U.S.C.A. § 2304. Compare the Jackson–Vanik Amendment conditioning trade benefits for communist countries on their permitting emigration. See Trade Act of 1974, § 402, 19 U.S.C.A. § 2432 (1976). See Restatement (Third) § 702, Reporters' Note 9. The U.S. imposed trade sanctions against South Africa for its policy of apartheid. See the Comprehensive Anti–Apartheid Act of 1986, 22 U.S.C.A. §§ 5001–5016. See Clarizio, Clements & Geetter, United States Policy Toward South Africa, 11 Hum. Rts. Q. 249 (1989). See also p. 175, for a discussion

of the sanctions imposed by states of the U.S. See generally Henkin, The Age of Rights, chap. 5 (1990).

In 1992 Congress enacted the Cuban Democracy Act, 22 U.S.C.A. §§ 6001–6010, which announces the policy of the U.S. "to seek a peaceful transition to democracy" in Cuba through the careful application of sanctions directed at the Castro government" and "to make clear to other countries that * * * the United States will take into account their willingness to cooperate in such a policy * * *." 22 U.S.C.A. § 6002. Sanctions against Cuba were strengthened with the Helms–Burton Act of 1996. See Chapters 10 and 13, pp. 816, 1108.

SECTION 2. REGIONAL HUMAN RIGHTS LAW

The Council of Europe and the Organization of American States have established comprehensive human rights regimes for those regions, parallel to, and in important respects more effective than, that of the United Nations. In 1981, African states moved toward a regional human rights system when the Organization of African Unity adopted the African [Banjul] Charter of Human and Peoples' Rights. The League of Arab States established a Commission on Human Rights in 1968, but as of the end of the century it appears to have remained inactive. For a comparative appraisal of regional human rights regimes, see Weston, Lukes & Hnatt, Regional Human Rights Regimes: A Comparison and Appraisal, 20 Vand. J. Transnat'l L. 585 (1987).

A. THE EUROPEAN HUMAN RIGHTS SYSTEM

Western European states were prominent in the development of international human rights under the auspices of the United Nations. Simultaneously, Western Europe saw the growth of European human rights as an important element in the political and economic rebirth of Western Europe after the Second World War. Western European governments saw in human rights the core of a common ideology that would promote European unity. Trust and friendly relations among the states of the region permitted the growth of institutions to help promote and support respect for rights within these states. With the Cold War, respect for human rights in the West also served to distinguish conditions there from totalitarian repression in the East.

Human rights in Europe drew on the burgeoning international human rights law and institutions and on constitutional traditions and developments within European countries (and the United States). Rights in Europe inspired and contributed to the development of human rights norms and institutions in the larger U.N. human rights universe.

THE EUROPEAN CONVENTION REGIME

The European Convention for the Protection of Human Rights and Fundamental Freedoms (213 U.N.T.S. 221, 1950) (European Convention) entered into force on September 3, 1953. It was drafted under the sponsorship of the Council of Europe (not to be confused with the European Union and its antecedents, see p. 659 and is open to accession by the member States of the Council. The Convention has been ratified by all forty-one Council members, but not all have ratified its various protocols. See Chart Showing Signatures and Ratifications of Conventions and Agreements Concluded Within the Council of Europe (Council of Europe 1999). Some states have ratified the European Convention subject to reservations and declarations of interpretation (e.g. France has made reservations relating to Articles 5, 6 and 15(1) and a declaration relating to Article 56).

After the Cold War ended, states in Central and Eastern Europe, including parts of the former Yugoslavia, moved to join the Council of Europe and have become parties to the European Convention. Respect for human rights, evidenced by membership in the Council and accession to the European Convention, has become a prerequisite for states aspiring to membership in the European Union.

1. The Rights and Freedoms Protected

There are sometimes significant differences in their formulation, but the substantive provisions of the European Convention are generally similar to those in the International Covenant on Civil and Political Rights. Some rights are in one of these instruments but not in the other. The European Convention includes: the right to life; freedom from torture and inhuman or degrading treatment; freedom from slavery, servitude or forced labor; liberty and security of person, and detention only in accordance with procedures prescribed by law; the right to a fair and public hearing in determining civil rights and obligations, or criminal charges; respect for privacy and family life; freedom of thought, conscience and religion; freedom of expression, peaceful assembly and association; the right to marry and found a family; freedom from invidious discrimination. The Convention provides that everyone whose rights are violated shall have an effective remedy.

Additions and other amendments to the Convention have been made periodically by protocols. Protocols have added protection for property, the right to an education, and an obligation on states to hold free elections (Protocol 1); a prohibition on the deprivation of liberty for inability to fulfil a contractual obligation; freedom of movement and residence, the right to leave any country (including one's own), freedom of expulsion from the country of one's nationality and a prohibition on the collective expulsion of aliens (Protocol 4). The adherence of a seventh party, in 1985, brought into force Protocol 6, prohibiting capital punishment in time of peace. Protocol 7 gives additional substantive protections–restrictions on the expulsion of aliens, the right to review of a criminal conviction by a higher tribunal, the right of a victim of a miscarriage of justice to be compensated, freedom from double jeopardy, and the equality of spouses in respect of marriage. Protocol 8, designed to expedite implementation procedures, came into force in 1990 and had 40 ratifications by 2000. Protocols 9 and 10, concerning procedures for bringing complaints before the Court, were superseded with the coming into force of Protocol 11 in November 1998 (discussed below).

At the beginning of the 21st century, the European Convention continues to differ from the International Covenant on Civil and Political Rights in some respects. Unlike the International Covenant (Article 1), the Convention contains no reference to a right of peoples to self-determination, or to "economic self-determination"; to the rights of persons belonging to ethnic, religious or linguistic minorities to enjoy their own culture, profess and practise their own religion, or use their own language (Article 27); the right to recognition everywhere as a person before the law (Article 16); and the right to equality before the law and equal protection of the law (Article 26). There is also no European counterpart to the International Covenant's requirement that parties prohibit war propaganda, or advocacy of national, racial, or religious hatred that constitutes incitement to discrimination (Article 20), nor is there explicit mention of the rights of the child (Article 24). Unlike the International Covenant, the European Convention protects property (Protocol 1, Article 1). The Convention provides that no one shall be deprived of the right to enter his own country (Protocol 4, Article 3), whereas the Covenant provides that no one shall be *arbitrarily* deprived of that right (International Covenant, Article 12(4)). The Convention provides explicitly that no one may be expelled from the territory of the state of which he is a national (Protocol 4, Article 3).

2. *The System of Implementation and Enforcement*

The authors of the European Convention constructed an elaborate institutional framework to supervise the observance of the rights listed in the Convention. This machinery consisted of an organ of inquiry and conciliation (the Commission), a political decision-making organ (the Committee of Ministers of the Council of Europe), and a judicial organ (the European Court of Human Rights).

Prior to November 1998, any claim by a state party under Article 24 of the European Convention, or by an individual under Article 25, was submitted to the Commission. The Commission determined the admissibility of applications, established the facts of each admitted case, sought to achieve a friendly settlement and, in the event of failure, drew up a report on the facts, stating the Commission's opinion as to whether the state had breached an obligation under the Convention. Such reports were submitted to the Committee of Ministers and to the states concerned. Within three months, the Commission, or a state whose national was alleged to be victim, or a state which referred the case to the Commission, or the state against which the complaint was lodged, could refer the case to the European Court of Human Rights (Article 48). In the original Convention there was no right of individual petition directly to the Court, but, in 1990, Protocol 9 opened access to the Court to individuals and groups who had lodged a complaint with the Commission (Protocol 9, Article 5). Once the Court had determined its jurisdiction over a case, it would consider whether it demonstrated a breach of the European Convention and issue its judgment accordingly. In the event that a case was not referred to the Court, the Committee of Ministers would issue its final decision, which was binding on the states concerned.

This three-tiered system established in the European Convention became increasingly over-burdened, with the number of applications registered annually with the Commission growing from 404 in 1981, to 2,037 in 1993, and to 4,750 by 1997. As Bratza and O'Boyle have written,

> The steadily increasing workload of the European Commission and Court of Human Rights over the years and the resulting problem of the length of Convention proceedings gave rise to reflection towards the end of the

> 1980's as to how the Convention's enforcement machinery could be streamlined. With the dramatic increase in the number of High Contracting Parties due to the developments in Eastern and Central Europe, reform of the Convention, as a means of preserving and building upon its achievements, became an urgent priority of the Council of Europe in the early 1990's.
>
> Discussion centred on whether adjustments and improvements should be made to the existing system or whether the existing Commission and Court should be merged to form a single Court of Human Rights. The proposal of a single Court was finally endorsed by a meeting of the Council of Europe's Heads of State and Government in the Vienna Declaration of 9 October 1993 and was given form by Protocol No. 11 to the Convention which was opened for signature on 11 May 1994.

Nicolas Bratza & Michael O'Boyle, The Legacy of the Commission to the New Court Under the Protocol No. 11, in The Birth of European Human Rights Law: Studies in Honor of Carle Aage Nygaard 377, 3 Eur. H.R. L.Rev. 272 (1997).

Bratza and O'Boyle have provided an overview of the new system introduced by Protocol 11:

> Protocol No. 11 provides for the establishment of a full-time single Court to replace the Convention's present enforcement machinery. * * *
>
> Other important changes brought about by the Protocol are as follows: (1) the right of individual petition is now mandatory and the Court will have jurisdiction over all inter-State cases;[2] (2) the decision-making role of the Committee of Ministers has been abolished. Its role will henceforth be limited to supervising the execution of the Court's judgements. All allegations of a violation of the Convention right will thus be adjudicated on by the Court; (3) judges of the Court will be full-time and elected for six-year terms rather than the present nine years. A retirement age of 70 has been introduced. There is no longer a prohibition on two judges having the same nationality. An express power of dismissal has also been introduced where a majority of two-thirds of the other judges consider that the judge has ceased to fulfil the required conditions; (4) the Protocol also expressly provides for the possibility of third-party intervention. The President of the Court may invite Contracting Parties not only to submit written comments but also to take part in hearings. However the opportunity has not been taken to add a specific provision concerning the power of the Court to order binding interim measures.
>
> The Court will sit in Committees, Chambers and a Grand Chamber comprising three, seven and seventeen judges respectively and occasionally in plenary. The Plenary Court will be responsible for appointing the Presidents of Chambers, constituting Chambers, adopting rules of procedure and the election of Presidents and Vice–Presidents of the Court. However it shall not hear cases. The new Court, in its various case-handling compositions, will have responsibility for determining all aspects

2. Article 34. However, the optional character of the right of individual petition has been retained in respect of overseas territories * * *.

of the admissibility and merits of registered applications. * * * Once an application is registered, a Judge Rapporteur will be assigned to it by a Chamber. The Rapporteur may consider that the case should be considered by a Committee of three judges. This Committee may, by a unanimous vote, declare individual cases inadmissible or strike cases off the list. If no such decision is taken by a Committee, the application will be referred to a Chamber which will decide on the admissibility and merits of the case. As under the present system, once a case has been declared admissible the Court will have the dual function of establishing the facts and placing itself at the disposal of the parties with a view to securing a friendly settlement. All inter-State cases must be decided on by a Chamber. Decisions on admissibility will be taken separately unless the Court in exceptional cases decides otherwise. Reasons must be given. The criteria of admissibility remain unchanged.

Where a case raises a serious question affecting the interpretation of the Convention or the Protocols or where the resolution of an issue before a Chamber might have a result inconsistent with a judgement previously delivered by the Court, the Chamber may relinquish jurisdiction to the Grand Chamber. However relinquishment cannot take place if one of the parties to the case objects. The Protocol also provides for the possibility of a re-hearing of the case before the Grand Chamber in exceptional cases at the request of any party within a period of three months from the date of judgment of the Chamber. This request shall be considered by a panel of five judges of the Grand Chamber and accepted "if the case raises a serious question affecting the interpretation or application of the Convention or the Protocols thereto, or a serious issue of general importance." The judgment of a Chamber thus only becomes final: (a) when the parties declare that they will not request that the case be referred to the Grand Chamber; or (b) three months after the date of the judgment if referral has not been requested; or (c) when the panel of five judges rejects a referral request.

Notes

1. The new system established in Protocol 11 was put in place in November 1998, after a one-year preparatory period following its ratification by all states parties to the European Convention. The new Court is composed of a number of judges equal to that of the states parties (in 2000, forty-one) and sits in permanent session. In 1999, the Court delivered 177 judgments, 63 of them by the Grand Chamber. 731 applications were declared admissible. For a discussion of the role of the Committee of Ministers in the new system under Protocol 11, see Klerk, Supervision of the Execution of the Judgments of the European Court of Human Rights: The Committee of Ministers' Role under Article 54 of the European Convention on Human Rights, 45 Neth. Int'l L. Rev. 65 (1998).

2. The new Court draws upon the practice and jurisprudence of the European Commission and the old Court, and the decisions of these bodies will continue to form part of the case-law interpreting the provisions of the Convention and Protocols. These include:

a. The Court's first action, in 1961, involved a complaint charging the Republic of Ireland with violations of Articles 5 and 6. In the Lawless Case,

[1961] Eur. Ct. H.R. Ser.A. no. 1, the Court described the kind of public emergency that would permit derogations from the Convention (Article 15) and found that detaining Lawless without a trial did not constitute a violation of the Convention. See p. 608 above.

b. Article 6 guarantees of a fair public trial, presumption of innocence, and right to legal counsel, have generated numerous cases. The Court has ruled on the reasonableness of time spent by prisoners in detention before trial and on the appropriate length of judicial proceedings. Neumeister Case, [1968] Eur.Ct. H.R. Ser. A. no. 5; Stogmuller Case, [1969] Eur. Ct. H.R. Ser. A. no. 7; Matznetter Case, [1969] Eur. Ct. H.R. Ser. A. no. 8. The Court found implicit in Article 6(1) a right of access to the courts, including a prisoner's right to obtain the assistance of counsel. Golder Case, [1975] Eur. Ct. H.R. Ser.A. no. 18.

In several cases during the 1980s and 1990s the Court looked with ill favor on lengthy trial proceedings and concluded that any unreasonable delay, not the fault of the defendant, violates Article 6(1). See the Eckle Case, [1982] Eur. Ct. H.R. Ser.A. no. 51; the Case of Foti and Others, [1982] Eur. Ct. H.R. Ser. A. no. 56; the Case of Albert and Le Compte, [1982] Eur. Ct. H.R. Ser.A. no. 81; the Maj Case, [1991] Eur. Ct. H.R Ser. A. no. 196–D. In 1999 the reconstituted Court found the Government in Italy to be in violation of Article 6(1) in 44 cases, because of the unreasonable length of criminal and civil court proceedings. See, e.g. Laino v. Italy, Application no. 33158/96, Judgment, 18 February 1999; Bottazzi v. Italy, Application no. 34884/97, Judgment, 28 July 1999; Gelli v. Italy, Application no. 37752/97, Judgment, 19 October 1999.

c. Claims brought under Articles 5 and 6 have provided the Court with opportunities to examine a number of issues concerning criminal practice and procedure in various states. See the Airey Case, [1980] Eur.Ct. H.R. Ser.A. no. 32 and the Artico Case, [1980] Eur. Ct. H.R. Ser.A. no. 37 (guarantee of legal counsel); the Adolf Case, [1982] Eur. Ct. H.R. Ser.A. no. 49 and the Minelli Case, [1983] Eur. Ct. H.R. Ser. A. no. 62 (innocent until proven guilty); the Barbera, Messegue and Jabardo Case, [1988] Eur. Ct. H.R. Ser.A. no. 146 (right to a fair trial).

d. The Court has scrutinized state acts alleged to have unreasonably deprived persons of liberty. See Guzzardi Case, [1980] Eur. Ct.H.R.Ser.A. no. 39 (Mafioso defendant confined on island); Winterwerp Case, [1980] Eur. Ct. H.R.Ser. A. no. 33 and Case of X v. The United Kingdom, [1981] Eur. Ct. H.R.Ser.A. no. 46 (procedures for confinement in mental institutions); Vagrancy Cases, [1971] Eur. Ct.H.R.Ser. A. no. 10 (jailing persons under vagrancy statutes); the Thynne, Wilson and Gunnell Case [1990] Eur. Ct. H.R.Ser. A. no. 190 (indeterminate prison sentence).

e. In several cases brought against Turkey, the Court considered violations of Articles 2, 3 and 5, in relation to disappearances, torture and ill-treatment in detention. See, e.g. Kurt [1998], 1998–III Eur. Ct. H.R. 1152; Aydin [1997] 1997–VI Eur. Ct. H.R. 1866.

f. The Court has considered alleged violations of Articles 11 and 14 relating to state actions discriminating against trade unions (see Belgium Police Case, [1975] Eur. Ct. H.R. Ser. A. no. 19, and Swedish Engine Driver's Union Case, [1976] Eur. Ct. H.R. Ser. A. no. 20), violations of the education guarantees in Article 2 (see Belgian Linguistic Cases, [1968] Eur. Ct. H.R. Ser. A. no. 4, and the Case of Campbell and Cosans, [1982] Eur. Ct. H.R. Ser.

A. no. 48), violations of the guarantee of freedom of expression in Article 10 (see the Sunday Times case, [1979] Eur. Ct. H.R. Ser. A. no. 28), violations of the guarantee of privacy in Article 8 (see the case of Silver and Others, [1983] Eur. Ct. H.R. Ser. A. no. 61, Malone Case [1984] Eur. Ct. H.R. Ser. A. no. 82, the Dudgeon Case, [1981] Eur. Ct. H.R. Ser. A. no. 45, the Kruslin case [1990] Eur. Ct. H.R. Ser. A. no. 176–A and the Huvig case [1990] Eur. Ct. H.R. Ser. A. no. 176–B) and the award of reparations as just satisfaction to an injured party under Article 50 (see Neumeister Reparation Case, [1974] Eur. Ct. H.R. Ser. A. no. 17).

g. In the *Soering* case the Court prohibited the extradition, by the United Kingdom to the United States, of a suspect charged with a capital offence because, if convicted, he might be sent to "death row". The Court found that, in the circumstances of the case, being held on "death row" for a significant period of time, awaiting execution, would violate the prohibition on torture, inhuman or degrading treatment or punishment contained in Article 3 of the European Convention. See p. 638 supra. Eventually, Soering was extradited when the U.S. agreed that he would be tried for a non-capital offence only. See Britain Extradites Soering, 6 Int'l Enforcement Reporter 26 (Issue 1, 1990). (Compare the *Short* case, in which the Netherlands Supreme National Court enjoined the Dutch military authorities from handing a member of the United States Armed Forces over to U.S. authorities pursuant to the Status of Forces Agreement between the Netherlands and the U.S. because if convicted he might be subject to the death penalty contrary to the Sixth Protocol to the European Convention on Human Rights to which the Netherlands was a party. The Court ruled that the Sixth Protocol took precedence over its obligations under the Status of Forces Agreement. Hoge Raad der Nederlanden [HR], 16 Rechtspraak van de Week [Rvd W] Nr. 76, 343 (1990) (Short v. Netherlands). See also the Opinion of the Netherlands Advocaat–General, reprinted in 29 I.L.M. 1375 (1990).)

3. The cases coming before the Court have continued to increase in number and variety, and include cases concerning the prohibition of forced labor, the right to respect for private and family life, home and correspondence, the right to marry, freedom of expression, the right to peaceful assembly, the right to trade union freedom, the right to effective remedy, the right to education, and the right to free elections. For a comprehensive listing of cases, see European Court of Human Rights, Aperçus: Survey of Activities 1959–1990 (1991); P. Kempees, A Systematic Guide to the Case–Law of the European Court of Human Rights, Vols. I and II (1960–1994) and Vol. III (1995–1996). See also Human Rights Case Digest (British Institute of Human Rights 1990–) and the website of the European Court, http://www.echr.coe.int. For reports of cases before the European Court, see the Human Rights Law Journal.

4. For discussion of the case-law, see Cassese et al., Human Rights and the European Community: Methods of Protection (1991); Cassese et al., Human Rights and the European Community: Substantive Law (1991); Janis, Kay & Bradley, European Human Rights Law: Text and Materials (1995). See generally Robertson & Merrills, Human Rights in Europe: A Study of the European Convention on Human Rights (1993); Harris, O'Boyle & Warbrick, Law of the European Convention on Human Rights (1995); The European System for the Protection of Human Rights (R. St. J. Macdonald, F. Matscher, & H. Petzold eds., 1993); Clapham, Human Rights and the European Community: A Critical Over-

view (1991); Van Dijk, Theory and Practice of the European Convention on Human Rights (1998).

THE EUROPEAN SOCIAL CHARTER

The Universal Declaration of Human Rights had declared civil, political, economic, social and cultural rights. In converting the Declaration into international agreements, the General Assembly divided these rights into a Covenant on Civil and Political Rights and another on Economic, Social and Cultural Rights. See p. 595 above. For similar reasons, the European Human Rights system developed a convention on civil and political rights–The European Convention for the Protection of Human Rights and Fundamental Freedoms–and concluded a separate Social Charter.

In 1961, the countries of Western Europe adopted the European Social Charter, 529 U.N.T.S. 89; it came into force on 26 February 1965. The following states have become parties: Austria, Belgium, Cyprus, Denmark, Finland, France, Germany, Greece, Iceland, Ireland, Italy, Luxembourg, Malta, The Netherlands, Norway, Portugal, Sweden, Spain, Turkey, and the United Kingdom.

The original Charter expresses the resolution of the parties "to make every effort in common to improve the standard of living and to promote the social well-being of both their urban and rural populations by means of appropriate institutions and action." In Part I, the parties "accept as the aim of their policy, to be pursued by all appropriate means, both national and international in character, the attainment of conditions in which the following rights and principles may be effectively realized." Part II lists undertakings in various categories, e.g., the right to work, the right to a fair remuneration, the right to bargain collectively, the rights of children, the right of employed women to protection, the right to Social Security, the right to social and medical assistance.

The Charter was revised in 1996, the parties recognizing "the advantage of embodying in a Revised Charter, designed progressively to take the place of the European Social Charter, the rights guaranteed by the Charter as amended, the rights guaranteed by the Additional Protocol of 1988 and to add new rights." E.T.S. No. 163. Part III of the Revised Charter provides:

> Article A—Undertakings
>
> 1. Subject to the provisions of Article B below, each of the Parties undertakes:
>
> a. to consider Part I of this Charter as a declaration of the aims which it will pursue by all appropriate means, as stated in the introductory paragraph of that part;
>
> b. to consider itself bound by at least six of the following nine articles of Part II of this Charter: Articles 1, 5, 6, 7, 12, 13, 16, 19 and 20;
>
> c. to consider itself bound by an additional number of articles or numbered paragraphs of Part II of the Charter which it may select, provided that the total number of articles or numbered paragraphs by which it is bound is not less than sixteen articles or sixty-three numbered paragraphs.

2. The articles or paragraphs selected in accordance with sub-paragraphs b and c of paragraph 1 of this article shall be notified to the Secretary General of the Council of Europe at the time when the instrument of ratification, acceptance or approval is deposited.

3. Any Party may, at a later date, declare by notification addressed to the Secretary General that it considers itself bound by any articles or any numbered paragraphs of Part II of the Charter which it has not already accepted under the terms of paragraph 1 of this article. Such undertakings subsequently given shall be deemed to be an integral part of the ratification, acceptance or approval and shall have the same effect as from the first day of the month following the expiration of a period of one month after the date of the notification.

4. Each Party shall maintain a system of labour inspection appropriate to national conditions.

IMPLEMENTATION AND ENFORCEMENT OF THE EUROPEAN SOCIAL CHARTER

in Human Rights (Henkin, Neuman, Orentlicher & Leebron eds.,1999) p. 598.

States Parties implement the European Social Charter * * * by domestic legislation where the matter is not one "normally left to agreements between employers or employers' organizations and workers' organizations." Article 33. The Charter also provides for international monitoring of compliance by Contracting Parties (Articles 21 to 29). While Parties undertake to consider themselves bound only by a selected number of the rights enumerated in Part II of the Charter, Member States are required to submit reports responding to detailed questionnaires in relation to both accepted and non-accepted provisions. These responses are initially reviewed by a Committee of Experts, independent specialists on social questions, joined by a representative from the International Labor Organization. The Committee reaches conclusions as to the domestic implementation of accepted Part II provisions, and comments also on those terms that are non-binding in respect of the particular Contracting Party. The Committee then submits its conclusions to the Governmental Committee of the Council of Europe, which presents its findings to the Committee of Ministers. The enforcement procedure, passing through several stages, often results in general recommendations directed at all states rather than criticism of individual states by the Committee of Ministers. This process has been characterized as leading to a "tug of war" between the Committee of Experts, backed by the Parliamentary Assembly, and the Committee of Ministers, "with the former urging the latter to demand more effective compliance by various government." Thomas Buergenthal, International Human Rights in a Nutshell 156 (1995).

The Revised European Social Charter (1996) takes important steps towards streamlining the Charter's supervisory mechanism. The most important changes strengthen the role and independence of the Committee of Experts by conferring on it, *inter alia*, the power to "assess from a legal standpoint the compliance of national law and practice with the obligations arising from the Charter for the Contracting Parties concerned." Protocol Amending the European Social Charter, Article 2. The Revised Charter also enlarges the Committee of Experts, gives greater powers to the Parliamentary Assembly, and makes the entire review process more transparent. The Additional Protocol to the European Social Charter, opened for signature in 1995, provides for collective complaints against alleged violations of the Charter and aims to reduce reliance on information from governments under the system of state reporting. The Additional Protocol also encourages the active participation of the Council's social partners as well as certain NGOs by allowing them to report Charter violations directly to the Committee of Experts in the form of a complaint. These developments have resulted in part from the limited efficacy of the Charter in its original form, from plans of the European Union to create a Social Charter of its own, and from the expansion of the Council of Europe to Eastern European Members. * * *

Notes

1. See generally, Harris, The European Social Charter (1984); Samuel, Fundamental Social Rights: Case Law of the European Social Charter (1997); Council of Europe, Revised European Social Charter: An Explanatory Report (Council of Europe Publications, 1996); Strasser, European Social Charter, in Encyclopedia of Public International Law, 291–295 (1995).

2. In 1989, the European Economic Communities (now the European Union) adopted a Community Charter of Fundamental Social Rights of Workers. "The Community Charter remains a programmatic and political document which has given flesh and bones to Community social policies; it will need to be revised also in the light of the achievements made so far in adopting legislation in various fields and in view of new emerging needs * * *" Silvana Sciarra, European Social Rights Policy Convergence, in The EU and Human Rights (Philip Alston ed., 1999) 473, 499. See also Watson, The Community Social Charter, 28 Common Mkt. L. Rev. 37 (1991).

THE EUROPEAN UNION AND HUMAN RIGHTS

The European Union is not formally party to the European Convention regime, but has developed its own role in the promotion and protection of human rights in Europe.

The European Court of Justice (ECJ), the highest judicial organ of the European Union, decides upon the validity of actions taken by other EU institutions, and determines whether actions taken by the member states conflict with Community law. It has given effect to some implied "fundamental," "basic" human rights in European Community law. The Court has also developed a doctrine by which provisions of Community law that are "directly effective" grant individual rights that must be upheld in national courts of member states. The treaties that form the basis of the EU contain a few express provisions that have a human rights character, such as those regarding freedom of movement of persons, non-discrimination, and voting rights. The ECJ has developed a jurisprudence that restricts the powers of the EU institutions and the powers of member states acting within the sphere of Community law, in order to ensure respect for additional fundamental human rights.

The European Court of Justice first made reference to the European Convention on Human Rights in the *Nold* judgment in 1974. * * *

While the Court of Justice had made reference in its judgments to human rights as a concept before the *Nold* decision it had not mentioned specifically the ECHR. In the *Nold* case the Court emphasised its commitment to fundamental human rights based on the constitutional traditions of the Member States * * *

The debate raging in Germany and which found expression in *Solange I* asked whether the transfer of competence to the Community can be exclusive if the result is a diminution of fundamental rights protection available to the individual under the national constitution. To this question, the German courts answered with a resounding no. The Italian Corte Costituzionale was also raising the same issue though less aggressively. France, a founding member of the Community, had finally ratified the ECHR on 3 May 1974. A response from the Court was called for. It had previously refused to consider the validity of Community acts in the light of national constitutions. The continuation of such a position would clearly not satisfy the not unreasonable concerns of national constitutional courts. If those courts were not satisfied, then the primacy of Community law, which was still a fairly new and uncertain concept, could be attacked. * * *

One of the most contentious issues * * * is the scope of the Community's responsibility and the Court's duty as regards human rights. The Court has carved out a very specific role for itself in the protection of human rights which appears designed to minimise potential overlap with the European Court of Human Rights. But as the scope of Community law continues to grow, this effort appears increasingly vain. However in so doing it has been criticised for failing to accept the challenge of human rights protection by limiting its scope of jurisdiction too severely.

Guild & Lesieur, The European Court of Justice on the European Convention on Human Rights: Who Said What, When? Introduction, xvii (1998).

Notes

1. See also The EU and Human Rights (Philip Alston ed., 1999); Alston & Weiler, An 'Ever Closer Union' in Need of a Human Rights Policy: The EU and Human Rights, 9 E.J.I.L. 658 (1999); Bermann, Goebel, Davey & Fox, Cases and Materials on European Community Law 142 (1993); The European Union and Human Rights (Neuwahl & Rosas ed. 1995); Weiler & Lockhart, "Taking Rights Seriously" Seriously: The European Court and Its Fundamental Rights Jurisprudence (Parts I and II), 32 Comm. Mkt. L. Rev. 51, 579 (1995).

2. In June 1999, the EU Heads of State or Government moved to establish a Charter of Fundamental Rights of the European Union. The European Council established an ad hoc body to draft the charter, with the objective of completing this task by the end of 2000. See European Council Decision on the Drawing up of a Charter of Fundamental Rights of the European Union, Presidency Conclusions, Cologne European Council 3 and 4 June 1999, SN 150/99 Annexes; see also, Affirming Fundamental Rights in the European Union, Time to Act: Report of the Expert Group on Fundamental Rights (European Commission, 1999). For the Charter as adopted December 7, 2000, see 40 I.L.M. 266 (2001).

HELSINKI: THE ORGANISATION FOR SECURITY AND COOPERATION IN EUROPE (OSCE) (THE HELSINKI FINAL ACT, 1975)

The human rights norms enunciated in the 1975 Helsinki Final Act are not strictly regional human rights law: it is not limited to Europe and it is not strictly law since all agreed that the Act was not legally binding. (See Chapter 7, pp. 462–466.) The Final Act (also known as the Helsinki Accords) was signed on August 1, 1975, by the leaders of 35 Eastern and Western European states, as well as the U.S. and Canada. It was the result of an interlude of Cold War detente and represented an important political bargain in which Western states accepted the political status quo in Europe and the Communist states made human rights commitments. See Human Rights, International Law, and the Helsinki Accord (Buergenthal, ed. 1977).

HENKIN, THE AGE OF RIGHTS

(1990) 57–58 (footnotes omitted).

At the Conference on Security and Cooperation in Europe the participating states agreed to discuss human rights together with other matters relating to security and cooperation. In the Final Act, the participants declared it to be among the principles guiding relations between them that they would respect human rights and fundamental freedoms and promote and encourage their effective exercise. In addition:

> In the field of human rights and fundamental freedoms, the participating States will act in conformity with the purposes and principles of the Charter of the United Nations and with the Universal Declaration of Human Rights. They will also fulfill their obligations as set forth in the international declarations and agreements in this field, including inter alia the International Covenants on Human Rights, by which they may be bound. (1(a)VII)

They also agreed to fulfill in good faith obligations under international law generally (1(a)X). Later in the act (Basket III) the participating states "make it their aim," "declare their readiness," and "express their intention" to implement cooperation in humanitarian and other fields, including human contacts, information, and cooperation and exchange in culture and in education. These human rights provisions were the condition and the price of other provisions of great political importance desired by other participants. Western participants saw them as the condition of and an integral aspect of détente at which the whole Final Act aimed.

While Helsinki was not intended to be a legally binding agreement, and does not add legally binding human rights obligations, it clearly precludes any suggestion that matters it deals with are within domestic jurisdiction and beyond the reach of appropriate inquiry and recourse.

Notes

1. The participants in the Helsinki Accords declared their resolve, in the period following the 1975 conference, to implement the provisions of the Final Act; they began this process through an exchange of views at a series of multilateral conferences in Belgrade (1977), Madrid (1979) and Vienna (1986), which largely became arenas for charges that members of the Soviet bloc were violating human rights. After the Cold War ended the then CSCE changed in character and focus. Successive meetings in 1989–91 at Paris, Vienna, Bonn, Copenhagen and Moscow reflected common agreement and commitment, and produced important documents on the Human Dimension of the CSCE. These documents, particularly the documents produced at the Copenhagen and Moscow meetings, elaborated the commitment to human rights in important detail and gave prominent emphasis to democracy as a major human right and as a foundation for other human rights. In 1995 the CSCE was renamed the Organization for Security and Co-operation in Europe (OSCE).

2. The OSCE began as a conference of states, without an institutional structure, but, since 1991, has "become operational rather than serve simply as a forum for discussion, dialogue, verbal confrontation, and adoption of documents." Brett, Human Rights and the OSCE, 18 Hum. Rts. Q. (1996) 668, 670. With the end of the Cold War, it has taken on new functions, through the creation of a High Commissioner for National Minorities in 1992, and the performance by the OSCE Office for Democratic Institutions and Human Rights of election, human rights and related monitoring functions. For example, in 1998, OSCE monitors were established in Kosovo, to verify withdrawal of Yugoslav military forces, and again in 1999 with the lead role in matters relating to institution-building, democratisation and monitoring, protecting and promoting human rights.

3. On the Helsinki system, see generally Buergenthal: Democratization and Europe's New Public Order, in CSCE and the New Blueprint for Europe 53 (Wyatt, ed. 1991); The Copenhagen CSCE Meeting: A New Public Order for Europe, 11 Hum. Rts. L.J. 217 (1990); CSCE Human Dimension: The Birth of a System, I Collected Course of the Academy of European Law 163 (No. 2, 1990). See also, The Conference on Security and Co-operation in Europe: Basic Documents, 1993–1995 (Arie Bloed ed., 1997); Lucas, The Conference on Security and Cooperation in Europe and the Post Cold War Era (1990); Monitoring Human Rights in Europe: Comparing International Procedures and Mechanisms (Arie Bloed, Liselotte Leicht, Manfred Nowak & Allan Rosas eds., 1993); The OSCE in the Maintenance of Peace and Security: Conflict Prevention, Crisis Management, and Peaceful Settlement of Disputes (Michael Bothe, Natalino Ronzitti & Allan Rosas eds., 1997).

B. THE INTER–AMERICAN HUMAN RIGHTS SYSTEM

Organizations of the states in the Western Hemisphere have been concerned with human rights since the Second World War. The Charter of the Organization of American States includes the provision: "Each State has the right to develop its cultural, political and economic life freely and naturally. In this free development the State shall respect the rights of the individual and the principles of universal morality" (originally Chapter III, Art. 13; now Chapter IV, Art. 16). These have been deemed to be words of legal obligation. Thomas & Thomas, The Organization of American States 223 (1963).

The American Declaration on the Rights and Duties of Man was adopted in 1948, seven months before the Universal Declaration. It is generally understood that the American Declaration was not intended to have legally binding character and has not acquired such character since. See LeBlanc, The OAS and the Promotion and Protection of Human Rights 13 (1977). But see pp. 668–669 infra.

In 1959, the Fifth Meeting of Consultation of Ministers of Foreign Affairs resolved that the Inter–American Council of Jurists should prepare a Convention on Human Rights, and create an Inter–American Court for the Protection of Human Rights. The Meeting decided also to organize an Inter–American Commission on Human Rights. The American Convention on Human Rights was signed in San Jose, Costa Rica on 22 November 1969, and came into force in June 1978. As of 2000, 24 states are parties to the Convention. (In May 1998 Trinidad and Tobago gave notice to the Secretary General of the O.A.S. of its denunciation of the Convention, pursuant to Article 78. See Chapter 7, pp. 540–544 on differences among human rights treaties concerning whether a right of withdrawal is permitted.)

Elections to the Inter–American Court of Human Rights created by the Convention first took place in May 1979. Terms are for six years and are staggered. Article 52 of the Convention permits nationals of all member states of the O.A.S. to serve on the Court, whether or not the member State is a party to the Convention. (Thomas Buergenthal of the United States—which is not a party to the Convention—served on the Court from 1979 to 1991 and as its Vice–President and President.)

1. The Rights and Freedoms Protected

Substantively, the American Declaration and the American Convention parallel the Universal Declaration and the International Covenant on Civil and Political Rights. The American Declaration, however, includes a chapter containing ten articles setting forth the individual's duties (compare Article 29(1) of the Universal Declaration). The American Convention protects the accepted political-civil rights, but some of them in terms significantly different from those in the International Covenant on Civil and Political Rights. (In the American Convention, for example, the right to life "shall be protected by law and, in general, from the moment of conception," Art. 4(1).) The protected rights include: the right to life, freedom from torture and inhuman treatment, freedom from slavery and servitude, the right to liberty and security, the right to a fair trial, freedom from retroactivity of the criminal law, the right to respect for private and family life, freedom of conscience and religion, freedom of thought and expression, freedom of assembly, freedom of association, freedom to marry and found a family, the right to property, freedom of movement, freedom from exile, prohibition of the collective expulsion of aliens, the right to participate in free elections, the right to an effective remedy if one's rights are violated, the right to recognition as a person before the law, the right to compensation for miscarriage of justice, the right of reply, the right to a name, the rights of the child, the right to a nationality, the right to equality before the law, the right of asylum. Like the European Convention but unlike the International Covenant, the American Convention includes protection for property, and freedom from exile and collective expulsion for aliens. Unlike both the International Covenant and the European

Convention, the American Convention recognizes a right of reply (to anyone injured by inaccurate or offensive statements or ideas) and the right of asylum.

2. *Protocols to the American Convention*

Unlike the European Convention, which anticipated amendment of and addition to its provisions by way of subsequent protocols (see p. 651 above), the O.A.S. did not contemplate that the American Convention would be continually altered. Nonetheless, two Additional Protocols have been adopted by the General Assembly of the O.A.S.

The American Convention does not include the right to an education or other economic-social rights, but commits the states parties, in Article 26, to work to achieve progressively "by legislation or other appropriate means, the full realization of the rights implicit in the economic, social, educational, scientific, and cultural standards set forth in the Charter of the Organization of American States. * * *" In 1988, the General Assembly of the O.A.S. adopted the Additional Protocol to the American Convention in the Area of Economic, Social and Cultural Rights (Protocol of San Salvador). OAS Treaty Series, No. 69. The states parties undertake to take measures to achieve full observance of the rights in the Protocol, which include: the right to work, the right to social security, the right to health, the right to a healthy environment, the right to adequate nutrition, the right to education. The implementation of the Protocol is monitored by the Inter–American Economic and Social Council and the Inter–American Council for Education, Science and Culture, which examine periodic reports submitted by the States Parties. Where a state party violates the rights contained in Article 8(a) (concerning the formation of trade unions), or Article 13 (concerning the right to education), the Inter–American Commission on Human Rights may intervene and, when applicable, the Inter–American Court, through the system of individual petitions (Protocol, Article 19). (See below.) The Protocol has been signed by 18 states and came into force in November 1999, after the eleventh ratification was deposited.

A second Additional Protocol to the Convention, adopted in 1990, obliges states parties not to apply the death penalty to any person subject to their jurisdiction. OAS Treaty Series, No. 73. As of 2000, seven States have ratified the Protocol.

3. *The System of Implementation and Enforcement*

The Inter–American Commission of Human Rights was created in 1960 and was elevated to the status of an organ of the O.A.S. in 1970. As such, its competence has been to "further respect" for human rights; the quoted words were interpreted to grant authority "to promote" but not "to protect" human rights. Almost immediately and for some years, however, an activist Commission read its mandate very broadly. In 1965, it was granted authority "to examine" private communications alleging violation of rights. The Commission has exercised its authority with mixed success, high in the Dominican Republic in 1965–66, least notable as regards Cuba and Haiti (which refused to cooperate with the Commission). See generally Harris & Livingstone, The Inter–American System of Human Rights (1998); Davidson, The Inter–American Human Rights System (1997); Buergenthal, Norris & Shelton, Protecting

Human Rights in the Americas (4th ed. 1996); Organization of American States, Basic Documents Pertaining to Human Rights in the Inter–American System (1988); Quiroga, The Battle of Human Rights: Gross, Systematic Violations and the Inter–American System (1988). See also Mower, Regional Human Rights: A Comparative Study of the West European and Inter–American Systems, (1991).

The Commission had been a controversial investigative body and advocate for human rights since its formation in 1960 under the authority of the O.A.S. With the coming into force of the American Convention, the Inter–American Commission acquired an additional judicial character and function not unlike that of the European Commission, and became one of two organs having "competence with respect to matters relating to the fulfillment of the commitments" made by States parties to the Convention (Article 33). The two functions of the Commission have sometimes appeared in tension—a tension which may affect the respect given its judgments. The European Commission, on the other hand, was formed as an enforcement arm of the European Convention and given only quasi-judicial functions, and its past role in the European human rights system is widely appreciated. The Inter–American Court of Human Rights is the second organ responsible for supervising adherence of states parties to the Convention. The enforcement duties of the Commission and Court are stated in Articles 46–61, and described in the chart below.

THE INTER-AMERICAN SYSTEM

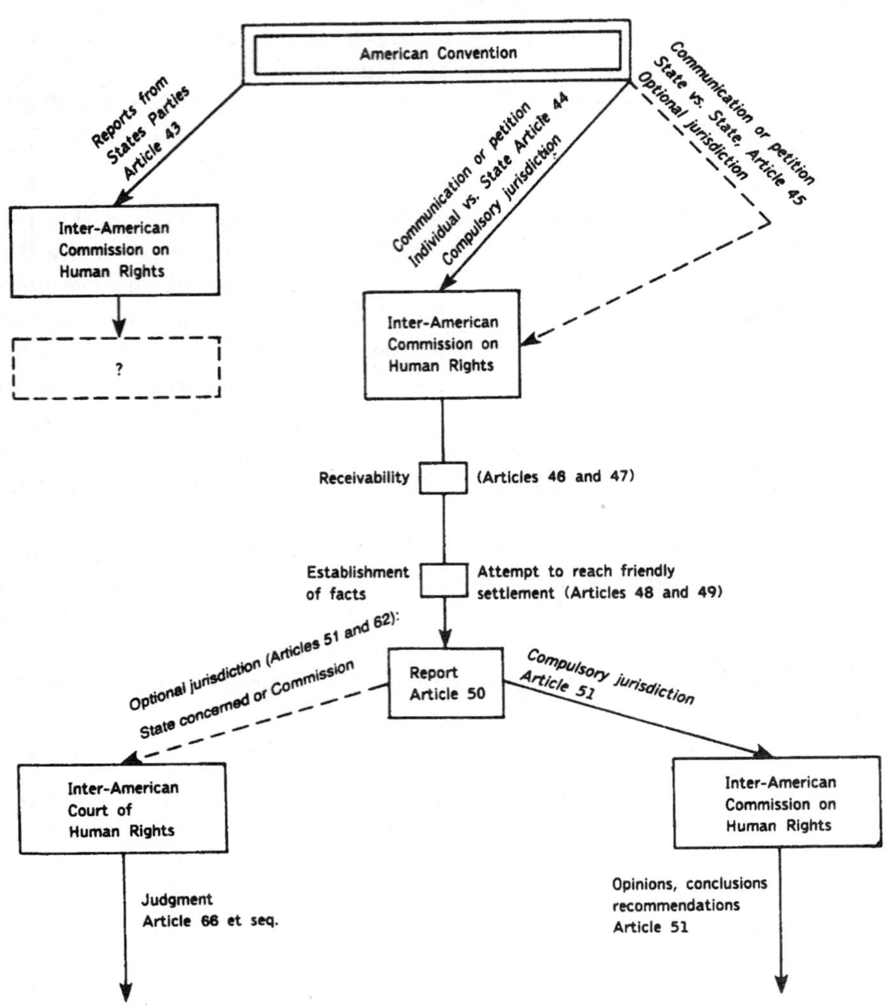

Vasak, International Dimensions of Human Rights 684 (1982)

[D10151]

Notes

1. The Inter–American Court of Human Rights was established in 1978. Twenty-one O.A.S. states have recognized the jurisdiction of the Court as binding and 20 are currently so bound: Costa Rica, Peru, Venezuela, Honduras, Ecuador, Argentina, Uruguay, Colombia, Guatemala, Suriname, Panama, Chile, Nicaragua, Trinidad and Tobago, Bolivia, Brazil, Dominican Republic, El Salvador, Haiti, Mexico and Paraguay (Trinidad and Tobago withdrew from the American Convention and its system of enforcement, effective May 1999, see p. 597 above). According to Article 62 of the Convention, any state party may accept the jurisdiction of the Court in a specific case.

Unlike the new European system under Protocol 11 (see p. 653 above), individuals remain unable to bring a complaint to the Inter–American Court, a subject of criticism of the Inter–American system. See Trindade, The Consolidation of the Procedural Capacity of Individuals in the Evolution of the International Protection of Human Rights: Present State and Perspectives at the Turn of the Century, 30 Colum. Human Rights L. Rev. 1 (1998).

2. The Inter–American Court issues both advisory opinions and decisions in contentious cases. Much of the jurisprudence of the Inter–American Court has been generated through advisory opinions, which may be rendered at the request of the Commission, or of any O.A.S member state. The Court's advisory opinions may provide interpretations not only of the Convention, but also of "other treaties concerning the protection of human rights in the American states" (Article 64).

3. The Court's advisory opinions include:

a. In response to developments in Guatemala, the Inter–American Commission on Human Rights requested the Court's opinion on whether the imposition of the death penalty by a state, for crimes for which such punishment was not provided in domestic law at the time of the adoption of the American Convention, constituted a violation of the Convention, even if the state had filed a reservation to the relevant provision in the Convention. The Court found that the Convention "imposes an absolute prohibition on the extension of the death penalty," and that a state party cannot apply the death penalty to additional crimes, even if a reservation to the relevant provision in the Convention had been entered at the time of ratification. I/A Court H.R., Restrictions to the Death Penalty (Arts. 4(2) and 4(4) American Convention on Human Rights), Advisory Opinion OC–3/83 of September 8, 1983, Ser. A No. 3. See Chapter 7, p. 495.

b. Responding to a request by Costa Rica, the Court advised that the compulsory licensing of journalists through mandatory membership in an association for the practice of journalism is incompatible with Article 13 of the American Convention on Human Rights if it denies a person access to the full use of the news media as a means of expressing opinions or imparting information. The Court also found that Costa Rica's proposed law requiring compulsory licensing of journalists would infringe Article 13 of the Convention because the law would prevent certain people from joining the association. See I/A Court H.R., Compulsory Membership in an Association Prescribed by Law for the Practice of Journalism (Arts. 13 and 29 American Convention on Human Rights), Advisory Opinion OC–5/85 of November 13, 1985, Ser. A No. 5.

c. Advising on an issue submitted by the Inter–American Commission, the Court has determined that exhaustion of local remedies is not required where an individual's indigence, or a general fear in the legal community to represent the individual, prevents the complainant from invoking local remedies. The Court also determined that where the state subject of the complaint demonstrates that there are local remedies, the complainant must show that the exceptions to exhaustion of local remedies within the Convention (Article 46(2)) apply and that the individual was prevented from obtaining the legal counsel necessary for the protection of rights guaranteed by the Convention. I/A Court H.R., Exceptions to the Exhaustion of Local Remedies (Art. 46(1), 46(2)(a) and 46(2)(b) American Convention on Human Rights), Advisory Opinion OC–11/90 of August 10, 1990, 12 Hum. Rts. L.J. 20 (1990).

d. In 1991, the Court declined to answer questions put to it by Costa Rica as to whether its draft legislation for the establishment of a Court of Criminal Appeals fulfilled the requirements of Article 8(2)(h) of the American

Convention on Human Rights (the right of appeal). The Inter–American Commission gave evidence that it had before it a number of cases involving alleged violations by Costa Rica of Article 8(2)(h). (In 1986, the Commission had given Costa Rica six months to rectify the situation in the hope that many of the cases could be resolved without further intervention by the Commission. By 1991, after a decision by the Supreme Court of Costa Rica that Article 8(2)(h) was self-executing, the legislation for the Court of Criminal Appeals had not yet been passed.) The Court held that a reply to the questions presented by Costa Rica could, in the guise of an advisory opinion, result in a determination of contentious cases not yet brought before the Court, without giving the victims of the alleged human rights abuses the opportunity to participate in the proceedings before the Court. I/A Court H.R., Advisory Opinion OC–12/91 of December 6, 1991, Compatibility of Draft Legislation with Article 8(2)(h) of the American Convention on Human Rights, 10 Annual Report of the Inter–American Court of Human Rights 114 (1991).

e. In 1993, the Commission requested an advisory opinion on the legal effects of a law promulgated by a state party to the Convention which manifestly violates the obligations of that state party under the Convention. This question was raised in light of Peru's re-introduction of the death penalty for the crime of terrorism, which ran contrary to Article 4 of the Convention. The Court found that the promulgation of such a law is a violation of the Convention and its enforcement by agents or officials of the state would give rise to international responsibility. See International Responsibility for the Promulgation and Enforcement of Laws in Violation of the Convention (Arts. 1 and 2 of the American Convention on Human Rights), Advisory Opinion OC–14/94, of December 9, 1994, Ser. A, No. 14 (1994).

f. In 1999, at the request of Mexico, the Court issued an advisory opinion concerning minimal judicial guarantees and due process in the framework of the death penalty, judicially imposed upon aliens who have not been informed of their right to communicate with or request the assistance of the consular authorities of their country. The Court found that "failure to observe a detained foreign national's right to information, recognized in Article 36(1)(b) of the Vienna Convention on Consular Relations, is prejudicial to the due process of law and, in such circumstances, imposition of the death penalty is a violation of the right not to be deprived of life 'arbitrarily,' as stipulated in the relevant provisions of the human rights treaties (American Convention on Human Rights, Article 4; International Covenant on Civil and Political Rights, Article 6), with the juridical consequences that a violation of this nature carries, in other words, those pertaining to the State's international responsibility and the duty to make reparation." See The Right to Information on Consular Assistance in the Framework of the Guarantees of the Due Process of Law, Advisory Opinion OC–16/1999, of October 1, 1999, Ser. A, No. 16 (1999). Cf. The Breard case, p. 216 above.

g. In response to a series of questions posed by the government of Peru relating to the Court's jurisdiction to issue advisory opinions, the Court found that it had advisory jurisdiction "with regard to any provision dealing with the protection of human rights set forth in any international treaty applicable in the American states, regardless of whether it be bilateral or multilateral, whatever be the principal purpose of such a treaty, and whether or not non-member states of the inter-American system are or have a right to become parties thereto." "Other Treaties" Subject to the Advisory Jurisdiction of the

Court (Art. 64 American Convention on Human Rights), Advisory Opinion OC–1/82 of September 24, 1982, Ser. A, No. 1.

h. In 1989, the Inter–American Court issued an advisory opinion on the legal effect to be given to the American Declaration on the Rights and Duties of Man. Colombia requested the Court to determine whether the Court had the authority under the Inter–American Convention on Human Rights to render advisory opinions interpreting the Declaration. The Court decided that it had such authority provided that the interpretation of the Declaration was necessary to resolve a question related to either the American Convention or one of the "other treaties" over which the Court has advisory jurisdiction. The Court noted that the American Declaration is an authoritative interpretation of the OAS Charter. Interpretation of the American Declaration of the Rights and Duties of Man in the Context of Article 64 of the American Convention on Human Rights, Advisory Opinion OC–10/89, July 14, 1989, Ser. A, No. 10.

What are the implications of the Court's advisory opinion in respect of the American Declaration on the Rights and Duties of Man, p. 663 above? Newman & Weissbrodt have translated the Spanish version of Court's opinion on the Declaration as concluding: "The fact that the Declaration is not a treaty does not * * * import the conclusion that it lacks legal effect, nor is the Court prevented from interpreting it * * *." Newman & Weissbrodt, International Human Rights 303 (1990).

Has the Court in effect expanded its advisory jurisdiction to include the customary international law of human rights? Does the advisory opinion on "other treaties", together with the Court's opinion on the American Declaration support the conclusion that the Court can also issue advisory opinions concerning other "non-binding resolutions," such as the Universal Declaration of Human Rights?

4. The Court's contentious cases include:

a. Beginning in 1987, the Court considered a series of cases submitted by the Inter–American Commission concerning disappearances in Honduras. The Court awarded compensation to the next of kin in two of the cases. I/A Court H.R., Velasquez Rodriguez Case, Compensatory Damages, Judgment of July 21, 1989 (Art. 63(1) American Convention on Human Rights) Ser. C, No. 7; I/A Court H.R., Godinez Cruz Case, Compensatory Damages, Judgment July 21, 1989 (Art. 63(1) American Convention on Human Rights) Ser. C, No. 8. In another case, the Court held that the responsibility of the Government of Honduras for the deaths of two Costa Rican citizens who had allegedly entered Honduras and disappeared had not been proved. I/A Court H.R., Fairen Garbi and Solis Corrales Case, Judgment of March 15, 1989, Ser. C. No. 6. In all three cases, the Court dealt with harassment and assassination of witnesses, finally indicating provisional measures ordering the Honduran government to do everything within its power to stop the harassment. The Court also considered a number of preliminary objections by Honduras, including failure to exhaust local remedies, and ruled that where a pattern of disappearances was proven, local remedies such as habeas corpus were non-existent or ineffective because of the failure of government officials to reveal the whereabouts of the victims and because of persistent harassment of persons trying to invoke local remedies. See, e.g., I/A Court H.R., Godinez Cruz Case, Judgment of January 20, 1989. Ser. C, No. 5., at 116. The Court also made strong statements on the burden and standard of proof to be applied in cases of wide-scale disappearances where the state subject of the complaint has most control over the evidence. See Godinez Cruz Case (above) and Velasquez Rodriguez Case, Judgment of July 29, 1988, 8 Annual Report of the Inter–American Court of Human Rights 35 (1988).

b. At the request of the Inter–American Commission, the Court ordered provisional measures to protect fourteen members of human rights organizations in Chunima, Guatemala. See Provisional Measures Requested by the Inter–American Commission on Human Rights with Regard to Guatemala (Chunima Case), Order of August 1, 1991, 10 Annual Report of the Inter–American Court of Human Rights 52 (1991). In 1990, the Court made a similar order in relation to a situation in Peru which was later corrected to the Court's satisfaction. See Provisional Measures Requested by the Inter–American Commission on Human Rights in the Matter of Peru (Bustios–Rojas Case), Order of January 17, 1991, 10 Annual Report of the Inter–American Court of Human Rights 15 (1991).

c. The Commission also brought to the Court a contentious case against Suriname concerning the killing of seven civilians by soldiers. Suriname claimed it was not responsible for the killings, but later, during the Court hearing, accepted responsibility. The Court retained jurisdiction in the case to decide on appropriate compensation to the next of kin. See Aloeboetoe et al. Case, Judgment of December 4, 1991, 10 Annual Report of the Inter–American Court of Human Rights 57 (1991). The Court also considered, and rejected, preliminary objections in two cases submitted to it by the Commission. See Gangaram Panday Case, Preliminary Objections, Judgment of December 4, 1991, 10 Annual Report of the Inter–American Court of Human Rights 64 (1991); and Neira Alegria et al. Case, Preliminary Objections, Judgment of December 11, 1991, 10 Annual Report of the Inter–American Court of Human Rights 75 (1991).

5. Contentious cases come to the Court by referral from the Inter–American Commission (see the chart on p. 666 above). The Commission itself is a source of jurisprudence interpreting the American Convention, whether or not complaints are later referred to the Court.

In the Abella case, the Commission interpreted and applied not only the American Convention, but also provisions of international humanitarian law and determined that common Article 3 of the Geneva Conventions of 1949 was applicable to combat between Argentinian military forces and a group of armed attackers, which lasted for a period of 30 hours. See *Abella v. Argentina*, Case 11.137, Inter–Am. Comm'n H.R. 271, OEA/ser.L/V/II.98, doc. 7 rev. (1997). (Compare the definition of an "armed conflict" given by the Appeals Chamber of the International Criminal Tribunal for the former Yugoslavia in the *Tadic* case, discussed below at p. 1061.)

6. Since 1980, the Inter–American Commission has heard several complaints against the United States alleging violations of the American Declaration of the Rights and Duties of Man, the American Convention on Human Rights, and of the customary law of human rights. See, e.g., the *"Baby Boy"* Case, Case No. 2141, Inter–Am.C.H.R. 25, OEA.Ser. L/V/II.54, doc. 9 rev. 1 (1981) *(Roe v. Wade* does not violate the right to life granted by American Declaration and the American Convention); The *Roach* Case, Case No. 9647, Inter–Am.C.H.R. 147, OEA/Ser. L/V/II.71, doc. 9 rev. 1 (1987) (U.S. death sentence for crime committed by juvenile under 18 is not a violation of a customary norm, although such a norm may be emerging); The *Celestine* case, Case No. 10,031, Inter–Am.C.H.R. res.

23/89, OEA/Ser. L./V/II.76, doc. 44 (1989) (facts did not establish that U.S. applied death penalty in racially discriminatory manner). There have also been charges before the Commission that the United States violated the Declaration and customary law when it invaded Panama in 1989, and when it interdicted vessels carrying Haitian asylum seekers on the high seas. *See Haitian Center for Human Rights v. United States*, Case 10.675, Inter-Am. Comm'n H.R. 550, OEA/ ser.L./V/II.95, doc. 7 rev. (1997).

7. For the jurisprudence of the Inter-American Court, see Systematization of the Contentious Jurisprudence of the Inter-American Court of Human Rights 1981–1991 (Inter-American Court of Human Rights, 1996). The Inter-American Human Rights Digest Project, based at American University's Washington College of Law, also compiles the jurisprudence of the Court and Commission. The first two volumes of the Digest, published in 1998, cover the Court from 1980 through 1997 and an on-line database is available. See also Davidson, The Inter-American Court of Human Rights (1998); Buergenthal, Norris & Shelton, Protecting Human Rights in the Americas: Selected Problems (4th ed. 1996); Shelton, The Jurisprudence of the Inter-American Court of Human Rights, 10 Am. U. J. Int'l L. & Pol'y 333 (1994); Frost, The Evolution of the Inter-American Court of Human Rights: Reflections of Present and Former Judges, 14 Hum. Rts. Q. 171 (1992); Grossman, Proposals to Strengthen the Inter-American System of Protection of Human Rights, 32 Germ.Y.B.Int'l L. 264 (1990).

C. THE AFRICAN HUMAN RIGHTS SYSTEM

For most of its existence, the Organization of African Unity (OAU) has been concerned with colonialism and its vestiges, with apartheid in South Africa, Namibia, and Rhodesia (now Zimbabwe), and the economic development of post-colonial African states. In 1979 the OAU decided to draft an African Charter on Human and Peoples' Rights.

The African Charter was drafted over a two-year period in Banjul, the Gambia. The Assembly of Heads of State and Government of the OAU adopted the Charter in 1981 and officially named it the "Banjul Charter." OAU Doc. CAB/LEG/67/3 rev. 5, reprinted in 21 I.L.M. 58 (1982). The Charter entered into force on October 21, 1986, after it was ratified by a majority of OAU member states. See generally Mbaye, Les Droits de L'Homme en Afrique (1992); Human Rights in Africa: Cross-Cultural Perspectives (An-Na'im & Deng, eds. 1990); Shivji, The Concept of Human Rights in Africa (1989); Howard, Human Rights in Commonwealth Africa (1986); Rembe, Africa and Regional Protection of Human Rights (1985); Eze, Human Rights in Africa (1984); See also Peter, Human Rights in Africa: A Comparative Study of the African Human and Peoples' Rights Charter and the New Tanzanian Bill of Rights (1990); Ben Salem, The African System of the Protection of Human and Peoples' Rights, 8 Interights Bull. 55 (1994); Amoah, The African Charter on Human and Peoples' Rights–An Effective Weapon for Human Rights?, 4 Afr. J. Int'l & Comp. L. 226 (1992). For a compilation of relevant documents, see Naldi, Documents of the Organization of African Unity (1992); The International Law of Human Rights in Africa: Basic Documents and Annotated Bibliography (Hamaleng-wa, Flinterman & Dankwa, eds. 1988).

1. The Rights and Freedoms Protected

The Banjul Charter speaks to both rights of individuals and of peoples, which states must recognise, as well as to the duties which every individual has "towards his family and society, the state and other legally recognized communities and the international community" (Article 27).

For individuals, the Charter protects the right to equal protection of the law; the right to life; freedom from slavery, torture and cruel, inhuman or degrading punishment and treatment; the right to liberty and freedom from arbitrary arrest or detention; the presumption of innocence in a criminal trial, and the right to counsel; freedom of conscience, profession, religion, expression, association, assembly and movement; the right to leave and return to one's own country; the right to seek and obtain asylum when persecuted; the right to participate freely in government; the right to property; the right to work under equitable and satisfactory conditions; the right to enjoy the best attainable state of physical and mental health; the right to an education; freedom from discrimination; prohibition of mass expulsion of aliens.

The Charter guarantees the right of "peoples" to existence and to self-determination. It specifically reserves to "colonized" or "oppressed" peoples the right to free themselves by resorting to any means recognized by the international community, and declares that all such peoples shall have the right to receive assistance from states parties to the Charter (Article 20). Also included is the right of peoples to economic, social and cultural development and the right to freely dispose of their wealth and natural resources. States parties are required to eliminate all forms of foreign economic exploitation. Peoples have the right to a "general satisfactory environment favorable to their development" (Article 24).

The Charter lists duties owed by a citizen to his state. They include the duty not to discriminate against others; to protect the family and respect and maintain parents; to serve the state and contribute to its defense; and to pay taxes in the interest of society.

2. *The System of Implementation and Enforcement*

The Charter establishes an African Commission on Human and Peoples' Rights to promote and ensure protection of human rights in Africa. The Commission is a body of independent experts whose mandate is generally three-fold: to promote respect for human rights through studies, seminars, conferences, the dissemination of information and cooperation with local agencies; to "ensure" the protection of human rights under conditions laid down by the Charter; and to interpret the provisions of the Charter (Article 45). Article 55 of the Charter has been interpreted to permit individuals and groups to petition the Commission concerning violations of its provisions by a state party. In addition, the Commission can consider that communications reveal a series of serious or massive violations of Charter rights and bring this to the attention of the OAU (Article 58). The Commission is therefore quasi-judicial in character, but only renders reports to the states concerned with a particular case and to the Assembly of Heads of State and Government. It is up to the states concerned, or the Assembly, to take any action in response to violations described in the reports. In these respects, the Commission is not unlike the human rights commissions of the European and American Conventions. See Welch, The African Commission on Human and Peoples' Rights: A Five Year Report and Assessment, 14 Hum. Rt.Q. 43 (1992); Odinkalu, The Individual Complaints Procedures of the African Commission on Human and

Peoples' Rights: A Preliminary Assessment, 8 Transnt'l L. & Contemp. Probs. 359 (1998); Ankumah, The African Commission on Human and Peoples' Rights: Practices and Procedures (1996).

The Charter does not create a court to which states or the Commission can refer cases when settlement is otherwise unattainable. This was considered a significant failure in the system of implementation and enforcement of Charter rights and the subject of a sustained advocacy campaign by many individuals and non-governmental organisations throughout the 1990s. In June 1998, the OAU Assembly adopted a Protocol to the Charter on the Establishment of an African Court on Human and Peoples' Rights. 1520 U.N.T.S., No. 26363. The Court will come into existence when 15 states have ratified the Protocol and will supplement the Commission as an additional tier of enforcement. See Naldi and Magliveras, Reinforcing the African System of Human Rights: The Protocol on the Establishment of a Regional Court of Human and Peoples' Rights, 16 Neth. Q. Hum. Rts. 431 (1998).

Note: Human Rights in the Arab World and in Asia

The Arab League, founded in 1945, decided in 1968 to establish a Permanent Arab Commission on Human Rights (Res. 2443, Sept. 3, 1968). Its essential aim is to promote respect for human rights, but provides no measures and creates no institutions to protect them. The Commission has focused on alleged human rights abuses by Israel in the occupied territories but not on human rights problems within the Arab States. See Boutros–Ghali, The League of Arab States, in Vasak, at 575; Rembe, Human Rights in Africa: Some Selected Problems (1984).

In 1994, the Council of the League of Arab States adopted the Arab Charter on Human Rights, but as of 2000 it has not come into force. The text of the Charter is set forth in 56 I.C.J. Rev. 57 (1996). The International Commission of Jurists summarizes its provisions in the following terms:

> The Charter generally embraces many components of the individual rights affirmed by the Universal Declaration of Human Rights (UDHR), including the right of non-discrimination between men and women. The Charter also endorses the collective right of self-determination and affirms some fundamental principles, particularly in the area of criminal law, which are necessary for the protection of the rights of the accused.
>
> Nevertheless, the Charter has many weaknesses. It affirms some, but not all, of the internationally recognised human rights. The most glaring omissions are those related to the freedom from slavery and the right to change one's religion. The omissions are perhaps based on the common assumption that these rights are not acknowledged in Islam.
>
> The Charter, moreover, minimises the scope of many of the rights it recognises and does not provide adequate remedies for their realisation. The introduction in the text of a distinction between citizens and others. is a cause for concern.
>
> The Charter also allows for rights to be further restricted and permits their derogation in times of public emergency. It establishes a monitoring mechanism that is inadequate to oversee the effective implementation of its provisions.

See also Rishmawi, The Arab Charter on Human Rights: A Comment, 10 Interights Bull. 8 (1996). An Arab Convention on the Prevention of Torture and

Inhuman or Degrading Treatment has also been drafted but, as of 2000, has not come into effect.

An Asian system for human rights protection did not exist as of 2000. The vast diversity of Asian countries, and differing attitudes about human rights as a general matter, did not conduce toward agreement on a regional system. See generally The East Asian Challenge for Human Rights (Bell & Bauer eds., 1999).

SECTION 3. THE HUMAN RIGHTS OF WOMEN

The ideology and the international law of human rights contemplate no distinction between the rights of men and the rights of women: women are human, equally human. And equality (including gender equality) and non-discrimination (including non-discrimination on the basis of gender) are cardinal tenets of the international law of human rights. See the Universal Declaration, Article 2; the International Covenant on Civil and Political Rights, Article 3; and the International Covenant on Economic, Social and Cultural Rights, Article 3 .

But societies and their laws continue to distinguish between men and women, and in law and practice equal respect for the equal human rights of women continues to suffer and to demand particular attention. International law includes a Convention on the Elimination of all Forms of Discrimination Against Women (not, notably, discrimination on the basis of gender), and a Committee on the same subject (see p. 675 below). The Convention includes unusual dispositions and obligations, including obligations to modify cultural patterns and eliminate stereotyped concepts that impair women's equality. Both the Convention and the Committee, though modeled upon the Convention on the Elimination of All Forms of Racial Discrimination and the Committee on the Elimination of All Forms of Racial Discrimination, suffer by comparison.

THE HUMAN RIGHTS OF WOMEN

In Human Rights, Henkin, Neuman, Orentlicher & Leebron (eds.) 1999, p. 358.

In the final decade of the twentieth century the human rights of women emerged as a major focus of international advocacy efforts. These efforts have had a significant impact on institutional responses to violations of women's human rights: The subject received prominent attention in the Declaration and Programme of Action adopted at the United Nations' World Conference on Human Rights in Vienna in 1993; the following year the UN Commission on Human Rights appointed a Special Rapporteur on Violence Against Women, and in 1995 the United Nations sponsored a World Conference on Women, in Beijing. During this same period various treaty bodies and international criminal tribunals issued key decisions clarifying gender-specific human rights protections.

* * *

The Universal Declaration expressed the equal human rights of men and women in the plainest possible terms. So, too, did the two Covenants, as well as the United Nations Charter, whose enumeration of Purposes of the Organization includes the following: "To achieve international cooperation in solving international problems of an economic, social, cultural, or humanitarian character, and in promoting and encouraging respect for human rights and for fundamental freedoms for all without distinction as to ... sex ...." (Article 1(3).) Like the U.N. Covenants, each of the comprehensive regional human rights treaties guarantees enjoyment of protected rights without discrimination on the basis of sex.

The customary law of human rights protects women and men equally, and it may also be a violation of customary law for any state, as a matter of state policy, to practice, encourage or condone systematic gender discrimination. See Restatement, Third, Foreign Relations Law of the United States, § 702, Comment *l*.

Yet despite these legal guarantees, women have long experienced gross inequalities in the enjoyment of fundamental rights. In many societies women remain subordinate in the home, in the family, in political processes, in social-sexual relations, in the enjoyment of property rights, in matters of employment and in the marketplace. In some countries, these inequalities are enshrined in law; in others, they reflect social, cultural and political resistance to legally-mandated assurances of equality.

Just as in the case of racial discrimination, it was thought necessary to adopt a special treaty dealing specifically with gender-based discrimination. In 1979, the UN General Assembly adopted the Convention on the Elimination of All Forms of Discrimination Against Women ("Women's Convention"), GA Res. 34/180, which entered into force two years later. But unlike the Convention on the Elimination of All Forms of Racial Discrimination, the Women's Convention has attracted numerous reservations, reflecting deeply ingrained historical, cultural and religious attitudes. * * *

Resistance to international protection of women's human rights is reflected also in the comparatively weak powers and procedures of the Committee on the Elimination of Discrimination Against Women (CEDAW), the treaty body that monitors States Parties' compliance with the Women's Convention.* In larger perspective, until relatively recently the human rights of women scarcely figured in international efforts to secure compliance with established standards. Instead, as many have noted, women's human rights were substantially ignored or marginalized in the principal international fora where human rights are promoted.

* * *

As its name implies, the central aim of the Women's Convention is to eliminate all forms of discrimination against women, which Article 1 defines as "any distinction, exclusion or restriction made on the basis of sex which has the effect or purpose of impairing or nullifying the recognition, enjoyment or exercise by women, irrespective of their marital status, on a basis of equality of men and women, of human rights and fundamental freedoms in the political, economic, social, cultural, civil or any other field."

* * * * [I]n 1999 the UN Commission on the Status of Women adopted an Optional Protocol to the Women's Convention. The protocol will expand CEDAW's supervisory powers * * *. [Editors' Note: See Note 2 on p. 677 for the status of this Optional Protocol as of 2000.]

While the convention's overall thrust is to ensure the enjoyment of rights in every sphere on a basis of equality between men and women, it also requires States Parties to take all appropriate measures "to ensure the full development and advancement of women." (Article 3.) Although this requirement is, to be sure, aimed at assuring the exercise and enjoyment of rights "on a basis of equality with men," it also conveys the distinct and important idea that the full development of women is a goal to be pursued in its own right.

Several other aspects of this convention are noteworthy. First, discrimination against women, which States Parties undertake to eliminate (Article 2), is defined in terms of distinctions, exclusions or restrictions that have the effect *or* purpose of impairing the enjoyment of rights on a basis of equality between men and women. Thus, even when it is not possible to establish discriminatory intent, a State Party might be responsible for a breach of the Women's Convention by virtue of practices that have a discriminatory effect. Second, the Women's Convention authorizes States Parties to undertake "temporary special measures"–measures that would be termed "affirmative action" programs in the United States context–to accelerate the achievement of de fact equality between men and women. (Article 4.)

One of the most distinctive features of the Women's Convention is its requirement that States Parties undertake affirmative steps to modify cultural patterns that impair the enjoyment of rights on a basis of equality of men and women. Article 5(a) requires States Parties "[t]o modify the social and cultural patterns of conduct of men and women, with a view to achieving the elimination of prejudices and customary and all other practices which are based on the idea of the inferiority or the superiority of either of the sexes or on stereotyped roles for men and women." Similarly, Article 10(c) requires States Parties to eliminate discrimination against women in the field of education by, *inter alia*, eliminating "any stereotyped concepts of the roles of men and women at all levels and in all forms of education by encouraging coeducation and other types of education which will help to achieve this aim and, in particular, by the revision of textbooks and school programmes and the adaptation of teaching methods."

Finally, perhaps more than any other human rights treaty, the Women's Convention embodies a vision of human rights in which the enjoyment of civil and political rights is indivisible from realization of economic, social and cultural rights. For example, Article 13 requires States Parties to take all appropriate measures to eliminate discrimination against women in the areas of economic and social life. To this end, States Parties must take measures to ensure that women enjoy the right to acquire bank loans, mortgages and other forms of financial credit on a basis of equality with men.

Notably, the Women's Convention is textually silent about violence against women, except in its requirement that States Parties take measures to suppress trafficking in women (Article 6). Nonetheless, CEDAW has interpreted the convention to prohibit violence against women and to require States Parties to take affirmative steps to prevent and punish such violence. * * *

In 1992, CEDAW adopted a General Recommendation on violence against women.

CEDAW, GENERAL RECOMMENDATION NO. 19, VIOLENCE AGAINST WOMEN

U.N. Doc. A/47/38 (1992).

8. The Convention applies to violence perpetrated by public authorities. Such acts of violence may breach that State's obligations under general international human rights law and under other conventions, in addition to breaching this Convention.

9. It is emphasized, however, that discrimination under the Convention is not restricted to action by or on behalf of Governments. * * * For example, under article 2(e) the Convention calls on States parties to take all appropriate measures to eliminate discrimination against women by any person, organization or enterprise. Under general international law and specific human rights covenants, States may also be responsible for private acts if they fail to act with due diligence to prevent violations of rights or to investigate and punish acts of violence, and for providing compensation. * * *

11. Traditional attitudes by which women are regarded as subordinate to men or as having stereotyped roles perpetuate widespread practices involving violence or coercion, such as family violence and abuse, forced marriage, dowry deaths, acid attacks and female circumcision. Such prejudices and practices may justify gender-based violence as a form of protection or control of women. The effect of such violence on the physical and mental integrity of women is to deprive them of the equal enjoyment, exercise and knowledge of human rights and fundamental freedoms. While this comment addresses mainly actual or threatened violence the underlying consequences of these forms of gender-based violence help to maintain women in subordinate roles and contribute to their low level of political participation and to their lower level of education, skills and work opportunities.

12. These attitudes also contribute to the propagation of pornography and the depiction and other commercial exploitation of women as sexual objects, rather than as individuals. This in turn contributes to gender-based violence. * * *

Notes

1. As of 2000, 165 States have ratified the Women's Convention. However, the Convention "has attracted the greatest number of reservations with the potential to modify or exclude most, if not all, of the terms of the treaty." Belinda Clark, The Vienna Convention Reservations Regime and the Convention on Discrimination Against Women, 85 A.J.I.L. 281, 317 (1991). See further references on reservations to the Convention at p. 489 in Chapter 7.

The United States signed the Convention in 1980. In 1994, the Foreign Relations Committee of the U.S. Senate recommended that the Senate consent to ratification with a series of reservations, understandings and declarations, but as of 2000 the Convention has not been brought to the Senate for action. See Proposed U.S. Reservations, Understandings and Declarations to the Convention on the Elimination of All Forms of Discrimination Against Women, 140 Cong. Rec. S13927–04 (1994).

2. On October 6, 1999, the U.N. General Assembly adopted the text of an Optional Protocol to the Women's Convention, which entered into force on

December 22, 2000. See G.A. Res. A/54/4, Oct. 6 1999, 39 I.L.M. 281 (2000). The Protocol provides for two procedures. Under Articles 2–7, the Committee (CEDAW) can consider communications submitted by individuals or groups of individuals under the jurisdiction of a state party who claim to be victims of a violation of any of the rights set forth in the Convention by that state party. Under Article 8, the Committee can initiate inquiries into situations of grave or systematic violations of women's rights. Only those states that have ratified the Protocol will be subject to these procedures.

3. What does the phrase "the human rights of women" mean? Henkin, Neuman, Orentlicher and Leebron, propose one way of approaching this question:

> Consider the following possibilities:
>
> *Human rights violations that are peculiar to women*, such as forced pregnancy. Forced pregnancy might violate a number of basic rights, such as the rights to physical integrity, family life, and privacy–*and* it is a type of violation of these rights that is peculiar to women.
>
> *Human rights violations to which women are especially–but not exclusively–vulnerable by virtue of their gender*, such as domestic violence.
>
> *Human rights violations that are gender-specific in the sense that they are committed or directed against women at least in part because they are women*, such as sexual violence. Unlike forced sterilization, sexual violence is not a violation of physical integrity that only women can experience. Neither, however, is gender beside the point in respect of this offence. Similarly, both boys and girls are potentially subject to genital mutilation, but no one would question that when girls are made to undergo this procedure in cultures where it is commonly practiced, they are subjected to it because they are female.
>
> CEDAW has defined "gender-based violence" in a manner that combines elements of the last two definitions. In its General Recommendation on Violence Against Women, CEDAW defined "gender-based violence" to include "violence that is directed against a woman because she is a woman or that affects women disproportionately." * * *
>
> In 1994 the UN Commission on Human Rights invited its Special Rapporteur on Torture, Professor Nigel Rodley, "to examine questions concerning torture directed disproportionately or primarily directed against women and conditions conducive to such torture, and to make appropriate recommendations concerning prevention of gender-specific forms of torture."

Henkin, Neuman, Orentlicher & Leebron (eds.), Human Rights (1999), p. 370.

See Report of the Special Rapporteur, Mr. Nigel S. Rodley, Submitted Pursuant of Commission on Human Rights Resolution 1992/32, U.N. Doc. E/CN.4/1995/34 (1995).

RAPE AND OTHER FORMS OF SEXUAL VIOLENCE

Rape as torture. The recognition of rape as a form of torture became a focus for many women's human rights activists in the 1980s and 1990s. In 1986, the Special Rapporteur on Torture of the U.N. Commission on Human Rights included rape in an enumeration of "methods of physical torture" in his first report to the Commission. Report by the Special Rapporteur, Mr. P. Kooijmans, appointed pursuant to Commission on Human Rights resolution

1985/33, U.N. Doc. E/CN.4/1986/15, p. 29 (1986). In 1995, the Inter–American Commission also concluded that "rape represents not only inhumane treatment that infringes upon physical and moral integrity under Article 5 of the Convention, but also a form of torture in the sense of Article 5(2) of that instrument." See Report on the Situation of Human Rights in Haiti, OEA/Ser.L/V/II.88, Doc. 10 rev. 9 (1995). See also Fernando Mejia Egocheaga and Raquel Martin de Mejia v. Peru, Case 10.970, Inter–Am. Comm'n H.R. 157, OEA/Ser. L/V/II.91, doc. 7 rev. (1996); I.C.T.Y., Prosecutor v. Delalic et al., Judgment, Nov. 16 1998, IT–96–21–T, at paras. 494–496 (finding that rape constitutes torture).

Rape as a war crime. In 1993, the U.N. Security Council established an international tribunal to prosecute those responsible for serious violations of international humanitarian law committed since 1991 in the territory of the former Yugoslavia (see Chapter 15). The International Criminal Tribunal for the former Yugoslavia (I.C.T.Y.) was created in response to the many reports of mass rapes, killings, and other abuses perpetrated in the course of "ethnic cleansing" in Bosnia and Herzegovina and there was considerable public pressure to ensure that the rapes were prosecuted as war crimes and the perpetrators punished. The Statute of the I.C.T.Y. confers subject-matter jurisdiction over two categories of war crimes, as well as over genocide and crimes against humanity. Rape is included explicitly only in the provisions relating to crimes against humanity. The I.C.T.Y. judges, however, have interpreted the provisions of the Statute to include rape as both a violation of the laws or customs of war and a grave breach of the Geneva Conventions of 1949 (rape as torture). See Prosecutor v. Delalic et al., Judgment, Nov. 16, 1998, IT–96–21–T, at para. 476, "There can be no doubt that rape and other forms of sexual assault are expressly prohibited under international humanitarian law." In 1994, the Security Council created a second international tribunal, with jurisdiction over crimes relating to the 1994 genocide in Rwanda. The Statute of the International Criminal Tribunal for Rwanda (I.C.T.R.) makes explicit reference to rape as a violation of Common Article 3 of the Geneva Conventions.

Notes

1. The Rome Statute for an International Criminal Court (ICC), adopted in July 1998, explicitly includes rape and other forms of sexual violence in its list of war crimes subject to the jurisdiction of the court. See Article 8(2)(b)(xxii) and (c)(vi) (enumerating, in addition to rape, "sexual slavery, enforced prostitution, forced pregnancy * * * [and] enforced sterilization" as war crimes).

2. On sexual violence as crimes within the jurisdiction of the I.C.T.Y. and I.C.T.R., see Kelly D. Askin, Sexual Violence in Decisions and Indictments of the Yugoslav and Rwandan Tribunals: Current Status, 93 A.J.I.L. 97 (1999); Patricia Viseur–Sellers, Emerging Jurisprudence on Crimes of Sexual Violence, in Symposium: War Crimes Tribunals: The Record and the Prospects, 13 Am. U. Int'l L. Rev. 1523 (1998). For a historical treatment of gender-specific war crimes, see Kelly D. Askin, War Crimes Against Women: Prosecution in International War Crimes Tribunals (1997); Theodor Meron, Rape as a Crime under International Humanitarian Law, 87 A.J.I.L. 424 (1993).

THE PUBLIC/PRIVATE DISTINCTION IN INTERNATIONAL LAW

The human rights of women, and particularly issues of violence against women, have highlighted distinctions in international law between the public and the private domains.

CHARLESWORTH, CHINKIN & WRIGHT, FEMINIST APPROACHES TO INTERNATIONAL LAW

85 A.J.I.L. 613, 625–29 (1991).

* * * Modern international law rests on and reproduces various dichotomies between the public and private spheres, and the "public" sphere is regarded as the province of international law. * * *

* * * One explanation feminist scholars offer for the dominance of men and the male voice in all areas of power and authority in the western liberal tradition is that a dichotomy is drawn between the public sphere and the private or domestic one. The public realm of the work place, the law, economics, politics and intellectual and cultural life, where power and authority are exercised, is regarded as the natural province of men; while the private world of the home, the hearth and children is seen as the appropriate domain of women. The public/private distinction has a normative, as well as a descriptive, dimension. Traditionally, the two spheres are accorded asymmetrical value: greater significance is attached to the public, male world than to the private, female one. The distinction drawn between the public and the private thus vindicates and makes natural the division of labor and allocation of rewards between the sexes. Its reproduction and acceptance in all areas of knowledge have conferred primacy on the male world and supported the dominance of men. * * *

The grip that the public/private distinction has on international law, and the consequent banishment of women's voices and concerns from the discipline, can be seen in the international prohibition on torture. [For further excerpts see p. 43 supra]

THE CHALLENGE OF CULTURAL RELATIVISM

The denial of women's human rights is often justified in terms of social and/or religious custom. Towards the end of the 20th century, tensions between women's rights and cultural relativism were manifested in particular in relation to issues of female genital mutilation. See Henkin, Neuman, Orentlicher & Leebron, Human Rights (1999), pp. 390–396; Hope Lewis, Between Irua and "Female Genital Mutilation": Feminist Human Rights Discourse and the Cultural Divide, 8 Harv. Hum. Rts. J. 1 (1995).

An issue related to questions of cultural relativism is that of how conflicts between rights should be resolved. As stated by Henkin, Neuman, Orentlicher and Leebron,

> some abridgements of women's human rights are justified in terms of religious doctrine mandating separate roles for men and women. In these circumstances, there may be a direct clash between the internationally-

protected right to manifest one's religious beliefs in community with others and the right not to be subjected to discrimination on the basis of sex. Even if one accepts in principle the claim that human rights are universal, this situation raises the question of how to resolve conflicts between and among rights each of which is internationally-protected.

Article 18(3) of the ICCPR provides that "[f]reedom to manifest one's religion or beliefs may be subject only to such limitations as are prescribed by law and are necessary to protect public safety, order, health, or morals or the fundamental rights and freedoms of others." Presumably, then, the Covenant permits some restrictions on religious practice if *necessary* to protect women's fundamental human rights and if those restrictions are prescribed by law. Still, this does not tell us how to determine whether particular forms of religious practice may–or must–be curbed to protect women's human rights.

Henkin, Neuman, Orentlicher & Leebron, Human Rights (1999), p. 396.

Notes

1. On the tension between freedom of religion and the human rights of women, see Abdullahi A. An–Na'im, Islamic Law, International Relations, and Human Rights: Challenge and Response, 20 Cornell Int'l L. J. 317 (1987); Donna Sullivan, Gender Equality and Religious Freedom: Toward a Framework for Conflict Resolution, 24 N.Y.U. J. Int'l L. and Pol. 795 (1992)

2. In 1981 the Human Rights Committee gave its view on a communication which raised the issue of conflict between the right of non-discrimination on the basis of sex and the cultural rights of a particular tribe. The author of the communication had lost her rights and status as an Indian, under Canadian law, and asserted that the relevant legislation was discriminatory on grounds of sex. The Committee did not directly confront this issue when finding that there had been a violation of her rights under Article 27 of the International Covenant of Civil and Political Rights. See *Lovelace v. Canada*, Human Rights Committee, 1981, U.N. Doc. CCPR/C/OP/1.

* * *

EPILOGUE: ASPIRATIONS AND REALITY

Adapted from Henkin, Human Rights: Ideology and Aspiration, Reality and Prospect, in Realizing Human Rights: Moving from Inspiration to Impact (Power & Allison, eds., 2000).

The Universal Declaration * * * internationalized the human rights idea and ideology, and rendered them of legitimate international concern. It placed human rights on the international political agenda and made it the subject of a growing corpus of international covenants, conventions and other treaties, and of an expanding customary international law of human rights. The Universal Declaration, and the national constitutional laws and the international law that it engendered, converted an easy colloquialism–"human rights"—into a catalogue of specific, defined rights–civil and political and economic and social. The international law and politics of human rights bred international institutions, and committed them as well as governments, non-governmental organizations, and innumerable individuals to the human rights ideology, and to promoting and ensuring respect for human rights for real people in real places.

The international norms and institutions that constitute international human rights have helped achieve, slowly, imperceptibly, an international culture of human rights, as well as a culture of human rights and constitutionalism within national societies. The edifice of norms and institutions has confirmed a significant erosion of state "sovereignty," and has established that how a state treats its inhabitants is not its own business only, but is of legitimate international concern. As a result, every human being–every one of more than six billion human beings–has a recognized, justified, claim to these rights, a claim upon his or her society and upon the international political system, to recognize, respect and ensure his or her human rights.

What difference has half a century of international human rights wrought in the lives of human beings? There have been differences–large and small, some immediate, some long-term; some concrete and demonstrable, some subtle and difficult to prove. In numerous countries on every continent, human rights are respected and ensured where they were not respected and ensured before the Second World War; hundreds of millions of human beings in Western Europe are now enjoying human rights they did not know fifty years ago. Constitutionalism and human rights have come to Eastern and Central Europe, to many countries in Latin America, to parts of Asia and Africa.

International human rights principles and obligations influence how governments behave in ways different from the influence of other international law and institutions. "Horizontal enforcement" of international norms–compliance induced by fear of retaliation–does not operate effectively in the law of human rights. But respect for human rights is enhanced by international monitoring and international criticism and various sanctions, as well as by criticism at home invoking international standards. International human rights norms and institutions deter violations and promote change.

Alas, there is another aspect to the human rights reality. The past half century—the age of rights—has not been free of genocide, crimes against humanity, war crimes, massive floods of refugees. Constitutionalism has not come to all countries in all corners of the world, and repressive regimes continue to jail opponents and suppress freedoms. Economic and social rights have not flourished for all, even in affluent societies. International norms have not prevented or deterred other violations; international institutions and powerful states have failed to respond promptly and adequately. But international human rights can be credited with what response there has been, however late and however inadequate. International human rights imbue all the continuing efforts to address the terrible violations.

In sum, the international human rights movement has established international human rights as a universal ideology. Every political society now must, in some way, attend to the rights of its people in its constitution, its laws and institutions. Every political society must answer for its human rights conditions to its own citizenry, to other governments, to the world. Many more societies than before 1948 have human rights systems, with fewer patterns of gross violation, and with institutions that help deter, prevent, remedy. Societies where these are absent or deficient are "abnormal," "under emergency," and are under continuing pressures to remedy. Where human rights systems become established, instances of retrogression are infrequent and perpetrators are under continuing pressure to recant and reform.

The condition of human rights leaves something to be desired in every society; in some societies human rights are grossly violated. But the idea and the ideology prevail. All human beings in all countries have claims to rights they did not have before the human rights movement. Hundreds of millions of human beings enjoy respect for their human rights because governments and societies have committed themselves to the idea and, perhaps, because they are monitored, shamed and deterred from violating human rights. No country can now say that the human rights of any human being subject to its jurisdiction are no one else's business. The world and its institutions may or may not respond, but they remain responsible.

In the 21st century, international law is no longer law reflecting only traditional state interests or values. International law now reflects also human values and addresses the human rights of individual human beings, all of them, of both genders and of all races.

Chapter 9

INTERNATIONAL RESPONSIBILITY AND REMEDIES

SECTION 1. GENERAL PRINCIPLES OF RESPONSIBILITY

If a state by its act or omission breaches an international obligation, it incurs international responsibility. If the consequence is an injury to another state, the delinquent state is responsible to make reparation or give satisfaction for the breach to the injured state. Thus when an internationally wrongful act occurs, it creates new legal relations between the states concerned. A state injured by a violation may seek redress by claims made through diplomatic channels or through a procedure of dispute settlement to which the states concerned have agreed. Under some circumstances, the injured state may take measures of self-help or counter-measures not involving use of force.

In the *Corfu Channel Case,* the International Court of Justice held Albania liable for certain omissions, in particular the absence of a warning of the danger of mines laid in her territorial waters. The International Court stated:

> These grave omissions involve the international responsibility of Albania. The Court therefore reaches the conclusion that Albania is responsible under international law for the explosions which occurred * * * and for the damage and loss of human life which resulted from them and that there is a duty upon Albania to pay compensation to the United Kingdom.

1949 I.C.J. 4 at 23.

In the much quoted words of the Permanent Court of International Justice:

> It is a principle of international law that the breach of an agreement involves an obligation to make reparation in an adequate form. Reparation therefore is the indispensable complement of a failure to apply a convention and there is no necessity for this to be stated in the convention itself.

Chorzów Factory Case (Jurisdiction), 1927 P.C.I.J., Ser. A, No. 9, p. 21.

As these statements indicate, responsibility arises whenever there is a breach of an international obligation, whatever its origin. There is no distinction in this respect between breach of an agreement or a violation of a rule of customary international law. Moreover, since any violation of an obligation resulting in injury to another state gives rise to international responsibility, the substantive grounds for such responsibility are as numerous and varied as the norms of international law.

International responsibility in the general sense is therefore distinct from the rules that determine the legality or illegality of conduct. The latter are sometimes described as "primary" rules, the breach of which is the source of responsibility. The general rules of responsibility are referred to as "secondary," inasmuch as they determine the legal consequences of failure to fulfill obligations established by the primary rules. See Report of the I.L.C., [1973] II Yb.I.L.C. 169–70. This does not mean, of course, that all breaches are treated in the same way. The gravity of a wrongful act and its consequences affect responsibility. Other distinctions are also relevant. But, in the language of the International Law Commission:

> [I]t is one thing to define a rule and the obligation it imposes, and another to determine whether there has been a breach of that obligation and what should be the consequences. Only the second aspect comes within the sphere of responsibility proper.

Id. at 170. See also Report of the I.L.C., 1999, G.A.O.R., 54th Sess., Supp. No. 10 (A/54/10) (hereinafter 1999 I.L.C. Report), pp. 98–100.

The material in this chapter deals with the general conditions under which a state may be held to have committed an internationally wrongful act which gives rise to international responsibility. It also deals with the consequences that an internationally wrongful act may have, such as the obligation of reparation and the procedures that may be used for redress. Specifically, the following questions are addressed:

— What is the "act of a state" under international law: when is an act or omission by human beings (individually or collectively) attributable to the state? (Section 2.)

— Is it a necessary element of a wrongful act that it include fault on the part of those responsible for the act? (Section 3.)

— Does breach of an international obligation by a state towards another state entail responsibility irrespective of actual injury or damage? (Section 3.)

— If a state violates a rule of customary law or a multilateral treaty, do all other states bound by the custom or treaty have a legal interest in the violation? (Section 3.)

— Should a distinction be made among wrongful acts based on the importance of the obligation violated? Should some violations of fundamental rules be treated as "international crimes"? (Section 4.)

— What circumstances generally preclude wrongfulness and responsibility for acts that are not in conformity with international obligations? Such circumstances may include prior consent of the injured state, distress, necessity, *force majeure,* self-defense. (Section 5.)

— Under what conditions may a state injured by a wrongful act take counter-measures that would otherwise be unlawful? (Section 6.)

— What requirements are imposed on a state responsible for a wrongful act? What are the forms of reparation? (Section 7.)

— What procedures are available for the injured state or injured persons to obtain remedies? (Section 8.)

I.L.C. Draft Articles on State Responsibility

Proposals for codification of rules of state responsibility have been before the International Law Commission since its first session in 1949, but as of 2000 this work is still in progress. Building on a series of valuable reports prepared by several eminent special rapporteurs, the I.L.C. provisionally adopted parts of Draft Articles on State Responsibility in stages during the 1970s, 1980s, and 1990s and a complete set of articles in 1996; these are reprinted in full in the Documents Supplement. Through the end of the 1990s and into 2000 and beyond, the Draft Articles have been the object of commentary and criticism on the part of governments and scholars; in the meantime, the I.L.C. has continued its examination of the topic.

Even though the Draft Articles remain in provisional form and it is unclear whether a formal treaty will ever result, they have already had a weighty influence on the jurisprudence of international tribunals. In the Case Concerning the Gabcikovo–Nagymaros Project, 1997 I.C.J. 7 at paras. 47–52 (see excerpts at pp. 709–711 and 715–716 infra), the International Court of Justice treated certain aspects of the Draft Articles as reflecting the customary international law of state responsibility. Other tribunals have likewise considered various parts of the Draft Articles and the I.L.C.'s commentary as authoritative expressions of customary law. See, e.g., the International Criminal Tribunal for the Former Yugoslavia in the *Blaskic* case, Case No. IT–95–14–AR108*bis* (Judgment of Appeals Chamber, Oct. 29, 1997), para. 26 at n. 34 (issue of who is an "injured State," with reference to Draft Article 40); and other cases referenced in this chapter.

The impact of the Draft Articles on states is less certain. Many governments have registered strenuous objections to some aspects of the Draft Articles, especially on international crimes and counter-measures. See, e.g., the U.S. Comments on the Draft Articles on State Responsibility, reprinted at 37 I.L.M. 468 (1998) (excerpted below under several of the topics to which the comments pertain), and the comments of various governments published at U.N. Doc. A/CN.4/488 and Add. 1–3. Governmental objections indicate skepticism about whether the more controversial aspects of the Draft Articles reflect state practice and/or *opinio juris*. For example, it is questionable whether any governments contemplating taking counter-measures against internationally wrongful acts (e.g., through economic sanctions) have believed that the limitations on counter-measures proposed in the Draft Articles reflect constraints that are already binding law (as opposed to suggestions for prospective law-making that states could accept or reject if the Draft Articles are eventually put forward in treaty form).

As of late 2000, the most recent version of the Draft Articles is a set provisionally adopted by the I.L.C.'s drafting committee in summer 2000. U.N. Doc. A/CN.4/L.600. (See also U.N. Doc. A/CN.4/L.602, as adopted by the Commission on second reading in 2001.) Some significant changes that would be made to provisions of the 1996 Draft are explained in the notes later in this chapter. See especially p. 701, note 9, on deletion of the concept of "international crimes" committed by states.

Notes

1. In considering the materials in this chapter, it will be important to keep in mind the themes from earlier chapters, such as the extent to which international law has been largely a state-centered system and pressures to change its state-centrism. Some critics of the Draft Articles on State Responsibility have argued that the very premises of the I.L.C. exercise ought to be challenged on this ground. As Philip Allott has written:

> Two especially vicious consequences result from using responsibility as a general and independent category in international law. First, it consecrates the idea that wrong-doing is the behavior of a general category known as "states" and is not the behavior of morally responsible human beings. It therefore obscures the fact that breaches of international law are attributable formally to the legal persons known as states but morally to the human beings who determine the behavior of states.
>
> Second, if responsibility exists as a legal category, it must be given legal substance. In particular, general conditions of responsibility have to be created which are then applicable to all rights and duties. The net result is that the deterrent effect of the imposition of responsibility is seriously compromised, not only by rationalizing it (the first vicious consequence) but also by leaving room for argument in every conceivable case of potential responsibility (the second vicious consequence). When lawyers leave room for argument there is much room for injustice.

State Responsibility and the Unmaking of International Law, 29 Harv. Int'l L.J. 1 (1988). Do you consider Allott's criticism well founded? Are the dangers he envisages likely consequences of the basic idea that an internationally wrongful act of a state entails the responsibility of the state?

2. For the history of the I.L.C.'s consideration of state responsibility, see the 1999 I.L.C. Report at pp. 91–95. The references therein to the reports of the special rapporteurs and the commentaries to the Draft Articles provide an entry point for research on the topic. A consolidated text of the commentaries has been compiled by the U.N. Secretariat from the 1973–1996 I.L.C. Reports: see Draft Articles on State Responsibility with Commentaries Thereto Adopted by the I.L.C. on First Reading, Doc. 97–02583 (Jan. 1997). Treatments by scholars include Spinedi & Simma (eds.), United Nations Codification of State Responsibility (1987); Rosenne (ed.), The International Law Commission's Draft Articles on State Responsibility (1991); and Bederman et al., State Responsibility in a Multiactor World, 1998 A.S.I.L. Proc. 291–312.

SECTION 2. THE ACT OF STATE UNDER INTERNATIONAL LAW RULES OF ATTRIBUTION

REPORT OF INTERNATIONAL LAW COMMISSION

[1973] II Yb.I.L.C. 161, 189.

(3) Since the State can act physically only through actions or omissions by human beings or human collectivities, the problems posed by this fundamental notion of the "act of the State" which have to be resolved in the present chapter have a common denominator. The basic task is to establish when, according to international law, it is the State which must be regarded as acting: what actions or omissions can in principle be considered as conduct of the State, and in what circumstances, such conduct must have been engaged in, if it is to be actually attributable to the State as a subject of international law. In that connexion, it must first of all be pointed out that, in theory, there is nothing to prevent international law from attaching to the State the conduct of human beings or collectivities whose link with the State might even have no relation to its organization; for example, any actions or omissions taking place in its territory could be considered acts of the State. In practice, however, we find that what is, as a general rule, attributed to the State at the international level are the acts of members of its "organization," in other words, the acts of its "organs" or "agents." This is the basic principle. The purpose of the present chapter of the draft will, in fact, be to define and complete this principle, to determine its scope and limitations and the derogations to which it is subject.

(4) From this point of view, once the basic rule has been laid down which attributes to the State the acts of its organs, the question arises whether the activities of certain categories of organs should be excluded from the "acts of the State." Another point to be considered is whether or not, in addition to the conduct of organs which form part of the State machinery, it is appropriate to attribute to the State, at the international level, the conduct of organs of public institutions other than the State itself, or of persons who, though not "organs" in the proper sense of the term, engage in what are in fact public activities, or of organs of another subject of international law placed at the disposal of the State in question. Attention will then be given to the question whether or not it is appropriate to regard as "acts of the State" the conduct of organs or, more generally, of persons whose activities are in principle attributed to the State, when such conduct is adopted in circumstances which cast doubt on the legitimacy of that attribution. This question arises, for example, where an organ exceeds its competence or acts contrary to the requirements of internal law concerning its activities. We next have to consider the treatment to be accorded to the conduct of private individuals acting solely in that capacity, and the basis on which the conduct of the State organs in connexion with acts by private individuals may be regarded as a source of responsibility. Lastly, consideration will be given to the case of the conduct of organs of other subjects of international law acting in the territory of the State and to problems relating to the retroactive attribution to a State of acts of a victorious insurrectionary movement.

Notes

1. For the rules of attribution drafted and adopted by the I.L.C., see Articles 5–15 of the Draft Articles on State Responsibility (1996), reprinted in the Documents Supplement. For the I.L.C.'s subsequent consideration, see 1999 I.L.C. Report, pp. 95–96. While aspects of the attribution articles have attracted interest and some debate (see below), they are not as controversial as other aspects of the Draft Articles to be considered later in this chapter.

2. Problems of attribution require that clear distinctions be made between matters governed by international law and matters governed by national law. The following examples are illustrative. Whether an entity (or a person) is an organ of the state is determined by national law. The fact that the organ's conduct is attributed to the state does not confer international status or personality on the organ. The criteria for determining attribution in international law are independent of those in national law. Hence, conduct may be internationally attributable to the state even when, in national law, there would be no such attribution. This may be the case, for example, for certain acts of private persons exercising functions of a governmental character without any authorization to do so. See Draft Articles 8 and 11(2) and I.L.C. commentary adopted in 1973–1975 (cited at 1996 I.L.C. Report, pp. 125–129).

Some governments and commentators have expressed concern that the Draft Articles could be construed as creating an "internal law loophole," so that a state might be able to evade international responsibility by virtue of how it had organized its internal affairs. See U.S. Comments on the Draft Articles, 37 I.L.M. 468, 484–485 (1998); Remarks by Clagett at the Panel on State Responsibility, 1998 A.S.I.L. Proc. 303–304. Is that a valid criticism of the formulation of the Draft Articles?

3. Does separation of powers within a national government affect attribution? As Draft Article 6 indicates (see Documents Supplement), it makes no difference in regard to attribution whether the organ was part of the executive, legislative, or judicial branch. Nor does it make any difference whether the organ had or had not any responsibility for foreign affairs. A state may be internationally accountable for officials performing entirely domestic duties, irrespective of whether their conduct had been endorsed or known to the officials charged with international matters.

4. Would attributing judicial conduct to the state run counter to the principle of independence of the judiciary or to the doctrine of *res judicata*? These tenets have been invoked in the past to negate attribution of judicial acts, but in recent years the responsibility of the state for acts of its judicial organs has been generally recognized. Thus, a state is responsible if a judgment denies immunity to an ambassador or is incompatible with an extradition treaty. If a judgment is not subject to appeal and is contrary to international law, an internationally wrongful act committed by a judicial organ is imputable to the state. On the other hand, if a judgment that is not appealable is contrary to national law, the state would not be responsible save in exceptional cases (for example, bad faith and discriminatory intent) where the "primary" international law rule was violated. See Jiménez de Aréchaga, International Responsibility, in Manual of Public International Law 550–53 (Sorensen, ed. 1968).

5. The doctrine of legislative (parliamentary) supremacy has no bearing on whether the acts of a legislative organ are attributable to the state. The Permanent Court has stated that from the standpoint of international law "municipal laws are merely facts which express the will and constitute the activities of states in the same manner as do legal decisions or administrative measures". Polish Upper Silesia Case, 1926 P.C.I.J. Ser. A, No. 7, p. 19.

Thus, if a state has incurred a treaty obligation which requires legislation, the failure of the legislature to enact such legislation results in responsibility of the state unless it took other means to fulfill the obligation. Moreover, the fact that, under national law, a legislative enactment prevails over a prior treaty obligation would not absolve the state from responsibility resulting from the non-performance of treaty obligations.

6. As Draft Article 6 makes clear, even a "subordinate organ" may engage in conduct attributable to a state. Would this be the case if recourse may be had to a superior organ to correct the wrongful or injurious conduct?

Should the probable availability of local remedies in cases of wrongful conduct affect the principle of attribution? For a discussion of the local remedies rule, see p. 734 infra.

7. Federal states have sometimes sought to deny responsibility for conduct of their constituent states and provinces. See Hyde, International Law 948 (2d rev. ed.). However, many arbitral awards have upheld attribution in cases involving injuries suffered by aliens. See Jiménez de Aréchaga, in Manual of Public International Law at 557. A federal state is also responsible for the fulfillment of treaty obligations in its entire territory irrespective of internal division of powers. Exceptions to this may be made in the treaty itself or in related circumstances. See Article 29 of Vienna Convention on the Law of Treaties.

8. Questions as to responsibility of a state for *ultra vires* acts of its officials, for conduct of private persons, and for acts of insurrectional movements have arisen mainly but not exclusively in regard to injuries to aliens. Some of these questions are dealt with in Chapter 10. A more general discussion of these problems of attribution will be found in the detailed commentary of the International Law Commission to Articles 10, 11, 14, 15. See I.L.C.Rep., [1975] II Yb.I.L.C. 61–106. See also The International Law Commission's Draft Articles on State Responsibility: Part I, Articles 1–35 (Rosenne ed. 1991); Caron, The Basis of Responsibility: Attribution and Other Transsubstantive Rules, in The Iran–United States Claims Tribunal: Its Contribution to the Law of State Responsibility (Lillich et al., eds., 1998).

9. In the Case Concerning U.S. Diplomatic and Consular Staff in Tehran, 1980 I.C.J. 3, at 29–37, the International Court of Justice considered the extent to which acts of student militants in seizing the U.S. Embassy, encouraged by the Ayatollah Khomeini as religious leader, would be imputable to the Iranian state. Although the Court did not find that the militants were acting as organs of the state, the responsibility of the state was nonetheless engaged by virtue of a variety of acts and omissions of state authorities.

10. State responsibility in relation to acts of private persons has become a notable issue in the human rights sphere. For example, when does a state incur responsibility on the international plane for failing to protect citizens from "death squads," or for ignoring domestic violence that results in death or serious injury to women and children? Recall the materials on these problems in Chapter 8, pp. 669–670, 677 (e.g., the Inter–American Court's *Velasquez Rodriguez* case). Do the

Draft Articles on State Responsibility offer a satisfactory conceptualization of this problem?

11. The Appeals Chamber of the International Criminal Tribunal for the Former Yugoslavia (I.C.T.Y.) resorted to "general rules on State responsibility" in order to determine whether the Bosnian Serb Army was acting as a de facto organ of the Federal Republic of Yugoslavia (Serbia–Montenegro). Prosecutor v. Tadic, No. IT–94–1–AR72, Judgment on Appeal from Conviction, July 15, 1999, at paras. 102–145. The Appeals Chamber discussed the international law of attribution and imputability in detail, with reference to the I.L.C. Draft Articles and further I.L.C. work through 1998. A noteworthy aspect of this discussion is the I.C.T.Y.'s critique of the judgment of the International Court of Justice in Military and Paramilitary Activities in and against Nicaragua, 1986 I.C.J. 14, where one issue had been whether actions of the Nicaraguan counter-revolutionaries (*contras*) were attributable to the United States. The I.C.T.Y. considered the I.C.J.'s "effective control" test enunciated in *Nicaragua* to be "unconvincing" in light of "the very logic of the entire system of international law on State responsibility," which the I.C.T.Y. thought should entail a "lower degree of control" than the *Nicaragua* test when the actors in question are organized military or paramilitary groups rather than unorganized individuals. Ibid., paras. 115–116, 124. In applying the lower standard, the Appeals Chamber concluded (at para. 162) that the Bosnian Serb armed forces were acting under the overall control of and on behalf of the Federal Republic of Yugoslavia.

Similar issues have been pending at the I.C.J. in two cases brought by Bosnia–Herzegovina and Croatia against the Federal Republic of Yugoslavia under the Genocide Convention. They have not yet been resolved in the several preliminary rulings entered in these cases. 1993 I.C.J. 3, 325; 1996 I.C.J. 595 (Bosnia–Herzegovina v. FRY); see also Application of the Convention on the Prevention and Punishment of the Crime of Genocide (Croatia v. FRY). It will be interesting to see whether, at the merits phase of these cases, the I.C.J. may be moved to reconsider its *Nicaragua* holding on attribution in light of the I.C.T.Y.'s critique in *Tadic*. Compare Zemanek, The Legal Foundations of the International System, 266 Rec. des Cours, 9, 259–262 (1997) (on attribution to states of acts of insurrectionary movements in Bosnia–Herzegovina).

SECTION 3. "FAULT," INJURY, AND THE REQUIREMENT OF LEGAL INTEREST

"Fault"

The element of "fault" is sometimes raised in connection with the assertion that every state has a general duty to prevent the use of its territory to cause significant harm to other states. Since many lawful activities within states may adversely affect neighboring states or common areas such as the high seas, the issue is presented whether an international responsibility to prevent harm should be conditioned on some element of fault such as negligence, lack of good faith, or intentional failure to comply with international standards. These issues have arisen mainly in connection with transboundary pollution of the atmosphere, rivers or other common waters. They also arise in respect of damage to the high seas and outer space. These matters of international environmental law are treated later in Chapter 17.

State responsibility in such cases has sometimes been considered under the principles of abuse of right or liability without fault. However, the trend has been to move away from these abstract and vague notions to defining conduct required of states to prevent harm to other states. Thus, the obligation to avoid harmful environmental damage has been stated as an obligation to take such measures as may be necessary to ensure that activities within the jurisdiction or control of a state conform to international rules and standards for the protection of the environment of other states or areas beyond national jurisdiction. See Restatement (Third) § 601. Many such obligations are specified in treaties relating to common waters and marine areas as well as to Antarctica and Outer Space. These "primary rules" of conduct determine the elements that are pertinent in deciding whether the obligation has been violated. Once a violation of such a primary rule is identified, the secondary rules of state responsibility determine the consequences of the violation.

Injury and Legal Interest

Does the breach of an obligation give rise to responsibility irrespective of injury caused to another state? It is sometimes said that the answer to this question depends on the primary rule of conduct, and that in the case of some primary rules, a breach does not occur unless and until injury occurs. For example, a state has a duty under international law to protect the embassy of a foreign government, but a breach of that obligation occurs only if the embassy suffers damage; negligence in protection is not itself a breach.

However, in the case of other kinds of primary rules, state responsibility may be engaged without tangible injury to another state. There may be situations where states claim to have suffered injury in a legal sense, even though they cannot point to specific material harm. Analytically, it is useful to distinguish between situations where harm *could* occur to a given state but remains inchoate at the time of the claim, and situations where the nature of the obligation is such that it is highly unlikely that any other state could ever be materially injured.

An extended discussion of the first kind of situation was given by a dispute settlement panel of the World Trade Organization in a case brought by the European Union against the United States. The EU complained that under Sections 301ff. of the U.S. Trade Act, the U.S. Trade Representative (U.S.T.R.) is empowered to take certain unilateral actions against other countries that the EU claimed would be incompatible with obligations under the GATT/WTO agreements. The United States defended against the petition on the grounds (*inter alia*) that the EU had suffered no injury, because the U.S.T.R. had not in fact imposed measures against the EU under this section. The EU responded that the very existence of the challenged legislation violated GATT/WTO obligations, even if it had not been applied against the EU and regardless of whether the EU had suffered injury. The dispute settlement panel wrote:

> * * * [U]nder traditional public international law, legislation under which an eventual violation could, or even would, subsequently take place, does not normally in and of itself engage State responsibility. If, say, a State undertakes not to expropriate property of foreign nationals without appropriate compensation, its State responsibility would normal-

ly be engaged only at the moment foreign property had actually been expropriated in a given instance. * * *

* * * In treaties which concern only the relations between States, State responsibility is incurred only when an actual violation takes place. By contrast, in a treaty the benefits of which depend in part on the activity of individual operators the legislation itself may be construed as a breach, since the mere existence of legislation could have an appreciable "chilling effect" on the economic activities of individuals.

* * * A law reserving the right for unilateral measures to be taken contrary to [WTO dispute settlement] rules and procedures may—as is the case here—constitute an ongoing threat and produce a "chilling effect" causing serious damage in a variety of ways. [The panel then discussed how that "chilling effect" might operate in the context of the economic decisions of individual operators.]

United States—Sections 301–310 of the Trade Act of 1974, WT/DS152/R (Dec. 22, 1999), paras. 7.80–7.81, 7.88, reprinted at 39 I.L.M. 452, 473–475 (2000). The panel went on to conclude, however, that although U.S. responsibility was prima facie engaged by the mere existence of GATT-illegal legislation on the statute books, the would-be responsibility was discharged by firm assurances tendered by the United States that the U.S.T.R. would not exercise its statutory discretion in a GATT-incompatible manner. Ibid., para. 7.126. See p. 221 supra.

The second type of situation concerns obligations which a state owes to treaty partners or to the international community as a whole, but which if breached would not typically cause actual injury to any other states. As the I.L.C. explained:

For examples we need only turn to the conventions on human rights or the majority of the international labour conventions. If one of these international obligations is violated, the breach thus committed does not normally cause any economic injury to the other States parties to the convention, or even any slight to their honour or dignity. Yet it manifestly constitutes an internationally wrongful act, so that if we maintain at all costs that 'damage' is an element in any internationally wrongful act, we are forced to the conclusion that any breach of an international obligation towards another State involves some kind of 'injury' to that other State. But this is tantamount to saying that the 'damage' which is inherent in any internationally wrongful act is the damage which is at the same time inherent in any breach of an international obligation.

I.L.C.Rep., [1973] II Yb.I.L.C. 183.

Does it follow from the examples given in the above passage, that the breach of an obligation by one state *always* infringes the rights of all other states to whom that obligation is owed? Are there not some obligations based on customary law or rules in multilateral treaties that may be violated with respect to one state (or a few states) without infringing the rights of all others bound? For example, the basic rule of territorial sovereignty binding on all states would be breached by one state entering illicitly the territory of another; but that breach does not infringe the rights of all other states or give rise to responsibility to them by the offending state. How do we distinguish these obligations from those referred to in the I.L.C. statement quoted above?

The International Court of Justice commented on this question in its judgment in the *Barcelona Traction Case*. We have already encountered this case in Chapter 6 (on corporate nationality) and Chapter 8 (on human rights as *erga omnes* obligations). The following excerpts from the Court's Judgment are pertinent to the point under discussion here:

CASE CONCERNING THE BARCELONA TRACTION, LIGHT AND POWER COMPANY, LIMITED (BELGIUM v. SPAIN), SECOND PHASE

International Court of Justice, 1970.
1970 I.C.J. 3.

33. When a State admits into its territory foreign investments or foreign nationals, whether natural or juristic persons, it is bound to extend to them the protection of the law and assumes obligations concerning the treatment to be afforded them. These obligations, however, are neither absolute nor unqualified. In particular, an essential distinction should be drawn between the obligations of a State towards the international community as a whole, and those arising vis-à-vis another State in the field of diplomatic protection. By their very nature the former are the concern of all States. In view of the importance of the rights involved, all States can be held to have a legal interest in their protection; they are obligations *erga omnes*.

34. Such obligations derive, for example, in contemporary international law, from the outlawing of acts of aggression, and of genocide, as also from the principles and rules concerning the basic rights of the human person, including protection from slavery and racial discrimination. Some of the corresponding rights of protection have entered into the body of general international law (Reservations to the Convention on the Prevention and Punishment of the Crime of Genocide, Advisory Opinion, I.C.J. Reports 1951, p. 23); others are conferred by international instruments of a universal or quasi-universal character.

35. Obligations the performance of which is the subject of diplomatic protection are not of the same category. It cannot be held, when one such obligation in particular is in question, in a specific case, that all States have a legal interest in its observance. In order to bring a claim in respect of the breach of such an obligation, a State must first establish its right to do so, for the rules on the subject rest on two suppositions:

> "The first is that the defendant State has broken an obligation towards the national State in respect of its nationals. The second is that only the party to whom an international obligation is due can bring a claim in respect of its breach." (Reparation for Injuries Suffered in the Service of the United Nations, Advisory Opinion, I.C.J. Reports 1949, pp. 181–82.)

(For additional excerpts, see pp. 441–448.)

Notes

1. The concept of *erga omnes* obligations expressed by the Court was endorsed by the International Law Commission and applied to the obligations, the breach of which constituted "international crimes." I.L.C.Rep., [1976] II (Pt.2) Yb.I.L.C. 95–122; see also [1985] II (Pt. 2) Yb.I.L.C. 25–27 (commentary on definition of "injured State" under Article 40(3) as including all states in the case of an international crime). For discussion of international crimes as proposed by the I.L.C., see Section 4 below. The Restatement (Third) also accepted the category of *erga omnes* obligations. It included in that category customary law obligations in respect of human rights and protection of the environment. See Restatement (Third) § 902.

2. Notwithstanding the apparent acceptance of the *erga omnes* concept, it has not generated substantial international litigation in the years since its enunciation in the *Barcelona Case.* Before *Barcelona* a similar idea had been asserted in a case brought in the International Court by Ethiopia and Liberia against South Africa for violation of the League of Nations mandate under which South Africa administered the territory of South West Africa. Ethiopia and Liberia asserted that as former members of the League they had a legal interest to vindicate the rights of that community of states in the mandate allegedly violated by South Africa. The Court in denying their legal standing referred to their claim as analogous to the *actio popularis* in Roman law under which a citizen could request the courts to protect a public interest. The Court observed that the *actio popularis* was "not known to international law at present * * * ." South West Africa Cases, 1966 I.C.J. 6 at 45.

3. When the Court subsequently endorsed the *erga omnes* conception in the *Barcelona Traction Case,* did it imply support of the right of any state to bring an action to protect a "public" or "collective" interest of the community? Such right, if recognized, would be similar to the *actio popularis.* However, on the international level the exercise of the right would require a jurisdictional basis. It could not be exercised unless the respondent state specifically agreed to jurisdiction or had consented in a treaty or by acceptance of compulsory jurisdiction under Article 36(2) of the Statute of the Court. See Chapter 11. Query whether it would contribute to wider law observance if every state could bring judicial action against a law violator (subject to jurisdictional requirements) for that state's infringement of collective interests. By increasing the class of potential plaintiffs, legal actions for breaches of law might become more common and thus enhance observance of norms that are in the interest of all states. On the other hand, would that very consequence make states more reluctant to submit in advance to jurisdiction of the Court? See discussion in Schachter, International Law in Theory and Practice 342–345 (1991); Schwelb, The Actio Popularis and International Law, 2 Isr. Yb. H.Rts. 47 (1972).

4. Recognition of *erga omnes* obligations has consequences beyond judicial proceedings. States considered to have a legal interest in vindicating important community or collective interests may assert that interest in relevant nonjudicial arenas such as international organs. Or, more important, they may take counter-measures unilaterally or jointly against offending states. (See Section 6 below.) Would such counter-measures strengthen compliance with basic rules of conduct? Is there a danger that in the absence of judicial control every state could "appoint itself as the avenger of the international community * * * in the name of higher

values as determined by itself" and thus add to international chaos? See P. Weil, Towards Relative Normativity in International Law, 77 A.J.I.L. 413, 433 (1983).

5. Under what circumstances would a state be regarded as having its rights infringed when another state breaches an obligation that applies generally to all states or to a large group of states under customary or treaty law? The International Law Commission has sought to answer this by giving a broad meaning to "injured states" in respect of breaches of customary law and multilateral treaties. Draft Article 40 suggests the following categories of "injured states" for purposes of responsibility:

— When the right infringed by the breach was established in favor of a state or group of states, those states are injured (Art. 40(2)(e)(i)). An example would be the state of nationality of an injured foreigner.

— When the infringement of the right affects the enjoyment of the right or the performance of obligations by other states, those other states are injured (Art. 40(2)(e)(ii)).

— Where the obligation was established to protect human rights and fundamental freedoms, all states are deemed to be injured by the breach (Art. 40(2)(e)(iii). The Commission observed that in this situation, the legal interests are not allocable to any particular state.

— Where a multilateral treaty has established a "collective interest" all parties are injured if the breach by one affects that interest (Art. 40(2)(f)).

— Lastly, all states are considered as "injured states" when the breach of the obligation is an international crime (Art. 40(3)).

See Documents Supplement and commentary at 1985 I.L.C. Report 54–59.

Note that the last three categories are in keeping with the principle of *erga omnes* obligations. What is the likely consequence of allowing all the states in these categories to invoke the responsibility of the offending state? Would it deter violations? Would the injured states be more likely to take countermeasures or bring charges in international bodies? Is there danger of abuse of these rights in the absence of controls by international judicial or political organs? See Charney, Third State Remedies in International Law, 10 Mich. J.Int'l L. 57 (1989). For differing perspectives, compare Damrosch, Enforcing International Law Through Non–Forcible Measures, 1997 Rec. des Cours 9, 50–54 (in favor of a broad construction of "injured state" in cases of human rights obligations), with Bederman, Article 40(2)(e) & (f) of the ILC Draft Articles on State Responsibility: Standing of Injured States Under Customary International Law and Multilateral Treaties, 1998 A.S.I.L. Proc. 291, 294 (arguing that the human rights provision is too expansively drafted). The U.S. Government has criticized this provision. See U.S. Comments, 37 I.L.M. 468, 483–484 (1998).

The provision adopted by the I.L.C. on second reading in 2001 embodies a simpler formulation that a state is entitled to invoke the responsibility of another state if the obligation breached is owed to the international community as a whole.

6. In its 1997 *Blaskic* ruling, p. 375 supra, the International Criminal Tribunal for the Former Yugoslavia spoke to the question of who would be an "injured state" in case of violation of the duty of states to cooperate with the Tribunal as required by Article 29 of its Statute. The I.C.T.Y. considered that this is an "obligation *erga omnes partes*," with a community interest in its fulfillment

that could be asserted by any member state of the United Nations. Ibid., para. 26 and n. 33. In this connection, the Tribunal referred to Article 40(2)(c) of the Draft Articles on State Responsibility, concerning the meaning of "injured state" in the case of an infringement of a "binding decision of an international organization." The I.C.T.Y. opined that if a breach of the duty to cooperate has been reported to the Security Council,

> each Member State of the United Nations may act upon the legal interest referred to; consequently it may request the State to terminate its breach of Article 29. In addition to this possible unilateral action, a collective response through other intergovernmental organizations may be envisaged. * * * It is appropriate to emphasise that this collective action:
>
> (i) may only be taken after a judicial finding has been made by the International Tribunal; and
>
> (ii) may take various forms, such as a political or moral condemnation, or a collective request to cease the breach, or economic or diplomatic sanctions.

SECTION 4. INTERNATIONAL CRIMES AND INTERNATIONAL DELICTS

INTERNATIONAL LAW COMMISSION DRAFT ARTICLES ON STATE RESPONSIBILITY

1996 I.L.C. Report 131.

ARTICLE 19

International Crimes and International Delicts

1. An act of a State which constitutes a breach of an international obligation is an internationally wrongful act, regardless of the subject-matter of the obligation breached.

2. An internationally wrongful act which results from the breach by a State of an international obligation so essential for the protection of fundamental interests of the international community that its breach is recognized as a crime by that community as a whole constitutes an international crime.

3. Subject to paragraph 2, and on the basis of the rules of international law in force, an international crime may result, *inter alia,* from:

(a) a serious breach of an international obligation of essential importance for the maintenance of international peace and security, such as that prohibiting aggression;

(b) a serious breach of an international obligation of essential importance for safeguarding the right of self-determination of peoples, such as that prohibiting the establishment or maintenance by force of colonial domination;

(c) a serious breach on a widespread scale of an international obligation of essential importance for safeguarding the human being, such as those prohibiting slavery, genocide, and apartheid;

(d) a serious breach of an international obligation of essential importance for the safeguarding and preservation of the human environment, such as those prohibiting massive pollution of the atmosphere or of the seas.

4. Any internationally wrongful act which is not an international crime in accordance with paragraph 2 constitutes an international delict.

Notes

1. An exposition of the authorities and reasons in support of the distinction between international crimes and delicts is included in the Report of the International Law Commission for 1976. I.L.C.Rep., [1976] II (Pt.2) Yb.I.L.C. 95–122. Draft Article 19 was approved unanimously by the International Law Commission in 1976. The discussion in the Commission and in its commentary emphasized that a wrongful act would be an international crime only if so recognized by the "international community as a whole." This did not mean unanimity according to the Commission members, but it did require agreement of "all the essential components of the international community." [1976] II (Pt.2) Yb.I.L.C. at 119. At that time, the "essential components" were considered to include the "Western countries" the "socialist countries" and the "Third World." Query whether these three categories are appropriate to describe the "essential components" of the international community today. Is it possible to define the international community in a way to express its pluralist character without requiring unanimity?

2. After its adoption by the I.L.C., Article 19 received mixed reactions in the Sixth (Legal) Committee of the U.N. General Assembly, with strong opposition from some governments. The United States, in particular, opposed the draft from the outset and has since reiterated its objections (see excerpts below). Several other Western and Latin American states also expressed objections to the draft article. Many of the supporters of Article 19, however, pointed out that the article did not provide for "penal responsibility" and that the question of the legal consequences of a crime of state was to be considered later in the Draft Articles. Most governments including the United States agreed that there were wrongful acts more serious than others because they affect fundamental common interests and that such violations may call for special legal consequences, but there is still no agreement on what those special consequences should be.

In its comments issued in response to the 1996 Draft Articles, the United States reaffirmed its objections to Article 19 in the following terms:

> *International Crimes*: * * * The concept of international crimes of state bears no support under the customary international law of state responsibility, would not be a progressive development, and would be unworkable in practice.
>
> State responsibility, as Professor Brownlie has pointed out, is "a form of *civil* responsibility". I. Brownlie, 1 *System of the Law of Nations: State Responsibility* 23 (1983) (emphasis added). *See also* 8 M. Whiteman, *Digest of International Law* 1215 (1967). * * *
>
> The notion that a state might additionally be subject to criminal responsibility for some delicts but not for others is foreign to the law of state responsibility. Indeed, the Commentaries adduce no international precedent to support the concept. Whether such breaches are called "crimes" or "exceptionally serious wrongful act[s]," they belong outside the framework of state responsibility. The United States continues to oppose the inclusion of a

concept of state crimes in the draft articles and would highlight the following difficulties:

> *Institutional redundancy*: Existing international institutions and regimes already contain a system of law for responding to violations of international obligations which the Commission might term "crimes." [E.g., the International Criminal Tribunals for the Former Yugoslavia and Rwanda.] * * *
>
> *Abstract and vague language*: * * * [S]pecific regimes of international law already govern particular violations referred to in article 19(3), so it is not clear how their enumeration in the draft articles adds anything to the law. These topics are enumerated with references that cloud rather than clarify meaning. * * * Highly subjective terms are used to qualify the topics; specific categories of crimes are encumbered with subjective qualifications ("of essential importance," "serious," "on a widespread scale", "massive") susceptible to any number of interpretations. * * *
>
> *The principle of individual responsibility*: * * * Practically, two regimes of responsibility—one for individuals and one for states—could help insulate the individual criminal from international sanction. Although some observers have found that state and individual criminal responsibility may coexist, an individual criminal may be emboldened to attempt to shift a degree of responsibility away from himself and to the state by resort to a provision for state crimes. To that extent, respect for the principles of war crimes tribunals at Nuremberg and the International Criminal Tribunals for the Former Yugoslavia and Rwanda will be undermined.

See U.S. Comments on the Draft Articles on State Responsibility, reprinted at 37 I.L.M. 468, 474–476 (1998).

3. Some countries, especially in Western Europe, questioned Article 19 because it implied the right of states not injured by the violation to take action against the violator. They observed this would open the way for unilateral action by powerful states ("self-appointed policemen") without any judicial determination of the crime. On the other hand, proponents of Article 19 emphasized the importance of recognizing that all states were affected by violations of rules of a fundamental character and every state should therefore be able to take countermeasures that were appropriate and proportionate to the violation. An intermediate position suggested by several states would recognize that non-injured states had a legal interest in crimes *erga omnes* but would require that the right be implemented within the framework of international institutions rather than unilaterally.

4. Note that Article 19 does not deal with the legal consequences of an international crime. That critical aspect was left to Part Two of the I.L.C. Draft Articles on State Responsibility. Some two decades after the adoption of Draft Article 19, the I.L.C. issued Draft Articles 51–53 specifying consequences of international crimes, including obligations for all states:

> not to recognize as lawful the situation created by the crime (Art. 53(a));
>
> not to render aid or assistance to the state which has committed the crime in maintaining the situation so created (Art. 53(b)); and
>
> to cooperate with other states in carrying out the above obligations and in the application of measures designed to eliminate the consequences of the crime (Arts. 53(c) and (d)).

See commentary at 1996 I.L.C. Report, pp. 164–170. The Commission stressed that these obligations "rest on the assumption of international solidarity in the face of an international crime. They stem from a recognition that a collective response by all States is necessary to counteract the effects of an international crime." 1996 Report, p. 170.

5. One consequence of an international crime, embodied in Draft Article 40(3), would be that if an act constitutes an international crime, all states would be considered "injured states," for purposes of taking counter-measures against the act. See p. 696 supra (on *erga omnes* violations) and pp. 723–724 infra (on counter-measures). In recognition of the controversy over the concept of international crimes, the Commission issued the following footnote to Article 40(3) upon adoption of the set of Draft Articles in 1996:

> "The term 'crime' is used for consistency with article 19 of Part One of the articles. It was, however, noted, that alternative phrases such as 'an international wrongful act of a serious nature' or 'an exceptionally serious wrongful act' could be substituted for the term 'crime,' thus, *inter alia*, avoiding the penal implication of the term.

See 1996 I.L.C. Report, p. 141.

6. Professor Weiler has suggested that the proponents of Article 19 had a "prophetic vision" by which they hoped to breathe new life into the U.N. Charter system which seemed at the time to have failed to deter the grave violations referred to in Article 19. Weiler wrote:

> The very acceptance of the concept of a Crime of State, "let loose" in the evolving international legal order and its law-making processes will, according to this prophetic vision, generate and prod the international community to evolve, flesh out and perfect whatever rudimentary regime of consequences is initially worked out.

J. Weiler, in International Crimes of State: A Critical Analysis of the ILC's Draft Article 19 on State Responsibility 332 (Weiler, Cassese, & Spinedi eds. 1989). In what ways could the concept of "international crimes" and a special regime of responsibility be fleshed out so as to strengthen international order?

7. In the light of U.N. actions in the 1990s (see pp. 727–728, 1006–1043 infra) can we expect that grave violations of essential rules such as those against aggression, genocide, and environmental devastation will be addressed by the U.N. Security Council and other international bodies that have competence to act under the Charter and other multilateral instruments? Would such "enforcement" measures by international organs be more likely if international law doctrine included the category of international crimes while leaving it to the institutionalized international community to take protective measures? Oppenheim's International Law 536 n. 14 (Jennings & Watts, eds., 9th ed. 1992) concludes that "unless the criminal responsibility of states is to be reduced to the vanishing point of law, its enforcement must be placed in the hands of impartial international agencies operating within the ambit of a politically organized international society." Does this suggest the need for a body more "impartial" than the U.N. Security Council?

8. The legislative history of Article 19 and the doctrinal and policy issues raised are well presented in a collective work edited by J. Weiler, A. Cassese, and M. Spinedi entitled International Crimes of State: A Critical Analysis of the ILC's Draft Article 19 on State Responsibility (1989). It includes contributions by 27 authoritative jurists. The bibliographical appendix lists 147 items on the subject up to 1987. See also Caron, State Crimes in the ILC Draft Articles on State

Responsibility, 1998 A.S.I.L. Proc. 307–312, and remarks by Crawford at 1998 A.S.I.L. Proc. 295–298.

9. As of late 2000, the concept of state crimes was set to disappear from the eventual final version of the Draft Articles. The drafting committee document eliminated Article 19 entirely, and governmental reactions in the U.N. Sixth (Legal) Committee indicated absence of support for restoring it. Instead of crimes, the 2001 draft would devote two articles to "serious breaches of obligations under peremptory norms of general international law" and the consequences of such breaches.

SECTION 5. CIRCUMSTANCES PRECLUDING WRONGFULNESS

Normally an act of state that is not in conformity with an international obligation is an internationally wrongful act entailing responsibility on the part of the state. However, under some special circumstances an inference of wrongfulness is precluded. The circumstances that are generally considered to have this effect are: consent, *force majeure* and fortuitous events, distress and necessity. Two other categories of state conduct may also be considered to exclude wrongfulness: self-defense and counter-measures. Counter-measures will be dealt with in the following section. Self-defense is treated in Chapter 12 on the use of force. The present section will deal with the other circumstances.

When any of these special circumstances is present, the obligation in question is not breached. "The act of the State in question cannot be characterized as wrongful for the good reason that, because of the presence of a certain circumstance, the State committing the act was not under an international obligation *in that case* to act otherwise." I.L.C.Rep., [1979] II (Pt.2) Yb.I.L.C. 108 (emphasis in original).

A. CONSENT

The International Law Commission proposed the following article on consent in the 1996 Draft Articles on State Responsibility:

Article 29. Consent

1. The consent validly given by a State to the commission by another State of a specified act not in conformity with an obligation of the latter State towards the former State precludes the wrongfulness of the act in relation to that State to the extent that the act remains within the limits of that consent.

2. Paragraph 1 does not apply if the obligation arises out of a peremptory norm of general international law. For the purposes of the present draft articles, a peremptory norm of general international law is a norm accepted and recognized by the international community of States as a whole as a norm from which no derogation is permitted and which can be modified only by a subsequent norm of general international law having the same character.

For the commentary, see [1979] II (Pt.2) Yb.I.L.C. 109–115. For the debate on whether to retain the article (or to delete it as proposed by the new special rapporteur, on the ground that the legal effect of consent belongs to the domain of primary rather than secondary rules), see 1999 I.L.C. Report at 160–163. The Commission in 2001 adopted the following formulation: "Valid consent by a State to the commission of a given act by another State precludes the wrongfulness of that act in relation to the former State to the extent that the act remains within the limits of that consent."

Notes

1. The entry of foreign troops into territory of another state which would normally be unlawful becomes lawful (as a rule) if it took place with the consent of that state. Many cases involving such entry of troops have occurred and a number were considered by the U.N. General Assembly and Security Council. The basic principle of consent as a legitimating factor was not challenged. Differences of opinion arose, however, on whether consent had been validly expressed on behalf of the state, whether rights of other states were violated, or whether a peremptory norm was infringed. Among such cases were those involving the entry of Soviet troops into Hungary (1956), Czechoslovakia (1968) and Afghanistan (1979), and the entry of U.S. troops into Lebanon (1958) and Grenada (1984). See Chapter 12. See also Schachter, The Right of States to Use Armed Force, 82 Mich.L.Rev. 1620 (1984); L. Doswald–Beck, The Legal Validity of Military Intervention By Invitation of the Government, 56 Brit. Y.B.I.L. 190 (1985); Hargrove, Intervention by Invitation, in Law and Force in the New International Order 113–126 (Damrosch & Scheffer eds., 1991).

Can a state consent in advance to the entry of foreign troops upon the occurrence of a condition such as the overthrow of its democratic government? When (if ever) would such consent be invalid because of conflict with a peremptory norm? Who (if anyone) could revoke or modify such consent? See Wippman, Treaty–Based Intervention: Who Can Say No? 62 U. Chicago L. Rev. 607 (1995).

Does consent require the support of the people? Is internal law decisive or are standards of international law relevant for determining the "will" of the state? These questions arise in several cases involving military intervention. See Chapter 12.

2. Many cases not involving military action also recognize that when a state entitled to observance of an obligation agrees to its non-observance, the other state does not commit a lawful act by such nonobservance. See Russian Indemnity Case, 3 U.N.R.I.A.A. 446.

3. May consent be implied or presumed? The I.L.C. considered that consent to be valid must be *"really expressed,"* but such expression may be by conduct as well as words. It cannot, however, be presumed. [1979] II (Pt.2) Yb.I.L.C. 112 (emphasis in original). Is it truly consent if there are elements of coercion? Would implicit threats of invasion invalidate consent? Would threats of economic retaliation?

4. Consent precludes the wrongfulness of an act only in relation to the state giving consent. However, an act consented to by one state may be a breach toward another state. Sending troops into one country may involve a breach to another (as for example where a treaty of neutralization is violated). Injury to nationals of a consenting state in violation of an international convention may also involve a breach toward other parties to the convention. The conventions on human rights are pertinent.

5. Note that the I.L.C. text considers that even freely given consent would not absolve a state from responsibility where the obligation was *jus cogens*. Does this involve an extension of the *jus cogens* principle beyond that laid down in the Vienna Convention on the Law of Treaties? See Articles 53 and 64 of the Convention on the Law of Treaties. The Commission bases its view on "logical principles" rather than on practice. I.L.C.Rep., [1979] II (Pt.2) Yb.I.L.C. 114. Would a government be free to consent to give up sovereignty and become a "protectorate" or province of another state? Can self-determination be asserted as *jus cogens* and a plebiscite demanded as a condition of state consent to giving up sovereign rights to another?

B. FORCE MAJEURE AND FORTUITOUS EVENT

Article 31 of the I.L.C. Draft Articles on State Responsibility reads:

> 1. The wrongfulness of an act of a State not in conformity with an international obligation of that State is precluded if the act was due to an irresistible force or to an unforeseen external event beyond its control which made it materially impossible for the State to act in conformity with that obligation or to know that its conduct was not in conformity with that obligation.
>
> 2. Paragraph 1 shall not apply if the State in question has contributed to the occurrence of the situation of material impossibility.

For the commentary, see [1979] II (Pt.2) Yb.I.L.C. 122–133. See also 1999 I.L.C. Report 175–178.

Notes

1. *Force majeure* and fortuitous events are frequently invoked as reasons for excluding wrongfulness. Although the use of the two terms is not uniform in practice, the situations covered by them have one common feature: "the State organs are involuntarily placed in a situation which makes it *materially impossible* for them either to adopt conduct in conformity with the requirements of an international obligation incumbent on their State or to realize that the conduct they are engaging in is not of the character required." I.L.C.Rep., [1979] II (Pt.2) Yb.I.L.C. 124.

2. Examples of such situations have often arisen when vessels or aircraft have entered the territory of another state without prior consent. Such entry may be due to bad weather or defects in function of equipment that made entry unavoidable or made it impossible for the pilot to know he had made an error. While such situations are not treated as international wrongs, disputes about them arise because facts and motives may not be verifiable. For example, the shooting down in 1983 by a Soviet military plane of a Korean passenger plane in flight over the U.S.S.R. in eastern Asia was followed by charges and counter-charges as to whether the plane had erroneously diverted from its course or had done so intentionally. If fortuitous events such as failure of equipment had been responsible for the pilot to go off course and not to know that, then the flight would not have been wrongful. See Report of the International Civil Aviation Organization on the case, 13 December 1983, 23 I.L.M. 937 (1984). The controversy about the facts continued after the foregoing report.

3. *Force majeure* has also been invoked as a ground for a state to avoid payment of its debt. Two cases that reached the Permanent Court of International

Justice involved pleas by debtor states that they were unable to pay in gold as required by the loan agreement. In both cases, the defense was unsuccessful on the ground that it was not in fact impossible for the states to pay in gold or equivalent value. See Case Concerning Serbian Loans, 1929 P.C.I.J., Ser. C., No. 16–III, pp. 211–29 and Case Concerning Brazilian Loans, 1929 P.C.I.J., Ser. A., No. 20/21, pp. 33–40.

Would *force majeure* in the sense of "material impossibility" apply when the debtor state could not pay without imposing severe hardships on its inhabitants? Would such condition be an "irresistible force"? If inability to pay had been caused by an unexpected collapse in prices of a commodity that was a major source of export earnings of the debtor state would the precipitating cause be regarded as a "fortuitous event"? See below for discussion of "distress" and "necessity" as possible grounds for non-payment.

4. In some cases the state claiming *force majeure* may have contributed to the occurrence of the event. It may, for example, have failed to provide adequate guidance to an aircraft that intruded into foreign territory. It would seem doubtful in that case that the state should be able to disclaim responsibility because of *force majeure*. See I.L.C.Rep., [1979] II (Pt.2) Yb.I.L.C. 125–26.

C. DISTRESS

Article 32 of the I.L.C. Draft Articles on State Responsibility reads:

> 1. The wrongfulness of an act of a State not in conformity with an international obligation of that State is precluded if the author of the conduct which constitutes the act of that State had no other means, in a situation of extreme distress, of saving his life or that of persons entrusted to his care.
>
> 2. Paragraph 1 shall not apply if the State in question has contributed to the occurrence of the situation of extreme distress or if the conduct in question was likely to create a comparable or greater peril.

For the commentary, see [1979] II (Pt.2) Yb.I.L.C. 133–136. See also 1999 I.L.C. Report 179–181.

An arbitral tribunal dealt with distress and related aspects of the I.L.C. Draft Articles in the following case:

RAINBOW WARRIOR (NEW ZEALAND v. FRANCE)

France–New Zealand Arbitration Tribunal, 1990.
82 I.L.R. 499.

[Using two high explosive devices, a team of French agents destroyed the *Rainbow Warrior,* a civilian vessel owned by Greenpeace International, at its moorings in Auckland Harbor, New Zealand on July 10, 1985. A serious dispute ensued between France, which requested the extradition of two captured agents (Major Alain Mafart and Captain Dominique Prieur), and New Zealand, which sought reparations for the incident. Unable to reach a settlement, France and New Zealand submitted their disagreements to the Secretary–General of the United Nations for binding arbitration.

The Secretary–General's ruling, issued on July 6, 1986, required France to pay reparations of US $7 million and to cease interfering in certain of New

Zealand's trade affairs with the European Economic Community. As to extradition, the Secretary General ordered that Mafart and Prieur be transferred to a French military facility on the isolated island of Hao in French Polynesia for a three-year period. The ruling stipulated that the two agents were "prohibited from leaving the island for any reason, except with the mutual consent of the two Governments." France and New Zealand formalized their understanding of the Secretary–General's ruling in an exchange of letters described as the "1986 Agreement" or the "First Agreement."

About five months after the transfer of the two agents to Hao, France asked New Zealand for permission to transport Major Mafart to a hospital in Paris to undergo urgent medical treatment for an abdominal pain of unknown cause. In the midst of negotiations to acquire New Zealand's consent, France transferred Mafart to Paris. After voicing strong objection to France's unilateral action, New Zealand sent a physician, Dr. R.S. Croxson, to Paris in order to examine Mafart. Although he expressed doubt as to the necessity of an emergency evacuation, Croxson confirmed that Mafart's medical condition required sophisticated tests that were unavailable in Hao. Croxson continued to observe Mafart on a regular basis; on February 12, 1988, he informed New Zealand that Mafart's medical condition no longer warranted his continued stay in Paris. Instead of returning Mafart to Hao, France declared him "repatriated for health reasons" on March 11, 1988.

A similar episode occurred with Captain Prieur. On May 3, 1988, France requested New Zealand's permission to transfer Prieur to Paris because she was pregnant. New Zealand asked to examine Prieur on Hao before consenting to the transfer. France agreed. However, when French authorities learned that Prieur's father was dying of cancer, they decided "for obvious humanitarian reasons" to fly her to Paris before arrangements to obtain New Zealand's consent were completed.

Soon thereafter, New Zealand and France submitted their dispute to an arbitral tribunal. New Zealand demanded (1) a declaration that France had breached its obligations by failing to obtain New Zealand's consent prior to the removal of Mafart and Prieur from Hao and (2) an order that France must return the two agents to the island for the balance of their three-year sentences. France denied international responsibility on the theories of *force majeure* and distress. The Tribunal commented as follows:]

CIRCUMSTANCES PRECLUDING WRONGFULNESS

76. Under the title "Circumstances Precluding Wrongfulness" the International Law Commission proposed in Articles 29 to 35 a set of rules which include three provisions, on *force majeure* and fortuitous event (Article 31), distress (Article 32), and state of necessity (Article 33), which may be relevant to the decision on this case. * * *

77. [T]here are several reasons for excluding the applicability of the excuse of force majeure in this case. As pointed out in the report of the International Law Commission, Article 31 refers to "a situation facing the subject taking the action, which leads it, as it were, despite itself, to act in a manner not in conformity with the requirements of an international obligation incumbent on it." Force majeure is "generally invoked to justify involuntary, or at least unintentional conduct"; it refers "to an irresistible

force or an unforeseen external event against which it has no remedy and which makes it 'materially impossible' for it to act in conformity with the obligation," since "no person is required to do the impossible." * * *

New Zealand is right in asserting that the excuse of force majeure is not of relevance in this case because the test of its applicability is of absolute and material impossibility, and because a circumstance rendering performance more difficult or burdensome does not constitute a case of force majeure. Consequently, this excuse is of no relevance in the present case.

78. Article 32 of the Articles drafted by the International Law Commission deals with another circumstance which may preclude wrongfulness in international law, namely, that of the "distress" of the author of the conduct which constitutes the act of the State whose wrongfulness is in question. * * * The commentary of the International Law Commission explains that " 'distress' means a situation of extreme peril in which the organ of the State which adopts that conduct has, at that particular moment, no means of saving himself or persons entrusted to his care other than to act in a manner not in conformity with the requirements of the obligation in question." * * * The question therefore is to determine whether the circumstances of distress in a case of extreme urgency involving elementary humanitarian considerations affecting the acting organs of the State may exclude wrongfulness in this case.

79. In accordance with the previous legal considerations, three conditions would be required to justify the conduct followed by France in respect to Major Mafart and Captain Prieur:

(1) the existence of very exceptional circumstances of extreme urgency involving medical or other considerations of an elementary nature, provided always that a prompt recognition of the existence of those exceptional circumstances is subsequently obtained from the other interested party or is clearly demonstrated.

(2) The reestablishment of the original situation of compliance with the assignment in Hao as soon as the reasons of emergency invoked to justify the repatriation had disappeared.

(3) The existence of a good faith effort to try to obtain the consent of New Zealand in terms of the 1986 Agreement.

THE CASE OF MAJOR MAFART

80. The New Zealand reaction to the French initiative for the removal of Major Mafart appears to have been conducted in conformity with the above considerations. * * *

81. The sending of Dr. Croxson to examine Major Mafart the same day of the arrival of the latter in Paris [implied] that if the alleged conditions of urgency justifying the evacuation were verified, consent would very likely have been given to what was until then a unilateral removal. * * * Dr. Croxson's first report, of 14 December 1987, accepts that Major Mafart needed "detailed investigations which were not available in Hao[.]" * * *

83. [Dr. Croxson's] sixth report, dated 12 February 1988, on the other hand, evidences that there was by that time a clear obligation of the French authorities to return Major Mafart to Hao, by reason of the disappearance of the urgent medical emergency which had determined his evacuation. This

report, together with the absence of other medical reports showing the recurrence of the symptoms which determined the evacuation, demonstrates that Major Mafart should have been returned to Hao at least on 12 February 1988, and that failure to do so constituted a breach by the French Government of its obligations under the First Agreement. * * *

88. Both parties recognized that the return of Major Mafart to Hao depended mainly on his state of health. Thus, the French Ministry of Foreign Affairs in its note of 30 December 1987 to the New Zealand Embassy referring to France's respect for the 1986 Agreement had said that Major Mafart will return to Hao when his state of health allowed.

Consequently, there was no valid ground for Major Mafart continuing to remain in metropolitan France and the conclusion is unavoidable that this omission constitutes a material breach by the French Government of the First Agreement. * * *

THE CASE OF CAPTAIN PRIEUR

89. As to the situation of Captain Prieur, the French authorities advised the New Zealand Government, on 3 May 1988, that she was pregnant, adding that a medical report indicated that "this pregnancy should be treated with special care * * *" The advice added that "the medical facilities on Hao are not equipped to carry out the necessary medical examinations and to give Mrs. Prieur the care required by her condition."

93. The facts * * *, which are not disputed, show that New Zealand would not oppose Captain Prieur's departure, if that became necessary because of special care which might be required by her pregnancy. * * *

94. On the other hand, it appears that during the day of 5 May the French Government suddenly decided to present the New Zealand Government with the fait accompli of Captain Prieur's hasty return for a new reason, the health of Mrs. Prieur's father, who was seriously ill, hospitalized for cancer. * * *

96. [D]uring the day of 5 May 1988, France did not seek New Zealand's approval in good faith for Captain Prieur's sudden departure; and accordingly, the return of Captain Prieur, who left Hao on Thursday, 5 May at 11:30 p.m. (French time) and arrived in Paris on Friday, 6 May, thus constituted a violation of the obligations under the 1986 Agreement. * * *

97. Moreover, France continued to fall short of its obligations by keeping Captain Prieur in Paris after the unfortunate death of her father on 16 May 1988. * * *

99. In summary, the circumstances of distress, of extreme urgency and the humanitarian considerations invoked by France may have been circumstances excluding responsibility for the unilateral removal of Major Mafart without obtaining New Zealand's consent, but clearly these circumstances entirely fail to justify France's responsibility for the removal of Captain Prieur and from the breach of its obligations resulting from the failure to return the two officers to Hao (in the case of Major Mafart once the reasons for their removal had disappeared). There was here a clear breach of its obligations and a breach of material character.

Notes

1. "Distress" differs from *force majeure* in that in case of distress, conformity with the obligation is possible but would result in loss of life. Distress has been invoked as an excuse when a frontier was violated by a vessel or aircraft to save lives in peril. See Lissitzyn, Treatment of Aerial Intruders, 47 A.J.I.L. 588 (1953). Multilateral conventions on the law of the sea and marine pollution contain exculpatory provisions for both *force majeure* and distress. See U.N. Convention on the Law of the Sea 1982, Article 18(2) and 39(1)(e); Convention on Prevention of Pollution by Oil 1954, 327 U.N.T.S. 8, Article V.

2. Would "distress" be a legitimate ground for a state to refuse to pay a debt if such payment would require so substantial a reduction in living standards as to cause starvation or higher rates of infant mortality? Leaders of some debtor countries have raised this issue.

D. NECESSITY

Article 33 of the I.L.C. Draft Articles on State Responsibility reads:

Article 33. State of necessity

1. A state of necessity may not be invoked by a State as a ground for precluding the wrongfulness of an act of that State not in conformity with an international obligation of the State unless:

(a) the act was the only means of safeguarding an essential interest of the State against a grave and imminent peril; and

(b) the act did not seriously impair an essential interest of the State toward which the obligation existed.

2. In any case, a state of necessity may not be invoked by a State as a ground for precluding wrongfulness:

(a) if the international obligation with which the act of the State is not in conformity arises out of a peremptory norm of general international law; or

(b) if the international obligation with which the act of the State is not in conformity is laid down by a treaty which, explicitly or implicitly, excludes the possibility of invoking the state of necessity with respect to that obligation; or

(c) if the State in question has contributed to the occurrence of the state of necessity.

For the commentary, see [1980] II (Pt.2) Yb.I.L.C. 34–52. See also 1999 I.L.C. Report 182–186.

Notes

1. Necessity as a ground for precluding wrongfulness differs from *force majeure* in that the latter involves material impossibility to conform with the obligation or to realize the conduct is contrary to the obligation. In that sense, *force majeure* involves an unintentional breach. A state of necessity, however, involves a deliberate act not to conform with the obligation. It is intentional conduct considered necessary to safeguard "an essential interest of the State against a grave and imminent peril" (Article 33). The state organs which have to

decide on the conduct to take are free to make a deliberate and fully conscious choice.

2. What are the "essential interests of the State" that justify breaking international obligations when such interests are endangered? The existence of the state is mentioned as one. Others suggested by the I.L.C. are: the maintenance of conditions in which essential services can function, the keeping of domestic peace, the survival of part of its population, the ecological preservation of all or some of its territory. I.L.C.Rep., [1980] II (Pt.2) Yb.I.L.C. 39–52.

The International Court of Justice dealt with "ecological necessity" in the following case:

CASE CONCERNING THE GABCIKOVO–NAGYMAROS PROJECT

International Court of Justice, 1997.
1997 I.C.J. 7.

[For the background of this case, see pp. 557–559 supra.]

49. The Court will now consider the question of whether there was, in 1989, a state of necessity which would have permitted Hungary, without incurring international responsibility, to suspend and abandon works that it was committed to perform in accordance with the 1977 Treaty and related instruments.

50. In the present case, the Parties are in agreement in considering that the existence of a state of necessity must be evaluated in the light of the criteria laid down by the International Law Commission in Article 33 of the Draft Articles on the International Responsibility of States that it adopted on first reading. [Quotation of Article 33 omitted.]

In its Commentary, the Commission defined the "state of necessity" as being

> "the situation of a State whose sole means of safeguarding an essential interest threatened by a grave and imminent peril is to adopt conduct not in conformity with what is required of it by an international obligation to another State" [Yb.I.L.C. 1980, Vol. II, Part 2, p. 34, para. 1].

It concluded that "the notion of state of necessity is ... deeply rooted in general legal thinking" (*ibid.*, p. 49, para. 31).

51. The Court considers, first of all, that the state of necessity is a ground recognized by customary international law for precluding the wrongfulness of an act not in conformity with an international obligation. It observes moreover that such ground for precluding wrongfulness can only be accepted on an exceptional basis. The International Law Commission was of the same opinion when it explained that it had opted for a negative form of words in Article 33 of its Draft

> "in order to show, by this formal means also, that the case of invocation of a state of necessity as a justification must be considered as really constituting an exception—and one even more rarely admissible than is the case with the other circumstances precluding wrongfulness ..." (*ibid.*, p. 51, para. 40).

Thus, according to the Commission, the state of necessity can only be invoked under certain strictly defined conditions which must be cumulatively satisfied; and the State concerned is not the sole judge of whether those conditions have been met.

52. In the present case, the following basic conditions set forth in Draft Article 33 are relevant: it must have been occasioned by an "essential interest" of the State which is the author of the act conflicting with one of its international obligations; that interest must have been threatened by a "grave and imminent peril"; the act being challenged must have been the "only means" of safeguarding that interest; that act must not have "seriously impair[ed] an essential interest" of the State towards which the obligation existed; and the State which is the author of that act must not have "contributed to the occurrence of the state of necessity". Those conditions reflect customary international law.

The Court will now endeavour to ascertain whether those conditions had been met at the time of the suspension and abandonment, by Hungary, of the works that it was to carry out in accordance with the 1977 Treaty.

53. The Court has no difficulty in acknowledging that the concerns expressed by Hungary for its natural environment in the region affected by the Gabcikovo–Nagymaros Project related to an "essential interest" of that State, within the meaning given to that expression in Article 33 of the Draft of the International Law Commission.

The Commission, in its Commentary, indicated that one should not, in that context, reduce an "essential interest" to a matter only of the "existence" of the State, and that the whole question was, ultimately, to be judged in the light of the particular case (see *Yearbook of the International Law Commission,* 1980, Vol. II, Part 2, p. 49, para. 32); at the same time, it included among the situations that could occasion a state of necessity, "a grave danger to . . . the ecological preservation of all or some of the [the] territory [of a State]" (*ibid.,* p. 35, para. 3); and specified, with reference to State practice, that "It is primarily in the last two decades that safeguarding the ecological balance has come to be considered an 'essential interest' of all States." (*Ibid.,* p. 39, para. 14.) * * *

54. The verification of the existence, in 1989, of the "peril" invoked by Hungary, of its "grave and imminent" nature, as well as of the absence of any "means" to respond to it, other than the measures taken by Hungary to suspend and abandon the works, are all complex processes. * * * Hungary on several occasions expressed, in 1989, its "uncertainties" as to the ecological impact of putting in place the Gabcikovo–Nagymaros barrage system, which is why it asked insistently for new scientific studies to be carried out.

The Court considered, however, that serious though these uncertainties might have been they could not, alone, establish the objective existence of a "peril" in the sense of a component element of a state of necessity. The word "peril" certainly evokes the idea of "risk"; that is precisely what distinguishes "peril" from material damage. But a state of necessity could not exist without a "peril" duly established at the relevant point in time; the mere apprehension of a possible "peril" could not suffice in that respect. It could moreover hardly be otherwise, when the "peril" constituting the state of necessity has at the same time to be "grave" and "imminent". "Imminence" is synonymous with "immediacy" or "proximity" and goes far beyond the concept of "possibility". As the International Law Commission emphasized in its commentary, the "extremely grave and imminent" peril must "have been a threat to the interest at the actual time" (*Yearbook of the International Law Commission,* 1980, Vol. II, Part 2, p. 49, para. 33). That does not exclude, in the view of the Court, that a "peril" appearing in the long term might be held to be "imminent" as soon as it is established, at the relevant point in time, that the realization of that peril, however far off it might be, is not thereby any less certain and inevitable. * * *

Both Parties have placed on record an impressive amount of scientific material aimed at reinforcing their respective arguments. The Court has given most careful attention to this material, in which the Parties have developed their opposing views as to the ecological consequences of the Project. It concludes, however, that, as will be shown below, it is not necessary in order to respond to the questions put to it in the Special Agreement for it to determine which of those points of view is scientifically better founded.

55. * * * The Court notes that the dangers ascribed to the upstream reservoir were mostly of a long-term nature and, above all, that they remained uncertain. * * * It follows that, even if it could have been established—which, in the Court's appreciation of the evidence before it, was not the case—that the reservoir would ultimately have constituted a "grave peril" for the environment in the area, one would be bound to conclude that the peril was not "imminent" at the time at which Hungary suspended and then abandoned the works relating to the dam.

56. * * * The Court also notes that, in these proceedings, Hungary acknowledged that, as a general rule, the quality of the Danube waters have improved over the past 20 years, even if those waters remained subject to hypertrophic conditions.

However "grave" it might have been, it would accordingly have been difficult, in the light of what is said above, to see the alleged peril as sufficiently certain and therefore "imminent" in 1989.

The Court moreover considers that Hungary could, in this context also, have resorted to other means in order to respond to the dangers that it apprehended. * * *

57. The Court concludes from the foregoing that, with respect to both Nagymaros and Gabcikovo, the perils invoked by Hungary, without prejudging their possible gravity, were not sufficiently established in 1989, nor were they "imminent"; and that Hungary had available to it at that time means of responding to these perceived perils other than the suspension and abandonment of works with which it had been entrusted. * * *

Notes

1. Necessity is similar to self-defense in that both involve a right to act to safeguard essential state interests. Self-defense involves a danger caused by the state acted against, in particular by that state's use or threat of armed force. In contrast, a state of necessity is independent of any conduct of the state injured by the violation of the obligation. For example, a state may invoke necessity to avoid payment of a financial debt on the ground the payment would clearly entail such

disruption of its public services as to jeopardize public order and economic life of the country. The Greek government offered this defense for its failure to pay awards of an arbitral tribunal to Belgium. Société Commercial de Belgique (Socobel) Case, P.C.I.J., Ser. C, No. 87, pp. 101, 141. The Belgian government questioned the fact of inability to pay and also declared that such inability, if verified, would only justify a suspension of payment, not a final discharge of the debt. The Court implicitly accepted the basic principle that, if verified, the inability of Greece to pay would justify nonpayment. P.C.I.J., Ser. A/B, No. 78, p. 19.

2. Would a "state of necessity" justify an incursion into foreign territory to rescue or protect endangered persons detained by hostile forces not under the control of the territorial state? Belgium advanced that ground to justify the entry of its parachutists into the Congo (later Zaire) in 1960 to protect endangered Belgian nationals. See McNemar, The Postindependence War in the Congo, in The International Law of Civil War, 244 (Falk ed., 1971). Other rescue actions such as those by Israel in Entebbe, Uganda (1976) and by the United States in Iran (1980) to free imprisoned hostages were justified on the ground of self-defense rather than necessity. See Schachter, International Law in the Hostage Crisis, in American Hostages in Iran 325 (Christopher et al., 1985). See Chapter 12.

3. In the context of the NATO intervention in Kosovo in 1999, some scholars argued that a justification on the ground of necessity was preferable to creating a new exception to the general prohibition on the use of force. See Chapter 12. Does Draft Article 33 provide any support for such an argument?

4. Does "necessity know no law"? Since "necessity" has been and can be used for inadmissible and often unstated purposes, should it not be excluded as a justification for violations of international obligations? Many leading jurists have so argued. Consider the views of Jiménez de Aréchaga & Tanzi:

> It may be concluded, therefore, that there is no general principle allowing the defence of necessity. There are particular rules of international law making allowance for varying degrees of necessity, but these cases have a meaning and a scope entirely outside the traditional doctrine. Thus, for instance, vessels in distress are allowed to seek refuge in a foreign port, even if it is closed; in the case of famine in a country, a foreign ship proceeding to another port may be detained and its cargo expropriated; neutral states may exercise the traditional right of angary with respect to foreign ships lying in their ports. In these cases—in which adequate compensation must be paid to the injured parties—it is not the doctrine of necessity which provides the foundation of the particular rules, but humanitarian considerations, which do not apply to the state as a body politic.

Jiménez de Aréchaga & Attila Tanzi, International State Responsibility in International Law: Achievements and Prospects 347, 355 (M. Bedjaoui ed., 1991). See also Brierly, The Law of Nations 403 (6th ed., Waldock, 1963).

5. Are there obligations in respect of which the plea of necessity should be excluded *a priori?* Article 33 excludes obligations based on *jus cogens* norms, particularly in cases of noncompliance with the prohibition of aggression. Some treaties also explicitly or implicitly exclude necessity as an excuse for nonperformance. The non-derogable provisions of human rights treaties cannot be infringed on grounds of necessity.

6. Should a state that justifiably invokes necessity be required nonetheless to pay compensation for material damage due to its violation of the obligation?

Such payment of compensation would not be reparation for "a wrongful act" but is there any reason why it could not be a separate "primary" obligation of the state that caused injury by its own deliberate act?

SECTION 6. COUNTERMEASURES AND SELF-HELP

A state injured by another state's violation of an international obligation is entitled to take measures against the offending state. Such unilateral measures are sometimes described as self-help or in recent usage as countermeasures. More specific legal terms are used to describe three different kinds of countermeasures; as follows:

(i) Reprisal refers to a countermeasure that would be unlawful if not for the prior illegal act of the state against which they were taken. Reprisals under traditional international law sometimes involved use of force but they also include nonforcible measures.

(ii) Reciprocal measures or measures "by way of reciprocity" refer to nonperformance by the injured state of its obligations toward the offending state when such obligations correspond to or are directly connected with the obligations breached.

(iii) Retorsion refers to countermeasures of the injured state against the offending state that are generally permissible in international law irrespective of the prior breach (for example, suspending diplomatic relations or bilateral aid).

The I.L.C. has striven over many years to formulate rules governing resort to countermeasures. The Draft Articles on State Responsibility now deal with the topic in Articles 30 and 47–50 (see Documents Supplement); see also the commentary at 1995 I.L.C. Report 144–173 and 1996 I.L.C. Report 153–164. They address countermeasures in the first two of the three senses identified above—that is, when the injured state takes measures that would otherwise violate its own legal obligations but may be justified as responses to the primary violations committed by another state.

The articles on countermeasures have proven to be among the most controversial of the Draft Articles, as they embody a series of compromises between arguably irreconcilable positions. On the one hand are those who would affirm the need for self-help measures in a world that does not yet have a central authority to deal with violations of the primary rules of international law. On the other hand are those who would emphasize the need for strict limitations on the use of self-help, in order to prevent abuses (especially by strong states against weaker ones) and to provide for procedural controls including dispute settlement.

The materials in this section address some of the areas of current controversy concerning countermeasures. The issues include:

— substantive conditions, including the requirement that countermeasures be proportional to the breach;

— efforts to formulate procedural conditions, such as a proposed linkage between countermeasures and compulsory dispute settlement;

— human rights and humanitarian considerations.

A. CONDITIONS FOR RESORTING TO COUNTERMEASURES (SELF-HELP)

The Restatement (Third) includes the following section on self-help:

§ 905. Unilateral Remedies

(1) Subject to Subsection (2), a state victim of a violation of an international obligation by another state may resort to countermeasures that might otherwise be unlawful, if such measures

(a) are necessary to terminate the violation or prevent further violation, or to remedy the violation; and

(b) are not out of proportion to the violation and the injury suffered.

(2) The threat or use of force in response to a violation of international law is subject to prohibitions on the threat or use of force in the United Nations Charter as well as to Subsection (1).

The I.L.C.'s Draft Articles on State Responsibility likewise provide in Article 49 that:

> Countermeasures taken by an injured State shall not be out of proportion to the degree of gravity of the internationally wrongful act and the effects thereof on the injured State.

Additionally, Article 50 of the Draft Articles would significantly qualify the rights of the injured state, by prohibiting an injured state from engaging in certain countermeasures, regardless of their proportionality. Article 50 reads as follows:

> An injured State shall not resort by way of countermeasures to:
>
> a. the threat or use of force as prohibited by the Charter of the United Nations;
>
> b. extreme economic or political coercion designed to endanger the territorial integrity or political independence of the State which has committed the internationally wrongful act;
>
> c. any conduct which infringes the inviolability of diplomatic or consular agents, premises, archives and documents;
>
> d. any conduct which derogates from basic human rights; or
>
> e. any other conduct in contravention of a peremptory norm of general international law.

Draft Article 48 would establish several further conditions of a procedural nature, including an obligation for prior negotiations (without prejudice to interim measures of protection necessary to preserve the injured state's rights), and requirements to proceed to compulsory dispute settlement and to suspend countermeasures while dispute settlement is in progress.

Proportionality and other substantive and procedural conditions on countermeasures have been addressed in several international judicial and arbitral decisions.

CASE CONCERNING THE GABCIKOVO–NAGYMAROS PROJECT

International Court of Justice, 1997.
1997 I.C.J. 7.

[For the background of this case, see pp. 557–559 supra. In the following excerpt, the Court considered Slovakia's contention that it was entitled to implement a significant variation from the original plan for the Danube River project, known as "Variant C," in response to Hungary's previous repudiation of the plans established by the 1977 Treaty between the parties.]

82. Although it did not invoke the plea of countermeasures as a primary argument, since it did not consider Variant C to be unlawful, Slovakia stated that "Variant C could be presented as a justified countermeasure to Hungary's illegal acts".

The Court has concluded, in paragraph 78 above, that Czechoslovakia committed an internationally wrongful act in putting Variant C into operation. Thus, it now has to determine whether such wrongfulness may be precluded on the ground that the measure so adopted was in response to Hungary's prior failure to comply with its obligations under international law.

83. In order to be justifiable, a countermeasure must meet certain conditions (see *Military and Paramilitary Activities in and against Nicaragua (Nicaragua v. United States of America), Merits, Judgment, I.C.J. Reports 1986,* p. 127, para. 249. See also *Arbitral Award of 9 December 1978 in the case concerning the Air Service Agreement of 27 March 1946 between the United States of America and France,* United Nations, *Reports of International Arbitral Awards (RIAA),* Vol. XVIII, pp. 443 *et seq.:* also Articles 47 to 50 of the Draft Articles on State Responsibility adopted by the International Law Commission on first reading * * *.

In the first place it must be taken in response to a previous international wrongful act of another State and must be directed against that State. Although not primarily presented as a countermeasure, it is clear that Variant C was a response to Hungary's suspension and abandonment of works and that it was directed against that State; and it is equally clear, in the Court's view, that Hungary's actions were internationally wrongful.

84. Secondly, the injured State must have called upon the State committing the wrongful act to discontinue its wrongful conduct or to make reparation for it. It is clear from the facts of the case, as recalled above by the Court (see paragraphs 61 *et seq.*) that Czechoslovakia requested Hungary to resume the performance of its treaty obligations on many occasions.

85. In the view of the Court, an important consideration is that the effects of a countermeasure must be commensurate with the injury suffered, taking account of the rights in question.

In 1929, the Permanent Court of International Justice, with regard to navigation on the River Oder, stated as follows:

> "[the] community of interest in a navigable river becomes the basis of a common legal right, the essential features of which are the perfect equality of all riparian States in the user of the whole course of the river

> and the exclusion of any preferential privilege of any one riparian State in relation to the others" (*Territorial Jurisdiction of the International Commission of the River Oder, Judgment No. 16, 1929, P.C.I.J., Series A, No. 23,* p. 27).

Modern development of international law has strengthened this principle for non-navigational uses of international watercourses as well, as evidenced by the adoption of the Convention of 21 May 1997 on the Law of the Non–Navigational Uses of International Watercourses by the United Nations General Assembly.

The Court considers that Czechoslovakia, by unilaterally assuming control of a shared resource, and thereby depriving Hungary of its right to an equitable and reasonable share of the natural resources of the Danube—with the continuing effects of the diversion of these waters on the ecology of the riparian area of the Szigetköz—failed to respect the proportionality which is required by international law. * * *

87. The Court thus considers that the diversion of the Danube carried out by Czechoslovakia was not a lawful countermeasure because it was not proportionate. It is therefore not required to pass upon one other condition for the lawfulness of a countermeasure, namely that its purpose must be to induce the wrongdoing State to comply with its obligations under international law, and that the measure must therefore be reversible.

* * *

Notes

1. Is proportionality a quantitative or qualitative concept? What understanding of proportionality did the I.C.J. apply in the *Gabcikovo* case? (A similar question can be asked about the *Air Services* arbitration which follows.) See Damrosch, Enforcing International Law Through Non–Forcible Measures, 269 Rec. des Cours 9, 57–60 (1997).

2. What is the basis for the suggestion (in paragraph 87 of *Gabcikovo*) that a countermeasure must be reversible? Would such a limitation rule out measures whose effects might persist after the measure itself had been removed?

CASE CONCERNING THE AIR SERVICES AGREEMENT BETWEEN FRANCE AND THE UNITED STATES, ARBITRAL AWARD OF DEC. 9, 1978

18 U.N.R.I.A.A. 417, 443–446.

[The United States claimed that France had violated the bilateral Air Services Agreement of 1946 by refusing to allow a smaller Pan Am plane to be substituted for a 747 aircraft in Pan Am flights to Paris via London. The French contended that the proposed change (a "change of gauge") was not authorized by the Agreement without French consent. The U.S. disagreed. After fruitless discussions, France compelled Pan Am to cease its flights to Paris. The U.S. protested and proposed arbitration. It also set in motion action under U.S. law to suspend the French flights to Los Angeles that were authorized by the 1946 Agreement and had been long established. The case was then submitted to arbitration under a *compromis* that put two questions to the tribunal: (1) did the U.S. carrier have the right to change gauge? (2) did the U.S. have the right to suspend French traffic to Los Angeles in retaliation for the suspension of Pan Am flights to Paris? The Tribunal answered both questions affirmatively.

[With respect to the second issue, France had questioned the U.S. right to retaliate on two grounds. First, it contended that retaliation was illegal because the Treaty provided for arbitration and the retaliatory measures were undertaken when the arbitral *compromis* was being negotiated. Second, it argued that the U.S. retaliation (the suspension of long-established Paris–Los Angeles flights of Air France) was grossly disproportionate to the French suspension of a new service from the United States via London to Paris. On these issues the Tribunal commented as follows:]

If a situation arises which, in one State's view, results in the violation of an international obligation by another State, the first State is entitled, within the limits set by the general rules of international law pertaining to the use of armed force, to affirm its rights through "counter-measures." (para. 81)

It is generally agreed that all counter-measures must, in the first instance, have some degree of equivalence with the alleged breach; this is a well-known rule. In the course of the present proceedings, both Parties have recognized that the rule applies to this case, and they both have invoked it. It has been observed, generally, that judging the "proportionality" of counter-measures is not an easy task and can at best be accomplished by approximation. In the Tribunal's view, it is essential, in a dispute between States, to take into account not only the injuries suffered by the companies concerned but also the importance of the questions of principle arising from the alleged breach. The Tribunal thinks that it will not suffice, in the present case, to compare the losses suffered by Pan Am on account of the suspension of projected services with the losses which the French companies would have suffered as a result of the counter-measures; it will also be necessary to take into account the importance of the positions of principle which were taken when the French authorities prohibited changes of gauge in third countries. (para. 83)

Can it be said that the resort to such counter-measures, which are contrary to international law but justified by a violation of international law allegedly committed by the State against which they are directed, is restricted if it is found that the Parties previously accepted a duty to negotiate or an obligation to have their dispute settled through a procedure of arbitration or of judicial settlement? (para. 84)

It is tempting to assert that when Parties enter into negotiations, they are under a general duty not to aggravate the dispute, this general duty being a kind of emanation of the principle of good faith. (para. 85)

Though it is far from rejecting such an assertion, the Tribunal is of the view that, when attempting to define more precisely such a principle, several essential considerations must be examined. (para. 86)

The Tribunal recalls the terms of Article VIII of the 1946 Agreement.

This Article provides for an obligation of continuing consultation between the Parties. In the context of this general duty, the Agreement establishes a clear mandate to the Parties to make good faith efforts to negotiate on issues of potential controversy; several other provisions of the Agreement and the Annex state requirements to consult in specific circumstances, when the possibility of a dispute might be particularly acute. Finally, Article X imposes on the Parties a special consultation requirement when, in spite of previous efforts, a dispute has arisen. (para. 88)

But the present problem is whether, on the basis of the above-mentioned texts, counter-measures are prohibited. The Tribunal does not consider that either general international law or the provisions of the Agreement allow it to go that far. (para. 89)

Indeed, it is necessary carefully to assess the meaning of countermeasures in the framework of proportionality. Their aim is to restore equality between the Parties and to encourage them to continue negotiations with mutual desire to reach an acceptable solution. In the present case, the United States of America holds that a change of gauge is permissible in third countries; that conviction defined its position before the French refusal came into play; the United States counter-measures restore in a negative way the symmetry of the initial positions. (para. 90)

It goes without saying that recourse to counter-measures involves the great risk of giving rise, in turn, to a further reaction, thereby causing an escalation which will lead to a worsening of the conflict. Counter-measures therefore should be a wager on the wisdom, not on the weakness of the other Party. They should be used with a spirit of great moderation and be accompanied by a genuine effort at resolving the dispute. But the Arbitral Tribunal does not believe that it is possible, in the present state of international relations, to lay down a rule prohibiting the use of counter-measures during negotiations, especially where such counter-measures are accompanied by an offer for a procedure affording the possibility of accelerating the solution of the dispute. (para. 91)

* * *

However, the lawfulness of such counter-measures has to be considered still from another viewpoint. It may indeed be asked whether they are valid in general, in the case of a dispute concerning a point of law, where there is arbitral or judicial machinery which can settle the dispute. Many jurists have felt that while arbitral or judicial proceedings were in progress, recourse to counter-measures, even if limited by the proportionality rule, was prohibited. Such an assertion deserves sympathy but requires further elaboration. If the proceedings form part of an institutional framework ensuring some degree of enforcement of obligations, the justification of counter-measures will undoubtedly disappear, but owing to the existence of that framework rather than solely on account of the existence of arbitral or judicial proceedings as such. (para. 94)

Besides, the situation during the period in which a case is not yet before a tribunal is not the same as the situation during the period in which that case is *sub judice*. So long as a dispute has not been brought before the tribunal, in particular because an agreement between the Parties is needed to set the procedure in motion, the period of negotiation is not over and the rules mentioned above remain applicable. This may be a regrettable solution, as the

Parties in principle did agree to resort to arbitration or judicial settlement, but it must be conceded that under present-day international law States have not renounced their right to take counter-measures in such situations. In fact, however, this solution may be preferable as it facilitates States' acceptance of arbitration or judicial settlement procedures. (para. 95)

The situation changes once the tribunal is in a position to act. To the extent that the tribunal has the necessary means to achieve the objectives justifying the counter-measures, it must be admitted that the right of the Parties to initiate such measures disappears. In other words, the power of a tribunal to decide on interim measures of protection, regardless of whether this power is expressly mentioned or implied in its statute (at least as the power to formulate recommendations to this effect), leads to the disappearance of the power to initiate counter-measures and may lead to an elimination of existing counter-measures to the extent that the tribunal so provides as an interim measure of protection. As the object and scope of the power of the tribunal to decide on interim measures of protection may be defined quite narrowly, however, the power of the Parties to initiate or maintain counter-measures, too, may not disappear completely. (para. 96)

As far as the action undertaken by the United States Government in the present case is concerned, the situation is quite simple. Even if arbitration under Article X of the Agreement is set in motion unilaterally, implementation may take time, and during this period counter-measures are not excluded: a State resorting to such measures, however, must do everything in its power to expedite the arbitration. This is exactly what the Government of the United States has done. (para. 98)

The Tribunal's Reply to Question (B) consists of the above observations as a whole. These observations lead to the conclusion that, under the circumstances in question, the Government of the United States had the right to undertake the action that it undertook under Part 213 of the Economic Regulations of the C.A.B. (para. 99)

Notes

1. Should a distinction be made between a counter-measure in the nature of reprisal and nonperformance of an obligation in response to a breach of the same or equivalent obligation by the other party? The latter has been referred to in international law jurisprudence as the principle of *inadimplenti non est adimplendum* (no performance is due to a nonperformer), described by Judge Anzilotti as "so just, so equitable, so universally recognized". Dissenting opinion in River Meuse Case, 1937 P.C.I.J., Ser. A/B, No. 70, p. 50 (1937). In the above *Air Services Case,* could the U.S. action to suspend flights to Los Angeles have been regarded as permissible nonperformance of an obligation similar to that allegedly breached by France? If so, would "necessity and proportionality" have been required? What criteria are relevant for differentiating nonperformance as a measure of reciprocity from nonperformance as a measure of self-help subject to limitations imposed by international law? For general discussion of reciprocity and unilateral remedies, see Zoller, Peacetime Unilateral Remedies 14–27 (1984).

2. Is a reprisal generally impermissible where an agreement between the parties provides for arbitration or judicial settlement? An affirmative answer was given by the *Institut de Droit International* in 1934, 38 Ann. de l'Inst. 709 (1934).

The International Law Commission also took that view in 1979, I.L.C.Rep. 319 (1979), as did Bowett, Economic Coercion and Reprisal of States, 13 Va.J.I.L. 1 (1972) and Dumbauld, Interim Measures of Protection in International Controversies 182–84 (1932). Why did the tribunal in the *Air Services Case* take a different position? See Damrosch, Retaliation or Arbitration—or Both?, 74 A.J.I.L. 785, 802, 807 (1980). Damrosch maintains that a victim state should not be required to "embark on lengthy and expensive litigation" before it may suspend its performance in the event of breach. Id. at 806. The "interplay and even escalation of responses before a dispute reaches a tribunal can serve important purposes." Id. at 807.

3. Article 48 of the I.L.C.'s Draft Articles on State Responsibility would require an injured state, prior to engaging in countermeasures, to "fulfil its obligation to negotiate provided for in article 54," without prejudice to its taking "interim measures of protection which are necessary to preserve its rights" (para. 1). The injured state would also be required to "fulfil the obligations in relation to dispute settlement arising under Part Three or any other binding dispute settlement procedure" and would have to suspend countermeasures while the dispute settlement procedure was being implemented in good faith (paras. 2–4).

Would the procedural preconditions of Article 48 give undue advantage to the wrongdoing state? Given the time-consuming nature of international dispute settlement mechanisms, is it fair to expect the injured state to defer the taking of counter-measures potentially for many years? Does Article 48 give the wrongdoing state an incentive to employ delaying tactics in negotiation? Would a fairer approach be to make the exhaustion of amicable settlement procedures a parallel obligation, rather than a precondition, for resort to countermeasures—that is, the injured state could take countermeasures until such time as the wrongdoing state agreed to a dispute settlement procedure? Or would the immediate imposition of countermeasures put the injured state in an unfair position of strength in any ensuing negotiations agreed to by the wrongdoing state?

4. The proposed linkage between countermeasures and dispute settlement has been one of the most contentious aspects of the Draft Articles. The current I.L.C. Special Rapporteur on State Responsibility, James Crawford, has taken a position against this linkage, on the ground that it would illogically give the state accused of a wrongful act an asymmetrical right to insist on compulsory dispute settlement concerning the countermeasures, while the allegedly injured state would have no corresponding right to compel the violator to arbitrate the primary illegality. See 1999 I.L.C. Report 194–199; Crawford, On Re–Reading the Draft Articles on State Responsibility, 1998 A.S.I.L. Proc. 295, 298–299. The U.S. government also objects to the conditioning of countermeasures on prior negotiation and compulsory arbitration. See U.S. Comments on Draft Articles on State Responsibility, 37 I.L.M. 468, 469–472 (1998).

In the formulation adopted by the I.L.C. in 2001, countermeasures "may not be taken if: the internationally wrongful act has ceased, and the dispute is pending before a court or tribunal which has the authority to make decisions binding on the parties," unless the responsible state "fails to implement the dispute settlement procedures in good faith."

5. When U.S. diplomats and other U.S. nationals were held as hostages in Tehran in 1979–1980, the U.S. took countermeasures by freezing (i.e., blocking) Iranian assets, to prevent Iran from withdrawing its funds in U.S. banks. The "freeze" continued after the U.S. instituted proceedings against Iran in the International Court of Justice. Other countermeasures such as a trade embargo

also were taken. The Court in its decision condemned Iran for allowing and condoning the seizure of the Embassy and detention of U.S. nationals. 1980 I.C.J. 3. It mentioned the U.S. countermeasures of an economic character but did not hold them to be wrongful. Id. at 17–18, 28–29. However, two judges (Soviet and Syrian nationals) declared that the U.S. blocking of Iranian assets was a coercive act aimed to influence the outcome of the dispute and therefore incompatible with the U.S. submission to the Court. United States Diplomatic and Consular Staff in Tehran Case, 1980 I.C.J. 3, 53–54, 63–65.

Should self-help measures be precluded during judicial proceedings "since they are designed to bring about the termination of the conflict without regard to the impartial determination the parties agreed to seek when they assented to the Tribunal's jurisdiction"? Stein, Contempt, Crisis and the Court, 76 A.J.I.L. 512 (1982). What if the tribunal is unable to protect the aggrieved State from injury during the pendency of the case? In the Tehran Hostages case, the Court's order for provisional measures of protection was ineffective. Is that why the Court refrained from criticizing the economic countermeasures taken by the United States in the Hostages case? See Schachter, International Law in the Hostage Crisis, in American Hostages in Iran, 325, 339–45 (Christopher et al., 1984).

6. The tribunal in the *Air Services Case* (supra) said that counter-measures must have "some degree of equivalence with the breach" (para. 83). This suggests a "tit for tat" response to a breach. But is that always permissible? Would the United States have had the right to hold Iranian diplomats as hostages because the Iranians held U.S. diplomats? Are not some countermeasures, although "equivalent," impermissible because contrary to peremptory norms or recognized humanitarian principles? How difficult, in practice, are the concepts of "proportionality" and "equivalence" to apply? Is it always possible to weigh the equivalence of countermeasures against the wrongful act?

7. May countermeasures against a state's wrongful conduct take the form of sanctions against individuals because they are nationals of the offending state? May the assets of individuals be frozen or seized on the ground that the state of which they are nationals has acted wrongfully? A U.S. Court held such action permissible with respect to Cuban nationals in the U.S. Sardino v. Federal Reserve Bank, 361 F.2d 106 (2d Cir.1966). The Court observed that "the Constitution protects the alien from arbitrary action by our government but not from reasonable response to such action by his own". Id. at 111. Does international law also impose a limit? For example if the state whose nationals were affected maintains that the "freeze" of assets was disproportionate or arbitrary, an international law issue would be raised. See Restatement (Third) § 905. Would retaliatory action against individuals for the wrongs of their states raise human rights issues based on invidious discrimination or disproportionate penalties? See Narenji v. Civiletti, 617 F.2d 745 (D.C.Cir.1979), upholding U.S. regulations that required Iranian students in the U.S. during the hostage crisis to report to the Immigration Service for a check on their compliance with their visas. U.S. legislation on countermeasures generally includes procedural provisions to protect individuals affected from arbitrary action. See Zoller, Enforcing International Law Through U.S. Legislation, 42–57 (1985).

8. There is considerable disagreement over whether states belonging to a so-called "self-contained regime"—defined generally as an international body creating both substantive obligations *and* special procedures in the event of a breach—may resort to countermeasures based on general international law in addition to the remedies specified by the regime's constitutive instrument. In the *Tehran*

Hostages case the International Court of Justice found that the regime of diplomatic law constituted a "self-contained regime," so that Iran's possibility of taking self-help measures against alleged breaches by U.S. personnel was limited to declaring them *personae non grata* and sending them home. 1980 I.C.J. 3, 40, at para. 86. Some commentators have found examples of "self-contained regimes" in the European Economic Community, in human rights systems such as the European Convention or the Covenant on Civil and Political Rights, or in trade agreements under the auspices of the World Trade Organization which embody dispute settlement procedures. Other commentators criticize the whole notion of "self-contained regimes." Compare Simma, Self–Contained Regimes, 16 Neth. Yb.I.L. 111 (1985) with Zemanek, The Legal Foundations of the International System, 266 Rec. des Cours 9, 235–236, 332 (1997).

The European Court of Justice has expressed the view that member states forfeited their freedom to engage in unilateral measures under the general international law of countermeasures as a consequence of joining the Community. However, Gaetano Arangio–Ruiz, former special rapporteur on state responsibility to the International Law Commission, has concluded otherwise:

> [A] State joining a so-called 'self-contained' regime does not thereby restrict—by a kind of autolimitation—the rights or *facultés* of unilateral reaction it possesses under general international law to such an extent as to render the accepted 'regime' unsusceptible of derogation or integration. Of course, any State accepting the 'regime' shall be bound, when confronted with a breach of a 'regime's' obligation on the part of another participating State, to react—if it wishes to react—first of all in conformity with the provisions of the relevant 'regime'.

Henkin also has stated, with respect to the principal human rights treaties, that the stipulated procedures were intended to supplement rather than to supplant remedies available under the general international law. Which view do you believe is most sound? Do states have an obligation, at a minimum, to utilize the express mechanisms of the "self-contained regime" simultaneously with any unilateral countermeasures?

9. An obligation of members of the GATT/WTO agreements (especially the Dispute Settlement Understanding) to refrain from unilateral countermeasures, pending authorization of sanctions as an outcome of dispute settlement, was explicated in the panel report in the 1999 *U.S.-Section 301* case, pp. 692–693 supra. Is this obligation a unique feature of the "self-contained regime" of the WTO, or does it have general applicability?

10. Must a state show injury in order to resort to countermeasures, or is a mere breach of international law sufficient for a state to act? Is there an inherent risk in a regime of countermeasures that a powerful nation could assume for itself a role as the "world's police" to enforce its own conception of the law? Riphagen, a former special rapporteur on state responsibility, has observed that the International Law Commission should "take the greatest care, in devising the conditions of lawful resort to such actions, to ensure that the factual inequalities among States do not unduly operate to the advantage of the strong and rich over the weak and needy." I.L.C.Rep. 327 (1991). Compare Damrosch, Enforcing International Law Through Non–Forcible Measures, 269 Rec. des Cours 9, 50–54 (on the application of the concept of "injured state" and "effects" for purposes of taking countermeasures in cases of human rights violations).

Riphagen also has noted that respect for humanitarian principles is another substantive restriction on resort to countermeasures. Other substantive limitations on countermeasures include the inviolability of specially protected persons (such as diplomatic envoys) and the obligations embodied in *jus cogens* and *erga omnes* norms. See Draft Article 50, paras. c, d, and e.

11. May a state other than an injured state take countermeasures? A variant on this question arose in 1999, when the European Union moved to interrupt air services to Yugoslavia in response to violations of human rights and humanitarian law in Kosovo. Assuming that this ban would otherwise have breached existing air services agreements in force with Yugoslavia, it could only be justified if the conditions for resort to countermeasures were met.

The I.L.C.'s drafting committee presented a new formulation in 2000 to cover the case of countermeasures by states other than an injured state. In situations of "serious breaches of essential obligations to the international community," any state could take countermeasures "in the interest of the beneficiaries of the obligation breached." Is this proposal an adequate solution where the "beneficiaries" are victims of human rights violations?

B. COUNTERMEASURES TO VIOLATION OF MULTILATERAL TREATY OR GENERAL CUSTOMARY LAW

As a rule a state injured by a breach of a multilateral treaty may suspend its performance of obligations toward the state that acted wrongfully. Article 60(2) of the Vienna Convention on the Law of Treaties provides that a party "specially affected by the breach may invoke it as a ground for suspending the operations of the agreement in whole or in part between itself and the defaulting state." A similar right of suspension by an injured state toward the violating state would seem appropriate in case of a breach of customary law. However, a number of exceptions to this broad right appear to be required. Consider the following:

1. Suspending performance of the obligation toward a defaulting state may adversely affect the rights of all other parties to the multilateral treaty. In that case the countermeasure would injure third states as well as the offending state. An example is a breach of a multilateral treaty concerning pollution. If a party suspends its restraints on pollution with respect to a state guilty of violation it almost surely will also injure other states parties to the treaty. In some cases, nonperformance may adversely affect a collective interest such as protection of the high seas, Antarctica or outer space. When a unilateral remedy against a violator by way of nonperformance would entail damage to a collective interest, there is good reason to bar unilateral nonperformance.

2. Where obligations are intended to protect individuals irrespective of nationality, to allow nonperformance as a retaliation for a breach would injure individuals who are the objects of protection. The Vienna Convention on the Law of Treaties does not allow for suspension of provisions for "the protection of the human person contained in treaties of a humanitarian character". Art. 60(5).

3. Multilateral treaties may provide expressly for responses to violations by collective decisions or other procedures. Such express stipulations are generally construed to exclude other responses by injured parties. See Restatement (Third) § 905, Comment *a*.

4. A violation of a peremptory rule of international law (e.g., on genocide, aggression, slave trade) obviously should not be a ground for an injured state or any state to suspend its compliance with that obligation. Other fundamental principles of international intercourse as, for example, immunities of diplomats, may have a similar status in this respect. A violation of diplomatic immunity by one state does not entitle the injured state to engage in similar violations.

The International Law Commission's Draft Articles on State Responsibility (Part Two) include provisions covering some of the above situations. See Draft Articles 47(3) and 50.

C. RETORSION

1. *Examples of Retorsion*

Retorsion as indicated above refers to retaliatory measures that an aggrieved state is legally free to take whether or not the offending state committed an illegal act. In practice, most retaliatory acts fall into this category. Typical examples of such retaliatory actions are rupture of diplomatic relations, cessation of trade in general or in specific items (e.g., strategic materials), curtailment of migration from the offending government, and denial of benefits available to the offending government. See Wild, Sanctions and Treaty Enforcement (1934); Lowenfeld, Trade Controls for Political Ends (2d ed. 1983); Zoller, Peacetime Unilateral Remedies (1984).

Retorsion is often an "equivalent" act of retaliation in response to an unfriendly act. For example, the expulsion of a diplomat is commonly followed by that diplomat's state declaring as *persona non grata* a diplomat of equivalent rank from the first state. The rupture of diplomatic relations falls within the scope of a state's discretion. It may follow an unfriendly act of another state that is not itself illegal (as, for example, an expulsion of nationals) or it may be a response to conduct considered unlawful. Trade boycotts or denial of trade benefits may similarly be directed against "unfriendly" acts or illegal conduct.

Whether or not they are effective in advancing their objectives depends on the particular circumstances. In many cases, economic boycotts or denial of specific benefits have not resulted in changing the policies of the offending states. This has been most evident when the target state's conduct is a manifestation of a basic political position. For example, the economic sanctions adopted by the United States against "unfriendly" regimes in China, Cuba, Iran, Libya and the U.S.S.R. are often considered to have failed to change the behavior of those states. See Doxey, International Sanctions in Contemporary Perspective (2d ed. 1996); Hufbauer, Schott & Elliott, Economic Sanctions Reconsidered (1990). However, some studies show that economic sanctions have probably influenced the offending state's behavior in a number of cases though it is difficult to say whether such sanctions were decisive in that respect. See Hufbauer et al. id. for analyses of more than a hundred cases of economic sanctions and their apparent effects. See also Damrosch, Enforcing International Law Through Non–Forcible Measures, 269 Rec. des Cours 9, 41–101 (1997).

U.S. legislation provides for retorsion in response to illegal acts in various situations:

— The first "Hickenlooper Amendment" directs the President to suspend foreign aid to any state that has nationalized properties of U.S. nationals without providing for compensation as required by international law. Foreign Assistance Act of 1961, as amended, 22 U.S.C.A. § 2370(e). See p. 818.

— The U.S. Foreign Assistance Act also denies assistance "to the government of any country which engages in a consistent pattern of gross violations of internationally recognized human rights," including torture, prolonged detention without charges "or other flagrant denial of the right to life, liberty and security of person". 22 U.S.C.A. § 2151h(a).

— Legislation on air carriers, fishermen, and taxation also prescribes measures against foreign states that violate treaty rights of the United States. See generally Zoller, Enforcing International Law Through U.S. Legislation (1985).

— Various restrictions are imposed under U.S. legislation against state sponsors of terrorism and states implicated in proliferation of weapons of mass destruction. See Iran and Libya Sanctions Act of 1996 and other measures discussed in Damrosch, Enforcing International Law Through Non-Forcible Measures, 269 Rec. des Cours 9, 81–91 (1997).

2. *Legal Limits on Retorsion*

Since states are generally free to refuse to trade with others or to deny benefits and to take other action that fails under the heading of retorsion, the question of their legality does not normally arise. However, their legality may be questioned when the countermeasures are directed to an unlawful end. Consider the example of a state discontinuing trade with an offending country and imposing as a condition for the resumption of trade a change in the internal or foreign policy of the offending state. Apropos of that example, Schachter has written:

> In that case, an otherwise discretionary act, the retorsion, is used as a means of coercing the object of that retorsion to give up its sovereign right, quite apart from the alleged violation of law that gave rise to the retorsion. There is good reason to consider such use of retorsion as illegal because of its improper objective. One may characterize it as an abuse of rights, but it is more precise to refer to a primary rule that precludes such coercion. The rule is expressed in the unanimously agreed Declaration of Principles of International Law Concerning Friendly Relations (adopted by the United Nations General Assembly in 1970) in the following language:
>
> > "No State may use or encourage the use of economic, political or any other type of measures to coerce another State in order to obtain from it the subordination of the exercise of its sovereign rights and to secure from it advantages of any kind."
>
> The fact that retorsion is used when the target of its use has violated an international law obligation would not legally entitle the government using it to demand that the offending State give up its sovereign rights. It is most unlikely that this broad principle will be challenged. However, its

application in actual cases is not always readily apparent except in rather extreme situations (such as a demand that the offending State change its government or cease relations with another State). Nonetheless, even acknowledging the impropriety of these "extreme" cases (which are by no means hypothetical) can be a significant step toward recognizing that in some cases otherwise legal acts may be rendered illicit because of the wrongful end sought.

Schachter, International Law in Theory and Practice 199 (1991).

Should acts of retorsion be subject to requirements of proportionality? In practice, retaliatory measures tend to have "a degree of equivalence" to the offense. Diplomatic or trade relations are rarely, if ever, suspended for minor or isolated offenses. While states are not legally required to maintain diplomatic or trade relations—or, in general, to be friendly—an "unfriendly act" that is disproportionate to an offense and causes substantial damage to another state may be viewed as "an abuse of rights" and therefore illegitimate. Oppenheim, International Law 345 (8th ed., Lauterpacht, 1955) concludes that states are legally precluded from taking measures that would otherwise be permitted if such measures "would inflict upon another State an injury which cannot be justified by a legitimate consideration of its own advantage". Is this general formulation of an "abuse of rights" principle verifiable as a rule of customary international law? If not, should it be favored as a rule *de lege ferenda?*

D. COLLECTIVE SANCTIONS

1. Counter-measures against an offending state for violation of an international obligation may be taken by aggrieved states through joint or parallel action. Such action, commonly called collective sanctions, have typically involved severance of diplomatic relations, trade boycotts and, in some cases, cessation of air or sea traffic. These measures, if not contrary to treaty obligations, fall within the discretionary authority of states (retorsion). Where they are contrary to treaty obligations or customary law obligations, they may be legally justified as reprisals by states injured by the offending state's violation. In several cases states not directly injured have joined in collective countermeasures on the ground that the violation affected a collective interest or a common concern of the international community. While such instances might have been characterized as responses to violations of *erga omnes* obligations, the states taking the action have rarely, if ever, explicitly referred to that doctrine. Nonetheless, their emphasis on the common concern of states in combatting such acts as aggression, terrorism or gross violations of human rights is in keeping with the concept of *erga omnes* obligations.

2. Trade restrictions and other retaliatory measures were taken by some states against Iran because of the seizure and detention of U.S. diplomats and other persons in Tehran in 1979–80. Although the Security Council had censured Iran for its breach of fundamental rules of diplomatic law, it had not called on states to take economic or diplomatic sanctions against Iran. The retaliatory actions were not challenged on legal grounds. On the seizure of the diplomats and Security Council action in that case, see the I.C.J. decision in Chapter 11, pp. 868–880.

3. Collective sanctions of a non-military character may be adopted by the U.N. Security Council as mandatory enforcement measures under Chapter VII of the U.N. Charter, particularly Article 41. Decisions of the Council under that article must be based on a determination of the existence of a threat to, or breach of, peace or an act of aggression. Article 39 of the Charter. The Council may then require U.N. members to sever economic and diplomatic relations and to interrupt, wholly or partially, all means of communication, including air, postal and radio traffic. Article 41. It may also order military action under Article 42. See Chapter 12. Collective sanctions under Article 41 were ordered by the Council in 1968 against the "illegal racist minority regime" in Southern Rhodesia (now Zimbabwe). S.C.Res. 253 (XXIII), (1968). See Chapter 12, p. 1010. In 1977 the Security Council also adopted a mandatory resolution under Chapter VII requiring all states to cease providing South Africa with arms and related material of all types. S.C.Res. 418 (XXXII), (1977). That resolution included a determination that the acts and policies of South Africa (in its maintenance of an illegal policy of *apartheid* constituted a threat to international peace and security.

4. Collective economic sanctions mandated by the U.N. Security Council became a frequent practice of the 1990s, in response to a wide range of violations of international law. Some of the most important sanctions episodes are:

— Almost immediately after the Iraqi invasion of Kuwait in August 1990, the Security Council imposed a sweeping trade and financial embargo on Iraq. S.C.Res. 661 (1990). As part of the terms of the cease-fire, sanctions remained in place pending Iraq's discharge of the obligations mandated by the Council, including supervised disarmament. S.C.Res. 687 (1991). As of 2000, the Iraq sanctions are still in place, as Iraq has not satisfied the Security Council's conditions.

— In May 1992, the Security Council declared trade sanctions and an oil embargo on Yugoslavia, comprising Serbia and Montenegro, in response to the savage conflict in Bosnia–Herzegovina and violations of international humanitarian law, such as "ethnic cleansing." S.C.Res. 757 (1992). The measures were tightened the following year, and the Bosnian Serb republic was also made a target of sanctions. S.C.Res. 820 (1993). U.N. sanctions were suspended and eventually ended in 1995–1996 as a result of the Dayton Agreement on a peace settlement for Bosnia–Herzegovina. S.C.Res. 1021, 1022 (1995), 1074 (1996).

— In 1992 and 1993, the Security Council mandated sanctions against Libya, to induce Libya to "demonstrate by concrete actions its renunciation of terrorism" and to surrender for trial before a United Kingdom or United States court the suspects in the 1988 explosion of Pan Am Flight 103 over Lockerbie, Scotland. S.C.Res. 731 (1992), 748 (1992), 883 (1993). These measures were suspended in 1999, when Libya turned over two suspects for trial in The Hague before Scottish judges. See Chapter 6, pp. 419–420, and Chapter 11, pp. 900–901.

— In 1993, the Security Council imposed mandatory sanctions against Haiti and its de facto government, including an embargo on oil and arms and police equipment and an assets freeze, because of the refusal of the de facto authorities to restore to power the legitimately elected president who had been overthrown in a 1991 military coup. S.C.Res. 841 (1993). These compulsory sanctions supported previous voluntary measures recommended by the Organization of American States. They were lifted following the return of President Aristide in fall 1994. S.C. Res. 944 (1994). (On the military aspects of this episode, see Chapter 12.)

— In 1997, the Security Council responded to a military coup in Sierra Leone with compulsory sanctions, including prohibitions on oil imports and military equipment as well as travel restrictions on the members of the military junta. S.C.Res. 1132 (1997). Some of the measures were lifted in 1998 (S.C.Res. 1156, 1171), but the situation remained unsettled through 2000.

— In 1998, an arms embargo was re-imposed against the Federal Republic of Yugoslavia (Serbia–Montenegro), because of its repressive actions in Kosovo. S.C.Res. 1160 (1998).

— In 1999, the Security Council imposed aviation and financial sanctions against the Taliban regime in Afghanistan, with the objective of ending support for international terrorists and inducing the Taliban to surrender for trial Usama bin Laden, who was under U.S. indictment for the August 1998 bombings of two U.S. embassies. S.C.Res. 1276 (1999).

These and other U.N.-organized sanctions are analyzed in Cortwright & Lopez, The Sanctions Decade: Assessing UN Strategies in the 1990s (2000). See also Damrosch, Enforcing International Law Through Non–Forcible Measures, 269 Rec. des Cours 9, 102–154 (1997). On the adverse humanitarian impacts that frequently result from sanctions, see also Damrosch, The Civilian Impact of Economic Sanctions, in Damrosch (ed.), Enforcing Restraint: Collective Intervention in Internal Conflicts (1993); Gibbons, Sanctions in Haiti: Human Rights and Democracy Under Assault (1999).

5. Obligatory collective sanctions have been held to be required, in at least one case, on the basis of a declaratory resolution of the U.N. Security Council. In 1970, the Security Council affirmed a General Assembly resolution that declared South Africa's mandate over South West Africa (Namibia) terminated. The Council then declared that the presence of South African authorities in Namibia was illegal and that their acts concerning Namibia were illegal and invalid. An advisory opinion of the International Court of Justice in 1971 held that all states are legally obliged to draw the consequences of the illegal presence of South Africa by not recognizing its administration or acts performed by it in the territory (with some exceptions required in the interest of the inhabitants). Advisory Opinion Concerning Namibia, 1971 I.C.J. 16. See p. 549.

Does this opinion of the Court indicate that all states may have a duty to take appropriate measures (particularly, non-recognition of illegal acts) when an offending state has committed a serious breach of law of concern to the international community? Does it depend on a binding decision by the Security Council?

SECTION 7. REPARATION FOR THE BREACH OF AN INTERNATIONAL OBLIGATION

JIMÉNEZ DE ARÉCHAGA, INTERNATIONAL LAW IN THE PAST THIRD OF A CENTURY

159 Rec. des Cours 285–287 (1978–I).

Leaving aside the possibility of sanctions which may be applied by an international organization in the event of international crimes, a State discharges the responsibility incumbent upon it for breach of an international obligation by making reparation for the injury caused.

Reparation is the generic term which describes the various methods available to a State for discharging or releasing itself from such responsibility. The forms of reparation may consist in restitution, indemnity or satisfaction.

The basic principles governing reparation were established by the Permanent Court of International Justice as follows:

> "* * * reparation must, as far as possible, wipe out all the consequences of the illegal act and re-establish the situation which would, in all probability, have existed if that act had not been committed. Restitution in kind, or, if this is not possible, payment of a sum corresponding to the value which a restitution in kind would bear; the award, if need be, of damages for loss sustained which would not be covered by restitution in kind or payment in place of it—such are the principles which should serve to determine the amount of compensation due for an act contrary to international law." P.C.I.J. Series A No. 17, pp. 47–48.

(1) Restitution

Restitution in kind is designed to re-establish the situation which would have existed if the wrongful act or omission had not taken place, by performance of the obligation which the State failed to discharge: revocation of the unlawful act, return of a property wrongfully removed or abstention from further wrongful conduct. The Permanent Court of International Justice implied, in the above passage, that restitution is the normal form of reparation and indemnity could only take its place if restitution in kind "is not possible".

Often, an arbitration agreement or *compromis* confers discretion on the arbitrator to select the most adequate form of reparation in a given case. In such cases, the tribunal will take into consideration the practical difficulties or inconveniences which may be involved in restitution in kind and select pecuniary compensation instead. The same discretion is vested in the International Court of Justice under Article 36(2) of its Statute. For these reasons, although restitution in kind remains the basic form of reparation, in practice, and in the great majority of cases, monetary compensation takes its place.

(2) Indemnity

This is "the most usual form of reparation" since "money is the common measure of valuable things." Since monetary compensation must, as far as possible, "wipe out all the consequences of the illegal act" and correspond "to the value which a restitution in kind would bear'', loss of profits are included and the value of a confiscated property must be determined at the time of payment and not at that of confiscation. The indemnity should compensate for all damage which follows as a consequence of the unlawful act, including "a profit which would have been possible in the ordinary course of events" but not prospective gains which are highly problematical, "too remote or speculative" or "possible but contingent and undeterminate damage." The basic test is the certainty of the damage. It is not essential that the damage should have already taken place for compensation to be recoverable. For instance, the future damaging consequences which will certainly result from nuclear fall-out warrant compensation even before the actual damage has occurred. Punitive or exemplary damages, inspired by disapproval of the unlawful act and as a measure of deterrence or reform of the offender, are incompatible with the basic idea underlying the duty of reparation. Imposition of such damages goes beyond the jurisdiction conferred on the International Court of Justice by its Statute and that normally attributed to arbitral tribunals, which are not invested "with a repressive power".

(3) Satisfaction

This third form of reparation is appropriate for non-material damage or moral injury to the dignity or personality of the State.

The forms of satisfaction must be considered, in contemporary law and practice, as limited to the presentation of official regrets and apologies, the punishment of the guilty minor officials and particularly the formal acknowledgment or judicial declaration of the unlawful character of the act.

The International Court of Justice, following the precedent of arbitral awards, has asserted that a judicial declaration of the unlawful character of an act constitutes "in itself appropriate satisfaction."

Notes

1. The I.L.C. Draft Articles on State Responsibility deal with the forms of reparation in Articles 42–45. See Documents Supplement. The Draft Articles also provide that the violating state must cease wrongful conduct (Article 41) and, where appropriate, provide guarantees of non-repetition (Article 46). For the commentary, see 1993 Yb.I.L.C., II (Part Two), 55–83.

Several aspects of the draft articles on reparation have elicited objections and controversy. See, e.g., U.S. Comments on the Draft Articles, 37 I.L.M. 468, 478–482 (1998). The United States and others have raised the concern that Article 44(2) might understate the damages allowable under international precedent, by providing only that interest "may" be recoverable, instead of specifying that interest is an integral element of making the claimant whole. The United States cited a decision of the Governing Council of the U.N. Compensation Commission (which is processing claims against Iraq), *Awards of Interest,* U.N. Doc. S/AC.26/1992/16 (1993), where the Commission held that "interest will be awarded from the date the loss occurred until the date of payment, at a rate sufficient to compensate successful claimants for the loss of use of the principal amount of the award." On the recoverability of lost profits and interest (Article 44), see Chapter 10, pp. 803–805.

The formulation adopted in 2001 is that interest "shall be payable when necessary in order to ensure full reparation."

2. Other aspects of the U.S. comments address proposed limitations on full reparation, e.g. where reparation might "depriv[e] the population of [the violating] State of its own means of subsistence" (Article 42(3)) or where restitution in kind might "seriously jeopardize the political independence of the State which has committed the internationally wrongful act." See 37 I.L.M. at 479 (1998). Can these proposed limitations be justified in terms of the fundamental human rights of the people of the violating state, who may bear little or no moral responsibility for the decisions of their regime to commit internationally wrongful acts? On these points, see Damrosch, Enforcing International Law Through Non–Forcible Measures, 269 Rec. des Cours 9, 60–61 (1997).

3. The issue of whether restitution-in-kind or indemnity should take precedence in the international law of reparations was faced squarely in Texaco Overseas Petroleum Co. and California Asiatic Oil Co. v. The Government of the Libyan Arab Republic, 17 I.L.M. 1 (1978); see pp. 148–153 supra and 790–798 infra. In reaching that issue, the sole arbitrator (Professor Dupuy) held, *inter alia,* that under international law, restitution-in-kind was the "normal sanction for non-performance of contractual obligations." Id. at 36. The award against the Government of Libya was rendered in defendant's absence; Libya did not participate in any stage of the proceedings. In fact, Libya had already stated that it would compensate the claimants. Rigaux, Des dieux et des héros, [1978] Revue Critique de Droit Int'l Privé 439–440. Several months after the Arbitrator announced his decision the parties settled their dispute for $152 million in crude oil; Von Mehren, Introductory Note, 17 I.L.M. 2 (1978).

A conclusion contrary to that in the *Texaco Case* was reached by Judge Lagergren in an earlier award rendered in BP v. Libya (Arbitral Award of Aug. 1, 1974 and Oct. 10, 1983). After extensive review of the authorities, Judge Lagergren decided that restitution would not be a proper remedy in case of confiscation of a concession in breach of the concession agreement. 53 I.L.R. 297, 34648 (1979).

Even if restitution-in-kind should be the preferred remedy for disputes based on treaties between states, query whether that principle should hold when a state contracts with individuals? Should an individual be able to invoke an "international contract law" to force a sovereign authority to act in a specified way with regard to activities within the authority's own territory?

4. Compensation may include both direct and indirect damage. In some cases, lost revenue may be included. But on the whole, rules as to calculation of damages, interest, loss of profits etc. are not clear. See Whiteman, Damages in International Law, 3 vols. (1943). In the 1990s, these issues have been presented in novel forms to the U.N. Compensation Commission which has been processing claims against Iraq arising out of Iraq's invasion of Kuwait. The U.N.C.C.'s jurisdiction is limited, however, to "direct" loss or damage. S.C.Res. 687 (1991), para. 16.

5. Should punitive or "exemplary" damages be awarded if the offense is serious and intentional or repetitive? There is some authority holding that punitive awards against states are not allowed. See Judge Parker's opinion in the *Lusitania Cases* (U.S. v. Germany 1923), 7 U.N.Rep. Int'l Arb. Awards 201 (1923). Should exception be made for an international crime? See Section 4 above. On the issue of punitive damages in international law, see Zemanek, The Legal Foundations of the International System, 266 Rec. des Cours 9, 270–271 (1997).

6. Since the primary obligation of the violating state is to undo the wrong and discontinue the acts that caused the violation, tribunals have occasionally issued orders directing the respondent state to take such steps. In the Iranian hostage case, the International Court of Justice ordered Iran to release the hostages and turn over the premises and archives of the U.S. Embassy to the protecting Power. 1980 I.C.J. 3, 45–46. Specific performance may be especially important in cases involving continuing environmental damage, an increasingly important topic of international claims. See Chapter 17. In the Gabcikovo–Nagymaros Case, 1997 I.C.J. 7, the parties had asked the Court to determine future conduct as well as the legal consequences of past conduct. The Court did so not by specifying the particular steps that either party would be required to take, but by instructing the parties to negotiate within the general framework of the legal principles that the Court had laid down, in order to implement a joint operational regime for the project in question. Id. at paras. 131–150.

SECTION 8. PROCEDURES TO IMPLEMENT OBLIGATIONS OF REPARATION

An injured state that is legally entitled to reparation from a state responsible for a wrongful act may bring a claim through diplomatic channels or through any procedure for dispute settlement to which the states have agreed. Diplomatic channels normally involve exchanges and negotiations between the parties. Dispute settlement procedures may be bilateral as, for example, through a commission composed of representatives of the two states. Other procedures of dispute settlement may involve third parties; either states or individuals. Dispute settlement procedures embrace a variety of arrangements provided for in existing treaties or ad hoc agreements. They include bilateral commissions, conciliation and mediation procedures, arbitration and judicial settlement. See Chapter 11.

Many claims commissions and arbitral tribunals have been established to deal with cases in which the violation of international obligations concerns the treatment of nationals or certain other persons of the injured state. Examples are the several claims commissions between Mexico and the United States and, more recently, the Iran–U.S. Claims Tribunal (established by treaty to adjudicate claims of U.S. nationals for injuries by Iran) and the U.N. Compensation Commission (established by the U.N. Security Council to determine claims against Iraq arising out of its invasion and occupation of Kuwait). See pp. 738–739 below and Chapter 10 on these and other claims tribunals. Another recent claims commission, with an innovative jurisdiction grounded in international law, is the Commission for Real Property Claims of Displaced Persons and Refugees, established by the 1995 Dayton Agreement as part of the peace settlement for Bosnia–Herzegovina. For an overview of recent developments concerning claims settlement, see Permanent Court of Arbitration, Institutional and Procedural Aspects of Mass Claims Settlement Systems (2000).

A. PROCEDURAL REQUIREMENTS

Claims and settlement procedures, although diverse in character, present a few common problems of a procedural character. They include the following:

1. *Standing to Make Claims*

States may present claims through diplomatic channels or to tribunals only if they have the requisite legal interest. As discussed above in Section 3, this depends on determining to whom the obligation is owed and on the meaning of "injury." Although the concept of certain *erga omnes* obligations has been recognized in principle, no judicial or arbitral proceeding has been identified where the claimant's standing was based on the *erga omnes* concept.

The issue of standing to bring a claim has been considered by the International Court of Justice in the Nottebohm Case (Liechtenstein v. Guatemala), 1955 I.C.J. 4; South West Africa Cases, 1966 I.C.J. 6; and the Barcelona Traction Case (Belgium v. Spain), 1970 I.C.J. 3. Cases concerning intervention by third parties have also considered the meaning of "legal interest". See Chapter 11.

Several international conventions allow *any* party to the convention to bring a case against another party for breach of an obligation, provided that both parties have accepted an optional protocol or clause to that effect. See, e.g., Convention on the Elimination of All Forms of Racial Discrimination, 660 U.N.T.S. 195 (1965).

An important feature of claims settlement practice in the period since the establishment of the Iran–U.S. Claims Tribunal is the trend toward creating vehicles for injured individuals or companies to present their own claims, not necessarily through the intermediation of their state of nationality. The U.N. Compensation Commission, for example, although generally requiring claims to be submitted by governments, has created special procedures for submission of claims "on behalf of persons who are not in a position to have their claims submitted by a Government" (e.g., stateless persons). See U.N.C.C., Provisional Rules for Claims Procedure, U.N. Doc. S/AC.26/1992/10, art. 5(2).

2. *Laches*

Whether international law includes a rule of laches has come up in several cases. An opinion of the U.S.-Mexican General Claims Commission stated that "no rule of international law put[s] a limit on * * * the presentation of an international claim to an international tribunal." George W. Cook Claim, 4 U.N.R.I.A.A. 3, 214. Some tribunals have denied remedies when the action was brought after a long lapse of time on the ground that the respondent government was placed in an unfair position in making its defense. See Ralston, The Law of Procedure of International Tribunals, 375–83 (1926) and Supplement 185–87 (1936). The *Institut de Droit International* concluded in 1925 that "it is left to the unfettered discretion of the international tribunal" to determine whether there has been undue delay. 32 Ann. de l'Inst. de Droit Int'l 558–60 (1925). An arbitral tribunal endorsed this principle in the *Ambatielos Case* when it denied a British contention that the claim of Greece should be rejected because of undue delay in its presentation. Ambatielos Case, Award of 1956, 12 U.N.R.I.A.A. 83, 103–04 (1963). Compare the materials at pp. 76–77 and 327–331 supra, on the issue of whether states can forfeit substantive rights through acquiescence, estoppel or prescription.

The trend in recent claims programs has been for the agreement or instrument establishing the tribunal (or its procedural rules) to set relatively brief time limits for receipt of claims once the tribunal is functioning: e.g., one year for the Iran–U.S. Claims Tribunal or the U.N. Compensation Commission. Such time limits facilitate processing of the claims and disbursement of any funds that may have been allocated for payment.

3. *Negotiation as a Prerequisite to Settlement Procedures*

Most agreements on dispute settlement provide that negotiation, consultation or "diplomacy" be resorted to before a claim can be submitted to a tribunal or other procedure for settlement. Even when that has not been specified in an agreement, tribunals have treated negotiation as an implied condition. As one court stated, a requirement that negotiation take place may be implied to show that a dispute actually exists and that "a difference of views is in question which has not been capable of being otherwise overcome" Chorzów Case (Interpretation of Judgments 7 and 8) 1927, P.C.I.J., Ser. A, No. 13, p. 10–11. Several cases have dealt with the meaning of the obligation to negotiate. In the *Mavrommatis Case* the Permanent Court of International Justice commented:

> "Negotiations do not of necessity always presuppose a more or less lengthy series of notes and despatches; it may suffice that a discussion has been commenced and * * * a deadlock is reached, or if finally a point is reached at which one of the parties definitely declares himself unable or refuses to give way."

1924 P.C.I.J., Ser. A, No. 2, p. 13.

The International Court of Justice in the *North Sea Continental Shelf Case* observed that

> the parties are under an obligation to enter into negotiation with a view to reaching an agreement * * *; they are under an obligation so to conduct themselves that the negotiations are meaningful, which will not be the case when either of them insists upon its own position without contemplating any modification of it.

1969 I.C.J. 3, 47–48.

What criteria may a court employ to determine whether a party that purports to be ready to negotiate and engages in discussion takes positions that it knows have no chance of acceptance? Can the court satisfy itself that negotiation in that case is a sham or futile?

4. *Exhaustion of Local Remedies*

A well-established rule of customary international law is that before a state can institute international proceedings for denial of rights to its nationals, remedies in local courts or administrative agencies must first have been exhausted. Although originally confined to the context of diplomatic protection of aliens, today international tribunals apply the "rule of local remedies" to the field of human rights as well. The rule confers on the host or respondent state an important initial role in the international dispute settlement process. C.F. Amerasinghe explains the justification for the rule as follows:

> The rule sprang up primarily as an instrument designed to ensure respect for the sovereignty of host States in a particular area of interna-

> tional dispute settlement. Basically this is the principal reason for its survival today and also for its projection into international systems of human rights protection. Whether in the modern law of diplomatic protection or in the conventional law of human rights protection, the raison d'être of the rule is the recognition given by members of the international community to the interest of the host State, flowing from its sovereignty, in settling international disputes of a certain kind by its own means before international mechanisms are invoked.

Local Remedies in International Law 359 (1990).

The "rule of local remedies" ensures that "the State where the violation has occurred should have an opportunity to redress it by its own means, within the framework of its own domestic legal system." Interhandel Case (Switzerland v. U.S.), 1959 I.C.J. 6. This requirement means that a remedy must be sought until the highest court rules on the issue. Exceptions to the exhaustion rule may be warranted where pursuit of local remedies would be "futile," e.g., where it is clear that the law is established by statute or precedent and that no court is competent to overrule it. What if it is clear that the courts are totally subservient to the executive who has taken the decision being challenged? See Panevezys Railway Case, 1939 P.C.I.J., Ser. A/B, No. 76, p. 18.

Are exceptions to the exhaustion of remedies rule warranted where the individual injured has only a transitory connection or none at all with the offending state? An example is that of a passenger in a plane shot down while in flight when that passenger had no link with the state. Should he be required to go to the courts of the offending state? The issue arose in a case brought by Israel against Bulgaria but the Court did not consider the Bulgarian contention that the injured Israeli had failed to seek remedies in Bulgarian courts. 1959 I.C.J. 127. Another example would involve an injury to a person in his own country caused by a space object or missile of a foreign state. Should that person be required to go to the courts of the responsible state before he or his state can claim damages? There is no such requirement in the Convention on Liability for Damage caused by Space Objects (1972); cf. art. IX.

For a recent discussion by the International Court of Justice of the rule of local remedies, see Case Concerning Elettronica Sicula S.p.A. (ELSI) (United States v. Italy), 1989 I.C.J. 15, 28 I.L.M. 1111, relevant portions of which are reprinted infra at p. 756 in Chapter 10.

5. *Manifestation of Consent to Third Party Settlement*

International claims "cannot in the present state of the law as to international jurisdiction be submitted to a tribunal except with the consent of the states concerned". Advisory Opinion of International Court of Justice on Reparation of Injuries, 1949 I.C.J. 177–78. Such consent may be manifested by agreements to general categories of cases such as agreements for claims commissions or arbitration. See Chapter 11 on jurisdictional clauses for arbitration and submission to jurisdiction of the International Court of Justice.

While the requirement of consent is unqualified, it has long been clear that consent need not be express but may be inferred from conduct conclusively establishing it. "The submission of arguments on the merits without making reservations in regard to the question of jurisdiction" has been held to confer the necessary consent. See Case Concerning Minorities in Upper Silesia, 1928 P.C.I.J., Ser. A, No. 16, p. 24. See also the Asylum Case (Colombia–Peru), 1950 I.C.J. 266, 267–68. The term *forum prorogatum* has been applied to jurisdiction based on conduct implying consent. See Chapter 11, p. 857. See also Rosenne, The Law and Practice of the International Court, 1920–1996 (1997) pp. 695–725.

B. ENFORCEMENT AND EXECUTION OF INTERNATIONAL AWARDS

Awards and orders of international tribunals holding states responsible for wrongful acts have generally been complied with. See Schachter, The Enforcement of International Judicial and Arbitral Awards, 54 A.J.I.L. 1 (1960). Cases of noncompliance have been relatively infrequent and nearly always based on objections by the defaulting state to the jurisdiction of the tribunal or on other grounds of nullity.

In cases of noncompliance the successful state may have recourse to national and international measures against the defaulting state.

1. *Execution Against Assets of Non-Complying State*

In the Tehran Hostages case, the International Court of Justice ruled that Iran was obliged to make reparation to the United States for the injury caused by the seizure and detention of U.S. nationals in Tehran. It left for future decision the determination of the form and amount, failing agreement of the parties. 1980 I.C.J. 45. Subsequently the parties reached agreement on settlement and no award of damages was requested by the United States.

If an award of monetary damages had been made by the Court and Iran did not comply, would the United States have been entitled to execute the award from the assets of the Iranian state and its agencies in the United States? Would such action have required a decision of the Security Council to give effect to the judgment in accordance with Article 94 of the U.N. Charter?

Or would execution by the United States have been a permissible act of self-help? Are the conclusions the same for binding arbitral awards as for judgments of the International Court of Justice?

Suppose the defaulting state had assets in a third state not a party to the dispute, would the successful state have been legally entitled to those assets to satisfy the judgment? Would the third state have been under a duty to transfer those assets? If no duty exists, would the third state be entitled to transfer the assets by recognizing the international award as binding and governed by principles of comity applicable to foreign judgments?

An affirmative answer to the latter question was suggested by the governments of France, the United Kingdom and the United States when they were faced with a demand that gold in their custody as fiduciaries and claimed by Albania should be used to pay the damages awarded by the International Court against Albania in the *Corfu Channel Case,* 1949 I.C.J. 4. The three governments were of the opinion that the required amount of gold could be paid to the United Kingdom to satisfy the Court's award provided that it was decided by arbitration that Albania was entitled to a share of the gold held by the three governments. Although the arbitrator did so decide, Italy contested the decision and then objected to the International Court determining the issue in the absence of Albania. 1949 I.C.J. 9, 10. In consequence the gold was not transferred to any of the claimants.

Whether or not the fiduciaries had the right to use the gold to meet the British claim to execution depends on their rights under the agreement delegating fiduciary powers to them. See Oliver, The Monetary Gold Decision in Perspective, 49 A.J.I.L. 216 (1955). The reasoning underlying the position of the fiduciary governments would support the right of a third state holding funds to meet a demand of a state entitled to execution under a binding decision of an international judicial or arbitral tribunal. See Schachter, The Enforcement of International Judicial and Arbitral Awards, 54 A.J.I.L. 1, 9–12 (1960).

2. Execution Through Domestic Courts of State in Which Funds of Judgment Debtor Are Located

In the case of *Socobel v. Greece,* a private Belgian company was awarded damages against Greece by an international arbitral tribunal. See 47 A.J.I.L. 508 (1953). When Greece did not pay, the Belgian company sought to attach funds of the Greek government in Belgium. The Belgian Court allowed an attachment as a conservatory action pending an *exequator* from the Belgian government certifying the validity and binding character of the arbitral award. The Belgian Court also held that the funds of Greece were not entitled to immunity against execution because they were related to business done by Greece in Belgium.

Can it be maintained that courts of a third state are under an obligation to recognize and enforce judgments of international tribunals that are binding on the parties in accordance with international law? Should it be regarded as a matter of comity? Would the municipal court have to ensure that competing claims are met? See M.E. O'Connell, 85 Proc. A.S.I.L. 439 (1991).

A separate question may be raised whether an award of a "non-national" tribunal is entitled to be treated as a foreign arbitral award made in a contracting state for purposes of recognition and enforcement under the U.N. Convention on Recognition and Enforcement of Arbitral Awards (the so-called New York Convention of 1958). See Paulsson, Arbitration Unbound: Award Detached from the Law of its Country of Origin, 30 I.C.L.Q. 358 (1981).

3. Enforcement Provisions in Multilateral Treaties

As indicated, the U.N. Charter provides that the Security Council may take measures to give effect to a judgment of the International Court when requested to do so. Article 94. No such action has been taken by the Council as of 2000. See Chapter 11.

The Convention on International Civil Aviation of 1944 also refers to possible noncompliance by a contracting state with a decision of the International Court or of an arbitral tribunal in a matter covered by the convention. The contracting states are obliged to exclude the airline of a contracting state from operating in their territory if the Council of the International Civil Aviation Organization has determined that the airline is not in compliance with the final decision of the International Court or arbitral tribunal. Article

87 of the Convention on International Civil Aviation. 61 Stat. 1180, 15 U.N.T.S. 295. See also Constitution of International Labor Organization, Article 33.

4. *Establishment of a Fund for Payment of Awards*

An unusual arrangement to ensure execution of awards was included in the Algiers Accords between the United States and Iran for arbitration of claims of nationals of each country against the other state arising out of debts, contracts, expropriations and other measures affecting property rights. Official claims of the United States arising out of contracts for goods and services were also covered. As part of the settlement agreement, a portion of the Iranian assets frozen in the United States was set aside to provide a fund out of which claims of U.S. nationals against Iran could be satisfied.

An earlier arrangement for funds to pay claims was the provision in the Peace Treaties of 1947 which gave the victorious states a right to retain the property of the enemy states situated in their territory and to liquidate such property for the purpose of paying claims which the government and their nationals had against the enemy country. See Mann, Enemy Property and the Paris Peace Treaties, 64 L.Q.Rev. 402 (1948).

The most recent and most complex arrangement to date is the U.N. Compensation Commission for claims against Iraq arising out of its invasion of Kuwait. A fund has been created under a system approved by the U.N. Security Council (the "oil-for-food" program), according to which Iraq is permitted to sell certain quantities of oil under international supervision, with the proceeds earmarked for specified purposes. See S.C.Res. 986 (1995); S.C.Res. 1111 (1997); S.C.Res. 1153 (1998). A portion of those proceeds is allocated to the payment of awards of the U.N. Compensation Commission. As of 2000, some $8.5 billion had already been awarded to small individual claimants, the bulk of which had been paid through the compensation fund, and considerable progress had been made on the large individual claims, corporate claims, and claims from governments and international organizations. See Wühler, The United Nations Compensation Commission, in Institutional and Procedural Aspects of Mass Claims Settlement Systems 17–18 (2000).

C. CLAIMS SETTLEMENT BY THE UNITED STATES

In 1794 the United States and Great Britain concluded the Jay Treaty under which several hundred claims based on maritime seizures were referred to a mixed commission for arbitration. See Hyde, International Law 1587–88 (1945). A number of arbitration cases involving the United States took place in the 19th century, one of the more notable being the U.S. claims against Great Britain for damage covered by the Confederate warship Alabama. See Hyde, id. at 1592–93.

Several claims commissions were established, beginning in 1868, to deal with U.S.-Mexican claims, mostly against Mexico but some against the U.S. The two U.S.-Mexico Claims Commissions set up in 1923 dealt with more than 6000 claims and in doing so created a significant body of case law on state responsibility. See Feller, The Mexican Claims Commissions 1923–1934 (1935).

After the Second World War, several lump-sum settlement agreements were made by the United States with countries in Europe and later with China. A Foreign Claims Settlement Commission was created in the United States to distribute funds received from foreign governments to the U.S. nationals entitled to receive them. The Commission has considered each claim separately and determined its validity and amount on the basis of "principles of international law, justice and equity." 22 U.S.C.A. §§ 1621–1645. See Weston, Lillich & Bederman, International Claims: Their Settlement by Lump Sum Agreements, 1975–1995 (1999).

As indicated above, the United States and Iran in the agreement known as the Algiers Accords established an arbitral tribunal to which some 3000 claims were submitted. The agreement is in 20 I.L.M. 223 (1981). See Chapter 10, p. 754. See also Aldrich, The Jurisprudence of the Iran–United States claims Tribunal (1996); Lillich, Magraw & Bederman (eds.), The Iran–United States Claims Tribunal: Its Contribution to the Law of State Responsibility (1998); Brower & Brueschke, The Iran–United States Claims Tribunal (1998); Caron & Crook (eds.), The Iran–United States Claims Tribunal and the Process of International Claims Resolution (2000).

The United States has settled some important recent claims on the basis of ad hoc agreement. Some such settlements have been made without formal acknowledgment of liability (that is, on a *ex gratia* basis). For example, the United States agreed to pay China $28 million in compensation for damage to the Chinese Embassy in Belgrade from the inadvertent NATO bombing during the Kosovo conflict of 1999. See "U.S. Agrees to Pay China $28 Million for Bombing," N.Y.Times, Dec. 16, 1999, p. A6, col. 1.

D. REMEDIES OF PRIVATE PERSONS FOR VIOLATIONS OF INTERNATIONAL LAW

The Restatement (Third), § 906, states:

> A private person, whether natural or juridical, injured by a violation of an international obligation by a state, may bring a claim against that state or assert that violation as a defense
>
> * * *
>
> b) in a court or other tribunal of that state pursuant to its law; or
>
> c) in a court or other tribunal of the injured person's state of nationality or of a third state, pursuant to the law of such state, subject to limitations under international law.

Notes

1. Is a state required by international law to provide a remedy to injured persons in its domestic courts for a violation of international law by that state? Schachter observes:

> There is no general requirement in international law that States provide such remedies. By and large, international law leaves it to them to meet their obligations in such ways as the state determines. * * * However, in some cases there are obligations of means—that is, specific requirements as to the procedures and agencies that are to be used for the fulfilment of obligations of

> result. Such obligations of means are specified in treaties of various kinds, particularly those which are intended to benefit private persons.
>
> * * * Some treaties require that individuals have a right to a remedy by a competent authority, leaving it to the State to decide whether that authority would be executive, administrative or judicial. In other cases, treaties do not expressly confer a right to judicial remedies, but an implication to that effect can be drawn.

Schachter, International Law in Theory and Practice 240 (1991) (footnotes omitted).

The Restatement (Third) declares in § 907, Comment *a*:

> International agreements, even those directly benefiting private persons, generally do not create private rights or provide for a private cause of action in domestic courts, but there are exceptions with respect to both rights and remedies * * *

2. Whether a treaty that says nothing about individual rights or remedies may be interpreted as conferring such rights or remedies may be easy to determine in some cases but difficult in others. For example, treaties concerned with rights of property by descent or inheritance have long been treated in the United States as conferring rights upon individuals. See Head Money Cases, 112 U.S. 580, 598, 5 S.Ct. 247, 28 L.Ed. 798 (1884). Similarly, treaties according nationals of the contracting states equal treatment have been construed to give individuals judicial remedies. See Asakura v. Seattle, 265 U.S. 332, 44 S.Ct. 515, 68 L.Ed. 1041 (1924). However, treaties concerned with the use of force such as the U.N. Charter, and other political treaties, have been interpreted as not conferring enforceable rights on individuals injured by violations. The courts in the United States have tended to deny relief either because the treaty was deemed not to confer individual rights or remedies, or on the ground that the issues raised were "political questions". See Chapter 3, pp. 205–212 on self-executing treaties and other issues relevant to judicial relief. On individual remedies for human rights violations, see Chapter 8, pp. 631–632.

3. For an example of a treaty provision expressly addressing individual remedies, see Article 2(3) of the International Covenant on Civil and Political Rights which obliges each state party to ensure "an effective remedy" to any person whose rights have been violated. It also requires that the right to such remedy be determined by "a competent authority provided for by the legal system of the state" and that the remedies granted be enforced by the state. See Schachter, The Obligation to Implement the Covenant in Domestic Law, in The International Bill of Rights 311 (Henkin ed. 1981).

4. Does international customary law require a state to provide a judicial remedy for an alien injured by a breach of international law? See Mann, The Consequences of an International Wrong in International and National Law, 48 Brit. Y.B.I.L. 1 (1975–76); cf. Banco Nacional de Cuba v. Chase Manhattan Bank, 658 F.2d 875 (2d Cir.1981). See generally Chapter 10.

5. Suits brought against foreign states may be barred by sovereign immunity unless such immunity has been waived. Whether a treaty conferring remedies to injured individuals constitutes a waiver is a matter of treaty interpretation. In the United States and other countries that have adopted the restrictive theory of immunity, suits against states may be brought in cases to which the immunity does not apply. See generally Chapter 14. Even where sovereign immunity applies, suit may sometimes be brought against a responsible official. See Restatement

(Third) § 131, Reporters' Note 4. Relief by a domestic court may also be barred in the United States by the act of state doctrine and related doctrines. See Chapter 3, p. 180.

6. Remedies in domestic courts are also limited by jurisdictional requirements. The forum state must have jurisdiction to adjudicate and the substantive law must be within its legislative jurisdiction. See further Chapter 13. Suits brought by foreign nationals may be limited by rules of the forum including the principle of *forum non conveniens.*

7. Suits against the United States require the consent of the United States. Such consent, by statute, to cover tort and contract claims, may include cases involving violations of international obligations. See Restatement (Third) § 907, Reporters' Note 2.

Chapter 10

STATE RESPONSIBILITY FOR INJURY TO ALIENS AND FOREIGN INVESTORS

SECTION 1. INTRODUCTION

Under ordinary circumstances, and in the absence of an international agreement to the contrary, a state is not obligated under international law to admit nationals of another state into its territory, and it incurs no international responsibility if it deports them. If aliens are admitted, they may be subjected to restrictions on the duration of their stay, where they may travel, and the activities in which they may engage. Similarly, a state may generally exclude a juridical entity (e.g., a corporation) organized under the laws of, or headquartered in, another state, or, if it is admitted, may regulate its activities.

Moreover, a national (whether an individual or juridical entity) of one state that comes within the territorial jurisdiction of another generally becomes subject to the legal regime applicable to nationals of that state, except to the extent that a special regime is applicable to aliens. For example, foreign nationals or foreign juridical entities may be excluded from engaging in various commercial or other gainful activity, from owning real property, from such civil and political rights as the right to vote or to hold public office, and from such duties as fulfilling a military service obligation. Generally, however, aliens' substantive and procedural rights are neither better nor worse than those of local nationals, and they do not carry with them the rights and protections they may enjoy under the law of the state of their nationality.

International agreements, such as treaties of friendship, commerce and navigation and bilateral investment treaties, often guarantee the right of persons of one contracting party to do business in the other state, subject to some restrictions but with the benefit of legal protection against specified non-commercial risks. Such agreements are discussed at pp. 805 to 813.

Even in the absence of an applicable international agreement, customary international law affords certain protection to alien individuals and foreign juridical entities under the principles of state responsibility discussed in Chapter 9. In essence, under customary international law alien individuals and juridical entities may properly seek from the state of their nationality, and it may properly accord, diplomatic protection against an act or omission by a foreign state causing injury to the alien that may give rise to international responsibility. A state is entitled to communicate with its national who is arrested or charged with a crime by another state, to give assistance and to have a representative present at the trial. The protecting state may intercede to protect its national's human rights, personal safety, property or other interests. See Restatement (Third) § 713, Comment *c*.

Under circumstances to be examined in this Chapter, if the alien individual or entity has suffered an injury as a result of a violation of a substantive rule of international law attributable to a foreign state, the state of the alien's nationality may assert, on the state-to-state level, a claim against the offending state that is based on the injury to the alien. Normally, the injured alien individual or entity must exhaust remedies under the legal system of the state to which the wrongful conduct is attributable. In the event such alien is unable to obtain redress for the injury under the laws of that state, what originated as the claim of the private party can be elevated to the international plane, provided that the state of which the private party is a national elects to assert a claim against the allegedly responsible state.

Most international claims are of this variety; they are derivative in the sense that they involve not a wrong inflicted directly on one state by another, but rather injury caused by one state to a national of another state. State responsibility arises only if the act or omission of the state causing the injury is wrongful under international law. The injury may be caused directly by action of the foreign state (for example, a physical injury to the person or confiscation of the property of an alien by an agent or organ of the state), or it may be caused by a failure of the state to provide redress for an injury inflicted on the alien by some private person (for example, a failure of the state to provide judicial remedies to an alien on whom a physical or economic injury has been inflicted by a resident of that state).

The customary international law of state responsibility for injury to alien individuals and the international law of human rights, examined in Chapter 8, which deals with the obligations of states to all human beings, not just to aliens, have developed separately. The latter reflects "general acceptance * * * that how a state treats individual human beings, including its own citizens, in respect of their human rights, is not the state's own business alone and therefore exclusively within its 'domestic jurisdiction,' but is a matter of international concern and a proper subject for regulation by international law." Restatement (Third) Part VII, Introductory Note.

Notwithstanding differences in the development and origins of the customary law of responsibility for injury to aliens and the law of human rights, there is a substantial overlap and a growing interrelationship between them. As stated by the Reporters of the Restatement (Third):

> The difference in history and in jurisprudential origins between the older law of responsibility for injury to aliens and the newer law of human rights should not conceal their essential affinity and their increasing convergence. The law of responsibility to aliens posited and invoked an international standard of justice for individuals, even if dogmas of the international system limited the application of that standard to foreign nationals. That standard of justice, like contemporary human rights law,

> derived from historic conceptions of natural law, as reflected in the conscience of contemporary mankind and the major cultures and legal systems of the world. As the law of human rights developed, the law of responsibility for injury to aliens, as applied to natural persons, began to refer to violation of their "fundamental human rights," and states began to invoke contemporary human rights norms as the basis for claims for injury to their nationals.

Id.

The law of state responsibility retains independent vitality in providing protection against injuries to individual aliens that do not rise to the level of violations of human rights and against injuries to juridical entities (such as privately owned corporations) that have no "human" rights.

When the wrongful conduct attributable to a state results in injury to a national of another state, although the underlying injury is to an alien individual or legal entity, the liability under international law runs from the responsible state to the state of which the injured alien or entity is a national. Thus, assertion of a claim based on state responsibility arising out of an injury to an alien requires the intercession of the state of which he is a national. The derivative nature of the state's claim based on injury to its national becomes important in connection with such matters as the measure of reparation and circumstances under which action by the national may effect a settlement or a waiver of any claim based on state responsibility. See p. 761. Because only the state of which the injured alien is a national may assert a claim against the offending state, the principles of nationality, discussed at pp. 425–450, play an important role in connection with state responsibility.

During the last 40 years or so, there have been a number of studies of the law of state responsibility for injury to aliens. One, with draft articles, was prepared for the International Law Commission by its Special Rapporteur, F.V. Garcia–Amador, and was considered by the Commission between 1956 and 1960. Beginning in 1962, a new Special Rapporteur, Roberto Ago, prepared a report for the Commission dealing with state responsibility in specific contexts. See Report of International Law Commission on the Work of its 32d Session, G.A.O.R., 35th Sess. Supp. No. 10 (A/35/10) (1980). Garcia–Amador's study and a draft convention with commentary prepared by Sohn and Baxter are contained in Garcia–Amador, Sohn & Baxter, Recent Codification of the Law of State Responsibility for Injuries to Aliens (1974). For a summary of the International Law Commission's work regarding state responsibility, see the International Law Commission Yearbook, Second Report of the Special Rapporteur on State Responsibility A/CN.4/498/Add.1–5, 53d Session (1999). In 1996, the I.L.C. adopted provisionally on first reading, draft articles on state responsibility which focused mainly on rules and procedures relating to state responsibility ("secondary rules") rather than on the principal focus of this chapter, the substantive principles ("primary rules"), breaches of which give rise to state responsibility. Report of the International Law Commission on the Work of its 48th Session, A/51/10 (1996), 37 I.L.M. 440 (1998) and Chapter 9 supra. See also Chapter 2, Part VII of the Restatement (Third), and Lillich, International Law of State Responsibility for Injury to Aliens (Lillich ed. 1983).

SECTION 2. CONFLICTING VIEWS ON BASIC PRINCIPLES

A. THE INTERNATIONAL MINIMUM STANDARD OF JUSTICE AND THE PRINCIPLE OF EQUALITY

The traditional view of the customary law of state responsibility as espoused by the United States and many other states, including, in particular, most of the industrialized states of the West, was summarized in 5 Hackworth at 471–72 as follows:

> * * * [R]esponsibility of the state * * * does not arise merely because an alien has been injured or has suffered loss within the state's territory. If the alien has suffered an injury at the hands of a private person, his remedy usually is against that person, and state responsibility does not arise in the absence of a dereliction of duty on the part of the state itself in connection with the injury, as for example by failure to afford a remedy, or to apply an existing remedy. When local remedies are available the alien is ordinarily not entitled to the interposition of his government until he has exhausted those remedies. * * * This presupposes the existence in the state of orderly judicial and administrative processes. In theory an unredressed injury to an alien constitutes an injury to his state, giving rise to international responsibility.
>
> If the alien receives the benefits of the same laws, protection, and means of redress for injuries which the state accords to its own nationals, there is no justifiable ground for complaint unless it can be shown that the system of law or its administration falls below the standard generally recognized as essential by the community of nations. The mere fact that the law and procedure of the state in which the alien resides differ from those of the country of which he is a national does not of itself afford justification for complaint. * * *

Elihu Root said:

> There is a standard of justice, very simple, very fundamental, and of such general acceptance by all civilized countries as to form a part of the international law of the world. The condition upon which any country is entitled to measure the justice due from it to an alien by the justice which it accords to its own citizens is that its system of law and administration shall conform to this general standard. If any country's system of law and administration does not conform to that standard, although the people of the country may be content or compelled to live under it, no other country can be compelled to accept it as furnishing a satisfactory measure of treatment to its citizens. * * *

Proceedings of the American Society of International Law 20–21, 22 (1910).

The relationship between the international minimum standard of justice and the principle of equality of aliens and nationals was highlighted in the diplomatic correspondence between the United States (represented by Secretary of State Cordell Hull) and Mexico on the obligation of Mexico under international law to compensate U.S. owners of agrarian properties expropriated by the Mexican government. Some excerpts that capture the substance and the flavor of the debate follow:

> *Secretary Hull to the Mexican Ambassador, July 21, 1938:* During recent years the Government of the United States has upon repeated occasions made representations to the Government of Mexico with regard to the continuing expropriation by Your Excellency's Government of agrarian properties owned by American citizens, without adequate, effective and prompt compensation being made therefor. * * *
>
> If it were permissible for a government to take the private property of the citizens of other countries and pay for it as and when, in the judgment of the government, its economic circumstances and its local legislation may perhaps permit, the safeguards which the constitutions of most countries and established international law have sought to provide would be illusory. Governments would be free to take property far beyond their ability or willingness to pay, and the owners thereof would be without recourse. We cannot question the right of a foreign government to treat its own nationals in this fashion if it so desires. This is a matter of domestic concern. But we cannot admit that a foreign government may take the property of American nationals in disregard of the rule of compensation under international law. * * *
>
> * * *
>
> *The Mexican Minister for Foreign Affairs to the American Ambassador, August 3, 1938:* * * * My Government maintains, on the contrary, that there is in international law no rule universally accepted in theory nor carried out in practice which makes obligatory the payment of immediate compensation, nor even of deferred compensation, for expropriations of a general and impersonal character like those which Mexico has carried out for the purpose of redistribution of the land. * * *
>
> * * *
>
> * * * Nevertheless Mexico admits, in obedience to her own laws, that she is indeed under obligation to indemnify in an adequate manner; but the doctrine which she maintains on the subject, is that the time and manner of such payment must be determined by her own laws. * * *
>
> The republics of our continent have let their voice be heard since the first Pan American Conference, vigorously maintaining the principle of equality between nationals and foreigners, considering that the foreigner who voluntarily moves to a country which is not his own, in search of a personal benefit, accepts in advance, together with the advantages which he is going to enjoy, the risks to which he may find himself exposed. It would be unjust that he should aspire to a privileged position * * *
>
> *Secretary Hull to the Mexican Ambassador, August 22, 1938:* * * * The Government of the United States merely adverts to a self-evident fact when it notes that the applicable and recognized authorities on international law support its declaration that, under every rule of law and equity, no government is entitled to expropriate private property, for whatever purpose, without provision for prompt, adequate, and effective payment therefor. * * *

The doctrine of equality of treatment, like that of just compensation, is of ancient origin. It appears in many constitutions, bills of rights and documents of international validity. The word has invariably referred to equality in lawful rights of the person and to protection in exercising such lawful rights. There is now announced by your Government the astonishing theory that this treasured and cherished principle of equality, designed to protect both human and property rights, is to be invoked, not in the protection of personal rights and liberties, but as a chief ground of depriving and stripping individuals of their conceded rights. It is contended, in a word, that it is wholly justifiable to deprive an individual of his rights if all other persons are equally deprived. * * *

19 Dep't of State, Press Releases 50–52, 136–37, 140, 143–44 (1938).

Notes

1. On March 18, 1938, the Mexican Government expropriated the properties in Mexico of certain foreign-owned oil companies operating there, including a number of U.S. companies. Mexico agreed in 1938 to the establishment of a joint commission to settle agrarian claims accumulated after 1927, and made a good faith down payment of $1 million. By the Mexico–United States Agreement of 1941, which resolved all prior agrarian and other claims exclusive of those arising out of the petroleum seizures, Mexico agreed to pay $40 million in annual installments, as against claims totaling more than $350 million. After voluminous diplomatic exchange, a Mexico–United States settlement of claims arising out of the expropriation of oil properties was finally achieved in 1942. The United States, on behalf of the U.S. oil companies that estimated the total value of their expropriated holdings at $260 million, settled for a sum approximating $24 million payable in installments over several years, plus interest at three per cent.

2. To the extent that a state violates the human rights of an alien protected under customary international law, the concept of equality of treatment ceases to have independent significance; an international human rights standard has become the authoritatively prescribed standard of justice for all human beings. See Restatement (Third) § 711, Comment *b*.

B. STATE RESPONSIBILITY FOR INJURIES TO ALIENS AS CUSTOMARY INTERNATIONAL LAW

During much of the post-World–War–II period, criticisms based on a variety of conceptual foundations were leveled at the traditional customary international law of state responsibility by representatives of many Latin American states, socialist states and states newly emerged from colonial domination in Africa and Asia.

For a considerable number of years, the International Law Commission tried unsuccessfully to reach agreement on a codification of the law of state responsibility for injury to aliens. Fundamentally differing views on the basic principles of state responsibility were the principal stumbling block. See Lillich, The Current Status of the Law of State Responsibility, in International Law of State Responsibility for Injuries to Aliens 16–21 (Lillich ed. 1983).

Efforts of the U.N. Centre and Commission on Transnational Corporations to develop a multilateral Code of Conduct on Transnational Corporations, discussed at p. 1623, also remained incomplete largely because of these fundamental differences. See Rubin, Transnational Corporations and International Codes of Conduct: A Study of the Relationship Between International Legal Cooperation and Economic Development, 10 Am. U. J. Int'l L. & Pol'y 1275 (1995). The 1985 Report of the Centre on Transnational Corporations on Work on the Formulation of the United Nations Code of Conduct on Transnational Corporations, E/C.10/1985/s/2, summarized as follows the views in opposition to the traditional view of state responsibility for injury to aliens supported by the United States and most other industrialized states, which embraces the international minimum standard of treatment that states must accord to aliens (footnotes omitted):

(ii) *Latin American views*

38. The theoretical foundations, as well as the practical implications of the traditional law of State responsibility, have been questioned by a number of Latin American officials and jurists. * * *

39. The basis of the objection, which was elaborated by [the Argentine jurist] Calvo, had two main elements. First, * * * that a sovereign independent State was entitled, by reason of the principle of equality, to complete freedom from interference in any form, whether by diplomacy or by force, from other States. Second, aliens were entitled to no greater rights and privileges than those available to nationals. * * * Thus, the Latin American response to the international minimum standard was the doctrine of national treatment. According to that doctrine, customary international law merely requires a host State to accord to aliens essentially the same rights as those enjoyed by nationals.

40. Latin American States sought to reinforce the [Calvo] doctrine by appropriate provisions in their national constitutions and laws and by "Calvo" clauses in concessions and other State contracts which enjoined aliens to seek redress exclusively in national courts. * * *

42. In sum, the impact of the Calvo doctrine * * * is reflected in the following propositions: (a) international law requires the host State to accord national treatment to aliens; (b) national law governs the rights and privileges of aliens; (c) national courts have exclusive jurisdiction over disputes involving aliens, who may therefore not seek redress by recourse to diplomatic protection; (d) international adjudication is inadmissible for the settlement of disputes with aliens. * * *

(iii) *Views of socialist countries*

43. The emergence of the socialist countries of Eastern Europe involved extensive nationalizations of private property, which challenged the philosophical assumptions underpinning the traditional doctrine of State responsibility. Although socialist countries subsequently undertook to pay compensation for nationalized foreign economic interests under lump-sum compensation settlements, they * * * rejected the traditional idea of an international minimum standard. Socialist countries maintain that the regulation of alien property falls exclusively within the province of national law.

44. * * * Accordingly, the treatment of a foreign company falls outside the purview of international law. This position is reinforced by the principle that international law is exclusively concerned with the

regulation of relations between States. Such a regime does not apply to relations between a State and an entity, such as a transnational corporation, which lacks international legal personality and is not a subject of international law. * * * Socialist countries thus reject the traditional doctrine of State responsibility which, in their view, was developed to protect foreign economic interests. * * *

(iv) *The emergence of new States*

46. The emergence of new nations from colonialism after the Second World War and their efforts to assert their economic independence and to restructure their internal economic systems has also had an impact on traditional principles of State responsibility. The new nations, especially in Africa and Asia, generally challenged the universal validity of those principles on the ground that they had been developed without their participation or consent. Furthermore, the principles of State responsibility were assailed as unjust, inequitable and essentially colonial in character. In fact, the application of those principles to the newly independent States was seen as perpetuating an exploitative system beneficial to the developed market economies.

Notes

1. In reviewing the materials that follow, it will be useful to keep in mind that in recent years the sharp edge of the debate over the basic principles of state responsibility for injury to aliens has been blunted as a result of pressures from a number of quarters. These have included the collapse of communism in the former U.S.S.R. and Eastern Europe and the effort in the states that emerged from that collapse to move toward privatization and market economies. This has been accompanied in the developing world by a growing recognition that moves toward freer markets and privatization of business are more likely to encourage economic development than continued reliance on government-owned enterprises and government-managed economies. Many developing countries have increasingly acknowledged that foreign private investment has an essential role to play in fostering economic development and that in order to encourage an inflow of foreign private investment and its concomitant technical and managerial know-how, it is necessary to enhance the legal security of foreign investment. The needs for capital in the developing world, the republics of the former U.S.S.R. and the states of Eastern Europe far exceed the available supply. The developing world and the states of Eastern Europe must therefore compete for scarce capital, and the competition has become all the keener as a result of the economic woes experienced during the late 1990s in Asia, Russia and Latin America. The compelling need in emerging economies of the world to attract foreign private capital has been accompanied by a widespread willingness on the part of developing countries to move beyond acerbic debates over doctrinal differences with respect to the basic principles of state responsibility and to consider more specific substantive and procedural arrangements to enhance the investment climate and legal security for foreign private investment. Both capital-importing and capital-exporting states have come to share a common interest in this enhancement. See note at p. 813 and Sarkar, The Legal Implications of Financial Sector Reform in Emerging Capital Markets, 13 Am. U. Int'l L. Rev. 705 (1998) and Steinberg, Emerging Capital Markets: Proposals and Recommendations for Implementation, 30 Int'l Law. 715 (1996).

2. Another issue to consider in connection with the materials that follow is to what extent does the development of the international law of human rights as a source of state responsibility have the potential for facilitating a reconciliation of the varying views as to the basic principles of state responsibility. Certain instances of action or inaction by agents of a state that fail to meet the international minimum standard of justice of the traditional law of state responsibility have been accepted as violations of the international law of human rights, deriving principally from the Universal Declaration on Human Rights and the Covenant on Civil and Political Rights. See p. 587. Indeed, there has developed a substantial overlap between state responsibility for violations of human rights of aliens and state responsibility for failure to accord a minimum standard of justice to aliens under traditional customary law principles, and to the extent of the overlap the operative rules may be regarded as having merged. See Restatement (Third) Part VII and Chapter 8.

C. CONFLICTING PRINCIPLES AS APPLIED TO TREATMENT OF ALIEN–OWNED PROPERTY

The issue framed during the 1930s in the United States–Mexico correspondence on the Mexican expropriations of agrarian properties, namely the scope of the obligation of a state under international law to compensate aliens whose property has been expropriated, became a particular focus of debates in the United Nations on the principles of state responsibility under customary law during the 1960s and 1970s. The U.N. General Assembly Resolution on Permanent Sovereignty over Natural Resources, G.A.Res. 1803, (XVII 1962), adopted by 87 votes to two, with 12 abstentions, provided that, in case of nationalization, the alien owner shall be paid "appropriate compensation, in accordance with the rules in force in the State taking such measures in the exercise of its sovereignty and in accordance with international law," and that "[f]oreign investment agreements freely entered into by or between sovereign States shall be observed in good faith." The United States unilaterally interpreted "appropriate" compensation to mean "prompt, adequate and effective." See Schwebel, The Story of the U.N. Declaration on Permanent Sovereignty over Natural Resources, 49 A.B.A.J. 463 (1963).

The Trade and Development Board of the U.N. Conference on Trade and Development (UNCTAD) adopted Resolution 88 (XII), 12 U.N. TDOR, Supp. 1 at 1, U.N. Doc TD/B/423 (1972) stating, in part, that it

> 2. *Reiterates* that * * * such measures of nationalization as States may adopt in order to recover their natural resources are the expression of a sovereign power in virtue of which it is for each State to fix the amount of compensation and the procedure for these measures, and any dispute which may arise in that connection falls within the sole jurisdiction of its courts, without prejudice to what is set forth in General Assembly resolution 1803 (XVII)* * *.

On December 17, 1973, the U.N. General Assembly adopted Resolution 3171, on Permanent Sovereignty over Natural Resources, (XXVIII 1973), which, after recalling, among others, its Resolution 1803 (XVII), stated, in part:

The General Assembly

* * *

> 3. *Affirms* that the application of the principle of nationalization carried out by States, as an expression of their sovereignty in order to safeguard their natural resources, implies that each State is entitled to determine the amount of possible compensation and the mode of payment, and that any disputes which might arise should be settled in accordance with the national legislation of each State carrying out such measures * * *

The vote was 109 in favor, one against (United Kingdom) and 17 abstaining (including the United States and most developed countries).

Then, on December 12, 1974, the General Assembly adopted Resolution 3281, the Charter of Economic Rights and Duties of States, (XXIX 1974). Chapter II, Art. 2(2) dealt with nationalization as follows:

> Each State has the right: * * *
>
> (c) To nationalize, expropriate or transfer ownership of foreign property, in which case appropriate compensation should be paid by the State adopting such measures, taking into account its relevant laws and regulations and all circumstances that the State considers pertinent. In any case where the question of compensation gives rise to a controversy, it shall be settled under the domestic law of the nationalizing State and by its tribunals, unless it is freely and mutually agreed by all States concerned that other peaceful means be sought on the basis of the sovereign equality of States and in accordance with the principle of free choice of means.

The vote on Article 2, Paragraph 2(c), was 104 in favor, 16 against (including the United States and many developed states) and six abstentions.

Lillich commented on the foregoing developments in the institutions of the United Nations in The Valuation of Nationalized Property in International Law, Vol. 3, 191–95 (1976), as follows (some footnotes omitted):

> The frontal assault on the substantive norms of Resolution 1803 (XVII) has coincided with a renewed attack on its procedural counterpart, the diplomatic protection of nationals abroad. Despite unsuccessful attempts during the past century, especially by the Latin American States, to restrict diplomatic protection, the Permanent Court of International Justice described this doctrine as "an elementary principle of international law," a view that has been reaffirmed by the International Court of Justice upon more than one occasion. Yet both the UNCTAD resolution [Resolution 88(XII), 12 U.N. TDOR, Supp. 1 at 1, U.N.Doc. TD/B/423 (1972)] and Resolution 3171 (XXVIII) purport to demolish, at least insofar as the nationalization of foreign-owned property is concerned, what one experienced observer has called "one of the most fundamental pillars of international law."[39] Abolishing the right of diplomatic protection, moreover, would emasculate whatever substantive norms governing compensation do exist * * *.
>
> That the sponsors and supporters of the UNCTAD resolution intended to immunize themselves from potential international responsibility is apparent from the language of their resolution, which states that "any

39. Freeman, Recent Aspects of the Calvo Doctrine and the Challenge to International Law, 40 A.J.I.L. 121, 122 (1946).

dispute'' concerning a State's nationalization of foreign-owned property ''falls within the sole jurisdiction of its courts * * * '' Similarly, Resolution 3171 (XXVIII) provides that ''any disputes which might arise should be settled in accordance with the national legislation of each State carrying out such measures,'' surely an open invitation to nationalizing States to enact measures making their domestic courts the final decision makers on the amount, if any, of ''possible'' compensation. Taken together, the two resolutions can be read as a thinly disguised attempt to endow the Calvo Doctrine, which maintains ''that aliens are not entitled to rights and privileges not accorded to nationals, and that therefore they may seek redress for grievances only before the local authorities,'' with limited international status. * * *

* * *

* * * [D]espite the fact that the Calvo Doctrine, both in general and as incorporated in the UNCTAD resolution and Resolution 3171 (XXVIII), is couched in procedural terms, the real issue involved is the international responsibility of the State. Its opponents simply do not want any question raised as to compliance with their international obligations; they do not wish to run the risks of an adverse award that might result from submission to arbitration. They wish to encourage foreign capital to invest and they would like foreign talent to assist in developing the country but they also wish to be completely free to take any measures they desire without being subject to a demand for compensation arising out of violations of rights. In brief, they would have the benefits of their bargain but not its obligations.

Note

It has been suggested ''that the opposing positions, when stated in the abstract, are in head-on contradiction, but the conflict may not be as sharp when the issues are placed in a more specific context. When a controversy arises over expropriation, it is almost certain that issues of fair treatment and 'appropriate' compensation will be raised within the negotiating or settlement framework established by the expropriating government. The argument then is not on the issue of national competence, but about the specific circumstances and the criteria to be applied.'' Schachter, The Evolving International Law of Development, 15 Colum. J. Transnat'l L. 1, 8 (1976). If this is so, the nationalizing government, even if committed ideologically to exclusive national competence, is likely to be influenced by principles followed in other countries and by their own perceived interest in maintaining the confidence of foreign investors. Thus, most compensation issues have been settled by negotiation or submitted to arbitration, not imposed by the courts of the expropriating states. Id. Moreover, as suggested above, in recent years, without necessarily abandoning their doctrinal positions on the law of state responsibility, many developing countries have moved toward encouraging foreign investment perceived to be needed for their economic development by improving the legal protection it enjoys and have adopted specific substantive and procedural measures toward this end that are inconsistent with the doctrinal positions they espoused in the debates of the 1960s and 1970s. These measures have included entry into hundreds of bilateral treaties for the protection of foreign investment, discussed at p. 808, adherence to the Convention for the Settlement of Investment Disputes Between States and Nationals of Other States, discussed at p. 1628, and participation in the Multilateral Investment Guaranty Agency, discussed at p. 1629.

SECTION 3. CONDITIONS TO AND PROCEDURAL ASPECTS OF ASSERTION OF A CLAIM OF STATE RESPONSIBILITY

A. GENERAL CONSIDERATIONS

International law imposes no duty on a state to press on the international level a claim based on injury caused by a foreign state to one of the former's nationals. Under the law of the United States, as well as most other states, the injured national has no legally enforceable right to compel his or her government to espouse the claim. See Borchard, The Diplomatic Protection of Citizens Abroad 355–98 (1915). Moreover, if the claim is espoused by the United States, it becomes an international claim and as such is appropriate for international negotiations between the United States and the state that has allegedly caused the injury. From the time it espouses the claim, the United States enjoys exclusive control over the handling and disposition of it.

In Administrative Decision V (United States v. Germany), Mixed Claims Commission, 1924, [1923–25] Administrative Decisions and Opinions 145, 190, 7 U.N.Rep. Int'l Arb. Awards 119, 152, Umpire Parker stated:

> In exercising such control [the nation] is governed not only by the interest of the particular claimant but by the larger interests of the whole people of the nation and must exercise an untrammeled discretion in determining when and how the claim will be presented and pressed, or withdrawn or compromised, and the private owner will be bound by the action taken. Even if payment is made to the espousing nation in pursuance of an award, it has complete control over the fund so paid to and held by it and may, to prevent fraud, correct a mistake, or protect the national honor, at its election return the fund to the nation paying it or otherwise dispose of it.

Thus, it is assumed that the Executive may waive or settle a claim by the United States against a foreign state based on its responsibility for an injury to a U.S. national despite the latter's objection (though there remain some open questions about the scope of executive claims settlement power; see Chapter 3 at pp. 231, 236–237.

A claim of state responsibility for injury to an alien is derivative in a number of respects. See Restatement (Third) § 713, Comment *a*. For example, the injured party enjoys broad rights to settle its claim against the foreign state *before* it is espoused by the state of which the claimant is a national and, by such settlement, preclude any claim by that state. Moreover, the injured person is generally required to exhaust possible remedies under the local law of the foreign state before the state of which the claimant is a national may assert a claim. See p. 755. In addition, the measure of compensation that may be recovered by the state is based on the injury to its national; reparation normally does not encompass any element of recompense for injury to the state itself. See p. 802.

The customary law of state responsibility developed primarily out of claims practice, negotiations and agreements concerning liability and compensation and by decisions of arbitral tribunals.

In some instances, the states concerned have agreed to a lump-sum settlement of all outstanding claims. See Lillich and Weston, International Claims: Their Settlement by Lump–Sum Agreements (1975). If not settled through negotiation, the states concerned might elect to submit the claim or claims to the International Court of Justice, to an arbitration established under a multilateral treaty such as the ICSID Convention discussed at p. 1628, to an ad hoc arbitral tribunal or to a special regime of arbitral tribunals established by the two states to hear specified categories of claims by nationals of one against the other. An example of the last approach is claims commissions established pursuant to international agreements, such as the General Claims Convention of 1923 between the United States and Mexico, 43 Stat. 1730, 4 Mallory 4441.

A more recent example is the Iran–United States Claims Tribunal established by the Algiers Accords in 1980, ending the Iranian hostage crisis. The crisis began on November 4, 1979, when Iranian militants seized the U.S. Embassy in Teheran, holding members of the U.S. diplomatic and consular staffs hostage for 444 days. As part of its efforts to obtain the release of the hostages, the Carter Administration froze assets of the Iranian Government in the United States. U.S. companies brought hundreds of lawsuits and effected judicial attachments of assets of the Government of Iran and its agencies. Eventually, the Algiers Accords between the United States and Iran were negotiated with the Algerian Government acting as intermediary. These Accords established procedures for the release of most frozen Iranian assets in exchange for the release of the U.S. hostages, lifted judicial attachments in return for the establishment of a Claims Tribunal, and created a Security Account from a portion of the frozen assets out of which the Tribunal was authorized to pay legitimate claims brought by U.S. nationals against Iran and by Iranian nationals against the United States.

Established at the Hague, the Tribunal consists of nine arbitrators, three appointed by the United States and three appointed by Iran. The six party-appointed arbitrators then chose three neutral arbitrators. The claims have been adjudicated by panels of three, two party-appointed and one neutral arbitrator.

As of February 1998, the Tribunal had received 3,952 claims and had concluded 3,918 cases by award, decision or order. Of those cases, the Tribunal has issued 584 awards and partial awards, totaling $2,140,348,092 for U.S. claimants and $1,010,986,784 for Iran and Iranian claimants. 13 No. 2 Mealey's Int'l Arb. Rep. (Feb. 1998). See also The Iran–United States Claims Tribunal: Its Contribution to the Law of State Responsibility (Lillich, Magraw & Bederman, eds., A.S.I.L. 1998), Aldrich, The Jurisprudence of the Iran–United States Claims Tribunal (1996). Brower, The Iran–United States Tribunal (Martinus Nijhoff 1998); Lillich, Iran–United States Claims Tribunal: Controversies, Cases and Contribution (1990); Westberg, International Transactions and Claims involving Government Parties: Case Law of the Iran–United States Claims Tribunal (1990). The Tribunal is still functioning in 2000.

Notes

1. Remedies available to a state whose national has suffered injury attributable to another state in violation of international law, including international claims procedures and other diplomatic steps or international responses, are discussed in Chapter 9. See also Restatement (Third) § 713. In the absence of a negotiated settlement, this state may invoke any measures provided for in a bilateral or multilateral treaty between the two states, including mediation, arbitration or adjudication. For example, bilateral treaties of friendship, commerce and navigation and bilateral investment treaties frequently provide for submission of controversies to international arbitration or, under some circumstances, to the International Court of Justice. See pp. 811 to 812. With respect to economic rights guaranteed to nationals of member states of the European Union, special remedies are available. See p. 401.

2. On December 28, 1998, the Republic of Guinea filed a state responsibility case against the Democratic Republic of Congo in the International Court of Justice. Guinea alleged that Ahmadou Sadio Diallo, a national of Guinea who had resided in the Republic of Congo for 32 years, was unlawfully imprisoned, without a trial, by the authorities of that state. It was also claimed that Diallo's investments, businesses and property were unlawfully expropriated. After Diallo attempted unsuccessfully, in local proceedings, to recover sums owed to him by companies owned by the government of the Congo and companies in which it was a shareholder, Guinea claims that, without judicial process, Diallo was expelled from the Republic of Congo. Guinea alleges a violation of "certain fundamental human rights, such as the principles that foreign nationals should be treated in accordance with the minimum standard of civilization, the obligation to respect the freedom and property of foreign nationals, and the right of foreign nationals accused of an offense to * * * a fair trial by an impartial court." A.S.I.L. Newsletter, March–April 1999, at 1, 3.

3. Disposition of claims made by or against the United States are summarized in 8 Whiteman, Digest of International Law 697–906 (1967) and later periodic Digests, and in the Current Practice section of the American Journal of International Law.

B. EXHAUSTION OF LOCAL REMEDIES

Generally a state may not espouse a claim based on injury inflicted on its national by another state unless its national has first exhausted all administrative and judicial remedies available in the defendant state. The rationale for this prerequisite is to give the allegedly responsible state an opportunity to remedy the wrong under its own domestic institutions before the claim can be elevated to the international plane. See generally Amerasinghe, Local Remedies in International Law (1990) and Trindade, The Application of the Rule of Exhaustion of Local Remedies in International Law (1983).

CASE CONCERNING ELETTRONICA SICULA S.P.A. (ELSI) (UNITED STATES OF AMERICA v. ITALY)

International Court of Justice, 1989.
1989 I.C.J. 15, 28 I.L.M. 1111.

[The United States instituted proceedings against Italy in respect of a dispute arising out of the requisition by the Government of Italy of the plant and related assets of Raytheon–Elsi S.p.A., previously known as Elettronica Sicula S.p.A. (ELSI), an Italian company. ELSI was 100 percent owned by the Raytheon Company ("Raytheon") and (to the extent of less than one percent of the ELSI shares) by Machlett Laboratories Incorporated ("Machlett"), a U.S. subsidiary of Raytheon. The United States alleged that the requisition deprived Raytheon of the right and capacity to conduct an orderly liquidation of ELSI's assets and resulted in losses to Raytheon of $12,679,000. The United States alleged that the requisition violated the Treaty of Friendship, Commerce and Navigation of 1948 and a Supplementary Agreement of 1951 between Italy and the United States. Following the requisition, ELSI's directors voted to file a voluntary petition in bankruptcy. In the bankruptcy proceedings conducted by an Italian court, what little remained of ELSI's assets after payment of bankruptcy administration expenses was distributed to creditors; Raytheon received nothing on its equity investment in ELSI and had to repay bank loans to ELSI that Raytheon had guaranteed. Prior to concluding on the merits that the actions of the Italian Government did not constitute breaches of the treaty or supplementary agreement, the Court discussed the contention by Italy that Raytheon had failed to exhaust its local remedies in Italy as follows (28 I.L.M. 1124–1128):]

48. It is common ground between the Parties that the Court has jurisdiction in the present case, under Article 36, paragraph 1, of its Statute, and Article XXVI of the Treaty of Friendship, Commerce and Navigation, of 2 June 1948 ("the FCN Treaty"), between Italy and the United States; which Article reads:

> Any dispute between the High Contracting Parties as to the interpretation or the application of this Treaty, which the High Contracting Parties shall not satisfactorily adjust by diplomacy, shall be submitted to the International Court of Justice, unless the High Contracting Parties shall agree to settlement by some other pacific means.

* * *

49. While the jurisdiction of the Chamber is not in doubt, an objection to the admissibility of the present case was entered by Italy in its Counter–Memorial, on the ground of an alleged failure of the two United States corporations, Raytheon and Machlett, on whose behalf the United States claim is brought, to exhaust the local remedies available to them in Italy. This objection, which the Parties agreed should be heard and determined in the framework of the merits, must, therefore, be considered at the outset.

50. The United States questioned whether the rule of the exhaustion of local remedies could apply at all to a case brought under Article XXVI of the

FCN Treaty. That Article, it was pointed out, is categorical in its terms, and unqualified by any reference to the local remedies rule; and it seemed right, therefore, to conclude that the parties to the FCN Treaty, had they intended the jurisdiction conferred upon the Court to be qualified by the local remedies rule in cases of diplomatic protection, would have used express words to that effect; as was done in an Economic Cooperation Agreement between Italy and the United States of America also concluded in 1948. The Chamber has no doubt that the parties to a treaty can therein either agree that the local remedies rule shall not apply to claims based on alleged breaches of that treaty; or confirm that it shall apply. Yet the Chamber finds itself unable to accept that an important principle of customary international law should be held to have been tacitly dispensed with, in the absence of any words making clear an intention to do so. This part of the United States response to the Italian objection must therefore be rejected.

51. The United States further argued that the local remedies rule would not apply in any event to the part of the United States claim which requested a declaratory judgment finding that the FCN Treaty had been violated. The argument of the United States is that such a judgment would declare that the United States' own rights under the FCN Treaty had been infringed; and that to such a direct injury the local remedies rule, which is a rule of customary international law developed in the context of the espousal by a State of the claim of one of its nationals, would not apply. The Chamber, however, has not found it possible in the present case to find a dispute over alleged violation of the FCN Treaty resulting in direct injury to the United States, that is both distinct from, and independent of, the dispute over the alleged violation in respect of Raytheon and Machlett. The case arises from a dispute which the Parties did not "satisfactorily adjust by diplomacy"; and that dispute was described in the 1974 United States claim made at the diplomatic level as a "claim of the Government of the United States of America on behalf of Raytheon Company and Machlett Laboratories, Incorporated". The Agent of the United States told the Chamber in the oral proceedings that "the United States seeks reparation for injuries suffered by Raytheon and Machlett". And indeed, as will appear later, the question whether there has been a breach of the FCN Treaty is itself much involved with the financial position of the Italian company, ELSI, which was controlled by Raytheon and Machlett.

52. Moreover, when the Court was, in the *Interhandel* case, faced with a not dissimilar argument by Switzerland that in that case its "principal submission" was in respect of a "direct breach of international law" and therefore not subject to the local remedies rule, the Court, having analysed that "principal submission", found that it was bound up with the diplomatic protection claim, and that the Applicant's arguments "do not deprive the dispute * * * of the character of a dispute in which the Swiss Government appears as having adopted the cause of its national * * *" *(Interhandel, Judgment, I.C.J. Reports 1959,* p. 28). In the present case, likewise, the Chamber has no doubt that the matter which colours and pervades the United States claim as a whole, is the alleged damage to Raytheon and Machlett, said to have resulted from the actions of the Respondent. Accordingly, the Chamber rejects the argument that in the present case there is a part of the Applicant's claim which can be severed so as to render the local remedies rule inapplicable to that part.

56. The damage claimed in this case to have been caused to Raytheon and Machlett is said to have resulted from the "losses incurred by ELSI's owners as a result of the involuntary change in the manner of disposing of ELSI's assets", and it is the requisition order that is said to have caused this change, and which is therefore at the core of the United States complaint. It was, therefore, right that any local remedy against the Italian authorities, calling in question the validity of the requisition of ELSI's plant and related assets, and raising the matter of the losses said to result from it, should be pursued by ELSI itself. In any event, both in order to attempt to recover control of ELSI's plant and assets, and to mitigate any damage flowing from the alleged frustration of the liquidation plan, the first step was for ELSI—and only ELSI could do this—to appeal to the Prefect against the requisition order. After the bankruptcy, however, the pursuit of local remedies was no longer a matter for ELSI's management but for the trustee in bankruptcy.

57. After the trustee in bankruptcy was appointed, he, acting for ELSI, by no means left the Italian authorities and courts unoccupied with ELSI's affairs. It was he who, under an Italian law of 1934, formally requested the Prefect to make his decision within 60 days of that request, which decision was itself the subject of an unsuccessful appeal by the Mayor to the President of Italy. On 16 June 1970, the trustee, acting for the bankrupt ELSI, brought a suit against the Acting Minister of the Interior and the Acting Mayor of Palermo, asking the court to adjudge that the defendants should

> "pay to the bankrupt estate of Raytheon–Elsi * * * damages for the illegal requisition of the plant machinery and equipment * * * for the period from April 1 to September 30, 1968, in the aggregate amount of Lire 2,395,561,600 plus interest * * *."

On 2 February 1973, the Court of Palermo * * * rejected the claim. The trustee in bankruptcy then appealed to the Court of Appeal of Palermo; which Court gave a judgment on 24 January 1974 which "partly revising the judgment of the Court of Palermo" ordered payment by the Ministry of the Interior of damages of 114,014,711 lire with interest. Appeal was taken finally to the Court of Cassation which upheld the decision of the Court of Appeal, by a decision of 26 April 1975.

58. It is pertinent to note that this claim for damages, as it came before the Court of Palermo in the action brought by the trustee, was described by that Court as being based *(inter alia)* upon the argument of the trustee in bankruptcy

> "that the requisition order caused an economic situation of such gravity that it immediately and directly triggered the bankruptcy of the company."

Similarly the Court of Appeal of Palermo had to consider whether there was a "causal link between the requisition order and the company's bankruptcy". It is thus apparent that the substance of the claim brought to the adjudication of the Italian courts is essentially the claim which the United States now brings before this Chamber. The arguments were different, because the municipal court was applying Italian law, whereas this Chamber applies international law; and, of course, the parties were different. Yet it would seem that the municipal courts had been fully seized of the matter which is the substance of the Applicant's claim before the Chamber. For both claims turn on the allegation that the requisition, by frustrating the orderly liquidation, triggered the bankruptcy, and so caused the alleged losses.

59. With such a deal of litigation in the municipal courts about what is in substance the claim now before the Chamber, it was for Italy to demonstrate that there was nevertheless some local remedy that had not been tried; or at least, not exhausted. This burden Italy never sought to deny. It contended that it was possible for the matter to have been brought before the municipal courts, citing the provisions of the treaties themselves, and alleging their violation. This was never done. In the actions brought before the Court of Palermo, and subsequently the Court of Appeal of Palermo, and the Court of Cassation, the FCN Treaty and its Supplementary Agreement were never mentioned. This is not surprising, for, as Italy recognizes, the way in which the matter was pleaded before the courts of Palermo was not for Raytheon and Machlett to decide but for the trustee. Furthermore, the local remedies rule does not, indeed cannot, require that a claim be presented to the municipal courts in a form, and with arguments, suited to an international tribunal, applying different law to different parties: for an international claim to be admissible, it is sufficient if the essence of the claim has been brought before the competent tribunals and pursued as far as permitted by local law and procedures, and without success.

60. The question, therefore, reduces itself to this: ought Raytheon and Machlett, suing in their own right, as United States corporations allegedly injured by the requisition of property of an Italian company whose shares they held, have brought an action in the Italian courts, within the general limitation—period (five years), alleging violation of certain provisions of the FCN Treaty between Italy and the United States; this mindful of the fact that the very question of the consequences of the requisition was already in issue in the action brought by its trustee in bankruptcy, and that any damages that might there be awarded would pass into the pool of realized assets, for an appropriate part of which Raytheon and Machlett had the right to claim as creditors?

* * *

62. * * * In the present case * * * it was for Italy to show, as a matter of fact, the existence of a remedy which was open to the United States stockholders and which they failed to employ. * * *

63. It is never easy to decide, in a case where there has in fact been much resort to the municipal courts, whether local remedies have truly been "exhausted". But in this case Italy has not been able to satisfy the Chamber that there clearly remained some remedy which Raytheon and Machlett, independently of ELSI, and of ELSI's trustee in bankruptcy, ought to have pursued and exhausted.

Notes

1. The Finnish Shipowners Case (Finland v. Great Britain), 3 U.N. Rep. Int'l Arbitral Awards, 1479 (1939), involved thirteen ships belonging to Finnish nationals that had been requisitioned and used by the British government in wartime from 1916–1917. The Finnish shipowners sought, and were denied, compensation under British law. The Finnish Government, believing the shipowners had ex-

hausted all local remedies, brought a claim on their behalf. The British Government, however, contended that the shipowners had not exhausted all local remedies, failing to appeal the decision of the Admiralty Transport Arbitration Board to the Court of Appeal. Sole Arbitrator Bagge disagreed, holding an attempted appeal would have been ineffective and unrealistic because the applicable law only allowed an appeal on points of law, not on findings of fact, such as the finding in this case that the ships had been requisitioned by Russia, not Great Britain. In sum, the Arbitrator held that there is no need to exhaust local remedies if it is established that such resort would be futile or that such remedies are nonexistent.

If an alien claimant loses on a point of law before a court of first instance, is there an obligation to appeal even if the appellate courts regard the applicable point of law as well settled? See the Panevezys–Saldutiskis Ry. Case (Estonia v. Lithuania), P.C.I.J., Ser. A/B, No. 76 (1939), in which the Court stated that if it could be substantiated that the highest Lithuanian court had already given a decision in a previous case adverse to the Estonian company's claim, there would be no need to appeal in order to satisfy the local remedies rule. Id. at 18. The Court held, however, that the highest Lithuanian court had not yet pronounced upon the applicable point of law, and the Estonian claim was rejected. Id. at 20–21. See Restatement (Third) § 713, Comment *f*, § 902, Comment *k*.

If it were shown that the Finnish shipowners had lost before the Arbitration Board because they had failed to call an available witness, would the Arbitrator have held that local remedies had been exhausted? See the Ambatielos Claim (Greece v. United Kingdom), 12 U.N.Rep. Int'l Arb. Awards 83, decided in 1956 by a special arbitral commission, which held that failure to call an essential witness in a British proceeding necessitated the rejection of a Greek national's claim. See also Bagge, Intervention on the Ground of Damage Caused to Nationals, with Particular Reference to Exhaustion of Local Remedies and the Rights of Shareholders, [1958] Brit. Y.B.I.L. 162, 167–68.

2. An exception to the local remedies rule may be applicable if "the state of the alien's nationality, which has espoused his claim, is asserting on its own behalf a separate and preponderant claim for direct injury to it arising out of the same wrongful conduct." Restatement (Second) § 208(c). See the Interhandel Case (Switzerland v. United States) (Preliminary Objections), 1959 I.C.J. 6.

C. STATE WAIVER OF EXHAUSTION OF LOCAL REMEDIES RULE

A state may waive the requirement of exhaustion of local remedies, allowing claims against it to be brought by another state directly to an international tribunal. See Article V of the Convention establishing the Mexico–United States General Claims Commission, Sept. 8, 1923, 43 Stat. 1730 T.S. 678, 4 Malloy 4441, providing that no claim should be "disallowed or rejected by the Commission by the application of the general principle of international law that the legal remedies must be exhausted as a condition precedent to the validity or allowance of any claim." Where two states have agreed to arbitrate existing disputes, will they be held impliedly to have waived the local remedies rule? Authority on this point is not uniform. Amerasinghe concludes that "it would seem the better view is that whether such treaties are signed before or after the disputes arise, no waiver of the local remedies may be generally implied," citing, inter alia, the *ELSI* case, p. 756. Amerasinghe, Local Remedies in International Law 258 (1990). Compare Garcia–Amador's view that "there can be no hard and fast rule applicable to every case, for it will always have to be ascertained whether the true purpose of the treaty was to exclude the application of the [local remedies] principle in the claim under consideration." Garcia–Amador, Sohn & Baxter, Recent Codification of the Law of State Responsibility for Injuries to Aliens (1974). An example involving an implied waiver is the Claims Settlement Declaration establishing the Iran–United States Claims Tribunal. The Declaration called for submission of claims by nationals of either party to arbitration "whether or not filed with any court" and stated that claims referred to the arbitration tribunal shall "be considered excluded from the jurisdiction of the courts of Iran or of the United States, or of any other court." Award No. 93–2–3 [1983], 4 Iran–U.S. Claims Tribunal Reports 102 (1983).

The implied waiver issue may also be presented if a state agrees in a contract with an alien to arbitrate any future dispute that may arise under the contract. There is substantial support for the position that there is generally an implied waiver in these circumstances although under certain circumstances the waiver may be subject to limitations. See Amerasinghe, supra at 260–268. Article 26 of the ICSID Convention, see p. 1628 infra, states as follows:

> Consent of the parties to arbitration under this Convention shall, unless otherwise stated, be deemed consent to such arbitration to the exclusion of any other remedy. A Contracting State may require the exhaustion of local administrative or judicial remedies as a condition of its consent to arbitration under this Convention.

The Report of the ICSID Executive Directors on the Convention comments that

> it may be presumed that when a State and an investor agree to have recourse to arbitration, and do not reserve the right to have recourse to other remedies or require prior exhaustion of other remedies, the intention of the parties is to have recourse to arbitration to the exclusion of any other remedy.

Doc. ICSID/2 at 10–11.

D. WAIVER BY ALIEN OF CLAIM OR RIGHT TO DIPLOMATIC PROTECTION

It is generally agreed that if an alien injured by a state in a manner wrongful under international law waives or settles the claim prior to diplomatic intervention by the state of which the alien is a national, then the waiver or settlement is effective as a defense on behalf of the respondent state, provided the waiver or settlement is not made under duress. The result appears to be different if the waiver or purported settlement is made by the alien after the alien's state has espoused the claim because that state enjoys exclusive control once it has asserted a claim against the respondent state. See Restatement (Third) § 713, Reporters' Note 6.

More troublesome problems have been raised by the efforts of Latin American states to avoid foreign diplomatic intervention on behalf of an injured alien through various devices, including waivers required of aliens in advance, which limit their rights to those available under domestic law and secured by domestic legal remedies. As noted above at p. 748, such efforts have been reflected in widespread adoption of statutory and constitutional provisions embodying the Calvo Doctrine.

A number of states have gone beyond the enactment of provisions of law embodying the Calvo Doctrine, by obligating aliens doing business under contract with the state to adhere to a so-called "Calvo clause." Under this clause, the alien must agree to submit all disputes to the courts of the host state and renounce all claims to diplomatic intercession by the state of which the alien is a national. Shea, The Calvo Clause 24 (1955).

An agreement between the North American Dredging Company and the Government of Mexico involved in the North American Dredging Co. Case (United States v. Mexico), General Claims Commission, 1926 [1927] Opinions of Commissioners, 21, 22, 4 U.N. Rep. Int'l Arb. Awards 26, 26–27 (1951), contained a Calvo clause requiring the contractor to submit solely to the laws of Mexico applicable to Mexican nationals and to waive all rights of diplomatic intercession by the United States with respect to the fulfillment of the contract. The Commission held that the contractor had not waived his right to protection by the United States in matters not connected with the "fulfillment, execution, or enforcement" of the contract, thereby retaining the right of his Government to extend protection to him against violations of international law. See also Mexican Union Railway, Ltd. Case (Great Britain v. Mexico), Mexico–Great Britain Claims Commission, 1930, 5 U.N. Rep. Int'l Arb. Awards 115, 120, in which the majority of the Commission stated their conviction that no person could "deprive the Government of his country of its undoubted right to apply international remedies to violations of international law committed to his hurt. For the Government the contract is *res inter alios acta*, by which its liberty of action can not be prejudiced." See Note, The Calvo Clause, 6 Texas Int'l L. Forum 289 (1971).

Insofar as the Calvo clause encompasses the duty of an alien to exhaust local remedies before a claim may arise under international law or diplomatic intervention properly be undertaken (see p. 755), the clause merely restates the otherwise existing obligations of the alien. See Lipstein, The Place of the Calvo Clause in International Law, [1945] Brit. Y.B.I.L. 130. The proper interpretation of the Calvo clause, the extent to which it may be given effect by an international tribunal, and the ability of a private individual to prevent his state from entering a claim on his behalf are discussed in Shea, supra, *passim*.

Notes

1. The United States and certain other states deny the validity of the Calvo Doctrine and the Calvo clause on the ground that the right of diplomatic protection is not the injured national's to waive. See [1976] Digest of U.S. Practice in Int'l Law 435. Is this position sound? Because the state's claim is essentially derivative, an individual can waive or settle any claim based on the injury attributable to the foreign state after the injury is incurred and before any intercession by the state of which the claimant is a national, and this waiver or settlement will defeat the state claim. See p. 753. To this extent, therefore, an agreement between a national and a foreign state can preempt the state's opportunity to assert a diplomatic claim for injury to its national. This being so, why can the injured national not also effectively defeat the state's right to

intervene before the fact through execution of an agreement containing a Calvo clause?

2. The parties to the International Convention on the Settlement of Investment Disputes between States and Nationals of Other States, 1965, T.I.A.S. No. 6090, 17 U.S.T. 1270, 575 U.N.T.S. 159, have agreed not to espouse diplomatically claims of their nationals in respect of disputes submitted to arbitration under the Convention. See p. 1628.

3. For further discussion of the Calvo clause see Manning–Cabrol, The Imminent Death of the Calvo Clause and the Rebirth of the Calvo Principle: Equality of Foreign and National Investors, 26 Law & Pol'y Int'l Bus. 1169 (1995); Wiesner, ANCOM: A New Attitude Toward Foreign Investment?, 24 U. Miami Inter–Am. L. Rev. 435 (1993); and Sunkel, Democratization, Economic Changes and Supranational Institutions in Latin America, 86 A.S.I.L. Proc. 25 (1992).

E. NATIONALITY OF CLAIMANT

A state may generally assert a claim against another state arising out of an injury to an individual or a juridical entity, such as a corporation, only if the injured party has the nationality of the claimant state. The principles governing the circumstances under which an individual or a corporation may be treated as a national of the claimant state for various purposes, including the law of state responsibility, have been examined in Chapter 6 at p. 425. A state allegedly responsible for an injury to an alien with multiple nationalities may refuse a claim or intercession by another state if the injured person (i) is also a national of the respondent state or (ii) is also a national of both a third state and the respondent state and the respondent state treats the person as its national for purposes of the conduct causing the injury. A state claim or intercession may not be refused, however, if the nationality of the claimant state is "dominant" as a result of the injured alien's stronger ties to that state based on all relevant factors, such as extended residence, family relationships and the like. See p. 436. Generally, no state may assert a claim or intercede diplomatically on behalf of a stateless person, but the human rights of a stateless person are protected under international human rights law, discussed at p. 768, which applies to all persons subject to a state's jurisdiction regardless of their nationality. Restatement (Third) § 713, Comments *d* and *e*.

If the nationality of a claimant changes after the injury on which the claim is based has occurred, or the claim is assigned to a person of another nationality, or the claimant dies and leaves heirs of a different nationality, is it likely that the claim will be espoused by any government? The position of the U.S. Department of State was formulated as follows by an Assistant Legal Adviser in 1960:

> * * * Under generally accepted principles of international law and practice, a claim may properly be espoused by one government against another government only on behalf of a national of the government espousing the claim, who had that status at the time the claim arose and continuously thereafter to the date of presentation of the claim. It has been the long-standing practice of the Department to decline to espouse claims which have not been continuously owned by United States nationals.

8 Whiteman 1243. See also 5 Hackworth 804–09. The rule, of course, may be modified by agreement between the governments of the claimant and the respondent states.

F. ATTRIBUTION OF CONDUCT TO A STATE

1. *Acts of De Jure Agents*

A state will be responsible for injury to the person or property of an alien only if the act or omission causing the injury is attributable to the state. The general rules relating to the attribution of conduct to the state have been considered in Chapter 9. In addition to being responsible for violations of its obligations under international law resulting from action or inaction of the executive, legislative or judicial branch of its government or the government of any political subdivision, a state may be responsible if the violation results from action or inaction by any "organ, agency, official, employee, or other agent of a government or of any political subdivision, acting within the scope of authority or under color of such authority." Restatement (Third) § 207. For commentary regarding attribution of conduct to a state, see Christenson, The Doctrine of Attribution in State Responsibility, in International Law of State Responsibility for Injuries to Aliens 321 (Lillich ed. 1983).

Notes

1. There is ample support in diplomatic practice and arbitral awards for attribution to the state of conduct of minor officials whether of the national government or political subdivisions. A well known example of attribution of the act of an official is the William T. Way Claim (United States v. Mexico), 4 U.N. Rep. Int'l Arbitral Awards 391 (1928). The United States–Mexico General Claims Commission held the state of Mexico responsible for the actions of a local mayor who had issued an invalid arrest warrant which led to the killing of a U.S. citizen by Mexican law enforcement authorities. The consistent practice of the United States has been to accept responsibility under international law for acts or omissions of agents of its political subdivisions and to require such acceptance by the national government of foreign states. The United States paid an indemnity to Italy because authorities of the City of New Orleans failed to prevent the lynching of Italian nationals being held for trial. Moore, Digest of International Law 837 (1906). Attribution of failure to act is discussed in Christenson, Attributing Acts of Omission to the State, 12 Mich. J. Int'l L. 312 (1991).

2. Article 10 of the 1996 Draft Articles on State Responsibility, prepared under the auspices of the International Law Commission, specifies that "conduct of an organ of a State, * * * such organ having acted in that capacity, shall be considered as an act of the State under international law even if, in the particular case, the organ exceeded its competence according to internal law or contravened instructions concerning its activity." 37 I.L.M. 440, 444; Report of the International Law Commission on the Work of its Forty–Eighth Session, U.N.G.A.O.R., 51st Sess., Supp. No. 10, U.N. Doc. A/51/10 (1996).

3. A state would be responsible for acts of an entity or a group that is not part of the governmental structure but has been empowered to exercise functions akin to those normally exercised by the state. The International Court of Justice held in the Case Concerning United States Diplomatic and Consular Staff in Tehran, 1980 I.C.J.Rep. 3, 29, that the conduct of the militants who had seized the

U.S. embassy and staff "might be considered as itself directly imputable to the Iranian State only if it were established that, in fact, * * * the militants acted on behalf of the State * * *."

4. Private persons employed by a state to abduct a person from the territory of another may have their conduct attributed to the state on whose behalf the abduction was conducted. See the *Eichmann* case, p. 1136. Private persons may also assume public functions in times of emergency. In these cases, there may be no formal link with the machinery of the state. As indicated in Article 8 of the International Law Commission's Draft Articles on State Responsibility, quoted in the Documents Supplement, the Commission considered that the state should bear responsibility if the persons were in fact exercising governmental authority and the circumstances justified such exercise.

2. *Acts of De Facto Agents*

CARON, THE BASIS OF RESPONSIBILITY: ATTRIBUTION AND OTHER TRANSSUBSTANTIVE RULES

in the Iran–United States Claims Tribunal: Its Contribution to the Law of State Responsibility 138–142 (1998)(footnotes omitted).

A clear provision in the internal law of the State involved that an actor de jure is a part of the government or is authorized to exercise elements of governmental authority provides a neat administrable rule of attribution. Beyond that * * *, however, the principal-agent relationship must be established on a case-by-case, de facto basis. The revolutionary institutions that arose after the [1979 Iranian] revolution in parallel to the official institutions squarely posed issues of de facto agency for the [Iran–United States Claims] Tribunal.

* * *

In *Yeager and Iran* * * * the issue was clearly presented. In that case, the claimant [an American businessman working for Bell Helicopter in Teheran] argued that he was constructively expelled from Iran by members of the "Revolutionary Guards" shortly after the success of the revolution in February 1979. For the Tribunal, "[t]he question then arises whether the acts at issue are attributable to Iran under international law." Describing the Revolutionary Guards and Committees, the Tribunal wrote:

> Many of the Ayatollah Khomeini's supporters were organized in local revolutionary committees, so called Komitehs, which often emerged from the "neighborhood committees" formed before the victory of the revolution. These Komitehs served as local security forces in the immediate aftermath of the revolution. It is reported that they made arrests, confiscated property, and took people to prisons * * * In May 1979, the Komitehs were officially recognized by decree under the name Revolutionary Guard. However, as early as 10 February 1979, groups loyal to the Ayatollah Khomeini were sometimes referred to as "Revolutionary Guards."

As to the attribution of the acts of the Revolutionary Guards in February 1979, the Tribunal, noting the differences between the de jure and de facto tests, concluded:

42. * * * While there is some doubt as to whether revolutionary 'Komitehs' or 'Guards' can be considered "organs" of the Government of Iran, since they were not formally recognized during the period relevant to this case, [attribution] of acts to the State is not limited to acts of organs formally recognized under internal law. Otherwise a State could avoid responsibility under international law merely by invoking its internal law. It is generally accepted in international law that a State is also responsible for acts of persons, if it is established that those persons were in fact acting on behalf of the State.

43. The Tribunal finds sufficient evidence in the record to establish a presumption that revolutionary 'Komitehs' or 'guards' after 11 February 1979 were acting on behalf of the new government * * *.

The Tribunal's holding regarding the Revolutionary Guards and Committees was subsequently followed in other cases.

Notes

1. Article 8 of the I.L.C.'s 1996 Draft Articles on State Responsibility deal with attribution of de facto agents as follows:

> The conduct of a person or group of persons shall * * * be considered as an act of the State under international law if:
>
> (a) it is established that such person or group of persons was in fact acting on behalf of that State; or
>
> (b) such person or group of persons was in fact exercising elements of the governmental authority in the absence of the official authorities and in circumstances which justified the exercise of those elements of authority.

37 I.L.M. 440, 444 (1998).

2. For further discussion of the attribution to the Government of Iran of de facto agents see Aldrich, What Constitutes a Compensable Taking of Property? The Decisions of the Iran–United States Claims Tribunal, 88 A.J.I.L. 585, 598–603 (1994).

G. CIRCUMSTANCES UNDER WHICH OTHERWISE UNLAWFUL CONDUCT CAUSING INJURY TO AN ALIEN IS NOT WRONGFUL

As discussed in Chapter 9 at p. 701, conduct attributable to a state causing damage to an alien that would otherwise violate international law may be found not to be wrongful because of special circumstances, such as force majeure, distress and necessity. In the context of state responsibility for injury to aliens, circumstances involving an exercise of the police power or power to regulate the state's currency may preclude finding the exercise of that power causing injury to an alien to be wrongful. For example, conduct that is reasonably necessary for the maintenance of public order, safety or health or the enforcement of laws of the state that do not depart from the international minimum standard of justice would normally not be violative of international law.

Conduct of a state reasonably necessary to control the value of its currency or to protect its foreign exchange resources is normally lawful even though it results in injury to an alien's economic interests, subject to the rules set down in the Articles of the International Monetary Fund if the state is a party thereto. See p. 1611. For example, devaluation of currency that results in an economic loss to an alien does not generally violate international law and the same is usually true with respect to application to an alien of a requirement that foreign funds held within the territory of the state be surrendered against payment in local currency at the official rate of exchange. Restatement (Second) § 198 (1965).

Moreover, conduct attributable to a state and causing injury to an alien will generally not be deemed wrongful if it is reasonably necessary to protect life or property in case of disaster or other serious emergency. See the discussion of distress and necessity at p. 704.

Conduct attributable to a state that would otherwise be lawful under the foregoing principles may not be so if it involves unreasonable discrimination against nationals of a state. See Restatement (Third) § 712, Comments *g* and *i* and discussion at pp. 778–779.

Application of the rules relating to circumstances under which a reasonable exercise of police powers or currency control preclude a finding of wrongfulness may be closely related to or may overlap determination of whether there has been a taking of property of an alien, which under customary international law principles would call for compensation to the injured alien. The line between a taking of property and permissible regulation of an alien is discussed at p. 785.

SECTION 4. SUBSTANTIVE BASES OF RESPONSIBILITY

A. GENERAL

RESTATEMENT (THIRD)

§ 711. State Responsibility for Injury to Nationals of Other States

A state is responsible under international law for injury to a national of another state caused by an official act or omission that violates

(a) a human right that, under § 701, a state is obligated to respect for all persons subject to its authority;

(b) a personal right that, under international law, a state is obligated to respect for individuals of foreign nationality; or

(c) a right to property or another economic interest that, under international law, a state is obligated to respect for persons, natural or juridical, of foreign nationality, as provided in § 712.

Comment:

a. Human rights, "denial of justice," and injury. * * * Any injury to an alien for which a state is responsible under this chapter has sometimes been characterized as a "denial of justice." More commonly the phrase "denial of justice" is used narrowly, to refer only to injury consisting of, or resulting from, denial of access to courts, or denial of procedural fairness and due process in relation to judicial proceedings, whether criminal or civil. As regards natural persons, most injuries that in the past would have been characterized as "denials of justice" are now subsumed as human rights violations under clause (a). Clauses (b) and (c) include injuries that are not commonly recognized as violations of human rights but for which a state is nonetheless responsible under international law when the victim is a foreign national. See Comment *e* and § 712.

b. International human rights as minimum standard. Under international law, a state is responsible for injury to foreign nationals resulting from violation of their internationally recognized human rights, as well as for injury resulting from violation of other interests for which international law provides special protections to foreign nationals. Under clause (a), the state is responsible for injury due to violation of those rights which the state is obligated to respect for all persons subject to its authority, whether pursuant to international human rights agreements to which it is party, or under the customary law of human rights (§ 702); aliens enjoy these rights equally with the state's own nationals. Clause (b) declares that, in respect of foreign nationals, a state is responsible also for injury due to violation of those internationally recognized * * * [personal] rights that may not fall under § 702 and would not be protected by international law as regards the state's own nationals in the absence of international agreement. Under clause (c), a state is responsible for injury to property and other economic interests of foreign nationals that may not be recognized as human rights, and that are protected for foreign juridical persons as well as for foreign individuals. See § 712. A foreign national may also enjoy other rights under special treaties, such as those of the European [Union]; under the Convention or the Protocol relating to the Status of Refugees * * *; under a treaty of friendship, commerce, and navigation [or bilateral investment treaty] between the state of his nationality and the state in which he resides or is present; or under the domestic law of the state of his residence or of another state.

c. Obligation to respect human rights of foreign nationals as customary law. A state's responsibility to individuals of foreign nationality under customary law includes the obligation to respect the civil and political rights articulated in the principal international human rights instruments—the Universal Declaration and the International Covenant on Civil and Political Rights—as rights of human beings generally * * *, but not political rights that are recognized as human rights only in relation to a person's country of citizenship, such as the right to vote and hold office, or the right to return to one's country. * * * Thus, a state party to the Covenant on Civil and Political Rights is responsible for any violation of any of its provisions in relation to any human being subject to its jurisdiction, regardless of the individual's nationality; but every state, whether or not a party to the Covenant, is responsible for denying to nationals of another state any right specified in the Covenant that is guaranteed by rules of customary law relating to the protection of foreign nationals. Customary law also holds a state responsible for "consistent patterns of gross violations" of human rights of any persons subject to its jurisdiction. § 702(g). As regards foreign nationals, however, a state is responsible even for a single violation of many of the civil and political rights proclaimed in the Universal Declaration (other than those applicable only to citizens), even if it is not "gross." See § 702, Comment *m*.

The Universal Declaration proclaims also certain economic, social, and cultural rights, later developed in the Covenant on Economic, Social and Cultural Rights. * * * The traditional responsibility of states under customary law does not include the obligation to extend such rights to foreign nationals. See Reporters' Note 2. Customary law, however, requires that foreign nationals be accorded the equal protection of the laws and forbids unreasonable distinctions between aliens and nationals. Distinctions between aliens and nationals in regard to some economic, social or cultural rights may not be unreasonable. See Restatement § 701, Comments *f* and *g* and Reporters' Note 3.

Notes

1. The Restatement Reporters state that "it is generally accepted that states may invoke recognized international human rights standards on behalf of their nationals; attempts to invoke protections going beyond international human rights standards, as in clauses (b) and (c) of this section, might be resisted by some states." Reporters' Note 1. The differences of view with respect to the content and doctrinal basis of the customary law of state responsibility and the lack of success in efforts at codification, discussed at p. 747, provide the backdrop for the Reporters' caveat with respect to acceptance of the protections reflected in clauses (b) and (c). To the extent that conduct causing injury to an alien constitutes a violation of a human right recognized in the Covenant on Civil and Political Rights or under customary international law, these differences of view appear to have been sapped of much of their significance.

2. Following the invasion by Iraq of Kuwait, the U.N. Security Council declared Iraq responsible under international law for its widespread violations of the human and property rights of nationals of Kuwait and many third countries caused by the invasion and occupation. S/RES/674 (1990), 29 I.L.M. 1561 (1990). Subsequently, the Security Council adopted Resolution 687 (1991), S/RES/687, 30 I.L.M. 847 (1991), paragraph 16 of which reaffirmed that responsibility and established institutions and procedures for processing, evaluating and payment of claims. In paragraph 17 of the resolution, the Council declared "that all Iraqi statements made since 2 August 1990 repudiating its foreign debt are null and void," and demanded that "Iraq adhere scrupulously to all of its obligations concerning servicing and repayment of its foreign debt." The Council also decided, in paragraph 18 of the resolution, "to create a fund to pay compensation for claims that fall within the scope of paragraph 16 * * * and to establish a Commission that will administer the fund."

In paragraph 19 of the resolution, the Security Council directed the Secretary General

> to develop and present to the Security Council for decision * * * recommendations for the fund to meet the requirement for the payment of claims established in accordance with paragraph 18 * * *, and for a programme to implement the decisions in paragraphs 16, 17 and 18 * * *, including: administration of the fund; mechanisms for determining the appropriate level of Iraq's contribution to the fund based on a percentage of the value of the exports of petroleum and petroleum products from Iraq not to exceed a figure to be suggested to the Council by the Secretary–General, taking into account

the requirements of the people of Iraq, Iraq's payment capacity as assessed in conjunction with the international financial institutions taking into consideration external debt service, and the needs of the Iraqi economy; arrangements for ensuring that payments are made to the fund; the process by which funds will be allocated and claims paid; * * * and the composition of the [Compensation] Commission. * * *

The United Nations Compensation Fund is administered by the United Nations Compensation Commission [UNCC], established by Security Council Resolution 692 (1991) of May 2, 1991, which functions under the authority of the Security Council. The Commission is charged with responsibility for dealing with a variety of complex administrative, financial, legal and policy issues, including the mechanism for determining the level of contribution by Iraq to the Fund; the allocation of funds and payments of claims; the procedures for evaluating losses, listing claims and verifying their validity; and resolving disputed claims. See Report of the Secretary General Pursuant to Paragraph 19 of Security Council Resolution 687 (1991) S/22559 2 May 1991, 30 I.L.M. 1706 (1991). The Security Council determined in Resolution 705 S/RES/705 (1991), on May 30, 1991, that the compensation to be paid by Iraq into the United Nations Compensation Fund shall not exceed 30 percent of the annual value of the exports of petroleum and petroleum products from Iraq. 30 I.L.M. 1715. See Report by the Secretary–General Pursuant to Paragraph 5 of Security Council Resolution 706 (1991), S/23006 4 September 1991, 30 I.L.M. 1722. Initially, Iraq refused to resume international sales of oil on the ground that the U.N. compensation arrangements constituted an interference in Iraq's internal affairs. After 1993, Iraqi oil sales authorized by the U.N. Security Council were resumed sporadically. In 1996, Dr. Norbert Wuhler, chief of legal services of the United Nations Compensation Commission, stated that if Iraqi oil sales were to return to their pre-Gulf War level, "it would be expected that Iraq's yearly revenue from oil sales would approach $20 to $21 billion; 30 percent would provide the UNCC $6 billion a year." 11 No. 10 Mealey's Int'l Arb. Rep. 19 (Oct. 1996). Sales at this level would make a substantial contribution to providing the UNCC with the funds necessary to satisfy the estimated $100 to $200 billion in losses caused by Iraq's violations of international law. See Owen, Note: Between Iraq and a Hard Place: The U.N. Compensation Commission and Its Treatment of Gulf War Claims, 31 Vand. J. Transnat'l L. 499 (1998).

Unfortunately, it did not prove to be the case that the allocated oil revenues would soon satisfy claimants. The fund grew more slowly and the enormous volume of claims took longer to process and pay than expected. The Compensation Fund generated by the "oil for food" program as of June 28, 1999, was $575 million, allowing the UNCC to expand its payments to successful claimants, 14 No. 7 Mealey's Int'l Arb. Rep. 15 (July 1999), including awarding $187.5 million to four corporate claimants in July 1998. These cases were chosen by the UNCC as "test" cases in hope that they would help resolve several legal issues that are relevant to deciding thousands of remaining corporate claims against Iraq. Alford, U.N. Commission Awards $187 Million Against Iraq, A.S.I.L. Newsletter, July–Aug. 1998, at 1,8. As of 2000, the UNCC had processed more than 2.5 million claims and had awarded more than $15.5 billion to successful claimants. Approximately 13,000 claims for $268 billion remained to be resolved by the UNCC's deadline for completion of mid–2003. See the UNCC website at http://www.unog.ch/uncc/status.htm. Mealey's International Arbitration Reports contain updates on the work of the UNCC, including commentary, as well as excerpts from current cases.

For further discussion of the U.N. Compensation Commission, see Bederman, The United Nations Compensation Commission and the Tradition of International Claims Settlement, 27 N.Y.U. J. Int'l L. & Pol. 1 (1994); Crook, The United Nations Compensation Commission—A New Structure to Enforce State Responsibility, 87 A.J.I.L. 144 (1993) and Lillich, Brower, Bettauer, Magraw, Glod and others, Panel Discussion on Claims Against Iraq: The U.N. Compensation Commission and Other Remedies, 86 A.S.I.L.Proc. 477–500 (1992).

B. DENIAL OF PROCEDURAL JUSTICE

The Restatement Reporters cite several examples of injuries that would be treated under traditional customary international law as unlawful failures to afford a minimum standard of justice to an alien and that under contemporary law would be accepted as violations of human rights under the Covenant on Civil and Political Rights or customary international law: (1) denials of due process in criminal proceedings (e.g., arbitrary arrest; unlawful or prolonged detention; unreasonably delayed or unfair trial; being tried twice for the same offense; denial of the right to defend oneself and confront witnesses or to communicate with representatives of one's government; and (2) arbitrary and unreasonable use of force by governmental representatives (e.g., excessive use of force by state officials; inhuman treatment and torture to elicit "confession"). Restatement (Third) § 711, Reporters' Note 2. A well known example is the B.E. Chattin Claim (United States v. Mexico), 4 U.N. Rep. Int'l Arbitral Awards 282 (1927). The Restatement Reporters further comment on the relevant state practice and decisions as follows:

> Claims were also made on behalf of aliens for other actions violating rights later recognized in the Universal Declaration [of Human Rights], such as freedom of speech, freedom of religion, freedom to travel within a country, and the right to marry or obtain a divorce. See, e.g., 8 Whiteman, Digest 402; L. of N. Doc. C.26.M.21. 1929, II, 32; Freeman 511. There is some authority in law to support such claims, but these freedoms might be restricted to resident aliens, and might be denied in time of national emergency.
>
> There were also claims for injury due to denial to foreign nationals of benefits enjoyed by nationals, such as social security or aid to indigents or incompetents, or due to other discrimination between aliens and nationals or against aliens of particular nationality. See 3 Hackworth 650–52; 8 Whiteman, Digest 387. International law forbids some such discriminations, but others are permitted. See § 712, Comments *f* and *i*. Compare the corresponding jurisprudence under the "equal protection" clause of the Fourteenth Amendment of the United States Constitution, § 722.
>
> There appears to be no record, however, of a state objecting to imprisonment of its nationals for debt, although that is prohibited by Article 11 of the Covenant on Civil and Political Rights. * * *

Restatement (Third) § 711, Reporters' Note 2.

There are denials of procedural justice that would be unlawful under customary international law but that would not rise to the level of human rights violations. An example would be denial of access to domestic courts in civil proceedings for the determination of an alien's rights. Van Bokkelen Case, 2 Moore, Int'l Arb. 1807 (1888). International agreements commonly guarantee reasonable access to a court or other tribunal on the same basis as nationals. See, e.g., Friendship, Commerce and Navigation Treaty between the United States and the Netherlands, March 27, 1956, art. V(1), 8 U.S.T. 2043, T.I.A.S. No. 3942, 285 U.N.T.S. 231. See also Council of Europe, Convention for the Protection of Human Rights and Fundamental Freedoms, art. 6(1), Eur. T.S. No. 5 (1950), Cmd. No. 8969 (T.S. No. 71) (1953), 213 U.N.T.S. 221; U.N. Universal Declaration of Human Rights, Art. 10 (1948), [1948] U.N.Yb.Hum. Rights 458; American Declaration of The Rights and Duties of Man, art. XVIII (1948), 43 A.J.I.L.Supp. 133, 136 (1949), U.N. Covenant on Civil and Political Rights arts. 9(3) and 14. Consider the relationship between state immunity, discussed at p. 1197, and denial of procedural justice. Can the dismissal of an action by an alien against the state on the ground of immunity give rise to a proper claim of denial of justice? See Restatement (Second) § 180(2) (1965).

It is well settled that mere error in a decision or relatively minor procedural irregularities do not constitute unlawful denials of procedural justice. The injustice must be egregious. The decision must be "so obviously wrong that it cannot have been made in good faith and with reasonable care," or "a serious miscarriage of justice" must otherwise be "clear." See e.g., Herrera v. Canevaro & Co., [1927–28] Ann.Dig. 219 (Sup. Ct. Peru). Examples of procedural insufficiencies or mistakes for which states have not been held responsible under international law include failure of a witness to take an oath, incorrect but good faith misapplication or misinterpretation of the law, and improper dismissal of a case for lack of jurisdiction (when another forum was available). Restatement (Third) § 711, Reporters' Note 2(B).

C. FAILURE TO PROTECT ALIENS OR TO APPREHEND AND PROSECUTE THOSE WHO WRONGFULLY INFLICT INJURY ON ALIENS

The Restatement (Second) § 183 provides: "A state is responsible under international law for injury to the person or property of an alien caused by conduct that is not itself attributable to that state, if

> (a) the conduct is either (i) criminal under the law of the state, (ii) generally recognized as criminal under the laws of states that have reasonably developed legal systems, or (iii) an offense against public order, and
>
> (b) either (i) the injury results from the failure of the state to take reasonable measures to prevent the conduct causing the injury, or (ii) the state fails to take reasonable steps to detect, prosecute, and impose an appropriate penalty on the person or persons responsible for the conduct if it falls within Clause (a)(i)."

The Restatement (Third) treats injuries to aliens of these types as violations of international law that fall short of violations of human rights and that are therefore covered by § 711(b). Restatement (Third) § 711, Reporters' Note 2(B).

Notes

1. In the Case Concerning United States Diplomatic and Consular Staff in Tehran, 1980 I.C.J. Rep. 3, 35–36, the I.C.J. held that after the U.S. Embassy was seized and diplomats had been held as hostages by the militants, the Iranian Government had a duty to make every effort to bring the hostage situation to a prompt end, which it clearly failed to fulfill.

2. In the William E. Chapman Claim (United States v. Mexico), the United States–Mexico General Claims Commission held Mexico liable for failure of Mexican authorities (i) to take appropriate steps to protect a U.S. Consul who was shot and seriously wounded in Puerto Mexico after threats to U.S. diplomatic and consular representatives had been communicated to Mexican authorities and (ii) to take proper steps to apprehend and punish the person who did the shooting. 4 U.N.Rep. Int'l Arb. Awards 632. See also Laura M.B. Janes Claim (United States v. Mexico), in which the General Claims Commission made an award based on the failure of the Mexican authorities to take prompt and effective action to apprehend and punish the killer of Janes. 4 U.N. Rep. Int'l Arb. Awards 82.

LILLICH & PAXMAN, STATE RESPONSIBILITY FOR INJURIES TO ALIENS OCCASIONED BY TERRORIST ACTIVITIES

26 Am.U.L.Rev. 217–221, 245–249, 276, 305–307 (1977) (footnotes omitted).

Scarcely a day passes without press reports of another act of transnational terrorism, whether it be an aerial hijacking like the June 1976 takeover of the Air France airliner flown to Uganda, a political kidnapping such as the spectacular seizure in December 1975 of the oil ministers from the Organization of Petroleum Exporting Countries (OPEC) in Vienna, or an indiscriminate act of violence designed to achieve publicity for its perpetrators or their cause. Such acts obviously present a serious challenge to the existing international legal order. At the outset, it has become apparent that, in Brian Jenkins' words, "[i]nternational law and the rules of warfare as they now exist are inadequate to cope with this new mode of conflict." * * *

* * * One important body of traditional international law which provides a significant, if in some cases relatively marginal, sanction against transnational terrorism is the law of state responsibility for injuries to aliens. * * *

Although rarely speaking directly to transnational terrorism, the norms governing state responsibility provide by analogy ample insights into how they might be applied in the terrorism context. In the first place, "such activities when emanating directly from the Government itself or indirectly from organizations receiving from it financial or other assistance or closely associated with it by virtue of the constitution of the State concerned, amount to a breach of International Law." Secondly, while the duty of a state to prevent the commission of acts injurious to foreign states, including acts injurious to their nationals as well, does not imply an obligation to suppress all inimical conduct by private persons or groups, "States are under a duty to prevent and suppress such subversive activity against foreign Governments as assumes the form of armed hostile expeditions or attempts to commit common crimes against life or property." Finally, even when a state does not incur responsibility for breach of the first two duties, it may render itself liable internationally as an "accessory-after-the-fact" if it "fails to take reasonable steps to apprehend and punish the wrongdoer, or if the punishment is so trivial as to be contemptuous of the wrong done to the alien." This duty to take reasonable steps to apprehend and punish arguably includes a duty to extradite if a state apprehends the wrongdoer but does not submit him to prosecution.

[The authors discuss in detail the authorities bearing on a state's responsibility for failure to prevent injuries to aliens and their property and conclude:]

That a state has a general duty under international law to prevent whenever possible injuries to aliens caused by ordinary individuals is apparent. * * * Moreover, that duty extends to injuries caused by terrorists. Yet the duty is not absolute, for states are not held accountable for all injuries to all aliens inflicted by such individuals. What is required is that they exercise "due diligence" with regard to the prevention of these injuries. That means essentially that states are to take all reasonable measures under the circumstances to prevent terrorist acts.

"Due diligence," in turn, depends upon certain basic assumptions about the ability of the state to fulfill its duty. First, it assumes that the state has the means to provide protection. If the state lacks such means, or if the possibility of providing protection is very remote, then frequently no responsibility for the injury will be imposed. * * *

Second, "due diligence" assumes that the state had the opportunity to prevent the act but failed to do so. In the terrorism context, opportunity would be linked most often to the question of some sort of prior notice. Where states have been put on actual notice or "alerted in good time" of an imminent threat of terrorism, another element to establish liability under the principles of state responsibility would be present. * * *

Having been put on notice, the final question becomes: what did the state do to avert the danger, or indeed could the danger have been averted? Here again the actions of the state are judged by their reasonableness under the circumstances. Where the state neglects or fails to take reasonable measures, responsibility will attach. In addition, where the state itself or its officials are involved in the promotion of terrorism, responsibility obviously runs directly to the state. * * * Failure to extradite transnational terrorists, while offering an attractive basis for claiming that a state responsibility norm has been violated, has not yet been recognized as a basis for such an international claim absent the existence of a treaty. Arguably, it should be, but at present states simply may have to "rely upon the goodwill of the requested state" in extraditing terrorists. Similarly, failure to apprehend and punish transnational terrorists, while also an attractive basis for imposing state responsibility obligations, has not been recognized as generating international liability in the absence of a treaty commitment condemning the particular terrorist act and creating a specific duty of prosecution or extradition.

* * *

[Lillich and Paxman conclude (at pp. 307–309) that a state may be held responsible for injury to aliens arising from, inter alia, its (a) subsidization and support of terrorists; (b) complicity with terrorists; (c) encouraging, counseling, and creating opportunity for terrorists; (d) failing to use due diligence to prevent terrorist acts; and (e) failure to apprehend or punish terrorists.]

Note

For discussion of international sanctions imposed upon states that support terrorist acts, and in particular the sanctions imposed on Libya by the U.N. Security Council in connection with the terrorist bombing of Pan Am 103 and UTA 772, see p. 419.

D. INJURY TO ECONOMIC INTERESTS OF ALIENS

1. Non–Commercial Risks of International Business

A principal focus of the law of state responsibility since the 1930s has been the extent to which it is a source of legal protection for the economic interests of alien investors against non-commercial risks. These risks have been discussed as follows in Pugh, Legal Protection of International Transactions Against Non–Commercial Risks, in Lawyer's Guide to International Business Transactions 301–311 (Surrey & Shaw eds., 1963) (footnotes omitted):

> International business transactions in many [developing] areas of the world involve an important measure of non-commercial risks. * * * To a large extent non-commercial risks are the inevitable results of the turbulent currents of political, economic and social change which are surging in these areas, and their existence is a fact of international business that sets operations in the developing countries off sharply from operations in the industrialized world. * * *
>
> What are these non-commercial risks? In their starkest forms they are familiar enough. Examples that jump to mind are expropriation by the foreign government without adequate compensation, violation by the foreign government of a concession or other agreement, imposition of foreign exchange restrictions that prevent remittance of profits abroad and import restrictions that prevent importation of necessary equipment or raw materials. While such events may be catastrophic in their impact on the foreign enterprise, they are, in a sense, simpler to isolate and to achieve a measure of protection against than less obvious factors that may be encountered.
>
> "Creeping expropriation" is a short-hand term that has gained wide currency to describe the great variety of more subtle measures that can be employed by a foreign government to interfere with business operations and impair the rights of the foreign investor. Residence and labor permits for key United States personnel or import permits for essential materials and equipment may be unreasonably delayed or refused. Taxes that discriminate in substance, if not in form, against foreign-owned business may be imposed. Profits may be restricted by governmental price controls or reduced as a result of governmentally subsidized competition. In these cases, the problem of securing legal protection is often aggravated by the difficulties of defining the violation of the foreigner's rights and of evaluating the amount of the loss that can be said to have resulted.

Beyond this, there is an area of risk of substantial loss to the foreign business resulting from local governmental interference against which no effective legal protection is possible. Governments in the developing countries commonly play a far more pervasive role in business operations than is usual in the industrialized countries of the West. * * * As a result of the extent of the local government's role in business operations in developing countries and the severe shortage of trained civil servants in many of these countries, the rights of the foreign businessman may be more seriously impaired through governmental inefficiency than through governmental design.

The non-commercial risks in international business transactions are particularly accentuated in the case in which the United States firm makes a direct investment abroad. Here substantial assets of the investor are exposed to expropriation or nationalization, or to requisition or damage in the event of war or insurrection. In addition, the investor faces the risk that currency restrictions will preclude remittance of profits home in U.S. dollars and the risk that if it should be decided to contract or abandon the venture, it may be impossible to repatriate in dollars some or all of the dollar capital originally invested. Devaluation of the local currency may seriously diminish the real return on the investment. * * *

* * *

Recognizing that non-commercial risks pose an important obstacle to foreign investment, most of the developing countries * * * have taken steps to grant special assurances to foreign investors against many of the more serious of these risks in an effort to encourage the desperately needed inflow of foreign private capital.

Such assurances may be negotiated on an ad hoc basis and embodied in a concession agreement or a guarantee agreement. In recent years, however, it has become increasingly common to find such assurances made available to the foreign investor pursuant to broad investment incentive programs. * * *

In terms of content, the benefits granted under the typical investment encouragement program go well beyond assurances against non-commercial risks. Typically, they include positive incentives such as tax reductions or holidays, assurances against tax increases, low interest loans supplied or guaranteed by the government, and establishment of tariff barriers to protect the investment from foreign competition. Of particular interest here is the extent to which such programs attempt to protect the foreign investor against non-commercial risks.

Since the primary focus of most investment incentive programs is on encouraging direct investments of foreign capital, their major concern is with the risks associated with such investment. Thus, the investment incentive program may include specific guarantees against expropriation without compensation. * * *

A basic feature of nearly every investment incentive program is guarantees with respect to the remittance of profits and the repatriation of capital. In some cases, the remittance of profits from an approved investment is guaranteed without limitation. In others, the guarantee may cover annual remittance of a certain percentage of profits or profits representing a certain percentage return on invested capital. In the case of guarantees with respect to repatriation of capital, it is common to find a fixed percentage of capital (for example, twenty percent) as the maximum which may be repatriated in any year with the additional limitation that there be no repatriation for an initial period of years. * * *

Where loans by the United States firm accompany an approved investment, assurances can commonly be obtained with respect to the availability and transferability of foreign exchange required for the interest and principal payments called for under an approved loan agreement.

* * *

Some capital-importing countries have accepted, either in ad hoc concession or guarantee agreements or under investment incentive programs, arbitration of disputes with foreign investors.

Note

The protection under customary international law against the non-commercial risks faced by foreign private parties making investments in, and supplying knowhow, goods and services to, developing countries is discussed in this chapter. Also discussed are bilateral investment treaties and treaties of friendship, commerce and navigation which afford varying degrees of legal protection against such risks and the role of U.S. courts and U.S. laws in providing legal security for international trade and investment. Other sources of existing and potential legal security against non-commercial risks are discussed in connection with international investment in Chapter 20 at p. 1617. National programs offering insurance against non-commercial risks and various multilateral efforts to improve the legal climate for private investment in developing countries, including the Convention on the Settlement of Investment Disputes and the Convention for a Multilateral Investment Guarantee Agency, are discussed in Chapter 20 at p. 1628 and p. 1629, respectively.

2. *Expropriation and Nationalization of Alien–Owned Property*

a. Introduction

During the last two decades many developing countries have moved toward privatization and freer economies in an effort to accelerate economic development. In addition, these states are now placing increased emphasis on attracting private investment from abroad, and in order to achieve success in this endeavor, it is essential to improve the legal security enjoyed by foreign investors. It is obviously incompatible with enhancing the legal security of private foreign investment and the confidence of potential investors for developing countries to attack the traditional customary international law rules of state responsibility that remain a significant source of legal security for the foreign investor. However, because, as discussed at p. 748, the doctrinal positions of the Latin American states, the socialist states and the developing states in Africa and Asia are deeply rooted, it has been impossible to fashion, in a code of binding rules, compromises on the basic rules of state responsibility that will command widespread support. Hence, there has been a shift of focus from the general substantive customary rules of state responsibility to specific mechanisms, both substantive and procedural, that will increase the legal protection of foreign investors in the developing world. For example, a large and growing number of developing states have embraced such arrangements as bilateral investment treaties according specific legal protections to foreign investors, discussed at p. 808, the concept of compulsory arbitration of investment disputes between investors and foreign states in which investments are made, discussed at p. 811, and insurance of foreign investments against non-commercial risks by bilateral and multilateral agencies, discussed at pp. 1617 and 1629. By focusing more narrowly on specific measures such as these, substantial progress in improving the legal security of foreign investments has been made.

Before turning to the areas in which there has been substantial recent progress, the current state of the substantive customary rules of state responsibility that protect the property rights of foreign investors can be usefully examined.

As discussed at p. 750, the United States has long maintained that a taking of property for public purposes is contrary to international law unless it is accompanied by "prompt, adequate and effective compensation." In contrast, the traditional Latin American view, subsequently espoused by many developing countries in Africa and Asia as well, was that the international legal obligation of the state to pay compensation to an alien whose property has been taken involves no more than a duty to compensate the alien to the extent that its own nationals are compensated under local law. Others would deny any international legal responsibility on the part of a state to pay compensation to an alien whose property has been taken. See p. 748.

Under certain circumstances, the taking of property will be wrongful under international law (with the result that a duty to make reparation will arise) quite independently of whether compensation has been paid. One case about which there is no room for dispute is when the taking violates a treaty. In the Case Concerning the Factory at Chorzów (Claim for Indemnity), P.C.I.J., Ser. A, No. 17 (1928), the Permanent Court held the taking to be in violation of the German–Polish Convention concerning Upper Silesia and that, accordingly, called for compensation equivalent to restitution of the property in kind. See p. 803. There is support for the view that a taking not for a public purpose would violate international law, see Restatement (Third) § 712(1)(a), and that a taking that involves discrimination against aliens is wrongful under international law. See Restatement (Third) § 712(1)(b).

The heart of the problem, however, has been to what extent does international law impose a duty to pay compensation in the event of a taking of alien property by a state that is for a public purpose, non-discriminatory and not violative of a treaty. Or to rephrase the question, to what extent must compensation be paid, if such a taking is to be lawful under international law?

RESTATEMENT (THIRD)

§ 712. Economic Injury to Nationals of Other States

A state is responsible under international law for injury resulting from:

(1) a taking by the state of the property of a national of another state that

(a) is not for a public purpose, or

(b) is discriminatory, or

(c) is not accompanied by provision for just compensation;

For compensation to be just under this Subsection, it must, in the absence of exceptional circumstances, be in an amount equivalent to the value of the property taken and be paid at the time of taking, or within a reasonable time thereafter with interest from the date of taking, and in a form economically usable by the foreign national. * * *

* * *

(3) other arbitrary or discriminatory acts or omissions by the state that impair property or other economic interests of a national of another state.

Notes

1. The public purpose requirement is included in the U.S. treaties of friendship, commerce and navigation, see p. 806, and bilateral investment treaties, see p. 808. Presumably because "public purpose" is a broad and undefined concept, challenges to expropriations on the ground that they are not for a public purpose have been rare. See Pellonpaa, Compensable Claims Before the Tribunal: Expropriation Claims, in The Iran–United States Claims Tribunal: Its Contribution to the Law of State Responsibility, 201–202 (A.S.I.L. 1998). The few decisions applying the rule have also involved a denial of compensation by the taking state. See, e.g., Walter Fletcher Smith, 2 U.N.Rep. Int'l Arb. 913 (1929); Banco Nacional De Cuba v. Sabbatino, 193 F.Supp. 375, 384 (S.D.N.Y.1961), aff'd, 307 F.2d 845 (2d Cir.1962), rev'd on other grounds, 376 U.S. 398, 84 S.Ct. 923, 11 L.Ed.2d 804 (1964). Article 10, paragraph (1)(a) of the Draft Convention on the Responsibility of States for Injuries to Aliens, prepared by Sohn and Baxter, provides that a taking is wrongful "if it is not for a public purpose clearly recognized as such by a law of general application in effect at the time of the taking," 55 A.J.I.L. 545, 553 (1961). The accompanying comment observes:

> * * * It is not without significance that what constitutes a "public purpose" has rarely been discussed by international tribunals and that in no case has property been ordered restored to its former owner because the taking was considered to be for other than a public purpose. This unwillingness to impose an international standard of public purpose must be taken as reflecting great hesitancy upon the part of tribunals and of States adjusting claims through diplomatic settlement to embark upon a survey of what the public needs of a nation are and how these may best be satisfied * * *. Id. at 555–56.

Consider a taking by a state of an alien's property for the personal use of an official of the state. See Restatement (Third) § 712, Comment *e*.

2. With respect to discrimination as a basis for finding a taking of an alien's property by a state to violate international law, it has been noted that "[d]iscrimination implies unreasonable distinction. Takings that invidiously single out property of persons of a particular nationality would be unreasonable; classifications, even if based on nationality, that are rationally related to the state's security or economic policies might not be unreasonable." Restatement (Third) § 712, Comment *f*.

b. Requirement of Compensation

The focus of most of the controversies relating to the law of expropriation is on the issue of compensation and whether that issue is to be determined under international law.

The proposition that compensation in the event of expropriation of the property of an alien must be determined under international law was reflected in U.N. General Assembly Resolution 1803 (XVII 1962) on Permanent Sovereignty over Natural Resources, p. 750, which refers to "appropriate compensation, in accordance with the rules in force in the State taking such measures in the exercise of its sovereignty and in accordance with international law."

However, an effort to undermine this position is reflected in subsequent resolutions adopted by various United Nations organs discussed at pp. 750–752, which reflected support among the socialist states, the Latin American countries and many developing countries for the proposition that the issue of compensation is to be determined not under international law but under the national law of the expropriating state.

In Resolution 3171 (XXVIII) on Permanent Sovereignty over Natural Resources, p. 750, adopted in 1974, the General Assembly refers to "possible compensation" and affirms that "any disputes which might arise should be settled in accordance with the national legislation of each State carrying out such measures."

The Charter of Economic Rights and Duties of States, p. 751, adopted by the U.N. General Assembly on December 12, 1974, (G.A.Res. 3281 (XXIX)), states that "appropriate compensation should be paid by the [expropriating] State, * * * taking into account its relevant laws and regulations and all circumstances that the State considers pertinent." However, settlement is to be under the domestic law of and in domestic tribunals of the nationalizing state unless it agrees to submit the matter to some other peaceful means of settlement.

The Restatement (Third) adopts the view maintained by the United States and many other states that the adequacy of compensation is a matter to be determined under international law. § 712, p. 778. This was also the position adopted by the arbitrator in Texaco Overseas Petroleum Company, et al. v. Libyan Arab Republic, 17 I.L.M. 1, 27–30(1978), who concluded that, unlike Resolution 3171 and the Charter of Economic Rights and Duties of States, Resolution 1803 (XVII) constituted authoritative evidence of customary international law because it was supported by states representing all geographical areas and all economic systems. See pp. 148–153. The question whether this view will ultimately prevail over the view that compensation should be determined solely by reference to the law of the expropriating state may remain open in the eyes of some developing states, but there has been a decided shift in recent years toward acceptance by a growing number of these states that expropriation disputes may properly be governed by international standards embodied in bilateral treaties. A significant manifestation of this shift is the large number of bilateral investment treaties entered into by over 80 developing states that specifically provide that full compensation must be paid to a foreign investor whose property has been expropriated. " * * * [I]t is not unreasonable to assume that as long as states want and need capital and technology from abroad, they will, on the whole, be prepared to give assurance in agreements and practice that they will abide by the requirements of international law in respect of compensation. Our experience to date tends to confirm this despite some UN speeches. States are more likely, of course, to accept this obligation when the foreign investor is perceived as beneficial and the interests of both sides are mutually reciprocal." Schachter, Compensation for Expropriation, 78 A.J.I.L. 121, 129–30 (1984).

It is also significant that in all of the arbitral decisions since 1971, the sole arbitrator or arbitral body has concluded that the issue of compensation was to be determined under customary international law or under the terms of a treaty where applicable. See Norton, A Law of the Future or a Law of the Past? Modern Tribunals and the International Law of Expropriation, 85 A.J.I.L. 474, 479–88 (1991).

c. *The Measure of Compensation*

Assuming that there is a duty under international law to pay compensation to an alien whose property is expropriated, the inquiry shifts to what is the proper measure of compensation due under international law.

Comment *d* to Restatement (Third) § 712 states:

> *d. Just compensation.* The elements constituting just compensation are not fixed or precise, but, in the absence of exceptional circumstances, compensation to be just must be equivalent to the value of the property taken and must be paid at the time of taking or with interest from that date and in an economically useful form.
>
> There must be payment for the full value of the property, usually "fair market value" where that can be determined. Such value should take into account "going concern value", if any, and other generally recognized principles of valuation.
>
> Provision for compensation must be based on value at the time of taking; as in United States domestic law, if compensation is not paid at or before the time of taking but is delayed pending administrative, legislative, or judicial processes for fixing compensation, interest must be paid from the time of taking.
>
> Compensation should be in convertible currency without restriction on repatriation, but payment in bonds may satisfy the requirement of just compensation if they bear interest at an economically reasonable rate and if there is a market for them through which their equivalent in convertible currency can be realized.
>
> Various forms of payment have been provided in negotiated settlements which would not be held to satisfy the requirement of just compensation, e.g., payment in nonconvertible currency that can be used for investment in productive assets in the taking state, or even payment in kind, as in the case of expropriation of investment in natural resources.
>
> In exceptional circumstances, some deviation from the standard of compensation set forth in Subsection (1) might satisfy the requirement of just compensation. Whether circumstances are so exceptional as to warrant such deviation, and whether in the circumstances the particular deviation satisfies the requirement of just compensation, are questions of international law. An instance of exceptional circumstances that has been

specifically suggested and extensively debated, but never authoritatively passed upon by an international tribunal, involves national programs of agricultural land reform. See Reporters' Note 3. A departure from the general rule on the ground of exceptional circumstances is unwarranted if (i) the property taken had been used in a business enterprise that was specifically authorized or encouraged by the state; (ii) the property was an enterprise taken for operation as a going concern by the state; (iii) the taking program did not apply equally to nationals of the taking state; or (iv) the taking itself was otherwise wrongful under Subsection (1)(a) or (b). * * *

Reporters' Note 3 adds:

The land reform exception has been supported on the ground that takings of agricultural land, unlike takings of mineral resources or of a going business concern, typically do not generate funds from which the government could make compensation. If a requirement of compensation fully in accord with the standard set forth in Subsection (1) would prevent the program, the obligation to compensate might be satisfied by a lower standard. Latin American states that have framed this exception have not denied that aliens had to be treated no less favorably than nationals as to compensation. * * *

Notes

1. The formulation that under international law compensation for expropriated property must be "adequate, prompt and effective" is sometimes referred to as the "Hull formula," in recognition of its assertion by Secretary of State Cordell Hull in his exchanges with the Mexican Government in 1938. See p. 746. The Hull formula has been consistently asserted by the United States in diplomatic exchanges and international tribunals to be the standard of compensation required under international law. Restatement (Third) § 712, Comment *c*. Thus, at the time of the adoption of U.N. General Assembly Resolution 1803 (XVII) in 1962, p. 750, the United States, after unsuccessfully proposing the Hull formula as the standard of compensation under international law, voted for the "appropriate compensation" formulation, but asserted the view that "appropriate" was the equivalent of the Hull formula. U.N. Doc. A/C.2/S.R. 850 at 327 (1962).

In fact, while the Hull formula has been incorporated in a large number of bilateral treaties negotiated by the United States and other capital-exporting states with a growing number of developing states, it has been rejected by many developing states and has not been adopted in multilateral agreements or declarations. Restatement (Third) § 712, Comment *c*. There is therefore dispute as to whether the Hull formula as such represents customary international law. Schachter, Compensation for Expropriation, 78 A.J.I.L. 121, 122–23 (1984). However, in 1985 Gann concluded that if one looks beyond the formulation articulated by arbitral tribunals to study the actual awards, there has been "little (if any) retreat in the level of protection to foreign investment afforded by tribunals since the 1965 Restatement." Gann, Compensation Standard for Expropriation, 23 Colum. J. Transnat'l L. 615, 616 (1985). In a 1991 review of arbitral decisions, including seven decisions rendered by Chambers of the Iran–United States Claims Tribunal and two disputes arbitrated under the auspices of the International Centre for Settlement of Investment Disputes (ICSID), Norton concluded that, with one exception, every arbitral tribunal that had considered the issue during the period from 1971 to 1991 had "affirmed that customary international law requires a state expropriating the property of a foreign national to pay the full value of that property measured, where possible, by the market price. * * * Although no tribunal has expressly invoked the Hull formula, the result has been the same." Norton, A Law of the Future or a Law of the Past? Modern Tribunals and the International Law of Expropriation, 85 A.J.I.L. 474, 488 (1991). It is significant that while Article 1110 of the North American Free Trade Agreement relating to compensation for expropriation does not use the terms "prompt," "adequate," and "effective," it effectively adopts this standard. Levy, NAFTA's Provision for Compensation in the Event of Expropriation: A Reassessment of the "Prompt, Adequate and Effective" Standard, 31 Stan.J.Int'l L. 423 (1995). See also Brower, 224 Rec. des Cours 123, 336–386 (1990).

2. To what extent is there a difference in substance between the formulation of "appropriate" compensation adopted in U.N. Resolution 1803 (XVII) and "just" compensation adopted by the Restatement (Third)? Consider the following comment by Schachter (footnotes omitted):

> * * * [A] case can be made for considering that just compensation should now be replaced by "appropriate compensation." Judge Jimenez de Arechaga, a former President of the International Court, has favored "appropriate" because in his view, "it conveys better [than 'just' or 'adequate'] the complex circumstances which may be present in each case." He also suggests that the concept brings in the principle of "unjust enrichment." There might also be a practical advantage to "appropriate compensation" because it has received the support of a great many capital-importing countries and these countries might then be more willing to accept the international obligation and international procedures for dispute settlement. On the other hand, the draft *Restatement,* taking a more traditional position, can justify its choice of "just" over "appropriate" by the fact that "just compensation" has been used widely in national constitutions (e.g., the Fifth Amendment), in legislation and in many treaties. It may also be said that "appropriate" would create uncertainty precisely because it would replace "just." It might then be argued—as does Jimenez de Arechaga—that "appropriate" allows for consideration of factors that would not be within the ambit of "just." For example, it might be considered "appropriate" to give weight to the needs and capabilities of the expropriating state. Some would consider this desirable, others unjust. * * *

Schachter, Compensation for Expropriation, 78 A.J.I.L. 121, 127–29 (1984).

3. Whether the formulation is "appropriate" or "just" compensation, there is obviously much room for disagreement and a large measure of flexibility for the tribunal or the negotiators called upon to resolve the issue of what level of compensation is called for in a particular case. Even under the Hull formula, there is ample room for disagreement concerning the precise meaning of the adjectives "adequate," "prompt" and "effective." It is equally clear that they are interrelated. For example, undue delay in payment or payment that cannot be converted into a usable economic benefit to the dispossessed alien can affect the "adequacy" of the compensation arrangements.

4. What criteria are or should be relevant or controlling in valuing the expropriated facilities for purposes of determining appropriate or just compensation? Consider use of book value, replacement value or fair market value of the expropriated assets or fair market value of the "going concern." To what extent should the value reflect lost future profits of the enterprise and other intangibles such as "good will" or managerial and technical knowhow? To what extent, if at

all, should adequacy of compensation be affected by other factors not bearing directly on current value of the expropriated business, such as the unavailability of foreign exchange with which to pay compensation in convertible currency, a history of large profits to the alien owners without commensurate benefits to the local economy, past environmental damage caused by the project and the ability of the expropriating state to pay? See Iran–United States Claims Tribunal, Aryeh v. Iran, Case No. 266, Chamber Three, Award No. 583–266–3 (1997); Ebrahimi v. Iran, Case Nos. 44, 46, 47, Chamber Three, Award No. 560–44/46/47/–3 (1995); Amoco International Finance Corp. v. Iran, Case No. 56, Chamber Three, Award No. 310–56–3 (1987). For further commentary see Leigh, Expropriation—standard of compensation under international law—lost profits as an element of damages—rejection of "discounted cash flow" method of valuation, 82 A.J.I.L. 358 (1988); Lillich, The Valuation of Nationalized Property in International Law 95 (1972).

5. To what extent does permitting payment in bonds meet the problem of the developing state that lacks the foreign exchange resources to pay adequate compensation in convertible currency? See Restatement (Third) § 712, Comment *d*, p. 781. Are there policy considerations that support under limited circumstances treating bonds as adequate compensation if their face amount, as opposed to their lower fair market value, equals the value of the property taken? What bearing does the currency in which the obligations to pay principal and interest are expressed have on this issue?

6. Although basic differences remain on such issues as the scope of the duty to compensate the alien whose property has been expropriated, there has been a palpable tendency to downplay issues like this one, on which compromise on the doctrinal level may not be possible, and to move on to adopting practical substantive and procedural measures that will contribute to the legal security of foreign investment in developing countries. The most significant of these from the point of view of substantive norms is the striking proliferation of bilateral investment treaties between developing and developed countries in which full compensation is required, often by specific reference to the Hull formula of prompt, adequate and effective compensation. See p. 808.

7. On September 25, 1992, the World Bank Group and the International Monetary Fund (IMF) published the Report to the Development Committee and Guidelines on the Treatment of Foreign Direct Investment, which is set forth at 31 I.L.M. 1366 (1992). The Development Committee is a Joint Ministerial Committee of the Boards of Governors of the IMF and the World Bank. Its approval and publication of the Report and Guidelines were particularly significant because of the almost universal membership of the sponsoring institutions and their central role in international development. In a foreword to the publication, the President of the World Bank Group indicated that the Development Committee agreed "without reservation" to call the guidelines to the attention of the member states. He further stated that the guidelines may "assist in the progressive development of international law in this important area." Id.

With respect to expropriation, Part IV of the Guidelines provides, in part, that "[a] State may not expropriate or otherwise take in whole or in part a foreign private investment in its territory, or take measures which have similar effects, except where this is done in accordance with applicable legal procedures, in pursuance in good faith of a public purpose, without discrimination on the basis of nationality and against the payment of appropriate compensation." The Guideline goes on to state that compensation will be deemed "appropriate" if it is "adequate, effective and prompt." Adequacy is generally to be based on the fair market value of the asset taken. Fair market value may be determined by a method agreed to by the expropriating state and the foreign investor or by a tribunal designated by them. In the event that such agreement is not achieved, the Guideline sets forth in detail the circumstances under which compensation will be deemed to be adequate, effective and prompt.

d. *What Constitutes a "Taking" of Property?*

Under certain circumstances an interference with an alien's property rights that falls short of an outright expropriation may constitute an effective or constructive taking of property that gives rise to an obligation on the part of the responsible state to compensate the alien whose property rights have thereby been impaired. "A 'taking of property' includes not only an outright taking of property but also any such unreasonable interference with the use, enjoyment, or disposal of property as to justify an inference that the owner thereof will not be able to use, enjoy, or dispose of the property within a reasonable period of time after the inception of such interference." Sohn & Baxter, Draft Convention on the International Responsibility of States for Injuries to Aliens, Art. 10, 55 A.J.I.L. 545, 553–54 (1961).

On the other hand, although conduct attributable to the state interferes with or impairs the alien's property rights, it may be deemed not to constitute a taking of his property because the conduct represents a reasonable exercise of the state's power to regulate matters related to public order, safety or health, its currency, foreign exchange resources, balance of payments or emergency situations. See p. 767.

In French v. Banco Nacional de Cuba, 23 N.Y.2d 46, 295 N.Y.S.2d 433, 242 N.E.2d 704 (1968), the plaintiff's assignor had invested in a Cuban farm in 1957 when the Cuban Government permitted foreign investors to turn the proceeds from their enterprises into U.S. dollars and exempted such proceeds from export tax. Under this regime, plaintiff's assignor acquired certificates executed by defendant bank and the Cuban Government's Currency Stabilization Fund stating he would receive for Cuban pesos from defendant bank U.S. $150,000 which would be exempt from the export tax. Thereafter, the Currency Stabilization Fund suspended processing of the certificates. Plaintiff, to whom the certificates were assigned, brought an action for $150,000, plus interest. The New York Court of Appeals held that the dishonoring of the certificates was an act of state, under the doctrine enunciated by the Supreme Court in *Banco Nacional De Cuba v. Sabbatino,* p. 181, according to which the courts of the United States will not (subject to the qualifications introduced by the Second Hickenlooper Amendment, see p. 190) inquire into the validity of acts of a foreign state within its territory. The Court observed, 295 N.Y.S.2d at 442–43:

> Indeed, if the act of state doctrine was decisive in the situation presented in the *Sabbatino* case, then, it must surely be so here again, unless the [Second] Hickenlooper Amendment requires a different result. In the present case, although there are circumstances which undoubtedly imposed serious losses upon the plaintiff's assignor, manifestly, they do not reach the level of an outright "taking" or "expropriation" with which the court was confronted in Sabbatino.

> The Government of Cuba * * * has actually done nothing more than enact an exchange control regulation similar to regulations enacted or promulgated by many other countries, including our own. * * * A currency regulation which alters either the value or character of the money to be paid in satisfaction of contracts is not a "confiscation" or "taking." * * * As one authoritative writer in the field has stated (Mann, Money in Public International Law, 96 Recueil Des Cours [1959] 1, 90), "[a] legislator who reduces rates of interest or renders agreements invalid or incapable of being performed or prohibits exports, or renders performance more expensive by the imposition of taxes or tariffs does not take property. Nor does he take property if he depreciates currency or prohibits payment in foreign currency or abrogates gold clauses. Expectations relating to the continuing intrinsic value of all currency or contractual terms such as the gold clause are, like favorable business conditions and good will, 'transient circumstances, subject to changes,' and suffer from 'congenital infirmity' that they may be changed by the competent legislator. They are not property, their change is not deprivation." * * *

The Court concluded that the Second Hickenlooper Amendment could not apply because there was no taking of property and therefore the act of state doctrine was controlling. See p. 193.

Notes

1. The following Comment accompanies Restatement (Third) § 712(1):

> *g. Expropriation or regulation.* Subsection (1) applies not only to avowed expropriations in which the government formally takes title to property, but also to other actions of the government that have the effect of "taking" the property, in whole or in large part, outright or in stages ("creeping expropriation"). A state is responsible as for an expropriation of property under Subsection (1) when it subjects alien property to taxation, regulation, or other action that is confiscatory, or that prevents, unreasonably interferes with, or unduly delays, effective enjoyment of an alien's property or its removal from the state's territory. Depriving an alien of control of his property, as by an order freezing his assets, might become a taking if it is long extended. A state is not responsible for loss of property or for other economic disadvantage resulting from bona fide general taxation, regulation, forfeiture for crime, or other action of the kind that is commonly accepted as within the police power of states, if it is not discriminatory, Comment *f*, and is not designed to cause the alien to abandon the property to the state or sell it at a distress price. As under United States constitutional law, the line between "taking" and regulation is sometimes uncertain. See Reporters' Note 6.

Compare the foregoing with the provisions concerning what constitutes a taking under the First Hickenlooper Amendment, 22 U.S.C.A. § 2370(e)(1), p. 818, and under the OPIC investment insurance program, p. 1617. Under the latter, a taking includes, *inter alia*, any action which is taken, authorized, ratified or condoned by the government of the project country which for a period of one year results in preventing the investor from "exercising effective control over the use or disposition of a substantial portion of its property or from constructing the Project or operating the same." Under this test, would appointment of a "receiver" to manage the enterprise constitute a "taking"?

For a decision of the I.C.J. rejecting the argument of the United States that the requisition of an Italian subsidiary of two related U.S. corporations constituted a taking of property without compensation which violated the terms of the United States–Italy Friendship, Commerce and Navigation Treaty of 1948 and a Supplementary Agreement of 1951, see Case Concerning Elettronica Sicula S.p.A. (ELSI) (United States v. Italy), 1989 I.C.J. 15, 28 I.L.M. 1111, at paras. 116–18.

For international arbitrations distinguishing a taking of property from lawful regulation, compare Harza Engineering Co. v. Islamic Rep. of Iran, 2 Iran–U.S.C.T.R. 499 (1982) (claim that the Iranian state bank had taken claimant's bank accounts by dishonoring claimant's check and frustrating its attempts to authenticate its officer's signature dismissed) and Computer Sciences Corp. v. Islamic Rep. of Iran, 10 Iran–U.S.C.T.R. (1986) (failure of Iranian bank to seek Iranian Central Bank permission for requested transfer of funds from Iranian Bank held a taking). Also compare the majority and concurring opinions in Starrett Housing Corp. v. Islamic Rep. of Iran, 4 Iran–U.S.C.T.R. 122, 23 I.L.M. 1090 (1984) (holding that appointment of a "temporary manager" of an Iranian firm previously controlled by Starrett rendered claimant's property rights so useless that they had effectively been taken). The extensive jurisprudence of the Iran–United States Claims Tribunal on when a compensable taking of property has occurred is discussed in Aldrich, What Constitutes a Compensable Taking of Property? The Decisions of the Iran–United States Claims Tribunal, 88 A.J.I.L. 585 (1994).

The "conceptional labyrinth that separates the so-called police power from the so-called power of eminent domain," is discussed in Weston, "Constructive Takings" under International Law: A Modest Foray into the Problem of "Creeping Expropriation", 16 Va.J.Int'l L. 101, 153–54 (1975). See also Christie, What Constitutes a Taking of Property Under International Law, [1962] Brit. Y.B.I.L. 307. For a discussion of possible remedies of foreign investors against bureaucratic overreaching in the P.R.C., see Weller, Note: The Bureaucratic Heavy Hand in China: Legal Means for Foreign Investors to Challenge Agency Action, 98 Col. L.Rev. 1238 (1998).

2. Article 21 of the Harvard Research Draft Convention on the Rights and Duties of Neutral States in Naval and Aerial War, 33 A.J.I.L.Supp. 167, 359 (1939), states: "A belligerent may, within its territory or within territory held in military occupation, in case of urgent necessity, requisition a neutral vessel privately owned and operated, or cargo owned by nationals of a neutral State, if the vessel or the cargo was brought into such territory voluntarily and not as the result of compulsion or pressure exercised by the belligerent or by an allied belligerent; provided that this privilege may be exercised by a belligerent only if it pays the fair market value, under prevailing conditions, of the vessel or cargo requisitioned." Article 22 states: "A belligerent has no duty to pay compensation for damage to a neutral vessel or other neutral property or persons, when such damage is incidental to a belligerent's act of war against the armed forces of its enemy and not in violation of the provisions of this Convention or of the law of war." Carnahan, Lincoln, Lieber, and the Laws of War: The Origins and Limits of the Principle of Military Necessity, 92 A.J.I.L. 213 (1998).

3. *Breach by a State of Its Contractual Undertaking to an Alien*

Contractual arrangements between states and aliens are a common phenomenon in international society. These arrangements may cover a great variety of matters. The agreements involved may be similar to agreements between private parties in a purely commercial context. A private supplier may sell goods or services to a foreign government or grant to it rights to patents or know-how under a licensing arrangement. Alternatively, they may involve special features related to the fact that the agreement is between an alien investor and a foreign government. A private company may enter into a concession agreement with a foreign government calling for the exploitation, development and marketing by the private company of mineral resources owned by the foreign government. A private investor may enter into a contractual arrangement with a foreign government pursuant to an investment incentive program under which an investment in productive facilities is made by the private investor in consideration for various guarantees and incentives provided by the foreign government. The undertakings made by the state under such varied arrangements differ widely and these differences may be relevant to the question of whether state responsibility under international law attaches as a result of its breach of a particular undertaking.

When does a breach of an undertaking by a state to an alien constitute a violation of international law? At one extreme, consider, in connection with the materials that follow, the validity of the position that because only states have rights and obligations under international law, a state can limit its exercise of sovereignty only by international agreement with another state or international organization, and consequently a state cannot limit its exercise of sovereignty by agreement with an alien.

At the other extreme, consider the view that the doctrine *of pacta sunt servanda* (agreements must be observed) as a rule of international law applies in the case of any agreement between a state and an alien relating to an investment or mineral concession. See, e.g., Schwebel, International Protection of Contractual Arrangements, 53 A.S.I.L. Proc. 266 (1959); Kissam & Leach, Sovereign Expropriation of Property and Abrogation of Concession Contracts, 28 Fordham L.Rev. 177, 194–214 (1959); Ray, Law Governing Contracts Between States and Foreign Nationals, 2 Institute on Private Investments Abroad 5 (1960). Does it follow from this view that contractual obligations assumed by a state are no less binding than treaty obligations?

a. Choice and Effect of Governing Law

A necessary first step in determining whether a breach or repudiation of a contractual obligation gives rise to state responsibility is to ascertain, in accordance with the principles of the conflict of laws (or private international law), what body of law (or bodies of law) governs questions of the validity, interpretation, and performance of the contract. As pointed out in the Saudi Arabia v. Arabian American Oil Company (Aramco) Arbitration Award, 27 Int'l L.Rep. 117, 165 (1958):

> It is obvious that no contract can exist *in vacuo,* i.e., without being based on a legal system. The conclusion of a contract is not left to the unfettered discretion of the Parties. It is necessarily related to some positive law which gives legal effects to the reciprocal and concordant manifestations of intent made by the parties. The contract cannot even be conceived without a system of law under which it is created. Human will can only create a contractual relationship if the applicable system of law has first recognized its power to do so.

Compare Sohn & Baxter, Responsibility of States for Injuries to the Economic Interests of Aliens, 55 A.J.I.L. 545, 569 (1961):

> [Every contract] draws its binding force, its meaning, and its effectiveness from a legal system, which must be so developed and refined as to be capable of dealing with the great range of problems to which the performance and violation of promises gives rise. *Pacta sunt servanda* is undoubtedly the basic norm of any system of law dealing with agreements, but the principle speaks on such a high level of abstraction that it affords little or no guidance in the resolution of concrete legal disputes relating to agreements. What is *pactum* and when and how and if it is to be *servandum* are questions which must be answered by a system of law capable of reacting in a sophisticated manner to these problems. What that system of law is can be determined by the private international law of the forum, whether national or international.

The choice of governing law problem can be quite complex in relation to an agreement between a state and an alien. In negotiating such an agreement, the parties are free under conflict of laws (or private international law) principles to designate the body or bodies of law that will govern the validity, interpretation and performance of the agreement and, if they so choose, to withdraw the agreement from the exclusive application of the law of the contracting state or any other domestic legal system. The generally unfettered freedom of the contracting state and the foreign private party to choose the governing law was reflected in a resolution adopted by the Institut de Droit International in 1979 stating that "[t]he parties may * * * choose as the proper law of the contract either one or several domestic legal systems or the principles common to such systems or the general principles of law or the principles applied in international economic relations, or international law, or a combination of these sources of law." Ann. Inst. de Droit Int'l Vol. 58 Part II at p. 195. National and international tribunals generally accept the choice by the contracting parties of governing law as binding, and it is only in the rare case that the parties, by design or inadvertence, fail to choose what law is to govern a significant contract. In connection with the materials that follow, consider what factors are likely to influence the negotiations on this issue.

In the absence of an explicit choice by a state and a foreign private party of the law or laws to govern their contract, the determination of governing law may be complicated by questions such as whether there should be a presumption in favor of the municipal law of the contracting state or whether reference of disputes under the agreement to an international arbitral tribunal implies a choice as to governing law or at least, as found by Arbitrator Cavin in the Sapphire–N.I.O.C. Arbitration, 13 I.C.L.Q. 987, 1011–15 (1964), a rejection of municipal law of the contracting state as controlling. See Lalive, Contracts Between a State or a State Agency and a Foreign Company, 13 I.C.L.Q. 987 (1964). Determining the governing law or the "proper law" of the contract may swing the door open to problems concerning the content of that law. For example, if municipal law of the contracting state is selected, does it encompass the municipal law relating to public or administrative contracts under which in certain circumstances the contracting state may not be bound if the public interest otherwise requires? Is it municipal law as it existed on the date of the agreement or as it may be amended from time to time? The parties may include a so-called "stabilization clause," stating that the agreement will be governed throughout its term by municipal law in force at the time the agreement is concluded. See p. 801. The purpose of a stabilization clause is to protect the foreign investor from risk of changes in municipal law detrimental to its interests.

The 1933 concession granted by Persia to the Anglo–Persian Oil Company provided that differences between the parties were to be settled by arbitration and that an award of the arbitrators was to be based on "the judicial principles contained in Article 38 of the Statute of the Permanent Court of International Justice." Does such a choice of law provision render international law directly applicable to the agreement? Does it follow that the agreement could not be altered or terminated by the application of municipal law? See Anglo–Iranian Oil Case, Pleadings, Oral Arguments and Documents 267, 268 (I.C.J.1952). Would such an agreement be subject to adjustment in accordance with fundamentally changed circumstances to the same extent that a treaty would? See p. 554.

TEXACO OVERSEAS PETROLEUM COMPANY ET. AL. v. LIBYAN ARAB REPUBLIC

International Arbitral Award, Jan. 19, 1977.

TRANSLATION OF AWARD ON THE MERITS IN FRENCH, JOURNAL DU DROIT INTERNATIONAL

Vol. 104, No. 2 (1977) at p. 350, 17 I.L.M. 1 (1978).

[On September 1, 1973 and February 11, 1974, Libya promulgated decrees purporting to nationalize all of the rights, interests and property of Texaco Overseas Petroleum Company ("TOPCO") and California Asiatic Oil Company ("CAOC") in Libya that had been granted to them jointly by the Government of Libya under 14 Deeds of Concession.

TOPCO and CAOC requested arbitration and appointed an arbitrator. The Libyan Government refused to accept arbitration and did not appoint an arbitrator. Pursuant to the arbitration provision in their Deeds of Concession, TOPCO and CAOC requested the President of the International Court of Justice to appoint a sole arbitrator to hear and determine the disputes. The Libyan Government opposed such request and filed a memorandum with the President contending, inter alia, that the disputes were not subject to arbitration because the nationalizations were sovereign acts.

After considering the Libyan Government's objections, the President of the International Court of Justice, on December 18, 1974, appointed René-Jean Dupuy, Secretary General of The Hague Academy of International Law and Professor of Law at the University of Nice, as the Sole Arbitrator. The Libyan Government did not participate in the subsequent proceedings.

On January 19, 1977, the Sole Arbitrator delivered an Award on the Merits in favor of TOPCO and CAOC. The Sole Arbitrator held that (a) the Deeds of Concession were binding on the parties, (b) by adopting the measures of nationalization the Libyan Government breached its obligations under the Deeds of Concession and (c) the Libyan Government was legally bound to perform the Deeds of Concession in accordance with their terms.

Following the rendering of the Award on the Merits, Libya, TOPCO and CAOC reached a settlement of their disputes. Libya agreed to provide TOPCO and CAOC over the next 15 months with $152 million of Libyan crude oil, and TOPCO and CAOC agreed to terminate the arbitration proceedings. The Sole Arbitrator's award on the merits stated, in part, as follows (footnotes omitted):]

1. The present arbitration arises out of 14 Deeds of Concession concluded between the competent Libyan Authorities (Petroleum Commission or Petroleum Ministry, depending on the date of the contracts) and the abovementioned companies * * *

* * *

22. * * * [T]he juridical value and, consequently, the binding nature of the Deeds of Concession in dispute can only be judged on the basis of the law which is applicable to them because it is obvious that, if—assuming arguendo—these contracts were governed by Libyan law, the result would have been that their binding nature could be affected *a priori* by legislative or regulatory measures taken within the Libyan national legal order * * *.

But the Deeds of Concession in dispute are not controlled by Libyan law or, more exactly, are not controlled by Libyan law alone. It is incontestable that these contracts were international contracts, both in the economic sense because they involved the interests of international trade and in the strict legal sense because they included factors connecting them to different states * * *.

23. What was the law applicable to these contracts? It is this particular question that the parties intended to resolve in adopting Clause 28 of the Deeds of Concession in a form which must be recalled here:

> "This concession shall be governed by and interpreted in accordance with the principles of the law of Libya common to the principles of international law and in the absence of such common principles then by and in accordance with the general principles of law, including such of those principles as may have been applied by international tribunals."

* * *

24. Two questions must therefore be decided by the Tribunal in order to rule on the binding nature of the Deeds of Concession which are in dispute:

— first question: Did the parties have the right to select the law which was to govern their contract?

— second question: Under what circumstances was the choice of law applicable and what consequence should be derived from the international character of the contracts?

25. The answer to this first question is beyond any doubt: all legal systems, whatever they are, apply the principle of the autonomy of the will of the parties to international contracts. * * *

* * *

36. Under what circumstances was the choice of applicable law made and what consequences should be derived therefrom as to the internationalization of the Deeds of Concession in dispute?

* * *

* * * [T]he internationalization of contracts entered into between States and foreign private persons can result in various ways which it is now time to examine.

41. a.a) At the outset, it is accepted that the reference made by the contract, in the clause concerning the governing law, to the general principles of law leads to this result. These general principles, being those which are mentioned in Article 38 of the Statute of the International Court of Justice, are one of the sources of international law: they may appear alone in the clause or jointly with a national law, particularly with the law of the contracting State.

* * *

42. International arbitration case law confirms that the reference to the general principles of law is always regarded to be a sufficient criterion for the internationalization of a contract. * * *

* * * The recourse to general principles is to be explained not only by the lack of adequate legislation in the State considered (which might have been the case, at one time, in certain oil Emirates). It is also justified by the need for the private contracting party to be protected against unilateral and abrupt modifications of the legislation in the contracting State: it plays, therefore, an important role in the contractual equilibrium intended by the parties.

* * *

44. b.b) Another process for the internationalization of a contract consists in inserting a clause providing that possible differences which may arise in respect of the interpretation and the performance of the contract shall be submitted to arbitration.

* * *

Even if one considers that the choice of international arbitration proceedings cannot by itself lead to the exclusive application of international law, it is one of the elements which makes it possible to detect a certain internationalization of the contract. The *Sapphire International Petroleum Ltd.* award is quite explicit: "If no positive implication can be made from the arbitral clause, it is possible to find there a negative intention, namely to reject the exclusive application of Iranian law" (35 Int'l L.R. 136 (1963), at 172); this is what led the arbitrator in that case, in the absence of any explicit reference to the law applicable, not to apply automatically Iranian law, thus dismissing any presumption in its favor. It is therefore unquestionable that the reference to international arbitration is sufficient to internationalize a contract, in other words, to situate it within a specific legal order—the order of the international law of contracts.

45. (c) A third element of the internationalization of the contracts in dispute results from the fact that it takes on a dimension of a new category of

agreements between States and private persons: economic development agreements * * *.

Several elements characterize these agreements: in the first place, their subject matter is particularly broad: they are not concerned only with an isolated purchase or performance, but tend to bring to developing countries investments and technical assistance, particularly in the field of research and exploitation of mineral resources, or in the construction of factories on a turnkey basis. Thus, they assume a real importance in the development of the country where they are performed: it will suffice to mention here the importance of the obligations assumed in the case under consideration by the concession holders in the field of road and port infrastructures and the training on the spot of qualified personnel. The party contracting with the State was thus associated with the realization of the economic and social progress of the host country.

In the second place, the long duration of these contracts implies close cooperation between the State and the contracting party and requires permanent installations as well as the acceptance of extensive responsibilities by the investor.

Finally, because of the purpose of the cooperation in which the contracting party must participate with the State and the magnitude of the investments to which it agreed, the contractual nature of this type of agreement is reinforced: the emphasis on the contractual nature of the legal relation between the host State and the investor is intended to bring about an equilibrium between the goal of the general interest sought by such relation and the profitability which is necessary for the pursuit of the task entrusted to the private enterprise. The effect is also to ensure to the private contracting party a certain stability which is justified by the considerable investments which it makes in the country concerned. The investor must in particular be protected against legislative uncertainties, that is to say the risks of the municipal law of the host country being modified, or against any government measures which would lead to an abrogation or rescission of the contract. Hence, the insertion, as in the present case, of so-called stabilization clauses: these clauses tend to remove all or part of the agreement from the internal law and to provide for its correlative submission to *sui generis* rules as stated in the *Aramco* award, or to a system which is properly an international law system. * * *

* * *

46. The Tribunal must specify the meaning and the exact scope of internationalization of a contractual relationship so as to avoid any misunderstanding: indeed to say that international law governs contractual relations between a State and a foreign private party neither means that the latter is assimilated to a State nor that the contract entered into with it is assimilated to a treaty.

47. This Tribunal * * * shall * * * consider as established today the concept that legal international capacity is not solely attributable to a State and that international law encompasses subjects of a diversified nature. If States, the original subjects of the international legal order, enjoy all the capacities offered by the latter, other subjects enjoy only limited capacities

which are assigned to specific purposes. * * * In other words, stating that a contract between a State and a private person falls within the international legal order means that for the purposes of interpretation and performance of the contract, it should be recognized that a private contracting party has specific international capacities. But, unlike a State, the private person has only a limited capacity and his quality as a subject of international law does enable him only to invoke, in the field of international law, the rights which he derives from the contract.

* * * [A]s stated by Professor Garcia Amador ("International Responsibility", 2 Y.B. Int'l L.Comm'n 1, U.N.Doc. A/CN.4/119 (1959), at 32):

> "* * * In the matter of contracts, the international personality and capacity of the individual [that is to say the private person, natural or fictitious] depend on the recognition granted to them by the State in its legal relations with him. Agreements which provide in one form or another for the application of a legal system or of principles alien to municipal law, or for the settlement of disputes by international means and procedures, differ from those governed exclusively by municipal law in that the contractual relation between a State and a private person is raised to an international plane, thus necessarily conferring upon that person the necessary degree of international personality and capacity."

Thus, the internationalization of certain contracts entered into between a State and a private person does not tend to confer upon a private person competences comparable to those of a State but only certain capacities which enable him to act internationally in order to invoke the rights which result to him from an internationalized contract.

* * *

49. * * * It is significant * * * that, in a formula in which it must be assumed that each term has been weighed, the parties concerned referred not to Libyan law itself, but to "the principles of Libyan law." Indeed, the parties thereby wanted to demonstrate that they intended the Arbitral Tribunal to base itself on the spirit of the Libyan law as expressed in the fundamental principles of that law, rather than by its rules which may be contingent and variable since these rules depended, in the last instance, on the unilateral will—even arbitrariness—of one of the contracting parties: hence, the reference which is also made to the principles of international law.

It follows that the reference made by the contracts under dispute to the principles of Libyan law does not nullify the effect of internationalization of the contracts which has already resulted from their nature as economic development agreements and recourse to international arbitration for the settlement of disputes. The application of the principles of Libyan law does not have the effect of ruling out the application of the principles of international law, but quite the contrary: it simply requires us to combine the two in verifying the conformity of the first with the second.

* * *

51. Applying the principles stated above, the Arbitral Tribunal will refer:

(1) On the one hand, as regards the principles of Libyan law: regardless of the source of Libyan law taken into consideration, whether we refer to the Sharia, the Sacred Law of Islam (a special reference should be made to Surah 5 of the Koran which begins with the verse: "O ye believers, perform your *contracts!*") or to the Libyan Civil Code which includes on this point two basic articles illustrating the value which Libyan law attaches to the principle of the respect for the word given:

— Article 147, under which "The contract makes the law of the parties. It can be revoked or altered only by mutual consent of the parties or for reasons provided by the law;"

— Article 148, under which "A contract must be performed in accordance with its contents and in compliance with the requirements of good faith,"

one is led to the same conclusion, that is: that Libyan law recognizes and sanctions the principle of the binding force of contracts.

(2) On the other hand, as regards the principles of international law: from this second point of view, it is unquestionable, as written by Professor Jessup * * * that the maxim " 'pacta sunt servanda' is a general principle of law; it is an essential foundation of international law."

No international jurisdiction whatsoever has ever had the least doubt as to the existence, in international law, of the rule *pacta sunt servanda:* it has been affirmed vigorously both in the *Aramco* award in 1958 and in the *Sapphire* award in 1963. One can read, indeed, in the *Sapphire* award, that "it is a fundamental principle of law, which is constantly being proclaimed by international Courts, that contractual undertakings must be respected. The rule 'pacta sunt servanda' is the basis of every contractual relationship" (35 Int'l L.R. 136 (1963), at 181). This Tribunal cannot but reaffirm this in its turn by stating that the maxim *pacta sunt servanda* should be viewed as a fundamental principle of international law.

52. The conformity, on this essential point, of the principles of Libyan law with the principles of international law relieves the Tribunal from discussing the matter further. * * *

* * *

[The arbitrator then considered whether the Deeds of Concession could be regarded as administrative contracts under civil law which the State would be entitled, under certain circumstances, to amend unilaterally or even abrogate in the public interest. The arbitrator concluded this position was untenable for two reasons. First, the Deeds of Concession did not meet the definition of administrative contracts under Libyan law. One element of this definition was that the contract confer upon the government rights and powers not usually found in a civil contract, such as the power to amend or abrogate the contract unilaterally if the public interest requires, or—in the terminology of French law—rights and powers going beyond the ambit of ordinary law *(clauses exorbitantes du droit commun).* * * *

The second reason cited by the arbitrator was that the distinction between administrative contracts and civil contracts was a creature of the

French legal system (and others based upon it) and it could not be regarded as a "principle of international law" or as a "general principle of law."]

* * *

61. * * * It is clear from an international point of view that it is not possible to criticize a nationalization measure concerning nationals of the State concerned, or any measure affecting aliens in respect of whom the State concerned has made no particular commitment to guarantee and maintain their position. On the assumption that the nationalizing State has concluded with a foreign company a contract which stems from the municipal law of that State and is completely governed by that law the resolution of the new situation created by nationalization will be subject to the legal and administrative provisions then in force.

62. But the case is totally different where the State has concluded with a foreign contracting party an internationalized agreement, either because the contract has been subjected to the municipal law of the host country, * * * applicable as of the effective date of the contract, and "stabilized" on that same date by specific clauses, or because it has been placed directly under the aegis of international law. Under these two assumptions, the State has placed itself within the international legal order in order to guarantee vis-à-vis its foreign contracting party a certain legal and economic status over a certain period of time. In consideration for this commitment, the partner is under an obligation to make a certain amount of investments in the country concerned and to explore and exploit at its own risks the petroleum resources which have been conceded to it.

Thus, the decision of a State to take nationalizing measures constitutes the exercise of an internal legal jurisdiction but carries international consequences when such measures affect international legal relationships in which the nationalizing State is involved.

* * *

67. * * * [T]he State, by entering into an international agreement with any partner whatsoever, exercises its sovereignty whenever the State is not subject to duress and where the State has freely committed itself through an untainted consent.

* * *

70. * * * Clause 16 of the Deeds of Concession contains a stabilization clause with respect to the rights of the concession holder. As consideration for the economic risks to which the foreign contracting parties were subjected, the Libyan State granted them a concession of a minimum duration of 50 years and, more specifically, containing a non-aggravation clause, Clause 16, which provided:

> "The Government of Libya will take all steps necessary to ensure that the company enjoys all the rights conferred by this concession. The contractual rights expressly created by this concession shall not be altered except by mutual consent of the parties."

Another paragraph was added to this provision under the Royal Decree of December 1961 and became an integral part of the contract on the basis of the Agreement of 1963. It provides:

> "This Concession shall throughout the period of its validity be construed in accordance with the Petroleum Law and the Regulations in force on the date of execution of the agreement of amendment by which this paragraph (2) was incorporated into the concession agreement. Any amendment to or repeal of such Regulations shall not affect the contractual rights of the Company without its consent."

71. Such a provision, the effect of which is to stabilize the position of the contracting party, does not, in principle, impair the sovereignty of the Libyan State. Not only has the Libyan State freely undertaken commitments but also the fact that this clause stabilizes the petroleum legislation and regulations as of the date of the execution of the agreement does not affect in principle the legislative and regulatory sovereignty of Libya. Libya reserves all its prerogatives to issue laws and regulations in the field of petroleum activities in respect of national or foreign persons with which it has not undertaken such a commitment. Clause 16 only makes such acts invalid as far as contracting parties are concerned—with respect to whom this commitment has been undertaken—during the period of applicability of the Deeds of Concession. Any changes which may result from the adoption of new laws and regulations must, to affect the contracting parties, be agreed to by them. This is so not because the sovereignty of Libya would be reduced, but simply by reason of the fact that Libya has, through an exercise of its sovereignty, undertaken commitments under an international agreement, which, for its duration, is the law common to the parties.

Thus, the recognition by international law of the right to nationalize is not sufficient ground to empower a State to disregard its commitments, because the same law also recognizes the power of a State to commit itself internationally, especially by accepting the inclusion of stabilization clauses in a contract entered into with a foreign private party.

73. Thus, in respect of the international law of contracts, a nationalization cannot prevail over an internationalized contract, containing stabilization clauses, entered into between a State and a foreign private company. The situation could be different only if one were to conclude that the exercise by a State of its right to nationalize places that State on a level outside of and superior to the contract and also to the international legal order itself, and constitutes an "act of government" ("acte de gouvernement") which is beyond the scope of any judicial redress or any criticism. * * * [For paragraphs 84–90, see excerpts in Chapter 2, pp. 148–153 supra.]

91. Therefore, one should note that the principle of good faith, which had already been mentioned in Resolution 1803 (XVII)[see p. 750], has an important place even in Resolution 3281 (XXIX) called "The Charter of Economic Rights and Duties of States". One should conclude that a sovereign State which nationalizes cannot disregard the commitment undertaken by the contracting State: to decide otherwise would in fact recognize that all contractual commitments undertaken by a State have been undertaken under a purely permissive condition on its part and are therefore lacking of any legal force and any binding effect. From the point of view of its advisability, such a

solution would gravely harm the credibility of States since it would mean that contracts signed by them did not bind them; it would introduce in such contracts a fundamental imbalance because in these contracts only one party—the party contracting with the State—would be bound. In law, such an outcome would go directly against the most elementary principle of good faith and for this reason it cannot be accepted.

[The arbitrator then analyzed at length Libyan law and international law relating to remedies for breach of contractual obligations and held that the injured complainants were entitled to *restitutio in integrum* and that Libya was required to perform specifically its contractual obligations with respect to the complainants, stating that] "* * * this Tribunal must hold that *restitutio in integrum* is, both under the principles of Libyan law and under the principles of international law, the normal sanction for non-performance of contractual obligations and that it is inapplicable only to the extent that restoration of the *status quo ante* is impossible * * *."

Notes

1. Consider the bases for what Professor Dupuy refers to as "internationalization" of the contract. What, if anything, does "internationalization" connote beyond the specific features on which the characterization is based? Does it imply that international remedies would be available to the private party for breach by the state that would not be available for violation by the state of other contracts? What, if anything, does the concept of internationalization contribute to the analysis of what law governs the contract? Dupuy makes clear that "internationalization" does not imply that the private party is assimilated to a state or the contract to a treaty. Is it more than a label for a contract between an alien and a state that is explicitly to be governed by international law (or general principles of law) rather than by the municipal law of the contracting state? Dupuy states that the private party under an internationalized contract is given "a limited capacity to invoke, in the field of international law, the rights that he derives from the contract." What is meant by invoking contractual rights "in the field of international law?"

2. Dupuy suggests that in the case of international development contracts, the contract may be "internationalized" whether or not there is an international arbitration clause or a clause selecting as the governing law a body of law other than that of the contracting state. Is there any basis for concluding that an international development contract involves obligations on the international level different from other contracts? See Fatouros, International Law and the Internationalized Contract, 74 A.J.I.L. 134–141 (1980). Consider the following (footnotes omitted):

> * * * [P]olitical and economic factors also bear in a more subtle way on the "internationalizing" of large-scale economic development agreements. The "host" state and the private company are not the only parties in interest; the home state of the company may be heavily involved and indeed often is. Its political, financial and other economic interests may be implicated in the concession or development agreement. The government may have urged the grant of the concession by the host government and encouraged the private firm to proceed. In many cases, it will have helped to provide financing directly or indirectly and it may have insured the company against political risks. In some cases, a bilateral treaty between the two states will apply to the

investment and impose obligations in that respect on the contracting state. Prosper Weil has observed that these relations are indicative of the international "enracinement" of many development agreements. He has suggested that this reality must be reflected in the relevant international law principles that apply on the inter-state level. This could mean that the Calvo doctrine espoused by many states would not apply so as to exclude the home state of the company from asserting its rights and interest in disputes concerning the contract and its performance. State practice confirms the role of the home states in extending diplomatic protection to private companies in cases of development agreements of a certain magnitude and salience. Host states tend to accept such "protection" as legitimate. In this sense, it may be said that the development agreements are "internationalized." But this is not the same as saying that they have become directly subject to international law or that their alleged breach by the state in itself involves a violation of international law.

In sum, we need to be cautious in employing the phrase "internationalized" contracts. We may use the term in a descriptive sense for contracts which have the transnational features we have discussed—namely, non-national governing law, non-national arbitration, or international economic and political significance. However, we cannot infer from these features that the contracts have been transposed to another "legal order" or that they have become subject to international law in the same way as a treaty between two States.

To be sure, the international law of State responsibility applies to these so-called international contracts just as it does to all other contracts and transactions between states and foreign nationals. The application of the rules of state responsibility will have to take cognizance of the special contractual provisions for non-national law and arbitration and also, when appropriate, the interest of the state to which the private party belongs. But these special features do not alter the basic principles of State responsibility applicable to injury to non-nationals resulting from contractual violations. * * *

Schachter, International Law in Theory and Practice 310–311 (1991).

b. *Breach of Undertaking as a Violation of International Law*

It is apparent from the foregoing that, under the applicable principles of conflict of laws (or private international law), the law governing the interpretation, validity and performance of the contract may be determined to be the municipal law of the contracting state, principles of law applied in common by two or more municipal law systems, principles of public international law, general principles of law, some other body of law, or some combination of these. Indeed, various aspects of the contractual relationship may be governed by different bodies of law.

Having determined the governing law, the problem shifts to seeking the content of that law as applied to the particular contractual undertaking involved. To what extent under the governing principles are contracting parties held to their undertakings under an inflexible application of *pacta sunt servanda?* To what extent, if at all, is either party afforded leeway in meeting its obligations? To what extent can the rights and duties of the parties be adjusted to meet changing conditions?

Then, assuming that a breach of contractual obligation by the contracting state is established under the law governing the agreement, when, in the absence of a treaty violation or a denial of procedural justice, will such a breach constitute a violation of international law thereby providing the substantive basis for a claim of state responsibility?

RESTATEMENT (THIRD)

§ 712. Economic Injury to Nationals of Other States

A state is responsible under international law for injury resulting from:

* * *

(2) a repudiation or breach by the state of a contract with a national of another state

(a) where the repudiation or breach is (i) discriminatory; or (ii) motivated by non-commercial considerations, and compensatory damages are not paid; or

(b) where the foreign national is not given an adequate forum to determine his claim of repudiation or breach, or is not compensated for any repudiation or breach determined to have occurred. * * *

Notes

1. Restatement (Third) § 712(2), Comment *h* states as follows:

Repudiation or breach of contract by state. A state party to a contract with a foreign national is liable for a repudiation or breach of that contract under applicable national law, but not every repudiation or breach by a state of a contract with a foreign national constitutes a violation of international law. Under Subsection (2), a state is responsible for such a repudiation or breach only if it is discriminatory, Comment *f*, or if it is akin to an expropriation in that the contract is repudiated or breached for governmental rather than commercial reasons and the state is not prepared to pay damages. A state's repudiation or failure to perform is not a violation of international law under this section if it is based on a bona fide dispute about the obligation or its performance, if it is due to the state's inability to perform, or if nonperformance is motivated by commercial considerations and the state is prepared to pay damages or to submit to adjudication or arbitration and to abide by the judgment or award.

With respect to any repudiation or breach of a contract with a foreign national, a state may be responsible for a denial of justice under international law if it denies to the alien an effective domestic forum to resolve the dispute and has not agreed to any other forum; or if, having committed itself to a special forum for dispute settlement, such as arbitration, it fails to honor such commitment; or if it fails to carry out a judgment or award rendered by such domestic or special forum. See Comment *j*.

A breach of contract by a state may sometimes constitute "creeping expropriation," Comment *g*, for example, if the breach makes impossible the continued operation of the project that is the subject of the contract.

For discussion of the treatment under international law of breaches by a state of different types of contracts, see Restatement (Third) § 712, Reporters' Notes 9 and 10.

2. The Guidelines on the Treatment of Foreign Direct Investment published by the World Bank Group and the IMF on September 25, 1992, 31 I.L.M. 1366 (1992), discussed at p. 1626, take the position that only under limited conditions may a state unilaterally terminate, amend or otherwise disclaim liability under a contract with a foreign private investor for other than commercial reasons. These conditions are that the action be taken (i) in accordance with applicable legal procedures, (ii) in pursuance in good faith of a public purpose, (iii) without discrimination on the basis of nationality, and (iv) against the payment of appropriate compensation. The appropriateness of compensation will be determined under the standards applicable to instances of expropriation. Guideline IV, Section 11, 31 I.L.M. 1383 (1992). See p. 784.

3. Agreements between states and foreign investors sometimes contain "stabilization clauses" stating that the law in force at the time of execution of the agreement will govern. An example was considered in the TOPCO Arbitration, p. 790. In addition to freezing tax laws and customs laws and other regulatory regimes that might adversely affect profitability of the project, these clauses are often intended to prevent repudiation of the contract or expropriation of the project. It has been argued that a state cannot be bound by such a clause because it would be inconsistent with its sovereignty. Saudi Arabia v. Aramco Award, 27 Int'l L.Rep. 117 (1958); Kuwait v. Aminol Award, 21 I.L.M. 976 (1982). The better view, however, seems to be that expressed by Professor Dupuy, namely that entering into such an undertaking is itself an exercise of sovereignty that is binding on the state. In the *Kuwait v. Aminol* decision, the tribunal concluded that the contract before it had such a long duration (i.e., 60 years) that the tribunal would not presume that the stabilization clause was intended to preclude nationalization unless that were expressly so stipulated, id. paras. 94–95, but decided that the stabilization clause had a legal effect in respect of nationalization by reinforcing requirements for proper indemnification as a condition of the taking. Id. para. 96. Under the formulation of § 712(2) of the Restatement (Third), if a state breaches a stabilization clause in an economic development agreement with a foreign private investor, for example, by imposing on the project exchange controls or tax increases that otherwise apply to nationals and aliens alike, would such a breach without more be a violation of international law? See Restatement (Third) § 712, Reporters' Note 10, where the view is expressed that "[i]f coupled with an arbitration clause, such a stabilization clause will be given effect by the arbitrator."

Liberian Eastern Timber Corporation (LETCO) v. Government of Liberia, 26 I.L.M. 647 (1987), an arbitration under the rules of the International Centre for the Settlement of Investment Disputes (ICSID), involved a timber concession agreement governed by Liberian law with a stabilization clause. The tribunal expressed the view that the stabilization clause must be respected. "Otherwise, the contracting state may easily avoid its contractual obligations by legislation. Such legislation action could only be justified by nationalization which [is for a bona fide public purpose, is nondiscriminatory and is accompanied by payment of appropriate compensation]" 26 I.L.M. 667 (1987).

4. Often under the investment incentive program of developing countries, instruments of approval are issued. Under a typical procedure, "the prospective investor must apply to the competent state agency, designated and quite often

created by the basic investment law, in order to have its investment approved or 'registered.' * * * The final instrument of approval is very often the product of extensive negotiations. By that instrument, the state grants to the investor some or all of the assurances and privileges provided for in the investment incentive law, while the investor undertakes certain obligations with respect to the form, amount, and other elements of the investment. The precise form of the instrument varies in the different countries. It is usually an act of the executive branch of government: an administrative decree, a decision of the cabinet or of certain ministers, or some other administrative act." Fatouros, Government Guarantees to Foreign Investors, 122–23 (1962). Do such unilateral undertakings by a state fall outside the area of "contract?" Fatouros concludes that such instruments "are of a mixed character, both contractual and noncontractual." Id. at 196; see the discussion id. at 192–209. If an undertaking constitutes no more than a unilateral act by the state, can a breach thereof constitute a breach of international law? To what extent are the principles in the contractual area applicable? Should general principles of estoppel come into play? See, e.g., MacGibbon, Estoppel in International Law, 7 I.C.L.Q. 468 (1958); Friedmann, Some Impacts of Social Organization on International Law, 50 A.J.I.L. 475, 506 (1956).

SECTION 5. REPARATION

When an act or omission attributed to a state causes injury to an alien in violation of international law, the state of which the injured alien is a national has, as against the responsible state, the remedies generally available between states for violation of customary international law, discussed in Chapter 9 at p. 729, and any special remedies available under an applicable treaty. Restatement (Third) § 713.

The violation of international law creates an obligation on the part of the delinquent to make reparation for the wrong to the state injured by the violation. Reparation may consist of an indemnity or money damages, restitution or satisfaction. See the discussion at p. 729. When a state asserts a claim based on responsibility of another state for an injury to one of its nationals, the state's claim is essentially derivative in nature, some of the implications of which have been discussed at p. 753. One of those noted is that, when a state's claim arises from an injury to one of its nationals, reparation often takes the form of a monetary payment measured by the damages suffered by its national; the injury to the dignity or sovereignty of the state is frequently treated as having only theoretical or symbolic significance. The Permanent Court of International Justice observed in the Case Concerning the Factory at Chorzów (Merits), P.C.I.J. Ser. A, No. 17, at 28 (1928):

> * * * Rights or interests of an individual the violation of which rights causes damage are always in a different plane to rights belonging to a State, which rights may also be infringed by the same act. The damage suffered by an individual is never therefore identical in kind with that which will be suffered by a State; it can only afford a convenient scale for the calculation of the reparation due to the State.

In unusual circumstances, reparation might also include additional monetary damages for the injury to the claimant state. For discussion of the relationship between the injury to an individual and to a state of which he is a national in fixing the measure of reparation, see Laura M.B. Janes Claim

(United States v. Mexico), [1927] Opinions of Commissioner 108, 4 U.N.Int'l Arb. Awards 82.

The entire reparation is paid to the claimant state and disbursed to its national claimants at its discretion. On the legal status of reparation received by the United States, see Opinion of J. Reuben Clark, Solicitor for the Department of State, 7 A.J.I.L. 382 (1913). See generally 3 Whiteman, Damages in International Law 203559 (1943) [Hereinafter cited as Whiteman, Damages]; 5 Hackworth 763–801.

In the *Chorzów Factory Case,* the Permanent Court of International Justice also indicated that:

> The essential principle contained in the actual notion of an illegal act—a principle which seems to be established by international practice and in particular by the decisions of arbitral tribunals—is that reparation must, as far as possible, wipe out all the consequences of the illegal act and reestablish the situation which would, in all probability, have existed if that act had not been committed. Restitution in kind, or, if this is not possible, payment of a sum corresponding to the value which a restitution in kind would bear; the award, if need be, of damages for loss sustained which would not be covered by restitution in kind or payment in place of it—such are the principles which should serve to determine the amount of compensation due for an act contrary to international law.

P.C.I.J. Ser. A, No. 17, at 41. In the majority of cases, restitution is impossible because of changed circumstances, and the reparation must consist of monetary compensation.

The Permanent Court also distinguished between the case in which the payment of "fair compensation" can render lawful under international law an expropriation or other taking of property (see p. 778) and the case in which the taking is wrongful under international law even if such compensation is paid. Id. at 46. In the former case, the Court indicated that the measure of compensation was the value of the property at the time of the taking plus interest to the date of the payment. The *Chorzów Factory Case* itself involved the latter because the taking there was in violation of a specific treaty prohibition against expropriation. The Court stated that in this situation the measure of damages was the value that the undertaking would have had at the time of indemnification had the expropriation not taken place, plus any losses sustained as a result of the expropriation. Id. at 48. Thus, the Court allowed damages for loss of profits realized between the seizure and the indemnification.

Reparation has been held to include compensation for lost profits when the violation of international law consists in tortious conduct resulting in loss or destruction of property if the profits were reasonably certain and not speculative. See 3 Whiteman, Damages at 1840–58. If the profits were speculative in view of the circumstances, they have generally not been included in the measure of reparation. In cases involving contract claims, lost profits may be allowed where they are reasonable and within the contemplation of the parties. See 3 Whiteman, Damages at 1858–66. When an arbitral tribunal is not permitted by the *compromis* to grant reparation for anticipated profits, or when it feels that the profits are too speculative to measure, it can normally grant interest in lieu of profits.

In claims for personal injuries, the measure of reparation is the loss to the individual claimant. Damages have included medical expenses, loss of earnings, George Henry Clapham Claim (Great Britain v. Mexico), 5 U.N.Rep. Int'l Arb. Awards 201, 203–04 (1931), pain and suffering, 1 Whiteman, Damages at 588–89, and mental anguish, Opinion in the Lusitania Cases (United States v. Germany), Mixed Claims Commission, [1923–25] Administrative Decisions and Opinions 17, 21–22, 7 U.N.Rep. Int'l Arb. Awards 32, 36–37 (1923). Damages may be reduced where the claimant has contributed to the injury. Lillie S. Kling Claim (United States v. Mexico), General Claims Commission, [1930–31] Opinions of Commissioners 36, 49–50, 4 U.N.Rep. Int'l Arb. Awards 575, 585 (1930). See Bederman, Contributory Fault and State Responsibility, 30 Va.J.Int'l L. 335 (1990).

Problems sometimes arise in attributing responsibility to the delinquent state for the damages suffered by an individual claimant. A state is ordinarily responsible only for the damages caused by its delinquency. Where the delinquency is a failure to apprehend and punish a private person who has injured an alien or his property, the offending state has not damaged the claimant except in so far as the state's delinquency prevents the claimant from bringing a damage action against the responsible person. If, as is often the case, an action against the private wrongdoer would be fruitless, the delinquent state has not caused any damage to the claimant. International tribunals have sometimes avoided such a result by finding that the delinquent state's lack of diligence in apprehending or punishing the private wrongdoer amounted to condoning the injury and imposed derivative liability on the state, or by finding that the claimant suffered "grief," "mistrust and lack of safety" resulting from the state's failure to apprehend or punish the wrongdoer. See Poggioli Case (Italy v. Venezuela), Ralston, Venezuelan Arbitrations of 1903, 847, 869, 10 U.N.Rep. Int'l Arb. Awards 669, 689; Laura M.B. Janes Claim (United States v. Mexico), General Claims Commission, [1927] Opinions of Commissioners 108, 120, 4 U.N.Rep. Int'l Arb. Awards 82. Under either theory damages have usually been measured by the loss suffered by the individual claimant rather than by the gravity of the state's delinquency. See 1 Whiteman, Damages at 39; Brierly, The Theory of Implied State Complicity in International Claims, [1928] Brit. Y.B.I.L. 42; Freeman, The International Responsibility of States for Denial of Justice 367–69 (1938). But cf. The William T. Way Claim (United States v. Mexico), 4 U.N.Rep. Int'l Arb. Awards 391 (1928); The "I'm Alone" Case (Canada v. United States), 3 U.N.Rep. Int'l Arb. Awards 1609 (1935); 1 Whiteman, Damages at 721–744, 788.

Another source of difficulty may arise in determining whether the delinquent state is liable for particular items of damage suffered by individual claimants. This problem may be presented particularly when the *compromis* conferring jurisdiction on an arbitral tribunal limits its jurisdiction to claims "resulting from" some specified event. Tribunals generally speak of "proximate cause" and tend to disallow damages which are "remote," "speculative," or not proximately caused by the delinquency. See Administrative Decision No. II, (United States v. Germany), Mixed Claims Commission, 1923, [1923–25] Administrative Decisions and Opinions 5, 12–13, 7 U.N.Rep. Int'l Arb. Awards 23, 29–30. Whatever particular damages will be allowed depends on the particular circumstances of each case. See 3 Whiteman, Damages at 1765–1874. For additional commentary on the issue of causation, see Borek,

Other State Responsibility Issues, in The Iran–United States Claims Tribunal: Its Contribution to the Law of State Responsibility 317 (A.S.I.L. ed. 1998).

International tribunals generally award interest either from the date of the obligation to make reparation or from the date of the award. The rate varies depending on the nature of the claim and on the rate of interest generally prevailing at the time and place of the injury. See 2 O'Connell at 1211–13; 1 Oppenheim at 353 n. 1; 3 Whiteman, Damages at 1913–2006. Tribunals frequently allow individual claimants the cost of preparing their claims. However, in the absence of an agreement to the contrary, the two governments involved bear their own costs in preparing or defending their claims and share the cost of the tribunal equally. 3 Whiteman, Damages at 2024–28.

SECTION 6. SUCCESSION TO INTERNATIONAL RESPONSIBILITY

Although the problem of state succession arises in other contexts, especially in connection with determining whether a successor state succeeds to rights and duties embodied in international agreements, see p. 568, it also arises in the context of state responsibility with the focus on the extent to which the successor state is responsible for violations of international law by the predecessor. See the discussion in Chapter 4 at p. 356.

SECTION 7. BILATERAL TREATIES

A. INTRODUCTION

A large number of bilateral treaties have been entered into between industrialized capital-exporting countries and developing countries that have as one of their objectives or as their sole objective increasing the legal protection to private parties of one of the contracting states that invest or engage in other business transactions in the other contracting state against non-commercial risks of the kinds discussed at p. 775. These treaties may be divided into two categories. The first encompasses treaties of friendship, commerce and navigation ("FCN treaties") which, as the title implies, cover a wide range of trade relations in addition to providing legal protection against non-commercial risks. The second category encompasses bilateral investment treaties concluded by capital-exporting countries with developing countries that focus specifically on protection of the foreign investor against specified non-commercial risks, such as the taking of the investor's property without compensation, discriminatory treatment, and, in some cases, breach or repudiation by a contracting state of contracts with nationals of the other contracting state. Many of these investment treaties have their roots in the Draft Convention on the Protection of Foreign Property prepared under the auspices of the Organization for Economic Cooperation and Development (OECD) and adopted in 1967 by the OECD Council, stating the belief that the Draft Convention would be useful in the preparation of bilateral agreements for the protection of foreign property. See p. 1621. Bilateral FCN and investment treaties are discussed generally in Bilateral Treaties for International Investment, International Chamber of Commerce (Paris 1977).

B. FRIENDSHIP, COMMERCE AND NAVIGATION TREATIES

During the 1950s and 1960s, the United States negotiated a network of bilateral treaties of friendship, commerce and navigation, designed primarily for the protection and encouragement of U.S. private trade and investment abroad. While the FCN program focused principally on developed countries, the United States did succeed in negotiating several FCNs with third world states. In total, the United States concluded forty FCN agreements, starting with the Republic of China in 1946 and ending with Togo and Thailand in 1966.* See Vandevelde, The Bilateral Investment Treaty Program of the United States, 21 Cornell Int'l L.J. 201, 206–207 (1988); American Bar Association, Commercial Treaty Index (1976); Wilson, U.S. Commercial Treaties and International Law (1960); Walker, Modern Treaties of Friendship, Commerce, and Navigation, 42 Minn.L.Rev. 805 (1958). For a detailed analysis of the U.S. FCN treaties see The Protection of Private Property Invested Abroad, Report by the Committee on International Trade and Investment, Section of International and Comparative Law, American Bar Association 39–58 (1963).

The United States–Pakistan Treaty of Friendship and Commerce, which entered into force on February 12, 1961, 12 U.S.T. 110, T.I.A.S. No. 4683, 404 U.N.T.S. 259, reflects the basic pattern of the post-World War II FCN treaties. The basic thrust of these agreements is to obligate each contracting state to grant at least national and most-favored-nation treatment to citizens and companies of the other contracting state. With respect to some activities, however, such as those related to national security, transport, utilities and exploitation of national resources, most-favored-nation treatment may be all that is guaranteed.

A number of the provisions of the Pakistan treaty are of particular significance to a U.S. investor. First, Article 6(3) prohibits discriminatory treatment as follows:

> Neither Party shall take unreasonable or discriminatory measures that would impair the legally acquired rights or interests within its territories of nationals and companies of the other Party in the enterprises which they have established, in their capital, or in the skills, arts or technology which they have supplied.

Second, with respect to expropriation, Article 6(4) of the treaty provides as follows:

> Property of nationals and companies of either Party shall not be taken within the territories of the other Party except for public purpose, nor shall it be taken without the prompt payment of just compensation. Such compensation shall be in an effectively realizable form and shall represent the full equivalent of property taken; and adequate provision shall have been made at or prior to the time of the taking for the determination and payment thereof.

* More than 40 countries have entered into FCN treaties with the United States: Argentina, Austria, Belgium, Bolivia, Brazil, Canada, Chile, Colombia, Denmark, Ecuador, Finland, Germany, Greece, Guatemala, Honduras, Iran, Ireland, Israel, Italy, Korea, Latvia, Liberia, Luxembourg, Nepal, Netherlands, Nicaragua, Norway, Oman, Pakistan, Paraguay, Spain, Suriname, Switzerland, Thailand, Togo, Tonga, Turkey, United Kingdom, Venezuela, Vietnam, and Yemen. The treaty with the Republic of China remains applicable with Taiwan.

Third, with respect to exchange restrictions on transfers of funds or financial instruments, Article 12 of the Pakistan treaty provides, in part, as follows:

* * *

(2) Neither Party shall impose exchange restrictions as defined in paragraph 5 of the present Article except to the extent necessary to prevent its monetary reserves from falling to a low level, to effect an increase in the reserves in order to bring them up to an adequate level, or both. It is understood that the provisions of the present Article do not alter the obligations either Party may have to the International Monetary Fund or preclude imposition of particular restrictions whenever the Fund specifically authorizes or requests a Party to impose such particular restrictions.

(3) If either Party imposes exchange restrictions in accordance with paragraph 2 of the present Article, it shall, after making whatever provision may be necessary to assure the availability of foreign exchange for goods and services essential to the health and welfare of its people, make reasonable provision for the withdrawal, in foreign exchange in the currency of the other Party, of: (a) the compensation referred to in Article 6, paragraph 4, (b) earnings, whether in the form of salaries, interest, dividends, commissions, royalties, payments for technical services, or otherwise, and (c) amounts for amortization of loans, depreciation of direct investments, and capital transfers, giving consideration to special needs for other transactions. If more than one rate of exchange is in force, the rate applicable to such withdrawals shall be a rate which is specifically approved by the International Monetary Fund for such transactions or, in the absence of a rate so approved, an effective rate which, inclusive of any taxes or surcharges on exchange transfers, is just and reasonable.

* * *

To what extent do these guarantees represent a significant measure of legal protection to a U.S. enterprise beyond that accorded under customary international law? Do they constitute meaningful limitations on a State's otherwise virtually untrammelled freedom to regulate its monetary policy? Do they lend any protection against currency depreciation or devaluation? Do they shift to the state imposing exchange controls a burden of justification that is to some extent susceptible of objective proof? See Fatouros, Government Guarantees to Foreign Investors 218 (1962). To what extent are the provisions on expropriation undermined by the foreign exchange provision escape clauses of Article 12(2) and (3)?

Articles 7 and 9 through 11 lend a limited measure of protection against various types of creeping expropriation, such as wage and labor controls, price controls, import and export restrictions, confiscatory taxation, or unfair competition from an enterprise owned by the local government or private interests. The treaty provides no protection, beyond the general assurance of national and most-favored-nation treatment against violation by a Contracting State of specific contractual or other undertakings made to an alien investor.

Some of the treaty provisions afford a measure of protection to the U.S. firm supplying knowhow to an enterprise in Pakistan under a license agreement, technical or managerial services agreement or some other contractual arrangement. Because the knowhow supplier's return is typically cast in the form of a current royalty or fee payment, the extent of the treaty protection against exchange restrictions that would inhibit or preclude the remittance of such payments in foreign exchange is of particular significance. Also, intellectual property rights (such as patents or trademarks) recognized under the laws of the Contracting State and owned by a U.S. enterprise would enjoy the same protection against expropriation and discriminatory treatment as other property. National and most-favored-nation treatment is accorded with respect to the obtaining and maintaining of patents, trademarks and other intellectual property.

The treaty does not provide for international judicial or arbitral enforcement of rights vested in private parties by its terms, but it does call for resolution of disputes between the Contracting States arising out of the treaty ultimately by recourse to the International Court of Justice if other means of settlement fail. Art. 23(2).

In evaluating the significance of the FCN treaties, one must consider not only their substantive coverage or lack of coverage but also the fact that the very existence of the treaty may reflect a favorable climate for U.S. trade and investment in the other contracting state. One must also keep in mind that relatively few FCN treaties have been concluded with the developing countries of Africa, Asia and Latin America, where the need for the protection they afford is often important. All such treaties, moreover, are terminable by either party on notice.

After the 1960s, the United States ceased negotiating FCN treaties with developing countries and shifted its efforts to negotiating reciprocal bilateral investment treaties which focus principally on providing the nationals of each contracting state with liberalized access to the market of the other contracting state and on providing enhanced legal protection against non-commercial risks.

Note

For discussion of the scope of various provisions of the 1948 U.S. FCN Treaty with Italy and a Supplementary Agreement of 1951, see Case Concerning Elettronica Sicula S.p.A. (ELSI) (United States v. Italy), 1989 I.C.J. 15, 28 I.L.M. 1111, the facts of which are summarized at p. ___. See also Murphy, The ELSI Case: An Investment Dispute at the International Court of Justice, 16 Yale J.Int'l L. 391 (1991).

C. BILATERAL INVESTMENT TREATIES (BITS)

Hundreds of bilateral investment treaties (BITs) have entered into force since the first such treaty was entered into by the Federal Republic of Germany and Pakistan in 1959. Salacuse, BIT by BIT: The Growth of Bilateral Investment Treaties and Their Impact on Foreign Investment in Developing Countries, 24 Int'l Law. 655, 657 (1990). All the major capital-exporting states, led by Germany, and more than 80 developing countries have become parties to BITs. In recent years, the United States has placed increasing reliance on them, usually denominated Treaties Concerning the Reciprocal Encouragement and Protection of Investments. As of 2000, there were BITs in force between the United States and about 30 countries* and a substantial number of additional BITs were awaiting ratification and others were being negotiated. The U.S. treaties differ from many entered into by European countries in that their purpose is not merely protection of investments but also ensuring free access (with limited exceptions) of investors of each contracting state to the markets of the other contracting state.

BITs typically grant rights to, and impose obligations on, both contracting states on a reciprocal basis. The treaties normally encompass such matters as general standards of treatment of foreign investment, protection against expropriation, compensation for losses from armed conflict or internal disorder, currency transfers and convertibility, and settlement of disputes. Treaties for the protection of foreign private investors in Kazakhstan, Romania and Russia represent radical departures from the past and reflect the dramatic change in the legal climate for foreign investment in those economies. Perhaps most striking, however, is the signing by the United States on November 14, 1991, of a treaty with Argentina, 31 I.L.M. 124 (1991), because Argentina, which has also signed treaties with Germany, Switzerland, Belgium/Luxembourg and the United Kingdom, agreed in the treaty with the United States to abandon the Calvo Doctrine and accept dispute settlement between the investor and the host government by binding arbitration under the rules of ICSID or UNCITRAL or other institution agreed to by the parties with no requirement for prior exhaustion of remedies in the host country. Article VII, 31 I.L.M. 132. Moreover, the treaty embodies the rule that expropriation must be accompanied by "prompt, adequate and effective compensation"—the Hull formula—which had been an anathema to most Latin American countries since the 1930s. Article IV(*l*), 31 I.L.M. at 131.

The U.S. BITs are exemplified by the Treaty with Argentina, which entered into force on November 14, 1991, which is included in the Documents Supplement.

1. *Standards of Treatment*

Most U.S. investment treaties, including that concluded with Argentina, call for according "fair and equitable treatment" to covered investments and, with a variety of exceptions and qualifications, provide for national treatment or most-favored-nation treatment, whichever is more favorable to the investor. Exceptions typically exclude sectors of the economy, such as public utilities, transport, and defense, that are not open to foreign investment.

2. *Expropriation*

A central feature of all of the investment treaties is the provisions relating to expropriation. All call for payment of full compensation, either invoking the Hull formula or some substantially equivalent formulation.

* These include Argentina; Armenia; Bangladesh; Bulgaria; Cameroon; Congo; Democratic Republic of the Congo; Egypt; Estonia; Georgia; Grenada; Kazakhstan; Kyrgyz Republic; Latvia; Moldova; Mongolia; Morocco; Pakistan; Panama; Poland; Romania; Senegal; Sri Lanka; Trinidad and Tobago; Tunisia; Turkey; and Ukraine. A Guide to the United States Treaties in Force, Bk II, 537–39 (Kavass 1999).

Many of these treaties go beyond the usual provisions of the FCN treaties by covering indirect takings of property of nationals of the other contracting state, and some cover violation of contractual undertakings given by a contracting state to a national of the other contracting state.

Article IV of the United States–Argentina Treaty, for example, provides in part, as follows:

> 1. Investments shall not be expropriated or nationalized either directly or indirectly through measures tantamount to expropriation or nationalization ("expropriation") except for a public purpose; in a non-discriminatory manner; upon payment of prompt, adequate and effective compensation; and in accordance with due process of law and the general principles of treatment provided for in Article II(2). Compensation shall be equivalent to the fair market value of the expropriated investment at the time the expropriatory action was taken or became known. Compensation shall be paid without delay; be fully realizable; and be freely transferable. In the event that payment of compensation is delayed, such compensation shall be paid in an amount which would put the investor in a position no less favorable than the position in which he would have been, had the compensation been paid immediately on the date of expropriation.
>
> 2. A national or company of either Party that asserts that all or part of its investment has been expropriated shall have a right to prompt review by the appropriate judicial or administrative authorities of the other Party to determine whether such expropriation and any compensation therefor conforms to the principles of this Article.

3. Losses from Armed Conflict or Internal Disorder

Most treaties provide that foreign investors will be accorded national and most-favored-nation treatment with respect to losses resulting from armed conflict, civil disturbance and the like. For example, Article IV(3) of the United States–Argentina Treaty, provides, in part, as follows:

> [n]ationals or companies of either Party whose investments suffer losses in the territory of the other Party owing to war, insurrection, civil disturbance or other similar events shall be accorded treatment by such other Party not less favorable than that accorded to its own nationals or companies or nationals or companies of any third country, whichever is the most favorable treatment, as regards any measures it adopts in relation to such losses.

For an ICSID arbitral award interpreting provisions of the Sri Lanka–United Kingdom Bilateral Investment Treaty concerning protection against losses owing to war or other armed conflict, revolution, a state of national emergency, revolt, insurrection or riot, see Asian Agricultural Products Ltd. v. Sri Lanka, 30 I.L.M. 580 (1990).

4. Transfers and Convertibility of Payments

Investment treaties typically include general provisions guaranteeing free transferability in convertible currency of "returns" on investment, broadly defined to include both remittance of current payments, such as interest, dividends, rents, royalties and service fees, and repatriation of capital, including gain from the sale of the investment. However, frequently there are qualifications which give the contracting party some flexibility to impose controls required to protect the value of its currency and its balance of payments. For example, Article 7 of The Netherlands–Philippines Treaty for the Promotion and Protection of Investment, Tractatenblad (Neth.) No. 86, 1985, provides:

> 1. Each Contracting Party shall in respect of investments permit nationals of the other Contracting Party the unrestricted transfer in free convertible currency of their investments and of the earnings from them to the country designated by those nationals, subject to the right of the former Contracting Party to impose equitably and in good faith such measures as may be necessary to safeguard the integrity and independence of its currency, its external financial position and balance of payments, consistent with its rights and obligations as a member of the International Monetary Fund.

Article V of the United States–Argentina Treaty does not accord comparable leeway to the host country:

> 1. Each Party shall permit all transfers related to an investment to be made freely and without delay into and out of its territory. Such transfers include: (a) returns; (b) compensation pursuant to Article IV; (c) payments arising out of an investment dispute; (d) payments made under a contract, including amortization of principal and accrued interest payments made pursuant to a loan agreement directly related to an investment; (e) proceeds from the sale or liquidation of all or any part of an investment; and (f) additional contributions to capital for the maintenance or development of an investment.
>
> 2. Except as provided in Article IV paragraph 1, transfers shall be made in a freely usable currency at the prevailing market rate of exchange on the date of transfer with respect to spot transactions in the currency to be transferred.* * *

5. *Settlement of Disputes*

Most recent U.S. BITs provide for two dispute settlement mechanisms: one to deal with disputes between a contracting state and a foreign investor and the other to deal with disputes between the two contracting states.

With respect to disputes in the first category, many recent treaties provide for eventual resolution of disputes under the rules and procedures of the International Centre for Settlement of Investment Disputes (ICSID). For example, Article VII of the United States–Argentina Treaty, provides, in part, as follows:

> 1. For purposes of this Article, an investment dispute is a dispute between a Party and a national or company of the other Party arising out of or relating to (a) an investment agreement authorization granted by that Party and such national or company; (b) an investment authorization granted by that Party's foreign investment authority * * * to such national or company; or (c) an alleged breach of any right conferred or created by this Treaty with respect to an investment.

2. In the event of an investment dispute, the parties to the dispute shall initially seek a resolution through consultation and negotiation. If the dispute cannot be settled amicably, the national or company concerned may choose to submit the dispute for resolution:

(a) to the courts or administrative tribunals of the Party that is a party to the dispute; or

(b) in accordance with any applicable, previously agreed dispute-settlement procedures; or

(c) in accordance with the terms of paragraph 3.

3. (a) Provided that the national or company concerned has not submitted the dispute for resolution under paragraph 2(a) or (b) and that six months have elapsed from the date on which the dispute arose, the national or company concerned may choose to consent in writing to the submission of the dispute for settlement by binding arbitration:

(i) to the International Centre for the Settlement of Investment Disputes ("Centre") established by the Convention on the Settlement of Investment Disputes between States and Nationals of other States, done at Washington, March 18, 1965 ("ICSID Convention"), provided that the Party is a party to such Convention; or

(ii) to the Additional Facility of the Centre, if the Centre is not available; or

(iii) in accordance with the Arbitration Rules of the United Nations Commission on International Trade Law (UNICTRAL); or

(iv) to any other arbitration institution, or in accordance with any other arbitration rules, as may be mutually agreed between the parties to the dispute.

(b) Once the national or company concerned has so consented, either party to the dispute may initiate arbitration in accordance with the choice so specified in the consent.

6. Significance of the Bilateral Investment Treaty Network

Salacuse sums up his evaluation of the bilateral investment treaties as follows:

Despite the lack of proof of [the treaties'] effectiveness, the BIT movement as a whole may be seen as part of an ongoing process to create a new international law of foreign investment to respond to the demands of the new global economy that has so rapidly emerged within the last few years. While the world has developed a relatively elaborate legal structure for trade in the form of the General Agreement on Tariffs and Trade [now including the World Trade Organization], it has yet to create similar structure for international investment. Such a multilateral arrangement, a General Agreement on Direct International Investment, is many years away and will only be achieved through a gradual step-by-step approach. * * * The BIT movement of the past thirty years has also been an important step in this direction. Although BITs themselves only bind the two countries concerned and are probably not sufficiently widespread to constitute customary international law, the process of study, consultation, discussion, and negotiation that has been part of the BIT movement has certainly laid a foundation for the creation of an international investment framework that may eventually attract the consensus of the nations of the world.

BIT by BIT: The Growth of Bilateral Investment Treaties and Their Impact on Foreign investment in Developing Countries, 24 Int'l Law., 655, 675 (1990) (footnotes omitted).

Salacuse cites, as an example of a multilateral investment treaty that has clearly been influenced by the bilateral treaties, the Agreement Among Brunei, Indonesia, Malaysia, The Philippines, Singapore, and Thailand for the Promotion and Protection of Investments, December 12, 1987, 27 I.L.M. 612 (1988). 24 Int'l Law. 675.

Note

For a discussion of bilateral investment treaties, see Guzman, Why LDCs Sign Treaties that Hurt Them: Explaining the Popularity of Bilateral Investment Treaties, 38 Va.J. Int'l L. 639 (1998); Kishoiyian, The Utility of Bilateral Investment Treaties in the Formulation of Customary International Law, 14 J. Int. L. Bus. 327 (1998); Vandervelde, The Political Economy of a Bilateral Investment Treaty, 92 A.J.I.L. 621 (1998); Dolzer & Stevens, Bilateral Investment Treaties (Nijhoff 1995); Alvarez, Vandevelde, Propp, Gunawardana and others, Panel Discussion on The Development and Expansion of Bilateral Investment Treaties, A.S.I.L. Proc. 532–557 (1992); Gann, The U.S. Bilateral Investment Treaty Program, 21 Stan.J. Int'l L. 373 (1985).

SECTION 8. PROTECTION UNDER U.S. LAW FOR INTERNATIONAL TRADE AND INVESTMENT

A. SOVEREIGN IMMUNITY, THE ACT OF STATE DOCTRINE, THE SECOND HICKENLOOPER AMENDMENT AND THE HELMS–BURTON ACT

A U.S. national seeking to obtain legal redress in U.S. courts for injury to property attributable to conduct of a foreign state or its instrumentality may be faced with a claim of sovereign immunity, discussed at p. 1197, as well as an invocation of the act of state doctrine, discussed at p. 180. To what extent does the Second Hickenlooper Amendment, at p. 190, which was enacted to preclude application of the act of state doctrine to certain takings of property in violation of international law, meaningfully improve the legal position of the U.S. national?

In connection with the materials on state immunity, the act of state doctrine and the Second Hickenlooper Amendment, consider under what circumstances a U.S. national can invoke the aid of U.S. courts if its property has been taken without compensation by a foreign state. What are the possibilities if the property seized is brought into the United States? How would the rights and remedies of the U.S. national be affected by whether the property is in the possession of the foreign state or some private party deriving its title through the foreign state? If the property does not find its way into the United States, under what circumstances, if any, could relief be obtained in U.S. courts?

Also consider under what circumstances a U.S. court can provide a remedy in the event of a breach of an investment guarantee contact, a mineral concession agreement or other international investment contract by a foreign state. See, generally, Mok, Comment: Expropriation Claims in United States Courts: The Act of State Doctrine, the Sovereign Immunity Doctrine, and the Foreign Sovereign Immunities Act. A Roadmap for the Expropriated Victim, 8 Pace Int'l L.Rev. 199 (1996).

Notes

1. Sovereign Immunity

Under customary international law and the U.S. Foreign Sovereign Immunities Act of 1976 (FSIA), 28 U.S.C.A. § 1602, foreign states are generally not immune from U.S. judicial jurisdiction insofar as their commercial activities are concerned so long as those commercial activities occur in or directly affect the United States. See p. 1204.

Moreover, with respect to takings of property by a foreign state, § 1605(a)(3) of the FSIA specifically provides that a state is not immune from U.S. jurisdiction to adjudicate with respect to property taken in violation of international law which is present in the United States in connection with a commercial activity carried on in the United States by the taking state. Section 1605(a)(2) of the FSIA eliminates immunity from suits arising out of a foreign state's "commercial activity" having a "direct effect" in the United States. As noted below and at p. 1242, sovereign immunity may be waived under § 1605(a)(1) of the FSIA.

2. The Act of State Doctrine

Even if a remedy in U.S. courts is not precluded by sovereign immunity as a result of the FSIA, the act of state doctrine may bar relief. A taking of a U.S. investor's property by a foreign state without compensation will almost always constitute an act of state, and a repudiation or breach of an investment contract or concession agreement may also be deemed a sovereign act.

The decision of the Supreme Court in the *Sabbatino* case at p. 181, involved a taking of property of a U.S. national by the government of a recognized state within its own territory that was alleged to have been in violation of a rule of customary international law as to which there was substantial controversy. The Court held that U.S. courts may not question the validity of a taking of property by a foreign government under those circumstances. The Supreme Court has not had occasion to decide a case involving a taking of property by a foreign state since *Sabbatino* in which one of those circumstances was not present.

While lower courts have applied the act of state doctrine to breach of contract by a foreign state, the Supreme Court has not decided the issue. See, e.g., Hewitt v. Speyer, 250 F. 367 (2d cir.1918) and French v. Banco Nacional de Cuba, 23 N.Y.2d 46, 295 N.Y.S.2d 433, 242 N.E.2d 704 (N.Y. 1968). The act of state doctrine is, however, subject to some clear and some arguable limitations and exceptions.

One clear exception is that provided by the Second Hickenlooper Amendment, discussed at p. 190, which precludes application of the act of state doctrine to a taking of property in violation of the principles of international law, including the principles of compensation set out in the First Hickenlooper Amendment, at p. 818.

After the reversal and remand by the Supreme Court in *Sabbatino* and enactment of the Second Hickenlooper Amendment, the *Sabbatino* case again came before the Second Circuit Court of Appeals. Banco Nacional de Cuba v. Farr, 383 F.2d 166 (2d Cir.1967), cert. denied, 390 U.S. 956, 88 S.Ct. 1038, 19 L.Ed.2d 1151 (1968). The Court of Appeals reaffirmed its prior decision rejecting the act of state defense and noted, in a dictum, that if the compensation standards of the statute were different from, they tended to be more exacting upon expropriating states than, the customary international law standards applied in the first *Sabbatino* case and reapplied in the second. 383 F.2d at 183–85.

If a suit based on a taking of property by a foreign state is brought under § 1506(a)(3) of the FSIA, the court may have to determine compliance with international law under that provision as well as under the Second Hickenlooper Amendment. It is unclear whether the court should apply the standards of customary international law or an applicable treaty or the more specific standards of the First Hickenlooper Amendment. See Restatement (Third) § 444, Comment *d*.

The scope of the Second Hickenlooper Amendment, however, is quite narrow. It is limited to actions asserting title to specific property within the United States. If the property taken is located in the United States, the plaintiff need not attach or reduce the property to possession, and, as long as it was in the United States when the action is commenced, it need not remain in the United States during the pendency of the action. Restatement (Third) § 444, Comment *e*. The Amendment does not, however, apply to claims for compensation for a taking of property or to assets of a nationalizing state not related to the taking on which the action is based that may come within the territory of the United States. See Banco Nacional de Cuba v. First National City Bank of New York, 270 F.Supp. 1004 (S.D.N.Y.1967), rev'd, 431 F.2d 394 (2d Cir.1970), rev'd, 406 U.S. 759, 92 S.Ct. 1808, 32 L.Ed.2d 466 (1972); French v. Banco Nacional de Cuba, 23 N.Y.2d 46, 295 N.Y.S.2d 433, 242 N.E.2d 704 (1968); compare Ramirez de Arellano v. Weinberger, 745 F.2d 1500 (D.C.Cir.1984), vac'd, 471 U.S. 1113, 105 S.Ct. 2353, 86 L.Ed.2d 255 (1985). The Amendment also has no application to cases involving breach of contractual obligations by a foreign state.

No President has made a determination that the foreign policy interests of the United States required application of the act of state doctrine in a case to which the Second Hickenlooper Amendment applied. However, in connection with the Algiers Accords containing the agreement between the United States and Iran of January 1981, the Carter Administration gave assurances that the courts would be advised that adjudication of claims brought by the government of Iran to recover property allegedly removed from Iran by the

Shah or his family should not be considered legally barred by the act of state doctrine.

A second clear exception to the act of state defense is that it generally does not apply to takings of property located outside the territorial jurisdiction of the taking state at the time of the taking, e.g., Republic of Iraq v. First National City Bank, 241 F.Supp. 567 (S.D.N.Y.1965), aff'd, 353 F.2d 47 (2d Cir.1965), cert. denied, 382 U.S. 1027, 86 S.Ct. 648, 15 L.Ed.2d 540 (1966). However, a court may give effect to an act of state even as to assets in the United States when it serves the policy objectives of the United States to do so. Banco Nacional de Cuba v. Chemical Bank New York Trust Co., 658 F.2d 903 (2d Cir.1981).

A third arguable exception to application of the act of state doctrine is that it should not be applied to property that is used in connection with commercial activity. In Alfred Dunhill of London, Inc. v. Republic of Cuba, 425 U.S. 682, 96 S.Ct. 1854, 48 L.Ed.2d 301 (1976), the Supreme Court held that repudiation by a Cuban state agency of an obligation to repay amounts paid by a U.S. importer of cigars did not constitute an act of state on the ground that an act of state implies a formal act of sovereignty. Four justices of the majority also expressed the view that an exception to the act of state doctrine should be applicable in the case of commercial transactions engaged in by a foreign state. This was based on the analogy of the commercial activity exception to the sovereign immunity doctrine and the fact that with respect to commercial transactions, unlike expropriation, there was broad international agreement as to the applicable rules, 425 U.S. at 695–706, 96 S.Ct. at 1861–1866. Four justices, however, declined to apply a commercial activity exception to the act of state doctrine. This exception, moreover, has been rejected by some lower courts. See, e.g., Braka v. Bancomer, S.N.C., 762 F.2d 222 (2d Cir.1985) and International Ass'n of Machinists and Aerospace Workers v. Organization of the Petroleum Exporting Countries (OPEC), 649 F.2d 1354 (9th Cir. 1981).

3. *The Helms–Burton Act*

In 1996, the U.S. Congress passed the Helms–Burton Act which provides, in part, that courts may not consider the "act of state" doctrine in regard to claims seeking to recover the property of U.S. nationals expropriated by Cuba since 1959. 22 U.S.C.A. § 6022; 35 I.L.M. 357. Title III provides a civil remedy in the form of monetary damages against any person that "traffics in property which was confiscated by the Cuban Government on or after January 1, 1959." Section 4 states that a person traffics in confiscated property if it "knowingly and intentionally * * * sells, transfers, distributes, dispenses, brokers, manages * * * engages in commercial activity using or otherwise benefiting from confiscated property." In contrast to the Second Hickenlooper Amendment, there are no limitations as to the location of the property. Additionally, Title IV of the Act imposes sanctions on individuals and corporations who do business with Cuba and thereby "traffic in confiscated property." The sanctions include denial of a U.S. visa to an individual, corporate officer, principal or shareholder in an entity involved with the confiscation or trafficking of such property and a spouse, minor child, or agent of such person. At present, the provisions in Title III and IV remain suspended by successive six-month presidential waivers. Washington Post, Jan. 16, 2000, at C3.

4. *Waiver of Immunity or Application of the Act of State Doctrine*

Another issue for the U.S. national seeking a recovery in U.S. courts to consider is whether there is a basis for arguing that the foreign state has waived its immunity or application of the act of state doctrine. Waiver of immunity is discussed at p. 1242, where it is noted that the FSIA distinguishes between (1) waiver of immunity from jurisdiction, (2) waiver of immunity with respect to execution and (3) waiver of immunity from attachment prior to the entry of judgment. Under the FSIA the first two may be effected either "explicitly or by implication," while the third waiver must be explicit.

Thus, under the FSIA, there is a relatively clear chart for the course needed to obtain a waiver of sovereign immunity in a contract between a U.S. person and a foreign sovereign.

Achieving an effective waiver by a foreign sovereign of the act of state doctrine, however, presents a more significant challenge—one that is of particular significance in connection with investment contracts between U.S. investors and foreign governments.

The courts have not generally been willing to apply the commercial activity exception applied in the sovereign immunity context to the act of state doctrine, and the FSIA does not purport to deal with act of state. However, although no court has yet definitively considered the matter, an explicit waiver of the act of state defense by the foreign government in its contract with the investor, if a feasible option in the context of the negotiations, may provide a measure of legal protection. For a comprehensive discussion of the act of state doctrine in the context of the enforceability of contracts between private parties and foreign governments in U.S. courts, see Ramsey, Acts of State and Foreign Sovereign Obligations, 39 Harv. Int'l L.J. 1 (1998).

5. *Enforceability of an International Arbitration Award*

In part because of the difficulties and uncertainties presented in enforcing a contractual obligation of a foreign sovereign in U.S. courts, some of which are touched on above, it is common for a U.S. investor to seek to have a provision calling for international arbitration of disputes included in its international concession agreement or other investment contract with a foreign state. As discussed at p. 811, many U.S. bilateral investment treaties provide for eventual resolution of disputes between a U.S. investor and the foreign state party to the BIT by arbitration under rules of ICSID, UNCITRAL or other arbitral body agreed to by the parties. An agreement to submit disputes to arbitration by the foreign state will not be defeated by a claim of immunity (which is waived by the agreement) or by the act of state doctrine. See, e.g., AGIP v. Popular Republic of the Congo, 21 I.L.M. 726 (1982); Texas Overseas Petroleum v. Libya, at p. 790. An award in favor of a U.S. claimant handed down by an international arbitration will be enforced by U.S. courts. Neither sovereign immunity, Restatement (Third) § 456(2)(b), nor the act of state doctrine, 9 U.S.C. § 15, bars such enforcement.

B. FIRST HICKENLOOPER AMENDMENT

FOREIGN ASSISTANCE ACT OF 1961, SECTION 301

77 Stat. 386 (1963), 78 Stat. 1013 (1964), as amended, 22 U.S.C.A. § 2370(e).

(e)(1) The President shall suspend assistance to the government of any country to which assistance is provided under this chapter or any other Act when the government of such country or any other government agency or subdivision within such country on or after January 1, 1962—

(A) has nationalized or expropriated or seized ownership or control of property owned by any United States citizen or by any corporation, partnership, or association not less than 50 per centum beneficially owned by United States citizens, or

(B) has taken steps to repudiate or nullify existing contracts or agreements with any United States citizen or any corporation or partnership, or association not less than 50 per centum beneficially owned by United States citizens, or

(C) has imposed or enforced discriminatory taxes or other exactions, or restrictive maintenance or operational conditions, or has taken other actions, which have the effect of nationalizing, expropriating, or otherwise seizing ownership or control of property so owned, and such country, government agency, or government subdivision fails within a reasonable time (not more than six months after such action, or, in the event of a referral to the Foreign Claims Settlement Commission of the United States within such period as provided herein, not more than twenty days after the report of the Commission is received) to take appropriate steps, which may include arbitration, to discharge its obligations under international law toward such citizen or entity, including speedy compensation for such property in convertible foreign exchange, equivalent to the full value thereof, as required by international law, or fails to take steps designed to provide relief from such taxes, exactions, or conditions, as the case may be; and such suspension shall continue until the President is satisfied that appropriate steps are being taken, and the provisions of this subsection shall not be waived with respect to any country unless the President determines and certifies that such a waiver is important to the national interests of the United States. Such certification shall be reported immediately to Congress.

Upon request of the President (within seventy days after such action referred to in subparagraphs (A), (B), or (C) of this paragraph), the Foreign Claims Settlement Commission of the United States * * * is hereby authorized to evaluate expropriated property, determining the full value of any property nationalized, expropriated, or seized, or subjected to discriminatory or other actions as aforesaid, for purposes of this subsection and to render an advisory report to the President within ninety days after such request. Unless authorized by the President, the Commission shall not publish its advisory report except to the citizen or entity owning such property. * * *

(2) [Second Hickenlooper Amendment, at p. 190.]

Note

Until amended by the Foreign Assistance Act of 1973, P.L. No. 93–183, 87 Stat. 722 (1973), to provide for waiver when certified by the President to be in the national interest, the First Hickenlooper Amendment, 22 U.S.C.A. § 2370(e)(1), dealing with suspension of foreign aid, contained a no-waiver clause. Prior to the 1973 change, the clause had been invoked only once, against Ceylon in 1963. In the case of the dispute between International Petroleum Company, Ltd. (IPC), a wholly owned subsidiary of Standard Oil of New Jersey, and Peru in 1969, the Nixon Administration strained to avoid applying it by finding that resort to Peruvian administrative remedies and ongoing negotiations constituted "appropriate steps" adequate to make invocation unnecessary. Even after those remedies had been exhausted and negotiations had broken down, the First Hickenlooper Amendment was not applied, and since then it has never been invoked. See Lillich, Requiem for Hickenlooper, 69 A.J.I.L. 97–100.

Chapter 11

DISPUTE SETTLEMENT

The topic of dispute settlement in international law raises threshold questions of concept and definition. Classic works on international law, and landmark treaties of the late 19th and early 20th century (e.g., the 1899 and 1907 Hague Conventions and 1928 General Act for the Pacific Settlement of International Disputes, and many bilateral treaties), identified the subject as "peaceful" or "pacific" settlement of disputes, thereby suggesting that legal mechanisms could help avoid war. Under this conceptualization, international law and legal institutions are understood as part of the array of available techniques for international conflict prevention and resolution. Yet despite the impressive proliferation of available dispute settlement mechanisms, the history of the 20th century shows that the most serious disputes have eluded legal resolution, and the root causes of conflict are often ones not amenable to solution by resort to international law.

While the U.N. Charter describes the International Court of Justice as "the principal judicial organ" of the United Nations and the U.N. is the most comprehensive peaceful settlement institution in terms of purposes and members, states have increasingly looked beyond the I.C.J. and other U.N. mechanisms for dispute resolution. A striking feature of the latter part of the 20th century has been the establishment of many new dispute settlement mechanisms, some of them sharing attributes and overlapping in jurisdiction with classic state-centered institutions such as the I.C.J., but others striking out in innovative new directions. Departures from the state-centric paradigm are a notable aspect of some of the new mechanisms, but others remain largely the creation and servant of states. The new bodies typically respond to a felt need for specialization in a given field–e.g., human rights, trade, law of the sea–with expert judges rendering decisions on increasingly complex and technical bodies of law. Though some might envisage these bodies as forming a kind of "system," there is no hierarchical relationship among them and no agreed method for harmonizing potential conflicts among their decisions. See generally Charney, Is International Law Threatened by Multiple Tribunals?, 271 Rec. des Cours 101 (1998); Symposium, The Proliferation of International Tribunals: Piecing Together the Puzzle, 31 N.Y.U.J.Int'l L. & Policy 679–933 (1999).

The multiplicity of international legal dispute settlement bodies in our era makes it an exciting time for the study and practice of international law.

New modes of international jurisdiction make it more likely than ever before that when disputes arise, there will be a forum available for their resolution–provided that the parties have the will to use it. As of the opening of the 21st century, it remains the case for basically all international legal institutions that jurisdiction is grounded in consent, given either in advance or once a dispute arises. Though there may be some harbingers of alternatives to the traditional consent paradigm (for example, recent developments in collective enforcement and international criminal jurisdiction discussed in Chapters 9 and 15), there is as yet no international court with general compulsory jurisdiction or with effective power to compel reluctant parties to submit to judicial authority. Because of the patchwork character of international dispute settlement, an important part of the international lawyer's craft is knowledge of the available forums and the scope of (and limitations on) their jurisdiction.

The subject of dispute settlement presupposes a concept of "dispute," or of the kinds of disputes amenable to resolution in the eyes of international law. As we will see shortly (pp. 825–26), the I.C.J. and other international legal bodies have developed and applied a legal definition of "dispute," which is a starting point for determining their jurisdiction. There is also extensive case law dealing with the recurrent objection that some kinds of disputes demand political rather than legal resolution.

The materials in this chapter begin with the framework set out in the U.N. Charter for dispute settlement "by peaceful means." We will survey a range of non-adjudicatory techniques, including negotiation, mediation, and facilities of regional and international organizations. We then turn to arbitration and adjudication, with emphasis on the I.C.J. as a classic model for adjudicatory settlement. The final section addresses the growing number of specialized tribunals, with attention to cross-cutting questions of structure, procedure, and implementation.

SECTION 1. THE OBLIGATION TO SETTLE DISPUTES BY PEACEFUL MEANS

A. THE CHARTER OBLIGATIONS

Article 2, paragraph 3 of the U.N. Charter provides:

> 3. All Members shall settle their international disputes by peaceful means in such a manner that international peace and security, and justice, are not endangered.

Article 33 of the Charter states:

> 1. The parties to any dispute, the continuance of which is likely to endanger the maintenance of international peace and security, shall, first of all, seek a solution by negotiation, enquiry, mediation, conciliation, arbitration, judicial settlement, resort to regional agencies or arrangements, or other peaceful means of their own choice.
>
> 2. The Security Council shall, when it deems necessary, call upon the parties to settle their dispute by such means.

Articles 34–38 of the Charter authorize the Security Council to recommend procedures and terms of settlement. Article 36(3) provides:

3. In making recommendations under this Article the Security Council should also take into consideration that legal disputes should as a general rule be referred by the parties to the International Court of Justice in accordance with the provisions of the Statute of the Court.

Notes

1. Does the obligation to settle disputes by peaceful means signify more than the obligation of Article 2(4) to avoid use of force or threat of force? Are states obliged to settle all their disputes or only those "the continuance of which is likely to endanger the maintenance of international peace and security" (Article 33)?

2. May the United Nations Security Council require a state to settle a dispute that the Council deems likely to endanger international peace? Compare the Council's authority under Chapter VI and Chapter VII of the Charter.

3. Does the obligation of Article 2(3) preclude a state from using force to vindicate its legal rights? See Chapter 12.

B. TREATY OBLIGATIONS OF PEACEFUL SETTLEMENT

Many treaties—multilateral and bilateral—have included obligations to settle disputes by peaceful means. Some cover broad categories of disputes; others refer to disputes of specified character.

1. The General Act of 1928

The most notable attempt to establish obligations of peaceful settlement of all disputes was the General Act for the Pacific Settlement of International Disputes adopted in Geneva by the League of Nations in 1928. It is sometimes referred to as the Geneva Act. Chapter I of the Act provides for the conciliation of legal disputes if the parties so agree; if they do not agree, or if conciliation fails, Chapter II requires the submission of the dispute to arbitration or to the Permanent Court of International Justice. Non-legal disputes are to be submitted to conciliation under Chapter I; if conciliation fails, the dispute is to be referred to an arbitral tribunal for settlement under Chapter III. A novel and striking aspect of Chapter III is its provision that, failing agreement to the contrary by the parties, the tribunal should decide the dispute *ex aequo et bono* if no rule of positive international law could dispose of the controversy. The significance of this provision is not clear, and its practical importance has not been great. In 1949, the General Assembly of the United Nations revised the Act in some minor respects, but previous adherences were not affected. Revised General Act, G.A.Res. 268 (IV) (1949).

The General Act was acceded to by 22 states but some states later denounced it. The 1949 Revised General Act has had only seven accessions. The United States did not become a party to either of the General Acts.

Whether the 1928 General Act was still in force has been questioned by parties in several cases before the International Court of Justice, including the Nuclear Tests Cases, 1974 I.C.J. 253; the Trial of Pakistani Prisoners of War Case, 1973 I.C.J. 328; and the Aegean Sea Continental Shelf Case, 1978 I.C.J. 3. The Court did not find it necessary to determine the present status of the 1928 Act. In the Case Concerning the Aerial Incident of 10 August 1999 (Pakistan v. India), 2000 I.C.J., 39 I.L.M. 1116 (Judgment on Jurisdiction),

Pakistan argued that British acceptance of the General Act in the interwar period carried over to both India and Pakistan, but the Court concluded that India had effectively rejected the General Act upon attaining independence. In view of its conclusion that India was not in any event bound by the General Act, the Court did not have to rule on whether the General Act survived the demise of the League of Nations.

2. *Other Dispute Settlement Treaties*

Between the two World Wars, many bilateral treaties were concluded providing for conciliation or arbitration of disputes between states. Generally, they exclude some categories of disputes such as those involving "vital interests" or domestic matters. The United States entered into about 20 bilateral treaties for conciliation and arbitration. Over 200 such treaties are reproduced in the U.N. Systematic Survey of Treaties for the Pacific Settlement of International Disputes 1928–1948 (1949).

After the United Nations Charter came into force, new treaties that dealt solely with peaceful settlement decreased sharply. Only 8 such treaties were concluded from 1949–1962. This is understandable, since the Charter itself includes obligations of pacific settlement. However, regional treaties were still thought to be useful to spell out obligations of dispute settlement and their implementation. In 1957, a European Convention on the Peaceful Settlement of Disputes was concluded, and in 1964 the African states concluded a Protocol on Conciliation and Arbitration to implement the general dispute settlement obligation in the Charter of African Unity. For texts, see U.N. Survey of Treaty Provisions for the Pacific Settlement of International Disputes 1949–1962 (1966). See also U.N. Handbook on the Peaceful Settlement of Disputes Between States (1992).

3. *Dispute Clauses in Treaties on Other Matters*

In addition to these specialized dispute settlement treaties, many treaties dealing with other matters contain broadly stated obligations to settle disputes through negotiation, conciliation, arbitration or judicial settlement. Some only repeat the U.N. Charter provisions. See, for example, the NATO Treaty of 1949, Articles 1 and 7 (34 U.N.T.S. 342). Multilateral agreements for regional cooperation, and numerous bilateral and multilateral treaties on economic matters, or transport and communications and social questions, have dispute settlement clauses applicable to differences arising under those treaties. For texts, see U.N. Survey, supra. Writing in 1976, Sohn noted that out of 17,000 treaties registered with the League of Nations or the United Nations, some 4,000 include compromissory clauses providing for the pacific settlement of disputes relating to the interpretation and application of the treaty itself. He writes:

> They present a rich and wondrous mosaic. The methods of settlement employed range from bilateral negotiations through conciliation and various forms of arbitration to reference to the International Court of Justice or other permanent tribunals.
>
> Some clauses take the form of a single sentence; others embody extensive codes of structural and procedural provisions, sometimes even offering alternative methods of settlement for different kinds of disputes.

Sohn, Settlement of Disputes Relating to the Interpretation and Application of Treaties, 136 Rec. des Cours 205, 259 (1976–II).

The United States is a party to more than 70 bilateral and multilateral treaties that include compromissory clauses providing for judicial settlement at the International Court of Justice. Morrison, Treaties as a Source of Jurisdiction Especially in U.S. Practice, in The International Court of Justice at a Crossroads 58, 61 (Damrosch ed., 1987). Many more U.S. treaties provide for another form of dispute settlement, such as arbitration.

Many of these clauses bind all disputants to submit to the procedure at the unilateral request of one of them. For example, the Multilateral Protocol for Regulating Poppy Cultivation and Opium Production of 1953 requires submission to the International Court of Justice "at the request of any of the parties to the dispute." Other clauses state simply that the dispute shall be submitted to arbitration or other means of settlement. While such clauses are mandatory, they require that all the parties to the dispute agree on the submission. The Antarctic Treaty, for example, says that "any dispute shall, with the consent of all parties to the dispute, be referred to the International Court of Justice for settlement."

The International Court of Justice and its predecessor, the Permanent Court of International Justice (P.C.I.J.), have considered the non-judicial remedies in compromissory clauses in a number of cases. An enlightening analysis of those cases is found in Scheffer, Non–Judicial Remedies and the Jurisdiction of the International Court of Justice, 27 Stan.J.Int'l L. 83 (1991).

The most common clauses in bilateral agreements provide for settlement through bilateral negotiations, consultation or other contacts of the parties. They do not involve third parties and therefore do not provide for binding decisions. Mixed commissions are often utilized. A contemporary example is the treaty between the United States and the Soviet Union on anti-ballistic missiles (ABM Treaty), 23 U.S.T. 3435, TIAS No. 7503, which provides for a Standing Consultative Commission to deal with questions of compliance under the treaty. See Caldwell, The Standing Consultative Commission, in Verification and Arms Control (Potter ed. 1985); Chayes & Chayes, The New Sovereignty: Compliance With International Regulatory Agreements 177, 207, 213 (1995) (on uses of Standing Consultative Commission in U.S.-Soviet arms control disputes).

Other clauses in bilateral treaties provide for reference to permanent organs or to arbitration and judicial settlement. See Sections 3 and 4.

Elaborate treaty provisions for dispute settlement are contained in the U.N. Convention on the Law of Sea of 1982 (UNCLOS). They include a variety of procedures for binding and non-binding decisions on disputes arising under the Convention and allow for considerable flexibility in the choice of procedures. However, every contracting party must signify, at the time it expresses its consent to be bound, its choice of the basic procedure or forum it is willing to accept. Part XV and Annexes V, VI, and VII of the Convention on the Law of the Sea, 1982. See Chapter 16. A major development following the entry into force of UNCLOS in 1994 is the establishment of the International Tribunal on the Law of the Sea: its judges were elected in 1996 and it began hearing cases in 1998. See pp. 913–919.

C. THE MEANING OF "DISPUTE"

The obligation of peaceful settlement applies to "disputes," not to all disagreements between states. A difference in views, or a sense of injury, does not necessarily mean that a dispute exists. International case-law and commentary have considered the term "dispute" as a term with a special legal meaning. The failure of an applicant to show the existence of a dispute has been a ground for rejecting cases brought to the International Court and its predecessor, the Permanent Court. See Electricity Company of Sofia, 1939 P.C.I.J. Ser. A/B, No. 77, 64, 83; Northern Cameroons Case, 1963 I.C.J. 15, 33–34; Nuclear Tests Cases, 1974 I.C.J. 253, 260, 270–271.

A dispute requires a degree of specificity and contestation. In the *Mavrommatis Case,* the International Court defined dispute "as a disagreement on a point of law or fact, a conflict of legal views or interests between two persons." 1924 P.C.I.J. Ser. A, No. 2, at 11–12.

There is authority that a disagreement is not a dispute if its resolution would not have any practical effect on the relations of the parties. In the *Northern Cameroons Case,* the International Court was faced with a disagreement on the interpretation of a United Nations trusteeship agreement that was no longer in force. Moreover, the applicant made no claim for reparation. In declining to adjudicate the claim, the Court said:

> The Court's judgment must have some practical consequences in the sense that it can affect existing legal rights or obligations thus removing uncertainty from their legal relations. No judgment on the merits in this case would satisfy these essentials of the judicial function.

1963 I.C.J. 15 at 33–34.

In the *Nuclear Tests Cases* brought by Australia and New Zealand against France, the majority of the Court considered that French government statements that the tests had ceased meant that a dispute between the parties no longer existed. 1974 I.C.J. 253 at 270–71. However, four dissenting judges noted that the claims and legal grounds advanced by the applicants were rejected by the French government on legal grounds. They said: "these circumstances in themselves suffice to qualify the present dispute as a 'dispute in regard to which the parties are in conflict as to their legal rights' and as a 'legal dispute' * * * ." Joint Dissenting Opinion of Judges Jiménez de Aréchaga, Dillard, Onyeama and Waldock, id. at 366. Compare the doctrine of "mootness" in U.S. domestic courts. For the Court's rejection of a subsequent attempt to revive these cases upon France's resumption of a different form of testing (underground rather than atmospheric), see Request for an Examination of the Situation in the Nuclear Tests Case (New Zealand v. France), Order of Sept. 22 1995, 1995 I.C.J. 288.

Is prior negotiation necessary to determine that a dispute exists? The P.C.I.J. declared in one of the *Chorzów Cases:* "The manifestation of a dispute in a specific manner, as for instance by diplomatic negotiations, is not required." But the Court added that it is "desirable" that a State should not summon another State to appear before the Court without having endeavored to make it clear that the difference between them "has not been capable of being otherwise overcome." 1927 P.C.I.J. Ser. A, No. 13, at 10–11.

The obligation to settle disputes by peaceful means is not limited to legal disputes. Neither the Charter provisions nor the other general treaty provisions requiring dispute settlement restrict the term "disputes" to legal disputes. The question of whether a dispute is "legal" arises when a treaty provides that a specific means of settlement shall be employed for legal disputes. Some treaties, for example, provide for settlement of non-legal disputes by conciliation or arbitration and for submission of legal disputes to the International Court. Although the International Court and other judicial tribunals are in a broad sense limited to deciding disputes on the basis of law, the parties to a dispute may refer a case to the International Court for a decision *ex aequo et bono* (see Article 38, para. 2, of the Statute). Apart from this exception, it seems clear from Article 38 that the Court must decide in accordance with international law. However, this does not preclude the Court from deciding an issue of fact "which if established would constitute a breach of an international obligation." Article 36(2) of the I.C.J. Statute.

Disputes regarding the interpretation or application of a treaty are recognized as essentially legal, even though they arise in political contexts and the legal question "forms only one element in a wider and long standing political dispute." Case Concerning the U.S. Diplomats in Tehran, 1980 I.C.J. 3, 19–20. In that case the Court found unacceptable the view that "because a legal dispute submitted to the Court is only an aspect of a political dispute, the Court should decline to resolve for the parties the legal question at issue between them." Id. See also Nicaragua v. United States, 1984 I.C.J. 392, 439–40 (Jurisdiction and Admissibility); Advisory Opinion on the Legality of the Threat or Use of Nuclear Weapons, 1996 I.C.J. 226, at para. 13, where the Court added that "the political nature of the motives which may be said to have inspired the request and the political implications that the opinion given might have are of no relevance in the establishment of its jurisdiction to give such an opinion." These cases are discussed below in Section 4 on the International Court. See also Restatement (Third) § 903, Comment *d*.

SECTION 2. NON-ADJUDICATORY PROCEDURES

A. NEGOTIATION

Negotiation is the dominant mode for settling disputes, or indeed for seeking to prevent them from arising in the first place. As a method that remains completely within the control of the parties, negotiation need not (and often does not) produce an outcome favoring the side with the stronger legal position. Nonetheless, in international as well as domestic matters, parties "bargain in the shadow of the law," and legal considerations are frequently relevant to the negotiating process.

A growing number of international cases deal with negotiation in the framework of international law, rather than mere power politics. An example is the obligation of parties to negotiate in good faith. In the *North Sea Continental Shelf Case,* the International Court said:

> The parties are under an obligation to enter into negotiations with a view to arriving at an agreement * * *. [T]hey are under an obligation so to conduct themselves that the negotiations are meaningful, which will

> not be the case when either of the parties insists upon its own position without contemplating any modification of it.

1969 I.C.J. 3, 47–48. In the *Gabcikovo-Nagymaros Project Case*, 1997 I.C.J. 92 at para. 139, the Court found the parties to be under a legal obligation to negotiate in order to consider in what way to fulfill all the multiple objectives of their 1977 treaty concerning works on the Danube River.

In the Nuclear Weapons Advisory Opinion, 1996 I.C.J. 226 at paras. 99–103, the Court interpreted Article VI of the Treaty on the Non–Proliferation of Nuclear Weapons, which contains an undertaking "to pursue negotiations in good faith on effective measures relating to the cessation of the nuclear arms race at an early date and to nuclear disarmament, and on a treaty on general and complete disarmament under strict and effective international control." The Court said (para. 99):

> The legal import of that obligation goes beyond that of a mere obligation of conduct; the obligation involved here is an obligation to achieve a precise result–nuclear disarmament in all its aspects–by adopting a particular course of conduct, namely, the pursuit of negotiations on the matter in good faith.

In the operative portion of its judgment (para. 2(F)), the Court unanimously held that there "exists an obligation to pursue in good faith *and bring to a conclusion* negotiations leading to nuclear disarmament in all its aspects under strict and effective international control." (Emphasis added.)

Notes

1. Many compromissory clauses provide that a dispute "not satisfactorily adjusted by diplomacy" (or negotiations) may be submitted upon unilateral application to an arbitral or judicial body. If such an application is submitted and the respondent objects to jurisdiction on the ground that negotiations have not been pursued or exhausted, should the tribunal accept, reject, or postpone its consideration of the issues presented to it? See, e.g., Border and Transborder Armed Actions (Nicaragua v. Honduras), Judgment on Jurisdiction and Admissibility, 1988 I.C.J. 69.

2. Multilateral negotiations in large international bodies and conferences obviously differ from negotiations between two states or among small groups. Where large numbers of participants are involved, blocs of like-minded states and coalitions of divergent groups generally play a significant role. Committees and working groups are often the principal arenas of negotiation. Leadership of some states or of individuals can be critical in reaching consensus. The chairmen of committees and secretariat personnel frequently seek compromise proposals. When the object is to achieve broad agreement, consensus procedures rather than voting are generally favored. Voting may however be resorted to for political ends. Several recent studies have thrown light on the complexities of multilateral negotiation. See Kaufmann, Conference Diplomacy (1968); Buzan, Negotiating by Consensus: Developments in Technique at the United Nations Conference on the Law of the Sea, 75 A.J.I.L. 324 (1981); Benedick, Ozone Diplomacy: New Directions in Safeguarding the Planet (1991).

On negotiation in general, see Merrills, International Dispute Settlement 1–26 (3rd ed. 1998) and references therein. See also Fisher & Ury, Getting to Yes:

Negotiating Agreement Without Giving In (2d ed. 1991); Cohen, Negotiating Across Cultures (rev. ed. 1997).

B. GOOD OFFICES, INQUIRY, MEDIATION, CONCILIATION

Good offices, inquiry, fact-finding, mediation, and conciliation all entail some form of third-party involvement in seeking a resolution of the dispute. Typically the parties to the dispute agree to receive third-party assistance but are not bound to accept the outcome of the process or the third party's proposals for a solution.

Good offices are frequently provided by the U.N. Secretary–General or another international leader to help the parties toward mutually acceptable terms of settlement. Fact-finding and inquiry include procedures under which an impartial third party investigates disputed facts and renders a report with conclusions: such investigations may go forward under the auspices of ad hoc or standing institutions, sometimes under the formal title of a "commission of inquiry." Under conciliation, the third party makes an impartial examination of the dispute and attempts to define the terms of a proposed settlement which the parties are invited (but not required) to accept.

Mediation is distinguished from conciliation and fact-finding in that the mediator is expected to have a more active role by furthering negotiation and interacting with the parties in the making of proposals for settlement. Techniques of mediation have been extensively studied by political scientists, historians, and social psychologists and a large body of research findings and analysis (along with historical and anecdotal narrative) is available. Flexibility and adaptation to the particular circumstances characterize the more successful efforts. Most observers agree that little would be gained by attempting to prescribe precise procedural rules or legal structures for mediation. On the other hand, detailed rules are available for conciliation, inquiry, and other structured procedures of dispute settlement, which the parties may draw on as appropriate.

Mediators, conciliators or other third-party facilitators may be individuals, committees, or institutional bodies. Heads of governments and experienced diplomats have often performed that role. In some cases, they can exercise leverage because of their ability to benefit or withhold benefits from the parties. They may have a representative role acting on behalf of the United Nations or an international regional agency. They may facilitate negotiation by providing information and ideas, by subdividing ("fractionating") issues, by offering services (such as monitoring compliance or providing resources), or even offering guarantees. Each dispute reveals its distinctive features and requires its own combination of methods

Notes

1. The 1899 and 1907 Hague Conventions for the Pacific Settlement of International disputes encouraged third parties to offer good offices and mediation. They also introduced procedures for commissions of inquiry to investigate and report on facts. Inquiries under the Hague Conventions include several episodes in which there had been exchange of fire or allegations of attack and the parties disagreed over exactly what had happened. For example, a commission of inquiry investigated the 1904 Dogger Bank incident, in which a Russian warship

had fired on a British fishing fleet in the mistaken belief that a Japanese torpedo attack was underway. Upon issuance of the report which concluded that there was no justification for opening fire, Russia paid an indemnity to Britain and the matter was considered closed. See Brierly, The Law of Nations 373–376 (6th ed. Waldock, 1963); Merrills, International Dispute Settlement 46–47 (3rd ed. 1998).

Fact-finding commissions under the Hague Conventions were utilized in several disputes of the early 20th century and a number of bilateral treaties provided for commissions of inquiry *(commissions d'enquête).* See Bar–Yaacov, The Handling of International Disputes By Means of Inquiry (1974); Report of the U.N. Secretary–General on Methods of Fact–Finding, U.N. Doc. A/5694 (1965) and A/6228 (1966); Merrills at 47–55 (3rd ed. 1998).

2. Early in the 20th century, the United States pursued a program of negotiating what became known as the "Bryan peace treaties," beginning with a 1914 treaty with Great Britain. The United States eventually concluded forty-eight "Bryan peace treaties," many of which are still in force. See 6 Hackworth at 5; Hyde at 1570–72; Report of the Secretary–General on Methods of Factfinding, U.N.Doc. A/5694, at 29–33 (May 1, 1964). The gist of the treaties was an agreement to refer "all disputes of every nature whatsoever" which could not be otherwise settled to a standing Peace Commission, consisting of one national and one non-national nominated by each party and a fifth member chosen by agreement.

The Bryan treaties lay dormant until the 1990s, when the United States and Chile agreed to submit a highly sensitive dispute to a commission constituted under the 1914 Bryan–Suárez Mujica Treaty. The dispute concerned the assassination in Washington, D.C. in 1976 of Orlando Letelier, a former Chilean Foreign minister in exile, and his American assistant. In the wake of both a domestic civil lawsuit brought by the victims' heirs against Chile, and a criminal investigation which revealed involvement of personnel of the Chilean intelligence service, the United States made an international claim against Chile. Chile denied responsibility but eventually offered to make an *ex gratia* payment corresponding to the sum that would have been payable if liability had been established. A commission was established under the Bryan treaty framework, which settled the amount of compensation to be paid. The United States and Chile accepted the outcome of this process in final settlement of their dispute over the Letelier assassination. See Chile–United States: Agreement to Settle Dispute Concerning Compensation for the Deaths of Letelier and Moffitt, 30 I.L.M. 422 (1991). For the award, see 31 I.L.M. 1 (1992); 88 I.L.R. 727.

3. On the General Act for the Pacific Settlement of International Disputes of 1928, the Locarno treaties of 1925, and the numerous other bilateral and multilateral conciliation conventions concluded between the wars, see generally 2 Oppenheim at 16–20, 88–96; Hyde at 1572–78. See also Habicht, Post–War Treaties for the Pacific Settlement of International Disputes (1931); U.N. Secretariat, Systematic Survey of Treaties for the Pacific Settlement of International Disputes, 1928–1948 (1949); U.N. Secretariat, A Survey of Treaty Provisions for the Pacific Settlement of International Disputes, 1949–1962 (1966). For a recent general survey, see J. Merrills, International Dispute Settlement (3rd ed. 1998).

4. Conciliation for dispute settlement is provided in the Vienna Convention on the Law of Treaties and the Vienna Convention on Succession of States in respect of Treaties. In both conventions, conciliation may be requested by any party to the dispute relating to the convention. The dispute is then referred to a conciliation commission which would seek to bring about an amicable settlement.

The commission may make proposals to the parties, but such proposals are not binding on the parties. See Kearney & Dalton, The Treaty on Treaties, 64 A.J.I.L. 495, 553–55 (1970); Lavalle, The Dispute Settlement Provisions of the Vienna Convention on Succession of States in Respect of Treaties, 73 A.J.I.L. 407 (1979). The U.N. Convention on the Law of the Sea of 1982 provides for compulsory (but non-binding) conciliation at the request of any party to a dispute relating to certain fisheries, scientific research and boundary questions. Article 297(3).

5. Conciliation procedures are also found in other multilateral treaties, including the Covenant on Civil and Political Rights (Article 42) and other human rights treaties. The objective of such procedures may be to reach an "amicable solution" or "friendly settlement" of a dispute under the treaty, without full-scale adjudication of the factual and legal issues. Compare the Case of Denmark v. Turkey, Friendly Settlement Judgment, European Court of Human Rights, Apr. 5, 2000, 39 I.L.M. 788 (2000) (case concerning allegations of torture of a Danish citizen in Turkey settled under Art. 38(1)(b) of European Convention as amended by Protocol No. 11).

6. Should the purely recommendatory character of a conciliation commission's proposals be reinforced by declaring in the rules that the parties are in no way bound or estopped by the findings of the commission? A proposal to this effect made by Fitzmaurice to the *Institut de Droit International* was not carried. See 2 Ann. de l'Institut de Droit Int'l 214 (1961). If a conciliation commission (e.g., under the Vienna Convention on the Law of Treaties) should find in favor of a state claiming invalidity of a treaty, would that finding furnish a good legal basis for that state to take steps to release it from the treaty commitment? Conversely, would a finding that there was no right to terminate estop a state from taking such action? It has been suggested that in determining the obligations of a party to the conciliation, the finding of the conciliator on the law and facts should be given weight but not treated as conclusive. Schachter, International Law in Theory and Practice 216 (1991).

7. Are conciliation commissions more effective if their procedure resembles that of negotiation (e.g., a round-table conference without rules of procedure)? Or is it generally desirable to have rules of procedure of a quasi-judicial nature? Both approaches have been followed in bilateral conciliation commissions. For consideration of the approaches, see 48–I Ann. de l'Institut de Droit Int'l 5 (1959), 49–II id., 214 (1961). When a commission faces a disagreement on a question of fact and seeks to interrogate witnesses or experts, should the proceedings be of a judicial nature? See Fox, Conciliation in International Disputes: The Legal Aspects, in Report of David Davies Memorial Institute 93 (1972). For general treatment of conciliation, see also Cot, International Conciliation (Eng. trans. 1972).

8. Several new mechanisms for conciliation and related procedures were introduced in the 1990s. Under U.N. auspices, a set of Model Rules for the Conciliation of Disputes Between States was approved: see U.N. Doc. A/50/33 (1995) and discussion in Merrills, International Dispute Settlement 79–80 (3rd ed. 1998). The Permanent Court of Arbitration has issued Optional Conciliation Rules (1996) and Optional Rules for Fact–Finding Commissions of Inquiry (1997), reprinted in Permanent Court of Arbitration, Basic Documents: Conventions, Rules, Model Clauses and Guidelines 153–184 (1998). The Organization for Security and Cooperation in Europe (O.S.C.E.) has likewise elaborated a Dispute Settlement Mechanism with elements of both mediation and conciliation, known as the Valletta Procedure, with enhancements subsequently adopted to induce resort to the available procedures. See Decision on Peaceful Settlement of Dis-

putes, 32 I.L.M. 551 (1993) and related instruments discussed in Merrills, pp. 80–83. The Stockholm Convention on Conciliation and Arbitration, also an O.S.C.E. instrument, came into force in 1994 with 12 European states as initial parties.

It remains to be seen whether any of these innovations of the 1990s will encourage greater resort to conciliation as a means of international dispute settlement. As an illustration of the relative underutilization of conciliation as a dispute settlement technique, only three of 63 disputes submitted to the World Bank's International Centre for Settlement of Investment Disputes (ICSID) took advantage of the Centre's conciliation facility, while the rest were arbitration cases (as reported in summary at 39 I.L.M. 966, 979 (2000)). What factors might disincline disputants toward the use of this technique?

MEDIATION IN RELATION TO INTERNATIONAL LAW AND LEGAL SETTLEMENT

Mediation of international disputes has frequently involved situations that for one reason or another could not be settled by resort to a legal institution or by application of international law. In a well-known example, mediation by the representative of the Pope, Cardinal Antonio Samoré, was able to bring about a definitive settlement of the dispute between Argentina and Chile concerning the Beagle Channel, after Argentina refused to accept the outcome of an arbitration that had awarded the disputed islands to Chile. The mediator could propose flexible approaches unavailable to the arbitrators, who were constrained to apply existing rules of international law to decide a boundary dispute. The mediator was able to defuse a crisis that could otherwise have led to war, by disaggregating the issues and finding a solution that respected both parties' genuine interests (separating possession of the island territories, of primary interest to Chile, from access to the maritime areas surrounding them, which was critical for Argentina). For discussion, see Laudy, The Vatican Mediation of the Beagle Channel Dispute: Crisis Intervention and Forum Building, in Words Over War: Mediation and Arbitration to Prevent Deadly Conflict (Greenberg, Barton & McGuinness, eds., 2000), pp. 293–320.

Recent literature on international conflict resolution explores the factors conducing toward successful mediation of international disputes. In a study of mediation sponsored by the Carnegie Commission on Preventing Deadly Conflict, published as Words Over War (Greenberg, Barton & McGuinness, eds., 2000), the editors pursue the theme of "whether mediators embraced or avoided concepts of international law," or more provocatively, whether substantive rules of international law might sometimes even impede the quest for just, sensible, and durable solutions to international conflict. See Greenberg, Barton & McGuinness, Introduction: Background and Analytical Perspectives, in Words Over War at pp. 1, 3–4, 7. They perceive some major problems with the existing rules and principles of international law, notably "zero-sum" notions of sovereignty which seem to discourage creative and pragmatic solutions to self-determination conflicts. Ibid., p. 13. After a review of a dozen case studies, including separatist conflicts and self-determination claims (Abkhazia, Bosnia, Croatia, Palestine), integrative processes (Cambodia, El Salvador, Northern Ireland, Rwanda, South Africa), and non-civil conflicts (Aral

Sea basin, Beagle Channel, North Korean nuclear proliferation), they conclude:

> The body of international law dealing with autonomy proved positively harmful. In those cases that confronted the intermixed questions of sovereignty, autonomy, confederation, self-determination, and independence, e.g., Abkhazia, Bosnia, Croatia, Northern Ireland, the legal debate stood in the way of effective dispute resolution. The legal concepts are too blunt to allow for political compromise; there is formally no such thing as partial sovereignty–even though, in practice, sovereignty is always limited by practical and formal international obligations and by responsibilities beyond the management of the nation-state. The absoluteness of the sovereignty concept often becomes an absolute barrier to agreement. * * *
>
> In other areas, international law has provided a framework, and may well have averted many disputes from ever reaching the conflict stage. Nevertheless, the technicalities of international law can create problems, as in the Beagle Channel dispute. * * * [R]esolution of the Beagle Channel dispute involved separating the treatment of rights over islands from the treatment of rights over associated exclusive economic zones in a way that was legally irrational but politically sensible. * * *
>
> In contrast to the performance of substantive international law, the performance of procedural international law has been excellent in essentially all the examples. Existing processes have successfully led to the availability of international mediators and a reasonable focus of discussion in almost all disputes studied. * * *
>
> The panel of legal experts who advised our group also pointed out the success of *emerging* principles of international law, which coincide with political science notions of democratic processes, transparency, and the right of the individual to security. Inherent in the substance of every mediated agreement were adherence to democratic procedures, fair elections, transparent governmental procedures, the primacy of the rule of law, and the promise of human rights to all individuals. Many of the agreements and subsequent implementation agreements incorporated specific international legal norms and covenants (e.g., the annexes of the Dayton Accords, the new South African constitution).
>
> A further surprise arises in connection with the application of international law during the follow-up to an agreement. As indicated above, we are now able (relatively) quickly and easily to incorporate international actions to assist in making an agreement work. This is exemplified by guarantees and UN forces, such as those in Cambodia and Croatia. * * *

Barton & Greenberg, Lessons of the Case Studies, in Words Over War 343, 358–359 (2000).

Notes

1. For other studies of interest, see J. Merrills, International Dispute Settlement 27–43 (3rd ed. 1998) (chapter on mediation); J. Bercovich (ed.), Resolving International Conflicts: The Theory and Practice of Mediation (1996); D. Pruitt and J. Rubin, Social Conflict: Escalation, Stalemate and Settlement (1986); I.W.

Zartman, Ripe for Resolution (1985); V. Pechota, Complementary Structures of Third Party Settlement in International Disputes (UNITAR Study), reprinted in Dispute Settlement Through the United Nations 149–220 (V. Raman ed., 1977); O. Young, The Intermediaries, Third Parties in International Crises (1967).

Notable recent instances of third-party mediation include the "Oslo channel" which produced the 1993 breakthrough in Israeli–Palestinian negotiations through active Norwegian efforts; agreements between Israel and its neighbors mediated by the United States (the Camp David agreement with Egypt in 1978; the peace treaty with Jordan concluded in Washington in 1995; and developments in the Israeli–Palestinian process, including the Wye River memorandum of 1998, leading to "final status" talks which were continuing with U.S. assistance through 2000). See, e.g., Bien, The Oslo Channel: Benefits of a Neutral Facilitator to Secret Negotiations, in Words Over War 109–138 (2000).

2. Third-party mediation has sometimes been carried out by non-governmental organizations and private individuals, as in the above example of papal mediation of the Beagle Channel dispute between Argentina and Chile. In 1993, a Roman Catholic lay society in Rome played a key role in bringing an end to a bloody civil war in Mozambique that had gone on for almost a decade. See C.R. Hume, The Mozambique Peace Process, in the Diplomatic Record 1993. The International Committee of the Red Cross and the Society of Friends (Quakers) have both carried out mediation efforts through "quiet diplomacy." Former heads of state and government, such as ex-U.S. President Jimmy Carter, have mediated solutions to several sensitive disputes (e.g, the 1994 dispute over North Korean compliance with non-proliferation obligations) while acting in a private capacity. See, e.g., Tang, The North Korean Nuclear Proliferation Crisis, in Words Over War 321–340 (2000).

For other examples and analysis, see Final Report of the Carnegie Commission on Prevention of Deadly Conflict (1998).

C. DISPUTE SETTLEMENT THROUGH THE UNITED NATIONS AND OTHER INTERNATIONAL ORGANIZATIONS

Preventive diplomacy and peacemaking by the United Nations are based on several Charter provisions, beginning with the principle of Article 2(3) that

> "All Members shall settle their international disputes by peaceful means in such a manner that international peace and security, and justice, are not endangered."

This unqualified language appears to oblige states to settle all their disputes with other states, whether or not their continuance endangers peace. In fact, there are numerous inter-state disputes that states feel no need to settle and that do not endanger peace. Note also that Article 2(3) requires that the settlement of a dispute shall not endanger "justice," a requirement that does not appear in Chapter VI on Pacific Settlement of Disputes.

Article 33 of Chapter VI also imposes an obligation of peaceful settlement, but here it refers to a dispute or situation "the continuance of which is likely to endanger the maintenance of international peace and security." This may suggest that a bilateral dispute would not be covered unless it threatened wider repercussions, but this limitation has not been recognized in practice.

Questions have arisen as to the responsibility of the Security Council under Article 34 to investigate any dispute or "situation" in order to determine whether the continuance of the dispute or situation is likely to endanger the maintenance of international peace and security. Developments of the 1990s leave little doubt that the Council is empowered to investigate situations involving internal conflict or mistreatment of inhabitants of a country as potential threats to peace and security. In a substantial number of cases the U.N. Security Council has authorized the Secretary–General to seek to facilitate settlement of internal disputes between competing factions in a country. It did so in respect to the former Belgian Congo (later Zaire) in 1961–1963. G. Abi–Saab, The United Nations Operation in the Congo, 1960–1964, 124–38 (1978). More recently, it did so in regard to Somalia in 1992–1993 (through several resolutions characterizing the internal situation of Somalia as a threat to peace and security); Haiti in 1993–1994; Sierra Leone since 1997 (continuing as of 2000); and various other cases. Since such peace-making efforts are increasingly associated with "peacekeeping" forces, the recent developments in this regard will be taken up in Chapter 12 on use of force.

Notes

1. Humanitarian assistance may facilitate dispute settlement in a situation where disorder and material shortages aggravate a conflict. The High Commissioner for Refugees, the Children's Fund (UNICEF), the World Food Program, the World Health Organization, and other humanitarian bodies have become an important part of many efforts to achieve settlement of conflict, along with non-governmental and private voluntary organizations.

2. The "Millennium Summit" of world leaders at U.N. headquarters in September 2000 provided the occasion for taking stock of U.N. involvement in efforts to settle a variety of dangerous disputes, and to assess potential institutional improvements. See generally Report of the Secretary-General on the Work of the Organization, U.N.Doc. A/55/1 (2000), pp. 5–12.

REGIONAL ORGANIZATIONS

Regional organizations such as the Organization of American States (O.A.S.), the Organization of African Unity (O.A.U.), the Arab League, the Organization for Security and Cooperation in Europe (O.S.C.E.), the Association of South–East Asian States (ASEAN), and others have also had active roles in non-adjudicatory dispute settlement. The conflicts in ex-Yugoslavia in the 1990s were dealt with through joint efforts of mediators appointed by the U.N. Secretary–General and the European Community/European Union. Efforts toward settlement of the civil war in El Salvador were carried out by representatives of the O.A.S. and the U.N. Secretary–General in 1991–1993, as were the efforts to restore democratic government in Haiti from 1991–1994. In regard to the conflict in Somalia, the U.N. efforts were joined by the O.A.U., the League of Arab States, and Organization of the Islamic Conference. The conflicts in the 1990s in Liberia, and in Sierra Leone continuing as of 2000, have included initiatives of a subregional organization, the Economic Community of West African States.

In some cases regional bodies have been perceived by one of the parties to the conflict as partial to the other and therefore as unsuitable for a mediatory role. From that standpoint the United Nations was preferred since its larger membership provided more assurance of even-handed treatment. Regional organizations also lack the resources and experience of the United Nations, particularly in regard to peacekeeping forces and large-scale fact-finding. The experiences of the 1990s in regard to the conflicts in ex-Yugoslavia, Somalia, and Haiti underlined the relative weakness of the respective regional bodies and the need for United Nations involvement. See generally Damrosch (ed.), Enforcing Restraint: Collective Intervention in Internal Conflicts (1993) and further discussion in Chapter 12.

It has often been suggested that regional (or sub-regional) machinery be used before recourse is had to the United Nations; indeed, Article 52(2) and (3) of the U.N. Charter would appear to express a preference for prior resort to dispute settlement through regional arrangements. There is little evidence that the regional bodies have been more effective in dealing with high-intensity conflicts. Even conceding that regional bodies may be better for dispute-settlement involving countries of the region, it is questionable whether the idea of regional primacy should deter or delay action in other bodies when it appears that regional measures will not be taken or are inadequate. As indicated above, joint efforts have been used in recent conflicts in ex-Yugoslavia, Somalia, El Salvador, and Haiti.

PUBLIC DEBATE AND PARLIAMENTARY DIPLOMACY IN DISPUTE SETTLEMENT

As a rule, negotiating mechanisms that are flexible and relatively informal are preferable for seeking resolution of difficult disputes. This is especially true when bargaining (i.e., the trading of concessions) is the dominant mode of negotiation. However, when there are marked disparities in bargaining strength, weaker parties will tend toward formal, rule-oriented structures or to larger forums in which they can obtain political support.

It is almost axiomatic that negotiation and mediation can be more effectively carried out in private rather than in public meetings. When institutional mechanisms provide generally for public meetings, it is often essential to use informal private negotiating mechanisms (as, for example, the Security Council consultations that are now standard procedures).

Notwithstanding the advantages of private negotiations, "parliamentary diplomacy" and public statements may help sometimes to further settlement by placing pressure on the parties. On the other hand, a public debate may complicate settlement procedures by increasing tensions, stimulating domestic rigidity, and adding ideological elements to the dispute.

Difficulties in determining who should be the parties to multilateral negotiation may require a variety of procedural stratagems, e.g., separate meetings, proxy representation, composite delegations, unofficial observers, etc. As questions of participation are often linked to substantive issues, the preliminary negotiations on the question of invitations and composition of delegations will often be partly determinative of the issues to be considered.

Notes

1. The role of international institutions in facilitating negotiation may be substantially reduced when the governing bodies adopt positions or express views in favor of one side. When an organization is perceived by the party as hostile, it loses its opportunity to act itself as a third-party intermediary or to have its officials perform that role. Does this imply that international bodies should renounce their role of expressing international policy or applying principles of law to particular situations? May their positions, when based on a general consensus, generate pressure for negotiation even though the organization does not act in a mediational role? These questions have been raised in major disputes brought to the United Nations when one side has been supported by large majorities in the General Assembly or Security Council.

In a report to U.N. Secretary–General Kofi Annan in August 2000, a panel commissioned to review all aspects of U.N. peacekeeping addressed this tension between organizational "impartiality" and the need to take a stand against evident violations of international law. See p. 1041, Note 3, in Chapter 12.

2. Post-settlement arrangements may influence the choice of settlement mechanisms. Mediators (whether governments or international organs) may contribute to the solution of the difficulties by accepting a role in security or economic arrangements to be carried out after an agreed settlement. For example, the U.N. may provide observers to supervise demilitarization. The World Bank played a key role in settling the Indus River dispute by providing development funds. Large-scale multilateral assistance is also relevant to major disputes over water management and other scarce resources. See Weinthal, Making Waves: Third Parties and International Mediation in the Aral Sea Basin, in Words Over War (2000), pp. 263–292. Prospects for settlement of the Israeli–Palestinian dispute depend in part on external commitments concerning economic as well as security assistance.

SECTION 3. ARBITRATION

A. ROLE OF ARBITRATION IN SETTLEMENT OF DISPUTES

Arbitration, in contrast to conciliation or mediation, leads to a binding settlement of a dispute on the basis of law. The arbitral body is composed of judges who are normally appointed by the parties but who are not subject to their instructions. The arbitral body may be established *ad hoc* by the parties or it may be a continuing body set up to handle certain categories of disputes. Arbitration differs from judicial settlement in that the parties have competence as a rule to appoint arbitrators, to determine the procedure and, to a certain extent, to indicate the applicable law.

The history of international arbitration can be traced as far back as ancient Greece, and its use as a means of peaceful settlement was frequent even during the Middle Ages. See generally Ralston, International Arbitration from Athens to Locarno 153–89 (1929). The process fell into disuse, however, until its revival in the nineteenth century by a series of arbitrations between the United States and the United Kingdom arising out of the Jay Treaty (1794) and the Treaty of Ghent (1814). See Simpson & Fox, International Arbitration 1–4 (1959); Hyde at 1587–88. A number of other international arbitrations occurred later in the nineteenth century, one of the most important of which concerned the claims of the United States against the United

Kingdom for damages arising out of the activities of the Confederate warship Alabama. See Simpson & Fox at 8–9; Hyde 1592–93. A system of rules and procedures was by this time gradually receiving general acceptance and in 1875 the *Institut de Droit International* completed an influential draft code of arbitral procedure. See Projet de règlement pour la procédure arbitrale internationale, I Ann. de l'Institut de Droit Int'l 126 (1877).

At the Hague Peace Conference of 1899 arbitration was one of the most important topics under discussion. The resulting Convention for the Pacific Settlement of International Disputes, 32 Stat. 1799, 2 Malloy 2016, contained, in addition to provisions on good offices, mediation, and inquiry, a number of articles on international arbitration, the object of which was stated in Article XV to be "the settlement of differences between States by judges of their own choice, and on the basis of respect for law." Article XVI set out the parties' recognition that, "[i]n questions of a legal nature, and especially in the interpretation or application of International Conventions," international arbitration was the "most effective, and at the same time the most equitable, means of settling disputes which diplomacy has failed to settle." Article XVIII specified that an agreement to arbitrate implied the legal obligation to submit to the terms of the award. The Convention did not impose any specific obligation to arbitrate; it merely attempted to set up institutions and procedures that could be utilized when and if two or more states desired to submit a dispute to arbitration.

Detailed rules on arbitral procedure were set out in the 1899 and 1907 Hague Conventions, and the so-called Permanent Court of Arbitration was established. The latter was in no sense a "permanent court"—it was, however, possible to convene a Court from among a permanent panel of arbitrators. Under the method of selection laid down by Article XLIV of the revised Convention of 1907, 36 Stat. 2199, 2 Malloy 2220, each party to the Convention was eligible to nominate a maximum of four persons "of known competency in questions of international law, of the highest moral reputation, and disposed to accept the duties of Arbitrator." When two states decided to refer a dispute to the Court, they could select two arbitrators from among those nominated by the states party to the Convention. Only one of those selected could be a national or a nominee of the selecting state. The four arbitrators would then choose an umpire. Detailed provision was made for the selection of an umpire if the arbitrators were unable to agree upon a single individual.

Since World War II, states have looked with less favor on the adoption of general multilateral conventions for compulsory arbitration. However, support for arbitration as a preferred means of adjudication still finds wide support among states. This was demonstrated in the U.N. Conference on the Law of the Sea by the preference for arbitration as the means to be used in default of any other choice of settlement machinery (see Chapter 16). Moreover, states continue to have recourse to arbitration on an *ad hoc* basis. In some cases, arbitration has been used even when hostilities between the parties had broken out. A successful example is the *Rann of Kutch Case* between India and Pakistan, decided in 1968, which involved a territorial dispute. For detailed account, see Wetter, The International Arbitral Process, vol. I, 250–275 (1979). More recently, the parties to the Dayton Agreement for settlement of the conflict in Bosnia–Herzegovina agreed to binding arbitration concerning the disputed territory known as the Brčko corridor. See note on p. 847.

Although arbitral awards are generally considered final and not subject to review in any other forum, there is a small set of state-to-state cases in which a party has asked the International Court of Justice to consider issues growing out of an arbitration. See Reisman, The Supervisory Jurisdiction of the International Court of Justice: International Arbitration and International Adjudication, 258 Rec. des Cours 9 (1996). On claims of nullity of an award, see pp. 847–851. Repudiation of arbitral awards has been relatively rare (with the Beagle Channel arbitration a notorious exception; see p. 831 above).

The texts of many international arbitral awards have been reprinted in volumes published by the United Nations, entitled Reports of International Arbitral Awards (U.N.R.I.A.A.). A full listing of public international law arbitrations from 1794 to 1989 can be found in Stuyt, Survey of International Arbitrations 1794–1989 (1990). International arbitral decisions also are published in International Legal Materials and in International Law Reports. See also Lauterpacht, Aspects of the Administration of International Justice 10–11 (1991) (listing numerous *ad hoc* arbitral decisions reported since 1945).

The Restatement (Third) deals with interstate arbitration in § 904.

Notes

1. The Permanent Court of Arbitration has been the venue for a few dozen cases in the century since the 1899 Hague Peace Conference. Although the cases may not seem numerous, some of them are classics of international law, such as the *Island of Palmas* arbitration (pp. 316–320 supra). See generally The Permanent Court of Arbitration: International Arbitration and Dispute Resolution: Summaries of Awards, Settlement Agreements and Reports (1999). Regular updates on P.C.A. activities are published in its annual reports.

In 1998, a dispute between Italy and Costa Rica over a loan agreement was arbitrated under P.C.A. auspices, and an award was rendered in a dispute between Eritrea and Yemen over sovereignty of a group of islands in the Red Sea; a second stage in the Eritrea–Yemen arbitration resulted in a judgment in December 1999. On the Eritrea–Yemen arbitration, see note by Reisman at 93 A.J.I.L. 668–682 (1999).

2. Recently, the P.C.A. has made significant strides toward greater flexibility in handling not just the kinds of state-to-state disputes contemplated under the 1899 and 1907 Hague Conventions, but also disputes involving other categories of parties. Toward this end, it has promulgated optional rules for arbitrating disputes when only one party is a state, as well as disputes between international organizations and states and between international organizations and private parties. See generally Permanent Court of Arbitration, Basic Documents: Conventions, Rules, Model Clauses and Guidelines (1998). In this respect, the P.C.A. is open to a significantly wider range of potential disputants than the International Court of Justice. Compare Section 4 infra.

3. Investment disputes typically involve a private investor on one side and a state party on the other. A facility for arbitrating such disputes is available through the World Bank's International Centre for the Settlement of Investment

Disputes (ICSID), which has handled some 60 arbitrations of this kind through 2000. See also pp. 1628–1629.

4. Arbitration is also provided for disputes between investors and states under Chapter 11 of the North American Free Trade Agreement (NAFTA). Several significant arbitral proceedings have been brought under those provisions. See, e.g., NAFTA Chapter 11 Arbitral Tribunal, Ethyl Corp. v. Government of Canada, Decisions of Nov. 28, 1997 and June 24, 1998, at 38 I.L.M. 700, 708 (1999).

5. Arbitrations between private parties of different nationalities, e.g. in commercial matters, may go forward under any of a number of available sets of rules, including those of the International Chamber of Commerce in Paris, the London Court of Arbitration, the American Arbitration Association, and various other facilities. Awards rendered in a state party to the New York Convention on the Recognition and Enforcement of Foreign Arbitral Awards, 21 U.S.T. 2517, T.I.A.S. 6997, 330 U.N.T.S. 3, may be enforced in accordance with that Convention.

The materials that follow address arbitration's general features, which are relevant regardless of whether the context is state-against-state, private party-against-state, or private-against-private arbitrations. (Special considerations flowing from the fact of an arbitration involving one or more state parties will be mentioned where relevant.) The diversity of parties that can participate in international arbitration is one factor distinguishing this form of "legal" dispute settlement from adjudication at the International Court of Justice. Compare Section 4.

B. THE UNDERTAKING TO ARBITRATE AND THE "COMPROMIS D'ARBITRAGE"

Generally, parties to a dispute undertake to submit the controversy to arbitration and, in the same instrument, specify the method by which the arbitral tribunal is to be constituted, the questions it is to answer, and the procedures by which it shall arrive at a decision. The undertaking to arbitrate may also appear as an independent agreement or as a part thereof. Standing by itself, the undertaking to arbitrate usually does not dispose of all the detailed questions that must be settled before arbitration actually takes place. It may, as a minimum, specify the manner in which the arbitrators are to be selected. Other questions remain to be answered by the parties in a subsequent agreement, sometimes called the *compromis d'arbitrage.* The contents of the *compromis* were described by the International Law Commission in Article 2 of its Model Rules on Arbitral Procedure:

> 1. Unless there are earlier agreements which suffice for the purpose, for example in the undertaking to arbitrate itself, the parties having recourse to arbitration shall conclude a *compromis* which shall specify, as a minimum:
>
> (a) The undertaking to arbitrate according to which the dispute is to be submitted to the arbitrators;
>
> (b) The subject-matter of the dispute and, if possible, the points on which the parties are or are not agreed;
>
> (c) The method of constituting the tribunal and the number of arbitrators.

2. In addition, the *compromis* shall include any other provisions deemed desirable by the parties, in particular:

(i) The rules of law and the principles to be applied by the tribunal, and the right, if any, conferred on it to decide *ex aequo et bono* as though it had legislative functions in the matter;

(ii) The power, if any, of the tribunal to make recommendations to the parties;

(iii) Such power as may be conferred on the tribunal to make its own rules of procedure;

(iv) The procedure to be followed by the tribunal; provided that, once constituted, the tribunal shall be free to override any provisions of the *compromis* which may prevent it from rendering its award;

(v) The number of members required for the constitution of a *quorum* for the conduct of the hearings;

(vi) The majority required for the award;

(vii) The time limit within which the award shall be rendered;

(viii) The right of the members of the tribunal to attach dissenting or individual opinions to the award, or any prohibition of such opinions;

(ix) The languages to be employed in the course of the proceedings;

(x) The manner in which the costs and disbursements shall be apportioned;

(xi) The services which the International Court of Justice may be asked to render.

This enumeration is not intended to be exhaustive. [1958] II Yb.I.L.C. 83. The parties to the *compromis* may confer jurisdiction on the arbitrators only to answer particular questions of law or fact, or they may give the tribunal power to decide on the merits a single controversy or a series of related disputes. One of the parties may admit liability, and the tribunal may therefore be asked only to determine damages. Any provision in the *compromis* relating to the law to be applied by the tribunal is essential to interpreting the award and to determining its value as a precedent. It is also important to note whether the award is to be accepted by the parties as final and binding or as merely advisory.

Questions of procedure not answered in the *compromis* must be settled by the tribunal. The *compromis* will normally give the tribunal the express power to perform this task, although it is often maintained that such a provision is unnecessary inasmuch as any arbitral tribunal has the inherent power to determine its procedures in a way not inconsistent with the *compromis*. Precedents established by past tribunals are often of great value, as are codes of procedure such as that prepared by the International Law Commission in 1958. For general information on the procedural aspects of arbitration, see Carlston, The Process of International Arbitration (1946); Simpson & Fox, International Arbitration 147 (1959); Merrills, International Dispute Settlement 88–105 (3rd ed. 1998).

Notes

1. "International law does not lay down hard and fast rules concerning the character or weight of evidence in international arbitrations or rules which closely approximate the technical rules followed in proceedings before domestic courts; admissibility of evidence and the weight to be attached to it is largely left to the arbitral tribunal. For the most part the rules followed by such tribunals are more elastic and more liberal than those generally followed by domestic courts." 6 Hackworth at 98. See generally Simpson & Fox at 192; Sandifer, Evidence before International Tribunals (rev. ed. 1975). See also White, The Use of Experts by International Tribunals (1965).

2. Bilateral treaties concluded between Western states often provide for the arbitration or judicial settlement of disputes arising out of the treaty. Article 27(2) of the Treaty of Friendship, Commerce and Navigation between the United States and Germany (1954), 7 U.S.T. 1839, provides, for example, as follows:

> Any dispute between the Parties as to the interpretation or the application of the present Treaty which the Parties do not satisfactorily adjust by diplomacy or some other agreed means shall be submitted to arbitration or, upon agreement of the Parties, to the International Court of Justice.

Such clauses have been inserted in many post-war commercial treaties concluded by the United States. See Wilson, United States Commercial Treaties and International Law 23 (1960). For a case in which the International Court of Justice held that a state was under a duty to submit to arbitration under the provisions of a bilateral treaty, see the Ambatielos Case (Greece v. United Kingdom), Merits: Obligation to Arbitrate, 1953 I.C.J. 10. For the ensuing arbitration and its result, see The Ambatielos Claim, 12 U.N.R.I.A.A. 83 (1956). For discussion and critique, see Reisman, The Supervisory Jurisdiction of the International Court of Justice: International Arbitration and International Adjudication, 258 Rec. des Cours at 70 (1996).

3. The five Paris Peace Treaties of 1947 provided, at the Soviet Union's insistence, for reference of disputes arising under the treaties to arbitral tribunals rather than to the International Court of Justice. Bulgaria, Hungary and Rumania were subsequently able to frustrate arbitration of disputes arising under the human rights provisions of the treaties by the simple expedient of refusing to appoint an arbitrator on their behalf. The International Court of Justice then ruled in an Advisory Opinion that the Secretary–General of the United Nations could not appoint a third arbitrator under the authority granted to him by the Peace Treaties until both parties to the dispute had appointed their arbitrators. 1950 I.C.J. 221. Article XLV of the Pact of Bogota, signed on April 30, 1948, contains an elaborate scheme designed to prevent the frustration of the arbitral procedure through a refusal by one party to appoint an arbitrator. 30 U.N.T.S. 55, 100.

For discussion of the species of arbitral clause under which a party could deliberately block arbitration by failing to appoint an arbitrator, and the suggestion that (at least in some kinds of interstate arbitrations) such clauses represent a policy choice for an "implicitly defeasible" rather than unqualified obligation to arbitrate, see Reisman, The Supervisory Jurisdiction of the International Court of Justice: International Arbitration and International Adjudication, 258 Rec. des Cours 168–175 (1996).

Most modern arbitration clauses (especially in the commercial sphere) provide for an appointing authority who can designate an arbitrator if a party's refusal to participate impedes the constitution of an arbitral tribunal.

4. Does arbitration always lead to a binding award? Consider Article 12 of the Air Transport Agreement between the United States and Italy, Feb. 6, 1948, 62 Stat. 3729, T.I.A.S. No. 1902, 73 U.N.T.S. 113:

> Except as otherwise provided in the present Agreement or its Annex, any dispute between the contracting parties relative to the interpretation or application of the present Agreement or its Annex, which cannot be settled through consultation, shall be submitted for an advisory report to a tribunal of three arbitrators, one to be named by each contracting party, and the third to be agreed upon by the two arbitrators so chosen, provided that such third arbitrator shall not be a national of either contracting party.
>
> * * * The executive authorities of the contracting parties will use their best efforts under the powers available to them to put into effect the opinion expressed in any such advisory report. * * *

On June 30, 1964, the two governments signed a *compromis* to establish an arbitral tribunal in accordance with Article 12 of their Air Transport Agreement. On July 17, 1965, the tribunal rendered a decision upholding the contentions of the United States, with the arbitrator designated by Italy filing a dissenting opinion. In June 1966, Italy denounced the bilateral agreement pursuant to Article 9 thereof. See 4 I.L.M. 974 (1965).

5. Normally, an arbitration agreement is limited to disputes between the parties to it. However, in some cases agreements have allowed third parties to bring claims. See, for example, Protocol between Germany and Venezuela (1903), Article VI, 9 U.N.R.I.A.A. 105–106. Mexico made a submission in a NAFTA arbitration between a U.S. company and the Canadian government, as permitted under Article 1128 of NAFTA. See 38 I.L.M. 708, 720–721 (1999).

C. PROBLEMS RELATING TO THE EFFECTIVENESS OF INTERNATIONAL ARBITRATION AGREEMENTS

Three persistent problems are related to international arbitration agreements: (1) the severability of an arbitration clause from the remainder of a contract or treaty, (2) the claim of denial of justice by refusal to arbitrate, and (3) the authority of a truncated international arbitral tribunal. These problems arise in public international arbitration between states or between a state and a private entity and in international commercial arbitration between private parties. See Schwebel, International Arbitration: Three Salient Problems (1987).

THE SEVERABILITY OF THE ARBITRATION AGREEMENT

The issue of severability arises when a contract or treaty containing an arbitration clause is claimed to be invalid or to have been terminated or suspended. In these circumstances it has been often argued that the nullification of the contract also vitiates the arbitral obligations of the parties. If the contract is invalid or no longer in force, it is claimed that the obligation to arbitrate fails with the agreement of which it is part. The argument against severability has been generally rejected on three principal grounds. First, an arbitration clause will ordinarily be comprehensive in terms and encompass "any dispute" arising out of or relating to the contract, including disputes over the validity of the agreement. See Delaume, Transnational Contracts: Applicable Law and Settlement of Disputes 59–61 (1985). Second, if one party could deny the other a right to arbitration by the mere allegation that the agreement lacked initial or continuing validity, then the simple expedient of declaring the agreement void would always be open to a party to avoid its arbitral obligation. Losinger & Co. Case, P.C.I.J., Ser. C, No. 78, 113–16 (1936). See Schwebel, International Arbitration 4 (1987). Third, it has been legally presumed that the parties to an agreement containing an arbitral clause conclude not one but two agreements: the principal substantive agreement and a second separable agreement providing for arbitration. Id., at 5. But see Wetter, Salient Features of Swedish Arbitrations Clauses, [1983] Y.B. of the Arbitration Institute of the Stockholm Chamber of Commerce 33, 35 ("such a conception is almost always very far from [the parties'] minds as well as from those of their legal advisors.").

Despite these arguments in favor of severability, it has been claimed that two situations may be inappropriate for its application. Where the issue is not whether the principal agreement is valid, but whether it was actually concluded at all, there may be room to challenge the existence of the arbitration clause. See Jennings, Nullity and Effectiveness in International Law, in Cambridge Essays in International Law 66–67 (1965). Second, where the issue is whether the agreement to arbitrate is valid, the decision of the arbitral tribunal on the matter may be reviewable in a national court. See, e.g., French Code of Civil Procedure, as amended by Decree No. 81–500 of 12 May 1981, reprinted in 20 I.L.M. 917–22 (1981). (For special considerations applicable to arbitrations involving state defendants, see Chapter 14.)

The major international arbitration agreements recognize the severability of the principal contract and an arbitration clause. The 1976 Arbitration Rules (Article 21(2)) adopted by the United Nations Commission on International Trade Law provide that "an arbitration clause which forms part of a contract and which provides for arbitration under these Rules shall be treated as an agreement independent of the other terms of the contract." See also the 1985 Model Law on International Commercial Arbitration (Article 16(1)) ("A decision by the arbitral tribunal that the contract is null and void shall not entail *ipso jure* the invalidity of the arbitration clause"); the Rules of the Court of Arbitration of the International Chamber of Commerce (Article 8(4)) ("the arbitrator shall not cease to have jurisdiction by reason of any claim that the contract is null and void * * * provided he upholds the validity of the agreement to arbitrate."); Resolution on Arbitration between States, State Enterprises or State Entities, and Foreign Enterprises, 63 Annuaire de L'Institut de Droit International 324 (1990–II) (Article 3(a)) ("Unless the arbitration agreement provides otherwise * * * [t]he arbitration agreement is separable from the legal relationship to which it refers * * * "). See further Schwebel, International Arbitration 13–23 (1987).

In the Appeal Relating to the Jurisdiction of the ICAO Council (Judgement), 1972 I.C.J. 46, the International Court of Justice addressed the issue of severability. In the case, India took the position that the Council of the International Civil Aviation Organization (ICAO) lacked jurisdiction under the 1944 Chicago Civil Aviation Convention and a Transit Agreement to hear Pakistan's complaint against India for prohibiting the flight of civil aircraft over Indian territory. India maintained that as the Convention and Transit Agreement had been terminated or suspended between India and Pakistan, those international agreements could not furnish the ICAO Council with a basis for jurisdiction. The Court rejected India's argument and held that a party to a treaty cannot defeat the provision for adjudication or arbitration that the treaty contains by contending that it has terminated the treaty. The Court stated:

> The acceptance of such a proposition would be tantamount to opening the way to a wholesale nullification of the practical value of jurisdictional clauses by allowing a party first to purport to terminate, or suspend the operation of a treaty, and then to declare that the treaty being now terminated or suspended, its jurisdictional clauses were in consequence void, and could not be invoked for the purpose of contesting the validity of the termination or suspension * * * Such a result, destructive of the whole object of adjudicability, would be unacceptable.

Id. at 64—65. See also Schwebel, International Arbitration (1987); Mann, The Consequences of an International Wrong in International and National Law, 48 Brit. Y.B.Int'l L. 60, n. 3 (1976–77).

In TOPCO v. Libya, Preliminary Award of 27 November 1975, 55 I.L.R. 389, Libya maintained before sole arbitrator René-Jean Dupuy that the arbitration clauses contained in Deeds of Concession were rendered void by the nationalization of the property subject to the Deeds. The arbitrator extensively canvassed international and municipal case law, as well as the opinion of publicists, in affirming the principle "of the autonomy or the independence of the arbitration clause. This principle * * * has the consequence of permitting the arbitration clause to escape the fate of the contract which it contains * * *." Id. at 407. For other aspects of this arbitration, see pp. 148–153, 790–798.

DENIAL OF JUSTICE BY REFUSAL TO ARBITRATE

Consider a situation where a contract between a state and an alien contains an arbitration clause that provides that arbitration shall be the exclusive remedy for the settlement of disputes but the state refuses to arbitrate. The question has been raised whether such a refusal constitutes a denial of justice under international law. See Mann, State Contracts and International Arbitration, 42 Brit. Y.B.Int'l L. 1 (1967). Mann concludes that:

> denial of justice in the strict and narrow sense of the term implied the failure to afford access to the tribunals of the respondent State itself. But there is no reason of logic or justice why the doctrine of denial of justice should not be so interpreted as to comprise the relatively modern case of the repudiation of an arbitration clause. The respondent State which, wilfully and as a result of its own initiative, has failed to implement an arbitration clause, can hardly allege that it has afforded justice in general or the agreed justice in particular, or complain that it is aggrieved by being held responsible for its own deliberate acts.

Id., at 27–28.

The Restatement (Third) § 712, Comment *h* declares that "a state may be responsible for a denial of justice under international law * * * if, having committed itself to a special forum for dispute settlement, such as arbitration, it fails to honor such commitment. * * * ''

Mann suggests a controversial exception for general legislation, not directed specifically at a contracting alien, adopted after the conclusion of the contract containing an arbitration clause. Mann maintains that a State which acts in accordance with the law cannot be said to frustrate the arbitration clause or commit a denial of justice. Schwebel, however, maintains that it is not state law but international law that protects the contractual relationship between a state and an alien. Schwebel claims "[i]f the alien's right to arbitration is negated by the contracting State, a wrong under international law ensues, whatever the law governing the contract, the arbitration agreement or the arbitral process, no less than a wrong under international law ensues if a State takes the property of an alien without just compensation whether or not the right to that property derives from its municipal law * * * The essential point is that international law sets up certain restraint upon the action which a State may legitimately take in its treatment of aliens." Schwebel, International Arbitration 66–67 (1987).

Sompong Sucharitkul, a member of the International Law Commission, has been critical of rules, including denial of justice, that would preclude a state from altering its obligations to arbitrate. He states that there is:

> nothing sacrosanct, nothing final about arbitration, least of all the peremptory character, the impossibility of derogation from an obligation to arbitrate. This would be more effective than international law, more powerful than supra-national law. It would be almost divine if once the State permits itself to submit to arbitration, it cannot allegedly derogate from this submission. However, it should be pointed out that the character of arbitration is itself voluntary, it is in itself extra-legal and conciliatory.

Sucharitkul, in Colloquium on International Trade Agreements 359, quoted in Schwebel, International Arbitration 107 (1987).

The claim of denial of justice by refusal to arbitrate has been raised by states at various times. In the arbitrations involving Texaco Overseas Petroleum Company (TOPCO) and California Asiatic Oil Company v. the Government of the Libyan Arab Republic, 53 I.L.R. 389; and Libyan American Oil Company (LIAMCO) v. Government of the Libyan Arab Republic, 62 I.L.R. 141, the United States delivered the following note of protest to Libya over its decrees affecting the interests of TOPCO and LIAMCO:

> The concession agreements governing the operations of the oil companies specifically provide * * * for arbitration of disputes not otherwise settled. * * * The United States Government understands that the companies in question have requested arbitration; it expects that the Government of the Libyan Arab Republic will respond positively to their request since failure to do so would constitute a denial of justice and an additional breach of international law.

[1975] Digest of United States Practice in International Law 490 (1976).

In Elf Aquitaine Iran v. National Iranian Oil Company, 11 Y.B. Commercial Arbitration 98 (1986), the sole arbitrator stated that "[i]t is a recognized principle of international law that a state is bound by an arbitration clause contained in an agreement * * * and cannot thereafter unilaterally set aside the access of the other party to the system envisaged by the parties in their agreement for the settlement of disputes." Id., at 104. The arbitrator concluded that "[t]he existing precedents demonstrate * * * that a government bound by an arbitration clause cannot validly free itself of this obligation by an act of its own will such as, for example, by changing its internal law, or by a unilateral cancellation of the contract or of the concession." This unpublished portion of the Preliminary Award of 1982 is reproduced in Schwebel, International Arbitration 101 (1987).

THE AUTHORITY OF TRUNCATED TRIBUNALS

The problem that arises in the case of a truncated arbitral tribunal is whether the tribunal has the power to issue a binding award when an arbitrator refuses to participate in the final award on his own initiative or on the instruction of a party, or when an arbitrator withdraws and a party fails to designate a replacement. This is a problem that has arisen in interstate arbitration and in arbitrations between states and aliens. Schwebel concludes that the weight of the law supports the authority of a truncated arbitral tribunal to render a binding award, but notes that the cases and the legal opinion of scholars are divided. Schwebel, International Arbitration 153 (1987). See also the extensive comments by members of the International Law Commission and other commentators on the authority of truncated tribunals, id., at 154–180.

The Iran–United States Claim Tribunal was confronted with the purposeful absence of arbitrators appointed by Iran. For example, in Case Number 17, 1 Iran–U.S. Claim Tribunal Rept. 415 (1982), Chamber Three of the Tribunal issued an award that was signed by only two of the three judges; the third judge from Iran, Judge Sani, informed the Tribunal that he would not sign the award because he had not been notified of the deliberative session of the Chamber during which the award was decided. One of the other judges responded that the case had been heard on September 1 and 2, 1982 and that during the following four months there had been numerous deliberations. Citing the *travaux préparatoires* of the UNCITRAL Rules, which the Iran–U.S. Claims Tribunal had incorporated into its own rules, the arbitrator signing the award contended that "under international law, Judge Sani cannot frustrate the work of the Chamber or the Tribunal by wilfully absenting himself and refusing to sign an award." Id., at 425. Similar absences of Iranian Judges occurred in nine other cases, but the Tribunal or the Chambers within it proceeded to give awards. Iran initially mounted a challenge to the awards in the courts of the Netherlands, but ultimately discontinued its claims. Schwebel maintains that in view of such discontinuance, "it may be concluded that Iran has acquiesced in the validity of those awards." Schwebel, International Arbitration: Three Salient Problems 253 (1987). See also Resolution on Arbitration between States, State Enterprises, or State Entities, and Foreign Enterprises, 63 Annuaire de L'Institut de Droit International 324 (1990–II) (Article 3(c)) ("A Party's refusal to participate in the arbitration, whether by failing to appoint an arbitrator pursuant to the arbitration agreement, or through the withdrawal of an arbitrator, or by resorting to other obstructionist measures, neither suspends the proceedings nor prevents the rendition of a valid award.").

Note

In the 1995 Dayton Accords (General Framework Agreement for Peace in Bosnia and Herzegovina, 35 I.L.M. 75 (1996)), the parties committed themselves to binding arbitration to resolve a dispute over the inter-entity boundary line between the Bosnian–Croat Federation on the one hand and the Republika Srpska on the other, in the strategically important area known as Brčko. Each of the two sides appointed an arbitrator, and (in the absence of agreement between those two on a third) a Presiding Arbitrator, Roberts B. Owen, was chosen by the President of the International Court of Justice as appointing authority. The Dayton Accords had envisioned the contingency of the tribunal being unable to reach a majority, and had provided that in that event, the decision of the Presiding Arbitrator would be final and binding. In each of three awards rendered in 1997, 1998, and 1999 respectively, only the Presiding Arbitrator signed the award. See 36 I.L.M. 396 (1997); 38 I.L.M. 534 (1999).

The Final Award is notable for its finding of massive failure of compliance on the part of the Serb authorities to meet the requirements of the previous awards, and for its ruling that non-compliance could be a ground for transferring the contested area entirely out of the territory of the non-complying side into the exclusive control of the other side. Other innovations include a regime for demilitarizing the corridor and setting up a structure to administer the area. See Introductory Note by Schreuer at 38 I.L.M. 534–535 (1999), commenting as follows:

> The Tribunal clearly assumed a public order function in deciding this case. Traditionally, arbitration is perceived as a mandate narrowly defined by the parties' agreement. Digression beyond this parameter is sometimes threatened by nullity. The Brčko Tribunal took a much broader view of its function. Despite its seemingly narrow task to determine the Inter–Entity Boundary Line, it took it upon itself to find the optimum solution as determined by the object and purpose of the Dayton Accords. It first created an international system of supervision and then a special neutral regime for the disputed area. The Tribunal took its mandate less from the disputing parties' agreement than from its role as an agent of the international community.

D. SOME SUBSTANTIVE PROBLEMS OF ARBITRATION

MODEL RULES ON ARBITRAL PROCEDURE

[1958] 2 Yb. I.L.C. 83.

* * *

ARTICLE 35

The validity of an award may be challenged by either party on one or more of the following grounds:

(a) That the tribunal has exceeded its powers;

(b) That there was corruption on the part of a member of the tribunal;

(c) That there has been a failure to state the reasons for the award or a serious departure from a fundamental rule of procedure;

(d) That the undertaking to arbitrate or the *compromis* is a nullity.

* * *

IN THE MATTER OF THE INTERNATIONAL TITLE TO THE CHAMIZAL TRACT

Award of the International Boundary Commission, 1911.
[1911] For.Rel. U.S. 573, 586, 597–98.

[The United States and Mexico attempted in the Treaty of Guadalupe Hidalgo of 1848 and in the Gadsden Treaty of 1853 to fix the boundary line between their respective territories. Because the Colorado and Rio Grande Rivers constantly shifted their channels, the two countries agreed in 1884 that the dividing line should continue to "follow the center of the normal channel" of each river, "notwithstanding any alterations in the banks or in the course of those rivers, provided that such alterations be effected by natural causes through the slow and gradual erosion and deposit of alluvium * * *." Other changes brought about by the force of the current, such as the sudden abandonment of an existing river bed and the opening of a new one ("avulsion"), were to produce no change in the dividing line, which should continue to follow the middle of the original channel bed, even though this should become wholly dry or obstructed by deposits. 24 Stat. 1011, 1 Malloy 1159. In 1889, an International Boundary Commission was created by agreement between the United States and Mexico and charged with the task of deciding whether changes in the course of the Colorado River and the Rio Grande had occurred "through avulsion or erosion" for the purposes of the 1884 treaty. 26 Stat. 1512, 1 Malloy 1167.

In 1895 a dispute arose over a tract of land in El Paso, Texas known as "El Chamizal." Each country claimed the entire tract. The Boundary Commission was unable to agree on the boundary line, and a convention was signed by the two governments on June 24, 1910, establishing a commission to "decide solely and exclusively as to whether the international title to the Chamizal tract is in the United States of America or Mexico." 36 Stat. 2481, 2483. In rendering the award, the Presiding Commissioner of the arbitral tribunal, with the Mexican Commissioner concurring in part, said:]

* * * [T]he Presiding Commissioner and the Mexican Commissioner are of opinion that the accretions which occurred in the Chamizal tract up to the time of the great flood in 1864 should be awarded to the United States of America, and that inasmuch as the changes which occurred in that year did not constitute slow and gradual erosion within the meaning of the Convention of 1884, the balance of the tract should be awarded to Mexico.

[The American Commissioner dissented. At the session of the Commission in which the award was read, the agent for the United States protested against the decision and award, *inter alia,* on the following grounds:]

1. Because it departs from the terms of submission in the following particulars:

a. Because in dividing the Chamizal tract it assumes to decide a question not submitted to the commission by the convention of 1910 and a question the commission was not asked to decide by either party at any stage of the proceedings;

b. Because it fails to apply the standard prescribed by the Treaty of 1884;

c. Because it applied to the determination of the issue of erosion or avulsion a ruling or principle not authorized by the terms of the submission or by the principles of international law or embraced in any of the treaties or conventions existing between the United States and Mexico;

d. Because it departs from the jurisdictional provision of the Treaty of 1889 creating the International Boundary Commission.

[Shortly after the Commission had adjourned, the United States notified Mexico that "[f]or the reasons set forth by the American commissioner in his dissenting opinion, and by the American agent in his suggestion of protest, [it did] not accept this award as valid or binding." [1911] For. Rel. U.S. 598. The United States suggested the negotiation of a new boundary convention to settle the matter, but Mexico declined on the ground that the matter had been finally adjudicated and that there remained only the admittedly difficult task of relocating the line of 1864.

No further action was taken until the conclusion in 1963 of a treaty by which the disputed territory was divided between the two countries. 15 U.S.T. 21, T.I.A.S. No. 5515, 505 U.N.T.S. 185. The agreement entered into force on January 14, 1964. See generally 3 Whiteman at 680–99. For a discussion of the controversy from a Mexican point of view, see Gomez Robledo, México y el Arbitraje Internacional 161 (1965). See also Carlston, The Process of International Arbitration 151–55 (1946).]

Note

Agreements to arbitrate have often formulated the issue as an "exclusive disjunction" (i.e., "either-or") permitting only one of two decisions. When arbitrators decide on a third solution, the result may be declared a nullity because of the deviation from the *compromis* (as in the *Chamizal Case*). In the much praised award in the *Island of Palmas Case* (p. 316 supra), the arbitrator, Huber, dealt with the issue squarely, asserting that the parties could not have intended him to return a *non liquet* (i.e., no decision). Is there not a danger that, if arbitrators depart from the compromissory restrictions, the decision will not be carried out? Would such decisions make states more reluctant to submit disputes to arbitration? One commentator, in discussing the dilemma of an arbitrator faced with an unsatisfactory either-or choice, suggested that "[o]nly if the alternative decisions available will be repudiated by the losing party * * * should a nondecision be delivered." Reisman, Nullity and Revision 550 (1971). Does this proposal involve, in effect, a modification of the *compromis* by implicit agreement of the parties?

Reisman later wrote:

> Arbitrators should resist the temptation to reconceive their roles as much broader and designed to resolve all outstanding conflicts between the parties. A variety of specific but limited roles in international law actually enriches it and increases its capacity to contribute to the resolution of disputes. Collaps-

ing all roles into one 'super' role actually impoverishes it and will have, as an unintended and unwanted result, a reduction on the part of States' willingness to submit issues to third-party decision.

258 Rec. des Cours 389–390 (1996).

FRAUD

HYDE, 2 INTERNATIONAL LAW CHIEFLY AS INTERPRETED AND APPLIED BY THE UNITED STATES

1640–42 (2d ed. 1945) (footnotes omitted).

In the cases of Weil and of La Abra Silver Mining Company before the American–Mexican Commission of July 4, 1868, when the United States discovered that, through fraud on the part of American claimants, it had been made the instrument of wrong towards a friendly State, by means of impositions upon the arbitral tribunal as well as upon itself, it repudiated the acts and made reparation.

The Department of State is rightly indisposed to seek enforcement of an award favorable to an American citizen, which is deemed unjust, by reason, for example, of the founding of the claim on the tortious conduct of the claimant, or of irregularities in the arbitral proceedings, or of the existence of documents adverse to the claimant and not submitted to the tribunal.

To quote Judge Ralston:

"The United States, upon a number of occasions, has seen fit to consent to the reopening of awards believed unjust. This was the case with the Venezuelan Claims Commission of 1866, whose awards were reopened and reviewed by the Commission of 1885, upon which sat two Americans and one Venezuelan. Awards under the Mexican treaty of 1848 were set aside by the courts in the case of the Gardiner claim, and were reviewed through act of Congress referring the Atocha claim to the Court of Claims. In the interest of rejected claims, Congress reopened two of the awards of the commission under the Chinese Claims Treaty of 1858, permitting the Attorney–General to decide one case finally and the Court of Claims the other. In the case of the *Caroline* the Secretary of State, against the protest of the claimant, returned to Brazil money which had been paid after a diplomatic settlement, and Congress appropriated a large sum to reimburse Brazil for moneys paid the United States representative, but which never reached the Treasury."

It will be observed that the foregoing discussions have reference to the attitude of the governments concerned rather than of arbitral tribunals upon which fraud may have been perpetrated by a litigating State.

In his decision of December 15, 1933, Mr. Justice Roberts, as Umpire in the cases of the Sabotage Claims against Germany, made the following statement:

"The petition, in short, avers the Commission has been misled by fraud and collusion on the part of witnesses and suppression of evidence on the part of some of them. The Commission is not *functus officio*. It still sits as a court. To it in that capacity are brought charges that it has been defrauded and misled by perjury, collusion, and suppression. No tribunal worthy of its name or of any respect may allow its decision to stand if such allegations are well-founded. Every tribunal has inherent power to reopen and to revise a decision induced by fraud. If it may correct its own errors and mistakes *a fortiori* it may, while it still has jurisdiction of a cause, correct errors into which it has been led by fraud and collusion."

The Commission exercising the jurisdiction which it undoubtedly possessed, on June 15, 1939, set aside, revoked and annulled an earlier decision of October 16, 1930, reached at Hamburg; and it went further, and, passing upon the merits of the claims, found that the liability of Germany had been established. * * *

Notes

1. If a tribunal's proceedings are not tainted by fraud, but the tribunal has arrived at a mistaken conclusion of law or fact, can its award be impeached on grounds of "essential error"? In the *Lehigh Valley Railroad Case* between U.S. and Germany (1940), the arbitral commission stated:

> Where the decision involves a material error the Commission not only has the power but is under a duty, upon a proper showing, to reopen and correct a decision to accord with the facts and applicable rules.

6 Hackworth at 132; see also Carlston, The Process of International Arbitration 185–192 (1946) (quoting and discussing treatment by *Trail Smelter* arbitral tribunal of contention of "essential error").

2. The distinction between "a mere error in law" that does not justify revision and "manifest" errors that could justify revision is a difficult one. Hyde suggested the following: "It is submitted that when the decision to which objection is made was based upon a supposition which it is inconceivable that the States at variance would, for any reason, have agreed for purposes of adjudication, to accept as a test of the propriety of the conduct of either, a sufficient ground for revision exists, the judicial error in such case being the misconception on the part of the court of the basis on which its conclusion was sought." Hyde at 1636.

3. A succinct analysis of case-law on scope of review of arbitral awards is contained in Reisman, Nullity and Revision 423–41 (1971).

E. THE IRAN–UNITED STATES CLAIMS TRIBUNAL

The most active arbitral tribunal in recent years has been the Iran–United States Claims Tribunal established under the Declaration of Algeria. 20 I.L.M. 223 (1981). It continues to function as of 2000, having already concluded and paid awards on more than 3000 claims of individuals, companies, and banks. The most significant items remaining on its docket are government-to-government claims.

The Tribunal, which has its seat at The Hague, has had jurisdiction over private claims of nationals of the United States against Iran and nationals of Iran against the United States, as well as over certain claims between the two governments. However, it may not decide claims arising under a contract which contained a forum-selection clause specifying the Iranian courts. In one of the earliest cases, the Tribunal ruled that it also has no jurisdiction over "direct" claims by one government against the nationals of the other. Case No. A/2, decision of 19 December 1981, reprinted in 21 I.L.M. 78 (1982).

The Tribunal consists of nine members, of which three are chosen by Iran, three by the U.S., and three by the six thus appointed. The arbitration rules of the United Nations Commission on International Trade Law (UNCITRAL) govern the appointment of arbitrators and the procedure of the Tribunal. See Baker & Davis, The UNCITRAL Arbitration Rules in Practice: The Experience of the Iran–United States Claims Tribunal (1992). If the parties fail to agree on any of the three arbitrators chosen jointly, according to these rules, the Secretary–General of the Permanent Court of Arbitration at The Hague shall designate an appointing authority who may exercise his discretion in appointing an arbitrator to the disputed position. Art. 7(b), UNCITRAL Arbitration Rules, 15 I.L.M. 701, 705 (1976). Pursuant to this provision, the Secretary–General designated the President of the Supreme Court of the Netherlands, Judge Moons, as the appointing authority. Appointments were made by him in several cases, including the appointment of the President of the Tribunal in 1985. In 1999, upon the resignation of Judge Moons as appointing authority, Judge Sir Robert Jennings of the United Kingdom was designated as the new appointing authority. He soon had to rule on a notice of challenge filed by Iran to the current president of the tribunal. See Iran–U.S. Claims Tribunal Appointing Authority, 94 A.J.I.L. 378–379 (2000).

The appointing authority also has the power to rule on challenges to the continued presence of a judge who refuses to withdraw and has done so in several cases. Articles 10–12, UNCITRAL Arbitration Rules. In the 1984 decision of the Tribunal on dual nationality (see Chapter 6, p. 439) the dissenting Iranian members declared that "[t]he composition of the so-called neutral arbitrators, itself the result of the imposed mechanism of the UNCITRAL Rules, is so unbalanced as to have made the Tribunal lose all credibility to adjudicate any dispute between the Islamic Republic of Iran * * * and the United States." Case No. A/18, decision of 6 April 1984, 5 Iran–U.S. Claims Tribunal Reports 251, 266.

All decisions and awards of the Tribunal are final and binding. They are enforceable against either government in the courts of any nation in accordance with its laws. A fund was also established in the Central Bank of the Netherlands for payment of the awards to U.S. claimants. See Chapter 9, p. 738.

The Tribunal is required to decide cases on the basis of respect for law, applying choice of law rules and principles of commercial and international law which it determines to be applicable. For a statement on the implications of this provision, see Damrosch, et al., Panel on Decisions of Iran–United States Claims Tribunal, 78 A.S.I.L.Proc. 221, 227–33 (1984). See also Khan, The Iran–United States Claims Tribunal: Controversies, Cases and Contribution (1990); Caron, The Nature of the Iran–United States Claims Tribunal and the Evolving Structure of International Dispute Resolution, 84 A.J.I.L. 104 (1990); Aldrich, The Jurisprudence of the Iran–United States Claims Tribunal (1996); Lillich, Magraw & Bederman (eds.), The Iran–United States Claims Tribunal (1998); Brower & Brueschke, The Iran–United States Claims

Tribunal (1998); Caron & Crook (eds.), The Iran–United States Claims Tribunal and the Process of International Claims Resolution (2000).

Tribunal decisions are published in a series entitled *Iran-United States Claims Tribunal Reports* (Grotius Press) and in two looseleaf services: *Iranian Assets Litigation Reporter* (Andrews Publications) and *Mealy's Litigation Reports: Iran Claims.* The more important decisions are reprinted in International Legal Materials and summarized in the Judicial Decisions section of the American Journal of International Law.

F. THE RECENT GROWTH OF INTERNATIONAL ARBITRATION

The tremendous growth of international commerce after the Second World War has led to a concomitant growth in the settlement of disputes arising from such commerce through arbitration. The leading institution in this field has been the International Court of Arbitration of the International Chamber of Commerce in Paris, France. Under its auspices and rules, a steadily growing number of disputes are settled. The United Nations Commission on International Trade Law has made international arbitration one of its preoccupations. It has developed the UNCITRAL Arbitration Rules that may be used both in *ad hoc* and institutionally supervised arbitration. Many arbitration institutions, including the American Arbitration Association (AAA), will administer arbitrations, under either their own rules or the UNCITRAL Rules. See Smit, The New International Arbitration Rules of the American Arbitration Association, 2 Am. Rev. Int'l Arb. 1 (1992). UNCITRAL has also developed a Model Law on International Commercial Arbitration, which has been adopted by a number of states in the United States and abroad. Developments in the field of international arbitration are addressed in the World Arbitration Reporter (Parker School of Foreign and Comparative Law, Columbia University) and the American Review of International Arbitration.

A most important advantage of international arbitration is that its awards are recognized and enforced in a large number of countries. As of 2000, the New York Convention on the Recognition and Enforcement of Foreign Arbitral Awards of June 10, 1958, 21 U.S.T. 2517, T.I.A.S. 6997, 330 U.N.T.S. 3, had been ratified by more than 120 states, including nearly all major commercial nations. This feature of international arbitration offers particular advantages in relations with foreign states. An arbitration clause in a contract with a foreign state ensures not only that there will be a forum to adjudicate any dispute that may arise under the contract, but also that any award rendered in such a dispute will be enforceable virtually anywhere in the world. In this respect, awards entitled to recognition and enforcement under the New York Convention enjoy more effective enforcement than other awards or judgments, including those of the International Court of Justice. On international arbitration generally, see A. Lowenfeld, International Litigation and Arbitration Ch. 4 (1993). Craig, Park, Paulsson & Reisman, International Commercial Arbitration (1997).

SECTION 4. THE INTERNATIONAL COURT OF JUSTICE

CHARTER OF THE UNITED NATIONS

[See Articles 92–96]

STATUTE OF THE INTERNATIONAL COURT OF JUSTICE

[See Articles 34–38]

Notes

1. The parties to the Statute include all members of the United Nations and one non-member (Switzerland) by resolution of the General Assembly pursuant to Article 93(2) of the United Nations Charter. The conditions upon which the Court is open to states which are not parties to the Statute are laid down in Security Council Resolution 9 of October 15, 1946, adopted pursuant to Article 35(2) of the Statute. See 1 SCOR, 2d Ser. No. 19, at 467–68.

2. There are fifteen judges on the Court elected by the Security Council and the General Assembly, each body voting separately. Nominations are made by national groups rather than by governments. See Articles 2–12 of the Statute. The judges may include no more than one national of any state. Judges serve for nine years, with 5 judges rotating off each three years. Judges may be re-elected and often are.

A "gentlemen's agreement" among members of the United Nations generally governs the distribution of seats among the various regions of the world. A practice has also evolved (consistent with the Security Council's role in elections) under which the permanent members of the Security Council generally do have judges of their nationality on the bench. Following the regular triennial elections held in November 1999 for the seats to be filled with effect from February 2000, the Court had 4 judges from western Europe (France, United Kingdom, Germany and the Netherlands), 2 from eastern Europe (Russian Federation and Hungary), 3 from Asia (China, Japan and Jordan), 3 from Africa (Algeria, Madagascar and Sierra Leone), 2 from Latin America (Venezuela and Brazil), and one from the United States.

On the practice for choosing judges, with particular reference to the role of the national groups "at one remove" from governments, see presentations by Abi–Saab and Damrosch on the topic "Ensuring the Best Bench: Ways of Selecting Judges," in Increasing the Effectiveness of the International Court of Justice (Peck & Lee, eds., 1997) at 165–206. On the way that the U.S. National Group has carried out consultations with professional organizations as recommended in Article 6 of the I.C.J. Statute, see Damrosch, The Election of Thomas Buergenthal to the International Court of Justice, 94 A.J.I.L. 579 (2000).

3. If a party in a case does not have a judge of its nationality, it may designate an *ad hoc* judge (Article 31).

Sometimes interesting issues arise concerning the use of *ad hoc* judges. For example, when the Federal Republic of Yugoslavia brought separate cases against

10 NATO member states concerning legality of use of force in the 1999 Kosovo crisis, Yugoslavia named its own judge *ad hoc* but objected to designation of judges *ad hoc* by certain of the respondents, on the ground that the bench already contained five judges from NATO respondent countries (France, Germany, the Netherlands, United Kingdom, United States). The Court, after deliberation, found that the nomination of judges *ad hoc* by the respective respondents in their own cases was justified at the provisional measures phase. See Case Concerning Legality of Use of Force (Yugoslavia v. Belgium), Request for the Indication of Provisional Measures, 1999 I.C.J., 1999 WL 1693067 (Order of June 2, 1999), para. 12, 38 I.L.M. 950, 954 (1999), and similar orders in the cases of Yugoslavia v. Canada, Yugoslavia v. Italy, Yugoslavia v. Spain, 38 I.L.M. at 1036, 1041 (para. 12); 1088, 1092 (para. 12); 1149, 1153 (para. 12). Portugal was sued but did not name a judge *ad hoc*. (Hungary, also a NATO member, had a judge on the bench but was not sued by Yugoslavia.)

4. The Court generally has decided cases by a full bench. It may, however, form chambers, composed of three or more judges to deal with a particular case or a category of cases (Articles 25–26). Ad hoc chambers have been used in a number of recent cases, including Gulf of Maine Area Case (Canada/U.S.), 1984 I.C.J. 246; Frontier Dispute (Burkina Faso/Mali), 1986 I.C.J. 554; ELSI Case (U.S./Italy), 1989 I.C.J. 15; Land, Island and Maritime Frontier Dispute (El Salvador/Honduras; Nicaragua intervening), 1992 I.C.J. 351. One of the controversial aspects of the use of chambers is the extent to which the parties may influence or control the selection of the judges. Judge Oda has noted that, although the jurisprudence of the Court is intended to reflect the diversity of the world's legal systems:

> In the case of all four of the ad hoc Chambers that have been constituted during recent years, consideration of "the main forms of civilization and the principal legal systems of the world" apparently was not in the minds of the parties in proposing the judges to sit on the Chamber or of the Court as a whole in electing the Chamber. Excluding national and ad hoc judges, the Chamber for the Gulf of Maine case had three Western European judges (from France, the Federal Republic of Germany and Italy); the Chamber for the Frontier Dispute (Burkina Faso v. Mali) case, one African (Algeria), one Eastern European (Poland) and one Latin American (Argentina); the Chamber for the Elettronica Sicula S.p.A. (ELSI) case (U.S./Italy), two Asians (India and Japan) and one Western European (United Kingdom) (one of the Asians was the then President of the Court); and the Chamber for the El Salvador/Honduras case, one Latin American (Brazil), one Asian (Japan) and one Western European (United Kingdom). This record suggests that no consistent geographical consideration has guided the choice of the judges of the Chambers. It may also be asked, when there are five main regions according to United Nations practice, by what criteria is the Court to choose three judges from among these five regions?

Shigeru Oda, Note and Comment, Further Thoughts on the Chambers Procedure of the International Court of Justice, 82 A.J.I.L. 556, 557 (1988). Do you agree that the objectivity, neutrality, and reputation of the Court is threatened by a system that allows the parties to have their dispute heard by an ad hoc chamber because they fear that the composition of the full court may not suit their goals? Consider an opposing view in favor of the use of chambers by Judge Schwebel:

> The workings of this process to date show that it affords the Court the opportunity to settle international disputes in a fashion that meets the needs of the parties and the international community, and does not detract from the

> integrity of the Court. It has not "fractionalized" or "regionalized" international law in any degree. It has not thrown into question the universal character of international law. It may be that sometimes the parties may desire, or settle upon, a Chamber of regional complexion; other times they will not. That happens in ad hoc arbitration as well.

Stephen Schwebel, Ad Hoc Chambers of the International Court of Justice, 81 A.J.I.L. 831, 850 (1987).

The Court also has a standing chamber of five judges to determine cases by summary procedure where speedy action is required (Article 29), and in 1993 a special Environmental Chamber was established.

5. All questions are decided by a majority vote of the judges present. In case of a tie the President has a casting vote (Article 55). The casting vote has been used in several of the Court's most controversial judgments, including the 1996 *Nuclear Weapons* advisory opinion where the judges were equally divided and President Bedjaoui (Algeria) cast the deciding vote. See p. 83.

6. For a comprehensive reference work on the I.C.J., see Rosenne, The Law and Practice of the International Court 1920–1996 (1997).

RECOURSE TO THE COURT

In its first half-century (1946–1996), the Court had just about 100 cases presented to it, of which 75 were under its contentious (state-to-state) jurisdiction and 22 were advisory opinion proceedings at the request of international organizations. It rendered 62 judgments, of which 39 were on the merits, and 23 advisory opinions. It also issued 298 orders, mostly of a procedural character but including some indicating provisional measures. See I.C.J. Yb. 1996–1997, p. 3.

Many of the judgments and advisory opinions have been of major significance for the clarification and development of international law. Nonetheless, international lawyers and students of international relations have noted and often deplored the fact that states have not chosen to submit most of their legal disputes to the Court. Even though resolutions have been adopted by unanimous votes in the General Assembly calling for greater use of the International Court, relatively few disputes are submitted to the Court.

The following comments sum up the reasons generally given for the reluctance of states to submit their disputes to the Court.

> It is no great mystery why they are reluctant to have their disputes adjudicated. Litigation is uncertain, time consuming, troublesome. Political officials do not want to lose control of a case that they might resolve by negotiation or political pressures. Diplomats naturally prefer diplomacy; political leaders value persuasion, manoeuvre and flexibility. They often prefer to "play it by ear," making their rules fit the circumstances rather than submit to pre-existing rules. Political forums, such as the United Nations, are often more attractive, especially to those likely to get wide support for political reasons. We need only compare the large number of disputes brought to the United Nations with the few submitted to adjudication. One could go on with other reasons. States do not want to risk losing a case when the stakes are high or be troubled with litigation in minor matters. An international tribunal may not inspire

> confidence, especially when some judges are seen as "political" or as hostile. There is apprehension that the law is too malleable or fragmentary to sustain "true" judicial decisions. In some situations, the legal issues are viewed as but one element in a complex political situation and consequently it is considered unwise or futile to deal with them separately. Finally we note the underlying perception of many governments that law essentially supports the *status quo* and that courts are not responsive to demands for justice or change.

Schachter, International Law in Theory and Practice 218 (1991).

A. JURISDICTION IN CONTENTIOUS CASES

The Court has two kinds of jurisdiction: to decide contentious cases between states and to render advisory opinions. Only states may be parties to a contentious case, not international organizations or private persons. The jurisdiction of the Court in contentious cases is based on the consent of the parties, express or implied (Article 36 of the Statute). Consent may be given *ad hoc* or by prior agreement in a treaty (Article 36(1)) or by accepting compulsory jurisdiction under Article 36(2). In the latter case, the case must be a "legal dispute." No such limitation is imposed in Article 36(1). However, Article 38 states that the function of the Court is to "decide in accordance with international law such disputes as are submitted to it." See Restatement § 903, Comment *d*.

Consent and reciprocity are the two bedrock principles of the Court's contentious jurisdiction. Consent is typically established by reference to the terms of the treaty or special agreement invoked under Article 36(1) or the unilateral declaration of acceptance under Article 36(2). Additionally, even if there is no preexisting agreement or declaration, a state may indicate its consent to be sued by pleading to the merits of a claim without raising any objections to jurisdiction. This last possibility, known as the principle of *forum prorogatum*, has been applied in the jurisprudence of both the Permanent Court and the present Court, as in the *Haya de la Torre* case, 1951 I.C.J. 71, where the Court observed:

> The Parties have in the present case consented to the jurisdiction of the Court. All the questions submitted to it have been argued on the merits, and no objection has been made to a decision on the merits. This conduct of the Parties is sufficient to confer jurisdiction on the Court. * * *

Reciprocity in an Article 36(1) case is usually found in the mutual obligations of the parties under the treaty invoked by the applicant. In an Article 36(2) case, however, the Court must determine whether both parties, by virtue of their unilateral declarations, have accepted "the same obligation." The Court's decisions establish that the respondent may invoke, by way of reciprocity, any material conditions that the applicant has placed on its own consent to jurisdiction. There is by now a considerable body of case law applying the principle of reciprocity. See, e.g., the *Nicaragua* case and notes at pp. 863–864 below.

Notes

1. Most of the Court's cases have been brought under compromissory clauses in treaties. Several have been based on the General Act for Peaceful Settlement (Section 1 supra). Others have been based on pre–1945 treaties that apply because the present International Court succeeded to the jurisdiction of the Permanent Court of International Justice under Article 37 of the Statute.

2. Nearly 250 treaties currently in force provide for resolution of disputes by the International Court. The United States is a party to more than 70 of them. See the Court's Yearbook and website for details.

3. A case brought under a treaty clause does not require a special agreement; it is begun by a unilateral application. Under a special agreement *(compromis)* the Court is limited to the questions put by the parties; under a treaty clause, the Court determines the relevant issues of law raised by the application. States that bind themselves by a treaty may be reluctant subsequently to adjudicate a particular case under that treaty. Some have refused to appear in such cases but nonappearance does not defeat jurisdiction. See Case Concerning U.S. Diplomatic and Consular Staff in Tehran, 1980 I.C.J. 3, pp. 868–879 below.

4. Some general multilateral conventions provide for compulsory jurisdiction through optional protocols such as those to the Vienna Conventions on Diplomatic Relations and on Consular Relations. Other conventions have jurisdictional clauses that allow any party to bring the dispute to the Court. Some of these conventions expressly allow reservations; others are silent on reservations but have had reservations made to them. See I.C.J. Advisory Opinion on Reservation to the Genocide Convention, Chapter 7. Some conventions exclude such reservations.

5. A few treaties give the Court "appellate jurisdiction." For example, the Convention on International Civil Aviation (1944) provides for appeals to the Court from decisions of the Council of the International Civil Aviation Organization (ICAO). See Case Between India and Pakistan Relating to Jurisdiction of ICAO Council, 1972 I.C.J. 46 (see Chapter 7, p. 551). The Court has also used its advisory jurisdiction to review judgments of international administrative tribunals. These cases have been brought by the organizations concerned under special procedures for advisory opinions and do not come within the contentious jurisdiction of the Court.

6. Relatively informal agreements between states for referring disputes to the Court may be sufficient for jurisdiction under Article 36(1). See the Fisheries Jurisdiction Cases, 1973 I.C.J. 3, 49 (discussed above at p. 559). Would an unsigned press communiqué expressing an intention to refer cases to the Court be adequate? The Court gave a negative reply in the Aegean Sea Continental Shelf Case, 1978 I.C.J. 3.

7. Many bilateral treaties include provisions for compulsory jurisdiction of disputes relating to the interpretation and application of the Treaty. Treaties of Friendship, Commerce and Navigation entered into by the United States with some 30 countries have such clauses. One was invoked by the United States in its case against Iran concerning the hostages in Tehran (discussed below) and another was invoked by Nicaragua in its proceeding against the United States for military and paramilitary activity against Nicaragua (infra).

The U.S.-Iranian treaty came before the Court again in the *Oil Platforms* case, 1996 I.C.J. 803; on that occasion Iran (which had ignored the Court in the *Tehran Hostages* case) sued the United States in relation to incidents occurring during the Iran–Iraq naval war of 1987–1988, when the U.S. military had destroyed certain Iranian oil platforms in the Persian Gulf which (according to the United States) had been used by the Iranian military to mount hostile attacks on neutral merchant shipping in the Gulf. Although Iran invoked several aspects of the bilateral treaty (known as the Treaty of Amity, Economic Relations, and Consular Rights), the Court confirmed jurisdiction only with respect to the Iranian contention that the U.S. conduct had interfered with freedom of navigation in violation of the treaty. Proceedings on the merits were still in progress as of 2000.

8. Article 36(1) also states that "the jurisdiction of the Court * * * comprises all matters specially provided for in the Charter of the United Nations." Are there any such matters? The only possible provision is Article 36(3) of the Charter which authorizes the Security Council to "recommend" that parties refer their disputes to the Court. However, as 7 judges declared in the Corfu Channel Case, 1949 I.C.J. 4, 31, a recommendation is an inadequate basis for compulsory jurisdiction. Is there room for the view that the Security Council may "decide" under Chapter VII of the Charter that a state must submit a dispute to the Court? Compare the Council's decisions under Chapter VII to create a compensation commission for claims against Iraq (p. 738) and to establish ad hoc criminal tribunals (Chapter 15 below).

COMPULSORY JURISDICTION UNDER THE OPTIONAL CLAUSE

Article 36(2) of the Statute provides:

> 2. The states parties to the present Statute may at any time declare that they recognize as compulsory *ipso facto* and without special agreement, in relation to any other state accepting the same obligation, the jurisdiction of the Court in all legal disputes concerning:
>
> a. the interpretation of a treaty;
>
> b. any question of international law;
>
> c. the existence of any fact which, if established, would constitute a breach of an international obligation;
>
> d. the nature or extent of the reparation to be made for the breach of an international obligation.

Article 36(3) of the Statute states:

> 3. The declarations referred to above may be made unconditionally or on condition of reciprocity on the part of several or certain states, or for a certain time.

As of 2000, 63 states were bound by declarations under Article 36(2). They are listed and their declarations are reprinted in the Yearbooks of the I.C.J. and also on the Court's website (www.icj-cij.org). Although for some periods of time certain groups of states (notably the Soviet bloc) had refrained from joining the optional clause system, this situation changed with the end of the Cold War, and the states accepting compulsory jurisdiction under Article

36(2) now come from all regions, including several of the post-Soviet and Eastern European states. Some declarations date from the period of the Permanent Court of International Justice: under Article 36(5) of the I.C.J. Statute, such declarations are deemed to be acceptances of the jurisdiction of the successor Court. The declarations of about a dozen more states are no longer effective, either because they have expired or have been withdrawn or terminated without being replaced. As summarized in the Restatement§ 903, Reporters' Note 2:

> Some of the declarations are without limit of time; others are for a specific period (usually five or ten years), in many instances with an automatic renewal clause. Many declarations reserve the right to terminate by a notice of withdrawal effective upon receipt by the Secretary–General of the United Nations. Some declarations specify that they apply only to disputes arising after the declaration was made or concerning situations or facts subsequent to a specified date. Seventeen declarations are without any reservation; the remaining declarations are accompanied by a variety of reservations. Many states have modified their reservations, some of them several times.
>
> The most common reservation excludes disputes committed by the parties to other tribunals or which the parties have agreed to settle by other means of settlement. Another common reservation excludes disputes relating to matters that are "exclusively" or "essentially" within the domestic jurisdiction of the declarant state; some of these reservations provide in addition that the question whether a dispute is essentially within the domestic jurisdiction is to be determined by the declaring state (a so-called "self-judging" clause). Several declarations exclude disputes arising under a multilateral treaty "unless all parties to the treaty affected by the decision are also parties to the case before the Court" or, more broadly, "unless all parties to the treaty are also parties to the case before the Court." Some reservations exclude disputes as to a particular subject, such as territorial or maritime boundaries or other law of the sea issues.
>
> A few declarations, using various formulas, exclude disputes arising out of hostilities to which the declarant state is a party; the most comprehensive of these reservations is that of India which excludes "disputes relating to or connected with facts or situations of hostilities, armed conflicts, individual or collective actions taken in self-defense, resistance to aggression, fulfillment of obligations imposed by international bodies, and other similar or related acts, measures or situations in which India is, has been or may in future be involved." A reservation of the United Kingdom made in 1957 excluded disputes "relating to any question which, in the opinion of the Government of the United Kingdom, affects the national security of the United Kingdom or of any of its dependent territories"; this clause was restricted in the United Kingdom's 1958 declaration to certain past disputes and was omitted in its 1963 declaration.
>
> An increasing number of states have added to their declarations clauses designed to avoid surprise suits by states that accept the Court's jurisdiction and immediately bring a case against another state. For

instance, some states have excluded any dispute that was brought before the Court by a party to a dispute less than 12 months after the party had accepted the jurisdiction of the Court with respect to that category of disputes. Many states have reserved the right to modify or terminate a declaration peremptorily by means of a notification to the Secretary–General of the United Nations, with effect from the moment of that notification.

SOME DECLARATIONS RECOGNIZING AS COMPULSORY THE JURISDICTION OF THE COURT

Guinea-Bissau

[Translation from the French] 7 VIII 89.

In accordance with Article 36, paragraph 2, of the Statute of the International Court of Justice, the Republic of Guinea–Bissau accepts as compulsory *ipso facto* and without special agreement, in relation to any other State accepting the same obligation, the jurisdiction of the Court in all legal disputes referred to in Article 36, paragraph 2, of the Statute thereof.

This declaration will remain in force until six months following the date on which the Government of Guinea–Bissau makes known its intention of terminating it.

New York, 7 August 1989.

(Signed) Raul A. DE MELO CABRAL,
Chargé d'affaires a.i.

United Kingdom of Great Britain and Northern Ireland

1 I 69.

1. I have the honour, by direction of Her Majesty's Principal Secretary of State for Foreign and Commonwealth Affairs, to declare on behalf of the Government of the United Kingdom of Great Britain and Northern Ireland that they accept as compulsory *ipso facto* and without special convention, on condition of reciprocity, the jurisdiction of the International Court of Justice, in conformity with paragraph 2 of Article 36 of the Statute of the Court, until such time as notice may be given to terminate the acceptance, over all disputes arising after 24 October 1945, with regard to situations or facts subsequent to the same date, other than:

(i) any dispute which the United Kingdom

(*a*) has agreed with the other Party or Parties thereto to settle by some other method of peaceful settlement; or

(*b*) has already submitted to arbitration by agreement with any State which had not at the time of submission accepted the compulsory jurisdiction of the International Court of Justice;

(ii) disputes with the government of any other country which is a Member of the Commonwealth with regard to situations or facts existing before 1 January 1969;

(iii) disputes in respect of which any other Party to the dispute has accepted the compulsory jurisdiction of the International Court of Justice only in relation to or for the purpose of the dispute; or where the acceptance of the Court's compulsory jurisdiction on behalf of any other Party to the dispute was deposited or ratified less than twelve months prior to the filing of the application bringing the dispute before the Court.

2. The Government of the United Kingdom also reserves the right at any time, by means of a notification addressed to the Secretary–General of the United Nations, and with effect as from the moment of such notification, either to add to, amend or withdraw any of the foregoing reservations, or any that may hereafter be added.

New York, 1 January 1969.

(Signed) L.C. GLASS

UNITED STATES OF AMERICA

26 VIII 46.

I, Harry S. Truman, President of the United States of America, declare on behalf of the United States of America, under Article 36, paragraph 2, of the Statute of the International Court of Justice, and in accordance with the Resolution of 2 August 1946 of the Senate of the United States of America (two-thirds of the Senators present concurring therein), that the United States of America recognizes as compulsory *ipso facto* and without special agreement, in relation to any other State accepting the same obligation, the jurisdiction of the International Court of Justice in all legal disputes hereafter arising concerning—

(a) the interpretation of a treaty;

(b) any question of international law;

(c) the existence of any fact which, if established, would constitute a breach of an international obligation;

(d) the nature or extent of the reparation to be made for the breach of an international obligation;

Provided, that this declaration shall not apply to—

(a) disputes the solution of which the parties shall entrust to other tribunals by virtue of agreements already in existence or which may be concluded in the future; or

(b) disputes with regard to matters which are essentially within the domestic jurisdiction of the United States of America as determined by the United States of America; or

(c) disputes arising under a multilateral treaty, unless (1) all parties to the treaty affected by the decision are also parties to the case before the Court, or (2) the United States of America specially agrees to jurisdiction; and

Provided further, that this declaration shall remain in force for a period of five years and thereafter until the expiration of six months after notice may be given to terminate this declaration.

(Signed) Harry S. TRUMAN

Done at Washington this fourteenth day of August 1946.

Notes

1. The U.S. acceptance of compulsory jurisdiction was terminated by President Reagan on October 7, 1985, with effect six months from that date. The termination was linked to the decision of the International Court in November 1984 in the case brought by Nicaragua against the United States for military and paramilitary activities in and against Nicaragua, 1984 I.C.J. 392. A summary of the case is at p. 880.

2. In explaining the motives for the decision to terminate acceptance of the compulsory jurisdiction clause, the Legal Adviser of the State Department observed that the United States had never successfully brought another state before the Court under the compulsory jurisdiction clause although it tried to do so several times. Sofaer, Statement to Senate Foreign Relations Committee, December 4, 1985, 86:2106 State Dept. Bull. 67 (1986). See p. 891 below. One reason he noted was that under the principle of reciprocity the respondent state could invoke the U.S. reservation involving matters essentially within domestic jurisdiction as determined by the United States, as was done by Bulgaria in 1960 in a case brought by the United States against Bulgaria for an aerial incident injuring U.S. nationals. See Gross, Bulgaria Invokes the Connally Amendment, 56 A.J.I.L. 357 (1962).

3. France brought a case against Norway based on the acceptance of compulsory jurisdiction by both states. The French declaration of acceptance contained a clause similar to that in the U.S. acceptance. Norway argued it had the right to rely on the restrictions in the French declaration and claimed that the matter fell within the national jurisdiction of Norway. The Court held that, in accordance with the condition of reciprocity, "Norway, equally with France, is entitled to except from the compulsory jurisdiction of the Court disputes understood by Norway to be essentially within its national jurisdiction". The French application was therefore rejected. The Court declared that it was not called upon to examine the validity of the reservation since the question of its validity was not presented by the issues in the proceedings inasmuch as both parties relied on the reservation. Case of Certain Norwegian Loans, 1957 I.C.J. 9. Judge Lauterpacht in a separate opinion maintained that a self-judging reservation was invalid and, if not separable, invalidated the acceptance of compulsory jurisdiction. 1957 I.C.J. 34. Similar views were expressed by Lauterpacht and three other judges in the Interhandel Case, 1959 I.C.J. 6 at 95; see also 1959 I.C.J. at 54, 75, 85.

4. Do the words of the clause in Article 36(2) that jurisdiction is accepted "in relation to any other state accepting the same obligation" mean that every acceptance impliedly includes a condition of reciprocity? Professor Edith Brown Weiss points out in an illuminating study of reciprocity that

> The current theory of reciprocity under the Optional Clause has three primary postulates. 1. Jurisdiction exists under the Optional Clause only to the extent that both parties have accepted a common commitment. 2. Determination of reciprocity takes place only at the moment the Court is seised of a case. 3. Reciprocity applies only to the scope and substance of the commitments, not to the formal conditions of their creation, duration or extinction.

E. Brown Weiss, Reciprocity and the Optional Clause, in the International Court at a Crossroads 82, 84 (Damrosch ed., 1987).

5. The United States argued in the 1984 *Nicaragua* case that it should benefit from an implied condition in Nicaragua's declaration permitting Nicaragua

to terminate its declaration at will with immediate effect. The Court refused to apply reciprocity to such temporal conditions of termination or modification, though the Court has recognized that the temporal conditions which exclude disputes prior to a given date are covered by reciprocity.

6. May a state that accepted compulsory jurisdiction withdraw such acceptance when it learns that a case is about to be brought against it? May a state accept compulsory jurisdiction to bring a specific case and immediately thereafter withdraw its acceptance to avoid being sued in another matter? Would such "hit-and-run" tactics be contrary to the principle of reciprocity or good faith?

7. When the United States terminated its acceptance, its spokesmen observed that a majority of judges in 1985 came from states that had not accepted compulsory jurisdiction and that only 47 countries in all had such acceptances. In what respect do these facts bear on the desirability or not of continued acceptance? Brown Weiss concluded that "acceptance of the compulsory jurisdiction of the Court by less than one-third of the countries that are parties to the Statute of the Court has not in practice resulted in significant inequities for those states that have accepted the Optional Clause" (loc. cit at 105).

8. In Fisheries Jurisdiction (Spain v. Canada), 1998 I.C.J. 432, Spain complained of Canada's arrest in 1995 of a Spanish trawler on the high seas outside Canada's exclusive economic zone in the regulatory area of the Northwest Atlantic Fisheries Organization (NAFO). In determining whether it had jurisdiction by virtue of the two parties' optional clause declarations, the Court had to interpret Canada's amended declaration filed May 10, 1994, which excluded "disputes arising out of or concerning conservation and management measures taken by Canada with respect to vessels fishing in the NAFO Regulatory Area * * * ." The Court affirmed its previous jurisprudence to the effect that "It is for each State, in formulating its declaration, to decide upon the limits it places upon its acceptance of the jurisdiction of the Court * * * ." 1998 I.C.J., para. 44. After close analysis of Canada's reservation in relation to the dispute in question, the Court concluded that the reservation was applicable and that the Court lacked jurisdiction to consider the dispute.

9. On April 26, 1999 the Federal Republic of Yugoslavia (Serbia–Montenegro) deposited a declaration of acceptance of compulsory jurisdiction under Article 36(2). On April 29, 1999 it initiated suit against ten NATO members, complaining that the bombing campaign concerning Kosovo which had begun on March 24, 1999 and which was then in progress was in violation of treaty obligations and general international law. Jurisdiction was asserted against some of the respondents under both Article 36(1) and Article 36(2) of the I.C.J. Statute: Article 36(1) was invoked as to the compromissory clause (Article IX) of the Genocide Convention, to which most of the respondents were parties, and Article 36(2) was invoked in relation to those NATO members (Belgium, Canada, the Netherlands, Portugal, Spain, the United Kingdom) that had accepted jurisdiction under Article 36(2)'s optional clause. In preliminary rulings dealing in the first instance with Yugoslavia's request for provisional measures (see p. 900 below), the Court held that it lacked prima facie jurisdiction to consider the request. A principal ground for the ruling concerning jurisdiction under Article 36(2) was that the dispute had already

arisen before Yugoslavia deposited its instrument of acceptance of optional clause jurisdiction. Case Concerning Legality of Use of Force (Yugoslavia v. Belgium), 1999 I.C.J., 1999 WL 1693067 and related cases, 38 I.L.M. 950 (1999).

OBJECTIONS TO JURISDICTION OR ADMISSIBILITY

NUCLEAR TESTS CASES (AUSTRALIA v. FRANCE) (NEW ZEALAND v. FRANCE)

International Court of Justice, 1974.
1974 I.C.J. 253, 457.

* * *

15. It is to be regretted that the French Government has failed to appear in order to put forward its arguments on the issues arising in the present phase of the proceedings, and the Court has thus not had the assistance it might have derived from such arguments or from any evidence adduced in support of them. The Court nevertheless has to proceed and reach a conclusion, and in doing so must have regard not only to the evidence brought before it and the arguments addressed to it by the Applicant, but also to any documentary or other evidence which may be relevant. It must on this basis satisfy itself, first that there exists no bar to the exercise of its judicial function, and secondly, if no such bar exists, that the Application is well founded in fact and in law.

* * *

16. The present case relates to a dispute between the Government of Australia [and of New Zealand] and the French Government concerning the holding of atmospheric tests of nuclear weapons by the latter Government in the South Pacific Ocean. Since in the present phase of the proceedings the Court has to deal only with preliminary matters, it is appropriate to recall that its approach to a phase of this kind must be, as it was expressed in the *Fisheries Jurisdiction* cases, as follows:

> "The issue being thus limited, the Court will avoid not only all expressions of opinion on matters of substance, but also any pronouncement which might prejudge or appear to prejudge any eventual decision on the merits." (I.C.J. Reports 1973, pp. 7 and 54.)

It will however be necessary to give a summary of the principal facts underlying the case.

* * *

18. As the United Nations Scientific Committee on the Effects of Atomic Radiation has recorded in its successive reports to the General Assembly, the testing of nuclear devices in the atmosphere has entailed the release into the atmosphere, and the consequent dissipation in varying degrees throughout the world, of measurable quantities of radio-active matter. It is asserted by Australia that the French atmospheric tests have caused some fall-out of this kind to be deposited on Australian territory; France has maintained in particular that the radio-active matter produced by its tests has been so

infinitesimal that it may be regarded as negligible, and that such fall-out on Australian territory does not constitute a danger to the health of the Australian population. These disputed points are clearly matters going to the merits of the case, and the Court must therefore refrain, for the reasons given above, from expressing any view on them.

* * *

51. In announcing that the 1974 series of atmospheric tests would be the last, the French Government conveyed to the world at large, including the Applicant, its intention effectively to terminate these tests. It was bound to assume that other States might take note of these statements and rely on their being effective. The validity of these statements and their legal consequences must be considered within the general framework of the security of international intercourse, and the confidence and trust which are so essential in the relations among States. It is from the actual substance of these statements, and from the circumstances attending their making, that the legal implications of the unilateral act must be deduced. The objects of these statements are clear and they were addressed to the international community as a whole, and the Court holds that they constitute an undertaking possessing legal effect. The Court considers that the President of the Republic, in deciding upon the effective cessation of atmospheric tests, gave an undertaking to the international community to which his words were addressed. It is true that the French Government has consistently maintained, for example in a Note dated 7 February 1973 from the French Ambassador in Canberra to the Prime Minister and Minister for Foreign Affairs of Australia, that it "has the conviction that its nuclear experiments have not violated any rule of international law," nor did France recognize that it was bound by any rule of international law to terminate its tests, but this does not affect the legal consequences of the statements examined above. The Court finds that the unilateral undertaking resulting from these statements cannot be interpreted as having been made in implicit reliance on an arbitrary power or reconsideration. The Court finds further that the French Government has undertaken an obligation the precise nature and limits of which must be understood in accordance with the actual terms in which they have been publicly expressed.

52. Thus the Court faces a situation in which the objective of the Applicant has in effect been accomplished, inasmuch as the Court finds that France has undertaken the obligation to hold no further nuclear tests in the atmosphere in the South Pacific.

53. The Court finds that no question of damages arises in the present case, since no such claim has been raised by the Applicant either prior to or during the proceedings, and the original and ultimate objective of Applicant has been to seek protection "against any further atmospheric test" * * *.

* * *

56. It may be argued that although France may have undertaken such an obligation, by a unilateral declaration, not to carry out atmospheric nuclear tests in the South Pacific Ocean, a judgment of the Court on this subject might still be of value because, if the judgment upheld the Applicant's contentions, it would reinforce the position of the Applicant by affirming the obligation of the Respondent. However, the Court having found that the

Respondent has assumed an obligation as to conduct, concerning the effective cessation of nuclear tests, no further judicial action is required. The Applicant has repeatedly sought from the Respondent an assurance that the tests would cease, and the Respondent has, on its own initiative, made a series of statements to the effect that they will cease. Thus the Court concludes that, the dispute having disappeared, the claim advanced by Australia no longer has any object. It follows that any further finding would have no *raison d'être.*

* * *

62. For these reasons,

THE COURT,

by nine votes to six,

finds that the claim of Australia no longer has any object and that the Court is therefore not called upon to give a decision thereon.

Notes

1. Does it make a difference whether the objective of Australia and New Zealand was to have the tests terminated from the date of its application or the date of the judgment? If the former, would the dispute have an object, e.g., a declaration of illegality as "satisfaction," or a basis for a future claim of damages? Can an issue be regarded as moot when it concerns the continued applicability of a rule of customary international law?

2. The Court considered it unnecessary to decide that it was properly seised of the dispute and had jurisdiction to entertain it since it found that the dispute had disappeared. Its action, in its view, rested on "inherent jurisdiction" to provide for orderly settlement of all matters in dispute. Consider the following comment in a joint dissenting opinion of 5 judges: "If the so-called 'inherent jurisdiction' is considered by the Court to authorize it to decide that France is now under an obligation to terminate atmospheric nuclear tests in the South Pacific Ocean, why does the 'inherent jurisdiction not also authorize it, on the basis of that same international obligation, to decide that the French Republic shall not carry out any further such tests". 1974 I.C.J. 325–26.

3. If the objective of Australia and New Zealand was to bring about a cessation of tests after the judgment, did the dispute cease when the French statements were made even if those statements did not amount to a legal undertaking? For a closely reasoned analysis of the meaning of "dispute" in this context, see Macdonald & Hough, The Nuclear Tests Case Revisited, 20 Germ. Y.B.I.L. 337 (1977). Other commentaries on the case include: Franck, Word Made Law, 69 A.J.I.L. 612–21 (1975); Lellouche, The Nuclear Tests Cases, 16 Harv. Int'l L.J. 614 (1975); McWhinney, International Law–Making and the Judicial Process: The World Court and the French Nuclear Tests Case, 3 Syracuse J.Int'l L. & Comm. 9 (1975). See also pp. 458–460 in Chapter 7.

4. More than 20 years after the decision in the principal case, New Zealand sought to reopen the matter in connection with France's resumption of underground nuclear testing in the South Pacific. The Court declined the request, on the ground that the previous case had concerned atmospheric rather than underground testing and that therefore the conditions for reopening the previous judgment were not fulfilled. See Request for an Examination of the Situation in

Accordance with Paragraph 63 of the Court's Judgment of 20 December 1974 in the Nuclear Tests (New Zealand v. France) Case, 1995 I.C.J. 288.

CASE CONCERNING UNITED STATES DIPLOMATIC AND CONSULAR STAFF IN TEHRAN (UNITED STATES OF AMERICA v. IRAN)

Order of Provisional Measures, 15 December 1979.
1979 I.C.J. 7.

REQUEST FOR THE INDICATION OF PROVISIONAL MEASURES

Having regard to the Application by the United States of America filed in the Registry of the Court on 29 November 1979, instituting proceedings against the Islamic Republic of Iran in respect of a dispute concerning the situation in the United States Embassy in Tehran and the seizure and holding as hostages of members of the United States diplomatic and consular staff in Iran;

1. Whereas in the above-mentioned Application the United States Government invokes jurisdictional provisions in certain treaties as bases for the Court's jurisdiction in the present case; whereas it further recounts a sequence of events, beginning on 4 November 1979 in and around the United States Embassy in Tehran and involving the invasion of the Embassy premises, the seizure of United States diplomatic and consular staff and their continued detention; and whereas, on the basis of the facts there alleged, it requests the Court to adjudge and declare:

(a) That the Government of Iran, in tolerating, encouraging, and failing to prevent and punish the conduct described in the preceding Statement of Facts [in the Application], violated its international legal obligations to the United States as provided by

—Articles 22, 24, 25, 27, 29, 31, 37 and 47 of the Vienna Convention on Diplomatic Relations,

—Articles 28, 31, 33, 34, 36 and 40 of the Vienna Convention on Consular Relations,

—Articles 4 and 7 of the Convention on the Prevention and Punishment of Crimes against Internationally Protected Persons, including Diplomatic Agents, and

—Articles II(4), XIII, XVIII and XIX of the Treaty of Amity, Economic Relations, and Consular Rights between the United States and Iran, and

—Articles 2(3), 2(4) and 33 of the Charter of the United Nations;

(b) That pursuant to the foregoing international legal obligations, the Government of Iran is under a particular obligation immediately to secure the release of all United States nationals currently being detained within the premises of the United States Embassy in Tehran and to assure that all such persons and all other United States nationals in Tehran are allowed to leave Iran safely;

(c) That the Government of Iran shall pay to the United States, in its own right and in the exercise of its right of diplomatic protection of its nationals, reparation for the foregoing violations of Iran's international legal obligations to the United States, in a sum to be determined by the Court; and

(d) That the Government of Iran submit to its competent authorities for the purpose of prosecution those persons responsible for the crimes committed against the premises and staff of the United States Embassy and against the premises of its Consulates;

2. Having regard to the request dated 29 November 1979 and filed in the Registry the same day, whereby the Government of the United States of America, relying on Article 41 of the Statute and Articles 73, 74 and 75 of the Rules of Court, asks the Court urgently to indicate, pending the final decision in the case brought before it by the above-mentioned Application of the same date, the following provisional measures:

(a) That the Government of Iran immediately release all hostages of United States nationality and facilitate the prompt and safe departure from Iran of these persons and all other United States officials in dignified and humane circumstances.

(b) That the Government of Iran immediately clear the premises of the United States Embassy, Chancery and Consulate of all persons whose presence is not authorized by the United States Chargé d'Affaires in Iran, and restore the premises to United States control.

(c) That the Government of Iran ensure that all persons attached to the United States Embassy and Consulate should be accorded, and protected in, full freedom within the Embassy and Chancery premises, and the freedom of movement within Iran necessary to carry out their diplomatic and consular functions.

(d) That the Government of Iran not place on trial any person attached to the Embassy and Consulate of the United States and refrain from any action to implement any such trial.

(e) That the Government of Iran ensure that no action is taken which might prejudice the rights of the United States in respect of the carrying out of any decision which the Court may render on the merits, and in particular neither take nor permit action that would threaten the lives, safety, or well-being of the hostages;

* * *

8. Whereas on 9 December 1979 a letter, dated the same day and transmitted by telegram, was received from the Minister for Foreign Affairs of Iran, which reads as follows:

* * *

I have the honour to acknowledge receipt of the telegrams concerning the meeting of the International Court of Justice on 10 December 1979, at the request of the Government of the United States of America, and to submit to you below the position of the Government of the Islamic Republic of Iran in this respect.

1. First of all, the Government of the Islamic Republic of Iran wishes to express its respect for the International Court of Justice, and for its distin-

guished members, for what they have achieved in the quest for just and equitable solutions to legal conflicts between States. However, the Government of the Islamic Republic of Iran considers that the Court cannot and should not take cognizance of the case which the Government of the United States of America has submitted to it, and in a most significant fashion, a case confined to what is called the question of the "hostages of the American Embassy in Tehran".

2. For this question only represents a marginal and secondary aspect of an overall problem, one such that it cannot be studied separately, and which involves, *inter alia,* more than 25 years of continual interference by the United States in the internal affairs of Iran, the shameless exploitation of our country, and numerous crimes perpetrated against the Iranian people, contrary to and in conflict with all international and humanitarian norms.

3. The problem involved in the conflict between Iran and the United States is thus not one of the interpretation and the application of the treaties upon which the American Application is based, but results from an overall situation containing much more fundamental and more complex elements. Consequently, the Court cannot examine the American Application divorced from its proper context, namely the whole political dossier of the relations between Iran and the United States over the last 25 years. This dossier includes, *inter alia,* all the crimes perpetrated in Iran by the American Government, in particular the *coup d'état* of 1953 stirred up and carried out by the CIA, the overthrow of the lawful national government of Dr. Mossadegh, the restoration of the Shah and of his régime which was under the control of American interests, and all the social, economic, cultural, and political consequences of the direct interventions in our internal affairs, as well as grave, flagrant and continuous violations of all international norms, committed by the United States in Iran.

4. With regard to the request for provisional measures, as formulated by the United States, it in fact implies that the Court should have passed judgment on the actual substance of the case submitted to it, which the Court cannot do without breach of the norms governing its jurisdiction. Furthermore, since provisional measures are by definition intended to protect the interests of the parties, they cannot be unilateral, as they are in the request submitted by the American Government.

In conclusion, the Government of the Islamic Republic of Iran respectfully draws the attention of the Court to the deep-rootedness and the essential character of the Islamic revolution of Iran, a revolution of a whole oppressed nation against its oppressors and their masters; any examination of the numerous repercussions thereof is a matter essentially and directly within the national sovereignty of Iran.

* * *

13. Noting that the Government of Iran was not represented at the hearing; and whereas the non-appearance of one of the States concerned cannot by itself constitute an obstacle to the indication of provisional measures;

14. Whereas the treaty provisions on which, in its Application and oral observations, the United States Government claims to found the jurisdiction of the Court to entertain the present case are the following:

(i) the Vienna Convention on Diplomatic Relations of 1961, and Article I of its accompanying Optional Protocol concerning the Compulsory Settlement of Disputes;

(ii) the Vienna Convention on Consular Relations of 1963, and Article I of its accompanying Optional Protocol concerning the Compulsory Settlement of Disputes;

(iii) Article XXI, paragraph 2, of the Treaty of Amity, Economic Relations, and Consular Rights of 1955 between the United States of America and Iran; and

(iv) Article 13, paragraph 1, of the Convention of 1973 on the Prevention and Punishment of Crimes against Internationally Protected Persons, including Diplomatic Agents;

* * *

18. Whereas, accordingly, it is manifest from the information before the Court and from the terms of Article I of each of the two Protocols that the provisions of these Articles furnish a basis on which the jurisdiction of the Court might be founded with regard to the claims of the United States under the Vienna Conventions of 1961 and 1963;

* * *

21. Whereas, therefore, the Court does not find it necessary for present purposes to enter into the question whether a basis for the exercise of its powers under Article 41 of the Statute might also be found under Article XXI, paragraph 2, of the Treaty of Amity, Economic Relations, and Consular Rights of 1955, and Article 13, paragraph 1, of the Convention on the Prevention and Punishment of Crimes against Internationally Protected Persons, including Diplomatic Agents, of 1973;

22. Whereas, on the other hand, in the above-mentioned letter of 9 December 1979 the Government of Iran maintains that the Court cannot and should not take cognizance of the present case, for the reason that the question of the hostages forms only "a marginal and secondary aspect of an overall problem" involving the activities of the United States in Iran over a period of more than 25 years; and whereas it further maintains that any examination of the numerous repercussions of the Islamic revolution of Iran is essentially and directly a matter within the national sovereignty of Iran;

23. Whereas, however important, and however connected with the present case, the iniquities attributed to the United States Government by the Government of Iran in that letter may appear to be to the latter Government, the seizure of the United States Embassy and Consulates and the detention of internationally protected persons as hostages cannot, in the view of the Court, be regarded as something "secondary" or "marginal," having regard to the importance of the legal principles involved; whereas the Court notes in this regard that the Secretary–General of the United Nations has indeed referred to these occurrences as "a grave situation" posing "a serious threat to international peace and security" and that the Security Council in resolution

457 (1979) expressed itself as deeply concerned at the dangerous level of tension between the two States, which could have grave consequences for international peace and security;

24. Whereas, moreover, if the Iranian Government considers the alleged activities of the United States in Iran legally to have a close connection with the subject-matter of the United States Application, it remains open to that Government under the Court's Statute and Rules to present its own arguments to the Court regarding those activities either by way of defence in a Counter–Memorial or by way of a counter-claim filed under Article 80 of the Rules of Court; whereas, therefore, by not appearing in the present proceedings, the Government of Iran, by its own choice, deprives itself of the opportunity of developing its own arguments before the Court and of itself filing a request for the indication of provisional measures; and whereas no provision of the Statute or Rules contemplates that the Court should decline to take cognizance of one aspect of a dispute merely because that dispute has other aspects, however important;

25. Whereas it is no doubt true that the Islamic revolution of Iran is a matter "essentially and directly within the national sovereignty of Iran;" whereas however a dispute which concerns diplomatic and consular premises and the detention of internationally protected persons, and involves the interpretation or application of multilateral conventions codifying the international law governing diplomatic and consular relations, is one which by its very nature falls within international jurisdiction;

26. Whereas accordingly the two considerations advanced by the Government of Iran in its letter of 9 December 1979 cannot, in the view of the Court, be accepted as constituting any obstacle to the Court's taking cognizance of the case brought before it by the United States Application of 29 November 1979;

27. Whereas in that same letter of 9 December 1979 the Government of Iran also puts forward two considerations on the basis of which it contends that the Court ought not, in any event, to accede to the United States request for provisional measures in the present case;

28. Whereas, in the first place, it maintains that the request for provisional measures, as formulated by the United States, "in fact implies that the Court should have passed judgment on the actual substance of the case submitted to it"; whereas it is true that in the *Factory at Chorzów* case the Permanent Court of International Justice declined to indicate interim measures of protection on the ground that the request in that case was "designed to obtain an interim judgment in favour of a part of the claim" *(Order of 21 November 1927, P.C.I.J., Series A, No. 12,* at p. 10); whereas, however, the circumstances of that case were entirely different from those of the present one, and the request there sought to obtain from the Court a final judgment on part of a claim for a sum of money; whereas, moreover, a request for provisional measures must by its very nature relate to the substance of the case since, as Article 41 expressly states, their object is to preserve the respective rights of either party; and whereas in the present case the purpose of the United States request appears to be not to obtain a judgment, interim

or final, on the merits of its claims but to preserve the substance of the rights which it claims *pendente lite;*

* * *

33. Whereas by the terms of Article 41 of the Statute the Court may indicate such measures only when it considers that circumstances so require in order to preserve the rights of either party;

34. Whereas the circumstances alleged by the United States Government which, in the submission of that Government, require the indication of provisional measures in the present case may be summarized as follows:

(i) On 4 November 1979, in the course of a demonstration outside the United States Embassy compound in Tehran, demonstrators attacked the Embassy premises; no Iranian security forces intervened or were sent to relieve the situation, despite repeated calls for help from the Embassy to the Iranian authorities. Ultimately the whole of the Embassy premises was invaded. The Embassy personnel, including consular and non-American staff, and visitors who were present in the Embassy at the time were seized. Shortly afterwards, according to the United States Government, its consulates in Tabriz and Shiraz, which had been attacked earlier in 1979, were also seized, without any action being taken to prevent it;

(ii) Since that time, the premises of the United States Embassy in Tehran, and of the consulates in Tabriz and Shiraz, have remained in the hands of the persons who seized them. These persons have ransacked the archives and documents both of the diplomatic mission and of its consular section. The Embassy personnel and other persons seized at the time of the attack have been held hostage with the exception of 13 persons released on 18 and 20 November 1979. Those holding the hostages have refused to release them, save on condition of the fulfilment by the United States of various demands regarded by it as unacceptable. The hostages are stated to have frequently been bound, blindfolded, and subjected to severe discomfort, complete isolation and threats that they would be put on trial or even put to death. The United States Government affirms that it has reason to believe that some of them may have been transferred to other places of confinement;

(iii) The Government of the United States considers that not merely has the Iranian Government failed to prevent the events described above, but also that there is clear evidence of its complicity in, and approval of, those events;

(iv) The persons held hostage in the premises of the United States Embassy in Tehran include, according to the information furnished to the Court by the Agent of the United States, at least 28 persons having the status, duly recognized by the Government of Iran, of "member of the diplomatic staff" within the meaning of the Vienna Convention on Diplomatic Relations of 1961; at least 20 persons having the status, similarly recognized, of "members of the administrative and technical staff" within the meaning of that Convention; and two other persons of United States nationality not possessing either diplomatic or consular status. Of the persons with the status of member of the diplomatic staff, four are members of the Consular Section of the Embassy;

(v) In addition to the persons held hostage in the premises of the Tehran Embassy, the United States Chargé d'Affaires in Iran and two other United States diplomatic agents are detained in the premises of the Iranian Ministry for Foreign Affairs, in circumstances which the Government of the United States has not been able to make entirely clear, but which apparently involve restriction of their freedom of movement, and a threat to their inviolability as diplomats;

* * *

38. Whereas there is no more fundamental prerequisite for the conduct of relations between States than the inviolability of diplomatic envoys and embassies, so that throughout history nations of all creeds and cultures have observed reciprocal obligations for that purpose; and whereas the obligations thus assumed, notably those for assuring the personal safety of diplomats and their freedom from prosecution, are essential, unqualified, and inherent in their representative character and their diplomatic function;

39. Whereas the institution of diplomacy, with its concomitant privileges and immunities, has withstood the test of centuries and proved to be an instrument essential for effective cooperation in the international community, and for enabling States, irrespective of their differing constitutional and social systems, to achieve mutual understanding and to resolve their differences by peaceful means;

40. Whereas the unimpeded conduct of consular relations, which have also been established between peoples since ancient times, is no less important in the context of present-day international law, in promoting the development of friendly relations among nations, and ensuring protection and assistance for aliens resident in the territories of other States; and whereas therefore the privileges and immunities of consular officers and consular employees, and the inviolability of consular premises and archives, are similarly principles deep-rooted in international law;

41. Whereas, while no State is under any obligation to maintain diplomatic or consular relations with another, yet it cannot fail to recognize the imperative obligations inherent therein, now codified in the Vienna Conventions of 1961 and 1963, to which both Iran and the United States are parties;

42. Whereas continuance of the situation the subject of the present request exposes the human beings concerned to privation, hardship, anguish and even danger to life and health and thus to a serious possibility of irreparable harm;

* * *

47. Accordingly,

THE COURT,

unanimously,

1. *Indicates,* pending its final decision in the proceedings instituted on 29 November 1979 by the United States of America against the Islamic Republic of Iran, the following provisional measures:

A. (i) The Government of the Islamic Republic of Iran should immediately ensure that the premises of the United States Embassy,

Chancery and Consulates be restored to the possession of the United States authorities under their exclusive control, and should ensure their inviolability and effective protection as provided for by the treaties in force between the two States, and by general international law;

(ii) The Government of the Islamic Republic of Iran should ensure the immediate release, without any exception, of all persons of United States nationality who are or have been held in the Embassy of the United States of America or in the Ministry of Foreign Affairs in Tehran, or have been held as hostages elsewhere, and afford full protection to all such persons, in accordance with the treaties in force between the two States, and with general international law;

(iii) The Government of the Islamic Republic of Iran should, as from that moment, afford to all the diplomatic and consular personnel of the United States the protection, privileges and immunities to which they are entitled under the treaties in force between the two States, and under general international law, including immunity from any form of criminal jurisdiction and freedom and facilities to leave the territory of Iran;

B. The Government of the United States of America and the Government of the Islamic Republic of Iran should not take any action and should ensure that no action is taken which may aggravate the tension between the two countries or render the existing dispute more difficult of solution;

2. *Decides* that, until the Court delivers its final judgment in the present case, it will keep the matters covered by this Order continuously under review.

CASE CONCERNING UNITED STATES DIPLOMATIC AND CONSULAR STAFF IN TEHRAN (UNITED STATES OF AMERICA v. IRAN)

Judgment of May 24, 1980.
1980 I.C.J. 3.

[The following summary is taken from the Yearbook of the International Court of Justice 1980 (at 119–25) with some excerpts from the Judgment:]

* * *

Iran took no part in the proceedings. It neither filed pleadings nor was represented at the hearing, and no submissions were therefore presented on its behalf. Its position was however defined in two letters addressed to the Court by its Minister for Foreign Affairs on 9 December 1979 and 16 March 1980 respectively. In these the Minister maintained *inter alia* that the Court could not and should not take cognizance of the case.

THE FACTS (PARAS. 11–32)

The Court expresses regret that Iran did not appear before it to put forward its arguments. The absence of Iran from the proceedings brought into operation Article 53 of the Statute, under which the Court is required, before finding in the Applicant's favour, to satisfy itself that the allegations of fact on which the claim is based are well founded.

In that respect the Court observes that it has had available to it, in the documents presented by the United States, a massive body of information from various sources, including numerous official statements of both Iranian and United States authorities. This information, the Court notes, is wholly concordant as to the main facts and has all been communicated to Iran without evoking any denial. The Court is accordingly satisfied that the allegations of fact on which the United States based its claim were well founded.

ADMISSIBILITY (PARAS. 33–44)

Under the settled jurisprudence of the Court, it is bound, in applying Article 53 of its Statute, to investigate, on its own initiative, any preliminary question of admissibility or jurisdiction that may arise.

On the subject of admissibility, the Court, after examining the considerations put forward in the two letters from Iran, finds that they do not disclose any ground for concluding that it could not or should not deal with the case. Neither does it find any incompatibility with the continuance of judicial proceedings before the Court in the establishment by the Secretary–General of the United Nations, with the agreement of both States, of a Commission given a mandate to undertake a fact-finding mission to Iran, hear Iran's grievances and facilitate the solution of the crisis between the two countries.

[The Court referred to the contention of Iran that the issues raised by the United States cannot be examined separately from the "overall problem" involving "more than 25 years of continual interference by the United States in the internal affairs of Iran". In response the Court commented that:]

* * * legal disputes between sovereign States by their very nature are likely to occur in political contexts, and often form only one element in a wider and long-standing political dispute between the States concerned. Yet never has the view been put forward before that, because a legal dispute submitted to the Court is only one aspect of a political dispute, the Court should decline to resolve for the parties the legal questions at issue between them. Nor can any basis for such a view of the Court's functions or jurisdiction be found in the Charter or the Statute of the Court: if the Court were, contrary to its settled jurisprudence, to adopt such a view, it would impose a far-reaching and unwarranted restriction upon the role of the Court in the peaceful solution of international disputes.

JURISDICTION (PARAS. 45–55)

Four instruments having been cited by the United States as bases for the Court's jurisdiction to deal with its claims, the Court finds that three, namely the Optional Protocols to the two Vienna Conventions of 1961 and 1963 on, respectively, Diplomatic and Consular Relations, and the 1955 Treaty of Amity, Economic Relations, and Consular Rights between the United States and Iran, do in fact provide such foundations.

[The Court noted that the Protocols provided for arbitration or conciliation before resort to the Court. However, it found that neither party had proposed arbitration or conciliation; consequently, they had no application. In any case "they are not to be understood as laying down a precondition of the applicability of the precise and categorical provision contained in Article I establishing the compulsory jurisdiction of the Court * * * " (para. 48). With regard to the 1955 Treaty of Amity, the Court referred to the dispute settlement clause which provides that any dispute "not satisfactorily adjusted by diplomacy shall be submitted to the International Court * * * " (Article XXI, para. 2). The Court observed that "the refusal of the Iranian government to enter into any discussion of the matter" meant "beyond any doubt" that there existed a "dispute not satisfactorily adjusted by diplomacy" (para. 51). The Court also observed in regard to the article in the 1955 treaty:]

While that Article does not provide in express terms that either party may bring a case to the Court by unilateral application, it is evident, as the United States contended in its Memorial, that this is what the parties intended. Provisions drawn in similar terms are very common in bilateral treaties of amity or of establishment, and the intention of the parties in accepting such clauses is clearly to provide for such a right of unilateral recourse to the Court, in the absence of agreement to employ some other pacific means of settlement.

* * *

MERITS, ATTRIBUTABILITY TO THE IRANIAN STATE OF THE ACTS COMPLAINED OF, AND VIOLATION BY IRAN OF CERTAIN OBLIGATIONS (PARAS. 56–94)

The Court has also, under Article 53 of its Statute, to satisfy itself that the claims of the Applicant are well founded in law. To this end, it considers the acts complained of in order to determine how far, legally, they may be attributed to the Iranian State (as distinct from the occupiers of the Embassy) and whether they are compatible or incompatible with Iran's obligations under treaties in force or other applicable rules of international law, while the Ayatollah declared that the detention of the hostages would continue until the new Iranian parliament had taken a decision as to their fate.

The Iranian authorities' decision to continue the subjection of the Embassy to occupation, and of its staff to detention as hostages, gave rise to repeated and multiple breaches of Iran's treaty obligations, additional to those already committed at the time of the seizure of the Embassy (1961 Convention: Arts. 22, 24, 25, 26, 27 and 29; 1963 Convention: *inter alia,* Art. 33; 1955 Treaty, Art. II(4)).

* * *

The Court finds that Iran, by committing successive and continuing breaches of the obligations laid upon it by the Vienna Conventions of 1961 and 1963, the 1955 Treaty, and the applicable rules of general international law, has incurred responsibility towards the United States. As a consequence, there is an obligation on the part of the Iranian State to make reparation for the injury caused to the United States. Since, however, the breaches are still continuing, the form and amount of such reparation cannot yet be determined.

At the same time the Court considers it essential to reiterate the observations it made in its Order of 15 December 1979 on the importance of the principles of international law governing diplomatic and consular relations. After stressing the particular gravity of the case, arising out of the fact that it is not any private individuals or groups that have set at naught the inviolability of an embassy, but the very government of the State to which the mission is accredited, the Court draws the attention of the entire international community to the irreparable harm that may be caused by events of the kind before the Court. Such events cannot fail to undermine a carefully constructed edifice of law, the maintenance of which is vital for the security and well-being of the international community.

(e) United States operation in Iran on 24–25 April 1980 (paras. 93 and 94)

With regard to the operation undertaken in Iran by United States military units on 24–25 April 1980, the Court says that it cannot fail to express its concern. It feels bound to observe that an operation undertaken in those circumstances, from whatever motive, is of a kind calculated to undermine respect for the judicial process in international relations. Nevertheless, the question of the legality of that operation can have no bearing on the evaluation of Iran's conduct on 4 November 1979. The findings reached by the Court are therefore not affected by that operation.

* * *

For these reasons, the Court gave the following decision:

"THE COURT,

1. By thirteen votes to two,

Decides that the Islamic Republic of Iran, by the conduct which the Court has set out in this Judgment, has violated in several respects, and is still violating, obligations owed by it to the United States of America under international conventions in force between the two countries, as well as under long-established rules of general international law;

2. By thirteen votes to two,

Decides that the violations of these obligations engage the responsibility of the Islamic Republic of Iran towards the United States of America under international law;

3. Unanimously,

Decides that the Government of the Islamic Republic of Iran must immediately take all steps to redress the situation resulting from the events of 4 November 1979 and what followed from these events, and to that end:

(a) must immediately terminate the unlawful detention of the United States Chargé d'affaires and other diplomatic and consular staff and other United States nationals now held hostage in Iran, and must immediately release each and every one and entrust them to the protecting Power (Article 45 of the 1961 Vienna Convention on Diplomatic Relations);

(b) must ensure that all the said persons have the necessary means of leaving Iranian territory, including means of transport;

(c) must immediately place in the hands of the protecting Power the premises, property, archives and documents of the United States Embassy in Tehran and of its Consulates in Iran;

4. Unanimously,

Decides that no member of the United States diplomatic or consular staff may be kept in Iran to be subjected to any form of judicial proceedings or to participate in them as a witness;

5. By twelve votes to three,

Decides that the Government of the Islamic Republic of Iran is under an obligation to make reparation to the Government of the United States of America for the injury caused to the latter by the events of 4 November 1979 and what followed from these events;

6. By fourteen votes to one,

Decides that the form and amount of such reparation, failing agreement between the Parties, shall be settled by the Court, and reserves for this purpose the subsequent procedure in the case.

Judge Lachs appended a separate opinion, and Judges Morozov and Tarazi dissenting opinions to the Judgment.

Notes

1. Was the Court justified in criticizing the attempt of the United States to rescue the hostages during the pendency of the case? Are measures of self-help, if otherwise legal, precluded when judicial proceedings are under way? One commentator suggests they are not permissible "for they are designed to bring about the termination of the conflict without regard to the impartial determinations the parties agreed to seek when they assented to the tribunal's jurisdiction." Stein, Contempt, Crisis and the Court, 76 A.J.I.L. 499, 512 (1982).

2. The Court's reprimand to the United States also referred to the Order of Provisional Measures, stating that no action was to be taken "which might aggravate the tension between the two countries." 1980 I.C.J. 43. Should Iran's failure to comply with the Court's order of provisional measures have relieved the United States of its duty to do so? Apparently the Court did not regard reciprocity as a condition of compliance. Assuming a state disobeys an order of provisional measures, may the Court impose penalties on that state? Should the Court have applied the equitable notion of "clean hands" to deny relief to a moving party (as the United States was)? Was it pertinent that Iran's non-compliance and continued violation of basic international law was relatively much more serious? See Schachter, International Law in the Hostages Crisis, in American Hostages in Iran 325, 344–45 (Christopher et al. eds., 1985).

3. Note that the Court did not pass upon the legality of the rescue mission under international law. The majority avoided taking issue with the U.S. position that the rescue was a justifiable self-help action because the individuals were in imminent danger of execution as evidenced by Iranian threats. Two dissenting judges, Tarazi (Syria) and Morozov (U.S.S.R.) considered that the United States was not entitled to reparations because of the rescue mission and the economic counter-measures taken against Iran. In their view these measures violated international law and the Court's provisional measures order. 1980 I.C.J. at 65.

4. Iran released the hostages in January 1981, seven months after the Court's judgment. Under the Declarations of Algeria by which Iran and the United States expressed their commitments for release of the hostages, withdrawal of sanctions and settlement of claims, the United States agreed to withdraw all

claims pending against Iran before the International Court of Justice. Para. 11 of Declaration of Algeria, 20 I.L.M. 223 (1981).

5. Iran's refusal to appear before the Court followed four earlier instances of non-appearance by respondent states. See p. 894 below.

CASE CONCERNING MILITARY AND PARAMILITARY ACTIVITIES IN AND AGAINST NICARAGUA (NICARAGUA v. UNITED STATES)

International Court of Justice, 1984.
1984 I.C.J. 169 (Provisional Measures).
1984 I.C.J. 392 (Jurisdiction).

[The following summary of the Court's decisions is taken from the Yearbook of the International Court of Justice 1984–85, pp. 135–47:]

On 9 April 1984 the Government of Nicaragua filed an Application instituting proceedings against the United States of America, accompanied by a request for the indication of provisional measures, in respect of a dispute concerning responsibility for military and paramilitary activities in and against Nicaragua. As basis for the jurisdiction of the Court it invoked [the] declaration[s] accepting the Court's jurisdiction deposited by the two States under Article 36 of the Statute of the Court.

On 13 April 1984, by a letter from its Ambassador to the Netherlands, the Government of the United States of America informed the Court that it had appointed an Agent for the purposes of the case while indicating its conviction that the Court was without jurisdiction to deal with the Application and was *a fortiori* without jurisdiction to indicate the provisional measures requested by Nicaragua.

Having heard the oral observations of both Parties on the request for provisional measures at public sittings on 25 and 27 April 1984, the Court held on 10 May 1984 a public sitting at which it delivered an Order (I.C.J. Reports 1984, p. 169) indicating such measures. The operative provisions of this Order are as follows:

"THE COURT,

A. Unanimously,

Rejects the request made by the United States of America that the proceedings on the Application filed by the Republic of Nicaragua on 9 April 1984, and on the request filed the same day by the Republic of Nicaragua for the indication of provisional measures, be terminated by the removal of the case from the list;

B. *Indicates,* pending its final decision in the proceedings instituted on 9 April 1984 by the Republic of Nicaragua against the United States of America, the following provisional measures:

1. Unanimously,

The United States of America should immediately cease and refrain from any action restricting, blocking or endangering access to or from Nicaraguan ports, and, in particular, the laying of mines;

2. By fourteen votes to one,

The right to sovereignty and to political independence possessed by the Republic of Nicaragua, like any other State of the region or of the world, should be fully respected and should not in any way be jeopardized by any military and paramilitary activities which are prohibited by the principles of international law, in particular the principle that States should refrain in their international relations from the threat or use of force against the territorial integrity or the political independence of any State, and the principle concerning the duty not to intervene in matters within the domestic jurisdiction of a State, principles embodied in the United Nations Charter and the Charter of the Organization of American States

IN FAVOUR; *President* Elias; *Vice-President* Sette–Camara; *Judges* Lachs, Morozov, Nagendra Singh, Ruda, Mosler, Oda, Ago, El–Khani, Sir Robert Jennings, de Lacharrière, Mbaye, Bedjaoui.

AGAINST: *Judge* Schwebel.

3. Unanimously,

The Governments of the United States of America and the Republic of Nicaragua should each of them ensure that no action of any kind is taken which might aggravate or extend the dispute submitted to the Court;

4. Unanimously,

The Governments of the United States of America and the Republic of Nicaragua should each of them ensure that no action is taken which might prejudice the rights of the other Party in respect of the carrying out of whatever decision the Court may render in the case; * * * "

* * *

On 15 August 1984, before the expiration of the time-limits allowed for the filing of pleadings relating to jurisdiction and admissibility, the Republic of El Salvador filed a Declaration of Intervention in the case under the terms of Article 63 of the Statute. In its Declaration, the Government of El Salvador stated that the purpose of its intervention was to enable it to maintain that the Court had no jurisdiction to entertain Nicaragua's application. In this connection, it referred to certain multilateral treaties on which Nicaragua relies in its dispute with the United States.

Having regard to the written observations on that Declaration submitted by the Parties in accordance with Article 83 of the Rules of Court, on 4 October 1984 the Court made an Order of which the operative provisions are as follows:

"THE COURT,

(i) By nine votes to six,

Decides not to hold a hearing on the Declaration of Intervention of the Republic of El Salvador.

IN FAVOUR: *President* Elias; *Vice-President* Sette–Camara; *Judges* Lachs, Morozov, Nagendra Singh, Oda, El–Khani, Mbaye, Bedjaoui.

AGAINST: *Judges* Ruda, Mosler, Ago, Schwebel, Sir Robert Jennings, de Lacharrière.

(ii) By fourteen votes to one,

Decides that the Declaration of Intervention of the Republic of El Salvador is inadmissible inasmuch as it relates to the current phase of the proceedings brought by Nicaragua against the United States of America.

IN FAVOUR: *President* Elias; *Vice-President* Sette–Camara; *Judges* Lachs, Morozov, Nagendra Singh, Ruda, Mosler, Oda, Ago, El–Khani, Sir Robert Jennings, de Lacharrière, Mbaye, Bedjaoui.

AGAINST: *Judge* Schwebel."

From 8 to 18 October 1984, the Court held nine public sittings during which speeches were made on behalf of Nicaragua and the United States on the questions of jurisdiction and admissibility. The Judge *ad hoc* appointed by Nicaragua under Article 31 of the Statute of the Court, Mr. C.-A. Colliard, participated in the work of the Court from this stage of the proceedings. (See p. 44.)

At a public sitting held on 26 November 1984, the Court delivered its Judgment (I.C.J. Reports 1984, p. 392). An analysis of the Judgment is given below.

Proceedings and Submissions of the Parties (paras. 1–11)

After recapitulating the various stages in the proceedings and setting out the submissions of the Parties (paras. 1–10), the Court recalls that the case concerns a dispute between the Government of the Republic of Nicaragua and the Government of the United States of America arising out of military and paramilitary activities in Nicaragua and in the waters off its coasts, responsibility for which is attributed by Nicaragua to the United States. In the present phase, the case concerns the Court's jurisdiction to entertain and pronounce upon this dispute, as well as the admissibility of Nicaragua's Application referring it to the Court (para. 11).

1. *The Question of the Jurisdiction of the Court to Entertain the Dispute (paras. 12–83)*

A. *The Declaration of Nicaragua and Article 36, Paragraph 5, of the Statute of the Court (paras. 12–51)*

To found the jurisdiction of the Court, Nicaragua relied on Article 36 of the Statute of the Court and the declarations accepting the compulsory jurisdiction of the Court made by the United States and itself.

The Relevant Texts and the Historical Background to Nicaragua's Declaration (paras. 12–16)

On 6 April 1984 the Government of the United States deposited with the Secretary–General of the United Nations a notification signed by the Secretary of State, Mr. George Shultz (hereinafter referred to as "the 1984 notification"), referring to the declaration of 1946, and stating that:

> "the aforesaid declaration shall not apply to disputes with any Central American State or arising out of or related to events in Central America, any of which disputes shall be settled in such manner as the parties to them may agree.
>
> "Notwithstanding the terms of the aforesaid declaration, this proviso shall take effect immediately and shall remain in force for two years, so

as to foster the continuing regional dispute settlement process which seeks a negotiated solution to the interrelated political, economic and security problems of Central America."

In order to be able to rely upon the United States declaration of 1946 to found jurisdiction in the present case, Nicaragua has to show that it is a "State accepting the same obligation" as the United States within the meaning of Article 36, paragraph 2, of the Statute.

For this purpose, it relies on a declaration made by it on 24 September 1929 pursuant to Article 36, paragraph 2, of the Statute of the Permanent Court of International Justice, the predecessor of the present Court, which provided that:

> "The Members of the League of Nations and the States mentioned in the Annex to the Covenant may, either when signing or ratifying the Protocol to which the present Statute is adjoined, or at a later moment, declare that they recognize as compulsory *ipso facto* and without special agreement, in relation to any other Member or State accepting the same obligation, the jurisdiction of the Court * * * "

in any of the same categories of dispute as listed in Article 36, paragraph 2, of the Statute of the present Court.

Nicaragua relies further on Article 36, paragraph 5, of the Statute of the present Court, which provides that:

> "Declarations made under Article 36 of the Statute of the Permanent Court of International Justice and which are still in force shall be deemed, as between the parties to the present Statute, to be acceptances of the compulsory jurisdiction of the International Court of Justice for the period which they still have to run and in accordance with their terms."

The Judgment recalls the circumstances in which Nicaragua made its declaration: on 14 September 1929, as a Member of the League of Nations, it signed the Protocol of Signature of the Statute of the Permanent Court of International Justice [1]: this Protocol provided that it was subject to ratification and that instruments of ratification were to be sent to the Secretary–General of the League of Nations. On 24 September 1929 Nicaragua deposited with the Secretary–General of the League a declaration under Article 36, paragraph 2, of the Statute of the Permanent Court which reads:

[Translation from the French]

> "On behalf of the Republic of Nicaragua I recognize as compulsory unconditionally the jurisdiction of the Permanent Court of International Justice.
>
> Geneva, 24 September 1929.
>
> *(Signed)* T.F. MEDINA."

The national authorities in Nicaragua authorized its ratification, and, on 29 November 1939, the Ministry of Foreign Affairs of Nicaragua sent a

1. While a State admitted to membership of the United Nations automatically becomes a party to the Statute of the International Court of Justice, a State member of the League of Nations only became a party to that of the Permanent Court of International Justice if it so desired, and, in that case, it was required to accede to the Protocol of Signature of the Statute of the Court.

telegram to the Secretary–General of the League of Nations advising him of the despatch of the instrument of ratification. The files of the League, however, contain no record of an instrument of ratification ever having been received and no evidence has been adduced to show that such an instrument of ratification was ever despatched to Geneva. After the Second World War, Nicaragua became an original Member of the United Nations, having ratified the Charter on 6 September 1945; on 24 October 1945 the Statute of the International Court of Justice, which is an integral part of the Charter, came into force.

The Arguments of the Parties (paras. 17–23) and the Reasoning of the Court (paras. 24–42)

This being the case, the United States contends that Nicaragua never became a party to the Statute of the Permanent Court and that its 1929 declaration was therefore not "still in force" within the meaning of the English text of Article 36, paragraph 5, of the Statute of the present Court.

In the light of the arguments of the United States and the opposing arguments of Nicaragua, the Court sought to determine whether Article 36, paragraph 5, could have applied to Nicaragua's declaration of 1929.

The Court notes that the Nicaraguan declaration was valid at the time when the question of the applicability of the new Statute, that of the International Court of Justice, arose, since under the system of the Permanent Court of International Justice a declaration was valid only on condition that it had been made by a State which had signed the Protocol of Signature of the Statute. It had not become binding under that Statute, since Nicaragua had not deposited its instrument of ratification of the Protocol of Signature and it was therefore not a party to the Statute. However, it is not disputed that the 1929 declaration could have acquired binding force. All that Nicaragua need have done was to deposit its instrument of ratification, and it could have done that at any time until the day on which the new Court came into existence. It follows that the declaration had a certain potential effect which could be maintained for many years. Having been made "unconditionally" and being valid for an unlimited period, it had retained its potential effect at the moment when Nicaragua became a party to the Statute of the new Court.

In order to reach a conclusion on the question whether the effect of a declaration which did not have binding force at the time of the Permanent Court could be transposed to the International Court of Justice through the operation of Article 36, paragraph 5, of the Statute of that body, the Court took several considerations into account.

As regards the French phrase *"pour une durée qui n'est pas encore expirée"* applying to declarations made under the former system, the Court does not consider it to imply that *"la durée non expirée"* (the unexpired period) is that of a commitment of a binding character. The deliberate choice of the expression seems to denote an intention to widen the scope of Article 36, paragraph 5, so as to cover declarations which have not acquired binding force. The English phrase "still in force" does not expressly exclude a valid declaration of unexpired duration, made by a State not party to the Protocol of Signature of the Statute of the Permanent Court, and therefore not of binding character.

With regard to the considerations governing the transfer of the powers of the former Court to the new one, the Court takes the view that the primary concern of those who drafted its Statute was to maintain the greatest possible continuity between it and the Permanent Court and that their aim was to ensure that the replacement of one Court by another should not result in a step backwards in relation to the progress accomplished towards adopting a system of compulsory jurisdiction. The logic of a general system of devolution from the old Court to the new resulted in the ratification of the new Statute having exactly the same effects as those of the ratification of the Protocol of Signature of the old Statute, i.e., in the case of Nicaragua, a transformation of a potential commitment into an effective one. Nicaragua may therefore be deemed to have given its consent to the transfer of its declaration to the International Court of Justice when it signed and ratified the Charter, thus accepting the Statute and its Article 36, paragraph 5.

Concerning the publications of the Court referred to by the Parties for opposite reasons, the Court notes that they have regularly placed Nicaragua on the list of those States that have recognized the compulsory jurisdiction of the Court by virtue of Article 36, paragraph 5, of the Statute. The attestations furnished by these publications have been entirely official and public, extremely numerous and have extended over a period of nearly 40 years. The Court draws from this testimony the conclusion that the conduct of States parties to the Statute has confirmed the interpretation of Article 36, paragraph 5, of the Statute, whereby the provisions of this Article cover the case of Nicaragua.

The Conduct of the Parties (paras. 43–51)

Nicaragua also contends that the validity of Nicaragua's recognition of the compulsory jurisdiction of the Court finds an independent basis in the conduct of the Parties. It argues that its conduct over 38 years unequivocally constitutes consent to be bound by the compulsory jurisdiction of the Court and that the conduct of the United States over the same period unequivocally constitutes its recognition of the validity of the declaration of Nicaragua of 1929 as an acceptance of the compulsory jurisdiction of the Court. The United States, however, objects that the contention of Nicaragua is inconsistent with the Statute and, in particular that compulsory jurisdiction must be based on the clearest manifestation of the State's intent to accept it. After considering Nicaragua's particular circumstances and noting that Nicaragua's situation has been wholly unique, the Court considers that, having regard to the source and generality of statements to the effect that Nicaragua was bound by its 1929 declaration, it is right to conclude that the constant acquiescence of that State in those affirmations constitutes a valid mode of manifestation of its intent to recognize the compulsory jurisdiction of the Court under Article 36, paragraph 2, of the Statute. It further considers that the estoppel on which the United States has relied and which would have barred Nicaragua from instituting proceedings against it in the Court, cannot be said to apply to it.

Finding: the Court therefore finds that the Nicaraguan declaration of 1929 is valid and that Nicaragua accordingly was, for the purposes of Article 36, paragraph 2, of the Statute of the Court, a "State accepting the same obligation" as the United States at the date of filing of the Application and could therefore rely on the United States declaration of 1946.

B. The Declaration of the United States (paras. 52–76)
The Notification of 1984 (paras. 52–66)

The acceptance of the jurisdiction of the Court by the United States on which Nicaragua relies is the result of the United States declaration of 14 August 1946. However, the United States argues that effect should be given to the letter sent to the Secretary–General of the United Nations on 6 April 1984 [see p. 882 above]. It is clear that if this notification were valid as against Nicaragua at the date of filing of the Application, the Court would not have jurisdiction under Article 36 of the Statute. After outlining the arguments of the Parties in this connection, the Court points out that the most important question relating to the effect of the 1984 notification is whether the United States was free to disregard the six months' notice clause which, freely and by its own choice, it has appended to its declaration, in spite of the obligation it has entered into vis-à-vis other States which have made such a declaration. The Court notes that the United States has argued that the Nicaraguan declaration, being of undefined duration, is liable to immediate termination, and that Nicaragua has not accepted "the same obligation" as itself and may not rely on the time-limit proviso against it. The Court does not consider that this argument entitles the United States validly to derogate from the time-limit proviso included in its 1946 declaration. In the Court's opinion, the notion of reciprocity is concerned with the scope and substance of the commitments entered into, including reservations, and not with the formal conditions of their creation, duration or extinction. Reciprocity cannot be invoked in order to excuse departure from the terms of a State's own declaration. The United States cannot rely on reciprocity since the Nicaraguan declaration contains no express restriction at all. On the contrary, Nicaragua can invoke the six months' notice against it, not on the basis of reciprocity, but because it is an undertaking which is an integral part of the instrument that contains it. The 1984 notification cannot therefore override the obligation of the United States to submit to the jurisdiction of the Court vis-à-vis Nicaragua.

The United States Multilateral Treaty Reservation (paras. 67–76)

The question remains to be resolved whether the United States declaration of 1946 constitutes the necessary consent of the United States to the jurisdiction of the Court in the present case, taking into account the reservations which were attached to the declaration. Specifically, the United States had invoked proviso (c) to that declaration, which provides that the United States acceptance of the Court's compulsory jurisdiction shall not extend to

> "disputes arising under a multilateral treaty, unless (1) all parties to the treaty affected by the decision are also parties to the case before the Court, or (2) the United States of America specially agrees to jurisdiction".

This reservation will be referred to as the "multilateral treaty reservation."

The United States argues that Nicaragua relies in its Application on four multilateral treaties, and that the Court, in view of the above reservation, may exercise jurisdiction only if all treaty parties affected by a prospective decision of the Court are also parties to the case.

The Court notes that the States which, according to the United States, might be affected by the future decision of the Court, have made declarations of acceptance of the compulsory jurisdiction of the Court, and are free, any time, to come before the Court with an application instituting proceedings, or to resort to the incidental procedure of intervention. These States are therefore not defenceless against any consequences that may arise out of adjudication by the Court and they do not need the protection of the multilateral treaty reservation (in so far as they are not already protected by Article 59 of the Statute). The Court considers that obviously the question of what States may be affected is not a jurisdictional problem and that it has no choice but to declare that the objection based on the multilateral treaty reservation does not possess, in the circumstances of the case, an exclusively preliminary character.

Finding: the Court finds that, despite the United States notification of 1984, Nicaragua's Application is not excluded from the scope of the acceptance by the United States of the compulsory jurisdiction of the Court. The two declarations afford a basis for its jurisdiction.

C. The Treaty of Friendship, Commerce and Navigation of 21 January 1956 as a Basis of Jurisdiction (paras. 77–83)

In its Memorial, Nicaragua also relies, as a "subsidiary basis" for the Court's jurisdiction in this case, on the Treaty of Friendship, Commerce and Navigation which it concluded at Managua with the United States on 21 January 1956 and which entered into force on 24 May 1958. Article XXIV, paragraph 2, reads as follows:

> "Any dispute between the Parties as to the interpretation or application of the present Treaty, not satisfactorily adjusted by diplomacy, shall be submitted to the International Court of Justice, unless the Parties agree to settlement by some other pacific means."

Nicaragua submits that this treaty has been and is being violated by the military and paramilitary activities of the United States as described in the Application. The United States contends that, since the Application presents no claims of any violation of the treaty, there are no claims properly before the Court for adjudication, and that, since no attempt to adjust the dispute by diplomacy has been made, the compromissory clause cannot operate. The Court finds it necessary to satisfy itself as to jurisdiction under the treaty inasmuch as it has found that the objection based upon the multilateral treaty reservation in the United States declaration does not debar it from entertaining the Application. In the view of the Court, the fact that a State has not expressly referred, in negotiations with another State, to a particular treaty as having been violated by the conduct of that other State, does not debar that State from invoking a compromissory clause in that treaty. Accordingly, the Court finds that it has jurisdiction under the 1956 Treaty to entertain the claims made by Nicaragua in its Application.

II. The Question of the Admissibility of Nicaragua's Application (paras. 84–108)

The Court now turns to the question of the admissibility of Nicaragua's Application. The United States contended that it is inadmissible on five separate grounds, each of which, it is said, is sufficient to establish such inadmissibility, whether considered as a legal bar to adjudication or as "a matter requiring the exercise of prudential discretion in the interest of the integrity of the judicial function".

The *first ground of inadmissibility* (paras. 85–88) put forward by the United States is that Nicaragua has failed to bring before the Court parties whose presence and participation is necessary for the rights of those parties to be protected and for the adjudication of the issues raised in the Application. In this connection, the Court recalls that it delivers judgments with binding force as between the Parties in accordance with Article 59 of the Statute, and that States which consider they may be affected by the decision are free to institute separate proceedings or to employ the procedure of intervention. There is no trace, either in the Statute or in the practice of international tribunals, of an "indispensable parties" rule which would only be conceivable in parallel to a power, which the Court does not possess, to direct that a third State be made a party to proceedings. None of the States referred to can be regarded as being in a position such that its presence would be truly indispensable to the pursuance of the proceedings.

The *second ground of inadmissibility* (paras. 89–90) relied on by the United States is that Nicaragua is, in effect, requesting that the Court in this case determines the existence of a threat to peace, a matter falling essentially within the competence of the Security Council because it is connected with Nicaragua's complaint involving the use of force. The Court examines this ground of inadmissibility at the same time as the *third ground* (paras. 91–98) based on the position of the Court within the United Nations system, including the impact of proceedings before the Court on the exercise of the inherent right of individual or collective self-defence under Article 51 of the Charter. The Court is of the opinion that the fact that a matter is before the Security Council should not prevent it from being dealt with by the Court and that both proceedings could be pursued *pari passu*. The Council has functions of a political nature assigned to it, whereas the Court exercises purely judicial functions. Both organs can therefore perform their separate but complementary functions with respect to the same events. In the present case, the complaint of Nicaragua is not about an ongoing war [or] armed conflict between it and the United States, but about a situation demanding the peaceful settlement of disputes, a matter which is covered by Chapter VI of the Charter. Hence, it is properly brought before the principal judicial organ of the United Nations for peaceful settlement. This is not a case which can only be dealt with by the Security Council in accordance with the provisions of Chapter VII of the Charter.

With reference to Article 51 of the Charter, the Court notes that the fact that the inherent right of self-defence is referred to in the Charter as a "right" is indicative of a legal dimension, and finds that if, in the present proceedings, it became necessary for the Court to judge in this respect between the Parties, it cannot be debarred from doing so by the existence of a procedure requiring that the matter be reported to the Security Council.

A *fourth ground of inadmissibility* (paras. 99–101) put forward by the United States is the inability of the judicial function to deal with situations involving ongoing armed conflict, since the resort to force during an ongoing armed conflict lacks the attributes necessary for the application of the judicial process, namely a pattern of legally relevant facts discernible by the means available to the adjudicating tribunal. The Court observes that any judgment on the merits is limited to upholding such submissions of the Parties as has been supported by sufficient proof of relevant facts and that ultimately it is the litigant who bears the burden of proof.

The *fifth ground of inadmissibility* (paras. 102–108) put forward by the United States is based on the non-exhaustion of the established processes for the resolution of the conflicts occurring in Central America. It contends that the Nicaraguan Application is incompatible with the Contadora process to which Nicaragua is a party.

The Court recalls its earlier decisions that there is nothing to compel it to decline to take cognizance of one aspect of a dispute merely because that dispute has other aspects *(United States Diplomatic and Consular Staff in Tehran* case, *I.C.J., Reports 1980,* p. 19, para. 36), and the fact that negotiations are being actively pursued during the proceedings is not, legally, any obstacle to the exercise by the Court of its judicial function *(Aegean Sea Continental Shelf* case, I.C.J. *Reports 1978,* p. 12, para. 29). The Court is unable to accept either that there is any requirement of prior exhaustion of regional negotiating processes as a precondition to seising the Court or that the existence of the Contadora process constitutes in this case an obstacle to the examination by the Court of Nicaragua's Application.

The Court is therefore unable to declare the Application inadmissible on any of the grounds the United States has advanced.

Findings (paras. 109–111)

* * *

Status of the Provisional Measures (para. 112)

The Court states that its Order of 10 May 1984 and the provisional measures indicated therein remain operative until the delivery of the final judgment in the case.

Operative Clause (para. 113)

"For these reasons,

THE COURT,

(1)(a) *finds,* by eleven votes to five, that it has jurisdiction to entertain the Application filed by the Republic of Nicaragua on 9 April 1984, on the basis of Article 36, paragraphs 2 and 5, of the Statute of the Court;

IN FAVOUR: *President* Elias; *Vice-President* Sette–Camara; *Judges* Lachs, Morozov, Nagendra Singh, Ruda, El–Khani, de Lacharrière, Mbaye, Bedjaoui; *Judge* ad hoc Colliard;

AGAINST: *Judges* Mosler, Oda, Ago, Schwebel and Sir Robert Jennings;

(b) *finds,* by fourteen votes to two, that it has jurisdiction to entertain the Application filed by the Republic of Nicaragua on 9 April 1984, in so far as that Application relates to a dispute concerning the interpretation or application of the Treaty of Friendship, Commerce and Navigation between the United States of America and the Republic of Nicaragua signed at Managua on 21 January 1956, on the basis of Article XXIV of that Treaty;

IN FAVOUR: *President* Elias; *Vice-President* Sette–Camara; *Judges* Lachs, Morozov, Nagendra Singh, Mosler, Oda, Ago, El–Khani, Sir Robert Jennings, de Lacharrière, Mbaye, Bedjaoui; *Judge* ad hoc Colliard;

AGAINST: *Judges* Ruda and Schwebel;

(c) *finds,* by fifteen votes to one, that it has jurisdiction to entertain the case;

IN FAVOUR: *President* Elias; *Vice-President* Sette–Camara; *Judges* Lachs, Morozov, Nagendra Singh, Ruda, Mosler, Oda, Ago, El–Khani, Sir Robert Jennings, de Lacharrière, Mbaye, Bedjaoui; *Judge* ad hoc Colliard;

AGAINST: *Judge* Schwebel;

(2) *finds,* unanimously, that the said Application is admissible."

Notes

1. Five judges dissented from that part of the Court's judgment relating to Nicaragua's 1929 declaration accepting compulsory jurisdiction. The dissenting judges considered that the declaration was not an "acceptance" within the meaning of Article 36(5) of the Court's statute inasmuch as it was not "in force" because it was never ratified. 1984 I.C.J. 461, 471, 514, 533, 558. Was the Court's use of the French text of Article 36(5) helpful to resolve the question of interpretation as to what is meant by "in force"? Was Nicaragua's "subsequent conduct" indicating its belief that it was bound by the 1929 declaration a valid reason to consider it bound? Was the U.S. objection a technical one that should not have overridden Nicaragua's assertion that it was bound?

2. Was the Court justified in denying the right of the United States to modify its acceptance on the ground that the six-month notice clause applied? Should that clause have been given effect even though Nicaragua had no similar clause in its acceptance and could have terminated it at any time? What does reciprocity mean in this connection? See opinions of dissenting Judges Ago and Jennings, 1984 I.C.J. 514, 533. See notes pp. 863–864 on reciprocity.

3. Two judges dissented from the finding of the Court that it had jurisdiction on the basis of a dispute settlement clause in the Treaty of Friendship, Commerce and Navigation of 1956. One of the dissenting judges, Judge Ruda of Argentina, considered that negotiation had not taken place and that such negotiation was a pre-condition of submission to the Court. Id. at 454. Judge Schwebel in a dissenting opinion declared that the bilateral treaty "is a purely commercial agreement whose terms do not relate to the use or misuse of force in international relations." He observed that the treaty expressly precluded its application to "traffic in arms" and to measures "necessary to protect the essential security interests" of a party. Schwebel, Dissenting Opinion, paras. 117–29. Other judges, however, noted that Nicaragua had alleged violations of specific provisions of the bilateral treaty (for example, that mining of ports and territorial waters and attacks on airports endangered traffic and trade in violation of the treaty), and that it would be up to Nicaragua to prove such treaty violations in the proceedings

on the merits. In their view, the allegations were sufficient to support a finding of jurisdiction. See, e.g., Ago, Separate Opinion, para. 2.

Compare the treatment of issues under a similar bilateral treaty in the *Oil Platforms* case, 1996 I.C.J. 803 (Iran v. U.S.), where allegations of unlawful use of force were likewise asserted under a treaty concerned with commerce and navigation. As noted above (p. 859), the Court did not accept the applicant's most sweeping jurisdictional contentions (e.g., that a treaty of "amity" should be read to reach claims involving military hostilities) but did confirm jurisdiction limited to the treaty provisions on navigation.

4. Was the Court justified in rejecting the U.S. argument, based on its reservation excluding disputes under a multilateral treaty unless all parties to the treaty affected by the decision were also parties to the case? The pleadings showed that El Salvador, Costa Rica and Honduras were involved in the charges and counter-charges. It was not clear that Nicaragua's complaint rested on multilateral treaties alone; Nicaragua had also argued violations of customary law on use of force. If so, would the U.S. reservation apply? Was the Court warranted in holding that this issue, as well as the question of whether Nicaragua's neighbors would be affected by the decision, could not be answered until the Court dealt with the merits? Judge Schwebel contended that the Court was nullifying the jurisdictional bar inserted by the United States in its acceptance. Schwebel, Dissenting Opinion, para. 71–72. See L. Damrosch, Multilateral Disputes, in The International Court of Justice at a Crossroads 376 (Damrosch ed., 1987).

5. Note the distinction in the Court's decision between jurisdiction and admissibility. A similar distinction was drawn in the *Tehran Hostages Case* (p. 868). Although the United States contended in the *Nicaragua Case* that the case was "inadmissible" on five separate grounds, the Court unanimously decided that the application was admissible. Is admissibility the same as "justiciability," that is, whether the dispute is a legal dispute capable of judicial determination? If the claim presents a legal question, is the Court entitled to abstain from acting on it because political issues are also involved, or because military hostilities are under way, or because the matter has been or is before the U.N. Security Council? Should a claim of self-defense be treated as justiciable? For a lively debate on these questions among international lawyers and public officials, see Proceedings of the American Society of International Law for 1985 and 1986.

6. About one year after the decision on jurisdiction and admissibility in the *Nicaragua Case,* the United States terminated its acceptance of compulsory jurisdiction, for reasons linked to the decision of the Court in *Nicaragua.* 24 I.L.M. 1742–45. See also statement of the Legal Adviser of the State Department to the Senate Foreign Relations Committee, extracts from which follow.

STATEMENT OF LEGAL ADVISER OF STATE DEPARTMENT, ABRAHAM D. SOFAER, TO SENATE FOREIGN RELATIONS COMMITTEE

December 4, 1985.
86 Dept. State Bull. 67, 70–71 (No. 2106, Jan.1986).

THE NICARAGUA CASE

* * *

Even more disturbing, for the first time in its history, the Court has sought to assert jurisdiction over a controversy concerning claims related to an ongoing use of armed force. This action concerns every state. It is inconsistent with the structure of the UN system. The only prior case involving use-of-force issues—the *Corfu Channel* case—went to the Court after the disputed actions had ceased and the Security Council had determined that the matter was suitable for judicial consideration. In the Nicaragua case, the Court rejected without a soundly reasoned explanation our arguments that claims of the sort made by Nicaragua were intended by the UN Charter exclusively for resolution by political mechanisms—in particular, the Security Council and the Contadora process—and that claims to the exercise of the inherent right of individual and collective self-defense were excluded by Article 51 of the Charter from review by the Court.

I cannot predict whether the Court's approach to these fundamental Charter issues in the jurisdictional phase of the Nicaragua case will be followed in the Court's judgment on the merits. Nevertheless, the record gives us little reason for confidence. It shows a Court majority apparently prepared to act in ways profoundly inconsistent with the structure of the Charter and the Court's place in that structure. The Charter gives to the Security Council—not the Court—the responsibility for evaluating and resolving claims concerning the use of armed force and claims of self-defense under article 51. With regard to the situation in Central America, the Security Council exercised its responsibility by endorsing the Contadora process as the appropriate mechanism for resolving the interlocking political, security, economic, and other concerns of the region.

Implications for U.S. National Security

The fact that the ICJ indicated it would hear and decide claims about the ongoing use of force made acceptance of the Court's compulsory jurisdiction an issue of strategic significance. Despite our deep reluctance to do so and the many domestic constraints that apply, we must be able to use force in our self-defense and in the defense of our friends and allies. We are a law-abiding nation, and when we submit ourselves to adjudication of a subject, we regard ourselves as obliged to abide by the result. For the United States to recognize that the ICJ has authority to define and adjudicate with respect to our right of self-defense, therefore, is effectively to surrender to that body the power to pass on our efforts to guarantee the safety and security of this nation and of its allies.

* * *

We recognize that this nation has a special obligation to support the ICJ and all other institutions that advance the rule of law in a world full of terror and disorder. Our belief in this obligation is what led us to set an example by accepting the Court's compulsory jurisdiction in 1946 and by continuing that acceptance long after it became clear that the world would not follow suit and that our acceptance failed to advance our interests in any tangible manner.

Yet, the President also is responsible to the American people and to Congress to avoid potential threats to our national security. The ICJ's decisions in the Nicaragua case created real and important additional considerations that made the continued acceptance of compulsory jurisdiction unacceptable, despite its symbolic significance. We hope that, in the long run, this action, coupled with our submission of disputes under article 36(1), will strengthen the Court in the performance of its proper role in the international system established by the UN Charter and the Court's own Statute.

Notes

1. Consider the contention in the above statement that the competence of the Security Council under Article 51 excludes adjudication by the Court of the legality of self-defense where the court has jurisdiction by virtue of a treaty provision or an acceptance under Article 36(2) rather than an agreed submission. The Council is authorized to take measures necessary to maintain peace and security. When it takes such measures, is a decision by the Council on the legality of the use of force implied? Is the Council an appropriate body to make legal determinations? Would a decision by the International Court on legality impose an obstacle (legal or political) to Council action? Suppose the Council is seized of the dispute but takes no action or does no more than request the parties to settle their dispute by peaceful means (as the Council did in the Nicaraguan case); should that decision deprive a state from seeking a judgment on the legality of the use of force by another state when that other state accepted jurisdiction in accordance with Article 36 of the statute of the Court? What if the respondent state is protected by the veto (its own or an ally's) from an adverse decision by the Council?

2. If the right of self-defense is non-justiciable (as implied by the Legal Adviser's comment on the right of the United States to decide the issue for itself), does that mean in effect that there is no legal restraint on use of force? Is it consistent with the notion of a legal right to exclude determination by a competent judicial body? If states have accepted compulsory jurisdiction of the Court by treaty or a declaration under Article 36(2) without excluding issues of self-defense or cases involving use of force, should the Court abstain from adjudicating the issue of self-defense? See Schachter, 80 A.S.I.L.Proc. 210 (1986).

3. Is there good reason to consider that the Court cannot generally decide factual issues concerning the use of force? See Judgment (Merits) in Nicaragua v. United States, 1986 I.C.J. 14 at 97–98 (Chapter 12). Even if the Court has a limited capacity to find the truth in cases of past or ongoing hostilities, does it follow that it should hold the case to be inadmissible? Would it be appropriate for the Court to consider the merits as argued by the parties and take account of difficulties in fact-finding as it decides what form of relief (if any) might be appropriate?

4. Consider the observation of the Legal Adviser (above) that "no state" can rely on the International Court to decide questions of illegal intervention "properly and fairly." Does that assume that the judges (or most of them) are incapable of deciding such issues "fairly and properly" because of political bias? Or does it suggest that the judicial process is unable to produce answers to the issues because the issues are not answerable by "judicial standards"?

On the objectivity of the Court, and related issues, see Schachter, International Law in Theory and Practice 43–46 (1991); Brown Weiss, Judicial Independence and Impartiality: A Preliminary Inquiry, in The International Court of Justice at a Crossroads 123–154 (Damrosch ed., 1987). On the question whether the Court may and should deal with cases involving use of force, see Schachter, Disputes Involving the Use of Force, in The International Court of Justice at a Crossroads 223–41; Gill, Litigation Strategy at the International Court (1989); Bilder, Judicial Procedures Relating to the Use of Force, 31 Va.J.Int'l L. 249 (1991).

NON–APPEARANCE

The United States appeared in the case brought against it by Nicaragua in order to contest jurisdiction and admissibility, but withdrew after the Court found it had jurisdiction. This was the first case of non-appearance after a finding of jurisdiction by the Court. In five prior cases, however, the respondent had declined to appear at all. These were: Iceland in 1972 *(Fisheries Cases)*, India in 1973 *(Case Concerning Prisoners of War)*, France in 1974 *(Nuclear Tests Cases)*, Turkey in 1976 (*Aegean Sea Continental Shelf Case*), and Iran in 1979 (*Tehran Hostages Case*). All five cases involved objections to jurisdiction at preliminary stages in connection with requests for provisional measures. The non-appearing states brought their objections to the notice of the Court by letters and other communications (like those of Iran in the hostages case, p. 868 above) that did not constitute official memorials or other documents called for by the Court's rules.

The Statute of the Court does not provide for entry of judgment by default. In the event that a party fails to appear or does not defend, Article 53 of the Statute requires the Court to satisfy itself that it has jurisdiction and, if so, that the claim of the applicant is well founded in fact and law. The Court has taken the position that it must examine the matter on its own and take "special care" to act with circumspection. Schachter argues that in effect this means that the non-appearing accused state acquires an advantage: it does not have to face questions by the Court, yet the Court takes special care to make sure its views are considered. The applicant state is handicapped since it cannot properly consider and answer arguments of the non-participating state. May the Court take any action against a state that boycotts the proceedings? See Schachter, International Law in Theory and Practice 230–231 (1991); Charney, Disputes Implicating the Institutional Credibility of the Court: Problems of Non–Appearance, Non–Participation, and Non–Performance, in The International Court of Justice at a Crossroads 288–319 (Damrosch ed., 1987); Thirlway, Non–Appearance Before the International Court of Justice (1985); Elkind, Non–Appearance Before the International Court of Justice: Functional and Comparative Analysis (1984); Fitzmaurice, The Problem of the Non–Appearing Defendant Government, 51 Brit. Y.B.I.L. 94–96 (1980).

The Institut de Droit International after some years of study and debate reached the following conclusions in a resolution adopted in 1991:

Article 1

> Each State entitled under the Statute to appear before the Court and with respect to which the Court is seized of a case is *ipso facto,* by virtue of the Statute, a party to the proceedings, regardless of whether it appears or not.

Article 2

> In considering whether to appear or to continue to appear in any phase of proceedings before the Court, a State should have regard to its duty to co-operate in the fulfillment of the Court's judicial functions.

Article 3

In the event that a State fails to appear in a case instituted against it, the Court should, if circumstances so warrant:

(a) invite argument from the appearing party on specific issues which the Court considers have not been canvassed or have been inadequately canvassed in the written or oral pleadings;

(b) take whatever other steps it may consider necessary, within the scope of its powers under the Statute and the Rules of Court, to maintain equality between the parties.

Article 4

Notwithstanding the non-appearance of a State before the Court in proceedings to which it is a party, that State is, by virtue of the Statute, bound by any decision of the Court in that case, whether on jurisdiction, admissibility, or the merits.

Article 5

A State's non-appearance before the Court is in itself no obstacle to the exercise by the Court of its functions under Article 41 of the Statute.

INTERVENTION AND OTHER "THIRD PARTY" ISSUES

A state may intervene in a case between other states in two kinds of situations. Under Article 62 of the Statute, a state which considers that "it has an interest of a legal nature in the case" may be permitted to intervene by the Court. The other situation applies when the state requesting intervention is a party to the convention which is before the Court. In that case the state has the right to intervene and if it uses that right, the treaty interpretation given by the Court will be binding on it. Article 63 of the Statute. The case-law on intervention is summarized in the Restatement (Third) § 903, Reporters' Note 7:

> In the Permanent Court of International Justice, there was only one case of intervention, by the Government of Poland in the Wimbledon Case, which involved the interpretation of the Peace Treaty of Versailles of 1919. P.C.I.J., ser. A, No. 1 at 11–13 (1923). In 1951, the International Court of Justice allowed Cuba to intervene in the Haya de la Torre Case between Colombia and Peru, which involved the interpretation of the 1928 Havana Convention on Asylum, to which Cuba was a party. [1951] I.C.J.Rep. 71, 76–77. In later cases involving permissive interventions under Article 62, the Court took a more restrictive attitude and refused to grant permission to intervene. See Nuclear Tests Cases, Reporters' Note 3, [1974] I.C.J.Rep. 530, 535 (Fiji's application to intervene lapsed when the proceedings were terminated because the main case "no longer has any object"); Case Concerning the Continental Shelf (Tunisia/Libyan Arab Jamahiriya) (Application of Malta for Permission to Intervene), [1981] I.C.J.Rep. 3, 19 (Malta's interests were no greater than those of other Mediterranean states, and her application was so restricted by various reservations that the decision in the case could not affect any of her legal interests); Case Concerning the Continental Shelf (Libyan Arab

Jamahiriya/Malta) (Application of Italy for Permission to Intervene), [1984] I.C.J.Rep. 3, 18–28 (to permit Italy to intervene would introduce a fresh dispute; Article 62 was not intended as an alternative means of bringing an additional dispute as a case before the Court); Case Concerning Military and Paramilitary Activities in and Against Nicaragua (Nicaragua v. United States) (Declaration of Intervention of the Republic of El Salvador), [1984] I.C.J.Rep. 215, 216 (although El Salvador's declaration invoked Article 63, this declaration addressed the substance of the dispute and was inadmissible at the stage of proceedings relating only to the Court's jurisdiction). Later, in a decision concluding that it had jurisdiction of the case, the Court noted that if Costa Rica, El Salvador, and Honduras should find that "they might be affected by the future decision of the Court" in the case, they would be free to institute proceedings against Nicaragua or resort to the incidental procedures for intervention under Articles 62 and 63 of the Statute. [1984] I.C.J.Rep. 392, 425. No further action was taken by Costa Rica or Honduras, but proceedings against them were instituted by Nicaragua in 1986. 25 Int'l Leg. Mat. 1290, 1293 (1986) (applications by Nicaragua); [1986] I.C.J.Rep. 548, 551 (procedural orders); [1987] *id.* 182 (order recording the discontinuance by Nicaragua of the proceedings against Costa Rica).

See also Sztucki, Intervention under Article 63 of the I.C.J. Statute in the Phase of Preliminary Proceedings: The Salvadoran Incident, 79 A.J.I.L. 1005 (1985); Damrosch, Multilateral Disputes, in The International Court of Justice at a Crossroads 376–400 (Damrosch ed., 1987); Chinkin, Third Parties in International Law (1993); Ruda, Intervention Before the International Court of Justice, in Fifty Years of the International Court of Justice (Lowe & Fitzmaurice, eds., 1996), at p. 487.

A less restrictive position was taken by a Chamber of the Court in allowing Nicaragua to intervene in a case between El Salvador and Honduras concerning their maritime frontier. The Chamber recognized that Nicaragua had a legal interest in the case by virtue of its co-ownership of the waters of the Gulf of Fonseca which was one area in dispute between the parties. The Chamber made it clear that its permission to Nicaragua to intervene did not make Nicaragua a party to the dispute. Maritime Frontier Case, 1990 I.C.J. 92, 133–34. Accordingly, Nicaragua would not be bound by the decision (or protected by it) under the terms of Article 59 of the Statute. It may be asked whether in view of Nicaragua's co-ownership of the waters in litigation, it should not have been treated as a party bound by the decision and protected by it. For a critical view of the Chamber's decision on this point, see D.W. Greig, Third Party Rights and Intervention Before the International Court, 32 Va.J.Int'l L. 285, 321–30 (1992). The Chamber's approach was followed by the full Court in addressing the application by Equatorial Guinea for permission to intervene in Land and Maritime Boundary (Cameroon v. Nigeria), with respect to the maritime boundary in the Gulf of Guinea. See Order of Oct. 21, 1999, reprinted at 39 I.L.M. 112 (2000).

The issue of third party participation came up before the International Court in a different way when it was argued that the two states parties to a treaty at issue were "necessary parties" and therefore their failure to intervene should preclude the Court from adjudicating the case. The case concerned the claim of Nauru that the three states that were trustees for Nauru under a U.N. trusteeship agreement breached their obligations by marketing Nauru's phosphate resources and failing to restore the property after the phosphate was removed. The Court ruled that the failure of the two trustees (New Zealand and the United Kingdom) to intervene did not bar Nauru from proceeding with its claim against Australia, the third trustee. Case Concerning Certain Phosphate Lands in Nauru, Preliminary Objection, 1992 I.C.J. 240. See generally Weeramantry, Nauru: Environmental Damage Under International Trusteeship (1992). Compare the Court's treatment of the "necessary party" issue in the Case Concerning East Timor, 1995 I.C.J. 90, discussed at p. 272 in Chapter 4, where the Court held that the absence of Indonesia barred Portugal's suit to invalidate a treaty between Australia and Indonesia concerning the offshore resources of the Timor Gap.

PROVISIONAL MEASURES OF PROTECTION

The Court has the "power to indicate, if it considers the circumstances so require, any provisional measures which ought to be taken to preserve the respective rights of the parties." Art. 41 of the Statute. This right is analogous to the common law interlocutory injunction under which parties may be enjoined from acting in a way to prejudice the outcome during the proceedings. The two criteria most often invoked for such provisional relief are urgency and irreparable injury. These criteria were satisfied in the *Tehran Hostages* and *Nicaragua* cases excerpted above. Compare the following materials:

AEGEAN SEA CONTINENTAL SHELF CASE (GREECE v. TURKEY)

International Court of Justice, 1976.
(Request for the Indication of Interim Measures of Protection)
1976 I.C.J. 3.

[In 1974, the Turkish Government began to explore for petroleum in submarine areas of the Aegean Sea claimed by Greece as part of the continental shelf appertaining to certain Greek islands. Following Greek protests and unsuccessful negotiations, Greece referred the matter simultaneously to the International Court and to the Security Council. In its application to the Court, Greece specified as a basis of jurisdiction the General Act of 1928 and a joint communiqué issued in 1975. Greece also requested that the Court indicate interim measures of protection under Article 41 of the Statute pending judgment on the merits. In particular, it requested that both countries be enjoined from conducting further exploration or research in the contested areas. The Court declined to indicate the interim measures of protection requested by Greece. The following excerpts are from its order of September 11, 1976:]

* * *

30. Whereas, according to the information before the Court, the seismic exploration undertaken by Turkey, of which Greece complains, is carried out by a vessel traversing the surface of the high seas and causing small explosions to occur at intervals under water; whereas the purpose of these

explosions is to send sound waves through the seabed so as to obtain information regarding the geophysical structure of the earth beneath it; whereas no complaint has been made that this form of seismic exploration involves any risk of physical damage to the seabed or subsoil or to their natural resources; whereas the continued seismic exploration activities undertaken by Turkey are all of the transitory character just described, and do not involve the establishment of installations on or above the seabed of the continental shelf; and whereas no suggestion has been made that Turkey has embarked upon any operations involving the actual appropriation or other use of the natural resources of the areas of the continental shelf which are in dispute;

31. Whereas seismic exploration of the natural resources of the continental shelf without the consent of the coastal State might, no doubt, raise a question of infringement of the latter's exclusive right of exploration; whereas, accordingly, in the event that the Court should uphold Greece's claims on the merits, Turkey's activity in seismic exploration might then be considered as such an infringement and invoked as a possible cause of prejudice to the exclusive rights of Greece in areas then found to appertain to Greece;

* * *

33. Whereas, in the present instance, the alleged breach by Turkey of the exclusivity of the right claimed by Greece to acquire information concerning the natural resources of areas of continental shelf, if it were established, is one that might be capable of reparation by appropriate means; and whereas it follows that the Court is unable to find in that alleged breach of Greece's rights such a risk of irreparable prejudice to rights in issue before the Court as might require the exercise of its power under Article 41 of the Statute to indicate interim measures for their preservation;

* * *

36. Whereas, independently of its request regarding the preservation of its rights, Greece requested the Court during the public sitting to indicate interim measures of protection in order to prevent the aggravation or extension of the dispute; whereas, before this request could be entertained, the Court would have to determine whether, under Article 41 of the Statute, the Court has such an independent power to indicate interim measures having that object; whereas, however, for the reasons now to be explained, the Court does not find it necessary to examine this point;

* * *

41. Whereas both Greece and Turkey, as Members of the United Nations, have expressly recognized the responsibility of the Security Council for the maintenance of international peace and security; whereas, in the abovementioned resolution, the Security Council has recalled to them their obligations under the United Nations Charter with respect to the peaceful settlement of disputes, in the terms set out in paragraph 39 above; whereas, furthermore, as the Court has already stated, these obligations are clearly imperative in regard to their present dispute concerning the continental shelf in the Aegean; and whereas it is not to be presumed that either State will fail to heed its obligations under the Charter of the United Nations or fail to heed

the recommendations of the Security Council addressed to them with respect to their present dispute;

* * *

42. Whereas, accordingly, it is not necessary for the Court to decide the question whether Article 41 of the Statute confers upon it the power to indicate interim measures of protection for the sole purpose of preventing the aggravation or extension of a dispute * * * .

Notes

1. What is the test of irreparable prejudice implicit in the Court's decision? Is it that any injury could be compensated by monetary payment to Greece? Would the acquisition of seismic information enable one party to have advantages in negotiating delimitation or joint venture agreements which would prejudice the other side? In view of this possibility, should Turkey have had the burden of showing that there would be no irreparable injury?

2. The Court did not find it necessary to pronounce on its jurisdiction as to the merits, even on a prima facie basis. However, several judges, in separate opinions, considered that the Court should have first decided the basic question of its own jurisdiction. For example, Judge Mosler stated that Article 41 was not "an independent source of jurisdiction on the same footing and quality as article 36. * * * In view of the provisional character of the requested order, it is sufficient that the Court when it actually indicates interim measures should have reached the provisional conviction based on a summary examination of the material before it * * * that it had jurisdiction on the merits of the case." Id. at 25. Judges Lachs, Morozov, Ruda, and Tarazi also regarded a finding of jurisdiction as essential; Tarazi and Morozov suggested a full finding on jurisdiction. In support of the majority, see Jiménez de Aréchaga 159 Rec. des Cours at 160–63; Elias, The International Court of Justice and the Indication of Provisional Measures of Protection (Amado Memorial Lecture 1978, published by United Nations). For a flexible approach to Article 41, see Mendelson, Measures of Protection in Cases of Contested Jurisdiction, 46 Brit. Y.B.I.L. 259 (1972–73).

3. To what extent must the Court be satisfied as to its jurisdiction before imposing provisional measures? As Judge Jiménez de Aréchaga said: "In cases where there is no reasonable probability, prima facie ascertained by the Court, of jurisdiction on the merits it would be devoid of sense to indicate provisional measures to ensure the execution of a judgment the Court will never render." Aegean Sea Case, 1976 I.C.J. 15. In the Fisheries Jurisdiction Case, the Court declared:

> On a request for provisional measures, the Court need not, before indicating them, finally satisfy itself that it has jurisdiction on the merits of the case, yet it ought not to act under Article 41 of the Statute of the Court if the absence of jurisdiction on the merits is manifest.

1972 I.C.J. 15–16. The Court has imposed provisional measures in several cases, including the Nicaragua Case, before determining definitively the issue of jurisdiction. Judge Schwebel, in a separate opinion in the Nicaragua Case (Provisional Measures Order), urged that the Court give parties time to argue issues of jurisdiction in depth and to take the necessary time itself to deliberate issues of jurisdiction in depth. 1984 I.C.J. 169 at 207 (Sep. Op. Schwebel).

The Court's provisional measures jurisprudence requires applicant to show a prima facie basis for jurisdiction. Where jurisdiction cannot be established even prima facie, provisional measures will be denied, no matter how urgent the matter or how serious the allegation of likely irreparable harm to applicant. Thus in the Kosovo cases of 1999, provisional measures were denied since applicant was not able to show a prima facie case for jurisdiction. Case Concerning Legality of Use of Force (Yugoslavia v. Belgium) and related cases, 1999 I.C.J. ___ (Order of June 2, 1999), 38 I.L.M. 950 (1999).

4. The possibility that the Court might find prima facie jurisdiction sufficient to sustain a provisional measures order, and then later determine that objections to jurisdiction were persuasive, has happened on occasion, including in the Anglo–Iranian Oil Company Case, 1951 I.C.J. 89 (Interim Protection Order) (interim measures granted), 1952 I.C.J. 93, 102–103 (Jurisdiction) (case dismissed for lack of jurisdiction).

A similar scenario unfolded in 1999–2000 under the dispute settlement provisions of the U.N. Convention on the Law of the Sea in the Southern Bluefin Tuna Cases (Australia and New Zealand v. Japan). There, the International Tribunal on the Law of the Sea, by a vote of 20–2, ordered Japan to observe on a provisional basis the last total allowable catch that had been agreed within the framework of the Convention on the Conservation of Southern Bluefin Tuna, pending arbitration of the dispute. ITLOS, Southern Bluefin Tuna Cases, Provisional Measures Order of Aug. 27, 1999, reprinted at 38 I.L.M. 1624 (1999). A year later, an arbitral tribunal agreed with Japan that the dispute was outside the compulsory jurisdiction provisions of the UNCLOS regime and could not be arbitrated without Japan's consent. The arbitral tribunal thereupon dissolved the provisional measures. See 39 I.L.M. 1359 (2000). For more on this interesting case, see Section 5 infra.

5. Interim measures of protection under Article 41 have been "indicated" by the International Court of Justice in various cases, including: the Anglo–Iranian Oil Case, 1951 I.C.J. 89; the Fisheries Jurisdiction Case, 1972 I.C.J. 12; Nuclear Tests Cases, 1973 I.C.J. 99, 135; United States Diplomatic and Consular Staff in Tehran, 1979 I.C.J. 23; Military and Paramilitary Activities In and Against Nicaragua, 1984 I.C.J. 4; Frontier Dispute (Burkina Faso/Mali), 1986 I.C.J. 3 (both sides requested the measures, after armed hostilities broke out in the disputed area); Application of the Genocide Convention (Bosnia–Herzegovina v. Federal Republic of Yugoslavia), 1993 I.C.J. 3, 325; and two separate cases concerning the Vienna Convention on Consular Relations, 1998 I.C.J. 248 (Paraguay v. U.S.) (Breard), and 1999 I.C.J. 9 (Germany v. U.S.) (La Grand).

They were refused in Interhandel, 1957 I.C.J. 105; Trial of Pakistani Prisoners of War, 1973 I.C.J. 328; Aegean Sea Continental Shelf, 1976 I.C.J. 3, p. 897 supra; the *Lockerbie* cases, 1992 I.C.J. 3, 15 (Libya v. U.K. and U.S.), pp. 419–420 supra and note 6 below), and Yugoslavia's applications against NATO member states growing out of the Kosovo situation, 1999 I.C.J., 38 I.L.M. 950 (1999), p. 855 supra.

See generally Merrills, Interim Measures of Protection in the Recent Jurisprudence of the International Court of Justice, 44 I.C.L.Q. 90 (1995).

6. In 1992, Libya requested that the Court impose provisional measures enjoining the United Kingdom and the United States from taking measures against Libya pursuant to a Security Council decision intended to induce Libya to surrender Libyans accused of terrorist activities to the two respondent countries. In particular, the individuals were accused of planting a bomb on Pan Am Flight

No. 103 that caused the plane to crash over Lockerbie, Scotland. Libya based its jurisdictional claim on the compromissory clause in the 1971 Montreal Convention on Suppression of Unlawful Acts Against Safety of Civil Aviation. Libya contended that the Convention recognized its right to prosecute the individuals accused of crimes covered by the Convention and its right not to surrender them to another country. The Court denied the Libyan request by eleven votes to five. The majority considered that the Security Council Resolution 745 (1992) requiring Libya to surrender the accused individuals imposed a legal duty on Libya and any indication of provisional measures would run "a serious risk of conflicting with the work of the Security Council." The Court noted that while it was not called on to determine definitively the legal effect of the Security Council resolution, the rights claimed by Libya were not "now" appropriate for protection by provisional measures. 1992 I.C.J. 3, 15.

7. Are provisional measures binding on the party or parties to whom they are addressed? The verbs of Article 41–"indicate" and "ought"–could suggest merely recommendatory authority. The language used by the Court in its provisional measures orders has often seemed hortatory ("should") rather than compulsory in character. Scholars have been divided as to whether the Court has power to order binding measures. Some have argued that such power can be inferred from the Charter and Statute taken as a whole, and that an obligation to give effect to an interim order is incumbent upon every party to the Statute, even if that party contests the jurisdiction of the Court over a particular claim. Other writers, and some governments, have maintained that the obligation of compliance attaches only to a final judgment on the merits and not to preliminary rulings made before the Court has decided challenges to its own jurisdiction. On these issues, see Oxman, Jurisdiction and the Power to Indicate Provisional Measures, in The International Court of Justice at a Crossroads 323 (Damrosch ed., 1987); Rosenne, The Law and Practice of the International Court of Justice 1920–1996 (1997) p. 1451.

In the Case Concerning the Vienna Convention on Consular Relations (Paraguay v. U.S.), 1998 I.C.J. 248, also known as the *Breard* case (pp. 216–219 above), the Court received the application approximately 10 days before a death sentence was to be carried out on a Paraguayan national convicted of capital murder by a Virginia court. On April 8, 1998, just a few days before the scheduled execution date, the Court entered a provisional measures order, the operative paragraph of which read:

> The United States should take all measures at its disposal to ensure that Angel Francisco Breard is not executed pending the final decision in these proceedings, and should inform the Court of all the measures which it has taken in implementation of this Order.

In an amicus curiae submission to the U.S. Supreme Court addressing (*inter alia*) the legal effect of this order in connection with Breard's petition for a stay of execution, the Solicitor–General of the United States said:

> As to the purportedly binding effect of the ICJ's order, there is substantial disagreement among jurists as to whether an ICJ order indicating provisional measures is binding. * * * The better reasoned position is that such an order is not binding. * * * The use of precatory language ("indicate," "ought to be taken," "suggested") instead of stronger language * * * strongly supports a conclusion that ICJ provisional measures are not binding.
>
> * * *

> Moreover, the ICJ itself has never concluded that provisional measures are binding on the parties to a dispute. That court has indicated provisional measures in seven other cases of which we are aware; in most of those cases, the order indicating provisional measures was not regarded as binding by the respondent. * * * The ICJ did not, in any of the final decisions in those cases, suggest that the failure of the respondent to comply with the indication of provisional measures had violated the court's earlier order.

The Supreme Court denied the stay of execution. On this episode in relation to I.C.J. provisional measures, see documentation and commentary in Agora: *Breard*, 92 A.J.I.L. 666–712 (1998), especially the comments by Henkin ("Provisional Measures, U.S. Treaty Obligations, and the States") and Vázquez ("*Breard* and the Federal Power to Require Compliance with ICJ Orders of Provisional Measures").

Similar issues came to the Court again in Germany's suit under the Vienna Convention on Consular Relations, known as the *LaGrand* case. An order in terms similar to the *Breard* order was entered on Germany's application, without hearing U.S. views. 1999 I.C.J. 9. Judge Schwebel questioned this ex parte procedure in his separate opinion. See 1999 I.C.J. at 21. The execution in Arizona took place the next day, without regard to Germany's position or the I.C.J. proceedings. For the point of view that there would have been time to hear both sides even under those urgent circumstances, see Rosenne, Controlling Interlocutory Aspects of Proceedings in the International Court of Justice, 94 A.J.I.L. 307, 310 n. 18 (2000). The legal effect of the provisional measures order was one issue raised by Germany in its pleadings and hearings on the merits held in late 2000. (Judgment was pending as of the time this casebook went to press.)

8. For a discussion of interim measures of protection in other international tribunals, see p. 917 in Section 5 below.

COUNTER–CLAIMS

As the Court observed in the *Tehran Hostages* case, at p. 872 (para. 24) above, Article 80 of the Rules of the Court provides for the filing of counter-claims. Until the 1990s, the International Court had little experience with counter-claims; but recently respondent states have availed themselves of this procedure, and the Court has thus had to consider issues arising under Article 80's requirement that a counter-claim be "directly connected with the subject-matter of the claim of the other party and that it comes within the jurisdiction of the Court."

Counter-claims have been held admissible in the following recent cases: Application of the Convention for the Prevention and Punishment of the Crime of Genocide (Bosnia–Herzegovina v. Yugoslavia), 1997 I.C.J. 243; Oil Platforms (Iran v. U.S.), 1998 I.C.J. 190; and Land and Maritime Boundary between Cameroon and Nigeria (Cameroon v. Nigeria), 1999 I.C.J. (Order of June 30, 1999). It is evident that applicant states will have to weigh the possibility of serious counter-claims entailing potentially heavy liabilities as part of the risk of initiating litigation.

B. ADVISORY OPINIONS

The Court may give an advisory opinion on "any legal question" requested by a body authorized by or in accordance with the U.N. Charter. See

Article 65 of the Statute of the Court. The Charter in Article 96 states that the General Assembly or the Security Council may request advisory opinions. In addition other organs of the United Nations may be so authorized by the General Assembly. Four organs of the United Nations and 16 specialized agencies have been authorized to request advisory opinions. A state may not request an advisory opinion. It may, however, request an authorized international organization to make such request.

As of 2000, the Court has rendered 25 advisory opinions and found itself without jurisdiction in one instance where a request was made (see p. 911). Fourteen opinions were in response to requests by the U.N. General Assembly, one (the *Namibia Case*) was requested by the Security Council and 2 by the Economic and Social Council. Three of the specialized agencies (UNESCO, WHO and IMCO) have also requested advisory opinions. Five advisory opinions were given at the request of the U.N. Committee on Applications for Review of Administrative Tribunal Judgments. This U.N. Committee was established in 1955 specifically for the purpose of requesting advisory opinions of the Court to review decisions of the U.N. Administrative Tribunal (UNAT). U.N.G.A.Res. 957(X) (1955). The I.C.J.'s supervisory jurisdiction over UNAT was recently abolished, by amendment to the UNAT Statute. See G.A. Res. 50/54 (1995); Reisman, The Supervisory Jurisdiction of the International Court of Justice, 258 Rec. des Cours at 392–393 (1996).

Although an advisory opinion has no binding effect in itself, some international agreements provide that disputes relating to the interpretation and application of the agreement shall be submitted to the Court for an opinion that will be accepted as binding by the parties to the dispute. One example is the following provision in the General Convention on Privileges and Immunities of the United Nations.

CONVENTION ON THE PRIVILEGES AND IMMUNITIES OF THE UNITED NATIONS

Adopted by the General Assembly, February 13, 1946.
1 U.N.T.S. 15.

Sec. 30. All differences arising out of the interpretation or application of the present convention shall be referred to the International Court of Justice, unless in any case it is agreed by the parties to have recourse to another mode of settlement. If a difference arises between the United Nations on the one hand and a Member on the other hand, a request shall be made for an advisory opinion on any legal question involved in accordance with Article 96 of the Charter and Article 65 of the Statute of the Court. The opinion given by the Court shall be accepted as decisive by the parties.

Notes

1. The Soviet Union and other Communist countries that were members of the United Nations filed reservations to the Convention on the Privileges and Immunities of the United Nations, denying the authority of the International Court to enter decisions without the consent of all parties to the dispute. The same states made similar reservations to the Convention on the Privileges and Immunities of the Specialized Agencies, adopted by the General Assembly on

November 21, 1947, 33 U.N.T.S. 261. See, e.g., Accession of Czechoslovakia, Dec. 29, 1966, 586 U.N.T.S. 246.

May the advisory jurisdiction of the Court be used in cases of disputes where one or more of the parties to the dispute does not consent to the Court's advisory jurisdiction? See the opinion of the Court in the *Western Sahara Case* below.

2. In Applicability of Article VI, Section 22, of the Convention on the Privileges and Immunities of the United Nations, 1989 I.C.J. 177, the United Nations Economic and Social Council (ECOSOC) requested an advisory opinion on behalf of the Sub–Commission on Prevention of Discrimination and Protection of Minorities. Article VI, Section 22 of the Convention on the Privileges and Immunities of the United Nations confers immunity on experts performing missions for the United Nations. In 1985, the Sub–Commission had appointed Mr. Mazilu, a Romanian national, as a special rapporteur and requested that he compile a report concerning human rights and youth. Mazilu had been expected to present his report in Geneva at the 1987 session of the Sub–Commission, but he failed to attend. After the U.N. made several unsuccessful attempts to contact Mazilu by mail, it became known that his Government had refused him permission to travel and that communications between him and the U.N. were being obstructed. In August 1988, Romania notified the U.N. that Mazilu was unable to finish his report because of his ill health. The Sub–Commission then requested the U.N. Secretary–General to attempt to establish contacts with the Romanian government over the matter. Romania responded that any attempt by the U.N. to intervene would be regarded as interference in the internal affairs of Romania and that the affair was an internal affair between a citizen and his government. It further maintained that Section 22 of the Convention did not apply to a special rapporteur and that, in any event, it did not apply to an expert in his country of residence or nationality, but only in countries to which he had been sent on a mission for the acts connected with that mission.

At this point ECOSOC requested the advisory opinion from the Court on the applicability of Section 22. Romania argued that the Court lacked jurisdiction to give an advisory opinion because of Romania's reservation to Section 30 of the Convention. The reservation was substantially identical to that of the Soviet Union referred to in note _ above. Romania argued that its consent was required for the Court to have jurisdiction to render an advisory opinion on the matter. The Court held unanimously that it had jurisdiction under Article 96 of the U.N. Charter and that Romania's reservation to Section 30 did not apply to advisory opinions. The Court reasoned that advisory opinions are not binding on states and, therefore, the consent of states are not required for jurisdiction. The Court noted, however, that in certain circumstances where consent was not required for jurisdiction, the Court might consider lack of consent as a compelling reason not to entertain the request for an advisory opinion. The Court nevertheless ruled that this exception was not available to Romania on the facts of the case. Having cleared the jurisdictional hurdle, the Court went on to hold that Section 22 applied to a special rapporteur in Mazilu's position and that persons eligible for immunity under the Convention could claim it in the states of which they were nationals or in which they were ordinarily resident, except where the state concerned had made specific reservations precluding its applicability and Romania had not made such a reservation. The Court also held that a special rapporteur retains immunity status until the tasks assigned have been completed.

3. Similar issues came to the Court, again on a request by ECOSOC, in Difference Relating to Immunity from Legal Process of a Special Rapporteur of

the Commission on Human Rights, 1999 I.C.J. 62 (Advisory Opinion of April 29, 1999). Mr. Dato' Param Cumaraswamy, a Malaysian lawyer, had been serving as a special rapporteur of the U.N. Commission on Human Rights, on the subject of Independence of Judges and Lawyers. In an interview with a magazine published in the United Kingdom and circulated in Malaysia, he was quoted with respect to his investigation of complaints that the Malaysian courts had been manipulated by business interests. He was then sued for defamation by Malaysian plaintiffs who had received favorable rulings in the cases in question. Although the U.N. Secretary–General certified that Cumaraswamy enjoyed immunity from process in national courts with respect to his functions as special rapporteur and that the interview in question had been given in that capacity, the Malaysian courts declined to honor the assertion of immunity.

The procedural posture of ECOSOC's request in the Cumaraswamy matter was different from the Mazilu case discussed in the preceding note, in that Malaysia as a party to the Convention on Privileges and Immunities had made no reservation to Section 30 comparable to that of Romania. The Court upheld its jurisdiction to give an advisory opinion and, by an overwhelming margin, sustained the immunity of the special rapporteur from any form of legal process arising out of his U.N. function. For more on the substance of the issues, see p. 1298 in Chapter 14.

WESTERN SAHARA CASE

International Court of Justice, Advisory Opinion, 1975.
1975 I.C.J. 12.

[For the facts of case, see Chapter 4, p. 320 supra]

The Court:

25. Spain has made a number of observations relating to the lack of its consent to the proceedings, which, it considers, should lead the Court to decline to give an opinion. These observations may be summarized as follows:

(a) In the present case the advisory jurisdiction is being used to circumvent the principle that jurisdiction to settle a dispute requires the consent of the parties.

(b) The questions, as formulated, raise issues concerning the attribution of territorial sovereignty over Western Sahara.

(c) The Court does not possess the necessary information concerning the relevant facts to enable it to pronounce judicially on the questions submitted to it.

* * *

28. In support of these propositions Spain has invoked the fundamental rule, repeatedly reaffirmed in the Court's jurisprudence, that a State cannot, without its consent, be compelled to submit its disputes with other States to the Court's adjudication. It has relied, in particular, on the application of this rule to the advisory jurisdiction by the Permanent Court of International Justice in the *Status of Eastern Carelia* case (P.C.I.J., Series B, No. 5), maintaining that the essential principle enunciated in that case is not modified by the decisions of the present Court in the cases concerning the Interpretation of Peace Treaties with Bulgaria, Hungary and Romania, First

Phase (I.C.J. Reports 1950, p. 65) and the Legal Consequences for States of the Continued Presence of South Africa in Namibia (South West Africa) notwithstanding Security Council Resolution 276 (1970) (I.C.J. Reports 1971, p. 16). Morocco and Mauritania, on the other hand, have maintained that the present case falls within the principles applied in those two decisions and that the *ratio decidendi* of the *Status of Eastern Carelia* case is not applicable to it.

* * *

31. In the proceedings concerning the Interpretation of Peace Treaties with Bulgaria, Hungary and Romania, First Phase, this Court had to consider how far the views expressed by the Permanent Court in the *Status of Eastern Carelia* case were still pertinent in relation to the applicable provisions of the Charter of the United Nations and the Statute of the Court. It stated, *inter alia*:

> "This objection reveals a confusion between the principles governing contentious procedure and those which are applicable to Advisory Opinions.
>
> "The consent of States, parties to a dispute, is the basis of the Court's jurisdiction in contentious cases. The situation is different in regard to advisory proceedings even where the Request for an Opinion relates to a legal question actually pending between States. The Court's reply is only of an advisory character: as such, it has no binding force. It follows that no State, whether a Member of the United Nations or not, can prevent the giving of an Advisory Opinion which the United Nations considers to be desirable in order to obtain enlightenment as to the course of action it should take. The Court's Opinion is given not to the States, but to the organ which is entitled to request it; the reply of the Court, itself an 'organ of the United Nations', represents its participation in the activities of the organization, and, in principle, should not be refused." (I.C.J. Reports 1950, p. 71.)

32. The Court, it is true, affirmed in this pronouncement that its competence to give an opinion did not depend on the consent of the interested States, even when the case concerned a legal question actually pending between them. However, the Court proceeded not merely to stress its judicial character and the permissive nature of Article 65, paragraph 1, of the Statute but to examine, specifically in relation to the opposition of some of the interested States, the question of the judicial propriety of giving the opinion. Moreover, the Court emphasized the circumstances differentiating the case then under consideration from the *Status of Eastern Carelia* case and explained the particular grounds which led it to conclude that there was no reason requiring the Court to refuse to reply to the request. Thus the Court recognized that lack of consent might constitute a ground for declining to give the opinion requested if, in the circumstances of a given case, considerations of judicial propriety should oblige the Court to refuse an opinion. In short, the consent of an interested State continues to be relevant, not for the Court's competence, but for the appreciation of the propriety of giving an opinion.

33. In certain circumstances, therefore, the lack of consent of an interested State may render the giving of an advisory opinion incompatible with the Court's judicial character. An instance of this would be when the circum-

stances disclose that to give a reply would have the effect of circumventing the principle that a State is not obliged to allow its disputes to be submitted to judicial settlement without its consent. If such a situation should arise, the powers of the Court under the discretion given to it by Article 65, paragraph 1, of the Statute, would afford sufficient legal means to ensure respect for the fundamental principle of consent to jurisdiction.

* * *

39. The above considerations are pertinent for a determination of the object of the present request. The object of the General Assembly has not been to bring before the Court, by way of a request for advisory opinion, a dispute or legal controversy, in order that it may later, on the basis of the Court's opinion, exercise its powers and functions for the peaceful settlement of that dispute or controversy. The object of the request is an entirely different one: to obtain from the Court an opinion which the General Assembly deems of assistance to it for the proper exercise of its functions concerning the decolonization of the territory.

* * *

42. Furthermore, the origin and scope of the dispute, as above described, are important in appreciating, from the point of view of the exercise of the Court's discretion, the real significance in this case of the lack of Spain's consent. The issue between Morocco and Spain regarding Western Sahara is not one as to the legal status of the territory today, but one as to the rights of Morocco over it at the time of colonization. The settlement of this issue will not affect the rights of Spain today as the administering Power, but will assist the General Assembly in deciding on the policy to be followed in order to accelerate the decolonization process in the territory. It follows that the legal position of the State which has refused its consent to the present proceedings is not "in any way compromised by the answers that the Court may give to the questions put to it" (Interpretation of Peace Treaties with Bulgaria, Hungary and Romania, First Phase, I.C.J. Reports 1950, p. 72).

* * *

47. The situation in the present case is entirely different from that with which the Permanent Court was confronted in the *Status of Eastern Carelia* case. Mauritania, Morocco and Spain have furnished very extensive documentary evidence of the facts which they considered relevant to the Court's examination of the questions posed in the request, and each of these countries, as well as Algeria and Zaire, have presented their views on these facts and on the observations of the others. The Secretary–General has also furnished a dossier of documents concerning the discussion of the question of Western Sahara in the competent United Nations organs. The Court therefore considers that the information and evidence before it are sufficient to enable it to arrive at a judicial conclusion concerning the facts which are relevant to its opinion and necessary for replying to the two questions posed in the request.

Notes

1. The *Eastern Carelia Case* to which the Court refers arose out of a dispute between Finland and the U.S.S.R. when the latter was not a member of the

League of Nations and refused to take any part in its proceedings or in the Court. For the Court's refusal to render an advisory opinion, see P.C.I.J., Ser. B, No. 5, p. 7 (1923).

2. The International Court also had occasion to consider its competence to render opinions in the absence of consent by states concerned in the Advisory Opinion on Interpretation of the Peace Treaties, referred to in the Western Sahara Opinion. Although the Court gave an advisory opinion that the three absent, non-consenting states (Bulgaria, Hungary, and Romania) were obliged to comply with the dispute-settlement clauses of the peace treaties, these states did not appoint members of the treaty commissions. In a subsequent opinion, the Court declared that their failure to make such appointments meant that the commissions could not function. 1950 I.C.J. 221.

3. In the instant case, the Court observed that "consent of an interested State continues to be relevant, not for the Court's competence, but for the appreciation of the propriety of giving an opinion." What circumstances would be relevant to "propriety" of giving an opinion requested by the General Assembly or Security Council? Would there have to be evidence of a genuine United Nations need for an opinion as distinct from the resolution of a dispute? Compare the two Nuclear Weapons advisory opinion requests, infra.

4. Where an advisory opinion proceeding entails elements of a dispute involving a particular state, should such a state be able to appoint a judge *ad hoc*? Compare the treatment of this issue in the *Namibia* advisory opinion request, 1971 I.C.J. 12, with *Western Sahara*, 1975 I.C.J. 12 at 16; and see the discussion in Merrills, International Dispute Settlement at 139 (3rd ed. 1998). Should Malaysia have had a judge *ad hoc* for the Cumaraswamy advisory opinion?

5. Would it be desirable for the General Assembly to authorize a special committee to request advisory opinions on legal disputes between states, provided that all states parties to the dispute should have consented to the procedure? It has been suggested that states would be willing to agree to nonbinding advisory jurisdiction in regard to disputes in which they would not accept the contentious jurisdiction of the Court. See Szasz, Enhancing the Advisory Jurisdiction of the World Court, in The Future of the International Court of Justice 499 (Gross ed., 1976).

6. Should use of the Court be encouraged, by having the General Assembly (through a committee) act as a conduit whereby regional and functional multinational bodies could submit requests for advisory opinions? A proposal has also been made that national courts be authorized to submit questions of international law which have come up before them to the I.C.J. for advisory opinions. See Jessup, The Price of International Justice 76–82 (1971).

7. Of the principal organs of the United Nations, the Secretary–General lacks authority to request advisory opinions. Proposals to confer such authority have been regularly made but not acted upon. What would be the advantages and disadvantages of expanding the reach of advisory opinion authority in this way?

8. For a valuable review of advisory opinions, see Pomerance, The Advisory Function of the International Court in the League and U.N. Eras (1973).

LEGALITY OF THE THREAT OR USE OF NUCLEAR WEAPONS

International Court of Justice, Advisory Opinion, 1996.
1996 I.C.J. 226.

[The General Assembly and the World Health Organization (WHO) both asked the I.C.J. for advisory opinions on slightly different questions concerning the legality of the threat or use of nuclear weapons. The Court agreed to give an advisory opinion to the General Assembly but declined to do so for the WHO. Excerpts from the opinion dealing with jurisdiction to reply to the General Assembly's request are reprinted below; for the treatment of the WHO's request, see the notes immediately following. Other aspects of the advisory opinion are considered in Chapters 2 and 12.]

10. The Court must first consider whether it has the jurisdiction to give a reply to the request of the General Assembly for an Advisory Opinion and whether, should the answer be in the affirmative, there is any reason it should decline to exercise any such jurisdiction.

The Court draws its competence in respect of advisory opinions from Article 65, paragraph 1, of its Statute. Under this Article, the Court

> "may give an advisory opinion on any legal question at the request of whatever body may be authorized by or in accordance with the Charter of the United Nations to make such a request".

11. For the Court to be competent to given an advisory opinion, it is thus necessary at the outset for the body requesting the opinion to be "authorized by or in accordance with the Charter of the United Nations to make such a request". The Charter provides in Article 96, paragraph 1, that:

> "The General Assembly or the Security Council may request the International Court of Justice to give an advisory opinion on any legal question." * * *

12. The question put to the Court has a relevance to many aspects of the activities and concerns of the General Assembly including those relating to the threat or use of force in international relations, the disarmament process, and the progressive development of international law. The General Assembly has a long-standing interest in these matters and in their relation to nuclear weapons. This interest has been manifested in the annual First Committee debates, and the Assembly resolutions on nuclear weapons; in the holding of three special sessions on disarmament (1978, 1982 and 1988) by the General Assembly, and the annual meetings of the Disarmament Commission since 1978; and also in the commissioning of studies on the effects of the use of nuclear weapons. In this context, it does not matter that important recent and current activities relating to nuclear disarmament are being pursued in other fora. * * *

13. The Court must furthermore satisfy itself that the advisory opinion requested does indeed relate to a "legal question" within the meaning of its Statute and the United Nations Charter. * * *

The question put to the Court by the General Assembly is indeed a legal one, since the Court is asked to rule on the compatibility of the threat or use of nuclear weapons with the relevant principles and rules of international law. To do this, the Court must identify the existing principles and rules, interpret them and apply them to the threat or use of nuclear weapons, thus offering a reply to the question posed based on law.

The fact that this question also has political aspects, as, in the nature of things, is the case with so many questions which arise in international life, does not suffice to deprive it of its character as a "legal question" and to "deprive the Court of a competence expressly conferred on it by its Statute" * * *. Whatever its political aspects, the Court cannot refuse to admit the legal character of a question which invites it to discharge an essentially judicial task, namely, an assessment of the legality of the possible conduct of States with regard to the obligations imposed upon them by international law [citations omitted]. * * *

The Court moreover considers that the political nature of the motives which may be said to have inspired the request and the political implications that the opinion given might have are of no relevance in the establishment of its jurisdiction to give such an opinion.

* * *

14. Article 65, paragraph 1, of the Statute provides: "The Court *may* give an advisory opinion ..." (Emphasis added.) This is more than an enabling provision. As the Court has repeatedly emphasized, the Statute leaves a discretion as to whether or not it will give an advisory opinion that has been requested of it, once it has established its competence to do so. * * *

The Court has constantly been mindful of its responsibilities as "the principal judicial organ of the United Nations" (Charter, Art. 92). When considering each request, it is mindful that it should not, in principle, refuse to give an advisory opinion. In accordance with the consistent jurisprudence of the Court, only "compelling reasons" could lead it to such a refusal [citations omitted]. There has been no refusal, based on the discretionary power of the Court, to act upon a request for advisory opinion in the history of the present Court; in the case concerning the *Legality of the Use by a State of Nuclear Weapons in Armed Conflict* [Ed.: see note 1 below on WHO request], the refusal to give the World Health Organization the advisory opinion requested by it was justified by the Court's lack of jurisdiction in that case. The Permanent Court of International Justice took the view on only one occasion that it could not reply to a question put to it, having regard to the very particular circumstances of the case, among which were that the question directly concerned an already existing dispute, one of the States parties to which was neither a party to the Statute of the Permanent Court nor a Member of the League of Nations, objected to the proceedings, and refused to take part in any way (*Status of Eastern Carelia, P.C.I.J., Series B, No. 5*).

[The Court next rejected contentions that it should not respond to the request because the question presented was vague and abstract, or because the Assembly had not explained the precise purposes for which it sought the advisory opinion.] * * *

17. It has also been submitted that a reply from the Court in this case might adversely affect disarmament negotiations and would, therefore, be contrary to the interest of the United Nations. The Court is aware that, no

matter what might be its conclusions in any opinion it might give, they would have relevance for the continuing debate on the matter in the General Assembly and would present an additional element in the negotiations on the matter. Beyond that, the effect of the opinion is a matter of appreciation. The Court has heard contrary positions advanced and there are no evident criteria by which it can prefer one assessment to another. That being so, the Court cannot regard this factor as a compelling reason to decline to exercise its jurisdiction.

18. Finally, it has been contended by some States that in answering the question posed, the Court would be going beyond its judicial role and would be taking upon itself a law-making capacity. It is clear that the Court cannot legislate, and, in the circumstances of the present case, it is not called upon to do so. Rather its task is to engage in its normal judicial function of ascertaining the existence or otherwise of legal principles and rules applicable to the threat or use of nuclear weapons. The contention that the giving of an answer to the question posed would require the Court to legislate is based on a supposition that the present *corpus juris* is devoid of relevant rules in this matter. The Court could not accede to this argument; it states the existing law and does not legislate. This is so even if, in stating and applying the law, the Court necessarily has to specify its scope and sometimes note its general trend.

19. In view of what is stated above, the Court concludes that it has the authority to deliver an opinion on the question posed by the General Assembly, and that there exist no "compelling reasons" which would lead the Court to exercise its discretion not to do so.

An entirely different question is whether the Court, under the constraints placed upon it as a judicial organ, will be able to give a complete answer to the question asked of it. However, that is a different matter from a refusal to answer at all.

Notes

1. In Legality of the Use by a State of Nuclear Weapons in Armed Conflict (Request of the World Health Organization), 1996 I.C.J. 66, the Court determined that it lacked jurisdiction to give the requested opinion. It interpreted Article 65 of its Statute and Article 96(2) of the Charter in the following way:

> Consequently, three conditions must be satisfied in order to found the jurisdiction of the Court when a request for an advisory opinion is submitted to it by a specialized agency: the agency requesting the opinion must be duly authorized, under the Charter, to request opinions from the Court; the opinion requested must be on a legal question; and this question must be one arising with the scope of the activities of the requesting agency * * * .

The Court found "no doubt" that the WHO had been duly authorized under Article 96(2) of the Charter to request advisory opinions. It also concluded (in terms similar to those in paragraph 13 of the advisory opinion excerpted above on the General Assembly request) that the matter involved a "legal question," notwithstanding the presence of political implications. As to the third condition, however, the Court concluded that the question posed did not arise "within the scope of [the] activities" of the WHO:

> 19. In order to delineate the field of activity or the area of competence of an international organization, one must refer to the relevant rules of the organization and, in the first place, to its constitution. From a formal standpoint, the constituent instruments of international organizations are multilateral treaties, to which the well-established rules of treaty interpretation apply. * * *

The Court examined the 22 subparagraphs of Article 2 of the WHO Constitution attributing functions to the organization, as well as the provisions of the preamble and Article 1 specifying its objectives in the sphere of public health:

> 21. Interpreted in accordance with their ordinary meaning, in their context and in the light of the object and purpose of the WHO Constitution, as well as of the practice followed by the Organization, the provisions of its Article 2 may be read as authorizing the Organization to deal with the effects on health of the use of nuclear weapons, or of any other hazardous activity, and to take preventive measures aimed at protecting the health of populations in the event of such weapons being used or such activities engaged in.
>
> The question put to the Court in the present case relates, however, *not to the effects* of the use of nuclear weapons on health, but to the *legality* of the use of such weapons *in view of their health and environmental effects.* Whatever those effects might be, the competence of the WHO to deal with them is not dependent on the legality of the acts that caused them. Accordingly, it does not seem to the Court that the provisions of Article 2 of the WHO Constitution, interpreted in accordance with the criteria referred to above, can be understood as conferring upon the Organization a competence to address the legality of the use of nuclear weapons, and thus in turn a competence to ask the Court about that.

The Court further found that to attribute to the WHO a general competence concerning legality of nuclear weapons would be inconsistent with the "principle of speciality" and the Charter system of specialized agencies:

> 26. * * * It follows from the various instruments mentioned above that the WHO Constitution can only be interpreted, as far as the powers conferred upon that Organization are concerned, by taking due account not only of the general principle of speciality, but also of the logic of the overall system contemplated by the Charter. If, according to the rules on which that system is based, the WHO has, by virtue of Article 57 of the Charter, "wide international responsibilities", those responsibilities are necessarily restricted to the sphere of public "health" and cannot encroach on the responsibilities of other parts of the United Nations system. And there is no doubt that questions concerning the use of force, the regulation of armaments and disarmament are within the competence of the United Nations and lie outside that of the specialized agencies. Besides, any other conclusion would render virtually meaningless the notion of a specialized agency; it is difficult to imagine what other meaning that notion could have if such an organization need only show that the use of certain weapons could affect its objectives in order to be empower to concern itself with the legality of such use. It is therefore difficult to maintain that, by authorizing various specialized agencies to request opinions from the Court under Article 96, paragraph 2 of the Charter, the General Assembly intended to allow them to seise the Court of questions belonging within the competence of the United Nations.
>
> For all these reasons, the Court considers that the question raised in the request for an advisory opinion submitted to it by the WHO does not arise

"within the scope of [the] activities" of that Organization as defined by its Constitution.

2. For commentary on aspects of the two opinions relating to the Court's exercise of its advisory jurisdiction, see Abi–Saab, On Discretion: Reflections on the Nature of the Consultative Function of the International Court of Justice, in International Law, the International Court of Justice and Nuclear Weapons 36–50 (Boisson de Chazournes & Sands, eds., 1999); Bothe, The WHO Request, in ibid., pp. 103–111; Leary, The WHO Case: Implications for Specialized Agencies, in ibid., pp. 112–127; see also Perez, The Passive Virtues and the World Court: Pro–Dialogic Abstention by the International Court of Justice, 18 Mich. J.I.L. 399 (1997).

SECTION 5. SPECIALIZED INTERNATIONAL TRIBUNALS

As indicated at the opening of this chapter, the institutions of international dispute settlement have multiplied rapidly in recent years; and with the creation of new tribunals has come an outpouring of new jurisprudence. Substantive aspects of the work of these bodies are taken up in the chapters to which they pertain–Chapter 8 for human rights, Chapters 9 and 10 for claims commissions, Chapter 15 for criminal tribunals, Chapter 16 for the institutions of the law of the sea, and Chapter 20 for the World Trade Organization and other institutions for disputes involving international economic law. We have also foreshadowed, in Chapter 2, some of the jurisprudential questions concerning the sources of law applied by these bodies and the prospects for coherence or inconsistency among their decisions.

The present section introduces the emerging subject of cross-institutional study of international tribunals, with illustrations from decisions of the late 1990s through 2000–the formative years for some of the new bodies.

A. "COMPULSORY" DISPUTE SETTLEMENT IN CERTAIN REGIMES?

As we have seen, the "compulsory" jurisdiction of the I.C.J. is in reality strictly optional, and only a fraction of potential disputes come with the ambit of this mode of international judicial authority.

An alternative possibility, increasingly embraced near the end of the 20th and the beginning of the 21st century, is the idea of regimes of compulsory dispute settlement for the subject-matter areas covered by certain general or regional multilateral treaties. The human rights area has become more fully "judicialized," especially in Europe, where acceptance of the competence of the European Court of Human Rights (for both state-to-state and individual petitions) has been made a condition of the inclusion of more states in ever more closely integrated European institutions. The 1982 U.N. Convention on the Law of the Sea (UNCLOS), which finally came into force in 1994, contains comprehensive dispute settlement provisions, so that in theory every sea dispute among the now more than 130 parties to this major treaty ought to be covered by one or another form of "compulsory" jurisdiction (with arbitration as the default mechanism). The 1994 agreements creating the World Trade Organization (W.T.O.) and its Dispute Settlement Body (D.S.B.) likewise represented significant progress toward comprehensive dispute settlement among now more than 140 states parties, notably by eliminating the possibility for a losing party to block adoption of a dispute settlement panel's report, so that the outcome of the new process should be conclusive.

These developments have presaged a real shift toward more genuinely "compulsory" forms of jurisdiction. Even so, gaps in compulsory authority have not been eliminated and some unexpected loopholes may be opening up. It has always been evident that the dispute settlement provisions of UNCLOS or the 1994 W.T.O. agreement could not bind parties that remained outside the underlying regime–for example, the United States for the law of the sea. But even among parties to some of these regimes, there has been disagreement over the scope of the undertakings to submit disputes to compulsory settlement.

In the area of trade disputes, the ink was hardly dry on the W.T.O. agreement setting up the D.S.B. before scholars began debating whether its output would be "binding" in a legal sense, as opposed to giving states a choice between compliance and noncompliance (followed by countermeasures). Compare Judith Hippler Bello, The WTO Dispute Settlement Understanding: Less is More, 90 A.J.I.L. 416 (1996) (arguing that W.T.O. is a system of voluntary compliance, under which states can elect not to comply with dispute settlement reports and suffer likely retaliation) with John H. Jackson, The W.T.O. Dispute Settlement Understanding–Misunderstandings on the Nature of Legal Obligation, 91 A.J.I.L. 60 (1997) (supporting obligatory character of GATT/W.T.O. rules and dispute settlement procedures). Certain states also intimated reliance on assertedly "self-judging" exceptions to W.T.O. dispute settlement competence, e.g. under the "national security" exemption of GATT Article XXI, thereby arguably jeopardizing the coherence of the third-party dispute settlement system (just as the Connolly Reservation and "vital interests" exceptions had done for I.C.J. compulsory jurisdiction, pp. 860–863). See Hannes L. Schloemann & Stefan Ohlhoff, "Constitutionalization" and Dispute Settlement in the W.T.O.: National Security as an Issue of Competence, 93 A.J.I.L. 424 (1999) (analyzing issue of GATT national security exception as a jurisdictional rather than substantive issue). Perhaps most important, several of the early rulings of the D.S.B. Appellate Body, such as the *Shrimp/Turtles* decision (noted in Chapters 17 and 20 below), were perceived in many quarters as showing the inadequacy of a trade dispute settlement regime for complex issues involving the intersection of trade law with environmental law or other systems.

One of the first cases to be heard under the UNCLOS dispute settlement procedures brought to the fore an unexpected difficulty in realizing what was supposed to have been a comprehensive system of binding dispute settlement. In general, under UNCLOS Part XV, states parties are under an obligation to settle their disputes under the Convention (Art. 279). An elaborate system of "compulsory procedures entailing binding decisions" is established, with a variety of mechanisms available among which states may choose an appropriate procedure (Arts. 286–296 and Annexes VI, VII, and VIII). Arbitration under Annex VII is the default option if a state has not made another election of if two disputants have not agreed on a procedure. The binding nature of dispute settlement is clearly specified in Article 296 (see Section 5.F below). Notwithstanding the apparently comprehensive and obligatory nature of these provisions, a gaping hole was revealed in the *Southern Bluefin Tuna Cases* of 1999–2000.

In the first phase of the *Southern Bluefin Tuna* procedure, Australia and New Zealand brought a complaint against Japan concerning overfishing of bluefin tuna stocks in the Southern Pacific. The International Tribunal for the Law of the Sea (ITLOS) prescribed provisional measures, ordering Japan to observe the last total allowable catch that had been agreed within the framework of a regional fisheries convention (the 1993 Convention on the Conservation of Southern Bluefin Tuna), pending resolution of the dispute under arbitration. In the second phase, however, Japan contested the jurisdiction of the arbitral tribunal to consider the merits of the claim, on the grounds that the dispute in reality arose not under UNCLOS but under the regional convention, and that UNCLOS dispute settlement was excluded because the parties had agreed to another means of settlement, namely consensual rather than compulsory submission. In a 4–1 decision, the arbitral tribunal agreed with Japan that it lacked jurisdiction to resolve the dispute. The tribunal had to interpret UNCLOS Articles 279–282, which deal with the relationship of dispute settlement under the Convention to other modes of settlement on which the parties may agree. The tribunal reasoned that the regional fisheries convention, which was at the core of the substantive dispute between the parties, contained its own dispute settlement provision, which required the consent of Japan to any arbitral submission. The tribunal's conclusion was that Article 16 of the regional convention "exclude[s] any further procedure" within the contemplation of UNCLOS Article 281(1). As the tribunal stated (at para. 62): "It thus appears to the Tribunal that UNCLOS falls significantly short of establishing a truly comprehensive regime of compulsory jurisdiction entailing binding decisions." *Southern Bluefin Tuna Cases*, Arbitral Award of Aug. 4, 2000, 39 I.L.M. 1359 (2000).

Although the full implications of the *Southern Bluefin Tuna* ruling will not be known until it becomes clear whether other arbitral tribunals or the ITLOS will follow its rationale, the decision has already sent ripples of disquiet through the segments of the international legal community that had envisioned the UNCLOS dispute settlement regime as a paradigm of compulsory dispute settlement.

Before leaving this topic, we should emphasize a distinction between compulsory jurisdiction—that is, an obligation *to submit* disputes to a stipulated mode of third-party legal settlement—and the binding quality of the decision that may result. Under a genuinely compulsory regime, there would be both an obligation to submit to jurisdiction and an obligation to carry out any eventual ruling. The two questions are, however, analytically different, and one form of obligation may exist without the other. See Section 5.F.

B. COMPOSITION OF TRIBUNAL

The I.C.J., as we have seen, has a standing bench of 15 geographically diverse members serving fixed renewable nine-year terms, supplemented as appropriate by one or more *ad hoc* judges chosen by parties who do not have a judge of their own nationality already on the bench. This system ensures that each litigant has a "voice" in the deliberations, though the judges are required to be independent (I.C.J. Statute, Art. 2) and therefore are not to take instruction from their state. Party-appointed arbitrators are likewise a typical feature of international arbitration.

The specialized international tribunals have made some notable departures from the I.C.J. model of judicial selection, while sometimes borrowing particular features (such as the principle of a representative bench). No tribunal to date has adopted the I.C.J. system of nominations by national groups "at one remove" from governments: rather, in general it is states parties to the treaty who make the nominations, and nominations are frequently restricted to the nationals of states parties. The electing authority may be a U.N. organ (as with the two existing ad hoc criminal tribunals; see Chapter 15), but more typically elections are reserved to the states parties to the treaty that establishes the tribunal. The constitutive instrument often specifies the subject-matter expertise required of judges: for example, for ITLOS, "recognized competence in the field of the law of the sea."

A split has emerged between tribunals that *do* follow the I.C.J. model of allowing national *ad hoc* judges, and those that take the opposite approach of requiring nonparticipation of judges of the nationality of the parties. The ITLOS, for example, has a provision for designation of *ad hoc* members (UNCLOS Annex VI, Art. 17). The W.T.O., by contrast, constructs its dispute settlement panels so that no member shall have the nationality of any of the disputants (unless the parties to the dispute otherwise agree). W.T.O. Dispute Settlement Understanding, Art. 8(3). If a developing country is in a dispute with a developed country, the developing country is entitled to request that the W.T.O. panel include at least one member from a developing country. Ibid., Art. 8(10).

C. STANDING

An important trend is the opening up of some dispute settlement procedures to parties other than states. This possibility has long been available in arbitral institutions (see p. 838), but the recent tendencies are for standing judicial institutions also to have facilities for disputes between private persons and states (or even between private parties). The human rights institutions illustrate this trend: see Chapter 8. In the law of the sea field, the ITLOS Statute provides that the tribunal "shall be open to State Parties" and also "open to entities other than States Parties in any case expressly provided for in Part XI [on deep seabed mining] or in any case submitted pursuant to any other agreement conferring jurisdiction on the Tribunal which is accepted by all the parties to that case." (UNCLOS Annex VI, Art. 30).

The W.T.O. D.S.B is restricted in its jurisdiction to disputes between states parties. Standing issues have arisen in some of the D.S.B.'s early cases: for example, in the *EC Bananas* dispute, the Appellate Body held that there was no requirement that a member have a "legal interest" in order to be allowed to initiate a complaint. European Communities–Regime for the Importation, Sale and Distribution of Bananas, WT/DS27/AB/R, paras. 132–133 (Sept. 25, 1997). Third states have been allowed to participate. See, e.g., United States–Tax Treatment for "Foreign Sales Corporation," WT/DS108/AB/R (Feb. 24, 2000) (intervention of Canada and Japan in proceeding initiated by European Union against United States).

A few specialized bodies have competence comparable to that of the I.C.J. to render advisory opinions at the request of specified entities. Notable in this regard is the Inter–American Court of Human Rights, which has a vibrant advisory jurisprudence. See Buergenthal, The Advisory Practice of the Inter–American Human Rights Court, 79 A.J.I.L. 1 (1985).

D. PROVISIONAL MEASURES

The authority of a tribunal to specify urgent measures to preserve the rights of the parties pending the litigation is an important procedural component of a mature dispute settlement system. We have already seen some of the difficulties in I.C.J. provisional measures jurisprudence, stemming from its incomplete patchwork of jurisdiction and from ambiguity as to whether parties are required to comply with interim orders. Some of the more recent tribunals benefit from the conferral of broader and clearer competence in this regard. For example, UNCLOS Article 290 and Annex VI Article 25 contain detailed specifications on provisional measures, including on the authority of the ITLOS to prescribe such measures pending the establishment of an arbitral tribunal. The ITLOS has already indicated provisional measures in several of its early cases, including *Southern Bluefin Tuna*, 38 I.L.M. 1624 (1999). In *M/V Saiga* (Saint Vincent and the Grenadines v. Guinea, Dec. 4, 1997), 37 I.L.M. 360 (1998), ITLOS ordered prompt release of an arrested vessel and crew, upon the posting of a reasonable bond. As noted above (p. 915), the measures entered by ITLOS in *Southern Bluefin Tuna* were later dissolved by the relevant arbitral tribunal, after that tribunal determined that the dispute did not fall under the compulsory dispute settlement procedures.

Regional human rights courts likewise have an active provisional measures jurisprudence. See generally Macdonald, Interim Measures in International Law, with Special Reference to the European System for the Protection of Human Rights, 52 Zeitschrift f. a. ö. R. 703–740 (1992).

E. APPELLATE REVIEW

The I.C.J. is a court of both first and last resort; there is no possibility of appeal from its judgments, and it has only a limited competence to act as a supervisory organ with respect to certain administrative or arbitral tribunals. See Reisman, The Supervisory Jurisdiction of the I.C.J., p. 838 above. With the increasing complexity and sophistication of international litigation, bifurcation of judicial functions between tribunals of first instance and organs of appellate review is becoming ever more necessary. Thus European regional institutions now include panels of first instance and appellate chambers. The two International Criminal Tribunals for Yugoslavia and Rwanda are structured with several trial chambers for each body, and a common appeals chamber to ensure coherence of jurisprudence.

The W.T.O. institutional changes have included the creation within the D.S.B. in late 1995 of an Appellate Body, consisting of seven members from different legal systems who serve fixed four-year terms, sitting in divisions of three members on a rotating basis. A set of Working Procedures for Appellate Review, WT/AB/WP/3 (Feb. 28, 1997) governs the mechanisms for appellate review. A general structural issue addressed in early rulings of the Appellate Body is the appropriate standard of review on appeal. In principle, the Appellate Body has considered that under Article 17 of the Dispute Settlement Understanding, its function is to consider issues of law and legal interpretation rather than new facts. See, e.g., Canada–Aircraft, WT/DS70/AB/R (Aug. 20, 1999); United States–Tax Treatment for "Foreign Sales Corporations," WT/DS108/AB/R (Feb. 24, 2000). In the latter proceeding, the Appellate Body also addressed whether new arguments can be raised on appeal (paras. 101–103).

F. COMPLIANCE

Along with the proliferation of international tribunals has come renewed attention to problems of compliance. Some constitutive instruments of international tribunals specify, in terms comparable to those applicable to the I.C.J. (U.N. Charter, Art. 94; I.C.J. Statute, Art. 59) that parties undertake to comply with the tribunal's decisions and that such decisions are binding on the parties (though not on third parties). See, e.g., UNCLOS Article 296, which provides:

> *Article 296. Finality and binding force of decisions*
>
> 1. Any decision rendered by a court or tribunal having jurisdiction under this section shall be final and shall be complied with by all the parties to the dispute.
>
> 2. Any such decision shall have no binding force except between the parties and in respect of that particulate dispute.

On the other hand, some tribunals, such as the U.N. human rights treaty bodies, may formally have only recommendatory competence even when acting in a quasi-adjudicatory capacity. But this formal shortfall may understate the authority of their decisions, which often enjoy a high degree of respect.

The comparative study of the "compliance pull" of international tribunals is becoming ever more interesting, as their growing output creates larger empirical bases for comparison. For an exploration of a theoretical framework for comparing compliance as between European and U.N. institutions, see Laurence Helfer & Anne–Marie Slaughter, Toward a Theory of Effective Supranational Adjudication, 107 Yale L.J. 273 (1997).

When compliance fails, some (but not many) of the tribunals have at least the theoretical possibility of enlisting assistance in enforcement from treaty parties or a coordinate institution. As noted, the U.N. Charter (Article 94(2)) provides for a prevailing party at the I.C.J. to seek an enforcement order from the Security Council, but this procedure has not yet been successfully invoked. Orders of the criminal tribunals could also theoretically be enforced by the Security Council under Chapter VII authority. Within the framework of the W.T.O., the sanction for noncompliance is authorized retaliation by the prevailing party (i.e., suspending an equivalent value of trade concessions).

Notes

1. For an overview of the multiplicity of new adjudicatory institutions, see Symposium Issue, The Proliferation of International Tribunals: Piecing Together the Puzzle, 31 N.Y.U. J. Int'l L. & Pol. 679–933 (1999). Current information about all international tribunals is maintained on the website of the Project on International Courts and Tribunals, www.pict-pcti.org.

2. On the dispute settlement institutions of the law of the sea, see International Tribunal for the Law of the Sea, Basic Texts (1998). See also Oda, Dispute Settlement Prospects in the Law of the Sea, 44 I.C.L.Q. 863 (1995); Rosenne, Establishing the International Tribunal for the Law of the Sea, 89 A.J.I.L. 806 (1995); Rosenne, International Tribunal for the Law of the Sea, 13 Int'l J. Marine & Coastal L. 487 (1998); Treves, Conflicts Between the International Tribunal for the Law of the Sea and the International Court of Justice, 31 N.Y.U. J. Int'l L. & Pol. 809 (1999).

3. The GATT/W.T.O. Dispute Settlement Understanding (Understanding on Rules and Procedures Governing the Settlement of Disputes) is reprinted at 33 I.L.M. 1125, 1226 (1994). On W.T.O. dispute settlement, see Palmeter & Mavroidis, Dispute Settlement in the World Trade Organization (1997); Petersmann, The GATT/WTO Dispute Settlement System (1997); presentations by Shoyer, Steger & Van den Bossche, and Cottier at the panel on WTO Dispute Settlement: Three Years in Review, 92 Proc. A.S.I.L. 75–91 (1998); Jackson, Fragmentation or Unification Among International Institutions: The World Trade Organization, 31 N.Y.U. J. Int'l L. & Pol. 823 (1999); Symposium: The First Five Years of the WTO, Part I: Review of the Dispute Settlement Understanding, 31 L. & Pol'y Int'l Bus. 565 (2000).

For a comprehensive study of dispute settlement under GATT prior to establishment of the W.T.O. D.S.B., see Hudec, Enforcing International Trade Law: The Evolution of the Modern GATT Legal System (1993).

Chapter 12

THE USE OF FORCE

SECTION 1. THE USE OF FORCE BETWEEN STATES

In principle, the international (interstate) system implies the autonomy and independence of every state, both its freedom from coercion and the integrity of its territory. All invasions of either a state's independence or of its territory have sometimes been subsumed in the term "intervention." The extreme form of intervention, of course, is resort to armed force to conquer another state's territory, sometimes even to swallow it and terminate its existence as a state. The present section considers the progression during the 19th and 20th century of efforts to prohibit transboundary attacks by one state against another. Section 2 then turns to uses of force in internal conflicts–intervention in civil wars and humanitarian intervention—while Section 3 considers collective uses of force. Section 4 takes up efforts to mitigate the devastation of war through restraints on weapons and on the conduct of warfare: that body of law is often referred to as the *jus in bello* (law in wartime), as contrasted to the *jus ad bellum* (the law of going to war).

A. THE TRADITIONAL LAW

The traditional law governing uses of force and resort to war was radically transformed by the U.N. Charter. In particular respects, however, it is not agreed whether the traditional law survived or was modified by the Charter. The traditional law as it relates to the permissible uses of force in peacetime is presented in Section 1A, followed by a review of efforts to prohibit war prior to the U.N. era (Section 1B). The changes effected by the Charter are discussed in Section 1C.

1. *Coercive Measures and Uses of Force Short of War*

States have traditionally utilized coercive measures short of war in attempting to prevail in disputes with other states. A variety of coercive measures may be encompassed within the term "retorsion," which refers to measures that are "unfriendly" but are not prohibited by international law, taken by one state against another in response to a perceived offense (whether or not the offense is a violation of an international norm). The severance of diplomatic relations is one such measure: since the maintenance of such relations is not required by international law, their severance is not contrary to international law. Other forms of retorsion include: the shutting of ports to vessels of an unfriendly state, imposition of travel restrictions or denial of entry visas for its nationals, suspension of foreign aid, revocation of tariff concessions not guaranteed by treaty (or other trade restrictions), or the display of naval forces near the waters of an unfriendly state. See Restatement (Third) § 203(3), § 905, Comment *a*; Stone, Legal Controls of International Conflict 288 (rev. ed. 1959). For an account of several acts of retorsion, see von Glahn, Law Among Nations[:] An Introduction to Public International Law 637–40 (6th ed. 1992). See also Chapter 9, pp. 724–726, on retorsion and nonforcible reprisals.

REPRISAL

HACKWORTH, DIGEST OF INTERNATIONAL LAW

Vol. 6, 154–55 (1943).

On October 19, 1914 a German official and two German officers from German Southwest Africa were killed at the Portuguese post of Naulilaa in Angola under the following circumstances: A party of Germans had crossed into Angola to discuss with the Portuguese authorities the importation of food supplies into German Southwest Africa. Due to difficulties in interpreting, misunderstandings arose between the parties. In the course of a discussion a Portuguese officer seized the bridle of a German official's horse and the official struck him. At that time a German officer drew his pistol. The Portuguese officer ordered his men to fire and the official and two officers were killed. Portuguese authorities subsequently interned the German interpreter and a German soldier. The authorities of German Southwest Africa did not communicate with the Portuguese authorities, but in alleged reprisal for the incident German troops attacked and destroyed certain forts and posts in Angola. These events took place prior to the entry of Portugal into the World War.

After the war, the Portuguese Government claimed damages on account of the incident. Alois de Meuron, a Swiss lawyer, was designated on August 15, 1920 as arbitrator to determine in conformance with paragraph 4 of the annex to articles 297–298 of the Treaty of Versailles the amount of the Portuguese claims. On February 9, 1928 two other arbitrators, both Swiss nationals, Robert Guex and Robert Fazy, were added to the tribunal. In an award rendered July 31, 1928 the arbitrators stated that the death of the German official and of the two German officers was not the consequence of an act contrary to the law of nations on the part of the Portuguese authorities. They declared that the *sine qua non* of the right to exercise reprisals is a motive furnished by a preliminary act contrary to the law of nations and that, even had such an act on the part of the Portuguese authorities been established, the German argument that the reprisals were justified would have been rejected because reprisals are only permissible when they have been preceded by an unsatisfied demand. The use of force, they stated, is only justified by necessity. They also stated that, even if it were admitted that the law of nations does not demand that reprisals be in approximate proportion to the offense, it would, nevertheless, certainly be necessary to consider as excessive and illegal reprisals out of all proportion to the act motivating them.

They found that there was obvious disproportion between the incident at Naulilaa and the reprisals which followed, and defined reprisals as follows:

> Reprisals are an act of self-help (Selbsthilfehandlung) on the part of the injured state, an act corresponding *after an unsatisfied demand* to an act contrary to the law of nations on the part of the offending state. They have the effect of momentarily suspending, in the relations between the two states, the observance of such or such a rule of the law of nations. They are limited by the experiences of humanity and the rules of good faith applicable in relations between state and state. They would be illegal if a preliminary act contrary to the law of nations had not furnished a reason for them. * * * [Translation.]

For the tribunal's full opinion, see 2 U.N.Rep. Int'l Arb. Awards 1011 (1949).

Note

Compare the Joint Resolution of April 22, 1914, relating to the U.S. occupation of Veracruz, which stated that "the President is justified in the employment of the armed forces of the United States to enforce his demands for unequivocal amends for certain affronts and indignities committed against the United States" by Mexico. The Resolution further stated that "the United States disclaims any hostility to the Mexican people or any purpose to make war upon Mexico." 38 Stat. 770. See 1 Hackworth at 151; 6 Hackworth at 152.

SELF–DEFENSE

THE CAROLINE

2 Moore, Digest of International Law 412 (1906).
Hyde, International Law 239 (1945).

[During an insurrection in Canada in 1837, the insurgents secured recruits and supplies from the American side of the border. There was an encampment of one thousand armed men organized at Buffalo, and located at Navy Island in Upper Canada; there was another encampment of insurgents at Black Rock, on the American side. The Caroline was a small steamer employed by these encampments. On December 29, 1837, while moored at Schlosser, on the American side of the Niagara River, and while occupied by some thirty-three American citizens, the steamer was boarded by an armed body of men from the Canadian side, who attacked the occupants. The latter merely endeavored to escape. Several were wounded; one was killed on the dock; only twenty-one were afterwards accounted for. The attacking party fired the steamer and set her adrift over Niagara Falls. In 1841, upon the arrest and detention of one Alexander McLeod, in New York, on account of his alleged participation in the destruction of the vessel, Lord Palmerston avowed responsibility for the destruction of the Caroline as a public act of force in self-defense, by persons in the British service. He therefore demanded McLeod's release. McLeod was, however, tried in New York, and acquitted. In 1842 the two Governments agreed on principle that the requirements of self-defense might necessitate the use of force. Mr. Webster, Secretary of State, denied, however, that the necessity existed in this particular case, while Lord Ashburton, the British Minister, apologized for the invasion of American territory. Said Mr. Webster in the course of a communication to the British Minister, August 6, 1842:]

The President sees with pleasure that your Lordship fully admits those great principles of public law, applicable to cases of this kind, which this government has expressed; and that on your part, as on ours, respect for the inviolable character of the territory of independent states is the most essential foundation of civilization. And while it is admitted on both sides that there are exceptions to this rule, he is gratified to find that your Lordship admits that such exceptions must come within the limitations stated and the terms used in a former communication from this department to the British plenipotentiary here. Undoubtedly it is just, that, while it is admitted that exceptions growing out of the great law of self-defense do exist, those exceptions should be confined to cases in which the "necessity of that self-defence is instant, overwhelming, and leaving no choice of means, and no moment for deliberation."

Notes

1. *Proportionality.* In an earlier letter to the British authorities, Mr. Webster included a requirement of proportionality: "It will be for [Her Majesty's Government] to show, also, that the local authorities of Canada, even supposing the necessity of the moment authorized them to enter the territories of the United States at all, did nothing unreasonable or excessive; since the act, justified by the necessity of self-defence, must be limited by that necessity, and kept clearly within it." Mr. Webster to Mr. Fox (April 24, 1841), 29 British and Foreign State Papers 1129, 1138 (1857).

2. *Self-defense under the U.N. Charter.* For the law as to self-defense since the U.N. Charter, see p. 955 infra. See generally Greenwood, Self–Defence and the Conduct of International Armed Conflict, in International Law at a Time of Perplexity: Essays in Honour of Shabtai Rosenne 273 (Dinstein, ed. 1989).

2. *War in Traditional International Law*

WAR AS A LAWFUL INSTRUMENT OF NATIONAL POLICY

OPPENHEIM, INTERNATIONAL LAW

Vol. 2, 177–78 (7th ed. Lauterpacht, 1952).

Prior to the General Treaty for the Renunciation of War the institution of war fulfilled in International Law two contradictory functions. In the absence of an international organ for enforcing the law, war was a means of self-help for giving effect to claims based or alleged to be based on International Law. Such was the legal and moral authority of this notion of war as an arm of the law that in most cases in which war was in fact resorted to in order to increase the power and the possessions of a State at the expense of others, it was described by the States in question as undertaken for the defence of a legal right. This conception of war was intimately connected with the distinction, which was established in the formative period of International Law and which never became entirely extinct, between just and unjust wars. At the same time, however, that distinction was clearly rejected in the conception of war as a legally recognised instrument for challenging and changing rights based on existing International Law. In the absence of an international legislature it fulfilled the function of adapting the law to changed conditions. Moreover, quite apart from thus supplying a crude substitute for a deficiency in international organisation, war was recognised as a legally admissible instrument for attacking and altering existing rights of States independently of the objective merits of the attempted change. As Hyde, writing in 1922, said: "It always lies within the power of a State * * * to gain political or other advantages over another, not merely by the employment of force, but also by direct recourse to war." International Law did not consider as illegal a war admittedly waged for such purposes. It rejected, to that extent, the distinction between just and unjust wars. War was in law a natural function of the State and a prerogative of its uncontrolled sovereignty.

Note

"It was not a cynic who once suggested that international law establishes order in unimportant matters but not in important ones. Doubtless, the comment referred in particular to the anomaly of international law before our times, which set up rules about international conduct in time of peace but did not forbid nations to commit the ultimate 'aggression' against international order, the resort to war. That incongruity had its explanations, principally in the failure of early attempts to distinguish just wars (to be permitted, even encouraged) from unjust wars (to be outlawed). Third nations also wished to avoid becoming involved in the wars of others and wished to go their way in relation to both belligerent sides without having to decide which was in 'the right.' And, in fact, one cannot say that the anomaly nullified international law. Indeed, nations were more likely to observe the international law of peace, knowing that if their interests were too gravely jeopardized they could go to war to vindicate them and establish a new basis for new relations in a revised international order with different international obligations." Henkin, How Nations Behave 135–36 (2d ed. 1979).

If states were not prepared to go to war in its legal sense, whether for reasons given by Henkin or for other reasons, they remained bound by the legal restraints on resort to force expressed in rules such as those on non-intervention, reprisal, and self-defense. See Waldock, The Regulation of the Use of Force by Individual States, 81 Rec. des Cours 457 (1952); Brownlie, International Law and the Use of Force by States 21 (1963).

THE STATE OF WAR IN INTERNATIONAL LAW

The concern of states to regulate the conduct and the impact of war was an early impetus to the development of international law. The first systematic international law treatise, that of Grotius, was entitled *De Jure Belli Ac Pacis (Of the Law of War and Peace).* International law writers postulated a dichotomy between war and peace and distinguished laws for nations at peace from laws for nations at war. "Belligerent" states, those at war, had the duty to observe the rules of war, and to respect the neutrality of non-belligerent states. These rules were designed to limit the spread of armed conflict and to promote a modicum of humanity in battle. Neutral states were expected to follow the relevant rules if they were to avoid the conflict. See p. 980 below.

In order to determine whether the rules of war or of neutrality applied it was necessary to determine whether a state of war existed between states.

Such a determination was not always easy to make. State practice during the nineteenth century suggests that a state of war resulted when one party declared war or intended a state of war to exist. This practice provided obvious advantages. If a state of war did not exist unless war was declared or intended, a state could refrain from declaring war so as to avoid the necessity of complying with the laws of war. Also, other nations could not then invoke the laws of neutrality. Some writers argued for an objective test, notably evidence of large-scale fighting. This view seemed more realistic as states began to initiate and engage in hostilities without formal declarations of war. For a critical discussion of the concept of war, see Grob, The Relativity of War and Peace (1949). On the difficulty of determining when armed hostilities constituted war, see Brownlie, International Law and the Use of Force by States 38–40 (1963). In cases of civil war, the concept of belligerency traditionally determined the application of the laws of war and neutrality: only when revolutionary factions attained the status of "belligerents" did the traditional laws come into play. In recent times, however, the practice of formally recognizing a state of belligerency fell into disuse. See p. 979 below.

Early in the twentieth century, new interest in defining war was stimulated by agreements to outlaw war as a method of settling disputes—the League of Nations Covenant and the Pact of Paris. See Treaty Providing for the Renunciation of War as an Instrument of National Policy (Kellogg–Briand Treaty), Aug. 27, 1928, p. 929 below. Without a workable definition of "war," the limitations imposed by these treaties upon the parties could not be determined. See Eagleton, The Attempt to Define War, [1933] Int'l Conciliation No. 291.

NEUTRALITY

OPPENHEIM, INTERNATIONAL LAW

Vol. 2, 653–54 (7th ed. Lauterpacht, 1952).

* * * Such States as do not take part in a war between other States are neutrals. The term "neutrality" is derived from the Latin *neuter*. Neutrality may be defined as the attitude of impartiality adopted by third States towards belligerents and recognised by belligerents, such attitude creating rights and duties between the impartial States and the belligerents. Whether or not a third State will adopt an attitude of impartiality at the outbreak of war is not a matter for International Law but for international politics. Therefore, unless a previous treaty stipulates it expressly, no duty exists for a State, according to International Law, to remain neutral when war breaks out. Every sovereign State, as an independent member of the Family of Nations, is master of its own resolutions, and the question of remaining neutral or not at the outbreak of war is, in the absence of a treaty stipulating otherwise, one of policy and not of law. However, all States which do not expressly declare the contrary by word or action are supposed to be neutral, and the rights and duties arising from neutrality come into existence, and remain in existence, through the mere fact of a State taking up an attitude of impartiality, and not being drawn into the war by the belligerents. A special assertion of intention to remain neutral is not, therefore, legally necessary on the part of neutral States, although they often expressly and formally proclaim their neutrality.

Notes

1. Neutrality was a legal status accorded to certain non-belligerents. In order to qualify for treatment as a neutral, a state had to assume an attitude of impartiality toward the belligerents. Policies adopted by the neutral state had to be applied equally to all parties at war. See Harvard Research in International Law, Draft Convention on Rights and Duties of Neutral States in Naval and Aerial War, 33 A.J.I.L. Spec. Supp. 175, 232–34 (1939); Eagleton, The Duty of Impartiality on the Part of a Neutral, 34 A.J.I.L. 99 (1940). In return for assuming the duty of impartiality toward belligerents, the neutral was guaranteed the inviolability of his territory and freedom from belligerent acts. On the early development of the law of neutrality, see Jessup & Deak, Neutrality, Volume I: The Origins (1935); 2 Oppenheim at 623–42; Örvik, The Decline of Neutrality 1914–1941 11–37 (1953); Hall, The Rights and Duties of Neutrals (1874). On the Declaration of Paris, see 2 Oppenheim at 460–63; Stone at 457; Smith, The Declaration of Paris in Modern War, 55 L.Q.Rev. 237 (1939).

2. The Hague Peace Conferences of 1899 and 1907 led to two conventions defining the rights of neutrals. See Convention Respecting the Rights and Duties of Neutral Powers and Persons in Case of War on Land, Oct. 18, 1907, 36 Stat. 2310, T.S. No. 540; Convention Concerning the Rights and Duties of Neutral Powers in Naval War, Oct. 18, 1907, 36 Stat. 2415, T.S. No. 545. As of 2000, about 30 states were parties to these conventions.

3. What were thought to be firm principles of the law of neutrality were repeatedly violated during the First and Second World Wars, particularly in regard to shipping, blockades and confiscation of properties. On long-range blockades generally, see Tucker, The Law of War and Neutrality at Sea 278–82, 316–17 (International Law Studies of the Naval War College, 1957); McDougal & Feliciano, Law and Minimum World Public Order 484–88 (1961); Alford, Modern Economic Warfare (International Law Studies of the Naval War College, 1963); Medlicott, The Economic Blockade (Vol. 1, 1952; Vol. 2, 1959). See also Smith, The Law and Custom of the Sea 131–37 (3d ed. 1959).

4. For discussion of neutrality under the U.N. Charter see p. 979–980.

B. PRE–UNITED NATIONS EFFORTS TO DISCOURAGE OR OUTLAW WAR

HAGUE CONVENTION II

CONVENTION RESPECTING THE LIMITATION OF THE EMPLOYMENT OF FORCE FOR THE RECOVERY OF CONTRACT DEBTS, SIGNED AT THE HAGUE, OCTOBER 18, 1907

36 Stat. 2241, T.S. 537.

ARTICLE 1

The contracting Powers agree not to have recourse to armed force for the recovery of contract debts claimed from the Government of one country by the Government of another country as being due to its nationals.

This undertaking is, however, not applicable when the debtor State refuses or neglects to reply to an offer of arbitration, or, after accepting the offer, prevents any *compromis* from being agreed on, or, after the arbitration, fails to submit to the award. * * *

THE LEAGUE OF NATIONS

BOWETT, THE LAW OF INTERNATIONAL INSTITUTIONS

17–18 (4th ed. 1982).

The creation of a league of States, dedicated to the maintenance of peace, had long been advocated in philosophical and juristic writings and in the aims of private organisations. The immediate source of the League of Nations was, however, a proposal introduced at the Peace Conference of Paris in 1919. In the drafting of the Covenant of the League the major powers played the decisive role; it emerged as a fusion of President Wilson's third draft and the British proposals emanating from the Phillimore Committee.

The League's objective was "to promote international co-operation and to achieve international peace and security." The system of collective security envisaged in the Covenant rested, essentially, on the notions of disarmament (Art. 8), pacific settlement of disputes and the outlawry of war (Arts. 11–15), a collective guarantee of the independence of each member (Art. 10), and sanctions (Arts. 16 and 17). The League's disarmament programme failed dismally. As envisaged in the Covenant, the pacific settlement of disputes likely to lead to a rupture of the peace was obligatory; parties to the dispute could choose to go to arbitration, judicial settlement or to the Council of the League. It was obligatory to accept the award or a unanimous report of the Council and an obligation on all members not to go to war with any State so accepting. The members agreed to respect and preserve the "territorial integrity and existing political independence" of all members against external aggression. War, as such, was not made illegal but only where begun without complying with the requirements of the Covenant with regard to prior resort to pacific settlement of the dispute. A State resorting to war in violation of its undertaking with regard to pacific settlement was deemed to have committed an act of war against all other members. Yet it was left to each member to decide whether a breach had occurred or an act of war had been committed, so that even the obligation to apply economic sanctions under Article 16(1) was dependent on the member's own view of the situation. Military sanctions could be recommended by the Council, but the decision on whether to apply them rested with each member.

Such was the system; in itself a not unworkable one. After an initial success in dealing with the Graeco–Bulgarian crisis of 1925, and a less spectacular achievement in the Chaco dispute of 1928, the League witnessed the invasion of Manchuria in 1931, the Italo–Abyssinian War of 1934–35, the German march into the Rhineland in 1936, into Austria in 1938, into Czechoslovakia in 1939, the Soviet Union's invasion of Finland in 1939 and, finally, the German invasion of Poland in 1939. Apart from half-hearted economic sanctions against Italy in 1935, no sanctions were ever really applied by the League. To this extent the failure of the League was due, not to the inadequacies of the Covenant, but to the apathy and reluctance of the member States to discharge their obligations.

COVENANT OF THE LEAGUE OF NATIONS, JUNE 28, 1919

1 Hudson International Legislation 1 (1931).

Article XVI

Should any Member of the League resort to war in disregard of its covenants under Articles 12, 13 or 15, it shall *ipso facto* be deemed to have committed an act of war against all other Members of the League, which hereby undertake immediately to subject it to the severance of all trade or financial relations, the prohibition of all intercourse between their nationals and the nationals of the covenant-breaking State, and the prevention of all financial, commercial or personal intercourse between the nationals of the covenant-breaking State and the nationals of any other State, whether a Member of the League or not.

It shall be the duty of the Council in such case to recommend to the several Governments concerned what effective military, naval or air force the Members of the League shall severally contribute to the armed forces to be used to protect the covenants of the League.

The Members of the League agree, further, that they will mutually support one another in the financial and economic measures which are taken under this Article, in order to minimise the loss and inconvenience resulting from the above measures, and that they will mutually support one another in resisting any special measures aimed at one of their number by the covenant-breaking State, and that they will take the necessary steps to afford passage through their territory to the forces of any of the Members of the League which are co-operating to protect the covenants of the League.

Note

Failure of the Covenant. The provisions of Article 16 of the Covenant were given their decisive test in the war between Italy and Abyssinia (Ethiopia). Italy invaded Abyssinia on October 3, 1935. Despite the absence of any procedural provisions in the Covenant, machinery for the implementation of Article 16 was swiftly devised. The League Council, after hearing the plea of Abyssinia, appointed a Committee of Six to draw up a report. On October 11, the Council adopted the report of the Committee which had found that the Italian Government had resorted to war in violation of the Covenant. Within sixteen days of the outbreak of war the League drew up a series of proposals suggesting to its members the implementation of embargoes extending to arms, financial credit, exports and imports and calling for mutual economic help to those innocent countries adversely affected by the embargo. The sanctions, however, fell short in many ways of those prescribed in Article 16 of the Covenant. Due to weakness and vacillation on the part of Britain and France, the export embargo did not extend to coal, steel and oil, the commodities most vital to Italy. The subsequent refusal of the League to take further measures when the initial sanctions proved inadequate exposed its impotence. In the face of British, French and Russian fears of war with Italy, the controversial oil embargo was never adopted.

The failure of the League to prevent the obvious aggression of Italy and to deal effectively with the aggressor undermined the credibility of a regime of international law under which war was to be abolished as an instrument of national policy. The standard used in assessing aggression is discussed in Wright, The Test of Aggression in the Italo–Ethiopian War, 30 A.J.I.L. 45 (1936). For a description of the League actions, see Spencer, The Italian–Ethiopian Dispute and the League of Nations, 31 A.J.I.L. 614 (1937). The relevant documents are set forth in League of Nations—Dispute Between Ethiopia and Italy, 30 A.J.I.L. Supp. 1 (1936).

On the League of Nations generally, see Walters, A History of the League of Nations (1960); Scott, The Rise and Fall of the League of Nations (1973); Joyce, Broken Star: The Story of the League of Nations, 1919–1939 (1978); Ostrower, Collective Insecurity: The United States and the League of Nations During the Early Thirties (1979); The League of Nations in Retrospect: Proceedings of the Symposium (1983); Northedge, The League of Nations: Its Life and Times, 1920–1946 (1986).

GENERAL TREATY FOR THE RENUNCIATION OF WAR (KELLOGG–BRIAND PACT)

August 27, 1928, 46 Stat. 2343, 94 L.N.T.S. 57.

Art. I. The High Contracting Parties solemnly declare in the names of their respective peoples that they condemn recourse to war for the solution of international controversies, and renounce it as an instrument of national policy in their relations with one another.

Art. II. The High Contracting Parties agree that the settlement or solution of all disputes or conflicts of whatever nature or of whatever origin they may be, which may arise among them, shall never be sought except by pacific means.

Notes

1. The Kellogg–Briand Pact became effective on July 24, 1929 and is still in force. Some new states (e.g., Barbados and Fiji) have adhered to it, and some of the new states of the former Yugoslavia (e.g., Bosnia–Herzegovina and Slovenia) specifically registered acceptance in the 1990s. (All the states of the former Soviet Union and former Yugoslavia could be considered bound on a continuity theory of succession; see pp. 584, 1082–1083.) As of 2000, more than 70 states are parties.

2. The "Saavedra Lamas Treaty," signed by certain American states at Rio de Janeiro on October 10, 1933, and by the United States in 1934, condemns wars of aggression and provides in Article 1 that "the settlement of disputes or controversies of any kind * * * shall be effected only by the pacific means which shall have the sanction of international law." 6 Hackworth at 9.

THE NUREMBERG CHARTER AND TRIALS

An International Military Tribunal was established at the end of World War II by the London Agreement among the United States of America, the French Republic, the United Kingdom of Great Britain and Northern Ireland, and the Union of Soviet Socialist Republics "for the trial of war criminals whose offenses have no particular geographical location whether they be accused individually or in their capacity as members of organizations or groups or in both capacities." The original indictment presented to the

Tribunal on October 6, 1945, charged the German defendants under Article VI of the Charter of the International Military Tribunal with committing Crimes against the Peace, War Crimes and Crimes against Humanity. An additional charge which merged with the others alleged that the defendants had planned and conspired to commit these same acts.

Crimes against the Peace were defined by Article VI as:

> planning, preparation, initiation, or waging of a war of aggression, or a war in violation of international treaties, agreements, assurances, or participation in a common plan or conspiracy for the accomplishment of any of the foregoing.

The Charter and the subsequent judgment never adopted a definition of aggressive war. Although the United States representative tried to have such a definition included in the Charter, his efforts were rebuffed. In the end, the Tribunal apparently accepted the argument that the acts perpetrated by Germany speak for themselves, and that under any seriously propounded definition of aggression the German leaders were guilty.

Since one of the central concerns of the Nuremberg Tribunal was the imputation of individual criminal responsibility, its use of the concept of aggressive war was influenced by the notion of a criminal conspiracy. Both the proof by the prosecution and the judgment of the Tribunal detail how the Nazi leaders in deliberate fashion planned the Second World War. The judgment describes the seizure of power by the Nazi Party, the intentions of its leaders, and finally the specific aggressive acts of the government. Aggressive war in these terms was the pursuit of an expansionist policy through deliberate criminal acts.

JUDGMENT OF THE INTERNATIONAL MILITARY TRIBUNAL

Nuremberg, Sept. 30, 1946, reprinted in 41 A.J.I.L. 186–218 (1946).

The charges in the Indictment that the defendants planned and waged aggressive wars are charges of the utmost gravity. War is essentially an evil thing. Its consequences are not confined to the belligerent states alone, but affect the whole world.

To initiate a war of aggression, therefore, is not only an international crime; it is the supreme international crime differing only from other war crimes in that it contains within itself the accumulated evil of the whole.

The first acts of aggression referred to in the Indictment are the seizure of Austria and Czechoslovakia; and the first war of aggression charged in the Indictment is the war against Poland begun on the 1st September 1939.

Before examining that charge it is necessary to look more closely at some of the events which preceded these acts of aggression. The war against Poland did not come suddenly out of an otherwise clear sky; the evidence has made it plain that this war of aggression, as well as the seizure of Austria and Czechoslovakia, was premeditated and carefully prepared, and was not undertaken until the moment was thought opportune for it to be carried through as a definite part of the preordained scheme and plan.

For the aggressive designs of the Nazi Government were not accidents arising out of the immediate political situation in Europe and the world; they were a deliberate and essential part of Nazi foreign policy.

From the beginning, the National Socialist movement claimed that its object was to unite the German people in the consciousness of their mission and destiny, based on inherent qualities of race, and under the guidance of the Fuehrer.

For its achievement, two things were deemed to be essential: The disruption of the European order as it has existed since the Treaty of Versailles, and the creation of a Greater Germany beyond the frontiers of 1914. This necessarily involved the seizure of foreign territories.

War was seen to be inevitable, or at the very least, highly probable, if these purposes were to be accomplished. The German people, therefore, with all their resources, were to be organized as a great political-military army, schooled to obey without question any policy decreed by the State.* * *

The Charter defines as a crime the planning or waging of war that is a war of aggression or a war in violation of international treaties. The Tribunal has decided that certain of the defendants planned and waged aggressive wars against 12 nations, and were therefore guilty of this series of crimes. This makes it unnecessary to discuss the subject in further detail, or even to consider at any length the extent to which these aggressive wars were also "wars in violation of international treaties, agreements, or assurances." * * *

The jurisdiction of the Tribunal is defined in the Agreement and Charter, and the crimes coming within the jurisdiction of the Tribunal, for which there shall be individual responsibility, are set out in Article 6. The law of the Charter is decisive, and binding upon the Tribunal. * * *

The Charter makes the planning or waging of a war of aggression or a war in violation of international treaties a crime; and it is therefore not strictly necessary to consider whether and to what extent aggressive war was a crime before the execution of the London Agreement. * * *

The question is, what was the legal effect of this [the Kellogg–Briand] Pact? The nations who signed the pact or adhered to it unconditionally condemned recourse to war for the future as an instrument of policy, and expressly renounced it. After the signing of the Pact, any nation resorting to war as an instrument of national policy breaks the Pact. In the opinion of the Tribunal, the solemn renunciation of war as an instrument of national policy necessarily involves the proposition that such a war is illegal in international law; and that those who plan and wage such a war, with its inevitable and terrible consequences, are committing a crime in so doing. War for the solution of international controversies undertaken as an instrument of national policy certainly includes a war of aggression, and such a war is therefore outlawed by the Pact. * * *

Notes

1. *Aggressive wars*. The Tribunal, following its Charter, distinguishes a war of aggression from one in breach of international agreements, but deals only briefly with the latter. Appendix C to the indictment sets out the various agreements which Germany is charged with having breached.

The defense argued on behalf of the German defendants that although a nation could not wage aggressive war without transgressing international law, it could use war as an instrument of self-defense, and that the nation itself must be the sole judge of whether its actions were in self-defense. If action in self-defense is permissible, who is to judge when a nation is an aggressor? Is it realistic to outlaw aggressive war without providing for a tribunal to arbitrate whether a particular course of conduct is aggressive? In rejecting the plea of self-defense, the Tribunal adopted the test stated in the *Caroline* case, p. 922.

The International Military Tribunal was criticized as necessarily biased since the victors could not impartially judge their adversaries. For example, it was pointed out that although the German "invasion" of Poland was found to be aggressive, this action by the Germans was executed in concert with the Union of Soviet Socialist Republics which was never accused of aggressive conduct before the International Military Tribunal. For a survey of the "aggressive" acts of the various governments, see Hankey, Politics, Trials and Errors 10–16 (1950).

It has also been argued that the question of aggression is so predominantly a political question that it should be settled through political means, not by a court. Instead of the Nuremberg procedure, should there have been a determination by the Allies that Germany was the aggressor, as a predicate for imposing harsh extra-legal measures against its leaders? Before the decision was taken to establish an international judicial tribunal, the alternative of summary execution of the top Nazi figures was advocated at the highest levels in several of the Allied governments, including the United Kingdom and the United States. On the counsels that overcame this advocacy, see Bass, Stay the Hand of Vengeance: The Politics of International War Crimes Tribunals 147–195 (2000).

Could a defeated nation ever hope to punish the leaders of a victorious aggressor nation? Would a victorious aggressor, or nations involved in wars where there is no clear victor, ever submit to the jurisdiction of an international tribunal with the possibility that their leaders might be declared perpetrators of crimes against the peace? See Chapter 15, p. 1370.

2. *The trial generally.* See, in general, Agreement for the Prosecution and Punishment of the Major War Criminals of the European Axis (the London Agreement), 59 Stat. 1544, 82 U.N.T.S. 279; Taylor, Nuremberg Trials, [1949] Int'l Conciliation No. 450, at 243; Memorandum submitted by the Secretary–General, The Charter and Judgment of the Nurnberg Tribunal, U.N.Doc. A/ACN. 4/5 (1949); Hankey, Politics, Trials and Errors (1950); Taylor, The Nuremberg Trials, 55 Colum. L.Rev. 488 (1955); Jackson, The Nurnberg Case (1947); Wright, The Law of the Nuremberg Trial, 41 A.J.I.L. 38 (1947); Finch, The Nuremberg Trial and International Law, 41 A.J.I.L. 20 (1947); Jessup, Crime of Aggression, 62 Pol. Sci. Q. 1 (1947); Schick, Crimes Against the Peace, 38 J.Crim. L. & Crim. 445 (1948). The Charter of the Tribunal—the underlying jurisdictional document—was annexed to the London Agreement, supra. For the Indictment, see U.S. Dep't of State, Trial of War Criminals 23 (Dep't of State pub. no. 2420, European Ser. No. 10, 1945). For an illuminating account by a principal prosecutor, see Taylor, The Anatomy of the Nuremberg Trials: A Personal Memoir (1992). For a convenient collection of materials concerning the trials, see Marrus, The Nuremberg War Crimes Trial 1945–46: A Documentary History (1997).

3. *Tokyo Tribunal.* A similar Tribunal was established in the Far East. For discussion of the Tokyo war crimes trials, in which several major Japanese leaders were found guilty and sentenced to death, see Keenan & Brown, Crimes against International Law (1950); Röling & Cassese, The Tokyo Trial and Beyond (1993).

For an alternative perspective, see Elizabeth Kopelman, Ideology and International Law: The Dissent of the Indian Justice at the Tokyo War Crimes Trial, 23 N.Y.U. J. Int'l L. & Pol. 373 (1991).

4. *Occupation trials.* The International Military Tribunals should not be confused with the tribunals convened by the various occupying powers under their own authority. The judgment of one of the latter tribunals is reproduced, in part at pp. 406–408 and 1325–1326.

5. *Nuremberg principles and Vietnam.* As noted in Chapter 5, pp. 405–409, a key Nuremberg principle, as endorsed by the U.N. General Assembly in 1946, is individual responsibility for the kinds of violations of international law at stake in the Nuremberg trials. There were several attempts to invoke the Nuremberg principles in relation U.S. involvement in the Vietnam war. In United States v. Mitchell, 246 F.Supp. 874 (D.Conn.1965), the defendant, charged with having failed to report for induction as ordered, defended on the ground, *inter alia,* that the war in Vietnam was a war of aggression within the meaning of the London Agreement, and that he would be responsible for participating even though ordered to do so. The trial court charged the jury that the agreement did not interfere "in any manner in respect to this defendant fulfilling his duty under this order." (Quoted at 386 U.S. 972, 87 S.Ct. 1162, 18 L.Ed.2d 132 (1967).) He was convicted and his conviction was affirmed, 369 F.2d 323 (2d Cir.1966); the Supreme Court denied certiorari, Douglas J. dissenting from the denial of certiorari with a brief opinion, 386 U.S. 972, 87 S.Ct. 1162, 18 L.Ed.2d 132 (1967). See also the dissenting opinion of Justices Stewart and Douglas from the denial of certiorari in Mora v. McNamara, 389 U.S. 934, 88 S.Ct. 282, 19 L.Ed.2d 287 (1967).

Most of the cases arising out of the Vietnam war raised issues under the U.S. Constitution, but some also addressed arguments that the United States was violating international law. Some courts rejected the substantive arguments; some declared them to be "political questions" and non-justiciable. See Sugarman, Judicial Decisions Concerning the Constitutionality of United States Military Activity in Indo–China, 13 Colum.J.Transnat'l L. 470 (1974). See also Henkin, Viet Nam in the Courts of the United States: "Political Questions," 63 A.J.I.L. 284 (1969). Compare Taylor, Nuremberg and Vietnam: An American Tragedy (1970).

6. *Nuremberg principles today.* On the efforts to establish a standing tribunal to prosecute crimes corresponding to those adjudged at Nuremberg, see Chapter 15. As of 2000, the establishment of an International Criminal Court appears imminent, but the provisions of its Statute will defer jurisdiction over the crime of aggression pending the adoption of a specific definition of the crime. The other Nuremberg crimes—war crimes and crimes against humanity—will fall within the I.C.C.'s jurisdiction as soon as the court comes into existence (once 60 states have ratified the Statute). See pp. 1367–1382.

C. THE UNITED NATIONS CHARTER

1. Overview

THE LAW OF THE CHARTER

The United Nations Charter laid the foundation of a "new world order" after the Allied victory in the Second World War. Originally an international agreement open only to states that had declared war against the Axis powers, it has become a universal agreement open to all states. Membership in the United Nations and adherence to the Charter have been the aim of virtually every entity that aspired to and achieved statehood. Since the United Nations is open only to states, acceptance for membership constitutes compelling proof of statehood. Among the community of states, Switzerland stands practically alone in declining to join the organization, having several times rejected by referendum proposals to support an application for U.N. membership (though Switzerland does participate in a variety of U.N. agencies and U.N.-sponsored treaties and activities).

The Charter prescribes international norms outlawing the threat or use of force, the principal norms on which the new order stands, and now universally recognized as *jus cogens*. Article 2(3) commits members to settle their disputes by peaceful means. By Article 2(4) member states undertake to refrain from the threat or use of force against the territorial integrity or political independence of other states or in any other manner inconsistent with the purposes of the United Nations. See p. 937.

The Charter not only outlaws "aggression" but also prohibits the "threat or use of force." Chapter VII of the Charter gives the U.N. Security Council authority to determine the existence of any threat to the peace, breach of peace or act of aggression and to make recommendations or decide what measures shall be taken to maintain or restore international peace or security. See p. 1009. By Article 51, "[n]othing in the present Charter shall impair the inherent right of individual or collective self-defence if an armed attack occurs * * * ." See p. 955.

THE UNITED NATIONS ORGANIZATION

The principal purpose of the United Nations Organization is "[t]o maintain international peace and security, and to that end: to take effective collective measures for the prevention and removal of threats to the peace, and for the suppression of acts of aggression or other breaches of the peace, and to bring about by peaceful means, and in conformity with the principles of justice and international law, adjustment or settlement of international disputes or situations which might lead to the breach of the peace * * * ." U.N. Charter, Article 1(1). The members of the U.N. conferred primary responsibility for the maintenance of international peace and security on the U.N. Security Council. Id., Article 24 and Chapter VII. The United Nations has other purposes as well, and organs of the U.N. other than the Security Council have responsibility to further those purposes (as well as some role in maintaining international peace and security). On the International Court of Justice as the U.N.'s principal judicial organ, see Chapter 11.

A general limitation on the purposes and powers of the United Nations is laid down in Article 2(7) of the Charter: "Nothing contained in the present Charter shall authorize the United Nations to intervene in matters which are essentially within the domestic jurisdiction of any state * * *;" this provision, however, "shall not prejudice the application of enforcement measures under Chapter VII." Id.

The General Assembly. All members of the United Nations are members of the General Assembly (Articles 9(1) and 18(1)). The General Assembly may discuss and make recommendations on any matters within the scope of the Charter (Article 10), but it may make recommendations on disputes or situations with regard to which the Security Council is exercising its powers only upon the Security Council's request (Article 12(1)). On the role of the General Assembly in peacekeeping, see pp. 1012–1013, 1028.

The Security Council. The Security Council consists of five permanent and—as a result of amendment—ten non-permanent members. The permanent members are China, France, Russia, the United Kingdom, and the United States. The non-permanent members are elected by the General Assembly for two-year terms with due regard to the contribution of members to the purposes of the U.N. and to equitable geographical distribution (Article 23(1)). The Security Council's principal task is to ensure international peace and security. The authority of the Security Council is set forth in Chapters V through VII of the Charter. Member States delegate to the Security Council "primary responsibility for the maintenance of international peace and security" (Article 24) and "agree to accept and carry out the decisions of the Security Council" (Article 25).

Article 52 of the Charter authorizes regional arrangements and agencies for dealing with matters relating to the maintenance of international peace and security. The Security Council may utilize regional arrangements for enforcement action under its authority (Article 53).

The Secretariat. The Secretariat is headed by the Secretary–General, who is appointed for a five-year term by the General Assembly upon the recommendation of the Security Council (Article 97). The Secretary–General may bring to the attention of the Security Council any matter that in his opinion may threaten international peace and security (Article 99).

THE LAW OF THE CHARTER DURING THE COLD WAR

For some 40 years the United Nations Organization and its activities were hampered, and often thwarted, by the Cold War. The Security Council was largely incapacitated in its principal role of maintaining international peace and security by lack of agreement (and by veto) of the permanent members. The Council did contribute to peacekeeping when the Big Powers agreed, but agreement was often elusive. As a consequence, the General Assembly sought to assume part of the Security Council's responsibility (see, e.g., the Uniting for Peace Resolution, G.A.Res. 337(V) (1950), G.A.O.R., 5th Sess., Supp. 20, at 10, discussed at p. 1012 infra), but it too was hampered by the Cold War and by the enlarged membership dominated by new, developing states.

The Cold War and its effects on the U.N. doubtless influenced the interpretation of the normative principles of the Charter and weakened compliance with those norms, but there was never a serious suggestion that the inability of the United Nations to maintain peace invalidated or impaired the Charter norms proscribing the threat or use of force. Those shortcomings did, however, increase reliance on Article 51's "inherent" right of self-defense. See pp. 955–973. The end of the Cold War has revived the Security Council, enabling it to play its intended role (e.g., in the Gulf War) and has encouraged the Council to extend its authority and activities (e.g., in the former Yugoslavia).

HENKIN, HOW NATIONS BEHAVE

137–38 (2nd ed. 1979).

Unlike the limited restraints in the Covenant of the League and the provisions of the Kellogg–Briand Pact, the Charter's prohibition on unilateral force was to apply universally: members were bound by it; they were to see to it that nonmembers also complied. For the first time, nations tried to bring within the realm of law those ultimate political tensions and interests that had long been deemed beyond control by law. They determined that even sincere concern for national "security" or "vital interests" should no longer warrant any nation to initiate war. They agreed, in effect, to forgo the use of external force to change the political status quo. Nations would be assured their fundamental independence, the enjoyment of their territory, their freedom—a kind of right to be let alone. With it, of course, came the corresponding obligation to let others alone, not to use force to resolve disputes, or even to vindicate one's "rights." Change—other than internal change through internal forces—would have to be achieved peacefully, by agreement. Henceforth there would be order, and international society could concentrate on meeting better the needs of justice and welfare.

This most political of norms has been the target of "realists" from the beginning. They have questioned whether it is viable, even whether it is clearly desirable. Some who approved the norm in 1945 began to ask later whether it was acceptable. A "realist" would suggest that the law could have worked only if the United States and the Soviet Union had been prepared to cooperate to enforce peace. A lawyer might ask whether the law remains law, according to the principle of *rebus sic stantibus,* when the assumptions on which it was based have failed, when the circumstances in which it was made and those for which it was contemplated have radically changed.

For me, the changing facts and faces of international law have not detracted from the validity of the law of the Charter and have only reinforced its desirability. Consider, first, the argument based on the failure of the original conception of the United Nations: it has not established an effective international police system; it has not developed and maintained machinery for peaceful settlement of disputes (making self-help unnecessary and undesirable). But the draftsmen of the Charter were not seeking merely to replace "balance of power" by "collective security"; they were determined, according to the Preamble, to abolish "the scourge of war." All the evidence is persuasive that they sought to outlaw war, whether or not the U.N. organization succeeded in enforcing the law or in establishing peace and justice. And none of the original members, nor any one of the many new members, has ever claimed that the law against the use of force is undesirable now that the United Nations is not what had been intended.

Notes

1. Henkin argues also that the other "changed circumstances"—the failure of Allied cooperation that gave way to the ideological confrontation of the Cold

War, the development and proliferation of terrible weapons of mass destruction, and the transformation of the political system by the emergence of new nations and the "Third World"—did not render Article 2(4) less valid or less desirable. Henkin, How Nations Behave 138–39 (2d ed. 1979). The revival of the Security Council has put an end to arguments that the Charter norms against the use of force (Articles 2(3) and 2(4)) may have been voided under the doctrine of *rebus sic stantibus* (p. 554), but its long dormant state encouraged arguments for inferring exceptions, for example to permit the use of force for humanitarian intervention or to defend or promote democracy. See p. 990.

On the continuing validity and viability of Article 2(4) during the Cold War, compare Franck, Who Killed Article 2(4)? Or Changing Norms Governing the Use of Force by States, 64 A.J.I.L. 809 (1970), with Henkin, The Reports of the Death of Article 2(4) Are Greatly Exaggerated, 65 A.J.I.L. 544 (1971). See also Henkin, How Nations Behave 146–53 (2d ed. 1979); Schachter, In Defense of International Rules on the Use of Force, 53 U.Chi. L.Rev. 113 (1986). For the impact of the Cold War on the interpretation of the law of the Charter, see pp. 977–978 infra. See also Henkin, The Use of Force: Law and U.S. Policy, in Right v. Might: International Law and the Use of Force 37, 38–41 (2d ed. 1991); Macdonald, The Use of Force by States in International Law, in International Law: Achievements and Prospects 715, 719–31 (Bedjaoui, ed. 1991).

2. U.S. actions, e.g., in Grenada, Nicaragua, and Panama, gave rise to charges that for the United States the law of the Charter was inapplicable when important national interests were at stake. Official U.S. representatives, however, continued to insist on the validity of the law of the Charter, and sought to justify U.S. actions under that law and to judge the actions of other states by that standard. But the United States withdrew from the proceedings brought against it by Nicaragua before the International Court of Justice. See p. 955.

3. Henkin concludes that even during the Cold War there were fewer violations of the Charter than was commonly assumed. The principal "wars" were civil wars with external involvement, as to which the law of the Charter did not speak clearly. See p. 984. The Cold War may have encouraged violations by smaller developing powers who expected that ideological conflict between the superpowers would incapacitate the Security Council and provide them immunity from other adverse consequences (e.g., the Iran–Iraq War 1981–1988 and wars between Ethiopia and its neighbors). See Henkin, How Nations Behave 112–118 (2nd ed. 1979).

The end of the Cold War led to different patterns of conflict and new types of external intervention, as in the former Yugoslavia. These have left their mark on international law. See pp. 989–1003.

2. *The Prohibition of the Use of Force*

CHARTER OF THE UNITED NATIONS

San Francisco, June 26, 1945.

* * *

ARTICLE 2

* * *

4. All Members shall refrain in their international relations from the threat or use of force against the territorial integrity or political independence

of any state, or in any other manner inconsistent with the Purposes of the United Nations.

* * *

SCHACHTER, INTERNATIONAL LAW IN THEORY AND PRACTICE

110–113 (1991) (footnotes omitted).

The basic provision restricting the use of force (or its threat) in international relations is Article 2, paragraph 4, of the Charter. * * *

The paragraph is complex in its structure and nearly all of its key terms raise questions of interpretation. We know that the principle was intended to outlaw war in its classic sense, that is, the use of military force to acquire territory or other benefits from another State. Actually the term "war" is not used in Article 2(4). It had been used in the League of Nations Covenant and the Kellogg–Briand Pact of 1928, but it had become evident in the 1930s that States engaged in hostilities without declaring war or calling it war. The term "force" was chosen as a more factual and wider word to embrace military action.

"Force" has its own ambiguities. It is sometimes used in a wide sense to embrace all types of coercion: economic, political and psychological as well as physical. Governments in the United Nations have from time to time sought to give the prohibition in Article 2(4) the wider meaning particularly to include economic measures that were said to be coercive. Although support was expressed by a great many states in the Third World for this wider notion, it was strongly resisted by the Western States. * * *

Even limited to armed force, the term raises questions of interpretation. Some center on the notion of "indirect" force. Does a State indirectly employ force when it allows its territory to be used by troops fighting in another country? Does a State use force when it provides arms to insurgents or to one side in a war? Does troop training as expert advice amount to indirect force? These questions have tended to be treated under the rubric of "intervention", a concept which has often been dealt with independently of Article 2(4) and defined as dictatorial interference by a State in the affairs of another State. However, Article 2(4) remains the most explicit Charter rule against intervention through armed force, indirect and direct, and it is pertinent to consider such actions as falling within the scope of the prohibition. * * *

* * *

A * * * basic question of interpretation is presented by the peculiar structure of the article. It is generally presumed that the prohibition was intended to preclude all use of force except that allowed as self-defence or authorized by the Security Council under Chapter VII. Yet the article is not drafted that way. The last 23 words contain qualifications. The article requires States to refrain from force or threat of force when that is "against the territorial integrity or political independence of any State" or "inconsistent with the purposes of the United Nations". If these words are not redundant, they must qualify that all-inclusive prohibition against force. Just how far they do qualify the prohibition is difficult to determine from a textual analysis alone.

The problem of interpretation has arisen in regard to two types of justification for the use of force. One such justification concerns the use of force solely to vindicate or secure a legal right. Thus it has been claimed that a State is allowed to use force to secure its lawful passage through waters of an international strait or to compel compliance with an arbitral or judicial award. One may extend this to other cases where a State considers that its rights have been violated. The textual argument based on the qualifying clause of Article 2(4) is that such force is not directed against the territorial integrity or political independence of the target state nor is it inconsistent with United Nations purposes. In its simplest form, it is the argument that force for a benign end does not fall within the qualifying language of Article 2(4). The argument, if accepted, would go a long way to cut down on the scope of Article 2(4). * * *

One answer to this argument is that the Charter itself requires that disputes be settled by peaceful means (Article 2, para. 3) and that the first declared purpose of the Charter is to remove threats to the peace and to suppress breaches of the peace. Consequently any use of force in international relations would be inconsistent with a Charter purpose. The only exceptions would be self-defense under Article 51 and military enforcement measures under Chapter VII.

A second answer is that any coercive incursion of armed troops into a foreign State without its consent impairs that State's territorial integrity, and any use of force to coerce a State to adopt a particular policy or action must be considered as an impairment of that State's political independence. On these premises it does not matter that the coercive action may have only a short-term effect nor does it matter that the end sought by the use of force is consistent with a stated purpose of the Charter. As long as the act of force involves a non-consensual use of a State's territory or compels a State to take a decision it would not otherwise take, Article 2(4) has been violated.

This position has been taken by the great majority of States and by most international lawyers. It finds support in the two decisions of the International Court of Justice concerned with the legality of the use of force[: *The Corfu Channel* case and the *Nicaragua* case].

Notes

1. Article 2(3) provides: "All Members shall settle their international disputes by peaceful means in such a manner that international peace and security, and justice, are not endangered." This is also a legal undertaking, but in practice it has been subordinated to Article 2(4). As long as a state does not resort to force, there has been no disposition to find a violation of law in failure to settle disputes peacefully, as by leaving them unsettled. Compare Chapter 11, pp. 821–822.

2. Unlike earlier efforts to outlaw "war" or "aggression," Article 2(4) does not mention either term. The framers avoided them because these terms lend themselves to circumvention. There could be hostilities without a declared war, and uses of force that did not acquire the character of war. Aggression had long resisted definition, and who was the aggressor could be falsified and might not

always be easy to determine. The framers also sought to outlaw even war as a "duel" by mutual consent, when neither side could properly be seen as aggressor.

The Charter was intended to outlaw war as well as all lesser uses of force, but the language used was not without ambiguity. Is only military force forbidden or does the prohibition include the use of "economic" force and other coercive measures? Is the threat of force forbidden only if a threat is expressed or clearly implied, or is it forbidden also to create threatening situations, as when one state builds up armed forces and armaments that could threaten another? Does the prohibition of the threat or use of force against the territorial integrity of another state forbid only force designed permanently to deprive another state of any part of its territory or does it also forbid any forcible invasion of another's territory however temporary? Does the prohibition of force against the "political independence" of another state forbid only force designed to end the latter's independence and render it a "puppet," or does it also bar force designed to coerce a state to act against its will, even once, in any circumstances? Is force forbidden even if its purpose is humanitarian, to save human lives, or to help a people achieve "self-determination?" Is the use of force permissible to install a legitimate, democratic government? Does Article 2(4) forbid a state to give military support to insurgents? to the incumbent government battling insurgents? to either side in a civil war? The relation of the prohibition in Article 2(4) to the right of self-defense (Article 51) is considered at p. 955 infra.

For a discussion of the meaning of Article 2(4), including many of the issues addressed in the following pages, see Schachter, The Right of States to Use Armed Force, 82 Mich. L.Rev. 1620 (1984). Schachter concludes (at 1633):

> Admittedly, the article does not provide clear and precise answers to all the questions raised. Concepts such as "force," "threat of force" or "political independence" embrace a wide range of possible meanings. Their application to diverse circumstances involves choices as to these meanings and assessments of the behavior and intentions of various actors. Differences of opinion are often likely even among "disinterested" observers; they are even more likely among those involved or interested. But such divergences are not significantly different from those that arise with respect to almost all general legal principles.
>
> The foregoing analysis shows that article 2(4) has a reasonably clear core meaning. That core meaning has been spelled out in interpretive documents such as the Declaration of Principles of International Law, adopted unanimously by the General Assembly in 1970. The International Court and the writings of scholars reflect the wide area of agreement on its meaning. It is therefore unwarranted to suggest that article 2(4) lacks the determinate content necessary to enable it to function as a legal rule of restraint.

On the modern prohibition of the use of force, see Law and Force in the New International Order (Damrosch & Scheffer, eds. 1991); Henkin, The Use of Force: Law and U.S. Policy, in Right v. Might: International Law and the Use of Force 37–69 (2nd ed. 1991); Walzer, Just and Unjust Wars (2d ed. 1992); Schachter, In Defense of International Rules on the Use of Force, 53 U.Chi. L.Rev. 113 (1986); Hoffmann, International Law and the Control of Force, in The Relevance of International Law 3466 (Deutsch & Hoffmann, eds., 1971); Falk, Legal Order in a Violent World (1968); Brownlie, International Law and the Use of Force by States (1963); McDougal & Feliciano, Law and Minimum World Public Order (1961); Stone, Legal Controls of International Conflict (1959).

3. During the drafting of Article 2(4), Brazil proposed including a prohibition against the use of "economic measures" against a state. See 6 Docs. of the U.N. Conf. on Int'l Org. 335. The proposal was rejected, but it is not clear whether the rejection reflected a belief that economic aggression was not included within the term "force" or whether "force" was a broad enough term to cover it without specific mention. Goodrich, Hambro and Simons state:

> It seems reasonable to conclude that while various forms of economic and political coercion may be treated as threats to the peace, as contrary to certain of the declared purposes and principles of the Organisation, or as violating agreements entered into or recognised principles of international law, they are not to be regarded as coming necessarily under the prohibition of Article 2(4), which is to be understood as directed against the use of armed force.

Goodrich, Hambro & Simons, Charter of the United Nations 49 (3rd ed. 1969). See p. 942 on the definition of aggression.

4. The Charter proscribes the use of force "against another state." Does it forbid also force against a non-sovereign entity? For a discussion of the issue in connection with British intervention in the Imamate of Oman, see the Verbatim Record of the Security Council, 12 SCOR (783d mtg) at 7, S/PV 783 (20 August 1957).

5. The Charter does not purport to make Article 2(4) binding on nonmember states, but Article 2(6) provides: "The Organization shall ensure that states which are not Members of the United Nations act in accordance with these Principles so far as may be necessary for the maintenance of peace and security." It is commonly accepted that in substance Article 2(4) has become a principle of customary law binding on all states, and has acquired the character of *jus cogens*. See Restatement (Third) § 102, Comment *k* and Reporters' Note 6. In the *Nicaragua* case, p. 955 infra, the International Court of Justice, after ruling that limitations on the Court's exercise of jurisdiction in the case precluded it from considering Nicaragua's claim under the U.N. Charter, went on to consider the claim under customary law which the Court held to be virtually identical to the law of the Charter as regards the use of force and the right of self-defense. See p. 956 below.

6. A violation of Article 2(4) is clearly a breach of international obligations to the victim of the threat or use of force. The International Court of Justice has said, moreover, that the principles of international law outlawing acts of aggression are obligations *erga omnes,* to the international community as a whole. See Barcelona Traction, Light and Power Company, Ltd., 1970 I.C.J. 3. See also Military and Paramilitary Activities in and against Nicaragua (Nicaragua v. United States) (Schwebel, J., dissenting), 1984 I.C.J. 169, 190.

For the argument that issues concerning Article 2(4) or the corresponding customary law are not justiciable before the International Court of Justice see p. 893 supra.

7. The term aggression does not appear in Article 2(4) of the Charter, but it appears in Article 1, which specifies that the purposes of the United Nations include maintenance of international peace and security, "and to that end: to take effective collective measures * * * for the suppression of acts of aggression or other breaches of the peace," as well as in Article 39, according to which the Security Council "shall determine the existence of any threat to the peace, breach of the peace, or act of aggression."

What is the relation of Article 39 to Article 2(4)? Is the Security Council's authority under Article 39 limited to situations caused by violations of Article 2(4)? See Goodrich, Hambro & Simons, Charter of the United Nations 306 (3rd ed. 1969). See further discussion of Article 39 in Section 3 at p. 1009.

DEFINING AGGRESSION

FRIEDMANN, THE CHANGING STRUCTURE OF INTERNATIONAL LAW

254–55 (1964).

* * * There is no reason to believe that the nations of the world could not theoretically agree on the concepts of "invasion," "armed attacks" or "blockade." Differences are primarily ones of objectives; they are essentially of a political and ideological, not of a logical, character. * * *

Basic disagreements can be reflected either in definitions so vague and ambiguous as to give effective liberty of action, or in a reluctance to entrust the decision to an impartial authority. The unwillingness of the nations, up to date, to entrust full authority over war and peace to the United Nations or to any international body, may be attributed to three major factors: (a) the continuing struggle between the conflicting demands of national sovereignty and international order, expressed in the claims and limitations of the national right of self-defence; (b) the development of means of destruction so swift and devastating that the traditional time lag between the development of an armed attack and the organisation of defence has become largely obsolete; (c) the enormously increased importance of political and ideological warfare, which has created new forms of "indirect" aggression, not amenable to the established criteria and definitions of aggression.

Note

At the San Francisco Conference, and for many years thereafter, the United States opposed the elaboration of a definition of aggression. President Truman summarized the United States position in his annual report to Congress, 1950:

> At the San Francisco Conference on International Organization (1945) there was a movement to insert a definition of aggression in the United Nations Charter. The United States opposed this proposal. It took the position that a definition of aggression cannot be so comprehensive as to include all cases of aggression and cannot take into account the various circumstances which might enter into the determination of aggression in a particular case. Any definition of aggression is a trap for the innocent and an invitation to the guilty. The United States position prevailed at San Francisco, and the Charter adopted a system whereby the appropriate U.N. organ, in the first instance the Security Council, would determine on the basis of the facts of a particular case whether aggression has taken place.

5 Whiteman, Digest of International Law 740 (1965).

On October 3, 1952, the Secretary–General, acting in compliance with G.A.Res. 599, submitted a comprehensive report on the question of defining aggression. U.N. Doc. A/2211. In 1967, the General Assembly decided to expedite the efforts to define aggression, and established a Special Committee on the

Question of Defining Aggression. See G.A.Res. 2330. The Committee finally adopted a definition by consensus in 1974 and recommended it for adoption by the General Assembly. See excerpts below (and full text in Documents Supplement):

RESOLUTION ON THE DEFINITION OF AGGRESSION

G.A.Res. 3314(XXIX) (1974), G.A.O.R. 29th Sess., Supp. 31, at 42 (footnotes omitted).

The General Assembly,

* * *

1. Approves the Definition of Aggression, the text of which is annexed to the present resolution;

* * *

3. Calls upon all States to refrain from all acts of aggression and other uses of force contrary to the Charter of the United Nations and the Declaration on Principles of International Law concerning Friendly Relations and Co-operation among States in accordance with the Charter of the United Nations [G.A.Res. 2625, 25 GAOR Supp. 28 (A/8028) at 121 (1970)];

4. Calls the attention of the Security Council to the Definition of Aggression, as set out below, and recommends that it should, as appropriate, take account of that Definition as guidance in determining, in accordance with the Charter, the existence of an act of aggression.

ANNEX

DEFINITION OF AGGRESSION

The General Assembly,

* * *

Recalling that the Security Council, in accordance with Article 39 of the Charter of the United Nations, shall determine the existence of any threat to the peace, breach of the peace or act of aggression and shall make recommendations, or decide what measures shall be taken in accordance with Articles 41 and 42, to maintain or restore international peace and security,

* * *

Believing that, although the question whether an act of aggression has been committed must be considered in the light of all the circumstances of each particular case, it is nevertheless desirable to formulate basic principles as guidance for such determination,

Adopts the following Definition of Aggression:

Article 1

Aggression is the use of armed force by a State against the sovereignty, territorial integrity or political independence of another State, or in any other manner inconsistent with the Charter of the United Nations, as set out in this Definition.

Explanatory note: In this Definition the term "State:"

(a) Is used without prejudice to questions of recognition or to whether a State is a Member of the United Nations;

(b) Includes the concept of a "group of States" where appropriate.

Article 2

The first use of armed force by a State in contravention of the Charter shall constitute *prima facie* evidence of an act of aggression although the Security Council may, in conformity with the Charter, conclude that a determination that an act of aggression has been committed would not be justified in the light of other relevant circumstances, including the fact that the acts concerned or their consequences are not of sufficient gravity.

Article 3

Any of the following acts, regardless of a declaration of war, shall, subject to and in accordance with the provisions of article 2, qualify as an act of aggression:

(a) The invasion or attack by the armed forces of a State of the territory of another State, or any military occupation, however temporary, resulting from such invasion or attack, or any annexation by the use of force of the territory of another State or part thereof;

(b) Bombardment by the armed forces of a State against the territory of another State or the use of any weapons by a State against the territory of another State;

(c) The blockade of the ports or coasts of a State by the armed forces of another State;

(d) An attack by the armed forces of a State on the land, sea or air forces, marine and air fleets of another State;

(e) The use of armed forces of one State which are within the territory of another State with the agreement of the receiving State, in contravention of the conditions provided for in the agreement or any extension of their presence in such territory beyond the termination of the agreement;

(f) The action of a State in allowing its territory, which it has placed at the disposal of another State, to be used by that other State for perpetrating an act of aggression against a third State;

(g) The sending by or on behalf of a State of armed bands, groups, irregulars or mercenaries, which carry out acts of armed force against another State of such gravity as to amount to the acts listed above, or its substantial involvement therein.

Article 4

The acts enumerated above are not exhaustive and the Security Council may determine that other acts constitute aggression under the provisions of the Charter.

Article 5

1. No consideration of whatever nature, whether political, economic, military or otherwise, may serve as a justification for aggression.

2. A war of aggression is a crime against international peace. Aggression gives rise to international responsibility.

3. No territorial acquisition or special advantage resulting from aggression is or shall be recognized as lawful.

Article 6

Nothing in this Definition shall be construed as in any way enlarging or diminishing the scope of the Charter, including its provisions concerning cases in which the use of force is lawful.

Article 7

Nothing in this Definition, and in particular article 3, could in any way prejudice the right of self-determination, freedom and independence, as derived from the Charter, of peoples forcibly deprived of that right and referred to in the Declaration on Principles of International Law concerning Friendly Relations and Co-operation among States in accordance with the Charter of the United Nations, particularly peoples under colonial and racist régimes or other forms of alien domination; nor the right of these peoples to struggle to that end and to seek and receive support, in accordance with the principles of the Charter and in conformity with the above-mentioned Declaration.

Article 8

In their interpretation and application the above provisions are interrelated and each provision should be construed in the context of the other provisions.

Notes

1. An explanatory note to Article 1 was included in the text of the Resolution. Explanatory notes to Articles 3 and 5 were included in the Report of the Special Committee on the Question of Defining Aggression, 29 GAOR, Supp. 19 (A/9619 and Corr. 1) at 5 (1974).

2. The United States acquiesced in the adoption of this definition. For its comments on the definition and on each of its articles, see the statement of Robert Rosenstock, the U.S. Representative to the Special Committee, 70 Dep't State Bull. 498 (1974). Have the fears the United States previously expressed in opposition to defining aggression been realized? Has the U.N. definition served any useful purpose?

3. There were two approaches to the definition of aggression during the years of debate in the United Nations. Some favored an "enumerative" definition that would include a list of the acts that constitute aggression; others favored a general definition similar to that of Article 2(4) of the Charter. The 1974 Resolution contains elements of both. Article 1 follows the general definition of the Charter, and limits the definition of aggression to armed force, despite the suggestion by a number of states that aggression includes other forms of hostile acts. Article 3, however, sets out a number of acts that constitute aggression and Article 4 indicates that the list is not exhaustive. The threat of force was not included in Article 1, and "[t]he economic, ideological and other modes of aggression were carefully considered * * * but the result was an interpretation that they did not fall within the term 'aggression' as it had been used in the Charter." Broms, The Definition of Aggression, 154 Rec. des Cours 299, 386 (1977–1). The 1974 Resolution has had mixed reviews on the ground that it

glosses over or avoids many disputed issues. See generally, Nyiri, The United Nations Search for a Definition of Aggression (1989); Stone, Conflict Through Consensus: UN Approaches to Aggression (1977); Ferencz, Defining Aggression, 2 vols. (1975); see also Bennett, A Linguistic Critique of the Definition of Aggression, 31 Germ.Y.B.Int'l L. 481 (1988); Brown–John, The 1974 Definition of Aggression: A Query, 15 Can.Y.B.Int'l L. 301 (1977); Garvey, The U.N. Definition of "Aggression": Law and Illusion in the Context of Collective Security, 17 Va.J.Int'l L. 177 (1977); Stone, Hopes and Loopholes in the 1974 Definition of Aggression, 71 A.J.I.L. 224 (1977). See also Ferencz, Can Aggression be Deterred by Law?, 11 Pace Int'l L. Rev. 301, 304 (1999).

4. The 1952 Report on the Question of Defining Aggression (cited p. 942) contained a suggestion that "unilateral action to deprive a State of the economic resources derived from the fair practice of international trade, or to endanger its economy" may be an act of aggression. U.N.Doc. A/2211 at 58. The concept of economic aggression was criticized by others as "liable to extend the concept of aggression almost indefinitely." Id. Economic coercion was not included in the 1974 Definition of Aggression but several resolutions have denounced such coercion as subverting sovereign rights. See, e.g., Article 32 of the Charter of Economic Rights and Duties of States, G.A.Res. 3281 (XXIX), reprinted in 14 I.L.M. 251 (1975); Declaration of the Principles of International Law Concerning Friendly Relations and Co-operation among States, G.A.Res. 2625 (XXV); Declaration on the Inadmissibility of Intervention in Domestic Affairs of States and the Protection of their Independence and Sovereignty, G.A.Res. 2131 (XX). Compare Article 16 of the Charter of the Organization of American States: "No State may use or encourage the use of coercive measures of an economic or political character in order to force the sovereign will of another State and obtain from it advantages of any kind." 119 U.N.T.S. 3, T.I.A.S. No. 2361, 2 U.S.T. 2394 (1948). For a defense of economic measures used for political purposes in the context of the Arab–Israeli dispute, see Shihata, Destination Embargo of Arab Oil: Its Legality under International Law, 68 A.J.I.L. 591 (1974). See generally, The Arab Oil Weapon (Paust & Blaustein, eds. 1977); Economic Coercion and the New International Economic Order (Lillich, ed. 1976); Almond, An Assessment of Economic Warfare: Developments from the Persian Gulf, 31 Va.J.Int'l L. 645 (1991); Edwards, The Iraqi Oil "Weapon" in the 1991 Gulf War: A Law of Armed Conflict Analysis, 40 Naval L.Rev. 105 (1992). On the use of economic force under Article 2(4) of the Charter, see p. [ ] supra.

5. On agreements procured by the use or threat of force, see Article 52 of the 1969 Vienna Convention on the Law of Treaties, discussed in Chapter 7 at p. 528.

6. On efforts to formulate a definition of aggression for applicability in criminal prosecutions against individuals, see Chapter 15 at p. 1370.

7. Under the above definition, would any first attack in strength across an international boundary constitute a *prima facie* case of aggression? Compare the difficulties in developing a workable and meaningful test of the "initiator" of war in political science and other disciplines. See Damrosch, Use of Force and Constitutionalism, 36 Colum. J. Transnat. L. 449, 460–465 (1997).

INDIRECT AGGRESSION

Charges of "indirect aggression" were not uncommon during the ideological conflict of the Cold War, and to some extent during the years of resistance to colonialism and of external support for "liberation movements." In the changed world order after the Cold War, instances of indirect aggression may be less frequent, but are not excluded.

FRIEDMANN, THE CHANGING STRUCTURE OF INTERNATIONAL LAW

262 (1964).

It is the increasingly numerous and important forms of attack upon the integrity of a state by other than the traditional means of military attack, usually styled "indirect" or "ideological" aggression, that give rise to problems of altogether different dimensions and that affect some of the foundations of traditional international law. These attacks range from many types of ideological and political propaganda and psychological warfare, by radio, by aerial leaflets, etc., to the organisation of subversive, political movements inside another country, the systematic infiltration of political agents, and the systematic economic strangulation of a regime by comprehensive trade boycott.

The legal problems arising from these important but often highly elusive forms of interference with the integrity of a state are further complicated by the fact that they are often intertwined with civil strife and the ensuing question whether assistance to one or both sides in a civil conflict, ranging from military assistance to the supply of arms, political and economic help, is permitted or prohibited by international law. In modern civil wars, military assistance to one or the other side may often be a means of deliberately supporting one political or social order as against another.

Notes

1. Brownlie writes:

> Charges of "aggression" are frequently based on allegations of military aid to, and control over, rebels in a civil war. If rebels are effectively supported *and controlled* by another state that state is responsible for a "use of force" as a consequence of the agency. Thus aid to rebels by foreign states has been held by the General Assembly to be inconsistent with the principles of the United Nations Charter, with implicit reference to Article 2, paragraphs 3 and 4. However, in cases in which aid is given but there is no agency established, and there is no exercise of control over the rebels by the foreign government, it is very doubtful if it is correct to describe the responsibility of that government in terms of a use of force or armed attack. Unfortunately the resolutions referred to above and the other relevant materials do not draw this distinction. The illegality of aid to rebel groups has been established in a variety of ways. It has been described as "intervention in the internal affairs of a state" and as "indirect aggression." In resolution 380(V) of 17 November 1950, the General Assembly included "fomenting civil strife" in its strong condemnation of aggression.

Brownlie, International Law and the Use of Force 370 (1963).

2. The 1952 Report of the Secretary–General on the Question of Defining Aggression (U.N.Doc. A/2211, Oct. 3, 1952) included extended discussion of "indirect aggression." See Section VII at 55. "The characteristic of indirect aggression appears to be that the aggressor state, without itself committing hostile

acts as a State, operates through third parties who are either foreigners or nationals seemingly acting on their own initiative. * * * The concept of indirect aggression has been construed to include certain hostile acts or certain forms of complicity in hostilities in progress." Id. at 56. The report also considered "cases of indirect aggression which do not constitute acts of participation in hostilities in progress, but which are designed to prepare such acts, to undermine a country's power of resistance, or to bring about a change in its political or social system." Id. at 55. Among examples proposed by spokesmen of various countries were: intervention in another state's internal or foreign affairs; violation of the political integrity of a country by subversive action; incitement to civil war; maintenance of a fifth column; ideological aggression and propaganda. Id. at 55–56.

The term "indirect aggression" is not included in the definition of aggression adopted by the General Assembly, but some elements in the definition may be deemed indirect, e.g., Art. 3(g), p. 944 supra. Note that Article 4 states that the acts enumerated in Article 3 are not exhaustive.

3. In Nicaragua v. United States, p. 955 below, 1986 I.C.J. 14 at 106–110, the International Court of Justice considered whether U.S. assistance to rebels seeking to overthrow the government of Nicaragua violated the rules of customary international law which it found to be essentially parallel to Article 2(4). Although the Court concluded that the U.S. actions were indeed violations of the prohibitions on use of force and intervention, it did not find a basis for attributing all the actions of the rebels to the U.S. government, since Nicaragua had not proved that the United States directly and effectively controlled their actions.

Some years later, the International Criminal Tribunal for the Former Yugoslavia expressed its disagreement with the *Nicaragua* court's "effective control" test and applied a different (lower) standard for attributing the conduct of a paramilitary group to a foreign government that had given it substantial support. Prosecutor v. Tadic, No IT–94–1–A, 38 I.L.M. 1518 (Judgment on Appeal from Conviction, July 15, 1999). However, the I.C.T.Y. was not considering "aggression" (or armed attack or intervention) but rather the different question of whether the conflict in Bosnia–Herzegovina was an "international" or "non-international" conflict for purposes of prosecution of an individual for war crimes. See p. 1062.

THREAT OF FORCE

Professor Schachter writes:

> What is meant by a "threat of force" has received rather less consideration [than what is meant by "the use of force"]. Clearly a threat to use military action to coerce a State to make concessions is forbidden. But in many situations the deployment of military forces or missiles has unstated aims and its effect is equivocal. However, the preponderance of military strength in some States and their political relations with potential target States may justifiably lead to an inference of a threat of force against the political independence of the target State. An examination of the particular circumstances is necessary to reach that conclusion, but the applicability of Article 2(4) in principle can hardly be denied. Curiously, it has not been invoked much as an explicit prohibition of such implied threats. The explanation may lie in the subtleties of power relations and the difficulty of demonstrating coercive intent. Or perhaps more realis-

tically, it may be a manifestation of the general recognition and tolerance of disparities of power and their effect in maintaining dominant and subordinate relationships between unequal States. However, such toleration, wide as it may be, is not without limits. A blatant and direct threat of force to compel another State to yield territory or make substantial political concessions (not required by law) would have to be seen as illegal under Article 2(4), if the words "threat of force" are to have any meaning.

Schachter, International Law in Theory and Practice 111 (1991) (footnotes omitted). See also Sadurska, Threats of Force, 82 A.J.I.L. 239 (1988); Report of the U.N. Secretary–General on the Question of Defining Aggression, U.N. Doc. A/2211 at 52 (Oct. 3, 1952), paras. 367–374.

Notes

1. In the Advisory Opinion on the Legality of the Threat or Use of Nuclear Weapons, 1996 I.C.J. 226, the Court addressed the "threat" aspect as follows:

> 47. In order to lessen or eliminate the risk of unlawful attack, States sometimes signal that they possess certain weapons to use in self-defence against any State violating their territorial integrity or political independence. Whether a signalled intention to use force if certain events occur is or is not a "threat" within Article 2, paragraph 4, of the Charter depends upon various factors. If the envisaged use of force is itself unlawful, the stated readiness to use it would be a threat prohibited under Article 2, paragraph 4. Thus it would be illegal for a State to threaten force to secure territory from another State, or to cause it to follow or not follow certain political or economic paths. The notions of "threat" and "use" of force under Article 2, paragraph 4, of the Charter stand together in the sense that if the use of force itself in a given case is illegal—for whatever reason–the threat to use such force will likewise be illegal. In short, if it is to be lawful, the declared readiness of a State to use force must be a use of force that is in conformity with the Charter. For the rest, no State–whether or not it defended the policy of deterrence–suggested to the Court that it would be lawful to threaten to use force if the use of force contemplated would be illegal.
>
> 48. Some States put forward the argument that possession of nuclear weapons is itself an unlawful threat to use force. Possession of nuclear weapons may indeed justify an inference of preparedness to use them. In order to be effective, the policy of deterrence, by which those States possessing or under the umbrella of nuclear weapons seek to discourage military aggression by demonstrating that it will serve no purpose, necessitates that the intention to use nuclear weapons be credible. Whether this is a "threat" contrary to Article 2, paragraph 4, depends upon whether the particular use of force envisaged would be directed against the territorial integrity or political independence of a State, or against the Purposes of the United Nations, or whether, in the event that it were intended as a means of defence, it would necessarily violate the principles of necessity and proportionality. In any of these circumstances the use of force, and the threat to use it, would be unlawful under the law of the Charter.

2. One criticism of the 1999 NATO intervention in Kosovo was that the United States and other NATO powers effectively gave the Yugoslav leadership an ultimatum that military force would be used against the Federal Republic of

Yugoslavia unless the negotiators agreed without delay to the terms of a peace settlement offered at Rambouillet, France, in February 1999. Would such "threat diplomacy" constitute a prohibited "threat of force" under Article 2(4)? See discussion by the Independent International Commission on Kosovo in its Kosovo Report (2000), excerpted at p. 1001 below. For more on the Kosovo intervention, see pp. 997–1003.

THREAT OR USE OF LIMITED FORCE

THE CUBAN MISSILE CRISIS, 1962

WHITEMAN, DIGEST OF INTERNATIONAL LAW

Vol. 4, 523–24 (1965).

On the evening of October 22, 1962, President John F. Kennedy announced that "This Government, as promised, has maintained the closest surveillance of the Soviet military buildup on the island of Cuba. Within the past week unmistakeable evidence has established the fact that a series of offensive missile sites is now in preparation on that imprisoned island." He added that "This urgent transformation of Cuba into an important strategic base—by the presence of these large, long-range, and clearly offensive weapons of sudden mass destruction—constitutes an explicit threat to the peace and security of all the Americas, in flagrant and deliberate defiance of the Rio Pact of 1947, the traditions of this nation and hemisphere, the Joint Resolution of the 87th Congress, the Charter of the United Nations, and my own public warnings to the Soviets on September 4 and 13 [1962]." On the following day, October 23, the Council of the Organization of American States, meeting as the Provisional Organ of Consultation, called for "the immediate dismantling and withdrawal from Cuba of all missiles and other weapons with any offensive capability" and recommended that "the member states, in accordance with Articles 6 and 8 of the Inter–American Treaty of Reciprocal Assistance [1947], take all measures, individually and collectively, including the use of armed force, which they may deem necessary to ensure that the Government of Cuba cannot continue to receive supplies which may threaten the peace and security of the Continent and to prevent the missiles in Cuba with offensive capability from ever becoming an active threat to the peace and security of the Continent."

On that same day—October 23, 1962—President Kennedy by Proclamation ordered the interdiction by U.S. forces of the delivery of offensive weapons to Cuba. The substantive portions of the Proclamation provided that in accordance with the resolution of the Organ of Consultation of the American Republics of October 23, 1962, "and to defend the security of the United States," the forces under the President's command were ordered, beginning at 2 p.m. Greenwich time October 24, 1962, to interdict the delivery of offensive weapons and associated matériel to Cuba. To enforce this order, the Secretary of Defense was ordered to take appropriate measures to prevent the delivery of the prohibited matériel to Cuba, "employing the land, sea and air forces of the United States in cooperation with any forces that may be made available by other American States." The Secretary of Defense was authorized to make designations "within a reasonable distance of Cuba, of prohibited or restricted zones and of prescribed routes." Further, the Proclamation specified:

> Any vessel or craft, which may be proceeding toward Cuba may be intercepted and may be directed to identify itself, its cargo, equipment and stores and its ports of call, to stop, to lie to, to submit to visit and search, or to proceed as directed. Any vessel or craft which fails or refuses to respond to or comply with directions shall be subject to being taken into custody. Any vessel or craft which it is believed is en route to Cuba and may be carrying prohibited matériel or may itself constitute such matériel shall, wherever possible, be directed to proceed to another destination of its own choice and shall be taken into custody if it fails or refuses to obey such directions. All vessels or craft taken into custody shall be sent into a port of the United States for appropriate disposition.
>
> In carrying out this order, force shall not be used except in case of failure or refusal to comply with directions, or with regulations or directives of the Secretary of Defense, issued hereunder, after reasonable efforts have been made to communicate them to the vessel or craft, or in case of self-defense. In any case, force shall be used only to the extent necessary.

Proclamation No. 3504, 47 Dep't State Bull. 717 (1962), 27 Fed. Reg. 10401 (1962).

Note

Was the U.S. action to impose a quarantine of Cuba a threat or use of force? against the territorial integrity or political independence of Cuba? of the Soviet Union? of states whose ships were prevented from going to Cuba? Was it "in any other manner inconsistent with the purposes of the United Nations?" See MacChesney, Some Comments on the "Quarantine" of Cuba, 57 A.J.I.L. 592, 596 (1963); Henkin, The UN and Its Supporters, 78 Pol. Sci. Q. 504, 527, 528 (1963). But see Wright, The Cuban Quarantine, 57 A.J.I.L. 546 (1963). Wright rejected the positions that the U.S. action was a "pacific blockade" under traditional international law, that it was permissible in self-defense under Article 51 (quoted below), and that it was justified under the authority of the Organization of American States, as officially argued by the State Department. (Note that the United States did not invoke a self-defense justification for the quarantine, but rather based its position on the O.A.S. authorization. See p. 1047.)

For the suggestion that international law was not "relevant" in the Cuban Missile Crisis, see Dean Acheson's statement at p. 39 supra. For defense of its relevance, see Henkin, How Nations Behave 279–302 (2d ed. 1979); Chayes, The Cuban Missile Crisis: International Crises and the Role of Law (1974, 1987).

INTERVENTION

The U.N. Charter does not speak to intervention by states (as distinguished from intervention by the U.N. "in matters which are essentially within the domestic jurisdiction of any state," which is precluded by Article 2(7)). Insofar as intervention is used strictly to refer to "dictatorial interference" by use or threat of force, p. 948 supra, it is to be considered in the light of the prohibition of Article 2(4). Other international instruments have inveighed against intervention, and several attempts have been made to define it with respect to nonforcible as well as forcible techniques (e.g., "economic coercion"). See, e.g., Declaration on the Inadmissibility of Intervention into the Domestic Affairs, of States, G.A. Res. 2131 (XX) (1965); Declaration on Principles of International Law Concerning Friendly Relations and Co-operation Among States in Accordance with the Charter of the United Nations, G.A. Res. 2625 (XXV) (1970) (Friendly Relations Declaration, reprinted in Documents Supplement). See generally Damrosch, Politics Across Borders: Nonintervention and Nonforcible Influence Over Domestic Affairs, 83 A.J.I.L. 1 (1989).

Intervention in civil conflicts and intervention for asserted "humanitarian" purposes will be addressed in Section 2 at pp. 980–1003 below.

INTERVENTION BY CONSENT

SCHACHTER, THE RIGHT OF STATES TO USE ARMED FORCE

82 Mich. L.Rev. 1620, 1644–45 (1984) (footnotes omitted).

A separate comment is called for by the kind of case presented by the request of the Governor–General of Grenada for military intervention by the United States and neighboring states [in 1983]. That request was premised on the "vacuum of authority" resulting from an attempted coup d'état and a danger of foreign intervention. A factual question was raised as to whether the Governor–General made his request prior to the intervention or whether it was "concocted" after the invasion had been agreed upon and set in motion. Another question was raised as to whether the Governor–General had the constitutional authority to make such a request. On both these points, there was reason to doubt that the Governor–General's "request" constituted an adequate legal justification for the armed intervention. However, apart from these questions specifically related to Grenada, there is the broader issue of principle concerning intervention on invitation of the government. * * * [I]n the absence of a civil war, recognized governments have a right to receive external military assistance and outside states are free to furnish such aid. But a problem arises if such outside military force is used to impose restrictions on the "political independence" of the country, as, for example, by limiting the choice of the population in regard to the composition of the government or the policies it should follow. In such cases, we would conclude that the foreign armies, though invited by the government, are using military force to curtail the political independence of the state, and therefore it is an action that contravenes article 2(4). A different conclusion may be reached when a foreign force is invited by the government to help put down an attempted coup or to assist in restoring law and order. This would not violate article 2(4). Recent examples include French and British military support of African governments facing internal disorder. The line between the two situations may not always be easy to draw. An initial intervention of a limited character may evolve into a more protracted use of foreign forces to repress internal democracy and political expression. There is good reason therefore to place a heavy burden on any foreign government which intervenes with armed forces even at the invitation of the constitutional authority to demonstrate convincingly that its use of force has not infringed the right of the people to determine their political system and the composition of their government. It cannot be assumed that governments will, as a rule, invite foreign interventions that leave the people entirely free to make their own political determinations, though on occasion this may be the case.

Notes

1. The U.S. action in Grenada implicated not only the issue of whether an appropriate Grenadan authority had consented to the intervention, but also whether military intervention might have been justified to protect U.S. nationals who were asserted to be in danger there. See p. 974 below. A similar combination of arguments was invoked concerning the U.S. intervention in Panama a few years later. Among the justifications claimed by the United States for the invasion of Panama in 1989, President Bush included the following:

> In the early morning of December 20, 1989, the democratically elected Panamanian leadership announced the formation of a government, assumed power in a formal swearing-in ceremony, and welcomed the assistance of the U.S. Armed Forces in removing the illegitimate Noriega regime.

Communication from the President of the United States Transmitting a Report on the Development Concerning the Deployment of United States Forces to Panama on December 20, 1989, House Doc. 101–127, 101st Cong., 2d Sess., at 1 (1990). In summing up the justifications for the invasion the President repeated that the deployment of U.S. forces "was welcomed by the democratically elected government of Panama." Id. at 2. See the President's letter to Congress, p. 967 infra.

It appears that several hours before the invasion began, a U.S. representative in Panama informed Guillermo Endara, who had apparently been the majority's choice in a recent election, that the invasion was about to take place. Endara was then taken to a U.S. military base in the Panama Canal Zone where the oath of office was administered to him. The United States did not claim that Endara invited the invasion or was asked to consent to it, or that if he had not done so the invasion would not have taken place. Did Endara's "welcome" of the invasion constitute an invitation by a government, justifying it under international law? Was it justified as a use of force to give effect to the wishes of the Panamanian people? See the discussion of the invasion of Panama, p. 966 infra. See also Hargrove, Intervention by Invitation and the Politics of the New World Order; Mullerson, Intervention by Invitation; Wedgwood, Commentary on Intervention by Invitation; and Ferencz, Commentary on What International Law Demands and How States Respond, all in Law and Force in the New International Order 111–185 (Damrosch & Scheffer, eds. 1991).

2. In the Nicaragua Case (Merits), the International Court of Justice said:

> As the Court has stated, the principle of non-intervention derives from customary international law. It would certainly lose its effectiveness as a principle of law if intervention were to be justified by a mere request for assistance made by an opposition group in another State—supposing such a request to have actually been made by an opposition to the régime in Nicaragua in this instance. Indeed, it is difficult to see what would remain of the principle of non-intervention in international law if intervention, which is already allowable at the request of the government of a State, were also to be allowed at the request of the opposition. This would permit any State to intervene at any moment in the internal affairs of another State, whether at

> the request of the government or at the request of its opposition. Such a situation does not in the Court's view correspond to the present state of international law.

Military and Paramilitary Activities in and Against Nicaragua (Nicaragua v. United States), 1986 I.C.J. 14, 126.

3. If an incumbent government has the right under international law to invite foreign troops into the country to help repel external or internal threats (compare pp. 956–959 and 985–987 below), may it also consent *in advance* to foreign intervention? Could it grant an irrevocable consent to future entry of foreign troops? Consider the following examples:

a. As a condition of ratification of the Panama Canal Treaties of 1977 (which provided *inter alia* for the return to Panama of full control over the Canal as of December 31, 1999), the United States insisted on reserving the right to take necessary steps, including by means of military force, to reopen the Canal if it should ever be closed in the future. Assuming that the government of Panama did properly agree to this condition (compare Chapter 7, p. 525 on challenges to consent to treaties and treaty reservations), could such agreement authorize the United States to take actions that would otherwise violate Article 2(4)'s prohibition on use of force? Could such consent endure in perpetuity?

b. Proposals have been made for an agreement among democratic governments that each would come to the aid of any other treaty partner, with military force if necessary, to resist or reverse any forcible attempt to overthrow such a government. It has also been suggested that consent to future external intervention to protect minorities or quell ethnic strife could be an important element in bringing about settlement of intractable ethnic conflicts. If a foreign military intervention would violate Article 2(4) in the absence of effective consent, may political leaders at a given time commit the country to receive a prospective intervention upon the occurrence of specified contingencies in the future? How might such consent thereafter be rescinded? For discussion of these and related problems, see, e.g., Farer, a Paradigm of Legitimate Intervention, in Damrosch (ed.), Enforcing Restraint: Collective Intervention in Internal Conflicts 316, 332 (1993); Wippman, Treaty–Based Intervention: Who Can Say No?, 62 U. Chicago L Rev. 607 (1995).

c. Upon intervening with military force in the Republic of Cyprus in 1974 (assertedly to protect the Turkish Cypriot minority on the island in the aftermath of a Greek-instigated coup), Turkey referred to a Treaty of Guarantee concluded when Cyprus attained independence in 1960. Under the Turkish interpretation, the treaty allowed the three guarantor powers–the United Kingdom, Greece, or Turkey–to intervene in the event of developments disrupting the agreed constitutional balance between the Greek and Turkish communities in Cyprus. Many governments and scholars have rejected the Turkish position that the Treaty of Guarantee could be interpreted to authorize unilateral forcible intervention, and have also considered that prospective consent to a use of force that would otherwise violate Article 2(4) could not validly be given in international law. Should Article 2(4) be understood as precluding any form of prospective consent? See discussion in Wippman, 62 U. Chicago L. Rev. at 635–648 (1995).

d. Could a potential settlement of the Israel–Palestinian conflict include a reservation to Israel of rights to send military forces into (or in airspace over) a future Palestinian state? Would the compatibility of such a provision with Article 2(4) depend on the contingencies in which such rights might be invoked, and/or on the purposes for which such forces might be used? See below on self-defense and anticipatory self-defense.

3. *The Self-Defense Exception: Article 51*

CHARTER OF THE UNITED NATIONS

San Francisco, June 26, 1945.

ARTICLE 51

Nothing in the present Charter shall impair the inherent right of individual or collective self-defence if an armed attack occurs against a Member of the United Nations, until the Security Council has taken measures necessary to maintain international peace and security. Measures taken by Members in the exercise of this right of self-defence shall be immediately reported to the Security Council and shall not in any way affect the authority and responsibility of the Security Council under the present Charter to take at any time such action as it deems necessary in order to maintain or restore international peace and security.

MILITARY AND PARAMILITARY ACTIVITIES IN AND AGAINST NICARAGUA (NICARAGUA v. UNITED STATES OF AMERICA)

1986 I.C.J. 14, 103–123.

[In 1984 the Republic of Nicaragua brought a case charging the United States with violations of customary and treaty law by military and paramilitary activities against Nicaragua. Nicaragua accused the United States of attacks on oil pipelines, storage and port facilities, and Nicaraguan naval patrol boats; the mining of Nicaraguan ports; violation of Nicaraguan air space; as well as training, arming, equipping, financing and supplying counter-revolutionary forces (known as the *contras*) seeking to overthrow the government of Nicaragua. Nicaragua claimed that these acts constituted violations of Article 2(4) of the U.N. Charter and corresponding principles of customary law. The United States withdrew from participation in the proceedings after the Court's adverse ruling on jurisdiction (see Chapter 11, pp. 880–894), but it made known its position that Nicaragua had supplied arms and given other support from its territory to armed opposition to the Government of El Salvador, and that U.S. actions were designed to interdict that support. The United States justified its activities against Nicaragua as acts in collective self-defense of El Salvador and of other Central American states allegedly threatened by Nicaraguan subversion.

Because of reservations in the U.S. declaration accepting the compulsory jurisdiction of the Court (see Chapter 11), the Court concluded that it could not consider the Nicaraguan claims under the U.N. Charter, but that the principles as to the use of force incorporated in the Charter "correspond, in essentials, to those found in customary international law." The Court proceeded to adjudicate Nicaragua's customary law claims accordingly (in effect construing Articles 2(4) and 51 of the Charter). The Court (by twelve votes to three) decided that by the actions in question the U.S. had breached its obligations under customary law not to use force against another state, not to intervene in the affairs of another state, and not to interrupt peaceful maritime commerce, and had breached its obligations under the Treaty of Friendship, Commerce and Navigation between the two states. The Court rejected claims that the Acts were justified as being in collective self-defense with the Government of El Salvador.

In its judgment the Court said:]

195. In the case of individual self-defence, the exercise of this right is subject to the State concerned having been the victim of an armed attack. Reliance on collective self-defence of course does not remove the need for this. There appears now to be general agreement on the nature of the acts which can be treated as constituting armed attacks. In particular, it may be considered to be agreed that an armed attack must be understood as including not merely action by regular armed forces across an international border, but also "the sending by or on behalf of a State of armed bands, groups, irregulars or mercenaries, which carry out acts of armed force against another State of such gravity as to amount to" *(inter alia)* an actual armed attack conducted by regular forces, "or its substantial involvement therein". This description, contained in Article 3, paragraph (*g*), of the Definition of Aggression annexed to General Assembly resolution 3314 (XXIX), may be taken to reflect customary international law. The Court sees no reason to deny that, in customary law, the prohibition of armed attacks may apply to the sending by a State of armed bands to the territory of another State, if such an operation, because of its scale and effects, would have been classified as an armed attack rather than as a mere frontier incident had it been carried out by regular armed forces. But the Court does not believe that the concept of "armed attack" includes not only acts by armed bands where such acts occur on a significant scale but also assistance to rebels in the form of the provision of weapons or logistical or other support. Such assistance may be regarded as a threat or use of force, or amount to intervention in the internal or external affairs of other States. It is also clear that it is the State which is the victim of an armed attack which must form and declare the view that it has been so attacked. There is no rule in customary international law permitting another State to exercise the right of collective self-defence on the basis of its own assessment of the situation. Where collective self-defence is invoked, it is to be expected that the State for whose benefit this right is used will have declared itself to be the victim of an armed attack.

196. The question remains whether the lawfulness of the use of collective self-defence by the third State for the benefit of the attacked State also depends on a request addressed by that State to the third State. A provision of the Charter of the Organization of American States is here in point: and while the Court has no jurisdiction to consider that instrument as applicable to the dispute, it may examine it to ascertain what light it throws on the content of customary international law. * * *

* * *

199. At all events, the Court finds that in customary international law, whether of a general kind or that particular to the inter-American legal system, there is no rule permitting the exercise of collective self-defence in the absence of a request by the State which regards itself as the victim of an armed attack. The Court concludes that the requirement of a request by the

State which is the victim of the alleged attack is additional to the requirement that such a State should have declared itself to have been attacked.

* * *

201. To justify certain activities involving the use of force, the United States has relied solely on the exercise of its right of collective self-defence. However the Court, having regard particularly to the non-participation of the United States in the merits phase, considers that it should enquire whether customary international law, applicable to the present dispute, may contain other rules which may exclude the unlawfulness of such activities. * * * [T]he Court must enquire whether there is any justification for the activities in question, to be found not in the right of collective self-defence against an armed attack, but in the right to take counter-measures in response to conduct of Nicaragua which is not alleged to constitute an armed attack. It will examine this point in connection with an analysis of the principle of non-intervention in customary international law.

* * *

211. The Court has recalled above (paragraphs 193 to 195) that for one State to use force against another, on the ground that that State has committed a wrongful act of force against a third State, is regarded as lawful, by way of exception, only when the wrongful act provoking the response was an armed attack. Thus the lawfulness of the use of force by a State in response to a wrongful act of which it has not itself been the victim is not admitted when this wrongful act is not an armed attack. In the view of the Court, under international law in force today—whether customary international law or that of the United Nations system—States do not have a right of "collective" armed response to acts which do not constitute an "armed attack". Furthermore, the Court has to recall that the United States itself is relying on the "inherent right of self-defence" (paragraph 126 above), but apparently does not claim that any such right exists as would, in respect of intervention, operate in the same way as the right of collective self-defence in respect of an armed attack. In the discharge of its duty under Article 53 of the Statute, the Court has nevertheless had to consider whether such a right might exist; but in doing so it may take note of the absence of any such claim by the United States as an indication of *opinio juris*.

* * *

229. The Court must thus consider whether, as the Respondent claims, the acts in question of the United States are justified by the exercise of its right of collective self-defence against an armed attack. The Court must therefore establish whether the circumstances required for the exercise of this right of self-defence are present and, if so, whether the steps taken by the United States actually correspond to the requirements of international law. For the Court to conclude that the United States was lawfully exercising its right of collective self-defence, it must first find that Nicaragua engaged in an armed attack against El Salvador, Honduras or Costa Rica.

230. As regards El Salvador, the Court has found (paragraph 160 above) that it is satisfied that between July 1979 and the early months of 1981, an intermittent flow of arms was routed via the territory of Nicaragua to the

armed opposition in that country. The Court was not however satisfied that assistance has reached the Salvadorian armed opposition, on a scale of any significance, since the early months of 1981, or that the Government of Nicaragua was responsible for any flow of arms at either period. Even assuming that the supply of arms to the opposition in El Salvador could be treated as imputable to the Government of Nicaragua, to justify invocation of the right of collective self-defence in customary international law, it would have to be equated with an armed attack by Nicaragua on El Salvador. As stated above, the Court is unable to consider that, in customary international law, the provision of arms to the opposition in another State constitutes an armed attack on that State. Even at a time when the arms flow was at its peak, and again assuming the participation of the Nicaraguan Government, that would not constitute such armed attack.

231. Turning to Honduras and Costa Rica, the Court has also stated (paragraph 164 above) that it should find established that certain trans-border incursions into the territory of those two States, in 1982, 1983 and 1984, were imputable to the Government of Nicaragua. Very little information is however available to the Court as to the circumstances of these incursions or their possible motivations, which renders it difficult to decide whether they may be treated for legal purposes as amounting, singly or collectively, to an "armed attack" by Nicaragua on either or both States. The Court notes that during the Security Council debate in March/April 1984, the representative of Costa Rica made no accusation of an armed attack, emphasizing merely his country's neutrality and support for the Contadora process (S/PV.2529, pp. 13–23); the representative of Honduras however stated that "my country is the object of aggression made manifest through a number of incidents by Nicaragua against our territorial integrity and civilian population" (ibid., p. 37). There are however other considerations which justify the Court in finding that neither these incursions, nor the alleged supply of arms to the opposition in El Salvador, may be relied on as justifying the exercise of the right of collective self-defence.

232. The exercise of the right of collective self-defence presupposes that an armed attack has occurred; and it is evident that it is the victim State, being the most directly aware of that fact, which is likely to draw general attention to its plight. It is also evident that if the victim State wishes another State to come to its help in the exercise of the right of collective self-defence, it will normally make an express request to that effect. Thus in the present instance, the Court is entitled to take account, in judging the asserted justification of the exercise of collective self-defence by the United States, of the actual conduct of El Salvador, Honduras and Costa Rica at the relevant time, as indicative of a belief by the State in question that it was the victim of an armed attack by Nicaragua, and of the making of a request by the victim State to the United States for help in the exercise of collective self-defence.

233. The Court has seen no evidence that the conduct of those States was consistent with such a situation, either at the time when the United States first embarked on the activities which were allegedly justified by self-defence, or indeed for a long period subsequently. So far as El Salvador is concerned, it appears to the Court that while El Salvador did in fact officially declare itself the victim of an armed attack, and did ask for the United States to exercise its right of collective self-defence, this occurred only on a date

much later than the commencement of the United States activities which were allegedly justified by this request. The Court notes that on 3 April 1984, the representative of El Salvador before the United Nations Security Council, while complaining of the "open foreign intervention practised by Nicaragua in our internal affairs" (S/PV.2528, p. 58), refrained from stating that El Salvador had been subjected to armed attack, and made no mention of the right of collective self-defence which it had supposedly asked the United States to exercise. Nor was this mentioned when El Salvador addressed a letter to the Court in April 1984, in connection with Nicaragua's complaint against the United States. It was only in its Declaration of Intervention filed on 15 August 1984, that El Salvador referred to requests addressed at various dates to the United States for the latter to exercise its right of collective self-defence (para. XII), asserting on this occasion that it had been the victim of aggression from Nicaragua "since at least 1980". In that Declaration, El Salvador affirmed that initially it had "not wanted to present any accusation or allegation [against Nicaragua] to any of the jurisdictions to which we have a right to apply", since it sought "a solution of understanding and mutual respect" (para. III).

234. As to Honduras and Costa Rica, they also were prompted by the institution of proceedings in this case to address communications to the Court; in neither of these is there mention of armed attack or collective self-defence. As has already been noted (paragraph 231 above), Honduras in the Security Council in 1984 asserted that Nicaragua had engaged in aggression against it, but did not mention that a request had consequently been made to the United States for assistance by way of collective self-defence. On the contrary, the representative of Honduras emphasized that the matter before the Security Council "is a Central American problem, without exception, and it must be solved regionally" (S/PV.2529, p. 38), i.e., through the Contadora process. The representative of Costa Rica also made no reference to collective self-defence. Nor, it may be noted, did the representative of the United States assert during that debate that it had acted in response to requests for assistance in that context.

235. There is also an aspect of the conduct of the United States which the Court is entitled to take into account as indicative of the view of that State on the question of the existence of an armed attack. At no time, up to the present, has the United States Government addressed to the Security Council, in connection with the matters the subject of the present case, the report which is required by Article 51 of the United Nations Charter in respect of measures which a State believes itself bound to take when it exercises the right of individual or collective self-defence. The Court, whose decision has to be made on the basis of customary international law, has already observed that in context of that law, the reporting obligation enshrined in Article 51 of the Charter of the United Nations does not exist. It does not therefore treat the absence of a report on the part of the United States as the breach of an undertaking forming part of the customary international law applicable to the present dispute. But the Court is justified in observing that this conduct of the United States hardly conforms with the latter's avowed conviction that it was acting in the context of collective self-defence as consecrated by Article 51 of the Charter. This fact is all the more noteworthy because, in the Security Council, the United States has itself

taken the view that failure to observe the requirement to make a report contradicted a State's claim to be acting on the basis of collective self-defence (S/PV.2187).

236. Similarly, while no strict legal conclusion may be drawn from the date of El Salvador's announcement that it was the victim of an armed attack, and the date of its official request addressed to the United States concerning the exercise of collective self-defence, those dates have a significance as evidence of El Salvador's view of the situation. The declaration and the request of El Salvador, made publicly for the first time in August 1984, do not support the contention that in 1981 there was an armed attack capable of serving as a legal foundation for United States activities which began in the second half of that year. The States concerned did not behave as though there were an armed attack at the time when the activities attributed by the United States to Nicaragua, without actually constituting such an attack, were nevertheless the most accentuated; they did so behave only at a time when these facts fell furthest short of what would be required for the Court to take the view that an armed attack existed on the part of Nicaragua against El Salvador.

237. Since the Court has found that the condition *sine qua non* required for the exercise of the right of collective self-defence by the United States is not fulfilled in this case, the appraisal of the United States activities in relation to the criteria of necessity and proportionality takes on a different significance. As a result of this conclusion of the Court, even if the United States activities in question had been carried on in strict compliance with the canons of necessity and proportionality, they would not thereby become lawful. If however they were not, this may constitute an additional ground of wrongfulness. On the question of necessity, the Court observes that the United States measures taken in December 1981 (or, at the earliest, March of that year—paragraph 93 above) cannot be said to correspond to a "necessity" justifying the United States action against Nicaragua on the basis of assistance given by Nicaragua to the armed opposition in El Salvador. First, these measures were only taken, and began to produce their effects, several months after the major offensive of the armed opposition against the Government of El Salvador had been completely repulsed (January 1981), and the actions of the opposition considerably reduced in consequence. Thus it was possible to eliminate the main danger to the Salvadorian Government without the United States embarking on activities in and against Nicaragua. Accordingly, it cannot be held that these activities were undertaken in the light of necessity. Whether or not the assistance to the *contras* might meet the criterion of proportionality, the Court cannot regard the United States activities summarised in paragraphs 80, 81 and 86, i.e., those relating to the mining of the Nicaraguan ports and the attacks on ports, oil installations, etc., as satisfying that criterion. Whatever uncertainty may exist as to the exact scale of the aid received by the Salvadorian armed opposition from Nicaragua, it is clear that these latter United States activities in question could not have been proportionate to that aid. Finally on this point, the Court must also observe that the reaction of the United States in the context of what it regarded as self-defence was continued long after the period in which any presumed armed attack by Nicaragua could reasonably be contemplated.

238. Accordingly, the Court concludes that the plea of collective self-defence against an alleged armed attack on El Salvador, Honduras or Costa Rica, advanced by the United States to justify its conduct toward Nicaragua, cannot be upheld; and accordingly that the United States has violated the principle prohibiting recourse to the threat or use of force by the acts listed in paragraph 227 above, and by its assistance to the *contras* to the extent that this assistance "involve[s] a threat or use of force" (paragraph 228 above).

Note

Judge Schwebel's dissent was based largely on his conclusion that Nicaragua's support of the insurgency in El Salvador was so extensive and persistent as to amount to an armed attack justifying collective self-defense by the United States, and that this warranted military activities not only in El Salvador but against Nicaraguan territory as well. Moreover, in his view, judgment for Nicaragua was unwarranted because it had pressed false testimony on the Court in a deliberate effort to conceal its wrongs. Schwebel voted with the majority holding that the United States violated customary law by failing to make known the existence and location of the mines it had laid.

Judge Oda objected to the Court's consideration of the Nicaraguan claim as arising under customary law. In his view, the U.S. reservation denied the Court jurisdiction of any proceeding based on a multilateral treaty, and even if the treaty and customary law could be disentangled, the Court could not entertain the case and decide it on principles of customary law. Moreover, the claim presented a political dispute, not a legal dispute under Article 36(2) of the Court's Statute.

Judge Jennings agreed with Oda that the U.S. multilateral treaty reservation must be respected and the Court could not exercise jurisdiction and apply customary law in lieu of the multilateral treaties. Therefore, he voted against the Court's decisions on the use of force, on intervention and on self-defense. However Jennings and Oda both joined the majority in holding that the laying of mines by the United States breached United States obligations under a bilateral treaty.

Seven of the judges who voted with the majority appended separate opinions dealing with various aspects of the judgment.

SCHACHTER, INTERNATIONAL LAW IN THEORY AND PRACTICE

141–46 (1991) (footnotes omitted).

A critical question affecting both law and policy on self-defense concerns the degree of uncertainty or indeterminacy that inheres in the proclaimed legal limits. Some indeterminacy results from the key standards of necessity and proportionality, concepts that leave ample room for diverse opinions in particular cases. Other sources of uncertainty can be traced to differing interpretations of the events that would permit forcible defensive action. Varying views have been advanced by governments and scholars relating to the kinds of illegal force that would trigger the right of an armed defensive response. While strong positions have been taken by nearly all States against "preventive" or "preemptive" war, some uncertainty remains as to threats of force that credibly appear as likely to result in imminent attack. Other issues, highlighted by the *Nicaragua* case, concern the illegal use of force through subversion, supply of arms, and logistic support of armed forces as sufficient ground for defensive response. It is not entirely clear to what extent self-defense responding to an armed attack embraces the use of force as a deterrent to future attacks. Nor is there agreement on the circumstances that would permit a State to intervene (or "counterintervene") in an internal conflict under the principle of collective self-defense. Even more unsettling is the uncertainty about the first use of nuclear weapons, the targeting of civilian centers and the proportionality of retaliatory action.

These controversial issues indicate that the rules of self-defense fall far short of a code of conduct that would provide precise "hard law" for many cases likely to arise. * * *

* * *

Notwithstanding its relative indeterminacy, self-defense as a legal norm can have an ascertainable relationship to the policies and actions of governments. The "defensist" principle namely, that self-defense is the only legitimate reason to use force against another State has been expressed as the strategic policy of most States. Evidence for this is not only found in governmental statements to international bodies, where they may be expected. Recent studies by political scientists and students of military strategy confirm the practical implication of defensist doctrine. When States proclaim the principle of self-defense as governing the use of force, they have a stake in its credibility to other States and to their own citizens. For such States to be credible, their weapons, training and contingent planning must reflect a defensist strategy. Their good faith can be tested by their willingness to consider ways to reduce threats and resolve conflicts without using force. Hence, a defensist posture is not merely one of restraint but a source of policy that goes beyond the essentially negative rules of the law. It has obvious implications for such protective activities as monitoring and inspection. It calls for limitations on weaponry and balance among adversaries. The danger that systems which purport to be defensive may be perceived as offensive and therefore "destabilizing" becomes a matter of central concern. The most obvious consequence of defensist doctrine is that States no longer consider that they may invade other States for objectives that were considered in prior periods as legitimate and appropriate. Thus, the naked use of force for economic gain, or to avenge past injustices, or civilize "inferior" people, or vindicate honor, or achieve "manifest destiny", is no longer asserted as national policy. Seen in the perspective of history, this is a profound change in the relations of States.

* * *

The more controversial questions of self-defense have been raised by actions and claims that would expand a State's right to use force beyond the archetypical case of an armed attack on the territory or instrumentality of that State. Such expanded conceptions of self-defense are exemplified by the following uses of force by States claiming self-defense:

(1) the use of force to rescue political hostages believed to face imminent danger of death or injury;

(2) the use of force against officials or installations in a foreign State believed to support terrorists acts directed against nationals of the State claiming the right of defense;

(3) the use of force against troops, planes, vessels or installations believed to threaten imminent attack by a State with declared hostile intent;

(4) the use of retaliatory force against a government or military force so as to deter renewed attacks on the State taking such action;

(5) the use of force against a government that has provided arms or technical support to insurgents in a third State;

(6) the use of force against a government that has allowed its territory to be used by military forces of a third State considered to be a threat to the State claiming self-defense;

(7) the use of force in the name of collective defense (or counterintervention) against a government imposed by foreign forces and faced with large-scale military resistance by many of its people.

* * * Nearly all the cases have been discussed in U.N. bodies and, although opinions have been divided, it is clear that most governments have been reluctant to legitimize expanded self-defense actions that go beyond the paradigmatic case. Thus, no U.N. resolution has approved the use of force in any of the cases that I have listed. In the few cases where resolutions were adopted that passed judgment on the legality of the action, they denied the validity of the self-defense claim. In many cases, resolutions were not adopted, but the majority of States that addressed the issue of lawfulness criticized the actions as contrary to the Charter. Few ventured to defend the legality of the self-defense claims. * * *

* * * [T]he general reluctance to approve uses of force under expanded conceptions of self-defense is itself significant. Such reluctance is evidence of a widespread perception that widening the scope of self-defense will erode the basic rule against unilateral recourse to force. The absence of binding judicial or other third-party determinations relating to the use of force adds to the apprehension that a more permissive rule of self-defense will open the way to further disregard of the limits on force. The refusal of the United States to take part in the proceedings of the International Court on the merits in the *Nicaragua* case and by its non-compliance with the judgment against it has given new emphasis to this point.

It is true that some international lawyers believe that legitimate self-defense should be construed more liberally. They argue that the absence of effective collective remedies against illegal force makes it necessary, indeed inevitable, that States take defensive action on the basis of their own perceptions of national interest and capabilities. In addition to the imperatives of national security, they cite the responsibility of powerful States to maintain international order. They call for a liberal construction of self-defense, stressing that the words of the Charter should be interpreted "in context" so as to yield "reasonable" meanings required by the "purpose and object" of the text. Unilateral acts that stretch the meaning of self-defense are treated as "State practice", although there is no general *opinio juris* to support their "acceptance as law". Conduct that violates text and earlier interpretations may be viewed as new or emerging law based on the efficacy of accomplished facts in shaping the law. Some of these arguments, if accepted, would extend the concept of self-defense so broadly as to allow almost any unilateral use of force taken in the name of law and order. There is no evidence that governments by and large would favor this result. On the contrary, the records of the United Nations, as already mentioned, show strong resistance to widening self-defense to permit force except where there has been an armed attack or threat of imminent attack. It does not seem likely that this resistance will disappear in the foreseeable future.

This does not mean, of course, that the law of self-defense will remain static. The kaleidoscopic events of our era will continue to create new pressures for resort to force. The role of international law cannot be limited to repeating the old maxims. What its role should be calls for further consideration.

Notes

1. During the years when the Security Council was largely neutralized, victims of an armed attack had to defend themselves indefinitely, alone or with the assistance of allies. In such circumstances, does the right of self-defense under Article 51 justify only such action as necessary to beat back the attack? Does it justify retaliation, limited perhaps by the principle of proportionality? Does it remove all the prohibitions of Article 2(4), so that the victim of an armed attack is in effect warranted in engaging in a "just war" against the aggressor, limited only by the traditional rules of war? May the victim carry the war to the territory of the aggressor? To the territories of allies of the aggressor? Are other states forbidden to help the aggressor? Obligated to help the victim?

If the victim of an armed attack, acting in lawful self-defense under Article 51, succeeds in conquering territory of the aggressor, is annexation of such territory lawful? See Chapter 4, p. 343.

2. The end of the Cold War and the revival of the Security Council raised additional questions about the relation of the right of self-defense to the authority of the Security Council and about the implications of the "until" clause of Article 51. How does the availability of the Security Council affect the right of self-defense? Apart from the reporting requirement of Article 51, is the victim of an armed attack expected to enlist the involvement of the Security Council (together with whatever steps the state may take in the exercise of its own "inherent right")? Can states continue to use armed force in self-defense after the Security Council is seized of the matter or after it has begun taking measures aimed at (but not yet successful in) restoring peace and security? Does the Article 51 right persist (or perhaps revive after a period of suspension) if the Security Council cannot definitively resolve the situation? See Section 3, p. 1022 on these issues in relation to Iraq's attack on Kuwait in 1990s and the continuation of Security Council measures against Iraq which remain in effect more than a decade after the attack.

3. Brownlie addressed the question of lawful defensive measures in the face of indirect aggression:

> In so far as there is a use of force by forces controlled by a foreign state, this may be met by lawful measures of self-defence including forcible measures proportionate to the danger. Yet it is very difficult in this context to say what are proportionate measures. In the case of sporadic incursions by armed

bands by land or sea effective measures may be taken to prevent incursion without any operations against the parent state. Interception may occur on the frontier or at the limit of territorial waters. However, preventive action has been taken against armed bands on a number of occasions and the legality of such action will depend on the status of anticipatory action in the modern law. More delicate problems arise in the case of the state which gives military aid to an aggressor, or which gives aid to, or exercises control over, rebel groups or other irregular forces. It is suggested that so far as possible defensive measures should be confined to the territory of the defending state and the hostile forces themselves unless there is clear evidence of a major invasion across a frontier which calls for extensive military operations which may not be confined merely to protecting the frontier line. The precise difficulty in the case of indirect aggression is to avoid major breaches of the peace of wide territorial extent arising from defensive measures based on vague evidence of foreign complicity.

In the present connexion it might be argued that "armed attack" in Article 51 of the Charter refers to a trespass, a direct invasion, and not to activities described by some jurists as "indirect aggression". But providing there is a control by the principal, the aggressor state, and an actual use of force by its agents, there is an "armed attack".

Brownlie, International Law and the Use of Force, 372–73 (1963).

4. In 1974, in response to a suggestion by Rostow that the United States endorse the right of reprisal under Article 51 of the United Nations Charter, Acting Secretary of State Kenneth Rush wrote:

[I]t is the established policy of the United States that a State is responsible for the international use of armed force originating from its territory, whether that force be direct and overt or indirect and covert. This equally is the announced policy of the United Nations, expressly reflected * * * in the General Assembly's resolution 2625 on Principles of International Law concerning Friendly Relations and Cooperation among States. The definition of aggression recently forwarded by a UN Special Committee to the General Assembly also maintains this accepted principle of international law.

You would add a complementary principle, namely, that where a State cannot or will not fulfill its international legal obligations to prevent the use of its territory for the unlawful exercise of force, the wronged State is entitled to use force, by way of reprisal, to redress, by self-help, the violation of international law which it has suffered.

As you know, resolution 2625 also contains the following categorical statement: "States have a duty to refrain from acts of reprisal involving the use of force." That injunction codifies resolutions of the Security Council which have so affirmed.

The United States has supported and supports the foregoing principle. Of course we recognize that the practice of States is not always consistent with this principle and that it may sometimes be difficult to distinguish the exercise of proportionate self-defense from an act of reprisal. Yet, essentially for reasons of the abuse to which the doctrine of reprisals particularly lends itself, we think it desirable to endeavor to maintain the distinction between acts of lawful self-defense and unlawful reprisals.

68 A.J.I.L. 736 (1974).

5. On April 14, 1986, the United States bombed targets in Libyan territory, killing both military and civilian persons and inflicting substantial damage. President Reagan announced that the United States had "launched a series of strikes against the headquarters, terrorist facilities, and military assets that support Muammar Qadhafi's subversive activities." The President's statement justified the action as being in response, in particular, to a bombing of a Berlin nightclub frequented by U.S. servicemen in which one was killed and many wounded. Reagan described the attack as "a mission fully consistent with Article 51 of the UN Charter. We believe that this preemptive action against terrorist installations will not only diminish Colonel Qadhafi's capacity to export terror, it will provide him with incentives and reasons to alter his criminal behavior." Presidential Statement of April 14, 1986, U.S. Dept. of State, Selected Documents No. 24.

Was the action of the United States justified as a use of force in self-defense under Article 51? Was it in response to an "armed attack against a member of the United Nations" within the meaning of that article? Note the reference to the bombing as a "preemptive action." (Compare pp. 968–971 on anticipatory self-defense.)

In October 1985 Israel launched an air attack on the Headquarters of the Palestine Liberation Organization (PLO) in Tunisia, in response to terrorist activities attributed to the PLO. The Security Council condemned the action as an "act of armed aggression * * * against Tunisian territory in flagrant violation of the Charter." S.C.Res. 573 (1985). The United States abstained. See 80 A.J.I.L. 165 (1986).

Compare the use or threat of force to apprehend alleged terrorists who are in another state's jurisdiction or control. In 1985, four United States military planes intercepted an Egyptian aircraft over the Mediterranean Sea, compelling it to land in Italy so that alleged terrorists aboard the aircraft could be prosecuted for seizing a vessel, taking hostages, and murder. Was the action lawful under the Charter? See Schachter, In Defense of International Rules on the Use of Force, 53 U.Chi. L.Rev. 113, 139–40 (1986); Cassese, Terrorism, Politics and Law: The Achille Lauro Affair (1989).

On April 14, 1993, it was reported that Kuwaiti authorities had thwarted a terrorist plot to assassinate former President George Bush while on a visit to Kuwait. An investigation by U.S. intelligence agencies concluded that the highest levels of the Iraqi government had directed its agents to carry out the assassination. On June 26, 1993, United States forces fired 23 Tomahawk missiles at Iraqi intelligence headquarters, from war ships stationed in the Persian Gulf and the Red Sea. At a special session of the Security Council, the U.S. representative said: "[T]his was a direct attack on the United States, an attack that required a direct United States response. Consequently, President Clinton yesterday instructed the United States armed forces to carry out a military operation against the headquarters of the Iraqi Intelligence Service in Baghdad. We responded directly, as we were entitled to do, under Article 51 of the United Nations Charter, which provides for the exercise of self defense in such cases."

Assuming the facts as reported, was the U.S. action justified under Article 51 as a response to an armed attack? Was it necessary? proportional? Was the U.S. action justifiable under Security Council resolutions relating to Iraq, pp. 1015, 1018–1020?

6. On December 20, 1989 the United States initiated military operations in Panama, with a deployment of 11,000 troops additional to 13,000 U.S. forces already present. The background to the invasion included a declaration by the

Panamanian National Assembly on December 15, 1989 that a state of war existed between Panama and the United States; an inflammatory anti-American speech given by Manuel Noriega (Panama's de facto president, who had refused to relinquish power after losing an election earlier in the year); and a series of violent attacks by Panama Defense Forces on U.S. military personnel and dependents in Panama, including the killing of a U.S. Marine officer and the beating of a U.S. naval officer on December 16, 1989.

President George Bush reported to the U.S. Congress that the "deployment of U.S. Forces is an exercise of the right of self-defense recognized in Article 51 of the United Nations Charter and was necessary to protect American lives in imminent danger and to fulfill our responsibilities under the Panama Canal Treaties. It was welcomed by the democratically elected government of Panama." See Report on the Development Concerning the Deployment of United States Forces to Panama, House Doc. 101–127, 101st Cong., 2d Sess. (1990).

Critics of the Panama invasion have concluded that the alleged justifications were not the real reasons for U.S. intervention and that its main purpose was to bring General Noriega to trial in the U.S. for conspiracy to smuggle drugs into the United States. However, assuming the facts and characterizations as alleged, was the Panama invasion justified under international law? Compare the article by the then Legal Adviser to the U.S. Department of State, Sofaer, The Legality of the United States Actions in Panama, 29 Colum.J.Trans. L. 281 (1991) and the letter to the President of the U.N. Security Council from the U.S. Permanent Representative to the United Nations. U.N.Doc. S/21035, with Henkin, The Invasion of Panama Under International Law: A Gross Violation, 29 Colum.J.Trans. L. 293 (1991). See also Agora: U.S. Forces in Panama: Defenders, Aggressors or Human Rights Activists, 84 A.J.I.L. 494 (1990).

One of the principal justifications invoked by President Bush appears to be the right of self-defense under Article 51. Do you agree? Was the invasion necessary? proportional? Are the U.S. justifications consistent with the opinion of the International Court of Justice in the *Nicaragua* case (Merits), p. 955 supra? In a detailed report, a committee of the Association of the Bar of the City of New York concluded that the legality of the intervention under existing standards of the law of self-defense was not established on the facts, as the existence of an "armed attack" (or anticipation of an imminent attack) and satisfaction of the requirements of necessity and proportionality were all in doubt. See Report, The Use of Armed Force in International Affairs: The Case of Panama, 47 Record A.B.C.N.Y. 604–738 (1992)

7. In August 1998, terrorist bombs exploded at U.S. embassy buildings in Nairobi, Kenya and Dar-es-Salaam, Tanzania, resulting in large loss of life. U.S. intelligence attributed the bombings to a terrorist network sustained by Osama bin-Laden, a wealthy Saudi Arabian national living in Afghanistan. About two weeks after the embassy explosions, U.S. cruise missiles struck facilities in Afghanistan and Sudan that were said to be part of bin-Laden's network. Some of the targets were alleged to be training camps for terrorists; in Sudan, one of the targets was supposedly a factory for chemicals to be used in chemical weapons (later reports identified it as a pharmaceutical plant). In justifying the cruise missile strikes, President Clinton invoked U.S. rights of self-defense; and the U.S. government notified the Security Council of the missile attacks, referring to Article 51. Does the action withstand scrutiny under Article 51? See Murphy, Contemporary Practice of the United States Relating to International Law, 93 A.J.I.L. 161–167 (1999).

ANTICIPATORY SELF–DEFENSE

During the nuclear confrontation of the Cold War the legal and political literature addressed the possibility of a nuclear "first strike" to preempt an impending nuclear attack and strategies to defend against such a horrific eventuality. With the end of the Cold War those debates lost some of their urgency, but it remains important to consider whether a state may act in anticipation that an attack (with weapons of mass destruction or even conventional weapons) may be impending.

SCHACHTER, THE RIGHT OF STATES TO USE ARMED FORCE

82 Mich. L.Rev. 1620, 1633–35 (1984) (footnotes omitted).

Our first question—whether self-defense requires an armed attack or whether it is permissible in anticipation of an attack—has given rise to much controversy among international lawyers. The text of article 51 does not answer the question directly. It declares that "[n]othing in the present Charter shall impair the inherent right of individual or collective self-defense if an armed attack occurs." On one reading this means that self-defense is limited to cases of armed attack. An alternative reading holds that since the article is silent as to the right of self-defense under customary law (which goes beyond cases of armed attack), it should not be construed by implication to eliminate that right. The drafting history shows that article 51 was intended to safeguard the Chapultepec Treaty which provided for collective defense in case of armed attack. The relevant commission report of the San Francisco Conference declared "the use of arms in legitimate self-defense remains admitted and unimpaired." It is therefore not implausible to interpret article 51 as leaving unimpaired the right of self-defense as it existed prior to the Charter. The main interpretive difficulty with this is that the words "if an armed attack occurs" then become redundant, a conclusion which should not be reached without convincing evidence that such redundant use was in keeping with the drafters' intention. The link with the Chapultepec Treaty provides a reason for the inclusion of the words "if an armed attack occurs" and explains why it was not said that self-defense is limited to cases of armed attack.

Much of the debate in recent years has focused on the consequences of adopting one or the other interpretation, especially in the light of the apprehension over nuclear missiles. Even as far back as 1946, the U.S. Government stated that the term "armed attack" should be defined to include not merely the dropping of a bomb but "certain steps in themselves preliminary to such action." In recent years, the fear that nuclear missiles, could, on the first strike, destroy the capability for defense and allow virtually no time for defense has appeared to many to render a requirement of armed attack unreasonable. States faced with a perceived danger of immediate attack, it is argued, cannot be expected to await the attack like sitting ducks. In response to this line of reasoning, others argue that the existence of nuclear missiles has made it even more important to maintain a legal barrier against preemptive strikes and anticipatory defense. It is conceded by them that states facing an imminent threat of attack will take defensive measures irrespective of the law, but it is preferable to have states make that choice governed by necessity than to adopt a principle that would make it easier for a state to launch an attack on the pretext of anticipatory defense.

Both of the foregoing positions express apprehensions that are reasonable. It is important that the right of self-defense should not freely allow the use of force in anticipation of an attack or in response to a threat. At the same time, we must recognize that there may well be situations in which the imminence of an attack is so clear and the danger so great that defensive action is essential for self-preservation. It does not seem to me that the law should leave such defense to a decision *contra legem.* Nor does it appear necessary to read article 51 in that way—that is, to exclude completely legitimate self-defense in advance of an actual attack. In my view it is not clear that article 51 was intended to eliminate the customary law right of self-defense and it should not be given that effect. But we should avoid interpreting the customary law as if it broadly authorized preemptive strikes and anticipatory defense in response to threats.

The conditions of the right of anticipatory defense under customary law were expressed generally in an eloquent formulation by the U.S. Secretary of State Daniel Webster in a diplomatic note to the British in 1842 * * * [on the *Caroline* episode, p. 922 above, in which he asserted] that self-defense must be confined to cases in which "the necessity of that self-defense is instant, overwhelming, and leaving no choice of means, and no moment for deliberation."

The Webster formulation of self-defense is often cited as authoritative customary law. It cannot be said that the formulation reflects state practice (which was understandably murky on this point when war was legal), but it is safe to say it reflects a widespread desire to restrict the right of self-defense when no attack has actually occurred. A recent case in point concerns the Israeli bombing of a nuclear reactor in Iraq in 1981, which the Israeli government sought to justify on the ground of self-defense. Israel cited the Iraqi position that it was at war with Israel and claimed that the reactor was intended for a nuclear strike. Many governments and the UN Security Council rejected the Israeli position. In the debates in the Security Council on this question, several delegates referred to the *Caroline Case* formulation of the right of anticipatory defense as an accepted statement of customary law. We may infer from these official statements recognition of the continued validity of an "inherent" right to use armed force in self-defense prior to an actual attack but only where such an attack is imminent "leaving no moment for deliberation."

Notes

1. Compare the following views:

(a) Under the Charter, alarming military preparations by a neighboring state would justify a resort to the Security Council, but would not justify resort to anticipatory force by the state which believed itself threatened.

The documentary record of the discussions at San Francisco does not afford conclusive evidence that the suggested interpretation of the words "armed attack" in Article 51 is correct, but the general tenor of the discussions, as well as the careful choice of words throughout Chapters VI and VII of the Charter relative to various stages of aggravation of dangers to the peace, support the view stated.

Jessup, A Modern Law of Nations 166–67 (1948) (footnotes omitted).

(b) It was to avoid and eliminate the political and military dangers of letting the nations judge by themselves the vital issues of attack and defence that the relevant provisions of the United Nations Charter were formulated. But the inability of the UN, as at present organised, to act swiftly has handed the power of decision back to the national states. * * * But while this immensely increases the necessity for a reliable international detection organisation and mechanism, in the absence of effective international machinery the right of self-defense must probably now be extended to the defence against a clearly imminent aggression, despite the apparently contrary language of Article 51 of the Charter. The dangers of such an interpretation should not be underestimated. It means that the United States or the Soviet Union may, on the basis of plausible but inaccurate information, send a bomber or missile force to the other country to destroy the force believed to be poised for aggression.

Friedmann, The Changing Structure of International Law 259–60 (1964) (footnotes omitted).

(c) If there were clear evidence of an attack so imminent that there was no time for political action to prevent it, the only meaningful defense for the potential victim might indeed be the pre-emptive attack and—it may be argued—the scheme of Article 2(4) together with Article 51 was not intended to bar such attack. But this argument would claim a small and special exception for the special case of the surprise nuclear attack; today, and one hopes for a time longer, it is meaningful and relevant principally only as between the Soviet Union and the United States * * * But such a reading of the Charter, it should be clear, would not permit (and encourage) anticipatory self-defense in other, more likely situations between nations generally.

Henkin, How Nations Behave 143–45 (2nd ed. 1979) (footnotes omitted).

(d) The United States was right in the Cuban Missile crisis not to say that the deployment of missiles in Cuba by the Soviet Union constituted an "armed attack" that would give rise to the right of self-defense. I agree that it would be too dangerous for the world community to allow unilateral uses of force simply because there were some deployments of weapons or modernization of weapons. On the other hand, to say that a nation has to be a sitting duck (to use Professor Myres McDougal's phrase) and wait until the bombs are actually dropping on its soil—that cannot be right either. When attack is initiated and is underway, even though the attacker has not actually arrived in the victim state, measures can be taken. There should be agreement on that principle.

But there are hard cases. Egyptian President Gamal Abdel Nasser announced the blockade of the Gulf of Aqaba in 1967; Israel attacked. I think most people felt that was justified self-defense. But when Israel attacked the nuclear reactor in Iraq in 1981, most people—maybe with the exception of McDougal and one or two others—argued that that went too far. And yet, if anticipatory self-defense cannot cover the Iraqi reactor case (and I have no doubt that nuclear reactor was not for peaceful purposes only), how are we going to deal with a Saddam Hussein who may be preparing to use weapons of mass destruction against his neighbors?

Gardner, Commentary on the Law of Self–Defense, in Law and Force in the New International Order 51–52 (Damrosch & Scheffer, eds. 1991).

A distinction has been suggested between "interceptive" and "anticipatory" self-defense: "interceptive, unlike anticipatory, self-defence takes place after the other side has committed itself to an armed attack in an ostensibly irrevocable way." Dinstein, War, Aggression and Self–Defense 190 (2d ed. 1994). Is this distinction helpful in clarifying the scope of legitimate self-defense?

2. The official justification of United States action in the 1962 Cuban missile crisis (p. 950 supra) did not invoke anticipatory self-defense, but some writers sought to justify the quarantine on that basis. See, e.g., MacChesney, Some Comments on the "Quarantine" of Cuba, 57 A.J.I.L. 592 (1963). For an opposing view, see Henkin, How Nations Behave 295–96 (2d ed. 1979). Some who argued against limiting the right to self-defense to cases where an armed attack occurs may have had in mind particularly a right to anticipate a nuclear attack. See, e.g., McDougal, The Soviet Cuban Quarantine and Self–Defense, 57 A.J.I.L. 597, 599–601 (1963).

3. In the *Nicaragua* case, 1986 I.C.J. 14 at 135, para. 269, the United States had based part of its collective self-defense claim on the proposition that Nicaragua had engaged in alarming conduct, including a massive build-up of armaments far in excess of what it needed for its own defense, which its neighbors could perceive as a threat to attack them. In addressing this contention (with the United States absent at the merits stage), the Court observed that in the absence of any limitations agreed upon by the states concerned, international law places no restrictions on the right of states to decide for themselves what level of weapons to maintain for their own security, and that this principle "is valid for all States without exception." Should this principle apply equally to weapons of mass destruction as well as conventional weapons? See the following note and materials below on nuclear weapons and self-defense.

4. In 1981, Israel bombed a nuclear reactor under construction in Iraq and sought to justify its action by claiming a right of "anticipatory" self-defense. Was the threat to Israel such as to bring it within a "liberal" reading of Article 51? Was the alleged Iraqi threat "immediate" within the formula or the spirit of *The Caroline?* Was it relevant that Iraq had continued to maintain that Iraq was in a state of war with Israel? See D'Amato, Israel's Air Strike Upon the Iraqi Nuclear Reactor, 77 A.J.I.L. 584 (1983); G. Fischer, Le bombardement par Israël d'un réacteur nucléaire irakien, 1981 Annuaire Français de Droit International 147. For a discussion of this action in the Security Council, see U.N.Docs. S/PV.2285–88, along with S.C.Res. (487), reprinted in 20 I.L.M. 993 (1981). Compare Alexandrov, Self–Defense Against the Use of Force in International Law 159–165, 296 (1996) (Israel's raid not justified on self-defense grounds) with McCormack, Self–Defense in International Law: The Israeli Raid on the Iraqi Nuclear Reactor 122–124, 238–239, 253–284 (1996). See also Walker, Anticipatory Collective Self–Defense in the Charter Era: What the Treaties Have Said, 31 Cornell I.L.J. 321 (1998).

Does the evidence developed in the 1990s of persistent Iraqi efforts to develop weapons of mass destruction cast the legal issues concerning anticipatory self-defense in any different light? On variations of self-defense arguments raised in connection with the December 1998 missile strikes against Iraq, see pp. 1021–1022.

SELF–DEFENSE AND NUCLEAR WEAPONS

When, if ever, might the use or threat of nuclear weapons be justified as a self-defensive measure? Strategic doctrine during and after the Cold War maintained that a credible threat of nuclear retaliation was the linchpin of deterrence, and that a posture of nuclear readiness had dissuaded any party from mounting a destabilizing attack with conventional or any other weapons. As part of the policy of deterrence, NATO has kept open the option of nuclear response to a large-scale attack with conventional weapons, as well as possibilities for certain uses of tactical nuclear weapons.

In Legality of the Threat or Use of Nuclear Weapons, 1996 I.C.J. 226, the International Court of Justice was asked by the General Assembly for an advisory opinion on the following question: "Is the threat or use of nuclear weapons in any circumstance permitted under international law?" In its opinion, the Court referred to certain constraints applicable to self-defense under Article 51 of the Charter and customary international law, including the requirements of necessity and proportionality (paras. 40–42), and observed:

> 42. The proportionality principle may thus not in itself exclude the use of nuclear weapons in self-defence in all circumstances. But at the same time, a use of force that is proportionate under the law of self-defence must, in order to be lawful, also meet the requirements of the law applicable in armed conflict which comprise in particular the principles and rules of humanitarian law.
>
> * * *
>
> 96. Furthermore, the Court cannot lose sight of the fundamental right of every State to survival, and thus its right to resort to self-defence, in accordance with Article 51 of the Charter, when its survival is at stake.
>
> Nor can it ignore the practice referred to as "policy of deterrence", to which an appreciable section of the international community adhered for many years. * * *

In the dispositive provisions of its ruling, the Court unanimously agreed (para. 105(2)C) that

> A threat or use of force by means of nuclear weapons that is contrary to Article 2, paragraph 4, of the United Nations Charter and that fails to meet all the requirements of Article 51, is unlawful.

The judgment also contained the following paragraph, adopted by an equally divided Court (seven votes to seven, by President Bedjaoui's casting vote) (para. 105(2)E):

> However, in view of the current state of international law, and of the elements of fact at its disposal, the Court cannot conclude definitively whether the threat or use of nuclear weapons would be lawful or unlawful in an extreme circumstance of self-defence, in which the very survival of a State would be at stake.

In dissent, Judge Schwebel (United States) referred to evidence suggesting that Iraq may have been deterred from using chemical weapons against coalition forces in the 1991 Gulf War because of a belief that the United States might respond with nuclear weapons. He criticized the Court for a disposition which left unanswered the ultimate question of permissibility of nuclear self-defense. See also pp. 77–87.

Note

On this aspect of the I.C.J. opinion, see Kohen, The Notion of "State Survival" in International Law, in Boisson de Chazournes & Sands (eds.), International Law, the International Court of Justice and Nuclear Weapons 293–314 (1999). For other references, see p. 87.

4. Claims of Permissible Use of Force for Benign Purposes

Article 2(4) of the Charter prohibits the use of force "against the territorial integrity or political independence of any state, or in any other manner inconsistent with the Purposes of the United Nations." There have been recurrent suggestions that the Charter should be interpreted to permit use of force for certain benign purposes, including: intervention to end or prevent gross violations of human rights; to protect one's nationals; to extricate hostages; to promote or maintain democracy, socialism or self-determination. With the possible exception of an "Entebbe principle" permitting the rescue of hostages, p. 975 infra, such claims remain highly contested. In Section 2 below we take up the debate over intervention in internal conflicts and the renewed controversy over humanitarian intervention in the wake of the Kosovo crisis of 1999. The remainder of this section deals with other asserted justifications based on the purpose for which force is used.

PROTECTION OF NATIONALS; RESCUE OF HOSTAGES

Intervention by a state to protect its nationals and ensure their humane treatment in another state was traditionally justified on the grounds of self-defense. Bowett, writing in 1958, took the position that such intervention to protect nationals had been lawful before the U.N. Charter as self-defense and remained lawful thereafter under Article 51. Bowett, Self–Defence in International Law 87–90 (1958). See also his later essay, The Use of Force for the Protection of Nationals Abroad, in The Current Legal Regulation of the Use of Force 39 (Cassese, ed. 1986). Friedmann wrote that:

> The conditions under which a state may be entitled, as an aspect of self-defense, to intervene in another state to protect its nationals from injury, were formulated by Professor Waldock in 1952 as follows: "There must be (1) an imminent threat of injury to nationals, (2) a failure or inability on the part of the territorial sovereign to protect them and (3) measures of protection strictly confined to the object of protecting them against injury" * * * This was invoked, among other reasons, by the British Government in support of its armed intervention in Egypt during the Suez Canal crisis of 1956. Since, unlike in the Dominican Republic in April, 1965, there was no breakdown of organized government in Egypt nor any physical threat to foreign nationals, the United States had much greater legal justification for its original, limited intervention in protec-

> tion of its nationals in the Dominican crisis than did Great Britain in the Suez crisis.

Friedmann, United States Policy and the Crisis of International Law, 59 A.J.I.L. 857, 867 n. 10 (1965). See generally, 1 Oppenheim's International Law 440–42 (9th ed. Jennings & Watts, eds. 1992). For the law prior to the Charter, see the opinion of Judge Huber in *The Spanish Zones of Morocco Claims,* 2 U.N.R.I.A.A. 615 (1925).

The right to intervene to protect nationals was one of the grounds invoked by the United States for its invasion of Grenada in 1983. See p. [ ] infra. See also Joyner, The United States Action in Grenada, 78 A.J.I.L. 131 (1984). It was also used as a justification by the U.S. for the invasion of Panama in 1989. See p. 967 above; see also Use of Force, Protection of Nationals—Deployment of U.S. Forces to Panama (U.S. Digest, Ch. 14, § 1), reprinted in 84 A.J.I.L. 545 (1990). Schachter suggests:

> Reliance on self-defence as a legal ground for protecting nationals in emergency situations of peril probably reflects a reluctance to rely solely on the argument of humanitarian intervention as an exception to Article 2(4) or on the related point that such intervention is not "against the territorial integrity or political independence" of the territorial State and that it is not inconsistent with the Charter. Many governments attach importance to the principle that any forcible incursion into the territory of another State is a derogation of that State's territorial sovereignty and political independence, irrespective of the motive for such intervention or its long term consequences. Accordingly, they tend to hold to the sweeping prohibition of Article 2(4) against the use or threat of force except where self-defence or Security Council enforcement action is involved.

Schachter, International Law in Theory and Practice 166–167 (1991) (footnotes omitted).

By no means have all writers agreed that the right to intervene to protect nationals survived the U.N. Charter. Professor Brownlie, for example, argues:

> * * *[I]t is very doubtful if * * * intervention [to protect nationals] has any basis in the modern law. The instances in which states have purported to exercise it, and the terms in which it is delimited, show that it provides infinite opportunities for abuse. Forcible intervention is now unlawful. It is true that the protection of nationals presents particular difficulties and that a government faced with a deliberate massacre of a considerable number of nationals in a foreign state would have cogent reasons of humanity for acting, and would also be under very great political pressure. The possible risks of denying the legality of action in a case of such urgency, an exceptional circumstance, must be weighed against the more calculable dangers of providing legal pretexts for the commission of breaches of the peace in the pursuit of national rather than humanitarian interest.

Brownlie, International Law and the Use of Force by States 301 (1963). See also Ronzitti, Rescuing Nationals Abroad through Military Coercion and Intervention on Grounds of Humanity 64 (1985). As regards the U.S. invasion of Panama in 1989, Henkin argues, *inter alia,* that the alleged protection of U.S. nationals could not be justified under Article 51 as a use of force in self-defense since no "armed attack" had occurred. Henkin, The Invasion of Panama Under International Law: A Gross Violation, 29 Colum.J.Transnat'l L. 293, 305–06 (1991). On Panama, see pp. 966–967.

A special case of protection of nationals is intervention to rescue nationals being held hostage and in mortal peril. Because this is a narrower category than intervention to protect nationals from situations of general instability or insecurity, the use of force in such circumstances seems more likely to be viewed as acceptable (or tolerable).

Consider the intervention by Israel in Uganda to release Israeli hostages from a hijacked plane at Entebbe, and the U.S. attempt to rescue U.S. hostages in Iran after the U.S. embassy was seized. Henkin maintains that in hostage situations there may be a limited right to intervene "to liberate hostages if the territorial state cannot or will not do so." Henkin, Use of Force: Law and U.S. Policy, in Right v. Might: International Law and the Use of Force 37, 41–42 (2nd ed. 1991). Henkin would not limit this protection to hostages that are nationals of the intervening state. Provided the "use of force is strictly limited to what is necessary to save lives," an intervening state could act to rescue its own nationals, the territorial state's nationals, or the nationals of a third state. Id. But see the Security Council debate on the Entebbe Incident, where the Israeli (and U.S.) representatives defended Israel's action as self-defense because the hostages were its nationals. U.N.Doc. S/PV.1939, at 5159 (July 1976), reprinted in 15 I.L.M. 1224 (1976).

INTERVENTION FOR DEMOCRACY

REISMAN, COERCION AND SELF-DETERMINATION: CONSTRUING CHARTER ARTICLE 2(4)

78 A.J.I.L. 642, 643–45 (1984) (footnotes omitted).

A sine qua non for any action—coercive or otherwise—I submit, is the maintenance of minimum order in a precarious international system. Will a particular use of force enhance or undermine world order? When this requirement is met, attention may be directed to the fundamental principle of political legitimacy in contemporary international politics: the enhancement of the ongoing right of peoples to determine their own political destinies. That obvious point bears renewed emphasis for it is the main purpose of contemporary international law: Article 2(4) is the means. The basic policy of contemporary international law has been to maintain the political independence of territorial communities so that they can continue to express their desire for political community in a form appropriate to them.

Article 2(4), like so much in the Charter and in contemporary international politics, rests on and must be interpreted in terms of this key postulate of political legitimacy in the 20th century. Each application of Article 2(4) must enhance opportunities for ongoing self-determination. Though all interventions are lamentable, the fact is that some may serve, in terms of aggregate consequences, to increase the probability of the free choice of peoples about their government and political structure. Others have the manifest objective and consequence of doing exactly the opposite. There is neither need nor justification for treating in a mechanically equal fashion Tanzania's intervention in Uganda to overthrow Amin's despotism, on the one hand, and Soviet intervention in Hungary in 1956 or Czechoslovakia in 196[8] to overthrow popular governments and to impose an undesired regime on a coerced population, on the other. Here, as in all other areas of law, it is important to remember that norms are instruments devised by human beings to precipitate desired social consequences. One should not seek point-for-point conformity to a rule without constant regard for the policy or principle that animated its prescription, and with appropriate regard for the factual constellation in the minds of the drafters.

Coercion should not be glorified, but it is naive and indeed subversive of public order to insist that it never be used, for coercion is a ubiquitous feature of all social life and a characteristic and indispensable component of law. The critical question in a decentralized system is not whether coercion has been applied, but whether it has been applied in support of or against community order and basic policies, and whether it was applied in ways whose net consequences include increased congruence with community goals and minimum order.

SCHACHTER, THE LEGALITY OF PRO–DEMOCRATIC INVASION

78 A.J.I.L. 645, 649–50 (1984).

The difficulty with Reisman's argument is not merely that it lacks support in the text of the Charter or in the interpretation that states have given Article 2(4) in the past decades. It would introduce a new normative basis for recourse to war that would give powerful states an almost unlimited right to overthrow governments alleged to be unresponsive to the popular will or to the goal of self-determination. The implications of this for interstate violence in a period of superpower confrontation and obscurantist rhetoric are ominous. That invasions may at times serve democratic values must be weighed against the dangerous consequences of legitimizing armed attacks against peaceful governments. It will be recalled that the International Court of Justice in the *Corfu Channel* case rejected the defense of the United Kingdom that it had used armed force in the cause of international justice. The Court's pronouncement on this bears repetition:

> The Court cannot accept such a line of defence. The Court can only regard the alleged right of intervention as the manifestation of a policy of force, such as cannot, whatever be the present defects in international organization, find a place in international law. Intervention is perhaps still less admissible in the particular form it would take here; for, from the nature of things, it would be reserved for the most powerful States, and might easily lead to perverting the administration of international justice itself.

The Court's measured phrases remind us of the historic realities of abuse by powerful states for supposedly good causes. It is no answer to say that invasions should be allowed where there is no abuse and only for the higher good of self-determination. In the absence of an effective international mechanism to restrain force, individual governments would have the latitude to decide on the "reality" of democracy and self-determination in various countries. The test one side would favor would not be acceptable to others. Ideological confrontations would sooner or later become clashes of power.

These considerations are so evident that we can be quite sure that governments will not adopt the suggested reinterpretation of Article 2(4) as law. Not even its espousal by a powerful state would make it law. In short, it is not, will not, and should not be law. Yet there is a reason for concern that the thesis has been put forward by an international lawyer of standing. In this period of tension and unilateral action, arguments such as those presented may influence policy in favor of armed intervention. The fragility of international organization enhances the danger. This is surely not the time for international lawyers to weaken the principal normative restraint against the use of force. The world will not be made safe for democracy through new wars or invasions of the weak by the strong.

Notes

1. *The "Reagan Doctrine."* In a speech on March 1, 1985, President Reagan said: "freedom movements arise and assert themselves. They're doing so on almost every continent populated by man—in the hills of Afghanistan, in Angola, in Kampuchea, in Central America * * * They're our brothers, these freedom fighters, and we owe them our help." See Reisman, Allocating Competences to Use Coercion in the Post–Cold War World: Practices, Conditions, and Prospects, in Law and Force in the New International Order 26, 34 n. 13 (Damrosch & Scheffer, eds. 1991). This and subsequent statements were interpreted as asserting the right of the United States (or any other state) to intervene by force to defend, maintain, restore or impose democratic government. See Kirkpatrick & Gerson, The Reagan Doctrine, Human Rights, and International Law, in Right v. Might: International Law and the Use of Force 19 (2nd ed. 1991); but see Henkin, The Use of Force: Law and U.S. Policy, in Right v. Might at 37, 44 (contending that the use of force for democracy could not be reconciled with Article 2(4)).

Support for democracy was implied by President Bush among his justifications for the 1989 invasion of Panama. See pp. 953, 966–967 supra.

2. *The "Brezhnev Doctrine."* During the Cold War, the Reagan doctrine's counterpart was the Soviet Union's Brezhnev doctrine, which had its genesis in the Soviet invasion of Czechoslovakia on September 25, 1968; it asserted the right of socialist states to intervene in another socialist state when socialism there was threatened. See the reported statement of Leonid Brezhnev on the occasion of the invasion of Czechoslovakia, reprinted in 7 I.L.M. 1323 (1968). The U.S.S.R. did not reassert the Brezhnev doctrine after Czechoslovakia, and some believe that the Soviet Union disavowed it in the Final Act of the Conference on Security and Cooperation in Europe (Helsinki 1975). The doctrine was unequivocally repudiated under Mikhail Gorbachev in the twilight of the Soviet period. See generally Müllerson & Scheffer, Legal Regulation of the Use of Force, in Beyond Confrontation: International Law for the Post–Cold War Era (Damrosch, Danilenko & Müllerson, eds., 1995), at 93, 95–96.

3. What are the implications of the Reagan and Brezhnev doctrines for the principle of "sovereign equality of states" enshrined in the U.N. Charter? The International Court of Justice appears to have rejected both doctrines in the *Nicaragua* case (Merits):

> The finding of the United States Congress also expressed the view that the Nicaraguan Government had taken "significant steps towards establishing a totalitarian Communist dictatorship". However the régime in Nicaragua be defined, adherence by a State to any particular doctrine does not constitute a violation of customary international law; to hold otherwise would make nonsense of the fundamental principle of State sovereignty, on which the whole of international law rests, and the freedom of choice of the political, social, economic and cultural system of a State. Consequently, Nicaragua's domestic policy options, even assuming that they correspond to the description given of them by the Congress finding, cannot justify on the legal plane the various actions of the [U.S.] complained of. The Court cannot contemplate the creation of a new rule opening up a right of intervention by one State against another on the ground that the latter has opted for some particular ideology or political system.

Military and Paramilitary Activities in and Against Nicaragua (Nicaragua v. United States), 1986 I.C.J. 14, 133.

4. During the years of decolonization there was some support for the view that states may intervene to promote the process of self-determination, as well as substantial criticism of that view. See Article 7 of the Resolution on the Definition of Aggression, p. 943 supra, which provides that nothing in the definition is intended to prejudice the "right to self-determination" and the right of "peoples forcibly deprived of that right * * * to struggle to that end and to seek and receive support, in accordance with the principles of the Charter and in conformity with the [Declaration on Friendly Relations]." G.A.Res. 3314 (XXIX) (1974). See also The Principle of Equal Rights and Self-Determination of Peoples in the Declaration on Principles of International Law Concerning Friendly Relations and Co-operation Among States in Accordance with the Charter of the United Nations, G.A.Res. 2625 (XXXV) (1970). Compare Reisman, Allocating Competences to Use Coercion in the Post-Cold War World, in Law and Force in the New International Order (Damrosch & Scheffer eds., 1991), at 26, 30–34, with Henkin's position:

> Self-determination as a justification for the use of force to end colonialism has lost its raison d'être, but some have invoked a people's right to "internal self-determination" to support the use of force by one state to preserve or impose democracy in another * * * Like the use of force to impose or maintain socialism or any other ideology, the use of force for democracy clearly would be contrary to the language of Article 2(4), to the intent of the framers, and to the construction long given to that article by the United States.
>
> At bottom, all suggestions for exceptions to article 2(4) imply that, contrary to the assumptions of the Charter's framers, there are universally recognized values higher than peace and the autonomy of states. In general, the claims of peace and state autonomy have prevailed.

Henkin, The Use of Force: Law and U.S. Policy, in Right v. Might: International Law and the Use of Force 37, 44 (2d ed. 1991).

5. Could democratic states agree among themselves to support their respective governments against any forcible *coup d'état*? For such a proposal, see Farer, A Paradigm of Legitimate Intervention, in Damrosch (ed.), Enforcing Restraint: Collective Intervention in Internal Conflicts (1993), at pp. 316, 332–333 (1993). See also Wippman, Treaty-Based Intervention: Who Can Say No?, 62 U.Chicago L. Rev. 607, 667–678 (1995).

6. After the end of the Cold War, issues of intervention to support democratic government took on a substantially different character, notably in the Haitian crisis of 1991–1994, which began with the overthrow of a democratically elected president and continued until the U.N. Security Council approved a multilateral military operation to bring about his restoration. This episode will be dealt with in Section 3 at p. 1038, together with other instances where the Security Council has identified a "threat to peace" emanating from internal conflicts.

As of 2000, unilateral claims of authority to use military force to change another state's regime had receded (at least by comparison to the controversies over the earlier Reagan and Brezhnev doctrines). Collective economic sanctions to counter antidemocratic coups or to bring pressure on abusive dictators to yield power had been organized in a variety of instances. See generally Damrosch, Enforcing International Law Through Non–Forcible Measures, 269 Rec. des Cours 9, 150–153 (1997) and p. 1039 below. It was unclear how the incoming U.S. administration of President George W. Bush would approach these issues (e.g., in connection with proposals to give military support to the Iraqi opposition).

7. See generally the essays on intervention against illegitimate regimes by Lukashuk, Franck, Burley and Nanda, in Law and Force in the New International Order 143–184 (Damrosch & Scheffer, eds. 1991); Schachter, Is There a Right to Overthrow an Illegitimate Regime, in Le Droit international au service de la justice et du développement: mélanges Michel Virally 423 (1991); Reisman, Old Wine in New Bottles: The Reagan and Brezhnev Doctrines in Contemporary International Law and Practice, 13 Yale J.Int'l L. 171 (1988); Henkin, The Use of Force: Law and U.S. Policy, in Right v. Might: International Law and the Use of Force 37 (2nd ed. 1991). See also Wippman, Defending Democracy Through Foreign Intervention, 19 Houston J.I.L. 659 (1997); Byers & Chesterman, "You the People:" Pro–Democratic Intervention in International Law, in Fox & Roth (eds.), Democratic Governance and International Law 259–292 (2000).

5. *Belligerency and Neutrality Under the Charter*

The U.N. Charter prohibits any threat or use of force, and presumably was designed also to abolish the state of war. If so, the concepts of belligerency and neutrality were also to be eliminated by the Charter. If the U.N. takes action against an aggressor, member states may be obliged to assist and cannot remain neutral. See Henkin, How Nations Behave 140 (2d ed. 1979); Norton, Between the Ideology and the Reality: The Shadow of the Law of Neutrality, 17 Harv. Int'l L.J. 249 at n. 7 (1976).

Unfortunately, the Charter did not put an end to large scale hostilities, however denominated, and issues about the rights and duties of both the participants in hostilities and of nonparticipants have continued to arise. Beginning with their attack on Israel in 1948, some Arab states claimed a state of war and belligerency as justification, e.g., for barring passage through the Suez Canal or international straits of Israeli vessels, and vessels of other states plying to and from Israel. For a rejection of this claim, see Security Council Resolution [2322?], at 3 (1951). The 1979 Peace Treaty between Egypt and Israel expressly terminated such a state of war. See Egypt–Israel Peace Treaty, March 26, 1979, 18 I.L.M. 362 (1979). Iraq has continued to claim it is in a state of war with Israel, having formally declared war against it. Israel characterized Iraq as a belligerent in its justification for bombing an Iraqi nuclear reactor. See p. 971 above. The Iran–Iraq war in the 1980s saw frequent invocation of the neutral-belligerent distinction, particularly as it relates to states that shipped oil from Iran. See Comment, Air Attacks on Neutral Shipping in the Persian Gulf: The Legality of the Iraqi Exclusion Zone and Iranian Reprisals, 8 Bost. Coll.Int'l & Comp. L.Rev. 517 (1985).

The "neutral state" continues to be mentioned in documents such as the Geneva Convention Relative to the Protection of Civilian Persons in Time of War (Art. 11), and the Geneva Convention Relative to the Treatment of Prisoners of War (Art. 11).

Note

Compare Henkin, Force, Intervention and Neutrality in Contemporary International Law, 57 A.S.I.L. Proc. 147, 159–161 (1963) with Deak, Neutrality Revisited, in Transnational Law in a Changing Society 137 (Friedmann, Henkin & Lissitzyn eds., 1972). See also Norton, Between the Ideology and the Reality: The Shadow of the Law of Neutrality, 17 Harv. Int'l L.J. 249 (1976).

On neutrality in relation to internal conflicts, see p. 983.

SECTION 2. INTERVENTION IN INTERNAL CONFLICTS

A notable feature of the post-Cold War era is the shift in conflict patterns away from interstate violence toward struggles taking place mainly within the borders of states. Of course, civil wars, revolutions, and ethnic strife are not new phenomena; and international law has long grappled with their implications for international order. Prior to the U.N. Charter, international law sought to constrain external involvement in civil wars, by limiting the support that outsiders could give to participants in an internal struggle. The doctrine of non-intervention was the principal heading under which such restraints were found (or claimed). The Charter period reaffirmed legal constraints on intervention in internal affairs, but there have been substantial pressures for change in the traditional law. With the savagery of some recent conflicts (e.g., Somalia, Rwanda, and former Yugoslavia in the 1990s), claims favoring a doctrine of "humanitarian intervention" have been given new urgency. If accepted, these claims could substantially alter what has been the dominant interpretation of the U.N. Charter through most of the late twentieth century. In this Section, we review these developments and consider the prospects for future evolution of the law. Our emphasis here is on interventions by states acting unilaterally; collective interventions will be addressed in Section 3.

A. THE TRADITIONAL LAW

Intervention by foreign powers in civil war and other domestic strife was regarded traditionally as a special form of foreign intervention, subject to the limitations imposed by international law on intervention generally. Even before the U.N. Charter, intervention in civil war was, for international law, a particularly troublesome form of intervention. Henkin writes:

> Not surprisingly, revolutionary movements sought external assistance for themselves, but condemned as intervention any assistance to the governments against which they were rebelling. Not surprisingly,

> governments (including those which themselves came to power by revolution) saw objectionable "intervention" when other nations supported rebellion, whether by financial, political, or military means. Not surprisingly, governments saw no objectionable "intervention" in financial, military, or political support for themselves, even to shore them up against possible rebellion.
>
> The result was that international society struggled to achieve consensus and law on such questions as: What kinds of assistance may be given to legitimate governments? At what point does such assistance cease to be permissible because the government's right and power to rule are being challenged? At what stage may nations begin to accord rebels limited rights as "insurgents"? When may they decide to accord them belligerent rights equal to those of the government previously in power? When may they recognize them as the legitimate government? What are the rights and duties of states in regard to one side or the other in full-blown civil war? The absence of international standards or procedures for recognition has left nations with wide discretion as to when and whom to recognize, which they are able to exploit for their own "interventionist" political interests.

How Nations Behave at 155 (2d ed. 1979).

The Spanish Civil War was a watershed for international law on intervention in civil war. In February of 1936, the Spanish Popular Front came to power in Spain through an electoral victory. Influential members of several rightist parties attempted to seize power without bloodshed, but when this effort failed, they started a revolt in Morocco headed by General Franco. From the start of hostilities, Germany and Italy intervened by transporting the rebel troops of General Franco to the mainland. The incumbent Republican government appealed for assistance. After initial vacillation, the French Cabinet decided not to intervene, but it did permit the private sale of arms to the Republican government. France's non-intervention policy appears to have been influenced by a fear of provoking Germany into more open intervention, leading to a world war. If France had been willing to provide the guns and ammunition sought by the Republican government, the rebellion might have been crushed.

At the initiative of Great Britain and France, an attempt was made to end intervention in the Spanish Civil War through the exchange of unilateral pledges by twenty-seven European governments. The agreements to prevent shipments of arms, ammunition and implements of war were to be supervised by the International Committee for the Application of the Agreement Regarding Non–Intervention in Spain. From its first meeting on September 9, 1936, until the middle of November, 1936, the Committee heard charges of intervention by the various powers. It is generally recognized that Germany and Italy violated the agreements on a major scale from the beginning. Although the Soviet Union maintained neutrality in the first stages of the war, it began to intervene in October, 1936, by sending significant quantities of equipment to the Republican Government.

The United States was not a party to the Non–Intervention Agreements, but it maintained a policy of strict neutrality, including an absolute embargo against the shipment of arms to Spain. The refusal of the United States to sell arms, combined with the non-intervention policy of the British and French, deprived the Spanish Republic of adequate armaments while the rebels received supplies from Germany and Italy.

The Non–Intervention Pact departed from the traditional doctrine that, in a civil war, the government but not the rebels may receive assistance from outside, at least until the rebels have been granted the status of belligerency. This status was never accorded to the Franco forces, who moved directly from rebels to full recognition as the government of Spain. Germany and Italy, while nominally parties to this Pact, not only violated it by providing massive supplies and armed contingents—of which the German bombing squadron that obliterated Guernica is the most notorious example—but they also circumvented the problem of inequality of status between government and rebels by recognizing the Franco rebels as the Government of Spain in November, 1936. This recognition came when the fall of Madrid was anticipated by many observers, but it has been criticized as premature recognition, forbidden by international law. (Compare p. 264 in Chapter 4.)

With the fall of Catalonia in February of 1939, the world concluded that the Spanish Civil War was over. France and Britain accorded official recognition to the government of General Franco on February 27; the United States extended recognition on April 1.

Notes

1. The classic analysis of the international law implications of the Spanish Civil War is Padelford, International Law and Diplomacy in the Spanish Civil Strife (1939). Friedmann has commented as follows:

> * * * A distinction has often been made between support for the incumbent government and support for insurgents, on the ground "that a foreign state commits an international delinquency by assisting insurgents in spite of being at peace with the legitimate government."[4] But since there is a very wide measure of discretion in the speed and manner in which any individual state may recognize insurgents in another state either as belligerents or as the legitimate government, the value of this distinction is highly doubtful. At most it may be said that, in extreme cases of foreign assistance to rebels in the guise of their immediate recognition as the legitimate government, at a time when they had no substantial control of the country, as was notably the case in the almost immediate recognition of the Franco government by Germany and Italy after the rebellion, is a thinly disguised interference in the affairs of another state, utterly at variance with established principles of recognition. Apart from such extreme cases, the parties in a civil strife seriously contesting the control of the country, must probably be taken as equals. Any, reasonably precise, definition of the rights and duties of other states with regards to the parties in a civil war is made extremely difficult by the fact that civil war usually arises from clashes of political philosophy and bitter social tensions, and that therefore the sympathies of governments and political groups outside the state torn by civil war are usually deeply engaged on one side or the other. This tends to mould legal interpretations of rights of intervention and duties of abstention even more in the direction of political

4. Oppenheim, International Law, Vol. 2 (7th ed., Lauterpacht, 1952), p. 660. See also Jessup, The International Problem of Governing Mankind (1947), p. 33 et seq.

> sympathies, than in other situations. Thus, in the Spanish Civil War from 1936–38, which deeply stirred official and non-official political opinion abroad, those favoring the cause of the incumbent Republican Government of Spain affirmed the widely supported doctrine that in the case of civil war, the legal government but not the insurgents are entitled to assistance, at least up to the point when the insurgents have become sufficiently established to attain the status of belligerency. This attitude was strengthened by the blatant intervention of Nazi Germany and Fascist Italy on the side of Franco, from the very outbreak of revolution. For reasons of policy rather than law, the Western governments came to treat both sides as equals, by concluding a non-intervention pact to which the Fascist Powers, as well as the Soviet Union, were also parties. This pact, based on the principle of abstention from assistance to either side proved a complete failure, not because of the underlying principle but because the Fascist Powers, and to a lesser extent the Soviet Union, ignored the obligations undertaken in the pact so that the disparity between the assistance granted to the Franco faction by states in league with him and the failure of the Republican Government to obtain aid from the Western Powers, became even greater. Legally, however, a case can be made for the theory underlying the nonintervention pact, provided, of course, that it is genuinely observed by all sides. Quincy Wright has contended, with powerful support in the legal literature, that "in a situation of civil strife, the state is temporarily inhibited from acting. A government beset by civil strife is not in a position to invite assistance in the name of the state."
> * * *

Friedmann, The Changing Structure of International Law 265–266 (1964) (some footnotes omitted).

Does the history of the Spanish Civil War illustrate the obsolescence of the traditional rule under which neutral governments are enjoined from assisting either side in a war by military supplies, but private manufacturers and traders are permitted to do so? Compare Friedmann, The Growth of State Control over the Individual and its Effect upon the Rules of International State Responsibility, 19 Br. Y.B.I.L. 118 (1938). Can a government disclaim responsibility for the movement of arms from its territory to any other power, or disclaim the power to regulate or interdict such supplies?

2. Supplying arms to a belligerent is one example of an act that may violate the neutral duty of impartiality. See p. 980 supra. The recruitment and training of troops in one state to launch an attack against another state is another example. Title 18 U.S.C.A. § 960 provides:

> Whoever, within the United States, knowingly begins or sets on foot or provides or prepares a means for or furnishes the money for, or takes part in, any military or naval expedition or enterprise to be carried on from thence against the territory or dominion of any foreign prince or state, or of any colony, district, or people with whom the United States is at peace, shall be fined not more than $3,000 or imprisoned not more than three years, or both.

In 1959, the Department of Justice asked the Department of State for its opinion whether an organization formed in California and called the "Tibetan Brigade," which reportedly intended to go into Tibet in order to "aid the Tibetans in their revolt against the Chinese Communist tyranny," might be acting in violation of 18 U.S.C.A. § 960. The Department of State replied that Communist China should not be considered a state within the meaning of the statute, since at the time the Communist régime was not recognized by the United States as the legitimate government. Furthermore the United States could not be considered at peace with Communist China. See 5 Whiteman 254–55.

Following the abortive action against the Castro régime by Cuban refugees and their sympathizers at the Bay of Pigs on April 15, 1961, the Attorney General of the United States stated that none of their activities had violated the neutrality laws of the United States. While conceding that the laws prohibit the departure from the United States of a group organized as a military expedition against a nation with whom the United States is at peace, he contended that the departure of several persons at the same time with the intent of joining an insurgent group was not criminal. 5 Whiteman 275–76.

The applicability of U.S. neutrality laws also became an issue with respect to private assistance for the Nicaraguan *contras* in the 1980s. See generally Dellums v. Smith, 573 F.Supp. 1489 (N.D.Cal.1983).

3. In 1989, the United Nations General Assembly adopted an International Convention against the Recruitment Use, Financing and Training of Mercenaries. See U.N.Doc. A/RES/44/34, reprinted in 29 I.L.M. 89 (1990). As of 2000, the Convention had 21 of the 22 signatures required to bring it into force.

B. CIVIL STRIFE AND THE UNITED NATIONS CHARTER

HENKIN, HOW NATIONS BEHAVE

155–57 (2d ed. 1979) (footnotes omitted).

When, in the U.N. Charter, the nations decided to outlaw wars and the use of force, they said nothing explicit about internal wars; clearly, they did not intend to prohibit revolution or civil war. The Charter, too, though it enshrines principles of "independence," "sovereign equality," and "self-determination," says nothing explicit about outside intervention in internal struggles. It is not commonly insisted that the Charter itself forbids intervention in internal wars by political and economic means. The question that has divided lawyers is whether the Charter provision that members shall not use or threaten force against the political independence or territorial integrity of another member forbids also intervention by force in a civil war.

* * *

Some lawyers have argued that, when nations come to the support of one side or the other in cases of independent insurrection or *bona fide* civil war, it is not a violation of the norms of the U.N. Charter but only of some customary rule against such intervention which, if it was ever sound, may not have recovered from the wounds it suffered in the Spanish Civil War. Many believed that there is no agreed norm forbidding active military support for the recognized government of a country, at least before rebellion has made great headway. The United States has invoked the right to give such aid to Greece, Lebanon, Nationalist China, and South Vietnam. The Soviet Union claimed a similar justification in Hungary. Some may even assert the right to recognize and support rebel causes, as in Angola (against Portugal), and even in the Congo in 1964–65. * * *

In our time, some forces for intervention have been particularly strong and unlikely to heed an uncertain law. The difficulties of defining and preventing "unlawful intervention" have been multiplied where domestic and international interests are entangled and internal conflicts have special international significance. There were interventions to help end colonialism, as when Tunisia actively supported the Algerian rebels, and when other nations supported rebels against Portuguese rule in Angola. The major interventions involved, of course, Communist expansionism and Western efforts to contain it.

INTERVENTION BY FORCE IN CIVIL WARS

SCHACHTER, THE RIGHT OF STATES TO USE ARMED FORCE

82 Mich. L.Rev. 1620, 1641–45 (1984) (footnotes omitted).

Foreign military interventions in civil wars have been so common in our day that the proclaimed rule of nonintervention may seem to have been stood on its head. Talleyrand's cynical quip comes to mind: "non-intervention is a word that has the same meaning as intervention." Indeed, virtually all the interventions that occur today are carried out in the name of nonintervention; they are justified as responses to prior interventions by the other side. No state today would deny the basic principle that the people of a nation have the right, under international law, to decide for themselves what kind of government they want, and that this includes the right to revolt and to carry on armed conflict between competing groups. For a foreign state to support, with "force," one side or the other in an internal conflict, is to deprive the people in some measure of their right to decide the issue by themselves. It is, in terms of article 2(4), a use of force against the political independence of the state engaged in civil war.

The states that intervene do not challenge this legal principle; they generally proclaim it as the basis for their "counter-intervention." They are often able to do so with some plausibility, because in almost every civil war the parties have sought and received some outside military support. A preeminent difficulty in applying the rule of nonintervention in these circumstances arises from the equivocal position of the established government. Other states are free as a general rule (in the absence of contrary treaties) to furnish arms, military training and even combat forces to that government at its request. On the other hand, they may not do the same for an opposing force; that would clearly violate the sovereignty and independence of the state.

Consequently, governments commonly receive foreign military aid and they may request more such aid when faced with an armed insurrection. At that point two questions arise: (1) is there an obligation to cease aid to the established regime because that now involves taking sides in an internal conflict? And (2) if such aid to the government constitutes foreign intervention, does it permit counter-intervention to support the other side? Concretely, if the Nicaraguan Sandinista regime receives Cuban and Soviet military supplies and advisors, is the United States free to support the armed opposition by training, arms and technical advice? An answer to the first question involves an assessment of the particular circumstances and of the presumption that the government is entitled to continued aid. The relevant general principle, in keeping with the concept of political independence and non-intervention, would be that when an organized insurgency occurs on a large scale involving a substantial number of people or control over significant areas of the country, neither side, government or insurgency, should receive outside military aid. Such outside support would be contrary to the right of the people to decide the issue by their own means. It would be immaterial whether the insurgency was directed at overthrow of the government or at secession (or autonomy) of a territorial unit.

The second and more difficult question is whether an illegal intervention on one side permits outside states to give military aid to the other party (whether government or insurrectionists). Such counter-intervention may be justified as a defense of the independence of the state against foreign intervention; it may then be viewed as "collective self-defense" in response to armed attack. True, it may also further "internationalize" a local conflict and increase the threat to international peace. The Vietnam War is the outstanding example. Despite the danger, the law does not proscribe such counter-intervention. It is not that two wrongs make a right but that the grave violation of one right allows a defensive response. The political solution is to avoid its necessity by a strict application of a nonintervention rule applied to both sides. To achieve this it is probably essential in most cases to have international mechanisms (peacekeeping forces or observer teams) to monitor compliance with a *cordon sanitaire* and a ban on assistance.

A related problem of practical importance is the clarification of what kinds of military aid qualify as illicit intervention. The UN resolutions on nonintervention leave this to ad hoc judgments, but a strong case can be made for the specifications of impermissible acts. Such specification would give more determinate content to the principle of nonintervention and, in that respect, strengthen it. In line with this view, the Institut de Droit International, in its resolution on nonintervention, has designated the following acts as impermissible when done to support either party in a civil war:

> (a) sending armed forces or military volunteers, instructors or technicians to any party to a civil war, or allowing them to be sent or to set out;
>
> (b) drawing up or training regular or irregular forces with a view to supporting any party to a civil war, or allowing them to be drawn up or trained;
>
> (c) supplying weapons or other war material to any party to a civil war, or allowing them to be supplied;
>
> * * *
>
> (e) making their territories available to any party to a civil war, or allowing them to be used by any such party, as bases of operations or of supplies, as places of refuge, for the passage of regular or irregular forces, or for the transit of war material. The last mentioned prohibition includes transmitting military information to any of the parties.

The Institut also declared that outside states should use "all means to prevent inhabitants of their territories, whether natives or aliens, from raising contingents and collecting equipment, from crossing the border or from embarking from their territories with a view to fomenting or causing a civil war." They also have a duty to disarm and intern any force of either party to a civil war which enters their territory. However, the Institut's resolution does not prohibit humanitarian aid for the benefit of victims of a civil war nor does it exclude economic or technical aid that is not likely to have a substantial impact on the outcome of a civil war. While it cannot be said that these declarations of the Institut are clearly existing law in every detail, they are a persuasive interpretation of the general rule against nonintervention and should influence state practice.

Two additional principles have been proposed for placing limits on counter-intervention. One is that the counter-intervention should be limited to the territory of the state where the civil war takes place. The fact that the prior intervention was illegal (i.e., in violation of the rule of non-intervention) would not justify legally the use of force by a third state in the violator's territory. This territorial limitation on counter-intervention has been observed in nearly all recent civil wars. However, it apparently has been abandoned by the United States insofar as its "counter-intervention" on the side of the El Salvador regime has extended to support of anti-Sandinista forces fighting on Nicaraguan soil. The United States had justified this action under the collective self-defense provision of article 51, presumably on the ground that Nicaragua has engaged in an armed attack on El Salvador. The United States also "counter-intervened" against Nicaragua by mining approaches to Nicaraguan ports. The legality of the U.S. actions has been challenged by Nicaragua in a case brought by it in April 1984 against the United States in the International Court of Justice. * * *

The second limitation arises from the principle of proportionality. It calls for limits on the technological level of weapons used in a counter-intervention. This is essentially a no-first-use rule. High-technology weapons of mass destruction should not be introduced into the internal conflict by any outside intervening state, whatever its right to intervene. On the whole, this rule of restraint has been followed in recent civil wars, though the Vietnam War involved exceptions. There is good reason to consider it as a legal restriction and not merely a prudential principle. It is, however, less clear that state practice conforms to a rule of proportionality in regard to the quantum of military aid on one side or the other. Proportionality would require some rough equivalence between the counter-intervention and the illicit aid given the other side. However, when an established regime faces a strong indigenous insurgency which has some outside aid, the counter-intervening government favoring the regime is likely to be under great pressure to give massive support to that regime, even if relatively minor aid from the outside is given to the insurgents. U.S. military aid to El Salvador is a current example. It demonstrates the difficulty of applying a principle of proportionality in the absence of agreed limits by both sides on the quantum and character of outside aid.

Notes

1. See generally Resolution on Principles of Non–Intervention of the Institute of International Law, 56 Annuaire de l'Institut de Droit International 119–56, 411–74 (1975, Wiesbaden Session) (resolution and accompanying reports and discussion); Vincent, Non-intervention and International Order (1974); J.N. Moore, Law and Civil War in the Modern World (1974); Bowett, Self–Defense in

International Law (1958); Falk, Legal Order in a Violent World, Part II (19), in Intervention in International Politics (Bull ed. 1984); Farer, Harnessing Rogue Elephants: a Short Discourse on Foreign Intervention in Civil Strife, 82 Harv. L.Rev. 511 (1969).

2. During the Cold War there were many instances of external participation in situations of internal disorder, strife or civil war: U.S. support for Greek and Turkish governments fighting Communist guerrilla bands (1947); the Soviet Union's interventions in Hungary (1956), Czechoslovakia (1968), and Afghanistan (1979); India in Bangladesh (1971); civil war in Lebanon (1958 and 1982); the sending of U.S. marines to the Dominican Republic (1965); internal and interstate war in the Horn of Africa; interventions in civil war in Angola and Southern Africa; Vietnam's invasion of Kampuchea to depose the Pol Pot regime (1979); external roles in civil war in El Salvador and Nicaragua (during most of the 1980s); French and Libyan involvement in civil war in Chad (1980s); and various other situations.

As to whether intervention in a state by one outside power justifies counter-intervention by another, see Cutler, The Right to Intervene, 64 Foreign Affairs 96 (1985). Compare Schachter, The Right of States to Use Armed Force, 82 Mich. L.Rev. at 1641–45; Schachter, In Defense of International Rules on the Use of Force, 53 U.Chi. L.Rev. 113, 120–21, 137–38 (1986); Henkin, The Use of Force: Law and U.S. Policy, in Right v. Might: International Law and the Use of Force 37, 50–65 (2d ed. 1991).

3. The most extensive involvement by the United States in foreign civil strife since World War II was in Vietnam. As Henkin has written:

> There are at least three possible models to characterize the Vietnam War and the U.S. role in it, and the judgment of international law will largely depend on which characterization it accepts.
>
> Model A saw the war as civil war within an independent South Vietnam, with North Vietnam an outside state helping one side, the United States another outside state helping the other. Military intervention in civil war was not acceptable under traditional international law, but that law may never have recovered from the wounds it suffered at many hands during the Spanish Civil War. On its face at least, such external intervention is not obviously a violation of Article 2(4) of the U.N. Charter as a use of force against the political independence or territorial integrity of another state, if the support was bona fide and the intervenor was not seeking to dominate the side it supported and establish a puppet regime. * * *
>
> A second view (Model B) also saw the war as civil war, not between the Vietcong and the Saigon Government in a separate independent South Vietnam, but within the single state of Vietnam, between North Vietnam and the Vietcong on one hand and Saigon forces on the other. In such a war, U.S. intervention, even bombing North Vietnam, was–again–perhaps a violation of traditional international norms against intervention in civil war, but not clearly of the U.N. Charter. * * *
>
> Officially, the United States saw the war in Vietnam in yet a third perspective (Model C). North Vietnam launched an armed attack against the territorial integrity and political independence of an independent country, the Republic of South Vietnam, using the Vietcong as its agent. This was a use of force in clear violation of Article 2(4) of the Charter. In the face of this armed attack, the Republic of South Vietnam had its inherent right of self-defense

> under Article 51 of the Charter, and the United States could come to its aid in collective self-defense–as indeed, it had obligated itself to do in the South East Asian Collective Defense Treaty. The United States and the Republic of South Vietnam had every right to carry the war to the territory of the aggressor in order to defeat the aggression; they could carry the war to the territory of any other countries that involved themselves in the aggression, or permitted the aggressor to use their territory for its aggressive purposes, *i.e.*, Laos and Cambodia.

Henkin, How Nations Behave 306–308 (2d ed. 1979) (footnotes omitted). In the Tonkin Gulf Resolution, H.J. Res. 1145, 78 Stat. 384 (1964), the U.S. Congress approved U.S. actions in support of a member of the Southeast Asia Collective Defense Treaty as, in effect, collective self-defense against aggression.

A convenient compendium of the principal documents and articles is contained in The Vietnam War and International Law (Falk ed. 1968–74). See also Falk, International Law and the United States Role in the Vietnam War, 75 Yale L.J. 1122 (1966); Moore, The Lawfulness of Military Assistance to the Republic of Vietnam, 61 A.J.I.L. 1 (1967); Falk's response at 76 Yale L.J. 1095 (1967); Falk, The Six Legal Dimensions of the Vietnam War (1968); J.N. Moore, Law and the Indo–China War (1972). Compare also their contributions to Symposium on the United States Military Action in Cambodia, 1970, in the Light of International and Constitutional Law, 65 A.J.I.L. 1 (1971).

4. Civil wars of the 1990s claimed millions of lives. More than two dozen such wars were in progress when the Carnegie Commission on Prevention of Deadly Conflict issued its Final Report in December 1997 (for illustrative figures, see the Final Report at pp. 11–22). A large portion of these wars involved the residue of arms transfers dating from the period of U.S.-Soviet confrontation, as well as the remnants of armies that had been proxies for one or the other superpower at an earlier time. Conflicts between ethnic groups likewise produced bloodshed on a staggering scale. On efforts to deploy techniques of international law to quell ethnic strife, see Wippman (ed.), International Law and Ethnic Conflict (1998); Ratner, Does International Law Matter in Preventing Ethnic Conflict?, 32 N.Y.U.J.Int'l L. & Pol. 591 (2000).

5. Emblematic of post-Cold War conflicts is the chaos that engulfed Congo (formerly Zaire; renamed Democratic Republic of Congo in 199_) with the collapse of the regime of Mobutu Sese Seko, who had ruled dictatorially for more than three decades until he was driven from power in 1997. A government headed by Laurent Kabila, who had ousted Mobutu, held power through January 2001, when Kabila was assassinated and replaced by his son, Joseph Kabila. Meanwhile, the regime based in the capital city, Kinshasa, lacked control of about half of the country (itself as large as Western Europe); rebels supported by several neighboring states continued in armed struggle against forces loyal to Kabila. While aspects of the conflict had economic motivations (related to Congo's valuable resources, which include diamonds, gold, timber and coffee), some of the outside parties maintained armed intervention for reasons related to their own security interests. Rwanda sent troops into Congo to pursue Rwandan Hutu extremists who had fled into Congolese territory after perpetrating massive genocide in Rwanda in 1994 (see p. 1035), and (together with Uganda and Burundi) Rwanda supported rebel forces that were threatening the Kabila government. Other African countries–Angola, Zimbabwe, and Namibia–also had troops in Congo, which had entered the country to bolster Laurent Kabila's forces and remained with the government's consent (or acquiescence).

In June 1999, Congo initiated suit at the International Court of Justice against Burundi, Rwanda, and Uganda, alleging of "acts of armed aggression perpetrated by [those states] on the territory of the Democratic Republic of the Congo, in flagrant violation of the United Nations Charter and of the Charter of the Organization of African Unity." The suits against Burundi and Rwanda were discontinued at Congo's request in January 2001. See Armed Activities on the Territory of the Congo (Democratic Republic of the Congo v. Burundi; Democratic Republic of the Congo v. Rwanda), 2001 I.C.J. (Order of Jan. 30, 2001). The suit against Uganda remains pending.

In February 2001, Joseph Kabila, appearing before the U.N. Security Council, "called for 'the armies of aggression' from Rwanda, Uganda and Burundi to withdraw from Congolese territory. He promised that other troops sent in by Zimbabwe, Angola and Namibia to shore up his father's government would leave later when stability was restored." At the same time, the acting U.S. ambassador to the U.N. said that "while Mr. Kabila's government had a right to demand that uninvited foreign forces depart, 'the governments of Rwanda and Uganda have a right under the U.N. charter to demand that Congolese territory not be used as a launching pad for attacks against their countries." See "Congo's New Leader, at the U.N., Pledges Talks With War Foes," N.Y. Times, Feb. 3, 2001, p. A7.

Do the materials in this Section on intervention in civil wars and the Definition of Aggression Resolution provide a legal framework for understanding the situation concerning foreign involvement in Congo's internal conflicts?

U.N. efforts to stabilize the situation in Congo have been unavailing. In 2000 the U.N. Security Council approved a peacekeeping force for Congo with an authorized strength of more than 5500 troops, but as of December 2000, when the Council renewed the six-month mandate for the force, only about 200 were in place. The dire security situation in the country was the main obstacle to deployment.

Against the background of conflict patterns of this type, international law in the late twentieth and early twenty-first centuries has been challenged to develop new approaches to the subject of intervention, with a view toward providing ideas and techniques for preventing and abating internal conflicts. The topic of humanitarian intervention, addressed immediately below, is one heading under which such consideration has been underway. Others will be taken up in Section 3 on collective uses of force.

C. HUMANITARIAN INTERVENTION

The legality of intervention for humanitarian reasons has been debated for decades and bears some resemblance to issues taken up earlier (p. 973) on permissible uses of force for benign purposes. In the sense used here, humanitarian intervention refers to uses of force by one state to protect persons within another state from massive atrocities such as genocide. There were various examples of such interventions in state practice in the nineteenth century, before a prohibition on the use of force had crystallized in international law. The lawfulness of humanitarian intervention in the U.N. Charter period has been much disputed, because it is difficult to reconcile such claims with the text of Article 2(4), with its negotiating history, or with subsequent U.N. efforts to clarify its meaning (as in the Friendly Relations Declaration or the Definition of Aggression Resolution). Similarly, it has not been clear that state practice or *opinio juris* could establish the existence of a customary law right of humanitarian intervention in the post-World War II period.

Developments near the end of the twentieth century brought renewed attention to the humanitarian intervention controversy. As hundreds of thousands lost their lives in brutal ethnic conflict in the former Yugoslavia, in Hutu-against-Tutsi massacres in Rwanda, in suppression of the self-determination movement in East Timor, and similar savagery in too many parts of the globe, there were growing demands for the outside world to become involved. Media attention—the so-called "CNN factor"—drew the spotlight to such situations and underscored the moral urgency of doing whatever could be done to stop the slaughter of innocents. Humanitarian aid to victims of manmade as well as natural disasters was delivered on several occasions in the 1990s with the help of outside military forces, as in Somalia (see p. 1032). It began to seem possible that external military interventions might be able to prevent or interrupt vast human tragedies, and if so, that international law should be interpreted (or reinterpreted, or revised) to permit rather than prohibit such uses of force.

The debates over humanitarian intervention took on a new dimension with the Kosovo crisis of 1999 (pp. 997–1003). Some political leaders and international lawyers explicitly embraced a humanitarian intervention rationale, in more expansive terms than had previously been acceptable under the dominant views of previous decades. Others, however, were reluctant to embrace a theory that could loosen the Charter's constraints on transboundary uses of force and provide a pretext for abusive interventions.

The materials that follow trace developments up to and after the Kosovo intervention. We will return to related questions in Section 3 on collective uses of force, since several of the humanitarian interventions of the 1990s had explicit Security Council authorization (and implicit multilateral approval was one of the claims proffered to justify NATO's action in Kosovo); also, it has often been contended that collective interventions can enjoy greater legitimacy in the eyes of international law than unilateral ones. Preliminary to turning to issues of collective intervention as presented in the post-Cold War era, we examine here the main trends in evaluating the lawfulness of unilateral humanitarian interventions.

EVALUATION UNDER THE U.N. CHARTER AND CUSTOMARY INTERNATIONAL LAW

SCHACHTER, INTERNATIONAL LAW IN THEORY AND PRACTICE

123–125 (1991) (footnotes omitted).

Apart from self-defense, the strongest claim to allowing an exception to the prohibition on armed force would appear to be the use of force to save the lives of innocent human beings threatened by massacres, atrocities, widespread brutality and destruction. * * *

In support, it has been argued that the renunciation of armed force could not have been intended to prevent such humanitarian interventions when other means, short of force, were proven ineffective. The interventions, if limited to humanitarian ends under conditions of necessity and proportionality, could not be against the territorial integrity or political independence of the State in question, nor could they be inconsistent with the purposes of the Charter. If the U.N. failed to take effective action and no other international body did, elementary humanitarian principles impose an obligation on States capable of taking protective measures to do so, including, if necessary the employment of armed forces in the troubled countries.

These arguments, appealing as they seem to be, have failed to win the explicit support of the international community of States or of any significant segment of that community. No United Nations resolution has supported the right of a State to intervene on humanitarian grounds with armed troops in a State that has not consented to such intervention. Nor is there evidence of State practice and related *opinio juris* on a scale sufficient to support a humanitarian exception to the general prohibition against non-defensive use of force.

It is true that, in a few cases, the action of an intervening army outside of its borders was seen as serving a humanitarian end because it saved innocent lives from death or injury. Whether these cases can be considered as precedents accepted as law is dubious, especially as no intervening state claimed a legal right based on that ground. Thus, when Indian troops acted to protect Bengalis in East Pakistan in 1971 from Pakistani troops, India asserted the action was necessary to protect its borders. * * * Despite much sympathy for the East Pakistan Bengalis, the great majority of States were clearly unwilling to legitimize India's armed action as a permissible exception to Article 2(4).

A second case that some lawyers have viewed as humanitarian intervention occurred when Tanzanian troops moved into Uganda following a Ugandan frontier incursion repulsed by Tanzania. Actually, Tanzania claimed self-defense rather than a right of humanitarian intervention. * * * Some African leaders criticized Tanzania's action but, understandably, many governments were not disposed to challenge its relatively benign occupation. It is hard to regard such non-action as accepting a right of unilateral intervention for humanitarian ends. What it does show is that governments hesitate to condemn a short-term military move against an egregious régime. * * *

A claim of humanitarian intent was used by Vietnam to support its armed action in Cambodia in 1978 against the Pol Pot forces. * * * The majority of States in the United Nations have rejected the Vietnamese contentions and called for the withdrawal of its troops.

* * *

Our sympathy for victims of atrocities should not obscure the lessons of past invasions claimed to be humanitarian. Past armed interventions, going back to 19th century incursions by imperial powers, have shown that intervening States have invariably had their own political agenda. They imposed conditions that were not freely chosen by the people of the country in question. They often obtained special advantages and exacerbated internal conflicts. It is hardly surprising that governments have refrained from adopting a general rule for humanitarian intervention. Indeed, I believe no government has actually declared itself as favoring so broad an exception to the rule against force.

Notes

1. Compare the following views:

a. "There is general agreement that, by virtue of its personal and territorial authority, a state can treat its own nationals according to discretion. But a substantial body of opinion and of practice has supported the view that there are limits to that discretion and that when a state commits cruelties against and persecution of its nationals in such a way as to deny their fundamental human rights and to shock the conscience of mankind, the matter ceases to be of sole concern to that state and even intervention in the interest of humanity might be legally permissible. However, the fact that, when resorted to by individual states, it may be—and has been—abused for selfish purposes tended to weaken its standing as a lawful practice."

1 Oppenheim's International Law 442–43 (9th ed., Jennings & Watts, eds. 1992) (footnotes omitted).

b. In a book titled Law and Civil War in the Modern World, Brownlie and Lillich had the following exchange:

> It is clear to the present writer that a jurist asserting a right of forcible humanitarian intervention has a very heavy burden of proof. Few writers familiar with the modern materials of state practice and legal opinion on the use of force would support such a view. In the first place, it is significant that the very small number of writers cited in support of this view by Lillich include two, McDougal and Reisman, who lean heavily on a flexible and teleological interpretation of treaty texts. Leading modern authorities who either make no mention of humanitarian intervention and whose general position militates against its legality, or expressly deny its existence include Brierly, Castrén, Jessup, Jiménez de Aréchaga, Briggs, Schwarzenberger, Goodrich, Hambro, and Simons, Skubiszewski, Friedmann, Waldock, Bishop, Sorenson, and Kelsen. In the lengthy discussions over the years in the United Nations bodies of the definition of aggression and the principles of international law concerning international relations and cooperation among states, the variety of opinions canvassed has not revealed even a substantial minority in favor of the legality of humanitarian intervention. The *Repertory of Practice of United Nations Organs* provides no support; nor does the International Law Commission's Draft Declaration of the Rights and Duties of States. The voluminous materials in Whiteman's *Digest* lack even a passing reference to humanitarian intervention. Counting heads is not, of course, a sound way of resolving issues of principle. However, quite apart from the weight of the opinion of experts cited above, it is the writer's view that these authorities are reporting and reflecting the universal consensus of government opinion and practice since 1945. Their views thus combine both policy in the sense of the reasonable expectations of states and the normative quality of rules based on *consensus*. With due respect to Lillich, it must be said that, if a new view is to be put forward, either it should be based on a much more substantial exposition of the practice, doctrine, and general development of the law relating to the use of force by states or the view should be offered *tout court* as a proposal to change existing law.

Brownlie, Humanitarian Intervention, in Law and Civil War in the Modern World 218–19 (Moore, ed., 1974) (footnotes omitted). Lillich replied:

> If, as Falk has remarked, "the renunciation of intervention does not substitute a policy of nonintervention; it involves the development of some form of collective intervention," then concomitantly the failure to develop effective international machinery to facilitate humanitarian interventions arguably permits a state to intervene unilaterally in appropriate situations. Writing a decade ago, Ronning wisely observed that "it is as useless to outlaw intervention without providing a satisfactory substitute as it was to outlaw war when no satisfactory substitute was available." He also posed the difficult question, which becomes more relevant every year, whether refusal to compromise on the principle of absolute non-intervention will not threaten the very principle itself. It can of course continue to be honored in countless declarations and protests, but if it does not square with the hard facts of international politics, that will be the extent of its honor. Although Brownlie does not consider this question, events during the past decade reveal a widening "credibility gap" between the absolute non-intervention approach to the Charter which he espouses and the actual practice of states.

Lillich, Humanitarian Intervention: A Reply to Dr. Brownlie and a Plea for Constructive Alternatives, in Law and Civil War in the Modern World 229, 247–248 (Moore, ed. 1974) (footnotes omitted). Does the revival of the U.N. Security Council since the end of the Cold War undercut Lillich's complaint about the lack of "effective international machinery?" See p. 1042 infra for a discussion of humanitarian intervention pursuant to U.N. authorization.

c. As state practice supporting humanitarian intervention as an exception to Article 2(4), Lillich and others have cited India's action in Bangladesh in 1971, the Vietnamese invasion of Cambodia in 1978, and the 1979 Tanzanian invasion of Uganda. Should these episodes be characterized instead as violations of the Charter? The British Foreign Office has stated:

> II.21. The state practice to which advocates of the right of humanitarian intervention have appealed provides an uncertain basis on which to rest such a right. Not the least this is because history has shown that humanitarian ends are almost always mixed with other less laudable motives for intervening, and because often the 'humanitarian' benefits of an intervention are either not claimed by the intervening state or are only put forward as an *ex post facto* justification of the intervention. * * * The two most discussed instances of alleged humanitarian intervention since 1945 are the Indian invasion of Bangladesh in 1971 and Tanzania's invasion of Uganda in 1979. But, although both did result in unquestionable benefits for * * * the people of East Bengal and Uganda, India and Tanzania were reluctant to use humanitarian ends to justify their invasion of a neighbor's territory. Both preferred to quote the right to self-defence under Article 51. And in each case the self-interest of the invading state was clearly involved.
>
> II.22. * * * [T]he overwhelming majority of contemporary legal opinion comes down against the existence of a right of humanitarian intervention, for three main reasons: first, the UN Charter and the corpus of modern international law do not seem specifically to incorporate such a right; secondly, state practice in the past two centuries, and especially since 1945, at best provides only a handful of genuine cases of humanitarian intervention, and, on most assessments, none at all; and finally, on prudential grounds, that the scope for abusing such a right argues strongly against its creation. * * * In essence, therefore, the case against making humanitarian intervention an exception to

the principle of non-intervention is that its doubtful benefits would be heavily outweighed by its costs in terms of respect for international law.

United Kingdom Foreign Office Policy Document No. 148, reprinted in 57 Brit. Y.B.Int'l L. 614 (1986). For the attitudes of other states towards humanitarian intervention, see Schachter, The Right of States to Use Armed Force, 82 Mich. L.Rev. 1620, 1628–33 (1984).

For the British government's different position expressed in the Kosovo crisis, see p. 1000.

2. For recent discussions of humanitarian intervention from various points of view, see the essays by Farer, Kartashkin, Meron and Damrosch, in Law and Force in the New International Order 185–223 (Damrosch & Scheffer, eds. 1991). See also Tesón, Humanitarian Intervention: An Inquiry into Law and Morality (2d ed. 1997); Murphy, Humanitarian Intervention (1996); Hoffmann et al., The Ethics and Politics of Humanitarian Intervention (1996); Müllerson & Scheffer, Legal Regulation of the Use of Force, in Beyond Confrontation: International Law for the Post–Cold War Era (Damrosch, Danilenko & Müllerson, eds., 1995), at pp. 93, 117–124. Earlier treatments include Humanitarian Intervention and the United Nations (Lillich, ed. 1973); Akehurst, Humanitarian Intervention, in Intervention in World Politics (Bull, ed. 1984); Franck & Rodley, After Bangladesh: The Law of Humanitarian Intervention by Military Force, 67 A.J.I.L. 275 (1973); Jhabvala, Unilateral Humanitarian Intervention and International Law, 21 Indian J.Int'l L. 208 (1981); Rodley, Human Rights and Humanitarian Intervention: The Case Law of the World Court, 38 Int'l & Comp. L.Q. 321 (1989); Scheffer, Toward a Modern Doctrine of Humanitarian Intervention, 4 Fla. Int'l L.J. 435 (1989). See also Restatement (Third) § 703, Comment *e*. Philosophical and political treatments include Rawls, The Law of Peoples 89–94 (1999); Walzer, Just and Unjust Wars 21–34, 51–73, 86–109 (3rd ed. 2000); Wheeler, Saving Strangers: Humanitarian Intervention in International Society (2000).

EFFORTS TO FORMULATE CRITERIA FOR HUMANITARIAN INTERVENTION

Writers supporting the legitimacy of humanitarian intervention generally agree that the scope for any such exception to the prohibition on use of force would have to be carefully circumscribed. Various sets of criteria have been formulated. Though they differ in their specifics, most would embody some or all of the following conditions:

—The violation of human rights would have to be extremely grave, e.g., genocide or similar atrocities on a mass scale, rather than lower-level breaches.

—There must be no other means of rectifying the violations: military force should be a last resort.

—The intervention should be supported (or at least not actively opposed) by those who would be its putative beneficiaries.

—The intervention should be conducted in full compliance with the laws of war (see Section 4) and with the least destructive means to achieve the objective of terminating the violations.

—The intervention should be calculated to cause less harm to the target state than would occur in the absence of intervention. (If the costs would outweigh the benefits, or if the probability of success is low, then there is probably not a good case for intervention on policy grounds. Some such considerations may also be relevant to legal and moral appraisal.)

—The intervenors should withdraw when the objective of terminating the violations is achieved.

Many writers would add that humanitarian intervention should preferably be carried out under the auspices of the United Nations or another appropriate multilateral institution; but if organizational capacity is lacking and international authorization cannot be obtained, unilateral intervention might be necessary. Some would also require the intervenor to report its actions to an international body and to be willing to allow its actions to be scrutinized after the fact for conformity to international law. As to these considerations, see below on the Kosovo crisis and further discussion on multilateral authority for intervention at pp. 1032–1043.

Notes

1. What level of human rights violations should be established before a humanitarian intervention would be considered justifiable? Should it be necessary to show that hundreds, perhaps thousands, of lives have already been lost? Would such a requirement run at cross-purposes with strategies designed to prevent massive violations before they reach catastrophic levels? On dilemmas of prevention, see Final Report of the Carnegie Commission on the Prevention of Deadly Conflict (1997); Jentleson (ed.), Opportunities Missed, Opportunities Seized: Preventive Diplomacy in the Post–Cold War Era (2000).

2. Should exhaustion of non-forcible means be a prerequisite to a legitimate humanitarian intervention? Most international law scholars stress that force should only be used as a last resort. But others consider that early intervention may be preferable for preventive purposes, and that delays while non-forcible alternatives are explored may only result in greater risks, costs, and bloodshed later on. The growing literature on prevention (note 1, supra) explores these difficulties.

3. Writers who accept humanitarian intervention sometimes demand "that there be no (overriding) selfish interests involved on the side of the intervenor; a demand formulated long ago by Rougier as that of *'désintéressement'* . . ." Verwey, Humanitarian Intervention Under International Law, 32 Neth. Int'l L.Rev. 357, 371 (1985). Critics of humanitarian intervention point out that many interventions undertaken with a purportedly humanitarian rationale have involved an ulterior motive on the intervenor's part, and that intervenors often pursue their own agenda in the target's territory long after achieving the supposed humanitarian objective. For example, Vietnam's 1979 intervention in Cambodia did not end with the ouster of the Khmer Rouge regime and indeed persisted into the 1990s. The likelihood of disingenuous or abusive invocations of a humanitarian rationale is one reason why many scholars reject the theory of humanitarian intervention in general:

> The fact that humanitarian intervention can serve as a pretext for achieving political objectives in another states argues strongly for invalidating multinational or unilateral missions altogether. But most norms of international law can be abused. Professor Higgins has aptly observed that "so have there been

countless abusive claims of the right to self-defence." That does not mean that the right to self-defence has ceased to exist.

Müllerson & Scheffer, Legal Regulation of the Use of Force, in Beyond Confrontation: International Law for the Post–Cold War Era 93, 124 (Damrosch, Danilenko & Müllerson eds., 1995), citing Rosalyn Higgins, Problems and Process: International Law and How We Use It 247 (1994). Does it matter that self-defense is a well-established doctrine of international law, while humanitarian intervention is hotly contested?

Could humanitarian intervention ever be wholly altruistic? Mixed motives and some degree of self-interest on the part of the intervenors would seem inevitable and not necessarily a bad thing. On the difficulties in devising a "principled" approach to humanitarian intervention, see Damrosch, The Inevitability of Selective Response? Principles to Guide Urgent International Action, in Kosovo and the Challenge of Humanitarian Intervention (Schnabel & Thakur, eds., 2000), at pp. 405–419.

4. Should an intervenor be expected to withdraw promptly? An intervening force may have to remain in place for a considerable period of time while the underlying causes of the humanitarian violations are being addressed. Precipitous withdrawal could quite likely lead to a renewal of genocide or other conditions that led to the intervention in the first place. On the prolonged presence of international forces in former Yugoslavia, see pp. 1039–1042.

5. Adam Roberts has commented that in "the long history of legal debates about humanitarian intervention, there has been a consistent failure to address directly the question of the methods used in such interventions." Roberts, NATO's Humanitarian War Over Kosovo, 41 Survival, No. 3, 102, 110 (1999). It has recently been suggested that perhaps humanitarian intervenors should be held to *higher* standards (e.g., of avoiding inadvertent civilian casualties) than would be required under the generally applicable laws of war (discussed in Section 4). On this point in relation to the intervention in Kosovo, see p. 1003.

6. Some have gone so far as to suggest not only a right, but perhaps even a duty, of humanitarian intervention. See Bettati & Kouchner, Le Devoir d'Ingérence (1987); Bettati, Le Droit d'Ingérence (1996).

THE KOSOVO INTERVENTION, 1999

Controversy over the international law of humanitarian intervention came to the fore with the multinational military intervention mounted by NATO countries against the Federal Republic of Yugoslavia (Serbia–Montenegro) concerning Kosovo in spring 1999. The intervention needs to be understood against the background of almost a decade of international efforts to alleviate the bloody ethnic conflicts in former Yugoslavia. Aspects of these efforts will be addressed in Section 3 below, under the heading of collective uses of force, where we take up the authority of the U.N. Security Council in relation to peacekeeping and enforcement. Although the Kosovo intervention had multinational participation, formal Security Council authorization was not conferred in advance. (On the Security Council's role in the Yugoslav conflict and arguments that the Security Council implicitly or retroactively authorized the NATO intervention in Kosovo, see p. 1042.) Given the lack of explicit Security Council imprimatur and doubts about the authority of NATO to act non-defensively within the territory of a non-member, the legal analysis of the military operation can begin by considering the Kosovo operation under the rubric of unilateral humanitarian intervention (in other words, with the unilateral intervenor being 13 NATO states acting jointly).

Kosovo had been an autonomous region within Serbia. A large majority of the population living in Kosovo (some 90%) was ethnic Albanian, and a small minority (perhaps 10%) was ethnic Serb. With the collapse of the socialist economic system of the former Yugoslavia at the end of the 1980s came increasing ethnic tensions (whipped up by nationalist politicians including the Serbian leader Slobodan Milosevic), revocation of Kosovo's autonomous status, and growing discrimination against the Albanians who were a minority within Serbia. The outbreak of ethnic violence in various parts of former Yugoslavia in the early 1990s was accompanied by increased repression of the Kosovar Albanians in Serbia. Although the conclusion of the Dayton Agreement for Peace in Bosnia–Herzegovina of December 1995 largely stabilized the ethnic conflicts among Serbs, Croats, and Bosnian Muslims, the situation of the Kosovar Albanians grew increasingly bleak in the late 1990s. The formation of the Kosovo Liberation Army (with a separatist agenda) led to an escalation of violence as Yugoslav forces cracked down on the KLA insurgency. In 1998 more than 230,000 Kosovar Albanians fled their villages to escape what the Security Council soon condemned as "the excessive and indiscriminate use of force by Serbian security forces and the Yugoslav Army." (S.C. Res. 1199, Sept. 23, 1998).

Despite the presence of an international verification force stationed in Kosovo with Security Council authorization from fall 1998 (S.C. Res. 1203, Oct. 24, 1998), Serb elements perpetrated an "ethnic cleansing" campaign aimed at driving Albanians out of Kosovo. Meanwhile, in January 1999, a "contact group" consisting of the United States, the United Kingdom, France, Germany, Italy and the Russian Federation convened talks at Rambouillet, France, with the participation of the Kosovar Albanians and the Yugoslav government, in an effort to reach a negotiated political settlement of the conflict. The Albanian side reluctantly agreed to the Rambouillet proposals (which were presented on a take-it-or-leave-it basis), but the Yugoslav side found them unacceptable. (Objectionable features included, among other things, provision for NATO implementation within Yugoslav territory.) Even as the talks foundered, a massacre of dozens of Albanian civilians in the Kosovo village of Rajak in February 1999 convinced NATO to move toward military intervention.

The apparent haste of the decision to proceed to a major military action is best understood in light of the desire of NATO leaders not to allow a replay of the tragedy of Bosnia–Herzegovina earlier in the 1990s, where "ethnic cleansing" went on for several years, with tremendous loss of life and civilian hardship, while the outside world weighed and adjusted the options. Thus, although the precise number of Albanians already killed or at risk as of February–March 1999 may not yet have reached a high toll (or was not known or knowable at the time), the record of the recent past gave reason to suspect that a massive humanitarian catastrophe would unfold if Milosevic's forces were left to their own devices.

On March 24, 1999, NATO began a bombing campaign against Serbia, with the proclaimed objective of protecting the Kosovar Albanians from further attacks at the hands of the Serbian forces. In the short term, however, the humanitarian disaster worsened as Serbs accelerated the "ethnic cleansing" of Albanians. The air war, which lasted for 78 days, was conducted from a height that kept NATO warplanes out of reach of ground fire but also made it difficult to carry out precision attacks on military targets; the results included several hundred civilian casualties (of Albanians as well as Serbs). Some blatant errors–such as the inadvertent bombing of the Chinese embassy in Belgrade, which had been misidentified as an intelligence facility for the Yugoslav military–compounded the perception of a flawed military operation.

Efforts to obtain an authoritative appraisal of the legal aspects of the NATO intervention were inconclusive at the time and afterwards. In the first days of the campaign, Russia introduced a Security Council resolution to condemn the NATO action as a "flagrant violation" of the U.N. Charter, but the resolution was defeated with only three votes in favor (Russia, China, and Namibia) and twelve against. U.N. Doc. S/PV.3989, at 6. While the bombing campaign was in progress, the Federal Republic of Yugoslavia (Serbia–Montenegro) brought separate suits at the International Court of Justice against 10 of the NATO members involved in the military action (Belgium, Canada, France, Germany, Italy, the Netherlands, Portugal, Spain, the United Kingdom, and the United States), in which Yugoslavia alleged:

> The Government of [the Kingdom of Belgium, and others *mutatis mutandis*], together with the Governments of other Member States of NATO, took part in the acts of use of force against the Federal Republic of Yugoslavia by taking part in bombing targets in the Federal Republic of Yugoslavia. In bombing the Federal Republic of Yugoslavia military and civilian targets were attacked. Great number of people were killed, including a great many civilians. Residential houses came under attack. Numerous dwellings were destroyed. Enormous damage was caused to schools, hospitals, radio and television stations, cultural and health institutions and to places of worship. * * *
>
> [B]y taking part in the bombing of the territory of the Federal Republic of Yugoslavia, the Kingdom of Belgium has acted against the Federal Republic of Yugoslavia in breach of its obligation not to use force against another State * * * .

Yugoslavia also sought provisional measures, which the Court denied in orders of June 2, 1999. (See discussion of jurisdictional and other aspects in Chapter 11, pp. 854–855, 864, 900.)

The various NATO states took different approaches to the legal issues involved in the military intervention. The United States did not issue a formal legal opinion, but U.S. leaders pointed to a variety of factors as supportive of the lawfulness of the NATO action. A few days before the commencement of the military action, the U.S. Department of State's spokesman said:

> There has been extensive consideration of the international legal issue with our NATO allies. We and our NATO allies have looked to numerous factors in concluding that such action, if necessary, would be justified–including the fact that Yugoslav military and police forces have committed serious and widespread violations of international law, and have used excessive and indiscriminate force in violation of international law. * * *

> * * * With Belgrade giving every indication that it will prepare a new offensive against Kosovar Albanians, we face the prospect of a new explosion of violence if the international community doesn't take preventative action. * * * Serb actions also constitute a threat to the region, particularly Albania and Macedonia and potentially NATO allies, including Greece and Turkey. In addition, these actions constitute a threat to the safety of international observers in Kosovo.
>
> On the basis of such considerations, we and our NATO allies believe there are legitimate grounds to threaten and, if necessary, use military force.

Murphy, Contemporary Practice of the United States Relating to International Law, 93 A.J.I.L. 628, 631 (1999).

The United Kingdom's Secretary of State for Defence, George Robertson, said: "We are in no doubt that NATO is acting within international law and our legal justification rests upon the accepted principle that force may be used in extreme circumstances to avert a humanitarian catastrophe." An earlier U.K. note of October 1998 had specified the position that "as matters now stand and if action through the Security Council is not possible, military intervention by NATO is lawful on grounds of overwhelming humanitarian necessity." (Quoted in Duke, Ehrhart & Karadi, The Major European Allies: France, Germany and the United Kingdom, in Kosovo and the Challenge of Humanitarian Intervention (Schnabel & Thakur, eds., 2000), at pp. 128, 137.) For the positions of other states, see the related chapters in the same volume (covering Italy, Greece and Turkey; Portugal, Belgium, Canada, and Spain; as well as Hungary, Poland and the Czech Republic which were new entrants to NATO; the Nordic countries in and out of NATO; Russia, China and India which were adamantly opposed to NATO's action; and others).

By early June 1999 the Milosevic government of Yugoslavia was ready to accept NATO's terms. A resolution formalizing the settlement of the conflict was soon adopted by the Security Council under Chapter VII of the U.N. Charter. S.C. Res. 1244 (June 10, 1999). The resolution demanded that the Federal Republic of Yugoslavia "put an immediate and verifiable end to violence and repression in Kosovo, and begin and complete verifiable phased withdrawal from Kosovo of all military, police and paramilitary forces according to a rapid timetable, with which the deployment of the international security presence in Kosovo will be synchronized." Significantly, Russia was willing to participate along with NATO military forces in the international security presence, known as KFOR. For more on the Security Council's role in the Kosovo crisis, see p. 1042.

Notes

1. On legal aspects of the Kosovo intervention, see editorial comments by Henkin, Wedgwood, Charney, Chinkin, Falk, Franck, and Reisman, at 93 A.J.I.L. 824–862 (1999); Simma, NATO, the UN and the Use of Force: Legal Aspects, 10 E.J.I.L. 1 (1999); Cassese, *Ex iniuria ius oritur*: Are We Moving Towards International Legitimation of Forcible Humanitarian Countermeasures in the World Community?, 10 E.J.I.L. 23 (1999); Catherine Guicherd, International Law and the War in Kosovo, 41 Survival, No. 2, 19–34 (1999); Roberts, NATO's "Humani-

tarian War'' Over Kosovo, 41 Survival, No. 3, 102–123 (1999); Charney, Anticipatory Humanitarian Intervention in Kosovo, 32 Vand. J. Transnat. L. 1231 (1999); and the contributions by Brownlie & Apperley, Chinkin, Greenwood, and Lowe, at 49 I.C.L.Q. 878–941 (2000). A valuable collection of essays, including legal perspectives, is Kosovo and the Challenge of Humanitarian Intervention (Schnabel & Thakur, eds., 2000). See also the Report of the Independent International Commission on Kosovo, Note 3 infra.

2. In his annual address to the U.N.General Assembly in September 1999, Secretary–General Kofi Annan said:

> While the genocide in Rwanda will define for our generation the consequences of inaction in the face of mass murder, the more recent conflict in Kosovo has prompted important questions about the consequences of action in the absence of complete unity on the part of the international community. * * * And to each side in this critical debate, difficult questions can be posed.
>
> To those for whom the greatest threat to the future of international order is the use of force in the absence of a Security Council mandate, one might ask—not in the context of Kosovo—but in the context of Rwanda: If, in those dark days and hours leading up to the genocide, a coalition of States had been prepared to act in defence of the Tutsi population, but did not receive prompt Council authorization, should such a coalition have stood aside and allowed the horror to unfold?
>
> To those for whom the Kosovo action heralded a new era when States and groups of States can take military action outside the established mechanisms for enforcing international law, one might ask: Is there not a danger of such interventions undermining the imperfect, yet resilient, security system created after the Second World War, and of setting dangerous precedents for future interventions without a clear criterion to decide who might invoke these precedents, and in what circumstances?

Report of the Secretary–General, 54 G.A.O.R., 4th Plen. Mtg., Sept. 20, 1999, U.N. Doc. A/54/PV.4. For other excerpts from the same address, see p. 7. See also U.N. Secretary–General Kofi Annan, The Question of Intervention: Statements by the Secretary–General (1999).

3. Following the Kosovo intervention, an independent international commission co-chaired by Richard Goldstone and Carl Tham prepared a comprehensive analysis of the situation. A chapter on "International Law and Humanitarian Intervention," puts forward an interpretation of the evolution of humanitarian intervention doctrine:

> This interpretation is situated in a gray zone of ambiguity between an extension of international law and a proposal for an international moral consensus. In essence, this gray zone goes beyond strict ideas of legality to incorporate more flexible views of legitimacy
>
> * * *
>
> One way to analyze the international law status of the NATO campaign is to consider legality a matter of degree. This approach acknowledges the current fluidity of international law on humanitarian intervention, caught between strict Charter prohibitions of non-defensive uses of force and more permissive patterns of state practice with respect to humanitarian interventions and counter-terrorist use of force. * * *

NATO and its supporters have wisely avoided staking out any doctrinal claims for its action either prior to or after the war. Rather than defining the Kosovo intervention as a precedent, most NATO supporters among international jurists presented the intervention as an unfortunate but necessary and reasonable exception. Nevertheless, NATO cannot hope to preclude states, and especially other regional organizations, from referring to its claims of intervention in Kosovo as a precedent. * * *

The Kosovo "exception" now exists, for better and worse, as a contested precedent that must be assessed in relation to a wide range of international effects and undertakings. Chief among these is that NATO * * * was widely viewed by many non-NATO countries as having independently waged a non-defensive war without having made sufficient effort to obtain proper authorization or to achieve a peaceful settlement. * * *

* * *

This situation supports the general conclusion that the NATO campaign was illegal, yet legitimate. Such a conclusion is related to the controversial idea that a "right" of humanitarian intervention is not consistent with the UN Charter if conceived as a legal text, but that it may, depending on context, nevertheless, reflect the spirit of the Charter as it relates to the overall protection of people against gross abuse. Humanitarian intervention may also thus be legitimately authorized by the UN, but will often be challenged legally from the perspective of Charter obligations to respect the sovereignty of states.

Allowing this gap between legality and legitimacy to persist is not healthy, for several reasons. Acknowledging the tension with most interpretations of international law either inhibits solidarity with civilian victims of severe abuse by territorial governments, or seriously erodes the prohibition on the use of force that the World Court and other authorities have deemed valid. * * * Therefore, although the Commission's finding is that the use of force by NATO in intervening in Kosovo is validated from the perspective of the legitimacy of the undertaking and its overall societal effects, the Commission feels that it would be most beneficial to work diligently to close the gap between legality and legitimacy in a convincing manner for the future.

The Commission is of the opinion that the best way to do this is to conceive of an emergent doctrine of humanitarian intervention that consists of a process of three phases:

- a recommended framework of principles useful in a setting where humanitarian intervention is proposed as an international response and where it actually occurs;
- the formal adoption of such a framework by the General Assembly of the United Nations in the form of a Declaration on the Right and Responsibility of Humanitarian Intervention, accompanied by UNSC interpretations of the UN Charter that reconciles such practice with the balance between respect for sovereign rights, implementation of human rights, and prevention of humanitarian catastrophe;
- the amendment of the Charter to incorporate these changes in the role and responsibility of the United Nations and other collective actors in international society to implement the Declaration on the Right and Responsibility of Humanitarian Intervention.

Independent International Commission on Kosovo, Kosovo Report: Conflict, International Response, Lessons Learned, Chapter 6 (2000) (footnotes omitted). The Commission then went on to elaborate a set of criteria for legitimacy, which overlap in large measure with those indicated at p. 995 above. A new and controversial idea, however, would be that

> There must be even stricter adherence to the laws of war and international humanitarian law than in standard military operations. This applies to all aspects of the military operation, including any post cease-fire occupation.

Elsewhere, the Commission observed:

> In effect, the Commission believes that a greater obligation is imposed on the intervening side to take care of the civilian population in a humanitarian campaign. The specific modalities of this higher standard of "military necessity" do not yet exist in any international agreement or United Nations declaration, but the Commission envisages this standard to be a flexible notion that complements the adaptation of legal constraints on the use of force to the realities of the early twenty-first century. The Commission believes that this proposal should be formalized in international law, perhaps in the form of a "Protocol III" to the Geneva Conventions.

On issues of application of the laws of war in the Kosovo conflict, see pp. 1062, 1077 in Section 4.

4. Is it worthwhile to propose formal codification of criteria for humanitarian intervention? Some believe that such codification would help clarify the legitimacy of such operations and discourage pretextual claims. Others fear that giving humanitarian intervention formal legal blessing would be more likely to encourage questionable military adventures. Compare Damrosch, Concluding Reflections, in Enforcing Restraint: Collective Intervention in Internal Conflicts 358–360 (Damrosch, ed., 1993) (contending that it would be premature and perhaps counterproductive to attempt to codify criteria for intervention), with the Kosovo Commission's initiative outlined in the preceding note.

For other recent reports (also spurred by the Kosovo events) proposing potential criteria for humanitarian intervention, see Danish Institute of International Affairs, Humanitarian Intervention: Legal and Political Aspects (1999); and a study sponsored by the government of the Netherlands, Advisory Council on International Affairs and Advisory Committee on Issues of Public International Law, Humanitarian Intervention (2000). In September 2000, the Canadian government launched an International Commission on Intervention and State Sovereignty, which plans to present its findings to the U.N. General Assembly in late 2001.

5. Is there a persuasive argument that different standards on intervention could apply in the European region? Compare Guicherd, International Law and the War in Kosovo, 41 Survival, No. 2, at 19, 29–30 (1999).

THE CHARTER'S CONTINUING RESTRAINTS ON THE UNILATERAL USE OF FORCE

SCHACHTER, THE RIGHT OF STATES TO USE ARMED FORCE

82 Mich. L.Rev. 1620–21, 1623–24, 1645–46 (1984).

When the United Nations (UN) Charter was adopted, it was generally considered to have outlawed war. States accepted the obligation to settle all disputes by peaceful means and to refrain from the use or threat of use of force in their international relations. Only two exceptions were expressly allowed: force used in self-defense when an armed attack occurs, and armed action authorized by the UN Security Council as an enforcement measure. These provisions were seen by most observers as the heart of the Charter and the most important principles of contemporary international law. They have been reaffirmed over and over again in unanimous declarations of the United Nations, in treaties and in statements of political leaders.

Yet as we are all acutely aware, there is widespread cynicism about their effect. Reality seems to mock them. Wars take place, countries are invaded, armed force is used to topple governments, to seize territory, to avenge past injustice, to impose settlements. Threats of force, open or implicit, pervade the relations of states. The menace of a nuclear holocaust hangs over all nations, great or small. Collective security, as envisaged in the Charter, has had little practical effect. Our personal lives are deeply affected by the expectation of violence, by the vast resources devoted to armaments, and perhaps most insidiously, by the belief that little can be done to replace force as the ultimate arbiter in conflicts between nations.

It is no wonder that the obligations of the Charter are widely seen as mere rhetoric, at best idealistic aspirations, or worse as providing a pretext or "cover" for aggression. This evaluation, devastating as it may appear for international law, cannot be dismissed or minimized. But there is the other aspect of reality. * * *

* * *

If we take the realistic view that governments deciding on the use of force take into account the diverse considerations referred to earlier—the probable costs and benefits, the responses of other states and the public, the effect on future claims by other states, the value of law-compliance to international order—we may conclude that the issue of permissibility under the law is a factor that would normally be considered. That this is often the case is shown, at least in some degree, by the fact that in virtually every case the use of force is sought to be justified by reference to the accepted Charter rules. While such justification may be no more than a rationalization of an action chosen solely on grounds of interest and power, the felt need to issue a legal justification is not without importance. It demonstrates that states require a basis of legitimacy to justify their actions to their own citizens and, even more, to other states whose cooperation or acquiescence is desired. The fact that claims of legitimacy are also self-serving does not mean that they do not influence conduct by the actors or by those to whom they are addressed. Even if we label those claims as hypocritical ("the tribute that vice pays to virtue"), they require credibility and for that reason must be confirmed by action. We need not treat this as a categorical imperative that holds good in every case in order to recognize that in a great many situations there is a link between conduct and the perceived restraints of law. Power and interest are not superseded by law, but law cannot be excluded from the significant factors influencing the uses of power and the perception of interests.

* * *

It would be a mistake to conclude that the international law of force is so vague and fragmentary as to allow governments almost unlimited latitude to use force. International texts and the legal positions taken by governments reveal a coherent body of principles that apply to a wide range of conduct involving armed force. These principles are grounded in two major interests, both widely accepted as basic to our international system. The first is the paramount interest in the sovereignty and independence of nation-states. The second is the common interest in restraints on the unbridled exercise of power. Such restraints are no longer seen as "mere" ideals. The fear of nuclear war and mass destruction has made them a prime necessity for survival.

It is true that the efficacy of law is limited because the system lacks effective central authority and is characterized by vast discrepancies in the power of states. Fear of nuclear devastation has not eliminated the Hobbesian element in that system. Powerful states may violate international obligations; they may do so with relative impunity or they may pay a price. But they also have a stake in stability and an acute sense of countervailing power. A decentralized legal system can operate because of these factors of self-interest and reciprocal reactions.

Moreover, the system is not wholly decentralized. As we have indicated, collective judgments are continuously being made both within and outside of formal institutions. Decisions of international bodies add both to the specificity and density of agreed law and affect the costs that result from illegitimate conduct. However inadequate this may seem in comparison to a mature national legal system, it should not be scorned as an element in maintaining peace. To consider its inadequacy a reason for ignoring the restraints can only add to the present insecurity. A world in which power and self-interest alone are expected to restrain force would not be a safer world. We may move dangerously in that direction by weakening existing law on the ground that it lacks impartial organs of application and enforcement. The best would then become the enemy of the good.

SECTION 3. COLLECTIVE USE OF FORCE

The League of Nations, the first "universal" organization established for the purpose of maintaining international peace, failed and effectively died in the Second World War. The reason for its failure was the unwillingness or inability of the principal world powers to resist Nazi–Fascist aggression, with subsidiary reasons commonly cited: the dominance of narrow nationalism among the Big Powers over their willingness to cooperate, the failure of the United States to participate, the unwillingness of France and Great Britain to act decisively to make the League work, suspicious hostility between them and the U.S.S.R. preventing cooperation against aggressive fascism.

The creation of the United Nations in 1945 embodied aspirations for a system that would effectively keep peace between nations. The U.N.'s experiences over more than half a century have been mixed. Since the end of the Cold War, it has been asked to take on increasingly ambitious tasks, including enforcement operations in the midst of internal conflicts and post-conflict peace-building. Alongside the United Nations (Section 3.A) are a variety of regional organizations and arrangements with the potential for carrying out complementary functions (Section 3.B).

A. THE UNITED NATIONS

The principal purpose of the United Nations is:

> To maintain international peace and security, and to that end: to take effective collective measures for the prevention and removal of threats to the peace, and for the suppression of acts of aggression or other breaches of the peace, and to bring about by peaceful means, and in conformity with the principles of justice and international law, adjustment or settlement of international disputes or situations which might lead to a breach of the peace;

Charter of the United Nations, Article 1(1).

The primary responsibility for achieving that purpose was lodged in the Security Council. (Article 24). The Security Council was given the authority to pursue that purpose by peaceful means (Chapter VI) and also if necessary by collective enforcement action (non-forcible or military) (Chapter VII). Additionally, the General Assembly as well as the Secretary–General were given authority which might be used for keeping the peace. See Articles 10–15 and 99.

1. The Collective Use of Force Under the Charter

The 51 states that signed the Charter of the United Nations in San Francisco on June 26, 1945, believed that the new Organization's principal function would be to maintain peace and security through an authoritative institution and process, including, if necessary, the use of collective force against an aggressor. To that end, the Charter entrusted executive authority and "primary responsibility" to the Security Council, and within the Council, to the five Permanent Members, whose unanimity is required for non-procedural decisions. By design, enforcement action under Chapter VII of the Charter cannot be taken against any Permanent Member, or against any state without the consent (or acquiescence) of all Permanent Members. Four of the five Permanent Members were the major Allied powers of World War II. Their collaboration was expected to lay the foundation for German and European reconstruction and for world-wide security from aggression. The fifth Permanent Member was China, the "awakening giant," expected to play a major role in the post-war world. Two of the world's great powers, Germany and Japan, were excluded as the recently defeated enemies.

By 1947, the Cold War had split the former Allies into opposing ideological blocs. This led to the partition of Germany. West Germany became a major ally of the United States, East Germany a satellite of the Soviet Union, and the mutual exercise of the veto in the Security Council long prevented either Germany from becoming a member of the United Nations. After the Communist takeover in China, the United States opposed the seating of the Communist government in any organ of the United Nations, so that the more than 700 million inhabitants of mainland China remained for more than two decades without effective representation in the United Nations. The incapacitation of one of the major pillars of the new organization—a security system built on the unified action of the world's five leading powers—shattered a second pillar; the Permanent Military Force envisaged in Articles 43–47 of the Charter could not be established because the major powers could not agree on the essentials of composition, command structure, territorial facilities, and conditions of action. The Korean War which began in 1950 evoked a response from U.N. organs, but not in the mode contemplated by U.N.'s founders. See pp. 1011–1013.

The void left by the absence of an international security system was temporarily, but only partly, filled by what may be called a "second phase" of collective security within the United Nations. After the collapse of the Charter's plan for a Security Council guided by the major powers acting in concert, an activist Secretary–General and a more engaged General Assembly gave the United Nations a general "watchdog" function in international conflicts and the power to undertake a "peacekeeping" role on an *ad hoc* basis (at least in some conflicts). The composition and function of these peacekeeping forces, however, were different from those of military forces envisaged under Chapter VII of the Charter. The peacekeeping forces were made up in the main of units from smaller states and they operated with the consent of the member states concerned. Their function was—and still is—to discourage hostilities, not to restore or maintain peace.

The "second phase" of United Nations collective security changed radically during the 1960s and 1970s. The principal reason was the explosive rate at which colonial and dependent territories attained statehood and almost automatic membership in the United Nations. This accentuated the discrepancy between power and responsibility. Under the original scheme of the Charter, the proliferation of new states would not have affected the predominance of the Security Council and the privileged position within the Council of the Permanent Members. But as the Security Council remained paralyzed, and as the functions and power of the General Assembly—in which each member has one vote—increased, a change in attitude of the major powers occurred as control slipped from their hands. This change was reflected in the crisis provoked by French and Soviet resistance to the advisory opinion of the International Court of Justice in *Certain Expenses of the United Nations,* see p. 1028 infra, a reaction against the increasing domination of the General Assembly by smaller and poorer states.

The policy of the United States also shifted in light of these trends. When, in 1950, the United States sponsored the "Uniting for Peace" resolution (p. 1012), which purports to confer on (or recognize in) the General Assembly powers to "recommend" collective measures when the Security Council is unable to act, the U.S. was still certain of a comfortable two-thirds majority in the General Assembly for action that it strongly sponsored. But that situation changed. In the aftermath of the Arab–Israeli war of June 1967, it was the Soviet Union—which had bitterly opposed the Uniting for Peace Resolution as usurping the functions of the Security Council—that invoked the Resolution when it failed to obtain a Security Council resolution condemning Israel as the aggressor, and it was the United States that opposed the convocation of the Assembly. In the General Assembly, neither the United States nor the U.S.S.R. thought it advisable to pursue its own draft resolution, and threw their support to conflicting resolutions introduced by smaller powers. The voting showed an almost even division among the members and it was not possible to obtain the required two-thirds majority.

Further political change brought further change to the United Nations. The continued proliferation of new states and the emergence of the "Third World" with substantial political solidarity; the acceptance of the People's Republic of China as the government of China to be represented in the U.N. and its aspirations to be the Big Power representative of the developing nations; conflict between the Soviet Union and China and improved relations between China and the United States—all further modified the U.N. peacekeeping system. It became possible for a combination of smaller members, sometimes with the support of one or both of the Communist powers, to authorize a United Nations operation to which the United States (and the United Kingdom) were opposed. In time, despite the stand earlier taken by the United States as to peacekeeping expenses, the U.S. and the U.K. began to see their interest in a voluntary rather than a compulsory assessment for the cost of all but basic administrative expenses for U.N. operations. That would help contain the power of the majority of non-Western and economically underdeveloped states in the General Assembly. At the same time, the U.N. majority was unwilling or unable to use the U.N. effectively. The U.N. played no role in the Vietnam War. It had little role in restoring or maintaining peace between African states such as Ethiopia and Somalia. It remained virtually irrelevant to the resolution of civil wars and other internal conflicts, even where they spilled out of national borders, and the result was largely determined by outsiders (e.g. Bangladesh in 1971; Angola in 1974; Western Sahara in 1975; Afghanistan in 1980; Chad in 1984).

A "third phase" of collective security in the United Nations began as the Cold War ended, with increased cooperation by the permanent members of the Security Council from the late 1980s into the 1990s and (with some qualifications) into the twenty-first century as well. This phase has been characterized by a new willingness and ability by the Security Council to fulfill its primary responsibility under the Charter for the maintenance of international peace and security, as seen in the Gulf War of 1990–91 and its aftermath, in modest but assertive measures in connection with the conflict in the former Yugoslavia throughout the 1990s, in the 1992–93 relief effort in Somalia, in authorizations from the Security Council to willing states to take military action in support of internationally approved purposes in Rwanda (1994), Haiti (1994), East Timor (1999), and elsewhere, and other actions presaging genuine enforcement of community interests.

In the 1990s, the Security Council moved well beyond the Charter's original understanding of "international" peace to a conception of "threats to peace" embracing some kinds of internal conflicts. When acting in its Chapter VII mode, the Council has been able to overcome Article 2(7)'s constraint on intervention in "matters which are essentially within the domestic jurisdiction of any state," as that article continues with the proviso that "this principle shall not prejudice the application of enforcement measures under Chapter VII." The Council has lent multilateral imprimatur to certain forcible interventions (e.g., for humanitarian purposes), thereby conferring legitimacy and legality that might otherwise have been lacking under the doctrines for evaluation of unilateral uses of force addressed in Section 2. In other instances where the permanent members have been unable to agree to grant specific authority (e.g., the Kosovo crisis of 1999), action has sometimes gone forward on a claim of implicit authorization flowing from previous resolutions.

The future of collective security and enforcement actions under Chapter VII of the Charter remains to be seen. Will cooperation continue? Will the Council's decision-making process avoid bias and the appearance of bias? Will the Security Council's structure, composition, and procedures, be reformed to reflect the world of the new century, with more (or different) permanent members? Will the authority and the mandate of the Security Council continue to expand? Will the U.N. mobilize the financial and political resources to enable it to meet the challenges that clamor for collective action, perhaps even use of force, against massive violations of human rights, ethnic strife, and floods of refugees?

THE SECURITY COUNCIL AND CHAPTER VII OF THE CHARTER

CHARTER OF THE UNITED NATIONS

San Francisco, June 26, 1945.

Action With Respect to Threats to the Peace, Breaches of the Peace, and Acts of Aggression

Article 39

The Security Council shall determine the existence of any threat to the peace, breach of the peace, or act of aggression and shall make recommendations, or decide what measures shall be taken in accordance with Article 41 and 42, to maintain or restore international peace and security.

Article 40

In order to prevent an aggravation of the situation, the Security Council may, before making the recommendations or deciding upon the measures provided for in Article 39, call upon the parties concerned to comply with such provisional measures as it deems necessary or desirable. Such provisional measures shall be without prejudice to the rights, claims, or position of the parties concerned. The Security Council shall duly take account of failure to comply with such provisional measures.

Article 41

The Security Council may decide what measures not involving the use of armed force are to be employed to give effect to its decisions, and it may call upon the Members of the United Nations to apply such measures. These may include complete or partial interruption of economic relations and of rail, sea, air, postal, telegraphic, radio, and other means of communication, and the severance of diplomatic relations.

Article 42

Should the Security Council consider that measures provided for in Article 41 would be inadequate or have proved to be inadequate, it may take such action by air, sea or land forces as may be necessary to maintain or restore international peace or security. Such action may include demonstrations, blockade, and other operations by air, sea, or land forces of Members of the United Nations.

Article 43

1. All Members of the United Nations, in order to contribute to the maintenance of international peace and security, undertake to make available to the Security Council, on its call and in accordance with a special agreement or agreements, armed forces, assistance, and facilities, including rights of passage, necessary for the purpose of maintaining international peace and security.

2. Such agreement or agreements shall govern the numbers and types of forces, their degree of readiness and general location, and the nature of the facilities and assistance to be provided.

3. The agreement or agreements shall be negotiated as soon as possible on the initiative of the Security Council. They shall be concluded between the Security Council and Members or between the Security Council and groups of Members and shall be subject to ratification by the signatory states in accordance with their respective constitutional processes.

Notes

1. See also Articles 2(6), 2(7), 9–12, 18, 23–25, 27, 34, 44–50, 103, 107 of the Charter.

2. The Security Council found threats to the peace, breaches of the peace or acts of aggression only rarely between 1945 and 1990, and only twice in that period did it act to impose compulsory measures under Chapter VII of the Charter: those were the cases of Southern Rhodesia and South Africa. Concerning Southern Rhodesia, see S.C Res. 217 (1965) (calling on the United Kingdom to quell the rebellion of the racist minority regime, using "appropriate measures which would prove effective"); S.C. Res. 221 (1966) (authorizing the United Kingdom "to prevent by the use of force if necessary" the arrival, in a third-country port, of vessels reasonably believed to be carrying contraband oil destined for Rhodesia); S.C. Res. 232 (1966) (imposing selective mandatory sanctions, including an arms embargo); S.C. Res. 253 (1968) (expanding sanctions). Concerning South Africa, see S.C. Res. 418 (1977) (imposing a mandatory arms embargo). On these measures, see Vera Gowland–Debbas, Collective Responses to Illegal Acts in International Law: United Nations Action in the Question of Southern Rhodesia (1990); Neta Crawford & Audie Klotz (eds.), How Sanctions Work: Lessons from South Africa (1999).

On the by now numerous determinations and actions under Chapter VII since 1990, see pp. 1013–1023, 1032–1043.

2. Collective Actions to Maintain or Restore International Peace and Security

The two major actions in which the Security Council has authorized the use of collective force in response to a transboundary attack are the Korean

War beginning in 1950 and the Persian Gulf War of 1990–1991. Additionally, both the Security Council and the General Assembly have approved the formation of peacekeeping forces under U.N. authority. Before the 1990s these forces mainly functioned with the consent of affected parties, but they have increasingly been placed on a Chapter VII footing as more and more ambitious tasks have been entrusted to them, as in former Yugoslavia in the 1990s. The Council has also approved military enforcement actions to be carried out by states, on newly expansive theories of "threats to peace" which have come to embrace humanitarian considerations in internal crises (with transboundary impacts being merely secondary effects of principally domestic conflicts).

KOREA

On June 25, 1950 North Korean forces invaded South Korea. A resolution adopted at an emergency meeting of the Security Council determined that the North Korean action constituted a breach of the peace and called for the immediate cessation of hostilities and the withdrawal of the North Korean units. S.C.Res. 82 (1950). There were no negative votes on the Council. (The Soviet delegate had been absent since January of 1950 because of a dispute over the representation of China.)

The Security Council met on June 27, 1950, and, having noted that "urgent military measures are required to restore international peace and security," recommended "that the Members of the United Nations furnish such assistance to the Republic of Korea as may be necessary to repel the armed attack and to restore international peace and security in the area." S.C.Res. 83 (1950). This resolution was the first collective security effort authorized under the Charter. Again, the Soviet delegate was absent and thus did not exercise a veto.

A Security Council resolution of July 7, 1950, requested the United States to appoint the commander of a unified command to which all Members were urged to provide assistance, including forces. The unified command was authorized to use the United Nations flag. S.C.Res. 84 (1950). The Soviet delegate returned to the Security Council on August 1, 1950, and blocked any further action by the Council. On October 7, 1950 the General Assembly, noting that the objectives of the Security Council had not yet been attained, established the United Nations Commission for the Unification and Rehabilitation of Korea. G.A.Res. 376(V) (1950). In view of the impasse in the Security Council produced by the threat of Soviet veto, the General Assembly also passed the "Uniting for Peace" Resolution, note 4 below.

The Korean conflict continued until the conclusion of an armistice agreement (T.I.A.S. No. 2782) at Panmunjom on July 27, 1953, between the Commander-in-Chief, United Nations Command, and the respective commanders of the North Korean and Communist Chinese forces. Although some of the principal provisions in the armistice agreement were not carried out and there were several incidents, hostilities did not resume. See Henkin, How Nations Behave at 77–79; Hoyt, The United States Reaction to the Korean Attack, 55 A.J.I.L. 45 (1961); Goodrich, Korea (1950); 5 Whiteman 102–09, 789–95, 1113–18 (1965).

Notes

1. *Abstention by a Permanent Member.* The U.S.S.R. long maintained that the Council's resolution recommending that states assist South Korea was illegal because it did not have the affirmative vote of all the permanent members of the Security Council. The practice of the Security Council since that time has rejected the Soviet position and established that abstention (or absence) does not constitute a veto. For example, in 1990, China, a permanent member, abstained from voting on Resolution 678, authorizing the use of force to expel Iraq from Kuwait, but the legality of the resolution or of the subsequent use of force has not been questioned. (China has also abstained on various other occasions in the 1990s when the Council has taken decisions on an expansive conception of "threats to peace" under Chapter VII; see below.) For the practice of the Council in respect of the veto, see Bailey, The Procedure of the U.N. Security Council 224–25 (2d ed. 1988); Kirgis, The Security Council's First Fifty Years, 89 A.J.I.L. 506, 510–511 (1995).

2. *Collective action or collective self-defense.* The resolutions passed by the Council in June and July of 1950 make no mention of Chapter VII of the Charter or of any specific Charter articles. Does that matter? Does the Security Council have power to make any recommendation whatsoever for the maintenance of international peace and security, or is it restricted to the specific measures set out in Chapter VII? See Dinstein, War, Aggression and Self–Defence (2d ed. 1994); Bowett, U.N. Forces 32–59 (1964); Goodrich, Korea 102–21 (1956). See also the advisory opinion of the International Court of Justice in *Certain Expenses of the United Nations,* p. 1028 infra. Some commentators have argued that the action taken in Korea is more appropriately characterized as an action taken in collective self-defense rather than an enforcement action under the Charter. See Stone, Legal Controls of International Conflict 234–237 (2nd ed. 1959). Was Article 51 of the Charter applicable even though neither North Korea nor South Korea was a member of the United Nations?

3. *Presidential authority.* President Truman sent U.S. armed forces to Korea, assumed the Unified Command and appointed General MacArthur to command the U.N. forces, all without seeking authorization from Congress. Did he act within his constitutional authority? Did the U.N. Charter, a treaty to which the United States is a party, supply the necessary authority since treaties are the law of the land and the President "shall take care that laws the be faithfully executed" (U.S. Const., Art. 2, sec. 2)? Was it relevant that the Council resolution was only a recommendation, not a mandatory decision legally binding on the United States? Some members of Congress questioned the President's authority but their objections were not pressed. 96 Cong. Rec. 9320 (daily ed. June 28, 1950). Congress in effect ratified the President's action through the appropriation of funds and by legislation. See Henkin, Congress, the President and the United Nations, 3 Pace Y.B.Int'l L. I (1991); compare Stromseth, Rethinking War Powers: Congress, the President, and the United Nations, 81 Georgetown L.J. 597, 620–640 (1993); Fisher, The Korean War: On What Legal Basis Did Truman Act?, 89 A.J.I.L. 21 (1995).

4. *Uniting for Peace Resolution.* In the Uniting for Peace Resolution, G.A. Res. 377, U.N. GAOR, 5th Sess., Supp. No. 20, at 10, U.N. Doc. A/1775 (1950), the General Assembly asserted authority to act in matters relating to international peace and security if the Security Council could not discharge its "primary" responsibility because of lack of unanimity among the permanent members. The

resolution provides that in the event of a threat to the peace, breach of the peace, or act of aggression to which the Security Council cannot respond,

> the General Assembly shall consider the matter immediately with a view to making appropriate recommendations to Members for collective measures, including in the case of a breach of the peace or act of aggression the use of armed force when necessary, to maintain or restore international peace and security.

After the Korean case, the resolution has had limited but significant application, notably with respect to the creation of the United Nations Emergency Force in the wake of the Suez crisis of 1956, p. 1026 below, and on other occasions as a basis for discussion of issues in the General Assembly. On the Uniting for Peace Resolution, see The Charter of the United Nations: A Commentary 235, 260–261 (Simma et al., eds., 1994). In the aftermath of the Kosovo events of 1999 (pp. 997–1003), some have urged a revival of the Uniting for Peace framework when the Security Council is immobilized.

IRAQ

The end of the Cold War and the thaw in relations between the United States and the Soviet Union resulted in a revitalized Security Council that faced its first major test when Iraq invaded Kuwait on August 2, 1990. The Security Council unanimously condemned the invasion and demanded that Iraq "withdraw immediately and unconditionally all its armed forces." S.C.Res. 660 (1990). On August 6, 1990, the Security Council acted under its compulsory powers to require sanctions against Iraq.

Security Council Resolution 661
August 6, 1990

The Security Council * * *

Acting under Chapter VII of the Charter of the United Nations, * * *

3. *Decides* that all States shall prevent:

(a) The import into their territories of all commodities and products originating in Iraq or Kuwait or exported therefrom after the date of the present resolution;

(b) Any activities by their nationals or in their territories which would promote * * * the export * * * of any commodities or products from Iraq or Kuwait; * * *

(c) The sale or supply by their nationals or from their territories * * * of any commodities or products, including weapons or any other military equipment * * * but not including supplies intended strictly for medical purposes, and, in humanitarian circumstances, foodstuffs, to any person or body in Iraq or Kuwait * * *

4. *Decides* that all States shall not make available to the Government of Iraq or to any commercial, industrial or public utility undertaking in Iraq or Kuwait any funds or any other financial or economic resources * * * except payments exclusively for strictly medical or humanitarian purposes

5. *Calls upon* all States, including States non-members of the United Nations, to act strictly in accordance with the provisions of the present resolution notwithstanding any contract entered into or licence granted before the date of the present resolution;

6. *Decides* to establish * * * a Committee of the Security Council consisting of all the members of the Council, to undertake the following tasks * * *

(a) To examine the reports on the progress of the implementation of the present resolution which will be submitted by the Secretary-General;

(b) To seek from all States further information regarding the action taken by them concerning the effective implementation of * * * the present resolution * * *

Note

This Security Council resolution provided a legal basis under U.S. law for implementation of the sanctions the Council had imposed. See the U.N. Participation Act, 22 U.S.C.A. § 287c.

Despite the economic and military embargo established by Resolution 661, some Iraqi ships were reported to be sailing in and out of Iraqi ports apparently carrying embargoed goods, and there was concern that some countries were violating the embargo. The United States took the position that Resolution 661 authorized the use of military force to stop Iraqi ships suspected of carrying prohibited cargo, but other states, including the Soviet Union, disputed that view. The United States took no action to enforce the sanctions until, after intensive negotiations, the Security Council adopted Resolution 665 authorizing the use of "measures commensurate to the specific circumstances as may be necessary * * * to halt all inward and outward maritime shipping in order to inspect and verify their cargoes and destinations and to ensure strict implementation of * * * resolution 661 * * *" S.C.Res. 665 (1991).

Later, the Security Council adopted Resolution 666 to ensure that permissible food shipments went to those most in need and not to the Iraqi military. The Council also adopted Resolution 670, directing states to take steps to ensure that their aircraft, and aircraft flying over their territory, were in compliance with Resolution 661. The Council also considered action it might take against states not complying with Resolution 661.

During the time the Security Council was engaged in implementing Resolution 661, there was a dramatic military buildup in the Persian Gulf. U.S. forces were rushed early to the Gulf area, and many troops entered Saudi Arabia pursuant to agreement between the two countries to deter and help defend Saudi Arabia against possible attack by Iraq. By the end of November 1990, it was reported, the U.S. had more than 250,000 military personnel in the region, part of a planned deployment of 400,000 troops by mid-January. Other states, including Egypt, Saudi Arabia, Britain, France, Argentina and Canada, had reportedly deployed between 200,000 and 250,000 troops. When

Iraq remained adamant in refusing to withdraw from Kuwait, the Security Council, on November 29, adopted Resolution 678 to authorize the use of military force to eject Iraq from Kuwait.

Security Council Resolution 678
November 29, 1990

The Security Council * * *

Noting that, despite all efforts by the United Nations, Iraq refuses to comply with its obligation to implement resolution 660 (1990) * * * in flagrant contempt of the Security Council,

Mindful of its duties and responsibilities under the Charter of the United Nations for the maintenance and preservation of international peace and security,

Determined to secure full compliance with its decisions,

Acting under Chapter VII of the Charter,

1. *Demands* that Iraq comply fully with resolution 660 (1990) and all subsequent relevant resolutions, and decides, while maintaining all its decisions, to allow Iraq one final opportunity, as a pause of goodwill, to do so;

2. *Authorizes* Member States co-operating with the Government of Kuwait, unless Iraq on or before 15 January 1991 fully implements, as set forth in paragraph 1 above, the foregoing resolutions, to use all necessary means to uphold and implement resolution 660 (1990) and all subsequent relevant resolutions and to restore international peace and security in the area;

3. *Requests* all States to provide appropriate support for the actions undertaken in pursuance of paragraph 2 of the present resolution;

4. *Requests* the States concerned to keep the Security Council regularly informed on the progress of actions undertaken pursuant to paragraphs 2 and 3 of the present resolution * * *.

As Iraq did not withdraw from Kuwait by the January 15, 1991 deadline set in Resolution 678, the military coalition supporting Kuwait began air strikes at that time. After an air war of several weeks and a ground war lasting a few more weeks, hostilities were suspended as noted in Resolution 686 (March 2, 1991), followed by terms for comprehensive settlement of the conflict in Resolution 687 (April 3, 1991). The latter resolution–the Council's most ambitious to date, sometimes called "the mother of all resolutions"—maintained economic sanctions on Iraq and detailed the conditions that Iraq would have to meet in order for sanctions to be lifted. It is excerpted and discussed below, together with issues in implementation of those conditions in the ensuing decade.

Notes

1. Schachter states that the action taken in the Gulf can be characterized either as one of collective self-defense authorized by the Security Council or as an

action taken under Article 42. Does the characterization have legal or practical consequences? See generally Schachter, United Nations Law in the Gulf Conflict, 85 A.J.I.L. 452–463 (1991).

For compilations of documents and references to literature, see The Kuwait Crisis: Basic Documents (Lauterpacht, Greenwood, Weller & Bethlehem, eds. 1991); Gulf War Legal and Diplomatic Documents, 13 Houston J. Int'l L. 281 (1991); Bibliography, The International Legal Implications of Iraq's Invasion of Kuwait: A Research Guide, 23 N.Y.U.J. Int'l L. & Pol. 231 (1991). See also Moore, The Gulf Crisis: Enforcing the Rule of Law (1992); Agora: The Gulf Crisis in International and Foreign Relations Law, 85 A.J.I.L. 63–109, 506–535 (1991); The Gulf War: The Law of International Sanctions, 85 A.S.I.L. Proc. 169 (1991); Quigley, The United States and The United Nations in the Persian Gulf War: New Order or Disorder?, 25 Cornell Int'l L.J. 1 (1992).

2. The Gulf War raised long dormant issues under Article 51 of the Charter. Article 51 provides that states may exercise the "inherent" right of individual or collective self-defense "until the Security Council has taken measures necessary to maintain international peace and security." Can the Council order the cessation of action taken in self-defense, despite the fact that it is an "inherent" right? Does the right to act in self-defense cease as soon as the Council is seized of the matter or only when the Council has taken measures? Will any action by the Council suspend the right to self-defense or does it come to an end only when the measures taken by the Security Council are successful and peace and security are restored? Who determines whether the measures taken have been effective? Once the Council has taken necessary measures, does the right of self-defense cease, or is it merely suspended, possibly to be revived at a later date? Professor Chayes has commented:

> Among the most important of the controverted questions—not because it was necessarily the most probable but because it throws the issues into sharpest relief—was the suggestion noted earlier that the United States was free, even in the absence of further provocation by Iraq or authorization by the Security Council, to use force against Iraq by virtue of some continuing right of collective self-defense emanating from the original attack on Kuwait. In other words, so the argument runs, the original deployments in Saudi Arabia and the Persian Gulf region were made in response to the armed attack on Kuwait and thus could be seen as an exercise of the inherent right of collective self-defense. The Security Council could be said to have acknowledged this position in its reference in Resolution 665 to "Member States co-operating with the government of Kuwait which are deploying maritime forces to the area." It rests with each of those states, perhaps in consultation with Kuwait and others whose forces were also at risk, to decide whether the measures taken in response to the Iraqi aggression were sufficient, and if not, what further action would be needed.
>
> The textual argument against this position, it seems to me, is very strong. Article 51 is not an affirmative grant of a right of self-defense but a statement of the situations in which the exercise of an "inherent right" is not precluded by the Charter. But those situations are subject to a limit of time. They endure only "until the Security Council has taken the measures necessary to maintain international peace and security."
>
> * * *

> In the larger scheme of the Charter, it is the Security Council that has "primary responsibility for the maintenance of international peace and security," which is recognized as primarily a political rather than a legal task. To carry out that responsibility, the Council, once seized of a matter under Chapter VII, must have the authority to make the political judgments as to the requirements of the situation and the measures necessary to deal with it. Security Council preemption, moreover, reinforces the fundamental objective of Article 2(4) and Article 51 to confine the permissible occasions for the unilateral use of force to the narrowest possible range, where it is immediately and universally apparent that armed response is required.
>
> * * *
>
> From the beginning of the Iraq–Kuwait crisis, as has been widely acknowledged, the Security Council worked "as it was supposed to work" according to the design of its framers. It cannot be argued that the Council failed to address the situation with appropriate gravity or to adopt measures with real impact or to strengthen those measures as the need became apparent. If the United Nations works as intended, judgments as to the ultimate objectives of U.N. action, the sufficiency of the measures to be taken, how long to wait for the sanctions to take effect, and the like are consigned to the Council, which acts by a majority of nine out of fifteen members, including the concurring or abstaining votes of the permanent members. In the process of reaching those decisions the United States necessarily has a very important voice. Indeed, there is both scope and need for American leadership. The United States can ensure by use of the veto that the Council will not act against its interests. But if the United States cannot induce the necessary number of other Security Council members to agree that additional measures involving the use of force are necessary, the Charter would clearly seem to preclude unilateral action.

Chayes, The Use of Force in the Persian Gulf, in Law and Force in the New International Order 3–7 (Damrosch & Scheffer, eds. 1991) (footnotes omitted). Compare Schachter's view:

> A Council decision that calls on an invader to withdraw and to cease hostilities is certainly a necessary measure, but it could not be intended to deprive the victim state of its right to defend itself when the invader has not complied with the Council's order. A reasonable construction of the provision in Article 51 would recognize that the Council has the authority to adopt a measure that would require armed action to cease even if that action was undertaken in self-defense. However, this would not mean that *any* measure would preempt self-defense. The intent of the Council as expressed in its decision would determine whether the right to use force in self-defense had been suspended by the Council.

Schachter, United Nations Law in the Gulf Conflict, 85 A.J.I.L. 452, 458 (1991). See also Greig, Self–Defence and the Security Council: What Does Article 51 Require?, 40 I.C.L.Q. 366 (1991); Gardner, Commentary on the Law of Self–Defense, in Law and Force in the New International Order (Damrosch & Scheffer, eds. 1991); Mullerson, Self–Defense in the Contemporary World, in Law and Force in the New International Order (Damrosch & Scheffer, eds. 1991).

3. Do the usual requirements for action taken in self-defense—necessity and proportionality—apply to an action authorized by the Council? Does the Council have the authority to suspend these requirements? See Implementing Limitations

on the Use of Force: The Doctrine of Proportionality and Necessity, 86 A.S.I.L.Proc. 39 (1992).

4. In Korea, the Security Council "recommended" that "member states" come to the defense of South Korea. In the Gulf War, the Council "authorized" military action by states cooperating with Kuwait. Are these differences of legal significance? In Korea the Security Council recommended a Unified Command controlled by the United States and authorized the use of the U.N. flag, while the Gulf War proceeded as an ad hoc coalition. The Security Council did not seek to exercise any control over the actions either in Korea or in the Gulf. Schachter states that "the problems of authority and control are almost certain to complicate any future large scale enforcement action." Schachter, International Law in Theory and Practice 398 (1991). This prediction has proven accurate, e.g. in Somalia in 1993 (p. 1034).

5. *Presidential authority.* As in the Korean War, the United States was the major power behind the coalition forces in the Gulf War. President Bush initially claimed constitutional authority to deploy and use forces pursuant to Security Council Resolution 678, without congressional approval. Members of Congress and many publicists denied that the President had the authority to commence hostilities without congressional authorization, especially in view of the War Powers Resolution. On the dispute between the President and the Congress, see U.S. Policy to Reverse Iraq's Occupation of Kuwait, 137 Cong. Rec. S323–04, 102d Cong., 1st Sess. (1991); The Situation in the Middle East[:] Expressing Sense of Congress that Congress Must Approve an Offensive Action against Iraq, 137 Cong. Rec. H390–01, 102d Cong., 1st Sess. (1991); see also the arguments in Dellums v. Bush, 752 F.Supp. 1141 (D.D.C.1990); Glennon, The Constitution and Chapter VII of the United Nations Charter, 85 A.J.I.L. 74 (1991); compare Franck & Patel, UN Police Action in Lieu of War: "The Old Order Changeth," 85 A.J.I.L. 63 (1991).

In the end, shortly before the January 15 deadline under Resolution 678, Congress gave the President the authority he requested in the Authorization for Use of Military Force Against Iraq Resolution, Pub. L. No. 102–1, 105 Stat. 3 (1991). This resolution does not specify an ending date and apparently confers continuing authority until such time as Iraq has come into compliance with the full series of U.N. Security Council resolutions. A decade later, it was still being actively invoked in recurrent military confrontations between the United States and Iraq. On uses of force against Iraq subsequent to the 1991 cease-fire, see below. On U.S. constitutional aspects, see Damrosch, The Clinton Administration and War Powers, 63 Law & Contemp. Prob. 125, 132 (2000).

Security Council Resolution 687
April 3, 1991

The Security Council * * *

Affirming the commitment of all Member States to the sovereignty, territorial integrity and political independence of Kuwait and Iraq, * * *

Conscious of the need to take the following measures acting under Chapter VII of the Charter, * * *

A

2. *Demands* that Iraq and Kuwait respect the inviolability of the international boundary * * *;

3. *Calls upon* the Secretary–General to lend his assistance to make arrangements with Iraq and Kuwait to demarcate the boundary between Iraq and Kuwait * * *;

B

5. *Requests* the Secretary–General, after consulting with Iraq and Kuwait, to submit within three days to the Security Council for its approval a plan for the immediate deployment of a United Nations observer unit to monitor the Khor Abdullah and a demilitarized zone, which is hereby established, extending ten kilometres into Iraq and five kilometres into Kuwait from the boundary * * *;

6. *Notes* that as soon as the Secretary–General notifies the Security Council of the completion of the deployment of the United Nations observer unit, the conditions will be established for the Member States cooperating with Kuwait in accordance with resolution 678 (1990) to bring their military presence in Iraq to an end consistent with resolution 686 (1991);

C

7. *Invites* Iraq to reaffirm unconditionally its obligations under the Geneva Protocol for the Prohibition of the Use in War of Asphyxiating, Poisonous or Other Gases, and of Bacteriological Methods of Warfare, signed at Geneva on 17 June 1925, and to ratify the Convention on the Prohibition of the Development, Production and Stockpiling of Bacteriological (Biological) and Toxin Weapons and on Their Destruction, of 10 April 1972;

8. *Decides* that Iraq shall unconditionally accept the destruction, removal, or rendering harmless, under international supervision of:

(a) All chemical and biological weapons and all stocks of agents and all related subsystems and components and all research, development, support and manufacturing facilities;

(b) All ballistic missiles with a range greater than 150 kilometres and related major parts, and repair and production facilities;

9. *Decides*, for the implementation of paragraph 8 above, the following:

(a) Iraq shall submit to the Secretary–General, within fifteen days of the adoption of the present resolution, a declaration of the locations, amounts and types of all items specified in paragraph 8 and agree to urgent, on-site inspection as specified below;

(b) The Secretary–General [shall develop a plan for a Special Commission to carry out immediate on-site inspection of Iraq's biological, chemical and missile capabilities, and for their destruction, removal or rendering harmless];

10. *Decides* that Iraq shall unconditionally undertake not to use, develop, construct or acquire any of the items specified in paragraphs 8 and 9 above and requests the Secretary–General, in consultation with the Special Commission, to develop a plan for the future ongoing monitoring and verification of Iraq's compliance with this paragraph * * *;

11. *Invites* Iraq to reaffirm unconditionally its obligations under the Treaty on the Non–Proliferation of Nuclear Weapons for 1 July 1968;

12. *Decides* that Iraq shall unconditionally agree not to acquire or develop nuclear weapons or nuclear-weapons-usable material or any subsys-

tems or components or any research, development, support or manufacturing facilities related to the above; * * * to place all of its nuclear-weapons-usable materials under the exclusive control, for custody and removal, of the International Atomic Energy Agency, with the assistance and cooperation of the Special Commission * * *; to accept * * * urgent on-site inspection and the destruction, removal or rendering harmless as appropriate of all items specified above; and to accept the plan discussed in paragraph 13 below for the future ongoing monitoring and verification of its compliance with these undertakings;

13. *Requests* the Director–General of the International Atomic Energy Agency * * * to carry out immediate on-site inspection of Iraq's nuclear capabilities * * *; to develop a plan * * * for the destruction, removal, or rendering harmless as appropriate of all items listed in paragraph 12 above; * * *

F

22. *Decides* that * * * upon Council agreement that Iraq has completed all actions contemplated in paragraphs 8, 9, 10, 11, 12 and 13 above, the prohibitions against the import of commodities and products originating in Iraq and the prohibitions against financial transactions related thereto contained in resolution 661 (1990) shall have no further force or effect; * * *

24. *Decides* that, in accordance with resolution 661 (1990) and subsequent related resolutions and until a further decision is taken by the Security Council, all States shall continue to prevent the sale or supply * * * to Iraq by their nationals, or from their territories or using their flag vessels or aircraft, of:

(a) Arms and related *matériel* of all types * * *;

(B) Items specified and defined in paragraphs 8 and 12 above * * *;

I

33. *Declares* that, upon official notification by Iraq to the Secretary–General and to the Security Council of its acceptance of the provisions above, a formal cease-fire is effective between Iraq and Kuwait and the Member States cooperating with Kuwait in accordance with resolution 678 (1990);

34. *Decides* to remain seized of the matter and to take such further steps as may be required for the implementation of the present resolution and to secure peace and security in the area.

Notes

1. In addition to the provisions excerpted above, Resolution 687 dealt with steps to facilitate the return of Kuwait property seized by Iraq (Part D, para. 15); to create a fund to pay compensation for claims for direct loss or injury resulting from Iraq's unlawful invasion and occupation of Kuwait, including environmental damage (Part E, paras. 16–19); to facilitate repatriation of all Kuwaiti and third-country nationals with the assistance of the International Committee of the Red Cross (Part G, paras. 30–31); and to renounce terrorism (Part H, para. 32). On the U.N. Compensation Commission established pursuant to Part E, see p. 738.

2. After the cease-fire in March 1991, there were reports of widespread attacks by Iraqi forces against Iraq's Kurdish and Shiite populations, causing

nearly two million refugees to flee towards the Turkish and Iranian borders. On April 5, 1991, the Security Council adopted Resolution 688, which, while recalling Article 2(7) of the Charter and reaffirming commitment to the sovereignty, territorial integrity and political independence of Iraq, condemned "the repression of the Iraqi civilian population in many parts of Iraq, including most recently in Kurdish populated areas, the consequences of which threaten international peace and security in the region," and demanded that Iraq cease the repression and allow "immediate access by international humanitarian organizations to all those in need of assistance in all parts of Iraq." Resolution 688 authorized the Secretary–General to pursue humanitarian efforts through U.N. agencies and to send a mission to the region, but did not explicitly authorize use of force to protect the refugees. See S.C.Res. 688 (1991), reprinted in 30 I.L.M. 858 (1991). See generally Weller (ed.), Iraq and Kuwait: The Hostilities and Their Aftermath (1993); U.N. Dep't of Public Information, The United Nations and the Iraq–Kuwait Conflict, 1990–1996 (1996).

In April, 1991, Britain, France and the United States sent forces into northern Iraq to create "safe havens" to which the Iraqi Kurdish refugee population could return. The United States stressed the humanitarian nature of the operation and invoked Resolution 688 "to establish several encampments in northern Iraq, where relief supplies * * * [would] be made available in large quantities and distributed in an orderly way." See Adelman, Humanitarian Intervention: The Case of the Kurds, 4 Int'l J. Refugee L. 4, 4–5 n. 1 (1992). The United States declared that "[a]dequate security [would] be provided at those sites by U.S., British and French ground forces, consistent with United Nations Resolution 688." Id. The United States, the United Kingdom and France and Britain also unilaterally declared a "no-fly zone" north of the 36th parallel in Iraq; and in August 1992, after renewed Iraqi attacks on Shiites in the southern marshes, they proclaimed another no-fly zone south of the 32nd parallel. No U.N. Security Council resolution specifically refers to such no-fly zones or explicitly confers authority to enforce them with military force.

Does Resolution 688 support these measures taken inside Iraq? See Stromseth, Iraq's Repression of Its Civilian Population: Collective Responses and Continuing Challenges, in Damrosch (ed.), Enforcing Restraint: Collective Intervention in Internal Conflicts 77–117 (1993); Murphy, Humanitarian Intervention: The United Nations in an Evolving World Order 165–198 (1996).

3. Since the 1991 ceasefire and continuing through the 1990s and into the 2000s, the United States and other states have taken recurrent military action in and over Iraqi territory. The no-fly zones are regularly policed by coalition aircraft using a Turkish base at Incirlik in proximity to northern Iraq, and from aircraft carriers in the Persian Gulf. Iraq has repeatedly tested the coalition forces' willingness to enforce the flight ban, and military confrontations have taken place repeatedly. The U.S. and other states have mounted air strikes or other military actions when Iraq has violated the terms of the cease-fire resolution, trespassed into Kuwait, renewed attacks on its Kurdish or Shiite populations, or otherwise acted in a hostile manner. In January 1993, U.S., British and French forces carried out air strikes in response to cease-fire violations, including unauthorized incursions into Kuwaiti territory and refusal to guarantee the safety and free movement of the Special Commission established under Resolution 687 (UNSCOM). The allies have reiterated this stance frequently thereafter (though by the late 1990s, France had dissociated itself from military enforcement of the no-fly zones).

4. Tensions over Iraq's refusal to allow UNSCOM to carry out its mandate to inspect and verify destruction of all capability for weapons of mass destruction escalated over the 1990s, culminating with the departure of the UNSCOM inspectors in 1998 and Iraq's refusal to permit them or a successor team to resume their functions. See generally Butler, The Greatest Threat: Iraq, Weapons of Mass Destruction, and the Crisis of Global Security (2000). In response to these Iraqi provocations, the United States and the United Kingdom undertook a series of air strikes in December 1998, and in the first eight months of 1999 they had flown more than 10,000 sorties and used more than 1000 bombs and missiles against more than 400 Iraqi targets. See Murphy, Contemporary Practice of the United States Relating to International Law: Continuation of Air Attacks and Sanctions Against Iraq, 94 A.J.I.L. 102–104 (2000); see also Murphy, Contemporary Practice, 93 A.J.I.L. 471 (1999).

Legal authority for use of military force in the post-cease-fire phase is disputed. The United States and its allies have relied on arguments derived from a combination of Resolutions 678, 687, 688 and other resolutions. For use of force to enforce Resolution 687 (which does not specify forcible enforcement or use terms such as "all necessary means" to confer such authority), one line of argument is that the authority granted in Resolution 678 never lapsed, or if that authority had been provisionally suspended upon conclusion of the cease-fire, it has revived by virtue of Iraq's violation of the conditions of Resolution 687 (or, alternatively, that Kuwait's inherent rights of collective self-defense in cooperation with other states have revived). These arguments rest in part on the position that Iraq is in material breach of the cease-fire resolution. (Compare p. 548 on issues of "material breach" in connection with armistice agreements.) For findings of "unacceptable and material breach," or "flagrant violation" of Resolution 687, see S/25081 (Jan. 8, 1993); S/25091 (Jan. 11, 1993); S.C. Res. 1134 (Oct. 23, 1997); S.C. Res. 1137 (Nov. 12, 1997); see also S.C. Res. 1154 (Mar. 2, 1998) (warning of "the severest consequences" should Iraq impede the inspectors) and accompanying statements. In Resolution 1205 (Nov. 5, 1998), the Council condemned Iraq's decision not to cooperate with UNSCOM but did not mention use of force.

For differing legal positions, compare Wedgwood, The Enforcement of Security Council Resolution 687: The Threat of Force Against Iraq's Weapons of Mass Destruction, 92 A.J.I.L. 724 (1998), with Lobel & Ratner, Bypassing the Security Council: Ambiguous Authorizations to Use Force, Cease–Fires and the Iraqi Inspection Regime, 93 A.J.I.L. 124 (1999). Lobel and Ratner argue that a valid claim of Security Council authorization to use force must be based on a resolution that is explicit, that clearly articulates the objectives and puts the Council in control, and that terminates with the establishment of a durable cease-fire unless explicitly extended by the Council.

5. As of 2000, Iraq had not met the conditions set by paragraph 22 of Resolution 687 for the lifting of the economic sanctions. The sanctions regime has thus been in effect for more than a decade, with dire effects on Iraq's civilian population. With the objective of alleviating the humanitarian impact of the sanctions, the Security Council approved an "oil-for-food" program, under which Iraq would be permitted to sell specified quantities of oil, with the proceeds earmarked for food, medicines, and other internationally approved purposes. See S.C. Res. 706 (1991); S.C. Res. 712 (1991); S.C. Res. 986 (1995). Iraq did not accept the terms of this program until 1996 and deliveries did not begin until 1997. The program has been periodically reauthorized, and sanctions have also been adjusted to allow redevelopment of power generation capability and the

purchase of spare parts for the oil industry. See, e.g., S.C. Res. 1111 (1997); S.C. Res. 1153 (1998); S.C. Res. 1210 (1998); S.C. Res. 1284 (1999).

On the humanitarian and other issues concerning sanctions, and the relationship of the Iraq sanctions to uses of force, see, e.g., Damrosch, The Civilian Impact of Economic Sanctions, in Damrosch (ed.), Enforcing Restraint: Collective Intervention in Internal Conflicts 274–315 (1993); Damrosch, Enforcing International Law Through Non–Forcible Measures, 269 Rec. des Cours 9, 108–121 (1997); Cortwright & Lopez, The Sanctions Decade: Assessing UN Strategies in the 1990s 37–61 (2000).

3. U.N. Peace Operations and "Coalitions of Willing States"

During the Cold War and the frustration of the Security Council, the principal U.N. contribution to international peace and security consisted of various forms of "peacekeeping"—efforts to prevent hostilities from erupting or resuming. The Security Council established some peacekeeping arrangements pursuant to its authority under Chapter VI. The General Assembly also exercised authority to recommend peacekeeping arrangements under Article 14. All the organs of the United Nations, including the Secretary–General, have contributed to peacekeeping by various forms of "preventive diplomacy."

The model of peacekeeping that evolved through innovations and improvisations of the U.N.'s early decades took on several salient features. In traditional peacekeeping, U.N. troops carry only light arms and are allowed to use force only in self-defense from attack or from armed interference with their mandate. They take up positions along a "thin blue line" between forces that have already agreed to stop fighting, and are present with the consent of the territorial state and the agreement of the parties to the conflict. They are expected to maintain strict neutrality and impartiality. Between 1945 and 1990, the United Nations initiated some 15 operations on this traditional model, as well as 10 missions involving unarmed observers.

Beginning in 1990, U.N. peace operations took on increasingly complex mandates of a qualitatively different character. Some operations in this "second generation" have involved the implementation of a comprehensive peace settlement in the aftermath of years or even decades of armed conflict; in these instances, U.N. forces have maintained order for a transitional period, administered elections, and supervised the inauguration of new institutions. In other cases, U.N. troops have entered in the absence of a firm peace settlement, with difficult and perhaps unachievable mandates and unintended "mission creep." The most ambitious of these undertakings have entailed as many as 20,000 troops, contributed by member states but serving under U.N. command. Table 12.1 presents summary information about both first- and second-generation operations:

As of early 2001, the following U.N. peacekeeping missions were in progress:[1]

United Nations Peacekeepers on Current Missions

Area of Deployment	Mission Name	Dates	Military Personnel[2]
Arab-Israel	UNTSO	1948-	142
India-Pakistan	UNMOGIP	1949-	46
Cyprus	UNFICYP	1964-	1,222
Syria	UNDOF	1974-	1,035
Lebanon	UNIFIL	1978-	5,716
Iraq-Kuwait	UNIKOM	Apr. 1991-	1,096
Western Sahara	MINURSO	Apr. 1991-	229
Georgia	UNOMIG	Aug. 1993-	104
Bosnia-Herzegovina	UNMIBH	Dec. 1995-	5[3]
Prevlaka [Bos.-Herz.]	UNMOP	Jan. 1996-	27
Kosovo	UNMIK	June 1999-	38[4]
Sierra Leone	UNAMSIL	Oct. 1999-	9,555
East Timor	UNTAET	Oct. 1999-	8,067
Dem. Rep. Congo	MONUC	Dec. 1999-	Auth. 5,537 Depl. 231
Ethiopia-Eritrea	UNMEE	July 2000-	Auth. 4,200 Depl. 3,571

[1] Source: United Nations, Dept. of Peacekeeping Operations, www.un.org/Depts/dpko

[2] Most U.N. peacekeeping missions include a combination of military and civilian personnel; and in some of the more recent missions, civilian police can be a significant component of the mission (sometimes larger in strength than the military component). As relevant to the present chapter, only the military personnel are shown in this table.

[3] The bulk of the international military force in Bosnia-Herzegovina is supplied not by the United Nations but by NATO pursuant to the Dayton Agreement. See p. 1041. In addition to the international military personnel, UNMIBH has 1,820 civilian police in Bosnia-Herzegovina.

[4] The bulk of the international military force in Kosovo is supplied not by the United Nations but by NATO and other countries pursuant to S.C. Res. 1244. See p. 1000. In addition to the international military personnel, UNMIK has 4,364 civilian police in Kosovo.

For legal purposes it is important to distinguish between operations organized and run by the United Nations (whether as classic or as complex peace operations), and operations undertaken by "coalitions of the willing" with Security Council approval. The enforcement operation against Iraq, as discussed above, was a "coalition of the willing" in support of Kuwait. Other "coalitions of the willing" include the Unified Task Force led by the United States in Somalia, the multinational intervention in Haiti (1994), *Opération*

Turquoise led by France in Rwanda (1994), the NATO implementation force in Bosnia–Herzegovina (1995–), and the intervention led by Australia in East Timor in 1999. Each of these had an authorizing resolution from the Security Council, but the United Nations did not control the national operations. In certain theaters, the parallel existence of U.N. peacekeeping forces and national forces operating as part of a "coalition of the willing" has led to confusion about their respective mandates and lines of authority and control. An example is the overlapping roles for the U.N. forces and U.N.-led Unified Task Force in Somalia, which came to an unhappy end. See pp. 1033–1034.

The materials that follow highlight some of the essential features of the most important U.N. peace operations, beginning with ones from the "first generation" whose mandate was to separate forces along an agreed cease-fire line, and then proceeding to the complex "second generation" operations of more recent years. Thereafter (Section 3.B) we turn to regional organizations and arrangements, which have assumed a significant share of responsibility for collective security and self-defense.

Note

Among the many works on U.N. peacekeeping, a good introduction is published by the United Nations as The Blue Helmets: A Review of United Nations Peace–Keeping (3rd ed. 1996). A series of U.N. "blue books" addresses specific conflicts, e.g., The United Nations and Rwanda, 1990–1996 (1996). A journal of International Peacekeeping has been published since 1994. Earlier references include: Durch (ed.), The Evolution of U.N. Peacekeeping: Case Studies and Comparative Analysis (1993); Durch & Blechman, Keeping the Peace: The United Nations in the Emerging World Order (1992); Fermann, Bibliography on International Peacekeeping (1992); White, The United Nations and the Maintenance of International Peace and Security (1990); Rikhye, United Nations and Peacekeeping: Results, Limits and Prospects (1988); James, Peacekeeping and International Politics (1990); Higgins, United Nations Peacekeeping 1946–79: Documents and Commentary, 4 vols. (1981); United Nations Peace–Keeping (Cassese, ed. 1978); Rikhye, Harbottle & Egge, The Thin Blue Line: International Peacekeeping and Its Future (1974); Bowett, United Nations Forces (1964); Heathcote, Peacekeeping by United Nations Forces (1963); Goodrich & Simons, The United Nations and the Maintenance of International Peace and Security (1955).

On "second-generation" peace operations, see Ratner, The New U.N. Peacekeeping: Building Peace in Lands of Conflict After the Cold War (1994). See also Carnegie Commission on the Prevention of Deadly Conflict, Final Report 63–67 (1997) and bibliography at 222–242. For an analytical bibliography, see Collins & Weiss, An Overview and Assessment of 1989–1996 Peace Operations Publications (Occasional Paper #28, Thomas J. Watson Jr. Institute for International Studies, 1997).

On delegations of Security Council authorities to coalitions of states, see Sarooshi, The United Nations and the Development of Collective Security: The Delegation by the U.N. Security Council of Its Chapter VII Powers (1999).

THE ARAB–ISRAELI CONFLICT: PEACEKEEPING IN SUPPORT OF CEASE–FIRE AND DISENGAGEMENT

After the cessation of fighting between Israel and the Arab states that followed the Israeli declaration of independence on May 14, 1948, friction with Egypt continued. The Egyptians had obstructed Israeli commerce through the Gulf of Aqaba and through the Suez Canal, and Israeli complaints to the Security Council on four occasions between 1950 and 1955 failed to achieve results. President Nasser then announced, on July 26, 1956, the nationalization of the Suez Canal Company. The principal shareholders of the latter were the United Kingdom and various private interests in the United Kingdom and in France.

On October 29, 1956, Israeli forces invaded Egypt, in concert with forces from the United Kingdom and France. On October 31, the Security Council approved by a vote of 7–2–2 a resolution introduced by Yugoslavia that placed the question before the General Assembly. As a procedural matter, the resolution was not defeated by the negative votes of France and the United Kingdom. See Article 27(2) of the Charter. The resolution (S.C.Res. 119) noted the grave situation created by the action against Egypt and called for the convocation of an emergency special session of the General Assembly pursuant to the "Uniting for Peace" Resolution.

On November 5, 1956, the General Assembly passed a resolution establishing "a United Nations Command for an emergency international Force to secure and supervise the cessation of hostilities." G.A.Res. 1000. By November 7, the fighting had stopped. On November 8, Major–General E.L.M. Burns of Canada was appointed Chief of the United Nations Command of the United Nations Emergency Force (UNEF). See U.N.Doc. A/3317. With Egyptian approval the UNEF was established on Egyptian territory. Israel indicated that "on no account" would she "agree to the stationing of a foreign force, no matter how called, in her territory or in any of the areas occupied by her." See U.N.Docs. A/3313 and A/3314; N.Y. Times, November 8, 1956, at 1, col. 2. See generally Friedmann & Collins, The Suez Canal Crisis of 1956, in Scheinman & Wilkinson, International Law and Political Crisis: An Analytic Casebook 91 (1968). After some delay and further resolutions of the U.N. General Assembly, on March 8, 1957, the Secretary–General confirmed full Israeli withdrawal behind the armistice lines.

Ten years later, on May 18, 1967, Egypt (then known as the United Arab Republic, or UAR) decided to terminate the presence of UNEF from the territory of the UAR and the Gaza Strip. The U.N. Secretary General U Thant accepted the authority of the UAR to take this action and instructed UNEF to withdraw. See Special Report of the Secretary–General, May 18, 1967, U.N.Doc. A/6669 (1967). The United States announced that it viewed with dismay the withdrawal of UNEF without action by either the General Assembly or the Security Council. See the letter of Ernest A. Gross challenging the legal right of the UAR to withdraw UNEF unilaterally and the propriety of the Secretary General's compliance. N.Y. Times, May 26, 1967 at 44.

As the UNEF troops withdrew, large UAR units took their place. Tension in the Middle East increased rapidly. Israeli Premier Eshkol warned that any interference with the freedom of Israeli shipping would be taken as an act of aggression. The efforts of the major powers to avert the outbreak of war were unavailing. On June 5, 1967, Israel, claiming attacks by its Arab neighbors, launched a major invasion of Arab territory. See U.N.Docs. S/PV 1347 at 3, 17–20; 1348 at 73–75 (1967). Within a week the Israeli troops were completely victorious and a large portion of Arab territory had been occupied. The Security Council's demand for an immediate cease-fire was eventually honored by the parties. Resolution 242, among other things, called for the withdrawal of Israeli forces "from territories" occupied by them. For the text of resolution 242 and other resolutions, see 6 I.L.M. 604–08 (1967). The efforts of the Soviet Union to have a resolution adopted requiring the withdrawal of Israeli troops were unsuccessful. See generally Bowie, The Suez Crisis 1956 (1974).

Despite Resolution 242, there was no progress towards a peaceful settlement, and Israel remained in control of the territories seized in the 1967 war. On October 6, 1973, Egyptian, Syrian and Iraqi forces launched a surprise attack on Israel, but after some initial successes they were repelled. Under pressure from the United States and the U.S.S.R., Israel agreed to withdraw its forces from Egyptian soil and disengagement agreements were signed between Israel–Egypt and Israel–Syria. The Security Council established another U.N. Emergency Force (UNEF II) to monitor disengagement between Egypt and Israel (S.C.Res. 340 (1973)), and the U.N. Disengagement Observer Force (UNDOF) (S.C.Res. 350 (1974)) for the buffer zone between Israel and Syria.

Israel also occupied southern Lebanon in retaliation for raids launched from bases of the Palestine Liberation Organization in that area. In 1978, the United Nations Interim Force in Lebanon (UNIFIL) was established to oversee the withdrawal of Israeli forces and assist the government of Lebanon in ensuring the return of its effective authority in the area. See S.C.Res. 425 and 426. UNIFIL was unable to fulfill its mandate completely but managed to reduce the level of violence and the risk of wider conflict between Israeli and Arab forces. In 1982 the Lebanese government asked France, Britain and the United States to send troops to bolster U.N. forces attempting to police a fragile ceasefire in Lebanon's civil war. Frequent attacks by the various militias culminated in a bomb attack on the U.S. troop barracks, killing 250 marines. Soon all Western troops were withdrawn and only the U.N. force remained.

In 1978–79, with U.S. support and intermediation, Israel and Egypt negotiated a peace treaty under which Israel agreed to withdraw from the Sinai, and Egypt agreed to end the state of war and to establish normal relations with Israel. The treaty was signed at Camp David on March 26, 1979. See 28 I.L.M. 362 (1979). Other Arab states rejected it, and a plan to have the agreement monitored by U.N. forces was abandoned because of Soviet opposition. Instead, a Multinational Force and Observers led by the United States has assisted in implementation of the Camp David agreement.

As of 2000, UNDOF and UNIFIL were still in place in the Middle East. UNDOF continues to monitor the Golan Heights buffer zone between Israel and Syria. In June 2000 Israel finally completed the withdrawal of its troops from Lebanon. See U.N. Doc. S/PRST/2000/21 (June 18, 2000). The Security Council has extended UNIFIL's mandate for successive 6-month periods. See, e.g., S/RES/1337 (Jan. 30, 2001).

Notes

1. As noted (p. 1007), France and the Soviet Union questioned the legality of U.N. assessments to pay for peacekeeping operations authorized by the General Assembly rather than by the Security Council. This objection pertained (*inter alia*) to UNEF I which the General Assembly had approved. In its advisory opinion on Certain Expenses of the United Nations, 1962 I.C.J. 151, the International Court of Justice concluded that the General Assembly had acted within the scope of its authority in recommending establishment of a peacekeeping force and approving its expenses. The opinion states in part:

Article 24 of the Charter provides:

"In order to ensure prompt and effective action by the United Nations, its Members confer on the Security Council primary responsibility for the maintenance of international peace and security * * * "

The responsibility conferred is "primary", not exclusive. This primary responsibility is conferred upon the Security Council, as stated in Article 24, "in order to ensure prompt and effective action." To this end, it is the Security Council which is given a power to impose an explicit obligation of compliance if for example it issues an order or command to an aggressor under Chapter VII. It is only the Security Council which can require enforcement by coercive action against an aggressor.

The Charter makes it abundantly clear, however, that the General Assembly is also to be concerned with international peace and security. Article 14 authorizes the General Assembly to "recommend measures for the peaceful adjustment of any situation, regardless of origin, which it deems likely to impair the general welfare or friendly relations among nations, including situations resulting from a violation of the provisions of the present Charter setting forth the purposes and principles of the United Nations." The word "measures" implies some kind of action, and the only limitation which Article 14 imposes on the General Assembly is the restriction found in Article 12, namely, that the Assembly should not recommend measures while the Security Council is dealing with the same matter unless the Council requests it to do so. Thus while it is the Security Council which, exclusively, may order coercive action, the functions and powers conferred by the Charter on the General Assembly are not confined to discussion, consideration, the initiation of studies and the making of recommendations; they are not merely hortatory. Article 18 deals with *"decisions"* of the General Assembly "on important questions". These "decisions" do indeed include certain recommendations, but others have dispositive force and effect. Among these latter decisions, Article 18 includes suspension of rights and privileges of membership, expulsion of Members, "and budgetary questions". * * *

By Article 17, paragraph 1, the General Assembly is given the power not only to "consider" the budget of the Organization, but also to "approve" it. The decision to "approve" the budget has a close connection with paragraph 2 of Article 17, since thereunder the General Assembly is also given the power to apportion the expenses among the Members and the exercise of the power of apportionment creates the obligation, specifically stated in Article 17, paragraph 2, of each Member to bear that part of the expenses which is apportioned to it by the General Assembly. When those expenses include expenditures for the maintenance of peace and security, which are not otherwise provided for, it is the General Assembly which has the authority to apportion the latter amounts among the Members. The provisions of the Charter which distribute functions and powers to the Security Council and to the General Assembly give no support to the view that such distribution excludes from the powers of the General Assembly the power to provide for the financing of measures designed to maintain peace and security.

2. *The Congo.* The Security Council and the General Assembly were both involved in authorizing peacekeeping in the Congo in 1960–64. Within a week of Congo's attaining independence from Belgium in 1960, there were mutinies in the Congolese army and attacks on Belgians and other Europeans. On July 8, Belgium dispatched troops to the Congo for the announced purpose of protecting its nationals. On July 11, the mineral-rich province of Katanga announced its secession. On July 12, President Kasavubu and Prime Minister Lumumba of the Republic of the Congo requested U.N. assistance in a telegram to the Secretary–General. See U.N.Doc. S/4382. On July 14, the Security Council approved a resolution authorizing the Secretary–General "to provide the Government of the Republic of the Congo with such military assistance as may be necessary until, through the efforts of the Congolese Government with the technical assistance of the United Nations, the national security forces may be able, in the opinion of the Government, to fully meet their tasks." S.C.Res. 143. The U.N. force is known by its French acronym, ONUC.

The Security Council became embroiled in a debate on the right of U.N. forces to enter Katanga. See the Secretary–General's memorandum of August 12, 1960, U.N.Doc. S/4417/Add.6. During September, the Soviet Union vetoed several resolutions that would have reaffirmed the power of the U.N. forces to maintain law and order. An impasse developed and continued until the adoption on September 17 of a United States-sponsored resolution (S.C.Res. 157) that called for an emergency meeting of the General Assembly as provided for in the "Uniting for Peace" Resolution. On September 20, the General Assembly passed a resolution confirming the functions of the U.N. forces and requesting the Secretary–General to continue his support of the Central Government of the Congo. G.A.Res. 1474.

Despite the presence of United Nations forces, civil strife in the Congo continued. On February 21, 1961, the Security Council reaffirmed its previous resolutions and urged that the United Nations act to prevent the occurrence of a civil war in the Congo. It called for the withdrawal of all foreign military personnel and called upon all states to take measures to prevent persons from joining the civil strife. The Council also urged the restoration of order through the convening of the Parliament and the reorganization of Congolese armed units. See S.C.Res. 161. Further resolutions of the Security Council were necessary before foreign mercenaries were removed, the secession of Katanga ended, and law and order restored. See U.N. Secretary–General, Report on the Withdrawal of the United Nations Force in the Congo and on other aspects of the United Nations operation, June 29, 1964, U.N.Doc. S/5784. Compare the withdrawal of the United Nations forces from the Congo with the withdrawal of forces from Egypt in 1967. Was the withdrawal of the forces in either case required by international law?

On the role of law in the crisis in the Congo, see Abi–Saab, The United Nations Operation in the Congo 1960–64 (1978). See also Miller (pseudonym for

Schachter), Legal Aspects of the United Nations Action in the Congo, 55 A.J.I.L. 1 (1961).

3. *U.N. Force in Cyprus.* After negotiations with Greece, Turkey, and representatives of the Greek and Turkish Cypriot communities, the United Kingdom granted independence to the Republic of Cyprus in 1960. Treaty concerning the Establishment of the Republic of Cyprus, August 16, 1960, 382 U.N.T.S. 8. Differences between the Greek and Turkish Cypriot communities soon manifested themselves during the drafting of constitutional provisions that were to guarantee the rights of the respective groups, and communal fighting broke out in late 1963. Although the conflict was domestic in character, the fact that each side was supported by a guarantor state (as established in the Treaty of Guarantee, 382 U.N.T.S. 8) gave the struggle international overtones. The Security Council considered the Cyprus situation from February 18 to March 4, 1964, and unanimously approved on the latter date a resolution establishing a United Nations Peace–Keeping Force in Cyprus (UNFICYP). S.C.Res. 186. UNFICYP was mobilized and in operation by March 27, 1964.

In August, 1964, fighting broke out and Turkey made several air attacks against Greek Cypriots. Turkey claimed that UNFICYP was unable to stop either the continued arming of the Greek community or its military offensive against the Turkish community. Widespread fighting ceased, but tensions remained high. In September, the Secretary–General reported that UNFICYP was able to maintain the peace, but that both sides were continuing to build their military strength.

In the following years, little progress was made toward the solution of the island's problems. Both sides remained armed and occasional, isolated fighting broke out. See generally Ehrlich, Cyprus 1958–1967 (1974). In 1974, the delicate balance was shattered when a coup by Greek officers overthrew President Makarios, apparently in a move toward uniting Cyprus with Greece. Turkish troops, however, invaded Cyprus and overthrew the rebel regime. The U.N. ordered a cease-fire, but by the time real cease-fire took hold Turkish troops controlled forty per cent of the island. President Makarios resumed control of the Government until he died, but the island remained effectively divided and efforts to resolve the dispute and reestablish an agreed unified government did not succeed. The presence of UNFICYP on Cyprus was still continuing as of 2000.

SECOND–GENERATION PEACEKEEPING: CAMBODIA

For many years, Cambodia suffered from civil war, interventions, genocide and other gross violations of human rights, and massive dislocations of its population. In March 1970, Cambodia's hereditary king, Norodom Sihanouk, was overthrown by General Lon Nol, who instituted authoritarian rule under the name of the Khmer Republic. In 1975, the Khmer Rouge gained control of Cambodia, renaming it Democratic Kampuchea, and attempted a total restructuring of Cambodian society, committing mass state-sponsored killing and other violations of human rights. In 1979, Vietnam invaded Cambodia and installed a régime known as the People's Republic of Kampuchea, which controlled most of Cambodia during the 1980s. After the Vietnamese invasion, four factions conducted a guerrilla war in an attempt to gain control of Cambodia.

In 1991, the four Cambodian warring factions endorsed a United Nations plan designed to help rebuild Cambodia and signed a number of agreements aimed at a comprehensive settlement. See Paris Conference on Cambodian Agreements Elaborating the Framework for a Comprehensive Political Settlement of the Cambodian Conflict, U.N.Doc. A/46/608 and S/233177, reprinted in 31 I.L.M. 174 (1992). Under the 1991 Paris Agreements the four warring factions agreed to create a Supreme National Council (SNC), composed of representatives of the factions, to act as the "unique * * * source of authority" and embody Cambodian sovereignty. The SNC delegated to the United Nations all authority necessary to ensure the implementation of the comprehensive settlement. In 1992, the United Nations set up the U.N. Transitional Authority (UNTAC) to monitor the disarmament of the four Cambodian factions and supervise free elections. UNTAC was comprised of over 20,000 personnel and was given substantial authority within Cambodia, including aspects of civil administration. In order to create a neutral environment for elections, the factions delegated to UNTAC control of five ministries and supervision of others, access to all governmental documents, and power to issue binding directives and replace personnel. See Ratner, The Cambodian Settlement Agreements, 87 A.J.I.L. 1 (1993).

Cambodia's first free and fair elections took place under UNTAC's supervision in May of 1993. Despite considerable violence in the preceding months, the elections unfolded without significant violence, disruptions or irregularities. After the election UNTAC worked to train the Cambodian army and other national institutions and assisted the constituent assembly in drafting a constitution compatible with human rights principles. UNTAC withdrew on schedule by the end of 1993, having successfully discharged its mandate. See generally Ratner, The United Nations in Cambodia: A Model for Resolution of Internal Conflicts?, in Damrosch (ed.), Enforcing Restraint: Collective Intervention in Internal Conflicts 241–273 (1993); Ratner, The New U.N. Peacekeeping (1994).

Note

The peace process showed signs of faltering in 1992 with the Khmer Rouge's refusal to disarm and to allow voter registration in areas it controlled and with its threats not to participate in the elections called for by the Accords. (The Khmer Rouge also engaged in hostilities against U.N. personnel.) In order to combat the Khmer Rouge's growing intransigence, the Security Council on November 30, 1992, called on states to prevent petroleum products from reaching the Khmer Rouge and requested states to respect a moratorium on the export of logs. S.C.Res 792 (1992). The Security Council indicated it would hold elections with or without the Khmer Rouge and expressed its intent to impose stronger sanctions if necessary. See generally Ratner, The Cambodian Settlement Agreements, 87 A.J.I.L. 1 (1993). The Security Council did not determine that the situation in Cambodia is a threat to international peace and security. Is there authority for the Security Council to impose sanctions without such a determination? Can the existence of a threat to international peace and security go without saying? On the sanctions against the Khmer Rouge, see Cortwright & Lopez, The Sanctions Decade: Assessing UN Strategies in the 1990s 135–145 (2000).

SOMALIA

In 1992, the Security Council authorized a United Nations Operation in Somalia (UNOSOM) to alleviate hunger and starvation there. S.C.Res. 733 (1992). On November 24 and November 30, 1992, the Secretary–General transmitted letters to the President of the Security Council reporting on the continuing deterioration of humanitarian conditions in Somalia, and on the civil strife between various factions and clans preventing UNOSOM from implementing the earlier Security Council mandate to provide relief assistance. See U.N.Docs. S/24859 and S/24868; S.C.Res. 733, 746, 751, 767 and 775 (1992). The Secretary–General urged military action pursuant to Article 39 of the Charter, to ensure that UNOSOM succeeded in its relief mission; in his opinion "no government exist[ed] in Somalia that could request and allow such use of force." U.N.Doc. S/24868, at 3. He emphasized that the purpose of the force would be to bring the violence against the international relief effort to an end and that in order to achieve this goal it would be necessary to disarm the various warring factions, irregular forces and gangs. On December 3, 1992 the Security Council adopted a resolution authorizing the use of "military forces" to establish "a secure environment for humanitarian relief operations in Somalia:"

Security Council Resolution 794
December 3, 1992

The Security Council * * *

Recognizing the unique character of the present situation in Somalia and *mindful* of its deteriorating, complex and extraordinary nature, requiring an immediate and exceptional response;

Determining that the magnitude of the human tragedy caused by the conflict in Somalia, further exacerbated by the obstacles being created to the distribution of humanitarian assistance, constitutes a threat to international peace and security * * *

* * *

Expressing grave alarm at the continuing reports of widespread violations of international humanitarian law occurring in Somalia * * *

* * *

Determined * * * to restore peace, stability and law and order with a view to facilitating the process of a political settlement under the auspices of the United Nations, aimed at national reconciliation in Somalia * * *

* * *

2. *Demands* that all parties, movements and factions in Somalia take all measures necessary to facilitate the efforts of the United Nations * * * and humanitarian organizations to provide humanitarian assistance to the affected population in Somalia;

* * *

5. *Strongly condemns* all violations of international humanitarian law occurring in Somalia * * * and *affirms* that those who commit or order the commission of such acts will be held individually responsible in respect of such acts;

* * *

7. *Endorses* the recommendation by the Secretary–General * * * that action under Chapter VII of the Charter * * * should be taken in order to establish a secure environment for humanitarian relief operations in Somalia as soon as possible;

8. *Welcomes* the offer by a Member State * * * concerning the establishment of an operation to create such a secure environment;

9. *Welcomes also* offers by other Member States to participate in that operation;

10. *Acting* under Chapter VII of the Charter of the United Nations, *authorizes* the Secretary–General and Member States cooperating to implement the offer referred to in paragraph 8 above to use all necessary means to establish as soon as possible a secure environment for humanitarian relief operations in Somalia;

11. *Calls* on all Member States which are in a position to do so to provide military forces and to make additional contributions, in cash or in kind, in accordance with paragraph 10 * * *;

12. *Authorizes* the Secretary–General and the Member States concerned to make the necessary arrangements for the unified command and control of the forces involved, which will reflect the offer referred to in paragraph 8 above;

13. *Requests* the Secretary–General and the Member States acting under paragraph 10 above to establish appropriate mechanisms for coordination between the United Nations and their military forces * * * .

Notes

1. There was little initial Somali resistance to the military intervention authorized by the Security Council for the protection of humanitarian aid. Would the authorization of force be within the authority of the Security Council under Chapter VII if taken in the face of active objection by a government in control of its territory? Would it be consistent with Article 2(7)? Did it matter that Somalia was perceived to be in a state of anarchy without an effective government? Was there a threat to the peace or a breach of the peace in Somalia within the meaning of Article 39 of the Charter? Is a determination of threat to international peace and security a prerequisite to Security Council action on humanitarian grounds? Is there any other legal basis for such action?

2. The "Member State" to which the cryptic paragraph 8 of Resolution 794 refers is the United States. The "necessary arrangements for the unified command and control of the forces involved" (para. 12) and "appropriate mechanisms for coordination between the United Nations and their military forces" (para. 13) led to confusion about the lines of authority between, on the one-hand, the U.S.-led Unified Task Force (which despite its acronym of UNITAF was independent of U.N. command and control), and on the other hand, UNOSOM II which was

authorized by the Security Council in Resolution 814 (Mar. 26, 1993) and operated under the control of the U.N. Secretary–General. There was also considerable disagreement about the respective mandates of the parallel endeavors. While the purpose of UNITAF was "to establish a secure environment for humanitarian relief operations," the resolution establishing UNOSOM II demanded that the Somali factions comply with undertakings on disarmament and also called for U.N. assistance to the people of Somalia in "the re-establishment of national and regional institutions and civil administration in the entire country" and in "the restoration and maintenance of peace, stability and law and order."

On June 5, 1993, 24 Pakistani peacekeepers serving under UNOSOM command were ambushed and killed. In response, the Security Council called on the Secretary–General "to take all necessary measures against all those responsible for the armed attacks * * * including to secure the investigation of their actions and their arrest and detention for prosecution, trial and punishment." S.C. Res. 837 (June 6, 1993), para. 5. A U.N. investigation subsequently found clear and convincing evidence that the leader of one of the Somali clans, General Mohammed Farah Aideed, had authorized the attack. The ensuing manhunt for General Aideed intensified the confrontation between his faction and U.S. and U.N. forces, culminating on October 3, 1993 with a devastating clash resulting in the deaths of 18 U.S. Army Rangers and at least 70 other U.S. casualties—and an even higher toll among Somali civilians. See Damrosch, Enforcing Restraint 378–382 (1993); Bowden, Black Hawk Down: A Story of Modern War (1999).

3. The backlash to the deaths of the U.S. Army Rangers in Somalia prompted the U.S. Congress to set a time-limit on the U.S. deployment. See Pub. L. 103–139, § 8151, 107 Stat. 1418, 1475 (1993). The limitation on funding the mission past March 31, 1994 contained the further proviso that "United States combat forces in Somalia shall be under the command and control of United States commanders under the ultimate direction of the President of the United States." 107 Stat. 1418, 1476. In fact, the U.S. forces had never been under U.N. command and were under U.S. control at all times, including when the fatal clashes occurred. The other participants in the U.S.-led multinational force withdrew their troops at approximately the same time as the United States.

Shortly after the completion of the U.S. withdrawal from Somalia, the Clinton Administration announced a set of guidelines for U.S. participation in U.N. peace operations, which became known as Presidential Decision Directive (PDD) 25. See United States: Administration Policy on Reforming Multilateral Peace Operations, 33 I.L.M. 705 (1994). The directive stated that the President would necessarily retain ultimate command authority, but that he could delegate operational control if appropriate to foreign commanders. The conditions for U.S. participation in any U.N. operation under PDD 25 include that the operation should enjoy support in Congress and among the public. Later, the Congress required that the President should give at least 15 days' advance notice before any Security Council vote to approve a peacekeeping operation.

On UNITAF's accomplishments, see Hirsch & Oakley, Somalia and Operation Restore Hope: Reflections on Peacemaking and Peacekeeping (1995). The U.N. role is described in the U.N. bluebook series, U.N. Dep't of Public Information, The United Nations and Somalia, 1992–1996 (1996). On disagreements between the United States and the U.N. Secretary–General, see Boutros–Ghali, Unvanquished 92–103 (1999). On problems of divided command, see Urquhart, Mission Impossible, N.Y. Review of Books, Nov. 18, 1999, pp. 26–29.

On U.S. domestic legal aspects, see Stromseth, Collective Force and Constitutional Responsibility: War Powers in the Post–Cold War Era, 50 U. Miami L. Rev. 145, 168–172 (1995); Damrosch, The Clinton Administration and War Powers, 63 Law & Contemp. Problems 125, 132–133 (2000).

4. Following the attacks on U.N. and U.S. forces in Somalia, the United Nations elaborated a Convention on the Safety of United Nations and Associated Personnel, 34 I.L.M. 482 (1994), which entered into force in 1999. The Rome Statute of the International Criminal Court (1998), Art. 8(2)(b)(iii), provides for the war crime of "[i]ntentionally directing attacks against personnel, installations, material, units or vehicles involved in a humanitarian assistance or peacekeeping mission in accordance with the Charter of the United Nations, as long as they are entitled to the protection given to civilians or civilian objects under the international law of armed conflict."

RWANDA

In a paroxysm of genocidal violence in spring 1994, approximately 800,000 people died in Rwanda. Most of the victims were of the Tutsi ethnic group, and most of the perpetrators were Hutu extremists, though some moderate Hutus were also killed at the outbreak of the genocide. The genocide took place despite the presence in Rwanda of a small U.N. peacekeeping force, UNAMIR, which the Security Council had authorized to assist in the implementation of a peace agreement between the Government of Rwanda (Hutu-dominated) and the Rwandese Patriotic Front (mainly but not exclusively Tutsis, with an exile base in Rwanda). See S.C. Res. 872 (1993). UNAMIR had begun deployment in late 1993 in difficult conditions, against a backdrop of increasing violence, with inadequate troop strength for the tasks at hand. The United States, still smarting from the debacle in Somalia in October 1993, was unwilling to commit significant resources to Rwanda and reluctant to exert leverage on others to do so. The Secretary–General had requested authority for a force of 5000 troops but the Security Council did not approve this request. Military experts later confirmed that a force of that size, with a proper mandate and adequately armed and trained, could have prevented the genocide. Nonetheless, UNAMIR's troop strength never exceeded 550. Included in that number was a battalion from Belgium, the former colonial power in Rwanda.

On April 6, 1994, a plane carrying Rwandan President Juvenal Habyarimana and the President of Burundi was shot down over Kigali, Rwanda while returning from a subregional summit. Almost immediately, Hutu extremists began executing a carefully-prepared plan for extermination of Tutsis and moderate Hutus who supported the peace process. Later investigations revealed that as early as January 11, 1994, UNAMIR's commander had urgently cabled U.N. headquarters with a warning from a government informant of a strategy to provoke the killing of Belgian peacekeepers and the Belgian battalion's withdrawal, to be followed by rapid extermination of Tutsi in Kigali. This warning elicited only a tepid response from New York at the time. In the event, on April 7, 10 Belgian peacekeepers who were guarding Rwandan Prime Minister Agathe Uwilingiyimana were killed, as was the Prime Minister herself. Thereafter, the Belgian government proceeded with a swift evacuation of the remainder of the Belgian contingent and indeed urged that

UNAMIR should collectively withdraw. Hutu-on-Tutsi violence unfolded with staggering rapidity and intensity in the following weeks.

On May 17, 1994, the Security Council adopted Resolution 918, which increased UNAMIR's authorized troop strength and imposed an arms embargo on Rwanda. Rwanda, which was sitting as a non-permanent member of the Security Council at the time, voted against the resolution. As late as July 25, UNAMIR still had only 550 troops (one-tenth of the authorized strength), and the Secretary–General was unable to induce states to contribute to the peacekeeping force.

Meanwhile, in late June 1994, France proposed to lead a multinational military operation in parallel to that of UNAMIR, in an effort to reestablish security and "safe humanitarian areas" in Rwanda. France requested that the Security Council authorize such an intervention under Chapter VII of the Charter, which was done in Resolution 929 (June 22, 1994), by a vote of 10 in favor with 5 abstentions (Brazil, China, New Zealand, Nigeria, and Pakistan). The intervention, known as *Opération Turquoise*, was authorized only for a two-month period. At the end of that time, with the situation largely stabilized, the participating countries withdrew their troops.

Notes

1. In 1999, U.N. Secretary–General Kofi Annan, who had been head of the U.N. Department of Peacekeeping Operations in 1994, requested an independent inquiry into U.N. actions in Rwanda in 1994. Ingvar Carlsson, former Prime Minister of Sweden, led this inquiry. The inquiry's report (available on the U.N. website) concludes in part:

> The overriding failure in the response of the United Nations before and during the genocide in Rwanda can be summarized as a lack of resources and a lack of will to take on the commitment which would have been necessary to prevent or to stop the genocide. UNAMIR, the main component of the United Nations presence in Rwanda, was not planned, dimensioned, deployed or instructed in a way which provided for a proactive and assertive role in dealing with a peace process in serious trouble. The mission was smaller than the original recommendations from the field suggested. It was slow in being set up, and was beset by debilitating administrative difficulties. It lacked well-trained troops and functioning materiel. The mission's mandate was based on an analysis of the peace process which proved erroneous, and which was never corrected despite the significant warning signs that the original mandate had become inadequate. By the time the genocide started, the mission was not functioning as a cohesive whole: in the real hours and days of deepest crisis, consistent testimony points to a lack of political leadership, lack of military capacity, severe problems of command and control and lack of coordination and discipline.
>
> * * *
>
> [I]t *is incomprehensible to the Inquiry that not more was done to follow-up on the information provided by the informant.* * * * Information received by a United Nations mission that plans are being made to exterminate any group of people requires an immediate and determined response * * * .
>
> * * *

[T]he *threat against the Belgian contingent should have been followed up* more clearly, not only in relation to the security of that particular contingent, but equally as part of the strategic discussions within the Secretariat and with the Security Council on the role of UNAMIR in Rwanda. The United Nations knew that extremists on one side hoped to achieve the withdrawal of the mission. * * *

Questions have been raised as to the wisdom of inviting Belgium, a former colonial power, to participate in UNAMIR. The threats against the Belgian contingent described in the Dallaire cable as well as on the radio and through other forms of propaganda, show the difficulties inherent in that participation. In the case of UNAMIR it must be said, however, that Belgium was providing well-equipped troops which were not being offered by others, and that both parties had accepted that they participate in the mission.

* * *

The Inquiry believes that it is essential to preserve the unity of United Nations command and control, and that troop contributing countries, despite the domestic political pressures which may argue the reverse, should refrain from unilateral withdrawal to the detriment and even risk of ongoing peacekeeping operations.

The loss of ten peacekeepers is a terrible blow to any troop contributing country. However, even if the Belgian Government felt that the brutal murder of its para-commandos and the anti-Belgian rhetoric in Rwanda at the time made a continued presence of its own contingent impossible, *the Inquiry finds the campaign to secure the complete withdrawal of UNAMIR difficult to understand.* * * * [T]he focus seems to have been solely on withdrawal rather than on the possibilities for the United Nations to act, with or without Belgium.

* * *

A general point about the need for political will is that such will must be mobilised equally in response to conflicts across the globe. *It has been stated repeatedly during the course of the interviews conducted by the Inquiry* * * * *that Rwanda was not of strategic interest to third countries and that the international community exercised double standards when faced with the risk of a catastrophe there compared to action taken elsewhere.*

* * *

Faced in Rwanda with the risk of genocide, and later the systematic implementation of a genocide, the United Nations had an obligation to act which transcended traditional principles of peacekeeping. In effect, there can be no neutrality in the face of genocide, no impartiality in the face of a campaign to exterminate part of a population. *While the presence of United Nations peacekeepers in Rwanda may have begun as a traditional peacekeeping operation to monitor the implementation of an existing peace agreement, the onslaught of the genocide should have led decision-makers in the United Nations* * * * *to realize that the original mandate, and indeed the neutral mediating role of the United Nations, was no longer adequate and required a different, more assertive response, combined with the means necessary to take such action.*

2. On the events in Rwanda, see Prunier, The Rwanda Crisis: History of a Genocide (1995); Murphy, Humanitarian Intervention: The United Nations in an

Evolving World Order 243–260 (1996); Gourevitch, We Wish to Inform You that Tomorrow We Will Be Killed with Our Families (1998).

HAITI

As described in Chapter 4 at p. 299, President Jean–Bertrand Aristide took office in early 1991 after an election that had been certified by U.N. and other international monitors as free and fair. On September 30, 1991, he was overthrown in a military coup. In addition to the diplomatic pressures from October 1991 forward (noted in Chapter 4), which included collective non-recognition of the usurping government by the Organization of American States and its members, the O.A.S. recommended economic sanctions to bring about the isolation of those who had illegally seized power in Haiti. The U.N. General Assembly likewise recommended measures supportive of the O.A.S. actions. When the regional, voluntary embargo had not achieved its objective as of June 1993, the locus of activity shifted to the U.N. Security Council, which imposed a mandatory embargo on oil and petroleum products and on arms and police equipment, as well as a freeze of the assets of the Haitian Government and *de facto* authorities. S.C. Res. 841 (June 16, 1993).

These measures went farther than any before in applying universal, mandatory and severe sanctions to influence a domestic political crisis over democratic governance. Initially, they seemed to have the desired effect of inducing the military rulers to begin serious negotiations over a transfer of power. On July 3, 1993, an agreement was reached at Governors Island, New York, according to which the Aristide government should have returned to power by October 30, 1993; a U.N. peacekeeping mission would have supervised the transition and assisted in reconstruction of the shattered nation. Following Resolution 841's formula, the Council suspended the compulsory sanctions in late August 1993, after the U.N. Secretary–General reported that the *de facto* authorities had begun implementing the Governors Island agreement. The illusion of good-faith compliance dissolved when the *de facto* rulers orchestrated a demonstration which blocked the disembarcation of the troop ship carrying the first deployment of the peacekeeping mission. On October 13, 1993, the Security Council reimposed the suspended sanctions. S.C. Res. 873. Unfortunately, this enforcement decision did not produce the desired results, nor did a series of supplementary measures adopted pursuant to further Security Council decisions in the first half of 1994, which expanded the sanctions to cover trade and financial assets. S.C. Res. 905 (Mar. 23, 1994); S.C. Res. 917 (May 6, 1994); S.C. Res. 933 (June 30, 1994).

The sanctions took a dire toll on Haiti's desperately poor people, prompting many of them to set sail in leaky boats for the United States and other neighboring countries. On July 31, 1994, the Security Council moved toward still more decisive action–the authorization of a "multinational force under unified command and control" which was empowered

> to use all necessary means to facilitate the departure from Haiti of the military leadership, consistent with the Governors Island Agreement, the prompt return of the legitimately elected President and the restoration of the legitimate authorities of the Government of Haiti, and to establish and maintain a secure and stable environment that will permit implementation of the Governors Island Agreement * * * .

S.C. Res. 940 (July 31, 1994). On September 19, 1994, as the initial units of this multinational force were on their way to Haiti from the United States, the *de facto* authorities finally allowed the transfer of power to the Aristide government to proceed.

Notes

1. Does the international law of the use of force require that non-forcible options be exhausted before the Security Council could authorize military force? See Damrosch, The Civilian Impact of Economic Sanctions, in Damrosch (ed.), Enforcing Restraint: Collective Intervention in Internal Conflicts 274, 299–301 (1993); Damrosch, Enforcing International Law Through Non–Forcible Measures, 269 Rec. des Cours 9, 139–153 (1997).

2. The Security Council resolutions stress the "unique and exceptional" nature of the Haitian crisis and draw attention to its regional context. How relevant were the regional treaties such as the O.A.S. Charter, which establish commitments to representative democracy? Do they provide grounds for limiting the Haitian "precedent" to the American region? (Note that several members of the Security Council denied that the episode could constitute a precedent for the future.) Could the O.A.S. have authorized a military intervention? Compare Acevedo, The Haitian Crisis and the OAS Response, in Damrosch (ed.), Enforcing Restraint, at 119, 138–140 (1993).

3. Did the Security Council need President Aristide's approval to authorize a military intervention to restore his government to power? Compare Malone, Decision–Making in the U.N. Security Council: The Case of Haiti, 1990–1997 (1998). See also Murphy, Humanitarian Intervention 260–281 (1996).

FORMER YUGOSLAVIA

The former Socialist Federal Republic of Yugoslavia had been composed of six republics (Slovenia, Croatia, Serbia, Montenegro, Bosnia–Herzegovina, and Macedonia) with ethnic populations of Serbs, Croats, Muslims, Slovenes, Albanians, Macedonians and other groups. Negotiations among the republics to achieve a loose federation of fully or semi-sovereign states failed, and further attempts to negotiate the political future and territorial integrity of the former Yugoslavia were unsuccessful. On June 25, 1991 Slovenia and Croatia declared their independence. On June 27, 1991, armed forces controlled by Serbia attacked the provisional Slovenian militia, which appealed for international assistance from the European Community (EC), the Conference on Security and Cooperation in Europe (CSCE), and the United Nations. By July 1991, Serbia had initiated hostilities in Croatia.

On September 25, 1991, the Security Council unanimously adopted Resolution 713 expressing support for the collective efforts of the EC and CSCE to bring about peace. The Council then decided under Chapter VII of the Charter "that all States shall, for the purposes of establishing peace and stability in Yugoslavia, immediately implement a general and complete embargo on all deliveries of weapons and military equipment to Yugoslavia until the Security Council decides otherwise * * * ." S.C.Res. 713 (1991). The Security Council did not invoke Article 2(4) and there was no suggestion that an international act of aggression had taken place. As noted in Chapter 4 p. 261), most of the former Yugoslav republics attained general international recognition in early 1992, so that what had begun as an internal conflict soon acquired transboundary character.

As ethnic fighting worsened during 1992–93, spilling over into Bosnia–Herzegovina, U.N. action remained modest and largely ineffective. The fighting continued to worsen in Croatia and Bosnia–Herzegovina, with atrocities and "ethnic cleansing." On May 30, 1992 the Security Council tightened its embargo with respect to Serbia and Montenegro, by prohibiting the import and export of commodities to or from these states. The Council also ordered that all air links with Serbia and Montenegro be severed. S.C.Res. 757 (1992). The Council had authorized creation of a U.N. Protection Force (UNPROFOR), initially as an interposition force between the Serbian and Croatian groups that had been fighting in Croatia, as one step within the framework of negotiations for an overall settlement. S.C. Res. 743 (Feb. 21, 1992); UNPROFOR's mandate was later extended to Bosnia–Herzegovina. On October 6, 1992, the Security Council banned military flights over Bosnia–Herzegovina. S.C.Res. 781 (1992). On November 16, 1992, in order to combat wide-spread violations of the Security Council's economic sanctions, the Council decided to impose a naval blockade of the Adriatic Sea and Danube River. S.C.Res. 787 (1992).

On December 11, 1992, the Security Council approved a deployment of 700 U.N. personnel to the former Yugoslavian republic of Macedonia. S.C. Res. 795. This was the first time that United Nations peacekeepers had been deployed in support of "preventive diplomacy" as called for by Secretary–General Boutros–Ghali in his Agenda for Peace, U.N. Doc. A/47/277, S/24111 (1992).

The series of Security Council resolutions adopted in 1992–1993 provided explicit legitimacy for a limited range of unilateral military activities on the part of states acting in support of the international efforts to promote peace in Yugoslavia, as well as for concerted multilateral force alongside UNPROFOR's peacekeeping objectives. These included: "all measures necessary" to ensure the delivery of humanitarian assistance (S.C. Res. 770, Aug. 13, 1992); forcible measures of enforcement of the economic sanctions, including forcible interdiction of vessels bound to or from the Federal Republic of Yugoslavia (S.C. Res. 820, April 17, 1993); measures to enforce the no-fly zone in Bosnia–Herzegovina, through operations toward that end in Bosnian airspace (S.C. Res. 816, Mar. 31, 1993); and the use of air power to support UNPROFOR in protecting the "safe areas" in Bosnia–Herzegovina (S.C. Res. 836, June 4, 1993).

In late spring and summer of 1995, an escalating series of events dramatically changed the dynamics of the conflict. NATO forces, acting to protect the U.N.-designated "safe areas" in Bosnia–Herzegovina, carried out air strikes against Bosnian Serb positions. In response, the Bosnian Serbs shelled the safe areas and seized more than 300 UNPROFOR troops as hostages. On July 11, 1995, Bosnian Serbs overran the Srebrenica "safe area," trapping some 430 Dutch members of UNPROFOR. The ensuing massacre of Muslim civilians at Srebrenica is said to be the worst atrocity in Europe since World War II.

In August 1995, Croatian government forces began a new offensive in the Krajina region of Croatia, displacing as many as 200,000 Serbs from the Krajina who fled into Serbia–Montenegro and Bosnia–Herzegovina. This offensive, together with renewed NATO airstrikes against the Bosnian Serb forces, motivated the Serbian side to agree to new peace talks. A cease-fire was reached on October 6, 1995, followed by several weeks of intensive peace negotiations under U.S. auspices at a military base near Dayton, Ohio. The result was the General Framework Agreement for Peace in Bosnia and Herzegovina, U.N. Doc. S/1995/999 (1995), which was initialed at Dayton and formally signed at Paris on December 14, 1995. See 35 I.L.M. 75 (1996). It was approved by the Security Council and placed on a Chapter VII footing in Resolution 1033 (Dec. 15, 1995).

The Dayton Agreement replaced UNPROFOR with a new force under NATO auspices, known as the Implementation Force or IFOR. IFOR was both substantially larger (up to 60,000 troops) and more robust in its mandate than UNPROFOR. In a slightly scaled-down version known as the Stability Force (SFOR), the NATO force has remained in Bosnia–Herzegovina and is still in place as of early 2001.

NATO's recognition as an enforcement organ of the Security Council, in the series of resolutions referred to above, was one basis for the contention that NATO had implicit authority to use force against the Federal Republic of Yugoslavia in the Kosovo crisis of spring 1999. See pp. 997–1003 and note 4 below.

Notes

1. See generally Weller, The International Response to the Dissolution of the Socialist Federal Republic of Yugoslavia, 86 A.J.I.L. 569 (1992); Steinberg, International Involvement in the Yugoslavia Conflict, in Damrosch (ed.), Enforcing Restraint: Collective Intervention in Internal Conflicts 27–75 (1993); Murphy, Humanitarian Intervention: The United Nations in an Evolving World Order 198–217 (1996); Ullman (ed.), The World and Yugoslavia's Wars (1996). On the negotiations for the Dayton Agreement, see Holbrooke, To End a War (1998). For references on the Kosovo conflict, see p. 1000.

2. A U.N. report on the fall of Srebrenica contains pointed criticisms of U.N. actions leading up to the disaster. In language cited and approved by the inquiry on Rwanda (p. 1036 above), the report concluded that "a deliberate and systematic attempt to terrorize, expel or murder an entire people must be met decisively with all necessary means, and with the political will to carry the policy through to its logical conclusion." Report of the Secretary–General Pursuant to General Assembly Resolution 53/55 (1998), U.N. Doc. A/54/549 (Nov. 15, 1999), sec. 502.

3. In a document known as the "Brahimi Report" (formally, the Comprehensive Review of the Whole Question of Peacekeeping Operations in All Their Aspects, U.N. Doc. A/55/305, S/2000/809 (Aug. 21, 2000), a panel chaired by the former foreign minister of Algeria made recommendations aimed at improving the U.N.'s capacity to respond to complex situations. A key paragraph addresses the need to rethink the rationale for certain of the hallmarks of "classical" peacekeeping (at p. ix; see also p. 9, para. 50):

> The Panel concurs that consent of the local parties, impartiality and the use of force only in self-defence should remain the bedrock principles of

> peacekeeping. Experience shows, however, that in the context of intra-State/transnational conflicts, consent may be manipulated in many ways. Impartiality for United Nations operations must therefore mean adherence to the principles of the Charter: where one party to a peace agreement clearly and incontrovertibly is violating its terms, continued equal treatment of all parties by the United Nations can in the best case result in ineffectiveness and in the worst may amount to complicity with evil. No failure did more to damage the standing and credibility of United Nations peacekeeping in the 1990s than its reluctance to distinguish victim from aggressor.

On follow-through to the Brahimi Report, see Security Council Res. 1327 (Nov. 13, 2000) ("On the Implementation of the Report of the Panel on United Nations Peace Operations").

4. As indicated at pp. 997–1000, the Security Council did not adopt a resolution explicitly authorizing "all necessary means" to enforce its previous resolutions with respect to Kosovo. Cf. Res. 1160 (March 31, 1998); Res. 1199 (Sept. 23, 1998); Res. 1203 (Oct. 24, 1998) (on arms embargo; deployment of Kosovo Verification Mission). Indeed, the language of those resolutions was crafted in awareness that Russia and China would not have approved use of force and were prepared to use their veto accordingly. Nonetheless, some governments and scholars have contended that those resolutions could be understood to convey implicit authority for use of force. See Murphy, Contemporary Practice of the United States Relating to International Law, 93 A.J.I.L. 628, 631–632 (1999). For commentary supportive of this line of argument, see, e.g., Wedgwood, NATO's campaign in Kosovo, 93 A.J.I.L. 835–837 (1999). Others have found implicit Security Council approval in the decisive rejection (by 3–12 vote) of Russia's draft resolution to condemn NATO's action. Some believe that the Council, in Resolution 1244 adopted at the end of the conflict (June 10, 1999), in effect retroactively validated the operation. See Henkin, Kosovo and the Law of "Humanitarian Intervention," 93 A.J.I.L. 831 (1999).

By contrast, other commentators see great difficulties with the argument for implicit authority derived from resolutions that not only do not specify authority for military action, but in context reflect an intent to approve non-forcible rather than forcible means. They observe that such a line of reasoning could have the detrimental effect of making permanent members less willing to approve non-forcible measures in the first place. On this point, see Independent International Commission, Kosovo Report, Chapter 6 (2000).

Could NATO have asked the General Assembly to authorize the Kosovo intervention, possibly by invoking the "Uniting for Peace" Resolution, p. 1012? On this question, the Independent Commission observed:

> the NATO states chose not to utilize the residual role of the General Assembly under the Uniting for Peace Resolution, because, even though there is no veto in the General Assembly, the sensitivity of non-Western states to interventionary claims of any sort made it unlikely that an authorization of force would have been endorsed by the required two-thirds majority.

5. In September 1999, the Security Council authorized the deployment to East Timor of a multinational force under unified command. Its objectives were to restore stability, to support a U.N. mission (UNAMET) that had been deployed to East Timor a few months earlier in order to supervise a referendum on independence (S.C. Res. 1246, June 11, 1999; S.C. Res. 1257, Aug. 3, 1999), and to

facilitate humanitarian assistance. S.C. Res. 1264 (Sept. 15, 1999). In August 1999, a large majority of East Timor's voters had endorsed independence from Indonesia. See p. 273. In a backlash against that vote, militias opposed to independence and element of the Indonesian military laid waste to the territory. The multinational force, known as INTERFET (International Force, East Timor), was led by Australia and included approximately 8000 troops from more than 15 countries. Although it entered the territory with Indonesia's content, the Security Council placed it on a Chapter VII footing. See Murphy, Contemporary Practice of the United States, 94 A.J.I.L. 105–108 (2000).

In October 1999 the Security Council established the United Nations Transitional Administration in East Timor (UNTAET), with sweeping governance powers in the territory. See S.C. Res. 1272 (Oct. 25, 1999) and UNTAET regulations reprinted at 39 I.L.M. 939 (2000).

On comparisons between the U.N. administrations in Kosovo under Resolution 1244 (1999) and in East Timor under Resolution 1272 (1999), and other post-conflict transitions, see the symposium on State Reconstruction after Civil Conflict, in 95 A.J.I.L. 1–119 (Jan. 2001).

B. REGIONAL ORGANIZATIONS

CHARTER OF THE UNITED NATIONS

San Francisco, June 26, 1945.

REGIONAL ARRANGEMENTS

Article 52

1. Nothing in the present Charter precludes the existence of regional arrangements or agencies for dealing with such matters relating to the maintenance of international peace and security as are appropriate for regional action, provided that such arrangements or agencies and their activities are consistent with the Purposes and Principles of the United Nations.

2. The Members of the United Nations entering into such arrangements or constituting such agencies shall make every effort to achieve pacific settlement of local disputes through such regional arrangements or by such regional agencies before referring them to the Security Council.

3. The Security Council shall encourage the development of pacific settlement of local disputes through such regional arrangements or by such regional agencies either on the initiative of the state concerned or by reference from the Security Council.

* * *

Article 53

1. The Security Council shall, where appropriate, utilize such regional arrangements or agencies for enforcement action under its authority. But no enforcement action shall be taken under regional arrangements or by regional agencies without the authorization of the Security Council * * *.

SCHACHTER, AUTHORIZED USES OF FORCE BY THE UNITED NATIONS AND REGIONAL ORGANIZATIONS

Law and Force in the New International Order, 65, 86–88.
(Damrosch & Scheffer, eds. 1991) (footnotes omitted).

The U.N. Charter recognizes in its Chapter VIII that regional arrangements and agencies are appropriate means for maintaining peace and security, provided that their activities are consistent with the purposes and principles of the Charter. Indeed, Article 52 of the Charter requires states to make every effort to achieve peaceful settlement of "local disputes" through regional arrangements or agencies before referring such disputes to the U.N. Security Council. The idea that disputes and threats to the peace involving states within a region should preferably be dealt with primarily by regional bodies has been an early and persistent influence. At San Francisco the Security Council was perceived as a forum of last resort when states were unable to resolve conflicts between them through the peaceful means listed in Chapter VI or through regional instrumentalities.

The Charter in Article 53 expressly directs the Security Council to utilize the regional arrangements or agencies covered by Chapter VIII for enforcement action where appropriate. The regional bodies are indirectly authorized to undertake enforcement action inasmuch as Article 53 states that they may not do so without the authorization of the Security Council. Thus the failure of the Council to grant permission for enforcement action would bar such action. A permanent member could therefore prevent enforcement action by a regional organization. Cases have come before the Security Council involving decisions of the Organization of American States (O.A.S.) to apply diplomatic and economic measures that were in the nature of sanctions as envisaged in Article 41 of the U.N. Charter. In these cases, the Council did not decide that those measures were covered by Article 53. The majority of members maintained that such non-forcible coercive measures were within the competence of individual states. Since states were free to sever trade or diplomatic relations, they could do so by concerted action under the aegis of a regional organization. The reasoning is not wholly compelling since concerted action by a regional body to impose sanctions of the kind contemplated in Chapter VII (Article 41) would appear to be within the meaning of enforcement action in Article 53.

* * *

Apart from collective self-defense, regional organizations may institute peacekeeping operations that do not involve coercive measures against a state. This has been done in a number of cases. However, it has not always been agreed that the regional peacekeeping operation has actually received the consent of the territorial sovereign. Questions of this kind have come up where it was uncertain who, if anyone, may legitimately grant such consent in the absence of effective and recognized governmental authority. This emerged as a problem when U.S. forces together with troops from several Caribbean countries intervened in Grenada, claiming *inter alia* that they had been authorized to do so by a regional body (the Organization of Eastern Caribbean

States) to bring peace and order to a country in a condition of anarchy. The General Assembly condemned the intervention as a violation of the Charter. However, there was no international criticism of a regional peacekeeping force of West African states that sought to bring an end to a bloody internal conflict in Liberia in 1990. This was clearly not an enforcement action or collective defense, nor was there an invitation from a government enjoying international recognition. A case of this kind would suggest an interpretation of peacekeeping by regional bodies that allows for a collective military intervention to help end an internal conflict when a government has been deposed or no longer has effective authority.

It is probable that peacekeeping actions and perhaps limited enforcement will be employed by regional organizations more frequently in the future. They are likely to be used to assist in monitoring and border patrol and perhaps to help to provide order to a country in internal conflict or near-anarchy.

1. The Inter–American System

The Inter–American system of collective security includes two principal international agreements: the 1947 Inter–American Treaty of Reciprocal Assistance (The Rio Treaty), 62 Stat. 1681, T.I.A.S. No. 2361, 21 U.N.T.S. 77, and the Charter of the Organization of American States (OAS Charter), 2 U.S.T. 2394, T.I.A.S. No. 2361, 119 U.N.T.S. 3. See in particular Articles 1, 3, 6, 8 & 9 of the Rio Treaty, and Articles 14–19, 24 & 25 of the OAS Charter. Also relevant are the 1933 Convention on the Rights and Duties of States (the Montevideo Convention) and the 1926 Convention for the Maintenance, Preservation, and Reestablishment of Peace. See 1 Garcia–Amador, The Inter–American System: Treaties, Conventions & Other Documents 261–326 (Pt. 2, 1983).

The Rio Treaty was an outgrowth of the Act of Chapultepec (Resolution on "Reciprocal Assistance and American Solidarity"), T.I.A.S. No. 1543 (1945). The Act contained a provision recognizing that aggression or the threat of aggression would warrant consultation among the American Republics with a view to collective measures of defense. The Charter of the Organization of American States entered into force for the United States on December 13, 1951. As of 2000, there were 35 member states in the Organization.

Notes

1. *Relationship with the United Nations.* A former legal adviser of the State Department described the relation as follows, in relation to an operation in the Dominican Republic:

> The appropriate relationship between the United Nations and regional organizations such as this one, the OAS, can be summarized in terms I think of six principles.
>
> One, the members of the United Nations pursuant to articles 33 and 52 of the charter should seek to deal with threats to the peace within a geographical region through regional arrangements before coming to the United Nations. This is precisely what the members of the OAS have done in the Dominican case.

Second, regional organizations should not of course take enforcement action without the authorization of the Security Council. But in the Dominican Republic the Organization of American States did not take the kind of action that would require Security Council approval.

Third, action taken by regional organizations must be consistent with the purposes and principles of the United Nations. This is obviously the case with the actions of the OAS in the Dominican Republic case.

Fourth, the Security Council should at all times be kept fully informed of actions undertaken by regional organizations. The OAS is keeping the Security Council fully informed; witness the report you have just had from Dr. Mora through Mr. Mayobre this afternoon. And the Council has also arranged to keep itself informed through a representative of the Secretary–General.

Fifth, the Security Council has the competence to deal with any situation which might threaten international peace and security. This competence is not at issue here.

But sixth, the Security Council should not seek to duplicate or interfere with action through regional arrangements so long as those actions remain effective and are consistent with our charter. The purposes of the United Nations Charter will hardly be served if two international organizations are seeking to do things in the same place with the same people at the same time.

As a matter of sound practice and the wise use of discretion, the Security Council under present conditions should keep itself fully informed but not undertake any activity, either diplomatic or on the ground, which would hinder the efforts and the responsibilities of the competent organization. It will serve the purposes of the United Nations Charter best if the OAS achieves what it has set out to accomplish, and that is to restore peace and achieve reconciliation so that the Dominican people can develop their own democratic institutions.

Stevenson, Principles of U.N.-OAS Relationship in the Dominican Republic, 52 Dep't State Bull. 975, 976–77 (1965).

David Scheffer adds:

Chapter VIII of the Charter (Articles 52–54) refers to enforcement action that may be taken by "regional arrangements or agencies." Although such regional arrangements typically would be established by treaty among its members (for example, the North Atlantic Treaty Organization and the Organization of American States), Chapter VIII is open to a more flexible interpretation encompassing arrangements which could fall short of formal treaty-based defense organizations. If it had exhibited more explicit organizational trappings, the multinational force that was created in 1990 to confront Iraqi aggression might have qualified for a Chapter VIII "arrangement" and therefore have been authorized by the Security Council to use military force pursuant to that chapter rather than Chapter VII. The fact that the principal participants (the United States, the United Kingdom, and France) of the multinational force arrayed against Iraq were from outside the Middle East might have appeared awkward in any such arrangement, but Chapter VIII does not necessarily limit the composition of regional arrangements to member states of the geographical region in question.

Scheffer, Commentary on Collective Security, in Law and Force in the New International Order 101, 107–08 (Damrosch & Scheffer, eds. 1991).

2. Meeker suggests that the Cuban quarantine of 1962 was justified under the Charter as an action taken by a "regional organization":

> It is clear that collective action for peace and security which the Security Council may take under Chapter VII does not contravene Article 2, paragraph 4. It is also clear that individual or collective self-defense against armed attack, in accordance with Article 51, does not violate the Charter. Here it may be noted that the United States, in adopting the defensive quarantine of Cuba, did not seek to justify it as a measure required to meet an "armed attack" within the meaning of Article 51. Nor did the United States seek to sustain its action on the ground that Article 51 is not an all-inclusive statement of the right of self-defense and that the quarantine was a measure of self-defense open to any country to take individually for its own defense in a case other than "armed attack." Indeed, as shown by President Kennedy's television address of October 22 and by other statements of the Government, reliance was not placed on either contention, and the United States took no position on either of these issues.
>
> The quarantine was based on a collective judgment and recommendation of the American Republics made under the Rio Treaty. It was considered not to contravene Article 2, paragraph 4, because it was a measure adopted by a regional organization in conformity with the provisions of Chapter VIII of the Charter. The purposes of the Organization and its activities were considered to be consistent with the purposes and principles of the United Nations as provided in Article 52. This being the case, the quarantine would no more violate Article 2, paragraph 4, than measures voted by the Council under Chapter VII, by the General Assembly under Articles 10 and 11, or taken by United Nations Members in conformity with Article 51.
>
> Finally, in relation to the Charter limitation on threat or use of force, it should be noted that the quarantine itself was a carefully limited measure proportionate to the threat and designed solely to prevent any further buildup of strategic missile bases in Cuba.

Meeker, Defensive Quarantine and the Law, 57 A.J.I.L. 523, 524 (1963).

For other expressions of this argument in support of the United States action, see Chayes, The Legal Case for U.S. Action in Cuba, 47 Dept. State Bull. 763 (1962); Chayes, The Cuban Missile Crisis (1974). Henkin expressed doubts about this justification. See Comment, in Chayes, The Cuban Missile Crisis 150–53 (1974); see also How Nations Behave 291–92 (2d ed. 1979).

3. The 1983 U.S. intervention in Grenada was said to be in response to a request for help from a group of Caribbean states called the Organization of Eastern Caribbean States. Is this group a regional organization within Article 52? Was the invasion of Grenada in 1983 by the United States and several Caribbean states a lawful "regional action" under the U.N. Charter? Moore argues:

> The Grenada mission by the OECS countries and Barbados, Jamaica and the United States is a paradigm of a lawful regional peacekeeping action under Article 52. It was undertaken in a context of civil strife and breakdown of government following the brutal murder of Maurice Bishop and members of his cabinet in an attempted coup. It was in response to a request for assistance in restoring human rights and self-determination from the only constitutional authority on the island, Governor–General Sir Paul Scoon. * * *

> Jointly requested or participated in by almost one-third of the membership of the Organization of American States, the Grenada mission is also consistent with the OAS Charter. * * * Articles 22 and 28 of the OAS Charter make clear that regional peacekeeping or defensive actions in accordance with special regional treaties do not violate the noninterventionist provisions. * * *
>
> Thus, on several grounds—request by lawful authority and action under "treaties in force" and "special treaties"—the peacekeeping and humanitarian protective action of the OECS in the Grenada mission is consistent with the Charter of the OAS. Moreover, since the Grenada mission is rooted in rights recognized by the UN Charter, under Article 137 of the revised Charter of the OAS, they could not be impaired by the OAS Charter in any event. Article 137 provides: "None of the provisions of this Charter shall be construed as impairing the rights and obligations of the Member States under the Charter of the United Nations."

J.N. Moore, Grenada and the International Double Standard, 78 A.J.I.L. 145, 154–59 (1984) (footnotes omitted).

Christopher Joyner disagrees:

> An especially intriguing facet of the entire diplomatic episode—and a second espoused legal justification as well—is that the United States was invited by at least five members of the Organization of Eastern Caribbean States (OECS) to intervene militarily into Grenada. Created in 1981, the OECS contains within its charter a quasi-collective security provision. * * *
>
> While "collective defence" as such is called for in the Treaty, nowhere is there stipulated the option to invite outside assistance against a member state. Further, it is difficult to fathom how a treaty among seven small states could legally promote an invasion by the United States against one of its own members at the behest of the others. To be sure, considerable doubt also exists about whether the invasion of Grenada is consistent with the original intent of the signers, or for that matter, those specified treaty provisions relating to "external defence" and "arrangements for collective security against external aggression."
>
> Several reasons rebut the use of this Treaty to legitimize U.S. intervention in Grenada. First, the United States is not a party to the Treaty and therefore legally lies outside the ambit of its concerns. (Interestingly enough, neither are Barbados and Jamaica, which also participated in the invasion.) Second, Article 8 specifically deals with "collective defence and the preservation of peace and security against external aggression." No external aggressor existed: Grenada, the state in question, was a Treaty member. In addition, the OECS Treaty makes no mention of any collective security or defensive measures to be taken against a member of the organization, should such an occasion arise. There is, in short, no provision for military action in instances other than those involving "external aggression, including mercenary aggression," and such a case was absent in the October 1983 Grenada episode. Joyner, Reflections on the Lawfulness of Invasion, 78 A.J.I.L. 131, 135–37, 142 (1984) (footnotes omitted).

See also the editorial comment, Vagts, International Law Under Time Pressure, 78 A.J.I.L. 169 (1984), and the communication by 9 Professors of Law, Boyle et al., International Lawlessness—Grenada, 78 A.J.I.L. 172 (1984).

4. On October 3, 1991, in response to the overthrow of the President of Haiti by military coup, the OAS unanimously recommended that its member states take "action to bring about the diplomatic isolation of those who hold power illegally in Haiti" and "suspend their economic, financial, and commercial ties * * * " OAS Doc. OEA/Ser. F/V.1/MRE/ RES. 1/91, corr. 1, paras. 5, 6 (1991). The trade embargo was strengthened on May 17, 1992. OAS Doc. OEA/Ser. F/V.1/MRE/ RES.3/92 (1992), reprinted in 86 A.J.I.L. 667 (1992). As discussed above (p. 1038, these measures were insufficient to end the crisis, and the U.N. Security Council authorized a military intervention in 1994. Some experts on the OAS consider it doubtful that the OAS could itself have authorized use of military force in the context of a strictly domestic political crisis. See Acevedo, The Haitian Crisis and the OAS Response, Damrosch, Enforcing Restraint: Collective Intervention in Internal Conflicts 119, 138–140 (1993).

However, in the Dominican Republic crisis, the OAS had adopted the following resolution on May 6, 1965:

> 1. To request governments of member states that are willing and capable of doing so to make contingents of their land, naval, air or police forces available to the Organization of American States, within their capabilities, and to the extent that they can do so, to form an inter-American force that will operate under the authority of this Tenth Meeting of Consultation.
>
> 2. That this Force will have as its sole purpose, in a spirit of democratic impartiality, that of cooperating in the restoration of normal conditions in the Dominican Republic, in maintaining the security of its inhabitants and the inviolability of human rights, and in the establishment of an atmosphere of peace and conciliation that will permit the functioning of democratic institutions.

4 I.L.M. 594 (1965), 59 A.J.I.L. 986 (1965), 52 Dep't State Bull. 862 (1965). Argentina, Bolivia, Brazil, Colombia, Costa Rica, Dominican Republic, El Salvador, Guatemala, Haiti, Honduras, Nicaragua, Panama, Paraguay, and the United States voted for the resolution. Chile, Ecuador, Mexico, Peru, and Uruguay voted against it, and Venezuela abstained.

5. On the OAS generally, see Thomas & Thomas, The Organization of American States (1963); Levin, The Organization of American States and the United Nations: Relations in the Peace and Security Field (1974); Lima, Intervention in International Law with Reference to the Organization of American States (1971); The Inter–American System: Treaties, Conventions and Other Documents: A Compilation (1983); The Organization of American States and International Law, 80 A.S.I.L.Proc. 1 (1986); cf., Acevedo, The Right of Members of the Organization of American States to Refer Their "Local Disputes Directly to the United Nations Security Council," 4 Am.U.J.Int'l L. & Pol'y 25 (1989); Caminos & Lavalie, New Departures in the Exercise of Inherent Powers by the UN and OAS Secretaries–General: The Central American Situation, 83 A.J.I.L. 395 (1989).

2. *Organization of African Unity (OAU)*

The heads of state of thirty-two African countries signed the Charter of the Organization of African Unity on May 25, 1963. 479 U.N.T.S. 39, 58 A.J.I.L. 873 (1964). The agreement entered into force on September 13, 1963. Article 2 of the Charter provides that the promotion of the unity and solidarity of the African states and the defense of the sovereignty, territorial integrity, and independence of these states shall be among the purposes of the Organization. The states agree to coordinate and harmonize their policies in several fields, among which is that of "defense and security." In Article 3, the agreement sets forth the following principles, to which the parties declare their adherence:

1. the sovereign equality of all Member States;
2. non-interference in the internal affairs of States;
3. respect for the sovereignty and territorial integrity of each State and for its inalienable right to independent existence;
4. peaceful settlement of disputes by negotiation, mediation, conciliation or arbitration;
5. unreserved condemnation, in all its forms, of political assassination as well as of subversive activities on the part of neighboring States or any other State; * * *

Article 20 authorizes the establishment of a Defense Commission.

The OAU's first opportunity to play a role in peacekeeping arose with the 1963 border dispute between Algeria and Morocco. A long-standing dispute over mineral-rich land flared up following Algerian independence in July 1962, and by October 1963 small skirmishes had yielded to military occupation of border towns and a general mobilization in Algeria. First attempts to arrange a cease-fire were not successful. The parties to the dispute were induced, however, to seek an all-African rather than a United Nations settlement as the result of a meeting arranged in Mali by Emperor Haile Selassie and President Modibo Keita. An extraordinary session of the OAU was convened, at which the Council of Ministers appointed an *ad hoc* commission and charged it with the tasks of ascertaining responsibility for the hostilities and of recommending a settlement. The commission met in Mali and in the Ivory Coast, receiving documents from both sides. On February 20, 1964, the two governments announced that an agreement had been reached. Withdrawal of forces was to take place, and a demilitarized zone was to be established. In April, prisoners were exchanged. The two states had reestablished diplomatic relations by May 1965, and the respective heads of state had met at the border.

The OAU has been less successful in dealing with subsequent problems within the sphere of its concern. It did not play an effective role in the dispute over the Western Sahara (see Chapter 4, p. [ ] supra), in efforts to curtail the atrocities of the Idi Amin regime in Uganda, or in resolving the long Rhodesian crisis before the creation of the State of Zimbabwe. Nor did the OAU play a role in the civil war in Chad. Peacekeeping troops were sent by individual African states.

Notes

1. In 1992, the OAU welcomed the United Nations military presence in Somalia to establish a secure environment for the distribution of relief aid but the Organization did not contribute to the military forces. See p. 1032 supra. In 1990, the OAU endorsed the peacekeeping efforts of the Economic Community of West African States (ECOWAS) in Liberia. On ECOWAS as a subregional organization and its role in African peacekeeping, see p. 1052 below.

2. On the OAU generally, see Documents of the Organization of African Unity (Naldi, ed. 1992); The Organization of African Unity, 1963–1988 (Akindele,

ed. 1988); Andemicael, The OAU and the UN: Relations Between the Organization of African Unity and the United Nations (1976); El Ayouty, The OAU After 10 Years: Comparative Perspectives (1975); Naldi, Peacekeeping Attempts by the Organization of African Unity, 34 Int'l & Comp. L.Q. 593 (1985); Ramphul, The Role of International and Regional Organizations in the Peaceful Settlement of Internal Disputes (With Special Emphasis on the Organization of African Unity), 13 Georgia J.Int'l & Comp. L. 371 (1983); M'Baye & Ndiaye, The Organization of African Unity, in The International Dimensions of Human Rights (Vasak, ed. 1982).

3. On a potential role for the OAU in African peacekeeping, compare S.C. Res. 1197 (Sept. 18, 1998) , encouraging the establishment of partnerships between states and regional and subregional organizations for purposes of peacekeeping and preventive action.

3. *Other regional and subregional bodies.*

a. The Arab League.

> The Arab League is a regional, political organisation of comprehensive aims. * * *
>
> * * *
>
> Under Article V [of the League Pact] the League Members renounce recourse to force to resolve disputes between them and, whilst they do not accept the jurisdiction of the Council of the League to mediate or arbitrate as compulsory over such disputes, if they do have recourse to the Council its decision is binding. In practice the League Council has used the more informal processes of conciliation on many occasions in dealing with inter-regional disputes, without any formal acceptance of the Council's jurisdiction under Article V. Indeed, in the Kuwait crisis in 1961, the Council established an Inter–Arab Force as a "peace-keeping" operation in view of the dispute between Kuwait and Iraq. The Council did the same in June 1976 in Lebanon.
>
> Under Article VI each Member has a right to summon the Council immediately in the event of aggression, whether by another League Member or an outside State. The Council may then, by unanimous vote (excepting the aggressor State), decide upon measures to check the aggression. This collective security function is further specified in a separate collective security pact, based upon Article 51 of the UN Charter and on the notion that aggression against any League Member is aggression against all; the pact entered into force on August 23, 1952, and established a Permanent Joint Defence Council and Permanent Military Commission. On the occasion of the Anglo–French aggression against Egypt in 1956, involving the landing of troops in Suez, the collective security machinery failed to bring assistance to Egypt. Prior to the Arab/Israeli war of June 1967, Egypt, Jordan and the PLA (Palestine Liberation Army) instituted a joint military command, although it is clear that no integration of armed forces comparable to that which has occurred in NATO and the Warsaw Pact has yet happened.

Bowett, The Law of International Institutions 229–231 (4th ed. 1982) (footnote omitted).

During the early days of the 1990 Persian Gulf crisis, the Arab League, in a bitterly divided vote, urged its members to participate in the military deployment approved by the Security Council to protect Saudi Arabia and other Arab states against Iraqi aggression. On the Arab League generally, see Pogany, The Arab League and Peacemaking in Lebanon (1987); Pogany, The League of Arab States: An Overview, 21 Bracton L.J. 41 (1989). For earlier works see Hassouna, League of Arab States and Regional Disputes (1975); MacDonald, League of Arab States (1965); Khalil, The Arab States and the Arab League (2 vol. 1962).

b. Association of South–East Asian Nations (ASEAN).

ASEAN is an organization comprised of rapidly developing nations in Southeast Asia; it includes Indonesia, Malaysia, the Philippines, Singapore, Thailand, Brunei and (since 1997) Myanmar (Burma). The 1967 Bangkok Declaration that brought the organization into existence declared that ASEAN was designed to improve the economic well-being of its members, but ASEAN has also a regional security component. The 1969 declaration provided that one of the purposes of the Association is to "promote regional peace and stability." It has been noted that all the members face threats from internal insurgency movements supported by external assistance and fear the power of Mainland China and Japan. See Krause, U.S. Economic Policy Toward ASEAN 5–6 (1982). See also Unger, ASEAN, in Negotiating World Order: The Artisanship and Architecture of Global Diplomacy, chap. 11 (1986).

Does either the Arab League or ASEAN qualify as a regional organizations within the meaning of Article 52? Compare generally Bowett, The Law of International Institutions 229 (4th ed. 1982), with Goodrich, Hambro & Simons, Charter of the United Nations 351 (3d ed. 1969).

c. Economic Community of West African States (ECOWAS)

The Economic Community of West African States, as the name implies, was established largely to promote the economic well-being of the states in its subregion. However, it has taken an active part in attempting to stabilize the chaotic situations in Liberia in the 1990s, and later in Sierra Leone, in the absence of any other institution willing to carry out peacekeeping there. Although the U.N. Security Council did not explicitly authorize ECOWAS to take "enforcement action" in Liberia under Article 53 of the Charter, approval could arguably inferred from certain resolutions and statements issued by or on behalf of the Council. See Wippman, Enforcing the Peace: ECOWAS and the Liberian Civil War, in Damrosch (ed.), Enforcing Restraint: Collective Intervention in Internal Conflicts 157, 184–187 (1993).

On the role of ECOWAS in Sierra Leone, see S.C. Res. 1132 (1997), para. 8, which refers to Chapter VIII of the Charter in authorizing ECOWAS to carry out implementing action.

NATO: NEW TASKS FOR A COLLECTIVE SELF–DEFENSE ARRANGEMENT?

During the decades of ideological conflict, bipolarism and the Cold War, groups of states established organizations principally for collective self-defense, but some had additional cooperative purposes. The most important politically was the North Atlantic Treaty Organization (NATO); the Communist bloc responded by establishing the Warsaw Pact. In other parts of the world groups of states established the Southeast Asia Treaty Organization (SEATO), the Central Treaty Organization (CENTO), and the ANZUS Council. Some of these organizations withered early; others lost their raison d'être with the end of the Cold War. NATO, however, metamorphosed in the 1990s from a defense alliance against the Soviet threat to an organ of enforcement, acting under U.N. authority to enforce Security Council resolutions in Bosnia–Herzegovina and to police the agreements reached at Dayton. In the Kosovo crisis of 1999, NATO claimed authority to act even without an explicit U.N. mandate, partly on the basis of inference from previous U.N. actions, but more generally to maintain security and advance humanitarian objectives in the European region.

The North Atlantic Treaty was signed in Washington on April 4, 1949, 63 Stat. 2241, T.I.A.S. No. 1964, 34 U.N.T.S. 243. The original parties were Belgium, Canada, Denmark, France, Iceland, Italy, Luxembourg, the Netherlands, Norway, Portugal, the United Kingdom, and the United States. It entered into force on August 24, 1949. Greece and Turkey acceded in 1951, 3 U.S.T. 43, T.I.A.S. No. 2390, 126 U.N.T.S. 350, and the Federal Republic of Germany in 1955, 6 U.S.T. 5707, T.I.A.S. No. 3428, 243 U.N.T.S. 308. France withdrew its military contingents from the NATO commands in 1966, but continued to be a member of NATO. Later decisions extended NATO membership to Spain (1981), T.I.A.S. No. 10564, and to Hungary, Poland, and the Czech Republic (protocols of accession signed December 16, 1997; entered into force December 4, 1998).

The Treaty states as its objectives collective self-defense (Articles 3–6) and also peaceful settlement of disputes involving a member (Article 1) and development of mutual relations, conditions of stability and well-being, and economic collaboration (Article 2).

A Council attends to implementation of the Treaty with such subsidiary bodies as may be necessary, including a European defense committee (Article 9). The defense committee was established, but in 1959 it was absorbed into the Council. The Council has established a number of other committees as well as the position of Secretary General, who is the Chairman of the Council and the administrative head of the organization.

The Treaty does not obligate a member to come to the aid of any other member when an armed attack occurs. A member need take only "such action as it deems necessary" to restore and maintain the security of the North Atlantic area (Article 5). The treaty also recognizes that each state's response must be in accord with its own constitutional processes (Article 11). Unified commands (Supreme Allied Commander in Europe and Supreme Commander for the North Atlantic) were formed with regional planning groups. Within the system of cooperation developed, there has been a substantial measure of integration. While there is no legal obstacle to a member state's withdrawing its forces from NATO commitments, in practice such withdrawal is difficult. Nevertheless, the absence of a legal obligation to come to a member state's defense kept alive concern about United States response in case of an armed attack in Europe.

Upon the disintegration of the Soviet bloc and collapse of the Warsaw Pact, NATO invited the new states of the former Soviet Union and Eastern Europe to join a "Partnership for Peace" for joint security activities. Almost all of them have done so, and, as noted, three former Warsaw Pact states–Hungary, Poland, and the Czech Republic–became full members of NATO effective in December 1998. They supported the NATO effort in Kosovo in 1999 and made military contributions thereto. See Talas & Valki, The New Entrants: Hungary, Poland, and the Czech Republic, in Kosovo and the Challenge of Humanitarian Intervention 201–212 (Schnabel & Thakur, eds., 2000).

Notes

1. On NATO generally, see NATO at 40: Confronting a Changing World (1990); NATO After Forty Years (1990); Schmitz, Defending the NATO Alliance: Global Implications (1987); Shea, NATO 2000: A Political Agenda for a Political Alliance (1990); Stromseth, The North Atlantic Treaty and European Security after the Cold War, 24 Cornell Int'l L.J. 479 (1991); Symposium, NATO and the European Community: Forging the Alliance, [1991] Detroit Coll. L.Rev. 279 (1991). For earlier analysis, see Stein & Hay, Law and Institutions in the Atlantic Area, 1031–1108 (1967); Moore, NATO and the Future of Europe (1958); Ball, NATO and the European Union Movement (1959). On the Conference on Security and Cooperation in Europe, see generally The Helsinki Process and the Future of Europe (Wells, ed. 1990); Flynn & Scheffer, Limited Collective Security, 80 For. Pol'y 77 (1990).

2. On NATO's "new strategic concept" adopted at a Washington summit just as the Kosovo war was beginning in April 1999, see NATO Handbook (2001) on NATO website at www.nato.int.

3. Standard treatises on international law and organization have traditionally treated NATO not as a regional organization under Chapter VIII of the U.N. Charter but as a defense alliance. Indeed, NATO did not typically act as a regional arrangement under Security Council authority within the meaning of Articles 52–54 (e.g., by making the kinds of reports expected under Article 54). Do the developments in former Yugoslavia in the 1990s suggest that NATO has become, in effect, a regional arrangement in Chapter VIII's terms? Or is it *sui generis*?

SECTION 4. THE LAW OF WAR AND THE CONTROL OF WEAPONS

A. THE LAWS OF WAR: INTERNATIONAL HUMANITARIAN LAW

The traditional rules of war addressed three subjects: the definition of war; the conduct of war (regulation of weapons, treatment of prisoners and injured participants, treatment of enemy nationals and their property, treatment of the populations of occupied territories, and protection for nonmilitary ships); and the relations between neutral states and belligerent states. Although war and acts of war, *per se,* were not unlawful, deviations from the laws of war (the *jus in bello*) were violations of international law. The adoption of the U.N. Charter and its provisions outlawing the use of force cast doubt on whether the state of war has remained part of international law and raised questions about the continued validity of conceptions of belligerency and neutrality. See p. 979–980 above. However, there has been universal agreement that "humanitarian law"—the rules governing the conduct of war—remain part of international law and are applicable in hostilities, lawful or unlawful under the Charter, and to both attackers and defenders against attack.

In describing the content of the laws of war one must consider the rationale of each rule, since the weapons and conditions addressed in the nineteenth and twentieth centuries have markedly changed. The originators could not foresee today's sophisticated lethal and non-lethal technologies. However, old norms, interpreted in light of the values they were designed to promote, may be applicable to modern warfare. Guerrilla wars, undeclared wars, and ethnic conflicts raise pertinent issues under these bodies of law as well. Indeed, rules which were not scrupulously observed in the total wars of the twentieth century may find application in today's more limited conflicts.

The interaction between the customary international law of war and formally codified treaties has been complex. Much of the law of war was codified at the Hague Peace Conferences of 1899 and 1907, then strengthened after the World Wars–notably through the four Geneva Conventions of 1949 (cited and discussed beginning at p. 1060)—and in 1977 with two additional protocols to the 1949 Geneva Conventions. These treaties have all received widespread multilateral adherence, and in most aspects—with some notable qualifications—they reflect contemporary customary international law. As of 2000, all 189 members of the United Nations as well as non-member Switzerland were parties to the four 1949 Conventions, making them among the most widely-ratified of international treaties. The 1977 additional protocols have also received impressive (although not universal) international support, with about 150 parties to each as of 2000. Although the United States had not ratified either of the 1977 protocols as of 2000, it does view many of their articles as reflecting customary international law or acceptable practice.

Enforcement of the laws of war took a leap forward in the 1990s with the creation of the war crimes tribunals for the former Yugoslavia and for Rwanda. The jurisprudence of those bodies has, in turn, contributed to the clarification of the "laws and customs of war" and the Hague-and Geneva-based treaty regime. The Rome Statute for the International Criminal Court adopted in 1998 builds on those initiatives with more specific formulations and new mechanisms for criminal enforcement. See Chapter 15; see also Meron, War Crimes Law Comes of Age (1998).

Increasingly sophisticated weaponry, as seen in the Iraq war of 1991 and the Kosovo conflict of 1999, has placed new demands on the laws of war. How do the rules apply in the era of so-called "smart bombs"? Are the distinctions between military and civilian targets meaningful? Can they be articulated with greater precision for stronger protection of civilians? Will they be observed? Can the "revolution in military affairs" and the "information warfare" of the computer age be addressed under the existing laws of war, or will new instruments be necessary?

Note

On the customary status of the laws of war and their interaction with treaty norms, see generally Meron, Human Rights and Humanitarian Norms as Customary Law (1989); Meron, The Continuing Role of Custom in the Formation of International Humanitarian Law, 90 A.J.I.L. 238 (1996). For the U.S. position on aspects of unratified treaties that are considered customary law, see U.S. Army, Operational Law Handbook 2000, Chapter 5. On the issues dissuading the United States and other states from ratification of Protocols I and II, see pp. 1063–1064.

On the evolution of the laws of war from the 1899 Hague Conference through the end of the twentieth century, see the Symposium: The Hague Peace Conferences, 94 A.J.I.L. 1–98 (2000) (essays by Aldrich, Chinkin, Caron, Vagts, Roach and Meron).

1. *Regulation of Weapons*

Classic conceptions of the use of weapons in war began with the proposition that the amount of force required to overpower the enemy may be used, but kinds and degrees of force that were not necessary for that military purpose were restricted by humanitarian principles. Agreements of the nineteenth and twentieth centuries that sought to limit the use of weapons focused on four types of armaments: (1) bullets; (2) poisons and poisoned weapons; (3) gases; and (4) aerial bombardment. These sought to limit the introduction of new techniques that appeared to be particularly destructive or inhumane. Generally, international agreements (such as the 1868 Declaration of St. Petersburg) attempted to eliminate weapons that cause unnecessary suffering. For example, mustard gas incapacitated soldiers but also burned flesh and internal organs; the dum-dum bullet expanded on impact, tearing great wounds in its victims. For the earliest treaty regulating bullets, see Declaration Renouncing the Use, in Time of War, of Explosive Projectiles under 400 Grammes Weight, Dec. 11, 1868, Hertslet, Treaties and Conventions between Great Britain and Foreign Powers 79 (1877). See also Declaration Respecting Expanding Bullets, July 29, 1899, [1907] Gr. Brit. T.S. No. 32; Scott (ed.), The Hague Conventions and Declarations of 1899 and 1907, at 227 (3d ed. 1918).

Concentrated aerial bombardment, introduced by Germany during the First World War and condemned by the Allies as inhumane, became the accepted practice of both sides during World War II. For an early but unsuccessful attempt to regulate aerial bombardment, see Declaration Prohibiting the Discharge of Projectiles and Explosives from Balloons, Oct. 18, 1907, 36 Stat. 2439, T.S.No. 546. The use of incendiary and explosive shells and bombs was another hazard that developed along with air power. Though they were widely condemned when used, attempts to eliminate them (and later, flamethrowers, fire and napalm) failed. Efforts to eliminate concentration bombing as practiced in World War II did not succeed at the time, and controversy about the applicability of legal constraints to strategic bombardment of populated areas continued through the era of the Vietnam war. Compare Spaight, Air Power and War Rights 259–95 (3d ed. 1947); Stone, Legal Controls of Armed Conflict 629–31 (rev. 3d. 1959); Bush, Review Essay, Nuremberg: The Modern Law of War and Its Limitations, 93 Colum. L. Rev. 2022, 2032 n. 34, 2085 (1993).

With the arrival of the nuclear age, the traditional international law of weapons regulation came under pressure for the development of new approaches. Efforts to restrain weapons of mass destruction–nuclear, chemical, biological, or other–will be dealt with in Section B below, under the heading of

Arms Control and Disarmament. In parallel to these efforts, many international lawyers advocated the application to nuclear weapons of doctrines rooted in the Hague and Geneva streams of humanitarian law. These issues were addressed, though not fully resolved, by the International Court of Justice in its Advisory Opinion on Nuclear Weapons, 1996 I.C.J. 226, at paras 74–95. In its opinion the Court distilled the essence of humanitarian law in terms which it envisioned as applicable to nuclear as well as conventional weapons:

> 78. The cardinal principles contained in the texts constituting the fabric of humanitarian law are the following. The first is aimed at the protection of the civilian population and civilian objects and establishes the distinction between combatants and non-combatants; States must never make civilians the object of attack and must consequently never use weapons that are incapable of distinguishing between civilian and military targets. According to the second principle, it is prohibited to cause unnecessary suffering to combatants: it is accordingly prohibited to use weapons causing them such harm or uselessly aggravating their suffering. In application of that second principle, States do not have unlimited freedom of choice of means in the weapons they use.
>
> The Court would likewise refer, in relation to these principles, to the Martens Clause, which was first included in the Hague Convention II with Respect to the Law and Customs of War on Land of 1899 and which has proved to be an effective means of addressing the rapid evolution of military technology. A modern version of that clause is to be found in Article 1, paragraph 2, of Additional Protocol I of 1977, which reads as follows:
>
> > "In cases not covered by this Protocol or by other international agreements, civilians and combatants remain under the protection and authority of the principles of international law derived from established custom, from the principles of humanity and from the dictates of public conscience."
>
> In conformity with the aforementioned principles, humanitarian law, at a very early stage, prohibited certain types of weapons either because of their indiscriminate effect on combatants and civilians or because of the unnecessary suffering caused to combatants, that is to say, a harm greater than that unavoidable to achieve legitimate military objectives. * * *
>
> 79. It is undoubtedly because a great many rules of humanitarian law applicable in armed conflict are so fundamental to the respect of the human person and "elementary considerations of humanity" as the Court put it in its Judgment of 9 April 1949 in the *Corfu Channel* case (*I.C.J. Reports 1949,* p. 22) that the Hague and Geneva Conventions have enjoyed a broad accession. Further these fundamental rules are to be observed by all States whether or not they have ratified the conventions that contain them, because they constitute intransgressible principles of international customary law.
>
> * * *

> 82. The extensive codification of humanitarian law and the extent of the accession to the resultant treaties, as well as the fact that the denunciation clauses that existed in the codification instruments have never been used, have provided the international community with a corpus of treaty rules the great majority of which had already become customary and which reflected the most universally recognized humanitarian principles. These rules indicate the normal conduct and behavior expected of States.

The Court did not, however, find it necessary to pronounce on whether these rules had attained the status of *jus cogens.* Id., para. 83. In the dispositive portion of its judgment, para. 105(2)D, the Court unanimously found that a threat or use of nuclear weapons "should * * * be compatible with the requirements of the international law applicable in armed conflict, particularly those of the principles and rules of international humanitarian law * * * ." For discussion of the aspects of the Court's opinion dealing with humanitarian law, see Matheson, The Opinions of the International Court of Justice on the Threat or Use of Nuclear Weapons, 91 A.J.I.L. 417, 427–434 (1997) and other references at p. 87. On the history of the Martens Clause (para. 78), see Meron, The Martens Clause, Principles of Humanity and Dictates of Public Conscience, 94 A.J.I.L. 78 (2000).

The destructive capabilities even of "conventional" weapons in the late twentieth and early twenty-first centuries have led to new developments in the legal regulation of weaponry, along with attempts to strength the implementation of traditional doctrines. The initiative to ban anti-personnel landmines is a notable contemporary manifestation of the drive begun in the nineteenth century to eradicate weapons that cannot discriminate between civilians and combatants or that cause unnecessary suffering. For other examples concerning weapons of mass destruction (nuclear, chemical or biological), see Section 4.B.

LANDMINES CONVENTION (1997)

The Landmines Convention of 1997–formally, the Convention on the Prohibition of the Use, Stockpiling, Production, and Transfer of Anti–Personnel Mines and on Their Destruction, opened for signature at Ottawa, December 3, 1997, 36 I.L.M. 1507 (1997)–is notable both for its substance and for the law-making process that brought it into being. Non-governmental organizations played an exceedingly influential role in the design of the Convention (also known as the Mine Ban Treaty), in the mustering of political pressure in support of the diplomatic conference that produced the final text in 1997, and thereafter for ratification and implementation. An unusually brisk pace of ratifications brought the treaty into force with effect from March 1, 1999. As of 2000, more than 100 states were parties.

The substantive obligations under the Landmines Convention include an international ban on the use, production, stockpiling and sale of anti-personnel mines, and the destruction of stockpiles and of mines in the ground in territories under the jurisdiction of states parties on specified timetables. No reservations to these obligations are permitted. Parties are required to report to the U.N. Secretary–General on their implementation measures (Art. 7).

Non-governmental organizations and civil society are also vigilantly monitoring the steps being taken (or not taken) by states parties, as well as by non-signatories and non-parties, in support of the Convention's objectives.

As of 2000, the United States had neither signed nor ratified the Landmines Convention; Russia and China also remained outside the treaty framework, as did several other important states. However, the United States has accepted a more limited treaty commitment restricting certain kinds of mines. See Convention on Prohibitions or Restrictions on the Use of Certain Weapons Which May Be Deemed to be Excessively Injurious or to Have Indiscriminate Effects, and its Protocol on Prohibitions or Restrictions on the Use of Mines, Booby–Traps and Other Devices (entered into force for the United States Sept. 24, 1995) and Amended Protocol II (ratified by the United States May 24, 1999); see also Matheson, The Revision of the Mines Protocol, 91 A.J.I.L. 158 (1997). The United States has also maintained a self-imposed restriction on exports of landmines since 1993 (extended by legislation through 2003) and has contributed significant resources and expertise to demining activities around the world. Between fiscal years 1993 and 1999 the United States contributed some $225 million to humanitarian demining in more than 30 countries. The United States has said it would consider eventually joining the Landmines Convention, provided that alternatives could be found to address specific military needs, especially on the Korean peninsula.

According to the International Campaign to Ban Landmines (a coalition of non-governmental organizations working for complete elimination of landmines), there has been a sharp drop in the number of new mines being laid and a sharp drop in exports of mines since the conclusion of the Mine Ban Treaty. NATO did not use anti-personnel mines as such in the Kosovo war of 1999 (but see note 4 below on cluster bombs), though landmines had been laid in many areas of former Yugoslavia between 1991 and 1999. Even so, millions of mines remain in the ground, not only in several dozen areas of ongoing armed conflict, but also in many countries where wars have ended. The practical problems of eliminating these stealthy killers are enormous and expensive.

Notes

1. Does the information above concerning the Landmines Convention support the position that a norm of customary international law has already come into existence to ban these weapons? Would the "persistent objector" rule apply in the case of the United States or other states that have declined to support the treaty-based norm?

2. The International Campaign to Ban Landmines has found that three signatories (Angola, Guinea–Bissau and Senegal) used landmines in 1998, after signing the treaty but before ratification. Would such use defeat the object and purpose of the treaty within the meaning of Article 18 of the Vienna Convention on the Law of Treaties?

3. For a compendium of current materials on landmines, including status of ratifications and implementation measures, see International Campaign to Ban Landmines, Landmine Monitor Report (annual volumes beginning in 1999). On the preparation of the Landmines Convention and the influence of non-govern-

mental organizations, see Thakur & Maley, The Ottawa Convention on Landmines: A Landmark Humanitarian Treaty in Arms Control?, 5 Global Governance 273 (1999); Anderson, The Ottawa Convention Banning Landmines, the Role of Non–Governmental Organizations and the Idea of International Civil Society, 11 E.J.I.L. 91 (2000). For analysis and critique of the positions of the United States and other countries, see Human Rights Watch, Clinton's Landmine Legacy (2000), and the respective country chapters of the Landmine Monitor Report.

4. Human rights groups claim that the high dud rate of cluster bombs turns these weapons into the equivalent of antipersonnel landmines, which lie in the ground until detonated on contact. Cluster bombs were dropped from high-flying aircraft in the 1999 Kosovo war and were also used with several kinds of delivery systems in the 1991 Gulf War. Should the 1997 Landmines Convention—or the general norm of humanitarian law requiring discrimination between combatants and civilians—be understood to restrict the use of such weapons? See, e.g., Human Rights Watch, Ticking Time Bombs: NATO's Use of Cluster Munitions in Yugoslavia (1999). A report prepared for the Prosecutor of the International Criminal Tribunal for the Former Yugoslavia found no legal basis for accusations that NATO's use of cluster bombs in the Kosovo campaign could constitute a criminal violation of the laws of war. See ICTY: Final Report to the Prosecutor by the Committee Established to Review the NATO Bombing Campaign Against the Federal Republic of Yugoslavia, 39 I.L.M. 1257, 1264–1265 (2000). The Independent Commission on Kosovo (p. 1001 supra) did not dispute this conclusion, "but nevertheless recommends that cluster bombs should never be used in any future undertaking under UN auspices or claiming to be a 'humanitarian intervention'." Kosovo Report, Chapter 6, text at n. 34 (2000).

5. For another recent treaty prohibition on a particularly harmful kind of weapon, see Protocol on Blinding Laser Weapons, Oct. 13, 1995, 35 I.L.M. 1218 (1996).

2. *International Humanitarian Law Concerning Combatants and Non–Combatants*

Alongside the norms restricting weaponry is the body of law governing treatment of combatants and non-combatants. The four Geneva Conventions of 1949 and the two 1977 additional protocols provide detailed codes in this regard. They are:

— Geneva Convention for the Amelioration of the Condition of the Wounded and Sick in Armed Forces in the Field, Aug. 12, 1949, 6 U.S.T. 3114, T.I.A.S. No. 3362, 75 U.N.T.S. 31 (Geneva Convention No. I)

— Geneva Convention for the Amelioration of the Condition of the Wounded, Sick, and Shipwrecked Members of the Armed Forces at Sea, Aug. 12, 1949, 6 U.S.T. 3217, T.I.A.S. No. 3363, 75 U.N.T.S. 85 (Geneva Convention No. II)

— Geneva Convention Relative to the Treatment of Prisoners of War, Aug. 12, 1949, 6 U.S.T. 3316, T.I.A.S. No. 3364, 75 U.N.T.S. 135 (Geneva Convention No. III)

— Geneva Convention Relative to the Protection of Civilian Persons in Time of War, Aug. 12, 1949, 6 U.S.T. 3516, T.I.A.S. No. 3365, 75 U.N.T.S. 287 (Geneva Convention No. IV)

— Additional Protocol Relating to the Protection of Victims of International Armed Conflicts, June 8, 1977, 1125 U.N.T.S. 3 (Protocol I)

— Additional Protocol Relating to the Protection of Victims of Non-International Armed Conflicts, June 8, 1977, 1125 U.N.T.S. 609 (Protocol II)

This set of rules applies differentially, depending on whether the conflict in question is "international" or "non-international." In general, stricter standards apply to conflicts of an international character. In the case of non-international (internal) conflicts, Article 3 common to all four Geneva Conventions ("Common Article 3") applies: it requires humane treatment of all persons not taking an active part in hostilities and prohibits various acts, including murder, torture, hostage-taking, and non-judicial punishments. (For full text of Common Article 3, see Document Supplement.) Protocol II (1977) establishes rules for non-international conflicts expanding upon those in Common Article 3; but a number of states (including the United States) have not ratified Protocol II, and its status as customary international law is uncertain. Compare Greenwood, Customary Law Status of the 1977 Geneva Protocols, in Humanitarian Law of Armed Conflict: Challenges Ahead 93–114 (1991).

For authoritative interpretations of the International Committee of the Red Cross on the Geneva Conventions and Protocols, see Pictet (ed.), Commentaries on the Geneva Conventions (1958, 1994); Sandoz et al., Commentary on the Additional Protocols of 8 June 1977 to the Geneva Conventions (1987). See also Best, Law and War Since 1945 (1994).

Notes

1. On what basis must the existence of an "armed conflict" be established, as a precondition to the applicability of the 1949 Geneva Conventions or the 1977 Protocols? What level of violence should such a requirement entail? What should be the scope of applicability in relation to hostilities that flare up, die down, recur, and perhaps subside again? What factors should be relevant in internal (as contrasted to international) armed conflicts? For the reasons why the states that drafted the Conventions and Protocols were relatively cautious in setting the thresholds for applicability (to exclude low-level disturbances or isolated incidents) and distinguishing between international and non-international conflicts, see Aldrich, The Laws of War on Land, 94 A.J.I.L. 42, 58–62 (2000).

In the 1995 *Tadic* Appeal on Jurisdiction, Case No. IT–94–1–AR72 (Oct. 2, 1995), the International Criminal Tribunal for the Former Yugoslavia discussed the preliminary issue of the existence of an armed conflict, in a context where defendant disputed whether there had been active hostilities in the area of the alleged crimes at the relevant time:

> 70. * * * [W]e find that an armed conflict exists whenever there is a resort to armed force between States or protracted armed violence between governmental authorities and organized armed groups or between such groups with a State. International humanitarian law applies from the initiation of such armed conflicts and extends beyond the cessation of hostilities until a general conclusion of peace is reached; or, in the case of internal conflicts, a peaceful settlement is achieved. Until that moment, international humanitarian law continues to apply in the whole territory of the warring

States or, in the case of internal conflicts, the whole territory under the control of a party, whether or not actual combat takes place there.

Applying the foregoing concept of armed conflicts to this case, we hold that the alleged crimes were committed in the context of an armed conflict. * * * Even if substantial clashes were not occurring in the Prijedor region at the time and place the crimes allegedly were committed–a factual issue on which the Appeals Chamber does not pronounce–international humanitarian law applies. It is sufficient that the alleged crimes were closely related to the hostilities occurring in other parts of the territories controlled by the parties to the conflict. * * *

2. The jurisprudence of the I.C.T.Y. now deals in depth with the distinction between international and non-international conflicts and the determination of which set of rules applies to the facts of the conflicts in former Yugoslavia. The 1995 *Tadic* appeal on jurisdiction, and the 1999 decision on Tadic's appeal of his conviction, both examine these issues at length. In the 1995 ruling, the I.C.T.Y.'s Appeals Chamber found that certain aspects of humanitarian law, notably the "grave breaches" system of the Geneva Conventions, would apply only to offenses committed in international armed conflicts, while other aspects could apply as well to internal conflicts. Case No. IT–94–1–AR72, paras. 79–85, 95–137 (Oct. 2, 1995). In the 1999 decision, the Appeals Chamber (overruling the trial chamber in this respect) found that the conflict entailed sufficient involvement of the Federal Republic of Yugoslavia in Bosnia–Herzegovina to bring into play the provisions of Geneva Convention No. IV on protecting civilians in times of international armed conflict, and likewise found that Bosnian Muslims in the hands of Bosnian Serbs were "protected persons" in the hands of a party of which they were not nationals under the Convention. The Appeals Chamber therefore found Tadic guilty of grave breaches of the Geneva Conventions. See Prosecutor v. Tadic, Case No. IT–94–1–A, paras. 68–171 (Judgment on Appeal from Conviction, July 15, 1999).

The jurisdiction of the International Criminal Tribunal for Rwanda is differently formulated. On the apparent assumption that the conflict was non-international in character, the Security Council specified that the I.C.T.R.'s jurisdiction over war crimes would be based on Common Article 3 of the 1949 Geneva Conventions and 1977 Protocol II (the "grave breaches" regime is thus not applicable). See Prosecutor v. Akayesu, Case No. ICTR–96–4–T, Judgment (Sept. 2, 1998), Section 6.5. *Akayesu* also held (Section 7.1) that civilians can in principle be criminally responsible for violations of the laws of war; but the trial chamber held that defendant's individual responsibility under Common Article 3 and Protocol II was not proved, although it did convict Akayesu (who had held the civilian post of *bourgmestre*) on charges of genocide and crimes against humanity.

3. In the developments in Kosovo beginning in 1998, at what point did the insurgency of the Kosovo Liberation Army and the counter-insurgency responses of the FRY fall within the scope of the Geneva Conventions? Was the conflict prior to NATO's entry international or non-international within the meaning of the I.C.T.Y.'s *Tadic* rulings? The I.C.T.Y. prosecutor maintained that she had jurisdiction to investigate allegations of violations of the laws of war in Kosovo and in due course did issue indictments in that regard: e.g., the indictment against Slobodan Milosevic issued in May 1999. Compare Security Council Resolutions 1160 (1998), 1199 (1998), and 1207 (1998) in relation to the I.C.T.Y.'s authority concerning violations of humanitarian law in Kosovo. See also Human Rights Watch, Humanitarian Law Violations in Kosovo 91–96 (1998).

4. It has been said that there "is no moral justification, and no truly persuasive legal reason, for treating perpetrators of atrocities in internal conflicts more leniently than those engaged in international wars." Meron, War Crimes Law Comes of Age 238 (1998). Similarly, there are strong arguments for establishing standards of protection that would apply in all situations, including those of internal violence falling short of "armed conflict" in the sense of the Geneva Conventions. On the progress toward promulgation of such a declaration of minimum humanitarian standards ("fundamental standards of humanity,") see Meron, International Criminalization of Internal Atrocities, 89 A.J.I.L. 554 (1995); Meron, The Humanization of Humanitarian Law, 94 A.J.I.L. 239, 274–275 (2000).

For an argument that humanitarian law should apply short of full-blown civil war, see Carrillo–Suárez, *Hors de Logique:* Contemporary Issues in International Humanitarian Law as Applied to Internal Armed Conflict, 15 Am. U. Int'l L. Rev. 1 (1999).

5. The Independent International Commission on Kosovo (p. 1001 supra) has suggested that standards for the conduct of armed conflict should be more exacting in the case of a war carried out for "humanitarian" purposes than in other kinds of conflicts. The Commission recommended that the International Committee of the Red Cross or another body should prepare a new legal convention to this effect, for applicability to U.N. peacekeeping or to humanitarian interventions.

On applicability of humanitarian law to U.N. operations, see U.N. Secretary–General, Bulletin on the Observance by U.N. Forces of International Humanitarian Law, U.N. Doc. ST/SGB/1999/13, reprinted in 38 I.L.M. 1656 (1999). See also Greenwood, International Humanitarian Law and United Nations Military Operations, 1 Y.B. Int'l Humanit. L. 3 (1998); Shraga, UN Peacekeeping Operations: Applicability of International Humanitarian Law and Responsibility for Operations–Related Damage, 94 A.J.I.L. 406 (2000).

6. Some aspects of humanitarian law apply in peacetime as well as in wartime. See, e.g., the Genocide Convention, Art. 1. In respect of crimes against humanity, it is important to distinguish between the substantive law, which is now generally understood to apply irrespective of the existence of armed conflict, and particular jurisdictional instruments which may be limited to such crimes committed in the course of armed conflict. For example, Article 5 of the I.C.T.Y Statute confers jurisdiction over crimes against humanity "when committed in armed conflict, whether international or internal in character." The Appeals Chamber of the I.C.T.Y. has explained that it is "a settled rule of customary international law that crimes against humanity do not require a connection to internal armed conflict * * * and may not require a connection between crimes against humanity and any conflict at all." Thus the Security Council "may have defined [crimes against humanity] more narrowly than necessary under customary international law." Prosecutor v. Tadic, Case No. IT–94–1–AR72, Appeal on Jurisdiction, para. 141 (Oct. 2, 1995); see also Appeal from Conviction, para. 251 (July 15, 1999). Compare Rome Statute for the International Criminal Court, Art. 7 (defining crimes against humanity without reference to armed conflict).

7. As of 2000, the United States had not ratified either Protocol I or Protocol II. Issues of concern to the United States (and other states) include provisions on wars of national liberation; application of rules on combatants and prisoner-of-war status to non-uniformed fighters; and prohibitions on belligerent reprisals. See generally Meron, The Time Has Come for the United States to Ratify Geneva Protocol I, 88 A.J.I.L. 678 (1994); Aldrich, The Laws of War on Land, 94 A.J.I.L.

42, 45–48, 57–58 (2000) and references therein. On the objection concerning belligerent reprisals and the debate over whether that prohibition might be (or become) customary international law, see Meron, The Humanization of Humanitarian Law, 94 A.J.I.L. 238, 249–251 (2000).

TREATMENT OF PRISONERS OF WAR AND THE SICK AND WOUNDED ON LAND AND AT SEA

Humanitarian treatment of prisoners of war was not emphasized until the second half of the nineteenth century. See 2 Oppenheim, International Law 367–396 (7th ed., Lauterpacht ed., 1952); Stone, Legal Controls of Armed Conflict 651–79 (1959). The Hague Regulations did not prevent many of the hardships that prisoners suffered during World War I, but they did provide an enlightened basis for regulation. Besides the failure to anticipate the problems that arose in World War I, the chief defects of the regulations were a lack of specificity and the absence of any enforcement procedures. After the First World War, a conference at Geneva adopted new, more elaborate rules. See Convention Relating to the Treatment of Prisoners of War, July 27, 1929, 47 Stat. 2021, T.S. No. 846, 118 L.N.T.S. 343. Like the prior rules, the new rules did not anticipate the new modes of warfare adopted in the world war that followed their acceptance.

The Third Geneva Convention is now the authoritative statement concerning prisoners of war. An outstanding innovation of the Convention, in addition to its application to all cases of declared war, is its partial application to all other armed conflicts, including internal wars. The Convention defines prisoners in a way calculated to include every person likely to be captured in hostilities. Full and primary responsibility for the treatment of prisoners of war falls upon the Detaining Power, not upon individuals. The Detaining Power is under a general obligation to treat prisoners humanely. They must receive maintenance and medical attention. Medical and scientific experiments are prohibited, as are reprisals for breaches of the laws of war other than breaches of the Convention itself. See Stone at 656 n. 21 (1959); 2 Oppenheim at 562 n. 3. Prisoners are to be treated alike, regardless of race, nationality, religious beliefs, or political opinions.

At the time of detention, the prisoner is required to give a minimum of information. He is not to be subjected to torture and may retain his personal effects. Conditions at the detention camps must meet standards provided in the Convention. The work that the prisoner is required to perform must not be inherently dangerous, humiliating, or directly connected with the operations of the war. The prisoner must be permitted contact with his family and correspondence privileges. Procedures must be established for registering complaints against the administration of the detention camp. Penal and disciplinary sanctions, including procedures for determining guilt, are prescribed by the Convention. Additional articles regulate repatriation and information to the outside regarding prisoners.

The Convention elaborates the idea of a Protecting Power appointed by mutual agreement, which determines whether the provisions of the conventions are being followed. When the belligerents are unable to agree upon such an appointment, the Detaining Power is required to request a neutral state, an impartial organization, or a humanitarian organization to substitute for the Protecting Power. Each contracting party undertakes to provide penal sanctions against persons who violate the established norms. Parties to the conventions are obligated to search out those persons alleged to have committed such breaches.

Many of the general provisions of the Third Geneva Convention on prisoners of war are incorporated into the First and Second Geneva Conventions with respect to the wounded and sick in armed forces in the field or at sea. On application of these rules in the 1991 Gulf conflict, see Meron, Prisoners of War, Civilians and Diplomats in the Gulf Crisis, 85 A.J.I.L. 104 (1991).

Notes

1. *Armed conflict at sea.* The laws of war have also included limitations in favor of merchant shipping. Unlike armed ships and other public vessels, an enemy merchant ship was not to be attacked unless it refused to submit to visit and capture. See generally 2 Oppenheim at 465–97; Stone at 571–607. These rules were widely disregarded in both World Wars, notably by submarines. Prohibitions on submarine warfare against merchant ships were made explicit between the wars. See Treaty for the Limitation and Reduction of Naval Armaments (London Naval Treaty of 1930), April 22, 1930, pt. IV, Art. 22, 46 Stat. 2858, 2881, T.S. No. 830, 112 L.N.T.S. 65, 88; 2 Hackworth at 690–95; 6 Hackworth at 466. After visit, a merchant vessel could be taken to port and adjudicated a prize, and thereafter its disposition was governed by municipal law. For a description of American prize practice, see Gilmore & Black, The Law of Admirality 40 (2d ed. 1975); 2 Whiteman at 1–138. Immunities have been granted to hospital ships, to vessels with religious, scientific, or philanthropic missions and also to coastal fishing boats.

2. On the current legal regime for naval conflicts, see San Remo Manual on International Law Applicable to Armed Conflicts at Sea (Louise Doswald–Beck ed., 1995); see also Roach, The Law of Naval Warfare at the Turn of Two Centuries, 94 A.J.I.L. 64 (2000).

3. In the *Nicaragua* case (Merits), the Court observed that the laying of mines in the waters of another state without any warning or notification is not only an unlawful act but also a breach of the principles of humanitarian law. The Court stated:

> [I]f a State lays mines in any waters whatever in which the vessels of another State have right of access or passage, and fails to give any warning or notification whatsoever, in disregard of the security of peaceful shipping, it commits a breach of the principles of humanitarian law underlying the specific provisions [Articles 3 and 4] of [Hague] Convention No. VIII of 1907. Those principles were expressed in the *Corfu Channel* case as follows:
>
> > "certain general and well recognized principles namely: elementary considerations of humanity, even more exacting in peace than in war" (I.C.J. Reports 1949, p. 22).

1986 I.C.J. 14, 112.

PROTECTION OF CIVILIANS IN WARTIME

The Fourth Geneva Convention governs protection of civilians in time of war. It comes into play during armed conflict when civilians ("protected persons") are in the hands of a party of which they are not a national. It prohibits violence to life and person and allows no distinction based on race, religion, or political opinion. It defines situations in which an alien may leave the territory of the belligerent and provides that the regulation of aliens who remain may deviate from the provisions regulating such aliens in peacetime only to the extent required by wartime control and security. Civilians must be allowed to receive relief, necessary medical care and religious comfort. They must be allowed to move from exposed areas. They may not be compelled to work on any task related to military operations and when working they must be accorded working conditions equal to those of the belligerent's nationals. There is also an elaborate set of rules regulating treatment of internees. See Stone, Legal Controls of International Conflicts 684–92 (1959).

When belligerent occupation has been established in accordance with the requirements of international law, the occupying power assumes broad legal powers that it would not have merely as a belligerent. These powers and reciprocal duties reflect the divergent and common interests of the occupying power and the local inhabitants. Both have a common interest in the maintenance of law and order. The occupying power desires to minimize the diversion of its resources from other war operations, while the local inhabitants want to conduct their lives without violence and undue coercion. Humane treatment of the inhabitants not only serves the values of decency, but is a precondition of administering the territory with a minimal expenditure of force. See McDougal & Feliciano, Law and Minimum World Public Order 790–808 (1961).

Belligerent occupation creates a complicated scheme of legal relations involving not only the occupant and the inhabitants, but also the temporarily ousted sovereign. Customary rules governing these relationships have been strongly influenced by the Hague Regulations and the Fourth Geneva Convention. For the purposes of the latter instrument, the fact that one of the parties to the conflict had violated a norm of international law in initiating hostilities would not affect the applicability of the Convention. The occupant is empowered to maintain order and utilize the resources of the country for its own military needs. The occupying power may not force the people to swear allegiance to it. The precise extent of its power is uncertain, particularly with respect to effecting changes in fundamental institutions. See Stone at 688–89, 723–32.

Ordinarily, an occupying power is expected to rely on the organs of the subservient government, such as the courts, for maintaining law and order. When these institutions prove inadequate, the belligerent may replace them with institutions of a military nature. In punishing war crimes or activity directed against the occupying power, the courts are forbidden to apply any retroactive law or to depart from the principle of proportionality in punishment. Death penalties are permissible in certain types of cases only. Collective penalties, intimidation, terrorism, taking of hostages and acts of reprisal against the civilian population are prohibited. Since, in reaction to a recalcitrant civilian population, an occupying power might well adopt penal measures without regard to these niceties, the practicality of such rules has been questioned. See McDougal & Feliciano at 797. Discrimination on the grounds of race, religion or political opinion is also forbidden. In general, all forcible mass transfers of population are prohibited, except where required by security or military necessity. The occupying power is also required to provide certain welfare services.

Notes

1. *Alien internment and property seizure in wartime.* Alien enemy control during the First and Second World Wars included internment of dangerous foreign nationals. Based on the experience at the outbreak of the First World War, the government increased the efficiency and incidence of internment at the beginning of the Second World War. On December 7, 1941, a presidential proclamation provided for the internment of Japanese nationals. Subsequent decrees applied to German, Italian, Hungarian, Bulgarian and Rumanian nationals. By October 5, 1943, 14,807 aliens had been taken into custody. See Hoover, Alien Enemy Control, 29 Iowa L.Rev. 398 (1944). Presidential authority for the supervision of enemy aliens is contained in 50 U.S.C.A. § 21. *Habeas corpus* was available to these persons, although the only justiciable question was whether they belonged to the category of persons designated by legislation as liable to seizure. See Brandon, Legal Control Over Resident Enemy Aliens in Time of War in the United States and in the United Kingdom, 44 A.J.I.L. 382 (1950).

Customary law permits the seizure of public enemy property and the prohibition of the withdrawal of private enemy property. At one time, belligerents were permitted to confiscate private as well as public enemy property, movable and immovable, including debts. This practice was reversed in respect of private property through treaties that provided that enemy subjects and private property could be withdrawn at the outbreak of war. The last case of outright confiscation of private property occurred in 1793. See 2 Oppenheim at 326. As to whether such confiscation today would violate customary international law, compare the treatment of private fishing vessels, The Paquete Habana, p. 62 supra.

In the early stages of the First World War, states scrupulously avoided confiscatory acts against enemy states, but most states eventually adopted exceptional war measures which, though not amounting to confiscation, inflicted great loss and injury. Regulation of enemy property has been recognized in the United States as within the war power of the federal government. See Hays, Enemy Property in America (1923); Gathings, International Law and American Treatment of Alien Enemy Property (1940); Council on Foreign Relations, The Postwar Settlement of Property Rights 16–22 (1945). Eight months after the United States entered the First World War, Congress passed the Trading with the Enemy Act, 40 Stat. 411 (1917). See 50 U.S.C.A.App. §§ 1–44 for the current authority. The Trading with the Enemy Act prohibited all trade with persons or firms resident within enemy territory or resident outside the United States and doing business within such territory or with nationals of an ally of an enemy state unless authorized by license. All business enterprises whose stock was held by enemies or allies of enemies, and all persons holding property of or indebted to enemies, were required to register with the Alien Property Custodian. At first empowered only to administer such property, the Alien Property Custodian was later authorized to manage and dispose of property. In the Second World War, government control of foreign-owned property was instituted more than a year before the entry of the

United States. Following the initial executive order relating to Norwegian and Danish property within the United States, the property of all the governments and nations of continental Europe (except Turkey), of Japan and of China was frozen. After the United States entered the war, the authority of the Secretary of the Treasury was widened to include liquidation or supervision of Axis-controlled business enterprises located in the United States. Nearly two years after the first freezing order, President Roosevelt established the Office of the Alien Property Custodian.

At the end of both the First and Second World Wars, the peace treaties included provisions giving nationals of the victorious states recourse against the vanquished states for loss of property. Nationals of the vanquished country, however, could apply only to their own states for compensation. See, e.g., Article 79 of the 1947 Peace Treaty with Italy, 61 Stat. 1245, T.I.A.S. No. 1648, 49 U.N.T.S. 1; Chapter 6, [Bonn] Convention on the Settlement of Matters Arising Out of the War and Occupation, 1952, 6 U.S.T. 4411, T.I.A.S. No. 3425, 332 U.N.T.S. 219; Tag v. Rogers, 267 F.2d 664 (D.C.Cir.1959), cert. denied, 362 U.S. 904, 80 S.Ct. 615, 4 L.Ed.2d 555 (1960); DeVries, The International Responsibility of the United States for Vested German Assets, 51 A.J.I.L. 18 (1957). On the treatment of enemy property, see generally Stone at 434–36; 2 Oppenheim at 326–32. On the practice during and after World War II, see Domke, Trading with the Enemy in World War II (1943); Domke, The Control of Alien Property (1947); Mann, Enemy Property and the Paris Peace Treaties, 64 L.Q.Rev. 492 (1948); Martin, The Treatment of Enemy Property under the Peace Treaties of 1947, 34 Grotius Soc.Trans. 77 (1948). The United States never recognized any obligation to compensate for the seizure of enemy property. In accordance with principles enunciated in the Potsdam and Paris agreements, the United States passed the War Claims Act of 1948, 62 Stat. 1240, which provided that owners of alien property seized during the Second World War would not be compensated.

2. On the treatment of the population of occupied territory, see Stone at 697–706, 723–26, 727–32; 2 Oppenheim at 438–56; McDougal & Feliciano at 732; von Glahn, The Occupation of Enemy Territory (1957); Gutteridge, The Protection of Civilians in Occupied Territory, 5 Y.B. World Aff. 290 (1951). See also Benvenisti, The International Law of Occupation (1993).

3. The extended occupation by Israel since the 1967 war of territories previously in Arab hands has raised some novel problems. See Roberts, Prolonged Military Occupation: The Israeli–Occupied Territories Since 1967, 84 A.J.I.L. 44 (1990). Israel has not acknowledged applicability of the Fourth Geneva Convention, claiming that that Convention applies only to territories that belonged to another sovereign state, and that in view of the termination of the British Mandate and the failure of the U.N. Partition Plan of 1947 which the Arab states rejected, the Geneva Convention does not formally apply. A discussion of the Israeli position is found in Blum, The Missing Reversioner: Reflections on the Status of Judea and Samaria, 3 Israel L.Rev. 279, 281–95 (1968). Israel has also argued that the prohibition on expulsion in the Fourth Geneva Convention applies only to mass displacement of population and does not forbid expulsion of individuals as a form of punishment or as a security measure. See generally, the debate between Falk and Weston, The Relevance of International Law to Palestinian Rights in the West Bank and Gaza: In Legal Defense of the Intifada, 32 Harv. Int'l L.J. 129 (1991). The U.N. called on Israel to cancel an order expelling a number of Palestinians from the West Bank in 1988 and from Gaza in 1992. See S.C.Res. 607 (1988) and Res. 799 (1992). U.N. organs, including the Security Council, General Assembly, and Commission on Human Rights, have frequently insisted that the

Fourth Geneva Convention does apply to the territories occupied by Israel and have called upon Israel to comply with its provisions. Cf. S.C. Res. 1322 (Oct. 7, 2000.) See discussion in Benvenisti & Zamir, Private Claims to Property Rights in the Future Israeli–Palestinian Settlement, 89 A.J.I.L. 295, 305–307 (1995).

The 1998 Rome Statute of the International Criminal Court, discussed at pp. 1367–1382, includes in the definition of "crimes against humanity" the following provisions (Art. 7(1), 7(2)(d)):

> 1. For the purpose of this Statute, "crime against humanity" means any of the following acts, when committed as part of a widespread or systematic attack directed against any civilian population, with knowledge of the attack: * * *
>
> (d) Deportation or forcible transfer or population; * * *
>
> 2. For the purpose of paragraph 1: * * *
>
> (d) "Deportation or forcible transfer of population" means forced displacement of the persons concerned by expulsion or other coercive acts from the area in which they are lawfully present, without grounds permitted under international law; * * *

and in the enumeration of "war crimes" the following provision (Art. 8(2)(b)(viii):

> The transfer, directly or indirectly, by the Occupying Power of parts of its own civilian population into the territory it occupies, or the deportation or transfer of all or parts of the population of the occupied territory within or outside this territory.

How might these provisions apply to expulsions of Palestinians from the occupied territories, or to Israeli settlements in the occupied territories?

4. The problem of protection of cultural property in wartime has received increasing attention, with the prominence in recent conflicts of wanton destruction of mosques, churches, statues, and other indicia of group identity and heritage. A 1954 Hague Convention for the Protection of Cultural Property in the Event of Armed Conflict, 249 U.N.T.S. 215, had approximately 90 parties in 2000 and more than 75 parties to its protocol. To strengthen existing protections, a Second Protocol to the 1954 Convention was adopted under the auspices of the United Nations Educational, Scientific and Cultural Organization (UNESCO) at The Hague in March 1999. See 38 I.L.M. 769 (1999).

5. For another recent initiative, see the Security Council's Resolution on the Protection of Civilians in Armed Conflict, S.C. Res. 1296 (2000), 39 I.L.M. 1022 (2000).

SEXUAL VIOLENCE IN WARTIME

The rape of women by belligerent or occupying forces has been a perennial atrocity addressed by international law in only general terms and not yet effectively deterred or punished. See Khushalani, Dignity and Honour of Women as Basic and Fundamental Human Rights 63–64 (1982); Meron, Rape as a Crime under International Humanitarian Law, 87 A.J.I.L. 424 (1993). An analogous atrocity has been the forced enrollment of women into brothels, as was done to Korean and other Asian women by Japan in the Second World War–a grievance remaining essentially unredressed through the end of the twentieth century. During the hostilities in the former Yugoslavia, it was reported that there had been as many as 20,000 cases of rape committed as a matter of state policy and strategy of war. The pattern continued with the use of rape against Kosovar Albanians in 1998–1999. See Human Rights Watch, Kosovo: Rape as a Weapon of "Ethnic Cleansing" (2000).

The Geneva Conventions contain provisions relevant to wartime sexual violence, e.g. in Article 27 of the Fourth Convention, which provides that "[w]omen shall be especially protected against any attack on their honour, in particular against rape, enforced prostitution, or any form of indecent assault," and in Common Article 3 (applicable to non-international conflicts) which prohibits "(a) violence to life and person, in particular murder of all kinds, mutilation, cruel treatment and torture * * * [and] (c) outrages upon personal dignity, in particular humiliating and degrading treatment * * * ." Protocol II (applicable to non-international conflicts) specifies in Article 4(2)(e) that "outrages upon personal dignity, in particular humiliating and degrading treatment, rape, enforced prostitution and any form of indecent assault" are prohibited at any time and in any place whatsoever. These formulations have been criticized, *inter alia* for being insufficiently explicit or comprehensive with respect to the diverse forms of sexual offenses, as well as for the references to "honour" and "dignity" which might seem to reflect patriarchal attitudes or to ignore the violent quality of rape. Another criticism is the omission of specific reference to sexual violence from the "grave breaches" provisions of the Geneva Conventions, thus leaving it a matter of inference that rape and other sexual offenses could be punishable as grave breaches by interpretation of the clauses on torture, "wilfully causing great suffering or serious injury to body or health," "unlawful confinement of a civilian," or another enumerated grave breach.

The jurisprudence of the International Criminal Tribunals for the Former Yugoslavia and for Rwanda now affirms that rape and other forms of sexual violence can indeed be prosecuted as grave breaches of the Geneva Conventions, as torture, as crimes against humanity, and even as genocide. In reaching these conclusions, the Tribunals have given specific readings to the general provisions of humanitarian law over which they have jurisdiction. Article 2 of the I.C.T.Y. Statute confers jurisdiction over grave breaches of the Geneva Conventions, in language taken verbatim from the Conventions themselves–neither adding to nor detracting from their wording and thus not explicitly referring to the diverse forms of sexual violence. Article 3 confers jurisdiction over violations of "the laws and customs of war" with a non-exclusive listing that likewise makes no specific mention of sexual violence. Article 4 recites verbatim the definition of genocide from the 1948 Genocide Convention. Article 5(g) on crimes against humanity does specify rape as a crime against humanity, when committed in armed conflict against a civilian population. The Statute of the International Criminal Tribunal for Rwanda incorporates Common Article 3 of the Geneva Conventions and Protocol II (applicable in non-international conflicts) as well as the Genocide Convention, and goes beyond the I.C.T.Y. definition by eliminating the "armed conflict" jurisdictional requirement for crimes against humanity. In interpreting these statutory provisions, the Tribunals have given a specific definition to the crime of rape in humanitarian law and have convicted defendants for perpetrating or being complicit in crimes of sexual violence.

The 1998 Rome Statute of the International Criminal Court is the most detailed codification to date of sexual and gender-based atrocities. Article 7(1) on crimes against humanity defines the crime to include "any of the following acts when committed as part of a widespread or systematic attack directed against any civilian population * * *:"

> (g) Rape, sexual slavery, enforced prostitution, forced pregnancy, enforced sterilization, or any other form of sexual violence of comparable gravity;

and subparagraph (h) also includes persecution on gender grounds (paragraph 3 states that the term " 'gender' refers to the two sexes, male and female, within the context of society"). The term "forced pregnancy is defined as

> * * * the unlawful confinement, of a woman forcibly made pregnant, with the intent of affecting the ethnic composition of any population or carrying out other grave violations of international law. This definition shall not in any way be interpreted as affecting national laws relating to pregnancy. (Art. 7(2)(f))

The provisions on war crimes (Art. 8(2)(b)) likewise specify as "serious violations" in international conflicts

> (xxii) Committing rape, sexual slavery, enforced prostitution, forced pregnancy, as defined in article 7, paragraph 2(f), enforced sterilization, or any other form of sexual violence also constituting a grave breach of the Geneva Conventions;

and a substantially similar provision is adopted for non-international conflicts (Art. 8(2)(e)(vi)) (substituting the term "serious violation of article 3 common to the four Geneva Conventions" in place of "grave breach of the Geneva Conventions").

Notes

1. For convictions in respect of crimes of sexual violence, see, e.g., Prosecutor v. Akayesu, Case. No. ICTR–96–4–T (Judgment, Sept. 2, 1998); Prosecutor v. Delalic, et al. (*Celebici* case), Case No. IT–96–21–T (Judgment, Nov. 16, 1998, affirmed on appeal, Feb. 2001); Prosecutor v. Furundzija, Case No. IT–95–17/1–A, Judgment on Appeal from Conviction (July 21, 2000); Prosecutor v. Kunarac (*Foca* case), Case No. IT–96–23–T, Judgment, Feb. 22, 2001. For commentary, see, e.g., Kelly Dawn Askin, War Crimes Against Women, Prosecution in International War Crimes Tribunals (1997); Askin, Sexual Violence in Decisions and Indictments of the Yugoslav and Rwandan Tribunals: Current Status, 93 A.J.I.L. 53 (1999).

The practical problems of prosecuting these crimes have been enormous, entailing not only all the obstacles familiar in domestic contexts (traumatized victims who may be reluctant to testify, defendants' efforts to put the victim's sexual history in issue or to insist that the victim's lack of consent must be affirmatively proved, and so on), but also the additional problems of securing evidence at great distance from the forum in the context of what may still be ongoing violence.

2. On the plight of the Korean comfort women, see Boling, Mass Rape, Enforced Prostitution, and the Japanese Imperial Army: Japan Eschews International Legal Responsibility?, 32 Colum. J. Transnat. L. 533 (1995). In December

2000, a nonofficial trial was held to focus attention on the continuing wrong of failure to acknowledge and make redress for their grievance. For discussion, see Chinkin, The Prosecutor and People of the Asian Pacific Region v. Emperor Hirohito and the Government of Japan, forthcoming in 95 A.J.I.L. (2001).

CHILDREN IN WAR

The Convention on the Rights of the Child, 1577 U.N.T.S. 3, deals in Article 38 with international humanitarian law as relevant to children and provides (Art. 38, paras. 2 and 3) for restrictions on participation in hostilities by, and recruitment into armed forces of, children who have not attained the age of 15 years. The 1998 Rome Statute of the International Criminal Court includes in the enumeration of war crimes "[c]onscripting or enlisting children under the age of fifteen years into the national armed forces or using them to participate activiely in hostilities." Art. 8(2)(b)(xxvi); the provision applicable to non-international armed conflicts, Art. 8(2)(e)(vii), is substantially similar, with application to "armed forces or groups" in lieu of "national armed forces." See also S.C. Res. 1261 (Aug. 25, 1999); Convention Concerning the Prohibition and Immediate Action for the Elimination of the Worst Forms of Child Labour, June 17, 1999, 38 I.L.M. 1207 (1999) (prohibiting compulsory recruitment of children in armed conflicts).

In May 2000, an Optional Protocol to the Convention on the Rights of the Child on the Involvement of Children in Armed Conflict was recommended by the U.N. Economic and Social Council, with the objective of raising the minimum age for children's participation from 15 to 18 years. U.N. Doc. A/54/L.84, 39 I.L.M. 1285 (2000). The Optional Protocol would enjoin states parties to take all feasible measures to ensure that those under age 18 do not take direct part in hostilities, and to ensure that they are not compulsorily recruited into a state's armed forces. States parties would also be expected to raise the minimum age for voluntary recruitment, by means of a binding declaration setting forth a minimum age.

3. The Law of War and Environmental Protection

PROTOCOL ADDITIONAL TO THE GENEVA CONVENTIONS RELATING TO THE PROTECTION OF VICTIMS OF INTERNATIONAL ARMED CONFLICT, DEC. 12, 1977 (PROTOCOL I)

1125 U.N.T.S. 3

ARTICLE 35—BASIC RULES

* * *

3. It is prohibited to employ methods or means of warfare which are intended, or may be expected, to cause widespread, long-term and severe damage to the natural environment.

* * *

ARTICLE 55—PROTECTION OF THE NATURAL ENVIRONMENT

1. Care shall be taken in warfare to protect the natural environment against widespread, long-term and severe damage. This protection includes a prohibition of the use of methods or means of warfare which are intended or may be expected to cause such damage to the natural environment and thereby to prejudice the health and survival of the population.

1977 CONVENTION ON THE PROHIBITION OF MILITARY OR ANY OTHER HOSTILE USE OF ENVIRONMENTAL MODIFICATION TECHNIQUES (ENMOD CONVENTION)

31 U.S.T. 333, T.I.A.S. No. 9614, 1108 U.N.T.S. 151.

ARTICLE I

1. Each State Party to this Convention undertakes not to engage in military or any other hostile use of environmental modification techniques having widespread, long-lasting or severe effects as the means of destruction, damage or injury to any other State Party.

2. Each State Party to this Convention undertakes not to assist, encourage or induce any State, group of States or international organization to engage in activities contrary to the provisions of paragraph 1 of this article.

ARTICLE II

As used in article I, the term 'environmental modification techniques' refers to any technique for changing—through the deliberate manipulation of natural processes—the dynamics, composition or structure of the Earth, including its biota, lithosphere, hydrosphere and atmosphere, or of outer space.

Notes

1. The United States has taken the position that Article 35(3) of Additional Protocol I (1977) "is too broad and ambiguous and is not a part of customary law." See Matheson, The United States Position on the Relation of Customary Law to the 1977 Protocols Additional to the 1949 Geneva Conventions, 2 Am. U.J.Int'l L. & Pol'y 419, 420–21 (1987).

In the Advisory Opinion on Nuclear Weapons, 1996 I.C.J. 226, at paras. 27–33, the International Court of Justice discussed Articles 35(3) and 55 of Protocol I, as well as other environmental treaties. The Court considered that these treaties could not have been intended to deprive states of their rights of self-defense, but that respect for the environment is "one of the elements that go to assessing whether an action is in conformity with the principles of necessity and proportionality." Para. 30. As for whether these obligations are embodied in customary law, the Court referred to Articles 35(3) and 55 of Protocol I as "powerful constraints for all the States having subscribed to these provisions" (para. 31), thereby apparently treating them only as treaty commitments rather than as obligations under customary international law.

2. The Conference of the Committee on Disarmament, which was the drafting body of the ENMOD Convention, appended four nonbinding "Under-

standings" in explanation of portions of the Convention. The understandings with regard to Articles I and II provide:

Understanding relating to Article 1

It is the understanding of the Committee that, for the purposes of this Convention, the terms "widespread", "long-lasting" and "severe" shall be interpreted as follows:

(a) "widespread": encompassing an area on the scale of several hundred square kilometres;

(b) "long-lasting": lasting for a period of months, or approximately a season;

(c) "severe": involving serious or significant disruption or harm to human life, natural and economic resources or other assets.

It is further understood that the interpretation set forth above is intended exclusively for this Convention and is not intended to prejudice the interpretation of the same or similar terms if used in connexion with any other international agreement.

Understanding relating to Article II

It is the understanding of the Committee that the following examples are illustrative of phenomena that could be caused by the use of environmental modification techniques as defined in Article II of the Convention: earthquakes; tsunamis; an upset in the ecological balance of a region; changes in weather patterns (clouds, precipitation, cyclones of various types and tornadic storms); changes in climate patterns; changes in ocean currents; changes in the state of the ozone layer; and changes in the state of the ionosphere.

It is further understood that all the phenomena listed above, when produced by military or any other hostile use of environmental modification techniques, would result, or could reasonably be expected to result, in widespread, long-lasting or severe destruction, damage or injury. Thus, military or any other hostile use of environmental modification techniques as defined in Article II, so as to cause those phenomena as a means of destruction, damage or injury to another State Party, would be prohibited.

It is recognized, moreover, that the list of examples set out above is not exhaustive. Other phenomena which could result from the use of environmental modification techniques as defined in Article II could also be appropriately included. The absence of such phenomena from the list does not in any way imply that the undertaking contained in Article I would not be applicable to those phenomena, provided the criteria set out in that Article were met.

As of 2000, the ENMOD Convention had been ratified by more than 65 states, including the United States, Great Britain and the former U.S.S.R.

3. During the 1991 Gulf War Iraqi forces reportedly opened valves at the Mina al-Ahamadi and Mina al-Gakr oil terminals and pumped large quantities of crude oil into the Persian Gulf. Toward the end of the conflict Iraq set massive fires in Kuwaiti oil fields. After the cease-fire, the Security Council adopted a resolution that declared Iraq was "liable under international law for any direct loss, damage, including environmental damage and the depletion of natural resources, or injury * * * as a result of Iraq's unlawful invasion and occupation of Kuwait." S.C.Res. 687, at ¶ 16, reprinted in 30 I.L.M. 846 (1991). Would Protocol I or the ENMOD Convention apply to Iraq's actions in the Gulf war? Professor Oxman writes:

The hard questions in considering environmental limitations on the conduct of armed conflict did not arise in Iraq's case. The fact that Iraq was an occupying power in Kuwait placed it under special obligations with respect to property located there. To most observers, both the oil spill and fires would represent precisely the kind of vindictive and wanton destruction that has long been excluded by the laws of war. This basic principle is manifested in many specific rules, such as the prohibition on pillage. Even if one could imagine some military advantages from the smoke and the oil slicks in impeding the adversary, the magnitude of the destruction done by the oil spill and the fires is wholly out of proportion to such military objectives. It violates one of the most fundamental principles of the law of armed conflict, namely the prohibition on damage that is excessive in relation to the military objectives involved.

As the Iraqi case demonstrates, many of the rules governing armed conflict that are designed to protect civilian lives, health, and property also have the collateral effect of protecting the environment. Moreover, increased knowledge of the environmental consequences of particular types of events affects the application of those rules, often broadening their restraining effect. To put it differently, military planners need to consider the effects of their actions on the environment if only because failure to do so may result in unlawful injury to civilians or non-military objects.

* * *

Both environmentalists and members of the armed forces would be justified in asking if myriad questions regarding the legality of virtually all modern methods or means of warfare should be resolved on the basis of the words *may be expected* and the words *widespread, long-term and severe.* Given the following "legislative history" in the official report on this ambiguous text, one wonders what the fuss is about anyway: "It appeared to be a widely shared assumption that battlefield damage incidental to conventional warfare would not normally be proscribed by this provision." *Long-term* was regarded as being "measured in decades," perhaps "twenty or thirty years * * * being a minimum."

Precisely because armed conflict is always bad for the environment, it would seem that any text attempting to deal with the problem of environmental restraints in a simple and sweeping fashion either would admonish us to think about and try to balance the competing values at stake, at best, or would descend into meaningless or hyperbole (undone by deft interpretations), at worst.

It makes more sense to assume the applicability of the general restraints of the laws of war, such as the principle of proportionality, and ask whether there are specific situations, not covered by rules restraining injuries to civilians and property, that require more detailed regulation. The Environmental Modification Convention, to which the United States is party, is an example of such an approach. That convention is regularly reviewed. If appropriate, such a review could become the occasion for discussion of these issues.

Specific rules regarding not only dams, dikes, and nuclear electric generating stations, but regarding the remnants of war, are set forth in Protocol I. Perhaps there is a need for other specific rules. Protocol I itself indicates that there may be other types of installations containing dangerous forces where attack should be closely regulated. Indeed, some installations may be dangerous precisely because they contain biological or chemical weapons, creating a direct collision between environmental and health concerns on the one hand and the traditional distinction between military and civilian targets on the other. Resolution of this conflict requires a risk/benefit analysis implied in the principle of proportionality. Whatever the command structure, one trusts that both operational and supervisory military and civilian officials participate in decisions involving potentially catastrophic targeting.

It is not easy to decide whether new rules are needed or desirable, not to mention negotiable in a helpful form. In this field, perhaps more so than in other fields of law, one must consider perverse effects. The practical impact of a particular protective legal rule may be to increase the likelihood of damage to an installation or site that would not otherwise have been a profitable object of attack.

Oxman, Environmental Warfare, 22 Ocean Dev. & Int'l L. 433, 433–436 (1991) (footnotes omitted).

On the environmental implications of the Gulf War, see Arkin, Durrant & Cherni, On Impact: Modern Warfare and the Environment—A Case Study of the Gulf War (1991); The Gulf War: Environment as a Weapon, 85 A.S.I.L.Proc. 214 (1991); Okorodudu–Fabara, Oil in the Persian Gulf War: Legal Appraisal of an Environmental Warfare, 23 St. Mary's L.J. 123 (1991); Robinson, International Law and the Destruction of Nature in the Gulf War, 21 Env'l Pol'y & L. 216 (1991); Szasz, Environmental Destruction as a Method of Warfare: International Law Applicable to the Gulf War, 15 Disarmament 128 (1992).

4. On the implications of the laws of war for the environment generally, see Environmental Protection and the Law of War: A Fifth Geneva Convention on the Protection of Environment in Time of Armed Conflict (Plant, ed.1992); Westing, Environmental Hazards of War: Releasing Dangerous Forces in an Industrialized World (1990); Almond, The Use of the Environment as an Instrument of War, 2 Y.B.Int'l Env'l L. 455 (1991); Blix, Arms Control Treaties Aimed at Reducing the Military Impact on the Environment, in Essays in International Law in Honour of Judge Manfred Lachs 704 (1984); Bothe, The Protection of the Environment in Times of Armed Conflict, 34 Germ. Y.B.Int'l L. 54 (1991); Drucker, The Military Commander's Responsibility for the Environment, 11 Env'l Ethics 135 (1989); Goldblat, Legal Protection of the Environment Against the Effects of Military Activities, 22 Bull. Peace Proposals 399 (1991); Singh, The Environmental Law of War and the Future of Mankind, in The Future of the International Law of the Environment 419 (Dupuy, ed.1985); Drumbl, Waging War Against the World: The Need to Move from War Crimes to Environmental Crimes, 22 Fordham Int'l L.J. 122 (1998).

5. Article 8(2)(b)(iv) of the Rome Statute for an International Criminal Court provides for the war crime of "intentionally launching an attack in the knowledge that such attack will cause * * * widespread, long-term and severe damage to the natural environment which would be clearly excessive in relation to the concrete and direct overall military advantage anticipated." The terms "widespread," "long-term," and "severe" correspond to terms in Protocol I and the ENMOD Convention, and the interpretations and understandings of those instruments may be relevant to the Rome Statute. Notably, however, the definition in the Rome Statute is conjunctive rather than disjunctive ("and" rather than "or"), so that each of the three requirements would presumably have to be established for purposes of individual criminal liability; and a high threshold for the individu-

al's state of mind ("intentionally * * * in the knowledge * * * ") would further limit the circumstances in which this provision could be applied. Compare the Elements of Crimes adopted by the I.C.C. Preparatory Committee in summer 2000. U.N. Doc. PCNICC/2000/INF/3/Add. 1.

6. In 1999, the Prosecutor of the International Criminal Tribunal for the Former Yugoslavia was asked by several states and non-governmental organizations to investigate whether the NATO intervention in Kosovo had caused environmental damage constituting a war crime. Allegations of environmental injury included the use by NATO of depleted uranium munitions which were said to have long-lasting detrimental effects. The Prosecutor's office concluded that there was no basis for opening an investigation into these allegations. The final report on this question took note of different standards for evaluating possible state breaches of customary international law on the one hand, and establishment of individual criminal responsibility for acts falling within the Tribunal's jurisdiction on the other hand. The report also observed that the International Court of Justice in the Advisory Opinion on Nuclear Weapons, 1996 I.C.J. 226 at para. 31, appeared to suggest that Article 35 of Protocol I (quoted above) may not represent customary international law. (Compare note 1 above.) See ICTY: Final Report to the Prosecutor by the Committee Established to Review the NATO Bombing Campaign Against the Federal Republic of Yugoslavia, 39 I.L.M. 1257, 1261–1264 (2000).

B. ARMS CONTROL AND DISARMAMENT

After the First World War, disarmament was high on the international agenda . The victorious nations imposed limitations on German rearmament and sought also to regulate their own armaments. The emphasis was on the weapons of the previous war. For example, revulsion at the use of mustard gas led to the Protocol for the Prohibition of the Use in War of Asphyxiating, Poisonous or Other Gases and of Bacteriological Methods of Warfare, June 17, 1925, 94 L.N.T.S. 65 (Geneva Gas Protocol). Disarmament conferences at Washington and London reached agreements establishing ratios on battleships for the major powers. See Washington Treaty for the Limitation of Naval Armament (1922), 43 Stat. 1655, T.S. No. 671, 25 L.N.T.S. 201; Treaty for the Limitation and Reduction of Naval Armaments (London Naval Treaty of 1930), April 22, 1930, 46 Stat. 2858, T.S. No. 830, 112 L.N.T.S. 65.

The emergence of nuclear weapons at the end of the Second World War gave urgency to the quest for means of eliminating or controlling them, along with other weapons of mass destruction. Arms control negotiations have never been long in abeyance, and a number of agreements to limit or regulate nuclear and other weaponry are in force. Many of these are multilateral treaties concluded within the framework of the United Nations, including:

— Antarctic Treaty, 12 U.S.T. 794, TIAS 4780, 402 UNTS 71

(Signed: 1 December 1959; entered into force: 23 June 1961.)

— Treaty banning nuclear weapon tests in the atmosphere, in outer space and under water (Limited Test Ban Treaty), 14 U.S.T. 1313, TIAS 5433, 480 UNTS 43

(Signed: 5 August 1963; entered into force: 10 October 1963.)

— Treaty on principles governing the activities of states in the exploration and use of outer space, including the moon and other celestial bodies (Outer Space Treaty), 18 U.S.T. 2410, TIAS 6347, 610 UNTS 205

(Signed: 27 January 1967; entered into force: 10 October 1967.)

— Treaty for the prohibition of nuclear weapons in Latin America (Treaty of Tlatelolco) and additional protocols, 22 U.S.T. 754, TIAS 7137, 634 UNTS 364; 33 U.S.T. 1792, TIAS 10147, 634 UNTS 362

(Signed: 14 February 1967; entered into force: 22 April 1968.)

— Treaty on the non-proliferation of nuclear weapons (Non–Proliferation Treaty), 21 U.S.T. 483, TIAS 6839, 729 UNTS 161

(Signed: 1 July 1968; entered into force: 5 March 1970.)

— Treaty on the prohibition of the emplacement of nuclear weapons and other weapons of mass destruction on the sea-bed and the ocean floor and in the subsoil thereof (Sea–Bed Treaty), 23 U.S.T. 701, TIAS 7337, 955 UNTS 115

(Signed: 11 February 1971; entered into force: 18 May 1972.)

— Convention on the prohibition of the development, production and stockpiling of bacteriological (biological) and toxin weapons and on their destruction (Biological Weapons Convention), 26 U.S.T. 583, TIAS 8062, 1015 UNTS 163

(Signed: 10 April 1972; entered into force: 26 March 1975.)

— Convention on the prohibition of military or any other hostile use of environmental modification techniques (ENMOD Convention), 31 U.S.T. 333, TIAS 9614, 1108 U.N.T.S. 151

(Signed: 18 May 1977; entered into force: 5 October 1978.)

— Convention on the prohibition of the development, production, stockpiling and use of chemical weapons and on their destruction (Chemical Weapons Convention), 32 I.L.M. 800 (1993)

(Signed: 13 January 1993; entered into force: 29 April 1997.)

— Comprehensive Nuclear Test Ban Treaty, U.N. Doc. A/50/1027, Annex, 35 I.L.M. 1439 (1996)

(Signed: 24 September, 1996; not in force as of 2000.)

— Convention on the prohibition of the use, stockpiling, production and transfer of anti-personnel mines and on their destruction (Landmine Treaty)

(Signed: 3 December 1997; entered into force: 1 March 1999.)

Other arms control agreements were, at least in the first instance, bilateral agreements between the United States and the Soviet Union (or, more generally, between Western allies on the one hand and Soviet bloc states on the other). These include:

— Agreement on measures to reduce the risk of outbreak of nuclear war between the U.S. and the USSR (U.S.–Soviet Nuclear Accidents Agreements), 22 U.S.T. 1590, TIAS 7186, 807 UNTS 57

(Signed: 30 September 1971; entered into force: 30 September 1971.)

— US–Soviet interim agreement on certain measures with respect to the limitation of strategic offensive arms (SALT I Interim Agreement), 23 U.S.T. 3462

(Signed: 26 May 1972; entered into force: 3 October 1972; no longer in force.)

— U.S.–Soviet treaty on the limitation of anti-ballistic missile systems (ABM Treaty), 23 U.S.T. 3435, TIAS 7503, 944 UNTS 13

(Signed: 26 May 1972; entered into force: 3 October 1972; Protocol signed 3 July 1974; entered into force: 25 May 1976.)

— U.S.–Soviet agreement on the prevention of nuclear war, 24 U.S.T. 1478, TIAS 7654

(Signed: 22 June 1973; entered into force: 22 June 1973.)

— U.S.–Soviet treaty on the limitation of underground nuclear weapons tests (Threshold Test Ban Treaty)

(Signed: 3 July 1974; entered into force: 11 December 1990.)

— U.S.–Soviet treaty on underground nuclear explosions for peaceful purposes (Peaceful Nuclear Explosions Treaty)

(Signed: 28 May 1976; protocol signed: 1 June 1990; both entered into force 11 December 1990.)

— Document on confidence-building measures and certain aspects of security and disarmament, included in the Final Act of the Conference on Security and Co-operation in Europe

(Signed: August 1975.)

— French–Soviet agreement on the prevention of the accidental or unauthorized use of nuclear weapons (French–Soviet Nuclear Accidents Agreement)

(Concluded through an exchange of letters on 16 July 1976 between the foreign ministers of France and the USSR; entered into force: 16 July 1976.)

— British–Soviet agreement on the prevention of an accidental outbreak of nuclear war (British–Soviet Nuclear Accidents Agreement)

(Signed: 10 October 1977; entered into force: 10 October 1977.)

— U.S.–Soviet strategic arms limitation treaty (SALT II)

(Signed: June 1979; never entered into force.)

— U.S.–Soviet treaty on the elimination of intermediate-range and shorter-range nuclear forces (Intermediate Nuclear Forces ("INF") Treaty), 27 I.L.M. 85 (1988), and related multilateral agreement regarding inspections, 27 I.L.M. 58 (1988)

(Signed: 8 and 11 December 1987; both entered into force: 1 June 1988.)

— U.S.–Soviet agreement on the destruction and non-proliferation of chemical weapons and on measures to facilitate the multilateral convention banning chemical weapons, 29 I.L.M. 932 (1990)

(Signed: 1 June 1990.)

— Treaty on conventional armed forces in Europe ("CFE"Treaty) (originally negotiated between members of NATO and the Warsaw Pact), 30 I.L.M. 1 (1991)

(Signed: 19 November 1990; entered into force: 9 November 1992.)

— U.S.–Soviet treaty on the reduction and limitation of strategic offensive arms (START Treaty), S. Treaty Doc. No. 102–20 (1991)

(Signed: 31 July 1991; see also multilateral protocol and related letters of 23 May 1992; both entered into force: 5 December 1994.)

— U.S.–Russian treaty on further reduction and limitation of strategic offensive arms (START II), S. Treaty Doc. No. 103–1 (1993)

(Signed: 3 January 1993; not in force as of 2000.)

— Document agreed among the States Parties to the Treaty on Conventional Armed Forces in Europe ("CFE Flank Agreement"), 36 I.L.M. 866 (1997); see also Senate resolution with conditions at 36 I.L.M. 980 (1997)

(Signed: 31 May 1996; entered into force: 15 May 1997)

— U.S.–Russian treaty on theater missile defense ("TMD")

(Signed: 1997; not in force as of 2000.)

REGULATION OF CHEMICAL AND BIOLOGICAL WEAPONS

The ban on poisonous weapons embodied in the 1925 Geneva Gas Protocol (p. 1077) was generally observed during World War II. Prohibitions were extended to biological weapons in the Convention on the Prohibition of the Development, Production and Stockpiling of Bacteriological (Biological) and Toxin Weapons and on Their Destruction, 26 U.S.T. 583, TIAS 8062 1015 U.N.T.S. 163, which was signed at Washington, London, and Moscow April 10, 1972 and entered into force in 1975.

In the 1980s and 1990s, however, disturbing evidence mounted of chemical weapons use during the Iran–Iraq War, both on a cross-boundary basis and by Iraq against its own Kurdish population. See reports of experts appointed by the U.N. Secretary–General, U.N. Docs. S/16433, S/17127, S/17130; U.N. Chronicle, at 3 (March 1984); id., at 24 (March 1985); McCormack, International Law and the Use of Chemical Weapons in the Gulf War, 21 Cal. W. Int'l L.J. 1 (1990–1991); Human Rights Watch, Iraq's Crime of Genocide: The Anfal Campaign Against the Kurds 262–265 and Appendix C (1995) (documenting chemical attacks against at least 60 Kurdish villages and the town of Halabja). By the 1990s (in the wake of further disclosures concerning Iraq's non-compliance with international obligations concerning weapons of mass destruction), the need for a stricter international regime with verification and sanctions had become clear.

On January 13, 1993, a new Convention on the Prohibition of the Development, Production, Stockpiling and Use of Chemical Weapons and on Their Destruction (Chemical Weapons Convention), 32 I.L.M. 800 (1993), was opened for signature and promptly signed by more than 120 states. It quickly garnered the ratifications necessary to bring it into force in April 1997. As of 2000, it has more than 140 states parties, including the United States. Several

Middle Eastern states have not signed, including Iraq, which as of 2000 remains under stringent international sanctions for its failure to comply with disarmament requirements imposed at the end of the 1991 Gulf War, including verification of destruction of chemical weapons.

Under the terms of the Chemical Weapons Convention, states parties are prohibited from using, producing or stockpiling poison gas or lethal chemical weapons, and are obliged to dispose of existing chemical weapons by the year 2010 at the latest. The treaty creates rigorous verification procedures implemented through a new Organization for the Prohibition of Chemical Weapons which has been established at The Hague and functioning since 1997. The implementation mechanisms include routine inspections at facilities that are declared to possess or use chemicals that may be precursors to weapons agents, and "challenge inspections" to guard against cheating.

Notes

1. Some concerns were expressed in the United States, prior to the Senate's advice and consent to ratification given in April 1997, that the inspection regime under the Chemical Weapons Convention (especially the system for challenge inspections) might pose constitutional problems, e.g. in light of the Fourth Amendment's requirements for searches and seizures or Fifth Amendment protections of private property. Another objection, based on a view of the original understanding of the Constitution's structural provisions, was that the treaty power should not be used to transfer enforcement powers to an international organization whose officials would not be accountable through constitutional processes. See Rotunda, The Chemical Warfare Convention: Political and Constitutional Issues, 15 Const. Commentary 131 (1998); Yoo, The New Sovereignty and the Old Constitution: The Chemical Weapons Convention and the Appointments Clause, 15 Const. Commentary 87 (1998). The Senate approved the treaty on the basis that there were no insuperable constitutional obstacles.

2. Does the widespread ratification of the Chemical Weapons Convention (see party list in Documents Supplement) indicate emergence of a customary norm coextensive with the normative provisions of the treaty? Is a non-party to the treaty (like Iraq) bound by such a norm? To what extent could implementation provisions be mobilized to press a non-party to comply with the normative provisions? On the treaty system in general, see Bothe, Ronzitti & Rosas (eds.), The New Chemical Weapons Convention: Implementation and Prospects (1998).

3. Could retaliation for chemical weapons use in kind, or with other weapons of mass destruction, ever be permissible? Compare Judge Schwebel's dissent in the Advisory Opinion on Legality of Use of Nuclear Weapons, p. 972. See also Müllerson, Missiles with Non–Conventional Warheads and International Law, 27 Israel Y.B.Human Rights 225, 226 n. 3 (1998). Compare Vienna Convention on the Law of Treaties, Art. 60(5), discussed at p. 547; and U.S. concerns about the prohibition on belligerent reprisals in Geneva Protocol I, p. 1063 note 7 supra.

4. The Missile Technology Control Regime, 26 I.L.M. 599 (1987), discussed in Müllerson, Missiles with Non–Conventional Warheads and International Law, 27 Israel Y.B. Human Rights 225, 243–249 (1998), now covers not only nuclear weapons delivery systems but also chemical and biological weapons delivery systems, and any surface-to-surface missile with a range over 150 km. See also Angelova, Note, Compelling Compliance with International Regimes: China and the Missile Technology Control Regime, 38 Colum. J. Transnat. L. 419 (1999).

NUCLEAR WEAPONS: POSSESSION, TESTING, USE

In 1961, the U.N. General Assembly passed a resolution declaring that the use of nuclear weapons is a violation of the U.N. Charter and of international law. Declaration on the Prohibition of the Use of Nuclear and Thermonuclear Weapons, G.A. Res. 1653 (XVI) (1961). The resolution was adopted by a vote of 55 to 20, with 26 abstentions. The United States, United Kingdom, France, Australia, Canada, China, and Italy were among the states voting no. The United States has strongly and repeatedly reiterated its view that the resolution does not reflect the state of international law.

The main Cold War antagonists, while avowing their own restraint, each recognized the possibility of use of nuclear weapons. The major powers insisted that they had to develop and retain nuclear weapons as a deterrent to the use of such weapons by other states, and to aggression with conventional weapons. Even some who insisted that the use of nuclear weapons was illegal or immoral conceded that it is not unlawful or immoral to keep them as a deterrent. Compare National Conference of Catholic Bishops, Pastoral Letter on War and Peace–Challenge of Peace: God's Promise and Our Response, reprinted in Castelli, The Bishops and the Bomb 274 (1983).

The major powers also recognized a shared interest in preventing the spread of nuclear weapons capability to other states. A significant milestone in this regard has been the Nuclear Non–Proliferation Treaty ("N.P.T."), 21 U.S.T. 483, TIAS 6839, 729 U.N.T.S. 161, which was signed in 1968 and entered into force in 1970. Under the N.P.T., the nuclear-weapon state parties undertake not to transfer to any recipient any nuclear weapons or or nuclear explosive devices or assist any non-nuclear-weapon state in acquiring them; and the non-nuclear-weapon states undertake not to acquire such weapons or devices. A safeguards system is established under the auspices of the International Atomic Energy Agency (I.A.E.A.) to verify that fissionable material is not diverted from peaceful uses to nuclear weapons or explosive devices. At the time, the nuclear-weapon states were the five declared nuclear powers: the United States, the Soviet Union, the United Kingdom, France, and China. A few threshold-nuclear states (notably India, Pakistan, and Israel) remained outside the N.P.T. framework. Others–Iraq and North Korea–undertook N.P.T. obligations, including I.A.E.A. safeguards, but came under strong suspicion of violating those undertakings. See pp. 539, 1022.

The initial duration of the N.P.T. was 25 years from entry into force. At a review conference held in May 1995, an indefinite extension was agreed.

Notes

1. The fragmentation of the Soviet Union into 15 independent republics has raised issues regarding succession to arms control treaties binding on the former Soviet Union. Bunn and Rhinelander discuss the application of a "continuity" theory of succession to the Soviet Union's arms control obligations, as contrasted to the "clean slate" rule frequently applied in decolonization situations (see Chapter 7, p. 577):

> * * * Application of the continuity rule would not make each former republic a nuclear-weapon state party to the NPT [Non–Proliferation Treaty]

just because the Soviet Union was such a party and the treaty applied throughout Soviet territory. Such a result would mean each could control nuclear weapons, which would be wholly inconsistent with the purpose of the treaty. The NPT was intended to hold the line at the number of nuclear-weapon states that had "manufactured and exploded a nuclear weapon or other nuclear explosive device prior to January 1, 1967." That was five: Britain, China and France as well as the Soviet Union and the United States.

The 1978 Vienna Convention [on Succession of States in respect of Treaties] contains an exception to the continuity rule if "it appears from the treaty or is otherwise established that the application of the treaty in respect of the successor State would be incompatible with the object and purpose of the treaty * * * ." Clearly, this exception is applicable to succession to the NPT by republics other than Russia. That means they are non-nuclear-weapon states under the NPT, and must join it in that capacity if they wish to become members.

What has happened in the former republics so far is consistent with this view. Tactical nuclear weapons from all the republics that had them other than Russia have been moved to Russia, except for some remaining in Belarus and Ukraine, and removal of these is promised before July 1, 1992. Strategic nuclear weapons exist only in Belarus, Kazakhstan and Ukraine besides Russia, and removal of the last of these from Kazakhstan is promised by 1999. Both Belarus and Ukraine have promised to join the NPT as non-nuclear-weapon states and to become nuclear-free zones. While Kazakhstan's position is more ambiguous, U.S. representatives are negotiating with it as well as with Belarus, Russia and Ukraine about further removal of nuclear weapons.

Bunn & Rhinelander, Who Inherited the Former Soviet Union's Obligations Under Arms Control Treaties with the United States? Memorandum to the Committee on Foreign Relations (10 March 1992). See also State Succession and Relations with Federal States, 86 A.S.I.L.Proc. 1, 6–10 (1992); and references in Chapter 7, p. 584.

On September 26, 1997, the U.S. Department of State issued a statement on a Memorandum of Understanding on Succession with respect to the Anti–Ballistic Missile Treaty:

[The ABM Treaty] was a bilateral agreement between [the U.S. and the USSR]. When the USSR dissolved at the end of 1991, and its constitutent republics became independent States, the only operationally-deployed ABM system was at Moscow, while a number of its early warning radars and an ABM test range were located outside of the Russian Federation. Although the ABM Treaty continues in force, it nevertheless has become necessary to reach agreement as to which New Independent States (NIS) would collectively assume the rights and obligations of the USSR under the Treaty.

The Memorandum of Understanding on Succession (MOUS) establishes that the Parties to the ABM Treaty shall be the United States, Belarus, Kazakhstan, the Russian Federation, and Ukraine. For the purposes of the MOUS and the ABM Treaty, the latter four states are considered to be the USSR Successor States. Pursuant to the MOUS provisions, the USSR Successor States collectively assume the rights and obligations of the USSR. * * *

It has been suggested in the U.S. Senate, however, that the ABM Treaty may not have survived dissolution of the USSR, and that new Senatorial advice and consent would be required in order to add new parties. See Murphy, Contemporary Practice of the United States Relating to International Law, 93 A.J.I.L. 910–912 (1999).

2. In an action against the Japanese government, Japanese citizens argued that the Japanese government had unlawfully waived their claims for damages resulting from the atomic bombs dropped at Hiroshima and Nagasaki by the United States in 1945. The court stated:

> [T]here is not an established theory among international jurists in connection with the difference of poison, poison gas, bacterium, etc. from atomic bombs. However, judging from the fact that the St. Petersburg Declaration declares that "* * * considering that the use of a weapon which increases uselessly the pain of people who are already placed out of battle and causes their death necessarily is beyond the scope of this purpose, and considering that the use of such a weapon is thus contrary to humanity * * *" and that article 23(e) of the Hague Regulations respecting War on Land prohibits "the employment of such arms, projectiles, and material as cause unnecessary injury," we can safely see that besides poison, poison-gas and bacterium the use of the means of injuring the enemy which causes at least the same or more injury is prohibited by international law. The destructive power of the atomic bomb is tremendous, but it is doubtful whether atomic bombing really had an appropriate military effect at that time and whether it was necessary. It is a deeply sorrowful reality that the atomic bombing on both cities of Hiroshima and Nagasaki took the lives of many civilians, and that among the survivors there are people whose lives are still imperilled owing to the radial rays, even today 18 years later. In this sense, it is not too much to say that the pain brought by the atomic bombs is severer than that from poison and poison-gas, and we can say that the act of dropping such a cruel bomb is contrary to the fundamental principle of the laws of war that unnecessary pain must not be given.

The Shimoda Case, Judgment of the Tokyo District Court, 7 Dec. 1963, reprinted in 8 Japanese Ann. Int'l L. 212, 241–42 (1964). See discussion of the Shimoda Case in the dissenting opinion of Judge Shahabuddeen in the Advisory Opinion on Nuclear Weapons, 1996 I.C.J. 226 at 375, 397.

3. The illegality of nuclear weapons under international law was raised in U.S. courts, without success, as a defense to criminal charges stemming from civil protests against such weapons. See United States v. Kabat, 797 F.2d 580 (8th Cir.1986), cert. denied, 481 U.S. 1030, 107 S.Ct. 1958, 95 L.Ed.2d 530 (1987); United States v. Montgomery, 772 F.2d 733 (11th Cir.1985); United States v. Brodhead, 714 F.Supp. 593 (D.Mass.1989). See also Boyle, Defending Civil Resistance Under International Law (1987); Lippman, Civil Resistance: Revitalizing International Law in the Nuclear Age, 13 Whittier L.Rev. 17 (1992); Citizen Initiatives under International Law, 82 A.S.I.L. Proc. 555 (1988). The illegality of such weapons was also asserted as a ground for challenging production and deployment of nuclear weapons. See United States v. Thompson, 90–10118, disposition (unpublished) tabled at, 931 F.2d 898 (9th Cir.1991); United States v. Allen, 760 F.2d 447 (2d Cir.1985). See also Pauling v. McElroy, 164 F.Supp. 390 (D.D.C.1958), aff'd, 278 F.2d 252 (D.C.Cir.1960), cert. denied, 364 U.S. 835, 81 S.Ct. 61, 5 L.Ed.2d 60 (1960); Greenham Women Against Cruise Missiles v. Reagan, 591 F.Supp. 1332 (S.D.N.Y.1984), aff'd, 755 F.2d 34 (2d Cir.1985).

4. *Limitations on Testing; Comprehensive Test Ban Treaty.* Efforts to control the spread of nuclear weapons have long focused on restricting the conditions for testing such weapons, with a view toward an ultimate ban on all forms of testing. Treaties and other instruments over some four decades established several kinds

of limitations, either on a general multilateral basis with widespread ratification or by special agreement among some or all of the declared nuclear powers. (See the listing of agreements at pp. 1077–1080 for the most significant of these undertakings.) Atmospheric testing was restricted under the Limited (Partial) Test Ban Treaty of 1963 which has been widely ratified (more than 125 adherences as of 2000). France did not become a party, however. As noted in earlier chapters, litigation at the International Court of Justice seeking a determination of unlawfulness of French atmospheric testing was dismissed in 1974, after France unilaterally announced an end to such testing. Nuclear Tests Cases (Australia and New Zealand v. France), 1974 I.C.J. 253, 457. See pp. 458, 865. Certain nuclear-weapons-free zones have also been established under the Treaties of Tlatelolco and Raritonga. See Thakur (ed.), Nuclear Weapons–Free Zones (1998).

On September 24, 1996 a Comprehensive Test Ban Treaty (CTBT) was opened for signature at the United Nations and was promptly signed by more than 135 states, including all five permanent members of the Security Council (who were at that time the only declared nuclear powers). See 35 I.L.M. 1439 (1996) for the list of initial signatories. Significantly, India and Pakistan did not sign; see below. The basic obligation of the CTBT is embodied in Article I, which provides:

> 1. Each State Party undertakes not to carry out any nuclear weapon test explosion or any other nuclear explosion, and to prohibit and prevent any such nuclear explosion at any place under its jurisdiction or control.
>
> 2. Each State Party undertakes, furthermore, to refrain from causing, encouraging, or in any way participating in the carrying out of any nuclear weapon test explosion or any other nuclear explosion.

The CTBT would also create a Comprehensive Nuclear Test–Ban Treaty Organization headquartered in Vienna, which would carry out verification activities under the treaty (Art. II). Verification mechanisms include international monitoring, consultation and clarification, on-site inspections, and confidence-building measures (Art. IV). States parties are also to implement the treaty through national measures, including adoption of prohibitions on nuclear testing anywhere on its territory or in any other place under its jurisdiction or control, or by any of its nationals (Art. III).

In signing the treaty on behalf of the United States, President Clinton declared that the signatures of the five declared nuclear powers and of the vast majority of other countries "will immediately create an international norm against nuclear testing even before the treaty formally enters into force." New York Times, Sept. 25, 1996, pp. A1, A6. He might have been referring to the potential impact of a multilateral normative treaty on international customary law (pp. 86, 115–117 supra), or to the obligation expressed in Article 18 of the Vienna Convention on the Law of Treaties for signatories to a treaty to refrain from undercutting its object and purpose prior to entry into force (pp. 475–477 supra). By its terms (Art. XIV), the CTBT can only enter into force after all states listed in its Annex 2 have ratified. That annex enumerates 44 states whose ratifications are required: they include all states with nuclear reactors. As of 2000, only 30 of those 44 states had ratified, out of about 70 states that had ratified in all (and about 160 that had signed). The United States, China and Israel had signed but not ratified; and India, Pakistan, and North Korea had neither signed nor ratified.

In October 1999, the U.S. Senate cast a negative vote (48–51) on a resolution to give advice and consent to ratification of the CTBT. The main objections expressed by opponents of the treaty included concerns about its verifiability and about whether a total test ban could impair the integrity of the U.S. nuclear deterrent. President Clinton insisted that the defeat in the Senate was only a temporary setback and that the treaty could be brought forward again at a more auspicious time. See Contemporary Practice of the United States Relating to International Law: Senate Rejection of the Comprehensive Test Ban Treaty, 94 A.J.I.L. 137–139 (2000).

Meanwhile, in spring 1998, first India and then Pakistan exploded nuclear weapons devices, thereby becoming the first states to do so since the CTBT had been opened for signature. They are also the first states—apart from the five permanent members of the Security Council–to have demonstrated overt nuclear weapons capability. On the motivations for the Indian and Pakistani tests in relation to the CTBT, see Thakur, Envisioning Nuclear Futures, 31 Security Dialogue 25 (2000).

C. THE LAWS OF WAR IN THE INTERNET ERA

It is an open question how the laws of war will apply to techniques of warfare in the age of cyberspace and "virtual war". The recent "revolution in military affairs" has produced a wide range of new technologies which could either exacerbate or alleviate the destructiveness of war. Potentially, more precise weapons could make it possible to discriminate more carefully between military and civilian objects, so that collateral damage to civilians might be minimized. "Non-lethal" military technologies–e.g, slippery foam to impede traffic, microwaves to disable electronic devices, pungent gases to disperse crowds–can assist combatants to direct their lethal fire against military forces and other military objectives, while avoiding civilian casualties. The legal issues surrounding such technologies are just beginning to be explored. See generally Council on Foreign Relations, Non–Lethal Technologies: Military Options and Implications xi, 11–13 (1995), and Nonlethal Technologies: Progress and Prospects 35 (1999) (noting possible concerns under treaties such as the Chemical Weapons Convention about certain non-lethal weapons). The possibilities for conducting remote warfare by computer, or using computer technologies to disable enemy capabilities while protecting one's own systems and infrastructure from comparable attacks, have opened up new avenues for legal inquiry.

The term "information warfare" (or "information operations") has come into use with respect to military techniques that target the opponent's information systems and infrastructure, including communications, weapons systems, command and control systems, intelligence systems, and civil infrastructure such as power grids and banking, as well as comparable defensive techniques. It has been suggested that some "information operations"–physical attacks on information systems, psychological operations, and jamming of radar and radio signals–are by now "traditional," and the application to them of the international laws of war is "reasonably well settled." See U.S. Department of Defense, Office of General Counsel, An Assessment of International Legal Issues in Information Operations 4 (1999). On the other hand, "[i]t will not be as easy to apply existing international law principles to *information attack*, a term used to describe the use of electronic means to gain access to or change information in a targeted information system without necessarily damaging its physical components," as by computer network attack, popularly known as "hacking". Ibid.

The difficulty in pinpointing the origin of computer network attack is one complication in seeking to apply traditional legal concepts to this new kind of activity. An attack emanating from a foreign state and targeting another state's military or other governmental computers could bring into play rights of self-defense under international law and principles of the humanitarian laws of war. On the other hand, "hacking" could be done by domestic as well as foreign actors and might have merely private rather than governmental objectives. Depending on the nature of the act, "hacking" could be addressed as a criminal matter rather than under the laws of war. (Negotiations for a convention on cybercrime were in progress as of 2000, under the auspices of the Council of Europe, with U.S. participation.) To the extent that information operations techniques are understood as weapons, aspects of the laws of war that regulate weaponry could come into play. More to the point, if a belligerent uses information techniques to cause injury, death and destruction to another belligerent, its actions could be evaluated under the humanitarian principles of the laws of war, including the principle of distinguishing between combatants and non-combatants, and the requirements of necessity and proportionality and of refraining from causing superfluous injury.

Notes

1. The 1999 Department of Defense legal study, cited above, has "Notes for Further Research" with bibliographic references at pp. 48–54. Other sources include: Kanuck, Information Warfare: New Challenges for Public International Law, 37 Harv. Int'l L.J. 5 (1996); Greenberg, et al., Information Warfare and International Law (1997); Sharp, Cyberspace and the Use of Force (1999); Schmitt, Computer Network Attack and the Use of Force in International Law: Thoughts on a Normative Framework, 37 Colum. J. Transnat. L. 885 (1999); Shulman, Discrimination in the Laws of Information Warfare, 37 Colum. J. Transnat. L. 939 (1999); Ignatieff, Virtual War: Kosovo and Beyond (2000); Walker, Information Warfare and Neutrality, 33 Vanderbilt J. Transnat. L. 1079 (2000); Schmitt & O'Donnell, Computer Network Attack and International Law (forthcoming in U.S. Naval War College, International Law Studies, vol. 76, 2001).

2. Would a new instrument to address legal regulation of information warfare be desirable? In 1998 the Russian Federation proposed a resolution inviting views on the "advisability of elaborating international legal regimes to ban the development, production, and use of particularly dangerous information weapons." The General Assembly thereafter adopted a resolution on "developments in the field of information and telecommunications in the context of international security," inviting multilateral consideration of information security issues. U.N. Doc. A/RES/53/70 (1999). The United States and the United Kingdom took the position that it is premature to consider international regulation of information operations as a security matter, and that the priority should be on measures against computer crime and terrorism. See U.N. Doc. A/54/213 (1999).

Chapter 13

BASES OF JURISDICTION

SECTION 1. JURISDICTION UNDER INTERNATIONAL LAW

A. JURISDICTION DEFINED: THE DIFFERENT FORMS OF JURISDICTION

The term jurisdiction is commonly used to describe authority to affect legal interests. Traditionally, three kinds of jurisdiction are distinguished: legislative, judicial, and executive or enforcement jurisdiction. It is generally recognized that rules of general import may be formulated not only by legislatures, but also by other institutions of government, such as administrative agencies, and even courts. For that reason, the Restatement (Third) prefers to use the term prescriptive instead of legislative jurisdiction. Similarly, recognizing that adjudicatory functions may be exercised by governmental institutions other than courts, the Restatement prefers the term jurisdiction to adjudicate over the term judicial jurisdiction. The Restatement distinguishes between jurisdiction to adjudicate and jurisdiction to enforce. It defines jurisdiction to adjudicate as "the authority of a state to subject particular persons or things to its judicial process" and jurisdiction to enforce as the authority of a state "to use the resources of government to induce or compel compliance with its law." Restatement, Part IV, Introductory Note. In the materials that follow, the terms legislative, judicial, and executive jurisdiction will be used interchangeably with the terms jurisdiction to prescribe, to adjudicate, and to enforce.

Jurisdiction may be defined on several levels. The legislative, judicial or executive powers of particular institutions must, in the first instance, be defined under municipal law. Municipal law may again operate on more than one level. For example, in the United States, the legislative, judicial, and executive powers of the federal branches of government are defined first in the Constitution. The federal Constitution sets limits beyond which the legislative, judicial, and executive branches of federal and state governments, in exercising their powers, may not go. Similarly, conflict of laws rules also define the limits of legislative, judicial, and executive jurisdiction. These limits may, but need not, be the same as those prescribed by constitutional law. Thus, a court in the United States may deny recognition to a foreign judgment or refuse to apply a foreign law because, under its conflicts rules, the foreign court or legislature sought to extend its jurisdiction too far; and it may do so, even if recognition of what the foreign institution did would not run afoul of constitutional limitations. See, e.g., Grubel v. Nassauer, 210 N.Y. 149, 103 N.E. 1113 (1913).

While, therefore, legislative, judicial, and executive jurisdiction already have to be defined on several levels under municipal law, international law provides still a different level. It defines the limits states and other international legal persons may not exceed in exercising jurisdiction. The extent to which the pertinent rules of international law are operative in municipal law systems depends, of course, on the status of international law within those systems. On this aspect, see Chapter 3. But, within the international system, rules of international law operate directly on the subjects of international law whose powers they delimit.

B. INTERNATIONAL LAW RULES OF JURISDICTION GENERALLY

International law has not yet developed a comprehensive set of rules defining with reasonable precision all forms of jurisdiction that may be exercised by states and other international legal persons. Rather, international law has given principal attention to the reach of a state's jurisdiction—legislative, judicial, or executive—in criminal matters.

The Restatement (Third) states in Comment *f* to § 403 that the criteria for jurisdiction to prescribe "apply to criminal as well as to civil regulation." But Reporters' Note 8 states that in "applying the principle of reasonableness, the exercise of criminal (as distinguished from civil) jurisdiction in relation to acts committed in another state may be perceived as particularly intrusive." However, Comment *b* to § 421, which deals with Jurisdiction to Adjudicate, states that it applies to the exercise of "criminal as well as of civil jurisdiction." The Restatement (Third) does not refer to judicial decisions or to other authority that broadly extend to jurisdiction in civil matters the limitations of international law on the exercise of criminal jurisdiction. The possibility that states could object on the grounds of international law to assertions of civil as well as criminal jurisdiction exists and may increase, as where civil plaintiffs act as "private attorneys-general" in matters affecting foreign state interests.

In recent times, foreign sovereigns have increasingly objected to the exercise of extraterritorial prescriptive jurisdiction through statutes that threaten both criminal and administrative and civil sanctions in the economic sphere. See Section 6 of this Chapter. Administrative and some forms of civil sanctions, such as injunctions and punitive damages, may, of course, affect the person on whom they are imposed as seriously as do criminal sanctions and may therefore be regarded as coming within the realm of criminal jurisdiction for the purposes here discussed. It may well be argued, however, that international law limitations on the exercise of administrative and civil jurisdiction are still in a stage of development and that broad generalizations should be treated with circumspection.

The exercise of executive jurisdiction in any form on the territory of another state is generally regarded as limited by international law, regardless of whether the enforcement measure is of a criminal or civil nature. See Sections 8–9 of this Chapter.

The classical view has been that a state does not have to establish a valid basis for its exercise of jurisdiction and that the burden of establishing that its exercise of jurisdiction violates international law rests upon the person asserting the violation. See the Lotus Case, p. 68 supra. More recently, the view has been espoused that, especially when it acts extraterritorially, a state must demonstrate affirmatively the existence of an appropriate basis of jurisdiction. An alternative view is that the exercise of all forms of jurisdiction is subject to an overall limitation of reasonableness. This is the position taken in the Restatement (Third) § 403. See also Schachter, International Law in Theory and Practice 258–261 (1991).

Thus far, international law, in defining the limits of jurisdiction, has concerned itself principally with defining the jurisdiction of states. However, as international entities with varying measures of international legal personality continue to develop, international law will increasingly have to concern itself with their jurisdiction. Indeed, the assertion by the European Economic Community of extraterritorial jurisdiction in antitrust matters and of powers in certain maritime areas makes it clear that international law will also play a significant role in defining the jurisdiction of international legal persons other than states. The permissible nature and scope of jurisdiction under international law may vary with the international legal person whose jurisdiction is at issue. As the International Court of Justice has taught in Reparation for Injuries Suffered in the Service of the United Nations, 1949 I.C.J. 174, p. 361 above, the powers of an international legal person are a function of the role it plays in the world community.

International tribunals that adjudicate crimes committed in the former Yugoslavia and Rwanda exercise adjudicatory jurisdiction, while applying rules that the United Nations had determined to be "beyond doubt part of customary international law" and therefore applicable to all states. These rules have been further defined in the elaboration of the Statute for the International Criminal Court and the clarification of its jurisdictional authority. See Chapter 15.

C. INTERNATIONAL LAW CRITERIA FOR DETERMINING JURISDICTION

1. *Basic Principles*

Under international law, the jurisdiction of a state depends on the interest that the state, in view of its nature and purposes, may reasonably have in exercising the particular jurisdiction asserted and on the need to reconcile that interest with the interests of other states in exercising jurisdiction. The nature and significance of the interests of a state in exercising jurisdiction depend on the relation of the transaction, occurrence, or event, and of the person to be affected, to the state's proper concerns.

Whatever happens on the territory of a state is of that state's primary concern (the territorial principle). A state also has a significant interest in exercising jurisdiction over persons or things that possess its nationality (the nationality principle) and in protecting its nationals (the passive personality principle). In addition, a state has an evident interest in protecting itself against acts, even if performed outside of its territory and by persons that owe it no allegiance, that threaten its existence or its proper functioning as a state (the protective principle). And, finally, certain activities are so universally condemned that any state has an interest in exercising jurisdiction to combat them (the universal principle).

RESTATEMENT (THIRD)

§ 402. Bases of Jurisdiction to Prescribe

Subject to § 403, a state has jurisdiction to prescribe law with respect to

(1) (a) conduct that, wholly or in substantial part, takes place within its territory;

(b) the status of persons, or interests in things, present within its territory;

(c) conduct outside its territory that has or is intended to have substantial effect within its territory;

(2) the activities, interests, status, or relations of its nationals outside as well as within its territory; and

(3) certain conduct outside its territory by persons not its nationals that is directed against the security of the state or against a limited class of other state interests.

§ 403. Limitations on Jurisdiction to Prescribe

(1) Even when one of the bases for jurisdiction under § 402 is present, a state may not exercise jurisdiction to prescribe law with respect to a person or activity having connections with another state when the exercise of such jurisdiction is unreasonable.

(2) Whether exercise of jurisdiction over a person or activity is unreasonable is determined by evaluating all relevant factors, including, where appropriate:

(a) the link of the activity to the territory of the regulating state, *i.e.*, the extent to which the activity takes place within the territory, or has substantial, direct, and foreseeable effect upon or in the territory;

(b) the connections, such as nationality, residence, or economic activity, between the regulating state and the person principally responsible for the activity to be regulated, or between that state and those whom the regulation is designed to protect;

(c) the character of the activity to be regulated, the importance of regulation to the regulating state, the extent to which other states regulate such activities, and the degree to which the desirability of such regulation is generally accepted;

(d) the existence of justified expectations that might be protected or hurt by the regulation;

(e) the importance of the regulation to the international political, legal, or economic system;

(f) the extent to which the regulation is consistent with the traditions of the international system;

(g) the extent to which another state may have an interest in regulating the activity; and

(h) the likelihood of conflict with regulation by another state.

(3) When it would not be unreasonable for each of two states to exercise jurisdiction over a person or activity, but the prescriptions by the two states are in conflict, each state has an obligation to evaluate its own as well as the other state's interest in exercising jurisdiction, in light of all the relevant factors, Subsection (2); a state should defer to the other state if that state's interest is clearly greater.

§ 404. Universal Jurisdiction to Define and Punish Certain Offenses

A state has jurisdiction to define and prescribe punishment for certain offenses recognized by the community of nations as of universal concern, such as piracy, slave trade, attacks on or hijacking of aircraft, genocide, war crimes, and perhaps certain acts of terrorism, even where none of the bases of jurisdiction indicated in § 402 is present.

Notes

1. The Restatement (Third) provides in § 403 for an overall limitation on the exercise of jurisdiction. This limitation, it is stated in Comment *a*, "has emerged as a principle of international law." To what extent is this statement borne out by the materials that follow? Is the imposition of this requirement likely to alleviate the problems that arise in cases of conflicts of jurisdiction? See Section 6 of this Chapter. Or would it be more appropriate to provide that national institutions should read this limitation into national law whenever possible?

2. Section 403 of the Restatement (Third) does not impose the limitation of reasonableness upon the exercise of jurisdiction on the basis of the universal principle. Is there no room for such a limitation when jurisdiction is exercised on that basis?

The extent to which recognized bases of jurisdiction provide the premises for the exercise of the various forms of jurisdiction will be considered in the sections that follow. Since each state is part of the world community, rules defining jurisdiction must take due account of the needs of that community and, specifically, of the need not to encroach unnecessarily on the interests of other members. This has been a significant consideration in delimiting in different fashion the extraterritorial reach of the various kinds of jurisdiction.

SECTION 2. JURISDICTION TO PRESCRIBE BASED ON THE TERRITORIAL PRINCIPLE

A. SCOPE

A state's territorial authority extends both horizontally and vertically. Traditionally, a state has exercised authority over its land territory for virtually all purposes. However, the measure of a state's authority over its maritime areas is more limited and decreases as the maritime areas become more distant from the state's shores. Similarly, although a state exercises its jurisdiction above as well as below the surface of its territory and maritime areas, the measure of its control decreases as the distance from the surface becomes greater. On the extent of land territory and authority below and above the surface, see Chapter 4. On the extent of maritime areas and related airspace, see Chapter 16. On jurisdiction in the air and outer space, see pp. 1123–1133 and Chapter 19.

Subject to the limitation that a state may exercise jurisdiction only in pursuit of purposes that are its proper concern, the territorial principle provides the premise for the exercise of jurisdiction not only with respect to transactions, persons, or things within the territory, but also with respect to certain consequences produced within the territory by persons acting outside it.

1. With Respect to Persons and Things Within the Territory

It is well settled that a state may exercise jurisdiction with respect to all persons or things within its territory. See, e.g., Marshall, C.J., in The Schooner Exchange v. McFaddon, 11 U.S. (7 Cranch) 116, 136, 3 L.Ed. 287 (1812), p. 1200 infra:

> The jurisdiction of the nation within its own territory is necessarily exclusive and absolute. It is susceptible of no limitation not imposed by itself. Any restriction upon it, deriving validity from an external source, would imply a diminution of its sovereignty to the extent of the restriction, and an investment of that sovereignty to the same extent in that power which could impose such restriction. All exceptions, therefore, to the full and complete power of a nation within its own territories, must be traced up to the consent of the nation itself.

2. With Respect to Persons and Things Without the Territory—Objective Territorial Principle

UNITED STATES v. ALUMINUM CO. OF AMERICA

United States Court of Appeals, Second Circuit, 1945.
148 F.2d 416.

Before L. HAND, SWAN AND A. HAND. CIRCUIT JUDGES.

[The complaint alleged that defendants Alcoa and Aluminum, Limited (a Canadian corporation formed to take over the properties of Alcoa outside the United States) had illegally conspired in restraint of domestic and foreign commerce with respect to the manufacture and sale of aluminum ingot. The Government's appeal from dismissal of its complaint, 44 F.Supp. 97 (S.D.N.Y. 1941), was referred to the Court of Appeals, because a quorum of six qualified Justices of the Supreme Court was wanting. One of the central issues in the case was whether the participation of Aluminum, Limited, in an "alliance" with a number of foreign producers constituted a violation of § 1 of the Sherman Act (15 U.S.C.A. § 1), which provides in relevant part that "every contract, combination * * * or conspiracy, in restraint of trade or commerce among the several States, or with foreign nations, is declared to be illegal." In the course of holding that "Limited" violated the Act, the court (per L. Hand, C.J.) stated:]

Whether "Limited" itself violated that section depends upon the character of the "Alliance." It was a Swiss corporation, created in pursuance of an agreement entered into on July 3, 1931, the signatories to which were a

French corporation, two German, one Swiss, a British, and "Limited." The original agreement, or "cartel," provided for the formation of a corporation in Switzerland which should issue shares, to be taken up by the signatories. This corporation was from time to time to fix a quota of production for each share, and each shareholder was to be limited to the quantity measured by the number of shares it held, but was free to sell at any price it chose. The corporation fixed a price every year at which it would take off any shareholder's hands any part of its quota which it did not sell. No shareholder was to "buy, borrow, fabricate or sell" aluminum produced by anyone not a shareholder except with the consent of the board of governors, but that must not be "unreasonably withheld." * * * However, * * * until 1936, when the new arrangement was made, imports into the United States were not included in the quotas. * * *

The agreement of 1936 abandoned the system of unconditional quotas, and substituted a system of royalties. Each shareholder was to have a fixed free quota for every share it held, but as its production exceeded the sum of its quotas, it was to pay a royalty, graduated progressively in proportion to the excess; and these royalties the "Alliance" divided among the shareholders in proportion to their shares. * * * Although this agreement, like its predecessor, was silent as to imports into the United States, when that question arose during its preparation, as it did, all the shareholders agreed that such imports should be included in the quotas. * * *

Did either the agreement of 1931 or that of 1936 violate § 1 of the Act? The answer does not depend upon whether we shall recognize as a source of liability a liability imposed by another state. On the contrary we are concerned only with whether Congress chose to attach liability to the conduct outside the United States of persons not in allegiance to it. That being so, the only question open is whether Congress intended to impose the liability, and whether our own Constitution permitted it to do so: as a court of the United States, we cannot look beyond our own law. Nevertheless, it is quite true that we are not to read general words, such as those in this Act, without regard to the limitations customarily observed by nations upon the exercise of their powers * * * . We should not impute to Congress an intent to punish all whom its courts can catch, for conduct which has no consequences within the United States. * * * On the other hand, it is settled law—as "Limited" itself agrees—that any state may impose liabilities, even upon persons not within its allegiance, for conduct outside its borders that has consequences within its borders which the state reprehends; and these liabilities other states will ordinarily recognize. * * * Restatement of Conflict of Laws § 65. It may be argued that this Act extends further. Two situations are possible. There may be agreements made beyond our borders not intended to affect imports, which do affect them, or which affect exports. Almost any limitation of the supply of goods in Europe, for example, or in South America, may have repercussions in the United States if there is trade between the two. Yet when one considers the international complications likely to arise from an effort in this country to treat such agreements as unlawful, it is safe to assume that Congress certainly did not intend the Act to cover them. Such agreements may on the other hand intend to include imports into the United States, and yet it may appear that they have had no effect upon them. That situation might be thought to fall within the doctrine that intent may be a substitute for performance in the case of a contract made within the United States; or it might be thought to fall within the doctrine that a statute should not be interpreted to cover acts abroad which have no consequence here. We shall not choose between these alternatives; but for argument we shall assume that the Act does not cover agreements, even though intended to affect imports or exports, unless its performance is shown actually to have had some effect upon them. Where both conditions are satisfied, the situation certainly falls within such decisions as United States v. Pacific & Arctic R. & Navigation Co., 228 U.S. 87, 33 S.Ct. 443, 57 L.Ed. 742; Thomsen v. Cayser, 243 U.S. 66, 37 S.Ct. 353, 61 L.Ed. 597, Ann. Cas. 1917D, 322 and United States v. Sisal Sales Corporation, 274 U.S. 268, 47 S.Ct. 592, 71 L.Ed. 1042. * * * It is true that in those cases the persons held liable had sent agents into the United States to perform part of the agreement; but an agent is merely an animate means of executing his principal's purposes, and, for the purposes of this case, he does not differ from an inanimate means; besides, only human agents can import and sell ingot.

Both agreements would clearly have been unlawful, had they been made within the United States; and it follows from what we have just said that both were unlawful, though made abroad, if they were intended to affect imports and did affect them.

[The Court went on to find that the 1936 agreement intended to set up a quota system for imports and that, absent a showing by "Limited" that imports were not in fact affected, the agreement violated § 1 of the Act.]

Notes

1. The territorial principle has not only been universally accepted by states, but it has had a significant development in modern times. This development has been a necessary consequence of the increasing complexity of the "act or omission" which constitutes crime under modern penal legislation. The "act or omission" need not consist of an isolated action or failure to act. Not infrequently it appears as an event consisting of a series of separate acts or omissions. These separate acts or omissions need not be simultaneous with respect to time or restricted to a single state with respect to place. Indeed, with the increasing facility of communication and transportation, the opportunities for committing crimes whose constituent elements take place in more than one state have grown apace. To meet these conditions, jurisdiction founded upon the territorial principle has been expanded in several ways.

> In the first place, national legislation and jurisprudence have developed the so-called subjective territorial principle which establishes the jurisdiction of the State to prosecute and punish for crime commenced within the State but completed or consummated abroad. * * *
>
> In the second place, national legislation and jurisprudence have developed the so-called objective territorial principle which establishes the jurisdiction of the State to prosecute and punish for crime commenced without the State but consummated within its territory. * * *

Harvard Research in International Law, Jurisdiction with Respect to Crime, 29 A.J.I.L.Supp. 435, 484, 487–488 (1935).

2. The objective territorial principle

> is often said to apply where the offence "takes effect" or "produces its effects" in the territory. In relation to elementary cases of direct physical injury, such as homicide, this is unexceptionable, for here the "effect" which is meant is an essential ingredient of the crime. Once we move out of the sphere of direct physical consequences, however, to employ the formula of "effects" is to enter upon a very slippery slope; for here the effects within the territory may be no more than an element of alleged consequential damage which may be more or less remote. * * * [T]o extend the notion of effects, without qualification, from the simple cases of direct physical injury to cases such as defamation, sedition, and the like, is to introduce a dangerous ambiguity into the basis of the doctrine. If indeed it were permissible to found objective territorial jurisdiction upon the territoriality of more or less remote repercussions of an act wholly performed in another territory, then there would be virtually no limit to a State's territorial jurisdiction.

Jennings, Extraterritorial Jurisdiction and the United States Antitrust Laws 33 Brit. Y.B.I.L. 146, 159 (1957).

3. The approach of the *Alcoa* case has been extended quite far. In Continental Ore Co. v. Union Carbide & Carbon Corp., 370 U.S. 690, 82 S.Ct. 1404, 8 L.Ed.2d 777 (1962), the plaintiff contended that a Canadian company, that had been appointed by the Canadian government as the exclusive wartime agent to purchase and allocate vanadium for Canadian industries, had violated the American antitrust laws by not purchasing vanadium from the plaintiff in Canada. The Supreme Court upheld the lower court's ruling that the Sherman Act extended its extraterritorial reach to this conduct and that the act of state doctrine was inapplicable since the incriminated conduct had not been required by the Canadian authorities. To the same effect, see United States v. The Watchmakers of Switzerland Information Center, Inc., 133 F.Supp. 40 (S.D.N.Y.1955).

4. Does the United States have jurisdiction to prescribe in regard to international drug trafficking in Panama that resulted in 2,141 pounds of cocaine being illegally brought into the United States? For an affirmative answer, see United States v. Noriega, 746 F.Supp. 1506 (S.D.Fla.1990), aff'd, 117 F.3d 1206 (11th Cir.1997), cert. denied, 523 U.S. 1060, 118 S.Ct. 1389, 140 L.Ed.2d 648 (1998). Did the manner in which U.S. forces seized Noriega in Panama have any bearing on the propriety of exercising jurisdiction? Compare United States v. Alvarez–Machain, p. 1187 infra.

RESTATEMENT (THIRD)

§ 415. Jurisdiction to Regulate Anti–Competitive Activities

(1) Any agreement in restraint of United States trade made in the United States, and any conduct or agreement in restraint of such trade that is carried out in significant measure in the United States, are subject to the jurisdiction to prescribe of the United States, regardless of the nationality or place of business of the parties to the agreement or of the participants in the conduct.

(2) Any agreement in restraint of United States trade that is made outside of the United States, and any conduct or agreement in restraint of such trade that is carried out predominantly outside of the United States, are subject to the jurisdiction to prescribe of the United States, if a principal purpose of the conduct or agreement is to interfere with the commerce of the United States, and the agreement or conduct has some effect on that commerce.

(3) Other agreements or conduct in restraint of United States trade are subject to the jurisdiction to prescribe of the United States if such agreements or conduct have substantial effect on the commerce of the United States and the exercise of jurisdiction is not unreasonable.

Notes

1. This section is part of a subchapter entitled "Principles of Jurisdiction Applied". Other sections in this subchapter deal with jurisdiction in tax, antitrust, and securities matters. See §§ 411–416.

2. Does the quoted provision reflect current law? Note that § 415(2) requires "some effect" and that § 415(3) requires "substantial effect" on United States commerce, as well as that the exercise of jurisdiction "is not unreasonable." Compare the *Hartford Fire* case below.

3. For applications of a "jurisdictional rule of reason," see Timberlane Lumber Co. v. Bank of America National Trust & Saving Ass'n, 549 F.2d 597 (9th Cir.1976). In this and other cases, the courts, applying the jurisdictional rule of reason, found it reasonable for the U.S. antitrust laws to reach conduct abroad. Do these cases support imposition of a requirement of reasonableness as a matter of international law? The difficulty of interest balancing by national courts has been duly noted. See Laker Airways v. Sabena et al., 731 F.2d 909, 951–52 (D.C.Cir. 1984):

> When one State exercises its jurisdiction and another in protection of its interests attempts to quash the first exercise of jurisdiction, it is simply impossible to judicially balance these totally contradictory and mutually negating actions.

See also British Airways Board v. Laker Airways (House of Lords, 1984), 23 I.L.M. 727 (1984); Schachter, International Law in Theory and Practice 260–261 (1991). On conflicts of jurisdiction, see Section 6 of this Chapter.

HARTFORD FIRE INSURANCE CO. v. CALIFORNIA

Supreme Court of the United States, 1993.
509 U.S. 764, 113 S.Ct. 2891, 125 L.Ed.2d 612 (footnotes omitted).

[The plaintiffs charged that the defendant insurers and reinsurers had violated American antitrust laws by agreeing to restrict the terms of coverage of commercial general liability insurance available in the United States. The defendants raised as defenses that the conduct complained of was insulated from antitrust liability by the McCarran–Ferguson Act and that, in any event, American antitrust laws did not cover conduct by the London insurers in Great Britain. The Supreme Court, per Justice Souter, rejected both defenses.]

Nineteen States and a number of private plaintiffs filed 36 complaints against the insurers involved in this course of events, charging that the conspiracies described above violated § 1 of the Sherman Act, 15 U.S.C. § 1. * * * The District Court * * * dismissed the three claims that named only certain London-based defendants, invoking international comity and applying the Ninth Circuit's decision in *Timberlane Lumber Co.* v. *Bank of America, N.T. & S. A.*, 549 F.2d 597 (1976).

The Court of Appeals reversed. * * * [A]s to the three claims brought solely against foreign defendants, the court applied its *Timberlane* analysis, but concluded that the principle of international comity was no bar to exercising Sherman Act jurisdiction.

We granted certiorari * * * to address the application of the Sherman Act to the foreign conduct at issue. * * *

* * *

Finally, we take up the question * * * whether certain claims against the London reinsurers should have been dismissed as improper applications of the Sherman Act to foreign conduct. * * *

At the outset, we note that the District Court undoubtedly had jurisdiction of these Sherman Act claims, as the London reinsurers apparently concede. See Tr. of Oral Arg. 37 ("Our position is not that the Sherman Act does not apply in the sense that a minimal basis for the exercise of jurisdiction doesn't exist here. Our position is that there are certain circumstances, and that this is one of them, in which the interests of another State are sufficient that the exercise of that jurisdiction should be restrained"). Although the proposition was perhaps not always free from doubt, see *American Banana Co. v. United Fruit Co.*, 213 U.S. 347, 29 S.Ct. 511, 53 L.Ed. 826 (1909), it is well established by now that the Sherman Act applies to foreign conduct that was meant to produce and did in fact produce some substantial effect in the United States. See *Matsushita Elec. Industrial Co. v. Zenith Radio Corp.*, 475 U.S. 574, 582, n. 6, 106 S.Ct. 1348, 1354, n. 6, 89 L.Ed.2d 538 (1986); *United States v. Aluminum Co. of America*, 148 F.2d 416, 444 (C.A.2 1945) (L. Hand, J.); Restatement (Third) of Foreign Relations Law of the United States § 415, and Reporters' Note 3 (1987) (hereinafter Restatement (Third) Foreign Relations Law); 1 P. Areeda & D. Turner, Antitrust Law ¶ 236 (1978); cf. *Continental Ore Co. v. Union Carbide & Carbon Corp.*, 370 U.S. 690, 704, 82 S.Ct. 1404, 1413, 8 L.Ed.2d 777 (1962); *Steele v. Bulova Watch Co.*, 344 U.S. 280, 288, 73 S.Ct. 252, 256, 97 L.Ed. 319 (1952); *United States v. Sisal Sales Corp.*, 274 U.S. 268, 275–276, 47 S.Ct. 592, 593–594, 71 L.Ed. 1042 (1927). Such is the conduct alleged here: that the London reinsurers engaged in unlawful conspiracies to affect the market for insurance in the United States and that their conduct in fact produced substantial effect. * * *

According to the London reinsurers, the District Court should have declined to exercise such jurisdiction under the principle of international comity. The Court of Appeals agreed that courts should look to that principle in deciding whether to exercise jurisdiction under the Sherman Act. * * * This availed the London reinsurers nothing, however. To be sure, the Court of Appeals believed that "application of [American] antitrust laws to the London reinsurance market 'would lead to significant conflict with English law and policy,'" and that "[s]uch a conflict, unless outweighed by other factors, would by itself be reason to decline exercise of jurisdiction." * * * But other factors, in the court's view, including the London reinsurers' express purpose to affect United States commerce and the substantial nature of the effect produced, outweighed the supposed conflict and required the exercise of jurisdiction in this litigation. * * *

When it enacted the Foreign Trade Antitrust Improvements Act of 1982 (FTAIA), 96 Stat. 1246, 15 U.S.C. § 6a, Congress expressed no view on the question whether a court with Sherman Act jurisdiction should ever decline to exercise such jurisdiction on grounds of international comity. See H.R.Rep. No. 97–686, p. 13 (1982) ("If a court determines that the requirements for subject matter jurisdiction are met, [the FTAIA] would have no effect on the court['s] ability to employ notions of comity . . . or otherwise to take account of the international character of the transaction") (citing *Timberlane*). We need not decide that question here, however, for even assuming that in a proper case a court may decline to exercise Sherman Act jurisdiction over foreign conduct (or, as Justice SCALIA would put it, may conclude by the employment of comity analysis in the first instance that there is no jurisdiction), international comity would not counsel against exercising jurisdiction in the circumstances alleged here.

The only substantial question in this litigation is whether "there is in fact a true conflict between domestic and foreign law." *Société Nationale Industrielle Aerospatiale v. United States Dist. Court*, 482 U.S. 522, 555, 107 S.Ct. 2542, 2562, 96 L.Ed.2d 461 (1987) (BLACKMUN, J., concurring in part and dissenting in part). The London reinsurers contend that applying the Act to their conduct would conflict significantly with British law, and the British Government, appearing before us as *amicus curiae*, concurs. * * * They assert that Parliament has established a comprehensive regulatory regime over the London reinsurance market and that the conduct alleged here was perfectly consistent with British law and policy. But this is not to state a conflict. "[T]he fact that conduct is lawful in the state in which it took place will not, of itself, bar application of the United States antitrust laws," even where the foreign state has a strong policy to permit or encourage such conduct. Restatement (Third) Foreign Relations Law § 415, Comment *j*; see *Continental Ore Co.*, *supra*, 370 U.S., at 706–707, 82 S.Ct., at 1414–1415. No conflict exists, for these purposes, "where a person subject to regulation by two states can comply with the laws of both." Restatement (Third) Foreign Relations Law § 403, Comment *e*.

Since the London reinsurers do not argue that British law requires them to act in some fashion prohibited by the law of the United States, * * * or claim that their compliance with the laws of both countries is otherwise impossible, we see no conflict with British law. See Restatement (Third) Foreign Relations Law § 403, Comment *e*, § 415, Comment *j*. We have no need in this litigation to address other considerations that might inform a decision to refrain from the exercise of jurisdiction on grounds of international comity.

Notes

1. Justice Scalia, joined by Justices O'Connor, Kennedy, and Thomas, dissented from the part of the Court's opinion excerpted above. Relying on the Restatement (Third) § 403 and various U.S. cases, the dissent emphasized the distinction between whether Congress has chosen to legislate extraterritorially in a given statute, and whether, assuming that it has, the legislation should nonetheless be interpreted to avoid conflicts with principles of international law:

> [Since *Alcoa,*] lower court precedent has also tempered the extraterritorial application of the Sherman Act with considerations of "international

> comity." [Citations to *Timberlane* and other cases omitted.] The "comity" they refer to is not the comity of courts, whereby judges decline to exercise jurisdiction over matters more appropriately adjudged elsewhere, but rather what might be termed "prescriptive comity": the respect sovereign nations afford each other by limiting the reach of their laws. That comity is exercised by legislatures when they enact laws, and courts assume it has been exercised when they come to interpreting the scope of laws their legislatures have enacted. It is a traditional component of choice-of-law theory. * * *
>
> In sum, the practice of using international law to limit the extraterritorial reach of statutes is firmly established in our jurisprudence. * * * Whether the Restatement precisely reflects international law in every detail matters little here, as I believe this case would be resolved the same way under virtually any conceivable test that takes account of foreign regulatory interests.

Upon applying the factors indicated in Restatement § 403, including Great Britain's comprehensive regulatory scheme governing the London reinsurance market, the dissent found it "unimaginable that an assertion of legislative jurisdiction by the United States would be considered reasonable, and therefore it is inappropriate to assume, in the absence of statutory indication to the contrary, that Congress has made such an assertion."

2. Does the principal case adequately distinguish between whether the United States could exercise legislative jurisdiction (under constitutional or international law) and whether the Sherman Act should be construed to reach the conduct complained of? Should the balancing test of the Restatement (Third) come into play only when the latter question is on the table? On the difficulties encountered in applying a balancing test, see Note 3, p. 1097 supra.

3. Is Justice Souter correct in stating that the decisive question is whether "a person subject to regulation by two states can comply with the laws of both"? What if the United Kingdom had enacted a statute forbidding the English insurers to comply with any antitrust decree issued by an American court? See Section 6, infra.

4. After the principal case, what is left of the balancing test as formulated in *Timberlane* (Note 3 on p. 1097)?

5. Does the Sherman Act reach conduct outside of the United States that is intended to affect and does affect activities of American companies, engaged in interstate and foreign commerce, insofar as these activities occur outside the United States? In Phillips Petroleum Inc. v. Heeremas, Civ. H98–1697, a district court judge in Texas said no. Is this ruling correct? No doubt, this novel issue will find its way into the appellate courts.

6. In still another variant, English insurers, acting as they did in the *Hartford Fire Insurance* case, had refused to insure an Australian asbestos producer for the types of risks for which coverage was sought in that case. The Australian producer commenced an action in the New Jersey court alleging a violation of the Sherman Act. Does that Act cover conduct abroad that is intended to affect and does affect an Australian producer who sells its products worldwide, including the United States, and seeks to increase coverage for the risks attending its American sales? On this case, see Lowenfeld, Forum Shopping, Antisuit Injunctions, Negative Declarations, and Related Tools of International Litigation, 91 A J.I.L. 314 (1997).

7. In W.S. Kirkpatrick & Co. v. Environmental Tectonics Corp., Int'l, 493 U.S. 400, 110 S.Ct. 701, 107 L.Ed.2d 816 (1990), the American plaintiff alleged that the American defendant had violated the Foreign Corrupt Practices Act of 1977 by bribing Nigerian officials in order to obtain a construction contract and that plaintiff had suffered damages as a consequence. The court ruled that the act of state doctrine did not preclude the plaintiff from recovering. No question was raised as to whether the 1977 Act could cover conduct and damages suffered in Nigeria. Of course, since the defendant was a U.S. corporation, jurisdiction could be justified on the basis of the nationality principle. See Section 3 infra.

8. Foreign governments continue to object to the extraterritorial application of U.S. antitrust laws. See, e.g., Griffin, Jurisdiction and Enforcement: Foreign Governmental Reactions to U.S. Assertion of Extraterritorial Jurisdiction, 6 Geo. Mason L. Rev. 505 (1998).

9. The North American Free Trade Agreement (NAFTA) of December 17, 1992, requires each nation to cooperate with the authorities of the other members to further the enforcement of their antitrust laws. See NAFTA Chapter 15, 32 I.L.M. 605, 663–664 (1993). For U.S. implementation, see the International Antitrust Enforcement Assistance Act, 108 Stat. 4597, 15 U.S.C.A. §§ 6201–6212 (1994).

10. On September 23, 1991, the Commission of the European Communities and the United States signed an Agreement Regarding the Application of Competition Laws. Upon a challenge by France, the European Court of Justice ruled that the agreement should have been concluded by the Council of the European Union. See Case C–327/91, France v. Commission, [1994] ECR I–3641. Nevertheless, the European Communities and the U.S. frequently cooperate in investigating cross-border conspiracies. See Microsoft Settles Accusations of Monopolistic Selling Practice 67 Antitrust & Trade Reg. Rep. (BNA) 106 (1994).

11. Whether the European Communities/European Union have embraced an extraterritorial theory of antitrust jurisdiction was for a long time uncertain. For some time, the Court of Justice avoided dealing with the problem of extraterritoriality by attributing the conduct of a subsidiary within the European Economic Community to its corporate parent and thereby finding the conduct of the parent to take place within the Community. The effect of this construction was to apply the E.E.C. Treaty extraterritorially in order to reach, among others, American enterprises outside of of the Community. See generally 2 Smit & Herzog, The Law of the European Economic Community § 85.19.

The E.C.J.'s *Wood Pulp* decision, Ahlstrom Osakeyhtio v. Commission, [1988] E.C.R 5193, involved the territorial scope of application of Article 85 of the Treaty of Rome concerning practices which have as their object or effect the restriction of competition within the common market. The European Commission charged certain U.S., Finnish, Swedish and Canadian firms and two of their export associations with fixing the price of wood pulp sold within the Community. The Court found the Commission's decision "not contrary to Article 85 of the Treaty or to the rules of public international law" on jurisdiction. Commentators have debated the extent to which this ruling applied an effects theory to agreements made outside the Community. Compare Griffin, EC and U.S. Extraterritoriality: Activism and Cooperation, 17 Fordham I.L.J. 353 (1994). More recently, the E.C.J. seems to have moved toward a view of the effects doctrine and reasonableness analogous to that of the U.S. Restatement §§ 402–403, in the *Gencor/Lonrho* case (1999), involving the merger of two South African companies with substantial European business. See Gencor Ltd. v. Commission of the European Communities,

Case T-102/96, E.C.J. Court of First Instance, Mar. 25, 1999. Also relevant is the practice of the European Commission as the Community's executive organ. In evaluating the Boeing/McDonnell Douglas merger and the Time Warner/AOL merger, the Commission considered how the amalgamations of these U.S. companies would affect competition within Europe. For commentary, see, e.g., Mavroidis, Some Reflections on the Extraterritorial Application of Laws 1–14, in Melanges Waelbroeack (1998).

UNITED STATES v. NIPPON PAPER INDUSTRIES CO. LTD.

United States Court of Appeals, First Circuit, 1997.
109 F.3d 1,
cert. denied, 523 U.S. 1044, 118 S.Ct. 685,
139 L.Ed.2d 632 (1998) (footnotes omitted).

SELYA, CIRCUIT JUDGE.

This case raises an important, hitherto unanswered question. In it, the United States attempts to convict a foreign corporation under the Sherman Act, a federal antitrust statute, alleging that price-fixing activities which took place entirely in Japan are prosecutable because they were intended to have, and did in fact have, substantial effects in this country. The district court, declaring that a criminal antitrust prosecution could not be based on wholly extraterritorial conduct, dismissed the indictment. *See United States v. Nippon Paper Indus. Co.*, 944 F.Supp. 55 (D.Mass.1996). We reverse.

I. JUST THE FAX

* * *

In 1995, a federal grand jury handed up an indictment naming as a defendant Nippon Paper Industries Co., Ltd. (NPI), a Japanese manufacturer of facsimile paper. The indictment alleges that in 1990 NPI and certain unnamed coconspirators held a number of meetings in Japan which culminated in an agreement to fix the price of thermal fax paper throughout North America. NPI and other manufacturers who were privy to the scheme purportedly accomplished their objective by selling the paper in Japan to unaffiliated trading houses on condition that the latter charge specified (inflated) prices for the paper when they resold it in North America. The trading houses then shipped and sold the paper to their subsidiaries in the United States who in turn sold it to American consumers at swollen prices. The indictment further relates that, in 1990 alone, NPI sold thermal fax paper worth approximately $6,100,000 for eventual import into the United States; and that in order to ensure the success of the venture, NPI monitored the paper trail and confirmed that the prices charged to end users were those that it had arranged. These activities, the indictment posits, had a substantial adverse effect on commerce in the United States and unreasonably restrained trade in violation of Section One of the Sherman Act, 15 U.S.C. § 1 (1994).

NPI moved to dismiss because, *inter alia*, if the conduct attributed to NPI occurred at all, it took place entirely in Japan, and, thus, the indictment failed to limn an offense under Section One of the Sherman Act. The government opposed this initiative on two grounds. First, it claimed that the law deserved a less grudging reading and that, properly read, Section One of the Sherman

Act applied criminally to wholly foreign conduct as long as that conduct produced substantial and intended effects within the United States. Second, it claimed that the indictment, too, deserved a less grudging reading and that, properly read, the bill alleged a vertical conspiracy in restraint of trade that involved overt acts by certain coconspirators within the United States. Accepting a restrictive reading of both the statute and the indictment, the district court dismissed the case. See *United States v. NPI*, 944 F.Supp. at 64–66. This appeal followed.

II. Analysis

We begin—and end—with the overriding legal question. Because this question is one of statutory construction, we review de novo the holding that Section One of the Sherman Act does not cover wholly extraterritorial conduct in the criminal context. See *United States v. Gifford*, 17 F.3d 462, 471–72 (1st Cir.1994).

* * *

B. The Merits.

Were this a civil case, our journey would be complete. But here the United States essays a criminal prosecution for solely extraterritorial conduct rather than a civil action. This is largely uncharted terrain; we are aware of no authority directly on point, and the parties have cited none.

Be that as it may, one datum sticks out like a sore thumb: in both criminal and civil cases, the claim that Section One applies extraterritorially is based on the same language in the same section of the same statute: "Every contract, combination in the form of trust or otherwise, or conspiracy, in restraint of trade or commerce among the several States, or with foreign nations, is declared to be illegal." 15 U.S.C. § 1. Words may sometimes be chameleons, possessing different shades of meaning in different contexts, *see, e.g., Hanover Ins. Co. v. United States*, 880 F.2d 1503, 1504 (1st Cir.1989), *cert. denied*, 493 U.S. 1023, 110 S.Ct. 726, 107 L.Ed.2d 745 (1990), but common sense suggests that courts should interpret the same language in the same section of the same statute uniformly, regardless of whether the impetus for interpretation is criminal or civil.

* * *

It follows, therefore, that if the language upon which the indictment rests were the same as the language upon which civil liability rests but appeared in a different section of the Sherman Act, or in a different part of the same section, we would be under great pressure to follow the lead of the *Hartford Fire* Court and construe the two iterations of the language identically. Where, as here, the tie binds more tightly—that is, the text under consideration is not merely a duplicate appearing somewhere else in the statute, but is the original phrase in the original setting—the pressure escalates and the case for reading the language in a manner consonant with a prior Supreme Court interpretation is irresistible. * * *

* * *

NPI and its amicus, the Government of Japan, urge that special reasons exist for measuring Section One's reach differently in a criminal context. We have reviewed their exhortations and found them hollow.

* * *

The Restatement. NPI and the district court, 944 F. Supp. at 65, both sing the praises of the Restatement (Third) of Foreign Relations Law (1987), claiming that it supports a distinction between civil and criminal cases on the issue of extraterritoriality. The passage to which they pin their hopes states:

> [I]n the case of regulatory statutes that may give rise to both civil and criminal liability, such as the United States antitrust and securities laws, the presence of substantial foreign elements will ordinarily weigh against application of criminal law. In such cases, legislative intent to subject conduct outside the state's territory to its criminal law should be found only on the basis of express statement or clear implication.

Id. at § 403 cmt. *f*. We believe that this statement merely reaffirms the classic presumption against extraterritoriality—no more, no less. After all, nothing in the text of the Restatement proper contradicts the government's interpretation of Section One.

* * *

Comity. International comity is a doctrine that counsels voluntary forbearance when a sovereign which has a legitimate claim to jurisdiction concludes that a second sovereign also has a legitimate claim to jurisdiction under principles of international law. See Harold G. Maier, *Extraterritorial Jurisdiction at a Crossroads: An Intersection Between Public and Private International Law*, 76 A.J. Int'l L. 280, 281 n. 1 (1982). Comity is more an aspiration than a fixed rule, more a matter of grace than a matter of obligation. In all events, its growth in the antitrust sphere has been stunted by *Hartford Fire*, in which the Court suggested that comity concerns would operate to defeat the exercise of jurisdiction only in those few cases in which the law of the foreign sovereign required a defendant to act in a manner incompatible with the Sherman Act or in which full compliance with both statutory schemes was impossible. *See Hartford Fire*, 509 U.S. at 798–99, 113 S.Ct. at 2910–11; *see also* Kenneth W. Dam, *Extraterritoriality in an Age of Globalization: The Hartford Fire Case*, 1993 Sup.Ct.Rev. 289, 306–07 (1993). Accordingly, the *Hartford Fire* Court gave short shrift to the defendants' entreaty that the conduct leading to antitrust liability was perfectly legal in the United Kingdom. *See Hartford Fire*, 509 U.S. at 798–99, 113 S.Ct. at 2910–11.

In this case the defendant's comity-based argument is even more attenuated. The conduct with which NPI is charged is illegal under both Japanese and American laws, thereby alleviating any founded concern about NPI being whipsawed between separate sovereigns. And, moreover, to the extent that comity is informed by general principles of reasonableness, *see* Restatement (Third) of Foreign Relations Law § 403, the indictment lodged against NPI is well within the pale. In it, the government charges that the defendant orchestrated a conspiracy with the object of rigging prices in the United States. If the government can prove these charges, we see no tenable reason why principles of comity should shield NPI from prosecution. We live in an age of international commerce, where decisions reached in one corner of the world can reverberate around the globe in less time than it takes to tell the tale. Thus, a ruling in NPI's favor would create perverse incentives for those who would use nefarious means to influence markets in the United States, rewarding them for erecting as many territorial firewalls as possible between cause and effect.

We need go no further. *Hartford Fire* definitively establishes that Section One of the Sherman Act applies to wholly foreign conduct which has an intended and substantial effect in the United States. We are bound to accept that holding. Under settled principles of statutory construction, we also are bound to apply it by interpreting Section One the same way in a criminal case. The combined force of these commitments requires that we accept the government's cardinal argument, reverse the order of the district court, reinstate the indictment, and remand for further proceedings.

Reversed and remanded.

LYNCH, CIRCUIT JUDGE (concurring).

The question presented in this case is whether Section One of the Sherman Act authorizes criminal prosecutions of defendants for their actions committed entirely outside the United States. Judicial precedents, culminating with the Supreme Court's decision in *Hartford Fire Insurance Co. v. California*, 509 U.S. 764, 113 S.Ct. 2891, 125 L.Ed.2d 612 (1993), conclusively establish that Section One's jurisdictional reach extends, in civil actions, to foreign conduct that is meant to produce, and does in fact produce, substantial effects in the United States. The next question to be asked is whether there is any persuasive reason to believe that, with regard to wholly foreign conduct, Section One in the criminal context is not co-extensive with Section One in the civil context.

In answering this second question, courts must be careful to determine whether this construction of Section One's criminal reach conforms with principles of international law. "It has been a maxim of statutory construction since the decision in *Murray v. The Charming Betsy*, 2 Cranch 64, 118, 2 L.Ed. 208 (1804), that 'an act of congress ought never to be construed to violate the law of nations, if any other possible construction remains.'"

* * *

This case does present a new interpretation. We are told this is the first instance in which the executive branch has chosen to interpret the criminal provisions of the Sherman Act as reaching conduct wholly committed outside of this country's borders.

Changing economic conditions, as well as different political agendas, mean that antitrust policies may change from administration to administration. The present administration has promulgated new Antitrust Enforcement Guidelines for International Operations which "focus primarily on situations in which the Sherman Act will grant jurisdiction and when the United States will exercise that jurisdiction" internationally. Brockbank, *The 1995 International Antitrust Guidelines: The Reach of U.S. Antitrust Law Continues to Expand*, 2 J. Int'l Legal Stud. 1, 22 (1996). The new Guidelines reflect a stronger enforcement stance than earlier versions of the Guidelines, and have been described as a "warning to foreign governments and enterprises that the [antitrust enforcement] Agencies intend to actively pursue restraints on trade occurring abroad that adversely affect American markets or damage American exporting opportunities." Id. at 21. The instant case is likely a result of this policy.

It is with this context in mind that we must determine if the exercise of jurisdiction occasioned by the decision of the executive branch of the United States is proper in this case. While courts, including this one, speak of determining congressional intent when interpreting statutes, the meaning of the antitrust laws has emerged through the relationship among all three branches of government. In this criminal case, it is our responsibility to ensure that the executive's interpretation of the Sherman Act does not conflict with other legal principles, including principles of international law.

That question requires examination beyond the language of Section One of the Sherman Act. It is, of course, generally true that, as a principle of statutory interpretation, the same language should be read the same way in all contexts to which the language applies. But this is not invariably true. New content is sometimes ascribed to statutory terms depending upon context. * * * Where Congress intends that our laws conform with international law, and where international law suggests that criminal enforcement and civil enforcement be viewed differently, it is at least conceivable that different content could be ascribed to the same language depending on whether the context is civil or criminal. It is then worth asking about the effect of the international law which Congress presumably also meant to respect.

The content of international law is determined "by reference 'to the customs and usages of civilized nations, and, as evidence of these, to the works of jurists and commentators.' "*Hilao v. Estate of Marcos*, 103 F.3d 789, 794 (9th Cir.1996) (quoting *The Paquete Habana*, 175 U.S. 677, 700, 20 S.Ct. 290, 299, 44 L.Ed. 320 (1900)); see also *Kadic v. Karadzic*, 70 F.3d 232 (2d Cir.1995). The Restatement (Third) of the Foreign Relations Law of the United States restates international law, as derived from customary international law and from international agreements to which the United States is a party, as it applies to the United States. See Restatement (Third) of the Foreign Relations Law of the United States §§ 1, 101 (1987) [hereinafter Restatement]. The United States courts have treated the Restatement as an illuminating outline of central principles of international law. See *Hartford Fire*, 509 U.S. at 799, 113 S.Ct. at 2910–11 (citing Restatement); *Hartford Fire*, 509 U.S. at 818, 113 S.Ct. at 2920 (Scalia, J., dissenting) ("I shall rely on the Restatement (Third) of Foreign Relations Law for the relevant principles of international law. Its standards appear fairly supported in the decisions of this Court construing international choice-of-law principles ... and in the decisions of other federal courts...."); *In re Maxwell Communication Corp.*, 93 F.3d 1036, 1047–48 (2d Cir.1996).

* * *

Comment *f* to Section 403 states that the principles of Sections 402 and 403 "apply to criminal as well as to civil regulation." Id. § 403 cmt. *f*. But, specifically naming the United States antitrust laws, the comment also says that for statutes that give rise to both types of liability, "the presence of substantial foreign elements will ordinarily weigh against application of criminal law." Id. The comment argues that legislative intent to apply these laws criminally should only be found on the basis of "express statement or clear implication." Id.

While the majority opinion accurately states that this comment is an expression of the clear statement rule, the comment also implies that there are special concerns associated with the imposition of criminal sanctions on foreign conduct. See also id. § 403 n. 8 ("In applying the principle of reasonableness, the exercise of criminal (as distinguished from civil) jurisdiction in relation to acts committed in another state may be perceived as particularly intrusive."). Indeed, most people recognize a distinction between civil and criminal liability; that the law of nations should do so as well is not surprising. And while *Hartford Fire* and earlier judicial decisions have found that the antitrust laws do apply, in the civil context, to foreign conduct, this antitrust common law is not the express statement of legislative intent that the Restatement suggests may be appropriate in the criminal context.

* * *

Notes

1. On the principal case, see Sulcove, The Extraterritorial Reach of the Criminal Provisions of U.S. Antitrust Laws: The Impact of United States v. Nippon Paper Industries, 19 U. Pa. J. Int'l Econ. L. 1067 (1998).

2. Since the court found that the conduct complained of was illegal under Japanese law, would it have been proper for the American court to stay the proceedings before it in order to give the Japanese authorities an opportunity to seek appropriate redress? Is there a doctrine of forum non conveniens in criminal cases? Should there be?

MODEL PENAL CODE

10 U.L.A. 433 (1974).

§ 1.03. Territorial Applicability

(1) Except as otherwise provided in this Section, a person may be convicted under the law of this State of an offense committed by his own conduct or the conduct of another for which he is legally accountable if:

(a) either the conduct which is an element of the offense or the result which is such an element occurs within this State; or

(b) conduct occurring outside the State is sufficient under the law of this State to constitute an attempt to commit an offense within the State; or

(c) conduct occurring outside the State is sufficient under the law of this State to constitute a conspiracy to commit an offense within the State and an overt act in furtherance of such conspiracy occurs within the State; or

(d) conduct occurring within the State establishes complicity in the commission of, or an attempt, solicitation or conspiracy to commit, an offense in another jurisdiction which also is an offense under the law of this State; or

(e) the offense consists of the omission to perform a legal duty imposed by the law of this State with respect to domicile, residence or a relationship to a person, thing or transaction in the State; or

(f) the offense is based on a statute of this State which expressly prohibits conduct outside the State, when the conduct bears a reasonable relation to a legitimate interest of this State and the actor knows or should know that his conduct is likely to affect that interest.

(2) Subsection (1)(a) does not apply when either causing a specified result or a purpose to cause or danger of causing such a result is an element of an offense and the result occurs or is designed or likely to occur only in another jurisdiction where the conduct charged would not constitute an offense, unless a legislative purpose plainly appears to declare the conduct criminal regardless of the place of the result.

(3) Subsection (1)(a) does not apply when causing a particular result is an element of an offense and the result is caused by conduct occurring outside the State which would not constitute an offense if the result had occurred there, unless the actor purposely or knowingly caused the result within the State.

(4) When the offense is homicide, either the death of the victim or the bodily impact causing death constitutes a "result," within the meaning of Subsection (1)(a) and if the body of a homicide victim is found within the State, it is presumed that such result occurred within the State.

(5) This State includes the land and water and the air space above such land and water with respect to which the State has legislative jurisdiction.

Note

Are these provisions compatible with international law?

OTHER EXTRATERRITORIAL ECONOMIC REGULATIONS: THE HELMS–BURTON ACT OF 1996 AND THE IRAN AND LIBYA SANCTIONS ACT

The Helms–Burton Act of 1996—officially the "Cuban Liberty and Democratic Solidarity (*Libertád*) Act—and the Iran and Libya Sanctions of the same year (ILSA) were adopted to deter persons in third countries from engaging in transactions involving investments or trade with the targeted countries. Both laws have been widely condemned by governments and international bodies as violations of international law because of their assertions of extraterritorial jurisdiction.

Title III of the Helms–Burton Act, Pub. L. No. 104–114, 110 Stat. 785 (Mar. 12, 1996), 22 U.S.C.A. §§ 6021–6091, 35 I.L.M. 357 (1996), enables United States nationals to recover civil damages in U.S. courts from any person or entity that has "trafficked" in property "confiscated" (i.e., expropriated without payment of compensation) by the Cuban government to which the U.S. national has a claim. "Trafficking" is broadly defined; it includes buying, selling, managing or otherwise benefiting from "confiscated" property. The law also provides that the Act of State doctrine shall not apply to any lawsuit brought under the civil remedy provision (§ 302(a)(6)). Title IV of the Helms–Burton Act authorizes U.S. officials to exclude aliens and their immediate families from the United States if the alien has been involved in the "trafficking" of property of a U.S. national that had been confiscated by Cuba.

The Iran and Libya Sanctions Act (ILSA), Pub. L. No. 104–172, 110 Stat. 1541 (Aug. 5, 1996), 35 I.L.M. 1273 (1996), requires sanctions to be imposed on any person or entity that engages in trade or makes investments that contribute to development of petroleum resources in Iran or Libya. These provisions were clearly meant to apply to foreign persons; U.S. nationals had been covered by earlier restrictions. The sanctions are in furtherance of counter-terrorism and non-proliferation policies.

Both acts were criticized by a large number of countries as violations of international law because they imposed penalties for actions outside of the United States that were legal in the countries under the applicable national law. Some states—including close allies of the United States—adopted blocking and clawback statutes to hinder the application of these statutes. The U.N. General Assembly adopted resolutions by a large majority condemning U.S. unilateral economic measures, *inter alia* because of the assertion of extraterritorial jurisdiction. The European Union protested the Helms–Burton Act diplomatically and complained about it at the World Trade Organization. Canada and Mexico raised objections under the North American Free Trade Agreement. A legal body, the Inter–American Juridical Committee (an organ of the Organization of American States), unanimously concluded that the Helms–Burton Act violated the international law of jurisdiction. It declared that "[a] prescribing State does not have the right to exercise jurisdiction over acts of 'trafficking' abroad by aliens under circumstances where neither the alien nor the conduct in question has any connection with its territory and where no apparent connection exists between such acts and the protection of its essential sovereign interests." The U.S. member of the committee, Keith Highet, voted for the declaration. See materials reprinted at 35 I.L.M. 397, 483, 1322, 1333 (1996).

The U.S. government rejected the legal arguments of the European and Latin American states. However, President Clinton issued a series of six-month waivers postponing the right to invoke the remedy under Title III of Helms–Burton. He declared that he would postpone that right as long as the U.S. allies continued their advocacy of democratic change in Cuba. See Statement by the President on Suspending Title III of the Helms–Burton Act, 36 I.L.M. 216 (1997). Nevertheless, the issue of the international legality of Helms–Burton (as well as ILSA) has remained a lively subject of dispute among governments and international lawyers.

Notes

1. Supporters of Helms–Burton have argued, citing judicial decisions in national courts, that a state which has taken property without just compensation does not acquire good title and consequently persons acquiring the property (or trafficking in it) are in the same legal position as one who obtains property from a thief. See Brice Clagett, Title III of the Helms–Burton Act is Consistent with International Law, 90 A.J.I.L. 434, 437 (1996); Malcolm Wilkey, "Helms–Burton:

Its Fundamental Basis, Validity and Practical Effect," ABA International Law News; compare F.A. Mann, Further Studies in International Law 186 (1990).

2. On the premise that a taking of property without just compensation violates international law, would a state (e.g., the United States) be entitled to give a civil remedy to the original owner (or successor in title) against the person who bought the property in question from the nationalizing state? Would this be justified as adjudicatory jurisdiction to enforce international law? Compare Sections 7–8 of this Chapter and Chapter 10, pp. 813–817. Is Helms–Burton comparable to the U.S. cases under the Alien Tort Claims Act (see Chapters 2 and 8, pp. 143, 647) where a foreign defendant could be held liable for acts abroad that are contrary to international customary law? Why have foreign states—even ones that share the U.S. position on legal requirements of compensation for expropriated property—reacted so negatively to Helms–Burton?

3. Should Helms–Burton penalties against traffickers for acts permitted in their countries be regarded as a type of secondary boycott that is (or should be) forbidden by international law? The United States declared its general opposition to secondary boycotts when the Arab states imposed a boycott against persons in other countries who had dealings with Israel. Do such "unfriendly" boycotts violate international law if intended to compel or influence the target state to change its domestic policy? See discussion on economic coercion supra pp. 940–941 and Damrosch, Politics Across Borders: Nonintervention and Nonforcible Influence Over Domestic Affairs, 83 A.J.I.L. 1 (1989). On Helms–Burton as a secondary boycott, see Lowenfeld, Congress and Cuba: The Helms–Burton Act, 90 A.J.I.L. 419 (1996); Clagett, A Reply to Professor Lowenfeld, id. at 641 (1996); Walker, The Legality of the Secondary Boycott Contained in the Helms–Burton Act Under International Law, 3 DePaul Dig. Int. L. 1134 (1997).

4. Could Helms–Burton and ILSA be justified by the "protective principle" of jurisdiction, infra p. 1134? Both acts refer to protecting the national security of the United States as a purpose of the legislation and its proponents consider the three target states as sources of terrorism against the United States. Is this consideration sufficient to justify measures against individuals in third countries whose economic activities may be beneficial to the target countries?

5. For additional readings, see Busby, Jurisdiction to Limit Third–Country Interaction with Sanctioned States: The Iran and Libya Sanctions and Helms–Burton Acts, 36 Colum. J. Transnat'l Law 621 (1998); Gierbolini, The Helms–Burton Act: Inconsistency with International Law and Irrationality at their Maximum, 6 J. Transnat'l L & Policy 289 (1997); Fairey, The Helms–Burton Act: The Effect of International Law on Domestic Implementation, 46 Am. U. L. Rev 1289 (1997); Brigitte Stern, Vers La Mondialisation Juridique? Les Lois Helms–Burton et D'Amato–Kennedy R.G.D.I.P. 1996, p. 4; European Union: Demarches Protesting the Cuban Liberty and Democratic Solidarity Act 35 I.L.M. 397 (1996); Tramhel, Helms–Burton Invites a Look at Counter–Measures, 30 Geo.Wash.J. Int'l L. & Econ. 317 (1996/7); Damrosch, Enforcing International Law Through Non–Forcible Measures, 269 Rec. des Cours 9, 63–78, 85–91 (1997); Report of the Committee on Inter–American Affairs, Domestic Legal Issues Concerning the Helms–Burton Act, 54 Record Ass'n Bar City N.Y. 515 (1999).

6. Notwithstanding their protests about exorbitant exercises of U.S. jurisdiction, some European states have purported to prescribe certain rules of law on a broad extraterritorial basis, affecting U.S. companies acting within U.S. territory

in accordance with U.S. law. For example, in November 2000 a French court ruled that French laws barring racist propaganda and sale of Nazi memorabilia would apply to the operations of Yahoo!, a U.S.-based Internet service provider; and it instructed Yahoo! to block access by French nationals to the auction section of its website. Yahoo! contended not only that it would be technologically impossible to prevent French nationals from reaching the website, but also that the First Amendment of the U.S. Constitution would prevent censorship of the content of the site. See "French Court Ruling Hits Yahoo!", Financial Times, Nov. 21, 2000, p. 1, and Editorial Comment, ibid., p. 20.

SECTION 3. JURISDICTION BASED ON NATIONALITY

A. JURISDICTION BASED ON NATIONALITY OVER NATURAL PERSONS

BLACKMER v. UNITED STATES

Supreme Court of the United States, 1932.
284 U.S. 421, 52 S.Ct. 252, 76 L.Ed. 375 (some footnotes omitted).

HUGHES, C.J.: The petitioner, Harry M. Blackmer, a citizen of the United States resident in Paris, France, was adjudged guilty of contempt of the Supreme Court of the District of Columbia for failure to respond to subpoenas served upon him in France and requiring him to appear as a witness on behalf of the United States at a criminal trial in that court. Two subpoenas were issued, for appearances at different times, and there was a separate proceeding with respect to each. The two cases were heard together, and a fine of $30,000 with costs was imposed in each case, to be satisfied out of the property of the petitioner which had been seized by order of the court. The decrees were affirmed by the Court of Appeals of the District [49 F.2d 523], and this Court granted writs of certiorari * * *.

The subpoenas were issued and served, and the proceedings to punish for contempt were taken, under the provisions of the Act of July 3, 1926, c. 762, 44 Stat. 835, U.S.C., tit. 28, §§ 711–718 (28 U.S.C.A. §§ 711–718). The statute provides that whenever the attendance at the trial of a criminal action of a witness abroad, who is "a citizen of the United States or domiciled therein," is desired by the Attorney General, or any assistant or district attorney acting under him, the judge of the court in which the action is pending may order a subpoena to issue, to be addressed to a consul of the United States and to be served by him personally upon the witness with a tender of traveling expenses. Sections 2, 3 of the act (28 U.S.C.A. §§ 712, 713). Upon proof of such service and of the failure of the witness to appear, the court may make an order requiring the witness to show cause why he should not be punished for contempt, and, upon the issue of such an order, the court may direct that property belonging to the witness and within the United States may be seized and held to satisfy any judgment which may be rendered against him in the proceeding. Sections 4, 5 (28 U.S.C.A. §§ 714, 715). Provision is made for personal service of the order upon the witness and also for its publication in a newspaper of general circulation in the district where the court is sitting. Section 6 (28 U.S.C.A. § 716). If, upon the hearing, the charge is sustained, the court may adjudge the witness guilty of contempt and impose upon him a fine not exceeding $100,000, to be satisfied by a sale of the property seized. Section 7 (28 U.S.C.A. § 717). This statute and the proceedings against the petitioner are assailed as being repugnant to the Constitution of the United States.

First. The principal objections to the statute are that it violates the due process clause of the Fifth Amendment. These contentions are: (1) That the "Congress has no power to authorize United States consuls to serve process except as permitted by treaty;" (2) that the act does not provide "a valid method of acquiring judicial jurisdiction to render personal judgment against defendant and judgment against his property;" (3) that the act "does not require actual or any other notice to defendant of the offense or of the Government's claim against his property;" (4) that the provisions "for hearing and judgment in the entire absence of the accused and without his consent" are invalid; and (5) that the act is "arbitrary, capricious and unreasonable."

While it appears that the petitioner removed his residence to France in the year 1924, it is undisputed that he was, and continued to be, a citizen of the United States. He continued to owe allegiance to the United States. By virtue of the obligations of citizenship, the United States retained its authority over him, and he was bound by its laws made applicable to him in a foreign country. Thus, although resident abroad, the petitioner remained subject to the taxing power of the United States. Cook v. Tait, 265 U.S. 47, 54, 56, 44 S.Ct. 444, 68 LEd. 895. For disobedience to its laws through conduct abroad, he was subject to punishment in the courts of the United States. United States v. Bowman, 260 U.S. 94, 102, 43 S.Ct. 39, 67 L.Ed. 149. With respect to such an exercise of authority, there is no question of international law,[6] but solely of the purport of the municipal law which establishes the duties of the citizen in relation to his own government. While the legislation of the Congress, unless the contrary intent appears, is construed to apply only within the territorial jurisdiction of the United States, the question of its application, so far as citizens of the United States in foreign countries are concerned, is one of construction, not of legislative power. American Banana Co. v. United Fruit Co., 213 U.S. 347, 357, 29 S.Ct. 511, 53 L.Ed. 826, 16 Ann. Cas. 1047; United States v. Bowman, supra; Robertson v. Labor Board, 268 U.S. 619, 622, 45 S.Ct. 621, 69 L.Ed. 1119. Nor can it be doubted that the United States possesses the power inherent in sovereignty to require the return to this country of a citizen, resident elsewhere, whenever the public interest requires it, and to penalize him in case of refusal. Compare Bartue and the Duchess of Suffolk's Case, 2 Dyer's Rep. 176b, 73 Eng. Rep. 388; Knowles v. Luce, Moore 109, 72 Eng. Rep. 473. What in England was the prerogative of the sovereign in this respect pertains under our constitutional system to the national authority which may be exercised by the Congress by virtue of the legislative power to prescribe the duties of the citizens of the United States. It is also beyond controversy that one of the duties which the citizen owes to his government is to support the administration of justice by

6. "The law of Nations does not prevent a State from exercising jurisdiction over its subjects travelling or residing abroad, since they remain under its personal supremacy." Oppenheim, International Law (4th Ed.) vol 1, § 145, p. 281; * * * Hyde, International Law, vol. 1, § 240, p. 424; Borchard, Diplomatic Protection of Citizens Abroad, § 13, pp. 21, 22.

attending its courts and giving his testimony whenever he is properly summoned. * * * And the Congress may provide for the performance of this duty and prescribe penalties for disobedience.

In the present instance, the question concerns only the method of enforcing the obligation. The jurisdiction of the United States over its absent citizen, so far as the binding effect of its legislation is concerned, is a jurisdiction in personam, as he is personally bound to take notice of the laws that are applicable to him and to obey them. United States v. Bowman, supra. But for the exercise of judicial jurisdiction in personam, there must be due process, which requires appropriate notice of the judicial action and an opportunity to be heard. For this notice and opportunity the statute provides. The authority to require the absent citizen to return and testify necessarily implies the authority to give him notice of the requirement. As his attendance is needed in court, it is appropriate that the Congress should authorize the court to direct the notice to be given, and that it should be in the customary form of a subpoena. Obviously, the requirement would be nugatory, if provision could not be made for its communication to the witness in the foreign country. The efficacy of an attempt to provide constructive service in this country would rest upon the presumption that the notice would be given in a manner calculated to reach the witness abroad. * * * The question of the validity of the provision for actual service of the subpoena in a foreign country is one that arises solely between the government of the United States and the citizen. The mere giving of such a notice to the citizen in the foreign country of the requirement of his government that he shall return is in no sense an invasion of any right of the foreign government and the citizen has no standing to invoke any such supposed right. While consular privileges in foreign countries are the appropriate subjects of treaties, it does not follow that every act of a consul, as, e.g., in communicating with citizens of his own country, must be predicated upon a specific provision of a treaty. The intercourse of friendly nations, permitting travel and residence of the citizens of each in the territory of the other, presupposes and facilitates such communications. In selecting the consul for the service of the subpoena, the Congress merely prescribed a method deemed to assure the desired result but in no sense essential. The consul was not directed to perform any function involving consular privileges or depending upon any treaty relating to them, but simply to act as any designated person might act for the government in conveying to the citizen the actual notice of the requirement of his attendance. The point raised by the petitioner with respect to the provision for the service of the subpoena abroad is without merit.

As the Congress could define the obligation, it could prescribe a penalty to enforce it. And, as the default lay in disobedience to an authorized direction of the court, it constituted a contempt of court, and the Congress could provide for procedure appropriate in contempt cases. * * *

Decrees affirmed.

Notes

1. In Skiriotes v. Florida, 313 U.S. 69, 61 S.Ct. 924, 85 L.Ed. 1193 (1941), the Supreme Court affirmed defendant's conviction for violation of a state statute making it criminal to use diving equipment in the taking of sponges off the coast

of Florida. Defendant had been arrested in Florida, but argued that the state had no power to try him because he had used the proscribed equipment while six miles from shore. The Court avoided the question of the extent of Florida's territorial waters, and, assuming from the record that Skiriotes was a citizen of the United States and of Florida, concluded that Florida might regulate the conduct of its "citizens" upon the high seas with respect to matters in which it had a legitimate interest and when there was no conflict with acts of Congress. Id. at 77.

2. A number of statutory provisions, in addition to that applied to *Blackmer*, apply specifically to the conduct or income of United States nationals abroad. See, e.g., 18 U.S.C.A. § 2381 (proscribing treason by anyone "owing allegiance to the United States" "within the United States or elsewhere"); 18 U.S.C.A. § 953 (punishing unauthorized attempts by "any citizen of the United States, wherever he may be," to influence a foreign government in its relations with the United States); 50 U.S.C.A.App. § 453 (requiring "every male citizen of the United States," *inter alia*, to register for military service). In the United Kingdom, statutes provide for the punishment of not only treason, but also homicide, bigamy, perjury, and other crimes, when committed abroad by a British subject. 10 Halsbury's Laws of England 322–24 (Simonds ed. 1955). See also 2 O'Connell at 898–99; 2 Hackworth at 203–06. India has provided that its criminal law applies to Indian nationals everywhere, no matter how minor the offense. Indian Penal Code § 4 (3d ed. Raju 1965). Non-common law states also claim comprehensive jurisdiction over crimes committed by nationals abroad. In France, for example, a citizen can be prosecuted in France for any *crime* (roughly equivalent to a felony) and many *délits* (misdemeanors) committed abroad. Code de Procédure Pénale, Art. 689 (Dalloz 1966); see Delaume, Jurisdiction over Crimes Committed Abroad: French and American Law, 21 Geo. Wash. L.Rev. 173 (1952); 1 Travers, Le Droit Pénal International 584–631 (1920). See also German Penal Code (Strafgesetzbuch) § 3 (German criminal law applicable to Germans whether act committed in Germany or abroad), § 4 (German criminal law applicable to persons acquiring German citizenship after criminal act has been committed).

3. Under what circumstances will a United States statute be held to apply to conduct by United States nationals taking place outside United States territory, when the statute does not expressly so provide? In United States v. Bowman, 260 U.S. 94, 43 S.Ct. 39, 67 L.Ed. 149 (1922), mentioned in *Blackmer*, the Supreme Court held that a statute punishing conspiracy to defraud a United States-owned corporation was applicable to conduct taking place on the high seas. The court stated that to limit the statute's scope to "the strictly territorial jurisdiction" would be greatly to curtail its usefulness and to leave open "a large immunity for frauds as easily committed by citizens on the high seas and in foreign countries as at home." In such cases, the Court continued, Congress had not "thought it necessary to make specific provision in the law that the *locus* shall include the high seas and foreign countries, but allows it to be inferred from the nature of the offense." Id. at 98. The conviction of three United States nationals was accordingly affirmed on the ground that they were "certainly subject to such laws as [the United States] might pass to protect itself and its property." Id. at 102. Cf. Steele v. Bulova Watch Co., 344 U.S. 280, 73 S.Ct. 252, 97 L.Ed. 319 (1952); Ramirez & Feraud Chili Co. v. Las Palmas Food Co., 146 F.Supp. 594 (S.D.Cal.1956), aff'd per curiam, 245 F.2d 874 (9th Cir.1957), cert. denied, 355 U.S. 927, 78 S.Ct. 384, 2 L.Ed.2d 357 (1958), construing the Lanham Act to reach infringement of trademarks by United States nationals in foreign countries but producing adverse economic effects in the United States. But cf. Vanity Fair Mills Inc. v. T. Eaton Co., 234 F.2d 633 (2d Cir.1956), cert. denied, 352 U.S. 871, 77 S.Ct. 96, 1 L.Ed.2d

76 (1956), reh. denied, 352 U.S. 913, 77 S.Ct. 144, 1 L.Ed.2d 120 (1956), holding that the Lanham Act did not provide a remedy for trademark infringement by a Canadian corporation in Canada, even though the infringement caused economic harm to plaintiff in the United States.

More recently, some lower courts have understood *Bowman* as grounded not only in the power of Congress to regulate conduct of U.S. nationals, but also in the power to protect state interests (in international law terms, the protective principle rather than the nationality principle). Thus, in United States v. Bin Laden, 92 F.Supp. 2d 189, 193–198 (S.D.N.Y.2000), where the indictment alleged that the defendants (who included foreign nationals) had conspired to bomb American facilities overseas, the court rejected the contention that U.S. statutes making it a crime to destroy property belonging to the United States should be construed as applicable only to U.S. nationals. On other jurisdictional issues in the *Bin Laden* case, see pp. 1122, 1135.

4. The statute involved in Blackmer v. United States, the principal case, is now codified as 28 U.S.C.A. § 1783, and is incorporated by reference into Fed. R.Civ. P. 45(b)(2) and Fed. R.Crim. P. 17(e)(2). It provides in relevant part that a United States court may order the issuance of a subpoena requiring the appearance as a witness of a "national or resident of the United States who is in a foreign country" if such testimony is "necessary in the interest of justice." Would the Court in the principal case have reached the same result if Blackmer had been an alien, domiciled in the United States? Is it unreasonable for a state to assert legislative jurisdiction over its domiciliaries when they are abroad? Compare Milliken v. Meyer, 311 U.S. 457, 462, 61 S.Ct. 339, 342, 85 L.Ed. 278 (1940) ("Domicile in the state is alone sufficient to bring an absent defendant within the reach of the state's jurisdiction for purposes of a personal judgment by means of appropriate substituted service.") The word "resident" in 28 U.S.C.A. § 1783 was, in the 1948 revision of the Judicial Code, substituted for "or domiciled therein." Would an alien's residence or domicile in the United States provide a reasonable basis for the assertion of legislative jurisdiction with regard to an act committed outside the United States? See Smit, International Aspects of Federal Civil Procedure, 61 Colum. L.Rev. 1031, 1048–49 (1961).

5. Once it is established that a defendant is a national of a state, may that state exercise jurisdiction over him? Does your answer depend on whether an international or national concept of nationality is applied? Cf. Grubel v. Nassauer, 210 N.Y. 149, 103 N.E. 1113 (1913) (denying recognition to an Austrian judgment rendered against an Austrian who had emigrated to the United States before the Austrian proceedings had been commenced). Would domicile be a more appropriate basis for jurisdiction? Cf. Friedmann, The Changing Structure of International Law 235–36 (1964). Should a distinction be drawn depending on whether civil or criminal jurisdiction is exercised?

6. It has been held that a state has jurisdiction to try and punish one of its nationals for an offense committed abroad even though he is also a national of the state in which the offense was committed. Coumas v. Superior Court, 31 Cal.2d 682, 192 P.2d 449 (1948); Tomoya Kawakita v. United States, 343 U.S. 717, 72 S.Ct. 950, 96 L.Ed. 1249 (1952).

B. JURISDICTION BASED ON NATIONALITY OVER LEGAL PERSONS

RESTATEMENT (THIRD)

§ 414. Jurisdiction with Respect to Activities of Foreign Branches and Subsidiaries

(1) Subject to §§ 403 and 441, a state may exercise jurisdiction to prescribe for limited purposes with respect to activities of foreign branches of corporations organized under its laws.

(2) A state may not ordinarily regulate activities of corporations organized under the laws of a foreign state on the basis that they are owned or controlled by nationals of the regulating state. However, under § 403 and subject to § 441, it may not be unreasonable for a state to exercise jurisdiction for limited purposes with respect to activities of affiliated foreign entities

(a) by direction to the parent corporation in respect of such matters as uniform accounting, disclosure to investors, or preparation of consolidated tax returns of multinational enterprises; or

(b) by direction to either the parent or the subsidiary in exceptional cases, depending on all relevant factors, including the extent to which

(i) the regulation is essential to implementation of a program to further a major national interest of the state exercising jurisdiction;

(ii) the national program of which the regulation is a part can be carried out effectively only if it is applied also to foreign subsidiaries;

(iii) the regulation conflicts or is likely to conflict with the law or policy of the state where the subsidiary is established.

(c) In the exceptional cases referred to in paragraph (b), the burden of establishing reasonableness is heavier when the direction is issued to the foreign subsidiary than when it is issued to the parent corporation.

Notes

1. The traditional rule is that a state has jurisdiction over legal persons organized under its laws. Many states, in addition, assert jurisdiction over legal persons whose principal place of business or registered office (*siège social*) is located in their territories, without encountering objections assertedly based on international law. States have further sought to regulate activities by legal persons organized or having their principal places of business abroad when these persons are owned or controlled by nationals. All three of these criteria can be found in United States law. See Restatement (Third) § 414, Reporters' Note 4. It is particularly the jurisdiction exercised over foreign legal persons owned or controlled by nationals that has led to objections by foreign states. See, e.g., the Soviet pipeline dispute, involving export prohibitions imposed by the United States pursuant to the Export Administration Act of 1979, 50 U.S.C.A. App. § 2404, upon "any person subject to the jurisdiction of the United States." The regulations issued to effectuate these prohibitions purported to extend their effect to foreign persons, not owned or controlled by United States persons, who had agreed, in licensing contracts concluded with United States persons, to abide by export prohibitions that might be promulgated by the United States. See, e.g., Export of Oil and Gas Equipment to the Soviet Union, Statement on Extension of U.S. Sanctions, 18 Weekly Comp. Pres. Doc. 820 (June 18, 1982). The European Economic Community and several of its member states protested and ordered persons in their territories to perform their contracts and deliver the pipeline materials to their Russian purchasers. See Legal Serv. E.C.Com., European

Communities: Comments on the U.S. Regulations Concerning Trade with the U.S.S.R., reprinted in 21 I.L.M. 891 (1982); N.Y. Times, Aug. 24, 1982, at D1, col. 3; N.Y. Times, July 23, 1982, at A1, col. 6 (government of France compelling all French companies to honor pipeline-related contracts with the Soviet Union); United Kingdom: Statement and Order Concerning the American Export Embargo with Regard to the Soviet Gas Pipeline (Aug. 2, 1982), reprinted in 21 I.L.M. 851 (1982) (British government order to four British companies with the largest pipeline contracts not to comply with the U.S. embargo). Were the European objections based on solid international law grounds? What if the "person subject to the jurisdiction of the United States" owns, but does not control, the foreign person? For a statement of the U.S. position, see Dam, Extraterritoriality and Conflicts of Jurisdiction, 1983 A.S.I.L.Proc. 370 (1983). See also the essays collected in 27 Ger. Y.B.I.L. 28–141 (1984).

2. Other areas in which the United States has endeavored to extend the extraterritorial reach of its legislation include shipping, tax, export control, anti-boycott legislation, foreign corrupt practices, and securities law. On such subjects, see Restatement (Third) § 414, Reporters' Notes 3–8. On the conflicts with foreign sovereigns that have arisen as a consequence, see Section 6 infra.

In McCulloch v. Sociedad Nacional de Marineros de Honduras, 372 U.S. 10, 83 S.Ct. 671, 9 L.Ed.2d 547 (1963), the Supreme Court refused to apply the National Labor Relations Act to maritime operations of foreign flag vessels employing alien seamen, even though the foreign corporations owning the vessels were wholly owned by American corporations and the vessels were operating in a regular course of trade between foreign and United States ports. The Court referred specifically to complications in international relations that might ensue from the application of the Act to such operations.

Compare United States v. Mitchell, 553 F.2d 996 (5th Cir.1977) (Marine Mammal Protection Act of 1972 held to protect animals only within U.S. territory and therefore inapplicable to U.S. citizens committing violations abroad) with United States v. King, 552 F.2d 833 (9th Cir.1976), cert. denied, 430 U.S. 966, 97 S.Ct. 1646, 52 L.Ed.2d 357 (1977) (conspiracy by U.S. citizens to distribute narcotics in Japan held a violation of 21 U.S.C.A. § 959 because defendants' intent was to import drugs into the U.S.).

3. On the extraterritorial reach of United States tax laws, see Restatement (Third) §§ 411–13. On the controversial "unitary tax" imposed by many states, see Container Corp. of America v. Franchise Tax Board, 463 U.S. 159, 103 S.Ct. 2933, 77 L.Ed.2d 545 (1983) (upholding the California unitary tax on a Delaware corporation, headquartered in Illinois); Restatement (Third) § 412, Reporters' Note 7. For the same issue in an international context, see Barclays Bank PLC v. Franchise Tax Board of California, 512 U.S. 298, 114 S.Ct. 2268, 129 L.Ed.2d 244 (1994) (upholding imposition of California income tax on the part of the worldwide income of a foreign multinational company that was attributed to California under a statutory formula).

On securities regulation, see Fox, Securities Disclosure in a Globalizing Market: Who Should Regulate Whom, 95 Mich. L. Rev. 696 (1998); Fox, The Political Economy of Statutory Reach: U.S. Disclosure Rules in a Globalizing Market for Securities, 97 Mich. L. Rev. 696 (1998); Choi & Guzman, National Laws, International Money: Regulation in a Global Capital Market, 65 Fordham L. Rev. 1855 (1997).

4. In Equal Employment Opportunity Commission v. Arabian American Oil Co., 499 U.S. 244, 111 S.Ct. 1227, 113 L.Ed.2d 274 (1991), the Supreme Court, per

Chief Justice Rehnquist, with Justices Marshall, Blackmun and Stevens dissenting, ruled that Title VII of the Civil Rights Act of 1964 did not apply extraterritorially to reach alleged discrimination (on the ground of race, religion, and national origin) by Aramco, a Delaware corporation, in regard to a U.S. citizen employed in Saudi Arabia. Application of a presumption that legislation generally has territorial scope (in the absence of a clear indication of congressional intent to legislate on an extraterritorial basis) led the Court to conclude that Congress did not intend to reach this conduct.

Shortly thereafter, Congress amended the Civil Rights Act to clarify its applicability to overseas operations of U.S. corporations, thereby overruling *EEOC v. Aramco.* Civil Rights Act of 1991, § 109, Pub. L. 102–166, 105 Stat. 1071, codified at 42 U.S.C. § 2000e(f); see Davila v. New York Hospital, 813 F.Supp. 977 (S.D.N.Y.1993).

5. May a state assert on the international level the rights of a corporation that neither is organized under its law nor has a principal office within its territory on the ground that the corporation is owned or controlled by shareholders who are nationals of the state? On this question, see the Barcelona Traction Case, 1970 I.C.J. 3, discussed in Chapter 10.

C. JURISDICTION BASED ON THE NATIONALITY OF THE VICTIM

(The Passive Personality Principle)

UNITED STATES v. FAWAZ YUNIS

United States Court of Appeals, District of Columbia Circuit, 1991.
288 U.S.App.D.C. 129, 924 F.2d 1086.

MIKVA, CHIEF JUDGE: Appellant Fawaz Yunis challenges his convictions on conspiracy, aircraft piracy, and hostage-taking charges stemming from the hijacking of a Jordanian passenger aircraft in Beirut, Lebanon. He appeals from orders of the district court denying his pretrial motions relating to jurisdiction, illegal arrest, alleged violations of the Posse Comitatus Act, and the government's withholding of classified documents during discovery. Yunis also challenges the district court's jury instructions as erroneous and prejudicial.

Although this appeal raises novel issues of domestic and international law, we reject Yunis' objections and affirm the convictions.

I. BACKGROUND

On June 11, 1985, appellant and four other men boarded Royal Jordanian Airlines Flight 402 ("Flight 402") shortly before its scheduled departure from Beirut, Lebanon. They wore civilian clothes and carried military assault rifles, ammunition bandoleers, and hand grenades. Appellant took control of the cockpit and forced the pilot to take off immediately. The remaining hijackers tied up Jordanian air marshals assigned to the flight and held the civilian passengers, including two American citizens, captive in their seats. The hijackers explained to the crew and passengers that they wanted the plane to fly to Tunis, where a conference of the Arab League was under way. The hijackers further explained that they wanted a meeting with delegates to the conference and that their ultimate goal was removal of all Palestinians from Lebanon.

After a refueling stop in Cyprus, the airplane headed for Tunis but turned away when authorities blocked the airport runway. Following a refueling stop at Palermo, Sicily, another attempt to land in Tunis, and a second stop in Cyprus, the plane returned to Beirut, where more hijackers came aboard. These reinforcements included an official of Lebanon's Amal Militia, the group at whose direction Yunis claims he acted. The plane then took off for Syria, but was turned away and went back to Beirut. There, the hijackers released the passengers, held a press conference reiterating their demand that Palestinians leave Lebanon, blew up the plane, and fled from the airport.

An American investigation identified Yunis as the probable leader of the hijackers and prompted U.S. civilian and military agencies, led by the Federal Bureau of Investigation (FBI), to plan Yunis' arrest. After obtaining an arrest warrant, the FBI put "Operation Goldenrod" into effect in September 1987. Undercover FBI agents lured Yunis onto a yacht in the eastern Mediterranean Sea with promises of a drug deal, and arrested him once the vessel entered international waters. The agents transferred Yunis to a United States Navy munitions ship and interrogated him for several days as the vessel steamed toward a second rendezvous, this time with a Navy aircraft carrier. Yunis was flown to Andrews Air Force Base from the aircraft carrier, and taken from there to Washington, D.C. In Washington, Yunis was arraigned on an original indictment charging him with conspiracy, hostage taking, and aircraft damage. A grand jury subsequently returned a superseding indictment adding additional aircraft damage counts and a charge of air piracy.

Yunis filed several pretrial motions, among them a motion to suppress statements he made while aboard the munitions ship. In *United States v. Yunis (Yunis I)*, 859 F.2d 953 (D.C.Cir.1988), this court reversed a district court order suppressing the statements, and authorized their introduction at trial. We revisited the case on a second interlocutory appeal relating to discovery of classified information, reversing the district court's disclosure order. *United States v. Yunis (Yunis II)*, 867 F.2d 617 (D.C.Cir.1989).

Yunis admitted participation in the hijacking at trial but denied parts of the government's account and offered the affirmative defense of obedience to military orders, asserting that he acted on instructions given by his superiors in Lebanon's Amal Militia. The jury convicted Yunis of conspiracy, 18 U.S.C. § 371 (1988), hostage taking, 18 U.S.C. § 1203 (1988), and air piracy, 49 U.S.C.app. § 1472(n) (1988). However, it acquitted him of three other charged offenses that went to trial: violence against people on board an aircraft, 18 U.S.C. § 32(b)(1) (1988), aircraft damage, 18 U.S.C. § 32(b)(2) (1988), and placing a destructive device aboard an aircraft, 18 U.S.C. § 32(b)(3) (1988). The district court imposed concurrent sentences of five years for conspiracy, thirty years for hostage taking, and twenty years for air piracy. Yunis appeals his conviction and seeks dismissal of the indictment.

II. Analysis

Yunis argues that the district court lacked subject matter and personal jurisdiction to try him on the charges of which he was convicted, that the indictment should have been dismissed because the government seized him in violation of the Posse Comitatus Act and withheld classified materials useful to his defense, and that the convictions should be reversed because of errors in the jury instructions. We consider these claims in turn.

A. Jurisdictional Claims

[The Court's discussion of the Hostage Taking Act has been omitted.]

* * *

Nor is jurisdiction precluded by norms of customary international law. The district court concluded that two jurisdictional theories of international law, the "universal principle" and the "passive personal principle," supported assertion of U.S. jurisdiction to prosecute Yunis on hijacking and hostage-taking charges. *See Yunis*, 681 F.Supp. at 899–903. Under the universal principle, states may prescribe and prosecute "certain offenses recognized by the community of nations as of universal concern, such as piracy, slave trade, attacks on or hijacking of aircraft, genocide, war crimes, and perhaps certain acts of terrorism," even absent any special connection between the state and the offense. See Restatement (Third) of the Foreign Relations Law of the United States §§ 404, 423 (1987) [hereinafter Restatement]. Under the passive personal principle, a state may punish non-nationals for crimes committed against its nationals outside of its territory, at least where the state has a particularly strong interest in the crime. See id. at § 402 comment *g*; *United States v. Benitez*, 741 F.2d 1312, 1316 (11th Cir.1984) (passive personal principle invoked to approve prosecution of Colombian citizen convicted of shooting U.S. drug agents in Colombia), *cert. denied*, 471 U.S. 1137 (1985).

Relying primarily on the Restatement, Yunis argues that hostage taking has not been recognized as a universal crime and that the passive personal principle authorizes assertion of jurisdiction over alleged hostage takers only where the victims were seized because they were nationals of the prosecuting state. Whatever merit appellant's claims may have as a matter of international law, they cannot prevail before this court. Yunis seeks to portray international law as a self-executing code that trumps domestic law whenever the two conflict. That effort misconceives the role of judges as appliers of international law and as participants in the federal system. Our duty is to enforce the Constitution, laws, and treaties of the United States, not to conform the law of the land to norms of customary international law. See U.S. CONST. art. VI. As we said in *Committee of U.S. Citizens Living in Nicaragua v. Reagan*, 859 F.2d 929 (D.C.Cir.1988): "Statutes inconsistent with principles of customary international law may well lead to international law violations. But within the domestic legal realm, that inconsistent statute simply modifies or supersedes customary international law to the extent of the inconsistency." *Id.* at 938. *See also Federal Trade Comm'n v. Compagnie de Saint–Gobain–Pont-à-Mousson*, 636 F.2d 1300, 1323 (D.C.Cir.1980) (U.S. courts "obligated to give effect to an unambiguous exercise by Congress of its jurisdiction to prescribe even if such an exercise would exceed the limitations imposed by international law").

To be sure, courts should hesitate to give penal statutes extraterritorial effect absent a clear congressional directive. See *Foley Bros. v. Filardo*, 336 U.S. 281, 285 (1949); *United States v. Bowman*, 260 U.S. 94, 98 (1922). Similarly, courts will not blind themselves to potential violations of international law where legislative intent is ambiguous. See *Murray v. The Schooner Charming Betsy,* 6 U.S. (2 Cranch) 64, 118 (1804) ("An act of congress ought never to be construed to violate the law of nations, if any other possible construction remains * * *."). But the statute in question reflects an unmistakable congressional intent, consistent with treaty obligations of the United States, to authorize prosecution of those who take Americans hostage abroad no matter where the offense occurs or where the offender is found. Our inquiry can go no further.

* * *

For the foregoing reasons, the convictions are

Affirmed.

Notes

1. A number of states have statutes asserting extraterritorial criminal legislative jurisdiction based on the victim's possessing their nationality. See the Lotus Case, p. 68 supra. It is disputed whether this is a permissible basis of jurisdiction, although objections to its exercise have not been made in recent years. See, e.g., Restatement (Third) § 402, Comment *g*; O'Connell, International Law 828–29 (2d ed. 1970) (tentatively accepting it); Brownlie, Principles of Public International Law 306 (5th ed. 1998) (calling it least justifiable of all bases); Mann, The Doctrine of Jurisdiction in International Law, 111 Rec. des Cours 39–41, 92–93 (1964–I) (noting that it has been severely criticized).

2. In 1984, the United States amended 18 U.S.C.A. § 7 to provide, in paragraph 7, that the "special maritime and territorial jurisdiction of the United States, as used in this title, includes * * * [a]ny place outside the jurisdiction of any nation with respect to an offense by or against a national of the United States". See also Restatement (Third) § 402, Comment *g*. Is this provision compatible with international law? Does it reflect sound legislative policy? Note that the section applies only to any place "outside the jurisdiction of any nation." For other amendments concerning "special maritime and territorial jurisdiction," see p. 1131.

In the *Achille Lauro* incident of 1985, a U.S. citizen, Leon Klinghoffer, was murdered by terrorists who seized an Italian-flag vessel in the Mediterranean and pushed him and his wheelchair into the sea. In the wake of this incident, Congress adopted a new provision for killing or serious bodily injury committed against "a national of the United States while such national is outside the United States." Omnibus Diplomatic Security and Antiterrorism Act of 1986, Pub. L. 99–399, codified at 18 U.S.C. § 2332. However, Congress deliberately decided not to extend such homicide jurisdiction to all such extraterritorial murders on a general passive personality theory of jurisdiction, but rather only to those of a specified nature, as follows:

> (e) *Limitation on prosecution.* No prosecution for any offense described in this section shall be undertaken by the United States except on written certification of the Attorney General * * * that, in the judgment of the certifying official, such offense was intended to coerce, intimidate, or retaliate against a government or a civilian population.

On September 13, 1994, another paragraph was added to 18 U.S.C. § 7, reading:

> (8) To the extent permitted by international law, any foreign vessel during a voyage having a scheduled departure from or arrival in the United

States with respect to an offense committed by or against a national of the United States.

Other recent enactments also assert U.S. criminal jurisdiction over certain international crimes that could be committed against U.S. nationals outside the United States. These include new statutes addressed to the use of weapons of mass destruction or the use of chemical weapons. See 18 U.S.C. §§ 2332a, 2332c. See Damrosch, Enforcing International Law Through Non–Forcible Measures, 269 Rec. des Cours 9, 222–225 (1997).

These statutes have been invoked in several recent prosecutions against foreign nationals for plots to attack U.S. citizens outside the United States. In United States v. Yousef, 927 F.Supp. 673 (S.D.N.Y.1996), involving a conspiracy to kill U.S. nationals abroad by means of bombing aircraft, the court upheld the sufficiency of the indictment and sustained extraterritorial jurisdiction (under § 2332 and other statutes) as reasonable and consistent with international and constitutional law, notwithstanding the fact that the plot was foiled and no U.S. citizens were injured. In United States v. Bin Laden, 92 F.Supp.2d 189 (S.D.N.Y. 2000), concerning the bombings of the U.S. embassies in Kenya and Tanzania in August 1998 and a broader conspiracy to kill U.S. nationals anywhere in the world, several of the statutes under which defendants were charged (18 U.S.C. §§ 2332, 2332a) relied at least in part on the passive personality principle. Although defendants challenged the sufficiency of the indictment on the ground that the United States has "traditionally rejected" the passive personality theory of jurisdiction, the district court disagreed, citing the Restatement, § 402, Comment *g* for the proposition that the passive personality principle is "increasingly accepted as applied to terrorist and other organized attacks on a state's nationals by reason of their nationality." 92 F.Supp. at 221; see also United States v. Rezaq, 328 U.S. App. D.C. 297, 134 F.3d 1121, 1133 (D.C.Cir.), cert. denied, 525 U.S. 834, 119 S.Ct. 90, 142 L.Ed.2d 71 (1998). See pp. 1115, 1135, 1284 on other aspects of the Bin Laden indictment.

3. A 1996 amendment to the Foreign Sovereign Immunity Act added subsection (7) to Section 1605(a), 28 U.S.C.A. § 1605(a)(7), which provides for non-immunity of certain foreign states (those that have been designated as state sponsors of terrorism) for acts of torture, extrajudicial killing, aircraft sabotage, or hostage-taking occurring outside of the United States, where the victim or claimant is national of the United States. On this provision, see Chapter 14, p. 1231. See also MacKusick, Human Rights vs. Sovereign Rights: The State–Sponsored Terrorism Exception to the Foreign Sovereign Immunities Act, 10 Emory Int'l L.Rev. 741 (1996); Damrosch, Enforcing International Law Through Non–Forcible Measures, 296 Rec. des Cours 9, 172–176 (1997).

4. The enactments referred to in Notes 2 and 3 indicate an increasing willingness on the part of the United States to accept the passive personality principle. On this development, see Tyler, Winning at the Expense of Law: The Ramifications of Expanding Counter–Terrorism Law Enforcement Jurisdiction Overseas, 14 Am.U.Int'l Rev. 1473 (1999); Robinson, United States Practice Penalizing International Terrorists Needlessly Undercuts Its Opposition to the Passive Personality Principle, 16 Boston U. Int'l L.J. 487 (1998).

D. JURISDICTION BASED ON THE NATIONALITY OF VEHICLES AND OBJECTS

1. *Maritime Vessels*

Vessels are usually considered to possess the nationality of the state whose flag they fly. But, as in the case of persons, international law requires that there be a "genuine link" between the state and the vessel. For discussion, see Chapter 16, pp. 1486–1489.

2. *Aircraft and Space Vehicles*

CONVENTION ON INTERNATIONAL CIVIL AVIATION

Signed at Chicago, December 7, 1944.
61 Stat. 1180, T.I.A.S. No. 1591, 15 U.N.T.S. 295.

Art. 17. Aircraft have the nationality of the State in which they are registered.

Art. 18. An aircraft cannot be validly registered in more than one State, but its registration may be changed from one State to another.

Art. 19. The registration or transfer of registration of aircraft in any contracting State shall be made in accordance with its laws and regulations.

Notes

1. As of 2000, this Convention was in force for 185 states, including the United States.

2. Whether Articles 17 and 19 of the Chicago Convention, and comparable provisions of earlier agreements, codify rules that would be customary international law in the absence of agreement is a debatable question, particularly in the context of the "genuine link" requirement of the International Court of Justice in the Nottebohm Case (p. 430 supra), and of the corresponding doctrine in the Law of the Sea (p. 1486 infra). Compare, e.g., McDougal et al. Law and Public Order in Space (1963) at 553–54, with Cheng, The Law of International Air Transport 130–31 (1962).

The International Civil Aviation Organization (ICAO) Legal Committee proposed amendments to the Chicago Convention that would transfer certain functions and duties from the state of registry to the state of the operator. See Fitzgerald, The International Civil Aviation Organization and the Development of Conventions on International Air Law (1947–1978), 3 Annals Air & Space L. 51, 75 (1978).

Article 77 of the Chicago Convention provides that "[t]he [ICAO] Council shall determine in what manner the provisions of this Convention relating to nationality of aircraft shall apply to aircraft operated by international operating agencies." The ICAO Council made this determination in 1968. See ICAO Doc. 8722–C/976 (1968). International organizations have chosen to operate their aircraft on a national basis. Fitzgerald at 75.

3. 49 U.S.C.A. § 140(f) provides that a certificate of aircraft registration with the United States shall be "conclusive evidence of nationality for international purposes."

TREATY ON PRINCIPLES GOVERNING THE ACTIVITIES OF STATES IN THE EXPLORATION AND USE OF OUTER SPACE, INCLUDING THE MOON AND OTHER CELESTIAL BODIES

Done at London, Moscow, and Washington, January 27, 1967.
18 U.S.T. 2410, T.I.A.S. No. 6347, 610 U.N.T.S. 205.

Art. 8. A State Party to the Treaty on whose registry an object launched into outer space is carried shall retain jurisdiction and control over such object, and over any personnel thereof, while in outer space or on a celestial body. Ownership of objects launched into outer space, including objects landed or constructed on a celestial body, and of their component parts, is not affected by their presence in outer space or on a celestial body or by their return to the Earth. Such objects or component parts found beyond the limits of the State Party to the Treaty on whose registry they are carried shall be returned to that State Party, which shall, upon request, furnish identifying data prior to their return.

Notes

1. As of 2000, 100 states had become parties to this Convention, including the United States.

2. The Convention on Registration of Objects Launched into Outer Space, 28 U.S.T. 695, T.I.A.S. No. 8480, 1023 U.N.T.S. 15, provides for registration of such objects with the Secretary–General of the United Nations. As of 2000, 42 states had become parties to the Convention.

3. For an interesting comment on choice of law in space, see Comment, "Oh I have slipped the surly bonds of earth: Multinational Space Stations and Choice of Law, 78 Calif. L.Rev. 1375 (1990).

CONVENTION ON INTERNATIONAL CIVIL AVIATION

Signed at Chicago, December 7, 1944.
61 Stat. 1180, T.I.A.S. No. 1591, 15 U.N.T.S. 295.

Art. 1. The contracting States recognise that every State has complete and exclusive sovereignty over the airspace above its territory.

* * *

Art. 5. Each contracting State agrees that all aircraft of the other contracting States, being aircraft not engaged in scheduled international air services shall have the right, subject to the observance of the terms of this Convention, to make flights into or in transit nonstop across its territory and to make stops for non-traffic purposes without the necessity of obtaining prior permission, and subject to the right of the State flown over to require landing. Each contracting State nevertheless reserves the right, for reasons of safety of flight, to require aircraft desiring to proceed over regions which are inaccessible or without adequate air navigation facilities to follow prescribed routes, or to obtain special permission for such flights.

Such aircraft, if engaged in the carriage of passengers, cargo, or mail for remuneration or hire on other than scheduled international air services, shall also, subject to the provisions of Article 7, have the privilege of taking on or discharging passengers, cargo, or mail, subject to the right of any State where such embarkation or discharge takes place to impose such regulations, conditions or limitations as it may consider desirable.

Art. 6. No scheduled international air service may be operated over or into the territory of a contracting State, except with the special permission or other authorisation of that State, and in accordance with the terms of such permission or authorisation.

Notes

1. The Convention goes on to provide a legal framework regulating flights of civil aircraft (excluding state aircraft, which include aircraft used in military, customs, and police services). Under Article 3 state aircraft are not permitted to fly over or land in the territory of a state without authorization by special agreement or otherwise.

2. Do aircraft enjoy a right of "innocent passage" through the airspace of a foreign state in the absence of the latter's express agreement? (On the right of innocent passage of vessels through a foreign state's territorial waters, see p. 1401, infra.) The International Air Services Transit Agreement (59 Stat. 1693, E.A.S. 487, 84 U.N.T.S. 389) grants limited transit and landing rights to scheduled aircraft. Would such aircraft have any rights in the airspace of a state that was not a party to the IAST Agreement or to a special bilateral agreement? As a matter of practice, no state concedes or claims a right of innocent passage for aircraft in the airspace of another state, absent international agreement. Statements made by delegates to the Geneva Conference on the Law of the Sea (1958) indicate a widespread conviction that aircraft enjoy no right of innocent passage, such comparable privileges as exist being solely the result of international agreement. See, e.g., 3 U.N.Conf. on the Law of the Sea, Off. Rec. 8, 104 (United Kingdom), 26 (United States), 90–91 (Canada) (1958); 1 id. at 336 (comments by International Civil Aviation Organization) (1958). This position was reaffirmed in the negotiations for the 1982 U.N. Convention on the Law of the Sea. See Chapter 16.

On rights of aircraft transiting airspace above a foreign state's territorial sea, or over international straits or archipelagic sea-lanes, see Chapter 16, pp. 1404–1412.

3. Does a right of "entry in distress" exist for aircraft? Article 25 of the Convention on International Civil Aviation provides: "Each contracting State undertakes to provide such measures of assistance to aircraft in distress in its territory as it may find practicable * * *." Whether the foregoing provision imposes any obligation with respect to state aircraft, or whether states not parties to the Chicago Convention are under any similar obligation with respect to aircraft of any type, are open questions. The ad hoc committee of the General Assembly on the peaceful uses of outer space, however, "considered that certain substantive rules of international law already exist concerning rights and duties with respect to aircraft and airmen landing on foreign territory through accident, mistake or distress. The opinion was expressed that such rules might be applied in the event of similar landings of space vehicles." U.N.Doc. A/4141, p. 67 (1959). A problem related to that of landing rights is raised when an aircraft enters another state's air space either because of navigational error or because it is forced by bad weather to do so. In 1946, five United States airmen were killed when their unarmed transport was shot down over Yugoslavia. The United States claimed

that the plane had been forced by bad weather to deviate from its course; Yugoslavia denied that there was bad weather in the vicinity of the incident and alleged that the aircraft had ignored landing signals. In paying an indemnity, "inspired by human feelings," to the United States on behalf of the families of the airmen, Yugoslavia reserved its position on the facts. See Lissitzyn, The Treatment of Aerial Intruders in Recent Practice and International Law, 47 A.J.I.L. 559, 569–73 (1953). Numerous subsequent disputes involving a number of Western and Soviet-bloc states were characterized by disagreement over factual issues such as the location of aircraft, the reason for their presence in foreign territory, and whether they had been warned to land. Id. at 573–85. The conclusion has been offered, however, that "there is a right of entry for all foreign aircraft, state or civil, when such entry is due to distress not deliberately caused by persons in control of the aircraft and there is no reasonably safe alternative. * * * Foreign aircraft and their occupants may not be subjected to penalties or to unnecessary detention by the territorial sovereign for entry under such circumstances or for entry caused by a mistake at least when the distress or mistake has not been due to negligence chargeable to the persons in control of the aircraft." Id. at 588–89. In July 1955, an Israeli passenger plane was shot down, with the loss of 58 lives, by Bulgarian aircraft after it had strayed from its course and penetrated Bulgarian territory. Attempts by Israel, the United Kingdom, and the United States to call Bulgaria to account in the International Court of Justice were defeated on jurisdictional grounds. See generally Gross, The Jurisprudence of the World Court: Thirty–Eighth Year (1959), 57 A.J.I.L. 751, 753–71 (1963). In May 1960, a United States U–2 reconnaissance plane was shot down while flying over the Soviet Union at an altitude of approximately 60,000 to 68,000 feet. The United States did not protest the Soviet action; nor did it protest the trial, conviction and imprisonment for espionage of the American pilot. When Soviet fire brought down a United States RB–47 two months later, however, the United States made vigorous protests on the ground that the aircraft had been over the high seas at the time of its interception. The Soviet Union claimed that the American plane had deliberately intruded into Soviet air space and had disobeyed an order to land. See Lissitzyn, Some Legal Implications of the U–2 and RB–47 Incidents, 56 A.J.I.L. 135 (1962).

4. On September 1, 1983, a Korean civil airplane, with 269 persons aboard, was shot down by the U.S.S.R. while flying without permission through Soviet airspace. Did the U.S.S.R. violate international law? Does the answer depend on (1) whether the plane was in Soviet airspace as the result of a navigational error or other inadvertence, (2) whether a proper directive to land had been given and disregarded, or (3) whether the plane was engaged in spying on Soviet military installations? See Note, Legal Argumentation in International Crises: The Downing of Korean Airlines Flight 007, 97 Harv. L.Rev. 1198 (1984).

CONVENTION ON INTERNATIONAL CIVIL AVIATION

Signed at Chicago, December 7, 1944.
61 Stat. 1190, T.I.A.S. No. 1591, 15 U.N.T.S. 295.

Art. 12. Each contracting State undertakes to adopt measures to insure that every aircraft flying over or maneuvering within its territory and that every aircraft carrying its nationality mark, wherever such aircraft may be, shall comply with the rules and the regulations relating to the flight and maneuver of aircraft there in force. Each contracting State undertakes to keep its own regulations in these respects uniform, to the greatest possible extent, with those established from time to time under this Convention. Over the high seas, the rules in force shall be those established under this Convention. Each contracting State undertakes to insure the prosecution of all persons violating the regulations applicable.

Notes

1. An aircraft took off from Rabat (Morocco) on October 22, 1956, carrying five representatives of the insurgent Algerian "Front de Liberation Nationale," who had been invited by the Sultan of Morocco to attend a conference in Tunis. The aircraft was registered in France, but owned and operated by a state-controlled Moroccan corporation. The pilots were French nationals. After refueling at Palma, the aircraft took off from Tunis, but was almost immediately ordered by the French government to direct its course toward Algiers. The pilot changed course accordingly, and the plane and its passengers were taken into custody upon arrival in Algeria. A strong protest from the Moroccan government accused France of an act of "pure piracy." France argued that the aircraft's registration in France justified the French action. See La Pradelle, L'enlèvement aérien des Chefs Fellagah, 19 Revue Generale de l'Air 235 (1956). The dispute was submitted to arbitration in 1958, but the tribunal adjourned after the Moroccan delegation walked out. Verplaetse, International Law in Vertical Space 73 (1960).

2. On whether a state may intercept a foreign aircraft over the high seas, see p. 1449.

CONVENTION ON OFFENCES AND CERTAIN OTHER ACTS COMMITTED ON BOARD AIRCRAFT

Opened for signature at Tokyo, September 14, 1963.
20 U.S.T. 2941, T.I.A.S. No. 6768, 704 U.N.T.S. 219.

Article 3

1. The State of registration of the aircraft is competent to exercise jurisdiction over offences and acts committed on board.

2. Each Contracting State shall take such measures as may be necessary to establish its jurisdiction as the State of registration over offences committed on board aircraft registered in such State.

3. This Convention does not exclude any criminal jurisdiction exercised in accordance with national law.

Article 4

A Contracting State which is not the State of registration may not interfere with an aircraft in flight in order to exercise its criminal jurisdiction over an offence committed on board except in the following cases:

(a) the offence has effect on the territory of such State;

(b) the offence has been committed by or against a national or permanent resident of such State;

(c) the offence is against the security of such State;

(d) the offence consists of a breach of any rules or regulations relating to the flight or manoeuvre of aircraft in force in such State;

(e) the exercise of jurisdiction is necessary to ensure the observance of any obligation of such State under a multilateral international agreement.

Notes

1. The Convention entered into force for the United States and eleven other states on December 4, 1969. As of 2000, more than 150 states have become parties. Omitted articles describe the powers of the aircraft commander to restrain persons while the aircraft is in flight and to disembark such persons and to deliver them to the authorities of a contracting state in whose territory the aircraft may land. The Convention also establishes procedures for the investigation of offenses and for the resolution of conflicts of jurisdiction. Article 11 obliges contracting states to "take all appropriate measures to restore control of [an] aircraft to its lawful commander or to preserve his control of the aircraft" in the event of an unlawful seizure by a person on board or an attempt at such seizure.

2. A Rumanian national, aboard a foreign aircraft en route to the United States, sexually accosted a nine-year old Norwegian girl. He was ruled subject to an American court's jurisdiction in United States v. Georgescu, 723 F.Supp. 912 (E.D.N.Y.1989). Is there a proper international law basis for this ruling?

CONVENTION FOR THE SUPPRESSION OF UNLAWFUL SEIZURE OF AIRCRAFT (HIJACKING)

Signed at The Hague, December 16, 1970.
22 U.S.T. 1641, T.I.A.S. No. 7192.

[See Articles 1–14]

Notes

1. As of 2000, this Convention had entered in force for 173 states, including the United States.

2. On September 23, 1971, a Convention for the Suppression of Unlawful Acts Against the Safety of Civil Aviation (Sabotage), 24 U.S.T. 564, T.I.A.S. No. 7570, was signed in Montreal, Canada. As of 2000, the Convention was in force for more than 165 states, including the United States. This Convention is in many respects similar to the 1970 Hague Convention, but is primarily designed to control attacks and sabotage against civil aircraft in flight and on the ground rather than "unlawful seizure" (hijacking). Article 1 of the 1971 Convention reads as follows:

1. Any person commits an offence if he unlawfully and intentionally:

(a) performs an act of violence against a person on board an aircraft in flight if that act is likely to endanger the safety of that aircraft; or

(b) destroys an aircraft in service or causes damage to such an aircraft which renders it incapable of flight or which is likely to endanger its safety in flight; or

(c) places or causes to be placed on an aircraft in service, by any means whatsoever, a device or substance which is likely to destroy that aircraft, or to cause damage to it which renders it incapable of flight, or to cause damage to it which is likely to endanger its safety in flight; or

(d) destroys or damages air navigation facilities or interferes with their operation, if any such act is likely to endanger the safety of aircraft in flight; or

(e) communicates information which he knows to be false, thereby endangering the safety of an aircraft in flight.

2. Any person also commits an offence if he:

(a) attempts to commit any of the offences mentioned in paragraph 1 of this Article; or

(b) is an accomplice of a person who commits or attempts to commit any such offence.

Article 2(b) of the Convention provides:

> an aircraft is considered to be in service from the beginning of the preflight preparation of the aircraft by ground personnel or by the crew for a specific flight until twenty-four hours after any landing; the period of service shall, in any event, extend for the entire period during which the aircraft is in flight as defined in paragraph (a) of this Article.

Article 2(a) is substantially identical with Article 3(1) of the 1970 Convention. Article 5 is similar to Article 4 of the 1970 Convention, but adds another clause: "(a) when the offence is committed in the territory of that State." There are some other differences between the two conventions. For the text of the 1971 Convention, see 10 I.L.M. 1151 (1971).

3. The Conventions of 1970 and 1971 were inspired by mounting international concern with the increasingly frequent hijacking of aircraft in flight and attacks upon aircraft on the ground as well as in flight. They greatly increased the permissible scope of state action in combatting hijackings.

4. The Tokyo and the Hague Conventions apply when an aircraft is unlawfully seized while "in flight." Article 1(3) of the Tokyo Convention defines an aircraft to be in flight from " * * * the moment when power is applied for purpose of takeoff until the landing run ends." Compare Article 3(1) of the Hague Convention.

5. On what bases of jurisdiction are the Hague, Tokyo, and Montreal Conventions premised? Does the grant of jurisdiction to any ratifying state within whose borders the alleged offender is found extend customary international law? Note that the Conventions obligate the state to exercise jurisdiction unless it agrees to extradite the accused to another state for purposes of prosecution.

6. Under Article 4 of the Hague Convention and Article 5 of the Montreal Convention, several states may have concurrent jurisdiction. May this lead to problems, since the Convention has no provision establishing the priority of their claims? See Abramovsky, Multilateral Conventions for the Suppression of Unlawful Seizures and Interference with Aircraft, Part I: The Hague Convention, 13 Colum.J.Transnat'l L. 381, 396 (1974) (concluding that the state in which the offender is apprehended would enjoy a primary de facto right to exercise jurisdiction).

In the *Lockerbie* cases at the International Court of Justice, Libya argued that it had no obligation under the Montreal Convention to surrender to the United States or the United Kingdom the two Libyan nationals who were suspected in the explosion of a U.S. aircraft en route to the United States over Lockerbie, Scotland. The International Court denied Libya's request for provisional measures to restrain the United States and the United Kingdom from pursuing sanctions against Libya in the U.N. Security Council. Questions of Interpretation and Application of the 1971 Montreal Convention arising from the Aerial Incident at Lockerbie (Libyan Arab Jamahiriya v. United Kingdom; Libyan Arab Jamahiriya v. United States), 1992 I.C.J. 3, 114; see also 1998 I.C.J. 9, 115 (Jurisdiction). The United States and the United Kingdom have maintained, inter alia, that the Montreal Convention did not contemplate that a state which may itself have been complicit in terrorist activity could shield its own nationals from prosecution by the states that would otherwise have jurisdiction and that were especially affected by the crime. Although Libya later surrendered the two accused for a special trial in The Hague that concluded in 2000, it did not abandon its I.C.J. claim for interpretation of the Montreal Convention. Briefing on the merits of that claim was still in progress as of 2000.

7. Since many hijackings are politically motivated, a state desiring to harbor fugitives might wish to claim the traditional exemption from extradition for "political offenses." See the discussion of this issue in Abramovsky, id. at 401–405 and Abramovsky, id., Part II: The Montreal Convention, 14 Colum. J.Transnat'l L. 296, 298–99 (1975). For more on the problem of "political offenses" in relation to aircraft hijacking and other terrorist crimes, see p. 1182.

8. Section 40106(b)(I) of Title 49 of the U.S.C.A. provides that the President may suspend the authority of any person to operate aircraft operating out of or with a foreign country that acts inconsistently with the Convention for the Suppression of Unlawful Seizure of Aircraft. See also 49 U.S.C.A. § 44907(d)(7) granting the Secretary of Transportation authority to withhold, revoke, or modify the operating authority of any nation that fails to maintain security measures provided for by the Convention on International Civil Aviation.

9. In June 1985, a TWA plane was hijacked on a flight from Cairo to Rome and forced to fly to various cities, ending up finally in Beirut. After the passengers had been discharged, the plane was blown up on the airfield in Beirut. N.Y. Times, June 15, 1985, Sec. 1, p. 1, col. 6. To what extent are any of the conventions discussed in this Section applicable to the activities of the hijackers? See United States v. Fawaz Yunis, 924 F.2d 1086 (D.C.Cir.1991) (finding the Hostage Taking Act, 18 U.S.C.A. § 1203, and the Antihijacking Act, 49 U.S.C.A.App. §§ 147(n), applicable to hijacking by an alien of a Jordanian plane with American passengers in Beirut). On this case, see also p. 1118 supra. The Hostage Taking Act 18 U.S.C.A. § 1203, was amended in 1988, 1994, and 1996. The 1994 amendment added the death penalty if the hostage taking results in death. The 1996 amendment expanded its coverage to conspiracy to take hostages.

10. On December 27, 1985, gunmen sprayed gunfire and detonated grenades in an airport lounge in Vienna. On the same day, gunmen did the same at the El–Al check-in counter at the Rome airport. Many persons, including Americans, were killed; many others were wounded. N.Y. Times, Dec. 28, 1985, Sec. 1, p. 1, col. 4. Are the provisions of any of the conventions discussed in this Section applicable? Does the United States have jurisdiction to prosecute the perpetrators? Would it be entitled to their extradition? On extradition, see Section 9 of this Chapter.

11. The Antihijacking Act of 1974, Pub. L. No. 93–366, amending the Federal Aviation Act of 1958, now codified at 49 U.S.C.A. § 40502(b)(2), gives the United States jurisdiction if a national of the U.S. was aboard the aircraft, an offender is a national of the U.S., or an offender is afterwards found in the United States. To what extent does international law permit the exercise of this jurisdiction?

12. In United States v. Cordova, 89 F.Supp. 298 (E.D.N.Y.1950), it was held that an aircraft was not a "vessel" within the meaning of 18 U.S.C.A. § 7(1) and that a United States Court therefore had no jurisdiction to try and punish a defendant accused of assaulting certain persons (including the pilot) on a United States aircraft flying over the high seas between Puerto Rico and New York. Congress thereupon amended 18 U.S.C.A. § 7 by an Act of July 12, 1952 (69 Stat. 589), adding a new subsection (5) so that the "special maritime and territorial jurisdiction of the United States" covers:

> Any aircraft belonging in whole or in part to the United States, or any citizen thereof, or to any corporation created by or under the laws of the United States, or any State, Territory, district, or possession thereof, while such aircraft is in flight over the high seas, or over any other waters within the admiralty and maritime jurisdiction of the United States and out of the jurisdiction of any particular State.

13. Note that 49 U.S.C.A. § 44102 permits the registration in the United States only of aircraft owned by citizens or lawful residents of the United States and not registered in any foreign country. United States citizens are not forbidden, however, to own or otherwise hold interests in aircraft that are registered in a foreign country. Under what circumstances, if any, might jurisdiction asserted by the United States on the basis of 18 U.S.C.A. § 7(5) supra be unlawful under international law? Does the same problem exist for jurisdiction asserted on the basis of 49 U.S.C.A. § 46501?

14. The U.S. statute on offenses committed on board aircraft, 49 U.S.C.A. § 46506, refers to the following sections in Title 18: assault (18 U.S.C.A. § 113(d), maiming (18 U.S.C.A. § 114), theft (18 U.S.C.A. § 661), receiving stolen property (18 U.S.C.A. § 662), murder (18 U.S.C.A. § 1111), manslaughter (18 U.S.C.A. § 1112), attempted murder or manslaughter (18 U.S.C.A. § 1113), robbery (18 U.S.C.A. § 2111), sexual assaults (18 U.S.C.A. §§ 2241 et seq).

TREATY ON PRINCIPLES GOVERNING THE ACTIVITIES OF STATES IN THE EXPLORATION AND USE OF OUTER SPACE, INCLUDING THE MOON AND OTHER CELESTIAL BODIES

Done at London, Moscow, and Washington, January 27, 1967.
18 U.S.T. 2410, T.I.A.S. No. 6347, 610 U.N.T.S. 205.

[See Articles 1–8 in Documents Supplement]

Notes

1. Would 18 U.S.C.A. § 7(5), quoted in Note 12 above, extend United States jurisdiction to a U.S. space shuttle in outer space or on a celestial body? On Dec. 21, 1981, Section 7 of Title 18 of the U.S.C.A. was amended to add paragraph 6, reading as follows:

> (6) Any vehicle used or designed for flight or navigation in space and on the registry of the United States pursuant to the Treaty on Principles Governing the Activities of States in the Exploration and Use of Outer Space, Including the Moon and Other Celestial Bodies and the Convention on Registration of Objects Launched into Outer Space, while that vehicle is in flight, which is from the moment when all external doors are closed on Earth

following embarkation until the moment when one such door is opened on Earth for disembarkation or in the case of a forced landing, until the competent authorities take over the responsibility for the vehicle and for persons and property aboard.

2. The Agreement on the Rescue of Astronauts, the Return of Astronauts, and the Return of Objects Launched into Outer Space, 19 U.S.T. 7570, T.I.A.S. No. 6599, 672 U.N.T.S. 119, came into force on December 3, 1968. By 2000, more than 110 states had become parties. See generally Houben, A New Chapter of Space Law, 15 Neth. Int'l L.Rev. 121 (1968); Christol, The Modern International Law of Outer Space 152 (1982). The Agreement provides, in part, as follows:

> Art. 1. Each Contracting Party which receives information or discovers that the personnel of a spacecraft have suffered accident or are experiencing conditions of distress or have made an emergency or unintended landing in territory under its jurisdiction or on the high seas or in any other place not under the jurisdiction of any State shall immediately:
>
> (a) Notify the launching authority or, if it cannot identify and immediately communicate with the launching authority, immediately make a public announcement by all appropriate means of communication at its disposal;
>
> (b) Notify the Secretary–General of the United Nations, who should disseminate the information without delay by all appropriate means of communication at his disposal.
>
> Art. 2. If, owing to accident, distress, emergency or unintended landing, the personnel of a spacecraft land in territory under the jurisdiction of a Contracting Party, it shall immediately take all possible steps to rescue them and render them all necessary assistance. It shall inform the launching authority and also the Secretary–General of the United Nations of the steps it is taking and of their progress. If assistance by the launching authority would help to effect a prompt rescue or would contribute substantially to the effectiveness of search and rescue operations, the launching authority shall co-operate with the Contracting Party with a view to the effective conduct of search and rescue operations. Such operations shall be subject to the direction and control of the Contracting Party, which shall act in close and continuing consultation with the launching authority.
>
> Art. 3. If information is received or it is discovered that the personnel of a spacecraft have alighted on the high seas or in any other place not under the jurisdiction of any State, those Contracting Parties which are in a position to do so shall, if necessary, extend assistance in search and rescue operations for such personnel to assure their speedy rescue. They shall inform the launching authority and the Secretary–General of the United Nations of the steps they are taking and of their progress.
>
> Art. 4. If, owing to accident, distress, emergency or unintended landing, the personnel of a spacecraft land in territory under the jurisdiction of a Contracting Party or have been found on the high seas or in any other place not under the jurisdiction of any State, they shall be safely and promptly returned to representatives of the launching authority.
>
> Art. 5. (1) Each Contracting Party which receives information or discovers that a space object or its component parts has returned to Earth in territory under its jurisdiction or on the high seas or in any other place not

under the jurisdiction of any State, shall notify the launching authority and the Secretary–General of the United Nations.

(2) Each Contracting Party having jurisdiction over the territory on which a space object or its component parts has been discovered shall, upon the request of the launching authority and with assistance from that authority if requested, take such steps as it finds practicable to recover the object or component parts.

(3) Upon request of the launching authority, objects launched into outer space or their component parts found beyond the territorial limits of the launching authority shall be returned to or held at the disposal of representatives of the launching authority, which shall, upon request, furnish identifying data prior to their return.

(4) Notwithstanding paragraphs 2 and 3 of this article, a Contracting Party which has reason to believe that a space object or its component parts discovered in territory under its jurisdiction, or recovered by it elsewhere, is of a hazardous or deleterious nature may so notify the launching authority, which shall immediately take effective steps, under the direction and control of the said Contracting Party, to eliminate possible danger of harm.

(5) Expenses incurred in fulfilling obligations to recover and return a space object or its component parts under paragraphs 2 and 3 of this article shall be borne by the launching authority.

Art. 6. For the purposes of this Agreement, the term "launching authority" shall refer to the State responsible for launching, or, where an international intergovernmental organization is responsible for launching, that organization, provided that that organization declares its acceptance of the rights and obligations provided for in this Agreement and a majority of the States members of that organization are Contracting Parties to this Agreement and to the Treaty on Principles Governing the Activities of States in the Exploration and Use of Outer Space, including the Moon and Other Celestial Bodies.

3. The Convention on International Liability for Damage Caused by Space Objects, 24 U.S.T. 2389, T.I.A.S. No. 7762, 961 U.N.T.S. 187, which as of 2000, had been ratified by more than 85 parties, provides for absolute liability of the launching state for damage caused by a space object on the surface of the earth or to aircraft in flight.

This Convention was invoked for the first time in January, 1978, when Canada billed the U.S.S.R. for six million dollars spent in locating and cleaning up radioactive debris from the disintegration of the Soviet's Cosmos 954. The Canadian claim is reproduced at 18 I.L.M. 899 (1979). Since then, the U.S.S.R. has paid. For a discussion of the legal issues involved, See Dembling, Cosmos 954 and The Space Treaties, 6 J. Space L. 129 (1978); Gorove, Cosmos 954; Issues of Law and Policy, id. at 137. See also Wilkins, Substantive Bases for Recovery for Injuries Sustained by Private Individuals as a Result of Fallen Space Objects, id. at 161; Christol, The Modern Law of Outer Space 59 (1982).

3. Other Things

The notion that inanimate things, like vessels and aircraft, may stand in a sufficiently close relationship to a particular state to provide a basis for the exercise of jurisdiction by that state over the thing and the persons using it naturally leads to the question whether this notion can be extended to other material, and perhaps even immaterial, things. For example, states may seek to exercise jurisdiction over artistic creations and cultural artifacts on the ground that they are part of the national patrimony. See, e.g., Convention on the Illicit Movement of Art Treasures, entered into force in April 24, 1972, for the United States on December 2, 1983, 823 U.N.T.S. 231, reprinted in 10 I.L.M. 289 (1971). American efforts to control beyond its borders the flow of technology created in the United States have also raised the question whether technology can be regarded as national so as to justify the exercise of jurisdiction on the basis of nationality by the state where it was created. For arguments against this basis for asserting jurisdiction, see Legal Serv. of the Comm'n of the European Communities, European Communities: Comments on the U.S. Regulations Concerning Trade with the U.S.S.R., reprinted in 21 I.L.M. 891 (1982), and further references concerning the Soviet pipeline dispute at p. 1116–1117.

SECTION 4. JURISDICTION BASED ON PROTECTION OF CERTAIN STATE, UNIVERSAL, AND OTHER INTERESTS

A. PROTECTIVE PRINCIPLE

RESTATEMENT (THIRD)

§ 402. Bases of Jurisdiction to Prescribe

Subject to § 403, a state has jurisdiction to prescribe law with respect to

(1) * * *

(2) * * *

(3) certain conduct outside its territory by persons not its nationals that is directed against the security of the state or against a limited class of other state interests.

Notes

1. In United States v. Archer, 51 F.Supp. 708 (S.D.Cal.1943), the court regarded the federal statute making it a crime for either an alien or a United States citizen to commit perjury before a diplomatic or consular office, 11 Stat. 61, 22 U.S.C.A. § 1203, [now 22 U.S.C.A. § 4221] as resting on the protective principle and convicted thereunder an alien who committed perjury before a vice consul in Mexico in connection with an application for a non-immigrant visa. See also United States v. Rodriguez, 182 F.Supp. 479 (S.D.Cal.1960), reversed on other grounds sub nom. Rocha v. United States, 288 F.2d 545 (9th Cir.1961), cert. denied, 366 U.S. 948, 81 S.Ct. 1902, 6 L.Ed.2d 1241 (1961).

2. Compare Restatement, (Third) § 402(3) with the following articles from the Harvard Research in International Law, Jurisdiction with Respect to Crime, 29 A.J.I.L.Supp. 435, 440 (1935):

> Art. 7. A state has jurisdiction with respect to any crime committed outside its territory by an alien against the security, territorial integrity or political independence of that state, provided that the act or omission which constitutes the crime was not committed in exercise of a liberty guaranteed the alien by the law of the place where it was committed.

Art. 8. A state has jurisdiction with respect to any crime committed outside its territory by an alien which consists of a falsification or counterfeiting, or an uttering or falsified copies or counterfeits, of the seals, currency, instruments of credit, stamps, passports, or public documents, issued by that state or under its authority.

3. In 1972, Israel amended its Penal Law to include the following provision:

> The courts in Israel are competent to try under Israeli law a person who has committed abroad an act which would be an offense if it had been committed in Israel and which harmed or was intended to harm the State of Israel, its security, property or economy or its transport or communications links with other countries.

Can this provision be supported by the protective principle? See Note, Extraterritorial Jurisdiction and Jurisdiction Following Forcible Abduction: A New Israeli Precedent in International Law, 72 Mich. L.Rev. 1087 (1974).

4. In U.S. v. Bin Laden, 92 F.Supp.2d 189 (S.D.N.Y.2000), the U.S. returned an indictment charging 15 defendants (including Bin Laden, who has not yet been apprehended, and six defendants who are in custody in the United States) with offenses under a number of federal statutes for acts committed abroad, including the bombing of the U.S. embassies in Kenya and Tanzania in August 1998. The court referred to the congressional intent that the Anti–Terrorism Act and several other relevant statutes were intended to reach conduct by foreign nationals on foreign soil, and concluded that the Anti–Terrorism Act was justified by the protective principle under international law. In response to a claim that due process requires minimum contacts with the United States, the court held that "if the extraterritorial application of a statute is justified by the protective principle, such application accords with due process." 92 F.Supp.2d at 220.

The court also noted that the embassy bombings involved murders of "internationally protected persons" (i.e., diplomats), and referred in this connection to the universality principle of jurisdiction under international law; see below. On the status of the embassy premises as relevant to U.S. authority to prescribe and enforce criminal law with respect to acts occurring there, see Chapter 14, p. 1284. In *Bin Laden*, the court concluded that the exercise of jurisdiction was sustainable on theories of passive personality, protective, and universal jurisdiction, but *not* on the subjective territorial principle for acts taking place on embassy premises. 92 F.Supp.2d at 215 n. 43. Thus the court dismissed certain counts of the indictment under two statutes, upon concluding that Congress did not intend the provisions on murder or maiming on federal lands to apply to embassy properties; but it upheld the remaining counts.

B. UNIVERSALITY PRINCIPLE

RESTATEMENT (THIRD) § 404

[See p. 1092 supra]

UNITED NATIONS CONVENTION ON THE LAW OF THE SEA

Art. 100

[See p. 1446 infra]

Note

"It has long been recognized and well settled that persons and vessels engaged in piratical operations on the high seas are entitled to the protection of no nation and may be punished by any nation that may apprehend or capture them. This stern rule of international law refers to piracy in its international-law sense and not to a variety of lesser maritime offenses so designated by municipal law." 2 Hackworth at 681. On piracy, see p. 1446 infra. For current U.S. law, see 18 U.S.C. §§ 1651–1653, 2280 (2000).

LETTER OF 15 JUNE 1960 FROM THE REPRESENTATIVE OF ARGENTINA TO THE PRESIDENT OF THE SECURITY COUNCIL

U.N. Doc. S/4336.

I have the honour, on the instructions of my Government, to request you to call an urgent meeting of the Security Council to consider the violation of the sovereign rights of the Argentine Republic resulting from the illicit and clandestine transfer of Adolf Eichmann from Argentine territory to the territory of the State of Israel, contrary to the rules of international law and the Purposes and Principles of the Charter of the United Nations and creating an atmosphere of insecurity and mistrust incompatible with the preservation of international peace.

An explanatory memorandum is attached. * * *

(Signed) Mario Amadeo
Ambassador

Explanatory Memorandum

In view of the failure of the diplomatic representations made by it to the Government of Israel the Argentine Government is now compelled, in defence of fundamental rights, to request that the case be dealt with by the Security Council, the case being in its view explicitly covered by the provisions of Article 34 and Article 35, paragraph 1, of the United Nations Charter.

The facts which have led to this situation are as follows:

1. Having learned from reports which had become known to world public opinion that Adolf Eichmann had been captured in Argentine territory by "volunteer groups" which transferred him to the territory of Israel and there delivered him to the authorities of that country, the Argentine Government approached the Government of Israel with a request for information in that connexion.

2. The Government of Israel, through its Embassy at Buenos Aires, replied to this request in a note of 3 June 1960 in which it stated that Eichmann had in fact been transferred to Israel from Argentine territory. After stating that Eichmann had consented to the transfer, the Government of Israel's note concluded with the statement that "if the volunteer group violated Argentine law or interfered with matters within the sovereignty of Argentina, the Government of Israel wishes to express its regret."

3. In view of the recognition of the authenticity of the facts reported in connexion with Eichmann's capture, the Argentine Government * * * made the most formal protest against the illegal act committed to the detriment of a fundamental right of the Argentine State, and requested appropriate reparation for the act, namely the return of Eichmann, for which it set a time-limit of one week, and the punishment of those guilty of violating Argentine territory. The Argentine Government stated that, failing compliance with this request, it would refer the matter to the United Nations.* * *

It is unnecessary to adduce further considerations in order to underline the gravity of the resulting situation. The illicit and clandestine transfer of Eichmann from Argentine territory constitutes a flagrant violation of the Argentine State's right of sovereignty, and the Argentine Government is legally justified in requesting reparation. That right cannot be qualified by any other considerations, even those invoked by the Government of Israel with regard to the importance attaching to the trial of a man accused of exterminations in concentration camps, although the Argentine Government and people understand those reasons to the full. Any contrary interpretation would be tantamount to approving the taking of the law into one's own hands and the subjecting of international order to unilateral acts which, if repeated, would involve undeniable dangers for the preservation of peace.

Before appealing to the Security Council, the Argentine Government endeavoured, in accordance with the Charter of the United Nations, to reach a satisfactory solution through the normal diplomatic channels of negotiation. In these endeavours the close friendship between Argentina and the State of Israel played a part. Those endeavours have, however, been without success. In these circumstances, the only remaining recourse is to the Security Council. A political question is involved which, apart from gravely prejudicing Argentine sovereignty, constitutes a precedent dangerous for international peace and security, for the maintenance of which the Security Council bears primary responsibility.

The Argentine Government hopes that the Security Council will attach to this question all the importance which it merits, and will take decisions involving just reparation for the rights violated.

Notes

1. On which bases of jurisdiction could Israel rely in its capture and execution of Eichmann? Is the fact that Israel did not exist as a state when Eichmann committed the acts for which he was prosecuted significant in this context?

2. Israel disputed the Council's competence to deal with the incident in a letter of June 21, 1960 (U.N.Doc. S/4341), stating that Argentina's unilateral allegations did not suffice to bring the dispute within the terms of Article 34 of the Charter and expressing the conviction that the difficulties between the two countries could best be settled by direct negotiations. At its 865th meeting on June 22, 1960, however, the Council included the matter in its agenda without objection. The Israeli representative was invited to take a seat at the Council table. For the debate, see U.N. Docs. S/P.V. 865–68; see also the summary contained in the Security Council's report to the General Assembly for the year

ending July 15, 1960, 15 GAOR Supp. 2 (A/4494), p. 19–24. On June 23, 1960, the Security Council adopted a resolution by eight votes to none, with two abstentions (Poland and the Soviet Union) and one member (Argentina) not participating in the vote. The operative parts of the resolution (S/4349) were as follows:

> *The Security Council,* * * *
>
> 1. *Declares* that acts such as that under consideration, which affect the sovereignty of a Member State and therefore cause international friction, may, if repeated, endanger international peace and security;
>
> 2. *Requests* the Government of Israel to make appropriate reparation in accordance with the Charter of the United Nations and the rules of international law * * *

3. On August 3, 1960, the following joint communiqué was published in Jerusalem and Buenos Aires:

> The Governments of Israel and the Republic of Argentina, animated by the wish to comply with the resolution of the Security Council of June 23, 1960, in which the hope was expressed that the traditionally friendly relations between the two countries will be advanced, have decided to regard as closed the incident that arose out of the action taken by Israeli nationals which infringed fundamental rights of the State of Argentina.

See Lord Russell of Liverpool, The Trial of Adolf Eichmann xvi-xvii (1962); Pearlman, the Capture and Trial of Adolf Eichmann 79 (1963); Papdates, The Eichmann Trial 60 n. 54 (1964). Eichmann was charged under the Nazis and Nazi Collaborators (Punishment) Law (5710–1950, No. 64, 4 Laws of the State of Israel 154) with commission of the following crimes in Germany or countries occupied by Germany during World War II—crimes against the Jewish people [§ 1(a)(1)], crimes against humanity [§ 1(a)(2)], war crimes [§ 1(a)(3)], and membership in a hostile organization [§ 3]—in the indictment of February 21, 1961. On December 11, 1961, the District Court of Jerusalem found Eichmann guilty on all counts of the indictment (Criminal Case No. 40/61). An appeal was dismissed on May 29, 1962 (Criminal Appeal No. 336/61). In the course of its Judgment, the court overruled the defense contention that there was no jurisdiction because the defendant had been captured in a foreign country in violation of international law. The court sustained the exercise of jurisdiction, inter alia on the basis of the universality principle. For a complete English translation of the judgments, see 36 Int'l L.Reports 5 (1968). A bibliography on the Eichmann trial is included in Mueller & Wise, eds., International Criminal Law 370–71 (1965).

4. On illegal capture and abduction, see also p. 1187 infra.

5. See also Matter of Demjanjuk, 612 F.Supp. 544 (N.D.Ohio 1985), approving a request for extradition to Israel of a person charged with crimes committed in Nazi concentration camps in Eastern Europe, even though the usual condition for extradition that the crimes had been committed in the territory of the requesting state was not met. The district court's decision in the *Demjanjuk* case was affirmed on appeal. 776 F.2d 571 (6th Cir.1985), cert. denied, 475 U.S. 1016, 106 S.Ct. 1198, 89 L.Ed.2d 312 (1986). After Demjanjuk had been tried in Israel, questions arose as to whether Demjanjuk was in fact the person who was accused of the crimes involved. This prompted an unusual order by the Court of Appeals issued *sua sponte* directing the United States to respond to reports that the prosecution had failed to disclose information to that effect.

REGINA v. BARTLE, BOW STREET STIPENDIARY MAGISTRATE AND COMMISSIONER OF POLICE, EX PARTE PINOCHET

United Kingdom, House of Lords
March 24, 1999

2 W.L.R. 827, 38 I.L.M. 581 (1999).

[In 1998, at the request of a Spanish investigating judge for extradition, a warrant was issued by an English magistrate for the arrest of Pinochet, a former head of state of Chile. The petition alleged that, while head of state of Chile, Pinochet had conspired with others to take hostage, torture, and kill numerous persons, including Spanish citizens. Pinochet was arrested and contended in the English courts that he was immune from arrest and could not properly be extradited. The House of Lord rendered judgment twice. The first judgment was vacated by the House of Lords itself on the ground that one of the law lords on the panel had failed to disclose his connection with Amnesty International, which had intervened in the case. In its second judgment, the House of Lords ruled that Pinochet could not claim immunity in regard to torture that had been made a universal crime by the International Convention Against Torture and other Cruel, Inhuman or Degrading Treatment or Punishment of 1984. This Convention, incorporated into English law by the Criminal Justice Act of 1988, effective as of September 29, 1988, effected an exception to the otherwise applicable immunity of present and former heads of state from criminal process.

On whether Pinochet was extraditable under the double criminality requirement imposed by the U.K.–Spain Extradition Treaty, the House of Lords ruled that the crime for which extradition was sought had to be a crime under both Spanish and U.K. law at the time of commission of the crime rather than at the time of extradition and that extradition could therefore be sought only for torture committed after 1988. The matter was referred back to the executive authorities and the lower courts for the proper processing of the request for extradition. Subsequently, Pinochet was permitted to return to Chile upon a finding that his poor health did not permit him to stand trial. The decisions rendered at the various stages of this proceedings can be found in 37 I.L.M. 1302 (1998) and 38 I.L.M. 68, 430, 489 and 581 (1999). The part of Lord Browne–Wilkinson's opinion dealing with whether the crimes alleged were crimes under English law follows. For other excerpts in this Chapter, see p. 1187. The part of his opinion with the immunity issue is reproduced in Chapter 14, at p. 1276 below.]

LORD BROWNE–WILKINSON

* * *

Torture

Apart from the law of piracy, the concept of personal liability under international law for international crimes is of comparatively modern growth. The traditional subjects of international law are states not human beings. But consequent upon the war crime trials after the 1939–45 World War, the international community came to recognise that there could be criminal liability under international law for a class of crimes such as war crimes and crimes against humanity. Although there may be legitimate doubts as to the legality of the Charter of the Nuremberg Tribunal, in my judgment those doubts were stilled by the Affirmation of the Principles of International Law recognised by the Charter of Nuremberg Tribunal adopted by the United Nations General Assembly on 11 December 1946. That Affirmation affirmed the principles of international law recognised by the Charter of the Nuremberg Tribunal and the judgment of the Tribunal and directed the Committee on the codification of international law to treat as a matter of primary importance plans for the formulation of the principles recognised in the Charter of the Nuremberg Tribunal. At least from that date onwards the concept of personal liability for a crime in international law must have been part of international law. In the early years state torture was one of the elements of a war crime. In consequence torture, and various other crimes against humanity, were linked to war or at least to hostilities of some kind. But in the course of time this linkage with war fell away and torture, divorced from war or hostilities, became an international crime on its own: see *Oppenheim's International Law* (Jennings and Watts edition) vol. 1, 996; note 6 to Article 18 of the *I.L.C. Draft Code of Crimes Against Peace*; Prosecutor v. Furundzija, Tribunal for Former Yugoslavia, Case No. 17–95–17/1–T. Ever since 1945, torture on a large scale has featured as one of the crimes against humanity: see, for example, U.N. General Assembly Resolutions 3059, 3452 and 3453 passed in 1973 and 1975; Statutes of the International Criminal Tribunals for former Yugoslavia (Article 5) and Rwanda (Article 3).

Moreover, the Republic of Chile accepted before your Lordships that the international law prohibiting torture has the character of jus cogens or a peremptory norm, i.e. one of those rules of international law which have a particular status. In *Furundzija* (supra) at para. 153, the Tribunal said:

> "Because of the importance of the values it protects, [the prohibition of torture] has evolved into a peremptory norm or jus cogens, that is, a norm that enjoys a higher rank in the international hierarchy than treaty law and even 'ordinary' customary rules. The most conspicuous consequence of this higher rank is that the principle at issue cannot be derogated from by states through international treaties or local or special customs or even general customary rules not endowed with the same normative force. * * * Clearly, the jus cogens nature of the prohibition against torture articulates the notion that the prohibition has now become one of the most fundamental standards of the international community. Furthermore, this prohibition is designed to produce a deterrent effect, in that it signals to all members of the international community and the individuals over whom they wield authority that the prohibition of torture is an absolute value from which nobody must deviate." (See also the cases cited in Note 170 to the Furundzija case.)

The jus cogens nature of the international crime of torture justifies states in taking universal jurisdiction over torture wherever committed. International law provides that offences jus cogens may be punished by any state because the offenders are "common enemies of all mankind and all nations have an equal interest in their apprehension and prosecution": *Demjanjuk v. Petrovsky* (1985) 603 F. Supp. 1468; 776 F. 2d. 571.

It was suggested by Miss Montgomery, for Senator Pinochet, that although torture was contrary to international law it was not strictly an international crime in the highest sense. In the light of the authorities to which I have referred (and there are many others) I have no doubt that long before the Torture Convention of 1984 state torture was an international crime in the highest sense. But there was no tribunal or court to punish international crimes of torture. Local courts could take jurisdiction: see *Demjanjuk* (supra); *Attorney–General of Israel v. Eichmann* (1962) 36 I.L.R. 5. But the objective was to ensure a general jurisdiction so that the torturer was not safe wherever he went. For example, in this case it is alleged that during the Pinochet regime torture was an official, although unacknowledged, weapon of government and that, when the regime was about to end, it passed legislation designed to afford an amnesty to those who had engaged in institutionalised torture. If these allegations are true, the fact that the local court had jurisdiction to deal with the international crime of torture was nothing to the point so long as the totalitarian regime remained in power: a totalitarian regime will not permit adjudication by its own courts on its own shortcomings. Hence the demand for some international machinery to repress state torture which is not dependent upon the local courts where the torture was committed. In the event, over 110 states (including Chile, Spain and the United Kingdom) became state parties to the Torture Convention. But it is far from clear that none of them practised state torture. What was needed therefore was an international system which could punish those who were guilty of torture and which did not permit the evasion of punishment by the torturer moving from one state to another. The Torture Convention was agreed not in order to create an international crime which had not previously existed but to provide an international system under which the international criminal—the torturer—could find no safe haven. Burgers and Danelius (respectively the chairman of the United Nations Working Group on the 1984 Torture Convention and the draftsmen of its first draft) say, at p. 131, that it was "an essential purpose [of the Convention] to ensure that a torturer does not escape the consequences of his act by going to another country."

The Torture Convention

Article 1 of the Convention defines torture as the intentional infliction of severe pain and of suffering with a view to achieving a wide range of purposes "when such pain or suffering is inflicted by or at the instigation of or with the consent or acquiescence of a public official or other person acting in an official capacity." Article 2(1) requires each state party to prohibit torture on territory within its own jurisdiction and Article 4 requires each state party to ensure that "all" acts of torture are offences under its criminal law. Article 2(3) outlaws any defence of superior orders. Under Article 5(1) each state party has to establish its jurisdiction over torture (a) when committed within territory under its jurisdiction, (b) when the alleged offender is a national of that state, and (c) in certain circumstances, when the victim is a national of that state. Under Article 5(2) a state party has to take jurisdiction over any alleged offender who is found within its territory. Article 6 contains provisions for a state in whose territory an alleged torturer is found to detain him, inquire into the position and notify the states referred to in Article 5(1) and to indicate whether it intends to exercise jurisdiction. Under Article 7 the state in whose territory the alleged torturer is found shall, if he is not extradited to any of the states mentioned in Article 5(1), submit him to its authorities for the purpose of prosecution. Under Article 8(1) torture is to be treated as an extraditable offence and under Article 8(4) torture shall, for the purposes of extradition, be treated as having been committed not only in the place where it occurred but also in the state mentioned in Article 5(1). * * *

Notes

1. On the Pinochet case, see also Ass'n Bar City of N.Y., Committees on International Human Rights and Inter–American Affairs, The English Patient and the Spanish Prisoner?, 55 Record 205 (2000); Bradley & Goldsmith, Pinochet and International Human Rights Litigation, 97 Mich.L.Rev. 2129 (1999); Wilson, Prosecuting Pinochet: International Crimes in Spanish Domestic Law, 2 Hum. Rts. Q. 927 (1999). Wedgwood, International Criminal Law and Augusto Pinochet, 40 Va.J.I.L. 829 (2000); Human Rights Watch, When Tyrants Tremble: The Pinochet Case (1999); Human Rights Watch, The Pinochet Precedent: How Victims Can Pursue Human Rights Criminals Abroad (2000). For a collection of materials concerning proceedings about Pinochet in Spain, the United Kingdom, France, and Belgium, see International Decisions, 93 A.J.I.L. 690–711 (1999).

2. Actions for international crimes against present or former government officials have given rise to pleas of immunity. In *Pinochet*, the immunity plea was rejected. See Chapter 14, p. 1276.

3. The U.S. Congress has enacted several statutes dealing with international crimes, but not all of them embrace a universal theory of jurisdiction. In the Genocide Convention Implementation Act, Pub. L. 100–106 § 1, 102 Stat. 3045 (Nov. 4, 1988), 18 U.S.C.A. § 1091 et seq., Congress chose to assert criminal jurisdiction only if the alleged genocide had been committed in the United States or by a national of the United States. (The Restatement and many other commentators, however, accept that universal jurisdiction over genocide is permissible under international law.) The War Crimes Act of 1996, Pub.L. 104–192, § 2(a), 110 Stat. 2104, 18 U.S.C.A. 2441 (Aug. 21, 1996) likewise stops short of universal jurisdiction. A notable U.S. assertion of universal jurisdiction is the Torture Convention Implementation Act of 1994, Pub. L. 103–236, Title V, Part A, § 506(a), 108 Stat. 463 (April 30, 1994), 18 U.S.C.A. § 2340 et seq. In § 2340A(b), Congress has established federal criminal jurisdiction over torture committed or attempted outside the United States if:

(1) the alleged offender is a national of the United States, or

(2) the alleged offender is present in the United States, regardless of the nationality of the victim or alleged offender.

On these acts, see Murphy, Civil Liability for the Commission of International Crimes as an Alternative to Criminal Persecution, 12 Harv. Hum. Rts. J. 1 (1999); Ballard, The Recognition and Enforcement of International Criminal Court Judgments in U.S. Courts, 29 Colum. Hum.R.L.Rev. 143 (1997); Ratner & Abrams, Accountability for Human Rights Atrocities in International Law (1997).

4. Note that the Restatement (Third) § 404 does not impose the limitation of reasonableness on the exercise of universal jurisdiction. Should it do so in cases in which there is another state that is better situated effectively to exercise its jurisdiction? On this question, see Schachter, International Law in Theory and

Practice 268 (1991). Does the possible absence of any link between the state exercising universal jurisdiction and the person over whom it is exercised require more extensive safeguards for the protection of that person? See id. at 269–70.

5. A trend toward actual national prosecutions on a universal theory seems to have picked up speed around the time of the *Pinochet* case. In addition to the third-country materials collected at 93 A.J.I.L. 690 (1999) (Note 1 supra), Germany has prosecuted for genocide in Yugoslavia on a universal theory. See State Attorney's Office v. Jorgic, Higher State Court of Dusseldorf, 2 StE 8/96 (1997), applying F.R.G. Penal Code § 220(a) on genocide. A "perfect, but also rare example of universal jurisdiction" is a warrant issued in Belgium "against a Rwandan responsible for massacres of other Rwandans in Rwanda." Meron, International Criminalization of Internal Atrocities, 89 A.J.I.L. 554, 577 (1995). Examples from a dozen or more countries are collected in a study by the Princeton Project on Universal Jurisdiction (forthcoming).

6. A number of recent multilateral conventions provide for punishment or extradition of persons guilty of specified crimes, such as hijacking, hostage taking, and terrorism, regardless of the absence of any of the traditional bases of jurisdiction other than the universality principle. On these conventions, see Section 3(D)(2) of this Chapter. Have the parties to these conventions in effect extended the universality principle to these crimes? Could they do so? See Schachter at 268.

7. For an argument in favor of expanding the universality principle of jurisdiction to terrorism and other offenses the community of nations widely condemns, see Randall, Universal Jurisdiction Under International Law, 66 Tex. L.Rev. 785 (1988). See also Note, Extraterritorial Jurisdiction Over Acts of Terrorism Committed Abroad: Omnibus Diplomatic Security and Antiterrorism Act of 1988, 72 Cornell L.Rev. 599; Comment, The Omnibus Diplomatic Security and Antiterrorism Act of 1986: Prescribing and Enforcing United States Law against Terrorist Violence Overseas, 37 UCLA L.Rev. 985 (1990).

8. Increasingly, jurisdiction to prosecute crimes punishable under the universal principle is assigned to international tribunals; see Chapter 15. To what extent are international and national jurisdiction in this area concurrent? May a national tribunal proceed in regard to an international crime when there is an international tribunal that has the authority to proceed? Does prosecution by one tribunal preclude prosecution by the other? On concurrent jurisdiction, the principle of complementarity, and protections against double jeopardy, see pp. 1334, 1381.

9. Is enforcement jurisdiction in regard to international crime universal? Can any state arrest a person accused of a universal crime wherever he may be found? Is there an obligation on a state where the universal criminal can be found to arrest the criminal and either prosecute him itself or deliver the criminal to the state or international tribunal that has issued an indictment? See p. 1168.

SECTION 5. JURISDICTION BASED ON AGREEMENT

Under international law, a state has jurisdiction to prescribe and enforce law in another state's territory to the extent provided by international agreement with the other state. The principle that jurisdiction may be conferred by agreement also underpins arrangements by which an international organization administers a territory for a temporary or transitional period.

Notes

1. By article II of the Hay–Bunau–Varilla Convention of 1903 (33 Stat. 234, T.S. No. 431) the United States was granted, "in perpetuity the use, occupation and control" of the Panama Canal Zone. Article III of this Convention provided that the United States was to exercise its rights as "if it were the sovereign of the territory within which said lands and waters are located to the entire exclusion of the exercise by the Republic of Panama of any such sovereign rights, power or authority." On this Convention, see Smit, The Panama Canal: A National or International Waterway?, 76 Colum. L.Rev. 965 (1976). By Treaties of Sept. 7, 1977, 16 I.L.M. 1022 (1977), the rights of the United States over the Canal Zone were substantially modified. The new Canal Treaty acknowledges "the Republic of Panama's sovereignty over its territory," stresses that Panama is the "territorial sovereign," declares the entire territory of Panama to be "under the flag of the Republic of Panama," and provides that Panama "shall reassume plenary jurisdiction over the former Canal Zone upon entry into force of this treaty." Canal Treaty, Preamble, para. (3), and arts. I(2), III(1), VII(*l*), and XI(1). What is the international legal effect of the quoted provisions? See Smit, The Proposed Panama Canal Treaties: A Triple Failure, 17 Colum.J.Transnat'l L. 1 (1978). On the return of the Canal to full Panamanian authority as of December 31, 1999, see pp. 954, 1410.

2. By an agreement of February 23, 1903, Cuba leased to the United States certain territory in Guantanamo for use by the latter as a naval station. Article III of the agreement recited the United States' recognition of Cuba's continuing "ultimate sovereignty" over the leased territory and Cuba's consent that the United States should exercise "complete jurisdiction and control over and within" the leased areas. 1 Malloy 358. A later agreement of the same year fixed the conditions of the lease and also provided for the mutual extradition of persons committing offenses against the laws of Cuba or the United States in areas under their respective control. 1 Malloy 360. Limited jurisdictional rights were granted to the United States when it leased naval and air bases in certain British territories during World War II. Article I of the agreement of March 27, 1941, 55 Stat. 1560, limited United States jurisdiction in the leased areas to "all the rights, power and authority * * * necessary for the establishment, use, operation and defence * * * or appropriate for their control." On leases of territory, see, in general, 1 O'Connell 361–63.

3. During the nineteenth and the early part of the twentieth centuries, a number of European states entered into agreements with weaker states, usually Asian or African, by which the latter relinquished their jurisdiction over individuals within their territory having the nationality of the other contracting parties, this jurisdiction being exercised instead by each state over its own nationals through special courts set up for the purpose. See 1 Oppenheim § 381 (8th ed. Lauterpacht 1955). On United States consular jurisdiction in Morocco, see Case Concerning Rights of Nationals of the United States of America in Morocco (France v. United States), 1952 I.C.J. 176; Nadelmann, American Consular Jurisdiction in Morocco and the Tangier International Jurisdiction, 49 A.J.I.L. 506 (1955). By a note of October 6, 1956 the United States relinquished its extraterritorial rights in Morocco, 35 Dep't St. Bull. 844 (1956). See Young, The End of American Consular Jurisdiction in Morocco, 51 A.J.I.L. 402 (1957).

4. Another example of jurisdiction based on agreement arises out of the trusteeship arrangements under Chapter XII of the United Nations Charter and the mandate system under the Covenant of the League of Nations. The trustee state, while not sovereign of the trust territory, has the power to prescribe and enforce rules of law. The powers of the trustee state have been exercised under the supervision of the Trusteeship Council of the United Nations. With the completion of the era of decolonization, the mandate and trusteeship system has been largely wound up. For important past applications, e.g. in the territory of Namibia, see pp. 549–551.

5. After World War II, the United States continued to control islands captured from Japan, including Okinawa and the other Ryukyu Islands. Article 3 of the 1951 Treaty of Peace with Japan gave to the United States, pending the creation, at the option of the United States, of a United Nations trusteeship administered by the United States, "the right to exercise all and any powers of administration, legislation and jurisdiction over the territory and inhabitants of these islands, including the territorial waters." 3 U.S.T. 3169, T.I.A.S. No. 2490, 136 U.N.T.S. 45. At the time the United States denied any intent of acquiring permanent possession of the islands and stated that Japan retained "residual sovereignty." 25:637 Dep't St. Bull. 455, 463 (1951). It asserted that the interests of peace and security justified its continued control of the islands. See 30:758 Dep't. St. Bull. 17 (1954); 3 Whiteman 595–600. A number of cases held that the United States did not acquire Okinawa and the Ryukyus. See United States v. Ushi Shiroma, 123 F.Supp. 145 (D.Hawaii 1954) (native of Okinawa held not to be a national of the United States; United States possesses de facto, not de jure, sovereignty); Burna v. United States, 240 F.2d 720 (4th Cir.1957) (Okinawa is a "foreign country" within meaning of Federal Tort Claims Act). By Agreement of June 17, 1971, 3 U.S.T. 3172, T.I.A.S. No. 2490, the United States relinquished in favor of Japan all rights it had under the 1951 Treaty of Peace over the islands.

6. States may also agree to exercise jurisdiction jointly over a territory. The resulting arrangement, the so-called condominium, may call for a joint or some form of divided administration of the conjoint sovereignty of the parties. Under one such agreement the United Kingdom and France governed the New Hebrides. Protocol respecting the New Hebrides, Aug. 6, 1914, [1922] Gr. Brit. T.S. 7, Cmd. at 1681, 10 L.N.T.S. 333. See generally 1 Oppenheim at 565–67; 1 O'Connell 360–31; El–Erian, Condominium and Related Situations in International Law (1952). In 1981, the New Hebrides declared their independence and were admitted to the United Nations as Vanuatu in September 1981.

7. By the Treaty of Uquair of 1922, Saudi Arabia and Kuwait agreed that a defined territory between the two states would be joint and common and that in this territory they would share equal rights (mashaa' or mushtaraqa). A similar treaty was concluded at the same time between Saudi Arabia and Iraq. In 1965, Saudi Arabia and Kuwait divided the joint territory into two parts, one of which was annexed to Kuwait and the other to Saudi Arabia. The 1965 Treaty preserved the interests each State had in the mineral resources in these parts, which it described as a one-half undivided interest. On these arrangements, see Lagoni, Oil and Gas Deposits Across National Frontiers, 73 A.J.I.L. 215 (1979); Onorato, Apportionment of an International Common Petroleum Deposit, 17 I.C.L.Q. 85 (1968). What rights does each of these states have to the mineral resources in these parts? In Getty Oil Co. v. Kuwait Petroleum Co. et al., Case No. 83 Civ. 0566 (S.D.N.Y.1983), Judge Pollack held that the parties were entitled to take equal parts of the oil in the ground and that, if one party took more, it had to account for the excess.

8. The United States Coast Guard stopped a Panamanian ship on the high seas, searched it, and found 20 tons of marijuana. Two crew members were prosecuted and convicted in a U.S. district court. Their conviction was upheld on the ground that Panama had agreed to the U.S. prosecution. United States v. Robinson, 843 F.2d 1 (1st Cir.1988), cert. denied, 488 U.S. 834, 109 S.Ct. 93, 102 L.Ed.2d 69 (1988).

9. In 1999, the United Nations embarked on two new initiatives to exercise prescriptive jurisdiction over territories under its (presumably temporary) administration, in Kosovo and East Timor. The Security Council authorized an interim administration in Kosovo and a transitional administration in East Timor under its Chapter VII authority, as discussed in Chapter 12. Although Chapter VII is compulsory in character, the U.N.'s authority to exercise prescriptive jurisdiction can be considered at least partly grounded in agreement, both because the states in question had consented to the U.N. Charter and because the authorities responsible for or controlling the territories (Federal Republic of Yugoslavia for Kosovo; Portugal *de jure* and Indonesia *de facto* for East Timor) agreed to terms of settlement which included temporary U.N. administration. Regulation No. 1999/1 of the U.N. Interim Administration Mission in Kosovo (UNMIK) declared that the laws applicable in the territory of Kosovo prior to March 24, 1999 would continue to apply for the time being; thereafter, new regulations were promulgated by the Special Representative of the Secretary–General, in an effort to bring the legal system up to international standards, including internationally recognized human rights. Compare U.N. Transitional Administration in East Timor (UNTAET), Regulation No. 2000/13, 39 I.L.M. 936 (2000), issued under the authority of the Special Representative of the Secretary–General pursuant to S.C. Res. 1272 (1999).

In the Comprehensive Review of the Whole Question of Peacekeeping Operations in All Their Aspects, U.N. Doc. A/55/305–S/2000/809 (Aug. 21, 2000) ("Brahimi Report"), the panel addressed some of its recommendations to "the challenge of transitional civil administration," with the Kosovo and East Timor examples in mind, stating (at p. 14):

> 79. Meanwhile, there is a pressing issue in transitional civil administration that must be addressed, and that is the issue of "applicable law." In the two locales where United Nations operations now have law enforcement responsibility, local judicial and legal capacity was found to be non-existent, out of practice or subject to intimidation by armed elements. Moreover, in both places, the law and legal systems prevailing prior to the conflict were questioned or rejected by key groups considered to be the victims of the conflicts. * * *
>
> 81. These missions' tasks would have been much easier if a common United Nations justice package had allowed them to apply an interim legal code to which mission personnel could have been pre-trained while the final answer to the "applicable law" question was being worked out. * * * [I]nterviews with researchers indicate that some headway toward dealing with the problem has been made * * *, emphasizing the principles, guidelines, codes and procedures contained in several dozen international conventions and declarations relating to human rights, humanitarian law, and guidelines for police, prosecutors and penal systems.
>
> 82. Such research aims at a code that contains the basics of both law and procedure to enable an operation to apply due process using international jurists and internationally agreed standards in the case of such crimes as

murder, rape, arson, kidnapping and aggravated assault. Property law would probably remain beyond reach of such a "model code," but at least an operation would be able to prosecute effectively those who burned their neighbours' homes while the property law issue was being addressed.

83. * * * [T]he Panel recommends that the Secretary–General invite a panel of international legal experts, including individuals with experience in United Nations operations that have transitional administration mandates, to evaluate the feasibility and utility of developing an interim criminal code, including any regional adaptations potentially required, for use by such operations pending the re-establishment of local rule of law and local law enforcement capacity.

AGREEMENT BETWEEN THE PARTIES TO THE NORTH ATLANTIC TREATY REGARDING THE STATUS OF THEIR FORCES

Signed at London, June 19, 1951.
4 U.S.T. 1792, T.I.A.S. No. 2846, 199 U.N.T.S. 67.

Article VII

1. Subject to the provisions of this Article,

(a) the military authorities of the sending State shall have the right to exercise within the receiving State all criminal and disciplinary jurisdiction conferred on them by the law of the sending State over all persons subject to the military law of that State;

(b) the authorities of the receiving State shall have jurisdiction over the members of a force or civilian component and their dependents with respect to offenses committed within the territory of the receiving State and punishable by the law of that State.

2. (a) The military authorities of the sending State shall have the right to exercise exclusive jurisdiction over persons subject to the military law of that State with respect to offences, including offences relating to its security, punishable by the law of the sending State, but not by the law of the receiving State.

(b) The authorities of the receiving State shall have the right to exercise exclusive jurisdiction over members of a force or civilian component and their dependents with respect to offences, including offences relating to the security of that State, punishable by its law but not by the law of the sending State.

(c) For the purposes of this paragraph and of paragraph 3 of this Article a security offence against a State shall include (i) treason against the State; (ii) sabotage, espionage or violation of any law relating to official secrets of that State, or secrets relating to the national defence of that State.

3. In cases where the right to exercise jurisdiction is concurrent the following rules shall apply:

(a) The military authorities of the sending State shall have the primary right to exercise jurisdiction over a member of a force or of a civilian component in relation to (i) offences solely against the property or security of that State, or offences solely against the person or property of another member of the force or civilian component of that state or of a dependent; (ii) offences arising out of any act or omission done in the performance of official duty.

(b) In the case of any other offence the authorities of the receiving State shall have the primary right to exercise jurisdiction.

(c) If the State having the primary right decides not to exercise jurisdiction, it shall notify the authorities of the other State as soon as practicable. The authorities of the State having the primary right shall give sympathetic consideration to a request from the authorities of the other State for a waiver of its right in cases where that other State considers such waiver to be of particular importance.

4. The foregoing provisions of this Article shall not imply any right for the military authorities of the sending State to exercise jurisdiction over persons who are nationals of or ordinarily resident in the receiving State, unless they are members of the force of the sending State.

5.(a) The authorities of the receiving and sending States shall assist each other in the arrest of members of a force or civilian component or their dependents in the territory of the receiving State and in handing them over to the authority which is to exercise jurisdiction in accordance with the above provisions.

(b) The authorities of the receiving State shall notify promptly the military authorities of the sending State of the arrest of any member of a force or civilian component or a dependent.

(c) The custody of an accused member of a force or civilian component over whom the receiving State is to exercise jurisdiction shall, if he is in the hands of the sending State, remain with that State until he is charged by the receiving State.

6.(a) The authorities of the receiving and sending States shall assist each other in the carrying out of all necessary investigations into offences, and in the collection and production of evidence, including the seizure and, in proper cases, the handing over of objects connected with an offence. The handing over of such objects may, however, be made subject to their return within the time specified by the authority delivering them.

(b) The authorities of the Contracting Parties shall notify one another of the disposition of all cases in which there are concurrent rights to exercise jurisdiction.

7.(a) A death sentence shall not be carried out in the receiving State by the authorities of the sending State if the legislation of the receiving State does not provide for such punishment in a similar case.

* * *

8. Where an accused has been tried in accordance with the provisions of this Article by the authorities of one Contracting Party and has been acquitted, or has been convicted and is serving, or has served, his sentence or has been pardoned, he may not be tried again for the same offence within the same territory by the authorities of another Contracting Party. However, nothing in this paragraph shall prevent the military authorities of the sending State from trying a member of its force for any violation of rules of discipline

arising from an act or omission which constituted an offence for which he was tried by the authorities of another Contracting Party.

9. Whenever a member of a force or civilian component or a dependent is prosecuted under the jurisdiction of a receiving State he shall be entitled-

(a) to a prompt and speedy trial;

(b) to be informed, in advance of trial, of the specific charge or charges made against him;

(c) to be confronted with the witnesses against him;

(d) to have compulsory process for obtaining witnesses in his favour, if they are within the jurisdiction of the receiving State;

(e) to have legal representation of his own choice for his defence or to have free or assisted legal representation under the conditions prevailing for the time being in the receiving State;

(f) if he considers it necessary, to have the services of a competent interpreter; and

(g) to communicate with a representative of the Government of the sending State and, when the rules of the court permit, to have such a representative present at his trial.

* * *

Notes

1. The NATO Status of Forces Agreement is supplemented by bilateral agreements between the United States and Canada (T.I.A.S. No. 3074), Denmark (T.I.A.S. No. 4002), Norway (T.I.A.S. No. 2950), Greece (T.I.A.S. No. 3649), the Netherlands (T.I.A.S. No. 3174) and Turkey (T.I.A.S. No. 3020). Iceland, although a member of NATO, is not a party to the Status of Forces Agreement; the status of United States forces in that country is regulated solely by bilateral agreement (T.I.A.S. No. 2295). Large numbers of United States military personnel are stationed in non-NATO countries; their status is usually regulated by bilateral agreement. See, e.g., the agreements with Korea (T.I.A.S. No. 6226), Japan (T.I.A.S. No. 4510), and Australia (T.I.A.S. No. 5349). Excerpts from other status of forces agreements are included in the appendices to Stanger, Criminal Jurisdiction over Visiting Armed Forces (Naval War College International Law Studies 1957–58) (1965). No agreement relating to the status of United States forces at the time they were present in South Vietnam has been made public. For detailed discussion of the operation of status of forces agreements to which the United States is a party, see Stanger at 141–266 and the annual Hearings before a Subcommittee of the Senate Committee on Armed Services to Review the Operation of Article VII of the NATO Status of Forces Treaty, Together with * * * Other Criminal Jurisdictional Arrangements (1954). See also Health, Status of Forces Agreements as a Basis for United States Custody of an Accused, 49 Mil. L.Rev. 45 (1970); Norton, United States Obligations Under Status of Forces Agreements: A New Method of Extradition?, 5 Ga.J.Int'l & Comp.L. 1 (1975); Schwenk, Jurisdiction of Receiving State Over Forces of Sending Under NATO Status of Forces Agreement, 6 Int'l Lawyer 525 (1972); Note, NATO Status of Forces Agreement not an Exclusive Remedy for Member of United States Forces or Civilian Component, 7 Vand.J.Transnat'l L. 5211 (1974). On status of military

forces generally, see Lazareff, Status of Military Forces Under Current International Law (1971).

2. The United States Supreme Court has, in a series of decisions, sharply limited the power of United States military authorities to try by court martial civilian employees or civilian dependents of members of United States forces. See Reid v. Covert; Kinsella v. Krueger, 354 U.S. 1, 77 S.Ct. 1222, 1 L.Ed.2d 1148 (1957); Kinsella v. United States ex rel. Singleton, 361 U.S. 234, 80 S.Ct. 297, 4 L.Ed.2d 268 (1960); Grisham v. Hagan, 361 U.S. 278, 80 S.Ct. 310, 4 L.Ed.2d 279 (1960); McElroy v. United States ex rel. Guagliardo, Wilson v. Bohlender, 361 U.S. 281, 80 S.Ct. 305, 4 L.Ed.2d 282 (1960).

WILSON v. GIRARD

Supreme Court of the United States, 1957.
354 U.S. 524, 77 S.Ct. 1409, 1 L.Ed.2d 1544.

PER CURIAM. Japan and the United States became involved in a controversy whether the respondent Girard should be tried by a Japanese court for causing the death of a Japanese woman. The basis for the dispute between the two Governments fully appears in the affidavit of Robert Dechert, General Counsel of the Department of Defense, an exhibit to a government motion in the court below, and the joint statement of Secretary of State John Foster Dulles and Secretary of Defense Charles E. Wilson, printed as appendices to this opinion.

Girard, a Specialist Third Class in the United States Army, was engaged on January 30, 1957, with members of his cavalry regiment in a small unit exercise at Camp Weir range area, Japan. Japanese civilians were present in the area, retrieving expended cartridge cases. Girard and another Specialist Third Class were ordered to guard a machine gun and some items of clothing that had been left nearby. Girard had a grenade launcher on his rifle. He placed an expended 30–caliber cartridge case in the grenade launcher and projected it by firing a blank. The expended cartridge case penetrated the back of a Japanese woman gathering expended cartridge cases and caused her death.

The United States ultimately notified Japan that Girard would be delivered to the Japanese authorities for trial. Thereafter, Japan indicted him for causing death by wounding. Girard sought a writ of habeas corpus in the United States District Court for the District of Columbia. The writ was denied, but Girard was granted declaratory relief and an injunction against his delivery to the Japanese authorities. 152 F.Supp. 21. The petitioners appealed to the Court of Appeals for the District of Columbia, and, without awaiting action by that court on the appeal, invoked the jurisdiction of this Court under 28 U.S.C. § 1254(1), 28 U.S.C.A. § 1254(1). Girard filed a cross-petition for certiorari to review the denial of the writ of habeas corpus. We granted both petitions. * * *

A Security Treaty between Japan and the United States, signed September 8, 1951, was ratified by the Senate on March 20, 1952, and proclaimed by the President effective April 28, 1952 [3 U.S.T. 3329, T.I.A.S. 2491]. Article III of the Treaty authorized the making of Administrative Agreements between the two Governments concerning "[t]he conditions which shall govern the disposition of armed forces of the United States of America in and about

Japan * * *" Expressly acting under this provision, the two Nations, on February 28, 1952, signed an Administrative Agreement covering, among other matters, the jurisdiction of the United States over offenses committed in Japan by members of the United States armed forces, and providing that jurisdiction in any case might be waived by the United States. This Agreement [3 U.S.T. 3341, T.I.A.S. 2492] became effective on the same date as the Security Treaty (April 28, 1952) and was considered by the Senate before consent was given to the Treaty.

Article XVII, paragraph 1, of the Administrative Agreement provided that upon the coming into effect of the "Agreement between the Parties to the North Atlantic Treaty regarding the Status of their Forces," [4 U.S.T. 1792, T.I.A.S. 2846] signed June 19, 1951, the United States would conclude with Japan an agreement on criminal jurisdiction similar to the corresponding provisions of the NATO Agreement. The NATO Agreement became effective August 23, 1953, and the United States and Japan signed on September 29, 1953, effective October 29, 1953, a Protocol Agreement [4 U.S.T. 1846, T.I.A.S. 2848] pursuant to the covenant in paragraph I of Article XVII.

Paragraph 3 of Article XVII, as amended by the Protocol, dealt with criminal offenses in violation of the laws of both Nations and provided:

> 3. In cases where the right to exercise jurisdiction is concurrent the following rules shall apply:
>
> (a) The military authorities of the United States shall have the primary right to exercise jurisdiction over members of the United States armed forces or the civilian component in relation to
>
> > (i) offenses solely against the property or security of the United States, or offenses solely against the person or property of another member of the United States armed forces or the civilian component or of a dependent;
> >
> > (ii) offenses arising out of any act or omission done in the performance of official duty.
>
> (b) In the case of any other offense the authorities of Japan shall have the primary right to exercise jurisdiction.
>
> (c) If the State having the primary right decides not to exercise jurisdiction, it shall notify the authorities of the other State as soon as practicable. The authorities of the State having the primary right shall give sympathetic consideration to a request from the authorities of the other State for a waiver of its right in cases where that other State considers such waiver to be of particular importance.

Article XXVI of the Administrative Agreement established a Joint Committee of representatives of the United States and Japan to consult on all matters requiring mutual consultation regarding the implementation of the Agreement; and provided that if the Committee " * * * is unable to resolve any matter, it shall refer that matter to the respective governments for further consideration through appropriate channels."

In the light of the Senate's ratification of the Security Treaty after consideration of the Administrative Agreement, which had already been signed, and its subsequent ratification of the NATO Agreement, with knowledge of the commitment to Japan under the Administrative Agreement, we are satisfied that the approval of Article III of the Security Treaty authorized the making of the Administrative Agreement and the subsequent Protocol embodying the NATO Agreement provisions governing jurisdiction to try criminal offenses.

The United States claimed the right to try Girard upon the ground that his act, as certified by his commanding officer, was "done in the performance of official duty" and therefore the United States had primary jurisdiction. Japan insisted that it had proof that Girard's action was without the scope of his official duty and therefore that Japan had the primary right to try him.

The Joint Committee, after prolonged deliberations, was unable to agree. The issue was referred to higher authority, which authorized the United States representatives on the Joint Committee to notify the appropriate Japanese authorities, in accordance with paragraph 3(c) of the Protocol, that the United States had decided not to exercise, but to waive, whatever jurisdiction it might have in the case. The Secretary of State and the Secretary of Defense decided that this determination should be carried out. The President confirmed their joint conclusion.

A sovereign nation has exclusive jurisdiction to punish offenses against its laws committed within its borders, unless it expressly or impliedly consents to surrender its jurisdiction. The Schooner Exchange v. M'Faddon, 7 Cranch 116, 136, 3 L.Ed. 287. Japan's cession to the United States of jurisdiction to try American military personnel for conduct constituting an offense against the laws of both countries was conditioned by the covenant of Article XVII, section 3, paragraph (c) of the Protocol that

> "* * * The authorities of the State having the primary right shall give sympathetic consideration to a request from the authorities of the other State for a waiver of its right in cases where that other State considers such waiver to be of particular importance."

The issue for our decision is therefore narrowed to the question whether, upon the record before us, the Constitution or legislation subsequent to the Security Treaty prohibited the carrying out of this provision authorized by the Treaty for waiver of the qualified jurisdiction granted by Japan. We find no constitutional or statutory barrier to the provision as applied here. In the absence of such encroachments, the wisdom of the arrangement is exclusively for the determination of the Executive and Legislative Branches.

The judgment of the District Court in No. 1103 is reversed, and its judgment in No. 1108 is affirmed. * * *

Note

The principal case has received renewed attention in connection with the controversy over potential U.S. participation in the prospective International Criminal Court (see Chapter 15, pp. 1376–1382). Although opponents object to the idea that members of the U.S. armed services might conceivably be vulnerable to prosecution by the I.C.C. for crimes committed in other countries, it has been pointed out that they are already subject to jurisdiction of the territorial state for certain crimes under the terms of Status of Forces Agreements and that the Supreme Court upheld constitutional challenges to that jurisdictional scheme in

Wilson v. Girard. For discussion, see Leigh, The United States and the Statute of Rome, 95 A.J.I.L. 124 (2001); Everett, American Servicemembers and the ICC, in Sewall & Kaysen (eds.), The United States and the International Criminal Court 137, 149 nn. 8, 20 (2000).

AGREEMENT BETWEEN THE UNITED NATIONS AND CYPRUS CONCERNING THE STATUS OF THE UNITED NATIONS PEACE-KEEPING FORCE IN CYPRUS

492 U.N.T.S. 57 (1964).

* * *

11. Members of the Force shall be subject to the exclusive jurisdiction of their respective national States in respect of any criminal offenses which may be committed by them in Cyprus.

12.(a) Members of the Force shall not be subject to the civil jurisdiction of the courts of Cyprus or to other legal process in any matter relating to their official duties. In a case arising from a matter relating to the official duties of a member of the Force and which involves a member of the Force and a Cypriot citizen, and in other disputes as agreed, the procedure provided in paragraph 38(b) shall apply to the settlement.

(b) In those cases where civil jurisdiction is exercised by the courts of Cyprus with respect to members of the Force, the courts or other Cypriot authorities shall grant members of the Force sufficient opportunity to safeguard their rights. If the Commander certifies that a member of the Force is unable because of official duties or authorized absence to protect his interests in a civil proceeding in which he is a participant the aforesaid court or authority shall at his request suspend the proceeding until the elimination of the disability, but for not more than ninety days. Property of a member of the Force which is certified by the Commander to be needed by him for the fulfillment of his official duties shall be free from seizure for the satisfaction of a judgment, decision or order, together with other property not subject thereto under the law of Cyprus. The personal liberty of a member of the Force shall not be restricted by a court or other Cypriot authority in a civil proceeding, whether to enforce a judgment, decision or order, to compel an oath of disclosure, or for any other reason. * * *

* * *

15. Military police of the Force may take into custody any Cypriot citizen committing an offence or causing a disturbance on the premises referred to in paragraph 19, without subjecting him to the ordinary routine of arrest, in order immediately to deliver him to the nearest appropriate Cypriot authorities for the purpose of dealing with such offence or disturbance.

16. The Cypriot authorities may take into custody a member of the Force, without subjecting him to the ordinary routine of arrest in order immediately to deliver him, together with any weapons or items seized, to the nearest appropriate authorities of the Force: (a) when so requested by the Commander, or (b) in cases in which the military police of the Force are unable to act with the necessary promptness when a member of the Force is

apprehended in the commission or attempted commission of a criminal offence that results or might result in serious injury to persons or property, or serious impairment of other legally protected rights.

* * *

18. The Commander and the Cypriot authorities shall assist each other in the carrying out of all necessary investigations into offences in respect of which either or both have an interest, in the production of witnesses, and in the collection and production of evidence, including the seizure and, in proper cases, the handing over, of things connected with an offence. The handing over of any such things may be made subject to their return within the time specified by the authority delivering them. Each shall notify the other of the disposition of any case in the outcome of which the other may have an interest or in which there has been a transfer of custody under the provisions of paragraphs 15 and 16 of these arrangements. The government will ensure the prosecution of persons subject to its criminal jurisdiction who are accused of acts in relation to the Force or its members which, if committed in relation to the Cypriot army or its members, would have rendered them liable to prosecution. The Secretary–General will seek assurances from Governments of Participating States that they will be prepared to exercise jurisdiction with respect to crimes or offences which may be committed against Cypriot citizens by members of their national contingents serving with the Force. * * *

Notes

1. Agreements were also concluded by the United Nations with Egypt, 260 U.N.T.S. 61, on the status of the United Nations Emergency Force (UNEF) in Egyptian territory, and with the Republic of the Congo, 414 U.N.T.S. 229, on the status of the United Nations Force in the Congo (ONUC). For comprehensive analysis and discussion, see Bowett, United Nations Forces (1964); Seyersted, United Nations Forces in the Law of Peace and War (1966).

2. As discussed in Chapter 12, peacekeepers are now present under authority of U.N. Security Council resolutions in more than a dozen countries, usually but not necessarily by agreement with the territorial state. Issues of jurisdiction to prescribe and enforce law with respect to the peacekeepers' conduct have arisen numerous times, including in relation to crimes of violence committed by members of the peacekeeping contingents against civilians in the territory in question. Generally, the sending state investigates and (if appropriate) prosecutes such allegations. For example, a Canadian court-martial heard charges in 1996 against a Canadian soldier arrested for aiding and abetting the torture of a Somali teenager who had been captured while attempting an intrusion into the Canadian camp during the peacekeeping deployment in Somalia; and an Italian commission investigated allegations of maltreatment and violence against Somali citizens on the part of Italian soldiers. See Young & Molina, International Humanitarian Law and Peace Operations: Sharing Canada's Lessons Learned from Somalia, 1 Y.B. Int'l Humanit. Law. 362–370 (1998); Boustany, *Brocklebank*: A Questionable Decision of the Court Martial Appeal Court of Canada, ibid., pp. 371–374; Lupi, Report by the Enquiry Commission on the Behaviour of Italian Peace–Keeping Troops in Somalia, ibid., pp. 375–379. See also Siekmann, The Fall of Srebrenica and the Attitude of Dutchbat from an International Legal Perspective, ibid., pp. 301–312. In 2000, a U.S. soldier with the Kosovo Force was charged with a sexual

attack on and murder of a Kosovar girl, convicted by a U.S. court-martial, and sentenced to life in prison without possibility of parole. See "Inquiry Into Abuse by G.I.'s in Kosovo Faults training," New York Times, Sept. 19, 2000, p. A10, col.1.

SECTION 6. CONFLICTS OF JURISDICTION

Bases of jurisdiction frequently overlap. For example, a state may, on the basis of the nationality principle, reach its nationals abroad, but the conduct of the nationals of that state may, on the basis of the territorial principle, also be within the jurisdiction of the foreign state in which these nationals act. Similarly, one state may have jurisdiction under the subjective territorial principle and another under the objective territorial or the protective principle.

These overlaps lead to particularly vexing problems when one of the states having jurisdiction prohibits conduct that the other state having jurisdiction commands. These problems are exemplified by United States v. The Bank of Nova Scotia, infra.

However, there may also be conflicts of jurisdiction when one state prohibits conduct that the other state does not command, but permits or encourages. In those cases, the permitting state, if it is sufficiently concerned, may turn the permission into a command. The inclination to do so becomes particularly strong if, as United States courts initially ruled, a United States court would not apply a coercive United States law extraterritorially if the foreign state where the conduct was required forbade it. Many of the so-called blocking statutes, p. 1163 infra, were enacted in an effort to accommodate nationals or residents subject to foreign extraterritorial prohibitions and provide them with a proper defense in American courts. As might have been expected, the response of American courts to the emergence of these statutes has been to limit, if not eliminate, the availability of this defense.

The imposition of the limitation of reasonableness by Restatement (Third) § 403 would reduce the area of overlap and, as a consequence, the possibility of conflicts of jurisdiction. But it would not eliminate the possibility of conflicts altogether. Indeed, it might aggravate the conflict by giving a state the opportunity to argue that reasonableness, and therefore international law, is on its side.

In an attempt to deal with these conflicts of jurisdiction, the Restatement (Third) provides its suggested solution in Section 441, reproduced infra. Whether its attempt is successful should be considered in the light of the materials that follow.

UNITED STATES v. THE BANK OF NOVA SCOTIA

United States Court of Appeals, Eleventh Circuit, 1982.
691 F.2d 1384, cert. denied, 462 U.S. 1119, 103 S.Ct. 3086, 77 L.Ed.2d 1348 (1983).

(Some footnotes omitted; others renumbered.)

Lewis R. Morgan, Senior Circuit Judge:

The Bank of Nova Scotia appeals from an order of the United States District Court for the Southern District of Florida holding the Bank of Nova

Scotia in civil contempt for failing to comply with an order of the court enforcing a grand jury subpoena duces tecum. The Bank of Nova Scotia (the Bank) presents three arguments against enforcing the subpoena. The Bank first contends that there were insufficient grounds to enforce the subpoena. The Bank also contends that enforcing the subpoena would violate due process. Finally, the Bank argues that the subpoena should not be enforced as a matter of comity between nations. We find that Bank's contentions to be without merit, and therefore we affirm the district court.

I. Facts

The Bank of Nova Scotia is a Canadian chartered bank with branches and agencies in forty-five countries, including the United States and the Bahamas. A federal grand jury conducting a tax and narcotics investigation issued a subpoena duces tecum to the Bank calling for the production of certain records maintained at the Bank's main branch or any of its branch offices in Nassau, Bahamas and Antigua, Lesser Antilles, relating to the bank accounts of a customer of the Bank.[1] The subpoena was served on the Bank's Miami, Florida agency on September 23, 1981. The Bank declined to produce the documents asserting that compliance with the subpoena without the customer's consent or an order of the Bahamian courts would violate Bahamian bank secrecy laws?[2] A hearing was held on the government's motion to compel the

1. The Bank investigated and found no documents which were requested located at its Antigua branch. Accordingly, that part of the subpoena is not in issue.

2. Banks and Trust Companies Regulations Act of 1965, 1965 Bah. Acts No. 64, as amended by the Banks and Trust Companies Regulation (Amendment) Act, 1980, 1980 Bah. Acts No. 3, and Section 19 of the Banks Act, III Bah. Rev. Laws, c. 96 (1965), as amended by the Banks Amendment Act 1980, 1980 Bah. Acts No.[ ]. Both Section 10 and Section 19 are identical. Section 10 of the Bank and Trust Companies Regulation Act as amended provides:

Preservation of secrecy

10.—(1) No person who has acquired information in his capacity as—

(a) director, officer, employee or agent of any licensee or former licenses;

(b) counsel and attorney, consultant or auditor of the Central Bank of The Bahamas, established under section 3 of the Central Bank of The Bahamas Act 1974, or as an employee or agent of such counsel and attorney, consultant or auditor;

(c) counsel and attorney, consultant, auditor, accountant, receiver or liquidator of any licensee or former licensee or as an employee or agent of such counsel and attorney, consultant, auditor, accountant, receiver or liquidator;

(d) auditor of any customer of any licensee or former licensee or as an employee or agent of such auditor;

(e) the Inspector under the provisions of this Act,

shall, without the express or implied consent of the customer concerned, disclose to any person any such information relating to the identity, assets, liabilities, transactions, accounts of a customer of a licensee or relating to any application by any person under the provisions of this Act, as the case may be, except-

(i) for the purpose of the performance of his duties or the exercise of his functions under this Act, if any; or

(ii) for the purpose of the performance of his duties within the scope of his employment; or

(iii) when a licensee is lawfully required to make disclosure by any court of competent jurisdiction within The Bahamas, or under the provisions of any law of The Bahamas.

—(2) Nothing contained in this section shall—

(a) prejudice or derogate from the rights and duties subsisting at common law between a licensee and its customer; or

(b) prevent a licensee from providing upon a legitimate business request in the normal course of business a general credit rating with respect to a customer.

—(3) Every person who contravenes the provisions of subsection (1) of this section shall be guilty of an offense against this Act and shall be liable on summary conviction to

Bank to comply with the subpoena on January 13, 1982. * * * The Bank also presented an affidavit showing that compliance with the subpoena could expose the Bank to prosecution under the Bahamian bank secrecy law. The affidavit also showed that the government could obtain an order of judicial assistance from the Supreme Court of the Bahamas allowing disclosure if the subject of the grand jury investigation is a crime under Bahamian law and not solely criminal under United States tax laws. The government did not make a showing that the documents sought are relevant and necessary to the grand jury's investigation.

After the district court entered an order compelling the Bank to comply with the subpoena, the Bank's Miami agent appeared before the grand jury and formally declined to produce the documents called for by the subpoena. The district court held the Bank in civil contempt and the Bank brings this appeal.

II. Relevance of the Documents

The Bank urges this court to follow the Third Circuit's holdings in In re Grand Jury Proceedings, 486 F.2d 85 (Schofield I), (3rd Cir.1973), and In re Grand Jury Proceedings, 507 F.2d 963 (Schofield II), (3rd Cir.1975), cert. denied, 421 U.S. 1015, 95 S.Ct. 2424, 44 L.Ed.2d 685 (1975), and require the government to show that the documents sought are relevant to an investigation properly within the grand jury's jurisdiction and not sought primarily for another purpose. * * *

The guidelines established by the Third Circuit in *Schofield* are not mandated by the Constitution; the Third Circuit imposed the requirements under that court's inherent supervisory power. *Schofield*, 486 F.2d at 89; *McLean*, 565 F.2d at 320. We decline to impose any undue restrictions upon the grand jury investigative process pursuant to this court's supervisory power. * * *

While it is true courts should not impinge upon the political prerogatives of the government in the sensitive area of foreign relations, Chicago and Southern Air Lines v. Waterman Steamship Corp., 333 U.S. 103, 111, 68 S.Ct. 431, 436, 92 L.Ed. 568 (1948), accepting the Bank's position would be a greater interference with foreign relations than the procedures employed here. In essence, the Bank would require the government to choose between impeding the grand jury's investigation and petitioning the Supreme Court of the Bahamas for an order of disclosure.

This court is cognizant that international friction has been provoked by enforcement of subpoenas such as the one in question. See, Restatement

a fine not exceeding fifteen thousand dollars or to a term of imprisonment not exceeding two years or to both such fine and imprisonment.

The government argues the Bank would not be successfully prosecuted by Bahamian authorities if it complied with the subpoena. In this regard it argues that because Section 10(2)(a) expressly preserves the common law relationship between bank and customers, the Bank is authorized to disclose the requested information. See Tournier v. National Provincial and Union Bank of England, [1924] 1 K.B. 461 (Banker may disclose banking information concerning a customer where the banker is compelled by law to disclose information); Barclay's Bank International, Ltd. v. McKinney, No. 474 (Bah. S.Ct. Feb. 16, 1979). Although the determination of foreign law is reviewable on appeal, F.R.Civ. P. 44.1, we shall assume for purposes of this appeal that the Bank will be subject to criminal sanctions in the Bahamas.

(Revised) of Foreign Relations Law of the United States § 420, Reporter's Note 1. See generally, Rio Tinto Zinc Corp. v. Westinghouse Electric Corp., [1978] A.C. 547, 616, 629–31, 639–40, 650 (H.L.) (criticizing the United States for claims of "jurisdiction over foreigners in respect to acts done outside the jurisdiction of that country"). But as recognized in United States v. First National City Bank, 379 U.S. 378, 384–85, 85 S.Ct. 528, 531–32, 13 L.Ed.2d 365 (1965), the various federal courts remain open to the legislative and executive branches of our government if matters such as this prove to have international repercussions. See, e.g., Convention on Double Taxation of Income, September 27, 1951. United States–Switzerland, 2 U.S.T. 1751, T.I.A.S. No. 2316 (Swiss–US Tax Treaty providing for exchange of information for, inter alia, the prevention of fraud.)

III. Due Process

The Bank contends that compliance with the subpoena would require it to violate the Bahamian bank secrecy law and therefore enforcing the subpoena and imposing contempt sanctions for noncompliance violates due process under Société Internationale pour Participations Industrielles v. Rogers, 357 U.S. 197, 78 S.Ct. 1087, 2 L.Ed.2d 1255 (1958). The Bank argues that once it has shown Bahamian law bars production of the documents and that it is a disinterested custodian of the documents due process prohibits enforcement of the subpoena. We disagree.

The Bank attempts to fashion a due process defense to the contempt proceedings because of its lack of purposeful involvement or responsibility in the subject matter before the court. In essence, the Bank asserts it is fundamentally unfair to require a "mere stakeholder" to incur criminal liability in the Bahamas. The Bank's position does not withstand analysis.

In *Société Internationale* a Swiss holding company brought an action to recover assets seized under the Trading with the Enemy Act. The district court had ordered production of certain banking records of a Swiss bank pursuant to the government's discovery request. The holding company failed to comply with the court's order, after good faith efforts were made to comply, on the grounds that compliance would violate Swiss penal laws. The district court then dismissed the suit with prejudice due to noncompliance with the production order. In reversing the district court, the Supreme Court did not erect an absolute bar to sanctions being imposed for noncompliance with summons or subpoenas whenever compliance is prohibited by foreign law. *Société Internationale*, 357 U.S. at 105–06, 78 S.Ct. at 1092–93; United States v. Vetco, Inc., 644 F.2d 1324, 1329 (9th Cir.1981), cert. denied, 454 U.S. 1098, 102 S.Ct. 671 (1981). *Société Internationale* held only that the sanction of outright dismissal of that plaintiff's complaint could not be imposed where that plaintiff had acted in good faith, was unable to comply because of foreign law, and was entitled to a hearing on the merits in order for the Trading with the Enemy Act to withstand constitutional challenge. *Société Internationale*, 352 U.S. at 211–12, 78 S.Ct. at 1095–96. Compare, National Hockey League v. Metropolitan Hockey Club, Inc., 427 U.S. 639, 96 S.Ct. 2778, 49 L.Ed.2d 747 (1976), and Roadway Express, Inc. v. Piper, 447 U.S. 752, 767 n. 14, 100 S.Ct. 2455, 2464 n. 14, 65 L.Ed.2d 488 n. 14 (1980). (emphasizing bad faith vs. inability to comply dichotomy). See United States v. Vetco, 644 F.2d at 1329–30. The Court left the district court free to impose other sanctions. *Société*

Internationale, 357 U.S. at 213, 78 S.Ct. at 1096. *Société Internationale* does not stand for the proposition that a lawfully issued grand jury subpoena may be resisted on constitutional grounds where compliance would violate foreign criminal law. See, e.g., United States v. Vetco, Inc., 644 F.2d at 1329; Ohio v. Arthur Andersen & Co., 570 F.2d 1370 (10th Cir.1978), cert. denied, 439 U.S. 833, 99 S.Ct. 114, 58 L.Ed.2d 129 (1978); SEC v. Banca Della Svizzera Italiana, 92 F.R.D. 111 (S.D.N.Y.1981).

The Bank has failed to bring itself within the holding of *Société Internationale*. The district court found the Bank had not made a good faith effort to comply with the subpoena in its order of June 11, 1982. Record at 140. The Bahamian government has not acted to prevent the Bank from complying with the subpoena. Finally, the Bank is not being denied a constitutionally required forum to recover confiscated assets?[3]

IV. Comity

The Bank's final contention is that comity between nations precludes enforcement of the subpoena. The Bank argues that the district court improperly analyzed this case under the balancing test of the Restatement (Second) of Foreign Relations Law of the United States § 40 (1965) adopted in In re Grand Jury Proceedings, United States v. Field, 532 F.2d 404 (5th Cir.1976), cert. denied, 429 U.S. 940, 97 S.Ct. 354, 50 L.Ed.2d 309 (1976).[4] The district court concluded that because compliance with the subpoena may cause the Bank to violate Bahamian penal laws, it was appropriate to follow the balancing test adopted in *Field*. Because we conclude this case is controlled by *Field*, we affirm the court below.

In *Field* contempt penalties were upheld against a nonresident alien who, having been subpoenaed to testify before a grand jury while present in the United States, refused to answer questions before the grand jury, despite the witness' assertion that the very act of testifying would subject him to criminal penalties in his country of residence. Id. at 405. The grand jury was investigating the use of foreign banks in evading tax enforcement. Field was an officer of a bank located in the Grand Cayman Islands, British West Indies, and was subpoenaed to testify about matters concerning his bank and its clients. Id. at 405–06. After balancing the competing interests of the United

3. It is difficult to fashion due process protections recognizing the differential argued by the Bank, i.e., stakeholder vs. participant. If fairness is the key, as is asserted here, then it seems hardly offensive to "traditional notions of fair play and substantial justice," Milliken v. Meyer, 311 U.S. 457, 463, 61 S.Ct. 339, 343, 85 L.Ed. 278 (1940), to subject entities who do business in the United States and thereby voluntarily bring themselves within the jurisdiction of our courts and legislatures to the burdens of United States law.

4. Section 40 reads:

Limitations on Exercise of Enforcement Jurisdiction

Where two states have jurisdiction to prescribe and enforce rules of law and the rules they may prescribe require inconsistent conduct upon the part of a person, each state is required by international law to consider, in good faith, moderating the exercise of its enforcement jurisdiction, in the light of such factors as

(a) vital national interests of each of the states,

(b) the extent and the nature of the hardship that inconsistent enforcement actions would impose upon the person,

(c) the extent to which the required conduct is to take place in the territory of the other state.

(d) the nationality of the person, and

(e) the extent to which enforcement by action of either state can reasonably be expected to achieve compliance with the rule prescribed by that state.

States and the Cayman Islands under the Restatement approach, the court affirmed the district court's imposition of contempt sanctions against Field. Id. at 407–09.

The situation before us is similar to that in *Field* in all material respects. The Bank has been subpoenaed while subject to the jurisdiction of our courts and has been required to disclose information before a grand jury even though the very fact of disclosure may subject the Bank to criminal sanctions by a foreign sovereign.

The Bank attempts to distinguish *Field* from the case before us on four grounds. The Bank first asserts that the Bank itself is not under investigation by the grand jury, unlike the situation in *Field*. See United States v. Payner, 447 U.S. 727, 100 S.Ct. 2439, 65 L.Ed.2d 468 (1980) (Castle Bank and Trust Company of Nassau, Bahamas under investigation in 1972 as part of narcotics investigation known as "Operation Trade Winds"). A careful reading of *Field* reveals that the fact that Castle Bank and Trust Company was under investigation did not affect the court's analysis. That court was concerned with the proliferation of foreign secret bank accounts utilized by Americans to evade income taxes and conceal crimes. In re Grand Jury Proceedings, United States v. Field, 523 F.2d at 407–08. The instant subpoena calls for the production of certain records relating to bank accounts of a United States citizen pursuant to a tax and narcotics investigation.

Second, the Bank argues this case is distinguishable from *Field* because documentary evidence is requested here rather than testimonial evidence as in *Field*. The distinction, while real, is immaterial. The case before us concerns the relations among nations; whether the subpoena will be enforced is a matter of international comity. Id. at 407. Comity is "a nation's expression of understanding which demonstrates due regard both to international duty and convenience and to the rights of persons protected by its own laws." Somportex Limited v. Philadelphia Chewing Gum Corp., 453 F.2d 435 (3d Cir. 1971), cert. denied, 405 U.S. 1017, 92 S.Ct. 1294, 31 L.Ed.2d 479 (1972). Whether the requested information is testimonial or documentary, the effect on the competing state interests will be the same. The deference accorded the Bahamian interest is not to be diminished by the form of the requested information.

Third, the bank argues this case is distinguishable from *Field* because the instant subpoena calls for information located in the Bahamas instead of the United States. This argument is without merit for two reasons. First, the disclosure to the grand jury will occur in this country. See United States v. Vetco, Inc., 644 F.2d at 1332. Second, the affront to the Bahamas occurs no matter where the information is originally located; the interest of the Bahamas in preserving the secrecy of these records is impinged by the fact of disclosure itself.

Finally, the Bank contends the government "could avoid rather than provoke disrespect for the sovereignty of a friendly nation" by pursuing the alternative of applying for an order of judicial assistance permitting disclosure from the Supreme Court of the Bahamas. Brief of Appellant at 18. See United States v. Vetco, Inc., 644 F.2d at 1332; United States v. First National City Bank, 396 F.2d 897 (2d Cir.1968); Restatement (Revised) of Foreign Relations Law of the United States § 420 (Tent. Draft No. 3, 1982). Applying for judicial assistance, however, is not a substantially equivalent means for obtaining production because of the cost in time and money and the uncertain likelihood of success in obtaining the order. According to the affidavit from a member of the Honorable Society of Lincoln's Inn, England, and of the Bahamas Bar, the Supreme Court of the Bahamas does not have power to order disclosure if the subject of the investigation is criminal only under the tax laws of the United States. Therefore, it is not clear to any degree of certainty that the Bahamian court would order disclosure of all the requested documents.[5]

The judicial assistance procedure does not afford due deference to the United States' interests. In essence, the Bank asks the court to require our government to ask the courts of the Bahamas to be allowed to do something lawful under United States law. We conclude such a procedure to be contrary to the interests of our nation and outweigh the interests of the Bahamas.

In *Field* the vital role of a grand jury's investigative function to our system of jurisprudence and the crucial importance of the collection of revenue to the "financial integrity of the republic" outweighed the Cayman Islands' interest in protecting the right of privacy incorporated into its bank secrecy laws. In re Grand Jury Proceedings. United States v. Field, 532 F.2d at 407–08. The United States' interest in the case before us has not been diminished since *Field* was decided. The Bank asserts the Bahamas' interest in the right of privacy; this interest is similarly outweighed. A Bahamian court would be able to order production of these documents. Banks and Trust Companies Regulation Act, 1965 Bah.Acts No. 64, § 10(I)(iii), as amended 1980 Bah. Acts No. 3. In addition, numerous officials, employees, attorneys, and agents of the Bank of Nova Scotia or the Central Bank of the Bahamas may disclose information regarding the account in the performance of their various functions under the Bank Act. Id. § 10(1)(a-e). It is incongruous to suggest that a United States court afford greater protection to the customer's right of privacy than would a Bahamian court simply because this is a foreign tribunal. In re Grand Jury Proceedings. United States v. Field, 535 F.2d at 408. A statute that is "hardly a blanket guarantee of privacy" does not present a Bahamian interest sufficient to outweigh the United States' interest in collecting revenues and insuring an unimpeded and efficacious grand jury process. See United States v. Payner, 447 U.S. 727, 731, 100 S.Ct. 2439, 2444, 65 L.Ed.2d 468 n. 4 (1980) (predecessor statute identical in relevant parts held not to create a reasonable expectation of privacy).

V. Conclusion

Absent direction from the Legislative and Executive branches of our federal government, we are not willing to emasculate the grand jury process whenever a foreign nation attempts to block our criminal justice process. It is unfortunate the Bank of Nova Scotia suffers from differing legal commands of separate sovereigns, but as we stated in *Field*:

> In a world where commercial transactions are international in scope, conflicts are inevitable. Courts and legislatures should take every reason-

5. The Bank conceded at oral argument that if the grand jury is conducting a tax investigation the documents could not be obtained through the judicial assistance procedure.

able precaution to avoid placing individuals in the situation [the Bank] finds [it]self. Yet, this court simply cannot acquiesce in the proposition that United States criminal investigations must be thwarted whenever there is conflict with the interest of other states.

In re Grand Jury Proceedings. United States v. Field, 535 F.2d at 410.

For the reasons stated above, the judgment entered by the district court is

Affirmed.

Notes

1. Initially, United States courts ruled that they would not require acts that would run afoul of the law of the foreign country in which they were to be performed. See, e.g., United States v. General Electric Co., 115 F.Supp. 835 (D.N.J.1953). See also Restatement (Third) § 441, Reporters' Notes 1 and 3. In United States v. First National City Bank, 396 F.2d 897 (2d Cir.1968), the Second Circuit stated, in dictum, that it would follow this rule even if the foreign prohibition was of a civil nature only. In this case, Citibank had argued that it should not be compelled to produce documents located in its German branch, because its disclosure would expose it to a civil damage suit in Germany. The Court ultimately ruled that Citibank had failed to show that this was a realistic danger.

2. Around the time these early decisions were rendered, foreign countries started to enact statutes forbidding, in specified circumstances, compliance with a foreign court order or law. Much cited examples are the Ontario Business Records Protection act, 1947 Ont. Rev. Stat. c. 54, and the Dutch Economic Competition Act of 1956, Staatsblad 1956, No. 401, § 39. For further examples, see Restatement (Third) § 442, Reporters' Note 4.

3. The response by American courts has been twofold. First, they have construed the pertinent foreign laws not to prohibit the conduct required by American law. See, e.g., First National City Bank of New York v. Internal Revenue Service, 271 F.2d 616 (2d Cir.1959), cert. denied, 361 U.S. 948, 80 S.Ct. 402, 4 L.Ed.2d 381 (1960); United States v. First National City Bank, 396 F.2d 897 (2d Cir.1968). It should be noted in this connection that the impact of blocking statutes, which prohibit the production of information in aid of foreign litigation, may be avoided by producing the information not in the foreign state but in the United States. These statutes generally do not prohibit that the person who possesses the information carry it to the state that requires its production. Once it has been carried to that state, its production can there be effectuated without running afoul of the prohibition. Cf. In re Anschuetz & Co., GmbH, 754 F.2d 602 (5th Cir.1985). Of course, a blocking statute might be construed to prohibit production in the state requiring production, but that would give it the very extraterritorial effect that is alleged to be objectionable to the state that enacted it.

4. The second type of response of American courts has taken the form of their being exacting in determining whether the person subject to the American command had made a good faith effort to avoid the foreign prohibition. The requirement that the person seeking to invoke a foreign prohibition as an excuse for non-compliance with an American command must make a good faith effort to avoid, or seek dispensation from, the foreign prohibition, finds a solid basis in the

Supreme Court's decision in Société Internationale Pour Participations Industrielles Et Commerciales, S.A. v. Rogers, 357 U.S. 197, 78 S.Ct. 1087, 2 L.Ed.2d 1255 (1958). See Note, Extraterritorial Discovery: An Analysis Based on Good Faith, 83 Colum.L.Rev. 1320 (1983).

5. In an effort to avoid being caught in the vise of conflicting demands, a number of litigants have sought the assistance of foreign courts in resisting the commands of American courts. This type of judicial confrontationism has not led to success for those who practiced it. A number of courts have issued injunctions enjoining litigants from complying with foreign court orders. See Marc Rich & Co. A.G. v. United States, 736 F.2d 864 (2d Cir.1984); see also Restatement (Third) § 403, Reporters' Note 7. But these injunctions have not proved effective. American courts, faced with foreign injunctions, have generally insisted upon compliance with their orders. See, e.g., Laker Airways, Ltd. v. Sabena, Belgian World Airlines, 731 F.2d 909 (D.C.Cir.1984). Their insistence has been facilitated by the circumstance that, in this game of judicial daring, the actual confrontation does not occur until the court that issued the injunction imposes sanctions for its disobedience. Thus far, no court has taken this ultimate step. Indeed, it is generally recognized that this type of judicial confrontation is to be avoided as incompatible with proper relations between members of the world community. See Restatement (Third) § 403, Reporters' Note 7. Cf. also British Airways Board v. Laker Airways, [1985] A.C. 58 (reversing an injunction enjoining Laker from pursuing an antitrust action in an American court).

6. The principal case reflects the now prevailing American response to foreign efforts to prohibit recourse to American procedures seeking information abroad. See also In re Grand Jury Proceedings, 691 F.2d 1384 (11th Cir.1982), cert. denied, 462 U.S. 1119, 103 S.Ct. 3086, 77 L.Ed.2d 1348 (1983); Remington Products, Inc. v. North American Philips Corp., 107 F.R.D. 642 (D.C.Conn.1985) (precluding reliance on Dutch blocking statute); Graco, Inc. v. Kremlin, Inc., 101 F.R.D. 503 (N.D.Ill.1984) (rejecting reliance on the French blocking statute). But see Reinsurance Co. v. Administratia Asigurarilor de Stat, 902 F.2d 1275 (7th Cir.1990). Cf. also In re Anschuetz & Co., GmbH, 754 F.2d 602 (5th Cir.1985). For a discussion of the steadily increasing number of foreign blocking statutes, see Restatement (Third) § 442, Reporters' Note 4. See also Lowe, Blocking Extraterritorial Jurisdiction: The British Protection of Trading Interests Act, 75 A.J.I.L. 257 (1981).

7. The Restatement (Third) § 442 deals in a separate section with conflicts of jurisdiction in obtaining disclosure abroad. As foreign enterprises increasingly become involved in American commerce, they increasingly are sued in American courts. When, in such actions, documents must be served, or disclosure obtained abroad, foreign states involved have, with growing measure, objected to the performance of the necessary procedural acts on their territory. These objections have often been defended as based on international law. The performance of such acts is, it has been argued, an infringement upon the foreign state's sovereignty. When the procedural act is performed by a private person, such as service by a person not a party over 18 years of age or a deposition before a private person agreed upon by the parties, the argument may be based on a misconception of American procedural rules. See Smit, International Cooperation in Civil Litigation: Some Observations on the Rules of International Law and Reciprocity, 9 Neth. Int. L.Rev. 137 (1963). Even if the procedural act is performed by a government official, in the absence of a clearly expressed objection, international law would not appear to be breached. The Supreme Court so ruled in Blackmer v. United States, 284 U.S. 421, 52 S.Ct. 252, 76 L.Ed. 375 (1932), p. 1111 supra. In

this case, involving service by an American consul of a subpoena on a United States citizen in Paris, Chief Justice Hughes stated that France could hardly be assumed to object to such service. On these problems generally, see Smit, International Aspects of Federal Civil Procedure, 61 Colum. L.Rev. 1031 (1961); Smit, International Litigation Under the United States Code, 65 Colum. L.Rev. 1015 (1965). For a decision dealing with the international law aspects of the making of service in proceedings before the Federal Trade Commission, see Federal Trade Commission v. Compagnie de Saint–Gobain–Pont-à-Mousson, 636 F.2d 1300 (D.C.Cir.1980). See also Restatement (Third) § 437, Reporters' Note 3; Oliver, International Law and Foreign Investigatory Subpoenas Sought to Be Enforced Without the Consent or Cooperation of the Territorial Sovereign: Impasse of Accommodation? 19 San Diego L.Rev. 409 (1982).

8. When the foreign objection takes the form of a statutory prohibition, conflicts of jurisdiction become aggravated. The Hague Conference on Private International Law has produced a Convention on Service of Judicial and Extrajudicial Documents Abroad and a Convention on the Taking of Evidence Abroad in Civil or Commercial Matters (23 U.S.T. 2555, T.I.A.S. No. 7444, 847 U.N.T.S. 231). While the purpose of these Conventions was to eliminate problems, they appear to have added to them. Foreign contracting states have argued that the Conventions preclude resort to otherwise available municipal law procedures. This position has been extensively discussed and litigated. See, e.g., Oxman, The Choice Between Direct Discovery and Other Means of Obtaining Evidence Abroad: The Impact of the Hague Evidence Convention, 37 U.Miami L.Rev. 733 (1983). See also Smit, International Control of International Litigation: Who Benefits?, 57 Law & Contemp. Prob. 25 (1994).

In Société Nationale Industrielle Aerospatiale v. U.S. District Court of Southern District Iowa, 482 U.S. 522, 107 S.Ct. 2542, 96 L.Ed.2d 461 (1987), the Supreme Court ruled the Hague Evidence Convention not to be exclusive. However, in Volkswagenwerk Aktiengesellschaft v. Schlunk, 486 U.S. 694, 108 S.Ct. 2104, 100 L.Ed.2d 722 (1988), the Court ruled The Hague Service Convention exclusive. The language of the Service Convention, the Court ruled, dictated this result. However, it significantly alleviated the impact of this ruling by finding that domestic rules could be used if the service on the foreign defendant were made in the United States. Why are foreign states so insistent upon a litigant's traveling the Convention route? Would the procedure not be more flexible if a litigant were left the choice between domestic and Convention rules?

9. The Restatement (Third) contains provisions dealing with conflicts of jurisdiction generally (§ 441) and in regard to disclosure (§ 442).

RESTATEMENT (THIRD)

§ 441. Foreign State Compulsion

(1) In general, a state may not require a person

(a) to do an act in another state that is prohibited by the law of that state or by the law of the state of which he is a national; or

(b) to refrain from doing an act in another state that is required by the law of that state or by the law of the state of which he is a national.

(2) In general, a state may require a person of foreign nationality

(a) to do an act in that state even if it is prohibited by the law of the state of which he is a national; or

(b) to refrain from doing an act in that state even if it is required by the law of the state of which he is a national.

Notes

1. To what extent do the materials in this Section provide support for these provisions as a matter of international or United States foreign relations law? What difference does it make whether they are the one or the other?

2. For discussion of the resolution of conflicts of jurisdiction arising from acts committed on foreign vessels in territorial waters, see p. 1502 infra.

3. For other decisions applying the Bank of Nova Scotia analysis, see e.g. Marsoner v. United States, 40 F.3d 959 (9th Cir.1994); U.S. v. Davis, 767 F.2d 1025 (2d Cir.1985); In re Anschuetz & Co. GmbH, 754 F.2d 602 (5th Cir.1985); In re Grand Jury Proceedings in Matter of Freeman, 708 F.2d 1571 (11th Cir.1983); In re Slaughter, 694 F.2d 1258 (11th Cir.1982); In re Grand Jury Proceedings, 694 F.2d 1256 (11th Cir.1982); In re Sealed Case, 263 U.S. App. D.C. 357, 825 F.2d 494 (D.C.Cir.1987). However, the Seventh Circuit has applied the doctrine after good faith efforts failed to obviate the foreign compulsion. Reinsurance Co. of America, Inc. v. Administratia Asigurarilor, 902 F.2d 1275 (7th Cir.1990). See also Note 6 on p. 1163.

4. Courts have ruled unanimously that the foreign compulsion doctrine cannot be invoked when either the person seeking disclosure or the one opposing it have failed to make good faith efforts to obtain dispensation from the foreign prohibition.

In Doe v. United States, 487 U.S. 201, 108 S.Ct. 2341, 101 L.Ed.2d 184 (1988), the prosecution sought disclosure from banks in the Cayman Islands and Bermuda of documents they might have relating to the target. The banks invoked foreign law that prohibited disclosure without the customer's consent. The district court ordered the person who was the target of the grand jury investigation to give his consent to the disclosure of whatever documents the banks might have. The target contended that the order, affirmed by the Fifth Circuit violated his Fifth Amendment privilege against self–incrimination. The Supreme Court affirmed. It ruled that the particular consent the target had been directed to provide did not constitute testimony by the target that the banks had records relating to him and therefore were not a testimonial statement by him. See also United States v. Rubin, 836 F.2d 1096 (8th Cir.1988) (Rubin could not complain of the district court's having quashed a subpoena seeking Cayman Island bank documents, since he could have obtained the documents by petitioning the Grand Court of the Cayman Islands). For a general discussion, see Browne, Extraterritorial Discovery: An Analysis Based on Good Faith, 83 Colum. L. Rev. 1320 (1983).

When good faith efforts to obtain dispensation have failed, some courts have applied the balancing test of the Restatement (Third) and denied disclosure. Reinsurance Co. of America, Inc. v. Administratia Asigurarilor, 902 F.2d 1275 (7th Cir.1990). To the same effect, see United States v. First Nat'l Bank of Chicago, 699 F.2d 341 (7th Cir.1983). But see Marsoner v. United States, 40 F.3d 959 (9th Cir.1994).

Some courts, after having ordered disclosure in disregard of a foreign prohibition, have refused to apply sanctions for non–compliance. See Cochran Consulting

v. Uwatec USA, 102 F.3d 1224 (Fed.Cir.1996). See also Reebok Int'l v. McLaughlin, 49 F.3d 1387 (9th Cir.1995).

5. Contractual stipulations may seek to avoid a state's exercising its legislative authority. A choice of law clause designating the law of another state as applicable seeks to do this directly. A choice of forum clause achieves this indirectly, when the foreign forum does not apply the local law. In both types of cases, the question arises whether the court of the state addressed will honor the reference to the foreign law or forum. Thus far, this has not been argued to raise a question of public international law. However, states may become gravely concerned when these clauses are used to avoid application of local law that is regarded as mandatory in the sense that its application cannot be affected by contractual stipulations. As global commerce expands and intensifies, this problem is likely to become more acute.

An excellent example is provided by Allen v. Lloyd's of London, 94 F.3d 923 (4th Cir.1996), in which it was contended by participants in Lloyd's insurance projects that the plan to reorganize Lloyd's in the face of claims for injuries caused by asbestos and similarly harmful products violated American securities laws. The court rejected these contentions in upholding choice of forum and choice of law clauses in the participants' [the so–called Names'] contracts which designated an exclusive English forum and English law as the applicable law. Eventually, all circuits that addressed the problem ruled the same way. See Richards v. Lloyd's of London, 135 F.3d 1289 (9th Cir.1998). For a general discussion, see Hall, No Way Out: An Argument Against Permitting Parties To Opt Out of U.S. Securities Laws In International Transactions, 97 Colum. L. Rev. 57 (1997).

SECTION 7. JURISDICTION TO ADJUDICATE

A state may not exercise its judicial functions within the territory of another state without the latter's consent. See Section 5 of this Chapter. Conversely, a state may normally exercise its judicial functions in regard to persons or things within its territory. Questions, analogous to those that have arisen in the area of legislative jurisdiction, may arise when a state exercises within its territory judicial authority over persons or things outside of its territory. These questions become particularly acute when the judicial authority is sought to be exercised over persons or things that have no reasonable relation to the state that seeks to exercise judicial jurisdiction.

However, many states have habitually exercised adjudicatory authority over persons outside of their borders in the absence of some contact that would be considered sufficient under due process limitations developed in the United States. Many states permit criminal prosecutions in absentia of the accused. And leading civil law countries exercise adjudicatory authority in civil cases on bases such as the nationality or residence of the plaintiff or the mere presence of unrelated property. For a more detailed discussion, see Rosenberg, Smit & Dreyfuss, Elements of Civil Procedure 226 (5th ed. 1990) and authorities cited. While these bases have been characterized as exorbitant or extraordinary, they have, thus far, not been asserted, on authoritative grounds, to be violative of international law.

The Restatement (Third) states that "increasingly, they [i.e., states] object to the improper exercise of jurisdiction [i.e. jurisdiction on an extravagant basis] as itself a violation of international principles." Section 421,

Introductory Note. Although the Restatement (Third) refers to no source supporting this statement, it would appear that good grounds exist for international law limitations on the exercise of a state's extraterritorial judicial jurisdiction, at least in criminal and administrative matters. For example, in the Alvarez–Machain case, see p. 1187 infra, it might be argued that prosecuting in the United States a person abducted in violation of international law constituted itself a violation of international law. See Note 2 p. 1195 infra. Whether the same is true in civil matters is considerably more doubtful.

The Restatement (Third) has attempted to formulate the proper criteria in the provisions set forth below.

RESTATEMENT (THIRD)

§ 421. Jurisdiction to Adjudicate

(1) A state may exercise jurisdiction through its courts to adjudicate with respect to a person or thing if the relationship of the state to the person or thing is such as to make the exercise of jurisdiction reasonable.

(2) In general, a state's exercise of jurisdiction to adjudicate with respect to a person or thing is reasonable if, at the time jurisdiction is asserted:

(a) the person or thing is present in the territory of the state, other than transitorily;

(b) the person, if a natural person, is domiciled in the state;

(c) the person, if a natural person, is resident in the state;

(d) the person, if a natural person, is a national of the state;

(e) the person, if a corporation or comparable juridical person, is organized pursuant to the law of the state;

(f) a ship, aircraft or other vehicle to which the adjudication relates is registered under the laws of the state;

(g) the person, whether natural or juridical, has consented to the exercise of jurisdiction;

(h) the person, whether natural or juridical, regularly carries on business in the state;

(i) the person, whether natural or juridical, had carried on activity in the state, but only in respect of such activity;

(j) the person, whether natural or juridical, had carried on outside the state an activity having a substantial, direct, and foreseeable effect within the state, but only in respect of such activity; or

(k) the thing that is the subject of adjudication is owned, possessed, or used in the state, but only in respect of a claim reasonably connected with that thing.

(3) A defense of lack of jurisdiction is generally waived by any appearance by or on behalf of a person or thing (whether as plaintiff, defendant, or third party), if the appearance is for a purpose that does not include a challenge to the exercise of jurisdiction.

§ 423. Jurisdiction to Adjudicate in Enforcement of Universal and Other Non–Territorial Crimes

A state may exercise jurisdiction through its courts to enforce its criminal laws that punish universal crimes or other non-territorial offenses within the state's jurisdiction to prescribe.

SECTION 8. JURISDICTION TO ENFORCE

§ 431. Jurisdiction to Enforce

(1) A state may employ judicial or nonjudicial measures to induce or compel compliance or punish noncompliance with its laws or regulations, provided it has jurisdiction to prescribe in accordance with §§ 402 and 403.

(2) Enforcement measures must be reasonably related to the laws or regulations to which they are directed; punishment for noncompliance must be preceded by an appropriate determination of violation and must be proportional to the gravity of the violation.

(3) A state may employ enforcement measures against a person located outside its territory

(a) if the person is given notice of the claims or charges against him that is reasonable in the circumstances;

(b) if the person is given an opportunity to be heard, ordinarily in advance of enforcement, whether in person or by counsel or other representative; and

(c) when enforcement is through the courts, if the state has jurisdiction to adjudicate.

Notes

1. Does this section purport to state a rule of American foreign relations law or of international law? The Introductory Note to this Section states that enforcement measures "are subject, under international law, to the requirement of reasonableness". Is this statement correct?

2. What is the effect of a state's having improperly exercised its executive jurisdiction on its subsequent exercise of judicial jurisdiction? If, for example, a state improperly seizes a person accused of a crime outside of its borders, may it nevertheless properly exercise judicial jurisdiction over this person in the United States? The traditional rule of international law is that of "*male captus, bene detentus*," i.e., that a person who has been improperly seized may nevertheless properly be tried. This rule has been argued to follow from the principle that, under international law, only the state in the territory of which the person was captured may complain of the improper exercise of executive jurisdiction. However, states have exercised judicial jurisdiction over persons improperly seized, even if the state in the territory of which they were seized objected. See p. 1187 supra. Furthermore, courts have generally sustained the exercise of judicial jurisdiction over persons improperly seized in a foreign country. Leading cases to this effect are Ker v. Illinois, 119 U.S. 436, 7 S.Ct. 225, 30 L.Ed. 421 (1886) and Frisbie v. Collins, 342 U.S. 519, 72 S.Ct. 509, 96 L.Ed. 541 (1952). The Second Circuit has grafted an exception upon the *Ker-Frisbie* doctrine in the case of a seizure abroad that was attended by brutality. United States v. Toscanino, 500 F.2d 267 (2d

Cir.1974). This decision appears to apply a rule of American rather than international law. In any event, the *Toscanino* rule has not been applied in cases that did not involve egregiously brutal conduct. See Restatement (Third) § 433, Reporters' Note 3; Note, Jurisdiction After International Kidnapping: A Comparative Study, 8 B.C.Int'l & Comp. L.Rev. 237 (1985). The *Ker-Frisbie* doctrine was reaffirmed in United States v. Alvarez–Machain, 504 U.S., 655, 112 S.Ct. 2188, 119 L.Ed.2d 441 (1992), reproduced at p. 1187 infra. The notes following that case explore the implications of the decision. See p. 1195 infra.

3. Is a state's judicial and executive jurisdiction more extensive in cases of the exercise of universal legislative jurisdiction than in other cases? May, in such cases, a state exercise executive jurisdiction on the territory of another state? Does the propriety of a state's exercising executive jurisdiction in such cases on the territory of another state depend on whether the person against whom the jurisdiction is exercised (a) is a national of the state exercising it, (b) performed the acts for which he is called to account within the territory of the state exercising it, (c) did the incriminated acts against a national of the state exercising it, or (d) is not called to account for his conduct by the state on the territory of which the jurisdiction is exercised?

KADIC v. KARADZIC

United States Court of Appeals, Second Circuit, 1995.
70 F.3d 232, cert. denied, 518 U.S. 1005, 116 S.Ct. 2524, 135 L.Ed.2d 1048 (1996).

(Some footnotes omitted; others renumbered.)

Jon O. Newman, Chief Judge:

Most Americans would probably be surprised to learn that victims of atrocities committed in Bosnia are suing the leader of the insurgent Bosnian-Serb forces in a United States District Court in Manhattan. Their claims seek to build upon the foundation of this Court's decision in Filártiga v. Peña-Irala, 630 F.2d 876 (2d Cir.1980), which recognized the important principle that the venerable Alien Tort Act, 28 U.S.C. §§ 1350 (1988), enacted in 1789 but rarely invoked since then, validly creates federal court jurisdiction for suits alleging torts committed anywhere in the world against aliens in violation of the law of nations. The pending appeals pose additional significant issues as to the scope of the Alien Tort Act: whether some violations of the law of nations may be remedied when committed by those not acting under the authority of a state; if so, whether genocide, war crimes, and crimes against humanity are among the violations that do not require state action; and whether a person, otherwise liable for a violation of the law of nations, is immune from service of process because he is present in the United States as an invitee of the United Nations.

These issues arise on appeals by two groups of plaintiffs-appellants from the November 19, 1994, judgment of the United States District Court for the Southern District of New York (Peter K. Leisure, Judge), dismissing, for lack of subject-matter jurisdiction, their suits against defendant-appellee Radovan Karadžić, President of the self-proclaimed Bosnian–Serb republic of "Srpska." Doe v. Karadžić, 866 F.Supp. 734 (S.D.N.Y.1994) ("Doe"). For the reasons set forth below, we hold that subject-matter jurisdiction exists, that Karadžić may be found liable for genocide, war crimes, and crimes against humanity in his private capacity and for other violations in his capacity as a state actor, and that he is not immune from service of process. We therefore reverse and remand.

BACKGROUND

The plaintiffs-appellants are Croat and Muslim citizens of the internationally recognized nation of Bosnia–Herzegovina, formerly a republic of Yugoslavia. Their complaints, which we accept as true for purposes of this appeal, allege that they are victims, and representatives of victims, of various atrocities, including brutal acts of rape, forced prostitution, forced impregnation, torture, and summary execution, carried out by Bosnian–Serb military forces as part of a genocidal campaign conducted in the course of the Bosnian civil war. Karadžić, formerly a citizen of Yugoslavia and now a citizen of Bosnia–Herzegovina, is the President of a three-man presidency of the self-proclaimed Bosnian–Serb republic within Bosnia–Herzegovina, sometimes referred to as "Srpska," which claims to exercise lawful authority, and does in fact exercise actual control, over large parts of the territory of Bosnia-Herzegovina. In his capacity as President, Karadžić possesses ultimate command authority over the Bosnian–Serb military forces, and the injuries perpetrated upon plaintiffs were committed as part of a pattern of systematic human rights violations that was directed by Karadžić and carried out by the military forces under his command. The complaints allege that Karadžić acted in an official capacity either as the titular head of Srpska or in collaboration with the government of the recognized nation of the former Yugoslavia and its dominant constituent republic, Serbia.

The two groups of plaintiffs asserted causes of action for genocide, rape, forced prostitution and impregnation, torture and other cruel, inhuman, and degrading treatment, assault and battery, sex and ethnic inequality, summary execution, and wrongful death. They sought compensatory and punitive damages, attorney's fees, and, in one of the cases, injunctive relief. Plaintiffs grounded subject-matter jurisdiction in the Alien Tort Act, the Torture Victim Protection Act of 1991 ("Torture Victim Act"), Pub.L. No. 102–256, 106 Stat. 73 (1992), codified at 28 U.S.C. §§ 1350 note (Supp. V 1993), the general federal-question jurisdictional statute, 28 U.S.C. §§ 1331 (1988), and principles of supplemental jurisdiction, 28 U.S.C. §§ 1367 (Supp. V 1993).

* * *

A. The Alien Tort Act

1. *General Application to Appellants' Claims*

The Alien Tort Act provides:

> The district courts shall have original jurisdiction of any civil action by an alien for a tort only, committed in violation of the law of nations or a treaty of the United States.

28 U.S.C. § 1350 (1988). Our decision in Filártiga established that this statute confers federal subject-matter jurisdiction when the following three conditions are satisfied: (1) an alien sues (2) for a tort (3) committed in violation of the law of nations (i.e., international law). 630 F.2d at 887; see also Amerada Hess Shipping Corp. v. Argentine Republic, 830 F.2d 421, 425 (2d Cir.1987), rev'd on other grounds, 488 U.S. 428, 109 S.Ct. 683, 102 L.Ed.2d 818 (1989). The

first two requirements are plainly satisfied here, and the only disputed issue is whether plaintiffs have pleaded violations of international law.

* * *

Filártiga established that courts ascertaining the content of the law of nations "must interpret international law not as it was in 1789, but as it has evolved and exists among the nations of the world today." Id. at 881; see also Amerada Hess, 830 F.2d at 425. We find the norms of contemporary international law by " 'consulting the works of jurists, writing professedly on public law; or by the general usage and practice of nations; or by judicial decisions recognizing and enforcing that law.' " Filártiga, 630 F.2d at 880 (quoting United States v. Smith, 18 U.S. (5 Wheat.) 153, 160–61, 5 L.Ed. 57 (1820)). If this inquiry discloses that the defendant's alleged conduct violates "well-established, universally recognized norms of international law," id. at 888, as opposed to "idiosyncratic legal rules," id. at 881, then federal jurisdiction exists under the Alien Tort Act.

Karadžić contends that appellants have not alleged violations of the norms of international law because such norms bind only states and persons acting under color of a state's law, not private individuals. In making this contention, Karadžić advances the contradictory positions that he is not a state actor, see Brief for Appellee at 19, even as he asserts that he is the President of the self-proclaimed Republic of Srpska, see Statement of Radovan Karadzic, May 3, 1993, submitted with Defendant's Motion to Dismiss. For their part, the Kadic appellants also take somewhat inconsistent positions in pleading defendant's role as President of Srpska, Kadic Complaint ¶ ¶ 13, and also contending that "Karadžić is not an official of any government," Kadic Plaintiffs' Memorandum in Opposition to Defendant's Motion to Dismiss at 21 n. 25.

* * *

We do not agree that the law of nations, as understood in the modern era, confines its reach to state action. Instead, we hold that certain forms of conduct violate the law of nations whether undertaken by those acting under the auspices of a state or only as private individuals. An early example of the application of the law of nations to the acts of private individuals is the prohibition against piracy. See United States v. Smith, 18 U.S. (5 Wheat.) 153, 161, 5 L.Ed. 57 (1820); United States v. Furlong, 18 U.S. (5 Wheat.) 184, 196–97, 5 L.Ed. 64 (1820). In The Brig Malek Adhel, 43 U.S. (2 How.) 210, 232, 11 L.Ed. 239 (1844), the Supreme Court observed that pirates were "hostis humani generis" (an enemy of all mankind) in part because they acted "without ... any pretense of public authority." See generally 4 William Blackstone, Commentaries on the Laws of England 68 (facsimile of 1st ed. 1765–1769, Univ. of Chi. ed., 1979). Later examples are prohibitions against the slave trade and certain war crimes. See M. Cherif Bassiouni, Crimes Against Humanity in International Criminal Law 193 (1992); Jordan Paust, The Other Side of Right: Private Duties Under Human Rights Law, 5 Harv.Hum.Rts.J. 51 (1992).

The liability of private persons for certain violations of customary international law and the availability of the Alien Tort Act to remedy such violations was early recognized by the Executive Branch in an opinion of

Attorney General Bradford in reference to acts of American citizens aiding the French fleet to plunder British property off the coast of Sierra Leone in 1795. See Breach of Neutrality, 1 Op. Att'y Gen. 57, 59 (1795). The Executive Branch has emphatically restated in this litigation its position that private persons may be found liable under the Alien Tort Act for acts of genocide, war crimes, and other violations of international humanitarian law. See Statement of Interest of the United States at 5–13.

The Restatement (Third) of the Foreign Relations Law of the United States (1986) ("Restatement (Third)") proclaims: "Individuals may be held liable for offenses against international law, such as piracy, war crimes, and genocide." Restatement (Third) pt. II, introductory note. The Restatement is careful to identify those violations that are actionable when committed by a state, Restatement (Third) § 702,[1] and a more limited category of violations of "universal concern," id. § 404,[2] partially overlapping with those listed in section 702. Though the immediate focus of section 404 is to identify those offenses for which a state has jurisdiction to punish without regard to territoriality or the nationality of the offenders, cf. id. § 402(1)(a), (2), the inclusion of piracy and slave trade from an earlier era and aircraft hijacking from the modern era demonstrates that the offenses of "universal concern" include those capable of being committed by non-state actors. Although the jurisdiction authorized by section 404 is usually exercised by application of criminal law, international law also permits states to establish appropriate civil remedies, id. § 404 cmt. b, such as the tort actions authorized by the Alien Tort Act. Indeed, the two cases invoking the Alien Tort Act prior to Filártiga both applied the civil remedy to private action. See Adra v. Clift, 195 F.Supp. 857 (D.Md.1961); Bolchos v. Darrel, 3 F.Cas. 810 (D.S.C.1795) (No. 1,607).

Karadžić disputes the application of the law of nations to any violations committed by private individuals, relying on Filártiga and the concurring opinion of Judge Edwards in Tel–Oren v. Libyan Arab Republic, 726 F.2d 774, 775 (D.C.Cir.1984), cert. denied, 470 U.S. 1003, 105 S.Ct. 1354, 84 L.Ed.2d 377 (1985). Filártiga involved an allegation of torture committed by a state official. Relying on the United Nations' Declaration on the Protection of All Persons from Being Subjected to Torture, G.A.Res. 3452, U.N. GAOR, U.N. Doc. A/1034 (1975) (hereinafter "Declaration on Torture"), as a definitive statement of norms of customary international law prohibiting states from permitting torture, we ruled that "official torture is now prohibited by the law of nations." Filártiga, 630 F.2d at 884 (emphasis added). We had no occasion to consider whether international law violations other than torture are actionable against private individuals, and nothing in Filártiga purports to preclude such a result.

* * *

2. Specific Application of Alien Tort Act to Appellants' Claims

In order to determine whether the offenses alleged by the appellants in this litigation are violations of the law of nations that may be the subject of Alien Tort Act claims against a private individual, we must make a particular-

1. Section 702 provides [quoted at p. 602].

2. Section 404 provides [quoted at p. 1092].

ized examination of these offenses, mindful of the important precept that "evolving standards of international law govern who is within the [Alien Tort Act's] jurisdictional grant." Amerada Hess, 830 F.2d at 425. In making that inquiry, it will be helpful to group the appellants' claims into three categories: (a) genocide, (b) war crimes, and (c) other instances of inflicting death, torture, and degrading treatment.

(a) *Genocide*. In the aftermath of the atrocities committed during the Second World War, the condemnation of genocide as contrary to international law quickly achieved broad acceptance by the community of nations. In 1946, the General Assembly of the United Nations declared that genocide is a crime under international law that is condemned by the civilized world, whether the perpetrators are "private individuals, public officials or statesmen." G.A.Res. 96(I), 1 U.N.GAOR, U.N. Doc. A/64/Add.1, at 188–89 (1946). The General Assembly also affirmed the principles of Article 6 of the Agreement and Charter Establishing the Nuremberg War Crimes Tribunal for punishing " 'persecutions on political, racial, or religious grounds,' " regardless of whether the offenders acted " 'as individuals or as members of organizations,' " In re Extradition of Demjanjuk, 612 F.Supp. 544, 555 n. 11 (N.D.Ohio 1985) (quoting Article 6). See G.A.Res. 95(I), 1 U.N.GAOR, U.N.Doc. A/64/Add.1, at 188 (1946).

The Convention on the Prevention and Punishment of the Crime of Genocide, 78 U.N.T.S. 277, entered into force Jan. 12, 1951, for the United States Feb. 23, 1989 (hereinafter "Convention on Genocide"), provides a more specific articulation of the prohibition of genocide in international law. The Convention, which has been ratified by more than 120 nations, including the United States, see U.S. Dept. of State, Treaties in Force 345 (1994), defines "genocide" to mean any of the following acts committed with intent to destroy, in whole or in part, a national, ethnical, racial or religious group, as such:

(a) Killing members of the group;

(b) Causing serious bodily or mental harm to members of the group;

(c) Deliberately inflicting on the group conditions of life calculated to bring about its physical destruction in whole or in part;

(d) Imposing measures intended to prevent births with the group;

(e) Forcibly transferring children of the group to another group.

Convention on Genocide art. II. Especially pertinent to the pending appeal, the Convention makes clear that "[p]ersons committing genocide . . . shall be punished, whether they are constitutionally responsible rulers, public officials or private individuals." Id. art. IV (emphasis added). These authorities unambiguously reflect that, from its incorporation into international law, the proscription of genocide has applied equally to state and non-state actors.

The applicability of this norm to private individuals is also confirmed by the Genocide Convention Implementation Act of 1987, 18 U.S.C. § 1091 (1988), which criminalizes acts of genocide without regard to whether the offender is acting under color of law, see id. § 1091(a) ("[w]hoever" commits genocide shall be punished), if the crime is committed within the United States or by a U.S. national, id. § 1091(d). Though Congress provided that the Genocide Convention Implementation Act shall not "be construed as creating any substantive or procedural right enforceable by law by any party in any proceeding," id. § 1092, the legislative decision not to create a new private remedy does not imply that a private remedy is not already available under the Alien Tort Act. Nothing in the Genocide Convention Implementation Act or its legislative history reveals an intent by Congress to repeal the Alien Tort Act insofar as it applies to genocide,[6] and the two statutes are surely not repugnant to each other. Under these circumstances, it would be improper to construe the Genocide Convention Implementation Act as repealing the Alien Tort Act by implication. * * *

Appellants' allegations that Karadžić personally planned and ordered a campaign of murder, rape, forced impregnation, and other forms of torture designed to destroy the religious and ethnic groups of Bosnian Muslims and Bosnian Croats clearly state a violation of the international law norm proscribing genocide, regardless of whether Karadžić acted under color of law or as a private individual. The District Court has subject-matter jurisdiction over these claims pursuant to the Alien Tort Act.

(b) *War crimes*. Plaintiffs also contend that the acts of murder, rape, torture, and arbitrary detention of civilians, committed in the course of hostilities, violate the law of war. Atrocities of the types alleged here have long been recognized in international law as violations of the law of war. See In re Yamashita, 327 U.S. 1, 14, 66 S.Ct. 340, 347, 90 L.Ed. 499 (1946). Moreover, international law imposes an affirmative duty on military commanders to take appropriate measures within their power to control troops under their command for the prevention of such atrocities. Id. at 15–16, 66 S.Ct. at 347–48.

After the Second World War, the law of war was codified in the four Geneva Conventions,[7] which have been ratified by more than 180 nations, including the United States, see Treaties in Force, supra, at 398–99. Common article 3, which is substantially identical in each of the four Conventions, applies to "armed conflict[s] not of an international character" and binds "each Party to the conflict ... to apply, as a minimum, the following provisions":

> Persons taking no active part in the hostilities ... shall in all circumstances be treated humanely, without any adverse distinction founded on race, colour, religion or faith, sex, birth or wealth, or any other similar criteria.
>
> To this end, the following acts are and shall remain prohibited at any time and in any place whatsoever with respect to the above-mentioned persons:
>
> (a) violence to life and person, in particular murder of all kinds, mutilation, cruel treatment and torture;

6. The Senate Report merely repeats the language of section 1092 and does not provide any explanation of its purpose. *See* S. Rep. 333, 100th Cong., 2d Sess., at 5 (1988), *reprinted at* 1988 U.S.C.C.A.N. 4156, 4160. The House Report explains that section 1092 "clarifies that the bill creates no *new* federal cause of action in civil proceedings." H.R. Rep. 566, 100th Cong., 2d Sess., at 8 (1988) (emphasis added). This explanation confirms our view that the Genocide Convention Implementation Act was not intended to abrogate civil causes of action that might be available under *existing* laws, such as the Alien Tort Act.

7. [Cited p. 1060.]

(b) taking of hostages;

(c) outrages upon personal dignity, in particular humiliating and degrading treatment;

(d) the passing of sentences and carrying out of executions without previous judgment pronounced by a regularly constituted court. . . .

Geneva Convention I art. 3(1). Thus, under the law of war as codified in the Geneva Conventions, all "parties" to a conflict—which includes insurgent military groups—are obliged to adhere to these most fundamental requirements of the law of war.

The offenses alleged by the appellants, if proved, would violate the most fundamental norms of the law of war embodied in common article 3, which binds parties to internal conflicts regardless of whether they are recognized nations or roving hordes of insurgents. The liability of private individuals for committing war crimes has been recognized since World War I and was confirmed at Nuremberg after World War II, see Telford Taylor, Nuremberg Trials: War Crimes and International Law, 450 Int'l Conciliation 304 (April 1949) (collecting cases), and remains today an important aspect of international law, see Jordan Paust, After My Lai: The Case for War Crimes Jurisdiction Over Civilians in Federal District Courts, in 4 The Vietnam War and International Law 447 (R.Falk ed., 1976). The District Court has jurisdiction pursuant to the Alien Tort Act over appellants' claims of war crimes and other violations of international humanitarian law.

(c) *Torture and summary execution*. In Filártiga, we held that official torture is prohibited by universally accepted norms of international law, see 630 F.2d at 885, and the Torture Victim Act confirms this holding and extends it to cover summary execution. Torture Victim Act §§ 2(a), 3(a). However, torture and summary execution—when not perpetrated in the course of genocide or war crimes—are proscribed by international law only when committed by state officials or under color of law. See Declaration on Torture art. 1 (defining torture as being "inflicted by or at the instigation of a public official"); Convention Against Torture and Other Cruel, Inhuman, or Degrading Treatment or Punishment pt. I, art. 1, 23 I.L.M. 1027 (1984), as modified, 24 I.L.M. 535 (1985), entered into force June 26, 1987, ratified by United States Oct. 21, 1994, 34 I.L.M. 590, 591 (1995) (defining torture as "inflicted by or at the instigation of or with the consent or acquiescence of a public official or other person acting in an official capacity"); Torture Victim Act §§ 2(a) (imposing liability on individuals acting "under actual or apparent authority, or color of law, of any foreign nation").

In the present case, appellants allege that acts of rape, torture, and summary execution were committed during hostilities by troops under Karadžić's command and with the specific intent of destroying appellants' ethnic-religious groups. Thus, many of the alleged atrocities are already encompassed within the appellants' claims of genocide and war crimes. Of course, at this threshold stage in the proceedings it cannot be known whether appellants will be able to prove the specific intent that is an element of genocide, or prove that each of the alleged torts were committed in the course of an armed conflict, as required to establish war crimes. It suffices to hold at this stage that the alleged atrocities are actionable under the Alien Tort Act, without regard to state action, to the extent that they were committed in pursuit of genocide or war crimes, and otherwise may be pursued against Karadžić to the extent that he is shown to be a state actor. Since the meaning of the state action requirement for purposes of international law violations will likely arise on remand and has already been considered by the District Court, we turn next to that requirement.

3. *The State Action Requirement for International Law Violations*

* * *

(b) Acting in concert with a foreign state. Appellants also sufficiently alleged that Karadžić acted under color of law insofar as they claimed that he acted in concert with the former Yugoslavia, the statehood of which is not disputed. The "color of law" jurisprudence of 42 U.S.C. §§ 1983 is a relevant guide to whether a defendant has engaged in official action for purposes of jurisdiction under the Alien Tort Act. See Forti v. Suarez–Mason, 672 F.Supp. 1531, 1546 (N.D.Cal.1987), reconsideration granted in part on other grounds, 694 F.Supp. 707 (N.D.Cal.1988). A private individual acts under color of law within the meaning of section 1983 when he acts together with state officials or with significant state aid. See Lugar v. Edmondson Oil Co., 457 U.S. 922, 937, 102 S.Ct. 2744, 2753–54, 73 L.Ed.2d 482 (1982). The appellants are entitled to prove their allegations that Karadžić acted under color of law of Yugoslavia by acting in concert with Yugoslav officials or with significant Yugoslavian aid.

B. The Torture Victim Protection Act

The Torture Victim Act, enacted in 1992, provides a cause of action for official torture and extrajudicial killing:

> An individual who, under actual or apparent authority, or color of law, of any foreign nation-
>
> (1) subjects an individual to torture shall, in a civil action, be liable for damages to that individual; or
>
> (2) subjects an individual to extrajudicial killing shall, in a civil action, be liable for damages to the individual's legal representative, or to any person who may be a claimant in an action for wrongful death.

Torture Victim Act § 2(a). The statute also requires that a plaintiff exhaust adequate and available local remedies, id. § 2(b), imposes a ten-year statute of limitations, id. § 2(c), and defines the terms "extrajudicial killing" and "torture," id. § 3.

By its plain language, the Torture Victim Act renders liable only those individuals who have committed torture or extrajudicial killing "under actual or apparent authority, or color of law, of any foreign nation." Legislative history confirms that this language was intended to "make[ ] clear that the plaintiff must establish some governmental involvement in the torture or killing to prove a claim," and that the statute "does not attempt to deal with torture or killing by purely private groups." H.R.Rep. No. 367, 102d Cong., 2d Sess., at 5 (1991), reprinted in 1992 U.S.C.C.A.N. 84, 87. In construing the terms "actual or apparent authority" and "color of law," courts are instructed to look to principles of agency law and to jurisprudence under 42 U.S.C. §§ 1983, respectively. Id.

* * *

Notes

1. For subsequent history, see, inter alia, Doe v. Karadzic, 176 F.R.D. 458 (S.D.N.Y.1997); Doe v. Karadzic, 192 F.R.D. 133 (S.D.N.Y.2000). Karadžić himself was absent throughout the subsequent proceedings and did not file papers in opposition to the plaintiffs' claim, which ultimately led Judge Leisure to rule that Karadžić had defaulted in the case. On August 10, 2000, in Kadic v. Karadzic, No. 93 Civ. 1163 (S.D.N.Y.), a federal jury in the Southern District of New York ruled in favor of the plaintiffs, who by this time had come to incorporate two non-profit organizations as well as twelve women and two children, and ordered Karadžić to pay $745 million in compensatory and punitive damages. A few weeks later, another jury in the Doe case entered an award of $4.5 billion. See "Jury in New York Orders Bosnian Serb to Pay Billions," New York Times, Sept. 26, 2000, p. A10, col.5.

2. On the principal case, see Enslen, Filartiga's Offspring: The Second Circuit Significantly Expands the Scope of the Alien Tort Claims Act with Its Decision in Kadic v. Karadzic, 48 Ala. L.Rev. 695 (1996).

3. Is female genital mutilation a tort under the Alien Tort Claim Act or the Torture Victim Protection Act? See Adam Karp, Genitorts in the Global Context, 18 Women's Rights L.Rep. 315 (1997). How is in personam competence obtained under these statutes?

4. The principal case does not involve the exercise of criminal legislative jurisdiction and raises the question of whether the exercise of civil jurisdiction is as limited as that of criminal jurisdiction. See United States v. Nippon Paper Industries Co., Ltd., p. 1102 supra.

5. On Karadzic's claim of immunity as a U.N. invitee in the principal case, see Chapter 14, p. 1313.

SECTION 9. EXTRADITION

A. GENERAL CONSIDERATIONS

Extradition is the surrender of an individual accused or convicted of a crime by the state within whose territory he is found to the state under whose laws he is alleged to have committed or to have been convicted of the crime. Until the nineteenth century the extradition of fugitives was rare and was a matter of sovereign discretion rather than of obligation. With the dramatic improvements in transportation in the nineteenth century, the number of criminals fleeing to foreign states increased and states began to conclude bilateral treaties providing for their extradition. In Factor v. Laubenheimer, 290 U.S. 276, 287, 54 S.Ct. 191, 193, 78 L.Ed. 315 (1933), the court noted that "[t]he principles of international law recognize no right to extradition apart from treaty. While a government may, if agreeable to its own constitution and laws, voluntarily exercise the power to surrender a fugitive from justice to the country from which he has fled * * * the legal right to demand his extradition and the correlative duty to surrender him to the demanding country exist only when created by treaty." In fact, the municipal law of many states prevents arrest and extradition of a fugitive except pursuant to a treaty operating as internal law or a statute providing for extradition. See 2 O'Connell 793–94; Valentine v. United States ex rel. Neidecker, 299 U.S. 5, 9, 57 S.Ct. 100, 102, 81 L.Ed. 5 (1936). In the United States, international extradition is governed by federal law. See 18 U.S.C.A. §§ 3181–3195. The States have no power to extradite fugitives to foreign countries. On extradition generally, see Restatement (Third) §§ 476–79; Bassiouni, International Extradition (2d ed. 1987).

Since most instances of extradition arise under bilateral or multilateral treaties, many of the problems raised by extradition are questions of treaty interpretation. Most bilateral treaties contain a list of acts for which a fugitive may be extradited. Multilateral and some bilateral treaties stipulate merely that the act for which extradition is sought be a crime in both the asylum and requisitioning states punishable by a certain minimum penalty, usually imprisonment for at least one year.

Depending on municipal law, extradition may be exclusively an executive function or may require a judicial hearing. The United States requires a judicial hearing of the evidence against the fugitive, 18 U.S.C.A. § 3184. Article IX of the 1972 Extradition Treaty between the United States and Great Britain provides that the extradition shall take place "only if the evidence be found sufficient according to the laws of the requested Party * * * to justify the committal for trial of the person sought if the offense of which he is accused had been committed in the territory of the requested Party * * *." 28 U.S.T. 227, T.I.A.S. No. 8468. "If, on such hearing, [the judge] deems the evidence sufficient to sustain the charge under the provisions of the proper treaty or convention, he shall certify the same, together with a copy of all the testimony taken before him, to the Secretary of State * * *." 18 U.S.C.A. § 3184. The Secretary of State then may grant or refuse extradition. See 4 Hackworth 49–50, 186ff. The function of the judicial hearing is to ensure that the proceedings comply with the applicable statutes and treaties. The decision of the committing magistrate on the sufficiency of the evidence is not subject to correction by appeal. Collins v. Miller, 252 U.S. 364, 369, 40 S.Ct. 347, 349, 64 L.Ed. 616 (1920). However, the fugitive may petition for a writ of habeas corpus to challenge the legality of his detention and may urge upon the Secretary of State that his extradition not be granted. See 4 Hackworth 174–75.

Notes

1. *Constitutionality of U.S. extradition statute.* In Lo Duca v. United States, 93 F.3d 1100 (2d Cir.), cert. denied, 519 U.S. 1007, 117 S.Ct. 508, 136 L.Ed.2d 399 (1996), the Court rejected the argument that the federal extradition statute, 18 U.S.C.A. § 3184, was unconstitutional since, in leaving the final decision to extradite to the Secretary of State, it assigned judicial power to the Executive Branch or, in the alternative, improperly assigned to the judiciary a role in making the executive decision to extradite. See also United States v. Luna, 165 F.3d 316 (5th Cir.), cert. denied, 526 U.S. 1126, 119 S.Ct. 1783, 143 L.Ed.2d 811 (1999).

In Parretti v. United States, 122 F.3d 758 (9th Cir.), rehearing en banc granted, 124 F.3d 1186 (1997), opinion withdrawn, appeal dismissed, en banc, 143

F.3d 508 (1998), cert. denied, 525 U.S. 877 119 S.Ct. 179, 142 L.Ed.2d 146 (1998), defendant raised both Fourth and Fifth Amendment challenges to his arrest on an extradition warrant pursuant to a treaty with France and the denial of bail pending extradition. The court initially held Article IV of the extradition treaty and 18 U.S.C.§ 3184 to be incompatible with the Fourth Amendment, to the extent that they provide for the issuance of "provisional arrest" warrants without independent judicial determinations of probable cause to believe the fugitive committed the offenses charged. The court further found that Parretti's detention without bail prior to the extradition hearing denied him due process of law. While the judicial proceedings were pending, Parretti fled the United States. The Ninth Circuit granted rehearing en banc, withdrew the panel's opinion, and dismissed the appeal. Since Parretti had become a fugitive from justice, the court did not address his constitutional claims in the rehearing en banc.

2. On April 24, 1996, the Congress amended Sections 3181 et. seq. of Title 18, Pub.L. No. 104–132, 120 Stat. 1280 (1996). The amendments made it possible to surrender foreign nationals who had committed crimes of violence against nationals of the United States without regard to the existence of any treaty of extradition.

3. On the respective roles under U.K. law of the extradition magistrate, the reviewing courts (including the House of Lords, with leave), and the Secretary of State, see the succinct explanation of Magistrate Bartle in Kingdom of Spain v. Pinochet, 38 I.L.M. 135 (2000).

THE PRINCIPLES OF SPECIALTY AND DOUBLE CRIMINALITY

According to the principle of specialty, the requisitioning state may not, without the permission of the asylum state, try or punish the fugitive for any crimes committed before the extradition except the crimes for which he was extradited. The permission of the asylum state is also required for the requisitioning state to re-extradite the fugitive to a third state. United States ex rel. Donnelly v. Mulligan, 74 F.2d 220 (2d Cir.1934). See also United States v. Rauscher, 119 U.S. 407, 7 S.Ct. 234, 30 L.Ed. 425 (1886); Harvard Research, at 213–19; Restatement (Third) § 478. Compare United States v. Alvarez–Machain, 504 U.S. 655, 112 S.Ct. 2188, 119 L.Ed.2d 441 (1992) (distinguishing *Rauscher*).

Difficult problems arise under the treaties that list extraditable crimes when the act committed by the fugitive is punishable in the requisitioning state and listed in the treaty, but not punishable in the asylum state because the law of the latter defines the crime differently. See The Eisler Extradition Case, 43 A.J.I.L. 487 (England 1949). In such a situation, if the asylum state applies its own law to define the crime, it may violate its obligations under the treaty. See 4 Hackworth 117–18. If the asylum state applies the law of the requisitioning state, it would be extraditing the fugitive for an act that was not an offense under its own law.

Under the requirement of "double criminality," extradition is available only when the act is punishable under the law of both states. The name of the offense and the elements that make it criminal need not be precisely the same, provided that the fugitive could be punished for the act in both states.

See Harvard Research in International Law, Draft Convention on Extradition, 29 A.J.I.L.Spec. Supp. 81–86 (1935); 1 Oppenheim 958; Re Clark, [1929] 3 D.L.R. 737. In Factor v. Laubenheimer, 290 U.S. 276, 54 S.Ct. 191, 78 L.Ed. 315 (1933), the Court approved extradition to Great Britain for the crime of receiving money knowing it to have been fraudulently obtained, even though the law of Illinois (where the fugitive was found) did not make such an act criminal. The Court stressed the fact that the offense was criminal under the laws of several of the States. For criticism, see Hudson, The Factor Case and Double Criminality in Extradition, 28 A.J.I.L. 274 (1934); cf. Borchard, The Factor Extradition Case, 28 A.J.I.L. 742 (1934). See also Restatement (Third) § 477, Comment *d*. In Peters v. Egnor, 888 F.2d 713 (10th Cir.1989), the British Theft Act and the American federal securities fraud statute were found "substantially analogous" and therefore to meet the requirement of dual criminality. In LoDuca v. United States, 93 F.3d 1100 (2d Cir.), cert. denied, 519 U.S. 1007, 117 S.Ct. 508, 136 L.Ed.2d 399 (1996), the court held that an Italian crime concerning an "association of mafia type" was substantially similar to U.S. crimes under the conspiracy statute and the Racketeer Influenced and Corrupt Organizations Act.

The principle of "double criminality" may also require that the act be punishable in both states at the time when it was committed. See the Pinochet case, p. 1139, and Note 2 infra. But see United States ex rel. Oppenheim v. Hecht, 16 F.2d 955 (2d Cir.1927), granting extradition for an act which was made criminal in the United States after it had been committed. Treaties frequently provide that extradition shall not take place if the prosecution of the fugitive is barred by a statute of limitations in either the asylum state or requisitioning state. See e.g., Extradition Treaty between the United States and Great Britain, Dec. 22, 1931, art. 5, 47 Stat. 2122, T.S. 849, 163 L.N.T.S. 59.

Special problems may arise when the crime for which extradition is sought was not committed on the territory of the state requesting extradition. In 1977, Abu Daoud, alleged to have participated in the massacre of Israeli athletes at the Munich Olympic Games, was arrested in France. Both West Germany and Israel sought his extradition. The *Chambre d'Accusation* of the Paris Court of Appeals, four days after Daoud's arrest, after a proceeding lasting only 20 minutes, released Daoud, and France expelled him to Algeria where he was accorded a hero's welcome. The ground given for rejection of the German request was that the request had not been "confirmed at the same time by diplomatic channel." The reasons for denial of the Israeli request were more complex. The Paris Court held that, at the time Daoud allegedly committed the crime, he could not have been prosecuted for it in France even if his victims had been French nationals, and that, therefore, he could not be extradited to Israel, even though Israeli law did permit his prosecution on the ground that the victims were Israeli citizens. The Paris Court also held that, although the French Penal Code was amended in 1975 to give France jurisdiction on the passive personality basis, this amendment could not be given retroactive effect. No reason was given why Daoud was not prosecuted in France for having entered on a false passport. On this case, see Liskofsky, The Abu Daoud Case: Law or Politics, 7 Is. Yb.H.Rtg. 66 (1977).

Notes

1. In United States v. Puentes, 50 F.3d 1567 (11th Cir.), cert. denied, 516 U.S. 933, 116 S.Ct. 341, 133 L.Ed.2d 239 (1995), the court took note of a split among the federal circuit courts as to whether a defendant has standing to raise a claim of violation of the principle of specialty (i.e., that he was prosecuted for a crime other than the one for which he had been extradited under a treaty), in the absence of affirmative protest from the state party to the treaty. The Eleventh Circuit concluded that the defendant had standing to raise the claim of a treaty violation, but he would lose that right if the state party waived its objection. The court then rejected the challenge on the merits.

2. The principle of double criminality was involved in the *Pinochet* extradition proceedings in the United Kingdom, pp. 1139, 1276. Both the requesting state (Spain) and the United Kingdom had ratified the 1984 Convention Against Torture and Other Cruel, Inhuman or Degrading Treatment or Punishment, which had become effective as domestic law in the United Kingdom by enactment of § 134 of the U.K. Criminal Justice Act on September 29, 1988 and had come into force for the United Kingdom with effect from December 8, 1988. Prior to 1988, however, there was no basis in U.K. law for extraterritorial jurisdiction over the crime of torture and thus no dual criminality in relation to Spain's prosecution. (Dual criminality would not have been a concern in respect of extradition to the territory where the torture was alleged to have taken place, namely Chile.) Lord Browne–Wilkinson's opinion stated on this point:

> [T]he principle of double criminality which requires an Act to be a crime under both the law of Spain and of the United Kingdom cannot be satisfied in relation to conduct before that date if the principle of double criminality requires the conduct to be criminal under United Kingdom law *at the date it was committed.* If, on the other hand, the double criminality rule only requires the conduct to be criminal under U.K. law *at the date of extradition* the rule was satisfied in relation to all torture alleged against Senator Pinochet whether it took place before or after 1988.

A majority of the House of Lords concluded that Pinochet could be extradited to Spain for crimes committed after the United Kingdom had implemented the Torture Convention, but not for earlier crimes.

The Spanish extradition request was based in part on the allegation that the crimes had been committed against Spanish nationals (passive personality jurisdiction), but also alleged crimes on a universal jurisdiction theory. Should extradition be limited to requests by states relying on the territorial, the subjective nationality, and the protective principle? If it is based on the universality principle, which of the states requesting extradition should be given preference? Should a state be permitted to deny extradition on the ground that it wishes to prosecute itself or has, in the exercise of prosecutorial discretion, decided not to prosecute? If none of these limitations apply, what prevents a single state from prosecuting, and demanding extradition for, crimes based on the universality principle? Note that subsequently to the Pinochet case, Spain requested extradition by Mexico for crimes alleged by committed in Argentina by Argentinian officials. See "Wide Net in Argentine Torture Case," New York Times, September 11, 2000, p. 6, col. 1.

EXEMPTION OF NATIONALS

Many extradition treaties contain provisions exempting nationals of the asylum state from extradition. A typical provision is that neither party shall be obligated to surrender its nationals, thus leaving the matter in the discretion of the asylum state. The policy, which is most commonly reflected in civil law jurisdictions, apparently stems from a feeling that individuals should not be withdrawn from the jurisdiction of their own courts. See Harvard Research, at 125. However, the courts in many civil law countries have broad jurisdiction to try and punish their nationals for crimes committed in other countries. See id. at 445; see also p. 1115. The United States surrenders its own nationals (unless exempted by treaty) as a matter of obligation, even in the absence of reciprocity. Charlton v. Kelly, 229 U.S. 447, 33 S.Ct. 945, 57 L.Ed. 1274 (1913). Great Britain generally surrenders nationals. See Extradition Act, 1870, 33 & 34 Vict. C. 52 § 26; 1 Oppenheim 956. Multilateral extradition conventions which recognize the principle of non-extradition of nationals generally provide that if the asylum state refuses to extradite a national it shall itself prosecute the person claimed. See e.g., Convention on Extradition, signed at Montevideo, Art. 2, 49 Stat. 3111, T.S. 882, 165 L.N.T.S. 45.

Constitutional restrictions on extradition of nationals have featured in the debates in some countries about cooperation with the International Criminals for Yugoslavia and Rwanda and the prospective International Criminal Court. See Chapter 15.

THE POLITICAL OFFENSE EXCEPTION

In the eighteenth century, extradition was frequently sought and granted for what are now termed political offenses. By the nineteenth century public opinion in Western Europe turned against the extradition of fugitives accused of only political offenses. Belgium, which enacted the first extradition law in 1833, incorporated the principle of non-extradition for political offenses into the law. Today, most treaties exempt fugitives accused of political offenses from extradition. Though the principle has been almost universally accepted, "political offenses" have never been precisely defined. The first attempt to delineate the principle was the "attentat" clause in many treaties, which provides that the murder of the head of a foreign government or a member of his family is not to be considered a political offense. See, e.g., Treaty of Extradition between the United States and Venezuela, Art. 3, 43 Stat. 1698, T.S. 675, 49 L.N.T.S. 435. Some treaties extend the exclusion to any murder or attempt on life in general. See, e.g., Extradition Treaty between Italy and Finland, 1928, Art. 3(3), 111 L.N.T.S. 295. However, in 1934 in the absence of such a clause in the applicable treaty, the Turin Court of Appeal refused to extradite the assassins of King Alexander of Yugoslavia to France on the ground that the crime was political. In re Pavelic, [1933–34] Ann. Dig. No. 158 (Italy).

In 1892, Switzerland adopted a law which provided that a crime was not to be considered political if it was primarily a common offense even though it had a political motivation or purpose. The decision on extradition was left to the highest Swiss Court. See 2 O'Connell 802; 1 Oppenheim 967. Some treaties provide that "[c]riminal acts which constitute clear manifestations of anarchism or envisage the overthrow of the bases of all political organizations" shall not be considered political offenses. Treaty of Extradition between the United States and Brazil, Art. V(6), 15 U.S.T. 2093, T.I.A.S. No. 5691, 532 U.N.T.S. 177. British and American courts have held that for an offense to be political it must be committed in furtherance of a political movement or in the course of a struggle to control the government of a state. In re Castioni, [1891] I Q.B. 149, 156, 166; In re Ezeta, 62 Fed. 972, 999 (D.C.Cal.1894). However, this strict rule has been relaxed to provide refuge for private individuals fleeing totalitarian states. See Regina v. Governor of Brixton Prison, Ex parte Kolczynski, [1955] I Q.B. 540 (1954). For a discussion of political offenses, see Regina v. Governor of Brixton Prison, Ex parte Schtraks, [1964] A.C. 556, 581–84, 587–92 (H.L.); Garcia Mora, Crimes Against Humanity and the Principle of Nonextradition of Political Offenders, 62 Mich. L.Rev. 927 (1964); Harvard Research at 107–19; Spanish–German Extradition Treaty case, [1925–26] Ann.Dig. No. 234 (Germany 1926). Treaties also frequently prohibit extradition for purely military offenses. See Convention on Extradition between the United States and Sweden, Art. V(4), 14 U.S.T. 1845, T.I.A.S. No. 5496, 494 U.N.T.S. 141.

The United States and the United Kingdom signed a Supplementary Extradition Treaty on June 25, 1985, T.I.A.S. No. 12,050, that excludes from the category of "political offenses" specified crimes of violence that are typically committed by terrorists (such as attacks by the so-called Irish Republic Army). Prior to the Supplementary Treaty, some courts had refused extradition for such crimes on the ground of the "political offense" exception. See, e.g., Matter of Doherty, 599 F.Supp. 270 (S.D.N.Y.1984); United States v. Doherty, 786 F.2d 491 (2d Cir.1986); see also Restatement (Third) § 478, Reporters' Note 6. The European Convention on the Suppression of Terrorism permits Council of Europe members not to regard as political similar offenses typically committed by terrorists. See Leich, Contemporary Practice of the United States Related to International Law, 79 A.J.I.L. 1045 (1985). In approving the Supplementary Treaty, the U.S. Senate required a modification to enable litigation of concerns that defendants might be subject to adverse treatment on the ground of race, religion, nationality or political opinion. For judicial application of the Supplementary Treaty, see p. 1185, Note 2.

CHALLENGES TO HUMAN RIGHTS PRACTICES IN THE REQUESTING STATE

The general rule in most extradition cases has been to reject defendants' efforts to resist extradition on the ground that they would be subjected to standards of procedural due process falling short of those in the requested state or would otherwise suffer unjust treatment following extradition. Courts have typically considered that the treaty obligation to extradite precludes such an inquiry, and that it is the responsibility of the executive branch in negotiating and implementing an extradition treaty (or the legislative branch in approving the treaty) to ensure adequate safeguards for the treatment of extraditees. Thus a "rule of judicial non-inquiry" has been applied under which the court considering an extradition request concerns itself only with whether the treaty standard for extradition is satisfied and does not usually entertain evidence about the quality of the justice system in the requesting state. (The Secretary of State may, however, consider such evidence in making the final discretionary decision whether to go forward with the surrender after the court has certified extraditability.)

Recently, however, some human rights challenges to extradition have proven successful, at least in relation to certain practices in the requesting state that the requested state considers to be contrary to fundamental human rights. There has now been a significant number of cases in which extradition has been withheld (or made subject to conditions) by virtue of differing positions in the requesting and requested state with respect to the death penalty and related practices. Other cases involve concerns about the practice of torture or other forms of cruel, inhuman or degrading treatment or punishment in the requesting state. On these and other human rights challenges, see generally Dugard & Van den Wyngaert, Reconciling Extradition with Human Rights, 92 A.J.I.L. 187 (1998) and the notes below.

Notes

1. In Ahmad v. Wigen, 910 F.2d 1063 (2d Cir.1990), stay denied, 497 U.S. 1054, 111 S.Ct. 23, 111 L.Ed.2d 835 (1990), the district court had held a hearing on defendant's habeas corpus petition, in which it took extensive testimony on whether a Palestinian defendant would receive a fair trial in Israel on allegations of a terrorist attack on a bus; after the hearing, the court denied defendant's habeas corpus petition. The Second Circuit affirmed the ruling that defendant was extraditable and confirmed the rationale underlying the "rule of judicial non-inquiry:"

> We have no problem with the district court's rejection of Ahmad's remaining argument to the effect that, if he is returned to Israel, he probably will be mistreated, denied a fair trial, and deprived of his constitutional and human rights. We do, however, question the district court's decision to explore the merits of this contention in the manner that it did. * * * A consideration of the procedures that will or may occur in the requesting country is not within the purview of a habeas corpus judge. * * * Indeed, there is substantial authority for the proposition that this is not a proper matter for consideration by the certifying judicial officer. * * * In Jhirad v. Ferrandina, supra, 536 F.2d at 484–85, we said that "[i]t is not the business of our courts to assume the responsibility for supervising the integrity of the judicial system of another sovereign nation." [Other citations omitted.]
>
> Notwithstanding the above described judicial roadblocks, the district court proceeded to take testimony from both expert and fact witnesses and received extensive reports, affidavits, and other documentation concerning Israel's law enforcement procedures and its treatment of prisoners. This, we think, was improper. The interests of international comity are ill-served by requiring a foreign nation such as Israel to satisfy a United States district judge concerning the fairness of its laws and the manner in which they are enforced. * * *

All the American judge has to find, the Court said, is that the evidence would support a reasonable belief that Ahmad was guilty of the crime charged.

2. In re Extradition of Smyth, 61 F.3d 711 (9th Cir.1995) cert. denied, 518 U.S. 1022, 116 S.Ct. 2558, 135 L.Ed.2d 1076 (1996), involved the application of the U.S.-U.K. Supplemental Extradition Treaty in a case involving a fugitive who had escaped from Maze Prison in Northern Ireland after conviction for attempted murder of a prison guard in Belfast. Article 3(a) of the Supplementary Treaty, added at the instance of the U.S. Senate, provides:

> Notwithstanding any other provision of this Supplementary Treaty, extradition shall not occur if the person sought establishes to the satisfaction of the competent judicial authority by a preponderance of the evidence that the request for extradition has in fact been made with a view to try or punish him on account of his race, religion, nationality or political opinions, or that he would, if surrendered, be prejudiced at his trial or punished, detained or restricted in his personal liberty by reason of his race, religion, nationality or political opinions.

The Circuit Court recognized this provision as a unique exception to the ordinary judicial non-inquiry rule. Finding that Smyth had not carried his burden of proof, the appellate court reversed the district court's ruling that Smyth would be subject to such discrimination and remanded for entry of an order allowing extradition.

3. Several cases have involved challenges to extradition to Hong Kong shortly before or after its incorporation into the People's Republic of China. Although a few courts have been sympathetic to defendants' claims that extradition should not go forward in light of the changeover, appellate courts have found defendants extraditable. See Lui Kin–Hong v. United States, 957 F.Supp. 1280 (D.Mass.), reversed, 110 F.3d 103 (1st Cir.1997), stay denied, 520 U.S. 1206, 117 S.Ct. 1491, 137 L.Ed.2d 816 (1997); Regina v. Secretary of State for the Home Department, Ex parte Launder, Nos. C.O. 2480/95, 0018/96 (Q.B. Div'l Ct. Aug. 6, 1996), reversed by the House of Lords, [1997] 1 W.L.R. 839. These and other cases are discussed in Dugard & Van den Wyngaert, 92 A.J.I.L. at 194 (1998).

4. *Extradition to death penalty jurisdictions.* In Soering v. United Kingdom, 161 Eur.Ct. H.R. (Ser. A) (1989), the European Court of Human Rights held that the United Kingdom would violate the human rights of a young man by extraditing him to face capital murder charges in the state of Virginia. The court acknowledged that international law does not prohibit the death penalty as such, but it found a serious risk that Soering would be subjected to inhuman or degrading treatment by virtue of what it termed the "death row phenomenon" of prolonged incarceration prior to execution of a death sentence. Soering was later extradited after receipt of assurances that the death penalty would not be applied.

In Ng v. Canada, U.N. Doc. CCPR/C/49/D/469/1991 (1993), 98 I.L.R.479, the U.N. Human Rights Committee found that extradition by Canada to the United States, where petitioner was to be subjected to the death penalty by means of asphyxiation in a gas chamber, was violative of Article 7 of the International Covenant on Civil and Political Rights prohibiting cruel, inhuman or degrading treatment or punishment. Cf. Kindler v. Canada, U.N. Doc. CCPR/C/48/D/470/1991 (1993), 98 I.L.R. 426 (since international law does not prohibit the death penalty, there was no obligation on the part of Canada to seek assurances from the United States that the death penalty would not be applied).

In United States v. Burns, 2001 SCC 7 (Sup. Ct. Canada, Feb. 15, 2001), the Supreme Court of Canada revisited its holdings in Kindler v. Canada (Minister of Justice), [1991] 2 S.C.R. 779, and Reference re Ng Extradition (Can.), [1991] 2 S.C.R. 858, in which it had held that there was no requirement of constitutional or international law to request assurances from the United States against application of the death penalty. In view of international trends toward abolition of the death penalty, and Canada's leadership role in initiatives toward that objective, the Court reinterpreted the Canadian Constitution's provisions on fundamental justice to require the Minister of Justice to obtain such assurances as a condition of extradition.

Meanwhile, an Italian court found that extradition could not be granted to a death penalty jurisdiction even if the executive branch of the requesting state gave assurances that the death penalty would not be sought. The court was apparently concerned that such assurances might not bind an independent branch of government, and interpreted its own fundamental law to preclude any involvement with surrendering the accused to a state where the death penalty was even a possibility. Venezia v. Ministero di Grazia e Giustizia, Italian Const. Ct., June 27, 1996, 79 Rivista di Diritto Internazionale 815 (1996), discussed in Bianchi, Case Note, 91 A.J.I.L. 727 (1997), and Dugard & Van den Wyngaert, 92 A.J.I.L. at 197, 206 n. 143 (1998).

5. Article 3 of the Convention Against Torture and Other Cruel, Inhuman or Degrading Treatment or Punishment, 23 I.L.M. 1027 (1984), in force for the United States since 1994, provides:

> 1. No State Party shall expel, return (*"refouler"*) or extradite a person to another State where there are substantial grounds for believing that he would be in danger of being subjected to torture.
>
> 2. For the purpose of determining whether there are such grounds, the competent authorities shall take into account all relevant considerations including, where applicable, the existence in the State concerned of a consistent patter of gross, flagrant or mass violations of human rights.

For discussion of this and comparable treaty provisions and litigation under them, see Dugard & Van den Wyngaert, Reconciling Extradition and Human Rights, 92 A.J.I.L. 187, 197–202 (1998).

TRANSFER TO A U.N. TRIBUNAL

In 1995, the President of the United States entered into an executive agreement with the International Criminal Tribunal for Rwanda (I.C.T.R.) "to surrender to the Tribunal * * * persons * * * found in its territory whom the Tribunal has charged with or found guilty of a violation or violations within the competence of the Tribunal." In 1996, Congress enacted Public Law 104–106 to implement the Agreement, Pub. L. 104–106, § 1342, 110 Stat. 486 (1996), by providing that federal extradition statutes are to apply to surrender of persons to the I.C.T.R. Elizaphan Ntakirutimana, a Rwandan pastor indicted on genocide charges by the I.C.T.R., sought to challenge his surrender by writ of habeas corpus, on the grounds that (1) the Constitution of the United States requires an Article II treaty for a surrender tantamount to extradition, (2) the request for surrender does not establish probable cause, (3) the U.N. Charter does not authorize the Security Council to establish the I.C.T.R., and (4) the I.C.T.R. does not protect fundamental rights guaranteed by the U.S. Constitution and international law. Although the first district judge to whom the matter was presented found his arguments persuasive and denied extradition, the government renewed its request successfully. On appeal, the court rejected all four bases for challenge. Ntakirutimana v. Reno,

184 F.3d 419 (5th Cir.1999), cert. denied, 528 U.S. 1135, 120 S.Ct. 977, 145 L.Ed.2d 929 (2000). The Secretary of State ordered the surrender and Ntakirutimana was delivered to the custody of the I.C.T.R. in March 2000.

B. ALTERNATIVES TO TREATY-BASED EXTRADITION: DEPORTATION, EXCLUSION, ABDUCTION

Where extradition is not possible because of the lack of a treaty or for some other reason, or where extradition is not feasible because of the time and expense involved, states have resorted to other methods of surrendering or recovering fugitives. If the fugitive is not a national of the asylum state, it may deport him as an undesirable alien or exclude him (i.e., deny him permission to enter the country). In either case, the fugitive may be turned over directly to the state that desires to prosecute him, or may be sent to a third state from which his extradition is possible. The United States and Mexico, and the United States and Canada, have frequently resorted to exclusion or deportation in order to deliver fugitives to each other without going through the process of extradition. See Evans, Acquisition of Custody over the International Fugitive Offender—Alternatives to Extradition: A Survey of United States Practice, 40 Brit. Y.B.I.L. 77 (1964).

UNITED STATES v. HUMBERTO ALVAREZ–MACHAIN

Supreme Court of the United States, 1992.
504 U.S. 655, 112 S.Ct. 2188, 119 L.Ed.2d 441.

(Some footnotes omitted; others renumbered.)

THE CHIEF JUSTICE delivered the opinion of the Court.

The issue in this case is whether a criminal defendant, abducted to the United States from a nation with which it has an extradition treaty, thereby acquires a defense to the jurisdiction of this country's courts. We hold that he does not, and that he may be tried in federal district court for violations of the criminal law of the United States.

Respondent, Humberto Alvarez–Machain, is a citizen and resident of Mexico. He was indicted for participating in the kidnap and murder of United States Drug Enforcement Administration (DEA) special agent Enrique Camarena–Salazar and a Mexican pilot working with Camarena, Alfredo Zavala–Avelar. The DEA believes that respondent, a medical doctor, participated in the murder by prolonging agent Camarena's life so that others could further torture and interrogate him. On April 2, 1990, respondent was forcibly kidnapped from his medical office in Guadalajara, Mexico, to be flown by private plane to El Paso, Texas, where he was arrested by DEA officials. The District Court concluded that DEA agents were responsible for respondent's abduction, although they were not personally involved in it. United States v. Caro–Quintero, 745 F.Supp. 599, 602604, 609 (C.D.Cal.1990).[1]

Respondent moved to dismiss the indictment, claiming that his abduction constituted outrageous governmental conduct, and that the District Court

1. Apparently, DEA officials had attempted to gain respondent's presence in the United States through informal negotiations with Mexican officials, but were unsuccessful. DEA officials then, through a contact in Mexico, offered to pay a reward and expenses in return for the delivery of respondent to the United States. United States v. Caro–Quintero, 745 F.Supp. 599, 602–604 (C.D.Cal.1990).

lacked jurisdiction to try him because he was abducted in violation of the extradition treaty between the United States and Mexico. Extradition Treaty, May 4, 1978, [1979] United States–United Mexican States, 31 U.S.T. 5059, T.I.A.S. No. 9656 (Extradition Treaty or Treaty). The District Court rejected the outrageous governmental conduct claim, but held that it lacked jurisdiction to try respondent because his abduction violated the Extradition Treaty. The district court discharged respondent and ordered that he be repatriated to Mexico. Caro–Quintero, supra, at 614.

The Court of Appeals affirmed the dismissal of the indictment and the repatriation of respondent, relying on its decision in United States v. Verdugo–Urquidez, 939 F.2d 1341 (C.A.9 1991), cert. pending, No. 91–670. 946 F.2d 1466 (1991). In Verdugo, the Court of Appeals held that the forcible abduction of a Mexican national with the authorization or participation of the United States violated the Extradition Treaty between the United States and Mexico.[2] Although the Treaty does not expressly prohibit such abductions, the Court of Appeals held that the "purpose" of the Treaty was violated by a forcible abduction, * * * which, along with a formal protest by the offended nation, would give a defendant the right to invoke the Treaty violation to defeat jurisdiction of the district court to try him. The Court of Appeals further held that the proper remedy for such a violation would be dismissal of the indictment and repatriation of the defendant to Mexico.

In the instant case, the Court of Appeals affirmed the district court's finding that the United States had authorized the abduction of respondent, and that letters from the Mexican government to the United States government served as an official protest of the Treaty violation. Therefore, the Court of Appeals ordered that the indictment against respondent be dismissed and that respondent be repatriated to Mexico. 946 F.2d at 1467. We granted certiorari, * * * and now reverse.

Although we have never before addressed the precise issue raised in the present case, we have previously considered proceedings in claimed violation of an extradition treaty, and proceedings against a defendant brought before a court by means of a forcible abduction. We addressed the former issue in United States v. Rauscher, 119 U.S. 407, 7 S.Ct. 234, 30 L.Ed. 425 (1886); more precisely, the issue of whether the Webster–Ashburton Treaty of 1842, 8 Stat. 576, which governed extraditions between England and the United States, prohibited the prosecution of defendant Rauscher for a crime other than the crime for which he had been extradited. Whether this prohibition, known as the doctrine of specialty, was an intended part of the treaty had been disputed between the two nations for some time. Rauscher, 119 U.S. at 411, 7 S.Ct., at 236. Justice Miller delivered the opinion of the Court, which carefully examined the terms and history of the treaty; the practice of nations in regards to extradition treaties; the case law from the states; and the writings of commentators, and reached the following conclusion:

"[A] person who has been brought within the jurisdiction of the court *by virtue of proceedings under an extradition treaty*, can only be tried for one

2. Rene Martin Verdugo–Urquidez was also indicted for the murder of agent Camarena. In an earlier decision, we held that the Fourth Amendment did not apply to a search by United States agents of Verdugo–Urquidez' home in Mexico. United States v. Verdugo–Urquidez, 494 U.S. 259, 110 S.Ct. 1056, 108 L.Ed.2d 222 (1990).

> of the offences described in that treaty, and for the offence with which he is charged in the proceedings for his extradition, until a reasonable time and opportunity have been given him, after his release or trial upon such charge, to return to the country from whose asylum he had been forcibly taken under those proceedings." Id., at 430, 7 S.Ct., at 246 (emphasis added).

In addition, Justice Miller's opinion noted that any doubt as to this interpretation was put to rest by two federal statutes which imposed the doctrine of specialty upon extradition treaties to which the United States was a party. * * * Unlike the case before us today, the defendant in Rauscher had been brought to the United States by way of an extradition treaty; there was no issue of a forcible abduction.

In Ker v. Illinois, 119 U.S. 436, 7 S.Ct. 225, 30 L.Ed. 421 (1886), also written by Justice Miller and decided the same day as Rauscher, we addressed the issue of a defendant brought before the court by way of a forcible abduction. Frederick Ker had been tried and convicted in an Illinois court for larceny; his presence before the court was procured by means of forcible abduction from Peru. A messenger was sent to Lima with the proper warrant to demand Ker by virtue of the extradition treaty between Peru and the United States. The messenger, however, disdained reliance on the treaty processes, and instead forcibly kidnapped Ker and brought him to the United States.[3] We distinguished Ker's case from Rauscher, on the basis that Ker was not brought into the United States by virtue of the extradition treaty between the United States and Peru, and rejected Ker's argument that he had a right under the extradition treaty to be returned to this country only in accordance with its terms. We rejected Ker's due process argument more broadly, holding in line with "the highest authorities" that "such forcible abduction is no sufficient reason why the party should not answer when brought within the jurisdiction of the court which has the right to try him for such an offence, and presents no valid objection to his trial in such court." * * *

In Frisbie v. Collins, 342 U.S. 519, 72 S.Ct. 509, 96 L.Ed. 541, rehearing denied, 343 U.S. 937, 72 S.Ct. 768, 96 L.Ed. 1344 (1952), we applied the rule in Ker to a case in which the defendant had been kidnapped in Chicago by Michigan officers and brought to trial in Michigan. We upheld the conviction over objections based on the due process clause and the Federal Kidnapping Act. * * *

The only differences between Ker and the present case are that Ker was decided on the premise that there was no governmental involvement in the abduction, 119 U.S. at 443, 7 S.Ct., 229; and Peru, from which Ker was abducted, did not object to his prosecution.[4] Respondent finds these differences to be dispositive, as did the Court of Appeals in Verdugo, 939 F.2d, at 1346, contending that they show that respondent's prosecution, like the prosecution of Rauscher, violates the implied terms of a valid extradition

3. Although the opinion does not explain why the messenger failed to present the warrant to the proper authorities, commentators have suggested that the seizure of Ker in the aftermath of a revolution in Peru provided the messenger with no "proper authorities" to whom the warrant could be presented. See Kester, Some Myths of United States Extradition Law, 76 Geo.L.J. 1441, 1451 (1988).

4. Ker also was not a national of Peru, whereas respondent is a national of the country from which he was abducted. * * *

treaty. The Government, on the other hand, argues that Rauscher stands as an "exception" to the rule in Ker only when an extradition treaty is invoked, and the terms of the treaty provide that its breach will limit the jurisdiction of a court. * * * Therefore, our first inquiry must be whether the abduction of respondent from Mexico violated the extradition treaty between the United States and Mexico. If we conclude that the Treaty does not prohibit respondent's abduction, the rule in Ker applies, and the court need not inquire as to how respondent came before it.

In construing a treaty, as in construing a statute, we first look to its terms to determine its meaning. Air France v. Saks, 470 U.S. 392, 397, 105 S.Ct. 1338, 1341, 84 L.Ed.2d 289 (1985); Valentine v. United States ex rel. Neidecker, 299 U.S. 5, 11, 57 S.Ct. 100, 103, 81 L.Ed. 5 (1936). The Treaty says nothing about the obligations of the United States and Mexico to refrain from forcible abductions of people from the territory of the other nation, or the consequences under the Treaty if such an abduction occurs. Respondent submits that Article 22(1) of the Treaty which states that it "shall apply to offenses specified in Article 2 [including murder] committed before and after this Treaty enters into force," 31 U.S.T., at 5073–5074, evidences an intent to make application of the Treaty mandatory for those offenses. However, the more natural conclusion is that Article 22 was included to ensure that the Treaty was applied to extraditions requested after the Treaty went into force, regardless of when the crime of extradition occurred.

More critical to respondent's argument is Article 9 of the Treaty which provides:

> "1. Neither Contracting Party shall be bound to deliver up its own nationals, but the executive authority of the requested Party shall, if not prevented by the laws of that Party, have the power to deliver them up if, in its discretion, it be deemed proper to do so.
>
> "2. If extradition is not granted pursuant to paragraph 1 of this Article, the requested Party shall submit the case to its competent authorities for the purpose of prosecution, provided that Party has jurisdiction over the offense." Id., at 5065.

According to respondent, Article 9 embodies the terms of the bargain which the United States struck: if the United States wishes to prosecute a Mexican national, it may request that individual's extradition. Upon a request from the United States, Mexico may either extradite the individual, or submit the case to the proper authorities for prosecution in Mexico. In this way, respondent reasons, each nation preserved its right to choose whether its nationals would be tried in its own courts or by the courts of the other nation. This preservation of rights would be frustrated if either nation were free to abduct nationals of the other nation for the purposes of prosecution. More broadly, respondent reasons, as did the Court of Appeals, that all the processes and restrictions on the obligation to extradite established by the Treaty would make no sense if either nation were free to resort to forcible kidnapping to gain the presence of an individual for prosecution in a manner not contemplated by the Treaty. Verdugo, supra, at 1350.

We do not read the Treaty in such a fashion. Article 9 does not purport to specify the only way in which one country may gain custody of a national of the other country for the purposes of prosecution. In the absence of an extradition treaty, nations are under no obligation to surrender those in their country to foreign authorities for prosecution. Rauscher, 119 U.S., at 411–412, 7 S.Ct. at 236; Factor v. Laubenheimer, 290 U.S. 276, 287, 54 S.Ct. 191, 193, 78 L.Ed. 315 (1933); cf. Valentine v. United States ex rel. Neidecker, supra, 299 U.S., at 8–9, 57 S.Ct., at 102 (United States may not extradite a citizen in the absence of a statute or treaty obligation). Extradition treaties exist so as to impose mutual obligations to surrender individuals in certain defined sets of circumstances, following established procedures. See 1 J. Moore, A Treatise on Extradition and Interstate Rendition, § 72 (1891). The Treaty thus provides a mechanism which would not otherwise exist, requiring, under certain circumstances, the United States and Mexico to extradite individuals to the other country, and establishing the procedures to be followed when the Treaty is invoked.

The history of negotiation and practice under the Treaty also fails to show that abductions outside of the Treaty constitute a violation of the Treaty. As the Solicitor General notes, the Mexican government was made aware, as early as 1906, of the Ker doctrine, and the United States' position that it applied to forcible abductions made outside of the terms of the United States–Mexico extradition treaty. Nonetheless, the current version of the Treaty, signed in 1978, does not attempt to establish a rule that would in any way curtail the effect of Ker. Moreover, although language which would grant individuals exactly the right sought by respondent had been considered and drafted as early as 1935 by a prominent group of legal scholars sponsored by the faculty of Harvard Law School, no such clause appears in the current treaty.[5]

Thus, the language of the Treaty, in the context of its history, does not support the proposition that the Treaty prohibits abductions outside of its terms. The remaining question, therefore, is whether the Treaty should be interpreted so as to include an implied term prohibiting prosecution where the defendant's presence is obtained by means other than those established by the Treaty. See Valentine, 299 U.S., at 17, 57 S.Ct., at 106 ("Strictly the question is not whether there had been a uniform practical construction denying the power, but whether the power had been so clearly recognized that the grant should be implied").

Respondent contends that the Treaty must be interpreted against the backdrop of customary international law, and that international abductions are "so clearly prohibited in international law" that there was no reason to include such a clause in the Treaty itself. Brief for Respondent 11. The international censure of international abductions is further evidenced, according to respondent, by the United Nations Charter and the Charter of the Organization of American States. Id., at 17, 57 S.Ct., at 106. Respondent does not argue that these sources of international law provide an independent basis

5. In Article 16 of the Draft Convention on Jurisdiction with Respect to Crime, the Advisory Committee of the Research in International Law proposed:

> "In exercising jurisdiction under this Convention, no State shall prosecute or punish any person who has been brought within its territory or a place subject to its authority by recourse to measures in violation of international law or international convention without first obtaining the consent of the State or States whose rights have been violated by such measures." Harvard Research in International Law, 29 Am. J. Int'l L. 442 (Supp 1935).

for the right respondent asserts not to be tried in the United States, but rather that they should inform the interpretation of the Treaty terms.

The Court of Appeals deemed it essential, in order for the individual defendant to assert a right under the Treaty, that the affected foreign government had registered a protest. Verdugo, 939 F.2d, at 1357 ("in the kidnapping case there must be a formal protest from the offended government after the kidnapping"). Respondent agrees that the right exercised by the individual is derivative of the nation's right under the Treaty, since nations are authorized, notwithstanding the terms of an extradition treaty, to voluntarily render an individual to the other country on terms completely outside of those provided in the Treaty. The formal protest, therefore, ensures that the "offended" nation actually objects to the abduction and has not in some way voluntarily rendered the individual for prosecution. Thus the Extradition Treaty only prohibits gaining the defendant's presence by means other than those set forth in the Treaty when the nation from which the defendant was abducted objects.

This argument seems to us inconsistent with the remainder of respondent's argument. The Extradition Treaty has the force of law, and if, as respondent asserts, it is self-executing, it would appear that a court must enforce it on behalf of an individual regardless of the offensiveness of the practice of one nation to the other nation. In Rauscher, the Court noted that Great Britain had taken the position in other cases that the Webster–Ashburton Treaty included the doctrine of specialty, but no importance was attached to whether or not Great Britain had protested the prosecution of Rauscher for the crime of cruel and unusual punishment as opposed to murder.

More fundamentally, the difficulty with the support respondent garners from international law is that none of it relates to the practice of nations in relation to extradition treaties. In Rauscher, we implied a term in the Webster–Ashburton Treaty because of the practice of nations with regard to extradition treaties. In the instant case, respondent would imply terms in the extradition treaty from the practice of nations with regards to international law more generally. Respondent would have us find that the Treaty acts as a prohibition against a violation of the general principle of international law that one government may not "exercise its police power in the territory of another state." Brief for Respondent 16. There are many actions which could be taken by a nation that would violate this principle, including waging war, but it cannot seriously be contended an invasion of the United States by Mexico would violate the terms of the extradition treaty between the two nations.

In sum, to infer from this Treaty and its terms that it prohibits all means of gaining the presence of an individual outside of its terms goes beyond established precedent and practice. * * * The general principles cited by respondent simply fail to persuade us that we should imply in the United States–Mexico Extradition Treaty a term prohibiting international abductions.

Respondent and his amici may be correct that respondent's abduction was "shocking," Tr. of Oral Arg. 40, and that it may be in violation of general international law principles. Mexico has protested the abduction of respondent through diplomatic notes, App. 33–38, and the decision of whether respondent should be returned to Mexico, as a matter outside of the Treaty, is a matter for the Executive Branch.[6] We conclude, however, that respondent's abduction was not in violation of the Extradition Treaty between the United States and Mexico, and therefore the rule of Ker v. Illinois is fully applicable to this case. The fact of respondent's forcible abduction does not therefore prohibit his trial in a court in the United States for violations of the criminal laws of the United States.

The judgment of the Court of Appeals is therefore reversed, and the case is remanded for further proceedings consistent with this opinion.

So ordered.

JUSTICE STEVENS, with whom JUSTICE BLACKMUN and JUSTICE O'CONNOR join, dissenting.

The Court correctly observes that this case raises a question of first impression. The case is unique for several reasons. It does not involve an ordinary abduction by a private kidnaper, or bounty hunter, as in Ker v. Illinois, 119 U.S. 436, 7 S.Ct. 225, 30 L.Ed. 421 (1886); nor does it involve the apprehension of an American fugitive who committed a crime in one State and sought asylum in another, as in Frisbie v. Collins, 342 U.S. 519, 72 S.Ct. 509, 96 L.Ed. 541 (1952). Rather, it involves this country's abduction of another country's citizen; it also involves a violation of the territorial integrity of that other country, with which this country has signed an extradition treaty.

A Mexican citizen was kidnaped in Mexico and charged with a crime committed in Mexico; his offense allegedly violated both Mexican and American law. Mexico has formally demanded on at least two separate occasions that he be returned to Mexico and has represented that he will be prosecuted and punished for his alleged offense. It is clear that Mexico's demand must be honored if this official abduction violated the 1978 Extradition Treaty between the United States and Mexico. In my opinion, a fair reading of the treaty in light of our decision in United States v. Rauscher, 119 U.S. 407, 7 S.Ct. 234, 30 L.Ed. 425 (1886), and applicable principles of international law, leads inexorably to the conclusion that the District Court, United States v.

6. The Mexican government has also requested from the United States the extradition of two individuals it suspects of having abducted respondent in Mexico, on charges of kidnapping. App. 39–66.

The advantage of the diplomatic approach to the resolution of difficulties between two sovereign nations, as opposed to unilateral action by the courts of one nation, is illustrated by the history of the negotiations leading to the treaty discussed in Cook v. United States, supra. The United States was interested in being able to search British vessels which hovered beyond the 3–mile limit and served as supply ships for motor launches which took intoxicating liquor from them into ports for further distribution in violation of prohibition laws. The United States initially proposed that both nations agree to searches of the other's vessels beyond the 3–mile limit; Great Britain rejected such an approach, since it had no prohibition laws and therefore no problem with United States vessels hovering just beyond its territorial waters. The parties appeared to be at loggerheads; then this Court decided Cunard Steamship Co. v. Mellon, 262 U.S. 100, 43 S.Ct. 504, 67 L.Ed. 894 (1923), holding that our prohibition laws applied to foreign merchant vessels as well as domestic within the territorial waters of the United States, and that therefore the carrying of intoxicating liquors by foreign passenger ships violated those laws. A treaty was then successfully negotiated giving the United States the right to seizure beyond the 3–mile limit (which it desired), and giving British passenger ships the right to bring liquor into United States waters so long as the liquor supply was sealed while in those waters (which Great Britain desired). Cook v. United States, supra.

Caro–Quintero, 745 F.Supp. 599 (C.D.Cal.1990), and the Court of Appeals for the Ninth Circuit, 946 F.2d 1466 (1991) (per curiam), correctly construed that instrument.

* * *

A critical flaw pervades the Court's entire opinion. It fails to differentiate between the conduct of private citizens, which does not violate any treaty obligation, and conduct expressly authorized by the Executive Branch of the Government, which unquestionably constitutes a flagrant violation of international law, and in my opinion, also constitutes a breach of our treaty obligations. Thus, at the outset of its opinion, the Court states the issue as "whether a criminal defendant, abducted to the United States from a nation with which it has an extradition treaty, thereby acquires a defense to the jurisdiction of this country's courts." Ante, at 2190. That, of course, is the question decided in Ker v. Illinois, 119 U.S. 436, 7 S.Ct. 225, 30 L.Ed. 421 (1886); it is not, however, the question presented for decision today.

The importance of the distinction between a court's exercise of jurisdiction over either a person or property that has been wrongfully seized by a private citizen, or even by a state law enforcement agent, on the one hand, and the attempted exercise of jurisdiction predicated on a seizure by federal officers acting beyond the authority conferred by treaty, on the other hand, is explained by Justice Brandeis in his opinion for the Court in Cook v. United States, 288 U.S. 102, 53 S.Ct. 305, 77 L.Ed. 641 (1933). That case involved a construction of a prohibition era treaty with Great Britain that authorized American agents to board certain British vessels to ascertain whether they were engaged in importing alcoholic beverages. A British vessel was boarded 11 1/2 miles off the coast of Massachusetts, found to be carrying unmanifested alcoholic beverages, and taken into port. The Collector of Customs assessed a penalty which he attempted to collect by means of libels against both the cargo and the seized vessel.

The Court held that the seizure was not authorized by the treaty because it occurred more than 10 miles off shore. The Government argued that the illegality of the seizure was immaterial because, as in Ker, the Court's jurisdiction was supported by possession even if the seizure was wrongful. Justice Brandeis acknowledged that the argument would succeed if the seizure had been made by a private party without authority to act for the Government, but that a different rule prevails when the Government itself lacks the power to seize. * * *

* * *

The Court's failure to differentiate between private abductions and official invasions of another sovereign's territory also accounts for its misplaced reliance on the 1935 proposal made by the Advisory Committee on Research in International Law. See ante, at 2194–2195, and n. 13. As the text of that proposal plainly states, it would have rejected the rule of the Ker case. The failure to adopt that recommendation does not speak to the issue the Court decides today. The Court's admittedly "shocking" disdain for customary and conventional international law principles, see ante, at 2195, is thus entirely unsupported by case law and commentary.

* * *

I suspect most courts throughout the civilized world will be deeply disturbed by the "monstrous" decision the Court announces today. For every Nation that has an interest in preserving the Rule of Law is affected, directly or indirectly, by a decision of this character. As Thomas Paine warned, an "avidity to punish is always dangerous to liberty" because it leads a Nation "to stretch, to misinterpret, and to misapply even the best of laws." To counter that tendency, he reminds us:

> "He that would make his own liberty secure must guard even his enemy from oppression; for if he violates this duty he establishes a precedent that will reach to himself."

I respectfully dissent.

Notes

1. It is a well-settled rule of international law that international agreements must be construed in accordance with good faith. See Chapter 7. Good faith is objective good faith; it imposes a standard of objective reasonableness. When a treaty is construed to accord with objective good faith, its provisions are supplemented by reference to the law, not to the subjective intentions of the parties. The pertinent question, in determining what the law requires, is not what the parties actually intended, but, instead, what they would have intended if they had thought of the possibility of including the lacking provision in the treaty. See Smit, Frustration of Contract: A Comparative Attempt at Consolidation, 58 Colum. L.Rev. 287 (1958). Is there any reasonable doubt that, if, at the time of the negotiation and conclusion of the Treaty, the parties had considered the possibility that either party would engage in abduction in violation of international law, they would have included in the Treaty a provision prohibiting this? Does the Court give any consideration to the possible implication of this prohibition on the basis of objective good faith rather than the parties' actual intentions?

2. The Court did not dispute that the forcible abduction of the accused from Mexico violated general international law. Should it also have considered whether the exercise of personal jurisdiction made possible by this forcible abduction constituted a violation of international law? Might the answer to that question depend on whether the abduction was effectuated by private persons or upon the direction of U.S. government officials? Is the notion of *male captus bene detentus* applicable in the latter case, which can more appropriately be described as *male captus male detentus*? See Glennon, State–Sponsored Abduction: A Comment on United States v. Alvarez–Machain, 86 A.J.I.L. 746 (1992).

3. Another question is whether the U.S. prosecutor and the Executive had the constitutional power to keep in custody and prosecute a person whose presence they had procured in violation of international law and elementary principles of proper governmental conduct. If they did not, would dismissal of the charges be the appropriate sanction? Cf. on this problem, M. Halberstam, In Defense of the Supreme Court Decision in Alvarez–Machain, 86 A.J.I.L. 736, 738–43 (1992).

4. Upon remand in the principal case, the district court granted an acquittal on the ground that the prosecution had failed to produce adequate proof of its charges. Thereafter, Alvarez–Machain brought a civil suit against the United States government and individuals involved in the abduction, including claims for "violation of the law of nations" within the meaning of the Alien Tort Claims Act,

28 U.S.C. § 1350. Although most of the claims were dismissed on defendants' motions in 1999, some issues remain to be resolved at trial. In its ruling on the motions, the district court concluded that state-sponsored transborder abductions do violate international law, as do arbitrary arrest and detention. See Murphy, Contemporary Practice of the United States Relating to International Law, 93 A.J.I.L. 892–894 (1999).

5. The decision in the principal case has generated widespread international criticisms. On November 23, 1994, the United States and Mexico signed a Treaty to Prohibit Transborder Abduction, requiring the prompt return of abducted persons and prohibiting the exercise of jurisdiction over them. The Treaty has not (yet) been ratified by the U.S. Senate. The Treaty may mark the emergence of a rule of customary international law prohibiting the exercise of jurisdiction over abducted persons. Would it make a difference whether the accused was abducted by private persons or agents of the prosecuting state? On these developments, see Jurisdiction Over Persons Abducted in Violation of International Law in the Aftermath of United States v. Alvarez–Machain, 5 U. Chi. L. Sch. Round Table 205 (1998).

6. For an instance in which FBI agents lured a person accused of hijacking a Jordanian airplane in Beirut with American passengers aboard onto a yacht in the Mediterranean with the promise of a drug deal and arrested him when the vessel entered international waters, see United States v. Fawaz Yunis, 924 F.2d 1086 (D.C.Cir.1991) (upholding the court's jurisdiction). If, in the principal case, the American anti-drug enforcement officers had lured the Mexican doctor to the United States, would international law have been violated? Would such a stratagem have been implicitly prohibited by the extradition treaty? On the Yunis arrest and related matters, see the series of articles by Lowenfeld, U.S. Law Enforcement Abroad, 83 A.J.I.L 880 (1989), 84 A.J.I.L. 444 (1990), and 84 A.J.I.L. 712 (1990).

Chapter 14

IMMUNITY FROM JURISDICTION

SECTION 1. JURISDICTIONAL IMMUNITIES OF FOREIGN STATES

Under international law, states and other international persons enjoy certain immunities from the exercise of jurisdiction. In addition, such immunities may be granted by municipal law. Of course, when an immunity exists under international law, its denial by municipal law may create a claim for violation of international law. But nothing prevents a state from granting more extensive immunities than those granted by international law. In states that do not recognize the supremacy of international law over national law, such as the United States, national law may grant a lesser measure of immunity than that prescribed by international law.

Consequently, in determining the jurisdictional immunities to which an international legal person is entitled, both international and municipal law must be studied. This is a circumstance worth noting, because both the United States and the United Kingdom have enacted statutes on this subject and other states are following their example.

Since jurisdiction may be exercised on the legislative, the judicial, and the enforcement level, immunities from jurisdiction may also operate on these three levels. However, traditionally, primary consideration has been given to immunity from judicial and enforcement jurisdiction.

Originally, jurisdictional immunities were regarded as being absolute. A state could invoke them, irrespective of the nature of its sovereign activities. This absolute form of immunity is based on the conception that all states are equal and that no one state may exercise authority over any other. It is aptly described by Chief Justice Marshall in The Schooner Exchange v. McFaddon, p. 1200 infra.

As states have become involved increasingly in commercial activities, the pressures towards limiting immunity have grown apace. As a consequence, the absolute approach to jurisdictional immunities has been forced into broad retreat. However, some states still embrace it, although their espousal of the absolute doctrine is frequently formal rather than substantive. While proclaiming that the absolute doctrine is part of prevailing international law, most of these countries have agreed that their instrumentalities engaged in commercial activities may be sued in foreign courts.

At present, a pragmatic functional approach has largely taken the place of the conceptual absolute one. Under this functional approach, the problems attendant upon exercising jurisdiction over a foreign state are balanced against the propriety of denying persons the benefits of exercising jurisdiction that they would enjoy if their claims were asserted against a private person rather than a foreign state. This functional approach has led to the emergence of a restrictive or relative doctrine. This restrictive doctrine denies immunity claimed by a foreign state in regard to an activity or property that is commercial rather than public or, as it is often expressed, that belongs to the sphere of *ius gestionis* rather than that of *ius imperii.* This development has greatly enhanced the significance of distinguishing between the three types of jurisdiction against which a plea of immunity is advanced. For since the factual premises for the exercise of these types of jurisdiction may differ, the propriety of a claim of immunity may depend on the particular form of jurisdiction from the exercise of which immunity is sought.

Problems of jurisdictional immunities arise when an action is brought in the tribunals of one state against another state or its instrumentalities or property. When such an action is brought, the first question that arises is whether the local tribunal has judicial jurisdiction over the foreign state. This question is one of immunity from judicial jurisdiction. The second question that arises is whether the forum has the authority to evaluate the foreign actor's conduct under the rules of law applicable to such conduct. This raises a question of immunity from legislative jurisdiction. This question has received scant attention. The third question that arises is when a foreign state or its property is immune from enforcement measures. This is a question of immunity from jurisdiction to enforce.

The efforts to restrict immunity from judicial jurisdiction are increasingly taking legislative form. The United States enacted the Foreign Sovereign Immunities Act (FSIA) in 1976, 90 Stat. 2891, 28 U.S.C.A. §§ 1330, 1332, 1391, 1441, 1602–1611. The FSIA was amended in 1988, 1996, 1998 and 2000. The 1988 amendments added provisions dealing with arbitration and admiralty cases, 28 U.S.C.A. §§ 1605(a)(6), 1605(b)-(d). Another amendment followed in 1996, which added Section 1605(a)(7) providing for non-immunity of foreign states that have been designated as state sponsors of terrorism, in specified actions for personal injury or death caused by torture, extrajudicial killing, aircraft sabotage, and hostage-taking. The 1998 and 2000 amendments dealt with execution of judgments under the new 1996 provision. See pp. 1231–1242. The United Kingdom enacted its State Immunity Act in 1978, 26 & 27 Eliz. 2, Ch. 33, 17 I.L.M. 1123. Canada enacted its Act to Provide for State Immunity in Canadian courts in 1982, 29, 30 & 31 Eliz. 2, Ch. 93, 21 I.L.M. 798 (1982). Australia, Pakistan, Singapore, and South Africa have enacted similar statutes. See U.N.Leg. Ser. U.N.Doc. ST/LEG/SER.B/20 (1982).

All of the statutes enacted thus far embrace a restrictive view of immunity. The provisions of the Foreign Sovereign Immunities Act of 1976 are treated in some detail below. On the U.K. State Immunity Act 1978, see Mann, The State Immunity Act 1978, 50 B.Y.I.L. 43 (1981); Bud, The State Immunity Act of 1978: An English Update, 13 Int. Law. 619 (1979); Delaume, The State Immunity Act of the United Kingdom, 73 A.J.I.L. 185 (1979); Shaw, The State Immunity Act of 1978, 128 N.L.J. 1136 (1978); Higgins, Recent Developments in the Law of Sovereign Immunity of the United Kingdom, 71

A.J.I.L. 423 (1977); Fox, Enforcement Jurisdiction, Foreign State Property and Diplomatic Immunity, 34 I.C.L.Q. 115 (1985); Davidson, State Immunity in the English Courts: A Lingering Death, 33 N.Ir. Legal Q. 171 (1982); Fox, State Immunity: The House of Lords Decision in I Congreso del Partido, 88 Law A.Rev. 94 (1982); Marasinghe, The Modern Law of Sovereign Immunity, 54 Mod. L.Rev. 664 (1991). On the Canadian Act, see Molot & Jewett, The State Immunity Act of Canada, 20 Can.Y.Int. L. 79 (1982); Jewett & Molot, State Immunity Act—Basic Principles, 61 Can. B.Rev. 843 (1983). On sovereign immunity policy in New Zealand, see Hastings, Sovereign Immunity in New Zealand, 1990 N.Z.L.J. 214 (1990).

The Council of Europe has developed a European Convention on State Immunity and Additional Protocol, Basel, May 16, 1972, 11 I.L.M. 470 (1972). This Convention enumerates the specific instances in which a contracting state is not immune from jurisdiction in the courts of another contracting state. These include the case in which a state "has on the territory of the State of the forum an office, agency or other establishment through which it engages, in the same manner as a private person, in an industrial, commercial or financial activity, and the proceedings relate to that activity" (Art. 7). On this Convention, see Sinclair, The European Convention on State Immunity, 22 I.C.L.Q. 254 (1973). See also Dellapenna, Foreign State Immunity in Europe, 5 N.Y.Int'l L.R. 51 (1992).

A general multilateral convention on sovereign immunity does not yet exist. The International Law Commission began preparing draft articles on the jurisdictional immunities of states and their property in 1978 and completed the first reading of the draft articles in 1986. See Report of the I.L.C., U.N. GAOR, 41st Sess., Supp. (No. 10) at 9–24, U.N. Doc. A/41/10 (1986), reprinted in [1986] 2. Y.B.Int'l L.Comm'n, U.N. Doc. A/CN.4/1986/Add.1 (Part 2); see also Greig, Specific Exceptions to Immunity Under the International Law Commission's Draft Articles, 38 I.C.L.Q. 560 (1989); Greig, Forum State Jurisdiction and Sovereign Immunity Under the International Law Commission's Draft Articles, 38 I.C.L.Q. 243 (1989); Schreuer, State Immunity: Some Recent Developments (1988). The Commission concluded the second reading of the draft articles in 1991. Report of the International Law Commission, U.N. GAOR, 46th Sess., Supp. (No. 10) at 11, U.N. Doc. A/46/10 (1991); see also 30 I.L.M. 1554 (1991). In 1998, the U.N. General Assembly called for a working group to consider recent developments of state practice and legislation and any other factors related to the issue since the adoption of the draft articles. G.A. Res. 53/98 (1998). See Report of the I.L.C., U.N. GAOR, 54th Sess., Supp. (No. 10) at 311–313, U.N. Doc. A/54/10 (1999), and Report of the Working Group on Jurisdictional Immunities of States and their Property, reprinted as an annex to the I.L.C.'s 1999 report, in U.N. Doc. A/54/10 at pp. 360–419. The main issues still under debate include: (1) the concept of a state for purposes of immunity (in particular in the case of federal states); (2) criteria for determining the commercial character of a contract or transaction (compare p. 1208 below on the "nature" and "purpose" tests); (3) the concept of a state enterprise or other entity in relation to commercial transactions (that is, the separate legal identity of such enterprises); (4) contracts of employment, especially for local employees; and (5) measures of constraint against state property (attachments and execution). The Commission's working group has also taken note that developments of the late 1990s may warrant revisiting the question of immunity in cases involving gross violations of human rights norms having the character of *jus cogens*. See ibid. at pp. 414–416. These developments include the *Pinochet* case, p. 1276 infra, and the U.S. FSIA amendments affecting certain claims for torture, extrajudicial killing, aircraft sabotage or hostage-taking. See p. 1231.

The main trend from the nineteenth through the twentieth and twenty-first centuries has been the gradual displacement of the absolute theory of sovereign immunity with a restrictive view.

A. THE ABSOLUTE FORM OF SOVEREIGN IMMUNITY

THE SCHOONER EXCHANGE v. McFADDON

Supreme Court of the United States, 1812.
11 U.S. (7 Cranch) 116, 3 LEd. 287.

[A libel was brought against the schooner Exchange by two American citizens who claimed that they owned and were entitled to possession of the ship. They alleged that the vessel had been seized on the high seas in 1810 by forces acting on behalf of the Emperor of France and that no prize court of competent jurisdiction had pronounced judgment against the vessel. No one appeared for the vessel, but the United States Attorney for Pennsylvania appeared on behalf of the United States Government to state that the United States and France were at peace, that a public ship (known as the Balaou) of the Emperor of France had been compelled by bad weather to enter the port of Philadelphia, and was prevented from leaving by the process of the court. The United States Attorney stated that, even if the vessel had in fact been wrongfully seized from the libellants, property therein had passed to the Emperor of France. It was therefore requested that the libel be dismissed with costs and the vessel released. The District Court dismissed the libel, the Circuit Court reversed (4 Hall's L.J. 232), and the United States Attorney appealed to the Supreme Court.]

MARSHALL, C.J.: * * * The jurisdiction of the nation within its own territory is necessarily exclusive and absolute. It is susceptible of no limitation not imposed by itself. * * *

This full and absolute territorial jurisdiction being alike the attribute of every sovereign * * * would not seem to contemplate foreign sovereigns nor their sovereign rights as its objects. One sovereign being in no respect amenable to another; and being bound by obligations of the highest character not to degrade the dignity of his nation, by placing himself or its sovereign rights within the jurisdiction of another, can be supposed to enter a foreign territory only under an express license, or in the confidence that the immunities belonging to his independent sovereign station, though not expressly stipulated, are reserved by implication, and will be extended to him.

This perfect equality and absolute independence of sovereigns, and this common interest impelling them to mutual intercourse, and an interchange of good offices with each other, have given rise to a class of cases in which every sovereign is understood to waive the exercise of a part of that complete exclusive territorial jurisdiction, which has been stated to be the attribute of every nation.

1st. One of these is admitted to be the exemption of the person of the sovereign from arrest or detention within a foreign territory. * * *

2d. A second case, standing on the same principles with the first, is the immunity which all civilized nations allow to foreign ministers. * * *

3d. A third case in which a sovereign is understood to cede a portion of his territorial jurisdiction is, where he allows the troops of a foreign prince to pass through his dominions. * * *

[The Court concluded that the territorial sovereign's license to foreign armies must be express, and not merely implied, but that a different rule applied in the case of foreign ships.] * * * If there be no prohibition, the ports of a friendly nation are considered as open to the public ships of all powers with whom it is at peace, and they are supposed to enter such ports and to remain in them while allowed to remain, under the protection of the government of the place. * * *

When private individuals of one nation spread themselves through another as business or caprice may direct, mingling indiscriminately with the inhabitants of that other, or when merchant vessels enter for the purposes of trade, it would be obviously inconvenient and dangerous to society, and would subject the laws to continual infraction, and the government to degradation, if such individuals or merchants did not owe temporary and local allegiance, and were not amenable to the jurisdiction of the country. * * *

But in all respects different is the situation of a public armed ship. She constitutes a part of the military force of her nation; acts under the immediate and direct command of the sovereign; is employed by him in national objects. He has many and powerful motives for preventing those objects from being defeated by the interference of a foreign state. Such interference cannot take place without affecting his power and his dignity. The implied license therefore under which such vessel enters a friendly port, may reasonably be construed, and it seems to the Court, ought to be construed, as containing an exemption from the jurisdiction of the sovereign, within whose territory she claims the rights of hospitality.

Upon these principles, by the unanimous consent of nations, a foreigner is amenable to the laws of the place; but certainly in practice, nations have not yet asserted their jurisdiction over the public armed ships of a foreign sovereign entering a port open for their reception.

Bynkershoek, a jurist of great reputation, has indeed maintained that the property of a foreign sovereign is not distinguishable by any legal exemption from the property of an ordinary individual, and has quoted several cases in which courts have exercised jurisdiction over causes in which a foreign sovereign was made a party defendant.

Without indicating any opinion on this question, it may safely be affirmed, that there is a manifest distinction between the private property of the person who happens to be a prince, and that military force which supports the sovereign power, and maintains the dignity and the independence of a nation. A prince, by acquiring private property in a foreign country, may possibly be considered as subjecting that property to the territorial jurisdiction; he may be considered as so far laying down the prince, and assuming the character of a private individual; but this he cannot be presumed to do with respect to any portion of that armed force, which upholds his crown, and the nation he is entrusted to govern. * * *

It seems then to the Court, to be a principle of public law, that national ships of war, entering the port of a friendly power open for their reception, are to be considered as exempted by the consent of that power from its jurisdiction.

* * *

The arguments in favor of this opinion which have been drawn from the general inability of the judicial power to enforce its decisions in cases of this description, from the consideration, that the sovereign power of the nation is alone competent to avenge wrongs committed by a sovereign, that the questions to which such wrongs give birth are rather questions of policy than of law, that they are for diplomatic, rather than legal discussion, are of great weight, and merit serious attention. But the argument has already been drawn to a length, which forbids a particular examination of these points. * * *

If the preceding reasoning be correct, the Exchange, being a public armed ship, in the service of a foreign sovereign, with whom the government of the United States is at peace, and having entered an American port open for her reception, on the terms on which ships of war are generally permitted to enter the ports of a friendly power, must be considered as having come into the American territory, under an implied promise, that while necessarily within it, and demeaning herself in a friendly manner, she should be exempt from the jurisdiction of the country. * * *

[Judgment of the Circuit Court reversed, and judgment of the District Court, dismissing the libel, affirmed.]

Notes

1. Early attempts to limit the scope of sovereign immunity to judicial jurisdiction came in cases involving claims arising from the operation of commercial vessels by foreign governments. However, in Berizzi Bros. Co. v. S.S. Pesaro, 271 U.S. 562, 46 S.Ct. 611, 70 L.Ed. 1088 (1926), the Supreme Court rejected the argument, accepted in a prior stage of the case by the District Court, that Italy was not entitled to immunity in an *in rem* proceeding brought to enforce a claim for cargo damage against a merchant vessel owned and operated by Italy.

2. In 1938, Lord Maugham, in Compania Naviera Vascongada v. S.S. Cristina, [1938] A.C. 485, 521–22, commented:

> Half a century ago foreign Governments very seldom embarked in trade with ordinary ships, though they not infrequently owned vessels destined for public uses, and in particular hospital vessels, supply ships, and surveying or exploring vessels. There were doubtless very strong reasons for extending the privilege long possessed by ships of war to public ships of the nature mentioned; but there has been a very large development of State-owned commercial ships since the Great War, and the question whether the immunity should continue to be given to ordinary trading ships has become acute. Is it consistent with sovereign dignity to acquire a tramp steamer and to compete with ordinary shippers and ship-owners in the markets of the world? Doing so, is it consistent to set up the immunity of a sovereign if, owing to the

want of skill of captain and crew, serious damage is caused to the ship of another country? Is it also consistent to refuse to permit proceedings to enforce a right of salvage in respect of services rendered, perhaps at great risk, by the vessel of another country? Is there justice or equity, or for that matter is international comity being followed, in permitting a foreign Government, while insisting on its own right of indemnity [*sic*], to bring actions in rem or in personam against our own nationals?

My Lords, I am far from relying merely on my own opinion as to the absurdity of the position which our Courts are in if they must continue to disclaim jurisdiction in relation to commercial ships owned by foreign Governments. The matter has been considered over and over again of late years by foreign jurists, by English lawyers, and by business men, and with practical unanimity they are of opinion that, if Governments or corporations formed by them choose to navigate and trade as shipowners, they ought to submit to the same legal remedies and actions as any other shipowner. This was the effect of the various resolutions of the Conference of London of 1922, of the conference of Gothenburg of 1923 and of the Genoa Conference of 1925. Three Conferences not being deemed sufficient, there was yet another in Brussels in the year 1926. It was attended by Great Britain, France, Germany, Italy, Spain, Holland, Belgium, Poland, Japan and a number of other countries. The United States explained their absence by the statement that they had already given effect to the wish for uniformity in the laws relating to State-owned ships by the Public Vessels Act, 1925 (1925 c. 428). The Brussels Conference was unanimously in favour of the view that in times of peace there should be no immunity as regards State-owned ships engaged in commerce; and the resolution was ratified by Germany, Italy, Holland, Belgium, Estonia, Poland, Brazil and other countries, but not so far by Great Britain. (Oppenheim, International Law, 5th ed., vol. i., p. 670.)

3. The Brussels Convention on the Unification of Certain Rules Relating to Immunity of State-owned Vessels, signed April 10, 1926, 176 L.N.T.S. 199, provides in Article 1 that "Seagoing vessels owned or operated by States, cargoes owned by them, and cargoes and passengers carried on Government vessels, and the States owning or operating such vessels, or owning such cargoes, are subject in respect of claims relating to the operation of such vessels or the carriage of such cargoes to the same rules of liability and to the same obligations as those applicable to private vessels, cargoes and equipments." The same procedures are to be available to enforce such liabilities and obligations as would be available in the case of privately owned merchant vessels and cargoes and their owners. These provisions do not apply, however, to warships and other vessels "used at the time a cause of action arises exclusively on Governmental and noncommercial service," nor shall such vessels be subject to seizure, attachment or other *in rem* proceedings. When such vessels are involved in controversies relating to collision, salvage, general average, repairs, supplies, or other contracts relating to the vessel, the claimant is entitled to institute proceedings in the courts of the state owning or operating the vessel, without that state being permitted to avail itself of its immunity. A supplementary protocol, signed May 24, 1934, prohibits attachment or seizure of vessels chartered by Governments for non-commercial service, without reference to the status of the vessel at the time the cause of action arose. In accordance with Article 7, the treaty ceased to have effect between belligerent states during World War II; it came into renewed force between Germany and most of the Allied Powers on November 1, 1953. Poland, which had ratified in 1936, denounced the Convention on March 17, 1952, and rejoined on July 16,

1976. Romania, which had joined on August 4, 1937, denounced on September 21, 1959. See Knauth's Benedict on Admiralty, Vol. 6A, Doc. 8–4, Sec. 8–38, 39 (7th ed. 1958 and 1988 Supp.), and [1976] Int'l Mar. Committee Documentation 235, 352, and succeeding years. The convention applies only as between parties to it; these were, as of 2000, Argentina, Belgium, Brazil, Chile, Cyprus, Denmark, Egypt, Estonia, France, Germany, Greece, Hungary, Italy, Libya, Luxembourg, Madagascar, Netherlands, Norway, Poland, Portugal, Somalia, Surinam, Sweden, Switzerland, Syrian Arab Republic, Turkey, United Kingdom, Uruguay, Zaire. As of 2000, the United States was still not a party to the Convention.

4. The Soviet Union and other communist states embraced a doctrine of absolute immunity premised on the notion that a state's immunity is the natural consequence of its sovereignty. To accommodate the needs of practice, the Soviet Union concluded a large number of bilateral treaties under which its trade delegations in foreign countries were subject to local jurisdiction with respect to their commercial activities.

In the United States, the problem was addressed by the Soviet Union's organizing a corporation formed under local law to conduct its commercial activities. See, generally, Triska & Slusser, The Theory, Law and Policy of Soviet Treaties, 324–33 (1962), and Sucharitkul, State Immunities and Trading Activities in International Law 152–61 (1959). Now that the formerly communist states have opted for a more market-oriented approach, they are likewise more inclined to the restrictive approach to sovereign immunity.

Between 1948 and 1958, the United States concluded fourteen treaties requiring that each party waive sovereign immunity for state-controlled enterprises engaged in commercial activities. The practice to include a provision to this effect was discontinued in 1958. See Setser, the Immunity Waiver for State–Controlled Business Enterprises in United States Commercial Treaties, 55 A.S.I.L. Proc. 89 (1961).

B. THE RESTRICTIVE FORM OF SOVEREIGN IMMUNITY

1. The "Commercial" Exception

LETTER OF ACTING LEGAL ADVISER, JACK B. TATE, TO DEPARTMENT OF JUSTICE, MAY 19, 1952

26 Dep't State Bull. 984 (1952).

The Department of State has for some time had under consideration the question whether the practice of the Government in granting immunity from suit to foreign governments made parties defendant in the courts of the United States without their consent should not be changed. The Department has now reached the conclusion that such immunity should no longer be granted in certain types of cases. In view of the obvious interest of your Department in this matter I should like to point out briefly some of the facts which influenced the Department's decision.

A study of the law of sovereign immunity reveals the existence of two conflicting concepts of sovereign immunity, each widely held and firmly established. According to the classical or absolute theory of sovereign immunity, a sovereign cannot, without his consent, be made a respondent in the courts of another sovereign. According to the newer or restrictive theory of sovereign immunity, the immunity of the sovereign is recognized with regard to sovereign or public acts *(jure imperii)* of a state, but not with respect to private acts *(jure gestionis)*. There is agreement by proponents of both theories, supported by practice, that sovereign immunity should not be claimed or granted in actions with respect to real property (diplomatic and perhaps consular property excepted) or with respect to the disposition of the property of a deceased person even though a foreign sovereign is the beneficiary.

The classical or virtually absolute theory of sovereign immunity has generally been followed by the courts of the United States, the British Commonwealth, Czechoslovakia, Estonia, and probably Poland.

The decisions of the courts of Brazil, Chile, China, Hungary, Japan, Luxembourg, Norway, and Portugal may be deemed to support the classical theory of immunity if one or at most two old decisions anterior to the development of the restrictive theory may be considered sufficient on which to base a conclusion.

The position of the Netherlands, Sweden, and Argentina is less clear since although immunity has been granted in recent cases coming before the courts of those countries, the facts were such that immunity would have been granted under either the absolute or restrictive theory. However, constant references by the courts of these three countries to the distinction between public and private acts of the state, even though the distinction was not involved in the result of the case, may indicate an intention to leave the way open for a possible application of the restrictive theory of immunity if and when the occasion presents itself.

A trend to the restrictive theory is already evident in the Netherlands where the lower courts have started to apply that theory following a Supreme Court decision to the effect that immunity would have been applicable in the case under consideration under either theory.

The German courts, after a period of hesitation at the end of the nineteenth century have held to the classical theory, but it should be noted that the refusal of the Supreme Court in 1921 to yield to pressure by the lower courts for the newer theory was based on the view that that theory had not yet developed sufficiently to justify a change. In view of the growth of the restrictive theory since that time the German courts might take a different view today.

The newer or restrictive theory of sovereign immunity has always been supported by the courts of Belgium and Italy. It was adopted in turn by the courts of Egypt and of Switzerland. In addition, the courts of France, Austria, and Greece, which were traditionally supporters of the classical theory, reversed their position in the 20's to embrace the restrictive theory. Rumania, Peru, and possibly Denmark also appear to follow this theory.

Furthermore, it should be observed that in most of the countries still following the classical theory there is a school of influential writers favoring the restrictive theory and the views of writers, at least in civil law countries, are a major factor in the development of the law. Moreover, the leanings of the lower courts in civil law countries are more significant in shaping the law than they are in common law countries where the rule of precedent prevails and the trend in these lower courts is to the restrictive theory.

Of related interest to this question is the fact that ten of the thirteen countries which have been classified above as supporters of the classical theory have ratified the Brussels Convention of 1926 under which immunity for government owned merchant vessels is waived. In addition, the United States which is not a party to the Convention, some years ago announced and has since followed, a policy of not claiming immunity for its public owned or operated merchant vessels. Keeping in mind the importance played by cases involving public vessels in the field of sovereign immunity, it is thus noteworthy that these ten countries (Brazil, Chile, Estonia, Germany, Hungary, Netherlands, Norway, Poland, Portugal, Sweden) and the United States have already relinquished by treaty or in practice an important part of the immunity which they claim under the classical theory.

It is thus evident that with the possible exception of the United Kingdom little support has been found except on the part of the Soviet Union and its satellites for continued full acceptance of the absolute theory of sovereign immunity. There are evidences that British authorities are aware of its deficiencies and ready for a change. The reasons which obviously motivate state trading countries in adhering the theory with perhaps increasing rigidity are most persuasive that the United States should change its policy. Furthermore, the granting of sovereign immunity to foreign governments in the courts of the United States is most inconsistent with the action of the Government of the United States in subjecting itself to suit in these same courts in both contract and tort and with its long established policy of not claiming immunity in foreign jurisdictions for its merchant vessels. Finally, the Department feels that the widespread and increasing practice on the part of governments of engaging in commercial activities makes necessary a practice which will enable persons doing business with them to have their rights determined in the courts. For these reasons it will hereafter be the Department's policy to follow the restrictive theory of sovereign immunity in the consideration of requests of foreign governments for a grant of sovereign immunity.

It is realized that a shift in policy by the executive cannot control the courts but it is felt that the courts are less likely to allow a plea of sovereign immunity where the executive has declined to do so. There have been indications that at least some Justices of the Supreme Court feel that in this matter courts should follow the branch of the Government charged with responsibility for the conduct of foreign relations.

In order that your Department, which is charged with representing the interests of the Government before the courts, may be adequately informed it will be the Department's practice to advise you of all requests by foreign governments for the grant of immunity from suit and of the Department's action thereon.

Notes

1. For a survey of cases in a variety of jurisdictions showing development of the restrictive theory from the mid-nineteenth to the mid-twentieth century, as

well as analysis of treaties and the opinions of scholars, see the decision of the Supreme Court of Austria in Dralle v. Republic of Czechoslovakia, [1950] I.L.R. 155. The Austrian court concluded that the classic (absolute) doctrine of immunity had lost its meaning in view of the growing commercial activities of states.

2. A private firm in Cologne sued the Empire of Iran in order to obtain payment of a bill for 292 DM ($73) rendered to the latter for repairs made on the heating system in the Iranian Embassy at the request of the Ambassador. The question of sovereign immunity was raised before the local court, which decided that the defendant, as a sovereign state, was immune under international law from German jurisdiction. The plaintiff appealed from this decision, and the case was referred to the Supreme Constitutional Court of the Federal Republic of Germany, which, after a comprehensive review of the authorities, reversed, stating:

> A summary evaluation of jurisprudence, of rules contained in treaties, of attempts at codification, and of the teachings of publicists, shows that unlimited state immunity can no longer be regarded as a rule of customary international law. One must agree with the Austrian Supreme Court, as it concluded in its decision of May 10, 1950 [the *Dralle* case] * * * "that it can no longer be said that, according to established international law, so-called acta gestionis are excluded from municipal jurisdiction." * * * Decision of April 30, 1963, 16 BVerfG 27, 16 N.J.W. 1732, 19 L.Z. 171.

3. In 1960, the Asian–African Legal Consultative Committee received the final report of the Committee on Immunity of States in Respect of Commercial and Other Transactions of a Private Character, in which India, Burma, Ceylon, Indonesia, Japan, Iraq, and the United Arab Republic had been represented. A delegation from Pakistan attended the 1960 session, as did an observer from Iran. The following are excerpts from the final report:

> All the delegations except that of Indonesia were of the view that a distinction should be made between different types of state activity and immunity to foreign states should not be granted in respect of their activities which may be called commercial or of private nature. The Indonesian delegate, however, adhered to the view that immunity should continue to be granted to all the activities of the foreign state irrespective of their nature provided they were carried on by the government itself. * * *
>
> The Committee having taken the view of all the delegations into consideration decided to recommend as follows: * * * (ii) A State which enters into transactions of a commercial or private character, ought not to raise the plea of sovereign immunity if sued in the courts of a foreign state in respect of such transactions. If the plea of immunity is raised it should not be admissible to deprive the jurisdiction of the Domestic Courts.
>
> * * * The Delegation of Indonesia dissented on the recommendation contained in clause (ii) which was agreed upon by all other Delegations.

The Indonesian Government summarized its views as follows:

> States should be immune from legal proceedings before Foreign Courts for all their acts, regardless of whether such acts are of a public or private character. * * *

Asian–African Legal Consultative Committee, Third Session, Colombo, 1960 (Secretariat of the Committee, New Delhi, India, n.d.), 66–69, 81.

4. On the restrictions upon sovereign immunity recognized by the 1991 Draft Articles of the International Law Commission, see 30 I.L.M. 1554 (1991).

FOREIGN SOVEREIGN IMMUNITIES ACT OF 1976

28 U.S.C.A. § 1602.

The Congress finds that the determination by United States courts of the claims of foreign states to immunity from the jurisdiction of such courts would serve the interests of justice and would protect the rights of both foreign states and litigants in United States courts. Under international law, states are not immune from the jurisdiction of foreign courts insofar as their commercial activities are concerned, and their commercial property may be levied upon for the satisfaction of judgments rendered against them in connection with their commercial activities. Claims of foreign states to immunity should henceforth be decided by courts of the United States and of the States in conformity with the principles set forth in this chapter.

Notes

1. What criteria determine whether the foreign state's activity or property is commercial rather than public? Are they criteria of international law, the law of the forum state, or the law of the foreign state? See also the Decision of April 30, 1963 of the German Constitutional Court, 16 BVerfG 63, 19 L.Z 175, p. 1207 supra (national law may be used to draw the distinction, but may not deviate from the views of the preponderance of states as to what belongs to the region of state authority in its narrow and proper sense).

2. In the United States, whether a foreign state's act is commercial is determined by reference to the Foreign Sovereign Immunities Act of 1976 (FSIA). Prior to the enactment of the FSIA, some argued that the purpose of the foreign state's act was determinative, while others looked at the nature of the act. For a discussion, see Victory Transport, Inc. v. Comisaria General de Abastecimientos y Transportes, 336 F.2d 354 (2d Cir.1964), cert. denied, 381 U.S. 934, 85 S.Ct. 1763, 14 L.Ed.2d 698 (1965). The Foreign Sovereign Immunities Act of 1976, 28 U.S.C.A. § 1603(d), provides the following definition:

> A "commercial activity" means either a regular course of commercial conduct or a particular commercial transaction or act. The commercial character of an activity shall be determined by reference to the nature of the course of conduct or particular transaction or act, rather than by reference to its purpose.

The Harvard Research in International Law, Competence of Courts in Regard to Foreign States, Art. 11, 25 A.J.I.L.Supp. 451, 597, provides that a state engages in a commercial activity when it "engages in an * * * enterprise in which private persons may engage." The Restatement (Third) § 451 adopts the latter criterion ("claims arising out of activities of the kind that may be carried on by private persons"). Which of these formulations is the most appropriate?

3. A number of authorities have approached the problem by seeking to determine what is political and considering all other activity commercial. See *Victory Transport,* Note 2, supra. The German Supreme Constitutional Court in its decision of April 30, 1963, p. 1207 supra, in which a private firm sued the Empire of Iran for non-payment of a bill allegedly incurred in the repair of the

Iranian Embassy's heating system, said: "It is obvious that the conclusion of such a contract does not fall within the core of the state's political authority." 16 BVerfG at 64, 19 L.Z. at 175. Compare the principle suggested by Lalive, L'Immunité de Juridiction des Etats et des Organisations Internationales, 84 Rec. des Cours 205, 285 (1953–III): "The foreign state enjoys jurisdictional immunity only for certain acts of public authority."

4. In 1960, the United States claimed immunity through diplomatic channels in a suit brought in Italy by an Italian company that had built sewers for the U.S. Logistic Command in Italy on the ground that the case arose from activity of the U.S. Government in its capacity as a sovereign. The Italian Court of Cassation upheld the decision below denying immunity on the ground that the transaction was of a private law nature even though done for a military purpose. Governo degli Stati Uniti di America c. Soc. I.R.S.A., [1963] Foro Ital. 1405, 47 Revista de Diritto Internazionale 484 (May 13, 1963).

The State Department, however, took the following position in 1962 with respect to a claim of immunity on behalf of the Industrial Bank of the Argentine Republic:

> [T]he activities for the defendant Bank in extending credits to private persons for the purpose of inducing them to invest in the economy of Argentina by bringing and operating their industrial plants there, importing raw materials for use therein, and constructing a plant to furnish hydroelectric power for such plants, even though the power plant was to be owned by the Government of Argentina, are all acts of a private nature *(jure gestionis)* for which the Bank is not entitled to claim sovereign immunity regardless of its relationship to the Government of Argentina. It may be assumed that all acts of a government whether of a public *(jure imperii)* or private nature *(jure gestionis)* are done for some public purpose. It is obvious, however, that this cannot be the criterion else the restrictive theory of sovereign immunity would be meaningless. It is the nature of the activity engaged in by the Government which is controlling and not whether it serves some public policy.

Letter to Argentine Embassy, dated April 19, 1962, concerning Mirabella v. Banco Industrial De La Republica Argentina, 38 Misc.2d 128, 237 N.Y.S.2d 499 (1963).

REPUBLIC OF ARGENTINA v. WELTOVER, INC.

Supreme Court of the United States, 1992.
504 U.S. 607, 112 S.Ct. 2160, 119 L.Ed.2d 394 (footnotes omitted).

JUSTICE SCALIA delivered the opinion of the Court.

This case requires us to decide whether the Republic of Argentina's default on certain bonds issued as part of a plan to stabilize its currency was an act taken "in connection with a commercial activity" that had a "direct effect in the United States" so as to subject Argentina to suit in an American court under the Foreign Sovereign Immunities Act of 1976, 28 U.S.C. § 1602 et seq.

I

Since Argentina's currency is not one of the mediums of exchange accepted on the international market, Argentine businesses engaging in foreign transactions must pay in U.S. dollars or some other internationally accepted currency. In the recent past, it was difficult for Argentine borrowers to obtain such funds, principally because of the instability of the Argentine currency. To address these problems, petitioners, the Republic of Argentina and its central bank, Banco Central (collectively Argentina), in 1981 instituted a foreign exchange insurance contract program (FEIC), under which Argentina effectively agreed to assume the risk of currency depreciation in cross-border transactions involving Argentine borrowers. This was accomplished by Argentina's agreeing to sell to domestic borrowers, in exchange for a contractually predetermined amount of local currency, the necessary U.S. dollars to repay their foreign debts when they matured, irrespective of intervening devaluations.

Unfortunately, Argentina did not possess sufficient reserves of U.S. dollars to cover the FEIC contracts as they became due in 1982. The Argentine government thereupon adopted certain emergency measures, including refinancing of the FEIC-backed debts by issuing to the creditors government bonds. These bonds, called "Bonods," provide for payment of interest and principal in U.S. dollars; payment may be made through transfer on the London, Frankfurt, Zurich, or New York market, at the election of the creditor. Under this refinancing program, the foreign creditor had the option of either accepting the Bonods in satisfaction of the initial debt, thereby substituting the Argentine government for the private debtor, or maintaining the debtor/creditor relationship with the private borrower and accepting the Argentine government as guarantor.

When the Bonods began to mature in May 1986, Argentina concluded that it lacked sufficient foreign exchange to retire them. Pursuant to a Presidential Decree, Argentina unilaterally extended the time for payment, and offered bondholders substitute instruments as a means of rescheduling the debts. Respondents, two Panamanian corporations and a Swiss bank who hold, collectively, $1.3 million of Bonods, refused to accept the rescheduling, and insisted on full payment, specifying New York as the place where payment should be made. Argentina did not pay, and respondents then brought this breach-of-contract action in the United States District Court for the Southern District of New York, relying on the Foreign Sovereign Immunities Act of 1976 as the basis for jurisdiction. Petitioners moved to dismiss for lack of subject-matter jurisdiction, lack of personal jurisdiction, and *forum non conveniens.* * * *

II

The Foreign Sovereign Immunities Act of 1976, 28 U.S.C. § 1602 *et seq.* (FSIA), establishes a comprehensive framework for determining whether a court in this country, state or federal, may exercise jurisdiction over a foreign state. Under the Act, a "foreign state *shall* be immune from the jurisdiction of the courts of the United States and of the States" unless one of several statutorily defined exceptions applies. § 1604 (emphasis added). The FSIA thus provides the "sole basis" for obtaining jurisdiction over a foreign sovereign in the United States. See *Argentine Republic v. Amerada Hess Shipping Corp.,* 488 U.S. 428, 434–439, 109 S.Ct. 683, 688–690, 102 L.Ed.2d 818 (1989). The most significant of the FSIA's exceptions—and the one at issue in this case—is the "commercial" exception of § 1605(a)(2), which provides that a foreign state is not immune from suit in any case "in which the action is based upon a commercial activity carried on in the United States by the foreign state; or upon an act performed in the United States in connection with a commercial activity of the foreign state elsewhere; or upon an act outside the territory of the United States in connection with a commercial activity of the foreign state elsewhere and that act causes a direct effect in the United States." § 1605(a)(2).

In the proceedings below, respondents relied only on the third clause of § 1605(a)(2) to establish jurisdiction, 941 F.2d, at 149, and our analysis is therefore limited to considering whether this lawsuit is (1) "based * * * upon an act outside the territory of the United States"; (2) that was taken "in connection with a commercial activity" of Argentina outside this country; and (3) that "cause[d] a direct effect in the United States." The complaint in this case alleges only one cause of action on behalf of each of the respondents, viz., a breach-of-contract claim based on Argentina's attempt to refinance the Bonods rather than to pay them according to their terms. The fact that the cause of action is in compliance with the first of the three requirements—that it is "based upon an act outside the territory of the United States" (presumably Argentina's unilateral extension)—is uncontested. The dispute pertains to whether the unilateral refinancing of the Bonods was taken "in connection with a commercial activity" of Argentina, and whether it had a "direct effect in the United States." We address these issues in turn.

A

Respondents and their *amicus,* the United States, contend that Argentina's issuance of, and continued liability under, the Bonods constitute a "commercial activity" and that the extension of the payment schedules was taken "in connection with" that activity. The latter point is obvious enough, and Argentina does not contest it; the key question is whether the activity is "commercial" under the FSIA.

The FSIA defines "commercial activity" to mean:

"[E]ither a regular course of commercial conduct or a particular commercial transaction or act. The commercial character of an activity shall be determined by reference to the nature of the course of conduct or particular transaction or act, rather than by reference to its purpose." 28 U.S.C. § 1603(d).

This definition, however, leaves the critical term "commercial" largely undefined: The first sentence simply establishes that the commercial nature of an activity does *not* depend upon whether it is a single act or a regular course of conduct, and the second sentence merely specifies what element of the conduct determines commerciality (*i.e.,* nature rather than purpose), but still without saying what "commercial" means. Fortunately, however, the FSIA was not written on a clean slate. As we have noted, see *Verlinden B.V. v. Central Bank of Nigeria,* 461 U.S. 480, 486–489, 103 S.Ct. 1962, 1967–1969, 76 L.Ed.2d 81 (1983), the Act (and the commercial exception in particular) largely codifies the so-called "restrictive" theory of foreign sovereign immunity first endorsed by the State Department in 1952. The meaning of "commercial" is the meaning generally attached to that term under the restrictive theory at the time the statute was enacted. * * *

This Court did not have occasion to discuss the scope or validity of the restrictive theory of sovereign immunity until our 1976 decision in *Alfred Dunhill of London, Inc. v. Republic of Cuba,* 425 U.S. 682, 96 S.Ct. 1854, 48 L.Ed.2d 301. Although the Court there was evenly divided on the question whether the "commercial" exception that applied in the foreign-sovereign-immunity context also limited the availability of an act-of-state defense, compare *id.,* at 695–706, 96 S.Ct., at 1861–1867 (plurality) with *id.,* at 725–730, 96 S.Ct., at 1875–1878 (Marshall, J., dissenting), there was little disagreement over the general scope of the exception. The plurality noted that, after the State Department endorsed the restrictive theory of foreign sovereign immunity in 1952, the lower courts consistently held that foreign sovereigns were not immune from the jurisdiction of American courts in cases "arising out of purely commercial transactions," *id.,* at 703, 96 S.Ct., at 1865–66; citing, *inter alia, Victory Transport, Inc. v. Comisaria General,* 336 F.2d 354 (C.A.2 1964), cert. denied, 381 U.S. 934, 85 S.Ct. 1763, 14 L.Ed.2d 698 (1965), and *Petrol Shipping Corp. v. Kingdom of Greece,* 360 F.2d 103 (CA2), cert. denied, 385 U.S. 931, 87 S.Ct. 291, 17 L.Ed.2d 213 (1966). The plurality further recognized that the distinction between state sovereign acts, on the one hand, and state commercial and private acts, on the other, was not entirely novel to American law. * * * The plurality stated that the restrictive theory of foreign sovereign immunity would not bar a suit based upon a foreign state's participation in the marketplace in the manner of a private citizen or corporation. 425 U.S., at 698–705, 96 S.Ct., at 1863–1866. A foreign state engaging in "commercial" activities "do[es] not exercise powers peculiar to sovereigns"; rather, it "exercise[s] only those powers that can also be exercised by private citizens." *Id.,* at 704, 96 S.Ct., at 1866. The dissenters did not disagree with this general description, see *id.,* at 725, 96 S.Ct., at 1875–1876. Given that the FSIA was enacted less than six months after our decision in *Alfred Dunhill* was announced, we think the plurality's contemporaneous description of the then-prevailing restrictive theory of sovereign immunity is of significant assistance in construing the scope of the Act.

In accord with that description, we conclude that when a foreign government acts, not as regulator of a market, but in the manner of a private player within it, the foreign sovereign's actions are "commercial" within the meaning of the FSIA. Moreover, because the Act provides that the commercial character of an act is to be determined by reference to its "nature" rather than its "purpose," 28 U.S.C. § 1603(d), the question is not whether the foreign government is acting with a profit motive or instead with the aim of fulfilling uniquely sovereign objectives. Rather, the issue is whether the particular actions that the foreign state performs (whatever the motive behind them) are the *type* of actions by which a private party engages in "trade and traffic or commerce," Black's Law Dictionary 270 (6th ed. 1990). See, *e.g., Rush–Presbyterian–St. Luke's Medical Center v. Hellenic Republic,* 877 F.2d 574, 578 (CA7), cert. denied, 493 U.S. 937, 110 S.Ct. 333, 107 L.Ed.2d 322 (1989). Thus, a foreign government's issuance of regulations limiting foreign currency exchange is a sovereign activity, because such authoritative control of commerce cannot be exercised by a private party; whereas a contract to buy army boots or even bullets is a "commercial" activity, because private companies can similarly use sales contracts to acquire goods, see, *e.g., Stato di Rumania v. Trutta* [1926] Foro It. 1 584, 585–586, 589 (Corte di Cass. del

Regno, Italy), translated and reprinted in part in 26 Am.J.Int'l L. 626–629 (Supp. 1932).

The commercial character of the Bonods is confirmed by the fact that they are in almost all respects garden-variety debt instruments: they may be held by private parties; they are negotiable and may be traded on the international market (except in Argentina); and they promise a future stream of cash income. We recognize that, prior to the enactment of the FSIA, there was authority suggesting that the issuance of public debt instruments did not constitute a commercial activity. *Victory Transport,* 336 F.2d, at 360 (dicta). There is, however, nothing distinctive about the state's assumption of debt (other than perhaps its purpose) that would cause it always to be classified as *jure imperii,* and in this regard it is significant that *Victory Transport* expressed confusion as to whether the "nature" or the "purpose" of a transaction was controlling in determining commerciality, *id.,* at 359–360. Because the FSIA has now clearly established that the "nature" governs, we perceive no basis for concluding that the issuance of debt should be treated as categorically different from other activities of foreign states.

Argentina contends that, although the FSIA bars consideration of "purpose," a court must nonetheless fully consider the *context* of a transaction in order to determine whether it is "commercial." Accordingly, Argentina claims that the Court of Appeals erred by defining the relevant conduct in what Argentina considers an overly generalized, acontextual manner and by essentially adopting a *per se* rule that all "issuance of debt instruments" is "commercial." See 941 F.2d, at 151 (" '[I]t is self-evident that issuing public debt is a commercial activity within the meaning of [the FSIA]' "), quoting *Shapiro v. Republic of Bolivia,* 930 F.2d 1013, 1018 (C.A.2 1991). We have no occasion to consider such a *per se* rule, because it seems to us that even in full context, there is nothing about the issuance of these Bonods (except perhaps its purpose) that is not analogous to a private commercial transaction.

Argentina points to the fact that the transactions in which the Bonods were issued did not have the ordinary commercial consequence of raising capital or financing acquisitions. Assuming for the sake of argument that this is not an example of judging the commerciality of a transaction by its purpose, the ready answer is that private parties regularly issue bonds, not just to raise capital or to finance purchases, but also to refinance debt. That is what Argentina did here: by virtue of the earlier FEIC contracts, Argentina was *already* obligated to supply the U.S. dollars needed to retire the FEIC-insured debts; the Bonods simply allowed Argentina to restructure its existing obligations. Argentina further asserts (without proof or even elaboration) that it "received consideration [for the Bonods] in no way commensurate with [their] value," Brief for Petitioners 22. Assuming that to be true, it makes no difference. Engaging in a commercial act does not require the receipt of fair value, or even compliance with the common-law requirements of consideration.

Argentina argues that the Bonods differ from ordinary debt instruments in that they "were created by the Argentine Government to fulfill its obligations under a foreign exchange program designed to address a domestic credit crisis, and as a component of a program designed to control that nation's critical shortage of foreign exchange." *Id.,* at 23–24. In this regard,

Argentina relies heavily on *de Sanchez v. Banco Central de Nicaragua,* 770 F.2d 1385 (C.A.5 1985), in which the Fifth Circuit took the view that "[o]ften, the essence of an act is defined by its purpose"; that unless "we can inquire into the purposes of such acts, we cannot determine their nature"; and that, in light of its purpose to control its reserves of foreign currency, Nicaragua's refusal to honor a check it had issued to cover a private bank debt was a sovereign act entitled to immunity. *Id.,* at 1393. Indeed, Argentina asserts that the line between "nature" and "purpose" rests upon a "formalistic distinction [that] simply is neither useful nor warranted." Reply Brief for Petitioners 8. We think this line of argument is squarely foreclosed by the language of the FSIA. However difficult it may be in some cases to separate "purpose" (*i.e.,* the *reason* why the foreign state engages in the activity) from "nature" (*i.e.,* the outward form of the conduct that the foreign state performs or agrees to perform), see *de Sanchez, supra,* at 1393, the statute unmistakably commands that to be done. 28 U.S.C. § 1603(d). We agree with the Court of Appeals, see 941 F.2d, at 151, that it is irrelevant *why* Argentina participated in the bond market in the manner of a private actor; it matters only that it did so. We conclude that Argentina's issuance of the Bonods was a "commercial activity" under the FSIA.

B

The remaining question is whether Argentina's unilateral rescheduling of the Bonods had a "direct effect" in the United States, 28 U.S.C. § 1605(a)(2). In addressing this issue, the Court of Appeals rejected the suggestion in the legislative history of the FSIA that an effect is not "direct" unless it is both "substantial" and "foreseeable." * * *

That suggestion is found in the House Report, which states that conduct covered by the third clause of § 1605(a)(2) would be subject to the jurisdiction of American courts "consistent with principles set forth in section 18, Restatement of the Law, Second, Foreign Relations Law of the United States (1965)." H.R.Rep. No. 94–1487, pp. 1, 19, U.S.Code Cong. & Admin. News 1976, pp. 6604, 6618 (1976). Section 18 states that American laws are not given extraterritorial application except with respect to conduct that has, as a "direct and foreseeable result," a "substantial" effect within the United States. Since this obviously deals with jurisdiction to *legislate* rather than jurisdiction to *adjudicate,* this passage of the House Report has been charitably described as "a bit of a *non sequitur,*" *Texas Trading & Milling Corp. v. Federal Republic of Nigeria,* 647 F.2d 300, 311 (C.A.2 1981), cert. denied, 454 U.S. 1148, 102 S.Ct. 1012, 71 L.Ed.2d 301 (1982). Of course the generally applicable principle *de minimis non curat lex* ensures that jurisdiction may not be predicated on purely trivial effects in the United States. But we reject the suggestion that § 1605(a)(2) contains any unexpressed requirement of "substantiality" or "foreseeability." As the Court of Appeals recognized, an effect is "direct" if it follows "as an immediate consequence of the defendant's * * * activity," 941 F.2d, at 152.

The Court of Appeals concluded that the rescheduling of the maturity dates obviously had a "direct effect" on respondents. It further concluded that that effect was sufficiently "in the United States" for purposes of the FSIA, in part because "Congress would have wanted an American court to entertain this action" in order to preserve New York City's status as "a preeminent commercial center." *Id.,* at 153. The question, however, is not what Congress "would have wanted" but what Congress enacted in the FSIA. Although we are happy to endorse the Second Circuit's recognition of "New York's status as a world financial leader," the effect of Argentina's rescheduling in diminishing that status (assuming it is not too speculative to be considered an effect at all) is too remote and attenuated to satisfy the "direct effect" requirement of the FSIA. *Ibid.*

We nonetheless have little difficulty concluding that Argentina's unilateral rescheduling of the maturity dates on the Bonods had a "direct effect" in the United States. Respondents had designated their accounts in New York as the place of payment, and Argentina made some interest payments into those accounts before announcing that it was rescheduling the payments. Because New York was thus the place of performance for Argentina's ultimate contractual obligations, the rescheduling of those obligations necessarily had a "direct effect" in the United States: Money that was supposed to have been delivered to a New York bank for deposit was not forthcoming. We reject Argentina's suggestion that the "direct effect" requirement cannot be satisfied where the plaintiffs are all foreign corporations with no other connections to the United States. We expressly stated in *Verlinden* that the FSIA permits "a foreign plaintiff to sue a foreign sovereign in the courts of the United States, provided the substantive requirements of the Act are satisfied," 461 U.S., at 489, 103 S.Ct., at 1969.

Finally, Argentina argues that a finding of jurisdiction in this case would violate the Due Process Clause of the Fifth Amendment, and that, in order to avoid this difficulty, we must construe the "direct effect" requirement as embodying the "minimum contacts" test of *International Shoe Co. v. Washington,* 326 U.S. 310, 316, 66 S.Ct. 154, 158, 90 L.Ed. 95 (1945). Assuming, without deciding, that a foreign state is a "person" for purposes of the Due Process Clause, cf. *South Carolina v. Katzenbach,* 383 U.S. 301, 323–324, 86 S.Ct. 803, 815–816, 15 L.Ed.2d 769 (1966) (States of the Union are not "persons" for purposes of the Due Process Clause), we find that Argentina possessed "minimum contacts" that would satisfy the constitutional test. By issuing negotiable debt instruments denominated in U.S. dollars and payable in New York and by appointing a financial agent in that city, Argentina " 'purposefully avail[ed] itself of the privilege of conducting activities within the [United States],' " *Burger King Corp. v. Rudzewicz,* 471 U.S. 462, 475, 105 S.Ct. 2174, 2183, 85 L.Ed.2d 528 (1985), quoting *Hanson v. Denckla,* 357 U.S. 235, 253, 78 S.Ct. 1228, 1240, 2 L.Ed.2d 1283 (1958).

* * *

We conclude that Argentina's issuance of the Bonods was a "commercial activity" under the FSIA; that its rescheduling of the maturity dates on those instruments was taken in connection with that commercial activity and had a "direct effect" in the United States; and that the District Court therefore properly asserted jurisdiction, under the FSIA, over the breach-of-contract claim based on that rescheduling. Accordingly, the judgment of the Court of Appeals is

Affirmed.

Notes

1. In what circumstances can a foreign state be sued in the United States on bonds it has issued? In the principal case, the Court stressed that the bonds were denominated in U.S. dollars and payable in New York. Would a clause in the bond declaring New York law applicable suffice? Would it be sufficient if the bonds were denominated in U.S. dollars and the holders were U.S. citizens or residents, but no place of payment were specified? How can a foreign state avoid being subjected to suit in the United States on bonds it has issued? Would a clause selecting a foreign forum be sufficient?

2. Would the New York court have had in personam competence under New York law if the FSIA had not supplied its own bases? Is it appropriate for the United States to subject a foreign state to suit in New York if the foreign state would not have been subject to suit if it had been a private entity? See Smit, Note 1 below.

3. In Foremost–McKesson, Inc. v. The Islamic Republic of Iran, 905 F.2d 438 (D.C.Cir.1990), the American plaintiff brought an action against Iran asserting that Iran had used its majority position in an Iranian corporate joint venture wrongfully to deprive plaintiffs of benefits to which it was entitled. Iran pleaded sovereign immunity. The Court ruled that Iran's alleged wrongful conduct was commercial and also found the requisite direct effect under the third clause of Section 1605(a)(2). The Court distinguished the case at bar from that adjudicated in Zedan v. Kingdom of Saudi Arabia, 849 F.2d 1511 (D.C.Cir.1988), in which it found the circumstance that the plaintiff had not received the contractually stipulated payment for work done in Saudi Arabia after his return to the United States not to produce the statutorily required effect in the United States. In the *Foremost* case, the complaint alleged a constant flow of capital, management personnel, engineering data, machinery and equipment between the United States and Iran. See also Texas Trading & Milling Corp. v. Federal Republic of Nigeria, 647 F.2d 300 (2d Cir.1981), cert. denied, 454 U.S. 1148, 102 S.Ct. 1012, 71 L.Ed.2d 301 (1982).

FOREIGN SOVEREIGN IMMUNITIES ACT OF 1976

[See 28 U.S.C.A. §§ 1602–06.]

Notes

1. On the Foreign Sovereign Immunities Act of 1976 generally, see Smit, The Foreign Sovereign Immunities Act of 1976: A Plea For Drastic Surgery, 1980 Proc. A.S.I.L. 49; Kahale & Vega, Immunity and Jurisdiction: Toward a Uniform Body of Law in Actions Against Foreign States, 18 Colum.J.Transnat'l L. 211 (1979); Brower, Bistline & Loomis, The Foreign Sovereign Immunities Act of 1976 in Practice, 73 A.J.I.L. 200 (1979); Carl, Suing Foreign Governments in American Courts: The United States Foreign Sovereign Immunities Act in Practice, 33 Southw. L.J. 1007 (1979); Delaume, Three Perspectives on Sovereign Immunity, 71 A.J.I.L. 379 (1977); Simmons, The Foreign Sovereign Immunities Act of 1976: Giving the Plaintiff his Day in Court, 46 Fordham L.Rev. 543 (1977); Von Mehren, The Foreign Sovereign Immunities Act of 1976, 17 Colum.L.Transnat'l L. 33 (1978); Hill, A Policy Analysis of the American Law of Foreign State Immunity, 50 Fordh. L.Rev. 155 (1981); Feldman, The United States FSIA of 1976 In Perspective: A Founder's View; 35 I.C.L.Q. 302 (1986); Lacroix, The Theory and Practice of the Foreign Sovereign Immunities Act: Untying the Gordian Knot, 5 Int'l Tax

& Bus. Law. 144 (1987); Foreign Governments in United States Court: [A Panel], 1991 Proc. A.S.I.L. 251.

2. On August 15, 2000, a Working Group of the International Litigation Committee of the Section of International Law and Practice of the American Bar Association published a Draft Report on the Foreign Sovereign Immunities Act, which recommends a number of amendments to the Act. The amendments proposed may be compared with those proposed in Smit, The Foreign Sovereign Immunities Act of 1976: A Plea for Drastic Surgery, 1980 Proc. A.S.I.L. 49.

3. Following the decision in Trendtex Trading Corp. v. Central Bank of Nigeria, [1977] 2 W.L.R. 356, in which the Court of Appeals held the restrictive doctrine to apply not only to *in rem,* but also to *in personam* cases, the United Kingdom enacted the State Immunity Act of 1978, 17 I.L.M. 1123 (1978).

4. The Report of the Senate Judiciary Committee states that the Foreign Sovereign Immunities Act codifies "the so-called 'restrictive' principle of sovereign immunity, as formerly recognized in international law." Sen. Rep. No. 94–1310, 94th Cong.2d Sess., p. 9 (1976). Is this an accurate statement?

5. Does Section 1604 properly reflect the developments in this area? In *Victory Transport,* p. 1208, note 2 *supra,* the Second Circuit stated: "Sovereign immunity is a derogation from the normal exercise of jurisdiction by the courts and should be accorded only in clear cases. * * * We are disposed to deny a claim of sovereign immunity * * * unless it is plain that the activity in question falls within one of the categories of strictly political or public acts * * * " Even before the Act was enacted, it had been stated that "a subtle shift has occurred—from a doctrine granting immunity unless the activity is 'commercial' to a doctrine denying immunity unless the activity is 'political'." Note, Sovereign Immunity of States Engaged in Commercial Activities, 65 Colum. L.Rev. 1086, 1100 (1965). See also Lord Denning in Rahimtoola v. Nizam of Hyderabad, [1958] A.C. 379, 422–23. See further, Note 3 supra. The Senate Judiciary Report on the Act states that, "since sovereign immunity is an affirmative defense which must be specially pleaded, the burden will remain on the foreign state to produce evidence in support of its claims of immunity." Sen. Rep. No. 94–1310, 94th Cong.2d Sess., p. 17 (1976). Is this statement supported by the text of the Act?

6. Why does Section 1605(a)(2) provide for non-immunity only if the action is based on a commercial activity carried on in, or having a substantial contact with, the United States or on an act performed or having a direct effect there? Should a foreign state, subject to suit in the United States under generally prevailing rules of adjudicatory authority, be allowed a plea of sovereign immunity because the commercial activity or act on which the claim for relief is based occurred abroad and caused no direct effect in, and had no substantial contact with, the United States? Does this provision improperly commingle rules of sovereign immunity and rules of judicial competence? See Section 1330(a) and (b) of the Act providing that, subject to certain qualifications, personal jurisdiction exists as to any claim for relief with regard to which the foreign state is not entitled to immunity under Sections 1605–1607.

7. In Yessenin–Volpin v. Novosti Press Agency, 443 F.Supp. 849 (S.D.N.Y. 1978), the court upheld a claim of immunity in an action alleging a libel in a publication distributed in the United States on the ground that the libel was not "an act outside of the territory of the United States in connection with a commercial activity of the foreign state elsewhere." Acknowledging that the act had produced a direct effect in the United States, the court held that it had not been performed "in connection with a commercial activity." Although Novosti did

engage in commercial activities, the court ruled that the publications in which the alleged libels appeared were official commentary of the Soviet government and therefore could not be regarded as published in the course of a commercial activity.

8. Do the activities of the Organization of Petroleum Exporting Countries, and specifically the fixing of crude oil prices, constitute a commercial activity? On this question, see International Ass'n of Machinists and Aerospace Workers v. OPEC, 477 F.Supp. 553 (C.D.Cal.1979), aff'd on act of state grounds, 649 F.2d 1354 (9th Cir.1981), cert. denied, 454 U.S. 1163, 102 S.Ct. 1036, 71 L.Ed.2d 319 (1982).

9. In Holden v. Canadian Consulate, 92 F.3d 918 (9th Cir.1996), cert. denied, 519 U.S. 1091, 117 S.Ct. 767, 136 L.Ed.2d 713(1997), the court held that an action for breach of contract of employment as "commercial officer" in the Canadian Consulate was based on a "commercial activity" within the meaning of the FSIA. The Court stressed that the plaintiff was not a civil servant or a foreign service officer.

10. For commentary on the effectiveness of the commercial activity exception in the FSIA, see Donoghue, Taking the "Sovereign" out of the Foreign Sovereign Immunities Act: A Functional Approach To The Commercial Activity Exception, 17 Yale J.Int'l L. 489 (1992); Vazquez, The Relationship Between The FSIA's Commercial Activity Exception And The Due–Process Clause, 1991 Proc. A.S.I.L. 257; Note, Nationalized and Denationalized Commercial Enterprises Under The Foreign Sovereign Immunities Act, 90 Colum. L.Rev. 2278 (1990).

2. *Other Restrictions Upon Immunity: Property, Non–Commercial Torts*

FOREIGN SOVEREIGN IMMUNITIES ACT OF 1976

[28 U.S.C.A. § 1605(a)(4), (5)].

a. Property Within the Forum State

Section 1605(a)(4) of the FSIA provides for denial of immunity in regard to claims to immovable property situated in the United States, irrespective of whether the property is of a commercial nature. This denial extends even to property used for diplomatic or consular purposes. See Sen. Rep. No. 94–1310, 94th Cong.2d Sess., p. 20 (1976).

Most courts and commentators have concluded that a foreign state's immunity from jurisdiction does not extend to proceedings for the determination of possession of, or an interest in, immovable or real property located in the territory of a state exercising jurisdiction. Restatement (Third) § 455(1) and (2). The reason usually given for this exception to state immunity is that real property, unless it is used for diplomatic or consular purposes, is "so indissolubly connected with the territory of a State that the State of the situs cannot permit the exercise of any other jurisdiction in respect thereof * * * " Harvard Research in International Law, Competence of Courts in Regard to Foreign States, Art. 9, 26 A.J.I.L.Supp. 451, 578 (1932). It has also been asserted that a state, by acquiring real property located in the territory of another state, voluntarily submits itself to the jurisdiction of the situs state (i.e., "waives" its immunity) in matters regarding its interests in the property. Storelli v. Government of the French Republic, [1923–24] Ann. Dig. 129 (Court of Rome, Italy, 1924); see also Restatement (Third) § 455, Comment *b*.

May a state rely on its immunity in order to resist eminent domain or other proceedings directed against its property by the state in which the property is located? Cf. Georgia v. City of Chattanooga, 264 U.S. 472, 44 S.Ct. 369, 68 L.Ed. 796 (1924). On the expropriation or requisition of a foreign state's chattels, see the position taken by the United States in 1941 in connection with the seizure of eighteen aircraft purchased in the United States by Peru. A memorandum prepared by the Legal Adviser's Office stated that "[e]very state undoubtedly possesses the right in case of emergency and subject to compensation to seize any foreign property on its territory." [1941] 7 For. Rel. 518. In proceedings before the Court of Claims, Switzerland did not argue that the United States had violated international law in requisitioning certain property belonging to the Swiss government. Swiss Confederation v. United States, 108 Ct.Cl. 388, 70 F.Supp. 235 (1947); Swiss Federal Railways v. United States, 125 Ct.Cl. 444, 112 F.Supp. 357 (1953).

According to the Senate Judiciary Committee Report, "[t]here is general agreement that a foreign state may not claim immunity when the suit against it relates to rights in property, real or personal, obtained by gift or inherited by the foreign state and situated or administered in the country where suit is brought." Sen. Rep. No. 94–1310, 94th Cong.2d Sess., p. 20 (1976). What is the basis for this denial of immunity?

b. Torts Within the Forum State

Section 1605(a)(5) denies immunity for most non-commercial torts causing "personal injury or death, or damage to or loss of property." As to the basis in international law for this denial of immunity, see Sen. Rep. No. 94–1310, 94th Cong., 2d Sess., pp. 20–21 (1976). On the scope of this provision, see Restatement (Third) § 454.

A prominent case involving this exception is Letelier v. Republic of Chile, 488 F.Supp. 665 (D.D.C.1980), judgment entered, 502 F.Supp. 259 (D.D.C. 1980). Chile was held not to be immune from suit in respect of an assassination by means of a car bombing that took place in the District of Columbia. For later proceedings involving an unsuccessful effort to execute the judgment against Chile's national airline, see 748 F.2d 790 (2d Cir.1984), cert. denied, 471 U.S. 1125, 105 S.Ct. 2656, 86 L.Ed.2d 273 (1985). The matter was finally settled by intergovernmental agreement. See materials at 30 I.L.M. 421 (1990); 31 I.L.M. 1 (1992), and p. 829 in Chapter 11. For another case involving allegations of political assassination within the forum, see Liu v. Republic of China, 892 F.2d 1419 (9th Cir.1989), cert. dismissed, 497 U.S. 1058, 111 S.Ct. 27, 111 L.Ed.2d 840 (1990) (federal choice of law rule points to California law on liability of Republic of China/Taiwan for acts of its agents resulting in a death in California).

c. Torts Outside the Forum State

From the beginning, section 1605(a)(5) was generally ruled inapplicable when the tort or injury occurred outside of the United States. See Persinger v. Islamic Republic of Iran, 729 F.2d 835 (D.C.Cir.1984), cert. denied, 469 U.S. 881, 105 S.Ct. 247, 83 L.Ed.2d 185 (1984) (detention of hostages in U.S.

embassy in Iran held not to have occurred in the United States); Asociacion de Reclamantes v. United Mexican States, 735 F.2d 1517 (D.C.Cir.1984), cert. denied, 470 U.S. 1051, 105 S.Ct. 1751, 84 L.Ed.2d 815 (1985); Australian Government Aircraft Factories v. Lynne, 743 F.2d 672 (9th Cir.1984), cert. denied, 469 U.S. 1214, 105 S.Ct. 1189, 84 L.Ed.2d 335 (1985); McKeel v. Islamic Republic of Iran, 722 F.2d 582 (9th Cir.1983), cert. denied, 469 U.S. 880, 105 S.Ct. 243, 83 L.Ed.2d 182 (1984); Harris v. VAO Intourist, 481 F.Supp. 1056 (E.D.N.Y.1979). But see De Sanchez v. Banco Central De Nicaragua, 515 F.Supp. 900 (E.D.La.1981) (conversion of a check drawn on a U.S. bank by foreign central bank is within this Section).

Notwithstanding these rulings, attempts to sue foreign states for wrongful conduct outside of the United States have continued. Initially, the courts resisted these attempts. See, e.g., Frolova v. U.S.S.R., 761 F.2d 370 (7th Cir.1985) (alleged violation of human rights did not occur in the United States). See also Siderman v. Republic of Argentina, 965 F.2d 699 (9th Cir.1992), cert. denied, 507 U.S. 1017, 113 S.Ct. 1812, 123 L.Ed.2d 444 (1993) (torture outside the United States does not confer jurisdiction under the FSIA). Attempts were then made to find a basis for jurisdiction outside of the FSIA, and, specifically, to base it on the Alien Torts Claims Act, as in Filartiga v. Pena–Irala, 630 F.2d 876 (2d Cir.1980), pp. 143, 647, where the defendant was a foreign state official rather than a foreign state. However, the Supreme Court has ruled that the FSIA is the sole basis for jurisdiction over foreign states. See the cases that follow.

ARGENTINE REPUBLIC v. AMERADA HESS SHIPPING CORP.

Supreme Court of the United States, 1989.
488 U.S. 428, 109 S.Ct. 683, 102 L.Ed.2d 818.

(Some footnotes omitted; others renumbered.)

CHIEF JUSTICE REHNQUIST delivered the opinion of the Court.

Two Liberian corporations sued the Argentine Republic in a United States District Court to recover damages for a tort allegedly committed by its armed forces on the high seas in violation of international law. We hold that the District Court correctly dismissed the action, because the Foreign Sovereign Immunities Act of 1976 (FSIA), 28 U.S.C. § 1330 *et seq.*, does not authorize jurisdiction over a foreign state in this situation.

Respondents alleged the following facts in their complaints. Respondent United Carriers, Inc., a Liberian corporation, chartered one of its oil tankers, the Hercules, to respondent Amerada Hess Shipping Corporation, also a Liberian corporation. The contract was executed in New York City. Amerada Hess used the Hercules to transport crude oil from the southern terminus of the Trans–Alaska Pipeline in Valdez, Alaska, around Cape Horn in South America, to the Hess refinery in the United States Virgin Islands. On May 25, 1982, the Hercules began a return voyage, without cargo but fully fueled, from the Virgin Islands to Alaska. At that time, Great Britain and petitioner Argentine Republic were at war over an archipelago of some 200 islands—the Falkland Islands to the British, and the Islas Malvinas to the Argentineans—in the South Atlantic off the Argentine coast. On June 3, United States officials informed the two belligerents of the location of United States vessels and Liberian tankers owned by United States interests then traversing the South Atlantic, including the Hercules, to avoid any attacks on neutral shipping.

By June 8, 1982, after a stop in Brazil, the Hercules was in international waters about 600 nautical miles from Argentina and 500 miles from the Falklands; she was outside the "war zones" designated by Britain and Argentina. At 12:15 Greenwich mean time, the ship's master made a routine report by radio to Argentine officials, providing the ship's name, international call sign, registry, position, course, speed, and voyage description. About 45 minutes later, an Argentine military aircraft began to circle the Hercules. The ship's master repeated his earlier message by radio to Argentine officials, who acknowledged receiving it. Six minutes later, without provocation, another Argentine military plane began to bomb the Hercules; the master immediately hoisted a white flag. A second bombing soon followed, and a third attack came about two hours later, when an Argentine jet struck the ship with an air-to-surface rocket. Disabled but not destroyed, the Hercules reversed course and sailed to Rio de Janeiro, the nearest safe port. At Rio Je Janeiro, respondent United Carriers determined that the ship had suffered extensive deck and hull damage, and that an undetonated bomb remained lodged in her No. 2 tank. After an investigation by the Brazilian Navy, United Carriers decided that it would be too hazardous to remove the undetonated bomb, and on July 20, 1982, the Hercules was scuttled 250 miles off the Brazilian coast.

Following unsuccessful attempts to obtain relief in Argentina, respondents commenced this action in the United States District Court for the Southern District of New York for the damage that they sustained from the attack. United Carriers sought $10 million in damages for the loss of the ship; Amerada Hess sought $1.9 million in damages for the fuel that went down with the ship. Respondents alleged that petitioner's attack on the neutral Hercules violated international law. They invoked the District Court's jurisdiction under the Alien Tort Statute, 28 U.S.C. § 1350, which provides that "[t]he district courts shall have original jurisdiction of any civil action by an alien for a tort only, committed in violation of the law of nations or a treaty of the United States." Amerada Hess also brought suit under the general admiralty and maritime jurisdiction, 28 U.S.C. § 1333, and "the principle of universal jurisdiction, recognized in customary international law." Complaint of Amerada Hess ¶ 5, App. 20. The District Court dismissed both complaints for lack of subject-matter jurisdiction, 638 F.Supp. 73 (1986), ruling that respondents' suits were barred by the FSIA.

A divided panel of the United States Court of Appeals for the Second Circuit reversed. 830 F.2d 421 (1987). The Court of Appeals held that the District Court had jurisdiction under the Alien Tort Statute, because respondents' consolidated action was brought by Liberian corporations, it sounded in tort ("the bombing of a ship without justification"), and it asserted a violation of international law ("attacking a neutral ship in international waters, without proper cause for suspicion or investigation"). *Id.,* at 424425. Viewing the Alien Tort Statute as "no more than a jurisdictional grant based on international law," the Court of Appeals said that "who is within" the scope of that grant is governed by "evolving standards of international law." *Id.,* at 425, citing *Filartiga v. Pena–Irala,* 630 F.2d 876, 880 (C.A.2 1980). The Court of Appeals reasoned that Congress' enactment of the FSIA was not meant to eliminate "existing remedies in United States courts for violations of international law" by foreign states under the Alien Tort Statute. 830 F.2d, at 426. The dissenting judge took the view that the FSIA precluded respondents' action. *Id.*, at 431. We granted certiorari, 485 U.S. 1005, 108 S.Ct. 1466, 99 L.Ed.2d 697 (1988), and now reverse.

* * *

We think that the text and structure of the FSIA demonstrate Congress' intention that the FSIA be the sole basis for obtaining jurisdiction over a foreign state in our courts. Sections 1604 and 1330(a) work in tandem: § 1604 bars federal and state courts from exercising jurisdiction when a foreign state is entitled to immunity, and § 1330(a) confers jurisdiction on district courts to hear suits brought by United States citizens and by aliens when a foreign state is not entitled to immunity. As we said in *Verlinden*, the FSIA "must be applied by the district courts in every action against a foreign sovereign, since subject-matter jurisdiction in any such action depends on the existence of one of the specified exceptions to foreign sovereign immunity." *Verlinden B.V. v. Central Bank of Nigeria*, 461 U.S. 480, 493, 103 S.Ct. 1962, 1971, 76 L.Ed.2d 81 (1983).

The Court of Appeals acknowledged that the FSIA's language and legislative history support the "general rule" that the Act governs the immunity of foreign states in federal court. 830 F.2d, at 426. The Court of Appeals, however, thought that the FSIA's "focus on commercial concerns" and Congress' failure to "repeal" the Alien Tort Statute indicated Congress' intention that federal courts continue to exercise jurisdiction over foreign states in suits alleging violations of international law outside the confines of the FSIA. Id., at 427. The Court of Appeals also believed that to construe the FSIA to bar the instant suit would "fly in the face" of Congress' intention that the FSIA be interpreted pursuant to " 'standards recognized under international law.' " Ibid., quoting H.R.Rep., at 14.

Taking the last of these points first, Congress had violations of international law by foreign states in mind when it enacted the FSIA. For example, the FSIA specifically denies foreign states immunity in suits "in which rights in property taken in violation of international law are in issue." 28 U.S.C. § 1605(a)(3). Congress also rested the FSIA in part on its power under Art. I, § 8, cl. 10, of the Constitution "[t]o define and punish Piracies and Felonies committed on the high Seas, and Offenses against the Law of Nations." See H.R.Rep., at 12; S.Rep., at 12. From Congress' decision to deny immunity to foreign states in the class of cases just mentioned, we draw the plain implication that immunity is granted in those cases involving alleged violations of international law that do not come within one of the FSIA's exceptions.

As to the other point made by the Court of Appeals, Congress' failure to enact a *pro tanto* repealer of the Alien Tort Statute when it passed the FSIA in 1976 may be explained at least in part by the lack of certainty as to whether the Alien Tort Statute conferred jurisdiction in suits against foreign states. Enacted by the First Congress in 1789, the Alien Tort Statute provides that "[t]he district courts shall have original jurisdiction of any civil action by an alien for a tort only, committed in violation of the law of nations or a treaty of the United States." 28 U.S.C. § 1350. The Court of Appeals did not cite any decision in which a United States court exercised jurisdiction over a foreign state under the Alien Tort Statute, and only one such case has come to our attention—one which was decided after the enactment of the FSIA.[1]

In this Court, respondents argue that cases were brought under the Alien Tort Statute against foreign states for the unlawful taking of a prize during wartime. Brief for Respondents 18–25. The Alien Tort Statute makes no mention of prize jurisdiction, and § 1333(2) now grants federal district courts exclusive jurisdiction over "all proceedings for the condemnation of property taken as a prize." In *The Santissima Trinidad,* 20 U.S. (7 Wheat.) 283, 353–354, 5 L.Ed. 454 (1822), we held that foreign states were not immune from the jurisdiction of United States courts in prize proceedings. That case, however, was not brought under the Alien Tort Statute but rather as a libel in admiralty. Thus there is a distinctly hypothetical cast to the Court of Appeals' reliance on Congress' failure to repeal the Alien Tort Statute, and respondents' arguments in this Court based on the principle of statutory construction that repeals by implication are disfavored.

We think that Congress' failure in the FSIA to enact an express *pro tanto* repealer of the Alien Tort Statute speaks only faintly, if at all, to the issue involved in this case. In light of the comprehensiveness of the statutory scheme in the FSIA, we doubt that even the most meticulous draftsman would have concluded that Congress also needed to amend *pro tanto* the Alien Tort Statute and presumably such other grants of subject-matter jurisdiction in Title 28 as § 1331 (federal question), § 1333 (admiralty), § 1335 (interpleader), § 1337 (commerce and antitrust), and § 1338 (patents, copyrights, and trademarks). Congress provided in the FSIA that "[c]laims of foreign states to immunity should *henceforth* be decided by courts of the United States in conformity with the principles set forth in this chapter," and very likely it thought that should be sufficient. § 1602 (emphasis added); see also H.R.Rep., at 12; S.Rep., at 11 (FSIA "intended to preempt any other State and Federal law (excluding applicable international agreements) for according immunity to foreign sovereigns").

For similar reasons we are not persuaded by respondents' arguments based upon the rule of statutory construction under which repeals by implication are disfavored. This case does not involve two statutes that readily could be seen as supplementing one another, see *Wood v. United States,* 41 U.S. (16 Pet.) 342, 363, 10 L.Ed. 987 (1842), nor is it a case where a more general statute is claimed to have repealed by implication an earlier statute dealing with a narrower subject. See *Morton v. Mancari,* 417 U.S. 535, 549–551, 94 S.Ct. 2474, 2482–2483, 41 L.Ed.2d 290 (1974). We think that Congress' decision to deal comprehensively with the subject of foreign sovereign immunity in the FSIA, and the express provision in § 1604 that "a foreign state shall be immune from the jurisdiction of the courts of the United States and of the States except as provided in sections 1605–1607," preclude a construction of the Alien Tort Statute that permits the instant suit. See *Red Rock v.*

1. *See Von Dardel v. Union of Soviet Socialist Republics,* 623 F.Supp. 246 (DC 1985) (alternative holding). The Court of Appeals did cite its earlier decision in *Filartiga v. Pena-Irala,* 630 F.2d 876 (1980), which involved a suit under the Alien Tort Statute by a Paraguayan national against a Paraguayan police official for torture; the Paraguayan Government was not joined as a defendant.

Henry, 106 U.S. 596, 601–602, 1 S.Ct. 434, 438–439, 27 L.Ed. 251 (1883); *United States v. Tynen*, 78 U.S. (11 Wall.) 88, 92, 20 L.Ed. 153 (1871). The Alien Tort Statute by its terms does not distinguish among classes of defendants, and it of course has the same effect after the passage of the FSIA as before with respect to defendants other than foreign states.

Respondents also argue that the general admiralty and maritime jurisdiction, § 1333(1), provides a basis for obtaining jurisdiction over petitioner for violations of international law, notwithstanding the FSIA. Brief for Respondents 42–49. But Congress dealt with the admiralty jurisdiction of the federal courts when it enacted the FSIA. Section 1605(b) expressly permits an *in personam* suit in admiralty to enforce a maritime lien against a vessel or cargo of a foreign state. Unless the present case is within § 1605(b) or another exception to the FSIA, the statute conferring general admiralty and maritime jurisdiction on the federal courts does not authorize the bringing of this action against petitioner.

Having determined that the FSIA provides the sole basis for obtaining jurisdiction over a foreign state in federal court, we turn to whether any of the exceptions enumerated in the Act apply here. These exceptions include cases involving the waiver of immunity, § 1605(a)(1), commercial activities occurring in the United States or causing a direct effect in this country, § 1605(a)(2), property expropriated in violation of international law, § 1605(a)(3), inherited, gift, or immovable property located in the United States, § 1605(a)(4), noncommercial torts occurring in the United States, § 1605(a)(5), and maritime liens, § 1605(b). We agree with the District Court that none of the FSIA's exceptions applies on these facts. * * *

Respondents assert that the FSIA exception for noncommercial torts, § 1605(a)(5), is most in point. * * * Section 1605(a)(5) is limited by its terms, however, to those cases in which the damage to or loss of property occurs *in the United States*. Congress' primary purpose in enacting § 1605(a)(5) was to eliminate a foreign state's immunity for traffic accidents and other torts committed in the United States, for which liability is imposed under domestic tort law. See H.R.Rep., at 14, 20–21; S.Rep., at 14, 20–21.

In this case, the injury to respondents' ship occurred on the high seas some 5,000 miles off the nearest shores of the United States. Despite these telling facts, respondents nonetheless claim that the tortious attack on the Hercules occurred "in the United States." They point out that the FSIA defines "United States" as including all "territory and waters, continental and insular, subject to the jurisdiction of the United States," § 1603(c), and that their injury occurred on the high seas, which is within the admiralty jurisdiction of the United States, see *The Plymouth*, 70 U.S. (3 Wall.) 20, 36, 18 L.Ed. 125 (1866). They reason, therefore, that "by statutory definition" petitioner's attack occurred in the United States. * * *

We find this logic unpersuasive. We construe the modifying phrase "continental and insular" to restrict the definition of United States to the continental United States and those islands that are part of the United States or its possessions; any other reading would render this phrase nugatory. Likewise, the term "waters" in § 1603(c) cannot reasonably be read to cover all waters over which United States courts might exercise jurisdiction. When it desires to do so, Congress knows how to place the high seas within the jurisdictional reach of a statute. We thus apply "[t]he canon of construction which teaches that legislation of Congress, unless contrary intent appears, is meant to apply only within the territorial jurisdiction of the United States." *Foley Brothers v. Filardo,* 336 U.S. 281, 285, 69 S.Ct. 575, 577, 93 L.Ed. 680 (1949); see also *Weinberger v. Rossi,* 456 U.S. 25, 32, 102 S.Ct. 1510, 1516, 71 L.Ed.2d 715 (1982). Because respondents' injury unquestionably occurred well outside the 3–mile limit then in effect for the territorial waters of the United States, the exception for noncommercial torts cannot apply.

The result in this case is not altered by the fact that petitioner's alleged tort may have had effects in the United States. Respondents state, for example, that the Hercules was transporting oil intended for use in this country and that the loss of the ship disrupted contractual payments due in New York. * * * Under the commercial activity exception to the FSIA, § 1605(a)(2), a foreign state may be liable for its commercial activities "outside the territory of the United States" having a "direct effect" inside the United States. But the noncommercial tort exception, § 1605(a)(5), upon which respondents rely, makes no mention of "territory outside the United States" or of "direct effects" in the United States. Congress' decision to use explicit language in § 1605(a)(2), and not to do so in § 1605(a)(5), indicates that the exception in § 1605(a)(5) covers only torts occurring within the territorial jurisdiction of the United States. Respondents do not claim that § 1605(a)(2) covers these facts.

We also disagree with respondents' claim that certain international agreements entered into by petitioner and by the United States create an exception to the FSIA here. * * * Respondents point to the Geneva Convention on the High Seas, Apr. 29, 1958, [1962] 13 U.S.T. 2312, T.I.A.S. No. 5200, and the Pan American Maritime Neutrality Convention, Feb. 20, 1928, 47 Stat. 1989, 1990–1991, T.S. No. 845. * * * These conventions, however, only set forth substantive rules of conduct and state that compensation shall be paid for certain wrongs. They do not create private rights of action for foreign corporations to recover compensation from foreign states in United States courts. Cf. *Head Money Cases,* 112 U.S. 580, 598–599, 5 S.Ct. 247, 253–254, 28 L.Ed. 798 (1884); *Foster v. Neilson,* 27 U.S. (2 Pet.) 253, 314, 7 L.Ed. 415 (1829). Nor do we see how a foreign state can waive its immunity under § 1605(a)(1) by signing an international agreement that contains no mention of a waiver of immunity to suit in United States courts or even the availability of a cause of action in the United States. We find similarly unpersuasive the argument of respondents and *Amicus Curiae* Republic of Liberia that the Treaty of Friendship, Commerce and Navigation, Aug. 8, 1938, United States–Liberia, 54 Stat. 1739, T.S. No. 956, carves out an exception to the FSIA. Brief for Respondents 52–53; Brief for the Republic of Liberia as *Amicus Curiae* 11. Article I of this Treaty provides, in pertinent part, that the nationals of the United States and Liberia "shall enjoy freedom of access to the courts of justice of the other on conforming to the local laws." The FSIA is clearly one of the "local laws" to which respondents must "conform" before bringing suit in United States courts.

We hold that the FSIA provides the sole basis for obtaining jurisdiction over a foreign state in the courts of this country, and that none of the enumerated exceptions to the Act apply to the facts of this case. The judgment of the Court of Appeals is therefore

Reversed.

[The concurring statement of Justice Blackmun, joined by Justice Marshall, has been omitted.]

Note

For a discussion of this decision, see Note, Obtaining Jurisdiction Over Foreign Sovereigns: The Alien Tort Statute Meets The Foreign Sovereign Immunities Act—Argentine Republic v. Amerada Hess Shipping Corp., 31 Harv. Int'l L.J. 368 (1990).

SAUDI ARABIA v. NELSON

Supreme Court of the United States, 1993.
507 U.S. 349, 113 S.Ct. 1471, 123 L.Ed.2d 47.

(Some footnotes omitted; others renumbered.)

JUSTICE SOUTER delivered the opinion of the Court.

The Foreign Sovereign Immunities Act of 1976 entitles foreign states to immunity from the jurisdiction of courts in the United States, 28 U.S.C. § 1604, subject to certain enumerated exceptions. § 1605. One is that a foreign state shall not be immune in any case "in which the action is based upon a commercial activity carried on in the United States by the foreign state." § 1605(a)(2). We hold that respondents' action alleging personal injury resulting from unlawful detention and torture by the Saudi Government is not "based upon a commercial activity" within the meaning of the Act, which consequently confers no jurisdiction over respondents' suit.

I

Because this case comes to us on a motion to dismiss the complaint, we assume that we have truthful factual allegations before us, see *United States* v. *Gaubert*, 499 U.S. 315, 327, though many of those allegations are subject to dispute * * *. Petitioner Kingdom of Saudi Arabia owns and operates petitioner King Faisal Specialist Hospital in Riyadh, as well as petitioner Royspec Purchasing Services, the hospital's corporate purchasing agent in the United States. * * * The Hospital Corporation of America, Ltd. (HCA), an independent corporation existing under the laws of the Cayman Islands, recruits Americans for employment at the hospital under an agreement signed with Saudi Arabia in 1973. * * *

In its recruitment effort, HCA placed an advertisement in a trade periodical seeking applications for a position as a monitoring systems engineer at the hospital. The advertisement drew the attention of respondent Scott Nelson in September 1983, while Nelson was in the United States. After interviewing for the position in Saudi Arabia, Nelson returned to the United States, where he signed an employment contract with the hospital, * * * satisfied personnel processing requirements, and attended an orientation session that HCA conducted for hospital employees. In the course of that program, HCA identified Royspec as the point of contact in the United States for family members who might wish to reach Nelson in an emergency. * * *

In December 1983, Nelson went to Saudi Arabia and began work at the hospital, monitoring all "facilities, equipment, utilities and maintenance systems to insure the safety of patients, hospital staff, and others." * * * He did his job without significant incident until March 1984, when he discovered safety defects in the hospital's oxygen and nitrous oxide lines that posed fire hazards and otherwise endangered patients' lives. * * * Over a period of several months, Nelson repeatedly advised hospital officials of the safety defects and reported the defects to a Saudi Government commission as well. * * * Hospital officials instructed Nelson to ignore the problems. * * *

The hospital's response to Nelson's reports changed, however, on September 27, 1984, when certain hospital employees summoned him to the hospital's security office where agents of the Saudi Government arrested him. The agents transported Nelson to a jail cell, in which they "shackled, tortured and bea[t]" him * * * and kept him four days without food * * * Although Nelson did not understand Arabic, government agents forced him to sign a statement written in that language, the content of which he did not know; a hospital employee who was supposed to act as Nelson's interpreter advised him to sign "anything" the agents gave him to avoid further beatings. * * * Two days later, government agents transferred Nelson to the Al Sijan Prison "to await trial on unknown charges." * * *

At the prison, Nelson was confined in an overcrowded cell area infested with rats, where he had to fight other prisoners for food and from which he was taken only once a week for fresh air and exercise. Ibid. Although police interrogators repeatedly questioned him in Arabic, Nelson did not learn the nature of the charges, if any, against him. * * * For several days, the Saudi Government failed to advise Nelson's family of his whereabouts, though a Saudi official eventually told Nelson's wife, respondent Vivian Nelson, that he could arrange for her husband's release if she provided sexual favors.

* * *

The District Court dismissed for lack of subject-matter jurisdiction under the Foreign Sovereign Immunities Act of 1976, 28 U.S.C. §§ 1330, 1602 *et seq.* * * *

The Court of Appeals reversed. 923 F.2d 1528 (C.A.11 1991). It concluded that Nelson's recruitment and hiring were commercial activities of Saudi Arabia and the hospital, carried on in the United States for purposes of the Act * * *. There was, the court reasoned, a sufficient nexus between those commercial activities and the wrongful acts that had allegedly injured the Nelsons: "the detention and torture of Nelson are so intertwined with his employment at the Hospital," the court explained, "that they are 'based upon' his recruitment and hiring" in the United States. * * *

II

The Foreign Sovereign Immunities Act "provides the sole basis for obtaining jurisdiction over a foreign state in the courts of this country." *Argentine Republic* v. *Amerada Hess Shipping Corp.*, 488 U.S. 428, 443 (1989). Under the Act, a foreign state is presumptively immune from the jurisdiction of United States courts; unless a specified exception applies, a federal court lacks subject-matter jurisdiction over a claim against a foreign state. *Verlinden B.V.* v. *Central Bank of Nigeria*, 461 U.S. 480, 488–489 (1983); see 28 U.S.C. § 1604; J. Dellapenna, Suing Foreign Governments and Their Corporations 11, and n. 64 (1988).

Only one such exception is said to apply here. The first clause of § 1605(a)(2) of the Act provides that a foreign state shall not be immune from the jurisdiction of United States courts in any case "in which the action is based upon a commercial activity carried on in the United States by the foreign state." The Act defines such activity as "commercial activity carried on by such state and having substantial contact with the United States," § 1603(e), and provides that a commercial activity may be "either a regular course of commercial conduct or a particular commercial transaction or act," the "commercial character of [which] shall be determined by reference to" its "nature," rather than its "purpose," § 1603(d).

There is no dispute here that Saudi Arabia, the hospital, and Royspec all qualify as "foreign state[s]" within the meaning of the Act. * * * For there to be jurisdiction in this case, therefore, the Nelsons' action must be "based upon" some "commercial activity" by petitioners that had "substantial contact" with the United States within the meaning of the Act. Because we conclude that the suit is not based upon any commercial activity by petitioners, we need not reach the issue of substantial contact with the United States.

We begin our analysis by identifying the particular conduct on which the Nelsons' action is "based" for purposes of the Act. See *Texas Trading & Milling Corp.* v. *Federal Republic of Nigeria*, 647 F.2d 300, 308 (C.A.2 1981), cert. denied, 454 U.S. 1148, 102 S.Ct. 1012, 71 L.Ed.2d 301 (1982); Donoghue, Taking the "Sovereign" Out of the Foreign Sovereign Immunities Act: A Functional Approach to the Commercial Activity Exception, 17 Yale J.Int'l L. 489, 500 (1992). Although the Act contains no definition of the phrase "based upon," and the relatively sparse legislative history offers no assistance, guidance is hardly necessary. In denoting conduct that forms the "basis," or "foundation," for a claim, see Black's Law Dictionary 151 (6th ed. 1990) (defining "base"); Random House Dictionary 172 (2d ed. 1987) (same); Webster's Third New International Dictionary 180, 181 (1976) (defining "base" and "based"), the phrase is read most naturally to mean those elements of a claim that, if proven, would entitle a plaintiff to relief under his theory of the case. * * *

We emphasized in *Weltover* that whether a state acts "in the manner of" a private party is a question of behavior, not motivation [quotation from *Weltover, supra,* omitted] * * *. We did not ignore the difficulty of distinguishing " 'purpose' (i.e., the *reason* why the foreign state engages in the activity) from 'nature' (i.e., the outward form of the conduct that the foreign state performs or agrees to perform)," but recognized that the Act "unmistakably commands" us to observe the distinction. 504 U.S., at 617, 112 S.Ct., at 2167 (emphasis in original). Because Argentina had merely dealt in the bond market in the manner of a private player, we held, its refinancing of the bonds qualified as a commercial activity for purposes of the Act despite the apparent governmental motivation. *Ibid.*

Unlike Argentina's activities that we considered in *Weltover*, the intentional conduct alleged here (the Saudi Government's wrongful arrest, imprisonment, and torture of Nelson) could not qualify as commercial under the restrictive theory. The conduct boils down to abuse of the power of its police by the Saudi Government, and however monstrous such abuse undoubtedly may be, a foreign state's exercise of the power of its police has long been understood for purposes of the restrictive theory as peculiarly sovereign in nature. See *Arango* v. *Guzman Travel Advisors Corp.*, 621 F.2d 1371, 1379 (C.A.5 1980); *Victory Transport Inc.* v. *Comisaria General de Abastecimientos y Transportes*, 336 F.2d 354, 360 (C.A.2 1964) (restrictive theory does extend immunity to a foreign state's "internal administrative acts"), cert. denied, 381 U.S. 934, 85 S.Ct. 1763, 14 L.Ed.2d 698 (1965); *Herbage* v. *Meese*, 747 F. Supp. 60, 67 (DC 1990), affirmance order, 292 U.S.App.D.C. 84, 946 F.2d 1564 (1991); K. Randall, Federal Courts and the International Human Rights Paradigm 93 (1990) (the Act's commercial-activity exception is irrelevant to cases alleging that a foreign state has violated human rights).[1] Exercise of the powers of police and penal officers is not the sort of action by which private parties can engage in commerce. "[S]uch acts as legislation, or the expulsion of an alien, or a denial of justice, cannot be performed by an individual acting in his own name. They can be performed only by the state acting as such." Lauterpacht, The Problem of Jurisdictional Immunities of Foreign States, 28 Brit.Y.B.Int'l L. 220, 225 (1952); see also *id.*, at 237.

The Nelsons and their *amici* urge us to give significance to their assertion that the Saudi Government subjected Nelson to the abuse alleged as retaliation for his persistence in reporting hospital safety violations, and argue that the character of the mistreatment was consequently commercial. One *amicus*, indeed, goes so far as to suggest that the Saudi Government "often uses detention and torture to resolve commercial disputes." Brief for Human Rights Watch as *Amicus Curiae* 6. But this argument does not alter the fact that the powers allegedly abused were those of police and penal officers. In any event, the argument is off the point, for it goes to purpose, the very fact the Act renders irrelevant to the question of an activity's commercial character. Whatever may have been the Saudi Government's motivation for its allegedly abusive treatment of Nelson, it remains the case that the Nelsons' action is based upon a sovereign activity immune from the subject-matter jurisdiction of United States courts under the Act.

* * *

1. The State Department's practice prior to the passage of the Act supports this understanding. Prior to the Act's passage, the State Department would determine in the first instance whether a foreign state was entitled to immunity and make an appropriate recommendation to the courts. See *Verlinden B.V.* v. *Central Bank of Nigeria*, 461 U.S. 480, 486–488, 103 S.Ct. 1962, 1967–1968, 76 L.Ed.2d 81 (1983). A compilation of available materials demonstrates that the Department recognized immunity with respect to claims involving the exercise of the power of the police or military of a foreign state. See Sovereign Immunity Decisions of the Department of State, May 1952 to January 1977 (M. Sandler, D. Vagts, & B. Ristau eds.), in 1977 Digest of United States Practice in International Law 1017, 1045–1046 (claim that Cuban armed guard seized cash from plaintiff at Havana airport); *id.*, at 1053–1054 (claim that Saudi militia fired on plaintiffs and caused personal and property damage).

Justice White points to an episode in which the State Department declined to recognize immunity with respect to a claim by Jamaican nationals, working in the United States, against the British West Indies Central Labour Organization, a foreign governmental agency. See id., at 1062–1063; *post,* at 1483, n. 3. In our view that episode bears little relation to this case, for the Jamaican nationals did not allege mistreatment by the police of a foreign state.

JUSTICE WHITE, with whom JUSTICE BLACKMUN joins, concurring in the judgment.

* * * The majority concludes that petitioners enjoy sovereign immunity because respondents' action is not "based upon a commercial activity." I disagree. I nonetheless concur in the judgment because in my view the commercial conduct upon which respondents base their complaint was not "carried on in the United States." * * * That, when the hospital calls in security to get even with a whistle-blower, it comes clothed in police apparel says more about the state-owned nature of the commercial enterprise than about the noncommercial nature of its tortious conduct.

[The statements of Justice Kennedy, with whom Justice Blackmun and Justice Stevens join as to Parts I–B and II, concurring in part and dissenting in part, and of Justice Blackmun, have been omitted.]

JUSTICE STEVENS, dissenting.

Under the Foreign Sovereign Immunities Act of 1976 (FSIA), a foreign state is subject to the jurisdiction of American courts if two conditions are met: The action must be "based upon a commercial activity" and that activity must have a "substantial contact with the United States." These two conditions should be separately analyzed because they serve two different purposes. The former excludes commercial activity from the scope of the foreign sovereign's immunity from suit; the second identifies the contacts with the United States that support the assertion of jurisdiction over the defendant.

* * *

Whether the first clause of § 1605(a)(2) broadly authorizes "general" jurisdiction over foreign entities that engage in substantial commercial activity in this country, or, more narrowly, authorizes only "specific" jurisdiction over particular commercial claims that have a substantial contact with the United States, petitioners' contacts with the United States in this case are, in my view, plainly sufficient to subject petitioners to suit in this country on a claim arising out of their nonimmune commercial activity relating to respondent. If the same activities had been performed by a private business, I have no doubt jurisdiction would be upheld. And that, of course, should be a touchstone of our inquiry; for as JUSTICE WHITE explains, * * * when a foreign nation sheds its uniquely sovereign status and seeks out the benefits of the private marketplace, it must, like any private party, bear the burdens and responsibilities imposed by that marketplace. I would therefore affirm the judgment of the Court of Appeals.

Notes

1. Justice Stevens' dissent states: "If the same activities had been performed by a private business, I have no doubt jurisdiction would be upheld." Nelson had responded to an advertisement for the hospital position in the United States and had signed his employment contract there. Would those facts have been sufficient to create in personam jurisdiction over Saudi Arabia under due process standards? See, e.g., Burger King Corp. v. Rudzewicz, 471 U.S. 462, 105 S.Ct. 2174, 85 L.Ed.2d 528 (1985). Could the activities alleged by Nelson have constituted a breach of an employment contract made in the United States? If so, should the

U.S. have exercised jurisdiction? Or does the use of the term "based on" in the FSIA (rather than "arising from," used in the typical long-arm statute) justify the result? Note that Nelson did not sue for breach of contract, possibly because the employment contract may have provided for the Saudi courts to be the exclusive forum. If the case had been based on a contract between private parties, would U.S. courts have construed an exclusive forum clause as covering the activities alleged and, in the affirmative case, have enforced it? Cf. M/S Bremen v. Zapata Off–Shore Co., 407 U.S. 1, 92 S.Ct. 1907, 32 L.Ed.2d 513 (1972).

2. If the FSIA had used the "arising from" terminology customarily used in long-arm statutes, would the result have been different? See Smit, The Foreign Sovereign Immunity Act of 1976: A Plea for Drastic Surgery, 1980 Proc. A.S.I.L. 49, 59.

3. In the principal case, could Saudi Arabia have relied on the act-of-state doctrine? See pp. 180–195.

4. In 1996, the FSIA was amended by addition of paragraph (a)(7) to the Section 1605, which now reads:

> (a) A foreign state shall not be immune from the jurisdiction of courts of the United States or of the States in any case—* * *
>
> (7) not otherwise covered by paragraph (2), in which money damages are sought against a foreign state for personal injury or death that was caused by an act of torture, extrajudicial killing, aircraft sabotage, hostage taking, or the provision of material support or resources (as defined in section 2339A of title 18) for such an act if such act or provision of material support is engaged in by an official, employee, or agent of such foreign state while acting within the scope of his or her office, employment, or agency, except that the court shall decline to hear a claim under this paragraph—
>
> (A) if the foreign state was not designated as a state sponsor of terrorism under section 6(j) of the Export Administration Act of 1979 (50 U.S.C. App. § 2405(j)) or section 620A of the Foreign Assistance Act of 1961 (22 U.S.C. § 2371) at the time the act occurred, unless later so designated as a result of such act; and
>
> (B) even if the foreign state is or was so designated, if—
>
> (i) the act occurred in the foreign state against which the claim has been brought and the claimant has not afforded the foreign state a reasonable opportunity to arbitrate the claim in accordance with accepted international rules of arbitration; or
>
> (ii) neither the claimant nor the victim was a national of the United States (as that term is defined in section 101(a)(22) of the Immigration and Nationality Act [8 USCA § 1101 (a)(22)]) when the act upon which the claim is based occurred.

5. After the 1996 amendment of the FSIA, could plaintiffs in a situation comparable to *Nelson* rely on Section 1605(a)(7)? (Note that Saudi Arabia has not been designated a state sponsor of terrorism within the meaning of that section.) If not, could they sue the persons who allegedly tortured them? Cf. Kadic v. Karadzic, 70 F.3d 232 (2d Cir.1995), p. 1169 supra. How might they obtain personal jurisdiction in such a case?

6. Since it is increasingly recognized that a state should not be immune from suit in regard to claims that arise from activities that states typically do not

engage in, should states be protected from suit in actions based on conduct that is generally recognized as improper state action? Should the international community be more intent upon exposing states to suits based on commercial conduct than to actions based on conduct that is universally regarded as offending basic notions of civilized conduct? Is it more embarrassing for a state to be held liable for torture than for commercial obligations?

7. Is there a defamation exception when adjudicatory authority is premised on commercial activities? In Bryks v. Canadian Broadcasting Corp., 906 F.Supp. 204 (S.D.N.Y.1995), the court answered affirmatively. See also Gregorian v. Izvestia, 871 F.2d 1515 (9th Cir.1989), cert. denied, 493 U.S. 891, 110 S.Ct. 237, 107 L.Ed.2d 188 (1989).

8. Is the FSIA applicable if the tortious conduct occurred wholly outside the United States, but the consequences were suffered in the United States? Compare Frolova v. Union of Soviet Socialist Republics, 761 F.2d 370 (7th Cir.1985) with Restatement Third § 454, Comment *e*.

ALEJANDRE v. REPUBLIC OF CUBA

United States District Court for the Southern District of Florida, 1997.
996 F.Supp. 1239.

(Some footnotes omitted; others renumbered.)

JAMES LAWRENCE KING, District Judge.

* * * The government of Cuba, on February 24, 1996, in outrageous contempt for international law and basic human rights, murdered four human beings in international airspace over the Florida Straits. The victims were Brothers to the Rescue pilots, flying two civilian, unarmed planes on a routine humanitarian mission, searching for rafters in the waters between Cuba and the Florida Keys.

As the civilian planes flew over international waters, a Russian built MiG 29 of the Cuban Air Force, without warning, reason, or provocation, blasted the defenseless planes out of the sky with sophisticated air-to-air missiles in two separate attacks. The pilots and their aircraft disintegrated in the mid-air explosions following the impact of the missiles. The destruction was so complete that the four bodies were never recovered.

The personal representatives of three of the deceased instituted this action against the Republic of Cuba ("Cuba") and the Cuban Air Force to recover monetary damages for the killings. One of the victims was not a U.S. citizen and his family therefore could not join in the suit. This is the first lawsuit to rely on recent legislative enactments that strip foreign states of immunity for certain acts of terrorism. Neither Cuba nor the Cuban Air Force has defended this suit, asserting through a diplomatic note that this Court has no jurisdiction over Cuba or its political subdivisions. A default was thus entered against both Defendants on April 23, 1997 pursuant to Rule 55(a) of the Federal Rules of Civil Procedure. Because this is a lawsuit against a foreign state, however, the Court may not enter judgment by default. Rather, the claimants must establish their "claim or right to relief by evidence that is satisfactory to the Court." 28 U.S.C. § 1608(e) (1994) * * *.

II. FINDINGS OF FACT

At trial, Plaintiffs presented extensive testimonial and documentary evidence in support of their claims. Because Cuba has presented no defense, the Court will accept as true Plaintiffs' uncontroverted factual allegations. * * *

Alejandre, Costa, and De la Peña were all members of a Miami-based humanitarian organization known as *Hermanos al Rescate*, or Brothers to the Rescue. The organization's principal mission was to search the Florida Straits for rafters, Cuban refugees who had fled the island nation on precarious inner tubes or makeshift rafts, often perishing at sea. Brothers to the Rescue would locate the rafters and provide them with life-saving assistance by informing the U.S. Coast Guard of their location and condition.

On the morning of February 24, 1996, two of Brothers to the Rescue's civilian Cessna 337 aircraft departed from Opa Locka Airport in South Florida. Costa piloted one plane, accompanied by Pablo Morales, a Cuban national who had once been a rafter himself. De la Peña piloted the second plane, with Alejandre as his passenger. Before departing, the planes notified both Miami and Havana traffic controllers of their flight plans, which were to take them south of the 24th parallel. The 24th parallel, well north of Cuba's twelve-mile territorial sea, is the northernmost boundary of the Havana Flight Information Region. Commercial and civilian aircraft routinely fly in this area, and aviation practice requires that they notify Havana's traffic controllers when crossing south through the 24th parallel. Both Brothers to the Rescue planes complied with this custom by contacting Havana, identifying themselves, and stating their position and altitude.

While the two planes were still north of the 24th parallel, the Cuban Air Force launched two military aircraft, a MiG–29 and a MiG–23, operating under the control of Cuba's military ground station. The MiGs carried guns, close range missiles, bombs, and rockets and were piloted by members of the Cuban Air Force experienced in combat. Excerpts from radio communications between the MiG–29 and Havana Military Control detail what transpired next: [transcript omitted]

The missiles disintegrated the Brothers to the Rescue planes, killing their occupants instantly and leaving almost no recoverable debris. Only a large oil slick marked the spot where the planes went down. The Cuban Air Force never notified or warned the civilian planes, never attempted other methods of interception, and never gave them the opportunity to land. The MiGs' first and only response was the intentional and malicious destruction of the Brothers to the Rescue planes and their four innocent occupants. Such behavior violated clearly established international norms requiring the exhaustion of all measures before resort to aggression against any aircraft and banning the use of force against civilian aircraft altogether.[1]

* * *

1. These norms have been codified in various international instruments. *See, e.g.*, Convention on International Civil Aviation, Dec. 7, 1944, 61 Stat. 1180, 15 U.N.T.S. 295 (both the United States and Cuba are parties to the Convention). The proscription on using force against civilian planes attaches even if they penetrate foreign airspace. *See, e.g.*, Kay Hailbronner, *Freedom of the Air and the Convention on the Law of the Sea*, 77 Am. J. Int'l L. 490, 514 (1983) ("Even if an order to land is deliberately disregarded, a civil unarmed aircraft that intrudes into foreign airspace may not be fired upon."). Common sense dictates that the negligible threat civilian planes may pose does not justify the possible loss of life.

III. Conclusions of Law

A. *Jurisdiction and Liability*

District courts have original jurisdiction to hear suits, not barred by foreign sovereign immunity, that are brought against foreign states. * * * Most recently, Congress crafted an additional, narrow exception to foreign sovereign immunity through the Anti–Terrorism and Effective Death Penalty Act of 1996 ("AEDPA"), Pub.L. No. 104–132, § 221, 110 Stat. 1214. AEDPA amended the FSIA to allow suits in U.S. courts against a foreign state that engages in acts of terrorism under certain specified circumstances. As a result, the FSIA now provides that a foreign state shall not be immune from the jurisdiction of U.S. courts in any case

> in which money damages are sought against a foreign state for personal injury or death that was caused by an act of torture, extrajudicial killing, aircraft sabotage, hostage taking, or the provision of material support or resources ... for such an act if such act or provision of material support is engaged in by an official, employee, or agent of such foreign state while acting within the scope of his or her office, employment, or agency.

28 U.S.C.A. § 1605(a)(7).[2] In addition, section 1605(a)(7) imposes the following requirements: (1) the U.S. must have designated the foreign state as a state sponsor of terrorism pursuant to section 6(j) of the Export Administration Act of 1979; (2) the act must have occurred outside the foreign state; and (3) the claimants and victims must have been U.S. nationals at the time the acts occurred.[3] Id. § 1605(a)(7)(A)-(B).

The record of this trial clearly establishes that all of these requirements have been met. First, the unprovoked firing of deadly rockets at defenseless, unarmed civilian aircraft undoubtedly comes within the statute's meaning of "extrajudicial killing." That term is defined in reference to its use in the Torture Victim Protection Act of 1991 ("TVPA"), which states that "the term 'extrajudicial killing' means a deliberated killing not authorized by a previous judgment pronounced by a regularly constituted court affording all the judicial guarantees which are recognized as indispensable by civilized peoples." 28 U.S.C. § 1350 note (1994). Cuba's actions in this case easily come within this definition. The occupants of the two civilian, unarmed planes received no warning whatsoever of their imminent destruction, much less the judicial process contemplated by the TVPA. *See Lafontant v. Aristide*, 844 F.Supp. 128, 138 (E.D.N.Y.1994) (finding that assassination of political opponent fell within statute's definition of extrajudicial killing).

2. The Court notes that it may retroactively apply AEDPA's amendments to the FSIA in this case. As part of AEDPA, the new exception to immunity was enacted on April 24, 1996. Yet the acts in question occurred in February 1996, two months before the FSIA was amended. AEDPA itself, however, addresses when its provisions are to become effective. It provides that the amendments to the FSIA "shall apply to any cause of action arising before, on, or after the date of the enactment of this Act." Pub.L. 104–132, § 221(c), 110 Stat. 1214. Therefore, the plain language of the statute evidences a clear Congressional intent to have section 1605(a)(7) apply retroactively. In cases such as this one, where "Congress has expressly prescribed the statute's proper reach[,] there is no need to resort to judicial default rules." *Landgraf v. USI Film Prods.*, 511 U.S. 244, 271, 114 S.Ct. 1483, 128 L.Ed.2d 229 (1994). Thus, Plaintiffs may rely on section 1605(a)(7)'s exception to immunity.

3. It is this last requirement that prevents the family of Pablo Morales, the fourth Brothers to the Rescue member who was killed, to take part in this suit. Pablo Morales was a Cuban national at the time of the incident.

Second, the Cuban Air Force was acting as an agent of Cuba when it committed the killings.[4] The evidence adduced at trial demonstrated how the pilots of the Cuban MiGs obtained authorization from state officials prior to the shootdown of each plane and hearty congratulations from those officials after the planes were destroyed.

Third, section 1605(a)(7)'s requirement that the foreign state have been designated as a state sponsor of terrorism has also been satisfied. Cuba was one of only seven states so designated at the time pursuant to the authority of the Export Administration Act of 1979. See 61 Fed.Reg. 12,927 (1996).

Fourth, the act occurred outside of Cuban territory. Plaintiffs have presented undisputed and competent evidence that the planes were shot down over international waters. As discussed above, the ICAO Report concluded that the planes were over international waters when they were destroyed. * * *

Finally, Plaintiffs and three of the four murdered pilots were U.S. citizens at the time of the shootdown. De la Peña and Costa were born in the United States, and Alejandre was a naturalized U.S. citizen. Plaintiffs were also U.S. citizens when the incident took place. Consequently, the facts of this case fall squarely within the requirements of section 1605(a)(7). Indeed, this is precisely the type of action for which Congress meant to provide redress by stripping terrorist states of immunity from the judgment of U.S. courts.

Having established an exception to foreign sovereign immunity, Plaintiffs base their substantive cause of action on a different statute, also enacted in 1996, entitled Civil Liability for Acts of State Sponsored Terrorism, Pub.L. 104–208, § 589, 110 Stat. 3009 (codified at 28 U.S.C.A. § 1605 note (West. Supp.1997)) ("Civil Liability Act"). The Civil Liability Act creates a cause of action against agents of a foreign state that act under the conditions specified in FSIA section 1605(a)(7). It thus serves as an enforcement provision for acts described in section 1605(a)(7). If Plaintiffs prove an agent's liability under this Act, the foreign state employing the agent would also incur liability under the theory of respondeat superior. *See Skeen* v. *Federative Republic of Brazil*, 566 F.Supp. 1414, 1417 (D.D.C.1983) (explaining that section 1605(a)(5) "is essentially a respondeat superior statute, providing an employer (the foreign state) with liability for certain tortious acts of its employees."). Because, as detailed above, Plaintiffs have presented compelling evidence that all of the relevant statutory requirements have been met, the Court finds that both the Cuban Air Force and Cuba are liable for the murders of Alejandre, Costa, and De la Peña. *Cf. Rafidain*, 15 F.3d at 242–43 (finding evidence sufficient to justify default judgment against foreign governmental entities); *de Letelier v. Republic of Chile*, 502 F.Supp. 259, 266 (D.D.C.1980) (finding evidence sufficient to justify default judgment against Republic of Chile for murder of Chilean ambassador).

B. *Damages*

The amount of damages that Plaintiffs may recover in this case is specified in the Civil Liability Act. It provides that an agent of a foreign state

4. The Cuban Air Force is clearly an agent of the Cuban state, as it acts on Cuba's behalf and subject to Cuba's control. See Archer v. Trans/American Servs., Ltd., 834 F.2d 1570, 1573 (11th Cir.1988); Restatement (Second) of Agency § 1 (1958) (defining agency relationship).

who commits an extrajudicial killing as described in FSIA section 1605(a)(7) shall be liable for "money damages which may include economic damages, solatium, pain and suffering, and punitive damages." 28 U.S.C.A. § 1605 note. Thus, the Cuban Air Force is liable for both compensatory and punitive damages. Under the theory of respondeat superior, Cuba is liable for the same amount of damages as its agent, with the exception of punitive damages, which the FSIA prohibits against foreign states. 28 U.S.C. § 1606.[5]

1. Compensatory Damages

[Discussion and calculations omitted.]

2. Punitive Damages

In addition to compensatory damages, punitive damages are explicitly permitted by the Civil Liability Act.[6] Because this is the first case to proceed to trial under this Act, however, there is no precedent to guide the Court in determining whether punitive damages are appropriate in this particular case, and if so, in what amount. Thus, the Court will look both to the traditional purpose behind awarding punitive damages and to analogous federal court cases addressing the role of punitive damages in cases of egregious international human rights violations.

The purpose of punitive, or exemplary, damages has traditionally been twofold. First, they may serve as a tool to punish truly reprehensible conduct. *See Paul v. Avril*, 901 F.Supp. 330, 336 (S.D.Fla.1994) (observing that exemplary damages are appropriate when defendant's actions are "malicious, wanton, and oppressive") * * *. In this way, the aggrieved plaintiff is given a socially acceptable avenue of retaliation, and, perhaps more importantly, the "punitive nature of exemplary awards also affords society a means of retribution for wrongs against the community interest." * * * Punitive damages are also an appropriate remedy in international law. As the Supreme Court has observed, "[A]n attack from revenge and malignity, from gross abuse of power, and a settled purpose of mischief ... may be punished by all the penalties which the law of nations can properly administer." *The Marianna Flora*, 24 U.S. (11 Wheat.) 1, 41, 6 L.Ed. 405 (1825).

The law also provides for awards of punitive damages upon the sound reasoning that they will deter others from committing similar acts. Courts reason that if a sizeable monetary sum over and above compensatory damages

5. Section 1606 of the FSIA, which determines the extent of liability in suits against a foreign state, provides in pertinent part: "The foreign state shall be liable in the same manner and to the same extent as a private individual under like circumstances; but a foreign state *except for an agency or instrumentality thereof* shall not be liable for punitive damages." 28 U.S.C. § 1606 (emphasis added). Thus, although punitive damages may not be assessed against the Republic of Cuba, they may be assessed against the Cuban Air Force. See *Gibbons v. Republic of Ireland,* 532 F. Supp. 668, 671 (D.D.C.1982); *de Letelier*, 502 F.Supp. at 266–67 (D.D.C. 1980).

6. The Court observes again that it may impose judgment and damages retroactively. First, Congress expressed its clear intent in AEDPA to allow suits against terrorist states for acts occurring before AEDPA's effective date. See [supra note 2]. Second, the Civil Liability Act and AEDPA's amendments to the FSIA are jurisdictional provisions, and as the Supreme Court has explained, "We have regularly applied intervening statutes conferring or ousting jurisdiction, whether or not jurisdiction lay when the underlying conduct occurred or when the suit was filed." *Landgraf*, 511 U.S. at 274. Finally, compensatory damages were already available against foreign states, and punitive damages were available against foreign governmental entities, long before changes to the FSIA made this suit possible. *See* 28 U.S.C. § 1606 (1994).

is assessed against the wrongdoer, he and others may be prevented from engaging in similar behavior in the future. * * *

Most courts faced with gross violations of international human rights have employed the tool of punitive damages to achieve these dual purposes. By granting large exemplary awards, courts have both expressed their condemnation of human rights abuses and attempted to deter other international actors from engaging in similar practices. Most of these cases have been brought pursuant to the authority of the Alien Tort Claims Act ("ATCA"), 28 U.S.C. § 1350, which allows aliens to sue in U.S. federal court for torts that violate "the law of nations or a treaty of the United States," and the more recently enacted TVPA, which establishes a cause of action against individuals for torture.

An early example is the seminal case of *Filartiga v. Pena–Irala*, 577 F.Supp. 860 (E.D.N.Y.1984), which addressed the propriety of punitive damages under the ATCA. * * *

> Chief among the considerations the court must weigh is the fact that this case concerns not a local tort but a wrong as to which the world has seen fit to speak. Punitive damages are designed not merely to teach a defendant not to repeat his conduct but to deter others from following his example. To accomplish that purpose this court must make clear the depth of the international revulsion against torture and measure the award in accordance with the enormity of the offense. Thereby the judgment may perhaps have some deterrent effect.

Id. at 866 (internal citation omitted). These considerations led the court to assess $5 million in punitive damages against the individual general for each plaintiff. Courts facing similar claims under the ATCA have followed *Filartiga*'s lead and awarded sizeable punitive damages. See Beth Stephens & Michael Ratner, *International Human Rights Litigation in U.S. Courts* 213–14 (1996). * * *

Part of the reason why punitive damages have been extensively awarded in cases brought under the ATCA is that they serve to redress conduct so heinous that it has been condemned by the world community. Punitive damages help reinforce "the consensus of the community of humankind," Filartiga, 577 F.Supp. at 863, that horrific abuses against the person will not be tolerated. Although, unlike claimants proceeding under the ATCA, Plaintiffs in this case do not have to prove a violation of international law in order to be entitled to damages, the Court finds that such an inquiry would be helpful in assessing the amount of punitive damages that should be awarded.

Like the torture in *Filartiga*, the practice of summary execution has been consistently condemned by the world community. A multitude of international agreements and declarations proclaim every individual's right not to be deprived of life wantonly and arbitrarily.[7] So widespread is the consensus

7. International instruments proscribing extrajudicial killings, to cite only a few, include the following: Universal Declaration of Human Rights, Dec. 10, 1948, art. 3, G.A. Res. 217A(III), U.N. Doc. A/810; International Covenant on Civil and Political Rights, Dec. 16, 1966, art. 6(1), G.A. Res. 2200, U.N. GAOR, 21st Sess., Supp. No. 16, U.N. Doc. A/6316, 999 U.N.T.S. 171; American Declaration of the Rights and Duties of Man, May 2, 1948, art. I, OEA/ser.L/V/II.23, doc. 21, rev. 6 (1979). Moreover, the international community's commitment to the peaceful resolution of disputes is fundamental to the structure of the United against extrajudicial killing that "every instrument or agreement that has attempted to define the scope of international human rights has 'recognized a right to life coupled with a right to due process to protect that right.' " *Xuncax*, 886 F.Supp. at 185 (citation omitted). The ban on extrajudicial killing thus rises to the level of *jus cogens*, a norm of international law so fundamental that it is binding on all members of the world community.[8] *See de Sanchez v. Banco Central de Nicaragua*, 770 F.2d 1385, 1397 (5th Cir.1985) ("[T]he standards of human rights that have been generally accepted—and hence incorporated into the law of nations ... encompass only such basic rights as the right not to be murdered, tortured, or otherwise subjected to cruel, inhuman or degrading punishment ... and the right not to be arbitrarily detained."); *Forti v. Suarez–Mason*, 672 F. Supp. 1531, 1542 (N.D.Cal.1987) ("The proscription of summary execution or murder by the state appears to be universal, is readily definable, and is of course obligatory."); *De Letelier*, 488 F. Supp. at 673 (stating that assassination is "clearly contrary to the precepts of humanity as recognized in both national and international law"); Restatement (Third) of Foreign Relations Law of the United States § 702(c) (1986) ("A state violates [customary] international law if, as a matter of state policy, it practices, encourages, or condones ... the murder or causing the disappearance of individuals.").

Cuba's extrajudicial killings of Mario T. De la Peña, Carlos Alberto Costa, and Armando Alejandre violated clearly established principles of international law. More importantly, they were inhumane acts against innocent civilians. The fact that the killings were premeditated and intentional, outside of Cuban territory, wholly disproportionate, and executed without warning or process makes this act unique in its brazen flouting of international norms. There appears to be no precedent for a military aircraft intentionally shooting down an unarmed, civilian plane. The Court must therefore fashion a remedy consistent with the unprecedented nature of this act. See *Filartiga*, 577 F.Supp. at 865 ("The nature of the acts is plainly important."). The Court finds that Plaintiffs have proven their clear entitlement to punitive damages. Based upon this record, the Court would be shirking its duty were it to refrain from entering a substantial punitive damage award for the dual purpose of (1) expressing the strongest possible condemnation of the Cuban government for its responsibility for commission of this monstrous act, and (2) deterring Defendants from ever again committing other crimes of terrorism.

* * *

* * * The record reflects that each MiG is worth approximately $45 million, and that the Cuban Air Force owns approximately 102 MiGs. The total value of this fleet, which is undoubtedly only a fraction of the Cuban Air Force's total assets, is therefore approximately $4.59 billion. The Court finds that 1% of this total, or $45.9 million, should be assessed against the Cuban Air Force for each of the killings. This figure is dictated by the unparalleled nature of Cuba's actions and comports with similar judgments against individ-

Nations Charter and to other international instruments. U.N. Charter, arts. 1, 2, 33, 39; *see also* Charter of the Organization of American States arts. 24–27, 3, para. I.

8. As the Ninth Circuit has explained, "Jus cogens norms, which are nonderogable and peremptory, enjoy the highest status within customary international law, are binding on all nations, and can not be preempted by treaty." *U.S. v. Matta–Ballesteros*, 71 F.3d 754, 764 n. 5 (9th Cir.1995), *cert. denied*, 519 U.S. 1118, 117 S.Ct. 965, 136 L.Ed.2d 850 (1997).

ual, non-governmental defendants. See Haslip, 499 U.S. at 19 (upholding punitive damages award that was more than four times amount of compensatory damages). Monetary damages, in whatever amount, can never adequately express the revulsion of this Court, and every civilized society, over these callous murders. Perhaps, however, this decision may serve in some small way as a deterrent to others in the future.

Accordingly, after a careful review of the record, and the Court being otherwise fully advised, it is

ORDERED and ADJUDGED that judgment is hereby entered on behalf of Plaintiffs and against Defendants the Republic of Cuba and the Cuban Air Force for total compensatory damages of $49,927,911. Further, judgment is hereby entered for Plaintiffs and against the Defendant the Cuban Air Force (only) as punitive damages, the sum of One Hundred Thirty Seven Million, Seven Hundred Thousand Dollars ($137,700,000). * * *

Notes

1. In the principal case, did the court consider whether, under due process standards, it had personal jurisdiction over the defendants? Even though the defendants had not appeared, should it have done so? Section 1608(e) provides that no judgment by default shall be rendered unless "the claimant establishes his claim or right to relief by evidence satisfactory to the court." Does the claimant's obligation under this provision cover establishing that the court has personal jurisdiction over the foreign state? The only contacts between the facts on which the claims were based and the United States were the U.S. nationalities of the plaintiffs and the U.S. registration of the plane. Were these contacts sufficient for due process purposes? See Notes at p. 1216 supra.

2. The Supreme Court has ruled that service of process and the exercise of judicial jurisdiction, when challenged under due process standards, must be determined by reference to applicable statutory provisions. See Wuchter v. Pizzutti, 276 U.S. 13, 48 S.Ct. 259, 72 L.Ed. 446 (1928) (service); Shaffer v. Heitner, 433 U.S. 186, 97 S.Ct. 2569, 53 L.Ed.2d 683 (1977) (jurisdiction). Does Section 1605(a)(7) identify circumstances that, under due process standards, are adequate to create personal jurisdiction?

3. Is there a basis for the U.S. exercise of legislative jurisdiction under Section 1605(a)(7)? Could the universality principle or the passive personality principle (or both) be applicable? See pp. 1118, 1134.

4. If a foreign state cannot validly claim immunity from jurisdiction for torture in the circumstances defined in Section 1605(a)(7), can it validly claim such immunity when it engages in torture in circumstances not defined in Section 1605(a)(7)? Should this Section be given a teleological interpretation or be narrowly limited? It has been argued that Section 1604 of the FSIA should have provided for non-immunity, except in statutorily defined circumstances. See Smit, The Foreign Sovereign Immunity Act of 1976: A Plea for Drastic Surgery, 1980 Proc. A.S.I.L. 49. See also Saudi Arabia v. Nelson, p. 1226 supra and Note 6 on p. 1231 supra.

5. It would appear that the drafters of Section 1605(a)(7) focused their attention on cases like Nelson and Amerada Hess, pp. 1220–1230 supra, which dealt with immunity, and failed to discern the problem of exercising personal jurisdiction in the statutorily defined circumstances.The FSIA's commingling of

rules of immunity and rules of personal jurisdiction criticized earlier (see Smit, Note 4 supra), naturally led to this oversight. If the FSIA had not attempted to define simultaneously the circumstances in which a foreign state could both be sued and not be entitled to immunity, would it have been possible to find general personal jurisdiction over Cuba on the basis of its non-immune activities in the U.S.? Cf. Helicopteros Nacionales de Colombia S.A. v. Hall, 466 U.S. 408, 104 S.Ct. 1868, 80 L.Ed.2d 404 (1984).

6. Before the addition of subsection (7) to Section 1605(a), (see p. 1231 supra) the estate of Alisa Michelle Flatow, who had been killed in a bombing attack on a bus in Israeli-occupied territory, brought an action against Iran, alleging that Iran had sponsored the attack. After the court had dismissed the action on the ground of Iran's immunity from suit, Congress reacted by two statutory measures. First, it added subsection (7) to Section 1605(a); and second, it enacted a provision called Civil Liability for Acts of State Sponsored Terrorism, Pub. L. 104–208, 110 Stat. 3009 (Sept. 30, 1996), reprinted at 28 U.S.C.A. § 1605 note (West 1997 Supp.), also known as the Flatow Amendment. Both of these enactments were first construed and applied in the *Alejandre* case, p. 1232 supra. Subsequently, under 28 U.S.C.A. § 1610(f), the plaintiffs in the *Alejandre* case were permitted to recover $97 million, representing compensatory damages, interest, and sanctions for non-compliance with discovery orders.

7. After enactment of these measures, the Flatow estate renewed its action against Iran. This action resulted in an award of $20 million for punitive damages. The court ruled that Section 1605(a)(7) applied retroactively and specifically addressed the issue of in personam jurisdiction. It ruled that "[S]overeign contacts, therefore, should be sufficient to sustain general jurisdiction over Defendants, at least for the purposes of 28 U.S.C.A. § 1605(a)(7)" and that "a foreign state that sponsors terrorist activities which cause[s] [sic] the death or personal injury of a United States national will invariably have sufficient contacts with the United States to satisfy Due Process." Flatow v. Islamic Republic of Iran, 999 F.Supp. 1, 23 (D.D.C.1998). On the Flatow estate's efforts to execute this judgment against Iranian-owned properties in the United States, see Flatow v. Islamic Republic of Iran, 67 F.Supp.2d 535 (D.Md.1999), affirmed, 225 F.3d 653 (4th Cir.2000), and discussion in Murphy, Contemporary Practice of the United States Relating to International Law, 95 A.J.I.L. 132, 134–139 (2001). See also Note 10 below.

8. In Rein v. Socialist People's Libyan Arab Jamahiriya, 995 F.Supp. 325 (E.D.N.Y.1998), affirmed, 162 F.3d 748 (2d Cir.1998), cert. denied, 525 U.S. 1003, 119 S.Ct. 2337, 144 L.Ed.2d 235 (1999), representatives of American nationals on Pan Am Flight 103 which crashed in Lockerbie, Scotland sued Libya as alleged sponsor of the plane's destruction. Libya appeared and moved to dismiss for lack of subject matter and in personam jurisdiction and failure to state a claim for relief; Libya also raised various constitutional defenses. The district court ruled that Section 1605(a)(7) had retroactive effect and denied the motion to dismiss. On interlocutory appeal, the Second Circuit found no constitutional infirmity in Congress's decision to make federal jurisdiction depend on the State Department's determination of whether a given foreign state is a sponsor of terrorism, especially since Libya had been so designated before Congress acted. Other issues were reserved for subsequent proceedings.

Would you have advised Libya to appear in order to challenge jurisdiction? Of the states covered by the state terrorism amendment, Libya is exceptional in having done so. Cuba, Iran, and Syria have all defaulted in actions brought against them under this section; Iraq filed an unsuccessful motion to dismiss in Daliberti v. Republic of Iraq, 97 F.Supp.2d 38 (D.D.C.2000), contending that the court lacked jurisdiction under the FSIA. See cases discussed in Murphy, supra Note 7, 95 A.J.I.L. at 135–137 (2001); see also 94 A.J.I.L. at 117–124 (2000). If a state appears to contest jurisdiction under the FSIA, is it bound by an adverse determination (unless it succeeds in having that determination reversed on appeal)?

9. On the decisions based on Section 1605(a)(7) and the Flatow Amendment, see Trent, An Unreasonable Act: The Extraterritorial Reach of the Cuban Liberty and Democratic Solidarity (Libertad) Act and Its Practical Implications, 10 N.Y. Int'l. L. Rev. 77 (1997); Early, Note, Flatow v. Islamic Republic of Iran and the Foreign Sovereign Immunity Act: Is Peace of Mind Enough?, 14 Conn. J. Int'l. L. 203 (1999); Glannon & Atik, Politics and Personal Jurisdiction: Suing State Sponsors of Terrorism Under the 1996 Amendments to the Foreign Sovereign Immunities Act, 87 Geo.L.J. 675 (1999).

10. Are the plaintiffs in the Alejandre, Flatow, and Rein cases likely to recover on their judgments? The plaintiffs in Alejandre sought to levy execution on debts owed by American enterprises to the Cuban Telephone Company, but the court of appeals vacated an order by the district court issuing writs of garnishment. The appellate court reasoned that the telephone company, although wholly owned by Cuba, was a separate entity. Alejandre v. Telefonica Larga Distancia de Puerto Rico, 183 F.3d 1277 (11th Cir.1999). The plaintiffs in Flatow also sought to execute against Alavi Foundation, an Iran-related organization. The district court quashed plaintiff's writ of execution and enjoined them from issuing any writ of execution in the future. Flatow v. Islamic Republic of Iran (Flatow II), 67 F. Supp.2d 535 (D.Md. 1999), aff'd. 225 F.3d 653 (4th Cir.2000). For discussion of these and related efforts, and of legislative initiatives to amend the FSIA again to enable plaintiffs to execute their judgments, see Murphy, supra, 94 A.J.I.L 117–124 (2000); 95 A.J.I.L. 137–139 (2001). See also p. 1268 infra.

On October 28, 2000, President Clinton signed new legislation providing for such execution but simultaneously exercised his statutory authority to waive the new provision, on the ground that attachments or executions against blocked assets "would impede the ability of the President to conduct foreign policy in the interest of national security * * *." 65 Fed. Reg. 66,483 (2000), cited in Murphy, 95 A.J.I.L. at 139. Should the President have authority to compromise the claims under such judgments as part of a process of eventually normalizing relations with Cuba, Iran and Libya?

11. In the Alejandre case, the Court developed the rules determining liability and remedies without reference to the conflict of laws rules prevailing in the state in which it was sitting. Should the Congress itself have formulated the applicable rules, in particular those relating to punitive damages to be imposed on a foreign state instrumentality, rather than leave this to the courts?

12. Also noteworthy is Section 1605(a)(7)(B) which conditions the claimant's right to pursue a claim under Section 1605(a)(7), when the conduct complained of occurred in the foreign state, on the claimant's having "afforded the foreign state a reasonable opportunity to arbitrate the claim in accordance with acceptable international rules of arbitration." Under this provision, the court would have to determine both what opportunity is "reasonable" and what "accepted international rules of arbitration" are. What advice should counsel for the claimant give when asked to formulate a proposal to the foreign state conforming to the requirements of this provision? Would a proposal to arbitrate under the Interna-

tional Rules of the American Arbitration Association or the Rules of the ICC International Court of Arbitration suffice? Or would the UNCITRAL Rules or the Rules of the Permanent Court of Arbitration be preferable? See Chapter 11, p. 853, on arbitration.

C. WAIVER OF IMMUNITY

FOREIGN SOVEREIGN IMMUNITIES ACT OF 1976

[See 28 U.S.C.A. §§ 1605(a)(1) and 1610.]

The Act distinguishes between three kinds of waiver: (1) waiver of immunity from jurisdiction (Section 1605(a)(1)); (2) waiver of immunity from attachment in aid of execution or from execution (Section 1610(a)-(c)); and (3) waiver of immunity from attachment prior to the entry of judgment (Section 1610(d)). In addition, counterclaims, regulated in Section 1607, may be regarded as a particular form of waiver. See p. 1246. The first two forms of waiver may be effectuated "either explicitly or by implication," while immunity from pre-judgment attachment may be waived only "explicitly." All three forms of waiver are effective "notwithstanding any withdrawal of the waiver which the foreign state may purport to effect except in accordance with the terms of the waiver."

In Siderman de Blake v. Republic of Argentina, 965 F.2d 699 (9th Cir.1992), cert. denied, 507 U.S. 1017, 113 S.Ct. 1812, 123 L.Ed.2d 444 (1993), the plaintiff sought to recover for torture and wrongful seizure of property by Argentine authorities. In response to Argentina's plea of sovereign immunity, the court ruled, *inter alia,* that Argentina had waived this defense by requesting the assistance of California state courts in proceedings conducted against the plaintiff in Argentina in pursuit of the very conduct that formed the basis for plaintiff's action:

> Here, we confront a situation where Argentina apparently not only envisioned United States court participation in its persecution of the Sidermans, but by its actions deliberately implicated our courts in that persecution. The Sidermans have presented evidence that a year after Jose, Lea and Carlos Siderman fled Argentina in fear for their lives, the Argentine military authorities altered the Tucuman provincial land records to show that they had held title only to 127, as opposed to 127,000 acres of land in the Province, and that in their last-minute efforts to raise cash they had thus sold property which did not belong to them. The Tucuman Public Prosecutor then initiated criminal proceedings against Jose Siderman for this "fraudulent" sale, and had the Tucuman Supreme Court enlist the aid of our courts, via a letter rogatory, in serving him with process. "The letter rogatory, dated May 11, 1980, informed the Presiding Judge of the Los Angeles Superior Court that criminal proceedings were pending against Jose Siderman in the Supreme Court of Tucuman. It requested the court's assistance in serving papers on Siderman, who was living in Los Angeles at the time. While the court complied with the request, the record is not clear as to the subsequent course of lawsuit. In their papers in support of jurisdiction, the Sidermans suggest that the Argentine military authorities sought to obtain Jose's return to Argentina in order to further torture and perhaps even to kill him." * * *

We conclude that the Sidermans have presented evidence sufficient to support a finding that Argentina has implicitly waived its sovereign immunity with respect to their claims for torture. The evidence indicates that Argentina deliberately involved United States courts in its efforts to persecute Jose Siderman. If Argentina has engaged our courts in the very course of activity for which the Sidermans seek redress, it has waived its immunity as to that redress.

Notes

1. A waiver may be contained in a treaty with a foreign state. On whether a waiver by treaty waives immunity from pre-judgment attachment, see p. 1258, Note 7 infra.

2. An explicit waiver may also be contained in a contract with a private party. See Sen. Rep. No. 94–1310, 94th Cong.2d Sess., p. 17 (1976). Can an explicit waiver also be effectuated by a unilateral act? What law determines the effectiveness of such a waiver? Can an effective waiver be included in a contract that is invalid under the applicable law?

3. Implicit waiver may be deduced from conduct signifying an intent to waive. A prominent example is the filing of a general appearance. See Flota Maritima Browning De Cuba, S.A. v. Motor Vessel Ciudad De La Habana, 335 F.2d 619 (4th Cir.1964) (holding ineffective an attempt to raise the plea of immunity at a later stage in the action). See also Flota Maritima Browning de Cuba, S.A. v. Snobl, 363 F.2d 733 (4th Cir.1966), cert. denied, 385 U.S. 837, 87 S.Ct. 82, 17 L.Ed.2d 71 (1966). Other examples are the signing of an arbitration clause, a forum selection clause, and a choice-of-law clause, and assertion of a counterclaim.

4. Can failure to appear be construed as a waiver? In Von Dardel On Behalf of Raoul Wallenberg et al. v. U.S.S.R., 623 F.Supp. 246 (D.D.C.1985), the Court gave an affirmative answer. After a default judgment was entered, the U.S.S.R. filed a special appearance and the court vacated its judgment 736 F.Supp. 1 (D.D.C.1990). But see Frolova v. U.S.S.R., 761 F.2d 370 (7th Cir.1985), in which the court raised the defense of sovereign immunity on its own motion. See also Subsection F, on Procedure for Claiming Immunity, p. 1259 infra.

5. The provision that a waiver may not be withdrawn except in accordance with its terms is designed to overrule legislatively decisions such as Rich v. Naviera Vacuba, S.A., 197 F.Supp. 710 (E.D.Va.1961), aff'd, 295 F.2d 24 (4th Cir.1961). See Sess., Rep. No. 94–1310, 94th Cong.2d Sess., p. 18 (1976).

6. In Foremost–McKesson, Inc. v. The Islamic Republic of Iran, 905 F.2d 438 (D.C.Cir.1990), Iran had answered that the action was barred by the Algiers Accord (Executive Order No. 12,294, 46 Fed. Reg. 14,111 (1981)). Foremost then pursued its claims before the Iran–United States Claims Tribunal. When this Tribunal had concluded its adjudication, Foremost revived its action. Iran then moved for leave to amend its answer to assert sovereign immunity. The Court rejected Foremost's argument that Iran had waived the immunity defense by failing to include it in its original answer. It ruled that, although a waiver could be implicit, Iran's original answer did not reflect an intention to forego the defense.

7. Can an ambassador extraordinary and plenipotentiary to the United Nations waive his state's immunity in an action brought on a promissory note executed by the ambassador on behalf of his state under a loan made by the plaintiff to finance the renovation of that state's permanent mission to the United

Nations? In First Fidelity Bank, N.A.v. The Government of Antigua & Barbuda Permanent Mission, 877 F.2d 189 (2d Cir.1989), the Second Circuit ruled that the ambassador's authority presented a question of fact to be determined upon a proper hearing. Neither the majority nor the dissent considered the relevance of the attorney for the foreign state's having signed the waiver, nor that it had been signed by the ambassador after the foreign state had negotiated a settlement with the plaintiff through the ambassador. Judge Newman dissented.

8. Must there be a nexus between the waiver and the U.S.? Cf. Proyecfin de Venezuela. S.A. v. Banco Industrial de Venezuela, 760 F.2d 390 (2d Cir.1985). Some courts have found that an agreement to arbitrate in a foreign country constitutes a general consent to suit on the award in the U.S. See S.A. Minaraçao da Trindade–Samitri v. Utah Int'l Inc., 576 F.Supp. 566 (S.D.N.Y.1983), aff'd, 745 F.2d 190 (2d Cir.1984). But others have limited the effect of the waiver to the place of arbitration chosen. See Ohntrup v. Firearms Center Inc., 516 F.Supp. 1281 (E.D.Pa.1981), aff'd 760 F. 2d 259 (3d Cir. 1985).

9. Implied waivers are not readily found. See, e.g., Creighton Ltd. v. Qatar, 181 F.3d 118 (D.C.Cir.1999), discussed infra. But selecting the application of U.S. law is generally construed as a waiver. See Eckert Int'l v. Fiji, 32 F.3d 77 (4th Cir.1994). It has been suggested that implied waiver should be found only when the person entitled to immunity participates in the litigation without objecting. See ABA Report of Aug. 15, 2000, Note 2 at p. 1217 supra. Do you agree?

THE EFFECT OF AN ARBITRATION AGREEMENT

On the circumstances in which an arbitration agreement may be regarded as a waiver of immunity, see Restatement (Third) § 456, Reporters' Note 3. Should an arbitration clause in an agreement between two states be treated in the same manner for this purpose as an arbitration clause in an agreement between a state and an individual? See the commentary on Art. 20 of the I.L.C. Draft Articles on State Immunity, p. 1199, which states that submission to arbitration by a state entails an implied acceptance of the supervisory jurisdiction of a court of another state otherwise competent to determine questions connected with the arbitration agreement. An agreement to submit to settlement pursuant to the Convention on the Settlement of Investment Disputes Between States and Nationals of Other States, 17 U.S.T. 1270, T.I.A.S. No. 6090, raises no question of waiver, since the decision of the tribunal has the force of a judgment in states adhering to the Convention (Art. 54(1)).

In 1988, the FSIA was amended to deal with problems that had arisen in regard to arbitration agreements to which a foreign state was a party. Subsection 6 was added to Section 1605(a) to permit an action to enforce such an arbitration agreement if "(A) the arbitration takes place or is intended to take place in the United States, (B) the agreement or award is or may be governed by a treaty or other international agreement in force for the United States calling for the recognition and enforcement of arbitral awards, (C) the underlying claim, save for the agreement to arbitrate, could have been brought in a United States court under this section or section 1607, or (D) [the waiver provision of § 1605(a)(1)] is otherwise applicable." The 1988 amendment also added subsection 6 to Section 1610(a) providing for execution of a judgment based on an arbitral award rendered against the foreign state, provided such execution not be inconsistent with the arbitration agreement. On the FSIA and arbitration agreements, see Kahale, New Legislation in the United States Facilitates Enforcement of Arbitral Agreements and Awards Against Foreign States, 6 J. Int'l Arb. 57 (1989).

Are the limitations of the amendment desirable? Restatement (Third) § 456(2)(b) provides that an agreement to arbitrate is a waiver of immunity from jurisdiction in an action to compel arbitration or to enforce the award. Is this the preferable rule?

Note

The impact of the FSIA's arbitration provisions was considered in Creighton Limited v. Qatar, 181 F.3d 118 (D.C.Cir.1999), which involved claims arising from a contract between Qatar and a Cayman Islands corporation with offices in Tennessee and Qatar to build a hospital in the Qatari capital. The corporation (Creighton) initiated an arbitration in France pursuant to an International Chamber of Commerce arbitration clause contained in that contract. The contract did not provide for the place of arbitration, but the I.C.C. designated Paris. An award was rendered for over $8 million. An attack on the award in France was rejected by the court of highest instance.

Creighton then sought enforcement of the award in the federal district court for the District of Columbia. Qatar raised as defenses (1) that the court lacked subject matter jurisdiction, (2) that defendant was entitled to sovereign immunity, and (3) that the court lacked in personam adjudicatory authority. The court of appeals rejected the first two defenses, but upheld the third. On the issues of subject matter jurisdiction and sovereign immunity, the court ruled that the agreement to arbitrate under the auspices of the I.C.C. International Court of Arbitration was not a waiver of immunity by implication within the meaning of Section 1605(a)(1) of the FSIA that rendered Qatar subject to suit in the United States. However, it did rule that Qatar was not immune from suit in the United States under Section 1605(a)(6) and that that section applied even though the contract was signed, and the arbitration commenced, before that section entered into effect. Nevertheless, although the FSIA provides in Section 1330(b) that U.S. courts have in personam competence over foreign states that are not entitled to sovereign immunity, the court ruled that there was a lack of constitutional power over Qatar under the Due Process Clause of the Fifth Amendment to the U.S. Constitution, because Qatar lacked the necessary minimum contacts with the United States.

The decision highlights once more the deficient structure of the FSIA, which applies the same criteria for determining the entirely different concepts of subject matter adjudicatory authority, sovereign immunity, and in personam adjudicatory authority. It also confirms the merits of the criticism that the FSIA has improperly jettisoned reliance on *in rem* forms of adjudicatory authority. See Smit, The Foreign Sovereign Immunity Act of 1976: A Plea for Drastic Surgery, 1980 Proc. A.S.I.L. 49, supra. In large part because of the deficient structure of the FSIA, the court reached a most questionable result.

In the first place, does it make sense to rule that a foreign state that has agreed to arbitrate disputes in a state that has ratified the 1958 New York Convention on the Recognition and Enforcement of Foreign Arbitral Awards has not waived its right to plead lack of personal jurisdiction in an action based on the award? In the second place, should not an American federal court, under the constitutional foreign relations power, have the authority to adjudicate actions brought under an agreement like the New York Convention against a foreign state, regardless of whether the foreign state is entitled to claim sovereign immunity? And third, in an action brought for recognition and enforcement of an arbitral award as against assets located in the United States by a plaintiff operating in the United States, it would appear entirely reasonable for a United States court to proceed with enforcement of the award. Surely, Section 1605(a)(6)(B) legislatively proclaims an important interest of the United States in having an American court entertain such an action. And the added interest of the plaintiff, whose offices are in the United States, would appear to render it eminently reasonable for the United States to exercise this limited form of jurisdiction. It might be argued that these factors would warrant the exercise of in rem, but not of in personam jurisdiction, and that the FSIA provides only for personal jurisdiction. If this were a dispositive answer, it would provide another argument for doing away with a legislative structure that has occasioned a wealth of unnecessary litigation. On all these questions, already anticipated at the birth of the FSIA, see Smit, loc cit. supra.

COUNTERCLAIMS

FOREIGN SOVEREIGN IMMUNITIES ACT OF 1976

28 U.S.C.A. § 1607.

COUNTERCLAIMS

In any action brought by a foreign state, or in which a foreign state intervenes, in a court of the United States or of a State, the foreign state shall not be accorded immunity with respect to any counterclaim—

(a) for which a foreign state would not be entitled to immunity under section 1605 of this chapter had such claim been brought in a separate action against the foreign state; or

(b) arising out of the transaction or occurrence that is the subject matter of the claim of the foreign state; or

(c) to the extent that the counterclaim does not seek relief exceeding an amount or differing in kind from that sought by the foreign state.

Notes

1. Subsection (a) is based upon article 1 of the European Convention on State Immunity, 11 I.L.M. 470 (1972).

2. Subsection (b) is inspired by the compulsory counterclaim rule of the Federal Rules of Civil Procedure, Fed.R.Civ.P. 13(a). See also Restatement (Third) § 456(2)(a)(i). Cf. also Alfred Dunhill of London, Inc. v. Republic of Cuba, 425 U.S. 682, 96 S.Ct. 1854, 48 L.Ed.2d 301 (1976).

3. Subsection (c) codifies the holding in National City Bank of New York v. Republic of China, 348 U.S. 356, 75 S.Ct. 423, 99 L.Ed. 389 (1955).

D. THE NATURE OF THE RESTRICTIONS ON IMMUNITY

1. The Relation Between Immunity From Legislative Jurisdiction And The Act of State Doctrine

Section 1605 of the FSIA speaks of immunity "from the jurisdiction of the courts." This type of immunity is distinguished from "immunity from attachment and execution" treated in Sections 1609–1611. The terminology used leaves uncertain whether the Act also deals with immunity from the exercise of legislative jurisdiction.

The Restatement (Third) § 461, Comment *h*, states that the FSIA "assumes that foreign states are not immune from United States jurisdiction to prescribe" in suits against foreign states that the Act permits. While the accuracy of this statement is subject to dispute (see p. 1249 infra), it leaves open whether foreign states are immune from jurisdiction to prescribe in all other cases.

The Act's failure to distinguish in specific terms between immunity from judicial jurisdiction and immunity from legislative jurisdiction may be explained by the circumstance that, once immunity from judicial jurisdiction is found, the court cannot reach the question of whether there is also immunity from legislative jurisdiction. Under the absolute doctrine of sovereign immunity, the question of immunity from legislative jurisdiction could therefore not arise.

But when the restrictive doctrine gained ground, the distinction became significant. This probably went largely unnoticed, because in most cases adjudicated by the courts the claim arose from, or was related to, the same commercial activity or property that, through seizure or attachment, provided the basis for the exercise of judicial jurisdiction. As a consequence, in such cases denial of immunity from judicial jurisdiction necessarily implied denial of immunity from legislative jurisdiction. However, this was not true in cases in which the commercial activity or property that provided the basis for the exercise of judicial jurisdiction was different from the activity or property from which the claim for relief arose.

This situation was presented in New York and Cuba Mail S.S. Co. v. Republic of Korea, 132 F.Supp. 684 (S.D.N.Y.1955), in which the attachment of funds of the Korean government on deposit in a New York bank provided the basis for the exercise of judicial jurisdiction, but the claim arose from a collision with defendant's vessel in Pusan, Korea. The State Department took the position that the funds were immune from attachment, but declined to suggest that the foreign state was entitled to claim immunity "inasmuch as the particular acts out of which the cause of action arose are not shown to be of purely governmental character." The State Department subsequently relinquished its position that a foreign state could claim immunity from judicial jurisdiction even if the property attached was commercial (see its statement in Stephen v. Zivnostenska Banka, Nat. Corp., 15 A.D.2d 111, 116, 222 N.Y.S.2d 128, 133–34 (1st Dep't 1961)), but the distinction it in effect made between immunity from judicial jurisdiction and immunity from legislative jurisdiction remained very much alive. Specifically, this distinction had to be made not only when an *in rem* type of action was brought and the property proceeded against had nothing to do with the claim for relief asserted (for another instance, see Chemical Natural Resources, Inc. v. Republic of Venezuela, 420 Pa. 134, 215 A.2d 864 (1966)), but also when a foreign state did substantial commercial business within the United States, but the claim for relief asserted did not arise from that business. Indeed, as American courts increasingly came to require a lesser and lesser measure of business done to support judicial competence in regard to unrelated claims (see, e.g., Bryant v. Finnish

Nat. Airline, 15 N.Y.2d 426, 260 N.Y.S.2d 625, 208 N.E.2d 439 (1965)), the possibility that judicial competence over foreign states would be premised on commercial activities unrelated to those from which the claim for relief arose became correspondingly larger.

It might therefore have been expected that the Foreign Sovereign Immunities Act of 1976 would pay particular attention to immunity from legislative jurisdiction. This, however, does not appear to be the case. The Act's failure to address immunity from legislative jurisdiction with particularity may be explained in part by the circumstance that the Act provides principally for *in personam* judicial competence in regard to claims that are related to the activity or to the act upon which judicial competence is based. See Title 28, Section 1330(b), in conjunction with Section 1605. However, while this type of specific competence is most likely to be the most frequent basis of judicial competence, the Act does provide for judicial competence in cases in which the claim asserted did not arise from the activity or act that provides the basis of competence. See Sections 1605(a)(3) and (b); see also the Notes following Saudi Arabia v. Nelson, p. 1230 supra. In addition, there may be circumstances in which a foreign state has waived immunity from judicial, but not immunity from legislative, jurisdiction. Cf. Restatement (Third) § 456, which distinguishes between waiver of immunity from judicial jurisdiction and waiver of immunity from attachment and deals separately with immunity from jurisdiction to prescribe, to adjudicate, and to enforce. In those cases, the question of whether the Act also deals with immunity from legislative jurisdiction therefore remains most pertinent. Endeavors to provide an answer to this question may take the following provision as a starting point.

FOREIGN SOVEREIGN IMMUNITIES ACT OF 1976

28 U.S.C.A. § 1606.

Extent of Liability

As to any claim for relief with respect to which a foreign state is not entitled to immunity under section 1605 or 1607 of this chapter, the foreign state shall be liable in the same manner and to the same extent as a private individual under like circumstances; but a foreign state except for an agency or instrumentality thereof shall not be liable for punitive damages; if, however, in any case wherein death was caused, the law of the place where the action or omission occurred provides, or has been construed to provide, for damages only punitive in nature, the foreign state shall be liable for actual or compensatory damages measured by the pecuniary injuries resulting from such death which were incurred by the persons for whose benefit the action was brought.

Notes

1. Is this provision to be read as providing that, once there is no immunity from judicial jurisdiction, the liability of the foreign state is to be determined on the assumption that the acts for which the foreign state is called to account were those of a private individual? If so, it would require rejection of claims of immunity from legislative jurisdiction in all cases in which there is no immunity from judicial jurisdiction.

Support for the view that denial of immunity from judicial jurisdiction implies denial of immunity from legislative jurisdiction may also be derived from Section 1605(a)(3) on expropriation. After all, the taking of property in violation of international law is rather typical of acts that are normally regarded as public rather than commercial. See *Victory Transport,* p. 1208 supra. It would, therefore, make little sense to deny immunity from judicial jurisdiction in an action "in which rights in property taken in violation of international law are in issue," unless the court were authorized to adjudicate such rights. Clearly, the court could do so only if it would not be barred from making such an adjudication by the act of state doctrine or a claim of immunity from legislative jurisdiction. For, if it would be so barred, Section 1605(a)(3) would encourage an action that would become an exercise in futility once the merits were reached.

The Senate Judiciary Committee Report on the Act states that since "* * * this section deals solely with issues of immunity, it in no way affects existing law on the extent to which, if at all, the 'act of state' doctrine may be applicable." Sen.Rep. No. 94–1310, 94th Cong.2d Sess., p. 19 (1976). The act of state doctrine applies typically in an action in which the validity or legality of an act of a foreign state performed within that state's territory is drawn into question. When applicable, it precludes American courts from judging the validity or legality of such an act. See, e.g., Oetjen v. Central Leather Co., 246 U.S. 297, 38 S.Ct. 309, 62 L.Ed. 726 (1917). The doctrine has also been extended to cases in which a foreign state, rather than a private party, invoked it to preclude examination of the validity or legality of its own sovereign act. Cf., e.g., Alfred Dunhill of London, Inc. v. Republic of Cuba, 425 U.S. 682, 96 S.Ct. 1854, 48 L.Ed.2d 301 (1976) at p. 187 supra. For a more detailed treatment of the act of state doctrine, see p. 180 supra. It would appear, however, that in such cases the reviewability of the act of a foreign sovereign should be determined by reference to rules of immunity from legislative jurisdiction rather than act of state. Not only are the reasons for abstaining from review of the act of a foreign state less weighty in cases between private parties, rules of immunity from legislative jurisdiction may be grounded in international law, while the act of state doctrine admittedly is a product of municipal lawmaking. See Banco Nacional de Cuba v. Sabbatino, 376 U.S. 398, 84 S.Ct. 923, 11 L.Ed.2d 804 (1964). See also Letelier v. Republic of Chile, 488 F.Supp. 665 (D.D.C.1980), in which the court rejected the argument that the officials who ordered the assassination of Letelier acted within Chile and were therefore covered by the act of state doctrine on the ground that "[t]o hold otherwise would totally emasculate the purpose and effectiveness of the Foreign Sovereign Immunities Act." (at 674).

On the relationship between the FSIA and the act of state doctrine, see Achebe, The Act of State Doctrine and Foreign Sovereign Immunities Act of 1976: Can They Coexist?, 13 Md.J.Int'l L. & Trade 247 (1989); Leacock, The Commercial Activity Exception To The Act Of State Doctrine Revisited: Evolution Of A Concept, 13 N.C.J.Int'l L. & Com. Reg. I (1988); Note, Act Of State And Sovereign Immunity: The Marcos Cases—Republic of the Philippines v. Marcos, 818 F.2d 1473; In re Grand Jury Proceedings, John Doe #700, 817 F.2d 1108 (4th Cir.1987); Republic of the Philippines v. Marcos, 806 F.2d 344 (2d Cir.1986); 29 Harv. Int'l L.J. 127 (1988). On the act of state doctrine and international business transactions under the FSIA, see Ebenroth & Teitz, Winning (Or Losing) By Default: The Act of State Doctrine, Sovereign Immunity And Comity In International Business Transactions, 19 Int'l Law. 225 (1985).

Whatever the proper analysis, the question of whether there is immunity from legislative jurisdiction will arise when the act of state doctrine does not apply. Not only does that doctrine not apply to acts done without the foreign sovereign's territory (see p. 187 supra); since the *Dunhill* decision, it also does not apply to commercial acts of the foreign state, even if performed inside its territory. Furthermore, the act of state doctrine does not apply in all cases in which the Hickenlooper amendment (see p. 190 supra) is applicable. In all of these situations, the question of whether, regardless of the act of state doctrine, the foreign sovereign may claim immunity from legislative jurisdiction must therefore be addressed.

The FSIA does not address that question in explicit terms. However, it may be argued that recognizing immunity from legislative jurisdiction in the situation covered by Section 1605(a)(3) would deprive this provision of its practical significance. On the other hand, the Act's legislative history, by acknowledging that the Act does not purport to affect act-of-state principles, gives potent support to the view that non-immunity from the jurisdiction of American courts does not necessarily imply non-immunity from the exercise of legislative jurisdiction. Under that view, immunity from legislative jurisdiction may be available to a foreign state in all cases in which the claim for relief arises from a foreign sovereign's public act other than the act that provides the basis for judicial competence.

The Restatement (Third) § 461 states that "A state is not immune from the jurisdiction to prescribe of another state except to the extent provided in respect of diplomatic and consular activities, §§ 464–66." Does this provision state prevailing international law? When, in an action brought against a foreign state which is not immune from judicial jurisdiction, a question arises as to the propriety of a governmental act of that foreign state either within or without that state's territory, is that state entitled to immunity from legislative jurisdiction?

2. The Senate Judiciary Report on the Act states: "The bill is not intended to affect the substantive law of liability." Sen. Rep. No. 94–1310, 94th Cong.2d Sess., p. 11 (1976). Is this statement borne out by the provisions of Section 1606? What about other provisions of the Act?

3. By reference to what law is an American court to determine whether the plaintiff suffered "actual or compensatory damages measured by the primary injuries * * * incurred by the persons for whose benefit the actions was brought," whether the persons referred to were the proper persons to bring the actions, and whether the damages "resulted" from the death? See Engle, Choosing Law For Attributing Liability Under The Foreign Sovereign Immunities Act: A Proposal For Uniformity, 15 Fordham Int'l L.J. 1060 (1991/92). Does it make any difference whether the action is pending in a state or federal court?

4. In Alejandre v. Cuba, p. [1232] supra, the district court awarded punitive damages against the Cuban Air Force for the shooting down above international waters of a plane registered in the United States and killing its crew. Was this award compatible with Section 1606? The Civil Liability Act, also known as the Flatow Amendment, enacted by Congress shortly after the addition of the subsection 1605(a)(7) of the FSIA, provides for the award of punitive damages. See Note [6] on p. [1240] supra.

2. *The Applicable Federal Common Law*

To what extent do the federal courts, when proceeding under the FSIA, have to apply federal common law? As made clear by Section 1606, the courts will have to put the appropriate constructions on its provisions. But this is not all. In almost every action under the FSIA, unless federal common law is deemed controlling, the court will have to determine the rights and obligations of the parties by reference to the law indicated by the proper conflict of law rules. Are these conflict of laws rules those of the state in which the federal court is sitting or judge-made federal conflict of laws rules? The usual rule is that a federal court should apply the conflict of laws rules of the state in which it sits. Klaxon Co. v. Stentor Electric Mfg. Co., 313 U.S. 487, 61 S.Ct. 1020, 85 L.Ed. 1477 (1941). However, there is, of course, a strong federal interest in the proper adjudication of cases involving foreign states. It is that interest that prompted enactment of the FSIA in the first place. And it is that interest that moved the court in Liu v. The Republic of China, 892 F.2d 1419 (9th Cir.1989) and Harris v. Polskie Linie Lotnicze, 820 F.2d 1000 (9th Cir.1987), to rule that in FSIA cases federal common law provides the applicable choice of law rule. The advantage of this approach is that it ensures that all American courts will apply the same law to disputes involving foreign states. This will, in turn, safeguard the federal interest in maintaining consistency in United States relations with foreign states. Indeed, a strong argument could be made for the federation's formulating its own rules for the resolution of disputes involving foreign states. The foreign relations power provides adequate constitutional support for such an approach. See Chapter 3 supra. And it would ensure that, in matters involving foreign nations, the United States would speak with a unitary voice.

E. THE ROLE OF THE EXECUTIVE BRANCH

FOREIGN SOVEREIGN IMMUNITIES ACT OF 1976

28 U.S.C.A. § 1602.

FINDINGS AND DECLARATION OF PURPOSE

* * * Claims of foreign states to immunity should henceforth be decided by courts of the United States and of the States in conformity with the principles set forth in this chapter.

In Ex parte Republic of Peru, 318 U.S. 578, 63 S.Ct. 793, 87 L.Ed. 1014 (1943), Chief Justice Stone, in ruling upon Peru's claim of sovereign immunity, stated:

> Here the State Department has not left the Republic of Peru to intervene in the litigation through its ambassador as in the case of *The Navemar* [303 U.S. 68, 58 S.Ct. 432, 82 L.Ed. 667 (1938)]. The department has allowed the claim of immunity and caused its actions to be certified to the district court through the appropriate channels. The certification and the request that the vessel be declared immune must be accepted by the courts as a conclusive determination by the political arm of the Government that the continued retention of the vessel interferes with the proper conduct of our foreign relations. Upon the submission of this certification to the district court, it became the court's duty, in conformity to established principles, to release the vessel and to proceed no further in the cause. * * *

In Republic of Mexico v. Hoffman (The Baja California), 324 U.S. 30, 65 S.Ct. 530, 89 L.Ed. 729 (1945), Chief Justice Stone, in affirming denial of a plea of sovereign immunity, stated:

> * * * More important, and we think controlling in the present circumstances, is the fact that, despite numerous opportunities like the present to recognize immunity from suit of a vessel owned and not possessed by a foreign government, this government has failed to do so. We can only conclude that it is the national policy not to extend the immunity in the manner now suggested, and that it is the duty of the courts, in a matter so intimately associated with our foreign policy and which may profoundly affect it, not to enlarge an immunity to an extent which the government, although often asked, has not seen fit to recognize.

Section 1602 is intended to free the courts from the obligation of absolute obedience to the executive. As stated in the Senate Judiciary Committee Report, "[a] principal purpose of this bill is to transfer the determination of sovereign immunity from the executive branch to the judicial branch. * * * The Department of State would be freed from pressures from foreign governments to recognize their immunity from suit and from any adverse consequences resulting from an unwillingness of the Department to support that immunity." Sen. Rep. 94–1370, 94th Cong.2d Sess. p. 9 (1976).

Notes

1. Does the Act intend to overrule the *Republic of Peru* and *Republic of Mexico* cases? If it does, how well does it express this intent? Can the Act constitutionally overrule these cases? Compare the action of the President in regard to claims upon Iran in Dames & Moore v. Regan, 453 U.S. 654, 101 S.Ct. 2972, 69 L.Ed.2d 918 (1981), discussed in Chapter 3, p. 231.

2. Does the Act preclude any role of the Executive in adjudication of claims of sovereign immunity? See Letter from the Legal Adviser of the State Department to the Attorney General (Nov. 10, 1976), 75 Dep't St. Bull. 649–50 (1976):

> * * * the Executive Branch will, of course, play the same role in sovereign immunity cases that it does in other types of litigation—e.g., appearing as *amicus curiae* in cases of significant interest to the Government. Judicial construction of the new statute will be of general interest to the Department of State, since the statute, like the Tate letter, endeavors to incorporate international law on sovereign immunity into domestic United States law and practice. If a court should misconstrue the new statute, the United States may well have an interest in making its views on the legal issues known to an appellate court. In addition, the Executive may wish to express its views to the courts in cases not covered by the Act.

3. Under the Act, may the Executive suggest upon the record that the foreign state claims sovereign immunity without taking a position on the claim? In Jackson v. People's Republic of China, 550 F.Supp. 869 (N.D.Ala.1982), China did not appear and the court entered a default judgment. After China made a special appearance and the United States filed an amicus curiae brief, 22 I.L.M. 1077 (1983), the court set aside the judgment. Jackson v. People's Republic of China, 596 F.Supp. 386 (N.D.Ala.1984), aff'd, 794 F.2d 1490 (11th Cir.1986), cert. denied, 480 U.S. 917, 107 S.Ct. 1371, 94 L.Ed.2d 687 (1987). For a discussion of practical difficulties encountered by a foreign state that did not wish to employ private counsel for this purpose, see Carl, Suing Foreign Governments in American Courts: The United States Foreign Sovereign Immunities Act in Practice, 33

Southw. L.J. 1007, 1056–57 (1979). The Executive may also suggest that a foreign state is not entitled to sovereign immunity in a given dispute. In Libyan American Oil Co. v. Socialist People's Libyan Arab Jamahirya, 482 F.Supp. 1175 (D.D.C. 1980), the district court ruled that a Libyan nationalization was a non-justiciable state action; on appeal, the United States filed an amicus curiae brief, reprinted at 20 I.L.M. 161 (1981), that sovereign immunity would not apply to this arbitration award enforcement case. The court of appeals vacated without opinion, 684 F.2d 1032 (D.C.Cir.1981).

4. The State Department continues to suggest immunity in cases of heads of state, their spouses and children, special envoys, and other foreign government officials. See the Notes following the Pinochet case, p. 1280 infra. Should the State Department refrain from doing so on the ground that the FSIA reflects a policy that it not become involved?

F. PROCEDURAL PROBLEMS

1. *Judicial Competence in Sovereign Immunity Cases*

SUBJECT MATTER COMPETENCE

1. Actions against foreign states

FOREIGN SOVEREIGN IMMUNITIES ACT OF 1976

28 U.S.C.A. § 1330(a)

(a) The district courts shall have original jurisdiction without regard to amount in controversy of any nonjury civil action against a foreign state as defined in section 1603(a) of this title as to any claim for relief in personam with respect to which the foreign state is not entitled to immunity either under sections 1605–1607 of this title or under any applicable international agreement.

* * *

28 U.S.C.A. § 1441(d)

Actions Removable Generally

(d) Any civil action brought in a State court against a foreign state as defined in section 1603(a) of this title may be removed by the foreign state to the district court of the United States for the district and division embracing the place where such action is pending. Upon removal the action shall be tried by the court without jury. Where removal is based upon this subsection, the time limitations of section 1446(b) of this chapter may be enlarged at any time for cause shown.

Notes

1. Is Section 1330(a) constitutional? In Verlinden B.V. v. Central Bank of Nigeria, 461 U.S. 480, 103 S.Ct. 1962, 76 L.Ed.2d 81 (1983), the Supreme Court reversed a decision by the Second Circuit Court of Appeals that there was no constitutional subject matter jurisdiction in the action brought by the Dutch plaintiff. The Supreme Court ruled that there was federal question jurisdiction

because the action arose under the FSIA. Is this reasoning persuasive? Or did *Verlinden* present a case of "protective" jurisdiction? See Smit, in International Contracts, Foreign Sovereign Immunity—American Style 255 (1981).

2. In which actions against a foreign state do the district courts have subject matter competence? What *in rem* actions can be brought in state courts? Can they be removed to a federal court? Recall that the Supreme Court has ruled that the FSIA provides the only bases for proceeding against a foreign state, Argentine Republic v. Amerada Hess Shipping Corp., p. 1220 supra. See Section 1610(d).

3. Is there ever a right to trial by jury in an action against a foreign state? The Act proceeds on the assumption that, since there is no right to trial by jury in an action against the U.S. Government, there is none in a suit against a foreign state. See Section 1441(d) (last sentence); cf. Sen. Rep. No. 94–1310, 94th Cong.2d Sess., p. 12 (1976). Does this conclusion necessarily follow? See Icenogle v. Olympic Airways, S.A., 82 F.R.D. 36 (D.D.C.1979) (holding plaintiff entitled to trial by jury in action against foreign corporation qualifying as "foreign state" under the Act).

Compare Ruggiero v. Compania Peruana de Vapores, 639 F.2d 872 (2d Cir.1981) (holding that denial of right to trial by jury does not violate Seventh Amendment), with Rex v. Compania Pervana de Vapores, S.A., 660 F.2d 61 (3d Cir.1981), cert. denied, 456 U.S. 926, 102 S.Ct. 1971, 72 L.Ed.2d 441 (1982) (holding foreign state instrumentality entitled to jury trial). Cf. also Williams v. Shipping Corp. of India, 653 F.2d 875 (4th Cir.1981), cert. denied, 455 U.S. 982, 102 S.Ct. 1490, 71 L.Ed.2d 691 (1982) (ruling absence of right to jury trial not to prevent removal from state court); Greeley v. KLM Royal Dutch Airlines, 85 F.R.D. 697 (S.D.N.Y.1980) (no jury trial in action removed under FSIA). See further Restatement (Third) § 458(4). On this question, see also Smit, The Foreign Sovereign Immunities Act of 1976: A Plea for Drastic Surgery, 1980 Proc.A.S.I.L. 49.

2. Actions by Foreign States

28 U.S.C.A. § 1332(a)(4)

Diversity of Citizenship

(a) The district courts shall have original jurisdiction of all civil actions where the matter in controversy exceeds the sum or value of $75,000, exclusive of interest and costs, and is between—

* * * (4) a foreign state, defined in section 1603(a) of this title [28 USCS § 1603(a)], as plaintiff and citizens of a State or of different States.

Note

A foreign state may bring an action in a federal court when the requirements of 28 U.S.C.A. § 1332(a)(4) are met. If the foreign state elects to bring the action in a state court, may it be removed to a federal court? Under 28 U.S.C.A. § 1441(b), unless that action asserts a claim arising under federal law, it may be removed by the defendant only if none of the defendants are citizens of the state in which the action is brought. It may therefore be crucial whether an action brought by a foreign state in a state court arises under federal law. If it does, any action involving a foreign state may be brought in, or removed to, a federal court, regardless of whether the foreign state is the plaintiff or the defendant. It would appear beyond question that this is the preferable rule. If the FSIA had been more skillfully drafted, it would straightforwardly have so provided. See Smit, The Foreign Sovereign Immunities Act of 1976: A Plea for Drastic Surgery, 1980 A.S.I.L.Proc. 49, 57. It does not so provide and, unfortunately, 28 U.S.C.A. § 1332(a)(4), which was added at the time of enactment of the FSIA, provides an argument against the preferable rule stated. For if any action involving a foreign state raises a question of federal law, this subsection would be superfluous.

As the law presently stands, however, it is possible to permit most actions involving a foreign state to be brought in, or removed to, a federal court while perhaps preserving some room for application of 28 U.S.C.A. § 1332(a)(4). The prevailing, and preferable, view is that, in cases involving foreign states, the applicable conflict of laws rules are federal. The Ninth Circuit has consistently so ruled. Liu v. The Republic of China, 892 F.2d 1419 (9th Cir.1989); Harris v. Polskie Linie Lotnicze, 820 F.2d 1000 (9th Cir.1987). Consequently, in all cases involving a foreign state in which it is necessary to apply conflict of laws rules, federal law must be applied. And such cases may therefore be removed to the federal court as arising under federal law, regardless of whether the foreign state is the plaintiff or the defendant.

It is only when an action brought by a foreign state raises no question of federal conflict of laws, that 28 U.S.C.A. § 1332(a)(4) retains its relevance. It may be difficult to conceive of such cases, since the very presence of a foreign state in the action would appear to necessitate reference to conflict of laws rules. However, this may well have escaped the notice of the legislature. After all, the applicability of conflict of laws rules often escapes notice. And it is certainly plausible that it escaped the notice of the draftsmen of the FSIA, which in many other respects appears deficient. Of course, if the view that the federal courts must apply federal law to all cases involving foreign states, regardless of conflict of laws rules, were adopted, all cases brought by foreign states could be brought in, or removed to, federal courts.

2. *In Personam Competence*

FOREIGN SOVEREIGN IMMUNITIES ACT OF 1976

28 U.S.C.A. § 1330(b) and (c).

ACTIONS AGAINST FOREIGN STATES

* * *

(b) Personal jurisdiction over a foreign state shall exist as to every claim for relief over which the district courts have jurisdiction under subsection (a) where service has been made under section 1608 of this title.

(c) For purposes of subsection (b), an appearance by a foreign state does not confer personal jurisdiction with respect to any claim for relief not arising out of any transaction or occurrence enumerated in sections 1605–1607 of this title.

Notes

1. Note that Section 1605(b) attempts to convert traditional *in rem* actions in admiralty into *in personam* actions. Is this merely window-dressing? See the

proviso at the end of Section 1605(b). The 1988 Amendments which added subsections (c) and (d) seek to eliminate the problems this attempted conversion occasioned. On these amendments, see Atkeson & Ramsey, 79 A.J.I.L. 770, 778 (1985). For a judicial circumvention of the forfeiture rule of Section 1605(b), see Velidor v. L/P/G Benghazi, 653 F.2d 812 (3d Cir.1981) (ruling that personal claim survives). For an application of Section 1605(b), see O'Connell Machinery Co. v. M.V. "Americana", 734 F.2d 115 (2d Cir.1984), cert. denied, 469 U.S. 1086, 105 S.Ct. 591, 83 L.Ed.2d 701 (1984); Note, The Limitation on Liens Against and the Arrest of State–Owned Ships: The Need for an Admiralty Foreign Sovereign Immunities Act, 57 Tul.L.Rev. 1274 (1983).

2. Was it desirable for the new Act to create its own bases of *in personam* competence or would it have been preferable to rely on generally prevailing bases? See Smit, p. 1231 supra. For decisions finding lack of *in personam* competence under the Act, see Carey v. National Oil Corp., 592 F.2d 673 (2d Cir.1979); Harris v. VAO Intourist, Moscow, 481 F.Supp. 1056 (E.D.N.Y.1979); Vencedora Oceanica Navigacion, S.A. v. Compagnie Nationale Algerienne De Navigation (C.N.A.N.), 730 F.2d 195 (5th Cir.1984); Upton v. Empire of Iran, 459 F.Supp. 264 (D.D.C. 1978), aff'd mem., 607 F.2d 494 (D.C.Cir.1979); Berkovitz v. Islamic Republic of Iran, 735 F.2d 329 (9th Cir.1984), cert. denied, 469 U.S. 1035, 105 S.Ct. 510, 83 L.Ed.2d 401 (1984) (all holding that in a personal injury case the direct effect within the meaning of Section 1605(a)(2) occurs at the place of injury). However, in other cases, the courts have been inclined to be more liberal. In Texas Trading & Milling Corp. v. Federal Republic of Nigeria, 647 F.2d 300 (2d Cir.1981), cert. denied, 454 U.S. 1148, 102 S.Ct. 1012, 71 L.Ed.2d 301 (1982), the issuance of letters of credit payable in New York on a sale transacted abroad was held sufficient to create competence under the Act. In addition, when a foreign state instrumentality engages in commercial activities within the United States, the courts have been more inclined to find the requisite direct effect in the United States in financial loss to a plaintiff in the United States resulting from a wrongful act abroad. See, e.g., Sugarman v. Aeromexico, Inc., 626 F.2d 270 (3d Cir.1980); Ministry of Supply, Cairo v. Universe Tankships, Inc., 708 F.2d 80 (2d Cir.1983); De Sanchez v. Banco Central De Nicaragua, 515 F.Supp. 900 (E.D.La. 1981). See further Restatement (Third) §§ 453–54.

3. Does Section 1605(a)(7), added in 1996, define a proper basis of *in personam* competence? See Alejandre v. Cuba, p. 1232 supra and Note 1 supra, following that case.

4. In an action against a foreign state, may *in personam* competence also be premised on a basis available under federal or state law not embodied in the Act? Cf. Fed. R.Civ. P. 4(e); Miller, Service of Process on State, Local, and Foreign Governments under Rule 4, 46 F.R.D. 101 (1969). For a negative answer, see Harris v. VAO Intourist Moscow, Note 4 supra. Cf. also the *Amerada Hess Shipping Co.* case supra, in which the Supreme Court ruled the bases of subject matter competence provided by the FSIA to be the only ones available.

5. Was it desirable to let the existence of *in personam* competence under Section 1330(b) depend on whether service has been properly made under Section 1608? For a negative answer, see Smit, Note 1, p. 1216 supra.

3. *In Rem Competence*

FOREIGN SOVEREIGN IMMUNITIES ACT OF 1976

28 U.S.C.A. § 1610(d).

EXCEPTIONS TO THE IMMUNITY FROM ATTACHMENT OR EXECUTION

(d) The property of a foreign state, as defined in section 1603(a) of this chapter, used for a commercial activity in the United States, shall not be immune from attachment prior to the entry of judgment in any action brought in a court of the United States or of a State, or prior to the elapse of the period of time provided in subsection (c) of this section, if—

(1) the foreign state has explicitly waived its immunity from attachment prior to judgment, notwithstanding any withdrawal of the waiver the foreign state may purport to effect except in accordance with the terms of the waiver, and

(2) the purpose of the attachment is to secure satisfaction of a judgment that has been or may ultimately be entered against the foreign state, and not to obtain jurisdiction.

Notes

1. Is a contractual waiver of "any sovereign immunity" an "explicit" waiver of immunity from attachment within the meaning of this provision? Or must the waiver provision state in so many words that the immunity waived includes immunity from pre-judgment attachment? How likely would it be for foreign lawyers to know of such a requirement and to include so explicit a provision?

2. If immunity from pre-judgment attachment has been waived explicitly, may an *in rem* action be brought against a foreign state or its property in a federal or state court? See Section 1610(d)(2) and (e).

3. Was it desirable to eliminate pre-judgment attachment? How likely are foreign states sued *in personam* to make their assets scarce when the time for execution arrives? See Smit, Note 1, p. 1216 supra. On whether attachments laid before the Act became effective continue their effect after the effective date of the Act, see, e.g., Amoco Overseas Oil Co. v. Compagnie Nationale Algerienne De Navigation, 459 F.Supp. 1242 (S.D.N.Y.1978), aff'd, 605 F.2d 648 (2d Cir.1979), National American Corp. v. Federal Republic of Nigeria, 448 F.Supp. 622 (S.D.N.Y.1978), aff'd, 597 F.2d 314 (2d Cir.1979).

4. Would a waiver of immunity contained in a contract concluded before the Act entered into force and at that time effectively waiving immunity from attachment become ineffective for failure of explicitness when the Act entered into force? Would an affirmative answer be compatible with the constitutional ban on the impairment of contracts?

5. The limitations imposed by the Act upon pre-judgment attachment raised significant problems at the time of the Iranian Hostage Crisis, when Iran announced the withdrawal of its funds from the United States. Most claimants laid attachments first and worried about the consequences later. The courts were understandably eager to find a proper legal basis for these attachments. See, e.g., Note 7 infra. Some litigants sought injunctions against debtors of Iran rather than

attachments. The President, in order to protect their rights, then issued an order freezing all such assets. The order was upheld in Dames & Moore v. Regan, 453 U.S. 654, 101 S.Ct. 2972, 69 L.Ed.2d 918 (1981), discussed in Chapter 3, p. 231. By the Algerian Accords, provision was made for U.S. claimants to present their claims to a United States–Iran Tribunal sitting in The Hague. Part of the frozen funds were released to Iran; another part was remitted to the custody of the Dutch Government with provision for payment out of these funds of awards rendered by the Tribunal. On this Tribunal, see pp. 739, 754.

6. An amendment was proposed permitting, under specified conditions, pre-judgment attachment against instrumentalities of a foreign state. See Atkeson & Ramsey, Proposed Amendments of the Foreign Sovereign Immunity Act, 79 A.J.I.L. 770, 776–77, 787 (1985). The conditions statutorily specified include the moving party's posting a bond of at least 50 percent of the value of the property attached. See proposed Section 1610(d)(i)(E), id. at 789. Is this an appropriate requirement? This proposed amendment was not adopted.

7. Does a waiver of immunity in a Treaty of Friendship, Commerce, and Navigation waive immunity from pre-judgment attachment? For an affirmative answer, see Behring International, Inc. v. Imperial Iranian Air Force, 475 F.Supp. 383 (D.N.J.1979), aff'd, 699 F.2d 657 (3d Cir.1983). Note that Section 1604 of the Act provides that a foreign state shall be immune from the jurisdiction of the courts "[S]ubject to existing international agreements."

4. *Service of Process*

FOREIGN SOVEREIGN IMMUNITIES ACT OF 1976

[See Section 1608(a), (b), and (c)]

Notes

1. Was it necessary to create special service provisions for actions against foreign states? Cf. Smit, Note 1, p. 1216 supra. See Petrol Shipping Corp. v. Kingdom of Greece, 360 F.2d 103 (2d Cir.1966) (holding that Federal Civil Rule 4 does not provide for service on a foreign state, but upholding service by mail under local district court rule); Hellenic Lines, Ltd. v. Moore, 345 F.2d 978 (D.C.Cir.1965) (holding improper service on the foreign state's ambassador in Washington); Caravel Office Building Co. v. The Peruvian Air Attache, 347 A.2d 280 (D.C.App.1975) (upholding service by registered mail on air attache as proper service on Peru); Alberti v. Empresa Nicaraguense De La Carne, 705 F.2d 250 (7th Cir.1983) (service by mail on foreign ambassador improper). In New England Merchants National Bank v. Iran Power Generation and Transmission Co., 495 F.Supp. 73 (S.D.N.Y.1980), the court permitted substituted service under Fed. R.Civ. P. 4(i). See also Note, Amenability of Foreign Sovereign to Federal In Personam Jurisdiction, 14 Va.J. Int'l L. 487, 489–91 (1974); Miller, Service of Process on State, Local, and Foreign Governments under Rule 4, Federal Rules of Civil Procedure, 46 F.R.D. 101, 121–22 (1969).

2. Was it desirable to let the availability of the form of service prescribed in Section 1608(a)(3) depend on the impossibility of making service under Section 1608(a)(1) and (2)? See Carl, Note 1, p. 1216 supra.

3. On August 24, 1967, the United States ratified the Convention on the Service Abroad of Judicial and Extrajudicial Documents in Civil or Commercial

Matters. As of 2000 the following countries had also ratified this Convention: Antigua & Barbuda, Bahamas, Barbados, Belarus, Belgium, Botswana, Bulgaria, Canada, China, Cyprus, Czech Republic, Denmark, Egypt, Estonia, Finland, France, Germany, Greece, Ireland, Israel, Italy, Japan, Republic of Korea, Latvia, Luxembourg, Malawi, the Netherlands, Norway, Pakistan, Poland, Portugal, Seychelles, Slovakia, Spain, Sweden, Switzerland, Turkey, the United Kingdom, and Venezuela. For a report on how this Convention has been working, see 28 I.L.M. 1556 (1989) and Weis, The Federal Rules and the Hague Conventions: Concerns of Conformity and Comity, 50 U.Pitt. L.Rev. 903 (1989). What is the relationship between the Convention's and the Act's provisions on service? See Smit, International Control of International Litigation: Who Benefits? 57 Law & Contemp. Probs. 26 (1994).

4. In 40 D 6262 Realty Corp. v. United Arab Emirates Government, 447 F.Supp. 710 (S.D.N.Y.1978), petitioners had affixed a notice of petition to the premises occupied by the defendant and had mailed a copy to the defendant's Permanent Mission. The Court held the service improper as not authorized by either Section 1608(a)(1), (a)(2), or (a)(3). Could the service have been held proper under the *Petrol Shipping* approach? See Note 1 supra. See also Gray v. Permanent Mission of the People's Republic of the Congo to the United Nations, 443 F.Supp. 816 (S.D.N.Y.1978) (holding insufficient under the Act service made upon the defendant's "secretary").

5. For the regulations of the Secretary of State prescribing the form of the notice of suit required by Section 1608(a)(3) and (4), see Title 22, CFR 93.1–93.2, 16 I.L.M. 159 (1977).

6. Section 1608(b) is inspired by Fed. R.Civ. P. 4(i). Would closer adherence to the Rule's provisions have been desirable? See Smit, Note 1, p. 1216 supra.

7. Courts are more likely to insist upon strict compliance with the FSIA service requirements when the defendant is a foreign state rather than an instrumentality. Compare Transaero v. La Fuerza Aerea Boliviana, 30 F.3d 148 (D.C.Cir.1994), cert. denied, 513 U.S. 1150, 115 S.Ct. 1101, 130 L.Ed.2d 1068 (1995) (requiring strict compliance when foreign state is served), with Straub v. A.P. Green, 38 F.3d 448 (9th Cir.1994) (substantial compliance is enough: the pivotal question is whether the defendant received actual notice (service not dispatched by court clerk)) and Sherer v. Construcciones Aeronauticas, S.A., 987 F.2d 1246 (6th Cir.1993), cert. denied, 510 U.S. 818, 114 S.Ct. 72, 126 L.Ed.2d 41 (1993) (no translation provided of summons and complaint).

5. *Procedures for Claiming Immunity*

A foreign state may be required to follow certain procedures in asserting its immunity, provided that these procedures do not unreasonably restrict its opportunity effectively to assert its immunity.

Notes

1. The Foreign Sovereign Immunities Act does not address the problem of how sovereign immunity is to be claimed.

2. For a ruling that a ship's master is not the proper person "to vindicate the owner's sovereignty," see The Gul Djemal, 264 U.S. 90, 44 S.Ct. 244, 68 L.Ed. 574 (1924).

3. On whether the Executive may suggest immunity on the record under the Act, see p. 1252 supra.

4. May the court raise the sovereign immunity defense on its own motion? The court did so in Frolova v. U.S.S.R., 761 F.2d 370 (7th Cir.1985) (on the ground that absence of sovereign immunity is a prerequisite to subject matter competence and may therefore be raised upon the court's own motion). But in Von Dardel on Behalf of Raoul Wallenberg et al. v. U.S.S.R., 623 F.Supp. 246 (D.D.C.1985), the Court construed the failure of the U.S.S.R. to appear and raise the defense as a waiver. When the U.S.S.R filed a special appearance, the judgment was vacated. 736 F.Supp. 1 (D.D.C.1990).

5. The appellate courts have ruled that a rejection by a district court of a claim to immunity is immediately appealable under the collateral order doctrine. See Foremost–McKesson v. Islamic Republic of Iran, 905 F.2d 438, 443 (D.C.Cir. 1990), and cases cited. See also Rein v. Socialist People's Libyan Arab Jamahiriya, 162 F.3d 748 (2d Cir.1998), cert. denied, 525 U.S. 1003, 119 S.Ct. 2337, 144 L.Ed.2d 235 (1999).

G. IMMUNITY FROM EXECUTION

FOREIGN SOVEREIGN IMMUNITIES ACT OF 1976

[See 28 U.S.C.A. §§ 1609–1611.]

Before the FSIA, the U.S. State Department took the position that the property of a foreign state was absolutely immune from execution. This position had also been adopted by American courts, the leading case being Dexter & Carpenter v. Kunglig Jarnvagsstyrelsen, 43 F.2d 705 (2d Cir.1930), cert. den., 282 U.S. 896, 51 S.Ct. 181, 75 L.Ed. 789 (1931). However, the United States position in this regard appeared not to be required by international law. Eminent authority supported the view that, under international law, the restrictive doctrine of immunity could properly be extended to deny immunity from execution to commercial, as distinguished from public, property of a foreign state. See, e.g., Lauterpacht, The Problem of Jurisdictional Immunities of Foreign States, 1951 Brit. Y.B.I.L. 220, 241–43; Lalive, L'Immunité de Juridiction des Etats et des Organisations Internationales, 84 Rec. des Cours 205, 274–75 (1953–III); Restatement, Second, Foreign Relations Law of the United States, § 69, Reporter's Note 2 (1965).

The FSIA changed prior United States practice and rulings by permitting execution on a foreign state's commercial property in the circumstances statutorily specified. It is to be noted that the commercial property upon which execution may be levied need not in all circumstances be used for the commercial activity from which the claims for relief arose. But cf. Section 1610(a)(2).

A proposed amendment to the Act that would substantially broaden execution permitted under the Act was not adopted. See Atkeson & Ramsey, Proposed Amendments to the Foreign Sovereign Immunities Act, 79 A.J.I.L. 770, 777–78 (1985). It would have permitted execution on any property belonging to an agency or instrumentality of a foreign state engaged in commercial activity in the United States when the judgment relates to a claim for which there is no immunity. Should the Act be amended to permit even broader execution? Does the decision that follows provide the proper approach?

FIRST NATIONAL CITY BANK v. BANCO PARA EL COMERCIO EXTERIOR DE CUBA

Supreme Court of the United States, 1983.
462 U.S. 611, 103 S.Ct. 2591, 77 L.Ed.2d 46.

(Some footnotes omitted; others renumbered.)

JUSTICE O'CONNOR delivered the opinion of the Court.

In 1960 the Government of the Republic of Cuba established respondent Banco Para el Comercio Exterior de Cuba (Bancec) to serve as "[a]n official autonomous credit institution for foreign trade * * * with full juridical capacity * * * of its own. * * *" Law No. 793, Art. 1 (1960), App. to Pet. for Cert.2d. In September 1960 Bancec sought to collect on a letter of credit issued by petitioner First National City Bank (now Citibank) in its favor in support of a contract for delivery of Cuban sugar to a buyer in the United States. Within days after Citibank received the request for collection, all of its assets in Cuba were seized and nationalized by the Cuban Government. When Bancec brought suit on the letter of credit in United States District Court [Feb. 1, 1961], Citibank counterclaimed [Mar. 8, 1961], asserting a right to set off the value of its seized Cuban assets. The question before us is whether Citibank may obtain such a setoff, notwithstanding the fact that Bancec was established as a separate juridical entity. [On July 7, 1961, Bancec filed a stipulation signed by the parties stating that Bancec had been dissolved and that its claim had been transferred to the Ministry of Foreign Trade, and agreeing that the Republic of Cuba may be substituted as plaintiff.] Applying principles of equity common to international law and federal common law, we conclude that Citibank may apply a setoff.

II

A

As an initial matter, Bancec contends that the Foreign Sovereign Immunities Act of 1976, 28 U.S.C. §§ 1602–1611 (FSIA), immunizes an instrumentality owned by a foreign government from suit on a counterclaim based on actions taken by that government. * * *

We disagree. The language and history of the FSIA clearly establish that the Act was not intended to affect the substantive law determining the liability of a foreign state or instrumentality, or the attribution of liability among instrumentalities of a foreign state. Section 1606 of the FSIA provides in relevant part that "[a]s to any claim for relief with respect to which a foreign state is not entitled to immunity * * *, the foreign state shall be liable in the same manner and to the same extent as a private individual under like circumstances * * *." The House Report on the FSIA states:

> "The bill is not intended to affect the substantive law of liability. Nor is it intended to affect * * * the attribution of responsibility between or among entities of a foreign state; for example, whether the proper entity of a foreign state has been sued, or whether an entity sued is liable in whole or in part for the claimed wrong." H.R.Rep. No. 941487, p. 12 (1976), U.S.Code Cong. & Admin. News 1976, pp. 6604, 6610.

Thus, we conclude that the FSIA does not control the determination of whether Citibank may set off the value of its seized Cuban assets against Bancec's claim.

B

We must next decide which body of law determines the effect to be given to Bancec's separate juridical status. Bancec contends that internationally recognized conflict-of-law principles require the application of the law of the state that establishes a government instrumentality—here Cuba—to determine whether the instrumentality may be held liable for actions taken by the sovereign.

We cannot agree. As a general matter, the law of the state of incorporation normally determines issues relating to the *internal* affairs of a corporation. Application of that body of law achieves the need for certainty and predictability of result while generally protecting the justified expectations of parties with interests in the corporation. See Restatement (Second) of Conflict of Laws § 302, Comments *a* & *e*, (1971). Cf. Cort v. Ash, 422 U.S. 66, 84, 95 S.Ct. 2080, 2090, 45 L.Ed.2d 26 (1975). Different conflicts principles apply, however, where the rights of third parties *external* to the corporation are at issue. See Restatement (Second) of Conflict of Laws, supra, § 301. To give conclusive effect to the law of the chartering state in determining whether the separate juridical status of its instrumentality should be respected would permit the state to violate with impunity the rights of third parties under international law while effectively insulating itself from liability in foreign courts. We decline to permit such a result.[1]

Bancec contends in the alternative that international law must determine the resolution of the question presented. Citibank, on the other hand, suggests that federal common law governs. The expropriation claim against which Bancec seeks to interpose its separate juridical status arises under international law, which, as we have frequently reiterated, "is part of our law * * * ." The Paquete Habana, 175 U.S. 677, 700, 20 S.Ct. 290, 299, 44 L.Ed. 320 (1900). As we set forth below, * * * the principles governing this case are common to both international law and federal common law, which in these circumstances is necessarily informed both by international law principles and by articulated congressional policies.

1. Pointing out that 28 U.S.C. § 1606, see supra, at 2597, contains language identical to the Federal Tort Claims Act (FTCA), 28 U.S.C. § 2674, Bancec also contends alternatively that the FSIA, like the FTCA, requires application of the law of the forum State—here New York—including its conflicts principles. We disagree. Section 1606 provides that "[a]s to any claim for relief with respect to which a foreign state is not entitled to immunity * * *, the foreign state shall be liable in the same manner and to the same extent as a private individual under like circumstances." Thus, where state law provides a rule of liability governing private individuals, the FSIA requires the application of that rule to foreign states in like circumstances. The statute is silent, however, concerning the rule governing the attribution of liability *among* entities of a foreign state. In Banco Nacional de Cuba v. Sabbatino, 376 U.S. 398, 425, 84 S.Ct. 923, 938, 11 L.Ed.2d 804 (1964), this Court declined to apply the State of New York's act of state doctrine in a diversity action between a United States national and an instrumentality of a foreign state, concluding that matters bearing on the Nation's foreign relations "should not be left to divergent and perhaps parochial state interpretations." When it enacted the FSIA, Congress expressly acknowledged "the importance of developing a uniform body of law" concerning the amenability of a foreign sovereign to suit in United States courts. H.R.Rep. No. 94–1487, p. 32 (1976). See Verlinden B.V. v. Central Bank of Nigeria, 461 U.S. 480, 489, 103 S.Ct. 1962, 1969, 76 L.Ed.2d 81 (1983). In our view, these same considerations preclude the application of New York law here.

III

A

Before examining the controlling principles, a preliminary observation is appropriate. The parties and *amici* have repeatedly referred to the phrases that have tended to dominate discussion about the independent status of separately constituted juridical entities, debating whether "to pierce the corporate veil," and whether Bancec is an "alter ego" or a "mere instrumentality" of the Cuban Government. In Berkey v. Third Avenue Ry. Co., 244 N.Y. 84, 155 N.E. 58 (1926), Justice (then Judge) Cardozo warned in circumstances similar to those presented here against permitting worn epithets to substitute for rigorous analysis.

> "The whole problem of the relation between parent and subsidiary corporations is one that is still enveloped in the mists of metaphor. Metaphors in law are to be narrowly watched, for starting as devices to liberate thought, they end often by enslaving it." Id., at 94, 155 N.E., at 61.

With this in mind, we examine briefly the nature of government instrumentalities.

Increasingly during this century, governments throughout the world have established separately constituted legal entities to perform a variety of tasks. The organization and control of these entities vary considerably, but many possess a number of common features. A typical government instrumentality, if one can be said to exist, is created by an enabling statute that prescribes the powers and duties of the instrumentality, and specifies that it is to be managed by a board selected by the government in a manner consistent with the enabling law. The instrumentality is typically established as a separate juridical entity, with the powers to hold and sell property and to sue and be sued. Except for appropriations to provide capital or to cover losses, the instrumentality is primarily responsible for its own finances. The instrumentality is run as a distinct economic enterprise; often it is not subject to the same budgetary and personnel requirements with which government agencies must comply.

These distinctive features permit government instrumentalities to manage their operations on an enterprise basis while granting them a greater degree of flexibility and independence from close political control than is generally enjoyed by government agencies. These same features frequently prompt governments in developing countries to establish separate juridical entities as the vehicles through which to obtain the financial resources needed to make large-scale national investments.

> "[P]ublic enterprise, largely in the form of development corporations, has become an essential instrument of economic development in the economically backward countries which have insufficient private venture capital to develop the utilities and industries which are given priority in the national development plan. Not infrequently, these public development corporations * * * directly or through subsidiaries, enter into partnerships with national or foreign private enterprises, or they offer shares to the public." Friedmann, Government Enterprise: A Comparative Analy-

sis, in Government Enterprise: A Comparative Study 303, 333–334 (W. Friedmann & J. Garner eds. 1970).

Separate legal personality has been described as "an almost indispensable aspect of the public corporation." Id., at 314. Provisions in the corporate charter stating that the instrumentality may sue and be sued have been construed to waive the sovereign immunity accorded to many governmental activities, thereby enabling third parties to deal with the instrumentality knowing that they may seek relief in the courts. Similarly, the instrumentality's assets and liabilities must be treated as distinct from those of its sovereign in order to facilitate credit transactions with third parties. Id., at 315. Thus what the Court stated with respect to private corporations in Anderson v. Abbott, 321 U.S. 349, 64 S.Ct. 531, 88 L.Ed. 793 (1944), is true also for governmental corporations:

> "Limited liability is the rule, not the exception; and on that assumption large undertakings are rested, vast enterprises are launched, and huge sums of capital attracted." Id., at 362, 64 S.Ct., at 537.

Freely ignoring the separate status of government instrumentalities would result in substantial uncertainty over whether an instrumentality's assets would be diverted to satisfy a claim against the sovereign, and might thereby cause third parties to hesitate before extending credit to a government instrumentality without the government's guarantee. As a result, the efforts of sovereign nations to structure their governmental activities in a manner deemed necessary to promote economic development and efficient administration would surely be frustrated. Due respect for the actions taken by foreign sovereigns and for principles of comity between nations, see Hilton v. Guyot, 159 U.S. 113, 163–164, 16 S.Ct. 139, 143, 40 L.Ed. 95 (1895), leads us to conclude as the courts of Great Britain have concluded in other circumstances[2]—that government instrumentalities established as juridical

2. The British courts, applying principles we have not embraced as universally acceptable, have shown marked reluctance to attribute the acts of a foreign government to an instrumentality owned by that government. In *I Congreso del Partido,* [1983] A.C. 244, a decision discussing the so-called "restrictive" doctrine of sovereign immunity and its application to three Cuban state-owned enterprises, including Cubazucar, Lord Wilberforce described the legal status of government instrumentalities:

> "State-controlled enterprises, with legal personality, ability to trade and to enter into contracts of private law, though wholly subject to the control of their state, are a well-known feature of the modern commercial scene. The distinction between them, and their governing state, may appear artificial: but it is an accepted distinction in the law of England and other states. Quite different considerations apply to a state-controlled enterprise acting on government directions on the one hand, and a state, exercising sovereign functions, on the other." Id., at 258 (citation omitted).

Later in his opinion, Lord Wilberforce rejected the contention that commercial transactions entered into by state-owned organizations could be attributed to the Cuban Government. "The status of these organizations is familiar in our courts, and it has never been held that the relevant state is in law answerable for their actions." Id., at 271. See also Trendtex Trading Corp. v. Central Bank of Nigeria, [1977] Q.B. 529, in which the Court of Appeal ruled that the Central Bank of Nigeria was not an "alter ego or organ" of the Nigerian Government for the purpose of determining whether it could assert sovereign immunity. Id., at 559.

In C. Czarnikow Ltd. v. Rolimpex, [1979] A.C. 351, the House of Lords affirmed a decision holding that Rolimpex, a Polish state trading enterprise that sold Polish sugar overseas, could successfully assert a defense of *force majeure* in an action for breach of a contract to sell sugar. Rolimpex had defended on the ground that the Polish Government had instituted a ban on the foreign sale of Polish sugar. Lord Wilberforce agreed with the conclusion of the court below that, in the absence of "clear evidence and definite findings" that the foreign government took the action "purely in order to extricate a state enterprise from contractual entities distinct and independent from their sovereign should normally be treated as such.

We find support for this conclusion in the legislative history of the FSIA.* * *

Thus, the presumption that a foreign government's determination that its instrumentality is to be accorded separate legal status is buttressed by this congressional determination. We next examine whether this presumption may be overcome in certain circumstances.

B

In discussing the legal status of *private* corporations, courts in the United States[3] and abroad,[4] have recognized that an incorporated entity—described by Chief Justice Marshall as "an artificial being, invisible, intangible, and existing only in contemplation of law"—is not to be regarded as legally separate from its owners in all circumstances. Thus, where a corporate entity is so extensively controlled by its owner that a relationship of principal and agent is created, we have held that one may be held liable for the actions of the other. See NLRB v. Deena Artware, Inc., 361 U.S. 398, 402–404, 80 S.Ct. 441, 443, 4 L.Ed.2d 400 (1960). In addition, our cases have long recognized "the broader equitable principle that the doctrine of corporate entity, recognized generally and for most purposes, will not be regarded when to do so would work fraud or injustice." Taylor v. Standard Gas Co., 306 U.S. 307, 322, 59 S.Ct. 543, 550, 83 L.Ed. 669 (1939). See Pepper v. Litton, 308 U.S. 295, 310, 60 S.Ct. 238, 246, 84 L.Ed. 281 (1939). In particular, the Court has consistently refused to give effect to the corporate form where it is interposed to defeat legislative policies. E.g., Anderson v. Abbot, 321 U.S., at 362–363, 64 S.Ct., at 537–538. * * *

liability," the enterprise cannot be regarded as an organ of the state. Rolimpex, he concluded, "is not so closely connected with the government of Poland that it is precluded from relying on the ban [on foreign sales] as government intervention. * * * " Id., at 364.

3. See 1 W. Fletcher, Cyclopedia of the Law of Private Corporations § 41 (rev. perm. ed. 1983) * * *.

4. In Case Concerning The Barcelona Traction, Light & Power Co., 1970 I.C.J. 3, the International Court of Justice acknowledged that, as a matter of international law, the separate status of an incorporated entity may be disregarded in certain exceptional circumstances:

> "Forms of incorporation and their legal personality have sometimes not been employed for the sole purposes they were originally intended to serve; sometimes the corporate entity has been unable to protect the rights of those who entrusted their financial resources to it; thus inevitably there have arisen dangers of abuse, as in the case of many other institutions of law. Here, then, as elsewhere, the law, confronted with economic realities, has had to provide protective measures and remedies in the interests of those within the corporate entity as well as of those outside who have dealings with it: the law has recognized that the independent existence of the legal entity cannot be treated as an absolute. It is in this context that the process of 'lifting the corporate veil' or 'disregarding the legal entity' has been found justified and equitable in certain circumstances or for certain purposes. The wealth of practice already accumulated on the subject in municipal law indicates that the veil is lifted, for instance, to prevent the misuse of the privileges of legal personality, as in certain cases of fraud or malfeasance, to protect third persons such as a creditor or purchaser, or to prevent the evasion of legal requirements or of obligations. * * *
>
> "In accordance with the principle expounded above, the process of lifting the veil, being an exceptional one admitted by municipal law in respect of an institution of its own making, is equally admissible to play a similar role in international law * * *." Id., at 38–39. * * *

C

We conclude today that similar equitable principles must be applied here. In National City Bank v. Republic of China, 348 U.S. 356, 75 S.Ct. 423, 99 L.Ed. 389 (1955), the Court ruled that when a foreign sovereign asserts a claim in a United States court, "the consideration of fair dealing" bars the state from asserting a defense of sovereign immunity to defeat a setoff or counterclaim. Id., at 365, 75 S.Ct., at 429. See 28 U.S.C. § 1607(c). As a general matter, therefore, the Cuban Government could not bring suit in a United States court without also subjecting itself to its adversary's counterclaim. Here there is apparently no dispute that, as the District Court found, and the Court of Appeals apparently agreed, see 658 F.2d, at 916, n. 4, "the devolution of [Bancec's] claim, however viewed, brings it into the hands of the Ministry [of Foreign Trade], or Banco Nacional," each a party that may be held liable for the expropriation of Citibank's assets. 505 F.Supp., at 425. See Banco Nacional de Cuba v. First National City Bank, 478 F.2d, at 194. Bancec was dissolved even before Citibank filed its answer in this case, apparently in order to effect "the consolidation and operation of the economic and social conquests of the Revolution," particularly the nationalization of the banks ordered by Law No. 891.[5] Thus, the Cuban Government and Banco Nacional, not any third parties that may have relied on Bancec's separate juridical identity, would be the only beneficiaries of any recovery.[6]

In our view, this situation is similar to that in the *Republic of China* case.

> "We have a foreign government invoking our law but resisting a claim against it which fairly would curtail its recovery. It wants our law, like any other litigant, but it wants our law free from the claims of justice." 348 U.S., at 361–362, 75 S.Ct., at 427 (footnote omitted).[7]

Giving effect to Bancec's separate juridical status in these circumstances, even though it has long been dissolved, would permit the real beneficiary of such an action, the Government of the Republic of Cuba, to obtain relief in our courts that it could not obtain in its own right without waiving its sovereign immunity and answering for the seizure of Citibank's assets–a seizure previously held by the Court of Appeals to have violated international law. We decline to adhere blindly to the corporate form where doing so would cause such an injustice. See Bangor Punta Operations, Inc. v. Bangor & Aroostook R. Co., supra, 417 U.S., at 713, 94 S.Ct., at 2584.

5. Law No. 930, the law dissolving Bancec, contains the following recitations: * * *

> "WHEREAS, the consolidation and the operation of the economic and social conquests of the Revolution require the restructuration into a sole and centralized banking system, operated by the State, constituted by the [Banco Nacional], which will foster the development and stimulation of all productive activities of the Nation through the accumulation of the financial resources thereof, and their most economic and reasonable utilization." * * *

6. The parties agree that, under the Cuban Assets Control Regulations, 31 CFR pt. 515 (1982), any judgment entered in favor of an instrumentality of the Cuban Government would be frozen pending settlement of claims between the United States and Cuba.

7. See also First National City Bank v. Banco Nacional de Cuba, 406 U.S., at 770–773, 92 S.Ct., at 1814–1816 (Douglas, J., concurring in result); Federal Republic of Germany v. Elicofon, 358 F.Supp. 747 (E.D.N.Y.1970), aff'd, 478 F.2d 231 (C.A.2 1973), cert. denied, 415 U.S. 931, 94 S.Ct. 1443, 39 L.Ed.2d 489 (1974). In *Elicofon,* the District Court held that a separate juridical entity of a foreign state not recognized by the United States may not appear in a United States court. A contrary holding, the court reasoned, "would permit nonrecognized governments to use our courts at will by creating 'juridical entities' whenever the need arises." 358 F.Supp., at 757.

Respondent contends, however, that the transfer of Bancec's assets from the Ministry of Foreign Trade or Banco Nacional to Empresa and Cuba Zucar effectively insulates it from Citibank's counterclaim. We disagree. Having dissolved Bancec and transferred its assets to entities that may be held liable on Citibank's counterclaim, Cuba cannot escape liability for acts in violation of international law simply by retransferring the assets to separate juridical entities. To hold otherwise would permit governments to avoid the requirements of international law simply by creating juridical entities whenever the need arises. * * * We therefore hold that Citibank may set off the value of its assets seized by the Cuban Government against the amount sought by Bancec.

IV

Our decision today announces no mechanical formula for determining the circumstances under which the normally separate juridical status of a government instrumentality is to be disregarded[8] Instead, it is the product of the application of internationally recognized equitable principles to avoid the injustice that would result from permitting a foreign state to reap the benefits of our courts while avoiding the obligations of international law. * * *

JUSTICE STEVENS, with whom JUSTICE BRENNAN and JUSTICE BLACKMUN join, concurring in part and dissenting in part.

Today the Court correctly rejects the contention that American courts should readily "pierce the corporate veils" of separate juridical entities established by foreign governments to perform governmental functions. Accordingly, I join Parts I, II, III–A, and III–B of the Court's opinion. But I respectfully dissent from Part III–C, in which the Court endeavors to apply the general principles it has enunciated. Instead I would vacate the judgment and remand the case to the Court of Appeals for further proceedings.

* * *

Of course, the Court may have reached a correct assessment of the transactions at issue. But I continue to believe that the Court should not decide factual issues that can be resolved more accurately and effectively by other federal judges, particularly when the record presented to this Court is so sparse and uninformative.[1]

8. The District Court adopted, and both Citibank and the Solicitor General urge upon the Court, a standard in which the determination whether or not to give effect to the separate juridical status of a government instrumentality turns in part on whether the instrumentality in question performed a "governmental function." We decline to adopt such a standard in this case, as our decision is based on other grounds. We do observe that the concept of a "usual" or a "proper" governmental function changes over time and varies from nation to nation. Cf. New York v. United States, 326 U.S. 572, 580, 66 S.Ct. 310, 313, 90 L.Ed. 326 (1946) (opinion of Frankfurter, J.) ("To rest the federal taxing power on what is 'normally' conducted by private enterprise in contradiction to the 'usual' governmental functions is too shifting a basis for determining constitutional power and too entangled in expediency to serve as a dependable legal criterion"); id., at 586, 66 S.Ct., at 316 (Stone, C.J., concurring); id., at 591, 66 S.Ct., at 318 (Douglas, J., dissenting). See also Friedmann, The Legal Status and Organization of the Public Corporation, 16 Law & Contemp. Prob. 576, 589–591 (1951).

1. Nor do I agree that a contrary result "would cause such an injustice." Ante, at 2603. Petitioner is only one of many American citizens whose property was nationalized by the Cuban Government. It seeks to minimize its losses by retaining $193,280.30 that a purchaser of Cuban sugar had deposited with it for the purpose of paying for the merchandise, which was delivered in due course. Having won this

Note

In Letelier v. Republic of Chile, 748 F.2d 790 (2d Cir.1984), it was held that a judgment rendered against Chile for damages resulting from the murder of the former Chilean Ambassador in Washington, D.C. could not be executed by levying on the assets of Linea Aerea Nacional–Chile, a corporation the stock of which is wholly owned by Chile. A similar decision was rendered in Alejandre v. Telefonica Larga Distancia, 183 F.3d 1277 (11th Cir.1999). See p. 1241.

H. POLITICAL SUBDIVISIONS AND INSTRUMENTALITIES OF A FOREIGN STATE ENJOYING IMMUNITY

Since the treatment of a foreign state differs from that of an instrumentality, see, e.g., 28 U.S.C.A. § 1608 (service requirements), 28 U.S.C.A. § 1391(f) (venue in the District Court of the District of Columbia for a foreign state), 28 U.S.C.A. § 1606 (punitive damages against an instrumentality), it is important to distinguish between the two. The FSIA's legislative history focuses on the entity's being able to sue or be sued, contract, and own property, in its own name. The courts have applied a "core function" test (see, e.g., Transaero, Inc. v. La Fuerza Aerea Boliviana, 30 F.3d 148 (D.C.Cir. 1994); Segni v. Commercial Office of Spain, 650 F.Supp. 1040 (N.D.Ill.1986)) and a "legal characteristics test" (see, e.g., Hyatt Corp. v. Stanton, 945 F.Supp. 675 (1996); Unidyne Corp. v. Aerolineas Argentinas, 590 F.Supp. 398 (E.D.Va.1984)).

The approach may differ when the issue is one of liability or of immunity from execution. An entity may be ruled a foreign state for liability purposes, but a separate entity for immunity purposes. See Hoffman, The Separate Entity Rule in International Perspective: Should State Ownership of Corporate Shares Confer Sovereign Status For Immunity Purposes?, 65 Tul. L. Rev. 535 (1991). Special problems arise when the entity is owned indirectly by the foreign state. See Griggs, International Law–The Foreign Sovereign Immunities Act: Do Tiered Corporate Subsidiaries Constitute Foreign States, 20 W. New Eng. L. Rev. 387 (1998). The prevailing view is that indirectly owned corporations come within the FSIA if the foreign state's ownership exceeds fifty percent. See, e.g., In re Air Crash Disaster Near Roselawn, Ind. On October 31, 1994, 96 F.3d 932 (7th Cir.1996) (pooling); Antoine v. Atlas Turner, Inc., 66 F.3d 105 (6th Cir.1995). But see Gates v. Victor Fine Foods, 54 F.3d 1457 (9th Cir.1995).

Another question is whether the status is to be determined as of the time the claim arose or the time the action was commenced. The prevailing view appears to be that the time of accrual of the claim is decisive. See, e.g., Peré v. Nuovo Pignone, 150 F.3d 477 (5th Cir.1998); General Elec. Capital Corp. v. Grossman, 991 F.2d 1376 (8th Cir.1993). Some courts have looked at the time of commencement of the action. See, e.g., Straub v. A. P. Green, 38 F.3d 448

lawsuit, petitioner will simply retain that money. If petitioner's contentions in this case had been rejected, the money would be placed in a fund comprised of frozen Cuban assets, to be distributed equitably among all the American victims of Cuban nationalizations. Ante, at 2602–2603, n. 24. Even though petitioner has suffered a serious injustice at the hands of the Cuban Government, no special equities militate in favor of giving this petitioner a preference over all other victims simply because of its participation in a discrete, completed, commercial transaction involving the sale of a load of Cuban sugar.

(9th Cir.1994). Others have ruled either time sufficient. See, e.g., Belgrade v. Sidex Int'l Furniture Corp., 2 F.Supp.2d 407 (S.D.N.Y.1998); Papapanos v. Lufthansa, 1995 Dist. Lexis 9163, ___ WL ___ (S.D. Fla.) (ruling that adoption of the time of commencement of the action approach does not preclude recourse to the other approach).

FOREIGN SOVEREIGN IMMUNITIES ACT OF 1976

[28 U.S.C.A. § 1603(a) and (b)].

DEFINITIONS

For purposes of this chapter—

(a) A "foreign state," except as used in section 1608 of this title, includes a political subdivision of a foreign state or an agency or instrumentality of a foreign state as defined in subsection (b).

(b) An "agency or instrumentality of a foreign state" means any entity–

(1) which is a separate legal person, corporate or otherwise, and

(2) which is an organ of a foreign state or political subdivision thereof, or a majority of whose shares or other ownership interest is owned by a foreign state or political subdivision thereof, and

(3) which is neither a citizen of a State of the United States as defined in section 1332(c) and (d) of this title, nor created under the laws of any third country.

* * *

Notes

1. The enumeration of entities comprehended within the term "foreign state" is intended to be exhaustive. Consequently, "[a]n entity which does not fall within the definitions of sections 1603(a) or (b) would not be entitled to sovereign immunity in any case before a Federal or State court." Sen. Rep. No. 94–1310, 94th Cong.2d Sess., p. 15 (1976).

2. Whether entities comprehended within the definition of foreign state are entitled to immunity depends on the other provisions of the Act. The scope of entitlement to immunity may depend on whether a foreign state or a political division or an instrumentality or agency thereof is involved. See Section 1610(b).

3. In Edlow Int'l Co. v. Nuklearna Elektrarna Krsko, 441 F.Supp. 827 (D.D.C.1977), an action against a Yugoslavian "workers organization" for brokerage fees in connection with a sale of uranium oxide was dismissed for want of subject matter competence under Section 1330(a), on the ground that the workers organization was not an "agency or instrumentality of a foreign state." Does this decision point up the undesirability of defining subject matter competence by reference to whether immunity is unavailable? See p. 1217 supra. The question of whether Novosti, a Soviet information agency, came within the definition of "foreign state" was raised in Yessenin–Volpin v. Novosti Press Agency, 443 F.Supp. 849 (D.N.Y.1978). The court, stressing the difficulty of applying the Act's definitions under "concepts which exist in socialist states such as the Soviet Union," held that "Novosti is either an organ of the U.S.S.R. or 'owned' by the U.S.S.R." For an analysis of these decisions, see Recent Development:Yessenin–

Volpin v. Novosti Press Agency and Edlow Int'l Co. v. Nuklearna Elektrarna Krsko, 5 B'klyn J.Int'l L. 191 (1979). But see Jugobanka A.D. Belgrade v. Sidex Int'l Furniture Corp., 2 F.Supp.2d 407 (S.D.N.Y.1998), which criticized *Edlow* for not following the plain language of the FSIA and ruled, inter alia, that entities of former communist societies were state agencies.

SECTION 2. IMMUNITIES OF STATE REPRESENTATIVES

A. GENERAL PRINCIPLES

The FSIA provides for the immunity of foreign states and political subdivisions and agencies and instrumentalities of a foreign state. According to the legislative history cited in Note 1 above, an entity that is not comprehended within the definitions of these entities given in Sections 1603(a) and (b) is not entitled to sovereign immunity. However, the FSIA does not deal with any immunity that might be claimed by foreign officials that are not entities within the FSIA's definitions. To the extent foreign officials are in the diplomatic or consular service of a foreign state, their immunities are prescribed by international agreements (the Vienna Conventions on Diplomatic and Consular Relations), general international law, and domestic law, as discussed in Sections 2C and 2D below. If they are state representatives to international organizations, their immunities are regulated by applicable international agreements and domestic law; see Section 2F. But if they are representatives of a foreign state that do not come within any of these categories, the extent of their immunity depends on either general international law or domestic law. As the materials that follow will demonstrate, the immunity that representatives of foreign states enjoy is a function of the nature of their office and the applicable international or domestic law.

In the following case, *Chuidian*, a U.S. court of appeals ruled that a foreign official was covered by the FSIA. In the *Pinochet* case, to be discussed in Section 2B below, the U.K. House of Lords applied the State Immunity Act 1978, which in turn refers to the Diplomatic Privileges Act 1964 to establish the relevant standards for immunities of a head of state. As these cases illustrate, it may be necessary to consult domestic law, as well as international treaties, customary law and general principles, in order to ascertain the rule of immunity applicable to a given individual.

CHUIDIAN v. PHILIPPINE NATIONAL BANK

United States Court of Appeals, Ninth Circuit, 1990.
912 F.2d 1095.

[Chuidian, a Philippine citizen, sued Daza, a Philippine citizen and an official of the Philippine government, after Daza instructed the Philippine National Bank (Bank) to dishonor a letter of credit issued by the Republic of the Philippines to Chuidian. Daza was a member of the Presidential Commission on Good Government (Commission), an executive agency created after the overthrow of former President Marcos and charged with recovering "ill-gotten wealth" accumulated by Marcos and his associates. In March 1986, acting pursuant to the Commission's authority, Daza instructed the Bank not to make payment on the letter of credit issued to Chuidian. According to

Daza, the Commission suspected that Marcos and Chuidian had entered into a fraudulent settlement of litigation to pay off Chuidian for not revealing certain facts about Marcos's involvement in Chuidian's business enterprises. As a result, the Commission wished to examine the propriety of the settlement, and, in order to secure payment in the event of a decision against Chuidian, needed to prevent payment under the letter of credit. In Chuidian's suit on the letter of credit, Daza moved to dismiss on grounds of sovereign immunity.]

III

The central issue in this appeal is whether Daza is entitled to sovereign immunity for acts committed in his official capacity as a member of the Commission. Daza argues that he qualifies as an "agency or instrumentality of a foreign state," 28 U.S.C. § 1603(b), and hence is entitled to immunity pursuant to the Act, 28 U.S.C. § 1604. Chuidian contends either that Daza is not covered by the Act, or, in the alternative, that this case falls within the exceptions to immunity expressly provided by the Act. *See* 28 U.S.C. §§ 1605–07. The government, in a "Statement of Interest of the United States," takes a third position. Under the government's view, Daza is not covered by the Act because he is an individual rather than a corporation or an association, but he is nevertheless entitled to immunity under the general principles of sovereign immunity expressed in the Restatement (Second) of Foreign Relations Law § 66(b).

A.

We initially consider whether the Act applies to an individual such as Daza acting in his official capacity as an employee of a foreign sovereign. Resolution of this issue necessitates a brief recitation of the evolution of the law of sovereign immunity.

* * * According to the Restatement, immunity extended to:

(a) the state itself;

(b) its head of state * * *;

(c) its government or any governmental agency;

(d) its head of government * * *;

(e) its foreign minister * * *;

(f) any other public minister, official, or agent of the state with respect to acts performed in his official capacity if the effect of exercising jurisdiction would be to enforce a rule of law against the state[.]

Restatement (Second), § 66.

In practice, however, the determination of whether a suit was barred under the principles of the Restatement was made not by the courts but by the State Department. * * *

During the 1970s, Congress became concerned that the law of sovereign immunity under the practice of the Tate letter was leaving immunity decisions subject to diplomatic pressures rather than to the rule of law. * * * As a result, in 1976 Congress enacted the Act, largely codifying the existing common law of sovereign immunity. The principal change envisioned by the statute was to remove the role of the State Department in determining immunity. Sovereign immunity could be obtained only by the provisions of the Act, and only by the courts interpreting its provisions; "suggestions" from the State Department would no longer constitute binding determinations of immunity. * * *

The Act is "the sole basis for obtaining [subject matter] jurisdiction over a foreign state in our courts." *Argentine Republic v. Amerada Hess Shipping Corp.,* 488 U.S. 428, 109 S.Ct. 683, 688, 102 L.Ed.2d 818 (1989) *(Amerada Hess)*; *Liu v. Republic of China,* 892 F.2d 1419, 1424 (9th Cir.1989). Therefore, if Daza is considered a "foreign state" for purposes of the Act, our decision on immunity must be based upon the provisions of that statute.

* * *

The government and Chuidian argue that the definition of "agency or instrumentality of a foreign state" in section 1603(b) includes only agencies, ministries, corporations, and other associations, and is not meant to encompass individuals. Such a reading draws some significant support from the legislative history of section 1603(b), which reads in part:

> The first criterion [section 1603(b)(1)] * * * is intended to include a corporation, association, foundation or any other entity which, under the law of the foreign state where it was created, can sue or be sued in its own name * * *.
>
> The second criterion [section 1603(b)(2)] requires that the entity be either an organ of a foreign state * * * or that a majority of the entity's shares or other ownership interest be owned by a foreign state. * * *
>
> As a general matter, entities which meet the definition of an "agency or instrumentality of a foreign state" could assume a variety of forms, including a state trading corporation, a mining enterprise, a transport organization such as a shipping line or airline, a steel company, a central bank, an export association, a governmental procurement agency or a department or ministry * * *

House Report at 6614.

This language from the House Report indicates that Congress was primarily concerned with *organizations* acting for the foreign state, and may not have expressly contemplated the case of *individuals* acting as sovereign instrumentalities. At least one court has so concluded. *Republic of the Philippines v. Marcos,* 665 F.Supp. 793, 797 (N.D.Cal.1987) *(Marcos)* ("The terminology of [section 1603(b)]—'agency', 'instrumentality', 'entity', 'organ'—makes it clear that the statute is not intended to apply to natural persons.").

Chuidian and the United States thus argue that Daza's immunity cannot be evaluated under the provisions of the Act. Chuidian argues that Daza therefore cannot be granted immunity: the Act provides the sole source of sovereign immunity, and Daza does not qualify under its definition of a foreign state. The government, on the other hand, urges us to apply the pre-Act common law of immunity. In its view, the Act replaces common law only in the context of "foreign states" as defined by section 1603(b); elsewhere—i.e., for entities covered by the common law but not covered by the Act—common law principles remain valid. The government further argues that

Daza is immune under the common law principles of the Second Restatement; Chuidian contends that even if the old common law applies, an exception to immunity is applicable.

We are persuaded by neither of these arguments. While section 1603(b) may not explicitly include individuals within its definition of foreign instrumentalities, neither does it expressly exclude them. The terms "agency," "instrumentality," "organ," "entity," and "legal person," while perhaps more readily connoting an organization or collective, do not in their typical legal usage necessarily exclude individuals. Nowhere in the text or legislative history does Congress state that individuals are *not* encompassed within the section 1603(b) definition; indeed, aside from some language which is more commonly associated with the collective, the legislative history does not even hint of an intent to exclude individual officials from the scope of the Act. Such an omission is particularly significant in light of numerous statements that Congress intended the Act to codify the existing common law principles of sovereign immunity. As pointed out above, pre–1976 common law expressly extended immunity to individual officials acting in their official capacity. If in fact the Act does not include such officials, the Act contains a substantial unannounced departure from prior common law.

The most that can be concluded from the preceding discussion is that the Act is ambiguous as to its extension to individual foreign officials. Under such circumstances, we decline to limit its application as urged by Chuidian and the government. We conclude that the consequences of such a limitation, whether they be the loss of immunity urged by Chuidian or the reversion to pre-Act common law as urged by the government, would be entirely inconsistent with the purposes of the Act.

It is generally recognized that a suit against an individual acting in his official capacity is the practical equivalent of a suit against the sovereign directly. *Monell v. Department of Social Services,* 436 U.S. 658, 690 n. 55, 98 S.Ct. 2018, 2035 n. 55, 56 L.Ed.2d 611 (1978) ("[O]fficial-capacity suits generally represent only another way of pleading an action against an entity of which an officer is an agent."); *Morongo Band of Mission Indians v. California State Board of Equalization,* 858 F.2d 1376, 1382 n. 5 (9th Cir.1988) ("A claim alleged against a state officer acting in his official capacity is treated as a claim against the state itself."), *cert. denied,* 488 U.S. 1006, 109 S.Ct. 787, 102 L.Ed.2d 779 (1989). Thus, to take Chuidian's argument first, we cannot infer that Congress, in passing the Act, intended to allow unrestricted suits against individual foreign officials acting in their official capacities. Such a result would amount to a blanket abrogation of foreign sovereign immunity by allowing litigants to accomplish indirectly what the Act barred them from doing directly. It would be illogical to conclude that Congress would have enacted such a sweeping alteration of existing law implicitly and without comment. Moreover, such an interpretation would defeat the purposes of the Act: the statute was intended as a comprehensive codification of immunity and its exceptions. The rule that foreign states can be sued only pursuant to the specific provisions of sections 1605–07 would be vitiated if litigants could avoid immunity simply by recasting the form of their pleadings.

Similarly, we disagree with the government that the Act can reasonably be interpreted to leave intact the pre–1976 common law with respect to foreign officials. Admittedly, such a result would not effect the sweeping changes which would accompany the rule suggested by Chuidian: the government merely proposes that immunity of foreign states be evaluated under the Act and immunity of individuals be evaluated under the (substantially similar) provisions of the Second Restatement. Nevertheless, such a rule would also work to undermine the Act.

The principal distinction between pre–1976 common law practice and post–1976 statutory practice is the role of the State Department. If individual immunity is to be determined in accordance with the Second Restatement, presumably we would once again be required to give conclusive weight to the State Department's determination of whether an individual's activities fall within the traditional exceptions to sovereign immunity. *See Ex Parte Peru,* 318 U.S. at 589, 63 S.Ct. at 800; Restatement (Second) § 69 note 1. As observed previously, there is little practical difference between a suit against a state and a suit against an individual acting in his official capacity. Adopting the rule urged by the government would promote a peculiar variant of forum shopping, especially when the immunity question is unclear. Litigants who doubted the influence and diplomatic ability of their sovereign adversary would choose to proceed against the official, hoping to secure State Department support, while litigants less favorably positioned would be inclined to proceed against the foreign state directly, confronting the Act as interpreted by the courts without the influence of the State Department.

Absent an explicit direction from the statute, we conclude that such a bifurcated approach to sovereign immunity was not intended by the Act. First, every indication shows that Congress intended the Act to be comprehensive, and courts have consistently so interpreted its provisions. *Amerada Hess,* 109 S.Ct. at 688 ("[T]he text and structure of the [Act] demonstrate Congress' intention that the [Act] be the *sole* basis for obtaining jurisdiction over a foreign state in our courts.") (emphasis added). Yet the rule urged by the government would in effect make the statute optional: by artful pleading, litigants would be able to take advantage of the Act's provisions or, alternatively, choose to proceed under the old common law.

Second, a bifurcated interpretation of the Act would be counter to Congress's stated intent of removing the discretionary role of the State Department. *See* House Report at 6605–06. Under the government's interpretation, the pre–1966 common law would apply, in which the State Department had a discretionary role at the option of the litigant. But the Act is clearly intended as a mandatory rather than an optional procedure. To convert it to the latter by allowing suits against individual officials to proceed under the old common law would substantially undermine the force of the statute. There is no showing that Congress intended such a limited effect in passing a supposedly comprehensive codification of foreign sovereign immunity.

Furthermore, no authority supports the continued validity of the pre–1976 common law in light of the Act. Indeed, the American Law Institute recently issued the Restatement (Third) of Foreign Relations Law, superseding the Second Restatement relied upon by the government in this action. The new restatement deletes in its entirety the discussion of the United States common law of sovereign immunity, and substitutes a section analyzing such issues exclusively under the Act. Restatement (Third) of Foreign Relations Law, §§ 451 *et seq.* (1986).

For these reasons, we conclude that Chuidian's suit against Daza for acts committed in his official capacity as a member of the Commission must be analyzed under the framework of the Act. We thus join the majority of courts which have similarly concluded that section 1603(b) can fairly be read to include individuals sued in their official capacity. *Kline v. Kaneko,* 685 F.Supp. 386, 389 (S.D.N.Y.1988) ("The [Act] does apply to individual defendants when they are sued in their official capacity."); *American Bonded Warehouse Corp. v. Compagnie Nationale Air France,* 653 F.Supp. 861, 863 (N.D.Ill.1987) ("Defendants Francois Bachelet and Joe Miller, sued in their respective capacities as employees of Air France [an instrumentality of the government of France], are also protected by the [Act]."); *Mueller v. Diggelman,* No. 82 CIV 5513 (S.D.N.Y.1983) (LEXIS, gen-fed library, dist. file) (judges and clerks of foreign court, sued in their official capacities, entitled to immunity under the Act); *Rios v. Marshall,* 530 F.Supp. 351, 371, 374 (S.D.N.Y.1981) (official of British West Indies Central Labour Organization, an instrumentality of the British West Indies, protected under the Act); *but see Marcos,* 665 F.Supp. at 797 (Act not applicable to Philippine solicitor general).

Notes

1. Is the court in the principal case correct in concluding that a foreign official who cannot be categorized as an agency or instrumentality cannot claim immunity? Note that Section 1603(b), in defining the concepts of agency and instrumentality, speaks of "entity."

2. Does it necessarily follow, as assumed by the court in the principal case, that recognition of immunity outside the scope of the FSIA restores the Department of State to its former role?

3. Should the Restatement (Third) have dealt with the immunity of foreign officials generally? Is a member of a foreign royal house entitled to immunity?

4. In 1988, the U.S. Department of State published its Guidance for Law Enforcement Officers with Regard to Personal Rights and Immunities of Foreign Diplomatic and Consular Personnel, 27 I.L.M. 1617 (1988).

5. For a ruling that the successor government could waive the former Philippines president's immunity, see In re Doe, 860 F.2d 40 (2d Cir.1988).

6. In the principal case, the court ruled that foreign officials are covered by the FSIA. The D.C. Circuit has taken the same approach. El–Fadl v. Central Bank of Jordan, 75 F.3d 668 (D.C.Cir.1996); Jungquist v. Sheikh Sultan Bin Khalifa Al Nahyan, 115 F.3d 1020 (D.C.Cir.1997). But some courts have denied immunity under the Alien Tort Act when the claim involves human rights abuses. See Xuncax v. Gramajo, 886 F.Supp. 162 (D.Mass.1995); Granville Gold Trust–Switzerland v. Commissione Del Fallimento/Interchange Bank, 928 F.Supp. 241 (E.D.N.Y.1996), aff'd 111 F.3d 123 (2d Cir.1997); Fitzpatrick, The Claim to Foreign Sovereign Immunity by Individuals Sued for International Human Rights Violations, 15 Whittier L. Rev. 465 (1994). On whether head of state immunity exists independently of the FSIA, see Dellapenna, Heads of State Immunity–FSIA–Suggestion by State Department: Lafontant v. Aristide, 88 A.J.I.L. 528 (1994).

B. HEADS AND FORMER HEADS OF STATE

REGINA v. BARTLE, BOW STREET STIPENDIARY MAGISTRATE AND COMMISSIONER OF POLICE, EX PARTE PINOCHET

United Kingdom, House of Lords, March 24, 1999
2 W.L.R. 827, 38 I.L.M. 581 (1999).

[For background on the *Pinochet* case and the House of Lords' treatment of issues of universal jurisdiction and extradition, see pp. 1139, 1182. The following excerpt from the opinion of Lord Browne–Wilkinson relates to the immunity issue. The opinions of the other Law Lords have been omitted.]

LORD BROWNE–WILKINSON:

STATE IMMUNITY

This is the point around which most of the argument turned. It is of considerable general importance internationally since, if Senator Pinochet is not entitled to immunity in relation to the acts of torture alleged to have occurred after 29 September 1988, it will be the first time so far as counsel have discovered when a local domestic court has refused to afford immunity to a head of state or former head of state on the grounds that there can be no immunity against prosecution for certain international crimes.

Given the importance of the point, it is surprising how narrow is the area of dispute. There is general agreement between the parties as to the rules of statutory immunity and the rationale which underlies them. The issue is whether international law grants state immunity in relation to the international crime of torture and, if so, whether the Republic of Chile is entitled to claim such immunity even though Chile, Spain and the United Kingdom are all parties to the Torture Convention and therefore "contractually" bound to give effect to its provisions from 8 December 1988 at the latest.

It is a basic principle of international law that one sovereign state (the forum state) does not adjudicate on the conduct of a foreign state. The foreign state is entitled to procedural immunity from the processes of the forum state. This immunity extends to both criminal and civil liability. State immunity probably grew from the historical immunity of the person of the monarch. In any event, such personal immunity of the head of state persists to the present day: the head of state is entitled to the same immunity as the state itself. The diplomatic representative of the foreign state in the forum state is also afforded the same immunity in recognition of the dignity of the state which he represents. This immunity enjoyed by a head of state in power and an ambassador in post is a complete immunity attaching to the person of the head of state or ambassador and rendering him immune from all actions or prosecutions whether or not they relate to matters done for the benefit of the state. Such immunity is said to be granted *ratione personae*.

What then when the ambassador leaves his post or the head of state is deposed? The position of the ambassador is covered by the Vienna Convention on Diplomatic Relations, 1961. After providing for immunity from arrest (Article 29) and from criminal and civil jurisdiction (Article 31), Article 39(1) provides that the ambassador's privileges shall be enjoyed from the moment he takes up post; and subsection (2) provides:

> "(2) When the functions of a person enjoying privileges and immunities have come to an end, such privileges and immunities shall normally cease at the moment when he leaves the country, or on expiry of a reasonable period in which to do so, but shall subsist until that time, even in case of armed conflict. However, with respect to acts performed by such a person in the exercise of his functions as a member of the mission, immunity shall continue to subsist."

The continuing partial immunity of the ambassador after leaving post is of a different kind from that enjoyed *ratione personae* while he was in post. Since he is no longer the representative of the foreign state he merits no particular privileges or immunities as a person. However in order to preserve the integrity of the activities of the foreign state during the period when he was ambassador, it is necessary to provide that immunity is afforded to his official acts during his tenure in post. If this were not done the sovereign immunity of the state could be evaded by calling in question acts done during the previous ambassador's time. Accordingly under Article 39(2) the ambassador, like any other official of the state, enjoys immunity in relation to his official acts done while he was an official. This limited immunity, *ratione materiae*, is to be contrasted with the former immunity *ratione personae* which gave complete immunity to all activities whether public or private.

In my judgment at common law a former head of state enjoys similar immunities, *ratione materiae*, once he ceases to be head of state. He too loses immunity *ratione personae* on ceasing to be head of state: see Watts, The Legal Position in International Law of Heads of States, Heads of Government and Foreign Ministers p. 88 and the cases there cited. He can be sued on his private obligations: Ex–King Farouk of Egypt v. Christian Dior (1957) 24 I.L.R. 228; Jimenez v. Aristeguieta (1962) 311 F. 2d 547. As ex head of state he cannot be sued in respect of acts performed whilst head of state in his public capacity: Hatch v. Baez [1876] 7 Hun. 596. Thus, at common law, the position of the former ambassador and the former head of state appears to be much the same: both enjoy immunity for acts done in performance of their respective functions whilst in office.

I have belaboured this point because there is a strange feature of the United Kingdom law which I must mention shortly. The State Immunity Act 1978 modifies the traditional complete immunity normally afforded by the common law in claims for damages against foreign states. Such modifications are contained in Part I of the Act. Section 16(1) provides that nothing in Part I of the Act is to apply to criminal proceedings. Therefore Part I has no direct application to the present case. However, Part III of the Act contains section 20(1) which provides:

> "Subject to the provisions of this section and to any necessary modifications, the Diplomatic Privileges Act 1964 shall apply to-
>
> (a) a sovereign or other head of state; * * *
>
> as it applies to a head of a diplomatic mission ..."

The correct way in which to apply Article 39(2) of the Vienna Convention to a former head of state is baffling. To what "functions" is one to have regard? When do they cease since the former head of state almost certainly never arrives in this country let alone leaves it? Is a former head of state's immunity limited to the exercise of the functions of a member of the mission, or is that again something which is subject to "necessary modification"? It is hard to resist the suspicion that something has gone wrong. A search was done on the parliamentary history of the section. From this it emerged that the original section 20(1)(a) read "a sovereign or other head of state who is in the United Kingdom at the invitation or with the consent of the Government of the United Kingdom." On that basis the section would have been intelligible. However it was changed by a Government amendment the mover of which said that the clause as introduced "leaves an unsatisfactory doubt about the position of heads of state who are not in the United Kingdom"; he said that the amendment was to ensure that heads of state would be treated like heads of diplomatic missions "irrespective of presence in the United Kingdom." The parliamentary history, therefore, discloses no clear indication of what was intended. However, in my judgment it does not matter unduly since Parliament cannot have intended to give heads of state and former heads of state greater rights than they already enjoyed under international law. Accordingly, "the necessary modifications" which need to be made will produce the result that a former head of state has immunity in relation to acts done as part of his official functions when head of state. Accordingly, in my judgment, Senator Pinochet as former head of state enjoys immunity *ratione materiae* in relation to acts done by him as head of state as part of his official functions as head of state.

The question then which has to be answered is whether the alleged organisation of state torture by Senator Pinochet (if proved) would constitute an act committed by Senator Pinochet as part of his official functions as head of state. It is not enough to say that it cannot be part of the functions of the head of state to commit a crime. Actions which are criminal under the local law can still have been done officially and therefore give rise to immunity *ratione materiae*. The case needs to be analysed more closely.

Can it be said that the commission of a crime which is an international crime against humanity and *jus cogens* is an act done in an official capacity on behalf of the state? I believe there to be strong ground for saying that the implementation of torture as defined by the Torture Convention cannot be a state function. This is the view taken by Sir Arthur Watts (supra) who said (at p. 82):

> "While generally international law . . . does not directly involve obligations on individuals personally, that is not always appropriate, particularly for acts of such seriousness that they constitute not merely international wrongs (in the broad sense of a civil wrong) but rather international crimes which offend against the public order of the international community. States are artificial legal persons: they can only act through the institutions and agencies of the state, which means, ultimately through its officials and other individuals acting on behalf of the state. For international conduct which is so serious as to be tainted with criminality to be regarded as attributable only to the impersonal state and not to the individuals who ordered or perpetrated it is both unrealistic and offensive to common notions of justice.

> "The idea that individuals who commit international crimes are internationally accountable for them has now become an accepted part of international law. Problems in this area—such as the non-existence of any standing international tribunal to have jurisdiction over such crimes, and the lack of agreement as to what acts are internationally criminal for this purpose—have not affected the general acceptance of the principle of individual responsibility for international criminal conduct."

Later, at p. 84, he said:

> "It can no longer be doubted that as a matter of general customary international law a head of state will personally be liable to be called to account if there is sufficient evidence that he authorised or perpetrated such serious international crimes."

It can be objected that Sir Arthur was looking at those cases where the international community has established an international tribunal in relation to which the regulating document expressly makes the head of state subject to the tribunal's jurisdiction: see, for example, the Nuremberg Charter Article 7; the Statute of the International Tribunal for former Yugoslavia; the Statute of the International Tribunal for Rwanda and the Statute of the International Criminal Court. It is true that in these cases it is expressly said that the head of state or former head of state is subject to the court's jurisdiction. But those are cases in which a new court with no existing jurisdiction is being established. The jurisdiction being established by the Torture Convention and the Hostages Convention is one where existing domestic courts of all the countries are being authorised and required to take jurisdiction internationally. The question is whether, in this new type of jurisdiction, the only possible view is that those made subject to the jurisdiction of each of the state courts of the world in relation to torture are not entitled to claim immunity.

I have doubts whether, before the coming into force of the Torture Convention, the existence of the international crime of torture as *jus cogens* was enough to justify the conclusion that the organisation of state torture could not rank for immunity purposes as performance of an official function. At that stage there was no international tribunal to punish torture and no general jurisdiction to permit or require its punishment in domestic courts. Not until there was some form of universal jurisdiction for the punishment of the crime of torture could it really be talked about as a fully constituted international crime. But in my judgment the Torture Convention did provide what was missing: a worldwide universal jurisdiction. Further, it required all member states to ban and outlaw torture: Article 2. How can it be for international law purposes an official function to do something which international law itself prohibits and criminalises? Thirdly, an essential feature of the international crime of torture is that it must be committed "by or with the acquiescence of a public official or other person acting in an official capacity." As a result all defendants in torture cases will be state officials. Yet, if the former head of state has immunity, the man most responsible will escape liability while his inferiors (the chiefs of police, junior army officers) who carried out his orders will be liable. I find it impossible to accept that this was the intention.

Finally, and to my mind decisively, if the implementation of a torture regime is a public function giving rise to immunity *ratione materiae*, this produces bizarre results. Immunity *ratione materiae* applies not only to ex-heads of state and ex-ambassadors but to all state officials who have been involved in carrying out the functions of the state. Such immunity is necessary in order to prevent state immunity being circumvented by prosecuting or suing the official who, for example, actually carried out the torture when a claim against the head of state would be precluded by the doctrine of immunity. If that applied to the present case, and if the implementation of the torture regime is to be treated as official business sufficient to found an immunity for the former head of state, it must also be official business sufficient to justify immunity for his inferiors who actually did the torturing. Under the Convention the international crime of torture can only be committed by an official or someone in an official capacity. They would all be entitled to immunity. It would follow that there can be no case outside Chile in which a successful prosecution for torture can be brought unless the State of Chile is prepared to waive its right to its officials' immunity. Therefore the whole elaborate structure of universal jurisdiction over torture committed by officials is rendered abortive and one of the main objectives of the Torture Convention—to provide a system under which there is no safe haven for torturers—will have been frustrated. In my judgment all these factors together demonstrate that the notion of continued immunity for ex-heads of state is inconsistent with the provisions of the Torture Convention.

For these reasons in my judgment if, as alleged, Senator Pinochet organised and authorised torture after 8 December 1988, he was not acting in any capacity which gives rise to immunity *ratione materiae* because such actions were contrary to international law, Chile had agreed to outlaw such conduct and Chile had agreed with the other parties to the Torture Convention that all signatory states should have jurisdiction to try official torture (as defined in the Convention) even if such torture were committed in Chile.

As to the charges of murder and conspiracy to murder, no one has advanced any reason why the ordinary rules of immunity should not apply and Senator Pinochet is entitled to such immunity.

For these reasons, I would allow the appeal so as to permit the extradition proceedings to proceed on the allegation that torture in pursuance of a conspiracy to commit torture, including the single act of torture which is alleged in charge 30, was being committed by Senator Pinochet after 8 December 1988 when he lost his immunity.

* * *

Notes

1. The House of Lords accepted as a basic premise that both present and past heads of state were immune from criminal process for acts performed in an official capacity while they were in office. But it ruled that the Torture Convention carved an exception from this rule for torture, since otherwise the Convention would be largely illusory. Does this reasoning necessarily apply in an extradition context? It could be argued that the Torture Convention cleared the way for the United Kingdom to prosecute Pinochet for torture notwithstanding his having been a head of state, but not for extraditing him to Spain.

2. Would Pinochet have been entitled to immunity if he had still been the head of state of Chile when arrested? On the reasoning of the House of Lords, the

Torture Convention should also effect an exception to immunity for incumbent heads of state. Would it be desirable to extend immunity to present heads of state *ratione personae*, regardless of the nature of the liability asserted, but *ratione materiae* only for acts performed in an official capacity for past heads of state, subject perhaps to the exception carved out by the House of Lords? In any event, should the immunity of heads of state, both present and former, be regulated by international agreement or local statute? Note that the U.S. Supreme Court held President Clinton subject to civil suit while he was serving as president. Clinton v. Jones. 520 U.S. 681, 117 S.Ct. 1636, 137 L.Ed.2d 945 (1997). Would President Clinton have been subject to suit if he had been sued in the United Kingdom?

3. Pinochet had also been made a Senator for life in Chile. Should he have been granted immunity for that reason? Is the time ripe for comprehensive regulation by international agreement or otherwise of immunity from suit of all the various kinds of officials who may be sued in a foreign country? Note that immunity might be provided to such officials by designating them as special envoys and requesting the receiving state to recognize them as such. See p. [ ] infra.

4. In the Pinochet case, it was argued that Pinochet had become head of state in an unconstitutional manner and that his designation as such was therefore legally ineffective. The House of Lords rejected the argument. Would it have had a better chance of acceptance if the Chilean Government had endorsed the argument? In fact, the Chilean government had strongly argued in favor of Pinochet's immunity in the United Kingdom and against his proposed extradition to Spain.

5. Could the President of the United States be arrested in the United Kingdom upon a request for extradition from Afghanistan or the Sudan for the extrajudicial killing of innocent civilians in the airstrikes he ordered in Afghanistan and the Sudan in 1998? Could the Prime Minister of Israel suffer the same fate on a request for his extradition by an Arab state for having condoned the torture of prisoners? Does it serve the needs of the international community to involve national courts, rather than international ones, in this type of exercise? Or should we recognize that, in the absence of effective international action against this type of misconduct, national courts are unlikely to serve a useful function?

6. On the Pinochet case generally, see p. [ ] supra. See also Woodhouse (ed.), The Pinochet Case: A Legal and Constitutional Analysis (2000). For an argument that a different analysis could apply if a similar suit arose in the United States, see Bradley & Goldsmith, *Pinochet* and International Human Rights Litigation, 97 Mich. L. Rev. 2129 (1999).

7. The FSIA does not deal with immunity from jurisdiction of a head of state. The Restatement (Second), Foreign Relations Law § 66 (1965), extended the sovereign immunity enjoyed by a foreign state to its head and members of its official party. However, the Restatement (Third) does not contain a similar provision. But cf. Restatement (Third) § 464, Comment *i* and Reporters' Note 13. The State Department, relying on "international authority" and "international custom," has continued issuing suggestions of immunity for heads of state after enactment of the FSIA. Are the courts free to disregard these suggestions? They have not done so. See, e.g., Psinakis v. Marcos (N.D.Cal.1975), 1975 Dig. U.S.Prac. Int'l 342, 344; Chong Boon Kim v. Kim Young (Haw. Cir. Ct.1963), 58 A.J.I.L. 186. Should the immunity of a head of state be co-extensive with that enjoyed by a state or with that enjoyed by a diplomatic or consular agent? On these problems,

see Note, Resolving the Confusion Over Head of State Immunity: The Defined Rights of Kings, 86 Colum. L.Rev. 169 (1986); Note, The Dictator, Drugs and Diplomacy by Indictment: Head–Of–State Immunity in United States v. Noriega, [683 F.Supp. 1373], 4 Conn.J.Int'l L. 729 (1989). President Noriega was ruled to lack immunity notwithstanding his holding a diplomatic passport in United States v. Noriega, 746 F.Supp. 1506 (S.D.Fla.1990).

8. In 1986, both Duvalier, then the President of Haiti, and Marcos, then the President of the Philippines, left their countries and took up residence abroad, Duvalier in France and Marcos in the United States. After their departure, actions were brought against them in the United States to recover large amounts assertedly wrongfully taken while they were President. Attachments were laid on assets allegedly owned by them in the United States. Switzerland, in a highly unusual move, instructed Swiss banks temporarily to freeze funds on deposit in the name of Duvalier. The following actions related to Duvalier's assets: Republic of Haiti v. Crown Charters, Inc. et al., 667 F.Supp. 839 (S.D.Fla.1987); In re Letter of Request for Judicial Assistance from the Tribunal Civil de Port-au-Prince, Republic of Haiti, 669 F.Supp. 403 (S.D.Fla.1987). The United States made available to the new Philippine government a list of assets Marcos had brought with him to Hawaii. To what extent are the doctrines of immunity from jurisdiction and act-of-state applicable? Marcos never resigned as president. Was he entitled to immunity as a former head of state? Should the opinion of the State Department be regarded as decisive? Cf. Republic of Philippines v. Westinghouse Elec. Corp., 821 F.Supp. 292 (D.N.J.1993).

9. The courts have generally deferred to State Department suggestions of immunity, which may be extended to a head of state, a prime minister (head of government), or other high-level officials. See Tannenbaum v. Rabin, 1996 WL 75283 (E.D.N.Y.); Saltany v. Reagan, 702 F.Supp. 319 (D.D.C.1988), aff'd, 886 F.2d 438 (D.C.Cir.1989), cert. denied, 495 U.S. 932, 110 S.Ct. 2172, 109 L.Ed.2d 501 (1990). Suggestions of immunity have also been issued in favor of family members of heads of state. See Kilroy v. Windsor, 81 I.L.R. 127 (1990) (Prince Charles); Kline v. Kaneko, 141 Misc.2d 787, 535 N.Y.S.2d 303 (Sup.Ct.1988) (wife of President of Mexico). Such immunity has been extended on a State Department suggestion even if the state itself would not have been immune. First Am. Corp. v. Sheikh Zayed Bin Sultan Al–Nahyan, 948 F.Supp. 1107 (D.D.C.1996).

10. An action was brought by four Chinese plaintiffs under the Alien Tort Claims Act alleging crimes against humanity, summary execution, arbitrary detention and torture at the time of the Tiananmen Square upheaval. Li Peng, China's prime minister at the time of the events, was served with process when he attended a U.N. meeting in New York in September 2000 as Chairman of the National People's Congress. Was he entitled to immunity from service as a present or former head of state or government, as an official attending the United Nations, or as a special envoy? See pp. 1291, 1313. Does it further the aims of the world community for one country to entertain suits of this kind? See Sullivan, Justice Tackles Rights Abuses Abroad, N.Y. Times, Sept. 3, 2000, p. A4, col. 3.

11. A French court ruled that Colonel Qaddafi of Libya did not enjoy head of state immunity in a prosecution for complicity in murder in the terrorist bombing of a French airliner. See "France: Go–Ahead to Try Qaddafi," N.Y. Times, Oct. 21, 2000, p. A6, col. 1.

C. DIPLOMATIC REPRESENTATIVES

HACKWORTH, DIGEST OF INTERNATIONAL LAW

Vol. 4, pp. 513–14 (1942).

In a letter of March 16, 1906 to the Secretary of Commerce and Labor, Secretary Root said:

> There are many and various reasons why diplomatic agents, whether accredited or not to the United States, should be exempt from the operation of the municipal law at [sic] this country. The first and fundamental reason is the fact that diplomatic agents are universally exempt by well recognized usage incorporated into the Common law of nations, and this nation, bound as it is to observe International Law in its municipal as well as its foreign policy, cannot, if it would, vary a law common to all. * * *
>
> The reason of the immunity of diplomatic agents is clear, namely: that Governments may not be hampered in their foreign relations by the arrest or forcible prevention of the exercise of a duty in the person of a governmental agent or representative. If such agent be offensive and his conduct is unacceptable to the accredited nation it is proper to request his recall; if the request be not honored he may be in extreme cases escorted to the boundary and thus removed from the country. And rightly, because self-preservation is a matter peculiarly within the province of the injured state, without which its existence is insecure. Of this fact it must be the sole judge: it cannot delegate this discretion or right to any nation however friendly or competent. It likewise follows from the necessity of the case, that the diplomatic agent must have full access to the accrediting state, else he cannot enter upon the performance of his specific duty, and it is equally clear that he must be permitted to return to the home country in the fulfillment of official duty. As to the means best fitted to fulfil these duties the agent must necessarily judge: and of the time required in entering and departing, as well as in the delay necessary to wind up the duties of office after recall, he must likewise judge.
>
> For these universally accepted principles no authority need be cited.

Notes

1. "It is enough that an ambassador has requested immunity, that the State Department has recognized that the person for whom it was requested is entitled to it, and that the Department's recognition has been communicated to the court." Carrera v. Carrera, 84 U.S.App. D.C. 333, 174 F.2d 496, 497 (1949).

The Diplomatic List maintained by the Department of State (the "Blue List") reflects only a ministerial act and not a determination by the executive of a right to immunity. See Trost v. Tompkins, 44 A.2d 226 (Mun.Ct. App. D.C.1945). Cf. also United States v. Dizdar, 581 F.2d 1031 (2d Cir.1978). Restatement (Third) § 464, Reporters' Note 1. See 22 U.S.C.A. § 254a-e, p. 1287 infra, and Haley v. State, 200 Md. 72, 88 A.2d 312 (1952) (immunity denied because official notice of defendant's status had not been communicated to Department of State). The State Department also maintains a "White List" of employees of diplomatic missions. See Carrera v. Carrera, supra; Restatement (Third) § 464, Reporters' Note 1.

Which members of a diplomat's family are entitled to immunity? See O'Keefe, Privileges and Immunities of the Diplomatic Family, 25 I.C.L.Q. 329 (1976).

2. In its 1958 articles on diplomatic privileges and immunities, which served as the basis for the Vienna Convention on Diplomatic Relations, the International Law Commission noted that diplomatic privileges and immunities had in the past been justified on the basis of the "extraterritoriality" theory or on the basis of the "representative character" theory. According to the former, the premises of the mission represented a sort of extension of the territory of the sending state; according to the latter, privileges and immunities were based on the idea that the diplomatic mission personified the sending state. The Commission then observed that a "third theory" appeared to be gaining ground in modern times; i.e., the "functional necessity" theory, "which justifies privileges and immunities as being necessary to enable the mission to perform its functions." The Commission stated that it had been guided by this third theory "in solving problems on which practice gave no clear pointers, while also bearing in mind the representative character of the head of the mission and of the mission itself." 2 Ybk. I.L.C. 95 (1958). What is the significance of the "functional necessity" theory to the scope and extent of diplomatic immunities? Does it imply an obligation on the part of the sending state to waive the immunity of one of its diplomatic agents in situations where it can be established that such waiver would not interfere with the functions of the mission? See Kerley, Some Aspects of the Vienna Conference on Diplomatic Intercourse and Immunities, 56 A.J.I.L. 88, 91–93 (1962). Compare Section 20 of the Convention on the Privileges and Immunities of the United Nations, infra. See Garretson, The Immunities of Representatives of Foreign States, 41 N.Y.U.L.Rev. 67, 71 (1966). For other support for the "functional necessity" theory of diplomatic immunities, see Restatement (Third) § 464, Comments *a*, *c*, and Reporters' Note 2; Harvard Research in International Law, Diplomatic Privileges and Immunities, 26 A.J.I.L.Supp. 15, 26 (Introductory Comment) (1932). This theory has become increasingly important as nations increase the size of their delegations, and as the number of nations and organizations appointing diplomats has grown. See Ling, A Comparative Study of the Privileges and Immunities of United Nations Member Representatives and Officials with the Traditional Privileges and Immunities of Diplomatic Agents, 33 Wash. & Lee L.Rev. 91 (1976).

3. The accepted view in recent years is that diplomatic premises and personnel enjoy immunity and inviolability but are not metaphoric extensions of the territory of the sending state. On rejection of the extraterritoriality theory in relation to embassy premises, see United States v. Bin Laden, 92 F.Supp.2d 189 (S.D.N.Y.2000), discussed in Chapter 13 at p. 1135. See also Paust, Non–Extraterritoriality of "Special Territorial Jurisdiction" of the United States: Forgotten History and the Errors of *Erdos*, 24 Yale J.I.L. 305 (1999).

4. Until 1978, diplomatic immunity was provided for by an Act of Congress enacted on April 30, 1790. This legislation extended civil and criminal immunity to all diplomats, diplomatic administrators, their family members and staff. By 1978, this amounted to over 30,000 individuals. The Department of State urged that this law be repealed in favor of legislation which would conform to the narrower provisions of the Vienna Convention on Diplomatic Relations, p. 1285 infra. On Sept. 30, 1978, the 95th Congress agreed by enacting the Diplomatic Relations Act, Pub. L. 95–393, 92 Stat. 808, which is codified at 22 U.S.C.A. § 254a-e and 28 U.S.C.A. § 1364. See p. 1287 infra.

5. Diplomatic agents are generally free to travel in the receiving state, subject to restrictions for national security reasons. Vienna Convention on Diplomatic Relations Art. 26. Travel restrictions had been imposed by the U.S.S.R. The United States retaliated, invoking Art. 47(2) of the Convention, which permits retaliation against a state that has interpreted the Convention restrictively. See Restatement (Third) § 464, Reporters' Note 5.

6. On diplomatic immunity generally, see Restatement (Third) §§ 464–66; Satow, Guide to Diplomatic Practice (5th ed. 1979); B. Sen, A Diplomat's Handbook on International Law and Practice (2d ed. 1979); Denza, Diplomatic Law: Commentary on the Vienna Convention on Diplomatic Relations (1976); Brown, Diplomatic Immunity: State Practice Under the Vienna Convention, 37 I.C.L.Q. 53 (1988).

VIENNA CONVENTION ON DIPLOMATIC RELATIONS

April 18, 1961.
23 U.S.T. 3227, TIAS No. 7502, 500 U.N.T.S. 95.

[See Articles 22–41.]

Notes

1. The Convention entered into force on April 24, 1964, after 22 states had deposited instruments of ratification. The United States ratified the Convention in 1972. As of 2000, 179 states were parties. For a full account and analysis of the proceedings in the conference that led to the adoption of the convention, see Kerley, Some Aspects of the Vienna Conference on Diplomatic Intercourse and Immunities, 56 A.J.I.L. 88 (1962).

2. Although Article 32(2) of the Vienna Convention provides that waiver "must always be express," it also provides in Article 32(3) that, when a diplomatic agent brings suit, waiver is implied as to a counterclaim directly related to the principal claim. Can the diplomat waive or only his state? See Note, Foreign Relations—Sovereign Immunity—Ambassador Status Is One Factor In Determining Agent's Authority To Waive Immunity. First Fidelity Bank v. Government of Antigua & Barbuda, 877 F.2d 189, 14 Suffolk Transnat'l L.J. 286 (1990). On waiver generally, see Restatement (Third) § 464, Reporters' Note 15.

3. For a study on abuse of diplomatic and consular privileges prompted by the killing of a U.K. policewoman by a member of the Libyan consular staff, see Higgins, U.K. Foreign Affairs Committee Report on the Abuse of Diplomatic Immunities and Privileges: Government Response and Report, 80 A.J.I.L. 135 (1986).

4. On the diplomatic courier and pouch, see Draft Articles on the Status of the Diplomatic Courier and the Diplomatic Bag Not Accompanied by Diplomatic Courier, Report of International Law Commission on Forty–First Session, U.N. Doc A/44/10, ch. II, paras. 17–72 (1989).

5. In Latin America, there have been a number of instances of granting asylum or refuge in diplomatic missions to political figures who have incurred the disfavor of the state in which the mission is established. The practice of granting diplomatic asylum is the subject of a number of Latin American Conventions on Asylum (Havana, 1928), (Montevideo, 1933), (Caracas, 1954), which provide for asylum only for political refugees and in cases of humanitarian concern. Even in those cases, the asylum may generally be granted only for limited time. The right

to grant diplomatic asylum is not recognized by the United States (2 Hackworth 622) or the United Kingdom (2 McNair, International Law Opinions 74–76 (1956)). In the Asylum Case, 1950 I.C.J. 266, the International Court of Justice observed:

> A decision to grant diplomatic asylum involves a derogation from the sovereignty of that State. It withdraws the offender from the jurisdiction of the territorial State and constitutes an intervention in matters which are exclusively within the competence of that State. Such a derogation from territorial sovereignty cannot be recognized unless its legal basis is established in each particular case.

Id. at 274–75. For other portions of the Asylum Case, see p. 87 supra. In 1956, the Department of State authorized the United States Legation in Budapest to grant refuge to Cardinal Mindszenty, threatened by the arrival of Soviet troops. He stayed there for many years. For other instances in which a U.S. Embassy has granted sanctuary to threatened persons, see 1978 Dig. of U.S.Prac. in Int'l L. 568–71; 75 A.J.I.L. 142–47 (1981). For a statement of U.S. policy, see Dep't State Bull., Oct. 1980 p. 50. If a refugee is granted diplomatic asylum, can he be forcibly removed by agents of the territorial state?

For a discussion of the relationship between Art. 41 of the Vienna Convention and the right of the embassy to grant asylum, see Note, Toward Codification of Diplomatic Asylum, 8 N.Y.U.J.Int'I L. & Pol. 435 (1976). See generally Restatement (Third) § 466, Comment *b* and Reporters' Note 3.

6. In what other ways may host nations protect diplomatic agents? Title 18 U.S.C.A. § 112 provides, in part, that "[w]hoever assaults, strikes, wounds, imprisons, or offers violence to a foreign official, official guest or internationally protected person or makes any other violent attack upon the person or liberty of such person," shall be subject to fine or imprisonment, or both. In addition, the statute prohibits demonstrations within one hundred feet of foreign government buildings, and makes the destruction or attempted injury to the property of a foreign government or of its officials a felony. The Act extends the jurisdiction of the United States to any offender found within its territory, irrespective of the nationality of the victim or the defendant, or the place where the crime was committed. The constitutionality of restrictions on picketing in the vicinity of an embassy was considered in Boos v. Barry, 485 U.S. 312, 108 S.Ct. 1157, 99 L.Ed.2d 333 (1988).

7. The United Nations has also been active in the area of protection of diplomats. On Dec. 14, 1973, the General Assembly adopted the Convention on the Prevention and Punishment of Crimes against Internationally Protected Persons, Including Diplomatic Agents. See 28 GAOR, Supp. 30, U.N.Doc. A/9030 (1973), 28 U.S.T. 1975, T.I.A.S. No. 8532, 1035 U.N.T.S. 167. As of 2000, the Convention has been ratified by more than 100 states, including the United States.

8. In the Iranian Hostage Case, p. 868 infra, the International Court of Justice granted both specific relief and damages for violation of the relevant provisions of the Vienna Conventions on Diplomatic Relations and on Consular Relations.

9. When the United States invaded Panama, President Noriega sought refuge in the mission of the Vatican in Panama. The United States negotiated with the Vatican emissary the terms of President Noriega's surrender.

DIPLOMATIC RELATIONS ACT

[See 22 U.S.C.A. § 254a-e]

Notes

1. This legislation was enacted on Sept. 30, 1978, and became effective 90 days later. For a discussion of the Act, see Note, 10 Case W.Res.J.I.L. 827 (1978).

2. Local communities sometimes object to the immunities, including the immunity from property taxes, diplomats enjoy. See, e.g., United States v. Glen Cove, 322 F.Supp. 149 (E.D.N.Y.1971), aff'd, 450 F.2d 884 (2d Cir.1971); Note, Immunity of Foreign Consulate Property from Real Property Taxation, 38 Albany L.Rev. 976 (1974).

3. What measures can properly be taken against illegal parking by diplomats? In New York City, the police tow illegally parked cars with diplomatic plates to the City pound, but release them without payment of a fine or a towing charge. Is this permissible under international law and applicable conventions?

4. Persons injured by diplomatic personnel traditionally have been denied relief under United States law. Section 254e directs the Director of the Office of Foreign Missions to require liability insurance of all mission members. This provision must be read in conjunction with 28 U.S.C.A. § 1364, which grants to the district courts competence, without regard to the amount in controversy, over all civil actions brought directly against the diplomats' insurer. See also the Department of State's Regulations on Compulsory Liability Insurance for Diplomatic Missions and Personnel, 22 CFR 151 et seq. (1980), 18 I.L.M. 871 (1979).

5. Section 254c allows the President to extend more or less favorable treatment on the basis of reciprocity. For an example, see Union of Soviet Socialist Republics–United States: Agreement on Privileges and Immunity of Embassy Staff, 17 I.L.M. 56 (1979).

6. In 1982, Congress adopted the Foreign Missions Act, 22 U.S.C.A. § 4301, authorizing the Secretary of State to determine the treatment to be extended to the mission of a foreign state. See Restatement (Third) § 464, Reporters' Note 5.

7. The immunities of a diplomat while in transit through the territory of a third state were long the subject of considerable controversy. See Harvard Research in International Law, Diplomatic Privileges and Immunities, 26 A.J.I.L.Supp. 15, 85–88 (Art. 15) (1932). See also Bergman v. De Sieyes, 170 F.2d 360 (2d Cir.1948) (immunity upheld) (opinion by L. Hand, C.J.). The article recommended by the Harvard Research provided that a third state should permit the transit of a diplomatic agent across its territory for the purpose of traveling to, or from, his post in the receiving state (whether or not the other end of his journey was the territory of the sending state), granting only such privileges and immunities as were necessary to facilitate the transit. These privileges and immunities would be subject to the conditions that the third state has recognized the government of the sending state and that it be informed of the agent's official character. Id.

The matter is now regulated by Article 40 of the Vienna Convention. If the Swiss ambassador to Cuba were ordered by his government to travel to the Swiss embassy in Ottawa in order to participate in a conference there, would he be entitled to the benefits of Article 40 while in transit through the United States? If the trip to Canada were for personal reasons (e.g., a vacation), would he be entitled to immunity? Compare United States v. Rosal, 191 F.Supp. 663 (S.D.N.Y. 1960).

D. CONSULS

VIENNA CONVENTION ON CONSULAR RELATIONS

Signed at Vienna, April 24, 1963.
21 U.S.T. 77, T.I.A.S. No. 6820, 596 U.N.T.S. 261.

[See Articles 41–55]

Notes

1. The U.N. Conference on Consular Relations adopted, on April 24, 1963, the Vienna Convention on Consular Relations and two optional protocols, one of which provides for settlement of disputes by the International Court of Justice. The Convention entered into force on March 19, 1967. As of 2000, the Convention had been ratified by 164 states, including the United States.

2. Article 5 of the Convention contains a list of consular functions. These cover a wide spectrum and include, among others, protecting in the receiving state the interests of the sending state and of its nationals; furthering the development of commercial, economic, cultural and scientific relations; ascertaining conditions and developments in the commercial, economic, cultural and scientific life of the receiving state; issuing passports, visas, and travel documents; helping and assisting nationals of the sending state; serving as a notary or civil registrar; assisting nationals in connection with decedents' estates, guardianships for persons lacking legal capacity and representation and preservation of rights before local tribunals; transmitting documents or executing letters rogatory or commissions to take evidence for courts of the sending state; exercising rights of supervision and inspection of vessels and aircraft of the sending state; and extending assistance to such vessels and aircraft and their crews, including conducting investigations and settling disputes.

Article 17 provides that a consular officer may be authorized to perform diplomatic acts without effect upon his consular status. Articles 3 and 70 deal with the performance of consular functions by diplomatic personnel. Other articles deal, *inter alia,* with the appointment and admission of consular officers, the *exequatur* (authorization from the receiving state admitting the head of a consular post to the exercise of his functions, no longer used by the United States), miscellaneous facilities and privileges to be granted by the receiving state, protocol matters, and the termination of consular functions.

Article 31, on the inviolability of consular premises, provides that authorities of the receiving state shall not enter "that part of the consular premises which is used exclusively for the purpose of the work of the consular post" except by permission, which may be "assumed" in the case of "fire or other disaster requiring prompt protective action." Article 31 of the Vienna Convention further provides that the consular premises and furnishings, as well as other post property, "shall be immune from any form of requisition for purposes of national defense or public utility," but then states that "if expropriation is necessary for such purposes," all possible steps shall be taken not to impede consular functions and that "prompt, adequate and effective compensation" shall be paid to the sending state. The latter clause was not included in the International Law

Commission draft articles, and the reason for its addition by the Conference is not clear. It has been stated that "[T]he trend before 1948 was to grant absolute consular immunity from military requisition and expropriation, irrespective of considerations of military defense or public utility," but that since World War II there are indications that expropriation or requisition of consular property may be permissible under conditions similar to those stated in Article 31 of the Vienna Convention. Lee, Consular Law and Practice 283–84 (1961).

3. In 1948, New York police authorities entered the Soviet Consulate General in order to provide medical assistance for, and to investigate the fall from a third-story window of a Soviet national who had refused to return to the Soviet Union. As a consequence of this and other incidents, consular relations between the United States and the Soviet Union were broken off. See Preuss, Consular Immunities: The Kasenkina Case, 43 A.J.I.L. 37 (1949), and compare Article 17 of the Consular Convention between the United States and the Soviet Union. The United States broke off consular relations with Communist China in 1950 when the latter requisitioned certain property serving as United States consular premises. 22 Dep't State Bull. 119 (1950). The United States resumed diplomatic relations with Communist China in 1979.

Notes

1. In Arcaya v. Páez, 145 F.Supp. 464 (S.D.N.Y.1956), aff'd per curiam, 244 F.2d 958 (2d Cir.1957), a Venezuelan citizen in exile for political reasons brought a libel action against the consul general of Venezuela in New York, alleging that defendant had disseminated defamatory information about plaintiff. After service of process, defendant was appointed alternate representative of Venezuela to the United Nations, with ambassadorial rank. The district court considered that the federal court had properly obtained jurisdiction of the subject matter under 28 U.S.C. § 1351, which gives exclusive jurisdiction to the federal courts over all actions against consuls. The question then became whether jurisdiction was ousted by virtue of defendant's subsequent appointment to a position entailing diplomatic immunity. (An accredited representative to the United Nations with the rank to which Páez was appointed is entitled to diplomatic privileges and immunities in the United States; see p. 1292.) The Department of State advised the court of the Executive's position that defendant's acquisition of diplomatic status would not defeat the court's previously acquired jurisdiction of the subject matter. The court was of the view that it should determine its own jurisdiction independently of the position of the Department of State, and upon making its own examination reached the same conclusion as the Department's on the matter.

Defendant further argued that his consular status entitled him to official acts immunity, and that the allegedly libelous statements had been uttered in the course of his official functions. The Venezuelan Ambassador wrote to the Department of State in support of this claim, asserting that Mr. Páez had written a letter to the New York Times and circulated information concerning Dr. Arcaya on official instructions from his government. The court concluded, however, that a consul's duties are mainly commercial and that a purported enlargement of his authority to act with immunity outside ordinary consular functions would have to have been recognized by the U.S. government, a contention not supported by the record of the U.S. government's communications in the case. The court thus denied the plea of consular immunity. Finally, the court concluded that the action should be stayed for the duration of defendant's appointment to the status of alternative representative to the United Nations with diplomatic rank.

2. Shortly after the decision in *Arcaya*, the Secretary of State informed the chiefs of foreign missions in the United States that:

> It has appeared to the Government of the United States that the functions and status of consular officers and employees, as determined by international law and practice and applicable treaties, are essentially incompatible with the functions and status of principal representatives to the United Nations and members of their staffs entitled to diplomatic privileges and immunities under the Headquarters Agreement between the United States and the United Nations, signed June 26, 1947.
>
> The Chiefs of Mission are accordingly advised that hereafter the Government of the United States must decline to recognize, in a consular capacity, or in any other non-diplomatic capacity, any person who is entitled to diplomatic immunity pursuant to Section 15 of the above-mentioned Headquarters Agreement. In the case of the several Governments who presently have one or more of their representatives in the United States recognized in a consular capacity and also accredited to the United Nations pursuant to Section 15 of the above-mentioned Headquarters Agreement, the Secretary of State would appreciate being advised, as soon as possible, whether the Government concerned prefers that the individual's exequatur or other consular recognition be revoked, or prefers to terminate, by appropriate notification to the Secretary General, his accreditation to the United Nations. * * *
>
> The Government of the United States will continue to recognize, in a dual capacity, members of diplomatic missions in Washington who also perform consular functions. The Government of the United States will also accept as consular officers and employees persons who from time to time may perform functions and duties in connection with their government's representation to the United Nations, provided that such officers and employees do not thereby become entitled to claim diplomatic immunity.

Dep't of State Circular of January 16, 1958, quoted in Lee at 190–91.

3. For a comparison of diplomatic and consular immunities, see Restatement (Third) § 466, Comment *a* and Reporters' Note 1. The principal difference is that consular personnel enjoy immunity only in regard to their official acts, while diplomatic personnel enjoy personal immunity. The State Department normally leaves to the court whether an act was done in the performance of official consular functions. The United States has bilateral consular conventions with a large number of countries. For a partial listing, and a brief discussion of their terms, see Restatement (Third) § 465, Reporters' Note 3.

4. As pointed out by the court in *Arcaya*, all civil actions and proceedings brought in the United States against consuls or vice consuls of foreign states must be brought in the federal district courts. 28 U.S.C.A. § 1351. The Supreme Court has held, however, that divorce proceedings may be brought against consuls in the state courts. Ohio ex rel. Popovici v. Agler, 280 U.S. 379, 50 S.Ct. 154, 74 L.Ed. 489 (1930). Until 1978, 28 U.S.C.A. § 1351, as it then read, was construed to render only the federal courts competent to hear cases against consular personnel. As a consequence, since the federal courts do not hear cases under state criminal law, consular personnel were in fact immune from prosecution under state law. This situation was changed when Congress, by the Diplomatic Relations Act of 1978, amended 28 U.S.C.A. § 1351 to make clear that it provided for exclusive federal competence only in civil cases. This statutory provision does not apply to members of the family of consular personnel. They remain subject to normal federal and state rules of judicial competence.

E. SPECIAL MISSIONS

In adopting a set of draft articles on diplomatic intercourse and immunities, the International Law Commission observed, in 1958, that these dealt only with permanent diplomatic missions and that it was desirable as well to clarify the status of "itinerant envoys, diplomatic conferences and special missions sent to a State for limited purposes." In 1960, the Commission adopted a preliminary set of draft articles on special missions and recommended that these be referred to the forthcoming Vienna Conference on Diplomatic Intercourse and Immunities. The Conference, however, decided that the draft articles were unsuitable for inclusion in the Vienna Convention and referred the articles back to the General Assembly, which in turn requested the International Law Commission to undertake further study of the problem. The Commission considered a revised draft and reexamined it in the light of comments from member states. See Report of the International Law Commission, 22 GAOR, Supp. No. 9 (A/6709/Rev. 1), at 2–4. On Dec. 8, 1969, the General Assembly approved a Convention on Special Missions, see G.A.Res 2530 (XXIV 1970) at 99. The Convention entered into force on June 21, 1985. As of 2000, there were 25 parties to the Convention; the United States had not become a party.

The Restatement (Third), in contrast to its predecessor, does not contain a provision recognizing that an official representative of a foreign state on special mission enjoys immunity to the extent required by the performance of his official duties. This immunity is now covered by the general provision on diplomatic immunity. See Restatement (Third) § 464, Comment *i* and Reporters' Note 13.

Notes

1. Although the United States has not ratified the Convention on Special Missions, could its provisions be regarded as reflecting general international law?

2. In 1998, Abba Sissoko was designated by The Gambia as a special envoy to the United States, and the U.S. embassy in The Gambia issued him a diplomatic visa. Subsequently, the United States, alleging that Sissoko had tried to bribe a U.S. customs official in a transatlantic phone conversation, requested his extradition from Switzerland and, having obtained his extradition, prosecuted him. The Gambia claimed that he was immune as a special envoy. The court rejected the plea on the ground that the State Department had not officially certified him as a special envoy. See United States v. Sissoko, 995 F.Supp. 1469 (S.D.Fla., 1997). Under international law, was official certification required? Or was the issuance of a diplomatic visa sufficient acknowledgment of Sissoko's status as a special envoy? Would it be advisable for the U.S. Department of State to promulgate rules to clarify situations like this one?

3. In October 2000 the Democratic Republic of the Congo filed an application against Belgium at the International Court of Justice, concerning an international arrest warrant issued on April 11, 2000 by a Belgian judge against Congo's acting minister for foreign affairs, seeking his extradition on allegations of grave violations of international humanitarian law. It appears from the application that Belgian law provides for universal jurisdiction in the case of grave breaches of the Geneva Conventions, crimes against humanity, and other serious offenses, and that the Belgian statute further provides that "the immunity conferred by a

person's official capacity does not prevent application of this Law." The application claims, inter alia, that Belgium violated international law by purporting to exercise enforcement jurisdiction over another state's foreign minister, and that the foreign minister should enjoy immunity equivalent to that of a diplomat under international law. Congo also requested the Court to enter an order of provisional measures of protection, on the ground that "the disputed international arrest warrant in effect prevents the [Congo's] Minister from departing that State for any other State where his duties may call him and, accordingly, from accomplishing his duties."

Should a foreign minister enjoy a level of immunity sufficient to enable him or her to carry on diplomatic relations by traveling to other states? Could a presumption of immunity be overcome in the case of exceptionally serious crimes, such as crimes against humanity?

F. REPRESENTATIVES TO INTERNATIONAL ORGANIZATIONS

CONVENTION ON THE PRIVILEGES AND IMMUNITIES OF THE UNITED NATIONS

Adopted by the General Assembly, February 13, 1946.
21 U.S.T. 1418, T.I.A.S. No. 6900, 1 U.N.T.S. 15.

* * *

Art. IV. § 11. Representatives of Members to the principal and subsidiary organs of the United Nations and to conferences convened by the United Nations, shall, while exercising their functions and during the journey to and from the place of meeting, enjoy the following privileges and immunities:

(a) Immunity from personal arrest or detention and from seizure of their personal baggage, and, in respect of words spoken or written and all acts done by them in their capacity as representatives, immunity from legal process of every kind;

(b) Inviolability for all papers and documents;

(c) The right to use codes and to receive papers or correspondence by courier or in sealed bags;

(d) Exemption in respect of themselves and their spouses from immigration restrictions, aliens registration or national service obligations in the state they are visiting or through which they are passing in the exercise of their functions;

(e) The same facilities in respect of currency or exchange restrictions as are accorded to representatives of foreign governments on temporary official missions;

(f) The same immunities and facilities in respect of their personal baggage as are accorded to diplomatic envoys, and also;

(g) Such other privileges, immunities and facilities not inconsistent with the foregoing as diplomatic envoys enjoy, except that they shall have no right to claim exemption from customs duties on goods imported (otherwise than as part of their personal baggage) or from excise duties or sales taxes.

§ 12. In order to secure, for the representatives of Members to the principal and subsidiary organs of the United Nations and to conferences convened by the United Nations, complete freedom of speech and independence in the discharge of their duties, the immunity from legal process in respect of words spoken or written and all acts done by them in discharging their duties shall continue to be accorded, notwithstanding that the persons concerned are no longer the representatives of Members.

* * *

§ 14. Privileges and immunities are accorded to the representatives of Members not for the personal benefit of the individuals themselves, but in order to safeguard the independent exercise of their functions in connection with the United Nations. Consequently a Member not only has the right but is under a duty to waive the immunity of its representative in any case where in the opinion of the Member the immunity would impede the course of justice, and it can be waived without prejudice to the purpose for which the immunity is accorded.

§ 15. The provisions of Sections 11, 12 * * * are not applicable as between a representative and the authorities of the state of which he is a national or of which he is or has been the representative.

§ 16. In this article the expression "representatives" shall be deemed to include all delegates, deputy delegates, advisers, technical experts and secretaries of delegations.

* * *

Notes

1. As of 2000, 139 states were parties to the Convention on the Privileges and Immunities of the United Nations. The United States ratified the Convention in 1970.

2. Section 15 of Article V of the Agreement between the United Nations and the United States Regarding the Headquarters of the United Nations, 61 Stat. 3416, T.I.A.S. No. 1676, 11 U.N.T.S. 11, provides as follows:

> (1) Every person designated by a Member as the principal resident representative to the United Nations of such Member or as a resident representative with the rank of ambassador or minister plenipotentiary,
>
> (2) such resident members of their staffs as may be agreed upon between the Secretary–General, the Government of the United States and the Government of the Member concerned,
>
> (3) every person designated by a Member of a specialized agency, as defined in Article 57, paragraph 2, of the Charter, as its principal resident representative, with the rank of ambassador or minister plenipotentiary, at the headquarters of such agency in the United States, and
>
> (4) such other principal resident representatives of Members to a specialized agency and such resident members of the staffs of representatives of a specialized agency as may be agreed upon between the principal executive officer of the specialized agency, the Government of the United States and the Government of the Member concerned,

> shall, whether residing inside or outside the headquarters district, be entitled in the territory of the United States to the same privileges and immunities, subject to corresponding conditions and obligations, as it accords to diplomatic envoys accredited to it. In the case of Members whose governments are not recognized by the United States, such privileges and immunities need be extended to such representatives, or persons on the staffs of such representatives, only within the headquarters district, at their residences and offices outside the district, in transit between the district and such residences and offices, and in transit on official business to or from foreign countries.

The United States insists that it may control the entry of aliens into the United States to safeguard its security. See Note 5, p. 1301 infra. The United States has in fact limited some representatives to a 25 mile radius over objections by their states. See Restatement (Third) § 470, Reporters' Note 2.

3. In 1986, the United States informed the U.S.S.R. that it would have to reduce the number of members of its mission, and those of Ukraine and Byelorussia, to the United Nations. The U.N. Secretary General referred the dispute to the appropriate U.N. Committee. It would appear to be covered by Article 15(2) of the Headquarters Agreement, Note 2 supra. If the dispute had arisen between the United States and the United Nations, it would have been subject to compulsory arbitration under Article 21 of the Headquarters Agreement.

4. Section 7(b) of the International Organizations Immunities Act, 22 U.S.C.A. § 288d(b), infra, accords representatives to international organizations, as well as officers and employees of such organizations, immunity "from suit and legal process relating to acts performed by them in their official capacity and falling within their functions as such representatives, officers, or employees."

On the immunities of representatives to international organizations, see generally Restatement (Third) § 470; Gross, Immunities and Privileges of Delegations to the United Nations, 16 Int'l Org. 483 (1962); Ling, Comparative Study of The Privileges and Immunities of UN Member Representatives and Officials with the Traditional Privileges and Immunities of Diplomatic Agents, 33 Wash. & Lee L.Rev. 91 (1976); Amerasinghe, Liability To Third Parties Of Member States Of International Organizations: Practice, Principle, and Judicial Precedent, 85 A.J.I.L. 259 (1991).

5. The privileges and immunities of member representatives to international organizations are treated in the Vienna Convention on the Representation of States in Their Relations with International Organizations of a Universal Character, U.N.Doc. No. A/CONF. 67/16, March 14, 1975 [not in force]. The United States abstained on the vote on the final text on the ground that the Convention would unduly expand privileges and immunities. See 1975 Dig. U.S.Prac. 38–40.

6. Is a representative to the United Nations entitled to the privileges and immunities of a diplomat *in transitu* while he travels to and from the Headquarters District? Does a comparison of the Vienna Convention with the Headquarters Agreement and the International Organizations Immunities Act, p. 1300 infra, reveal any significant advantages enjoyed by diplomatic agents in transit through the United States over representatives to the United Nations? See Hearings Before the Subcommittee of the Senate Committee on Foreign Relations, on Executive H, 88th Cong., 1st Session (Vienna Convention on Diplomatic Relations), 89th Cong., 1st Sess. at 15–16 (1965).

7. 28 U.S.C.A. § 1351, as amended by the Diplomatic Relations Act of 1978, gives the district courts exclusive original competence over all civil actions against

diplomatic personnel. It is apparently intended also to cover members to missions to international organizations, such as the United Nations and the Organization of American States. See Restatement (Third) § 470, Reporters' Note 4.

8. A number of decisions by American courts have given effect to the immunity from legal process of representatives to international organizations. See, e.g., Anonymous v. Anonymous, 44 Misc.2d 14, 252 N.Y.S.2d 913 (N.Y.Family Ct.1964) and cases cited in Restatement (Third) § 470, Reporters' Note 2.

SECTION 3. IMMUNITIES OF INTERNATIONAL ORGANIZATIONS, THEIR AGENTS, OFFICIALS, AND INVITEES

The modern law relating to the immunities of international organizations has developed principally from the experience of the League of Nations and the International Labor Organization, although some aspects of its origin can be traced back into the nineteenth century. This body of law began as little more than "a general principle resting on the questionable analogy of diplomatic immunities; it has become a complex body of rules set forth in detail in conventions, agreements, statutes and regulations." Jenks, International Immunities XXXV (1961). As the scope and importance of the activities of international organizations have increased in the postwar world, so have the extent and significance of their immunities and those of their officials. The bases for their immunities differ in important respects from those for the granting of jurisdictional immunities to foreign states. Like states, international organizations require jurisdictional immunities in order to carry on their functions without interference from municipal courts and administrators; unlike states, however, international organizations do not enjoy a long history of respect for their authority or the means of taking reciprocal reprisals against infringements of that authority. Two main questions are raised in the following materials: In what essential respects do the immunities of international organizations differ from those of states? To what extent is the trend towards limiting the immunities of states likely to apply to international organizations? As a corollary to the latter question, what procedures and practices can organizations adopt that will forestall abuse and consequent criticism and curtailment of their immunities?

CONVENTION ON THE PRIVILEGES AND IMMUNITIES OF THE UNITED NATIONS

Adopted by the General Assembly, February 13, 1946.
21 U.S.T. 1418, T.I.A.S. No. 6900, 1 U.N.T.S. 15.

[See Articles II and V]

Notes

1. In an *Aide-Mémoire* to the Permanent Representative of a Member State of October 27, 1963, the Secretary-General of the United Nations gave the following legal opinion concerning the proposed accession by that State to the Convention subject to a reservation denying to any United Nations official (or an expert on mission for the United Nations) of that state's nationality any privilege or immunity under the Convention, 1963 U.N. Jur'l Yb. 188:

1. * * *

2. In the opinion of the Secretary–General, a closer examination of the true legal operation of this reservation, as so interpreted, will leave no doubt that it is incompatible with the United Nations Charter. * * *

3. Numerous privileges and immunities specified in article V are not ordinarily understood to have practical application as between an official of the United Nations and his Government of nationality. Such an official will have no occasion, unless in rare circumstances, to require immunity from immigration restrictions in his own country, or privileges in respect of exchange facilities, or repatriation facilities in time of international crisis; he cannot by definition require immunity from alien registration, and it would be exceptional for him to have reason to claim duty-free entry for his personal effects on taking up his post in the country.

4. The situation is quite otherwise in the matter of his official acts, and it is here that the reservation cannot be reconciled with the Charter. Section 18(a) in article V requires that officials of the United Nations be "immune from legal process in respect of words spoken or written and all acts performed by them in *their official capacity*" (emphasis supplied). It follows that your country, in proposing the reservation quoted above, has (no doubt unintentionally) reserved the right to prosecute United Nations officials of its nationality for words spoken or written or for any acts performed by them in their official capacity, indeed for actions which are in effect the acts of the Organization itself. It would equally be the consequence of the reservation that your country would be reserving jurisdiction to its national courts to entertain private lawsuits against its citizens for acts performed by them as officials of the United Nations.

5. Article 105 of the Charter provides in its second paragraph that officials of the Organization shall "enjoy such privileges and immunities as are necessary for the independent exercise of their functions in connection with the Organization." Likewise, by the second paragraph of Article 100 each Member of the United Nations "undertakes to respect the exclusively international character of the responsibilities of the Secretary–General and the staff." It needs no argument to demonstrate that the reservation by a Member of the right, even in the abstract, to exercise jurisdiction over the official acts of the United Nations staff, either through its courts or through other organs or authorities of the State, would be incompatible with the independent exercise and exclusively international character of the responsibilities of such officials of the Organization. This derogation from the clear terms of the Charter would in no way be affected by the common nationality of the international official and the prosecuting authority. The Secretary–General cannot believe that the legal effect of the reservation in question, although indisputable when examined in this light, was consciously intended.

2. Absent special agreement or legislation in each Member State, would the United Nations be entitled to the privileges and immunities of Article 105 of the Charter?

Before the United States acceded to the Convention in 1970, were the substantive obligations of the Convention nonetheless binding on the United States? The Legal Counsel, speaking as the representative of the Secretary–General of the United Nations, stated in 1968:

> With regard to the legal framework of the regime of privileges and immunities of the United Nations, * * * in the first place, Article 105 of the Charter accorded such privileges and immunities as were "necessary." By paragraphs 1 and 2, it imposed an obligation on all Members of the United Nations to accord such privileges and immunities as were necessary for the fulfillment of the purposes of the Organization or for the independent exercise of the functions of representatives and officials, irrespective of whether or not they had acceded to the Convention. In accordance with paragraph 3, the purpose of the Convention was merely to determine the details of the application of the first two paragraphs of the same Article. In the second place, the Convention, in determining the details of certain privileges and immunities, in effect provided the minimum privileges and immunities which the Organization required in all Member States. Additional privileges and immunities necessary for special situations, such as at the Headquarters in New York or for peace-keeping or development missions in various areas of the world, were provided for by special agreements. In the third place, ninety-six Member States had acceded to the Convention while, in most of the remaining Member States as well as in some nonmember States, the provisions of the Convention had been made applicable by special agreements. It could thus be said that in the nearly twenty-two years since the adoption of the Convention by the General Assembly, the standards and principles of the Convention had been so widely accepted that they had now become a part of the general international law governing the relations of States and the United Nations.

Annual Report of the Secretary–General, 23 GAOR, Supp. I (A/7201), at 208–09 (1968) (summary record).

As of 2000, 106 States, but not the United States, had become parties to the companion Convention on the Privileges and Immunities of the Specialized Agencies, adopted by the General Assembly on November 21, 1947, 33 U.N.T.S. 261, which provides in detail for the immunities of organizations related to the United Nations under Articles 57 and 63 of the Charter. The constitutions of many of these organizations, however, provide themselves for some degree of immunity, as do the constituent instruments of many non-related organizations. See, e.g., Article 16 of the Constitution of the Food and Agriculture Organization, T.I.A.S. No. 4803, and the other provisions cited in Jenks, International Immunities 3–5 (1961). What might account for the United States' failure to accede to this convention on privileges and immunities? See the provisions of the International Organizations Immunities Act, p. 1300 infra, and the Headquarters Agreement, p. 1293 supra.

3. Unlike the Charter, the Covenant of the League of Nations provided only for the immunity of League officials (in addition to representatives of members of the League), who were to be entitled to "diplomatic privileges and immunities" when they were "engaged on the business of the League." The only protection intended for the League itself was a provision that League property was to be "inviolable." Covenant, Art. 7(4), (5). On the relevance of the experience of the League and the International Labour Organisation to the development of the immunities of the United Nations and other postwar organizations, see Jenks at 12–16. A *modus vivendi* was entered into by the League and the Swiss Federal Government on September 18, 1926, by which Switzerland recognized that the League possessed international personality and legal capacity and that it could not "in principle, according to the rules of international law, be sued before the Swiss Courts without its express consent." The archives and premises of the League

were recognized as inviolable, and certain customs and fiscal exemptions were granted. In addition, the League's staff was granted certain immunities from Swiss civil and criminal jurisdiction. See Hill, Immunities and Privileges of Officials of the League of Nations 14–23, 138–98 (1947).

4. The Permanent Court of International Justice began to sit at The Hague in 1922. The government of the Netherlands gave effect to the immunities and privileges of the judges envisaged by Article 19 of the Court's Statute and to the immunities and privileges of Court officials envisaged by Article 7(4) of the Covenant in a series of regulations; these were replaced in 1928 by an agreement between the Dutch Foreign Minister and the President of the Court, in which judges and officials continued to be assimilated to corresponding diplomatic representatives and officials. Hill at 21–23; see generally id. at 50–57, and the 1928 Agreement and supplementary rules, id. at 199–202 (Annex III), 1 Hudson, International Legislation 597 (1931). On the status of the International Court of Justice, see Articles 19, 32(8), and 42(3) of the Statute, the site agreement between the Netherlands and the President of the Court, 8 U.N.T.S. 61, and the recommendations contained in the General Assembly Resolution 90, U.N.Doc. A/64/Add. I at 176–79 (1946). The Court as an institution continues to be assimilated to the diplomatic corps. For discussion, see 5 Repertory of Practice of United Nations Organs 362–66 (1955); Jenks at 93–95. The privileges and immunities of other international tribunals, including the European Court of Human Rights and the Court of Justice of the European Communities, are discussed id. at 95–101.

5. The immunities of international organizations and their officials and premises, archives, documents and communications are treated in Restatement (Third) § 467–470. On these immunities generally, see Jenks, International Immunities (1961) and Bowett, The Law of International Institutions (3d ed. 1975).

6. In 1999 the International Court of Justice gave an advisory opinion on the immunity of a special rapporteur of a U.N. body, in relation to national judicial proceedings in his own country. See Difference Relating to Immunity from Legal Process of a Special Rapporteur of the Commission on Human Rights, 1999 I.C.J. 62, 38 I.L.M. 873 (1999). The circumstances were as follows:

Dato Param Cumaraswamy, a Malaysian lawyer, was appointed by the U.N. Commission on Human Rights (an organ of the U.N. Economic and Social Council (ECOSOC)) to serve as its Special Rapporteur on the Independence of Judges and Lawyers. In an interview with a U.K.-based magazine circulated in Malaysia, he commented on his investigation into complaints that certain business and corporate interests had manipulated the Malaysian courts to influence decisions in their favor. Four defamation lawsuits were then filed in Malaysia by plaintiffs who had been beneficiaries of such favorable rulings. The Malaysian courts from the trial level through two levels of appeals declined to give effect to Cumaraswamy's immunity from legal process, as asserted by the U.N. Secretary–General in relation to matters falling within the Special Rapporteur's U.N. functions. The Secretary–General had certified that the allegedly defamatory words were spoken in the course of Cumaraswamy's U.N. responsibilities.

In its request for an advisory opinion, ECOSOC asked the I.C.J. to advise on the applicability of Article VI, Section 22 of the Convention on the Privileges and Immunities of the United Nations to the circumstances of the case and on Malaysia's legal obligations. The Court observed that Cumaraswamy was an expert on mission, "and that such experts enjoy the privileges and immunities provided for under the General Convention in their relations with States parties, including those of which they are nationals or on the territory of which they reside." (Para. 46.) The Court stated:

> 51. Article VI, Section 23, of the General Convention provides that "[p]rivileges and immunities are granted to experts in the interests of the United Nations and not for the personal benefit of the individuals themselves." In exercising protection of United Nations experts, the Secretary–General is therefore protecting the mission with which the expert is entrusted. * * *
>
> 52. The determination whether an agent of the Organization has acted in the course of the performance of his mission depends upon the facts of a particular case. In the present case, the Secretary–General, or the Legal Counsel of the United Nations on his behalf, has on numerous occasions informed the Government of Malaysia of his finding that Mr. Cumaraswamy had spoken the words quoted in the article * * * in his capacity as Special Rapporteur of the Commission and that he consequently was entitled to immunity from "every kind" of legal process.
>
> 53. * * * [T]he Secretary–General was reinforced in this view by the fact that it has become standard practice of Special Rapporteurs of the Commission to have contact with the media. This practice was confirmed by the High Commissioner for Human Rights who * * * wrote that: "it is more common than not for Special Rapporteurs to speak to the press about matters pertaining to their investigations, thereby keeping the general public informed of their work."

The Court concluded that the Government of Malaysia had an obligation, under Article 105 of the Charter and the General Convention, to inform its courts of the Secretary–General's position; and that the Secretary–General's finding of immunity created a presumption "which can only be set aside for the most compelling reasons and is thus to be given the greatest weight by national courts." (Paras. 61–62.)

On the *Cumaraswamy* advisory opinion, see the case note by Peter Bekker case at 93 A.J.I.L. 913–923 (1999); Charles H. Brower II, International Immunities: Some Dissident Views on the Role of Municipal Courts, 41 Va. J.I.L. 1, 41–57 (2000).

7. Can an international or national tribunal summon an international peacekeeper to testify about crimes witnessed in the course of his official responsibilities? The International Criminal Tribunal for the Former Yugoslavia considered its authority to making binding orders for production of evidence in the *Blaskic* case (Case No. IT–95–14–AR108*bis*, Judgment on Request of Croatia for Review of Subpoena Decision, 1997); the Appeals Chamber concluded that the Tribunal does have competence to issue such orders to individuals serving under U.N. authority. See p. 375.

In the *Akayesu* case, General Roméo Dallaire, the Canadian head of U.N. peacekeeping forces in Rwanda, testified before the International Criminal Tribunal for Rwanda under a waiver of immunity issued by the U.N. Secretary–General, at defendant's request. Prosecutor v. Akayesu, Case No. ICTR–96–4–T (Judgment, Sept. 2, 1998), para. 1.4.1 (noting decision of Nov. 19, 1997 on motion to subpoena a witness and grant of leave to U.N. Secretariat witness to make a statement on lifting of immunity). General Dallaire's testimony was also requested before national parliamentary bodies and other inquiries in Belgium, Canada, and France. Should the Secretary–General have waived immunity so that the U.N.

commander could testify in national inquiries about the circumstances of the 1994 genocide, in relation to national peacekeeping forces serving under international authority?

8. On immunities of international organizations and their personnel, see Bekker, The Legal Position of Intergovernmental Organizations (1994); Singer, Jurisdictional Immunity of International Organizations: Human Rights and Functional Necessity Concerns, 36 Va. J.I.L. 53 (1995); Schermers & Blokker, International Institutional Law (1995); Amerasinghe, Principles of the Institutional Law of International Organizations (1996); Frey & Frey, The History of Diplomatic Immunity 577–578 (1999); Charles H. Brower II, International Immunities: Some Dissident Views on the Role of Municipal Courts, 41 Va. J.I.L. 1, 41–57 (2000); Reinisch, International Organizations Before National Courts (2000).

INTERNATIONAL ORGANIZATIONS IMMUNITIES ACT

[See 22 U.S.C.A. § 288a-e]

Notes

1. For the international organizations designated as entitled to the benefits of the International Organizations Immunities Act, see the table following 22 U.S.C.A. § 288, supplemented by executive orders appearing in the Federal Register and in Title 3 of the Code of Federal Regulations.

2. 22 U.S.C.A. §§ 288f(1)–288f(2) authorize the President to extend to the European Space Agency and the Organization of Eastern Caribbean States as well as to the Organization of African Unity respectively the privileges of the International Organizations Immunities Act. 22 U.S.C.A.§§ 288g–288k permit the extension of the privileges and immunities enjoyed by accredited diplomatic missions to the Organization of American States, the Commission of European Communities, and the Liaison Office of the People's Republic of China, the International Development Law Institute and Hong Kong Economic and Trade Offices.

3. On the immunity of the European Space Agency from suit in German courts, see the judgments of the European Court of Human Rights in Waite & Kennedy v. Germany, Application No. 26083/94, and Beer & Regan v. Germany, Application No. 28934/95 (E.C.H.R., Feb. 18, 1999), discussed in the case note by August Reinisch at 93 A.J.I.L. 933–938 (1999).

4. Legislation concerning the legal status, privileges and immunities of the United Nations and the specialized agencies, as well as of other international organizations, has been enacted in many states. See the statutes, regulations and other instruments collected in Legislative Texts and Treaty Provisions concerning the Legal Status, Privileges and Immunities of International Organizations, ST./LEG/SER.B/10, 11 (1959, 1961), as supplemented by extracts reproduced in successive issues, beginning in 1962, of the United Nations Juridical Yearbook. Legislation has been enacted in the United Kingdom that is comparable in scope to that of the United States. See the International Organizations (Immunities and Privileges) Act, 1950 (14 Geo. 6, c. 14), and 7 Halsbury's Laws of England § 586 for the organizations designated by Order in Council as entitled to the benefits of the Act. For a case applying the Act, see Zoernsch v. Waldock, [1964] 2 All E.R. 256 (C.A.) (suit against a member and the secretary of the European Commission of Human Rights for alleged "negligence and corruption in running the business * * * of the Commission * * * ").

5. Problems concerning the immunities and privileges of international organizations are particularly likely to arise in those states in which the organizations have their headquarters, or in which they carry on extensive activities. The "Headquarters Agreement" between the United States and the United Nations was authorized by Congress on August 4, 1947, 61 Stat. 756, and entered into force on November 21, 1947, T.I.A.S. No. 1676, 61 Stat. 3416. In addition to provisions concerning the privileges and immunities of representatives of members of the United Nations, discussed at p. 1292, the Headquarters Agreement contains the following Article guaranteeing the communication and transit privileges of the Organization, its officials, and representatives of members:

> Art. IV. § 11. The federal, state or local authorities of the United States shall not impose any impediments to transit to or from the headquarters district of (1) representatives of Members or officials of the United Nations, or of specialized agencies as defined in Article 57, paragraph 2, of the Charter, or the families of such representatives or officials, (2) experts performing missions for the United Nations or for such specialized agencies, (3) representatives of the press, or of radio, film or other information agencies, who have been accredited by the United Nations (or by such a specialized agency) in its discretion after consultation with the United States, (4) representatives of non-governmental organizations recognized by the United Nations for the purpose of consultation under Article 71 of the Charter, or (5) other persons invited to the headquarters district by the United Nations or by such specialized agency on official business. The appropriate American authorities shall afford any necessary protection to such persons while in transit to or from the headquarters district. This section * * * does not impair the effectiveness of generally applicable laws and regulations as to the operation of means of transportation.
>
> § 12. The provisions of Section 11 shall be applicable irrespective of the relations existing between the Governments of the persons referred to in that section and the Government of the United States.

In the joint resolution that authorized the President to conclude the Headquarters Agreement, it was provided in Section 6 (61 Stat. at 767) that nothing in the agreement should be construed as "in any way diminishing, abridging, or weakening the right of the United States to safeguard its own security and completely to control the entrance of aliens into any territory of the United States other than the headquarters district and its immediate vicinity, * * * and such areas as it is reasonably necessary to traverse in transit between the same and foreign countries." For the 1953 dispute involving the application of this provision by the United States, see infra.

Article III of the Agreement (§§ 7–10) deals with "Law and Authority in the Headquarters District." The Headquarters District is itself inviolable, and United States officials may not enter the district in order to perform official duties, nor may legal process be served there, without the consent of the Secretary–General, but the United Nations is obligated to prevent the Headquarters District from becoming a refuge (§ 9). Federal, state and local law apply within the district (§ 7), except insofar as inconsistent with United Nations regulations made "for the purpose of establishing therein conditions in all respects necessary for the full exercise of its [the Organization's] functions" (§ 8). The United Nations is given no enforcement jurisdiction other than that inherent in its power to deny entry to or expel persons from the District (§ 10). For a discussion and summary of regulations promulgated by the U.N., pursuant to the Headquarters Agreement, see 5 Repertory of Practice of United Nations Organs 340–42 (1955). See People v. Coumatos, 32 Misc.2d 1085, 224 N.Y.S.2d 507 (Gen. Sess. N.Y.Co., 1962) (prosecution for grand larceny committed by United Nations employee in Headquarters District; held, defendant not entitled to immunity, and New York law applicable within District in absence of inconsistent United Nations regulations). The United States has also concluded a headquarters agreement with the Organization of American States (181 U.N.T.S. 147), and Switzerland has such agreements with a large number of organizations. See Jenks, International Immunities 7 (1961). The United Nations has concluded a number of special headquarters agreements on behalf of its economic commissions, political missions (such as those in Korea, Egypt, Lebanon, Jordan, and the Congo), and technical assistance missions in various countries. See id. at 8–10. Numerous agreements have also been concluded in connection with the stationing of United Nations forces. See p. 1153 supra.

6. How do the privileges and immunities of the United Nations in the United States, as contained in the International Organizations Immunities Act and in the Headquarters Agreement, compare to those specified in the Convention on the Privileges and Immunities of the United Nations, supra? To what extent does the immunity enjoyed by the United Nations and its officials differ from that enjoyed by a foreign state and its officials? To what extent do the limitations imposed by the International Organizations Immunities Act on the immunities and privileges of United Nations officials who are United States citizens go beyond the limitations of the Convention?

LUTCHER S.A. CELULOSE E PAPEL v. INTER-AMERICAN DEVELOPMENT BANK

United States Court of Appeals, District of Columbia Circuit, 1967.
127 U.S.App. D.C. 238, 382 F.2d 454.

BURGER, CIRCUIT JUDGE. Appellants brought suit in the District Court for damages and injunctive relief claiming that the Bank had violated loan agreements with Lutcher S.A. Celulose e Papel by participating in loans made to competitors of Lutcher. This appeal followed the District Court's denial of preliminary injunctive relief and the grant of the Bank's motion to dismiss on the ground that the Bank is immune from suit and that the complaint failed to state a claim for which relief could be granted.

Appellant Lutcher S.A. is a Brazilian corporation organized in 1959 to engage in lumbering operations and the processing of paper pulp; F. Lutcher Brown is president and majority shareholder of Lutcher S.A.

Appellee is an international lending institution established in 1959 by joint action and subscription of the United States of America and all Latin American nations, Cuba excepted. Its stated purpose is "to contribute to the acceleration of the process of economic development of the member countries, giving priority to those loans and guarantees that will contribute most effectively to their economic growth."

The complaint alleges that from 1961 to 1964 the Bank made loans to Lutcher aggregating $8,700,000. In the same period it also made loans aggregating $5,000,000 to another Brazilian corporation engaged in lumbering and pulp processing, Papel e Celulose Catarinense Ltda., referred to as the Klabin group. Klabin operated the largest pulp and paper facility in Brazil and had a "monopoly in the newsprint industry." The Bank also made loans of $15,500,000 to another borrower to expand the largest pulp and paper and newsprint facility in Chile. These loans were made over Brown's protests that the Bank had inaccurate information about the state of the pulp market in Brazil and in Latin America and that these loans could jeopardize Lutcher's financial and competitive position.

In 1965 the Klabin group came to the Bank to obtain clearances to enable it to borrow additional funds from other sources, and Lutcher again urged the Bank to study the market situation. The Bank stated it would have an independent study made. In reliance on this, Appellants' complaint continues, Lutcher made payments owed the Bank. But in February, 1966, it is claimed, the Bank decided not to have a market study made. It appearing that the Bank was about to approve the Klabin request, Appellants brought this action to enjoin the Bank from doing so and to recover damages.

Appellants allege that the Bank "knowingly carried out wrongful acts with reckless disregard" for Appellants by lending to competitors and breached "an implied obligation" not to hinder Lutcher in fulfilling its contract with the Bank. The complaint alleges the Bank "impliedly warranted" to act "prudently" in considering loan applications from applicants in competition with Lutcher. Appellants view the duty of the Bank in these terms: "As a Development bank, the Inter–American Bank should have assisted Lutcher S.A. and by all means avoided any direct action detrimental to Lutcher S.A." They also claim that the Bank breached the 1965 agreements to make a market study, in reliance upon which Lutcher had incurred new debts and taken actions which it might otherwise not have taken.

Appellee contends, apart from argument on the merits, that it is immune from suit by virtue of specific legislation. The International Organizations Immunities Act provides that international organizations may be designated by the President so that they "shall enjoy the same immunity from suit and every form of judicial process as is enjoyed by foreign governments, except to the extent that such organizations may expressly waive their immunity for the purpose of any proceedings or by the terms of any contract." In 1960 President Eisenhower designated the Bank an international organization entitled to immunity, hence the question of the Bank's immunity turns on whether it has waived immunity from suit.

The answer in this case must be found in the Agreement establishing the Bank. The relevant provision is paragraph 1, Section 3 of Article XI; it provides:

> "Actions may be brought against the Bank only in a court of competent jurisdiction in the territories of a member in which the Bank has an office, has appointed an agent for the purpose of accepting service or notice of process, or has issued or guaranteed securities."

This provision is hardly a model of clarity; Appellants argue it constitutes a waiver of immunity. The Bank urges that such an interpretation "would wipe out Section 2(b) of the Immunities Act," a result which it says can be avoided by interpreting the provision as only a partial waiver, allowing suit by bondholders, creditors, and beneficiaries of its guarantees, on the theory that in such cases vulnerability to suit contributes to the effectiveness of the Bank's operation.

Unless this provision is read as merely describing the available forum for such suits and actions as to which waiver had been otherwise made, it must itself be a waiver of immunity. We do not read it as a venue provision for actions resulting from individual waivers; rather it is a provision waiving immunity and laying venue for the suits permitted. The terms are clear that "actions may be brought against the Bank"; had the drafters intended this clause to be only a venue provision, the language would more likely have provided, in essence, that actions brought against the Bank pursuant to any waiver of immunity could be brought in certain named courts. We conclude the absence of such limitation was purposeful. The subscribing nations were certainly alert to the problem and it was entirely appropriate to resolve the immunity question in the organic law of the Bank rather than leave it to case-by-case decision. That this was a deliberate choice is indicated by the title of Article XI, "Status, Immunities and Privileges," and the fact that the second paragraph of Section 3 expressly prohibits suits by members. The drafters thus manifested full awareness of the immunity problem and we conclude they must have been aware that they were waiving immunity in broad terms rather than treating narrowly a venue problem. * * *

In 1960 President Eisenhower issued, as we noted, his Executive Order qualifying the Bank for immunities available under the terms of the International Organizations Immunities Act. In 1962 President Kennedy amended President Eisenhower's Order by another Order, which is entitled as intended "to provide for an exception to the Inter–American Development Bank's immunity from suit specified in the International Organizations Immunities Act."This Order added the following clause to the Eisenhower Order:

> *"Provided,* That such designation shall not be construed to affect in any way the applicability of the provisions of Section 3, Article XI, of the Articles of Agreement of the Bank. * * * "

As amended, the Order tracks the Orders qualifying the International Finance Corporation and the World Bank. Its effect could only have been to reinforce the waiver of immunity. * * *

The Bank contends that, while Section 3 does waive immunity, it does so only with respect to suits brought by "bondholders, and other like creditors and the beneficiaries of its guarantees." The Bank seems to rest its argument on a broad assurance that it knows "the purpose and effect of the complex of statutory, international agreement and executive order provisions is this." The distinction made by the Bank is surely not necessary, as the Bank suggests it is, to preserve Section 2(b) of the Immunities Act, since that section expressly contemplates waiver.

There is an indication in Section 3 that bondholders have a special status under the agreement. The status conferred however is not that of the Bank's waiver of immunity, but rather the Bank's willingness to defend suits where it "has issued or guaranteed securities" even though venue might not otherwise lie in that jurisdiction. The status is conferred in the phrase which is disjunctively connected with other phrases laying venue "in the territories of a member in which the Bank has an office, has appointed an agent for purpose of accepting service or notice of process, or has issued or guaranteed securities."

In fact, there are two features of Section 3 that militate against the Bank's argument. First, the drafters of the Agreement indicated that when they wanted to make an exception to waiver of immunity they knew how to do so. Prudently concerned with possible interference in bank operations by member countries, the drafters explicitly and expressly provided in paragraph 2 of Section 3 that *members* could not sue the Bank. This insured that members would not, in the Bank's words, intrude into "essential policy decisions * * * entrusted to its officers and Board." Second, the drafters stated that the Bank could be sued "in the territories of a member in which the Bank has an office, has appointed an agent for the purpose of accepting service or notice of process, or has issued or guaranteed securities." They must have contemplated that the Bank would establish offices in the areas intended to be served. Provision for suit in *any* member country where the Bank has an office must have been designed to facilitate suit for some class other than creditors and bondholders, i.e., borrowers; creditors suing to enforce bond obligations would more likely sue in United States Courts.

It is true, as the Bank argues, that the Agreement of the Asian Development Bank limits suit to "cases arising out of or in connection with the exercise of its powers to borrow money, to guarantee obligations, to buy and sell or underwrite the sale of securities" and that the Treasury Department stated that the Asian Bank's "immunities, exemptions and privileges * * * are similar to those embodied in the charters of the World Bank and the Inter–American Development Bank." The Department was indeed correct; the agreements of the Inter–American Bank and the Asian Bank are similar with respect to "immunities, exemptions and privileges." But similar does not mean identical, and the difference in language with respect to immunity from suit—only one of many privileges and immunities treated in the two agreements—is quite significant. Article 50 of the Asian Bank Agreement provides:

> 1. The Bank *shall enjoy immunity* from every form of legal process, *except in cases arising out of or in connection with the exercise of its powers to borrow money,* to guarantee obligations, or to buy and sell or underwrite the sale of securities, in which cases actions may be brought against the Bank in a court of competent jurisdiction in the territory of a country in which the Bank has its principal or a branch office, or has appointed an agent for the purpose of accepting service or notice of process, or has issued or guaranteed securities. (Emphasis added.)

Section 3 of Article XI of the Inter–American Bank Agreement states:

> "*Actions may be brought* against the Bank only in a court of competent jurisdiction in the territories of a member in which the Bank has an office, has appointed an agent for the purpose of accepting service or notice of process, or has issued or guaranteed securities." (Emphasis added.)

The Asian Bank Agreement explicitly reserves immunity except for certain situations, which are specifically spelled out. The Inter–American Bank Agreement has no reservation of immunity and mentions no category of cases in paragraph one in which the Bank cannot be sued. After this difference, the language of the two provisions becomes very similar, but the difference is a clear and telling one. It is quite impossible to argue in the face of it that the

Inter–American Bank's Agreement implicitly provides an immunity which the Asian Bank's Agreement explicitly sets forth. * * *

There is no support in the common law doctrine of sovereign immunity for the Bank's argument. The doctrine has developed around the nature and function of the defendant, not the type of action a particular suit represents. No case is cited to us in which the immunity of the sovereign, be it domestic or foreign, depended on the identity of the suitor.

Even if we accepted the rationale of the distinction urged by the Bank as relevant to waiver, it would not necessarily yield the result desired by the Bank. There is no reason to believe that suits by creditors are less harassing to Bank management, or less expensive than are other kinds of suits. Just as it is necessary for the Bank to be subject to suits by bondholders in order to raise its lending capital, it may be that responsible borrowers committing large sums and plans on the strength of the Bank's agreement to lend would be reluctant to enter into borrowing contracts if thereafter they were at the mercy of the Bank's good will, devoid of means of enforcement. Suits by non-member creditors can affect the management of the Bank just as much as suits by borrowers—perhaps more; the Bank may have market power with respect to borrowers that would enable it to insist on loan contracts insulating its management functions, which it may not have with respect to creditors. * * *

[The court of appeals then concluded that the complaint does not state a cause of action for which relief is available.]

Notes

1. To what extent should an international organization having competence to influence "delicate, complex issues of international economic policy" be entitled to the deference accorded by courts in the United States and other countries to foreign states when the latter act within their territory or otherwise within their competence in international law so as to give effect to important public interests? Compare Banco Nacional de Cuba v. Sabbatino, p. 181 supra. Would a foreign state have been entitled to immunity under circumstances comparable to those present in the principal case?

2. In Curran v. City of New York, 191 Misc. 229, 77 N.Y.S.2d 206 (Sup.Ct. 1947), aff'd, 275 App.Div. 784, 88 N.Y.S.2d 924 (N.Y.App.Div.1949), a taxpayer brought suit against the City of New York, Trygve Lie, Secretary–General of the United Nations, and others in order to set aside city action making possible the location of U.N. headquarters in New York. The Secretary–General appeared specially and moved for the dismissal of the complaint against him on the ground that the court had no jurisdiction because he was being sued in respect of acts performed by him in his official capacity, citing sections 2(b) [22 U.S.C.A. § 288a(b)] and 7(b) [22 U.S.C.A. § 288d(b)] of the International Organizations Immunities Act, p. 1300 supra. The United States Attorney brought to the court's attention the State Department's certification of "the immunity of the United Nations and of Lie as its Secretary General," and requested that the service of process on him be vacated and the complaint dismissed for lack of jurisdiction. The court so ruled. Compare Westchester County on Complaint of Donnelly v. Ranollo, 187 Misc. 777, 67 N.Y.S.2d 31 (City Ct. New Rochelle 1946), in which the personal chauffeur of the Secretary–General was charged with speeding while

driving the latter on official business. Immunity was claimed on the basis of section 7(b) of the International Organizations Immunities Act, on the ground that the defendant had been performing an act in his official capacity and within his functions, but the court held that the Act and the Charter conferred immunity only upon "those personnel whose activities are such as to be necessary to the actual execution of the purposes and deliberations of the United Nations as distinguished from those household servants and personnel who merely serve the personal comfort, convenience or luxury of the delegates and Secretariat who actually perform the true functions of the Organization." 187 Misc. at 781, 67 N.Y.S.2d at 35. In the absence of State Department certification that immunity was in the public interest, the court refused to grant immunity except upon a trial of the issue of fact, i.e., whether defendant had been acting in his official capacity and within his functions. For criticism of the *Ranollo* case, see Preuss, Immunity of Officers and Employees of the United Nations for Official Acts: The Ranallo [*sic*] Case, 41 A.J.I.L. 555 (1947); Jenks, International Immunities 119 (1961). Although the State Department subsequently indicated that it thought immunity should be granted, the United Nations decided not to press the claim of immunity and to pay the fine. Preuss at 557. Following this case, the United Nations no longer claimed immunity in respect of traffic violations for its drivers or other officials driving in the course of duty. Jenks at 119.

3. The Diplomatic Relations Act, 22 U.S.C.A. § 254e, extends the requirement of compliance with the Director of the Office of Foreign Missions' regulations on liability insurance to the individuals described in Section 19 of the Convention on Privileges and Immunities of the United Nations. Article V, section 15, of the Headquarters Agreement, p. 1293 supra, makes representatives to the United Nations subject to the same obligation. The State Department regulations on this subject may be found at 22 CFR 151 et seq. (1980); 18 I.L.M. 871 (1979).

Prior to the adoption of these provisions, immunity had usually been waived in those accident cases involving United Nations vehicles for which a settlement could not be reached; furthermore, a 1946 resolution of the General Assembly had instructed the Secretary–General to ensure that the drivers of official United Nations vehicles, as well as staff members who owned or operated cars, carry liability insurance. G.A.Res. 22E (1946). See also Jenks at 119–20.

4. In United States v. Coplon, 84 F.Supp. 472 (S.D.N.Y.1949), espionage activities by a Soviet employee of the Secretariat were held not to fall within the categories set up by the International Organizations Immunities Act or the United Nations Charter. Defendant himself, not the Secretariat, had claimed immunity.

How can the United States proceed against one of the officials entitled, under the Convention, to complete immunity? See Articles 18 and 19 of the Convention, supra, and compare 22 U.S.C.A. § 288d. See Jenks at 30.

If the United Nations, or an official entitled to immunity, were to initiate legal proceedings in a United States court, would the defendant have the right to assert a counterclaim? See Restatement (Third) § 469, Reporters' Note 4.

5. In addition to the possibility that an international organization will waive its immunity or that of one of its officials from suit in a municipal court, there may be available to a private claimant certain procedures within the organization by which judicial redress may be obtained. The Administrative Tribunals of the United Nations and of the International Labour Organisation are competent "to determine disputes between international organisations and their officials and persons claiming through such officials concerning the terms of appointment and tenure of officials and the rights of officials and pensioners under the applicable

staff and pension regulations." Jenks at 161. The ILO Tribunal was originally the League of Nations Tribunal and has been granted by agreement jurisdiction in respect of the World Health Organisation, the Food and Agriculture Organisation, UNESCO, the International Telecommunication Union, the World Meteorological Organisation, the European Organisation for Nuclear Research, the International Atomic Energy Agency, and GATT. By agreement the U.N. Administrative Tribunal has jurisdiction over the International Civil Aviation Organization and the International Maritime Organization. See further Jessup, Transnational Law 82–94 (1956), particularly on the law applied by the Tribunals. In 1954, the International Court of Justice ruled in an advisory opinion that the General Assembly did not have the right to refuse to give effect to a compensation award made by the United Nations Administrative Tribunal. Effect of Awards of Compensation Made by the United Nations Administrative Tribunal (Advisory Opinion), 1954 I.C.J. 47. The United Nations has adopted the practice of including arbitration clauses in its commercial contracts. Jessup at 100.

For recent discussion of the Administrative Tribunals in relation to considerations of immunity from national jurisdiction, see Charles H. Brower II, International Immunities: Some Dissident Views on the Role of Municipal Courts, 41 Va. J.I.L. 1, 75–91 (2000).

6. Does the restrictive doctrine also apply to international organizations? Cf. Broadbent v. OAS, 628 F.2d 27 (D.C.Cir.1980) (the U.S. argued to this effect, but the court did not reach the issue); Tuck v. Pan American Health Organization, 668 F.2d 547 (D.C.Cir.1981) (issue not reached, since there would be immunity in any event); Mendaro v. The World Bank, 717 F.2d 610 (D.C.Cir.1983) (finding immunity in suit of former employee). See generally Restatement (Third) § 467, Reporters' Note 4; Glenn et al., Immunities Of International Organizations, 22 Va.J.Int'l L. 247 (1982); Oparil, Immunity Of International Organizations In United States Courts: Absolute Or Restrictive? 24 Vand. J.Transnat'l L. 689 (1991).

7. For a recent holding that the immunity of the World Bank from taxation in the District of Columbia did not extend derivatively to the Bank's food service contractor, see International Bank for Reconstruction and Development v. District of Columbia, 171 F.3d 687 (D.C.Cir.1999), 38 I.L.M. 818 (1999).

ADMISSION OF REPRESENTATIVES OF NON-GOVERNMENTAL ORGANIZATIONS ENJOYING CONSULTATIVE STATUS

Legal Opinion of the Secretariat of the United Nations.
April 10, 1953, U.N.Doc. E/2397.

2. [T]he Women's International Democratic Federation, a non-governmental organization in consultative relationship with the Council in Category B, designated Mrs. Margarette Rae Luckock as its representative to attend the seventh session of the Commission on the Status of Women, which adjourned on 3 April 1953, and thereafter to attend the current session of the Economic and Social Council. The World Federation of Trade Unions, a non-governmental organization in consultative relationship with the Council in Category A, designated Mr. Jan Dessau as its representative to attend the current session of the Council. Both representatives made application for a visa at appropriate United States Consulates and the Secretariat of the Economic and Social Council made notification to the United States Mission to the United Nations of these applications, in accordance with established procedures.

3. The representative of the United States reported to the Economic and Social Council at its 679th plenary meeting on 9 April 1953 that his Government had found it impossible to grant these applications. He explained the position of his Government as follows:

> In denying these applications, my Government has found it necessary to invoke the right to safeguard its security which it reserved to itself in Section 6 of the Joint Resolution (Public Law 357) of the 80th Congress, which authorized the United States to enter into the Headquarters Agreement, and in the note of its Representative, dated November 21, 1947, bringing the Headquarters Agreement into effect.

4. Section 11(4) of the Headquarters Agreement provides: [p. 1301 supra].

5. Section 13(a) of the Headquarters Agreement reads as follows:

> (a) Laws and regulations in force in the United States regarding the entry of aliens shall not be applied in such manner as to interfere with the privileges referred to in Section 11. When visas are required for persons referred to in that Section, they shall be granted without charge and as promptly as possible.

6. These are the only provisions in the Headquarters Agreement bearing upon the right of transit to the Headquarters District on the part of properly designated representatives of non-governmental organizations. Nothing in the text of the Headquarters Agreement reserves to the United States the authority to deny a visa to any of the classes of persons specified in Section 11. Indeed, Section 13(d) specifies that, *except* as provided above, "* * * the United States retains full control and authority over the entry of persons or property into the territory of the United States * * *"

7. By Joint Resolution (Public Law 357—80th Congress) the Senate and House of Representatives of the United States Congress authorized the President of the United States to bring the Headquarters Agreement into effect on the part of the United States.

8. Section 6 of the Joint Resolution stated that nothing in the Agreement should be construed as in any way diminishing, abridging or weakening the right of the United States to safeguard its own security and completely to control the entry of aliens into any territory of the United States other than the Headquarters District and its immediate vicinity, and such areas as it was reasonably necessary to traverse in transit between the same and foreign countries.

9. The Secretary–General of the United Nations was authorized to bring the Headquarters Agreement into force by the General Assembly, which approved the text of the Agreement in its resolution 169(II). But in the event that the provision in section 6 of the Joint Resolution had been intended by the United States to constitute a reservation, it was never made known to the General Assembly as such, and it was never considered by the General Assembly nor accepted by it.

* * *

12. Finally, even if the United States had intended to formulate a reservation, it would not appear from a reading of section 6 of the Joint Resolution that it could have application to the present cases. It refers to

control by the United States of the entrance of aliens into any territory of the United States *other than* the Headquarters District, its immediate vicinity, and the necessary area of transit.

13. It appears from the foregoing that persons falling within the classes referred to in section 11 of the Headquarters Agreement are entitled to transit to and from the Headquarters District, and that this right of transit has not been made the subject of any reservation.

Notes

1. As a result of negotiations between the Secretary–General and the United States government, it was agreed that the Headquarters Agreement was not to be used as a cover for activities directed against United States security. It was recognized that the United States (1) had a right to grant visas "valid only for transit to and from the Headquarters District and sojourn in its immediate vicinity;" (2) had the authority "to make any reasonable definition, consistent with the purposes of the Agreement, of the 'immediate vicinity' of the Headquarters District, of the necessary routes of transit, and of the time and manner of expiration of the visas following the completion of official functions;" and (3) had a right to deport persons abusing the privileges of residence in activities outside their official capacity. On the other hand, with respect to "aliens in transit to the Headquarters District exclusively on official business of, or before, the United Nations," it was recognized that "the rights of the United States are limited by the Headquarters Agreement to those mentioned." As for borderline cases, i.e., where there might be evidence that a person was coming to the United States for purposes detrimental to United States security, the United States gave assurances that "timely" decisions would be made at "the highest levels," and that the Secretary–General would be kept informed. Report by the Secretary–General to the Economic and Social Council, July 27, 1953, U.N.Doc.E/2492 at 23. The possibility of submitting future disputes to arbitration, as provided in the Headquarters Agreement, was discussed in the Council as the only alternative to a failure of negotiations. See Liang, The Question of Access to the United Nations Headquarters of Representatives of Non–Governmental Organizations in Consultative Status, 48 A.J.I.L. 434, 445–50 (1954).

2. Henrique Galvão, a former colonial officer under the Salazar regime in Portugal, had been convicted by a Portuguese court of involuntary manslaughter in connection with the seizure of a vessel on which he made his way to Brazil, where he was received as a political refugee. In a letter of Nov. 4, 1963, he requested a hearing before the Fourth Committee for the purpose of proposing a solution to problems of Portuguese administration in Angola. U.N.Doc.A/C.4/600/Add.5. The Fourth Committee requested an opinion as to the legal implications of the possible appearance before it of Mr. Galvão. The Legal Opinion of the Secretariat of the United Nations of November 15, 1963, U.N.Doc. A/C.4/621; 1963 U.N.Jur'l Ybk. 164, stated as follows:

* * *

> 4. Apart from police protection * * * the obligations imposed on the host Government by the Headquarters Agreement are limited to assuring the right of access to the Headquarters and an eventual right of departure. The Headquarters Agreement does not confer any diplomatic status upon an individual invitee because of his status as such. He therefore cannot be said to

be immune from suit or legal process during his sojourn in the United States and outside of the Headquarters district.

5. Two other provisions of the Headquarters Agreement serve to reinforce the right of access to the Headquarters. Section 13(a) specifies that the laws and regulations in force in the United States regarding the *entry* of aliens shall not be applied in such manner as to interfere with the privilege of transit to the Headquarters district. This provision, however, clearly assures admission to the United States without conferring any other privilege or immunity during the sojourn. Similarly, section 13(b) interposes certain limitations on the right of the host Government to require the departure of persons invited to the Headquarters district while they continue in their official capacity; but this plainly relates to restrictions on the power of deportation and not, conversely, on a duty to bring about departure. Moreover, section 13(d) makes clear that, apart from the two foregoing restrictions, "the United States retains full control and authority over the entry of persons or property into the territory of the United States and the conditions under which persons may remain or reside there."

6. It is thus clear that the United Nations would be in no position to offer general assurances to Mr. Galvão concerning immunity from legal process during his sojourn in the United States. It might be that individual citizens of the United States might have civil causes of action against him and could subject him to service of process. While the Federal Government might have no intention, and might lack jurisdiction, to initiate any criminal proceedings against him, it is a known fact that there are legal limitations on the powers of the executive branch of the United States Government to ensure against any type of proceeding by another branch of the Government, including the judicial branch.

7. Moreover, * * * the attention of the Committee has already been invited to the possibility that extradition proceedings might be instituted against Mr. Galvão during his presence in this country. By an Extradition Convention of 7 May 1908 between Portugal and the United States persons may be delivered up who are charged, among other crimes, with piracy or with mutiny or conspiracy by two or more members of the crew or other persons on board of a vessel on the high seas, for the purpose of rebelling against the authority of the captain of the vessel, or by fraud or violence taking possession of the vessel, or with assault on board ships upon the high seas with intent to do bodily harm, or with abduction or detention of persons for any unlawful end. The extradition is also to take place for the participation in any of such crimes as an accessory before or after the fact. The Convention contains the usual exception for any crime or offence of a political character, or for acts connected with such crimes or offences (Articles II and III).

* * *

9. There is no precedent in the history of the Headquarters Agreement which would indicate whether an application of Federal Regulations restricting departure of an alien, by reason of proceedings against him not related to his presence at the United Nations, would constitute an impediment to transit "from the Headquarters district" within the meaning of section 11 of the Agreement. There is likewise no precedent which would indicate whether compliance by the Federal Government with the terms of an extradition treaty would conflict with the right of transit of an invitee from the Head-

quarters district. In this connexion it is important to note that what the United States Government has undertaken not to do, by the terms of section 11, is to "impose" any impediment to transit from the Headquarters. To the extent that the presence of Mr. Galvão in the United States might in one manner or another give rise to proceedings against him by operation of existing law in relation to preexisting facts (such as previous activities on his part), it could be argued that this did not constitute an action taken by the Government to impose an impediment on his departure.* * *

* * *

11. In these circumstances, it must be recognized that a situation could arise by which the Fourth Committee was deprived of the advantage of receiving oral testimony from Mr. Galvão. Should he not be prepared to attend because of the inability of the host Government to confer upon him a general immunity, it is clear that his abstention from appearing would be his own, and not the affirmative imposition of an impediment to his transit. For it might only be at the moment of his attempted departure from the United States that an arbitrable dispute could arise as to whether he was entitled to depart notwithstanding proceedings which might in the meantime have been instituted against him. * * *

On November 14, 1963 the Fourth Committee approved Galvão's request for a hearing and decided to request the Secretary–General to consult with the United States government "with a view to ensuring that petitioners coming to the United States for the purpose of testifying before a committee should enjoy the necessary protection during their transit to and from the Headquarters district." 18 U.N.GAOR, 4th Comm. 324–25 (1963). Galvão appeared before the Committee on December 9, 1963, id. at 525–529, and apparently left the United States without incident on the following day. See 3 I.L.M. 169 (1964).

Is the Secretariat's interpretation of the Headquarters Agreement open to criticism? See the debate in the Fourth Committee on November 13, 1963, 18 U.N.GAOR, 4th Comm. 305–09 (1963), quoted in part at 1963 U.N.Jur'l Yb. 16667 n. 7. Note that Section 27 of the Headquarters Agreement provides that the agreement "shall be construed in the light of its primary purposes to enable the United Nations at its headquarters in the United States, fully and efficiently to discharge its responsibilities and fulfill its purposes." 61 Stat. at 3434. Compare the Secretariat's note to the Under–Secretary for Economic and Social Affairs, November 26, 1963, 1963 U.N.Jur'l Yb. 167, in which it is stated that "[t]he essential element in the right of access [to meetings of U.N. organs and to offices of the U.N.] is that representatives of governments, officials of the Organization and other persons invited on official business shall not be impeded in their transit to or from the United Nations offices in connection with meetings or other activities in which they are entitled to participate." It was further noted that the Secretary–General had taken the position that derogation from "the foregoing principles of access * * * would be disruptive to the functioning of United Nations organs and contrary to the clear obligations of Member States under the Charter." Id. at 168.

3. For the status of Permanent Observers at the United Nations of nonmember states, see the Legal Counsel's memorandum to the Acting Secretary–General, August 22, 1962, 1962 U.N.Jur'l Ybk. 237. Cf. Pappas v. Francisci, 119 N.Y.S.2d 69 (Sup.Ct.1953) (Italian observer held not entitled to immunity).

4. In Kadic v. Karadzic, 70 F.3d 232 (2d Cir.1995), cert. denied, 518 U.S. 1005, 116 S.Ct. 2524, 135 L.Ed.2d 1048 (1996), discussed at pp. 1169–1177 supra, defendant was the political leader of the Bosnian Serb republic. While present in New York City as an invitee of the United Nations, he was personally served with the summons and complaints in two civil actions under the Alien Tort Claims Act, in which it was alleged that he was responsible for atrocities committed against Bosnian Muslim and Croat women. Karadzic claimed that service of process was defective and that he was immune from suit, inter alia by virtue of his presence in New York to participate in U.N. meetings. In the portion of its opinion dealing with these issues, the court said in part:

> The Headquarters Agreement provides for immunity from suit only in narrowly defined circumstances. * * *
>
> Counsel for the United Nations has also issued an opinion stating that although the United States must allow United Nations invitees access to the Headquarters District, invitees are not immune from legal process while in the United States at locations outside of the Headquarters District. See *In re Galvao*, [1963] U.N. Jur.Y.B. 164 (opinion of U.N. legal counsel); *see also Restatement (Third)* § 469 reporter's note 8 (U.N. invitee "is not immune from suit or legal process outside the headquarters district during his sojourn in the United States"). * * *
>
> Karadzic nonetheless invites us to fashion a federal common law immunity for those within a judicial district as a United Nations invitee. He contends that such a rule is necessary to prevent private litigants from inhibiting the United Nations in its ability to consult with invited visitors. * * *
>
> Karadzic also endeavors to find support for a common law of immunity in our decision in [Klinghoffer v. S.N.C. Achille Lauro, 937 F.2d 44 (2d Cir. 1991)]. Though, as noted above, *Klinghoffer* declined to extend the immunities of the Headquarters Agreement beyond those provided by its express provisions, the decision applied immunity considerations to its construction of New York's long-arm statute * * *.
>
> Despite the considerations that guided *Klinghoffer* in its narrowing construction of the general terminology of New York's long-arm statute as applied to United Nations activities, we decline the invitation to create a federal common law immunity as an extension of the precise terms of a carefully crafted treaty that struck the balance between the interests of the United Nations and those of the United States.

5. In Askir v. Boutros-Ghali, 933 F.Supp. 368 (S.D.N.Y. 1996), plaintiff sought to sue certain U.N. officials for unlawful possession of his property in Somalia during the peacekeeping and humanitarian operations there. The court found the U.N. defendants to be immune and dismissed the claims for lack of subject-matter jurisdiction. Should the immunity questions have been addressed under an absolute or a restrictive (or functional) theory?

Chapter 15

INTERNATIONAL CRIMINAL LAW

SECTION 1. INTRODUCTION

The scope of international criminal law has been delineated in a variety of ways. See, e.g., Schwarzenberger, The Problem of an International Criminal Law, 3 Current Legal Problems 263–296 (1950) and M.C. Bassiouni, 1 International Criminal Law: Crimes 1–9 (2d ed. 1998). The core of the topic encompasses serious crimes under customary international law or treaty for which an individual may be prosecuted and punished and the institutions that may be involved in enforcement and prosecution of these crimes. Some crimes, such as piracy and slave trading, have long been recognized under customary international law. Many more have been defined in multilateral treaties, and some of these treaty crimes enjoy such widespread acceptance and *opinio juris* that they are considered to be a part of customary law binding on all states, even those not party to the treaty concerned. Examples would include war crimes constituting grave breaches of the 1949 Geneva Conventions, genocide and official torture. Many other crimes, including various acts of terrorism, are defined in multilateral treaties but may not have met the threshold requirements to qualify as crimes under customary international law.

The institutions involved in enforcement and prosecution of crimes under international law may include national or international institutions or both. But at present it is national institutions that play the dominant role in enforcing international criminal law. In many cases in which conduct is a crime under international law, it is also a crime under domestic law, and it may be investigated and prosecuted by national enforcement authorities and adjudicated in national courts.

In a very limited category of cases, alleged crimes under international law, often involving serious violations of internationally protected human rights, may be investigated and prosecuted before one of the ad hoc international tribunals set up by the U.N. Security Council, which now exist for the former Yugoslavia and Rwanda. In such cases, if delivered to the custody of the tribunal, the accused will be tried and, in the event of conviction, will be punished by that tribunal. Eventually, some of these crimes may be investigated and prosecuted before a permanent international criminal court. In July 1998, at a U.N. diplomatic conference in Rome, 120 nations voted to approve the Rome Statute of the International Criminal Court that would have jurisdiction in specified circumstances to prosecute individuals for certain serious crimes under international law. The Statute, which the United States voted against but later signed, will become effective upon ratification by 60 states. See p. 1367.

An important part of international criminal law as just described is international humanitarian law, a name that has been used traditionally to denote the international law relating to crimes under the laws of war, particularly as codified in the 1949 Geneva Conventions. See pp. 1060–1072 in Chapter 12. In recent years, the trend has been to use the term humanitarian law more broadly. For example, the U.N. Security Council resolution establishing the international criminal tribunal for the former Yugoslavia referred to it as the tribunal for the "prosecution of persons responsible for serious violations of international humanitarian law." U.N. Doc. S/RES/808 (1993). Similar terminology is used in the U.N. Security Council resolution establishing the international tribunal for Rwanda. U.N. Doc. ITR/3/REV. 1 (1995). In these instances, international humanitarian law is used to encompass the law relating to genocide and crimes against humanity as well as the law relating to war crimes. It might also be used to cover the law relating to aggression and other crimes under international law committed during international or internal conflict that involve egregious violations of human rights.

Although most of international criminal law is focused on individual responsibility, also appropriate for study in the context of international criminal law is possible state criminal responsibility. Indeed, in an early essay, international criminal law was construed to encompass only the question of the criminal responsibility of states. Schwarzenberger, supra at p. 1314. A central question is whether conduct by a nation-state itself may ever be regarded as a crime under international law, and, if so, what the implications of such a characterization would be. For discussion of this issue in relation to the International Law Commission's Draft Articles on State Responsibility, see Chapter 9, pp. 697–701.

Another important area, increasingly considered in connection with international criminal law, encompasses crimes under domestic law (like money-laundering) that have transnational implications and the institutions and procedures involved in enforcement and prosecution of these transnational crimes. Although this area is analytically distinct from the international criminal law that involves crimes under customary international law or international treaty, there is a considerable area of overlap. Indeed, crimes under international law are often crimes under domestic law as well, and national, not international, institutions are usually involved in their enforcement and prosecution.

With the advent of the U.N. Tribunals and the prospective permanent international criminal court, issues have arisen as to the relationship (or "complementarity") between international criminal tribunals and national courts in dealing with crimes that are potentially subject to the jurisdiction of both. To what extent does the jurisdiction of the international criminal tribunal complement or supplant the jurisdiction of national courts? Quite different resolutions of this issue have been adopted in the Statutes of the ad hoc Tribunals for the Former Yugoslavia and Rwanda, on the one hand, and the Rome Statute for the International Criminal Court, on the other. See pp. 1334 and 1375.

In the case of both international and national criminal courts, there must be a proper jurisdictional basis under international law for the exercise of criminal jurisdiction. The jurisdictional bases under international law are discussed in Chapter 13. They become particularly significant when a nation-state seeks to enforce its criminal statutes extraterritorially. If extraterritorial enforcement of a state's criminal statutes, such as those dealing with international drug trafficking and money laundering, is to be lawful under international law, the legislature's assertion of criminal jurisdiction in relation to extraterritorial conduct must have a jurisdictional basis that is accepted under international law.

Assuming a proper international jurisdictional nexus, a state may attempt to enforce its criminal statute extraterritorially against a person abroad. If a state has indicted for a transnational crime under its domestic law an individual who is present in a foreign state, the indicting state may seek to have the accused extradited by the foreign state to the custody of the former. The mechanism of extradition, which may be available under bilateral or multilateral agreements, whether the crime has transnational ramifications or not, is discussed in Chapter 13. Moreover, elaborate bilateral and multilateral arrangements have been adopted by states to enable and promote mutual assistance in criminal investigations and prosecutions. These often play a role in connection with investigation by national authorities and prosecution in national courts of crimes under international law and crimes under domestic law with transnational implications. Mechanisms analogous to these are being developed to provide international extradition or rendition of accused persons and mutual assistance in support of the existing and proposed international criminal tribunals.

In this chapter, the principal emphasis will be placed on crimes under international law for which individuals may be punished either by national or, in exceptional cases, international tribunals vested with competence.

A. THE ROLE OF NATIONAL COURTS IN APPLYING INTERNATIONAL CRIMINAL LAW

For hundreds of years there have been some crimes under customary international law for which individuals could be tried and, if convicted, punished in national courts. Piracy and slave trading are time-honored examples. See, e.g., United States v. Smith, 18 U.S. (5 Wheat.) 153, 5 L.Ed. 57 (1820). Under the U.S. Constitution, Congress is vested with "power to define and punish Piracies and Felonies committed on the High Seas and Offenses against the Law of Nations." U.S. Const. Art. 1, § 8(10). In the *Smith* case, the Supreme Court held that Smith had properly been convicted under an act of Congress that criminalized "piracy, as defined by the law of nations;" Congress had adequately defined the crime by incorporating by reference the definition of piracy under customary international law. 18 U.S. at 158; 5 L.Ed. at 58.

Another example of crimes under customary international law is war crimes under the laws of war. In Ex parte Quirin, 317 U.S. 1, 63 S.Ct. 1, 87 L.Ed. 3 (1942), the Supreme Court held that Congress had, by enacting the Articles of War, explicitly provided that U.S. military tribunals have jurisdiction to try individuals for offenses against the laws of war. The case involved the trial and conviction of a group of spies (one, a U.S. national, and the others, German nationals) who were put ashore with explosives in the United States by German submarines during World War II. The Court stated:

> * * * Similarly by the reference in the 15th Article of War to "offenders or offenses that . . . by the law of war may be triable by such military commissions", Congress has incorporated by reference, as within the jurisdiction of military commissions, all offenses which are defined as such by the law of war * * * and which may constitutionally be included within that jurisdiction. Congress had the choice of crystallizing in permanent form and in minute detail every offense against the law of war, or of adopting the system of common law applied by military tribunals so far as it should be recognized and deemed applicable by the courts. It chose the latter course.
>
> * * * The spy who secretly and without uniform passes the military lines of a belligerent in time of war, seeking to gather military information and communicate it to the enemy, or an enemy combatant who without uniform comes secretly through the lines for the purpose of waging war by destruction of life or property, are familiar examples of belligerents who are generally deemed not to be entitled to the status of prisoners of war, but to be offenders against the law of war subject to trial and punishment by military tribunals. * * *
>
> Such was the practice of our own military authorities before the adopting of the Constitution, and during the Mexican and Civil Wars.

317 U.S. at 30–31, 87 L.Ed. at 47–50.

The four Geneva Conventions of 1949 on the laws of war authorize any state party (including a belligerent state) to try individuals (including members of enemy forces) who are alleged to have committed grave breaches specified in the conventions. Geneva Convention for the Amelioration of the Condition of the Wounded and Sick in Armed Forces in the Field, 6 U.S.T. 3114, T.I.A.S. 3362,75 U.N.T.S. 31, Art. 49; Geneva Convention for the Amelioration of the Condition of Wounded, Sick and Shipwrecked Members of Armed Forces at Sea, 6 U.S.T. 3114, T.I.A.S. 3363, 75 U.N.T.S. 85, Art. 50; Geneva Convention Relative to the Treatment of Prisoners of War, 6 U.S.T. 3316, T.I.A.S. 3364, 75 U.N.T.S. 135. Art. 129; Geneva Convention Relative to the Protection of Civilian Persons in Time of War, 6 U.S.T. 3516, T.I.A.S. 3365,75 U.N.T.S. 287, Art. 146, all entered into force Oct. 21, 1950. An individual member of a belligerent's military force who violates the laws of war may also be tried by a military tribunal of that state.

Certain flagrant violations of human rights, such as genocide and officially conducted or sanctioned torture, have more recently been defined in multilateral treaties and appear to have emerged as crimes under customary international law. See Convention on the Prevention and Punishment of the Crime of Genocide, 78 U.N.T.S. 277, entered into force Jan. 12, 1951; Convention against Torture and Other Cruel, Inhuman or Degrading Treatment or Punishment, G.A. Res. 39/46, annex, 39 U.N. GAOR Supp. (No. 51) at 197, U.N. Doc. A/39/51 (1984), entered into force June 24, 1987. Other international crimes for which individuals may be held responsible have also been identified in treaties. Many of these crimes are related to international terrorism, such as aircraft hijacking, aircraft sabotage, and hostage-taking.

See p. 1128. These treaties require that state parties treat the proscribed conduct as a serious crime. In addition, if a party obtains custody of an alleged perpetrator, it must either (i) investigate, and, if the facts warrant, prosecute the suspect or (ii) extradite the suspect to another state that has a basis for exercising jurisdiction and that has requested extradition. These treaties are often considered to embody an application of the universality principle as among the state parties, because custody of the suspect is the only relevant nexus; there is no requirement that the offence be committed within the state's territory, by its national or against its national. Other crimes that have been established under multinational treaty include apartheid and crimes against internationally protected persons, such as diplomats and officials of international organizations.

In the absence of international tribunals with broad jurisdiction over crimes under international law, it is left to national courts to try individuals who have committed such crimes. There is ample authority for the proposition that a national court may try an individual who has committed a crime under customary international law or international treaty as long as there is a jurisdictional basis under international law for doing so. Individual trials by national courts also normally presuppose that the conduct that is considered criminal under customary international law or treaty has also been designated as a crime under domestic law. This can occur if the international law is automatically incorporated as part of domestic law or, as is required in the case of the United States, legislation has been enacted which specifies the crime under international law as a crime under U.S. law.

A number of prosecutions of perpetrators of atrocities committed by prominent Nazis and collaborators during the World War II period have been carried out by national courts subsequent to the Nuremberg trials. Most celebrated was the trial in Israel in 1961 of Adolf Eichmann, who played an important role in implementing the Holocaust. Eichmann was kidnapped by Israeli agents in Argentina, brought to Israel, tried and convicted for the crimes under Israeli law, including crimes against the Jewish people, crimes against humanity and war crimes. 36 I.L.R. 5 (1968). See pp. 1136–1138 in Chapter 13. Also, Klaus Barbie in 1987, Paul Touvier in 1994, and Maurice Papon in 1998, were convicted by French courts of crimes against humanity committed during World War II. National courts, moreover, have played a growing role in trying individuals for alleged atrocities committed in Bosnia and Rwanda. A number of Serbs have been convicted by German courts of crimes committed in the former Yugoslavia. For example, Nikola Jorgic was convicted on 30 counts of murder and 11 counts of genocide and was sentenced to life in prison in September 1997 and Maxim Sokolovic was convicted of complicity in genocide and sentenced to nine years in prison in November 1999.

The case that has produced the greatest international furor in recent years is the attempt by the Government of Spain to have Augusto Pinochet, former dictator of Chile, extradited from the United Kingdom, where he had traveled for medical treatment, to be tried in Spain for crimes under international law committed in Chile. The Law Lords of the U.K. House of Lords held that Pinochet could be extradited to be tried for the crime of torture, as defined in the International Convention Against Torture and under the U.K. Criminal Justice Act of 1988. However, the U.K. Home Secretary ultimately declined to extradite because of Pinochet's failing health and Pinochet was allowed to return to Chile. See p. 1139.

In the United States, civil suits under the Alien Tort Act, enacted in 1789, 28 U.S.C. § 1350, have been brought to recover damages against individuals for violations of internationally protected human rights. For such an action brought against Radovan Karadzic, leader of the Bosnian Serbs during the ethnic cleansing in the former Yugoslavia that began in 1991, see Kadic v. Karadzic, 70 F.3d 232 (2d Cir.1995), rehearing den., 74 F.3d 377 (1996), in which the court of appeals held that Karadzic could be found civilly liable for genocide, war crimes and crimes against humanity. See pp. 1169, 1177.

As discussed in Chapter 13, p. 1088 supra, a nation-state's jurisdiction to extend its authority to apply law to persons, things and conduct beyond its frontiers is frequently divided into jurisdiction to legislate or prescribe law, jurisdiction to enforce its law and jurisdiction to adjudicate matters involving the application of its law. Restatement (Third) § 401. The jurisdiction (i) of a state's legislature or other law-making institutions to prescribe laws designating conduct with international dimensions to be criminal, (ii) of its executive instrumentalities to enforce those laws by investigating, arresting and prosecuting the alleged perpetrators, and (iii) of its judicial or administrative authorities to adjudicate violations and impose punishment on convicted individuals, is subject to requirements imposed by public international law concerning whether there is a proper jurisdictional basis under international law for the extraterritorial exercise of jurisdiction concerned. It is possible for the U.S. Congress to define conduct outside the United States as a crime under U.S. law, even in the absence of a jurisdictional basis recognized under international law for this exercise of jurisdiction to prescribe. U.S. courts will normally attempt to construe federal criminal statutes having extraterritorial effect in a way that will comply with jurisdictional standards of international law, but if the intent of Congress to apply a statute extraterritorially is in conflict with those standards, the courts will apply the statute as written. Violation of international law by an act of Congress provides no defense to the accused. See, e.g., United States v. Fawaz Yunis, 924 F.2d 1086, (D.C.Cir. 1991), at pp. 1118, 1121 in Chapter 13.

Efforts by the U.S. government to exercise enforcement jurisdiction by arresting an accused outside the United States may also violate international law if they are carried out in excess of accepted jurisdictional limits or infringe upon another state's territorial jurisdiction. However, in the *Alvarez-Machain* case, at p. 1187, the U.S. Supreme Court upheld the exercise of criminal jurisdiction over a Mexican national who was kidnaped in Mexico by agents of the United States without the consent of the Mexican government, notwithstanding the international law violation. See Mitchell, English–Speaking Justice: Evolving Responses to Transnational Forcible Abduction After Alvarez–Machain, 29 Cornell Int'l L.J. 383 (1996) and pp. 1187–1196 in Chapter 13.

B. THE ROLE OF INTERNATIONAL CRIMINAL TRIBUNALS

Individuals have long been tried and punished for commission of crimes under customary international law and international treaty in national courts, usually on the basis of national legislation criminalizing the conduct and imposing penalties. However, the first instances in the twentieth century of trial of individuals for crimes under customary international law by multinational tribunals were the trials of German and Japanese war criminals by the Nuremberg and Tokyo tribunals established after World War II. Agreement for the Prosecution and Punishment of the Major War Criminals of the European Axis and Charter of the International Military Tribunal, 59 Stat. 1544, 82 U.N.T.S. 280, entered into force Aug. 8, 1945. Although these tribunals, which are discussed at p. 1322, were established by the victorious nations, the trials established precedents for treating crimes against peace, crimes against humanity and war crimes as crimes under international law for which individuals could be tried, convicted and punished by specifically constituted multinational tribunals. The principles of international law adopted in the Charter and Judgment of the Nuremberg Tribunal were later affirmed by the U.N. General Assembly. Res. 95(I) of the U.N. General Assembly (Dec. 11, 1946). See p. 1327.

In 1948, the General Assembly asked the International Law Commission to study the desirability and possibility of establishing an international judicial organ for the trial of persons charged with genocide or other crimes over which jurisdiction will be conferred upon that organ by international conventions. Report of the International Law Commission on the Work of its First Session, 12 April to 9 June 1949 (A/925). The Commission was further requested to consider the possibility of establishing a Criminal Chamber of the International Court of Justice. Id. The Cold War, however, effectively precluded any real progress toward creation of an international criminal tribunal. It took an end to the Cold War and inhuman atrocities in the former Yugoslavia, beginning in 1991, to bring about the creation of the first truly international tribunal to try individuals accused of crimes under international law.

In 1993, the U.N. Security Council established an international tribunal for the prosecution of persons responsible for serious violations of international humanitarian law committed in the territory of former Yugoslavia since 1991 (International Criminal Tribunal for the former Yugoslavia, or I.C.T.Y.). U.N. Doc. S/RES/808, S/RES/827 (1993). See p. 1332. Not long thereafter, the slaughter by Hutu extremists of more than half a million Tutsis and moderate Hutus in Rwanda led to the decision by the Security Council to set up a comparable international tribunal to prosecute individuals responsible for genocide and other serious violations of international humanitarian law in Rwanda during 1994. (International Criminal Tribunal for Rwanda, or I.C.T.R.) See p. 1352.

Building upon the work of the International Law Commission (I.L.C.) over many years, which culminated in preparation of a draft statute for a permanent international criminal court in 1994, the U.N. General Assembly created a Preparatory Committee which met beginning in 1996 to review the I.L.C. draft and to prepare a statute for a permanent international court. On July 17, 1998, a diplomatic conference in Rome approved and opened for signature and ratification the Rome Statute for the International Criminal Court (I.C.C.). U.N. Doc. A/CONF. 183/90. See p. 1367.

SECTION 2. INTERNATIONAL CRIMINAL LAW AND HUMAN RIGHTS

As discussed in Chapter 8, the international law of human rights includes the body of international law that relates to the protection of individuals against violations by their own or another government of rights that are recognized and protected under customary international law or international agreement. Violations of human rights occurring within a nation-state may justify action by the United Nations and other nation-states aimed at discouraging, suppressing or penalizing their commission.

The areas of international criminal law identified above intersect and implicate the international law of human rights at a number of points. First, crimes under international law for which an individual may be held responsible under domestic or international law (or under both) will often constitute a violation of internationally protected human rights. In this sense, international human rights are the normative foundation for an important part of international criminal law. International criminal law and the institutions that enforce it have as a central thrust the vindication and protection of internationally protected human rights. Genocide, crimes against humanity, officially authorized or sanctioned torture and serious war crimes represent egregious violations of human rights recognized and protected under international law. It is the importance of basic human rights, such as the right to life and security of the person and the right to be free from slavery, torture and other inhuman or degrading treatment, that is the moral imperative that underlies the legitimacy of criminalizing their violation. Second, in investigating, arresting, detaining and prosecuting an individual for international conduct made a crime under domestic or international law, national and international law enforcement officials and tribunals must respect and uphold the human rights of the accused to due process, a public trial, the presumption of innocence and a right to appeal that are guaranteed by international human rights law, including the International Covenant on Civil and Political Rights. See Chapter 8. Third, conduct by a state that violates fundamental international norms, such as the prohibition in Article 2(4) of the U.N. Charter against aggression, constitutes what some scholars would characterize as a crime under international law. Whether or not such conduct can properly entail criminal responsibility under international law, it may well violate human rights protected under international law.

SECTION 3. THE NUREMBERG AND TOKYO CRIMINAL TRIBUNALS

AGREEMENT FOR THE PROSECUTION AND PUNISHMENT OF THE MAJOR WAR CRIMINALS OF THE EUROPEAN AXIS POWERS AND CHARTER OF THE INTERNATIONAL MILITARY TRIBUNAL

Done at London, Aug. 8, 1945.
Entered into force, Aug. 8, 1945; for the United States, Sept. 10, 1945.
59 Stat. 1544, 82 U.N.T.S. 279.

CHARTER OF THE INTERNATIONAL MILITARY TRIBUNAL

* * *

II. JURISDICTION AND GENERAL PRINCIPLES

Article 6.

The Tribunal established by the Agreement referred to in Article 1 hereof for the trial and punishment of the major war criminals of the European Axis countries shall have the power to try and punish persons who, acting in the interests of the European Axis countries, whether as individuals or as members of organizations, committed any of the following crimes:

The following acts, or any of them, are crimes coming within the jurisdiction of the Tribunal for which there shall be individual responsibility:

(a) CRIMES AGAINST PEACE: namely, planning, preparation, initiation or waging of a war of aggression, or a war in violation of international treaties, agreements or assurances, or participation in a common plan or conspiracy for the accomplishment of any of the foregoing;

(b) WAR CRIMES: namely, violations of the laws or customs of war. Such violations shall include, but not be limited to, murder, ill-treatment or deportation to slave labor or for any other purposes of civilian population of or in occupied territory, murder or ill-treatment of prisoners of war or persons on the seas, killing of hostages, plunder of public or private property, wanton destruction of cities, towns or villages, or devastation not justified by military necessity;

(c) CRIMES AGAINST HUMANITY: namely, murder, extermination, enslavement, deportation, and other inhumane acts committed against any civilian population, before or during the war; or persecutions on political, racial or religious grounds in execution of or in connection with any crime within the jurisdiction of the Tribunal, whether or not in violation of the domestic law of the country where perpetrated.

Leaders, organizations, instigators, and accomplices participating in the formulation or execution of a common plan or conspiracy to commit any of the foregoing crimes are responsible for all acts performed by any persons in execution of such plan.

* * *

IV. Fair Trial for Defendants

Article 16.

In order to ensure fair trial for the Defendants, the following procedure shall be followed:

(a) The Indictment shall include full particulars specifying in detail the charges against the Defendants. A copy of the Indictment and of all the documents lodged with the Indictment, translated into a language which he understands, shall be furnished to the Defendant at a reasonable time before the Trial.

(b) During any preliminary examination or trial of a Defendant he shall have the right to give any explanation relevant to the charges made against him.

(c) A preliminary examination of a Defendant and his Trial shall be conducted in, or translated into, a language which the Defendant understands.

(d) A Defendant shall have the right to conduct his own defense before the Tribunal or to have the assistance of Counsel.

(e) A Defendant shall have the right through himself or through his Counsel to present evidence at the Trial in support of his defense, and to cross-examine any witness called by the Prosecution.

Notes

1. Those who negotiated the Nuremberg Charter, including Justice Robert H. Jackson of the U.S. Supreme Court, who became Chief U.S. Prosecutor, and U.S. Secretary of War Henry Stimson, had three principal objectives: to treat wars of aggression as crimes under international law, to treat atrocities against civilians as "crimes against humanity" and to achieve these ends through a trial that would uphold the rule of law by protecting the rights of the defendants to due process. Official Records of the General Assembly, Forty-ninth Session, Supplement No. 10 (A/49/10), para. 90–91. By its existence and the manner in which it was conducted, the trial had to exemplify the hope that at long last the conscience of mankind might hold those individuals responsible for aggression and atrocities to account under the rule of law. As stated by Justice Jackson in his opening statement to the International Military Tribunal (IMT):

> The privilege of opening the first trial in history for crimes against the peace of the world imposes a grave responsibility. The wrongs which we seek to condemn and punish have been so calculated, so malignant, and so devastating, that civilization cannot tolerate their being ignored, because it cannot survive their being repeated. That four great nations, flushed with victory and stung with injury, stay the hand of vengeance and voluntarily submit their captive enemies to the judgment of the law is one of the most significant tributes that power has ever paid to reason.

2 Trial of the Major War Criminals 99 (1947).

2. The IMT consisted of four judges, one representing each of France, the United Kingdom, the U.S.S.R., and the United States. The Tribunal indicted and tried 24 top Nazis, not including Adolf Hitler, Joseph Goebbels and Heinrich Himmler, who had committed suicide when Soviet troops entered Berlin. Of those

indicted, 21 were actually tried before the IMT, and 18 were convicted. Those convicted included, among others, Hermann Goering (Hitler's designated successor); Rudolf Hess (Hitler's Deputy for Nazi Party Affairs); Joachim von Ribbentrop (Foreign Minister); Julius Streicher (editor of the anti-Semitic paper, Der Stuermer); and Admiral Karl Doenitz (chief of the Navy). Of the 18 convicted, 11 were sentenced to death by hanging and seven were given prison terms ranging from 10 years to life. Martin Bormann (Hess's successor who played a key role in the Holocaust) was convicted in absentia and sentenced to death (but his whereabouts and fate remain shrouded in mystery). International Military Tribunal (Nuremberg), Judgment and Sentences, Oct. 1, 1946, 41 A.J.I.L. 172, 331–33 (1947).

In the Tokyo Trials before the International Military Tribunal for the Far East (IMTFE), 25 Japanese leaders were tried and 23 convicted. Seven, including Prime Minister Tojo and Admiral Yamashita (chief of the Navy), were executed; 16 were sentenced to life in prison.

A series of subsequent trials, involving less prominent figures also took place at Nuremberg and elsewhere in Germany between 1946 and 1949. Those trials were conducted under Control Council Law No. 10. The Control Council was the body, comprised of representatives of France, the United Kingdom, the U.S.S.R., and the United States, that governed occupied Germany. In the U.S. occupation zone of Germany, trials were conducted before U.S. judges. One of these trials, involving important German judges and legal officials, was depicted in the award-winning film, Judgment at Nuremberg (1961).

3. Among the important principles relating to individual responsibility for crimes under international law addressed by the Judgment of the IMT were those dealing with the accused's official position and obedience to law or to orders of a superior. On those issues the Judgment stated, in part, as follows:

> The principle of international law, which under certain circumstances protects the representatives of a state, cannot be applied to acts which are condemned as criminal by international law. The authors of these acts cannot shelter themselves behind their official position in order to be freed from punishment in appropriate proceedings. Article 7 of the Charter expressly declares:
>
>> The official position of Defendants, whether as heads of State, or responsible officials in Government departments, shall not be considered as freeing them from responsibility, or mitigating punishment.
>
> On the other hand, the very essence of the Charter is that individuals have international duties which transcend the national obligations of obedience imposed by the individual state. He who violates the laws of war cannot obtain immunity while acting in pursuance of the authority of the state if the state, in authorizing action, moves outside its competence under international law.
>
> It was also submitted on behalf of most of these defendants that in doing what they did they were acting under the orders of Hitler, and therefore cannot be held responsible for the acts committed by them in carrying out these orders. The Charter specifically provides in Article 8:
>
>> The fact that the Defendant acted pursuant to order of his Government or of a superior shall not free him from responsibility, but may be considered in mitigation of punishment.

> The provisions of this article are in conformity with the law of all nations. That a soldier was ordered to kill or torture in violation of the international law of war has never been recognized as a defense to such acts of brutality, though, as the Charter here provides, the order may be urged in mitigation of the punishment. The true test, which is found in varying degrees in the criminal law of most nations, is not the existence of the order, but whether moral choice was in fact possible.

International Military Tribunal (Nuremberg) Judgment and Sentences, 41 A.J.I.L. 172, 221 (1947).

4. For further discussion of individual responsibility under international law before the Nuremberg and Tokyo tribunals, see Tomuschat, International Criminal Prosecution: The Precedent of Nuremberg Confirmed, in Clark & Sann, The Prosecution of International Crimes 18 (1996); Pritchard, The International Military Tribunal for the Far East and Its Contemporary Resonances, 149 Mil. L. Rev. 25 (1995); and Sunga, Individual Responsibility in International Law for Serious Human Rights Violations (1992).

TRIALS OF WAR CRIMINALS BEFORE THE NUREMBERG MILITARY TRIBUNALS UNDER CONTROL COUNCIL LAW NO. 10, 1946–1949, VOL. III (1951)

"The Justice Case" (Case No. 3), Opinion and Judgment, 954, 955, 964, 970–972, 974–975, 979, 983–984.

The defendants claim protection under the principle *nullum crimen sine lege,* though they withheld from others the benefit of that rule during the Hitler regime. Obviously the principle in question constitutes no limitation upon the power or right of the Tribunal to punish acts which can properly be held to have been violations of international law when committed. By way of illustration, we observe the C.C.Law 10, article II, paragraph 1(b), "War Crimes," has by reference incorporated the rules by which war crimes are to be identified. In all such cases it remains only for the Tribunal, after the manner of the common law, to determine the content of those rules under the impact of changing conditions.

Whatever view may be held as to the nature and source of our authority under C.C.Law 10 and under common international law, the *ex post facto* rule, properly understood, constitutes no legal nor moral barrier to prosecution in this case.

Under written constitutions the *ex post facto* rule condemns statutes which define as criminal, acts committed before the law was passed, but the *ex post facto* rule cannot apply in the international field as it does under constitutional mandate in the domestic field. Even in the domestic field the prohibition of the rule does not apply to the decisions of common law courts, though the question at issue be novel. International law is not the product of statute for the simple reason that there is as yet no world authority empowered to enact statutes of universal application. International law is the product of multipartite treaties, conventions, judicial decisions and customs which have received international acceptance or acquiescence. It would be sheer absurdity to suggest that the *ex post facto* rule, as known to constitutional states, could be applied to a treaty, a custom, or a common law decision of an international tribunal, or to the international acquiescence which follows the event. To have attempted to apply the *ex post facto* principle to judicial decisions of common international law would have been to strangle that law at birth. As applied in the field of international law, the principle *nullum crimen sine lege* received its true interpretation in the opinion of the IMT in the case versus Goering, et al. The question arose with reference to crimes against the peace, but the opinion expressed is equally applicable to war crimes and crimes against humanity. The Tribunal said:

> In the first place, it is to be observed that the maxim *nullum crimen sine lege* is not a limitation of sovereignty, but is in general a principle of justice. To assert that it is unjust to punish those who in defiance of treaties and assurances have attacked neighboring states without warning is obviously untrue, for in such circumstances the attacker must know that he is doing wrong, and so far from it being unjust to punish him, it would be unjust if his wrong were allowed to go unpunished. * * *

[For other excerpts from this case, see pp. 406–408 in Chapter 6.]

Notes

1. Although the Nuremberg and Tokyo trials formed the foundation for development of much of the contemporary principle of individual responsibility for crimes under international law, they have not escaped criticism. A bias was built into the IMT Charter itself. It authorized only prosecution of war criminals of the "European Axis countries." Charter of the International Military Tribunal (IMT), in Agreement for the Prosecution and Punishment of the Major War Criminals of the European Axis (London Agreement), 58 Stat. 1544, E.A.S. No. 472, 82 U.N.T.S. 280, Aug. 8, 1945. The murder of thousands of Polish officers by Soviet forces in the Katyn Forest near Smolensk, the allied fire bombing of Dresden and the dropping of the atomic bombs on Hiroshima and Nagasaki, Japan, are among the events that suggest the victors may not have been free of culpability. The IMT convicted Germans for invading Poland but refused to admit evidence of the Soviet Union's secret agreement with Hitler to divide Poland. Admiral Doenitz was convicted on different and lesser charges after evidence was adduced that one of the charges against him, sinking nonmilitary ships without warning, was essentially similar to the practice of the U.S. Navy in the Pacific. Does the partiality inherent in a tribunal established by the victors impugn the legal validity of the IMT's judgment and sentences? Does it undercut the moral legitimacy of the Tribunal?

2. To what extent did the goal of the framers of the IMT Charter to establish crimes against peace and crimes against humanity as crimes under international law conflict with the basic principle of criminal justice prohibiting *ex post facto* prosecutions (*nullum crimen sine lege; nulla poena sine lege*)? In the case of acts labeled crimes against humanity, such as mass murder, the acts concerned were crimes under every legal system. They were "internationalized" by the IMT Charter, but it hardly seems unfair to the defendants to be prosecuted and punished for such acts. Could the same be said for crimes against peace or aggression? Soldiers had not been prosecuted for the act of planning, initiating or participating in an act of aggression from the Peace of Westphalia in 1648 to the Nuremberg trials. Aggression had not been characterized as a crime under international law until the IMT Charter did so. Does the IMT Judgment quoted in *The Justice Case* deal persuasively with this issue?

SECTION 4. U.N. EFFORTS TOWARD THE CODIFICATION OF INTERNATIONAL CRIMINAL LAW

AFFIRMATION OF THE PRINCIPLES OF INTERNATIONAL LAW RECOGNIZED BY THE CHARTER OF THE NUREMBERG TRIBUNAL

Adopted by the U.N. General Assembly, Dec. 11, 1946.
U.N.G.A. Res. 95(I), U.N.Doc. A/236 (1946), at 1144.

The General Assembly,

Recognizes the obligation laid upon it by Article 13, paragraph 1, subparagraph a, of the [U.N.] Charter, to initiate studies and make recommendations for the purpose of encouraging the progressive development of international law and its codification;

Takes note of the Agreement for the establishment of an International Military Tribunal for the prosecution and punishment of the major war criminals of the European Axis signed in London on 8 August 1945, and of the [IMT] Charter annexed thereto, and of the fact that similar principles have been adopted in the Charter of the International Military Tribunal for the trial of the major war criminals in the Far East, proclaimed at Tokyo on 19 January 1946;

Therefore,

Affirms the principles of international law recognized by the Charter of the Nürnberg Tribunal and the judgment of the Tribunal;

Directs the Committee on the Codification of International Law established by the resolution of the General Assembly of 11 December 1946, to treat as a matter of primary importance plans for the formulation, in the context of a general codification of offences against the peace and security of mankind, or of an International Criminal Code, of the principles recognized in the Charter of the Nürnberg Tribunal and in the judgment of the Tribunal.

Note

The efforts of the U.N. International Law Commission (I.L.C.) to develop a draft code of crimes beginning in 1950 have been reviewed in Chapter 6 at pp. 410–411. On July 5, 1996, the I.L.C. adopted the final text of 20 articles constituting a Draft Code of Crimes against the Peace and Security of Mankind. Report of the International Law Commission on the Work of its Forty–Eighth Session, U.N. Doc. A/51/10; 1996–II(2) Y.B.I.L.C. The Rome Statute of the International Criminal Court includes definitions of genocide, war crimes and crimes against humanity and builds upon the definitions of these crimes reflected in the 1996 Draft Code of Crimes. For the text of the Draft Code, see the Documents Supplement. Excerpts from the I.L.C.'s commentary follow.

DRAFT CODE OF CRIMES AGAINST THE PEACE AND SECURITY OF MANKIND

Report of the International Law Commission on Its Forty–Eighth Session. U.N. GAOR, 51st Sess., Supp. No. 10, at 9. U.N. Doc. A/51/10 (1996).

[Article 2(3)(a) embodies the principle of individual responsibility for crimes against the peace and security of mankind. It also treats as responsible an individual who orders commission of such a crime if it is committed or attempted (Art. 2(3)(b)); fails to prevent or repress commission of such a crime in specific circumstances (Art. 2(3)(c)); aids, abets or otherwise assists commission of such a crime (Art. 2(3)(d)); participates in planning or conspiring to commit such a crime (Art. 2(3)(e)); incites another to commit such a crime if it is committed (Art. 2(3)(f)); or attempts to commit such a crime even if it does not occur independent of his intentions (Art. 2(3)(g)). The Commentary to Article 2 states, in part, as follows:]

(14) Subparagraph (e) is intended to ensure that high-level government officials or military commanders who formulate a criminal plan or policy, as individuals or as co-conspirators, are held accountable for the major role that they play which is often a decisive factor in the commission of the crimes covered by the Code. This principle of individual responsibility is of particular importance for the crimes set forth in articles 17 to 20 [genocide, crimes against humanity, crimes against U.N. personnel and war crimes] which by their very nature often require the formulation of a plan or a systematic policy by senior government officials and military commanders. Such a plan or policy may require more detailed elaboration by individuals in mid-level positions in the governmental hierarchy or the military command structure who are responsible for ordering the implementation of the general plans or policies formulated by senior officials. The criminal responsibility of the mid-level officials who order their subordinates to commit the crimes is provided for in subparagraph (b). Such a plan or policy may also require a number of individuals in low-level positions to take the necessary action to carry out the criminal plan or policy. The criminal responsibility of the subordinates who actually commit the crimes is provided for in subparagraph (a). Thus, the combined effect of subparagraphs (a), (b) and (e) is to ensure that the principle of criminal responsibility applies to all individuals throughout the governmental hierarchy or the military chain of command who contribute in one way or another to the commission of a crime set out in articles 17 to 20.

(15) The principle of individual criminal responsibility for formulating a plan or participating in a common plan or conspiracy to commit a crime was recognized in the Nürnberg Charter (article 6), the Genocide Convention (article III, paragraph (b)) and the Statutes of the International Criminal Tribunals for the former Yugoslavia (article 7, paragraph 1 (planning)) and Rwanda (article 6, paragraph 1 (planning)). The Commission also recognized conspiracy as a form of participation in a crime against peace in the Nürnberg Principles * * *.

* * *

Article 5—Order of a Government or a superior

The fact that an individual charged with a crime against the peace and security of mankind acted pursuant to an order of a Government or a superior does not relieve him of criminal responsibility, but may be considered in mitigation of punishment if justice so requires.

Commentary

* * *

(3) Article 5 addresses the criminal responsibility of a subordinate who commits a crime while acting pursuant to an order of a Government or a superior. The government official who formulates a criminal plan or policy and the military commander or officer who orders the commission of a criminal act in the implementation of such a plan or policy bear particular responsibility for the eventual commission of the crime. However, the culpability and the indispensable role of the subordinate who actually commits the criminal act cannot be ignored. Otherwise the legal force and effect of the prohibition of crimes under international law would be substantially weakened by the absence of any responsibility or punishment on the part of the actual perpetrators of these heinous crimes and thus of any deterrence on the part of the potential perpetrators thereof.

(4) The plea of superior orders is most frequently claimed as a defence by subordinates who are charged with the type of criminal conduct covered by the Code. Since the Second World War the fact that a subordinate acted pursuant to an order of a government or a superior has been consistently rejected as a basis for relieving a subordinate of responsibility for a crime under international law. In this regard, the Nürnberg Charter provided in article 8 that "The fact that the Defendant acted pursuant to order of his Government or of a superior shall not free him from responsibility, but may be considered in mitigation of punishment if the Tribunal determines that justice so requires." Most of the major war criminals tried by the Nürnberg Tribunal raised as a defence the fact that they were acting pursuant to the orders of their superior. The Nürnberg Tribunal rejected the plea of superior orders as a defence * * *. The defence of superior orders has been consistently excluded in the relevant legal instruments adopted since the Nürnberg Charter, including the Tokyo Tribunal Charter (article 6), Control Council Law No. 10 (article 4) and, more recently, the Statutes of the International Criminal Tribunals for the former Yugoslavia (article 7) and Rwanda (article 6).

* * *

(5) Notwithstanding the absence of any defence based on superior orders, the fact that a subordinate committed a crime while acting pursuant to an order of his superior was recognized as a possible mitigating factor which could result in a less severe punishment in the Nürnberg Charter and the subsequent legal instruments referred to in the preceding paragraph. The mere existence of superior orders will not automatically result in the imposition of a lesser penalty. A subordinate is subject to a lesser punishment only when a superior order in fact lessens the degree of his culpability. For example, a subordinate who is a willing participant in a crime irrespective of an order of his superior incurs the same degree of culpability as if there had been no such order. In such a situation, the existence of the superior order

does not exert any undue influence on the behaviour of the subordinate. In contrast, a subordinate who unwillingly commits a crime pursuant to an order of a superior because of the fear of serious consequences for himself or his family resulting from a failure to carry out that order does not incur the same degree of culpability as a subordinate who willingly participates in the commission of the crime. The fact that a subordinate unwillingly committed a crime pursuant to an order of a superior to avoid serious consequences for himself or his family resulting from the failure to carry out that order under the circumstances at the time may justify a reduction in the penalty that would otherwise be imposed to take into account the lesser degree of culpability. The phrase "if justice so requires" is used to show that even in such cases the imposition of a lesser punishment must also be consistent with the interests of justice. * * * Thus, the court must weigh the seriousness of the consequences that in fact resulted from the order having been carried out, on the one hand, and the seriousness of the consequences that would have most likely resulted from the failure to carry out the order under the circumstances at the time, on the other. At one end of the scale, the court would have no reason to show any mercy for a subordinate who committed a heinous crime pursuant to a superior order in the absence of an immediate or otherwise significant risk of serious consequences resulting from the failure to comply with that order. At the other end of the scale, a court may decide that justice requires imposing a lesser punishment on a subordinate who committed a serious crime pursuant to a superior order only to avoid an immediate or otherwise significant risk of equally or more serious consequences resulting from a failure to comply with that order.

(6) * * * The text of the article is based on the relevant provisions contained in the Nürnberg Charter and the Statutes of the International Criminal Tribunals for the former Yugoslavia and Rwanda. * * *

Article 6—Responsibility of the superior

The fact that a crime against the peace and security of mankind was committed by a subordinate does not relieve his superiors of criminal responsibility, if they knew or had reason to know, in the circumstances at the time, that the subordinate was committing or was going to commit such a crime and if they did not take all necessary measures within their power to prevent or repress the crime.

Commentary

(1) Military commanders are responsible for the conduct of members of the armed forces under their command and other persons under their control. This principle of command responsibility was recognized in the 1907 Hague Convention and reaffirmed in subsequent legal instruments. It requires that members of the armed forces be placed under the command of a superior who is responsible for their conduct. A military commander may be held criminally responsible for the unlawful conduct of his subordinates if he contributes directly or indirectly to their commission of a crime. A military commander contributes directly to the commission of a crime when he orders his subordinate to carry out a criminal act, such as killing an unarmed civilian, or to refrain from performing an act which the subordinate has a duty to perform, such as refraining from providing food for prisoners of war which results in their starvation. * * * A military commander also contributes indirectly to

the commission of a crime by his subordinate by failing to prevent or repress the unlawful conduct. * * *

(2) The criminal responsibility of a military commander for failing to prevent or repress the unlawful conduct of his subordinates was not provided for in the Nürnberg Charter or recognized by the Nürnberg Tribunal. However, this type of criminal responsibility was recognized in several judicial decisions after the Second World War. The United States Supreme Court, in the Yamashita case, gave an affirmative answer to the question whether the laws of war imposed on an army commander a duty to take such appropriate measures as were within his power to control the troops under his command and prevent them from committing acts in violation of the laws of war. The court held that General Yamashita was criminally responsible because he had failed to take such measures. Similarly, the United States Military Tribunal, in the German High Command Trial, stated that "Under basic principles of command authority and responsibility, an officer who merely stands by while his subordinates execute a criminal order of his superiors which he knows is criminal, violates a moral obligation under International Law. By doing so, he cannot wash his hands of international responsibility". * * * For its part, the Tokyo Tribunal decided that it was the duty of all those on whom responsibility rested to secure proper treatment of prisoners and to prevent their ill-treatment.

(3) * * * This article recognizes that a military commander has a duty to prevent and to suppress violations of international humanitarian law committed by his subordinates. This article also recognizes that a military commander has a duty, where appropriate, to initiate disciplinary or penal action against alleged offenders who are his subordinates. The principle of individual criminal responsibility under which a military commander is held responsible for his failure to prevent or repress the unlawful conduct of his subordinates is elaborated in article 86 of Additional Protocol I [to the 1949 Geneva Conventions]. This principle is also contained in the Statutes of the International Criminal Tribunals for the former Yugoslavia (article 7) and Rwanda (article 6).

* * *

Article 7—Official position and responsibility

The official position of an individual who commits a crime against the peace and security of mankind, even if he acted as head of State or Government, does not relieve him of criminal responsibility or mitigate punishment.

* * *

Commentary

(3) In accordance with this provision, the Nürnberg Tribunal rejected the plea of act of State and that of immunity which were submitted by several defendants as a valid defence or ground for immunity:

> It was submitted that ... where the act in question is an act of State, those who carry it out are not personally responsible, but are protected by the doctrine of the sovereignty of the State. In the opinion of the Tribunal, [this submission] must be rejected. ... The principle of international law, which under certain circumstances, protects the representative

of a State, cannot be applied to acts which are condemned as criminal by international law. The authors of these acts cannot shelter themselves behind their official position in order to be freed from punishment in appropriate proceedings. . . .

(4) The official position of an individual has been consistently excluded as a possible defence to crimes under international law in the relevant instruments adopted since the Nürnberg Charter, including the Tokyo Tribunal Charter (article 6), Control Council Law No. 10 (article 4) and, more recently, the Statutes of the International Criminal Tribunals for the former Yugoslavia (article 7) and Rwanda (article 6). * * *

Note

For discussion of the Draft Code of Crimes against the Peace and Security of Mankind see Rayfuse, The Draft Code of Crimes against the Peace and Security of Mankind, 8 Crim. L.F. 43 (1997); Broomhall, Developments in Criminal Law and Criminal Justice: Looking Forward to the Establishment of an International Criminal Court: Between State Consent and the Rule of Law, 8 Crim.L.F. 317 (1997); McCormack & Simpson, The International Law Commission's Draft Code of Crimes against the Peace and Security of Mankind: An Appraisal of the Substantive Provisions, 5 Crim.L.F. 1 (1994).

SECTION 5. U.N. TRIBUNAL FOR THE FORMER YUGOSLAVIA

A. BACKGROUND

The disintegration of the former Yugoslavia and the ensuing interethnic hostilities of the early 1990s have been discussed in previous chapters, as have the substantive rules of humanitarian law applicable to the international and internal dimensions of the conflict (see pp. 259, 1060). In seeking for ways to respond to the violence, the Security Council laid the groundwork for eventual criminal prosecution and punishment of those responsible for serious violations of international criminal law.

On July 13, 1992, the U.N. Security Council, in adopting Resolution 764, reaffirmed that "all parties to the Yugoslav conflict must comply with international humanitarian law, particularly the Geneva Conventions of 1949, and that persons who commit or order the commission of grave breaches of those conventions are individually responsible for war crimes." U.N. Doc. S/RES 764 (1992). On October 6, 1992, the Security Council adopted Resolution 780, in which it requested the Secretary–General to establish an impartial Commission of Experts to examine and report to the Secretary–General on the evidence of grave breaches of the Geneva Conventions and other violations of international humanitarian law committed in the former Yugoslavia. U.N. Doc. S/RES/780, para. 2 (1993). The Commission's first interim report concluded that grave breaches and other violations of international humanitarian law had been committed in the territory of the former Yugoslavia. U.N. Doc. S/25274 (1993). The Commission concluded that "ethnic cleansing" had been carried out in the former Yugoslavia "by means of murder, torture, arbitrary arrest and detention, extra-judicial executions, rape and sexual assault, confinement of civilian population in ghetto areas, forcible removal, displacement and deportation of civilian population, deliberate military attacks or threats of attacks on civilians and civilian areas, and wanton destruction of property." U.N. Doc. S/25274 at 16, para. 56. The report defined "ethnic cleansing" as "rendering an area ethnically homogeneous by using force or intimidation to remove persons of given groups from the area." Id. at 16, para. 55. Moreover, the Commission concluded that this practice of ethnic cleansing involved crimes against humanity and could constitute the crime of genocide as defined in the Convention on the Prevention and Punishment of the Crime of Genocide, 78 U.N.T.S. 277. Id. The Commission concluded this report by discussing the concept of establishing an ad hoc international criminal tribunal in relation to crimes in the territory of the former Yugoslavia.

On February 22, 1993, the Security Council adopted Resolution 808, in which it determined that the widespread violation of international humanitarian law in the former Yugoslavia constituted a threat to international peace and security and decided to establish an international tribunal for the former Yugoslavia (I.C.T.Y.). U.N. Doc. S/RES/808 (1993). Creation of the Tribunal was intended to put an end to the crimes, bring the responsible persons to justice, and thereby contribute to the restoration and maintenance of peace. Resolution 808 also requested the Secretary–General, to prepare and submit a report "on all aspects of this matter, including specific proposals, and, where appropriate, options for the effective and expeditious implementation of [the above decision] * * *." Id. The Secretary–General's report, which was submitted on May 3, 1993, examined existing rules of international humanitarian law and international criminal law and the legal basis for the establishment of the I.C.T.Y. and discussed the I.C.T.Y.'s structure. Report of the Secretary–General Pursuant to Paragraph 2 of Security Council Resolution 808 (1993), U.N. Doc. S/25704, Corr.1 and Add.1 (1993), reprinted at 32 I.L.M. 1163. The Secretary–General's report included a draft statute for the I.C.T.Y. with commentary. See Documents Supplement.

On May 25, 1993, the Security Council unanimously adopted Resolution 827, which established "an international tribunal for the sole purpose of prosecuting persons responsible for serious violations of international humanitarian law committed in the territory of the former Yugoslavia between 1 January 1991 and a date to be determined by the Security Council upon the restoration of peace" and to this end adopted the Statute of the International Tribunal (annexed to the Secretary–General's report mentioned in the preceding paragraph). U.N. Doc. S/RES/827 (1993). Resolution 827 provides that "all States shall cooperate fully with the International Tribunal and its organs in accordance with the present resolution and the Statute of the International Tribunal." Id. The I.C.T.Y. is located in The Hague in the Netherlands.

Note

During the Security Council's deliberations following the unanimous vote adopting Resolution 827, the representative of the People's Republic of China stated that China's vote in favor of the resolution "should not be construed as our endorsement of the legal approach involved," that "an international tribunal should be established by concluding a treaty so as to provide a solid legal foundation for it and ensure its effective functioning," and that to adopt the statute by Security Council resolution "is not in compliance with the principle of State judicial sovereignty." S.C. Res 827, U.N. Doc. S/RES/827 (1993). What factors appear to underlie the reservations of the PRC's representative about the legitimacy of the Tribunal under international law? What arguments can be made in support of such legitimacy? See Prosecutor v. Tadic, Case No. IT–94–1–AR72, Decision on Interlocutory Appeal on Jurisdiction (Oct. 2, 1995), paras. 32–37, 55–60, and excerpts at pp. 1342–1349.

B. COMPOSITION AND RULES OF THE TRIBUNAL

In September 1993, the U.N. General Assembly elected eleven judges from among twenty-three candidates nominated by the Security Council. (The size of the Tribunal was later expanded to 14 judges, sitting in three trial chambers of three judges and one appeals chamber of five judges; and in November 2000 the Security Council further expanded the Tribunal's capacity by establishing a pool of ad litem judges. See S/RES/1329 (2000).) On February 11, 1994, the I.C.T.Y. adopted Rules of Procedure and Evidence (hereinafter referred to as the "Rules") for the Tribunal. 33 I.L.M. 484 (1994). The Rules, which are excerpted in the Documents Supplement, came into force on March 14, 1994 and have been periodically amended. (For the latest version, see I.C.T.Y. website at www.un.org/icty.)

The I.C.T.Y. Rules deal with nine distinct areas: (1) General Provisions; (2) Primacy of the Tribunal; (3) Organization of the Tribunal; (4) Investigations and Rights of Suspects; (5) Pre–Trial Proceedings; (6) Proceedings Before Trial Chambers; (7) Appellate Proceedings; (8) Review Proceedings; and (9) Pardon and Commutation of Sentence.

The Rules are historically significant as a result of the novelty of the I.C.T.Y. and because of their potential precedential value in connection with the possible future establishment of a permanent International Criminal Court. The following is a brief summary of some of the more notable Rules.

Part One provides that the working languages of the I.C.T.Y. are English and French and that an accused shall have the right to use his own language and that the I.C.T.Y. shall bear the expenses of interpretation and translation. Rule 3.

Part Two deals with the relationship between the I.C.T.Y. and national courts, which frequently will have concurrent jurisdiction. The concept of "complementarity" is often used to denote the relationship between international and national courts. Compare note 7 on p. 1381. The I.C.T.Y. Statute provides for primacy of the I.C.T.Y.'s jurisdiction. When it appears to the I.C.T.Y. Prosecutor that a crime within the I.C.T.Y.'s jurisdiction is or has been the subject of investigation or criminal proceedings in a national jurisdiction, the Prosecutor may propose that the appropriate Trial Chamber of the I.C.T.Y. formally request a national court to defer to the competence of the International Tribunal. Such deferral may be requested if the national proceedings: (1) characterize the act(s) under investigation as an ordinary crime; (2) exhibit a lack of impartiality or independence or are designed to shield the accused from international criminal responsibility; or (3) concern matters closely related to significant factual or legal questions that may have implications for investigations or prosecutions before the Tribunal. Rule 9. The Rules also provide that should a state fail to respond adequately to a request for deferral, the Trial Chamber may request the President to report the matter to the Security Council. Rule 11. Measures to be adopted once the matter has been reported to the Security Council would be determined by the Council.

Part Three establishes the organizational structure of the I.C.T.Y. and provides for several trial chambers and one appellate chamber of judges, the I.C.T.Y.'s Presidency, the Registry, and the Prosecutor. Additionally, the Rules establish the Bureau, comprised of the President, Vice–President and the Presiding Judges of the Trial Chambers, which oversees all major questions relating to the functioning of the Tribunal. Rule 23.

Article 22 of the Statute provides for the protection of victims and witnesses and states that protective measures shall include, but not be limited to, the conduct of *in camera* proceedings and the protection of the victim's identity. Rule 34 establishes a Victims and Witnesses Unit, which is charged with recommending protective measures for victims and witnesses in accordance with Article 22 of the Statute, and providing counseling and support for them, particularly in cases of rape and sexual assault.

Part Four empowers the Prosecutor, in the conduct of an investigation, to seek the assistance of any state authority or any relevant international body including the International Criminal Police Organization ("INTERPOL"). Rule 39. Rule 40 provides that the Prosecutor may request any State to provisionally arrest a suspect; to seize physical evidence; and to take all necessary measures to prevent the escape of a suspect or an accused, injury to or intimidation of a victim or witness, or the destruction of evidence. Rule 42 provides that suspects have (1) the right to assistance of counsel of their choice or appointment of counsel in case of indigence, (2) the right to free assistance of an interpreter, and (3) the right to be informed of these rights in a language the suspect can understand. Note that these rights attach to a *suspect*, in contrast to the U.S. criminal system in which such rights attach to an individual who is in custody and/or accused of a crime.

Part Five, in addition to setting forth the procedures for issuance of indictments, establishes the procedures for issuing and executing arrest warrants. Rule 55 provides that the Registrar shall transmit a warrant for the arrest of an accused to the national authorities of the state in whose territory or under whose jurisdiction the accused resides or was last known to be located. The Peace Agreement for Bosnia–Herzegovina (sometimes called the "Dayton Peace Accords"), which was brokered by the United States and the European Union and signed by the presidents of Bosnia-Herzegovina, Croatia, and the Federal Republic of Yugoslavia (Serbia-Montenegro) on December 14, 1995, has resulted in somewhat more effective measures for enforcing arrest warrants. U.S. Department of State Dispatch Supplement, Volume 7, Number 1. With the objective of bringing to justice those guilty of genocide, crimes against humanity and war crimes, the Peace Agreement provides that NATO troops implementing peace in Bosnia are empowered to arrest any indicted war criminals they encounter. A substantial number of indicted individuals have been arrested by NATO-led Stabilization Force (SFOR) troops. Additionally, the Agreement provides that indicted war criminals will not be allowed to hold office or serve in the military in Bosnia. This provision prevented Bosnian Serb leader Radovan Karadzic and the Bosnian Serb military commander, General Ratko Mladic, from retaining their positions. Both have been indicted by the I.C.T.Y., but neither had been arrested as of December 31, 2000.

In the event that a state fails to execute an arrest warrant and personal service of the indictment is not effected, the President may notify the Security Council. Rules 59 and 61(E). In the event of such a failure, and if all reasonable steps have been taken to effect personal service and inform the accused of the indictment, a Judge of the Tribunal may order the Prosecutor to submit the indictment to the Trial Chamber in open court, together with all the evidence that was before the Judge who initially confirmed the indictment. Additionally, the Trial Chamber may issue an international arrest warrant in respect of the accused which is transmitted to all states. Rule 61(D). An international arrest warrant would make it impossible for the accused to travel abroad openly without facing risk of arrest.

Part Five also sets forth specific provisions for disclosure of evidence by the Prosecutor to the defense, reciprocal disclosure of the defense, and disclosure of exculpatory evidence. In exceptional circumstances, the Prosecutor may request a Trial Chamber to order the non-disclosure of the identity of victims or witnesses to protect them until they are brought under the protection of the Tribunal. Subject to measures taken for the protection of victims or witnesses provided for under Rule 75, the identity of those protected must be disclosed in sufficient time prior to the trial to permit adequate time for the defense to prepare. Rules 66–69.

Part Six governs the proceedings before a Trial Chamber. Rule 74 provides that a Trial Chamber may grant leave to any state, organization or person to appear before it and make submissions on any issue the Chamber specifies. Nongovernmental organizations (NGOs) concerned with respect for human rights have made extensive use of this rule. Additionally, Rule 74 may be used to enable victims to have appropriate representation throughout the proceedings.

Rule 89 sets forth the general provisions relating to submission of evidence before a Trial Chamber, stating that Trial Chambers are not bound by national rules of evidence and that, unless otherwise provided, the Chamber shall apply rules of evidence that will best promote a fair determination of the matter before it. This general mandate is subject to various specific exceptions. Rule 95 provides that evidence obtained by means which cast substantial doubt on its reliability will not be admissible. Rule 96 provides special rules of evidence for trying charges involving sexual assault.

Part Seven sets forth procedures for appeals. Either the accused or the Prosecutor may appeal a decision of a Trial Chamber. Rule 115 provides that a party may move the Appeals Chamber to admit additional evidence which was not available to the moving party at trial. The Appeals Chamber may permit the presentation of such evidence if it considers that the interests of justice so require.

Part Eight sets forth procedures for review where a new fact has been discovered which was not known to the moving party at trial or appeal and could not have been discovered through the exercise of due diligence. Rule 119. The Prosecutor has one year after the final judgment has been pronounced within which to make this motion; however, no comparable limitation applies to the defense.

Part Nine provides procedures for pardons and commutation of sentences. Rule 123 provides that if, according to the domestic law of a state in which a convicted person is imprisoned, the convicted person is eligible for pardon or commutation of sentence, the state shall notify the Tribunal of such eligibility. Rule 125 sets forth the standards by which the President, in consultation with the Judges, will determine whether pardon or commutation is appropriate.

C. THE WORK OF THE I.C.T.Y.

At the I.C.T.Y.'s inaugural meeting in late 1993, Antonio Cassese was elected President of the Tribunal and judges were assigned to the chambers. At the second session in early 1994, the judges adopted the Rules of Procedure and Evidence. At the third session of the I.C.T.Y. in April–May 1994, the Tribunal amended the Rules with respect to sexual assault cases. Under amended Rule 96(ii), no corroboration of the victim's testimony is required, and consent is not allowed as a defense under specified circumstances, including threats of violence, duress or psychological oppression. Moreover, evidence of prior sexual conduct of the victim is not admissible. U.N. Doc. IT/32/Rev.7 (1996).

Article 18 of the Statute of the I.C.T.Y. vests in the Prosecutor the authority to prepare indictments. Rules 47 through 53 set forth the procedures for the preparation and issuance of indictments. Rule 47 provides that once the Prosecutor is satisfied that sufficient evidence exists to provide reasonable grounds for believing that a suspect has committed a crime within the jurisdiction of the Tribunal, the Prosecutor must prepare and forward to the Registrar an indictment, together with supporting material, for confirmation by a Judge. Upon receipt of the indictment and supporting material, and after the Judge has heard the Prosecutor's presentation of any additional material in support of any count, the Judge may confirm or dismiss each count. The dismissal of a count in an indictment does not preclude the Prosecutor from subsequently bringing a new indictment based upon the acts underlying the dismissed count if there is supporting evidence for a new indictment. Rule 50 provides that the Prosecutor may amend an indictment, without leave, at any time before its confirmation, and thereafter with leave of the Judge who confirmed it or, if at trial, with leave of the Trial Chamber. Rule 53 provides that the Judge may delay public disclosure of the indictment until it is served on the accused, if such an order for delay is in the interests of justice. A number of indictments issued in secret appear to have facilitated arrests of accused individuals in Bosnia and elsewhere.

Justice Richard J. Goldstone, Judge of the Appellate Division of the Supreme Court of South Africa, was appointed I.C.T.Y. Prosecutor by the Security Council, effective August 15, 1994. Justice Goldstone was replaced as the I.C.T.Y.'s Prosecutor by Canadian Justice Louise Arbour of the Ontario Court of Appeal in 1996. In 1999, Justice Arbour resigned to take a seat on the Canadian Supreme Court. Justice Arbour was replaced on September 15, 1999, by the Swiss Federal Attorney General and Public Prosecutor, Carla Del Ponte.

On July 25, 1995, the Tribunal handed down public indictments involving 24 individuals. Most of these were members of the Bosnian Serb military and police forces as well as politicians and detention camp commanders accused of atrocities. Dr. Radovan Karadzic, the leader of the Bosnian Serbs, and General Ratko Mladic, the commander of the Bosnian Serb military, were the highest ranking officials to be indicted prior to the indictment in 1999 of Slobodan Milosevic, President of Serbia, and four other Serbian officials. Karadzic and Mladic are alleged to be responsible for the internment of thousands of Bosnian Muslims and Croats in detention facilities where they were subjected to widespread acts of physical and psychological abuse and to inhuman conditions. Karadzic and Mladic have been charged with genocide committed with intent to destroy, in whole or in part, a national, ethnic or religious group. In early November 1995, the Tribunal amended the indictments against Karadzic and Mladic to include genocide for allegedly orchestrating the slaughter in July of up to 8,000 Bosnian Muslims in the town of Srebrenica, which had been designated a U.N.-protected safe area under the protection of a lightly armed Dutch contingent of the UNPROFOR. Also indicted was Milan Martic, leader of the breakaway Croatian Serbs in the region of Krajina, who was charged with ordering attacks on three Croatian cities, including the firing of cluster-bombs into the center of Zagreb.

On November 13, 1995 six Bosnian Croat leaders were indicted for war crimes and crimes against humanity, which allegedly were carried out on such a large scale and widespread basis, and implemented in such a systematic fashion, that they effectively destroyed or removed almost the entire Muslim civilian population in the Lasva River Valley. The indicted individuals included Tihofil Blaskic and Dario Kordic, who were charged with commanding troops that leveled 14 towns in the Lasva River Valley and with involvement in the 1993 massacre at Ahmici, in which an estimated 120 people were killed and scores of homes were burned. Blaskic was chief of staff of the Croatian Defense Council, a Bosnia-based fighting force. Kordic was chairman of the Croatian Democratic Union, which was the political arm of the militia, and was the Bosnian counterpart of Croatia's ruling Democratic Union led by Franjo Tudjman, then President of Croatia.

While Article 21(4)(d) of the I.C.T.Y.'s statute prohibits trials in absentia, provision is made under Rule 55 for proceedings preliminary to issuance of an international arrest warrant and, in fact, the first evidentiary proceeding before the Tribunal began on October 13, 1995, in connection with the issuance of an international arrest warrant for Dragan "Jenki" Nikolic, who had previously been indicted for crimes against humanity between June and September 1992 in connection with running a concentration camp at Susika in Serb-controlled northwestern Bosnia. Nikolic was accused, inter alia, of killing eight Muslim detainees at the camp, torturing ten others and deportation, confinement and persecution of more than 500 civilians. The court, presided over by French Judge Claude Jorda, heard testimony concerning how Nikolic allegedly raped a number of women and murdered, beat and tortured other civilians. After hearing the evidence, the court issued an international arrest warrant for Nikolic on October 20, 1995. The warrant was delivered to the Bosnian and Serbian authorities. One objective of the proceeding and the arrest warrant was to increase international pressure to bring about Nikolic's arrest if and when he crossed an international border and was identified. In fact, Nikolic has since been arrested and was in the custody of the I.C.T.Y. in 2000.

Eleven individuals had been publicly indicted by the I.C.T.Y. for genocide as of the end of 2000. The first prosecution for genocide was aborted when, before judgment was rendered, the accused, Milan Kovacevic died. In another case, Goran Jelesic, who called himself the Serb "Adolf," was convicted of 31 counts of war crimes and crimes against humanity committed at the Serb-run Luka prison camp. The judgment detailed the grisly way in which Jelisic's Serbian and Croatian victims were beaten, mutilated and executed before being dumped into a river or mass grave. On December 14, 1999, in pronouncing the 40–year sentence, the longest imposed by the Tribunal up to that time (longer sentences have been imposed subsequently), Presiding Judge Claude Jorda cited the "repugnant, bestial and sadistic nature" of Jelisic's crimes. Jelisic was acquitted of the charge of genocide because the prosecution failed to prove the existence of the necessary intent to destroy an ethnic or religious group. "War Crimes Tribunal Sentences Bosnian Serb to a 40–Year Term," N.Y. Times, December 15, 1999, at A5. The Prosecutor has appealed this acquittal. Six individuals were being tried or awaiting trial for genocide and three (including Karadzic and Mladic) remained at large as of early 2001.

Atrocities in the former Yugoslavia entered a new phase in January 1999 when the Serbs initiated an ethnic cleansing campaign directed against ethnic Albanians in Kosovo. The massacre of more than 45 ethnic Albanians in Racak in mid-January drew international condemnation. In February, peace talks were initiated in Rambouillet, France. In mid-March, after the Kosovar–Albanian delegation agreed to accept the limited autonomy proposed in the negotiations but the Serbs refused, the peace talks were adjourned. Serbian forces then massed in and around Kosovo and began an offensive against ethnic Albanians and the Kosovo Liberation Army (KLA). On March 24, 1999, NATO initiated airstrikes against Serb targets, and the Serbs promptly launched a military and police assault against the ethnic Albanians in almost every city and town in Kosovo. Over 10,000 ethnic Albanians are estimated to have been killed and hundreds of thousands were displaced from their homes, most of which were pillaged and destroyed. The NATO bombing campaign lasted 78 days before Serbian officials accepted the NATO peace plan on June 3, 1999, and, on June 9, Serb forces began their withdrawal from Kosovo. On June 12, 1999, NATO troops arrived. Thereafter, more than 100,000 Serbs and Gypsies fled Kosovo amid reprisal killings by ethnic Albanians.

The Prosecutor of the I.C.T.Y., Louise Arbour, initially and consistently took the position that crimes allegedly committed in Kosovo were within the jurisdiction of the Tribunal. Investigation of alleged crimes was difficult because prior to the end of the NATO bombing campaign, the Tribunal's investigators were denied access to Kosovo. However, NATO allies, including particularly the United States and the United Kingdom, made classified intelligence available to the I.C.T.Y.'s prosecutors.

On May 27, 1999, the I.C.T.Y. Prosecutor announced the indictment of Slobodan Milosevic (President of the Federal Republic of Yugoslavia) and four other Serbian leaders (Milan Milutino, Vice–President of the Republic of Serbia; Nikola Sainovic, Deputy Prime Minister of the Federal Republic of Yugoslavia; Dragoljub Ojdanic, Chief of the General Staff of the armed forces of the Federal Republic of Yugoslavia and Vlajko Stojiljkovic, Minister of Internal Affairs of the Republic of Serbia) for crimes against humanity—more specifically, murder of over 340 identified individuals, forced deportation and persecution of 740,000 Kosovo Albanians—and violations of the laws and customs of war. The 42–page indictment had been confirmed by a judge of the I.C.T.Y. on May 24, 1999. The indictment encompasses only crimes allegedly committed in Kosovo beginning in 1999, but in the light of further investigation may be expanded to cover crimes allegedly committed earlier in Bosnia. This was the first instance in modern times of an indictment by an international criminal tribunal of a sitting head of state.

International arrest warrants were issued for all five and were transmitted to all U.N. member states and to Switzerland. The warrants are accompanied by an order of the I.C.T.Y. requesting all states to search for and to freeze any and all assets under their jurisdiction owned by the indicted leaders. The purpose of the order was to prevent foreign assets being used for the purpose of evading justice and to permit effective restitution to be made if the individuals are convicted.

As of late 2000, nearly 100 persons had been indicted publicly by the Tribunal. Of the indicted individuals, 34 were in the custody of the I.C.T.Y. or under house arrest awaiting trial, being tried, or serving sentences. Of those publicly indicted, 30 remained at large. The excess of those indicted over those in custody or at large was attributable to deaths, acquittal or dismissal of charges. A number of appeals were pending. As noted above, an unknown number of secret indictments had been issued as a means of facilitating arrest. Six suspects had been arrested by the NATO-led Stabilization Force (SFOR) troops under secret indictments. Fifteen indictees had been convicted and sentenced; one had been acquitted. Ten trials were under way.

Notes

1. A serious shortcoming of the I.C.T.Y. has been its inability to bring to justice high-level individuals who have been indicted. In an effort to increase the likelihood that the leaders responsible for the atrocities committed in Bosnia would be brought to justice, the U.S. State Department offered rewards of up to $5 million for information leading to the arrest or conviction of individuals indicted by the I.C.T.Y., including Milosevic, Karadzic and Mladic.

The first high ranking military commander to be convicted by the I.C.T.Y. was Croatian General Tihomar Blaskic. He was convicted on March 3, 2000, of crimes against humanity, war crimes and grave breaches of the Geneva Convention for the Protection of Civilian Persons in Time of War. He was sentenced to 45 years in prison, the longest sentence yet imposed. The Tribunal stated, "The Republic of Croatia did not content itself with merely remaining a spectator on the sidelines or even seek simply to protect its borders * * *. It intervened in the conflict, pitting Muslims and Croats of central Bosnia against each other." Simons, War Crimes Tribunal Sentences Croatian General to 45 Years, N.Y. Times, March 4, 2000, at A6.

In June 2001, Milosevic was arrested by authorities of the Federal Republic of Yugoslavia and transferred to The Hague.

2. In May 1998, the I.C.T.Y. decided to withdraw indictments against 14 at-large Bosnian Serbs. These indictees had been charged with atrocities against Bosnian Muslim and Croat civilian prisoners held at the Omarska and Keraterm camps outside Prijedor. The Tribunal's announcement stated that the decision to withdraw the charges was not based on a lack of evidence, but to enable the

Tribunal to reallocate its available resources in a manner that would allow it to respond fairly and expeditiously to a much larger than anticipated number of trials and maintain its investigative focus on persons who held higher levels of responsibility or who were alleged to have been personally responsible for exceptionally brutal or otherwise extremely serious offenses. In withdrawing the indictments, the Prosecutor reserved the right to pursue the same or other charges against the 14 accused in the event of a change in circumstances and offered assistance to national jurisdictions that in good faith pursued charges of violations of international humanitarian law against any of them.

3. On November 16, 1998, the I.C.T.Y. convicted two Bosnian Muslims and one Bosnian Croat for crimes of murder, torture and rape committed while they were running the Celebici prison camp in 1992. This was the first time Bosnian Muslims had been convicted of atrocities against Serbs. The two Bosnian Muslims, Hazim Delic and Esad Landzo, were sentenced to prison terms of 20 years and 15 years, respectively. The Bosnian Croat, Zdravco Mucic, was sentenced to seven years. Delic was found guilty of committing two murders and "calculated cruelty," including rape, against prisoners. The tribunal found Landzo guilty of three murders, and cited his "perverse pleasure in the infliction of pain and suffering." The I.C.T.Y. found Mucic responsible for nine murders and for allowing guards "to commit the most heinous of offenses without taking any disciplinary action." The I.C.T.Y. set an important precedent in holding that acts of rape may constitute torture under customary law. Also, the conviction of Mucic marked the first time since the Nuremberg and Tokyo trials following World War II that anyone had been found guilty by an international tribunal for the actions of subordinates.

4. On December 3, 1998, Serb General Radislav Krstic was arrested by the U.S. troops in the NATO-led SFOR in Bosnia. Krstic had been indicted secretly for genocide and crimes against humanity. Krstic is the highest ranking person yet detained by the I.C.T.Y. and the first military leader. Krstic reported directly to Ratko Mladic, Bosnian Serb military commander. The charges against Krstic are based on his role as commander of the Drina Corps, which in July 1995 brushed aside Dutch UNPROFOR peacekeepers and attacked the Muslim town of Srebrenica in eastern Bosnia. They allegedly separated male Croatian inhabitants from women and children and slaughtered thousands, mostly men and boys. More than 8,000 were killed or are missing.

Krstic pleaded not guilty to charges of genocide and crimes against humanity. The arrest of General Krstic is particularly significant because the I.C.T.Y. has been criticized for using its limited and strained resources to prosecute individuals much farther down the chain of command.

Another notable arrest of a high ranking individual, Serbian General Momir Talic, was made by Austrian authorities. Talic, who had been secretly indicted by the I.C.T.Y., was arrested while attending a conference in Vienna. On December 20, 1999, retired General Stanislav Galic, commander of the Bosnian Serb forces that besieged Sarajevo and slaughtered more than 10,000 of its trapped, largely Muslim, population from 1992 to 1994, who had also been indicted under seal, was arrested by British SFOR troops in Banja Luka, in the Serbian entity of Republika Srpska in Bosnia. Both Talic and Galic have been transferred to the custody of the I.C.T.Y.

On April 3, 2000, Momcilo Krajisnik, former Serbian representative on Bosnia's tripartite presidency and head of the Bosnian Serb delegation to the Dayton peace negotiations, was arrested and transferred to the I.C.T.Y. by French

NATO troops. Krajisnik had been secretly indicted for genocide, crimes against humanity and war crimes. He is the highest ranking Bosnian Serb in custody. Simon, NATO Troops Seize a Top Serb Facing War Crime Charge, New York Times, April 4, 2000, at A1.

5. The rules and procedures of the I.C.T.Y. are an amalgam of common law and civil law features. What are the most significant departures from criminal law procedures based in the common law tradition? For general background, see Criminal Procedure: A Worldwide Study (Bradley ed. 1999).

PROSECUTOR v. TADIC

International Criminal Tribunal for the
Former Yugoslavia, Appeals Chamber
Case No. IT–94–1–AR72.
Decision on Interlocutory Appeal on
Jurisdiction, Oct. 2, 1995.
35 I.L.M. 32 (1996) (footnotes omitted).

[The first individual to be tried by the I.C.T.Y. was Dusko Tadic. The trial was noteworthy as the first war crimes trial before an international tribunal since the Nuremberg and Tokyo trials of German and Japanese war criminals. Tadic, a Serb, was accused of committing atrocities at the Serb-run Omarska concentration camp in northwestern Bosnia–Herzegovina in 1992. Tadic emigrated to Germany in late 1992 after the Omarska camp was closed. He was arrested there on the basis of information supplied by Muslim émigrés who had witnessed some of Tadic's alleged crimes. The Tribunal requested the German Government on November 8, 1994 to surrender Tadic to the Tribunal for trial. After authorizing legislation was enacted, this surrender was effected. In the indictment, Tadic was charged with the commission of multiple war crimes and crimes against humanity at the Omarska camp. He had allegedly beaten prisoners to death, raped at least one woman, participated in sexual mutilation of a man, and forced people to crawl like pigs and drink from puddles.

Tadic was tried by a Trial Chamber headed by Judge Gabrielle Kirk McDonald, a former U.S. district court judge. The initial contention of Tadic's defense was that the I.C.T.Y. was without jurisdiction to try him because the U.N. Security Council exceeded its authority by creating the Tribunal. On August 10, 1995, the trial court dismissed Tadic's challenge to the Tribunal's jurisdiction. This decision was appealed to the Appeals Chamber of the Tribunal. A portion of Appeals Chamber's decision on the preliminary jurisdictional issues is set forth below; for other excerpts, see p. 372.]

Before: Judge Cassese, Presiding; Judges Li, Deschenes, Abi–Saab, and Sidhwa.

4. Article 25 of the Statute of the International Tribunal * * * (hereinafter Statute of the International Tribunal)) adopted by the United Nations Security Council opens up the possibility of appellate proceedings within the International Tribunal. This provision stands in conformity with the International Covenant on Civil and Political Rights which insists upon a right of appeal * * *.

* * *

C. Grounds Of Appeal

* * *

* * * [T]he arguments developed by Appellant [attacking the jurisdiction of the International Tribunal] * * * are offered under the following headings:

a) unlawful establishment of the International Tribunal;

b) unjustified primacy of the International Tribunal over competent domestic courts;

c) lack of subject-matter jurisdiction.

* * *

II. Unlawful Establishment of the International Tribunal

* * *

As no * * * limitative text appears in the Statute of the International Tribunal, the International Tribunal can and indeed has to exercise its "*compétence de la compétence*" and examine the jurisdictional plea of the Defence, in order to ascertain its jurisdiction to hear the case on the merits.

20. It has been argued by the Prosecutor, and held by the Trial Chamber that:

> "[T]his International Tribunal is not a constitutional court set up to scrutinise the actions of organs of the United Nations. It is, on the contrary, a criminal tribunal with clearly defined powers, involving a quite specific and limited criminal jurisdiction. If it is to confine its adjudications to those specific limits, it will have no authority to investigate the legality of its creation by the Security Council."

(Decision at Trial, at para. 5; see also paras. 7, 8, 9, 17, 24, passim.)

There is no question, of course, of the International Tribunal acting as a constitutional tribunal, reviewing the acts of the other organs of the United Nations, particularly those of the Security Council, its own "creator." It was not established for that purpose, as is clear from the definition of the ambit of its "primary" or "substantive" jurisdiction in Articles 1 to 5 of its Statute.

But this is beside the point. The question before the Appeals Chamber is whether the International Tribunal, in exercising this "incidental" jurisdiction, can examine the legality of its establishment by the Security Council, solely for the purpose of ascertaining its own "primary" jurisdiction over the case before it.

* * *

Obviously, the wider the discretion of the Security Council under the Charter of the United Nations, the narrower the scope for the International Tribunal to review its actions, even as a matter of incidental jurisdiction. Nevertheless, this does not mean that the power disappears altogether, particularly in cases where there might be a manifest contradiction with the Principles and Purposes of the Charter.

22. In conclusion, the Appeals Chamber finds that the International Tribunal has jurisdiction to examine the plea against its jurisdiction based on the invalidity of its establishment by the Security Council.

2. Is The Question At Issue Political And As Such Non–Justiciable?

* * *

25. The Appeals Chamber does not consider that the International Tribunal is barred from examination of the Defence jurisdictional plea by the so-called "political" or "non-justiciable" nature of the issue it raises.

* * *

(b) Can The Security Council Establish A Subsidiary Organ With Judicial Powers?

37. The argument that the Security Council, not being endowed with judicial powers, cannot establish a subsidiary organ possessed of such powers is untenable: it results from a fundamental misunderstanding of the constitutional set-up of the Charter. Plainly, the Security Council is not a judicial organ and is not provided with judicial powers (though it may incidentally perform certain quasi-judicial activities such as effecting determinations or findings). The principal function of the Security Council is the maintenance of international peace and security, in the discharge of which the Security Council exercises both decision-making and executive powers.

38. The establishment of the International Tribunal by the Security Council does not signify, however, that the Security Council has delegated to it some of its own functions or the exercise of some of its own powers. Nor does it mean, in reverse, that the Security Council was usurping for itself part of a judicial function which does not belong to it but to other organs of the United Nations according to the Charter. The Security Council has resorted to the establishment of a judicial organ in the form of an international criminal tribunal as an instrument for the exercise of its own principal function of maintenance of peace and security, i.e., as a measure contributing to the restoration and maintenance of peace in the former Yugoslavia.

* * *

(c) Was The Establishment Of The International Tribunal an Appropriate Measure?

39. The third argument is directed against the discretionary power of the Security Council in evaluating the appropriateness of the chosen measure and its effectiveness in achieving its objective, the restoration of peace.

Article 39 leaves the choice of means and their evaluation to the Security Council, which enjoys wide discretionary powers in this regard; and it could not have been otherwise, as such a choice involves political evaluation of highly complex and dynamic situations.

It would be a total misconception of what are the criteria of legality and validity in law to test the legality of such measures ex post facto by their success or failure to achieve their ends (in the present case, the restoration of peace in the former Yugoslavia, in quest of which the establishment of the

International Tribunal is but one of many measures adopted by the Security Council).

40. For the aforementioned reasons, the Appeals Chamber considers that the International Tribunal has been lawfully established as a measure under Chapter VII of the Charter.

4. Was The Establishment Of The International Tribunal Contrary To The General Principle Whereby Courts Must Be "Established By Law"?

41. Appellant challenges the establishment of the International Tribunal by contending that it has not been established by law. The entitlement of an individual to have a criminal charge against him determined by a tribunal which has been established by law is provided in Article 14, paragraph 1, of the International Covenant on Civil and Political Rights. It provides:

> "In the determination of any criminal charge against him, or of his rights and obligations in a suit at law, everyone shall be entitled to a fair and public hearing by a competent, independent and impartial tribunal established by law."

(ICCPR, art. 14, para. 1.)

* * *

Appellant argues that the right to have a criminal charge determined by a tribunal established by law is one which forms part of international law as a "general principle of law recognized by civilized nations," one of the sources of international law in Article 38 of the Statute of the International Court of Justice. In support of this assertion, Appellant emphasises the fundamental nature of the "fair trial" or "due process" guarantees afforded in the International Covenant on Civil and Political Rights, the European Convention on Human Rights and the American Convention on Human Rights. Appellant asserts that they are minimum requirements in international law for the administration of criminal justice.

* * *

* * * Appellant takes the position that, given the differences between the United Nations system and national division of powers, discussed above, the conclusion must be that the United Nations system is not capable of creating the International Tribunal unless there is an amendment to the United Nations Charter. We disagree. It does not follow from the fact that the United Nations has no legislature that the Security Council is not empowered to set up this International Tribunal if it is acting pursuant to an authority found within its constitution, the United Nations Charter. As set out above (paras. 28–40) we are of the view that the Security Council was endowed with the power to create this International Tribunal as a measure under Chapter VII in the light of its determination that there exists a threat to the peace.

In addition, the establishment of the International Tribunal has been repeatedly approved and endorsed by the "representative" organ of the United Nations, the General Assembly: this body not only participated in its setting up, by electing the Judges and approving the budget, but also expressed its satisfaction with, and encouragement of the activities of the International Tribunal in various resolutions. * * *

45. * * * [Another] possible interpretation of the requirement that the International Tribunal be "established by law" is that its establishment must be in accordance with the rule of law. This appears to be the most sensible and most likely meaning of the term in the context of international law. For a tribunal such as this one to be established according to the rule of law, it must be established in accordance with the proper international standards; it must provide all the guarantees of fairness, justice and even-handedness, in full conformity with internationally recognized human rights instruments.

* * *

As noted by the Trial Chamber in its Decision, there is wide agreement that, in most respects, the International Military Tribunals at Nuremberg and Tokyo gave the accused a fair trial in a procedural sense (Decision at Trial, at para. 34). The important consideration in determining whether a tribunal has been "established by law" is not whether it was pre-established or established for a specific purpose or situation; what is important is that it be set up by a competent organ in keeping with the relevant legal procedures, and that it observes the requirements of procedural fairness.

* * *

46. An examination of the Statute of the International Tribunal, and of the Rules of Procedure and Evidence adopted pursuant to that Statute leads to the conclusion that it has been established in accordance with the rule of law. The fair trial guarantees in Article 14 of the International Covenant on Civil and Political Rights have been adopted almost verbatim in Article 21 of the Statute. Other fair trial guarantees appear in the Statute and the Rules of Procedure and Evidence. For example, Article 13, paragraph 1, of the Statute ensures the high moral character, impartiality, integrity and competence of the Judges of the International Tribunal, while various other provisions in the Rules ensure equality of arms and fair trial.

47. In conclusion, the Appeals Chamber finds that the International Tribunal has been established in accordance with the appropriate procedures under the United Nations Charter and provides all the necessary safeguards of a fair trial. It is thus "established by law."

48. The first ground of appeal: unlawful establishment of the International Tribunal, is accordingly dismissed.

III. Unjustified Primacy of the International Tribunal Over Competent Domestic Courts

* * *

50. [The primacy of the International Tribunal over national courts] is established by Article 9 of the Statute of the International Tribunal * * *

Appellant's submission is material to the issue, inasmuch as Appellant is expected to stand trial before this International Tribunal as a consequence of a request for deferral which the International Tribunal submitted to the Government of the Federal Republic of Germany on 8 November 1994 and which this Government, as it was bound to do, agreed to honour by surrendering Appellant to the International Tribunal. (United Nations Charter, art. 25, 48 & 49; Statute of the Tribunal, art. 29.2(e); Rules of Procedure, Rule 10.)

In relevant part, Appellant's motion alleges: "[The International Tribunal's] primacy over domestic courts constitutes an infringement upon the sovereignty of the States directly affected". * * *

* * *

55. Article 2 of the United Nations Charter provides in paragraph 1: "The Organization is based on the principle of the sovereign equality of all its Members."

In Appellant's view, no State can assume jurisdiction to prosecute crimes committed on the territory of another State, barring a universal interest "justified by a treaty or customary international law or an opinio juris on the issue." * * *

Based on this proposition, Appellant argues that the same requirements should underpin the establishment of an international tribunal destined to invade an area essentially within the domestic jurisdiction of States. In the present instance, the principle of State sovereignty would have been violated. * * *.

* * *

56. * * * Appellant's plea faces several obstacles, each of which may be fatal, as the Trial Chamber has actually determined.

Appellant can call in aid Article 2, paragraph 7, of the United Nations Charter: "Nothing contained in the present Charter shall authorize the United Nations to intervene in matters which are essentially within the domestic jurisdiction of any State [* * *]". However, one should not forget the commanding restriction at the end of the same paragraph: "but this principle shall not prejudice the application of enforcement measures under Chapter VII." (United Nations Charter, art. 2, para. 7.)

Those are precisely the provisions under which the International Tribunal has been established. Even without these provisions, matters can be taken out of the jurisdiction of a State. In the present case, the Republic of Bosnia and Herzegovina not only has not contested the jurisdiction of the International Tribunal but has actually approved, and collaborated with, the International Tribunal * * *.

As to the Federal Republic of Germany, its cooperation with the International Tribunal is public and has been previously noted.

The Trial Chamber was therefore fully justified to write, on this particular issue:

> "[I]t is pertinent to note that the challenge to the primacy of the International Tribunal has been made against the express intent of the two States most closely affected by the indictment against the accused—Bosnia and Herzegovina and the Federal Republic of Germany. The former, on the territory of which the crimes were allegedly committed, and the latter where the accused resided at the time of his arrest, have unconditionally accepted the jurisdiction of the International Tribunal

> and the accused cannot claim the rights that have been specifically waived by the States concerned. To allow the accused to do so would be to allow him to select the forum of his choice, contrary to the principles relating to coercive criminal jurisdiction."

(Decision at Trial, at para. 41.)

57. This is all the more so in view of the nature of the offences alleged against Appellant, offences which, if proven, do not affect the interests of one State alone but shock the conscience of mankind.

* * *

58. The public revulsion against similar offences in the 1990s brought about a reaction on the part of the community of nations: hence, among other remedies, the establishment of an international judicial body by an organ of an organization representing the community of nations: the Security Council. This organ is empowered and mandated, by definition, to deal with trans-boundary matters or matters which, though domestic in nature, may affect "international peace and security" (United Nations Charter, art 2.(1), 2.(7), 24, & 37). It would be a travesty of law and a betrayal of the universal need for justice, should the concept of State sovereignty be allowed to be raised successfully against human rights. Borders should not be considered as a shield against the reach of the law and as a protection for those who trample underfoot the most elementary rights of humanity. In the *Barbie* case, the Court of Cassation of France has quoted with approval the following statement of the Court of Appeal:

> "[* * *] by reason of their nature, the crimes against humanity [* * *] do not simply fall within the scope of French municipal law but are subject to an international criminal order to which the notions of frontiers and extradition rules arising therefrom are completely foreign. (*Fédération Nationale de Déportés et Internés Résistants et Patriotes And Others v. Barbie*, 78 International Law Reports 125, 130 (Cass. crim. 1983).)

Indeed, when an international tribunal such as the present one is created, it must be endowed with primacy over national courts. Otherwise, human nature being what it is, there would be a perennial danger of international crimes being characterised as "ordinary crimes" (Statute of the International Tribunal, art. 10, para. 2(a)), or proceedings being "designed to shield the accused," or cases not being diligently prosecuted (Statute of the International Tribunal, art. 10, para. 2(b)).

If not effectively countered by the principle of primacy, any one of those stratagems might be used to defeat the very purpose of the creation of an international criminal jurisdiction, to the benefit of the very people whom it has been designed to prosecute.

59. The principle of primacy of this International Tribunal over national courts must be affirmed; the more so since it is confined within the strict limits of Articles 9 and 10 of the Statute and Rules 9 and 10 of the Rules of Procedure of the International Tribunal.

The Trial Chamber was fully justified in writing:

> "Before leaving this question relating to the violation of the sovereignty of States, it should be noted that the crimes which the International Tribunal has been called upon to try are not crimes of a purely domestic nature. They are really crimes which are universal in nature, well recognized in international law as serious breaches of international humanitarian law, and transcending the interest of any one State. The Trial Chamber agrees that in such circumstances, the sovereign rights of States cannot and should not take precedence over the right of the international community to act appropriately as they affect the whole of mankind and shock the conscience of all nations of the world. There can therefore be no objection to an international tribunal properly constituted trying these crimes on behalf of the international community."

(Decision at Trial, at para. 42.)

60. The plea of State sovereignty must therefore be dismissed.

[The Tribunal then rejected Appellant's contention that he had a right to be tried by his national courts under his national laws, stating, in part, as follows:]

63. The objection founded on the theory of *jus de non evocando* [right not to have case removed from its natural judge] was considered by the Trial Chamber which disposed of it in the following terms:

> "Reference was also made to the *jus de non evocando*, a feature of a number of national constitutions. But that principle, if it requires that an accused be tried by the regularly established courts and not by some special tribunal set up for that particular purpose, has no application when what is in issue is the exercise by the Security Council, acting under Chapter VII, of the powers conferred upon it by the Charter of the United Nations. Of course, this involves some surrender of sovereignty by the member nations of the United Nations but that is precisely what was achieved by the adoption of the Charter." (Decision at Trial, at para. 37.)

No new objections were raised before the Appeals Chamber, which is satisfied with concurring, on this particular point, with the views expressed by the Trial Chamber.

64. For these reasons the Appeals Chamber concludes that Appellant's second ground of appeal, contesting the primacy of the International Tribunal, is ill-founded and must be dismissed.

[Discussion by the Appeals Chamber upholding the decision of the Trial Chamber that it had subject-matter jurisdiction under the Statute of the I.C.T.Y. is omitted.]

Notes

1. After resolution of the jurisdictional issues by the decision of the Appeals Chamber excerpted above, the Trial Chamber proceeded to hear the Tadic case on the merits. In May 1997, following seven months of hearings, Dusko Tadic was found guilty in a 300–page judgment of 11 counts of war crimes and crimes against humanity, including taking part in Serb attacks on his home town of Kozarac and other villages and herding the inhabitants into camps like the Omarska camps where they were beaten and kept in inhuman conditions. Prose-

cutor v. Dusko Tadic, Case No. IT–94–1–T, Opinion and Judgment, May 7, 1997. Tadic was sentenced to 20 years in prison. Tadic appealed his conviction to the Appeals Chamber. Id., Sentencing Judgment, July 15, 1997. The prosecutor also appealed. The Appeals Chamber found Tadic guilty of additional crimes and increased his sentence to 25 years. Id., Appeals Judgment, July 15, 1999, 38 I.L.M. 1518 (1999) and Sentencing Judgment, Nov. 11, 1999, 39 I.L.M. 117 (2000). The Tribunal subsequently adjusted this to 20 years because Tadic had spent five years in investigative custody. Tadic's case, which began on May 7, 1996, was finally concluded on January 26, 2000.

For a narrative of the case through the trial, see Scharf, Balkan Justice: The Story Behind the First International War Crimes Trial Since Nuremberg (1997). For critical legal commentary, see Alvarez, Rush to Closure: Lessons of the Tadic Judgment, 96 Mich. L. Rev. 2031 (1998).

2. The Bosnia Peace Agreement of December 14, 1995, 35 I.L.M. 75, 90 (1996), states as follows in Article IX:

> The Parties shall cooperate fully with all entities involved in implementation of this peace settlement, as described in the Annexes to this Agreement, or which are otherwise authorized by the United Nations Security Council, pursuant to the obligation of all Parties to cooperate in the investigation and prosecution of war crimes and other violations of international humanitarian law.

The Peace Agreement also provides that persons indicted by the Tribunal for crimes against humanity are ineligible to stand for election. The Agreement was implemented with the support of 60,000 members of the NATO-led Stabilization Force (SFOR), including a large U.S. contingent.

3. What are the factors that bear on the necessity or desirability of proceeding with the trial by the I.C.T.Y. of individuals indicted for crimes falling within the Tribunal's competence? Consider the following comment on the Tadic case:

> * * * If there is any hope of a durable settlement in Bosnia and the former Yugoslavia, it rests upon breaking the cycle of retaliation. "Crime has a name and a face," wrote Bertolt Brecht. By putting a name and a face to Balkan crimes, courts may help to avert collective guilt and mass reprisals. "Someone must pay," says the Omarska survivor Mulharem Besic, "so others don't. If they can bring the instigators to justice, then we might be able to live together with Serbs again."

Crane–Engel, "Germany vs. Genocide," New York Times Magazine, October 20, 1994, at p. 59.

4. One complication presented by the Tribunal's request for the extradition of Tadic was that Germany, like most countries, including the United States, had at the time the I.C.T.Y. was established no legal mechanism for turning over an accused to an international criminal tribunal. Extradition (discussed in Chapter 13) had been developed to deliver an accused or convicted persons to another state, not to an international tribunal. Germany amended its law to make possible the surrender to the I.C.T.Y. of Tadic and others similarly situated. A number of other countries, including the United States, France, Spain, Italy and the Netherlands, have also enacted legislation that permits surrender of individuals indicted for serious violations of humanitarian law to an international tribunal with jurisdiction. All member states of the United Nations are obligated under Article 25 of the Charter to accept and carry out decisions of the Security Council. Security Council Resolution 827 (1993) requires all member states to cooperate

fully with the Tribunal and to take "any measures necessary under their domestic law to implement" this Resolution and the I.C.T.Y.'s Statute.

5. The I.C.T.Y.'s procedural and substantive jurisprudence has developed rapidly to cover many areas concerning protection of the respective rights of defendants, on the one hand, and victims and witnesses on the other hand; application of cross-cutting issues in criminal law, such as the requisite state of mind for conviction of the crimes charged; defenses of justification or excuse arising from claims of duress or necessity; and sentencing policies.

In the *Erdemovic* case, No. IT–96–22, defendant entered a plea of guilty which he subsequently sought to set aside after the imposition of sentence. In a series of thoughtful opinions, the judges of the Appeals Chamber considered the nature of a guilty plea in the context of an international criminal tribunal; the blending of elements of common-law and civil-law forms of criminal procedure in the Statute and Rules of the I.C.T.Y; the defenses of duress and necessity; and other interconnected problems.

In the *Blaskic* case, No. IT–95–14, the Appeals Chamber addressed itself to problems in obtaining documentary and testimonial evidence needed for the prosecution or defense of a case. In other cases, including *Tadic* (Appeal from Judgment of Conviction, July 15, 1999), the Appeals Chamber considered the defendant's contention that the procedural framework for obtaining evidence and conducting the trial was so disadvantageous to the defense as to amount to denial of his right to a fair trial; it rejected this contention.

Several cases have involved a weighing of defendant's fair trial rights in relation to the interests of victims and witnesses. The Statute and Rules provide for measures to protect victims and witnesses, and the Tribunal has applied these to safeguard witness identities from the public and, in exceptional cases, even from the defendant. These measures have provoked intense debate between those who see them as appropriate to prevent retraumatization of victims and perhaps even additional harm to them or their families, and those who question whether they are compatible with due process for defendants. For different perspectives, see Christine Chinkin, International Tribunal for the Former Yugoslavia: Amicus Curiae Brief on Protective Measures for Victims and Witnesses, 7 Crim. L.F. 179 (1996); Chinkin, Due Process and Witness Anonymity, 91 A.J.I.L. 75 (1997); Monroe Leigh, Witness Anonymity Is Inconsistent with Due Process, 91 A.J.I.L. 80 (1997). The Trial Chambers and Appeals Chamber have considered these matters in, among others, the *Tadic* case (supra); the so-called "Foca" indictment (Prosecutor v. Kunarac, Decision Granting Protective Measures for Witness FWS–191); and the *Furundzija* case, No. IT–95–17/1–A (Appeals Chamber, Judgment, July 21, 2000). In the latter case, a dispute arose over whether the Prosecutor should have disclosed to the defense certain materials concerning counseling that a witness had received at a treatment center in Bosnia–Herzegovina; the defense sought to impugn her testimony as arguably affected by post-traumatic stress disorder. On this and related matters, see Kelly Dawn Askin, Sexual Violence in Decisions and Indictments of the Yugoslav and Rwandan Tribunals: Current Status, 93 A.J.I.L. 97, 110–115 (1999).

Some defendants have raised challenges to the legality of the manner of their apprehension in unsuccessful efforts to defeat the Tribunal's jurisdiction. See Prosecutor v. Dokmanovic, No. IT–95–13a-PT, Decision on Motion for Release by the Accused (1997); Scharf, The Prosecutor v. Dokmanovic: Irregular Rendition and the ICTY, 11 Leiden J.I.L. 369 (1998); Murphy, Progress and Jurisprudence of the International Criminal Tribunal for the Former Yugoslavia, 93 A.J.I.L. 57, 75–

76 (1999). The latter article also contains a helpful thematic review of the Tribunal's jurisprudence.

6. For further discussion of the I.C.T.Y., see Bass, Stay the Hand of Vengeance: The Politics of War Crimes Tribunals 206–275 (2000); Goldstone, For Humanity: Reflections of a War Crimes Investigator (2000); Meron, War Crimes Law Comes of Age 210–227 (1998); Morris & Scharf, An Insider's Guide to the International Criminal Tribunal for the Former Yugoslavia: Documentary History and Analysis (2 vols., 1995). See also Mills, War Crimes in the 21st Century, 3 Hofstra L. & Pol'y Symp. 47 (1999); Brown, Nationality and Internationality in International Humanitarian Law, 34 Stan. J. Int'l L. (1998); Scharf, *Prosecutor v. Dusko Tadic*: An Appraisal of the First International War Crimes Trial Since Nuremberg, in Conceptualizing Violence: Present and Future Developments in International Law, 60 Alb. L. Rev. 861 (1997); Isenberg, Genocide, Rape, and Crimes Against Humanity: An Affirmation of Individual Accountability in the Former Yugoslavia in the Karadzic Actions, 60 Alb. L. Rev. 1051 (1997); Schmandt, Peace with Justice: Is It Possible for the Former Yugoslavia?, 30 Tex. Int'l L.J. 335 (1995); and Saunders, The World's Forgotten Lesson: The Punishment of War Criminals in the Former Yugoslavia, 8 Temp. Int'l & Comp. L.J. 357 (1994).

SECTION 6. U.N. TRIBUNAL FOR RWANDA

A. BACKGROUND

Rwanda has experienced recurrent outbreaks of ethnic conflict between the Hutus (who have comprised approximately 85% of the population), and the Tutsis (less than 15%). In April 1994, shortly after the assassination of Hutu President Juvenal Habyarimana of Rwanda, Hutu extremist troops, militia and mobs launched a genocidal wave of murder and rape against the Tutsi minority and Hutu moderates. Between April and July 1994, at least half a million and perhaps 800,000 or more Tutsis and moderate Hutus were killed. For background on the conflict, see Prunier, The Rwanda Crisis: History of a Genocide (1997); Gourevitch, We Wish to Inform You That Tomorrow We Will Be Killed with Our Families: Stories from Rwanda (1998). See also the discussion of humanitarian law in internal conflicts at p. 1062 in Chapter 12.

On November 8, 1994, the U.N. Security Council decided to set up an ad hoc tribunal similar to the I.C.T.Y. to prosecute individuals responsible for genocide and other serious violations of international humanitarian law in the territory of Rwanda during 1994.

SECURITY COUNCIL RESOLUTION 955

S/RES/955, 33 I.L.M. 1598 (1994).

The Security Council,

* * *

Expressing once again its grave concern at the reports indicating that genocide and other systematic, widespread and flagrant violations of international humanitarian law have been committed in Rwanda,

Determining that this situation continues to constitute a threat to international peace and security,

Determined to put an end to such crimes and to take effective measures to bring to justice the persons who are responsible for them,

Convinced that in the particular circumstances of Rwanda, the prosecution of persons responsible for serious violations of international humanitarian law would enable this aim to be achieved and would contribute to the process of national reconciliation and to the restoration and maintenance of peace,

Believing that the establishment of an international tribunal for the prosecution of persons responsible for genocide and the other above-mentioned violations of international humanitarian law will contribute to ensuring that such violations are halted and effectively redressed,

Stressing also the need for international cooperation to strengthen the courts and judicial system of Rwanda, having regard in particular to the necessity for those courts to deal with large numbers of suspects,

Considering that the Commission of Experts established pursuant to resolution 935 (1994) should continue on an urgent basis the collection of information relating to evidence of grave violations of international humanitarian law committed in the territory of Rwanda and should submit its final report to the Secretary–General by 30 November 1994,

Acting under Chapter VII of the Charter of the United Nations,

1. Decides hereby, having received the request of the Government of Rwanda (S/1994/1115), to establish an international tribunal for the sole purpose of prosecuting persons responsible for genocide and other serious violations of international humanitarian law committed in the territory of Rwanda and Rwandan citizens responsible for genocide and other such violations committed in the territory of neighbouring States, between 1 January 1994 and 31 December 1994 and to this end to adopt the Statute of the International Criminal Tribunal for Rwanda annexed hereto;

2. Decides that all States shall cooperate fully with the International Tribunal and its organs in accordance with the present resolution and the Statute of the International Tribunal and that consequently all States shall take any measures necessary under their domestic law to implement the provisions of the present resolution and the Statute, including the obligation of States to comply with requests for assistance or orders issued by a Trial Chamber under Article 28 of the Statute, and requests States to keep the Secretary–General informed of such measures;

* * *

VOTE: 13–1–1 (Rwanda against; China abstaining).

Notes

1. In a statement to the U.N. Security Council on November 21, 1994, the U.S. Permanent Representative to the U.N. Security Council, Madeleine K. Albright stated, in part:

> The investigation of genocide is, indeed, very grim work. But we have a responsibility to see that the International Tribunal for Rwanda can accomplish its objective—one that this Council increasingly recognizes—to hold

individuals accountable for their violations of international humanitarian law. As evident in the former Yugoslavia, in Rwanda there is an equal need to forge harmony among ethnic groups by bringing to justice the individuals who committed such heinous crimes, regardless of their position in society.

In closing, let me express my government's hope that the step we have taken here today can promote both justice and national reconciliation, lest the Rwandan people be unable to escape the memory of madness and barbarism they have just lived through.

S/1994/1321.

2. In the light of the creation of the International Criminal Tribunal for Yugoslavia in 1993, the Security Council was pressed to overcome criticisms of "Eurocentrism" by responding to the dire events in Rwanda in 1994 with comparable instruments. This was one factor encouraging the establishment of the Rwandan Tribunal. For further discussion see Von Sternberg, A Comparison of the Yugoslavian and Rwandan War Crimes Tribunals: Universal Jurisdiction and the Elementary Dictates of Humanity, 22 Brook. J. Int'l L. 111 (1996). See also Wang, The International Tribunal for Rwanda: Opportunities for Clarification, Opportunities for Impact, 27 Colum.Hum.Rts. L. Rev. 177 (1995).

3. As noted in paragraph 1 of Resolution 955, the Government of Rwanda had initially requested creation of an international tribunal. However, as also noted above, Rwanda (which happened to occupy a non-permanent seat on the Security Council in 1994), voted against the final formulation of Resolution 955, partly because the statute annexed to the resolution did not authorize the death penalty to be imposed on those convicted of genocide by the Tribunal.

In parallel to the international proceedings, Rwanda has gone forward with a wholesale program of arrest and detention of genocide suspects: indeed, approximately 125,000 (roughly 10% of the adult male Hutu population) had been detained through the late 1990s. In 1996 Rwanda enacted legislation to facilitate the processing of this overwhelming number of cases. National trials have gone forward, and in some genocide cases the death penalty has been imposed and carried out.

On the relationship between the international and national proceedings in respect of Rwanda, see Dubois, Rwanda's National Criminal Courts and the International Tribunal, 321 Int'l Rev. Red Cross 717 (1997); Alvarez, Crimes of State/Crimes of Hate: Lessons from Rwanda, 24 Yale J.Int'l L. 365 (1999); Drumbl, Rule of Law Amid Lawlessness: Counseling the Accused in Rwanda's Domestic Genocide Trials, 29 Colum. Hum. Rts. L. Rev. 545 (1998); Drumbl, Punishment, Postgenocide: From Guilt to Shame to *Civis* in Rwanda, 75 N.Y.U. L. Rev. 1221 (2000).

B. STRUCTURE OF THE INTERNATIONAL TRIBUNAL FOR RWANDA (I.C.T.R.)

The Statute of the I.C.T.R. mirrors closely the I.C.T.Y. Statute. Differences between the subject matter jurisdiction of the two tribunals derive from the fact that the conflict in Rwanda was essentially internal, whereas the conflict in the former Yugoslavia was in part international. Thus, the competence of the I.C.T.R. encompasses genocide, crimes against humanity, and serious violations of common article 3 of the Geneva Conventions of August 12, 1949 and Additional Protocol II thereto of June 8, 1977, but not grave breaches of the Geneva Conventions or war crimes under the 1907 Hague Convention because the latter are implicated only in international conflict.

Like the I.C.T.Y., the institutions of the I.C.T.R. include a Presidency, a Registrar and several trial chambers of three judges. The I.C.T.R. and the I.C.T.Y. have the same five-judge Appeals Chamber. Also, both tribunals are served by a single prosecutor (as of 2000, the former Swiss federal prosecutor, Carla Del Ponte).

C. THE WORK OF THE I.C.T.R.

In February 1995, the Security Council selected Arusha, Tanzania, as the site for the Tribunal. The organization of the Tribunal was handicapped, however, by the dire financial straits of the United Nations, which in October 1995 imposed a freeze on new spending for its activities worldwide. This slowed construction of the I.C.T.R.'s facilities and the hiring of staff, including investigators and prosecutors.

Although the identities of many of the Hutu leaders who instigated the murders are known, they left little or no paper record (unlike the Nazis of World War II Germany). Thus, guilt must be established through testimony—a daunting challenge in the light of the limited resources of the Tribunal and the number of witnesses who failed to survive.

Despite these obstacles, the Tribunal for Rwanda held its first sessions in Arusha and indicted eight individuals on December 12, 1995. The indictments reflect the policy of investigating and indicting the persons who held positions of authority in relation to the mass killings and rapes in Rwanda in mid–1994, including individuals who either gave orders leading to the atrocities or were in positions of control and knew what was about to transpire and took no steps to prevent it.

In July 1997, seven genocide suspects were arrested in Kenya, including Jean Kambanda, Rwandan Prime Minister when the massacres were initiated. All were transferred to the custody of the Tribunal. In May 1998, Kambanda pleaded guilty to genocide and was sentenced to life in prison. In September 1998, the I.C.T.R. convicted Jean–Paul Akayesu, the former *bourgmestre* (mayor) of Taba, Rwanda, of genocide, public incitement to commit genocide, and crimes against humanity (murders, torture, rape and other inhumane acts).

PROSECUTOR v. JEAN–PAUL AKAYESU

SUMMARY OF JUDGMENT
Delivered on September 2, 1998.
ICTR–96–4–T
37 I.L.M. 1399 (1999).

* * *

2. The Judgment, which is already available in French and English, the two official languages of the Tribunal, is a voluminous document of almost three hundred pages. The Chamber therefore considers that it would be appropriate to limit its delivery to a summary of the content of its Judgment and its Verdict as regards the guilt of Jean–Paul Akayesu on each count with which he is charged.

* * *

9. Jean–Paul Akayesu, a Rwandan national, was born in 1953. He is married, with five children. Prior to becoming *bourgmestre* of Taba commune, in the prefecture of Gitarama, in Rwanda, he was a teacher, then an inspector of schools. Akayesu entered politics in 1991, during the establishment of the *Mouvement Démocratique Républicain* (MDR), of which he is one of the founding members. He was Chairman of the local wing of the MDR in Taba commune, which a vast majority of the population joined. In April 1993, Akayesu, whose candidacy was supported by several key figures and influential groups in the commune, was elected *bourgmestre* of Taba. He held that position until June 1994, when he fled Rwanda.

10. Based on the evidence submitted to it, the Chamber notes that, in Rwanda, the *bourgmestre* was traditionally treated with a lot of deference by the people and that he had extensive powers. Akayesu appears to have discharged his various responsibilities relatively well until the period of the events described in the Indictment and to have been a respected *bourgmestre*.

11. In the opinion of the Chamber, the Defence case, in essence, is that he did not commit, order to be committed or in any way aid and facilitate the acts with which he is charged in the Indictment. Akayesu concedes, nonetheless, that massacres aimed mainly at the Tutsi took place in Taba commune in 1994. The Defence argues that Jean–Paul Akayesu was helpless to prevent the commission of such acts, because the balance of force in the commune was in favour of the Interahamwe [Hutu militia], who were under the strict authority of one Silas Kubwimana. The Defence argues further that the Accused was allegedly so harassed by the Interahamwe that he himself had to flee Taba temporarily. It submits that as soon as the massacres became widespread, the Accused was stripped of all authority and lacked the means to stop the killings. The Defence stated further that Jean–Paul Akayesu could not be required to be a hero, to lay down his life in futile attempt to prevent the massacres. As concerns acts of sexual violence and rape which were allegedly committed in Taba, Jean–Paul Akayesu maintains that he never heard of them and considers that they never even took place.

* * *

14. Even though the number of victims is yet to be known with accuracy, no one can reasonably refute the fact that widespread killings took place during this period throughout the country. Dr. Zachariah, who appeared as an expert witness before this Tribunal, described the piles of bodies he saw everywhere, on the roads, on the footpaths and in rivers and, particularly, the manner in which all these people had been killed. He saw many wounded people who, according to him, were mostly Tutsi and who, apparently, had sustained wounds inflicted with machetes to the face, the neck, the ankle and also to the Achilles' tendon to prevent them from fleeing. Similarly, the testimony of Major–General Dallaire, former Commander of UNAMIR [U.N. peacekeeping mission in Rwanda], before the Chamber indicated that, from 6 April 1994, the date of the crash that claimed the life of President Habyarimana, members of FAR [Rwandan Armed Forces] and the Presidential Guard were going into houses in Kigali that had been previously identified in order to kill. Another witness, the British cameraman, Simon Cox, took photographs of bodies in various localities in Rwanda, and mentioned identity cards strewn on the ground, all of which were marked "Tutsi."

15. Consequently, in view of these widespread killings the victims of which were mainly Tutsi, the Trial Chamber is of the opinion that the first requirement for there to be genocide has been met, to wit, killing and causing serious bodily harm to members of a group. The second requirement is that these killings and serious bodily harm be committed with the intent to destroy, in whole or in part, a particular group targeted as such.

16. In the opinion of the Chamber, many facts show that the intention of the perpetrators of these killings was to cause the complete disappearance of the Tutsi people. In this connection, Alison DesForges, a specialist historian on Rwanda, who appeared as an expert witness, stated as follows: "on the basis of the statements made by certain political leaders, on the basis of songs and slogans popular among the interahamwe, I believe that these people had the intention of completely wiping out the Tutsi from Rwanda so that—as they said on certain occasions—their children, later on, should not know what a Tutsi looked like, unless they referred to history books." This testimony given by Dr. DesForges was confirmed by two prosecution witnesses, who testified separately before the Tribunal that one Silas Kubwimana said during a public meeting chaired by the Accused himself that all the Tutsi had to be killed so that someday Hutu children would not know what a Tutsi looked like. Dr. Zachariah also testified that the Achilles' tendons of many wounded persons were cut to prevent them from fleeing. In the opinion of the Chamber, this demonstrates the resolve of the perpetrators of these massacres not to spare any Tutsi. Their plan called for doing whatever was possible to prevent any Tutsi from escaping and, thus, to destroy the whole group. Dr. Alison DesForges stated that numerous Tutsi corpses were systematically thrown into the River Nyabarongo, a tributary of the Nile, as seen, incidentally, in several photographs shown in court throughout the trial. She explained that the intent in that gesture was "to send the Tutsi back to their origin," to make them "return to Abyssinia," in accordance with the notion that the Tutsi are a "foreign" group in Rwanda, believed to have come from the Nilotic regions.

17. Other testimonies heard, especially that of Major–General Dallaire, also show that there was an intention to wipe out the Tutsi group in its entirety, since even newborn babies were not spared. Many testimonies given before the Chamber concur on the fact that it was the Tutsi as members of an ethnic group who were targeted in the massacres. General Dallaire, Doctor Zachariah and, particularly, the Accused himself, unanimously stated so before the Chamber.

18. Numerous witnesses testified before the Chamber that the systematic checking of identity cards, on which the ethnic group was mentioned, made it possible to separate the Hutu from the Tutsi, with the latter being immediately arrested and often killed, sometimes on the spot, at the roadblocks which were erected in Kigali soon after the crash of the plane of President Habyarimana, and thereafter everywhere in the country.

* * *

20. Consequently, the Chamber concludes from all the foregoing that it was, indeed, genocide that was committed in Rwanda in 1994, against the Tutsi as a group. The Chamber is of the opinion that the genocide appears to have been meticulously organized. In fact, Dr. Alison DesForges testifying

before the Chamber on 24 May 1997, talked of "centrally organized and supervised massacres." Some evidence supports this view that the genocide had been planned. First, the existence of lists of Tutsi to be eliminated is corroborated by many testimonies. In this respect, Dr. Zachariah mentioned the case of patients and nurses killed in a hospital because a soldier had a list including their names. * * *

22. Having said that, the Chamber then recalled that the fact that genocide was, indeed, committed in Rwanda in 1994, and more particularly in Taba, cannot influence it in its findings in the present matter. It is the Chamber's responsibility alone to assess the individual criminal responsibility of the Accused, Jean–Paul Akayesu, for the crimes alleged against him, including genocide, for which the Prosecution has to show proof. Despite the indisputable atrociousness of the crimes and the emotions evoked in the international community, the judges have examined the facts adduced in a most dispassionate manner, bearing in mind that the accused is presumed innocent.

23. The Chamber then turned to the question of assessment of evidence. The evidence produced by the parties to the case was mainly testimonial. Yet, human testimony often has the shortcoming of being eminently fragile and fallible. The Chamber considered the credibility of the testimonies, all the more so as three problems were posed: firstly, the fact that most of the witnesses directly experienced the terrible events they were narrating, and that such trauma could have an impact on their testimonies; secondly, the impact of cultural and social factors on communication with the witnesses; and thirdly, the difficulties in interpreting the statements made by the witnesses, most of whom spoke in Kinyarwanda. Despite the difficulties experienced, the Chamber wishes, in this regard, to thank each witness, once again, for his/her deposition at the hearing and commends the strength and courage of survivors, who have narrated the extremely traumatic experiences they had, sometimes rekindling extremely painful emotions. Their testimonies were invaluable to the Tribunal in its search for the truth on the events that happened in Taba commune in 1994.

24. The Chamber then ruled on the admissibility of some evidence. It concluded, in essence, in accordance with the Statute and Rules of Procedure and Evidence, that the Chamber applies the rules which in its view best favour a fair determination of the matter before it and are consonant with the spirit and general principles of law. It noted, in particular that when only one testimony is presented on a fact, it is not bound to apply the adage, *Unus Testis, Nullus Testis*, whereby corroboration of evidence is required if it is to be admitted. The Chamber determined to freely assess the probative value of all relevant evidence. The Chamber had thus determined that in accordance with Rule 89, any relevant evidence having probative value may be admitted into evidence, subject to it being in accordance with the requisites of a fair trial. The Chamber also found that hearsay evidence is not inadmissible per se, but that such evidence should be considered with caution.

25. Having made all these preliminary remarks, the Chamber dealt with the specific facts of the case. It rendered its detailed factual conclusions, by scrupulously analyzing, for each fact, all the related prosecution and defence testimonies, including that of the accused himself. It emerges that for each of

the events described in paragraphs 12 to 23 of the Indictment, the Chamber is convinced beyond a reasonable doubt of the following:

26. The Chamber finds that, as pertains to the acts alleged in paragraph 12, it has been established that, throughout the period covered in the Indictment, Akayesu, in his capacity as *bourgmestre*, was responsible for maintaining law and public order in the commune of Taba and that he had effective authority over the communal police. Moreover, as "leader" of Taba commune, of which he was one of the most prominent figures, the inhabitants respected him and followed his orders. Akayesu himself admitted before the Chamber that he had the power to assemble the population and that they obeyed his instructions. It has also been proven that a very large number of Tutsi were killed in Taba between 7 April and the end of June 1994, while Akayesu was *bourgmestre* of the Commune. Knowing of such killings, he opposed them and attempted to prevent them only until 18 April 1994, * * * after which he not only stopped trying to maintain law and order in his commune, but was also present during the acts of violence and killings, and sometimes even gave orders himself for bodily or mental harm to be caused to certain Tutsi, and endorsed and even ordered the killing of several Tutsi.

27. With regard to the acts alleged in paragraphs 12 (A) and 12 (B) of the Indictment [alleging crimes against humanity], the Prosecutor has shown beyond a reasonable doubt that between 7 April and the end of June 1994, numerous Tutsi who sought refuge at the Taba Bureau communal were frequently beaten by members of the Interahamwe on or near the premises of the Bureau communal. Some of them were killed. Numerous Tutsi women were forced to endure acts of sexual violence, mutilations and rape, often repeatedly, often publicly and often by more than one assailant. Tutsi women were systematically raped, as one female victim testified to by saying that "each time that you met assailants, they raped you." Numerous incidents of such rape and sexual violence against Tutsi women occurred inside or near the Bureau communal. It has been proven that some communal policemen armed with guns and the accused himself were present while some of these rapes and sexual violence were being committed. Furthermore, it is proven that on several occasions, by his presence, his attitude and his utterances, Akayesu encouraged such acts, one particular witness testifying that Akayesu, addressed the Interahamwe who were committing the rapes and said that "never ask me again what a Tutsi woman tastes like." In the opinion of the Chamber, this constitutes tacit encouragement to the rapes that were being committed.

* * *

29. As regards the facts alleged in paragraphs 14 and 15 of the Indictment, it is established that in the early hours of 19 April 1994, Akayesu joined a gathering in Gishyeshye and took this opportunity to address the public; he led the meeting and conducted the proceedings. He then called on the population to unite in order to eliminate what he referred to as the sole enemy: the accomplices of the Inkotanyi; and the population understood that he was thus urging them to kill the Tutsi. Indeed, Akayesu himself knew of the impact of his statements on the crowd and of the fact that his call to fight against the accomplices of the Inkotanyi would be understood as exhortations to kill the Tutsi in general. * * *

[The summary then recounts the evidence on the basis of which the Chamber determined whether the Prosecutor had proved the acts alleged in the indictment.]

37. Having made its factual findings, the Chamber analysed the legal definitions proposed by the Prosecutor for each of the facts. It thus considered the applicable law for each of the three crimes under its jurisdiction, which is all the more important since this is the very first Judgement on the legal definitions of genocide on the one hand, and of serious violations of Additional Protocol II of the Geneva Conventions, on the other. Moreover, the Chamber also had to define certain crimes which constitute offences under its jurisdiction, in particular, rape, because to date, there is no commonly accepted definition of this term in international law.

38. In the opinion of the Chamber, rape is a form of aggression the central elements of which cannot be captured in a mechanical description of objects and body parts. The Chamber also notes the cultural sensitivities involved in public discussion of intimate matters and recalls the painful reluctance and inability of witnesses to disclose graphic anatomical details of the sexual violence they endured. The Chamber defines rape as a physical invasion of a sexual nature, committed on a person under circumstances which are coercive. Sexual violence, including rape, is not limited to physical invasion of the human body and may include acts which do not involve penetration or even physical contact. The Chamber notes in this context that coercive circumstances need not be evidenced by a show of physical force. Threats, intimidation, extortion and other forms of duress which prey on fear or desperation may constitute coercion.

39. The Chamber reviewed Article 6(1) of its Statute, on the individual criminal responsibility of the accused for the three crimes constituting *ratione materiae* of the Chamber. Article 6(1) enunciates the basic principles of individual criminal liability which are probably common to most national criminal jurisdictions. Article 6(3), by contrast, constitutes something of an exception to the principles articulated in Article 6(1), an exception which derives from military law, particularly the principle of the liability of a commander for the acts of his subordinates or "command responsibility". Article 6(3) does not necessarily require the superior to have had knowledge of such to render him criminally liable. The only requirement is that he had reason to know that his subordinates were about to commit or had committed and failed to take the necessary or reasonable measures to prevent such acts or punish the perpetrators thereof.

40. The Chamber then expressed its opinion that with respect to the crimes under its jurisdiction, it should adhere to the concept of notional plurality of offences (cumulative charges) which would render multiple convictions permissible for the same act. As a result, a particular act may constitute both genocide and a crime against humanity.

41. On the crime of **genocide**, the Chamber recalls that the definition given by Article 2 of the Statute is echoed exactly by the Convention for the Prevention and Repression of the Crime of Genocide. The Chamber notes that Rwanda acceded, by legislative decree, to the Convention on Genocide on 12 February 1975. Thus, punishment of the crime of genocide did exist in Rwanda in 1994, at the time of the acts alleged in the Indictment, and the

perpetrator was liable to be brought before the competent courts of Rwanda to answer for this crime.

42. Contrary to popular belief, the crime of genocide does not imply the actual extermination of a group in its entirety, but is understood as such once any one of the acts mentioned in Article 2 of the Statute is committed with the specific intent to destroy "*in whole or in part*" a national, ethnical, racial or religious group. Genocide is distinct from other crimes inasmuch as it embodies a special intent or *dolus specialis*. Special intent of a crime is the specific intention, required as a constitutive element of the crime, which requires that the perpetrator clearly seek to produce the act charged. The special intent in the crime of genocide lies in "the intent to destroy, in whole or in part, a national, ethnical, racial or religious group, as such."

43. Specifically, for any of the acts charged under Article 2(2) of the Statute to be a constitutive element of genocide, the act must have been committed against one or several individuals, because such individual or individuals were members of a specific group, and specifically because they belonged to this group. Thus, the victim is chosen not because of his individual identity, but rather on account of his being a member of a national, ethnical, racial or religious group. The victim of the act is therefore a member of a group, targeted as such; hence, the victim of the crime of genocide is the group itself and not the individual alone.

44. On the issue of determining the offender's specific intent, the Chamber considers that intent is a mental factor which is difficult, even impossible, to determine. This is the reason why, in the absence of a confession from the Accused, his intent can be inferred from a certain number of presumptions of fact. The Chamber considers that it is possible to deduce the genocidal intent inherent in a particular act charged from the general context of the perpetration of other culpable acts systematically directed against that same group, whether these acts were committed by the same offender or by others. Other factors, such as the scale of atrocities committed, their general nature, in a region or a country, or furthermore, the fact of deliberately and systematically targeting victims on account of their membership of a particular group, while excluding the members of other groups, can enable the Chamber to infer the genocidal intent of a particular act.

45. Apart from the crime of genocide, Jean–Paul Akayesu is charged with complicity in genocide and direct and public incitement to commit genocide.

46. In the opinion of the Chamber, an Accused is **an accomplice in genocide** if he knowingly aided and abetted or provoked a person or persons to commit genocide, knowing that this person or persons were committing genocide, even if the Accused himself lacked the specific intent of destroying in whole or in part, the national, ethnical, racial or religious group, as such.

47. Regarding the crime of **direct and public incitement to commit genocide**, the Chamber defines it mainly on the basis of Article 91 of the Rwandan Penal Code, as directly provoking another to commit genocide, either through speeches, shouting or threats uttered in public places or at public gatherings, or through the sale or dissemination, offer for sale or display of written material or printed matter in public places or at public gatherings or through the public display of placards or posters, or by any

other means of audiovisual communication. The moral element of this crime lies in the intent to directly encourage or provoke another to commit genocide. It presupposes the desire of the guilty to create, by his actions, within the person or persons whom he is addressing, the state of mind which is appropriate to the commission of a crime. In other words, the person who is inciting to commit genocide must have the specific intent of genocide: that of destroying in whole or in part, a national, ethnical, racial or religious group, as such. The Chamber believes that incitement is a formal offence, for which the mere method used is culpable. In other words, the offence is considered to have been completed once the incitement has taken place and * * * is direct and public, whether or not it was successful.

48. The second crime which comes within the jurisdiction of the Tribunal and of which Jean–Paul Akayesu is charged is that of crimes against humanity. On the law applicable to this crime, the Chamber reviewed the case law on this crime, from the judgements rendered by the Nuremberg and Tokyo Tribunals to more recent cases, including the Touvier and Papon cases in France notably, and the Eichmann trial in Israel. It indicated the circumstances under which the charge of crimes against humanity would be leveled, as provided for by Article 3 of the Statute, under which the act must be committed as part of a widespread or systematic attack directed against a civilian population on discriminatory grounds.

49. The third crime on which the Chamber rendered its conclusions is that for which it has competence pursuant to article 4 of the Statute, which provides that the Tribunal is empowered to prosecute persons committing or ordering to be committed serious violations of Article 3 common to the Geneva Conventions of 12 August 1949 for the protection of War Victims, and of the Additional Protocol II thereto of June 8 1977. The said Article 3 common to the Geneva Conventions extends a minimum threshold of humanitarian protection as well to all persons affected by a non-international conflict, a protection which was further developed and enhanced in the 1977 Additional Protocol II. The Chamber decided to analyse separately, the respective conditions of applicability of Article 3 Common to the Geneva Conventions and the Additional Protocol II thereto. It then analysed the conflict which took place in Rwanda in 1994 in the light of those conditions and concluded that each of the two legal instruments was applicable in this case. Furthermore, the Chamber is of the opinion that all the norms set forth under article 4 of its Statute constitute a part of customary International Law. It finally recalled that the violation of the norms defined in article 4 of the Statute may, in principle, commit criminal responsibility of civilians and that the Accused belongs to the category of individuals who could be held responsible for serious infringement of international humanitarian law, particularly for serious violations of article 3 common to the Geneva Conventions and the Additional Protocol II thereto.

50. On the basis of the factual findings just shown, the Chamber delivered the following legal findings.

51. With regard to count one on genocide, the Chamber having regard, particularly, to the acts described in paragraphs 12(A) and 12(B) of the Indictment, that is, rape and sexual violence, the Chamber wishes to underscore the fact that in its opinion, they constitute genocide in the same way as

any other act as long as they were committed with the specific intent to destroy, in whole or in part, a particular group, targeted as such. Indeed, rape and sexual violence certainly constitute infliction of serious bodily and mental harm on the victims * * * and are even, according to the Chamber, one of the worst ways of inflicting harm on the victim as he or she suffers both bodily and mental harm. In light of all the evidence before it, the Chamber is satisfied that the acts of rape and sexual violence described above were committed solely against Tutsi women, many of whom were subjected to the worst public humiliation, mutilated, and raped several times, often in public, in the Bureau Communal premises or in other public places, and often by more than one assailant. These rapes resulted in physical and psychological destruction of Tutsi women, their families and their communities. Sexual violence was an integral part of the process of destruction, specifically targeting Tutsi women and specifically contributing to their destruction and to the destruction of the Tutsi group as a whole.

52. The rape of Tutsi women was systematic and was perpetrated against all Tutsi women and solely against them. A Tutsi woman, married to a Hutu, testified before the Chamber that she was not raped because her ethnic background was unknown. As part of the propaganda campaign geared to mobilizing the Hutu against the Tutsi, the Tutsi women were presented as sexual objects. Indeed, the Chamber was told, for an example, that before being raped and killed, Alexia, who was the wife of the Professor, Ntereye, and her two nieces, were forced by the Interahamwe to undress and ordered to run and do exercises "in order to display the thighs of Tutsi women." The Interahamwe who raped Alexia said, as he threw her on the ground and got on top of her, "let us now see what the vagina of a Tutsi woman tastes like." As stated above, Akayesu himself, speaking to the Interahamwe who were committing the rapes, said to them: "don't ever ask again what a Tutsi woman tastes like."

53. On the basis of the substantial testimonies brought before it, the Chamber finds that in most cases, the rapes of Tutsi women in Taba, were accompanied with the intent to kill those women. Many rapes were perpetrated near mass graves where the women were taken to be killed. A victim testified that Tutsi women caught could be taken away by peasants and men with the promise that they would be collected later to be executed. Following an act of gang rape, a witness heard Akayesu say: "tomorrow they will be killed" and they were actually killed. In this respect, it appears clearly to the Chamber that the acts of rape and sexual violence, as other acts of serious bodily and mental harm committed against the Tutsi, reflected the determination to make Tutsi women suffer and to mutilate them even before killing them, the intent being to destroy the Tutsi group while inflicting acute suffering on its members in the process.

54. The Chamber has already established that genocide was committed against the Tutsi group in Rwanda in 1994, throughout the period covering the events alleged in the Indictment. Owing to the very high number of atrocities committed against the Tutsi, their widespread nature not only in the commune of Taba, but also throughout Rwanda, and to the fact that the victims were systematically and deliberately selected because they belonged to the Tutsi group, with persons belonging to other groups being excluded, the Chamber is also able to infer, beyond reasonable doubt, the genocidal intent of

the accused in the commission of the above-mentioned crimes; to the extent that the actions and words of Akayesu during the period of the facts alleged in the Indictment, the Chamber is convinced beyond reasonable doubt, on the basis of evidence adduced before it during the hearing, that he repeatedly made statements more or less explicitly calling for the commission of genocide. Yet, according to the Chamber, he who incites another to commit genocide must have the specific intent to commit genocide: that of destroying in whole or in part, a national, ethnical, racial, or religious group, as such.

55. In conclusion, regarding Count One on genocide, the Chamber is satisfied beyond reasonable doubt that these various acts were committed by Akayesu with the specific intent to destroy the Tutsi group, as such. Consequently, the Chamber is of the opinion that the acts alleged in paragraphs 12, 12A, 12B, 16, 18, 19, 20, 22 and 23 of the Indictment, constitute the crimes of killing members of the Tutsi group and causing serious bodily and mental harm to members of the Tutsi group. Furthermore, the Chamber is satisfied beyond reasonable doubt that in committing the various acts alleged, Akayesu had the specific intent of destroying the Tutsi group as such.

56. Regarding Count Two, on the crime of complicity in genocide, the Chamber indicated supra that, in its opinion, the crime of genocide and that of complicity in genocide were two distinct crimes, and that the same person could certainly not be both the principal perpetrator of, and accomplice to, the same offence. Given that genocide and complicity in genocide are mutually exclusive by definition, the accused cannot obviously be found guilty of both these crimes for the same act. However, since the Prosecutor has charged the accused with both genocide and complicity in genocide for each of the alleged acts, the Chamber deems it necessary, in the instant case, to rule on Counts 1 and 2 simultaneously, so as to determine, as far as each proven fact is concerned, whether it constituted genocide or complicity in genocide.

[The summary then reviews the other counts of the indictment and explains the basis for finding Akayesu also guilty of crimes against humanity and direct and public incitement to commit genocide.]

63. With regard to Counts 13 and 14, relating to the acts described in paragraphs 12A and 12B of the indictment and which it considers proven, the Chamber is also satisfied beyond a reasonable doubt that they constitute acts of rape and other inhumane acts, committed as part of a widespread and systematic attack against a civilian population on ethnic grounds and therefore constitute a crime against humanity. Consequently, the Chamber finds the Accused individually criminally liable for the said acts described in counts 13 and 14 and for having through his presence tacitly abetted their commission.

64. With respect to Counts 6, 8, 10, 12 and 15, Akayesu is charged with violations of Common Article 3 of the Geneva Conventions of 1949 in counts 6, 8, 10 and 12, and with violations of Common Article 3 of the Geneva Conventions and of Additional Protocol II thereto of 1977 under count 15. The Chamber finds that it has been established beyond reasonable doubt that there was an armed conflict not of an international character between the Government of Rwanda and the RPF [Rwandan Patriotic Front] at the time of the facts alleged in the Indictment, and that the said conflict was well within the provisions of Common Article 3 and of the Additional Protocol II.

The Chamber however finds that the Prosecution has failed to show beyond reasonable doubt that Akayesu was a member of the armed forces and that he was duly mandated and expected, in his capacity as a public official or agent or person otherwise vested with public authority or a de facto representative of the Government, to support and carry out the war effort.

* * *

Notes

1. Akayesu was sentenced to imprisonment for life.

2. In January 2000, Alfred Musema, a former tea factory manager, was convicted by the I.C.T.R. of genocide and crimes against humanity, including extermination and rape. Musema was found to have led Hutu killers into the factory where Tutsi workers had taken refuge, raped a Tutsi girl and encouraged four others to rape her as well. This was the I.C.T.R.'s seventh conviction. Musema was sentenced to life. See Prosecutor v. Musema, Case No. ICTR–96–13–T (Judgment, Jan. 27, 2000). As of 2000, the Tribunal had indicted 45 individuals, including ten former ministers of the Hutu government; suspects in custody in Arusha included the most prominent of the alleged organizers of the genocide, many of whom were arrested in third countries and extradited to the Tribunal. Musema had been arrested in Switzerland. The trial of a second Rwandan mayor, Ignace Bagilishema, former mayor of Mabanza, who was arrested in South Africa and extradited to the I.C.T.R., was in progress in 2000. He was charged with genocide, crimes against humanity and war crimes.

3. In February 1999, two former Rwandan ministers, Eliezer Niyitegeka, Information Minister, and Casimir Bizimungu, Minister of Health, were arrested in Kenya and transferred into the custody of the I.C.T.R. in Arusha. On July 23, 1999, Kenyan authorities arrested Georges Ruggiu, a Belgian journalist whose broadcasts had urged Hutus to kill Tutsis and Hutu moderates. Ruggiu, the first non-Rwandan to be indicted by the I.C.T.R., pleaded guilty to the crime of direct and public incitement to commit genocide and a crime against humanity (persecution). He was sentenced in June 2000 to two concurrent twelve-year sentences. See Prosecutor v. Ruggiu, Case No. ICTR–97–32–1, Judgement and Sentence (June 1, 2000), 39 I.L.M. 1338 (2000).

In November 1999, the I.C.T.R. decided to release a genocide suspect, Jean–Bosco Barayagwiza, due to lapse of time (one and one-half years) between arrest and charging. Initially, the Tribunal held that the delay had infringed Barayagwiza's human rights. The Prosecutor called for reconsideration of the ruling, and on March 31, 2000, the Appeals Chamber revised its position. See Barayagwiza v. Prosecutor, Case No. ICTR–97–19–AR72 (Mar. 31, 2000).

4. A Rwandan (Hutu) clergyman, Elizaphan Ntakirutimana, who had been indicted by the I.C.T.R., was arrested in 1996 in Texas by federal marshals. A 1996 agreement between the United States and the U.N. Tribunals, incorporated in legislation by Congress, provides for rendition by the United States of indicted individuals to the Tribunal issuing the indictment. Ntakirutimana is alleged to have urged men, women and children to take refuge in a church and hospital to escape the ethnic slaughter in progress. He then allegedly returned with a band of Rwandan soldiers who murdered hundreds of people who had sought sanctuary at his urging. N.Y. Times, Dec. 12, 1997, p. 1, col. 1. A divided Court of Appeals

affirmed the denial of Ntakirutimana's petition for a writ of habeas corpus and cleared the way for his rendition. Ntakirutimana v. Reno, 184 F.3d 419 (5th Cir.1999), cert. denied, 528 U.S. 1135, 120 S.Ct. 977, 145 L.Ed.2d 929 (2000). The Secretary of State approved the rendition in March 2000, marking the first instance of transfer of an indicted criminal by the United States to an international criminal tribunal. Ntakirutimana has pleaded not guilty before the I.C.T.R.

5. In August 1999, a woman, Pauline Nyiramasuhuko, a former Rwandan Minister of Family and Women's Affairs, was indicted by the I.C.T.R. and charged with genocide and with rape as a crime against humanity. The rape charge is based on allegations that she knew her subordinates were raping Tutsi women and failed to take reasonable and necessary measures to stop or punish them. It was the first time a woman has been indicted by an international tribunal and charged with rape in violation of international humanitarian law.

In August 1999, two additional former Rwandan cabinet ministers, Prosper Mugiraneza, Minister of Civil Service and Justin Mugenzi, Minister for Commerce, pleaded not guilty to charges of genocide. A third, Jerome Bicamumpaka, had a not guilty plea entered for him by the Court.

6. Can trials in an international tribunal such as the one for Rwanda contribute in a meaningful way to reconciliation in a post-conflict situation? For differing perspectives, compare the Alvarez and Drumbl articles cited in Note 3 on p. 1354, and Akhavan, Justice and Reconciliation in the Great Lakes Region of Africa: The Contribution of the International Criminal Tribunal for Rwanda, 7 Duke J. Comp. & Int'l L. 325 (1997); Schabas, Justice, Democracy and Impunity in Post–Genocide Rwanda: Searching for Solutions to Impossible Problems, 7 Crim. L.F. 523 (1996).

7. For detailed treatment of the I.C.T.R., see Virginia Morris & Michael P. Scharf, The International Criminal Tribunal for Rwanda (1998).

8. Following the experiences of the I.C.T.Y. and I.C.T.R., international tribunals have been proposed for several other ongoing or post-conflict situations, including Cambodia, East Timor, and Sierra Leone. See generally Ratner & Abrams, Accountability for Human Rights Atrocities in International Law: Beyond the Nuremberg Legacy (1997) (assessment of various accountability mechanisms, with particular reference to Khmer Rouge atrocities in Cambodia). On plans for Sierra Leone, see S.C. Res. 1315 (2000); Report of the Secretary–General on the Establishment of a Special Court for Sierra Leone, U.N. Doc. S/2000/915 (2000). Some of these proposals have included alternatives for combining national and international justice, e.g. by constituting a criminal tribunal with a mix of national and international judges. As of 2000, the proposals were still under negotiation or discussion with the respective governments (and/or authorities in control) in the territories in question.

The creation of a International Criminal Court in the future (see next section) could obviate the need for protracted negotiations over the terms of reference of new ad hoc tribunals. However, since the I.C.C. Statute (which is not in force as of 2000) will cover only crimes committed after the Statute enters into force, demands for ad hoc bodies could continue for some years to come.

SECTION 7. ROME STATUTE OF THE INTERNATIONAL CRIMINAL COURT

A. INTRODUCTION

U.N. efforts to prepare a draft statute for a permanent international criminal court have been reviewed above (pp. 410, 1327). These efforts approached culmination with the convening of an international conference of plenipotentiaries in Rome on June 15, 1998. As anticipated, negotiations at Rome on a number of basic issues were difficult and intense. In the end, enough compromises were devised to produce approval of the Rome Statute of the International Criminal Court on July 17, 1998 by a vote of 120 states in favor and seven opposed. The United States voted against approval, as did China and Israel which explained reasons for their opposition, and four other states that did not declare themselves publicly. On the Rome conference and its outcome, see generally Roy S. Lee (ed.), The International Criminal Court: The Making of the Rome Statute: Issues, Negotiations, Results (1999) (on final vote, see p. 26 n. 48); Bartram S. Brown, The Statute of the ICC: Past, Present, Future, in Sarah B. Sewall & Carl Kaysen (eds.), The United States and the International Criminal Court 61–84 (2000) (on final vote, see p. 81 n. 19); see also Philippe Kirsch & John T. Holmes, The Rome Conference on an International Criminal Court: The Negotiating Process, 93 A.J.I.L. 2 (1999); Mahnoush Arsanjani, The Rome Statute of the International Criminal Court, 93 A.J.I.L. 22 (1999).

Excerpts from the Rome Statute are set forth in the Documents Supplement. The Statute remained open for signature until December 31, 2000. As of that date, it had been signed by 139 states and had been ratified by 27 states. It will come into effect upon ratification by 60 states. The United States and Israel were among the states that signed the Statute on the last day; but President Clinton stated in connection with the U.S. signature that he would not recommend going forward with ratification for the time being.

President Clinton had early indicated support, in principle, for a permanent international criminal court. E.g., Remarks at University of Connecticut, 1995 Pub. Papers 1597. The Department of Defense, however, mounted a vigorous campaign in opposition which was based primarily on the concern that U.S. military personnel serving abroad might be subjected to politicized prosecution for alleged war crimes over the objection of the United States.

In receiving an honorary doctorate of law from the University of Witwatersrand, Johannesburg, South Africa, in 1998 U.N. Secretary–General Kofi Annan commented, in part, as follows on the Rome Statute:

> The work of * * * [the U.N.] Tribunals [for the former Yugoslavia and Rwanda], though still incomplete, has been a milestone in the age-long struggle to end the "culture of impunity"; to prove that, when crimes occur of such magnitude that they are rightly dubbed "crimes against humanity," humanity is not without recourse.
>
> Tomorrow, in Arusha, a historic landmark will be passed when the Rwanda Tribunal announces the first judgment ever given by an international court in a case of genocide.

Moreover, the establishment of those two Tribunals was an essential step on the road to Rome. In Rome, six weeks ago, it was my privilege to hand over to the Italian Government the Rome Statute of the International Criminal Court.

In Rome, for five weeks before that, diplomats and lawyers from 160 States had been working day and night to draft that Statute. * * * It was a prodigious achievement.

Divergent and sometimes diametrically opposed national criminal laws and procedures had to be reconciled. Small States had to be reassured that the Statute would not give more powerful ones a pretext to override their sovereignty. Others had to be convinced that the pursuit of justice would not interfere with the vital work of making peace.

That last point, I know, was a concern for many of you here in South Africa.

Your recent history has been marked by some appalling crimes, which have been painfully chronicled and exposed in the hearings of your Truth and Reconciliation Commission. You have confronted the legacy of the past by offering amnesty, even to the worst offenders, provided they were willing to make a full confession under the eyes of the whole nation, in the presence of the surviving victims.

The world has followed those dramatic hearings, with wonder and on the whole with admiration. But now some people have tried to use them as an argument against the International Criminal Court. They have suggested that in the future such an exemplary process of national reconciliation might be torpedoed, since the Statute empowers the Court to intervene in cases where a State is "unwilling or unable" to exercise its national jurisdiction.

Ladies and Gentlemen, that argument is a travesty.

The purpose of that clause in the Statute is to ensure that mass murderers and other arch-criminals cannot shelter behind a State run by themselves or their cronies, or take advantage of a general breakdown of law and order. No one should imagine that it would apply to a case like South Africa's, where the regime and the conflict which caused the crimes have come to an end, and the victims have inherited power. It is inconceivable that, in such a case, the Court would seek to substitute its judgment for that of a whole nation which is seeking the best way to put a traumatic past behind it and build a better future.

Some people seem to imagine that this Court will be composed of frivolous or malicious people, roaming the world in search of opportunities to undermine a peace process here, or prosecute a peacekeeper there.

Nothing could be more improbable.

The judges and prosecutors, according to the Statute, will be persons of high moral character, with extensive competence and experience either in criminal law and procedure, or in relevant areas of international law.

They will be chosen by secret ballot in an Assembly of all States that have signed and ratified the Statute, and at least 60 States must have done so before the Court can come into existence.

So if any States are worried that the judges or prosecutors of this Court may be inclined to malice, or frivolity, or bias, by far their best remedy is to sign and ratify the Statute, and to ensure that as many like-minded States as possible do the same.

South Africa, I am delighted to say, was one of the first States to grasp this vital point. It was one of 39 States that signed the Statute on the very first day. That fact provides the most convincing answer to those who think the Court would somehow interfere with a South African-style process of Truth and Reconciliation.

I was equally delighted, though not surprised, to find Richard Goldstone [a South African judge and former Prosecutor for the U.N. Tribunals] in the forefront of the Court's defenders after the Statute was signed. In a characteristically trenchant essay, published in Time magazine, he recalled the vital role of the United States in setting up the Nuremberg tribunal after World War Two, and in supporting the two existing Tribunals for the former Yugoslavia and Rwanda. He issued a call to the United States to join its closest allies in supporting the new International Court, and so to "resume its position of leadership on behalf of international justice."

As he rightly said, "the United States does have an understandable and legitimate interest in ensuring that such a court would not unfairly subject American citizens to politicized complaints." But he was equally right when he went on to say that "the careful procedures and demanding qualifications for the selection of the prosecutor and judges * * * will serve as an effective check against irresponsible behaviour."

* * *

U.N. Doc. SG/SM/6686 (Sept. 1, 1998).

B. STRUCTURE AND JURISDICTION OF THE INTERNATIONAL CRIMINAL COURT

Under Article 1 of the Rome Statute, the International Criminal Court (I.C.C.) will be a permanent institution vested with competence to try individuals indicted for the most serious crimes of international concern specified in Article 5. Article 1 also provides that the Court "shall be complementary to national criminal jurisdictions." The I.C.C. will be established in The Hague in the Netherlands and will have a relationship with the United Nations to be established by agreement approved by the Assembly of States Parties to the Statute.

Article 5 of the Statute provides as follows:

1. The jurisdiction of the Court shall be limited to the most serious crimes of concern to the international community as a whole. The Court has jurisdiction in accordance with this Statute with respect to the following crimes:

   (a) The crime of genocide;

   (b) Crimes against humanity;

   (c) War crimes;

   (d) The crime of aggression.

2. The Court shall exercise jurisdiction over the crime of aggression once a provision is adopted in accordance with articles 121 and 123 defining the crime and setting out the conditions under which the Court shall exercise jurisdiction with respect to this crime. Such a provision shall be consistent with the relevant provisions of the Charter of the United Nations.

Note

As implied by Article 5(2), the I.C.C. will have jurisdiction to try individuals for the crime of aggression only if the state parties are able to agree on a definition of the crime and on the conditions that would have to be fulfilled before the I.C.C. could exercise jurisdiction over it and then to adopt such a provision under the articles on amendment of the Statute. A key issue will be the role of the U.N. Security Council. For example, would a finding by the U.N. Security Council that an act of aggression has been committed be part of the definition of the crime or be a condition precedent to an exercise of the Court's jurisdiction to indict and try an individual for the crime?

As of 2000, the I.C.C.'s Preparatory Commission had been unable to finalize a proposed definition for this purpose. Compare the 1974 General Assembly Resolution on the Definition of Aggression (G.A. Res. 3314), excerpted and discussed in Chapter 12 at p. 943. In what respects might that definition be unsuitable for application in the context of individual criminal responsibility? What should be the significance of Security Council action (or inaction) in a potential criminal matter?

C. CRIMES WITHIN THE JURISDICTION OF THE COURT

ROME STATUTE OF THE INTERNATIONAL CRIMINAL COURT

Adopted by the U.N. Diplomatic Conference of Plenipotentiaries on the Establishment of an International Criminal Court. A/CONF.183/9, July 17, 1998.

Article 6
Genocide

For the purpose of this Statute, "genocide" means any of the following acts committed with intent to destroy, in whole or in part, a national, ethnical, racial or religious group, as such:

(a) Killing members of the group;

(b) Causing serious bodily or mental harm to members of the group;

(c) Deliberately inflicting on the group conditions of life calculated to bring about its physical destruction in whole or in part;

(d) Imposing measures intended to prevent births within the group;

(e) Forcibly transferring children of the group to another group.

Article 7
Crimes against humanity

1. For the purpose of this Statute, "crime against humanity" means any of the following acts when committed as part of a widespread or systematic attack directed against any civilian population, with knowledge of the attack:

(a) Murder;

(b) Extermination;

(c) Enslavement;

(d) Deportation or forcible transfer of population;

(e) Imprisonment or other severe deprivation of physical liberty in violation of fundamental rules of international law;

(f) Torture;

(g) Rape, sexual slavery, enforced prostitution, forced pregnancy, enforced sterilization, or any other form of sexual violence of comparable gravity;

(h) Persecution against any identifiable group or collectivity on political, racial, national, ethnic, cultural, religious, gender as defined in paragraph 3, or other grounds that are universally recognized as impermissible under international law, in connection with any act referred to in this paragraph or any crime within the jurisdiction of the Court;

(i) Enforced disappearance of persons;

(j) The crime of apartheid;

(k) Other inhumane acts of a similar character intentionally causing great suffering, or serious injury to body or to mental or physical health.

[Paragraphs 2 and 3, which contain definitions of many of the key terms used in Article 7(1), are not reprinted here; they are contained in the Documents Supplement.]

Article 8
War crimes

[Omitted portions set forth in the Documents Supplement]

1. The Court shall have jurisdiction in respect of war crimes in particular when committed as a part of a plan or policy or as part of a large-scale commission of such crimes.

2. For the purpose of this Statute, "war crimes" means:

(a) Grave breaches of the Geneva Conventions of 12 August 1949, namely, any of the following acts against persons or property protected under the provisions of the relevant Geneva Convention:

(i) Willful killing;

(ii) Torture or inhuman treatment, including biological experiments;

(iii) Willfully causing great suffering, or serious injury to body or health;

(iv) Extensive destruction and appropriation of property, not justified by military necessity and carried out unlawfully and wantonly;

(v) Compelling a prisoner of war or other protected person to serve in the forces of a hostile Power;

(vi) Willfully depriving a prisoner of war or other protected person of the rights of fair and regular trial;

(vii) Unlawful deportation or transfer or unlawful confinement;

(viii) Taking of hostages.

(b) Other serious violations of the laws and customs applicable in international armed conflict, within the established framework of international law, namely, any of the following acts:

[Subparagraphs (i) through (xxvi) list the covered crimes.]

(c) In the case of an armed conflict not of an international character, serious violations of article 3 common to the four Geneva Conventions of 12 August 1949, namely, any of the following acts committed against persons taking no active part in the hostilities, including members of armed forces who have laid down their arms and those placed hors de combat by sickness, wounds, detention or any other cause:

(i) Violence to life and person, in particular murder of all kinds, mutilation, cruel treatment and torture;

(ii) Committing outrages upon personal dignity, in particular humiliating and degrading treatment;

(iii) Taking of hostages;

(iv) The passing of sentences and the carrying out of executions without previous judgment pronounced by a regularly constituted court, affording all judicial guarantees which are generally recognized as indispensable.

(d) Paragraph 2(c) applies to armed conflicts not of an international character and thus does not apply to situations of internal disturbances and tensions, such as riots, isolated and sporadic acts of violence or other acts of a similar nature.

(e) Other serious violations of the laws and customs applicable in armed conflicts not of an international character, within the established framework of international law, namely, any of the following acts:

[subparagraphs (i) through (xii) list the covered crimes.]

(f) Paragraph 2(e) applies to armed conflicts not of an international character and thus does not apply to situations of internal disturbances and tensions, such as riots, isolated and sporadic acts of violence or other acts of a similar nature. It applies to armed conflicts that take place in the territory of a State when there is protracted armed conflict between governmental authorities and organized armed groups or between such groups.

3. Nothing in paragraphs 2(c) and (d) shall affect the responsibility of a Government to maintain or re-establish law and order in the State or to defend the unity and territorial integrity of the State, by all legitimate means.

Note

In order to clarify the definitions of the crimes encompassed in Articles 6, 7 and 8, Article 9(1) provides that Elements of Crimes shall be prepared to assist the Court in interpreting those crimes. Article 9(2) goes on to establish the following procedures:

Amendments to the Elements of Crimes may be proposed by:

(a) Any State Party;

(b) The judges acting by an absolute majority;

(c) The Prosecutor.

Such amendments, to be drafted at meetings of the Preparatory Commission, will become effective upon adoption by a two-thirds majority of the members of the Assembly of States Parties.

The Elements of Crimes were finalized in June 2000 and adopted at the fifth session of the I.C.C.'s Preparatory Commission on June 30, 2000. See U.N. Doc. PCNICC/2000/INF/3/Add.1. The Elements of Crimes deal with such matters as (for example) the perpetrator's knowledge and intent in relation to the acts in question; the connection of the perpetrator's actions to the actions of others (e.g., to interpret the term "widespread or systematic attack directed against any civilian population" in Article 7's definition of crimes against humanity); and the meaning of terms such as "forcibly" (which is not restricted to physical force, but may include threat of force or coercion). The elements of the crime of rape and other sexual crimes are defined in detail, drawing on the jurisprudence of the I.C.T.Y. and I.C.T.R. in cases such as *Akayesu* discussed above.

D. CONDITIONS TO THE EXERCISE OF JURISDICTION

ROME STATUTE OF THE INTERNATIONAL CRIMINAL COURT

Adopted by the U.N. Diplomatic Conference of Plenipotentiaries on the Establishment of an International Criminal Court. A/CONF.183/9, July 17, 1998.

Article 12
Preconditions to the exercise of jurisdiction

1. A State which becomes a Party to this Statute thereby accepts the jurisdiction of the Court with respect to the crimes referred to in article 5.

2. In the case of article 13, paragraph (a) or (c), the Court may exercise its jurisdiction if one or more of the following States are Parties to this Statute or have accepted the jurisdiction of the Court in accordance with paragraph 3:

(a) The State on the territory of which the conduct in question occurred or, if the crime was committed on board a vessel or aircraft, the State of registration of that vessel or aircraft;

(b) The State of which the person accused of the crime is a national.

3. If the acceptance of a State which is not a Party to this Statute is required under paragraph 2, that State may, by declaration lodged with the Registrar, accept the exercise of jurisdiction by the Court with respect to the crime in question. * * *

Article 13
Exercise of jurisdiction

The Court may exercise its jurisdiction with respect to a crime referred to in article 5 * * * if:

(a) A situation in which one or more of such crimes appears to have been committed is referred to the Prosecutor by a State Party in accordance with article 14;

(b) A situation in which one or more of such crimes appears to have been committed is referred to the Prosecutor by the Security Council acting under Chapter VII of the Charter of the United Nations; or

(c) The Prosecutor has initiated an investigation in respect of such a crime in accordance with article 15.

Article 14
Referral of a situation by a State Party

1. A State Party may refer to the Prosecutor a situation in which one or more crimes within the jurisdiction of the Court appear to have been committed requesting the Prosecutor to investigate the situation for the purpose of determining whether one or more specific persons should be charged with the commission of such crimes.

2. As far as possible, a referral shall specify the relevant circumstances and be accompanied by such supporting documentation as is available to the State referring the situation.

Article 15
Prosecutor

1. The Prosecutor may initiate investigations *proprio motu* on the basis of information on crimes within the jurisdiction of the Court.

2. The Prosecutor shall analyze the seriousness of the information received. For this purpose, he or she may seek additional information from States, organs of the United Nations, intergovernmental or non-governmental organizations, or other reliable sources that he or she deems appropriate, and may receive written or oral testimony at the seat of the Court.

3. If the Prosecutor concludes that there is a reasonable basis to proceed with an investigation, he or she shall submit to the Pre–Trial Chamber a request for authorization of an investigation, together with any supporting material collected. Victims may make representations to the Pre–Trial Chamber, in accordance with the Rules of Procedure and Evidence.

4. If the Pre–Trial Chamber, upon examination of the request and the supporting material, considers that there is a reasonable basis to proceed with an investigation, and that the case appears to fall within the jurisdiction of the Court, it shall authorize the commencement of the investigation, without prejudice to subsequent determinations by the Court with regard to the jurisdiction and admissibility of a case.

5. The refusal of the Pre–Trial Chamber to authorize the investigation shall not preclude the presentation of a subsequent request by the Prosecutor based on new facts or evidence regarding the same situation.

6. If, after the preliminary examination referred to in paragraphs 1 and 2, the Prosecutor concludes that the information provided does not constitute a reasonable basis for an investigation, he or she shall inform those who

provided the information. This shall not preclude the Prosecutor from considering further information submitted to him or her regarding the same situation in the light of new facts or evidence.

Article 16
Deferral of investigation or prosecution

No investigation or prosecution may be commenced or proceeded with under this Statute for a period of 12 months after the Security Council, in a resolution adopted under Chapter VII of the Charter of the United Nations, has requested the Court to that effect; that request may be renewed by the Council under the same conditions.

Article 17
Issues of Admissibility

1. Having regard to paragraph 10 of the Preamble and article 1, the Court shall determine that a case is inadmissible where:

(a) The case is being investigated or prosecuted by a State which has jurisdiction over it, unless the State is unwilling or unable genuinely to carry out the investigation or prosecution;

(b) The case has been investigated by a State which has jurisdiction over it and the State has decided not to prosecute the person concerned, unless the decision resulted from the unwillingness or inability of the State genuinely to prosecute;

(c) The person concerned has already been tried for conduct which is the subject of the complaint, and a trial by the Court is not permitted under article 20, paragraph 3;

(d) The case is not of sufficient gravity to justify further action by the Court.

2. In order to determine unwillingness in a particular case, the Court shall consider, having regard to the principles of due process recognized by international law, whether one or more of the following exist, as applicable:

(a) The proceedings were or are being undertaken or the national decision was made for the purpose of shielding the person concerned from criminal responsibility for crimes within the jurisdiction of the Court referred to in article 5;

(b) There has been an unjustified delay in the proceedings which in the circumstances is inconsistent with an intent to bring the person concerned to justice;

(c) The proceedings were not or are not being conducted independently or impartially, and they were or are being conducted in a manner which, in the circumstances, is inconsistent with an intent to bring the person concerned to justice.

3. In order to determine inability in a particular case, the Court shall consider whether, due to a total or substantial collapse or unavailability of its national judicial system, the State is unable to obtain the accused or the necessary evidence and testimony or otherwise unable to carry out its proceedings.

Article 18
Preliminary Rulings Regarding Admissibility

1. When a situation has been referred to the Court pursuant to article 13(a) and the Prosecutor has determined that there would be a reasonable basis to commence an investigation, or the Prosecutor initiates an investigation pursuant to articles 13(c) and 15, the Prosecutor shall notify all States Parties and those States which, taking into account the information available, would normally exercise jurisdiction over the crimes concerned. * * *

2. Within one month of receipt of that notice, a State may inform the Court that it is investigating or has investigated its nationals or others within its jurisdiction with respect to criminal acts which may constitute crimes referred to in article 5 and which relate to the information provided in the notification to States. At the request of that State, the Prosecutor shall defer to the State's investigation of those persons unless the Pre–Trial Chamber, on the application of the Prosecutor, decides to authorize the investigation.

3. The Prosecutor's deferral to a State's investigation shall be open to review by the Prosecutor six months after the date of deferral or at any time when there has been a significant change of circumstances based on the State's unwillingness or inability genuinely to carry out the investigation.

4. The State concerned or the Prosecutor may appeal to the Appeals Chamber against a ruling of the Pre–Trial Chamber, in accordance with article 82, paragraph 2. The appeal may be heard on an expedited basis.

* * *

Article 124
Transitional Provision

Notwithstanding article 12, paragraph 1, a State, on becoming a party to this Statute, may declare that, for a period of seven years after the entry into force of this Statute for the State concerned, it does not accept the jurisdiction of the Court with respect to the category of crimes referred to in article 8 [war crimes] when a crime is alleged to have been committed by its nationals or on its territory. A declaration under this article may be withdrawn at any time. The provisions of this article shall be reviewed at the Review Conference convened in accordance with article 123, paragraph 1 [seven years after entry into force of the Statute].

E. THE UNITED STATES' POSITION

DAVID J. SCHEFFER, U.S. AMBASSADOR–AT–LARGE FOR WAR CRIMES ISSUES, TESTIMONY BEFORE THE SUBCOMMITTEE ON INTERNATIONAL OPERATIONS OF THE U.S. SENATE FOREIGN RELATIONS COMMITTEE

105th Congress, 2d Session, July 23, 1998, at 10, 13–15.

Mr. Chairman, the U.S. delegation certainly reduced exposure to unwarranted prosecutions by the international court through our successful efforts to build into the treaty a range of safeguards that will benefit not only us but also our friends and allies. But serious risks remain because of the document's provisions on jurisdiction.

Our position is clear: Official actions of a non-party state should not be subject to the court's jurisdiction if that country does not join the treaty, except by means of Security Council action under the U.N. Charter. Otherwise, the ratification would be meaningless for governments. In fact, under such a theory, two governments could join together to create a criminal court and purport to extend its jurisdiction over everyone, everywhere in the world. There will necessarily be cases where the international court cannot and should not have jurisdiction unless the Security Council decides otherwise. The United States has long supported the right of the Security Council to refer situations to the court with mandatory effect, meaning that any rogue state could not deny the court's jurisdiction under any circumstances. We believe this is the only way, under international law and the U.N. Charter, to impose the court's jurisdiction on a non-party state. In fact, the treaty reaffirms this Security Council referral power. Again, the governments that collectively adopt this treaty accept that this power would be available to assert jurisdiction over rogue states.

Second, as a matter of policy, the United States took the position in these negotiations that states should have the opportunity to assess the effectiveness and impartiality of the court before considering whether to accept its jurisdiction. At the same time, we recognized the ideal of broad ICC jurisdiction. Thus, we were prepared to accept a treaty regime in which any state party would need to accept the automatic jurisdiction of the court over the crime of genocide, as had been recommended by the International Law Commission in 1994. We sought to facilitate U.S. participation in the treaty by proposing a 10–year transitional period following entry into force of the treaty and during which any state party could "opt-out" of the court's jurisdiction over crimes against humanity or war crimes. We were prepared to accept an arrangement whereby at the end of the 10–year period, there would be three options—to accept the automatic jurisdiction of the court over all of the core crimes, to cease to be a party, or to seek an amendment to the treaty extending its "opt-out" protection. We believe such transition period is important for our government to evaluate the performance of the court and to attract a broad range of governments to join the treaty in its early years. While we achieved the agreement of the Permanent Members of the Security Council for this arrangement as well as appropriate protection for non-party states, other governments were not prepared to accept our proposal. In the end, an opt-out provision of seven years for war crimes only was adopted.

Unfortunately, because of the extraordinary way the court's jurisdiction was framed at the last moment, a country willing to commit war crimes could join the treaty and "opt out" of war crimes jurisdiction for seven years while a non-party state could deploy its soldiers aboard and be vulnerable to assertions of jurisdiction.

Further, under the amendment procedures, states parties to the treaty can avoid jurisdiction over acts committed by their nationals or on their territory for any new or amended crimes. This is protection we successfully sought. But as the jurisdiction provision is now framed, it purports to extend jurisdiction over non-party states for the same new or amended crimes.

The treaty also creates a *proprio motu* or self-initiating prosecutor who, on his or her own authority with the consent of two judges, can initiate investigations and prosecutions without referral to the court of a situation either by a government that is party to the treaty or by the Security Council. We opposed this proposal, as we are concerned that it will encourage overwhelming the court with complaints and risk diversion of its resources, as well as embroil the court in controversy, political decision-making, and confusion.

In addition, we are disappointed with the treatment of the crime of aggression. We and others had long argued that such a crime had not been defined under customary international law for purposes of individual criminal responsibility. We also insisted, as did the International Law Commission in 1994, that there had to be direct linkage between a prior Security Council decision that a state had committed aggression and the conduct of an individual of that state. The statute of the court now includes a crime of aggression, but leaves it to be defined by a subsequent amendment to be adopted seven years after entry into force. There is no guarantee that the vital linkage with a prior decision by the Security Council will be required by the definition that emerges, if in fact a broadly acceptable definition can be achieved. We will do all we can to ensure that such linkage survives.

We also joined with many other countries during the years of negotiation to oppose the inclusion of crimes of terrorism and drug crimes in the jurisdiction of the court on the grounds that this could undermine more effective national efforts. We had largely prevailed with this point of view only to discover on the last day of the conference that the Bureau's final text suddenly stipulated, in an annexed resolution that would be adopted by the conference, that crimes of terrorism and drug crimes should be included within the jurisdiction of the court, subject only to the question of defining the relevant crimes at a review conference in the future. This last minute insertion in the text greatly concerned us and we opposed the resolution with a public explanation. We said that while we had an open mind about future consideration of crimes of terrorism and drug crimes, we did not believe that including them will assist in the fight against these two evil crimes. To the contrary, conferring jurisdiction on the court could undermine essential national and transnational efforts, and actually hamper the effective fight against these crimes. The problem, we said, was not prosecution, but rather investigation. These crimes require an ongoing law enforcement effort against criminal organizations and patterns of crime, with police and intelligence resources. The court will not be equipped effectively to investigate and prosecute these types of crimes.

Finally, we were confronted on July 17th with a provision stipulating that no reservations to the treaty would be allowed. We had long argued against such a prohibition and many countries had joined us in that concern. We believed that as a minimum there were certain provisions of the treaty, particularly in the field of state cooperation with the court, where domestic constitutional requirements and national judicial procedures might require a reasonable opportunity for reservations that did not defeat the intent or purpose of the treaty.

Mr. Chairman, the Administration hopes that in the years ahead other governments will recognize the benefits of potential American participation in the Rome treaty and correct the flawed provisions in the treaty.

In the meantime, the challenge of international justice remains. The United States will continue as a leader in supporting the common duty of all law-abiding governments to bring to justice those who commit heinous crimes in our own time and in the future. The hard reality is that the international court will have no jurisdiction over crimes committed prior to its actual operations. So more ad hoc judicial mechanisms will need to be considered. We trust our friends and allies will show as much resolve to pursue the challenges of today as they have to create the future international court.

Notes

1. The Rome Conference established a Preparatory Commission for the I.C.C., consisting of states that have signed the Rome Statute and others invited to participate. The Commission is empowered to prepare proposals for the practical arrangements for the establishment and operation of the Court. These arrangements include such matters as (a) rules of procedure and evidence; (b) elements of the crimes covered by the Court's jurisdiction; (c) relationship agreement between the Court and the United Nations; (d) a headquarters agreement between the I.C.C. and the country in which the Court is established; (e) financial regulations and first-year budget; and (f) rules of procedure for the Assembly of States Parties. Although it voted against the Rome Statute, the United States has participated in the meetings of the Preparatory Commission. As noted (p. 1373), the Preparatory Commission adopted the Elements of Crimes on June 30, 2000, and also completed the Rules of Procedure and Evidence at the same session. See U.N. Doc. PCNICC/2000/INF/3/Add.2.

The Commission is also directed to prepare proposals for a provision on aggression, including the definition and elements of the crime of aggression and the conditions under which the I.C.C. could exercise its jurisdiction with regard to this crime. The Commission is to submit such proposals to the Assembly of States Parties at a Review Conference to be convened seven years after the Statute takes effect, with the objective of obtaining agreement on provisions relating to the crime of aggression for inclusion of the Statute.

2. If U.S. military personnel were to be involved in a U.N. peace-keeping mission abroad and were to be accused of committing a crime covered by the Rome Statute in a state that is party to the Statute, under what circumstances, if any, could those personnel be prosecuted before the I.C.C.? What if the crime were committed within a state that is not a party? Could such personnel be prosecuted even if the United States were not a party to the Statute? During the negotiations at the Rome Conference, the United States pressed hard to make prosecution before the I.C.C. contingent on a referral to the Court by the U.N. Security Council on which the United States enjoys a veto.

3. Is it anomalous, as Ambassador Scheffer maintains, that a state bent on committing war crimes could join the treaty and "opt out" of the Court's war crimes jurisdiction for seven years while forces of a non-party could participate in a foreign peace-keeping mission and be vulnerable to war crimes prosecution?

4. Ambassador Scheffer has stated that "[a] fundamental principle of international law is that only states that are party to a treaty should be bound by its terms," citing Arts. 34–38 of the Vienna Convention on the Law of Treaties, 1155 U.N.T.S. 331. Scheffer, The United States and the International Criminal Court, 93 A.J.I.L. 12, 16 (1999). He goes on to note that under Article 12 of the Treaty, the I.C.C. may exercise jurisdiction over anyone (even non-nationals of a party)

anywhere in the world if either the state in which the crime was committed or the state of the accused's nationality consents. Id. Does the theory of universal jurisdiction for genocide, crimes against humanity and war crimes justify such an exercise of jurisdiction by the I.C.C.? Are there procedural safeguards, such as the requirements for a determination of admissibility, the primacy accorded to national jurisdictions and possible deferral of I.C.C. jurisdiction at the behest of the Security Council that adequately protect U.S. military or civilian personnel from prosecution before the I.C.C.?

5. In the final hour of the last meeting of the Committee of the Whole at the Rome Conference on July 17, 1998, the United States unsuccessfully moved adoption of an amendment to Article 12, which would have stated, in part:

> 1. With respect to States not party to the Statute, the Court shall have jurisdiction over acts committed in the territory of a State not party, or committed by officials or agents of a State not party in the course of official duties and acknowledged by the State as such, only if the State or States in question have accepted jurisdiction in accordance with this article.

A/CONF.183/L.1/l.90.

Suppose the Preparatory Commission were to accept a "procedural" rule proposal by the United States that no national of a non-party state acting in an official capacity can physically be surrendered to the I.C.C. without the consent of that non-party state or unless the Security Council has otherwise determined that the national be subjected to the jurisdiction of the court. Would such a rule be likely to meet the objectives of the United States and to be acceptable by the states that have signed the Rome Statute?

On August 2, 2000, Ambassador Scheffer, commenting on the U.S. position in the negotiations in the Preparatory Commission, stated, in part, as follows:

> Our fundamental concern has been articulated to other governments and narrowed to one point, which is the exposure of American service members and government officials to surrender to this court during that period of time that we are a non-party to the treaty. That's the only issue on the table now. We don't believe it's justifiable to subject our service members to the jurisdiction of this court while we are a non-party to the treaty. And it is only realistic to assume that for a number of years, at least, we will be a non-party.* * *
>
> So all we're trying to do at this point in these negotiations is to ensure that if there is an attempt to request the surrender of an American service member or government official to the International Criminal Court while we are a non-party to the court, that we have the right to either consent or object and thus prevent that actual surrender to the court.
>
> If that can be resolved—and I think there's reason to resolve it, because I think that will strike the right balance at this moment in time, at this time in history, between our obligations for international peace and security and involvement in humanitarian missions and the pursuit of international justice—then we'll be in a position to cooperate with the court even as a non-party.

State Department Briefing on 10th Anniversary of Iraq's Invasion of Kuwait, August 2, 2000.

The U.S. posture with respect to the I.C.C. was complicated by the introduction during the summer of 2000 of S. 2726 by Senator Jesse Helms and H.R. 4654, by Representative Tom DeLay, which contained the American Servicemembers' Protection Act of 2000. This proposed legislation would, among other things, prohibit use of federal funds to support the I.C.C. and military aid to any country that has ratified the I.C.C. treaty, with exceptions only for NATO and major non-NATO allies. Moreover, it would require that the U.N. Security Council grant immunity to U.S. personnel as a condition to their participation in U.N.-authorized military activity. The Clinton Administration opposed the bills, and the legislation was not enacted as of 2000.

6. For analysis of the U.S. objections to the I.C.C., see the collection of essays in The United States and the International Criminal Court (Sewall & Kaysen eds., 2000). Some of the viewpoints include: Ruth Wedgwood, "The Constitution and the ICC," at pp. 119–136; Robinson O. Everett, "American Servicemembers and the ICC," at pp. 137–151 (concluding that complementarity principle, though not an absolute protection, would largely address U.S. concerns; and recommending that Congress should enact any necessary amendments to the Uniform Code of Military Justice and other federal laws to ensure that the United States has properly perfected its own jurisdiction over any crimes for which U.S. nationals might arguably be prosecuted by the I.C.C.); and William L. Nash, "The ICC and the Deployment of U.S. Armed Forces," at pp. 153–164 (Major General, U.S. Army, Retired, who was commander of a multinational division supporting the Dayton Peace Accords in northeastern Bosnia–Herzegovina, finds pragmatic reasons for concluding that it would be prudent to work with the I.C.C. rather than to oppose it).

Some opponents of the I.C.C. argue that the Rome Statute contains inadequate safeguards for defendants' rights, in comparison to the U.S. Bill of Rights: one example is the absence of provisions for jury trial; another is the fact that the prosecution as well as the defense could appeal from adverse rulings. Supporters point out, however, that although there may be some differences between U.S. procedural protections and those embodied in the Rome Statute, the latter fully satisfies modern human rights standards and is at least as protective of defendants' rights as the U.S. Constitution. See, e.g., Wedgwood, supra at pp. 121, 123 (noting that the prosecution would have to advise a suspect of rights even in noncustodial interrogation, while under U.S. law the *Miranda* warnings are required only in custodial settings and concluding that "the most persuasive answer is that there is no forbidding constitutional obstacle to U.S. participation in the treaty"); see also Monroe Leigh, The United States and the Statute of Rome, 95 A.J.I.L. 124, 130–131 (2001) ("the list of due-process rights guaranteed by the Rome Statute is, if anything, somewhat more detailed and comprehensive than those in the American Bill of Rights. Not better, but more detailed.").

7. Compare the provisions of the Rome Statute dealing with the relationship between the proposed I.C.C. and national courts with those dealing with the relationship between the I.C.T.Y. and I.C.T.R. and national courts. What are the factors that underlie the differences between the handling of this "complementarity" issue? Are the differences likely to contribute to the ratification and the eventual effective functioning of the I.C.C. if the Rome Statute comes into force as currently drafted? Note that under Article 17, a case will be deemed inadmissible if the case "is being investigated or prosecuted by a State which has jurisdiction over it." Does "jurisdiction," as used in Article 17, mean jurisdiction to prescribe (or legislate) or jurisdiction to enforce or adjudicate or both? If a U.S. national is in the custody of another state or of the I.C.C., the distinction could be of controlling significance. See Paust, The Reach of ICC Jurisdiction Over Non–Signatory Nationals, 33 Vand.J.Trans. L. 1 (2000).

8. Can the Rome Statute be persuasively criticized for making it difficult to prosecute crimes committed in domestic civil wars occurring in non-party states?

9. The use of nuclear, biological, and chemical weapons and other weapons of mass destruction is not mentioned in the list of war crimes. What factors underlay this decision?

10. For further discussion of the proposed international criminal court, see Lee (ed.), The International Criminal Court: The Making of the Rome Statute: Issues, Negotiations, Results (1999); Scheffer, the United States and the International Criminal Court, 93 A.J.I.L. 12 (1999); Blakesley, Jurisdiction, Definition of Crimes, and Triggering Mechanisms, 25 Denv. J. Int'l L. & Pol'y 233 (1997); Broomhall, Developments in Criminal Law and Criminal Justice: Looking Forward to the Establishment of an International Criminal Court: Between State Consent and the Rule of Law, 8 Crim. L.F. 317 (1997); Broms, The Establishment of an International Criminal Court, in Dinstein & Tabory, War Crimes in International Law 214 (1996); and Rebane, Extradition and Individual Rights: The Need for an International Criminal Court to Safeguard International Rights, 19 Fordham Int'l L.J. 1636 (1996).

Chapter 16

THE LAW OF THE SEA

"A law of the sea is as old as nations, and the modern law of the sea is virtually as old as modern international law. For three hundred years it was probably the most stable and least controversial branch of international law. It was essentially reaffirmed and codified as recently * * * as 1958. By 1970 it was in disarray." Henkin, How Nations Behave 212 (2d ed. 1979).

In 1982, after years of negotiation, there was again general agreement on the legal regime that should govern the seas, reflected in the Law of the Sea Convention of that year. One aspect, however—the law governing mining on (and in) the sea-bed beyond national jurisdiction—continued to be controversial, with the United States among the few dissenting and abstaining. A compromise on that issue by a special agreement concluded in 1994 led the U.S. government to announce that it would move to adhere to the Convention and to the 1994 Agreement. As of 2000, however, the U.S. Senate has not given its consent to ratification and the United States is not yet a party to the 1982 Convention.

The history of the law of the sea reflects a continuing struggle between states that asserted special rights in vast areas of the sea and other states that insisted on the freedom to navigate and fish in all the ocean spaces. Exceptions to the freedom of the seas (*mare liberum*) developed slowly, as coastal states pressed for control over marine traffic and resources near their shores. Important inroads on the freedom of the seas, principally in favor of coastal states, and the definition of "high seas" in the 1982 Convention on the Law of the Sea as "the area beyond national jurisdiction," suggest that it may be useful to examine coastal state rights before dealing with the seas "beyond national jurisdiction."

After stating basic principles (Section 1), Section 2 of this Chapter traces the development of the rights of coastal states as exceptions to the freedom of the seas, culminating in codification in the Law of the Sea Convention of 1982 which permits coastal states to exercise authority over a "territorial sea," "the continental shelf," and an "exclusive economic zone." Section 3 sets forth the law of the extensive areas of the sea that remain "beyond national jurisdiction," are subject to "the regime of the high seas," and are open to all for reasonable use, with due consideration for the rights of other states to use them similarly. Three smaller but important subjects (the marine environment, scientific research, and the settlement of sea disputes) are considered in

Sections 4 through 6. Section 7 closes this Chapter with a discussion of the law that applies in all parts of the sea to the instrument that first opened the seas to human voyagers—the ship.

Note

The Law of the Sea is commonly used to describe that part of international law that deals with the relations, activities and interests of states involving the sea. It is distinct from other branches of sea-related law. Admiralty or maritime law, for example, deals primarily with relations, activities and interests of private persons involved in the transport by sea of passengers or goods. Those relations are generally governed by the domestic law of states, but various aspects are now regulated by international agreement. The International Maritime Organization (IMO) has included among its concerns maritime safety and marine pollution, and the Law of the Sea Convention contains some rules of maritime law as well—for example, those relating to penal jurisdiction in the event of collision.

SECTION 1. BASIC PRINCIPLES

A. SOURCES AND RECENT HISTORY

The law of the sea was largely customary law until it was codified and developed by the International Law Commission in a major undertaking culminating in the first United Nations Conference on the Law of the Sea in 1958. That Conference adopted four conventions: on the Territorial Sea and the Contiguous Zone (15 U.S.T. 1606, T.I.A.S. No. 5639, 516 U.N.T.S. 205); on the High Seas (13 U.S.T. 2312, T.I.A.S. No. 5200, 450 U.N.T.S. 82); on the Continental Shelf (15 U.S.T. 471, T.I.A.S. No. 5578, 499 U.N.T.S. 311); and on Fishing and Conservation of the Living Resources of the High Seas (17 U.S.T. 138, T.I.A.S. No. 5969, 559 U.N.T.S. 285).

As of 2000, the 1958 Convention on the High Seas has 57 parties; the Territorial Sea Convention has 51 parties; the Continental Shelf Convention, 57; the Fishing and Conservation Convention, 37. The United States signed and ratified all the 1958 conventions. Insofar as the 1958 Conventions codify customary law, they reflect law binding also on states that have not adhered to them. The 1958 conventions also have contributed to the continuing development of customary law. Compare the North Sea Continental Shelf Cases, p. 92.

In the 1960s, technological, economic, and political developments pressed for substantive changes in the law of the sea and for a new recodification of the law. The result was a new, comprehensive convention, the U.N. Convention on the Law of the Sea of 1982. Understandably, the negotiations of a new, comprehensive convention, and the pressures that inspired that activity, discouraged additional adherence to the 1958 conventions, but did not render them moot or unimportant. The 1958 conventions continue to govern states parties who have not acceded to the 1982 Convention (notably the United States, which did not sign the 1982 Convention and, as of 2000, has not acceded to it). The 1958 conventions continue to govern states parties to them who are also parties to the later Convention, except insofar as a provision in the latter is inconsistent with and supersedes the earlier provision. The 1958 conventions are also guides to the customary law of the sea governing states not parties to any convention.

The move toward a new recodification of the law of the sea was inspired by the proliferation of new states who did not participate in the earlier codification, and by a desire to respond to the promises of technological developments. Specifically, initiatives in the U.N. General Assembly, beginning in 1967, to deal with the resources of the sea-bed "beyond national jurisdiction" led to the Third U.N. Law of the Sea Conference, at which virtually the whole of the law of the sea was reexamined. The Conference began in 1973, and after eight years of negotiation (with active U.S. participation), it produced the Draft Convention on the Law of the Sea (Informal Text), A/CONF.62/WP.10/Rev.3 (1980). However, the Reagan Administration, which had taken office in the United States in 1981, proposed a number of changes to the Draft Convention, particularly with regard to the sea-bed mining provisions. These U.S. proposals were largely rejected by the Conference and the final draft of the Convention was approved on April 30, 1982, by a vote of 130 states in favor, 4 against, and 17 abstentions. The four states voting against adopting the Convention were the United States, Israel, Turkey and Venezuela.

The new Convention, containing 320 articles and nine annexes (with 125 additional articles), A/CONF.62/122 (1982), reprinted in 21 I.L.M. 1245 (1982), was signed in Jamaica, December 10, 1982, by 119 states.

After the Convention was finalized, the United States accepted many of its provisions as authoritative, but maintained its opposition to certain aspects and insisted that until those problems were solved the United States would not be able to join the Convention. In 1983 President Reagan proclaimed a 200–mile Exclusive Economic Zone for the United States, an act he said was in accord with the existing maritime law and practice as confirmed by the 1982 Convention. The President's statement read in part:

> The United States has long been a leader in developing customary and conventional law of the sea. Our objectives have consistently been to provide a legal order that will, among other things, facilitate peaceful, international uses of the oceans and provide for equitable and effective management and conservation of marine resources. The United States also recognizes that all nations have an interest in these issues. * * *
>
> [T]he convention * * * contains provisions with respect to traditional uses of the oceans which generally confirm existing maritime law and practice and fairly balance the interests of all states.
>
> Today I am announcing three decisions to promote and protect the oceans interests of the United States in a manner consistent with those fair and balanced results in the convention and international law.
>
> First, the United States is prepared to accept and act in accordance with the balance of interests relating to traditional uses of the oceans—such as navigation and overflight. In this respect, the United States will recognize the rights of other states in the waters off their coasts, as reflected in the convention, so long as the rights and freedoms of the United States and others under international law are recognized by such coastal states.

> Second, the United States will exercise and assert its navigation and overflight rights and freedoms on a worldwide basis in a manner that is consistent with the balance of interests reflected in the convention. The United States will not, however, acquiesce in unilateral acts of other states designed to restrict the rights and freedoms of the international community in navigation and overflight and other related high seas uses.
>
> Third, I am proclaiming today an exclusive economic zone in which the United States will exercise sovereign rights in living and nonliving resources within 200 nautical miles of its coast.

83 Dep't State Bull. No. 2075 at 70–71 (1983).

The failure of the United States to support the final text of the Convention resulted in uncertainty as to the status of the Convention before it went into force, and as to the state of the law of the sea in relation to states that do not become parties to the Convention. The United States appeared ready to accept as customary law virtually all the provisions except those relating to mining in the deep sea-bed. Many states, however, especially developing states, argued that the Convention was a "package deal" reflecting not only compromises as to the terms of particular articles, but "trade-offs" between articles and subjects. In particular, they insisted that they had agreed to provisions favorable to the interests of developed states (notably the United States) in some sections of the treaty, in order to achieve agreement on the provisions wanted by the developing states, notably the regime for deep sea-bed mining. Consequently, they argued, sections desired by the developed states cannot be treated as reflecting agreed customary law unless the entire treaty—including the deep sea-bed regime—is recognized as customary law. Nevertheless, all agreed that many provisions of the 1982 Convention duplicate provisions in the 1958 conventions, and many other provisions are clearly established customary law of the sea.

The Restatement (Third), Part V, Introductory Note, concludes:

> For purposes of this Restatement, therefore, the Convention as such is not law of the United States. However, many of the provisions of the Convention follow closely provisions in the 1958 conventions to which the United States is a party and which largely restated customary law as of that time. Other provisions in the LOS Convention set forth rules that, if not law in 1958, became customary law since that time, as they were accepted at the Conference by consensus and have influenced, and came to reflect, the practice of states. See § 102, Reporters' Note 2. In particular, in March 1983 President Reagan proclaimed a 200–nautical-mile exclusive economic zone for the United States and issued a policy statement in which the United States in effect agreed to accept the substantive provisions of the Convention, other than those dealing with deep sea-bed mining, in relation to all states that do so with respect to the United States. Thus, by express or tacit agreement accompanied by consistent practice, the United States, and states generally, have accepted the substantive provisions of the Convention, other than those addressing deep sea-bed mining, as statements of customary law binding upon them apart from the Convention. See Case Concerning Delimitation of the Maritime Boundary of the Gulf of Maine (Canada/United States), [1984] I.C.J.Rep. 246, 294 (the provisions of the LOS Convention concerning the

continental shelf and the exclusive economic zone "were adopted without any objections" and may "be regarded as consonant at present with general international law on the question"). In a few instances, however, there is disagreement whether a provision of the Convention reflects customary law. See, *e.g.*, § 514, Reporters' Note 4, and § 515, Comment *b*. Some provisions of the Convention, notably those accepting particular arrangements for settling disputes, clearly are not customary law and have not been accepted by express or tacit agreement.

In the *Gulf of Maine Case*, a Chamber of the International Court of Justice stated:

> Turning lastly to the proceedings of the Third United Nations Conference on the Law of the Sea and in the final result of that Conference, the Chamber notes in the first place that the Convention adopted at the end of the Conference has not yet come into force and that a number of States do not appear inclined to ratify it. This, however, in no way detracts from the consensus reached on large portions of the instrument and, above all, cannot invalidate the observation that certain provisions of the Convention, concerning the continental shelf and the exclusive economic zone, were adopted without any objections.

1984 I.C.J. 53. See also *Case Concerning Continental Shelf* (Libya v. Malta), 1985 I.C.J. 13, 30 (it is the clear duty of the Court to consider if relevant, provisions of the 1982 Law of the Sea Convention that are binding as rules of customary law); *Case Concerning the Arbitral Award of 31 July 1989* (Guinea–Bissau v. Senegal), 1990 I.C.J. 64, 72 (guidance may be found in the 1982 Convention, although it has not yet entered into force) (Evensen, J., separate opinion); *Case Concerning Passage Through the Great Belt* (Finland v. Denmark) (application for provisional measures), 1991 I.C J. 12, 13 (account has to be taken of the provisions of the 1982 Law of the Sea Convention that reflect customary law).

In referring to the Convention, therefore, it may be desirable to note the continuity between the 1982 Convention and its antecedents.

For discussions of the Third LOS Conference, see Law of the Sea: United States Policy Dilemma (Oxman, Caron & Buderi, eds. 1983); Allott, Power Sharing in the Law of the Sea, 77 A.J.I.L. 1 (1983). For a collection of documents on the Third Law of the Sea Conference, see Platzöder, Third United Nations Conference on the Law of the Sea: Documents, 18 vols. (1982–1988). For the perspectives of different states on the Third Law of the Sea Conference and on the law of the sea generally, see The International Law of the Sea (Blishchenko & Gureyev, eds. 1988); The Law of the Sea: Problems from the East Asian Perspective (Park & Park, eds. 1987); Szekely, Latin America and the Development of the Law of the Sea (1986); Singh, The United Nations Convention on the Law of the Sea (1985); Rembe, Africa and the International Law of the Sea (1980); El–Hakim, The Middle Eastern States and the Law of the Sea (1979). On the law of the sea generally, see New Directions in the Law of the Sea, 11 vols. (Nordquist et al., eds.); O'Connell, The Law of the Sea (Shearer ed. 1982); The Law of the Sea in the 1990s: A Framework for Further Cooperation (Kuribayashi & Miles eds. 1992); A Handbook on the New Law of the Sea (Dupuy ed. 1991). For an indication of provisions of the 1982 Convention that do not apply to the

United States, or whose applicability is in doubt, see Restatement (Third), Part V, Introductory Note, n. 4.

The number of states that have adhered to the 1982 Convention grew steadily, though a number of states saw no reason to adhere to the Convention as long as the United States (and other industrialized states) did not join, especially since the implementation of key sections of the Convention depended on the financial and technological commitment of those states.

The United States maintained its opposition and non-adherence into the 1990s, despite continuing international pressures and domestic voices urging change and compromise. In November 1992, an independent panel of U.S. experts concluded:

> Fundamental United States interests would be served by removing the obstacles to widespread ratification of the 1982 United Nations Convention on the Law of the Sea. U.S. interests in the Convention include those related to the use and protection of the oceans, international trade and economic growth, as well as national interests in order, stability, and orderly change in international relations.

The panel went on to enumerate fundamental U.S. interests in security, in free movement of trade and communications, and in the environment, as supporting ratification of the 1982 Convention. See also Panel on the Law of Ocean Uses, United States Interests in the Law of the Sea Convention, 88 A.J.I.L. 167 (1994).

The 1990s also brought radical changes in the political context of the Convention and in underlying economic assumptions. In particular, it became clear that deep sea-bed mining would not in fact be economical for a long time, perhaps for decades, and that no country had any economic reason (and few have political reasons) for proceeding with sea-bed mining. Doubt as to the economic viability of deep sea-bed mining muted the debate about its legality. The changed world order following the end of the Cold War also largely overtook the ideological differences that underlay some of the compromises of the "package deal" behind important provisions of the Convention; the general commitment to "privatization" and free market principles, and democracy, also may have outdated some of the provisions to which the United States objected.

In the early 1990s, the Secretary–General of the United Nations undertook informal negotiations with a view to removing the obstacles to widespread ratification of the Convention (especially in the deep sea-bed mining provisions of Part XI of the Convention and its annexes). The Clinton Administration in the United States was pressed to re-examine the U.S. position. The various efforts to compromise differences and to meet objections, notably those of the United States, so as to achieve general acceptance of the 1982 Convention, bore fruit in 1994. Consultations resulted in an "Agreement Relating to the Implementation of Part XI of the United Nations Convention on the Law of the Sea of 10 December 1982," and a resolution of the U.N. General Assembly by which the Assembly would adopt the Agreement and urge states to adhere to it and to the Convention. The General Assembly adopted the resolution and the annexed Agreement on July 28, 1994, by 121 in favor, none against, and 7 abstentions. The Agreement was signed promptly by many states, including the United States.

For the text of the Agreement and a summary of the modifications which the Agreement and its Annex effected in the law and institutions of sea-bed mining, see the Documents Supplement and pp. 1461–1472 below.

As of 2000, 135 states have become party to the Convention, and 100 of these states have become party to the 1994 Agreement. The United States announced that it would ratify the 1982 Convention and the 1994 Agreement modifying it, and President Clinton requested the consent of the U.S. Senate to ratification. As of 2000, however, the Senate has not given its consent.

B. THE PRINCIPLES OF FREEDOM AND "COMMONAGE"

For hundreds of years after Hugo Grotius prevailed in his famous controversy with John Selden (see Historical Introduction), international law saw the seas as belonging to everyone or to no one, and *mare liberum* was the fundamental principle of the law of the seas (although subject in war to the laws of war, p. 1064 supra). With that principle of freedom—or beneath it—has been the concept of commonage, that the sea belonged to everyone, or to no one. In particular, unlike land, the sea could not be acquired by nations and made subject to national sovereignty. That status and that principle applied throughout the seas. Exceptions, principally in favor of coastal states, developed slowly, and historically, at least, were seen—and resisted—as carved out of the commonage, as derogations from freedom. Zones of "national jurisdiction" for the coastal states—the territorial sea, the continental shelf, the exclusive economic zone—are later developments, some very recent, creating distinctions between them and the rest of the seas and giving the latter the distinguishing label, the "high seas."

HENKIN, CHANGING LAW FOR THE CHANGING SEAS

Uses of the Seas 69, 70–71 (Gullion ed. 1968).

Freedom of the seas has meant freedom to use the seas, and no uses have been barred. The principal use has been navigation—for fishing, trade, travel, war. In time, the seas began to lend themselves to tunneling, laying of cables, submarine travel, scientific research. Today, the seas are a principal area of military deployment and manoeuvre and harbor "permanently" sophisticated military weapons and equipment. The seas have recreational and scientific importance. They have long been a repository for waste, recently also for atomic waste. Unless modified, the principle of freedom would presumably apply also to future uses—to transportation, sojourn, or other human activity in the waters below or on the sea bed.

Freedom has extended also to the air above the seas and it, too, has been open to all for aviation and its various purposes. There has been no agreement, however, as to "who owns the seabed," as to whether the "commonage" of the seas applies as well to the seabed and its subsoil. Some have urged that the seas are not subject to national acquisition only because that would interfere with freedom, particularly for navigation, but there is no similar reason for denying national acquisition and sovereignty in the seabed and its subsoil.

Freedom of the seas, and the principle that they belong to all, or none, has meant also freedom for all nations to exploit sea resources, principally to fish and to keep one's catch. Those who insisted that the seas were common property might have had difficulty explaining why individual nations could appropriate the fish that belonged to all. But the theoretical questions bothered only theoreticians. Fishing was older than international law; no nation had any interest in insisting that fishing was generally prohibited; besides, the fish reproduced themselves and seemed plentiful and inexhaustible. Even when it proved that fish were not in fact always and everywhere plentiful and inexhaustible, the freedom to fish in the seas at large survived unimpaired. It seemed unlikely that a different rule would apply as man began to extract other resources, organic or inorganic, from the waters, or to the waters themselves, although questions might arise if new processes for extraction required major, "permanent" installations that unduly interfered with navigation or other established rights.

Again, there has been disagreement as to whether the resources on or beneath the seabed are similarly subject to appropriation by anyone. * * * If, however, it is now (or will soon be) possible for any nation to extract a wealth of oil and manganese in parts of the sea far from any coast, may it lawfully do so, and, if so, on what terms, subject to what limitations? Or are these minerals the property of all, not to be extracted at all without the consent of "the community," and only on its terms?

SECTION 2. DEROGATIONS FROM "COMMONAGE" IN FAVOR OF COASTAL STATES

The territorial sea resulted from early recognition that the coastal state had special interests in waters adjacent to its shores for some purposes; in time, the various interests combined into "sovereignty" over a "territorial sea." See Jessup, The Law of Territorial Waters and Maritime Jurisdiction (1927). Coastal states also claimed the need to protect their territorial interests (or their territorial sea) against acts outside the territorial sea. A "contiguous zone" in which the coastal state could act against smugglers developed early; later, some claimed rights to act against polluters or "pirate broadcasters." There developed also a right for the coastal state of "hot pursuit," even on the high seas, of violators of its special zones and interests.

Preference or exclusive rights for the coastal state to natural resources in or beneath waters adjacent to the coast (but beyond the territorial sea) developed more recently; the 1945 Truman Proclamation justified the doctrine of the continental shelf in the interest of conservation and as "reasonable and just." See p. 1422 infra. Other coastal states thought it reasonable and just that the coastal state have preferred or exclusive fishing rights in coastal areas even beyond the territorial sea, leading to an exclusive economic zone, with exclusive rights for the coastal state in all natural resources of their "patrimonial sea." See pp. 1434–1437.

The 1982 Convention completed a process of development in the customary law of the seas that confirmed authority for coastal states, but different authority in different coastal zones.

RESTATEMENT (THIRD) § 511

Subject to §§ 512–15, a coastal state may exercise jurisdiction over the following coastal zones:

(a) The territorial sea: a belt of sea that may not exceed 12 nautical miles, measured from a baseline which is either the low-water line along the coast, or the seaward limit of the internal waters of the coastal state or in the case of an archipelagic state the seaward limit of the archipelagic waters;

(b) The contiguous zone: a belt of sea contiguous to the territorial sea that may not extend beyond 24 nautical miles from the baselines from which the breadth of the territorial sea is measured;

(c) The continental shelf: the sea-bed and subsoil of the submarine areas that extend beyond the coastal state's territorial sea

(i) throughout the natural prolongation of the state's land territory to the outer edge of the continental margin, subject to certain limitations based on geological and geographical factors; or

(ii) to a distance of 200 nautical miles from the baselines from which the breadth of the territorial sea is measured, where there is no continental margin off the coast or where the continental margin does not extend to that distance;

(d) The exclusive economic zone: a belt of sea beyond the territorial sea that may not exceed 200 nautical miles from the baselines from which the breadth of the territorial sea is measured.

Comment:

a. Different coastal state authority in different zones. The authority of the coastal state is different in the different zones defined in this section. The coastal state exercises sovereignty in the territorial sea; limited policing rights in the contiguous zone; sovereign rights over the natural resources of the continental shelf and over economic exploitation of the exclusive economic zone; and limited jurisdiction within the exclusive economic zone with regard to marine scientific research, the protection and preservation of the marine environment, and artificial islands and certain installations and structures. *Compare* § 512 and § 513 *with* § 514 and § 515. With respect to matters falling within its authority in the particular zone, the coastal state generally has jurisdiction to prescribe, to adjudicate, and to enforce by nonjudicial measures, but such jurisdiction is not necessarily exclusive. See Introductory Note to Part IV.

* * *

d. Exercise of coastal state jurisdiction optional. Under international law, every coastal state is entitled to exercise authority in areas of the sea adjacent to its coast, as indicated in this chapter. There is, however, no duty for a state to assert or exercise such authority or to do so to the fullest extent permissible. The United States, for instance, has refused to extend its territorial sea beyond three miles, to claim certain areas as historic waters, or to draw straight baselines in certain areas where its coast is deeply indented or where there is a fringe of islands along the coast, thus diminishing the sea areas to which its jurisdiction could have been extended. See United States v. California, 381 U.S. 139, 167–68, 175, 85 S.Ct. 1401, 1416–17, 1421, 14 L.Ed.2d 296 (1965); United States v. Louisiana, 394 U.S. 11, 72–73, 89 S.Ct. 773, 806–807, 22 L.Ed.2d 44 (1969). See also Reporters' Notes 3, 4, and 5.

In respect of coastal zones other than the continental shelf, the jurisdiction of the coastal state and the limits and content of that jurisdiction depend on a proclamation or other express act by the state, but the rights of the coastal state in the continental shelf are automatic and do not depend on exercise or assertion of authority. *Compare* Article 77(3) of the LOS Convention *with* Articles 3, 33, 47, and 57.

e. Internal waters and ports. Internal waters are waters wholly or largely surrounded by a state's land territory, as well as sea waters on the landward side of the baseline of the territorial sea or of the archipelagic waters. 1958 Convention on the Territorial Sea and the Contiguous Zone, Article 5(1); LOS Convention, Articles 8(1) and 50. Under international law, a coastal state's sovereignty over its land territory extends to its internal waters, including bays. See Comment *f.* A state also has complete sovereignty over its seaports, but there are special rules for roadsteads and offshore terminals. 1958 Convention on the Territorial Sea, Article 9; LOS Convention, Articles 12, 60, 218, and 220.

A. THE TERRITORIAL SEA

U.N. CONVENTION ON THE LAW OF THE SEA (1982)

1833 U.N.T.S. 3, U.N. Doc. A/CONF. 62/122; 21 I.L.M. 1261 (1982).

ARTICLE 2

Legal Status of the Territorial Sea, of the Air Space Over the Territorial Sea and of its Bed and Subsoil

1. The sovereignty of a coastal State extends, beyond its land territory and internal waters and, in the case of an archipelagic State, its archipelagic waters, to an adjacent belt of sea, described as the territorial sea.

2. This sovereignty extends to the air space over the territorial sea as well as to its bed and subsoil.

3. The sovereignty over the territorial sea is exercised subject to this Convention and to other rules of international law.

Note

The analogous articles in the 1958 Convention on the Territorial Sea and the Contiguous Zone (Articles 1 and 2) do not include the reference to archipelagic states. The 1982 Convention contains a new Part IV, Articles 46–54, prescribing specially for such states. See p. 1399 below.

1. Definition and Delimitation: Historic Development

After state claims to vast expanses of ocean had ceased, during the seventeenth century, to obtain international respect in law or in practice, there remained the idea that a littoral state might properly claim special interests in at least certain areas of adjacent waters, the inviolability of which was necessary to its safety and protection. The doctrine of the territorial sea is traditionally regarded as having been based on the maxim laid down by the Dutch jurist Bynkershoek in the early eighteenth century, that a state's dominion extended only so far out to sea as its cannon would reach; this, in turn, is regarded as having given rise to the doctrine of a three-mile belt of territorial waters, three miles supposedly being the approximate range of eighteenth-century, shore-based cannons. See Walker, Territorial Waters: The Cannon Shot Rule, 22 Brit.Y.B.I.L. 210, 213–22 (1945). This rule did not involve a continuous belt of waters, but merely constructed zones or "pockets" of adjacent sea within which, during wars, prizes could not be taken without violating a duty owed to the neutral state. In the North, however, the German jurist Pufendorf envisaged as early as 1672 a maritime belt for defensive purposes (id. at 224), and Denmark (which had at various times claimed the whole ocean between Iceland and Norway, as well as the Baltic Sea) claimed, for certain purposes, a belt of waters adjacent to her territories and measured in leagues. Under pressure from other states, Denmark was forced in 1745 to reduce her jurisdiction for neutrality purposes to one league, but this was the Scandinavian league of four nautical miles and not the three-mile league used in the rest of Europe. Kent, The Historical Origins of the Three–Mile Limit, 48 A.J.I.L. 537, 538–45 (1954).

The doctrine of a continuous belt of territorial sea, one league or three marine miles wide, received its first explicit statement in 1782, on the basis of the Italian writer Galiani's conclusion that it would be unreasonable for the neutrality of particular waters to depend on whether or not forts were built on the adjacent shores, and on the range of the guns which might be mounted therein. Walker at 228–29. Galiani's proposal of a standard three-mile limit probably had no relation to the actual or supposed range of contemporary cannons, but simply represented a convenient standard measure, just as had the league in the North. The cannon shot tradition, however, was to linger for many years in diplomatic practice and in writings on international law.

The first acceptance in state practice of the three-mile belt of territorial sea occurred in 1793, when the United States, forced to define its neutral waters in the war between France and Great Britain, proposed that the belligerents should respect United States neutrality up to "*the utmost range of a cannon ball*, usually stated at one sea league," this being the smallest breadth claimed by any state. 1 Moore, Digest of International Law 702–703 (1906). France and Great Britain agreed, and the three-mile limit was subsequently applied in British and United States prize courts. See Walker at 230 n. 1.

Thereafter, the three-mile limit was applied for a number of purposes, and states came to rely on the comprehensive notion of the territorial sea as a basis for the exercise of, *inter alia*, fishing, police, and revenue jurisdiction. After inclusion in a number of European treaties regulating fishing rights, and after adoption by a number of Asian and South American states, the three-mile limit was world-wide by the end of the nineteenth century, with comparatively few exceptions.

In time, the traditional association of the three-mile limit with the cannon shot doctrine was rendered obsolete. But state practice remained apparently fairly constant up to and during the first three decades of the twentieth century, though there was considerable, deep-rooted dissatisfaction with the three-mile territorial sea. Especially after the 1945 Truman proclamations with regard to the continental shelf and the conservation of fisheries, many states extended their claims to six or twelve miles, or even more. See 28 Dep't St.Bull. 486–87 (1953).

In 1951, pursuant to a recommendation of the General Assembly, the International Law Commission began work on the regime of the territorial sea. Although substantial progress was made in most areas, this body also failed to reach agreement on the breadth of the territorial sea. The Geneva Conference on the Law of the Sea in 1958 failed to achieve the two-thirds majority that was necessary for decision on a definite limit of territorial waters. But there was agreement (Article 24) that the contiguous zone, "a zone of high seas contiguous to its territorial sea," may not extend beyond twelve miles from shore, which implied that the territorial sea was to be at most something less than twelve miles wide.

The failure of the 1958 Conference to reach agreement on the two most important problems before it—the breadth of the territorial sea and the extent of fishing rights in the contiguous zone—motivated the decision to convene a second Conference on the Law of the Sea in 1960. But a compromise proposal at the Conference failed to receive the necessary two-thirds approval. Second U.N. Conf. on the Law of the Sea, Off.Rec. Summary Rec. 30 (1960). The United States and the United Kingdom emphasized that the non-acceptance of the compromise proposal left the legal situation where it had been prior to the Conference, and stated their intention to continue to adhere to the three-mile limit and not to recognize any larger claim as valid against them without their agreement. See generally Dean, The Second Geneva Conference on the Law of the Sea, 54 A.J.I.L. 751 (1960). After 1960, with the continuing proliferation of states and the emergence of the "Third World," the drive for a twelve-mile territorial sea became stronger and the opposition to it eroded. The United States indicated its readiness to accept the twelve-mile zone, provided passage through international straits were assured. See p. [1261] infra. But developing coastal states no longer saw widening the territorial sea beyond twelve miles as the way to extending their exclusive jurisdiction over resources and joined to develop instead the concept of a far-wider "patrimonial sea" or "exclusive economic zone." See pp. [1291–92] infra.

BREADTH OF THE TERRITORIAL SEA

U.N. CONVENTION ON THE LAW OF THE SEA (1982)

1833 U.N.T.S. 3, U.N.Doc. A/CONF. 62/122; 21 I.L.M. 1261 (1982).

ARTICLE 3

Every State has the right to establish the breadth of its territorial sea up to a limit not exceeding 12 nautical miles, measured from baselines determined in accordance with this Convention.

* * *

ARTICLE 5

Except where otherwise provided in this Convention, the normal base-line for measuring the breadth of the territorial sea is the low-water line along the coast as marked on large-scale charts officially recognized by the coastal State.

Notes

1. The 1982 Convention laid to rest the long controversy as to the breadth of the territorial sea, which could not be resolved in the negotiations on the 1958 Conventions, or at the Second United Nations Conference on the Law of the Sea in 1960, convened specially for that purpose. But coastal states that had pressed for a wide territorial sea, some up to 200 (or more) miles, did so particularly to obtain exclusive fishing rights; and during the years of negotiations leading up to the 1982 Convention, coastal states began to claim large exclusive fishing zones. Increasing acceptance of such zones and the move to a 200 mile Exclusive Economic Zone (see p. 1434 infra) eliminated the pressure for a large territorial sea and led to acceptance of the 12 mile limit on the territorial sea.

2. Under the 1982 Convention a state "has the right" to establish a territorial sea "to a limit not exceeding" 12 miles. The United States had refrained from extending its own territorial sea beyond three miles, perhaps in the hope of inducing others to exercise similar restraint. In 1988, however, President Reagan issued a Proclamation declaring that "[t]he territorial sea of the United States henceforth extends to 12 nautical miles from the baselines of the United States determined in accordance with international law." Presidential Proclamation on the Territorial Sea of the United States, December 27, 1988, reprinted in 28 I.L.M. 284 (1989).

The legal significance of the Proclamation was the source of some uncertainty. In United States v. One Big Six Wheel, 987 F.Supp. 169 (E.D.N.Y.1997), the court determined that the 1988 Presidential Proclamation "had only a limited legal effect [, and] Congress had to enact legislation in order to implement the expansion of the territorial sea with respect to international law." However, the Second Circuit, in In re: Air Crash Off Long Island, 209 F.3d 200 (2d Cir., 2000), made clear that such implementing legislation was not necessary. In that case, the court held that the Death on the High Seas Act (DOHSA) did not govern damage claims stemming from the death of the 230 passengers who died in the crash of TWA Flight 800 on July 17, 1996. The crash occurred approximately eight nautical miles south of Long Island. The court reaffirmed the lower court's decision that the "high seas" are waters beyond the territorial sea, and since the Proclamation extended the territorial sea to 12 miles, the deaths did not occur on the high seas, and DOHSA did not apply.

3. As of the 1990s, state practice had taken a marked swing from three miles to twelve miles as the width most commonly claimed. The 1982 Convention probably states the present customary law, and claims beyond 12 miles doubtless will be challenged.

4. Important consequences for the maritime right of innocent passage (and for aircraft, which have no right of innocent passage over the territorial sea) flow from the extension of the territorial sea to 12 miles. The United States representative at the 1958 Geneva Conference pointed out:

> One of the merits of the three mile limit was that it was safest for shipping. Many landmarks still used for visual plotting by small craft were not visible

> at a range of 12 miles; only 20 per cent of the world's lighthouses had a range that exceeded that distance; radar navigation was of only marginal utility beyond 12 miles; and many vessels (which frequently did not want to enter the territorial sea) did not carry sufficient cable or appropriate equipment to anchor at the depths normally found outside the 12 mile-limit. * * * One further objection to extending the territorial sea was that, in time of war, a neutral state would have greater difficulty in safeguarding the broader belt of territorial waters against the incursions of ships of belligerents.

III 1958 Sea Conference Records 26. See also *Fisheries Jurisdiction Case* (Jurisdiction), 1973 I.C.J. 3, 28 n. 8 (Fitzmaurice, J. dissenting) (broader territorial sea presents difficulty for states in the discharge of their territorial sea responsibilities of policing; marking channels, reefs and other obstacles; giving notice of dangers to navigation; and providing rescue services).

5. The method of measuring the territorial sea involves highly technical geographical considerations and was long controversial. See, for example, *Fisheries Case* (United Kingdom v. Norway), 1951 I.C.J. 116. In response to intensified exploitation of Norwegian coastal waters by British fishing vessels, the Norwegian government had issued a decree in 1935 which delimited Norway's northern territorial waters on the basis of straight baselines drawn along the most seaward points on the islands ("skjaergaard") which line the coast. Contending that international law required the baseline to be the actual low-water mark (except in the case of bays), the United Kingdom instituted proceedings in the International Court of Justice after its negotiations with Norway had failed. There was no objection to Norway's use of four miles as the breadth of its territorial sea, in view of Norway's historic claim to a four-mile territorial sea. The Court prefaced its decision with a discussion of the geographic and economic characteristics of the coastal regions of the Norwegian mainland, as well as of the "skjaergaard" of some 120,000 islands, rocks, and reefs, in the course of which it stressed the pronounced indentations and convolution of the coast and the dependence of the local population on fishing as a means of survival. The Court found, by a vote of ten to two, that the method of delimitation used by Norway was not contrary to international law, and, by a vote of eight to four, that the baselines drawn by the 1935 Decree did not violate international law.

The *Fisheries Case* has been often cited as denying the claims of coastal states to determine their own jurisdiction. The Court said (at 132): "The delimitation of the sea areas has always an international aspect; it cannot be dependent merely upon the will of the coastal State as expressed in its municipal law." The *Fisheries Case* is also cited to support the principle that a state is not bound by a rule of customary international law if it expressed dissent while the law was developing. See 1951 I.C.J. at 131. See Chapter 2, p. 100.

6. The 1982 Convention generally follows the 1958 Convention as to the method of measuring the territorial sea. See in particular Article 5 (normal baseline) and Article 7 (straight baselines). A new Article 6 provides that for islands situated on atolls or having fringed reefs, the baseline is the seaward low-water line of the reef. Where the coastline is highly unstable, Article 7(2) permits the coastal state to select the appropriate points along such baselines which remain effective until changed by the coastal state. Article 11 adds that "[o]ff-shore installations and artificial islands shall not be considered as permanent harbour works" to be regarded as part of the coast for the purpose of delimiting the territorial sea. Article 14 adds that "[t]he coastal state may determine

baselines in turn by any of the methods provided for in the foregoing articles to suit different conditions."

7. In 1965, the United States Supreme Court resolved a dispute between the Federal Government and the State of California over the definition of "inland waters" on the California coast. United States v. California, 381 U.S. 139, 85 S.Ct. 1401, 14 L.Ed.2d 296 (1965). The United States had ceded various submerged lands to coastal states under the Submerged Lands Act of 1953. See [p. 1285] below. Under the Act, the United States owned the lands "lying seaward of the ordinary low-water mark, and outside of the inland waters, extending seaward three nautical miles * * *." The Court applied the recently "settled" international rule defining inland waters, contained in the Convention on the Territorial Sea and the Contiguous Zone (T.I.A.S. No. 639), which had been ratified by the United States. The provision of the 1958 Convention used by the Court is carried over into the 1982 Law of the Sea Convention unchanged (Art. 10).

In United States v. Alaska, 503 U.S. 569, 112 S.Ct. 1606, 118 L.Ed.2d 222 (1992), the Supreme Court pointed out that in *United States v. California* it held that "international law recognized the seaward expansion of sovereignty through artificial additions to the coastline." As between state and federal government, however, the Court in the Alaska case upheld the power of the Secretary of the Army to condition a permit to build an artificial addition on the Alaskan coastline, on Alaska's stipulation that the construction would not alter the location of the existing federal-state boundary. See also United States v. Alaska, 521 U.S. 1, 117 S.Ct. 1888, 138 L.Ed.2d 231 (1997).

On jurisdiction over internal waters and ports, and the law governing islands, see pp. 1392, 1400, 1496–1504.

BAYS

If an area of sea meets the legal requirements to be considered a bay, it becomes internal waters so that there is no right of innocent passage. See p. 1401 infra.

Attempts to establish, for international legal purposes, a geographic definition for bays occurred with some frequency during the nineteenth century, especially in the Anglo–French Fisheries Convention of 1839 and in the North Sea Fisheries Convention of 1882 (both of which provided that the mouth of a "bay" might be no more than ten miles wide in order for the coastal state to claim exclusive fishing rights therein). At the same time, however, a number of states claimed, on historic or other grounds, bays the openings of which were of greater width. A 24–mile closing line was adopted in the 1958 Geneva Convention.

The 1982 Convention, Art. 10, retains the 24–mile closing line adopted in Article 7 of the 1958 Convention and is identical with that Convention in other respects, too.

The Restatement (Third) § 511, Comment *f*, states:

> A coastal state may designate a bay as its internal waters if it has prescribed characteristics. It must be a well-marked indentation in the coast, not a mere curvature. Its area must be as large as, or larger than, that of the semicircle whose diameter is a line drawn across the mouth of the indentation. The closing line of a bay is drawn between its natural

entrance points; the line may not exceed 24 nautical miles, but a 24–mile line may be drawn within the bay in such manner as to enclose the maximum area of water that is possible with a line of that length. 1958 Convention on the Territorial Sea and the Contiguous Zone, Article 7; LOS Convention, Article 10.

In addition, international law recognizes "historic" bays that have been considered internal waters even though they do not satisfy criteria for a bay. 1958 Convention on the Territorial Sea and the Contiguous Zone, Article 7(6); LOS Convention, Article 10(6).

Article 7(6) of the 1958 Convention on the Territorial Sea and Contiguous Zone provides that states were free to claim so-called "historic" bays even if these did not meet the geographic criteria of the rest of Article 7. For background, see [1962] 11 Yb.I.L.C. 1. Article 10(6) of the 1982 Convention says only that its provisions do not apply to historic bays.

In the *Continental Shelf Case* (Libya v. Tunisia), 1982 I.C.J. 18, the Court noted that historic bays had been purposefully left for later consideration when Article 7 of the 1958 Convention was drafted and that the 1982 Convention had failed to address the issue. The Court concluded:

> It seems clear that the matter continues to be governed by general international law which does not provide for a '*single régime*' for 'historic waters' or 'historic bays,' but only for a particular régime for each of the concrete, recognised cases of 'historic waters' or 'historic bays.'

1982 I.C.J. at 73.

The United States has long characterized "bays" according to two principles: a geographic test, based on a maximum closing line of ten miles and a minimum area of enclosed waters, or an "historic" test. If either principle applied, the U.S. would consider the waters a bay and internal waters of the United States. Delaware and Chesapeake Bays have long been considered as forming part of the internal waters of the United States. 1 Moore, Digest of International Law 735–39, 741–42 (1906). Other important "historic" bays are the Bay of Chaleurs, Conception Bay, and Miramichi Bay (all Canadian). Canada claims as well all of Hudson's Bay, but this claim has been disputed by the United States. See, in general, 4 Whiteman at 233–58. It should be noted that some "historic" bays may now be able to qualify as geographic bays under the liberalized criteria adopted in Article 7 of the 1958 Convention and Article 10 of the 1982 Convention.

Another controversial claim to an historic bay is Libya's claim to the Gulf of Sidra. That claim and its rejection by the United States played a role in a 1981 incident in the Gulf where United States jets shot down two Libyan fighters that were challenging the presence of United States ships in Gulf waters and United States jets in the airspace above. In 1986, the United States again engaged Libyan forces in the Gulf when a naval fleet crossed the Libyan-set boundary to assert the right to innocent passage in waters beyond 12 miles from the Libyan shore. See 87 Dept. State Bull. 69 (1987); Blum, The Gulf of Sidra Incident, 80 A.J.I.L. 668 (1986).

On bays generally, see Westerman, The Juridical Bay (1987); Bouchez, The Regime of Bays in International Law (1964); Scovazzi, Bays and Straight Baselines in the Mediterranean, 19 Ocean Dev. & Int'l L. 401 (1988); Goldie,

Historic Bays in International Law: An Impressionistic Overview, 11 Syracuse J.Int'l L. & Com. 211 (1984).

The 1982 Convention includes a special regime requiring cooperation by states bordering "enclosed or semi-enclosed seas," defined as "a gulf, basin, or sea surrounded by two or more States and connected to the open seas by a narrow outlet or consisting entirely or primarily of the territorial seas and exclusive economic zones of two or more coastal States." (Part IX, Arts. 122–23.)

ARCHIPELAGOES AND ARCHIPELAGIC STATES

In a note of December 12, 1955 to the United Nations, the Philippine government declared its position that "all waters around, between and connecting the different islands belonging to the Philippine Archipelago irrespective of their widths or dimensions, are necessary appurtenances of its land territory, forming an integral part of the national or inland waters, subject to the exclusive sovereignty of the Philippines," and that other water areas (specified in the Spanish cession of 1898 to the United States, and in other United States agreements) were considered as territorial waters. 4 Whiteman at 282–83. On December 14, 1957, the Indonesian government stated that the "Indonesian archipelago" had historically been considered as an "entity," and that all waters "around, between and connecting" the islands of the archipelago were consequently to be considered as "inland or national waters subject to the absolute sovereignty of Indonesia." The peaceful passage of foreign vessels was guaranteed to the extent they did not infringe Indonesian sovereignty or security. Id. at 284. The United States refused to recognize the validity of the Philippine and Indonesian claims and Australia and Japan refused to recognize the validity of the Indonesian claim. Id. at 283–85. In Civil Aeronautics Board v. Island Airlines, Inc., 235 F.Supp. 990 (D.Hawaii 1964), aff'd, 352 F.2d 735 (9th Cir.1965), it was held that each island of the Hawaiian archipelago had its own territorial sea and that the intervening waters were high seas. For the State Department position in *Island Airlines*, see 4 Whiteman at 281. See also Dellapenna, The Philippines Territorial Water Claim in International Law, 5 J.L. & Econ.Dev. 45 (1970).

The problems of security, communications and fishing faced by the Philippines and Indonesia were countered by the interests of other states in the use of the intervening waters and their airspace for international transport (and, to a lesser extent, for fishing of their own). See, generally, McDougal & Burke, The Public Order of the Oceans 411–15 (1962). If no special consideration were given to the facts that a group of islands was relatively close-knit and under the sovereignty of a single state, it might be expected that each constituent island would be entitled to its own territorial sea and that the archipelago as a whole would be entitled to no extraordinary jurisdiction over intervening waters.

The claims of archipelagic states were largely accepted in the 1982 Convention which in Articles 46 and 47 defines archipelagoes and permits the drawing of straight archipelagic baselines under specified terms. The territorial sea, contiguous zone, exclusive economic zone, and the continental shelf of an archipelagic state are measured from these baselines (Art. 48). The archipelagic state has sovereignty over all the waters enclosed by these baselines as well as over the airspace, seabed and subsoil (Art. 49). But archipelagic states agree to respect existing agreements with other states and traditional fishery rights and other activities of immediately adjacent neighboring states and submarine cables laid by other states (Art. 51). There is a right to innocent passage within archipelagic waters (Art. 52). The archipelagic state may designate sea lanes and air routes suitable for continuous and expeditious passage, analogous to those established by states bordering international straits. See p. 1407 infra. All ships and aircraft have the right of "archipelagic sea lane passage" (Art. 53).

On archipelagoes generally, see United Nations, Analytical Studies on the Law of the Sea Convention–Archipelagic States (1990); Rajan, The Legal Regime of Archipelagos, 29 Germ.Y.B.Int'l L. 441 (1987); Herman, The Modern Concept of Off–Lying Archipelago in International Law, 23 Can. Y.B.Int'l L. 172 (1985); Tolentino, Archipelagoes under the Convention on the Law of the Sea, 28 Far Eastern L.Rev. 1 (1984); Coquia, Development of the Archipelagic Doctrine as a Recognized Principle of International Law, 58 Philippine L.J. 13 (1983).

ISLANDS

U.N. CONVENTION ON THE LAW OF THE SEA (1982)

1833 U.N.T.S. 3, U.N.Doc. A/CONF. 62/122; 21 I.L.M. 1261 (1982).

ARTICLE 121

Régime of islands

1. An island is a naturally formed area of land, surrounded by water, which is above water at high tide.

2. Except as provided for in paragraph 3, the territorial sea, the contiguous zone, the exclusive economic zone and the continental shelf of an island are determined in accordance with the provisions of this Convention applicable to other land territory.

3. Rocks which cannot sustain human habitation or economic life of their own shall have no exclusive economic zone or continental shelf.

Notes

1. According to the Conciliation Commission in the *Jan Mayen Case*, reprinted in 20 I.L.M. 797 (1981), the 1982 Convention "reflect[s] the present status of international law," with respect to islands. The 1982 Convention's definition repeats that of the 1958 Convention, but restricts the conditions under which an island may have an exclusive economic zone and continental shelf. See Jaywardene, The Regime of Islands in International Law (1990).

2. Small islands have become increasingly important because of the possibility of exploiting gas and oil resources in the sea-bed of their adjacent waters. In the South China Sea, for example, the People's Republic of China, Taiwan, Vietnam, the Philippines and Malaysia have been in dispute over the Paracel Islands and Spratly Islands for many years for this reason. China and Vietnam have engaged in hostilities over their competing claims to the Spratly Islands and in 1992 China reportedly stationed military forces on the Islands over the protests of the other

claimants. See generally Johnston & Valencia, Pacific Ocean Boundary Problems: Status and Solutions (1991); Bennett, The People's Republic of China and the Use of International Law in the Spratly Islands Dispute, 28 Stan.J.Int'l L. 425 (1992); Chang, China's Claim of Sovereignty over Spratly and Paracel Islands: A Historical and Legal Perspective, 23 Case W.Res.J.Int'l L. 399 (1991). See also p. 326 in Chapter 4.

In *Case Concerning the Land, Island and Maritime Frontier Dispute* (El Salvador v. Honduras: Nicaragua intervening), 1992 I.C.J. 351, the Court put an end to a century-old territorial dispute between El Salvador and Honduras; the Court held, among other things, that El Salvador is entitled to possession of the islands in the Gulf of Fonseca. In *Case Concerning Maritime Delimitation and Territorial Questions Between Qatar and Bahrain* (Qatar v. Bahrain), Qatar instituted proceedings against Bahrain in "respect of certain disputes between the two States relating to sovereignty over the Hawar Islands, sovereign rights over the shoals of Dibal and Qit'at Jaradah, and the delimitation of the maritime areas of the two States." Order, 1992 I.C.J. 237. See also the arbitral decision in the Case Concerning Delimitation of Maritime Areas Between Canada and the French Republic, involving the delimitation of the continental shelf off Canada and the French islands of St. Pierre and Miquelon, reprinted in 31 I.L.M. 1149 (1992).

See also Charney, "Rocks That Cannot Sustain Human Habitation," 93 A.J.I.L. 863 (1999).

2. *Passage Through the Territorial Sea*

a. Innocent Passage

U.N. CONVENTION ON THE LAW OF THE SEA (1982)

1833 U.N.T.S. 3, U.N.Doc. A/CONF. 62/122; 21 I.L.M. 1261 (1982).

ARTICLE 17

Right of Innocent Passage

Subject to this Convention, ships of all States, whether coastal or land-locked, enjoy the right of innocent passage through the territorial sea.

ARTICLE 18

Meaning of Passage

1. Passage means navigation through the territorial sea for the purpose of:

(a) traversing that sea without entering internal waters or calling at a roadstead or port facility outside internal waters; or

(b) proceeding to or from internal waters or a call at such roadstead or port facility.

2. Passage shall be continuous and expeditious. However, passage includes stopping and anchoring, but only in so far as the same are incidental to ordinary navigation or are rendered necessary by *force majeure* or distress or for the purpose of rendering assistance to persons, ships or aircraft in danger or distress.

ARTICLE 19

Meaning of Innocent Passage

1. Passage is innocent so long as it is not prejudicial to the peace, good order or security of the coastal State. Such passage shall take place in conformity with this Convention and with other rules of international law.

2. Passage of a foreign ship shall be considered to be prejudicial to the peace, good order or security of the coastal State if in the territorial sea it engages in any of the following activities:

(a) any threat or use of force against the sovereignty, territorial integrity or political independence of the coastal State, or in any other manner in violation of the principles of international law embodied in the Charter of the United Nations;

(b) any exercise or practice with weapons of any kind;

(c) any act aimed at collecting information to the prejudice of the defence or security of the coastal State;

(d) any act of propaganda aimed at affecting the defence or security of the coastal State;

(e) the launching, landing or taking on board of any aircraft;

(f) the launching, landing or taking on board of any military device;

(g) the loading or unloading of any commodity, currency or person contrary to the customs, fiscal, immigration or sanitary laws and regulations of the coastal State;

(h) any act of wilful and serious pollution contrary to this Convention;

(i) any fishing activities;

(j) the carrying out of research or survey activities;

(k) any act aimed at interfering with any systems of communication or any other facilities or installations of the coastal State;

(*l*) any other activity not having a direct bearing on passage.

ARTICLE 20

Submarines and Other Underwater Vehicles

In the territorial sea, submarines and other underwater vehicles are required to navigate on the surface and to show their flag.

Notes

1. "The right of innocent passage seems to be the result of an attempt to reconcile the freedom of ocean navigation with the theory of territorial waters. While recognizing the necessity of granting to littoral states a zone of waters along the coast, the family of nations was unwilling to prejudice the newly gained freedom of the seas. As a general principle, the right of innocent passage requires no supporting argument or citation of authority; it is firmly established in international law." Jessup, The Law of Territorial Waters and Maritime Jurisdiction 120 (1927).

2. The 1982 Convention spells out in detail the kinds of laws and regulations relating to innocent passage that the coastal state may adopt. "Such laws and regulations shall not apply to the design, construction, manning or equipment of foreign ships unless they are giving effect to generally accepted international rules or standards" (Art. 21(2)). Article 22 authorizes the coastal state to establish sea lanes and traffic separation schemes, especially for ships carrying nuclear or other dangerous or toxic substances. The duties of the coastal state are also given greater specificity. It may not discriminate against the ships of any state or against ships carrying cargoes to, from or on behalf of any state (Art. 24(*l*)(b)). As under the 1958 Convention, "the coastal state shall give appropriate publicity to any dangers to navigation, of which it has knowledge * * * " (Art. 24(2)). Is that requirement less stringent than that suggested in the *Corfu Channel Case*, 1949 I.C.J. 4? By Article 26 the coastal state may not levy charges for passage, only for any specific service rendered the ship, and without discrimination.

3. For a suggestion that the right to "innocent passage" was not violated by a United States military search and seizure of a United States vessel in foreign territorial waters, see United States v. Conroy, 589 F.2d 1258 (5th Cir.1979), cert. denied, 444 U.S. 831, 100 S.Ct. 60, 62 L.Ed.2d 40 (1979), discussed at Note 5, p. 1507 below.

4. A warship's right of innocent passage under customary law was unclear. Jessup concluded in 1927 that "the sound rule seems to be that they [warships] should not enjoy an absolute legal right to pass through a state's territorial waters any more than an army may cross the land territory." The Law of Territorial Waters and Maritime Jurisdiction 120 (1927). The Hague Codification Conference confined itself to observing that states ordinarily "will not forbid the passage of foreign warships" and "will not require a previous authorisation or notification." 24 A.J.I.L.Supp. 246 (1930). For a collection of views, see 4 Whiteman at 404–17.

The 1958 Convention on the Territorial Sea and the Contiguous Zone provides:

> Article 23. If any warship does not comply with the regulations of the coastal State concerning passage through the territorial sea and disregards any request for compliance which is made to it, the coastal State may require the warship to leave the territorial sea.

The 1982 Convention, Article 30, repeats the 1958 Convention but adds the word "immediately."

Did the inclusion of Article 23 in the 1958 Convention imply that warships have a right of innocent passage through a foreign state's territorial sea? See Slonim, The Right of Innocent Passage and the 1958 Geneva Conference on the Law of the Sea, 5 Colum. J. Transnat'l L. 96 (1966). Is it persuasive, with respect to the innocent passage of warships, that Article 14(6) of the 1958 Convention and Article 20 of the 1982 Convention provide that "submarines are required to navigate on the surface and to show their flag"? The 1982 Convention places warships and other government ships operated for non-commercial purposes in the same subsection of a section entitled "Innocent Passage in the Territorial Sea." The right of innocent passage is set forth in a subsection applicable to all ships. See Delupis, Foreign Warships and Immunity for Espionage, 78 A.J.I.L. 53 (1984). See also Jin, The Question of Innocent Passage of Warships after the UNCLOS 111, 13 Marine Pol'y 56 (1989); Oxman, The Regime of Warships under the United Nations Convention on the Law of the Sea, 24 Va.J.Int'l L. 809 (1984); Sadurska, Foreign Submarines in Swedish Waters: The Erosion of an International Norm, 10 Yale J.Int'l L. 34 (1984).

5. The Restatement (Third) § 512 states:

Subject to § 513, the coastal state has the same sovereignty over its territorial sea, and over the air space, sea-bed and subsoil thereof, as it has in respect of its land territory.

b. International Straits

CORFU CHANNEL CASE (UNITED KINGDOM v. ALBANIA)

International Court of Justice, 1949.
1949 I.C.J. 4.

[The United Kingdom sought to hold Albania responsible for damage caused to British warships by mines moored in the Corfu Channel in Albanian territorial waters. Albania, in turn, charged that, on another occasion, British warships had passed through the channel without the permission of Albanian authorities, and sought satisfaction.]

* * *

To begin with, the foundation for Albania's responsibility, as alleged by the United Kingdom, must be considered. On this subject, the main position of the United Kingdom is to be found in its submission No. 2: that the minefield which caused the explosions was laid between May 15th, 1946, and October 22nd, 1946, by or with the connivance or knowledge of the Albanian Government.

The obligations incumbent upon the Albanian authorities consisted in notifying, for the benefit of shipping in general, the existence of a minefield in Albanian territorial waters and in warning the approaching British warships of the imminent danger to which the minefield exposed them. Such obligations are based, not on the Hague Convention of 1907, No. VIII, which is applicable in time of war, but on certain general and well-recognized principles, namely: elementary considerations of humanity, even more exacting in peace than in war; the principle of the freedom of maritime communication; and every State's obligation not to allow knowingly its territory to be used for acts contrary to the rights of other States.

In fact, Albania neither notified the existence of the minefield, nor warned the British warships of the danger they were approaching.

* * *

In fact, nothing was attempted by the Albanian authorities to prevent the disaster. These grave omissions involve the international responsibility of Albania.

The Court therefore reaches the conclusion that Albania is responsible under international law for the explosions which occurred on October 22nd, 1946, in Albanian waters, and for the damage and loss of human life which resulted from them, and that there is a duty upon Albania to pay compensation to the United Kingdom.

* * *

In the second part of the Special Agreement, the following question is submitted to the Court:

> (2) Has the United Kingdom under international law violated the sovereignty of the Albanian People's Republic by reason of the acts of the Royal Navy in Albanian waters on the 22nd October and on the 12th and 13th November 1946 and is there any duty to give satisfaction?

The Court will first consider whether the sovereignty of Albania was violated by reason of the acts of the British Navy in Albanian waters on October 22nd, 1946.

On May 15th, 1946, the British cruisers Orion and Superb, while passing southward through the North Corfu Channel, were fired at by an Albanian battery in the vicinity of Saranda. It appears from the report of the commanding naval officer dated May 29th, 1946, that the firing started when the ships had already passed the battery and were moving away from it; that from 12 to 20 rounds were fired; that the firing lasted 12 minutes and ceased only when the ships were out of range; but that the ships were not hit although there were a number of "shorts" and of "overs". An Albanian note of May 21st states that the Coastal Commander ordered a few shots to be fired in the direction of the ships "in accordance with a General Order founded on international law."

The United Kingdom Government at once protested to the Albanian Government, stating that innocent passage through straits is a right recognized by international law. There ensued a diplomatic correspondence in which the Albanian Government asserted that foreign warships and merchant vessels had no right to pass through Albanian territorial waters without prior notification to, and the permission of, the Albanian authorities. This view was put into effect by a communication of the Albanian Chief of Staff, dated May 17th, 1946, which purported to subject the passage of foreign warships and merchant vessels in Albanian territorial waters to previous notification to and authorization by the Albanian Government. The diplomatic correspondence continued, and culminated in a United Kingdom note of August 2nd, 1946, in which the United Kingdom Government maintained its view with regard to the right of innocent passage through straits forming routes for international maritime traffic between two parts of the high seas. The note ended with the warning that if Albanian coastal batteries in the future opened fire on any British warship passing through the Corfu Channel, the fire would be returned.

* * *

It is, in the opinion of the Court, generally recognized and in accordance with international custom that States in time of peace have a right to send their warships through straits used for international navigation between two parts of the high seas without the previous authorization of a coastal State, provided that the passage is innocent. Unless otherwise prescribed in an international convention, there is no right for a coastal State to prohibit such passage through straits in time of peace.

The Albanian Government does not dispute that the North Corfu Channel is a strait in the geographical sense; but it denies that this Channel belongs to the class of international highways through which a right of passage exists, on the grounds that it is only of secondary importance and not even a necessary route between two parts of the high seas, and that it is used almost exclusively for local traffic to and from the ports of Corfu and Saranda.

It may be asked whether the test is to be found in volume of traffic passing through the Strait or in its greater or lesser importance for international navigation. But in the opinion of the Court the decisive criterion is rather its geographical situation as connecting two parts of the high seas and the fact of its being used for international navigation. Nor can it be decisive that this Strait is not a necessary route between two parts of the high seas, but only an alternative passage between the Aegean and the Adriatic Seas. It has nevertheless been a useful route for international maritime traffic. * * *

* * *

Having regard to these various considerations, the Court has arrived at the conclusion that the North Corfu Channel should be considered as belonging to the class of international highways through which passage cannot be prohibited by a coastal State in time of peace.

On the other hand, it is a fact that the two coastal States did not maintain normal relations, that Greece had made territorial claims precisely with regard to a part of Albanian territory bordering on the Channel, that Greece had declared that she considered herself technically in a state of war with Albania, and that Albania, invoking the danger of Greek incursions, had considered it necessary to take certain measures of vigilance in this region. The Court is of opinion that Albania, in view of these exceptional circumstances, would have been justified in issuing regulations in respect of the passage of warships through the Strait, but not in prohibiting such passage or in subjecting it to the requirement of special authorization.

Notes

1. The *Corfu Channel* decision has been criticized for giving insufficient weight to functional considerations, i.e., failing to balance "the interest which the coastal state has in its own territorial sea against that which the international maritime community has in traversing that passage." 1 O'Connell at 563.

2. Article 16(4) of the 1958 Convention provides:

> There shall be no suspension of the innocent passage of foreign ships through straits which are used for international navigation between one part of the high seas and another part of the high seas or the territorial sea of a foreign state.

The International Law Commission, in its final version of the predecessor of Article 16(4), limited the right of passage through straits to those which are "normally used for international navigation between two parts of the high seas." [1956] II Yb.I.L.C. 273. In the First Committee, however, the word "normally" was deleted and the article was further amended to its present form by a vote of 31–30–10, over vigorous objection by the Arab states. (Prior to the occupation of the Sinai Peninsula by Israeli forces in 1967, Egypt and Saudi Arabia controlled the Straits of Tiran which provided the sole access to the Gulf of Aqaba, on which Israel has several miles of frontage.) 3 U.N.Conf. on the Law of the Sea, Off.Rec. 93–96,100 (1958). Several Arab states, however, entered reservations to this provision.

For materials on the problem of the Gulf of Aqaba, see 4 Whiteman at 465–480.

3. By the terms of the Treaty of Lausanne (Convention relating to the Régime of the Straits, signed at Lausanne, July 24, 1923, 28 L.N.T.S. 115), the Dardanelles and the Bosphorus came under the supervision of an international commission, the only one of its type ever to function. Vessels of commerce were to be allowed free passage in time of war and in peace, but limits were placed on the number of naval vessels permitted to transit the Straits into the Black Sea; Turkey was permitted to take defensive measures against enemy ships in time of war (Annex to Art. 2 of the Treaty of Lausanne), but the Straits were demilitarized (Art. 4). The Straits Commission functioned as a supervisor of transit, assuring that warships could pass through the Straits without undue hindrance, upon occasion making representations to Turkey on this subject. The Commission was terminated upon conclusion of the Montreux Convention of 1936 (Convention concerning the Régime of the Straits, signed at Montreux, July 20, 1936, entered into force Nov. 9, 1936, 173 L.N.T.S. 213, 7 Hudson, International Legislation 386 (1941)). The Montreux Convention transferred the functions of the Straits Commission to Turkey (Art. 24), the littoral state, which thus reasserted its sovereignty. Restrictions on the number of warships transiting the Straits into the Black Sea were maintained. Turkey assumed responsibility for assuring free passage. Free and unlimited navigation for merchant vessels was retained (Art. 2), but Turkey was granted the right to remilitarize the Straits. The Montreux Convention was to remain in force for twenty years from the date of its entry into force, and was subject to denunciation upon two years' notice after 1956; the right of free transit for merchant vessels is to continue without time limitation. Apparently, none of the parties had sought to denounce the Convention. See 4 Whiteman at 417–47; see also Baxter, The Law of International Waterways 159–68 (1964).

THE 1982 CONVENTION AND INTERNATIONAL STRAITS

In response to pressures to widen the territorial sea (p. 1394 supra), the United States and several other powers indicated a willingness to accept a twelve-mile territorial sea provided they were assured passage through international straits. They were not content with mere rights of "innocent passage" through such straits since there had been disagreement as to whether warships were entitled to innocent passage, and submarines were explicitly required to surface; also, the meaning of innocent passage had been disputed and in any event left passing vessels substantially at the mercy of the coastal state. The result was a new regime for international straits with a right of "transit passage."

TRANSIT PASSAGE

U.N. CONVENTION ON THE LAW OF THE SEA (1982)

1833 U.N.T.S. 3, U.N.Doc. A/CONF. 62/122; 21 I.L.M. 1261 (1982).

ARTICLE 37

Scope of This Section

This section applies to straits which are used for international navigation between one part of the high seas or an exclusive economic zone and another part of the high seas or an exclusive economic zone.

Article 38

Right of Transit Passage

1. In straits referred to in article 37, all ships and aircraft enjoy the right of transit passage, which shall not be impeded; except that, if the strait is formed by an island of a State bordering the strait and its mainland, transit passage shall not apply if there exists seaward of the island a route through the high seas or through an exclusive economic zone of similar convenience with respect to navigational and hydrographical characteristics.

2. Transit passage means the exercise in accordance with this Part of the freedom of navigation and overflight solely for the purpose of continuous and expeditious transit of the strait between one part of the high seas or an exclusive economic zone and another part of the high seas or an exclusive economic zone. However, the requirement of continuous and expeditious transit does not preclude passage through the strait for the purpose of entering, leaving or returning from a State bordering the strait, subject to the conditions of entry to that State.

3. Any activity which is not an exercise of the right of transit passage through a strait remains subject to the other applicable provisions of this Convention.

Article 39

Duties of Ships and Aircraft During Transit Passage

1. Ships and aircraft, while exercising the right of transit passage, shall:

(a) proceed without delay through or over the strait;

(b) refrain from any threat or use of force against the sovereignty, territorial integrity or political independence of States bordering the strait, or in any other manner in violation of the principles of international law embodied in the Charter of the United Nations;

(c) refrain from any activities other than those incident to their normal modes of continuous and expeditious transit unless rendered necessary by *force majeure*, or by distress;

(d) comply with other relevant provisions of this Part.

2. Ships in transit passage shall:

(a) comply with generally accepted international regulations, procedures and practices for safety at sea, including the International Regulations for Preventing Collisions at Sea;

(b) comply with generally accepted international regulations, procedures and practices for the prevention, reduction and control of pollution from ships.

3. Aircraft in transit passage shall:

(a) observe the Rules of the Air established by the International Civil Aviation Organization as they apply to civil aircraft; state aircraft will normally comply with such safety measures and will at all times operate with due regard for the safety of navigation;

(b) at all times monitor the radio frequency assigned by the competent internationally designated air traffic control authority or the appropriate international distress radio frequency.

ARTICLE 40

Research and Survey Activities

During transit passage, foreign ships, including marine scientific research and hydrographic survey ships, may not carry out any research or survey activities without the prior authorization of the States bordering straits.

Notes

1. The 1982 Convention provides that bordering states may designate sea lanes and prescribe traffic separation schemes where necessary to promote safe passage (Art. 41), and may make laws and regulations for safety, regulation of traffic, prevention of pollution and fishing, enforcing customs, immigration, fiscal and sanitary laws (Art. 42). User states and border states shall by agreement cooperate in navigation and safety aids and prevention of pollution from ships (Art. 43). International straits not covered by this regime (see Art. 36) shall be governed by "innocent passage" which shall not be suspended (Art. 45).

2. Does the "transit passage" regime modify the rules governing the exercise of civil and criminal jurisdiction of the coastal state in its territorial sea, p. [1336] infra?

INTERNATIONAL CANALS

"The right of free passage through international straits is a product of state practice hardening into customary international law and thence into treaty. The right of free passage through interoceanic canals is a consequence of the opening of each waterway to usage by the international community. It is the origin of the right in a series of individual grants which distinguishes the law relating to canals from the law of straits. The privilege of free passage through the three major interoceanic canals, Suez, Panama, and Kiel, has been created in each case by a treaty to which the territorial sovereign, acting freely or under the pressure of other powers, has been a party." Baxter, The Law of International Waterways 168–69 (1964).

The right of free passage through the Suez Canal is usually said to be founded on the Convention of Constantinople of 1888 (79 Brit. & For. State Papers 18, reprinted in 3 A.J.I.L.Supp. 123 (1909)), although some writers maintain that the international character of the canal had already been established by concessions of 1854 and 1866. The Convention was signed by Great Britain, Germany, France, Austria–Hungary, Italy, the Netherlands, Russia, Spain, and the Ottoman Empire (then holding sovereignty over Egypt); after the Canal's nationalization in 1956, Egypt reaffirmed its obligations under the Convention (265 U.N.T.S. 299; 272 U.N.T.S. 225). The Convention provides in Article I that the Canal "shall always be free and open, in time of war as in time of peace, to every vessel of commerce or of war, without distinction of flag," and in Article IV that "no right of war, no act of hostility, nor any act having for its object the obstruction of the free navigation of the Canal, shall be committed in the Canal and its ports of access, as well as within a radius of three marine miles from those ports, even though the Ottoman Empire should be one of the belligerent Powers." The Convention also includes restrictions on warships and fortifications. In practice, rights under Article I have usually been regarded as granted to all states whether or not they adhere to the Convention. See 1 O'Connell at 643–48; Baxter at 89–91, 169–70, 183 n. 162. During the two World Wars, the United Kingdom justified measures inconsistent with the Convention as necessary to prevent the Canal's destruction; after 1948, Egypt justified anti-Israeli restrictions on the basis of its "inherent" right of self-defense. See 1 O'Connell at 647–48; Gross, Passage Through the Suez Canal of Israel-bound Cargo and Israel Ships, 51 A.J.I.L. 530 (1957). The Suez Canal was opened to Israel-bound cargoes pursuant to the Egypt–Israel Peace Treaty, Art. 5 (28 I.L.M. 362 (1979)).

The regime of the Panama Canal was governed by the Hay–Pauncefote Treaty of 1901 between the United States and Great Britain (32 Stat.1903), the rules of which were expressly stated to be "substantially as embodied in the Convention of Constantinople." The agreement provided in Article III that "the canal shall be free and open to the vessels of commerce and of war of all nations observing these Rules, on terms of entire equality, so that there shall be no discrimination against any such nation, or its citizens or subjects, in respect of the conditions or charges of traffic, or otherwise." The foregoing language was substantially reproduced in the 1903 treaty by which the United States acquired the Canal Zone from Panama. See Baxter at 170–71.

The Panama Canal Treaties were replaced by new ones concluded in 1977. See 16 I.L.M. 1022 and 1040 (1977). By Article 2 of the new Panama Canal Treaty, 33 U.S.T. 39, T.I.A.S. 10030, 1280 U.N.T.S. 3, the treaty terminated at noon, Panama time, December 31, 1999. The United States returned the Canal to Panama at that time. A companion treaty known as the Neutrality Treaty, which is of unlimited duration, commits both the United States and Panama to maintain the permanent neutrality of the Canal and the access to it of vessels of all flags.

The Kiel Canal had not, prior to the Treaty of Versailles of 1919, been held out by Germany as an international waterway open without restriction to all states. Article 380 of the Treaty of Versailles, however, provided that "the Kiel Canal and its approaches shall be maintained free and open to the vessels of commerce and of war of all nations at peace with Germany on terms of entire equality." 112 Brit. & For. State Papers 1, 189. The Permanent Court of International Justice, in the Case of the S.S. Wimbledon, P.C.I.J., Ser. A, No. 1 (1923), referred to the Canal as "an international waterway * * * for the benefit of all nations of the world" (id. at 22), even though only twenty-eight states were parties to Article 380. In 1936, Germany denounced Article 380 without effective protest from other states.

The legal position of states that are not parties to treaties guaranteeing passage through international canals has been rationalized by the doctrine of "international servitudes," by the "third-party beneficiary" concepts drawn from municipal law, by the theory that certain treaties are "dispositive" in nature in the sense that they create "real rights" that attach to a territory and are therefore not dependent on the treaty which created them, and by analogy to treaties, such as the United Nations Charter, that have an objective, legislative character, in that they create international status that must be recognized by all states, whether contracting parties or not. Baxter states that "the preferable theory concerning the rights of nonsignatories is that a state may, in whole or in part, dedicate a waterway to international use, which dedication, if relied upon, creates legally enforceable rights in favor of the shipping of the international community. A treaty, a unilateral declaration—perhaps even a concession—may be the instrument whereby the dedication is effected. Its form is not important; what is important is that it speaks to the entire world or to a group of states who are to be the beneficiaries of the right of free passage." Baxter at 182–83. See generally 2 Hackworth at 769; 3 Whiteman at 10761; Baxter, The Law of International Waterways, *passim* (1964); 1 O'Connell at 640–51.

c. *Archipelagic Sea–Lane Passage*

RESTATEMENT (THIRD) § 513(4)

(4) In archipelagic waters, (a) all ships have the right of innocent passage; and (b) all ships and aircraft enjoy the right of archipelagic sea lanes passage.

Comment:

* * *

k. Archipelagic sea lanes passage. Under Subsection (4), foreign ships (and aircraft) enjoy the right of passage through designated archipelagic sea lanes (and air routes), which must include all normal passage routes used for international navigation or overflight. Where there are two routes of similar convenience between the same entry and exit points, only one needs to be designated. The sea lanes and air routes are to be designated by agreement between the archipelagic state and the competent international organization (principally IMO). LOS Convention, Article 53. Such passage is generally subject to the same standards as transit passage through straits, Article 54, but the Convention explicitly provides that archipelagic sea lanes passage is allowed in "the normal mode"; for instance, submarines may travel under water. *Compare* Articles 38(2) and 39(1)(c) with 53(3). If the archipelagic state has not designated archipelagic sea lanes or routes, "the right of archipelagic sea lanes passage may be exercised through the routes normally used for international navigation." *Id.* Article 53(12). In archipelagic waters other than the designated sea lanes, ships of all states enjoy the right of innocent passage similar to the one they possess in the territorial sea, except in inland waters delimited by straight lines drawn across mouths of rivers, bays, and entrances to ports. See *id.* Articles 50 and 52(1).

Notes

1. Restatement (Third) § 513, Reporters' Note 4 states:

Acceptance by the major maritime states of the concept of archipelagic state was conditional on acceptance of the right of archipelagic sea lanes passage. Such sea lanes are defined in detail in Article 53 of the LOS Convention. The main rules relating to international straits apply, with such modifications as may be necessary, to archipelagic sea lanes passage. See LOS Convention, Arts. 46–54.

2. In 1992, the Japanese government came under intense pressure not to use the Strait of Malacca, one of the world's most heavily traveled sea lanes, to transport a large quantity of plutonium to Japan. As a result, vessels transporting the plutonium followed a high seas route instead. Was Japan entitled to use the Strait of Malacca? See Restatement (Third) § 513(3), Comment *j*, and Reporters' Note 3. See also de Yturriaga, Straits Used for International Navigation (1991); Langdon, The Extent of Transit Passage: Some Practical Anomalies, 14 Marine Pol'y. 130 (1990); Mahmoudi, Customary International Law and Transit Passage, 20 Ocean Dev. & Int'l. L. 157 (1989); Caminos, The Legal Regime of Straits in the 1982 United Nations Convention on the Law of the Sea, 205 Rec. des Cours 9 (1987); Valencia & Marsh, Access to Straits and Sealanes in Southeast Asian Seas: Legal, Economic and Strategic Considerations, 16 J. Maritime L. & Com. 513 (1985).

3. The Contiguous Zone

CHURCH v. HUBBART

Supreme Court of the United States, 1804.
6 U.S. (2 Cranch) 187, 2 L.Ed. 249.

[The brigantine Aurora, an American vessel, was seized "four or five leagues" off the coast of Brazil by Portuguese authorities, for alleged illicit trade with the shore. To recover the loss, the vessel's owner sued on two insurance policies issued by the defendant. Each policy, however, had excluded losses arising out of illicit trade with the Portuguese. The insurer relied on the exclusions, but the plaintiff argued, *inter alia,* that a seizure so far from shore was unlawful because it was outside the Portuguese territorial jurisdiction. The Circuit Court directed a verdict for the insurer, and the owner appealed. In the course of his opinion, Chief Justice Marshall stated:]

That the law of nations prohibits the exercise of any act of authority over a vessel in the situation of the Aurora, and that this seizure is, on that account, a mere marine trespass, not within the exception, cannot be admitted. To reason from the extent of protection a nation will afford to foreigners, to the extent of the means it may use for its own security, does not seem to be perfectly correct. It is opposed by principles which are universally acknowledged. The authority of a nation, within its own territory, is absolute and exclusive. The seizure of a vessel, within the range of its cannon, by a foreign force, is an invasion of that territory, and is a hostile act which it is its duty to repel. But its power to secure itself from injury may certainly be exercised beyond the limits of its territory. Upon this principle, the right of a belligerent to search a neutral vessel on the high seas, for contraband of war, is universally admitted, because the belligerent has a right to prevent the injury done to himself, by the assistance intended for his enemy: so too, a nation has a right to prohibit any commerce with its colonies. Any attempt to violate the laws made to protect this right, is an injury to itself, which it may prevent, and it has a right to use the means necessary for its prevention. These means do not appear to be limited within any certain marked boundaries, which remain the same, at all times and in all situations. If they are such as unnecessarily to vex and harass foreign lawful commerce, foreign nations will resist their exercise. If they are such as are reasonable and necessary to secure their laws from violation, they will be submitted to. * * *

If this right be extended too far, the exercise of it will be resisted. It has occasioned long and frequent contests, which have sometimes ended in open war. The English, it will be well recollected, complained of the right claimed by Spain to search their vessels on the high seas, which was carried so far, that the *guarda costas* of that nation seized vessels not in the neighborhood of their coasts. This practice was the subject of long and fruitless negotiations, and at length, of open war. The right of the Spaniards was supposed to be exercised unreasonably and vexatiously, but it never was contended, that it could only be exercised within the range of the cannon from their batteries. Indeed, the right given to our own revenue cutters, to visit vessels four leagues from our coast, is a declaration that, in the opinion of the American government, no such principle as that contended for has a real existence. Nothing, then, is to be drawn from the laws or usages of nations, which gives to this part of the contract before the court, the very limited construction which the plaintiff insists on, or which proves that the seizure of the Aurora, by the Portuguese governor, was an act of lawless violence.

The argument that such act would be within the policy, and not within the exception, is admitted to be well founded. That the exclusion from the insurance of "the risk of illicit trade with the Portuguese," is an exclusion only of that risk, to which such trade is by law exposed, will be readily conceded. It is unquestionably limited and restrained by the terms "illicit trade." No seizure, not justifiable under the laws and regulations established by the crown of Portugal, for the restriction of foreign commerce with its dependencies, can come within this part of the contract, and every seizure which is justifiable by those laws and regulations, must be deemed within it.

[The judgment below was reversed, and a new trial ordered, because the trial court had admitted improperly authenticated documents.]

Notes

1. Marshall, writing in 1804, suggested that a state's power to secure itself from injury may be exercised beyond the limits of its territory, and that the means "do not appear to he limited within any certain marked boundaries." In time, however, the coastal state's rights to act were confined to a limited contiguous zone. Might the coastal state have authority to act beyond the contiguous zone for some purposes? See pp. 1416–1421. Compare the right of a coastal state to act against "pirate broadcasting" from the high seas. See p. 1447.

2. "The exercise of jurisdiction in contiguous zones of the high seas becomes necessary in view of the inadequacy under modern conditions of any reasonable breadth of territorial waters; whatever we may regard as the breadth of marginal sea now accepted under international law, there are occasions and purposes for which jurisdiction must be exercised farther out from shore. This differs from an attempt to declare such areas territorial waters subject to the full sovereignty of the coastal state." Bishop, The Exercise of Jurisdiction for Special Purposes in High Seas Beyond the Outer Limit of Territorial Waters (paper prepared for the sixth conference of the Inter-American Bar Ass'n., 1949), reprinted. in 99 Cong. Rec. 2493 (1953).

3. What is the scope of the proposition that a state may exercise such jurisdiction on the high seas as is "reasonable and necessary" to prevent the violation of its laws? Does a privilege to prevent violations encompass the privilege to punish attempted violations or past violations?

U.N. CONVENTION ON THE LAW OF THE SEA (1982)

1833 U.N.T.S. 3, U.N.Doc. A/CONF. 62/122; 21 I.L.M. 1261 (1982).

ARTICLE 33

Contiguous Zone

1. In a zone contiguous to its territorial sea, described as the contiguous zone, the coastal State may exercise the control necessary to:

(a) prevent infringement of its customs, fiscal, immigration or sanitary laws and regulations within its territory or territorial sea;

(b) punish infringement of the above laws and regulations committed within its territory or territorial sea.

2. The contiguous zone may not extend beyond 24 nautical miles from the baselines from which the breadth of the territorial sea is measured.

Notes

1. Article 24 of the 1958 Convention was essentially the same except that there the outer-limit of the zone was set at twelve miles. See also Restatement (Third) § 513, Comment *f*.

Article 24 of the 1958 Convention was based on a text adopted by the International Law Commission at its eighth session in 1956. The Commission's commentary on the article provided:

> (1) International law accords States the right to exercise preventive or protective control for certain purposes over a belt of the high seas contiguous to their territorial sea. It is, of course, understood that this power of control does not change the legal status of the waters over which it is exercised. These waters are and remain a part of the high seas and are not subject to the sovereignty of the coastal State, which can exercise over them only such rights as are conferred on it by the present draft or are derived from international treaties.
>
> (2) Many States have adopted the principle that in the contiguous zone the coastal State may exercise customs control in order to prevent attempted infringements of its customs and fiscal regulations within its territory or territorial sea, and to punish infringements of those regulations committed within its territory or territorial sea. The Commission considered that it would be impossible to deny to States the exercise of such rights.
>
> (3) Although the number of States which claim rights over the contiguous zone for the purpose of applying sanitary regulations is fairly small, the Commission considers that, in view of the connexion between customs and sanitary regulations, such rights should also be recognized for sanitary regulations.
>
> (4) The Commission did not recognize special security rights in the contiguous zone. It considered that the extreme vagueness of the term

"security" would open the way for abuses and that the granting of such rights was not necessary. The enforcement of customs and sanitary regulations will be sufficient in most cases to safeguard the security of the State. In so far as measures of self-defence against an imminent and direct threat to the security of the State are concerned, the Commission refers to the general principles of international law and the Charter of the United Nations.

(5) Nor was the Commission willing to recognize any exclusive right of the coastal State to engage in fishing in the contiguous zone. * * *

[1956] 11 Yb.I.L.C. 294–95. The Commission's decision not to include "immigration" as one of the matters over which a coastal state could exercise jurisdiction outside its territorial waters was overruled at the Geneva Conference. 3 U.N.Conf. on the Law of the Sea, Off.Rec. 181–82, 198–99 (1958). See generally Mason, Alien Stowaways, the Immigration and Naturalization Service and Shipowners, 12 Tulane Mar.L.J. 361 (1988).

In United States v. F/V Taiyo Maru, 395 F.Supp. 413 (D.Me.1975), a Japanese ship was found fishing illegally and was seized in the United States exclusive fishing zone, nine miles offshore and beyond the then three mile territorial sea limit. The defendants argued that the seizure was not permitted by Article 24 of the 1958 Convention, but the court held that the list in Article 24 of purposes for which a contiguous zone may be established is not exhaustive. Id., at 419. See also United States v. Postal, 589 F.2d 862, 876 n. 20 (5th Cir.1979), cert. denied, 444 U.S. 832, 100 S.Ct. 61, 62 L.Ed.2d 40 (1979); Ridell, Hot Pursuit from a Fisheries Zone, 70 A.J.I.L. 95 (1976).

2. What is the scope of the authority permitted to the coastal state in the contiguous zone? May a coastal state prescribe rules with which foreign vessels in the contiguous zone must comply? Would such rules have to relate to infringement of customs, fiscal, immigration or sanitary interests within the coastal state's territory or territorial sea? May a coastal state enforce such rules against foreign ships while the latter are in the contiguous zone? What is the scope of jurisdiction to "prevent" violations within the coastal state's territory or territorial sea? Might legitimate "preventive" measures include the arrest of a smuggling vessel or the confiscation of contraband? Would the Portuguese action upheld in Church v. Hubbart, supra, be allowable under the 1982 Convention? See McDougal & Burke,The Public Order of the Oceans 608–630 (1962); Lowe, The Development of the Contiguous Zone, 52 Brit.Y.B.I.L. 109 (1981); Varghese, Territorial Sea and Contiguous Zone: Concept and Development, 9 Cochin U.L.Rev. 436 (1985); Symonides, Origin and Legal Essence of the Contiguous Zone, 20 Ocean Dev. & Int'l L. 203 (1989).

3. In 1988, the United States extended its territorial sea to 12 miles, see p. 1395 supra, and on September 2, 1999 the contiguous zone was extended, by Presidential Proclamation 7219, to 24 nautical miles, the limit permitted under Article 33 of the 1982 Convention.

4. In comparison to the flexible standard laid down in Church v. Hubbart, supra, and in light of the considerations that necessitate the exercise of jurisdiction beyond territorial waters, how satisfactory is the Convention Article? "It should be observed," said Hyde, "that the privilege * * * is not measured by exact limits and might be rendered illusory if it were. The geographical features of the coasts of maritime States vary so greatly that needed privileges of self-protection on the high sea are not alike and do not lend themselves to arrangements that lay down uniform geographical or linear tests." 1 Hyde 462. See also McDougal &

Burke, supra at 606–07; Jessup, The United Nations Conference on the Law of the Sea, 59 Colum.L.Rev. 234, 244 (1959).

5. Since the 1982 Convention now provides for a 200 mile exclusive economic zone (p. 1437 infra) and defines the continental shelf as extending even beyond that zone in some cases (p. 1424 infra), has the significance of the contiguous zone changed?

CUSTOMS ZONES, HOVERING, AND HOT PURSUIT

From the early part of the eighteenth century, the United Kingdom enforced laws sometimes referred to as "hovering acts" which authorized the search and seizure, on the high seas at varying distances (up to eight or even 100 leagues) from the coast, of British and foreign ships suspected of having an intention to smuggle goods ashore. See Masterson, Jurisdiction in Marginal Seas With Special Reference to Smuggling 1–162 (1929); Jessup, The Law of Territorial Waters and Maritime Jurisdiction 77–79 (1927). No state protested these acts, and Sir William Scott defended them in the case of Le Louis, 2 Dodson Adm.Rep. 210, 245 (1817), as founded on the "common courtesy" and "common convenience" of nations. The United States and a number of Latin American countries, on becoming independent, adopted similar customs zones, usually of twelve miles, and some European states also authorized seizures outside territorial waters. Jessup at 80–91, see also Masterson at 175–206. In 1876, however, the United Kingdom reversed its policy and, in repealing the "hovering acts," took the position that a state could not, under international law, exercise jurisdiction on the high seas against vessels of other states. Jessup at 79. The new British doctrine gained the adherence of some other states, notably Germany and Japan, but the United States and a number of other countries continued to regard contiguous zone jurisdiction in customs matters as a right sanctioned by state practice. Brierly; The Law of Nations 205 (6th ed. Waldock 1963).

Prior to the advent of Prohibition—the laws implementing the 18th Amendment to the U.S. Constitution prohibiting "the manufacture, sale, or transportation of intoxicating liquors within, the importation thereof into, or the exportation thereof from the United States"—the United States did not attempt to board foreign vessels beyond the three-mile territorial sea except when the vessel was bound for the United States, or when it had been caught violating United States laws in the territorial sea and was then "hotly pursued." See Cook v. United States, 288 U.S. 102, 112–13, 53 S.Ct. 305, 308–09, 77 L.Ed. 641 (1933). The widespread smuggling of liquor, after 1920, from British and other ships led Congress to provide, in the Tariff Act of 1922, that even foreign vessels not bound for the United States might be boarded, searched, and seized beyond the three-mile limit. Hyde, 780–82. It nevertheless continued to be the consistent United States policy to release vessels seized beyond this limit which had not been bound for the United States, except in cases where it appeared that the vessel had already been in contact with the shore. See Cook v. United States, supra. The "shore contact" rule was applied in The Grace and Ruby, 283 Fed. 475 (D.Mass.1922), to justify forfeiture of a British schooner seized outside the three-mile limit but which had used its boat and members of its crew to assist in ferrying liquor ashore. A British protest was answered by the State Department with a reference to the incident of the Araunah, in which the United Kingdom had acquiesced in a Russian seizure on the high seas of a British vessel engaged in illegal seal hunting by means of its canoes operating close to the shore. [1922] 1 For.Rel.U.S. 592–93. In the Henry L. Marshall, 286 Fed. 260 (S.D.N.Y.1922), aff'd, 292 Fed. 486 (2d Cir.1923), cert. denied, 263 U.S. 712, 44 S.Ct. 38, 68 L.Ed. 519 (1923), the "shore contact" rule was applied even though contact was made through shore-based boats, rather than the ship's own. Although the ship was ostensibly of British registry, the United Kingdom did not press a protest because the registration had been fraudulently obtained; the State Department nevertheless vigorously asserted the validity of the principle involved. [1923] 1 For.Rel.U.S. 163–64; Jessup at 251–53.

The United States and the United Kingdom finally entered into a treaty in 1924, 43 Stat. 1761, under which the United Kingdom agreed not to protest restrictions imposed on British vessels by the United States within an hour's sailing distance from the latter's coast, and the United States agreed that it would not enforce the Prohibition laws against liquor carried by British vessels in United States waters as sealed cargo destined for foreign ports or as sea stores. Similar treaties were concluded between the United States and other countries. See 1 Hackworth at 678–79. In 1925, the northern European coastal states (from Norway and Denmark to the U.S.S.R.) concluded the Treaty of Helsingfors, 42 L.N.T.S. 75, 4 Whiteman 489, which authorized, as among the parties, a twelve-mile contiguous zone off their respective coasts for the purpose of suppressing contraband traffic in liquor.

In the Anti–Smuggling Act of 1935, 49 Stat. 517, Congress provided that the President, upon finding that vessels hovering beyond the twelve-mile limit of "customs waters" were assisting or threatening to assist "the unlawful introduction or removal into or from the United States of any merchandise or person," might declare a "customs-enforcement area" extending not more than one hundred miles from the vicinity of the offending vessels and not more than fifty miles from the outward limit of United States customs waters (i.e., not more than sixty-two miles from the United States coastline). Within such a customs-enforcement area, United States customs officers were to have the same enforcement powers (including the power of seizure and arrest) as they would have at any place in the United States. The Act expressly disclaimed the intention to authorize jurisdiction in violation of any international agreement, and the provisions relating to customs-enforcement areas were not regarded in the United States as in themselves authorizing the violation of customary rules of international law. See generally Jessup, The Anti–Smuggling Act of 1935, 31 A.J.I.L. 101 (1937). Only five such zones were established, Briggs, The Law of Nations 375 (2d ed. 1952), and the only seizure made under the 1935 Act that provoked a protest from a foreign government did not involve a customs-enforcement area but a conspiracy. In The Reidun, 14 F.Supp. 771 (E.D.N.Y.1936), libels were dismissed against a Norwegian vessel seized in New York for having transshipped liquor while 500 to 600 miles from the nearest point of the United States customs waters or enforcement areas on the ground that the place of transshipment was not "adjacent to the customs waters of the United States" within the meaning of the Anti–Smuggling Act. However, an amended libel which charged that the vessel had been fitted out in Belgium for the purpose of smuggling, in violation of Section 3(a) of the Act was subsequently sustained. 15 F.Supp.

112 (E.D.N.Y.1936). The court stated: "Congress may very well have intended to mete out punishment to those who conspire outside of the territorial jurisdiction to violate laws of the nation by subjecting them to apprehension or punishment when found within the jurisdiction. If the *Reidun* was fitted out as alleged and did cause merchandise to be smuggled into the United States in defiance of its revenue laws, it ran the hazard of punishment by coming within the customs enforcement areas." Id. at 113. Does the foregoing rationale express a theory of territorial and maritime jurisdiction, or does it depend upon some other principle? Compare United States v. Aluminum Company of America, supra p. 1093. The Norwegian Government protested the seizure of the *Reidun*, and the vessel was released upon that government's assurances that it would take steps to prevent Norwegian vessels from violating United States revenue laws.

How does the contiguous zone provision in the 1982 Convention affect a coastal state's enforcement of its customs laws? Could the United States proclaim a "customs-enforcement area" pursuant to the Anti–Smuggling Act if this area extended beyond the contiguous zone? Could a coastal state board and search a foreign vessel hovering beyond its territorial sea but within the contiguous zone? If contraband or false manifests were found, could the coastal state order the forfeiture of the vessel or of its cargo? Would such an order be "punitive" or "preventive" action, within the meaning of the contiguous zone provision? Does that provision exclude the application of the "shore contact" doctrine to ships beyond the contiguous zone? Within the contiguous zone, does the "shore contact" rule add anything to the coastal state's ability to enforce its customs laws?

For the United States program to interdict vessels suspected of bringing undocumented aliens to the United States, see p. 1449 below.

RIGHT OF HOT PURSUIT

U.N. CONVENTION ON THE LAW OF THE SEA (1982)

1833 U.N.T.S. 3, U.N.Doc. A/CONF. 62/122; 21 I.L.M. 1261 (1982).

ARTICLE 111

1. The hot pursuit of a foreign ship may be undertaken when the competent authorities of the coastal State have good reason to believe that the ship has violated the laws and regulations of that State. Such pursuit must be commenced when the foreign ship or one of its boats is within the internal waters, the territorial sea or the contiguous zone of the pursuing State, and may only be continued outside the territorial sea or the contiguous zone if the pursuit has not been interrupted. It is not necessary that, at the time when the foreign ship within the territorial sea or the contiguous zone receives the order to stop, the ship giving the order should likewise be within the territorial sea or the contiguous zone. If the foreign ship is within a contiguous zone, as defined in article 33, the pursuit may only be undertaken if there has been a violation of the rights for the protection of which the zone was established.

2. The right of hot pursuit shall apply *mutatis mutandis* to violations in the exclusive economic zone or on the continental shelf, including safety zones

around continental shelf installations, of the laws and regulations of the coastal State applicable in accordance with this Convention to the exclusive economic zone or the continental shelf, including such safety zones.

3. The right of hot pursuit ceases as soon as the ship pursued enters the territorial sea of its own country or of a third State.

4. Hot pursuit is not deemed to have begun unless the pursuing ship has satisfied itself by such practicable means as may be available that the ship pursued or one of its boats or other craft working as a team and using the ship pursued as a mother ship are within the limits of the territorial sea, or, as the case may be, within the contiguous zone or the exclusive economic zone or above the continental shelf. The pursuit may only be commenced after a visual or auditory signal to stop has been given at a distance which enables it to be seen or heard by the foreign ship.

5. The right of hot pursuit may be exercised only by warships or military aircraft, or other ships or aircraft clearly marked and identifiable as being on government service and specially authorized to that effect.

6. Where hot pursuit is effected by an aircraft:

(a) The provisions of paragraphs 1 to 4 shall apply *mutatis mutandis*:

(b) The aircraft giving the order to stop must itself actively pursue the ship until a ship or aircraft of the coastal State, summoned by the aircraft, arrives to take over the pursuit, unless the aircraft is itself able to arrest the ship. It does not suffice to justify an arrest outside the territorial sea that the ship was merely sighted by the aircraft as an offender or suspected offender, if it was not both ordered to stop and pursued by the aircraft itself or other aircraft or ships which continue the pursuit without interruption.

7. The release of a ship arrested within the jurisdiction of a State and escorted to a port of that State for the purposes of an inquiry before the competent authorities may not be claimed solely on the ground that the ship, in the course of its voyage, was escorted across a portion of the exclusive economic zone or the high seas, if the circumstances rendered this necessary.
* * *

Notes

1. This provision essentially repeats that in Article 23 of the 1958 Convention on the High Seas except for the addition of paragraph 2 extending the doctrine of hot pursuit, *mutatis mutandis*, to violations in the exclusive economic zone or on the continental shelf. See pp. 1436, 1441 infra. See Restatement (Third) § 513, Comment *g*.

2. How does the right of "hot pursuit" relate to a coastal state's rights in the contiguous zone? See generally Allen, Doctrine of Hot Pursuit: A Functional Interpretation Adaptable to Emerging Maritime Law Enforcement Technology and Practices, 20 Ocean Dev. & Int'l. L. 30 (1989); Poulantzas, The Right of Hot Pursuit in International Law (1969).

COASTAL STATE AUTHORITY IN OTHER "ZONES"

a. Security Zones

The Preparatory Committee for the Hague Codification Conference of 1930 recommended, as a basis of discussion, that a coastal state might exercise jurisdiction on the high seas adjacent to territorial waters to prevent "interference with its security by foreign ships." 2 Conference for the Codification of International Law, Bases of Discussion 34 (1930). However, the Conference itself reached no agreement on the subject. Similarly, the 1958 Geneva Conference considered but did not adopt a proposal on security jurisdiction.

State practice and the views of writers prior to 1958 in the matter of security zones were inconclusive. In reliance on the principle of reasonableness advanced in Church v. Hubbart, p. 1412 supra, it might be urged that "a neutral State may reasonably demand that belligerent operations at sea be conducted at such a distance from its territory as may be necessary in order to safeguard it from injury or interference." Hyde at 2348. During World War I, a number of South American states had proposed a declaration by the American Republics that belligerents must refrain from hostile acts within a "reasonable" distance from the shores. Id. After the outbreak of World War II in 1939, the Foreign Ministers of the American Republics issued the "Declaration of Panama," 1 Dep't. State Bull. 331 (1939), which enunciated the "inherent right" of the American states "to have those waters adjacent to the American continent * * * free from the commission of any hostile act by any non-American belligerent * * *." Such waters were defined by a system of straight lines which extended in many places several hundred miles out from the shore. See generally Fenwick, The Declaration of Panama, 34 A.J.I.L. 116 (1940). In response to an inquiry regarding the propriety of the Declaration under international law, the Department of State called the Declaration "a practical measure designed to maintain certain vital interests," and a "statement of principle, based on the inherent right of self-protection rather than a formal proposal for the modification of international law." 7 Hackworth at 703–704. The zone was also defended on the ground of its "inherent reasonableness." The battle in 1939 involving the Graf Spee, and certain other engagements, occasioned a joint protest by the American Republics to the belligerent powers. The replies were alike in rejecting the right of the American states to impose a modification of international law upon other states without their consent. 7 Hackworth at 704–708. The Naval War College affirmed the right of the belligerent states not to recognize the binding nature of the Panama Declaration, calling the latter "without precedent" in the extent of neutral waters for which it called. U.S. Naval War College, International Law Situations 80 (1939).

What is the effect of war, or armed conflict not labeled "war," on the jurisdiction which a state may exercise in adjacent waters? During the Algerian war, French forces intercepted on the high seas a number of vessels suspected of carrying arms destined for Algerian revolutionaries. Germany protested the interception of its vessels as a violation of international law. 4 Whiteman at 513–14. To what extent is the literal application of the Conventions subject to temporary suspension in time of crisis not amounting to war or even armed conflict, but affecting a nation's security? Did the United States have the right in meeting the threat posed by the installing of Soviet missiles in Cuba (see p. 950) in October, 1962 to intercept on the high seas vessels bound for Cuba? To what extent and under what conditions may a state use areas of the high seas for activities that require the exclusion of unauthorized vessels? May a state forbid foreign vessels to enter an area in which it is conducting tests of nuclear weapons or guided missiles? See generally 4 Whiteman 553–631; McDougal & Schlei, The Hydrogen Bomb Tests in Perspective: Lawful Measures for Security, 64 Yale L.J. 648 (1955). Compare Margolis, The Hydrogen Bomb Experiments and International Law, 64 Yale L.J. 629 (1955). Compare Nuclear Tests (Australia v. France, New Zealand v. France), 1974 I.C.J. 253, 535.

The Restatement (Third) § 511, Comment *k*, states that "[i]nternational law has not recognized coastal state assertions of special zones to protect security * * *."

b. Air Defense Zones

Some states have asserted the right to create air identification zones extending far beyond the contiguous zone. Restatement (Third) § 521, Reporters' Note 2 states:

> *Overflight and air defense*. The United States has established air defense areas, air defense identification zones (ADIZ), and, for Alaska, a distant early warning identification zone (DEWIZ). Some of these zones extend several hundred miles into the sea. Pilots entering these zones are obliged to report promptly and to provide specified data to United States authorities; a foreign aircraft not complying with this requirement is not permitted to enter the air space of the United States. See 14 C.F.R. § 99.23. Similar zones have been established by other states. These zones have been generally accepted. It is uncertain, however, whether a coastal state can apply such regulations to aircraft passing through its declared air defense zone but not planning to enter its airspace. See Note, "Air Defense Identification Zones: Creeping Jurisdiction in the Airspace," 18 Va.J.Int'l L. 485 (1978); 4 Whiteman, Digest of International Law 496–97 (1965). See also § 511, Comment *k*.

c. Anti–Pollution Zones

In 1970, Canada declared an "anti-pollution" zone up to 100 nautical miles from her Arctic coast, forbade pollution in that zone, imposed penalties and civil liability for violations (including unintentional violations), and authorized comprehensive regulation and inspection of vessels to prevent pollution. 18–19 Elizabeth 11, c. 47 (1969–70), reprinted in 9 I.L.M. 543 (1970). See Henkin, Arctic Anti–Pollution: Does Canada Make–or Break–International Law?, 66 A.J.I.L. 131 (1971).

Pollution control is now the subject of a number of conventions, and is dealt with in the 1982 Convention, Part XII, "Protection and Preservation of the Marine Environment." See p. 1476 infra. The Restatement concludes that international law has not yet recognized coastal state authority in a special zone to protect the environment. Restatement (Third) § 511, Comment *k*.

B. ECONOMIC RESOURCES BEYOND THE TERRITORIAL SEA

SCHACHTER, INTERNATIONAL LAW IN THEORY AND PRACTICE

275–77 (1991).

Viewed from a lawyer's perspective, the first notable action in derogation of the *res communis* was the claim by the United States in 1945 to full sovereignty over the continental shelf. That claim expressed in the Truman Proclamation has been generally seen as the start of the process of territorial expansion in ocean space. The shelf was claimed by the United States as an extension of the land-mass of the adjacent State and thus naturally appurtenant to it. Over a decade or so, the United States position was adopted by others and then embodied in the 1958 Geneva Convention on the Continental Shelf. It did not give rise to controversy since the extension of national authority over the shelf did not impinge very much on the traditional uses of the seas—fishing and navigation. * * * What was important as technology developed were the hydrocarbon resources, oil and gas, that were found and exploited on the shelf. These resources are still the most valuable of the resources of the sea * * *.

Although the appropriation of the shelf by coastal States did not appear to challenge the freedom of the seas, it had an influence on the claims made in the 1940s and 1950s by some coastal States to exclusive rights to fish or to engage in whaling in a 200–mile zone off their coasts [see p. 1434 below] * * *. In due course, the demands for preferential and exclusive fishing zones spread to other coastal countries and were more vigorously expressed. * * *

Note

Demands for special rights of protection for coastal states were followed by claims of preferential rights to resources. Such rights were embodied in treaties and given judicial imprimatur in the fisheries cases involving Iceland decided by the International Court in 1974 [see p. 1434 below]. In a short period of time preferential rights evolved into exclusive rights over a fishing zone generally of 200 miles. In the course of the ten-year period of negotiation of the United Nations Convention on the Law of the Sea, these zones became the 200–mile exclusive economic zones in which coastal states exercised "sovereign rights" over all resources. The principle of the exclusive economic zone was gradually given legal force by unilateral acts of coastal states and received acceptance as a major principle of the new Convention.

1. *The Continental Shelf*

POLICY OF THE UNITED STATES WITH RESPECT TO THE NATURAL RESOURCES OF THE SUBSOIL AND SEA BED OF THE CONTINENTAL SHELF

Presidential Proclamation 2667, September 28, 1945.
10 Fed.Reg. 12303 (1945).

WHEREAS the Government of the United States of America, aware of the long range world-wide need for new sources of petroleum and other minerals, holds the view that efforts to discover and make available new supplies of these resources should be encouraged; and

WHEREAS its competent experts are of the opinion that such resources underlie many parts of the continental shelf off the coasts of the United States of America, and that with modern technological progress their utilization is already practicable or will become so at an early date; and

WHEREAS recognized jurisdiction over these resources is required in the interest of their conservation and prudent utilization when and as development is undertaken; and

WHEREAS it is the view of the Government of the United States that the exercise of jurisdiction over the natural resources of the subsoil and sea bed of the continental shelf by the contiguous nation is reasonable and just, since the effectiveness of measures to utilize or conserve these resources would be contingent upon cooperation and protection from the shore, since the continental shelf may be regarded as an extension of the land-mass of the coastal nation and thus naturally appurtenant to it, since these resources frequently form a seaward extension of a pool or deposit lying within the territory, and since self-protection compels the coastal nation to keep close watch over activities off its shores which are of the nature necessary for utilization of these resources;

NOW, THEREFORE, I, HARRY S. TRUMAN, President of the United States of America, do hereby proclaim the following policy of the United States of America with respect to the natural resources of the subsoil and sea bed of the continental shelf.

Having concern for the urgency of conserving and prudently utilizing its natural resources, the Government of the United States regards the natural resources of the subsoil and sea bed of the continental shelf beneath the high seas but contiguous to the coasts of the United States as appertaining to the United States, subject to its jurisdiction and control. In cases where the continental shelf extends to the shores of another State, or is shared with an adjacent State, the boundary shall be determined by the United States and the State concerned in accordance with equitable principles. The character as high seas of the waters above the continental shelf and the right to their free and unimpeded navigation are in no way thus affected.

Notes

1. A White House press release issued on the same day as the Truman Proclamation noted that "[g]enerally, submerged land which is contiguous to the continent and which is covered by no more than 100 fathoms (600 feet) of water is considered as the continental shelf." 4 Whiteman 758. See, in general, 4 Whiteman at 752–64. On President Truman's proclamation, also issued on September 28, 1945, relating to the conservation and protection of fishing resources in areas of the high seas contiguous to United States waters, see 4 Whiteman at 945–62. See p. 1435 infra.

2. In 1951, in the *Abu Dhabi* case, Lord Asquith of Bishopstone concluded that the doctrine of the continental shelf was unknown to international law in 1939 and had not yet become part of the corpus of international law in 1951. See 1 I.C.L.Q. 247 (1952).

The International Law Commission adopted draft articles on the continental shelf and related subjects at its third session in 1951. In its commentary to Article 2 (providing that the continental shelf was "subject to the exercise by the coastal State of control and jurisdiction for the purpose of exploring it and exploiting its natural resources"), the Commission noted that "though numerous proclamations have been issued over the past decade, it can hardly be said that such unilateral action has already established a new customary law." [1951] 2 Yb.I.L.C. 141–42. See also Kunz, Continental Shelf and International Law: Confusion and Abuse, 50 A.J.I.L. 828, 829, 832 (1956).

Compare the suggestion made in the North Sea Continental Shelf cases that emerging customary law "became crystallized in the adoption of the Continental Shelf Convention," p. 1426 infra.

DEFINITION OF THE CONTINENTAL SHELF

U.N. CONVENTION ON THE LAW OF THE SEA (1982)

1833 U.N.T.S. 3, U.N.Doc. A/CONF. 62/122; 21 I.L.M. 1261 (1982).

Article 76

1. The continental shelf of a coastal State comprises the sea-bed and subsoil of the submarine areas that extend beyond its territorial sea throughout the natural prolongation of its land territory to the outer edge of the continental margin, or to a distance of 200 nautical miles from the baselines from which the breadth of the territorial sea is measured where the outer edge of the continental margin does not extend up to that distance.

* * *

3. The continental margin comprises the submerged prolongation of the land mass of the coastal State, and consists of the sea-bed and subsoil of the shelf, the slope and the rise. It does not include the deep ocean floor with its oceanic ridges or the subsoil thereof.

Notes

1. The 1958 Convention contained the following definition of the continental shelf:

> Art. 1. For the purpose of these articles, the term "continental shelf" is used as referring (a) to the seabed and subsoil of the submarine areas adjacent to the coast but outside the area of the territorial sea, to a depth of 200 metres or, beyond that limit, to where the depth of the superjacent waters admits of the exploitation of the natural resources of the said areas; (b) to the seabed and subsoil of similar submarine areas adjacent to the coasts of islands.

The wide expansion of the definition of the continental shelf in the 1982 convention as compared with the 1958 Convention is related to the acceptance of the exclusive economic zone of 200 miles, p. 1437 infra.

2. Sections 4–7 of Article 76 of the 1982 Convention provide for defining the outer edge of the continental margin wherever it extends beyond 200 nautical miles. It shall not exceed 350 miles from the baseline or 100 nautical miles from the 2500 meter isobath. (Only the 350 mile limit applies on submarine ridges,

Article 76(6).) A Commission on the Limits of the Continental Shelf is to be established which shall make recommendations to coastal states, but the limits established by the coastal state "taking into account these recommendations" shall be final and binding. Article 76(8).

Do states not party to the 1982 Convention need to take into account recommendations of the Commission? If they do not, can they claim the expanded provision of Article 76 on the basis of customary law? Compare Note 3 below.

3. States generally were prepared to accept a very wide continental shelf, but the geographically disadvantaged states sought to share in as much of the continental shelf as exceeded the 200 mile zone which would accrue to coastal states under the new Exclusive Economic Zone. The 1982 Convention, Article 82, provides:

> 1. The coastal State shall make payments or contributions in kind in respect of the exploitation of the non-living resources of the continental shelf beyond 200 nautical miles from the baselines from which the breadth of the territorial sea is measured.
>
> 2. The payments and contributions shall be made annually with respect to all production at a site after the first five years of production at that site. For the sixth year, the rate of payment or contribution shall be 1 per cent of the value or volume of production at the site. The rate shall increase by 1 per cent for each subsequent year until the twelfth year and shall remain at 7 per cent thereafter. Production does not include resources used in connection with exploitation.
>
> 3. A developing State which is a net importer of a mineral resource produced from its continental shelf is exempt from making such payments or contributions in respect of that mineral resource.
>
> 4. The payments or contributions shall be made through the Authority, which shall distribute them to States Parties to this Convention, on the basis of equitable sharing criteria, taking into account the interests and needs of developing States, particularly the least developed and the landlocked among them.

Can a state not party to the Convention claim that the extended definition of the continental shelf is customary law if it does not accept also the obligations of Article 82? See Restatement (Third) Introductory Note to Part V. See generally Jewett, The Evolution of the Legal Regime of the Continental Shelf, 22 Can. Y.B.Int'l L. 153 (1984), and 23 Can.Y.B.Int'l L. 201 (1985).

DELIMITATION OF THE CONTINENTAL SHELF BETWEEN STATES

THE NORTH SEA CONTINENTAL SHELF CASES

International Court of Justice, 1969.
1969 I.C.J. 3, 38, 53.

[In 1966, a dispute arose between the Federal Republic of Germany on one side and the Netherlands and Denmark on the other concerning the delimitation of the boundaries of their respective continental shelves in the North Sea. The United Kingdom had concluded agreements with Norway, Denmark and the Netherlands on the boundaries of their respective continental shelf claims. Denmark, the Netherlands and Germany, however, had not agreed with each other on boundaries in the eastern part of the North Sea. On March 31, 1966, Denmark and the Netherlands reached agreement on the boundary line between their respective claims. This line, based on the principle of the "equidistant line," begins at a point on the boundary line separating the United Kingdom's shelf from the eastern half of the North Sea, and extends to a point off the coast of West Germany, thus preventing Germany from extending its continental shelf to the United Kingdom boundary line in the middle of the North Sea. The Federal Republic of Germany is not a party to the Convention on the Continental Shelf.

[Special agreements were concluded between the Federal Republic of Germany and the Netherlands and between the Federal Republic of Germany and Denmark providing for the submission to the International Court of Justice of the disagreement between Germany and its neighbor states over the proper delimitation of the continental shelf in the North Sea.

[The Court rejected the argument of Denmark and the Netherlands that the rule of equidistance has *a priori* character of inherent necessity because it gave expression to, and translated into linear terms, a principle of proximity inherent in the basic concept of the continental shelf, causing every part of the shelf to appertain to the nearest coastal state and to no other. It then considered the contention of Denmark and the Netherlands that although prior to the 1958 Geneva Conference, continental shelf law was only in the formative stage, and state practice lacked uniformity, yet "the process of the definition and consolidation of the emerging customary law took place through the work of the International Law Commission, the reaction of governments to that work and the proceedings of the Geneva Conference"; and that this emerging customary law became "crystallized in the adoption of the Continental Shelf Convention by the Conference." The Court rejected this contention as applied to this issue, stating:]

Whatever validity this contention may have in respect of at least certain parts of the Convention, the Court cannot accept it as regards the delimitation provision (Article 6), the relevant parts of which were adopted almost unchanged from the draft of the International Law Commission that formed the basis of discussion at the Conference. The status of the rule in the Convention therefore depends mainly on the processes that led the Commission to propose it. These processes have already been reviewed. * * * [T]he Court considers this review sufficient for present purposes also, in order to show that the principle of equidistance, as it now figures in Article 6 of the Convention, was proposed by the Commission with considerable hesitation, somewhat on an experimental basis, at most *de lege ferenda*, and not at all *de lege lata* or as an emerging rule of customary international law. This is clearly not the sort of foundation on which Article 6 of the Convention could be said to have reflected or crystallized such a rule.

[The Court buttressed this conclusion by pointing out that Article 6 was one of the provisions in respect of which Article 12 permitted any state to attach a reservation on signing, ratifying or acceding. The Court further concluded that neither the effect of the Geneva Convention nor state practice since its signing justified the inference that delimitation according to the principle of equidistance rises to the level of a mandatory rule of customary law. See the excerpt of the Court's opinion at p. 92 supra. Having decided that neither the equidistance method nor any other method of delimitation was obligatory, the Court stressed as the basic applicable legal principles (1) that delimitation must be the object of agreement between the states concerned and (2) that such agreement must be arrived at in accordance with equitable principles. In its judgment (eleven votes to six) the Court stated:]

[T]he principles and rules of international law applicable to the delimitation as between the Parties * * * are as follows:

(1) delimitation is to be effected by agreement in accordance with equitable principles, and taking account of all the relevant circumstances, in such a way as to leave as much as possible to each Party all those parts of the continental shelf that constitute a natural prolongation of its land territory into and under the sea, without encroachment on the natural prolongation of the land territory of the other;

(2) if, in the application of the preceding sub-paragraph, the delimitation leaves to the Parties areas that overlap, these are to be divided between them in agreed proportions or, failing agreement, equally, unless they decide on a régime of joint jurisdiction, user, or exploitation for the zones of overlap or any part of them;

[I]n the course of the negotiations, the factors to be taken into account are to include:

(1) the general configuration of the coasts of the Parties, as well as the presence of any special or unusual features;

(2) so far as known or readily ascertainable, the physical and geological structure, and natural resources, of the continental shelf areas involved;

(3) the element of a reasonable degree of proportionality, which a delimitation carried out in accordance with equitable principles ought to bring about between the extent of the continental shelf areas appertaining to the coastal State and the length of its coast measured in the general direction of the coastline, account being taken for this purpose of the effects, actual or prospective, of any other continental shelf delimitations between adjacent States in the same region.

Note

The Court's disposition of the cases is criticized in Friedmann, The North Sea Continental Shelf Cases, 64 A.J.I.L. 229 (1970). For other aspects of the Court's opinion see Chapter 2, p. 92 supra.

U.N. CONVENTION ON THE LAW OF THE SEA (1982)

1833 U.N.T.S. 3, U.N.Doc. A/CONF. 62/122; 21 I.L.M. 1261 (1982).

ARTICLE 83

Delimitation of the Continental Shelf Between States With Opposite or Adjacent Coasts

1. The delimitation of the continental shelf between States with opposite or adjacent coasts shall be effected by agreement on the basis of international law, as referred to in Article 38 of the Statute of the International Court of Justice, in order to achieve an equitable solution.

2. If no agreement can be reached within a reasonable period of time, the States concerned shall resort to the procedures provided for in Part XV.

3. Pending agreement as provided for in paragraph 1, the States concerned, in a spirit of understanding and co-operation, shall make every effort to enter into provisional arrangements of a practical nature and, during this transitional period, not to jeopardize or hamper the reaching of the final agreement. Such arrangements shall be without prejudice to the final delimitation.

4. Where there is an agreement in force between the States concerned, questions relating to the delimitation of the continental shelf shall be determined in accordance with the provisions of that agreement.

Notes

1. Article 83 (and the identical Article 74 dealing with delimitation of exclusive economic zones) reflect the inability of states to achieve a formula for maritime boundary delimitation between continental shelves or exclusive economic zones of different states. The inability to agree has resulted in numerous arbitrations and adjudications to delimit maritime boundaries. Between 1969 and 1984 the International Court of Justice heard three maritime boundary cases, two by a full court and one by a chamber: *Continental Shelf* (Tunisia/Libya), 1982 I.C.J. 18; 1985 I.C.J. 192; *Continental Shelf* (Libya/Malta), 1985 I.C.J. 13; and *Gulf of Maine* (U.S/Canada, chamber). By 2000, six additional cases on delimitation had been brought to the Court: *Arbitral Award of 31 July 1989* (Guinea–Bissau v. Senegal), 1991 I.C.J. 53; *Land, Island and Maritime Frontier Dispute* (El Salvador v. Honduras: Nicaragua intervening) (Merits), 1992 I.C.J. 351; *Maritime Delimitation in the Area Between Greenland and Jan Mayen* (Denmark v. Norway), 1993 I.C.J. 38; *Maritime Delimitation Between Qatar and Bahrain* (Qatar v. Bahrain), 1995 I.C.J. 6; *Land and Maritime Boundary Between Cameroon and Nigeria* (Cameroon v. Nigeria: Equatorial Guinea intervening) (Prelim. Objections), 1998 I.C.J. 275; and *Maritime Delimitation Between Nicaragua and Honduras in the Caribbean Sea* (Nicaragua v. Honduras), Order of 21 March 2000. See also *Case Concerning Passage Through the Great Belt* (Finland v. Denmark) (Provisional Measures), 1992 I.C.J. 348.

The *North Sea Continental Shelf Cases*, p. 1425 above, and the *Continental Shelf Case* between Libya and Tunisia, relied on "equitable principles" to divide a shelf where there was no interruption in the natural prolongation of the coasts, but gave no clear guidelines as to the applicable principles. The Court did not try to elucidate equitable principles, beyond a few statements such as that parties should not refashion nature and that special effects or circumstances could be taken into account.

In the *Gulf of Maine Case*, the Chamber seemed to abandon any quest for principles to apply to delimitation cases generally. The Chamber said (1984 I.C.J. 246 at 299):

> 111. A body of detailed rules is not to be looked for in customary international law * * * and not [to be tested] by deduction from preconceived ideas. It is therefore unrewarding, especially in a new and still unconsolidated field like that involving the quite recent extension of the claims of States to areas which were until yesterday zones of the high seas, to look to general international law to provide a ready-made set of rules that can be used for

solving any delimitation problems that arise. A more useful course is to seek a better formulation of the fundamental norm, on which the Parties were fortunate enough to be agreed, and whose existence in the legal convictions not only of the Parties to the present dispute, but of all States, is apparent from an examination of the realities of international legal relations.

112. The Chamber therefore wishes to conclude this review * * * by attempting a more complete and, in its opinion, more precise reformulation of the "fundamental norm" already mentioned. For this purpose it will, *inter alia*, draw also upon the definition of the "actual rules of law * * * which govern the delimitation of adjacent continental shelves–that is to say, rules binding upon States for all delimitations" which was given by the Court in its 1969 Judgment in the North Sea Continental Shelf cases (I.C.J Reports 1969, pp. 46–47, para. 85). What general international law prescribes in every maritime delimitation between neighbouring States could therefore be defined as follows:

(1) No maritime delimitation between States with opposite or adjacent coasts may be effected unilaterally by one of those States. Such delimitation must be sought and effected by means of an agreement, following negotiations conducted in good faith and with the genuine intention of achieving a positive result. Where, however, such agreement cannot be achieved, delimitation should be effected by recourse to a third party possessing the necessary competence.

(2) In either case, delimitation is to be effected by the application of equitable criteria and by the use of practical methods capable of ensuring, with regard to the geographic configuration of the area and other relevant circumstances, an equitable result.

The Chamber concluded that, in the absence of agreement, states will have to seek third party determination of maritime boundaries. No principle applies in the absence of agreement. (The equidistance line, for example, cannot be applied in the absence of agreement.)

As for the principles that should guide the third party, the Chamber said:

There has been no systematic definition of the equitable criteria that may be taken into consideration for an international maritime delimitation, and this would in any event be difficult *a priori* because of their highly variable adaptability to different concrete situations * * * Here again the essential consideration is that none of the potential methods has intrinsic merits which would make it preferable to another in the abstract * * *. Above all there must be willingness to adopt a combination of different methods whenever that * * * may be relevant in the different phases of the operation and with reference to different segments of the line.

Id. at pp. 312, 315.

All these I.C.J. cases indicate that in applying equitable principles, geography is the primary concern; economic conditions and environmental concerns are excluded. Nevertheless, geography was "modified" to some extent to achieve a more equitable result. The concavity of the Federal Republic of Germany's coast was taken into account in the *North Sea Cases*. A line dictated by the general direction of the coasts was modified by the presence of islands in the *Libya-Tunisia Case*. The proportionality of the coasts was considered in the *Gulf of Maine Case*.

The International Court of Justice Chamber in *Gulf of Maine* also looked for the first time at a unitary boundary for both the shelf and the water column. While it reiterated the dual character of its task throughout the opinion, the Chamber did not indicate how the line it drew would be different if it were delimiting the shelf only. It seemed to imply that in the absence of a clear, natural division in the continental shelf between adjacent states, it will be possible to divide both water column and shelf using the same principles. Again, the exact nature of those principles remains unclear. Compare Restatement (Third) § 511. See generally, International Maritime Boundaries (Charney & Alexander, eds., 1993); Evans, Relevant Circumstances and Maritime Delimitation (1989); Weil, The Law of Maritime Delimitations—Reflections (1989); Jagota, Maritime Boundary (1984). See also Charney, Ocean Boundaries Between Nations: A Theory for Progress, 78 A.J.I.L. 582 (1984); Charney, Progress in International Maritime Boundary Delimitation, 88 A.J.I.L. 227 (1994); Charney, Maritime Delimitation in the Area between Greenland and Jan Mayen (Denmark v. Norway) 88 A.J.I.L. 105 (1994).

2. In its 1994 submittal to the Senate recommending approval of the Law of the Sea Convention, the U.S. Department of State explained the provisions of the Convention relevant to maritime boundary delimitation with respect to the continental shelf and other potentially overlapping areas. The letter of submittal noted that the United States has 28 maritime boundary situations with its neighbors, of which ten have been negotiated or adjudicated in whole or in part, and that the U.S. positions are fully consistent with the rules reflected in the Convention. See Message from the President of the United States transmitting U.N. Convention on the Law of the Sea, Senate Treaty Doc. 103–39, 103rd Cong., 2d Sess. 88–90 (1994) (discussing 1984 *Gulf of Maine* decision resolving the boundary with Canada; treaties already approved with Mexico, Venezuela (on boundary with Puerto Rico and U.S. Virgin Islands), Cook Islands/New Zealand (on boundary with American Samoa), and the Russian Federation; and pending treaties with Cuba and the United Kingdom (concerning Virgin Islands).

3. For discussion of the awards of an arbitral tribunal in a 1998–2000 dispute between Eritrea and Yemen including questions of delimitation of maritime boundaries, see Reisman, Eritrea–Yemen Arbitration, 93 A.J.I.L. 668 (1999), 94 A.J.I.L. 721 (2000).

4. On the regulation of common fishing stocks or shared off-shore hydrocarbon deposits between states, see generally Ong, Joint Development of Common Offshore Oil and Gas Deposits: "Mere" State Practice or Customary International Law?, 93 A.J.I.L. 771 (1999).

5. In the United States, controversy over the continental shelf has centered chiefly upon the rights of the federal government as opposed to those of the coastal states. In 1947, the Supreme Court held that the United States was "possessed of paramount rights in, and full dominion and power over, the lands, minerals and other things" underlying the Pacific Ocean seaward of the low-water mark on the coast of California and outside of inland waters, to the extent of three nautical miles, and that California had "no title thereto or property interest therein." United States v. California, 332 U.S. 19, 67 S.Ct. 1658, 91 L.Ed. 1889 (1947), reh'g denied, 332 U.S. 804, 805, 68 S.Ct. 20, 21, 92 L.Ed. 382 (Decree) (1947). In United States v. Louisiana, 339 U.S. 699, 70 S.Ct. 914, 94 L.Ed. 1216 (1950), the Court followed the *California* decision and held that the United States possessed identical rights over areas underlying the Gulf of Mexico, to the extent (27 miles from the coast) claimed by Louisiana. Noting that the one difference

between Louisiana's claim and the earlier claim of California was that the former state claimed rights "twenty-four miles seaward of the three-mile belt," the Court (per Douglas, J.) stated: "If, as we held in California's case, the three-mile belt is in the domain of the Nation rather than that of the separate States, it follows *a fortiori* that the ocean beyond that limit also is. The ocean seaward of the marginal belt is perhaps even more directly related to the national defense, the conduct of foreign affairs, and world commerce than is the marginal sea." 339 U.S. at 705. On the same day as the *Louisiana* decision, the Court held that Texas had no interest in the undersea areas contiguous to its coast, even though Texas argued that it had acquired both proprietary and sovereign rights in a 9–mile marginal belt prior to annexation by the United States. United States v. Texas, 339 U.S. 707, 70 S.Ct. 918, 94 L.Ed. 1221 (1950), reh'g denied, 340 U.S. 907, 71 S.Ct. 277, 95 L.Ed. 656 (1950). The United States was held to be possessed of paramount rights in, and full dominion and power over, the undersea areas extending to the edge of the continental shelf in the Gulf of Mexico first claimed by Texas in 1947. 339 U.S. at 715–20; 340 U.S. at 900–901.

On May 22, 1953, Congress passed the Submerged Land Act, 67 Stat. 29, 43 U.S.C.A. §§ 1301–15, by which the United States relinquished to the coastal states all of its rights in submerged lands within certain geographical limits, and confirmed the rights of the United States beyond those limits. The Act defined the areas relinquished to the states in terms of state boundaries as they existed at the time a state became a member of the Union, but not extending beyond three geographic miles in the Atlantic and Pacific Oceans or beyond three marine leagues (9 miles) in the Gulf of Mexico. On August 7, 1953, Congress approved the Outer Continental Shelf Lands Act, 67 Stat. 462, 43 U.S.C.A. §§ 1331–46, which provided for the jurisdiction of the United States over the "outer Continental Shelf" (defined as areas seaward of those relinquished to the states by the Submerged Lands Act) and authorized the Secretary of the Interior to lease such areas for exploitation purposes. In United States v. States of Louisiana, Texas, Mississippi, Alabama and Florida, 363 U.S. 1, 80 S.Ct. 961, 4 L.Ed.2d 1025, 80S.Ct. 961 (1960), the United States sought a declaration that it was entitled to full dominion and power over the undersea areas underlying the Gulf of Mexico that were more than three geographic miles seaward from the coast, and extending to the edge of the continental shelf. The State Department took the position that it could not accept an interpretation of the Submerged Lands Act that would result in recognition of state claims to "marginal seas of a greater breadth than 3 marine miles." 4 Whiteman at 62. The Court held that the Government's contention that state claims to historic seaward boundaries of more than three miles conflicted with national policy on the three-mile limit rested "on an oversimplification of the problem" inasmuch as the Submerged Lands Act allowed state claims of up to three marine leagues for "purely domestic purposes." 363 U.S. at 33, 80 S.Ct. at 980. Turning to the historic claims of the coastal states, the Court concluded that Texas was entitled, as against the United States, to the areas underlying the Gulf of Mexico to a distance of three leagues from her coast. Id. at 64. Florida was also held, on other grounds, to be entitled to a three-marine-league belt of land under the Gulf of Mexico, seaward from its coast. United States v. Florida, et al., 363 U.S. 121, 129, 80 S.Ct. 961, 4 L.Ed.2d 1025 (1960). The other Gulf states were held not to be entitled to rights in submerged lands lying beyond three geographic miles from their respective coasts. 363 U.S. at 79, 82. See further United States v. Louisiana, 394 U.S. 1, 11, 89 S.Ct. 768, 773, 22 L.Ed.2d 36, 44 (1969); 420 U.S. 529, 95 S.Ct. 1180, 43 L.Ed.2d 373 (1975) (Special Master's Report accepted and decree issued); 422 U.S. 13, 95 S.Ct. 2022, 44 L.Ed.2d 652

(1975) (supplemental decision). See also United States v. California, 381 U.S. 139, 85 S.Ct. 1401, 14 L.Ed.2d 296 (1965) discussed at p. 1397, note 7.

In United States v. Maine, 420 U.S. 515, 95 S.Ct. 1155, 43 L.Ed.2d 363 (1975), the Supreme Court held that the right to explore and exploit the sea bed beyond 3 miles belonged to the federal government, not to the defendants, the original states of the Union that had claimed these rights by succession to Great Britain.

6. In United States v. Ray, 423 F.2d 16 (5th Cir.1970), the Court of Appeals for the Fifth Circuit granted the United States a decree enjoining private persons, American citizens, from establishing a "new sovereign country" on two coral reefs on the continental shelf of the United States (outside its claimed territorial sea) without finding that these reefs were the property of the United States. The Court held that the structures interfered with the exclusive rights of the United States to exploit the reefs under the Geneva Convention on the Continental Shelf and the Outer Continental Shelf Lands Act.

But in Treasure Salvors, Inc. v. Unidentified Wrecked and Abandoned Sailing Vessel, etc., 569 F.2d 330, 339 (5th Cir.1978), the Court of Appeals denied the United States sovereign rights to an abandoned vessel found by a private person on the continental shelf, since U.S. interests in the shelf were only for the purpose of exploring it and exploiting its natural resources.

Compare the 1982 Convention, Article 73, on coastal state jurisdiction in the exclusive economic zone p. 1440 infra. For the right of "hot pursuit" as applied to violation of the continental shelf, see the 1982 Convention, Article 111(2), p. 1441 infra. See Feldman and Colson, The Maritime Boundaries of the United States, 75 A.J.I.L. 729 (1981).

THE CONTINENTAL SHELF AND THE RIGHTS OF COASTAL STATES

U.N. CONVENTION ON THE LAW OF THE SEA (1982)

1833 U.N.T.S. 3, U.N.Doc. A/CONF. 62/122; 21 I.L.M. 1261 (1982).

Article 77

Rights of the Coastal State in the Continental Shelf

1. The coastal State exercises over the continental shelf sovereign rights for the purpose of exploring it and exploiting its natural resources.

2. The rights referred to in paragraph 1 are exclusive in the sense that if the coastal State does not explore the continental shelf or exploit its natural resources, no one may undertake these activities without the express consent of the coastal State.

3. The rights of the coastal State over the continental shelf do not depend on occupation, effective or notional, or on any express proclamation.

4. The natural resources referred to in this Part consist of the mineral and other non-living resources of the sea-bed and subsoil together with living organisms belonging to sedentary species, that is to say, organisms which, at the harvestable stage, either are immobile on or under the sea-bed or are unable to move except in constant physical contact with the sea-bed or the subsoil.

ARTICLE 78

Legal Status of the Superjacent Waters and Airspace and the Rights and Freedoms of Other States

1. The rights of the coastal State over the continental shelf do not affect the legal status of the superjacent waters or of the air space above those waters.

2. The exercise of the rights of the coastal State over the continental shelf must not infringe, or result in any unjustifiable interference with navigation and other rights and freedoms of other States as provided for in this Convention.

Notes

1. Articles 77 and 78 are essentially the same as Articles 2 and 3 of the 1958 Convention on the Continental Shelf, except that the latter identified the waters above the shelf as "high seas". Compare the Exclusive Economic Zone, p. [1291] infra. Article 78(2) covers in part what is in Article 5(1) of the 1958 Convention.

2. Restatement (Third) § 511, Comment *b,* states:

> *"Sovereignty" and "sovereign rights."* A state has complete sovereignty over the territorial sea, analogous to that which it possesses over its land territory, internal waters, and archipelagic waters. See § 512; LOS Convention, Article 2(1). See also the 1958 Convention on the Territorial Sea and the Contiguous Zone, Article 1(1). The sovereignty over the territorial sea is subject, however, to the right of innocent passage for foreign vessels (id. Articles 1(2) and 14(1); LOS Convention, Articles 2(3) and 17; see § 513(1) and (2)). The territorial sea within a strait or adjacent to archipelagic waters is also subject to the right of transit passage or archipelagic sea lanes passage (LOS Convention, Articles 38 and 53(1); see § 513(3) and (4)).
>
> "Sovereign rights," which a coastal state enjoys in its exclusive economic zone and on its continental shelf, are functional in character, limited to specified activities. In the continental shelf, the coastal state exercises sovereign rights only "for the purpose of exploring it and for exploiting its natural resources," both living and nonliving. See § 515; 1958 Convention on the Continental Shelf, Article 2; LOS Convention, Article 77. In the exclusive economic zone, a coastal state has sovereign rights "for the purpose of exploring and exploiting, conserving and managing the natural resources, whether living or nonliving, of the waters superjacent to the sea-bed and its subsoil," as well as "with regard to other activities for the economic exploitation and exploration of the zone, such as the production of energy from the water, currents and winds." See § 514; LOS Convention, Article 56(1)(a). In addition, international law confers on the coastal state limited jurisdiction in that zone for some other purposes, *e.g.*, with respect to marine scientific research and the protection and preservation of the marine environment, and artificial islands and certain installations and structures. *Id.* Articles 56(1)(b) and 60.

3. Article 79 of the 1982 Convention, like Article 4 of the 1958 Convention, recognizes the rights of other states to lay and maintain cables and pipelines subject to reasonable measures of the coastal state for the exploration of the continental shelf. The 1982 Convention provision also permits the coastal state to take reasonable measures to control pollution from pipelines, and requires the

consent of the coastal state to the delineation of the course for laying pipelines. States laying pipelines shall pay due regard to cables or pipelines already in position.

2. *The Exclusive Economic Zone (EEZ)*

EXCLUSIVE ECONOMIC ZONE: ANTECEDENTS

Long before the law of the sea conventions, coastal states claimed exception to the rule of *mare liberum*. Coastal state claims that led to the development of the territorial sea, see p. [1240], were inspired in significant part by the desire for exclusive rights in the resources of that part of the sea, principally its fish. Coastal states also asserted a right to enforce measures of conservation outside their territorial sea designed to maintain the supply of fish for the benefit of national fisheries. See 3 Gidel, Le Droit International Public de la Mer 465 (1934).

A series of new claims by coastal states arose between 1945 and 1958, some to wide fishing zones, some to territorial sea (although these, too, may have been designed principally as a way to claim more fish and sea-bed resources). Considering the economic importance to many states of offshore fishing resources, it was not surprising that these countries early began to invoke the customs laws of the United States and other states as justifying, by analogy, attempts to exercise jurisdiction over fishing areas adjacent to territorial waters. Indeed, the parallel was invoked, although not without criticism, in the United States Congress as early as 1937 to justify proposals for a far-reaching appropriation of certain high seas fisheries. The Truman Proclamation asserting the exclusive jurisdiction of the coastal state to the mineral resources of the continental shelf beyond the territorial sea inevitably encouraged other coastal states to claim exclusive rights to fish in waters beyond the territorial sea.

Iceland's attempt to extend its fisheries jurisdiction from 12 to 50 miles was opposed in the International Court of Justice by the United Kingdom, whose vessels had fished off the Icelandic coast for centuries. In the *Fisheries Jurisdiction Case*, 1974 I.C.J. 3, the Court acknowledged an increasing and widespread acceptance of preferential fishing rights for coastal states. The Court said, however, that such rights are not absolute and could not imply the extinction of the concurrent rights of other states, particularly states that had historic claims to fish in particular waters. The Court concluded that Iceland could not unilaterally exclude the United Kingdom from its historic fishing grounds. The Court declared also that the two countries had an obligation to resolve their dispute by negotiation.

For years the United States resisted claims by other coastal states to large exclusive fishing zones, and strenuously supported claims by its nationals to fish in distant waters outside the territory of other states. For its part as a coastal state, the United States itself claimed only a limited conservation zone.

To deal with the problems of conservation and disputes rising from unilateral claims, the Geneva Conference of 1958 adopted a Convention on Fishing and Conservation of the Living Resources of the High Seas, 17 U.S.T.

138, T.I.A.S. 5960, 559 U.N.T.S. 285. The Convention provides in Article 6 that a coastal state has a "special interest in the maintenance of the productivity of the living resources in any area of the high seas adjacent to its territorial sea," and may thus take the initiative in prescribing measures of conservation (which must be non-discriminatory and based on "appropriate" scientific findings, and the need for which must be "urgent"). See generally 4 Whiteman at 768–77; Bishop, The 1958 Geneva Convention on Fishing and Conservation of the Living Resources of the High Seas, 62 Colum.L.Rev. 1202 (1962). On September 28, 1945, President Truman issued a proclamation asserting that the United States would consider it proper "to establish conservation zones in those areas of the high seas contiguous to the coasts of the United States." The United States would regulate fishing activities of its own nationals unilaterally, and those of foreign nationals by agreement with their states. 10 Fed. Reg. 12304 (1945), 4 Whiteman 945–62.

In time, however, in response to pressure from other coastal states and its own fishing interests, the United States began to assert fishing zones of its own. In 1966, Congress established a "Contiguous Fishery Zone" of 12 miles (9 miles beyond its territorial sea). Pub.L. 89–658, Oct. 14, 1966, 80 Stat. 908, 16 U.S.C.A. § 1091.

FISHERY CONSERVATION AND MANAGEMENT ACT OF 1976

16 U.S.C.A. § 1801 et seq.

Title I—Fishery Management Authority of the United States

Sec. 101. Fishery Conservation Zone

There is established a zone contiguous to the territorial sea of the United States to be known as the fishery conservation zone. The inner boundary of the fishery conservation zone is a line coterminous with the seaward boundary of each of the coastal States, and the outer boundary of such zone is a line drawn in such manner that each point on it is 200 nautical miles from the baseline from which the territorial sea is measured.

Sec. 102. Exclusive Fishery Management Authority

The United States shall exercise exclusive fishery management authority, in the manner provided for in this Act, over the following:

(1) All fish within the fishery conservation zone.

(2) All anadromous species throughout the migratory range of each such species beyond the fishery conservation zone; except that such management authority shall not extend to such species during the time they are found within any foreign nation's territorial sea or fishery conservation zone (or the equivalent), to the extent that such sea or zone is recognized by the United States.

(3) All Continental Shelf fishery resources beyond the fishery conservation zone.

Sec. 103. Highly Migratory Species

The exclusive fishery management authority of the United States shall not include, nor shall it be construed to extend to, highly migratory species of fish.

* * *

TITLE IV—MISCELLANEOUS PROVISIONS

Sec. 401. Effect on Law of the Sea Treaty

If the United States ratifies a comprehensive treaty, which includes provisions with respect to fishery conservation and management jurisdiction, resulting from any United Nations Conference on the Law of the Sea, the Secretary, after consultation with the Secretary of State, may promulgate any amendment to the regulations promulgated under this Act if such amendment is necessary and appropriate to conform such regulations to the provisions of such treaty, in anticipation of the date when such treaty shall come into force and effect for, or otherwise be applicable to, the United States.

Notes

1. In Title II, the Fishery Conservation and Management Act provides for foreign fishing pursuant to existing or future agreements, essentially on the basis of reciprocity.

2. In United States v. F/V Taiyo Maru, 395 F.Supp. 413 (D.Me.1975), the U.S. District Court upheld the right of hot pursuit from the contiguous fisheries zone. The court held that Articles 23 and 24 of the 1958 Convention on the High Seas do not forbid a coastal state to establish a contiguous fisheries zone (up to 12 miles) or to conduct hot pursuit from such a zone. For a critical comment, see Ciobanu, Hot Pursuit From a Fisheries Zone: A Further Comment on United States v. Fishing Vessel Taiyo Maru No. 28; United States v. Kawaguchi, 70 A.J.I.L. 549 (1976); Ridell, Hot Pursuit from a Fisheries Zone, 70 A.J.I.L. 95 (1976).

On hot pursuit from the exclusive economic zone, see p. 1441 infra.

3. Henkin writes:

> Developed maritime states early resisted coastal-state expansion. As distant fishing states, they rejected the notion that a coastal state might exclude them from wide coastal zones in which they had long fished. They feared, too, "creeping jurisdiction." Already they had seen how exclusive mining rights for coastal states on the continental shelf (beyond their territorial sea) had created pressures for exclusive fishing rights for coastal states in wide zones beyond the territorial sea. Developed maritime states feared that if the coastal state acquired exclusive fishing rights, its jurisdiction would continue to expand to other uses and would interfere also with navigation, scientific research, and military uses in wide coastal zones.
>
> But developed maritime states are also coastal states and have important national interests that stood to gain from coastal-state expansion. They had some sympathy with the economic needs of poor coastal states. They were reluctant to confront developing coastal states (supported by the rest of the Third World), especially since the latter had effective "possession" of the coastal areas and could seize them (or threaten to seize them) unilaterally.

> Pressed from without and by national interests from within, they acquiesced in the concept of an exclusive economic zone. (This, in fact, unleashed domestic forces that pressed unilateral expansion. While the conference was in process, the United States Congress declared a 200–mile fishing zone for the United States.)

Henkin, How Nations Behave 217 (2d ed. 1979) (footnotes omitted).

THE EXCLUSIVE ECONOMIC ZONE IN THE 1982 CONVENTION

Extensive pressure from states with varying interests at stake led the Law of the Sea Convention to adopt the exclusive economic zone:

> The drive to extend coastal-state jurisdiction has come particularly from Latin–American states. * * * [F]ishing states have pressed for monopoly over fish equivalent to that enjoyed by their neighbors over coastal minerals. Within the general campaign of the poorer states for change in the international economic system and its law, and the general reexamination of the law of the sea that has followed upon Malta's initiative, mining and fishing states in Latin America have joined to propose a "patrimonial sea" of 200 miles in which the coastal state would have exclusive rights to all resources. A group of African states has also proposed such an "exclusive economic zone."

Henkin, Politics and the Changing Law of the Sea, 89 Pol.Sci.Q. 56–57 (1974). See generally Orrego Vicuña, The Exclusive Economic Zone: Regime and Legal Nature under International Law (1989); Kwiatkowska, The 200 Mile Exclusive Economic Zone in the New Law of the Sea (1989); Attard, The Exclusive Economic Zone in International Law (1987); Charney, The Exclusive Economic Zone and Public International Law, 15 Ocean Dev. & Int'l L. 233 (1985); Hollick, The Origins of 200–Mile Offshore Zones, 71 A.J.I.L. (1977).

U.N. CONVENTION ON THE LAW OF THE SEA (1982)

1833 U.N.T.S. 3, U.N.Doc. A/CONF. 62/122; 21 I.L.M. 1261 (1982).

Article 55

Specific Legal Regime of the Exclusive Economic Zone

The exclusive economic zone is an area beyond and adjacent to the territorial sea, subject to the specific legal regime established in this Part, under which the rights and jurisdictions of the coastal State and the rights and freedoms of other States are governed by the relevant provisions of this Convention.

Article 56

Rights, Jurisdiction and Duties of the Coastal State in the Exclusive Economic Zone

1. In the exclusive economic zone, the coastal State has:

(a) sovereign rights for the purpose of exploring and exploiting, conserving and managing the natural resources, whether living or non-living, of the sea-bed and subsoil and the superjacent waters, and with regard to other activities for the economic exploitation and exploration of the zone, such as the production of energy from the water, currents and winds;

(b) jurisdiction as provided for in the relevant provisions of this Convention with regard to:

(i) the establishment and use of artificial islands, installations and structures;

(ii) marine scientific research;

(iii) the protection and preservation of the marine environment;

(c) other rights and duties provided for in this Convention.

2. In exercising its rights and performing its duties under this Convention in the exclusive economic zone, the coastal state shall have due regard to the rights and duties of other States and shall act in a manner compatible with the provisions of this Convention.

3. The rights set out in this article with respect to the sea-bed and subsoil shall be exercised in accordance with Part VI.

Article 57

Breadth of the Exclusive Economic Zone

The exclusive economic zone shall not extend beyond 200 nautical miles from the baselines from which the breadth of the territorial sea is measured.

Article 58

Rights and Duties of Other States in the Exclusive Economic Zone

1. In the exclusive economic zone, all States, whether coastal or land-locked, enjoy, subject to the relevant provisions of this Convention, the freedoms referred to in article 87 of navigation and overflight and of the laying of submarine cables and pipelines, and other internationally lawful uses of the sea related to these freedoms, such as those associated with the operation of ships, aircraft and submarine cables and pipelines, and compatible with the other provisions of this Convention.

2. Articles 88 to 115 and other pertinent rules of international law apply to the exclusive economic zone in so far as they are not incompatible with this Part.

3. In exercising their rights and performing their duties under this Convention in the exclusive economic zone, States shall have due regard to the rights and duties of the coastal State and shall comply with the laws and regulations adopted by the coastal State in accordance with the provisions of this Convention and other rules of international law in so far as they are not incompatible with this Part.

Notes

1. In 1983, President Reagan established an exclusive economic zone for the United States by proclamation, asserting rights over living and nonliving resources in accordance with the 1982 Convention. 19 Weekly Compilation of Presidential Documents 383 (1983), 83 Dep't State Bull. No. 2075 at 70–71 (1983),

22 I.L.M. 464 (1983). See p. 1385 above. For the conclusion that the EEZ is now customary law, see Restatement (Third) § 514, Comment *a*. If the EEZ is customary law, does it supersede the 1976 Act of Congress, p. 1435 above as law of the United States? See Chapter 3, p. 171 above.

2. Article 74 of the 1982 Convention, dealing with delimitation of exclusive economic zones between states with opposite or adjacent coasts, is identical with Article 83 which deals with delimitation of the continental shelf. See p. 1427 above. Delimitation problems in the exclusive economic zone and the shelf are generally the same, and are sometimes considered together.

3. The Restatement (Third) § 514, Comment *c*, states:

> *Rights of coastal state in exclusive economic zone*. The coastal state does not have sovereignty over the exclusive economic zone but only "sovereign rights" for a specific purpose—the management of natural resources and other economic activities. See § 511, Comment *b*. The coastal state's authority (called "jurisdiction" in the LOS Convention) is even more limited with respect to artificial islands in the exclusive economic zone and such installations and structures as may be required for economic purposes, and with respect to marine scientific research and the protection of the marine environment. See Comments *g-i*. These grants of power are further circumscribed by rules contained in Parts V, XII, and XIII of the Convention, which in large part have already become law by custom and tacit agreement. Among these are rules requiring coastal states to ensure that their laws and regulations for the prevention, reduction, and control of pollution from vessels conform and give effect to generally accepted international rules and standards, to adjust their enforcement measures to the gravity of the violation, and to impose only monetary penalties.
>
> While there is no provision in the Law of the Sea Convention with respect to salvage activities in the exclusive economic zone, the implication in Article 303 of that Convention seems to be that the coastal state may regulate such activities only in the 24–mile contiguous zone. See § 521, Reporters' Note 6.

4. Tuna, a commercially valuable fish, is found both on the high seas and in the exclusive economic zones of many states. As a "highly migratory species," it is covered by Article 64 of the 1982 Convention (See Annex 1 to the Convention). The United States maintains that under this article, and under customary law, a coastal state does not have exclusive rights over tuna in its exclusive economic zones. The United States Fishery Conservation and Management Act of 1976, extending U.S. exclusive authority over fish within the 200–mile zone, excludes tuna, though not other migratory species. However, other coastal states have asserted exclusive authority over tuna within their EEZ and have seized U.S. vessels fishing for tuna within their zones without their authorization. In retaliation the United States has imposed embargoes on the import of fish from these countries. Several South Pacific island states and Mexico have been seriously affected.

Is it plausible to regard tuna and other highly migratory species as "non-residents" and therefore not a resource of the EEZ? Is the United States correct in construing the obligation to cooperate in Article 64 of the LOS Convention as precluding exclusive rights of the coastal state in respect of highly migratory species? See Hey, The Regime for the Exploitation of Transboundary Marine Fisheries Resources (1989); Munro, Extended Jurisdiction and the Management of Pacific Highly Migratory Species, 21 Ocean Dev. & Int'l L. 289 (1990); Weld, Critical Evaluation of Existing Mechanisms for Managing Migratory Pelagic

Species in the Atlantic Ocean, 20 Ocean Dev. & Int'l L. 285 (1989); Kelly, The Law of the Sea: The Jurisdictional Dispute Over Highly Migratory Species of Tuna, 26 Colum.J.Transnat'l L. 475 (1988); Burke, Highly Migratory Species in the New Law of the Sea, 14 Ocean Dev. & Int.L.J. 273 (1983); Oda, Fisheries Under the United Nations Conventions on the Law of the Sea, 77 A.J.I.L. 739 (1984).

Assuming that the law recognizes an exclusive right to tuna in the EEZ, is the United States a "persistent dissenter" entitled to an exception from that principle? See Chapter 2, p. 102. Is it relevant that the United States has not asserted an exception in its law for highly migratory species other than tuna?

5. In the exclusive economic zone, the coastal state is given exclusive rights with regard to artificial islands, installations and structures (Art. 60). It is responsible for conservation of living resources (Art. 61). Article 62 establishes the objective of "optimum utilization." See also the special provisions for stocks occurring within two or more economic zones (Art. 63); highly migratory species (Art. 64), anadromous stocks (Art. 66) and catadromous species (Art. 67). Exploitation of marine mammals is left to regulation by the coastal state (or an international organization) (Art. 65). Sedentary species are governed by the regime of the continental shelf (Art. 77(4)).

If the coastal state does not have the capacity to harvest the entire allowable catch, it shall give access to other states taking into account the "need to minimize economic dislocation in States whose nationals have habitually fished in the zone or which have made substantial efforts in research and identification of stocks," (Art. 62(3)). In particular, there is a right to participate by land-locked states in the region (Art. 69), and states with "special geographical characteristics," having no zone of their own or one unable to supply the needs of their population (Art. 70). But developed land-locked states are entitled to participate only in the economic zones of developed coastal states of the region (Arts. 69(4), 70(5)). Articles 69–70 do not apply when the coastal state's economy is "overwhelmingly dependent" on the exploitation of the living resources of its exclusive economic zone (Art. 71).

Article 73 provides:

> 1. The coastal State may, in the exercise of its sovereign rights to explore, exploit, conserve and manage the living resources in the exclusive economic zone, take such measures, including boarding, inspection, arrest and judicial proceedings, as may be necessary to ensure compliance with the laws and regulations enacted by it in conformity with this Convention.
>
> 2. Arrested vessels and their crews shall be promptly released upon the posting of reasonable bond or other security.
>
> 3. Coastal State penalties for violations of fisheries regulations in the exclusive economic zone may not include imprisonment, in the absence of agreements to the contrary by the States concerned, or any other form of corporal punishment.
>
> 4. In cases of arrest or detention of foreign vessels the coastal State shall promptly notify, through appropriate channels, the flag State of the action taken and of any penalties subsequently imposed.

6. Is the exclusive economic zone "high seas"? Does it matter? See Articles 55 and 58 supra; also Article 86, p. 1442 below. Compare Article 3 of the 1958 Convention on the Continental Shelf: "The rights of the coastal State over the

continental shelf do not affect the legal status of the superjacent waters as high seas, or that of the airspace above those waters."

The Restatement (Third) § 514, Comments *b*, *d* and *e* state:

> *b. Relation of exclusive economic zone to high seas.* The LOS Convention does not explicitly designate the exclusive economic zone as part of the high seas. See § 521, Comment *a*. According to the United States and other maritime states, however, the Convention reflects the general understanding that, as a matter of customary law as well as under the Convention, the rights and freedoms of other states in the zone, set forth in Subsection (2), are the same as on the high seas. See Comment *e*. As to matters not expressly covered by this section, any conflict that might arise between the interests of a coastal state and those of any other state concerning their respective rights and duties in the exclusive economic zone should be resolved "on the basis of equity and in the light of all the relevant circumstances, taking into account the respective importance of the interests involved to the parties as well as to the international community." LOS Convention, Article 59. Special procedures for settling such disputes are provided in the Convention, but will not apply to states not parties. Id. Article 297(1).
>
> * * *
>
> *d. Rights of other states in exclusive economic zone.* In the exclusive economic zone of any state, all other states may exercise most high seas freedoms, such as those of navigation, overflight, and laying of submarine cables and pipelines (§ 521), but their right to participate in fishing is subject to the special rights of the coastal state under Subsection (1). The rights of other states with respect to operation of ships, aircraft, and submarine cables and pipelines are both qualitatively and quantitatively the same as the rights recognized by international law for all states on the high seas. See Subsection 2.
>
> *e. Due regard to rights and duties of other states.* The Convention explicitly applies to the exclusive economic zone the principle of customary international law that in exercising its rights a state must do so with due regard to the rights of other states. The coastal state must exercise its rights and perform its duties under Subsection (1) with due regard to the rights and duties of other states under Subsection (2). LOS Convention, Article 56(2). Other states must exercise their rights and perform their duties under Subsection (2) with due regard to the rights of the coastal state under Subsection (1). Id. Article 58(3).

7. On the right of hot pursuit from the EEZ, the 1982 Convention Art. 111(2) provides:

> The right of hot pursuit shall apply *mutatis mutandis* to violations in the exclusive economic zone or on the continental shelf, including safety zones around continental shelf installations, of the laws and regulations of the coastal State applicable in accordance with this Convention to the exclusive economic zone or the continental shelf, including such safety zones.

See generally, Korolera, The Right to Hot Pursuit from the Exclusive Economic Zone, 14 Marine Pol'y 137 (1990).

8. On the protection of the marine environment, including the environment of the EEZ, see Section 4, p. 1476 infra. On marine scientific research, including research in the EEZ, see Section 5, p. 1481 infra.

SECTION 3. THE REGIME OF THE HIGH SEAS

Once, all the seas were governed by a regime characterized by principles of commonage and freedom. See p. 1389 supra. The emergence of the concept of the territorial sea, followed by other special zones and privileges for coastal states, reduced the areas subject to that regime (now distinctively called the "high seas") and created additional exceptions to its principles of commonage and freedom. Under the law emerging from the Third U.N. Law of the Sea Conference, the extent of the "high seas" is reduced by further concessions to coastal states—by a wider territorial sea and recognition of archipelagic states, and the special status of the Exclusive Economic Zone. Even the high seas as thus reduced are subject to additional rights for coastal states, as in the special-purpose zones described above, the coastal state's rights in its continental shelf where it is under the "high seas" because it extends beyond the 200 mile economic zone, and new regimes for pollution control and scientific research.

Subject to these limitations, the regime of the high seas continues to be characterized by commonage and freedom, but commonage does not necessarily mean, as it used to, that all states are free to take the resources of the sea and the sea-bed, and freedom is subject to increasing international regulation.

DEFINITION OF "HIGH SEAS"

U.N. CONVENTION ON THE LAW OF THE SEA (1982)

1833 U.N.T.S. 3, U.N.Doc. A/CONF. 62/122; 21 I.L.M. 1261 (1982).

ARTICLE 86

The provisions of this Part apply to all parts of the sea that are not included in the exclusive economic zone, in the territorial sea or in the internal waters of a State, or in the archipelagic waters of an archipelagic State. This article does not entail any abridgement of the freedoms enjoyed by all States in the exclusive economic zone in accordance with article 58.

Note

Compare Article 1 of the 1958 Convention on the High Seas which defined "high seas" as "all parts of the sea that are not included in the territorial sea or in the internal waters of a State." For the status of the EEZ under the 1982 Convention, see p. 1437 above.

A. THE PRINCIPLE OF FREEDOM

U.N. CONVENTION ON THE LAW OF THE SEA (1982)

1833 U.N.T.S. 3, U.N.Doc. A/CONF. 62/122; 21 I.L.M. 1261 (1982).

ARTICLE 87

Freedom of the High Seas

1. The high seas are open to all States, whether coastal or land-locked. Freedom of the high seas is exercised under the conditions laid down by this

Convention and by other rules of international law. It comprises, *inter alia*, both for coastal and land-locked States:

(a) Freedom of navigation;

(b) Freedom of overflight;

(c) Freedom to lay submarine cables and pipelines, subject to Part VI;

(d) Freedom to construct artificial islands and other installations permitted under international law, subject to Part VI;

(e) Freedom of fishing, subject to the conditions laid down in section 2;

(f) Freedom of scientific research, subject to Parts VI and XIII.

2. These freedoms shall be exercised by all States, with due consideration for the interests of other States in their exercise of the freedom of the high seas, and also with due consideration for the rights under this Convention with respect to activities in the Area.

Article 88

Reservation of the High Seas for Peaceful Purposes

The high seas shall be reserved for peaceful purposes.

Article 89

Invalidity of Claims of Sovereignty Over the High Seas

No State may validly purport to subject any part of the high seas to its sovereignty.

Article 90

Right of Navigation

Every State, whether coastal or land-locked, has the right to sail ships under its flag on the high seas.

Notes

1. Articles 87–90 of the 1982 Convention essentially repeat Articles 2 and 4 of the 1958 Convention, subject to exceptions consequent upon recognition of a wide continental shelf (Part VI), and the provisions relating to scientific research (Part XIII).

2. Warships and other vessels owned or operated by a government in "non-commercial service" on the high seas have complete immunity from the jurisdiction of any other state. 1982 Convention Arts. 95, 96. Is the same rule applicable to aircraft? Compare Chapter 13, p. 1125 above.

3. All states, including land-locked states, have the right to freedom of navigation. Article 3 of the 1958 Convention gave states without seacoast free access to the sea, pursuant to agreement, by transit through the territory of the coastal state and access to its ports. The 1982 Convention extends and expands such rights in Part X, Articles 124–132.

B. LIMITATIONS ON FREEDOM

HENKIN, CHANGING LAW FOR THE CHANGING SEAS

Uses of the Seas 69, 72, 74–75 (Gullion ed. 1968).

Like all law, the various laws of the seas may be seen as derogations from the principle of freedom. The freedom of the sea is, of course, subject to general law that applies at sea as elsewhere, for example rules protecting persons and property, or the law of the U.N. Charter outlawing war and other uses of force. There are limitations in special laws and agreements that have applied only, or especially, at sea—for example, those against piracy or slave-running, or wartime limitations on trade between neutrals and belligerents.

* * *

The Law of "Conflicting Uses"

Freedom of the seas for all has meant of course that no state was free to exclude others. From the beginning, too, freedom had to give way to "conflicting uses"—if only between two vessels seeking to ply the same waters, or nations competing to fish in the same area. As uses of the sea grew, the possibilities of conflict grew. Even navigation and fishing had to accommodate each other. Later, ships had to watch out for cables, and recently for oil derricks, sea mounts, scientific buoys; submarines might run afoul of diving gear, installations on the seabed or military detection equipment. Nuclear tests prevented all other uses in large areas of seas for short periods. Other military uses, operations and pollutions might bar other uses for long times.

Early, as freedom led to conflict, conflict led to some regulation. Friendly nations began to leave each other alone, to develop navigation lanes, rules of navigation, laws about collisions and other mishaps at sea. General recognition of the special rights of coastal states helped to reduce conflict. As regards fishing, in particular, in some areas and for some species, there grew a network of international agreements designed to accommodate the claims of coastal states and of others, of states with historical rights and of newcomers, and to make some provision for conservation. Infrequently, nations also entered agreements determining their respective rights in other resources, for example, the 1942 agreement between Great Britain and Venezuela with respect to mineral resources in the Gulf of Paria.

Some law grew also to regulate conflicts between different uses. The law developed principles of priority and some general standards of conduct. Traditionally, navigation has been a preferred use, and interferences with navigation (in time of peace) have been strongly resisted. (That nuclear tests at sea interfered with navigation, albeit temporarily, was a principal argument of those who considered them illegal.) "Reasonableness" has frequently been invoked as the standard of behavior: There may be "reasonable" interferences with some uses to promote others; when uses conflict there must be a "reasonable" balancing of interests to determine which use is to be preferred.

Conflicting uses are also the subject of agreement. In the nineteenth century agreements provided for the protection of oceanic cables. The 1958 Geneva conventions on the law of the sea, while codifying the principle of freedom, also included basic provisions to regulate conflicting uses. The Convention on the Continental Shelf, for example, provides that, subject to its right to take "reasonable measures" to explore the shelf and exploit its mineral resources, the coastal state may not interfere with laying cables or pipelines. Mining "must not result in any unjustifiable interferences with navigation, fishing or the conservation of the living resources of the sea." Installations and safety-zones around them must not interfere with "recognized sea lanes essential to international navigation." Mining must not "result in any interference with fundamental oceanographic or other scientific research carried out with the intention of open publication." And research on and concerning the continental shelf requires the consent of the coastal state but such consent shall be normally granted.

Notes

1. For an examination of the law of navigation and its relation to other uses, see Bouchez, Ocean Navigation: International Legal Aspects, International Law Association, Report of the 56th Conference, New Delhi, 330 (1976).

2. See generally Krueger, Artificial Islands and Offshore Installations, International Law Association, Report of the 57th Conference, Madrid, 396 (1978). See also Pontavice, Rapport Concernant les Aspects Juridiques de l'Exploitation des Maisons sous la Mer, International Law Association, Report of the 57th Conference, Madrid, 343 (1978).

PROHIBITED ACTIVITIES

a. Slave Transport

U.N. CONVENTION ON THE LAW OF THE SEA (1982)

1833 U.N.T.S. 3, U.N.Doc. A/CONF. 62/122; 21 I.L.M. 1261 (1982).

ARTICLE 99

Prohibition of the Transport of Slaves

Every State shall adopt effective measures to prevent and punish the transport of slaves in ships authorized to fly its flag and to prevent the unlawful use of its flag for that purpose. Any slave taking refuge on board any ship, whatever its flag, shall *ipso facto* be free.

Note

There are a number of conventions outlawing slavery and slave trade. It has been urged that these are also violations of customary law and indeed are international crimes. See Chapter 8, p. 602 above.

b. *Piracy*

U.N. CONVENTION ON THE LAW OF THE SEA (1982)

1833 U.N.T.S. 3, U.N.Doc. A/CONF. 62/122; 21 I.L.M. 1261 (1982).

Article 100

Duty to Co-operate in the Repression of Piracy

All States shall co-operate to the fullest possible extent in the repression of piracy on the high seas or in any other place outside the jurisdiction of any State.

Article 101

Definition of Piracy

Piracy consists of any of the following acts:

(a) Any illegal acts of violence, detention or any act of depredation, committed for private ends by the crew or the passengers of a private ship or a private aircraft, and directed:

(i) On the high seas, against another ship or aircraft, or against persons or property on board such ship or aircraft;

(ii) Against a ship, aircraft, persons or property in a place outside the jurisdiction of any State;

(b) Any act of voluntary participation in the operation of a ship or of an aircraft with knowledge of facts making it a pirate ship or aircraft;

(c) Any act of inciting or of intentionally facilitating an act described in subparagraphs (a) and (b).

Article 105

Seizure of a Pirate Ship or Aircraft

On the high seas, or in any other place outside the jurisdiction of any State, every State may seize a pirate ship or aircraft, or a ship taken by piracy and under the control of pirates, and arrest the persons and seize the property on board. The courts of the State which carried out the seizure may decide upon the penalties to be imposed, and may also determine the action to be taken with regard to the ships, aircraft or property, subject to the rights of third parties acting in good faith.

Notes

1. The 1982 Convention Articles 100, 101 and 105 repeat Articles 14, 15, and 19, of the 1958 Convention on the High Seas.

2. "It has long been recognized and well settled that persons and vessels engaged in piratical operations on the high seas are entitled to the protection of no nation and may be punished by any nation that may apprehend or capture them. This stern rule of international law refers to piracy in its international-law sense and not to a variety of lesser maritime offenses so designated by municipal law." 2 Hackworth at 681.

3. An increasing number of cases of piracy have been reported in recent years, especially in the waters of Southeast Asia (e.g., the Gulf of Thailand, the Malacca Straits, and the Sulu and Celebes Seas). See Dzurek, Piracy in Southeast Asia, 32 Oceanus 65–70 (Winter 1989–90); Rubin, The Law of Piracy (2d ed. 1998).

4. On piracy, see generally Dubner, The Law of International Sea Piracy (1980); Boulton, The Modern International Law of Piracy: Content and Contemporary Relevance, 7 Int'l Relations 2493 (1981–83); Restatement (Third) § 522, Comment *c*, Reporters' Note 2. For earlier writings, see Harvard Research in International Law, Piracy, 26 A.J.I.L.Supp. 739 (1932); 2 Moore, Digest of International Law 951–79 (1906); 2 Hackworth at 681–95; Dickinson, Is the Crime of Piracy Obsolete?, 38 Harv.L.Rev. 334 (1925); Lenoir, Piracy Cases in the Supreme Court, 25 J.Crim.L. & Crim'y 532 (1934); Johnson, Piracy in Modern International Law, 43 Trans. Grot.Soc'y 63 (1957). See also In re Piracy Jure Gentium, [1934] A.C. 586 (attempt to commit a "piratical robbery" is equivalent to piracy under the law of nations). The municipal law of a number of states provides for the punishment of so-called *delicta juris gentium* other than piracy on the same basis as the latter. See Harvard Research in International Law, Jurisdiction with Respect to Crime, 29 A.J.I.L.Supp. 435, 569–72 (1935).

5. The 1982 Convention defines piracy to include acts against aircraft, but covers only acts by the crew or the passengers of a private aircraft, committed for "private" ends. For acts by others, see the Convention for the Suppression of Unlawful Seizure of Aircraft, the Anti–Hijacking Act of 1974, and the Hostage–Taking Act of 1984, pp. 1118–1122, 1128–1131.

c. Uses Impinging on Coastal State Interests: Offshore "Pirate" Broadcasting

In the late 1950s, a number of unauthorized radio and television stations operated in international waters in the North, Baltic, and Irish Seas. These stations, situated on fixed platforms or on ships flying foreign "flags of convenience," were a multiple source of irritation to the governments of the coastal states to which their broadcasts were directed: they used unauthorized wave lengths, evaded the payment of royalties due to holders of copyright on the material used (largely popular music), evaded income and other taxes, and either broke the monopoly of the coastal state's government on broadcasting or violated its prohibition of commercial broadcasting. In 1962, Belgium and the four continental Scandinavian countries enacted legislation directed at nationals of those states engaged in or assisting offshore broadcasting. See Hunnings, Pirate Broadcasting in European Waters, 14 I.C.L.Q. 410, 417–21 (1965). In view of the insufficiency of such laws to deal with stations owned and manned by foreigners, and because of the reluctance of some states to take direct unilateral action against stations operating off their shores, the Council of Europe opened for signature in early 1965 a convention intended to deal with the problem. In brief, the European Agreement for the Prevention of Broadcasts Transmitted from Stations Outside National Territories requires contracting states to make punishable under domestic law the operation of, or collaboration with, unauthorized broadcasting stations located outside national territories, and to apply such legislation to nationals and to foreigners otherwise within their jurisdiction. The Agreement applies only to stations situated "on board ships, aircraft, or any other floating or airborne objects" and thus does not cover stations installed on fixed platforms; it expressly provided, however, that nothing in the agreement prevents a party from applying the provisions thereof to such platforms. In December 1964, the Netherlands enacted the North Seas Installations Act and took action thereunder to silence a radio-television station operated from an artificial structure by individuals of undisclosed nationality and identity. Van Panhuys & van Emde Boas, Legal Aspects of Pirate Broadcasting: A Dutch Approach, 60 A.J.I.L. 303, 303–04 (1966). In 1967 the United Kingdom also enacted legislation to prohibit and punish "pirate" broadcasting. The Marine, & c., Broadcasting (Offences) Act, 1967, 1967 Ch. 41, enacted July 14, 1967, makes it unlawful to broadcast from a ship, aircraft or structure registered in the United Kingdom or located in United Kingdom tidal or "external" waters (defined as the "whole of the sea adjacent to the United Kingdom which is within the seaward limits of territorial waters adjacent thereto"). The statute makes the owner, master, operator, or one who procures the act of broadcasting (including supplying of equipment, food or advertising) liable to punishment of three months' imprisonment and/or fine of 400 pounds. The statute bases jurisdiction to prescribe and punish on territorial jurisdiction over the territorial waters or on citizenship of the persons responsible for the broadcast.

Unauthorized broadcasting from the high seas is dealt with in the 1982 Convention, Art. 109:

> 1. All States shall co-operate in the suppression of unauthorized broadcasting from the high seas.
>
> 2. For the purposes of this Convention, "unauthorized broadcasting" means the transmission of sound radio or television broadcasts from a ship or installation on the high seas intended for reception by the general public contrary to international regulations, but excluding the transmission of distress calls.
>
> 3. Any person engaged in unauthorized broadcasting may be prosecuted before the court of:
>
> (a) the flag State of the ship;
>
> (b) the State of registry of the installation;
>
> (c) the State of which the person is a national;
>
> (d) any State where the transmissions can be received; or
>
> (e) any State where authorized radio communication is suffering interference.
>
> 4. On the high seas, a State having jurisdiction in accordance with paragraph 3 may, in conformity with article 110, arrest any person or ship engaged in unauthorized broadcasting and seize the broadcasting apparatus.

What of unauthorized broadcasting from the exclusive economic zone to the territory of the state whose zone it is? to other territories? See generally Robertson, The Suppression of Pirate Radio Broadcasting: A Test Case for Control of International Activities Outside National Territory, 45 L. & Contemp. Probs. 71 (1982).

ACTION TO PROTECT AGAINST FORBIDDEN ACTIVITIES

International law permits all states to protect the common interests in the high seas against unlawful activities. The law authorizes some measures by coastal states.

U.N. CONVENTION ON THE LAW OF THE SEA (1982)

1833 U.N.T.S. 3, U.N.Doc. A/CONF. 62/122; 21 I.L.M. 1261 (1982).

ARTICLE 110

1. Except where acts of interference derive from powers conferred by treaty, a warship which encounters on the high seas a foreign ship, other than a ship entitled to complete immunity in accordance with articles 95 and 96, is not justified in boarding her unless there is reasonable ground for suspecting:

(a) That the ship is engaged in piracy;

(b) That the ship is engaged in the slave trade;

(c) That the ship is engaged in unauthorized broadcasting and the warship has jurisdiction under article 109;

(d) That the ship is without nationality; or

(e) That, though flying a foreign flag or refusing to show its flag, the ship is, in reality, of the same nationality as the warship.

2. In the cases provided for in paragraph 1, the warship may proceed to verify the ship's right to fly its flag. To this end, it may send a boat, under the command of an officer, to the suspected ship. If suspicion remains after the documents have been checked, it may proceed to a further examination on board the ship, which must be carried out with all possible consideration.

3. If the suspicions prove to be unfounded, and provided that the ship boarded has not committed any act justifying them, it shall be compensated for any loss or damage that may have been sustained.

4. These provisions shall apply *mutatis mutandis* to military aircraft.

5. These provisions shall also apply to any other duly authorized ships or aircraft clearly marked and identifiable as being on government service.

Notes

1. This article duplicates Article 22 of the 1958 Convention, but adds the clauses on unauthorized broadcasting, vessels without nationality, and paragraphs 4 and 5.

2. In 1981, President Reagan issued a proclamation addressing "the continuing problem of migrants coming to the United States, by sea, without necessary entry documents * * * ." The Proclamation instructed the Secretary of State "to enter into, on behalf of the United States, cooperative arrangements with appropriate foreign governments for the purpose of preventing illegal migration to the United States by sea." The Coast Guard was to be instructed to "enforce the suspension of the entry of undocumented aliens and the interdiction of any vessel carrying such aliens in waters beyond the territorial sea of the United States." The order applied to vessels of the United States, vessels without nationality, and

vessels of foreign nations with whom the United States has entered into arrangements authorizing the United States to stop and board such vessels. The Attorney General, in consultation with other departments, was instructed to "take whatever steps are necessary to ensure the fair enforcement of our laws relating to immigration" and "the strict observance of our international obligations concerning those who genuinely flee persecution in their homeland." See Presidential Proclamation No. 4865, 46 Fed.Reg. 48, 107 (Sept. 29, 1981), reprinted at 8 U.S.C. § 1182.

By an exchange of letters the week before the proclamation issued, the United States entered into a cooperative arrangement with the government of Haiti. In effect, the parties agreed that the United States may do what the President's Proclamation instructed the Coast Guard to do, including to board Haitian vessels, investigate, detain a vessel and the persons aboard it, and return the vessel and the persons aboard it to Haiti.

Challenges to the program on the ground that it violated the obligations of the United States under the Protocol to the Refugee Convention, and the rights of individuals under the U.S. Constitution and laws, were rejected in Haitian Refugee Center, Inc. v. Gracey, 600 F.Supp. 1396 (D.D.C.1985), aff'd, 809 F.2d 794 (D.C.Cir.1987).

The United States policy of interdiction on the high seas was continued after the Haitian government was overthrown by military coup in 1991 and a large number of Haitians attempted to seek asylum in the United States. On May 24, 1992, President Bush issued Executive Order 12807 requiring the Coast Guard to "enforce the suspension of entry of undocumented aliens by sea and the interdiction of any defined vessel carrying such aliens" in waters "beyond the territorial sea of the United States." Ex. Order 12807, §§ 2(a) and 2(d), 57 Fed.Reg. 23 1933 (May 24, 1992). Pursuant to that order, the Coast Guard intercepted boatloads of Haitian asylum seekers and returned them to Haiti without making a determination as to whether they were refugees under Article 33 of the Refugee Convention. See p. 622 in Chapter 8 for discussion of Sale v. Haitian Centers Council, 509 U.S. 155, 113 S.Ct. 2549, 125 L.Ed.2d 128 (1993), which rejected the Haitians' challenges to the interdiction program.

Does international law permit the United States to protect against illegal immigration by boarding vessels on the high seas? Does the consent of the flag state matter? Can the United States establish a ring of military vessels on the high seas to keep vessels suspected of carrying asylum seekers from leaving their home state's territorial waters or from entering U.S. territorial waters?

C. MILITARY USES OF THE HIGH SEAS

The seas have never been far from military strategy and planning and from concern for national security in war or Cold War, even in peace. With advancing technology, the seas became a locus also for new weapons and new uses. Even in Cold War the antagonists were concerned to seek advantage and support in international law, in customary law or in applicable treaties; they were also willing to explore the possibility of agreement on arms control, even on some disarmament.

The 1982 Convention was concluded during the Cold War. The end of the Cold War doubtless reduced but did not end the military importance of the Convention's provisions governing the military uses of the high seas.

HENKIN, CHANGING LAW FOR THE CHANGING SEAS

Uses of the Seas 69, 84–86 (Gullion ed. 1968).

The law governing military uses at sea can be importantly affected by changes in law of general applicability, for example by agreements eliminating or controlling the use of some weapon. In a different way new agreement on a wider territorial sea may effectively bar military vessels and equipment from additional areas of sea, and even a wider continental shelf will tend to discourage military uses there. In deep sea, too, a general law aimed at other uses can affect military uses as well.* * *

Suggestions for new law about the military uses in particular take different forms and have different goals. Some have written about the need to protect, even promote, military uses, at least "defensive" ones: for example, law could expressly permit, and protect against violation by others, national "hardened" submarine rocket installations, fixed submarine maintenance facilities, research and communications stations, storage depots, repair works, or other submarine "strategic areas." Similarly, some foresee the need for regulating "traffic" in submarine military vehicles as they increase in quantity and mobility.

Usually, suggestions for regulating military uses propose various forms of disarmament or arms control in the sea. (Suggestions for protecting submarine military installations would also have some arms control qualities since they would require identification and disclosure of the installations.) Arms control proposals take different forms. One kind is typified by a proposal to establish a sea-wide network of buoys and equipment for detecting and tracking submarines . The network might be operated by some international authority. Most proposals would demilitarize or exclude particular weapons from all or parts of the sea. Recently attention has focused in particular on the seabed: some have proposed that it be wholly demilitarized, while others would at least exclude weapons of mass destruction. Supporters of such proposals usually invoke the precedent of outer space, where by U.N. resolution and subsequent treaty, nations agreed not to place weapons of mass destruction in orbit around the earth, on celestial bodies, or anywhere in space. (Antarctica, too, has been reserved by treaty for peaceful purposes only and nuclear explosions have been barred there for any purposes. The Spitsbergen Treaty of 1920 also barred militarization of that area.) But, again, in these and other cases, nations forewent what they did not yet have, had never relied on, perhaps could not appreciate. In the sea, military vessels and weapons are an integral and dominant element of national defense, for many nations; submarine-based missiles, indeed, are key weapons in global strategy, on which deterrence, security and perhaps world peace depend. Precedents and analogies apart, the United States surely will not give up its Navy and its submarine-based missiles, except–theoretically–in some final stage of general and complete disarmament.

On the other hand, it is not out of the question to consider the demilitarization of some parts of the sea, the elimination or control of some weapons or some uses. (Nuclear-testing underwater and in the atmosphere–including the air space above the seas–is forbidden by the Nuclear Test Ban of 1963.) While demilitarizing the seabed without demilitarizing the sea might contribute little to peace and military stability, it might forestall fixed military complexes and atomic "caches" that would be more difficult to eliminate or control later; it might also serve as another small step to slow down the arms race. Whether such proposals are feasible and acceptable is not clear. The ambiguous content of the term "demilitarization" would be especially discouraging. There is no indication that nations have already stationed weapons of mass destruction on the seabed or that the right to do so looms large in future plans for national deterrence systems. On the other hand, the United States, and probably the Soviet Union, apparently have considerable, sophisticated "military equipment" on the seabed, e.g., submarine detection devices. It is unlikely that the United States would agree to sacrifice them, and it is not clear that any agreement to that end could be effectively monitored. Proposals that would bar the seabed to weapons of mass destruction might also entail inspection problems, and a system to verify a ban on such weapons might interfere with submarine detection systems and perhaps other uses of the seabed. For these and other reasons some believe that, unlike outer space, proposals for controlling arms in the sea or on the seabed cannot be simple, and would hold more promise in a context of negotiation about disarmament rather than about the law of the sea.

It seems unlikely, then, that the United States would agree to a U.N. resolution "demilitarizing" the seabed; it might also be reluctant to agree to exclude weapons of mass destruction.* * *

Notes

1. The testing of nuclear weapons on the high seas gave rise to substantial debate. See p. [1021] above. In 1963, the United States, Britain, and the Soviet Union adhered to the Treaty Banning Nuclear Weapons Tests in the Atmosphere, In Outer Space and Under Water, 480 U.N.T.S. 43. See also the Treaty on the Prohibition of the Emplacement of Nuclear Weapons and Other Weapons of Mass Destruction on the Seabed and the Ocean Floor and in the Subsoil Thereof, 23 U.S.T. 701, T.I.A.S. No. 3337. In the absence of a treaty provision prohibiting it, may states test nuclear weapons on the high seas? The 1982 Convention limits the use of the high seas to "peaceful purposes." (Article 88). Does weapons testing of any sort on the high seas violate this provision?

2. See Treves, Military Installations, Structure, and Devices on the Seabed, 74 A.J.I.L. 808 (1980); Treves, La notion d'utilisation des espaces marins à des fins pacifiques dans le nouveau droit de la mer, 1980 Annuaire Français 687; Truver, The Law of the Sea and the Military Use of the Oceans in 2010, 45 La.L.Rev. 1221 (1985). On the laws of war generally, see Chapter 12; on war and neutrality in relation to the law of the sea, see p. 1065.

D. EXPLOITATION OF RESOURCES BEYOND NATIONAL JURISDICTION

1. Mineral Resources of the Seabed

Derogations from "freedom of the seas" and from the principles of "commonage," reflected in the law of the sea since World War II, were changes inspired largely by the desire of technologically-advanced coastal states, such as the United States, to explore and exploit the resources of the sea, as by "distant fishing" and, in particular, by mining the mineral resources of the sea-bed and sub-soil off their shores beyond the territorial sea. Technologically-advanced states were content with *laissez-faire,* the freedom to exploit the commonage. New, developing states, sought to establish the sea-bed beyond national jurisdiction as "the common heritage of mankind," to be developed by "mankind," through institutions governed by "democratic principles" (generally one state, one vote). They wished also that the "haves" contribute generously to the costs of exploitation by "mankind," and provide mankind with access to the relevant technology, even technology that is privately owned.

These differences, though compromised during years of negotiation leading to the 1982 Convention, persisted through 12 years of additional delay in bringing the Convention into effect, until bridged by the 1994 "Agreement Relating to the Implementation of Part XI of the United Nations Convention on the Law of the Sea of 10 December of 1982." (The differences are not yet definitively resolved, since, as of 2000, the United States has not yet ratified the 1982 Convention as modified by the 1994 Agreement.)

The 1994 Agreement became possible when the end of the Cold War largely eliminated the political elements in the controversy, and greater realism dispelled the rosier dreams of the developing states. The developing world recognized that the sea-bed beyond national jurisdiction was far from ready for exploitation and would not soon produce the wealth of which they had dreamed. But a new regime is ready.

BACKGROUND TO THE 1982 CONVENTION ON THE SEA–BED

HENKIN, LAW FOR THE SEA'S MINERAL RESOURCES

49–51, 58–59 (1968).

However the continental shelf is defined, exploitation of mineral resources is or will soon be possible in the sea beyond. The major legal issue that is developing is who is–or should be–entitled to exploit these resources, on what basis, under what limitations. In general terms, the issue is between *laissez-faire* for interested states (subject to any "ground rules" they may agree on) and control by the international community. * * *

* * *

Two general attitudes are already in evidence. One insists that the sea's resources have always been "for the taking" and there is no reason why those who can take them should give up their right. In the long run, moreover–and in the less long run too–all of mankind will benefit if the sea's mineral resources are extracted as quickly, as efficiently, as economically as possible. What is called for, then, is law that will induce the technologically-advanced nations and their nationals to explore the ocean bed energetically and to begin to extract its minerals. This means law that imposes few limitations on national initiative, that assures to enterprising nations the fruits of their labor (as is just and reasonable), that affords them protection against encroachment and unfair competition. To achieve such law one need only reaffirm traditional legal concepts in favor of those who proceed to dig against any who come later. One could also adapt much of the law that protects sea-going vessels, giving to any installation the protection of the "flag it flies."

* * *

The opposing view would argue that now is the time to lay down the basic principles that will shape the law of the future. As in regard to outer space, now is the time for "preventive law" to avoid certain evils. As mankind stands at the threshold of a new environment, before egotistic national interests form and vest, it is important to accept legal principles and establish international machinery to assure that there will not be an international "race" or conflict for the sea's wealth; that the resources that belong to all will not be grabbed for the selfish profit of a few; that the new environment will serve to reduce rather than widen the gulf between rich nations and poor.

* * *

Those who favor substantial *laissez-faire* (principally the technologically advanced nations) will not be eager to have a strong international organization with substantial authority. If they feel compelled to accept some international body in principle they will seek to assure that its organization and its powers and functions leave maximum autonomy to individual states. Most nations, on the other hand, will not see themselves as major entrepreneurs in the sea and will seek an organization with as much control as possible over the activities of the states that will be the principal "miners."

Probably they would settle for a regime that includes some international organization reflecting some international authority and provides some revenue for international purposes.

MORATORIUM ON EXPLOITATION OF RESOURCES OF THE DEEP SEA–BED

G.A.Res. 2574D (XXIV) (1969).

The General Assembly * * * [d]eclares that, pending the establishment of the aforementioned international regime:

> (a) States and persons, physical or juridical, are bound to refrain from all activities of exploitation of the resources of the area of the seabed and ocean floor, and the subsoil thereof, beyond the limits of national jurisdiction;
>
> (b) No claim to any part of that area or its resources shall be recognized.

[The vote on the Moratorium Resolution was 62–28–28; the United States challenged the statement of international law reflected in the resolution and the authority of the Assembly to declare a "moratorium."]

DECLARATION OF PRINCIPLES GOVERNING THE SEA–BED AND THE OCEAN FLOOR, AND SUBSOIL THEREOF, BEYOND THE LIMITS OF NATIONAL JURISDICTION

G.A.Res. 2749 (XXV) (1970).

The General Assembly,

Recalling its resolutions 2340 (XXII) of 18 December 1967, 2467 (XXIII) of 21 December 1968 and 2574 (XXIV) of 15 December 1969, concerning the area to which the title of the item refers,

Affirming that there is an area of the sea-bed and the ocean floor, and the subsoil thereof, beyond the limits of national jurisdiction, the precise limits of which are yet to be determined,

Recognizing that the existing legal régime of the high seas does not provide substantive rules for regulating the exploration of the aforesaid area and the exploitation of its resources,

Convinced that the area shall be reserved exclusively for peaceful purposes and that the exploration of the area and the exploitation of its resources shall be carried out for the benefit of mankind as a whole,

Believing it essential that an international régime applying to the area and its resources and including appropriate international machinery should be established as soon as possible,

Bearing in mind that the development and use of the area and its resources shall be undertaken in such a manner as to foster healthy development of the world economy and balanced growth of international trade, and to minimize any adverse economic effects caused by fluctuation of prices of raw materials resulting from such activities,

Solemnly declares that:

1. The sea-bed and ocean floor, and the subsoil thereof, beyond the limits of national jurisdiction (hereinafter referred to as the area), as well as the resources of the area, are the common heritage of mankind.

2. The area shall not be subject to appropriation by any means by States or persons, natural or juridical, and no State shall claim or exercise sovereignty or sovereign rights over any part thereof.

3. No State or person, natural or juridical, shall claim, exercise or acquire rights with respect to the area or its resources incompatible with the international régime to be established and the principles of this Declaration.

4. All activities regarding the exploration and exploitation of the resources of the area and other related activities shall be governed by the international régime to be established.

* * *

Notes

1. The concept of the "common heritage of mankind" adopted in the Declaration (and later confirmed in Article 136 of the 1982 Convention) is usually attributed to Ambassador Arvid Pardo of Malta (deceased during early 2000) who in 1967 proposed the subject of sea-bed mining for consideration by the General Assembly. See U.N.Doc. A/6695 (1967). See also de Marffy, The Pardo Declaration and the Six Years of the Sea–Bed Committee, in 1 A Handbook on the New Law of the Sea 141 (Dupuy, ed. 1991). The concept was expressed earlier, including in a statement by President Johnson: "We must ensure that the deep seas and the ocean bottoms are, and remain, the legacy of all human beings." 2 Weekly Compilation of Presidential Documents 930, 931 (1966).

On the common heritage of mankind generally, see Postyshev, The Concept of the Common Heritage of Mankind: From New Thinking to New Practice (Chalyan, trans. 1990); Kiss, Conserving the Common Heritage of Mankind, 59 Revista Juridica de la Universidad de Puerto Rico 773 (1990); Joyner, Legal Implications of the Concept of the Common Heritage of Mankind, 35 I.C.L.Q. 191 (1986); Shraga, The Common Heritage of Mankind: The Concept and Its Application, 15 Annales d'Etudes Internationales 45 (1986); Van Hoof, Legal Status of the Common Heritage of Mankind, 7 Grotiana 49 (1986).

2. Restatement (Third) § 523, Reporters' Note 2 states:

> *Sea-bed mining under customary international law.* Even before the development of the doctrine of the continental shelf and of the concept of the exclusive economic zone (§§ 514–15), there was disagreement, then largely theoretical, as to who owns the sea-bed beyond a state's territorial sea, whether any state could acquire sovereignty or title therein, and whether a state or private person could lawfully exploit the resources of that sea-bed or subsoil and appropriate them to its own use. Discovery in the 1960s of vast mineral resources ("manganese nodules," containing also nickel, copper and cobalt) on the floor of the deep ocean beyond the continental shelves, and the development of technology for obtaining access to these resources, led to three different views as to the applicable law. It was generally agreed that these minerals are the common heritage of mankind (Declaration of Principles Governing the Sea–Bed and the Ocean Floor, and the Subsoil Thereof, Beyond the Limits of National Jurisdiction, adopted by G.A.Res. 2749 (XXV) 25 U.N. GAOR Supp. No. 28, at 24, paras. 1–4, 9 (1970)), but there was disagreement on the application of this concept. Some considered that these minerals could be exploited only by or on behalf of mankind, not by any state or person for its own account; under this view, exploitation would be lawful only pursuant to a generally accepted international agreement. Others argued that, unless a state has agreed otherwise, it may exploit the resources of the sea-bed freely, and the first claimant in any area is entitled to exclude all others from mining there. See, *e.g.,* Ely, "The Law Governing the Development of Undersea Mineral Resources," 1 Offshore Technology Conference Proc. 19–42 (1969). A third view, which has been accepted by this Restatement, is that like the fish of the high seas the minerals of the deep sea-bed are open to anyone to take. Consequently, any state is entitled to extract and keep them. But no state may conduct or authorize mining operations on an exclusive basis or in such a way as effectively to appropriate large areas of the sea-bed in violation of Subsection (1)(a). See Subsection l(b)(i). It would therefore not be permissible for any mining enterprise to reserve for itself an area of some 25,000 square

miles (equal to the area of Belgium and the Netherlands combined) or more, as some enterprises have suggested.

An analogy may be made also to the law of finds as applied to shipwrecks, the finder having the exclusive right to bring up the find, and others being obliged to stay a reasonable distance away. See, e.g., Hener v. United States, 525 F.Supp. 350, 354 (S.D.N.Y.1981).

3. Beginning in 1972, bills were introduced in the United States Congress which would authorize the licensing of United States nationals to mine the deep seabed in areas beyond national jurisdiction, and recognize the rights of nationals of other states on the basis of reciprocity. Initially, the Executive Branch opposed passage of such legislation on the ground that it would prejudice the negotiation of an international regime at the Law of the Sea Conference. However, as the Conference dragged on, the U.S. Administration, in 1977, endorsed passage of interim legislation which would authorize licensing pending the conclusion of a comprehensive law of the sea treaty.

The Deep Seabed Hard Mineral Resources Act, Pub.L. No. 96–283, 94 Stat. 553, enacted in 1980, explicitly adopted the United States position that, in the absence of a supervening treaty, states had the right to mine the seabed as an aspect of the freedom of the seas, and that national licensing would not be an assertion of sovereignty of ownership over any part of the seabed. The Act recognizes the character of seabed resources as the common heritage of mankind, and provides for the establishment of an international revenue-sharing fund. Congress's declared purpose in adopting the Act was to provide "assured and nondiscriminatory access" as well as "security of tenure" to U.S. nationals seeking to exploit deep seabed resources. While the act was declared to be transitional pending U.S. adherence to an agreement resulting from the Law of the Sea Conference or any other multilateral treaty concerning the deep seabed, it establishes that any regulation issuing as a result of its passage not inconsistent with subsequent treaties shall remain valid.

Other states enacted similar interim legislation, and the Provisional Understanding Regarding Deep Seabed Mining, signed by the United States and seven other parties in 1984, adopted a preliminary scheme for resolving overlapping claims to deep seabed mining areas.

The legality of unilateral legislation, "interim" or otherwise, was challenged by the Group of 77 essentially on the legal grounds reflected in the majority vote on the Moratorium Resolution. See Letter dated 23 April 1979 from the Group of Legal Experts on the Question of Unilateral Legislation Addressed to the Chairman of the Group of 77, U.N.Doc. A/CONF. 62/77. See also Vicuña, National Laws on Seabed Exploitation (1979).

4. The dispute over the Moratorium Resolution reflected deeper and larger controversy over the character of the regime that is to govern seabed mining; the Moratorium Resolution was an early staking-out of legal positions to support bargaining in the negotiations to come at the Third U.N. Law of the Sea Conference. While all states had agreed that the resources of the seabed were the common heritage of mankind, they disagreed sharply as to how mankind was to reap the benefits of that heritage, consequently also on the principles that should govern exploitation, and the organization and role of any international seabed authority. The developed states sought essentially an international licensing system: an international authority would issue licenses to governments (or to their nationals), collecting fees or royalties that might go to international development purposes. The international authority would be organized to reflect the

dominant interests of the states that had the capital, and the technology necessary to support exploitation, and to assure its limited function. The developing states, represented by the "Group of 77" (which actually included more than 100 developing states), sought a regime whereby the exclusive right to mine the seabed beyond national jurisdiction would be vested in the international Sea–Bed Authority which would establish an Enterprise for that purpose. They wished an authority organized principally on the basis of majority-rule by states of equal voting authority. Some developing states also sought to assure that seabed minerals would not compete with land-based minerals which they produced and exported.

In 1976, a compromise was proposed which would establish a "parallel" system, one set of mining sites to be exploited by states (or their corporations), the other by an operating arm of the Authority—the Enterprise. The developed states would also provide the Enterprise with capital and technology to enable the Enterprise to carry out its first exploitation. Differences continued, however, as to the organization of the Sea–Bed Authority. There was agreement in principle on a Council (with weighted representation) and an Assembly (with equal representation), as in the United Nations. The developed states, however, insisted on "assured access" to their part of the system, and wished to allocate authority to make certain that the Assembly, which they could not control, could not interfere with such access. The developing states continued to press for effective control by the majority through the Assembly.

In 1980, a compromise was reached on the decision-making powers of the organs of the Authority, methods for insuring, and the terms for, transfer of capital and technology to the Enterprise, the criteria for licensing and taxing of state-owned and private mining companies, and limitations on seabed mining to protect land-based sources. Review of the system in 15–25 years was agreed to.

By 1981 the new Convention was all but complete, and a vote on the final version was scheduled for April 1982. However, in 1981 the new Reagan Administration in the United States said it wanted major changes in the treaty before it would sign it, but though some changes were made, the controversial sea-mining provisions were largely retained.

The deep seabed regime is set forth in the 1982 Convention in Part XI, Arts. 133–85, and in Annexes III and IV. The Reagan Administration announced that it would not sign the Convention. See p. 1385 above.

SEA–BED MINING UNDER THE 1982 CONVENTION

U.N. CONVENTION ON THE LAW OF THE SEA (1982)

1833 U.N.T.S. 3, U.N.Doc. A/CONF. 62/122; 21 I.L.M. 1261 (1982).

Article 136

Common Heritage of Mankind

The Area and its resources are the common heritage of mankind.

Article 137

Legal Status of the Area and Its Resources

1. No State shall claim or exercise sovereignty or sovereign rights over any part of the Area or its resources, nor shall any State or natural or

juridical person appropriate any part thereof. No such claim or exercise of sovereignty or sovereign rights nor such appropriation shall be recognized.

2. All rights in the resources of the Area are vested in mankind as a whole, on whose behalf the Authority shall act. These resources are not subject to alienation. The minerals recovered from the Area, however, may only be alienated in accordance with this Part and the rules, regulations and procedures of the Authority.

3. No State or natural or juridical person shall claim, acquire or exercise rights with respect to the minerals recovered from the Area except in accordance with this Part. Otherwise, no such claim, acquisition or exercise of such rights shall be recognized.

Article 138

General Conduct of States in Relation to the Area

The general conduct of States in relation to the Area shall be in accordance with the provisions of this Part, the principles embodied in the Charter of the United Nations and other rules of international law in the interests of maintaining peace and security and promoting international cooperation and mutual understanding.

Article 139

Responsibility to Ensure Compliance and Liability for Damage

1. States Parties shall have the responsibility to ensure that activities in the Area, whether carried out by States Parties, or state enterprises or natural or juridical persons which possess the nationality of States Parties or are effectively controlled by them or their nationals, shall be carried out in conformity with this Part. The same responsibility applies to international organizations for activities in the Area carried out by such organizations.

2. Without prejudice to the rules of international law and Annex III, article 22, damage caused by the failure of a State Party or international organization to carry out its responsibilities under this Part shall entail liability; States Parties or international organizations acting together shall bear joint and several liability. A State Party shall not however be liable for damage caused by any failure to comply with this Part by a person whom it has sponsored under article 153, paragraph 2(b), if the State Party has taken all necessary and appropriate measures to secure effective compliance under article 153, paragraph 4, and Annex III, article 4, paragraph 4.

3. States Parties that are members of international organizations shall take appropriate measures to ensure the implementation of this article with respect to such organizations.

Article 140

Benefit of Mankind

1. Activities in the Area shall, as specifically provided for in this Part, be carried out for the benefit of mankind as a whole, irrespective of the geographical location of States, whether coastal or land-locked, and taking into particular consideration the interests and needs of developing States and of peoples who have not attained full independence or other self-governing

status recognized by the United Nations in accordance with General Assembly resolution 1514(XV) and other relevant General Assembly resolutions.

2. The Authority shall provide for the equitable sharing of financial and other economic benefits derived from activities in the Area through any appropriate mechanism, on a non-discriminatory basis, in accordance with article 160, paragraph 2(f)(i).

Notes

1. The Restatement (Third) § 523, Reporters' Note 3, summarizes the sea-bed regime of the 1982 Convention as follows:

> *Sea-bed regime of LOS Convention.* Under the LOS Convention, any deep sea-bed mining would have to be conducted in accordance with rules, regulations, and procedures to be drafted by a Preparatory Commission, and to be adopted and from time to time revised by the International Sea–Bed Authority that will start functioning as soon as 60 states ratify the Convention. * * * The Authority would function through: (a) an Assembly, in which all the members might participate and which would act as the "supreme organ" of the Authority with power to establish "general policies"; (b) a Council of 36 members, seats on which are guaranteed for some states, including "the largest consumer" of minerals derived from the area (the United States, as of 1986) and three Eastern European states, with power to establish "specific policies" and to approve "plans of work" for each mining project; and (c) an "Enterprise," with a separate legal personality, which will carry out mining activities in the area, either directly or through joint ventures with national or private companies. During an interim 25–year period and within defined, strict limits, the Authority would be entitled to establish a production ceiling in order to protect the economies and export earnings of developing countries engaged in the production of certain minerals against the adverse economic effects of sea-bed production.
>
> To facilitate the work of the Enterprise, each applicant for a mining contract would have to present to the Authority two mining sites of equal estimated mining value; the Authority would designate one of them as reserved for the Enterprise, which would be allowed to relinquish it to a developing country. The applicant would also have to arrange for the transfer to the Enterprise (or to a developing country exploiting a reserved area) on fair and reasonable terms and conditions, to be determined in case of disagreement by commercial arbitration, the technology that the contractor would be using in its sea-bed mining activities. A contractor would have a choice between two methods of payment to the Authority * * *.
>
> Since the activities in the deep sea-bed area are to be carried out "for the benefit of mankind as a whole," taking into particular consideration the interests and needs of developing states and of peoples who have not yet attained full independence or self-government, the Authority would have the task of ensuring that such states will share equitably in the financial and other economic benefits derived from these activities. As the Enterprise is not likely to have sufficient funds at the beginning to exploit a reserved site, it was agreed (in Annex IV to the Convention, Art. 11 (3)) that states parties to the Convention would make available to it the necessary funds for one site, in accordance with the scale of assessments for the United Nations general budget. Such funds (estimated at more than one and a half billion dollars in

1986) would be provided half in the form of long-term interest-free loans, and half by guarantee of debts incurred by the Enterprise in raising the remainder. * * *

2. The Restatement (Third) § 523, Reporters' Note 4, also sets forth the U.S. objections to the Convention regime as of the 1980s:

> *United States objections to Convention regime.* When the Third United Nations Conference on the Law of the Sea approved the Convention, the United States cast a negative vote (Introductory Note to this Part). In explaining that vote, a spokesman for the United States said that the text was unacceptable as it would deter future development of deep sea-bed mineral resources, because of lack of certainty with regard to the granting of mining contracts, the artificial limitations on sea-bed mineral production, and the imposition of burdensome financial requirements; would not give the United States an adequate role in the decision-making process; would allow amendments to the Convention to enter into force for the United States without its approval; would provide for mandatory transfer of private technology related to sea-bed mining; and would allow the transfer of a portion of funds received from the miners by the International Sea–Bed Authority to national liberation movements. Statements by President Reagan and Ambassador Malone on July 9 and August 12, 1982, respectively, 18 Weekly Comp. of Pres. Docs. 887 (1982), U.S. Dep't of State, Current Policy No. 416 (1982). In a later statement the White House characterized the deep sea-bed mining regime of the Convention as "hopelessly flawed," and announced that the United States would not participate in the work of the Preparatory Commission established by the Conference to draft regulations for sea-bed mining. The Law of the Sea Convention, White House Office of Policy Information, Issue Update No. 10 (April 15, 1983), at 8.

3. In 1994, John R. Stevenson and Bernard H. Oxman, both of whom had been active members of the U.S. delegation to the U.N. Conference on the Law of the Sea, wrote on "The Future of the United Nations Convention on the Law of the Sea." 88 A.J.I.L. 488 (1994). They wrote as the Convention was about to enter into force, and before the 1994 Agreement modifying Part XI was concluded. Their article was both a strong plea for ratification of the Convention, and a justification of the Convention under several headings including: international security, trade and communications, protecting the marine environment, scientific research, and coastal resources.

CHANGES IN THE LAW OF SEA–BED MINING UNDER THE 1994 AGREEMENT

In 1994, consultations under the auspices of the U.N. Secretary–General sought agreement to modify Part XI of the 1982 Convention to meet the principal objections of the industrialized nations. The consultations proceeded with urgency, in view of the fact that the 1982 Convention was about to enter into force following the deposit of the 60th instrument of ratification. (UNCLOS, Art. 308.) The result was the "Agreement Relating to the Implementation of Part XI of the United Nations Convention on the Law of the Sea of 10 December 1982," signed July 29, 1994 and endorsed as an annex to a resolution of the U.N. General Assembly (G.A. Res. 48/263, 1994) (adopted with 121 states in favor, none opposed, and seven abstentions):

The General Assembly,

Prompted by the desire to achieve universal participation in the United Nations Convention on the Law of the Sea of 10 December 1982 (hereinafter referred to as the "Convention") and to promote appropriate representation in the institutions established by it,

Reaffirming that the seabed and ocean floor and subsoil thereof, beyond the limits of national jurisdiction (hereinafter referred to as the "Area"), as well as the resources of the Area, are the common heritage of mankind,

Recalling that the Convention in its Part XI and related provisions (hereinafter referred to as "Part XI") established a regime for the Area and its resources,

* * *

Recognizing that political and economic changes, including in particular a growing reliance on market principles, have necessitated the re-evaluation of some aspects of the regime for the Area and its resources,

* * *

Considering that the objective of universal participation in the Convention may best be achieved by the adoption of an agreement relating to the implementation of Part XI,

* * *

2. *Reaffirms* the unified character of the United Nations Convention on the Law of the Sea of 10 December 1982;

3. *Adopts* the Agreement relating to the implementation of Part XI of the United Nations Convention on the Law of the Sea of 10 December 1982 (hereinafter referred to as the "Agreement"), the text of which is annexed to the present resolution;

4. *Affirms* that the Agreement shall be interpreted and applied together with Part XI as a single instrument;

5. *Considers* that future ratifications or formal confirmations of or accessions to the Convention shall represent also consent to be bound by the Agreement and that no State or entity may establish its consent to be bound by the Agreement unless it has previously established or establishes at the same time its consent to be bound by the Convention;

6. *Calls upon* States which consent to the adoption of the Agreement to refrain from any act which would defeat its object and purpose;

* * *

11. *Urges* all States and entities referred to in article 3 of the Agreement to consent to its provisional application as from 16 November 1994 and to establish their consent to be bound by the Agreement at the earliest possible date;

12. *Also urges* all such States and entities that have not already done so to take all appropriate steps to ratify, formally confirm or accede to the Convention at the earliest possible date in order to ensure universal participation in the Convention.

* * *

The Agreement entered in force on July 28, 1996. By its terms, it is to be interpreted and applied together with Part XI of the Convention as a single instrument. In case of conflict with the provisions of Part XI, the 1994 Agreement prevails. States ratifying the Convention after July 1994 are bound by the Agreement. As of 2000, 100 parties to the 1982 Convention, including the European Community, are bound by the Agreement. States that had ratified the 1982 Convention prior to the adoption of the Agreement have to establish their consent to be bound by the Agreement separately. As of 2000, 36 such states apply the Agreement de facto, without having expressed formal consent to be bound by it.

AGREEMENT RELATING TO THE IMPLEMENTATION OF PART XI OF THE UNITED NATIONS CONVENTION ON THE LAW OF THE SEA OF 10 DECEMBER 1982

Annex to UNGA Res. 48/263, A/48/950 (1994).

Article 1

Implementation of Part XI

1. The States parties to this Agreement undertake to implement Part XI in accordance with this Agreement.

2. The annex forms an integral part of this Agreement.

Article 2

Relationship Between This Agreement and Part XI

1. The provisions of this Agreement and Part XI shall be interpreted and applied together as a single instrument. In the event of any inconsistency between this Agreement and Part XI, the provisions of this Agreement shall prevail. * * *

Article 4

Consent to be Bound

1. After the adoption of this Agreement, any instrument of ratification or formal confirmation of or accession to the Convention shall also represent consent to be bound by this Agreement.

2. No State or entity may establish its consent to be bound by this Agreement unless it has previously established or establishes at the same time its consent to be bound by the Convention. * * *

Annex

Section 1. Costs to States Parties and Institutional Arrangements

* * *

2. In order to minimize costs to States Parties, all organs and subsidiary bodies to be established under the Convention and this Agreement shall be cost-effective. * * *

* * *

6.(a) An application for approval of a plan of work for exploration shall be considered by the Council * * * subject to the following:

[provisions on pioneer investor regime omitted]

* * *

Section 2. The Enterprise

* * *

2. The Enterprise shall conduct its initial deep seabed mining operation through joint ventures. * * * If joint-venture operations with the Enterprise accord with sound commercial principles, the Council shall issue a directive * * * providing for [the functioning of the Enterprise independently of the Secretariat of the Authority].

3. * * * States Parties shall be under no obligation to finance any of the operations in any mine site of the Enterprise or under its joint-venture arrangements.

4. The obligations applicable to contractors shall apply to the Enterprise. * * *

* * *

Section 3. Decision–Making

[Procedures are specified so that "chambers" of states with particular interests have a substantial voice in important decisions.]

* * *

Section 4. Review Conference

The provisions relating to the Review Conference in article 155, paragraphs 1,3 and 4, of the Convention shall not apply. * * *

Section 5. Transfer of Technology

1. * * * [T]ransfer of technology for the purposes of Part XI shall be governed by the following principles:

(a) The Enterprise, and developing States wishing to obtain deep seabed mining technology, shall seek to obtain such technology on fair and reasonable commercial terms and conditions on the open market, or through joint-venture arrangements.

* * *

Section 6. Production Policy

1. The production policy of the Authority shall be based on the following principles:

(a) Development of the resources of the Area shall take place in accordance with sound commercial principles;

(b) The provisions of the General Agreement on Tariffs and Trade, its relevant codes and successor or superseding agreements, shall apply with respect to activities in the Area;

(c) In particular, there shall be no subsidization of activities in the Area except as may be permitted under the agreement referred to in subparagraph (b). * * *

* * *

Section 8. Financial Terms of Contracts

1. The following principles shall provide the basis for establishing rules, regulations and procedures for financial terms of contracts:

(a) The system of payments to the Authority shall be fair both to the contractor and to the Authority and shall provide adequate means of determining compliance by the contractor with such a system.

* * *

MESSAGE FROM THE PRESIDENT OF THE UNITED STATES TRANSMITTING UNITED NATIONS CONVENTION ON THE LAW OF THE SEA AND THE AGREEMENT RELATING TO THE IMPLEMENTATION OF PART XI OF THE UNITED NATIONS CONVENTION ON THE LAW OF THE SEA

Sen. Treaty Doc. No. 103–39, pp. vii-viii (Oct. 7, 1994).

* * *

The achievement of a widely accepted and comprehensive law of the sea convention—to which the United States can become a Party—has been a consistent objective of successive U.S. administrations for the past quarter century. However, the United States decided not to sign the Convention upon its adoption in 1982 because of objections to the regime it would have established for managing the development of seabed mineral resources beyond national jurisdiction. While the other Parts of the Convention were judged beneficial for U.S. ocean policy interests, the United States determined the deep seabed regime of Part XI to be inadequate and in need of reform before the United States could consider becoming Party to the Convention.

Similar objections to Part XI also deterred all other major industrialized nations from adhering to the Convention. However, as a result of the important international political and economic changes of the last decade—including the end of the Cold War and growing reliance on free market principles—widespread recognition emerged that the seabed mining regime of the Convention required basic change in order to make it generally acceptable. As a result, informal negotiations were launched in 1990, under the auspices of the United Nations Secretary–General, that resulted in adoption of the Agreement on July 28, 1994.

The legally binding changes set forth in the Agreement meet the objections of the United States to Part XI of the Convention. The United States and all other major industrialized nations have signed the Agreement.

The provisions of the Agreement overhaul the decision-making procedures of Part XI to accord the United States, and others with major economic interests at stake, adequate influence over future decisions on possible deep seabed mining. The Agreement guarantees a seat for the United States on the critical executive body and requires a consensus of major contributors for financial decisions.

The Agreement restructures the deep seabed mining regime along free market principles and meets the U.S. goal of guaranteed access by U.S. firms to deep seabed minerals on the basis of reasonable terms and conditions. It eliminates mandatory transfer of technology and production controls. It scales back the structure of the organization to administer the mining regime and links the activation and operation of institutions to the actual development of concrete commercial interest in seabed mining. A future decision, which the United States and a few of its allies can block, is required before the organization's potential operating arm (the Enterprise) may be activated, and any activities on its part are subject to the same requirements that apply to private mining companies. States have no obligation to finance the Enterprise, and subsidies inconsistent with GATT are prohibited.

The Agreement provides for grandfathering the seabed mine site claims established on the basis of the exploration work already conducted by companies holding U.S. licenses on the basis of arrangements "similar to and no less favorable than" the best terms granted to previous claimants; further, it strengthens the provisions requiring consideration of the potential environmental impacts of deep seabed mining.

The Agreement provides for its provisional application from November 16, 1994, pending its entry into force. Without such a provision, the Convention would enter into force on that date with its objectionable seabed mining provisions unchanged. * * * Further, the Agreement provides flexibility in allowing States to apply it provisionally in accordance with their domestic laws and regulations.

In signing the agreement on July 29, 1994, the United States indicated that it intends to apply the agreement provisionally pending ratification. Provisional application by the United States will permit the advancement of U.S. seabed mining interests by U.S. participation in the International Seabed Authority from the outset to ensure that the implementation of the regime is consistent with those interests, while doing so consistent with existing laws and regulations. * * *

OXMAN, THE 1994 AGREEMENT AND THE CONVENTION

88 A.J.I.L. 687, 688–695 (1994) (footnotes omitted).

It may be instructive to consider how the 1994 Agreement responds to the problems identified and the concerns expressed by the United States when it sought, without success, to change Part XI in 1982.

U.S. policy regarding the 1982 Convention, as enunciated by the Reagan administration, may be summarized as follows. "While most provisions of the draft convention are acceptable and consistent with U.S. interests, some major elements of the deep seabed mining regime are not acceptable." The

United States "has a strong interest in an effective and fair Law of the Sea treaty which includes a viable seabed mining regime." It was "not seeking to change the basic structure of the treaty" or "to destroy the system" but "to make it work for the benefit of all nations to enhance, not resist, seabed resource development." If negotiations could fulfill six key objectives with respect to the deep seabed mining regime, the "Administration will support ratification" of the Convention. It was the administration's "judgement that, if the Presidents' objectives as outlined are satisfied, the Senate would approve the Law of the Sea Treaty."

The six objectives identified by President Reagan required a deep seabed mining regime that would:

- Not deter development of any deep seabed mineral resources to meet national and international demand;
- Assure national access to these resources by current and future qualified entities to enhance U.S. security of supply, to avoid monopolization of the resources by the operating arm of the international authority, and to promote the economic development of these resources;
- Provide a decision making role in the deep seabed regime that fairly reflects and effectively protects the political and economic interests and financial contributions of participating states;
- Not allow for amendments to come into force without approval of the participating states, including, in our case, the advice and consent of the Senate;
- Not set other undesirable precedents for international organizations; and
- Be likely to receive the advice and consent of the Senate. In this regard, the convention should not contain provisions for the mandatory transfer of private technology and participation by and funding for national liberation movements.

How the 1994 Agreement responds to U.S. objections and U.S. requirements may be considered under several headings.

Decision Making

Like many international organizations, the International Sea–Bed Authority established by the Convention will have an Assembly in which all parties are represented, a Council of limited membership, and specialized elected organs also of limited membership.

1982 text: While all specific regulatory powers with regard to deep seabed mining are reposed exclusively or concurrently in the Council, Article 160 gives the Assembly "the power to establish general policies."

Problem: "Policymaking in the seabed authority would be carried out by a one-nation, one-vote assembly."

Response: The 1994 Agreement qualifies the general policy-making powers of the Assembly by requiring the collaboration of the Council. It also provides: "Decisions of the Assembly on any matter for which the Council also has competence or on any administrative, budgetary or financial matter shall be based on the recommendations of the Council." The Assembly may either approve the recommendations or return them.

Problem: "The executive council which would make the day-to-day decisions affecting access of U.S. miners to deep seabed minerals would not have permanent or guaranteed representation by the United States."

Response: The new Agreement guarantees a seat on the Council for "the State, on the date of entry into force of the Convention, having the largest economy in terms of gross domestic product." That state is the United States.

1982 text: Consensus on the thirty-six-member Council is required for such matters as proposing treaty amendments; adopting rules, regulations and procedures; and distributing financial benefits and economic adjustment assistance. Other substantive Council decisions require either a two-thirds or three-quarters vote.

Problem: The "United States would not have influence on the council commensurate with its economic and political interests." * * *

Response: The new Agreement establishes "chambers" of states with particular interests. Two four-member chambers of the Council are likely to be effectively controlled by major industrial states, including the United States (which is guaranteed a seat in one of those chambers). The Agreement provides that "decisions on questions of substance, except where the Convention provides for decisions by consensus in the Council, shall be taken by a two-thirds majority of members present and voting, provided that such decisions are not opposed by a majority of any one of the chambers." Any three states in either four-member chamber may therefore block a substantive decision for which consensus is not required.

The Agreement further specifies: "Decisions by the Assembly or the Council having financial or budgetary implications shall be based on the recommendations of the Finance Committee." The United States and other major contributors to the administrative budget are guaranteed seats on the Finance Committee, and the committee functions by consensus.

This approach to voting enables interested states (including the United States) to block undesirable decisions. Because blocking power encourages negotiation of decisions desired by and acceptable to the states principally affected, it enhances affirmative as well as negative influence.

Production Limitation

Problem: "The United States believes that its interests ... will best be served by developing the resources of the deep seabed as market conditions warrant. We have a consumer-oriented philosophy. The draft treaty, in our judgment, reflects a protectionist bias which would deter the development of deep seabed mineral resources." Specifically, the "treaty would impose artificial limitations on seabed mineral production" and "would permit discretionary and discriminatory decisions by the Authority if there is competition for limited production allocations." The production ceiling is undesirable as a matter of principle and precedent, and the process for allocating production authorizations is a significant source of uncertainty and discriminatory treatment impeding guaranteed access to minerals by qualified miners.

Response: The new Agreement specifies that the provisions regarding the production ceiling, production limitations, participation in commodity agreements, production authorizations and selection among applicants "shall not apply." In their place, the Agreement incorporates the market-oriented GATT restrictions on subsidies. It prohibits "discrimination between minerals derived from the [deep seabed] and from other sources," and specifies that the rates of payments by miners to the Authority "shall be within the range of those prevailing in respect of land-based mining of the same or similar minerals in order to avoid giving deep seabed miners an artificial competitive advantage or imposing on them a competitive disadvantage."

Technology Transfer

Problem: "Private deep seabed miners would be subject to a mandatory requirement for the transfer of technology to the Enterprise and to developing countries." This provision was considered burdensome, prejudicial to intellectual property rights, and objectionable as a matter of principle and precedent.

Response: The new Agreement declares that the provisions on mandatory transfer of technology "shall not apply." It substitutes a general duty of cooperation by sponsoring states to facilitate the acquisition of deep seabed mining technology, "consistent with the effective protection of intellectual property rights," if the Enterprise (the operating arm of the Sea–Bed Authority) or developing countries are unable to obtain such technology on the open market or through joint-venture arrangements.

Access

Problem: "The draft treaty provides no assurance that qualified private applicants sponsored by the U.S. Government will be awarded contracts. It is our strong view that all qualified applicants should be granted contracts and that the decision whether to grant a contract should be tied exclusively to the question of whether an applicant has satisfied objective qualification standards."

Response: The new Agreement eliminates the provisions for choice among qualified applicants. Access will be on a first-come, first-served basis. The qualification standards for mining applicants are to be set forth in rules, regulations and procedures adopted by the Council by consensus and "shall relate to the financial and technical capabilities of the applicant and his performance under any previous contracts." If the applicant is qualified; if the application fee is paid; if procedural and environmental requirements are met; if the area applied for is not the subject of a prior contract or application; and if the sponsoring state would not thereby exceed maximum limits in the Convention, "the Authority shall approve" the application. Its failure to do so will be subject to arbitration or adjudication.

* * *

The new Agreement accords important "grandfather" rights to the U.S. consortia that already have made investments under the U.S. Deep Seabed Hard Mineral Resources Act. They are deemed to have met the necessary financial and technical qualifications if the U.S. Government, as the sponsoring state, certifies that they have made the necessary expenditures. They are also entitled to arrangements "similar to and no less favorable than" those accorded investors of other countries that registered as pioneers with the Preparatory Commission prior to entry into force of the Convention.

Problem: U.S. objectives "would not be satisfied if minerals other than manganese nodules could be developed only after a decision was taken to promulgate rules and regulations to allow the exploitation of such minerals."

Response: The new Agreement requires the Council of the Authority to adopt necessary rules, regulations and procedures within two years of a request by a state whose national intends to apply for the right to exploit a mine site. This applies to manganese nodules or any other mineral resource. If the Council fails to complete the work on time, it must give provisional approval to an application based on the Convention and the new Agreement, notwithstanding the fact that the rules and regulations have not been adopted.

The Enterprise

Problem: "The treaty would give substantial competitive advantages to a supra-national mining company—the Enterprise." It "creates a system of privileges which discriminates against the private side of the parallel system. Rational private companies would, therefore, have little option but to enter joint ventures or other similar ventures with the operating arm of the Authority, the Enterprise, or with developing countries. Not only would this deny the United States access to deep seabed minerals through its private companies because the private access system would be uncompetitive but, under some scenarios, the Enterprise could establish a monopoly over deep seabed mineral resources."

Response: The new Agreement provides: "The obligations applicable to contractors [private miners] shall apply to the Enterprise." It requires the Enterprise to conduct its initial operations through joint ventures "that accord with sound commercial principles," and delays the independent functioning of the Enterprise until the Council decides that those criteria have been met. The Agreement does not exclude the Enterprise either from the principle that mining "shall take place in accordance with sound commercial principles" or from its prohibitions on subsidies. It specifies that the "obligation of States Parties to fund one mine site of the Enterprise . . . shall not apply and States Parties shall be under no obligation to finance any of the operations in any mine site of the Enterprise or under its joint-venture arrangements." The Agreement also eliminates mandatory transfer of technology to the Enterprise and the potentially discriminatory system for issuing production authorizations.

The Agreement makes clear that a private miner may contribute the requisite "reserved area" to the Enterprise at the time the miner receives its own exclusive exploration rights to a specific area (thus minimizing its risk and investment). That miner has "the right of first refusal to enter into a joint-venture arrangement with the Enterprise for exploration and exploitation of" the reserved area, and has priority rights to the reserved area if the Enterprise itself does not apply for exploration or exploitation rights to the reserved area within a specified period.

Finance

Problem: "The treaty would impose large financial burdens on industrialized countries whose nationals are engaged in deep seabed mining and financial terms and conditions which would significantly increase the costs of mineral production."

Response: The new Agreement halves the application fees for either exploration or exploitation to $250,000 (subject to refund to the extent the fee exceeds the actual costs of processing an application), and eliminates the detailed financial obligations of miners set forth in the 1982 text, including the million-dollar annual fee. Financial details would be supplied, when needed, by rules, regulations and procedures adopted by the Council by consensus, on the basis of general criteria that, for example, would link the rates to those prevailing for mining on land, and prohibit discrimination or rate increases for existing contracts.

With respect to state parties, in addition to eliminating any requirement that states contribute funds to finance the Enterprise or provide economic adjustment assistance to developing countries, the new Agreement provides for streamlining and phasing in the organs and functions of the Authority as needed, and for minimizing costs and meetings. Budgets and assessments for administrative expenses are subject to consensus procedures in the Finance Committee and approval by both the Council and the Assembly.

Regulatory Burdens

Problem: "The new international organization would have discretion to interfere unreasonably with the conduct of mining operations, and it could impose potentially burdensome regulations on an infant industry."

Response: The substantive changes set forth in the new Agreement, including the elimination of production limitations, production authorizations and forced transfer of technology, and the relaxation of diligence requirements, substantially narrow the area of potential abuse. The new procedural provisions, including voting arrangements in the Council of the Finance Committee, and restrictions on the Assembly, decrease the risk of unreasonable regulatory decisions. As indicated in its Preamble and in the General Assembly resolution adopting it, the new Agreement is the product of a marked shift, throughout the world, from statist and interventionist economic philosophies toward more market-oriented policies. Taken together, the new provisions and new attitudes give reason to expect the system to operate in accordance with the provisions of the Convention and the Agreement guaranteeing the miner exclusive rights to a mine site, security of tenure, stability of expectations and title to minerals extracted, and according the miner and its sponsoring state extensive judicial and arbitral remedies to protect those rights.

What cannot be supplied in advance by any blueprint for a deep seabed mining regime is the measure of confidence born of experience with a system in operation.

Distribution of Revenues

1982 text: The Convention authorizes the equitable sharing of surplus revenues from mining, "taking into particular consideration the interests and needs of the developing States and peoples who have not attained full independence or other self-governing status."

Problem: "The convention would allow funding for national liberation groups, such as the Palestine Liberation Organization and the South West Africa People's Organization."

Response: Political developments in Africa and the Middle East have mitigated this problem. Moreover, distribution to such groups would be a practical impossibility unless the Sea–Bed Authority's revenues from miners and from the Enterprise exceeded both its administrative expenses and its assistance to adversely affected land-based producers, and would be possible then only if the Council decided by consensus to include such groups in the distribution of surplus revenues. A decision on distribution of surplus funds would also be subject, under the new Agreement, to a consensus in the Finance Committee.

Review Conference

Problem: "A review conference would have the power to impose treaty amendments on the United States without its consent."

Response: The new Agreement declares that the provisions in Part XI relating to the review conference "shall not apply." Amendments to the deep seabed mining could not be adopted without U.S. consent.

Notes

1. As of 2000, 135 states are parties to the 1982 Convention as modified by the 1994 Agreement. The United States has not yet ratified it. The Convention was submitted to the U.S. Senate for its advice and consent to ratification on October 7, 1994, but the Senate Foreign Relations Committee has yet to hold hearings, despite the priority given to ratification by the Departments of State and Defense.

2. For analysis of legal aspects of the 1994 Agreement, see (in addition to the Oxman article excerpted above), the contributions by Professors Sohn and Charney to "Law of the Sea Forum: The 1994 Agreement on Implementation of the Seabed Provisions of the Convention on the Law of the Sea," 88 A.J.I.L. 696–714 (1994).

CUSTOMARY LAW OF THE SEABED

For states not party to the Convention, customary law would remain applicable. The Restatement summarizes the customary law as it was understood in the mid–1980s:

RESTATEMENT (THIRD) § 523

(1) Under international law,

(a) no state may claim or exercise sovereignty or sovereign or exclusive rights over any part of the sea-bed and subsoil beyond the limits of national jurisdiction, or over its mineral resources, and no state or person may appropriate any part of that area;

(b) unless prohibited by international agreement, a state may engage, or authorize any person to engage, in activities of exploration for and exploitation of the mineral resources of that area, provided that such activities are conducted

(i) without claiming or exercising sovereignty or sovereign or exclusive rights in any part of that area, and

(ii) with reasonable regard for the right of other states or persons to engage in similar activities and to exercise the freedoms of the high seas;

(c) minerals extracted in accordance with paragraph (b) become the property of the mining state or person.

(2) Under the law of the United States, a citizen of the United States may engage in activities or exploration for, or exploitation of, the mineral resources of the area of the sea-bed and subsoil beyond the limits of national jurisdiction only in accordance with a license issued by the Federal Government pursuant to law or international agreement.

Notes

1. The Restatement "restates the customary international law that applies before the Convention goes into effect, and would apply thereafter to non-parties." Restatement (Third) Introductory Note to Part V. Query whether the subsequent entry into force of the Law of the Sea Convention as modified by the 1994 Agreement, and the widespread (near-universal, with the exception of the United States and a few other states) ratification of those instruments has effectively produced a change in the customary law.

2. The Restatement analogizes mining in the deep sea-bed to fishing in high-seas waters. See § 523, Comment *b*.

3. The Restatement (Third) § 523, Comment *c* states:

> *c. Mining by persons.* Under customary international law, any person, natural or juridical, engaged in activities on the high seas is normally subject to the jurisdiction of the flag state of the ship used for such activity or of the state of which such person is a national. See, e.g., LOS Convention, Article 97 (jurisdiction in collisions on the high seas). A private person may engage in the activities indicated in Subsection (1)(b) only when properly licensed by a state. A state issuing such licenses is obligated to assure that the person licensed respects the rules set forth in this section, and is responsible for any violation by such person.

2. Living Resources

FISHING ON THE HIGH SEAS

The freedom to fish is the oldest freedom of the sea and remains an essential freedom in the regime of the high seas. The 1982 Convention confirms the "freedom of fishing" for all states and their nationals, but also recognizes the need to regulate and conserve living marine resources, including fish.

U.N. CONVENTION ON THE LAW OF THE SEA (1982)

1833 U.N.T.S. 3, U.N.Doc. A/CONF. 62/122; 21 I.L.M. 1261 (1982).

Article 116

Right to Fish on the High Seas

All States have the right for their nationals to engage in fishing on the high seas subject to:

(a) their treaty obligations;

(b) the rights and duties as well as the interests of coastal States provided for, inter alia, in article 63, paragraph 2, and articles 64 to 67; and

(c) the provisions of this section.

Article 117

Duty of States to Adopt With Respect to Their Nationals Measures for the Conservation of the Living Resources of the High Seas

All States have the duty to take, or to co-operate with other States in taking, such measures for their respective nationals as may be necessary for the conservation of the living resources of the high seas.

Article 118

Co-operation of States in the Conservation and Management of Living Resources

States shall co-operate with each other in the conservation and management of living resources in the areas of the high seas. States whose nationals exploit identical living resources, or different living resources in the same area, shall enter into negotiations with a view to taking the measures necessary for the conservation of the living resources concerned. They shall, as appropriate, co-operate to establish subregional or regional fisheries organizations to this end.

Notes

1. The problem of regulating fishing in order to prevent the continuing depletion of fish stocks as a result of overfishing, overcapacity, or inadequate conservation and management, has long been an important international concern. The Law of the Sea Convention was intended to provide a framework on which more detailed regional agreements could be established. Because the 1982 Convention contains only very general provisions on the conservation of fish stocks in the high seas, regional organizations were established, including the Northwest Atlantic Fisheries Organization (NAFO); the International Commission for the Conservation of Alaska Tunas (ICCAT); and a Commission for the Conservation of Antarctic Living Marine Resources (CCALMR). For a statement of the U.S. position on the problem of fishing by vessels of countries that are not members of such organizations, see statement of Mary Beth West, Deputy Assistant Secretary of State, in Contemporary Practice of the United States, 93 A.J.I.L. 470, 494 (1999).

On fisheries management under the 1982 Convention generally, see Burke, Implications for Fisheries Management of U.S. Acceptance of the 1982 Convention on the Law of the Sea, 89 A.J.I.L. 792 (1995).

2. On June 27, 1996, the Senate voted its advice and consent to ratification of the Agreement for the Implementation of the Provisions of the United Nations Convention on the Law of the Sea of 10 December 1982 Relating to the Conservation and Management of Straddling Fish Stocks, with Annexes, adopted at New York on August 4, 1995, by consensus of the U.N. Conference on Straddling Fish Stocks and Highly Migratory Stocks. The Senate's consent was subject to one declaration (registering the Senate's lack of enthusiasm for treaties containing "no-reservation" clauses). See 90 A.J.I.L. 647 (1996).

The Straddling Fish Stocks Agreement requires, among other things, compatibility between conservation and management measures established for the high seas and those adopted by coastal states in their areas of national jurisdiction; it requires also that regional cooperation measures be observed by all states parties. As of 2000, there were 59 signatories, but only 24 ratifications/accessions. In 1997, a U.N. General Assembly resolution, co-sponsored by the United States, G.A. Res. A/52/L.28, U.N. GAOR, 52d Sess. (1997), urged prompt ratification of the Agreement and its observance provisionally.

3. In the late 1980s, the use of "driftnets" by some East Asian countries, such as Japan and the Republic of Korea, caused controversy. (Driftnets are gillnets or other combinations of nets over 2.5 kilometers in length and sometimes stretching up to 40 kilometers.) Many states charged that the use of driftnets seriously depletes stocks of commercial fish and indiscriminately traps and kills porpoises, seabirds and a wide variety of fish not sought by fishermen. International efforts to ban the use of driftnets in fishing resulted in the 1989 Convention for the Prohibition of Fishing with Long Driftnets in the South Pacific and United Nations General Assembly Resolution 44/225, which recommends that "[i]mmediate action should be taken to reduce progressively large-scale pelagic driftnet fishing activities...." In July 1990, it was reported that Japan and China would suspend and ban driftnet fishing. See Johnson, The Driftnetting Problem in the Pacific Ocean: Legal Consideration and Diplomatic Options, 21 Ocean Dev. & Int'l L. 5 (1990).

4. In 1998, in *Fisheries Jurisdiction* (Spain v. Canada), the International Court of Justice decided that it lacked jurisdiction over a dispute arising out of Canada's seizure of a Spanish fishing vessel on the high seas outside Canada's exclusive economic zone. In the opinion justifying its conclusion, the Court had occasion to consider the term "conservation and management measures" (which was used by Canada in excluding certain disputes from its acceptance of the Court's compulsory jurisdiction), by comparison to similar terms in Articles 117–118 of the 1982 Convention. While the suit was pending, Canada and the European Community signed an Agreed Minutes on the Conservation and Management of Fish Stocks, which resolved some (but not all) of the underlying dispute. See the discussion of the decision in 93 A.J.I.L. 502, 505 (1999).

5. On August 27, 1999, the International Tribunal for the Law of the Sea, in response to a dispute between Australia and New Zealand on one side and Japan on the other, concerning the conservation of the population of southern bluefin tuna, issued several provisional orders to prevent damage to joint fisheries. The Tribunal noted that there was no disagreement between the parties that the stock of southern bluefin tuna was severely depleted. It recognized that there is scientific uncertainty regarding measures to be taken to conserve the stock, but considered that, in the circumstances, the parties should act prudently and cautiously to ensure that serious harm to the stock of southern bluefin tuna is prevented. The Tribunal ordered that the parties ensure that their annual catches

did not exceed the levels to which they had last agreed, and that the parties refrain from conducting experimental fishing program until the dispute is arbitrated. See Southern Bluefin Tuna (New Zealand v. Japan; Australia v. Japan, Order on Provisional Measures (ITLOS Cases Nos. 3 and 4), International Tribunal for the Law of the Sea, August 27, 1999, reported in 94 A.J.I.L. 150, 2000 (by Barbara Kwiatkowska). The suit was later dismissed for lack of jurisdiction by an arbitral tribunal and the provisional measures order was vacated. See pp. 915, 917 in Chapter 11.

6. On conservation and protection of highly migratory species and marine mammals generally, see Lones, The Marine Mammal Protection Act and the International Protection of Cetaceans: A Unilateral Attempt to Effectuate Transnational Conservation, 22 Vand.J.Transnat'l L. 997 (1989); Davis, International Management of Cetaceans under the New Law of the Sea Convention, 3 Bost. U.Int'l L.J. 484–488 (1985). Kindt & Wintheiser, The Conservation and Protection of Maritime Mammals, 7 U.Hawaii L.Rev. 301 (1985); Nafziger, Global Conservation and Management of Marine Mammals, 17 San Diego L.Rev. 591 (1980). See also p. 1439 for discussion of highly migratory species in relation to the Exclusive Economic Zone, and Chapter 17, p. 1533, on protection of endangered species including marine mammals.

SECTION 4. THE MARINE ENVIRONMENT

Marine pollution has received special attention in international law. This is readily understandable, since pollution of the marine environment, and especially the oceans, affects all users. The rapid growth of maritime traffic in recent years has increased pollution of the marine environment. In addition, dumping of noxious and harmful substances, including radioactive materials, oil spills from wells in maritime areas, and tanker disasters have added substantially to marine pollution. All of these developments have enhanced concern for the marine environment and produced international and national measures for its protection. The 1958 Convention on the High Seas contains a number of provisions seeking to ensure safety at sea and to prevent pollution by discharges of oil and radioactive waste. 13 U.S.T. 2312, T.I.A.S. No. 5200, 450 U.N.T.S. 82 (Art. 10, 24–25). The 1982 Law of the Sea Convention includes provisions that deal not only with the types of pollution addressed in the 1958 Convention, but also with pollution from land-based sources and pollution through the atmosphere. The Third U.N. Law of the Sea Conference concentrated on rules governing land-based sources of marine pollution, pollution from continental shelf activities and from deep sea-bed mining, and dumping. Most significantly, the 1982 Convention on the Law of the Sea gave coastal states, particularly port states, power to enforce international rules and to do so against foreign vessels, but made special provision for the settlement of disputes that might result. The protection of the marine environment has been addressed not only as part of the law of the sea, but also in the context of environmental protection generally. Problems of pollution by ships have been treated specially by the International Maritime Consultative Organization (IMCO), now the International Maritime Organization (IMO).

U.N. CONVENTION ON THE LAW OF THE SEA

1833 U.N.T.S. 3, U.N. Doc. A/CONF.62/122; 21 I.L.M. 1261 (1982).

Article 194

Measures to Prevent, Reduce and Control Pollution of the Marine Environment

1. States shall take, individually or jointly as appropriate, all measures consistent with this Convention that are necessary to prevent, reduce and control pollution of the marine environment from any source, using for this purpose the best practicable means at their disposal and in accordance with their capabilities, and they shall endeavour to harmonize their policies in this connection.

2. States shall take all measures necessary to ensure that activities under their jurisdiction or control are so conducted as not to cause damage by pollution to other States and their environment, and that pollution arising from incidents or activities under their jurisdiction or control does not spread beyond the areas where they exercise sovereign rights in accordance with this Convention.

3. The measures taken pursuant to this Part shall deal with all sources of pollution of the marine environment. These measures shall include, inter alia, those designed to minimize to the fullest possible extent:

(a) the release of toxic, harmful or noxious substances, especially those which are persistent, from land-based sources, from or through the atmosphere or by dumping;

(b) pollution from vessels, in particular measures for preventing accidents and dealing with emergencies, ensuring the safety of operations at sea, preventing intentional and unintentional discharges, and regulating the design, construction, equipment, operation and manning of vessels;

(c) pollution from installations and devices used in exploration or exploitation of the natural resources of the sea-bed and subsoil, in particular measures for preventing accidents and dealing with emergencies, ensuring the safety of operations at sea, and regulating the design, construction, equipment, operation and manning of such installations or devices;

(d) pollution from other installations and devices operating in the marine environment, in particular measures for preventing accidents and dealing with emergencies, ensuring the safety of operations at sea, and regulating the design, construction, equipment, operation and manning of such installations or devices.

4. In taking measures to prevent, reduce or control pollution of the marine environment, States shall refrain from unjustifiable interference with activities carried out by other States in the exercise of their rights and in pursuance of their duties in conformity with this Convention.

5. The measures taken in accordance with this Part shall include those necessary to protect and preserve rare or fragile ecosystems as well as the

habitat of depleted, threatened or endangered species and other forms of marine life.

Notes

1. Article 220 provides for coastal state enforcement of international standards. A port state may act against vessels that have violated national laws which accord with the Convention or other international standards, while passing through the territorial sea or exclusive economic zone. When there are "clear grounds for believing" that a vessel navigating the territorial sea has committed a violation in the territorial sea, the coastal state may inspect the vessel and arrest it. When there is clear ground for believing that a vessel navigating in the territorial sea or the exclusive economic zone committed a violation in the economic zone, the coastal state may require the vessel to give relevant information; if the information is refused or if the information given is "manifestly at variance" with the facts and there has been substantial discharge and significant pollution of the environment, the coastal state may physically inspect the vessel; if the violation has resulted in major damage or threat of damage to the coastal state's interest, the state may cause proceedings to be taken in accordance with its laws.

2. Other articles of the 1982 Convention require states not to transfer damage from one area to another, or transform one type of pollution into another (Art. 195); to control pollution from the use of technologies or the introduction of alien or new species (Art. 196). Article 197 requires states to cooperate on a global or regional basis to elaborate international standards consistent with this Convention. States must immediately notify other states likely to be affected, and appropriate international organizations, of any pollution or imminent danger of pollution (Art. 198).

Later sections provide that states are liable under international law for failure to fulfil their obligations to protect the marine environment, and must assure recourse under their legal systems for prompt and adequate compensation and other relief for pollution by persons under their jurisdiction (Art. 235). The provisions of the Convention dealing with the environment do not apply to state-owned or state-operated vessels or aircraft used on noncommercial service (Art. 236).

3. Section 603 of the Restatement (Third), which is based on the provisions of the 1982 Convention of the Law of the Sea, Arts. 194, 207–212, 217 and 220, applies the general environmental principles of Section 601 of the Restatement (Third) to marine pollution.

4. In using "the best practicable means at their disposal," (Art. 194(1)), states must regulate pollution not only from land-based sources, but also from vessels. The latter regulation includes proper regulation of design, construction, and equipment of vessels flying the state's flag, as well as navigational routing. See Art. 194(3)(b) and 211 of the 1982 Convention. States must also adopt proper measures to protect the marine environment from pollution caused by deep seabed mining (Arts. 194(3)(c) and (d) and 208) and from noxious emissions by aircraft (Art. 212).

5. Collisions involving large tankers led to revisions in 1960 and 1974 of international conventions dealing with safety at sea. See International Convention for the Safety of Life at Sea (SOLAS), London, June 17, 1960, 16 U.S.T. 185,

T.I.A.S. No. 5780, 536 U.N.T.S. 27; Nov. 1, 1974, 32 U.S.T. 47, T.I.A.S. No. 9700. See further Restatement (Third) § 603, Reporters' Note 2.

6. The Torrey Canyon disaster, in which the United Kingdom destroyed a tanker without the consent of the flag state, prompted adoption of the International Convention Relating to Intervention on the High Seas in Cases of Oil Pollution Casualties, 1969, 26 U.S.T. 765, T.I.A.S. No. 8068. In 1973, the Convention was broadened to extend coverage to specific substances other than oil.

7. Oil pollution of the seas is regulated by the International Convention for the Pollution of the Sea by Oil, London, May 12, 1954, 12 U.S.T. 2989, T.I.A.S. No. 4900, 327 U.N.T.S. 3., which was amended 1962 and 1969, 17 U.S.T. 1523, T.I.A.S. No. 6109, 600 U.N.T.S. 332; 28 U.S.T. 1205, T.I.A.S. No. 8505. This Convention is superseded by the 1978 Protocol Relating to the International Convention for the Prevention of Pollution from Ships, as between parties to that protocol.

The Convention on the Prevention of Marine Pollution by Dumping of Wastes and other Matter, December 29, 1972, 26 U.S.T. 2403, T.I.A.S. No. 8165, 1046 U.N.T.S. 120, prohibits dumping of high level radioactive waste and makes dumping of other radioactive waste subject to special permit by national authorities. The Convention is superseded by the 1996 Protocol to the Convention on the Prevention of Marine Pollution by Dumping of Wastes and other Matter, adopted on November 7, 1996, 36 I.L.M. 1 (1997), for all parties that join the protocol.

On the Convention see Finn, Ocean Disposal of Radioactive Wastes: The Obligation of International Cooperation to Protect the Marine Environment, 21 Va.J.Int'l L. 621 (1981); Duncan, The 1972 Convention on the Prevention of Marine Pollution by Dumping of Wastes at Sea, 5 J.Mar.L. & Com. 299 (1973–74). On the 1996 Protocol, see Brown Weiss et al, International Environmental Law and Policy, 760–767 (1998).

Discharges other than dumping are the subject of the International Convention for the Prevention of Pollution from Ships (MARPOL), London, November 2, 1973, 12 I.L.M. 1319 (1973). The Protocol of 1978 relating to the International Convention for the Prevention of Pollution from Ships incorporates with modifications the provisions of the 1973 Convention, including its annexes and protocol. The protocol entered into force December 31, 1988. In addition, there are a number of special and regional conventions. See Kay & Jacobson, Environmental Protections: The International Dimension (1983); Hakappaa, Marine Pollution in International Law 75 (1981); Trinagenis, International Control of Marine Pollution (1980); Restatement (Third) Sec. 603, Reporters' Note 5.

8. In United States v. Locke, 529 U.S. 89, 120 S.Ct. 1135, 146 L.Ed.2d 69 (2000), also known as the *Intertanko* case, the U.S. Supreme Court found that the federal regulatory scheme governing oil tankers preempted the regulations of Washington State on tanker design, equipment, and operation, which the state had sought to justify on the grounds of its interest in preventing marine pollution. The Court took note of "a significant and intricate complex of international treaties and maritime agreements bearing upon the licensing and operation of vessels," including the International Convention for Prevention of Pollution from Ships and other agreements to which the United States is a party. In the procedural context of the case, the Court did not find it necessary to decide whether any specific international agreement had preemptive force over state law (though it left that question open for possible later consideration). It resolved the issues before it on the basis of the existence of a comprehensive federal statutory

and regulatory regime governing tankers, which precluded the possibility of parallel state regulation.

9. On the protection of the marine environment generally, see Brown Weiss et al., International Environmental Law and Policy 747–777 (1998); Charney, The Marine Environment and the 1982 United Nations Convention on the Law of the Sea, 28 Int'l Lawyer 879 (1994); Brown, Maritime Oil Pollution Literature: An Annotated Bibliography, 13 J.Mar.L. & Com. 373 (1982); Tharpes, International Environmental Law: Turning the Tide on Marine Pollution, 20 U.Miami Inter–Am.L.Rev. 579 (1989); M'Gonigle, "Developing Sustainability" and the Emerging Norms of International Environmental Law: The Case of Land–Based Marine Pollution Control, 28 Canadian Y.B.Int'l L. 169 (1990); Shaw et al., The Global Environment: A Proposal to Eliminate Marine Oil Pollution, 27 Nat.Resources J. 157 (1987); Gold, Marine Pollution Liability After "Exxon Valdez": The U.S. "All-or-Nothing" Lottery, 22 J.Mar.L. & Com. 423 (1991); Boyle, Marine Pollution Under the Law of the Sea Convention, 79 A.J.I.L. (1985); Kindt, Marine Pollution and the Law of the Sea (4 vol. with supplements, loose-leaf, first published in 1986). See also Kari Hakapää, Vessel–Source Pollution in the U.N. Law of the Sea Convention: Some Assessment as of Today, in *Liber Amicorum* Bengt Broms, Finnish Branch of the International Law Association No. 9 (1999).

THE EEZ AND THE ENVIRONMENT

RESTATEMENT (THIRD) § 514, COMMENT i

Protection and preservation of marine environment. With respect to its exclusive economic zone, a coastal state has jurisdiction to adopt laws and regulations for the enforcement of "generally acceptable international rules and standards established through the competent international organization or general diplomatic conference for the prevention, reduction, and control of pollution from ships of other states. A coastal state can also enforce its own laws and regulations adopted in accordance with applicable international rules and standards, with respect to a violation occurring within its territorial sea or exclusive economic zone. LOS Convention, Articles 211(5) and 220(1). Ordinarily, such enforcement takes place when the ship accused of the violation is voluntarily within a port or at an offshore terminal of the state concerned.

If the coastal state has clear grounds for believing that a foreign ship has violated applicable international rules, or the supplementary laws or regulations of the coastal state, in the exclusive economic zone, and the ship is not in port but is navigating in the exclusive economic zone or territorial sea of the coastal state, that state may require the ship to give information regarding its identity and its port of registry, its last and next port of call, and other relevant information required to establish whether a violation has occurred. If a violation has resulted in a substantial discharge causing significant pollution of the marine environment, and the ship has refused to give information or the information supplied is manifestly at variance with the evident factual situation, the coastal state may undertake physical inspection of the ship for matters relating to the violation. If the discharge causes or threatens to cause major damage to the coastline or related interests of the coastal state, or to any resources of its territorial sea or exclusive economic zone, the coastal state may, if the evidence warrants it, institute proceedings including detention of the ship in accordance with its laws. But the ship must be allowed to proceed on its journey as soon as it has furnished appropriate bond or other financial security. Id. Article 220(2)-(7).

Alternatively, in case of a discharge from a ship in violation of generally applicable international rules and standards, the flag state, the coastal state in whose coastal waters the discharge occurred, or the state damaged or threatened by the discharge, may request another state, in whose port or offshore terminal the ship has voluntarily stopped, to undertake investigations and, where warranted by the evidence, to impose penalties on the violators. If the aggrieved state requests it, the port state must transfer the records of the investigation to the coastal state and terminate its proceedings. In addition, any port state proceedings to impose penalties must be suspended if the flag state decides to institute proceedings against the ship in its own courts; but the coastal or port state that has instituted the original proceedings need not suspend them if they relate to an event involving major damage to the coastal state or if the flag state in question "has repeatedly disregarded its obligations to enforce effectively the applicable international rules and standards in respect of violations committed by its vessels." Id. Articles 218 and 228. See also § 512, Reporters' Note 7; § 604, Comments *d* and *e*.

SECTION 5. MARINE SCIENTIFIC RESEARCH

Under the 1958 Conventions, marine scientific research was unrestricted on the high seas but subject to the control of the coastal state in its territorial sea. Research on the continental shelf also required coastal state consent, but the 1958 Convention on the Continental Shelf provided that consent should not normally be withheld (Arts. 5(1), 5(8)). In practice, coastal states have withheld their consent despite the latter provision; and since 1958 virtually no research has been done on any state's continental shelf by foreign scientists. Some states further restricted research by applying the consent requirement to the superjacent waters as well.

At the Third Law of the Sea Conference, scientific research was the subject of intense negotiation, with the United States taking the lead in challenging coastal state control both on the continental shelf and in the exclusive economic zone. See 1982 Convention, Part XIII.

The 1982 Convention does not change the status of research in the territorial sea or on the high seas. (See Art. 143 on marine scientific research in the area beyond national jurisdiction, and Part XIII, especially Arts. 245, 256, 257). As to the EEZ, the United States sought in the negotiations a regime that would not subject research to coastal state constraints. The developing countries, however, viewed control of scientific research as crucial for protecting their interests in the resources of the economic zone and the continental shelf; the views of the developing states prevailed. Coastal state consent is required for research in the exclusive economic zone and on the continental shelf (Art. 246). The coastal state shall normally grant consent unless the research falls into certain categories, e.g., is related to resource use (Art. 246(5)). See also Art. 296(2), whereby the coastal state is not obliged to submit to settlement under Part XV, section 2, disputes arising out of the exercise by the coastal state of its discretion under Article 246 or of its right to suspend research under Article 253. Compare also Article 297(2)(b), providing for conciliation in these two cases.

U.N. CONVENTION ON THE LAW OF THE SEA (1982)

1833 U.N.T.S. 3, U.N.Doc. A/CONF. 62/122; 21 I.L.M. 1261 (1982).

Article 245

Marine Scientific Research in the Territorial Sea

Coastal States, in the exercise of their sovereignty, have the exclusive right to regulate, authorize and conduct marine scientific research in their territorial sea. Marine scientific research therein shall be conducted only with the express consent of and under the conditions set forth by the coastal State.

Article 246

Marine Scientific Research in the Exclusive Economic Zone and on the Continental Shelf

1. Coastal States, in the exercise of their jurisdiction, have the right to regulate, authorize and conduct marine scientific research in their exclusive economic zone and on their continental shelf in accordance with the relevant provisions of this Convention.

2. Marine scientific research in the exclusive economic zone and on the continental shelf shall be conducted with the consent of the coastal State.

3. Coastal States shall, in normal circumstances, grant their consent for marine scientific research projects by other States or competent international organizations in their exclusive economic zone or on their continental shelf to be carried out in accordance with this Convention exclusively for peaceful purposes and in order to increase scientific knowledge of the marine environment for the benefit of all mankind. To this end, coastal States shall establish rules and procedures ensuring that such consent will not be delayed or denied unreasonably.

4. For the purposes of applying paragraph 3, normal circumstances may exist in spite of the absence of diplomatic relations between the coastal State and the researching State.

5. Coastal States may however in their discretion withhold their consent to the conduct of a marine scientific research project of another State or competent international organization in the exclusive economic zone or on the continental shelf of the coastal State if that project:

(a) is of direct significance for the exploration and exploitation of natural resources, whether living or non-living;

(b) involves drilling into the continental shelf, the use of explosives or the introduction of harmful substances into the marine environment;

(c) involves the construction, operation or use of artificial islands, installations and structures referred to in articles 60 and 80;

(d) contains information communicated pursuant to article 248 regarding the nature and objectives of the project which is inaccurate or if the researching State or competent international organization has outstanding obligations to the coastal State from a prior research project.

6. Notwithstanding the provisions of paragraph 5, coastal States may not exercise their discretion to withhold consent under subparagraph (a) of that paragraph in respect of marine scientific research projects to be undertaken in accordance with the provisions of this Part on the continental shelf, beyond 200 nautical miles from the baselines from which the breadth of the territorial sea is measured, outside those specific areas which coastal States may at any time publicly designate as areas in which exploitation or detailed exploratory operations focused on those areas are occurring or will occur within a reasonable period of time. Coastal States shall give reasonable notice of the designation of such areas, as well as any modifications thereto, but shall not be obliged to give details of the operations therein.

7. The provisions of paragraph 6 are without prejudice to the rights of coastal States over the continental shelf as established in article 77.

8. Marine scientific research activities referred to in this article shall not unjustifiably interfere with activities undertaken by coastal States in the exercise of their sovereign rights and jurisdiction provided for in this Convention.

RESTATEMENT (THIRD) § 514, REPORTERS' NOTE 6

United States policy concerning scientific research. In the oceans policy statement accompanying the 1983 proclamation on the exclusive economic zone (Reporters' Note 5 and § 511, Reporters' Note 7), President Reagan announced that the United States elected not to assert the right, recognized by international law, of "jurisdiction over marine scientific research within such a zone," in view of "the United States interest in encouraging marine scientific research and avoiding any unnecessary burdens." Nevertheless, the United States will recognize the right of other coastal states over marine scientific research within their exclusive economic zones "if that jurisdiction is exercised reasonably in a manner consistent with international law."

SECTION 6. SETTLEMENT OF SEA DISPUTES

The 1982 Convention includes a complex set of provisions for resolving various disputes under the Convention. In several instances, agreement on a means of resolving disputes was indispensable to achieving agreement on the underlying substantive principles. The dispute settlement provisions are found in general in Part XV (Articles 279–299) and Annex VI, which contains the Statute for the International Tribunal for the Law of the Sea (ITLOS), as well as in Annex V on conciliation, Annex VII on arbitration, and Annex VIII on special arbitration.

In submitting the Convention to the Senate, the U.S. government explained the dispute settlement provisions as follows:

> The Convention establishes a dispute settlement system to promote compliance with its provisions and ensure that disputes are settled by peaceful means. The system applies to disputes between States and, with

respect to deep seabed mining, to disputes between States or miners and the Authority. The dispute settlement procedures of the Convention are:

> Flexible, in that Parties have options as to the appropriate means and fora for resolution of their disputes;
>
> Comprehensive, in that the bulk of the Convention's provisions can be enforced through binding mechanisms; and
>
> Accommodating of matters of vital national concern, in that they exclude certain sensitive categories of disputes (e.g., disputes involving EEZ fisheries management) from binding dispute settlement; they also permit a State Party to elect to exclude other such categories of disputes (e.g., disputes involving military activities) from binding dispute settlement.

The dispute settlement system of the Convention advances the U.S. policy objective of applying the rule of law to all uses of the oceans. As a State Party, the United States could enforce its rights and preserve its prerogatives through dispute settlement under the Convention, as well as promote compliance with the Convention by other States Parties. At the same time, the procedures would not require the United States to submit to binding dispute settlement matters such as military activities or the right to manage fishery resources within the U.S. EEZ.

See Sen. Treaty Doc. 103–39 (Oct. 7, 1994), p. 1465 supra, at pp. 83–84.

Notes

1. For comparison of LOS dispute settlement procedures with those in other fields, and of the ITLOS with other tribunals, see Chapter 11.

2. Restatement (Third), Introductory Note to Part V at n. 6, states:

> The provisions of the LOS Convention establishing new institutions and a system for the settlement of disputes arising under the Convention are not customary international law and will not become law for the United States unless the United States becomes a party to the Convention. See, *e.g.*:
>
> Section 502, Comment *f*. Where a state suffers a loss due to the failure of the flag state to exercise proper control, a special dispute settlement mechanism is provided in Part XV of the Convention.
>
> Section 511, Reporters' Note 8. A special procedure to resolve continental shelf issues is to be established. (Art. 76(8).)
>
> Section 514, Comments *b*, *j*, and Reporters' Note 2; § 515, Reporters' Note 2. Under the Convention there is a special procedure for settling certain disputes between coastal and other states as to their respective rights and duties in the exclusive economic zone. (Art. 297.)
>
> Section 517, Comment *e*, and Reporters' Note 3. The Convention provides for submission of certain maritime boundary disputes to a conciliation commission. (Art. 298(1)(a).)
>
> In addition to effecting changes in the substantive rules governing mining in the deep sea-bed, the Convention establishes institutions and procedures that are binding only on parties to the Convention. See § 523, Comment *e*, and Reporters' Note 3.

3. Under the 1982 Convention, as modified by the 1994 Agreement (p. 1463 supra), there might well be disputes between states party to the Convention and a state not a party that proceeds to exploit resources of the deep seabed, or to issue permits to private companies to do so. The Convention provides for the settlement of disputes between parties (Articles 187(a) and 188(1)), and Resolution II, para. 5(c), but makes no provision for disputes with non-parties. It has been suggested that the General Assembly might be asked to submit such a question to the International Court of Justice for an advisory opinion. See Restatement (Third) § 523, Reporters' Note 2.

4. During 1997 the ITLOS established two special seven-member Chambers, one a Chamber on Fisheries Matters and the other a Chamber on the Marine Environment. The Chamber on Fisheries Matters will be available to hear any disputes which parties agree to submit to it concerning the conservation and management of marine living resources. The Chamber on the Marine Environment was established to provide a forum to settle disputes relating to the protection and preservation of the marine environment. On the ITLOS generally, see Rosenne, Establishing the International Tribunal for the Law of the Sea, 89 A.J.I.L. 806 (1995).

5. In November 1997 the Registrar of the Tribunal received the first application instituting a case before the Tribunal. (This followed almost immediately after the adoption of the Rules of the Tribunal and one year after its inauguration.) The application to institute proceedings was put forward by Saint Vincent and the Grenadines against the Government of Guinea with regard to the alleged arrest of the *M/V Saiga* off the coast of West Africa. Saint Vincent and the Grenadines requested the Tribunal to order the prompt release of the *M/V Saiga*, its cargo and crew detained in Conakry, Guinea. The vessel was allegedly attacked by representatives of the Guinean Government who shot at the ship and eventually arrested the vessel and its crew.

The application, based on Article 292 of the UNCLOS, alleged that Guinea did not comply with the requirements of the Convention for prompt release of the vessel or its crew and, that the parties, both of whom are party to the Convention, did not agree within ten days from the time of detention to submit the case to another court or Tribunal. On December 4, 1997 the full Tribunal ruled unanimously that the Court had jurisdiction, and, by a vote of twelve to nine, the court ordered Guinea to release the vessel and the crew with the deposit of U.S. $400,000 as security. See p. 1488 below.

6. On July 30, 1999, Australia and New Zealand filed a request for the prescription of provisional measures (interim injunction) with the Registrar of the Tribunal. The dispute between Australia and New Zealand on one side and Japan on the other concerned the conservation of the population of Southern Bluefin Tuna. See above, p. 1475.

7. On the settlement of sea disputes generally, see Adede, The System for Settlement of Disputes under the United Nations Convention on the Law of the Sea[:] A Drafting History and Commentary (1987); Expert Panel on the Law of Ocean Uses, U.S. Policy on the Settlement of Disputes in the Law of the Sea, 81 A.J.I.L. 438 (1987); Hakapää, Some Observations on the Settlement of Disputes in the New Law of the Sea, in Essays on International Law 57 (Finnish Branch of the ILA, 1987); Oda, Some Reflections on the Dispute Clauses in the United Nations Convention on the Law of the Sea, in Essays in Honor of Judge Manfred Lachs 645 (Makarczyk, ed. 1984). See also Janis, The Law of the Sea Tribunal and the ICJ[:] Some Notions about Utility, 16 Marine Pol'y 102 (1992); And see,

Charney, Comment: The Implications of Expanding International Dispute Settlement Systems: the 1982 Convention on the Law of the Sea, 90 A.J.I.L. 69 (1996); Noyes, Law of the Sea Dispute Settlement: Past, Present, and Future, 5 ILSA J. Int'l & Comp. L. 301 (1999).

SECTION 7. THE LAW OF OCEAN VESSELS

The principal uses of the sea have required vessels. Small vessels were individual property but larger vessels tended to be public property and enjoyed privileges and immunities. See Chapter 14. In time, all vessels that plied the seas came to enjoy the protection of the state and acquired "nationality," usually reflected in documents of registration and the right to fly the state flag. Both the 1958 and 1982 Conventions place the law as to ships in the context of the law governing the high seas. The nationality and status of ships and the rights and duties of the flag state, however, have application as well in places other than the high seas. See also Restatement (Third) § 501.

A. THE NATIONALITY OF VESSELS

U.N. CONVENTION ON THE LAW OF THE SEA (1982)

1833 U.N.T.S. 3, U.N.Doc. A/CONF. 62/122; 21 I.L.M. 1261 (1982).

Article 90

Right of Navigation

Every State, whether coastal or land-locked, has the right to sail ships flying its flag on the high seas.

Article 91

Nationality of Ships

1. Every State shall fix the conditions for the grant of its nationality to ships, for the registration of ships in its territory, and for the right to fly its flag. Ships have the nationality of the State whose flag they are entitled to fly. There must exist a genuine link between the State and the ship.

2. Every State shall issue to ships to which it has granted the right to fly its flag documents to that effect.

Article 92

Status of Ships

1. Ships shall sail under the flag of one State only and, save in exceptional cases expressly provided for in international treaties or in this Convention, shall be subject to its exclusive jurisdiction on the high seas. A ship may not change its flag during a voyage or while in a port of call, save in the case of a real transfer of ownership or change of registry.

2. A ship which sails under the flags of two or more States, using them according to convenience, may not claim any of the nationalities in question with respect to any other State, and may be assimilated to a ship without nationality.

Notes

1. Convention Articles 90–92 are essentially the same as Articles 4–6 of the 1958 Convention on the High Seas. In the 1958 Convention (Art. 5), however, the following was added to the "genuine link" requirement: "in particular, the State must effectively exercise its jurisdiction and control in administrative, technical and social matters over ships flying its flag." In the 1982 Convention that clause is no longer attached to the "genuine link" requirement, but is included among the duties of the flag state (Article 94). That article includes also the duty to ensure safety at sea, extending and giving greater specificity to what is provided in Article 10 of the 1958 Convention. *Inter alia,* Article 94 provides for inquiry into "every marine casualty or incident of navigation * * * causing loss of life or serious injury to nationals of another State or serious damage to shipping or installations of another State or to the marine environment."

2. The requirement of a "genuine link" between the flag state and the ship has been a source of uncertainty. The report of the Senate Committee on Foreign Relations explaining the same clause in the 1958 Convention said:

> The International Law Commission did not decide upon a definition of the term "genuine link." This article as originally drafted by the Commission would have authorized other states to determine whether there was a "genuine link" between a ship and the flag state for purposes of recognition of the nationality of the ship.
>
> It was felt by some states attending the Conference on the Law of the Sea that the term "genuine link" could, depending upon how it was defined, limit the discretion of a state to decide which ships it would permit to fly its flag. Some states, which felt their flag vessels were at a competitive disadvantage with vessels sailing under the flags of other states, such as Panama and Liberia, were anxious to adopt a definition which states like Panama and Liberia could not meet.
>
> By a vote of 30 states, including the United States, against 15 states for, and 17 states abstaining, the provision was eliminated which would have enabled states other than the flag state to withhold recognition of the national character of a ship if they considered that there was no "genuine link" between the state and the ship.
>
> Thus, under the Convention on the High Seas, it is for each state to determine how it shall exercise jurisdiction and control in administrative, technical and social matters over ships flying its flag. The "genuine link" requirement need not have any effect upon the practice of registering American built or owned vessels in such countries as Panama or Liberia. The existence of a "genuine link' between the state and the ship is not a condition of recognition of the nationality of a ship; that is, no state can claim the right to determine unilaterally that no genuine link exists between a ship and the flag state. Nevertheless, there is a possibility that a state, with respect to a particular ship, may assert before an agreed tribunal, such as the International Court of Justice, that no genuine link exists. In such event, it would be for the Court to decide whether or not a "genuine link" existed.

Executive Report No. 5–Law of the Sea Conventions, 106 Cong.Rec. 11189, 11190 (86th Cong., 2d Sess., May 26, 1960). See generally McDougal & Burke, The Public Order of the Oceans 1013–15, 1033–35, 1073–75, 1080–82, 1087–88, 1137–39 (1962). Compare Boczek, Flags of Convenience 276–83 (1962). See also Flags of

Convenience–Study by the Maritime Transport Committee of OECD, reproduced in ILO Doc. JMC/21/4, Joint Maritime Commission 21st session, Nov.-Dec. 1972; UNCTAD Secretariat, Economic Consequences of the Existence or Lack of a Genuine Link between Vessel and Flag of Registry, UNCTAD Doc. TB/B/C. 4/168 (1977); also, generally, Osieke, Flags of Convenience Vessels: Recent Developments, 73 A.J.I.L. 604 (1979).

3. What is a "genuine link"? Is a ship owned by a national or domiciliary of the flag state bound to the flag state by a "genuine link"? What if the shipowner is a corporation created under the law of the state of registry, the shares of which are held by foreign interests, or if the ship is owned in part by foreign interests and in part by domestic interests? Is a ship that is required by the law of the state of registry to carry a crew made up in whole or in part of nationals of that state connected to the latter by a "genuine link"? If only the officers are required to be nationals? For a summary and discussion of legislation regulating the nationality of ships, see Boczek, Flags of Convenience 39–53 (1962). Is there anything in the *Nottebohm Case*, p. 430 that helps to explain the application of the "genuine link" requirement to the nationality of vessels? To what extent do the criteria specified by the Court as relevant to the existence of a "genuine link" between an individual and a state also apply to the existence of a "genuine link" between a vessel and a state? What different policy considerations may be applicable? See McDougal & Burke at 1029–33; Boczek at 119–24.

The Restatement (Third) § 501, Comment *b*, states:

> *"Genuine link."* In general, a state has a "genuine link" entitling it to register a ship and to authorize the ship to use its flag if the ship is owned by nationals of the state, whether natural or juridical persons, and the state exercises effective control over the ship. In most cases a ship is owned by a corporation created by the state of registry. However, in determining whether a "genuine link" with the state of registry exists, the following additional factors are to be taken into account: whether the company owning the ship is owned by nationals of the state; whether the officers and crew of the ship are nationals of the state; how often the ship stops in the ports of the state; and how extensive and effective is the control that the state exercises over the ship.
>
> Although international law requires a genuine link between the ship and the registering state, the lack of a genuine link does not justify another state in refusing to recognize the flag or in interfering with the ship. A state may, however, reject diplomatic protection by the flag state when the flag state has no genuine link with the ship. If another state doubts the existence of a genuine link, for instance, because there is evidence that the flag state has not been exercising its duties to control and regulate the ship (see § 502), it may request that the flag state "investigate the matter and, if appropriate, take any action necessary to remedy the situation." LOS Convention, Article 94(6); § 502, Comment *f*.

See also McConnell, Darkening Confusion Mounted Upon Darkening Confusion: The Search for the Elusive Genuine Link, 16 J.Mar.L. & Comm. 365 (1985).

4. "Genuine link" and its relevance for the duties of the flag ship under the 1982 Convention were considered in the *M/V "Saiga"* (No. 2) (Saint Vincent and the Grenadines v. Guinea), Judgement (ITLOS Case No. 2).

On October 27, 1997, the *M/V Saiga,* an oil tanker provisionally registered in Saint Vincent and the Grenadines, which was serving as a bunkering vessel off the coast of West Africa, supplied gas oil to three fishing vessels licensed by Guinea to fish in its 200–mile exclusive economic zone (EEZ). The refueling occurred within Guinea's EEZ about 22 miles off the island of Alcatraz. The next day Guinean patrol boats fired on, boarded, and arrested the *Saiga* off the coast of Sierra Leone, beyond the southern limit of Guinea's EEZ. Two persons on board suffered gunshot wounds. The *Saiga* was brought to Conakry, where the ship and crew were detained, the cargo of gas oil was removed, and the master was prosecuted for customs violations. In its first full case on the merits, the International Tribunal for the Law of the Sea found that Guinea's actions violated the U.N. Convention on the Law of the Sea and awarded damages to Saint Vincent and the Grenadines. Oxman & Bantz: Judgment of the International Tribunal for the Law of the Sea on Legality of Seizure of a Bunkering Ship at Sea and Prosecution of its Master for Customs Violations, 94 A.J.I.L. 140 (2000).

5. For a comprehensive discussion of the effect of the rise of "flag of convenience" shipping (i.e., the registration for economic reasons of foreign owned vessels in countries such as Panama, Liberia, and Honduras–sometimes referred to as the "Panlibhon" group) on the traditional rule that only the state of registration could set the requirements for and subsequently question a ship's right to its registry and flag, see Boczek, supra. See also McDougal & Burke, supra, ch. 8. See also Constitution of the Maritime Safety Committee of the Inter–Governmental Maritime Consultative Organization (Advisory Opinion), 1960 I.C.J. 150; Osieke, Flags of Convenience Vessels: Recent Developments, 73 A.J.I.L. 604 (1979); Resolution of UNCTAD Committee on Shipping. TD/B/C.4 (S–III) Misc. 2 at 23, 31 (1981); Juda, World Shipping, UNCTAD and the New International Economic Order, 35 Int'l Org. 493 (1981); Goldie, Environmental Catastrophes and Flags of Convenience–Does the Present Law Pose Special Liability Issues, 3 Pace Y.B.Int'l L. (1991); Momtaz, The High Seas, in 1 A Handbook on the New Law of the Sea 402–06 (Dupuy, ed. 1991); Egiyan, "Flag of Convenience" or "Open Registration" of Ships, 14 Marine Pol'y 106 (1990); Bergstrand & Doganis, The Impact of Flags of Convenience (Open Registries), in The Law of the Sea and International Shipping: Anglo–Soviet Post-UNCLOS Perspectives 413 (Butler ed., 1985); Restatement (Third) § 501, Reporters' Note 7.

6. Numerous bilateral commercial treaties provide that the nationality of a vessel is to be determined in accordance with the law of the state under whose flag it sails. The United States has treaties containing such a provision with Honduras (Dec. 7, 1927, 45 Stat. 2618, T.S. 764) and Liberia (Aug. 8, 1938, 54 Stat. 1739, T.S. 956), two states having large flag-of-convenience fleets. For a discussion of comparable treaty provisions, see Boczek, Flags of Convenience at 95–100. Could the United States refuse to recognize a Liberian flag vessel as entitled to various privileges specified in the United States–Liberia treaty of commerce on the ground that the ship had no "genuine link" with Liberia?

B. JURISDICTION OVER VESSELS

1. Requisition and Control of National Vessels

In 1917, the British Government informed the Netherlands that it intended to requisition a number of vessels which, although owned by Dutch corporations and registered in the Netherlands, were "in reality British" because British nationals owned the shares of the controlling corporations. The Netherlands Government delivered a strong protest, asserting that it alone had the right to requisition vessels flying the Dutch flag. In reply, the British Government changed its position, noting, that it did not seek to rely upon the fact of British ownership or control but upon the recognized right of a belligerent to requisition neutral ships present in its territory. 111 Brit. & For.St.Pap. 465–69 (1917–18). The British–Dutch exchange is often cited as support for the general proposition that under international law, the right to requisition ships rests with the state of registry. Rienow, The Test of the Nationality of a Merchant Vessel 100–102 (1937); Boczek, Flags of Convenience 195–97 (1962). It is also admitted, however, that a state of "ultimate ownership" is entitled to requisition foreign-flag vessels with the consent or acquiescence of the country of registry, and the United States apparently expects that those states under whose "flags of convenience" many United States-owned vessels sail will acquiesce in the vessels' transfer to United States control and registry, either or both, in the event of an emergency requiring such transfer. See generally Boczek, supra at 188–208. If the state of registry should resist the transfer of its vessels to the control of another state, the latter could still requisition these or other vessels, whether or not owned by its nationals, which it finds *within its territory*. See generally, on the "right of angary," 6 Hackworth at 638–55. Boczek suggests that requisition by a state of national-owned vessels found on the high seas or in foreign ports might be justified, even without the consent of the flag state, on the ground that the latter is unable to afford the vessels adequate protection against the dangers of hostilities. Boczek, supra at 207. See 49 Stat. 2015, as amended, 46 U.S.C.A. § 1242, providing for the requisition of vessels owned by United States citizens.

Note

It has been stated that it is "unquestioned practice that the state which is responsible for a ship's conformity with international law has a competence equal to its responsibility and may control the movement and activities of its ships as its interpretation of community obligations and its national policies require." McDougal & Burke, The Public Order of the Oceans 1066 (1962). What is the significance in this context of national ownership? Could a state enforce penalties against a foreign-flag vessel found within its territory on the ground that the owner was one of its nationals and had failed to exercise control over the vessel in accordance with applicable legislation?

2. *Jurisdiction Over Acts Committed on National Vessels*

RIGHTS AND DUTIES OF THE FLAG STATE

RESTATEMENT (THIRD) § 502

(1) The flag state is required

(a) to exercise effective authority and control over the ship in administrative, technical, and labor matters; and

(b) (i) to take such measures as are necessary to ensure safety at sea, avoid collisions, and prevent, reduce, and control pollution of the marine environment, and

(ii) to adopt laws and regulations and take such other steps as are needed to conform these measures to generally accepted international standards, regulations, procedures, and practices, and to secure their implementation and observance.

(2) The flag state may exercise jurisdiction to prescribe, to adjudicate, and to enforce, with respect to the ship or any conduct that takes place on the ship.

Notes

1. Compare the extent of United States jurisdiction asserted in 18 U.S.C.A. § 7(1), providing that the "special maritime and territorial jurisdiction of the United States" includes:

> The high seas, any other waters within the admiralty and maritime jurisdiction of the United States and out of the jurisdiction of any particular State, and any vessel belonging in whole or in part to the United States or any citizen thereof, or to any corporation created by or under the laws of the United States, or of any State, Territory, District, or possession thereof, when such vessel is within the admiralty and maritime jurisdiction of the United States and out of the jurisdiction of any particular State.

Does 18 U.S.C.A. § 7(1) purport to assert United States jurisdiction over crimes committed on foreign-flag vessels owned in whole or in part by a citizen of the United States? See Rienow, The Test of the Nationality of a Merchant Vessel 193–213 (1937); Restatement (Third) § 403, Reporters' Note 9; § 502, Reporters' Note 4. In United States v. Keller, 451 F.Supp. 631 (D.C.Puerto Rico 1978), the court stated that the determination of the citizenship of the owner of a vessel is a mixed question of law and fact, but did not indicate which considerations were legal and which factual.

2. A 1984 Amendment extended this jurisdiction to space vehicles, and to "Any place outside the jurisdiction of any nation with respect to an offense by or against a national of the United States." See Pub.L. 98–473, Title 11, § 1210, 98 Stat. 2164 (1984). See Chapter 13, p. 1121.

3. In 1994, Section 7(8) was added to the special maritime and territorial jurisdiction of the United States as part of the Violent Crime Control and Law Enforcement Act of 1994, Pub. L. No. 103–322, § 120002, 108 Stat. 2021 (Sept. 13, 1994). Section 7(8) extends the special maritime jurisdiction of the United States to include: "to the extent permitted by international law, any foreign vessel during any voyage having a scheduled departure from or arrival in the United States with respect to an offense committed by or against a national of the United States." 18 U.S.C. § 7(8). See Chapter 13, Section 3.C [Passive Personality Jurisdiction].

In United States v. Ioan Pizdrint, Jr., 983 F.Supp. 1110 (M.D.Fl., 1997), the court found that jurisdiction was proper over an assault and battery committed by a non-American on board the *M/V Celebration*, a vessel operating under the flag of Liberia, against an American, while on the high seas. Although the court based its ruling on the principle of effects jurisdiction, see supra Chapter 13, Section 2.A.2, it recognized the government's argument that jurisdiction may be predicated on Section 7(8) as meritorious. In support of its conclusion that the assault and battery had effect in the United States, and that exercising jurisdiction would not be unreasonable, the court found that: the *M/V Celebration* engaged in substantial business in the United States and regularly operated in United States territory;

the vessel originated and terminated its voyage in the United States; and the majority of its passengers were American citizens.

Events on board the *M/V Celebration* while it was located on the high seas were again important in United States v. Roberts, 1 F.Supp. 2d 601 (E.D.La.). In *Roberts*, a claim of sexual abuse was made against another non-American. In this instance, however, the court explicitly based its holding that jurisdiction was proper under both 18 U.S.C.A. §§ 7(1) and 7(8).

4. Article 97 of the 1982 Convention provides:

> 1. In the event of a collision or any other incident of navigation concerning a ship on the high seas, involving the penal or disciplinary responsibility of the master or of any other person in the service of the ship, no penal or disciplinary proceedings may be instituted against such person except before the judicial or administrative authorities either of the flag State or of the State of which such person is a national.
>
> 2. In disciplinary matters, the State which has issued a master's certificate or a certificate of competence or license shall alone be competent, after due legal process, to pronounce the withdrawal of such certificates, even if the holder is not a national of the State which issued them.
>
> 3. No arrest or detention of the ship, even as a measure of investigation, shall be ordered by any authorities other than those of the flag State.

Article 97 of the 1982 Convention is identical to Art. 11 of the 1958 Convention on the High Seas. The effect of this article is to overrule in part the holding of the Permanent Court of International Justice in the *Lotus Case,* p. [63] supra. To some extent, this result had already been achieved by the parties to the International Convention for the Unification of Certain Rules Relating to Penal Jurisdiction in Matters of Collisions and Other Incidents of Navigation, signed at Brussels on May 10, 1952. 439 U.N.T.S. 233 (entered into force Nov. 20, 1955). See [1956] II Yb.I.L.C. 281.

5. In October 1985, terrorists captured the Italian cruise ship *Achille Lauro* in the Mediterranean Sea near Egypt, held its passengers hostage and killed an American on board before surrendering to Egypt. See 85 Dep't State Bull. 74 (Dec.1985). Italy asserted jurisdiction over the hijackers because the offenses took place on an Italian ship. The United States asserted jurisdiction based on 18 U.S.C.A. § 1203, the section of the U.S. Criminal Code that implements the Convention Against the Taking of Hostages, a treaty negotiated in 1979 and effective for the United States in 1985. The Convention authorizes a state to assert jurisdiction over hostage-takers on three bases, in addition to the normal territorial jurisdiction: (1) if it is the state of nationality or residence of the hijackers; (2) if it is the state whose activity was sought to be coerced; or (3) if it is the state of the nationality of the hostages. Pursuant to 18 U.S.C.A. § 1203, which adopts the bases of jurisdiction authorized by the Convention, the United States asserted jurisdiction on the basis that a number of the hostages—including the one killed—were U.S. nationals.

Since the United States had no statute that would make it a crime to murder a United States national on the high seas, could the United States have prosecuted the hostage-takers for murder had Italy transferred them to United States control?

For other issues raised by the incident, see McGinley, The Achille Lauro Affair, 52 Tenn.L.Rev. 691 (1986); Schachter, In Defense of International Rules on the Use of Force, 53 U.Chi.L.Rev. 113, 138–41 (1986). And see Chapter 12, p. 966.

6. Regina v. Leslie, 8 Cox Crim.Cas. 269 (Ct.Crim.App.1860), involved the question whether a conviction for false imprisonment could be sustained against the master of an English merchant ship who, under contract with the Chilean Government, transported to England a group of persons who had been banished from Chile and who were placed aboard the ship by Chilean Government officials while the ship was in Chilean waters. After indicating that the conviction could not be sustained for what was done in Chilean waters because the Chilean Government could "justify all that it did within its own territory" and the defendant merely acted as its agent, the Court sustained the conviction for acts committed on the high seas, stating:

> * * * It is clear that an English ship on the high seas, out of any foreign territory, is subject to the laws of England, and persons, whether foreign or English, on board such ship are as much amenable to English law as they would be on English soil. In Reg. v. Sattler (7 Cox Crim.Cas. 431), this principle was acted on so as to make the prisoner, a foreigner, responsible for murder on board an English ship at sea. The same principle has been laid down by foreign writers on international law. * * *

3. *Jurisdiction Over Acts Committed on Foreign Vessels in the Territorial Sea*

a. *Jurisdiction of the Coastal State*

(1) Vessels in Innocent Passage

THE DAVID

United States–Panama Claims Commission, 1933.
[1933–1934] Ann.Dig. 137.

The Facts.—On May 11, 1923, the steamer *Yorba Linda*, belonging to the General Petroleum Corporation, an American corporation, collided with the steamer *David*, belonging to the Compañia de Navegación Nacional, Panama. The latter Company started an action in the Court of Panama in respect of the alleged negligence of *The Yorba Linda* and obtained judgment for 27,-103.50 balboas. This action was not begun by personal service but by service through publication, as permitted by Articles 470–473 of the Judicial Code of Panama. The Petroleum Company never appeared, but was represented by an attorney designated by the Court who offered no evidence. The judgment remained unsatisfied. Fifteen days after its confirmation by the Supreme Court of Panama the Petroleum Company issued a writ *in rem* of the United States District Court of the Canal Zone against *The David* and her owners, alleging that the collision had taken place in territorial waters of the United States and that it had been caused by the negligence of *The David*. The Marshal of the District Court thereupon arrested *The David* within a few hundred yards of Flamenco Island, and between that island and the San José Rock, which lies off the Pacific entrance to the Panama Canal. The judge of the District Court held the arrest to be valid, and the parties promptly settled the action. The terms of the settlement were that the Petroleum Company should pay to the Navegación Company the sum of $16,250, that the writ against *The David* should be discharged, and that the Panamanian judgment be canceled.

Before the Commission it was alleged that the arrest of *The David* had been illegal as, first, it had taken place outside the territorial waters of the Canal Zone and, secondly, the vessel had been in innocent passage at the time and therefore immune from arrest even if within territorial waters. Damages were claimed in respect of the loss occasioned by the settlement and for the injury to the standing of the Navegación Company which the proceedings in the District Court had occasioned.

Held (by the majority): that the claim must be disallowed as the arrest had been made within territorial waters. The fact that the vessel had been in innocent passage did not confer on her any immunity.

I. *Jurisdiction over Ships in Innocent Passage.*—The question whether or not the arrest was lawful even if within the territorial waters of the Canal Zone was argued at great length by the parties. Upon this question the Commission said:

> The general rule of the extension of sovereignty over the three-mile zone is clearly established. Exceptions to the completeness of this sovereignty should be supported by clear authority. There is a clear preponderance of authority to the effect that this sovereignty is qualified by what is known as the right of innocent passage, and that this qualification forbids the sovereign actually to prohibit the innocent passage of alien merchant vessels through its territorial waters.
>
> There is no clear preponderance of authority to the effect that such vessels when passing through territorial waters are exempt from civil arrest. In the absence of such authority, the Commission cannot say that a country may not, under the rules of international law, assert the right to arrest on civil process merchant ships passing through its territorial waters.

U.N. CONVENTION ON THE LAW OF THE SEA (1982)

1833 U.N.T.S. 3, U.N.Doc. A/CONF. 62/122; 21 I.L.M. 1261 (1982).

ARTICLE 27

Criminal Jurisdiction on Board a Foreign Ship

1. The criminal jurisdiction of the coastal State should not be exercised on board a foreign ship passing through the territorial sea to arrest any person or to conduct any investigation in connection with any crime committed on board the ship during its passage, save only in the following cases:

(a) if the consequences of the crime extend to the coastal State;

(b) if the crime is of a kind to disturb the peace of the country or the good order of the territorial sea;

(c) if the assistance of the local authorities has been requested by the master of the ship or by a diplomatic agent or consular officer of the flag State; or

(d) if such measures are necessary for the suppression of illicit traffic in narcotic drugs or psychotropic substances.

2. The above provisions do not affect the right of the coastal State to take any steps authorized by its laws for the purpose of an arrest or investigation on board a foreign ship passing through the territorial sea after leaving internal waters.

3. In the cases provided for in paragraphs 1 and 2, the coastal State shall, if the master so requests, notify a diplomatic agent or consular officer of the flag State before taking any steps, and shall facilitate contact between such agent or officer and the ship's crew. In cases of emergency this notification may be communicated while the measures are being taken.

4. In considering whether or in what manner an arrest should be made, the local authorities shall have due regard to the interests of navigation.

5. Except as provided in Part XII or with respect to violations of laws and regulations adopted in accordance with Part V, the coastal State may not take any steps on board a foreign ship passing through the territorial sea to arrest any person or to conduct any investigation in connection with any crime committed before the ship entered the territorial sea, if the ship, proceeding from a foreign port, is only passing through the territorial sea without entering internal waters.

ARTICLE 28

Civil Jurisdiction in Relation to Foreign Ships

1. The coastal State should not stop or divert a foreign ship passing through the territorial sea for the purpose of exercising civil jurisdiction in relation to a person on board the ship.

2. The coastal State may not levy execution against or arrest the ship for the purpose of any civil proceedings, save only in respect of obligations or liabilities assumed or incurred by the ship itself in the course or for the purpose of its voyage through the waters of the coastal State.

3. Paragraph 2 is without prejudice to the right of the coastal State, in accordance with its laws, to levy execution against or to arrest, for the purpose of any civil proceedings, a foreign ship lying in the territorial sea or passing through the territorial sea after leaving internal waters.

Notes

1. Articles 27–28 of the 1982 Convention essentially duplicate Articles 19–20 of the 1958 Convention, but add the introductory clause to Section 5 referring to laws against pollution (Part XII of the 1982 Convention) and those protecting the Exclusive Economic Zone (Part V).

2. The extent to which foreign government-owned vessels used for commercial purposes should be subject to the coastal state's civil and criminal jurisdiction while in innocent passage was a question which caused difficulties in the International Law Commission and in the First Law of the Sea Conference. The Commission had expressly adopted the restrictive principle of the Brussels Convention of 1926 concerning the immunity of such ships. See p. 1497 infra. The U.S.S.R. and Czechoslovakian members opposed this decision. [1956] 2 Yb.I.L.C. 276. In the First Committee, a Rumanian amendment which would have preserved the immunities of state-owned commercial ships from coastal state civil

jurisdiction was defeated. 3 U.N.Conf. on the Law of the Sea, Off.Rec. 132 (1958). The Commission draft was overwhelmingly approved by the Plenary Meeting of the Conference (62–9–4). Four delegations of the Soviet bloc based their negative votes on the absolute theory of state immunity. 2 id. at 66. Reservations to the 1958 Convention have been entered by the Communist states to the articles permitting coastal states to exercise civil jurisdiction over state trading vessels. Articles 27–28, of the 1982 Convention, however, appear under the subheading: "Rules Applicable to Merchant Ships and Government Ships Operated for Commercial Purposes."

(2) Vessels in Port

Restatement (Third) § 512, Reporters' Note 3 states:

> *Access to ports.* It has been said that, as no civilized state has "the right to isolate itself wholly from the outside world," there is "a corresponding obligation imposed upon each maritime power not to deprive foreign vessels of commerce of access to all of its ports." 1 Hyde, International Law Chiefly as Interpreted and Applied by the United States 581 (2d ed. 1945). The LOS Convention does not mention a right of access of ships to foreign ports, but the customary law on the subject, as reflected in a number of international agreements, has been confirmed by at least one international decision. Thus, the Statute on the International Regime of Maritime Ports of 1923, confirmed the freedom of access to maritime ports by foreign vessels on condition of reciprocity; but it allows the coastal state "in exceptional cases, and for as short a period as possible," to deviate from this provision by measures which that state "is obliged to take in case of an emergency affecting the safety of the state or the vital interest of the country." 58 L.N.T.S. 285, 301, 305; 2 Hudson, International Legislation 1162 (1931). Although this Statute has been ratified by less than 30 states and the United States is not a party to it, the Statute has been accepted as reflecting a customary rule of international law. An arbitral tribunal, relying on this Statute, stated that "[a]ccording to a great principle of international law, ports of every State must be open to foreign merchant vessels and can only be closed when the vital interests of a State so require." Saudi Arabia v. Arabian American Oil Company (ARAMCO), Award of August 23, 1958, 27 Int'l L.Rep. 117, 212 (1963).
>
> The Institute of International Law has considered this issue in 1898, 1928, and 1957, and each time, after a heated discussion, it affirmed the right of access to ports, subject to various conditions. In 1898, the Institute agreed that, as a general rule, access to ports "is presumed to be free to foreign ships," except when a state, "for reasons of which it is sole judge," declares its ports, or some of them, closed "when the safety of the State or the interest of the public health justifies the order," or when it refuses entrance to ships of a particular nation "as an act of just reprisal." Resolutions of the Institute of International Law 144 (J. Scott ed. 1916). In 1928, the Institute stated that, as a general rule, access to ports "is open to foreign vessels," but, as an exception and for a term as limited as possible, "a state may suspend this access by particular or general measures which it is obliged to take in case of serious events touching the safety of the state or the public health"; it also confirmed the exception in case of reprisals. Institut de Droit International, Tableau

Général des Résolutions, 1873–1956, at 102 (Wehberg ed. 1957); 22 Am.J.Int'l L. 844, 847 (1928). In 1957, the Institute distinguished between internal waters and ports, and pointed out that a coastal state may deny access to internal waters, "[s]ubject to the rights of passage sanctioned either by usage or by treaty," but should abstain from denying such access to foreign commercial vessels "save where in exceptional cases this denial of access is imposed by imperative reasons." On the other hand, the Institute declared that "it is consistent with general practice of States to permit free access to ports and harbors by such vessels. [1957] 2 Annuaire de l'Institut de Droit International 485–86. For discussion, see id. 171, 180, 194–98, 202–09, 212–22, 253–67; for the text of the 1957 resolution, see also 52 Am.J.Int'l L. 103 (1958).

It seems, therefore, that it is now generally accepted that "in time of peace, commercial ports must be left open to international traffic," and that the "liberty of access to ports granted to foreign vessels implies their right to load and unload their cargoes; embark and disembark their passengers." Colombos, The International Law of the Sea 176 (6th ed. 1967). But see Khedivial Line, S.A.E. v. Seafarers' International Union, 278 F.2d 49, 52 (2d Cir.1960) (plaintiff presented no precedents showing that "the law of nations accords an unrestricted right of access to harbors by vessels of all nations"); Lowe, "The Right of Entry into Maritime Ports in International Law," 14 San Diego L.Rev. 597, 622 (1977) ("the ports of a State which are designated for international trade are, in the absence of express provisions to the contrary made by a port State, presumed to be open to the merchant ships of all States," and they "should not be closed to foreign merchant ships except when the peace, good order, or security of the coastal State necessitates closure").

* * *

States may impose, however, special restrictions on certain categories of ships. For instance, the Convention on the Liability of Operators of Nuclear–Powered Ships, Brussels, 1962, provides that nothing in that Convention "shall affect any right which a Contracting State may have under international law to deny access to its waters and harbours to nuclear ships licensed by another Contracting State, even when it has formally complied with all the provisions" of that Convention. Art. XVII, 57 Am.J.Int'l L. 268 (1963). See also Reporters' Note 1. In 1985, New Zealand denied to United States nuclear ships access to its ports. See 21 Weekly Comp.Pres.Docs. 147 (1985). A directive of the Council of the European Economic Community regulates the entry into Community ports of oil, gas, and chemical tankers, Dec. 21, 1978, 22 O.J. Eur.Comm. (No. L. 33) 33 (1979); amended Dec. 11, 1979, id. (No. L. 315) 16 (1979). Access to ports by other categories of vessels (e.g., fishing vessels) may also be subject to various restrictions.

A coastal state can condition the entry of foreign ships into its ports on compliance with specified laws and regulations.

* * *

The principles governing international aviation differ from those governing shipping; landing rights as well as overflight rights have to be specifically conferred. See § 513, Comment *i*.

On access to U.S. coastal waters and ports, see Restatement (Third) § 512, Reporters' Note 4.

WILDENHUS' CASE

Supreme Court of the United States, 1887.
120 U.S. 1, 7 S.Ct. 385, 30 L.Ed. 565.

[Wildenhus, a Belgian national, killed another Belgian national below the deck of the Belgian vessel of which they were both crew members, which was at the time of the slaying moored to a dock in Jersey City. The local police authorities arrested Wildenhus, charging him with the killing, and held two other crew members as witnesses. The Belgian consul applied for a writ of habeas corpus, citing Article 11 of the treaty of March 9, 1880 (21 Stat. 776) between Belgium and the United States, which provided: "The respective consuls-general, consuls, vice-consuls and consular agents shall have exclusive charge of the internal order of the merchant vessels of their nation, and shall alone take cognizance of all differences which may arise, either at sea or in port, between the captains, officers and crews, without exception, particularly with reference to the adjustment of wages and the execution of contracts. The local authorities shall not interfere except when the disorder that has arisen is of such a nature as to disturb tranquillity and public order on shore, or in the port, or when a person of the country or not belonging to the crew shall be concerned therein." The Circuit Court refused to order the release of the prisoners, and the consul appealed to the Supreme Court.]

WAITE, C.J. * * * By sections 751 and 753 of the Revised Statutes the courts of the United States have power to issue writs of *habeas corpus* which shall extend to prisoners in jail when they are in "custody in violation of the constitution or a law or treaty of the United States," and the question we have to consider is whether these prisoners are held in violation of the provisions of the existing treaty between the United States and Belgium.

It is part of the law of civilized nations that, when a merchant vessel of one country enters the ports of another for the purposes of trade, it subjects itself to the law of the place to which it goes, unless, by treaty or otherwise, the two countries have come to some different understanding or agreement; for, as was said by Chief Justice Marshall in The Exchange, 7 Cranch, 144: "It would be obviously inconvenient and dangerous to society, and would subject the laws to continual infraction, and the government to degradation, if such * * * merchants did not owe temporary and local allegiance, and were not amenable to the jurisdiction of the country." * * * And the English judges have uniformly recognized the rights of the courts of the country of which the port is part to punish crimes committed by one foreigner on another in a foreign merchant ship. Regina v. Cunningham, Bell, Cr.Cas. 72; S.C. 8 Cox, Crim.Cas. 104; Regina v. Anderson, 11 Cox, Crim.Cas. 198, 204; S.C.L.R. 1 Cr.Cas. 161, 165; Regina v. Keyn, 13 Cox, Crim.Cas. 403, 486, 525; S.C. 2 Exch.Div. 63, 161, 213. As the owner has voluntarily taken his vessel, for his own private purposes, to a place within the dominion of a government other than his own, and from which he seeks protection during his stay, he owes that government such allegiance, for the time being, as is due for the protection to which he becomes entitled.

From experience, however, it was found long ago that it would be beneficial to commerce if the local government would abstain from interfering with the internal discipline of the ship, and the general regulation of the rights and duties of the officers and crew towards the vessel, or among themselves. And so by comity it came to be generally understood among civilized nations that all matters of discipline, and all things done on board, which affected only the vessel, or those belonging to her, and did not involve the peace or dignity of the country, or the tranquillity of the port, should be left by the local government to be dealt with by the authorities of the nation to which the vessel belonged as the laws of that nation, or the interests of its commerce should require. But, if crimes are committed on board of a character to disturb the peace and tranquillity of the country to which the vessel has been brought, the offenders have never, by comity or usage, been entitled to any exemption from the operation of the local laws for their punishment, if the local tribunals see fit to assert their authority. Such being the general public law on this subject, treaties and conventions have been entered into by nations having commercial intercourse, the purpose of which was to settle and define the rights and duties of the contracting parties with respect to each other in these particulars, and thus prevent the inconvenience that might arise from attempts to exercise conflicting jurisdictions.

The first of these conventions entered into by the United States after the adoption of the constitution was with France, on the fourteenth of November, 1788, (8 St. 106), article 8 of which is as follows: "The consuls or vice-consuls shall exercise police over all the vessels of their respective nations, and shall have on board the said vessels all power and jurisdiction in civil matters in all the disputes which may there arise. They shall have entire inspection over the said vessels, their crew, and the changes and substitutions there to be made, for which purpose they may go on board the said vessels whenever they may judge it necessary. Well understood that the functions hereby allowed shall be confined to the interior of the vessels, and that they shall not take place in any case which shall have any interference with the police of the ports where the said vessels shall be."

It was when this convention was in force that the cases of *The Sally* and *The Newton* arose * * *. The Sally was an American merchant vessel in the port of Marseilles, and the Newton a vessel of a similar character in the port of Antwerp, then under the dominion of France. In the case of *The Sally,* the mate, in the alleged exercise of discipline over the crew, had inflicted a severe wound on one of the seamen, and, in that of *The Newton,* one seaman had made an assault on another seaman in the vessel's boat. In each case the proper consul of the United States claimed exclusive jurisdiction of the offense, and so did the local authorities of the port; but the council of state, a branch of the political department of the government of France to which the matter was referred, pronounced against the local tribunals, "considering that one of these cases was that of an assault committed in the boat of the American ship Newton by one of the crew upon another, and the other was that of a severe wound inflicted by the mate of the American ship Sally upon one of the seamen for having made use of the boat without leave." This was clearly because the things done were not such as to disturb "the peace or tranquillity of the port." Wheat.Elem. (3d Ed.) 154. The case of *The Sally* was simply a quarrel between certain of the crew while constructively on board the vessel, and that of *The Newton* grew out of a punishment inflicted by an officer on one of the crew for disobedience of orders. Both were evidently of a character to affect only the police of the vessel, and thus within the authority expressly granted to the consul by the treaty.

[The Court then analyzed a number of treaties subsequently entered into by the United States, and concluded that these treaties either impliedly, or as in the case of the Belgian treaty under consideration explicitly] gave the consuls authority to cause proper order to be maintained on board, and to decide disputes between the officers and crew, but allowed the local authorities to interfere if the disorders taking place on board were of such a nature as to disturb the public tranquillity, and that is substantially all there is in the convention with Belgium which we have now to consider. This treaty is the law which now governs the conduct of the United States and Belgium towards each other in this particular. Each nation has granted to the other such local jurisdiction within its own dominion as may be necessary to maintain order on board a merchant vessel, but has reserved to itself the right to interfere if the disorder on board is of a nature to disturb the public tranquillity.

* * * [T]he only important question left for our determination is whether the thing which has been done—the disorder that has arisen—on board this vessel is of a nature to disturb the public peace, or, as some writers term it, the "public repose," of the people who look to the state of New Jersey for their protection. If the thing done—"the disorder," as it is called in the treaty—is of a character to affect those on shore or in the port when it becomes known, the fact that only those on the ship saw it when it was done, is a matter of no moment. Those who are not on the vessel pay no special attention to the mere disputes or quarrels of the seamen while on board, whether they occur under deck or above. Neither do they, as a rule, care for anything done on board which relates only to the discipline of the ship, or to the preservation of order and authority. Not so, however, with crimes which from their gravity awaken a public interest as soon as they become known, and especially those of a character which every civilized nation considers itself bound to provide a severe punishment for when committed within its own jurisdiction. In such cases inquiry is certain to be instituted at once to ascertain how or why the thing was done, and the popular excitement rises or falls as the news spreads, and the facts become known. It is not alone the publicity of the act, or the noise and clamor which attends it, that fixes the nature of the crime, but the act, itself. If that is of a character to awaken public interest when it becomes known, it is a "disorder," the nature of which is to affect the community at large, and consequently to invoke the power of the local government whose people have been disturbed by what was done. The very nature of such an act is to disturb the quiet of a peaceful community, and to create, in the language of the treaty, a "disorder" which will "disturb tranquillity and public order on shore or in the port." The principle which governs the whole matter is this: Disorders which disturb only the peace of the ship or those on board are to be dealt with exclusively by the sovereignty of the home of the ship, but those which disturb the public peace may be suppressed, and, if need be, the offenders punished, by the proper authorities of the local jurisdiction. It may not be easy at all times to

determine to which of the two jurisdictions a particular act of disorder belongs. Much will undoubtedly depend on the attending circumstances of the particular case, but all must concede that felonious homicide is a subject for the local jurisdiction; and that, if the proper authorities are proceeding with the case in a regular way the consul has no right to interfere to prevent it. * * *

The judgment of the circuit court is affirmed.

Notes

1. If the local police and judicial authorities may decide for themselves whether a particular incident "disturbs the peace of the port," even though there is no actual disturbance, can it be said that the "peace of the port" doctrine ever allows the foreign vessel to claim immunity as of right? The British view is that "the subjection of the ship to the local criminal jurisdiction is * * * complete and that any derogation from it is a matter of comity in the discretion of the coastal state." Brierly, The Law of Nations 223 (6th ed. Waldock 1963). When the United States prohibition laws were held in Cunard S.S. Co. v. Mellon, 262 U.S. 100, 43 S.Ct. 504, 67 L.Ed. 894 (1923) to be applicable to foreign vessels temporarily in United States ports, the protests of foreign governments were based almost entirely on appeals to comity. Jessup, The Law of Territorial Waters and Maritime Jurisdiction 221–28 (1927). For general discussions of criminal jurisdiction over visiting foreign vessels, see id. at 144–94; Stanger, Criminal Jurisdiction over Visiting Armed Forces 43–54 (Naval War College International Law Studies 1957–1958) (1965).

2. As the Chief Justice indicates in *Wildenhus' Case,* states customarily resort to international agreements in order to reconcile potential conflicts of jurisdiction that might arise from the presence of merchantmen in foreign ports. The Consular Convention of 1951 between the United States and the United Kingdom (3 U.S.T. 3426, T.I.A.S. No. 2494, 165 U.N.T.S. 121) provides in Article 22(2):

> Without prejudice to the right of the administrative and judicial authorities of the territory to take cognizance of crimes or offenses committed on board the vessel when she is in the ports or in the territorial waters of the territory and which are cognizable under the local law or to enforce local laws applicable to vessels in ports and territorial waters or persons and property thereon, it is the common intention of the High Contracting Parties that the administrative and police authorities of the territory should not, except at the request or with the consent of the consular officer,
>
> (a) concern themselves with any matter taking place on board the vessel unless for the preservation of peace and order or in the interests of public health or safety, or
>
> (b) institute prosecutions in respect of crimes or offenses committed on board the vessel unless they are of a serious character or involve the tranquillity of the port or unless they are committed by or against persons other than the crew.

Compare the 1982 Convention Article 27.

3. "It may be doubted whether in the absence of a concession by treaty, the territorial sovereign is deterred by the operation of any rule of international law from exercising through its local courts jurisdiction over civil controversies be-

tween masters and members of a crew, when the judicial aid of its tribunals is invoked by the latter, and notably when a libel *in rem* is filed against the ship. It is to be observed, however, that American courts exercise discretion in taking or withholding jurisdiction according to the circumstances of the particular case. Their action in so doing is not to be regarded as indicative of any requirement of public international law." Hyde at 742–43. On the application of the doctrine of *forum non conveniens* in litigation involving foreign merchant vessels and seamen, see The Ester, 190 Fed. 216 (E.D.S.C.1911) (summary of United States practice); Bickel, The Doctrine of Forum Non Conveniens as Applied in the Federal Courts in Matters of Admiralty, 35 Cornell L.Q. 12 (1949).

After the court has decided to retain a case for decision, whether in the exercise of its sound discretion or in compliance with legislative mandate, it must decide whether the forum's jurisdiction to prescribe shall be deemed to have been exercised so that United States law applies to the issue presented. See, e.g., McCulloch v. Sociedad Nacional de Marineros de Honduras, 372 U.S. 10, 83 S.Ct. 671, 9 L.Ed.2d 547 (1963); Lauritzen v. Larsen, 345 U.S. 571, 73 S.Ct. 921, 97 L.Ed. 1254 (1953).

The United States has not ordinarily applied its law to events and transactions aboard foreign vessels. In Lauritzen v. Larsen, the U.S. Supreme Court rejected the applicability to a foreign vessel of the Jones Act, providing for compensation to seamen for injury suffered in the course of their employment. "By usage as old as the Nation, such statutes have been construed to apply only to areas and transactions in which American law would be considered operative under prevalent doctrines of international law." Lauritzen v. Larsen, 345 U.S. 571, 577, 73 S.Ct. 921, 926, 97 L.Ed. 1254, 1265 (1953):

> International or maritime law in such matters as this does not seek uniformity and does not purport to restrict any nation from making and altering its laws to govern its own shipping and territory. However, it aims at stability and order through usages which considerations of comity, reciprocity and long-range interest have developed to define the domain which each nation will claim as its own. Maritime law, like our municipal law, has attempted to avoid or resolve conflicts between competing laws by ascertaining and valuing points of contact between the transaction and the states or governments whose competing laws are involved. The criteria, in general, appear to be arrived at from weighing of the significance of one or more connecting factors between the shipping transaction regulated and the national interest served by the assertion of authority. It would not be candid to claim that our courts have arrived at satisfactory standards or apply those that they profess with perfect consistency. But in dealing with international commerce we cannot be unmindful of the necessity for mutual forbearance if retaliations are to be avoided; nor should we forget that any contact which we hold sufficient to warrant application of our law to a foreign transaction will logically be as strong a warrant for a foreign country to apply its law to an American transaction.

Id. at 582, 73 S.Ct. at 928, 97 L.Ed. at 1267–68.

In listing and weighing the various factors connecting a particular incident to different states, the Court said: "[I]t is significant to us here that the weight given to the ensign overbears most other connecting events in determining applicable law. * * * [The law of the flag] must prevail unless some heavy counterweight appears." Id. at 585–86, 73 S.Ct. at 930, 97 L.Ed. at 1269–70.

But a tendency to find a "heavy counterweight" in Jones Act cases has become apparent. Hellenic Lines Ltd. v. Rhoditis involved injury to a Greek seaman on a ship flying the Greek flag, registered in Greece, and owned by a Panamanian corporation which was a subsidiary of a Greek corporation. But the Greek corporation had its principal offices in the United States and 95 percent of its shares were owned by a Greek citizen who was a permanent resident of the United States. The Court of Appeals said: "The Hero's flag is more symbolic than real . * * * Courts need not elevate symbols over reality. We therefore pierce the corporate veil and conclude that the Hero's flag is merely one of convenience." 412 F.2d 919, 923 (5th Cir.1969). The U.S. Supreme Court affirmed, 398 U.S. 306, 90 S.Ct. 1731, 26 L.Ed.2d 252 (1970), three justices dissenting.

In *Rhoditis,* the injury took place while the vessel was in an American port, although that factor did not appear to weigh heavily in the court's conclusion. In Antypas v. Cia. Maritima San Basilio, SA, 541 F.2d 307 (2d Cir.1976), cert. denied, 429 U.S. 1098, 97 S.Ct. 1116, 51 L.Ed.2d 545 (1977), where the injury took place on the high seas, the court applied the Jones Act on the basis of substantial contacts with the United States. But see De Oliveira v. Delta Marine Drilling Co., 707 F.2d 843 (5th Cir.1983), reh'g denied, 715 F.2d 577; Perez & Compania (Cataluna), S.A. v. Triton Pacific Maritime Corp., 826 F.2d 1449 (5th Cir.1987).

4. Vessels in distress that enter the territorial waters of a state in search of refuge or as a result of *force majeure* or other necessity are generally exempt from the jurisdiction of the port state. See Kate A. Hoff Claim (United States v. Mexico, 1929), 4 U.N.R.I.A.A. 444 (1951). However, "if the vessel or those on board commit an offense against the local law subsequent to the entry in distress, the littoral state's power to punish is undiminished." Harvard Research in International Law, Draft Convention on the Law of Territorial Waters, 23 A.J.I.L.Spec.Supp. 241, 299 (1929). On the right of entry in distress, see generally Jessup, The Law of Territorial Waters and Maritime Jurisdiction 194–208 (1927); 2 Hackworth at 277–82; 2 O'Connell at 685–87. On the right of entry into ports in general, see Lowe, The Right of Entry into Maritime Ports in International Law, 14 San Diego L.Rev. 597 (1977). See also Restatement (Third) § 512, Comment *c*, Reporters' Note 3.

5. Restatement (Third) § 512, Reporters' Notes 5 and 6 state:

> 5. *Jurisdiction over foreign vessels in port.* Once a commercial ship voluntarily enters a port, it becomes subject to the jurisdiction of the coastal state. Cunard S.S. Co. v. Mellon, 262 U.S. 100, 124, 43 S.Ct. 504, 507, 67 L.Ed. 894 (1923); Benz v. Compania Naviera Hidalgo, S.A., 353 U.S. 138, 142, 77 S.Ct. 699, 1 L.Ed.2d 709 (1957). See § 502, Comment *d*.
>
> The coastal state "may out of considerations of public policy choose to forego the exertion of its jurisdiction or to exert the same in only a limited way, but this is a matter resting solely within its discretion." Cunard S.S. Co. v. Mellon, supra, at 124, 43 S.Ct. at 507.
>
> * * *
>
> Jurisdiction over foreign vessels in port is frequently limited by bilateral agreement. See, e.g., United States–United Kingdom Consular Convention, 1951, Art. 22, 3 U.S.T. 3426, T.I.A.S. No. 2494, 165 U.N.T.S. 121.
>
> The authority of the coastal state generally applies to ships "voluntarily in port," not to ships driven to take refuge in a port by *force majeure* or other necessity. See Kate A. Hoff Claim (United States v. Mexico, 1929), 4 R.Int'l Arb. Awards 444 (1951); but see Cushin and Lewis v. The King, [1935]

Can.Exch. 103, [1933–34] Ann.Dig. 207 ("putting into port under constraint does not carry any legal right to exemption from local law or local jurisdiction"). See also statement by Secretary Webster, August 1, 1842, 2 Moore, Digest of International Law 353, 354 (1906).

For a study of the treatment by different states of foreign merchant vessels in port, see reports by the UNCTAD Secretariat, U.N.Docs. TD/B/C.4/136 (1975) and TD/B/C.4/158 (1977).

6. *Warships and other government ships operated for noncommercial purposes.* A warship (§ 501, Reporters' Note 1) in a foreign port must comply with the laws and regulations of the coastal state relating to navigation and safety. See LOS Convention, Art. 21(*l*) and (4); see also Harvard Research in International Law, The Law of Territorial Waters, 23 Am.J.Int'l L.Spec.Supp. 328 (1929). For an example of such legislation, see the Spanish order of March 23, 1958, Art. 6, U.N. Legislative Series, National Legislation and Treaties Relating to the Law of the Sea 145, 148 (U.N.Pub. ST/LEG/SER.B/19) (1980). If any such ship does not comply with port regulations, the flag state is internationally responsible for any damage caused, and the ship may be required to leave the port. See LOS Convention, Arts. 30–31.

The coastal state has no jurisdiction over offenses committed on board foreign warships or other government ships operated for non-commercial purposes. See Bustamante Code of Private International Law, Havana, 1928, Art. 300, 86 L.N.T.S. 111, 4 Hudson, International Legislation 2279, 2323 (1931). (The United States is not a party to this instrument.) Under international law, government-owned vessels not used for commercial purposes enjoy immunity from arrest, attachment, or execution. See § 457, Reporters' Note 7. But there is no immunity for a foreign public vessel from a maritime lien based upon a commercial activity of the foreign state. See § 455(4) and Reporters' Note 3 thereto.

b. Jurisdiction of the Flag State

UNITED STATES v. FLORES

Supreme Court of the United States, 1933.
289 U.S. 137, 53 S.Ct. 580, 77 L.Ed. 1086.

JUSTICE STONE: By indictment found in the District Court for Eastern Pennsylvania it was charged that appellee, a citizen of the United States, murdered another citizen of the United States upon the Steamship Padnsay, an American vessel, while at anchor in the Port of Matadi, in the Belgian Congo, a place subject to the sovereignty of the Kingdom of Belgium, and that appellee, after the commission of the crime, was first brought into the Port of Philadelphia, a place within the territorial jurisdiction of the District Court. * * * [T]he Padnsay, at the time of the offense charged, was unloading, being attached to the shore by cables, at a point 250 miles inland from the mouth of the Congo river.

The District Court * * * sustained a demurrer to the indictment and discharged the prisoner on the ground that the court was without jurisdiction to try the offense charged. 3 F.Supp. 134. The case comes here by direct appeal * * *.

Sections 273 and 275 of the Criminal Code, 18 U.S.C. §§ 452, 454 (18 U.S.C.A. §§ 452, 454), define murder and fix its punishment. Section 272, upon the construction of which the court below rested its decision, makes punishable offenses defined by other sections of the Criminal Code, among other cases, "when committed within the admiralty and maritime jurisdiction of the United States and out of the jurisdiction of any particular State on board any vessel belonging in whole or in part to the United States" or any of its nationals. And by section 41 of the Judicial Code, 28 U.S.C. § 102 (28 U.S.C.A. § 102), venue to try offenses "committed upon the high seas, or elsewhere out of the jurisdiction of any particular State or district," is "in the district where the offender is found, or into which he is first brought." As the offense charged here was committed on board a vessel lying outside the territorial jurisdiction of a state * * *, and within that of a foreign sovereignty, the court below was without jurisdiction to try and punish the offense unless it was within the admiralty and maritime jurisdiction of the United States.

Two questions are presented on this appeal, first, whether the extension of the judicial power of the federal government "to all Cases of admiralty and maritime Jurisdiction," by article 3, § 2, of the Constitution confers on Congress power to define and punish offenses perpetrated by a citizen of the United States on board one of its merchant vessels lying in navigable waters within the territorial limits of another sovereignty; and second, whether Congress has exercised that power by the enactment of section 272 of the Criminal Code under which the indictment was found.

[The Court held that Congress had the constitutional power to define and punish crimes on American vessels in foreign waters, and that the language of the statute making it applicable to offenses committed on an American vessel outside the jurisdiction of a state "within the admiralty and maritime jurisdiction of the United States" was broad enough to include crimes in the "territorial waters" of a foreign country. Mr. Justice Stone continued:]

It is true that the criminal jurisdiction of the United States is in general based on the territorial principle, and criminal statutes of the United States are not by implication given an extraterritorial effect. United States v. Bowman, 260 U.S. 94, 98, 43 S.Ct. 39, 67 L.Ed. 149; compare Blackmer v. United States, 284 U.S. 421, 52 S.Ct. 252, 76 L.Ed. 375. But that principle has never been thought to be applicable to a merchant vessel which, for purposes of the jurisdiction of the courts of the sovereignty whose flag it flies to punish crimes committed upon it, is deemed to be a part of the territory of that sovereignty, and not to lose that character when in navigable waters within the territorial limits of another sovereignty. * * * Subject to the right of the territorial sovereignty to assert jurisdiction over offenses disturbing the peace of the port, it has been supported by writers on international law, and has been recognized by France, Belgium, and other continental countries, as well as by England and the United States. * * *

A related but different question, not presented here, may arise when jurisdiction over an offense committed on a foreign vessel is asserted by the sovereignty in whose waters it was lying at the time of its commission, since for some purposes, the jurisdiction may be regarded as concurrent, in that the courts of either sovereignty may try the offense.

There is not entire agreement among nations or the writers on international law as to which sovereignty should yield to the other when the jurisdiction is asserted by both. See Jessup, the Law of Territorial Waters, 144–193. The position of the United States exemplified in Wildenhus's Case, 120 U.S. 1, 7 S.Ct. 385, 30 L.Ed. 565, has been that at least in the case of major crimes, affecting the peace and tranquillity of the port, the jurisdiction asserted by the sovereignty of the port must prevail over that of the vessel. * * *

This doctrine does not impinge on that laid down in United States v. Rodgers [150 U.S. 249, 14 S.Ct. 109, 37 L.Ed. 1071 (1893)], that the United States may define and punish offenses committed by its own citizens on its own vessels while within foreign waters where the local sovereign has not asserted its jurisdiction. In the absence of any controlling treaty provision, and any assertion of jurisdiction by the territorial sovereign, it is the duty of the courts of the United States to apply to offenses committed by its citizens on vessels flying its flag, its own statutes, interpreted in the light of recognized principles of international law. So applied the indictment here sufficiently charges an offense within the admiralty and maritime jurisdiction of the United States and the judgment below must be reversed.

Notes

1. Compare the 1982 Convention, Art. 94 (duties of the flag state) and Art. 97 (penal jurisdiction in matters of collision), p. 1492 supra, with Restatement (Third) § 502 (rights and duties of flag state), p. 1490 supra.

2. See the 1982 Convention, Art. 27 (criminal jurisdiction on board a foreign ship) and Art. 28 (civil jurisdiction in relation to foreign ships), p. 1494 and p. 1495, supra.

3. Would the Court have reached the same result if the defendant had not been a United States national? In Regina v. James Anderson, 11 Cox Crim.Cas. 198 (Ct.Crim.App.1868), an American crewman serving on a British vessel had been convicted of murder committed on board the vessel while the latter was in the Garonne River in France, about forty-five miles from the sea and about 300 yards from the nearest bank. The court upheld the conviction despite defendant's argument that the court had no jurisdiction, pointing out that although "the prisoner was subject to the American jurisprudence as an American citizen, and to the law of France as having committed an offense within the territory of France, yet he must also be considered as subject to the jurisdiction of British law, which extends to the protection of British vessels, though in ports belonging to another country." Id. at 204 (Bovill, C.J.)

4. In United States v. Reagan, 453 F.2d 165 (6th Cir.1971), the defendant was accused of killing a fellow seaman on an American vessel in a German harbor. The Court said in part:

> Since there is no "controlling treaty provision" the resolution of the question before us turns upon whether there has been "any assertion of jurisdiction by the territorial sovereign." It is our view that there was no "assertion of jurisdiction" by Germany and, therefore, that the district court was not without jurisdiction.
>
> The record shows that Reagan was taken into custody by German authorities on December 16, 1966, and judicially committed to a German mental institution on December 17, 1966, when his ship went to sea. He was subsequently released (after the return of the *SS Thunderbird* to port) and on

> April 5, 1967 the appropriate local court refused to issue a warrant for Reagan's arrest requested by the local prosecutor, finding that there was no probable cause for the issuance of such a warrant. The German court had before it the results of a rather extensive police investigation.
>
> * * * We do not believe that this preliminary proceeding constituted an "assertion of jurisdiction" by the local sovereign which would operate to oust the jurisdiction of the flag sovereign. It would appear that for whatever its reasons, the German court declined to "assert jurisdiction" within the meaning of *Flores,* supra. The application of the doctrine of "concurrent jurisdiction" is based on principles of comity. Assertion by the court below of its own jurisdiction in no way infringed upon the jurisdiction of the German court. The appropriate German authorities carefully scrutinized the matter and no formal charges were ever brought. There was no determination of Reagan's guilt or innocence. A different case would be presented if Reagan had been brought to trial in Germany or perhaps even if he had been indicted in Germany. We hold that the district court did have proper subject matter jurisdiction.

Id. at 171.

5. In March 1920, Charles Vincenti, a citizen of the United States, was arrested while on an American motorboat in British territorial waters off Bimini, Bahama Islands, British West Indies, by a special officer of the Department of Justice and by two internal-revenue agents holding a warrant against him for unlawful sale of liquor in Maryland and was taken back to the United States, although the motorboat was fired upon and pursued by British officials. Subsequently, the Department of State informed the British Ambassador that–

> * * * you will observe that the persons who arrested Vincenti and forcibly removed him from the Biminis Islands, acted on their own initiative and without the knowledge or approval of this Government in any way, and have been reprimanded and indefinitely suspended for their participation in the affair. Furthermore, it appears that Vincenti's bail has been exonerated and all proceedings subsequent to his unlawful arrest have been revoked. The incident is greatly regretted by this Government and I trust that the steps taken to make amends for it are entirely satisfactory to your Government.

The Ambassador replied that the action taken by the Government was satisfactory. 1 Hackworth 624 (1940).

What circumstances distinguish the jurisdiction exercised by the United States in the Vincenti affair from that exercised in United States v. Flores, supra?

In United States v. Conroy, 589 F.2d 1258 (5th Cir.1979), cert. denied, 444 U.S. 831, 100 S.Ct. 60, 62 L.Ed.2d 40, the court held that the United States Coast Guard had the authority to search an American vessel in foreign territorial waters. In that case the local government had agreed to the search but the court suggested that permission of the local government was not required. Id. at 1268. See also p. 1403, Note 3 supra.

For the application of U.S. constitutional principles to searches and seizures at sea, and the relation of constitutional principles to applicable principles of the international law of the sea, see Henkin, The Constitution at Sea, 36 Maine L.Rev. 201 (1984). Compare the *Alvarez-Machain* and the *Verdugo* cases p. 177 supra.

* * *

Note

A symposium published in 2000, edited by Christopher Joyner (and dedicated to Arvid Pardo), addresses "The Law of the Sea in the New Millennium: Neglected and Unresolved Issues." 31 Ocean Development & International Law, Nos. 1–2 (2000). The symposium identifies the following "neglected or unresolved" issues: Military Uses of Ocean Space and the Law of the Sea in the New Millennium; Straight Baselines: The Need for a Universally Applied Norm; Historic Salvage Law Revisited; Rethinking the Legal Status of Sunken Warships; Marine Conservation versus International Free Trade: Reconciling Dolphins with Tuna and Sea Turtles with Shrimp; Acoustic Pollution in the Oceans: The Search for Legal Standards; Designing the Ocean Policy Future: An Essay on How I Am Going To Do That; Emerging Law of the Sea Issues in the Antarctic Maritime Area: A Heritage for the New Century?

At the birth of a new century, the Law of the Sea is much changed from what it was in the middle of the 20th century, after the Second World War. What had been essentially customary law has been codified, first in the 1958 Conventions and then, comprehensively, in the U.N. Convention on the Law of the Sea of 1982. The Law of the Sea is once again generally resolved: even the law governing mining the sea-bed and subsoil beyond coastal state jurisdiction (which had been a major focus of controversy and which delayed the coming into force of the Convention for many years) is now generally agreed law, thanks to the 1994 Agreement modifying Part XI of the 1982 convention. See p. 1463 above. (But mining in the sea-bed beyond national jurisdiction remains a distant prospect.) As compared with the law as it was at the end of the Second World War, and with its codification in the 1958 conventions, the law of the new century finds the authority and jurisdiction of coastal states much enlarged, including a wider territorial sea, a 200–mile exclusive economic zone, a continental shelf often of quite large dimension. Enlarged coastal state authority diminishes "the commonage," and the projected complex of institutions for mining the sea-bed will subject the commonage to a novel regulatory regime. Inevitably, enlarged authority for coastal states has brought issues of delimitation between zones and shelves of different states. The Law of the Sea has given birth to new institutions, including a complex of tribunals, chambers, and procedures for the settlement of disputes. The International Court of Justice and other bodies with general jurisdiction are also busy interpreting and implementing the law.

Chapter 17

PROTECTING THE ENVIRONMENT

SECTION 1. THE EMERGING INTERNATIONAL LAW OF THE ENVIRONMENT

The Greening of International Law

The emergence of international environmental law as a distinctive legal regime was a notable development of the late 20th century. It responded to a heightened awareness of the degradation of air, water and natural resources throughout the world. This was not entirely novel. International legal measures of one kind or another had long been taken to prevent or alleviate pollution or accidents affecting more than one state. In the past half-century, the increased apprehension of world-wide dangers arising from the growth of population, industry and technology highlighted the interrelationship of phenomena that endangered human well-being and the natural order. Popular movements and scientific bodies pressed governments to take remedial measures over a wide range of human activity. The United Nations responded in the Stockholm conference of 1972 following years of study and discussion on a global basis. The Conference unanimously declared in Principle 21 that all states are responsible for ensuring "that the activities within their jurisdiction and control do not cause damage to the environment of other states or areas beyond the limits of national jurisdiction." Stockholm Declaration on the Environment, U.N. Publication E. 73 II A.14 (1973). At the same time and in the same provision the declaration recognized the "sovereign right of states to exploit their own resources pursuant to their own environmental policies" in accordance with the Charter and the principles of international law. Thus, typically of U.N. resolutions, this provision embraced the competing principles of international responsibility and national sovereignty. The declaration also called on states "to develop further the international law regarding liability and compensation for the victims of pollution and other environmental damages."

Customary law and general principles of law

Although the term "environmental law" was rarely used until recently, international law had long taken cognizance of environmental injuries in various situations. Pollution of shared rivers, marine oil spills, and transfrontier fumes were among the environmental problems dealt with through international agreements and principles of international responsibility. General principles of law were applied to disputes that had environmental aspects.

For example, the International Court of Justice in the Corfu Channel Case of 1949, pp. 133, 1404 supra, faced with a dispute over mines that endangered international navigation, referred to certain "general and well-recognized principles" that supported "every state's obligation not to allow its territory to be used for acts contrary to the rights of other states." Corfu Channel Case (Merits), 1949 I.C.J. 4, 22.

The international law concept of "abuse of rights" was sometimes invoked to condemn state behavior harmful to the environment of other states. The same principle has been expressed in the maxim *sic utere tuo ut alienum non laedas* (usually simply referred to as *sic utero tuo*). Its literal meaning is "use your own so as not to injure another." It has often been applied to situations of pollution or drainage of a shared waterway.

The basic principle of territorial integrity has also been invoked as a legal ground for condemning activities that caused injurious substances to enter other states. Other principles have been cited as legal grounds for preventing or reducing transboundary pollution. A Dutch scholar, Lammers, has listed 27 such principles and concepts bearing on transboundary pollution. Lammers, Pollution of International Watercourses 556–580 (1984).

The main non-official bodies of international lawyers have adopted resolutions that broadly assert state obligations to prevent or abate transboundary environmental damage. See, for example, Institut de Droit International, Resolution on Responsibility and Liability under International Law for Environmental Damage, 67 (II) Yearbook 487 (1998); Restatement (Third) § 601. In the 1990s international governmental conferences played a leading role in declaring principles and objectives of environmental protection—notably, the Rio Conference on Environment and Development in 1992, often referred to as the Earth Summit (see below).

The Object and Scope of International Environmental Law

Governments have justified their environmental law mainly as protective of human health and well-being. Many environmentalists see this as unjustifiably anthropocentric. They favor extending the concept of environmental harm to include injury or interference with the natural order whether or not harmful to humans. Protection of other species and the physical aspects of the earth and or extra-terrestrial objects should also be protected regardless of injury to human beings. Sometimes referred to as "deep ecology," or the "holistic approach," this conception has found international legal recognition in conventions that protect other species and works of nature. It has even been proposed that natural objects such as trees or mountains should have "standing" to obtain legal protection. Actually a number of treaties do extend protection to natural features and non-human species (for example, the Convention on International Trade in Endangered Species, CITES, see below) though for political reasons they may be justified as benefits to human beings. For example, the 1992 Convention on Biological Diversity, see below, is justified both for its protection of the natural order and for its indirect benefits to human beings.

Harm in Environmental Law

A wide range of situations fall within the concept of environmental harm. However, not every interference or detrimental impact on the environment is regarded as "harm" in its international law meaning. At least four conditions are required. First, the harm must result from human activity. Floods or storms unless causally attributable to human action do not fall within the legal concept of environmental harm. Second, the environmental injury must, as a general rule, result from a physical consequence of the causal human activity. Declines or increases in the price of commodities would not be regarded as environmental harm even if they adversely affect crops or indirectly impact on land or water management. A third condition requires, as a general rule, that the physical environmental impact extend beyond national boundaries of the source state. Destruction of a forest entirely within national territory would not be an international environmental harm unless its physical consequence was harmful to another state or to a common area or climate. A fourth condition requires that the environmental harm be substantial or appreciable (a term used in the International Law Commission reports, see Barboza, Sixth Report on International Liability, U.N. Document A/CN4/428, at 41 (1990).) This condition would include harm to humans and also in some cases (as indicated earlier) substantial harm to "nature"—that is, to other species or national features.

The Significance of Risk

Attempts to formulate general rules for environmental obligations usually link harm and risk. States are enjoined to take steps to prevent appreciable (or substantial or significant) harm and to minimize the risk (i.e. the probability of such harm occurring). Proposed measures draw attention to two different types of situations. The first is one in which a disaster of great magnitude could occur though the probability of such occurrence is low. The meltdown of a nuclear plant or an oil tanker running aground are examples where the risk is not high but the harm that results is great, perhaps catastrophic. In the second type of situation (such as automobile exhaust in cities), the probability of extensive harm is high but the effects on an individual are relatively minor and often undetected. In this situation the diffuse nature of the harmful effects together with the recognized benefits to the population as a whole tend to reduce the felt need for restrictions and precautionary measures. In contrast, cases in which the concentrated damage is high, even though the probability of occurrence is low, are more readily seen to require regulation.

Economic and social factors generally have a substantial effect on judgments of risk and harm. A poor community faced by food shortages and lack of economic opportunities will tend to minimize the harm to the environment. In fact, the great divide in present international environmental debates is between the developed countries that emphasize the need to reduce environmental dangers and the developing countries concerned about meeting food and health necessities along with economic development even if environmental risks occur.

Obligation of Due Care and the Precautionary Principle

A central principle of environmental law is an implicit obligation of states to exercise due care to prevent and minimize injury to other states. The Restatement (Third) § 601 asserts that a state is legally obligated to take such measures "as may be practicable under the circumstances, to ensure that activities within its jurisdiction or control are conducted so as not to cause significant injury to the environment of another state or of areas beyond the limits of national jurisdiction." The International Law Commission draft articles dealing with transboundary harm "arising out of acts not prohibited by international law" would require states to prevent or, where necessary, minimize the risk of transboundary harm. The duty of prevention is qualified: the measures must be "appropriate and practicable." International Law Commission, International Liability for Injurious Consequences Arising out of Acts Not Prohibited by International Law, draft Article 8; Barboza, Sixth Report on International Liability, U.N. Document A/CN4/428, paragraph 311 (1990). In recent years, this obligation has been expressed as the "precautionary principle," which broadly would require states to take preventive measures even without prior proof that the failure to employ such measures will cause appreciable harm of an environmental character. The Rio Declaration of 1992 stated that this approach shall be applied by states according to their capabilities. "Where there are threats of serious or irreversible damage, lack of full scientific certainty shall not be used as a reason for postponing cost-effective measures to prevent environmental degradation." (Principle 15). In some contexts, the precautionary principle places the burden of proof on a state to show that its activity or product would not cause significant harm. See Section 7 on genetically modified organisms below. On the role of prevention in the field of environmental protection see also the International Court of Justice's decision in the *Gabcikovo-Nagymaros Case* (Hungary v. Slovakia), 1997 I.C.J. 7, reprinted in 37 I.L.M. 162 (1998); and Article 13 of the Institut de Droit International's Resolution on Responsibility and Liability under International Law for Environmental Damage, 67 (II) Yearbook 487, 501 (1998).

The concept of a precautionary principle has received broad support among European countries but the United States has expressed its opposition to the principle unless it is significantly qualified. One "model" text proposes that preventive measures need not be taken if the overall cost and loss of benefits from such measures would exceed the benefit that the preventive action would produce in the long run. See Barboza, Article 11.

For in-depth treatment of the concept and its application, see articles in Freestone & Hay (eds.), The Precautionary Principle and International Law: The Challenge of Implementation (1996).

Duty to Inform, Assess, Consult

The duty of a source state to inform others of impending harm to them or of the risk of such harm is a corollary of the obligation to prevent and minimize harm to other countries. The principle would apply to situations that have a fair probability of causing heavy damage in the event of a serious accident. For example, the transport of dangerous materials should require notification to the governments of states that could be injured by accidents or operational difficulties. Normal development activities such as hydroelectric projects or oil drilling may have extraterritorial environmental consequences. Sewage disposal that results in polluted water is a common example. The *Trail Smelter* case (see below) imposed liability for the harm resulting to the United States from fumes of a plant in Canada. The evident risk of transborder damage in some situations would justify prior notice and consultations between the source state and the potentially affected state. Joint commissions as used for international rivers may also provide a practical means for surveillance and consultation regarding environmental threats in other trans-border situations. See Schachter, Sharing the World's Resources, 71–73 (1977). On the International Joint Commission, set up by Canada and the United States in 1909, see Francis, Binational Cooperation for Great Lakes Water Quality: A Framework for the Groundwater Connection, 65 Chi.-Kent L.Rev. 359 (1989). For more on such duties in the context of international watercourses, see Chapter 18.

International Responsibility and Civil Liability

International responsibility and civil liability have been basic concepts in the formation of international environmental law but usage has varied as to their meaning and application. In keeping with general international law usage, international (i.e. state) responsibility arises as a consequence of a state's breach of an obligation established under international law and of its duty to re-establish the original position or pay compensation. An international obligation to compensate may also arise from violation of a rule of international law imposing strict responsibility for harm, irrespective of fault.

The concept of civil liability is applicable to operators (whether private or governmental) who are assigned liability under domestic law or governing rules of international law. State responsibility and operator liability each serve corrective justice by shifting loss from an innocent victim to the causal agent. They also give teeth to rules of prevention and mitigation. From an economist's point of view, liability internalizes the costs of environmental damage, thus tending to promote more efficient use of resources. The "polluter pays" principle has been widely supported by governments and environmentalists on the double ground of fairness and efficiency. The principle has also been cited to support the contention that the richer developed countries should pay a major share of cleaning up the global environment since they were the source of most of the pollution.

The issue of strict liability has also been raised by the International Law Commission in its project on "the international liability of states for injurious consequences arising out of acts not prohibited by international law." Begun in 1978, it quickly became apparent that the general topic would have its principal application in the environmental area where appreciable harm resulted from activities not prohibited by international law." The I.L.C. had not adopted a draft as of 2000. The tendency in the Commission was to recognize a state's obligation to compensate an "injured state" for appreciable harm caused by its activities even if those activities were legally permissible. Such reparation would be determined as a rule by negotiation between the "source" and injured states, guided by criteria of an equitable character. It is uncertain whether a multilateral treaty will emerge on this subject but the I.L.C. draft proposals may well influence bilateral agreements and specialized regimes established by states. A related I.L.C. study of transboundary damage from hazardous activities was also still in progress as of 2000.

Issues of state responsibility and civil liability for environmental damage also raise questions of the legal effect of standards adopted by international bodies which are neither treaty nor customary law obligations. Such standards constitute the bulk of environmental rules; they range from detailed, precise standards of safety to broad requirements of due care. The Restatement (Third) § 601 (1)(a) declares that states are obligated to conform to such "generally accepted international rules and standards." Failure to do so may be viewed as wrongful conduct—not as violations of law but as falling short of the "due care" or the precautionary approach required of states in regard to activities creating a significant risk of transborder environmental injury. One of the advantages of this approach is that it focuses on the particular circumstances of the activity in question rather than judging the activity in general.

Professor Schachter comments generally on the limitations of liability:

> Interesting as problems of liability are, we should not overlook its limitations in regard to major areas of environmental damage. Liability is a feasible mechanism when damage is identifiable, traceable to a state of origin and reasonably foreseeable by that state. It is thus appropriate for discrete accidents such as oil spills and chemical disasters. It is also applicable to specific activities that foreseeably carry risks resulting from continued activities such as sewage disposal or toxic-waste deposits. It may be appropriate for a large-scale hydrological project affecting rivers or groundwater. On the other hand, it would be difficult, and perhaps impossible, to apply liability in its normal sense to the vast number of environmental harms that result from routine economic and social life, such as the use of automobiles and air conditioners, burning coal, cutting timber and grazing cattle. These activities may create enormous damage in the aggregate over time, but they have numerous sources and are aspects of beneficial, and even necessary, features of society. The numbers of injured are countless, dispersed in many places, and the losses imposed cannot be adequately calculated or assigned. The remedy of legal liability is clearly not practicable, at least not in the commonly understood sense of claims by injured states against state sources. However, there is room for international remedial action that would take account of the relative responsibility of states for contributing to the problems. This might be done, as has been proposed, by establishing an international trust fund to take measures of reparation and prevention in cases of global or regional problems. The states most responsible for the environmental injury would bear relatively heavy costs of such funds, limited by their ability to pay. This would not be liability in its legal sense, but it would serve the aim of reparation and give weight to the responsibility of the states from which the damage emanated.

Schachter, International Environmental Law, 44 J. Int'l Aff., 457, 488–489 (1991).

In general, liability for environmental harm is based on the injurious consequences to individuals or to property in the territory of an affected state. Both the Stockholm and Rio Declarations refer to liability and compensation for the victims of pollution and of other environmental damages. A similar position is taken in nearly all the agreements providing for liability. An exception is found in the 1988 Convention on Regulation of Antarctic Mineral Resources. It provides liability for damage to the "Antarctic environment or dependent or associated ecosystems."

A similar principle may be appropriate for environmental harm to the oceans or other areas beyond national jurisdiction. A corollary would accord juridical standing to every state on the assumption of the common interest in the "global commons" i.e., the high seas, outer space or the global atmosphere. On this premise, any state may lodge a claim for damage as a result of pollution, whether or not the damage affected its nationals or territory.

Sustainable Development

The United Nations Conference on Environment and Development (UNCED), the Rio Earth Summit, in 1992 recognized that the environment and development must be addressed in their mutual relationship and that many internal developments affect the international environment. Population growth, the depletion of the ozone layer, deforestation, desertification, and preservation of biological diversity provide ready examples. At the Rio Earth Summit, several instruments were approved: the Rio Declaration on Environment and Development (27 non-binding principles); a Non-Legally Binding Authoritative Statement of Principles for a Global Consensus on the Management, Conservation and Sustainable Development of all Types of Forests; and Agenda 21, an "action plan" on sustainable development to guide the policies of governments into the next century, as well as the Framework Convention on Climate Change and the Biodiversity Convention discussed below.

The principle of "sustainable development" had been defined earlier, in the report *Our Common Future* of the World Commission on Environment and Development (the so-called Brundtland Commission), as "development that meets the needs of the present without compromising the ability of future generations to meet their own needs." Our Common Future 8–9, 43 (1987). The International Court of Justice, in a 1997 decision involving construction on the Danube, saw the "need to reconcile economic development with protection of the environment * * * aptly expressed in the concept of sustainable development." Case Concerning the Gabcikovo–Nagymaros Project (Hungary v. Slovakia), 1997 I.C.J. 7, reprinted in 37 I.L.M. 1652 (1998). See below, Section 2. In his separate opinion, Judge Weeramantry examines several international instruments and examples of state practice which lead him to conclude that sustainable development has world-wide acceptance as a normative concept. 1997 I.C.J. 92–95. The principle of sustainable development was included in Article 3 of the Framework Convention on Climate Change and the Kyoto Protocol to the Convention, discussed below. For further information on the principle see Brown Weiss et al., International Environmental Law and Policy 53–58 (1998); Robinson, Legal Structure and Sustainable Development: Comparative Environmental Law Perspectives on Legal Regimes for Sustainable Development, 3 Wid. L. Symp. J. 247 (1998). On the Earth Summit and the preparatory work that preceded it, see Gardner, Negotiating Survival: The Road from Rio (1992); Organization Summary: International Union for the Conservation of Nature and Natural Resources: The Issue of Sustainable Development, 7 Colo.J.Int'l Envt'l L. & Pol'y 213 (1996).

Environment and Human Rights

There is growing movement towards recognition of a human right to a safe environment. Although no legally binding international instrument deals specifically with the nexus between environmental protection and human rights, a Draft Declaration of Principles on Human Rights and the Environment was drafted in 1994 by a United Nations group of experts on human rights and environmental protection. See Popovic, In Pursuit of Environmental Human Rights: Commentary on the Draft Declaration of Principles on Human Rights and the Environment, 27 Colum. H.R. L.Rev. 487 (1996). Furthermore, Article 2 of the Institut de Droit International's Resolution on Environment, adopted in Strasbourg in 1997, states: "Every human being has the right to live in a healthy environment." Institut de Droit International, 67(II) Yearbook 477, 479 (1998). Judge Weeramantry, in his separate opinion to the 1997 I.C.J. *Gabcikovo* decision, stated: "The protection of the environment is likewise a vital part of contemporary human rights doctrine, for it is a sine qua non for numerous human rights such as the right to health and the right to life itself. It is scarcely necessary to elaborate on this, as damage to the environment can impair and undermine all the human rights spoken of in the Universal Declaration and other human rights instruments." 37 I.L.M. 162, 204.

Two cases in federal courts under the U.S. Alien Tort Claim Act (28 U.S.C. § 1350) suggested the possibility of connections between environmental concerns and human rights. In Doe v. Unocal Corp., 963 F.Supp. 880 (1997), the U.S. District Court for the Central District of California considered a claim brought against the corporation UNOCAL for alleged human rights violations in connection with the construction of an oil pipeline in Burma. Although the claim initially survived a motion to dismiss, defendants' motion for summary judgment was later granted. 110 F.Supp.2d 1294 (C.D.Cal. 2000). In Aguinda v. Texaco, 945 F.Supp. 625 (S.D.N.Y.1996), claims were brought by indigenous people for environmental damage resulting from Texaco's exploitation of oil fields in Ecuador; the district court dismissed on grounds of forum non conveniens and comity but the judgment was reversed and the case sent back to the district court. Jota v. Texaco, 157 F.3d 153 (1998). See Shelton, General Developments, 8 Y.B. Int'l Env. L. 126, at 131–132 (1997). The relationship between human rights and environmental protection has also been recognized by the European Court of Human Rights. In Balmer–Schafroth and others v. Switzerland, 67/1996/686/876 (Aug. 26, 1997) the Court considered a challenge to the Swiss government's decision to extend a license to operate a nuclear plant under Article 6 of the European Convention on Human Rights (right to a hearing). The Court found that the plaintiffs had not shown that the plant exposed them personally to danger that was specific, serious and imminent. In Guerra and others v. Italy, 116/1996/735/932 (Feb. 19, 1998), the plaintiffs, who lived close to a chemical factory, claimed, first, that the Italian Government had failed to provide them with information about the risks of the factory, and second, that the state had violated its alleged obligation to prevent the effects of toxic emissions. The Court rebuffed the first, but upheld the second argument holding that "severe environmental pollution may affect individuals' well-being and prevent them from enjoying their homes in such a way as to affect their private and family life adversely." Therefore, the Court found that the Italian Government had not fulfilled its obligation to secure plaintiff's right to respect for private and family life under Article 8 of the Convention.

In the European context, the 1997 European Convention for the Protection of Human Rights and Dignity of Human Beings with regard to the Application of Biology and Medicine, E.T.S. No. 164, and its 1998 Protocol on the Cloning of Human Beings, E.T.S. No. 168, take into account the accelerating developments in biology and medicine and the need to protect human dignity against possible misuse of biology and medicine. As of 2000, the Convention had 28 signatories and 6 parties and had entered into force on December 15, 1999. The Protocol, with 28 signatories and 5 ratifications, entered into force in early 2001.

Some national constitutions have also granted protection of environmental rights. For a compilation, see Brown Weiss et al., International Environmental Law and Policy, at 415–417 (1998). For general discussion see Beanal v. Freeport–McMoRan, Inc., 969 F.Supp. 362 (E.D.La.1997); Boyle & Anderson (eds.), Human Rights Approaches to Environmental Protection (1996); Gormley, The Legal Obligation of the International Community to Guarantee a Pure and Decent Environment: The Expansions of Human Rights Norms, 3 Geo. Int'l Env. L.Rev. 85 (1990); Tay, Human Rights, Culture, and the Singapore Example, 41 McGill L.J. 743 (1996); Taylor, From Environmental to Ecological Human Rights: A New Dynamic in International Law? 10 Geo. Int'l Env. L.Rev. 279 (1998).

The Challenge to the Legitimacy of International Environmental Law

As international environmental law has developed, many issues raised (notably climate change) have become divisive and political. Some have questioned the legitimacy of international environmental rules that lack general consensus of states and approval of the peoples affected. As Daniel Bodansky has written, "First, the coming generation of environmental problems will probably require more expeditious and flexible lawmaking approaches, which do not depend on consensus among states. Second, to the extent that international environmental law is beginning to have significant implications for non–or substate actors (who have not consented to it directly), rather than just for the relations among states, state consent may for them have little legitimating effect.* * * Its lack of transparency and accountability will become increasingly problematic." Bodansky, The Legitimacy of International Governance: A Coming Challenge for International Environmental Law? 93 A.J.I.L. 596, 606 (1999).

SECTION 2. TRANSBORDER ENVIRONMENTAL HARM

TRAIL SMELTER CASE

(U.S. v. Canada)
3 U.N. Rep. Int. Arb. Awards 1911 (1941).

[The case was decided by a Special Arbitral Tribunal under a convention which required the application of the "law and practice followed in dealing with cognate questions in the United States of America as well as international law and practice." 3 U.N.Rep.Int'l Arb.Awards 1905, 1908. The arbitration grew out of air pollution from sulphur dioxide fumes emitted by a smelter plant at Trail, British Columbia, owned by a Canadian corporation. In a previous decision the Special Arbitral Tribunal had found that the fumes caused damage in the State of Washington during the period from 1925 to 1937. In holding Canada responsible and directing injunctive relief and payment of an indemnity, the Tribunal stated, id. at 1963–64:]

As Professor Eagleton puts it (Responsibility of States in International Law, 1928, p. 80): "A State owes at all times a duty to protect other States against injurious acts by individuals from within its jurisdiction." * * * These and many others have been carefully examined. International decisions, in various matters, from the Alabama case onward, and also earlier ones, are based on the same general principle, and, indeed, this principle, as such, has not been questioned by Canada. But the real difficulty often arises rather when it comes to determine what, *pro subjecta materie*, is deemed to constitute an injurious act.

* * *

No case of air pollution dealt with by an international tribunal has been brought to the attention of the Tribunal nor does the Tribunal know of any such case. The nearest analogy is that of water pollution. But, here also, no decision of an international tribunal has been cited or has been found.

There are, however, as regards both air pollution and water pollution, certain decisions of the Supreme Court of the United States which may legitimately be taken as a guide in this field of international law, for it is reasonable to follow by analogy, in international cases, precedents established by that court in dealing with controversies between States of the Union or with other controversies concerning the quasi-sovereign rights of such States, where no contrary rule prevails in international law and no reason for rejecting such precedents can be adduced from the limitations of sovereignty inherent in the Constitution of the United States.

[The Tribunal then discussed Missouri v. Illinois, 200 U.S. 496, 26 S. Ct. 268, 50 L.Ed. 572 (1906), New York v. New Jersey, 256 U.S. 296, 41 S. Ct. 492, 65 L.Ed. 937 (1921), and New Jersey v. New York, 283 U.S. 473, 51 S.Ct. 519, 75 L.Ed. 1176 (1931), dealing with water pollution, and Georgia v. Tennessee Copper Company, 206 U.S. 230, 27 S.Ct. 618, 51 L.Ed. 1038 (1907) and Georgia v. Tennessee Copper Company, 237 U.S. 474, 35 S.Ct. 631, 59 L.Ed. 1054 (1915), dealing with air pollution, and concluded: "[U]nder the principles of international law, as well as of the law of the United States, no State has the right to use or permit the use of its territory in such a manner as to cause injury by fumes in or to the territory of another or the properties or persons therein, when the case is of serious consequence and the injury is established by clear and convincing evidence." Id. at 1965. The Tribunal described in detail the measures of control to be imposed upon the Trail Smelter. These measures included the maintenance of meteorological and sulphur emission records and the specification of maximum hourly emission of sulphur dioxide under various conditions.]

Notes

1. Does the *Trail Smelter* case endorse a standard of strict liability? Compare the language of this decision with that of the Restatement (Third) § 601.

2. A Convention on Long–Range Transboundary Air Pollution was adopted in Geneva on November 13, 1979, T.I.A.S. No. 10541, 18 I.L.M. 1442 (1979). The purpose of the Convention is "to limit, and, as far as possible, gradually reduce and prevent air pollution including long-range air pollution." The principal means provided for are research and exchange of information. As of 2000, the Convention

was in force for 45 states, including the United States. Protocols to the Convention followed in 1984 on financing, in 1985 on the reduction of sulphur emissions or their transboundary fluxes by at least 30%, in 1988 on the control of emissions of nitrogen oxides or their transboundary fluxes, in 1991 on the control of emissions of volatile organic compounds or their transboundary fluxes, in 1994 on further reduction of sulphur emissions, in 1998 on heavy metals and on persistent organic pollutants, and in 1999 on abatement of acidification, eutrophication and ground level ozone.

3. The principal United States statutes dealing with transfrontier pollution are the Clean Water Act, 33 U.S.C.A. §§ 1251–1387, and the Clean Air Act, 42 U.S.C.A. §§ 7401–42 (1977). The former Act applies to transfrontier pollution on condition of reciprocity. The Clean Air Act has similar provisions. In 1980, Canada revised its Clean Air Act of 1971 to create reciprocity required by its counterpart. CanStat., ch. 45, Sec. 21.1(19) (1980–81). For actions taken under these Acts, the Acid Precipitation Act of 1980 (42 U.S.C.A. §§ 8901–05, 8911–12), and other measures dealing with transborder pollution, see Restatement (Third) § 601, Reporters' Note 8.

THE CHERNOBYL NUCLEAR PLANT EXPLOSION

On April 26, 1986, an explosion occurred at the Chernobyl atomic power plant near Kiev in the U.S.S.R. The explosion caused radioactive substances to be released into the atmosphere. It was not until three days later, when significantly higher levels of radioactivity were found in Scandinavian countries, that the U.S.S.R. acknowledged that an explosion had occurred. However, it failed to disclose any particulars as to the nature of the occurrence and the extent of the release of radioactive substances. It was not until eleven days later, when increased levels of radioactive attributed to the Chernobyl explosion were found as far away as Japan, that Pravda published an official account. This account acknowledged that the release of radioactive substances continued, but "avoided discussion to the amount of radioactivity released, its potential effects, the doses that residents may have been exposed to in the hours or days before they were evacuated, or the dangers posed by the accident." N.Y. Times, May 6, 1986, Sec. A, at 1, col. 6, at 6, col. 1. Many foreign countries filed protests with the U.S.S.R., complaining that it had failed properly to inform them of the accident. Did the U.S.S.R. have an international obligation to inform potentially affected countries of the occurrence of the accident and its potential effects? Compare Art. 198 of the Law of the Sea Convention (1982) which provides that a state, damaged or in imminent danger of being damaged by pollution, "shall immediately notify other States it deems likely to be affected by such damage, as well as the competent international organizations." See also Arts. 204–06 of the Convention requiring monitoring of, and reporting on, activities likely to pollute the marine environment. Are these provisions applicable by analogy? If the United States learned of the explosion by remote sensing, was it under an international obligation to notify potentially affected states of dangers created by the incident, as soon as it obtained the information? Was the U.S.S.R. internationally liable for the injuries suffered in other states as a result of the explosion? Would the destruction of contaminated vegetables and milk by public officials in affected states be "significant injury"? Would the Ukraine be liable, if the injuries suffered as a result of the explosion were to manifest themselves only many years later? Would it be under an international obligation to discontinue the practices that led to the accident and to adopt measures to avoid its reoccurrence? Would the United States, in a similar situation, be under any such obligations, if the nuclear plant were privately owned? See generally Sands, Chernobyl: Law and Communication: Transboundary Nuclear Pollution: The Legal Materials (1988); Malone, The Chernobyl Accident: A Case Study in International Law Regulating State Responsibility For Transboundary Nuclear Pollution, 12 Colum.J.Env.L. 203 (1987); Note, After Chernobyl: Liability For Nuclear Accidents Under International Law, 12 Colum.J.Transnat'l L. 647 (1987).

Soon after the Chernobyl explosion the International Atomic Energy Agency (IAEA) adopted two conventions, the Convention on Assistance in Case of a Nuclear Accident or Radiological Emergency, 25 I.L.M. 1377 (1986), and the Convention on Early Notification of a Nuclear Accident, 25 I.L.M. 1370 (1986).

CASE CONCERNING THE GABCIKOVO–NAGYMAROS PROJECT (HUNGARY v. SLOVAKIA)

International Court of Justice.
1997 I.C.J. 7, reprinted in 37 I.L.M. 162 (1998).

[Hungary and Slovakia entered into a treaty in 1977 for construction of a system of dams and other works on the Danube River in their territories and to reroute waters of the river by way of a canal. After disputes arose, Hungary terminated the treaty and eventually the two states submitted the case to the Court. Hungary argued that because of fundamentally changed circumstances (see pp. 557–559 in Chapter 7) and "ecological necessity" it rightfully terminated the treaty. The Court rejected the Hungarian argument and held that the parties were obliged to negotiate to implement the treaty in accordance with its terms. The Court's opinion contained several references to the importance of environmental concerns. It quoted the following statement made by the Court in its Advisory Opinion on the Legality of the Threat or Use of Nuclear Weapons of 1996 (1996 I.C.J. 226, reprinted in 25 I.L.M. 809): "[T]he existence of the general obligation of States to insure that activities within their jurisdiction and control respect the environment of other States or of areas beyond national control is now part of the corpus of international law relating to the environment." Para. 53. It referred to "new means and standards" which states must take into account even when continuing activities begun in the past. "The need to reconcile economic development with protection of the environment is aptly expressed in the concept of sustainable development." Para. 140. The Court also noted "Hungary's basic right to an equitable and reasonable sharing of the resources of an international watercourse." Para. 78. Judge Weeramantry, in a separate opinion, noted that the principle of sustainable development is a part of modern international law which reaffirms that there must be both development and environmental protection. Paras. 205, 207 and 213 of the separate opinion of Judge Weeramantry.]

Notes

1. The International Court's opinion referred to a "great number of instruments dealing with the environment" but did not mention any. However, it quoted from scholarly works that referred to sustainable development and environmental necessity in general terms. Does the Court's opinion and Judge Weeramantry's eloquent commentary support the conclusion that "sustainable development" can be applied as a legal concept sufficiently determinate to enable a tribunal to decide specific disputes? See articles in 8 Y.B. Int'l Env.L. (1997) by Bourne, Boyle, Canelas de Castro, Klabbers and Stec & Eckstein.

2. In its opinion, the International Court stated that "[t]he awareness of the vulnerability of the environment and the recognition that environmental risks have to be assessed on a continuous basis have become much stronger in the years since the Treaty's conclusion." Does this suggest that apart from the treaty obligation there is a general obligation to conduct environmental risk assessments? Is there an obligation to conduct such assessments on an ongoing basis and to do so in accordance with emerging norms relating to the environment?

3. An interesting aspect of the Court's decision is its bearing on domestic political controversy in the countries concerned. The internal opposition to the treaty project particularly within Hungary was blocked by the decision of the I.C.J. that the treaty survived all changes and challenges. Neither government could unilaterally revoke the treaty, whatever the internal political demands. One writer concludes: "Treaties thus serve as trump cards in the domestic political game * * * A treaty is the ultimate guarantee for the durability of the deal struck between different domestic groups at the time of its ratification * * *." Benvenisti, Domestic Politics and International Resources: What Role for International Law?, in Michael Byers (ed.), The Role of Law in International Politics (2000). May the obligation of due care and the precautionary principle mentioned by the I.C.J. in the *Gabcikovo* case require states to take account of local interests and actions? For further discussion on the *Gabcikovo* case see Bekker, Gabcikovo–Nagymaros Project: International Court of Justice Judgment on Continuing Effect of 1977 Treaty between Czechoslovakia and Hungary regarding Danube River Project, 92 A.J.I.L. 273 (1998).

4. International disputes about transnational resources and environmental restraints will often involve differences among domestic interest groups. May the obligation of due care and the precautionary principle mentioned by the I.C.J. in the *Gabcikovo* case require states to take account of local interests and actions? See Benvenisti, supra.

5. In 1993, the International Court of Justice established a Chamber on Environmental Matters. The Court stated that the decision was taken in view of the developments in the field of International Environmental Law and the need to be prepared to the fullest possible extent to deal with any environmental case falling within its jurisdiction. 4 Y.B. Int'l Env. L. 484 (1993). As of 2000, the Chamber had still not been used.

SECTION 3. MILITARY WEAPONS AND WARFARE: ENVIRONMENTAL ISSUES

The International Court of Justice discussed international environmental law in its Advisory Opinion on the Legality of the Threat or Use of Nuclear Weapons. The following paragraphs of this opinion relate to environmental law.

ADVISORY OPINION ON THE LEGALITY OF THE THREAT OR USE OF NUCLEAR WEAPONS

International Court of Justice.
1996 I.C.J. 226, 241–243.

27. In both their written and oral statements, some States furthermore argued that any use of nuclear weapons would be unlawful by reference to existing norms relating to the safeguarding and protection of the environment, in view of their essential importance.

Specific references were made to various existing international treaties and instruments. These included Additional Protocol I of 1977 to the Geneva Conventions of 1949, Article 35, paragraph 3, of which prohibits the employment of "methods or means of warfare which are intended, or may be expected, to cause widespread, long-term and severe damage to the natural environment"; and the Convention of 18 May 1977 on the Prohibition of Military or Any Other Hostile Use of Environmental Modification Techniques, which prohibits the use of weapons which have "widespread, long-lasting or severe effects" on the environment (Art. 1). Also cited were Principle 21 of the Stockholm Declaration of 1972 and Principle 2 of the Rio Declaration of 1992 which express the common conviction of the States concerned that they have a duty

> "to ensure that activities within their jurisdiction or control do not cause damage to the environment of other States or of areas beyond the limits of national jurisdiction".

These instruments and other provisions relating to the protection and safeguarding of the environment were said to apply at all times, in war as well as in peace, and it was contended that they would be violated by the use of nuclear weapons whose consequences would be widespread and would have transboundary effects.

28. Other States questioned the binding legal quality of these precepts of environmental law; or, in the context of the Convention on the Prohibition of Military or Any Other Hostile Use of Environmental Modification Techniques, denied that it was concerned at all with the use of nuclear weapons in hostilities; or, in the case of Additional Protocol I, denied that they were generally bound by its terms, or recalled that they had reserved their position in respect of Article 35, paragraph 3, thereof.

It was also argued by some States that the principal purpose of environmental treaties and norms was the protection of the environment in time of peace. It was said that those treaties made no mention of nuclear weapons. It was also pointed out that warfare in general, and nuclear warfare in particular, were not mentioned in their texts and that it would be destabilizing to the rule of law and to confidence in international negotiations if those treaties were now interpreted in such a way as to prohibit the use of nuclear weapons.

29. The Court recognizes that the environment is under daily threat and that the use of nuclear weapons could constitute a catastrophe for the environment. The Court also recognizes that the environment is not an abstraction but represents the living space, the quality of life and the very health of human beings, including generations unborn. The existence of the general obligation of States to ensure that activities within their jurisdiction and control respect the environment of other States or of areas beyond national control is now part of the corpus of international law relating to the environment.

30. However, the Court is of the view that the issue is not whether the treaties relating to the protection of the environment are or are not applicable during an armed conflict, but rather whether the obligations stemming from these treaties were intended to be obligations of total restraint during military conflict.

The Court does not consider that the treaties in question could have intended to deprive a State of the exercise of its right of self-defence under international law because of its obligations to protect the environment. Nonetheless, States must take environmental considerations into account when assessing what is necessary and proportionate in the pursuit of legitimate military objectives. Respect for the environment is one of the elements that go to assessing whether an action is in conformity with the principles of necessity and proportionality.

This approach is supported, indeed, by the terms of Principle 24 of the Rio Declaration, which provides that:

> "Warfare is inherently destructive of sustainable development. States shall therefore respect international law providing protection for the environment in times of armed conflict and cooperate in its further development, as necessary."

31. The Court notes furthermore that Article 35, paragraph 3, and 55 of Additional Protocol I provide additional protection for the environment. Taken together, these provisions embody a general obligation to protect the natural environment against widespread, long-term and severe environmental damage; the prohibition of methods and means of warfare which are intended, or may be expected, to cause such damage; and the prohibition of attacks against the natural environment by way of reprisals.

These are powerful constraints for all the States having subscribed to these provisions.

32. General Assembly resolution 47/37 of 25 November 1992 on the "Protection of the Environment in Times of Armed Conflict" is also of interest in this context. It affirms the general view according to which environmental considerations constitute one of the elements to be taken into account in the implementation of the principles of the law applicable in armed conflict: it states that "destruction of the environment, not justified by

military necessity and carried out wantonly, is clearly contrary to existing international law." Addressing the reality that certain instruments are not yet binding on all States, the General Assembly in this resolution "*[a]ppeals* to all States that have yet done so to consider becoming parties to the relevant international conventions."

In its recent Order in the *Request for an Examination of the Situation in Accordance with Paragraph 63 of the Court's Judgement of 20 December 1974 in the* Nuclear Tests (New Zealand v. France) *Case,* the Court stated that its conclusion was "without prejudice to the obligations of States to respect and protect the natural environment" (*Order of 22 September 1995, I.C.J. Reports 1995*, p. 306, para. 64). Although that statement was made in the context of nuclear testing, it naturally also applies to the actual use of nuclear weapons in armed conflict.

33. The Court thus finds that while the existing international law relating to the protection and safeguarding of the environment does not specifically prohibit the use of nuclear weapons, it indicates important environmental factors that are properly to be taken into account in the context of the implementation of the principles and rules of the law applicable in armed conflict.

Notes

1. For discussion of other aspects of the Advisory Opinion see Chapter 2 at pp. 77–87. On environmental aspects, see 7 Y.B. Int'l Env. L. 360 (1996).

2. Environmental issues were raised in a case brought by New Zealand against France relating to nuclear tests conducted by France. 1995 I.C.J. 288. New Zealand requested a reexamination of an earlier judgment but the Court rejected the request. The dissenting judges, Weeranmantry and Palmer (ad hoc judge) discussed several issues based on international environmental law. See Brown Weiss, International Environmental Law and Policy, 288–310 (1998).

3. Wartime conduct detrimental to the environment has been considered by the U.N. Compensation Commission (U.N.C.C.) hearing claims against Iraq growing out of the 1990–1991 invasion of Kuwait. See, e.g., U.N.C.C. Decision 40 Concerning the Well Blowout Control Claim, S/AC.26/Dec.40 (1996) (Dec. 18, 1996).

SECTION 4. PROTECTING THE ATMOSPHERE AND CLIMATE

Scientific reports on the destruction of the ozone layer by chemicals and on climate change due to emissions of greenhouse gases, which cause global warming, have led states to adopt treaty regimes dealing with the protection of the atmosphere and the protection against climate changes. These regimes are an important complement to the general principles of international environmental law. As Professor Schachter underlines: "No-one expects that all these injurious activities can be eliminated by general legal fiat, but there is little doubt that international legal restraints can be an important part of the response." Schachter, International Law in Theory and Practice 365 (1991).

A. OZONE PROTECTION REGIME

The stratospheric ozone protection regime began to form as the threat from ozone depletion to human life and to the environment came to be understood. See Jurgielewicz, Global Environmental Change and International Law: Prospects for Progress in the Legal Order 177–178 (1996); Nanda, International Environmental Law & Policy 210–11 (1995). Scientific reports in the 1970s and 1980s showed that certain chemicals, such as chlorofluorocarbons (CFC) released by human activities into the stratosphere (used for example in refrigerators and air conditioners) deplete the ozone layer, inhibiting its Ultraviolet-radiation-blocking function. For the scientific background see Brown Weiss et al., International Environmental Law and Policy 642–648 (1998). Responding to such findings, states began to take action to address the problem of ozone depletion.

In 1981, the United Nations Environment Programme (UNEP) created the Ad Hoc Working Group of Legal and Technical Experts for the Preparation of a Global Framework Convention for the Protection of the Ozone Layer. The work of the Ad Hoc Working Group led in 1985 to the adoption of the Vienna Convention for the Protection of the Ozone Layer, in force for the United States since Sept. 22, 1988. T.I.A.S. 11097; Treaty Doc. No. 9, 99th Cong., 1st Sess. (1985), reprinted in 26 I.L.M. 1529. The Convention created a framework for international cooperation in research, monitoring and exchange of information with respect to ozone depletion, but did not prescribe any concrete obligation for the member states to curb their production or use of ozone depleting chemicals.

Two years later in 1987, the Montreal Protocol on Substances that Deplete the Ozone Layer imposed quantitative limits on the production and consumption of CFCs and halons. S. Treaty Doc.100–10, reproduced in 26 I.L.M. 1550 (1987). The Protocol entered into force on January 1, 1989. As of 2000, it had 172 parties, among them the United States.

MONTREAL PROTOCOL ON SUBSTANCES THAT DEPLETE THE OZONE LAYER

1522 U.N.T.S. 3, 26 I.L.M. 1550 (1987).

ARTICLE 2

Control Measures

1. Each party shall ensure that for the twelve-month period commencing on the first day of the seventh month following the date of the entry into force of this Protocol, and in each twelve-month period thereafter, its calculated level of consumption of the controlled substances in Group I of Annex A does not exceed its calculated level of consumption in 1986. By the end of the same period, each Party producing one or more of these substances shall ensure that its calculated level of production of the substances does not exceed its calculated level of production in 1986, except that such level may have increased by no more than ten per cent based on the 1986 level. Such increase shall be permitted only so as to satisfy the basic domestic needs of the Parties operating under Article 5 [developing countries] and for the purposes of industrial rationalization between Parties.

* * *

5. Any Party whose calculated level of production in 1986 of the controlled substances in Group I of Annex A was less than twenty-five kilotonnes may, for the purposes of industrial rationalization, transfer to or receive from another Party, production in excess of the limits set out in paragraphs 1, 3 and 4 provided that the total combined calculated levels of production of the Parties concerned does not exceed the production limits set out in this Article. Any transfer of such production shall be notified to the secretariat, no later than the time of the transfer.

* * *

9. (a) Based on the assessments made pursuant to Article 6, the Parties may decide whether:

(i) adjustments to the ozone depleting potentials specified in Annex A should be made and, if so, what adjustments should be; and

(ii) further adjustments and reductions of production or consumption of the controlled substances from 1986 levels should be undertaken and, if so, what the scope, amount and timing of any such adjustments and reductions should be.

* * *

(c) In taking such decisions, the Parties shall make every effort to reach agreement by consensus. If all efforts at consensus have been exhausted, and no agreement reached, such decisions shall, as a last resort, be adopted by a two-thirds majority vote of the Parties present and voting representing at least fifty per cent of the total consumption of the controlled substances of the Parties.

(d) The decisions, which shall be binding on all Parties, shall forthwith be communicated to the Parties by the Depository. Unless otherwise provided in the decisions, they shall enter into force on the expiry of six months from the date of the circulation of the communication by the Depository.

* * *

Article 8

Non-compliance

The Parties, at their first meeting, shall consider and approve procedures and institutional mechanisms for determining non-compliance with the provisions of this Protocol and for treatment of Parties found to be in non-compliance.

Notes

1. The Montreal Protocol, adjusted and amended in London (1990) and in Copenhagen (1992), caps each party's production and consumption of certain ozone depleting chemicals with a view to reduction and eventual elimination of the substances identified as harmful to the stratospheric ozone layer. The Protocol provides for a differential treatment of developing states who, for example, were given a longer period of time to achieve compliance. Moreover, to attract developing countries, the second meeting of Parties at Copenhagen established a Multilat-

eral Fund to provide financial and technical aid to developing States involved in the ozone protection regime.

2. In 1992, at the meeting in Copenhagen, the member states adopted a procedure for noncompliance with provisions of the Protocol. Fourth Meeting Annexes IV and V. The Implementation Committee is charged to examine complaints against member states allegedly in violation of the Protocol. The reports are studied by the Meetings of the Parties which alone have the authority to decide whether measures shall be taken. The possible measures, enumerated under Annex V, are "appropriate assistance", "issuing cautions" and "suspension of rights and privileges including those concerned with industrial rationalization, production, consumption, trade, transfer of technology, financial mechanism, and institutional arrangements." Annex V (A), (B) and (C). Read the text of the Protocol cited above. Besides the procedure for noncompliance, what other provisions support the effectiveness of the Protocol?

For further discussion on the ozone protection regime and its implementation see Brown Weiss et al., International Environmental Law and Policy 641–676 (1998); Benedick, Ozone Diplomacy: New Directions in Safeguarding the Planet (1991); Caron, Protection of the Stratospheric Ozone Layer and the Structure of International Environmental Law Making, 14 Hastings Int'l & Comp.L.Rev. 755 (1991); Jachtenfuchs, The European Community and the Protection of the Ozone Layer, J.Comm. Mkt. Studies 261 (1991); Lawrence, Technology Transfer Funds and the Law–Recent Amendments to the Montreal Protocol on Substances that Deplete the Ozone Layer, 4 J.Env.L. 15 (1992); Shimberg, A Review of Major Provisions: Stratospheric Ozone and Climate Protection: Domestic Legislation and the International Process, 21 Env. L. 2175 (1991); Stewart, Stratospheric Ozone Protection: Changes Over Two Decades of Regulation, 7 Nat.Resources & Env't 24 (1992); Werksman, Compliance and Transition: Russia's Non–Compliance Tests the Ozone Regime, Zeitschrift für ausländisches öffentliches Recht und Völkerrecht, 750 (1996); Note, The Montreal Protocol and Recent Developments to Protect the Ozone Layer, 15 Harv.Env.L.Rev. 275 (1991); Note, Progress Toward a Healthy Sky: An Assessment of the London Amendments to the Montreal Protocol on Substances that Deplete the Ozone Layer, 16 Yale J.Int'l L. (1991).

B. PROTECTION AGAINST CLIMATE CHANGE

Global warming is another environmental phenomenon that is becoming the subject of its own regime. The climate change regime began to take shape in 1992 at the United Nations Conference on Environment and Development in Rio de Janeiro where states adopted the Framework Convention on Climate Change, reprinted at 31 I.L.M. 849 (1992). As of 2000, 180 countries were parties to the Convention. Global warming results from the accumulation of carbon dioxide and other greenhouse gases in the atmosphere. On the scientific and political background see Brown Weiss et al., International Environmental Law and Policy, 677–700 (1998). The Convention was intended as a first step to combat global warming by returning emissions of certain greenhouse gases to their 1990 levels by the year 2000. In a system of "common but differentiated responsibilities", the Convention requires all member states to cooperate in controlling, reducing and preventing particular gases but imposes the obligation to limit their emissions only on industrialized countries (Annex I). The general ideas of the Convention are highlighted in its preamble.

Notes

1. Article 4(2) of the Framework Convention on Climate Change establishes only a reduction "aim" for the industrialized states but does not impose binding emission targets or timetables. As of November 1998, only 4 industrialized states had succeeded in reducing their emissions. At the first conference of the parties to the Convention held in Berlin in 1995, the parties found the commitments made in the Convention inadequate and established in the so-called "Berlin Mandate" a process to strengthen the commitments through a protocol with the goal of imposing emission targets and of elaborating measures to reduce emissions.

2. In Kyoto in 1998, over 160 parties to the United Nations Framework Convention on Climate Change agreed on a Protocol to the Convention, reprinted at 37 I.L.M. 22 (1998), that provides for legally binding emission reduction targets for industrialized countries coupled with innovative mechanisms for transboundary emission reduction cooperation. The overall reduction target for industrialized countries is about 5.2% from their emission levels in 1990 until 2008–2012, but the targets vary among states owing to differences in energy production and consumption profiles. Thus, the concept results in targets ranging from an 8% reduction for the European Union to a 10% increase in the emission levels of Iceland. See Breidenich et al., Current Development: The Kyoto Protocol to the United Nations Framework Convention on Climate Change, 92 A.J.I.L. 315, 320 (1998).

KYOTO PROTOCOL TO THE UNITED NATIONS FRAMEWORK CONVENTION ON CLIMATE CHANGE

37 I.L.M. 22 (1998).

Article 6

1. For the purpose of meeting its commitments under Article 3, any Party included in Annex I may transfer to, or acquire from, any other such Party emission reduction units resulting from projects aimed at reducing anthropogenic emissions by sources or enhancing anthropogenic removals by sinks of greenhouse gases in any sector of the economy, provided that:

(a) Any such project has the approval of the Parties involved;

(b) Any such project provides a reduction in emissions by sources, or an enhancement of removals by sinks, that is additional to any that would otherwise occur;

(c) It does not acquire any emission reduction units if it is not in compliance with its obligations under Articles 5 and 7; and

(d) The acquisition of emission reduction units shall be supplemental to domestic actions for the purposes of meeting commitments under Article 3.

2. The Conference of the Parties serving as the meeting of the Parties to this Protocol may, at its first session or as soon as practicable thereafter, further elaborate guidelines for the implementation of this Article, including for verification and reporting.

* * *

ARTICLE 12

1. A clean development mechanism is hereby defined.

2. The purpose of the clean development mechanism shall be to assist Parties not included in Annex I in achieving sustainable development and in contributing to the ultimate objective of the Convention, and to assist Parties included in Annex I in achieving compliance with their quantified emission limitation and reduction commitments under Article 3.

3. Under the clean development mechanism:

(a) Parties not included in Annex I will benefit from project activities resulting in certified emission reductions; and

(b) Parties included in Annex I may use the certified emission reductions accruing from such project activities to contribute to compliance with part of their quantified emission limitation and reduction commitments under Article 3, as determined by the Conference of the Parties serving as the meeting of the Parties to this Protocol.

4. The clean development mechanism shall be subject to the authority and guidance of the Conference of the Parties serving as the meeting of the Parties to this Protocol and be supervised by an executive board of the clean development mechanism.

5. Emission reductions resulting from each project activity shall be certified by operational entities to be designated by the Conference of the Parties serving as the meeting of the Parties to this Protocol, on the basis of:

(a) Voluntary participation approved by each Party involved;

(b) Real, measurable, and long-term benefits related to the mitigation of climate change; and

(c) Reductions in emissions that are additional to any that would occur in the absence of the certified project activity.

* * *

ARTICLE 17

The Conference of the Parties shall define the relevant principles, modalities, rules and guidelines, in particular for verification, reporting and accountability for emissions trading. The Parties included in Annex B may participate in emissions trading for the purposes of fulfilling their commitments under Article 3 of this Protocol. Any such trading shall be supplemental to domestic actions for the purpose of meeting quantified emission limitation and reduction commitments under that Article.

Notes

1. Article 24 provides that fifty-five ratifications are needed for the Protocol to enter into force. They have to include industrialized states, which accounted in total for at least 55% of the total carbon dioxide emissions for 1990 of the industrialized states. At a conference in Bonn, in November 1999, the parties could not agree to take concrete steps with regard to the implementation of the Protocol, although most countries expressed their wish for the Protocol to take

effect by 2002. The criticism of the Protocol points out that the threat of global warming cannot be averted without engaging developing countries in the process, that is to say, without requiring those countries to meet emission targets as well. The annual emissions of developing countries such as China, India and Brazil, are projected to surpass annual emissions of industrialized countries early in this century. Besides this, states failed to agree on a non-compliance mechanism and on "emission trading". See Ministers Vow to Control Greenhouse Gases, N.Y. Times, Nov. 6, 1999, at A5. What is the reason for not imposing binding targets on developing countries?

2. Article 16*bis* of the Protocol states that "Parties included in Annex B [industrialized countries] may participate in emissions trading for the purposes of fulfilling their commitments under Article 3." Such trading is to be "supplemental to domestic actions." The "principles, modalities, rules and guidelines, in particular for verification, reporting and accountability for emissions trading" are to be defined by the Conference of the Parties. Neither the Fourth Conference of the Parties in late 1998 in Buenos Aires nor the Fifth Conference in Bonn in November 1999 led to such a definition. Emissions trading might allow industrialized countries to buy credits from other (industrialized) countries, willing to reduce greenhouse emissions further than the treaty requires, to achieve their own reduction targets. Besides this, industrialized countries might get credits by assisting other countries to reduce their emissions. At the Conference in Bonn, Kazakhstan, underlining that it had succeeded in reducing its emissions, tried to become an "Annex I country" but was turned down.

3. Many developed countries (including the United States) and economies in transition support emissions trading, since it would allow reductions to take place in a more cost-effective manner. Criticism, especially from the developing countries, points out that trading would enable wealthy countries to buy their way out of their obligations to reduce greenhouse emissions at home. The European Union therefore wants to limit the industrialized states' right to "buy" credits in other countries to 50% of the state's total obligation. What are the advantages and disadvantages of the trading system? Should there be limits to the trading of emissions?

4. In Bonn, the parties agreed to meet in November 2000 in the Netherlands again to discuss the open questions of the climate change regime; but the meeting held in The Hague did not resolve the controversies. For further information on the regime see Breidenich et al., Current Development: The Kyoto Protocol to the United Nations Framework Convention on Climate Change, 92 A.J.I.L. 315 (1998); Brown Weiss et al., International Environmental Law and Policy 677–746 (1998); Harris, Common but Differentiated Responsibility: The Kyoto Protocol and United States Policy, 7 N.Y.U. Env. L.J. 27 (1999); Nanda, The Kyoto Protocol on Climate Change and the Challenges to Its Implementation: A Commentary, 10 Colo. J. Int'l Env. L. & Pol'y 319 (1999); Wiener, Global Environmental Regulation: Instrument Choice in Legal Context, 108 Yale L.J. 677 (1999).

5. Related to climate change is the growing problem of desertification. On international measures to combat desertification, see p. 1552 in Chapter 18 on fresh water resources.

SECTION 5. BIODIVERSITY AND ENDANGERED SPECIES

Traditionally, international environmental law dealt only with the protection of particular endangered species but not with the conservation of the ecosystem. Biodiversity became subject to a regime when the U.N. Conference on Environment and Development at Rio de Janeiro, in 1992, adopted the Convention on Biological Diversity. 31 I.L.M. 818 (1992). Under the Convention, "Biological diversity means the variability among living organisms from all sources including, inter alia, terrestrial, marine and other aquatic ecosystems and the ecological complexes of which they are part; this includes diversity within species, between species and of ecosystems." Article 2.

CONVENTION ON BIOLOGICAL DIVERSITY

31 I.L.M. 818 (1992).

ARTICLE 1: *Objectives*

The objectives of this Convention, to be pursued in accordance with its relevant provisions, are the conservation of biological diversity, the sustainable use of its components and the fair and equitable sharing of the benefits arising out of the utilization of genetic resources, including by appropriate access to genetic resources and by appropriate transfer of relevant technologies, taking into account all rights over those resources and to technologies, and by appropriate funding.

* * *

ARTICLE 3: *Principle*

States have, in accordance with the Charter of the United Nations and the principles of international law, the sovereign right to exploit their own resources pursuant to their own environmental policies, and the responsibility to ensure that activities within their jurisdiction or control do not cause damage to the environment of other States or of areas beyond the limits of national jurisdiction.

Notes

1. The responsibility provision of Article 3 contains a basic principle established earlier in the *Trail Smelter* case. 3 U.N.Rep.Int.Arb.Awards 1911, at 1965 (1941). What is the significance of this provision for the biodiversity regime? Is it codificatory or progressive development? Compare the language of Article 3 of the Convention with that of the *Trail Smelter* decision and that of the Restatement (Third) § 601.

2. The Convention on Biological Diversity establishes a monitoring system for biological diversity and provides for national *in situ* and *ex situ* conservation measures. Each Party is obliged to set up a system of protected areas "where special measures need to be taken to conserve biological diversity." Article 8. For the purpose of complementing these *in situ* measures, each Party must adopt measures for *ex situ* conservation of components of biological diversity outside their natural habitat. Furthermore, the Convention provides for national reports

on implementing measures and their effectiveness, national strategies, plans or programs to protect biodiversity, and environmental impact assessments of projects for adverse effects on biodiversity. In 1992, the United States refused to sign the Convention, especially because Articles 16(3) and 19(2), which require a transfer of technology, would risk the loses of intellectual property protection and might encourage global pirating. One year later, the U.S. accepted an interpretive statement saying that the United States understands that "the Convention requires all Parties to ensure that access or transfer of technology is consistent with the adequate and effective protection of intellectual property rights." See U.S. Treaty Doc. 103–20, Nov. 16, 1993, VI–VII. As of 2000, 176 countries had become parties to the Convention. The United States had not ratified the Convention as of 2000.

3. For further discussion on the biodiversity regime see Brown Weiss et al., International Environmental Law and Policy 927–979 (1998); Hunter, et al., International Environmental Law and Policy 956–1007 (1998); Bodansky, International Law and the Protection of Biological Diversity, 28 Vand. J. Transnatl. L. 623 (1995); IUCN Environmental Law Center, A Guide to the Convention on Biological Diversity (1994); Jacoby et al., Recognizing Property Rights in Traditional Biocultural Contribution, 16 Stan. Env. L.J. 74 (1997); McConnell, The Biodiversity Convention: A Negotiating History (1996); Perlman et al., Biodiversity: Exploring Values and Priorities in Conservation (1997).

CONVENTION ON INTERNATIONAL TRADE IN ENDANGERED SPECIES OF WILD FAUNA AND FLORA

27 U.S.T. 1087, T.I.A.S. No. 8249, 993 U.N.T.S. 243, 12 I.L.M. 1085 (1973).

ARTICLE II: *Fundamental Principles*

1. Appendix I shall include all species threatened with extinction which are or may be affected by trade. Trade in specimens of these species must be subject to particularly strict regulation in order not to endanger further their survival and must only be authorized in exceptional circumstances.

2. Appendix II shall include:

a) all species which although not necessarily now threatened with extinction may become so unless trade in specimens of such species is subject to strict regulation in order to avoid utilization incompatible with their survival; and

b) other species which must be subject to regulation in order that trade in specimens of certain species referred to in sub-paragraph (a) of this paragraph may be brought under effective control.

3. Appendix III shall include all species which any Party identifies as being subject to regulation within its jurisdiction for the purposes of preventing or restricting exploitation, and as needing the cooperation of other parties in the control of trade.

4. The Parties shall not allow trade in specimens of species included in Appendices I, II, III except in accordance with the provisions of the present Convention.

Article III: *Regulation of Trade in Specimens of Species included in Appendix I*

1. All trade in specimens of species included in Appendix I shall be in accordance with the provisions of this Article.

2. The export of any specimen of a species included in Appendix I shall require the prior grant and presentation of an export permit. An export permit shall only be granted when the following conditions have been met:

(a) a Scientific Authority of the State of export has advised that such export will not be detrimental to the survival of that species;

(b) a Management Authority of the State of export is satisfied that the specimen was not obtained in contravention of the laws of that State for the protection of fauna and flora;

(c) a Management Authority of the State of export is satisfied that any living specimen will be so prepared and shipped as to minimize the risk of injury, damage to health or cruel treatment; and

(d) a Management Authority of the State of export is satisfied that an import permit has been granted for the specimen.

* * *

Article VIII: *Measures to be Taken by the Parties*

1. The Parties shall take appropriate measures to enforce the provisions of the present Convention and to prohibit trade in specimens in violation thereof. These shall include measures:

(a) to penalize trade in, or possession of, such specimens, or both; and

(b) to provide for the confiscation or return to the State of export of such specimens.

Notes

1. In 1997, elephants were re-transferred from Appendix I to Appendix II for the purpose of limited trade in ivory between Botswana, Namibia and Zimbabwe and Japan. For a general overview on the Convention and its background see Brown Weiss, et al., International Environmental Law and Policy, 981–983 (1998). See also Glennon, Has International Law Failed the Elephant?, 84 A.J.I.L. 1 (1990).

2. Particular species, such as whales, fur seals, polar bears, dolphins as well as migratory species have been subject to specific agreements. After two International Conventions for the Regulation of Whaling in 1931, 49 Stat. 3079, T.S. 880, and in 1964, 161 U.N.T.S. 2/24, the International Whaling Commission adopted a moratorium on all commercial whaling in 1982, to which Norway objected. On the whaling problem see Martin & Brennan, Enforcing the International Convention for the Regulation of Whaling: The Pelly and Packwood–Magnuson Amendments, 17:2 Den. J. Intl. L. & Poly. 293 (1989); Birnie, Problems Concerning Conservation of Wildlife including Marine Mammals in the North Sea, Intl. J. Estuarine & Coastal L. 252 (1990); Hankins, The United States' Abuse of the Aboriginal Whaling Exception: A Contradiction in United States Policy and a Dangerous Precedent for the Whale, 24 U.C. Davis L. Rev. 489 (1990); D'Amato & Chopra, Whales: Their Emerging Right to Life, 85 A.J.I.L. 21 (1991).

Problems exist also with regard to the protection of fur seals and polar bears. As the 1957 Interim Convention on Conservation of North Pacific Fur Seals, 8

U.S.T. 2283, T.I.A.S. No. 3948, 314 U.N.T.S. 105, was not extended in 1984, the North Pacific fur seals are only subject to national laws such as the Fur Seal Act of 1966, 16 U.S.C. § 1151. Antarctic seals are protected under the 1964 Agreed Measures for the Conservation of Antarctic Fauna and Flora, 17 U.S.T. 991, T.I.A.S. 6058, the 1972 Convention for Conservation of Antarctic Seals, 29 U.S.T. 441, T.I.A.S. 8826, reprinted in 11 I.L.M. 251, and the 1991 Protocol on Environmental Protection to the Antarctic Treaty, 30 I.L.M. 1455, which entered into force on January 14, 1998. Polar bears are included in Appendix II of the Convention on International Trade in Endangered Species (see supra) and are protected, in addition, through the Agreement on the Conservation of Polar Bears, 27 U.S.T. 3018, T.I.A.S. 8409. Dolphins are threatened by "driftnetting", a fishing technology used in the Pacific to catch tuna by means of large nets which cause a high unintended catch of dolphins and other species. For information on the driftnetting controversy see Johnston, The Driftnetting Problem in the Pacific Ocean: Legal Considerations and Diplomatic Options, 21 Ocean Dev. & Int'l L.J. 5 (1990); McDorman, The GATT Consistency of U.S. Fish Import Embargoes to Stop Driftnet Fishing, and Save Whales, Dolphins and Turtles, 24 Geo. Wash. J. Int'l L. & Econ. 477 (1991); Brown Weiss, International Environmental Law and Policy 1026–1031 (1998).

4. A Bonn Convention on the Conservation of Migratory Species of Wild Animals protects animals that migrate between countries or between areas of national jurisdiction and the sea. 19 I.L.M. 15 (1980).

5. Regional agreements dealing with the protection of endangered species complement the already mentioned international agreements. Of particular interest are the American Convention on Nature Protection and Wildlife Preservation in the Western Hemisphere of 1940, T.S. 981, Bevans 630, U.N.T.S. 193; the 1968 African Convention on the Conservation of Nature and Natural Resources, 1001 U.N.T.S. 3 (1968); the 1985 ASEAN Agreement on the Conservation of Nature and Natural Resources, not yet in force; and the European Declaration on the Conservation of Flora, Fauna and Their Habitat of 1988, ECE/ENVWA/20 (1991).

SECTION 6. ENVIRONMENT AND TRADE

Developing countries remain wary that developed countries may be using environmental concerns as a non-tariff barrier. See Chang, An Economic Analysis of Trade Measures to Protect the Global Environment, 83 Geo. L.J. 2121 (1995); Goldman, Resolving the Trade and Environment Debate: In Search of a Neutral Forum and Neutral Principles, 49 Wash. & Lee L.Rev. 1279 (1992); Reinstein, Trade and Environment: The Case for and Against Unilateral Actions, Sustainable Development and International Law (Lang, ed. 1995); Schoenbaum, International Trade and Protection of the Environment: The Continuing Search for Reconciliation, 91 A.J.I.L. 268 (1997); Steinberg, Trade–Environment Negotiations in the EU, NAFTA, and WTO: Regional Trajectories of Rule Development, 91 A.J.I.L. 231 (1997); Esty, Greening the GATT, Trade Environment and the Future, (1993); Wiener, Essay: On the Political Economy of Global Environmental Regulation, 87 Geo. L.J. 749 (1999).

A. TRADE DISPUTES AND PROTECTION OF ENDANGERED SPECIES

Environmental issues have arisen in a number of international trade disputes before the World Trade Organization. In the so-called Tuna/Dolphin dispute, the United States banned the import of tuna caught by Mexican fisherman without proper regard for dolphins. In 1991, this ban was ruled incompatible with the GATT. See Dispute Settlement Panel Report on United Nations Restrictions on Imports of Tuna, 4 World Trade Materials 20 (1992), 30 I.L.M. 1594 (1991). In the Shrimp Turtle case seven years later, a W.T.O. Panel came to the same result with regard to the U.S. import ban of shrimp from India, Malaysia, Pakistan and Thailand. See WT/DS58/R; (98–1710), May 15, 1998. On the appeal by the United States, this decision was partially overturned by the Appellate Body. WT/DS58/AB/R;(98–3899); AB–1998–4. In its decision of October 12, 1998, the Appellate Body made reference to major international environmental conventions, especially to the Convention on Trade in Endangered Species and the Convention on the Conservation of Migratory Species of Wild Animals, and held that the trade restraints imposed by the U.S. regime served a legitimate environmental objective and were not incompatible with the GATT. However, the Appellate Body found that, while the environmentally based trade restraints were not themselves contrary to the GATT, the United States had contravened the GATT by applying those restraints unilaterally in a discriminatory manner. The Appellate Body accepted the amicus curiae briefs of three groups of non-governmental organizations from the U.S. submission (para. 79–91). See pp. 392–394 in Chapter 5. Concluding its decision the Appellate Body underlined (paras. 185–186):

> We wish to underscore what we have not decided in this case. We have not decided that the protection and preservation of the environment is of no significance to Members of the WTO. Clearly it is. We have not decided that the sovereign nations that are Members of the WTO cannot adopt effective measures to protect endangered species, such as sea turtles. Clearly they can and should. And we have not decided that sovereign states should not act together bilaterally, plurilaterally or multilaterally, either within the WTO or in other international fora, to protect endangered species or to otherwise protect the environment. Clearly they should and do.
>
> What we *have* decided in this appeal is simply this: although the measure of the United States in dispute in this appeal serves an environmental objective that is recognized as legitimate under paragraph (g) of Article XX of the GATT 1994, this measure has been applied by the United States in a manner which constitutes arbitrary and unjustifiable discrimination between Members of the WTO, contrary to the requirements of the chapeau of Article XX. For all of the specific reasons outlined in this Report, this measure does not qualify for the exemption that Article XX of the GATT 1994 affords to measures which serve certain recognized, legitimate environmental purposes but which, at the same time, are not applied in a manner that constitutes a means of arbitrary or unjustifiable discrimination between countries where the same conditions prevail or a disguised restriction on international trade. As we emphasized in *United States—Gasoline*, WTO Members are free to adopt their own policies aimed at protecting the environment as long as, in so doing, they fulfill their obligations and respect the rights of other Members under the *WTO Agreement*.

Notes

1. Some environmental groups have accused the W.T.O. of ignoring the environmental impact of its decision that the U.S. import ban on shrimp was incompatible with GATT requirements. In December 1999, at a meeting of the W.T.O. in Seattle, representatives of all member states faced strong protest by environmentalists calling for the W.T.O. to weigh environmental impact more heavily when making trade decisions. "Behind the Hubbub in Seattle," N.Y. Times, Dec. 1, 1999, at p. 14. However, this decision is the first to indicate that the W.T.O. could accept a concern to protect environmental integrity as an adequate justification for the imposition by a state of unilateral restrictions on the trade of a particular good.

2. For further discussion on the shrimp turtle decision see Stewart & Burr, Trade and Domestic Protection of Endangered Species: Peaceful Coexistence or Continued Conflict? The Shrimp–Turtle Dispute and the World Trade Organization, 23 Wm. & Mary Env. L. & Pol'y Rev. 109 (1998); Robinson, Legal Structure and Sustainable Development: Comparative Environmental Law Perspectives on Legal Regimes for Sustainable Development, 3 Wid. L. Symp. J. 247 (1998).

B. INTERNATIONAL MOVEMENTS OF HAZARDOUS WASTE

International movements of hazardous waste are subject to the Basel Convention on the Control of Transboundary Movements of Hazardous Wastes and their Disposal. U.N.Doc. UNEP/IG. 80–3 (1989), 28 I.L.M. 649 (1989). The Basel Convention entered into force May 5, 1992. 1673 U.N.T.S. 57. As of 2000, the Convention had more than 140 parties. The United States, the world's largest hazardous waste generator, is a signatory but has not yet become a party. On the Basel Convention see Hagen & Housman, The Basel Convention, in The Use of Trade Measures in Select Multilateral Environmental Agreements (UNEP 1995); Hunter et al., International Environmental Law and Policy 862–873 (1998). In addition to this international regime, national regulations of transboundary shipment and export of hazardous waste play a significant role. On the U.S. regulation, specifically the U.S. Resource Conservation and Recovery Act, 42 U.S.C. § 6901–6992 (1998), see Belenky, U.S. Hazardous Waste Export Regulations and International Law, 17 Berkeley J.Int'l L. 95, 120–124 (1999).

SECTION 7. GENETICALLY MODIFIED ORGANISMS

Whether biotechnology involving the release of genetically modified organisms (GMOs) threatens the environment has become an issue for governments and international organizations. A Protocol on Biosafety, the first global regime regulating trade in GMOs, was adopted on January 29, 2000 and is to enter into force after ratification by 50 states. As the negotiations began in Cartagena, Colombia, the protocol is referred to as the Cartagena Protocol. The biosafety regime is a protocol to the 1992 Convention on Biological Diversity. Consequently a state that has not become a party to the Convention (for example the United States) cannot become a party to the Protocol. Nevertheless, a state not party to the Protocol will have to comply with its provisions when exporting to states parties to the Protocol.

The Biosafety Protocol allows its member states to bar imports of genetically altered seeds, microbes, animals and crops they regard as a threat to their environment. But the Protocol provides no requirement that shipments of genetically altered products identify the specific variety, a provision proposed by Europeans. The United States and Canada refused to agree to that requirement, claiming it would harm international trade in safe foods. In the last years, European resistance to American food products (about half the soybeans and one third of the corn grown in the U.S. in 1999 contained foreign genes making the crops resistant to herbicides or insects) has caused significant U.S. export losses. See "130 Nations Agree On Safety Rules For Biotech Food," N.Y. Times, Jan. 30, 2000, at 1, 8.

The Protocol requires exporting states to apply for advance permission from the importing country before shipping of a particular living GMO (seeds, living fish for example) meant for release into the environment. Such advance permission is not required for exports of agricultural commodities meant for eating or processing, hence not released into the environment. After a crop has been approved for commercial use in one country, that country is obliged to send information about it to an Internet-based biosafety clearinghouse. Other countries are then free to decide whether or not they are willing to accept the imports. The aim is to ensure that recipient countries have both the opportunity and the capacity to assess risks involving the products of genetic modification. This may be viewed as an application of the precautionary principle allowing a state to take action to protect itself even if there is no scientific certainty that the (barred) import of a GMO would be dangerous. The Protocol does not apply to human pharmaceuticals.

For comments, see Kendall, et al. Bioengineering of Crops: Report of the World Bank Panel on Transgenic Crops (World Bank, 1997); Rissler & Mellon, Perils Amidst the Promise: Ecological Risks of Transgenic Crops in a Global Market (Union of Concerned Scientists, 1993); Baram et al., Symposium: Transgenic Agriculture: Biosafety and International Trade, 4 Boston U.J.Sci. & Tech. L. 4 (1998); Graziano, Biosafety Protocol: Recommendations to Ensure the Safety of the Environment, 7 Colo.J.Int'l L & Pol'y 179 (1996). For an overview see Hunter et al., International Environmental Law and Policy 997–1005 (1998). For the text as well as the status of the Biosafety Protocol see <www.biodiv.org>.

Chapter 18

INTERNATIONAL WATERCOURSES

International watercourses present complex issues since they are not entirely within a state's exclusive control, nor are they considered the common property of all states. Multiple sovereigns have thus claimed the use and allocation of international watercourses. These claims for use originally related to navigation. Recent years however have highlighted other uses, notably for irrigation, power, flood control, industry, waste disposal, and domestic purposes; while claims to be safeguarded from pollution have taken on equal importance. As freshwater is an essential but limited natural resource incapable of substitution, the various uses and needs of states set the stage for competing claims and potential conflicts. Resolving these claims and conflicts involves the normative concepts and principles that are considered in the following materials.

SECTION 1. CONCEPT AND SCOPE

Surface waters and groundwaters flow without respect for political boundaries. Nearly 300 rivers are shared by two or more countries. Water is vital to life, yet freshwater accounts for only 2.5% of the earth's water. Because most of this freshwater is trapped in polar ice caps, glaciers, and deep underground aquifers, less than 1% of all freshwater is actually available for use. Via the hydrologic cycle, the total quantity of water on earth remains relatively unchanged. However, changes in water use, along with population growth, increasing consumption, unequal distribution of water supplies, and continuing pollution, make a finite resource prone to intensified conflicts among states sharing watercourses. See Gleick (ed.), Water in Crisis (1993); Green Cross Int'l, National Sovereignty and International Watercourses (2000).

When water such as a channel, lake bed or aquifer flows only in a state's territory, a state maintains sovereignty and effective control over the water. However, when such waters are shared among two or more states, their rights and obligations are at issue. In the 18th and 19th centuries, these issues related mainly to navigation. The Congress of Vienna, with its Final Act of 1815 in Articles 108 and 109, recognized that riparian states had equal rights of navigation on rivers which "separate" (i.e., contiguous or boundary rivers) or "cross" (i.e., successive rivers) two or more states. 1 Hertslet, The Map of

Europe By Treaty, No. 27 at 269–270 (1875). Although such rights of navigation were usually contained in treaties for particular rivers, the Permanent Court of International Justice referred to "the principles governing international fluvial law in general" and concluded that riparian states shared a "community of interest." This therefore served as "the basis of a common legal right" whose "essential features * * * are the perfect equality of all riparian States in the user [sic] of the whole of the course of the river and the exclusion of any preferential privilege of any one riparian State in relation to the others." Case Concerning the International Commission of the River Oder, P.C.I.J. Ser. A, No. 23, at 26–27 (1929).

As industrial, hydroelectric, agricultural and domestic water uses gained importance, the international law governing the allocation and use of non-navigational watercourses evolved. The scope of the law's application was initially limited to international rivers, but as the physical linkages of a hydrologic system were increasingly recognized, a more comprehensive approach developed to include concepts such as the drainage basin and the watercourse system, including both surface waters and groundwaters, and the various components through which water flows. As noted by Professor Schachter, "the interplay of economic, technological, and normative factors is producing new legal concepts and arrangements that combine ideas of distributive justice and of practical resource management." Schachter, Sharing the World's Resources 65 (1977). Theories dealing with the allocation and use of watercourses such as absolute territorial sovereignty and absolute territorial integrity have given way to the principle of equitable utilization, and to such policies as integrated water resources management and an ecosystem approach. These theories and their implications are further discussed in Section 3, dealing with the 1997 United Nations Convention on the Law of the Non–Navigational Uses of International Watercourses.

SECTION 2. USE AND DIVERSION

LAKE LANOUX CASE

Arbitration between France and Spain.
24 I. L. R. 101, at 127–128, 130, 140 (1961).
Award of Nov. 16, 1957.

[The case arose out of a treaty between France and Spain of 1866 relating to the flow of boundary water which safeguarded the right of Spain to the natural flow of water into the River Carol, an outlet of Lake Lanoux. A French proposal to use the lake waters for hydroelectric generation was objected to by Spain, because it would change the natural flow. Spain claimed that, under the treaty, prior agreement was necessary before the works could proceed. The arbitral tribunal found that the treaty would not be violated by France, since it would provide the previous quantity of water. The tribunal also acknowledged that whenever works are planned on a state's part of a transboundary river, that state must take into consideration other states' interests and genuinely try to reconcile these interests with their own. The parties also argued on the basis of customary law and the tribunal acknowledged that the treaty should be interpreted by taking into account "international common law." The opinion of the tribunal on legal principles in the absence of agreement includes the following passages relating to the duty to negotiate:]

11. In effect, in order to appreciate in its essence the necessity for prior agreement, one must envisage the hypothesis in which the interested States cannot reach agreement. In such case, it must be admitted that the State which is normally competent has lost its right to act alone as a result of the unconditional and arbitrary opposition of another State. This amounts to admitting a "right of assent," a "right of veto," which at the discretion of one State paralyzes the exercise of the territorial jurisdiction of another.

That is why international practice prefers to resort to less extreme solutions by confining itself to obliging the states to seek, by preliminary negotiations, terms for an agreement, without subordinating the exercise of their competence to the conclusion of such an agreement. Thus, one speaks, although often inaccurately, of the "obligation of negotiating an agreement." In reality the engagements thus undertaken by States take very diverse forms and have a scope which varies according to the procedures intended for their execution: but the reality of the obligations thus undertaken is incontestable and sanctions can be applied in the event, for example, of an unjustified breaking off of the discussions, abnormal delays, disregard of the agreed procedures, systematic refusals to take into consideration adverse proposals or interests, and, more generally, in cases of violation of good faith.

* * *

13. * * * International practice reflects the conviction that States ought to strive to conclude such agreements: there would thus appear to be an obligation to accept in good faith all communications and contacts which could, by a broad comparison of interests and good will, provide States with the best conditions for concluding agreements. * * *

But international practice does not so far permit more than the following conclusions: the rule that States may utilize the hydraulic power of international watercourses only on condition of a prior agreement between the interested States cannot be established as a custom, even less as a general principle of law.* * *

* * *

23. * * * As a matter of form, the upstream State has, procedurally, a right of initiative; it is not obliged to associate the downstream State in the elaboration of its schemes. If, in the course of discussions, the downstream State submits schemes to it, the upstream State must examine them, but it has the right to give preference to the solution contained in its own scheme provided it takes into consideration in a reasonable manner the interests of a downstream State.

CASE CONCERNING THE GABCIKOVO–NAGYMAROS PROJECT (HUNGARY v. SLOVAKIA)

1997 I.C.J. 7.
reprinted in 37 I.L.M. 162 (1998).

[Under a 1977 treaty between Hungary and Czechoslovakia (Slovakia became an independent state in 1993), a system of dams and other works were to be constructed on approximately 200 kilometers of the Danube River forming, for the most part, the border between Hungary and Slovakia. The main objectives of the treaty included hydroelectric production, flood protection and improved navigation. In 1989, Hungary stopped working on the project, citing economic and environmental reasons. After negotiations between the two countries failed to resolve the matter, Czechoslovakia considered possible alternatives and decided upon "Variant C." Hungary unilaterally terminated the treaty in May 1992, claiming that Variant C would adversely affect Hungary's access to the Danube's waters. By October 1992, Czechoslovakia began work on "Variant C," thus damming the Danube River within its territory. The following excerpts pertain to the allocation, use and diversion of an international watercourse.]

78. Moreover, in practice, the operation of Variant C led Czechoslovakia to appropriate, essentially for its use and benefit, between 80 and 90 per cent of the waters of the Danube before returning them to the main bed of the river, despite the fact that the Danube is not only a shared international watercourse but also an international boundary river.

Czechoslovakia submitted that Variant C was essentially no more than what Hungary had already agreed to and that the only modifications made were those which had become necessary by virtue of Hungary's decision not to implement its treaty obligations. It is true that Hungary, in concluding the 1977 Treaty, had agreed to the damming of the Danube and the diversion of its waters into the bypass canal. But it was only in the context of a joint operation and a sharing of its benefits that Hungary had given its consent. The suspension and withdrawal of that consent constituted a violation of Hungary's legal obligations, demonstrating, as it did, the refusal by Hungary of joint operation; but that cannot mean that Hungary forfeited its basic right to an equitable and reasonable sharing of the resources of an international watercourse.

The Court accordingly concludes that Czechoslovakia, in putting Variant C into operation, was not applying the 1977 Treaty but, on the contrary, violated certain of its express provisions, and, in so doing, committed an internationally wrongful act.

* * *

85. * * *

In 1929, the Permanent Court of International Justice, with regard to navigation on the River Oder, stated as follows:

> "[the] community of interest in a navigable river becomes the basis of a common legal right, the essential features of which are the perfect equality of all riparian States in the user of the whole course of the river and the exclusion of any preferential privilege of any one riparian State in relation to the others" (Territorial Jurisdiction of the International Commission of the River Oder, Judgment No. 16, 1929, P.C.I.J., Series A, No. 23, p. 27).

Modern development of international law has strengthened this principle for non-navigational uses of international watercourses as well, as evidenced by the adoption of the Convention of 21 May 1997 on the Law of the Non–

Navigational Uses of International Watercourses by the United Nations General Assembly.

The Court considers that Czechoslovakia, by unilaterally assuming control of a shared resource, and thereby depriving Hungary of its right to an equitable and reasonable share of the natural resources of the Danube—with the continuing effects of the diversion of these waters on the ecology of the riparian area of the Szigetköz—failed to respect the proportionality which is required by international law.

86. Moreover, as the Court has already pointed out (see paragraph 78), the fact that Hungary had agreed in the context of the original Project to the diversion of the Danube (and, in the Joint Contractual Plan, to a provisional measure of withdrawal of water from the Danube) cannot be understood as having authorized Czechoslovakia to proceed with a unilateral diversion of this magnitude without Hungary's consent.

* * *

147. Re-establishment of the joint régime will also reflect in an optimal way the concept of common utilization of shared water resources for the achievement of the several objectives mentioned in the Treaty, in concordance with Article 5, paragraph 2, of the Convention on the Law of the Non–Navigational Uses of International Watercourses, according to which:

> "Watercourse States shall participate in the use, development and protection of an international watercourse in an equitable and reasonable manner. Such participation includes both the right to utilize the watercourse and the duty to cooperate in the protection and development thereof, as provided in the present Convention." (General Assembly Doc. A/51/869 of 11 April 1997.)

* * *

150. Reparation must, "as far as possible", wipe out all the consequences of the illegal act. In this case, the consequences of the wrongful acts of both Parties will be wiped out "as far as possible" if they resume their co-operation in the utilization of the shared water resources of the Danube, and if the multi-purpose programme, in the form of a co-ordinated single unit, for the use, development and protection of the watercourse is implemented in an equitable and reasonable manner. What it is possible for the Parties to do is to re-establish co-operative administration of what remains of the Project. * * *

Note

For other aspects of this case, see pp. 557–559, 709–711 above.

SECTION 3. UNITED NATIONS CONVENTION ON THE LAW OF THE NON–NAVIGATIONAL USES OF INTERNATIONAL WATERCOURSES

The 1997 U.N. Watercourses Convention, G.A. Res. 51/229, U.N. GAOR, 51st Sess., 99th plen. mtg., May 21, 1997, Annex, U.N. Doc. A/RES/51/229

(1997), reprinted in 36 I.L.M. 700 (1997), was based on the International Law Commission's draft articles on the Law of the Non-Navigational Uses of International Watercourses, initiated in the 1970s and transmitted to the U.N. General Assembly for consideration in 1994. See G.A. Res. 2669 (XXV), U.N. G.A.O.R., 25th Sess., Supp. No. 28, at 127, U.N. Doc. A/8028 (1970); Report of the International Law Commission on the work of its forty-sixth session, U.N. GAOR, 49th Sess., Supp. No. 10, at 197–326, U.N. Doc. A/49/10 (1994) [hereinafter I.L.C. Report 1994]. In order to address the diversity characterizing individual watercourses and the human needs they serve, the International Law Commission developed a framework convention intended to establish general principles and rules for the use and management of international watercourses. This approach provides a legal blueprint and encourages states to enter into specific agreements regarding the watercourses they share. Consequently, the principles contained in the framework convention may be adjusted to tailor an agreement suitable for a specific watercourse and its watercourse states. As of 2000, the Convention on the Law of the Non-Navigational Uses of International Watercourses had 16 signatories and 8 ratifications, and had yet to enter into force. Its key elements concerning equitable utilization, no harm, and prior notification, however, are to a large extent codification of existing norms. Furthermore, the Convention's other provisions, functioning *de lege ferenda*, may be instrumental in generating new norms.

For the Working Group negotiations of the U.N. Convention on the Law of the Non-Navigational Uses of International Watercourses, see U.N. G.A.O.R., 51st Sess., Summary Records of the Sixth Committee, U.N. Docs. A/C.6/51/SR.12–SR.25 and A/C.6/51/SR.51–SR.62 (1996–1997). The Convention was adopted by the General Assembly with a vote of 103 in favor, 3 against (Burundi, China and Turkey), and 27 abstentions. Subsequently, Belgium (which had earlier abstained), Nigeria and Fiji informed the U.N. Secretariat that they had intended to vote in favour. For the voting record and explanations of vote, see U.N. G.A.O.R., 51st Sess., 99th plen. mtg., Verbatim Record, U.N. Doc. A/51/PV.99 (1997).

See generally McCaffrey & Sinjela, Current Developments: The 1997 United Nations Convention on International Watercourses, 91 A.J.I.L. 97 (1998); Brown Weiss et al., International Environmental Law and Policy, 861–909 (1998); Tanzi, The Completion of the Preparatory Work for the U.N. Convention on the Law of International Watercourses, 21 Nat. Res. F., 239–245 (1997); International Water Law: Selected Writings of Professor Charles B. Bourne (Wouters ed., 1997); Idris & Sinjela, The Law of the Non-Navigational Uses of International Watercourses, 3 Afr. Y.B. Int'l L. 183–203 (1995); Malgosia Fitzmaurice–Lachs, The Law of Non-Navigational Uses of International Watercourses—The International Law Commission Completes its Draft, 8 Leiden J. Int'l L 361–375 (1995); Caflisch, The Law of International Waterways and Its Sources, in Essays in Honour of Wang Tieya, 115 (R.St.J. Macdonald, ed. 1993). See also Godana, Africa's Shared Water Resources: Legal and Institutional Aspects of the Nile, Niger and Senegal River Systems (1985); The Law of International Drainage Basins (Garretson, Hayton & Olmstead eds. 1967); Berber, Rivers in International Law (1959).

ARTICLE 1

Scope of the present Convention

1. The present Convention applies to uses of international watercourses and of their waters for purposes other than navigation and to measures of protection, preservation and management related to the uses of those watercourses and their waters.

2. The uses of international watercourses for navigation is not within the scope of the present Convention except insofar as other uses affect navigation or are affected by navigation.

ARTICLE 2

Use of terms

For the purposes of the present Convention:

(a) "Watercourse" means a system of surface waters and groundwaters constituting by virtue of their physical relationship a unitary whole and normally flowing into a common terminus;

(b) "International watercourse" means a watercourse, parts of which are situated in different States;

(c) "Watercourse State" means a State Party to the present Convention in whose territory part of an international watercourse is situated, or a Party that is a regional economic integration organization, in the territory of one or more of whose Member States part of an international watercourse is situated;

(d) "Regional economic integration organization" means an organization constituted by sovereign States of a given region, to which its member States have transferred competence in respect of matters governed by the present Convention and which has been duly authorized in accordance with its internal procedures, to sign, ratify, accept, approve or accede to it.

Notes

1. Article 2(a) defines the hydrological and geographical scope of 1997 Watercourses Convention. In the 1966 Helsinki Rules on the Uses of the Waters of International Rivers prepared by the International Law Association (a non-governmental body), a drainage basin approach was followed: "An international drainage basin is a geographical area extending over two or more States determined by the watershed limits of the system of waters, including surface and underground waters, flowing into a common terminus." International Law Association [I.L.A.], Report of the Fifty–Second Conference, Art. 2 at 485 (1966). Professor Schachter noted that "[t]he use of the drainage basin as a territorial unit for sharing does more than delimit a geographical area; it brings within the scope of shareability the whole system of surface and underground hydrological linkages which affect the availability and quantity of water." Schachter, Sharing the World's Resources 65 (1977).

Some scholars have suggested that the term "watercourse" represents a regression in international law from the drainage basin approach. See, e.g., Caron, The Frog That Wouldn't Leap: The International Law Commission and Its Work on International Watercourses, 3 Colo. J. Int'l Env. L. & Pol'y. 269 (1992).

However, "watercourse" in Article 2(a) of the 1997 Watercourses Convention is not used in a restrictive sense, but instead refers "to the hydrologic system composed of a number of different components through which water flows * * * [including] rivers, lakes, aquifers, glaciers, reservoirs and canals. So long as these components are interrelated with one another, they form part of the watercourse. * * * Thus, water may move from a stream into the ground under the stream bed, spreading beyond the banks of the stream, then re-emerge in the stream, flow into a lake which empties into a river, be diverted into a canal and carried to a reservoir, etc. Because the surface and groundwaters form a system, and constitute by virtue of their physical relationship a unitary whole, human intervention at one point in the system may have effects elsewhere within it." I.L.C. Report 1994 at 200–201; see also McCaffrey & Sinjela, Current Developments: The 1997 United Nations Convention on International Watercourses, 91 A.J.I.L. 97 (1998). What significance, if any, in the watercourse definition does the modifier "normally" have with regard to the phrase "flowing into a common terminus"? Do the Danube and the Rhine Rivers form a watercourse because at certain times of the year, water flows from the Danube River as groundwater into the Rhine River via Lake Constance?

2. Article 2(c) defines a "watercourse state" relying on the geographical criterion "part of an international watercourse." This definition is more in line with hydrologic reality since the traditional term "riparian" only refers a state's territory which "touches a river flowing on the surface," while the term "watercourse state" takes into account instances where state X's groundwaters contribute substantially to a river's surface waters in states Y and Z, yet they never reach the surface of state X. See also 1966 Helsinki Rules, commentary to Article 3. In this scenario, which states are riparian and/or watercourse states?

3. Emerging trends indicate an integrated use and management of all water resources, including confined groundwaters. For instance, the consolidated I.L.A. Rules on International Water Resources now includes in Article 2(2): "The water of an aquifer that is intersected by the boundary between two or more States is international groundwater and such an aquifer with its water forms an international basin or part thereof. Those States are basin States whether or not the aquifer and its water form with surface waters part of a hydraulic system flowing into a common terminus." I.L.A., Report of the Committee on Water Resources Law, London, at 4 (2000).

Would confined groundwaters be within the purview of the 1997 Watercourses Convention? In regions such as the Middle East, these waters are significant water resources. See Israeli–Palestinian Declaration of Principle on Interim Self–Government Arrangements, Sept. 13, 1993, Annex III, para. 1, 32 I.L.M. 1525; Interim Agreement on the West Bank and the Gaza Strip, Sept. 28, 1995 (Annex III, art. 40), 36 I.L.M. 551; Ximena Fuentes, The Utilization of International Groundwater in General International Law, in The Reality of International Law: Essays in Honour of Ian Brownlie 177–198 (Goodwin–Gill & Talmon, eds., 1999) and K. P. Scanlan, The International Law Commission's First Ten Articles on the Law of Non–Navigational Uses of International Watercourses: Do They Adequately Address All the Major Issues of Water Usage in the Middle East?, 19 Fordham Int'l L. J. 2224 (1996).

ARTICLE 3

Watercourse agreements

1. In the absence of an agreement to the contrary, nothing in the present Convention shall affect the rights or obligations of a watercourse

State arising from agreements in force for it on the date on which it became a party to the present Convention.

2. Notwithstanding the provisions of paragraph 1, parties to agreements referred to in paragraph 1 may, where necessary, consider harmonizing such agreements with the basic principles of the present Convention.

3. Watercourse States may enter into one or more agreements, hereinafter referred to as "watercourse agreements", which apply and adjust the provisions of the present Convention to the characteristics and uses of a particular international watercourse or part thereof.

4. Where a watercourse agreement is concluded between two or more watercourse States, it shall define the waters to which it applies. Such an agreement may be entered into with respect to an entire international watercourse or any part thereof or a particular project, programme or use except insofar as the agreement adversely affects, to a significant extent, the use by one or more other watercourse States of the waters of the watercourse, without their express consent.

5. Where a watercourse State considers that adjustment and application of the provisions of the present Convention is required because of the characteristics and uses of a particular international watercourse, watercourse States shall consult with a view to negotiating in good faith for the purpose of concluding a watercourse agreement or agreements.

6. Where some but not all watercourse States to a particular international watercourse are parties to an agreement, nothing in such agreement shall affect the rights or obligations under the present Convention of watercourse States that are not parties to such an agreement.

Note

Over 3,600 treaties dealing with water use since 805 A.D. have been identified by the United Nations. For a survey of recent state practice, see Food and Agriculture Organization (F.A.O.) of the U.N., Treaties Concerning the Non–Navigational Uses of International Watercourses, Africa, F.A.O. Legislative Study No. 61 (1997); F.A.O., Treaties Concerning the Non–Navigational Uses of International Watercourses—Asia, F.A.O. Legislative Study No. 55 (1995); F.A.O., Treaties Concerning the Non–Navigational Uses of International Watercourses—Europe, F.A.O. Legislative Study No. 50 (Stefano Burchi ed., 1993); U.N. Dep't of Technical Cooperation for Dev., Treaties Concerning the Utilization of International Water Courses for Other Purposes than Navigation—Africa, U.N. Sales No. E/F.84.I.I.A.7 (1984); F.A.O., Systematic Index of International Water Resources Treaties, Declarations, Acts and Cases by Basin, Legislative Study No. 15 (1978); Legislative Texts and Treaty Provisions concerning the Utilization of International Rivers for other Purposes than Navigation, U.N. Doc. ST/LEG/Ser.B/12, U.N. Sales No. 63.V.4 (1963).

Article 4

Parties to watercourse agreements

1. Every watercourse State is entitled to participate in the negotiation of and to become a party to any watercourse agreement that applies to the entire

international watercourse, as well as to participate in any relevant consultations.

2. A watercourse State whose use of an international watercourse may be affected to a significant extent by the implementation of a proposed watercourse agreement that applies only to a part of the watercourse or to a particular project, programme or use is entitled to participate in consultations on such an agreement and, where appropriate, in the negotiation thereof in good faith with a view to becoming a party thereto, to the extent that its use is thereby affected.

Article 5

Equitable and reasonable utilization and participation

1. Watercourse States shall in their respective territories utilize an international watercourse in an equitable and reasonable manner. In particular, an international watercourse shall be used and developed by watercourse States with a view to attaining optimal and sustainable utilization thereof and benefits therefrom, taking into account the interests of the watercourse States concerned, consistent with adequate protection of the watercourse.

2. Watercourse States shall participate in the use, development and protection of an international watercourse in an equitable and reasonable manner. Such participation includes both the right to utilize the watercourse and the duty to cooperate in the protection and development thereof, as provided in the present Convention.

Notes

1. If the Lake Lanoux case were decided today under the 1997 Watercourses Convention, would the outcome be the same?

2. According to a theory of absolute territorial sovereignty (the so-called Harmon Doctrine), a state possessed an unlimited right to use the water in its territory irrespective of the effects on others, but had no right to demand the water's continued flow from other states. However, it has also been argued that a state has the right to the continuation of the water's full natural flow from an upstream state. The I.L.C.'s, as well as the I.L.A.'s, studies on watercourses indicate that these two theories have been largely repudiated. For discussion of the Harmon Doctrine, see McCaffrey, The Harmon Doctrine One Hundred Years Later: Buried, Not Praised, 36 Nat. Resources J. 725 (1996)).

Article 5 expresses the well-established principle of equitable utilization. Equitable utilization employs "the concept of equitable shares in the uses of waters, thus leaving behind the vexatious and unproductive concern over 'ownership' of the perpetually transient waters." [1982] 2 Y.B. I.L.C., at 76, para. 50, U.N. Doc. A/C.N.4/SER.A/1982/Add.1 (Part 1). As noted by the International Law Commission, "the scope of a State's rights of equitable utilization depends on the facts and circumstances of each individual case, and specifically on a weighing of all relevant factors," including those provided in Article 6 (I.L.C Report 1994, at 221). See also Helsinki Rules on the Uses of the Waters of International Rivers, I.L.A., Report of the Fifty–Second Conference, at 477 (1966). States negotiating the 1997 Watercourses Convention added to Article 5(1) the words "and sustainable" and "taking into account the interests of the watercourse States concerned;" what effects do these additions have on the Article? How does this Article interplay with the provisions on protection, preservation and management, particularly Articles 20—23?

For a survey of evidence supporting the doctrine of equitable utilization as a general rule of law, see [1982] 2 Y.B.I.L.C., at 75–82, paras. 43–72, U.N. Doc. A/CN.4/SER.A/1982/Add.1(Part 1); and [1986] 2 Y.B.I.L.C. at 103–130, paras. 75–168, U.N. Doc. A/CN.4/SER.A/1986/Add.1 (Part 1). See also Bourne, The Primacy of the Principle of Equitable Utilization in the 1997 Watercourses Convention, 35 Can. Y.B. Int'l L. 215–232 (1997); Ximena Fuentes, The Criteria for the Equitable Utilization of International Rivers, 67 Brit. Y.B. Int'l L., 337–412 (1996).

3. Article 5(2) calls for equitable participation which recognizes that "cooperative action by watercourse States is necessary to produce maximum benefits for each of them, while helping to maintain an equitable allocation of uses and affording adequate protection to the watercourse States and the international watercourse itself." I.L.C. Report 1994, at 220. In the Case Concerning the Gabcikovo–Nagymaros Project, p. 1540 above, the International Court of Justice discusses the right to an equitable and reasonable share of the resources of an international watercourse, and quotes Article 5(2) of the 1997 Watercourses Convention. How does this concept of equitable participation affect a state's unilateral action regarding an international watercourse?

Article 6

Factors relevant to equitable and reasonable utilization

1. Utilization of an international watercourse in an equitable and reasonable manner within the meaning of article 5 requires taking into account all relevant factors and circumstances, including:

(a) Geographic, hydrographic, hydrological, climatic, ecological and other factors of a natural character;

(b) The social and economic needs of the watercourse States concerned;

(c) The population dependent on the watercourse in each watercourse State;

(d) The effects of the use or uses of the watercourses in one watercourse State on other watercourse States;

(e) Existing and potential uses of the watercourse;

(f) Conservation, protection, development and economy of use of the water resources of the watercourse and the costs of measures taken to that effect;

(g) The availability of alternatives, of comparable value, to a particular planned or existing use.

2. In the application of article 5 or paragraph 1 of this article, watercourse States concerned shall, when the need arises, enter into consultations in a spirit of cooperation.

3. The weight to be given to each factor is to be determined by its importance in comparison with that of other relevant factors. In determining what is a reasonable and equitable use, all relevant factors are to be considered together and a conclusion reached on the basis of the whole.

ARTICLE 7

Obligation not to cause significant harm

1. Watercourse States shall, in utilizing an international watercourse in their territories, take all appropriate measures to prevent the causing of significant harm to other watercourse States.

2. Where significant harm nevertheless is caused to another watercourse State, the States whose use causes such harm shall, in the absence of agreement to such use, take all appropriate measures, having due regard for the provisions of articles 5 and 6, in consultation with the affected State, to eliminate or mitigate such harm and, where appropriate, to discuss the question of compensation.

Notes

1. The obligation not to cause significant harm contained in Article 7 was a major source of controversy during the negotiations of 1997 Watercourses Convention. The International Law Commission (I.L.C. Report 1994, at 236) had envisioned in Article 7 "a process aimed at avoiding significant harm as far as possible while reaching an equitable result in each concrete case," yet upstream and downstream states differed on its applications. The equitable utilization rule of Article 5 was seen by upstream states as granting more flexibility in making new uses of their watercourses; while the no harm rule of Article 7 was favored by downstream states because it would afford these states greater protection of their established uses.

A United Nations report concerning the 1997 Watercourse Convention contained the following statement of understanding as regards Article 7(2): "In the event such steps as are required by article 7(2) do not eliminate the harm, such steps as are required by article 7(2) shall then be taken to mitigate the harm." Report of the Sixth Committee convening as the Working Group of the Whole, at 5, U.N. Doc. A/51/869 (1997). What is the significance of the word "nevertheless" in Article 7(2)? Does Article 7(2) set an additional obligation of due diligence besides the implicit requirement of due diligence contained in Article 7(1)?

2. One commentator has noted that "[b]y refraining from assigning property rights to existing allocations, this formula [contained in Article 7] emphasizes the necessity of negotiation, and thus increases the likelihood of equitable, optimal and environmentally sound outcomes." See Benvenisti, Collective Action in the Utilization of Shared Freshwater: The Challenges of International Water Resources Law, 90 A.J.I.L. 384, 404 (1996). However, in view of the broad scope of factors to be considered in Article 6, do they provide sufficient guidance for practical solutions? Article 6 allows for the consideration of additional factors; what other factors should be included?

Since water rights are mainly local in their effects, should negotiating states include participation by local representatives? Would this better ensure that a watercourse agreement under Article 3(4) does not "adversely affect[]" another watercourse state's use?

3. If state X's agricultural use conflicts with state B's hydroelectric use, how would the conflict be resolved taking into account the articles of the 1997 Watercourses Convention? Would the no harm rule of Article 7 override equitable utilization, as found in Articles 5 and 6? Does it matter whether state X is an

upstream or downstream state? What if state X and state B share a contiguous river?

ARTICLE 8

General obligation to cooperate

1. Watercourse States shall cooperate on the basis of sovereign equality, territorial integrity, mutual benefit and good faith in order to attain optimal utilization and adequate protection of an international watercourse.

2. In determining the manner of such cooperation, watercourse States may consider the establishment of joint mechanisms or commissions, as deemed necessary by them, to facilitate cooperation on relevant measures and procedures in the light of experience gained through cooperation in existing joint mechanisms and commissions in various regions.

ARTICLE 9

Regular exchange of data and information

1. Pursuant to article 8, watercourse States shall on a regular basis exchange readily available data and information on the condition of the watercourse, in particular that of a hydrological, meteorological, hydrogeological and ecological nature and related to the water quality as well as related forecasts.

2. If a watercourse State is requested by another watercourse State to provide data or information that is not readily available, it shall employ its best efforts to comply with the request but may condition its compliance upon payment by the requesting State of the reasonable costs of collecting and, where appropriate, processing such data or information.

3. Watercourse States shall employ their best efforts to collect and, where appropriate, to process data and information in a manner which facilitates its utilization by the other watercourse States to which it is communicated.

Notes

1. Under Articles 8 and 9, cooperation leading to the regular exchange of data and information ensures that a watercourse state has the necessary facts to enable its compliance with the obligations under Articles 5, 6 and 7 vis-à-vis other watercourse states. In regions where states are politically at odds or security factors exist, how viable is such cooperation? Would the establishment of joint mechanisms or commissions mentioned in Article 8(2) be feasible in such situations? In circumstances such as armed conflict or the absence of diplomatic relations, Article 30 acts as a general saving clause and provides for cooperation through any acceptable "indirect procedures" I.L.C. Report 1994 at 251, 317–318. India and Pakistan, despite three full-scale wars and numerous conflicts between them, have not interfered in the operations of a joint Indian–Pakistani water management administration. See Dellapenna, Treaties as Instruments for Managing Internationally Shared Water Resources: Restricted Sovereignty vs. Community of Property, 26 Case W. Res. J. Int'l L. 30–31 (1994).

There exist, however, varying capabilities between and among states for monitoring and collecting data on a watercourse's condition. Satellite technology gives states the ability to construct an accurate picture of other states' water flows, regardless of information exchange. How will this technological capability transform relations and cooperation among states?

2. A valuable resource is the Transboundary Freshwater Dispute Database (T.F.D.D., <http://terra.geo.orst.edu/users/tfdd/>), a digitized delineation of the world's international river basins. T.F.D.D. uses a definition of "river basin" similar to the 1997 Watercourses Convention's definition of "watercourses." See Wolf, et. al., International River Basins of the World, 15 Int'l J. Water Resources Dev. at n. 5 (1999). The T.F.D.D. contains a searchable database of summaries and full text of more than 150 water-related treaties, from 1874 to the present, as well fourteen case-studies of international water conflict resolution, news files concerning acute water-related disputes, and descriptions of indigenous methods of water conflict resolution.

3. Jordan, the Palestinian Authority and Israel, in 1996, finalized the first regional water agreement in the Middle East. How were highly politicized water issues turned into concrete technical and academic components that served as the basis of negotiations? See Trolldalen, Troubled Waters in the Middle East: The Process Towards the First Regional Water Declaration between Jordan, Palestinian Authority, and Israel, 21 Natural Resources F. 101 (1997) and Gamal Abouali, Natural Resources under Occupation: The Status of Palestinian Water Under International Law, 10 Pace Int'l L. Rev. 411 (1998).

4. A recent project, which uses the 1997 Watercourses Convention as a basis, is the Nile River Basin Cooperative Framework Project. United Nations Development Programme, Project Documents, U.N Docs. RAB/96/008, RAF/96/024, and GLO/98/115 (1997–1998). The Nile River watercourse, including the White and Blue Niles, is shared by ten states—Burundi, Congo, Egypt, Eritrea, Ethiopia, Kenya, Rwanda, Sudan, Tanzania and Uganda—half of which rank among the world's ten poorest countries. This project aims to develop a legal and institutional framework for cooperation among the riparian basin states. An acceptable framework for cooperation may then pave the way for equitable and legitimate uses of the Nile River Basin's water resources. The first draft of the Cooperative Framework produced during October 1999 in Uganda presents options which closely follow the language of the 1997 Watercourses Convention's general principles, rights and obligations. See also Carroll, Note, Past and Future Legal Framework of the Nile River Basin, 12 Geo. Int'l Env. L. Rev. 269 (1999).

5. For further reading about other international watercourses, see Cunningham, Comment, Do Brothers Divide Shares Forever? Obstacles to the Effective Use of International Law in Euphrates River Basin Water Issues, 21 U. Pa. J. Int'l Econ. L. 131 (2000); Salman & Uprety, Hydro–Politics in South Asia: A Comparative Analysis of the Mahakali and the Ganges Treaties, 39 Nat. Res. J. 295 (1999); Hyman, Under the Danube Canopy: the Future of International Waterway Law, 23 Wm. & Mary Env. L. & Pol'y. Rev. 355 (1998); Lopez, Note, Border Tensions and the Need for Water: an Application of Equitable Principles to Determine Allocation from the Rio Grande to the United States and Mexico, 9 Geo. Int'l Env. L. Rev. 489 (1997).

Article 10

Relationship between different kinds of uses

1. In the absence of agreement or custom to the contrary, no use of an international watercourse enjoys inherent priority over other uses.

2. In the event of a conflict between uses of an international watercourse, it shall be resolved with reference to articles 5 to 7, with special regard being given to the requirements of vital human needs.

Notes

1. The report concerning the 1997 Watercourse Convention contained the following statement of understanding as regards Article 10: "In determining 'vital human needs', special attention is to be paid to providing sufficient water to sustain human life, including both drinking water and water required for production of food in order to prevent starvation." Report of the Sixth Committee convening as the Working Group of the Whole, at 5, U.N. Doc. A/51/869 (1997).

Professor Knauth made the following comment more than forty years ago: "In the present state of national rivalries and political jealousies, it is not to be hoped that there could be a sort of declaration of a Human Right to the present benefit of water." Report of the Forty-eighth Conference of the International Law Association, New York, 1958, at 96 (1959). Read the Universal Declaration of Human Rights, particularly Article 25, and the Convention on the Rights of the Child, particularly Article 24(2)(c). Is a human right to water implied by the right to life? If so, what are the implications of such a right? See McCaffrey, A Human Right to Water: Domestic and International Implications, 5 Geo. Int'l Env. L. R. 1 (1992).

See the U.N. Convention to Combat Desertification in those Countries Experiencing Serious Drought and/or Desertification, (1954 U.N.T.S. 3, Oct. 14, 1994), which has 167 parties as of 2000, and the Protocol on Water and Health to the 1992 Convention on the Protection and Use of Transboundary Watercourses and International Lakes (June 17, 1999, U.N. ECOSOC Doc. MP.WAT–AC.1–1999).

2. The Constitution of the Republic of South Africa (Act 108 of 1996) in its Bill of Rights includes: "Everyone has the right to have access to sufficient food and water." (Section 27(1)(b).) This right to water is further elaborated in the new South African Water Law which recognizes the National Government as public trustee of the nation's water resources, so that it "must ensure that water is protected, used, developed, conserved, managed and controlled in a sustainable manner, for the benefit of all persons and in accordance with its constitutional mandate." See Republic of South Africa, National Water Bill, ch.1, sec. 3(1). Since the South African Bill of Rights is enforceable and justiciable, any person may approach a court to enforce a right contained therein, either on his or her own behalf, or on the behalf of another person or body, or in the public interest. See Bill of Rights, sec. 38. In a brief for a test case on the right to water before the South African Courts, what would your legal arguments entail?

3. Would recognition of a "human right" to water bear on the allocation of water for industrial and agricultural use?

Article 11

Information concerning planned measures

Watercourse States shall exchange information and consult each other and, if necessary, negotiate on the possible effects of planned measures on the condition of an international watercourse.

ARTICLE 12

Notification concerning planned measures with possible adverse effects

Before a watercourse State implements or permits the implementation of planned measures which may have a significant adverse effect upon other watercourse States, it shall provide those States with timely notification thereof. Such notification shall be accompanied by available technical data and information, including the results of any environmental impact assessment, in order to enable the notified States to evaluate the possible effects of the planned measures.

Notes

Articles 11–19 concern "Planned Measures." These articles, in contrast to Article 9, deal with the provision of information on an ad hoc basis. The procedures contained in Articles 12–19 "are triggered by the criterion that measures planned by a watercourse State may have 'a significant adverse effect' upon other watercourse States." I.L.C. Report 1994, at 260. How is this threshold different from Article 7's "significant harm" standard? What is the purpose of having two different thresholds?

ARTICLE 20

Protection and preservation of ecosystems

Watercourse States shall, individually and, where appropriate, jointly, protect and preserve the ecosystems of international watercourses.

ARTICLE 21

Prevention, reduction and control of pollution

1. For the purpose of this article, "pollution of an international watercourse" means any detrimental alteration in the composition or quality of the waters of an international watercourse which results directly or indirectly from human conduct.

2. Watercourse States shall, individually and, where appropriate, jointly, prevent, reduce and control the pollution of an international watercourse that may cause significant harm to other watercourse States or to their environment, including harm to human health or safety, to the use of the waters for any beneficial purpose or to the living resources of the watercourse. Watercourse States shall take steps to harmonize their policies in this connection.

3. Watercourse States shall, at the request of any of them, consult with a view to arriving at mutually agreeable measures and methods to prevent, reduce and control pollution of an international watercourse, such as:

(a) Setting joint water quality objectives and criteria;

(b) Establishing techniques and practices to address pollution from point and non-point sources;

(c) Establishing lists of substances the introduction of which into the waters of an international watercourse is to be prohibited, limited, investigated or monitored.

ARTICLE 23

Protection and preservation of the marine environment

Watercourse States shall, individually and, where appropriate, in cooperation with other States, take all measures with respect to an international watercourse that are necessary to protect and preserve the marine environment, including estuaries, taking into account generally accepted international rules and standards.

Notes

1. During the negotiations of the 1997 Watercourse Convention, a proposal had been made to replace Article 20's wording "preserve the ecosystem" with "maintain the ecological balance." Do these terminologies essentially have the same meaning or is one more restrictive than the other? Which wording is more in line with the 1992 Convention on Biological Diversity? For further reading on ecosystem integrity and water law, see Tarlock, International Water Law and the Protection of River System Ecosystem Integrity, 10 B.Y.U. J. Pub. L. 181 (1996).

2. Is the "precautionary principle" of environmental law (see Chapter 17, p. 1511 inherent in Article 20 or Article 21(2)? If so, what are the obligations or duties imposed? Under Article 21(2), the obligations of prevention, reduction and control apply to pollution "that may cause significant harm to other watercourse States or to their environment"; the International Law Commission comments that this "is a specific application of the general principles contained in articles 5 and 7." I.L.C. Report 1994 at 291. How do Article 5's equitable utilization and Article 7's no harm rule interplay with Article 21(2)? Is pollution that falls below the Article 21(2) "significant harm" threshold necessarily covered by Article 20 or Article 23? For background reading on pollution and international watercourses, see Lammers, Pollution of International Watercourses (1984).

3. The U.N. Economic Commission for Europe (E.C.E.) Convention on the Protection and Use of Transboundary Watercourses and International Lakes, March 17, 1992, U.N. Doc. ENVWA–R.53 and Add.1, reprinted in 31 I.L.M. 1312 (1992) entered into force as of October 6, 1996 and as of 2000, has 28 European states and the European Community as parties. Compare this Convention, particularly Articles 1, 2 and 3, with the 1997 Watercourses Convention. If a state became a party to both of these Conventions, are their provisions mutually compatible? For a comprehensive analysis of the scope, interrelationship and implications of these two Conventions see Tanzi, Report of the U.N./E.C.E. Task Force on Legal and Administrative Aspects: Comparing two United Nations Conventions on Water, U.N. Doc. ECE/ENHS/NONE/00/2 (2000).

ARTICLE 27

Prevention and mitigation of harmful conditions

Watercourse States shall, individually and, where appropriate, jointly, take all appropriate measures to prevent or mitigate conditions related to an international watercourse that may be harmful to other watercourse States, whether resulting from natural causes or human conduct, such as flood or ice conditions, water-borne diseases, siltation, erosion, salt-water intrusion, drought or desertification.

ARTICLE 28

Emergency situations

1. For the purposes of this article, "emergency" means a situation that causes, or poses an imminent threat of causing, serious harm to watercourse States or other States and that results suddenly from natural causes, such as floods, the breaking up of ice, landslides or earthquakes, or from human conduct, such as industrial accidents.

2. A watercourse State shall, without delay and by the most expeditious means available, notify other potentially affected States and competent international organizations of any emergency originating within its territory.

3. A watercourse State within whose territory an emergency originates shall, in cooperation with potentially affected States and, where appropriate, competent international organizations, immediately take all practicable measures necessitated by the circumstances to prevent, mitigate and eliminate harmful effects of the emergency.

When necessary, watercourse States shall jointly develop contingency plans for responding to emergencies, in cooperation, where appropriate, with other potentially affected States and competent international organizations.

ARTICLE 32

Non-discrimination

Unless the watercourse States concerned have agreed otherwise for the protection of the interests of persons, natural or juridical, who have suffered or are under a serious threat of suffering significant transboundary harm as a result of activities related to an international watercourse, a watercourse State shall not discriminate on the basis of nationality or residence or place where the injury occurred, in granting to such persons, in accordance with its legal system, access to judicial or other procedures, or a right to claim compensation or other relief in respect of significant harm caused by such activities carried on in its territory.

Notes

1. Articles 27–28 concerning "Harmful Conditions and Emergency Situations" apply to events such as the January 2000 spill of approximately 100,000 cubic meters of liquid and suspended waste at the Aurul gold and silver producing plant in Baia Mare, Romania. This toxic spill released an estimated 100 tons of cyanide, as well as heavy metals into the Sasar River, flowing into the Lapus River before joining the Somes River which crosses the border with Hungary. Through the Somes River joining the Tisza River, the pollution then flowed through Hungary and into the Federal Republic of Yugoslavia, reaching the Danube River upstream of Belgrade. The pollution continued a further 1,200 km before entering the Black Sea. At the Danube delta, the cyanide plume was still measurable one month later and 2,000 km from the toxic spill's source.

A United Nations assessment team investigating this toxic spill found that the breach in Aurul's retention dam "was probably caused by a combination of inherent design deficiencies in the process, unforeseen operating conditions and bad weather." Although timely information exchange and measures taken by

Romanian, Hungarian and Yugoslavian authorities mitigated and reduced the risk and impact of the spill, acute transboundary pollution will potentially have "a severe negative impact on biodiversity, the rivers' ecosystem, drinking water supply and socio-economic conditions of the local population." U.N. Environment Program, Office for the Coordination of Humanitarian Affairs, Spill of Liquid and Suspended Waste at the Aural S.A. Pretreatment Plant in Baia Mare, Assessment Mission Romania, Hungary & Federal Republic of Yugoslavia, U.N. Doc. ST/OCHA/DRB/2000/17 (2000).

The U.N. assessment team did not address the question of liability and compensation related to the toxic spill and its consequences. However, it was expected that claims for compensation would be brought against the Romanian company.

2. Would Article 32 enable a Jordanian farmer, who can establish that his or her livelihood is ruined, or under serious threat of ruin due to Israel's withdrawal of water from Lake Tiberias, to have standing to sue Israel in an Israeli court for compensation? If a fisherman in the Persian Gulf could show that his or her catch was seriously reduced because of the run-off from irrigated fields in Turkey, would the fisherman be able to claim compensation or other relief in Turkey?

3. See also Boos–Hersberger, Transboundary Water Pollution and State Responsibility: The Sandoz Spill, 4 Ann. Surv. Int'l & Comp. L. 103 (1997); McClatchey, Chernobyl and Sandoz One Decade Later: The Evolution of State Responsibility for International Disasters 1986–1996, 25 Ga. J. Int'l & Comp. L. 659 (1996).

SECTION 4. WATERCOURSE BOUNDARIES

A state has sovereignty over its natural resources within its territory; however, as discussed in the previous section, obligations exist when a resource such as a watercourse flows beyond the border into another state. Determining where the boundary lies and which waters are within the territory of a state depends upon whether a successive or contiguous watercourse is involved. With successive watercourses, in the absence of an agreement, the border is along the shortest line connecting the points where the opposite states' borders intersect the banks of a river. See generally Marson, Boundary Waters, in 10 Encycl. Pub. Int'l L. 26 (Bernhardt ed., 1987); Caflisch, Règles Générales du Droit des Cours d'Eau Internationaux, 219 Rec. des Cours (1989–VII) 9, 66 (1992); Bouchez, The Fixing of Boundaries in International Boundary Rivers, 12 I.C.L.Q. 789 (1963).

With contiguous or boundary watercourses, in absence of an agreement, generally the thalweg (i.e., main channel) establishes the boundary of a navigable watercourse, while the median line establishes the boundary of a non-navigable watercourse. See, e.g., 1 Oppenheim's International Law 664–665 (Jennings & Watts ed., 1992); cf. Caflisch, The Law of International Waterways and Its Sources, in Essays in Honour of Wang Tieya 115, 120 (Macdonald, ed. 1993).

These rules are widely accepted as customary law but disputes have arisen as to their application in particular cases.

Notes

1. One source of dispute, not uncommon, may arise when the channel of navigation shifts due to natural forces, such as gradual erosion or deposit of alluvium (i.e., accretion), or as in some cases, due to abrupt changes—known as "avulsion"—forming a new channel. In the case of the gradual change, the boundary shifts with the change; whereas in the case of avulsion, where the watercourse suddenly changes, the boundary remains the same. See Case Concerning Land, Island and Maritime Frontier Dispute (El Salvador/Honduras: Nicaragua intervening), 1992 I.C.J. 351, para. 308. The U.S. Supreme Court has applied this distinction similarly in riparian boundary disputes between states of the United States. See, e.g., Louisiana v. Mississippi, 516 U.S. 22, 116 S.Ct. 290, 133 L.Ed.2d 265 (1995); Arkansas v. Tennessee 246 U.S. 158 (1918). See also Caflisch, The Law of International Waterways and Its Sources, in Essays in Honour of Wang Tieya, 115, 120 (Macdonald, ed. 1993). Caflisch questions whether general custom may be deduced from the various riparian treaties that define boundaries in terms of particular geographical conditions.

2. A notably acrimonious dispute between the United States and Mexico lasting more than a century arose from the constant shifting of channels in the Rio Grande and Colorado rivers. After some forty years of controversy, an International Boundary Commission was created by the two states in 1889 to decide whether changes in these rivers had occurred through avulsion or erosion. Subsequently, a dispute concerning a tract of land in El Paso ("El Chamizal") was submitted to an arbitral commission to determine the international boundary. The United States refusal to comply with the El Chamizal award remained a sore point of relations with Mexico until a treaty was concluded in 1963 dividing the disputed area between the two countries. For a summary of the dispute relating to the arbitral commission award, see p. 848 above.

3. Navigational watercourses may have more than one navigable channel, thus raising the question of which is to be the main channel (i.e., the thalweg) for determining the boundary. The International Court of Justice faced this issue in a boundary dispute between Botswana and Namibia decided in December 1999. Case Concerning Kasikili/Sedudu Island, 1999 I.C.J., reprinted at 39 I.L.M. 310 (2000). In this case, an island in the river resulted in two channels, each claimed by one of the parties to be the main channel—that is, the thalweg.

The Court examined an 1890 Treaty which locates the dividing line between Great Britain's and Germany's spheres of influence in the " 'main channel' of the River Chobe; however, neither this, nor any other provision of the Treaty, furnishes criteria enabling that 'main channel' to be identified. It must also be noted that the English version refers to the 'centre' of the main channel, while the German version uses the term 'thalweg' of that channel (*Thalweg des Hauptlaufes*)." Para. 21. The Court's opinion discussed various meanings of "thalweg" in treaties and usage with examples such as "the most suitable channel for navigation," "the line of deepest soundings," or the "median line." The Court, noting that the parties had used the term "main channel," applied that concept by taking into account the flow of water, the bed profile configuration, the channels' depth, width and navigability, and particularly, "the line of deepest soundings" in the northern channel of the River Chobe. The result favored Botswana by 11 votes to 4. See also p. 327 in Chapter 4.

Chapter 19

OUTER SPACE AND POLAR REGIONS

SECTION 1. THE LAW OF OUTER SPACE AND CELESTIAL BODIES

A. OUTER SPACE AS *RES COMMUNIS*

Even before the advent of space flights, international lawyers and governments considered whether space beyond the atmosphere could be claimed as state territory and where the upper boundary of a state's dominion should be drawn. One early view was that state territory should extend upwards as far as the state would exercise its control. A radically different proposal was that outer space and the celestial bodies be regarded as *res communis* and, like the high seas, not subject to appropriation by any state. Schachter, Legal Aspects of Space Travel, 1 J. Brit. Interplanetary Society 14 (Jan. 1952), and "Who Owns the Universe" in Across the Space Frontier 118–131 (C. Ryan ed., 1952).

The United Nations took up the question of the legal status of space in 1957 and agreed in 1963 (without dissent) on the principle of non-appropriability of outer space and the celestial bodies. It did so, first, in a "Declaration of Legal Principles" adopted without objection in 1963. G.A. Res 1962 (XVII). These principles were incorporated in a Treaty on Principles Governing the Activities of States in the Exploration and Use of Outer Space, Including the Moon and other Celestial Bodies (18 U.S.T. 2410, T.I.A.S. No. 6347, 610 U.N.T.S. 205). This treaty, known as the Outer Space Treaty, was concluded by the three space powers in 1967—the United States, U.S.S.R. and the United Kingdom—and has been accepted by over 100 states. It includes the following provisions:

> Art. 1. The exploration and use of outer space, including the moon and other celestial bodies, shall be carried out for the benefit and in the interests of all countries, irrespective of their degree of economic or scientific development, and shall be the province of all mankind.
>
> Outer space, including the moon and other celestial bodies, shall be free for exploration and use by all States without discrimination of any kind, on a basis of equality and in accordance with international law, and there shall be free access to all areas of celestial bodies.
>
> There shall be freedom of scientific investigation in outer space, including the moon and other celestial bodies, and States shall facilitate and encourage international co-operation in such investigation.

Art. 2. Outer space, including the moon and other celestial bodies, is not subject to national appropriation by claim of sovereignty, by means of use or occupation, or by any other means.

Notes

1. The Outer Space Treaty is in force for over 100 states. It is also generally agreed by legal scholars and governments that the earlier Declaration of Legal Principles expresses general customary law, binding on all states. See Bin Cheng, United Nations Resolutions on Outer Space: Instant International Customary Law?, 5 Indian J. Int'l L. 23 (1965).

2. Neither the treaty nor the declaration defines outer space or celestial bodies. See below for issues raised.

3. Following the adoption of the treaty, the United Nations continued to discuss international legal issues raised by activities in outer space. As of 2000 the U.N. General Assembly had adopted the following multilateral treaties, all of which have entered into force:

— Convention on the Rescue of Astronauts, the Return of Astronauts and the Return of Objects Launched into Outer Space, 19 U.S.T. 7570, 672 U.N.T.S. 119 (1968)

— Convention on Liability for Damage Caused by Space Objects, 24 U.S.T. 2389, 961 U.N.T.S. 187 (1972)

— Convention on Registration of Objects Launched into Outer Space, 28 U.S.T. 695, 1023 U.N.T.S. 15 (1975)

— Agreement Concerning the Activities of States on the Moon and Other Celestial Bodies, 1363 U.N.T.S. 3, 18 I.L.M. 1434 (1979). (This treaty has not been ratified by the major space powers. As of 2000, it had only 9 states parties.)

B. WHERE DOES OUTER SPACE BEGIN? IS A DEFINITION NECESSARY?

Recognition of outer space as a distinct legal category presupposes an agreed definition or at least criteria for distinguishing the realm of non-appropriable space from the sovereign realm of state territory. One suggestion was to base demarcation on technical criteria such as the upper limit of air flight (about 84 km) or, alternatively the lowest altitude (perigee) at which satellites can remain in orbit. These criteria raised doubts because of possible technical developments that would result in changing the "boundary" depending on technical variations (e.g. rockets, or orbits with low perigees). A contrary proposal would base legal rights on the functional character of the space vehicles and avoid space limits.

For some years, the issue did not give rise to practical disputes. Vehicles intended for space probes or orbital flights traversed the airspace of foreign states without objection. It was inferred that state practice supported a right of free access to space but it was questionable that many states would accept an explicit recognition of a right to enter their air space without express or implied permission. Governments managed to avoid the issue until 1976 when the "equatorial" states claimed sovereign rights over that segment of the "geostationary orbit" above their territories. For discussion, see K. Gorove &

E. Kamenetskaya, Tensions in the Development of the Law of Outer Space, in Damrosch, Danilenko & Mullerson (eds.), Beyond Confrontation: International Law for the Post–Cold War Era 225, 243–248, 269–271 (1995).

C. RIGHTS TO THE GEOSTATIONARY ORBIT

In the Declaration of Bogota of 1976, nine equatorial states asserted that in the absence of an agreed definition of outer space, the special character of the geostationary orbit in relation to the territorial states supported the right of the underlying territorial state to exercise sovereign rights over the orbit. The arguments by the equatorial states noted the dependence of the orbital satellites on the gravitational pull of the earth and therefore on that part of the globe "beneath" the orbit positions. The equatorial states also contended that the states currently operating satellites in the orbit were seeking to appropriate a part of outer space contrary to the international treaty. These arguments were rejected by a large number of states but there was some support for granting the equatorial states special privileges while denying their claim of sovereign right. Some governments have suggested that the rights to the geostationary orbit should be decided by the International Telecommunication Union as the international body competent to regulate the frequency spectrum. For a comprehensive review of these issues, see U.N. Doc. A/AC.105/C. 2/7 (1970) and U.N. Doc. A/AC.105/C.2/7 Add. 1 (1977). For recent discussion and references, see K. Gorove & E. Kamenetskaya, supra, at 234–238, 263–264 (1995).

Notes

1. Do the principles of non-appropriability and of free access to space result in giving the few technically advanced states permanent orbital positions that come close to an appropriation of a part of outer space?

2. Is it in the interest of the international community and equitable development to provide an opportunity for developing states to utilize the locations on the geostationary orbit that have been pre-empted by the "space powers"? The International Telecommunications Union (I.T.U.), the specialized agency charged with assignment of radio frequencies, has responded to the demands of the less developed states by allocating frequencies on the geostationary orbit to every state regardless of its present ability to put a satellite into that orbital slot. However, the increased demand for frequencies and orbital positions continues to place pressure on the I.T.U. and other international telecommunications agencies. For general discussion of issues, see M.L. Smith, International Regulation of Satellite Telecommunications (1990); Lyall, Posts and Telecommunications, in 2 United Nations Legal Order 813–817 (O. Schachter & C. Joyner, eds., 1995); Steinhardt, Outer Space, in 2 Schachter & Joyner at 764–766; N. Jasentuliyana, A Survey of Space Law as Developed by the United Nations, in Perspectives on International Law 373–6 (N. Jasentuliyana ed., 1995)

D. MILITARY USES OF SPACE AND THE REQUIREMENT OF PEACEFUL PURPOSES

In the 1967 Outer Space Treaty the states parties have undertaken not to place in orbit any objects carrying nuclear weapons or other weapons of mass destruction (Art. 4, para. 1). The treaty also requires that the moon and other celestial bodies be used exclusively for peaceful purposes (para 2). These provisions have not excluded military uses of outer space. In fact, the principal users of space technology are the military services of major powers. See Ivan Vlasic, Space Law and the Military Applications of Space Technology, in Perspectives on International Law 385–410 (N. Jasentuliyana ed., 1995).

Query: Should the requirement of "peaceful purposes" bar all military use or should space uses be limited—as contended by the U.S.—to "non-aggressive uses"?

Some governments have construed the "peaceful uses" provision of the Outer Space Treaty as a norm that should exclude all military applications, but the major military powers have rejected this position. See Vlasic supra. The 1991 Gulf War was characterized as the "first space war" by the U.S. Air Forces Chief of Staff, who observed that the "full range of modern military assets was applied * * * Seven imaging satellites made an average of 12 daily passes over the theatre of operations", facilitating bombing and other attacks by the U.S. forces. See Vlasic supra, p. 388. Such orbital "imaging" was not regarded as violating the express restrictions of the Space Treaty even though the "imaging" was used to guide bombings and other uses of weapons.

E. FREEDOM OF USE AND LEGAL LIMITS ON USE

The Outer Space Treaty of 1967 expressly recognizes that outer space and celestial bodies "shall be free for use and exploration by all States * * * on a basis of equality and in accordance with international law." Art. 1. Whether freedom of use should be limited by international law has given rise to controversy in respect of two activities involving space satellites: (1) remote sensing and photographing of a foreign state's territory, and (2) direct broadcast satellites that send television images to receivers in countries around the world. Both activities have been challenged and the issues considered by the U.N. Committee on Outer Space and its Legal Subcommittee.

With respect to remote sensing, the less developed countries argued for an obligation to obtain the prior consent of the sensed state before data based on the sensing could be obtained or disseminated. The principle of "sovereignty over natural resources" was invoked as a *jus cogens* doctrine. In opposition the developed states argued for freedom of use and of dissemination of data on a non-discriminatory basis. The United Nations Legal Subcommittee on Outer Space devoted 15 years in an effort to reach agreement on principles and in 1986 the General Assembly adopted a set of principles based on consensus. G.A. Res. 41/65. The principles did not require prior consent of the sensed states thus satisfying the United States and other space powers. However, several principles met the interests of sensed states. For example, Principle IV declared that remote sensing activities shall "be conducted on the basis of respect for the principle of full and permanent sovereignty of all States and peoples over their own wealth and resources. * * * Such activities shall not be conducted in a manner detrimental to the legitimate rights and interests of sensed states." The sensed states were also given a right to be consulted so as to enhance their participation and to receive data "that may be useful to states affected by natural disasters." Although sensed states are supposed to be given special consideration (as indicated), the principles do not require their prior consent as to either the sensing or the distribution of data. See

Steinhardt, Outer Space, in Schachter & Joyner, 2 United Nations Legal Order 778–80 (1995); C. Christol, Remote Sensing and International Space Law, 16 J. Space Law 21 (1988).

F. DIRECT BROADCASTING SATELLITES

A conflict between the principle of freedom of use in outer space and sovereign rights has also arisen in respect of direct television broadcasting by space satellites. Many states have maintained that prior consent of the receiving state is legally required for such broadcasts directed into their territory. In 1982 the U.N. General Assembly adopted a resolution by a large majority (108 to 13, with 13 abstentions) which declared that any state planning an international direct television broadcasting satellite service should consult with receiving states and should only establish the service in agreement with any receiving state that so requested. The United States and Western European states voted against the restriction because of this provision which they contended violated the Outer Space Treaty as well as the human right to seek, receive and impart information (Article 19 of the Universal Declaration of Human Rights).

Query: Should the principle of territorial integrity and the recognized right of a state to control entry into its territory apply to broadcasts from space satellites directed to the people in that state? Have targeted states an international legal right to block or interfere with the reception of such broadcasts in order to protect their political and cultural values? Should interference be considered as a violation of freedom of space? See Steinhardt, supra; C. Christol, The Modern International Law of Space 606–719 (1982); Doyle, Space Law and the Geostationary Orbit, 17 J. Space Law 13 (1989).

G. LIABILITY FOR ACCIDENTS

An international body of tort law for outer space emerged with the 1967 Outer Space Treaty and the Liability Convention of 1972, 24 U.S.T. 2389, 961 U.N.T.S. 187. Under the Outer Space Treaty, liability attaches to harm in space, earth and air space caused by private as well as governmental actors. The 1972 Liability Convention provides for a dual system of liability depending on where the damage occurs. Strict liability is imposed for damages on the surface of the earth and to aircraft in flight. Fault-based liability applies for damages that occur "elsewhere than on the surface of the earth" to a space object or to persons or property on board a space object belonging to another launching state (Art. III). The term "launching state" is broadly defined to apply to any space launched from its territory even if the government had no control over the launch or the object causing harm.

The Liability Convention was applied in 1974 after a Soviet satellite, Cosmos 95U, fell from orbit scattering radioactive debris over parts of Canada. Canada submitted a claim for compensation asserting damages in excess of fourteen million dollars. The Soviet Union eventually paid three million dollars, which Canada accepted in full payment.

Canada's claim was based not only on the Liability Convention but specifically also on "relevant international agreements" and "general principles of international law," The development of a private commercial space industry has raised concerns about damage and interest in strengthening the international liability regime.

Private sector space activity has also brought to the forefront questions of intellectual property rights and insurance. See Böckstiegel, Commercial Space Activities: Their Growing Influence on Space Law, XII Annals of Air & Space Law 175 (1987); Neagos, Commercial Space Transportation XVI Annals of Air & Space Law 393 (1991).

H. CONTAMINATION AND ENVIRONMENTAL DAMAGE IN SPACE

The possibility of contaminating outer space and the celestial bodies was noted in Article IX of the 1967 Outer Space Treaty which enjoined states parties to conduct exploration so as to avoid "harmful contamination and also adverse changes in the environment of the Earth resulting from the introduction of extraterrestrial matter." Although this language refers generally to harmful contamination, the United States and some other state parties consider that the harmful contamination prohibition is limited to the atmosphere of the earth. Moreover, a Senate report on ratification of the 1967 treaty declares that the prohibition on harmful contamination pertains only to the physical non-electronic damage that space activities may cause to citizens or property of a state. Treaty on Outer Space, S. Exec. Doc. No. 8, 90th Cong., lst Sess. 5 (1967). Some governments have expressed concern over environmental threats in space—including space debris and nuclear-powered satellites—and questions have been raised in the U.N. committees concerned with both the technical and legal aspects of outer space.

The interest generated by reports of "waste" and potential environmental damage has given rise to proposals for more legal restraints. See O. Portree & J. Loftus, Orbital Debris and Near–Earth Environmental Management: A Chronology (1993); Vereshchetin, Next Steps in International Space Law, in N. Jasentuliyana op. cit at 476–477. There are many thousands—probably millions—of pieces of debris in space. "Most are large enough to cause catastrophic damage or produce mission-degrading effects in the case of a collision with an active spacecraft." Ibid.

Query: Is the Liability Convention adequate for meeting the space debris problem? See generally Jasentuliyana, Environmental Aspects of Space Activities, in 27 Colloquium on the Law of Outer Space 390 (1984). On proposals to deal with space debris and other environmental concerns, see K. Gorove & E. Kamenetskaya, supra, pp. 238–243, 264–269 (1995).

I. TELECOMMUNICATIONS: THE INSTITUTIONAL FRAMEWORK APPLICABLE TO OUTER SPACE

The civilian application of space technology is principally in the area of telecommunications. Global and regional regulatory bodies have been established through international agreements and organizational arrangements. These bodies engage in rule-making and allocation of frequencies. The International Telecommunications Union (I.T.U.), a specialized agency of the U.N., is the principal regulatory agency for non-military space communication. It has long functioned as the international instrument for allocating and managing the radio spectrum. With the advent of space satellite communication, the I.T.U. was chosen as the agency to set aside radio frequencies for satellite use and to regulate the technical functioning of the communication satellites so as to avoid interference that would adversely affect the satellite systems. One of the most challenging tasks for the I.T.U. was the allocation of frequencies on the geostationary orbit for direct broadcast satellites. The Union acting through its Administrative Radio Conferences in 1977 and 1983 achieved an agreed allocation of frequency positions. However, in regard to the geostationary orbit, demands are continuously made for re-allocation and new assignments of orbital positions.

In addition to the I.T.U., several other international bodies have been established by governments to manage and regulate international communication satellites. The most important is INTELSAT, a commercial cooperative of more than 130 countries, which provides commercial communication services on a non-discriminatory basis to all areas of the world. Agreement relating to INTELSAT of 1971 (entered into force in 1973), 23 U.S.T. 3813, 4091, 10 I.L.M. 909. See M.L. Smith, International Regulation of Satellite Telecommunications (1990).

Another important international body was established for managing maritime satellite services by an international convention that entered into force in 1979, 31 U.S.T. 1, T.I.A.S. 9605. Known as INMARSAT (originally the International Maritime Satellite Organization), it has been extended to land and air mobile communications services as well as maritime services. INMARSAT is the first organization initially constituted by intergovernmental treaty to make the transition to privatized form: since 1999, it has been a limited liability company under U.K. law. Although little has been written about it in international law journals, INMARSAT performs essential services in respect to mobile communication services on land, sea and in the air, including handheld cellular telephone service utilizing space satellites. See www.inmarsat.org. The remarkable explosion of such space-based communication throughout the world has been facilitated by the international regulatory bodies that are an important, if little known, segment of the contemporary international legal system.

SECTION 2. THE POLAR REGIONS

HACKWORTH, DIGEST OF INTERNATIONAL LAW

Vol. 1, pp. 456–58 (1940).

On January 29, 1934 the British Ambassador in Washington addressed a note to the Secretary of State, reading in part as follows:

> The United States Government will doubtless be aware that an expedition to the Antarctic led by Admiral Byrd left New Zealand on December 12th for a base in Ross Dependency which was established on his previous expedition in 1928–1929. * * *
>
> His Majesty's Government in New Zealand understand that the expedition has the official backing of the United States Government and in these circumstances they feel it necessary to state that their attention has been drawn to articles in certain newspapers reporting that it is intended to establish a post office at Admiral Byrd's base in Ross Dependency and that certain members of the expedition were before

leaving the United States formally sworn in before the Postmaster General of the United States with the object of acting as postmasters at this post office. It is also understood that special stamps in connection with the expedition have been issued by the United States Government, and it has been reported that these will be used to frank letters posted at the expedition's base. While His Majesty's Government in New Zealand recognise that some allowance must be made for the absence of ordinary postal facilities in Ross Dependency, they would point out that if a United States post office were to be officially established in the dependency, or if the United States Government were to sanction the use of United States postage stamps there without permission from the sovereign Power, such acts could not be regarded otherwise than as infringing the British sovereignty and New Zealand administrative rights in the dependency as well as the laws there in force.

Although it is understood that the expedition is operating a wireless station in Ross Dependency, no license for such a station was applied for, and similarly although it is understood that United States aircraft are being imported into the dependency for the purpose of making flights in or over its territory, the competent authorities received no application for permission for such flights. Since on his previous expedition Admiral Byrd established a wireless station at his base and carried aircraft to the dependency, and was not then required to obtain a license or formal permission he may have thought it unnecessary to do so on this occasion. His Majesty's Government in New Zealand are indeed willing to regard their offer of facilities as covering now, as on the previous expedition, permission both for the wireless station and for the flights over the dependency, but they would nevertheless point out that they would have preferred prior application to have been made to the competent authority by or on behalf of the expedition in accordance with the relevant legislation applicable. * * *

[On February 24, 1934, the State Department replied, indicating it was unnecessary to discuss the "interesting questions" contained in the British note and reserving "all rights which the United States or its citizens may have with respect to this matter." On November 14, 1934 the following was stated in an informal note to the British Ambassador:]

It is understood that His Majesty's Government in New Zealand bases its claim of sovereignty on the discovery of a portion of the region in question. While it is unnecessary to enter into any detailed discussion of the subject at this time, nevertheless, in order to avoid misapprehension, it is proper for me to say, in the light of long established principles of international law, that I can not admit that sovereignty accrues from mere discovery unaccompanied by occupancy and use.

In reply, the following note, dated December 27, was handed to the Secretary of State by the British Ambassador on December 29:

With reference to the letter which you were so good as to address to me on November 14th last, I have the honour, under instructions from His Majesty's Principal Secretary of State for Foreign Affairs, at the instance of His Majesty's Government in New Zealand to inform you that the supposition that the British claim to sovereignty over the Ross

Dependency is based on discovery alone, and, moreover, on the discovery of only a portion of the region, is based on a misapprehension of the facts of the situation.

2. The Dependency was established and placed under New Zealand Administration by an Order in Council of 1923 in which the Dependency's geographical limits were precisely defined. Regulations have been made by the Governor General of New Zealand in respect of the Dependency and the British title has been kept up by the exercise in respect of the Dependency of administrative and governmental powers, e.g., as regards the issue of whaling licenses and the appointment of a special officer to act as magistrate for the Dependency.

3. * * * As regards Mr. Anderson's present mission, they understand that he is carrying letters to which are, or will be, affixed special stamps printed in the United States and that these stamps are to be cancelled and date-stamped on board the Expedition's vessel. They also understand that these stamps are intended to be commemorative of the Byrd Expedition and have been issued as a matter of philatelic interest.

4. In the above circumstances His Majesty's Government in New Zealand have no objection to the proposed visit of Mr. Anderson. They must, however, place it on record that, had his mission appeared to them to be designed as an assertion of United States sovereignty over any part of the Ross Dependency or as a challenge to British sovereignty therein, they would have been compelled to make a protest.

WHITEMAN, DIGEST OF INTERNATIONAL LAW

Vol. 2, pp. 1250–53 (1963).

In a note dated June 16, 1955, to the Secretary of State, the Australian Ambassador at Washington stated:

> I have the honour to refer to my letter of 11th March, 1949, depositing with the Government of the United States the Australian Instrument of Ratification of the Convention of the World Meteorological Organization signed at Washington, D.C. on 11th October, 1947.
>
> I wish to inform you that the Australian Government has now decided, by virtue of its membership of the World Meteorological Organization, to apply the Convention to the Australian Antarctic Territory which does not maintain its own meteorological service.

In his reply dated January 30, 1956, the Secretary of State, after acknowledging receipt of the Australian Ambassador's note and summarizing its contents, stated:

> My Government wishes to point out, as it has on previous occasions, that it does not recognize any claims so far advanced in the Antarctic and reserves all rights accruing to the United States out of activities of nationals of the United States in the area. * * *

[The American Embassy in Santiago delivered the following aide memoire to the Foreign Minister of Chile on August 2, 1955:]

> The Government of the United States of America notes Chilean law 11,846 was promulgated on June 17, 1955. That law purports to incorpo-

rate into Chilean provincial administration those areas claimed by Chile in the Antarctic. The Government of the United States wishes to reiterate that it has recognized no claims advanced with respect to the Antarctic by other countries and that it reserves all rights of the United States with respect to the area.

[The Department of State replied in like manner on November 5, 1956, to a Chilean memorandum transmitting a copy of a Decree implementing the above law.]

[On May 14, 1958, the Legal Adviser of the Department of State, Loftus Becker, said in the course of testimony before the Special Committee on Space and Astronautics of the United States Senate:]

> * * * There [in Antarctica], for many, many years, the United States has been engaged in activities which under established principles of international law, without any question whatsoever, created rights upon which the United States would be justified in asserting territorial claims. I mean by that, claims to sovereignty over one or more areas of the Antarctic.
>
> Notwithstanding this fact, the United States has not asserted any claim of sovereignty over any portion of Antarctica, although the United States has, at the same time, made it perfectly plain that it did not recognize any such claims made by other States.
>
> Nonetheless, the United States has been consistent in asserting that under international law and practice, its activities in the Antarctic Continent have entitled it to rights in that area which it has at all times expressly reserved.
>
> It is the position of the United States Government, and one well founded in international law, that the fact that the United States has not based a claim of sovereignty over one or more areas of Antarctica, upon the basis of the activities it has engaged in there, in no way derogates from the rights that were established by its activities.

A. THE "SECTOR THEORY" AS APPLIED IN POLAR REGIONS

LAUTERPACHT, SOVEREIGNTY OVER SUBMARINE AREAS

1950 Brit. Y.B.Int'l L. 376, 427.

Some aspects of the doctrine of contiguity also underlie the claims to Arctic and Antarctic regions put forward by a number of states—such as Great Britain, Canada, New Zealand, France, Russia, and Norway—in so far as it is based on the so-called sector principle. By virtue of that principle areas have been claimed which are embraced by the projection northwards or southwards, as the case may be, of the areas bordering the respective maritime territories. While with regard to the Arctic these areas are, in a sense, contiguous to the territories of the states concerned, in the case of the Antarctic the contiguity is distinctly symbolic. In some cases an element of uncertainty is added to the situation by the fact that the territory claimed as the base of the sector is claimed by virtue of discovery. This applies, for instance, to Adélie Land claimed by France. While New Zealand has dissented from the suggestion that the Ross Dependency is claimed by virtue of discovery alone, the "effective settlement" of it has taken place largely by "display of State activity" in the wider sense such as issuing licenses and appointment of magistrates. Essentially, notwithstanding the controversial differences of the geographical features of the Arctic and Antarctic in relation to the mainland from which they project, the claims to them are based—in so far as they are based on legal grounds—on some as yet undefined kind of contiguity, variously referred to also as proximity, region of attraction, and continuity. It is of interest to note that when the Russian claim to Arctic islands was first put forward in 1916 it referred to them as constituting "an extension northward of the continental tableland [shelf] of Siberia."

ACADEMY OF SCIENCES OF THE U.S.S.R., INTERNATIONAL LAW

190–93 (1961).

Status of the Arctic. The state territory of countries adjacent to the Arctic and having polar sectors in the Arctic includes all lands and islands lying within these sectors.

The term "polar sector of a State adjacent to the Arctic" means the expanse of which the base line is the coast of the given State, the apex the North Pole and the limits to either side the meridians from the North Pole to the eastern and western frontiers of the State.

It is in theory and practice recognized that all lands and islands discovered, as well as those which may be discovered in the future within the polar sector adjacent to the coast of a given State constitute part of that State's state territory. * * *

The status of the Soviet sector was determined by a Decree of the Central Executive Committee and the Council of People's Commissars of the Soviet Union, dated April 15, 1926. This laid down that all lands and islands discovered, as well as those which may be discovered in the future, lying between the Arctic coast of the Soviet Union, the North Pole and the meridians 32°4′35″ East and 168°49′30″ West, are Soviet territory. An exception was made for islands which on April 15, 1926 the Soviet Union recognized as foreign state territory (that is, the eastern islands of the Spitzbergen Archipelago lying between 32° and 35° East and which are under the jurisdiction of Norway).

There are many reasons for the division of Arctic territories into sectors. The States which have sectors in the Arctic are linked with the North Pole by an almost uninterrupted chain of islands or by a cap of almost unbroken ice which creates continuity between their mainland territory and their polar sectors.

The Arctic polar regions are sources of livelihood for the inhabitants of the coastal areas and are of exceptional economic importance to the State concerned. In the case of the Soviet Union, the Arctic regions are also of great importance from the point of view of defense, owing to their proximity to important centres.

The Arctic polar sectors have been substantially developed by the countries concerned and are partially settled. The Soviet people have played a particularly important part in the development of the Arctic. The study of the Arctic, including many areas lying outside the Soviet sector, has been a result of many centuries of consistent effort by Russian navigators and scientists, and of hard work and considerable material expenditure by the Soviet State and people.

Status of Antarctica. Interest in Antarctica began to develop at the end of the 19th century * * *.

The division of Antarctica into sectors gave rise to a prolonged conflict between Britain on the one hand and Argentina and Chile on the other.

The struggle of the capitalist States to partition Antarctica shows that the unilateral absorption of Antarctic territories is not an acceptable solution to the problem of the Antarctic regime. The problem of Antarctica can be justly solved only on an international basis, in a manner taking account of the special characteristics of its position.

Unlike those in the Arctic, sectors in Antarctica have no base lines, that is, the coast of the States claiming sectors. The mainland of Antarctica is thousands of miles away from other continents. Antarctica is of great importance to all countries, including the Soviet Union. From its waters come more than 90 per cent of the world's whale catch. * * *

The shortest intercontinental air routes may in the future lie across Antarctica. Finally, Antarctica is of interest to all countries including the Soviet Union, as a centre for important scientific research and observations. * * *

Notes

1. The Norwegian Government in 1930 expressed its disapproval of the sector theory. The U.S. Minister to Norway informed the Department of State, in connection with a Norwegian expedition in the Antarctic:

> The Minister for Foreign Affairs told me the other day that Norway has no intention of annexing territory charted by the *Norvegia* but that it would object to applying the sector principle to the south polar regions * * *.

1 Hackworth 463.

Subsequently, the American Legation at Oslo advised the Department of State that, by a note of Nov. 5, 1930, the Norwegian Government had recognized the sovereignty of Canada over the Arctic islands known as "Sverdrup's Islands". The Minister added that Norway did not thereby acknowledge the so-called sector principle "which means the direct extension of Canada's borders converging to the North Pole." Id. at 465.

2. The United States has long disputed certain Canadian claims in Arctic areas, including Canadian assertion of sovereignty over waters and waterways in the Arctic archipelago. Canada has insisted that icebreakers proceeding through the Northwest Passage must first obtain consent to transit from the Canadian government, while the U.S. Coast Guard has from time to time sent icebreakers through the Passage without prior consultation or consent. See Howson, Breaking the Ice: The Canadian–American Dispute Over the Arctic's Northwest Passage, 26

Colum. J. Transnat. L. 337 (1988); see also p. 76 supra. Though the two countries have endeavored to reach pragmatic accommodations, neither has relinquished its legal position on the underlying principle.

The shrinking of the polar ice cap and growing attractiveness of polar routes for shipping and air traffic have drawn renewed attention to fundamental legal questions of authority to control access and regulate activity in the Arctic. Canada has promulgated a Polar Code to regulate shipping north of the 60th parallel and also controls airspace in the area. While most shipping and air lines follow Canadian rules, the United States and major European shipping countries maintain that the relevant legal regime is transit passage through international straits (see Chapter 16, pp. 1407–1409, and that Canada has no authority to withhold consent to transit or to exercise broad unilateral regulatory jurisdiction for environmental or other reasons. "See Arctic Shortcut for Shipping Raises New Fears in Canada," N.Y. Times, July 29, 2000 pp. A1, A6.

3. On June 14, 1991, the eight Arctic States (Canada, Denmark, Finland, Iceland, Norway, Sweden, the U.S.S.R., and the United States) adopted the Arctic Environmental Protection Strategy. See 30 I.L.M. 1624 (1991). The objectives of this Strategy are to protect the Arctic environment and the indigenous peoples. The participating states commit themselves to meet periodically and to co-operate in achieving the Strategy's objectives. In 1996 the Arctic states (with the Russian Federation in place of the U.S.S.R.) signed a Declaration on the Establishment of the Arctic Council to provide a permanent framework for overseeing activities in the Arctic. Significantly, the region's indigenous peoples are brought into the framework, through acceptance of the organizations representing the majority of circumpolar indigenous peoples as permanent participants in the Arctic Council. See 35 I.L.M. 1382 (1996).

4. See generally Legal Regimes of the Arctic: A Panel, 82 A.S.I.L.Proc. 315 (1988); Nature Protection in the Arctic: Recent Soviet Legislation, 41 Int'l & Comp. L.Q. 366 (1992).

B. ANTARCTICA

Influenced perhaps by the momentum generated during the International Geophysical Year of 1957–58, during which scientific expeditions from many countries conducted research and experiments in Antarctica without regard to questions of territorial sovereignty, a conference called by the United States of those states having substantial interests in that continent succeeded in producing the Antarctic Treaty, signed on December 1, 1959, 12 U.S.T. 794, 402 U.N.T.S. 71. The most important provision of the treaty states that Antarctica "shall be used for peaceful purposes only" (Art. I), and, to that end, the treaty prohibits military installations, maneuvers, and weapons tests, including nuclear explosions of all kinds. The free exchange of scientific information and personnel is provided for (Art. III), and provision is made for the meeting at suitable intervals of representatives of contracting states in order to formulate and recommend measures in furtherance of the objectives of the treaty (Art. IX). In addition to other articles dealing with mutual inspection of Antarctic activities and installations by the contracting parties and with the exercise of jurisdiction over certain Antarctic personnel, the treaty provides in Article IV:

1. Nothing contained in the present Treaty shall be interpreted as:

(a) a renunciation by any Contracting Party of previously asserted rights of or claims to territorial sovereignty in Antarctica;

(b) a renunciation or diminution by any Contracting Party of any basis of claim to territorial sovereignty in Antarctica which it may have whether as a result of its activities or those of its nationals in Antarctica, or otherwise;

(c) prejudicing the position of any Contracting Party as regards its recognition or non-recognition of any other State's right or claim or basis of claim to territorial sovereignty in Antarctica.

2. No acts or activities taking place while the present Treaty is in force shall constitute a basis for asserting, supporting or denying a claim to territorial sovereignty in Antarctica or create any rights of sovereignty in Antarctica. No new claim, or enlargement of an existing claim, to territorial sovereignty in Antarctica shall be asserted while the present Treaty is in force.

The Treaty contains no general provision governing jurisdiction over persons in Antarctica. It entered into force on June 23, 1961. As of 2000, the Treaty was in force for 44 states, including the United States. The Treaty may be amended at any time by unanimous vote of the contracting parties. At the expiration of thirty years from the date of entry into force, any of the original contracting parties may call for a conference of all contracting parties. The conference may amend the Treaty by majority vote. Failure to ratify any amendment constitutes withdrawal from the Treaty.

In 1980, the Convention on the Conservation of Antarctic Marine Living Resources, which came into force in 1982, was adopted. This Convention prescribes rather rigorous guidelines for the harvesting of any species. The target species is krill, a crustacean of about two inches that is the principal food of great whales and was thought, because of its being rich in protein and minerals, to be able to provide a major source of food for man and domestic animals. More recently, the interest in krill has abated.

Following adoption of the 1982 Convention on the Law of the Sea, the status of Antarctica was placed on the agenda of the 1983 General Assembly by some Third World nations. The question raised was whether Antarctica should be under the control of the parties to the Antarctica Treaty System or be part of the common heritage of mankind to be developed for the benefit of all nations. The parties to the Antarctica Treaty System responded by inviting India and Brazil to become Consultative Parties and subsequently accepted China and Uruguay. They also invited all states that had acceded to the Treaty to send observers to their meetings and to participate in the discussions, but successfully resisted the creation of a U.N. Committee on Antarctica.

In June 1991, the Antarctic Treaty states approved the Protocol on Environmental Protection to the Antarctic Treaty (the Madrid Protocol), 30 I.L.M. 1455 (1991). The Protocol has been called the most comprehensive multilateral agreement on the international protection of the environment. See Blay, New Trends in the Protection of the Antarctic Environment: The 1991 Madrid Protocol, 86 A.J.I.L. 377 (1992). One of its most important features is the imposition of a moratorium on mining. It also contains comprehensive provisions for the conservation of Antarctic marine living resources. This Protocol had been preceded by the Final Act and Convention on The Regulation of Antarctic Mineral Resource Activities, of June 2, 1988, 27 I.L.M. 859 (1988), by which the contracting states imposed substantial limitations on mineral resource activities in Antarctica. The United States ratified the Protocol in 1997 and it entered into force in 1998.

Notes

1. See generally Bernhardt, Sovereignty in Antarctica, 5 Calif. W.Int'l L.J. 297 (1975); Chopra, Antarctica in the United Nations: Rethinking the Problems and Prospects, 80 A.S.I.L. Proc. 269 (1986); Joyner, The United States and Antarctica: Rethinking the Interplay of Law and Interests, 20 Cornell Int'l L.J. 65 (1987); Scott, Protecting United States Interest in Antarctica, 26 San Diego L.Rev. 575 (1989); Hinkley, Protecting American Interests in Antarctica: The Territorial Claims Dilemma, 39 Naval L.Rev. 43 (1990).

2. The Antarctic Treaty also prohibits, in Article 5, the disposal of radioactive waste in Antarctica.

3. For additional measures seeking to protect the Antarctic environment, see Convention for the Conservation of Antarctic Seals, London, June 1, 1972, 29 U.S.T. 441, T.I.A.S. No. 8826, which, as of 2000, was in effect for 16 states, including the United States; and the Convention on the Conservation of Antarctic Marine Living Resources, Canberra, May 20, 1980, 33 U.S.T. 3476, T.I.A.S. No. 10240, which, as of 2000, was in force for some 30 parties, including the United States and the European Economic Community.

4. For recent writings on Antarctica, see, e.g., Blay et al., Antarctica After 1991 (1989); Trofimov, Legal Status of Antarctica (1990); Redgwell, Antarctica, 39 I.C.L.Q. (1990); Bentham, Antarctica: A Minerals Regime, 8 J. Energy & Nat. Resources L. 120 (1990); Suter, Antarctica: Private Property or Public Heritage? (1991); Sahurier, The International Law of Antarctica (1991); Shepherd, The United States' Actions in Antarctica: The Legality, Practicality, and Morality of Applying the National Environmental Policy Act, 14 Geo. Mason U.L. Rev. 373 (1991); Bondareff, The Congress Acts to Protect Antarctica, 1 Terr. Sea J. 223 (1991); Delhi, Antarctica: An International Laboratory, 18 B.C.Envtl.Aff. L.Rev. 423 (1991); Redgwell, Antarctica, 40 I.C.L.Q. 976 (1991); Herber, Mining or World Park? A Politico–Economic Analysis of Alternative Land Use Regimes in Antarctica, 31 Nat. Resources J. 839 (1991); Poole, Liability For Environmental Damage in Antarctica, 10 J. Energy & Nat. Resources 246 (1992); Stokke & Vidas (eds.) Governing the Antarctic: The Effectiveness and Legitimacy of the Antarctic Treaty System (1997); Joyner, Governing the Frozen Commons: The Antarctic Regime and Environmental Protection (1998); Joyner, The Legal Status and Effect of Antarctic Recommended Measures, in D. Shelton (ed.), Commitment and Compliance 164–196 (2000); Vidas (ed.), Protecting the Polar Marine Environment (2001).

Chapter 20

INTERNATIONAL ECONOMIC LAW AND ORGANIZATIONS

SECTION 1. INTRODUCTION

International economic law has been defined as "all the international law and international agreements governing economic transactions that cross state boundaries or otherwise have implications for more than one state, such as those involving movement of goods, funds, persons, intangibles, technology, vessels or aircraft." Restatement (Third) Part VIII, Introductory Note. While this definition is broad enough to encompass international law and agreements affecting private parties in their commercial, financial and economic dealings, this Chapter will focus on the international law and agreements that apply primarily or exclusively to states.

The principal role of the aspects of international economic law here discussed is to restrict or regulate the broad range of actions in the economic sphere states may take that may affect other states' interests or the interests of their nationals. Illustrations would include a state's imposition of taxes, exchange controls, tariffs, import quotas, export subsidies, environmental controls or safety regulations.

This is an area dominated by international agreements; little customary law affecting economic relations has developed beyond the customary law related to state responsibility for injury to the economic interests of aliens and foreign investors examined in Chapter 10. The broad areas principally affected by these international agreements are international trade, international monetary affairs and international investment. Of these, trade and monetary relations have been subjected to substantial regulation by multilateral agreements, the most important of which are the General Agreement on Tariffs and Trade (GATT), the Agreement establishing the World Trade Organization (WTO), and the Articles of Agreement of the International Monetary Fund (IMF). International investment has been the subject of a network of bilateral agreements. These include bilateral treaties of friendship, commerce and navigation and bilateral investment treaties for the encouragement and protection of foreign investment, under which specified legal protection is accorded to property and contractual interests of foreign investors, and bilateral investment guaranty arrangements, which provide insurance for investments against noncommercial risks.

An important multilateral step toward encouraging investment in developing countries was the agreement creating the International Centre for the Settlement of Investment Disputes which affords arrangements for mediation or arbitration of disputes between foreign investors and states in which investments are made. See p. 1628. Another significant multilateral measure was the Convention establishing the Multilateral Investment Guarantee Agency, which provides insurance for international investments against non-commercial risks that complements bilateral insurance programs. See p. 1629.

There have been a number of significant but as yet unsuccessful efforts to develop multilateral regimes regulating the treatment of foreign investments. Some have taken the form of guidelines on the treatment of international investment published by the OECD and the World Bank Group. See pp. 1622 and 1626. Others have taken the form of proposed binding rules. The OECD published a Draft Convention on the Protection of Private Property in 1967. See p. 1621. The U.N. Commission and Centre on Transnational Corporations attempted over a number of years to develop a draft Code of Conduct on Transnational Corporations aimed at setting standards for the conduct of transnational corporations as well as for their treatment by host countries. More recently, an unsuccessful attempt was made under the auspices of the OECD to draft a multilateral investment agreement (MAI). See p. 1626. The most important multilateral agreements now in force that regulate international investment, as such, have been those establishing regional economic communities, most importantly, the European Union and NAFTA.

Other multilateral agreements establish a variety of international banking and finance institutions, such as the World Bank (and its affiliates, the International Development Association and the International Finance Corporation) and regional development banks, which support international private investment either by providing loans to developing countries themselves or providing part of the financing for projects that involve an investment of private capital from abroad.

In addition to the network of multilateral and bilateral agreements and multilateral institutions, informal groupings of states have played an important role in international economic relations. The two most prominent have been the Group of 77 and the Group of Seven.

The Group of 77 is a grouping of the developing countries of Africa, Asia and Latin America, which has grown in number far beyond the original 77. The Group of 77 functions as a kind of caucus for its participants with respect to their common economic and political concerns. Many of the concerns of the Group of 77 were reflected in the formulation of the so-called New International Economic Order (NIEO), which advocated, among other things, a state's right to expropriate property of aliens without being obligated under international law to pay compensation, greater support for commodity prices, and tariff preferences for the products exported by developing countries. The NIEO was embodied in the U.N. Charter of Economic Rights and Duties of States, U.N.Doc. A/Res./3281 (XXIX 1975), 14 I.L.M. 251 (1975), which was adopted by the U.N. General Assembly over the objection of the United States and other industrialized states. See p. 780.

The Group of 77 has often voted as a bloc in U.N. institutions. The Group's impact has been particularly pronounced in the proceedings of the

U.N. Conference on Trade and Development. See p. 1591. The influence of the Group of 77, which was relatively powerful in the 1960s and 1970s, has waned in recent years. Severe economic problems in the developing countries, including the Third World debt crisis, declines in commodity prices and the economic crises in a number of Asian and Latin American countries have diminished the collective impact of the Group's efforts to foster reform of the world's economic arrangements in favor of the developing world. Competition for capital generated by Eastern European countries and the republics of the former Soviet Union has also eroded the capacity of the developing countries to achieve enhancement of their economic development through collective action.

The Group of Seven (G–7) is an informal grouping of seven major industrialized countries which include Canada, France, Germany, Italy, Japan, the United Kingdom and the United States. (With the addition of Russia, the group is referred to as the Group of Eight.) The heads of state of these countries come together with the head of the European Union in annual summit meetings to discuss issues of common concern, principally in the economic, environmental and financial spheres, and to develop cooperative approaches. The finance ministers and central bank governors of the G–7 countries also meet on a regular basis to discuss and coordinate economic policies, including policies affecting interest rates and exchange rates. The role of the G–7 and G–8 is discussed in Hajnal, The G7/G8 System: Evolution, Role and Documentation (1999); Bergsten, Global Economic Leadership and the Group of Seven (1996); Funabashi, Managing the Dollar: From the Plaza to the Louvre (2d ed. 1989) and Destler & Henning, Dollar Politics: Exchange Rate Policy Making in the United States (1989).

SECTION 2. INTERNATIONAL TRADE LAW

A. THE GENERAL AGREEMENT ON TARIFFS AND TRADE AND THE WORLD TRADE ORGANIZATION

The United States' dominant economic position immediately after World War II gave it the power to lead a restructuring of post-war world trade aimed at eliminating the crippling protectionist measures of the inter-war period. Its position was that a liberalized system of international trade, based on non-discrimination and elimination of trade barriers, was essential to world economic well-being. The rules governing world trade were to be developed and enforced by an international trade organization, one part of a system of economic cooperation through international economic institutions, which were to include the World Bank and the IMF.

It was evident, looking back at the inter-war period, that protectionism and balance of payments problems could have disastrous effects on domestic economies. This factor was borne in mind in the planning for the new international trade system which was to develop after World War II. It seemed necessary to build in safeguards to ensure that a return to a system of free trade would not produce phenomena similar to those of the early 1930s.

To achieve a rational re-ordering of world trade mechanisms, an international conference on trade and employment was held at Havana in the winter of 1947–1948. The Conference approved the Charter of an International Trade

Organization (ITO) which included agreements on six topics: commercial policy; restrictive business practices; commodity agreements; employment; economic development and international investment; and a constitution for a new United Nations agency in the field of international trade. The Charter represented the first attempt to state and apply uniform principles of fair dealing to both private and state enterprises involved in international trade. Significantly, the Charter recognized the special position of developing countries by permitting them to impose restrictions on trade in the form of preferences and import quotas to protect "infant industries." The ITO Charter, however, never came into existence, as a result mainly of American and British opposition. See Gardner, Sterling-Dollar Diplomacy (2nd ed. 1969).

The demise of the ITO did not create a complete void in the area of international trade relations. Shortly before the Havana Conference, negotiations had been completed for a General Agreement on Tariffs and Trade (GATT). The GATT represented the first global commercial agreement in history. It had originally been conceived as a temporary device, to remain in effect until the ITO Charter became effective.

The GATT incorporated the code of commercial policy that was to have been part of the ITO structure. In pursuance of its principal purpose of reducing tariffs and other barriers to world trade, the GATT combined the bilateral approach to trade negotiations with the unconditional most-favored nation (MFN) principle (according to which the most favorable benefits accorded by one nation to another are available to all other nations). The MFN principle had the effect of multilateralizing any concessions contained in bilateral agreements by making them available to all members of the GATT. A significant modification of this principle was the agreement on unilateral preferences for less developed countries. See generally Curzon, Multilateral Commercial Diplomacy (1965).

The original GATT itself never entered into force. Instead, it was given effect pursuant to, and to the extent prescribed by, a Protocol of Provisional Application of Oct. 30, 1947, 61 Stat. pts. 5, 6, T.I.A.S. No. 1700, 55 U.N.T.S. 308, which became effective on January 1, 1948. This Protocol was concluded because it was desired to have the GATT in force as soon as possible, and the delay attendant upon the necessary legislative action in participating states made provisional application desirable. When the ITO did not come into existence, the GATT, applied under the Protocol, became the principal instrument for regulating international trade.

The original GATT is now often referred to as GATT 1947 to distinguish it from the GATT adopted in 1994. GATT 1947 was the sponsor of eight rounds of major tariff and trade negotiations. The sixth, the so-called Kennedy Round, produced tariff reductions of 50 percent on a broad range of products, an anti-dumping code, and special exceptions for less developed countries. The seventh round, the Tokyo Round, was concluded in 1979. In this Round, the focus was shifted to non-tariff barriers and nine agreements were adopted, including codes covering such matters as subsidies, unification of anti-dumping rules, customs valuation, discrimination against foreign goods in government purchasing, countervailing duties and quality specifications that operate to burden foreign imports. See Agreements Reached in the Tokyo

Round of Multilateral Trade Negotiations, H.D. 96–153, 96th Cong., 1st Sess. (1979).

The eighth round of trade agreement negotiations under the auspices of the GATT, the so-called Uruguay Round, was signed on April 15, 1994. During the negotiations the parties agreed not to take any trade-restricting or distorting measures and to dismantle such measures inconsistent with the GATT, and to establish a permanent trade body, the World Trade Organization (WTO). Although the negotiations, which involved more than 100 states, addressed a broad range of matters, the principal substantive achievements of GATT 1994 fell into four areas. The first was the "market access negotiations" in which individual countries made binding commitments to reduce or eliminate specific tariffs and non-tariff barriers to merchandise trade. The second was the "initial commitments" on liberalization of trade in services. The third was a set of rules requiring a minimum level of protection for intellectual property. The fourth was adoption of enhanced dispute-resolution mechanisms.

The GATT 1947 lacked a permanent formal administrative structure. The GATT referred only to action by the contracting states. The action was generally restricted to fact-finding and mediation. "Over its history, however, the GATT has evolved procedures and institutional practices, and a web of obligations requiring states to submit their actions in respect of trade to international scrutiny, to negotiate about them, and to consider the likely reactions of other states. While some GATT obligations have not been meticulously observed at the margin, overall the Agreement constitutes the prevailing norm of international trade among member states." Restatement (Third) Part VIII, Chapter 1, Introductory Note. The absence of a permanent administrative body was remedied by establishing the WTO in 1994.

1. *Outline of the GATT and the WTO*

JACKSON, DAVEY AND SYKES, LEGAL PROBLEMS OF INTERNATIONAL ECONOMIC RELATIONS

289–292, 302–304 (Third Edition 1995).

The end of the eight-year Uruguay Round of trade negotiations in 1994 brought a profound change in the legal structure of the institutions for international trade. Since 1947, the General Agreement on Tariffs and Trade (the General Agreement or GATT) was the principal international multilateral treaty for trade, although technically it was only in force "provisionally." In theory, the General Agreement did not establish an "organization," although in practice GATT operated like one. The Uruguay Round results create a new and better defined international organization and treaty structure—a World Trade Organization (WTO)—to carry forward GATT's work. Some have suggested that this is the most significant result of the Uruguay Round, and that it is part of a series of circumstances (including economic integration in Europe and North America) which may be the most profound change in international economic institutions since the Bretton Woods Conference of 1944.

* * *

The General Agreement is a treaty which deals almost entirely with trade in products. The Uruguay Round for the first time has produced a comparable treaty for trade in services (broadly defined) and a new treaty dealing with intellectual property. These three treaties form the core and bulk of the substantive international rules which will be administered by the WTO. What do these treaties provide?

GATT 1947 & 1994: The General Agreement on Tariffs and Trade, completed in late 1947 and amended and embellished with a variety of treaty instruments (about 200), provides an important "code" of rules applying to government actions which regulate international trade. The basic purpose of the General Agreement is to constrain governments from imposing or continuing a variety of measures which restrain or distort international trade. Such measures include tariffs, quotas, internal taxes and regulations which discriminate against imports, subsidy and dumping practices, state trading, as well as customs procedures and a plethora of other "non-tariff measures" which discourage trade. The basic objective of the rules is to "liberalize trade" * * *. An additional and very important rule is the "MFN" or Most Favored Nation Clause of Article I, which provides that government import or export regulations should not discriminate between other countries' products. Likewise Article III establishes the "national treatment" obligation of non-discrimination against imports. Article II establishes that the tariff limits expressed in each contracting party's "schedule of concessions" shall not be exceeded. The thrust of the General Agreement is to channel all "border protection" against imports into the tariff, and provide for agreements for tariff reductions, which are "bound" in the schedules and reinforced by Article II rules and the rest of the agreement.

The General Agreement also has a number of exceptions, such as those for national security, health and morals, safeguards or escape clauses (for temporary restraint of imports), free trade agreements, and the like, plus a "waiver" power.

The WTO annex 1A incorporates a document labelled GATT 1994 which is essentially GATT 1947 as amended and changed through the Uruguay Round, along with all the ancillary agreements pertaining to GATT 1947, as modified.

GATS: The General Agreement on Trade in Services resulted from negotiations in the Uruguay Round on one of the "new subjects." The word "services" embraces more than a hundred different service sectors, such as banking, tourism, communications, medical, legal, insurance, brokerage, transport, etc. Many of these sectors are difficult and complex to regulate. The policy makers of the 1980's felt that developing world economic trends making services an even larger portion of international and national markets necessitated some type of multilateral rule structure comparable to that for goods, to inhibit a growing tendency of governments to limit competition with restrictions and protectionist measures. The trade negotiators naturally tended to use analogies to GATT rules to try to regulate services, although sometimes the analogies may not work too well. Nevertheless, the GATS agreement has counterpart provisions to MFN and national treatment. It also has a system of "schedules of concessions." The GATS, however, also includes rules on competition and monopoly policy (anti-trust) and government procurement. It contains exceptions clauses similar to GATT's on safeguards, health and morals, and national security. It also includes clauses on "transparency," calling for openness and publication of information affecting traders.

TRIPS: The Agreement on Trade–Related Aspects of Intellectual Property Rights is designed to provide rules requiring governments to ensure a certain minimum level of protection for patents, copyrights, industrial designs, trademarks, business secrets and similar matters. It refers to some of the major intellectual property treaties (such as the Berne Convention concerning copyrights and the Paris Convention on patents). One of the major goals of proponents of this agreement was to add a measure of "enforceability" through a GATT-type dispute settlement system to intellectual property norms. Rules included in this agreement also require governments to provide civil and administrative procedures and remedies for rights-holders to pursue. This agreement also has clauses concerning MFN treatment, national treatment and transparency, as well as exceptions for national security.

Added to these three major substantive agreements, are the WTO Charter itself, an understanding on dispute settlement provisions, a "TPRM–Trade Policy Review Mechanism," and an annex with four so-called "plurilateral agreements." A chart showing the relationship follows:

WTO CHARTER

Annex 1: Multilateral Agreements

Annex 1A: GATT 1994 (including side agreements, understandings and the Marrakesh Protocol)

Annex 1B: GATS

Annex 1C: TRIPS

Annex 2: Dispute Settlement Rules

Annex 3: Trade Policy Review Mechanism

Annex 4: Plurilateral Agreements (optional)

Annex 4A: Civil Aircraft

Annex 4B: Government Procurement

Annex 4C: Dairy

Annex 4D: Bovine Meat

By adhering to the WTO Charter, countries become subject to all of the annexed agreements, except the plurilateral agreements, adherence to which is optional. There are also, as part of the April 1994 Final Act that established the WTO structure, an assortment of appended Ministerial Decisions, Declarations, Understandings and Recommendations.

* * *

It is important to realize that the WTO is not an ITO (the 1948 International Trade Organization). The ITO Charter included five sizeable chapters filled with substantive rules concerning international economic behavior, plus a chapter with an elaborate set of institutional clauses. The WTO Charter by comparison, is a "mini-charter," relatively spare regarding institutional measures and containing no substantive rules, although large texts of such matter are included in Annexes. This overall structure of the WTO is itself significant. It suggests a spirit of flexibility, which allows for texts to be added or subtracted over time and for the evolution of institutions necessary for implementation of the rules.

* * *

The WTO Charter is confined to institutional measures, but the charter explicitly outlines four important annexes which technically contain thousands of pages of substantive rules. Indeed it is reported that the total "package" of the text of the Uruguay Round results weighs 385 pounds and consists of over 22,000 pages, including annexes and schedules, etc.

The annex structure is important; the different annexes have different purposes and different legal impacts:

Annex 1 contains the "Multilateral Agreements," which comprise the bulk of the Uruguay Round results and which are all "mandatory," in the sense that these texts impose binding obligations on all members of the WTO. This reinforces the single package idea of the negotiators, departing from the Tokyo Round approach of "pick and choose" side texts, or "GATT à la carte." As outlined above, the Annex 1 texts include:

Annex 1A consists of GATT 1994, which includes the revised General Agreement with new understandings, side agreements on 12 topics ranging from agriculture to preshipment inspection, and the vast "schedules of tariff concessions" that make up the large bulk of pages in the official treaty text. The schedule for each of the major trading countries, the U.S., Japan, and the European Union, constitutes a volume of printed tariff listings. There are a number of "side agreements," some originating from the Tokyo Round results (as revised in the Uruguay Round). * * *

* * *

Annex 1B consists of the General Agreement on Trade in Services (GATS), which also incorporates a series of schedules of concessions (* * *).

Annex 1C consists of the Agreement on Trade–Related Aspects of Intellectual Property (TRIPS) (* * *).

Annex 2 has the dispute settlement rules, which are obligatory on all members, and which form (for the first time) a unitary dispute settlement mechanism covering all the agreements listed in Annex 1, Annex 2 and Annex 4 (i.e., all but the TPRM procedures) (* * *).

Annex 3 establishes the Trade Policy Review Mechanism (TPRM), by which the WTO will review the overall trade policies of each member on a periodic and regular basis, and report on those policies. The approach is not supposed to be "legalistic," and questions of consistency with WTO and Annex obligations are not the focus; rather the focus is the general impact of the trade policies, both on the country being examined and on its trading partners.

Annex 4 contains the four agreements which are "optional," termed "plurilateral agreements." This is a slight departure from the single package ideal, but the agreements included tend to be either targeted to a few industrial countries, or to be more "hortatory" in nature without real legal impact. The four agreements deal with government procurement * * *, trade in civil aircraft * * *, bovine meat and dairy products. Clearly this annex, which may be added to, leaves open some important flexibility for the WTO to evolve and redirect its attention and institutional support for important new subjects that may emerge during the next few decades.

* * *

Unlike the General Agreement, the WTO Charter clearly establishes an international organization, endows it with legal personality, and supports it with the traditional treaty organizational clauses regarding "privileges and immunities," secretariat, director general, budgetary measures, and explicit authority to develop relations with other inter-government organizations and, important to some interests, non-government organizations. The charter prohibits staff of the Secretariat from seeking or accepting instructions from any government "or any other authority external to the WTO."

* * *

There is strong indication in various parts of the WTO Charter to promote a sense of legal and practice continuity with GATT. Except as otherwise provided, the WTO and the Multilateral Trade Agreements shall "be guided by the decisions, procedures and customary practices followed by [GATT 1947]." Art. XVI:1. The secretariat of the GATT 1947 will generally become the WTO secretariat.

* * *

The governing structure of the WTO follows some of the GATT 1947 model, but departs from it substantially. At the top there is a "Ministerial Conference," which meets not less often than every two years. Next there is not one, but four "Councils." The "General Council" has overall supervisory authority, including responsibility for carrying out many of the functions of the Ministerial Conference between Ministerial Conference sessions. Presumably, the "General Council" will meet at least as often as the GATT Council, which met monthly (with some exceptions). In addition, however, there is a Council for each of the Annex 1 agreements, thus:

Council for Trade in Goods

Council for Trade in Services, and

Council for Trade–Related Aspects of Intellectual Property Rights

A "Dispute Settlement Body" (DSB) is established to supervise and implement the dispute settlement rules in Annex 2. The General Council is authorized to perform the DSB tasks. Likewise there is a TPRM Body for the Trade Policy Review Mechanism.

Notes

1. On the GATT generally, see Bhala, International Trade Law: Cases and Materials (1996); Jackson, Davey & Sykes, Legal Problems of International Economic Relations, Chapter 6 (3d ed. 1995); Stephan, The New International Law—Legitimacy, Accountability, Authority and Freedom in the New Global Order, 70 U.Colo.L.Rev. 1555 (1999); Jackson, Fragmentation or Unification Among International Institutions: The World Trade Organization, 31 N.Y.U.J.

Int'l L. & Pol. 823 (1999); Hudec, Enforcing International Trade Law (1993); Hudec, The GATT Legal System and World Trade Diplomacy (2d ed. 1990); and Jackson, The World Trading System: Law and Policy of International Economic Relations (2nd ed. 1997).

2. The WTO was established on January 1, 1995, with its headquarters in Geneva, Switzerland. Its membership includes 141 countries. A substantial number of additional states, including the People's Republic of China, have applied for membership. The WTO administers WTO trade agreements; provides a forum for trade negotiations; handles trade disputes; monitors national trade policies; and provides technical assistance and training for developing countries. The WTO succeeded the GATT as the principal legal institution of the multilateral trading system. The WTO's rules cover most aspects of world trade in goods and services, and the WTO is also the primary international forum for negotiating and settling disputes on all trade matters. At a highly publicized meeting in Seattle late in 1999, which was beset by demonstrations by the U.S. labor movement, environmentalist groups and others and riven by a growing divide between developing and developed countries, the WTO failed to reach agreement on an agenda for the next round of trade negotiations.

3. The GATT has not been a direct source of rights for private parties. See § 3(f) of the Trade Agreements Act of 1979, 19 U.S.C.A. § 2504(d). However, many provisions of U.S. trade legislation mirror international obligations contained in the GATT or its related codes and confer rights on private parties affected by imports. U.S. exporters, however, must seek intercession by the U.S. Trade Representative to obtain benefits of the GATT with respect to import restraints imposed by foreign states. See § 301 of the Trade Act of 1974, 19 U.S.C.A. § 2411.

4. GATT Article XXIV(12) binds each party to take "reasonable measures" to ensure observance of the GATT by regional and local governments. In the United States, prior state legislation has been held to be superseded by the GATT to the extent inconsistent with it. See, e.g., Bethlehem Steel Corp. v. Board of Comm'rs, 276 Cal.App.2d 221, 80 Cal.Rptr. 800 (1969). Compare Crosby v. National Foreign Trade Council, 530 U.S. 363, 120 S.Ct. 2288, 147 L.E. 2nd 352 (2000), at p. 175 above.

2. *Tariffs*

By virtue of Article I of the GATT, under which each member state undertakes to grant MFN treatment, and Article II, under which each agrees to adhere to the tariffs listed in the schedules it has negotiated under the GATT, tariff reduction negotiations have, as noted above, been multilateralized through a series of negotiating rounds, in which states balance the concessions they make against all concessions they receive from whatever party grants them. The Article III national treatment obligation that imports shall be treated no worse than domestically produced goods under internal tax or regulatory regimes applies domestically the non-discriminatory principle reflected in MFN treatment.

In addition to the MFN obligation of Article I, the GATT also imposes MFN treatment with respect to such matters as marks of origin (Art. IX(*l*)), quantitative restrictions (Art. XIII(1)), and export controls on goods in short supply (Art. XX(j)). There are certain specific exceptions to these MFN obligations under specified circumstances, including preferences for developing countries and for customs unions and free trade areas.

Notes

1. A party to the GATT is obligated not to increase a tariff to a level above the rate to which it is committed by the tariff's inclusion in a schedule to which the party is committed. A tariff is "bound" when a state has filed with the WTO a commitment not to increase it or to lower it. The binding process occurs principally at the negotiating rounds conducted by the parties. A state may withdraw a "binding" if it negotiates substantially similar equivalent concessions on other products of interest to the principal beneficiaries of the original binding. Art. XXVIII. See Restatement (Third) § 803. Article XXVIII provides that periodically a state may modify or withdraw any concession by agreement with the contracting party with which it was originally negotiated and with any other party determined to have "a principal supplying interest." This is a party that "had, over a reasonable period of time prior to the negotiations, a larger share in the market of the applicant contracting party than a contracting party with which the concession was initially negotiated." Art. XXVIII, Note 4.

2. The MFN principle is stated in § 126 of the Trade Act of 1974, 19 U.S.C.A. § 2136(a). Sections 401–10 of the Act, 19 U.S.C.A. §§ 2431–2439, deny MFN treatment to Communist states unless a commercial agreement is in effect and limit the authority of the President to enter into such agreements. MFN treatment has been extended by the United States by a series of bilateral agreements to the People's Republic of China. Restatement (Third) § 802, Reporters' Note 2. The trade agreement negotiated in November 1999 between the United States and the PRC would extend permanent MFN treatment to the PRC. In this agreement, the name MFN is changed to Normalized Trade Relations (NTR). This agreement was approved by Congress in fall 2000, thereby removing one of the last obstacles to participation by the PRC in the WTO and GATT.

3. The national treatment obligation of Article III, which is also found in most U.S. bilateral investment (BIT) treaties and bilateral friendship, commerce and navigation (FCN) treaties, discussed at pp. 806–813, forbids discrimination against imported goods once they have passed tariff and other similar barriers. Problems in this area arise typically when the more favorable treatment of domestically produced goods results from domestic measures, such as labeling requirements, technical standards requirements, and anti-pollution rules, that may be regarded as not seeking to grant domestic producers a competitive advantage, but instead as pursuing other domestic policies. Article XX of the GATT, in an effort to permit fair accommodation of competing interests, provides for potentially broad exceptions from national treatment. However, since the legislative motive is not always apparent, ambiguous situations can easily arise. See, e.g., the Federal Trade Commission ruling of April 1979, requiring animals formerly designated as "Minks, Japanese" to be designated in the future as "Japanese Weasels." On national treatment generally, see Jackson, World Trade and the Law of GATT c. 12 (1969); Jackson, Davey & Sykes, Legal Problems of International Economic Relations 501–558 (3d ed. 1995).

3. Classification and Valuation

The effective tariff burden on imported goods is determined not only by the tariff rate, but also by other factors, such as customs classification and valuation for customs purposes. For example, in Western Stamping Corp. v. United States, 417 F.2d 316 (C.C.P.A. 1969), the issue was whether a toy typewriter was to be classified as a typewriter, which was duty-free, or as a toy, subject to 35 percent ad valorem duty, with the court upholding its classification as a typewriter.

In an effort to eliminate disparate treatment as a result of classification differences, the Harmonized Commodity Description and Coding System, also called the "Harmonized System," was incorporated in a multilateral convention effective January 1, 1988, to which the United States is a party. The Harmonized Tariff Schedule of the United States (HTS) was enacted by subtitle B of title I of the Omnibus Trade and Competitiveness Act of 1988, which came into effect in January 1, 1989. 100 P.L. 418, 102 Stat. 1107, 19 U.S.C. § 3001 (1999). The U.S. HTS is based on the Harmonized System.

Under the Uruguay Round Agreement on Implementation of Article VII of GATT 1994 (Agreement on Customs Valuation) the primary basis for determining customs value is "transaction value," i.e. the price actually paid or payable for the goods sold for export to the country of import, provided that there are no restrictions or conditions that would affect that price and provided that buyer and seller are not related. This price must be adjusted for certain specific elements that form part of the value for customs purposes and are incurred by the buyer but are not included in the price actually paid, such as packing costs, sales commissions, royalties or license fees borne by the buyer. The rules giving effect to this broad principle are quite detailed. The Agreement on Customs Valuation will obligate all WTO members to observe uniform rules for custom valuation and therefore produce greater uniformity in valuation methodology, although not necessarily in customs values determined.

Note

For discussion of these issues see Uruguay Round Trade Agreement, Statement of Administrative Action, Agreement on Customs Valuation, H.R. Doc. No. 316, 103d Cong., 2d Sess., Vol. 1, 896–7 (September 27, 1994); Bhala, International Trade Law: Cases and Materials 432–89 (Michie 1996); and Jackson, Davey & Sykes, Legal Problems of International Economic Relations 403–411 (3d ed. 1995).

4. Quantitative Restrictions

Quantitative restrictions on imports (quotas) are prohibited by Article XI(1) of GATT 1947, subject to some important exceptions. Under Article XI(2)(c) import restrictions are permitted in the case of "any agricultural or fisheries product" in support of programs that attempt to restrict domestic output of the product in question or of some closely related product, provided that such programs do not alter the proportion of imports to domestic production that would otherwise obtain.

Quantitative restrictions are authorized, under specified conditions, by Articles XII and XIII (or by Article XVIII:B with respect to less developed states) for states in critical balance of payments difficulties. Under GATT 1994, WTO members are obligated to end their use of balance of payments measures as soon as possible and to use the least trade-disruptive measures.

Quantitative restrictions are also permitted for certain law enforcement purposes, such as prevention of deceptive practices, protection of public morals, national treasures or human or animal health. Art. XX. Quantitative restrictions may also be imposed in escape clause cases, but not in countervailing duty or anti-dumping cases.

No quantitative restriction may be applied to imports of one party unless it is similarly applied to all third countries, and quotas must be allocated among supplying states so as to preserve the shares of imports they might be expected to have but for the restrictions. Art. XIII. See Restatement (Third) § 804, Comment *a*.

Notes

1. U.S. law authorizes imposition of quotas when needed under a variety of circumstances, including injury caused by import competition, relief from unfair trade practices and safeguarding national security. The United States has imposed quotas under Section 22 of the Agricultural Adjustment Act, 7 U.S.C.A. § 624, on certain agricultural commodities, such as dairy products, cotton, sugar and peanuts. Other developed countries have used quotas usually justified by injury from imports or unfair trade practices. See Jackson, Davey & Sykes, Legal Problems of International Economic Relations 431–33 (3d ed. 1995).

2. Some controversies over excessive imports of certain products, such as automobiles, have been settled by voluntary quantitative limits on exports. Such quotas have not been regarded as violative of Article XI of the GATT because the exporting country has consented. Restatement (Third) § 804, Reporters' Note 4.

5. Indirect Barriers to Imports

The GATT also prohibits indirect restraints on imports. Article II states that "internal taxes and other regulations and requirements affecting local sale * * * purchase, transportation, distribution or use of products * * * should not be applied * * * so as to afford protection to domestic production." Parties are called upon to minimize the burden of import formalities. This obligation has been implemented in a series of codes on such matters as technical standards, customs procedures and formalities, and government procurement.

Note

State-trading enterprises are enjoined to act in connection with imports and exports solely in accordance with non-discriminatory commercial considerations. Art. XVII. With respect to imports to be used by the government itself, however, only "fair and equitable treatment" for products of other states is required, and non-commercial government purchases are exempt from the national treatment principle of Article III.

6. Subsidies and Countervailing Duties

Countervailing duties on imports that have benefited from an export subsidy are authorized by Article VI(6) of the GATT, provided that the effect of the subsidization is "such as to cause or threaten material injury" to or "to retard materially the establishment of a domestic industry." The countervailing duty may not exceed the amount of the subsidy.

An important result of the Uruguay Round was adoption of the Agreement on Subsidies and Countervailing Measures (SCM Agreement). 103 P.L.

465, 108 Stat. 4809, 19 U.S.C.A. § 1677 and § 3571 (Dec. 8, 1994). It is binding on all WTO members and replaces the 1979 Subsidies Code of the Tokyo Round. The SCM Agreement addresses two related topics: multilateral disciplines regulating the provision of subsidies and the use of countervailing measures to offset injury caused by subsidized imports. The Agreement substantially tightens the restraints on use of subsidies to encourage exports or discourage imports. Previously, the only effective U.S. remedy for export subsidies was the imposition of countervailing duties (CVD) on subsidized products imported into the United States. The SCM Agreement coupled with the WTO dispute-resolution procedures provide substantive and procedural tools for addressing subsidized competition anywhere.

The SCM Agreement contains a specific definition of "subsidy," building on two basic elements: (1) a "financial contribution" by a government or any public body within a government's territory and (2) a consequent conferral of "a benefit" which operates directly or indirectly to increase exports of any product from, or reduce imports of any product into, the territory of a WTO member.

The SCM Agreement establishes three categories of subsidies and subsidy remedies: (1) subsidies that are prohibited ("red light" subsidies); (2) subsidies that may be challenged in WTO dispute-resolution procedures and subjected to domestic countervailing duties if they cause adverse trade effects ("yellow light" and "dark amber" subsidies); and (3) subsidies that are nonactionable and cannot be subject to domestic countervailing duties if they are structured to meet criteria intended to limit their potential for causing trade distortions ("green light" subsidies). A Subsidies Committee is established to administer the SCM Agreement rules.

Notes

1. For a summary of the SCM Agreement, see Uruguay Round Trade Agreement, Statement of Administrative Action, Agreement on Subsidies and Countervailing Measures, H.R. Doc. No. 316, 103d Cong., 2d Sess., Vol. 1, 911–923 (September 27, 1994)(U.S. Statement of Administrative Action).

2. The SCM Agreement provides expeditious procedures for resolving disputes concerning prohibited (red light) subsidies. A panel or the Appellate Body need only find that a government is granting a prohibited subsidy. If such a finding is made, the Dispute Settlement Body of the WTO must authorize countermeasures if the subsidy is not terminated promptly. SCM Agreement, Art. 4.

3. For a description of the SCM Agreement provisions concerning "yellow", "dark amber" and "green" light subsidies, see The U.S. Statement of Administrative Action at pp. 915–921.

4. Special rules applicable to developing countries are described in the U.S. Statement of Administrative Action at pp. 921–922, in part, as follows:

> Article 27 [of the SCM Agreement] applies multilateral subsidy disciplines to developing countries for the first time. Developing countries with annual GNP per capita at or above $1,000 must phase out all export subsidies progressively over eight to ten years, unless the Subsidies Committee extends the period. Each developing country also must phase out export subsidies in a

given product sector over two years, whenever its share of world trade in that sector reaches 3.25 percent during two consecutive years. For least-developed countries and countries with GNP per capita below $1,000, the phase-out period for export subsidies for competitive products will be eight years. Developing countries will be allowed a five-year phase-out period, and the least-developed countries an eight-year period, to eliminate prohibited import substitution subsidies.

* * * A member may challenge a developing-country subsidy in WTO dispute settlement proceedings if the subsidy nullifies or impairs tariff concessions or other GATT obligations (such as displacing or impeding exports into the developing country's market) or causes injury to a domestic industry in the challenging country. Developing countries will be exempt from WTO (but not domestic CVD) subsidy remedies for notified, time-limited subsidies linked to programs to privatize state-owned firms.

5. A controversy involving the prohibition on export subsidies focused on provisions of the U.S. Internal Revenue Code that permitted deferral of U.S. tax on certain export-related income of a U.S. corporation that qualified as a domestic international sales corporation (DISC). A GATT panel found that the DISC provisions created a subsidy not permitted by the GATT and the report was adopted by the GATT Council in 1981. 16 J. World Trade L. 361–62 (1982). The issue was defused in 1984 when the DISC provisions were largely but not entirely supplanted by provisions granting tax reductions to the export-related income of a foreign sales corporation (FSC) that is organized under foreign law and has substantial foreign activities. 28 U.S.C.A. §§ 921–927. See Jackson, The Jurisprudence of International Trade: The DISC Case in GATT, 72 A.J.I.L. (1978).

6. On October 12, 1999, a WTO Dispute Settlement Body panel (DSB) issued a final report on the EU complaint against the U.S. laws granting tax benefits to FSCs. The EU complaint alleged that the tax reductions accorded to U.S. FSCs were illegal export subsidies. The dispute panel, formed in September 1998, ruled that the benefits available under the FSC rules violated the SCM Agreement and the Agreement on Agriculture, which prohibit subsidies contingent upon export performance. The panel report gave the United States until October 1, 2000, to comply with these agreements. Tax Notes International, December 20, 1999, at p. 2292. This decision has been affirmed by a WTO appeals panel. United States–Tax Treatment for Foreign Sales Corporations, WTO Appellate Body, WT/DS108/AB/R, 24 February 2000 (00–0675). In 1999, the FSC provisions produced estimated tax savings to U.S. businesses of $4 billion. See Kahn, U.S. Loses Dispute on Export Sales, N.Y. Times, February 24, 2000, at A1. It was also estimated that $1 of every $4 of U.S. exports of goods and services was channeled through FSCs. Daily Tax Reports (BNA) 228 DTR G–3, November 29, 1999.

On November 15, 2000, the President signed into law the FSC Repeal and Extraterritorial Income Exclusion Act of 2000, P.L. 106–519 ("2000 Act"). The 2000 Act replaces the FSC regime with an exclusion from the gross income of a U.S. taxpayer for certain foreign trade income. As a result, the excluded income is exempt from U.S. tax. In an apparent effort to sidestep the WTO DSB ruling that the FSC benefits were contingent on exports, the exclusion is not limited to income from U.S. exports, does not require the use of a foreign corporation and permits the manufacturing to be done outside the United States. In general, the exclusion regime appears to be an attempt to align the Code more closely than the FSC provisions with the territorial systems used by some of the European countries. The ironic result is that the change increases the tax benefit to U.S.

taxpayers and adds an estimated $1.5 billion to the projected $25 billion five-year cost of the FSC benefits. Bus. Week, Sept. 4, 2000 at p. 103. Perhaps not surprisingly, the EC has objected to the new U.S. regime and on November 17, 2000, asked the WTO to approve retaliatory sanctions against U.S. products worth more than $4 billion to compensate the EC for damages allegedly suffered by the EC as a result of the FSC tax benefits accorded to U.S. exporters. On November 17, 2000, the EC also requested that a WTO dispute settlement panel rule on whether the extraterritorial income exclusion that replaces the FSC provisions is in compliance with the WTO agreements that prohibit export subsidies. In announcing this step, the EC stated:

> The new legislation continues to provide a significant illegal export subsidy to more than half of total US exports, to the direct detriment of European companies. Furthermore, the legislation maintains in place the FSC regime at least until the year 2002, despite the WTO ruling and implementation deadlines. * * *

EC, Dispute Settlement: United States—Tax Treatment for "Foreign Sales Corporations" (Nov. 17, 2000). The EC also contends that the new legislation makes the tax benefits contingent on use of at least 50 percent domestic rather than imported materials, which the EC argues is also illegal under the SCM Agreement. Arbitration on the amount of sanctions the EC may impose as a result of noncompliance of the FSC regime with WTO Agreements has been suspended pending the outcome of the compliance dispute relating to the extraterritorial income exclusion.

7. *Dumping and Anti–Dumping Duties*

Article VI(1) of the GATT defines "dumping" as sales below "normal value." Normal value means the price of the same product when destined for consumption in the producing state. In the absence of such a price, it means the price charged with respect to exports to third countries or the cost of production, whichever is higher.

The GATT authorizes the imposition by the importing state of an anti-dumping duty to equal the full amount of the margin of dumping, but Article 8(1) of the Anti–Dumping Code, to which the United States is a party, states that it is desirable that the duty be lower if adequate to remove the injury. Agreement on the Implementation of the General Agreement on Tariffs and Trade (Anti–Dumping Code 1979), 31 U.S.T. 4919, T.I.A.S. No. 9650. See also Trade Agreement Act of 1979, 19 U.S.C.A. § 2503.

Notes

1. Especially in the case of enterprises owned by a government, the same product may benefit from an export subsidy and may be sold at a price falling within the dumping definition. Both countervailing duties and anti-dumping duties may be imposed in respect of the same product, but not in such a way as to provide a duplicate response to a single effect of a foreign practice. Restatement (Third) § 806, Comment *a*.

2. The U.S. Anti-dumping Act of 1916 has been charged by the EU as being in violation of the WTO rules. In February 1999, the WTO established a panel to review whether the Act runs counter to anti-dumping agreements. The Act allows remedies for dumping in addition to anti-dumping duties and does not accommo-

date WTO investigation procedures. The United States has responded that the Act is essentially moribund, having no more than a de minimis effect on trade. Antidumping Law Challenge Stalled, 16 Int'l Trade Rep. (BNA) 1572 (Sept. 29, 1999).

8. *Emergency Action to Protect Domestic Producers*

Article XIX—the escape clause of the GATT—provides that a party may suspend or withdraw a concession with respect to a product if it finds that, as a result of unforeseen developments and of concessions given, the product is being imported into its territory in such increased quantities and under such conditions as to cause or threaten serious injury to its domestic producers. Such suspension or withdrawal may be taken only in case of emergency and only for so long as necessary to deal with it. A party must give advance notice to other parties and to states having a substantial interest as exporters and, except in critical circumstances, is required to consult with the parties primarily affected before taking action. Art. XIX(2). Any party injured by the action may respond by suspending substantially equivalent concessions on imports from the state resorting to the escape clause action.

Note

The GATT provides a number of alternatives to invoking the escape clause mechanism. Tariff concessions may be renegotiated at specified intervals under Article XXVIII. Exporting and importing parties may enter into an orderly marketing agreement so long as third parties are not adversely affected. Under Article XVII(4)(a) developing states may restrict imports temporarily to aid domestic industries.

9. *Customs Unions and Free Trade Areas*

Under Article XXIV of the GATT, two or more parties may form a customs union or a free trade area, provided that (i) the resulting tariffs and other restrictions on trade with other states are not on the whole higher or more restrictive than the general incidence of duties and restrictions previously applicable in the territory of the customs union or free trade area and (ii) duties and other restrictions on substantially all trade within the territory of the union or area are eliminated. Participating states must follow procedures specified in Article XXIV for notifying the WTO, consultation with the contracting states, and negotiation with particularly affected states.

Notes

1. A customs union is a grouping of states in which duties and trade restrictions are eliminated with respect to internal trade while the same duties and trade restrictions are applied by all members of the union to imports from all other states (the common external tariff). The European Union is the leading example. Other examples include the Andean Common Market (ANCOM), and the Central American Common Market (CACM). A free trade area also involves eliminating duties and restrictions on trade within the area, but each member is free to determine its own duties and restrictions with respect to trade with nonmembers. An example is the North American Free Trade Agreement (NAFTA), p. 1590 note 4. At the signing of the NAFTA with Canada and Mexico on

December 17, 1992, President Bush expressed the hope that the Agreement would eventually encompass all of the Western Hemisphere. In the meantime, efforts to establish free trade areas or common markets are progressing in Latin America and the Caribbean on other fronts under the auspices of the Andean Pact Organization, MERCOSUR (Argentina, Bolivia, Chile and Uruguay) and the Caribbean Community (CARICOM). Moreover, the Treaty Establishing the African Economic Community, signed on June 3, 1991, 30 I.L.M. 1241 (1991), involving the 51 member states of the Organization of African Unity, called for creation of a free trade area within 10 years. Similar developments have occurred in Southeast Asia with Japan and the United States indicating interest in participating in arrangements that would eventually include all Pacific Rim countries. The Association of Southeast Asian Nations (ASEAN), including Brunei Darussalam, Indonesia, Malaysia, Philippines, Singapore, and Thailand entered into agreements on January 28, 1992, to establish an ASEAN Free Trade Area (AFTA) within 15 years. The centerpiece is a common effective preferential tariff applicable to goods originating in ASEAN member states. 31 I.L.M. 506 (1992).

2. In 1985, the United States and Israel entered into an agreement establishing a bilateral free trade area. Under the agreement all duties have been eliminated. Agreement on the Establishment of a Free Trade Area Between the Government of the United States and the Government of Israel, signed April 22, 1985. Shortly thereafter, it was approved by Congress. Pub. L. No. 99–47, 99 Stat. 82.

3. The Canada–United States Free Trade Agreement (CUSFTA) became effective on January 1, 1989. 27 I.L.M. 281 (1988). With this agreement, the United States and Canada created a free trade area involving the largest volume of trade between any two nations. During the first year of the agreement, trade between the two countries increased by $30 billion. See Baker, The Canada–United States Free Trade Agreement, 23 Int'l Law. 37 (1989). The United States implemented the Agreement in the United States–Canada Free Trade Agreement Implementation Act of 1988, Pub. L. No. 1(100)–449, 102 Stat. 1851, 19 U.S.C. § 2112 (1988).

The principal goal of the Canada–United States agreement was the elimination of tariffs and other barriers to free trade between the two countries. More specifically, the agreement expanded some of the parties' basic obligations under the GATT, created new obligations with respect to trade in services, and established new dispute-resolution mechanisms.

4. Pursuant to special authorization by Congress, a NAFTA between Canada, Mexico and the United States entered into effect in 1994. See North American Free Trade Implementation Act, Pub. L. 103–182, 107 Stat. 2057 (1993). NAFTA calls for phasing out barriers to trade in goods and services in North America, eliminating specified barriers to investment, and strengthening the protection of intellectual property rights. As tariffs and other trade barriers are eliminated, the NAFTA will create a massive open market involving over 360 million people and over $6 trillion in annual output. NAFTA replaced CUSFTA.

10. Special Treatment of Developing States

Article XVII of the GATT allows states with "low standards of living" and in "the early stages of development" to depart from their obligations under the GATT by imposing tariffs or quotas, granting subsidies or by taking other measures to protect domestic industries or their balance of payments.

Moreover, in 1971, the parties to the GATT granted a general waiver to permit developed countries to make tariff concessions to developing states that they did not grant to other states. BISD, 18th Supp. p. 24 (1972).

Notes

1. It has been the position of the United States that it is contrary to the GATT for a developing state to grant a preference to a developed state in return for a preference granted to it. It also seems contrary to the GATT for a developed state to grant a preference to one developing state but not to others. Restatement (Third) § 810, Comment *b*.

2. Restatement (Third) § 810, Comment *c* states:

> Title V of the Trade Act of 1974 authorizes a Generalized System of Preferences, adopted in response to the GATT waiver of 1971. That legislation, renewed in 1984, authorizes the President to designate states as eligible to introduce eligible goods free of duty or subject to reduced duties. * * * Further, products of the following categories of states are ineligible for GSP treatment: members of the Organization of Petroleum Exporting Countries and similar cartel arrangements; states affording trade preferences to developed states other than the United States; states refusing to cooperate with the United States in narcotics control; states refusing to honor awards resulting from arbitrations with United States citizens; states that have expropriated investments or otherwise impaired the rights of United States investors in violation of international law, as defined in the Hickenlooper Amendment (§ 712, Reporters' Note 2), unless the President determines that designation of the state will be in the national economic interest of the United States. Products likely to damage domestic industries * * * are ineligible for GSP benefits. The goods that may be exempt from duty are limited to a fixed amount per year per country for any product category, adjusted for changes in the gross national product of the United States. In addition, if imports of any product from any country reach or exceed 50 percent of all imports of that product, then (subject to stated exceptions) duty-free imports of that product shall cease.

The Generalized System of Preferences (GSP) is codified, as amended, at 19 U.S.C. §§ 2461–2466 (1994).

3. Developing countries have contended that the GATT's basic structure disfavors them and tends to keep in place tariff protection that is biased against imports of manufactured products from developing countries. In addition, they have argued that developed countries have increased non-tariff barriers against manufactured goods from developing countries. These complaints led developing nations to sponsor the creation of the UNCTAD, which first met in 1964 and since has become a permanent institution affiliated with the U.N. General Assembly. See Pestieau & Henry, Non–Tariff Barriers as a Problem in International Development 39–96 (The Canadian Economic Policy Committee, Montreal 1972). Trade issues are discussed both in the WTO (formerly the GATT) and UNCTAD.

4. Six core organizations are working together with the Least Developed Countries (LDCs) to coordinate their trade assistance programs through an Integrated Framework (IF) for Trade–Related Technical Assistance to these countries. These agencies are the IMF, the International Trade Centre (ITC), UNCTAD, the U.N. Development Programme (UNDP), the World Bank, and the WTO. LDCs can invite other multilateral and bilateral development partners to

participate in the IF process. The IF is a concrete result of the WTO Plan of Action for the Least Developed Countries, agreed at the Ministerial Conference of WTO in December 1996. The six agencies have agreed to develop and apply it on a case-by-case basis to meet the needs identified by individual LDCs, to assist them to enhance their trade opportunities, to respond to market demands and to better integrate them into the multilateral trading system.

11. Commodity Agreements

One of the most significant factors in the economic development of many developing countries is the extent to which they depend on income from exports of primary commodities. Apart from making long-term attempts to diversify their economies, developing countries have therefore sought to stabilize commodity prices through bilateral or multilateral commodity agreements.

There have been three types of commodity agreements. The first of these—exemplified by the International Wheat Agreement—obligates importers and exporters to buy or sell certain guaranteed quantities at a price fluctuating between stipulated maximum and minimum prices. The second type—exemplified by the International Natural Rubber Agreement—establishes an international buffer stock administered by an authority which seeks to stabilize prices by buying the commodity whenever the price falls below a certain minimum and selling when it rises above it. The third type—exemplified by the International Coffee Agreement—seeks to assure equitable export shares between competing producers of a commodity in surplus production by allocating export quotas and obligating the participating importers to limit their imports from non-participants.

Article XX(h) of the GATT permits parties to enter into commodity agreements, provided that they are open to participation by both exporting and importing states and are designed to assure the availability of supplies adequate to meet demand at stable prices. See Art. XXXVIII(2)(a).

Notes

1. The United States has been party to commodity agreements relating to coffee, cotton, jute, natural rubber, sugar, tropical timber, wheat and wine. See Restatement (Third) § 811, Reporters' Note 2 and Khan, The Law and Organization of International Commodity Agreements (1982). The United States signed the International Natural Rubber Agreement on April 23, 1996. S. Treaty Doc. No. 27, 104th Cong., 2d Sess. (1996). See also Foli, Note: International Coffee Agreements and The Elusive Goal of Price Stability, 4 Minn.J.Global Trade 79 (1995).

2. There has been considerable pressure from developing countries for protection against commodity price fluctuations. See, e.g., Brown, Developing Countries in the International Trade Order, 14 N.Ill.U.L.Rev. 347 (1994) and Kreinin & Finger, A Critical Survey of the New International Economic Order, 10 J. World Trade L. 493 (1976). One consequence has been the establishment of a Compensatory Finance Facility under the IMF upon which developing states may draw by showing the impact on their economy of commodity price fluctuations and expressing willingness to accept the IMF's conditions. See p. 1605 and Finger & Derose, The Compensatory Finance Facility and Export Instability, 14 J. World Trade L. 14 (1980). In recent years, most negotiations concerning commodity agreements have been conducted under the auspices of UNCTAD.

12. Export Controls

A party to the GATT is not permitted to impose quantitative restrictions on exports to achieve economic advantage for its products. See Articles I(1)(MFN), XI, XIII, XX, XXI. Other export controls, even if discriminatory, do not generally violate the GATT. Moreover, controls to prevent "critical shortages" of foodstuffs or other temporary essential products (Art. XI) and controls essential to the acquisition or distribution of products in short supply (Art. XX(j)) are specifically permitted under certain circumstances. These exceptions are very broad, and in any event, the GATT does not prohibit export taxes.

Article XXI of the GATT provides a general exception to all GATT obligations for measures taken by a state that are "necessary for the protection of its essential security interests." * * * Under the protection of this provision, the United States has operated a system for controlling exports of strategic materials (and technology) to potential adversaries. See generally Jackson, Davey & Sykes, Legal Problems of International Economic Relations 961 (3d ed. 1995). The United States has also used export controls to deter conduct by foreign states deemed inimical to U.S. interests.

Notes

1. Most of the OPEC states participating in the oil embargo imposed against the United States and the Netherlands in 1973 were not parties to the GATT.

2. Could export controls implemented by the United States alone or collectively with other states violate principles of international law other than those contained in the GATT? Can they violate the provisions of bilateral treaties of friendship, commerce and navigation treaties or bilateral investment treaties to which the United States is party? See p. 807. Can a state injured by a violation of international law by another state lawfully resort to a boycott? See Restatement (Third) § 812, Reporters' Note 1. Multilateral export controls sanctioned by the U.N. Security Council, such as those imposed on Libya because of its acquiescence in acts of terrorism, see p. 419, are lawful. See Diggs v. Shultz, 470 F.2d 461 (D.C.Cir.1972), cert. denied, 411 U.S. 931, 93 S.Ct. 1897, 36 L.Ed.2d 390 (1973).

12. Dispute Resolution

GATT PRESS SUMMARY, NEWS OF THE URUGUAY ROUND 29–31

(April 5, 1994).

* * *

Understanding on Rules and Procedures Governing the Settlement of Disputes

The dispute settlement system of the GATT is generally considered to be one of the cornerstones of the multilateral trade order. The system has already been strengthened and streamlined as a result of reforms agreed to following the Mid–Term Review Ministerial Meeting held in Montreal in December 1988. Disputes currently being dealt with by the Council are subject to these new rules, which include greater automaticity in decisions on the establishment, terms of reference and composition of panels, such that these decisions are no longer dependent upon the consent of the parties to a dispute.

The Uruguay Round Understanding on Rules and Procedures Governing the Settlement of Disputes (DSU) will further strengthen the existing system significantly, extending the greater automaticity agreed in the Mid–Term Review to the adoption of the panels' and a new Appellate Body's findings. Moreover, the DSU will establish an integrated system permitting WTO Members to base their claims on any of the multilateral trade agreements included in the Annexes to the Agreement establishing the WTO. For this purpose, a Dispute Settlement Body (DSB) will exercise the authority of the General Council and the Councils and committees of the covered agreements.

The DSU emphasizes the importance of consultations in * * * dispute resolution, requiring a Member to enter into consultations within 30 days of a request for consultations from another Member. If after 60 days from the request for consultations there is no settlement, the complaining party may request the establishment of a panel. Where consultations are denied, the complaining party may move directly to request a panel. The parties may voluntarily agree to follow alternative means of dispute settlement, including good offices, conciliation, mediation and arbitration.

Where a dispute is not settled through consultations, the DSU requires the establishment of a panel, at the latest, at the meeting of the DSB following that at which a request is made, unless the DSB decides by consensus against establishment. The DSU also sets out specific rules and deadlines for deciding the terms of reference and composition of panels. * * *

Panels normally consist of three persons of appropriate background and experience from countries not party to the dispute. The Secretariat will maintain a list of experts satisfying the criteria.

Panel procedures are set out in detail in the DSU. It is envisaged that a panel will normally complete its work within six months or, in cases of urgency, within three months. Panel reports may be considered by the DSB for adoption 20 days after they are issued to Members. Within 60 days of their issuance, they will be adopted, unless the DSB decides by consensus not to adopt the report or one of the parties notifies the DSB of its intention to appeal.

The concept of appellate review is an important new feature of the DSU. An Appellate Body will be established, composed of seven members, three of whom will serve on any one case. An appeal will be limited to issues of law covered in the panel report and legal interpretations developed by the panel. Appellate proceedings shall not exceed 60 days from the date a party formally notifies its decision to appeal. The resulting report shall be adopted by the DSB and unconditionally accepted by the parties within 30 days following its issuance to Members, unless the DSB decides by consensus against its adoption.

Once the panel report or the Appellate Body report is adopted, the party concerned will have to notify its intentions with respect to implementation of adopted recommendations. If it is impracticable to comply immediately, the party concerned shall be given a reasonable period of time, the latter to be decided either by agreement of the parties and approval by the DSB within 45 days of adoption of the report or through arbitration within 90 days of adoption. In any event, the DSB will keep the implementation under regular surveillance until the issue is resolved.

Further provisions set out rules for compensation or the suspension of concessions in the event of non-implementation. Within a specified time-frame, parties can enter into negotiations to agree on mutually acceptable compensation. Where this has not been agreed, a party to the dispute may request authorization of the DSB to suspend concessions or other obligations to the other party concerned. The DSB will grant such authorization within 30 days of the expiry of the agreed time-frame for implementation. Disagreements over the proposed level of suspension may be referred to arbitration. In principle, concessions should be suspended in the same sector as that in issue in the panel case. If this is not practicable or effective, the suspension can be made in a different sector of the same agreement. In turn, if this is not effective or practicable and if the circumstances are serious enough, the suspension of concessions may be made under another agreement.

One of the central provisions of the DSU reaffirms that Members shall not themselves make determinations of violations or suspend concessions, but shall make use of the dispute settlement rules and procedures of the DSU.

* * *

Note

The flowchart on page 1596 illustrates the various stages of the panel process that may be involved under the WTO dispute resolution procedures. You may retrieve this flowchart at www.wto.org/english/thewto_e/whatis_e/tif_e/disp2_e.htm

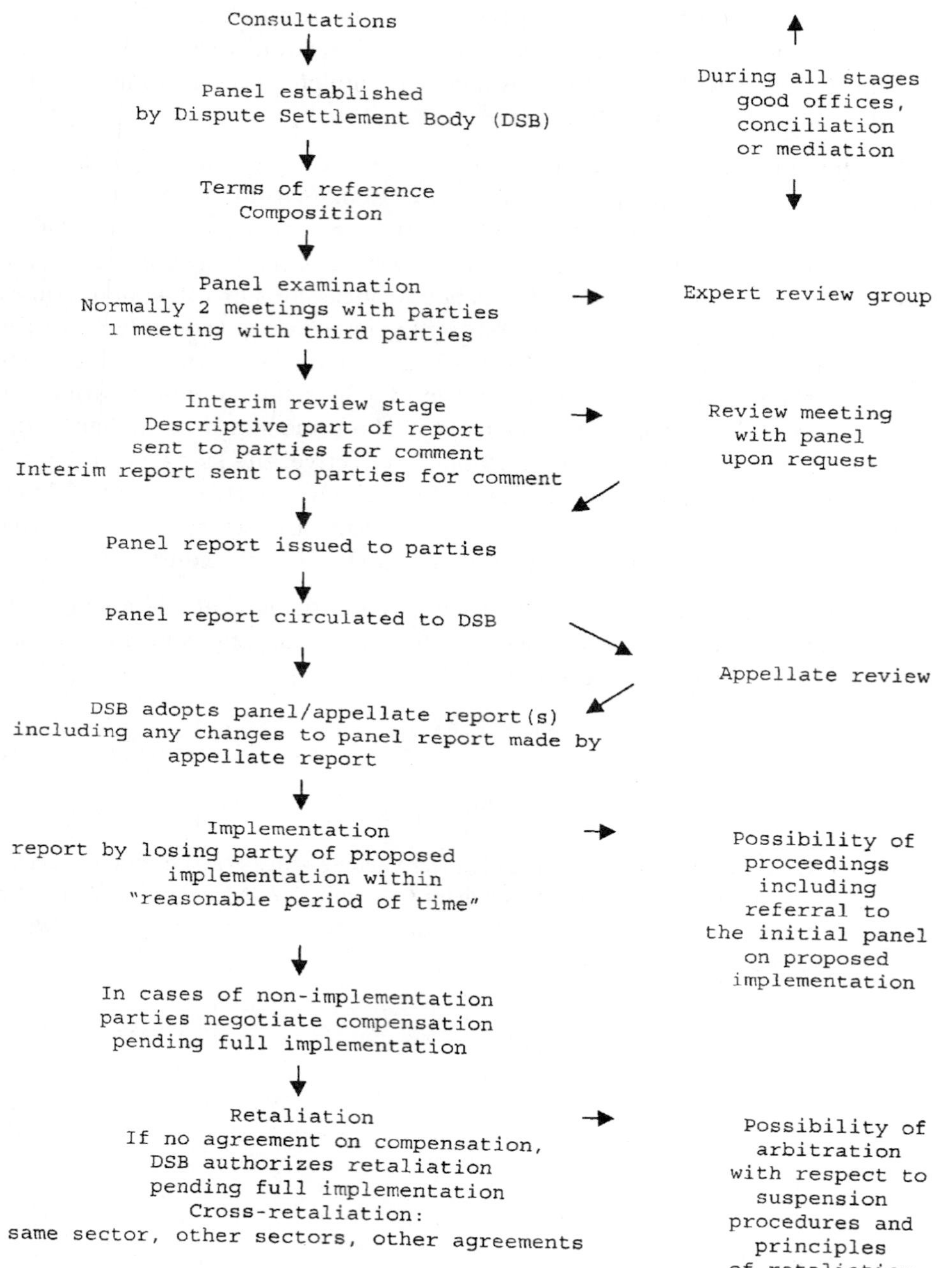

SECTION 3. INTERNATIONAL MONETARY LAW

A. THE INTERNATIONAL MONETARY SYSTEM: THE BRETTON WOODS INSTITUTIONS

With the 1920s came the desire to restore the gold-standard-based monetary system that had existed before World War I. However, the exchange rates established did not take account of the divergence between price of goods and production costs that had occurred since 1913, and the effort failed due to Great Britain's departure from the gold standard in 1931 and the Great Depression in the United States in the 1930s. The depression of the next decade caused low economic activity in the major industrial countries, resulting in a drop in imports, the collapse of commodity prices, and a decline in international trade. To counter the reduced ability to buy foreign goods in exchange for exports, many countries reduced their reserves of gold and international currencies to a low level. To protect these reserves, countries imposed restrictions on citizens' freedom to buy abroad, devised multiple currency systems with more favorable exchange rates for preferred transactions and less favorable for others, held down market values by official purchases and unilaterally devalued their currencies to secure competitive advantages. Exchange rates were chaotic as each country freely modified its currency's rate to stimulate its own exports and protect its own import-substitutive industries in implementation of the dominant "beggar-thy-neighbor" policy of the time.

To avoid a post-World War II slump, the United States and Great Britain conceived of the idea for a conference on international monetary cooperation in the early 1940s. This culminated in a multinational Conference held in Bretton Woods, New Hampshire in 1944, at which two international institutions were created, the International Monetary Fund (IMF or the Fund) and the International Bank for Reconstruction and Development (IBRD or World Bank). The purposes of the IMF were to establish a framework for a multilateral system of international payments and a mechanism to prevent significant fluctuations in currency exchange rates; to provide short-or medium-term funds for states needing reserves; to develop and administer a code of conduct for states in international monetary matters; and to serve as a forum for discussion and resolution of international financial and monetary issues. The purpose of the IBRD was to mobilize economic resources for long-term economic development.

Another goal of the Bretton Woods institutions was the promotion of orderly change through expansion of trade, increasing levels of employment and income, and development of the resources of each member. The Fund and IBRD could be consulted on problems and give technical assistance with respect to monetary, financial and development issues. The immediate consequences of the Conference were the elimination of wartime restrictions and discriminatory practices and the stimulation of post-war trade expansion.

Note

See Ciorciari, A Prospective Enlargement of the Roles of the Bretton Woods Financial Institutions in International Peace Operations, 22 Fordham Int'l L.J. 292 (1998) and Jackson, Managing the World Economy: Fifty Years After Bretton Woods, 142–143 (Kenen, ed. 1994).

B. THE INTERNATIONAL MONETARY FUND

1. Introduction

One of the principal purposes of the IMF was to provide financing to countries for redress of temporary balance of payments problems under appropriate conditions. Resort to previously utilized methods of exchange and payments restrictions, restrictive trade measures, export subsidies or competitive exchange rate practices was outlawed. The Articles of Agreement of the Fund provided the formal rules for an international monetary system. Member quotas supplied the resources for the Fund from which members could borrow; exchange controls on international payments were prohibited except on capital payments needed to ease balance of payments burdens; exchange rates were pegged to a "par value" in gold; and national gold and currency reserves were augmented so that short-run deficits would not end in domestic deflation and unemployment. As of 2000, 183 states were members of the IMF, including the People's Republic of China.

Since its founding the IMF has been a leading forum for the discussion of international financial and monetary matters, and it has served as a source of reserves made available to members to enable them to correct international payment imbalances without resorting to measures that might adversely affect other members, subject to conditions imposed by the Fund that have affected economic and monetary policies of the states assisted in important ways. The code of conduct embodied in the Bretton Woods Agreement lasted for about 25 years, but was fundamentally altered in 1971, when the United States announced that it would no longer assure the convertibility of the U.S. dollar into gold (at $35 per ounce) or other reserve assets.

Article IV of the Bretton Woods Agreement had created a system of fixed par values for the currencies of member states, which could be changed only with the concurrence of the Fund and only under conditions of "fundamental disequilibrium." All currency values were fixed in terms of gold and member states undertook through intervention in exchange markets to maintain the value of their currencies within one percent of parity. After the United States abandoned convertibility of the U.S. dollar into gold or other reserve assets and after some efforts to retain a par value system based on realigned exchange rates, the international monetary system shifted in early 1973 to a system of floating exchange rates in which major states no longer undertook to maintain any specific exchange rate with other currencies or gold.

During the period from 1971 to 1976, the institutional arrangements of the Bretton Woods Agreement were basically retained, as were many aspects of the code of conduct, including the provisions related to exchange controls, p. ___ infra. In January 1976, an agreement was reached amending the Articles of the IMF principally to revise Article IV to accommodate and reflect the floating exchange rate system.

The principal source of financial resources for the IMF is the capital subscriptions or quotas of its members. These quotas are now expressed in Special Drawing Rights, called SDRs, described at p. 1601 infra, created by the Fund as a supplement to existing international reserve assets.

The financial assistance provided by the Fund to its members is accomplished through purchases of currency. In drawing from the Fund, a member buys freely convertible currencies of other members with its own currency. Upon repayment (usually within three to five years) the member repurchases its own currency with currencies acceptable to the Fund. As of FY 2000, the IMF had credits and loans outstanding of 50.4 billion in SDRs (about $66.5 billion U.S. dollars). The arrangements through which convertible currencies are purchased by member states for their own currency and their own currency is subsequently repurchased by them involve what are called regular and special facilities described at p. 1604 infra.

During the period from 1979 through 1985, the IMF was heavily involved in assisting developing country members to deal with problems resulting from dramatic increases in international debt, oil prices and interest rates. Between mid–1982 and the end of 1984, the Fund lent SDR 22 billion in support of adjustment programs in 70 member countries. In addition, it helped arrange financial packages for debtor members from governments, commercial banks and other financial institutions. On occasion the Fund would request commercial banks to commit new loans before the Fund approved adjustment programs and provided financing for debtor countries from its own resources. Each dollar of Fund financing was estimated to "unlock" from four to seven dollars of new loans and refinancing from governments and commercial banks. By April 1985, 21 Fund members had agreed with commercial banks to restructure $150 billion (20 percent) of the bank debt of developing countries. The willingness of commercial banks to accept lower spreads, longer repayment periods and grace periods under these rescheduling arrangements was materially enhanced by the effectiveness of adjustment efforts undertaken by debtor states with support from the resources of the Fund.

During the early 1990s, the IMF committed its resources to three principal areas. First, it assisted those member countries whose economies were disrupted by the invasion of Kuwait by Iraq and the Gulf War in adjusting the resulting payments imbalances. Second, it provided both financial and technical assistance to the Eastern European countries in transition from centrally planned to market-based economies. In particular, it supplied policy advice, technical assistance, and balance of payments financing in support of macroeconomic and structural reform programs in these countries. Third, it continued its efforts to assist its poorest members in achieving economic growth.

The Asian financial crisis that erupted in July 1997 in Thailand, and its subsequent global reverberations, dominated the IMF's work in the two-year period ended April 30, 1999. The crisis—the global consequences of which continued after the end of the financial year—also prompted a record level of IMF lending, adding immediacy to the need to strengthen the financial resources of the institution to enable it to continue playing a fully effective role in the globalized world economy. The crisis also led to the creation of a new lending facility (the Supplemental Reserve Facility); stepped-up work on strengthening the conduct of IMF surveillance; and, more generally, to the elaboration of a framework for strengthening the architecture of the international monetary system. Separately, the IMF undertook an extensive review of its concessional lending facility for low-income countries, the Enhanced Structural Adjustment Facility (ESAF), and continued its work aimed at ensuring the uninterrupted availability of financial resources for the ESAF. Together with the World Bank and other creditors, the IMF made important headway in implementing the initiative to reduce the external debt burden of a number of heavily indebted poor countries (the HIPC Initiative).

In its 2000 fiscal year (ended on April 30, 2000), the Fund focused on strengthening the international monetary and financial system and on enhancing its support for its poorest member countries. A stronger global financial architecture is widely seen as essential for helping countries both benefit from, and better cope with, the pressures of economic globalization—pressures that were given voice in public demonstrations against the IMF and World Bank at their April 2000 meetings. The IMF has recognized that its own adaptation is critical for helping it (i) deal more effectively with potential turbulence in emerging market economies, (ii) assist countries in transition from central planning to market-oriented systems, and (iii) promote growth and reduce poverty in the world's poorest countries. As stated in its 2000 Annual Report, the IMF took steps in a variety of areas during the year to transform its operations. These included:

> • increasing the transparency of members' policies and of IMF activities, in large part by releasing an unprecedented amount of information;
>
> • developing and strengthening international standards of good practice, and assessing members' observance of the standards;
>
> • helping member countries strengthen their financial systems, and better evaluating financial sector risks and vulnerabilities;
>
> • involving the private sector in preventing and resolving financial crises;
>
> • improving its capacity to reduce poverty in the poorest countries * * * by transforming the former Enhanced Structural Adjustment Facility into the Poverty Reduction and Growth Facility, which makes poverty reduction a key element of a growth-oriented strategy; and
>
> • enhancing the joint IMF–World Bank Initiative for Heavily Indebted Poor Countries to provide faster, broader, and deeper debt relief.
>
> These reforms took into account, as never before, the IMF's role in relation to other international institutions and groups—notably the World Bank, but also the Financial Stability Forum (FSF), the Bank for International Settlements (BIS), other Basel-based groups, the World Trade Organization (WTO), the Organization for Economic Cooperation and Development (OECD), and others.

Annual Report, 2000 at 1–2.

Note

For discussion of the development and functioning of the IMF, see, e.g., Griffith–Jones, Stabilizing Capital Flows to Developing Countries: The Role of Regulation in Regulating International Business 161–82 (Picciotto & Mayne eds., 1999); Gwin & Feinberg, The International Monetary Fund in a Multipolar World: Pulling Together (1989); de Vries, Balance of Payments Adjustments, 1945 to 1986: The IMF Experience (1987); Gold, Developments in the International Monetary System, the International Monetary Fund and International Monetary Law since 1971, 174 Rec. des Cours 107 (1982); de Vries, The International Monetary Fund, 1972–1982: Cooperation on Trial (1985); Edwards, International Monetary Collaboration (1985); Lowenfeld, The International Monetary System (2d ed. 1984). Reviews of the Fund's operations are contained in the Fund's annual reports. Official actions by the Fund (including decisions of the Board of Governors and Executive Directors) are published in Selected Decisions of the International Monetary Fund.

2. *The Main Features of the IMF Articles*

Under the Articles, each member of the Fund is assigned a quota, which reflects its relative position in the world's economy. One quarter of the quota (including any increases) had generally to be paid in gold (under the original Articles) or must (under the amended Articles) be paid in SDRs or convertible currencies specified by the Fund. The other three quarters may be paid in the member's own currency. Quotas may be changed with the member's consent and overall quotas are reviewed at intervals of not more than five years.

In January 1998, the Board of Governors increased IMF quotas by 45 percent from SDR 146 billion to SDR 212 billion. In January 1999, the consent of the 85 percent majority of member countries needed for the quota increase to become effective was secured. As of 2000, the United States remained, as it has been from the outset, the largest quotaholder in the Fund at 18.25 percent.

The member's required contribution to the resources of the Fund, the amounts of its drawing rights and its voting power are geared to its quota. The bulk of IMF resources is provided by these quota subscriptions, but the IMF may borrow in order to supplement its reserves.

The first amendment to the Articles in 1969 gave the Fund the authority to issue Special Drawing Rights (SDRs), the first international reserve asset to be created by a decision of the international community. See p. 1607. The SDRs are allocated to particular members by the Board of Governors in order to supplement existing reserve assets. Parties can engage in SDR transactions when one member needs currency for balance of payments outflows only with the Fund's approval and its designation of a member to receive SDRs in exchange for currency.

Training and technical assistance to members are available in various forms and are directed largely to assisting developing countries in establishing policies aimed at rectifying their balance of payments problems. The IMF Institute provides training facilities to officials of member governments. Technical advisory assistance aimed at establishing or strengthening national monetary systems is provided by experts, upon request by member countries, through the activities of the Central Banking Service. Experts are generally assigned for periods of one year and are responsible solely to the institution to which they are assigned. The IMF Fiscal Affairs Department provides technical assistance on tax policy.

3. *Structural Framework*

a. Organization

The Fund is composed of the Board of Governors, the Executive Directors, and the Managing Director and staff. Nearly all powers originally vested in the Board have now been delegated to the Executive Directors. The Board meets once a year in conjunction with the annual meeting of the World Bank, with each country represented by a Governor (usually the Minister of Finance or President of the Central Bank) and an alternate.

The Executive Directors supervise the day-to-day management of the Fund. There are 24 Executive Directors, five of whom are appointed by the five countries having the largest quotas (United States, Japan, Germany,

France, and United Kingdom) and 19 elected at two-year intervals by the remaining members. The Articles provide for two Executive Directors to be elected by the American Republics not entitled to appoint (XII(3)(b)(iv)), but since 1956 an additional Director has been elected by them. No provision is made for representation of other regional groups, but in practice countries with homogeneous interests have combined to form fairly stable combinations in order to muster the prescribed minimum number of votes necessary to elect an Executive Director. In addition, the number of appointed Directors may be augmented by one or two if during the two years preceding an election the six member countries with the largest quotas do not include the two members that have provided the largest absolute amounts of currency used by the Fund in its activities (Art. XII(3)(c)).

The Managing Director of the Fund is selected by the Executive Directors for an initial term of five years. He is Chairman of the Executive Directors and participates in meetings of the Board of Governors, is chief of the Fund's operating staff and, under the direction of the Executive Directors, manages the ordinary business of the Fund.

b. Voting

The IMF was one of the first post-war international organizations to provide for unequal voting power. Each member is allotted the same basic number of votes (250) in recognition of the equality of states and to give adequate voice to all members. Additional votes are allocated in proportion to a country's quota, expressed since 1972 in SDRs (one vote for each SDR 100,000 of quota). As of November 2, 1999, there were a total of 2,142,564 votes, the largest allotment being 371,743 votes held by the United States and the smallest being 275 held by the Marshall Islands.

The voting scheme applies to the Board of Governors and the Executive Directors. The Articles are silent on the relationship between the Executive Directors and the group of members which they represent. The degree to which the Executive Directors wish to adhere to the advice of members is left to their discretion. Votes are cast as a unit by the Executive Director concerned.

When the Articles were agreed upon, the idea of weighted voting was accepted. The assumption was that a country's voice in an international financial organization should be related to its contributions to the organization's resources. Most decisions taken by the Board of Governors or the Executive Directors are adopted by a simple majority of the votes cast. However, for more important decisions, a larger majority is required. Broadly, a 70 percent majority of the total voting power is needed to resolve such operational issues as rates of charges on the use of the Fund's resources and the rate of interest on holdings of SDRs. An 85-percent majority (often referred to as a "high" majority) is required to decide certain particularly important matters, such as those concerned with the structure of the Fund, changes in quotas, the allocation of SDRs, and the disposition of the Fund's gold. The United States alone, or the members of the European Union or the group of developing countries voting together, can veto proposals subject to a high majority. In practice, formal votes are rarely taken by the Executive Directors. In most cases, decisions are taken by consensus.

Note

In response to claims by developing countries that they had inadequate voting power, the size of the Board of Executive Directors was increased in order to give them greater representation, and increased emphasis has been placed on the involvement of all members in Fund decisions.

4. The Shift from Fixed to Floating Exchange Rates

Under the original agreement, each nation undertook to maintain a "par value" in gold for its currency and to convert foreign official holdings of its currency into gold or the currency of the holder. Spot transactions of exchange had to take place within a prescribed margin of parity relationships, and governments intervened in the exchange markets to maintain the par values of their currencies. Changes in par values were allowed only when "fundamental disequilibria" in balance of payments made it necessary.

Gold was the main reserve asset of the system. But gold convertibility turned out to be inadequate. The supply needed for monetary purposes was not available due to the limited production of gold and the growth of individual and commercial uses. Differences between the official and private market led to official sales in private markets, speculation, and pressure for change in official prices. Countries purchased dollars in order to finance transactions, since the growth in capital transactions was not satisfied by the gold reserves alone. Eventually, par values no longer reflected the changes that had occurred in the relations among countries, as the rapid growth of Japan and Europe created imbalances in payments.

At the time of the Bretton Woods Conference, the dollar was the most widely used currency. To obtain additional liquidity in the system, countries maintained their par values through intervention of the dollar because the United States was willing to buy and sell gold for officially held dollars. The dollar became overvalued as other countries did not make needed adjustments, and the United States accumulated short term debt abroad. Dependence on the dollar led to a United States balance of payments deficit that in 1971 was three times the value of United States gold holdings.

The late 1960s saw the revaluation or devaluation of a number of widely used currencies, such as the pound sterling, French franc, and Deutsche mark. In May 1971, the mark and Dutch guilder were allowed to float without government intervention to maintain stable rates. In August 1971, the United States suspended the convertibility of the dollar into gold or other reserve assets. This act was followed by the decision of several other countries to allow their currencies to float.

The Articles did not provide for floating exchange rates, and floating was in fact generally a violation of the obligation to keep transactions within a prescribed margin (Art. XV, sec. 2). However, the Fund tolerated floating rates. At first, the Fund merely refrained from voicing formal objection, but thereafter it allowed access to its resources by those members permitting floating rates. Floating came to be viewed as the best remedy for inflation that could not be controlled in the short run and useful in accomplishing the transition to different parity levels.

In reacting to the chain of events in the early 1970s, the Fund merely noted the circumstances accounting for the actions of the members, emphasized their obligation to collaborate with the Fund to promote exchange stability, welcomed the expressed intent of the members to resume compliance with their obligations as soon as circumstances permitted, and stated that the Fund would remain in close consultation with them. No sanction was brought to bear on the members; instead, attention was turned to reforming the system to adapt it to the needs of a changed world situation. It was recognized that governments could not maintain stable rates due to hostilities in the Middle East, petroleum price increases, labor unemployment and inflation.

5. *Revision of the System*

An Interim Committee established in 1974 to devise a new monetary system proposed amendments in the Jamaican Agreement of 1976. These were approved by the Board of Governors and submitted to the legislative bodies of member countries.

The amendments provide for elimination of the central role of gold by abolishing its official price, eliminating all requirements for its use in Fund transactions, and empowering the Fund to dispose of its gold holdings. Quotas were expanded, and the required "high" majority of 85 percent for decisions of major policy significance in the Fund was established. This was intended to ensure wide support for such decisions and protect the concerns of the major industrial countries. Further expansion of the Fund's financing ability was provided for by a temporary 45 percent expansion of access to regular facilities, liberalization of the Compensatory Finance Facility (recently renamed the "Compensatory and Contingency Financing Facility" (CCFF)), and expansion of SDR uses.

New exchange rate provisions replaced the par value system, legalizing such practices as floating and allowing members to choose their own exchange arrangements. A general obligation was imposed on members to collaborate with the Fund and each other to assure orderly exchange arrangements and promote a stable exchange rate system. The Fund was given authority for surveillance over the policies of members and the adoption of principles of guidance for such policies.

Note

The revised Articles of Agreement of the International Monetary Fund, Second Amendment, April 30, 1976, 29 U.S.T. 2203, T.I.A.S. No. 8937 entered in force for the United States on April 1, 1978.

6. *Use of IMF Resources by Member States*

Members of the Fund may apply to use the resources of the Fund to assist in dealing with balance of payments problems. Freely convertible funds, for example U.S. dollars, pounds sterling, or Japanese yen, are sold by the Fund to the member state for its own currency subject to the member's agreement to repurchase its own currency within a stated period (normally three to five years) for other currencies acceptable to the Fund and subject to conditions negotiated with the Fund concerning the economic policies to be pursued by the member during that period.

Drawings on the resources of the IMF are usually made in "tranches" representing one quarter of the drawing member's quota. The Fund's credit under its so-called regular facilities is made available in four segments or tranches of 25 percent each of the member's quota. A drawing that raises the Fund's holdings of the member's currency by 25 percent of its quota is a first credit tranche purchase, from 25 to 50 percent is a second credit tranche purchase, and so on through the fourth credit tranche. Since one quarter of the member's quota was actually contributed by it in reserve assets, a drawing of the first credit tranche ("reserve tranche") is in effect a drawing against the assets it has contributed. A drawing of the first credit tranche requires only that a member demonstrate reasonable efforts to overcome its balance of payments difficulties. Performance criteria and charges are not applied and repurchases are normally required in 3¼ to 5 years, while drawings under subsequent credit tranches are subject to charges and conditions that are usually increasingly restrictive for each successive tranche.

Conditions for drawings in excess of the first reserve tranche may be negotiated at the time of an actual drawing or, as is frequently the case, in advance, in connection with a stand-by arrangement. A stand-by is an arrangement under which the member is assured that it will be able to draw on the resources of the IMF up to a stated amount within a stated period of up to 3 years on the basis of conditions and understandings negotiated with the Fund at the time the stand-by arrangement is effected. Stand-by arrangements focus on macroeconomic policies, such as fiscal, monetary, and exchange rate policies, aimed at overcoming balance of payments difficulties. Performance criteria to assess policy implementation, such as budgetary and credit ceilings, reserve and external debt targets, and avoidance of restrictions on current payments and transfers, are applied during the period of the arrangement, and purchases (or drawings) are made in installments. Repurchases are made in 3¼ to 5 years.

Under extended arrangements, the Fund supports medium-term programs that generally run for 3 years (up to 4 years in exceptional circumstances) and that are aimed at overcoming balance of payments difficulties stemming from macroeconomic and structural problems. Typically, a program states the general objectives for the three-year period and the policies for the first year; policies for subsequent years are spelled out in annual reviews. Performance criteria are applied, and repurchases are made in 4½ to 10 years, except in the case of purchases made with resources borrowed under the enlarged access policy.

Special Facilities. The Fund provides funding for special purposes through a broad range of so-called special facilities, such as the Compensatory Finance Facility and the Supplemental Reserve Facility referred to above. The resources of these facilities are not part of the Fund's general resources but are administered by the Fund as a service to members. For that reason, the constraints that the Articles place on nondiscriminatory use of the Fund's resources do not apply to these facilities. A variety of special facilities have been created, some of which have been terminated or permitted to lapse after their particular purposes have been served. In the mid–1970s the Fund created two such facilities—the Oil Facility Subsidy Account and the Trust Fund—and in 1980 set up the Supplementary Financing Facility Subsidy Account. The Oil Facility Subsidy Account assisted Fund members most seriously affected by oil price increases. Other examples are special facilities that have been established to help deal with protracted balance of payments problems of low-income countries.

A structural adjustment facility (SAF) set up in 1986 enables the Fund to provide resources on concessional terms to support medium-term macroeconomic adjustment and structural reforms in low-income countries facing protracted balance of payments problems. The member develops and updates a medium-term policy framework for a three-year period. Within this framework, detailed yearly policy programs are formulated and are supported by SAF arrangements, under which annual loan disbursements are made. The programs include quarterly benchmarks to assess performance. The rate of interest on SAF loans is 0.5 percent, and repayments are called for in 5 1/2 to 10 years.

An enhanced structural adjustment facility (ESAF) was set up in 1987. Its objectives, conditions for eligibility, and program features are similar to those under SAF arrangements. However, ESAF arrangements differ in the scope and strength of structural policies adopted, and in terms of access levels, monitoring procedures, and sources of funding.

Under the SAF and ESAF programs, the member country must submit a policy framework paper (PFP) prepared by the member's national authorities, the World Bank and the Fund. The PFP outlines the member's economic and structural objectives, the strategy to achieve these objectives and the proposed financing to support the strategy. Because the PFP requires more formal coordination between the World Bank and the Fund, it incorporates strategies both to alleviate payments imbalances and to address long-term issues of structural adjustment and sector policies as well as analyses of the social impact of the strategies.

As noted above, in FY 2000, the ESAF was transformed into the Poverty Reduction and Growth Facility, which is intended to focus on poverty reduction in the poorest countries.

Notes

1. In April 1999, the IMF instituted Contingent Credit Lines (CCLs) to provide financial support for well-managed economies. The CCLs are designed as a crisis-prevention mechanism when economies are faced with financial market contagions. IMF Annual Report, 1999.

2. "Conditionality" refers to the policies members are expected to follow when they use Fund resources to assist in dealing with balance of payments deficits. The basic concept has been described as follows:

> The Fund attaches to the use of its resources a degree of conditionality sufficient to provide confidence that the borrowing member will overcome its balance of payments difficulties and be able to repurchase its currency from the Fund without undue strain during the specified period. The degree of conditionality thus depends largely on the character of the member's balance of payments problem. If the problem results from temporary factors, such as a cyclical decline in export earnings, the member need only continue its existing policies until the situation returns to normal. On the other hand, if the difficulty is caused by deep-seated factors, such as a persistent deterioration

> in the terms of trade, excessive domestic demand, cost-price distortions, including overvaluation of the domestic currency, or a permanent decline in net capital inflows, the member's policies need to be changed.
>
> The member describes in a letter of intent the policies it intends to implement in order to have access to the Fund's resources under [drawing or] stand-by * * * arrangements. This letter normally contains a summary of the member's policy objectives with respect to its balance of payments, economic growth, and movements in the general price level, as well as an outline of measures being adopted to achieve these objectives.

The Role and Function of the International Monetary Fund 47–49 (Washington 1985).

In recent years there has been increased cooperation between the World Bank and the IMF. As a consequence, members applying for assistance have faced the challenge of cross-conditionality. Cross-conditionality refers to the arrangement under which a borrowing country is required to accept conditions of one financial institution as a precondition for financial support of the other. Although the cross-conditions do not appear as explicit preconditions, they have become a regular practice resulting from increased collaboration between the World Bank and the IMF. The cross-conditionality arrangements, moreover, may involve a variety of financial institutions in addition to the World Bank and the IMF, including commercial banks and export credit agencies. For example, a commercial bank may condition its loan on the borrower's ability to draw under a stand-by arrangement from the IMF. See Kremmydas, The Cross–Conditionality Phenomenon—Some Legal Aspects, 23 Int'l Law. 651, 654 (1989) and Feinberg, The Changing Relationship Between the World Bank and the International Monetary Fund, 42 Int'l Org. 551, 556 (1988).

3. Comment *e* to Restatement (Third) § 821 states:

> The basic condition for use of the Fund's resources is that they must be used in a manner consistent with the Articles of Agreement. Except for drawings within the member's reserve tranche * * * and drawings under certain special facilities, the Fund will examine the economic situation and policies of a member state prior to approval of a drawing or stand-by. The Fund may negotiate arrangements with the state's authorities with respect to economic policies to be pursued by the state during the period the drawing or stand-by is outstanding. Such arrangements are not international agreements in the sense that non-compliance is a breach of an international obligation. * * * However, an unjustified failure to live up to an arrangement with the Fund in connection with a drawing or stand-by may be a basis for non-renewal of a stand-by or for limitations on future drawings, and failure to achieve performance criteria in a stand-by arrangement may interrupt the right to make further drawings thereunder.

4. SDRs are reserve assets created from time to time by decision of the IMF and allocated to member states that participate in the Special Drawing Rights Department in proportion to their quotas. SDRs were created in response to an anticipated shortage of world reserves and were intended to be a supplemental source of reserves independent of the production of gold or of balance of payments deficits of reserve currency states, especially the United States. The shortage of reserves did not develop and as of March 1992 SDRs constituted about 2.2 percent of all reserves, but SDRs have continued to be used not only as an asset that Fund members can use to comply with their reserve asset subscription obligations, but also to settle official balances between states.

Under the original Bretton Woods regime when the U.S. dollar was pegged at 35 U.S. dollars to the ounce of gold, an SDR equalled one U.S. dollar. Since the advent of floating exchange rates, the SDR has been calculated daily with reference to the market exchange rates of the currencies of the five member states (France, Germany, Japan, United Kingdom and United States) with the largest exports of goods and services during the period 1985–1989. The use of the SDR has grown not only in transactions involving the IMF and in official intergovernmental settlements but also as a unit of account in other international state and private agreements, including loans, construction and mining agreements and limitations on the liability of owners of ships, aircraft and other carriers. See Gold, The SDR in Treaty Practice: A Checklist, 22 I.L.M. 209 (1983).

7. *Obligations of Member States*

a. Exchange Arrangements

Article IV specifies the members' obligations with respect to exchange arrangements. There is a general obligation on each member to collaborate with the Fund and with other members to promote orderly exchange arrangements and a stable system of exchange rates. Members are also obligated to pursue economic and financial policies that promote orderly economic growth with reasonable price stability and to foster orderly underlying economic and financial conditions. In addition, they are required to avoid exchange rate and other policies that prevent effective balance of payments adjustment or provide an unfair competitive advantage over other members.

Under the amended IMF Articles, member states may adopt any exchange arrangement consistent with orderly economic growth and reasonable price stability, provided that it is not linked to gold and does not involve multiple currency practices or discriminate against the currency of any other member state without the approval of the Fund.

Members may choose among a variety of exchange arrangements. For example, they may peg the value of their currency to that of another currency or to the SDR or some other composite measure or they may enter into cooperative arrangements, under which they maintain the value of their currency in relation to the value of the currency or currencies of other members within the same group. Members must notify the Fund promptly of any change in their exchange arrangements.

Many members have pegged their currencies to the U.S. dollar or the euro or other currency of a major trading and financial partner because of the convenience and certainty that pegging offers to those involved in international transactions and in international planning. A second group of states has pegged their currency to various composites of currencies, such as the SDR. These tend to be countries with diversified trade patterns which find that the composites reduce the effect of fluctuations among the values of the major currencies on the prices of imports and exports. A third group maintains the value of their individual currencies within a predetermined range of other currencies in the group. Most of the remaining members use a managed floating system which permits smoother and more rapid adjustments to payments imbalances.

Notes

1. Comment *a* to Restatement (Third) § 821(1) states, in part:

> While the provisions of the original Articles of Agreement requiring members to maintain a par value for their currencies have been eliminated from the amended Articles * * *, the principle that exchange rates are a subject of international concern is maintained * * *. Under Article IV(2) of the amended Articles, each member state must notify the Fund of the exchange arrangements it intends to apply and of any changes in those arrangements. Notification need not be given in advance of their implementation, but must be given promptly thereafter. Members are expected to respond to questions from the Fund and, on request, to consult with the Fund on these arrangements and on the effect they may have on other member states or on the international economy as a whole.

2. Prohibited discriminatory arrangements would include, for example, permitting foreign currency operations to be undertaken for transactions in some currencies but not in others. Prohibited multiple exchange practices include official action causing exchange rate spreads and cross-rate quotations to differ unnecessarily from those that arise in the marketplace.

For a discussion of the amendments to, and the functioning of, Article IV, see Gold, Strengthening the Soft International Law of Exchange Arrangements, 77 A.J.I.L. 443–489 (1983).

b. Consultation and Cooperation

Article IV(3)(b) of the amended Articles requires the Fund to exercise "firm surveillance over the exchange rate policies of members" and to adopt "specific principles for the guidance of all members with respect to those policies."

Each member is required to furnish relevant information and to consult with the Fund periodically (usually every 12 months) with respect to its exchange rate policies. The results are reported to the Executive Board by the Managing Director. The Managing Director may initiate further discussions with a member state if so directed by the Executive Board or on his or her own initiative. Summaries of the country reports prepared by the IMF staff are published as Press Information Notices and are posted on the IMF's internet website (www.imf.org).

"Exchange rate policies" with respect to which the member states must inform and consult with the Fund clearly extend beyond the "exchange arrangements" provided for in Article IV(2), and include, for example, member states' intervention (or not) in foreign exchange markets, the level of government borrowing or lending for balance of payments purposes, and restrictions on or incentives to current transactions or capital transfers.

Other obligations to consult relate to specific matters, such as drawings, exchange restrictions and use of SDRs. In addition to its regular consultations, the Fund holds special consultations as necessary with those countries whose policies have a major influence on the world's economy.

Notes

1. Article IV(1) of the amended Articles refers to "the orderly underlying conditions that are necessary for financial and economic stability," and the 1977 Decision on Surveillance, Ex. Bd. Decision No. 5392 (77/63), April 29, 1977, Selected Decisions of the IMF 10, 13 (10th issue 1983), states that the Fund's appraisal of a member's exchange rate policies "shall be made within the framework of a comprehensive analysis of the * * * economic policy strategy of the member, and shall recognize that domestic as well as external policies can contribute to timely adjustment of the balance of payments."

2. The 1977 Decision on Surveillance also states that members (i) shall avoid manipulating exchange rates in order to prevent effective balance of payments adjustments (an obligation contained in Article IV(1) of the Amended Articles); (ii) should intervene in the exchange market if necessary to counter disorderly conditions in the exchange value of their currency; and (iii) should take into account in their intervention policies the interests of other member states. It is unclear to what extent items (ii) and (iii) are obligatory, but compliance can at least be the subject of consultations and negotiations with respect to drawing on the IMF resources.

3. The following cautionary note concerning the liberalization of capital flows encouraged by IMF policies has been sounded by Picciotto:

> * * * Since the 1930s, capital markets and financial intermediation have been largely national, and the postwar regime supervised by the IMF aimed to liberalize only current account payments. However the ability of TNCs [transnational corporations] to manage their internal cross-border payments undermined the distinction between current and capital accounts, and the emergence of the Eurocurrency markets and of the system of "offshore" finance dominated by TNCs and their banks created a vast pool of "hot money" and inevitably led to currency floating. During the 1980s the developed countries ended exchange controls and began to reform their rules to make it easier for domestic banks and savings institutions * * * to lend and invest abroad. By the early 1990s, financial liberalization became more general, and the rapid-growth countries of East Asia and Latin America, as well as former communist countries offering apparently promising investment opportunities, became identified as "emerging markets". However, the resulting boom in short-term portfolio capital flows was very uneven (many countries in Africa and elsewhere had little inflow, or even net outflows) and extremely volatile. Peaking at $104bn in 1993, portfolio capital flows to emerging markets fell to less than a quarter of that level in 1995 due to the Mexican *peso* crisis, but rebounded to $50bn in 1996 * * *.
>
> The financial crisis sparked off in Asia in 1997 led to an even more dramatic reversal, with drastic economic and social repercussions. The spreading contagion of financial volatility led to proposals through the IMF and elsewhere for "strengthening the architecture of the international financial system"; but * * * these were aimed essentially at increasing the availability of information (transparency) and tightening supervision, intending to facilitate continued liberalization. * * * [However,] the inherent volatility of such short-term flows requires more serious consideration of regulatory requirements that can act as a brake on both inflows and outflows. Although some of

these can, in principle, be introduced unilaterally by states, the competition to attract capital is such that some coordination is necessary. * * *

Yet powerful voices in New York, London and Washington still press for the facilitation of unrestricted international capital flows. Unrestricted capital flows were a basic principle of the MAI [proposed Multilateral Agreement on Investment: see p. 1626], and were also proposed (although rejected on this occasion) as a condition for the $18bn U.S. commitment to the new IMF facility in October 1998. * * *

The experience of 1997–8, when many countries which had liberalized capital flows suffered economic disaster, while others such as China and India which had retained controls fared much better, revived the case for capital controls. It also cast a large shadow over the project to extend the IMF's aims and jurisdiction to liberalization of capital flows, which, combined with the MAI [which never came into effect] and the liberalization of financial services under the WTO, would have created a single global capital market under the aegis of the IMF * * *.

Picciotto, Introduction: What Rules for the World Economy? in Regulating International Business 7–9 (Mayne & Picciotto eds., 1999).

c. Exchange Restrictions: Current and Capital Transactions

Under Article VI(3) of the Articles, members are permitted to exercise such controls as are necessary to regulate international movements of capital (e.g., investments in and repatriation of equity capital and making and repayment of long-term loans), but not in a manner that will restrict payments for current transactions. Article VIII provides that member states that agree to accept its provisions are not permitted to restrict payments for current transactions (e.g., payment of the sales price for imported products, fees for services, royalties for the licensing of patents, interest on debt obligations, and dividends on corporate stock) without prior approval of the Fund.

Notes

1. Article XIV of the Articles of Agreement permits a member state when it joins the Fund to declare that it intends to maintain restrictions on current transactions for a transitional period (with no limit on the duration thereof). Such a member is obligated to endeavor to withdraw the restrictions on current payments as soon as conditions permit and to consult with the Fund periodically to that end. Imposition of new restrictions, reimposition of a previously terminated restriction, and a decision of a state no longer to accept the obligations of Article VIII, require prior approval of the Fund.

2. For a case holding that approval by the Fund of restrictions on current payments after their imposition is sufficient compliance with the approval requirement of Article VIII, see Callejo v. Bancomer, S.A., 764 F.2d 1101 (5th Cir.1985) (act of state doctrine applied with respect to Mexican exchange controls; their imposition did not violate IMF Articles).

d. Sanctions

A variety of sanctions is provided for in the Articles. The Fund's primary method of securing compliance with member's obligations under the Articles is through consultations with officials of the offending state. The Fund can informally communicate its views or present a report to a member. Art. XII, sec. 8; Art. V, sec. 5. A report can be published about a member's condition, Art. XII, sec. 8, or a "general scarcity" of the currency of a country in surplus can be declared, Art. VII, sec. 1. Punitive rates may be imposed when the use of resources rises to an excessive level. Art. V, sec. 8(c) and (d). A member may be declared ineligible to use new resources, SDR rights may be suspended, or the member's withdrawal compelled. See Article XXVI, sec. 2(a); Article V, sec. 5; Article VI, sec. 1; Article XIV, sec. 3; Article XXVI, sec. 2(c). A Third Amendment of the Articles of Agreement, effective on November 11, 1992, adopted Article XXVI, sec. 2(b), which added a sanction short of compulsory withdrawal. It permits suspension of a member's voting and related rights by a decision taken by a 70–percent majority of the total weighted voting power, if a member, having previously been held ineligible to use the resources of the Fund, continues to fail to comply with its obligations under the Articles. The IMF has used its powers to impose sanctions cautiously. This has led to claims that the IMF lacks sufficient effective influence over its members and has led to suggestions for additional more flexible sanctions.

e. Enforceability of Agreements Violating Lawful Exchange Controls

Art. VIII(2)(b) provides that "exchange contracts which involve the currency of any member and which are contrary to the exchange control regulations of that member maintained or imposed consistently with this agreement should be unenforced in the territories of any member." This clause has been interpreted by the Fund to prohibit disregard of such regulations on traditional conflict of law grounds or grounds of public policy *(ordre public)*. Controversy exists as to whether these interpretations are binding on courts of member states. See Williams, Extraterritorial Enforcement of Exchange Control Regulations under IMF Agreement, 15 Va.J.Int'l.L. 319 (1975). Judicial interpretations also differ as to the content of the key terms used in the clause, such as "exchange contract," "involve," and "exchange control regulations." The European courts have given these words broad scope, while U.S. courts generally have not. See French v. Banco Nacional de Cuba, 23 N.Y.2d 46, 295 N.Y.S.2d 433, 242 N.E.2d 704 (1968), where the act of state doctrine was applied rather than Art. VIII, with the result that the regulations of a nonmember country inconsistent with the Fund Agreement were enforced in a New York court. But in Banco Frances e Brasileiro S.A. v. Doe, 36 N.Y.2d 592, 370 N.Y.S.2d 534, 331 N.E.2d 502 (1975), the New York Court of Appeals embraced an expansive application of the Article based upon a perceived policy of broad cooperation embodied in the IMF Agreement. The Court held it would entertain an action for rescission of currency exchange contracts and damages in tortious fraud and deceit arising from alleged violations of Brazil's exchange control regulations. A month later, the same court concluded that New York substantive law controlled due to New York's "paramount interest in the outcome" as the "financial capital of the world," and then stated that Art. VIII did not encompass a claim dealing with a letter of credit which was held not to constitute an "exchange contract". J. Zeevi & Sons, Ltd. v. Grindlays Bank (Uganda) Ltd., 37 N.Y.2d 220, 229, 371 N.Y.S.2d 892, 898, 333 N.E.2d 168, 174 (1975), cert. denied, 423 U.S. 866, 96 S.Ct. 126, 46 L.Ed.2d 95 (1975). Moreover, loan agreements have been held not to constitute "exchange contracts" covered by Article VIII(2)(b), see, e.g., Libra Bank Ltd. v. Banco Nacional De Costa Rica, 570 F.Supp. 870, 900 (S.D.N.Y.1983). See Note, The IMF and New York Courts, 9 Vand.J.Trans. L. 199 (1976); Note, Enforcement of Foreign Exchange Control Regulations in Domestic Courts, 70 A.J.I.L. 101 (1976). With respect to the meaning of "exchange contracts" and other key terms of Article VIII(2)(b), see Gold, The Fund Agreement in the Courts, Vol. II 393–427 (1982).

Some of the principal U.S., U.K. and German cases and the perceived inconsistency between the governmental recognition of the economic cooperation objectives of the IMF and the judicial disregard of them by the courts of a number of members, including the United States and the United Kingdom, are discussed in Ebke, Article VIII, Section 2(b), International Monetary Cooperation, and the Courts, 23 Int'l Law. 677 (1989). See also Gold, Exchange Controls and External Indebtedness: Are the Bretton Woods Concepts Still Workable?, 7 Hous.J.Int'l L. I (1984).

SECTION 4. INTERNATIONAL INVESTMENT LAW

A. INTRODUCTION

Private foreign direct investment in developing countries brings in capital, generates employment, and is an important means of facilitating technical and managerial know-how transfers and foreign market access. Through training of local staff, foreign direct investment helps to transfer product and process technologies and contributes to the development of local management and marketing skills. Thus, flows of privately owned investment resources into developing countries are often a powerful fuel for economic growth and development.

The sea change in the area of economic development is the recognition throughout much of the developing world that economic development can proceed much more vigorously in a private-enterprise-free-market environment than in an environment dominated by state-owned enterprises and central planning. As a consequence, developing countries are increasingly recognizing the myriad benefits of private foreign direct investment and are taking steps to promote it.

In the 1990s, private foreign direct investment in developing countries increased dramatically overall but it tended to be concentrated in a relatively limited number of countries. 1999 Annual Report of the International Finance Corporation (IFC) at p. 4.

The challenges posed by enhancing sustainable economic development of developing countries were rendered more daunting by the financial crises in a number of Asian countries and Russia, which produced reverberations in important developing countries in Latin America and elsewhere. Ameliorative measures focused principally on the IMF. A key objective of the IMF and most developed states has been to restore the flow of private capital and debt financing into investment in the developing world.

In recent years much attention has been focused on economic globalization—the organization of productive facilities, procurement of raw materials and components, sales and supply of services, on a worldwide basis—and it has been increasingly recognized that international trade and international investment are inextricably linked in the globalization process as well as in promotion of economic development. Thus far, however, international investment has been subject to considerably less international regulation than international trade and monetary relations.

The scope of basic regulation of direct foreign investment has tended to deal with some or all of the following:

a. The right of establishment or the obligation to permit foreign investors freedom of entry into the local economy.

b. National treatment of foreign investors, i.e., treatment of foreign investors as favorably as domestic investors.

c. Most-favored-nation treatment of foreign investors, i.e., investors of one foreign country must be treated as favorably as investors from any other foreign country.

d. Rules providing enhanced legal security for foreign investors.

e. Mechanisms for settlement of disputes between foreign investors and the host government.

Unlike international trade relations, which are subject to an international legal regime under the GATT and the WTO, and international monetary relations, which are subject to a legal regime administered principally by the IMF, international investment is not regulated by a cohesive international legal regime.

Regulation of the right of establishment encompasses both the host state's right to restrict the access of foreign investors to certain spheres of economic activity and its duty to ensure access to others. Another aspect of the right of establishment involves ensuring fair and equitable treatment of foreign investment, one aspect of which may involve according national and most-favored-nation treatment, subject only to carefully circumscribed exceptions. Another topic is the regulation of the conduct of multinational or transnational enterprises and their relations with home and host countries. International accounting standards, regulation of anti-competitive or corrupt practices, labor standards, and labor-management relations are included among the topics related to the conduct of transnational corporations that have been of concern. Regulation of international tax matters, such as transfer pricing within a multinational enterprise, which can result in artificial shifting of income to reduce international tax burdens and to deprive the host state of its rightful share of tax revenues, has also been on the transnational enterprise agenda. A matter of particular concern to the foreign investor in the developing world is the extent of legal protection accorded to the foreign investment under the laws of the host government and under international law.

Many bilateral and multilateral international agreements have significant impact on international investment. At present, the most extensively used device to embody an international legal regime aimed at promoting and providing protection to foreign investment is the network of BITs, discussed at p. 808. These are designed to provide specific legal protection against the non-commercial risks that often accompany an investment made by a private investor in a foreign country, especially in a country in which economic or political instability may be present. Many of these treaties, including, in particular, those entered into by the United States, also seek to ensure broadened access to foreign markets for U.S. investment. The principal contribution of these treaties to enhancing the legal protection of the foreign investor has been to provide substantive rules regarding such matters as the capital-importing state's obligation to provide non-discriminatory and national, and often most-favored-nation, treatment to foreign investments and to pay adequate compensation in the event of expropriation. Many of the treaties have also contained procedural protection in the form of mandatory submission of disputes between the investor and the capital-importing state to binding international arbitration.

Many efforts looking toward multilateral regulation and protection of investment have been made. See pp. 1621 to 1637. However, the only binding multilateral arrangements (aside from regional arrangements, such as the EU and NAFTA) are those relating to settlement of investment disputes under the auspices of the International Centre for the Settlement of Investment Disputes (ICSID), the agreement establishing the Multilateral Investment Guaranty Program administered by the Multilateral Investment Guaranty Agency (MIGA), and the GATT and WTO. See pp. 1628 to 1637.

The increasing integration of trade and investment is an important aspect of GATT and the WTO, and it heralds an increasing role of the WTO in international investment issues. For example, the GATS deals, in the area of services, with the right of establishment and the treatment of foreign investors once established—two central features of the regulation of investment. In addition, the Agreement on Trade–Related Aspects of Intellectual Property Rights (TRIPs Agreement) deals with the protection of intellectual property of foreign investors. Moreover, members of the WTO are expected to examine provisions on investment policy related to the liberalization of trade in the years ahead.

Regional arrangements also play an increasingly important role in connection with international investment. The leading example is the group of agreements establishing the European Union. The EU regime involves extensive regulation of cross-border investments within the Union and now extends to most of Western Europe. The EU rules encompass such matters as the right of establishment, regulation of transfers of capital, technology and services, cross-border mergers, and regulation of competition.

Significant multilateral efforts focused more specifically on regulation of investment flows from developed to developing countries have not as yet enjoyed success. The efforts that have failed have included attempts to formulate multilateral codes for the regulation and protection of private investment abroad, discussed at p. 1621, and for the regulation of transnational corporations, discussed at p. 1623. There have been a number of regional multilateral agreements governing the legal protection of foreign investment, which have not yet had a significant impact. Like the EU, NAFTA, discussed at p. 1590 note 4, moves beyond the removal or reduction of most barriers to flows of goods and services to deal with transborder investment. As a result, a North American investment regime is developing based on the principle of national treatment. See Eden, The Emerging North American Investment Regime, 5 Transnat. Corporations No. 3 at 61 (1996).

MERCOSUR also incorporates investment rules along with trade liberalization which is its principal focus. The ASEAN leaders have agreed to study the creation of an ASEAN free investment area. The agenda of APEC (Asian Pacific Economic Cooperation) also includes international investment. See Ruggiero, Foreign Direct Investment and the Multilateral Trading System. 5 Transnat. Corporations, No. 1 at 1 (1996).

It may be that the extensive network of BITs, the multilateral WTO Agreements, the agreements establishing ICSID and MIGA, and the small number of regional multilateral investment treaties will eventually evolve over time into broadly based multilateral arrangements for the regulation and protection of international investment; or possibly some of the norms embodied in bilateral and regional agreements will evolve into norms of customary international law. Such evolution is likely to extend over a period of years, but there is evidence that the pace of efforts to regulate and improve the legal security of international investment is quickening, spurred by the compelling need to attract private capital and know-how from abroad on the part of developing countries of the Third World and the countries in Eastern Europe and the former Soviet Union that are moving from communism and managed economies toward freer economies and privatization.

In addition to the treaties regulating certain aspects of international investment and the as yet unsuccessful efforts to produce multilateral agreements regulating and providing legal protection for international investment, there have been efforts to develop guidelines for the conduct and treatment of international investment. Although not intended to articulate binding norms, such guidelines may nonetheless prove to be building blocks for the eventual development of regulatory schemes. One significant effort in this regard has been the Guidelines for Multinational Enterprises promulgated by the Governments of the OECD Member States. See p. 1622.

Another significant straw in the wind was the 1992 Report to the Development Committee of the World Bank Group and the IMF entitled Legal Framework for the Treatment of Foreign Investment, which includes a set of Guidelines on the Treatment of Foreign Direct Investment. The Report and Guidelines were published by the World Bank Group on September 25, 1992. Legal Framework for the Treatment of Foreign Investment (Volume II: Guidelines), Washington, D.C. The International Bank for Reconstruction and Development/The World Bank, 1992, reproduced at 31 I.L.M. 1363 (1992). The Guidelines suggest the appropriateness of providing broad legal protection for direct foreign investment against non-commercial risks. They are discussed at p. 1626.

Agreement between the state of the private investor's nationality and the host state on substantive principles of customary international law relating to protection of foreign investment has often not been attainable because of basic doctrinal differences on the applicable rules. See p. 777. Even when this has been the case, host governments have increasingly been willing to accept the procedural device of submitting investment disputes to binding international arbitration, and to this end many developing states have become parties to the Convention on the Settlement of Investment Disputes Between States and Nationals of Other States, p. 1628, which established the ICSID. In the frequent cases in which compulsory international arbitration of investment disputes between investors and host governments is not mandated by a treaty, binding arbitration may be available because the host state and the investor have agreed on an ad hoc basis to arbitration of such disputes under the rules of the ICSID, UNCITRAL, the International Chamber of Commerce, or some other international arbitral regime.

One widely used technique for closing the gaps that remain in the substantive and procedural protection that the foreign investor enjoys against non-commercial risks is the bilateral investment insurance schemes that have been provided by many developed states with respect to certain investments made by their nationals in selected developing countries. The U.S. foreign investment insurance program, which is administered by the Overseas Private Investment Corporation (OPIC), is discussed in the following section.

In addition to bilateral investment insurance arrangements, there have been a variety of multilateral efforts toward this end. The most successful of these to date has been the Multilateral Investment Guarantee Agency (MIGA), discussed at p. 1629, established under the auspices of the World Bank with extensive participation by developing as well as developed states. See generally the 2000 MIGA Annual Report.

B. OPIC INVESTMENT GUARANTIES

1. The Overseas Private Investment Corporation (OPIC)

The OPIC administers a program of insurance and guaranties for U.S. private investments in less developed countries against certain non-commercial risks. OPIC, a self-supporting corporation wholly owned by the U.S. Government, was created in 1969 to take over the functions of the Investment Guaranty Program of the Agency for International Development (AID). 22 U.S.C.A. §§ 2191–200.

The OPIC investment insurance program provides insurance protection against three specific types of non-commercial or political risk: inconvertibility of foreign currency into dollars; expropriation of investment by the host government; and war, revolution, insurrection and politically motivated civil strife, terrorism, and sabotage. The loan guaranty program is broader, offering protection against any default, whether for commercial or political reasons. In addition to these two main activities, OPIC operates several special programs that insure U.S. financial institutions, cross-border leasing investments, oil and gas and natural resources ventures, and contractors and exporters against both non-commercial (or political) and some commercial risks.

OPIC's investment insurance is available to U.S. citizens; to corporations, partnerships or other associations created under the laws of the United States or of any state or territory which are substantially beneficially owned by U.S. citizens; and to foreign businesses that are wholly-owned* by any of the above. A U.S. corporation qualifies as "substantially beneficially owned" if a majority of each class of its issued and outstanding stock is beneficially owned by U.S. citizens.

Only investments in "less developed friendly countries" are eligible for insurance, and insurance will not be granted unless the United States and the

* In the case of foreign corporations, only 95% U.S. ownership is required.

host government have previously entered into an agreement (usually through an exchange of diplomatic notes) for the institution of the program. The U.S. model agreement is set forth in the Documents Supplement. The purpose of these agreements is to provide, in advance, orderly procedures for the handling of claims, the transfer of foreign currencies and other issues that are likely to arise between the two governments. The agreements generally provide that OPIC may offer insurance coverage to eligible investors in projects that are approved by the foreign host government, that the rights of the United States as assignee and subrogee of the insured will be recognized and that any disputes arising from the agreement or the guaranty program will be resolved by negotiation or, if necessary, by impartial international arbitration.

The investment must be new or must constitute a significant expansion, modernization or development of an existing enterprise. No fixed form of eligible investment is prescribed; for example, eligible investments may take the form of conventional debt or equity, contribution of goods or services, licensing agreements, certain technical assistance and construction contracts, or special arrangements such as contractual joint ventures. OPIC insurance covers both initial investment and rights under related securities or contracts, and may usually be obtained for retained earnings or accrued interest, up to a dollar limit equal to the insurance coverage on the initial investment.

OPIC may not issue insurance for investments that are likely to cause the investor to reduce the number of employees in the United States because U.S. production is being replaced by production of the foreign investment of the same product for the same market as the investor's U.S. production. Investments need not be tied to U.S. procurement, but substantial procurement in other developed countries may jeopardize eligibility for coverage. The developmental benefit to the host country is also a factor in determining eligibility, as is the extent to which the host government fosters private economic activity. Finally, preference is given to investments by smaller U.S. firms and to investments in the poorest of developing countries.

The insured is required to bear at least 10 percent of the total risk of loss; thus, all OPIC insurance is limited to 90 percent of a proposed investment. Loans and leases from financial institutions to unrelated third parties are eligible for 100 percent insurance of principal and interest. OPIC Program Handbook, April 1999. For certain investments, OPIC has chosen to limit coverage even further. Insurance for large equity investments, particularly in extractive industries, is typically limited to 75 percent of the total equity investment, but may be reduced to as little as 50 percent. Parent-to-subsidiary loans may usually be insured only for 85 percent of their value, although exceptions are made for small business.

Insurance contracts are written for a maximum of 20 years with premiums payable annually. The premium rates charged by OPIC vary with the nature of the investment and the coverage but do not vary depending on the country in which the investment is made, whatever the level of political risk may be.

When an investor makes a claim, OPIC determines its validity and the amount that is due the investor; disputes between OPIC and the investor are submitted to binding arbitration. As a result of one such arbitration OPIC was found liable to International Telephone & Telegraph Corporation, Sud America, for cash payments and note guarantees totaling $95 million in connection with the nationalization of I.T.T. property by the Chilean government.

a. Inconvertibility Coverage

In essence, OPIC's convertibility insurance assures the investor that any rights or guarantees with respect to convertibility and repatriation of earnings and capital which the investor enjoys at the time of the original investment will continue for the life of the contract.

The convertibility guaranty for earnings on the investment or for the return of the investment may be invoked in three situations:

(a) when the investor is prevented from converting his local currency into U.S. dollars for a period of thirty days by direct operation of law, decree, regulation, or affirmative administrative determination (i.e., outright blockage);

(b) when the investor is prevented from converting his local currency into U.S. dollars by the failure for 60 days of the applicable government authorities to grant a duly submitted application for transfer (i.e., passive blockage achieved through governmental inaction); and

(c) when the investor is permitted to convert his local currency into U.S. dollars, but only at a discriminatory rate of exchange which is less than 99 percent of the reference rate, which is generally the official exchange rate for the type of transfer involved (e.g., dividend remittance).

In these situations, OPIC will pay the investor in dollars a sum equal to 99 percent of the dollar equivalent of the investor's inconvertible local currency.

The insurance affords no protection against the effects of currency devaluation or inflation. Local currency held by the investor for more than 18 months is not eligible for reimbursement. In addition, the investor cannot invoke the guaranty to alleviate the effect of any exchange regulation or practice that was in effect when the contract was executed.

Inconvertibility coverage is available both for debt and equity; however, some debt insurance incorporates a 10 percent or 15 percent first loss deductible.

Payment of claims under convertibility insurance is made by OPIC in dollars against delivery to it of the local currency. In most cases, the exchange rate used to determine payment is the effective free market rate of exchange, or, if no effective market exists, the rate at which other U.S. investors convert local currency into dollars for remittance of earnings.

b. Expropriation Coverage

OPIC's expropriation coverage provides compensation in dollars to the U.S. investor if the host government subjects his property to "expropriatory action" with or without compensation. "Expropriatory action" is defined to include not only outright nationalization, but also less drastic actions sometimes termed "creeping expropriation." The OPIC Contract of Insurance

(OPIC Form 234 KGT 12–70) (Second Revision) defines expropriatory action as:

> any action which is taken, authorized, ratified or condoned by the Government of the Project Country, commencing during the Insurance Period, with or without compensation therefor, and which for a period of one year directly results in preventing:
>
> (a) the Investor from receiving payment when due in the currency specified of amounts which the Foreign Enterprise owes the Investor on or in respect of the Securities; or
>
> (b) the Investor from effectively exercising its fundamental rights with respect to the Foreign Enterprise either as shareholder or as creditor, as the case may be, acquired as a result of the Investment; provided, however, that rights acquired solely as a result of any undertaking by or agreement with the Government of the Project Country shall not be considered fundamental rights merely because they are acquired from such undertaking or agreement; or
>
> (c) the Investor from disposing of the Securities or any rights accruing therefrom; or
>
> (d) the Foreign Enterprise from exercising effective control over the use or disposition of a substantial portion of its property or from constructing the Project or operating the same; or
>
> (e) the Investor from repatriating, and from exercising effective control in the Project Country over, amounts received in respect of the Securities as Investment Earnings or Return of Capital, which action commences within the eighteen (18) months immediately succeeding such receipt.

* * *

Under this broad definition, the investor enjoys significant protection against foreign government interference with its property rights that falls short of an outright and permanent taking. The Contract treats a partial loss under sections (a) to (d) as a total loss and provides that the investor must assign all its property rights in the investment and any claims or causes of action connected therewith to OPIC before receiving compensation.

The investor and the foreign enterprise must take all reasonable measures, including administrative and judicial proceedings in the host country, to prevent or contest the expropriatory action. However, an investor may not invoke the guaranty when subjected to a non-discriminatory increase in taxation, or to a non-discriminatory regulatory measure that is reasonably related to a valid regulatory purpose, despite any adverse effect on the investor's profits.

c. *War, Revolution, Insurrection and Civil Strife Coverage*

This basic coverage provides compensation for the loss of an investor's interest in the tangible property of the foreign enterprise if the loss is directly caused by war, revolution or insurrection. In addition, coverage is available for civil strife, terrorism and sabotage. The Contract covers hostile acts of any national or international organized force, and acts of any organized revolutionary or insurrectionary forces, including acts of sabotage. The Contract also covers damage which is a direct result of actions taken to combat or defend against an actual or anticipated act of war, revolution, insurrection, civil strife, terrorism or sabotage.

Compensation under insurance for equity investment, certain debt, and construction service contracts is measured by the depreciated book value of the covered property, but is limited to the lesser of (a) the repair or replacement cost of the property or (b) the diminution in the fair market value of the property. Loan insurance contracts generally cover the debt obligation itself and compensate the lender for the amount of any defaulted installments of principal or interest. These contracts are limited, however, by a first-loss deductible borne by the insured.

Note

See generally Betancourt, OPIC Political Risk Insurance for Infrastructure Projects in Emerging Markets, 745 PLI/Comm 179 (October 1996); Perry, A Model for Efficient Foreign Aid: The Case for the Political Risk Insurance Activities of the Overseas Private Investment Corporation, 36 Va. J. Int'l L. 511 (1996); Fitzgerald, U.S. Government Assistance to Exporters: The Role of the Overseas Private Investment Corporation, 789 PLI/Comm 833 (October 1–2, 1992); Stillwell, Encouraging Investment in LDC's: The United States Investment Guaranty Program, 8 Brooklyn J.Int'l L. 365 (1982); T. Meron, OPIC Investment Insurance Is Alive and Well, 73 A.J.I.L. 104–111 (1978); and T. Meron, Investment Insurance in International Law (1976).

C. MULTILATERAL EFFORTS TO PRODUCE INVESTMENT CODES

1. Background

In view of the wide gulf between the doctrinal positions adopted by various groups of states in the post-World War II period, and particularly between the developed and the developing countries, it is not surprising that efforts to codify the law of state responsibility for injury to the economic interests of aliens have been fruitless. See p. 777.

The OECD prepared a Draft Convention on the Protection of Foreign Property. The Draft Convention was adopted on October 12, 1967, by the Council of the OECD, with Spain and Turkey abstaining. In the Resolution adopting the Draft Convention, the Council stated that it considered the Draft Convention to embody "recognized principles relating to the protection of foreign property, combined with rules to render [them] more effective," and that it commended the Draft Convention "as a basis for furthering and rendering more effective the application of these principles." Among the provisions were the following:

> Art. 2. Each Party shall at all times ensure the observance of undertakings given by it in relation to property of nationals of any other Party.
>
> Art. 3. No Party shall take any measures depriving, directly or indirectly, of his property a national of another Party unless the following conditions are complied with: (i) The measures are taken in the public

> interest and under due process of law; (ii) The measures are not discriminatory; and (iii) The measures are accompanied by provision for the payment of just compensation. Such compensation shall represent the genuine value of the property affected, shall be paid without undue delay, and shall be transferable to the extent necessary to make it effective for the national entitled thereto.

In view of these provisions and the doctrinal positions then embraced by most developing countries, it is hardly surprising that the Convention did not attract support in the developing countries in 1967. See pp. 777 to 785.

In 1976, the OECD adopted a Declaration on International Investment and Multinational Enterprises, to which were annexed Guidelines for Multinational Enterprises. The OECD Governments jointly recommended to multinational enterprises operating in their territories the observance of the Guidelines. The basic premise of the OECD Guidelines, most recently amended in summer 2000 (reprinted at 40 I.L.M. 237 (2000)), is that multinational enterprises can bring substantial benefits to the economies of home and host countries but their transnational activities, organization and financial resources transcend the capacity of individual states to regulate and may lead to abuses of economic power and conflicts with national policy objectives. The Guidelines for Multinational Enterprises relate to such matters as encouraging positive contributions to the economic and social policies of home and host countries, timely disclosure of meaningful information concerning their operations and finances, avoidance of anti-competitive activities, respect for national employment and industrial relations laws and policies and environmental protection regimes. OECD Member States are to cooperate concerning national treatment of foreign-controlled enterprises, conflicting requirements imposed on multinational enterprises by governments in different countries and international investment incentives and disincentives. See Annex 1 to Declaration of June 21, 1976 by Governments of OECD Member Countries on International Investment and Multinational Enterprises, in OECD, The OECD Declaration and Decisions on International Investment and Multinational Enterprises: Basic Texts 9 (1992), as amended by OECD Council Decision of July 19, 2000, OECD Doc. C(2000)96/FINAL, on OECD website at www.oecd.org. There have also been a number of regional efforts to develop multilateral investment regimes. The most important is the regime established for the European Union. Another example is the Uniform Code on Andean Multinational Enterprises. 30 I.L.M. 1296 (1991).

The most significant steps toward development of multilateral investment regimes in the last two decades have been the work on the Code of Conduct on Transnational Corporations, resulting in a 1990 draft Code, which is discussed in the following section, and the Guidelines on the Treatment of Foreign Direct Investment published by the World Bank Group in 1992, which is discussed at p. 1626. Another recent development has been the unsuccessful effort to negotiate a draft Multilateral Agreement on Investment (MAI) under the auspices of the OECD, which is discussed at p. 1626.

There has, however, been an extensive proliferation of bilateral investment agreements providing protection for private investment in developing countries.

Broadly based multilateral efforts have been channeled into avenues with more immediate productive potential than investment codes. The leading examples are the Convention on the Settlement of Investment Disputes Between States and Nationals of Other States, which established ICSID, discussed at p. 1628, and the Convention Establishing the MIGA, discussed at p. 1629.

2. *U.N. Code of Conduct on Transnational Corporations*

A multilateral effort supported by many developing countries to articulate principles intended, among other things, to regulate international investment and to deal with legal protections against certain non-commercial risks was carried out under the auspices of the U.N. Commission and Centre on Transnational Corporations. The principal focus of their efforts was on the activities of multinational corporations and on developing a Code of Conduct on Transnational Corporations.

The Commission (consisting of 48 members) and the Centre were established by the U.N. Economic and Social Council in November of 1974. The Centre served as a focal point for all matters related to transnational corporations and acted as secretariat to the Commission. The broad objectives of the Centre's activities were to further the understanding of the nature of transnational corporations and of their political, legal, economic and social effects on home and host countries and in international relations, particularly between developed and developing countries; to secure effective international arrangements aimed at enhancing the contribution of transnational corporations to national development goals and world economic growth, while controlling and eliminating their negative effects; and to strengthen the negotiating capacity of host countries.

In 1975 the Centre began work on the Code of Conduct and shortly thereafter initiated a project on establishment of international standards of accounting and reporting by transnational corporations. The Centre also prepared numerous studies of the role of transnational corporations and their impact on economic development and international trade and finance. See, e.g., Transnational Corporations in World Development, Third Survey, E/C. 10/1984/2, and Transnational Corporations in South Africa and Namibia, E/C.10/1984/10. The Centre also attempted to assist and enhance through its research activities and technical assistance, the negotiating capabilities of developing countries in their dealings with transnational corporations. See Measures Strengthening the Negotiating Capacity of Governments in their Relations with Transnational Corporations. Joint Ventures among Firms in Latin America, E/C.10/1982/15.

The basis for the conclusion that there was a need for a Code of Conduct on Transnational Corporations was summarized as follows in the 1985 Report of the Centre on Transnational Corporations on Work on the Formulation of the United Nations Code of Conduct on Transnational Corporations, E/C. 10/1985/s/2 at pp. 6–7 (hereinafter cited as "1985 Report on Code of Conduct"

> * * * It is essential at the outset to restate basic arguments that have established the need for the code. Broadly speaking, this need rests on the evolutionary nature of international norms, the desire to minimize

the negative effects of the operations of transnational corporations and the desire to maximize their positive contributions to economic growth and development in the context of an interdependent world. Together, these three considerations establish a commonality of interest among all States in adopting a code of conduct which, in a balanced manner, sets out the rights and expectations of the international community with regard to transnational corporations.

* * *

* * * Thus, a broad commonality of interests exists in establishing standards of behaviour, and in encouraging the observance of those standards, through which frictions and conflicts disruptive and costly for all parties involved can be reduced. Naturally, a framework which is based on and promotes that convergence of interests in an interdependent world cannot be established unilaterally or bilaterally. Rather, it has to be negotiated on a multilateral basis, taking into account the interests of all parties concerned.

While agreement was eventually reached within the Commission on Transnational Corporations in 1990 on a draft Code of Conduct, agreement was possible only by papering over basic disputed issues through adoption of language that is broad and abstract enough to accommodate the competing positions without resolving the underlying differences. The President of the forty-sixth session of the General Assembly convened a round of informal consultations on the Code on July 21–23, 1992. The conclusion reached was that no consensus was possible on the draft Code.

The completion of the Code in a satisfactory manner was frustrated by disagreements on a number of fundamental issues. Perhaps the most basic was the relevance of customary international law to the norms to be established under the Code. The 1985 Report on the Code of Conduct commented as follows on this issue, at pp. 12–13:

25. There are at least two different schools of thought on this matter. The first maintains that the code should allow for the applicability of customary international legal principles in relevant areas to amplify or qualify the broad standards enunciated in the code. According to this view, the applicability of international law to the relations between States and transnational corporations is not limited to international obligations expressly founded on conventions, treaties or other international agreements. In addition, customary international law is seen as prescribing principles and rules with respect to such matters as jurisdiction over transnational corporations, permanent sovereignty of States over their natural wealth and resources, renegotiation of State contracts, nationalization and compensation, non-discriminatory treatment of transnational corporations, diplomatic protection of aliens and alien property, and procedures for the settlement of disputes between Governments and transnational corporations. It follows that the provisions of the code would not derogate from the application of those customary principles of international law, subject of course to the express undertakings of the

States concerned under conventions, treaties and other international agreements concluded by such States. * * *

26. The second school of thought questions the existence of universally recognized principles of customary international law governing the treatment of transnational corporations or foreign investors. Adherents to that school maintain that this area falls primarily within the purview of national law, subject to international legal norms and specific undertakings and obligations expressly stipulated in international instruments, such as codes of conduct and conventions, treaties and other international agreements, to which the States concerned have freely subscribed. * * *

Another difficult issue was to what extent, if at all, preferential treatment for developing countries should be reflected in exceptions to the general requirement that foreign investors be accorded at least national treatment, for example, to permit developing countries to grant special incentives to the development of domestic industries.

Other issues related to the extent to which transnational corporations and developing states should be free in their contractual relationships to make an unrestricted choice of governing law and of the forum for the settlement of disputes. Another source of controversy was whether, in the event of expropriation, the expropriating state is obligated to pay compensation under international law. Paragraph 57 of the 1990 draft Code of Conduct states unhelpfully that "compensation is to be paid by the State concerned, in accordance with the applicable legal rules and principles." With respect to the transfer of payments relating to investments, many developing country delegations objected to inclusion of a provision, supported by various developed countries, stating that transnational corporations should generally be permitted to transfer without restriction all payments related to their investments, including repatriation of capital, remittance of dividends, and payment of royalties under licensing arrangements and technical assistance fees. Many developing countries objected to the "without restriction" formulation, noting that transfer of payments should explicitly be made subject to host country exchange control laws and regulations. See 1985 Report on Code of Conduct at pp. 12–33. The 1990 draft does not restrict the imposition of exchange controls by host countries.

In the 1990 draft of the Code of Conduct a number of key provisions, such as paragraph 57 referred to above, incorporate vague formulations that reflect rather than resolve disagreements between groups of governments on basic issues. See letter dated 31 May 1990 from the Chairman of the reconvened special session of the Commission on Transnational Corporations to the President of the Economic and Social Council. E/1990/94 12 June 1990. In general, the provisions deal with standards rather than regulatory rules and are quite abstract. Efforts to complete the Code for submission to the General Assembly seem dead for the foreseeable future. The activities of the Centre on Transnational Corporations have been transferred to the Division on Investment, Technology and Enterprise Development of UNCTAD.

3. *World Bank Guidelines for the Treatment of Foreign Investment*

REPORT TO THE DEVELOPMENT COMMITTEE [OF THE WORLD BANK GROUP AND THE IMF] ON THE LEGAL FRAMEWORK FOR THE TREATMENT OF FOREIGN INVESTMENT

[Report and Guidelines I through VI in the Documents Supplement].

Note

The Report to the Development Committee of the World Bank Group (IBRD, IFC, ICSID and MIGA) and the IMF and the Guidelines on the Treatment of Foreign Direct Investment were approved and published by the Committee on September 25, 1992. The Committee agreed "without reservation" to call the Guidelines to the attention of the member states of the institutions involved. In publishing the Report and Guidelines, the President of the World Bank Group stated that they "should be of great relevance to the continuous efforts in our member countries to improve investment climates and facilitate greater investment flows." In addition, they "may also assist in the progressive development of international law in this important area." 31 I.L.M. 1366 (1992). The fact that the Guidelines were developed and published by the World Bank Group and the IMF, the principal institutions enjoying virtually universal membership that are centrally involved in international development, implies that the Guidelines have the potential to influence significantly the progressive development of international law in this area. The changed attitude of many developing countries toward legal protection for foreign private direct investment is reflected in some of the differences between the 1990 Draft Code of Conduct on Transnational Corporations, discussed at p. 1623, and the OECD Guidelines for Multinational Enterprises as amended through 2000. The OECD Declaration on International Investment and Multinational Enterprises and Guidelines are included in the Documents Supplement.

4. *OECD Multilateral Agreement on Investment (MAI)*

Efforts to draft a MAI were initiated in 1995 under the auspices of the OECD. Generally, the objectives of the MAI were to eliminate barriers to foreign investment and to strengthen investor protection. The cornerstone of the draft was the principle of non-discrimination, under which the host country would be required to accord foreign investors the more favorable of either national or MFN status, subject to identified general and country-specific exceptions or reservations. These exceptions would be covered by a standstill obligation, under which no new exceptions or reservations would be allowed once the MAI came into effect for a state. Unlike the bilateral investment treaties (BITs), which generally cover only direct investment, the MAI would have included portfolio investment. Moreover, direct investment would have been defined broadly to include "(vi) intellectual property rights; (vii) rights conferred pursuant to law or contract such as concessions, licenses, authorisations, and permits; (viii) any other tangible and intangible, movable and immovable property, and any related property rights, such as leases, mortgages, liens and pledges." MAI Draft Article II (2).

Like most BITs, the draft MAI contained protections for foreign investors from expropriation, including provisions calling for non-discrimination, due process and payment of prompt, adequate, effective and fully transferable compensation. The draft MAI would have gone beyond most BITs in calling for transparency of laws, regulations, procedures, agreements and decisions affecting foreign investment. Reflecting unresolved issues, the draft contained alternative provisions restricting the lowering of labor, health, safety or environmental standards to attract an inflow of foreign investment.

The OECD planned to finalize the agreement for signature at its annual meeting in April 1998. Major unresolved matters, such as taxation of foreign-owned assets, U.S. trade sanction laws, and the European Union insistence on granting its own investors special treatment, prevented final agreement. Certain non-governmental organizations strongly opposed the agreement because of a potential reduction in labor and environmental standards. Others also suggested that the OECD is not an appropriate forum for a wide ranging multilateral investment agreement because its focus does not include human rights issues. See Charnovitz, The Globalization of Economic Human Rights, 25 Brooklyn J. Int'l L. 113 (1999) and Verhoosel, Foreign Direct Investment and Legal Constraints on Domestic Environmental Policies: Striking a "Reasonable" Balance Between Stability and Change, 29 Law & Policy in Int'l Bus. 451, 473 (1998). In addition, the MAI was perceived as dealing principally with the concerns of its 29 members (mostly developed) countries, rather than with the needs of non-member developing countries. See Picciotto, A Critical Assessment of the MAI, in Regulating International Business 82–105 (Picciotto & Mayne eds. 1999).

In December 1998, the OECD suspended negotiations on the MAI indefinitely. Future efforts to conclude a multilateral investment agreement seem likely to be spearheaded by the WTO, the members of which include a broad representation of developing as well as developed countries.

Note

Consider the following comment:

> * * * The growing financial and economic crises, which had begun in Asia, reinforced the view that the MAI was one of the dying gasps of the laissez-faire neo-liberal agenda which had dominated the 1980s. The sweeping liberalization obligations envisaged in the MAI, covering every type of short-term and speculative transaction as well as longer-term direct investment, aimed to "discipline" or restrict national state regulation, thus weakening state capacity. Its strong rights for investors, backed by binding arbitration, were not balanced by any responsibilities.
>
> Increased global economic integration and interdependence needs to be underpinned by a strengthened international regulatory framework. Measures are needed to curb the excessive volatility of short-term capital flows, and while international direct investment by TNCs has been the motor of growth in some countries, it is not always beneficial and should not go unregulated. Indeed, TNCs themselves have helped create and foster the system of offshore centres and tax havens which has contributed so much to financial volatility, tax evasion and money laundering. A broader framework is needed, which should aim to strengthen international cooperative arrangements to combat

avoidance and evasion of tax as well as other regulations. It should put sustainable development at its heart, should be bottom-up and aimed at building the regulatory capacity of governments, and create responsibilities as well as rights for investors and firms. * * * As the debate on investment regulation has shifted away from the OECD and to wider forums, these issues should come to the fore. * * *

Mayne & Picciotto, Preface, in Regulating International Business vii (Mayne & Picciotto eds., 1999).

D. MACHINERY FOR SETTLEMENT OF INVESTMENT IISPUTES

CONVENTION ON THE SETTLEMENT OF INVESTMENT DISPUTES BETWEEN STATES AND NATIONALS OF OTHER STATES

Washington, March 18, 1965.
17 U.S.T. 1270, T.I.A.S. No. 6090, 575 U.N.T.S. 159.

[Articles 25–55 in the Documents Supplement]

Notes

1. The International Centre for the Settlement of Investment Disputes (ICSID) was established on October 14, 1966, by the entry into force of the Convention on the Settlement of Investment Disputes between States and Nationals of Other States. 17 U.S.T. 1270, T.I.A.S. No. 6090, 575 U.N.T.S. 159. As of 2000, the Convention had been signed by 148 states and ratified or acceded to by 133, including many developing countries. For a brief description of the Convention, see Broches, The Convention on the Settlement of Investment Disputes: Some Observations on Jurisdiction, 5 Colum.J.Transnat'l L. 263 (1966).

2. ICSID is an autonomous international organization. However, it has close links with the World Bank. All of ICSID's members are also members of the Bank. Unless a government makes a contrary designation, its Governor for the Bank sits *ex officio* on ICSID's Administrative Council. The Vice President and General Counsel of the Bank has consistently been elected by the Administrative Council to serve as ICSID's Secretary General. The expenses of the Secretariat are financed out of the Bank's budget, although the costs of individual proceedings are borne by the parties involved. For the U.S. implementing legislation, see Convention on the Settlement of Investment Disputes Act of 1966, 80 Stat. 344 (1966), 22 U.S.C.A. § 1650–1650(a).

3. ICSID provides facilities for the conciliation and arbitration of investment disputes between Contracting States and Nationals of other Contracting States. As of 2000, 38 such disputes had been resolved and 27 were pending under the Convention. Parties to ICSID proceedings have included the governments of 32 different countries from each of the major regions of the world and nationals of a dozen other countries. The disputes have involved a variety of different kinds of investment in the agricultural, banking, construction, energy, health, industrial, mining and tourism sectors.

4. Recourse to ICSID conciliation and arbitration is entirely voluntary. However, once the parties have consented to arbitration under the ICSID Convention, neither can unilaterally withdraw its consent. Moreover, all ICSID members, whether or not parties to the dispute, are required by the Convention to recognize

and enforce ICSID arbitral awards. Provisions calling for ICSID arbitration of disputes are commonly found in investment contracts between governments of member countries and investors from other member countries. Advance consents by governments to submit investment disputes to ICSID arbitration can also be found in some investment laws and in hundreds of bilateral investment treaties. Arbitration under the auspices of ICSID is similarly one of the mechanisms for the settlement of investment disputes under four multilateral trade and investment treaties (the North American Free Trade Agreement, the Energy Charter Treaty, the Cartagena Free Trade Agreement and the Colonia Investment Protocol of MERCOSUR).

5. What advantages do you perceive from the point of view of the capital-exporting and the capital-importing states to this approach to the problem of providing legal security for international investments as compared with the other alternatives? The use of the arbitration procedural mechanism side-steps the doctrinal differences on the applicable rules of state responsibility that have long frustrated efforts to obtain broad agreement on the applicable substantive rules. The problem of determining the substantive rights and duties of the parties (bypassed in the Convention) remains but is finessed unless and until a controversy arises. Is the Convention likely to facilitate the resolution of this problem to the extent ICSID arbitration becomes necessary in specific cases? What advantages are gained by providing for compulsory arbitration through a multilateral convention?

E. MULTILATERAL INVESTMENT INSURANCE

A third approach to multilateral protection of foreign investments has been directed toward creation of an international agency to insure investments in the less developed countries against noncommercial risks and to provide advisory services to assist member countries in creating a more attractive climate for private foreign investment. See International Bank for Reconstruction and Development, Multilateral Investment Insurance (March, 1962) [hereinafter cited as "World Bank Report"]. After more than two decades of effort, in October 1985, the Board of Governors of the World Bank opened for signature a Convention Establishing the MIGA. The structure and operations of MIGA are described in MIGA. Review 2000 (November 2000).

Many of the problems inherent in the investment code approach also burdened the insurance proposals. In fact, some of the proposals called for incorporation of an investment code as an integral part of the insurance plan. One major problem was the definition of the risks to be covered. Too broad a definition might result in a high rate of successful claims and impair the financial stability of the agency. On the other hand, a broad definition might be considered by the capital-importing states as an unwarranted infringement of their freedom of action. Too narrow a definition could make the insurance unattractive to investors able to take advantage of the various national insurance programs, such as the OPIC insurance program of the United States described above.

The scope of membership and of liability for losses also raised difficult questions. Participation by both capital-importing and capital-exporting countries was favored over participation by the latter alone. Many of the proposals called for the capital-importing countries to share in the capital contributions and consequently in any losses not covered by premium income. Presumably, the fact that the capital-importing states would participate in risks would encourage them to avoid acts against foreign investments. However, as a practical matter they would frequently have little or no control over convertibility and war risks. In addition, there would be little incentive for the capital-importing states to participate in such a program because they could derive the same benefits from the existing national programs without sharing the risks. World Bank Report at 20–22.

Under the national insurance programs, the insuring government, subrogated to the rights of an investor whose claim has been paid, can engage in negotiations and employ the entire range of its diplomatic power to recover from the host government. Additionally, the insuring government can settle the dispute on a basis other than a purely monetary settlement. On the other hand, a multilateral agency whose sole function is to administer the insurance program could not agree to other than a monetary settlement. If a host government proved unwilling to negotiate a settlement or to submit to arbitration, the agency's only sanction would be publicity or a refusal to write further insurance in that country.

Ultimately the proposals adopted were reflected in the 1985 Convention Establishing MIGA. The Convention is designed to encourage the flow of investment to and between developing countries by issuing guarantees against non-commercial risks and by carrying out various investment promotional and advisory activities. The Convention became effective upon ratification by at least five Category One countries (developed countries) and at least fifteen Category Two countries (developing countries), subscribing to at least one third (about $360 million) of MIGA's capital. In April 1988, MIGA was formally constituted and became the newest member of the World Bank Group (along with the Bank, IDA, IFC and ICSID). As of 2000, 165 states had signed the Convention, 152 states had become full members with a number of applications pending, the subscribed capital of MIGA exceeded $1.3 billion, and the agency was operating profitably. MIGA's annual premium income reached about $30 million, representing 20 percent annual growth over the preceding five years, and its assets increased from $232 to $721 million. MIGA's primary objective is to meet insurance needs that are developmental but not yet adequately served by other private or public sector providers. Its current priority areas are providing political risk guarantees with respect to (i) poorer developing countries eligible for assistance from the International Development Agency, especially in Africa, (ii) investments between developing (Category Two) countries, (iii) small- and medium-sized enterprises and (iv) complex infrastructure projects. MIGA Review 2000 at p. iv. For a discussion of the background and purposes of the Convention, see Shihata, The Multilateral Investment Guarantee Agency, 20 Int'l Law. 485 (1986). See also Shihata, MIGA: A Fresh Investment for Cooperation, 26 EFTA Bull. 67 (1985). In addition, the World Bank has published an extensive commentary (approved by the Bank's Executive Directors) on the Convention in a single volume with the Convention (hereafter cited as the "Commentary").

The MIGA Convention differs from earlier proposals, including a draft prepared by the OECD in 1965, 5 I.L.M. 96 (1966), in a number of respects:

(1) MIGA provides a broader framework, going beyond investment insurance, for international economic policy coordination between capital-importing countries, capital-exporting countries and foreign investors;

(2) While earlier proposals were focused on investment flows from developed to developing countries, MIGA is also expected to promote investment flows between developing countries;

(3) Political oversight of, and financial responsibility for, MIGA are shared by both home and host countries; and

(4) There are a number of safeguards to ensure the host governments' control over investment activities in their territories and provisions requiring MIGA to work toward improving investment conditions through agreements with those countries.

Thus, in pursuance of its overall objective of encouraging flows of investments for productive purposes to developing countries, MIGA is called upon to "promote mutual understanding and confidence between host governments and foreign investors, heighten awareness of investment opportunities and increase information, knowledge and expertise related to the investment process. More particularly, MIGA will insure eligible investments against losses resulting from non-commercial risks and carry out various research and promotional activities." Commentary at p. 6.

MIGA can insure new investment or investments for expansion, modernization or restructuring of existing enterprises. The investment, however, must involve nationals of member countries and must be located in a developing country.

Eligible investments are described in the Commentary as follows:

18. Article 12 defines the type of investments eligible for cover by the Agency. This provision endeavors to strike a balance between the need to preserve the Agency's scarce capital to promote flows of direct investment and the need to assure future flexibility by allowing the Board to extend coverage to other types of investment. It is envisaged that the Agency will focus on guaranteeing * * * equity investment, different forms of direct investment, and medium-to long-term loans made or guaranteed by owners of equity in the enterprise concerned (so-called equity-type or sponsored loans). The term "direct investment" is a generic term whose precise scope will have to be determined by the Board. The Board is expected to be guided by the International Monetary Fund's definition of foreign direct investment as an "investment that is made to acquire a lasting interest in an enterprise operating in an economy other than that of the investor, the investor's purpose being to have an effective voice in the management of the enterprise." The Board may consider as direct investment such new forms of investment as service and management contracts as well as franchising, licensing, leasing, and production-sharing agreements where the investor's return depends on the performance of the enterprise. In any case, it is immaterial whether the investment is made in monetary form or in kind such as the contribution of machinery, service, technical processes and technology.

> 19. Article 12(b) gives the Board flexibility, in the future, to extend the Agency's coverage to other forms of investment. It authorizes the Board, by special majority, to extend coverage to any medium-or long-term form of investment except loans which are not related to a specific investment covered or to be covered by the Agency. * * * Because the coverage of the Agency is restricted to investments, exports will be covered * * * only to the extent that they represent a contribution to a specific investment. * * *
>
> 21. To serve its objective without undermining its financial viability, the Agency will limit its guarantees to sound investments. It should satisfy itself that the investment concerned will contribute to the economic and social development of the host country, comply with the laws and regulations of that country, and be consistent with the country's declared development objectives. It should also be satisfied that appropriate investment conditions, including the availability of fair and equitable treatment and legal protection, will apply to the investment concerned (Article 12(d)). In case no such protection is assured under the laws of the host country or under bilateral investment treaties, the Agency will issue the guarantee only after it reaches agreement with the host country pursuant to Article 23(b)(ii) or otherwise on the treatment to be extended to the investments covered by the Agency. Investments guaranteed by the Agency should also be new, that is implemented subsequent to the registration of the application for the guarantee by the Agency (Article 12(c)). The exclusion of pre-existing investments would not bar the Agency from covering investments made to develop an existing investment or from covering the reinvestment of earnings which could otherwise be transferred outside the host country. * * *
>
> 22. To qualify for a guarantee, investors who are natural persons must be nationals of members other than the host country. If investors are juridical persons, they must be incorporated and have their principal place of business in a member country other than the host country or have the majority of their capital owned by a member country or its nationals, other than the host country or its nationals. Privately and publicly owned investments are eligible as long as they are operated on a commercial basis (Article 13(a)(iii)). It is expected, however, that the bulk of guaranteed investments will be privately owned.

Id. at 6–8.

MIGA's Investment Guaranty Guide describes the four basic types of investment guarantees against non-commercial risks as follows:

> (1) Transfer Restriction. Protects against losses arising from an investor's inability to convert local currency (capital, interest, principal, profits, royalties, and other remittances) into foreign exchange for transfer outside the host country. The coverage insures against excessive delays in acquiring foreign exchange caused by host government action or failure to act, by adverse changes in exchange control laws or regulations, and by deterioration in conditions governing the conversion and transfer of local currency. Currency devaluation is not covered.
>
> On receipt of the blocked local currency from an investor, MIGA pays compensation in the currency of its Contract of Guarantee.

(2) Expropriation. Protects against loss of the insured investment as a result of acts by the host government that may reduce or eliminate ownership of, control over, or rights to the insured investment. In addition to outright nationalization and confiscation, "creeping" expropriation—a series of acts that, over time, have an expropriatory effect—is also covered.

Coverage is available on a limited basis for partial expropriation (e.g., confiscation of funds or tangible assets). Bona fide, non-discriminatory measures taken by the host government in the exercise of legitimate regulatory authority are not covered.

For total expropriation of equity investments, MIGA pays the net book value of the insured investment. For expropriation of funds, MIGA pays the insured portion of the blocked funds. For loans and loan guaranties, MIGA insures the outstanding principal and any accrued and unpaid interest.

Compensation will be paid upon assignment of the investor's interest in the expropriated investment (e.g., equity shares or interest in a loan agreement) to MIGA.

(3) Breach of Contract. Protects against losses arising from the host government's breach or repudiation of a contract with the investor. In the event of an alleged breach or repudiation, the investor must be able to invoke a dispute resolution mechanism (e.g., an arbitration) in the underlying contract and obtain an award for damages. If, after a specified period of time, the investor has not received payment or if the dispute resolution mechanism fails to function because of actions taken by the host government, MIGA will pay compensation.

(4) War and Civil Disturbance. Protects against loss from damage to, or the destruction or disappearance of, tangible assets caused by politically-motivated acts of war or civil disturbance in the host country, including revolution, insurrection, coups d'état, sabotage, and terrorism. For equity investments, MIGA will pay the investor's share of the least of the book value of the assets, of their replacement cost, or of the cost of repair of damaged assets. For loans and loan guaranties, MIGA will pay the insured portion of the principal and interest payments in default as a direct result of damage to the assets of the project caused by war and civil disturbance.

War and Civil Disturbance coverage also extends to events that, for a period of one year, result in an interruption of project operations essential to overall financial viability. This type of business interruption is effective when the investment is considered a total loss; at that point, MIGA will pay the book value of the total insured equity investment. For loans and loan guaranties, MIGA pays the insured portion of the principal and interest payments in default as a result of business interruption caused by covered events.

MIGA Investment Guarantee Guide 1–2 (1998).

With respect to Host Country Approval and Subrogation, the Commentary states:

> 25. Article 15 provides that the Agency will not conclude any contract of guarantee before "the host government has approved the issuance of the guarantee by the Agency against the risks designated for cover." Any host government may withhold its approval. This enables the host country to evaluate a proposed investment before giving its consent. The Agency is expected to establish procedures for obtaining consents under this provision. These may include requesting approvals on a no objection basis (Article 38(b)). Although the approval of the home country of the investor is not required, it would not be appropriate for the Agency to cover an investment if informed by the investor's home country that it would be financed with funds transferred outside such country in violation of its laws.
>
> 26. Article 18(a) provides that where the Agency compensates or agrees to compensate an investor under a contract of guarantee, it assumes the rights that the investor acquired against the host country as a result of the event giving rise to the claim against the Agency. Subrogation is an accepted principle of insurance law. It provides for the assignment of an existing claim from the guaranteed investor to the Agency and the Agency as subrogee acquires the same rights as the investor had. The contracts of guarantee will define the terms and conditions of subrogation. * * * Article 18(b) provides for the recognition of the Agency's right of subrogation by all members.
>
> 27. Under Article 18(c), the Agency has the right to treatment as favorable as would be given the holder of the guarantee with respect to the use and transfer of local currencies of host countries received by the Agency as subrogee. In addition, the Agency is authorized to use these currencies for the payment of its administrative expenditures or other costs and is directed to seek to enter into agreements with host countries on other uses of these currencies if they are not freely usable. * * *

Id. at 8–9.

MIGA has international juridical personality and functions autonomously with a Council of Governors (one from each member), a Board of Directors elected by the Council and a President elected by the Board. The voting arrangements involve parity between Category One (developed) and Category Two (developing) states on the assumption that all members of the World Bank eventually become members of MIGA.

Typically, MIGA issues a guarantee for a maximum of 15 years at a rate of premium between 0.3 and 1.5 percent of the guaranteed amount per year. MIGA can cover up to 90 percent of the amount of an eligible investment with a maximum coverage limit of $50 million. MIGA is enjoined to cooperate with and seek to complement the activities of other investment insurers. To this end, MIGA has the authority to enter into reinsurance and coinsurance agreements for eligible investments with both private and public investment insurers.

MIGA is expected to meet its liabilities from premium income and other income, including return on investments. In addition to relying on the capital subscriptions of member states, MIGA is authorized to underwrite investments sponsored by member countries on the basis of a special "Sponsorship Trust Fund" kept apart from MIGA's own funds and sustained by states electing to serve as sponsoring countries. This "sponsorship window" is a particularly interesting innovation because it has no financial ceiling and it permits coverage in countries other than Category Two developing countries.

Shihata has summed up the role of MIGA as follows (footnotes omitted):

> MIGA is not envisaged as only an insurance mechanism. MIGA will also seek to stabilize and improve investment climates in its developing member countries and thus stimulate investment flows to these countries. This mandate is reflected in a number of the provisions of the Convention. It is reinforced by MIGA's institutional structure and internal dynamics.
>
> In the past, the need for fair and stable investment conditions has been emphasized from the point of view of investors and their home countries. However, host countries clearly serve their national interests by providing sound investment conditions. Their ability to attract badly needed resources and to bargain for better terms and conditions is obviously strengthened by the availability of better investment climates in their territories. The establishment of an international development institution, financed and controlled jointly by developed and developing countries, manifests the common interest in creating a favorable investment climate in the latter countries.
>
> Frequently, issues related to foreign investment have also become intermingled with the political interests of home and host countries. As a result, investment disputes often became highly politicized. MIGA seeks to remove the disputes from the political arena and ensure that they will be resolved only on the basis of legal and economic criteria. It is explicitly prohibited from interfering in the political affairs of its members. Moreover, MIGA's internal dynamics will result in its playing an important role as an intermediary between investors and host countries. To attract business and generate revenues, it must offer effective guarantee protection and pay claims which are justified. To minimize underwriting losses, * * * [when claims] occur, [MIGA must] secure recovery from the host country whenever possible. Recovery procedures could jeopardize MIGA's good relations with developing member countries which could easily curtail MIGA's operations by denying their approval for further guarantees. Therefore MIGA must ensure that the goodwill of member countries is not lost and that their common interest in the Agency's functioning prevails over the conflicting interests in a particular dispute.
>
> The competing pressures will force MIGA to cover risks that are unlikely to invite adverse host governmental action which could give rise to claims. At the same time, MIGA will have to ensure that these investments are accorded stable and predictable treatment. * * *
>
> Where disputes nevertheless arise between investors and host countries, MIGA will become involved in the process of conflict resolution in a way that will place it in a unique position to facilitate an amicable settlement. The Convention indeed directs MIGA to encourage such settlements. In the case of disputes, MIGA's assessment, based on the broad information available to it, together with its worldwide experience, is likely to moderate the conflicting claims of an investor and a host country and increase the likelihood of a settlement.

> Another way in which MIGA may encourage host governments and investors to arrive at amicable settlements is to reduce the financial burden of any settlements by accepting the local currency of the host country on a temporary basis and paying the investor out of its own funds in freely usable currency. MIGA might then, under an agreement with the host country, sell the local currency to the World Bank, other international institutions, companies importing goods from the host country, or to the host government itself over a period of time and restore its financial position accordingly. MIGA might also facilitate the settlement by paying the investor in cash and accepting debt instruments from the government as reimbursement. As a variant of this approach, MIGA could persuade the investor to accept installments rather than insisting on a cash payment by backing the government's commitments with its guarantee. In view of its developmental mandate and policy interests, MIGA can be anticipated to facilitate settlements amicably at least as successfully as some of the national agencies have done. In this, as well as in all its other activities, MIGA will be serving its broad mandate of encouraging additional investment flows among its members and to developing countries in particular.

Shihata, The Multilateral Investment Guaranty Agency, supra at 495–97.

Notes

1. Since its inception, MIGA's guarantees have facilitated cumulative direct foreign investment of nearly $39 billion in 76 developing countries. MIGA's guarantees in those countries have totaled over $7.5 billion. MIGA has also entered into reinsurance agreements with private insurers and has established a Cooperative Underwriting Program (CUP), which has substantially reduced its net exposure. The CUP is designed to encourage private insurers to offer political risk reinsurance for projects in developing countries that are members of MIGA. While a private insurer might not wish to assume political risk in a host country on its own, it may be willing to do so in conjunction with MIGA. The CUP is a "fronting" arrangement, whereby MIGA is the insurer-of-record and issues a Contract of Guarantee for the entire amount of insurance requested by an investor, but retains only a portion of the exposure for its own account. The remainder is underwritten by one or more private reinsurers using MIGA's contract wording. The premium rates, claims payments, and recoveries are all shared on a pari passu basis.

2. Where, in MIGA's opinion, appropriate investment conditions do not exist, it seeks to enter into a legal protection agreement with the potential host country on the treatment of investments guaranteed by it. Shihata, The Multilateral Investment Guarantee Agency supra, at 491. Article 23(b)(ii) of the Convention states that such agreements "will assure that the Agency * * * has treatment at least as favorable as that guaranteed by the member concerned for the most favored investment guarantee agency or State in an agreement related to investment." When an investment insured by MIGA is located in a country that has concluded a legal protection agreement with the Agency, the provisions of any bilateral or multilateral investment treaty to which the host country is a party apply to the insured investment, even if the country from which the investment originates has not concluded an investment treaty with the host country. Although MIGA—not the investor—is the beneficiary of the most favorable treat-

ment, the investor benefits indirectly from the protection granted by MIGA. Furthermore, since the legal protection agreement enhances the overall investment climate in a developing host country, it also serves the host country's interests.

3. MIGA carries out promotional activities, such as conducting research, providing information, policy advice and technical assistance to member governments, including, for example, advice on the drafting of investment codes and investment incentive programs. Convention Art. 23(a).

4. MIGA's objective is to complement national and regional programs rather than compete with them. It therefore focuses on guaranteeing investments from members without an investment guaranty program, co-guaranteeing investments from members with national and regional agencies, providing reinsurance for national and regional agencies, guaranteeing investments that fail eligibility tests of the national and regional program concerned and guaranteeing investments financed by investors from a number of member countries. It also participates in arrangements for reinsurance with private insurers in member states.

5. The voting arrangements in the MIGA are unique and are described as follows in the Commentary:

> 63. The voting structure of the Agency reflects the view that Category One and Category Two countries have an equal stake in foreign investment, that cooperation between them is essential, and that both groups of countries should, when all eligible countries become members, have equal voting power (50/50). It is also recognized that a member's voting power should reflect its relative capital subscription. The Convention, therefore, provides that each member is to have 177 membership plus one subscription vote for each share of stock held by it (Article 39(a)). The number of membership votes is computed so as to ensure that if all Bank members joined the Agency, developing countries as a group would have the same voting power as developed countries as a group. * * *

Commentary at p. 18.

6. The first claim in 12 years of operation was filed against MIGA in March 1999. The claim was brought by an investor in Indonesia, as a consequence of the postponement of a power project. MIGA and the host government made intensive efforts to find a solution that would be acceptable to all parties involved. MIGA paid the claim on June 16, 2000; negotiations with Indonesia continue.

*

Index

References are to Pages

B

References are to Pages

D

E

I

J

K

L

O

Q

R

References are to Pages

T

Y

Z

†